FAMOUS
FIRST FACTS

Other titles by Joseph Nathan Kane in the Wilson Facts Series

Facts About the Presidents, Sixth Edition

**Other titles by Joseph Nathan Kane, Steven Anzovin & Janet Podell
in the Wilson Facts Series**

Facts About the States, Second Edition

Other H. W. Wilson titles by Steven Anzovin & Janet Podell

Old Worlds to New: The Age of Exploration and Discovery (authors)
Speeches of the American Presidents (editors)

Other titles in the Wilson Facts Series

Facts About American Immigration (forthcoming)
Facts About the American Wars
Facts About the British Prime Ministers
Facts About Canada, Its Provinces and Territories
Facts About China (forthcoming)
Facts About the Cities, Second Edition
Facts About the Congress
Facts About the Supreme Court of the United States
Facts About the Twentieth Century (forthcoming)
and
Famous First Facts, International Edition (forthcoming)

JOSEPH NATHAN KANE
STEVEN ANZOVIN & JANET PODELL

FAMOUS FIRST FACTS
Fifth Edition

A Record of First Happenings, Discoveries,

and Inventions in American History

The H. W. Wilson Company
New York ◆ Dublin
1997

Library of Congress Cataloging-in-Publication Data

Kane, Joseph Nathan Kane, 1899–
    Famous first facts / by Joseph Nathan Kane, Steven
Anzovin, Janet Podell.—5th ed.
        p.   cm.
    Includes indexes.
    ISBN 0-8242-0930-3
    1. Encyclopedia and dictionaries. I. Anzovin,
Steven. II. Podell, Janet. III. Title.
AG5.K315   1997
031.02—dc21   97-31252
                                                         CIP

Printed in the United States of America

06 05 04 03 02 01 00 99   10 9 8 7 6 5 4 3 2

The H. W. Wilson Company
950 University Avenue
Bronx, NY 10452

http://www.hwwilson.com

Contents

Preface

Joseph Nathan Kane's *Famous First Facts* has been the standard record of notable American firsts since the publication of the original edition in 1933. This new revised edition, the first in 17 years, retains the special flavor of Mr. Kane's language. Among reference book compilers, Mr. Kane is second to none, and the esteem in which he is held by librarians and readers alike made it imperative to keep as much as possible to his style and his way of doing things. Were it not for Mr. Kane's persistence and diligence, *Famous First Facts* would not have become the highly respected compendium that it is today.

The genesis of *Famous First Facts* can be traced to Mr. Kane's career as a freelance, self-syndicated journalist. Intending to write a book about the history of American inventions, he spent the better part of each year from 1922 to 1932 traveling throughout the United States, visiting libraries and museums, seeking out inventors and achievers or their descendants, and talking with virtually everyone he met. The task was an enormous one, made even more difficult by conflicting patent claims and inadequate records. Mr. Kane personally researched each and every one of the 3,000 facts that would eventually find their way into the first edition of *Famous First Facts,* spending innumerable hours poring over public documents and newspaper clippings and conducting interviews around the country. After completing his manuscript, submitting it to publishers, and amassing a total of 11 rejections, he approached Halsey W. Wilson, then president of the H. W. Wilson Company, which Mr. Wilson had founded in 1898. Initially unconvinced of the merits of Mr. Kane's proposal, Mr. Wilson was ultimately persuaded to publish the first edition of *Famous First Facts* after receiving multiple requests for the book from reference librarians to whom Mr. Kane had shown portions of his manuscript.

In the preface to the first edition, Mr. Kane wrote that his intention was not "to remold public conceptions, but merely to present impartial facts" and thereby "replace romantic history with commonplace truth." His efforts were applauded by information seekers everywhere. "It was surely a happy inspiration that set Joseph Nathan Kane at the task of producing so intriguing a volume," a reviewer for the *New York Times* wrote in 1933, "and a dogged resolution of almost superhuman force that kept him at work so incessantly grilling until it was finished." The success of the original edition of *Famous First Facts* led to a new career for Mr. Kane. He served as the host of a radio program entitled *Famous First Facts* in 1938–39, was a leading provider of questions (and answers) to the nation's most popular radio and television quiz shows from 1945 to 1957, and became the originating author of additional titles in the Wilson Facts Series, namely *Facts About the Presidents* and *Facts*

About the States. The popularity of *Famous First Facts* also resulted in a supplement in 1935, a second edition in 1950, a third in 1964, a fourth in 1981, and now, the fifth edition. With each new edition Mr. Kane revised entries as necessary and added new firsts. He also added four indexes, enabling readers to find information by year, by days of the month, by personal names, and by city (or state when the city was unknown).

The entries in this fifth edition of *Famous First Facts*, including 1,000 new firsts, represent the entire range of American history, from the earliest known human activity in the area that is now the United States to current social, cultural, and scientific developments. Much of the material in the previous edition was consolidated to make room for the events of the recent past. The format of the book has been reorganized for easier access. Related entries are now grouped together under main subject categories, which are divided as necessary into subcategories. In addition, an entirely new Subject Index has been created for this fifth edition. A more detailed discussion of the new classification system and the five indexes is presented in the section entitled How to Use This Book, which appears on the following page.

We would like to extend our gratitude to Michael Schulze, director of General Publications for the H. W. Wilson Company, for initiating this project and for giving us the opportunity to carry on the *Famous First Facts* tradition. We thank senior editor Hilary Claggett, managing editors Gray Young and Joseph Sora, and manager of library specifications Christopher Monell for their strong support. Thanks are also due to the many institutions, agencies, organizations, and librarians who responded so helpfully to our inquiries, and to the individuals who sent us information about their accomplishments.

JANET PODELL AND STEVEN ANZOVIN
Amherst, Massachusetts
November 1997

How to Use This Book

Related entries in this book are grouped together under main subject categories, which are arranged alphabetically. Where appropriate, the main subject categories are divided into subcategories, which are also arranged alphabetically. For example, the main category *Religion* is divided into eight subcategories, including *Buddhist, Catholic, Jewish, Protestant,* and *Various.* The subcategory *Protestant,* in turn, lists a number of miscellaneous and general entries and is then divided into *Anabaptist, Baptist, Episcopal, Lutheran, Methodist,* and so on. Three levels of categories (*Religion—Protestant—Methodist*) are the maximum allowed. A complete list of the subject categories appears in the Expanded Contents, which begins on page xi.

Within this structure of classification, the entries are arranged chronologically. This arrangement has the advantage of enabling the reader to get a sense of how and when a field of endeavor developed. Each entry begins with a four-digit indexing number, starting with number 1001, and an introductory phrase, referred to here as an entry head, in boldface type (for example, **1836. Novel by a writer born in America**). Please note that this four-digit indexing number does not indicate the year in which an event took place. Instead, the date can be found in the text of the entry.

To find a specific entry, the reader can turn either to the Expanded Contents or to one of the five indexes printed at the back of the volume. Four of these—Index by Years, Index by Days, Index to Personal Names, and the Geographical Index—have been continued from previous editions. The new one is the Subject Index, which lists alphabetically all entry heads as well as key words representing particular populations (for example, *African-American* and *Woman*). The Subject Index also includes many firsts that appear as part of longer entries and thus do not have entry heads of their own (for example, *Movie closeup,* which appears in the text under the boldface entry head **Movie to be copyrighted**). The creation of the Subject Index has permitted the elimination of space-consuming cross-references from the main text. In all five indexes, entries are identified by the four-digit indexing number, which appears in italics.

History is a complicated subject, and classification is an inexact science. In the many cases in which entries were classifiable under more than one subject category, priorities were established that will quickly become evident to the reader. *Education,* for instance, takes priority over other possible subject categories for classifying academies run by branches of the armed forces, which appear under *Education—Military,* rather than in the *Military* category. Similarly, naval hospitals and army dentists appear under *Medicine—Military.*

Expanded Contents

Famous First Facts

A

AGRICULTURE

1001. Agricultural fair held annually was authorized by the director and council of New Netherlands (now New York) on September 30, 1641. They "ordained that henceforth there shall be held annually at Fort Amsterdam a Cattle Fair on the 15th of October; and a fair for Hogs on the 1st of November. Whosoever hath any things to sell or to buy can regulate himself accordingly."

1002. Agricultural experiment farm was established on 10 acres set aside by Savannah, GA, in 1735. A skillful botanist was appointed "to collect the seeds of drugs and dying-stuffs in other countries in the same climate, in order to cultivate such of them as shall be found to thrive well in Georgia."

1003. Agricultural experiment station operated by a state was the Connecticut Agricultural Experiment Station, established in Connecticut by an act approved on July 20, 1875. Orange Judd, editor and proprietor of the *American Agriculturist,* offered $1,000, and the trustees of Wesleyan University at Middletown, CT, offered the free use of the chemical laboratory of the university's Orange Judd Hall on condition that the legislature appropriate $2,800 per year for two years. The appropriation was made on October 1, 1875, and work began on January 1, 1876. Professor Wilbur Olin Atwater was the first director.

1004. Farm bureau was the Broome County Farm Bureau, established on March 20, 1911, in Binghamton, NY. The bureau's first officer was John H. Barron, an agent of the Department of Agriculture, who worked in cooperation with the State College of Agriculture at Cornell University, the Binghamton Chamber of Commerce, and the Delaware, Lackawanna and Western Railway. On May 24, 1913, an act appropriating $25,000 for assisting the farm bureaus was passed by New York, the first state to pass an act of this kind.

1005. Soil conference of importance was the International Congress of Soil Science that met in Washington, DC, June 13–22, 1917. Delegates from over 20 countries were present.

1006. Payment by the Federal Crop Insurance Corporation was a payment of $129.32 made on April 14, 1939, to John F. Biggs of Floydada, TX, to compensate him for the total loss of his share in a 52-acre wheat crop. The corporation was established under the Agricultural Adjustment Act of 1938. Its purpose was to insure wheat yields against natural hazards such as drought, flood, hail, winterkill, lightning, insect infestation, and plant diseases.

AGRICULTURE—CROPS

1007. Crop limitation law enacted by a colony was passed on October 16, 1629, by the Virginia General Assembly. Act Five limited the planting of tobacco.

1008. Crop surplus destruction ordered by a government was ordered on January 6, 1639, by the Virginia General Assembly: "Tobacco by reason of excessive quantities made, being so low that the planters could not subsist by it or be enabled to raise more staple commodities or pay their debts, enacted that the tobacco of that year be viewed by sworn viewers and the rotten and unmerchantable, and half the good to be burned, so the whole quantity made would come to 1,500,000 pounds without stripping and smoothing."

1009. Indigo crop was planted and harvested in South Carolina prior to 1690, when a petition was presented by Governor Seth Sothell to the Lords Proprietors asking that the inhabitants of South Carolina might be allowed to "pay their rents in the most valuable and merchantable produce of their lands" and enumerating such products as silk, cotton, rice, and indigo. Indigo, from which blue dye is derived, was not a successful crop until Elizabeth Lucas Pinckney began cultivating it on her family's two South Carolina plantations in 1740.

1010. Hemp to be exported was shipped to England in 1730. It consisted of 50 hundredweight of hemp raised in New England and Carolina, and 3 hundredweight from Virginia.

AGRICULTURE—CROPS—continued

1011. Seed business regularly established was organized on January 7, 1784, by David Landreth in Philadelphia, PA. Previously, seeds had been imported from Europe or saved from each crop by individual farmers. The firm, incorporated in 1904 as the D. Landreth Seed Company, later became a subsidiary of the Robert Buist Company, founded in Philadelphia in 1828.

1012. Alfalfa is supposed to have been introduced into California in 1854 from Chile, but John Spurrier described alfalfa (which he called "lucerne") in his book *The Practical Farmer*, which was dedicated to Thomas Jefferson and published at Wilmington, DE, in 1793.

1013. Vineyard that was successful was established on August 28, 1798, by John James Dufour on a tract of land consisting of about 630 acres situated 25 miles from Lexington, KY. He called it "The First Vineyard." Dufour was one of the pioneer viticulturists in America. Attempts to establish vineyards had been made as early as 1619 in Virginia.

1014. Guano for use as a soil fertilizer was imported from Peru in 1832. Guano is the deposits of droppings of sea birds and bats, found in caves or above ground in areas where there is little or no rain.

1015. Agricultural seed distribution on a national scale was undertaken in 1836–37 by the Commissioner of Patents, Henry Leavitt Ellsworth, at his own expense and without congressional authorization. In 1838 the cost was $126.40. In 1839 about 30,000 packets were distributed, the expense being about $1,000. Yearly seed distribution continued until 1923.

1016. Synthetic fertilizer was developed by Professor James Jay Mapes, who experimented with fertilizers in 1847 on his 20-acre farm at Newark, NJ. He applied for a patent in 1849 on a superphosphate of lime made from charred bone (the waste products of sugar refineries), to which were added sulfate of ammonia and Peruvian guano. The patent was granted on November 22, 1859.

1017. Irrigation law enacted by Congress was the act of July 26, 1866, which ruled that control of waterways was a matter of state control subject to "local customs, laws and decisions of the court."

1018. Jute culture was introduced by the Department of Agriculture in 1869–70. A quantity of seed was imported from France and India and planted from the Carolinas to Texas.

1019. Fruit spraying was done in 1878 when an apple grower in Niagara County, NY, sprayed his apple trees with Paris green for the control of canker worms.

1020. Sweet potato was brought to California in 1888 by John B. Avila, a native of the Portuguese Azores. Avila planted a 20-acre plot of *Ipomoea batatas,* a species originally native to Central and South America that was probably introduced to Europe by Christopher Columbus.

1021. Tung trees (*Aleurites fordii*) successfully grown for tung oil were planted in 1905 by the U.S. Plant Introduction Garden, Chico, CA. The seeds had been forwarded by David Fairchild, chief of the Division of Plant Exploration and Introduction, Department of Agriculture, who had received them from L.S. Wilcox, consul general at Hankow, China.

1022. Hybrid seed corn shipment was sold to Samuel Ramsay, Jacobsburg, OH, on April 13, 1916, by Funk Brothers Seed Company, Bloomington, IL. The price was $15 a bushel.

1023. Japanese beetle appeared in Riverton, NJ, in 1916. Its grubs were believed to have arrived in the roots of imported nursery stock.

1024. Soybean processing plant that was commercially successful was built by Augustus Eugene Staley in Decatur, IL, in 1922. The beans were run through an expeller, which removed the oil to within 4 percent, and the residue was sold to the feed industry for use in commercial animal feeds or to farmers, who mixed the meal with other ingredients as a protein supplement for livestock.

1025. Corn-husking championship was held on November 24, 1924, on a farm near Alleman, Polk County, IA. There were six contestants. The winner was Fred Stanek of Webster County, IA, who husked 1,891 pounds in 90 minutes.

1026. Fruit tree patent was issued on February 16, 1932, to James E. Markham and assigned to the Stark Brothers Nurseries and Orchards Company of Louisiana, MO. The patent was obtained on a peach tree, the fruit of which ripened later than ordinary peaches.

1027. Kenaf fiber was planted commercially in July 1951 at Belle Glade, FL, by the American Kenaf Fiber Corporation. One and a half million pounds were harvested that year and sold at 30 cents a pound to the Commodity Credit Corporation for the Munitions Board. Kenaf is a 10-foot plant whose soft fibers are a substitute for jute, burlap, and paper.

1028. Genetically altered plants were approved for outdoor testing by the Department of Agriculture in 1986. The cultivars were high-yield tobacco plants.

AGRICULTURE—CROPS—COTTON

1029. Cotton crop exported to England consisted of eight bales from Charleston, SC, which were seized by the custom house in England in 1764 on the grounds that the American colony could not have produced so much.

1030. Cotton gin to separate the seed from the cotton was invented in 1792 by Eli Whitney at Mulberry Grove, a plantation near Savannah, GA, possibly using ideas furnished by his financial patron, Catherine Littlefield Greene. He formed a partnership with Greene's second husband, Phineas Miller, to manufacture the gin, but his model was stolen by dishonest manufacturers who produced many units. Although Whitney received a patent on March 14, 1794, he was unable to stop the infringement of his rights because the gin was so successful, greatly increasing cotton production in the South. The patent was not renewed when it expired because of the power exerted by those who had been enriched by Whitney's invention.

1031. Cottonseed hulling machine was invented by John Lineback of Salem, NC, and patented by him on March 31, 1814.

1032. Cotton boll weevil was introduced into the United States from Central America about 1892, probably through Brownsville, TX. The weevil is a species of beetle that causes extensive crop damage but is immune to most insecticides.

1033. Mechanical cotton picker of importance was the Rust Cotton Picker, a horse-drawn picker built by John Daniel Rust in Weatherford, TX, in 1928. In 1929 it was rebuilt into a self-propelled model powered by a Model T motor. In 1935 a tractor model was built, and in 1937 an improved model picked 13 bales of cotton in one day.

1034. Cotton acreage reduction payment was made on July 28, 1933, to William E. Morris of Nueces County, TX, who was presented with a check for $517 by President Franklin Delano Roosevelt for having plowed under 47 acres of his cotton crop. In addition, he was given an option on 23.5 bales of cotton at six cents a pound.

1035. Cotton crop commercially produced entirely by machinery from planting to baling, with the exception of a few incidental hours of hand labor, was grown during the year 1944 on 28 acres owned by Hopson Planting Company of Clarksdale, MS. The soil was prepared, crop-seeded, and cultivated by machines, the weeds eradicated by flame, and the crop harvested by a mechanical picker.

AGRICULTURE—CROPS—HYDROPON-ICS

1036. Description of hydroponic agriculture was included in William Frederick Gericke's article "Aquaculture, A Means of Crop Production," published in December 1929 in the *American Journal of Botany.* The term "hydroponics" for soilless crop production was first used in Gericke's article "Hydroponics—Crop Production in Liquid Culture Media," published on February 12, 1937, in *Science.* Early attempts at hydroponic growing of crops had used sand beds, mounted over tanks containing nutrient solutions, to hold the plantings.

1037. Private hydroponic garden where vegetables and flowers were grown in nutrient-enriched water was created in 1931 by William Frederick Gericke at his home in Berkeley, CA.

1038. Commercial production of plants in water instead of soil was undertaken by the firm of Vetterle and Reinelt of Capitola, CA, in February 1934. The company constructed a greenhouse 100 by 33 feet, with 100 tanks. The first planting consisted of about 2,000 begonias, which, as a result of precise regulation of humidity and food supply, grew more rapidly than if soil-planted. On October 12, 1935, the growers set out tomato plantings that grew to 15 feet in height within six to eight months.

1039. Commercial hydroponicum on a large scale was established in Montebello, CA, on December 5, 1935, by Ernest Walfrid Brundin and Frank Farrington Lyon, who installed a water-circulating system. They obtained a patent on December 1, 1936, on a "system of water culture" and incorporated the company on October 19, 1937, as the Chemi-Culture Company.

AGRICULTURE—FARM EQUIPMENT

1040. Greenhouse was erected by James Beekman in New York City in 1764. It is claimed that Andrew Faneuil erected a glass house at Boston, MA, prior to 1737.

AGRICULTURE—FARM EQUIPMENT—
continued

1041. Plow patent was granted on June 26, 1797, to Charles Newbold, a farmer of Burlington County, NJ. The plow was of solid cast iron, excepting the handles and beam, and consisted of a bar, a sheath, and a moldplate. It was the first cast-iron plow made. The invention did not meet with great success, as many farmers believed that the iron poisoned the land.

1042. Plow with interchangeable parts was patented by John Jethro Wood of Poplar Ridge, NY, on September 1, 1819. His plow substituted cast iron for the wooden moldboard, landside, and standard. In this it was similar to the solid cast-iron plow patented in 1797 by Charles Newbold.

1043. Reaper machine that worked was invented by Henry Ogle in 1826. It consisted of a straight scythe blade that moved against a series of triangular fingers. The cut grain fell on a collecting board.

1044. Reaper machine that was practical was built by Cyrus Hall McCormick in 1831 and demonstrated at a public trial in a field near Walnut Grove, VA. The owner of the field feared that the machine would rattle the heads off his wheat and stopped the demonstration. Another neighbor whose ground was more level invited McCormick to his field, where the machine worked splendidly, cutting six acres of wheat in half a day—as much as six men would have done. The reaper was patented on June 21, 1834, but farmers remained suspicious of it, and McCormick did not make his first sale until 1841. He began manufacturing it on a large scale in Chicago, IL, in 1847.

1045. Steel plow with a steel moldboard was made in 1837 by John Deere, a blacksmith, who tested it on the farm of Lewis Crandall, near Grand Detour, IL. Deere used steel from a broken saw blade. In 1843, he imported rolled steel from England, which cost about $300 a ton. In 1847 he began manufacturing the plows in Moline, IL, using steel produced by the Jones and Quiggs Steel Works, Pittsburgh, PA. His company was incorporated in 1868 as Deere and Company.

1046. Threshing machine to employ steam was patented by John A. Pitts and Hiram Abial Pitts of Winthrop, ME, who received a patent on December 29, 1837, on a "machine for threshing or cleaning grain." The machine separated grain from the straw and chaff.

1047. Seeding machine that was practical was invented by Joseph Gibbons of Adrian, MI, who received a patent on August 25, 1840. His machine was a grain drill with cavities to deliver seed and a device for regulating the volume. An earlier gravity-fed device, patented by Eliakim Spooner of Vermont on January 25, 1799, was not practical.

1048. Grain elevator operated by steam to transfer and store grain for commercial purposes was designed by Robert Dunbar and made by Jewett and Root for Joseph Dart, Buffalo, NY, in 1842. The first cargo of corn was unloaded on June 22, 1843, from the *South America*.

1049. Plow for pulverizing the soil was patented by George Page of Washington, DC, who received a patent for it on August 7, 1847. Page's design used a revolving single disk on the side of the plow.

1050. Beehive with removable frames was patented by Lorenzo Lorraine Langstroth, a former pastor in Oxford, OH, on October 5, 1852. Langstroth's hive design revolutionized beekeeping because it was the first that allowed bees to build combs on wooden frames that could be removed, stripped of honey and wax, and then replaced. His key discovery was the "bee space," the minimum air space that bees would not bridge with wax or bee glue. By setting up his frames at this distance, he prevented the bees from building connections between them. This allowed him to remove one frame at a time without damaging the adjacent frames, and enabled him to maximize the amount of honeycomb in the hive.

1051. Silo on record was constructed by Fred L. Hatch in 1873 in McHenry County, IL.

1052. Fence made of woven wire was constructed in 1883 by John Wallace Page on his farm in Lenawee County, MI. The fence was made of wires that were interlaced horizontally and vertically. There were so many calls for similar fences from Page's neighbors that he opened a factory in Adrian, MI.

1053. Tractor with an endless chain was invented by Charles Dinsmoor of Warren, PA, who received a patent for it on November 2, 1886. The endless-chain tractor, or track-type tractor, did not become a commercial and practical reality until Benjamin Holt of the Holt Manufacturing Company of Stockton, CA, produced one in 1906 and proceeded to build and sell them in quantities.

1054. Steam tractor was made by Daniel Best of San Leandro, CA, in 1886. One of his Best tractors was loaded on a car at San Leandro on February 8, 1889.

1055. Gasoline tractor was manufactured in 1892 by John Froelich of Froelich, IA. On September 6, 1892, he shipped one of his tractors to Langford, SD, where it was employed from September 24 to November 16 in threshing. It had a Van Duzen vertical single-cylinder gasoline engine mounted on wooden beams to operate a J.I. Case threshing machine. In 1893, Froelich formed the Waterloo Gasoline Traction Engine Company, Waterloo, IA, which was later acquired by the John Deere Plow Company.

1056. Rotating milking platform was the Rotolactor, invented by Henry W. Jeffers and installed on November 13, 1930, in the lactorium of the Walker Gordon Laboratory Company at Plainsboro, NJ. It permitted 1,680 cows to be milked in 7 hours by means of a revolving platform that brought them into position with the milking machines.

1057. Diesel-powered tractor offered on the market was the Caterpillar Diesel Tractor, manufactured by the Caterpillar Tractor Company, Peoria, IL. It was a track-type, weighed 24,390 pounds, and developed 68 maximum drawbar horsepower. It was powered with a four-cylinder, four-cycle diesel engine. The first one was delivered in October 1931.

AGRICULTURE—FISH

1058. Oyster propagation under state auspices began in Rhode Island, which in June 1779 set aside part of the public domain for the cultivation and propagation of oysters.

1059. Fish hatchery to breed salmon was an experimental laboratory established in 1864 under the supervision of James B. Johnson. He imported from Europe salmon eggs, which were hatched in his New York City laboratory.

1060. Fish hatchery run by the federal government was established in 1872 at Bucksport, ME, under the supervision of Charles Grandison Atkins, for the propagation of Atlantic salmon. It was a joint activity, with the cooperation of state agencies of Maine, Massachusetts, and Connecticut, and was a continuation of experiments initiated by these agencies in 1871. It was later moved to East Orland, ME.

1061. Goldfish hatchery successfully operated was established in the summer of 1899 by Eugene Curtis Shireman in Martinsville, IN. The hatchery started with 200 goldfish and eventually bred millions of goldfish annually. It was incorporated in 1924 as Grassyfork. Public interest in goldfish began in 1878, when Rear Admiral Daniel Ammen of the Navy presented the U.S. Fish Commission with goldfish that had been brought over from Japan.

AGRICULTURE—FLOWERS

1062. Japanese cherry trees were a gift to the United States from the people of Tokyo, Japan. The first shipment arrived in 1909 but had to be destroyed because of insect infestation. A second shipment was planted in 1912 in Potomac Park, Washington, DC.

1063. Plant patent was awarded to Henry F. Bosenberg of New Brunswick, NJ, on August 18, 1931. It covered a climbing rose named New Dawn that blooms successively throughout the season instead of in June only, as does its parent, Dr. Van Fleet.

1064. Tetraploid flower produced by the use of chemicals was publicly exhibited by David Burpee of the W. Atlee Burpee Company, Philadelphia, PA, on January 29, 1940, at the New York City Flower Show. A marigold was treated with colchicine, a chemical extracted from the roots of the fall crocus, with the result that it was one and a half times as large in diameter as the Guinea Gold from which it started.

AGRICULTURE—LIVESTOCK

1065. Branding law enacted by a colony was enacted on February 5, 1644, by Connecticut. It provided that all cattle and swine older than six months be earmarked or branded before May 1, 1644, and that the marks be registered. The penalty for violation was five shillings a head, two of which were paid to informers.

1066. Pounds for stray livestock were required by Connecticut on May 1650. It decreed "that there shall be one sufficient pound or more made and maintained in every town and village within this jurisdiction, for the impounding of all swine and cattle as shall be found in any cornfield or other inclosure."

1067. Partridge propagation was encouraged in 1790 when Richard Bache, son-in-law of Benjamin Franklin, stocked his plantation at Beverly, NJ, with partridges. Four years previously, General Lafayette of France had sent a few partridges to George Washington.

AGRICULTURE—LIVESTOCK—*continued*

1068. Egg incubator for hatching chickens by artificial heat was patented on March 30, 1843, by Napoleon E. Guerin of New York City, who invented a "mode of distributing steam heat, purifying air, etc."

1069. Poultry show was the Grand Show of Domestic Poultry and Convention of Fowl Breeders and Fanciers, held on November 15–16, 1849, at the Public Garden, Boston, MA, with 1,423 specimens in 219 cages. More than 10,000 persons attended.

1070. Fur-bearing animals raised commercially were minks reared in Oneida County, NY, in 1866 by H. Ressegue. Prices of skins were high, and live animals for breeding stock brought $30 a pair.

1071. Ostrich farm was established at South Pasadena, CA, by Edwin Cawston in 1886. He imported 50 ostriches from Africa, 18 of which survived the trip and were landed at Galveston, TX, in 1886. In order to discourage the exportation of ostriches from Africa, an export tax of $500 was placed on each ostrich and $25 on each egg, but this shipment escaped the tax, as the boat sailed from Africa a few hours before it went into effect.

1072. Alligator farm was established in 1892 at Anastasia Island, St. Johns County, FL, by George Reddington.

1073. Goat show was held on September 15–27, 1913, at Exhibition Park, Rochester, NY, in connection with the sixth annual Rochester Industrial Exposition. Pedigreed goats were exhibited at the show, which was sponsored by the Standard Milch Goat Breeders' Association of North America.

1074. Chinchilla farm that was successful was established on February 22, 1923, at Los Angeles, CA, by Mathias Farrell Chapman with 11 chinchillas imported from Peru and Chile. The farm, which was later moved to Inglewood, CA, contained about 1,300 animals.

1075. Radio broadcast of a livestock auction took place at the International Livestock Exposition, Chicago, IL, on December 18, 1924. The auction, which sold pigs, sheep, lamb, and cattle, was broadcast by WLS, Chicago, IL, on 345-meter wavelength.

AGRICULTURE—LIVESTOCK—CATTLE

1076. Cattle to be imported were brought over form Dover, England, in March 1624 by Edward Winslow, governor of the Plymouth Colony in Massachusetts. Cows were raised principally for their hides; secondly, for meat; and only very incidentally for their milk.

1077. Cattle to be exported were 16 steers shipped from Savannah, GA, in 1755. It is possible that prior shipments were made, but there is no record of them.

1078. Cattle fair was held on October 1, 1810, in Pittsfield, MA. It was promoted by Elkanah Watson and was known as the Berkshire Cattle Show. There were 383 sheep, 20 bulls, and 15 yoke of oxen entered for premiums amounting to $70. After the fair, there was a grand procession a half mile long of 60 yoke of prime oxen.

1079. Cattle of the Guernsey breed were imported in 1831, when one bull and two heifers arrived at Boston, MA. They were taken to the farm of General Moody Adams Pillsbury at Guernsey Island, Lake Winnepesaukee, NH.

1080. Cattle that were purebred shorthorns were imported by the Ohio Company for Importing English Cattle, which was organized in Chillicothe, OH, on November 2, 1833. To further purebred strains, the society sent Felix Renick to England, where he purchased seven bulls and 12 cows on May 20, 1834. They were shipped to Philadelphia, PA, and driven overland to Chillicothe, OH, where they arrived in June 1834. Two years later, on October 29, 1836, Renick's Indian Creek Farm held the first public auction sale of purebread shorthorns, selling 43 head of cattle for $34,540, an average of $803 apiece.

1081. Cattle of the Aberdeen-Angus breed were brought to the United States in 1873 by George Grant of Victoria, KS, who imported four bulls, two of which were exhibited the same year at Kansas City, MO. The bulls, imported from Scotland, were crossed with native longhorn Texas cattle.

1082. Cattle of the Afrikaaner breed were imported on December 11, 1931, when 16 bulls and 13 cows and heifers arrived in New York City from Capetown, South Africa. They were held in quarantine until March 9, 1932, at the Department of Agriculture's Animal Quarantine Station, Clifton, NJ. William Henry Black, in charge of Beef Cattle Investigations, Bureau of Animal Industry, selected the cattle and had complete supervision until their arrival at their final destination, King Ranch, Kingsville, TX, on March 14, 1932.

1083. Artificial animal breeding cooperative organization was Breeding Unit No. 1 of the New Jersey Holstein-Friesian Cooperative Association, organized on May 16, 1938, in Hunterdon, Somerset, and Warren Counties, NJ. Dr. James Arnold Henderson was in charge. The original membership consisted of 102 dairymen, who entered 1,050 Holstein cows.

AGRICULTURE—LIVESTOCK—SHEEP

1084. Sheep were imported into America in 1609, when the London Company brought over a shipment to Jamestown, VA.

1085. Sheep of the Merino breed were imported in 1802 by Colonel David Humphreys, United States Minister to Spain, who shipped 100 of them from Lisbon, Portugal, to Derby, CT. In 1809 they were valued at $1,500 each. It is also recorded that in 1793 three merino sheep were smuggled in by William Foster, but they were eaten.

1086. Sheep of the Karakul breed were imported in 1908 from Russia on the S.S. *Esthonia.* The shipment consisted of five rams and 10 ewes. After arriving in New York City, they were placed in quarantine at Athenia, NJ, before being shipped to the ranch of Dr. C.C. Young at Holliday, TX.

AGRICULTURE—ORGANIZATIONS

1087. Agriculture society was the Philadelphia Society for the Promotion of Agriculture, which was organized on March 1, 1785. Meetings were scheduled every two months. Earlier, in 1781, the New Jersey Society for Promoting Agriculture, Commerce and Arts had undertaken the promotion of agriculture as one of its functions.

1088. Horticultural society was the New York Horticultural Society, founded in 1818. It existed about 15 years. The first permanent organization was the Pennsylvania Horticultural Society, organized on November 24, 1827, in Philadelphia, PA, with a membership of 53. Horace Binney was the first president. The first exhibition open to the public was held on June 6, 1829.

1089. Agriculture organization (national) was the National Grange of the Patrons of Husbandry, which was organized in Washington, DC, December 4, 1867, with William Saunders of the Department of Agriculture as master and Oliver Hudson Kelley, a native of Boston, MA, as secretary. This was the first important cooperation undertaken by farmers. The movements and meetings of the society were carried on in secret.

1090. Cattle club to promote Jersey cattle was the American Jersey Cattle Club, formed on July 1868, at Newport, RI, by 43 dairymen who signed a tentative constitution. The first annual meeting was held on April 5, 1869, at the Astor House, New York City. The group's object was to record and perpetuate the breed of Jersey cattle. The first president was Samuel J. Sharpless of Philadelphia, PA.

1091. Dairy association (state) was the Vermont Dairymen's Association, organized on October 27, 1869, at Montpelier, VT.

1092. Cattle club to promote Guernsey cattle was the American Guernsey Cattle Club, formed on March 1, 1876, at the home of Augustus Ward, Farmington, CT. A permanent organization was effected on February 7, 1877, when 11 men from five states met in New York City. The first annual meeting was held on December 19, 1877.

AMERICANA

1093. Letter containing a description of America was probably written by the explorer Christopher Columbus, who sailed on August 3, 1492, from the harbor of Palos, Spain, with three small caravels and about 90 men, and returned 224 days later, on March 14, 1493, to Lisbon, Portugal. From Lisbon, he dispatched two letters of identical content, one to Raphael Sanchez and the other to Luis de Santangel.

1094. Use of "America" as a geographical designation was made by the German mapmaker Martin H. Waldseemüller, also called Ilacomilus or Hylacomylus, in his book *Cosmographiae Introductio,* published in April 1507 at St. Dié in the Vosges Mountains of Alsace. The book contained an account by the Italian explorer Amerigo Vespucci of his discoveries in South America. Waldseemüller coined the name in his honor.

1095. Letters written in English in America are claimed to be the four letters of Ralph Lane, the first commander of Raleigh's first colony at Roanoke Island, NC. The letters were written on August 12, 1585, from Porte Ferdynando. They were not published until 1860.

1096. Document known to have been printed in America was the "Oath of a Free Man," printed in March 1639 by the Stephen Day Press, Cambridge, MA. It was a one-page sheet that read: "I doe solemnly bind myself in the sight of God, that when I shall be called to give my voice touching any subject of this State, in which Freemen are to deal, I will give my vote and suffrage as I shall judge in mine own conscience may best conduce and tend to the publick weal of the body, without respect of persons, or favour of any man."

1097. Use of the name United States instead of United Colonies was authorized on September 9, 1776, by the Second Continental Congress: "That in all continental commissions and other instruments where heretofore the words, 'United Colonies' have been used, the style be altered, for the future, to the 'United States.'"

AMERICANA—*continued*

The colonies were first definitely proclaimed to be united in a resolution adopted by the Second Continental Congress on June 7, 1775: "On motion, resolved, that Thursday, the 20th of July next, be observed throughout the Twelve United Colonies as a day of humiliation, fasting and prayer." Only 12 of the 13 colonies were represented because Georgia did not send delegates to the First and Second Continental Congresses.

1098. Use of "American" as an adjective instead of "United States" was officially recommended by John Hay, secretary of state, who instructed American diplomatic and consular officers under date of August 3, 1904, to adopt it. The adjective form of designation is not used in strictly formal documents and in notarial acts performed by consular officers; instead, the full name of the country is given, as, for example: Government of the United States of America, Embassy of the United States of America.

AMERICANA—DOCUMENTS—CONSTITUTION

1099. Constitution to declare that "the foundation of authority is in the free consent of the people" was the first constitution of colonial Connecticut, known as the "fundamental orders," drawn up by Roger Ludlow and adopted on January 14, 1639, in Hartford, CT, by representatives of Wethersfield, Windsor, and Hartford. Ludlow was influenced by a sermon delivered May 31, 1638, by the Reverend Thomas Hooker at Hartford's Center Church.

1100. Written constitution adopted by a community of American-born freemen is known as the "Articles of the Watauga Association." It was written in May 1772 by colonists from North Carolina and Tennessee who formed an independent civil government called the Watauga Commonwealth.

1101. Constitution adopted by a state was that of Massachusetts, adopted on May 16, 1775, by the Provincial Congress of Massachusetts. The motto of the state was *Ense petit placidam sub libertate quietem* ("with the sword she seeks peace under liberty"). The constitution was temporary. A new one was framed in Boston on September 1, 1779, and was completed on March 2, 1780, and ratified by a two-thirds vote. John Hancock served as the first governor under the permanent constitution.

1102. Articles of Confederation were adopted on November 15, 1777, and were formally engrossed on July 9, 1778, in Philadelphia, PA. South Carolina was the first of the 13 states to ratify them, on February 5, 1778, and Maryland was the last, on January 30, 1781. The articles were formally announced to the public on March 1, 1781.

1103. Printed copies of the Constitution were printed from plates engraved by Jacob Shallus, assistant clerk of the Pennsylvania Assembly, who received $30 for the work. Sixty proof sheets were printed August 1–3, 1787, and laid before the Constitutional Convention on August 6.

1104. Constitution of the United States was signed at the conclusion of the Constitutional Convention, which met at Philadelphia, PA, from May 25, 1787, to September 17. Of the original 55 delegates, only 41 remained to the conclusion, and three of them refused to sign. It was agreed that the Constitution would become binding on the 13 former colonies when it was ratified by nine states. This took place on June 21, 1788, when the legislature of New Hampshire approved ratification by a 57-47 vote. The Constitution was declared to be in effect on March 4, 1789.

1105. Newspaper to publish the Constitution was the *Pennsylvania Packet and Daily Advertiser,* Philadelphia, PA, published by John Dunlap and David C. Claypoole. The text of the Constitution was published in the issue dated September 19, 1787.

1106. State to ratify the federal Constitution was Delaware, on December 6, 1787. The constitution was ratified on December 6 and signed on December 7 by all 30 members of the Constitutional Convention. Thomas Collins, who was president of Delaware at that time, automatically became the first state governor.

1107. Constitutional amendments were drawn up by James Madison and were declared in force on December 15, 1791, having been passed by both houses of Congress and ratified by the required number of states. These 10 amendments are collectively known as the Bill of Rights. The first of them established religious freedom, freedom of speech and press, the right to assemble, and the right to petition the government. The amendments were submitted to the states by the First Congress on September 25, 1789. The first state to ratify was New Jersey, which acted on November 20,

1789. Originally 12 amendments were passed by both houses, but two of them—on the proportionment of representatives and on compensation—failed to secure the requisite number of state ratifications.

1108. Constitutional amendment proposal to bear the signature of a president was an amendment that would have prevented Congress from banning or regulating slavery in the states. It was signed by President Abraham Lincoln on March 2, 1861, in the hope of averting a civil war. It read: "No amendment shall be made to the Consitution which will authorize or give to Congress, the power to abolish or interfere, within any State, with the domestic institutions thereof, including that of persons held to labor or service by the laws of said State." The proposal was not ratified.

1109. Constitutional amendment submitted to the states for repeal was the 18th Amendment, also known as the Prohibition Amendment, which had banned alcoholic drinks. The amendment became law on January 16, 1920, after it was ratified by 36 states. It prohibited the manufacture, sale, or transportation of intoxicating liquors within the United States. A bill to repeal the amendment was passed in the Senate by a 63–23 vote on February 16, 1933, and in the House by a 289–121 vote on February 20. The 72nd Congress then offered it as a proposal to state constitutional conventions. The first state to ratify was Michigan, on April 10, 1933. It was followed by 35 others, and the 21st Amendment, repealing the 18th Amendment, was declared ratified on December 5, 1933.

AMERICANA—DOCUMENTS—DECLARATION OF INDEPENDENCE

1110. Declaration of independence by citizens of an American colony was formally made on July 12, 1774, in the First Presbyterian Church in Carlisle, PA, at a meeting of freeholders and freemen from the several townships. The Reverend John Montgomery presided. A similar statement was the Mecklenburg Declaration of Independence, adopted by local citizens on May 20, 1775, in Charlotte, Mecklenburg County, NC.

1111. Declaration of rights was passed by the First Continental Congress in Philadelphia, PA, on October 14, 1774, and was known as the "Declaration and Resolves of the First Continental Congress." It stated that the the colonists "are entitled to life, liberty and property; and they have never ceded to any foreign power whatsoever a right to dispose of either without their consent."

1112. Declaration of independence by a colonial government was made on April 12, 1776, when the Provincial Congress in session at Halifax, NC, by unanimous action empowered the delegates to the Continental Congress to concur with delegates of other provinces in declaring independence from Great Britain.

1113. Signer of the Declaration of Independence was John Hancock of Massachusetts, president of the Continental Congress, who signed it on July 4, 1776, in Philadelphia, PA. It was also signed on that date by secretary Charles Thomson, who was not a delegate. The parchment copy was signed by the delegates on August 2, 1776.

1114. Printing of the Declaration of Independence was done on July 5, 1776, in Philadelphia, PA, by John Dunlop in a folio broadside and distributed the same day. On July 4, Congress, acting as a Committee of the Whole, approved the Declaration and ordered that it be printed and that copies be "sent to the several assemblies, conventions and committees or counsels of safety and to the several commanding officers of the Continental troops that it be proclaimed in each of the United States and at the head of the army."

1115. Newspaper to publish the Declaration of Independence was the *Pennsylvania Evening Post* of Philadelphia, PA, which printed the text in its edition of July 6, 1776.

1116. Public reading of the Declaration of Independence took place on July 8, 1776, when Colonel John Nixon, delegated by the high sheriff of Philadelphia, read it in the old State House yard (now Independence Square). The "Liberty Bell," which bore the biblical inscription "Proclaim liberty throughout all the land unto all the inhabitants thereof," was rung to call the citizens together to hear the reading.

AMERICANA—FLAG

1117. American flag saluted by a foreigner was the Continental Union flag flown by the brig *Andrea Doria* at St. Eustatius, Dutch West Indies, on November 16, 1776. It was saluted by Johannes de Graeff, governor of the colony. The brig was captained by Nicholas Biddle, who had been sent to St. Eustatius to transport arms and ammunition for the American army.

1118. American flag to represent the United States was formally adopted as the National Standard by Congress on June 14, 1777. Except for the adding of a new star for each new state and changes in the arrangement of the stars, the flag displayed today is the same as the first flag. Claims have been made that the first flag

AMERICANA—FLAG—*continued*

was made by Betsy Ross (Elizabeth Griscom Ross) in her little shop at 239 Arch Street, Philadelphia, PA, at the request of George Washington, Robert Morris, and Colonel George Ross, for the Continental Congress.

1119. American flag displayed on a man-of-war was flown in Portsmouth Harbor, NH, when a group of young women presented to Captain John Paul Jones a flag they had made, using cloth taken from their own and their mothers' gowns. Captain Jones raised it to the mast of his ship, the *Ranger,* on July 4, 1777.

1120. American flag flown in battle was carried on September 3, 1777, by a detachment of light infantry and cavalry under General William Maxwell at Cooch's Bridge, DE, where they met an advance guard of British and Hessian troops under Generals Richard Howe, Charles Cornwallis, and Wilhelm von Knyphausen.

1121. American flag on the high seas was carried by Captain Thomas Thompson of the American sloop *Raleigh,* who, on September 4, 1777, was engaged in an encounter with a British vessel.

1122. American flag saluted by a foreign nation was flown from the top mast of the *Ranger,* under the command of Captain John Paul Jones. The *Ranger* sailed for France on November 1, 1777, with dispatches announcing the surrender of British general John Burgoyne. On February 14, 1778, the *Ranger* saluted the French flag in the harbor of Quiberon, France, with 13 guns. The salute was returned by Admiral La Motte Piquet with nine guns.

1123. Ship to carry the American flag around the world was the *Columbia,* a 212-ton vessel under Captain Kendrick that sailed from Boston, MA, on September 30, 1787, on a fur-trading mission to Canada. It was accompanied by the sloop *Washington,* under Captain Robert Gray, who exchanged commands with Captain Kendrick and completed the trip, returning to Boston on August 9, 1790. The trip took nearly three years and covered a distance of 41,899 miles. The crew explored the Queen Charlotte Islands and discovered the straits of Juan de Fuca and the mouth of the Columbia River.

1124. Changes in the American flag to be authorized by Congress were passed by Congress on January 13, 1794, an "act making an alteration in the flag of the United States" and providing "that from and after the first day of May 1795, the Flag of the United States be fifteen stripes, alternate red and white; and that

the union be fifteen stars, white, in a blue field." The change was made so that Vermont and Kentucky would be represented on the flag. A law passed on April 4, 1818, reduced the number of stripes to 13 to represent the original 13 states, as in the first American flag, and provided one star for each state. A new star was to be added on the Fourth of July following the admission of each new state.

1125. American flag flown over a fortress of the Old World was flown on April 27, 1805, when Lieutenant Presley Neville O'Bannon of the Marines raised the colors over the Tripolitan fortress at Darna, on the north coast of Africa (now in Libya).

1126. American flag flown over a schoolhouse was flown in May 1812 over the log schoolhouse at Catamount Hill, Colrain, MA. It was cut and made by Rhoda Shippee, Mrs. Lois Shippee, Mrs. Sophia Willis, and Mrs. Stephen Hale at the home of Captain Amasa Shippee, who instructed the women in the arrangement of the stars and stripes.

1127. Naval vessel to display the American flag around Cape Horn was the *Essex,* a frigate commanded by Captain David Porter, which left the Delaware capes on October 27, 1812, with a crew of 287 and 32 marines, and arrived at Valparaiso, Chile, on March 14, 1813. The ship had been launched on September 30, 1799, by Enos Briggs, Salem, MA. The flag was presented to the United States and accepted by Captain Edward Preble on December 17, 1799. It was sold at public auction on June 6, 1837.

1128. Battle flag was that of the Confederate Army, adopted on March 4, 1861, by the Confederate Convention in Montgomery, AL. It set a blue St. Andrew's Cross and 13 stars against a red field. The battle flag was adopted after the Battle of Bull Run (July 16–21, 1861), in which soldiers were confused by the similarities between the Confederate flag, which consisted of seven stars and three stripes, and the stars and stripes of the Union flag.

1129. American flag made of American bunting to fly over the Capitol in Washington, DC, was hoisted on February 24, 1866. It was 21 feet by 12 feet and was made by the United States Bunting Company, Lowell, MA. It was presented to the Senate by the company.

1130. American flag displayed from the right hand of the Statue of Liberty in honor of an individual was flown on June 13, 1927, designated as Lindbergh Day, in honor of Charles Augustus Lindbergh's transatlantic solo flight. The flag was hoisted to the peak of the right arm of the Statue of Liberty in unison with the raising of the Post Flag and the discharge of the Morning Gun at Governors Island, and was lowered in unison with Post Retreat ceremonies.

1131. American flag to orbit the earth was carried in the capsule of the satellite *Discoverer 8,* which was launched on August 10, 1960, by the Air Force at Vandenberg Air Force Base, CA. A 300-pound reentry capsule was ejected on August 11, 1960, on the 17th orbit and was recovered the same day by the U.S.S. *Haiti Victory,* whose frogmen used a helicopter. The flag was presented to President Dwight David Eisenhower on August 15, 1960. The orbital time of the satellite was 94.1 minutes; its perigee was 161 miles, its apogee 436 miles.

AMERICANA—SEAL

1132. Design for the Great Seal of the United States was suggested by Benjamin Franklin, Thomas Jefferson, and John Adams in 1776, and showed the Jews escaping from the pursuing Egyptian army across the divided Sea of Reeds. The motto, taken from the biblical Book of Maccabees, read: "Rebellion to tyrants is obedience to God." The design that was ultimately accepted for the federal seal was made by William Barton and adopted on June 20, 1782. It shows a spread eagle, bearing on its breast a shield with 13 red and white stripes, with an olive branch in its right talon and 13 arrows in its left. In its beak is a ribbon bearing the legend *E pluribus unum* ("from many, one"). Over the head of the eagle is a golden light breaking through a cloud surrounding 13 stars that form a constellation on a blue field.

1133. Impression made by the Great Seal of the United States was made on September 16, 1782, on the upper left corner of a document authorizing General George Washington to negotiate and sign an agreement with the British for the exchange, subsistence, and better treatment of prisoners of war. The document bore the signatures of John Hanson, president of the Continental Congress, and Charles Thomson, secretary.

ANIMALS

1134. Cat domestically bred in America was probably the American shorthair cat. It is believed to descend from cats brought to the New World by the early European explorers.

1135. Wolf bounty was granted under authority of the General Assembly held at James City, VA, on October 5, 1646. It was signed by Sir William Berkeley, Knight Governor, and provided that "what person soever shall after publication hereof kill a wolfe and bring in the head to any commissioner, upon certificate of said communication to the county court, he or they shall receive one hundred pounds of tobacco for so doing to be raised out of the County where the wolfe is killed."

1136. Lion was exhibited on November 26, 1716, in Boston, MA, by Captain Arthur Savage. A notice in a Boston newspaper invited the public to Savage's house on Brattle Street, "where is to be shewn by William Nichols, a Lyon of Barbary, with many other rarities, the like never before in America."

1137. Camel was an "African camel ... 7 feet high and 12 feet long," exhibited in Boston, MA, and advertised in the *Boston Gazette* of October 2, 1721.

1138. Polar bear was Ursa Major, a nine-month-old cub caught in Davis Strait, on the western coast of Greenland, which was exhibited on January 18, 1733, at Clark's Wharf, North End of Boston, MA. It was brought by Captain Atkins from Greenland and kept in a large cage. It was shipped to London on February 27, 1734.

1139. Monkey trained to perform was "a creature called a Japanese, of about two feet high, his body resembling a human body in all parts except the feet and tail," exhibited on February 25, 1751, at the house of Edward Willet, New York City. Admission of a shilling was charged for the performance, in which the monkey walked a tightrope, exercised a gun, and danced.

1140. Rat of record was observed in Boston, MA, in 1775. It was a rat of the common European domestic variety (*Rattus norvegicus*), also called the brown rat or Norway rat.

1141. Mule born in the United States was bred from a jackass sent to President George Washington. The exportation of full-blooded jacks from Spain was prohibited, but King Charles III of Spain, learning of Washington's interest, sent him two jacks and two jennets, which arrived in Boston, MA, on October 26, 1785.

ANIMALS—*continued*

1142. Elephant arrived in New York City on the *America* on April 13, 1796, from Bengal, India. She was two years old, 6.5 feet high, and was exhibited by Jacob Crowninshield at the corner of Beaver Street and Broadway. The elephant's habits were described as follows: "It eats thirty pounds of rice besides hay and straw—drinks all kinds of wine and spirituous liquors, and eats every sort of vegetable; it will also draw a cork from a bottle with its trunk."

1143. Leopard was exhibited on February 2, 1802, by Othello Pollard, near the Columbian Museum, Boston, MA. An admission fee of 25 cents was charged to see the "import from Bengal."

1144. Rhinoceros was exhibited on September 13, 1826, at Peale's Museum and Gallery of the Fine Arts, New York City. Advertisements stated that "its body and limbs are covered with a skin so hard and impervious that he fears neither the claws of the tiger nor the proboscis of the elephant; it will turn the edge of a scimitar and even resist the force of a musket ball." The exhibit, scheduled to close on October 13, was extended to November 25.

1145. Camels imported for military purposes were landed on May 14, 1856, at Indianola, TX. Lieutenant David Dixon Porter of Chester, PA, brought them from Izmir, Turkey, on the *Supply,* a Navy storeship. The shipment consisted of 34 camels—one more than left Smyrna. On March 3, 1855, Congress had appropriated $30,000 to the War Department for the purchase and importation of camels and dromedaries to be employed for military purposes.

1146. Camel race took place on April 7, 1864, at Agricultural Park, Sacramento, CA. The proceeds obtained from the sale of tickets were used to aid the poor.

1147. Cat show was held at Madison Square Garden, New York City, on May 8–11, 1895. Over 200 cats were exhibited in cages. The owners could take their cats home overnight upon payment of a $5 bond guaranteeing they would be brought back the following day. Prizes and money were awarded for each class—for example, the best litter of kittens, the best homeless cat.

1148. Pronghorn antelope bred and reared in captivity was born in the City Park Zoo, Denver, CO, in 1903. The event was noted by Theodore Roosevelt, who congratulated the zoo director, Alfred Hill.

1149. Platypus was publicly exhibited on July 15, 1922, at the Bronx Zoo, New York City. It arrived at San Francisco, CA, from Australia.

1150. Musk ox born in captivity was a calf born on September 5, 1925, at the Bronx Zoo, New York City.

1151. Frog-jumping jubilee was held at Angels Camp, Calaveras County, CA, on May 19–20, 1928, in commemoration of Mark Twain's famous story, "The Celebrated Jumping Frog of Calaveras County." Fifty-one frogs were entered in the contest. "The Pride of San Joaquin," a frog owned by Louis R. Fischer of Stockton, CA, was the winner with a jump of 3 feet 4 inches.

1152. Reindeer born in the United States was a jet-black calf born on May 31, 1929, at Lodgepole Ranch, the estate of Otis Emerson Dunham at North Beverly, MA.

1153. Cow flown in an airplane was Elm Farm Ollie, a Guernsey, who went aloft on February 18, 1930, with a corps of reporters. She was milked during the flight and the milk was sealed in paper containers and parachuted over St. Louis, MO.

1154. Giant panda was Su-Lin, imported from China by Mrs. William H. Harkness, Jr., on the *President McKinley.* It weighed about five pounds when it arrived at San Francisco, CA, December 18, 1936. Su-Lin died on April 1, 1938, in the Brookfield Zoo, Chicago, IL, which had purchased it for $8,750.44. Giant pandas, though bearlike in appearance, are related to raccoons. They were first discovered in China in November 1936.

1155. Okapi was imported on August 4, 1937, when it arrived at New York City. It was 21 months old, weighed 235 pounds, and was 49 inches tall at the shoulder. It resembled a cross between a zebra and a giraffe, and had a mahogany-red body with white stripes on its buttocks and upper legs. It consumed eight bananas, four heads of cabbage, three bunches of carrots, and six liters of condensed milk and water daily. It was captured in the Belgian Congo and shipped on July 22, 1937, on the Red Star liner *Pennland,* under the personal care of Dr. William Reid Blair, director of the Bronx Zoo, New York City, to which it was delivered.

1156. Porpoise born in captivity was born dead on February 14, 1940, at Marineland, FL.

1157. King cobra snakes born in captivity in the United States were hatched on July 4, 1955, at the Bronx Zoo, New York City. The parent snakes were mated on March 10, 1955, and on April 25, the female snake laid 41 eggs. Nine eggs hatched, the first on July 4 and the last on July 12. The infant cobras were mottled white and brown and felt leathery to the touch.

1158. Dugong arrived at the Steinhart Aquarium, San Francisco, CA, on November 16, 1955, and was on display until December 27, 1955, when it died. The dugong is a sea mammal similar to a manatee.

1159. Gorilla born in captivity in the United States was Colo, born on December 22, 1956, at the zoo in Columbus, OH. She weighed 3.25 pounds and was the offspring of Baron (11 years old, 380 pounds) and Christiana (9 years old, 260 pounds).

1160. Gerenuk born in the United States was born on September 30, 1963, at the Bronx Zoo in New York City. The gerenuk (*Litocranius walleri*) is a reddish-brown gazelle-like antelope indigenous to eastern Africa.

1161. Orca born in captivity was a six-foot, 125-pound calf born on February 28, 1977, at Marineland, Los Angeles, CA. She was the offspring of Cork, a 16-year-old, 11-ton orca. Orcas are also known as killer whales.

1162. Zebra mussels were accidentally introduced from Europe in the mid-1980s. The first specimen of the prolific shellfish (*Dreissena polymorpha*) was identified in 1988 in Lake St. Clair, near Detroit, MI. The mussels quickly spread through Lake Erie into Lake Ontario and connected bodies of water, replacing native species and causing damage to underwater structures and marine equipment.

1163. Killer bees entered the United States from Mexico in October 1990. More properly called Africanized honeybees, the aggressive species, a hybrid of European honeybees and African honeybees, had been migrating north since their origin in Brazil in 1956. By the 1990s, they had caused more than 1,000 human deaths.

ANIMALS—BIRDS

1164. Sparrows were imported in 1850 under the auspices of Nicholas Pike and other directors of the Brooklyn Institute, Brooklyn, NY (now part of New York City), for the purpose of protecting shade trees from foliage-eating caterpillars. Eight pairs of English, or house, sparrows (*Passer domesticus*) were imported. The birds were kept in cages until liberated in the spring of 1851. They did not thrive, and in 1852 a larger number were imported.

1165. Bird for which a definite crossing of the Atlantic was recorded was a common tern (*Sterna hirundo*) that was banded at Eastern Egg Rock, ME, on July 3, 1913, and found dead in August 1917 at the mouth of the Niger River, West Africa.

1166. Ptarmigan hatched and reared in captivity was hatched on July 24, 1934, at Ithaca, NY, from one of 10 eggs obtained from Churchill, Manitoba, Canada, by Arthur Augustus Allen, professor of ornithology, Cornell University, Ithaca, NY. The ptarmigan was 110 days old when it died of enterohepatitis.

1167. Snow goose bred in captivity was hatched in 1934 in the City Park Zoo, Denver, CO.

1168. Quetzal bird (*Pharomacrus costaricensis*) was imported on October 4, 1940, by Dr. Victor Wolfgang Von Hagen, New York City, who had captured it. It was exhibited at the Bronx Zoo, New York City, for three days before being acquired by the St. Louis Zoo, St. Louis, MO. It was a male, three years old, pigeon-sized, with a crimson breast, emerald back and head, jet black wings, a black-and-white tail, and a green train about a yard long. On October 29, 1937, Von Hagen had brought back nine young quetzals, which were shown at the Bronx Zoo until April 1939, when the last one died.

1169. Whooping crane born in captivity was Dawn, a six-inch-tall crane born on May 28, 1975, at the Rare and Endangered Bird Research Center, Laurel, MD.

ANIMALS—DOGS

1170. Dog domestically bred was the American foxhound. All dogs of this breed descend from a pack of foxhounds imported from England by Robert Brooke, who settled in Maryland in 1650. The dogs were later crossed with other hound breeds from England, Ireland, and France.

1171. Dog show of importance was held at the Hippodrome (Gilmore's Garden), 26th Street and Madison Avenue, New York City, on May 8, 1877, under the auspices of the Westminster Kennel Bench Show of Dogs. Charles Lincoln was superintendent of this show, at which there were 1,191 entries.

1172. Dog license law enacted by a state was "an act for the better protection of lost and strayed animals and for securing the rights of the owners thereof," passed on March 8, 1894, by New York. It authorized the American Society for the Prevention of Cruelty to Animals to carry out the provisions of the law and collect a $2 annual fee for dogs in cities with populations over 1.2 million. Unlicensed dogs were to be destroyed if not redeemed within 48 hours.

ANIMALS—DOGS—*continued*

1173. Dogs trained to guide the blind in the United States were taught at The Seeing Eye, Nashville, TN, in 1928. The Seeing Eye was incorporated as a nonprofit association on January 9, 1929. Mrs. Harrison Eustis was the first president. The organization moved to Morristown, NJ, in May 1929. Buddy, the first Seeing Eye dog to guide a blind person in this country, was a shepherd dog brought over from Vevey, Switzerland, in June 1928 by Morris S. Frank.

ANIMALS—HORSES

1174. Horses arrived with the Spanish conquerors in the 16th century. The first horses in the English colonies were imported in April 1629 by the Massachusetts Bay Colony. The agreement made by Matthewe Cradock, first governor of the company, required that "such cattle, both horses, mares, cowes, bulls, and goates, as are shipped by Mr. Cradock, are to bee devyded in equall halfes twixt him & the Companie."

1175. Horse that was a thoroughbred is claimed to have been Bulle Rock, who was imported into Virginia in 1730. He was foaled in 1717 and was a son of Darley Arabian and the mare Byerly Turk. Another horse for which the same claim has been made was Spark, who was presented to Lord Baltimore by the Prince of Wales, the father of George III. Lord Baltimore gave Spark to Governor Samuel Ogle of Maryland about 1750.

1176. Morgan horse was named after its owner, Justin Morgan. It was foaled in 1789 in Randolph, VT, and got by True Briton, also known as Beautiful Bay. It died in 1821.

1177. Trotting horse was Messenger, a gray horse 15 hands 3 inches high, foaled in 1780. He was imported from England and arrived in Philadelphia, PA, in May 1788. He was buried with military honors on January 28, 1808.

1178. Horseshoe manufacturing machine was patented on November 23, 1835, by Henry Burden of Troy, NY, who received subsequent patents in 1843, 1857, and 1862. His machine produced a completed horseshoe from a rod of iron that was fed into it. It produced shoes more rapidly and uniformly than the traditional method of hand production on a forge.

1179. Percheron horse importation was attempted by Edward Harris of Moorestown, NJ, in 1839. Four horses were obtained from France, but only one, a mare, survived the trip. Two stallions and two mares were subsequently imported. One of the stallions, Diligence, was credited with 400 foals.

1180. Horse show was the Upperville Colt and Horse Show, Upperville, VA, established in 1853 by Colonel Richard Hunter Dulany. Shows were held annually in June until the Civil War. The first show after the war was held on November 10, 1869.

1181. Horse show of national scope was held at Madison Square Garden, New York City, October 22–26, 1883, by the National Horse Show Association of America. There were 187 exhibitors with 623 entries. Cornelius Fellowes was the first president of the association.

1182. Horse farm operated by the federal government was the United States Morgan Horse Farm, Middlebury, VT, established in 1907 on 400 acres donated by Colonel Joseph Battell of Middlebury. The first 270 acres of land were deeded to the United States by Battell on February 1, 1907. Horse breeding under the Bureau of Animal Industry began in December 1904 as a cooperative enterprise with the Colorado Experiment Station to develop an American utility horse.

1183. Transcontinental solo trip on horseback by a woman was made by Nan Jane Aspinwall, who left San Francisco, CA, on September 1, 1910, carrying a letter from Mayor Patrick Henry McCarthy to Mayor William Jay Gaynor of New York City. She covered 4,500 miles in 301 days, 108 of which were spent traveling. She arrived in New York City on July 8, 1911.

1184. Forest horse born in the United States was Pepin, sired by Charlemagne and foaled by Siegling on May 18, 1956, at the Chicago Zoological Park, Brookfield, IL. This extinct forest breed had been re-created by a program of crossbreeding that involved more than 300 Iceland ponies, Shetland ponies, Dartmoor ponies, Norwegian duns, Hanover coach horses, feral horses from Patagonia, and Koniks of Poland. Forest horses were first imported into the United States in 1955.

1185. Haflinger horse was imported by Tempel Smith of Spring Grove, IL, who imported 17 horses, including 10 mares, three stallions, two fillies, and two colts, on August 18, 1958. They arrived in New York Harbor from Austria. The Haflinger is compactly built, longer than it is tall, with a height of 140 to 150 centimeters at the withers.

ANIMALS—ZOOS AND AQUARIUMS

1186. Zoo was the Philadelphia Zoological Garden, Philadelphia, PA, which was under the management of the Zoological Society of Philadelphia. The garden was opened to the public on July 1, 1874. Feature attractions were the bear pit and the lion house.

1187. Aquarium with an inland saltwater environment was installed by Marshall McDonald in Chicago, IL, for the 1893 World's Columbian Exposition. Medals were conferred upon him by Belgium, Britain, France, Germany, and Russia for his efforts to increase and better the hatching and propagation of fish.

1188. Zoo habitat constructed of simulated rock formations without bars was started in 1915 at the City Park Zoo, Denver, CO, and was completed in 1918 at a cost of $60,000. Colored concrete and steel were used to simulate a mountain habitat. The floors of the enclosures were on ground level or above the outside walkway. The area was designed and supervised by Victor Borcherdt, the director of the zoo.

1189. Radio broadcast from a zoo took place at 3:30 P.M. on April 21, 1930, from the Bronx Zoo, New York City. Dr. Claude Willard Leister, curator of educational activities, was master of ceremonies. The program was broadcast by National Broadcasting Company radio station WEAF, New York City.

1190. Aquarium for large marine animals was Marineland, 18 miles south of St. Augustine, FL, built at an approximate cost of $500,000. Ground was broken on May 15, 1937, and the dedication and formal opening took place on June 23, 1938. The marine studios consisted of two adjacent open-air steel and concrete tanks (one rectangular, 100 feet by 40 feet, and 18 feet deep; the other circular, 75 feet in diameter and 11 feet deep) with 200 portholes.

1191. Zoo with twilight conditions was dedicated on April 3, 1973, in Highland Park, Pittsburgh, PA, by the Pittsburgh Zoological Society. The zoo contained six ecological niches depicting nocturnal and diurnal scenes from various regions around the world. The same degree of lighting prevailed both day and night.

ARTS—ARCHITECTURE

1192. Landscape architect was John Reid, gardener to Sir George Mackenzie of Rosebaugh, lord advocate under Charles II. Reid left Aberdeen, Scotland, on August 28, 1683, on the *Exchange,* accompanied by his wife and three daughters, and landed at Staten Island, NY (now part of New York City), on December 19, 1683.

1193. Architect and engineer who worked professionally was Benjamin Henry Latrobe, born on May 1, 1764, near Leeds, England. After studying architecture in London, he left for America in 1795 and went into private practice in Virginia in 1796. Among his early projects was the design of Philadelphia's first water system. He is also credited with introducing to America the Gothic and Greek Revival styles of architecture. Latrobe is best known for his work on the Capitol Building in Washington, DC. His designs include the Hall of the House (now Statuary Hall), the Old Senate Chamber, and the Old Supreme Court Chamber.

1194. Architect who was a woman was Louise Blanchard Bethune, who opened an independent office in 1881 in Buffalo, NY. She was the first woman member of the American Institute of Architects, elected to full membership on September 15, 1890. The first woman to receive an architectural patent was Harriet Morrison Irwin, sister-in-law of General Stonewall Jackson, who in 1869 patented her design for a two-story hexagonal house, with all rooms connected by an airy central hallway. The house was built on West Fifth Street in Charlotte, NC.

ARTS—ART—ARTISTS

1195. Artist to come to America was Jacques Le Moyne de Morgues, a cartographer attached to the French Huguenot expedition to Florida under René Goulaine de Laudonnière. They sailed from Havre de Grace, France, on April 20, 1564, and reached Florida (then called New France) on June 22, remaining until September 20, 1565, when the Spanish destroyed their settlement and killed its inhabitants. Le Moyne's work consisted principally of scenic and historical views.

1196. Artist in the English colonies was the English painter and cartographer John White, who came to North Carolina in 1585 as part of Sir Walter Raleigh's expedition. He recorded Native American life in his paintings and made maps of the coast as far south as Florida. He returned in 1587 as governor of Raleigh's Roanoke colony, which disappeared while White

ARTS—ART—ARTISTS—*continued*

was back in England getting supplies. Among the vanished colonists was Virginia Dare, the first child of European descent known to have been born in America, who was White's grandchild.

1197. Pastelist was Henrietta Johnston of Charlestown, SC, who was active between 1707 and 1720. She worked with colored chalk. Her subjects were principally colonial women of South Carolina. Her most celebrated piece of work, done in 1718, was a portrait entitled *His Excellency Robert Johnson Captain General, Governor and Commander-in-Chief in and over His Majesty's Province of Carolina.*

1198. Painter to obtain a public commission was Gustavus Hesselius. His painting *The Last Supper,* an oil on canvas, 117.5 inches wide and 35 inches high, was commissioned on September 5, 1721, by the Vestry of St. Barnabas' Church, Queen Anne's Parish, Prince Georges County, MD. It was put in place as an altarpiece on November 26, 1722. Hesselius was paid "£17 currt. money" for the painting and installation. It was also the first important commission in America for a painting with more than one figure.

1199. Mezzotint engraving was a portrait of Cotton Mather about 13.5 by 10 inches, made by Peter Pelham in 1727.

1200. Artist of importance to be born in America was John Singleton Copley, the great portraitist, who was born in Boston, MA, in 1738, and emigrated to England in 1774. He painted many of the prominent people of his era, including Samuel Adams, John Adams, John Quincy Adams, John Hancock, and the King and Queen of England. He is credited with more than 269 oil paintings, 35 crayons, and 14 miniatures.

1201. Commercial artist who was successful was Matthew Pratt, who painted signboards in Philadelphia, PA, in 1768. From 1764 to 1768 he had been an art student in London, where he studied under the American expatriate artist Benjamin West.

1202. Artist of American birth to head the Royal Academy of London was Benjamin West, who became president of the Royal Academy on March 24, 1792, succeeding Sir Joshua Reynolds. Born on October 10, 1738, near Springfield, PA, he went to Italy in 1760 for three years of study and afterward settled in London, where he gained fame as a painter of historical subjects. In 1772 he became historical painter to King George III.

1203. Landscape painter of renown was Thomas Cole, born in 1801 in England and recognized as the founder of American landscape painting. The leader of the Hudson Valley School of artists, Cole specialized in painting the scenery of New York State. His later works were often done in a grandiose neoclassical style.

1204. Painting movement was the Hudson River School, a group of American landscape painters who were active between 1825 and 1875. Their main subject was the Hudson River valley and other grand vistas of the American landscape. Among the most important members of the school were Thomas Cole, Albert Bierstadt, Asher Brown Durand, Samuel Finley Breese Morse, and Frederick Edwin Church.

1205. Artists' organization (national) was the National Academy of Design, whose first president was the inventor and artist Samuel Finley Breese Morse. It was organized on January 18, 1826, by 15 members of the New York Drawing Association, which had been formed on November 8, 1825, in New York City.

1206. Etcher of skill was William Dunlap of New York City, a painter who studied under Benjamin West in London and whose success in 1830 inspired others to practice the art of etching. He was also a prominent playwright and historian.

1207. Sculptor to obtain a federal commission was John Frazee. A federal appropriation of $400 was granted to him on March 2, 1831, for a bust of John Jay for the Supreme Court, Washington, DC.

1208. Sculptor of renown was Hiram Powers of Vermont, who got his start as a sculptor in a waxworks museum. His chief sculptures were produced from 1835 to 1873. In addition to neoclassical statues entitled *Eve Disconsolate, Greek Slave, Proserpine, Il Penseroso, A Californian,* and *An American,* he made busts of George Washington for Louisiana, of John Caldwell Calhoun for South Carolina, and of Daniel Webster for Boston. His busts of Benjamin Franklin and Thomas Jefferson were installed in the Capitol in Washington, DC. He also made busts of John Quincy Adams, Andrew Jackson, Chief Justice John Marshall, Martin Van Buren, and other distinguished Americans.

1209. Artist of renown who was African-American was Henry Ossawa Tanner. Born in Pittsburgh, PA, in 1859, Tanner studied with Thomas Eakins and was best known for his genre scenes depicting African-American life. He died in 1937. He was the subject of the first major solo show of work by an African-American artist, a 90-piece exhibition co-sponsored by the National Collection of Fine Arts and the Frederick Douglass Institute that opened in Washington, DC, in 1969 and traveled to seven other major American museums.

ARTS—ART—ARTWORKS

1210. Cave paintings known to have been made in what is now the United States were painted in caves near the Pecos River in southwest Texas circa 1970 B.C.E. The caves had been inhabited for more than 3,000 years when the paintings were made, and continued to be inhabited until the arrival of the Spanish in the 16th century. The date of the paintings was established using a technique developed by Marvin Rowe, Marian Hyman, and Jon Russ of Texas A&M University that separates organic materials in the paint from inorganic substances in the rock.

1211. Painting of an American scene by a European painter was painted near what is now St. Augustine, FL, on June 27, 1564, by Jacques Le Moyne de Morgues, a cartographer who accompanied the French Huguenot expedition to Florida under René Goulaine de Laudonnière. The work, titled *Laudonnierus et Rex Athore ante Columnam a Praefecto Prima Navigatione Locatam Quamque Venerantur Floridenses,* was painted in gouache and metallic pigments on vellum. It shows Laudonnière being welcomed by a party of Native Americans led by Chief Athore.

1212. Self-portrait from the English colonies known to exist was painted circa 1670 by Captain Thomas Smith, a Puritan mariner of Boston, MA. The painting, in a style taken from Dutch portraiture, shows Smith resting his hand on a skull, which in turn rests on a poem that discusses Smith's own death.

1213. Caricature was Nathaniel Hurd's *The True Profile of the Notorious Doctor Seth Hudson,* published in 1762 in Boston, MA. It depicted Dr. Hudson in the pillory and Howe, his assistant, at the whipping post, in punishment for forging paper money.

1214. Lithograph was *A Water Mill,* by Bass Otis of Philadelphia, PA, published July 1819 in the *Analectic Magazine.*

1215. Marble statuary group executed by an American was *The Chanting Cherubs,* designed in 1830 by Horatio Greenough for James Fenimore Cooper. The subject was suggested by a portion of a Raphael painting but incurred hostility because of the nudity of the figures.

1216. Chromolithograph was made in 1861 of John Banvard's painting *The Orison,* which depicted the interior of the St. Eustace convent in Italy. It was 16 by 24 inches and was chromo-lithographed by Sarony, Major and Knapp. Proofs were $10, prints $5.

1217. Abstract paintings by a modern artist were the work of Arthur Dove, born in Geneva, NY. In 1910, he created a series of six paintings on linen, such as *Nature Symbolized, No. 1,* that took their inspiration from landscape but showed no clearly recognizable representational forms.

1218. Cover of the *Saturday Evening Post* by Norman Rockwell appeared on the issue dated May 20, 1916. It depicted a boy pushing a baby carriage past a group of jeering pals. Rockwell, a native New Yorker who became famous for his anecdotal scenes of small-town American life, painted 319 more covers for the magazine. The last appeared in 1963.

1219. Bas relief of stainless steel in large size was created by Isamu Noguchi and unveiled on April 29, 1940, over the entrance to the Associated Press Building, New York City. It was 17 by 22 feet and depicted five figures, one using a pad and pencil, and the other four using a teletype, telephone, wirephoto, and a camera, respectively.

1220. Artwork to incorporate lightning was *Lightning Field* by Walter de Maria, completed in 1977 and located 200 miles southwest of Albuquerque, NM. The artist installed 400 polished stainless steel lightning rods in a field one mile long and one kilometer wide. In stormy weather the rods attracted lightning to create a spectacular electrical display.

1221. Painting by an African-American artist to hang in the White House was *Dunes at Sunset, Atlantic City,* an 1885 landscape painting by Henry Ossawa Tanner. The painting was purchased for $100,000 by the White House Historical Association in 1996 and was put on display in the Green Room.

ARTS—ART—ENGRAVINGS

1222. Woodcut was a likeness of the Reverend Richard Mather, the leader of Congregationalism in the Massachusetts Bay Colony, made just prior to his death in April 1669. The engraver, John Foster, cut away from the surface of a flat wooden block those parts which were to appear white in the print, leaving the actual design in raised outline on the block. The print was 5 by 6 inches.

1223. Engraving of any artistic merit was a line-engraving copperplate portrait of Increase Mather, made in 1701 by Thomas Emmes. It was used as a frontispiece to a sermon, "The Blessed Hope," published in Boston, MA, in 1701 by Timothy Green for Nicholas Boone.

1224. Historical print engraved in America was *A Prospective Plan of the Battle Fought Near Lake George,* which presented a bird's-eye view showing the march of troops at the left, the camp and battle at the right, and Forts William Henry and Edward in the upper right-hand corner. It was a hand-colored line engraving by Thomas Johnston after a painting by Samuel Blodget, and was printed by Richard Draper in Boston, MA, in 1755.

1225. Engraving to achieve popularity was *The Bloody Massacre Perpetrated in King Street, Boston, on March 5, 1770,* which was engraved, printed, and sold by Paul Revere. It depicted the shooting of five Americans in Boston, MA, by British troops—the famous Boston Massacre—and has appeared in countless children's textbooks and general works on American history.

1226. Wood engraving made with an engraving tool known as the burin, making use of the intaglio "white line," was a tobacco stamp made by Alexander Anderson in June 1793 in New York City. The following year, he made a wood engraving for a book, *The Looking-Glass for the Mind; or Intellectual Mirror* by William Durell, translated from Arnaud Berquin's *L'Ami des Enfants.*

1227. Halftone engraving was made by Stephen Henry Horgan and appeared in the *New York Daily Graphic* on March 4, 1880. It was entitled *Scene in Shantytown, NY.* The basis of the invention was a screen gradated from transparency to opacity.

ARTS—ART—EXHIBITIONS

1228. Modern art exhibition of importance opened at the 69th Regiment Armory in New York City on February 17, 1913. The controversial exhibition, organized chiefly by the American modernist painter Arthur Bowen Davies, scandalized the public with such avant-garde works as Marcel Duchamp's *Nude Descending a Spiral Staircase.* More than 250,000 visitors received their first look at paintings by Paul Cèzanne, Paul Gauguin, Vincent van Gogh, Edward Hopper, Henri Matisse, John Marin, Charles Sheeler, and others.

1229. Native American art exhibition of importance was the Exposition of Indian Tribal Arts, a traveling show assembled by artist John Sloan and writer Oliver La Farge in 1931. The highlight of the show was the collection of Navajo textiles of the Classic Period, worth up to $1,000 apiece at the time. The first major museum show of Native American art took place in 1940 at the Museum of Modern Art, New York City.

1230. Art auction televised on a coast-to-coast circuit was held on April 27, 1960, for the benefit of the 30th Anniversary Fund of the Museum of Modern Art, New York City. It originated at the Parke-Bernet Galleries, New York City, and was seen in New York, Chicago, Dallas, and Los Angeles through TNT Theatre Network Television.

1231. Exhibition of the *Mona Lisa* in the United States took place on January 8, 1962, in the National Gallery of Art, Washington, DC. The painting, Leonardo da Vinci's masterpiece of 1506, was owned by the Louvre, in Paris. The loan of the painting was arranged by First Lady Jacqueline Kennedy and André Malraux, the French minister of culture. On the first day, 2,000 dignitaries were allowed to view the painting. The exhibition was opened to the public on January 9 and received 518,535 viewers during its three-week stay. The *Mona Lisa* was then moved to the Metropolitan Museum of Art in New York City, where it was seen by 1,077,051 visitors.

ARTS—DANCE

1232. Ballet was presented on February 7, 1827, as part of the play *The Deserter,* at the Bowery Theatre, New York City. The dancer, Madame Francisquy Hutin, wore a gauze dress. An observer wrote in the *New York Clipper:* "A sort of subdued expression of fear and terror simultaneously rose from the ladies present, and at the next instant, as if inspired by one idea, they fled from the house."

1233. Tap dancer of renown was William Henry Lane of Providence, RI, an African-American entertainer who went by the stage name Juba during the 1840s. Billed as "The Wonder of the World, Juba . . . the King of All Dancers," Lane derived his tapping style by combining fast steps from jigs and reels with West African *giouba*, a kind of step-dance. He was the first African-American to headline a troupe of white dancers. Bill "Bojangles" Robinson, born Luther Robinson in Richmond, VA, in 1878, was the first dancer to bring tap into modern stage and film entertainment.

1234. Modern dancer was Isadora Duncan, born Angela Duncan in 1878 in San Francisco, CA. She trained in classical ballet, but rejected it in favor of a personal, freely interpretive style, often based on Greek classical art, that attempted to synthesize music, poetry, and natural imagery into a symbolism of movement. She preferred to dance barefoot, wearing a loose, flowing tunic and scarves. In 1899 she left the United States and traveled to England, Germany, and, in 1905, Russia, where she met her greatest success. Her only important tour of the United States, in 1922, was a complete failure.

1235. Ballet choreographer of international renown to work in the United States was George Balanchine, born Georgi Meilitonovitch in 1904 in Russia. Balanchine defected from the Soviet Union in 1924 to join Sergei Pavlovich Diaghilev's Ballets Russes. He settled in 1933 in New York City, where he cofounded the School of American Ballet with Lincoln Kirstein. In 1948 he became artistic director and principal choreographer of the New York City Ballet. Balanchine's works, of which there were more than 100, were noted for their abstract themes and simplicity of movement.

1236. Ballet on an American theme by an American choreographer that was set to American music and performed by an American ballet company was *Billy the Kid*, a work depicting the violent career of the Western folk hero. The choreographer was Eugene Loring of Milwaukee, WI. The music was composed by Aaron Copland. The ballet was first performed at the Chicago Civic Opera House on October 9, 1938, by Lincoln Kirstein's Ballet Caravan.

1237. Copyright registered for a choreographic score was presented on microfilm by Hanya Holm, New York City, and registered on February 25, 1952, as an unpublished dramatic-musical composition. It was a complete score of her choreography for Cole Porter's musical comedy *Kiss Me, Kate,* which opened on December 30, 1948, at the Century Theater, New York City. The score was recorded in Labanotation, the notation system invented by Rudolf Laban.

1238. Ballet transmitted by satellite to be shown in the United States was the Royal Ballet's "The Royal Ballet Salutes the U.S.A.," hosted by Gene Kelly from Covent Garden, London, and broadcast over WNEW-TV, New York City, at 8 P.M. on July 22, 1978, and at 3 P.M. on July 23. The program was a Metromedia Television–British Broadcasting Company television coproduction and was sponsored by the Irving Trust Company.

ARTS—DRAMA

1239. Theatrical performance by nonprofessional actors was *The Bare and The Cubb,* a satire by Philip Alexander Bruce, which was performed on August 27, 1665, at Accomack, VA. The actors, Cornelius Watkinson, Philip Howard, and William Darby, were accused of sedition and were summoned to appear in court on November 16, 1665, "in those habiliments that they then acted in and give a draught of such verses or other speeches and passages which were then acted by them." They were found not guilty, and Edward Martin, who had informed on them, was ordered "to pay all the expenses of the presentment."

1240. Play of note written by an American and produced in America was *Gustavus Vasa,* a tragedy by Benjamin Colman. Harvard College students gave a performance of it in 1690 in Cambridge, MA.

1241. Play written in America that was printed was Governor Robert Hunter's *Androboros,* a biographical farce in three acts, printed in 1714 by William Bradford in New York City. The text contained 27 pages, quarto size. Androboros means "maneater." New York City was disguised in the play as Monoropolis, meaning "Fool's town."

1242. Play presented by professional players was given at the New Theatre, New York City, on December 6, 1732. It was *The Recruiting Officer,* by the Irish dramatist George Farquhar. The part of Worth was played by Thomas Heady, a barber.

ARTS—DRAMA—*continued*

1243. Play by William Shakespeare produced in America is supposed to have been *Richard III,* which was presented at the Nassau Street Theatre, New York City, on March 5, 1750, by Walter Murray and Thomas Kean. The play was "altered" by the poet Colley Cibber. The performance began at 6:30 P.M. Admission to the pit was five shillings and to the gallery three shillings.

1244. Benefit performance of a play was given on January 7, 1751, at the Nassau Street Theatre, New York City, for Walter Murray, one of the managers. It was advertised in the December 31, 1750, issue of the *Weekly Post-Boy:* "By his Excellency's Permission (for the benefit of Mr. Murray). On Monday, the seventh of January, will be performed, a comedy, called, 'A Bold Stroke For A Wife,' (being the last time of its being perform'd this season) to which will be added, an Entertainment called 'The Devil To Pay, Or, The Wives Metamorphos'd.'"

1245. Playwright to write professionally was William Dunlap, who wrote or adapted 63 dramatic pieces, many of which appeared at the Park Theatre, New York City. His first comedy, *Modest Soldier, or Love in New York,* was written in a few weeks in 1787. He went bankrupt in 1805. He was also a painter and a historian. His books included *The History of The American Theatre,* published in 1832.

1246. Play by an American writer to be successfully presented by an established company on a regular stage was Royall Tyler's five-act play *The Contrast.* It was first produced on April 16, 1787, at the John Street Theatre, New York City, by the American Company under the management of Lewis Hallam and John Henry. It depicted the contrast between the meretricious standards of the fashionable world and the simple, straightforward ideals of the true American. The play was published in 1790 for Thomas Wignell in Philadelphia, PA, by Prichard and Hall.

1247. Play about a Native American written by an American was James Nelson Barker's *The Indian Princess, or La Belle Sauvage,* a three-act operatic melodrama on the life of Pocahontas, based on Captain John Smith's *General History of Virginia.* It was first produced on April 6, 1808, at the Chestnut Street Theatre, Philadelphia, PA.

1248. Play performed 1,000 times was *The Gladiator,* a five-act tragedy in blank verse, set in ancient Rome. It was written by Dr. Robert Montgomery Bird and was first performed on September 26, 1831, at the Park Theatre, New York City, with Edwin Forrest as Spartacus. By 1853 it had been performed 1,000 times.

1249. Aquatic play was *The Pirate's Signal, or The Bridge of Death,* presented on July 4, 1840, at the Bowery Theatre, New York City. At the end of the fifth act, at the upper entrance of the stage, a full-rigged ship appeared, floated on water down to the footlights, turned, and went up the stage and off at the upper entrance.

1250. Chinese theatrical performance was offered by the Tong Hook Tong Dramatic Company under the management of Mr. Likeoon, Norman Assing, and Tong Chick at the American Theatre, Sansom Street, San Francisco, CA, on October 18, 1852. The company consisted of 123 performers and musicians who were shareholders in the theatrical enterprise. The performance contained four parts: *The Eight Genii Offering Their Congratulations to the High Ruler Yuk Hwang on His Birthday, Too Tsin Made High Minister by the Six States, Parting at the Bridge of Parkew of Kwan Wanchang and Tsow,* and *Defeated Revenge.*

1251. Play in which a horse race was run on stage was *Herne, the Hunter,* presented on February 18, 1856, in the Old Broadway Theatre, 326-328 Broadway, New York City. A chariot pulled by six horses was used. Many injuries occurred. One horse caused the collapse of a platform, another fell off the proscenium onto spikes, and there were many similar mishaps. The theater had 4,000 seats with no backs and room for 500 spectators to stand. Admission was 25 cents.

1252. Musical with an American theme and original score was *Evangeline, the Belle of Acadia,* first performed at Niblo's Theatre, New York City, on July 27, 1874. It was based on Henry Wadsworth Longfellow's poem "Evangeline." The book and lyrics were by J. Cheever Goodwin. It ran for two weeks and featured bare-legged dancing. George K. Fortesque was the female impersonator playing the ponderous Catherine.

1253. Play presented by a Jewish professional acting troupe was *Die Hexe (The Sorceress),* by Arthur Firzer, which was staged by the Hebrew Opera and Dramatic Company at the Bowery Garten Theater, 113 Broadway, New York City, on September 25 and 27, 1880. It was directed by Leon Golubok, the 17-year-old comedian who played the part of the 80-year-old witch. An advertisement of August 12, 1882, stated that a performance would be given for the benefit of 10 poor Russian immigrant families.

1254. Greek play produced in Greek was *Oedipus Tyrannus* by Sophocles. It was presented at Harvard University, Cambridge, MA, in May 1881. George Riddle played the part of Oedipus.

1255. Yiddish theater performance took place in New York City on August 18, 1882, when a Yiddish acting troupe from Russia staged a performance of *Koldunya (The Witch),* by Abraham Goldfaden, at Turner Hall on East Fourth Street. The cast included Boris Thomashefsky, who afterwards became one of the leaders of New York's thriving Yiddish theater scene.

1256. Musical comedy written by African-Americans for African-American performers was *A Trip to Coontown,* a musical comedy in two acts by Bob Cole and Billy Johnson, produced at the Third Avenue Theatre at 31st Street in New York City on April 4, 1898. Cole played the part of the tramp Willie Wayside, and Johnson played Jim Flimflammer, the bunco steerer.

1257. Drama broadcast on radio was *The Wolf,* by Eugene Walter, broadcast on August 3, 1922, by station WGY, Schenectady, NY. The two-and-a-half-hour performance was directed by Edward H. Smith.

1258. Play of full length by an African-American writer to be performed in New York City was *Appearances,* by Garland Anderson, a three-act protest against lynching, which was produced on October 13, 1925, at the Frolic Theatre atop the New Amsterdam Theatre, New York City. It was produced by Lester W. Sager and lasted 23 performances.

1259. Puppet show to be televised was a two-minute symbolic one-act play with puppet characters, produced on August 21, 1928, by WOR, Newark, NJ, a radio station owned by L. Bamberger and Company of Newark. In the play, a character symbolizing "Creative Genius" produced an apparatus that brought forth "The Spirit of Television," a winged sprite holding a globe. Sight and sound were synchronized. Viewers heard the narrator and musical accompaniment through earphones.

1260. Play to be shown on television was *The Queen's Messenger,* by J. Hartley Manners, presented on September 11, 1928, by radio station WGY of the General Electric Company, Schenectady, NY. The telecast was under the direction of Mortimer Stewart, with Izetta Jewell and Maurice Randall as the principal performers. The performance went out on three wavelengths, the picture on 379.5 meters and 21.4 meters and the voices on 31.96 meters. Several semicommercial 24-line receivers were set up in the WGY studios. Three cameras were used. The image was 3 by 3 inches.

1261. Drama broadcast on radio from a ship at sea was heard over the WABC Columbia network on July 1, 1933, when a radio version of a new motion picture was presented in the main salon of the Furness-Bermuda liner *Queen of Bermuda* on a weekend cruise to the mid-Atlantic. The movie from which the radio version was prepared was *Lady for a Day,* adapted from the short story by Damon Runyon.

1262. Drama broadcast on radio from a regular stage with full scenery and a cast in costume was *Roses and Drums,* a dramatic story of the unsuccessful Union attempt in 1864 to capture Jefferson Davis and free the Union prisoners from Libby Prison. It was presented by WABC, New York City, on September 24, 1933.

1263. Theatrical presentation sponsored by the federal government was *The Family Upstairs,* first produced on January 30, 1934, by a cast of players operating under the Civil Works Administration at the Central School of Business and Arts, New York City. An appropriation of $28,000 for wages was made on January 12, 1934. The project was under the direction of Margaret Smith. Other plays were presented later the same day. By March 25, 1934, 864,000 persons had witnessed 576 performances of 17 plays produced under this program in 107 schools, clubs, and museums.

1264. Musical comedy broadcast on radio with specially composed music was *The Gibson Family,* sponsored by the Procter and Gamble Company of Cincinnati, OH, and introduced over the National Broadcasting Company network on September 15, 1934. The comedy was composed by Arthur Schwartz and the lyrics were written by Howard Dietz. The musical comedy was booked for a 39-week period and was broadcast from station WEAF, New York City.

ARTS—DRAMA—*continued*

1265. Lighting designer for the stage was Jean Rosenthal of New York City, who devised a dramatic lighting plan in 1937 for a production of *Julius Caesar* at Orson Welles's Mercury Theatre. Until then, lighting in stage productions was arranged for the sole purpose of illuminating the action, rather than for dramatic effect. Rosenthal also invented a notation system for recording the placement and use of lights that allowed the original lighting plan for a play or dance performance to be duplicated in subsequent productions.

1266. Broadway play shown in a television version with its original cast was Rachel Crothers's comedy *Susan and God,* presented on June 7, 1938, over station W2XBS. The play was produced by the Radio Corporation of America in cooperation with John Golden, the Broadway producer. Featured in the cast were Gertrude Lawrence, Paul McGrath, and Nancy Coleman, then playing in *Susan and God* at the Plymouth Theater, New York City. Exact replicas of the stage settings were built for the telecast from the National Broadcasting Company's studio in the RCA building, New York City. The first to be televised in color was James Matthew Barrie's *Peter Pan,* starring Mary Martin as Peter Pan and Cyril Ritchard as Captain Hook, which was telecast on March 7, 1955, from 7:30 to 9:30 P.M. by WRCA, Channel 4, New York City, on *Producer's Showcase.* It could also be seen in black and white on the NBC network.

1267. Play on Broadway in which an African-American actress had a starring role was *Mamba's Daughters,* a play by Dorothy and DuBose Heyward, in which the blues singer Ethel Waters played the leading role. The play opened in New York City in January 1939. Waters took 17 curtain calls on opening night.

1268. Musical comedy to be shown on television was a performance of "Topsy and Eva—Television Edition," presented on July 25, 1939, by station W2XBS of the National Broadcasting Company, New York City. The entertainers who appeared on the program were the Duncan sisters, Billy Kent, Florence Auer, Winfield Hoeney, Edwin Vail, the Southernaires, and the Chansonettes.

1269. Musical comedy written for television was *The Boys from Boise,* produced by the Charles M. Storm Company for *Esquire* magazine on September 28, 1944, over WABD, New York City. The program was directed by Ray Nelson.

1270. Play by an African-American woman to appear on Broadway was *Raisin in the Sun,* by Lorraine Hansberry, which opened on March 11, 1959, at the Ethel Barrymore Theatre, New York City. It was a story about an African-American family living in the Southside area of Chicago and starred Sidney Poitier, Ruby Dee, and Claudia McNeil.

1271. Musical to run for more than 3,000 performances was *Fiddler on the Roof,* based on stories by the Yiddish writer Sholem Aleichem (pen name of Sholem Yakov Rabinowitz). It opened on September 22, 1964, at the Imperial Theatre, New York City, and ran for 3,242 performances. Zero Mostel took the part of Tevye. It was presented by Harold Prince, with choreography by Jerome Robbins, music by Jerry Bock, lyrics by Sheldon Harnick, and book by Joseph Stein.

1272. Rock musical was *Hair, An American Tribal Love-Rock Musical,* which opened at the Public Theater in New York City on October 29, 1967. The composer was Galt MacDermott. The musical, which appeared during the Vietnam War, carried an antiwar message and aroused some controversy for its glorification of "hippie" values, including a nude scene at the end of the first act. The production moved to Broadway's Biltmore Theatre in April 1968.

ARTS—DRAMA—ACTORS

1273. Actor of American birth was John Martin, who appeared at the Old Southwark Theatre, Philadelphia, PA, on March 13, 1790, in a play entitled *Douglas.*

1274. English actor of note to perform in America was George Frederick Cooke of Covent Garden, London, who made his debut on November 21, 1810, as Richard III in the play of the same name at the Park Theatre, New York City, before 2,000 people. His manager, Thomas Apthorpe Cooper, paid him $125 a week for 10 months, a traveling fee of 25 cents per mile, and expenses. Cooke died in New York City on September 26, 1812.

1275. Actor to receive curtain applause was Edmund Kean, the famous English actor, who appeared in a group of special performances in Boston, MA, in 1821.

1276. Actor to appear abroad was James Henry Hackett, who made his English debut on April 5, 1827, at Covent Garden, London. He had made his professional debut the previous year in New York City.

1277. Actors' home was the Forrest Home, Philadelphia, opened on October 2, 1876. The property consisted of 90 acres of farmland and 20 acres of lawn. The first superintendent was Joseph McArdle.

ARTS—MUSIC

1278. Music society of importance was the St. Cecilia Society of Charleston, SC, organized in 1737 as an amateur concert society and formally organized in 1762 to give annual concerts and balls.

1279. Musical instrument dealer was Michael Hillegas, who opened a shop in Philadelphia, PA, in 1759. On December 13, 1759, he advertised instruments, music, and musical supplies in the *Pennsylvania Gazette*. Musical instruments, however, had been sold previously and were advertised for sale at a dancing school in Boston, MA, in 1716.

1280. Music printed in a magazine was "The Hill Tops, a New Hunting Song," printed in the April 1774 issue of the *Royal American Magazine or Universal Repository of Instruction and Amusement*, published by Isaiah Thomas in Boston, MA.

1281. Music publishers to deal exclusively in music were John C. Moller and Henri Capron of Philadelphia, PA, whose publishing business was established in 1790. They also had a music store and offered musical instruction.

1282. Singing contest in America took place in 1790 in Dorchester, MA, between the singers of the First Parish of Dorchester and the singing society of Stoughton. The Stoughtonians began with Jacob French's "Heavenly Vision," the author of which was their fellow townsman. When they finally sang Handel's *Hallelujah Chorus* without books, the Dorchestrians gave up the contest and gracefully acknowledged defeat.

1283. Music festival is claimed to have been given in Boston, MA, to celebrate the signing of the Treaty of Ghent, which ended the War of 1812 between the United States and Great Britain. The treaty was signed on December 25, 1814. The news reached Boston on February 13, 1815. A concert of sacred music was played on February 16 at the Reverend Dr. Baldwin's house in Boston. It included the first part of Haydn's *Creation,* Handel's *Hallelujah Chorus,* parts of Handel's *Judas Maccabeus,* and the Dettingen *Te Deum* and *Ode to St. Cecilia's Day.*

1284. Music by Native Americans to be recorded were two disk recordings of "Indian Songs," both titled "Three Melodies from the Ghost Dance." They were listed in the first catalog, dated November 1, 1894, of the United States Gramophone Company, Washington, DC. No examples of these recordings are known to have survived.

1285. Organists' society (national) was the American Guild of Organists, organized on April 13, 1896. One hundred and forty-five organists, called founders, were enrolled by December 31, 1896. Gerrit Smith was the first warden and Dr. Henry Granger Hanchett, inventor of the third pedal, the first secretary. The first branch chapter was organized in Philadelphia, PA, on June 10, 1902. The first convention was held on December 29–30, 1914, in New York City.

1286. Music society for the protection of composers and song writers was the American Society of Composers, Authors and Publishers, which was formed on February 13, 1914, in New York City. The object of the society was to protect the copyrighted musical compositions of its members against illegal public performance for profit and other forms of infringement, and to collect license fees for authorized performances in public amusement establishments for distribution among its members. The society was an unincorporated voluntary association and was affiliated with similar societies functioning in foreign countries. George Maxwell was the first president.

ARTS—MUSIC—CLASSICAL AND JAZZ

1287. Concert with documentation was "a concert of music on sundry instruments" held at six o'clock at Peter Pelham's "great room" near the Sun Tavern in Boston, MA, on December 30, 1731. Tickets cost five shillings each.

1288. Oratorio performance was a presentation of George Frideric Handel's *Messiah* on December 25, 1818, by the Handel and Haydn Society, Boylston Hall, Boston, MA, with a chorus of approximately 200 singers. The soloists were the Misses Sumner and Bennett, Mr. J. Sharp, and Master White. Benjamin Holt, the president of the society, conducted the concert.

1289. Oratorio by an American was John Knowles Paine's *Oratorio of St. Peter,* performed on June 3, 1873, at the City Hall, Portland, ME, by the Haydn Society of Portland, assisted by eminent artists from abroad and the 41-member Harvard orchestra of Cambridge, MA.

ARTS—MUSIC—CLASSICAL AND JAZZ
—*continued*

1290. Symphonic work by an American composer was the Symphony in C minor, Opus 23, by John Knowles Paine, presented in January 1876 in Boston, MA, by Theodore Thomas and his orchestra.

1291. Telephone concert held long-distance was held on March 31, 1877, at Steinway Hall, New York City. Music played in Philadelphia, PA, was heard by means of Elisha Gray's so-called Transmission of Music by Telegraph. The audience heard "Home, Sweet Home," "The Last Rose of Summer," "Yankee Doodle," and other songs.

1292. Performance of *The Stars and Stripes Forever* by John Philip Sousa took place at the Academy of Music in Philadelphia, PA, on May 14, 1897. Sousa's greatest march was such a smashing success that the audience asked to hear it twice more. One newspaper account praised it as "stirring enough to rouse the American eagle from his crag and set him to shriek exultantly while he hurls his arrows at the aurora borealis." Some musicologists believe the march was first performed in public in Augusta, ME, on May 1, two weeks earlier.

1293. Sheet music to sell millions of copies was "Maple Leaf Rag," a ragtime composition for piano by composer Scott Joplin, who was then living in Sedalia, MO. It was published in 1899.

1294. Jazz record sold to the public was recorded by the Original Dixieland Jass Band, a group of five white musicians led by cornetist Nick La Rocca, the son of an Italian cobbler. The session was recorded on a Victor 78 disk by the Victor Company in New York City in February 1917. It featured two tunes, "Dixieland Jass Band One-Step" and "Livery Stable Blues," in which La Rocca made his horn sound like a horse whinnying.

1295. Radio broadcast of a concert from an airplane took place on April 14, 1922, from a Fokker airplane over New York City. The plane was piloted by Belvin W. Maynard, an ordained Baptist minister. Jeanette Vreeland, a lyric soprano, was the performer. She was introduced by Thais Magrane, chairman of the American Legion Auxiliary. The program was intended to raise money for the Veterans Mountain Camp, Tupper Lake, NY, a home for tubercular ex-servicemen. It was relayed by telephone to the camp's New York offices at the Hotel Astor.

1296. Symphonic work to require an airplane propeller was *Ballet Méchanique,* written by the New Jersey–born composer George Antheil in 1922, when he was 22 years old. The score called for player pianos, automobile horns, and other mechanical contraptions, among them an airplane propeller. The work was premiered in Paris in 1926 and was first presented in the United States on April 10, 1927, at Carnegie Hall, New York City.

1297. Symphony on an African-American folk theme was the Symphony No. 1, known as the *Negro Folk Symphony,* composed by the African-American conductor William Levi Dawson. It was first presented on November 14, 1934, by the Philadelphia Orchestra under the direction of Leopold Stokowski at the Academy of Music, Philadelphia, PA.

1298. Jazz concert at Carnegie Hall in New York City took place on January 17, 1938, when Benny Goodman and His Orchestra played with guest performers Jess Stacy, Count Basie, and members of the Basie and Duke Ellington orchestras.

1299. Symphonic concert to be shown on television was transmitted on March 20, 1948, by the Columbia Broadcasting System. At 5 P.M., Eugene Ormandy conducted the Philadelphia Symphony Orchestra in a concert televised by WCAU-TV, Philadelphia, PA, on CBS. At 6:30 P.M. that same day, Arturo Toscanini conducted the NBC Symphony Orchestra in an all-Wagner concert televised by WNBT-TV, New York City, over the National Broadcasting Company system.

1300. Musical composition consisting entirely of silence was *4′33″,* a piece by avant-garde composer John Cage. The score, composed in 1952, was entirely blank. It was meant to be "performed" by a musician sitting silently for 4 minutes and 33 seconds in front of a piano or any other instrument. Cage's intent was to employ the ambient sounds in the concert hall as his "music."

1301. Jazz composition to appear on the Top 40 charts was pianist Dave Brubeck's instrumental piece *Take Five,* which entered the Top 40 popular music chart published by the trade newspaper *Billboard* on October 23, 1961. It eventually reached No. 25.

ARTS—MUSIC—MUSICAL INSTRUMENTS

1302. Chimes and bells were manufactured by Benjamin Hanks, who came to America in 1699, settling in Plymouth, MA, and then in Litchfield, CT. He also manufactured the first tower clocks and the first self-winding clock, a "machine that winds itself up by help of the air and will continue to do so without any other aid or assistance."

1303. Organs were brought to the United States in 1700 by the Episcopal Church of Port Royal, PA, and the Gloria Dei Church of Philadelphia, PA, a Swedish Lutheran church. Priority is claimed for each.

1304. Organ built in the United States was constructed by Johann Gottlob Klemm, also known as John Clemm, of Philadelphia, PA, who proposed building an organ on June 1, 1739, for Trinity Church, New York City. His proposition was accepted, and in May 1740 the pipe organ was installed in the West Gallery. It had three manuals and 26 stops: 10 in the great organ, 10 in the choir, and six in the swell. It cost about £520.

1305. Carillon was installed in the belfry of the Old North Church (now Christ Church), Boston, MA, in 1745. Eight bells were ordered in 1744 from Abell Rudhall's foundry, Gloucester, England, by Thomas Gunther, who put up a bond to guarantee payment. They were shipped on the *Two Friends* on March 9, 1745, the total cost being £560, four shillings, 10 pence.

1306. Trombone was played at the funeral of a child on November 15, 1754, at Bethlehem, PA. Trombones were also used on March 30, 1755, in the church's Easter services.

1307. Harpsichord was made by John Harris. It was called a spinet and was described in the *Boston Gazette* of September 18, 1769. It had only three or four octaves. Each jack was provided with a little spur of goose-quill that plucked the thin wire to cause vibration.

1308. Iron piano frame was made in 1837 in Boston, MA, by Jonas Chickering. It was designed to resist the tremendous tension of the modern piano without allowing the wires to deflect from pitch.

1309. Melodeon patent was granted to C. Austin of Concord, NH, on June 19, 1849. The melodeon was a small kind of reed organ and employed a suction bellows worked by treadles that drew the air through the reeds.

1310. Piano wire was produced at the factory of Ichabod Washburn, Grove Street, Worcester, MA, in 1850. This plant was later part of the Washburn and Moen Manufacturing Company, afterward absorbed by the American Steel and Wire Company.

1311. Calliope was invented by Joshua C. Stoddard of Worcester, MA, who on October 9, 1855, received a patent on a "new musical instrument to be played by the agency of steam or highly compressed air." He formed the American Steam Music Company in Worcester, MA, in 1855.

1312. Grand piano with a cast-metal plate designed to withstand the pull of high-tension strings was invented by the German-American piano maker Henry Engelhard Steinweg in 1859. The new grand piano, manufactured in Steinweg's New York City factory, yielded a fuller tone than earlier instruments. Steinweg began calling himself Steinway beginning in 1865, and his company became Steinway & Sons.

1313. Zither factory was established by Franz Schwartzer in Washington, MO, in 1866. In the first 20 years, he sold about 3,000 zithers, ranging in price from $50 to $500.

1314. Electric organ was built by Hilborne Lewis Roosevelt in 1876, and installed in Chickering Hall, Fifth Avenue and 18th Street, New York City. It was operated by storage batteries. It had 31 ranks: 10 in the great organ, eight in the swell organ, five in the solo organ, three in the echo organ, and five in the pedal organ.

1315. Organ with color display was invented by Bainbridge Bishop of New Russia, NY, who obtained a patent on January 16, 1877, on an "attachment for key-board musical instruments" for typifying musical sounds by the display of colors.

1316. Player piano was invented by John McTammany, Jr., of Cambridge, MA, who received a patent on June 14, 1881, on a "mechanical musical instrument." He constructed a mechanism for automatic playing of organs using narrow sheets of perforated flexible paper that governed the notes to be played.

1317. Player piano that was completely automatic was the Angelus, made by the Wilcox and White Company, Meriden, CT, in February 1897. It was invented by Edward H. Leveaux of Surrey, England. Leveaux obtained a British patent on February 27, 1879, and an American patent on October 4, 1881, on an "apparatus for storing and transmitting motive power."

ARTS—MUSIC—MUSICAL INSTRU-
MENTS—*continued*

1318. Saxophone production was undertaken in 1888 by Charles Gerard Conn, Elkhart, IN. The instruments were made of brass, had two octave keys, and descended to B-flat. Originally they were used only by military bands.

1319. Clarinet made exclusively of metal was manufactured by Charles Gerard Conn of Elkhart, IN, who obtained a patent on August 27, 1889, on a "clarionet." Previously, all clarinets had been made of wood. Conn's clarinet was made with double metal walls in the old Albert system.

1320. Pneumatic piano player that was practical was the Pianola, invented in 1896 by Edwin S. Votey of Detroit, MI, who received a patent on May 22, 1900. His original model was larger than the piano to which it was attached. The patent was for an attachment of practical and economical construction that could be applied to and removed from any piano. It was introduced by the Aeolian Company.

1321. Music synthesizer powered by electricity was the Telharmonium, also known as the Dynamophone, invented by Thaddeus Cahill and first demonstrated publicly in 1906 at Telharmonic Hall in New York City. The huge, 200-ton instrument, consisting of 140 dynamos and tone mixers powered by electrically driven gears, was controlled by an organ-style keyboard and foot pedals. When the player pressed the keys, current produced by the dynamos was converted into musical tones. The machinery itself was so noisy it had to be placed in the basement of the building. The sound was transmitted by telephone lines to subscribing restaurants, hotels, and homes, marking the first use of electronic equipment to distribute music.

1322. Sousaphone was manufactured by the C.G. Conn Company, Elkhart, IN, from designs suggested by John Philip Sousa. The first models had the bell pointing up. The first instrument with the bell in front was made in 1908.

1323. Modern carillon was installed in the Church of Our Lady of Good Voyage, Gloucester, MA, and blessed by Cardinal O'Connell on July 2, 1922. The bells and apparatus, weighing 28,000 pounds, were made and installed by John Taylor and Company, Loughborough, England, and consisted of 31 bells, the largest weighing 2,826 pounds. They were played for the first time by carillonneur George B. Stevens.

1324. Pipeless organ was invented by Laurens Hammond, who received a patent on April 24, 1934, covering 74 claims. The organ was manufactured by the Hammond Clock Company, Chicago, IL, and was first exhibited at the Industrial Arts Exposition, New York City, on April 15, 1935. The organ consisted of a two-manual console with pedal clavier and an electric power cabinet. It had neither reeds, pipes, nor vibrating parts. It weighed 275 pounds and cost less than one cent an hour to operate.

1325. Electric guitar to be widely marketed was the Rickenbacker Electro Spanish guitar of 1935, designed by Adolph Rickenbacker (also spelled Rickenbacher), George Beauchamp, and Doc Kauffman of the Electro Company, Los Angeles, CA. It was made of cast Bakelite, a synthetic resin, and featured a one-piece body, molded fittings, and a bolt-on neck. A patent was filed by Beauchamp in 1936 and granted in 1939. Credit for the first electric guitar of any kind is claimed by several inventors. Between 1920 and 1924, acoustical engineer Lloyd Loar experimented with microphone pickups for acoustic guitars, and in the early 1930s he designed for the Vivi-Tone company an acoustic-electric Spanish-neck guitar made out of solid wood. Les Paul electrified acoustic guitars in 1929 using a phonograph needle. George Beauchamp patented the electrified Fry Pan Hawaiian guitar, which was made of solid aluminum, in 1931, the same year that Dobro introduced its own electric solid-body Hawaiian guitar.

1326. Musical instrument capable of making any audible sound was the RCA Electronic Music Synthesizer, developed at the Columbia–Princeton Electronic Music Center in New York City in 1955. It could generate electronically all the physical characteristics of any sound and produce an infinite variety of sound combinations. The instrument was operated by a teleprinter-style alphanumeric keyboard.

ARTS—MUSIC—MUSICIANS AND COM-
POSERS

1327. Composer born in America was Francis Hopkinson, one of the signers of the Declaration of Independence, who was born in Philadelphia, PA, in 1737 and graduated in 1757 from the College of Philadelphia. He was also a lawyer, judge, and writer of political commentary and satire. His first important song was "My Days Have Been So Wondrous Free," composed in 1759, one of the earliest secular compositions extant. In 1763, his book *A Collection of Psalm Tunes, with a few anthems and* *hymns, some of them entirely new, for the use of the United Churches of Christ Church and St. Peter's Church in Philadelphia* was printed by W. Dunlop, Philadelphia, PA. He was the author of the first book of secular songs by an American-born composer, *Seven Songs for the Harpsichord or Forte Piano,* published in 1788.

1328. Musician born in America to achieve fame in Europe was the pianist Louis Moreau Gottschalk, who in 1852 gave concerts in the leading music centers of the world. Born in New Orleans, LA, in 1829, he exhibited an interest in music at the age of four and played an organ in church when he was six. In April 1845 he appeared in Paris, in 1846–47 in Italy, and in 1850 in Switzerland. He was also a composer who wrote piano pieces, songs, symphonies, and other instrumental and orchestral works.

1329. Composer born in America to win an international reputation was Edward Alexander MacDowell, born in New York City in 1861. A protege of Franz Liszt, MacDowell wrote symphonic poems, concertos, orchestral suites, songs, and piano sonatas, including *Woodland Sketches,* composed in 1896, and *Sea Pieces,* composed in 1898. He taught at Columbia University, New York City, from 1896 to 1904.

1330. Singer whose voice was broadcast over radio was Eugenia H. Farrar, whose voice was broadcast by Lee De Forest on December 16, 1907, from the Brooklyn Navy Yard, Brooklyn, New York City, on the occasion of the departure of Admiral Robley Dunglison Evans on a cruise with the fleet.

1331. Composer of jazz music was William Christopher "W.C." Handy, whose *Memphis Blues* was composed in 1911 and published on September 27, 1912. An African-American born in Florence, AL, he was known as the "father of the blues," having composed numerous other pieces in that idiom, among them *St. Louis Blues* and *Beale Street Blues.*

1332. Composer of gospel music of importance was Thomas Andrew Dorsey, born in 1899 in Villa Rica, GA. Known as "the father of gospel music," Dorsey began his career as a blues pianist and songwriter with the stage name of Georgia Tom and was later a church choir director in Chicago, IL. In 1926, after the death of a close friend, he composed "If You See My Savior, Tell Him That You Saw Me," considered the first true gospel song. Dorsey's achievement was to bring a strong blues and ragtime sound to religious song. Among his best-known compositions are "Take My Hand, Precious Lord," "The Lord Will Make a Way Somehow," and "Peace in the Valley."

1333. Opera prima donna who was African-American was Caterina Jarboro, who appeared on July 22, 1933, as Aida, the Ethiopian slave, in Giuseppe Verdi's opera *Aida,* presented by Alfredo Salmaggi's Chicago Opera Company at the New York Hippodrome, Sixth Avenue and 43rd Street, New York City.

1334. Opera composer who was a woman and who conducted her work in a major opera house was Ethel Leginska (Ethel Legins), whose opera *Gale* was sung on November 23, 1935, by the Chicago City Opera Company, Chicago, IL. It was a one-act arrangement of a Cornish legend adapted from *The Haunting* (1922) by Catharine Amy Dawson-Scott. It was performed by an all-American cast including John Charles Thomas, Frank Forest, Julia Peters, and Helen Bertush.

1335. Bluegrass musician of renown was William Smith "Bill" Monroe, the "father of bluegrass music," born 1911 in Rosine, KY. In 1939, Monroe formed a band called the Blue Grass Boys and developed the blend of Appalachian melodies, folk music, and jazz that came to be called bluegrass. He wrote more than 500 songs, including the classic bluegrass tune "Blue Moon of Kentucky." In 1983 he received the first Grammy Award in the category of Best Bluegrass Recording from the National Academy of Recording Arts and Sciences.

1336. Opera singer who was African-American to sing a white role with a white cast was Robert Todd Duncan, a baritone of Washington, DC, who first appeared as Tonio in *I Pagliacci* on September 28, 1945, and as Escamillo in *Carmen* on September 30, 1945, in the New York City Opera Company's presentation at the City Center of Music and Drama, New York City. Both operas were included in the 1945 fall season. *I Pagliacci* was performed five times and *Carmen* seven.

1337. Gospel singer of importance was Mahalia Jackson, born in New Orleans, LA, in 1911. Jackson began singing in a church children's choir when she was four years old. Her first recording, "I Will Move On Up A Little Higher," issued in 1946, sold close to 2 million copies. Of her total of 31 recordings, 12 sold more than one million copies. Her rendition of "We Shall Overcome" became the unofficial anthem of the civil rights movement of the 1960s.

ARTS—MUSIC—MUSICIANS AND COMPOSERS—*continued*

1338. Metropolitan Opera singer who was African-American was Marian Anderson, contralto, who sang the role of the fortune teller Ulrica in Giuseppe Verdi's *Un Ballo in Maschera*, presented on January 7, 1955, at the Metropolitan Opera House, New York City.

1339. Metropolitan Opera orchestra conductor who was African-American was Henry Lewis, who conducted Giacomo Puccini's *La Bohème* on October 16, 1972, in New York City.

1340. Metropolitan Opera orchestra conductor who was a woman was Sarah Caldwell, who conducted *La Traviata* by Giuseppi Verdi on January 13, 1976. The cast included Beverly Sills as Violetta, Stuart Burrows as Alfredo, and William Walker as Germont.

ARTS—MUSIC—OPERA

1341. Opera performed in America was Colley Cibber's ballad opera *Flora, or Hob in the Well*, presented on February 18, 1735, at the Courtroom, Charleston, SC. It was advertised in the *South Carolina Gazette* and was shown with a pantomime entertainment billed as *The Adventure of Harlequin Scaramouche*.

1342. Opera performed by a professional visiting troupe was *The Beggar's Opera*, a three-act burlesque by John Gay, performed on December 3, 1750, by the Walter Murray and Thomas Kean Company at the Nassau Street Theatre, New York City. The principal songs were "Let Us Take to the Road," "Lillibullero," "Green Sleeves," "Hither Dear Husband," and "When a Wife's in a Pout." Entertainment was presented between the acts.

1343. Comic opera written for the American stage was Andrew Barton's *The Disappointment, or The Force of Credulity*, a satirical comedy in two acts with a prologue and epilogue, inspired by "the infrequency of dramatic compositions in America, the necessity of contributing to the entertainment of the city, and to put a stop (if possible) to the foolish and pernicious practice of searching after supposed hidden treasures." The satire was directed against seekers of the pirate Blackbeard's treasure. The opera contained 18 songs and was arranged with seven scenes in the first act and five in the second. A performance was scheduled to take place on April 20, 1767, in Philadelphia, PA, but at the last moment the work was withdrawn for fear of offending. The libretto, published later that year in New York City, was the first opera libretto published in America.

1344. Opera of a serious nature produced in America was James Hewitt's *Tammany, or The Indian Chief*, based on the book by Anne Julia Kemble Hatton. The opera was produced on March 3, 1794, by Charles Ciceri, under the auspices of the Tammany Society, by the Old American Company at the John Street Theatre, New York City.

1345. Opera by an American composer was *The Archers, or the Mountaineers of Switzerland*, about the exploits of William Tell, which was performed in New York City on April 18, 1796, with a libretto by William Dunlap and music by Benjamin Carr. The first one of importance was *Leonora*, a lyrical drama in three acts with a libretto by Joseph Reese Fry and music by William Henry Fry, which was performed on June 4, 1845, at the Chestnut Street Theatre, Philadelphia, PA. The plot was based on Bulwer-Lytton's *The Lady of Lyons*. It was sung in English and had a chorus of 75 and an orchestra of 50.

1346. Italian opera to be produced in the United States in Italian, with Italian singers, was Gioacchino Antonio Rossini's *Il Barbiere di Siviglia*, performed on November 29, 1825, at the Park Theatre, New York City. The libretto was by Cesare Sterbini. The singers were Manuel de Populo Vicente, De Rosich, Manuel Crivelli, Maria Felicita Garcia, and Manuel Garcia, Jr. The orchestra of 25 musicians was conducted by Nathaniel De Luce. Performances were given at 7:30 P.M. The prices were listed as follows: boxes, $2.00; orchestra, $1.00; gallery, 25 cents. Twenty-three performances were given. The largest receipts for a single performance were $1,962, and the smallest $250.

1347. Opera produced at the Metropolitan Opera House in New York City was Charles François Gounod's *Faust*, sung in Italian on October 22, 1883. Augusto Vianesi was the conductor. Faust was sung by Italo Campanini, Mephistopheles by Franco Novara, Valentin by Giuseppe Del Puente, Wagner by Ludovico Contini, Siebel by Sofia Scalchi, Marthe by Louise Lablache, and Marguerite by Christine Nilsson. Admission was priced at $6 for orchestra stalls, $3 for the balcony, and $2 for the family circle.

1348. Opera composed by a woman to be performed at the Metropolitan Opera House was the one-act opera *Der Wald*, by the English composer Dame Ethel Mary Smyth, performed on March 11, 1903, in New York City. Alfred Hertz was the conductor. Johanna Gadski sang Roschen, and Georg Anther sang Heinrich.

1349. Opera by an American composer to be performed at the Metropolitan Opera House in New York City was *The Pipe of Desire,* by Frederick Shepherd Converse, which was produced on March 18, 1910. The libretto was by George Edward Barton. The cast included Riccardo Martin, Louise Homer, Clarence Whitehill, Leonora Sparkes, Lillia Snelling, Glenn Hall, and Herbert Witherspoon. The opera had been produced previously in Boston in 1906.

1350. Opera broadcast over the radio in its entirety was presented on May 19, 1921, during Music Week, from the Auditorium, Denver, CO. A municipal chorus of 150 voices presented *Martha* over station 9ZAF. The first by a professional cast was *Samson et Dalila* by Camille Saint-Saëns, broadcast on November 14, 1921, over station KYW, Chicago, IL, from the Chicago Auditorium. Lucien Muratore and Marguerite D'Alvarez were the leads; Giorgio Polacco conducted. The Metropolitan Opera House's first full opera broadcast was Engelbert Humperdinck's *Hansel and Gretel,* presented on December 25, 1931, through the National Broadcasting Company, New York City. Editha Fleischer was Hansel, Queena Mario was Gretel, and Karl Riedel conducted.

1351. Opera house established by a city was the War Memorial Opera House of San Francisco, CA, which opened on October 15, 1932, with a performance of *Tosca* by the San Francisco Opera Company.

1352. Opera to be televised in its entirety was Engelbert Humperdinck's *Hansel and Gretel,* presented on December 23, 1943, by WRGB of the General Electric Company, Schenectady, NY.

1353. Opera to be televised from the Metropolitan Opera House was Giuseppe Verdi's *Otello,* a three-and-a-half-hour performance that was televised on November 29, 1948, over WJZ-TV, New York City. It was sponsored by the Texaco Company. It starred Licia Albanese, Ramon Vinay, Leonard Warren, Martha Lipton, John Garris, and Nicola Moscona and was conducted by Fritz Busch. Milton Cross was the commentator. The telecast was also seen at network outlets in Philadelphia, Baltimore, Washington, and Boston. On March 10, 1940, station W2XBS, New York City, presented a condensed version of the first act of Ruggiero Leoncavallo's opera *I Pagliacci,* performed by members of the Metropolitan Opera Company and broadcast from a Radio City studio.

1354. Opera written for television was *Amahl and the Night Visitors,* by Gian-Carlo Menotti, first televised on December 24, 1951, by the National Broadcasting Company from WNBT-TV, New York City. The program was sponsored by Hallmark Greeting Cards. Thomas Schippers was the conductor and Chet Allen, a 12-year-old boy soprano, the featured singer. The opera tells the story of the Three Wise Men and the miraculous cure of a disabled boy.

ARTS—MUSIC—ORCHESTRAS AND ENSEMBLES

1355. Orchestra was the Collegium Musicum of Bethlehem, PA, formed in 1744. There were 14 players, including two first violins, two second violins, two violas, two flutes, two trumpets, two French horns, one cello, and one double bass. The orchestra believed to have been the original Philharmonic Orchestra was founded about 1810–11 in Boston, MA, by Johann Christian Gottlieb Graupner. Its last concert was given at the Pantheon, Boylston Square, Boston, on November 24, 1824.

1356. Orchestra in a theater was employed in 1750 at the Nassau Street Theater, located between John Street and Maiden Lane, New York City. The instruments were German flutes, horns, and drums. The theater, a two-story gabled structure, was illuminated by a chandelier made of a barrel hoop through which a dozen nails were driven to serve as candle holders. It had 10 box seats at eight shillings each, 161 pit seats at five shillings each, and 121 gallery seats at three shillings each. The stage was set five feet above the floor level.

1357. College orchestra was founded at Harvard University, Cambridge, MA. The minutes record that "at a meeting held on March 6, 1808, by a number of students of Harvard University, they unanimously agreed to institute a society for their mutual improvement in instrumental music." It was known as the Pierian Sodality, as it was not the custom then for any extracurricular activity to take the name of a college. The orchestra is now known as the Harvard University Orchestra.

1358. Orchestra of international stature was the Philharmonic Society of New York, later called the New York Philharmonic. On December 7, 1842, the 63-member orchestra gave its first public performance in New York City's Apollo Room, playing Beethoven's Fifth Symphony. Ureli Corelli Hill was the conductor.

1359. Chamber music ensemble was the Mendelssohn Quintette Club of Boston, MA. Its first concert was given at Chickering Hall on December 14, 1849.

ARTS—MUSIC—ORCHESTRAS AND EN-
SEMBLES—*continued*

1360. School band was formed in 1857 by the
Boston Asylum and Farm School for Indigent
Boys, located on Thompson Island in Boston
Bay, MA. Musical sounds were produced by
singing through paper-covered combs. Later,
three violins, a bass violin, saxhorn, cornopean,
and drum were added. Beginning in 1859, the
band participated in street parades in Boston
and elsewhere. In 1860 they had 14 brass
pieces and a bass drum. On June 10, 1907, the
name of the school was changed to the Farm
and Trades School and in 1956 to Thompson
Academy.

1361. Community chorus was established in
1912 in Rochester, NY, by Harry Barnhart,
who appeared by permission of the mayor of
Rochester at a band concert at the Convention
Hall, where he introduced the idea of community singing.

1362. City orchestra supported by taxes was
the Baltimore Symphony Orchestra, Baltimore,
MD, formed in 1915 with a Board of Estimate
appropriation of $6,000. It was managed by
Frederick R. Huber, who took office on July
13, 1915, as the municipal director of music.
The first concert master was J.C. van Hulsteyn,
the first soloist Mabel Garrison, and the first
conductor Gustav Strube. The first concert was
presented on February 11, 1916.

**1363. Orchestra from the United States to
make a European tour** was the Symphony Society of New York, which sailed for Europe on
April 22, 1920. Under the leadership of Walter
Johannes Damrosch, 34 concerts were given in
21 cities in France, Italy, Belgium, Holland,
and England. The first concert was given on
May 4, 1920, at the Paris Opera House. The
last was given on June 20, 1920, at the Royal
Albert Hall, London. The Symphony Society
merged with the New York Philharmonic on
March 30, 1928, to form the Philharmonic Society of New York, with Arturo Toscanini as
conductor in chief.

1364. Radio orchestra was the Detroit News
Orchestra of Detroit, MI, a 16-piece symphonic
ensemble that began broadcasting on May 28,
1922. It was composed principally of members
of the Detroit Symphony Orchestra. Otto
Krueger, piccolo player, was the conductor. The
broadcasts were sponsored by the Detroit Bank
on station WWJ.

**1365. Symphony orchestra devoted exclusive-
ly to radio broadcasting** was the National
Broadcasting Company (NBC) Symphony Orchestra, formed on November 13, 1937. The
conductor was Arturo Toscanini. The orchestra
made its debut at 10 P.M. on December 25,
1937, over the NBC stations WEAF and WJZ,
New York City. The program consisted of the
first symphony of Johannes Brahms, Wolfgang
Amadeus Mozart's G minor symphony, and
Antonio Vivaldi's *Concerto Grosso.*

ARTS—MUSIC—POPULAR MUSIC

1366. Song to hit No. 1 in the pop charts was
Tommy Dorsey's "I'll Never Smile Again,"
sung by Frank Sinatra. Pop music record charts
for single songs were published by the music
trade newspaper *Billboard* beginning on July
20, 1940.

**1367. Record album to hit No. 1 in the pop
charts** was Nat King Cole's *King Cole Trio.*
Pop music record charts for albums were published by the music trade newspaper *Billboard*
beginning on March 24, 1945.

1368. Rock and roll song was probably
"Rocket 88," recorded in 1951 by Jackie
Brenston for Chess Records, Chicago, IL.

**1369. Rock and roll song to hit No. 1 in the
pop charts** was "Rock Around the Clock,"
recorded by Bill Haley and the Comets, one of
the first all-white acts to play rock and roll. It
was recorded on April 12, 1954, and reached
No. 1 on June 29, 1955.

1370. Performance by a British rock group
was a televised set by the Beatles on the CBS
variety series *The Ed Sullivan Show,* broadcast
on February 7, 1964, from New York City. The
Beatles performed their top single "I Want to
Hold Your Hand" from their album *Meet the
Beatles,* which, at the time, was the fastest-
selling album in American history.

1371. Rock and roll broadcast on FM radio
took place on April 7, 1967, in San Francisco,
CA, on KMPX-FM, a foreign-language station.
The disk jockey, Tom Donahue, played a program of San Francisco–area psychedelic rock
and other underground music.

1372. Rock music festival was the Monterey
International Pop Festival, held on June 15–18,
1967, at the Monterey, CA, fairgrounds. Promoter Alan Pariser and booking agent Ben Sha-
piro assembled the largest roster of rock and
soul acts up to that time, including the Who,
the Grateful Dead, Otis Redding, Jefferson Air-

plane, Big Brother and the Holding Company with Janis Joplin, and the Jimi Hendrix Experience. More than 50,000 fans attended the nonprofit event, which inaugurated a decade of ever-larger rock festivals.

1373. Rap album to attract a mass audience was *Run-D.M.C.*, recorded by the rap group of the same name. Run-D.M.C.'s members were "Jam Master" Jason Mizell, Joseph "Run" Simmons, and "MC" Darryl "D" McDaniels, all of New York City. The album was released by Profile Records in June 1984 and went gold on December 17 of that year.

ARTS—MUSIC—SONGS

1374. Patriotic song to achieve national popularity was "Yankee Doodle," written in 1755 by Dr. Richard Shuckburgh, regimental surgeon to General Edward Braddock, commander in chief of the British forces during the French and Indian War. The verses were written at Albany, NY, and set to an ancient English tune, "The World Turned Upside Down." Shuckburgh intended to ridicule the "homely clad colonials," but the song was taken up by the colonists themselves, and was played at the victory celebration in Yorktown in 1781 when Lord Cornwallis surrendered at the end of the Revolutionary War.

1375. Secular song by a composer born in America was "My Days Have Been So Wondrous Free," composed in 1759 by Francis Hopkinson of Philadelphia, PA. It was based on a poem by Thomas Parnell. Despite its popularity, it was not published until the 20th century.

1376. Patriotic song by an American was "The Liberty Song," also known as "In Freedom We're Born," published by John Mein and John Fleming in July 1768 in Boston, MA. The lyrics were by John Dickinson, set to the tune of "Hearts of Oak" by William Boyce of London. The words were published in the *Boston Gazette* of July 18, 1768.

1377. War song was "Chester," composed in 1778 by William Billings of Boston, MA. The song was published in Billings's *The Singing Master's Assistant, or Key to Practical Music,* printed by Draper and Folsom, Boston, in 1778. "Chester" contains the following chorus: "Let tyrants shake their iron rod; / And Slav'ry clank her galling chains, / We fear them not; / We trust in God, / New England's God forever reigns."

1378. Orchestral song to be printed contained parts for a first viol, a second viol, a first clarinet, a second clarinet, E-flat horns, and other instruments, and was tipped in after page 186 of the *Massachusetts Magazine,* published in Boston, MA, in March 1791. The song was "The Death Song of an Indian Chief," by Hans Gram of Boston. It was based upon *Ouabi,* a tale of the Native Americans in four cantos by "Philenia, a lady of Boston" (Sarah Wentworth Apthorp Morton).

1379. Secular song hit with words and music by an American was "The Ministrel's Return from the War," by John Hill Hewitt, composed in Greenville, SC, in 1825. It was published in 1827 by James L. Hewitt and Company, Boston, MA, but was not copyrighted, as its importance was not anticipated.

1380. Performance of "America the Beautiful" in a public took place on July 4, 1832, in the Park Street Church, Boston, MA, where it was sung by the schoolchildren of Boston. The song was written on a scrap of paper in half an hour by Dr. Samuel Francis Smith, a Baptist minister. The original manuscript is in the Harvard University Library.

1381. Song popular in the Confederate States was "I Wish I Was in Dixie's Land" (better known as "Dixie"), written and composed by Daniel Decatur Emmett, a Northerner, expressly for Bryant's Minstrels, who performed at 472 Broadway, New York City. It was announced as a plantation song and dance. According to some sources, it was based on a song of lament sung by the slaves of a Dutch planter named Dixye, who sold them away to a farmer in Piedmont County, South Carolina, after trying unsuccessfully to grow tobacco in Harlem, New Amsterdam (the future New York City). The song was introduced by Emmett on April 4, 1859, at Mechanics Hall, New York City, and was published by Firth Pond and Company, New York City. It was sung at the inauguration of Jefferson Davis as president of the Confederate States on February 18, 1861.

1382. Taps played as a military signal, indicating "lights out" at night and "farewell" at military funerals, was originally played on a drum, whence its name. The musical form of "Taps," which is performed as a bugle call and also as a song, was written toward the beginning of July 1862 in a Union Army camp. General Daniel Butterfield wrote the music on the back of a torn envelope and whistled the tune to Oliver Willcox Norton, bugler and aide-de-camp of General Strong Vincent, commander of the

ARTS—MUSIC—SONGS—continued

83rd Regiment Pennsylvania Volunteers of the Army of the Potomac. They were resting in camp at Harrison's Landing on the James River in Virginia, immediately after the seven days of fighting near Richmond.

1383. Civil rights anthem to achieve fame was "We Shall Overcome." It was originally published in Chicago, IL, in May 1945 as a gospel song, "I'll Overcome Someday," with music by Atrong Twigg and revised lyrics and music by Kenneth Morris. The tune was based on the melody of a hymn dating from the colonial era. The words were adapted from another hymn that included the line: "If in my heart, I do not yield, I'll overcome some day." African-American workers sang the song on a picket line in Charleston, SC, in 1945. The song became the anthem of the civil rights movement in the 1960s.

AVIATION

1384. Aviation law enacted by a state was passed by Connecticut on June 8, 1911. It required all airships to be registered, for a $5 fee, and all applicants for a pilot's license to be tested, for a fee not more than $25. A license to operate and direct airships was required by each pilot, for a $2 fee. The law also established a penalty for noncompliance of a $100 fine and six months' imprisonment. An earlier law, passed by Tennessee in 1905, authorized a tax on aircraft, but did not attempt to regulate or control aircraft.

1385. Aviation department of a state government was established on May 10, 1927, when the Connecticut legislature authorized the organization of the Connecticut Department of Aviation, the first independent state department for the control and regulation of aeronautics in the United States. Offices were opened on July 1, 1927, at Brainard Field, Hartford, CT.

1386. Pressure suit was flight-tested by aviator Wiley Hardeman Post in his plane, the *Willie Mae,* at Wright Field, Dayton, OH, in August 1934. Post was preparing for an air race from London, England, to Melbourne, Australia, in October and planned to fly most of the trip in the stratosphere. At that altitude, he needed to breathe pressurized oxygen to stay alive. After two tries, a workable suit was designed and sewn by engineer Russell Colley of the B.F. Goodrich Company. It was constructed of two layers of fabric, a balloon-like rubber layer containing the pressurized oxygen and an outer layer that protected the balloon and controlled its shape. Post wore a modified diver's helmet over his head.

AVIATION—AIRPLANES

1387. Airplane accident that was fatal occurred on September 17, 1908, at Fort Myer, Arlington Heights, VA, when a propeller blade struck an overhead wire because a fitting to which the guy wire was attached had worn through. Thomas Etholen Selfridge of the Army died from a skull fracture and Orville Wright received multiple hip and leg fractures.

1388. Airplane sold commercially was the *Gold Bug,* delivered by Glenn Hammond Curtiss to the New York Aeronautical Society at Hammondsport, NY, for $5,000 on June 16, 1909. Flying instructions were given to two members.

1389. Airplane purchased by the federal government was a Wright biplane that was given its first official flight on July 30, 1909, and accepted from Orville and Wilbur Wright of Dayton, OH, on August 2. The purchase price was $25,000, but a bonus of $5,000 was given because the specified speed, 40 miles per hour in still air, was exceeded. The plane, built at Dayton, was powered by a 25-horsepower motor. It was 28 feet long, with a wingspan of 36 feet 4 inches, and weighed 740 pounds (gross weight, 1,200 pounds). Its top speed was 44 miles per hour. It was known as *Miss Columbia.* Lieutenant Frank Purdy Lahm and Wilbur Wright made the first flight under government ownership at College Park, MD, on October 8, 1909.

1390. Monoplane was the Walden III, invented by Dr. Henry W. Walden and test-flown at Mineola, NY, on December 9, 1909. It was equipped with a 1909 Anzani three-cylinder motor that developed 22 horsepower and flew at a speed of 52 miles per hour.

1391. Hydroplane that was successful was the *Flying Fish,* which was flown by its inventor, Glenn Hammond Curtiss, at San Diego, CA, on January 26, 1911.

1392. Airplane accident in a solo military airplane that was fatal took the life of Second Lieutenant George E. Maurice Kelly of the Signal Corps, who crashed to the ground in a Curtiss airplane about 7:30 A.M. on May 10, 1911, in San Antonio, TX. He suffered a fractured skull and was rushed to Fort Sam Houston Hospital, where he died one hour later.

1393. Airplane accident involving a woman that was fatal took the life of Julia Clark of Denver, CO, who was killed on June 17, 1912, at the Illinois State Fair Grounds, Springfield, IL, when her Curtiss biplane struck the limb of a tree and turned over while she was circling the field at 40 miles per hour on her first flight. Her death was the 151st in heavier-than-air aircraft.

1394. Airplane with ailerons was an 850-pound biplane that attained a speed of 40 miles per hour. The engine was in the rear and was connected to two large propellers by a chain drive. It was built by William Whitney Christmas of Washington, DC, who obtained a patent on a flying machine on May 5, 1914, and assigned it to the Christmas Aeroplane Company of Washington, DC. On December 18, 1923, the federal government paid $100,000 for the patent.

1395. Airplane with a fuselage of molded plywood was the *Whistling Bill*, a two-place fighter, built in 1918 by the Curtiss Aeroplane and Motor Company, Garden City, NY. The fuselage was made of four longitudinal sheets of Haskelite, three-ply birch plywood, steamed and formed to contour in a concrete die. The cooling radiators were of the tubular type, located on the sides of the fuselage. The plane was of 400 horsepower, carried two .30-caliber machine guns, and had a sea-level speed of 170 miles per hour. It was designed by Charles Kirkham.

1396. Corporation to own its own airplane for transportation of its executives was the Standard Oil Company of Indiana, which paid $47,709 to the Stout Metal Aircraft Division of the Ford Motor Company, Detroit, MI, for a *Stanolind,* a 600-horsepower trimotor monoplane. The first flight was made on May 21, 1927, from Detroit to Chicago. The plane had a complete set of double controls, could carry 4,000 pounds, and could accommodate two pilots, one mechanic, and eight passengers.

1397. Stabilized airplane in commercial use was the Curtiss Condor No. 5, built in 1931 by the Curtiss Aeroplane and Motor Company in its factory at Garden City, NY. The plane was powered by two liquid-cooled 12-cylinder engines, 650 horsepower, and was equipped with both a Sperry stabilizer and an automatic pilot, which were placed in a box under the pilot's seat. The airplane carried 18 passengers, two pilots, and a hostess, and was operated by the Eastern Air Transport airlines between New York City and Miami, FL.

1398. Plastic bonded airplane to be awarded a Type certificate by the Civil Aeronautics Administration was an open two-place tandem low-wing full-cantilever type monoplane built by the Timm Aircraft Corporation, Van Nuys, CA, in July 1940. It was approved on April 5, 1941. It was a training plane, the fuselage, wings, and all control surfaces of which were fabricated from a special material formed by binding several laminations of plywood with liquid plastic and pressing in a precision mold to the exact contour and size desired. The entire airplane structure contained less than 7 percent aluminum.

1399. Jet airplane designed and built in the United States was the XP-59, an Airacomet, built by the Bell Aircraft Corporation, Buffalo, NY, and flown for the first time on October 1, 1942, at a secret testing base in Muroc, CA, by Robert Morris Stanley. It was rated over 400 miles per hour and in excess of 40,000 feet. The higher the altitude (up to a certain maximum), the faster it flew. It employed two turbojet engines built by the General Electric Company from designs made by Group Captain Frank Whittle, the British inventor. The fuel was generally kerosene, although anything that burned could be used as a substitute. There was no propeller.

1400. Gas-turbine propeller-driven airplane was the XP-81, a fighter, designed and produced by Consolidated Vultee Aircraft Corporation at Vultee Field, Downey, CA, and first flight-tested on February 11, 1945, at the Army Air Force base in Muroc, CA. Its wingspan was 50 feet 6 inches and its fuselage 44 feet 8 inches long. It weighed 19,500 pounds and traveled at a speed greater than 500 miles per hour. In the nose was a propeller-driven gas turbine built by the General Electric Company. Between the cockpit and the tail was a jet engine, also built by General Electric.

1401. Twin-engine pressurized airplane was the Convair Liner, a 40-passenger airliner equipped with two 2,400-horsepower Pratt and Whitney engines that reached a speed of 300 miles per hour. Its wingspan was 91 feet 11 inches, its length 74 feet 8 inches, and its height 26 feet 11 inches. The Convair's jet exhaust propulsion provided additional speed. The plane was produced at the Consolidated Vultee Aircraft Corporation plant at San Diego, CA. It was first test-flown on March 16, 1947.

AVIATION—AIRPLANES—*continued*

1402. Airplane with a delta wing was the Convair Model 7002, built by the Consolidated Vultee Aircraft Corporation in Downey, CA, and San Diego, CA. It was 42 feet 5 inches long, 17 feet 8 inches high, and had a 31 foot 3 inch wingspan. The wing had a 60-degree sweepback on its leading edge and had elevons on its straight trailing edge. The plane was powered by a single-jet Allison J33-A 29 engine. It made its first flight on September 18, 1948, at Muroc, CA (later Edwards Air Force Base). It was delivered to the Air Force on May 14, 1949, and designated XF 92A.

1403. Jet airplane used for commercial transport that was built in the United States was the Boeing Stratoliner Model 707, first tested July 15, 1954, by Alvin M. Johnston at Renton, WA, where it was built by the Boeing Airplane Company. It had four Pratt and Whitney J-57 engines with more than 10,000 pounds of thrust. It weighed 190,000 pounds and cost about $20 million. It was designed to carry about 150 passengers across the Atlantic Ocean at a speed of 550 miles per hour. The first transport was delivered on August 16, 1958, to Pan American Airways.

1404. Airplane disaster involving more than 100 persons occurred on June 30, 1956, when a Trans World Airlines Super Constellation en route from Los Angeles to Kansas City collided with a United Air Lines DC-7 traveling from Los Angeles to Chicago and Newark. The accident took place over the Grand Canyon in Arizona. There were 128 deaths.

1405. Jumbo jet was the Boeing 747, introduced for flight service by the Boeing Company of Seattle, WA, in 1970. The wide-bodied, two-decked aircraft was taller than a six-story building and could carry up to 490 passengers, more than could easily be handled by the terminal facilities of the time. The first 747s went into transatlantic service for Pan American Airlines beginning on January 21, 1970.

1406. Human-powered aircraft that was successful was the *Gossamer Condor*, designed and built by a team under the direction of Paul MacCready, an aeronautical engineer living in Pasadena, CA. The ultra-lightweight craft was constructed primarily of cardboard, piano wire, aluminum tubing, and Mylar plastic sheeting. The power was supplied by the pilot, who continuously pushed a set of bicycle pedals. On August 23, 1977, bicyclist Bryan Allen pedaled over a three-mile course to win the $50,000 Kremer Prize, awarded for milestones in hu-

man-powered flight. On June 12, 1979, another MacCready design, the *Gossamer Albatross*, became the first human-powered aircraft to cross the English Channel. Allen piloted the plane from Folkestone, England, to Cap Gris-Nez, France, in 2 hours 55 minutes.

1407. Ornithopter that succeeded in flying was designed by Jeremy Harris of the Battelle Memorial Institute, Columbus, OH, and James DeLaurier, a professor of aerospace engineering at the University of Toronto. In late 1991, after 20 years of work, they designed and flew the world's first true ornithopter, an 8.6-pound aircraft that flapped its wings and flew like a bird. The model ornithopter was made of wood, Kevlar, and carbon composites, and was radio-controlled. Its one-horsepower piston engine powered 10-foot wings made of three hinged panels. The first flight lasted 11.5 minutes.

AVIATION—AIRPLANES—COMMERCIAL SERVICE

1408. Hydroplane service started on January 1, 1914, between St. Petersburg, FL, and Tampa, FL. The planes were built by the Benoist Aircraft Company and were operated by the St. Petersburg–Tampa Airboat Line. Two round-trip flights were made daily. The regular round-trip fare was $10. Mayor Abram Cump Phiel of St. Petersburg paid $400 for the first round trip. The planes flew 80 feet above the water across Tampa Bay, an air distance of 18 miles, in 23 minutes.

1409. Hydroplane international service was established by Aeromarine Airways on November 1, 1920, on a route from Key West, FL, to Havana, Cuba. The service employed two hydroplanes, each with the capacity to carry three people. The fare was $50. Mail was also carried.

1410. Airplane scheduled passenger flight at night was made on April 1, 1927, when a three-engine Fokker of the Colonial Air Transport Company took off for Boston, MA, from Hadley Field, NJ, then the only lighted airport with a lighted runway.

1411. Transcontinental daily air-rail passenger service began at 5 P.M. on June 14, 1929, when a New York Central train left New York City. At Cleveland, OH, the passengers switched to a Universal Air Express Lines flight, which brought them to Garden City, KS. There they boarded a Santa Fe Railroad train to Los Angeles, CA, arriving at 9:15 A.M. on June

17, 1929. The total time for the trip was 62 hours 15 minutes. For the occasion, Mayor James John Walker of New York City sent a bottle of water to Mayor George Edward Cryer of Los Angeles.

1412. Airline flight attendant who was a woman was Ellen Church, a nurse from Cressbill, IA. In May 1930, she made her first flight between San Francisco, CA, and Cheyenne, WY, on Boeing Air Transport, a forerunner of United Air Lines. Requirements for the job were that she be not older than 25, not taller than 5 feet 4 inches, and that her weight be 115 pounds or less. The salary was $125 a month for 100 hours of flying. The first African-American woman hired as a flight attendant was Ruth Carol Taylor, a graduate nurse from Ithaca, NY, who made her first flight on February 11, 1958, from Ithaca to New York City on Mohawk Airlines.

1413. Airplane sleeping berths were introduced by American Airways of Chicago, IL, in March 1933. Each berth was made by folding two of the plane's chairs to form a cot. The first airplane with nonconvertible sleeping berths was placed in service on October 5, 1933, by Eastern Air Transport on the route between Atlanta, GA, and New York City. The plane was a Curtiss-Wright Condor and was designed to contain eight berths and five seats, but on the initial trip only two berths were installed, an upper and a lower. The berths were 6 feet 5 inches long and 2 feet 4 inches wide. The first passengers to occupy the berths were the air ace Captain Edward Vernon Rickenbacker and Alexander Strong. The plane was equipped in the company's shops at the Atlanta Municipal Airport, where the first trip started.

1414. Transport airplane designed for transoceanic service was the *Pan American Clipper,* a 19-ton flying boat powered by four Hornet air-cooled, geared, and supercharged engines, each developing 750 horsepower. It was an all-metal monoplane, 68 feet long, with a wingspread of 118 feet 2 inches. It carried within its hull and in the wings and pontoons a fuel load of more than 8.5 tons, adequate for a flight range of 3,500 miles. Under the command of Captain Edwin Charles Musick, the first Clipper took off April 16, 1935, at 6:50 P.M. from San Francisco, CA, and arrived 12:59 P.M. on April 17 at Pearl Harbor, Honolulu, HI, covering 2,301 air miles in 18 hours 39 minutes. The return trip was begun on April 22, 1935, at 8:59 P.M. from Pearl Harbor, and the transport landed at Alameda, CA, on April 23, at 5:59 P.M.

1415. Transatlantic commercial airplane service over the "southern route" was initiated by the 41.5-ton *Dixie Clipper* of Pan American Airways, commanded by Captain Robert Oliver Daniel Sullivan. It left Port Washington, NY, on June 28, 1939, at 1:59 P.M., with 12 crew members and 22 passengers. It was powered by four 1,550-horsepower Wright Cyclone engines. Stops were made at Horta, in the Azores, and at Lisbon, Portugal. The plane landed at Marseilles, France, on June 30, 1939, at 8:21 A.M. The fare was $375.

1416. Round-the-world commercial airplane service began on June 17, 1947, when a Pan American airplane commanded by Hugh Gordon left La Guardia Field, New York City, with 21 passengers and a crew of 10. The route, 22,297 miles, was via Newfoundland, London, Istanbul, Karachi, Manila, Bangkok, Calcutta, Shanghai, Tokyo, Guam, Wake, Honolulu, and San Francisco. The first trip took 309 hours 21 minutes, with 101 hours 32 minutes of actual flying time. Round-trip fare for the world flight was $1,700.

1417. Cargo airlines licensed by the Civil Aeronautics Board were the Flying Tiger Line, Slick Airways, United States Airlines, and Airnews, which were issued licenses on April 29, 1949, effective June 24, 1949.

1418. Year in which air traffic volume exceeded first-class rail traffic volume was 1951, when scheduled United States domestic, territorial, and local-service (feeder) carriers flew 10,556,139,000 revenue passenger-miles, compared with parlor and sleeping car traffic of 10,225,525,000 miles on Class One railroads.

1419. Airline to install rear-facing passenger seats aboard its planes was North American Airlines, Burbank, CA. The first flight of a plane equipped with these seats was made from Burbank to La Guardia Field, New York City, on June 1, 1953.

1420. Transcontinental nonstop eastbound airplane service was inaugurated on October 19, 1953, when a Trans World Airlines Lockheed Super-Constellation took off from International Airport, Los Angeles, CA, at 7:09 P.M. It arrived at Idlewild International Airport, New York City, at 6:26 A.M. New York time on October 20. On westward flights, a stopover at Chicago was made.

AVIATION—AIRPLANES—COMMER-
CIAL SERVICE—*continued*

1421. Transcontinental nonstop two-way airplane service was instituted on November 29, 1953, by American Airlines, using Douglas DC-7s, between International Airport, Los Angeles, CA, and Idlewild International Airport, New York City, a distance of 2,540 miles. The eastbound flight was scheduled for 7 hours 15 minutes and the westbound flight for 7 hours 55 minutes.

1422. Transcontinental jet airplane passenger service began on January 25, 1959, when a four-engine American Airlines Boeing 707 made the trip between Los Angeles, CA, and New York City with 112 passengers and eight-member crew in 4 hours 3 minutes 3 seconds. The plane was piloted by Captain Charles Macatee of Huntington, NY. The fare was $158.85 one way plus tax and $301.90 round-trip plus tax.

1423. Airline to carry 100 million passengers was American Airlines, New York City, which selected pioneering aviator Lieutenant General James Harold Doolittle, chairman of the board of Space Technology Laboratories, Los Angeles, as the national symbol of the 100,000,000th passenger and presented him with a crystal bowl on December 28, 1961.

1424. Transatlantic supersonic jet service to serve civilian passengers in the United States began operations on May 24, 1976, with the arrival of two Concorde jet airplanes at Dulles International Airport, Washington, DC. One plane had departed from Paris, the other from London. Passengers on the Concorde were able to cross the Atlantic in a mere three hours. Supersonic flights between France and New York City began on October 19, 1977.

AVIATION—AIRPLANES—FLIGHTS

1425. Airplane model to make a sustained flight under its own power was Samuel Pierpont Langley's model No. 5, which was tested on May 6, 1896, on the shores of the Potomac River. This unmanned model "aerodrome" weighed 26 pounds, was 16 feet in length, and had four cambered single-tier wings, each about 14 feet from tip to tip. It was driven by a one-horsepower steam engine. It was catapulted from a platform 20 feet above the water and flew a distance of about 0.75 miles, remaining aloft 1.5 minutes during one of its flights. As the fuel was exhausted, the plane descended gently to the water. It was picked up, dried off, refueled, and relaunched the same afternoon. This was the first flight

anywhere in the world of a mechanically propelled machine that was heavier than air. Langley predicted that airplanes would eventually be used to carry humans, but his friends and the press scoffed.

1426. Airplane flight took place on December 17, 1903, at Kill Devil Hills, near Kitty Hawk, NC, with Orville Wright at the controls of a motor-powered airplane he had built with his brother Wilbur. The plane, which weighed 745 pounds and had a four-cylinder, 12-horsepower engine, was launched from a monorail after a 35- to 40-foot run. It remained aloft for 12 seconds and covered 120 feet. Three subsequent flights took place that day, of which the longest covered 852 feet in 59 seconds. The average speed was 31 miles per hour. Some historians respect the claim of Gustave Whitehead, who is said to have made four flights, one of which covered a distance of 1.5 miles, in his airplane *No. 21* on August 14, 1901, near Bridgeport, CT.

1427. Airplane endurance flight exceeding one hour was made on September 9, 1908, by Orville Wright, who flew a Wright airplane with a Wright motor at Fort Myer, VA, for 1 hour 2 minutes 15 seconds.

1428. Intercity airplane flight by a U.S. military officer was made on July 30, 1909, by Lieutenant Benjamin Delahauf Foulois, who flew with Orville Wright as the pilot from Fort Myer, VA, to Alexandria, VA. They traveled 10 miles at an altitude of 600 feet, averaging 42 miles per hour, thereby establishing three world records for distance, speed, and altitude.

1429. Night flight in an airplane was made by Walter Richard Brookins on April 18, 1910, at Montgomery, AL.

1430. Airplane round trip made in one day between two large cities took place on June 13, 1910, when Charles Keeney Hamilton, flying in a Curtiss biplane equipped with a Curtiss motor, made the round trip between Governors Island, New York City, and Philadelphia, PA. He left Governors Island at 7:36 A.M. and arrived at Front Street and Erie Avenue, Philadelphia, at 9:26 A.M. The average speed for his flight of 1 hour 50 minutes was 46.92 miles per hour. He left Philadelphia at 11:33 A.M. and, after a detour, landed at South Amboy, NJ, at 12:54 P.M., in a swamp instead of on a green. He repaired a broken spark plug, reascended at 6:17 P.M., and landed at Governors Island at 6:40 P.M. The flying time for the round trip was 3 hours 34 minutes. For this accomplishment he won a $10,000 prize offered by the *New York Times* and the *Philadelphia Ledger*.

1431. Airplane to fly higher than a mile in altitude was a Wright biplane flown by Walter Richard Brookins to an altitude of 6,234 feet on July 9, 1910, over Atlantic City, NJ. The gasoline gave out when he descended to 5,800 feet and the engine stopped, but Brookins glided the airplane to safety. He was in the air 1 hour 2 minutes 35 seconds. For his feat he won a $5,000 prize offered by the Atlantic City Aero Club.

1432. Airplane flight over water was made by Glenn Hammond Curtiss, who on August 31, 1910, flew in his biplane over Lake Erie from Euclid Beach Park, Cleveland, OH, to Cedar Point, Sandusky, OH. He flew at an altitude between 400 and 500 feet. The trip took 78 minutes nonstop over a distance of 70 miles.

1433. Airplane flight from a ship was made on November 14, 1910, when Eugene Burton Ely, a civilian pilot of the Curtiss Company, took off from the bow of the scout cruiser *Birmingham,* anchored at the Hampton Roads Yacht Clubhouse at Willoughby spit, and flew through fog and rain to Hampton Roads, VA. The runway was 83 feet long with a 5-degree slope, allowing only a 26-foot takeoff, as the length of the plane was 57 feet. Ely won a $5,000 prize.

1434. Airplane flight to the deck of a carrier was made on January 18, 1911, by Eugene Burton Ely of San Francisco, CA, who took off at 10:45 A.M. from Selfridge Field, Camp Selfridge, CA, flew 13 miles, and landed on a sloped wooden platform 130 feet long and 50 feet wide above the deck of the cruiser *Pennsylvania* in San Francisco Harbor. Ropes and sandbags were used to stop the airplane. Its speed was 35 miles per hour.

1435. Airplane rescue at sea took place on January 30, 1911, 10 miles from Havana, Cuba. John Alexander Douglas McCurdy had been flying from Key West, FL, to Camp Columbia, Havana, making the first sea flight out of sight of land, when his biplane developed engine trouble as a result of a faulty oil connection. He landed the plane on the sea, where its pontoons kept it afloat, and within four minutes was picked up by the destroyer *Terry.*

1436. Hydroplane flight to and from a ship was made by Glenn Hammond Curtiss from North Island, San Diego, CA, to the U.S.S. *Pennsylvania* in the Pacific Ocean on February 17, 1911. He landed alongside the ship and was hoisted aboard before starting out on the return trip.

1437. Airplane flight under a bridge was made on June 27, 1911, by Lincoln Beachey, who flew in the rain in a 60-horsepower Curtiss biplane at Niagara Falls, NY, as a stunt for the international carnival. He took off from a baseball field on the American side of the Niagara River, crossed over the American Falls and the Horseshoe Falls at an altitude of 2,000 feet, and flew under the steel arch bridge, 168 feet high and 100 feet wide, at a height of some 15 feet above the water. He then flew down the gorge almost to the Whirlpool Rapids at a speed of 60 miles per hour and landed on the Canadian side. About 150,000 spectators witnessed the flight, which Beachey repeated two days later.

1438. Airplane rescue at sea by another airplane was made by Hugh Robinson on August 14, 1911. Pilot Rene Simon had been flying over Lake Michigan in a monoplane and dived down to wave to some motorboats. Unable to rise, he crashed into the lake. Robinson, in a Curtiss hydroplane, flew over to Simon and found him in his floating plane smoking a cigar. Robinson hailed several people in motorboats, and they towed Simon and his monoplane to the shore.

1439. Transcontinental airplane flight made in stages was made by Calbraith Perry Rodgers, who left Sheepshead Bay, NY, on September 17, 1911, in his Burgess-Wright biplane and spent 49 days en route to California, arriving in Pasadena on November 5. He was followed by a special train carrying spare parts. The distance was 3,417 miles, which he covered in 70 hops. His actual flying time was 3 days 10 hours 14 minutes. His best day's coverage was 231 miles and his best single flight was 133 miles, from Stovall, CA, to Imperial Junction, CA. Weather was responsible for the loss of 11 days, and 13.5 days were consumed in making repairs. On November 12, at Compton, CA, he crashed and was badly injured, but on December 10 he continued the journey.

1440. Transcontinental eastbound airplane flight made in stages was made by Robert Grant Fowler, who left Los Angeles, CA, on October 19, 1911, in a Model B Wright biplane equipped with a 30-horsepower four-cylinder Wright engine. He made 65 landings in California, Arizona, New Mexico, Texas, Louisiana, Alabama, Georgia, and Florida, and landed at Jacksonville, FL, on February 8, 1912.

AVIATION—AIRPLANES—FLIGHTS—
continued

1441. Airplane round-trip flight over water was made by Glenn Luther Martin in a biplane on May 10, 1912. The trip was made in 37 minutes at an altitude in excess of 2,000 feet for an approximate distance of 31 miles over the Pacific Ocean from Newport Bay, CA, to Avalon, Santa Catalina Island, CA. The return flight was from Santa Catalina Island via San Pedro and down the coast to Newport Bay, covering 45 miles in 51 minutes. An inflated tire tube on the fuselage served as a life preserver.

1442. Airplane takeoff from a hotel roof was made by a Curtiss biplane at 2:35 P.M., June 11, 1912. In a light rain, Silas Christoferson took off from the Multnomah Hotel, Portland, OR, on a 170-foot board runway built over obstructions. Christoferson, who had not yet won his pilot's license, crossed the Williamette and Columbia rivers on the flight.

1443. Airplane loop-the-loop was made by Lincoln Beachey at North Island, San Diego, CA, on November 18, 1913. When he reached an altitude of 1,000 feet, he brought his machine up with a swoop and a moment later was flying head downward. The loop was completed at the 300-foot level. On November 28 he made a triple loop.

1444. Airplane flight longer than 500 miles was made by Ruth Law, who flew a two-year-old obsolete Curtiss biplane 590 miles from Chicago, IL, to Hornell, NY, on November 19, 1916. She left at 8:25 A.M. and arrived at 2:10 P.M. in 5 hours 45 minutes' flying time. She landed and refueled and continued on to Binghamton, NY. Law, an accomplished stunt flyer, was the first American woman to fly at night. She and her husband later ran a three-plane flying troupe, Ruth Law's Flying Circus.

1445. Transatlantic hydroplane flight made in stages began on May 8, 1919, in Rockaway, NY. A hydroplane commanded by Lieutenant Commander Albert Cushing Read left Rockaway in company with two others that failed to finish the trip. Stops were made at Trepassey, Newfoundland; Horta and Ponta Delgada, in the Azores; and Lisbon, Portugal. The final destination, Plymouth, England, was reached on May 31. The total distance was 4,500 miles.

1446. Airplane flight between New York and Alaska was made by four United States planes of the Alaskan Flying Expedition that left Mitchel Field, NY, on July 15, 1920, and arrived at Nome, AK, on August 25. The return trip began in Nome on August 29 and ended at Mitchel Field on October 20, with 16 stops en route. The distance was 4,345 miles each way. The average flying speed of the trip was 80 miles per hour. The expedition commander was Captain St. Clair Streett.

1447. Transcontinental airplane flight made within 24 hours was made by Lieutenant William Devoe Coney of the 91st Aero Squadron, who took off from Rockwell Field, San Diego, CA, at 7 P.M., February 21, 1921. He was forced down at Bronte, TX, by a snowstorm. He completed his flight at Pablo Beach, Jacksonville, FL, on February 24 at 7:27 A.M. He covered 2,079 miles in an elapsed time of 36 hours 27 minutes and a flying time of 22 hours 27 minutes.

1448. Airplane to fly faster than 200 miles per hour was piloted by Lieutenant Lester James Maitland on October 14, 1922, at the national airplane meet at Selfridge Field, Mount Clemens, MI. Maitland flew a Curtiss pursuit plane with a 375-horsepower engine at a speed of 216.1 miles per hour for 50 kilometers.

1449. Transcontinental nonstop airplane flight was made by Lieutenants Oakley G. Kelly and John A. Macready of the Navy Air Service. On May 2, 1923, the pilots, flying a Fokker T2 monoplane equipped with a Liberty engine, took off from Roosevelt Field, NY, at 11:36 P.M. They arrived at Rockwell Field, Coronado Beach, CA, at 12:26 P.M. the next day, covering a distance of 2,700 miles in 26 hours 50 minutes.

1450. Transatlantic solo airplane flight was made by Charles Augustus Lindbergh on May 20, 1927, from New York to Paris. He flew about 3,610 miles in 33 hours 32 minutes in the *Spirit of St. Louis,* a Ryan monoplane equipped with a single 225-horsepower Wright Whirlwind motor. He left Roosevelt Field, NY, at 7:52 A.M. on May 20 and arrived at 5:24 P.M. New York time the following day at Le Bourget field, Paris.

1451. All-blind airplane flight was made on September 24, 1929, at Mitchel Field, NY, by Lieutenant James Harold Doolittle in a two-seater Consolidated-Wright biplane. He made a complete flight in an enclosed cockpit without seeing the ground or any part of the airplane except an illuminated instrument board. From takeoff to landing, only flight instruments were used. Doolittle was guided by a radio beacon. Lieutenant Benjamin Kelsey accompanied him in the event of an emergency.

1452. Airplane catapulted from an airship was a Vought two-seater observation plane that was released on May 20, 1930, from the airship *Los Angeles*. It was piloted by Lieutenant Commander Charles Ambrose Nicholson, who flew it to the carrier *Saratoga*.

1453. Transcontinental solo airplane flight by a woman was made by Laura Ingalls, who left Roosevelt Field, NY, on October 5, 1930, in a Moth biplane. She made nine stops before reaching Glendale, CA, on October 9. The flight took 30 hours 27 minutes. The return flight, which began on October 18, lasted 25 hours 35 minutes. Ingalls was also the first female pilot to make a nonstop transatlantic flight westbound. Her Wasp-powered Lockheed Orion monoplane, the *Auto da Fé*, left Floyd Bennett Field, Brooklyn, New York City, on July 10, 1935, and arrived at Burbank, CA, 18 hours 19.5 minutes later.

1454. Transpacific nonstop airplane flight was made by Clyde Pangborn and Hugh Herndon, Jr., who landed at Wenatchee, WA, on October 5, 1931, having flown from Sabishiro, Japan, a distance of 4,458 statute miles, in 41 hours 13 minutes. They flew in a single-motored 425-horsepower Bellanca monoplane. This was the last lap of their round-the-world trip.

1455. Transatlantic solo airplane flight by a woman was made by Amelia Earhart, a native of Atchison, KS, who left Harbor Grace, Newfoundland, Canada, at 5:50 P.M. on May 20, 1932, and arrived at Londonderry, Ireland, at 8:46 A.M. on May 21. She flew 2,026 miles in 14 hours 56 minutes. Her flight took place exactly five years after that of Charles Augustus Lindbergh, the first pilot to make a solo transatlantic crossing.

1456. Transcontinental nonstop airplane flight by a woman was accomplished by Amelia Earhart. She took off from Los Angeles, CA, on August 24, 1932, at 1:26 P.M., in her red Wasp-powered Lockheed airplane, and arrived at the Newark, NJ, Metropolitan Airport, at 11:32 A.M. She flew approximately 2,600 miles in 19 hours 5 minutes.

1457. Round-the-world solo airplane flight was made by Wiley Hardeman Post in a Lockheed Vega monoplane, the *Winnie Mae*. He took off from Floyd Bennett Field, New York City, on Saturday, July 15, 1933, at 5:10 A.M. and landed in Berlin, Germany, at 6:55 A.M. the following day, after a flight of 25 hours 45 minutes. Other stops were at Konigsberg, Moscow, Novosibirsk, Irkutsk, Rukhlovo, Khabarovsk, Flat, Fairbanks, and Edmonton. Post returned to Floyd Bennett Field on July 22 at 11:59:30 P.M., making the round-the-world circuit of 15,596 miles in 7 days 18 hours 49 minutes, of which 115 hours 36 minutes 30 seconds was flying time. His airplane was equipped with a Sperry automatic pilot and a directional radio. Post had previously made a round-the-world flight in the *Winnie Mae*, accompanied by Harold Gatty. Starting from Roosevelt Field, NY, on June 23, 1931, they covered a total of 15,474 miles before returning on July 1 after an elapsed time of 8 days 15 hours 51 minutes. Post was thus the first man to fly around the world twice.

1458. Transcontinental flight made by African-Americans in their own airplane was made by Charles Alfred Anderson of Bryn Mawr, PA, holder of a transport license, and Dr. Albert Ernest Forsythe of Atlantic City, NJ, a privately licensed pilot. They took off from Bader Airport, Atlantic City, on July 17, 1933, at 2:49 A.M. and arrived at Los Angeles, CA, on July 19 at 5:30 P.M.

1459. Train of airplanes soared from Floyd Bennett Field, NY, on August 2, 1934, at 10:44 A.M. It consisted of a Wright-Eaglerock airplane, piloted by Elwood Keim, that towed three gliders, which were piloted by Jack O'Meara, Dr. Roswell Earl Franklin, and Stanley Smith. The gliders were to be released from the train at Philadelphia, Baltimore, and Washington. The flight was arranged by the Lustig Sky Train Corporation, and each glider carried about 75 pounds of mail. Because of heavy winds, the air train was forced down at Philadelphia at 1:20 P.M.

1460. Transpacific solo airplane flight by a woman was made by Amelia Earhart. She left Wheeler Field, Honolulu, HI, at 10:15 P.M. on January 11, 1935, and arrived at the Oakland Airport, Oakland, CA, at 4:31 P.M. the next day, covering 2,408 miles in 18 hours 16 minutes at an average speed of 133 miles per hour.

AVIATION—AIRPLANES—FLIGHTS—
continued

1461. Transatlantic round-trip airplane flight from the United States was made in the *Lady Peace* by Richard Merrill and Harry Richman, who left Floyd Bennett Field, NY, on September 2, 1936, at 4:37 A.M., and made a forced landing on September 3 at about 10:30 A.M. at Llwyncelyn, Carmarthenshire, Wales, 175 miles from Croydon Airdrome. The return trip was made from Southport, England, on September 13. The plane crash-landed at Musgrave Harbor, Newfoundland, Canada, about 100 miles from Harbor Grace, and returned to New York City a week later.

1462. Round-the-world flight by a commercial airplane was made by the *Pacific Clipper*, of Pan American Airways, which left San Francisco, CA, on December 2, 1941, under Captain Robert Ford, with a 10-man crew, and returned to New York City on January 6, 1942. The plane covered 31,500 miles in a flying time of 209.5 hours. Because of war conditions, the return trip from New Zealand was over the Coral Sea, Netherlands East Indies, Indian Ocean, Java Sea, Bay of Bengal, Arabian Sea, Persian Gulf, Red Sea, the Nile and Congo rivers, overland to West Africa, thence to Brazil, and finally to New York.

1463. Airplane human pickup was accomplished on September 5, 1943, at the Clinton County Army Air Base at Wilmington, OH. Captain Norman Rintoul was the pilot. His plane was equipped with an electric reeling motor and a hook from which was suspended a 185-foot nylon rope half an inch thick. With this equipment, he succeeded in hoisting up paratrooper First Lieutenant Alexis Doster of Washington, DC.

1464. Jet-propelled landing on an aircraft carrier was made on November 6, 1945, by Ensign Jake C. West in an FR-1 Fireball on the escort aircraft carrier *Wake Island* off San Diego, CA. The Fireball, a Ryan-built navy fighter plane, was powered by both a turbojet and a conventional reciprocating engine, and normally used its reciprocating power plant for takeoff and landing, switching over to the jet as either an exclusive or a supplementary propulsive force once it was in the air. As West was landing, the reciprocating engine power failed, and he landed using jet power.

1465. Transcontinental round-trip airplane flight made within 24 hours was made on June 12, 1946, by a jet-propelled P-80 Shooting Star fighter plane. The pilots were Colonel Leon Gray of Casa Grande, AZ, Major Robin Olds of Beverly Hills, CA, and Lieutenant Jack Richardson of Oklahoma City, OK. They flew from March Field, CA, to Andrews Field, MD, in 5 hours 31 minutes, with a 34-minute stop at Oklahoma City to refuel, and returned in 6 hours 45 minutes, with stops to refuel at Scott Field, IL, and Midland, TX. The trip of approximately 4,540 miles was made in 12 hours 15 minutes. Total elapsed time, including a drive to Washington, DC, for lunch, was 14 hours 51 minutes.

1466. Jet airplane to land on a ship was an FD-1 Phantom, piloted by Lieutenant Commander James J. Davison, which landed on July 21, 1946, on the deck of the aircraft carrier *Franklin D. Roosevelt* 60 miles east of Cape Henry, VA. It was designed and built by the McDonnell Aircraft Corporation of St. Louis, MO, and had a service ceiling over 7 miles and a top speed in excess of 500 miles per hour. It was a single-seat, low-wing monoplane of conventional monocoque design, with twin axial-flow Westinghouse turbojet engines built into the wing roots. Total weight with full combat load was less than 10,000 pounds. The wings folded electrically and when rigged for stowage the plane was 16 feet wide.

1467. Transatlantic flight by a robot airplane was done by the Skymaster, an Army C-54 four-engine military transport that took off from Stephensville, Newfoundland, Canada, on September 22, 1947, and arrived 10 hours and 15 minutes later at Brise Norton, England, near London, a distance of 2,400 miles. The robot piloting device was not touched after the throttles were opened to start the airplane. The plane carried 14 persons, including Colonel James Milligan Gillespie, the pilot and commander.

1468. Airplane to fly faster than the speed of sound was piloted by Major Charles Elwood "Chuck" Yeager, who flew a Bell X-1, an army rocket airplane, at Edwards Air Force Base, Muroc, CA, on October 14, 1947. The rocket engine was built by Reaction Motors, Rockaway, NJ. The plane attained the speed of 750 miles per hour (Mach 1.06) and an altitude of 70,140 feet. Alcohol and liquid oxygen were used as fuel, forced into the burners by gaseous nitrogen. The plane was equipped with rockets that could keep it in the air only 10 minutes. It had to be dropped from a bomber while at a high altitude. Official announcement of the achievement was withheld until June 10, 1948. The first woman to break the sound barrier was Jacqueline Cochran, who flew a North American F-86 Saber over Edwards Air Force Base on May 18, 1953, at the speed of 760 miles per hour.

1469. Transatlantic eastward flight by jet airplane was made on July 20, 1948, by 16 Lockheed P-80 Shooting Stars that flew from Mount Clemens, MI, to Odiham, England, under the command of Colonel David Carl Schilling, of Raleigh, NC, commander of the 56th Fighter Group. They traveled a distance of 4,283 miles in 10 hours 40 minutes. Stops were made at Goose Bay, Labrador; Bluie West Two, Greenland; Keflavik, Iceland; and Stornoway, in the Outer Hebrides, off Scotland.

1470. Round-the-world nonstop flight by an airplane was made in 94 hours 1 minute by a B-50 Superfortress, *Lucky Lady II,* under the command of Captain James Gallagher. The plane left Carswell Air Force base, Fort Worth, TX, on February 26, 1949, at 11:21 A.M. It carried a crew of 14 and averaged 249 miles per hour on its 23,452-mile trip. It was refueled four times in the air by B-29 tanker planes and landed on March 2, 1949, at 9:22 A.M.

1471. Airplane to fly with a load of 100,000 pounds was an XC-99 Convair that took off from Carswell Air Base, Fort Worth, TX, on April 15, 1949, with a cargo of zinc alloy for use in aircraft tooling. B.A. Erickson was pilot and F. Keen was copilot. The transport, built by the Convair division of General Dynamics Corporation, San Diego, CA, was designed to carry 400 fully armed men or 300 litter patients with their attendants.

1472. Transatlantic airplane flight carrying 100 people was *The Champ,* a four-engine Air Force C-74 Globemaster, 82 tons, built by the Douglas Company, Santa Monica, CA. It was commanded by Captain John M. Kelly of West Palm Beach, FL. The plane took off at 3:35 P.M. from Mobile, AL, on November 17, 1949, with 103 persons aboard, including 90 Air Force replacement personnel and a crew of 13. It landed at Marham, England, at 7:35 P.M. on November 18. Total flying time was 23 hours.

1473. Transatlantic nonstop jet airplane flight was made on September 22, 1950, by Colonel David Carl Schilling of Raleigh, NC, commanding officer of the 31st Escort Wing, who flew from Manston, England, to the Air Force base at Limestone, ME, a distance of 3,300 miles, in a single-engine F-84E Republic

Thunderjet. The flight took 10 hours 1 minute. Schilling made three aerial refueling contacts with Air Force tanker planes. Lieutenant Colonel William D. Ritchie, who also took off in an F-84, was forced to bail out over Labrador, Canada.

1474. Jet airplane passenger trip was made on January 10, 1951. An Avro Jetliner four-engine turbojet piloted by Donald Howard Rogers took off from Chicago, IL, at 11:07 A.M. and arrived at New York City in 1 hour 42 minutes, setting a new speed record of 442 miles per hour.

1475. Transpacific nonstop jet airplane flight was made on July 29, 1952, by a four-jet RB-45 Tornado bomber from Elmendorf Air Force Base, which crossed from Anchorage, AK, to Yokota Air Base, Japan, a distance of 3,460 miles, in 9 hours 50 minutes, at an average speed of 350 miles per hour. The plane was refueled twice in flight by B-29 tanker aircraft. The flight was under the command of Major Louis H. Carrington of Austin, TX.

1476. Transatlantic nonstop jet airplane eastward flight was made by two Boeing B-47 Stratojets of the Strategic Air Command's 306th Medium Bombardment Wing, based at MacDill Air Force Base, Tampa, FL, on April 7, 1953. The flight was made from Limestone, ME, to Fairford, England, in 5 hours 38 minutes, a distance of 3,120 miles, at an average speed of 555 miles per hour. The lead plane was piloted by Colonel Michael Norman Wright McCoy.

1477. Passenger to circle the world on commercial airlines in less than 100 hours was Major Horace C. Boren of Dallas, TX, who arrived at Idlewild International Airport, New York City, on June 25, 1953, having completed a round-the-world flight in 99 hours 16 minutes. Boren stopped at 19 airports on his 21,000-mile flight.

1478. Transcontinental round-trip solo flight between sunrise and sunset was made on July 23, 1953, by Lieutenant Commander George H. Whisler, Jr. Whisler took off from the Naval Air Station, Norfolk, VA, in a Grumman F9F-6 Cougar jet fighter at 5:18 A.M., 17 minutes after sunrise. After stops at the Naval Air Station in Memphis, TN, and Webb Air Force Base, Big Spring, TX, he arrived at the Naval Air Station at North Island, San Diego, CA, at 9:05 A.M. On the return trip, he flew a Douglas F3D-2 Skyknight all-weather jet fighter, departing from San Diego at 9:55 A.M., refueling at the Naval Air Station in Dallas, TX, and arriving

AVIATION—AIRPLANES—FLIGHTS—
continued

at the Norfolk, VA, airfield at 7:15 P.M., just before sunset. His elapsed flight time was 13 hours 57 minutes, with a flying time of 11.2 hours. The total distance covered was 4,930 statute miles. The flights in both directions were delivery trips for new planes.

1479. Round-the-world flight over the North Pole on a regularly scheduled air route began on November 15, 1954, when the Scandinavian Airlines System, using DC-6B planes, inaugurated simultaneous service in both directions between Copenhagen, Denmark, and Los Angeles, CA. The eastbound flight, with 40 passengers, left International Airport, Los Angeles, CA, at 8:23 P.M. Greenwich Mean Time and arrived at Copenhagen on November 16 at 8:18 P.M. G.M.T., an elapsed time of 23 hours 55 minutes (20 hours 38 minutes' flying time) for the 5,800 miles. The westbound flight was made in 24 hours 11 minutes' flying time (27 hours' elapsed time).

1480. Round-the-world nonstop flight by a jet airplane was made by three B-52 Air Force Stratofortress bombers, which flew 24,325 miles in 45 hours 19 minutes at an average speed of 525 miles per hour under the command of Major General Archie J. Old, Jr., of the 15th Air Force. The takeoff was from Castle Air Force Base, Merced, CA, on January 16, 1957, and the landing was made at March Air Base, Riverside, CA, on January 18. The planes were refueled in flight by KC aerial tankers. Each eight-engine jet carried a crew of nine. The route was via Newfoundland, French Morocco, Saudi Arabia, the coasts of India and Ceylon, the Philippines, and Guam.

1481. Solar-powered long-distance airplane flight took place on December 3, 1979, when the *Solar Challenger* flew for 22 minutes over six miles of desert near Marana, AZ. The pilot was Janice Brown. The 210-pound aluminum and plastic aircraft drew power from 16,000 lightweight solar cells on its wings. On July 7, 1980, the *Solar Challenger,* with Stephen R. Ptacek at the controls, became the first solar-powered plane to cross the English Channel.

1482. Round-the-world nonstop airplane flight without refueling took place from December 15 to December 23, 1986, when Richard Rutan and Jeana Yeager circled the globe in *Voyager,* a front-and-rear-propeller plane constructed mainly of plastic. The 216-hour, 24,986-mile circumnavigation began and ended

at Edwards Air Force Base, Muroc, CA. Most of the fuel supply was stored in the plane's wings. The plane decreased in weight from 9,750 to 1,858 pounds as the fuel was consumed.

AVIATION—AIRPLANES—MILITARY

1483. Naval airplane was the Curtiss Amphibian Triad with dual controls, delivered July 1911. It was purchased with funds from a $25,000 congressional appropriation passed on March 4, 1911, "for experimental work in the development of aviation for naval purposes." The plane was tested at Lake Keuka, Hammondsport, NY. The first naval pilots were Lieutenants Theodore Gordon Ellyson and John Henry Towers.

1484. Airplane outfitted with a machine gun was a Wright biplane, flown at College Park, MD, on May 7, 1912, by pilot Lieutenant Thomas de Witt Milling. It was equipped with a Lewis machine gun manned by Charles de Forest Chandler of the Army Signal Corps.

1485. Airplane in actual military operation by the United States Army was used in March 1916, when the 1st Aero Squadron, composed of 11 officers, 82 enlisted men, one civilian mechanic, and eight JN airplanes, was ordered to proceed to Casa Grandes, Mexico, for active duty with the punitive expedition against Pancho Villa commanded by General John Joseph Pershing. Airplanes had been previously used, though not in combat, in February 1913, when the Army Aviation School at Augusta, GA, was transferred to Texas City, TX, for the purpose of providing aviation for ground troops stationed on the Mexican border to prevent disorders.

1486. Fighter plane was the Kirkham Fighter, designed by Charles Kirkham, manufactured by the Curtiss Aeroplane and Motor Company, Garden City, NY, and tested at Garden City on August 19, 1918, when it attained a speed of 162 miles per hour. It established a world's record on October 11, 1918, when it made a ceiling climb of 26,300 feet.

1487. Fighter plane equipped with a cannon was the P-39 (Airacobra), tested by pilot Jimmy Taylor at Wright Field, Dayton, OH, on April 6, 1938. It was built by the Bell Aircraft Corporation at the Niagara Falls Airport, Niagara Falls, NY. The armament consisted of a 37mm cannon located on the fuselage center line, with the gun barrel projecting through the reduction gearbox and propeller hub; two .50-caliber machine guns in the forward fuselage; and four .30-caliber free-firing machine guns installed in pairs in each outer wing panel.

1488. Naval patrol bomber launched like a ship was the *Mars,* a 140,000-pound XPB2M-1 made by the Glenn L. Martin Company and launched on November 8, 1841, at Baltimore, MD. The keel was laid August 22, 1940. The bomber had a 200-foot wingspan and four engines of 2,000 horsepower each. It was the first flying boat accorded Navy keel-laying and launching ceremonies.

1489. Jet-propelled fighter plane to be accepted by the Army Air Force for combat purposes was the P-80 Shooting Star, designed by Clarence L. Johnson and constructed in 143 days by the Lockheed Aircraft Corporation, Burbank, CA. It had a wingspan of 38 feet 10.5 inches, an overall length of 34 feet 6 inches, and a height of 11 feet 4 inches. The first flight was made on January 1944. In February 1945, the Army declared that it had been perfected for actual combat.

1490. Rocket airplane for military use was the MX-324, built by the Northrop Aircraft, Hawthorne, CA, and flown July 5, 1944, by Harry Crosby, pilot. It had a prone cockpit in which the pilot lay flat to withstand the pull. An Aerojet XCAL-200 rocket motor was used with monoethylaniline as fuel. The craft was known as the Rocket Ram. It was originally tested as a glider on October 2, 1943, by John Myers.

1491. Bomber plane with the Flying Wing design was the Northrop XB35, built by Northrop Aircraft, which took off from Northrop Field, Hawthorne, CA, on June 25, 1946, and made a successful flight of 85 miles to the Army Air Force base at Muroc, CA. It weighed 209,000 pounds in gross overload condition and had a 172-foot wingspan with a 53-foot overall length. It had an operational range of about 10,000 miles and could carry 56,000 pounds of bombs.

1492. Rocket plane for manned supersonic flight built in the United States was the Army XS-1, manufactured by the Bell Aircraft Corporation, Buffalo, NY. The craft was an orange-colored needle-nose plane 31 feet long, with a 28-foot wingspan and a 210-pound engine. It carried both fuel and oxygen. After a series of glide tests, the XS-1 made its first powered flight on December 9, 1946, when it was released from a B-29 bomber at 25,000 feet. It remained aloft 19 minutes, seven of which were under power. The test pilot, Chalmers Goodlin of New Alexandria, PA, landed the plane at the army air field in Muroc, CA.

1493. Stealth aircraft used in combat were deployed in the early hours of December 20, 1989, during the U.S. invasion of Panama. On December 23, 1989, the Department of Defense, Washington, DC, said that two F-117A Stealth bombers, aircraft equipped with advanced sensor-evasion technology, had bombed a barracks in the Panama City area.

AVIATION—AIRPLANES—TECHNOLOGY

1494. Gyroscope that was successful in automatically stabilizing aircraft was demonstrated by Lawrence B. Sperry and Lieutenant Patrick Nelson Lynch Bellinger in August 1913 at Lake Keuka, Hammondsport, NY, in a Curtiss-F boat. Stabilization was longitudinal and lateral.

1495. Radio compass on a naval airplane was used on July 7, 1920, when a Curtiss F-5-L naval seaplane flew from Norfolk, VA, to the battleship *Ohio,* 95 miles at sea, and returned, guided entirely by radio signals.

1496. Airplane refueling attempt in midair was made at Rockwell Field, Coronado, CA, on June 27, 1923, at 4:43 A.M., from a De Havilland plane piloted by Air Corps Captain Lowell Herbert Smith, with Air Corps Lieutenant John Paul Richter as receiver of fuel. A 40-foot hose encased in steel wire was lowered to the fuel-receiving plane. After refueling in flight, the planes remained aloft 37 hours 15 minutes 14.8 seconds.

1497. Wind tunnel for testing airplane parts was completed in the summer of 1927 at the Langley Field Laboratory of the National Advisory Committee for Aeronautics, Langley Field, VA. The tunnel permitted the full-scale testing of engines and propellers, engine nacelles, wing combinations, and fuselages. It had an airstream 20 feet in diameter that traveled at speeds up to 110 miles per hour. A high-speed jet wind tunnel that allowed the testing of airfoils at a wind speed of about 600 miles per hour was completed on June 29, 1929.

1498. Airplane diesel engine was manufactured by the Packard Motor Car Company of Detroit, MI, in 1928. It was an air-cooled nine-cylinder 225-horsepower radial engine that weighed 510 pounds. It was used in a Stinson Detroiter airplane and made its first flight on September 19, 1928.

AVIATION— AIRPLANES— TECHNOLO-GY—*continued*

1499. Automatic pilot on an airplane was installed on a Gates-Day Standard J5 airplane operated by the Pennsylvania-Central Airlines. It was first used on October 8, 1929, on a flight from Cleveland, OH, to Pittsburgh, PA, under the command of Captain Trow Sebree. Automatic pilot, an instrument which can be set to take over and relieve the pilot, was developed by William Green.

1500. Flight trainer for airplane pilots was the Link Trainer, a mechanical-electrical device complete with hooded cockpit, controls, and a full complement of flight instruments. The trainer simulated conditions in an aircraft without leaving the ground. It was invented by Edwin Albert Link. The first sale was made in 1929 to the Link Flying School, Binghamton, NY. It was adopted by the Navy in 1931 and by the Army Air Corps in 1934.

1501. Full-scale wind tunnel for testing airplanes was placed in operation on May 27, 1931, at the Langley Research Center of the National Advisory Committee for Aeronautics, Langley Field, VA. It was 30 feet high and 60 feet wide. The jet of air in the tunnel was moved by two propellers 35 feet 5 inches in diameter up to a speed of 110 miles per hour. Each propeller was driven by a 4,000-horsepower electric motor. In 1936, a new tunnel was constructed with an air speed up to 600 miles per hour.

1502. Airplane propeller blade of hollow steel made from a single piece of steel tubing was placed in mass production by the American Propeller Corporation, Toledo, OH, in June 1942. The process was developed at the Lycoming Division of the Aviation Corporation, Williamsport, PA. Over 80,000 hollow steel propeller blades were made from tubing in three years.

AVIATION—AIRPORTS

1503. Airport owned by a city was the Tucson Municipal Airport, located east of Tucson, AZ. The first plane landed on November 20, 1919, and was piloted by "Swede" Myerhofer.

1504. Airport runway illumination was attempted on August 21, 1923, when 42 landing fields on the Chicago–Iowa City–Omaha–North Platte–Cheyenne route were lit by 30 six-inch electric arc beacons which made complete revolutions three times a minute. The lights were of 5.3 million candlepower and were visible for 50 miles.

1505. Airport owned by a county was the Kern County Airport, Bakersfield, CA, developed in 1925 under the auspices of the Kern County Chamber of Commerce near Highway 99, about a mile west of the present site of Meadows Field.

1506. International airplane passenger station was established at Meacham Field, Key West, FL, in 1927. The airport consisted of a small frame building that served as the station and an even smaller frame building that served as a radio shack. Maintenance facilities were housed in an old fort nearby. Federal health, customs, and immigration officials came to the station when notified of the arrival or departure of a plane. The first flight to use the station was a Pan American World Airways flight on October 28, 1927.

1507. Airport manager who was a woman was Laurette Schimmoler, appointed on May 28, 1932, at Port Bucyrus, OH, at a salary of $510 a year.

1508. Civilian airport owned and operated by the federal government was the Washington National Airport, Washington, DC, opened for regular traffic on June 16, 1941. The cornerstone of the Terminal Building was laid by President Franklin Delano Roosevelt on September 28, 1940. The Civil Aeronautics Administration was in charge, and John Groves was the manager.

1509. Airport fog disposal unit was accepted by test on March 29, 1949, by the Los Angeles Airport, Los Angeles, CA. It consisted of 392 oil burners installed alongside runways. During World War II, the system was used in England and known as FIDO, Fog Investigation and Disposal Operation.

1510. Jetway was installed on July 29, 1959 at International Airport, San Francisco, CA. It was a self-powered telescopic corridor that extended from 44 to 107 feet and swung into place to connect the terminal with aircraft, to protect passengers from wind and weather as they boarded or disembarked. The jetway could be extended from the terminal building to the aircraft door in less than 60 seconds.

1511. Airport baggage scanning system that converted electronic data to a visible X-ray format was the Pep-720 baggage X-ray system manufactured by Princeton Electronic Products, New Brunswick, NJ. The first system to be installed was ordered by the Army's Picatinny Arsenal on August 9, 1971.

AVIATION—AIRSHIPS

1512. Airship was designed and built by Caesar Spiegler. The flight was scheduled for July 3, 1878, with John Wise of Lancaster, PA, as the pilot. The dirigible was of the cigar shape and supported a wicker-cage partition with a door and window.

1513. Airship disaster occurred on May 23, 1908, at Berkeley, CA, when the cigar-shaped balloon invented by John A. Morrell collapsed and exploded, injuring the inventor and 15 passengers. The airship was 450 feet long and 46 feet in diameter at the center and was powered by six gasoline engines that generated 200 horsepower each.

1514. Airship ordered by the federal government was designed by Glenn Hammond Curtiss and built by Captain Thomas Scott Baldwin. It was 96 feet long, 19.5 feet in diameter, carried 19,500 cubic feet of hydrogen, and had a 10-foot wooden propeller and a 20-horsepower Curtiss engine. The body was covered by two layers of Japanese silk with vulcanized rubber. It was demonstrated to government representatives at Fort Myer, VA, on August 18, 1908, with Baldwin acting as pilot and Curtiss as engineer. It was subsequently purchased from Captain Baldwin and used by the Signal Corps at Omaha, NE. Its engine, the first water-cooled engine that Curtiss made, is now in the National Museum. It averaged 19.61 miles per hour and stayed aloft two hours. It was sold for $5,737.50.

1515. Transatlantic airship flight was attempted by Walter Wellman on October 15, 1910, when he and his companions left Atlantic City, NJ, in a nonrigid dirigible, *The America,* en route to Ireland. The dirigible was 228 feet long, with a 52-foot diameter. They were forced down by storms and fogs after flying 1,008 miles in 71.5 hours. The crew was rescued about 375 miles east of Cape Hatteras, NC.

1516. Navy airship was the DN1, a twin-engine nonrigid 115,000-cubic-foot dirigible. The envelope was built at New Haven, CT, and the car at Boston, MA. It was acquired under contract of June 1, 1915, at a cost of $45,636. It was too overweight to leave the ground and the twin engine was replaced with a single engine. The first flight was made at Pensacola, FL, in April 1917. Only three flights were made, as the airship was damaged in handling and was not worth repairing.

1517. Airship to land on a roof was the A4, a 160-foot dirigible with a 95,000-cubic-foot gas capacity, which took off from the Wingfoot Lake Naval Air Station near Akron, OH, on May 23, 1919, and landed on a 30-by-30-foot platform on the roof of the Statler Hotel in Cleveland, OH. Two of the five passengers alighted, one of them Ralph Hazlett Upson, designer of the dirigible. The pilot was James Shade.

1518. Stowaway on an aircraft was William Ballantyne, a rigger, a member of the original crew of the British dirigible R-34. Ballantyne and two other men had been laid off in order to lighten the load for a transatlantic crossing to America, but Ballantyne stowed away on the flight. The R-34 left East Fortune, Scotland, at 2 A.M. on July 2, 1919, and arrived at 9:45 A.M. at Roosevelt Field, Long Island, NY, on July 6.

1519. Airship filled with helium gas was the semirigid cigar-shaped Navy dirigible C-7. It contained 181,000 cubic feet of gas and was powered by two motors. It was tested on December 1, 1921, at Hampton Roads Base, Hampton Roads, VA, and on December 4 made a round trip from Hampton Roads to Washington, DC. Lieutenant Commander R.F. Wood was the pilot.

1520. Transcontinental airship flight was made by the C2, which left Langley Field, Newport News, VA, on September 14, 1922, and arrived at Ross Field, Arcadia, CA, on September 23. The dirigible was 192 feet long, 64 feet wide, and 67 feet high, and contained 172,000 cubic feet of hydrogen gas. It was powered by two 150-horsepower Wright motors and commanded by Major Harold A. Strauss and Captain George W. McEntire. On October 17, during the return trip, the bag ripped while the airship was being towed out of the hangar at San Antonio, TX, causing an explosion which injured seven of the eight-man crew.

1521. Rigid airship and the first of the zeppelin type to use helium gas was *Shenandoah*—"daughter of the stars"—which was launched on August 20, 1923, and tested in flight on September 4, 1923, at Lakehurst, NJ. In 1924 it made the first transcontinental flight by a dirigible, leaving Lakehurst on October 7 under the command of Lieutenant Commander Zachary Lansdowne, arriving at San Diego, CA, on October 11, and finishing the return trip at Lakehurst on October 25. On September 3, 1925, it was destroyed in a storm over Caldwell, OH. Lansdowne and 14 members of the crew were killed.

AVIATION—AIRSHIPS—*continued*

1522. Airship with an enclosed cabin was the nonrigid dirigible *Pilgrim,* a 51,000-cubic-foot airship built by the Goodyear Tire and Rubber Company, Akron, OH. The car was fitted close to the envelope. The first flight was made on June 3, 1925, with John Maloney Yolton as pilot.

1523. Airship transfer of mail to a train was effected on June 15, 1928, by an Air Corps blimp piloted by Lieutenants Karl S. Axtater and Edward H. White, who flew directly over an Illinois Central train near Scott Field, Belleville, IL, with a sack of mail suspended on a rope. The blimp dipped low enough to permit the railroad mail clerk to reach up and remove the sack. The blimp was a "C"-type dirigible, 210 feet long, with a crew of six.

1524. Airship made completely of metal was the ZMC-2, which was constructed by the Detroit Aircraft Corporation, Detroit, MI, and delivered to the Navy. It was tested at Grosse Ile Airport, Grosse Ile, MI, on August 19, 1929, and was manned by Captain William E. Kepner and a crew of four who stayed aloft 49 minutes 55 seconds. The ship was 149 feet 5 inches long and 52 feet 8 inches in diameter and had a displacement of 202,200 cubic feet of helium gas. Its weight, empty, was 9,115 pounds. It carried a total load of 12,242 pounds. A congressional resolution signed by President Calvin Coolidge on June 24, 1926, had appropriated $300,000 toward its construction.

1525. Airship passenger transfer to an airplane was effected on August 29, 1929, at the Cleveland, OH, Air Show, when Lieutenant Calvin Bolster descended a ladder of metal girders lowered from the keel of the dirigible *Los Angeles* and boarded a plane flown by Navy Lieutenant Adolphus W. Gorton. The ladder ended in a hook which was attached to a hawser stretched between two uprights on the top wing of the plane.

1526. Airship for private commercial operation was delivered on May 22, 1930, by the Goodyear Zeppelin Corporation of Akron, OH, to the New England Airship Company of Bedford, MA. It was chartered by Bird and Son of East Walpole, MA, and as a goodwill messenger made 1,380 flights, carrying more than 6,000 passengers in less than five months.

1527. Airship to land and take off from an oceangoing steamship was the nonrigid dirigible *Mayflower,* a blimp of the Goodyear Fleet. On July 31, 1930, as the S.S. *Bremen* reached New York City, the *Mayflower* lowered itself to the deck and picked up a passenger, Paul Weeks Litchfield, president of the Goodyear Tire and Rubber Company. The railings of the ship were covered with mattresses to prevent the dirigible's sides from being punctured. The *Mayflower* was 128 feet long and 37 feet wide and contained 86,000 cubic feet of gas. The deck of the *Bremen* was 85 feet long and 36 feet wide.

1528. Airship that was certified by the Federal Aviation Administration was *Skyship 600,* built by Airship Industries, which received certification on May 9, 1989. The $6 million airship first flew in 1984. Prior to 1987, the FAA set no criteria for lighter-than-air craft.

AVIATION—AUTOGIROS

1529. Autogiro flown in America was a C8 Mark II designed and built by Juan de la Cierva of Madrid, Spain, the inventor of the autogiro. It was remodeled from an English biplane. It was first flown at Pitcairn Field, Willow Grove, PA, on December 19, 1928, by Harold Frederick Pitcairn, who subsequently formed the Pitcairn-Cierva Autogiro Company of America to manufacture autogiros in this country. This first import was presented to the Smithsonian Institution in Washington, DC, in 1931.

1530. Autogiro licensed for commercial use was the Pitcairn PCA-2, built by the Pitcairn Aircraft Company, Willow Grove, PA, which received the Approved Type Certificate on April 2, 1931. It had two seats in tandem, the front one designed for two people. Its Wright Whirlwind 300-horsepower engine had a cruising speed of 24 miles per hour. The four-bladed rotor was 43 feet in diameter and each blade was fitted with a hydraulic damper. The plane had both drag and flapping hinges, and weighed 2,094 pounds empty, 2,598 pounds fully loaded.

1531. Transcontinental autogiro flight was made by John MacDonald Miller, who left Pitcairn Field, Willow Grove, PA, in *The Missing Link* on May 14, 1931. Many stops were made en route to California to exhibit the machine. The autogiro landed on May 28, 1931, at the North Island Naval Air Station, San Diego, CA, and May 29, 1931, at Los Angeles Municipal Airport.

1532. Transcontinental autogiro flight by a woman was made on May 29, 1931, by Amelia Earhart, who took off in a Pitcairn PCA-2 from Newark Airport, NJ, and landed at Los Angeles, CA, on June 7, 1931. In December 1930 she had become the first woman pilot to fly solo in an autogiro and the first pilot of either sex to fly an autogiro with passengers.

1533. Autogiro owned by the federal government was the XOP-1, an experimental rotary-wing Navy aircraft, ordered at a cost of $29,500 from the Pitcairn Aircraft Company on January 22, 1931. It was delivered on June 1, 1931, to Washington, DC, and flown at the Anacostia Station, where it remained aloft for 30 minutes. It had a 300-horsepower Wright J-6 motor, a speed of 123 miles per hour, and a ceiling of 16,400 feet. It was a two-seater and weighed 2,807 pounds.

1534. Autogiro to land and take off from a ship was an XOP-1 built by the Pitcairn Aircraft Company. It made three successful landings and takeoffs on September 23, 1931, using the airplane carrier U.S.S. *Langley* off Norfolk and Cape Henry, VA, as its base. Navy Lieutenant Alfred Melville Pride of the experimental division of the Hampton Roads Naval Air Base made the first flight and three subsequent flights, each with a different passenger. No landing crew was required.

AVIATION—BALLOONS

1535. Balloon flight was made by Edward Warren, 13 years old, on June 24, 1784, at Baltimore, MD. Warren went up in Peter Carnes's balloon, 35 feet in diameter and 30 feet high, made of silk of various colors. The air was rarefied by a cylindrical stove of iron suspended under the balloon. Carnes attempted a flight on July 17, 1784, at Philadelphia, but the balloon burst into flames.

1536. Balloon flight in which a presidential order was carried was a 40-minute flight made by Jean Pierre Blanchard of France, who left Philadelphia, PA, at 10:16 A.M. on January 9, 1793, in the presence of President George Washington and other officials. He was permitted the use of the Walnut Street Prison courtyard at Germantown, Philadelphia, PA. The roar of artillery announced the moment of his departure. President Washington presented him with an order "To all to whom these presents shall come" directing that he be allowed "to pass in such direction and to descend in such

places as circumstances may render most convenient." The balloon reached about one mile in altitude. He landed in Deptford Township, Gloucester County, NJ, about 15 miles away. It was his 45th ascension.

1537. Balloon flight by an aeronaut born in America was made by Charles Ferson Durant, the first American to make aeronautics his profession. On September 9, 1830, he gave an exhibition in a balloon that he had constructed at his own home, flying from Castle Garden, New York City, to Perth Amboy, NJ. Durant was the first person to land on board a ship, a feat that he performed in Chesapeake Bay on the *Independence*. For his accomplishment he was awarded a gold medal in 1836 by the American Institute.

1538. Transatlantic crossing attempted by a balloon took place on October 6, 1873, when the 300,000-cubic foot *Daily Graphic*, built by John Wise and funded by the *New York Daily Illustrated Graphic* newspaper, was launched in Capitoline Gardens, Brooklyn, NY (now part of New York City). Instead of a basket, the balloon carried a lifeboat supported by two slings. The crew consisted of Captain Washington Harrison Donaldson, George Ashton Lunt, and a newspaperman, Alfred Ford. The balloon left the earth at 9:19 A.M. A few hours later it ran into a storm. The crew jumped off at 1:15 P.M. near New Canaan, CT.

1539. Balloon pilot who was a woman was Mary H. Myers, who flew a balloon in 1880 at Little Falls, NY. Myers performed at fairs as Carlotta, the Lady Aeronaut. In 1886 she rose to a height of four miles—a world altitude record—in a balloon filled with natural gas.

1540. Balloon to land on a building was flown by A. Roy Knabenshue on June 30, 1905. He flew a distance of three miles in 25 minutes and landed on a 10-story building in Toledo, OH. After a 15-minute pause, he returned the airship to its starting point.

1541. Balloon flight to rise higher than 100,000 feet was made by the Winzen Research Balloon as part of Project Manhigh. It rose from Crosby, MN, on August 19, 1957, and descended at Elm Lake, SD, the following day, having reached an altitude of 101,516 feet during its 32 hours in the stratosphere. For approximately 26 hours its altitude was over 90,000 feet. Major David Goodman Simons, medical officer of the Air Force, was awarded the Distinguished Flying Cross for this flight on August 24, 1957.

AVIATION—BALLOONS—*continued*

1542. Balloon flight powered by solar energy was made at 8:30 A.M. on May 16, 1973, by Tracy Barnes, president of the Balloon Works, Statesville, NC. Barnes flew in the *Solar Fire-Fly,* a 203,129-cubic-foot tetrahedron, or inverted pyramid. It used only solar energy to fly and did not employ a lifting gas or heat-producing device. The heat of the sun's rays was absorbed by the dark skin, and the solar energy dilated the air within the balloon, creating its buoyancy. The flight began at the soccer field of the University of North Carolina, Charlotte, NC, and lasted about 10 minutes.

1543. Transatlantic balloon flight began on August 11, 1978, when Ben Abruzzo, Larry Newman, and Maxie Leroy Anderson, all of Albuquerque, NM, left Presque Isle, ME, in a helium-filled balloon, the *Double Eagle II.* They reached Paris on August 17 after a journey lasting 137 hours 18 minutes.

1544. Transcontinental nonstop balloon flight was made by Maxie Leroy Anderson and his son, Kris Anderson, of Albuquerque, NM, who took off from San Francisco at 12:30 A.M. on May 8, 1980, in the *Kitty Hawk,* a 75-foot-tall helium-filled plastic balloon, bound for Kitty Hawk, NC. They flew 3,100 miles—a straight distance of 2,817 miles—and landed on May 11 outside Matane, Quebec, on the Gaspé peninsula, more than 1,000 miles north of their original destination.

1545. Transatlantic solo balloon flight was completed on September 18, 1984, by Air Force Colonel Joe Kittinger. Flying the *Rosie O'Grady,* a 101,000-cubic-foot helium balloon, Kittinger navigated from Caribou, ME, to Montenotte, Italy, a flight of 3,543 miles, in 86 hours.

AVIATION—GLIDERS

1546. Glider flight was made by John Joseph Montgomery on March 17, 1884, from a hillock south of the valley of Otay, CA. The weight of the first glider was only 30 pounds and that of its rider 130 pounds. It traveled about 600 feet. Although Montgomery did not receive full recognition for his work at the time, probably because of lack of publicity, he nevertheless gained the title "Father of Gliding."

1547. Glider with cambered wings was invented in 1895 by Octave Chanute, who made about 2,000 glider flights without accident in 1896 and 1897 from his base at Miller's Station, IL, near Chicago.

1548. Glider released from an airship was piloted by Lieutenant Ralph Stanton Barnaby of the Navy. The glider was cast loose on January 31, 1930, at Lakehurst, NJ, from the *Los Angeles,* commanded by Lieutenant Commander Herbert Victor Wiley, at an altitude of 3,000 feet. A perfect landing was made in 12 minutes.

1549. Glider flight indoors in "dead air" was made on March 2, 1930, when Harry Kuchins, a member of the St. Louis, MO, Glider Club, flew a glider inside the St. Louis Terminal building at a Boy Scout circus. The glider had been used by Colonel Charles Augustus Lindbergh in June 1929.

1550. Seaplane glider to be piloted in the air was loosed from a seaplane on March 15, 1930, at Port Washington, NY. It was built at Roosevelt Field, NY, and was fashioned after a flying boat. The first seaplane glider pilot was Frank Monroe Hawks, whose achievement was duplicated later the same day by Robert Atwater, flying a German-built converted glider.

1551. Transcontinental glider tow began on March 30, 1930, when Captain Frank Monroe Hawks took off from Lindbergh Field, San Diego, CA, in the *Eagle,* also known as the *Cloud-Hopping Choo Choo,* a glider designed for the Texas Company by Professor Roswell Earl Franklin of the University of Michigan. The glider was attached by a towline to a single-motor biplane piloted by J.D. "Duke" Jernigin, Jr. Stops were made at Tucson, AZ, Sweetwater, TX, Tulsa, OK, East St. Louis, IL, Columbus, OH, and Buffalo, NY. The glider landed in the rain before 15,000 people on April 6, 1930, at Van Cortlandt Park, New York City. Flying time was 36 hours 47 minutes.

1552. Rocket glider flight that was successful was made at Atlantic City, NJ, on June 4, 1931, by William G. Swan. The 200-pound glider was equipped with pontoons. When it was up in the air, the pilot turned on a switch to ignite the rockets. He made a 1,000-foot hop at a 100-foot altitude. The next day he made an eight-minute flight at an altitude of 200 feet, using the full power of 12 rockets.

1553. Glider entirely built of plywood and plastic was Model BM-5, built by Bowlus Sailplanes, San Fernando, CA. Mock-up tests were begun on December 1, 1941, an Army Air Force contract was obtained on January 20, 1942, and the prototype was flown in May 1942. The contract was terminated prior to delivery of the finished models and construction was suspended.

1554. Amphibious seaplane glider was the XL-Q-1, manufactured by the Bristol Aeronautical Corporation, New Haven, CT, and flown on January 16, 1943, at the Navy Yard, Philadelphia, PA. It was designed as a troop transport and cargo carrier by the National Aircraft factory under Commander Ralph Stanton Barnaby at the Navy Yard. The glider was taken aloft behind a Catalina seaplane and released. It had an all-wood body, was 40 feet long with a 72-foot wingspan, and carried 12 men and their equipment.

1555. Glider commercial freight service was inaugurated on April 24, 1946, by Winged Cargo of Philadelphia, PA. Colonel Fred Paul Dollenberg took off from Northeast Airport, Philadelphia, in a DC-3 Air Liner that towed a Waco glider at the end of a nylon towrope. The plane carried 5,000 pounds of freight and the glider 3,500 pounds. The average speed of the flight was 150 miles per hour. The first stop was at Miami, FL, with other stops at Havana, Cuba, and San Juan, Puerto Rico. Paul Myers Aubin piloted the glider.

1556. Powered soaring glider commercially licensed was the *Dragonfly*, designed by William Hawley Bowlus and built by the Nelson Aircraft Corporation, San Fernando, CA. The glider was licensed by the Civil Aeronautics Administration on October 15, 1946. It was a strut-braced high-wing monoplane with a 47-foot 4-inch wingspan. It had a four-cylinder, two-cycle pusher engine that developed 25 horsepower at 3,900 revolutions per minute.

AVIATION—HELICOPTERS

1557. Helicopter that was successful was the VS-300, constructed in October and November 1939 by Vought-Sikorsky Aircraft, Stratford, CT. A flight of 15 minutes and 3 seconds was made on July 18, 1940, by Igor Ivan Sikorsky at Stratford, CT, with a single main rotor powered by a 70-horsepower Franklin engine. The helicopter had three auxiliary tail rotors for control, one turning in a vertical plane for rudder control and the other two turning in a horizontal plane on outriggers on either side of the tail.

1558. Helicopter commercially designed was the S-51, a four-passenger helicopter designed and built by the Sikorsky Aircraft Division of the United Aircraft Corporation, Bridgeport, CT, which made its initial flight on February 16, 1946. It received its Approved Type Certificate from the Civil Aeronautics Authority on March 26, 1946. It cruised at 80 miles per hour and had a range of 150 miles with pilot, three passengers, and 70 pounds of baggage.

1559. Helicopter with a twin engine was the XHJD-1, built by the McDonnell Aircraft Corporation, St. Louis, MO, and tested in March 1946 at the Lambert–St. Louis Municipal Airport. Two 450-horsepower Pratt and Whitney Wasp Jr. engines, mounted midway on the pylons extending from the fuselage, turned two 40-foot blade rotors in opposite directions. The helicopter could carry a 3,000-pound load, operating on either one or both of the engines. It could take off or land vertically, hover motionless, and fly forward, backward, or sideways. The span from rotor tip to rotor tip was 81 feet.

1560. Helicopter licensed for commercial use by the Civil Aeronautics Administration was a Bell 47B able to cruise at speeds of 1 to 100 miles per hour, fly forward, backward, or sideways, ascend or descend vertically, and hover. License No. 1 was granted on March 8, 1946, to the *New York Journal-American*, New York City, which used the helicopter for news coverage and photo delivery.

1561. Helicopter with a fully servo-controlled intermeshing rotor was the K-125, built by the Kaman Aircraft Corporation, Bloomfield, CT. It made its initial flight in January 1947 at Windsor Locks, CT.

1562. Helicopter to deliver material across a picket line was used on March 9, 1947, by the Cornell-Dubilier Electric Corporation, New Bedford, MA. Seven hourly landings were made with supplies of raw materials. The helicopter was hired from the New England Helicopter Service.

1563. Helicopter hoist rescue took place off the coast of Fairfield, CT, in 1946. A Sikorsky R-5 helicopter equipped with an experimental hydraulic hoist was used to rescue two oil workers who were stranded on a barge that was being pounded against a reef by hurricane-force winds. Jimmy Viner, a nephew of helicopter pioneer Igor Sikorsky, piloted the helicopter, assisted by Jackson Beighle.

1564. Ramjet helicopter was the Little Henry, built by the McDonnell Aircraft Corporation, St. Louis, MO, for the Air Force and tested on May 5, 1947, by Charles Raymond Wood, Jr., at Lambert Field, St. Louis. It weighed 310 pounds and had a two-blade rotor, two tip ramjets weighing 10 pounds each, a small rudder and an open steel-tube structure supporting the pilot, fuel tanks, and controls. It had a forward speed of 50 miles per hour and a 300-pound lifting capacity.

AVIATION—HELICOPTERS—*continued*

1565. Heliport commercial base in a major city was Heliport No. 1 at Pier 41, New York City, leased from the Department of Marine Aviation by the Metropolitan Aviation Corporation. The seadrome was 161 by 60 feet. The first flight was May 18, 1949, the official opening of service, when pilot George Callahan and passenger Deputy Mayor John James Bennett flew in a Bell 47-B with a 605-pound payload capacity.

1566. Gas-turbine helicopter or turborotor was the Navy K-225, built by the Kaman Aircraft Corporation, Bloomfield, CT, and tested on December 10, 1951, at Bradley Field, Windsor Locks, CT. It was powered by a Boeing 502-2 gas turbine developing 175 horsepower for continuous operation. The turbine was manufactured by the Boeing Airplane Company, Seattle, WA. The first twin turborotor was the HTK-1, built by Kaman Aircraft and flown March 26, 1954, at Bloomfield. It had two 190-horsepower Boeing 502-2 gas turbines manufactured by the Boeing Airplane Company, Seattle, WA. They produced 380 horsepower and could be used separately or simultaneously.

1567. Helicopter fully operated by remote control was the HTK-1, built by the Kaman Aircraft Corporation, Bloomfield, CT. In July 1953, at Windsor Locks, CT, it took off and landed, flew backward, sideways, and forward, and hovered at varying altitudes, speeds, and distances in compliance with commands from a remote-control station. The signals were sent by radio from a ground station to controls in the drone.

1568. Helicopter passenger service was instituted by New York Airways on July 9, 1953, at 9:15 A.M., when two passengers were transported between La Guardia Airport and Idlewild Airport, both in New York City. Twelve passengers were carried the first day. The captain was Jack S. Gallagher and the flight attendant was Neils Johnson. Freight service had been inaugurated on October 1, 1947, by Los Angeles Airways, which carried mail in the San Fernando Valley, CA.

1569. Military heliport was the Fort Eustis Heliport, Felker Field, Fort Eustis, VA, dedicated December 7, 1954. The field was named for Warrant Officer Alfred Charles Felker, a graduate of the first army helicopter pilot course, who was killed in an airplane flight in February 1953. The heliport was built in the shape of a huge wheel, with 600-foot runways forming the spokes and a circular taxiway composing the rim. The first commanding officer was Lieutenant Colonel Robert C. Spiedel, Jr.

1570. Aerocycle was built by De Lackner Helicopters, Mount Vernon, NY, and tested at Camp Kilmer, NJ, by the Army, which bought 12 on December 29, 1955. The aerocycle weighed about 200 pounds, carried a load of about 300 pounds, and had a top speed of 65 miles per hour and a range of about 150 miles. Handlebars controlled the ascent and descent, the pilot steering by leaning in the direction he wanted to go. The machine had helicopter blades, rose vertically, and was powered by a 41-horsepower outboard motor mounted above pontoons.

1571. Human-powered helicopter was developed by students at the California Polytechnic State University in San Luis Obispo, CA. The pedal-powered aircraft, which was constructed of graphite-epoxy, wood, and mylar, featured a 140-foot-long rotor driven by props at each end. It was named the Da Vinci 3, after Leonardo da Vinci, who first conceived of a rotary-wing flying vehicle. On December 10, 1989, in the school's gymnasium, the Da Vinci 3 made its first flight, which lasted 6.8 seconds and reached a height of seven inches.

AVIATION—HELICOPTERS—FLIGHTS

1572. Helicopter flight of importance was made on June 16, 1922, by Henry Adler Berliner at College Park, MD, before representatives of the U.S. Bureau of Aeronautics. The machine raised itself three times to the height of seven feet. It had two lifting propellers in the front, the forward motion being obtained by tilting a propeller in the rear of the fuselage.

1573. Helicopter flight of one-hour duration was made on April 15, 1941, by Igor Ivan Sikorsky, who hovered aloft in a Vought-Sikorsky VS-300 for 1 hour 5 minutes 14.5 seconds over Sniffen's Point, Stratford, CT. The main lift was supplied by a three-bladed propeller 28 feet in diameter. On May 6, 1941, the helicopter hovered over a tennis court for 1 hour 32 minutes 26.1 seconds.

1574. Helicopter flight from water was made on April 17, 1941, by Igor Ivan Sikorsky at Stratford, CT, in a Vought-Sikorsky VS-300 helicopter mounted on rubber bags so that it could land and take off on either land or water.

1575. Long-distance helicopter flight was made in a two-place XR-4 Air Force helicopter designed by Igor Ivan Sikorsky, which took off on May 13, 1942, from Stratford, CT. It flew at low altitudes a distance of 761 miles and landed at Wright Field, Dayton, OH, on May

17, making 16 stops en route. Actual flying time was 16 hours 10 minutes. Charles Lester Morris, test pilot of Sikorsky Aircraft Division of the United Aircraft Corporation, was the pilot.

1576. Transatlantic helicopter flight was made by the Air Force Air Rescue Service in two H-19 (S-55) helicopters that left Westover Air Force Base, MA, on July 15, 1952, and arrived at the Air Force base at Wiesbaden, Germany, on August 4, after 51 hours 55 minutes of elapsed flight time. Leader of the flight was Captain Vincent Howard McGovern of Springfield, NJ, who with copilot Harry Celestine Jeffers of Newark, OH, piloted the project ship, *Hop-A-Long*. The accompanying aircraft, *Whirl-O-Way,* was piloted by First Lieutenant Harold W. Moore of Cincinnati, OH, and copiloted by Major George Okie Hambrick of Carter, OK. The 3,410-mile Atlantic crossing was made in 42 hours 25 minutes.

1577. Helicopter refueling flight that was successful was accomplished at Fort Rucker, AL, on August 14, 1956, when an Army twin-rotary H-21 helicopter manufactured by the Vertol Aircraft Corporation, Morton, PA, was refueled from a fixed-wing tanker.

1578. Transcontinental nonstop helicopter flight was made from Miramar Naval Air Station, San Diego, CA, on August 23, 1956, to Washington, DC, a distance of 2,610 miles, in 31 hours 40 minutes, by a twin-rotored H21. The helicopter was refueled four times in flight and twice while hovering. The crew was headed by Major Hugh Gaddis of Tulsa, OK. The helicopter, produced by the Vertol Aircraft Corporation of Morton, PA, weighed 3,300 pounds.

1579. Round-the-world helicopter flight was made by two Americans, Ross Perot, Jr., and Jay Coburn, in a helicopter called *The Spirit of Texas*. The flight began on September 1, 1982, and ended on September 30. It lasted 29 days 3 hours 8 minutes 13 seconds.

AVIATION—PARACHUTES

1580. Parachute jump from a balloon was made by Charles Guille, who ascended on August 2, 1819, from Vauxhall Gardens, New York City, in a wicker basket decorated with flowers and suspended from a 25,000-cubic-foot prepared-silk balloon that cost $3,000. Avoiding a squall, he jumped from a height of two miles with an umbrella-shaped parachute and fell 300 feet before it expanded. He drifted

across the East River and in 15 minutes was out of sight, landing at New Bushwick, NY, on Long Island, four miles from the city. He carried two phials of hartshorn and cologne water to counteract dizziness.

1581. Parachute jump from an airplane was made on March 1, 1912, by Captain Albert Berry from a Benoist Pusher plane piloted by Antony Jannus, at Jefferson Barracks, St. Louis, MO. Berry jumped from an altitude of 1,500 feet while the plane was traveling at 50 miles per hour.

1582. Parachute jump from an airplane by a woman was made by Georgia Broadwick, 18 years old, on June 21, 1913, over Griffith Field, Los Angeles, CA, from an airplane piloted by Glenn Martin and flying at a 1,000-foot altitude and a speed of 30 miles per hour. After a 100-foot drop, her 11-pound silken parachute opened and she landed in a barley field.

1583. Parachute known as the "free parachute" was developed by the Army Air Corps under the direction of Major Edward L. Hoffman. With this type of parachute, the operator jumps before pulling the rip cord. The first person to jump with the manually operated chute was Leslie Le Roy Irvin, who jumped on April 28, 1919, from a de Havilland DH-9 biplane at an altitude of 1,500 feet, flying at a speed of 100 miles per hour over McCook Field, Dayton, OH. He broke his ankle when he struck the ground. Floyd Smith was at the controls. Later Irvin founded the Irving Air Chute Company. His name was spelled incorrectly on the incorporation papers.

1584. Caterpillar Club member was John Boettner, pilot of the *Wing Foot* balloon of the Goodyear Tire and Rubber Company, Akron, OH, who parachuted 1,200 feet to safety on July 21, 1919, while his balloon crashed into a building at La Salle Street and Jackson Boulevard, Chicago, IL. The crash resulted in the death of three persons and injuries to 28. "Caterpillar Club" is a name used to designate those persons whose lives have been saved by parachute jumps from aircraft in distress.

1585. Pilot to bail out of a disabled airplane was Lieutenant Harold R. Harris, chief of the flying section of McCook Field, Dayton, OH, who jumped from a Loening monoplane on October 20, 1922, 2,000 feet over North Dayton, before his plane crashed.

AVIATION—PARACHUTES—*continued*

1586. Caterpillar Club member who was a woman was Irene McFarland, who jumped from her plane on June 28, 1925, over Grissard Field, Cincinnati, OH. She was testing a parachute that was packed in a container fastened to the plane, so that when she jumped her weight would cause the container to break and permit the parachute to slip and blow out. Officials also required her to use an army parachute. She jumped and her parachute jammed, suspending her under the fuselage, from which she swung like a pendulum. She could not release herself and Lieutenant Watson, her pilot, could not land. He motioned to her to release the army parachute, which she did, the force breaking the cords that held her tied to the airplane.

1587. Caterpillar Club members who were father and son were Paul Fisk Collins, who jumped on November 19, 1928, north of Brookville, PA, and Lieutenant Paul Liske Collins, who jumped on February 11, 1944, 50 miles south of Fairbanks, AK.

1588. Parachute jump from an autogiro was made on November 15, 1931, by Frankie Hammond, a parachute jumper from West Paterson, NJ, who jumped from a Pitcairn Autogiro at an air circus at Curtiss Essex Airport, Caldwell, NJ. The air show was for the benefit of the family of Keyport pilot Victor Brooks, who was killed on November 1, 1931, when his plane crashed during a race at Stanhope, NJ.

1589. Parachute tower for training jumpers was a free-drop tower built April 1935 in Hightstown, NJ, by the Safe Parachute Jump Company. The tower was 125 feet high, with a horizontal arm at the top capable of being rotated 360 degrees.

1590. Parachute fatality in the Army occurred on March 6, 1941, at Fort Benning, Columbus, GA, when Sergeant Floyd S. Beard, age 28, of Coleman, GA, a parachutist of Company C of the 501st Parachute Battalion, participated in a mass jump with 35 others. His parachute failed to function and he fell 750 feet to his death.

1591. Parachute jump using a nylon parachute was made on June 6, 1942, from an airplane at Brainard Field, Hartford, CT, by Adeline Gray, parachute rigger of the Pioneer Parachute Company, Manchester, CT.

1592. Pilot to bail out of an airplane flying at supersonic speed was George Franklin Smith of Manhattan Beach, CA, who was propelled into the air when his seat automatically detached itself from an F-100A Super Sabre Jet fighter on February 26, 1955, above the Los Angeles International Airport, Los Angeles, CA. He was flying at an altitude of 6,500 feet at the supersonic speed of 777 miles per hour. His clothes were cut to ribbons, and his socks, helmet, and oxygen mask were stripped off. He felt deceleration of 40 Gs, so that his organs weighed 40 times their normal weight. He landed in the ocean and was rescued by a passing boat off Laguna Beach, CA. He was hospitalized for about six months.

1593. Parachute jumper snagged by airplane in midair was Charles M. Alexander, a test parachutist for the Pioneer Parachute Company, Manchester, CT, who jumped from a single-engine Cessna 180 airplane at 10,000 feet on August 29, 1966, above the Sussex County Airport, Georgetown, DE. When he reached 9,000 feet, his parachute was snagged by a C-122 transport plane, piloted by Captain Arnold Olsen, that was traveling at 120 miles per hour. Alexander was taken aboard safely. The snag was done on purpose, to demonstrate a method of rescuing airmen who bail out over enemy territory.

AVIATION—PILOTS

1594. Pilot from the United States to establish an airplane altitude record was Louis Paulhan, who flew a Farman biplane on January 12, 1910, to a height of 3,967 feet at an aviation meet at Los Angeles, CA. About 50,000 spectators witnessed his flight, which lasted 50 minutes 46.2 seconds. His descent was made in 7 minutes 30 seconds.

1595. Pilot licensed by the Aero Club of America was Glenn Hammond Curtiss of Hammondsport, NY, who received License No. 1 on June 8, 1911.

1596. Pilot licensed by the Aero Club of America who was a woman was Harriet Quimby, a New York City journalist, who passed the test on August 1, 1911, and received License No. 37. She was followed two weeks later by Matilde Moisant. Both joined the exhibition team founded by Moisant's brother, John Moisant. Quimby was the first woman to cross the English Channel in a plane, on April 16, 1912. She was killed three months later when she was thrown out of her plane during an air meet in Boston. The first American woman to make a solo flight was Blanche Scott, whose training airplane left the ground on September 2, 1910, despite the throttle block applied to it by Glenn Hammond Curtiss, Scott's instructor.

1597. Pilot who was an African-American woman was Bessie Coleman of Chicago, IL, the daughter of an African-American mother and a Native American father. Refused permission to enroll in aviation courses in the United States, she received her training in France and Germany and qualified for an international pilot's license. From 1922 until her death in a plane crash in 1926, she did exhibition stunt flying in air shows across the United States.

1598. Glider pilot's license issued by the National Aeronautic Association was awarded to Leonard A. Wiggins, Akron, OH, on October 7, 1930. He was the first to receive both the "A" license (for a flight of one-minute duration with two S curves and normal landing) and the "B" license (for a starting, 360-degree turn both to the left and the right).

1599. Glider license awarded to a woman by the National Aeronautic Association was No. 10 Class "A," issued to Maxine Dunlap on February 5, 1931. Requirements were a flight of one-minute duration with two S curves and a normal landing.

1600. Pilot to fly a regularly scheduled airmail transport who was a woman was Helen Richey, who flew from Washington, DC, to Detroit, MI, via Pittsburgh and Cleveland on December 31, 1934. She was appointed a copilot by Central Airlines and flew a Tri-Motored Ford 12-passenger transport.

1601. Airplane instructor's license issued under the Civil Aeronautics Authority, created by the Civil Aeronautics Act of June 23, 1938, was a rerated license issued to Arthur J. Banks, Atlanta, GA, on September 27, 1939. The first woman licensed was Evelyn Pinckert Kilgore, San Bernardino, CA, who received her license on October 13, 1939. In the early days, "instructor" could be written on a private pilot's license after 200 hours of flight.

1602. Father and son to become commercial airline pilots were Captain E. Hamilton Lee and his son First Officer Robert E. Lee. Captain Lee was employed on July 1, 1927, by Boeing Air Transport, which later became United Air Lines. Robert E. Lee was employed as a first officer on May 19, 1941. Both did their team flying between San Francisco and Los Angeles, CA.

1603. Test pilot who was a woman was Alma Heflin, who made her first production test flight November 12, 1941, for the Piper Aircraft Corporation, Lock Haven, PA.

1604. Pilot on a scheduled passenger line who was African-American was Perry H. Young of Orangeburg, SC, who was hired as a flight crewman on December 17, 1956, by New York Airways, New York City. He started regular passenger flights on February 1, 1957, as a copilot in a 12-passenger S-58 helicopter between New York International, La Guardia, and Newark, NJ, airports.

1605. Pilot to fly a million miles in a jet airplane was Melvin C. Garlow of Alexandria, VA, who flew his millionth mile on March 7, 1959. His first jet flight was made on January 1955 in a Capital Viscount.

1606. Pilot on a regularly scheduled major airline who was a woman was Emily H. Warner. She was hired by Frontier Airlines on January 29, 1973, as the second officer (co-pilot) on a Boeing 737.

AVIATION—PILOTS—MILITARY

1607. Army pilot to fly solo in an airplane was Second Lieutenant Frederic Erastus Humphreys, who on October 26, 1909, at College Park, MD, made two circuits of the field in three minutes. He was followed by Lieutenant Frank Purdy Lahm, who went six times around and made some small circles as well, remaining aloft 13 minutes. Lieutenant Humphreys then resumed his solo flying for eight minutes.

1608. Pilot to fire a gun from an airplane was Lieutenant Jacob Earl Fickel of the 29th Infantry, who fired rifle shots at a target on August 20, 1910, at the Sheepshead Bay Race Track, New York City, from a single-seater Curtiss plane piloted by Glenn Hammond Curtiss.

1609. Aviator who was African-American was Eugene Bullard, born in Columbus, GA, on October 9, 1894. After immigrating to France, he joined the French Army and received his flying certification on May 5, 1917. His first flight, a reconnaissance mission over the city of Metz, took place on September 8. Bullard was credited with one confirmed "kill," a German Pfalz he shot down over Verdun in November 1917.

1610. Army pilot to win a victory over an enemy airplane was First Lieutenant Stephen W. Thompson of the 1st Aero Squadron, who downed an Albatross pursuit plane on February 5, 1918, at Saarbrucken, Germany.

AVIATION—PILOTS—MILITARY—*continued*

1611. Ace of Aces from the United States was Captain Edward Vernon Rickenbacker of Columbus, OH, who was credited with 26 victories, including 22 airplanes and four balloons. His first victory took place in the Baussant region, in the Toul sector, France, on April 29, 1918, and his last in the St. Juvin region, on October 30, 1918.

1612. Ace to fly under American colors was Lieutenant Douglas Campbell, who shot down a German pilot on April 14, 1918. His fifth victory, which qualified him as an ace, occurred on May 31, 1918.

1613. Navy ace in World War I was David Sinton Ingalls of the Naval Aviation Forces, who, while attached to the 213th Squadron of the British Royal Air Force, "alone and in conjunction with other pilots shot down at least four enemy aeroplanes and one or more enemy balloons." He was awarded the Distinguished Flying Cross by the British Government on October 25, 1918, and the Distinguished Service Medal by the United States on November 11, 1920. He served as assistant secretary of the Navy for aeronautics from March 1929 to March 1932.

1614. Pilot to die because of a lack of oxygen was Captain Hawthorne C. Gray of the Army Air Corps, who took off from Scott Field, Belleville, IL, on November 4, 1927, in a balloon that rose to 40,000 feet. Despite his oxygen mask, he died because he was unable to open a reserve oxygen cylinder. He was found near Sparta, TN, about 310 miles from Belleville, in the basket of his balloon.

1615. Air hero in World War II was Second Lieutenant George S. Welch of Wilmington, DE, who shot down four Japanese airplanes at Oahu, HI, during the surprise attack on Pearl Harbor on December 7, 1941. He was awarded the Distinguished Service Cross on December 16, and received the congratulations of President Franklin Delano Roosevelt at the White House on May 25, 1942. In 33 months, he shot down 18 enemy aircraft.

1616. Ace in World War II was First Lieutenant Boyd David Wagner of Johnstown, PA. While serving in the Army Air Corps in the Philippines, Wagner was attacked on December 13, 1941, by five Japanese pursuit planes. He shot two planes out of the air and machine-gunned 12 on the ground, leaving five burning. He was awarded the Distinguished Service Cross.

1617. Navy ace in World War II was Lieutenant Edward Henry O'Hare. On February 20, 1942, in the southwest Pacific, alone and single-handed, he attacked nine twin-engine Japanese heavy bombers, shot down five, and damaged a sixth in an action of about five minutes' duration.

1618. Naval Reserve flier who was African-American was Jesse Leroy Brown of Hattiesburg, MI, who was commissioned an ensign on April 15, 1949. He crashed on December 4, 1950, near the Changjin Reservoir in Korea. He was the first African-American flier in the Naval Reserve to be killed in combat. On March 18, 1972, a Knox-class ocean destroyer escort, the *Jesse L. Brown,* was named in his honor at the Avondale Shipyards, Westwego, LA. It was the first naval ship to be named for an African-American naval officer.

1619. Marine Corps jet ace in Korea was Major John F. Bolt of Sanford, FL, who led a four-plane Saber flight in an attack on four enemy fighters east of Sinuiju, Korea, on November 18, 1950, on his 37th mission, and downed his fifth and sixth MIG-15s. He first qualified as an ace in World War II, when he shot down six Zekes between September 23, 1943, and January 4, 1944, while serving with Boyington's Black Sheep Squadron.

1620. Ace to fly a jet was Captain James Jabara of Wichita, KS, a member of the Fourth Fighter Interceptor Wing, who shot down his fifth and sixth enemy MiG jet airplanes on May 20, 1951, in battle over Sinuiju, northwest Korea. He was flying an F-86 Sabre Jet airplane. He eventually defeated 15 MiGs over Korea and became the second triple jet ace.

1621. Triple jet ace was Captain Joseph Christopher McConnell, Jr., who shot down 16 MiG-15s in his F-86 Sabre Jet. On May 18, 1953, he downed three in one day. He completed 106 missions in Korea. On August 10, 1953, a residence known as Appreciation House was presented to him by his neighbors in Apple Valley, CA, who built it in 45 hours. He was killed on August 25, 1954, at Edwards Air Force Base, Muroc, CA, while testing a new plane, an F-86 H.

1622. Navy ace in Korea was Lieutenant Guy Bordelon, who achieved his fifth victory on July 17, 1953, in a World-War-II-vintage propeller-driven F-4U Corsair. He was awarded the Navy Cross.

1623. Pilot of an airplane to qualify as an astronaut by attaining a 50-mile altitude was Major Robert Michael White of the Air Force, who piloted his X-15 rocket airplane to an altitude of 314,750 feet on July 17, 1962. He was launched from a B-52 at Edwards Air Force Base, Muroc, CA, and landed on Rogers Dry Lake after a flight lasting about 11 minutes. He was awarded astronaut wings on July 18, 1962. White was the fifth to qualify as an astronaut, having been preceded by Alan B. Shepard, Jr., Virgil Grissom, John H. Glenn, and Scott Carpenter.

1624. Air Force ace in Vietnam was Captain Richard Stephen Ritchie of Reidsville, NC, who downed his fifth MIG-21 aircraft in North Vietnam on August 28, 1972, in an air-to-air missile battle southwest of Hanoi. He flew an F-4 Phantom with the 555th Tactical Fighter Squadron of the 432d Tactical Reconnaissance Wing based in Thailand. His other "kills" occurred May 10th, May 31st, and two on July 8, 1972.

1625. Pilot who was a woman to die in a combat zone was Army Major Marie T. Rossi-Cayton, whose supply helicopter crashed on March 1, 1991, over Iraq during the Gulf War. In 1992, Rossi-Cayton was inducted into the Army Aviation Hall of Fame, becoming the first woman so honored.

1626. Pilot of a B-52 bomber who was a woman was Air Force Second Lieutenant Kelly Jean Flinn. In 1996, she flew Secretary of the Air Force Dr. Sheila Widnall in a Boeing B-52 strategic bomber stationed at Minot Air Force Base in Minot, ND.

AWARDS—ARTS

1627. Photographer to receive the John Simon Guggenheim Memorial Foundation award was Edward Weston of Los Angeles, CA, who received a $2,500 grant for his series of photographic documents of the West. Announcement of the award was made on March 28, 1937. The photographs, taken with an 8-by-10-inch camera using panchromatic film, were used as illustrations for *California and the West,* by Charis Wilson Weston and Edward Weston, published by Duell, Sloan and Pearce, New York City, in 1940.

1628. Emmy awards for excellence in television were presented by the National Academy of Television Arts and Sciences on January 25, 1949, at the Hollywood Athletic Club, Los Angeles, CA. Walter O'Keefe was the host. Most of the awards were won by programs originating at station KTLA, Los Angeles, CA, including the award for the most popular television program, *Pantomine Quiz Time;* the award for the most outstanding television personality, Shirley Dinsdale and her puppet Judy Splinters; and the award for the best film made for television, *The Necklace,* which appeared on the KTLA series *Your Show Time.* KTLA won an additional award for outstanding overall achievements in 1948.

1629. Grammy awards for musical recordings were awarded in 1958 by the National Academy of Recording Arts and Sciences, Burbank, CA. The winning single recording was *Nel Blu Dipinto Di Blu (Volare)* by Domenico Modugno. The winning album was *The Music From Peter Gunn* by Henry Mancini.

AWARDS—ARTS—OSCARS

1630. Oscar for best picture was awarded to *Wings,* an aviation adventure released by Paramount Pictures in 1927. It was directed by William A. Wellman and starred Clara Bow, Charles "Buddy" Rogers, Richard Arlen, and Gary Cooper. The award was presented to Wellman by the Academy of Motion Picture Arts and Sciences in Hollywood, CA, on May 16, 1929.

1631. Oscars for best acting were presented to Emil Jannings *(The Last Command, The Way of All Flesh)* and Janet Gaynor *(Seventh Heaven, Street Angel, Sunrise)* by the Academy of Motion Picture Arts and Sciences in Hollywood, CA, on May 16, 1929, "for the best acting in pictures released in Los Angeles, CA, between August 1, 1927, and July 31, 1928." Ten similar awards and two special awards were presented to others for excellence in allied fields, such as cinematography, art direction, engineering effects, and direction.

1632. Oscars for best movie director were given to Frank Borzage for the drama *Seventh Heaven* and Lewis Milestone for the comedy *Two Arabian Knights.* The awards were presented by the Academy of Motion Picture Arts and Sciences in Hollywood, CA, on May 16, 1929.

1633. Oscar awarded to a performer who was African-American was won by Hattie McDaniel, who played Scarlett O'Hara's "mammy" in the movie version of Margaret Mitchell's *Gone With the Wind.* The award, for the best performance by a supporting actress, was presented by the Academy of Motion Picture Arts and Sciences on February 29, 1940, in Hollywood, CA. The first African-American performer to win the Oscar for best actor was Sidney Poitier, who played an itinerant construction worker in *Lilies of the Field.* He received his Oscar on April 13, 1964.

AWARDS—ARTS—OSCARS—*continued*

1634. Oscar winners who were father and son were Walter Huston, who won the best supporting actor award, and his son, John Huston, who won the award for the best director, both for *The Treasure of Sierra Madre.* The film also received the award for best screenplay. The presentations were made in Hollywood, CA, on March 24, 1949, by the Academy of Motion Picture Arts and Sciences.

1635. Oscar winners who were husband and wife were Sir Laurence Olivier, who received the award on March 24, 1949, for his performance in *Hamlet,* and his wife, Vivien Leigh, who received hers on February 29, 1940, for her performance as Scarlett O'Hara in *Gone With the Wind.* On March 20, 1952, she received a second Oscar for her part as Blanche du Bois in *A Streetcar Named Desire.*

1636. Oscar movie awards ceremony to be telecast took place on March 19, 1953, when pick-ups of the 25th ceremony of the Academy of Motion Picture Arts and Sciences were made from New York City and Hollywood, CA, and broadcast over 174 stations. Oscar winners included *The Greatest Show on Earth* for best picture, Gary Cooper as best actor for his performance in *High Noon,* and Shirley Booth as best actress for her performance in *Come Back, Little Sheba.* The first color telecast of the Academy Awards took place in 1966.

1637. Oscar for best picture awarded to a movie that was independently produced was won by *Marty,* the 1955 film version of a television play by Paddy Chayefsky. The film was produced by an independent company founded by Burt Lancaster and Harold Hecht.

1638. Oscar for best picture awarded to an X-rated movie was given to *Midnight Cowboy,* a 1969 film directed by John Schlesinger and starring Jon Voight and Dustin Hoffman.

AWARDS—CIVILIAN

1639. Carnegie Hero Fund Commission award granted to a woman was given to 17-year-old Ernestine F. Atwood. On August 22, 1904, while boating in Boston Harbor, she dived off her rowboat and rescued Harry M. Smith, a coachman, who was trapped under a float 200 feet from shore.

1640. National Geographic Society gold medal was the Hubbard medal, presented on December 15, 1906, in Washington, DC, by President Theodore Roosevelt to Commander Robert Edwin Peary for his Arctic explorations. On December 15, 1909, Peary received a second medal for his discovery of the North Pole the previous April 6. The first woman to receive the Hubbard medal was Anne Morrow Lindbergh, copilot and radio operator of the Charles A. Lindbergh Aerial Survey, on March 31, 1934. The National Geographic Society awarded a special gold medal on June 21, 1932, to Amelia Earhart for her achievement in becoming the first woman to make a solo transatlantic flight.

1641. Aviation trophy was awarded by the magazine *Scientific American* in New York City in 1908. It was valued at $2,500. It was to become the property of the flyer taking it three years in succession, the conditions for winning to be changed each year according to the progress of aviation. Flights were to be made before official witnesses at a preannounced time and place. Glenn Hammond Curtiss was the first trophy winner. His first flight for the trophy was made at 7:30 P.M. on July 4, 1908, at Hammondsport, NY, in his *June Bug* at a speed of 40 miles per hour. The *June Bug* was equipped with an eight-cylinder air-cooled Curtiss engine with a six-foot propeller on the rear of its crankshaft.

1642. Air Mail Flyer's Medal of Honor was presented to Mal Bryan Freeburg on December 13, 1933, by President Franklin Delano Roosevelt. On April 12, 1933, while Freeburg was flying a trimotor plane, an outward propeller broke and the vibration loosened a motor, which lodged in a wing strut and damaged the landing gear. He flew over the Mississippi River, banked his plane, and shook the motor free so that it would fall in the river and not endanger anyone. He then flew 25 miles to an emergency field and landed safely. The Air Mail Flyer's Medal was authorized on February 14, 1931.

1643. Presidential Unit Citation award in peacetime was made by President Dwight David Eisenhower on August 8, 1958, to the crew of the submarine *Nautilus* for its voyage from June 8 to August 5, 1958, across the top of the world from the Bering Sea to the Greenland Sea, passing submerged beneath the geographic North Pole. Her crew was entitled to wear a citation ribbon and a special clasp in the form of a golden *N.*

1644. Presidential Citizen Medal was presented on May 14, 1973, to the widow of Roberto Walker Clemente, star outfielder of the Pittsburgh Pirates, who was killed December 31, 1972, in the crash of a DC-7 four-engined cargo plane off San Juan International Airport, San Juan, PR, while delivering aid to victims of the earthquake in Managua, Nicaragua. The medal was established by executive order on November 13, 1969, by President Richard Milhous Nixon for "citizens of the United States of America who have performed exemplary deeds of service for their country or their fellow citizens."

1645. Charles Stark Draper Prize for engineering and technology was awarded in February 1990 to Robert N. Noyce and Jack S. Kilby, who, working independently, invented the integrated circuit and developed its commercial potential. The $350,000 prize, which included a gold medal, was established by the National Academy of Engineering in 1989 to honor engineers who contribute "to the advancement of human welfare and freedom."

AWARDS—FOREIGN

1646. Copley Medal awarded to an American was presented to Benjamin Franklin of Philadelphia, PA, in 1753 for his "curious experiments and observations on electricity." The medal, the highest distinction given by England for scientific research, was awarded by the Royal Society of London.

1647. Albert Medal presented to a person born in America was awarded on June 10, 1884, to James Buchanan Eads for his plan for deepening the Mississippi River as far as the mouth of the Ohio River by jetties. The Albert Medal was established in 1862 in memory of Prince Albert, consort of Queen Victoria, and was awarded by the (British) Society for the Encouragement of Arts, Manufactures and Commerce.

1648. Croix de Guerre awarded to an African-American in the American Army was given to Private Henry Johnson, 369th Infantry, 93rd Division, on May 24, 1918, with the following citation: "Being on double sentry duty at night, was attacked by twelve Germans. He shot one and seriously wounded two others with his bayonet. Even though he had been three times wounded at the beginning of the action by revolver bullets and grenades, he went to the assistance of his wounded comrade, who was about to be carried off by the enemy, and continued the combat until he put the Germans to flight. It was a splendid example of courage and energy."

AWARDS—GOVERNMENT

1649. Medal awarded by the Continental Congress was granted to General George Washington for his exploit of March 17, 1776, in compelling the British forces to evacuate Boston, MA. The date of the resolution authorizing the medal was March 25, 1776. It was struck in Paris. The obverse showed Washing-

ton in profile. The reverse showed Washington and his officers on horseback viewing the town of Boston in the distance with the British fleet in view under sail. The medal was not presented to Washington until 1786.

1650. Medal awarded by the Continental Congress to a foreigner was a silver medal presented to Lieutenant Colonel François Louis Teisseidre de Fleury, who commanded the first of the storming parties in the assault upon Stony Point, NY, on July 15, 1779. He was the first man to enter the main fort and strike the British flag with his own hands. Fleury, who had been in the French military service, joined the Continental Army in 1777. The date of the congressional resolution was July 26, 1779, and the presentation was made on October 1.

1651. Medal awarded to an American food producer was the Great Council Medal, which was awarded in 1851 to Gail Borden, Jr., of Elizabethport, NY, at the Great International Exposition in London for his invention of the meat biscuit. A 1-pound meat biscuit contained a nutrient value of 5 pounds of meat and 10 ounces of flour and retained its original flavor and value for years. The biscuit was eagerly accepted by explorers, travelers, troops, etc., who needed rations packed as compactly as possible.

1652. Congressional medal awarded to a physician was presented to Frederick Henry Rose of the British Navy. In April 1858, in Jamaica, yellow fever broke out on the U.S.S. *Susquehanna*. Rose offered his services and sailed to New York with the stricken crew. On May 11, 1858, Congress authorized a gold medal to be presented to him for his kindness and humanity to the officers and crew.

1653. Lifesaving medal awarded by the Treasury Department as authorized by act of June 20, 1874, was given on June 19, 1876, to Lucian M. Clemons, keeper of the United States Lifesaving Service Station at Marblehead, OH, for saving men from the schooner *Consuelo* on May 1, 1875. The award was established for "persons who should thereafter endanger their own lives in saving or endeavoring to save the lives of others from the perils of the sea within the United States or upon any American vessel."

1654. Interstate Commerce Commission Medal of Honor was a bronze medal awarded on December 5, 1905, to George H. Poell of Grand Island, NE. On June 26, 1905, while a fireman on the St. Joseph and Grand Island Railway, he climbed out on the pilot of his engine and rescued a child on the tracks. Poell

AWARDS—GOVERNMENT—*continued*
was seriously injured and one foot had to be amputated. The medal was authorized by act of Congress of February 23, 1905, for presentation to those "who shall hereafter, by extreme daring, endanger their own lives in saving, or endeavoring to save lives from any wreck, disaster or grave accident, or in preventing or endeavoring to prevent" accidents. Four degrees were established: chief commander, commander, officer, and legionnaire.

1655. Medal of Technology awarded to a woman was won by Rear Admiral Grace Murray Hopper in 1991, when she was 85. During World War II, Hopper was assigned by the Navy to the Bureau of Ordnance Computation Project at Harvard University, Cambridge, MA. Later she became a senior mathematician for the Eckert-Mauchly Corporation in Philadelphia, PA, working on UNIVAC, the world's first fully electronic commercial computer. In 1955, she developed a prototype compiler, a computer language for automatically generating programs in the low-level machine code understood by a computer's central processing unit. This was the basis for COBOL (Common Business Oriented Language), the first widely used programming language for business. The medal is the highest award for technological achievement awarded by the federal government.

AWARDS—MILITARY

1656. Purple Heart was awarded to Sergeants Daniel Bissell, William Brown, and Elijah Churchill of Connecticut regiments, decorated on May 9, 1783, for singularly meritorious action in the Revolutionary War. They were entitled "to wear on facings over the left breast, the figure of a heart in purple cloth or silk, with narrow lace or binding." The Order of the Purple Heart, a decoration for "military merit," was established by George Washington on August 7, 1782, at Newburgh, NY, and was the first honor badge for enlisted men and noncommissioned officers.

1657. Military campaign medal was the Dewey Medal, authorized by act of Congress of June 3, 1898, to be presented to all officers and men under the command of Commodore George Dewey who participated in the Battle of Manila Bay on May 1, 1898. Unlike medals suspended from ribbons, this bronze medal was suspended from a bar that bore the design of an American eagle with its wings spread over the sea.

1658. Pilot to receive the Congressional Medal of Honor was Second Lieutenant Frank Luke, for extraordinary heroism in action at Murvaux, France, September 12–15, 1918, when he destroyed eight enemy balloons in four days. The award was made on April 14, 1919, and was posthumously presented at Phoenix, AZ, on May 29, 1919, to his father, Frank Luke, Sr. Luke was a member of the 27th Aero Squadron when he was killed in action. He is officially credited with 18 victories, a record that was surpassed in World War I only by Captain Edward Vernon Rickenbacker.

1659. Navy Cross awarded to a Coast Guard officer in World War II was presented on June 4, 1942, to Lieutenant Maurice D. Jester, who, while in command of the 165-foot Coast Guard *Icarus* off the Carolina coast, sank an enemy submarine, captured the commanding officer, his first mate, and 31 members of the crew, and brought them as prisoners to Charleston, SC.

1660. Distinguished Service Cross awarded in enemy-occupied territory was presented on July 11, 1942, to Captain Charles C. Kegelman of El Reno, OK, for "his heroism, his flying skill, his intimate knowledge of his equipment and his great coolness and judgment in action" against the enemy on July 4, 1941. Although one motor in his aircraft was shot to pieces, the tail riddled with bullets, and a hole made in the cabin, he saved his aircraft and his crew. His rank was raised to that of major on July 9, 1942.

1661. Navy–Marine Corps Medals for Heroism awarded to Marines were awarded to Sergeant Norman C.S. Pearson of Minneapolis, MN, and Corporal Gordon Miller of Cincinnati, OH, who risked their lives to save a gunner sergeant imprisoned in a fallen and burning airplane. They were specially commended on September 21, 1942, by Lieutenant General Thomas Holcomb, commandant of the Marine Corps, and promoted a grade.

1662. Silver Star Medal awarded to a civilian was presented by General Douglas MacArthur to Vern Haugland, Associated Press correspondent, on October 3, 1942. He was a passenger on an army airplane forced to descend in New Guinea during World War II. After 43 days in the jungle, he reached civilization.

1663. Soldier's Medal awarded to a woman was conferred on nurse Edith Greenwood on June 21, 1943, for heroism in saving the lives of her patients in a fire in a station hospital near Yuma, AZ, on April 17, 1943. A Soldier's Medal was presented on November 17, 1943, at Allied Headquarters, Algiers, to Private Margaret Helen Maloney of Rochester, NY, a member of the Women's Army Corps, for rescuing Private Kenneth J. Jacobs from a pool of burning gasoline.

1664. Distinguished Service Cross awarded to an animal was authorized under General Order No. 79 of the 3rd Infantry Division dated October 24, 1943, and conferred by Major General Lucian Truscott on Chips, a half-shepherd and half-husky dog owned by Mr. and Mrs. Edward Wren of Pleasantville, NY, for "courageous action in singlehandedly eliminating a dangerous machine-gun nest and causing surrender of the crew." The award was rescinded on February 3, 1944, after a War Department circular dated January 19, 1944, prohibited the awarding of decorations to animals.

1665. Army officer to receive the three highest decorations for valor in combat in one war was Captain Maurice L. Britt of Lonoke, AR, an infantry officer of the Third Battalion. He was the recipient of the Silver Star for action in Acerno, Italy, in 1943; the Medal of Honor for action in November 7–12, 1943, at Mount Rotundo, Italy; and the Distinguished Service Cross on December 7, 1944, by Major General Frank L. Walker. Britt received numerous other decorations, including the Purple Heart with three Oak Leaf clusters and the Military Cross of the British Empire.

1666. Presidential citation to an entire division was made on March 15, 1945, to the 101st Airborne Division, the heroes of Bastogne, by General Dwight David Eisenhower, somewhere on the western front. From December 18 to December 27, 1944, the division withstood tremendous odds during the Battle of the Bulge.

1667. Air Force Medal of Honor for action in the Korean War was awarded posthumously to Major Louis J. Sebille of Chicago, IL, who was killed on August 5, 1951, in an F-51 Mustang which he crashed into the ground amid a group of enemy armored vehicles near Hamchang, Korea. The award was presented to his widow, Mrs. Elizabeth J. Sebille, on August 24, 1951, at March Air Force Base, Riverside, CA.

1668. Navy–Marine Corps Medal for Heroism awarded to a woman was presented on August 7, 1953, to Staff Sergeant Barbara Olive Barnwell, of Pittsburgh, PA, Marine Corps Reserve, in Washington, DC. She saved Private First Class Frederick G. Romann from drowning on June 7, 1952, at Onslow Beach, Camp Lejeune, NC.

1669. Silver Star Medal awarded to a navy chaplain for gallantry was presented on April 18, 1968, to Lieutenant Richard M. Lyons, a Roman Catholic priest, who braved enemy fire to administer last rites to wounded marines during the battle for Hue, South Vietnam.

AWARDS—MILITARY—MEDAL OF HONOR

1670. Medal of Honor action took place February 13–14, 1861, at Apache Pass, AZ, when Colonel Bernard John Dowling Irwin, assistant surgeon, "voluntarily took command of troops and attacked and defeated the hostile Indians (Chiricahua) he met on the way." This action occurred before the medal was authorized on July 12, 1862. The award was made on January 21, 1894.

1671. Medal of Honor awarded to a member of the Naval Service was given to John Williams, captain of the maintop of the U.S.S. *Pawnee* during an attack on Matthias Point on June 26, 1861. A congressional act of December 21, 1861, authorized 200 Naval Service medals for gallantry in action and other seamanlike qualities during the Civil War. The first awards were made to 36 recipients by General Order No. 11 of April 3, 1863. The act of March 3, 1915, extended the provisions to include the Navy, the Marine Corps, and the Coast Guard.

1672. Medal of Honor awarded to a Marine in the Civil War was presented to Sergeant John Freeman Mackie by Commander Henry Rolando under authorization of General Order No. 17 dated July 10, 1862. During the attack on Fort Darling at Drewrys Bluff, James River, VA, on May 15, 1862, Mackie rallied the Marine Guard on the U.S.S. *Galena* after the entire 3rd Division was killed or wounded. He cleared the deck and resumed the action without awaiting orders.

1673. Medal of Honor of the Army was authorized on July 12, 1862, to be given in the name of Congress "to such non-commissioned officers and privates as shall most distinguish themselves by their gallantry in action and other soldier-like qualities during the present insurrection." The first award was made to six mem-

AWARDS—MILITARY—MEDAL OF HONOR—*continued*

bers of a raiding party of 20 who in 1862 penetrated the Confederate lines for more than 200 miles and destroyed bridges and tracks between Chattanooga, TN, and Atlanta, GA. A congressional act of March 3, 1863, authorized the award to commissioned officers as well. It is conferred upon those who have distinguished themselves in actual conflict with the enemy by gallantry and intrepidity at the risk of life beyond the call of duty.

1674. Medal of Honor winner to receive two awards was Thomas W. Custer, Second Lieutenant, Company B, 6th Michigan Cavalry, who was awarded the medal on May 3, 1865, for the capture of a flag at Namozine Church, VA, on May 10, 1863, and a second medal on May 26, 1865, for his heroism at Sailors Creek, VA, on April 6, 1865, when he jumped his horse over the enemy's works and captured two stands of colors despite the fact that his horse was shot under him and he received a severe wound.

1675. Medal of Honor awarded to a Jewish soldier was conferred upon Sergeant Leopold Karpeles of Springfield, MA, of Company E, 57th Massachusetts Infantry, who, while serving as flag bearer, rallied the retreating troops at the Battle of the Wilderness, near Fredericksburg, VA, on May 6, 1864, and persuaded them to check the enemy's advance. The award was authorized July 12, 1864, and the date of issue was April 30, 1870.

1676. Medal of Honor awarded to an African-American soldier in the Spanish-American War was issued on June 23, 1899, to Private George Henry Wanton, Troop M, 10th U.S. Cavalry, who voluntarily went ashore at Tayabacoa, Cuba, on June 30, 1898, "in the face of the enemy and aided in the rescue of his wounded comrades, this after several previous attempts at rescue had been frustrated."

1677. Medal of Honor awarded to an African-American soldier in the Civil War was issued on May 23, 1900, to Sergeant William Harvey Carney for his bravery on July 18, 1863, while a member of Company C, 54th Massachusetts Colored Infantry, at Fort Wagner, SC. He was wounded twice while planting the flag on a parapet and removing it when the troops fell back under a fierce fire in which he was severely wounded. He was discharged on June 30, 1864, with disability.

1678. Medal of Honor awarded in World War I was presented in Washington, DC, on May 21, 1919, to Ernest August Janson, gunnery sergeant, who served under the name of Charles F. Hoffman, of Brooklyn, New York City, in the 49th Company, 5th Regiment, 2nd Division, Marine Corps. On June 6, 1918, near Chateau-Thierry, France, he saw 12 enemy soldiers with light machine guns and bayoneted two of them, forcing the others to flee and abandon their guns.

1679. Medal of Honor awarded in World War II was posthumously awarded to Second Lieutenant Alexander Ramsey "Sandy" Nininger, Jr., for heroism in action in the vicinity of Abucay, Bataan, Philippine Islands, on January 12, 1942. It was presented on February 10, 1942, at Tampa, FL, to his father, Alexander Ramsey Nininger. The first Medal of Honor awarded to a Marine in World War II was presented posthumously to First Lieutenant George "Ham" Hammon Cannon of Ann Arbor, MI, battery commander of Battery H, 6th Defense Battalion Fleet Marine Force, Marine Corps, on March 14, 1942. He was mortally wounded by shell fire on December 7, 1941, at the bombardment of Sand Island, Midway Islands, by Japanese forces, and refused to be evacuated from his post until his own men who had been wounded by the same shell were evacuated. He continued to direct the reorganization of his command post until he was forcibly removed. He died from loss of blood.

1680. Medal of Honor awarded posthumously to a Coastguardsman killed in action in World War II was awarded to Signalman First Class Douglas Albert Munro of South Cle Elum, WA, who was killed on September 27, 1942, while leading five Higgins boats from the seaplane tender *Ballard* to the beach to engage in the evacuation of a battalion of 500 marines trapped by enemy forces at Point Cruz, Guadalcanal. The medal was presented by President Franklin Delano Roosevelt on May 27, 1943, to Munro's mother, Mrs. James Munro.

1681. Medal of Honor awarded to a conscientious objector was presented on October 12, 1945, to Private First Class Desmond T. Doss of Lynchburg, VA, for outstanding bravery as a medical corpsman on Okinawa in specific acts between April 29 and May 21, 1945.

1682. Medal of Honor awarded to a chaplain was presented to Reverend Timothy O'Callahan, of Cambridge, MA, on January 23, 1946, at Washington, DC. He gave the last rites, organized rescue parties, and carried ammunition when the U.S.S. *Franklin* was set afire by an aerial bombing by kamikaze pilots on March 19, 1945, off the Japanese coast.

1683. Medal of Honor awarded to a soldier of Japanese ancestry was conferred upon Private First Class Sadao S. Munemori of Company A, 100th Infantry Battalion, 442nd Combat Team, for action near Seravezza, Italy, on April 5, 1945, when he knocked out two machine guns with grenades and saved the lives of two of his companions by diving on an exploding grenade. The medal was presented posthumously on March 13, 1946, to his mother, Mrs. Nawa Munemori.

1684. Medal of Honor awarded in the Korean War was presented on September 30, 1950, to Major General William Frische Dean of Berkeley, CA, commanding general of the 24th Infantry Division, who at the battle for Taejon on July 20–21, 1950, personally and alone attacked an enemy tank while armed with only a hand grenade. Other recipients at the ceremony were Private First Class Melvin L. Brown of Mahaffey, PA, and First Lieutenant Frederick F. Henry of Clinton, OK. Posthumous awards were also made to Sergeant Charles W. Turner of Boston, MA, and Master Sergeant Travis E. Watkins of Gladewater, TX. The first Medal of Honor given to a Marine in the Korean War was presented to Lieutenant Henry Alfred Commiskey of Hattiesburg, MS, who killed seven enemy soldiers in hand-to-hand combat, armed only with a pistol, on September 20, 1950, near Yongdungpo, outside Seoul, Korea. The medal, the 30th medal award of the Korean War, was presented on August 1, 1951, by President Harry S. Truman at the White House, Washington, DC.

1685. Medal of Honor awarded to a helicopter pilot was conferred posthumously upon Lieutenant (j.g.) John Kelvin Koelsch of Hudson, NY, on April 8, 1955, and presented to his next of kin on August 3, 1955. On July 3, 1951, Koelsch and Aviation Machinist Mate George M. Neal volunteered to rescue James V. Wilkins from North Korea. They took off in a helicopter without fighter escort. The helicopter was shot down and the three men were captured a few days later. Koelsch died of malnutrition and dysentery in a Korean prisoner-of-war camp on October 16, 1951.

1686. Medal of Honor awarded in the Vietnam war was presented on December 5, 1964, to Army Captain Roger Hugh Donlon of Saugerties, NY. He was wounded four times (in the stomach, leg, shoulder, and face) at Nam Dong, about 20 miles from the Laotian frontier. The award was the first since the Korean War, the first in a counterinsurgency effort, and the first to a soldier with a friendly foreign force engaged in an armed conflict in which the United States was not a belligerent.

1687. Medal of Honor awarded posthumously in the Vietnam War to an African-American soldier was awarded to Private First Class Milton Lee Olive III, of Company B, 503rd Infantry, 173rd Airborne Brigade, who was killed on October 22, 1965, when he grabbed an enemy hand grenade and fell on it to save the lives of four companions. The presentation was made to his father by President Lyndon Baines Johnson in Washington, DC, on April 21, 1966.

1688. Medal of Honor awarded to a Seabee was presented posthumously on September 13, 1966, in Washington, DC, to Marvin Glen Shields of Port Townsend, WA, for heroism in the 14-hour battle at Dongzoal, Vietnam, on June 10, 1965, during which he saved the lives of many of his companions. The medal was accepted by his widow, Joan Elaine Shields.

1689. Medals of Honor awarded to African-American servicemen for service in World War II were awarded on January 13, 1996, by President William Jefferson Clinton at a ceremony in the White House, Washington, DC. None of the 1.7 million African-Americans who served in World War II had received a Medal of Honor despite the many documented cases of bravery that were presented to officials of the armed forces. Of the seven servicemen who received the medal at the ceremony, the only one still alive was Vernon Baker, a 77-year-old retired career Army officer. Medals were awarded posthumously to Staff Sergeant Edward A. Carter, Jr., of Los Angeles, First Lieutenant Charles L. Thomas of Detroit, Private George Watson of Birmingham, AL, First Lieutenant John R. Fox of Boston, Private First Class Willy F. James, Jr., of Kansas City, KS, and Staff Sergeant Ruben Rivers of Tecumseh, OK.

AWARDS—NOBEL PRIZES

1690. Nobel Prize awarded to an American was the Nobel Peace Prize, granted in 1906 to President Theodore Roosevelt for his service in the cause of peace in concluding the treaty between Russia and Japan at the end of the Russo-Japanese War. The Nobel Prizes, established by the Swedish inventor Alfred Nobel, are awarded annually in six fields to individuals or institutions whose accomplishments have been of great benefit to humanity. The first Nobel Prizes were awarded in 1901.

1691. Nobel Prize for physics awarded to an American was granted in 1907 to Albert Abraham Michelson of the University of Chicago, Chicago, IL, "for his optical instruments of precision, and the spectroscopic and metrologic investigations which he carried out by means of them."

1692. Nobel Prize for chemistry awarded to an American was granted in 1914 to Theodore William Richards of Harvard University, Cambridge, MA, "in recognition of his accurate determination of the atomic weight of a large number of chemical elements." The prize of 146,900 Swedish kroner was presented on November 12, 1915, in Stockholm.

1693. Nobel Prize for physiology or medicine awarded to an American citizen was granted in 1930 to Austrian-born bacteriologist and immunologist Karl Landsteiner, who had become an American citizen the previous year, after having worked for six years at the Rockefeller Institute for Medical Research, New York City. He won the prize for discovering the four blood groups: A, B, AB, and O. This discovery made safe blood transfusions possible.

1694. Nobel Prize for literature awarded to an American was granted in 1930 to Sinclair Lewis "for his great and living art in painting life, with a talent for creating types with wit and humor." The first American woman to win the prize was Pearl Sydenstricker Buck, author of *The Good Earth* and other novels about China. She received it on December 10, 1938, at the Concert House, Stockholm, Sweden.

1695. Nobel Peace Prize awarded to an American woman was granted to Jane Addams, the pioneering social worker who founded Hull House in Chicago, IL, to serve the city's poor residents. She received the award jointly with Dr. Nicholas Murray Butler, president of Columbia University, for her leading role in the women's peace movement. She chaired the Woman's Peace party in 1915, presided over the Women's International League

for Peace and Freedom from 1919 to 1929, and helped to found the American Civil Liberties Union in 1920. The award was accepted for Addams and Butler in Oslo, Norway, on December 10, 1931, by Hoffman Phillips, U.S. minister to Norway. The first woman to receive the peace prize was Bertha von Suttner of Austria in 1905.

1696. Nobel Prize shared by an American husband and wife was the Nobel Prize for physiology or medicine, awarded to Dr. Carl Ferdinand Cori and Dr. Gerty Theresa Cori of the Washington University School of Medicine, St. Louis, MO, who discovered how sugar in the human system is coverted into glycogen through an enzyme or biological catalyst called phosphorylase. The award was announced on October 23, 1947. The Coris shared the prize with Dr. Bernardo Alberto Houssay of the Buenos Aires Institute of Biology and Experimental Medicine, who was recognized for his work on the relation between the pancreas and the pituitary gland.

1697. Nobel Peace Prize awarded to an African-American was awarded to Dr. Ralph Johnson Bunche, whose mediations in 1948 and 1949 during Israel's war of independence resulted in an armistice settlement. On December 10, 1950, in Oslo, Norway, he received the Nobel Medal and diploma and a cash award equivalent to $31,674.

1698. Nobel Peace Prize awarded to a professional soldier was awarded to General George Catlett Marshall on December 10, 1953, at Oslo University, Oslo, Norway. Marshall was the chief of staff of the Army during World War II and the sponsor of the postwar European Recovery Program, popularly known as the Marshall Plan.

1699. Nobel Prize winner to receive awards in two different categories was Dr. Linus Carl Pauling of the California Institute of Technology, Pasadena, CA, who was presented with the 1954 award for chemistry in Stockholm, Sweden, and the 1962 Peace Prize in Oslo, Norway. The awards were worth $35,000 and $50,000 respectively. Pauling was also the first (and remains the only) person to have received two unshared Nobel Prizes. The first person of any nationality to win awards in two different categories was French physicist Marie Curie, who won the prize for physics in 1903 and the prize for chemistry in 1911 (she shared the former with two other physicists).

1700. Nobel Prize in economic sciences was granted in 1970 to Paul Anthony Samuelson, born in Gary, IN, in 1915. Samuelson, a presidential economic advisor during the Kennedy and Johnson administrations, won the award for improving the analytical methods used in economic theory. He was the author of the classic textbook *Economics,* published in 1948. The first scientists of any nationality to receive this prize, established in 1968, were Norwegian economist Ragnar Frisch and Dutch economist Jan Tinbergen, who were jointly awarded the first prize, in 1969.

1701. Nobel Prize winner to win twice in the same field was physicist John Bardeen of Champaign, IL. He and two co-winners, Dr. William Shockley and Dr. William Houser Bralton, received the Nobel Prize for physics in Stockholm, Sweden, on December 10, 1956, for their work on semiconductors and the discrepancy of the transistor effect. Bardeen also shared the 1972 prize with Leon N. Cooper and John Robert Schrieffer for their explanation of superconductivity leading to more efficient transmission of electrical power.

1702. Year in which Nobel Prizes were won by Americans in five of six categories was 1976. On December 10, 1976, in Stockholm, Sweden, King Carl XVI Gustaf presented medals to William Nunn Lipscomb, Jr., in chemistry; Saul Bellow, literature; Milton Friedman, economics; Baruch Samuel Blumberg and Daniel Carleton Gajdusek, medicine; Burton Richter and Samuel Chao Chung Ting, physics. The Nobel Peace Prize went to Mairead Corrigan and Betty Williams of Northern Ireland.

1703. Nobel Prize for literature awarded to an African-American writer was awarded in 1993 to the novelist Toni Morrison for the beauty of her language, as the Swedish Academy attested in its citation: "She delves into the language itself, a language she wants to liberate from the fetters of race. And she addresses us with the luster of poetry." Morrison, born in 1931, won the Pulitzer Prize in 1988 for her novel *Beloved.*

AWARDS—PULITZER PRIZES

1704. Pulitzer Prize awarded to a newspaper reporter was won by Herbert Bayard Swope of the *New York World* for his stories on the internal situation in the German empire. The $500 award was announced by Columbia University, New York City, on June 4, 1917.

1705. Pulitzer Prize for a newspaper editorial was won by an editorial by Frank Herbert Simonds that was published in the *New York Tribune* on May 7, 1916, the first anniversary of the sinking of the *Lusitania.* The $500 award was announced by Columbia University, New York City, on June 4, 1917.

1706. Pulitzer Prize for fiction was won by *His Family,* by Ernest Poole, published in 1917 by the Macmillan Company, New York City. It was about a New York man and his three daughters. The $500 award was announced by Columbia University, New York City, on June 4, 1917.

1707. Pulitzer Prize awarded to a newspaper was given to the *New York Times.* The award was presented on June 5, 1918, at the graduation ceremony at Columbia University, New York City.

1708. Pulitzer Prize for drama was awarded to *Why Marry?,* a three-act comedy by Jesse Lynch Williams and produced by Selwyn and Company. It opened on December 25, 1917, at the Astor Theatre, New York City. It starred Nat C. Goodwin as Uncle Everett, Lotus Robb as Jean, Edmund Breese as John, and Harold West as Rex. It was adapted for the stage from a 1914 novel entitled *And So They Were Married.* The award was announced on June 3, 1918, and awarded on June 5.

1709. Fiction writer to win the Pulitzer Prize twice was Booth Tarkington, who won the 1919 award for his novel *The Magnificent Ambersons* and the 1921 award for *Alice Adams.* Both prizes were awarded in New York City.

1710. Pulitzer Prize for an editorial cartoon was awarded to "On the Road to Moscow" by Rollin Kirby, which appeared on August 5, 1921, in the *New York World.* The award of the $500 prize was announced on May 21, 1922.

1711. Pulitzer Prize for a novel written by a woman was presented in 1921 to Edith Newbold Jones Wharton for her novel *The Age of Innocence,* published in 1920 by D. Appleton and Company.

1712. Pulitzer Prize awarded to a musical was given to the two-act comedy *Of Thee I Sing* by George Simon Kaufman, Morrie Ryskind, George Gershwin, and Ira Gershwin, on May 2, 1932. It was produced by Sam H. Harris at the Music Box Theatre, New York City, on December 26, 1931, and starred Victor Moore as Alexander Throttlebottom and William Gaxton as John P. Wintergreen. It played for 441 performances.

AWARDS—PULITZER PRIZES—*continued*

1713. Poet to win a Pulitzer Prize four times was Robert Frost, who was awarded the prize in New York City on May 3, 1943, for *A Witness Tree*. His other awards were in 1924 for *New Hampshire: A Poem with Notes and Grace Notes,* in 1931 for *Collected Poems,* and in 1937 for *A Further Range.*

1714. Writer to win the Pulitzer Prize in both fiction and poetry was Robert Penn Warren, who won the fiction award for *All the King's Men* in 1947 and the poetry award for *Promises: Poems 1954–1956* in New York City in 1958.

1715. Poet who was an African-American woman to win the Pulitzer Prize was Gwendolyn Brooks of Chicago, IL, who received the award on May 1, 1950, for *Annie Allen,* a collection of poems about a woman as daughter, wife, and mother.

1716. Writer to win a Pulitzer Prize four times for drama was Eugene Gladstone O'Neill, who was awarded the prize for the fourth time on May 6, 1957, for his play *Long Day's Journey into Night.* His other awards were in 1920 for *Beyond the Horizon,* in 1922 for *Anna Christie,* and in 1928 for *Strange Interlude.* Robert Emmet Sherwood won three Pulitzer Prizes for drama—for *Idiot's Delight* in 1936, *Abe Lincoln in Illinois* in 1939, and *There Shall Be No Night* in 1941—and the Pulitzer Prize for biography in 1949, for *Roosevelt and Hopkins: An Intimate History.*

1717. Pulitzer Prize awarded to a comic book was a special prize in journalism that was awarded in 1990 to *Maus,* by Art Spiegelman. *Maus* used the comic-book format to recount the experiences and suffering of Spiegelman's father and mother during the Holocaust, with Jews depicted as mice and Nazis as cats.

1718. Pulitzer prize awarded to a science book was awarded in 1991 to *The Ants,* a comprehensive guide to myrmecology by biologists Edward O. Wilson and Bert Holldobler, both of Harvard University, Cambridge, MA. Wilson was the first scientist to win two Pulitzer prizes. His first was for *On Human Nature* (1979).

AWARDS—SPORTS—AMATEUR

1719. Athlete to win the James E. Sullivan Memorial Trophy for outstanding amateur athlete of the year was golfer Robert Tyre "Bobby" Jones of Atlanta, GA. The award was made by the Amateur Athlete Union of the United States on December 16, 1930. The selecting committee of 600 considered 150 nominations. Jones received 1,625 votes, more than twice that of the runner-up. The award was presented on February 26, 1931, at the Medinah Athletic Club in Chicago, IL.

1720. Athlete who was African-American to win the James E. Sullivan Memorial Trophy was Malvin Greston "Mal" Whitfield of the Los Angeles Athletic Club, a half-miler, who was the first choice on 252 of 657 ballots cast by a nationwide tribunal of sports authorities and tabulated on December 30, 1954. Whitfield set the Olympic record for 800 meters in London in 1948 and held the world 880-yard record and the 600-yard indoor record. The trophy, presented annually since 1930 by the Amateur Athletic Union, is the top award for amateur athletes in the United States.

1721. Athlete who was an African-American woman to win the James E. Sullivan Memorial Trophy was Wilma Rudolph of Clarksville, TN. The presentation was made on February 23, 1962, at the New York Athletic Club, New York City. Rudolph won three gold medals in track at the 1960 Olympic Games in Rome.

AWARDS—SPORTS—BASEBALL

1722. Baseball players to win the Most Valuable Player award in the major leagues were Frank "Wildfire" Schulte of the Chicago Cubs and Ty Cobb of the Detroit Tigers, who won in 1911.

1723. Baseball player who was African-American to win the Most Valuable Player award in the major leagues was Jackie Robinson, second baseman of the National League's Brooklyn Dodgers, New York City, who won the Kenesaw Mountain Landis Memorial plaque on November 18, 1949, from the Baseball Writers Assocation. The first African-American player in the American League to win the award was Elston Howard, catcher for the New York Yankees, on November 7, 1963.

1724. Baseball player to win Most Valuable Player award in both major leagues was Frank Robinson. He was elected on November 22, 1961, by the Baseball Writers Association for his efforts as an outfielder with the National League's Cincinnati Reds. and again on November 8, 1966, unanimously, for services with the American League's Baltimore Orioles.

AWARDS—SPORTS—FOOTBALL

1725. Football player to win the Heisman Trophy for excellence in college football was University of Chicago halfback John J. "Jay" Berwanger, who received the award from former University of Pennsylvania coach and football innovator John Heisman at the Downtown Athletic Club in New York City in 1935. The winner was chosen by sportswriters and sportscasters. The trophy, designed by Frank Eliscu of Brooklyn, New York City, was a bronze casting 21 inches high on a black onyx base and weighed approximately 70 pounds. It depicted a ball carrier with right hand extended to stiff-arm an opponent. Warren Mulrey of Fordham University was the model. The first casting cost $250. After Heisman's death in 1936, the name of the trophy was changed to the Heisman Memorial Trophy.

1726. Football player who was African-American to win the Heisman Memorial Trophy was Ernie Davis, halfback of Syracuse University, named on November 28, 1961, and presented with the award on December 6, 1961, at the Downtown Athletic Club, New York City. The Heisman trophy is awarded annually to the outstanding college player in the United States.

B

BOOKS

1727. Book written in America was *A True Relation of Such Occurrences and Accidents of Noate as Hath Happened in Virginia Since the First Planting of That Collony,* printed for I. Tappe in 1608 in London. The author was Captain John Smith, who used the pseudonym Th. Watson. A plain, unadorned account of hardships, it is generally regarded as more reliable than his later work *A Generall Historie of Virginia* (1624), which includes the romantic, and possibly fabricated, tale of his rescue by Pocahontas.

1728. Book published in America was the *Bay Psalm Book,* printed by Stephen Day of Cambridge, MA, the first colonial printer. Its full title was *The Whole Booke of Psalmes, Faithfully Translated into English Metre whereunto is prefixed a Discourse declaring not only the lawfullness, but also the necessity of the heavenly ordinance of singing scripture psalmes in the Churches of God.* The book, 5.5 by 7 inches, contained 296 pages and was published in July 1640. It was a new metrical version of the psalms, a revision of those of Sternhold and Hopkins. Seventeen hundred copies were printed and sold for 20 pence each, netting a profit of almost £80. This was also the first hymnbook published in America.

1729. Children's book was John Cotton's catechism *Milk for Babes, Drawn out of the Breasts of Both Testaments, Chiefly for the Spiritual Nourishment of Boston Babes in either England: But may be of like use for any children,* printed by Stephen Day in Cambridge, MA, 1641–45.

1730. Book intended for circulation in the English colonies was Martin Luther's *Little Catechism,* translated into the Algonkian Native American language in 1656 by Johannes Campanius, a clergyman, who dedicated it to King Karl X Gustav of Sweden. It contained 132 pages of text and 27 pages of dictionary. About 600 copies of the book were printed in 1696, 40 years later, in Stockholm, Sweden, by Thomas Campanius Holm, Campanius's grandson. The title was *Lutheri Cathechismus oswersatt pä American-Virginiste Sprätet.* It was intended for missionary work among the Native Americans in the colony of New Sweden, in what is now New Jersey and Delaware, and also contained a small vocabulary in the Algonkian language.

1731. Bookbinder was John Ratliffe of Massachusetts, who in 1663 was commissioned to bind missionary John Eliot's Algonkian translation of the Bible. His job was to "take care of the binding of 200 of them strongly and as speedily as may bee with leather, or as may bee most serviceable for the Indians." On August 30, 1664, he sent a letter to the Commissioners of New England stating that he was not well satisfied with the fees paid him for binding, and that three shillings four pence was the lowest price at which he could bind books.

BOOKS—*continued*

1732. Book privately printed was John Eliot's *Communion of Churches; or, The Divine Management of Gospel-Churches by the Ordinance of Councils, Constituted in Order According to the Scriptures*, printed in 1665 by Marmaduke Johnson, Cambridge, MA. It contained 40 pages. It was not for general sale.

1733. Miniature book was William Secker's *A Wedding Ring, fit for the Finger, or the Salve of Divinity on the Sore of Humanity. With directions to those men that want wives, how to choose them; and to those women that have husbands, how to use them.* The book contained 92 pages and was published in 1705 in Boston, MA, by T. Green for Nicholas Buttolph. The size was approximately 2 by 3.5 inches. It was a reprint of a work published in 1658 in London.

1734. Book of folio size other than lawbooks was Samuel Willard's *A Compleat Body of Divinity in Two Hundred and Fifty Expository Lectures on the Assembly's Shorter Catechism wherein the doctrines of the Christian religion are unfolded, their truth confirm'd ... etc.*, published posthumously in 1726 in Boston, MA, by Bartholomew Green and Samuel Kneeland. It contained 1,000 pages printed in two columns. There is an error in pagination, as the work was printed by two presses.

1735. Shorthand book was printed in 1728 by S. Keimer in Philadelphia, PA, and was offered as a premium to anyone purchasing three shillings' worth of useful books.

1736. Translation of a classic was Marcus Porcius Cato's *Moral Distichs Englished in Couplets*, which was translated by James Logan, president of the Council and chief justice of the province of Philadelphia. It was printed and sold in 1735 by Benjamin Franklin, Philadelphia, PA, for one shilling. It consisted of 24 pages of precepts of morality and moral apothegms. An announcement in the pages of the *Pennsylvania Gazette* of December 11 and December 18, 1735, stated that it was "very proper to be put into the Hands of Young Persons."

1737. Book plate by an American engraver of which there is any record was made by Nathaniel Hurd of Boston, MA, in 1740 for Thomas Dering.

1738. Book made with American paper, ink, and type was *The Impenetrable Secret*, printed and sold by Story and Humphreys in 1775 in Philadelphia. It was advertised on June 23, 1775, in the *Pennsylvania Mercury* as "just published and printed with types, paper and ink manufactured in this Province."

1739. Bibliography of Americana in English was *Bibliotheca Americana; or a Chronological Catalogue of the most curious and interesting books, pamphlets, state papers, etc. upon the subject of North and South America, from the earliest period to the present in print*, published in 1789 in London for J. Debrett. It contained 271 pages and included an introductory study on the state of literature in North and South America.

1740. Anthology of American literature was *American Poems, Selected and Original*, 304 pages, compiled by Elihu Hubbard Smith, published in 1793 in Litchfield, CT, by [Thomas] Collier and [David] Buel. An earlier anthology, *Select Poems on Various Occasions, Chiefly American*, printed by S. Hall, Boston, MA, in 1787, contained English as well as American poems.

1741. Book with color plates was *The City of Philadelphia in the State of Pennsylvania North America as it appeared in the year 1800*, consisting of twenty-eight plates drawn and engraved by W. Birch and Son, published on December 31, 1800, in Philadelphia, PA. It was a large oblong folio containing 26 separate views drawn and engraved and two preliminaries. It was originally issued in 14 numbers (two parts) in wrappers. It sold for $28 uncolored, $41.50 hand-tinted in unbound boards, and $44.50 bound.

1742. Type specimen book from an American type foundry is said to be that of Archibald Binny and James Ronaldson in Philadelphia, PA. It was printed in 1809 by Fry and Kammerer and titled *A Specimen of Metal Ornaments cast at the Letter Foundry of Binny and Ronaldson, Philadelphia*. Type faces were not shown, but about 100 ornaments were illustrated. In 1812, Binny and Ronaldson published *A Specimen of Printing Types*, in which type faces were shown.

1743. Stereotyped book was *The Larger Catechism*, which bore on the title page "The first book ever stereotyped in America. Stereotyped and printed by J. Watts and Company, New York, June 1813." The process was introduced by John Watts and was a combination of the systems of Firmin Didot and Charles Mahon, Earl of Stanhope.

1744. Pamphlet produced from a steel plate engraving was Jacob Perkins and Gideon Fairman's *Running Hand Stereographic Copies*, published in 1815 by Charles Whipple, Newburyport, MA. It contains a title page and seven pages of text that contain samples of handwriting.

1745. Book on Americanisms was John Pickering's *A Vocabulary, or Collection of Words and Phrases Which Have Been Supposed to Be Peculiar to the United States of America; to which is prefixed an essay on the present state of the English language in the United States,* a 206-page book published in 1816 by Cummings and Hilliard, Boston, MA.

1746. Book commercially bound in cloth was the fourth edition of Charlotte Anne Waldie Eaton's *Rome in the Nineteenth Century; containing a complete account of the ruins of the ancient city, the remains of the middle ages, and the monuments of modern times,* republished in 1827 by J. and J. Harper, New York City. It was first published in 1820 in Edinburgh and reprinted in 1822, 1823, and 1826.

1747. Book for the blind was the *Gospel of St. Mark,* published in 1833 in Philadelphia, PA, by the Pennsylvania Institution for the Instruction of the Blind. It was printed in embossed roman letters, upper and lower case. Jacob Snider, Jr., recording secretary of the Pennsylvania Institute, proposed the publication and the funds were donated by Nathan Dunn and Edward Coleman.

1748. Book jacket was designed by John Keep for *The Keepsake; a Gift for the Holidays,* published in 1833 in New York City. It was variously called a book cover jacket, a book jacket, a dust cover, a dust jacket, and a wrapper.

1749. Book on vellum was George Allen's *The Life of Philidor, Musician and Chess Player,* published in 1863 by E.H. Butler and Company, Philadelphia, PA. Only two copies of the regular edition were printed on vellum. Four copies of a 16-page pamphlet entitled *The First Plymouth Patent, Granted June 1, 1621,* edited by Charles Deane and published in Cambridge, MA, were printed on vellum in 1854.

1750. Book showing photographs of movements in sequence was *An Electro-Photographic Investigation of Consecutive Phases of Animal Movements,* by Eadweard Muybridge, begun in 1872, completed in 1885 and published in 11 volumes under the auspices of the University of Pennsylvania in 1887. The 781 plates, comprising 20,000 figures of men, women, children, animals, and birds, were printed by the Photo-Gravure Company of New York.

1751. Book manuscript that was typewritten was the manuscript of *The Adventures of Tom Sawyer,* by Mark Twain (Samuel Langhorne Clemens). It was typed on a Remington typewriter in Hartford, CT, in 1875. *Life on The Mississippi* was also typewritten the same year. Twain did not publicize his use of the typewriter, as he did not want to write testimonials or explain the operation of the machine to the curious.

1752. Book set by linotype was *The Tribune Book of Open Air Sports,* edited by Henry Hall and published in 1887 by the Tribune Association, New York City. The foreword states, "This book is printed without type—being the first product in book form of the Mergenthaler machine which wholly supersedes the use of movable type."

1753. Book series of small-size paperbacks was the Little Blue Books, 3.5 by 5 inches, published in 1919 by Haldeman-Julius Publications, Girard, KS. The books, priced at five cents each, contained from 32 to 128 pages; most were 64 pages. The first two booklets were *The Rubaiyat of Omar Khayyam* and *The Ballad of Reading Gaol* by Oscar Wilde. By 1931, 1,666 titles had been printed. By 1874, more than 300 million books had been sold.

1754. Book completed entirely by one man was *Old Papermaking,* by Dr. Dard Hunter, published in 1923 by the author at Chillicothe, OH. It consisted of 140 pages 9 by 11.5 inches in size and was printed on handmade paper from linen and cotton cloth. Not only was Dr. Hunter the author, but he manufactured the paper, designed the book, cut and cast the type, and printed and bound the sheets.

1755. Book bound with preprinted offset cloth was Gertrude Stein's *Portraits and Prayers,* a 264-page book published on November 7, 1934, by Random House, New York City. The cover showed a portrait of Gertrude Stein made at her home in Belignin, France, by Carl Van Vechten. The cloth was supplied by Columbia Mills, Syracuse, NY.

1756. Book set into type completely by electronic composition was *The Long Short Cut,* a 192-page suspense novel by Andrew Garve, which was published by Harper and Row, New York City, in April 1968. The type was composed and pages were produced by means of an electronic beam projected on the face of a high-resolution cathode ray tube at speeds of up to 600 characters per second. The book was produced by Haddon Craftsmen of Scranton, PA, who used an RCA Videocomp and computer system installed at Video Graphic Systems, Hauppauge, NY.

BOOKS—AGRICULTURE AND GARDENING

1757. Agricultural book was *The Husbandman's Guide: In Four Parts. Part First. Containing many Excellent Rules for Setting and Planting of Orchards, Gardens and Woods, the times to Sow Corn, and all sorts of Seeds. Part Second. Choice Physical Receipts for divers dangerous Distempers in Men, Women and Children. Part Third. The Experienc'd Farrier.... Part Fourth. Certain rare Receipts to make Cordial Waters, Conserves, Preserves.* It was a 107-page reprint of an English book and was published in 1710 for Eleazar Phillips by John Allen, Boston, MA.

1758. Agricultural book distinctly American was *Essays upon Field Husbandry in New England,* by Jared Eliot. It consisted of six essays, originally printed separately, which were printed and sold by Edes and Gill in Boston, MA, in 1760.

1759. Fruit culture treatise was *A Treatise on the Culture and Management of Fruit Trees; in which a new method of pruning and training is fully described. Together with observations on the diseases, defects and injuries in all kind of fruit and forest trees,* by William Forsyth, published for J. Morgan in 1802 in Philadelphia, PA. The book also contained *An Introduction and Notes Adapting the Rules of the Treatise to the Climates and Seasons of the United States* by William Cobbett.

1760. Gardener's manual was the *Young Gardener's Assistant, containing a catalogue of garden and flower seeds, with practical directions under each head, for the cultivation of culinary vegetables and flowers, also directions for cultivating fruit trees, the grape vine, etc.,* by Thomas Bridgeman, published in 1835 in New York City.

1761. Herd book for livestock was the *American Herd Book, containing pedigrees of short horn cattle to which is prefixed a concise history, of English and American short horns,* 240 pages, edited by Lewis Falley Allen and published in 1846 in Buffalo, NY.

1762. Cranberry treatise was B. Eastwood's *A Complete Manual for the Culture of the Cranberry, with a Description of the Best Varieties,* published in 1856 by C.M. Saxton and Company, New York City. It contained 120 pages and described the location of patches, preparation of soils, planting of vines, diseases, picking, and so on.

1763. Agriculture bureau scientific publication was *A Report on the Chemical Analysis of Grapes,* a four-page leaflet by Charles Mayer Wetherill, Ph.D., M.D., dated October 15, 1862, printed by the Government Printing Office, Washington, DC.

BOOKS—ALMANACS

1764. Almanac was *An Almanak for the Year of Our Lord, 1639, Calculated for New England,* by William Peirce, printed in 1638 at Cambridge, MA, by Stephen Day's Cambridge Press. The months began with March.

1765. Nautical almanac was Samuel Stearns's *The Universal Kalendar, Comprehending the Landsman's and Seaman's Almanack for the Year 1783,* published on December 29, 1782, in Boston, MA, by Benjamin Edes and Son.

1766. Almanac with a continuous existence was *The Farmer's Almanack, Calculated on a New and Improved Plan, for the Year of Our Lord 1793; Being the First After Leap Year, and Seventeenth of the Independence of America,* founded by Robert Bailey Thomas of Sterling, MA, and printed at the Apollo Press in Boston, MA, by Belknap and Hall in 1792. The price was sixpence a copy, four shillings a dozen, 40 shillings a gross. Three thousand copies were printed. In 1832, the title was changed to *The Old Farmer's Almanac.*

BOOKS—BOOK CATALOGS AND INDEXES

1767. Book catalog of a college was Harvard's *Catalogus Eorum Qui in Collegio Harvardino ... Alicujus Gradus Laurea Donati Sunt,* printed in 1697 in Boston, MA, by Bartholomew Green and John Allen.

1768. Catalog of the Library of Congress was *A Catalogue of Books, Maps, and Charts, Belonging to the Library of the Two Houses of Congress,* printed in 1802 by William Duane, Washington, DC.

1769. Book publishers' catalog was *The Catalogue of All the Books Printed in the United States, with the prices and places where published.* It was printed in January 1804 for the booksellers of Boston, MA, and contained 80 pages. It sold for 10 cents. The books were classified according to subjects: law, physic, divinity, Bibles, miscellanies, schoolbooks, and singing books. The first book catalog to contain the combined trade lists of American publishers in uniform size was *The American Bookseller's Complete Reference Trade List and Alphabetical Catalogue of Books Published in This*

Country with the Publishers' and Authors' Names and Prices Arranged in Classes for Quick and Convenient Reference, 232 pages, compiled by Alexander Vietts Blake and published in 1847 by Simeon Ide, Claremont, NH.

1770. Index to books was the *American Book Circular,* published in 1843 by Wiley and Putnam, New York City. It contained 64 pages, of which 55 were devoted to a list of 1,172 original works in 2,474 volumes. It classified "some of the most important and recent American publications."

1771. Periodical index was *An Alphabetical Index to Subjects Treated in the Reviews and Other Periodicals to Which No Indexes Have Been Published,* edited by William Frederick Poole and issued in 1848 by George Palmer Putnam in New York City. This was the forerunner of the famous *Poole's Index to Periodical Literature,* first shown in September 1853 at a library convention in New York City.

1772. Catalog of government publications was *A Descriptive Catalogue of the Government Publications of the U.S.—Sept. 5, 1774–March 4, 1881,* compiled by order of Congress. The work was given to printer Benjamin Perley Poore on March 1, 1883, and was finished in 1885. It was arranged chronologically with a general index and was published by the Government Printing Office, Washington, DC.

1773. Catalog of first American editions of American authors was the *Catalogue of First Editions of American Authors, Poets, Philosophers, Historians, Statesmen, Essayists, Dramatists, Novelists, Travellers, Humorists, etc.,* published in 1885 by Leon and Brother, booksellers, of New York City. It consisted of 58 pages and listed the various American authors in alphabetical order and the current prices for first editions of their works. In addition to the regularly issued catalog, there were also interleaved copies on handmade paper.

1774. Monthly cumulative index of books was the *Cumulative Book Index,* published in February 1898 by Morris and Wilson, Minneapolis, MN. It listed nine pages of books published during January 1898. The cumulative feature was begun a few months later, when all the books listed in previous issues were cumulated in one alphabet.

1775. Union catalog of books in American libraries was begun in 1901, when the Librarian of Congress authorized the exchange of printed catalog cards between the Library of Congress and other libraries holding books for which no Library of Congress cards were available. The catalog combined all holdings of the Library of Congress together with the holdings of over 600 other libraries in one author alphabet.

1776. Union catalog of books in a state library was undertaken in 1909 by the California State Library, Sacramento, CA. The catalog covered periodicals available in California libraries and was later extended to books.

BOOKS—BOOKSELLING

1777. Bookseller of importance was Hezekiah Usher, who started in business in Cambridge, MA, in 1639. He later obtained a monopoly on printing the laws of the General Court of Massachusetts and superintended the publications of the London Society for the Propagation of the Gospel Among the Indians.

1778. Book auction was authorized on April 18, 1662, by the Court of Burgomasters and Schepens of New Amsterdam, which declared that "Anna Claas Croezens, widow of Daniel Litschoe, deceased, requests by petition to be allowed to sell by the Baliff some books which she has belonging to Sir Henry Moedy, as according to obligation she has a claim on him for a considerable sum."

1779. Book auction catalog was mentioned in the *Boston News Letter,* Boston, MA, on May 18, 1713: "On Thursday next, the 28th current being the day after the election, there will be exposed to sale by public vendue or outcry at the house of Mr. Ambrose Vincent, silk dyer in Wings Lane, Boston, a good collection of books, to be seen at the said house two days before the sale, etc. Catalogues will be posted at public places."

1780. Book auction printed catalog was *A Catalog of Curious and Valuable Books Belonging to the Late Reverend and Learned Mr. Ebenezer Pemberton, Consisting of Divinity, Philosophy, History, Poetry and Generally Well Bound,* which described the books "to be sold by auction at the Brown Coffee House in Boston, Mass." on July 2, 1717, at 3 P.M. The catalog was printed by B. Green in 1717 and was obtainable free at the shop of Samuel Gerrish, bookseller.

BOOKS—BOOKSELLING—*continued*

1781. Fiction best seller was *Charlotte, a Tale of Truth,* by Susanna Haswell Rowson, an actress at the New Theatre, Philadelphia, PA, and the author of several previous novels. *Charlotte* was printed by D. Humphreys for M. Carey, Philadelphia, PA, in two volumes in 1794. An English edition of *Charlotte* was printed in London in 1790. Later it was entitled *Charlotte Temple.* About 200 editions have been printed.

1782. Booksellers' organization was the American Company of Booksellers, organized on June 7, 1801, in New York City "to improve quality, to avoid interference, to discontinue importations, to favor a literary fair, to recommend correspondence and to promote the general interest." The first president was Mathew Carey of Philadelphia, PA.

1783. Book fair was held in the Coffee House on Beaver Street, New York City, on June 1, 1802, to display offerings of publishers and booksellers. Hugh Gaines was chairman. This literary fair was attended by 46 booksellers and proved so successful that the following year a similar one was held in Philadelphia, PA, after which the fairs alternated between those cities.

1784. Antiquarian bookseller was established on July 10, 1830, in Boston, MA, by Samuel Gardner Drake, who specialized in writing about Native Americans.

1785. Publishing society was the Seventy-Six Society, organized on September 5, 1854, in Philadelphia, PA. Its *Collections* dealt solely with subjects pertaining to the American Revolution. Henry J. Williams was president.

1786. Mass-market paperback book was a work of fiction entitled *Malaeska: Indian Wife of the White Hunter,* by Mrs. Ann S. Stephens. It was published by Irwin P. Beadle and Company, New York City, and first advertised on June 7, 1860, in the *New York Tribune* as "Beadle's Dime Novels No. 1."

1787. Bookseller's guide was *The American Bookseller's Guide,* published monthly by the American News Company, New York City. The first issue was dated January 7, 1869. It was issued free to every publisher, bookseller, news dealer, music dealer, and stationer in the United States and Canada. The price to librarians and others not engaged in the trade was $1 a year.

1788. Nonfiction best seller other than a textbook or purely theological work was *In His Steps, or What Would Jesus Do?* by the Reverend Charles Monroe Sheldon. It was written in the winter of 1896 and was a utopian fantasy of what the world might be like if people lived literally according to the teachings of Jesus. It was read by the author a chapter at a time to his Sunday evening congregation in the Central Congregational Church, Topeka, KS. He sold the story for $75 to the Chicago *Advance* and it was printed as a serial in 1897. As only parts of the serial were sent to the copyright office, the copyright was declared defective. Over 8 million copies in various editions were published by different publishers.

1789. Book-of-the-Month Club selection was *Lolly Willowes, or the Loving Huntsman,* by Sylvia Townsend Warner, published by Viking Press, which was distributed to 4,750 members of the club on April 16, 1926. The club was established in New York City in April 1926 by Harry Scherman, with Robert Haas as president. The original book judges were Dorothy Canfield, Heywood Broun, Henry Seidel Canby, William Allen White, and Christopher Morley.

1790. Paperback publisher in the United States whose entire line was bound in paper was Pocket Books, launched by Robert de Graff in New York City in 1935. The first books issued by the company included reprints of *Wuthering Heights,* by Emily Bronte, *Five Great Tragedies,* by William Shakespeare, *The Murder of Roger Ackroyd,* by Agatha Christie, and *Bambi,* by Felix Salten. They were sold for a quarter each on newsstands and drugstore racks.

1791. Instant book compiled in haste and rushed to the bookstores after an event of major importance was *FDR: A Memorial,* published by Pocket Books, New York City, in April 1945, a few days after the death of President Franklin Delano Roosevelt. It was also the first book written for publication as a paperback. Previously, paperbound editions were reprints of books that had already been published in hardcover.

1792. Book censorship board established by a state was appointed by Georgia in March 1953 under authority of an act approved on February 19, 1953, with the power to make recommendations for prosecution. The first chairman of the three-member committee was James Wesberry. Newspapers were not subject to review or censorship.

BOOKS—BUSINESS

1793. Business manual was John Hill's *The Young Secretary's Guide; or a Speedy help to learning,* based on an English work and printed by Bartholomew Green and John Allen for S. Phillips in 1703 in Boston, MA. It contained 192 pages of instructions on writing business and social letters, punctuation rules, a dictionary of "hard words," and examples of bonds, bills, letters of attorney, deeds of sale, mortgage forms, warrants of attorney, deeds of gift, bills of sale, bills of exchange, assignments, and so on.

1794. Insurance book of importance was *Ways and Means for the Inhabitants of Delaware to Become Rich, wherein the several growths and products of these countries are demonstrated to be a sufficient fund for a flourishing trade,* 65 pages, printed in Philadelphia, PA, in 1725, by S. Keimer. The author was Francis Rawle, who advocated the establishment by the legislature of an insurance office in Philadelphia for the purpose of providing marine insurance for merchants.

1795. Credit report book was prepared by Sheldon P. Church and published anonymously in 1844 in New York City. It was distributed to subscribers only and contained commercial information about merchants in southern and midwestern states.

BOOKS—DICTIONARIES

1796. Native American dictionary was *A Key into the Language of America, or an help to the language of the natives in that part of America called New England; together with briefe observations of the customes, manners and worships, etc., of the aforesaid natives,* by Roger Williams, the founder of Providence, RI. Williams prepared it on shipboard en route to Southampton, England, and it was published by Gregory Dexter, London, in 1643.

1797. Dictionary published in the United States was *The Royal Standard English Dictionary; the First American Dictionary, Carefully Revised and Corrected, from the Fourth British Edition,* by William Perry, lecturer in the Academy at Edinburgh, which was printed in 1788 in Worcester, MA, by and for Isaiah Thomas. It sold for seven shillings and contained 596 pages, including an appendix listing proper names in the Bible. There were 38 lines to a page, in double columns, and brief definitions, usually no longer than one line. The dictionary was dedicated to the American Academy of Arts and Sciences.

1798. Pocket dictionary was William Perry's *The Royal Standard English Dictionary, in which the words are ... rationally divided into syllables, accurately accented, their parts of speech properly distinguished,* 596 pages, printed in 1788 by Isaiah Thomas, Worcester, MA. It was dedicated to the American Academy of Arts and Sciences and was based upon a British edition.

1799. Agricultural dictionary published in the United States was Samuel Deane's *The New England Farmer; or, georgical dictionary: containing a compendious account of the ways and methods in which the most important art of husbandry, in all its branches is, or may be practised to the greatest advantage in this country,* a 335-page double-column book, published in 1790 by Isaiah Thomas in Worcester, MA. It was copyrighted on September 13, 1790, in the 3rd Massachusetts District.

1800. Dictionary of the English language compiled by an American was Noah Webster's *A Compendious Dictionary of the English Language. In which 5,000 words are added to the number found in the best English compends; the orthography is in some instances corrected: the pronunciations marked by an accent or other suitable direction; and the definitions of many words amended and improved.* The dictionary was 408 pages long and was published in 1806 at New Haven, CT, by Sidney's Press for Hudson and Goodwin.

1801. Hebrew dictionary was Clement Clarke Moore's *A Compendious Lexicon of the Hebrew Language in Two Volumes; Volume 1, containing an explanation of every word which occurs in the Psalms with notes; Volume 2, being a lexicon and grammar of the whole language,* printed and sold in 1809 by Collins and Perkins, New York City.

1802. Military dictionary was *A Military Dictionary, or explanation of the several systems of Discipline of different kinds of troops, infantry, artillery and cavalry, the principles of fortification and all the modern improvements in the science of tactics,* by William Duane, a retired lieutenant colonel, published in 1810 in Philadelphia, PA. It contained 748 pages.

1803. Rhyming dictionary was *A Rhyming Dictionary, containing all the perfect rhymes of a different orthography, and allowable rhymes of a different sound, throughout the language, with authorities for the usage of them from our best poets,* published in 1823 by F. and R. Lockwood, New York City. It was an American edition of John Walker's *A Dictionary of the English language answering at once the purposes of rhyming, spelling and pronouncing on a plan not hitherto attempted,* first published in London in 1775.

1804. Medical dictionary was *A Dictionary of Medical Science* by Robley Dunglison, published in 1833 in Philadelphia, PA.

BOOKS—DICTIONARIES—*continued*

1805. Dictionary of American law was John Bouvier's *A Law Dictionary Adapted to the Constitution and Laws of the United States of America and of the Several States of the American Union With References to the Civil and Other Systems of Foreign Law.* It was published in two volumes in Philadelphia, PA, in 1839.

1806. Phonetic dictionary was the *Phonetic Dictionary of the English Language adapted to the present state of literature and science, with pronouncing vocabularies of classical, scriptural and geographical names,* 776 pages, compiled by Daniel S. Smalley and published by Longley Brothers, phonetic publishers, Cincinnati, OH, in 1855.

1807. Bohemian dictionary was the *Dictionary of Bohemian and English Languages,* compiled by Karel Jonas and published in Racine, WI, in 1876. It contained 626 pages.

1808. Dictionary compiled by a woman was *The Language of Fashion,* edited by Mary Brooks Picken, published on February 2, 1940, in New York City. It contained 8,000 terms and 600 illustrations relating to clothing.

1809. Mongolian dictionary was *Mongolian Vocabulary (Modern Khalkha Language),* compiled by Dorothy A. Troxel of the Army Map Service and published in January 1953 as Army Technical Manual TM 30–537.

1810. Medical slang dictionary was the *Dictionary of Medical Slang and Related Esoteric Expressions,* 207 pages long, by Jacob Edward Schmidt, published in 1959 in Springfield, IL.

BOOKS—DIRECTORIES

1811. Thesis directory was a broadside, "A List of Theses at the Commencement of Harvard College," published in 1642 by Stephen Day, Cambridge, MA. No copy is known to exist.

1812. Trade directory was *Aitken's General American Register, and the Gentleman's and Tradesman's Complete Annual Account Book and Calendar for ... 1773.* It was printed by J. Crukshank for Robert Aitken in Philadelphia, PA, in 1772–73, and contained 110 unnumbered pages. The contents included a calendar, an account book for the year, a list of public officers of the various colonies, and space for memoranda.

1813. City directory was *Macpherson's Directory for the City and Suburbs of Philadelphia Extending to Prime Street, Southward; and Maiden Street, Northward; and From the River Delaware to Tenth Street Westward,* published on October 1, 1785, by John Macpherson. It was printed by Francis Bailey at Loick's Head, 65 Market Street, Philadelphia, PA, and contained 6,250 names, of which 686 were subscribers. William Bradford of Philadelphia also published a directory of that city the same year. It contained 83 pages with 43 names to the page, making a total of 3,569 names.

1814. American gazetteer was compiled by Jedidiah Morse and was printed in 1795 in Boston, MA, by Isaiah Thomas and Ebenezer T. Andrews. It was titled *American Universal Geography, or a View of the Present State of All the Empires, Kingdoms, States and Republics in the Known World, and of the United States of America in Particular.* It contained 7,000 different subjects, "exhibiting in alphabetical order a much more full and accurate account than has been given of States, Provinces, Counties, Cities, Towns, etc."

1815. Gazetteer of the world was *Lippincott's Pronouncing Gazetteer of the World,* which was published in 1854 by Lippincott, Grambo and Company of Philadelphia, PA. It contained 1,364 pages.

1816. Postal directory was *A List of Post Offices in the United States with the Names of the Postmasters on the first of July 1855, also the Principal Regulations of the Post Office Department,* compiled by Daniel Tompkins Leech of the Post Office Department and printed by George S. Gideon, Washington, DC, in 1855. It contained 146 pages of directory, 48 pages of regulations, and six pages of miscellaneous material.

1817. Congressional directory published by the federal government was authorized by act of February 14, 1865, and published in 1865 for the first session of the 39th Congress. It was compiled by Benjamin Perley Poore. In addition to a roster of congressmen, the 57-page directory contained information about Washington banks, insurance companies, hotels, express offices, churches, railroads, steamboats, and mail service.

1818. Telephone directory was issued on February 21, 1878, by the New Haven District Telephone Company, New Haven, CT. It listed about 50 names.

1819. Yellow pages telephone directory was published in Cheyenne, WY, in 1883. The directory contained listings for businesses. It was printed on yellow paper and bound into a residential telephone directory,

1820. Social register published was the *Society List and Club Register for the Season of 1886-7,* compiled by the Society List Publishing Company, New York City. It cost $3 and contained 381 pages, of which 276 pages contained lists of marriages, deaths, and subscription balls, and a directory of clubs and names, while 105 pages were devoted to advertisements.

1821. Telephone directory with internet addresses was issued for Westchester County, NY, in February 1997 by Nynex, a New York regional telephone utility company serving New York and New England. The directory included names, addresses, phone numbers, fax numbers, e-mail addresses, and World Wide Web addresses. Similar information had been provided by on-line computerized directories beginning in 1995.

BOOKS—EDUCATION

1822. Spelling book was printed by Stephen Day in 1643 in Cambridge, MA.

1823. Schoolbook was the *New England Primer* of 1689–90. It was "printed by R. Pierce for, and sold by Benjamin Harris, at the London Coffee-House," Boston, MA.

1824. Textbook printed in America was Thomas Dilworth's *A New Guide to the English Tongue,* a combined reader, speller, and grammar, published in London in 1740 and reprinted by Benjamin Franklin's press in 1747 in Philadelphia, PA. It went through 26 editions before 1792. Dilworth was one of the first to provide word lists for spelling. Prior to this time, spelling had been taught incidentally with reading, using the Bible as an advanced reader.

1825. Teaching methodology book was Christopher Dock's *Schul-ordnung; or A Simple and Thoroughly Prepared School-Management clearly setting forth not only in what manner children may best be taught in the branches usually given at school, but also how they may be well instructed in the knowledge of godliness.* The book was completed on August 3, 1750, but was not published until 20 years later. The preface was dated March 27, 1770. It was originally written in German and was printed by Christopher Saur in Germantown, PA.

1826. Book advocating spelling reform was *A Scheme for a New Alphabet and Reformed Mode of Spelling; with Remarks and Examples,* written by Benjamin Franklin in 1768. He advocated dropping C, J, Q, W, X, and Y from the alphabet and substituting six other characters so "that there be no distinct sounds in the language without letters to express them."

1827. Education book was the Reverend Samuel Read Hall's *Lectures to Teachers on School Keeping,* which was published in 1829 in Boston, MA, by Richardson, Lord and Holbrook. Ten thousand copies were purchased by the State of New York.

1828. Kindergarten manual was Edward Wiebe's *The Paradise of Childhood: A Manual for Self-Instruction in Friedrich Froebel's Educational Principles, and a Practical Guide to Kinder-Gartners,* printed in 1869 by Milton Bradley and Company, Springfield, MA. It was intended primarily for kindergarten teachers. Much of the material was translated from the German of Froebel, Marenholtz, Goldammer, and Morgenstern. The manual contained 86 pages and 74 full-page plates of illustrations.

1829. Typewriting primer was *Ted and Polly,* by Ralph Haefner, published in November 1933 by the Macmillan Company, New York City, and intended for use in first and second grades by children aged five to eight. The material in the book had been tried out two years previously in various schools.

BOOKS—ENCYCLOPEDIAS

1830. Encyclopedia printed in the United States was a reproduction of the third edition of the *Encyclopaedia Britannica,* originally published in Edinburgh between the years 1788 and 1797. The American reprint, however, was not called *Encyclopaedia Britannica,* but *Encyclopaedia; or a Dictionary of Arts, Sciences, and Miscellaneous Literature.* It consisted of 18 volumes and was completed in 1798 by Thomas Dobson in Philadelphia, PA. The first volume appeared in 1790 and contained 799 pages and 31 plates.

1831. Agricultural encyclopedia was Anthony Florian Madinger Willich's *The Domestic Encyclopedia, or A Dictionary of Facts, and useful knowledge, comprehending a concise view of the latest discoveries, inventions and improvements, chiefly applicable to rural and domestic economy.* The encyclopedia was a five-volume set, published in Philadelphia, PA, in 1804 by William Young Birch and Abraham Small. It had originally appeared in England.

BOOKS—ENCYCLOPEDIAS—*continued*

1832. Encyclopedia compiled by American editors was the *Encyclopedia Americana,* edited by Francis Lieber. The set consisted of 13 volumes, of which the first was issued in 1829 and the last in 1833. It was published in Philadelphia, PA.

1833. Medical encyclopedia was the *American Cyclopedia of Practical Medicine and Surgery; A Digest of Medical Literature,* edited by Isaac Hays, surgeon to Wills' Hospital and physician to the Philadelphia Orphan Asylum, published by Carey, Lea and Blanchard, Philadelphia, PA. Only two volumes of the work were published, covering "A to Azygores": Volume 1, 1834, 560 pages, and Volume 2, 1836, 589 pages.

1834. Braille encyclopedia was the *World Book Encyclopedia,* copyrighted in 1959 by the American Printing House for the Blind, Louisville, KY. The braille edition, comprising 30,467 pages, consisted of 145 volumes, which were issued between 1961 and 1972. Captions of illustrations were added to the text.

BOOKS—FICTION

1835. Story serialized in a newspaper appeared in Samuel Keimer's *Pennsylvania Gazette* in Philadelphia in 1729. It was entitled "Religious Courtship" and was written by Daniel Defoe, author of *Robinson Crusoe.* It was reprinted from his book of the same title, published in 1722 in London.

1836. Novel by a writer born in America was *The Life of Harriot Stuart,* by Charlotte Ramsay Lennox, published in two volumes in London in 1751. The author, whose father was a British army officer, was born in 1720 in New York State and moved to England at the age of 15. This novel, her first, was a semiautobiographical romance. Samuel Johnson, the eminent English writer and lexicographer, was a personal friend of hers, and celebrated the book's publication by throwing an all-night party.

1837. Work of satirical fiction was a 16-page pamphlet by Francis Hopkinson entitled *A Pretty Story, Written in the Year of Our Lord 2774 by Peter Grievous, Esquire, ABCDE. Velunti in Speculo.* It was a political satire on the administration of the British colonies in North America and the causes of the American Revolution. It was printed in Williamsburg, VA, in 1774 by John Pinkney, for the benefit of Clementine Rind's children.

1838. Novel by an American writer to be translated into a foreign language was *Adventures of Alonso: Containing Some Striking Anecdotes of the Present Prime Minister of Portugal* (Sebastião José de Carvalho e Mello, Marquis de Pombal) by "A Native of Maryland, some years resident in Lisbon." The work is attributed to Thomas Atwood Digges of Warburton Manor, MD. The original edition consisted of two volumes, 148 pages and 129 pages, and was printed for John Bew in London in 1775. It was published in Leipzig, Germany, in 1787 by Schwickert as *Alonzo's Abenteur.*

1839. Novel by an American writer to be published in America was *The Power of Sympathy or the Triumph of Nature Founded in Truth,* dedicated "to the young ladies of America." It was printed in 1789 in Boston, MA, by Isaiah Thomas and Company and sold at the company's bookstore, 45 Newbury Street. Publication was announced in the *Independent Chronicle* of January 21, 1789. The novel appeared in two volumes of 138 and 158 pages. No author's name appeared on the first edition. Later editions bore the name of Mrs. Sarah Wentworth Apthorp Morton, but literary scholars attribute the novel to William Hill Brown. Brown, the son of a Boston clockmaker who had emigrated from England, was a friend of the Apthorp family and embarrassed them by including in his novel a thinly disguised version of a real event, the seduction and suicide of one of the daughters.

1840. Novel published in America to be republished in England was Royall Tyler's *The Algerine Captive; or the Life and Adventures of Doctor Updike Underhill; Six Years a Prisoner among the Algerines,* originally published in 1797 in Walpole, NH.

1841. Historical novel was James Fenimore Cooper's *The Spy,* the story of an itinerant peddler who spies for George Washington during the Revolution. It was published in 1821. The New York–born author, then 32, wrote it after making a bet with his wife that he could pen a more exciting story than the English novel she was reading at the time.

1842. Novel about whaling was *Miriam Coffin; or, The Whale-Fishermen,* by Massachusetts author Joseph C. Hart, written in 1834. The novel was set in Nantucket and New Bedford.

1843. Novel by an American to depict Native Americans in a realistic manner was *The Yemassee*, written in 1835 by South Carolina author William Gilmore Simms. Simms, a planter, politician, and leading secessionist, wrote more than 80 books, most of which concern some aspect of South Carolina history and manners. *The Yemassee* describes the Yemassee rebellion of 1715–18.

1844. Detective story to achieve popularity was Edgar Allan Poe's "The Murders in the Rue Morgue," published in April 1841 in *Graham's Magazine*, Philadelphia, PA.

1845. Novel by an African-American writer was William Wells Brown's *Clotel, or the President's Daughter, a Narrative of Slave Life in the United States,* the story of a slave woman represented as the housekeeper of Thomas Jefferson. In the novel one of the woman's two daughters drowns herself in the Potomac River to elude pursuing slavers. The book was published in London in 1853, and reprinted with slight changes in 1864 in Boston, MA, under the title of *Clotelle, A Tale of the Southern States.* It was published by James Redpath, contained 104 pages, and sold for 10 cents.

BOOKS—FOOD AND DRINK

1846. Cookbook was *The Compleat Housewife: or Accomplished Gentlewoman's Companion. Being a collection of upwards of Five Hundred of the most approved Receipts fit either for private Families, or such Publick-Spirited Gentlewomen as would be beneficent to their poor Neighbours,* published in 1742 in Williamsburg, VA, by William Parks. It was modeled after a cookbook printed by Mrs. E. Smith in England.

1847. Cookbook by an American author was Amelia Simmons's *American Cookery, or the Art of Dressing Viands, Fish, Poultry and Vegetables, and the Best Modes of Making Puff-Pastes, Pies, Tarts, Puddings, Custards and Preserves, and All Kinds of Cakes, from the Imperial Plumb to Plain Cake—Adapted to This Country, and All Grades of Life.* It was printed for the author in 1796 by Hudson and Goodwin in Hartford, CT, and contained 46 pages.

1848. Distilling book was Michael August Krafft's *American Distiller, or The Theory and Practice of Distilling, according to the latest discoveries and improvements, including its most important methods of constructing stills and of rectification.* It contained 219 pages and six plates and was printed in 1804 by Thomas Dobson, Philadelphia, PA. The book was dedicated to Thomas Jefferson.

1849. Canning book was a translation of Francois Appert's *L'Art de Conserver, pendant plusieurs années, toutes les substances animales et végétales,* published in 1812 by David Longworth, New York City.

BOOKS—GRAMMARS

1850. Native American grammar was John Eliot's *The Indian Grammar Begun; or, An Essay to Bring the Indian Language into Rules, for the Help of Such as Desire to Learn the Same, for the Furtherance of Gospel Among Them,* published in Cambridge, MA, in 1666 by Marmaduke Johnson. It was written in the language of the Massachusetts peoples and consisted of 66 pages of text. About 500 copies were printed.

1851. Primer in a Native American dialect was *The Indian Primer; or, The Way of Training Up of Our Indian Youth in the Good Knowledge of God, in the Knowledge of the Scriptures and in an Ability to Read,* by John Eliot. It was printed in the Algonkian language spoken by the Native Americans of Massachusetts and was published in Cambridge, MA, in 1669 by Marmaduke Johnson. A similar edition by Eliot is believed to have been published in 1653–54 by Samuel Green, Cambridge, MA, but no known copies are in existence.

1852. Latin grammar textbook was *A Short Introduction to the Latin Tongue. For the use of the lower forms in the Latin School. Being the Accidence abbridg'd and compiled in that most easy and accurate method, wherein the famous Mr. Ezekiel Cheever taught and which he found the most advantageous by seventy years' experience.* It was prepared by Ezekiel Cheever, master of the Boston Latin School, and published in 1709 in Boston, MA, by Bartholomew Green "for Benj. Eliot at his shop under the Town-house." It contained 64 pages and was 3 by 6 inches.

1853. English grammar by an American was *A Short English Grammar, an Accidence to the English Tongues,* by Hugh Jones, professor of mathematics at the College of William and Mary, Williamsburg, VA. It was published in London in 1724.

1854. Hebrew grammar was *Dickdook Leshon Gnebreet: A Grammar of the Hebrew Tongue, being an essay to bring the Hebrew Grammar into English, to facilitate the instruction of all those who are desirous of acquiring a clear idea of this primitive tongue by their own studies,* by Judah Monis, an instructor in Hebrew at Harvard College. It was 94 pages long, printed with type imported from England, and was published in 1735 in Boston, MA.

BOOKS—GRAMMARS—*continued*

1855. Spanish grammar was *A Short Introduction to the Spanish Language; to which is added a vocabulary of familiar words for the more speedy improvement of the learner: with a preface shewing the usefulness of this language particularly in these parts*, by Garrat Noel, printed in New York City by James Parker in 1751.

1856. English grammar by an American published in America was Samuel Johnson's *The First Easy Rudiments of Grammar, Applied to the English Tongue. By one who is extremely desirous to promote good literature in America, and especially a right English Education. For the Use of schools*, 36 pages. It was published in 1765, in New York City by "J. Holt, near the Exchange in Broad Street." Dr. Johnson was the first president of King's College (now Columbia University).

1857. French grammar written and printed in America was *A New French and English Grammar, wherein the principles are methodically digested, with useful notes and observations, explaining the terms of grammar, and further improving its rules*, by John Mary, instructor at Harvard College. It was printed in 1784 by John Norman, Boston, MA, and sold by the author.

1858. Hebrew spelling book was *The Hebrew Reader: Hebrew and English Designed as an Easy Guide to the Hebrew Tongue for Jewish Children and Self-instruction*, by Isaac Leeser, printed by Haswell, Barrington and Haswell at Philadelphia, PA, in 1838. It contained 48 pages.

BOOKS—HISTORY

1859. History book of the colonial era was *A True Relation of such occurrences and accidents of noate as hath hapned in Virginia since the first planting of that Collony, which is now resident in the south part thereof, tille the last return from thence*, by Th. Watson for J. Tappe, published in London in 1608. Watson was a pseudonym for Captain John Smith.

1860. History of New England was Edward Johnson's *A History of New-England From the English Planting in the yeere 1628 untill, the yeere 1652, Declaring the Form of Their Government, Civil, Military and Ecclesiastique*, a 236-page book also known as *The Wonder-Working Providence of Sions Saviour in New England*, was published in London in 1654. The first history of New England to be published in New England was *New England's Memoriall, or a Brief Relation of the Most Memorable and Remarkable Passages of the Providence of God, Manifested to the Planters of New England in America: With Special Reference to the First Colony Therefore, Called New Plimouth*, published by Nathaniel Morton, secretary to the court for the Jurisdiction of New Plymouth. It was printed in 1669 in Cambridge, MA, by S. Green and M. Johnson, for John Usher of Boston, MA.

1861. Law history book published was William Penn's *The Excellent Priviledge of Liberty and Property being the birth-right of the freeborn subjects of England. Containing 1. Magna Charta, with a learned comment upon it. 2. The confirmation of the charters of the Liberties of England and of the Forrest, made in the 35th year of Edward the first. 3. A statute made the 34 Edw. 1. commonly called De Tallageo non concedendo; wherein all fundamental laws, liberties and customs are confirmed. With a comment upon it. 4. An abstract of the pattent granted by the king to William Penn and his heirs and assigns for the province of Pennsylvania. 5. And lastly, the charter of liberties granted by the said William Penn to the freemen and inhabitants of the province of Pennsylvania and territories thereunto annexed, in America.* A sextodecimo book containing 83 pages, it was printed by William Bradford in Philadelphia, PA, in 1687.

1862. History book by a Jewish author of ancient times was a 1719 reprint of the third edition of *The Wars of the Jews; in two books, with the most deplorable history of the siege and destruction of the City of Jerusalem epitomized from the works of Flavius Josephus, published in London in 1717.* The reprint was published by Samuel Kneeland and Nicholas Buttolph in Boston, MA.

1863. History of medicine was printed in New York City in 1769 by Hugh Gaine. It was entitled *A Medical Discourse, or An Historical Inquiry into the ancient and present State of Medicine: The Substance of which Was delivered at opening the Medical School in the City of New York*, by Peter Middleton, M.D., professor of the theory of physic in King's College (now Columbia University). It contained a two-page dedication and 72 pages of text.

1864. Genealogy of an American family to be published separately was a 24-page pamphlet published in Hartford, CT, in 1771 by Ebenezer Watson. It was Luke Stebbins's *The Genealogy of the Family of Mr. Samuel Stebbins and Mrs. Hannah Stebbins, His Wife from the Year 1707 to 1771 with their names, time of their births,* marriages, and deaths of those that are deceased. In *The Memoirs of Captain Roger Clap*, 38 pages, published by Bartholomew Green in Boston, MA, in 1731, there was a 10-page supplement by James Blake, Jr., containing "a short account of the author and his family. Written by one that was acquainted therewith." Clap's family consisted of his wife and their six children.

1865. American history book of importance whose author was a woman was a three-volume narrative history of the Revolutionary War entitled *History of the Rise, Progress, and Termination of the American Revolution, Interspersed with Biographical, Political and Moral Observation*, by Mercy Otis Warren. It was published in Boston, MA, in 1805.

1866. History of printing was Isaiah Thomas's *History of Printing in America, with a Biography of Printers, and an Account of Newspapers*, published in two volumes in 1810 in Worcester, MA.

1867. Comic history of the United States was *A Diverting History of John Bull and Brother Jonathan*, a 135-page book by Hector Bull-Us (pseudonym of James Kirke Paulding), published in 1812 in New York City by Inskeep and Bradford.

1868. Political history book was *A Political and Civil History of the U.S.A. from the year 1763 to the close of the administration of President Washington in March, 1797 including a summary view of the political and civil state of the North American colonies, prior to that period*, by Timothy Pitkin. It was published in two volumes by Hezekiah Howe and Durrie and Peck in 1828 at New Haven, CT.

1869. Genealogical collective work was Farmer's *Genealogical Register of the First Settlers of New England*, published in 1829 by John Farmer in Lancaster, MA.

1870. Theater history of importance was *A History of the American Theatre*, by William Dunlap, published in 1832 in New York City by J. and J. Harper. It contained 430 pages.

1871. History of African-Americans of a scholarly nature was *A History of the Negro Race in America from 1619 to 1880*, by George Washington Williams. The two-volume work was published in 1883. Williams, a pastor, journalist, and lawyer, was also the first African-American representative to serve in the Ohio legislature.

BOOKS—LAW

1872. Law book of colonial laws was *The Book of the General Lawes and Libertyes concerning the inhabitants of the Massachusets, collected out of the records of the General Court for the several years wherein they were made and established and now revised by the same Court and disposed into an Alphabetical order and published by the same Authoritie in the General Court held at Boston the fourteenth of the first month Anno 1647*. The work was published in Cambridge, MA, in 1648 and sold by Hezekiah Usher in Boston, MA.

1873. Insurance law treatise was a reprint of an English book, *A System of the Law of Marine Insurances; with three chapters on bottomry, on insurance on lives and on insurances against fire*, by Sir James Alan Park, published in Philadelphia, PA, in 1789.

1874. Law report was Ephraim Kirby's *Reports of Cases Adjudged in the Superior Court of the State of Connecticut from the year 1785 to May 1788 with some determinations in the Supreme Court of Errors*, published in 1789 by Collier and Adam, Litchfield, CT. It consisted of 456 pages of text, 12 pages of index, and a five-page list of subscribers. Volume 1 of Harris and McHenry's *Maryland Reports*, published in 1809, reported cases from as far back as 1658.

1875. Law book containing laws enacted by more than one session of Congress without regard to whether or not they had been subsequently repealed prior to publication was *The Laws of the United States of America. Vol 1. Containing the Federal Constitution; the Acts of the Three Sessions of the First Congress; The Treaties Existing Between the United States and the Foreign Nations, and the Several Indian Tribes. Also the Declaration of Independence and Sundry Resolves and Ordinances of Congress Under the Confederation. The whole collated with and corrected by the original rolls in the Office of the Secretary of State, agreeably to a resolve of Congress, passed February 18, 1791. To which is added a complete index*, 592 pages, printed in 1791 and sold by Francis Childs and John Swaine, New York City.

1876. Law book of federal laws was *Acts passed at a Congress of the United States of America, begun and held at the City of New York, on Wednesday the fourth of March 1789, being the acts passed at the first session of the First Congress of the United States, to wit, New Hampshire, Massachusetts, Connecticut,*

BOOKS—LAW—*continued*

New York, New Jersey, Pennsylvania, Delaware, Maryland, Virginia, South Carolina and Georgia, which eleven states ratified the Constitution of Government for the United States. The book contained 486 pages and was published in Hartford, CT, in 1791 by Barzillai Hudson and George Goodwin.

1877. Law text was George Caines' *An Enquiry into the Law-Merchant of the United States; or Lex Mercatoria Americana; on Several Heads of Commercial Importance*, a 648-page book published in 1802 by Abraham and Arthur Stansbury, New York City.

1878. Digest of American law was *An Abridgement of the Laws of the United States or a complete digest of all such acts of Congress as concern the United States at large, to which is added an appendix containing all existing treaties, the Declaration of Independence, the Articles of Confederation, the rules and articles for the government of the army and the ordinance for the government of the territory north-west of Ohio*. It was edited by William Graydon and published in Harrisburg, PA, in 1803. It contained 650 pages.

1879. Medical jurisprudence treatise accepted as authoritative was Theodoric Romeyn Beck's *Elements of Medical Jurisprudence*, a two-volume work published in 1823 in Albany, NY.

1880. Law book of federal laws then in force was *The Public Statutes at Large of the United States of America, from the organization of the government in 1789 to March 3, 1845, arranged in chronological order with references to the matter of each act and to the subsequent acts on the same subject, and copious notes of the decisions of the Courts of the United States construing those acts and upon the subjects of the laws with an index to the contents of each volume*. The first volume, containing 777 pages, was published in 1845 in Boston, MA, by Charles C. Little and James Brown. It was edited by Richard Peters. Publication was authorized by act of March 3, 1845, "a resolution to authorize the Attorney General to contract for copies of a proposed edition of the laws and treaties of the United States."

BOOKS—MATHEMATICS

1881. Arithmetic book printed in America was James Hodder's *Arithmetick; or that necessary art made most easy. Being explained in a way familiar to the capacity of any that desire to learn it in a little time*, printed by James Franklin, Boston, MA, in 1719 for S. Phillips. It had originally been published in London in 1661.

1882. Arithmetic book by an American-born author was Isaac Greenwood's *Arithmetick—Vulgar and Decimal with the Application Thereof to a Variety of Cases in Trade and Commerce*, which was published in 1729 in Boston, MA, by S. Kneeland and T. Green for T. Hancock at the Sign of the Bible and Three Crowns in Ann Street. It contained 158 pages, four pages of index, and four pages of advertisements.

1883. Algebra book was *Arithmetic, or the art of ciphering, according to the coins, measures and weights of New York, together with a short treatise on algebra*, a Dutch textbook by Pieter Venema, printed by John Peter Zenger in 1730 in New York City. The Dutch title was *Arithmetica of Cyffer-Konst, Volgens de Munten Maten en Gewigten, te Nieu York, gebruykelyk als mede een kort ontwerp van de Algebra*.

1884. Slide rule book was Thomas Abel's *Subtensial Plain Trigonometry, Wrought with a Sliding-Rule, with Gunter's Lines: and also arithmetically in a very concise manner. And this method apply'd to Navigation and Surveying, to which is added, 1. Mensuration of masons work, 2. A solution of rota, or Aristotle's wheel. 3. A brief discourse upon gravity*, printed in 1761 by Andrew Stuart, Philadelphia, PA. It contained 86 pages and seven folding plates.

1885. Algebra book by an American-born author was Nicholas Pike's *A New and Complete System of Arithmetic, composed for the use of the citizens of the United States*, published in 1788 by John Mycall, Newburyport, MA. It contained 512 pages, of which 39 were devoted to algebra.

BOOKS—MEDICINE

1886. Medical pamphlet was published on January 21, 1677. It was a treatise on smallpox entitled *Brief Rule to Guide the Common People of New England how to Order themselves and theirs in the Small Pocks or Measles*. It was published in Boston, MA, by Thomas Thacher and consisted of a single sheet 15.5 by 10.5 inches.

1887. Hydrotherapy book was *The Curiosities of Common Water; or, the advantages thereof, in preventing and curing many distempers. Gather'd from the writings of several eminent physicians, and also from more than forty years experience to which are added some rules for preserving health by diet*, by John Smith, C.M., reprinted in 1723 by Samuel Keimer, Philadelphia, PA, from a London edition of 1712. It contained 47 pages. The first entirely American hydrotherapy book was *On Baths and Mineral*

Waters by Dr. John Bell, printed in two volumes in 1831 in Philadelphia, PA. Volume 1 (374 pages) was "a full account of the hygienic and curative powers of cold, tepid, warm, hot and vapour baths and of sea bathing." Volume 2 (158 pages) was "a history of the chemical composition and medicinal properties of the chief mineral springs of the United States and Europe."

1888. Epidemiology report was *The Practical History of a New Epidemical Eruptive Military Fever, with an Angina Ulcusulosa which prevailed in Boston, New-England in the years 1735 and 1736,* a 24-page thesis by William Douglass, M.D., printed and sold by Thomas Fleet at the Sign of the Heart and Crown in Cornhill, Boston, MA, in 1736. "This distemper did emerge 20th May 1735 in Kingston Township, fifty miles eastward from Boston, and affected one-fourth of the inhabitants."

1889. Pleurisy book was John Tennent's *An Essay on the Pleurisy,* 46 pages, printed in 1736 by William Parks, Williamsburg, VA.

1890. Dissection report appeared in 1750. It was a report by Dr. John Bard and Dr. Peter Middleton, who dissected the body of Hermanus Carroll, a criminal executed for murder, in New York City.

1891. Medical education book was printed by William Bradford, Philadelphia, PA, in 1765. It contained 63 pages of text and was entitled *A Discourse Upon the Institution of Medical Schools in America,* by John Morgan, M.D., professor of the theory and practice of medicine in the College of Philadelphia. The discourse was delivered at a public anniversary commencement held in the College of Philadelphia in May 1765, and was prefaced by "The Author's Apology for attempting to introduce the regular mode of practicing Physic in Philadelphia."

1892. Medical ethics book was *A Discourse Upon the Duties of a Physician, with Some Sentiments on the Usefulness and Necessity of a Public Hospital, delivered before the President and Governors of King's College (now Columbia University) at the commencement held on the 16th of May, 1769. As advice to those gentlemen who then received the first medical degrees conferred by that university,* by Samuel Bard, M.D., and printed by A. and J. Robertson, New York City, in 1769. It consisted of 18 printed pages.

1893. Surgery manual was *Plain, Concise Practical Remarks on the Treatment of Wounds and Fractures; to which is added a short appendix on camp and military hospitals; principally designed for the use of young military surgeons in North America,* 92 pages, printed in 1775 by John Holt, New York City. The author was Dr. John Jones, professor of surgery in King's College (now Columbia University), New York City.

1894. Croup report was "Cases of the Angina Trachealis with the Mode of Cure," published in 1781 by Hugh Gaine, New York City. It consisted of a report made to William Hunter, M.D., by Richard Bayley, surgeon, based on observations dating from April 1774.

1895. Army medical book was *A Journal of the Practice of Medicine, Surgery and Pharmacy in the Military Hospitals of France, published by order of the King. Reviewed and digested by M. De Horne, under the inspection of the Royal Society.* The 120-page octavo book, printed in 1790 by J.M. McLean and Company, New York City, was translated from the French by Joseph Browne and consisted of one volume. The French edition, consisting of seven volumes, was published from 1782 to 1788.

1896. Anatomy book was *A Compendious System of Anatomy,* published in 1792 by Thomas Dobson in Philadelphia, PA. It contained 438 pages and 12 anatomical plates and was divided into six parts covering osteology, the muscles, the abdomen, the thorax, the brain and nerves, and the senses. The text was an extract from the American edition of the *Encyclopaedia Britannica.* The first anatomy book written as such, also published in Philadelphia by Dobson, was *A System of Anatomy for the Use of Students of Medicine,* by Dr. Caspar Wistar, professor of anatomy at the medical school of the University of Pennsylvania from 1808 to 1818. The book contained 422 pages.

1897. Pediatrics monograph was Charles Caldwell's *An Attempt to Establish the Original Sameness of Those Phenomena of Fever, (Principally confined to Infants and Children) Described by Medical Writers Under the Several Names of Hydrocephalus Internus, Cynanche Trachealis and Diarrhoea Infantum,* a thesis presented on May 17, 1796, for a degree at the University of Pennsylvania Medical School, Philadelphia, PA. It was published in Philadelphia by Thomas Dobson.

BOOKS—MEDICINE—*continued*

1898. Gastroenterology treatise was *An Experimental Inquiry into the Principles of Nutrition and the Digestive Processes,* a 48-page graduation thesis submitted by John Richardson Young at the University of Pennsylvania, Philadelphia, PA. It was published by Eaken and Mecum, Philadelphia, PA, in 1803.

1899. Hemophilia treatise was prepared by Dr. John Conrad Otto of Philadelphia, PA, who stated that the hemorrhagic tendency was transmitted through the females to the males but that the females were not susceptible themselves. His report appeared in 1803 in the *Medical Repository & Review of American Publications on Medicine and Surgery,* and was entitled "An Account of an Haemorrhagic Disposition Existing in Certain Families." The magazine was published in New York City.

1900. Obstetrics book was Samuel Bard's *A Compendium of the Theory and Practice of Midwifery,* a 239-page book published in 1807 by Collins and Perkins, New York City. It contained "practical instructions for the management of women during pregnancy, in labor, and in child-bed, calculated to correct the errors, and to improve the practice of midwives as well as to serve as an introduction to the study of this art for students and young practitioners."

1901. Medical book by a navy medical officer was *Observations on the Means of Preserving the Health of Soldiers and Sailors; and on the Duties of the Medical Department of the Army and Navy; with remarks on hospitals and their internal arrangement,* by Edward Cutbush. It was printed by Thomas Dobson in Philadelphia, PA, in 1808. It contained 336 pages and a 14-page supplement by Dr. Benjamin Rush.

1902. Hydrophobia book was James Thacher's *Observations on Hydrophobia, Produced by the Bite of a Mad Dog or Other Rabid Animal,* published in 1812 by Joseph Avery at Plymouth, MA.

1903. Psychiatry book was *Medical Inquiries and Observations Upon the Diseases of the Mind,* by Benjamin Rush, M.D., which was published by Kimber and Richardson, Philadelphia, PA, in 1812. This comprehensive book on mental illness contained 367 pages plus four pages listing books issued by the publishers. Dr. Rush was professor of the institutes and practice of medicine and of clinical practice at the University of Pennsylvania.

1904. Therapeutics book was *Discourses on the Elements of Therapeutics and Materia Medica,* published in 1817 in Philadelphia, PA, by Nathaniel Chapman.

1905. Ophthalmology book was *A Treatise on the Diseases of the Eye; Including the Doctrines and Practice of the Most Eminent Modern Surgeons, and Particularly those of Professor [George Joseph] Beer,* by Dr. George Frick, ophthalmic surgeon to the Baltimore General Dispensary, Baltimore, MD. It was published by Fielding Lucas, Jr., and printed by John D. Toy in Baltimore in 1823. It consisted of 320 pages.

1906. Homeopathic treatise was Christian Friedrich Samuel Hahnemann's *Geist der Homöopathischen Heil-Lehre,* translated by Dr. Hans Birch Gram and published as a 24-page pamphlet entitled *The Characteristic of Homöopathia.* The book was issued in December 1825 by J. and J. Harper, New York City.

1907. Pathology textbook was *A Treatise on Pathological Anatomy,* published in Philadelphia, PA, in 1829. It contained 460 pages. The author was William Edmonds Horner, who in 1831 was appointed professor of anatomy in the medical school of the University of Pennsylvania, Philadelphia.

1908. Phrenology book was *Outlines of Phrenology* by Johann Gaspar Spurzheim, M.D., of the universities of Vienna and Paris, licentiate of the Royal College of Physicians of London. It was published in 1832 by Marsh, Capen and Lyon, Boston, MA. It was divided into three sections covering general principles of phrenology, special facilities of the mind, and practical applications of phrenology.

1909. Cranioscopy book was Dr. Samuel George Morton's *Crania Americana; or A Comparative View of the Skulls of Various Aboriginal Nations of North and South America to Which Is Prefixed an Essay on the Varieties of the Human Species,* published in 1839 by J. Dobson, Philadelphia, PA. It was a tall folio containing a five-page preface, 297 pages of text, and four blank sheets. It had 71 full pages of lithograph plates.

1910. Embalming book was *History of Embalming, and of Preparations in Anatomy, Pathology and Natural History; including an account of a new process for embalming,* 264 pages, published in 1840 in Philadelphia, PA, by Judah Dobson. It was a translation by Richard Harlan, M.D., of a book by Jean Nicolas Gannal that had been published in 1838 in Paris.

1911. Bronchitis treatise was published in 1846 by Horace Green, professor of theory and practice of medicine at the New York Medical College. It was entitled *Treatise on the Diseases of the Air Passages comprising an Inquiry into the History, Pathology, Causes and Treatment of those affections of the Throat called Bronchitis, Chronic Laryngitis, Clergyman's Sore Throat.*

1912. Psychiatry textbook was *A Manual of Psychological Medicine,* by John Charles Bucknill and Daniel Hack Tuke, published in Philadelphia, PA, in 1858. It contained 536 pages. The chapters on history, nosology, description, and statistics were written by Tuke; the chapters in the last half of the book on diagnosis, pathology, and treatment of insanity, as well as the appendix of cases, by Bucknill.

1913. Chiropody book was *Surgical and Practical observations on the Diseases of the Human Foot,* by Issachar Zacharie, published in 1860 in New York City.

1914. Electrotherapy book was Dr. Alfred Charles Garratt's *Electro-Physiology and Electro-Therapeutics, showing the best methods for the medical uses of electricity,* 712 pages, published in 1860 by Ticknor and Fields, Boston, MA.

1915. Neurology textbook was Dr. William Alexander Hammond's *The Diseases of the Nervous System,* edited by Dr. Thaddeus M.B. Cross and published in 1871 in New York City. It was divided into five sections covering diseases of the brain, spinal cord, cerebrospinal system, nerve cells, and peripheral nerves. The book consisted of Hammond's lectures delivered at the New York State Hospital for Diseases of the Nervous System and Bellevue Hospital Medical College, New York City.

1916. Allergy book was Morrill Wyman's *Autumnal Catarrh—Hay Fever,* published in 1872 by Hurd and Houghton, New York City. It was dedicated to Jeffries Wyman, professor of anatomy at the Harvard University School of Medicine, and contained 173 pages and three maps.

1917. Dermatology treatise was *The Atlas of Skin Diseases* by Dr. Louis Adolphus Duhring, professor of skin diseases at the medical school of the University of Pennsylvania. The first section was published in 1876 in Philadelphia, PA.

1918. Bacteriology textbook was *Bacteria,* by Dr. Antoine Magnin, translated from the French by George Miller Sternberg, M.D., surgeon of the Army. The 227-page book was published in 1880 by Little, Brown and Company, Boston, MA.

1919. Neurasthenia book was George Miller Beard's *A Practical Treatise on Nervous Exhaustion (Neurasthenia); Its symptoms, nature, sequences and treatment.* It contained 198 pages and was published in 1880 by M. Wood and Company, New York City. Beard's first article on this subject appeared on April 29, 1869, in the *Boston Medical and Surgical Journal.*

1920. Pediatrics book of importance was Dr. Luther Emmett Holt's *The Care and Feeding of Children, a Catechism for the Use of Mothers and Children's Nurses,* 66 pages, published in 1894 by D. Appleton and Company, New York City. It was dedicated to Mrs. Chapin, "the founder of the first training school for nurses of infants in America."

1921. Aviation medicine book was *Aviation Medicine,* 241 pages, by Dr. Louis Hopewell Bauer, commandant of the School of Aviation Medicine. The book was published by Williams and Wilkins Company, Baltimore, MD, in 1926.

BOOKS—MEDICINE—DENTISTRY

1922. Dentistry book that was strictly American was Richard Cort Skinner's *A Treatise on the Human Teeth, Concisely Explaining Their Structure and Cause of Disease and Decay,* copyrighted in 1801 by Johnson and Stryker, New York City. It contained 26 pages and sold for 30 cents. Originally published in 1794, it claimed to obviate every disease of the teeth and gums. The first dentistry book to become popular was Josiah Foster Flagg's *The Family Dentist: Containing a Brief Description of the Structure, Formation, Diseases and Treatment of the Human Teeth,* 82 pages, printed and published in 1822 in Boston, MA, by Joseph W. Ingraham.

1923. Dental surgery textbook was *A System of Dental Surgery in three parts: 1. Dental surgery as a science; 2. Operative dental surgery; 3. Pharmacy connected with dental surgery,* by Samuel Sheldon Fitch, a surgeon dentist of Philadelphia, PA. The work, which contained 568 pages, was published in 1829 in New York City by G. and C.H. Carvill.

BOOKS—MEDICINE—DENTISTRY—*continued*

1924. Orthodontia treatise to be printed was *An Essay on the Importance of Regulating the Teeth of Children Before the Fourteenth Year; or the Period of Life when the Second Set of Teeth Become Perfectly Developed,* by Solyman Brown, M.D., which was printed in 1841 in New York City.

1925. Dental hygienists' book was *Mouth Hygiene,* compiled and edited by Dr. Alfred Civilion Fones and associate editors Robert Hallock Wright Strang and Edward Cameron Kirk. It was a course of instruction for dental hygienists and consisted of 530 pages with 278 illustrations and seven plates. It was published by Lea and Febiger, Philadelphia and New York, in 1916.

BOOKS—MEDICINE—PHARMACEUTICALS

1926. Pharmacopoeia was the work of Dr. William Brown, physician-general to the hospitals of the United States, who wrote it for the use of the Military Hospital of the Army at Lititz, PA. It was entitled *Pharmacopoeia simpliciorum et efficaciorum, in usum nosocomii militaris.* It was entirely in Latin and was published in Philadelphia, PA, in 1778. There were 32 pages. The page size was 4.25 by 2.5 inches.

1927. Herbal book was Samuel Stearns's *The American Herbal or Materia Medica wherein the virtues of the mineral, vegetable and animal productions of North and South America are laid open,* printed in 1801 in Walpole, NH, by David Carlisle for Thomas and Thomas and the author. It contained 360 pages.

1928. Pharmacopoeia prepared by a medical association for the use of its members was authorized October 3, 1805, by the Massachusetts Medical Society, Boston, MA. It contained 286 pages and was edited by Dr. James Jackson and Dr. John Collins Warren. It was published in 1808 in Boston, MA, as *The Pharmacopoeia of the Massachusetts Medical Society.*

1929. Pharmaceuticals book was the *American Dispensatory, Containing the Operations of Pharmacy, Together With the Natural, Chemical, Pharmaceutical and Medical History of the Different Substances Employed in Medicine,* by John Redman Coxe. It was printed in 1806 in Philadelphia, PA, by A. Bartram for Thomas Dobson. It was a simplified arrangement of Dr. Duncan's *Edinburgh New Dispensatory,* and contained 787 pages and six plates. The first

entirely American pharmaceuticals book was *Dispensatory of the United States of America,* 1092 pages, published in 1833 in Philadelphia, PA, by Grigg and Elliot. It was prepared by Dr. George Bacon Wood, professor of materia medica and pharmacy, and Dr. Franklin Bache, professor of chemistry, both of the Philadelphia College of Pharmacy.

1930. General pharmacopoeia was *The Pharmacopoeia of the United States of America.* It was published on December 15, 1820, in both English and Latin by Wells and Lilly of Boston, MA, and copyrighted by Ewer and Bedlington of Boston. It listed 217 drugs. It consisted of 274 pages printed on rather porous paper, 6 by 10 inches. The chairman in charge of the work was Dr. Lyman Spalding, who had proposed the work on January 8, 1817, to the New York County Medical Society.

BOOKS—MUSIC

1931. Hymnbook published in America was Stephen Day's *The Whole Booke of Psalmes, Faithfully Translated into English Metre whereunto is prefixed a Discourse declaring not only the lawfullness, but also the necessity of the heavenly ordinances of singing scripture psalmes in the Churches of God,* better known as the *Bay Psalm Book.* It was published in July 1640 in Cambridge, MA, and was the first book of any kind published in America.

1932. Music book printed with bars was *The Grounds and Rules of Musick Explained; or, an Introduction to the art of singing by note. Fitted to the Meanest Capacities. Recommended by Several Ministers,* by the Reverend Thomas Walter of Roxbury, MA. It was an oblong book containing 19 pages of songs with the reverse pages blank, and was printed in 1721 by James Franklin, Boston, MA.

1933. Vocal instruction book was *A Very Plain and Easy Introduction to the Art of Singing Psalm-tunes; with the cantus or trebles of twenty-eight psalm-tunes, contrived in such a manner as that the learner may attain the skill of singing them, with the greatest ease and speed imaginable,* by John Tufts, pastor of Newburyport, MA. It was printed by James Franklin for Samuel Gerrish in Boston, MA, in 1721. Letters took the place of notes on the staff, with F, S, L, substituting for fa, sol, la, and so on.

1934. Music book by an author born in America was *Urania; or a Choice Collection of Psalm-Tunes, Anthems, and Hymns, in Two, Three and Four parts; the whole peculiarly adapted to the use of churches and private families—to which are prefix'd the plainest and most necessary rules of Psalmody,* by James Lyon, A.B. It was published in 1761 in Philadelphia and contained 198 songs in its 220 pages.

1935. Music book printed from type was *The Psalms of David, with the ten commandments, creed, Lord's prayer, etc. In Metre, also the catechism, confession of faith, liturgy etc.,* printed by James Parker, New York City, in 1767. It had 479 pages and contained all 150 psalms, translated from the Dutch for the use of the Reformed Protestant Dutch Church of the city of New York. It was edited by Francis Hopkinson and had a preface by Johannes Ritzema. The type for the music notes was obtained from Amsterdam, Holland.

1936. Book of music by a composer born in America was *The New England Psalm-Singer or American Chorister containing a number of psalm tunes, anthems, and canons in four and five parts,* composed by William Billings. It was printed by Edes and Gill, Boston, MA, in 1770, consisted of 112 pages, and sold for eight shillings.

1937. Songbook of secular songs was Alexander Reinagle's *A Selection of the Most Favorite Scots Tunes,* published in August 1787 by Thomas Dobson, Philadelphia, PA.

1938. Songbook of secular songs by a composer born in America was Francis Hopkinson's *Seven Songs for the Harpsichord or Forte Piano,* which was dedicated to George Washington and published in 1788 by Thomas Dobson, Philadelphia, PA. An advertisement in the *Federal Gazette* stated: "These songs are composed in an easy familiar style, intended for young practitioners on the harpsichord or forte piano, and is the first work of this kind attempted in the U.S."

1939. Music book for children was the *Juvenile Lyre: or Hymns and Songs, Religious, Moral and Cheerful, set to appropriate music, for the use of primary and common schools,* by Lowell Mason, published in 1831 by Richardson, Lord and Holbrook, Boston, MA. It contained 61 songs and was copyrighted February 1, 1831, in the District of Massachusetts.

1940. Catalog of recordings on disk was offered by the United States Gramophone Company, Washington, DC, the successor to Emile Berliner's American Gramophone Company. Dated November 1, 1894, the single-sheet catalog listed selections of band, instrumental, vocal, and folk music. Each disk sold for 60 cents, about half the cost of a cylinder recording.

1941. Ragtime instruction book was Ben Harney's *Rag-Time Instructor,* published by M. Witmark and Sons, New York City, in 1897. It was billed as "the only work published giving full instructions how to play rag-time music on the piano." It contained 12 pages and cost 50 cents. Harney was the composer of "Mister Johnson Turn Me Loose," "You've Been a Good Old Wagon, But You've Done Broke Down," and other pieces.

BOOKS—POETRY

1942. Poetry translation prepared in America was made by George Sandys, treasurer of the Virginia Company, who made his translation while he was a member of the English colony at Jamestown, VA. His translation of Ovid's *Metamorphoses* was published in 1626 in London as *Ovid's Metamorphoses Englished, Mytholized and Represented in Figures.* A second edition was published in 1632, to which was added a translation of Virgil's *Aeneid.*

1943. Poetry collection by an American poet was Anne Dudley Bradstreet's volume *Several Poems compiled with great variety of Wit and Learning, full of delight; wherein especially is contained a compleat Discourse, and Description of the Four Elements, Constitutions, Ages of Man, Seasons of the Year, together with an exact Epitome of the Three first Monarchyes, Viz. The Assyrian, Persian, Grecian, and beginning of the Romane Common-wealth to the end of their last King: With diverse other pleasant & serious Poems. By a Gentlewoman in New-England.* The book was published in Massachusetts in 1640. Bradstreet was born in Northampton, England, circa 1612 and came in 1630 to Massachusetts, where her husband later served as governor.

1944. Poetry collection by an American poet who was a man was *New Englands Crisis, or a Brief Narrative of New Englands Lamentable Estate at present, compar'd with the former (but few) years of Prosperity. Occasioned by many unheard of Crueltyes practised upon the Persons and Estates of its united Colonyes, without respect of Sex, Age or Quality of Persons, by the Barbarous Heathen thereof.* The

83

BOOKS—POETRY—*continued*

author was Benjamin Tompson, who was graduated from Harvard College, Cambridge, MA, in 1662. This work, a 31-page book of poems about King Philip's War, was published in 1676 in Boston, MA. It was printed and sold by John Foster.

1945. Poem to be printed in a newspaper was "The Seminary at Quebeck," a Latin poem published on December 24, 1705, in the *Boston News Letter*. It was four lines long and described a fire whose flames engulfed a church: *Gallica crux aequam flammam sentive coacta est.*

1946. Poetry collection by an African-American woman was *Poems on Various Subjects, Religious and Moral*, published in London in 1773 and dedicated to the Countess of Huntingdon. Wheatley was born in Africa, possibly in Senegal, about 1753. She was kidnapped by slavers as a child and taken to Boston, MA, where she became personal servant to the wife of tailor John Wheatley. She began to write in English at the age of 13. Her first poem, "An Elegiac Poem on the Death of George Whitefield," was published in 1770. The first African-American woman known to have written poetry was Lucy Terry Prince, a resident of Deerfield, MA, who wrote a poem in August 1746 commemorating a Native American raid on the town.

1947. Poem to win national acclaim was Henry Wadsworth Longfellow's *Song of Hiawatha*, which was published in book form on November 10, 1855, by Ticknor and Fields, Boston, MA. In four weeks 10,000 copies were sold, and in 18 months, 30,000.

BOOKS—RELIGION

1948. Sermon to be printed was "The Sin and Danger of Self-Love, a Discourse," based on the text from I Cor.10:24, "Let no man seek his own; But every man another's wealth." It was delivered on December 9, 1621, by Robert Cushman in Plymouth, MA, in "an assembly of His Majesty's faithful subjects, there inhabiting," and was printed in London in 1622. It was reprinted by S. Kneeland, Boston, MA, in 1724.

1949. Latin book written in New England was *Responsio ad totam quaestionum syllogen a clarissimo viro domino Guilielmo Apollonio, ecclesiae middleburgensis pastore, propositam,* written by John Norton and published in 1648 in London. The preface was by John Cotton.

1950. Theological treatise of importance was *Vier kleine doch ungemeine und sehr nützliche Tractätlein,* by Francis Daniel Pastorius, published in 1690 in Germantown, PA. It contained an outline of the saints, an account of the bishops and saints, and a review of the church councils and the bishops and patriarchs of Constantinople.

1951. Book of Common Prayer in the Mohawk language was *The morning and evening prayer, the litany, church catechism, family prayers, and several chapters of the Old and New Testament, translated into the Mahaque Indian language by Lawrence Claesse, interpreter to William Andrews, Missionary to the Indians from the Honourable and Reverend the Society for the Propagation of the Gospel in Foreign Parts.* The book contained 115 pages and was published in 1715 by William Bradford in New York City.

1952. Catalog of theological and biblical literature appeared in Cotton Mather's *Manuductio Ad Ministerium; directions for a candidate of the ministry, wherein first, a right foundation is laid for his future improvement, and, then, rules are offered for such a management of his academical and preparatory studies, and thereupon, for such a conduct after his appearance in the world, as may render him a skilful and useful minister of the gospel.* The work was printed in 1726 for Thomas Hancock and sold at his shop in Ann Street, Boston, MA. It contained 151 pages and a catalog for a young student's library.

1953. German book printed in America was Johann Conrad Beissel's *Das Buchlein vom Sabbath*, printed in Philadelphia, PA, in 1728 by Andrew Bradford.

1954. Jewish prayer book published in America was *Prayers for Shabbath, Rosh-Hashanah and Yom Kippur, or the Sabbath, the beginning of the year and the Day of Atonements; with the Amidah and Musaph of the Moadim, or Solemn Seasons according to the order of the Spanish and Portuguese Jews,* translated by Isaac Pinto and printed for him in 1766 (the year 5526 according to the Hebrew calendar) by John Holt, New York City. The book contained 196 pages.

1955. Episcopal catechism published after the separation of the American synod from the British church was *The ABC with the Church of England Catechism. To which are annexed, prayers used in the academy of the Protestant Episcopal Church in Philadelphia. Also a Hymn on the Nativity of our Saviour; and an-*

other for Easterday. It was 12 pages long and was printed in 1785 by Young, Stewart and M'Cullough in Philadelphia, PA. On page six, instead of the words "king" and "him," dotted lines were printed so that the title of the head of government could be written in.

1956. Unitarian prayer book was *A Liturgy, Collected Principally From the Book of Common Prayer, for the use of the first Episcopal Church in Boston; together with the Psalter or Psalms of David,* compiled by the Reverend James Freeman and printed in 1785 by Peter Edes of Boston, MA, for King's Chapel, Boston.

1957. Publisher of denominational religious books was the Methodist Book Concern, organized at a conference in the John Street Methodist Episcopal Church, New York City, in May 1789. The Reverend John Dickins advanced the capital, $600, from his private savings and started publishing in Philadelphia, PA. The first book issued was *The Christian's Pattern,* John Wesley's version of Thomas à Kempis's *Imitation of Christ.*

1958. Hebrew book other than the Bible published in America was *Abne Yehoshua* ("Stones of Joshua"), by Joshua Ben Mordecai ha-Cohen Falk, published in 1860 in New York City. It contained 108 pages.

BOOKS—RELIGION—BIBLES

1959. Bible translated into a Native American language was finished in 1661 by John Eliot, the "Apostle to the North American Indians." It was entitled *The New Testament of Our Lord and Saviour Jesus Christ* and bore a dedication in English to England's King Charles II. It contained 130 printed leaves without pagination and two title pages, one in English and the other in the Algonkian language. The text was in double columns with marginal references. In 1663 *The Holy Bible, Containing the Old Testament and the New, Translated into the Indian Language* was printed in quarto size and contained 540 leaves. Both Bibles were "ordered to be printed by the Commissioners of the United Colonies in New England, at the charge and with the consent of the corporation in England for the propagation of the gospel amongst the Native Americans in New England," and were printed in Cambridge, MA, by Samuel Green and Marmaduke Johnson.

1960. Bible concordance was a reprint of an edition published in London in 1643. It was published in Cambridge, MA, in 1683. In 1720 it was published as the *Cambridge Concordance* by Samuel Newman of Cambridge, MA.

1961. Bible printed in German was printed by Christopher Sower in Germantown, PA, in 1743, from the text of the 32nd Halle edition, with type obtained from Frankfurt, Germany. Its abbreviated title was *Biblia Das ist; Die Heilige Schrift altes und Neues Testaments, Nach der Deutschen Uebersetzung D. Martin Luthers.*

1962. Bible printed in English was printed by Robert Aitken of Philadelphia, PA, in 1782. It was entitled *The Holy Bible, containing the Old and New Testaments—newly translated out of the original tongues; and with the former translations diligently compared and revised.* The frontispiece noted that it was "printed and sold by R. Aitken, at Pope's Head, Three doors above the Coffee House, in Market Street, Philadelphia, PA, 1782." It was a duodecimo of 353 pages without pagination. The venture, though authorized by Congress on September 21, 1782, was financially unsuccessful. The New Testament alone was printed in 1781 by Aitken.

1963. Catholic Bible in English was a 990-page quarto printed by Carey, Stewart and Company, Philadelphia, PA, in 1790. It was printed from new type cast in the foundry of John Baine, Philadelphia, and was intended to be issued in 48-page sections every Saturday. The first section was issued on December 12, 1789. The title was *The Holy Bible, translated from the Latin Vulgate: diligently compared with the Hebrew, Greek and other editions, in divers languages; and first published by the English College at Douai, anno 1609. Newly revised and corrected, according to the Clementine edition of the Scriptures, with annotations for elucidating the principal difficulties of Holy Writ.* It was based on the New Testament published in 1582 in Reims, France, and the Old Testament published in Douai, Flanders, in 1609.

1964. Bible in folio size to be illustrated was *The Holy Bible, containing the Old and New Testaments: With the Apocrypha. Translated out of the original tongues and with the former translations diligently compared and revised by the special command of King James I of England,* published in 1791 by Isaiah Thomas, Worcester, MA. It was 8.875 by 11.5 inches and contained 1,012 pages and about 50 plates.

1965. Greek Testament was *The New Testament in Greek,* 478 pages, printed in 1800 by Isaiah Thomas, Worcester, MA.

BOOKS—RELIGION—BIBLES—*continued*

1966. Bible translated into English was *The Holy Bible, containing the old and new covenant, commonly called the Old and New Testament; translated from the Greek,* issued in four volumes with unnumbered pages. It was printed in Philadelphia, PA, by Jane Aitken in 1808. It was copyrighted on September 12, 1808, in the District of Pennsylvania by the translator, Charles Thomson, who had been secretary to the Continental Congress.

1967. Bible in Hebrew published in America was *Biblia Hebraica,* printed in 1814 by Thomas Dobson, Philadelphia, PA, from type imported from Amsterdam, Holland.

1968. Bible for the blind in embossed form using the old line letter system was issued in 1835 by the American Bible Society, New York City. This society was also the first to supply the blind with the Bible in New York Point, and in the more recent Braille.

1969. Phonetic Bible was *The New Testament of Our Lord and Saviour Jesus Christ, translated out of the original Greek, and with the former translations diligently compared and revised,* by Andrew Comstock, M.D. It contained 397 pages and was published in 1848 in Philadelphia, PA. Comstock used a character for each of the 38 elementary sounds and six compound letters. The text was set in double columns.

1970. Bible translation by a woman was made by Julia Evelina Smith of Glastonbury, CT, and published in Hartford, CT, in 1876 by the American Publishing Company. The full title was *The Holy Bible, containing the Old and New Testaments: translated literally from the original tongues.* The book contained 1,168 pages.

BOOKS—RELIGION—HYMNBOOKS

1971. Lutheran hymnbook in English was Johann Christoff Kunze's *A Hymn and Prayer Book for the Use of Such Lutheran Churches as Use the English Language,* printed and sold by Hurlin and Commardinger, 450 Pearl Street, New York City, in 1795. Its 300 pages contained 240 hymns, 70 of which were of English origin. Kunze was the senior of the Lutheran clergy in New York State. A Lutheran hymnbook in German, *Erbauliche Lieder-Sammlung zum Gottesdienstlichten Gebrauch in den Vereinigten Evangelisch-Lutherischen Gemeinken in Nord-America,* was published in 1786 in Germantown, PA. It contained 707 hymns compiled by the Reverend Henry Melchior Muhlenberg. It was copyrighted on October 2, 1786, by Peter Leibert and Michael Billmeyer.

1972. Hymnbook with music was the ninth edition of *The Psalms, Hymns & Spiritual Songs of the Old and New Testament; Faithfully Translated into English Meetre. For the Use, Edification and Comfort of the Saints in publick and private especially in New England,* 420 pages, printed in 1798 by Bartholomew Green and J. Allen, Boston, MA, for Michael Perry. The book contained 13 tunes.

1973. Hymnbook compiled by an African-American editor was *A Collection of Spiritual Songs and Hymns, Selected from Various Authors,* published in Philadelphia, PA, in 1801. The compiler was Richard Allen, the first African-American minister in the Methodist Church and the founder of the African Methodist Episcopal Church.

BOOKS—SCIENCE AND TECHNOLOGY

1974. Paleontology report was prepared by the Reverend Cotton Mather in 1713. The subject was three teeth and a 17-foot thigh bone that had been unearthed in Albany, NY, in 1705, and which Mather thought to be the remains of a race of giants. The report was read before the Royal Society of London in 1714. On the basis of his scientific work *Curiosa Americana,* Mather was elected a member of the Royal Society, the first American to receive this distinction.

1975. Logic book was William Brattle's *Compendium Logicae Secundum Principia, D. Renati Cartesii Plerumque Efformatum, et Catechistice Propositum,* published in Boston, MA, in 1735. The text was in Latin and contained 64 pages.

1976. Chemistry textbook was Benjamin Rush's *Syllabus of a Course of Lectures on Chemistry,* published in 1770 in Philadelphia, PA.

1977. Engineering book was a translation of Louis André de la Mamie de Clairac's *L'Ingénieur de Compagne; or Field Engineer.* It contained 256 pages and a variety of copperplates. It was translated by Major Lewis Nicola and was published in 1776 by Robert Aitken, Philadelphia, Pa.

1978. Geography book was Jedidiah Morse's *Geography Made Easy, being a short but comprehensive system of that useful and agreeable science,* a 214-page duodecimo published in 1784 in New Haven, CT, by Meigs, Bowen and Dana.

1979. Botany book by an American-born author and printed in this country was *Arbustrum Americanum; the American Grove, or an alphabetical catalogue of forest trees and shrubs, natives of the American United States ... also some hints of their uses in medicines, dyes and domestic economy,* 174 pages, by Humphry Marshall of Chester County, PA, published in 1785 by Joseph Crukshank, Philadelphia, PA.

1980. Chemistry laboratory manual was James Woodhouse's *Young Chemist's Pocket Companion,* a 56-page book that contained about 100 experiments. It was published in 1797 in Philadelphia, PA.

1981. Geology book of importance was *Observations on the Geology of the United States,* which was read by William Maclure on January 20, 1809 before the American Philosophical Society. It was published in revised form in 1817 in Philadelphia, PA, and contained the first chart of United States territory that divided the land into rock types. It was the first true geological map of any part of North America and one of the world's earliest geological maps. Maclure was a wealthy businessman and amateur geologist who emigrated from Scotland and became a citizen in 1796. He is considered the first American geologist of note.

1982. Mineralogy textbook was *An Elementary Treatise on Mineralogy, being an introduction to the study of these sciences, and designed for the use of pupils,—for persons attending lectures on these subjects,—and as a companion for travellers in the United States of America,* by Parker Cleaveland, professor of mathematics and natural philosophy at Bowdoin College. It was published in 1816 by Cummings and Hilliard, Boston, MA, and printed by Hilliard and Metcalf at the University Press, Cambridge, MA. The book contained 668 pages and six illustrated plates.

1983. Geology textbook was *The Index to the Geology of the Northern States,* by Amos Eaton, which was published in 1818 in Leicester, MA.

1984. Entomology book was Thomas Say's *American Entomology, or Descriptions of the Insects of North America,* three volumes, published in Philadelphia, PA, by Samuel Augustus Mitchell. The first volume was published in 1824, the second in 1825, and the third in 1828. Each contained 18 plates.

1985. Astronomical observations book was James Melville Gillis's *Astronomical Observations made at the Naval Observatory, Washington, under Orders of the Honorable Secretary of the Navy, Dated August 13, 1838.* It contained 671 pages and was a catalog of 1,248 stars. It was printed in Washington, DC.

1986. Photography book was *The History and Practice of the Art of Photography: or, the Production of Pictures Through the Agency of Light, Containing All the Instructions Necessary for the Complete Practice of the Daguerrean and Photogenic Art, Both on Metallic Plates and on Paper,* by Henry Hunt Snelling, published by G.P. Putnam, New York City, in 1849. It contained 139 pages of text.

1987. Aviation book was John Wise's *A System of Aeronautics, Comprehending Its Earliest Investigations, and Modern Practice and Art; Designed as a History for the Common Reader, and Guide to the Student of the Art,* 310 pages, published in three parts in 1850 at Philadelphia by Joseph A. Speel.

1988. Mechanics textbook was *The Elements of Analytical Mechanics,* 445 pages, by William Holmes Chambers Bartlett, professor of natural and experimental philosophy at the U.S. Military Academy, West Point, NY, published by A.S. Barnes and Company, New York City, in 1853.

1989. Sociology treatise was *A Treatise on Sociology; Theoretical and Practical,* by Henry Hughes of Mississippi. It was 292 pages long and was published in Philadelphia, PA, in 1854.

1990. Forestry book was Franklin Benjamin Hough's *Elements of Forestry; designed to afford information concerning the planting and care of forest trees for ornament or profit and giving suggestions upon the creation and care of woodlands with the view of securing the greatest benefit for the longest time, particularly adapted to the wants and conditions of the United States.* It contained 381 pages and was published in 1882 by R. Clarke and Company, Cincinnati, OH.

1991. Ecology book of wide influence was *Silent Spring* by biologist Rachel Louise Carson. The book, published in 1962 by the Houghton Mifflin Company, Boston, MA, detailed the harm to wildlife caused by the widespread use of the persistent pesticide DDT. It is credited with launching the environmental movement in the United States.

BOOKS—SPORTS AND GAMES

1992. Fencing book was Edward Blackwell's *A Compleat System of Fencing; or the art of defence, in the use of the small sword; wherein the most necessary parts thereof are plainly laid down; chiefly for gentlemen, promoters and lovers of that science in North America,* printed in 1734 by William Parks, Williamsburg, VA. It was based on Henry Blackwell's *The English Fencing Master,* published in London in 1705.

1993. Fishing treatise was a 22-page pamphlet, *A Discourse Utter'd In Part at Ammauskeeg Falls in the Fishing Season 1739,* by Joseph Seccombe ("Fluviatulis Piscator"), parish minister in Kingston, NH, published in 1743 in Boston, MA, by Samuel Kneeland and Timothy Green. It was dedicated "to the honourable Theodore Atkinson, Esq., and others, the worthy patrons of the fishing at Ammauskeeg."

1994. Sports book of importance was *The Sportsman's Companion, or, an essay on shooting; illustratiously shewing in what manner to fire at birds of game, in various directions and situations—and, directions to gentlemen for the treatment and breaking their own pointers and spaniels.* The book was published in 1783 in New York City.

1995. Chess book was *Chess Made Easy—New Comprehensive Rules For Playing the Game of Chess with Examples from Philidor, Cunningham, etc. to which is prefixed a pleasing account of its origin; some interesting anecdotes of several exalted personages who have been admirers of it; and the Morals of Chess written by the ingenious Dr. Franklin.* It contained 106 pages, including eight pages of advertisements, and was printed and sold in 1802 by James Humphreys of Philadelphia, PA. Evidently it was a reprint of an English edition.

1996. Gymnastics book was *Gymnastics for Youth; or a practical guide to healthful and amusing exercises for the use of schools,* by Johann Christoph Friedrich Guts Muths, translated from the original work in German, but erroneously credited to Christian Gotthelf Salzmann. It was published in 1802 by William Duane, Philadelphia, PA. It was illustrated with copper plates and contained 432 pages.

1997. Horse race pacing register was the *American Race-Turf Register, Sportsman's Herald and General Stud Book; containing the pedigrees of the most celebrated horses, mares, and geldings that have distinguished themselves as pacers on the American turf,* 602 pages, by Patrick Nisbett Edgar, published in 1833 in New York City.

1998. Baseball book was Robin Carver's *The Book of Sports,* published in 1834 in Boston, MA, by Lilly, Wait, Colman, and Holden. It was based on an English edition of the *Boy's Own Book.*

1999. Whist rule book was *The Whist Player's Hand Book, containing most of the maxims of the old school and several new ones exemplified by opposite cases; with a method of acquiring a knowledge of the principles on which they are grounded to which are added observations on short whist, also the games of Boston and euchre.* The book was written by Thomas Matthews and published in 1844 in Philadelphia, PA, by Isaac M. Moss. It contained 96 pages, 75 of which were devoted to whist.

2000. Billiards book was *Billiards Without a Master: a full and complete set of rules for the government of the game of billiards and the various games of pool, etc; hints to players, advice to amateurs, keepers of saloons, etc.,* by Michael Phelan, containing 127 pages and 50 copperplate diagrams. It was published in 1850 in New York City by D.D. Winant.

2001. Horse race trotting register was John Hankins Wallace's *American Trotting Register, containing all that is known of the pedigrees of trotting horses, their ancestors and descendants, with a full record of all published performances in which a mile was trotted or paced in 2.40 or less, from the earliest dates till the close of 1868,* a 504-page book published in 1871 in New York City.

2002. Football book was *American Football,* by Walter Chauncey Camp, published in 1891 by Harper and Brothers, New York City. It contained 175 pages with 31 portraits.

2003. Golf book was *Golf in America,* a practical manual by James Parrish Lee, published on May 25, 1895, by Dodd, Mead and Company, New York City. It consisted of 194 pages and a frontispiece.

2004. Crossword puzzle book was the *Crossword Puzzle Book,* published by Simon and Schuster, New York City, on April 18, 1924. It was edited by Prosper Buranelli, F. Gregory Hatswick, and Margaret Petherbridge. It was an anthology of 50 puzzles from the *New York World.*

2005. Book on the game of bridge was *Laws of Contract Bridge 1927,* which was adopted and issued by the Whist Club, New York City. It was published by John C. Winston Company, New York City, and contained 57 pages. The rules became effective on September 15, 1927. The game was invented in 1925 by Harold Stirling Vanderbilt.

2006. Book on the game of bridge by a championship team was *The Four Aces System of Contract Bridge*, 302 pages, published in 1935 by Random House, New York City. It contained an introduction by the game's founder, Harold Stirling Vanderbilt, and new international contract bridge laws and scoring chart. The Four Aces team, formed in August 1933, consisted of Oswald Jacoby, David Burnstine, Howard Schenken, and Michael T. Gottlieb, and had won 11 of 13 major championship events.

BOOKS—VARIOUS

2007. Masonic book was printed and published by Benjamin Franklin in Philadelphia in 1734. It was advertised from May 9 to May 30, 1734, in the *Pennsylvania Gazette*. It was an American edition of Anderson's *Constitutions of the Freemasons; containing the History, Charges, Regulations, etc., of that most Ancient and Right Worshipful Fraternity*.

2008. Philosophy book printed in America was *Elementa Philosophica: Containing Chiefly, Noetica, or Things Relating to the Mind or Understanding: and Ethica, or Things Relating to the Moral Behaviour*, by Samuel Johnson. It contained 103 pages and was printed in 1752 in Philadelphia, PA, by Benjamin Franklin and D. Hall.

2009. Architecture book printed in America was Abraham Swan's *British Architect; or the Builders Treasury of Staircases*, published in 1775 by Robert Bell in Philadelphia, PA, for J. Norman. It was a reprint of the edition published in London in 1745.

2010. Military field strategy manual was Roger Stevenson's *Military Instructions for Officers detached in the field, containing a scheme for forming a corps of a partisan, illustrated with plans of the manoeuvres necessary in carrying on the Petite Guerre*. The 232-page book was printed in 1775 by Robert Aitken, Philadelphia, PA.

2011. Military drill manual was Baron von Steuben's *Regulations for the Order and Discipline of the Troops of the United States*, 154 pages, printed in 1779 in Philadelphia, PA, by Melchior Styner and Charles Cist.

2012. Book advocating voting rights for women was a reprint of *A Vindication of the Rights of Women, with Strictures on Political and Moral Subjects*, by Mary Wollstonecraft Godwin, 276 pages, printed in 1792 in Philadelphia, PA, by William Gibbons. Another edition, of 340 pages, was published in Boston, MA, by Peter Edes with a slight subtitle variation. The book was originally published in England in 1790.

2013. Maternity book was *Letters to Married Women on Nursing and the Management of Children*, by Dr. Hugh Smith, published in 1792 in Philadelphia, PA, by Mathew Carey. It contained 167 pages on subjects such as birthmarks, miscarriages, mother's milk, nursing, and weaning. It was printed from the sixth London edition.

2014. Coast survey book was Captain Lawrence Furlong's *The American Coast Pilot, containing the courses and distance from Boston to all the principal harbours, capes and headlands included between Passamaquady and the Capes of Virginia with directions for sailing into, and out of, all the principal ports and harbours, with the sounding on the coast*, 121 pages, printed in March 1796 in Newburyport, MA, by Edward March Blunt and Angier March.

2015. Architecture book distinctly American was *The Country Builders' Assistant; containing a collection of new designs of carpentry and architecture*, by Asher Benjamin. It contained 30 plates and was printed in 1797 by Thomas Dickman, Greenfield, MA.

2016. Guide to parliamentary rules of order was Thomas Jefferson's *A Manual of Parliamentary Practice, for the Use of the Senate of the United States*, a 199-page book, printed in 1801 by Samuel Harrison Smith in Washington, DC.

2017. Cryptography book was *A Dictionary to enable any two persons to maintain a correspondence with a secrecy, which is impossible for any other person to discover*, a 48-page book published anonymously in 1805 in Hartford, CT.

2018. Magic lantern book was *The Expositor, or Many Mysteries Unravelled; delineated in a series of letters between a friend and his correspondent, comprising the learned pig, invisible lady and acoustic temple, philosophical swan penetrating spy glasses, optical and magnetic, and various other curiosities on similar princi-*

BOOKS—VARIOUS—*continued*

ples; also a few of the most wonderful feats as performed by the art of legerdemain, with some reflections on ventriloquism, by William Frederick Pinchbeck. It was 100 pages long and was printed in Boston, MA, in 1805.

2019. Book on child-rearing was *The Maternal Physician; A Treatise on the Nurture and Management of Infants, from the Birth until Two Years Old, Being the Result of Sixteen Years' Experience in the Nursery,* published in Philadelphia, PA, in 1810 by "An American Matron."

2020. Railroad treatise was John Stevens's *Documents Tending to Prove the Superior Advantages of Rail-ways and Steam-Carriages Over Canal Navigation,* printed in 1812 by T. and J. Swords, 160 Pearl Street, New York City. Stevens proposed to build a railroad from Albany to Buffalo, NY, laying the track on wooden stringers capped with wrought-iron plate.

2021. Fireworks book was *A System of Pyrotechny, comprehending the theory and practice with the application of chemistry, designed for exhibition and for war, adapted to the military and naval officer, the man of science and the artificer.* The book contained 612 pages, including a 44-page introduction. It was written by James Cutbush, acting professor of chemistry and mineralogy at the U.S. Military Academy, and was published by Clara F. Cutbush in Philadelphia, PA, in 1825.

2022. Transportation report was William Strickland's *Reports on Canals, Railways, Roads and Other Subjects made to the Pennsylvania Society for the Promotion of Internal Improvement,* a 51-page pamphlet containing 72 engraved plates, published in 1826 by H.C. Carey and I. Lea, Philadelphia, PA.

2023. Antislavery book was published in Boston, MA, in 1833 by Allen and Ticknor. It was written by Lydia Maria Francis Child and entitled *An Appeal in Favor of That Class of Americans Called Africans.*

2024. Tourist guide for train travelers was *The Traveller's Guide Through the State of New York, Canada, etc., embracing a general description of the city of New York; the Hudson River Guide, and the fashionable tour to the springs and Niagara Falls: with steam-boat, rail-road, and stage routes, accompanied by correct maps.* It was 72 pages long and was published in 1836 by J. Disturnell, New York City. It contained a folded map of New York

State and another of the Hudson River vicinity, lists of canal routes, stage routes, and railroad routes, lists of railroads, cemeteries, monuments, colleges, museums, hotels, amusements, and other notable places, and a general description of New York City.

2025. Tourist guide with train schedules showing the arrival and departure times of trains was Doggett's *United States Railroad and Ocean Steam Navigation Guide, Illustrated with a map of the United States, showing the working lines of Railroad,* published in September 1847 by John Doggett, Jr., of New York City. It contained 132 pages and a folding map and sold for 12.5 cents.

2026. Postage stamp catalog was compiled by A.C. Kline, 824 Walnut Street, Philadelphia, PA, in 1862. It listed 1,500 varieties of stamps. Its title was *The Stamp Collector's Manual, Being a complete guide to the collectors of American and Foreign postage and despatch stamps.*

2027. Patent list was the *Official Gazette of the U.S. Patent Office,* issued weekly, which gave the numbers, titles, and claims of the patents issued during the week immediately preceding, together with the names and addresses of the patentees. The first issue was dated January 3, 1872.

2028. Comic books containing colored cartoons that had previously been published in newspapers were published in 1904 by Cupples and Leon, New York City. The books were 10 inches high and 15 inches long, contained 40 pages, and retailed for 75 cents. The titles of some of the books were *Alphonse and Gaston and Their Friend Leon* and *Happy Hooligan* by Frederick Burr Opper, *The Naughty Adventures of Vicious Mr. Jack* by James Swinnerton, and *The Katzenjammer Kids* by Rudolph Dirks. The first comic book containing original material was *More Fun,* published in 1935 by National Periodical Publications, which later became Detective Comics (DC). In June 1938, DC began issuing *Superman,* the first comic book starring a superhero. Superman was the brainchild of writer Jerry Siegel and artist Joe Shuster, both of whom were high school students in Cleveland, OH.

2029. Talking book for blind listeners was a collection of eight phonograph records of patriotic documents. It was issued in July 1934 by the American Foundation for the Blind, New York City, and was intended to be played on a specially designed phonograph. The Declaration of Independence and the Constitution of the United States were recorded on four double-faced records. The other four contained George Washington's Farewell Address to the Continental Army and his letter to the Congress of the United States.

2030. Comic book versions of literary works were created by Albert Kanter, founder of the Gilberton Company. In 1940, Kanter began publishing *Classic Comics,* a line of great books in comic-book format that proved popular with GIs. The name was changed to *Classics Illustrated* in 1947. Among the works adapted were *Moby Dick, Frankenstein,* and *Romeo and Juliet.*

BOOKS—WRITERS

2031. Writer to work professionally who was a woman was Hannah Adams, born in Medfield, MA, in 1755. Her income from this source was very limited. Her first book, *Alphabetical Compendium of the Various Sects which Have Appeared from the Beginning of the Christian Era to the Present Day,* appeared in 1784.

2032. Writer whose livelihood was obtained exclusively by writing was Charles Brockden Brown of New York and Philadelphia. His first book was *Alcuin, a Dialogue,* one of the earliest known works by an American to champion the rights of women. It was published anonymously and was first announced on April 28, 1798, by T. and J. Swords, New York City. His first novel was *Wieland, or the Transformation,* the first American example of the Gothic horror novel, which was published in New York City in 1798.

2033. Humor writer who was a woman was Frances Miriam Berry Whitcher, who contributed humorous pieces to Joseph Clay Neal's *Saturday Gazette* in 1846 under the nom de plume "Frank." Her "Widow Bedott" papers, republished in book form in 1855, sold over 100,000 copies.

2034. Poet laureate of the United States was Robert Penn Warren, who was named the country's first official poet laureate on February 26, 1986, in Washington, DC, by the Librarian of Congress, Daniel J. Boorstin. Warren was born in Guthrie, KY, in 1905 and won three Pulitzer Prizes, two for volumes of poetry and one for his 1946 novel *All the King's Men.* The first woman to hold the post was Mona Van Duyn, designated in 1992, the sixth person to receive that honor. The first African-American poet laureate, named in 1993, was Rita Dove, who in 1985 had become the second African-American woman to win a Pulitzer Prize for poetry.

BUILDINGS—BUILDING MATERIALS

2035. Slate used for roofing material was obtained from Delta, PA, and Cardiff, MD, in 1734 by William and James Reese.

2036. Brick roofing tile was manufactured in 1735 by Hüster, a German tile maker in Montgomery County, PA.

2037. Rivet production on a commercial scale was attempted by Josiah Gilbert Pierson, who invented a "coldheader machine" on which he obtained a patent on March 23, 1794. His heading machine was a massive affair, with a heavy framework anchored to the floor and a large flywheel that operated on the toggle principle. His factory was located in New York City, on the later site of the New York Produce Exchange.

2038. Ball bearing commercial installation was made on October 30, 1794, on the weathervane topping the steeple of the Evangelical Lutheran Church of the Holy Trinity, Lancaster, PA. The bearings were of the antifriction roller type, with a pin through them.

2039. Natural cement rock was discovered in 1818 by Canvass White near Fayetteville, Onondaga County, NY. He obtained a patent on a cement manufacturing process, which he sold to New York State for $10,000.

2040. Angle iron was rolled in 1819 by Samuel Leonard at the Union Rolling Mill, on the Monongahela River at Pittsburgh, PA. The mill had four puddling furnaces.

2041. Concrete was patented as a building material by canal engineer Canvass White in 1820. His patent covered the use of cement made from "hydraulic lime" for underwater structures. Concrete mined in New York State's Madison, Cayuga, and Onondaga counties was first used in the construction of the Erie Canal that same year.

2042. Wall and floor tiles were manufactured in 1845 by Abraham Miller, 7th and Zane streets, Philadelphia, PA. In 1810, he had succeeded Andrew Miller, who had conducted a pottery in Sugar Alley since 1791.

2043. Cork manufacturer is said to have been William King, whose factory in Brooklyn, NY (now part of New York City), produced cork products from 1850 to 1860.

2044. Cement was introduced into the United States from England about 1870. Because of its weight it was brought over as ballast. American portland cement was invented by David Oliver Saylor of Allentown, PA, who perfected a process for making hydraulic cement from argillo-

BUILDINGS—BUILDING MATERIALS—
continued

magnesium and argillo calcareous limestone and received a patent on September 26, 1871. European cement was regarded as superior and it was not until 1897 that the use of American cement exceeded the use of cement imported from Europe.

2045. Corkboard patent to be issued on pure corkboard was granted to John T. Smith of Brooklyn, NY (now part of New York City), on July 14, 1891. Manufacture was begun in Brooklyn in 1894 by Stone and Duryea. Cork covering was produced first, followed by the manufacture of pure corkboard.

2046. Cork for covering steam pipes was manufactured in the United States in 1894 by Stone and Duryea of Brooklyn, NY (now part of New York City). The company moved to Bridgeport, CT, in 1896 and the following year produced cork covering for cold pipelines. It was succeeded by the Nonpareil Cork Manufacturing Company, which in turn was purchased by the Armstrong Cork Company in 1904.

2047. Rock wool insulation factory was the Crystal Chemical Works, Alexandria, IN, opened on June 1, 1897, by Charles Corydon Hall, who melted limestone rock in a specially designed water-jacketed cupola. The rock was blown by steam pressure into fine wool-like threads for use as insulating material. The Johns Manville Corporation acquired the works in 1929.

2048. Impregnated corkboard was made in 1900 by the Armstrong Cork Company of Pittsburgh, PA. It was produced in a specially constructed plant in Beaver Falls, PA. The business grew rapidly until the "composition" corkboard gave way entirely to pure corkboard insulation.

2049. Plywood commercially produced was marketed by the Portland Manufacturing Company in 1905 in St. Johns (now Portland), OR. They sold plywood panels of Oregon pine, and later of Columbian pine and Douglas fir. Plywood contains an odd number of veneer sheets bonded together, with the grain of each at right angles to the sheets above and below. Laminated sheets, all having the grain in the same direction, had been made earlier.

2050. Sound-absorbing material made of rigid insulating board was invented by Carl Gebhard Muench of St. Paul, MN, who obtained a patent on September 14, 1915, on a "thermo non-conductor" known as Insulite. The invention consisted of a rigid thermal insulation with groundwood screenings as a fiber source.

The first board machine built to make a fibrous board in one thick continuous layer was installed in International Falls, MN, where production was started on May 15, 1914. Sugarcane bagasse was also found to be a satisfactory fiber for making insulation board. It was first used on August 10, 1921, in Marrero, LA, by the Celotex Corporation of Chicago, IL.

2051. Cornstone was made at the Iowa State College, Ames, IA, in 1922. Also called Maizolith, it was made principally from corncobs and cornstalks and was harder than the hardest wood and several times stronger than the strongest wood. It ranged in color from golden tan to ebony. It was used as a structural material when great strength rather than weight was desired.

2052. Building in which wrought-iron window sashes were installed was the new plant of the Pittsburgh Plate Glass Company in Crystal City, MO, where the Mesker Brothers Iron Company of St. Louis placed 70,000 square feet of sash in 1929.

BUILDINGS—BUILDING MATERIALS— BRICK

2053. Brick kiln in America was established in Salem, MA, in 1629.

2054. Fire brick was made by the Salamander Works of Woodbridge, NJ, in 1825. Although definite records are not obtainable, it is believed an attempt was made to manufacture fire bricks in 1812.

2055. Fire brick to withstand high heat was manufactured in 1841 by the Mount Savage Fire Brick Works of Mount Savage, MD, later the Union Mining Company of Allegany County, MD.

2056. Terra cotta was manufactured by James Renwick in 1853 in New York City. He conceived the idea of introducing terra cotta as a building material and a substitute for cut stone work.

2057. Brick machine for the production of soft mud bricks was designed and built by Henry Martin in 1857 and installed in Hartford, CT. The clay was pushed from the press box through a die or jack mold into sanded wooden molds by a process similar to the method of pressing the clay by hand into wood or steel molds.

2058. Terra cotta factory to be successful was established by J.N. Glover in Louisville, KY, in 1867. After a series of successive changes of locale and management, it gradually developed into the Northwestern Terra Cotta Company, Chicago, IL.

2059. Insulating brick was supplied to the trade by the Armstrong Cork Company of Lancaster, PA, in June 1913 under the trade name Nonpareil Insulating Brick. This brick was used in high-temperature equipment such as industrial furnaces, ovens, oil stills, blast furnaces, stoves, and similar apparatus. Diatomaceous earth was pulverized and mixed with finely ground cork, and a small quantity of clay was added for a binder. It was molded into brick form and then fired. The cork was consumed, leaving the finished brick terra-cotta in color and extremely cellular in structure. Because of the many small voids left when the particles of cork were burned out, and because of a large amount of noncirculating air, the ability of the brick to hold heat was exceptionally high.

2060. Lightweight brick was developed in 1927 by Charles Frederick Burgess of the C.F. Burgess Laboratories, Madison, WI. It was porous, one-fifth the weight of ordinary brick, and yet resistant to the entrance of water. It floated in water and had adequate compressive strength for use in all types of buildings for load-bearing walls.

BUILDINGS—COMMERCIAL

2061. Arcade was the Philadelphia Arcade, which extended from Chestnut Street through to Carpenter Street between Sixth and Seventh streets, Philadelphia, PA. It was erected by the Arcade Company, of which John Haviland was architect. The cornerstone was laid on May 3, 1826, and the building finished in September 1827. The cost of construction was $112,000; $42,500 was paid for the land.

2062. Building designed to be used by artists was the Tenth Street Studio Building in New York City, owned by businessman James Boorman Johnston. Johnston purchased a plot of land on 10th Street between Fifth and Sixth Avenues in Greenwich Village and hired architect Richard Morris Hunt to design a building to house artists' studios and galleries. Individual studios were arranged around a large central exhibition hall where new paintings could be shown to other tenants and collectors. The building opened in 1858. Among the artists who rented space there were Frederick Edwin Church, Sanford Gifford, Albert Bierstadt, Winslow Homer, and William Merritt Chase.

2063. Boardwalk was dedicated on June 26, 1870, at Atlantic City, NJ. To finance it, $5,000 was obtained by the sale, at a 10 percent discount, of scrip which could be used to pay taxes. The boardwalk was eight feet wide and a mile long. It was built in eight-foot col-lapsible sections, which for 18 years were removed in September and stored for the winter. The idea for the boardwalk was conceived by a hotel man, Jacob Keim of the Chester County House, and Alexander Boardman, a railroad conductor on the Camden and Atlantic Railroad.

2064. Air rights lease was made by the New York Central Railroad Company in February 1910 to the Grand Central Palace, New York City, for $30,000 a year. The Palace was permitted to build its structure over the New York Central Railroad tracks. The idea of selling air rights over real estate was originated by Ira A. Place.

2065. Air-conditioned office building was the Milam Building, San Antonio, TX, which opened on January 1, 1928. The building was 21 stories high, contained nearly 3 million cubic feet of space, and had 247,779 square feet of gross floor area. It was the first building in the world in which the air conditioning was a part of the original construction.

2066. Circular office building was the Capitol Tower, Hollywood and Vine streets, Los Angeles, CA, dedicated April 6, 1956. It was 150 feet high, with 13 stories, and had a diameter of 92 feet. Above the roof was a 90-foot spire from which a beacon light flashed the word *Hollywood* in Morse code. Welton Becket was the architect.

2067. Commercial building with solar heating was the Solar Building, a single-story building in Albuquerque, NM. The heating system, designed by Frank Hillman Bridgers and Donald Paxton, was completed on August 1, 1957. One wall of the building, which was sheathed in glass tilted to face the sun, collected heat from the sun's rays. The heat warmed panels containing water, which flowed through a conventional heating system.

BUILDINGS—CONSTRUCTION

2068. Brick building was erected in 1633 in the fort of New Amsterdam (the future New York City) as a residence for Wouter Van Twiller, the fifth Dutch governor. Several other brick structures were erected within the fort. The bricks were imported from Holland.

2069. Log cabins were constructed by the Swedish immigrants who built New Sweden, NJ (near the present site of Trenton), in 1638. Each cabin contained one room, about 12 feet by 14 feet, that housed a family and, in cold weather, its livestock.

BUILDINGS—CONSTRUCTION—*continued*

2070. Marble building of importance was the Bank of the United States, Philadelphia, PA, incorporated February 25, 1791. The building was designed by Samuel Blodget, although he was not an architect, and built in 1791.

2071. Building in all-Gothic architecture was Trinity Episcopal Church, New Haven, CT, designed by Ithiel Town of New Haven in 1814. It had seamfaced traprock with brownstone trim.

2072. Building of fireproof construction was the Fireproof Building, which was designed and built by Robert Mills in 1822–23 on Meeting Street, between Queen and Broad streets, Charleston, SC. It was built for the preservation of the county records and was a stone and iron structure. Even the window sashes were made of iron.

2073. Split-level buildings were the Elfreth houses, three brownstone buildings on South Third Street, built in 1830 in Philadelphia, PA. The rooms in the rear were higher than those in the front.

2074. Building heated by steam was the Eastern Hotel in Boston, MA, erected in 1845. Small wrought-iron pipes conveyed the steam and the heat was diffused by coils of pipe. The firm of Walworth and Nason (later known as the Walworth Company), founded by James Jones Walworth and Joseph Nason, established a plant in Boston in 1842 for the purpose of "warming and ventilating buildings by means of steam and hot water apparatus." At first they used hot water for the system, converting to steam in 1844.

2075. Monolithic concrete building was the Milton House, Milton, WI, a two-story hotel built in 1845 by Joseph Goodrich on the corduroy road between Chicago, IL, and Madison, WI. It replaced a log house built in 1837 and a frame building built in 1839. The walls were 18 inches thick. A hexagonal tower three stories high served as a lookout for the approach of Native Americans.

2076. Building constructed wholly of cast iron was a factory five stories high that was built by James Bogardus at the corner of Centre and Duane streets in New York City in May 1848.

2077. Building in which wrought-iron beams were used was erected for Harper and Brothers in New York City in 1854. Wrought-iron beams were rolled for the first time in the United States in 1854 at the Trenton Iron Works, Trenton, NJ, of which Peter Cooper was the principal owner. These beams were intended for the Cooper Union building in New York City, but they were not ready in time, as it took two years to prepare them. They were seven inches deep, weighed 81 pounds per yard, and were of the type known as deck beams. Previously, cast-iron beams had been used in construction work.

2078. Heating system to heat buildings from a central station was installed in Lockport, NY, in 1877 by Birdsall Holly. He ran a steam line through a trench for a distance of 100 feet from his house to an adjoining property and found that the heat was not lost by being carried through pipes. He subsequently formed the Holly Steam Combination Company, whose first plant was located at Elm and South streets, Lockport. The company was later operated by the New York State Electric and Gas Corporation, Lockport division.

2079. Building shaped like an elephant was James V. Lafferty's structure the Elephant, which was built in the form of an elephant with a covering of tin painted to resemble elephant hide. It was built in 1882 in Cedar Grove in Atlantic City, NJ, as an attraction to promote his real estate surrounding it. The hind legs contained a spiral staircase that led into a large room handsomely fitted with carved wood, where photographs and models of the property for sale were displayed. The front legs contained staircases leading to the eyes, through which the ocean was visible. The howdah, which was 65 feet above the sand, served as an observation tower. The structure cost $25,000 to build.

2080. Steel-frame building was the Tacoma Building in Chicago, IL, completed in 1887. It was designed by Holabird and Roche and built by George Allon Fuller. This building embodied the principles upon which all modern skyscrapers are designed and erected.

2081. Revolving door was invented by Theophilus Van Kannel of Philadelphia, PA, who obtained a patent on August 7, 1888, on a "storm door structure." The first building to install a revolving door was an office building in Philadelphia.

2082. Steel-frame residence was the Copper House, built in 1890 at Shore Road and 88th Street in the Bay Ridge section of Brooklyn, NY (now part of New York City). The house was constructed with copper sheets riveted to the exterior. It was built by Niels Poulson, who resided in it from 1890 until his death in 1911.

2083. Building with caisson foundations was the Manhattan Life Insurance Company building, New York City, opened on May 1, 1894. The bridge caissons were sunk by pneumatic process. They were made of steel in varying size, from 9.6 inches in diameter to 25 by 21 feet square fitted with concrete. The 16-story building had a 67-foot frontage and seven elevators, five hydraulic and two electric. The architects were Francis Henry Kimball and George Kramer Thompson.

2084. Building with an all-marble dome was the Rhode Island State House in Providence, RI, occupied by the General Assembly and other state officers beginning on January 1, 1901. Ground was broken on September 16, 1895, and the cornerstone was laid on October 15, 1896. The architects were McKim, Mead and White, and the builders were Norcross Brothers, Worcester, MA. The dome was made of 327,000 cubic feet of white Georgia marble, and was 94 feet high. The diameter of the dome below the top of the gallery was 70 feet; the diameter above the top of the gallery, 56 feet; and the diameter of the dome proper, 50 feet.

2085. Building with a large-scale clear-span dome was built in 1901 in West Baden (formerly Mile Lick), IN, by Colonel Lee Sinclair, a businessman and entrepreneur. Sinclair, who operated a resort near the town's sulfur springs, contracted with architect Harrison Albright and engineer Oliver J. Westcott to build the 708-room West Baden Springs Hotel complex, which featured a clear-span dome 130 feet high and 200 feet in diameter. The dome had no pillars, but was supported at the rim by 24 steel ribs weighing 8.5 tons each. The ribs were attached to the supporting walls by pivots that moved on tracks, thus allowing for thermal expansion and contraction of the dome. The hotel opened on September 1, 1902. It was the largest freestanding domed structure in the world until the opening of the Houston Astrodome in 1965.

2086. Building of pressed structural steel was a two-story, 14-room building designed and built in June 1907 by the Taft-Howell Company of Cornwall Landing, NY, for the Tuxedo Park Association, Tuxedo Park, NY. The pressed steel, known by its trade name, Metal Lumber, was developed by Harry Merrill Naugle, chief engineer of the Berger Manufacturing Company, Canton, OH. The building had structural members substituting in every detail for what normally would be wood studs and joists in balloon frame construction for dwellings.

2087. Automatic swinging doors operated by a photoelectric cell were installed in Wilcox's Pier Restaurant, West Haven, CT. The Stanley Works of New Britain, CT, completed the installation on June 19, 1931. The "magic eye" provided fully automatic control and operation of swinging doors between the main dining room and kitchen.

2088. Building with prefabricated walls of mosaic concrete was built by the Earley Process Corporation, Washington, DC, on the Colesville Pike, north of Washington. It was completed in February 1935. The walls of the house consisted of 32 panels, each 2 inches thick, approximately 9 feet high, and 4 to 10 feet wide, heavily reinforced with electrically welded steel mesh that was fireproof, weatherproof, and waterproof. Color and texture were determined by the color of the crushed quartz and quartz sand used in the concrete.

2089. All-glass windowless structure was the Owens-Illinois Glass Company's packaging laboratory at Toledo, OH, completed on January 15, 1936. Eighty thousand translucent water-clear hollow glass blocks weighing about 150 tons were used in the two-story building, which had 39 rooms and an aggregate floor area of 20,000 square feet. The blocks were manufactured at the company's plant in Muncie, IN, and were a part of the structural strength of the building.

2090. Building built completely inside a factory and ready for occupancy, and the first building floated across a river, was a 41-ton five-room house and garage, 32 by 42 feet, fully equipped with furnace, cooling system, laundry, and plumbing, and partly furnished. It was built by the firm of R.G. Le Tourneau, Peoria, IL. It was towed across the Illinois River on its own bottom from Peoria to the Le Tourneau test farm in East Peoria, IL, on September 17, 1938.

2091. Aluminum-faced building was the Alcoa Building, Pittsburgh, PA, a 30-story, 410-foot skyscraper, completed on August 1, 1953, for the Aluminum Company of America and dedicated on September 15, 1953. The exterior walls were thin stamped aluminum panels, 6 by 12 feet, bolted to angles on the spandrel beams and backed up with four inches of perlite-concrete sprayed on slotted aluminum lath and reinforcing bars. It had 183,000 square feet of exterior wall area. About 3 million pounds of aluminum were used. The elevators were of all-aluminum construction, the electrical wiring and conductors all-aluminum, and the plumbing 65 percent aluminum.

BUILDINGS—CONSTRUCTION—*continued*

2092. Building with its roof supported by cables was the J.S. Dorton Arena, in Raleigh, NC, which was completed and dedicated in 1953. The saddle-shaped roof was suspended on a network of cables that extended crosswise from the 90-foot parabolic arch. The 14-foot-wide arches reached a maximum height of 90 feet. They crossed each other at about 26 feet above ground, then extended into a tunnel below the surface at the east and west ends. The weight of the roof was equalized by tension cables, with 14-foot 2-inch strands connecting each end of the parabola through the stress tunnel. The roof was suspended in a way that eliminated any necessity for structural steel supports and presented no obstructions of view from any seat.

2093. Civic center with an aluminum geodesic dome was the Virginia Beach Convention Center, Virginia Beach, VA, opened on May 15, 1957. It was renamed the Alan B. Shepard Convention Center on July 28, 1961.

2094. Geodesic dome of substantial size was the Climatron, which opened in 1960 at the Missouri Botanical Garden in St. Louis, MO. The dome housed a tropical rainforest display, including streams, waterfalls, and some 1,200 species of plants in a natural setting. A geodesic dome is comprised of a complex network of triangles that form a roughly spherical surface. It is the structure with the highest ratio of enclosed area to external surface area. The geodesic dome was the invention of visionary architect and engineer Richard Buckminster Fuller, who received patents on it in 1947 and 1954. Fuller's original geodesic dome was constructed in Carbondale, IL, where he was a professor at Southern Illinois University.

2095. Building of large size with a retractable roof was the Civic Arena and Exhibit Hall, a stainless steel dome structure in Pittsburgh, PA, that was dedicated on September 17, 1961. The roof, which had no interior support, was divided radially into eight leaves, two of which were stationary and six of which rotated about a pin at the top as they rolled along curved rails laid on a reinforced concrete ring girder. There were approximately 2,950 tons of structural steel in the roof. The dome was constructed to open or close electrically in 2.5 minutes. It was nearly circular, 415 feet in diameter and 136 feet high at center. The arena could accommodate 13,000 spectators at a basketball game and 15,000 at a rally. It occupied a five-acre site and cost $22 million. The first event held there was the Ice Capades, September 18–30, 1961.

2096. Elliptical office building was the $40 million Phoenix Mutual Building of the Phoenix Mutual Life Insurance Company, constructed as a part of the urban renewal project on Constitution Plaza, Hartford, CT. It contained 13 floors, each about 13,000 square feet. It measured 225 feet from end to end and 87 feet across at the widest point. It was designed by Wallace Kirkman Harrison and Max Abramovitz and was completed in November 1963. George A. Fuller was the contractor.

BUILDINGS—CONSTRUCTION—SKYSCRAPERS

2097. Building with a high steeple was Trinity Church, New York City, which was begun on October 17, 1839, and dedicated on May 21, 1846, Ascension Day. The steeple was 284 feet above Broadway. The staircase to the top of the steeple had 308 steps, "with suitable resting places provided," and reached a point 34 feet below the peak. The Trinity spire was the highest point until 1894, when the Manhattan Life Insurance Company erected a 16-story building and tower that thrust its pinnacle 60 feet higher.

2098. Skyscraper was a 10-story steel-skeleton building erected by the Home Insurance Company of New York at La Salle and Adams streets, Chicago, IL. Designed by Major William Le Baron Jenney, it was started on May 1, 1884, and completed in the fall of 1885. It was constructed of marble and flanked by four columns of polished granite supporting a marble balcony. Two additional stories were added to it later. A steel frame supported the entire weight of the walls, instead of the walls themselves carrying the weight of the building.

2099. Skyscraper higher than 750 feet in height was the Woolworth Building in New York City. It measured 791.5 feet high, 947 feet above sea level at high tide. At the time, it was the tallest structure in the world, with the exception of the Eiffel Tower in Paris. It was formally opened on April 24, 1913, at 7:30 P.M., when President Woodrow Wilson at the White House, Washington, DC, pressed a telegraph key that rang a bell in the engine room and dining hall and lit the electric lights on the 55 floors. The architect was Cass Gilbert.

2100. Skyscraper higher than 1,250 feet was the Empire State Building, New York City, 102 stories high. It was dedicated on May 1, 1931, by President Herbert Clark Hoover, who pressed a button from the White House in Washington, DC, that switched on the lights. It was 1,250 feet high and cost about $52 million.

The builder was Colonel William Aiken Starrett; the architect, William Frederick Lamb; the engineer, Homer Gage Balcom. In 1950, a 222-foot television sending-tower was constructed on the roof.

2101. Skyscraper of bronze and glass was the Seagram Building, a 519-foot structure, 38 stories high, at 375 Park Avenue, New York City. It contained 3,650,000 square feet of glass divided into 3,800 windows. The steel framework was put together with high-tensile steel bolts instead of steel rivets. Mies van der Rohe and Philip Johnson were the architects and Kahn and Jacobs the associated architects, with the George A. Fuller Company the general contractor. The highest point of steel construction was reached on December 17, 1956. The building was completed in November 1957.

2102. Skyscraper higher than 1,400 feet in height was the 110-story Sears Building of Sears Roebuck and Company, measuring 1,454 feet high, located on Jackson Boulevard between Adams and Franklin streets in Chicago, IL, which was topped out on May 4, 1973, and completed in 1974.

BUILDINGS—ELEVATORS AND ESCALATORS

2103. Elevator was a platform elevator made by Henry Waterman in 1850 in his shop on Duane Street, New York City. The elevator was installed in a building owned by Hecker and Brother, millers, at 203 Cherry Street, New York City, where it was used it to hoist barrels upstairs.

2104. Elevator with safety devices to prevent the car from falling in case the ropes should break was made by Elisha Graves Otis in 1853 and exhibited by him the same year at the Crystal Palace Exposition in New York City. The first such elevator was delivered on September 20, 1853, to Benjamin Newhouse, 275 Hudson Street, New York City.

2105. Elevator with a completely enclosed car for conveying passengers to the upper floor of a building was installed in 1857 by Elisha Graves Otis in the store of E.V. Haughwout, at the corner of Broadway and Broome Streets, New York City.

2106. Escalator patent was obtained by Nathan Ames of Saugus, MA, on August 9, 1859, on an improvement in revolving stairs. Steps or stairs were arranged upon an inclined endless belt or chain. Another escalator design was patented by Jesse W. Reno in March 1892. His Reno Inclined Elevator, an inclined conveyor belt with rubber cleats, was first installed at the Old Iron Pier on Coney Island, NY (now part of New York City), in 1896.

2107. Elevator in a hotel was installed in the six-story Fifth Avenue Hotel, New York City, which opened on August 23, 1859. The elevator operated on the principle of an Archimedean screw. It was viewed and inspected by Albert Edward, Prince of Wales, on October 11, 1860.

2108. Elevator in an office building was installed in 1868 in the original Equitable Life Assurance Society building, located on lower Broadway, New York City.

2109. Electric elevator successfully operated was installed in 1889 by Otis Brothers and Company in the Demarest Building, Fifth Avenue and 33rd Street, New York City.

2110. Escalator of the modern type was manufactured by the Otis Elevator Company of New York City in 1900 and placed on exhibit at the Paris Exposition the same year. It was installed in 1901 in the Eighth Street store of Gimbel Brothers, Philadelphia, PA. The trade name Escalator was registered on May 29, 1900.

2111. Elevator with two cars operated separately on different levels in the same shaftway was made by the Westinghouse Electric and Manufacturing Company and placed in regular service in its main office building in East Pittsburgh, PA, in 1931. The upper elevator was an express. When it was on the main floor, the local was in the basement. Precautions were taken to prevent a collision in the shaft. The service was announced on January 13, 1931.

2112. Double-deck elevator was installed in January 1932 by the Otis Elevator Company in the Sixty Wall Tower building, New York City. It served 30 floors and traveled at a speed of 1,000 feet per minute. There were eight double-decked cars that stopped at two floors at the same time. The building was formally opened on May 13, 1932.

BUILDINGS—ELEVATORS AND ESCA-
LATORS—*continued*

2113. Elevator with electronic signal controls
was installed by the Otis Elevator Company in
April 1948 at the Universal Pictures Building,
New York City, after several years of experiment and development. Eight elevators, four local and four express, served the building's 22
stories. When a passenger touched a landing
button, the call was registered by an electronic
tube, which lit up to show that it had been activated. The stopping of the cars in response to
these calls, the canceling of the calls as they
were answered, and the operation of the cars
were all controlled by means of electronic circuits.

BUILDINGS—GOVERNMENT

2114. Statehouse was a building on Duke of
Gloucester Street, Williamsburg, VA, in which
the General Assembly met. The building was
erected in 1698 by Governor Francis Nicholson, who was the first person to apply the term
"capitol" to a government building.

**2115. Building erected in the United States
for public use** under the authority of the federal government was a structure for the U.S.
Mint. This was a plain brick edifice on the east
side of Seventh Street, near Arch, in Philadelphia, PA. The mint was established by the act
of April 2, 1792, an "act establishing a mint
and regulating the coins of the United States."
The cornerstone was laid by David Rittenhouse,
director of the Mint, on July 31, 1792.

**2116. Building erected in Washington, DC,
by the federal government** was the White
House, originally known as the Executive Mansion. It was modeled after the palace of the
Duke of Leinster in Ireland and was designed
by James Hoban. The cornerstone was laid on
October 13, 1792. The Executive Mansion was
first occupied by President John Adams in
1800, and the first New Year's reception there
was held on January 1, 1801. The mansion was
burned by the British in 1814, during the War
of 1812, and only the four walls were left
standing. It was restored in 1818. In order to
obliterate the marks of fire, the stones were
painted white. Since that time, the Executive
Mansion has been known as the White House.
When Adams first took occupancy, there was
only a path through an elder swamp leading
from the President's house to the Capitol.

2117. Building known as a Quonset hut was
built for the Navy in September 1941 at Quonset Point air station, Greenwich, RI, by the
Great Lakes Steel Corporation, Stran-Steel Division, Detroit, MI. The structures were built
around a framework of Stran-Steel members, a
light steel building material distinguished by a
patented groove into which nails could be driv-
en. They were officially designated by the
Navy as Navy Arch-Rib Huts.

**2118. Building containing 6.5 million square
feet of usable space** was the Pentagon, Arlington, VA, built of reinforced concrete faced with
Indiana limestone, and completed on January
15, 1943, at a cost of about $83 million. It is
five stories high; each facade is 921 feet long;
and each floor has a different color scheme. It
has five rings of buildings intersected by 10
corridors. The length of the corridors is 17.5
miles. It covers 34 acres of land, with a five-
acre pentagonal court in the center and 204
acres of lawns and terraces. It accommodates
the headquarters of the Department of Defense.
It was designed by George Edwin Bergstrom of
Los Angeles, CA.

**2119. Federal government building built to
withstand a nuclear attack** was the laboratory
for the Armed Forces Institute of Pathology,
Walter Reed Army Medical Center, Washington, DC, which was occupied on March 13,
1955, and dedicated by President Dwight David
Eisenhower on May 23. The eight-story reinforced concrete bomb-resistant building contained eight floors, five above ground and three
underground. It had a gross area of approximately 215,000 square feet and a net usable
area of 130,000 square feet. It was constructed
by the Cramer-Vollmerhousen Company of
Washington, DC.

**2120. Air-conditioned public elementary
school** was the Belaire School, San Angelo,
TX, which was opened in October 1955. The
school, containing eight classrooms, was completely air-conditioned.

2121. Circular school building was St. Patrick
Central High School, Kankakee, IL, opened on
February 6, 1956. It was a two-story building,
200 feet in diameter, that housed classrooms
and a gymnasium unit accommodating 2,000
spectators. It was connected to a small rectangular wing containing the administrative offices
and library. The total cost of the school was
$736,592. Belli and Belli of Chicago, IL, were
the architects.

2122. Underground school was the Abo Elementary School, Artesia, NM, built underground in 1976 for safety from radiation and the effects of fallout. The roof was at ground level. The school was heated and air-conditioned during school hours. It had 16 teaching stations, a large library media center, and a multipurpose room with tables and seats that folded up into the wall. There were no distractions or outside noises, the lighting was near perfect, and the acoustics were excellent.

BUILDINGS—RESIDENTIAL

2123. Summer home was the manor house erected in 1769 on the 4,000-acre tract of John Wentworth, last royal colonial governor of New Hampshire (1767–75). It was located on the shore of Lake Wentworth, Wolfeboro, NH.

2124. Tenement house was built in New York City in 1833 on Water Street, on a site later within the limits of Corlears Park. It was four stories high, with arrangements for one family on each floor. This was the beginning of the system of grouping many homes under one roof. A tenement is any house, or part of a house, occupied by three or more families living independently of each other and doing cooking on the premises. The term generally refers to buildings where the rents are low and the living conditions are substandard.

2125. Apartment house with a modern layout was erected in New York City in 1869. It was known as the Stuyvesant Apartments and was located at 142 East 18th Street. Every floor contained four apartment suites, each with a kitchen, dining room, parlor, and bedrooms, plus a servant's room and a dumbwaiter. The fifth and top floor was arranged for artists' studios. The annual rental for the apartments varied from $1,200 to $1,800 each; $200 was charged for the studios. The architect was Richard Morris Hunt; the owner, Rutherford Stuyvesant.

2126. Apartment house cooperative was the Gramercy, a 10-story apartment house at 34 Gramercy Park, New York City, constructed by James Campbell for the Gramercy Company. Each apartment was adjudged equal to a certain number of shares. Apartments sold for $4,500 to $8,000. The property, which became ready for occupancy in September 1883, was managed by seven trustees. The building had three hydraulic elevators and a restaurant on an upper floor that was leased in October 1883 to Louis Sherry.

2127. Apartment house to occupy a square city block was the Belnord Apartment House, a 12-story building in New York City, which became ready for occupancy on October 15, 1909. It was bounded by 86th Street on the south, 87th Street on the north, Broadway on the west, and Amsterdam Avenue on the east. At the time, it was the largest apartment house in the world. Its area was 64,614 square feet, with an interior court of 22,033 square feet. It contained six separate passenger elevators and 178 suites, each with 7 to 11 rooms and two to four baths. Every room was an outside room. Annual rentals ranged from $2,100 upwards. Philip Hiss and H. Hobart Weekes were the architects.

2128. House completely heated by solar energy was built in Dover, MA, and occupied on December 24, 1948. The house trapped the sun's energy through a unit consisting of a black sheet-metal collector behind two panes of glass. The solar heat was stored in a "heat bin" containing an inexpensive sodium compound. Electric fans blew the stored heat through vents as desired. The experiments were sponsored by Amelia Peabody. The house was designed by Eleanor Raymond and the heating system was developed by Dr. Maria Telkes.

2129. House with solar heating and radiation cooling was built by Raymond Whitcomb Bliss in Tucson, AZ. The system, built at a cost of nearly $4,000 for labor and materials, was placed in operation on January 15, 1955. A large slanting slab of steel and glass converted the sunlight into heat, which was brought into the house by ducts. The same fans, controls, and ducts were used for summer cooling.

2130. House with a built-in nuclear bomb shelter was exhibited on May 24, 1959, at Hi-Tor Woods, Pleasant Hills, PA. It was built by the Obie Construction Company, Pittsburgh, PA, and contained a fully equipped underground integral shelter, with bunks to sleep four persons, sanitary facilities, a food storage area and refrigerator, a transoceanic radio, a first-aid kit, a weather-warning device, a Geiger counter, a fire extinguisher, and other equipment. The main part of the shelter was 22 feet long and 8 feet wide. Another section contained an auxiliary power plant, heating equipment, an air filtering system, and an oxygen tank. The walls were made of concrete blocks 10 inches thick; lead was used for insulation against radiation. The shelter had a concrete escape tunnel.

BUILDINGS—SECURITY

2131. Mortised lock was introduced in 1835 by Philos Blake and Eli Whitney Blake of Blake Brothers, Westville, CT.

2132. Burglar alarm was installed by Edwin Thomas Holmes on February 21, 1858, in Boston, MA. The releasing of a spring by the opening of a door or window made a contact that caused a short circuit of the wires.

2133. Pin-tumbler cylinder lock was invented by Linus Yale, Jr., of Newport, NY, who obtained a patent on January 29, 1861, for his design. The pin-tumbler cylinder lock with a thin, flat key, still the basis for many combination locks today, was the most successful of Yale's many lock inventions, which included the first dial combination bank lock and a double bank lock that required two keys to open.

2134. Burglar alarm system in which the protected premises were connected by wire to a central office system that was immediately apprised of entry was installed by the Holmes Burglar Alarm Company, New York City, in 1872. The alarms served safe cabinets and bank vaults specifically, instead of providing general protection for stores and houses.

2135. Time lock was manufactured by Sargent and Greenleaf, Rochester, NY, and installed in May 1874 on the vault of the First National Bank of Morrison, IL. James Sargent of Rochester, NY, obtained a patent on July 20, 1875, on a "time-lock" and another on September 25, 1877, on "combined time-locks, and bolt-works for safes."

2136. Burglar alarm operated by ultrasonic or radio waves using the Doppler effect was the Alertronic, invented by Samuel Bagno of New York City, who obtained a patent on October 13, 1953, on a movement detection system for intruders or fire. It was manufactured by the Alertronic Corporation of Long Island City, NY (part of Queens, New York City), and was first sold in June 1950. Reflected waves of 19,000 cycles a second, pitched too high for normal human ears, were recorded through a microphone into an alarm, generally stationed at a convenient location. The noise made by an intruder, having a slightly different frequency, would cause the alarm gong to sound.

C

CHILDREN

2137. Orphanage was established in New Amsterdam (now New York City) in June 1654. Fifty orphan children were sent from Holland in order to help populate Manhattan Island. They arrived on the *Pereboom* and the *Gelderse Blom*. A resolution was passed and signed by the colony's administrator, Peter Stuyvesant, on November 9, 1654, "to hire the house of Mr. [Isaac] Allerton and lodge there the children sent over by the Poor-masters." This orphanage also received the orphan children of the early colonists.

2138. Toy distribution center was opened on September 24, 1832, at the New York University community center, New York City. The organizers collected and repaired old toys for distribution to children. The first director was Mrs. Ida Cash.

2139. Vacation fund to send poor children to the country was established in 1847 by the Reverend William Augustus Muhlenberg, rector of the Church of the Holy Communion, New York City.

2140. Baby carriage was made by Charles Burton in 1848 in New York City. Protests were heard because the people wheeling them showed a tendency to hit pedestrians. Burton moved to England, where he opened a factory and obtained orders for his "perambulator" from Queen Victoria, Queen Isabella II of Spain, and the pasha of Egypt. The first baby carriage factory to be successfully operated was started in 1858 in Leominster, MA, under the name of F.W. and F.A. Whitney. This later became the F.A. Whitney Carriage Company. The carriages had two wheels, with a long tongue and a supporting standard in front, and were made of wood. In the first year, 75 carriages were built.

2141. Baby show was held at Springfield, OH, on October 5, 1854, more in a spirit of jest than with serious intent. It met with instant favor and 127 babies were entered. The prize baby was the 10-month-old daughter of William Ronemus of Vienna, OH, who was awarded a silver plate service including a large salver worth $300. Three other prizes were awarded.

2142. Gyroscopes for use as toys to be commercially manufactured were made by the Holbrook Apparatus Company, Hartford, CT, in June 1857. They were made of iron and sold for $2.

2143. Camp for boys that stressed outdoor recreation was Camp Comfort, Welch's Point, Milford, CT, established in August 1861, when Frederick William Gunn, founder of the Gunnery School, took 50 boys on a two-week camping trip. The camp was organized again in August 1863 and in August 1865. In 1867 Gunn started another camp at Point Beautiful on Lake Waramaug, Washington, CT, which operated for a two-week period in August for 12 successive years.

2144. Playground was erected in Boston, MA, in 1886 in the yard of the Children's Mission. Three piles of yellow sand were brought there. The first Boston school appropriation for playgrounds was made in 1899.

2145. Teddy bear was created in 1902 by Morris Michtom, a Russian-born toymaker from Brooklyn, New York City. Michtom took a liking to a political cartoon that showed President Theodore Roosevelt refusing to shoot a bear cub, and he put the cartoon in the window of his store along with a stuffed toy bear with button eyes. He began manufacturing the "Teddy's Bear" in 1903. The same cartoon independently inspired a German toymaker, Margaret Stieff, to market a similar bear beginning in 1904.

2146. Child welfare congress was the International Congress in America for the Welfare of the Child, held on March 10–17, 1908, in Washington, DC, under the auspices of the National Congress of Mothers. President Theodore Roosevelt addressed the congress.

2147. Child delinquency law enacted by a state was passed on April 28, 1909, by Colorado. The law made it illegal to "encourage, cause or contribute to the dependency, neglect or delinquency of a child."

2148. Scouting organization for girls was the Girl Guides, founded on March 12, 1912, in Savannah, GA, by Juliette Gordon Low and adapted from the Girl Guides organization in England. The name was changed to Girl Scouts in 1913. The first Girl Guide was Mrs. Low's niece, Daisy Gordon. Another scouting organization, the Camp Fire Girls, was developed by Mrs. Luther Halsey Gulick at her camp at Lake Sebago, ME, and was made public on March 17, 1912. The group's watchword was "Wohelo," made from the first two letters of each of the words Work, Health, and Love.

2149. Boy Scouts of America uniformed troop was organized at the Central YMCA, Troy, NY, in the fall of 1911. The uniform was designed by Charles M. Connally of Troy and has since become standard equipment. The Boy Scouts of America, an organization for boys from nine years upward, was founded by Daniel Carter Beard, the author of *Boy Pioneers and Sons of Daniel Boone,* who took his inspiration from the Boy Scouts movement that had recently begun in England. It was incorporated in Washington, DC, on February 8, 1910, and was granted a federal charter by an act of Congress of June 15, 1916. The first Eagle Scout was Arthur Rose Eldred of the Oceanside, NY, troop, who received this distinction on August 21, 1912. Others may have qualified at about the same time, but his name is the first recorded.

2150. Youth hostel was opened on December 27, 1934, in Northfield, MA, as the headquarters of the American Youth Hostels organization, incorporated on March 15, 1934, in Hartford, CT. The organization was the 18th member of the International Youth Hostels. Isabel and Monroe Smith were appointed directors of the American group.

2151. Diapers that were disposable were Boaters, invented in 1950 by a New York City mother, Marion Donovan. They consisted of an absorbent pad attached to a waterproof backing and were fastened on the baby with snaps. The first mass-market disposable diapers were Pampers, introduced in Peoria, IL, by Procter and Gamble of Cincinnati, OH, in 1961. They cost 10 cents each. After consumers complained about the price, the company withdrew them from the market and reintroduced them in Sacramento, CA, in 1966 for six cents each. The first disposable diapers with adhesive tabs to replace safety pins were Kimbies, made by Kimberly-Clark, Dallas, TX, in the early 1970s. Procter and Gamble's Luvs, introduced in 1976, were the first to come with an elastic fit.

2152. Barbie doll was invented in 1959 by Ruth and Eliot Handler, the founders of Mattel, a toy company in El Segundo, CA. The plastic doll, designed to appeal to fashion-conscious girls, was named after their daughter Barbara. They also introduced a male doll to serve as Barbie's boyfriend; he was named after their son Ken. The first human-sized Barbie was released by Mattel in 1992. It was three feet tall and sized to fit real girls' clothes.

CHILDREN—*continued*

2153. Toy action figure was G.I. Joe, introduced in February 1964 by Hasbro, Pawtucket, RI. It cost $2.49. It was the first mass-market doll intended exclusively for boys and, despite predictions to the contrary, was a great success, especially during the Vietnam War years.

2154. Baby carrier to be mass-produced was the Snugli, a corduroy pouch that could be strapped on a parent's front or back. It was created by Ann Moore, a Peace Corps volunteer from Colorado who observed traditional African infant carriers when she was in Togo in the early 1960s. Moore patented the Snugli in 1977.

CHILDREN—BIRTHS

2155. Child born of European parents on American soil was Snorri, the son of Thorfinn Karlsefni and Gudrid, widow of Leif Eriksson's brother Thorstein Eriksson. They were among 160 volunteers from Iceland who arrived in America circa 1007 to colonize a region they called Vinland, which had been explored by Leif Eriksson some years before. Historians have placed Vinland in various parts of the Atlantic coast, including Nova Scotia, Maine, and Massachusetts.

2156. Child born of English parents in America was Virginia Dare. She was born at Roanoke Island, in the future state of North Carolina, on August 18, 1587, and was the daughter of Ananias Dare and Eleanor (White) Dare. Her maternal grandfather was John White, governor of the colony. Only the first nine days of her life are known to history. Her parents were part of a group of 150 settlers, including 25 women and children, who left England on May 8, 1587, in three vessels. They landed at Cape Hatteras on July 22 and cruised up what is now Pamlico Sound to the "iland called Roanoac." Two vessels returned to England immediately. The third, with John White aboard, sailed for England on August 27, nine days after Virginia Dare's birth, to acquire more supplies. When White returned in 1590, the colonists had vanished and their fort was in ruins.

2157. Child born of English parents in New England was Peregrine White, born on board the *Mayflower* off Cape Cod harbor on November 20, 1620. He was the son of Susanna and William White.

2158. Child born of African-American parents in America was William Tucker, born in Elizabeth City, VA, to Antoney and Isabell, two of the first 20 Africans to arrive in Jamestown in 1619 and the first Africans to marry. William was baptized in Jamestown in 1624.

2159. Birth registration law enacted by a state was passed by Georgia on December 19, 1823. It required the "clerks of the court of ordinary, in each county respectively to enter and register in a book" the dates of births of all persons upon due proof made by affidavit or oath. The clerk was entitled to charge 25 cents for each registration.

2160. Child born in an airplane was the daughter of Mr. and Mrs. T.W. Evans, born on October 28, 1929, in a transport plane over Miami, FL.

2161. City law requiring reporting of premature births was passed on March 5, 1935, by Chicago, IL. It required physicians to report the birth of all premature babies within an hour after the birth. A supplemental item was added to the official birth certificate to show whether or not a baby was born prematurely.

2162. Birth registration uniform numbering system was adopted on March 18, 1948, by the American Association of Registration Executives and was approved on August 30 by the Council on Vital Records and Vital Statistics. The system was inaugurated on January 1, 1949. It required each birth certificate to be assigned a three-part number. The first number identified the state—101 for Alabama, 102 for Arizona, 103 for Arkansas, and so on. The second number referred to the year, and the third number to the order of the birth in the state's record. The lowest number in the classification was given to Leonard Blake Gunnells of Prattville, AL, whose name was the first on the roll of the first county in Alabama's alphabetical county list. His number was 101-49-000001.

2163. Birth to be shown on closed-circuit television was shown in color on June 14, 1951, as part of the American Medical Association meeting at Atlantic City, NJ. Two thousand physicians and their families watched the birth of Michael Gallagher, who weighed 9 pounds 12 ounces.

2164. Birth to be televised for the public took place on December 2, 1952, and was televised by KOA, Denver, CO, over 49 stations of the National Broadcasting Company. The birth was that of Gordon Campbell Kerr, who weighed 5 pounds 7 ounces, and was delivered by cesarean section in the hospital delivery room of the

Colorado General Hospital of the University of Colorado Medical School, Denver. The parents were Lillian Kerr and John R. Kerr of Denver. The telecast was part of the "March of Medicine" program presented in conjunction with the annual clinical meeting of the American Medical Association.

2165. Test for newborn health was the Newborn Scoring System, invented by Dr. Virginia Apgar, professor of anesthesiology at Columbia University, New York City, and introduced in 1952. Commonly known as the Apgar Score, the test allows attendants at a birth to identify problems with the baby's breathing, circulation, muscle tone, reflexes, and color.

2166. Child born in the United States through in vitro fertilization was Elizabeth Jordan Carr, born on December 28, 1981, at Norfolk Hospital, Norfolk, VA. Assisting in the fertilization process were Howard and Georgeanna S. Jones of the In Vitro Fertilization Clinic, Eastern Virginia Medical School, Norfolk. In this procedure, an ovum extracted from a woman is placed in a glass dish and mixed with sperm. (The term *in vitro* means "in glass" in Latin.) The resulting embryo is implanted in the uterus of the mother, who then becomes pregnant. The world's first child produced by in vitro fertilization was Louise Brown, conceived in Bristol, England, on January 1, 1979.

2167. Trial of a surrogate mother for refusing to give up her baby took place in New Jersey in 1987, when Mary Beth Whitehead of Brick Township was sued by William and Elizabeth Stern of Tenafly for breach of contract. Whitehead had signed a contract with the Sterns in which she agreed to accept $10,000 as compensation for undergoing artificial insemination, carrying the pregnancy to term, and giving up all parental rights. She changed her mind after giving birth to the baby, who was known in court records as "Baby M." On March 31, 1987, the trial judge upheld the legality of the contract, but his decision was overturned on February 3, 1988, by the state supreme court, which ruled unanimously that commercial contracts for surrogate motherhood were illegal. A lower court allowed the Sterns to retain custody of the baby, but gave visiting rights to the mother.

2168. Ban on surrogate motherhood enacted by a state was signed into law on June 27, 1988, by Governor James J. Blanchard of Michigan. The act made it illegal for women to enter into contracts that require them to bear other people's children in exchange for money.

2169. Grandmother to give birth to her own grandchild in the United States was 42-year-old librarian Arlette Schweitzer of Aberdeen, SD. Schweitzer's daughter, Christa Uchytil, age 22, had been born without a uterus. Ova taken from Christa were fertilized with sperm from her husband Kevin and implanted in Schweitzer's uterus at the University of Minnesota Hospital and Clinic in Minneapolis, MN. On October 12, 1991, she gave birth to twins named Chad and Chelsea.

CHILDREN—BIRTHS—MULTIPLES

2170. Siamese twins to attain fame were brought to Boston, MA, by Robert Hunter on August 16, 1829. They were known as Chang and Eng. They were born on April 15, 1811, in Bangesau, Siam, of a Chinese father and a Chinese-Siamese mother. They were joined at the waist by a cartilaginous band about four inches long and eight inches in circumference. They grew to be about 5 feet 2 inches in height, and, since they faced in the same direction, could walk, run, and swim. They were exhibited throughout the United States and later in Europe. They were married in April 1843 to two sisters, Sarah and Adelaide Yates. Chang had 10 children and Eng nine children. They died within three hours of each other on January 17, 1874. The name "Siamese twins," meaning twins whose bodies are connected in any of a variety of ways, is derived from them.

2171. Sextuplets recorded were three boys and three girls born on September 8, 1866, in Chicago, IL, to James and Jennie A. Lewis Bushnell. The midwife was Priscilla Bancroft and the attending physician was Dr. James Edwards. One of the sextuplets, Lucy, died at the age of two months, and one, Laberto, died at eight months. Of the surviving four, Norberto died at 68, and three—Alberto, Alice Elizabeth, and Alincia—were over 70 when they died. There was a previous report, in the *Boston Medical and Surgical Journal* of 1847, of the birth of sextuplets on June 27, 1846, to Mrs. Marr of Phipsburg, ME, but the report may have been a hoax.

2172. Quintuplets recorded were five boys born on February 13, 1875, in Watertown, WI, to Mrs. Edna Beecham Kanouse, wife of Edward Cole Kanouse. All five died within two weeks. There are earlier, unverified claims for quintuplet births in Mars Bluff, SC, in 1776 and in Monticello, IL, in 1800.

CHILDREN—BIRTHS—MULTIPLES—*continued*

2173. Quadruplets to graduate from college were the Keys sisters, Leota, Mary, Mona, and Roberta, who received B.A. degrees from Baylor University, Waco, TX, on May 31, 1937. They were born on June 4, 1914.

2174. Quadruplets delivered by cesarean operation were Maureen, Kathleen, Eileen, and Michael Cirminello, born to Mr. and Mrs. Joseph Cirminello on November 1, 1944, in Philadelphia, PA. The cesarean section was performed under spinal anesthesia. The obstetrician in charge was Dr. John Calvin Ullery of Upper Darby, PA.

2175. Siamese twins separated successfully by surgery were Carolyn Anne and Catherine Anne Mouton, daughters of Ashton and Rosa Mouton. The girls were born in Lafayette, LA, on July 22, 1953. Their lower intestines were connected and their lower spinal bone structure and dural membrane were joined. On September 17, 1953, a team of 15 doctors worked for more than two hours at the Ochsner Foundation Hospital, New Orleans, LA, to separate them. The operation was successful, and on October 14 they were discharged from the hospital.

2176. Quintuplets to live more than five years were a boy (James Andrew) and four girls (Mary Ann, Mary Catherine, Mary Magdalen, and Mary Margaret), born within over the course of 63 minutes to Mr. and Mrs. Andrew J. Fischer of Aberdeen, SD, on September 14, 1963, in St. Luke's Hospital. They weighed approximately 2.5 to 4 pounds each. The physician was Dr. James Barbos.

2177. Quintuplets to survive infancy who were African-American were the Gaither quints, Joshua, Brandon, Ashlee, Renee, and Rhealyn. They were born in 1983 to Suzanne and Sidney Gaither of Indianapolis, IN. Dr. Frank Johnson was the attending obstetrician.

2178. Septuplets were born on May 21, 1985, in Orange, CA, to Patti Frustaci, a 30-year-old schoolteacher. It was the largest multiple birth in the history of the United States. One child was stillborn and three more died within a month. Two boys and one girl survived. Frustaci and her husband later filed a malpractice suit against her doctors and the infertility clinic where she had been treated.

2179. Triplets born several weeks apart were delivered to Delvonda and Bernard Boldin of Florida. The first triplet, Kenard, was born on November 23, 1995. He weighed 1 pound 4 ounces and required emergency care. Doctors gave Delvonda drugs to stop her labor and stitched her cervix closed to allow the other babies more time to develop. Two daughters, each weighing less than two pounds, were born by cesarean section 23 days later.

CITIES AND TOWNS

2180. Curfew bell was introduced by Wilhelm Kieft, the third governor of New Netherlands (later New York City). In 1638 he instituted the custom of ringing the church bell nightly at nine o'clock to announce the hour of resting; every morning and evening to call persons to and from labor; and on Thursdays to summon prisoners to court.

2181. City incorporated in the colonies was Georgeana (now York), ME. On December 2, 1631, Sir Ferdinando Gorges received a grant of 24,000 acres on both sides of the Agamenticus, or York, River and founded a town named after the river on April 10, 1641. The name was changed to Georgeana when the city was incorporated on March 1, 1642, and was later changed again to York. The charter embraced a territory of 21 square miles and the inhabitants were formed into a body politic. This was the first English charter for a city in America. Kittery, ME, was the first and oldest town in the state, but Georgeana was incorporated as a city rather than as a town.

2182. Communistic settlement with a religious basis was a monastic commune established in the colony of Ephrata, eight miles from Lancaster, PA, in 1733 by Johann Conrad Beissel. A convent for women was similarly established. The group, known as the Ephrata Society, was an offshoot of the Dunkards (also known as Brethren or German Baptists).

2183. Town built by free African-Americans in an area now in the United States was Fort Mose, near St. Augustine, FL. In 1738, Spanish authorities established a free militia of 100 former slaves, including men, women, and children, who had escaped from British territory in what is now Georgia. They built Fort Mose, a 65-foot-square structure in the salt marshes north of St. Augustine. In 1740 they were driven away by a British attack, but rebuilt and enlarged the fort in 1752. In 1763, when Spanish Florida was ceded to England, the residents of Fort Mose moved to Cuba. The fort was declared a national historic landmark in 1994.

2184. Intercity stagecoach service was inaugurated on November 9, 1756, between Philadelphia, PA, and New York City by John Butler, Francis Holman, John Thompson, and William Waller.

2185. Milestones between cities were set by the directors of an insurance company known as The Philadelphia Contributionship for the Insurance of Houses from Loss by Fire. On February 17, 1761, they agreed "to apply their fines (a forfeiture of one shilling for not meeting precisely at the hour appointed, and two shillings for total absence) in purchasing Stones to be erected on the Road leading from Philadelphia toward Trenton, the distance of a mile one from another with the Number of miles from Philadelphia, to be cut in each stone, and Tho. Wharton and Jacob Lewis are requested to Contract for the same." On May 15, 1764, at five o'clock in the morning, the two men started out from Front and Market streets, taking with them the Surveyor General of the Province, and planted a stone at the end of every mile. They planted the 29th milestone near the edge of the Delaware River, and gave their two remaining stones to be planted on the Jersey side of the road to New York.

2186. Town named for George Washington was a North Carolina town originally known as Forks of Tar River, which had been founded on November 20, 1771, by James Bonner. It changed its name to Washington in 1775 and was incorporated in 1782. The first town to be incorporated under the name of Washington was a town in Wilkes County, GA, that was incorporated on January 23, 1780.

2187. City founded by an African-American pioneer was Chicago, which got its start in 1779 when a trading post was established on the shore of Lake Michigan. The trader was Jean Baptiste Point du Sable, a settler from Haiti whose mother was Haitian and father French. In 1800 he sold his lands to John Kinzie for $1,200 and moved to Missouri to farm. By 1834, prime waterfront property in Chicago sold for more than $20,000 an acre.

2188. Town founded by a woman was Tangipahoa, LA, settled in 1806 by Rhoda Holly Singleton Mixon, who came from South Carolina accompanied by her daughters and slaves. Her grandchildren sold their property in 1869.

2189. Communistic settlement that was not religious was established at New Harmony, IN, in 1825, by the utopian thinker Robert Owen and his associates, who purchased for approximately $150,000 the village that had been founded by the German pietist George Rapp in 1805. It had about 1,000 members and existed until May 1827.

2190. City carriage service ran along Broadway in New York City from Wall Street to Bleecker Street in what is now Greenwich Village. The proprietor was A. Brower. The first vehicle to run along the route was an open carriage, which was replaced in 1829 by the Sociable, a closed carriage pulled by two horses. It sat on double-deck springs and was so high off the ground that passengers had to climb six steps to get inside. Ten passengers could be accommodated on its long sideways seats. The fare was one shilling.

2191. Village improvement society with a long-term existence was the Laurel Hill Association of Stockbridge, MA, founded by Mary Gross Hopkins. The society was organized on August 24, 1853, "to improve and ornament the streets and public parts of Stockbridge, by planting and cultivating trees and doing such other acts as shall tend to improve and beautify the village."

2192. Cow town was Abilene, KS. In the late 1860s, Abilene was the terminus of the Kansas Pacific Railway. In 1867, Illinois cattleman Joseph Geating McCoy bought the entire town for $2,400 and turned it into a central shipping depot for cattle driven north from rural Texas along the Chisholm Trail. The first rail shipment took place on September 5, 1867, when 20 Kansas Pacific Railway cars full of Texas longhorns embarked for slaughterhouses in Kansas City and Chicago. The first year, 35,000 head of cattle were shipped through Abilene.

2193. African-American town in continuous existence is Nicodemus, KS, the oldest town entirely populated by African-American residents and the only such town west of the Mississippi. A tiny settlement with 50 permanent residents, it was founded in 1877 and was named after an African prince who was reputed to be the first slave to buy his freedom. The town was designated a national historic landmark in 1976.

CITIES AND TOWNS—*continued*

2194. Settlement house in a poor city neighborhood was the University Settlement, established by Stanton Coit in 1886 in a Forsythe Street tenement, New York City. The idea was that intellectuals would settle in a slum area and by living and working with their tenement neighbors would be able to help them raise their standard of living. Playgrounds were provided for children, instruction in English was given to immigrants, and other educational programs were established.

2195. Enclave was established at Fairhope, Baldwin County, AL, by the Fairhope Industrial Association, composed of seven men who purchased 135 acres in the town for $771 on January 5, 1895, and an additional 200 acres for $250 at a later date. The association was succeeded by the Fairhope Single Tax Corporation, incorporated on August 9, 1904, which owned about 4,000 acres, three-fourths of which was under lease. The association paid all taxes, and leaseholders paid only rent for the land.

2196. Tract housing development was Concrest, a development of 100 identical six-room houses near East Rochester, NY. It was built by Kate Gleason, a local machine-shop saleswoman turned contractor, beginning in 1913. Gleason had seen car engines mass-produced on an assembly line and decided to apply the method to the construction of low-cost housing.

2197. City in miniature was Tiny Town, in Grant Beach Park, Springfield, MO. It was built on June 6, 1925, by 10,000 children under the direction of William H. Johnson, on a carefully prepared townsite of five acres, with avenues, electric lights, and water mains, all to a scale of one inch to one foot. The town had 1,200 miniature structures, covering every aspect of a modern city. Schoolchildren served as the officers of the town, which had the manager-commission form of government. Conceived and constructed as an incentive to building, Tiny Town boosted building permits in Springfield from a $280 daily average for the 90 days preceding its exhibition to $1,843 per day for the 90 days immediately following. Six years before the townsite was selected, a miniature village was exhibited by Johnson on the floor of the convention hall in Springfield.

2198. Retirement colony was dedicated on October 23, 1936, at Roosevelt Park, Millville, NJ. The project, which was completed on January 1, 1937, contained seven houses for couples, which rented for $7 a month; six houses for single people, which rented for $5; and a community house. The city of Millville supplied the land, which had been taken over for taxes; the federal government's Works Progress Administration supplied $34,571. The city collected rent and agreed to keep the houses in repair. Residents received $15 monthly from the state under the Old Age Assistance Act. The plan was originated by Effie Morrison, deputy director of the Cumberland County Welfare Board.

2199. Planned suburban development was Levittown, NY, a tract of 17,447 identical four-room houses constructed between 1947 and 1951 on former potato fields in Nassau County, Long Island, by builder William Jaird Levitt. Along with the houses, which sold initially for $7,990 each, Levittown contained seven village greens and shopping centers, 14 playgrounds, nine swimming pools, two bowling alleys, and a town hall. Levittown and other suburban developments were built to meet the need for housing by veterans of World War II who returned home to marry and start families. Levitt was a Navy Seabee during the war and adapted the Seabees' rapid construction techniques in his developments.

2200. Private housing development designed as a complete community was LeFrak City, in Queens, New York City, a 40-acre complex containing high-rise apartment buildings, an office park, schools, stores, and recreational facilities. It was built by Samuel Jayson LeFrak, a real estate developer, and was opened in 1961. The complex cost $150 million to build and contained 5,000 apartments housing 25,000 people.

2201. Year in which the average price of a new house topped $100,000 was 1984. In May of that year, the average price of a new single-family house was $101,000.

CITIES AND TOWNS—GOVERNMENT

2202. City government using the commission plan originated in Galveston, TX, in 1901 as an emergency measure following a disastrous flood. The legislature granted Galveston a charter on April 19, 1901, and the system went into operation on September 18. Under this form, large powers both legislative and executive are vested in a single group of officers, elected by the whole body of voters within the city without regard to political party.

2203. City manager was Charles Edward Ashburner of Richmond, VA, who on April 2, 1908, was elected general manager by the city council of Staunton, VA. He opened his office on April 15, 1908. His first year's salary was $2,000; the second year's, $2,500. He served until July 1911.

2204. City government using the manager plan was adopted by Sumter, SC, in June 1912, when the voters, in a regular election, adopted the manager-commission form of government. The commission was composed of a mayor and two councilmen, all elected at large. The commission employed a city manager to whom active administration of the affairs of the city was entrusted and who was accountable to the commission.

2205. Zoning ordinance was put into effect in New York City on July 25, 1916, in the wake of concern over the unprecedented size of the 39-story Equitable Building, erected in lower Manhattan in 1915. The ordinance restricted the height and mass of skyscrapers and required buildings to be set back from the street, with the amount of setback calculated from the height and area of the building site. The total floor area of skyscrapers was also limited to no more than 12 times the area of the building site.

CITIES AND TOWNS—MAYORS

2206. City mayor elected by popular vote was Cornelius Van Wyck Lawrence, a Democrat, who defeated Gulian Crommelin Verplanck, a Whig, in the three-day election held on April 8–10, 1834, in New York City. There were 34,988 votes cast, of which 17,573 were for Lawrence, 17,393 for Verplanck, and 22 for others. Seven other municipal officers were also elected. Previously, mayors had been chosen by a board of the Common Council.

2207. Mayor who was a woman was Susanna Medora Salter, elected mayor of Argonia, KS, on April 4, 1887. Her name was submitted without her knowledge by the Woman's Christian Temperance Union, and she did not know that she was a candidate until she went to the polls and found her name listed on the ballot. Although only 27 years of age, she received a two-thirds majority of the votes. She served one year for $1. The first woman to serve as a mayor with a town council consisting entirely of women was Mrs. Mary D. Lowman, elected in April 1888 in Oskaloosa, KS. Her council consisted of Sadie Balsley, Millie Golden, Emma Hamilton, Carrie Johnson, and Hannah Morse.

2208. Mayor of a major city who was a Socialist was Emil Seidel, who served as mayor of Milwaukee, WI, from April 1910 to April 1912.

2209. Mayor of a major city who was African-American was Carl Burton Stokes, a Democrat, elected on November 7, 1967, by the citizens of Cleveland, OH. He was sworn in on November 13, 1967, in the City Council Chamber. Also in 1967, Walter E. Washington was elected mayor of Washington, DC, and Richard G. Hatcher was elected mayor of Gary, IN. The first African-American mayor of a major city in the South was Maynard Jackson, who was elected mayor of Atlanta, GA, on October 16, 1973.

2210. Mayor of a major city who was a woman was Patience Sewell Latting, sworn in on April 13, 1971, as mayor of Oklahoma City, OK. Her salary was $2,000 a year. The city's population exceeded 366,000. The first woman to be elected mayor of a city with a population over 500,000 was Janet Gray Hayes of San Jose, CA, elected on November 6, 1974, on the Democratic ticket.

2211. Mayor of a major city who was of Mexican descent was Henry Gabriel Cisneros, who was elected mayor of San Antonio, TX, on April 4, 1981.

2212. Mayor of New York City who was African-American was David N. Dinkins, 63, the Manhattan borough president, who was elected on November 7, 1989, as a Democrat. He served one term. He was defeated in his 1993 bid for reelection by Republican candidate Rudolph Giuliani, whom he had beaten in 1989.

CITIES AND TOWNS—STREETLIGHTS

2213. Gas streetlights were installed in 1806 in Newport, RI, on Pelham Street, in front of the residence of David Melville. He patented his apparatus for making coal gas on March 18, 1813, about which time several important installations were made.

2214. Gas streetlights throughout a city were installed in Baltimore, MD, by the Gas Light Company in 1817. On June 19, 1816, the mayor and council authorized the company, whose officers included the artist Rembrandt Peale, to lay pipes for the manufacture and distribution of gas "to provide for more effectually lighting the streets, squares, lanes and alleys of the city of Baltimore." Coal gas was used. The first street was lighted on February 17, 1817. The first engineer of the company was David Pugh.

CITIES AND TOWNS—STREETLIGHTS—
continued

2215. Electric arc streetlights were made by Charles Francis Brush and were used in the Public Square, Cleveland, OH, on April 29, 1879. Twelve lamps of the carbon variety—two carbon points slightly separated—were used. The current jumped from carbon to carbon, giving off a dazzling white light.

2216. Electric streetlight installed in a city was installed in Wabash, IN. On February 2, 1880, the city appropriated $100 to the Brush Electric Light Company of Cleveland, OH, to install a light on the dome of the courthouse. On March 31, four lights, each over 4,000 candlepower, were placed on a staff above the courthouse, and on April 8 a further payment of $1,800 was authorized.

2217. Automatic streetlight system in which the lights individually turn themselves on and off was installed in New Milford, CT, on March 2, 1949, by the Connecticut Light and Power Company, New Milford, CT. Each streetlight was equipped with an electronic device that used a photoelectric cell. A total of 190 photoelectric-controlled streetlights were installed on approximately seven miles of streets by November 1949.

2218. Fluorescent electric lighting to be installed on every street of a city in accordance with illuminating engineering code levels was installed in Brookings, SD. The project, started in 1953, was completed in 1958.

CITIES AND TOWNS—STREETS

2219. Street-sweeping service was instituted in 1757 in Philadelphia, PA, by Benjamin Franklin, who reported: "After some inquiry, I found a poor industrious man who was willing to undertake keeping the pavement clean by sweeping it twice a week, carrying off the dirt from before the neighbors' doors, for the sum of six pence per month, to be paid by each house."

2220. Street-cleaning machine of importance was employed by Philadelphia, PA, on December 15, 1854. According to a contemporary account, it consisted of "a series of brooms on a cylinder about two feet six inches wide, attached to two endless chains, running over an upper and lower set of pulleys, which are suspended on a light frame of wrought iron behind a cart, the body of which is near the ground. As the cart wheels revolve, a rotary motion is given to the pulleys conveying the endless

chains, and series of brooms attached to them; which being made to bear on the ground successively sweep the surface and carry the soil up an incline or carrier plate, over the top of which it is dropped into the cart."

2221. Snow-melting apparatus was patented by Nicholas H. Borgfeldt of New York City on April 6, 1869. The device combined a sieve and a heated surface. A mass of snow was subdivided into flakes by a sieve and then melted by a heated surface. The system was not practical.

2222. Underground burial of electric wires to be required by a state was mandated under a law enacted on June 14, 1884, by New York. It required that "all telegraph, telephonic and electric light wires and cables in any incorporated city having a population of 500,000 or over ... be placed under the surface of the streets, lanes and avenues." It also specified that telegraph poles be removed by November 1, 1885. Overhead wires had killed hundreds of people in New York City alone.

2223. Snow-melting apparatus using pipes embedded in the sidewalk was installed by Best and Company, a department store in New York City, which installed a system of 15 coils comprising 4,530 feet of pipe. A solution of about 67 percent water and 33 percent antifreeze by volume was circulated as protection against freezing temperatures as low as five degrees below zero. The system was tested on December 8, 1946, and was put into operation during a blizzard on December 26.

CITIES AND TOWNS—WATER AND
    SEWAGE

2224. Water supply system built for a city was built in Boston, MA, by the Water Works Company in 1652. A series of wooden pipes was used to convey the water from nearby springs to a central reservoir, which was only 12 feet square.

2225. Water pumping plant was installed in Bethlehem, PA, on May 27, 1755. Water from a spring was pumped through wooden pipes into a 70-foot-high water tower. The plant was constructed by Hans Christopher Christiansen.

2226. Waterworks system to use cast-iron pipes was installed by Philadelphia, PA, in 1817. The pipeline was 400 feet long and 4.5 inches in diameter. The pipes were imported from England and were so much superior to the old wooden water pipes that the Watering Committee decided to adopt them. In 1818 the committee resolved to make all future installations with cast-iron pipe.

2227. Drinking water conduit to be built underwater was built in 1848 by the Water Department of Boston, MA. It was constructed on the shore, floated into place, and sunk into a prepared trench below the surface of the channel under the Dover Street Bridge, the Warren Avenue Bridge, the Chelsea Street South Bridge, and the Chelsea Street North Bridge. The wooden tunnels were approximately 4 feet 8.5 inches in diameter and some 50 feet or more in length. They contained cast-iron pipes 20 inches in diameter that carried drinking water from central Boston to the South Boston, Charlestown, and Chelsea sections of the city. All these pipes were in use before 1852.

2228. Underground city sewer system was begun in Chicago, IL, in 1856 on the grid pattern. The sewers were of circular cross sections ranging from 3 to 6 feet in diameter and had brick walls 8.5 inches thick. Branch sewers were two feet in diameter, and the hose drains were four-inch and six-inch pipes or boxes made of wood planks. Manholes were provided every 100 feet, and in general the slope or gradient was 1 foot in 500. By June 30, 1860, about 46 miles had been completed. Single uncoordinated sewers had been used earlier.

2229. Dual sewer system for sewage and storm water was built in Brooklyn, NY (now a borough of New York City), in 1857 by Colonel Julius Adams. The size and capacity were scientifically calculated to care for a rainfall intensity of one inch per hour.

2230. Sewage-disposal system separate from the city water system was built in Memphis, TN, under the direction of George Edwin Waring, beginning on January 21, 1880. Within four months, he had installed a system comprising 18 miles of pipe, with 152 flush tanks and four-inch connecting drains. The pipes were for sewage only and were kept constantly cleansed with water and well ventilated. Six-inch vitrified pipes emptied into larger pipes, which in turn emptied into increasingly larger ones until 20-inch pipes were used. An independent and separate set of pipes was provided for disposing of storm water. The total cost of 20 miles for the two main sewers, including labor, materials, engineering, superintending, and incidentals, was about $137,000. A similar system was adopted at about the same time by Pullman, IL (now a part of Chicago).

2231. Plumbing law enacted by a state was enacted on May 30, 1881, by Illinois. It was "an act for the regulation and inspection of tenement and lodging houses or other places of habitation." In cities with a population of 50,000 or more, plumbers were required to receive a written certificate of instruction from the commissioner before commencing work on buildings. They were also required to work according to a prepared plan. Violations were punishable by a fine of not less than $100 for the first offense and $10 a day for noncompliance.

2232. Sewer district established by a city was the Sanitary District of Chicago, IL, authorized on November 5, 1889, by referendum vote to construct and operate the sewage system for the protection of the public water supply. Murray Nelson was the first president.

2233. Sewage disposal by chemical precipitation was undertaken in Worcester, MA, which installed the system in 1890. It used six chemical precipitation settling basins, each 66.67 by 100 by 7 feet. The raw sewage was screened and then treated with milk of lime. It was passed through a mixing channel into the six settling basins in series. The detention period was approximately six hours. After being quiescent for a few hours, the top water was drawn off, and the sludge was run to a six-inch centrifugal pump and discharged into lagoons.

2234. Water filtration system for bacterial purification of a city water supply was the Lawrence Filter, Lawrence, MA, designed by Hiram Francis Mills and completed in September 1893. It was an open filter of 2.75 acres that purified water from the Merrimack River by slow sand filtration. The idea dates from 1873, when an English-type slow sand filter was built at Poughkeepsie, NY, from plans prepared by James Pugh Kirkwood.

2235. Drinking water supply to be chemically treated with chlorine compounds on a practical scale was the water supply of Jersey City, NJ, which was chlorinated in 1908 under the supervision of George Arthur Johnson.

2236. Water supply to be fluoridated in order to reduce tooth decay was the water system of Grand Rapids, MI. Fluoridation started on January 25, 1945, with the addition of one part of fluoride ion to each million parts of water passing through the water treatment plant.

2237. Seawater conversion plant that was practical was opened on May 8, 1961, by the Office of Saline Water, Department of the Interior, at Freeport, TX. It was dedicated on June 21 by President John Fitzgerald Kennedy, who pressed a switch installed in his office at Washington, DC. The plant was set up to produce about a million gallons of water a day at a cost of $1 to $1.25 per 1,000 gallons.

CIVIL RIGHTS AND SLAVERY

2238. African slaves in America arrived in 1581 at the Spanish colony of St. Augustine, FL. They belonged to King Philip II of Spain. The first slaves in the English colonies in America were introduced in Jamestown, VA, in August 1619 by a Dutch man-of-war that sold 20 kidnapped Africans to the planter colonists. They were treated as indentured servants, since slavery was not legalized in Virginia for several decades. Forms of slavery were also practiced among Native American peoples from ancient times.

2239. Slavery emancipation law enacted by a colony was enacted by Rhode Island. It was one of several "Acts and Orders made at the General Court of Election held at Warwick, RI, this 18th day of May, anno 1652." It contained the following provision: "No blacke mankind or white ... [may be] forced by covenant bond or otherwise to serve any man or his assignes longer than ten years, or until they come to be 24 years of age, if they be taken in under 14, from the time of their coming within the Liberties of the Collonie, and at the end or terme of ten years ... [are to be set] free, as is the manner with the English servants. And that man that will not let them goe free, or shall sell them away elsewhere, to that end that they may be enslaved to others for a long time, he or they shall forfeit to the Collonie forty pounds."

2240. Protest against slavery of importance was made on February 18, 1688, by the German Friends, or Quakers, at a meeting in Germantown, PA. They protested against the "traffic in the bodies of men" and considered the question of the "lawfulness and unlawfulness of buying and keeping Negroes." Some of the protesters were Francis Daniel Pastorius, Dirck op den Graeff, Abraham op den Graeff, and Gerhard Hendricks.

2241. Rebellion of African-American slaves in a colony occurred on April 6, 1712, in New York City. Six whites were killed. The militia was called out to suppress the revolt. Twenty-one African-American slaves (some accounts say 12) were executed by hanging, and 6 committed suicide.

2242. Slave importation ban enacted by a colony was passed on June 13, 1774, by the Rhode Island General Assembly in Newport, RI. It provided that "no Negro or mulatto slave shall be brought in to this colony, and in case any slave shall be brought in, he or she shall be, and are hereby, rendered immediately free, so far as respects personal freedom, and the enjoyment of private property, in the same manner as the native Indians."

2243. Abolition organization was the Society for the Relief of Free Negroes Unlawfully Held in Bondage, formed on April 14, 1775, in Philadelphia, PA. The first president was John Baldwin. The society was incorporated in 1789 as the Pennsylvania Society for Promoting the Abolition of Slavery and for the Relief of Free Negroes Unlawfully Held in Bondage and for Improving the Condition of the African Race.

2244. Slavery emancipation law enacted by a state was enacted by Vermont, whose constitution of July 2, 1777, provided that "no male person born in this country or brought from over sea, ought to be holden by law, to serve any person as a servant, slave or apprentice, after he arrives to the age of twenty-one years, nor female, in like manner, after she arrives to the age of eighteen years, unless they are bound by their own consent, after they arrive to such age, or bound by law, for the payment of debts, damages, fines, costs or the like."

2245. Slave to be emancipated was Elizabeth Freeman, known as Mum (or Marm) Bett, who was owned by Hannah Hogeboom Ashley, the wife of Colonel John Ashley of Sheffield, MA. In 1780, Hannah Ashley endeavored to strike Lizzie, Elizabeth's sister, with a red-hot kitchen shovel. Elizabeth interfered and received the blow on her arm, where she was scarred for life. She ran away to the home of lawyer Theodore Sedgwick, whom she had seen at the Ashley house discussing the rights of man with a group of Sheffield notables, and obtained his help in suing for her freedom. The case was tried in Great Barrington, MA, on August 21, 1781. The jury granted her freedom. She died on December 28, 1829, and was buried in the Sedgwick family plot.

2246. Slavery ban enacted for a territory of the United States was prepared by Nathan Dane of Massachusetts and enacted on July 13, 1787, by the Continental Congress. The law prohibited slavery forever within the borders of the Northwest Territory, a region east of the Mississippi River, north of the Ohio River, south and west of the Great Lakes, and west of Pennsylvania.

2247. Fugitive slave law enacted by Congress was passed on February 12, 1793. It required the forcible return of slaves who had escaped. The law stated: "No person held to service or labor in one state, under the laws thereof, escaping into another, shall, in consequence of any law or regulation therein, be discharged from such service or labor, but shall be delivered up on claim of the party to whom such service or labor may be due."

2248. National convention of African-Americans assembled at Bethel African Methodist Episcopal Church, Philadelphia, PA, on September 15, 1830. It was attended by delegates from seven states. Bishop Richard Allen presided. The convention was organized to protest the work of the American Colonization Society, which was calling for the return to Africa of free African-Americans.

2249. Slave rebellion after the Revolution on a large scale took place beginning August 21, 1831, in Southampton County, VA. It was led by Nat Turner, an African-American slave and religious visionary who believed that he was divinely chosen to lead his fellow slaves to freedom. With seven accomplices, Turner killed his owner, Joseph Travis, and the Travis family in their sleep, then led more than 70 followers in a two-day revolt in which 55 to 60 whites were killed. State militiamen and armed whites confronted the rebels near Jerusalem, VA, and killed as many as 100 slaves, a number of whom had not taken part in the rebellion. Turner escaped, but was caught six weeks later and hanged on November 11.

2250. Senator elected on an antislavery ticket was John Parker Hale of New Hampshire, who was elected on June 9, 1846, for the six-year term that began on March 4, 1847. Previously, he had served as a Democrat in the House of Representatives from March 4, 1843, to March 3, 1845.

2251. School for freed slaves was established by the American Missionary Association at Fortress Monroe, VA, on September 17, 1861, with an African-American teacher, Mary S. Peake.

2252. Emancipation proclamation made by President Abraham Lincoln was the Preliminary Emancipation Proclamation, issued on September 22, 1862, to take effect on January 1, 1863. It declared that "all Persons held as Slaves" in all the Confederate states, excepting a number of counties under federal control, were to be considered "forever Free." It also enjoined members of the federal armed forces from returning fugitive slaves to their owners. The Emancipation Proclamation in its final form was signed on January 1, 1863.

2253. Ku Klux Klan meeting took place in 1865 in Pulaski, TN. It was originally founded as a social organization, but quickly became a terrorist group that tried to enforce white supremacy by means of intimidation and violence. The first Grand Wizard was the Confederate general Nathan Bedford Forrest.

2254. Civil rights law enacted by Congress was an "Act to Protect all Persons in the United States in their Civil Rights and Furnish the Means of Their Vindication," enacted on April 9, 1866, during the first session of the 39th Congress. The act conferred citizenship upon African-Americans.

2255. Jim Crow law intended specifically to discriminate against African-Americans was enacted by the Tennessee legislature in 1875 and was struck down as unconstitutional in 1880 by a federal circuit court. In 1881, Tennessee passed another law that segregated African-American passengers on railroads, establishing a precedent that was quickly imitated by other Southern states. The constitutionality of Jim Crow laws was upheld on May 18, 1896, by the Supreme Court in the case of *Plessy v. Ferguson*. The result was a flurry of state laws that segregated everything from restaurants to drinking fountains. The term "Jim Crow" was borrowed from a character in a minstrel show.

2256. Lynching ban enacted by a state was a statute approved on December 20, 1893, by Georgia, "an act to prevent mob violence in this state, to prescribe a punishment for the same, to provide a means for carrying this act into effect, to punish a failure to comply with its requirements, and for other purposes." Violators were guilty of a felony punishable by imprisonment of up to 20 years. If death resulted, a murder charge could be instituted.

2257. Federal administrator who was an African-American woman was Mary Jane McLeod Bethune, born in Mayesville, SC, in 1875, the daughter of slaves. On June 24, 1936, she was named director of the Negro Division of the National Youth Administration by President Franklin Delano Roosevelt, thus becoming the first African-American woman to receive a major federal appointment. In 1904, Bethune founded the Daytona Normal and Industrial Institute for Negro Girls, later known as Bethune-Cookman College, located in Daytona Beach,

CIVIL RIGHTS AND SLAVERY—*continued*

FL. She was also the founder and first president of the National Council of Negro Women. In 1991, her home and offices in Washington, DC, were designated a national historic landmark.

2258. Year in which there were no reported lynchings of African-Americans was 1952. Record-keeping began in 1881.

2259. Mass boycott by civil rights protesters took place in Montgomery, AL, over a period of 381 days in 1955–56, when the African-American residents of the city refused to ride the municipal buses. The boycott was organized to protest the arrest on December 1, 1955, of an African-American seamstress, Rosa Parks, for refusing to give up her seat to a white passenger, as required by law. The protest was led by a young minister, the Reverend Dr. Martin Luther King, Jr. Eventually the city agreed to treat all riders equally and to hire African-Americans as bus drivers.

2260. Civil rights sit-in occurred on February 1, 1960, when four African-American freshmen from the Agricultural and Technical College in Greensboro, NC—Joseph McNeil, Izell Blair, Franklin McCain, and David Richmond—sat down at the lunch counter of the Woolworth's in Charlotte, NC. They were protesting the store's policy of refusing to allow African-American customers to sit down. The students were denied service but sat at the counter until closing time. Within weeks, similar "sit-in" protests were held in other Southern cities.

2261. State law to end de facto segregation in schools was "an act providing for the elimination of racial imbalance in the public schools," enacted in Massachusetts on August 18, 1965.

2262. Black Power advocate was Stokely Carmichael, chairman of the Student Nonviolent Coordinating Committee, based in Atlanta, GA. In June 1966 he issued a call urging African-Americans to reject integration as a goal of the civil rights movement and to adopt militant action instead of the pacifist methods of Martin Luther King, Jr.

CLOTHING

2263. Umbrella is believed to have been used in Windsor, CT, in 1740. It produced a riot of merriment and derision, with the neighbors parading after the user, carrying sieves balanced on broom handles. Umbrellas were invented by Jonas Hanway, a British merchant and philanthropist.

2264. Gloves manufactured in commercial quantities were made in 1809 by Talmadge Edwards of Johnstown, NY, whose small shop employed home-based stitchers.

2265. Circus tights are believed to have been introduced in 1828 by Nelson Hower, a bareback rider in the Buckley and Wicks Show, as the result of a mishap. The performers wore short jackets, knee breeches, and stockings, but Hower's costume failed to arrive and he appeared for the show in his long knit underwear.

2266. Shirt factory of importance was established in Boston, MA, in 1848 by Oliver Fisher Winchester.

2267. Bloomers were introduced at Lyceum Hall in Seneca Falls, NY, on July 19, 1848, during the First Woman's Rights Convention. They were long, full, ankle-length pants covered by a skirt that reached below the knees. The designer of the garment was Elizabeth Smith Miller, a well-to-do New York City housewife who wanted something practical to wear while she was gardening. The name was derived from the woman who first wore them in public, Amelia Jenks Bloomer, editor of the feminist magazine *Lily,* who was interested in reforming women's restrictive clothing customs.

2268. Blue jeans were invented in 1853 by Levi Strauss, a 20-year-old German Jewish immigrant and dry goods salesman. Strauss had arrived three years earlier in San Francisco, CA, where he began making sturdy canvas pants for gold miners. He called them "bibless overalls." In 1853 he opened a pants factory on California Street and switched to indigo-dyed denim fabric. Another characteristic feature of blue jeans, copper rivets to reinforce stress points, were the idea of Jacob Davis, a Russian Jewish tailor. They were added to Strauss's jeans, called Levis, in 1877.

2269. Bustle was patented by Alexander Douglas of New York City, who obtained a patent on April 21, 1857, on an "improvement in bustles," making them adjustable so that the size could be increased or decreased.

2270. Earmuffs were invented in 1873 by Chester Greenwood of Farmington, ME, who commenced manufacturing them commercially the following year. He obtained a patent on March 13, 1877, on what he called "ear mufflers."

2271. Corset manufactured by a factory as a health item rather than a fashion article was made July 1874 by Warner Brothers, a partnership of Dr. Ira DeVer Warner and Dr. Lucien Calvin Warner, in McGraw, NY. The corset combined three garments in one—a corset, a skirt supporter, and self-adjusting pads—and had shoulder straps.

2272. Tuxedo coat was worn to the Autumn Ball at the Tuxedo Club in Tuxedo Park, NY, on October 10, 1886. Pierre Lorillard IV, heir to a tobacco fortune and the biggest landowner in town, asked his tailor to create four new formal black jackets modeled after the tailless red wool coats worn by English fox hunters. Lorillard declined to wear the result, but his son Griswold Lorillard and three of his friends did, along with waistcoats of scarlet satin, and the look caught on.

2273. Ready-made clothing for children was introduced in New York City by Louis Borgenicht, a Jewish immigrant from Poland who sold household goods out of a pushcart. He and his wife began sewing aprons and dresses for children in 1889.

2274. Dress made of spun glass was made in 1893 for Georgia Cayven, who ordered 12 yards of glass cloth at $25 a yard from the E.D. Libbey Glass Company, Toledo, OH. The cloth was produced at the company's exhibit at the World's Columbian Exposition, Chicago, IL. The dress made from the cloth was not practical for wearing purposes.

2275. Uniforms for working women were made by Henry A. Dix, born Henry Dickstein in the Ukraine. Dix and his wife were shopkeepers in Millville, NJ, who went into business sewing ready-made dresses for women. In 1896 they switched their three factories to the production of uniforms for nurses, waitresses, maids, and saleswomen.

2276. Brassiere patent was granted in November 1914 to Mary Phelps Jacobs (later known as Caresse Crosby), a New York socialite, for the Backless Brassiere, which was designed to be worn under a sheer evening gown. Her original model was made of two white handkerchiefs, a length of satin ribbon, and some cord. In 1915 she sold her patent rights to the Warner Brothers Corset Company of Bridgeport, NY, for $1,500. Standardized sizes for bras were introduced in the 1920s by dressmaker Ida Kaganovich Rosenthal, a Russian-Jewish immigrant who founded the Maidenform company.

2277. Swimsuit of stretch fabric was made by the Portland Knitting Mills, Portland, OR, in 1915, using a lightweight woolen rib-knit cloth invented by Carl Jantzen, a Danish immigrant who was a partner in the company. He designed a body-hugging athletic costume for the Portland rowing team that was quickly adopted by swimmers. Bathing suits previously consisted of baggy clothes that covered the swimmer from neck to ankle.

2278. Nylon stockings went on sale on May 15, 1940, "Nylon Day," at selected stores throughout the country. The merchandise was fought over by mobs of shoppers reacting to advertisements by the manufacturer of nylon, E.I. Du Pont de Nemours and Company of Wilmington, DE, which announced that nylon stockings, unlike silk, would be virtually indestructible. This was the first use of a synthetic fabric for an article of clothing. By the end of 1940, 36 million pairs of nylon stockings had been sold.

2279. Suits for men made of Dacron were introduced on May 8, 1951, by the Hart, Schaffner and Marx Company. They were made of 8–8.5 ounce fabric, consisting of 55 percent Dacron and 45 percent worsted, produced by Deering, Milliken and Company, New York City, under the brand name of Visa.

2280. Clothing designer of international renown who was born in the United States was Roy Halston Frowick, born in Des Moines, IA, in 1932. He began his career as a milliner in Chicago, IL, and introduced his first complete line of women's apparel at Bergdorf Goodman in New York City in 1966, using the name Halston. In 1968 he became the first American designer to have his own freestanding couture establishment. He ceased to design professionally in 1984 and died of AIDS on March 26, 1990.

2281. Sports bra was invented in 1978 by Lisa Zobian-Lindahl, a runner, and Hinda Miller, a professional costume designer, both of Vermont. The product was called the Jogbra. The original consisted of two modified jock straps sewn together. Early commercial versions of the Jogbra were purchased for the permanent collections of the Smithsonian Institution, Washington, DC, and the Costume Collection of the Metropolitan Museum of Art, New York City.

CLOTHING—COLLARS

2282. Detachable collar was made in 1825 in Troy, NY, by Hannah Lord Montague, who, tired of washing her husband's shirts merely because the collar was dirty, took scissors and performed the amputation that created a new style in men's apparel.

2283. Collar manufacturer to make detachable collars was Ebenezer Brown, who started in Troy, NY, in 1829. He hired a number of women to make, wash, and iron the collars, giving in payment merchandise from his retail store, located at 285 River Street. These collars, which were known as string collars because they were tied about the neck with a string, were placed in paper boxes 16 or more inches in length, and were sold in his store.

2284. Collar factory for the manufacture of men's linen collars and shirtfronts was established by Orlando Montague and Austin Granger, under the firm name of Montague and Granger, in Troy, NY, in 1833.

2285. Paper collar was invented by Walter Hunt of New York City, who obtained a patent for it on July 25, 1854. He used a thin white cotton muslin and coated both sides with very thin white paper, with a layer of paste interposed between them. The collars were then varnished with a colorless bleached shellac that made them proof against perspiration; they could be wiped clean with a damp cloth.

CLOTHING—FASTENERS

2286. Buttons of pewter or block tin were manufactured in 1790 in Waterbury, CT, by Henry, Silas, and Samuel Grilley, three brothers who established a small factory on Waterbury's Bunker Hill. The buttons were cast in molds. The eyes were originally cast of the same material. Later, wire eyes were used.

2287. Gilt buttons to be commercially manufactured were produced in 1802 by Abel Porter and Company of Waterbury, CT. This concern later developed into the Scovill Manufacturing Company of Waterbury, CT.

2288. Cloth-covered buttons were made by hand in Easthampton, MA, in 1826 by Mrs. Samuel Williston, who was the first to introduce their use commercially in the United States. Her husband formed a partnership with Joel Hayden, who invented the first machine for making covered buttons. The partnership lasted until 1848, when Williston bought out his partner and conducted the business alone.

2289. Hooks and eyes were successfully manufactured in 1836 in Waterbury, CT, by Holmes and Hotchkiss.

2290. Buttons of freshwater pearl were manufactured in Muscatine, IA, in 1890 by John F. Boepple, assisted by William Molis and R. Kerr. The pearl was obtained from domestic freshwater clam shells.

2291. Slide fastener was invented by Whitcomb L. Judson of Chicago, IL, who obtained a patent on August 29, 1893, on a clasp locker for shoes. His design consisted of two metal chains made up of hook-and-eye locks that were fastened together by the movement of a slider. The patents were assigned to the Universal Fastener Company in Illinois. The fasteners were first manufactured in 1893 by the Automatic Hook and Eye Company of Meadville, PA, through the efforts of Colonel Lewis Walker. They jammed frequently and were not widely used.

2292. Zipper was invented about 1906 by Gideon Sundback of Hoboken, NJ, an inventor of Swedish ancestry, who obtained a patent on April 29, 1913, on "separable fasteners." His design consisted of two flexible tapes, each of which carried a row of metal teeth with tiny hooks, and a slider that locked the two rows of hooks together. This fastener was improved upon by later patents obtained on March 20 and October 16, 1917, which were assigned to the Hookless Fastener Company of Meadville, PA, under the name "Talon." The first manufactured garments to incorporate zippers were rubber boots made by the B.F. Goodrich Company in 1923. The term "zipper" was coined by the English novelist Gilbert Frankau, who saw the device at a promotional luncheon and exclaimed: "Zip! It's open! Zip! It's closed!" The first fashion designer to use zippers was Elsa Schiaparelli, who added them to garments in her 1930 collection.

CLOTHING—HATS

2293. Hat factory is believed to have been established in Danbury, CT, in 1780 by Zadoc Benedict. He employed one journeyman and two apprentices whose total output was about 18 hats a week. They were made from rabbit and beaver fur and sold for $6 to $10 apiece. They were described as being "without elegance, being heavy, rough and unwieldy."

2294. Straw hats were made in June 1798 by 12-year-old Betsey Metcalf of Providence, RI. She plaited seven strands of oat straws into braid and fashioned them into bonnets, which she trimmed with ribbons. The hats were lined with pink satin and sold for $1 to $1.25.

2295. Derby hat was manufactured by James Henry Knapp of Knapp and Gilliam, South Norwalk, CT, in 1850. The first derbies were sold to New York jobbers Henderson and Bird, who sold 18 each of brown and black to a retail store on Broadway and Ninth Street, New York City. An English clerk suggested "Derby," after the famous English horse race, as the name of the hat. The word is pronounced "darby" in England and "derby" in the United States.

2296. Felt hats for women were introduced in New York City in 1851 by John Nicholas Genin, who took low-crowned soft black hats, fastened the left side of the brim of each to the crown, and ornamented it with a black feather. Prior to this time, women wore bonnets. Genin created the new style to celebrate the arrival of Lajos Kossuth, the Hungarian patriot, who arrived in New York City on December 5, 1851, on board the *Mississippi.*

2297. Cowboy hat was the invention of hatmaker John B. Stetson of Philadelphia, PA. In 1860, he designed the original wide-brimmed, high-crowned "10-gallon" hat to appeal to wealthy cattle ranchers who ordered their clothing back east. Before the Stetson, cowboys wore no special headgear.

CLOTHING—SHOES

2298. Shoes to be manufactured were made in 1628 by Thomas Beard, who came over on the *Mayflower.* Prior to that date, shoes were imported from England. The colonists also learned from the Native Americans how to make moccasins, which were so well liked that as early as 1650 they were exported to England.

2299. Shoe measuring stick was introduced as early as 1657. A dispute arose in court with regard to shoe sizes, and the court was informed that William Newman of Stamford, CT, "hath an instrument in his hand, which he brought out of England, which is thought to be right to determine the question between the buyer and the seller." The court "did ordain that the said instrument should be procured and sent to New Haven."

2300. Shoe peg was invented by Joseph Walker of Hopkinton, MA, in 1818. Prior to his invention, all shoe soles were sewn.

2301. Rubber shoe manufacturer was Leverett Candee, who established the L. Candee Shoe Factory in Hamden, CT, in 1842. He used the Goodyear vulcanizing patent. Prior attempts had been made in 1823 and 1831 to manufacture rubber footwear out of gum elastic, but the shoes were not serviceable. They melted and produced offensive odors.

2302. Shoe pegging machine was operated by Charles D. Bigelow at his shop in Jacob Street, New York City, in the "Swamp" district, in 1852.

2303. Shoe manufacturing machine was the McKay stitching machine, which revolutionized shoe manufacturing methods. It was invented by Lyman Reed Blake of Abington, MA, who obtained patents on July 6, 1858. The upper was lasted upon the insole by means of tacks driven through the insole and clinched against the steel bottom of the last. The outsole was then attached to the insole and upper by the McKay sewing machine, which made a chain stitch through and through to the inside of the shoe. The surface of the insole was then covered by a lining. The machine was introduced in the factory of William Porter and Sons, Lynn, MA, in 1861. It was probably operated by foot power.

2304. Snowshoe production for commercial purposes was undertaken in 1862 in Norway, ME, by Alanson Millen Dunham, Jr.

2305. Rubber shoe heel was made in Lowell, MA, by Humphrey O'Sullivan. He obtained a patent on January 24, 1899, on a "safety-heel."

2306. Running shoes of the modern variety were introduced in 1962 by New Balance, Boston, MA, a company that specialized in orthopedic shoes. Known as Tracksters, they featured a one-piece rippled sole and a rubber shock-absorber in the heel.

2307. Sneakers with rubber soles and plain cloth uppers were sold from the early 1870s by Charles Goodyear of New York City, who developed the vulcanized rubber shoe sole, and by many other footwear companies. The first brand of sneakers was Keds, introduced in 1916 by the United States Rubber Company, the successor to Goodyear's shoe company. The first Keds had black soles and high-top brown canvas uppers, mimicking leather shoes. The name was a combination of "kids" and *ped,* the Latin word for "foot."

COMMERCE

2308. Bankruptcy act was the act of Congress of April 4, 1800, "to establish a uniform system of bankruptcy in the United States." It contained 64 sections and applied to "any merchant or other person residing within the United States, actually using the trade of merchandise, by buying and selling in gross, or by retail, or dealing in exchange as a banker, broker, factor, underwriter or marine insurer." It was repealed in December 1803. It did not permit voluntary bankruptcy and applied to traders only.

2309. Metric system usage to be approved by Congress was approved on July 28, 1866. The act provided that it "shall be lawful throughout the United States of America to employ the weights and measures of the metric system."

2310. Boycott law enacted by a state was passed on September 26, 1903, by Alabama, "to prohibit boycotting, unfair lists, picketting, or other interference with the lawful business or occupation of others, and to provide a penalty therefor." The law declared it a misdemeanor for two or more persons to conspire to prevent persons from carrying on a lawful business, to print or circulate stickers, cards, etc., and to use threats. The penalty was a fine of not less than $50 nor more than $500, or imprisonment of not more than 60 days at hard labor.

2311. Consumer protection law enacted by Congress was "an act forbidding the importation, exportation or carriage in interstate commerce of falsely or spuriously stamped articles of merchandise made of gold or silver or their alloys." It was enacted on June 13, 1906.

2312. Consumer protection medical alert listing medical quacks, manufacturers of spurious "cure-alls," peddlers of nostrums, "inventors" of worthless diets and exercises, and others who prey on the ill and the gullible was started in January 1930 by the New York City Department of Health and is said to be the first of its kind in the world. The "rogue's gallery" was compiled by the National Better Business Bureau, at the suggestion of Special Deputy Health Commissioner Edward Fisher Brown.

2313. Resale price maintenance law enacted by a state was California's Fair Trade Act, approved on May 8, 1931, which provided "that the buyer will not resell [a] commodity except at the price stipulated by the vendor." The title of the act is "an act to protect trade-mark owners, distributors and the public against injurious and uneconomic practices in the distribution of articles of standard quality under a distinguished trade-mark, brand or name."

2314. Installment sales law enacted by a state to protect consumers in practically all types of time sales was signed by Governor William Averell Harriman of New York on April 17, 1957. It placed a limit on credit service charges, required all charges to be clearly itemized, and prohibited fine print in the contracts.

2315. Product liability lawsuit to result in a criminal trial was filed by the relatives of three women who were killed in 1978 in an auto accident involving a Ford Pinto. The Ford Motor Company was charged with reckless homicide for knowingly selling vehicles that were unsafe. On March 13, 1981, a jury in Winimac, ID, found the company not guilty.

COMMERCE—ADVERTISING

2316. Patent medicine advertisement appeared in the 1692 *Boston Almanack,* printed by Benjamin Harris and John Allen: "That Excellent Antidote against all manner of Gripings called Aqua anti torminales, which if timely taken, it not only cures the Griping of the Guts, and the Wind Cholick; but preventeth that woful Distemper of the Dry Belly Ach; With printed directions for the use of it. Sold by Benjamin Harris at the London-Coffee House in Boston. Price three shillings the half pint Bottle."

2317. Newspaper advertisement appeared from May 1 to May 8, 1704, in the *Boston News-Letter,* Boston, MA. Three ads occupied four inches in a single column. The only display was a two-line initial letter in the text and the word "Advertisement" above the ads. One offered "At Oysterbay on Long Island in the Province of New York ... a very good Fulling Mill to be Let or Sold, as also a Plantation, having on it a large new Brick house, and other good house by it for a Kitchin and workhouse, etc." Another offered a reward for the capture of a thief and the return of certain wearing apparel, and the third was a notice of the loss of two anvils.

2318. Medicine advertisement in booklet form was *A Short Treatise of the Virtues of Dr. Bateman's Pectoral Drops: The Nature of the Distemper They Cure, and the Manner of Their Operation.* It contained 36 pages, including 15 pages of testimonials and a four-page abstract of the royal patent granted to the inventor, Benjamin Okell, and his associates. The catalog was originally printed by J. Cluer in Bow-Churchyard, London, and was reprinted by John Peter Zenger in New York in 1731. The medicine was sold wholesale and retail by James Wallace of New York City, for cases of "the rheumatism, stone and gravel pains, colds, agues, and fevers, gout, jaundice, ailments of the breast, and asthmas."

2319. Magician's advertisement appeared on March 18, 1734, in the *New York Weekly Journal.* It announced that on that day Joseph Broome would "perform Wonders of the World by Dexterity of Hand" at the home of Charles Sleigh, on Duke Street, New York City, and invited "all to be Spectators of his Ingenuity." The admission fees were one shilling, ninepence, and sixpence.

2320. Newspaper advertisement across two columns appeared in the *New York Weekly Journal,* New York City, on July 18, 1743, announcing the exhibition of a musical automaton imported from England—the first automaton seen in this country. It was also the first advertisement to occupy a half-page space in a periodical.

2321. Price sheet for commodities was the *South-Carolina Price-Current,* a broadside issued by Crouch and Gray, commission merchants, Charleston, SC, on a sheet 6 by 12 inches, two columns wide. The first known copy, that of July 30, 1774, listed 168 commodities with their prices.

2322. Advertising agency was opened in 1841 in Philadelphia, PA, by Volney B. Palmer, who thus became the first commercial advertising agent.

2323. Premiums given away with merchandise were successfully introduced by Benjamin Talbert Babbitt of New York City in 1865, to help him sell soap in wrappers. People felt that they were paying extra for the wrappers, so he printed the word "coupon" on them and offered to give away a "beautiful lithograph picture" for 10 coupons. Eventually his company ran a premium department, which carried as many as a thousand different items in stock.

2324. Trademark for food registered by the Patent Office was granted in 1867 to William Underwood and Company of Boston, MA. The mark depicted a red devil and was printed on the packaging for Underwood's canned "deviled entremets," or deviled meats, introduced the same year.

2325. Newspaper premiums were chromolithograph pictures, offered between 1870 and 1881 by the *Christian Union,* edited by Henry Ward Beecher. They were credited with raising the paper's circulation from 10,000 to 100,000. Premiums were also offered by the *New York*

Recorder, New York City, whose issue of March 25, 1893, printed the first of a series of coupons offering 17-by-25-inch color reproductions of celebrated paintings. Ten different subjects were offered, any one of which could be had for 20 coupons. Coupons and bonus prizes were also offered for ad insertions; prizes included a $10 gold piece, five silver watches, and 10 plush ottomans.

2326. Bandwagon used for the distribution of samples and advertising matter was employed in 1871 by Benjamin Talbert Babbitt, who used eight imported white Arabian stallions to pull the wagon. The band was seated on top of the wagon. His slogan, "For All Nations," was prominently featured on advertising cards over the doors of Broadway streetcars in New York City. Babbitt had the distinction of being one of the first to advertise in streetcars and buses.

2327. Trading stamp was originated in 1891 by Thomas Alexander Sperry, who in 1896 organized the Sperry and Hutchinson Company of Bridgeport, CT. The company was incorporated in 1900. Trading stamps were issued by merchants as an incentive to customers. The more a customer spent, the greater the number of trading stamps earned. Books of collected stamps could be exchanged for free merchandise.

2328. Trademark character impersonated by an actor as an advertising ploy was Aunt Jemima. The original Aunt Jemima was a character in a song. Chris Rutt, the inventor of the first ready-made pancake mix, borrowed the name to represent his product because he thought it suggested the image of an expert family cook. In 1893, when the Davis Milling Company, manufacturers of the mix, set up a promotional booth at the World's Columbian Exposition in Chicago, IL, it hired a local woman named Nancy Green to cook pancakes for visitors. Green continued to play the role for the rest of her life.

2329. Full-page magazine advertisement for a food product was printed in several national magazines in 1894. The product was Van Camp Pork and Beans, manufactured by the Van Camp Seafood Company of Indianapolis, IN. The ad offered a sample can for six cents.

2330. Truth-in-advertising law enacted by a state was "an act to regulate the sale of merchandise and to prevent misleading and dishonest representations in connection therewith," passed by New York on April 30, 1898. Those whose advertisements are "intended to have the appearance of an advantageous offer, which is untrue or calculated to mislead, shall be guilty of a misdemeanor."

COMMERCE—ADVERTISING—*continued*

2331. Car advertisement in a specialty magazine appeared in *Scientific American* on July 30, 1898. It was a one-column advertisement by the Winton Motor Car Company, Cleveland, OH, under the caption "Dispense with a Horse."

2332. Car advertisement in a national magazine of general circulation appeared in the *Saturday Evening Post* on March 31, 1900. The W.E. Roach Company of Philadelphia, PA, ran an ad featuring its slogan, "Automobiles That Give Satisfaction."

2333. Radio commercial was sponsored by the Queensboro Realty Corporation, Jackson Heights, NY, on August 28, 1922, over station WEAF, the experimental station of the American Telephone and Telegraph Company, New York City. The advertising rate was $100 for 10 minutes. Listeners heard H.M. Blackwell speak for 10 minutes about Hawthorne Court, a dwelling in Jackson Heights.

2334. Skywriting advertisement exhibition took place at noon over Times Square, New York City, on November 28, 1922. The skywriting was done by Captain Cyril Turner of the Royal Air Force, who spelled out the message "Hello, U.S.A. Call Vanderbilt 7200" in letters a half mile high at an altitude of 10,000 feet. The message resulted in 47,000 telephone calls in 2.5 hours. The letters were written upside down in white smoke released from the rear of the airplane. The vapors formed when oil hit a hot exhaust pipe. The release of the oil was controlled by levers.

2335. Radio network program sponsored by commercial advertising was "The Eveready Hour," first broadcast on February 12, 1924, from station WEAF, New York City, to stations WCAP, Washington, DC, and WJAR, Providence, RI, under the sponsorship of the National Carbon Company.

2336. Newspaper advertisement scented with perfume was issued on March 25, 1937, by the *Daily News,* Washington, DC. It contained a one-page advertisement of the Peoples Drug Stores featuring flowers.

2337. Skywriting advertisement written at night was exhibited by Andy Stinis of the Skywriting Corporation of America over New York City on September 18, 1937, when he wrote the words "Green River" for Oldtyme Distillers. The vapors were the same as those used in daytime skywriting and showed only when the moon was bright.

2338. Radio show sponsored by a cooperative of commercial advertisers was "Thirty Minutes in Hollywood," first broadcast on October 10, 1937, by station KHJ, Hollywood, CA, over the Mutual Broadcasting System. It was broadcast for 26 weeks in 72 cities, and paid for by 48 commercial sponsors on a prorated cost basis. The orchestra was conducted by Tommy Tucker; the masters of ceremonies were George Jessel and Norma Talmadge. The guest star on the first program was Eddie Cantor.

2339. Radio news program sponsored by a cooperative of commercial advertisers was broadcast in November 1937 by Fulton Lewis, Jr., from station WOL, Washington, DC, under the direction of William B. Dolph. Individual sponsors in different cities bore the expenses on a cooperative basis.

2340. Radio advertising contract for FM broadcasts was signed on December 9, 1940, by the Longines Watch Company and provided for the broadcasting of Longines time signals by W2XOR, New York, for 26 weeks beginning on January 1, 1941. FM stands for "frequency modulation."

2341. Television commercial that was sanctioned by the Federal Communications Commission and legally broadcast on a commercial station was aired on July 1, 1941, by WNBT, the National Broadcasting Company affiliate in New York City. During a break in a game between the Dodgers and the Phillies at Ebbets Field in Brooklyn, New York City, the camera focused in on a ticking Bulova watch while an announcer read the time. The Bulova Watch Company was billed $9 for the airtime and station charges. Advertisements not sanctioned by the FCC had been appearing on noncommercial stations for at least a decade.

2342. Department store sales demonstrations using television on a large scale were staged at Gimbel Brothers, Philadelphia, PA, from October 24 to November 14, 1945, with RCA-Victor equipment. Approximately 25,000 people viewed the demonstrations at the auditorium and at 20 television sites placed at strategic locations on the seven floors of the department store. There were 11 daily demonstrations lasting about 10 minutes and showing millinery, home furnishings, shoes, scarves, furs, nursery furniture, toys, curtains, interior decorating, and hair styling.

2343. Movie trailer to be shown on television appeared on September 20, 1946, on WNBT-TV, New York City. It advertised a Columbia Pictures film, *The Jolson Story.*

2344. Television show to be sponsored by a commercial advertiser was "Geographically Speaking," sponsored by the Bristol-Myers Company and broadcast on October 27, 1946, on WNBT, New York, and WPTZ, Philadelphia. The first in color was Colgate Palmolive's *Colgate Comedy Hour,* telecast on November 22, 1953, from the Colonial Theater, New York City, by WNBT-TV, New York City, on the NBC network from 8 to 9 P.M. It starred Donald O'Connor, Corinne Calvet, Ralph Bellamy, Dorothy Dandridge, and Sidney Miller.

2345. Newspaper advertisement that looked three-dimensional was published on June 12, 1953, in the *Daily Freeman,* Waukesha, WI. A decorating company, Hale-Frame Associates, used a full page to advertise carpets. A cardboard cutout with red and blue lenses with which to view the three-dimensional effect was supplied with the newspaper.

2346. Television commercial in color to appear on a local show was commissioned on March 9, 1954, by Castro Decorators, New York City, in a contract with WNBT-TV, New York City, for spot announcements. The first telecast was on August 6, 1954.

2347. Newspaper advertisement printed on aluminum foil appeared in the *Milwaukee Sentinel,* Milwaukee, WI, on March 18, 1958. It was a lamination of Reynolds aluminum foil on one side and paper on the other. The foil side was printed in seven colors at the gravure plant of the Reynolds Metal Company in St. Louis, MO, while the paper side was printed by the *Sentinel* in one color and black.

2348. Advertisement on a space vehicle was carried in 1993 on the side of the Conestoga rocket that launched the Commercial Experiment Transporter (COMET), the first private space mission. COMET and the Conestoga booster were built and managed entirely by a consortium of commercial companies, with partial funding by the National Aeronautics and Space Administration. The ad was for *The Last Action Hero,* an action film starring Arnold Schwarzenegger and released by Columbia Pictures. The ad space was sold by Michael F. Lawson of Space Marketing in Atlanta, GA, the first company to specialize in space-based promotion. Russian space vehicles had already been carrying advertisements for four years.

COMMERCE—ADVERTISING—SIGNS

2349. Electric sign of large dimensions was designed and constructed by the Edison General Electric Company and installed in June 1892 on the wall of a nine-story building near Broadway and 23rd Street, New York City. The sign occupied a surface area 60 by 68 feet and was composed of 107 galvanized iron boxes varying in height from 3 to 6 feet. The front of each box was cut out to form the desired letter. Inside the boxes were 1,457 16-candlepower Edison bulbs in red, blue, green, and frosted white. The sign read: "BUY HOMES ON / LONG ISLAND / SWEPT BY OCEAN BREEZES / MANHATTAN BEACH / ORIENTAL HOTEL / MANHATTAN HOTEL / GILMORE'S BAND / BROCK'S FIREWORKS." Current was supplied by the Edison Electric Illuminating Company. The sign was illuminated from dusk to 11 P.M. One line went on at a time until all the lights were on, then all the lights went out and the cycle began again.

2350. Neon advertising sign was installed on a marquee at the Cosmopolitan Theatre, 59th Street and Columbus Circle, New York City, in July 1923. This sign advertised the theatrical production *Little Old New York,* in which Marion Davies played the leading role. A patent on this tube was granted to George Claude of Paris on January 19, 1915.

2351. Electric flashing sign installed was the Motogram, placed in service on the four sides of the *New York Times* building, New York City, on November 6, 1928, when election returns were flashed. The system was invented by Francis E.J. Wilde of Meadowmere Park, NY, who obtained a patent on May 3, 1927, on an "electric sign control" designed "to permit changing of sign without interruption." It was installed by the Motorgram Corporation, New York City, and was 360 feet long and 5 feet high. It had 14,800 lamps, 88,000 soldered connections, 1,386,000 feet of wire, and 39,000 contact brushes that created 21,925,664 lamp flashes an hour.

2352. Electric sign showing an animated cartoon was displayed April 28, 1937, by Douglas Leigh on the front of a building on Broadway, New York City. It contained 2,000 bulbs and presented a four-minute show depicting, among other things, a cavorting horse and ball-tossing cats.

COMMERCE—ARBITRATION

2353. Arbitration law enacted by a colony was "an act for the more easy and effectually finishing of controversies by arbitration," passed at the legislative session held from October 11 to November 2, 1753, in New Haven, CT. Three arbitrators were appointed, one by each side and one by the court. The court was granted power to levy and collect the awards.

2354. Arbitration tribunal was established by the Chamber of Commerce, New York City, on May 3, 1768, and consisted of seven members. It was charged with adjusting "any differences between parties agreeing to leave such disputes to this Chamber." A different committee was appointed for each meeting.

2355. Arbitration law enacted by a state was passed on December 15, 1778, by the General Assembly of Maryland, in Annapolis, which ruled that "it shall be lawful to and for such court to give judgment upon the award of the person or persons to whom such submission and reference shall be made."

2356. Arbitration law enacted by Congress was "an act to make valid and enforceable written provisions or agreements for arbitration of disputes arising out of contracts, maritime transactions or commerce among the States or Territories or with foreign nations," approved on February 12, 1925.

COMMERCE—BUSINESS EQUIPMENT

2357. Fireproof safe worthy of the name was the Salamander Safe, invented by Charles A. Gayler of New York City, who obtained a patent on April 12, 1833, on a "fire-proof iron chest." It consisted of two chests, one within the other, with a space between to "inclose air or any non-conductors of heat."

2358. Annunciator was invented by Seth Fuller of Boston, MA, who obtained a patent on December 26, 1833. It was installed at the Tremont House hotel, Boston, MA, and was known as "hanging bells." There were 140 bells, which occupied a space 57 feet long, 6 feet high, and 1 foot deep. A small hammer hitting a gong caused the sound and vibrated a card showing a number corresponding with the room number. Each bell was in a glass-enclosed box. The annunciator was placed in operation when the hotel opened on October 16, 1829.

2359. Safe deposit vault was opened on June 5, 1865, by the Safe Deposit Company of New York, 140–146 Broadway, New York City. Four vaults were located on the ground floor of the building and were constantly guarded. One of the vaults was devoted exclusively to the reception of deposits of valuable articles, for which the rates ranged from $1.50 to $2.50 per year for every $1,000 represented. The three other vaults contained individual safe deposit vaults, which cost from $30 to $40 annually. Each subscriber was provided with an individual key to open his vault box.

2360. Cash carrier system was invented by David Brown of Lebanon, NJ, who obtained a patent on July 13, 1875, on "an apparatus for transmission of goods, packages, etc." It had a wire rail with endless rope pulleys. William Stickney Lamson installed it in his ladies' furnishing store in Lowell, MA, in February 1879. By means of two overhead wires, a small basket was conveyed from the salesman to the cashier. In the spring of 1881, he organized the Lamson Consolidated Store Service Company to manufacture these carriers for others, and in January 1882 he incorporated the Lamson Cash Railway Company.

2361. Stenotype device for printing a legible text in the English alphabet at a high reporting speed was invented by John Celinergos Zachos of New York City, who received a patent on April 11, 1876, on a "typewriter and phonotypic notation." The type was fixed on eighteen shuttle bars, several of which might be simultaneously placed in position. The impression was given by a plunger common to all the bars.

2362. Electric turnstile with a rachet was used at the Philadelphia Centennial, Philadelphia, PA, which opened on May 10, 1876. The attendant released the brake by foot pressure to allow visitors to enter. The number of turns was registered on a machine in the central office.

2363. Cash register was invented in 1879 by James J. Ritty, a businessman from Dayton, OH, who while on a trip to Europe observed the workings of a recording device on the steamship that marked the revolutions of the ship's propeller and gave the officers an accurate daily record of the speed of the boat. Back in the United States, he invented a machine for registering receipts of cash and totaling them. It was not accurate, but the following year, 1880, he produced a machine that gave some evidence of being practical. In 1884 the National Cash Register Company took over the business.

2364. Electric tabulating machine was invented by Dr. Herman Hollerith of New York City, who received a patent on January 8, 1889, on a system of recording separate statistical items by means of holes, or combinations of holes, punched in cards, and then counting or tallying such statistical items either separately or in combination by means of electrical counters operated by electromagnets, the circuits being controlled by the perforated cards. The first extensive use of the electric tabulating system was in the compilation of the statistics of population for the 11th federal census, in 1890.

2365. Addressograph was invented in 1892 by Joseph Smith Duncan of Sioux City, IA. The first model consisted of a hexagonal wood block upon which was glued rubber type torn from rubber stamps. The block revolved, advancing a new name and address to the printing point and inking the type simultaneously at each operation. This model was never marketed. The model "Baby 'O'" was put into production on July 26, 1893, in a small back room in the old Caxton Building on Dearborn Street, Chicago, IL.

2366. Public locker plant was established in 1903 by A.G. Eames of the Chico Ice and Cold Storage Company, Chico, CA. Individual lockers, each with a lock and key, were rented to the public. The company was purchased in 1913 by the Union Ice Company of San Francisco, CA.

2367. Multigraph was invented by Harry Christian Gammeter of Cleveland, OH, who obtained a patent on March 10, 1903, on a "duplicating machine." It was the first successful machine designed to simplify the printing processes, so that the ordinary layman could print from type, either with ribbon or with ink. Commercial manufacture was undertaken on December 12, 1902, by the American Multigraph Sales Company, Cleveland, OH.

2368. Punchboards were manufactured by Charles A. Brewer and Sons, Chicago, IL. They were patented on January 17, 1905, as "vending devices" by Charles A. Brewer and Clinton G. Scannell of Chicago.

2369. Coin-operated locker was invented by Willis S. Farnsworth of Petaluma, CA, who received a patent on March 7, 1911, which he assigned to the Coin Controlled Lock Company. He also secured a patent jointly with William H. Reed on a coin receptacle "magazine-hinge and conveyor" on the same date. The insertion of a coin in a slot released a key to open and close the locker.

2370. Photographic copying machine was known by the trade name Photostat and was commercially manufactured in 1910 by the Eastman Kodak Company, Rochester, NY, under the supervision of John S. Greene of the Photostat Corporation. It photographed the subject to be copied directly upon a roll of sensitized paper and eliminated the necessity for the use of any glass plate or film negative. It was capable of making a print 11.5 by 14 inches. The process was not new, but was simplified.

2371. Shopping cart was the invention of Sylvan N. Goldman, the owner of the Standard Food Stores chain of Oklahoma City, OK. Seeking a way to make it easier for consumers to buy larger quantities of goods, Goldman got the idea for a folding basket on wheels after seeing a pair of folding chairs atop a wheeled dolly. After several months of tinkering, he introduced the finished design into his stores in June 1937.

2372. Copy made by xerography was made by Chester Floyd Carlson, a research physicist from New York City. Xerography is the process of making dry paper copies based on principles of photoconductivity and electrostatics. While doing some work in the patent office for P.R. Mallory and Company, an electronics firm, Carlson saw the need for a high-volume copying process that was more economical and easier to handle than photostats and carbon copies. On October 22, 1938, in Astoria, Queens, New York City, Carlson made the first electrophotographic image on wax paper pressed against an electrostatically charged, sulfur-coated zinc plate dusted with fine dark powder. The image consisted of the message "10-22-38 Astoria." Carlson patented the process, which he called xerography, on October 6, 1942.

2373. Bar code scanner was invented by Bernard Silver and N.J. Woodland, who in 1949 filed a patent application entitled "Classifying Apparatus and Method." It described techniques for creating machine-readable product identification codes. The first bar code scanner in commercial use was installed by Sylvania General Telephone on the Boston and Maine Railroad in 1961. The unit read red, white, blue, and black bars that identified gravel train cars and commuter cars. The first scanner used in a retail store was installed in a Kroger supermarket in Cincinnati, OH, in 1967.

COMMERCE—BUSINESS EQUIPMENT—
continued

2374. Copy machine that was commercially successfully was the Model 914, introduced in 1950 by the Haloid Company of Rochester, NY. An earlier Haloid copier, the Model A, was too slow and complicated to be successful. In 1961, Haloid changed its name to the Xerox Corporation.

COMMERCE—BUSINESS EQUIPMENT—
　ADDING MACHINES

2375. Adding machine to employ depressible keys was made by Du Bois D. Parmelee of New Paltz, NY, who received a patent for it on February 5, 1850. He called his machine a "calculator." It was neither practical nor widely used.

2376. Adding machine to print totals and subtotals was made in 1872 by Edmund D. Barbour of Boston, MA. His machine, which was called a "calculating machine," was not practical.

2377. Adding machine absolutely accurate at all times was the "Comptometer," which was invented by Dorr Eugene Felt of Chicago, IL, in November 1884. Felt entered into partnership with Robert Tarrant to produce the machine. Until 1902, this machine was the only multiple-order key-driven calculator on the market.

2378. Adding machine successfully marketed was invented by William Seward Burroughs of St. Louis, MO. In January 1886 he incorporated his business as the American Arithmometer Corporation of St. Louis, MO, with an authorized capitalization of $100,000. This company was acquired on January 16, 1905, by the Burroughs Adding Machine Company, organized under the laws of Michigan with a capital stock of $5 million.

COMMERCE—BUSINESS EQUIPMENT—
　SCALES

2379. Platform scale was built in St. Johnsbury, VT, in 1830 by Thaddeus Fairbanks. It was patented on June 30, 1831, by Erastus and Thaddeus Fairbanks. Previously, even-balance and steelyard types of scales had been used.

2380. Automatic computing pendulum scale was invented by Allen De Vilbiss, Jr., of Toledo, OH, who received a patent on the fan-type automatic computing scale on May 22, 1900. In 1899 he organized the De Vilbiss Scale Company, which later developed into the Toledo Scale Company. This company was the first to produce an adjustable automatic indicator controller for bringing the hand to a quick stop. It was also the first to produce a commercially successful computing scale of the gravity type; first to invent a cylinder platform scale to replace the hanging cylinder scale; first to produce a commercially successful automatic-dial portable scale; first to produce auto truck scales with lever pivots all on the same plane, to permit the use of a shallow pit; first to produce a double-pendulum counterbalance with a floating fulcrum; first to produce a built-in automatic electric lighting system with a ribbon switch that did not hold the scale off zero; and first to produce a device for locking the pendulum and tare beam lever for safety in loading the scale.

COMMERCE—BUSINESS EQUIPMENT—
　TIME RECORDERS

2381. Key time recorder was invented by Willard L. Bundy of Auburn, NY, who obtained a patent on November 20, 1888. A key bearing the workman's number was inserted in the mechanism, which printed both the number and the time on a paper tape. Bundy formed the Bundy Manufacturing Company, which later became a division of IBM Corporation.

2382. Dial time recorder was invented in 1888 by Dr. Alexander Dey of Glasgow, Scotland, who obtained a U.S. patent on September 24, 1889. Numbers assigned to the various employees appeared around the circumference of a large ring on the front of the machine. A pivoted pointer arm was pressed into a guide hole, which caused the machine to print the time opposite the number on a prepared sheet. In 1893, Alexander Dey formed the Dey Patents Company of Syracuse, NY, along with his two brothers, John and Robert, who operated a department store in Syracuse. The company later changed its name to the Dey Time Register Company.

2383. Card time recorder was invented by Daniel M. Cooper of Rochester, NY, who received a patent on October 30, 1894. The employee pressed a lever on the machine to record the time on specially printed cards divided by horizontal lines into seven equal spaces for the days of the week. The recorder, known as the Rochester, was manufactured by the Willard and Frick Manufacturing Company.

COMMERCE—BUSINESS EQUIPMENT—TYPEWRITERS

2384. Typewriter was patented on July 23, 1829, by William Austin Burt of Mount Vernon, MI, who received a patent on his invention of a "typographer." The first letter written on the machine was sent by John P. Sheldon, editor of the *Michigan Gazette,* Detroit, MI, to Martin Van Buren, secretary of state, on May 25, 1829.

2385. Typewriter that was practical was invented in 1867 by Christopher Latham Sholes, who also coined the word "type-writer." The machine was patented on June 23, 1868, and was known commercially as The Type-Writer. This machine had a movable carriage, a lever for turning paper from line to line, and a converging type bar. The keyboard, similar to that of a piano, had two rows of black walnut keys with letters painted in white. The machine had all the letters in capitals, figures from 2 to 9, a comma, and a period. It was manufactured by E. Remington and Sons of Ilion, NY, under contract dated March 1, 1873. The first machine was completed on September 12, 1873. A few years later, the firm sold its typewriter business to Wyckoff, Seamans and Benedict, who afterward organized the Remington Typewriter Company.

2386. Typewriter ribbon was patented on September 14, 1886, by George K. Anderson of Memphis, TN.

2387. Portable typewriter was the Blickensderfer, which was patented on April 12, 1892, by George C. Blickensderfer of Stamford, CT.

2388. Typewriter to produce a line of writing visible as it was being typed was invented by Herman L. Wagner of Brooklyn, NY (now part of New York City), who obtained a patent on it on May 16, 1893. This machine went through an experimental period with the Wagner Typewriter Company and then was sold to John T. Underwood, who had been associated with Wagner's father in the ribbon and carbon business of John Underwood and Company. The Underwood Typewriter Company, incorporated in March 1895, undertook the manufacture of Wagner's machine in New York City.

2389. Correction fluid for typewriters was Liquid Paper, invented in 1951 by Bette Nesmith Graham, an executive secretary at the Texas Bank and Trust Company in Dallas, TX, who saved erasing time by applying a dab of white tempera waterbase paint over her typing mistakes. Her bottled version of the paint was originally called "Mistake Out." Changes to the formula made it quick-drying and virtually invisible.

2390. Electric portable typewriter was manufactured by Smith-Corona, Syracuse, NY. It was announced on October 9, 1956, and placed on sale on February 4, 1957. It weighed about 19 pounds and retailed at $190.

2391. Typewriter without type arms was the Selectric typewriter, introduced in 1961 by International Business Machines, Armonk, NY. Designed by Eliot Fette Noyes, it utilized an interchangeable element about the same size and shape as a golf ball with an entire font of type embossed on its surface. The ball moved parallel to a stationary platen and oriented itself to hit the ribbon with each letter typed. The Selectric was faster and less likely to jam than conventional electric typewriters with type arms.

2392. Typewriter that could retype text automatically was an adaptation of the Selectric typewriter. In 1964, the IBM Corporation, Armonk, NY, began selling a magnetic tape recorder and controller device that attached to certain Selectric models. The device recorded each keystroke of the typist. When played back, the tape caused the Selectric to retype the text automatically. It was the first crude word processor. The combined unit cost $10,000.

COMMERCE—BUSINESS EQUIPMENT—VENDING MACHINES

2393. Vending machine that dispensed liquid automatically was patented on December 16, 1884, by William Henry Fruen of Minneapolis, MN. When a coin was inserted in the slot, a uniform supply of liquid was released from a reservoir.

2394. Vending machine to dispense postage stamps was manufactured in 1892 by the United States Postage Stamp Delivery Company, Boston, MA, of which Carroll Davidson Wright was president. It was a quartered-oak case 20 inches high, 9.75 inches wide, and 5.4 inches deep. Upon insertion of a nickel, it delivered a capsule containing four cents' worth of stamps and a coupon that could be redeemed for merchandise from advertisers.

COMMERCE—BUSINESS EQUIPMENT—
VENDING MACHINES—*continued*

2395. Vending machine to operate automatically without the aid of plungers or indicators was produced by the Pulver Company, Rochester, NY, in 1897. The machine dispensed gum for a penny a package.

2396. Vending machine to sell food from bulk was the Automatic Clerk, a wooden cabinet six feet high, which dispensed hot peanuts in bags. The machine was equipped with a heater and a weighing device. It was invented in 1897 by T.S. Wheatcraft of Rush, PA.

2397. Vending machine law enacted by a city was approved by Omaha, NE, on May 10, 1898, by Mayor Frank Edward Moores. The law made all vending machines subject to a $5 permit fee.

2398. Valeteria for pressing and storing clothes was made by the United States Hoffman Machinery Corporation and displayed on September 19, 1951, in the lobby of the Bulkley Building, Cleveland, OH. The device had a control unit equipped with a telephone and a series of lockers in which garments could be hung. It was designed to open doors, accept payments, and give correct change without any manual aid. It was based on an invention of Ross L. Timms of Akron, OH.

2399. Newspaper vending machine to deliver a single copy with the insertion of the proper coins was the NewsVend, manufactured by the United Sound and Signal Company, Columbia, PA, and leased on March 20, 1954, to the *Chicago Tribune,* the *New York Journal American,* the *New York Mirror,* the *Philadelphia Bulletin,* and the *Washington Times-Herald.* It had 30 compartments, each capable of holding any size paper or magazine up to 300 pages, and was available in any coin combination, returning pennies or nickels in change when required. All newspaper vending machines prior to this time had a mechanism that unlocked a single compartment, allowing dishonest customers to remove more than one copy.

2400. Vending machine to dispense fresh flowers was placed in the Grand Central Terminal, New York City, on October 20, 1961, by the Automated Flowers Company, Greenwich, CT. It was six feet high, three feet wide, and two feet deep. The machine, which was manufactured by Wittenborg of Denmark, was a self-contained refrigerated unit that required no plumbing.

2401. Vending machine for art was the Vend'art machine, invented by Ona Linquist. Linquist reconditioned ice cream vending machines from the 1950s and filled them with inexpensive original artworks commissioned from working artists. The first Vend'art machine was installed in a Greenwich Village movie theater in New York City in 1985.

COMMERCE—CORPORATIONS

2402. Commercial corporation was the New York Fishing Company, which was chartered on January 8, 1675, by the Governor and Council of New York, acting for the Duke of York "for settleing a fishery in these parts." Shares of the capital stock were £10 each.

2403. Corporate body chartered by a special act of Congress was the President, Directors and Company of the Bank of the United States, chartered on February 25, 1791, by the First Congress, in session in New York City.

2404. Holding companies authorized by a state were authorized by New Jersey in a law passed on April 4, 1888. It provided that it was "lawful for any corporation of this state, or of any other state, doing business in this state and authorized by law to own and hold shares of stocks and bonds of corporations of other states, to own and hold and dispose thereof in the same manner and with all the rights, powers and privileges of individual owners of shares of the capital stock and bonds or other evidences of indebtedness of corporations of this state."

2405. Corporation with a capitalization of $1 billion was the United States Steel Corporation. It was incorporated on February 25, 1901, and was ready for business on April 1, 1901, with an authorized capitalization of $1.4 billion. The original member companies were the Carnegie Company, Federal Steel Company, National Steel Company, National Tube Company, American Steel and Wire Company of New Jersey, American Tin Plate Company, American Steel Hoop Company, American Sheet Steel Company, Lake Superior Consolidated Iron Mines, and American Bridge Company. The first president was Charles M. Schwab.

2406. Corporation with a net income of more than $1 billion in one year was the General Motors Corporation, Detroit, MI, whose net income in 1955 was $1,189,477,082 (9.6 percent of net sales amounting to $12,443,277,420). It exceeded $1.5 billion in 1963, with a net income of $1,591,823,085 (9.7 percent of net sales of $16,494,818,184). In 1965, net income exceeded $2 billion, with the corporation reporting a net income of $2,125,606,400 (10.3 percent of net sales of $20,733,982,295).

2407. Fortune 1000 company to be owned and chaired by a woman was the Warnaco Group of New York City, a company specializing in women's apparel. Linda Wachner headed a $480 million leveraged buyout of Warnaco in 1986 and proceeded to turn it into one of the most profitable companies in the industry.

COMMERCE—EXPOSITIONS

2408. Manufacturers' fair was held in the Masonic Hall, New York City, on October 24, 1828, under the auspices of the American Institute in the City of New York. The institute was incorporated on May 2, 1829, to encourage and promote domestic industry in the United States in agriculture, commerce, manufacturing, and the arts.

2409. World's fair was held in New York City in 1853, modeled after the 1851 World's Fair held in London. The exposition, sponsored by the Association for the Exhibition of the Industry of All Nations, was held at Reservoir Square, in a specially erected two-story building with an area of 249,691 square feet that occupied the space from 40th Street to 42nd Street and between Fifth and Sixth avenues. The exposition was opened by President Franklin Pierce on July 14, 1853. Admission was 50 cents for a single ticket, $2.50 monthly, $10 per person; children under 12 were admitted for 25 cents each. The building was destroyed by fire on October 5, 1858.

2410. Centennial exhibition was the International Exhibition, which occupied 236 acres in Fairmount Park, Philadelphia, PA. It opened on May 10, 1876, and was host to 76,172 cash customers and 110,500 free customers. It closed on November 10, 1876. It attracted 60,000 exhibitors and 9,010,916 visitors.

2411. Electrical show was held in Philadelphia, PA, from September 2 to October 11, 1884, and was known as the Electrical Exhibition and National Conference of Electricians. It was sponsored by the Franklin Institute, and was held in the Pennsylvania Railroad Station, 32nd and Market streets. There were 216 exhibitors and 282,779 paid admissions.

2412. Advertising show to be held annually took place May 3–9, 1906, in Madison Square Garden, New York City. Its slogan was "If your business isn't with advertising, advertise it for sale."

2413. Women's World Fair was held in Chicago, IL, April 18–25, 1925, to demonstrate women's progress in 70 industries. At the Chicago World's Fair of 1893, women's handicrafts had been featured only at the sewing exhibit. The Women's World Fair was officially opened by Grace Coolidge, the wife of President Calvin Coolidge.

2414. Fashion show to be shown on television took place on May 17, 1939, at the Ritz-Carlton Hotel, New York City. Renee Macready was the fashion coordinator. It was shown on WNBT-TV, New York City, in cooperation with the Swiss Fabric Group and the Ostrich Feather Group.

2415. World's Fair that was financially successful was the Century 21 Exposition, held from April 21 to October 21, 1962, in Seattle, WA. It was opened by remote control by President John Fitzgerald Kennedy in conjunction with a speech he transmitted by telephone from Palm Beach, FL. The fair paid for its entire operating expenses, had a surplus of about a million dollars, and left a number of very valuable buildings and improvements on the site of the present Seattle Center.

COMMERCE—FISHING AND WHALING

2416. Commercial fishery is believed to have been established at Medford, MA. On April 17, 1629, the colonists were given instructions to let the fish "be well saved with the said salt, and packed up in hogsheads; and send it home by the 'Talbot' or 'Lion's Whelpe.'" The industry flourished and on May 28, 1639, received "salt, lines, hooks, knives, boots, etc., for the fishermen." Fishing had also been attempted elsewhere by the first colonists.

2417. Whaling industry established by a city was organized on March 7, 1644, by Southampton, NY, a town on the coast of Long Island where whales were often cast ashore. The town was divided into four wards of 11 persons each to attend to the whales. Two persons from each ward were employed to cut them up so that each inhabitant obtained an equal portion. A whaling franchise was granted to a Mr. Whiting in 1647 for the waters of Long Island Sound between Stonington, CT, and Montauk Point, NY.

COMMERCE—FISHING AND WHALING—*continued*

2418. Sperm whale captured at sea was captured in 1711 by a whaling vessel out of Nantucket, MA. This was the beginning of an industry that numbered over 700 vessels by 1846.

2419. Whaling expedition on record set sail from Nantucket, MA, about 1715. Six sloops, of 30 to 40 tons burden each, returned with cargoes amounting to 600 barrels of oil and 11,000 pounds of bone, the total value of which was £1,100 sterling. There were whaling trips by single boats prior to this expedition.

2420. Ship sunk by a whale was the whaler *Essex,* which sailed from Nantucket, MA, on August 12, 1819, headed for the whaling grounds off the coast of Chile. According to the account of first mate Owen Chase, on November 20, 1820, the *Essex* was hunting sperm whales at latitude 0 degrees 40 minutes S, longitude 119 degrees W, when an enraged bull whale rammed the ship twice and capsized it. The crew escaped in open boats, but only five of them survived the 4,500-mile journey to Peru, which took 83 days. The story of the *Essex* was one of the inspirations for Herman Melville's novel *Moby-Dick.*

COMMERCE—HOTELS

2421. Building built to serve as a hotel was the City Hotel, with 70 rooms, opened in 1794 on Broadway, just below Wall Street, New York City.

2422. Hotel recognized as a modern first-class hotel was the Tremont House in Boston, MA, which celebrated its opening with an elaborate dinner on October 16, 1829. It covered 12,839 square feet and contained 170 rooms. The rate was $2 a day, including four meals. Travelers were permitted to rent a single private room instead of having to double up with strangers. Other innovations at the Tremont House were a key for each room, a washbowl, a pitcher, a free cake of soap for every guest, and gaslights. In addition, the Tremont was the first hotel outfitted with plumbing, including indoor bathrooms and toilets. It had eight "privies" and eight bathing rooms in the basement, to which there was a separate entrance. The kitchen and laundry had cold running water. Each of the two cisterns in the attic contained three hogsheads of rainwater, one for the baths and the other for various outlets. The plumbers were Thomas Philpott and Thomas Pollard. The cornerstone of the hotel was laid July 4, 1828, by Samuel Turell Armstrong, president of the Massachusetts Charitable Mechanic Association.

2423. Hotel with safe deposit boxes was the New England Hotel, Boston, MA. In 1866, Lambert Maynard, the manager, purchased a Salamander safe in which he installed compartments with individual locks.

2424. Hotel that was fireproof was the Palmer House, Chicago, IL, opened in November 1873 by Potter Palmer. The building cost approximately $2 million, the land $1 million, and the furnishings $500,000. It replaced the Palmer House that had been destroyed by fire on October 8, 1871, a year after it opened.

2425. Hotel for women was the Women's Hotel, New York City, founded by Alexander Turney Stewart and inspected by 20,000 visitors on its opening day, April 2, 1878. It was a nine-story building of brick, iron, and stone built around a courtyard, 197 feet by 205 feet in area and 155 feet high, with five steam elevators. Guests could choose from among 115 large rooms at $12 a week, 34 medium-sized rooms at $10, and 354 small rooms at $7 a week, board included. The main dining room accommodated 600 diners and also supplied meals to be taken out. Breakfast was 35 cents, lunch 25 cents, dinner 50 cents. There were 250 servants. The cost of the hotel was $3.7 million. Any profit was to be used to reduce the rates and any deficit was covered by a fund. On June 8, 1878, it became a commercial hotel accommodating both sexes.

2426. Hotel to install electric lights was the Prospect House, Blue Mountain Lake, NY. In 1881 the electricity was installed, but the lights were not entirely dependable. On October 12, 1882, the Duke of Veranga and his party arrived after dark to celebrate Columbus Day. As they were shown to their rooms the lights went out, but after a slight delay the lights went on again. The hotel was owned by Howard M. Durant and operated by George Tunnicliffe. The name was later changed to the Eutowana.

2427. Hotel transported from one location to another was the Brighton Beach Hotel, Brooklyn, NY (now part of New York City), which was moved 600 feet inland, the operation taking place from April 3 to July 29, 1888. The hotel was jacked up on railroad cars on 24 parallel tracks and moved by six locomotives in two teams of three each. The building, which was 500 feet long and weighed 6,000 tons, was moved 124 feet the first day.

2428. Hotel with individually controlled air conditioning and heating in every room was the St. Regis Hotel, New York City, opened on September 4, 1904. Six dynamos operated six metallic fans, each seven feet in diameter. The building cost approximately $4 million, $5.5 million when equipped.

2429. Motel was the Motel Inn, built in 1924 on Neil Cook's property on the north side of San Luis Obispo, CA, and opened on December 12, 1925. Arthur S. Heineman was the architect. The building featured a sign with flashing lights that alternated the letters *H* and *M* preceding the letters *otel* to spell out "Hotel" and "Motel." It had accommodations for 160 guests in individual chalets with garage, bathroom, and telephone.

2430. Hotel to install radio reception with two selective channels was Hotel Statler of Boston, MA, which on May 10, 1927, broadcast programs free to guests from a central control room. Thirteen hundred rooms were originally equipped with individual headsets. Later, loudspeakers were placed in the rooms.

2431. Hotel at an airport was the Oakland Airport Inn, in Oakland, CA, built by the Board of Port Commissioners. It was opened on July 15, 1929, and operated by the Interstate Company.

2432. Holiday Inn was opened in 1952 on U.S. Highway 70 in Memphis, TN. The owner was Kemmons Wilson. It was the first motel with all the major features of a modern motel chain: a swimming pool, air conditioning and television in every room, free ice, and no charge for children under 12.

2433. Hotel to establish a heliport was the Western Hills Hotel, Fort Worth, TX. The heliport, 150 feet by 190 feet, surfaced with asphalt paving, was formally opened on May 20, 1953. It was privately owned but was intended for public use and was licensed by the city of Fort Worth on May 20, 1953, and approved by the Civil Aeronautics Administration. It was built by the E.M. Moore Construction Company, Fort Worth.

2434. Hotel built over a pier was the Flagship Hotel, Galveston, TX, opened on June 30, 1965. The hotel, containing 240 rooms, was built on a pier 1,500 feet long and 340 feet wide, extending into the Gulf of Mexico.

2435. Horse motel was opened on June 10, 1967, by Wayne Biggs at Marshfield, MO. It was 100 feet long and 89 feet wide, with an addition of 24 by 48 feet on the back side. The price was $7 a night with feed and care, or $5 for lodging. About 40 horses could be accommodated in one night.

2436. Dog hotel was the Kennelworth, opened on November 12, 1975, in New York City by Leo Wiener. The 116 air-conditioned rooms had different color schemes and were built around a circular court. They measured 28, 37, and 55 feet square and rented for $10, $12, and $14 a day, respectively. Proof of distemper and rabies shots was required.

2437. Undersea hotel was Jules' Undersea Lodge, located at the bottom of 30-foot-deep Bora Bora Lagoon off Key Largo, FL. The hotel was opened in 1987 by Gary Gerberg, who renovated a former marine research station into a luxury hotel for up to six people. For $195 to $295 a night, guests could stay in an 8- by- 10-foot bedroom complete with a refrigerator, television, VCR, and compact-disc player. Each room also had a 42-inch porthole for viewing marine life. The hotel had its own air supply. Guests could use special air hoses to go diving without bulky tanks, but standard diving gear was required to get to the hotel from the surface.

COMMERCE—LAUNDRIES

2438. Laundry was established in 1835 by Independence Starks, a manufacturer of Troy, NY, at 66 North Second Street, to wash and press the products of his own factory and of nearby collar makers.

2439. Chinese laundry opened in 1851 in San Francisco, CA. Most of its customers were gold miners. California miners had been sending their dirty clothes to Chinese laundries in Hawaii since the beginning of the Gold Rush in 1849.

2440. Commercial power laundry came into existence in 1851 when the Contra Costa Laundry was established in Leona Heights, Oakland, CA. A 10-horsepower donkey engine bought from a ship captain served as a crude form of washing machine.

2441. Rough-dry laundry service was started by W.M. Barnes in 1892 in Philadelphia, PA, and in 1893 in Pittsburgh, PA.

COMMERCE—LAUNDRIES—continued

2442. Laundromat was installed by J.F. Cantrell in a "washateria" in Fort Worth, TX, on April 18, 1934. Four electric washing machines were rented by the hour to those who wished to do their laundry. Hot water and electricity were supplied, but users were obliged to furnish their own soap.

COMMERCE—MILLIONAIRES

2443. Millionaire with a fortune greater than $100 million was Cornelius Vanderbilt, who was born in Staten Island, NY (now part of New York City), in 1794. As a boy, Vanderbilt worked on a ferry in New York harbor, and later entered the steamboat and shipping business. His strategy of cutting rates below those of his competitors earned him $20 million by 1860. He followed the same practice after entering the railroad business in 1865 and within two years gained control of the New York Central Railroad. At his death in 1877, his estate was valued at more than $100 million.

2444. Millionaire who was an African-American woman was Sarah Breedlove, who, under her married name, Madame C.J. Walker, founded the first successful cosmetics company that catered exclusively to African-American customers. She invented the first hair-straightening tonic and began selling it to African-American women in Denver, CO, in 1906. Within five years, she had opened two factories and expanded her business nationally, using uniformed saleswomen to sell her line of grooming products door-to-door. The company moved to Indianapolis, IN, in 1910.

2445. Billionaire was John Davison Rockefeller, born in 1839 in Richford, NY. In 1863 he established an oil refinery that became the Standard Oil Company of Ohio. Rockefeller bought out most of his competitors and came to dominate the U.S. oil-refining industry. In 1899 he consolidated his companies into the Standard Oil Company of New Jersey, which became the target of a celebrated antitrust lawsuit by the federal government in 1911. Rockefeller retired in 1911 with a fortune estimated at well over a billion dollars.

COMMERCE—ORGANIZATIONS

2446. Chamber of Commerce was incorporated on March 13, 1770, under a royal charter from King George III. Its motto was *Non nobis nate solum* ("not born for ourselves alone"). The Chamber of Commerce of the United States was founded in 1912 by approximately 500 representatives of commercial organizations, trade associations, and individual establishments, who were invited to participate in a series of discussions by President William Howard Taft and Secretary of Commerce and Labor Charles Nagel. The headquarters of the Chamber of Commerce of the United States was dedicated on May 20, 1925.

2447. Credit protection group was the Merchants' Vigilance Association, formed in 1842 by importers and commission houses in New York City. The association distributed reports prepared by Sheldon P. Church. William C. Dusenbury, who later formed the Mercantile Agency of Woodward and Dusenbury, was the secretary.

2448. Chamber of commerce established by a state was the New York Chamber of Commerce, formed on April 5, 1868, by 20 merchants at a meeting at Fraunces Tavern, New York City, for "promoting and encouraging commerce, supporting industry, adjusting disputes relative to trade and navigation, and procuring such laws and regulations as may be found necessary for the benefit of trade in general." John Cruger was the first president.

2449. Measurement organization (national) to improve systems of weights and measures was the American Metrological Society, formed on December 30, 1873, at Columbia University, New York City, by Wolcott Gibbs, Frederick Augustus Porter Barnard, and Hubert Anson Newton.

2450. Business organization for African-Americans (national) was the National Negro Business League, founded in Boston, MA, on August 23, 1900, by Booker T. Washington. Four hundred delegates from 34 states attended the founding conference, which promoted the growth of African-American–owned businesses. Washington was elected the first president of the organization.

2451. Rotary Club meeting took place on February 23, 1905, in Chicago, IL. The group's founder was a lawyer, Paul Percy Harris, who invited three friends, a coal dealer, a tailor, and a mining engineer. Meetings were held in each member's place of business in rotation, so that each could obtain some knowledge of the others' businesses. A convention of 16 Rotary clubs met in Chicago in August 1910 to form a national association. An international association was formed in August 1912 in Duluth, MN, to provide charters for Winnipeg, Canada, and London, England. The constitution was revised in June 1922, when Rotary International was adopted as the group's new name.

2452. Advertising association to combat business abuses by advancing truth and fair practice in business was the Vigilance Committee of the Advertising Club of New York, New York City, organized at a meeting called on December 1911 by Lewellyn E. Pratt, program committee chairman.

2453. Junior chamber of commerce was organized on October 13, 1915, as the Young Men's Progressive Civic Association, St. Louis, MO. In 1918, the name was changed to the Junior Chamber of Commerce. On January 21, 1921, delegates from 24 cities assembled in St. Louis to establish the United States Junior Chamber of Commerce. The first national convention was held in St. Louis on June 17–19, 1920. Henry Giessenbier, Jr., was elected president.

COMMERCE—RESTAURANTS

2454. Gourmet restaurant was Delmonico's of New York City, founded by two Swiss-born brothers, Giovanni and Pietro Del-Monico, in 1827. At first the brothers ran a wine, coffee, and chocolate shop on Williams Street in the Battery section of Manhattan. In 1831 they opened a "Restaurant François." By the 1860s, under the direction of Lorenzo Delmonico and principal chef Charles Ranhofer, the restaurant had become a mecca for well-to-do Americans seeking the best food and wine. Unable to thrive under Prohibition, when alcoholic beverages were banned, Delmonico's closed its doors on May 21, 1923.

2455. Chinese restaurant was the Macao and Woosung, opened in 1849 in San Francisco, CA, by Norman Asing, a Chinese-American businessman from Charleston, SC. Most Chinese restaurants of the period identified themselves by flying small yellow flags, as was traditional in China.

2456. Ornamented soda fountain for restaurants was made of white Italian marble and produced in 1858 by Gustavus D. Dows of Lowell, MA. It was adorned with spread eagles perched on the syrup cocks. In 1862, Dows invented the double-stream draft arm and cock, which allowed the choice of a large or small stream. In 1863, Dows embarked on the manufacture of these fountains, which he sold for $225 each. His first patent was obtained on January 25, 1870.

2457. Lunch wagon was introduced in Providence, RI, in 1872 by Walter Scott. He drove a wagon to a location on Westminster Street, where he sold coffee, sandwiches, pies, and cakes. In order to comply with Board of Health regulations and to secure running water, the op-erators of lunch wagons obtained desirable vacant sites where they hooked up to a water supply. Individual wagons were constructed until 1887, when they were commercially manufactured in Providence, RI, by Ruel B. Jones, who also operated a chain of lunch wagons.

2458. Self-service restaurant was opened on September 4, 1885, at 7 New Street, New York City, opposite the New York Stock Exchange. It was called the Exchange Buffet.

2459. Cafeteria was opened in 1895 in Chicago, IL, on Adams Street between Clark and La Salle streets, by Ernest Kimball. In 1899 he moved it to the basement of the New York Life Building, where it was located until 1925.

2460. Penny restaurant where most items were sold for one cent was opened by Bernarr Adolphus Macfadden at 487 Pearl Street, New York City, in the winter of 1900. In 1901 he opened a larger one. He continued opening branches and by 1906 he had 30 in operation. They were known as the Macfadden Physical Culture Restaurants.

2461. Restaurant with an automatic arrangement for vending food was the Automat Restaurant, which was opened by the Horn and Hardart Baking Company at 818 Chestnut Street, Philadelphia, PA, on June 9, 1902. The mechanism, which cost $30,000, was imported from Germany, where the patents were acquired from their Swedish originators. The company then opened a chain of Automat restaurants in cities across the nation, including New York City, where a branch opened in 1912 at 1515 Broadway. These Automats used a different mechanism that was patented and manufactured by Horn and Hardart. Customers were presented with an array of little compartments, each containing a dish of prepared food visible through a glass door. When the customer dropped a nickel in the proper slot, the door popped open, allowing the customer to remove the dish. The compartments were refilled from behind by restaurant workers.

2462. Pizzeria was G. Lombardi, which opened on Spring Street in New York City in 1905 (some give the date as 1895). The first deep-dish, Chicago-style pizza was created in 1943 by Ike Sewell and Ric Riccardo of Pizzeria Uno, Chicago, IL.

2463. Franchise chain was Howard Johnson's. The chain got its start in 1925, when Howard Dearing Johnson, the proprietor of a drugstore in Quincy, MA, began making ice cream with a hand-held crank to sell at the soda fountain. Unable to finance additional restaurants on his

COMMERCE—RESTAURANTS—*continued*

own, he began franchising his name and the formulas for his ice cream and other specialties. The first restaurant to which he granted a franchise, in 1932, was on Cape Cod. Eventually, the chain had 600 restaurants across the country. Johnson's innovations included the use of a central commissary to supply all franchisees with food of consistent quality and the siting of diners along highways.

2464. McDonald's restaurant was opened by Ray Kroc on April 15, 1955, in Des Plaines, IL. The idea for a fast-food restaurant originated with two brothers in the restaurant business, Richard and Maurice McDonald of San Bernardino, CA, who granted a franchise to Kroc, a milkshake-supplies salesman. In 1961, Kroc bought out the brothers for $14 million. By the 1980s, he had built McDonald's into a multi-billion-dollar, multinational burger empire that was widely considered America's most successful modern export. The original drive-up building in Des Plaines was replaced by a modern design that retained the building's golden arch, which became the symbol of the corporation.

2465. Revolving restaurant was The Top of the Needle, located at the 500-foot level of the 600-foot-high steel and glass tower dedicated on May 22, 1961, at the Century 21 Exposition, Seattle, WA. It contained 260 seats and revolved 360 degrees in an hour. Above the restaurant was an observation deck and above that a beacon. It was designed by John Graham and Company.

2466. Singles bar was T.G.I. Fridays, opened on First Avenue in New York City by Alan Stillman on March 15, 1965. It was the first bar specifically intended as a place for unmarried professionals to meet one another.

2467. Cyber cafe was the Electronic Cafe International, founded by video artists Sherrie Rabinowitz and Kit Galloway. It opened in Santa Monica, CA, in 1988 and offered computers with modems and other telecommunications gear for the use of patrons, plus a coffeehouse menu and artistic events. The first kosher cyber cafe, the IDT Megabite Cafe in New York City's diamond district, opened in the spring of 1997.

COMMERCE—SHIPPING

2468. Royal navigation act affecting the American colonies was passed by the English Parliament in 1651. The law allowed a three-year exemption from duty for all merchandise for the English-American plantations, on the condition that no colonial vessel could carry American produce to a foreign port. Except for intercolonial trade, all goods were to be carried in English ships.

2469. Customhouse in colonial America was established in Yorktown, VA. It was built about 1706 by Richard Ambler, who occupied it as "Collector of Ports for Yorktown" in 1720. At this period Yorktown was the port of entry for New York, Philadelphia, and other northern cities. A tombstone in Hampton, VA, badly obliterated but decipherable, reads "Peter Heyman, Collector of his Majesty's custom, died April 29, 1700." He is presumed to have been one of the early collectors of customs at Yorktown.

2470. Embargo act of the Continental Congress was the nonimportation act enacted on October 14, 1774. It stated: "After the first day of December next, there be no importation into British America, from Great Britian or Ireland, of any goods, wares or merchandize whatsoever, or from any other place of any such goods, wares or merchandize."

2471. Drawback legislation enacted by Congress was Sections 3 and 4 of the Tariff Act of July 4, 1789. It provided that dutiable merchandise imported into the United States that was reexported within a year was entitled to a refund of 99 percent of the duty paid. In lieu of a drawback of the duties imposed on the importation of salt employed and expended in the fish industry, an allowance of five cents was granted on the exportation of every quintal of dried fish and on every barrel of pickled fish or salted provision. From August 1, 1789, to December 31, 1790, drawback to the amount of $10,582 was allowed on dried and pickled fish.

2472. Navigation act enacted by Congress was approved on July 20, 1789. It imposed a duty on the tonnage of vessels.

2473. Export report by the federal government covered the fiscal year ending September 30, 1791. The exports for the year amounted to $19 million, of which $18.5 million was for domestic merchandise and $512,041 for foreign goods. The imports for the same period amounted to $29.2 million, an excess of imports over exports of more than $10 million.

2474. Standardization of weights and measures for customs was established by Congress in an act dated March 2, 1799, which required the surveyor of customs of each port to standardize his measures to comply with the customs clause requiring "all duties, imposts, and excises [to] be uniform throughout the United States."

2475. Embargo act enacted by Congress was passed by Congress by a vote of 82–44 and approved by President Thomas Jefferson on December 22, 1807. The act required all American ships to refrain from international commerce. It was repealed on March 1, 1809. A later act substituted a requirement of nonintercourse with Great Britain and France.

2476. Year in which exports exceeded imports was the fiscal year ending September 30, 1811. The difference amounted to an excess of $7.9 million. Exports of domestic merchandise were worth $45.3 million and of foreign merchandise $16 million, making a grand total of exports of $61.3 million. The imports amounted to $53.4 million.

2477. Transatlantic passenger line was the Black Ball Line, which ran regularly scheduled runs from New York City to Liverpool beginning on January 5, 1818, when the 400-ton *James Monroe* left New York Harbor. The line's other original ships were the *Amity,* the *Courier,* and the *Pacific.* The company was founded by New York merchant Isaac Wright and four partners, each of whom put up $25,000 in capital. They promised monthly crossings "on a certain day in every month throughout the year." Before that time, passengers had to book passage on a cargo ship and wait until the hold was full and the ship was ready to sail. During the first nine years, the Black Ball Line averaged 23 days for the transatlantic crossing.

2478. Coastal shipping service was established in 1831 by Thomas Lowery Servoss. He outfitted five packet ships that ran regularly between New York City and New Orleans.

2479. Express delivery service was organized on February 23, 1839, by William Frederick Harnden of Boston, MA, who arranged for delivery service between Boston and New York City. The service was advertised to begin on March 4, 1839. The first shipment was a few suitcases. Shipments were made via the Boston and Providence Railway and Long Island Sound Steamboat.

2480. Warehouse legislation enacted by Congress was passed by Congress on August 6, 1846. This act permitted duty-free storage of imported merchandise in warehouses owned or leased by the federal government, the duty to be paid upon withdrawal of the merchandise within a specified time of not more than one year. Another act, passed on March 28, 1854, extended bonded storage privileges to private warehouses approved by the secretary of the treasury. These warehouses were required to have proper customs officers in charge or to have joint custody with customs officers of all merchandise.

2481. Docks owned by a state were acquired by California by an act approved on April 24, 1863, "an act to provide for the improvement and protection of the wharves, docks and water front in the city and county of San Francisco." Three commissioners, one elected by the state, one elected by the city, and one appointed by the Senate and Assembly at a joint session, formed the Board of State Harbor Commissioners "to construct new wharves, to keep in good repair seawalls, embankments, wharves, piers, landings and thoroughfares for the advancement of commerce."

2482. Year-round railroad shipments of dressed beef were made in 1877 by Gustavus Franklin Swift of Swift and Company, who shipped meat from Chicago, IL, in 10 refrigerated cars built to his own specifications. The beef was hung from racks, and the floor was covered with boxes and cases.

2483. Interstate commerce act enacted by Congress was approved on February 4, 1887, and was popularly known as the Cullom Act. Its principal objects were "to secure just and reasonable charges for [railroad] transportation; to prohibit unjust discrimination in the rendition of like services under similar circumstances and conditions; to prevent undue preferences to persons, corporations or localities; to inhibit greater compensation for shorter than for longer distances over the same lines; and to abolish combinations for the pooling of freights." The act established the Interstate Commerce Commission, which was organized on March 31, 1887.

2484. Intercity trucking service began on October 29, 1904, when William B. Chenoweth placed a six-cylinder motor truck in service between Colorado City, CO, and Snyder, TX.

COMMERCE—SHIPPING—*continued*

2485. Shipment of merchandise by airplane was delivered to the Morehouse-Martens Company of Columbus, OH, by pilot Philip Parmelee. The shipment contained five bolts of Rajah silk manufactured by Rogers and Thompson of New York City and valued at $600. Parmelee took possession of the silk after it arrived in Dayton, OH, and brought it to Columbus in a Wright biplane, landing at the old Columbus Driving Park. The silk was cut up and the pieces were stamped with the legend, "This silk is a piece of the first merchandise ever carried in an airplane—Dayton to Columbus, November 7, 1910." The distance of 60 miles was made in 56 minutes. The delivery was a publicity stunt for which $5,000 was paid. The shipping rate was $71.42 a pound.

2486. Free port was opened on February 1, 1937, at Stapleton, Staten Island, New York City, under authority of a congressional act "to provide for the establishment, operation and maintenance of foreign-trade zones in ports of entry of the United States, to expedite and encourage foreign commerce, and for other purposes," approved on June 18, 1934. The port embraced an 18-acre tract around New York Municipal Piers Nos. 12, 13, 15, and 16, and was operated as a public utility by the Department of Docks, New York City, under the supervision of the Customs Service. Foreign merchandise was admitted in bond without payment of import duties. The first superintendent was John McKenzie.

2487. Containerized shipping was invented by Malcolm McLean of Maxton, NC, the owner of McLean Trucking, a large freight-trucking firm. He developed a large shipping container that could be packed with goods at the factory, hauled by truck to a port facility, carried on specially fitted ships to a port terminal, offloaded from the ship, and hitched directly to trucks or loaded on freight cars for cross-continental transport, all without unpacking the container's contents. McLean's first containership, the *Ideal X*, left the port of Newark, NJ, on April 25, 1956. The first containership facility was the Elizabeth–Port Authority Marine Terminal, operated by the Port of New York Authority. It opened for business on August 15, 1962, when Sea-Land Service's S.S. *Elizabethport* docked in Newark Bay, Elizabeth, NJ, on the south side of the Elizabeth Channel, south of Port Newark. During its first year, the facility handled 1.5 million tons of cargo on 242 vessels and employed 730 people, who earned a total of more than $4 million.

2488. Ship to transport fresh orange juice in stainless-steel tanks was the S.S. *Tropicana*, 8,000 tons, which left Port Canaveral, FL, on February 16, 1957, and arrived on February 19 at Whitestone, NY, 56 hours later. The first shipment was made by Fruit Industries of Bradenton, FL, and consisted of 650,000 gallons.

2489. Airborne express delivery service was Federal Express, founded in 1972 in Memphis, TN, by Frederick W. Smith. With $72 million in financing, Smith purchased eight aircraft and a fleet of trucks to deliver packages overnight to selected locations in the United States. Package deliveries began in April 1973. Federal Express delivered its first letters in 1981.

COMMERCE—STORES

2490. Cooperative store for consumers was organized in 1830 in New York City by William Bryan, treasurer of a cooperative in Brighton, England. He established a store in New York City that sold articles to members at prices generally below those prevailing at retail outlets.

2491. Department store was opened by Adam Gimbel, a German Jewish immigrant who began his career peddling household goods on foot in the Mississippi Valley. In 1842, he opened a store in Vincennes, IN, that offered a wide variety of goods under one roof, along with a money-back guarantee of satisfaction. Gimbel's seven sons imported the idea to cities across the country.

2492. Department store to occupy a city block was Alexander Turney Stewart's A.T. Stewart and Company department store, which opened in New York City in 1860. It occupied the block between 9th and 10th streets and between Broadway and Fourth Avenue.

2493. Chain store organization with a long existence was the Great Atlantic and Pacific Tea Company, better known as A&P. George Huntington Hartford was in the hide and leather business in New York City in 1857, and in 1859 he added tea to his merchandise. In 1864 he originated the Great American Tea Company, which developed into the Great Atlantic and Pacific Tea Company in 1869. He remained president of the firm until his death on August 29, 1917. Despite the name, the first store on the Pacific Coast was not opened until January 1930. The stores later became a chain of supermarkets.

2494. Mail-order business was established by Aaron Montgomery Ward in 1872 in a 12-by-14-foot room at 825 North Clark Street, Chicago, IL, with $2,400 capital, one-third of which was advanced by George R. Thorne. The first catalog consisted of a single-sheet price list, 8 by 12 inches, without illustrations. It was issued on August 18, 1872, and inaugurated a money-back guarantee policy. In 1873, the catalog was increased to four pages and listed 394 items. Afterward, catalogs with descriptive pictures were issued and a 15-cent charge made for them. The first free catalogs, more than 3 million weighing four pounds each, were mailed in 1904.

2495. Store with fixed prices was the Mechanic's Store, opened in Sacramento, CA, in 1874 by David Lubin, a Polish Jewish immigrant. Traders and storekeepers usually bargained with their customers. Lubin's innovation was to mark each item of merchandise with a fixed price based on its value plus a small profit. Lubin went on to found the International Institute for Agriculture, which promoted cooperation and information exchange among the farmers and growers of 45 member nations and was later absorbed into the United Nations Food and Agriculture Organization.

2496. Five-cent store was opened in Utica, NY, on February 22, 1879, by Frank Winfield Woolworth. The store was a great disappointment as its sales after a few weeks were as low as $2.50 a day. Woolworth moved his store in June 1879 to Lancaster, PA, where it proved a success. He came up with the idea for a five-cent store on September 24, 1878, in Watertown, NY, when he originated a "five-cent table" in the store of Moore and Smith during the week of the county fair. The first joint venture of the Woolworth brothers in Harrisburg, PA, was called the "Great 5 Cent Store."

2497. Cooperative store at a college was the Harvard Cooperative Society, Cambridge, MA. The store was managed by students and sold merchandise to members at prices below retail. The store's constitution was presented on February 28, 1882, and by March 15 it had 400 subscribers. The plan was proposed by Charles Hayden Kip. Frank Bolles was the first president.

2498. Discount clothing store was Filene's Automatic Bargain Basement, which opened in Boston, MA, in 1909. It was owned by a Prussian-American merchant, William Filene, and his sons Edward P. Filene and Abraham Lincoln Filene. The store sold discount apparel and dry goods.

2499. Drive-in gas station was opened by the Gulf Refining Company on December 1, 1913, at the intersection of Baum Boulevard and St. Clair Street, Pittsburgh, PA. The station remained open all night and provided free crankcase service. Thirty gallons of gasoline were sold the first day. Frank McLaughlin was the first manager.

2500. Self-service grocery store was the Piggly Wiggly in Memphis, TN, founded by Clarence Saunders in 1916. The store had four aisles containing 605 items. Saunders patented the idea in 1917.

2501. Shopping center in a suburban business area planned to cater exclusively to customers with cars was the Country Club Plaza, Kansas City, MO, built by Jesse Clyde Nichols from the master plan drawn by Edward Buehler Delk on April 22, 1922. Construction began in November 1922, and the first tenant moved in in March 1923. The center occupied 40 acres and had 150 stores, a 2,000-seat auditorium, and a parking lot for 5,500 automobiles.

2502. Shopping mall was Country Club Plaza, built in 1922 by J.C. Nichols as part of a new residential development on the outskirts of Kansas City, MO. Customers had to drive to get there, as it was not accessible by public transportation. The first shopping plaza in which the stores faced in toward the promenade, rather than out toward the access road, was the Highland Park Shopping Village in Dallas, TX, built in 1931.

2503. Cooperative store operated by women was the Montgomery Farm Women's Cooperative Market, Bethesda, MD, incorporated in August 1932 by 29 women.

2504. Self-service supermarket was the Big Bear Super Market, Elizabeth, NJ, which was opened in 1932 in an empty car factory by Robert M. Otis and Roy O. Dawson. It was the first large discount self-service grocery store. Meats, produce, canned and packaged foods, radios, automobile accessories, and paints, all at cut prices, were displayed on long pine tables.

2505. Liquor stores run by a state government were established by Pennsylvania in 1933. An act was passed by a special session of the legislature and signed by Governor Gifford Pinchot on November 29, 1933. On January 2, 1934, 90 stores were opened in various parts of the state, stocked and ready to do business.

COMMERCE—STORES—*continued*

2506. Keedoozle store was opened in Memphis, TN, on May 15, 1937, by the Keedoozle Corporation of Memphis, TN, of which Clarence Saunders was president. Sample merchandise was displayed behind rows of tiny glass windows. The customer made purchases by inserting a notched rod into a keyhole beside the items desired. The mechanism automatically recorded the selections. The merchandise was automatically collected and wrapped when the insertion of the key in a final slot released the contents to a conveyor for wrapping. *Keedoozle* is a coined word for "key-does-all."

2507. Department store to hold a public art auction was Gimbel Brothers, New York City, on November 14 and 15, 1941, when 303 items were auctioned by the Kende Galleries. The sales totaled $12,066.

2508. Retail store whose sales in one day exceeded $1 million was the R.H. Macy Company, New York City, whose sales on December 7, 1944, exceeded $1 million. On December 14, 1957, they first exceeded $2 million; on December 18, 1965, $3 million; and on December 18, 1967, $4 million.

2509. Food-O-Mat was installed in the Grand Union Company store in Carlstadt, NJ, on May 24, 1945. It was invented by Lansing Peter Shield. The patented merchandise display fixture operated on a gravity-feed, rear-load principle. Stockmen working behind the unit placed cans, jars, and packages on inclined runways with the labels upright. The items reached the shopper with the brand name uppermost. As the customer picked out an item, another slid in place by gravity.

2510. Department store to sell apartments was Gimbel Brothers, Philadelphia, PA, which on January 13, 1953, invited the public to the furniture floor to see full-size furnished duplicates of Philadelphia's first cooperative apartments. Over a million dollars' worth of apartments were contracted for on the first day.

2511. Department store to sell insurance of various types was Carson Pirie Scott and Company, Chicago, IL. The first sale was made on September 29, 1953, on a wedding present and personal effects floater for $2,500. The premium was $20.

2512. Enclosed climate-controlled suburban shopping mall was Southdale, in the Minneapolis suburb of Edina, MN, opened in 1956. Designed by Victor Gruen, it had two levels and a central "garden court." The arrangement was copied by thousands of similar projects in suburbs across the country.

2513. Pedestrian shopping mall was constructed in 1959 along a section of Burdick Street in downtown Kalamazoo, MI, which thereafter called itself "Mall City, U.S.A." Based on a design by Victor Gruen of Victor Gruen Associates, the mall was intended to protect the town's commercial center from the threat posed by large suburban malls, but the attempt was a failure. The lack of parking drove customers away and led to the decline of the stores that lined the mall. Gruen had designed a pedestrian mall for Fort Worth, TX, seven years earlier, in 1952, but it was never built.

2514. Wal-Mart store was opened in 1962 by Samuel Moore Walton of Kingfisher, OK. Wal-Mart went public in 1970 and became the largest retailer in American history.

COMMERCE—TRUSTS AND MONOPOLIES

2515. Trade monopoly was the fur trade established in Vermont by the explorer Samuel de Champlain, acting as the agent of fur dealers in France. In 1609, he set up trading operations in the Lake Champlain area with the local Hurons and Algonkians. The first trade monopoly among manufacturers was probably the United Company of Spermaceti Candlers, formed by nine New England spermaceti candle manufacturers in 1761. The group set a maximum price at which whale oil products could be sold.

2516. Price regulation agreement by colonists was signed by 21 coopers of New York City on December 17, 1679. The coopers agreed upon "the Rate and Prizes of Caske, this is to Say, for every Dry halfe Baril one shilling Six Pence." The agreement concluded: "And Wee, the Under Written, Doo Joyntly and Seavorally Bind ourselves, that for Every one that shall sell any cask Beefore mentioned under the Rate or Prizes above, Sd., that for every Such Default ffivety Shillinges he or they shall pay for use of the poore, as Wittnes our hands, this 17th Day of December, 1679." The coopers' action was condemned and they were brought to trial in the Council Chamber on January 8, 1680. The compact was annulled and the following verdict issued: "They are adjudged guilty, all that have signed the Contract, and are To pay each 50s, & either of them in publick employ to be dismist. The paym't to be to the Church or pious uses."

2517. Price regulation law enacted by a colony was enacted by Rhode Island at Providence on December 31, 1776. It was "an act to prevent monopolies and oppression by excessive and unreasonable prices for many of the necessaries and conveniencies of life, and for preventing engrossers, and for the better supply of our troops in the army with such necessaries as may be wanted." The law regulated prices on farm labor, beef, hides, shoes, cotton, sugar, salt, coffee, cheese, butter, beans, peas, potatoes, pork, wool, flannel, towcloths, flax, tallow, rum, molasses, oats, stockings, wheat, rye, maize, salted pork, and similar commodites. Lawbreakers were assessed fines equivalent to the value of the merchandise. The fines were distributed equally to the state and to informers.

2518. Trust was the salt trust, organized on November 10, 1817, by the salt manufacturers of Kanawha, WV. It went into active operation on January 1, 1818, at the Kanawha Salt Company. It was formed for the purpose of controlling the quantity of salt manufactured, the method of manufacture, the packing, and the production. The company disbanded on January 1, 1822.

2519. Trade association of importance was the American Brass Association, which was organized in the Naugatuck Valley of Connecticut in February 1853. Headquarters were opened in Waterbury, CT. The original object of the association was to regulate prices, but in 1856 it also attempted to regulate production. The association ceased to function in 1869.

2520. Antitrust law enacted by a state was an act "to prevent monopolies in the transportation of freight, and to secure free and fair competition in the same," approved on February 23, 1883, by Alabama. The first general law was passed on March 9, 1889, by Kansas, "to declare unlawful trusts and combinations in restraint of trade and products, and to provide penalties therefor."

2521. Antitrust law enacted by Congress was an "act to protect trade and commerce against unlawful restraints and monopolies," passed by Congress on July 2, 1890. It provided that "every contract combination in the form of trust or otherwise, or conspiracy, in restraint of trade or commerce among the several states, or with foreign nations, is hereby declared to be illegal." The act is popularly known as the Sherman Act.

2522. Price regulation law enacted by a state was enacted by Louisiana and approved on July 2, 1908, by Governor Jared Young Sanders. It prohibited "unfair commercial discrimination between different sections, communities, cities, or localities in the State of Louisiana or unfair competition therein."

2523. Blue-sky laws enacted by a state were passed by Kansas on March 10, 1911, "for the regulation and supervision of investment companies and providing penalties for the violation thereof."

2524. Cartel of corporations listed by that name was the Pacific Coast Gasolene Cartel. The cartel was an association of the companies selling 95 percent of the gasoline in the states of California, Washington, Oregon, Arizona, and Nevada, and the territories of Hawaii and Alaska. The agreement, which regulated competition, was approved by the secretary of the interior on February 13, 1934. A committee of seven persons was chosen to manage the activities of the cartel. The first chairman was Ralph Kenneth Davies of San Francisco, director of the Standard Oil Company of California, who was elected on February 24, 1934. The government representative on the board was William Herbert Eaton. The cartel became effective on March 1, 1934, but was abandoned before the end of the month.

2525. Company to pay a fine of $100 million for a price-fixing scheme was the Archer Daniels Midland Company, Decatur, IL, a maker of agricultural commodities. The Justice Department imposed the fine on the company on October 14, 1996, as a penalty for conspiring with other companies to fix the prices of two food additives, lysine and citric acid. The company admitted the charges. It was by far the largest such fine up to that time.

COMPUTERS—HARDWARE

2526. Computing device with electronic components was constructed in 1930 by Vannevar Bush, a professor at the Massachusetts Institute of Technology, Cambridge, MA. His "differential analyzer" used vacuum tubes in which numerical values could be stored as voltages. Bush, who later served as science advisor to President Franklin Delano Roosevelt, also designed the "memex device," an electromechanical information appliance. The memex, which was never built, presaged many of the features of the personal computer and the Internet.

COMPUTERS—HARDWARE—*continued*

2527. Computer bug was an actual bug, a moth that got into the circuits of a Mark II computer at Harvard University, Cambridge, MA. On September 9, 1945, the moth was located by Grace Murray Hopper and her assistants and was removed with tweezers. The moth is preserved in the Naval Museum at Dahlgren, VA. The computer terms "bug" and "debug" do not derive from this incident, however. The use of "bug" to refer to a defect in an apparatus or its operation dates from the early 1800s.

2528. Electronic computer was the Electronic Numerical Integrator and Computer (ENIAC), designed and built under the direction of J. Presper Eckert, Jr., and John W. Mauchly of the Moore School of Electrical Engineering at the University of Pennsylvania, Philadelphia, PA. It was given its first public demonstration on February 14, 1946. The ENIAC was subsequently used by the Army Ordinance Department at Aberdeen, MD. It was housed in a room 30 by 50 feet, contained approximately 18,000 vacuum tubes, and required 130 kilowatts per hour to operate.

2529. Electronic computer for commercial use was the UNIVAC I (Universal Automatic Computer), introduced by J. Presper Eckert, Jr., and John W. Mauchly in 1951, and manufactured by the Remington Rand Corporation, Philadelphia, PA. It was demonstrated and dedicated at the Bureau of the Census in Philadelphia on June 14, 1951. The key to its success was the use of inexpensive magnetic tape for data input and output. It could retain a maximum of 1,000 separate numbers, accept information contained on magnetic tape at the rate of more than 10,000 characters per second, add, subtract, multiply, divide, sort, collate, and take square and cube roots as needed. More than 50 units were sold in all.

2530. Electronic computer with solid-state components was developed in 1958 by Remington Rand Univac, a division of the Sperry Rand Corporation, at the company's laboratories in Philadelphia, PA, and was built at Ilion, NY. Because solid-state elements such as transistors, Ferractor amplifiers, and magnetic cores were used in its construction, the computer occupied about one-sixth the space of its predecessor, the UNIVAC, though it had 100 times the capacity and 10 times the speed.

2531. Mobile computer center was established by Remington Rand Univac, a division of the Sperry Rand Corporation, New York City, which equipped a motor van with a UNIVAC Solid-State 90 computer. The first assignment was undertaken on March 27, 1961, for the Douglas Aircraft Corporation, Charlotte, NC.

2532. Supercomputer was the Control Data 6600, designed by a team under Seymour R. Cray at a division of the Control Data Corporation located in Chippewa Falls, MN. The CDC 6600, introduced in August 1963, was far faster than competing mainframe computers of the time. It was purchased by the military to simulate nuclear explosions and break Soviet codes. Scientists also used the 6600 and later Cray-designed supercomputers to model complex phenomena such as hurricanes and the formation of galaxies.

2533. Minicomputer that was commercially successful was the PDP-8, introduced by the Digital Equipment Corporation of Maynard, MA, in 1965. The $18,000 minicomputer was smaller and less expensive than competing mainframe computers, but was almost as powerful. It was purchased primarily by institutions, smaller businesses, and researchers.

2534. Computer modem that was practical was demonstrated by John van Geen at the Stanford Research Institute, Stanford, CA, in 1966. A modem, short for "modulator/demodulator," is a device that converts digital computer information to a signal that can be transmitted to another computer over a telephone line. Van Geen's acoustical coupler modem design was able to receive data signals accurately over telephone lines despite random noise and static, a problem that earlier modem researchers had been unable to solve.

2535. Computer mouse was invented by Douglas Engelbart of the Palo Alto Research Center, Palo Alto, CA. A mouse is a hand-operated pointing device that enables the computer user to manipulate text or images on a computer screen. Prior to the mouse, the user interacted with the computer screen by typing commands on a keyboard. Engelbart first publicly demonstrated a three-button mouse in San Francisco in 1968.

2536. Floppy disk was developed in 1971 by researcher Alan Shugart for the International Business Machines Corporation of Armonk, NY. The eight-inch disk was made of polyester sheet coated with fine magnetic particles and encased in a cardboard sleeve. It was the first form of digital information storage that was cheap, portable, and high-density.

2537. Personal computer was the Altair 8800, sold in kit form beginning on December 19, 1974, when it was featured on the cover of the January 1975 issue of *Popular Electronics* magazine. It was developed by Edward Roberts at Micro Instrumentation and Telemetry Systems (MITS) of Albuquerque, NM. The kit cost $397. The first personal computer that was commercially successful was the Commodore PET, developed by Commodore Business Machines of Westchester, PA, and marketed to consumers beginning in early 1977. It sold for $595. The Apple II, developed by Steven Jobs and Steven Wozniak of Apple Computer, Cupertino, CA, is often considered the first successful PC, but it was not released until later in 1977.

2538. Voice reader for reading printed matter aloud was invented by Raymond Kurzweil. It was first demonstrated publicly on January 13, 1976, and was tested by the National Federation for the Blind. The machine, manufactured by Kurzweil Computer Products, Cambridge, MA, converted ordinary printed materials, including books, magazines, and typewritten correspondence, directly into spoken English at 150 words per minute. It used a camera to scan the pages into a computer that analyzed the letters and pronounced them.

2539. Optical computer that stored its programs and processed information entirely by means of light rather than electricity was demonstrated by electrical engineers Harry F. Jordan and Vincent P. Heuring of the University of Colorado, Boulder, CO, in January 1993. The complex array of lasers, switches, and optical fibers was the size of a small car and had the computing ability of a 1960s-era minicomputer. Its limited memory rendered it unable to perform complex calculations.

2540. Holographic data storage system was demonstrated by Lambertus Hesselink, John Heanue, and Matthew Bashaw of Stanford University, Stanford, CA, in the summer of 1994. It was a crystal the size of a large lump of sugar in which was stored a digitized image of the "Mona Lisa." Hesselink founded a company named Optitek to commercialize the invention, which had the potential to store information more compactly than any current data storage system.

2541. Teraflop computer capable of performing a trillion mathematical operations per second was the Janus, built by the Intel Corporation, Santa Clara, CA. The computer, housed in 84 cabinets, contained 9,072 Pentium Pro processors and had hundreds of billions of bytes of memory, enough to generate simulations of complex and massive events in four dimensions with extreme detail. It was installed in July 1997 at Sandia National Laboratories in Albuquerque, NM. The cost was $55 million.

COMPUTERS—NETWORKS

2542. Military computer network was SAGE (Semi-Automatic Ground Environment), a network for U.S. air defense. Developed in 1958 by researchers at the Massachusetts Institute of Technology, Cambridge, MA, SAGE provided computer communications over telephone lines for 27 regional command centers controlling more than 100 radar and surface-to-air missile sites.

2543. Large commercial computer network was the SABRE airline reservation system, developed in 1964 by the International Business Machines Corporation, Armonk, NY, for American Airlines. SABRE allowed airlines and travel agents to check schedules and book reservations for passengers on any participating airline.

2544. General-purpose computer network was ARPANET, a data communications network developed by J.C.R. Licklider, Robert Taylor, and other researchers for the Department of Defense's Advanced Research Projects Agency. The first ARPANET link was put into service on November 21, 1969. It connected a computer in the computer science department at the University of California at Los Angeles with a laboratory computer at the Stanford Research Institute, Stanford, CA. Over the next decade, ARPANET grew to include many government and university computers. In 1973, Dr. Vinton Cerf and Robert E. Kahn were commissioned by the federal government to create a national computer network for military, governmental, and institutional use. The network was based on ARPANET sites and employed packet-switching, flow-control, and fault-tolerance techniques developed by ARPANET. This was the origin of the Internet.

COMPUTERS—OPERATING SYSTEMS

2545. Computer operating system for multiple users that was practical was Unix, developed by Ken Thompson, Dennis Ritchie, and Rudd Canaday of Bell Telephone Labs, Holmdel, NJ, between April and June of 1969. A full working implementation of Unix was demonstrated in the summer of 1970 on a Digital Equipment PDP-11/20. The first written documentation for Unix was the *Unix Programmer's Manual*, dated November 3, 1971. Be-

COMPUTERS—OPERATING SYSTEMS—
continued

cause it allowed any number of users to access a computer at one time, and because it was relatively easy to program, Unix became the preferred operating system for large academic and engineering computer installations.

2546. Personal computer operating system was CP/M (Control Program for Microcomputers), developed by Gary Kildall in 1974. The first version was the CP/M-80 operating system, which simplified the tasks of writing and debugging software for Intel 8080-compatible microprocessors. It was the first operating system suited to computer hobbyists. A version of CP/M was available for the Altair 8800, the first personal computer.

2547. Graphical user interface for a commercial computer was used in the Star, developed by the Xerox Corporation at its Palo Alto Research Center, Palo Alto, CA, and put on the market in 1981. The Star had many of the interface features later incorporated into nearly all personal computers, including a mouse input device and a screen with icons, windows, and menus.

COMPUTERS—SOFTWARE

2548. Computer graphics software was Sketchpad, invented by Ivan Sutherland for his doctoral thesis at the Massachusetts Institute of Technology, Cambridge, MA, in 1963. An artist using Sketchpad could draw geometric shapes directly on a computer screen with a lightpen and then interactively modify them to create a finished design.

2549. Computer-aided design (CAD) software was DAC (Design Augmented by Computer), a system developed jointly in 1964 by the General Motors Corporation of Detroit, MI, and the International Business Machines Corporation of Armonk, NY. The DAC system was geared to automobile prototyping. It was first used to design the trunk lids for GM's 1965 line of Cadillacs.

2550. Educational computer programming language was BASIC (Beginner's All-purpose Symbolic Instruction Code), invented by John Kemeny and Thomas Kurtz of Dartmouth College, Dartmouth, NH, as a simple programming language for student instruction. It was introduced in 1965 and soon gained wide popularity with hobbyists.

2551. Computer programming language for children was Logo, invented by Seymour Papert at the Massachusetts Institute of Technology, Cambridge, MA, in 1967. With Logo, children could write simple programs to make a mechanical turtle move around on the floor.

2552. Commercial software for personal computers was a program that enabled the Altair 8800 personal computer to understand software written in the BASIC computer language. It was developed in 1975 by William Henry Gates III, age 19, and Paul Gardner Allen, age 22, in Seattle, WA. Microsoft, the company they founded to market the software, was the world's first personal computer software company.

2553. Interactive multimedia authoring program was HyperCard, written by William Atkinson for Apple Computer of Cupertino, CA, and introduced for the Macintosh computer in September 1987. HyperCard enabled computer users who were unfamiliar with programming to create their own information databases with hypertextual links, audio-visual effects, and true interactivity.

2554. Educational multimedia CD-ROM was *Mixed-Up Mother Goose,* published by Sierra Online of Bellevue, WA, in the spring of 1991. The disc featured animated Mother Goose characters with digitized voices. It sold for $59.95.

2555. Computer software application on Digital Video Disc was the PhoneDisc PowerFinder USA ONE, an electronic phone directory for the entire United States, announced by Digital Directory Assistance, Bethesda, MD, on January 18, 1996. It contained on a single digital video disc, or DVD, information that previously required the storage capacity of six CD-ROM discs.

CONGRESS

2556. Session of Congress took place in New York City from March 4, 1789, to September 29, 1789. The 13 states were represented by 26 senators and 65 representatives. The largest number of representatives from any state was 10, from Virginia. The first quorum of the House of Representatives met on April 1, when 30 members were present, and the first Senate quorum assembled on April 6. The final session in New York City was held on August 12, 1790. The capital was then moved to Philadelphia, PA. The first session to meet in Philadelphia was held on December 6, 1790, and the final session on May 14, 1800. The act of April 24, 1800, provided for the removal of the govemment to Washington, DC, and on November 17, 1800, the second session of the Sixth Congress convened there. On February 27, 1801, Congress assumed jurisdiction over the District of Columbia.

2557. Joint meeting of the Senate and the House of Representatives was held on April 6, 1789, in the Senate Chamber, New York City. The House of Representatives attended the opening of the Senate session and the counting by the Senate of the electoral votes for president and vice president in the country's first presidential election. The electoral votes were cast as follows: George Washington 69, John Adams 34, Samuel Huntingdon 2, John Jay 9, John Hancock 4, Robert H. Harrison 6, George Clinton 3, John Rutledge 6, John Milton 2, James Armstrong 1, Edward Telfair 1, and Benjamin Lincoln 1.

2558. Congressional act was "An Act to regulate the Time and Manner of administering certain Oaths," which was approved by President George Washington on June 1, 1789. The first Congress (March 4, 1789–March 3, 1791) enacted 118 acts, comprising 94 public acts, 14 public resolutions, 8 private acts, and 2 private resolutions.

2559. Congressional act declared unconstitutional by the Supreme Court was the act of September 24, 1789, which authorized the Supreme Court to issue writs of mandamus (written orders) to American courts and public officials. The Court's ruling held that this statute extended the Supreme Court's powers beyond what was specified in the Constitution.

2560. Congressional investigation was authorized on March 27, 1792, after troops under the command of Major General Arthur St. Clair were defeated by Native American forces near the Ohio-Indiana border on November 4, 1791. The House of Representatives, by a vote of 44–10, resolved "that a committee be appointed to inquire into the causes of the failure of the late expedition under Major General St. Clair; and that the said committee be empowered to call for such persons, papers and records as may be necessary to assist their inquires." The seven-member committee, which was headed by Thomas Fitzsimons, a Federalist of Pennsylvania, absolved St. Clair and ruled that his defeat "can in no respect be imputed to his conduct either at any time before or during the action." St. Clair nonetheless resigned his army command, retaining his post as governor of the Northwest Territory.

2561. Special session of Congress was held on May 15, 1797, in Philadelphia, PA. President John Adams had issued a proclamation on March 25 for convening the Senate and the House of Representatives to consider the difficulty with France.

2562. Congress in which 1,000 bills were introduced was the 22nd Congress, held from December 5, 1831, to July 16, 1832 (226 days) and December 3, 1832, to March 2, 1833 (91 days). Of the 976 bills and 24 joint resolutions introduced, 462 were passed, comprising 175 public acts, 16 public resolutions, 270 private acts, and 1 private resolution.

2563. Congressional lobbyist who was a woman was Dorothea Lynde Dix, who in the 1840s and 1850s championed the care of the indigent insane. On June 23, 1848, she presented a petition to Congress for a grant of 5 million acres for "the relief and support of the indigent insane in the United States." By courtesy of Congress, a special alcove in the Capitol Library was set apart for her use, where she could converse with members.

2564. Body to lie in state in the Capitol rotunda was that of Senator Henry Clay, who died in Washington, DC, at the age of 75 on June 29, 1852. His body was placed in the rotunda, where it was displayed July 1, 1852, prior to interment in Lexington Cemetery, Lexington, KY.

2565. Officer to preside over both of the branches of Congress was Schuyler Colfax of Indiana, who served as speaker of the House of Representatives in the 38th, 39th, and 40th Congresses (March 4, 1863–March 3, 1869), and who presided over the Senate as President Ulysses Simpson Grant's vice president (March 4, 1869–March 3, 1873).

2566. Congress to appropriate $1 billion was the 52nd Congress, which lasted from March 4, 1891, to March 3, 1893. It appropriated $507,376,398 in the first session for the fiscal year 1893 and $519,535,293 in the second session for the fiscal year 1894. The appropriations included funds for the postal service, payable from postal revenues, and estimated permanent annual appropriations, including sinking-fund requirements.

2567. Radio broadcast of an open session of Congress took place on December 3, 1923, from noon to 12:45 P.M., during the first session of the 68th Congress. The swearing-in ceremony was broadcast by radio station WRC, Washington, DC, from the Senate. Three newly elected senators—Alva Blanchard Adams of

CONGRESS—*continued*

Colorado, a Democrat; Magnus Johnson of Minnesota, a member of the Farmer-Labor Party; and Porter Hinman Dale of Vermont, a Republican—were sworn in alphabetically. The session adjourned in memory of the recently deceased senators whose seats they were taking—Samuel Danford Nicholson, Knute Nelson, and William Paul Dillingham, respectively.

2568. Congress to enact more than 1,000 laws was the 70th Congress, which met from March 4, 1927, to March 3, 1929. It enacted 1,722 acts, comprising 1,037 public acts, 108 public resolutions, 568 private acts, and 9 private resolutions.

2569. Physician to Congress was Dr. George Wehnes Calver, a retired rear admiral. He reported for duty at the Capitol in Washington, DC, on December 8, 1928, in response to a resolution of the 70th Congress, passed December 4, requesting the secretary of the Navy to detail a medical officer to be in attendance at the sessions of Congress. His title was "the attending physician."

2570. Congress in session a full year was the third session of the 76th congress, in session from January 3, 1940, to January 3, 1941, a total of 366 days. The first session of the 77th Congress lasted 365 days, from January 3, 1941, to January 2, 1942.

2571. Congressional opening session to be televised was the joint session of the 80th Congress that met on January 3, 1947. The proceedings were televised by the major networks.

CONGRESS—COLONIAL ERA

2572. Colonial congress met at Albany, NY, from June 19 to July 11, 1754, to form a plan of union and to negotiate a treaty with the Six Nations of the Iroquois. Seven colonies attended. Massachusetts Bay sent four delegates, New Hampshire four, New York four, Pennsylvania four, Connecticut three, Maryland two, and Rhode Island two.

2573. Continental Congress session began on September 5, 1774, at Carpenters' Hall, Philadelphia, PA. The participants were 44 delegates from 11 colonies. Delegates from Georgia and North Carolina did not attend until later sessions. The Congress adjourned on October 26, 1774, recommending another session to begin on May 10, 1775, in Philadelphia, PA.

2574. President of the Continental Congress was Peyton Randolph, a delegate from Virginia, who was elected on September 5, 1774, the day the Congress assembled. He resigned on October 22, 1774, to attend the Virginia State Legislature, and his place was taken on the same day by Henry Middleton of South Carolina.

2575. Continental Congress assembly to be opened with prayer was held on September 7, 1774, at Carpenters' Hall, Philadelphia, PA. The Reverend Jacob Duche, an Episcopalian minister, rector of Christ Church, appeared in his canonicals, attended by his clerk. The morning service of the Episcopal Church was read, with the clerk making the responses. The Psalter for the seventh day of the month includes the 35th Psalm, wherein David prays for protection against his enemies: "Plead my cause, O Lord, with them that strive with me; fight against them that fight against me." The rector concluded with an appeal so heartfelt that Congress gave him a vote of thanks.

CONGRESS—HOUSE OF REPRESENTATIVES

2576. Session of the House of Representatives met in New York City on March 4, 1789. It was attended by four delegates from Massachusetts, three from Connecticut, four from Pennsylvania, one from Virginia, and one from South Carolina. Meetings were constantly called and adjourned for lack of a quorum. The first quorum gathered on April 1, 1789, and the first business transacted was the balloting for the office of speaker of the House.

2577. Clerk of the House of Representatives was John James Beckley of Virginia, who served from April 1, 1789, to May 15, 1797, in the First through the Fifth Congresses, and from January 10, 1803, to October 26, 1807, in the Seventh through the 10th Congresses.

2578. Speaker of the House was Frederick Augustus Conrad Muhlenberg of Pennsylvania, who served as speaker in the First Congress from April 1, 1789, to October 23, 1791, and in the Third Congress from December 2, 1793, to December 6, 1795. He represented Pennsylvania in the House from March 4, 1789, to March 3, 1797.

2579. Congressional committee was the Committee on Elections, a standing committee, appointed on April 2, 1789, to determine the eligibility and rights of admission of those who had been elected. It was resolved "that a committee be appointed to prepare and report such standing rules and orders of proceedings as may be proper to be observed."

2580. Congressional chaplain was the Reverend William Linn, a Presbyterian minister, who served in the First Congress from May 1, 1789, to December 10, 1790.

2581. House of Representatives filibuster to delay legislative action occurred on June 11, 1790, when Elbridge Gerry of Massachusetts and William Loughton Smith of South Carolina made long speeches during consideration of the resolution to change the seat of government.

2582. Congressional apportionment of representatives under the Constitution was authorized by act of April 14, 1792, an "act for apportioning representatives among the several states according to the first enumeration." The first apportionment was made in 1793. It was based on the results of the first decennial census, the census of 1790, and provided for 106 representatives, one for every 33,000 of population. The first Congress, which met before this apportionment was made, had consisted of 65 representatives, one for every 30,000.

2583. Brawl in the House of Representatives took place in Philadelphia, PA, on January 30, 1798, when Matthew Lyon of Vermont had an argument with Roger Griswold of Connecticut and spat in Griswold's face. A resolution was introduced to expel Lyon. Lyon acted as his own attorney and defended himself in the proceedings, which lasted from January 30 to February 12, 1798, and occupied practically all the attention of the House. The resolution was carried by a vote of 52 to 44, but because expulsion requires a two-thirds vote, Lyon was not expelled.

2584. Congressional caucus was held secretly in 1800 by the Federalist party at the instigation of Alexander Hamilton for the purpose of reelecting President John Adams in the third presidential election. The Democratic-Republicans later held their own caucus and nominated Thomas Jefferson. Adams and Jefferson each received 73 electoral votes, whereupon the election was turned over to the House of Representatives. After 37 ballots taken between February 11 and 17, 1801, the House elected Thomas Jefferson of Virginia as president and Aaron Burr of New York as vice president. The first congressional caucus to meet openly, rather than in secret, was held on February 25, 1804, by the Democratic-Republicans, who nominated Thomas Jefferson. Jefferson received 162 of the 176 electoral votes.

2585. Congressional chaplain who was Catholic was Father Charles Constantine Pise, ordained in 1825, who served the 22nd Congress from March 4, 1831, to March 3, 1832.

2586. Gag rule in the House of Representatives was adopted on May 26, 1836, when the House voted 117 to 68 to ban any consideration of the contentious subject of slavery. The resolution read: "Whereas it is extremely important and desirable that the agitation of this subject should be finally arrested, for the purpose of restoring tranquility to the public mind, your committee respectfully recommend the adoption of the following additional resolution: Resolved that all petitions, memorials, resolutions, propositions, or papers, relating in any way, or to any extent whatever, to the subject of slavery, or the abolition of slavery, shall without being either printed or referred, be laid upon the table, and that no further action whatever shall be had thereon."

2587. Rabbi to open the House of Representatives with prayer was Rabbi Morris Jacob Raphall, rabbi of Congregation B'nai Jeshurun, New York City, who delivered the invocation on February 1, 1860, at the first session of the 36th Congress.

2588. African-American preacher to deliver a sermon in the House of Representatives was the Reverend Dr. Henry Highland Garnet, pastor of the 15th Street Presbyterian Church, Washington, DC. President Abraham Lincoln, with the unanimous consent of his Cabinet and the two congressional chaplains, arranged for the special Sunday morning service. The chaplain of the House, the Reverend William Henry Channing, extended an invitation to Dr. Garnet to preach a sermon commemorating the triumph of the Union Army and the deliverance of the country from chattel slavery. He delivered the sermon on Sunday, February 12, 1865, to a crowded chamber. He was also the first African-American allowed in the House, as previously African-Americans had been forbidden to enter the grounds.

2589. Congressional committee headed by a woman was the District of Columbia Affairs Committee, of which Mary Teresa Hopkins Norton, a Democrat of Jersey City, NJ, became the chairman on December 15, 1931. She served until June 22, 1937, when she became the chairman of the House Committee on Labor.

2590. Congressional page who was female was Gene Cox, 13 years old, the daughter of Representative Edward Eugene Cox of Georgia, who served on January 3, 1939, the first day of the 76th Congress, and received a check for $4 for her services.

CONGRESS—HOUSE OF REPRESENTA-
TIVES—*continued*

2591. Congressional standing committee headed by an African-American was the Committee on Expenditures in the Executive Departments, to which William Levi Dawson of Chicago, IL, was appointed on January 18, 1949.

2592. Congressional page who was African-American was Frank Mitchell, age 15, of Springfield, IL, who was appointed on August 14, 1965, by Representative Paul Findley, Republican of Illinois.

2593. Vote in the House of Representatives to be tallied by machine took place on March 3, 1971, when 391 votes were cast on a motion to pass the Wright Patman amendment to delete an interest rate section in a proposed piece of debt-ceiling legislation. Representatives displayed a green card if they were in favor, a red card if they were against. The name of the voter appeared on each card. There were 180 green cards and 211 red.

2594. Vote in the House of Representatives to be recorded electronically took place on January 23, 1973, when 331 members recorded their presence at a quorum call. Forty-four voting stations were located throughout the House Chamber. Each member placed a personalized plastic identification card in one of the vote stations to vote yea, nay, or present. A large panel on the south wall of the room, above the Speaker's podium, displayed the names of all the representatives and indicated their presence by means of light signals. The recorder, which cost $1.1 million, was designed by Dr. Frank B. Ryan, director of the House Information Systems.

2595. Bilingual report of a congressional committee was the 215-page report of a hearing that took place on March 28, 1978, at Miami, FL. It was entitled *Needs of the Hispanic Elderly, hearing before the Select Committee on Aging, House of Representatives, Ninety-Fifth Congress, second session,* and was simultaneously printed in Spanish under the title *Las Necesidades de los Ancianos Hispanos.*

CONGRESS—HOUSE OF REPRESENTA-
TIVES—REPRESENTATIVES

2596. Congressional representative appointed to a presidential cabinet was James Madison of Virginia, who served in Congress from March 4, 1789, to March 3, 1797, and as Thomas Jefferson's secretary of state from May 2, 1801, to March 3, 1809.

2597. Congressional representative who was Catholic was Thomas FitzSimons of Pennsylvania, who was elected as a Federalist to the first three Congresses. He served from March 4, 1789, to March 3, 1795. Another Catholic, Charles Carroll of Maryland, also served in the First Congress.

2598. Congressional representative who was Jewish was Israel Jacobs, who was elected by Pennsylvania to sit in the Second Congress. He served from March 4, 1791, to March 3, 1793. (There were two men named Israel Jacobs from Pennsylvania, and confusion exists as to which one served.) The next was Lewis Charles Levin, representative from Pennsylvania, who was elected as a candidate of the American Party and served from March 4, 1845, to March 3, 1851.

2599. Congressional representative to serve before his 25th birthday in contravention of the constitutional requirement was William Charles Cole Claiborne of Tennessee, a Jeffersonian Democrat, who served from March 4, 1797, to March 3, 1801. He was born in Sussex County, VA, in 1775.

2600. Congressional representative to be refused a seat was John Bailey of Canton, MA, an Independent, who was elected in 1823. He was excluded on the ground that he was not a resident of the district he purported to represent. An election was held to fill the resulting vacancy, and Bailey ran and won again. He was seated on December 13, 1824, was reelected three times, and served to March 3, 1831.

2601. Congressional representative who was a Catholic priest was Father Gabriel Richard, 56, who served as a nonvoting delegate from the Michigan Territory from March 4, 1823, to March 3, 1825. He was ordained a priest in France on October 15, 1790, and served as a missionary in Detroit, MI.

2602. Brothers to serve as representatives in Congress simultaneously were the three Washburn brothers, each of whom represented a different state. Israel Washburn, Jr., of Maine, served two terms as a Whig and three terms as a Republican, from March 4, 1851, to January 1, 1861. Elihu Benjamin Washburne of Illinois, who spelled his name with a final *e,* served as a Whig from March 4, 1853, to March 6, 1869. Cadwallader Colden Washburn of Wisconsin served as a Republican from March 4, 1855, to March 3, 1861. The three brothers served simultaneously as congressmen from March 4, 1855, to January 1, 1861. Another brother, William Drew Washburn of Minnesota, served as a Republican from March 4, 1879, to March 3, 1885.

2603. Congressional representative who was African-American was Joseph Hayne Rainey of Georgetown, SC, a Republican, who was sworn in on December 12, 1870, to fill the vacancy caused by the action of the House of Representatives in declaring the seat of Benjamin Franklin Whittemore vacant. Rainey served 10 years, until March 3, 1879. The first African-American representative from a northern state was Oscar Stanton De Priest of Chicago, IL, a Republican, who served from March 4, 1929, to January 3, 1935. The first from the Democratic Party was Arthur Wergs Mitchell of Illinois, who served from January 3, 1935, to January 3, 1943.

2604. Congressional representative to serve a single day was George Augustus Sheridan of Lake Providence, LA, elected as a Liberal on November 5, 1872, to the 43rd Congress, which ran from March 4, 1873, through March 3, 1875. He finally took his seat on March 3, 1875, the last day of the session, after an unsuccessful challenge by Pinckney Benton Stewart Pinchback.

2605. Congressional representative of Italian ancestry was Francis Barretto Spinola, Democrat of New York, who served from March 4, 1887, to April 14, 1891.

2606. Congressional representative elected by prohibitionists was Kittel Halvorson, born in Telemarken, Norway, who was elected as the candidate of the Farmers' Alliance and the prohibitionists. He served as a representative from Minnesota from March 4, 1891, to March 3, 1893.

2607. Congressional representative who was a Socialist was Victor Louis Berger of Wisconsin, who served from March 4, 1911, to March 3, 1913, in the 62nd Congress. He was elected to the 66th and 67th congresses, but was not permitted to take his seat. He was subsequently elected to the 68th, 69th, and 70th congresses and served from March 4, 1923, to March 3, 1929.

2608. Congressional representative to attend college after his term of service was George Arthur Bartlett, a Democrat from Nevada, who served from March 4, 1907, to March 3, 1911. On August 18, 1911, he enrolled as a freshman in the University of Nevada, Reno, NV. He had already been graduated from the law department of Georgetown University, Washington, DC.

2609. Congressional representative who was a woman was Jeannette Rankin, who was elected as a Republican from Montana and served from March 4, 1917, to March 4, 1919, and from January 3, 1941, to January 3, 1943. She was the first representative to vote twice against entry into war, on April 6, 1917, and December 8, 1941.

2610. Congressional representative who was a mother was Winnifred Sprague Mason Huck, a Republican from Chicago, IL, who was elected on November 7, 1922, to fill the vacancy caused by the death of her father, William Ernest Mason, on June 16, 1921. She served from November 20, 1922, to March 3, 1923, in the 67th Congress.

2611. Congressional representative to serve 18 terms who was a woman was Edith Frances Nourse Rogers, a Republican representing the 5th District of Massachusetts, who served in the 69th through the 86th Congresses, from December 7, 1925, to September 10, 1960. Her husband, John Jacob Rogers, who died on March 28, 1925, served from March 4, 1913, to his death.

2612. Congressional representative who had been an actress was Helen Gahagan Douglas, Democrat of California, who served from January 3, 1945, to January 3, 1951.

2613. Mother and son simultaneously elected to Congress were Ohio Republicans elected on November 4, 1952, to serve in the 83rd Congress. Frances Payne Bolton, 67, represented Ohio's 22nd District, and had served since February 27, 1940, when she was elected to fill the vacancy caused by the death of her husband, Chester Castle Bolton. Her son, Oliver Payne Bolton, 35, represented Ohio's 11th District.

2614. Congressional representative of Indian ancestry was Dalip Singh Saund, a Democrat representing the 29th district of California, who was born in Amritsar, India. He was elected on November 6, 1956, and reelected in 1958 and 1960. He was the first congressional representative of Asian descent.

2615. Congressional representative reelected after serving a prison term was Thomas Joseph Lane, a Democrat of Massachusetts, who was elected to the 77th Congress at a special election on December 30, 1941, and served eight terms before being convicted of income tax evasion and sentenced to four months in jail. He served his sentence in the Federal Correctional Institution, Danbury, CT, from May 7, 1956, to September 4, 1956. He was subsequently elected on November 6, 1956, to serve his ninth term.

CONGRESS—HOUSE OF REPRESENTATIVES—REPRESENTATIVES—*continued*

2616. Congressional representative of Japanese ancestry was Daniel Ken Inouye, 34, a Democrat, who was elected on July 28, 1959, by Hawaii, which was about to become the 50th state. He was a veteran of World War II, in which he lost an arm. In 1962, Inouye was elected to the Senate, becoming the first Japanese-American senator. The first woman of Japanese ancestry to serve in the House of Representatives was Patsy Takemoto Mink, Democrat of Hawaii, who served from January 4, 1965, to January 3, 1975.

2617. Congressional representative who was an African-American woman was Shirley Anita St. Hill Chisholm, a Democrat, who was elected on November 5, 1968, from New York City's 12th District, in the Bedford-Stuyvesant section of Brooklyn. She was sworn in on January 3, 1969, and was reelected six times, leaving the House of Representatives in 1982. The first female African-American representative from a southern state was Barbara Charline Jordan, elected as a Democrat from the 18th District of Texas in 1972. Jordan, who held degrees in political science, history, and law, had served in the Texas state senate from 1966 to 1972. In 1976 she became the first African-American speaker to deliver the keynote speech at a Democratic National Convention.

2618. Congressional representative of Puerto Rican ancestry was Herman Badillo, a Democrat, who was born on August 21, 1929, in Caguas, Puerto Rico. He was elected on November 3, 1970, by the 21st district of New York. He served in the 92nd, 93rd, 94th, and 95th congresses and resigned on December 31, 1977.

2619. Congressional candidate elected while missing was Thomas Hale Boggs, Democrat of Louisiana and House majority leader, who was elected to his 15th term on November 7, 1972. He had been missing since October 16, when the small plane in which he was a passenger disappeared. He was declared dead, and his wife, Corinne Claiborne "Lindy" Boggs, was elected in his stead on March 20, 1973.

2620. Congressional representative to give birth while holding office was Yvonne Braithwaite Burke, 41, Democrat of California, who gave birth to a daughter, Autumn Roxanne Burke, in Los Angeles, CA, on November 23, 1973. She had been elected to the 93rd Congress on November 7, 1972, and reelected to serve in the 94th and 95th congresses. Previously, she was the first African-American woman to be elected to the General Assembly of California.

2621. Congressional representative who was a grandmother was Millicent Hammond Fenwick, a Republican of New Jersey, who was elected to the 94th Congress on November 5, 1974, and was reelected to two subsequent terms. She was born on February 25, 1910. She had eight grandchildren.

2622. Congressional representatives to marry each other were Martha Elizabeth Keys, Democrat of Kansas, and Andrew Jacobs, Jr., Democrat of Indiana. Both were elected on November 5, 1974, to the 94th Congress. They were married on January 3, 1976, at Topeka, KS. He had first been elected on November 3, 1964, and had served in the 89th, 90th, 91st, and 92nd congresses; he was subsequently elected to the 95th and 96th Congresses. She was reelected to serve in the 95th Congress.

2623. Congressional representative of Polish ancestry was Barbara Ann Mikulski of Maryland, a Democrat, who was elected on November 2, 1976 and reelected on November 7, 1978.

CONGRESS—SENATE

2624. Session of the Senate met in New York City on March 4, 1789. The only members present were Senators John Langdon and Paine Wingate of New Hampshire, William Samuel Johnson and Oliver Ellsworth of Connecticut, William Maclay and Robert Morris of Pennsylvania, Caleb Strong of Massachusetts, and William Few of Georgia. Various sessions were called but had to be adjourned because no quorum was present. The first session of the Senate at which there was a quorum was held on April 6, 1789, at which meeting John Langdon of New Hampshire was elected president pro tempore.

2625. Senate president pro tempore was John Langdon of New Hampshire, who held the office on April 6, 1789, during the counting of the votes for president and vice president in the first presidential election. April 6 was the first occasion on which a Senate quorum assembled. The counting resulted in the election of George

Washington as president and the runner-up, John Adams, as vice president. Since the Constitution provides that the vice president shall act as president of the Senate, Adams took over the office on April 21, 1789.

2626. Special session of the Senate was held on March 4, 1791, at the Senate Chamber, Philadelpia, PA. It was summoned by President George Washington to transact urgent business: the nomination of district supervisors, of military officers, and of the various officers necessary to put the federal government into operation in the newly admitted state of Vermont.

2627. Senate filibuster took place February 11–21, 1811, to disrupt the Senate's debate over the Bank of the United States. The filibuster was not continuous, as other business was transacted during the period. The bank's charter had been approved on February 25, 1791. The Senate's first continuous filibuster extended from February 18, 1841, to March 11, 1841. The topic was the dismissal of the printers of the Senate and the election of a public printer.

2628. Senate hearing witness who was a woman was Elizabeth Cady Stanton, who addressed the Senate District Committee on January 20, 1869, in a plea to save the women of the District of Columbia from being debarred from voting.

2629. Senate whip was Senator James Hamilton Lewis of Illinois, who was appointed on May 28, 1913, by the Democratic Party to see that Democrats were present or paired at every roll call. The first whip of the Republican Party was Senator James Wolcott Wadsworth of New York, who served one week in 1915 until Senator Charles Curtis of Kansas was named his successor.

2630. Senate election in which neither candidate was seated after a recount was the election of November 2, 1926, in Pennsylvania. William Bauchop Wilson, a Democrat, was narrowly defeated by William Scott Vare, a Republican, who presented his credentials as senator-elect for the term beginning March 4, 1927. The Senate, on December 6, 1929, decided by a vote of 58–22 that Vare was not entitled to the seat. Governor John Stuchell Fisher appointed Joseph Ridgway Grundy, a Republican, to the vacant seat. Grundy served from December 11, 1929, to December 1, 1930.

2631. Radio broadcast from the Senate chamber in the Capitol building, Washington, DC, was made on March 4, 1929, in connection with the inauguration ceremonies of President Herbert Clark Hoover. The retiring vice president, Charles Gates Dawes, and the incoming vice president, Charles Curtis, were both heard.

2632. Senate parliamentarian was Charles Lee Watkins, who was formally appointed on July 1, 1937, although he had served as parliamentarian and journal clerk since July 1, 1935, and in other capacities in the Senate since July 16, 1914. He resigned on January 1, 1965, and was designated parliamentarian emeritus by Senate Resolution No. 4 on January 4, 1965.

2633. Senate filibuster to last for more than 24 hours was conducted by Senator James Strom Thurmond, Democrat of South Carolina, who spoke against civil rights legislation for 24 hours and 18 minutes on August 28–29, 1957.

2634. Senate election race in which both candidates were women was held on November 8, 1960, in Maine. Incumbent Margaret Chase Smith, Republican, defeated Lucia Marie Cormier, Democrat, by a vote of 255,890 to 159,809.

2635. Photograph of the Senate in session that was authorized was taken on September 24, 1963, by National Geographic Society photographers for the U.S. Capitol Historical Society, Washington, DC. It showed the Senate during the debate on the nuclear test ban treaty.

2636. Senate page who was African-American was Lawrence Wallace Bradford, Jr., age 16, of New York City, who was appointed by Senator Jacob Javits of New York on April 13, 1965.

2637. Senate proceeding to be shown on television was the installation ceremony for Nelson Aldrich Rockefeller of New York, who was sworn in as the 41st vice president of the United States on December 19, 1974, in the Senate chamber, Washington, DC, immediately after being confirmed. He was selected by President Gerald Rudolph Ford on August 20, 1974, 11 days after Ford took office following the resignation of President Richard Milhous Nixon.

CONGRESS—SENATE—SENATORS

2638. Senator who was Catholic was Daniel Carroll, a Federalist of Maryland, who served from March 4, 1789, to March 3, 1791. His brother was John Carroll, the first Catholic bishop in the United States.

CONGRESS—SENATE—SENATORS—*continued*

2639. Senator appointed by a governor was John Walker of Virginia, who was appointed on March 31, 1790, by Governor Beverley Randolph. Walker was appointed to the Senate to fill the vacancy caused by the death of William Grayson. He produced his credentials, took his seat April 26, 1790, and served until November 9, 1790, when James Monroe was elected to fill the unexpired term ending March 3, 1791.

2640. Senators elected but not seated were William Blount and William Cocke of Tennessee, elected by the Tennessee legislature, who presented their credentials on May 9, 1796. They were refused seats because Tennessee was not admitted to the Union until June 1, 1796. They were elected again on August 2, 1796, and took their seats on December 6, 1796.

2641. Senator to be impeached was William Blount, the first senator from Tennessee, who was elected on August 2, 1796, and served from December 6, 1796, until July 8, 1797, when he was expelled. The trial was held from December 17, 1798, to January 14, 1799, when the vice president announced the decision of the High Court of Impeachment that the charges were dismissed for want of jurisdiction. Blount was accused of entering into a conspiracy with British officers to divert part of Louisiana from Spain to Great Britain, "a high misdemeanor, entirely inconsistent with his public trust and duty as a Senator." While the case was in progress in Washington, DC, Blount was elected to serve in the Tennessee state senate, and at the opening session in 1798 was chosen to be its speaker.

2642. Senator to serve in contravention to the age limit was Henry Clay of Kentucky, who served from November 19, 1806, to March 3, 1807. He was born on April 12, 1777, in Hanover County, VA, and was 29 years 221 days old when he took office, although the Constitution states that "no person shall be a Senator who shall not have attained to the age of thirty years."

2643. Senator to be censured was Timothy Pickering, a Federalist of Massachusetts, and a former postmaster general, secretary of war, and secretary of state. On January 2, 1811, the Senate approved a motion to censure him, by a vote of 20 to 7. The motion stated that Pickering, who "read from his place certain documents confidentially communicated by the President of the United States to the Senate, the injunction of secrecy having been removed, has, in so doing, committed a violation of this body." He served in the Senate from March 4, 1803, to March 3, 1811, and in the House of Representatives from March 4, 1813, to March 3, 1817.

2644. Father and son who were senators at the same session were Henry Dodge of Wisconsin and his son Augustus Caesar Dodge of Iowa, who sat together from December 7, 1848, to February 22, 1855, in the 30th to 33rd Congresses. Previously they had served as delegates to the House of Representatives in the 27th and 28th Congresses, from March 4, 1841, to March 3, 1845, prior to the statehood of their territories. Henry Dodge continued to serve in the Senate until March 3, 1857.

2645. Senator to serve three states was James Shields of Illinois, Minnesota, and Missouri. He was elected as a Democrat to serve Illinois in the 33rd Congress for the term commencing March 4, 1849. His election was declared void because he had not been a citizen for the requisite number of years. He was then reelected for the same term and served from October 27, 1849, to March 3, 1855. In the 35th Congress, he represented Minnesota, serving from May 12, 1858, to March 3, 1859. He was elected by Missouri on January 22, 1879, to fill the vacancy caused by the death of Lewis Vital Bogy, and served in the 44th Congress from January 27, 1879, to March 3, 1879.

2646. Senator who was returned to the Senate after being defeated for the presidency was Henry Clay of Kentucky, who served in the Senate in 1806–07 and 1810–-11, spent many years in the House of Representatives and as secretary of state, served again in the Senate from 1831 to 1842, ran unsuccessfully for president as the candidate of the Whig Party in the election of November 5, 1844, and was returned to the Senate on March 4, 1849, serving until 1852.

2647. Senator who was Jewish was Judah Philip Benjamin of New Orleans, LA, who was elected to the Senate in 1852 and reelected in 1856. He resigned his seat in 1861, after Louisiana seceded from the Union, and was appointed attorney general of the Confederacy and then its secretary of war. A previous senator of Jewish descent was David Levy Yulee, a Democrat from Florida who had converted to Christianity. He served from 1845 to 1851 and again from 1855 to 1861.

2648. Senator to address the Senate in military uniform was Edward Dickinson Baker, Republican of Oregon. On August 11, 1861, he was drilling his regiment at Meridian Hill when he was summoned to refute Senator John Breckinridge, Democrat of Kentucky, who was speaking against a proposal to send troops against the South. Baker did not have time to change into civilian attire but removed his sword prior to delivering his speech. He was killed at the Battle of Balls Bluff, VA, on October 21, 1861.

2649. Senator who was African-American was Hiram Rhoades Revels, Republican of Natchez, MS, who was elected to the Senate on January 20, 1870, by the legislature of Mississippi for the unexpired term beginning March 4, 1865, and ending March 3, 1871. He was sworn in on February 25, 1870. After his Senate service he became president of Alcorn Agriculture and Mechanical College in Lorman, MS. The first African-American senator to serve a full term was Blanche Kelso Bruce, Republican of Mississippi, who served from March 4, 1875, to March 3, 1881. He had been born a slave in Virginia.

2650. Senator who was Native American was Charles Curtis of Kansas, who served from January 23, 1907, to March 3, 1913, and from March 4, 1915, to March 3, 1929, when he resigned to assume the vice presidency under President Herbert Clark Hoover.

2651. Senator who was a woman was Rebecca Latimer Felton, a Democrat, who was appointed temporarily to the Senate by Governor Thomas William Hardwick of Georgia on October 3, 1922, to fill the vacancy caused by the death of Thomas Edward Watson. The first woman to be elected to the Senate was Hattie Ophelia Wyatt Caraway, a Democrat from Jonesboro, AR, who was appointed in November 1931 to fill the vacancy caused by the death of her husband, Senator Thaddeus Horatio Caraway, and who was elected in her own right on January 12, 1932, and reelected in 1938. The first woman to be elected without first having been appointed was Margaret Chase Smith, Republican of Maine and a former member of the House of Representatives, who was elected to the 81st Congress on September 13, 1948.

2652. Senator who was a Latino was Dennis Chavez, Democratic senator of New Mexico from 1935 to 1962.

2653. Senator who was a woman who had previously served in the House of Representatives was Margaret Chase Smith of Skowhegan, ME, a Republican, who was elected on June 3, 1940, to the 76th Congress to fill the vacancy caused by the recent death of her husband, Representative Clyde Harold Smith. She was reelected to the 77th and the three succeeding congresses, serving from June 3, 1940, to January 3, 1949. She was elected to the Senate for the term beginning January 3, 1949, and served until January 3, 1973, having been defeated for reelection in 1972.

2654. Senator to win a seat that had been occupied by his father and his mother was Russell Long of Louisiana, who was elected on November 2, 1948, and sworn in on December 31, 1948, for the term expiring January 2, 1951. His father, Huey Pierce Long, the boss of the Democratic party machine in Louisiana, was elected on November 4, 1930, and took the oath of office on January 25, 1932. He was assassinated in 1935. Rose McConnell Long, wife of Huey Long and mother of Russell Long, was appointed on January 31, 1936, to fill the seat left vacant by the assassination. She served until January 2, 1937.

2655. Senator who had been a newspaper reporter was Blair Moody, a Democrat, who served in the Washington bureau of the *Detroit News* for 18 years (1933–51). He was appointed to a vacant Senate seat on April 23, 1951, by Governor Gerhard Mennen Williams of Michigan and was sworn in on April 25, on which date Vice President Alben William Barkley called upon him to preside over the Senate.

2656. Three brothers from one family to serve in the Senate were the three sons of Joseph Patrick Kennedy and Rose Kennedy of Boston, MA: John Fitzgerald Kennedy, senator from Massachusetts, who was sworn in on January 3, 1953; Edward Moore Kennedy, also from Massachusetts, who was sworn in on January 9, 1963; and Robert Francis Kennedy, senator from New York, who was sworn in on January 3, 1965.

2657. Senator of Chinese ancestry was Hiram Leong Fong, a Republican of Chinese ancestry who was elected on July 29, 1959, by Hawaii, which joined the Union on August 21. He was sworn in on August 24. His parents, emigrants from China, were laborers on sugar plantations. He was the first senator of Asian descent.

CONGRESS—SENATE—SENATORS—*continued*

2658. Senator who was African-American to be elected by popular vote was Edward William Brooke, the attorney general of Massachusetts, who was elected on November 8, 1966, by a plurality of approximately 439,000 votes. He was seated on January 10, 1967.

2659. Senator to act in the movies was Everett McKinley Dirksen of Illinois, who appeared in *The Monitors,* a satire released on October 9, 1969. It was a 91-minute film produced by Bell and Howell Productions in association with Commonwealth United Entertainment. The film depicted a pacifistic nonviolent United States dominated from the White House down by a horde of robot-like young men in bowlers. It featured Ed Begley as the president, Keenan Wynn as the general, and Larry Storch as the colonel.

2660. Senator who had been an astronaut was John Herschel Glenn, Jr., of New Concord, OH, the first astronaut to orbit the earth, who was elected as a Democrat on November 5, 1974. He was the pilot of the Mercury spacecraft *Friendship,* launched on February 20, 1962, by an Atlas booster. He made three orbits in 4 hours 55 minutes and landed east of the Bahamas in the Atlantic Ocean.

2661. Senator who was an African-American woman was Carol Mosely Braun, a Democrat from Chicago, IL, who was elected on November 3, 1992.

CONTROLLED SUBSTANCES

2662. Twelve-step rehabilitation program was Alcoholics Anonymous, founded in New York City on June 10, 1935, by recovering alcoholics William "Bill W." Wilson and Dr. Robert H. Smith. They devised a plan to help alcoholics control their addiction through guided group discussion and confession, reliance on a "higher power," and a gradual return to sobriety. The first high school chapter of Alcoholics Anonymous was started in 1988 in Pacific Palisades, CA, by Palisades High School psychologist Linda Levine.

CONTROLLED SUBSTANCES—ALCOHOL

2663. Beer was brewed at Sir Walter Raleigh's Roanoke colony in the future state of North Carolina in 1587. According to Thomas Hariot's account, "Wee made of the same [pagatowr, or maize] ... some mault, whereof was brued as good ale as was to bee desired. So likewise by the help of hops thereof may bee made as good beere."

2664. Brewery to remain in business for 200 years was Francis Perot's Sons Malting Company of Philadelphia, PA. The original concern was established in 1687 by Anthony Morris 2nd in Philadelphia, on the east side of Front Street, below Walnut, facing the Delaware River. The concern descended from father to son for eight generations.

2665. Cocktail is said to have been served in 1776 by Betsy Flanagan, a barmaid in Halls Corners, Elmsford, NY, who decorated the bar with tail feathers. An inebriate called for a glass of "those cocktails," so she prepared a mixed drink, and inserted one of the feathers.

2666. Bourbon whiskey was distilled from corn in 1789 by a Baptist minister, Elijah Craig, in the bluegrass country of Kentucky. The area was later renamed Bourbon County.

2667. Lager beer was manufactured in Philadelphia, PA, in 1840 by John Wagner, who had an eight-barrel kettle in his home. It was stored in a cellar under the brewhouse.

2668. Grape vines planted in California for wine-making were planted in Buena Vista, CA, in 1857 by Count Agoston Haraszthy de Moksa, who imported Tokay, Zinfandel, and Shiras grape varieties from his native Hungary. These were the first varietal grapevines in the United States. In 1861, at the request of the California State Legislature, de Moksa imported 100,000 cuttings of 300 varieties of European wine grapes.

2669. Oyster cocktail is attributed to a miner who appeared at a California bar about 1866 and ordered a whiskey cocktail and a plate of California raw oysters. After drinking the cocktail, he placed the oysters in the same glass with some tomato catsup, Worcestershire sauce, and pepper sauce, and ate them with great gusto. The bartender, seizing on the idea, marketed a new product which sold for "four bits" (50 cents) per glass and which has since been called an oyster cocktail.

2670. Martini was mentioned in O.H. Byron's *The Modern Bartender's Guide,* published in New York in 1884. A martini is a cocktail made of gin or vodka and vermouth, with a dash of bitters. The origin of the name is in dispute. Byron called the drink a "Martinez" and described it as a Manhattan (a whiskey cocktail sweetened with vermouth) but made with gin rather than whiskey. It was first called a "Martini" in Henry Johnson's 1888 book

How to Mix Drinks in the Present Style. The martini did not become "dry" until after World War I, when it became the fashion to use unsweetened French vermouth instead of the sweet Italian variety.

2671. Beer in cans for retail sale was packed by the Krueger Brewing Company at Newark, NJ, and placed on sale in Richmond, VA, on January 24, 1935.

CONTROLLED SUBSTANCES—ALCO-HOL—TEMPERANCE AND PROHIBITION

2672. Alcohol prohibition enforcement officers were authorized by proclamation of Sir Francis Wyatt, governor of Virginia, on June 21, 1622: "We do ordaine an officer for that purpose to be sworne in every plantacion, to give information of all such, as shalbe so disordered: the moiety of the forfeitures to be given the sd officer so informing, or for default in him to any other that shall informe, and the other to the publique Threasury."

2673. Liquor reform movement was undertaken by the Dutch Reformed Church on Manhattan Island in 1623. It maintained a strong position against liquor, particularly with regard to excessive use.

2674. Alcohol temperance law enacted by a colony was signed on March 5, 1623, by Governor Sir Francis Wyatt of Virginia and 32 others. It provided that "the proclamations for swearing and drunkenness set out by the Governor and Counsell are confirmed by this assembly, and it is further ordered that the churchwardens shall be sworne to present them to the commanders of every plantation and that the forfeitures shall be collected by them to be for publique uses."

2675. Temperance organization was formed in 1789 by the farmers of Litchfield County, CT. Their pledge read in part: "We do hereby associate and mutually agree that hereafter we will carry on our business without the use of distilled spirits as an article of refreshment, either for ourselves or for those whom we employ; and that, instead thereof, we will serve our workmen with wholesome food and the common simple drinks of our production."

2676. Alcohol prohibition law enacted by a state was passed by Tennessee on January 26, 1838. The bill, an "act to repeal all laws licensing tippling houses," provided that "all persons convicted of the offense of retailing spirituous liquors shall be fined at the discretion of the court" and that the fines and forfeitures be used for the support of common schools.

2677. Temperance society for women (state) was the New York Women's State Temperance Society, founded on April 20, 1852, at a convention held in Rochester, NY, principally through the efforts of Susan Brownell Anthony. Approximately 500 women attended.

2678. Temperance society for women (national) was the National Woman's Christian Temperance Union, organized in the Second Presbyterian Church, Cleveland, OH, on November 18–20, 1874. The first president was Mrs. Annie T. Wittenmyer of Philadelphia, PA. The World Woman's Christian Temperance Union, an outgrowth of the national group, was organized at a convention held from October 31 to November 3, 1883, in Detroit, MI.

2679. Alcohol abuse programs required in schools by the federal government was put into place under a law enacted in 1882. The law, the first in the world, required "temperance education" to be included in the standard course of studies in public schools. Temperance education became mandatory in Washington, DC, in 1886. By 1900, similiar laws had been enacted by all the states.

2680. Anti-saloon organization was the Anti-Saloon League, established on May 24, 1893, in the Oberlin College library building, Oberlin, OH. The group was founded by Howard Hyde Russell and 15 members of the Oberlin Temperance Alliance. The purpose of the society was to force the Ohio saloons out of business and to preach the benefits of temperance. On June 23, 1893, the Anti-Saloon League of the District of Columbia was formed in Washington, DC, with Major Samuel Hamilton Walker as the first president.

2681. National anti-saloon league was the Anti-Saloon League of America, formed December 17–18, 1895, at the Calvary Baptist Sunday School, Washington, DC, by a coalition of the Anti-Saloon League of the District of Columbia, the Anti-Saloon League of Ohio, and 45 other local temperance organizations. The first president was Hiram Price.

2682. Alcohol prohibition vote taken in Congress that showed the House of Representatives with a dry majority was taken on December 22, 1914. The representatives voted 197–189 in favor of a resolution to provide a constitutional amendment banning the manufacture and sale of intoxicating beverages. The resolution, offered by Representative Richmond Pearson Hobson of Alabama, failed to win the necessary two-thirds majority.

CONTROLLED SUBSTANCES—ALCO-
HOL—TEMPERANCE AND PROHIBI-
TION—*continued*

2683. State to ratify the Prohibition Amendment to the Constitution was Mississippi, which ratified it on January 8, 1918. The amendment had been submitted by Congress to the legislatures of the states on December 18, 1917. Ratification by three-fourths of the states is required for any amendment to the Constitution. Nebraska became the 36th state to ratify the amendment on January 16, 1919. On January 29, the secretary of state proclaimed the amendment effective as of January 16, 1920. In 1933 it became the first constitutional amendment to be repealed.

2684. Alcohol prohibition law enacted by Congress forbidding the sale of intoxicating liquors except for export was the Wartime Prohibition Act, passed on November 21, 1918.

CONTROLLED SUBSTANCES—DRUGS

2685. Narcotics tariff enacted by Congress was enacted by the Tariff Act of August 30, 1842, which placed a levy of 75 cents a pound on opium. Prior to this act, opium was exempted from duty by the act of July 14, 1832, and the act of March 2, 1833. The McKinley Tariff Act of October 1, 1890, provided for an internal revenue tax of $10 a pound upon all opium manufactured in the United States for smoking purposes, and limited the manufacture to United States citizens.

2686. Narcotics ban enacted by Congress was enacted on February 9, 1909. The act made it illegal to import opium and opium derivatives into the United States, except for medicinal purposes.

2687. Drug control law enacted by Congress was the Harrison Narcotics Act of 1914, sponsored by Representative Francis Burton Harrison of New York. It required sellers of narcotic drugs to register with the Internal Revenue Service.

2688. Drug treatment center for addicts established by Congress was the U.S. Narcotics Farm at Lexington, KY, which covered 11 acres of a 1,050-acre plot. The cornerstone was laid on July 29, 1933, and the building was dedicated on May 25, 1935, by the Public Health Service. The first occupants were received on May 29, 1935. Dr. Lawrence Kolb was the first director.

2689. Marijuana ban enacted by Congress was the Marijuana Traffic Act of 1937, which banned the possession, cultivation, and sale of the marijuana plant and its products. It was signed into law by President Franklin Delano Roosevelt on August 2, 1937.

2690. Drug treatment center for minors offering full-scale long-term treatment was the Riverside Hospital, North Brother Island, New York City, which was converted for the purpose in November 1951. The first patients were received on July 1, 1952. The first superintendent was Dr. Jerome Louis Leon.

2691. Narcotics ban enacted by a state was enacted by Nevada on March 19, 1965. It stated that "the possession of dangerous drugs without a prescription is punishable as a gross misdemeanor upon first and second conviction and is punishable as a felony upon third conviction, and exempting physicians, dentists, chiropodists, veterinarians, pharmacists, manufacturers, wholesalers, jobbers and laboratories, and exempting ranchers under certain conditions."

2692. Methadone program for the rehabilitation of heroin addicts was established in New York City in 1964 by Vincent P. Dole and Marie Nyswander of Rockefeller University. Dole was awarded the Albert Lasker Medical Research award in 1988 for his work. Methadone, a synthetic opiate that blocks the euphoria of heroin and causes less severe withdrawal, was developed by German chemists during World War II.

2693. Drug control chief appointed by the federal government was William J. Bennett, the former secretary of education, who was named to the newly created post of director of national drug control policy by President George Bush in 1989. The press quickly gave Bennett the informal title of "drug czar." At the time, an estimated 14.5 million Americans were using illegal drugs at least once a month. Bennett's plan, announced on September 5, 1989, included new policing efforts funded by the federal government.

CONTROLLED SUBSTANCES—TOBAC-CO

2694. Tobacco cultivation was undertaken at Jamestown, VA, in 1612 by John Rolfe, the future husband of Pocahontas, who had arrived from England with 107 other settlers on May 13, 1607. Rolfe was the first settler to come up with a method of curing tobacco, which made it possible to grow tobacco crops for export to England.

2695. Tobacco tax enacted by a colony was authorized on October 3, 1632, by the Massachusetts Court of Assistants and General Court, which ruled in Boston "that no person shall take any tobacco publicly, under pain of punishment; also that everyone shall pay 1d. for every time he is convicted of taking tobacco in any place, and that any Assistant shall have power to receive evidence and give order for the levying of it, as also to give order for the levying of the officer's charge. This order to begin the tenth of November next."

2696. Antismoking law enacted by a colony was the work of Willem Kieft, the third governor of New Netherlands (later New York City). In 1637, he introduced an ordinance to outlaw tobacco use and trade everywhere in the colony. On May 25, 1647, the colonial legislature of Connecticut passed a law forbidding smoking on the streets or in nearby fields, but permitted citizens to indulge freely at home, as long as no more than one other person "who useth and drinketh the same weed" was present.

2697. Tobacco tax enacted by Congress was levied in 1794, but after two years it was abandoned. A similar attempt was made in 1812 and repealed in 1816. The first federal tobacco tax for internal revenue purposes was levied by an act of Congress of July 1, 1862.

2698. Cigarette tax was levied by the United States under an act of Congress of June 30, 1864. The system of placing stamps on each package to indicate payment of tax was inaugurated in 1868.

2699. Cigarette tax enacted by a state was established on April 11, 1921, when Iowa enacted a tax applicable to cigarettes, cigarette papers, and cigarette tubes. The tax on cigarettes was one mill on each cigarette ($1 per 1,000). This act repealed an existing law prohibiting the sale of cigarettes in Iowa.

2700. Smoking ban on airplane flights went into effect on April 23, 1988. In compliance with rules issued by the Federal Aviation Administration, airlines banned smoking on domestic passenger flights lasting less than two hours, with the exception of chartered flights and travel club flights. Northwest Airlines voluntarily banned smoking on domestic passenger flights of all durations. The first commercial domestic air service that was entirely smoke-free, including the cockpit, was inaugurated by Delta Air Lines of Atlanta, GA, which banned smoking on all flights beginning January 1, 1995.

2701. Tobacco sales to minors to be restricted by federal regulations were restricted as of February 28, 1997. The Food and Drug Administration implemented restrictions on retailers that required them to check the ages of all customers younger than 27 to prevent persons under 18 years of age from buying tobacco. Store owners caught selling cigarettes and other tobacco products to minors faced federal fines of $250 per violation. All states already had laws banning the sale of tobacco to persons under 18.

CONTROLLED SUBSTANCES—TOBACCO—SMOKING PRODUCTS

2702. Cigar factory of importance was established by Simeon Viets in 1810 in West Suffield, CT. He employed 15 women and a foreman. His popular brands were Windsors and Long Nines.

2703. Cigar bands of special interest was prepared for cigars distributed at a dinner given by the Common Council of the City of New York on September 2, 1858, at the Metropolitan Hotel, New York City, to honor Cyrus West Field and the officers of the U.S. steam frigate *Niagara* and the British steamship H.B.M. *Gorgon* who had completed the laying of the transatlantic telegraph cable on August 5, 1858. The cigar bands, which were printed in black ink, depicted Field.

2704. Corncob pipe commercial manufacture was undertaken in 1869 by Henry Tibbe of Washington, MO, who used plaster of paris to fill uneven surfaces in the pipe. He obtained a patent on July 9, 1878, on a "smoking pipe made of corncob, in which the interstices are filled with a plastic self-hardening cement." In 1872 he was joined by his son, Anton A. Tibbe, and they later incorporated as the Missouri Meerschaum Company.

2705. Cigarette-manufacturing machine was the Hook machine, which was invented by Albert H. Hook of New York City in 1872, but which did not come into practical commercial use until 1882. In 1875, 50 million cigarettes were made, according to revenue collection figures. The Hook machine was granted a patent on November 7, 1876. It unspooled a continuous ribbon of paper into which tobacco was fed before the edges were passed over a gummed wheel. The result was a very long cigarette that was afterwards cut into separate cigarettes.

2706. Cigar-rolling machine that was practical was invented by Oscar Hammerstein of New York City, who obtained a patent for it on February 27, 1883.

COURTS

2707. Juvenile court was the Juvenile Court of Cook County, known as the Chicago Juvenile Court, authorized on April 21, 1899, and opened on July 1, 1899, with Richard Stanley Tuthill as judge. This was the first juvenile court in the world. During the first year, about 2,300 cases were heard. Cases involving girls were tried by a female judge, Mary Margaret Bartelme, beginning on March 3, 1913.

2708. Night court was opened in New York City on September 1, 1907. It was a magistrates' court, the Jefferson Market Court at Ninth Street and Sixth Avenue, presided over by Charles Nathan Harris. Sessions were held from 8 P.M. to 3 A.M. until September 1, 1910, when the closing hour was fixed at 1 A.M.

2709. Domestic relations court was established in Buffalo, NY, in 1909 by Simon Augustine Nash, judge of Police Court, who privately heard domestic relations cases in his chambers instead of in open court. A state law approved on May 29, 1909, formally established the City Court of Buffalo, and the domestic relations division was opened on January 1, 1910.

2710. Small claims court was a state court for small debtors, authorized on March 15, 1913, by Kansas, to deal with cases involving not more than $20. Plaintiffs and defendants appeared without legal representation. Judges served without fee, pay, or award and were not required to be lawyers. Appeals could be taken to the district court. The first court was at Topeka, KS, with W.H. Kemper as judge. The first city conciliation tribunal for small claims was the Conciliation Branch of the Municipal Court of Cleveland, OH, also established on March 15, 1913. The complainant could not be represented by counsel but had to present his own case. Strict rules of evidence and procedure were waived. The judgment rendered had the same force and effect, and was as binding, as a judgment rendered in any court of record.

COURTS—FEDERAL

2711. Attorney of the United States was Samuel Sherburne, Jr., of New Hampshire, who was appointed United States attorney in and for the New Hampshire District on September 26, 1789. Twelve other attorneys, one for each state district, were appointed on the same date.

2712. Claims court established by the federal government was established by an act "to establish a court for the investigation of claims against the United States," signed on February 24, 1855, by President Franklin Pierce. It required the appointment by the president, with the consent of the Senate, of three judges with life tenure. President Pierce appointed Isaac Blackford of Indiana and John James Gilchrist of New Hampshire on March 3, 1855, and George P. Scarborough of Virginia on May 8, 1855. The judges received $4,000 annually. The court was organized on May 11, 1855, with Judge Gilchrist as presiding judge. It was reorganized by act of March 3, 1863. Until March 3, 1887, it was the only court in which cases could be prosecuted against the government.

2713. Commerce court established by the federal government was established by act of Congress on June 18, 1910. A presiding judge and five associates were appointed by President William Howard Taft for terms that extended from one to five years. The court was organized on February 8, 1911, and opened on February 15 in Washington, DC. Appeal of its decisions could be made only to the Supreme Court. Because of various abuses, the court was abolished on December 31, 1913.

2714. District attorney who was a woman was Annette Abbott Adams, who served as U.S. district attorney in the Northern California District from July 25, 1918, to June 26, 1920.

2715. Television eyewitness allowed to testify in a federal court was Mrs. Sophie Eisenberg of Brooklyn, New York City, who testified in U.S. Federal Court, New York City, on January 29, 1951, before Judge Irving Robert Kaufman. The lawsuit before the court had been brought by Jonas Walvisch of New York City, who had been a spectator at a hockey game between the Montreal Canadiens and the New York Rangers at Madison Square Garden on March 16, 1947. Walvisch accused Emile "Butch" Bouchard, the captain of the Canadiens, of hitting him, and sued him for $75,000. Mrs. Eisenberg testified that she was watching the game on television when she saw Bouchard hit Walvisch. The spectator, however, lost his suit.

2716. District attorney who was African-American was Cecil Francis Poole, who was sworn in July 6, 1961, at San Francisco, as attorney for the northern district of California. He retired February 3, 1970. Previously, four African-Americans had served as United States attorney in the U.S. Virgin Islands, which are territorial possessions of the United States.

2717. Courtroom verdict to be televised was delivered on March 14, 1964, at the 3rd Criminal District Court of Dallas County, Dallas, TX. The telecast took place from 12:37 to 2 P.M. Judge Joseph Brantley Brown sentenced Jack Ruby (Jacob L. Rubenstein) to die in the electric chair for the murder with malice of Lee Harvey Oswald, the alleged assassin of President John Fitzgerald Kennedy, on November 24, 1963. The broadcast was pooled by the Columbia Broadcasting System, sent to New York City, and shared with the NBC and ABC networks.

COURTS—JUDGES

2718. Judge to be impeached was Nicolas More, chief justice of colonial Philadelphia. He fell under such displeasure that the assembly on May 15, 1685, presented 10 charges of impeachment against him to the council. Among other offenses he was charged with "assuming to himself an unlimited and arbitrary power in office." He was expelled on June 2, 1685, but the council refused to sanction the impeachment proceedings.

2719. Federal judge to be impeached was John Pickering, judge of the U.S. District Court for the district of New Hampshire, who was removed from office after his conviction by the Senate on March 12, 1804, on charges of drunkenness, profanity, and violence on the bench. The vote was 19–7.

2720. Justice of a state supreme court who was African-American was Jonathan Jasper Wright of Beaufort, SC, who served as one of the three members of the court from February 2, 1870, to December 1, 1877. The first African-American chief justice of a state supreme court was James Benton Parsons, who became chief justice of the Illinois Supreme Court on April 18, 1975.

2721. Justice of the peace who was a woman was Esther Hobart Morris of South Pass City, WY, who was appointed on February 17, 1870, by the county commissioners.

2722. Judge to impose the death penalty who was a woman was Florence Ellinwood Allen, a judge of the Court of Common Pleas of the County of Cuyahoga, Cleveland, OH. She gave a sentence of death by electrocution to Frank Motto, who had been convicted by a jury on a charge of first-degree murder on May 14, 1921. The sentence was carried out on August 20, 1921.

2723. State supreme court justice who was a woman was Florence Ellinwood Allen of Cleveland, OH, who was elected on December 16, 1922, to the Ohio Supreme Court.

2724. State supreme court in which all the judges were women was the Special Supreme Court of Texas, appointed by Governor Pat Morris Neff on January 8, 1925. When an application for writ of error in the case of *W.T. Johnson, et al. v. J.M. Darr, et al.,* from El Paso County (a Woodmen of the World case), reached the Supreme Court of Texas, all three judges found themselves disqualified to consider it and immediately certified their disqualifications to the governor as required by law. The governor appointed Hortense Ward of Houston as special chief justice and Hattie L. Henenberg of Dallas and Ruth Brazzil of Galveston as special associate justices. The case was decided on May 23, 1925, affirming the judgment of the Court of Civil Appeals.

2725. Justice on the federal bench who was a woman was Genevieve Rose Cline of the U.S. Customs Court, New York, who was appointed on May 4, 1928, by President Calvin Coolidge. The first justice of the Circuit Court of Appeals who was a woman was Florence Ellinwood Allen, nominated on March 6, 1934, by President Franklin Delano Roosevelt to fill the vacancy brought about by the death of Judge Smith Hickenlooper. She was sworn in on April 9, 1934. She served in the sixth judicial court.

2726. Judge who was an African-American woman was Jane Matilda Bolin, who on July 22, 1939, was appointed judge of the Court of Domestic Relations by Mayor Fiorello La Guardia of New York City. She was also the first African-American woman to graduate from Yale Law School and the first to be admitted to the New York City bar. The first African-American woman to be elected to a judgeship, rather than appointed, was Edith Spurlock Sampson, elected associate judge of the Municipal Court of Chicago, IL, on November 8, 1962, and sworn in on December 3, 1962. She became an associate judge of the Circuit Court of Cook County, Chicago, IL, on January 1, 1964.

2727. Judge on the federal bench who was African-American was Irvin Charles Mollison of Chicago, IL, sworn in and inducted as a judge of the U.S. Customs Court on November 3, 1945, in New York City. The first African-American justice of the Circuit Court of Appeals was William Henry Hastie, former governor of the U.S. Virgin Islands, who was unanimously confirmed by the Senate on July 19,

COURTS—JUDGES—*continued*

1950, for a recess appointment to the Third Judicial Circuit (Pennsylvania, New Jersey, Delaware, and the Virgin Islands). He was sworn in by Chief Judge John Biggs, Jr., in Philadelphia, PA.

2728. Judge of Chinese ancestry was Delbert E. Wong, appointed to the municipal bench of Los Angeles, CA, by Governor Edmund Brown in 1959.

2729. Judge of a federal district court who was African-American was Judge James Benton Parsons, who was sworn in on September 22, 1961, at Chicago, IL, as a U.S. district judge for the Northern District of Illinois. His appointment had been confirmed by the Senate on August 30, 1961. The first African-American woman to serve as judge of a federal district court was Constance Baker Motley, nominated by President Lyndon Baines Johnson on April 4, 1966, confirmed on August 30 by the Senate Judiciary Committee, and sworn in at the U.S. Court House, Foley Square, New York City on September 9, 1966. She served in the Southern District of New York. In 1982 she was appointed chief judge. Previously, she had been the first African-American woman elected to the New York State Senate.

2730. State supreme court chief justice who was a woman was Lorna Elizabeth Lockwood of Douglas, AZ, who was elected as chief justice of the Arizona Supreme Court by unanimous vote of the other justices on January 8, 1965, as chief justice of the Arizona Supreme Court. She served as chief justice from 1965 to 1975. She had been elected an associate justice of the court in 1961.

2731. Judge who had served time in prison was Robert A. "Bob" Young, who was elected to serve the term from January 3, 1977, to December 31, 1983, as judge of the Justice Court, Loomis, CA. He had been convicted at the age of 19 of stealing a credit card out of the mail and had served 20 months in federal prison and four years on parole. He was graduated from law school in 1970 and after a two-year investigation was admitted to the bar.

2732. Judge of the U.S. Court of Appeals who was an African-American woman was Amalya Lyle Kearse of New York City, who was sworn in on June 27, 1979, by Chief Judge Irving Robert Kaufman at the U.S. Court of Appeals, New York City.

COURTS—JURIES

2733. Grand jury convened on September 1, 1635, at New Towne (now Cambridge), MA, to investigate accusations against persons charged with crimes and indict them for trial before a petit jury if there was sufficient evidence.

2734. Jury composed of women was ordered by the General Provinciall Court at the session held on September 22, 1656, at Patuxent, MD. The jury was composed of seven married women and four single women who tried Judith Catchpole for the murder of her child. The order read: "Whereas Judith Catchpole being brought before the Court upon Suspicion of Murdering a Child which She is accused to have brought forth, and denying the fact or that She ever had Child, the Court hath ordered that a Jury of able women be Impannelled and to give in their Verdict to the best of their Judgment whether She the said Judith hath ever had a Child or not." The jury's verdict was "not guilty" and the court ordered that "the said Judith Catchpole be acquitted of that charge unless further evidence appear."

2735. Interracial jury composed of both white and African-American jurors was the grand jury that indicted Jefferson Davis, the president of the Confederacy, on a treason charge on May 8, 1866. The petit jury in this case was the second interracial jury. Davis, his wife, and their four children were captured at Irwinville, GA, on May 10, 1865, by Lieutenant Colonel Benjamin Dudley Pritchard, commanding the 4th Michigan Cavalry. Davis was imprisoned and indicted for treason. In 1867 he was released on bond. The case was finally brought to trial on December 3, 1868, in the Circuit Court of the United States at Richmond, VA, before Judges Salmon Portland Chase and John Curtiss Underwood, but was dismissed because of President Andrew Johnson's general amnesty proclamation, issued on December 25, 1868. The charge was dropped by the district attorney on February 15, 1869.

2736. Jury school was opened on January 16, 1937, by Judge William Clark, U.S. District Court, District of New Jersey, in the Post Office Building, Newark, NJ. The first class was attended by 150 men and women. About 2,500 persons, mostly women, attended the course, which was designed to acquaint citizens with courtroom procedure and duties of jurors in considering evidence. The school was disbanded on December 10, 1937.

2737. Grand jury foreman who was a woman was Julia Isabelle Sims of Newark, NJ, who served on the federal grand jury in the U.S. District Court for the District of New Jersey in session at Newark from April 6, 1937, to October 19, 1937. Judge William Clark presided.

COURTS—MILITARY

2738. Court-martial in a colony was held on August 24, 1676, in Newport, RI, by Governor Walter Clarke, Deputy Governor John Crayton, and their assistants. Edmund Calverly was the attorney general. Quanpen, a Native American sachem also known as Sowagonish, was found guilty of participation in King Philip's War against the colonists and ordered shot on August 26. Others who had participated in the war were sentenced to various penalties.

2739. Court-martial by the Army was held on January 20, 1778, in Cambridge, MA. Colonel David Henley, commanding officer of the American troops in Cambridge, was accused "of a general tenor of language and conduct heinously criminal as an officer, and unbecoming a man, of the most indecent, violent, vindictive severity against unarmed men, and of intentional murder." The trial was concluded on February 25, when Henley was found not guilty. Brigadier General John Glover was the presiding officer at the trial.

2740. Court-martial at which the judges included enlisted men was convened at 8:30 A.M. on February 1, 1949, in Heidelberg, Germany, to try Private First Class Andrew D. Byrd of Orlando, FL, and Private First Class Oscar B. Gannon of Hanging Rock, OH, on the charge of premeditated murder of a German civilian and assault on another in a brawl. The military court consisted of four sergeants and six officers. The defendants were convicted on February 3 of manslaughter and sentenced to serve seven years of hard labor and to receive dishonorable discharges.

2741. Court-martial of an officer for collaborating with his captors was held on September 23, 1954, at Fort Sheridan, IL. A court of eight colonels and three lieutenant colonels sentenced Lieutenant Colonel Harry Fleming, reserve officer, of Racine, WI, to "involuntary discharge" for collaborating with Communists during the Korean War. On February 8, 1957, the Court of Military Appeals upheld the conviction and agreed with the court-martial and military board of review.

COURTS—SUPREME COURT

2742. Supreme Court of the United States consisted of Chief Justice John Jay of New York (1789–95), and associate justices John Rutledge of South Carolina (1789–91), William Cushing of Massachusetts (1789–1810), James Wilson of Pennsylvania (1789–98), John Blair of Virginia (1789–96), and Robert Hanson Harrison of Maryland (1789–90). The appointments were made by President George Washington on September 24, and confirmed by the Senate on September 26. The Judiciary Act of 1789, which implemented the clause in the Constitution providing for the Supreme Court, was passed on September 24. It provided for six justices, four of whom constituted a quorum. The first session began on February 1, 1790, in the Royal Exchange Building on Broad Street, New York City, and lasted 10 days. Two sessions were held each year, beginning on the first Monday of February and of August.

2743. Supreme Court clerk was John Tucker of Boston, MA, appointed on February 3, 1790. It was required "that he reside and keep his office at the seat of the national government, and that he do not practice, either as an attorney or a counsellor in this court, while he shall continue to be clerk of the same."

COURTS—SUPREME COURT—DECISIONS

2744. Supreme Court decision was *West v. Barnes,* tried in the August 1791 term. The motion was refused, as "writs of error made by clerk of the circuit court for Rhode Island district to remove causes to this court from inferior courts, can regularly issue only from the clerk's office of court." No cases were argued during the first four terms of the court (February 1790, August 1790, February 1791, August 1791).

2745. Supreme Court decision in a matter between states was the result of a bill in equity between New York and Connecticut in the term that began on August 5, 1799. Chief Justice Oliver Ellsworth presided. The decision read: "As the state of New York was not a party to the suit, nor interested in the decision of these suits, an injunction ought not to issue."

2746. Supreme Court decision voiding an act of Congress was *Marbury vs. Madison,* which was heard in the term beginning on February 3, 1803, and concerned the congressional act of September 24, 1789. President John Adams appointed William Marbury justice of the peace. President Thomas Jefferson instructed Secretary of State James Madison not to deliver the commission.

COURTS—SUPREME COURT—DECISIONS—*continued*

2747. Supreme Court decision establishing the power of the federal government as greater than that of the individual states was made on February 20, 1809, when Chief Justice John Marshall, in *United States v. Judge Peters,* rendered an opinion sustaining the federal power and ordered a writ of mandamus issued to carry a previous decree into effect. Judge Richard Peters of the U.S. District Court of Pennsylvania had decreed that a certain sum of prize money be paid to a Mr. Olmstead of Connecticut for his capture of a British sloop during the Revolutionary War. The state of Pennsylvania refused to recognize Olmstead's claim, and the state militia was called out to stop a federal marshal from serving the judge's order. The Supreme Court decided that a state legislature of a state cannot annul the judgment or determine the jurisdiction of a federal court.

2748. Supreme Court decision declaring a state law unconstitutional was made on March 16, 1810, in the case of Robert Fletcher of Amherst, NH, who bought 13,000 acres of land for $3,000 on May 14, 1803, from John Peck of Boston, MA. The court ruled that Georgia's rescinding act violated the contract clause of Article 1, Section 10, of the Constitution. Chief Justice John Marshall decided that "the Union has a constitution, the supremacy of which all acknowledge, and which imposes limits to the legislation of the several states, which none claim a right to pass."

2749. Supreme Court decision reversing the ruling of a state supreme court was rendered in 1813 in the case of *Fairfax's Devisee v. Hunter's Lessee.* The case concerned the Virginia estate of a wealthy loyalist, Lord Thomas Fairfax, which had been confiscated by Virginia during the Revolutionary War. The Virginia Court of Appeals held that the confiscation was illegal. A writ of error was obtained and the case was argued as *Martin v. Hunter's Lessee.* The Supreme Court in 1816 unanimously sustained the validity of the 25th section of Chapter 20 of the act of September 24, 1789, which established the judicial system and established for all time the right of the Supreme Court to review the determinations of the highest state courts in cases involving the Constitution and federal laws or treaties.

2750. Supreme Court decision in a commerce case was *Thomas Gibbons v. Aaron Ogden,* for which the opinion was written by Chief Justice John Marshall in February 1824. The decision determined that navigation from one state to another is a form of interstate commerce. It reversed a lower court ruling that prevented Gibbons from sailing his steamboats in New York State waters.

2751. Supreme Court decision in a state boundary case was made in 1846, when Chief Justice Roger Brooke Taney ruled that a bill "should be dismissed upon the ground that this court under the Constitution of the United States have not the power to try such a question between states, or redress a wrong, even if the wrong is proved to have been done." On March 16, 1832, Rhode Island, the complainant, had petitioned the Supreme Court to settle a boundary controversy with Massachusetts.

COURTS—SUPREME COURT—JUDGES

2752. Supreme Court chief justice was John Jay of New York, who was appointed by President George Washington on September 24, 1789. His appointment was confirmed on September 26, 1789, and he served until June 29, 1795.

2753. Supreme Court nominee who was rejected by the Senate was William Paterson of New Jersey, who was nominated on February 20, 1793, by President George Washington. His name was sent to the Senate for approval on February 27, but he was rejected on a technicality (he had been serving as senator from New Jersey when the office of associate justice was created). On March 4, 1793, Washington renominated Paterson under a recess appointment. He was confirmed, and served from March 14, 1793, to September 9, 1806.

2754. Supreme Court chief justice whose nomination was not confirmed was John Rutledge of South Carolina, a Federalist, who was appointed chief justice by President George Washington during the adjournment of Congress. He served at a salary of $4,000 a year beginning on July 1, 1795, and presided at the August 1795 term. On December 15, 1795, the Senate rejected the nomination. Rutledge had served as an associate justice from September 26, 1789, to March 5, 1791, at a salary of $3,500 a year, and had resigned to become chief justice of South Carolina.

2755. Supreme Court chief justice who had been a congressional representative was John Marshall of Virginia, who served in the House of Representatives from March 4, 1799, to June 7, 1800, and as chief justice from Febuary 4, 1801, to July 6, 1835, when he died.

2756. Supreme Court chief justice to serve in a presidential cabinet was John Marshall of Virginia, who was chief justice from February 4, 1801, to July 6, 1835. For the first month, until March 4, 1801, he continued to serve as President John Adams's secretary of state, the job he had held since June 1800.

2757. Supreme Court justice to be impeached was Samuel Chase, against whom charges were brought on March 12, 1804, by the House of Representatives. The accusation consisted of eight articles, of which the majority had to do with high-handed conduct displayed by Chase in two treason and sedition trials. There were also political reasons for the impeachment, which was encouraged by President Thomas Jefferson. The trial began on January 30, 1805. Chase was acquitted and served until his death on June 19, 1811, at the age of 70.

2758. Supreme Court justice who had been a representative in Congress was Gabriel Duvall of Maryland, who served in the House of Representatives from November 11, 1794, to March 28, 1796, and as associate justice from February 3, 1812, to January 15, 1835.

2759. Supreme Court chief justice who was Catholic was Roger Brooke Taney of Frederick, MD, who was appointed by President Andrew Jackson to succeed John Marshall. He served from March 28, 1836, until his death on October 12, 1864.

2760. Supreme Court nominee to die before taking office was Edwin McMasters Stanton, appointed by President Ulysses Simpson Grant on December 20, 1869, and confirmed the same day by a vote of 46 to 11. Stanton died on December 24.

2761. Supreme Court justice to be appointed chief justice was Edward Douglass White, who was appointed associate justice on March 12, 1894, and chief justice on December 12, 1910. He took his seat on December 19 and served until May 2, 1921, a week before his death. In 1795, President George Washington had appointed former associate justice John Rutledge to be chief justice, but the appointment was rejected by the Senate after Rutledge had already served during one session.

2762. Supreme Court justice who was Jewish was Louis Dembitz Brandeis of Boston, MA, who was appointed on January 28, 1916, by President Woodrow Wilson. The nomination was confirmed by the Senate on June 1, 1916, and Brandeis was sworn in on June 3. He served until 1939. The first Jewish woman to serve on the Supreme Court was Ruth Bader Ginsburg of the U.S. Appeals Court for the District of Columbia, nominated by President William Jefferson Clinton on June 14, 1993. She filled the seat vacated by Justice Byron White. She was the second woman to serve on the Supreme Court and the first Jewish justice since the resignation of Abe Fortas in 1969.

2763. Supreme Court justice who was African-American was Thurgood Marshall of Maryland, appointed on June 13, 1967, by President Lyndon Baines Johnson. He was confirmed by the Senate by a vote of 69–11 on August 30, 1967, and sworn in on September 1 in a private ceremony. He was publicly sworn in at the opening ceremony of the new term on October 2, 1967. He was the 96th justice.

2764. Supreme Court justice to participate in a television program was Hugo LaFayette Black, who was interviewed in his home at Alexandria, VA, on December 3, 1968, for CBS News by Eric Sevareid and Martin Agronsky.

2765. Supreme Court justice who was a woman was Sandra Day O'Connor of Arizona, nominated as an associate justice by President Ronald Reagan on July 7, 1981. The Senate approved her appointment by a vote of 99–0 on September 21. O'Connor took her seat on September 25 after taking the oath of office administered by Chief Justice Warren E. Burger.

CRIME

2766. Kidnapping is recorded in a letter dated July 8, 1524, from Giovanni da Verrazano, the Florentine explorer, to Francis I, king of France. The letter, which was sent from Dieppe, France, chronicled Verrazano's discoveries in America. Verrazano relates that in 1524 his crew "tooke a [Native American] childe from ... [an] olde woman to bring into France, and going about to take ... [a] young woman which was very beautiful and of tall stature, they could not possibly, for the great outcries that she made, bring her to the sea; and especially having great woods to pass through and being farre from the ship, we purposed to leave her behinde, beareing away the childe only."

CRIME—*continued*

2767. Slander proceedings were instituted on September 17, 1607, by John Robinson, who accused Edward Maria Wingfield, the first governor of the colony at Jamestown, VA, "of having said he, with others, consented to run awaye with the shallop to Newfoundland." A verdict was rendered in favor of Robinson.

2768. Pirate on the Atlantic seaboard was Dixie Bull, an English colonist who had received a grant of land at York, ME. In June 1632, while he was away in Penobscot Bay, a French pinnace arrived and seized his shallop and stock of "coats, ruggs, blanketts, bisketts, etc." Bull avenged himself by becoming a pirate and looting Bristol, ME.

2769. American "Robin Hood" was a thief named Tom Cook, born in 1741 in Westborough, MA. For years, Cook stole from the rich and gave to the poor in scores of New England towns. He called himself "the Leveller." He was finally caught roasting a stolen goose in an abandoned schoolhouse in Brookline, MA. As punishment, Cook was offered the choice of staying in jail or running the gauntlet between two rows of his former victims, all of whom were armed with whips. He chose the gauntlet, which he survived.

2770. Street gangs were formed in the New York City slums beginning about 1785. The members were young tradesmen who claimed various streets as their territory and fought one another over these claims. The first organized gang of street criminals was the Forty Thieves, formed by Edward Coleman in 1826 in Five Points, an Irish slum neighborhood in lower Manhattan. The gangs of Five Points began the custom of having identifiable clothing, hand signals, and rituals.

2771. Conscience fund for people with nagging consciences was started in 1811 during President James Madison's administration by an unknown person who claimed to have defrauded the government and the Treasury of $5 and who wanted to pay it. Other deposits in that year increased the total to $250. No further deposits were received until 1827, when $6 was forwarded. The largest amount collected in one year was received in 1950, when $370,285 was sent in. For statistical and accounting purposes, funds are listed as "Miscellaneous Receipts."

2772. Piracy law enacted by Congress was "an act to protect the commerce of the United States and punish the crime of piracy," enacted on March 3, 1819. Offenders convicted by a circuit court could be punished by death.

2773. Bank robbery occurred on Saturday, March 19, 1831, when two doors of the City Bank, Wall Street, New York City, were opened by duplicate keys. The bank was robbed of $245,000. An Englishman named Edward Smith (alias Edward Jones, alias James Smith, alias James Honeyman) was indicted by the grand jury and arraigned on May 2, 1831, at the Court of General Sessions. On May 11 he was sentenced to five years of hard labor at Sing Sing. Over $185,000 of the loot was recovered.

2774. Train robbery of a disabled train took place on May 5, 1865, when an Ohio and Mississippi Railroad train en route from St. Louis, MO, to Cincinnati, OH, overturned at North Bend, OH, 14 miles from Cincinnati, and was robbed by looters.

2775. Bank and train robbery gang that was well organized was the James Gang, which operated in Missouri after the Civil War. The gang included the James brothers, Frank and Jesse, and the Younger brothers, Cole, James, and Robert. Their first bank holdup took place on February 13, 1866, at the Clay County Savings and Loan Association in Liberty, MO. The cashiers, brothers Greenup and William Bird, were locked in the bank's vault, while the robbers joked that "all birds should be caged." They made off with $60,000 in currency and securities. It was the first of more than 26 raids by the James Gang that yielded more than $500,000 in loot.

2776. Train robbery of a train in motion took place on October 6, 1866, when Frank Sparks, John Reno, and Simeon Reno boarded an Ohio and Mississippi Railroad baggage and express car while it was getting into motion and threw off two safes, one containing $15,000 and the other $30,000. The second safe was recovered. The bandits were arrested, freed on bail, and never tried, although they were later convicted of other crimes.

2777. Tong organized crime gang was the Kwong Dock Tong of San Francisco, CA, organized about 1870. Tongs were secret societies formed by Chinese immigrants. The first tong war broke out in 1873 as a result of an attack made on Ming Long, a member of the Kwong Dock Tong, by Low Sing, a member of the Suey Sing Tong. The dispute arose in connection with the gangs' traffic in forced prostitution. At Ross Valley and Waverly Place, San Francisco, the two factions met by appointment and began shooting. Six members of the Kwong Dock Tong were wounded, three of them fatally, and one of the Suey Sing Tong men was killed.

2778. Airplane bombing raid by criminals occurred on November 12, 1926, during a Prohibition feud between rival illicit beer and rum factions, the Sheltons and the Birgers, in Williamson County, IL. A plane swooped low and dropped three crude bombs on the farmhouse of Charles Birger. They failed to explode, which probably saved the lives of Birger and his companions, for the marksmanship of the flyer was unusually good.

2779. Armored truck holdup was staged on March 11, 1927, by the Flatheads gang, about seven miles from Pittsburgh, PA, on the Bethel Road on the way to Coverdale. An armored truck carrying a $104,250 payroll of the Pittsburgh Terminal Coal Company blew up when it drove over a mine planted under the roadbed by the bandits. Five guards were badly injured.

2780. Organized crime massacre of national notoriety was the St. Valentine's Day Massacre, which took place in Chicago, IL, on February 14, 1929. In a gangland struggle for control of the Chicago trade in bootleg liquor, gunmen in the employ of mobster Al Capone machinegunned seven members of the George "Bugs" Moran gang in a garage on North Clark Street.

2781. Airplane bombing raid by a mercenary soldier took place in 1929, when Patrick Murphy, an American pilot in the pay of Mexican rebels, dropped bombs on Naco, AZ. Murphy apologized to the United States, claiming that he had meant to bomb the town of Naco in Sonora, Mexico, just across the border, but he bombed the American town several more times anyway. When the 1929 Mexican revolution collapsed, Murphy disappeared.

2782. Mobster convicted for tax evasion was Alphonse Capone, better known as Al Capone, who ruled Chicago's illicit beer and liquor trade during Prohibition. Capone's crime organization netted him more than $100 million a year in the late 1920s, little of which he declared to the government. On October 24, 1931, he was sentenced in a federal court in Chicago to 11 years' imprisonment and a $50,000 fine for failing to pay $231,000 in federal income taxes.

2783. Ten Most Wanted list was issued by the Federal Bureau of Investigation in March 1950 at the urging of the International News Service, which asked the FBI for information on mostwanted fugitives for a series of articles. It was largely a publicity stunt, but one that paid off: Two of the men were caught within the month, based on tips from the public. The first woman to be placed on the Ten Most Wanted list was Ruth Eisemann-Schier, accused in the kidnapping for ransom of Barbara Jane Mackle from a motel in Decatur, GA, on December 17, 1968. Mackle was found alive about 80 hours after the abduction, buried in a box underground. Eisemann-Schier was arrested in Norman, OK, on March 5, 1969, convicted, and sentenced to a seven-year prison term.

2784. Skyjacking of a commercial American airplane took place on May 1, 1961, during the flight of a National Airlines twin-engine Convair CV 440 from Miami, FL, to Key West, FL. The plane left Marathon, FL, at 3:23 P.M. with eight passengers. The crew consisted of pilot Francis X. Riley, copilot J.T. Richardson, and flight attendant Inez Barlow. A passenger named Antillo Ortiz, using the name El Pirata Cofresi, threatened the crew and passengers with a pistol and a knife. The plane landed in Havana and returned to Key West at 8:35 P.M., 4.5 hours late. The string of airplane highjackings that followed were dubbed "skyjackings" by the press and led to the U.S.'s first air piracy law, passed in September 1961.

2785. Skyjacking law enacted by Congress was "an act to amend the Federal Aviation Act of 1958 to provide for the application of federal criminal law to certain events occurring on board aircraft in air commerce," enacted on September 5, 1961, and signed by President John Fitzgerald Kennedy. It made hijacking punishable by death or not less than 20 years imprisonment. Carrying a concealed or dangerous weapon was subject to a fine of $1,000 or imprisonment of not more than one year, or both.

2786. Murder to be shown live on television took place at 12:20 P.M. on November 24, 1963, in the police headquarters at Dallas, TX. While television news cameras were rolling, a Dallas police officer brought in Lee Harvey Oswald, the alleged assassin of President John Fitzgerald Kennedy. Oswald was in the process of being transferred to the county jail. A man in the crowd stepped forward and fired a concealed pistol at Oswald, killing him. The crime was witnessed by millions of people. The murderer was Jack Ruby (Jacob L. Rubenstein), a Dallas nightclub owner.

CRIME—*continued*

2787. Skyjacking in which the skyjacker disappeared took place on November 24, 1971, when D.B. Cooper commandeered a Northwest Airlines plane at 11 P.M. He parachuted near Woodland, WA, into a raging thunderstorm with winds up to 200 miles per hour and the temperature at seven degrees below zero, wearing only a light business suit. He escaped with 10,000 $20 bills. He was never found, and it is believed that he was killed.

2788. Poisoning of store merchandise known to have resulted in numerous deaths took place in and around Chicago, IL. In a three-day period from September 29 to October 1, 1982, seven people died after taking Tylenol, a brand of acetaminophen, which they had bought at local drugstores and supermarkets. A murderer who was never apprehended had removed the bottles from store shelves, opened them, added cyanide to the capsules of Tylenol, and replaced them in the stores. The poisonings led to the introduction of wraps and seals on all pharmaceutical products and many other products as well.

2789. Computer hacker to be convicted was Donald Burleson, the former director of computer security at a Texas insurance firm, USPA and IRA of Fort Worth, TX. Three days after Burleson was fired in 1985, the company discovered that 168,000 sales records had been erased from its computer system. Burleson used a type of computer virus called a "logic bomb" or "worm" to destroy the computer data. In September 1988, a Fort Worth jury convicted him on third-degree felony charges and sentenced him to seven years' probation and an $11,800 fine.

2790. Bombing of a skyscraper by foreign terrorists occurred at 12:18 P.M. on February 26, 1993, when a truck bomb exploded in the parking garage of the World Trade Center in New York City. The bomb left a crater 200 feet wide and and caused interior walls and floors of the twin towers to collapse, but the main structures were not seriously damaged. Six people were killed and several hundred were injured. Some 50,000 people were evacuated from the buildings in a rescue effort that disrupted the city's economy and transportation. An FBI manhunt led to the arrest and eventual conviction of several suspects from the Middle East, including the radical Islamic cleric Sheik Omar Abdel Rahman, who surrendered outside a mosque in Brooklyn, New York City, on July 2, 1993.

2791. Bombing by domestic terrorists resulting in large loss of life occurred at 9:02 A.M. on April 19, 1995, when a massive truck bomb destroyed the Alfred P. Murrah Federal Building in Oklahoma City, OK. One hundred sixty-eight people were killed, including 19 children, and an estimated 850 were injured. The rescue effort lasted two weeks and involved more than 12,000 volunteers, one of whom was killed by falling debris. A nationwide manhunt resulted in the arrest of Timothy McVeigh and Terry Nichols, both of whom had connections to the far-right militia movement.

CRIME—DEATH PENALTY

2792. Execution in America was that of John Billington, one of the signers of the Pilgrims' compact, who was hanged in Plymouth, MA, on September 30, 1630. He was "arraigned, and both by grand and petie jurie found guilty of willful murder, by plaine and notorious evidence, and was for the same accordingly executed. This, as it was the first execution amongst them, so was it a matter of great sadness unto them. He way-laid a young man, one John Newcomin (about a former quarele), and shote him with a gune, whereof he dyed."

2793. Execution for witchcraft on record was that of Achsah Young of Massachusetts, who was hanged as a witch on May 27, 1647, although some histories of New England state that the first accused witch to be executed was Margaret Jones of Charlestown, MA, hanged in 1648.

2794. Electrocution experiment was performed in Philadelphia, PA, by Benjamin Franklin, who described his findings in 1773 in a letter to Barbeau Dubourg and Thomas Francois Dalibard. Current from six Leyden jars was used to electrocute chickens, a 10-pound turkey, and a lamb.

2795. Execution by the Army occurred on June 27, 1776. A guard, Thomas Hickey, plotted with others to capture George Washington and deliver him to Sir William Howe. Hickey was tried, convicted, and hanged in New York City. The execution took place at a field near Bowery Lane in the presence of 20,000 persons, including an armed assembly of all the off-duty officers and men of four brigades.

2796. Death penalty ban by a state was enacted by Pennsylvania on April 22, 1794. The law abolished all executions except in cases of murder in the first degree. Michigan enacted a general ban on the death penalty on May 4, 1846, except in cases of treason against the state.

2797. Execution for slave trading carried out by the federal government was the hanging of Nathaniel Gordon at the Tombs prison, New York City, on February 21, 1862. He had been tried and convicted of piracy under the law of May 15, 1820, which defined slave trading as piracy. Gordon, a native of Portland, ME, was the captain of the *Erie*. His ship was stopped by the U.S. *Mohican* about 50 miles off the African coast and was found to be carrying 890 Africans, including 600 children, to a slave market. The captives were released in Liberia and Gordon's ship was brought to New York City, where his trial was held.

2798. Execution of a woman by hanging by the federal government took place on July 7, 1865. The condemned woman was Mary Eugenia Surratt, the proprietor of a boarding-house in Washington, DC. Her son was a friend of the actor John Wilkes Booth and met with him and other plotters in the boarding-house to plan the assassination of President Abraham Lincoln. The assassination was carried out on April 14, 1865. Mrs. Surratt was arrested and tried for conspiracy by a military commission of nine army officers headed by Major General David Hunter. The trial began on May 9 and ended on June 30 with a conviction and the death sentence. Four conspirators, including Mrs. Surratt, were hanged on July 7. Her guilt is still a subject of controversy. Her son was brought to trial, but the government failed to obtain an indictment, and he was released.

2799. Execution by electrocution was that of William Kemmler, alias John Hart, who died on August 6, 1890, at Auburn Prison, Auburn, NY. He had been convicted of the first-degree murder of Matilda Ziegler. The electric chair used at the prison was invented by Dr. Alphonse David Rockwell. An autopsy was performed three hours after the execution under the direction of Dr. Carlos Frederick MacDonald. The first woman to be executed by electrocution was Martha M. Place of Brooklyn, New York City, who was electrocuted at Sing Sing Prison, Ossining, NY, on March 20, 1899, for the murder of her stepdaughter Ida.

2800. Execution by lethal gas took place on February 8, 1924, in Carson City, NV. The executed man was a Chinese gang member, Gee Jon, who had been convicted of killing a rival tong man. Lethal gas as a means of execution had been adopted by Nevada on March 28, 1921.

2801. Execution for kidnapping was imposed by the Circuit Court of Kansas City, MO, on July 27, 1933. Walter H. McGee was found guilty by a jury of having kidnapped Mary McElroy, daughter of the city manager of Kansas City. The prosecutor was Assistant County Prosecutor Michael W. O'Hern. The court applied a congressional act of May 18, 1934, regarding interstate kidnapping.

2802. Death penalty authorized by federal law made the killing of a federal officer a mandatory capital offense. The law was enacted on May 18, 1934. The first man executed under the law was George W. Barrett, for the murder of federal agent Nelson Bernard Klein in College Corner, IN, on August 16, 1935. He was tried before U.S. District Judge Robert C. Baltzell, convicted on December 14, 1935, and hanged on March 24, 1936, at the Marion County Jail, Indianapolis, IN.

2803. Execution of an organized crime leader in the electric chair was that of Louis Buchalter, better known as Louis Lepke, the head of Murder Incorporated, a gang of mob assassins based in New York City. Lepke surrendered to FBI chief J. Edgar Hoover on August 24, 1939, to face a charge of union racketeering. Under a secret agreement, he pleaded guilty to a lesser charge and was sentenced to a 14-year term in the federal penitentiary at Fort Leavenworth, KS. After New York State authorities found out from a mob informer about Lepke's career of murder, he was tried again and sentenced to death. On March 4, 1944, Lepke went to the electric chair at Sing Sing Prison in Ossining, NY.

2804. Execution carried out by the federal government for the killing of an FBI agent took place at Sing Sing Prison, Ossining, NY, on August 12, 1954, when Gerhard Puff was electrocuted. He had been convicted of killing Joseph Brock, an agent of the Federal Bureau of Investigation, in a gun battle in New York City on July 26, 1952. Brock had been attempting to arrest Puff for participating in the robbery of $62,650 from the Johnson County National Bank and Trust Company of Prairie Village, KS. He was confined for 15 months in the death house and his execution was postponed five times pending various appeals.

CRIME—DEATH PENALTY—*continued*

2805. Lethal injection as a method of execution was authorized on May 10, 1977, by Oklahoma. The law provided that "the punishment of death must be inflicted by continuous, intravenous administration of a lethal quantity of an ultrashort-acting barbiturate in combination with a chemical paralytic agent until death is pronounced by a licensed physician according to accepted standards of medical practice."

2806. Execution by lethal injection took place on December 7, 1983, in the state penitentiary at Huntsville, TX. Charles Brooks, Jr., who had been convicted of murdering an auto mechanic, received an intravenous injection of sodium pentathol, the barbiturate also known as truth serum.

CRIME—DUELS

2807. Duel of which there is any record took place on June 18, 1621, between two servants of Stephen Hopkins, one of the leaders of the Plymouth Colony. Governor William Bradford's decision was rendered as follows: "The Second Offense is the first Duel fought in New England, upon a Challenge at Single Combat with Sword and Dagger between Edward Dotey and Edward Leister, Servants of Mr. Hopkins; Both being wounded, the one in the Hand, the other in the Thigh; they are adjudg'd by the whole Company to have their Head and Feet tied together, and so to lie for 24 hours, without Meat or Drink; which is begun to be inflicted, but within an Hour, because of their great Pains, at their own and their Master's humble request, upon Promise of better Carriage, they are Released by the Governor."

2808. Dueling law enacted by a state was an "act to prevent the evil practice of duelling," passed by the Fourth General Assembly held at Knoxville, TN, and signed on November 10, 1801, by Governor Archibald Roane.

2809. Duel in which a future president of the United States participated took place on May 30, 1806, at Harrison's Mills on the Red River, Logan County, KY, when Andrew Jackson shot and killed Charles Dickinson. The combatants stood 24 feet apart. Dickinson fired first. The shot broke a couple of Jackson's ribs and grazed his breastbone. Despite the injury, Jackson fired and killed Dickinson. It was one of a hundred duels and brawls in which Jackson is said to have participated. Jackson served as president of the United States from March 4, 1829, to March 3, 1837.

2810. Duel between representatives in Congress was held on the famous Bladensburg, MD, dueling field in 1808, when George Washington Campbell of Tennessee shot Barent Gardenier of New York through the body. Gardenier had accused Congress of being under the influence of France, which Campbell denied, at the same time assailing Gardenier with a torrent of personal abuse. Gardenier challenged him to a duel, was wounded, and after his recovery returned to his attacks with more animosity than before. Campbell served in Congress from October 17, 1803, to March 3, 1809; Gardenier served from March 4, 1807, to March 3, 1811.

CRIME—PRISONS

2811. Prison was constructed in 1676 in Nantucket, MA. The court hired William Bunker on November 16, 1676, to keep the prison for one year and agreed to pay him "foeur pounds, halfe in wheat, the other in other graine."

2812. Prison reform society to bring about changes in prison administration was the Philadelphia Society for Alleviating the Miseries of Public Prisons, formed on May 8, 1787, in the German School House on Cherry Street, Philadelphia, PA, by Philadelphia Quakers. The first president was William White. A similar organization for war prisoners was the Philadelphia Society for Relieving Distressed Prisoners Owing to the War of Independence, organized on February 7, 1776, which ceased operations in September 1777.

2813. Prison to have individual cells for prisoners was the Walnut Street prison in Philadelphia, PA, built in 1773, which was remodeled in 1790 in accordance with the act of April 5, 1790, of the Pennsylvania General Assembly. The remodeled prison contained 24 cells, each six feet wide, eight feet long, and seven feet high. The prisoners were kept in solitary confinement and were not allowed to leave their cells. The prison held about 110 prisoners.

2814. Federal law exempting debtors from prison on processes issuing from a United States court amounting to less than $30 was "an act for the relief of persons imprisoned for debt," passed on May 28, 1796. On February 28, 1839, an act of Congress prohibited imprisonment for debt by a United States court in states where such imprisonment had been abolished.

2815. State law abolishing imprisonment for debt was passed by Kentucky on December 17, 1821.

2816. Prison treadmill was completed on September 7, 1822, for the New York City Prison. The treadmill was designed to be operated by eight to 16 persons and to grind 40 to 50 bushels of maize daily. The wheel was 5 feet 2 inches in diameter. The treadmill was placed in operation on September 23, 1822, in a two-story building 60 feet in length and 30 feet wide, with a garret that served as a granary. The idea for the treadmill was suggested to Stephen Allen, the mayor of New York, by Isaac Collins, one of the managers of the Society for the Prevention of Pauperism, and Stephen Greelet.

2817. Reformatory for juvenile deliquents was the New York House of Refuge, New York City, which officially opened on January 1, 1825, with three boys and six girls. It was under the supervision of the Society for the Reformation of Juvenile Offenders in the City of New York. The first president was Cadwallader David Colden. On April 9, 1825, the state authorized a grant of $2,000 annually for the next five years.

2818. Branding punishment by a federal court was imposed at Pensacola, FL, in 1844. Jonathan Walker, a ship captain, was convicted of stealing seven slaves, whom he carried into his 30-foot schooner. He set sail on June 23, 1844, intending to go to Nassau, but was captured by the U.S. steamer *General Taylor* and taken to Pensacola on July 20. He was imprisoned, tried in the District Court, and placed in the pillory on the public highway to be pelted with rotten eggs. He was sentenced to one year in jail for each of the seven slaves and was fined $600 for each slave plus all the costs of the trial. The initials SS, for "slave stealer," were branded on the palm of his right hand.

2819. Prison matrons for guarding women prisoners were appointed in 1845 through the efforts of the American Female Guardian Society. Four were assigned to Blackwell's Island, NY, and two the City Prison, New York City.

2820. Reformatory for boys established by a state was the reformatory school at Westborough, MA, later known as the Lyman School for Boys. It was authorized on April 9, 1847.

2821. Military prison on an island was Fort Jefferson, Monroe County, FL. Construction was begun in 1846 on an island in the Gulf of Mexico, 60 miles from Key West. It was a six-sided masonry structure with a huge courtyard in the center. The sides were 1,000 feet long, 80 feet high, and 60 feet thick. On January 19, 1861, it was garrisoned for the first time by Brevet Major Lewis Golding Arnold, 2nd U.S. Artillery, with four officers and 62 men. The fort had not been completed and was barely defensible. A prison for the confinement of U.S. military prisoners was established at Fort Jefferson in 1863. The prison, often called Dry Tortugas, was maintained during the Civil War.

2822. Probation officer for juvenile delinquents to be hired by a state was hired under a Massachusetts law enacted on June 23, 1869. The law required the governor to appoint a visiting agent at $2,500 a year to work for the welfare and redemption of delinquents, rather than for their punishment. The visiting agent or his deputies were directed to visit all children maintained wholly or in part by the Commonwealth of Massachusetts once every three months.

2823. Prison built for women and managed by women was the Indiana Reformatory Institution for Women and Girls, Indianapolis, IN, which received its first 17 prisoners on October 8, 1873. The first superintendent was Sarah J. Smith. In 1907 the name was changed to the Indiana Women's Prison. Beginning in January 1877, all members of the Board of Trustees were women.

2824. Reformatory for women established by a state was the Reformatory Prison for Women, Sherborn, MA, opened November 7, 1877. The first superintendent was Eudora Clark Atkinson and the first resident physician was Dr. Eliza Maria Mosher. The part of Sherborn in which the reformatory was located was annexed to the town of Framingham, MA, in 1925.

2825. Probation system for criminals of all ages was legally established as a judicial policy by Boston, MA, in 1878 and by Massachusetts in 1880. This was the first such system in the world.

2826. Penitentiary building opened by the federal government was the Federal Penitentiary at Atlanta, GA, which was authorized in 1899 and completed in January 1902. The Federal Penitentiary at Leavenworth, KS, was authorized earlier, on March 3, 1891, but was not completed until February 1, 1906.

2827. Prison organized into community groups was Auburn Prison, Auburn, NY. In 1914, a Mutual Welfare League of prisoners was created on an experimental basis to assume the responsibility of discipline in the prison.

CRIME—PRISONS—*continued*

2828. Prisoners in a federal penitentiary to be employed in industry produced cotton duck for mail bags and other purposes at the Cotton Duck Mill operated by the Federal Penitentiary in Atlanta, GA, whose first loom started on July 11, 1919. The building covered an area of almost three acres. In the first year, 386,414 yards of duck were produced. The mill was authorized by act of Congress on July 10, 1918, which appropriated $650,000 for equipment and $150,000 as working capital. A wage system for inmates, established on April 29, 1921, set up a wage fund of two cents per yard that was divided among the inmates in proportion to their number of hours of service.

2829. Prison established by the federal government for women was the Federal Industrial Institution for Women, Alderson, WV, established by act of Congress in 1926 and opened the same year. The first superintendent was Dr. Mary Belle Harris, sworn in on March 12, 1925. The compound contained 17 two-story brick dormitories, each designed to accommodate 30 persons, and built on the college plan. They cost over $2 million and occupied 500 acres of land. There were no prison walls or guards.

2830. Prison commissioner who was a woman was Anna Moscowitz Kross, who was sworn in on January 1, 1954, as commissioner of correction, New York City. The first woman to direct a state prison system was Ward E. Murphy, who became director of the Maine Bureau of Corrections at Augusta, ME, in July 1970.

2831. Prison guard who was a woman to serve in a maximum security prison for men was Joan Wyatt Stewart of Burlington, IA, who was appointed correction officer on February 1, 1973, in the Iowa State Penitentiary, Fort Madison, IA.

2832. Year in which the prison population exceeded 1 million was 1994, according to an announcement made by the Justice Department on October 27 of that year. The increase in prisoners made the United States second in the world to Russia with regard to incarceration rates.

CRIME—TREASON

2833. Treason trial by a colony was held on May 7, 1634, when the Virginia Assembly heard complaints against Sir John Harvey, governor of Virginia. On April 28, 1635, he was removed from the governorship as a traitor and replaced by Captain John West. Harvey was returned to England, where his case was considered. On April 2, 1636, he returned to assume his post, which he held until November 1639.

2834. Colonist hanged for treason was Jacob Leisler, who led an insurrection against Governor Francis Nicholson of New York in 1689 "for the preservation of the Protestant religion" and in behalf of the sovereigns William and Mary. Through trickery, the aristocratic party regained power and in a manifestly unfair trial convicted Leisler of treason. He was hanged on May 16, 1691, from a scaffold erected in City Hall Park.

2835. Citizen of the United States to be hanged for treason was William Bruce Mumford, a retired gambler. During the Civil War, Captain Theodorus Bailey was sent by Admiral David Glasgow Farragut to New Orleans, LA, where he hoisted the American flag over the mint on April 28, 1862. After the troops left, Mumford tore down the flag. On May 1, General Benjamin Franklin Butler arrived in New Orleans with 2,000 troops and took possession of the St. Charles Hotel. A crowd gathered in front of it, among them Mumford, who boasted of his exploit in humbling the "old rag of the United States." Mumford was arrested, tried under the direction of the provost marshal of the district of New Orleans, convicted, and hanged on June 7, 1862.

2836. Peacetime death sentence for espionage was imposed on April 5, 1951, by Judge Irving Robert Kaufman of the U.S. District Court, Southern District, who sentenced Ethel and Julius Rosenberg to death for passing secret information about nuclear weapons to the Soviet Union. The trial began on March 6, 1951, and the jury rendered its verdict of guilty on March 29. The chief witness was Ethel Rosenberg's brother David Greenglass, an army sergeant who admitted that he had given them the information. The Rosenbergs were electrocuted on June 19, 1953, at Sing Sing Prison, Ossining, NY. They were the first native-born Americans executed for espionage by order of a civilian court.

D

DEATH

2837. Lead coffins used in the New World were three caskets dating from the 17th century. Archeologists found them at St. Mary's City, MD, in the ruins of the first Catholic church built in England's North American colonies. They contained the remains of former Maryland governor Philip Calvert, his first wife, and his infant daughter by his second wife. Calvert died in 1661.

2838. Cannibal of note was John Johnston, a trapper, army scout, and lawman in the Wyoming territory around 1840 to 1890. He was known as Liver-Eating Johnston for his habit of killing members of the Crow tribe and consuming their livers. Native Americans called him Abaroka Dabiek, or Crow Killer. Johnston claimed that he was taking revenge for the murder of his pregnant Chinook wife by a Crow raiding party. After killing some 250 to 300 Crow, he made peace with them and was made the blood brother of a prominent chief.

2839. Funeral home operated on the cooperative plan was the Collingwood Memorial, Toledo, OH, which opened on September 15, 1930. The expenses of operation were divided equally by the concerns using the building, thereby enabling funeral services to be provided more cheaply.

2840. Right-to-die society was the National Society for the Legalization of Euthanasia, formed on January 14, 1938, in New York City with the Reverend Charles Francis Potter as president. The society was incorporated as the Euthanasia Society of America on November 30, 1938.

2841. Freezing of a corpse for future resuscitation took place in January 1967. Robert F. Nelson and others interested in cryonics used dry ice to freeze the body of James H. Bedford, a retired psychology professor.

2842. Probate delay law enacted by a state eliminating red tape in probating wills was enacted on June 22, 1973, by Wisconsin, an "act relating to establishing a procedure for informal administration of estates."

2843. Right-to-die law enacted by a state was the Natural Death Act of California, enacted on September 30, 1976, which allowed physicians of terminally ill patients to withhold life-sustaining procedures under certain conditions.

2844. Suicidal person to jump off the Empire State Building and live was 26-year-old Thomas Helms, who attempted to commit suicide by jumping from the observation deck on the 86th floor of the Empire State Building in New York City on December 22, 1977. Helms landed on a narrow ledge on the 85th floor, about 20 feet lower down. He was knocked unconscious for half an hour, but was not seriously injured.

2845. Death by suicide machine occurred in Detroit, MI, on June 4, 1990, when Janet Adkins of Portland, OR, took her own life using a device that administered a fatal dose of drugs when she pushed a button. The machine was invented by Dr. Jack Kevorkian, the crusader for doctor-assisted suicide. Kevorkian was on hand to assist Adkins, who suffered from Alzheimer's disease. Michigan was selected as the site because at that time the state had no law prohibiting doctor-assisted suicide.

2846. Space burial took place on April 21, 1997, when small samples of the ashes of 24 people, including Timothy Leary and Gene Roddenberry, were carried into space along with Spain's first communications satellite. Leary, a psychologist famous for his espousal of psychedelic drugs, died on May 31, 1996. His final request was for "one last far-out trip." Roddenberry, who created the "Star Trek" television series, died on October 24, 1991. The remains were ejected in lipstick-sized capsules that were expected to orbit the earth for up to 10 years before burning up in the atmosphere.

DEATH—AUTOPSY

2847. Autopsy was performed in Florida in 1536 on Philippe Rougement (Felipe de Rojamón), 22 years old, a victim of the plague or scurvy.

2848. Autopsy officially recorded took place at Salem, MA, in September 1639. In his *History of New England,* John Winthrop wrote: "This boy was ill-disposed, and his master gave him unreasonable correction and used him ill in his diet. After the boy gate a bruise on his head, so as there appeared a fracture in his skull, being dissected after his death." Marmaduke Perry of Salem was arraigned for the death of his apprentice.

2849. Autopsy with verdict of a coroner's jury was recorded in Maryland on September 24, 1657. The surgeon received his fee of "one hogshead of tobacco" for "dissecting and viewing the corpse" of an African-American slave thought to have been murdered by his master.

DEATH—AUTOPSY—*continued*

2850. Autopsy performed by a woman physician on a male corpse was performed by Dr. Bethenia Owens-Adair at Roseburg, OR, in 1870 and verified by six physicians. She was a graduate of two courses of medical lectures and had completed the course of study at the Eclectic School of Medicine, Philadelphia, PA.

DEATH—CEMETERIES

2851. Jewish cemetery was established in New York City by Congregation Shearith Israel, the first Jewish congregation in America, in 1656. The plot occupied a piece of ground in the section now known as Chatham Square. It was consecrated on February 22, 1656.

2852. National cemetery was established in Washington, DC, in a section of Christ Church known as the Washington Parish Burial Ground. Records show that burials were made in 1804, but the date of the deed is recorded as March 31, 1812. In 1816, the federal government, seeking a burial place "for the interment of members of Congress, any heads of General Government and members of their familes," accepted the cemetery from the vestry of Christ Church. Located at 18th and E streets, SE, it is more familiarly known as the Congressional Cemetery and occupies 30 acres alongside the Anacostia River.

2853. Federal cemetery to contain graves of both Union and Confederate soldiers was opened in Springfield, MO, by act of Congress dated March 3, 1911. Part of it was formerly a Confederate cemetery maintained by the state of Missouri, which deeded it to the federal government on June 21, 1911. A stone wall separates the graves of the Confederate troops from those of the Union soldiers. The cemetery contains over 3,100 graves.

2854. Burial at the Tomb of the Unknown Soldier in the National Cemetery at Arlington, VA, took place on November 11, 1921. President Warren Gamaliel Harding, accompanied by practically every prominent government officer, attended the services and the unveiling of the national shrine, which was built to honor the large number of American soldiers who lost their lives in World War I but whose bodies were never identified.

2855. Foreign servicewomen interred in the Arlington National Cemetery in Arlington, VA, were Section Officers Monica M. Daventry of Worcester, England, and Ruth P. Watson of Hampstead, England, members of the British Women's Auxiliary Air Force, interred on November 19, 1942. Returning from duty, they were killed in an automobile accident. American soldiers served as pallbearers and 12 Waves as honorary pallbearers.

DEATH—CREMATION

2856. Cremation was that of Henry Laurens of Charleston, SC, an export merchant and delegate to the Continental Congress who served on diplomatic missions in France and England after the Revolutionary War. He died on December 8, 1792. His will read as follows: "I solemnly enjoin it upon my son as an indispensable duty that, as soon as he conveniently can after my decease, he cause my body to be wrapped in twelve yards of tow cloth, and burnt until it is entirely consumed, and then, collecting my ashes, deposit them wherever he may see proper."

2857. Crematory was erected by Francis Julius LeMoyne on his grounds in Washington, PA, in 1876. It was the only crematory in the United States until 1884. The first body incinerated was that of Baron Joseph Henry Louis de Palm, on December 6, 1876. LeMoyne died of diabetes on October 14, 1879, and two days later was cremated in his own crematory.

2858. Crematory established by a state government was authorized by New York on May 21, 1888, when $20,000 was appropriated to build and equip a crematory on Swinburne Island in New York Harbor. It was built by Dr. Miles Lewis Davis of Lancaster, PA. In 1889, bodies buried at the Quarantine cemetery at Sequine's Point were disinterred and cremated.

DISASTERS

2859. Flood of which there is any known record was the flooding of the Mississippi River in 1543, which was observed by the Spanish explorer Hernando de Soto. He noted that the river began overflowing its banks on March 18 and continued until it crested on April 20. By the end of May, the flood had receded.

2860. Hurricane of record occurred on August 15, 1635, when a cyclonic storm ravaged the Plymouth colony.

2861. Earthquake description is contained in *History of the Plymouth Plantation* by William Bradford, the colony's first governor. The earthquake occurred on Friday, June 1, 1638, at 2 P.M. at Plymouth, MA, and is described in part as follows: "However, it was very terrible for the time; and as the men were set talking in the house, some women and others were without the doors, and the earth shooke with the violence as they could not stand without catching hold of the posts and pails that stood next them, but the violence lasted not long. And about halfe an hower, or less, came an other noyse & shaking, but neither so loud nor strong as the former, but quickly passed over, and so it ceased." In 1638 several Native Americans described to Roger Williams, founder of Providence, RI, an earthquake that had occurred there in 1558. No accurate record exists prior to this date.

2862. Cyclone of record occurred on August 27, 1667, at Jamestown, VA. According to one observer, it produced "such violence that it overturned many houses burying in the ruins much goods and many people, beating to the grounds such as were any ways employed in the fields, blowing many cattle that were near the sea or rivers, into them, whereby unknown numbers have perished, to the great affliction of all people .... the sea swelled twelve foot above the normal eight, drowning the whole country before it, with many of the inhabitants, their cattle and feed."

2863. Tornado of record occurred at New Haven, CT, on June 10, 1682, about 2:30 P.M. Sir Walter Raleigh's Virginia colonists are believed to have seen a tornado off the coast of North Carolina on June 23, 1586.

2864. Volcanic eruption for which a date can be estimated occurred at Cinder Cone, in the Lassen Peak district of California, about 1694.

2865. Drought of record occurred in New England in 1727, when there was hardly any rainfall from the second week of April through the middle of July.

2866. Hailstone shower of record that was fatal took place on May 8, 1784, at Winnsborough, SC, when "an extraordinary shower of hail, attended with thunder and lightning," killed several people, as well as sheep and fowl.

2867. Earthquake of consequence to be recorded was felt on August 31, 1886, throughout the eastern part of the United States. The epicenter was 15 miles northwest of Charleston, SC, where 41 people died, 90 percent of the city's 6,956 brick buildings were damaged, and nearly all of its 14,000 chimneys were broken off at the roof. Altogether, the earthquake claimed some 100 lives. A series of earthquakes beginning on December 16, 1811, were the most severe in U.S. history—they changed the course of the Mississippi River and created many new lakes—but the epicenter was in a sparsely populated region and caused no known casualties.

2868. Dam disaster of great consequence occurred on May 31, 1889, at Johnstown, PA, when the South Fork Dam burst and flooded the city with a wall of water reaching 75 feet high and half a mile wide. The flood caused 2,205 deaths and property damage of about $10 million. The dam had held back the waters of Conemaugh Lake, which was about 2.5 miles long and 1.5 miles wide, with an average depth of 50 feet.

2869. Tornado disaster on a large scale occurred on March 18, 1925, when tornados struck Indiana, Illinois, Kentucky, and Tennessee. Over the course of three hours, 689 people died, 13,000 were injured, and $16–18 million worth of damage occurred.

2870. Volcanic eruption to be broadcast on radio was the eruption of the Mount Kilauea volcano in Hawaii. The sound was transmitted via short wave by station KGU, Honolulu, HI, whose wires extended 3.5 miles from the mouth of the volcano to the transmitter. The broadcast was picked up in San Francisco and relayed to WJZ, New York City, where it was heard at 4:15 P.M. on December 28, 1931. Thomas A. Jaggar, a volcanologist, likened the sound of the erupting volcano to the roar of Niagara Falls and reported that in six days about 260,000 cubic feet of lava had been disgorged.

2871. Volcano known to claim human life in the contiguous 48 states was Mount St. Helens, located in the Cascade Range of Washington state. During the massive eruption of May 18, 1980, 61 people were asphyxiated by the rain of hot ash, buried by pyroclastic flows of superheated gas and mud, or drowned in flash floods.

2872. Year when half of the nation's agricultural counties were designated disaster areas was 1988. By the end of June, much of the United States was suffering through the worst drought in five decades.

DISASTERS—EPIDEMICS

2873. Smallpox epidemic of importance occurred in 1616–17 and swept away the Native Americans of New England from the Penobscot River to Narragansett Bay, reducing the fighting force from 3,000 to some 50 men. About a century later, in May 1721, an outbreak of smallpox killed up to a quarter of the population of Boston, MA, and nearby cities.

2874. Influenza epidemic occurred in 1733 and was most serious in Philadelphia, PA, and New York City. About three-fourths of the entire population was affected.

2875. Medical record of an epidemic was Benjamin Rush's *An Account of the Bilious Remitting Yellow Fever, as It Appeared in the city of Philadelphia, in the year 1793.* The book, which had 363 pages, was printed in 1794 by Thomas Dobson in Philadelphia, PA. About 4,000 people died between August and November 1793.

2876. Cholera epidemic occurred in 1832. Individual cases are said to have developed in several cities, but the real force of the epidemic was manifested in the larger cities such as New York City, Boston, MA, and Philadelphia, PA. The first case in New York City appeared on June 28, 1832. From July 5 to August 29, 5,835 cases developed, of which 2,251 resulted in death. On July 21, New York City reported 311 cases and 100 deaths.

2877. Poliomyelitis epidemic occurred in Vermont in 1894. Between June 17 and September 1, 123 cases appeared in Rutland and Wallingford. The first major urban polio epidemic took place in the summer of 1916 in New York City, where 9,000 children were stricken and 2,400 died.

2878. AIDS epidemic began in the spring of 1981, when the first cases were reported to the Centers for Disease Control in Atlanta, GA, by doctors in San Francisco and New York City. The initial patients were all young, previously healthy homosexual men who died from rare opportunistic illnesses because their immune systems had been suppressed. AIDS stands for "acquired immunodeficiency syndrome."

DISASTERS—FIRES

2879. Fire of serious consequence that was recorded occurred on November 27, 1676, when there "burned down to the ground 46 dwelling houses, besides other buildings, meeting house, etc.," in Boston, MA. Three years later, on August 8, 1679, another Boston fire destroyed 80 dwellings and 70 commercial buildings, the damage amounting to almost $1 million.

2880. Fire in a mine was chronicled by the Reverend Charles Beatty in 1765. He reported that a fire had been burning for at least a year in a coal mine known as Spot Hill, the opening of which was somewhere between the Point Bridge and the Smithfield Street Bridge, on the south side of the Monongahela River in that part of Pittsburgh now known as Mount Washington.

2881. Fire of great destructive force took place in New York City on December 16, 1835, when 600 buildings were demolished, entailing a loss of over $20 million.

2882. Fire in an oil well occurred on April 17, 1861, when the Little and Merrick well on the Buchanan farm near Rouseville, PA, at Oil Creek, caught fire shortly after it gushed. It burned for three days and 19 persons lost their lives. The well produced about 3,000 barrels a day.

2883. Forest fire of consequence that was recorded occurred on October 8, 1871, at Peshtigo, WI, north of Green Bay. The fire, which was eight to 10 miles wide, destroyed 1.28 acres of timberland. The forests were dry, since there had been no rain for three months.

E

EDUCATION—ADULT

2884. Lyceum for adult education was founded by Josiah Holbrook in Millbury, MA, in October 1826. Its purpose was to afford adults an opportunity for mutual improvement through association and study, stimulate an interest in the schools, and contribute to the training of teachers and the dissemination of knowledge through libraries and museums. The Millbury Lyceum became part of the American Lyceum Association when it was organized on May 4, 1831, in New York City by delegates from Maine, Massachusetts, and New York.

2885. Chautauqua organization meeting took place on August 4, 1874, in Fair Point, NY, when the organization was founded by the first Sunday School Teachers Assembly at the suggestion of John Heyl Vincent and Lewis Miller. On August 10, 1878, home study courses were offered and the name Chautauqua Literary and Scientific Circle adopted.

2886. Correspondence course of a serious nature was offered by the Literary and Scientific Circle of the Chautauqua Institution, which was organized on August 10, 1878. A correspondence School of Theology was organized and in 1881 received its charter. On March 30, 1883, the Chautauqua College of Liberal Arts was given a charter by the legislature of the State of New York, conferring full authority to grant diplomas and to confer the usual college and university degrees.

2887. Night school for immigrants was run by Henrietta Szold in Baltimore, MD, beginning in 1889. Szold, a teacher in a school for girls, taught English to Jewish refugees from czarist Russia. The first semester's enrollment was 50 students. The classes were taken over by the Baltimore board of education in 1898.

2888. Correspondence school for workers was started through the initiative of Thomas Jefferson Foster, proprietor and editor of the *Shenandoah Herald,* Shenandoah, PA, who issued a course in the fundamentals of coal mine development and operation as a way of educating workers. The first student was enrolled on October 16, 1891. The name was later changed to the International Correspondence Schools, with headquarters at Scranton, PA.

2889. Continuation school for adults established by a state government was the Racine Continuation School, Racine, WI, which opened on November 3, 1911, to offer evening instruction to adults, as well as to children from 14 to 16 years of age who had permits to work.

EDUCATION—AGRICULTURE

2890. Agriculture professor at a college was Samuel Latham Mitchill, who was appointed by Columbia College, New York City, on July 9, 1792, as professor of natural history, chemistry, agriculture, and the other related sciences. Part of his course included the "theory of vegetation and application of its principles to practical agriculture, nutrition and food of plants, with the history of manures, multiplication, dissemination and habitations of plants. Chemical history of various vegetable products, Sap, Gum, Resin, Farina, etc., with their preparation and application to the uses of man. Vegetable colors, vegetable poisons, baking, brewing, tanning, etc."

2891. Agricultural college to be chartered by a state was the Farmers High School of Pennsylvania, incorporated on April 13, 1854. The school opened on February 16, 1859. In the first session, 119 students were admitted. The Bachelor of Scientific and Practical Agriculture degree was awarded to those who completed a four-year course and submitted a dissertation. The name was changed on May 6, 1862, to the Agricultural College of Pennsylvania. Another state agricultural school, the Agricultural College of Michigan in Lansing, MI, received its charter later, in 1855, but opened sooner, on May 13, 1857.

2892. Land grant for an agricultural college was proposed by Justin Smith Morrill, congressman from Vermont. He advocated giving each state an allotment of land, the income from which should be used to support at least one agricultural college in each state. The bill was vetoed by President James Buchanan in 1857, but was signed by President Abraham Lincoln on July 2, 1862, after certain modifications had been made. It was known as the Morrill Act.

2893. Farmers' institute sponsored by a state was held by the Massachusetts State Board of Agriculture in Springfield, MA. The institute opened on December 8, 1863, and continued for four days. Lectures and discussions pertaining to agriculture occupied the meetings.

2894. Farmers' institute sponsored by a college was held on November 14, 1868, by the Kansas State Agricultural College, now the Kansas State College of Agriculture and Applied Science, at the Riley County Courthouse, Manhattan, KS. Local arrangements for the institute were made by the Riley County Agricultural Society.

2895. Land grant college for African-American students was the Alcorn Agricultural and Mechanical College in Rodney, MS, which was established by the state of Mississippi in 1871. The original name was Alcorn University. Under the Morrill Act of 1862, which gave each state an allotment of land on which to build an agricultural college, Mississippi received scrip for 210,000 acres, which it disposed of for $188,928. Three-fifths of the sum went to Alcorn University and the remaining two-fifths went to support the University of Mississippi.

EDUCATION—AGRICULTURE—*continued*

2896. Animal husbandry professor at a college was John Alexander Craig of the Wisconsin Agricultural Experiment Station, University of Wisconsin, Madison, WI, who served from 1890 to 1897. His specialty was sheep husbandry.

2897. Dairy school at a college was opened on January 3, 1890, by the College of Agriculture, University of Wisconsin, Madison, WI, to supplement courses in testing milk and farm churning. The first instructor in charge of dairying was Professor John Wright Decker. The first year, the organized course was attended by only two students, but the following year 70 registered from nine states and Canada. Dairy certificates were awarded to those who passed the full course and had been in practical charge of a creamery or cheese factory for two seasons.

EDUCATION—ARTS

2898. School for music teachers for music teachers was the Boston Academy of Music, Boston, MA, founded on January 8, 1833. Samuel Atkins Eliot was the first president. The faculty consisted of Lowell Mason and George James Webb. The school used the teaching method that had been developed by the Swiss educator and reformer Johann Heinrich Pestalozzi.

2899. Music school authorized to confer degrees was established about 1835 by Oramel Whittlesey in Salem, CT. It was successively known as Mr. Whittlesey's Music School, Music Vale Seminary, and the Normal Academy of Music. The first degree was conferred about 1849.

2900. Music instruction in a public school was conducted by Lowell Mason in November 1837 at the Hawes School, South Boston, MA. On August 28, 1838, the school board voted that a committee on music be instructed to contract with a teacher of vocal music for the several public schools of Boston. Mason was appointed and served from 1838 to 1841. He was in charge of four assistants.

2901. Music convention of singing teachers was attended by 96 men and 42 women from 10 states and was held August 16–25, 1838, in Boston, MA. Colonel Asa Barr of New Braintree, MA, was president.

2902. Fine arts department in a college was the School of Fine Arts, Yale University, New Haven, CT, which was established in 1864 and opened in 1869 with four students under John Ferguson Weir, appointed professor of painting and design. Until 1891, when the school's first Bachelor of Fine Arts degree was awarded to Josephine Miles Lewis, certificates were given to those who completed the three-year course. The College of Fine Arts at Syracuse University, Syracuse, NY, established June 24, 1873, was the first college fine arts department to grant degrees.

2903. Architecture department at a college was established on February 20, 1865, by the Massachusetts Institute of Technology, Boston, MA. William Robert Ware was the first head of the department and received the title of professor.

2904. Music chair at a college was established at Harvard University, Cambridge, MA, on August 30, 1875, when John Knowles Paine was appointed professor of music. On March 29, 1862, he had been appointed instructor in music, and on June 2, 1873, assistant professor. He served until his death, on April 25, 1906.

2905. Drama school devoted exclusively to training performers for the professional stage was the Lyceum School of Acting in New York City, which was founded by Franklin Haven Sargent on October 1, 1884. It was renamed the American Academy of Dramatic Arts in 1890.

2906. Ceramics school was started by Ohio State University, Columbus, OH, in 1894 under the guidance and direction of Professor Edward Orton, Jr.

2907. Organ school was the Guilmant Organ School, New York City, established in 1899 by Dr. William Crane Carl and Dr. Howard Duffield. The school was named for the French organist Alexandre Guilmant.

2908. School of modern dance was the Denishawn Dance School, founded in 1915 in New York City by dancers Ruth St. Denis (born Ruth Dennis) and Ted Shawn. St. Denis's dances, based on Asian models, and Shawn's works incorporating Native American themes strongly influenced the early course of modern dance in America. A second Denishawn School was founded in Los Angeles in 1920. Shawn also founded the first all-male dance company in the United States, Ted Shawn and His Men Dancers.

2909. Dance major at a college was approved on November 11, 1926, by the Wisconsin Board of Regents and offered in the Department of Physical Education of Women, University of Wisconsin, Madison, WI. Margaret Newell H'Doubler was appointed chairman of the program.

2910. Drama school at a college that was operated in association with a professional theater was the Mohawk Drama Festival and Institute of the Theater, which offered its first courses on July 2, 1935, at Union College, Schenectady, NY. Seventy students enrolled in the intensive eight-week course, which covered history, theory, and practice. The director was Dr. Thomas Herbert Dickinson. Four plays were presented: *The Merry Wives of Windsor, Lysistrata, Rip Van Winkle,* and *Master of the Revels.* The course concluded on August 24, 1935, when 25 certificates of meritorious achievement were awarded. The school was chartered by the Regents of the University of the State of New York in 1938.

2911. Cartooning school giving courses in the production of animated cartoons was the Hastings School of Animation, New York City, organized February 1938. Instruction began in April 1938.

2912. Radio production course at a college was part of a four-year combined program in liberal arts and radio leading to the degree of Bachelor of Arts, offered by New York University in September 1939 in the Washington Square College of Arts and Science. The course included instruction in writing, speaking, announcing, planning and production, news broadcasting, and broadcasting of special events.

2913. Television production course at a college was offered on September 26, 1940, in evening sessions at New York University, New York City. The instructor was Thomas H. Hutchinson of the National Broadcasting Company. The first day course was given by the School of Speech, Marquette University, Milwaukee, WI, in the fall of 1951. Fourteen students registered for instruction in programing, administrative duties, and coordination of writing, staging, directing, and acting. The course was conducted by Colby Lewis, assistant program manager of WTMJ-TV, Milwaukee.

2914. Film professorship at a college was established by the Washington Square College of Arts and Sciences of New York University, New York City, on May 26, 1941, when the appointment of Robert Gessner as assistant professor of motion pictures was approved for the term beginning on September 1, 1941. The title for the position was variously changed to professor of television, motion pictures and radio, and to professor of cinema.

2915. Ballet technique course at a college was offered at Texas Christian University, Fort Worth, TX, in 1949, when instructor David Preston taught a class of 18 freshmen in the fall semester.

2916. Belly-dancing course at a college was "Body Conditioning Through the Art of Oriental Belly Dance," a noncredit course consisting of six lessons, offered in August 1973 by the University of Texas at Arlington, TX. The instructor was Germaine Brown, known professionally as Chastity Fox. Sixty enrollees paid the $25 fee.

EDUCATION—BUSINESS

2917. Business school was opened in Rochester, NY, in 1842 by George Washington Eastman, and was named the Eastman Commercial College.

2918. Business economics course at a college was established by the University of Louisiana (now Tulane University), New Orleans, LA, in 1849. It was conducted by Professor James Dunwoody Brownson De Bow under the title "Commerce, Political Economy, and Statistics."

2919. Business school at a college was the Wharton School of Commerce and Finance in Philadelphia, PA, established in 1881 by the University of Pennsylvania through a $100,000 gift of Joseph Wharton.

2920. Industrial corporation course at a college was offered by Dr. Amos Griswold Warner, lecturer on political and economic science, at the University of Nebraska, Lincoln, NE, in 1888–89. It was entitled "Private Corporations; Origin, history and present status of joint stock concerns, including railroads."

2921. Advertising school was established in 1920 by the members of the Poor Richard Club in their clubhouse in Philadelphia, PA. A diploma was awarded for the completion of the two-year course. In 1924, the name was changed to the Charles Morris Price School of Advertising and Journalism of the Poor Richard Club.

EDUCATION—BUSINESS—*continued*

2922. Business history chair at a college was the Isidor Straus Professorship of Business History, established in 1923 by the Graduate School of Business Administration, Harvard University, Cambridge, MA. The first incumbent was Norman Scott Brien Gras, appointed in 1927.

2923. Radio advertising course at a college was instituted by the School of Business and Civic Administration of the City College of New York on September 28, 1930, under the direction of Frank Atkinson Arnold, director of development of the National Broadcasting Company. The class consisted of 62 students.

EDUCATION—COLLEGES AND UNIVERSITIES

2924. College proposed in America was the College of William and Mary, proposed in 1617. In 1618 the London Company set aside 10,000 acres for the college and the following year the General Assembly at Virginia petitioned to have workmen sent to erect buildings for it at the town of Henrico. However, it was not incorporated until February 8, 1693, when it received a charter from King William III of England and was named the College of William and Mary, to be established in Williamsburg, VA. Instruction was begun about 1696 and the first graduation exercises were held in 1700, nearly six decades after Harvard's first commencement.

2925. College founded in America was Harvard College, established in 1636 by the General Court of Massachusetts Bay. On September 8, 1636, the Court appropriated £400 for the project, and in 1637 it appointed 12 of the principal men of the colony "to take orders for a college at New Towne." The institution was originally given the name Cambridge College. It was renamed in 1638 in honor of the Reverend John Harvard, who bequeathed the college about £800 and 300 books. Nathaniel Eaton was appointed the first master of the College and Henry Dunster the first president. The first building, erected in 1637, was known as "The Indian Collidge." It was made of brick and was 30 feet long and 200 feet wide. The first commencement was held on September 23, 1642, when the B.A. degree was conferred on nine graduates.

2926. College charter granted by the Crown under the Seal of the Privy Council was "their Majesties Royal College of William and Mary" in Williamsburg, VA, the charter for which was granted on February 8, 1693. The college was also the first to receive a coat of arms from the College of Heralds.

2927. College to have a full faculty was the College of William and Mary, Williamsburg, VA. On February 27, 1729, the college realty was transferred from the trustees to the faculty, which consisted of a president, six professors, an usher, and a writing master.

2928. College charter granted by a governor with only the assent of his council was issued on October 22, 1746, to 12 trustees of the College of New Jersey (now Princeton University), Princeton, NJ, by Governor John Hamilton, president of His Majesty's Council. The college opened the fourth week of May 1747. The first commencement was held on November 9, 1748. The Reverend Jonathan Dickinson was the first president.

2929. Academy to offer a broader curriculum than was taught in grammar schools was the Academy and College of Philadelphia, founded in 1749 in Philadelphia, PA, by Benjamin Franklin, who became its president. The academy opened on August 13, 1751, and offered English, mathematical, and classical courses of study. Seven men were graduated on May 17, 1757, at the first commencement, six as Bachelors of Arts and one as Master of Arts.

2930. College to confer medals as prizes was the College of William and Mary at Williamsburg, VA. In 1770 Lord Botetourt, governor of Virginia, presented two gold medals, one to be awarded to the best student in philosophy, the other to the best student in classics.

2931. College to use the honor system during examinations was the College of William and Mary, Williamsburg, VA, in 1779.

2932. College with an elective system of study was the College of William and Mary, Williamsburg, VA. In 1779 students were permitted to choose the subjects they wanted to pursue.

2933. University legally designated as such was the University of the State of Pennsylvania, Philadelphia, PA. The original name of the institution was the College of Philadelphia. It was designated a university on November 27, 1779, by the Pennsylvania legislature. Since 1791, the name has been University of Pennsylvania. It is a privately endowed institution, not a state university. Whether it was in fact a university before it was designated as one, and whether it was the first institution to merit being called a university, are questions of definition.

2934. College named after George Washington was Washington College in Washington College, TN, founded in 1780 by the Reverend Dr. Samuel Doak, who became its first president. On April 24, 1783, it was chartered as Martin Academy by North Carolina, of which Tennessee was then a part. A second charter was received on March 31, 1785, from the state of Franklin, which was never officially recognized. A third charter, received on July 8, 1795, changed the name to Washington College. The name was proposed to the legislature of the "Territory of the United States South of the River Ohio" by General John Sevier.

2935. State university to be chartered was the University of Georgia, Athens, GA. Although it was chartered on January 27, 1785, it was not opened to students until 1801. The first state university actually opened was the University of North Carolina, Chapel Hill, NC, which began operating on February 13, 1795.

2936. City college was the College of Charleston, Charleston, SC, which was founded in 1770, chartered on March 19, 1785, and opened in 1790 with the Reverend Robert Smith as the first principal. On December 20, 1837, it became a municipal university under municipal control. It opened on April 1, 1838, with 16 students. The first president was the Reverend Dr. William Theophilus Brantley, pastor of the Baptist Church.

2937. College founded as a Methodist institution was Cokesbury College, Abingdon, MD, named in honor of Bishops Thomas Coke and Francis Asbury. The building was 108 feet long, 40 feet wide, and three stories high. The first headmaster was the Reverend Mr. Heath. The foundation sermon was delivered on June 5, 1785, and the building was opened on December 6, 1787.

2938. College founded as a Catholic institution was Georgetown College, Washington, DC, established on January 23, 1789, and opened on November 15, 1791. The first student to register was William Gaston of Newberne, NC. Authority to grant degrees was authorized by act of Congress of March 1, 1815.

2939. College that was nondenominational was Blount College, Knoxville, TN (now the University of Tennessee), chartered on September 10, 1794. The charter provided that the college "take effectual care that students of all denominations may and shall be admitted to the equal advantages of a liberal education and to the emoluments and honors of the college, so that they shall receive a like, fair, generous and equal treatment during their residence therein." The first president was Samuel Carrick. The second nondenominational college was Union College, Schenectady, NY, chartered on February 25, 1795, whose charter required that the majority of the 24 trustees "shall not at any time be composed of persons of the same religious sect or denomination." The Reverend John Blair Smith assumed office as the first president on December 8, 1795.

2940. Land grant university was Ohio University, Athens, OH, which was chartered on February 18, 1804, and opened on June 1, 1808, with three students. Governor Edward Tiffin presided at the first trustees' meeting. The first president was the Reverend Jacob Lindley. A contract dated October 27, 1787, between the Ohio Company of Associates and the federal government provided that the rental derived from land belonging to Ohio's townships should be set aside for the support of a university.

2941. College entrance requirement other than Greek, Latin, and arithmetic was geography, which was required in 1807 for admission to Harvard College, Cambridge, MA.

2942. College founded as a Quaker institution was the Haverford School, Haverford, PA, which opened on October 28, 1833, under the sponsorship of members of the Society of Friends. The first superintendent was Samuel Hilles. The name was changed to Haverford College in 1856.

2943. College to enroll women and men on equal terms was Oberlin Collegiate Institute, Oberlin, OH, which opened on December 3, 1833, with 44 students, 29 men and 15 women. Equal status was granted to women on September 6, 1837, when 30 men matriculated along with four women: Elizabeth Smith Prall of New York City, Caroline Mary Rudd of Huntington, CT, Mary Hosford of Oberlin, OH, and Mary Fletcher Kellogg of Jamestown, NY. In 1841, the first three of these women graduated with the B.A. degree, having pursued a classical course equivalent to that at Yale. On March 21,

EDUCATION—COLLEGES AND UNIVERSITIES—*continued*

1850, the name of the school was changed to Oberlin College. It was the first school to advocate the abolition of slavery and to accept African-American men and women on equal terms with white students.

2944. College for women was Mount Holyoke College, South Hadley, MA, chartered on February 11, 1836, and opened on November 8, 1837, as the Mount Holyoke Female Seminary, with 80 students who paid $64 a year for tuition and board. They were required to do cooperative household tasks. The first principal was Mary Lyon, who served until 1849. The first commencement, at which four women were graduated, was held on August 23, 1838. Another women's college chartered in 1836 was Wesleyan College, Macon, GA, originally known as the Georgia Female College, which graduated its first class of 11 women on July 16, 1840. An earlier claim is made for the Elizabeth Female Academy, Washington, MS, which existed from 1818 to 1843.

2945. Masonic college was the Masonic College of Missouri, opened for enrollment on May 12, 1844, near Philadelphia, Marion County, MO. It later moved to Lexington, MO. The cost for tuition was $15 a session and for board and washing $25, with the maximum cost $85 a year. The first president was J. Worthington Smith, who was also professor of moral philosophy.

2946. College to prohibit discrimination because of race, religion, or color was Cooper Union for the Advancement of Science and Art, New York City, whose deed of trust, dated April 29, 1851, prohibited discrimination in the acceptance of students for reasons of race, creed, or color. Peter Cooper was the first president.

2947. College professor who was a woman and who was accorded the same privileges as male professors was Rebecca Mann Pennell, professor of physical geography, drawing, natural history, civil history, and didactics, who was appointed in September 1852 by Antioch College, Yellow Springs, OH. She conducted classes when the college opened on October 5, 1853. Other institutions employed women but did not allow them to attend faculty meetings.

2948. University on the Pacific Coast was Willamette University, Salem, OR. It was organized on February 1, 1842, as the Oregon Institute, offering only elementary work, and opened on August 13, 1844, with five students. On January 12, 1853, it was chartered as a university by the Oregon Territorial Legislature. The Oregon Institute was continued as a preparatory school.

2949. College for African-American students was the Ashmun Institute, Chester County, PA, which was chartered by act of the legislature of Pennsylvania on April 29, 1854, to give theological, classical, and scientific training to African-Americans. It was named after Jehudi Ashmun, the reorganizer of the colony of Liberia. It opened on January 1, 1857. The first president was John Pym Carter. The charter was amended in 1866, changing the name to Lincoln University.

2950. College to sponsor an endowed lecture series was the Union Theological Seminary, New York City, which on May 20, 1865, established the Morse Lectureship on the Relationship of the Bible to Any of the Sciences. The series was named in memory of the founder's father, Samuel Finley Breese Morse. The first lecture series was given in 1866 by Professor Arnold Guyot on "The First Chapter of Genesis." An endowed series known as the Elias P. Ely Lectureship on the Evidences of Christianity had previously been established by the same institution, but lectures were not given until 1867.

2951. University for African-American students with undergraduate, graduate, and professional schools was Howard University, Washington, DC, founded on November 20, 1866, as the Howard Theological Seminary. On January 8, 1867, the name was changed to Howard University. On May 1, 1867, the teacher-training department and the preparatory department opened in a leased frame structure with five students, all children of the trustees. It was incorporated on March 2, 1867, by act of Congress, which authorized the establishment of the teacher-training, preparatory, collegiate, theological, medical, law, and agricultural departments. The first president was the Reverend Charles Brandon Boynton. The first African-American president was Dr. Mordecai Wyatt Johnson of Charleston, WV, whose service began on September 1, 1926.

2952. State university supported by a direct property tax was the University of Michigan, Ann Arbor, MI. An act of the state legislature approved on March 15, 1867, assessed all taxable property one twentieth of a mill on each dollar of value, to be used for the use, aid, and maintenance of the university. The funds paid to the university in 1867 totalled $15,398.

2953. State university to grant equal privileges to women was Indiana University, Bloomington, IN. Sarah Parke Morrison, who was graduated in 1869, was the first woman to enter the school and the first to receive a degree from it.

2954. State college for women was the Mississippi Industrial Institute and College, established in Columbus, MS, by act of the Mississippi legislature on March 12, 1884. The first graduation exercises took place in June 1889, at which time 10 A.B. degrees were conferred. The first president was Dr. Richard Watson Jones. In 1920 the name was changed to the Mississippi State College for Women.

2955. Graduate school for women was Bryn Mawr College, Bryn Mawr, PA, which was organized in 1884 and formally opened on October 23, 1885. From its inception, Bryn Mawr offered graduate work leading to the M.A. and Ph.D. degrees, in addition to undergraduate programs.

2956. College for women to affiliate with a university was the H. Sophie Newcomb Memorial College, established on October 11, 1886, in New Orleans, LA. The college affiliated with Tulane University, also in New Orleans, in October 1887.

2957. Academic costume standardization for colleges was advocated by Gardner Cotrell Leonard of Albany, NY, in "The Cap and Gown in America," an article in the December 1893 issue of *University Magazine*. On May 16, 1895, a commission composed of representatives from various colleges and universities assembled at Columbia University, New York City, and drew up a code. A Bureau of Academic Costume was chartered July 2, 1902, at Albany, NY, by the Regents of the University of the State of New York "to maintain a register of statutes, codes, and usages, designs and descriptions of the articles of academic costume and regalia with their correct color, materials, qualities, sizes, proportions and the arrangement thereof."

2958. College for women founded as a Catholic institution was the College of Notre Dame of Maryland, Baltimore, MD, which opened on September 2, 1895. The first commencement was held on June 14, 1899, when four bachelor of arts degrees and two bachelor of literature degrees were awarded. Charles Joseph Bonaparte, a grandnephew of Napoleon, was the commencement speaker, his subject being "The Significance of the Bachelor's Degree."

2959. Finnish college was Suomi College, in Hancock, MI, which opened on September 8, 1896. Founded and supported by people of Finnish descent with the goal of preserving the Finnish religious heritage and culture, it was operated by the Finnish Evangelical Lutheran Church. Enrollment in the first semester of the two-year college was 15 men and 7 women. Fees were $10 for the fall term and $15 for the spring term; room and board cost $2 a week. The first rector was Juho Kustra Nikander. In 1904 Suomi became a theological seminary.

2960. University press was founded in 1899 by the Johns Hopkins University, Baltimore, MD. Its first publication was the *American Journal of Mathematics*.

2961. Rhodes Scholars took up residence at Oxford University, England, in 1904. The will of the British financier and industrialist Cecil Rhodes, dated July 1, 1899, established three-year scholarships to Oxford for outstanding students from the United States, Germany, and British colonies. The first year, 43 awards were made to students from 43 different states. The first African-American student to receive a Rhodes scholarship was Alain Le Roy Locke of Pennsylvania, who studied philosophy at Oxford's Hertford College from 1907 to 1910. He received his A.B. degree in 1908 from Harvard University.

2962. Technical college for women was Simmons College, Boston, MA, which was chartered in 1899 by the provisions of the will of John Simmons, a Boston merchant who died in 1870. The college opened in 1902 and the first class was graduated on June 13, 1906, when 32 B.S. degrees were conferred. The first president was Henry Lefavour.

2963. College under Jewish auspices that was nonsectarian was Dropsie College for Hebrew and Cognate Learning of Philadelphia, PA, chartered on June 6, 1907. The college was founded in accordance with the will of Moses Aaron Dropsie, who directed "that in the admission of students there shall be no distinction on account of creed, color or sex." The first president of the college was Dr. Cyrus Adler.

EDUCATION—COLLEGES AND UNIVERSITIES—*continued*

2964. University for African-American students founded as a Catholic institution was Xavier University, New Orleans, LA, which conferred five A.B. degrees on June 6, 1928. It had opened on September 27, 1915, as a high school. A two-year program to educate teachers was opened on September 24, 1917. The college department opened on September 13, 1925, with Sister Mary Frances as the first dean. The first president was the Reverend Edward Brunner, S.S.J.

2965. College of liberal arts and sciences founded as a Jewish institution was Yeshiva College, Amsterdam Avenue and 186th Street, New York City, chartered on March 29, 1928, by the board of Regents of the University of the State of New York. The first graduating class, consisting of 19 members, received bachelors' degrees on June 16, 1932. The first president was Rabbi Dr. Bernard Revel. On November 16, 1945, the college became Yeshiva University and was authorized to establish new graduate and undergraduate schools and to confer 15 kinds of degrees.

2966. College to use the unit-cost plan was Rollins College of Winter Park, FL, which adopted it in September 1933. The plan, which was recommended by President Hamilton Holt, required the operating expenses of the college to be divided by the estimated number of students in order to ascertain the individual cost for each student. In the first year of operation, each student was required to pay $1,350 to cover the cost of board, room, and tuition.

2967. College principally for war veterans was Champlain College, Plattsburgh, NY, opened on September 16, 1946. It was operated by the Associated Colleges of Upper New York, a corporation created by legislative act effective April 1, 1946, which also opened Mohawk College in Utica, NY, and Sampson College, in Sampson, NY, opened on October 23, 1946. The president was Asa Smallidge Knowles.

2968. College for women founded as a Jewish institution was Stern College for Women, New York City, which opened on September 13, 1954, with 33 students. The first graduation took place on June 19, 1958, when 26 B.A. degrees were awarded. The first president was Dr. Samuel Belkin.

2969. College on a Native American reservation was Navajo Community College, established in Tsaile, AZ, in 1969.

2970. College whose tuition fees were based on family income was Beloit College, in Beloit, WI, which adopted the plan on October 11, 1971, for the term beginning in September 1972. Tuition in 1972–73 for families with no other children in college varied from $500 for those with an adjusted income of less than $7,000 to $1,650 for those with an adjusted income of $30,000 or more.

EDUCATION—COLLEGES AND UNIVERSITIES—ADMINISTRATION

2971. College president who was a woman was Frances Elizabeth Willard, professor of science at the Northwestern Female College, Evanston, IL. In February 1871, when the school was reorganized as the Evanston College for Ladies, she became president. All the members of the faculty and all the trustees were women. On June 25, 1873, the college was incorporated into Northwestern University as the Woman's College, with Miss Willard as the dean. The first woman to become president of a university was Hanna Holborn Gray, who became head of the University of Chicago on October 6, 1978.

2972. Dean of the faculty at a college was Martha Carey Thomas, one of the four women in the world at that time to hold the Ph.D. degree, who was appointed at the January 1884 meeting of the trustees of Bryn Mawr College, Bryn Mawr, PA.

2973. Dean of students at a college was appointed at Whitman College, Walla Walla, WA, in 1901. Benjamin Harrison Brown, professor of physics and chemistry, was appointed dean of men, and Dr. Louis Francis Anderson, professor of Greek, was appointed dean of women.

2974. Dean of a university graduate school who was a woman was Dr. Frieda Wunderlich, elected on January 4, 1939, as dean of the Graduate Faculty of Political and Social Science, part of the New School for Social Research, New York City.

2975. President of a major university who was African-American was Clifton Reginald Wharton, Jr., who on January 2, 1970, became the 14th president of Michigan State University, East Lansing, MI, which had an enrollment of about 44,000.

EDUCATION—COLLEGES AND UNIVERSITIES—DEGREES

2976. Bachelor of Arts degree was conferred on September 23, 1642, by Harvard College, Cambridge, MA, on nine graduates: Tobias Barnard, Samuel Bellingham, Nathaniel Brewster, John Bulkley, George Downing, William Hubbard, Henry Saltonstall, John Wilson, and Benjamin Woodbridge.

2977. Doctor of Philosophy degree was awarded in 1861 by Yale University, New Haven, CT, to three graduates: Eugene Schuyler, James Morris Whiton, and Arthur Williams Wright. The degree had been authorized on July 24, 1860.

2978. Doctor of Philosophy degree awarded to an African-American scholar was granted to Edward Alexander Bouchet by Yale University, New Haven, CT, in 1876, in physics. His thesis was entitled *Measuring Refractive Indices*. Bouchet was also the first African-American to be elected to Phi Beta Kappa, the national scholastic fraternity. He was graduated from Yale in 1874.

2979. Doctor of Philosophy degree awarded to a woman by an American university was granted by Boston University, Boston, MA, on June 6, 1877, to Helen Magill. The title of her dissertation was *The Greek Drama*. She received her A.B. degree in 1875 from Swarthmore College.

2980. College diploma made of silver was issued on May 18, 1934, by the Colorado School of Mines, in Golden, CO. Made of sterling silver, measuring approximately 5 inches by 5.75 inches, and 0.02 inches thick, the diplomas were signed with a stylus by the president, Dr. Melville Fuller Coolbaugh.

2981. College degree awarded to a ventriloquist's dummy was conferred on August 28, 1938, by the School of Speech of Northwestern University, Evanston, IL, on the dummy Charlie McCarthy during the regular Edgar Bergen-Charlie McCarthy hour in the Chicago studios of the National Broadcasting Company. The school's dean, Ralph Dennis, awarded the dummy the degree of Master of Innuendo and Snappy Comeback.

2982. College commencement exercises in a prison were held on January 20, 1975, in the Jackson State Prison, Jackson, MI. Twenty associate degrees were conferred by Jackson Community College.

EDUCATION—COLLEGES AND UNIVERSITIES—FRATERNITIES

2983. Scholastic fraternity at a college was Phi Beta Kappa, founded on December 5, 1776, at William and Mary College, Williamsburg, VA, with a nucleus of 50 members. In December 1779 it authorized the establishment of branches at Yale and Harvard. The first chapter to be established at an African-American university was formed on April 4, 1953, at Fisk University, Nashville, TN. Goodrich Cook White, president of the United Chapters of Phi Beta Kappa, presented the charter to eight charter members and two foundation members, both Fisk alumni. On April 8, 1953, a chapter was established at Howard University, Washington, DC.

2984. Social fraternity at a college was Kappa Alpha, established on November 26, 1825, at Union College, Schenectady, NY. The first initiation was held on December 3, 1825. The first presiding officer was David White.

2985. Fraternity house at a college was occupied in 1839 by the Williams Chapter (Alpha Chapter of Massachusetts) of the Kappa Alpha Society at Williams College, Williamstown, MA. The chapter was founded on October 29, 1833, and used various quarters until 1839, when it hired a frame structure two stories high, an annex to the residence of Captain James Meachem. The first floor supplied space for social gatherings and a banquet room. A winding stair led to the second story, planned expressly for secret meetings.

2986. College secret society for women was the Adelphean Society, organized on May 15, 1851, at Wesleyan College, Macon, GA, with 16 charter members whose motto was "We live for one another." The founder was Eugenia Tucker Fitzgerald. The name was changed to Alpha Delta Phi Sorority in 1904, at which time the society had 60 active members and 3,000 alumnae. In 1913 it changed its name to the Alpha Delta Pi Sorority.

2987. Professional fraternity at a college was Theta Xi, founded on April 29, 1864, at the Rensselaer Polytechnic Institute, Troy, NY. Membership was confined to students of engineering and science. The fraternity was an offspring of Sigma Delta, a local society at Rensselaer Polytechnic Institute.

EDUCATION—COLLEGES AND UNIVERSITIES—FRATERNITIES—*continued*

2988. Sorority at a college was Kappa Alpha Theta, which was founded on January 27, 1870, at Indiana Asbury University, now DePauw University, in Greencastle, IN. The first sorority for African-American students was Alpha Kappa Alpha, founded on January 15, 1908, at Howard University, Washington, DC, by Ethel Hedgeman Lyle. The first president was Lucy Slowe.

2989. National college fraternity for African-American men was Alpha Phi Alpha, formed on December 4, 1906, by members of a social study club formed in 1905. The first president was George B. Kelley. The first chapter was started at Cornell University, Ithaca, NY, and the second, in 1908, at Howard University, Washington, DC.

EDUCATION—COLLEGES AND UNIVERSITIES—PROGRAMS

2990. College literary society was the Cliosophic Society, founded at Princeton University, Princeton, NJ, in 1765. The first coeducational literary society at a college was the Alethezetean Society of Antioch College, Yellow Springs, OH, founded in December 1853. The society was disbanded in 1855 by vote of the faculty.

2991. College alumni association established for any considerable period without suspending operations was the Society of Alumni of Williams College, Williamstown, MA, formed on September 1821. The first president was Dr. Asa Burbank of the class of 1797. The first full-time paid secretary of a college alumni association was Ralph C. McAllister, whose position was created on June 30, 1897, by the University of Michigan, Ann Arbor, MI, to foster service on the part of the alumni for the university.

2992. College course without Greek or Latin was established in 1824 by Geneva College (now Hobart College), Geneva, NY. The course, known as the "English Course," was designed "for the practical business of life by which the Agriculturist, the Merchant and the Mechanic may receive a practical knowledge of what genius and experience have discovered, without passing through a tedious course of Classical studies." The first course diploma, in English, was awarded in 1827 to Henry Smith Attwater.

2993. College summer school was established at Mount Union College, Alliance, OH. Lewis Miller of Akron, OH, presented the idea to the faculty in February 1870 and the summer school was started as a part of a four-term system in June 1870.

2994. College entrance plan using certified schools in which admission was based on the credentials of the applicant's preparatory school rather than the credentials of the applicant was the Michigan System, originated by Henry Simmons Frieze and introduced in September 1871 at the University of Michigan, Ann Arbor, MI. A student who graduated from an approved school was admitted without the necessity of taking individual examinations.

2995. College program of study abroad was introduced by Boston University, Boston, MA, which entered into reciprocal agreement on February 11, 1875, with the National University, Athens, Greece, and the Royal University, Rome, Italy. Students could attend these universities and have their credits applied towards degrees at their home institution. The first program offering a junior year abroad was instituted by the University of Delaware, Newark, DE, in 1923, when Professor Raymond Watson Kirkbride took a group of eight students to France for work at the University of Paris.

2996. Honors program offered by a university was held in September 1882 at the University of Michigan, Ann Arbor, MI. The program enabled students to take required work for two years and then, under faculty committee direction, to proceed within a limited range of subjects in a specialized course. Students who exhibited a thorough knowledge in their special fields were given bachelor's degrees or master's degrees upon passing a cumulative examination and completing a thesis.

2997. College extension courses granting college credits were offered on January 1, 1893, by the University Extension Division in the Class-Study Department of the University of Chicago, Chicago, IL, "with credit ... given in the books of the University to properly qualified students who completed any course of instruction." Twenty-five academic or secondary school courses and 40 college courses were given. Admission requirements were the same as those of other parts of the university. The first director of the Extension Division was George Henderson.

2998. College varsity sports program in which letters were awarded was established on January 29, 1904, at the University of Chicago, Chicago, IL, by Amos Alonzo Stagg. It was known as the "order of the 'C.'" Since then, practically all colleges and high schools have established similar organizations. The practice of awarding blankets to lettermen who had completed their competition was initiated by Stagg at the University of Chicago following the football season of 1904. This practice has also been widely copied.

2999. College foreign-language house was Deutsches Haus, a four-story brick building at Columbia University, New York City, opened in 1911. The first director was Rudolph Tombs, Jr. The house was suggested by Columbia's president, Nicholas Murray Butler.

3000. College comprehensive senior examination program was adopted on May 26, 1913, by the faculty of Whitman College, Walla Walla, WA. Beginning with the class of 1914, every student graduated from Whitman College was required to pass an examination, either oral or oral and written, given by a committee of the faculty in the student's department and covering the entire field of study in student's major subject. The written examinations ran from 6 to 10 hours and the orals from 1 to 3.

3001. College to dispense with credits, hours, points, and grades was Olivet College, Olivet, MI, which on October 1, 1934, substituted a system proposed by its president, Joseph Brewer. The system divided the college into junior and senior divisions and required candidates for the degree of Bachelor of Arts to have at least three years of instruction and to pass preliminary and final examinations. It also opened lectures to all members of the college without distinction and assigned tutors to guide each student's course while investing the responsibility for acquiring an education with the student.

3002. College classes intended to combat the influence of communism were instituted on December 4, 1935, by St. Joseph's College, Philadelphia, PA. More than 1,200 students registered for the courses, the only charge being a registration fee of one dollar. College credits were not given, but certificates of completion were issued. The president of the college was the Very Reverend Thomas Joseph Higgins.

3003. College to offer courses to railroad commuters was Adelphi University, in Garden City, NY, which offered graduate courses in business statistics, microeconomic analysis, accounting, marketing, and the legal environment of business on trains of the Long Island Railroad between Huntington, NY, and New York City, beginning on October 18, 1971. The commuting classrooms contained swivel chairs, audiovisual systems, blackboards, and microphones. The fee was the same as on the campus, $246 for each three-point course, plus train fare. The Master of Business Administration degree was awarded on completion of the two-year program, which consisted of three classes a week for eight weeks, or two a week for 12 weeks. The 66-minute class began at 5:56 A.M. from Huntington; the 77-minute return-trip class from New York City began at 5:56 P.M. The courses, for which Adelphi received a $20,000 grant from the Long Island Trust Company, were under the direction of Dr. Peter Berman and Dean Julius Liff.

3004. College to offer athletic scholarships to women was the University of Miami, in Coral Gables, FL, which offered full-tuition scholarships, each worth $2,400 a year, to 15 athletes. The first recipient was Terry Williams of Homestead, FL, on May 5, 1973.

EDUCATION—COLLEGES AND UNIVERSITIES—STUDENTS

3005. College student to work his way through college was Zechariah Brigden, 14 years old, who was graduated from Harvard College, Cambridge, MA, in 1657. He earned money by "ringing the bell and waytinge."

3006. College graduate who was Native American was Caleb Cheeshahteaumuck, the son of a Narragansett sachem of Holmes Hole in Martha's Vineyard, MA, who was graduated from Harvard College, Cambridge, MA, in 1665. He died of tuberculosis shortly after his graduation.

3007. Protest by college students of record was instigated in 1766 by Asa Dunbar, a student at Harvard College, Cambridge, MA. Dunbar complained about the food and raised the chant "Behold, our butter stinketh!" He was condemned for "the sin of insubordination" and responded by leading several followers off-campus to eat their breakfasts. Dunbar grew up to become the grandfather of the transcendentalist writer Henry David Thoreau.

EDUCATION—COLLEGES AND UNIVERSITIES—STUDENTS—*continued*

3008. College graduate who was Jewish was Isaac Abrahams, who was graduated from King's College (later called Columbia College), New York City, in 1774, receiving the A.B. degree. He delivered a Latin oration at the commencement exercises. Judah Monis, the Italian-born son of Portuguese Marranos (hidden Jews), was granted the degree of Master of Arts by Harvard College in 1720, probably on the strength of a manuscript that he had prepared on teaching Hebrew grammar. After his conversion to Christianity in 1722 he was appointed to the Harvard faculty as instructor in Hebrew.

3009. College graduate who was African-American was Alexander Lucius Twilight, who was graduated from Middlebury College, Middlebury, VT, in 1823 with a B.A. degree.

3010. College graduate who was an African-American woman was Lucy Ann Stanton of Cleveland, OH, who was graduated on December 8, 1850, from Oberlin College, Oberlin, OH, receiving the Bachelor of Literature degree.

3011. Chinese graduate of an American college was Yung Wing, who entered Yale University, New Haven, CT, in 1850 and was graduated on June 13, 1854, with a B.A. degree. He had been one of a group of three Chinese students who were brought to the United States in April 1847 by the Reverend Samuel Robbins Brown, head of the Morrison School, the first English-language school in China, to study at the Monson Academy, Monson, MA. They were the first Chinese students in the United States. Yung Wing later went on to serve as associate minister in the first Chinese embassy to the United States, which opened in Washington, DC, in October 1878.

3012. Graduate student who was a woman to receive a university fellowship was Harriet Elizabeth Grotecloss, who was awarded the Sage Fellowship in Entomology and Botany by Cornell University, Ithaca, NY, on June 19, 1884. The fellowship had a stipend of $400 per year, payable in six installments, and provided free tuition for graduate study.

3013. Student government at a college was the Bryn Mawr Self-Government Association, chartered on February 23, 1892, by the trustees, subjecting student conduct outside the classrooms at Bryn Mawr, PA, to student rulings.

3014. College student to receive assistance from the federal government as the child of a deceased veteran was George A. Turner, 19, of Brooklyn, New York City, who enrolled at the University of Oklahoma. He was the son of William G. Turner, who died in 1954 at the age of 43 from a disability incurred during the Normandy invasion in World War II. The law authorizing such grants was enacted by Congress on June 29, 1956, "to establish an educational assistance program for children of servicemen who died as a result of a disability or disease incurred in line of duty during World War One, World War Two, or the Korean conflict." It authorized the Veterans Administration to pay a subsistence grant of up to $110 a month not in excess of 36 months to a son or daughter between the ages of 18 and 23.

3015. Campus takeover by student protesters took place in September 1964 and was known as the Free Speech Movement. Students at the University of California, Berkeley, CA, occupied the administration building as a protest against the university's decision to ban various political activities on campus. More than 800 demonstrators were arrested by order of Governor Edmund G. Brown. Further building takeovers followed, as well as a general strike by faculty members and graduate students that shut down the university. The ban was rescinded.

EDUCATION—DISABILITIES

3016. School for children with mental disabilities was the Massachusetts School for the Idiotic and Feeble-Minded Youth, created through the efforts of Dr. Samuel Gridley Howe and established by a legislative resolution, approved on May 8, 1848, which appropriated $2,500 a year for three years. The first students were received on October 1, 1848. The name was later changed to the Massachusetts School for the Feeble-Minded and then to the Walter E. Fernald State School, named for Dr. Walter Elmore Fernald, the first resident superintendent.

3017. Private school for children with disabilities was planned in 1861 by a Miss Cornelia and Dr. James Knight. It was opened on May 1, 1863, at the Hospital for the Ruptured and Crippled, New York City, under the auspices of the New York Society for the Relief of the Ruptured and Crippled.

3018. Kindergarten for children with disabilities was opened at the Alta Settlement House, Cleveland, OH, in 1900.

3019. Public school for children with disabilities was the Tilden School, Chicago, IL, opened in 1900, with Emma Haskell as teacher. A horse-drawn wagon was used to transport the children.

3020. Outdoor school for children with tuberculosis was the Meeting Street School, Providence, RI, which opened on January 27, 1908, as the Fresh Air School. Marie E. Powers was teacher and principal. Dr. Ellen R. Stone was the superintendent. Twenty children were in the first class, which comprised grades one through eight. Hot lunches furnished by the school supplemented lunches brought by the children.

3021. Intelligence test in a school for children with mental retardation was the Binet-Simon Test. It was introduced in August 1908 by Dr. Henry Herbert Goddard, director of research in the New Jersey Training School for Feeble-Minded Boys and Girls in Vineland, NJ, to determine the degree of retardation of children in the institution.

3022. Public school classes for children with epilepsy were organized in January 1935 in a small school building in Detroit, MI. In 1936 the courses were transferred to the White Special School, one of the divisions of Special Education of the Detroit Public Schools. The first teachers were Alice Mortimore and Edith Sargent.

EDUCATION—DISABILITIES—BLINDNESS

3023. School for blind students was the New England Asylum for the Blind, Boston, MA, incorporated on March 2, 1829. The school was founded by Dr. John Dix Fisher and opened under Dr. Samuel Gridley Howe in August 1832 with six pupils. In 1839, the name changed to the Perkins Institution and the Massachusetts Asylum for the Blind in honor of Thomas Handasyd Perkins, who in 1833 offered his Boston home for a school building, along with the open grounds around it. The school later moved to Watertown, MA, and was known as the New England Institution for the Education of the Blind.

3024. State school for blind students was the Ohio Institution for the Blind, authorized on April 3, 1837, and opened on July 4, 1837, with five pupils, in the Presbyterian Church, Columbus, OH, in the presence of 900 people. Anson W. Penniman was the first teacher and William Chapin the first superintendent. In 1902, the name was changed to the Ohio State School for the Blind.

3025. School for blind students to adopt the Braille system was the Missouri School for the Blind, St. Louis, MO. In 1859, Dr. Simon Pollak, a trustee of the school, introduced the system directly from Paris with a change in three letters. The system was adapted for use in music, spelling, etymology, and other subjects.

3026. School for blind African-American students was the State School for the Blind and the Deaf, opened in Raleigh, NC, on January 4, 1869, with 26 pupils.

3027. Kindergarten for blind children was established by the Perkins Institution and Massachusetts School for the Blind in Roxbury, MA, in 1887. The kindergarten was authorized on March 15, incorporated as a separate department of the school on March 30, and opened on May 2 with 10 children. The plan was proposed by Michael Anagnos, who became the first director.

3028. Eye conservation class for the education of schoolchildren with seriously defective vision opened on April 3, 1913, at the Thornton Street School, Boston, MA. Helen L. Smith was the teacher.

3029. Correspondence school to offer instruction in Braille was the Hadley Correspondence School for the Blind, Winnetka, IL, founded by William Aaron Hadley. In August 1921 the school offered courses in English grammar, business correspondence, Bible study, and instruction in reading Braille printing.

EDUCATION—DISABILITIES—DEAFNESS

3030. Instruction for deaf students was given by the Reverend John Stanford in 1807 in the Almshouse, New York City. This instruction continued for about a year. Stanford's title was Chaplain to the Humane and Criminal Institutions. In 1817 a meeting was held at his home to organize the New York Institution for the Deaf, now the New York School for the Deaf, which opened in 1818.

3031. Oral school for deaf students was started at Cobbs, Chesterfield County, VA, in 1815 by Colonel William Bolling with John Braidwood as instructor, but it lasted only two years. The Clarke School for the Deaf, which was founded in 1867 in Northampton, MA, was the first permanent oral school for deaf students. It originated in 1865 in a small experimental school in Chelmsford, MA, founded by Harriet Rogers, who was its first principal.

EDUCATION— DISABILITIES— DEAFNESS—continued

3032. School for deaf students to be established on a permanent basis was the Connecticut Asylum for the Education and Instruction of Deaf and Dumb Persons, which opened on April 15, 1817, in Hartford, CT, with seven pupils. In May 1819, the name was changed to the American Asylum. The school was financed through the generosity of a few men, one of whom, Dr. Mason Fitch Cogswell, had a deaf daughter, Alice. Thomas Hopkins Gallaudet, the first principal, inaugurated the system of teaching with the collaboration of a Frenchman, Laurent Clerc. Sign language and finger spelling were the means of communication.

3033. College for deaf students was the National Deaf Mute College, Washington, DC, a department of the Columbia Institution for the Instruction of the Deaf, Dumb, and Blind, incorporated on February 16, 1857. On April 8, 1864, the parent school, now called the Columbia Institution for the Deaf, was authorized by a special act of Congress to confer degrees. The first graduate received his diploma in 1866. The name of the college was changed in 1894 to Gallaudet College in honor of Thomas Hopkins Gallaudet, who was the first principal of the first school for the deaf in America. His son, Dr. Edward Miner Gallaudet, served as president of the college from 1864 to 1910.

3034. Visible speech method of instruction for deaf students was used by the Horace Mann School in Boston, MA, in 1871. It was a form of phonetic writing invented by Alexander Melville Bell to show graphically any sound made by the human voice, and was used to facilitate pronunciation of foreign languages. The teachers at Horace Mann were instructed in the system by Bell's son, Alexander Graham Bell.

3035. Lipreading instruction for deaf people was given by Sarah Warren Keeler, a teacher at the Institution for the Improved Instruction of Deaf Mutes in New York City, who advertised lipreading lessons for adults in 1882. She lectured on the subject in 1884 and published her method in 1894. The first successful lipreading school for adults was established by Lillie Eginton Warren in 1890 in New York City. She obtained a patent in 1903 on a "means for teaching of the facial expressions which occur in speaking."

3036. Lipreading tournament held nationally was held on June 23, 1926, in Philadelphia, PA, during the seventh annual meeting of the American Federation of Organizations for the Hard of Hearing.

EDUCATION—ELEMENTARY

3037. School run by missionaries in America was a classical school briefly operated by Spanish Franciscan priests in St. Augustine, FL, in 1606.

3038. School for colonial children in America is the subject of some dispute. A school is known to have been established by the Dutch West India Company on Manhattan Island in 1633, with Adam Roelantsen as its first master. Instruction was given in Dutch prior to 1775. In 1783 the school became known as the Collegiate School (formally the School of the Collegiate Reformed Dutch Church in the City of New York), the oldest school still in existence in the United States. Claims for earlier informal schools have been made on behalf of Jamestown, VA, where African-American and Native American children were taught in 1620, and the Pilgrim settlement at Plymouth, MA, where instruction was given to the children of colonists circa 1621.

3039. Free school funded by an endowment in the American colonies was the Syms-Eaton Academy, founded in Hampton, VA, in 1634 by Benjamin Syms (or Symmes). He donated "two hundred acres of land on Poquoson River with the milk and increase of eight cows for the maintenance of a learned and honest man to keep upon the said grounds a free school." In 1805 the name was changed to the Hampton Academy. Another early free school with an endowment was the Free Schoole in Roxburie, established in Roxbury, MA, in 1645. It was incorporated in 1789 as the "Grammar School in the Easterly Part of the Town of Roxbury."

3040. Public school with a continuous existence was the Boston Public Latin School for boys, established on February 13, 1635, and supported by voluntary contributions. The first schoolmaster was Philemon Pormort. Its original purpose was to prepare boys for the ministry by enabling them to "obtain a knowledge of the Scriptures and by acquaintance with the Ancient Tongues qualify them to discern the true sense and meaning of the original, however corrupted by false glosses."

3041. Property tax established by a colony to support public schools was established by vote of Dorchester, MA, on May 20, 1639: "It is ordered the 20th of May 1639, that there shall be a rent of twenty pounds a year for ever imposed upon Tomsons Island to be paid by every person that hath property in the said island according to the proportion that any such person shall from time to time enjoy and possess there."

3042. Catholic school was founded circa 1640 by the Jesuits at St. Mary's City, MD. The Catholic parochial school system is considered by some historians to have originated in a school started by St. Mary's Church, Philadelphia, PA, in 1782, while others date its beginnings from 1809, when Elizabeth Ann Bayley Seton, the first Catholic saint born in America, founded a school near Baltimore, MD.

3043. Compulsory education law in a colony was passed by Massachusetts on June 14, 1642. It stated: "This Court, taking into consideration the great neglect of many parents and masters in training up their children in learning and labor and other imployments which may be profitable to the common wealth, so hereupon order and decree, that in every towne the chosen men appointed for managing the prudentiall affayers of the same shall henceforth stand charged with the care of the redresse of this evil ... and for this end ... they shall have power to take account from time to time of all parents and masters, and of their children, concerning their calling and imployment of their children."

3044. School committee was elected in Dorchester, MA, in 1645. The members were elected for life, although the town reserved the right to remove any of them for "weighty reasons." They had charge of everything that pertained to the betterment of the school.

3045. Colonial law requiring towns to hire teachers and construct schools was passed on November 11, 1647, by Massachusetts. It "ordered that every township in this jurisdiction, after the Lord hath increased them to the number of fifty householders, shall then forthwith appoint one within their town to teach all such children as shall resort to him to write and read, whose wages shall be paid either by the parents or masters of such children, or by the inhabitants in general." Towns of 100 families were required to "set up a grammar school, the master thereof being able to instruct youths so far as they may be fitted for the university."

3046. Evening school for working children was established in New Amsterdam (now New York City) in 1661. Fees and regulations for instruction were contained in a report, *Instructions and Rules for Schoolmaster, Evert Pietersen*, which was drawn up by the burgomasters on November 4, 1661.

3047. Town trust fund for education was created by Burlington, NJ, in 1682. The assembly provided that a valuable island situated in the Delaware River above Burlington, and known as Matinicunk Island, "remain to and for the use of the town of Burlington ... for the maintaining of a school for the education of youth."

3048. Blackboards for use in schools were introduced in 1714 by Christopher Dock of Skippack, PA. Dock, an immigrant from Germany, was the author of the first book on teaching methodology to be published in America.

3049. School for Native Americans to be permanently established was founded in 1720 in Williamsburg, VA, through the generosity of Robert Boyle, the eminent English scientist and formulator of Boyle's Law. To house the school, the Brafferton Building was erected at the College of William and Mary in 1723. The building was named after Boyle's estate in Yorkshire, England, which provided revenue from rents to support the school.

3050. School for Protestant girls was a boarding school established by Countess Benigna von Zinzendorf at Germantown, PA, in 1742, exclusively for girls of the Moravian Church. By 1800 this had become a noted seminary. It eventually became the Moravian College for Women.

3051. Land set-aside for schools authorized by the Continental Congress was authorized by an ordinance of May 20, 1785: "There shall be reserved the lot No. 16 of every township for the maintenance of public schools within said township." This applied to the Western Reserve (now Ohio) and other unsurveyed lands to the west. A new system of surveying was established, with the land laid out in townships six miles square, subdivided into 36 numbered sections, each a mile square. Section No. 16 was popularly known as the "school section."

3052. Superintendent of schools hired by a state was Gideon Hawley, who was appointed state superintendent of common schools by New York in 1812. He began serving on January 14, 1813. An act was passed on April 15, 1814, making him secretary of the New York State Board of Regents at a salary of $400 a year. He was removed in 1821 because of political machinations, and the secretary of state was authorized to act as superintendent. In 1854 New York created the job of superintendent of public instruction.

EDUCATION—ELEMENTARY—*continued*

3053. Catholic school for Native Americans was the St. Regis Seminary, Florissant, MO, which opened on May 11, 1824, under the direction of Father Van Quickenborne. It was located in three buildings that cost about $2,000 to build. There were 40 to 60 students. It closed on June 30, 1831.

3054. Tax enacted by a state to support public schools was "an act providing for the establishment of free schools," enacted on January 15, 1825, by Illinois. It provided for a common school in each county, open to every class of white citizens between the ages of 5 and 21 years and supported by a tax of $2 of every $100 and five-sixths of the interest from the school fund.

3055. Superintendent of schools hired by a city was Roswell Willson Haskins, who was appointed "city superintendent of common schools" in 1836 by Buffalo, NY. He resigned before the end of the year, as the law was imperfect and restrictions hampered his work.

3056. Board of education established by a state was established by Massachusetts on April 30, 1837. The first secretary of the board, later designated as commissioner, was the educational reformer Horace Mann. He was appointed on June 29, 1837, and received $1,000 a year.

3057. Handwriting teaching system widely used in schools was developed by Platt Rogers Spencer of East Fishkill, NY, between 1846 and 1850. Spencer based his ornate, rounded, strongly slanted letters on esthetic ideals he derived from Greek philosophy. He established "Spencerian" business colleges—the first schools to specialize in business communications—throughout the country. His handwriting copybooks and textbooks were used in the schools of 42 states.

3058. School to provide separate classrooms for each class was established in 1846 in Quincy, MA.

3059. Compulsory education law enacted by a state was approved on May 18, 1852, by Governor George Sewall Boutwell of Massachusetts. It prescribed that children must attend school "between the ages of eight and fourteen years" for 12 weeks in the year, 6 of which must be consecutive.

3060. Physical education classes in elementary schools were required in 1853 in Boston, MA, where school officials ruled that "every scholar shall have daily in the forenoon and afternoon some kind of physical exercise."

3061. Truancy law enacted by a state was "an act to provide for the care and instruction of idle and truant children," enacted by New York on April 12, 1853. A $50 fine was levied against parents whose children between the ages of 5 and 15 were absent from school.

3062. Public school for Chinese-American children was established in September 1859 in the basement of the Chinese Chapel, San Francisco, CA. James Denman was the superintendent of schools. The school had an enrollment of 67 boys and 8 girls, but the average daily attendance was only 12. The school was suspended in June 1860 and was reopened as an evening school.

3063. Boarding school on a Native American reservation was the Yakima Agency Boarding School, opened in November 1860 in the buildings of old Fort Simco on the Yakima Reservation, WA, under provision of the treaty with the Yakima Nation of June 8, 1855, proclaimed on April 18, 1859. James H. Wilbur was appointed superintendent of teaching. There were 25 pupils the first year.

3064. School for African-American children established by a state was the Snowden School of Alexandria, VA. It was authorized by act of the legislature on July 11, 1870, and was under the guidance of William Frank Powell. It had only a short existence.

3065. School of prominence for Native American children was opened on November 1, 1879, at the old Army Barracks, Carlisle, PA, with 147 students. It was supported by private funds until March 3, 1881, when Congress appropriated $1,000 to pay Captain Richard Henry Pratt's salary as director. The school taught useful trades. The schoolwork did not go above the eighth grade, but students who were graduated were assisted in continuing their studies under the supervision of the school. At the end of the first year, 196 students were enrolled, 139 boys and 57 girls.

3066. Country day school was the Country School for Boys of Baltimore, MD, a private school that opened in September 1897. The first headmaster was Frederick Winsor.

3067. School to use platoon organization was the Central School, Bluffton, IN, established in September 1899 under the direction of William Wirt. The curriculum was arranged so that specific times were allotted for study, work, and play. In September 1902 the system was extended to the three elementary schools in the city.

3068. Trial of a teacher for violating a state ban on teaching the theory of evolution took place in July 1925. John Thomas Scopes, a high school science teacher in Dayton, TN, was convicted of breaking a law passed by the Tennessee legislature and signed on March 23, 1925, by Governor Austin Peay. It provided that "it shall be unlawful for any teacher in any of the universities, normal and all other public schools of the state which are supported in whole or in part by the public school funds of the state to teach any theory that denies the story of the Divine creation of man as taught in the Bible, and to teach instead that man has descended from a lower order of animals." Scopes was prosecuted by William Jennings Bryan and defended by Clarence Darrow. He was fined $100. The conviction was later overturned on technical grounds.

3069. Elementary schools to use closed-circuit televisions in teaching were eight public schools in Washington County, MD, which began using a closed-circuit system in September 1956. The schools served about 6,000 pupils. The system was expanded in September 1963, when all 45 public schools in the county were linked to the television circuit. The Fund for the Advancement of Education and the Ford Foundation contributed about $200,000 a year to the project over a five-year period. The equipment, worth $300,000, was provided by 75 manufacturers through the Electronics Industries Association.

3070. Federal aid program for primary and secondary schools was the Elementary and Secondary School Act, signed into law by President Lyndon Baines Johnson on April 11, 1965. The act allocated $1.3 billion for school districts according to the number of needy children they contained, and included funds for parochial and private schools.

3071. Teacher testing requirement to be enacted by a state was enacted by Arkansas, which passed a law in 1983 requiring all teachers in public skills to pass an examination of basic teaching skills. Teachers who failed the exam lost their state teaching licenses. Ninety percent of Arkansas teachers passed the first administration of tests in 1985.

EDUCATION—ELEMENTARY—PRE-SCHOOLS

3072. Nursery school was established in New York City in 1827 by the Infant School Society of the City of New York, founded on May 23, 1827, "to relieve parents of the laboring classes from the care of their children while engaged in the vocations by which they live, and provide for the children a protection from the weather, from idleness and the contamination of evil example besides affording them the means of early and efficient education." Children from 18 months to 5 years of age were accommodated, 448 receiving attention over the course of two years. Joanna Bethune was the first director.

3073. Kindergarten was established in Boston, MA, in 1868 by Elizabeth Palmer Peabody, who employed the Friedrich Froebel system of education used in Germany. An informal kindergarten group had been formed in December 1856 by Margarethe Meyer Schurz, wife of General Carl Schurz, in her home at Watertown, WI, for six children, two of whom were her own.

3074. Public school kindergarten that was successful was authorized on August 26, 1873, by the Board of Education of St. Louis, MO, and opened September 1873 in the Des Peres School, with an enrollment of 42. Susan Elizabeth Blow was the teacher. Dr. William Torrey Harris was the superintendent of schools.

3075. Free kindergarten was the Florence Kindergarten, which opened on January 3, 1876, in Florence, MA, in the home of its founder, Samuel Lapham Hill. The school was later known as the Hill Institute.

EDUCATION—ENVIRONMENT

3076. Forestry school at a college was established on September 19, 1898, at Cornell University, Ithaca, NY, as the New York State College of Forestry. Dr. Bernhard Eduard Fernow was director and dean. The law under which this school was established was signed by Governor Frank Swett Black on April 8, 1898, making New York the first state to establish a forestry course. The activities of the school were suspended in 1903. Lectures on forestry and tree culture were given at Yale University in 1873 and at Cornell in 1874.

3077. Forestry school operated privately to give scientific training in the care and preservation of shade trees was a department of the Davey Tree Expert Company, Kent, OH, incorporated on February 9, 1909. The first president was John Davey.

3078. Game management chair at a college was established by the University of Wisconsin, Madison, WI, in August 1933, at which time Aldo Leopold was appointed to fill the post. The primary aim was to provide facilities for graduate research and a clearinghouse for the development of game production as a new use

185

EDUCATION—ENVIRONMENT—*continued*
for Wisconsin land. The University of Michigan had established a school of conservation in 1927 and the University of Iowa had created the position of director of game research in 1932.

EDUCATION—HIGH SCHOOLS

3079. School for the higher education of women was the Middlebury Female Seminary, started by Emma Hart Willard in 1814 in her home in Middlebury, VT. The curriculum included academic subjects as well as household management. In 1819 she moved to Waterford, NY, and established the Waterford Academy. She had hoped for state aid, but no funds were appropriated. However, the citizens of Troy, NY, provided funds for a building, and in 1821 she opened the Troy Female Seminary, afterwards known as the Emma Willard School. Her book *Plan for Improving Female Education* was published in 1819.

3080. High school was the English Classical School, opened in May 1820 in Boston, MA. The name was changed in 1824 to the English High School. Admittance was open to boys at least 12 years of age who were "well acquainted with reading, writing, English grammar in all its branches, and arithmetic, as far as simple proportions."

3081. High school for girls was established in 1826 in Boston, MA, but was abolished in 1828. Instead, the course of study in the elementary schools was advanced.

3082. High school night classes were authorized in Ohio on March 16, 1829. Accordingly, three evening schools for boys opened in Cincinnati in November 1840. In 1855, schools for girls were also opened.

3083. Commercial high school was operated as part of an already established school in Pittsburgh, PA, in 1868.

3084. Business high school was the Washington Business High School, Washington, DC, authorized on June 11, 1889, by the Board of Education. It opened on September 22, 1890, in an unused grade school building of seven rooms. Allan Davis was the first principal.

3085. County high school was the Dickinson County Community High School, Chapman, KS, opened in September 1889. The first building was constructed entirely of limestone at a cost of $12,000. Enrollment the first year was 137. S.M. Cook, who taught mathematics, Latin, and Greek, was the first principal.

3086. Vocational high school for girls was the Trade School for Girls, Boston, MA, opened in July 1904 as a summer experiment in training. Subjects taught were plain sewing, advanced sewing, dressmaking, millinery, machine operating, trade design, and domestic science. Florence M. Marshall was principal.

3087. Junior high school was the Indianola Junior High School, Columbus, OH, opened on September 7, 1909. On July 6, 1909, the Columbus Board of Education directed Superintendent of Schools Jacob A. Shawan "to organize the new Indianola School primarily as a junior high school, with the 7th, 8th, and 9th grades as a unit, and only to admit such of the first six grades as might be necessary to relieve the neighboring districts." The ninth grade offered courses in English, German, algebra, elementary science, physical geography, manual training, domestic science, general history, and government of Ohio.

3088. Sex education program for high schools to be presented in a citywide system of public schools began in Chicago, IL, in 1913. It was devised by Ella Flagg Young, the superintendent of schools, who convinced the School Management Committee, a subcommittee of the Board of Education, to institute for all students in the city's secondary schools a series of lectures on "sex hygiene."

3089. Aviation course in a high school was instituted by Haaren High School, New York City, in September 1929, with 11 students under the direction of William Arnheim. In September 1931 an aviation annex was organized and the 833 boys enrolled in the aviation course were transferred to this building. In 1944, there were 3,500 students enrolled.

3090. Driving course in a high school was offered at State College High School, State College, PA, from February 17 to June 11, 1934. It included both classroom work and behind-the-wheel training. The first instructor was Amos Earl Neyhart. Students who completed the course received Pennsylvania automobile operators' licenses.

3091. Public high school to specialize in the performing arts was the School of Performing Arts, a division of the Metropolitan Vocational High School, New York City, opened on September 13, 1948. Dr. Franklin J. Keller was the first principal. The school was conducted on the usual secondary school basis. However, half the time was given to practical work in the arts (music, dance, theater, and broadcasting) and the other half to college preparatory academic courses, with a diploma at the end of three years to those who had come from junior high schools and at the end of four years of study to those from eight-year elementary schools.

3092. High school for pregnant teenage girls was the Educational Center of District 12, opened on June 23, 1967, in the Lincoln Hospital Neighborhood Maternity Center, New York City. The school opened with approximately 75 students and had a staff of one administrator, one guidance counselor, and five subject teachers. It was organized and started by project coordinator Martha Neilson for the Board of Education of the City of New York.

3093. Japanese high school in the United States opened in Sweetwater, TN, in May 1989. The fully accredited private school, called the Tennessee Meiji Gakuin, was a boarding school for the children of Japanese executives living in the United States. It was built by Tokyo's Meiji Gakuin University on the site of the former Tennessee Military Institute. The cost for a year's tuition, room, and board was $17,000.

EDUCATION—HUMANITIES

3094. School of modern history at a college was established at the College of William and Mary, Williamsburg, VA, in 1803.

3095. Ancient and modern history chair at a college was the McLean Professorship at Harvard College, Cambridge, MA, which was endowed in 1823 under the will of John McLean and established in 1838. The first incumbent was Professor Jared Sparks. The first integrated course in ancient and modern history at a women's college was given by Professor Woodrow Wilson at Bryn Mawr College, Bryn Mawr, PA, in 1885. The histories of Greece and Rome were taken as representative of ancient history, and of France and England as representative of medieval and modern history. The object was to "keep the student mindful of the broad views of history in which the events in the lives of individual nations stand related."

3096. American history chair at a college was established by the University of Pennsylvania, Philadelphia, PA, in 1850. The first incumbent was William Bradford Reed.

3097. Journalism course at a college was given in 1869 by Professor Willard Fiske at Washington University (later Washington and Lee University), Lexington, VA. The idea was introduced by General Robert Edward Lee. A knowledge of shorthand and telegraphy was required, as well as practical experience in the university printing office.

3098. Bibliography course at a college was offered in 1878 by the University of Michigan at Ann Arbor, MI. Raymond Cazallis Davis, the librarian, gave a lecture once a week during November and December.

3099. Library school at a college was the School of Library Economy at Columbia University, New York City, which opened on January 5, 1887, through the efforts of Melvil Dewey. The school was transferred on April 1, 1889, to Albany, NY, where it was placed under the direction of the State University of New York as the New York State Library School. The first session was held on April 10, 1889, and the first public commencement and conferring of degrees took place on July 8, 1891. In 1926 the school was returned to Columbia University, where it was united with the Library School of the New York Public Library to form the School of Library Service, Columbia University.

3100. Public speaking department at a college was established in December 1892 at the University of Michigan, Ann Arbor, MI, with Thomas Clarkson Trueblood as professor of elocution and oratory. Similar courses had been given in 1887, but without departmental status.

3101. College course in the contemporary novel was given by Professor William Lyon Phelps at Yale University, New Haven, CT, in the academic year 1895–96. The course was called "Modern Novels" and was elected by 250 juniors and seniors.

3102. Journalism school at a college offering a degree in journalism was opened on September 14, 1908, at the University of Missouri, Columbia, MO. Enrollment for the school year 1908–09 was 97, including 84 men and 13 women. The first degree, a Bachelor of Science in Journalism, was awarded in 1909 to Charles Arnold. The first dean was Walter Williams.

3103. Marriage course at a college was given by Professor Ernest Rutherford Groves in 1924 at the University of North Carolina, Chapel Hill, NC.

3104. Book course at a college was taught in the fall of 1926 at Rollins College, Winter Park, FL, by Dr. Edwin Osgood Grover, professor of books. The first instruction was given on September 22. The idea of a "professorship of books" was first suggested by Ralph Waldo Emerson in his essay "Books," which appeared in the *Atlantic Monthly* issue of January 1858.

EDUCATION—HUMANITIES—*continued*

3105. Theater and dramatic criticism course at a college to award a Ph.D. degree was established by the Department of Drama, Yale University, New Haven, CT, on September 24, 1934. The first degrees were awarded to George Riley Kernodle, John Huber McDowell, and Virginia More Roediger on June 23, 1937. The normal minimum time required for the course was four full years of study and research. The first professor of the history of the drama was Allardyce Nicoll.

3106. Archival course at a college was "Archives and Historical Manuscripts," offered beginning on September 29, 1938, by Columbia University, New York City, under Dr. Solon Justus Buck, director of publications, National Archives, Washington, DC.

3107. Archivist training program at a college was offered beginning on September 25, 1940, by the School of Public Affairs, American University, Washington, DC.

3108. Science fiction course at a college was offered at the City College of New York, New York City, in 1953. It was taught by Samuel Moskowitz.

EDUCATION—HUMANITIES—LANGUAGES

3109. Hebrew instruction at a college was given to divinity students by the president and tutors of Harvard College, Cambridge, MA, in 1636. A chair of Hebrew and Oriental languages was endowed in 1655. The curriculum of 17th-century Harvard required students to study Hebrew and related languages one day each week for a total of three years. The Hebrew requirement was lifted in 1817.

3110. French instruction at a college was offered in 1733 at Harvard College, Cambridge, MA. Louis Langloiserie was appointed instructor.

3111. German instruction at a college was given by William Creamer at the University of Pennsylvania, Philadelphia, PA, from 1754 to July 11, 1755.

3112. School of modern languages at a college was established by the College of William and Mary, Williamsburg, VA, in 1779.

3113. English grammar instruction at a college was offered in 1795 at the University of North Carolina, Chapel Hill, NC.

3114. Italian instruction at a college was given at the College of William and Mary, Williamsburg, VA, in 1799 by Carlo Bellini, professor of modern languages.

3115. Comparative philology chair at a college was established by Lafayette College, Easton, PA, in 1856. The first professor was Francis Andrew March.

3116. Chinese language and literature lectureship at a college was created by Yale University, New Haven, CT, in 1877. Samuel Wells Williams, Commodore Oliver Hazard Perry's secretary and interpreter in Japan, was the lecturer.

3117. Esperanto course at a college was offered by Clark University, Worcester, MA, on September 16, 1908. Dr. Robert Mowry Bell taught the course, which offered "a brief outline of the grammar, and some practice in reading the new universal language."

3118. Foreign language course broadcast on radio took place on March 21, 1924, when station WJZ, New York City, operating on a 455-meter wavelength, offered French lessons in cooperation with the Berlitz School of Languages.

3119. Yiddish professorship at a college was established on February 11, 1952, at Columbia University, New York City. The first incumbent was Uriel Weinreich, associate professor of Yiddish language, literature, and culture.

EDUCATION—LAW

3120. Law instruction at a college was offered by King's College (now Columbia University), New York City, in 1755. The fourth year of study was described as containing, among other things, "the Chief Principles of Law and Government together with History, Sacred and Profane."

3121. Law school at a college was established in 1779 at the College of William and Mary, Williamsburg, VA. Professors did not receive a stipulated amount from the college but were paid by the students attending the course. The first professor was George Wythe, who was appointed professor of law and police on December 4, 1779. The first college law school to be permanently organized was the Harvard College School of Law, Cambridge, MA, which was opened in 1817.

3122. Law school operated privately was opened in Litchfield, CT, in 1784 by Judge Tapping Reeve. He conducted it alone in a building near his home until 1789. The session was from 14 to 18 months, for which a tuition fee of $100 was charged for the first year and $60 for the balance of the course. About a dozen students were enrolled the first year.

3123. Law school at a university to admit women was the St. Louis Law School, now the School of Law, Washington University, St. Louis, MO. In 1869, two women students matriculated. One, Phoebe W. Couzins of St. Louis, was graduated from the school on June 15, 1871. Both eventually became members of the bar.

3124. Law school graduate who was a woman was Ada H. Kepley of Effingham, IL, who was graduated from the Union College of Law, Chicago, IL, on June 30, 1870.

3125. Law school where the entire faculty was 65 years of age or over and had retired from other teaching positions was the Hastings College of the Law, University of California, San Francisco, CA, founded in 1878. It engaged the first overage professor in 1940, during World War II, on an emergency basis, and made two other appointments in the mid-40s before the policy was permanently established in 1948.

3126. Foreign service school in a college was the School of Comparative Jurisprudence and Diplomacy of George Washington University, Washington, DC, which opened on November 15, 1898. It was discontinued as a separate school in 1913, though courses continued to be given by Columbian College. In September 1928, training in foreign service and governmental theory and administration was reestablished as a separate branch under the School of Government.

3127. Editor in chief of a law review who was a woman was Mary Honor Donlon, a student at the Cornell Law School, Ithaca, NY, who edited three issues of the *Cornell Law Quarterly* that were published in November 1919, January 1920, and March 1920.

3128. Civil rights chair at a college was established at Lafayette College, Easton, PA, through the gift of Fred Morgan Kirby. The first lectures were given in February 1921 by Professor Herbert Adams Gibbons.

EDUCATION—MEDICINE

3129. Anatomy lectures to medical students were given by Dr. William Shippen at the College of Philadelphia, PA, from 1762 to 1765. Public lectures on anatomy were given in Boston, MA, in 1789 by John Jeffries, but public opinion was so much against his policy of dissecting bodies that at the second lecture a mob invaded the lecture room and carried off the body of a convict on which he was demonstrating. Further lectures were stopped as a result of public animosity.

3130. Midwifery professor at a college was Dr. John Van Brugh Tennent, appointed professor of midwifery at King's College (now Columbia University), New York City, in 1767.

3131. Physician to receive a Bachelor of Medicine degree was John Archer, who was the first of 10 students to be graduated on June 21, 1768, from the University of Pennsylvania, Philadelphia, PA. The university required a three-year waiting period before its medical graduates could return and receive the degree of Doctor of Medicine. Four of the 10 did so in 1771. The first M.D. degree was awarded in 1770 by King's College (now Columbia University), New York City, which required only one year to elapse before a student could return and for the M.D. degree. At both schools, the applicant for the higher degree was required to write a thesis in Latin or an inaugural dissertation and defend it satisfactorily before the faculty.

3132. Pharmacy professorship at a college was established in 1789 in Philadelphia, PA, at the Medical School of the College of Philadelphia (merged in 1791 with the University of Pennsylvania), when Dr. Samuel Powel Griffitts was appointed professor of materia medica and pharmacy. The first professorship devoted entirely to pharmacy was established in 1844 by the Maryland College of Pharmacy (now part of the University of Maryland), Baltimore, MD. David Stewart was appointed to the chair of theory and practice of pharmacy.

3133. Nurses' training was given by Dr. Valentine Seaman of the New York Hospital, New York City, who gave lectures on anatomy, physiology, the care of children, and midwifery from 1798 to 1817. The first class consisted of 24 nurses.

3134. Medical jurisprudence course at a college was given by Dr. James Stringham, professor of medical jurisprudence at the College of Physicians and Surgeons, Columbia University, New York City, from 1813 to 1817. Prior to this appointment he served as professor of chemistry.

3135. Clinical instruction and bedside demonstration were introduced in 1818 by Alexander Hodgdon Stevens. It is said that in his operations as surgeon of the New York Hospital he often purposely avoided the neatness deemed so essential by other surgeons, in order to show his students that it was not essential to the recovery of the patient, provided the surgeon's skill and rapidity of manipulation were great enough.

EDUCATION—MEDICINE—*continued*

3136. Hygiene lectures at a college were delivered in 1818 by Dr. James Jackson, Hersey professor of the theory and practice of physic, at Harvard College, Cambridge, MA. The committee decided on October 8, 1818, "that he be required to deliver a number of lectures on subjects relating to the care and preservation of health, and that they be this year delivered to the members of the two upper classes, at the hour appointed on Friday for a public lecture to those classes." The first professor of public hygiene was Dr. Thomas Bevan, appointed in 1868 by Northwestern University, Chicago, IL.

3137. Ophthalmology course at a college was established in 1823 at the Ophthalmic Clinic, Baltimore General Dispensary, University of Maryland, Baltimore, MD. The first professor of ophthalmology was Elkanah Williams, who was appointed by the Miami Medical College of Cincinnati, OH, in 1865.

3138. Clinic for teaching medical students was established in 1840 by Dr. Willard Parker, professor of surgery in the College of Physicians and Surgeons, New York City. He opened a dispensary where outpatients were brought to be examined and treated in the presence of the medical students.

3139. Pathology chair at a college was established at Harvard University, Cambridge, MA, in 1847, when John Barnard Sweet Jackson was appointed professor of pathological anatomy and curator of the Warren Museum. The professorship was endowed by George Cheyne Shattuck in 1854. The first chair of modern pathology (after the field had been revolutionized by Louis Pasteur and his successors) was established in 1883 by Johns Hopkins University, Baltimore, MD. The first incumbent was Professor William Henry Welch.

3140. Physiology and hygiene courses at a liberal arts college were given in 1853 at Antioch College, Yellow Springs, OH. The college opened on October 5, 1853. Instruction was supervised by Professor Rebecca Mann Pennell and Acting Professor John Wesley Hoyt, M.D.

3141. Pediatrics professor at a college was Dr. Abraham Jacobi, a Jewish immigrant from Germany, who lectured at the College of Physicians and Surgeons (now part of Columbia University), New York City, in 1857. He was appointed professor of infant pathology and therapeutics in 1860 and held the post of clinical professor of pediatrics from 1870 to 1899.

3142. Laryngology instruction at a college was offered regularly by the Medical Department of the University of the City of New York in the autumn of 1861. Dr. Louis Elsberg lectured on the laryngoscope and diseases of the throat and larynx in 1863–64. From 1869 to 1873 he was clinical professor of diseases of the throat and from 1873 to 1881 professor of diseases of the throat and laryngology.

3143. Orthopedics chair at a college was established by Bellevue Hospital Medical College, New York City, in 1861. The first incumbent was Dr. Lewis Albert Sayre.

3144. Dermatology chair at a college was established by Harvard University, Cambridge, MA, in 1871. The first incumbent was Dr. James Clarke White, instructor in medical chemistry, who later became the first president of the American Dermatological Association.

3145. Medical chemistry course at a college was offered in 1871 by Dr. Edward Stickney Wood, assistant professor of chemistry, at the Harvard Medical School, Cambridge, MA.

3146. Analytical chemistry course requirement for pharmacy students was required by the Maryland College of Pharmacy (now part of the University of Maryland), Baltimore, MD, incorporated in 1841. The chair of analytical chemistry was established on March 20, 1872, and Dr. William Simon was the first professor to occupy it.

3147. Pharmacist who was a woman to receive a degree from a pharmacy college was Susan Hayhurst of St. Michael's, MD, who graduated on March 16, 1883, from the Philadelphia College of Pharmacy with the Ph.G. degree. She went on to receive her M.D. degree in 1857 from the Female Medical College of Pennsylvania. She was the first female physician to graduate from a pharmacy college.

3148. Psychology professor at a college was James McKeen Cattell, who was appointed professor of psychology at the University of Pennsylvania, Philadelphia, PA, in 1888.

3149. Bacteriology courses at a college were given by the Hygienic Laboratory of the University of Michigan, Ann Arbor, MI. The laboratory was established in 1887, and the first class in bacteriology was instituted by Dr. Victor Clarence Vaughan and Dr. Frederick George Novy in January 1889. Classes were in session four hours daily for three months. In 1890–91 bacteriology became a required course for medical students. The first bacteriology lectures for medical school students were given in 1885 by Harold Clarence Ernst at the Harvard Medical School, Cambridge, MA.

3150. Psychiatric institute organized for research and the training of physicians was the Pathological Institute, New York City, established by New York State on May 12, 1896. Dr. Ira Van Gieson was the first director. The name was changed in 1909 to the New York State Psychiatric Institute and Hospital. In 1927 it became the Psychiatric Department of the Columbia University–Presbyterian Hospital Medical Center and was housed in a new building dedicated December 3–4, 1929.

3151. Professor at a first-class medical school who was a woman was Dr. Florence Rena Sabin, who served on the faculty of the Johns Hopkins University School of Medicine, Baltimore, MD. She was appointed special fellow in anatomy in 1901 and became associate professor of anatomy in 1905 and professor of histology in 1917. She was the first woman to teach there and was also the first female member of the National Academy of Sciences.

3152. Hydrotherapy chair at a college was established in the Department of Materia Medica, College of Physicians and Surgeons, Columbia University, New York City, in 1907. Dr. Simon Baruch was appointed professor of hydrotherapy in March 1907.

3153. Optometry courses at a college were given at Columbia University, New York City, which offered a two-year program beginning on September 28, 1910, following enactment of legislation by New York State on March 31, 1909, which required that optometrists be licensed. Instruction was given by Andrew Jay Cross, instructor in theoretic optometry, Frederick Albert Woll, and Charles F. Prentice, instructor in practical optics. Members of the university's departments of physics and mathematics gave instruction in those subjects to the optometry students.

3154. Medical research chair at a college was the John Herr Musser chair, established in 1910 by the School of Medicine, University of Pennsylvania, Philadelphia, PA. The first incumbent was Professor Richard Mills Pearce.

3155. Occupational therapy course at a college was given in 1913 by the Milwaukee-Downer College of Milwaukee, WI. The subjects included psychology, physiology, sociology, design, metal work, leather work, and textile craft. Two students enrolled. The form of treatment called occupational therapy "includes any occupation, mental or physical, which is definitely prescribed and guided for the distinct purpose of contributing to, or hastening recovery from diseases or injury."

3156. Plastic surgery professor at a college was Dr. Joseph Eastman Sheehan, who was appointed to that post in 1926 by the New York Postgraduate Medical School and Hospital, New York City.

3157. History of medicine department at a college with a full salaried professor and staff was the Institute of the History of Medicine, inaugurated on October 18, 1929, by Johns Hopkins University, Baltimore, MD. Dr. William Henry Welch was the first professor of the history of medicine and Dr. Stephen d'Irsay was associate.

3158. Anesthesiology professor at a college was Dr. Virginia Apgar, who was appointed by Columbia University, New York City, in 1949. Apgar had previously spent 11 years as director of anesthesiology at an affiliated institution, Columbia–Presbyterian Medical Center.

EDUCATION—MEDICINE—SCHOOLS

3159. Medical college was the College of Philadelphia Department of Medicine, now the University of Pennsylvania School of Medicine, which was established in Philadelphia, PA, on May 3, 1765, principally through the efforts of Dr. William Shippen, Jr., and Dr. John Morgan, who became professor of the theory and practice of physick and professor of anatomy and surgery, respectively. The school was started in a wooden building known as Surgeons' Hall. At the first commencement, held on June 21, 1768, the first medical diplomas (Bachelor of Medicine) issued in America were presented to the 10 members of the graduating class.

3160. Pharmacy college was the Philadelphia College of Apothecaries, established on February 23, 1821, at a meeting at Carpenters' Hall, Philadelphia, PA. Dr. Samuel Jackson was appointed professor of materia medica and pharmacy and Dr. Gerardt Troost professor of chemistry. Charles Marshall was elected president. The first class was held on November 9, 1821. The school was renamed the Philadelphia College of Pharmacy in 1822 and conferred the Ph.G. degree on its first three graduates on November 28, 1826. This was not the first time that degrees were granted to pharmacists: The University of Pennsylvania awarded honorary Master of Pharmacy degrees to 16 practicing apothecaries on April 5, 1821.

EDUCATION—MEDICINE—SCHOOLS—
continued

3161. Homeopathy school was the North American Academy of the Homeopathic Healing Art, founded on April 10, 1835, in Allentown, PA. The school was known as the Allentown Academy. The degree of Doctor of Homoeopathia was conferred upon graduates. Instruction was in German. Constantine Hering, who came to Philadelphia in 1832 from Germany, was the first president and principal instructor.

3162. Dental college was the Baltimore College of Dental Surgery, organized in Baltimore, MD, in 1839 and formally opened on November 3, 1840, with five students. The faculty consisted of H. Willis Baxter, M.D., professor of anatomy and physiology; Thomas E. Bond, Jr., M.D., professor of special pathology and therapeutics; Chapin Aaron Harris, M.D., professor of practical dentistry; and Horace Henry Hayden, M.D., professor of dental physiology and pathology. This college is now the School of Dentistry, University of Maryland, Baltimore.

3163. Homeopathy college was the Homeopathic Medical College of Pennsylvania, Philadelphia, PA, incorporated on April 8, 1848. The regular course started with 15 students on November 6, 1848, and concluded on March 1, 1849. Six students graduated at the commencement exercises held on March 29, 1849. Dr. Walter Williamson was the dean of the college.

3164. Medical school for women was the Boston Female Medical School, Boston, MA, which was organized through the initiative of Samuel Gregory. It opened on November 1, 1848, with 12 pupils and 2 teachers. On May 24, 1856, the school was incorporated as the New England Female Medical College, with power to confer degrees. In 1874 it was absorbed by the Boston University School of Medicine, founded the previous year as a school of homeopathy, which thus became the first coeducational medical school in the world.

3165. Medical college on the Pacific Coast was the Medical Department of the University of the Pacific, opened at Santa Clara, CA, in 1858 by Dr. Elias Samuel Cooper.

3166. Nursing school to award a diploma was the School of Nursing of the Woman's Hospital of Philadelphia, PA, chartered on March 22, 1861. The first diploma was awarded in 1865. The first nurse known to have received the diploma was Harriet N. Phillips.

3167. Dental school to be associated with a medical school and the first to be permanently established by a university was the Harvard School of Dental Medicine, Boston, MA, established on July 17, 1867. The first class began on November 4, 1868, with 16 students. Dr. Nathan Cooley Keep was the first dean, as well as the first professor of mechanical dentistry.

3168. Optometry school was the Illinois College of Optometry, Chicago, IL, founded in 1872 by George W. McFatrich, M.D., author of *Correction for Myopia,* who taught refraction. In 1907, Dr. William B. Needles founded the Needles Institute of Optometry, Kansas City, MO. These schools merged under the name of the Northern Illinois College of Optometry, chartered in 1927.

3169. Nursing school for African-American students was the Spelman Seminary, Atlanta, GA, founded in 1881 by Sophia Booker Packard and Harriet E. Giles of Boston, MA, as the Atlanta Baptist Female Seminary. A nurses' training department was established in 1886 in a two-room frame building set apart to serve as an infirmary and known as the Everts Ward. The first nurse received her certificate in 1888. The name of the school was changed in 1924 to Spelman College.

3170. Osteopathy school was the American School of Osteopathy, chartered in Kirksville, MO, on May 10, 1892. The founders were Dr. Andrew Taylor Still and Dr. William Smith. It opened on October 3, 1892, in a little frame cottage with an enrollment of about 20 students. Its purpose, according to the articles of incorporation, was "to improve our system of surgery, midwifery, and treatment of general diseases—the adjustment of the bones is the leading feature of this school." Eighteen diplomas were granted to the first graduating class on March 2, 1894.

3171. Navy medical school was the Naval Laboratory and Department of Instruction, opened on August 1, 1893, at the U.S. Naval Hospital, Brooklyn, NY (now a borough of New York City). The first director was Henry M. Wells, appointed on August 21, 1893, with the relative rank of captain. An unofficial school had been authorized on May 19, 1823, and opened at the Navy Yard Hospital, Philadelphia, under the direction of Dr. Thomas Harris of Philadelphia's Pennsylvania Hospital, who taught naval hygiene, military surgery, customs and usage of the naval service, and so on. The secretary of the navy appropriated $400 for the support of the school, whose expenses were paid by Dr. Harris from his own income. The school was discontinued by order of January 31, 1843.

3172. Chiropractic school was the Palmer School of Chiropractic, Davenport, IA, which opened in 1900. It was established by Daniel David Palmer.

3173. Nursing school at a college was the School of Nursing, University of Minnesota, Minneapolis, MN, authorized by the Board of Regents on October 1, 1908, and established on March 1, 1909, through the efforts of Dr. Richard Olding Beard. The first director of the school was Bertha Erdmann.

3174. Chiropody school of note was the New York School of Chiropody, organized in 1910 by members of the Pedic Society of the State of New York. On January 1, 1913, it became the First Institute of Podiatry, with Dr. Maurice J. Lewi as president. Its first graduating class, in 1913, consisted of 13 men and 1 woman. On November 16, 1939, it became affiliated with Long Island University, awarding the degree of Pod.D. (Doctor of Podiatry).

3175. Chiropody school at a college opened on September 20, 1915, at Temple University, Philadelphia, PA, where a chiropody clinic at the Garretson Hospital, an annex to Temple Hospital, had already been established. Four students completed the 34-week course in June 1916 and received the degree of M.Cp. The course was later changed to cover four years and lead to the degree of D.S.C. (Doctor of Surgical Chiropody). Dr. Frank Adoniram Thompson was the first dean of the school, and Dr. W. Ashton Kennedy and Dr. James Richardson Bennie were the first professors of chiropody.

3176. Army nursing school was the Army School of Nursing, authorized on May 25, 1918, by Secretary of War Newton Diehl Baker as a division of the surgeon general's office under the Medical Department of the Army. The first class of 402 graduates completed the course at Walter Reed Hospital, Washington, DC, on June 16, 1921. A three-year program of study was prescribed, with advanced credits offered to graduates of approved courses. The first dean of the school was Annie Warburton Goodrich. The school was discontinued on August 12, 1931.

3177. Hygiene and public health school at a college was established in 1916 at Johns Hopkins University, Baltimore, MD, under an endowment from the Rockefeller Foundation "for the advancement of knowledge and the training of investigators, teachers, officials and other workers" in the general field of hygiene and public health. This school was opened on October 1, 1918, with Dr. William Henry Welch as its first director.

3178. Medical center devoted to teaching, treatment, and research was the Columbia–Presbyterian Medical Center, on 168th Street west of Broadway, New York City, which opened on March 6, 1928. It had a library of 100,000 books and was designed to serve 600 students.

3179. Medical college founded as a Jewish institution was the Albert Einstein College of Medicine of Yeshiva University, New York City, which offered instruction on September 12, 1935, to 56 men and women, although only one floor of the six-story building was completed. Dr. Marcus David Kogel was the first dean.

EDUCATION—MEDICINE—VETERINARY

3180. Veterinary college was the Boston Veterinary Institute, Boston, MA, incorporated on April 28, 1855. The first president was Daniel Denison Slade, M.D. Courses were given in anatomy, physiology, chemistry, pharmacy, and the theory and practice of medicine and surgery.

3181. Veterinary college of importance was the New York College of Veterinary Surgeons, New York City, incorporated on April 6, 1857. It did not go into active operation until 1865. The course of study, which embraced comparative anatomy, was given in two sections of five months each. The tuition fee was $135, of which $5 was for matriculation fees, $100 for lecture fees, $5 for the dissecting room fee, and $25 for the diploma. The president of the school was Eben Mason. The school had professors of histology, anatomy, physiology, theory and practice, surgical pathology, and operative surgery.

3182. Veterinary department at a college was the Department of Veterinary Science of Cornell University, Ithaca, NY, which offered courses by Professor James Law beginning on October 7, 1868.

EDUCATION— MEDICINE— VETERINARY—continued

3183. Veterinary school established by a state was established on May 23, 1879, by the Board of Trustees of Iowa State College at Ames, IA. Lectures were given on veterinary anatomy, physiology, materia medica, pathology, disease and treatment, surgery, sanitary science, and practice. The first class of the veterinary school was graduated in 1880. The school was the first veterinary school in the United States to inaugurate a four-year program and the first to require as prerequisites for entrance diplomas from a high school and college.

EDUCATION—MILITARY

3184. Military school was the American Literary, Scientific and Military Academy, founded by Captain Alden Partridge in Norwich, VT, on August 6, 1819. The cadets were required to wear uniforms, and received instruction in fencing, military drawing, topography, "the Laws of Nations, Military Law ... the construction of Marine Batteries, Artillery duty, the Principles of Gunnery ... etc." The first class entered on September 4, 1820. The first cadet enrolled was Cyril Pennock of Hartford, VT. No specific time for completing the course was required, but the enrollment period varied from one to six years according to the student's ability. The name was changed on November 6, 1834, to Norwich University. In March 1866, the buildings were destroyed by fire and the school was moved to Northfield, VT.

3185. Military school established by a state was the Virginia Military Institute, Lexington, VA, established as an independent school at the Lexington Arsenal by act of March 29, 1839. It was governed by a board of visitors appointed by the governor, subject to approval by the state senate. The first corps of 28 cadets was mustered into service on November 11, 1839. The first superintendent was Professor (later Major General) Francis Henney Smith, who served until January 1, 1890.

3186. Military school operated by a church was the Catonsville Military Academy, founded in 1845 by Libertius Van Bokkelen in Catonsville, MD, and affiliated with St. Timothy's Protestant Episcopal Church.

3187. Bicycle corps of cadets was organized in 1894 by Colonel Royal Page Davidson and was made up of cadets in the Northwestern Military Academy, Lake Geneva, WI. It was composed of 16 bicycles, each equipped with special clips for carrying rifles and other equipment. One of the feats of the corps was a maneuver in which the riders put themselves and their bicycles, which when fully loaded with equipment weighed 54 pounds each, over a 16-foot wall in 2 minutes 48 seconds. The corps made numerous long cross-country trips, including a three-week journey from Chicago, IL, to Washington, DC, in June 1897 to deliver a message to the secretary of war.

3188. Airplane flying school was opened by the Curtiss Exhibition Company at Lake Keuka, Hammondsport, NY, in September 1910. It gave military officers free instruction in flying. Glenn Hammond Curtiss was the instructor. The first army officer assigned to take the course was Captain Paul N. Beck, who became the first military aviator. The Navy Department also sent officers for instruction in flying.

3189. Military service academies' enrollment of women was authorized by an act of Congress of October 7, 1975, "to insure that female individuals shall be eligible for appointment and admission to the service academics beginning with appointments to such academy for the class beginning in calendar year 1976."

EDUCATION—MILITARY—AIR FORCE

3190. Air Force academy was authorized on April 1, 1954. Temporary headquarters were established on July 11, 1955, at the Lowry Air Force Base, Denver, CO, where 306 candidates were sworn in. The first commandant was Lieutenant General Hubert Reilly Harmon. A $135 million academy was built at Colorado Springs, CO, and received its first cadets on August 29, 1958. The first graduating class of 207 cadets was commissioned on June 3, 1959. First in the graduating class was Bradley Clark Hosmer of Dunseith, ND. The four-year course consisted of 1,548 hours of the humanities, 1,629 hours of science, and 2,178 hours of airmanship.

3191. Air Force Academy graduate who was Native American was Leo Johnson of Fairfax, OK, who was one of the 297 graduates of the academy, Colorado Springs, CO, on June 6, 1962. He went on to earn the Air Force Commendation Medal as a pilot.

3192. Air Force Academy graduates who were African-American were Charles Vernon Bush, Isaac Sanders Payne IV, and Roger Bernard Sims, who were graduated from the academy in Colorado Springs, CO, on June 5, 1963, and received the Bachelor of Science degree.

3193. Air Force Academy cadets who were women were admitted to the academy at Colorado Springs, CO, on June 28, 1976, when 155 women were enrolled.

EDUCATION—MILITARY—ARMY

3194. Army academy was the United States Military Academy, established at West Point, NY, by act of Congress of March 16, 1802, for the purpose of educating and training young men in the theory and practice of military science. The first superintendent was Jonathan Williams.

3195. West Point graduate who was Jewish was Simon Magruder Levy of Maryland, who was appointed a cadet for his good conduct as orderly sergeant at the Battle of Maumee Rapids, August 20, 1794. He was one of the two cadets in the first graduating class on October 12, 1802, and was commissioned a second lieutenant in the Corps of Engineers. He resigned from the Army on September 30, 1805, because of ill health and died in 1807 in Georgia. The first Jewish woman to graduate from West Point was Cadet Donna Maller of Cockeysville, MD, one of 13 Jewish cadets who were graduated and commissioned on June 4, 1980, in a class of 831 men and 63 women.

3196. West Point graduates were Joseph Gardner Swift of Massachusetts and Simon Magruder Levy of Maryland. Both men were graduated from the U.S. Military Academy at West Point, NY, on October 12, 1802, and were appointed to the rank of second lieutenant. They were the only students to graduate of the original class of 10, which consisted of 5 men from Massachusetts and 1 each from Connecticut, Maryland, Missouri, New York, and Virginia. Levy, who was also the first Jewish graduate of West Point, resigned from the Army in 1805 because of ill health. Swift was brevetted a brigadier general on November 11, 1813, for his heroism in the battle at Chrystler's Field in upper Canada. On February 19, 1814, he was promoted to brigadier general for his meritorious service in the defense of New York in the War of 1812. He became head of the Military Academy in 1816 and retired from the Army on November 12, 1818. He died in 1865.

3197. West Point graduate killed in action was George Ronan, killed fighting against Native American allies of the British in the War of 1812. On August 15, 1812, he was mortally wounded during Captain Nathan Heald's desperate battle near Fort Chicago, IL, against a vastly superior force of Native Americans. Before he died, he killed two Native Americans in hand-to-hand fighting.

3198. West Point graduate who was Native American was David Moniac, a member of the Creek nation, who graduated and was commissioned a second lieutenant in 1822. He was killed in Florida in 1836 in the Battle of Wahoo Swamp, during the Army's campaign against the Seminoles. He had attained the rank of major.

3199. West Point graduate who was African-American was Henry Ossian Flipper, born a slave on March 29, 1856, in Thomasville, GA. He was a cadet from May 20, 1873, to June 14, 1877. He was appointed a second lieutenant in the 10th Cavalry on June 15, 1877, and remained in service until June 30, 1882, when he was dismissed for conduct unbecoming an officer and a gentleman. In December 1976, the Army reviewed his court-martial charge and changed his discharge record from dishonorable to honorable. The first African-American admitted to West Point was James Webster Smith, who was appointed by Congressman Solomon Lafayette Hoge and who reported on May 31, 1870.

3200. Army war college was authorized by the War Department on November 27, 1901, to furnish advanced military instruction to regularly commissioned army officers, using $20,000 that had been authorized by Congress on May 26, 1900. The first president was Major General Samuel Baldwin Marks Young. The first class of 16 officers was convened on November 1, 1904, and terminated on May 31, 1905. Classes were held in rented quarters until June 20, 1907, when a permanent building was opened in Washington, DC.

3201. West Point graduates who were Chinese nationals were Ying Shing Wen and Ting Chia Chen, who enrolled at West Point on June 15, 1905, and were graduated on June 11, 1909. As they were foreigners, they were not commissioned.

3202. Army school for chaplains was the Army Chaplain School, Fort Monroe, VA, organized on February 9, 1918. Instruction was offered in military law, international law, and military science and tactics. The school was moved to Camp Taylor, KY, on April 9, 1918.

3203. Movie for training soldiers utilized by the Army was *School of the Soldier,* produced by the Bray Pictures Corporation of New York City at West Point, NY, in 1917.

EDUCATION—MILITARY—ARMY—*continued*

3204. Army language school began courses in Japanese on November 1, 1941, at Crissey Field, Presidio of San Francisco, CA. After moving to other locations, it was settled at the Presidio of Monterey, CA, in June 1946. In 1953 the school offered courses in 24 languages.

3205. West Point instructor who was a woman was Elizabeth Matthew Lewis, who taught a course entitled "Introduction to Fine Arts, including art history, appreciation and related activities," beginning on February 1, 1968. She had served since November 6, 1967, as fine arts librarian.

3206. Army War College graduates who were women were Lieutenant Colonel Frances V. Chaffin of Washington, DC, and Lieutenant Colonel Shirley Rowell Heinze of Houston, TX, of the Women's Army Corps, who were graduated on June 16, 1969, in a class of 224, at Carlisle, PA.

3207. West Point cadets who were women were accepted for admission on March 9, 1976, and enrolled on July 7, 1976. The graduating class on May 28, 1980, contained 62 women, who were commissioned second lieutenants.

3208. West Point cadet who was a woman to graduate at the top of her class was 21-year-old Rebecca Marier of New Orleans, LA, who was graduated from the United States Military Academy on June 3, 1995. She topped a class of 858 men and 130 women.

EDUCATION—MILITARY—COAST GUARD

3209. Coast Guard officers' training school was the Revenue Cutter Service School of Instruction, which was opened on July 31, 1876, in New Bedford, MA. The classes were held on board the revenue cutter *J.C. Dobbin,* which sailed on its first practice cruise on May 25, 1877, under Captain J.A. Henriques. In 1914 the name was changed to the Revenue Cutter Academy, and later, with the creation of the Coast Guard, to the Coast Guard Academy.

3210. Coast Guard Academy graduate who was African-American was Merle James Smith, Jr., of Baltimore, MD, part of the class of 113 cadets who were graduated on June 8, 1966. The ceremony was held at Jones Field, New London, CT. His commission was presented to him by his father, a colonel in the regular Army.

3211. Coast Guard Academy graduates who were women were 14 cadets who were graduated on May 21, 1980, in a class of 156. They were among a group of 38 women who had entered the Coast Guard Academy in New London, CT, on June 28, 1976, their admission having been authorized by a law enacted in October 1975. Completion of the four-year course entitled them to receive the bachelor of science degree in engineering and commissions as ensigns and second lieutenants at a salary of $660 a month. The first of the women to be graduated was Jean Marie Butler of Hershey, PA, since the graduates were called in alphabetical order.

EDUCATION—MILITARY—NAVY

3212. Naval officers' training school was established on December 10, 1815, at the Navy Yard, Charlestown, MA. It was under the guidance of Commodore William Bainbridge, whose expertise as a naval leader had been demonstrated in the war with Tripoli.

3213. Naval academy was established at Windmill Point, Fort Severn, Annapolis, MD, on a nine-acre site that was transferred on August 15, 1845, from the War Department to the Navy Department. It was known as the Naval School and officially opened on October 10, 1845, with 56 students. The first superintendent was Commander Franklin Buchanan. As most of the midshipmen had already served some time at sea or otherwise in the Navy, the course of instruction varied in length, depending on the dates of their appointments. On July 1, 1850, the name was changed to the U.S. Naval Academy. The following year, the academy instituted a standard four-year program. The first official graduation was held on June 10, 1854. From May 9, 1861, to September 9, 1865, while Maryland was part of the Confederacy, the academy was transferred to Newport, RI.

3214. Naval Academy graduate who was Japanese was Zun Zow Matzmulla, admitted on December 8, 1869, under the act of Congress of July 27, 1868, authorizing the secretary of the Navy "to receive for instruction not exceeding six persons to be designated by the government of the Empire of Japan." Matzmulla completed the course in 1873.

3215. Naval Academy graduate to attain the rank of rear admiral was Edward Simpson, who was graduated in 1846 in the first class. He became a lieutenant in 1855, a lieutenant commander in 1862, a commander in 1865, a commodore in 1878, and a rear admiral in 1884.

3216. Naval war college was established at Coaster's Harbor Island, Newport, RI, on October 6, 1884, by order of the Secretary of the Navy. Commander Stephen Bleecker Luce was the first superintendent. The college opened on September 3, 1885. It offered naval officers an 11-month course in military science, the art of naval warfare, and marine international law. On January 11, 1889, the college was consolidated with the Torpedo Station on Goat Island in Newport harbor.

3217. Naval air training school was the Navy Aeronautic Station, Pensacola, FL, opened on December 1, 1914, under the command of Captain Henry Croskey Mustin. The first staff consisted of three instructors and a dozen mechanics. The name was later changed to the Naval Air Station. From 1911 to 1914, flight training was given at a camp at Greensbury Point, near Annapolis, MD.

3218. Navy school for chaplains was the Chaplains' School, Naval Operating Base, Norfolk, VA, which held its first session on February 23, 1942.

3219. Naval Academy graduate who was African-American was Wesley Anthony Brown of Washington, DC, who graduated on June 3, 1949, and received his commission as ensign. The first African-American midshipman at the Academy was James Henry Conyers of South Carolina, who attended from September 21, 1872, to November 11, 1873, but who did not graduate.

3220. Naval War College students who were African-American were Commander Samuel Lee Gravely, Jr., of Richmond, VA, who attended the School of Naval Warfare for senior officers, and Lieutenant Commander George Irwin Thompson of Los Angeles, CA, who attended the School of Naval Command and Staff for mid-career officers. Both schools were given at the Naval War College, Newport, RI, from August 16, 1963, to June 17, 1964.

3221. Naval Academy students who were women were admitted on July 6, 1976, when 80 women were admitted. The first female midshipman at the Academy to graduate at the top of her class was Kristine Holderied, who graduated on May 23, 1984.

3222. Naval War College president who was a former prisoner of war was Vice Admiral James Bond Stockdale, who served as president from October 13, 1977, to August 22, 1979. He was graduated from the U.S. Naval Academy, Annapolis, MD, on June 5, 1946. While serving during the Vietnam War, he parachuted from his stricken A-4 jet over North Vietnam and was captured. He endured 2,714 days of imprisonment, during which he was kept in solitary confinement for three years, suffering torture on numerous occasions. He was released on February 12, 1973, and on October 13, 1977, was promoted to the rank of vice admiral. In the presidential election of 1992, he was the running mate of the Texas businessman Ross Perot.

EDUCATION—ORGANIZATIONS

3223. Education association was the Middlesex County Association for the Improvement of Common Schools, organized on May 1799 in Middletown, CT, by the Reverend William Woodbridge, who served as its first president.

3224. Educational association (national) was the American Institute of Instruction, formed at a preliminary meeting held March 15–19, 1830, and organized August 19–21, 1830, at a convention at Boston, MA, attended by delegates from 15 states. The first president was Francis Wayland, Jr., president of Brown University.

3225. Teachers' organization (national) was the National Teachers Association, which was organized on August 26, 1867, at a national convention attended by representatives of state teachers' associations, who met in the Hall of the Controllers of the Public Schools in Philadelphia, PA. The organization was intended "to elevate the character and advance the interest of the profession of teaching and to promote the cause of popular education in the United States." John L. Enos was chairman. At the convention held in Cleveland, OH, on August 15, 1870, the name was changed to the National Education Association.

3226. Parent-teacher assocation was the Froebel Society of Brooklyn, NY (now part of New York City), founded in 1884 to further the "advancement of educational interests and the promotion of self-culture." It was named for the German educator Friedrich Wilhelm August Froebel.

3227. Parent-teacher association (national) was the National Congress of Mothers, organized on February 17, 1897, in Washington, DC, by Alice McLellan Birney and Phoebe Apperson Hearst at a meeting attended by 2,000 persons. At the annual meeting of March 9, 1908, the name was changed to the National Congress of Mothers and Parent-Teacher Associations. On May 9, 1924, the name was changed to the National Congress of Parents and Teachers.

EDUCATION— ORGANIZATIONS— *continued*

3228. International federation of students was the Pan American Student League, founded in New York City in 1920 to promote understanding among young people throughout the Americas. The first U.S. delegate to the group's International Council, and its first president, was Philip Leonard Green. The first secretary was J. Antonio Reyes of Peru.

EDUCATION—SCIENCE AND TECHNOLOGY

3229. Botany professor at a college was Adam Kuhn, who was appointed in January 1768 by the Philadelphia College, Philadelphia, PA. He occupied his post for 21 years. His schooling was obtained in Sweden under Linnaeus.

3230. Chemistry professor at a college was Benjamin Rush, one of the signers of the Declaration of Independence. He gave lectures in chemistry at the Philadelphia Medical School, Philadelphia, PA, as early as 1769.

3231. Mineralogy instruction at a college was given in 1786 by Dr. Benjamin Waterhouse at Rhode Island College, Providence, RI.

3232. Civil engineering course at a college was given in 1819 at Norwich University, Norwich, VT. The university was founded by Captain Alden Partridge on August 6, 1819, as the American Literary, Scientific and Military Academy. Courses in civil engineering included the construction of roads, canals, locks, and bridges, as well as architecture. The name was changed to Norwich University in 1834. In March 1866 the buildings were destroyed by fire and the college was moved to Northfield, VT.

3233. Engineering college was the Rensselaer School, Troy, NY, founded on November 5, 1824, and opened on January 3, 1825. The first class of 10 students was graduated on April 26, 1826, with the degree of A.B. The first civil engineering degree was awarded in October 1835. Amos Eaton was senior professor and the first director. The name of the school was changed to Rensselaer Institute in 1832 and to Rensselaer Polytechnic Institute in 1861.

3234. Applied chemistry professor at a college was Benjamin Silliman, Jr., who in 1846 was appointed to teach at the new Yale Analytical Laboratory, Yale University, New Haven, CT.

3235. Chemical laboratory at a college was opened at Boylston Hall, Harvard University, Cambridge, MA, in 1858. Josiah (Joseph) Parsons Cooke, author of numerous chemical books, was in charge of instruction.

3236. Mines school at a college was opened on November 15, 1864, in the basement of the Columbia University building on East 49th Street, New York City. The first professor of mines and metallurgy was Thomas Egleston, who was appointed on February 1, 1864. It was through his efforts that the plan of the school was proposed and carried out.

3237. Paleontology chair at a college was established by Yale University, New Haven, CT, in 1866, and was held by Professor Othniel Charles Marsh from that date to 1899. He was the first professor of vertebrate paleontology.

3238. Entomology professor at a college was Hermann August Hagen, who taught at Harvard University, Cambridge, MA, from 1870 to 1893.

3239. Electrical engineering school at a college was established on September 21, 1883, by the College of Engineering, Cornell University, Ithaca, NY. The college offered a four-year program leading to the degree of Bachelor of Science. Instruction was given in the theory of electricity; the construction and testing of telegraph lines, cables, and instruments; dynamo machines; and civil and mechanical engineering. Dr. Andrew White pledged his own resources for the school.

3240. Biology course offered at a college was conducted by Edmund Beecher Wilson, professor of biology at Bryn Mawr College, Bryn Mawr, PA, beginning on September 23, 1885. Five lectures were given weekly, with eight hours of laboratory practice. The students examined the structure of typical animals and plants, first of familiar species, then of unicellular organisms, working thence progressively upward and taking the higher animals and plants, and ending with the embryological development of the chick. An advanced class was engaged in the study of animal morphology. Lectures on specific phases of biology had, however, been given earlier.

3241. College graduate in geology who was a woman was Lou Henry Hoover, who received her degree in geology from Stanford University, Palo Alto, CA, in 1898. She translated Agricola's classical mining work *De Re Metallica* with her husband, Herbert Hoover, the future president, who had received his bachelor's degree in geology from Stanford three years earlier.

3242. Climatology professor at a college was Robert De Courcy Ward, appointed in 1910 by Harvard University, Cambridge, MA.

3243. Oil and gas production course at a college was offered by the School of Engineering, University of Pittsburgh, Pittsburgh, PA, in 1912–13. The course was given by Professor Roswell Hill Johnson.

3244. Aeronautical engineering course at a college was given in 1913 by the Department of Naval Architecture and Marine Engineering, Massachusetts Institute of Technology, Cambridge, MA. Lectures in aeronautics were given in 1912 and 1913. The first regular instructor in aeronautical engineering was appointed in 1913. The aerodynamic laboratory was placed in operation and a graduate course was established leading to the degree of Master of Science in Aeronautical Engineering in 1914.

3245. Geography school at a college was the Clark Graduate School of Geography, Clark University, Worcester, MA, which opened in the fall of 1921. Dr. Wallace Walter Atwood, president of the university, was appointed director of the school and professor of physical and regional geography.

3246. Petroleum refining course at a college was offered by the School of Mines, University of Pittsburgh, Pittsburgh, PA, in 1922–23 under the direction of Dr. Warren Fred Faragher.

3247. Micropaleontology course at a college was given by Professor Jesse James Galloway at Columbia University, New York City, starting on September 25, 1924. It covered the principles of paleontology, classification and nomenclature, the use of paleontological literature, and the identification of small forms with the microscope.

3248. Nuclear engineering course at a college was established by the North Carolina State College of Agriculture and Engineering of the University of North Carolina, Raleigh, NC, under the direction of Dr. Clifford Keith Beck, head of the physics department. The first students were accepted and enrolled on June 12, 1950.

3249. Team to achieve a perfect score in the International Mathematical Olympiad were the six members of the 1994 U.S. team, drawn from the more than 350,000 high school students who took the American School Mathematics Examination that year. The 35th International Mathematical Olympiad was held in Hong Kong in July 1994. The U.S. team, all boys, scored a perfect 42 points in the two-day, nine-hour test of algebra, geometry, and number theory. Students from 68 other countries competed, including the favored Chinese and Russian teams, which took second and third place. The U.S. coach was Walter Mientka of the University of Nebraska, Lincoln, NE.

EDUCATION—SOCIAL SCIENCES

3250. Political economy course at a college was given at the College of William and Mary of Williamsburg, VA, in 1784.

3251. Political economy chair at a college was established at Harvard University, Cambridge, MA, in 1871. The first professor was Charles Franklin Dunbar. An earlier chair in moral philosophy and political economy was established in 1818 at Columbia College, New York City, with Professor John McVickar the first occupant.

3252. Sociology professor at a college was Albion Woodbury Small, appointed professor and head of the Department of Sociology at the University of Chicago, Chicago, IL, effective October 1, 1892. Small held the position until his retirement on October 1, 1925. He was also dean of the Graduate School of Arts and Literature from 1905 to 1923. A course in sociology had been offered at Bryn Mawr College in 1892 by Franklin Henry Giddings, associate professor of political science.

3253. Urban planning instruction at a college was offered in 1909 by Harvard University, Cambridge, MA, under James Sturgis Pray, professor of landscape architecture. In the fall of 1929, the Charles Dyer Norton Chair of Regional Planning was founded by a gift from James F. Curtis, and a separate School of City Planning was set up requiring a bachelor's degree for entrance and giving a Master of City Planning degree. The first degrees of Master in Landscape Architecture were conferred on June 18, 1925, and the first degrees of Master of City Planning on June 18, 1931.

3254. Civic design chair at a college was established by the University of Illinois, Urbana, IL, in 1912 as part of the landscape development program inaugurated in 1897 by Joseph Cullen Blair, in charge of the Department of Horticulture. The first incumbent of the chair was Professor Charles Mulford Robinson, who served as professor of civic design from September 1, 1913, until his death on December 30, 1917.

3255. Citizenship and public affairs school at a college was opened on October 3, 1924, by Syracuse University, Syracuse, NY, through the generosity of George Holmes Maxwell. The first dean was William Eugene Mosher.

EDUCATION—SOCIAL SCIENCES—*continued*

3256. Propaganda course at a college was given by Professor Harold Dwight Lasswell of the Department of Political Science, University of Chicago, Chicago, IL, in 1927. It was entitled "Political Opinion and Propaganda."

3257. Industrial and labor relations school at a college was the New York State School of Industrial and Labor Relations, Cornell University, Ithaca, NY, opened for registration on November 2, 1945. Irving McNeil Ives was the first dean.

EDUCATION—TEACHING

3258. Teacher training school was the Concord Academy, Concord, VT, opened on March 11, 1823, by the Reverend Samuel Read Hall, who conducted it as a teachers' seminary until 1830.

3259. Model laboratory school at a college for student teaching was a three-story building opened on October 31, 1838, by Lafayette College, Easton, PA, and was known as West College. Its cost of $2,230 was paid by the college's president, George Junkin.

3260. Teacher training school established by a state was the Normal School in Lexington, MA, which opened on July 3, 1839, with three pupils. Free tuition was offered to those who completed the one-year course and planned to teach in Massachusetts. Cyrus Pierce was the first principal. The school was started on the initiative of the educational reformer Horace Mann with the help of Edmund Dwight, who offered $10,000 on condition that the Commonwealth appropriate the same amount to be expended by the Board of Education in qualifying teachers for common schools. That amount was appropriated on April 19, 1838. On December 15, 1853, the school moved to Framingham, MA.

3261. Teachers' institute was held at Hartford, CT, in October 1839, when 26 male teachers attended a six-week course sponsored by Henry Barnard and received the "opportunity of critically reviewing the studies which they will be called upon to teach, with a full explanation of all the principles involved." Among the authorities who gave instruction were Charles Davies in higher mathematics and Thomas Hopkins Gallaudet in composition and school government.

3262. Teaching methodology course at a college was offered beginning on December 1, 1841, when Alfred Saxe was appointed professor of normal instruction at Wesleyan University, Middletown, CT, for a term of two years "to prepare teachers more perfectly for the business of instruction." No tuition charge was made for the course, which was a one-year program of study.

3263. Teacher training school at which students conducted practice classes was the Oswego Training School for Primary Teachers, Oswego, NY, established on May 1, 1861, with an enrollment of nine students. Dr. Edward Austin Sheldon, who served from 1861 to 1897, was the first principal. On March 4, 1863, the New York legislature passed "an act for the support of a training school for primary teachers" that appropriated $3,000 for two years, calculated on an attendance of 50 pupils. On March 27, 1867, the state acquired the Oswego school as a state normal school and changed its name to the Oswego State Normal and Training School.

3264. Teacher training school principal who was a woman was Anna Callender Brackett, who on January 5, 1863, took charge of the St. Louis Normal School, St. Louis, MO.

3265. Education department at a college was the Collegiate Department of Education, created by the University of Iowa, Iowa City, IA, in 1873, along with the first professorship of education. The department absorbed the university's former Normal Department, which had been in operation since 1855. A temporary department of education had been created by New York University in New York City in 1832.

EDUCATION—THEOLOGICAL

3266. Divinity professor at a college was Edward Wigglesworth, appointed on January 24, 1722, to the Thomas Hollis Professorship of Divinity at Harvard College, Cambridge, MA. He served until his death on January 16, 1765.

3267. Theology school was founded by the Dutch Reformed Church in 1784 with the appointment of Dr. John Henry Livingston of the Collegiate Church of New York City as professor of theology. In 1810, Livingston went to New Brunswick, NJ, under an agreement that allowed the school to share the campus of Queen's College (later Rutgers University). The theology school was named the New Brunswick Theological Seminary. The two institutions were not corporately connected and retained separate identities.

3268. Catholic seminary was St. Mary's Seminary and College, in Roland Park, Baltimore, MD. It was established on July 10, 1791, when Francis Charles Nagot, the first superintendent, arrived in Baltimore with three priests and and five students. It became a pontifical university on May 1, 1822, when Pope Pius VII granted it the right and privilege of conferring degrees in divinity. The first degrees were granted on January 24, 1824.

3269. Theology school that was nonsectarian was the Divinity School of Harvard College, Cambridge, MA, organized as a separate department of the college in 1816, although the faculty of the Divinity School was not appointed until 1819. Six students were graduated in 1817. Degrees were not conferred by the Divinity School until 1870. Theology had been taught since the opening of Harvard College.

3270. Theology school graduate who was African-American was Theodore Sedgwick Wright, born in Providence, RI, in 1797, who was graduated from the Princeton Theological Seminary, Princeton, NJ, in 1828. He was ordained in February 1829 and served for 18 years as pastor of the First Colored Presbyterian Church in New York City.

3271. Theological school that was multisectarian and presented regular courses by scholars representing different denominations was the Boston Theological Seminary, Boston, MA, which opened in September 1867 with Catholic, Methodist, and Presbyterian professors, as well as faculty members of other faiths.

3272. Theological college for Jews was Maimonides College, Philadelphia, PA, which opened on October 27, 1867. It was sponsored by the Hebrew Education Society of Philadelphia and the Board of Delegates of American Israelites. The founder and first president was Rabbi Isaac Leeser, who also served as professor of homiletics, belles lettres, and comparative theology. It offered a five-year course leading to Bachelor's and Doctor of Divinity degrees. Tuition was $100, and board and lodging $200 per year. Dr. Marcus Jastrow was provost. The college closed in 1873.

3273. Theological school to admit women as students was the Boston University School of Theology, Boston, MA, founded on March 30, 1871, when the Boston Theological Seminary united with Boston University. The first female student matriculated on September 25, 1872. The first B.D. (Bachelor of Divinity) degree awarded to a woman was granted to Anna Oliver on June 7, 1876.

3274. Rabbinical college for the Reform Jewish movement was Hebrew Union College, established on October 3, 1875, in Cincinnati, OH, through the efforts of Dr. Isaac Mayer Wise, who served as president from 1875 to 1900. The first graduation was held on July 11, 1883.

3275. Missionary training school was the Missionary Training College for Home and Foreign Missionaries and Evangelists, New York City, founded 1882 and formally opened on October 1, 1883, with an enrollment of four students. The course consisted of one year of study, including courses in English, Christian evidences, Bible study and interpretation, church history, and Christian life and work. The school was founded by Dr. Albert Benjamin Simpson, who was the first president. The name was changed to the Missionary Training Institute in April 1894.

3276. Yeshivah for Jewish religious study was Yeshivah Etz Chaim, founded in 1886 in New York City. It was not a congregational school, as previous Jewish schools had been, but an independent institution supported by an Orthodox Jewish community organization, the Hebra Machzikei Yeshivat Etz Chaim. It offered religious and secular studies at the elementary level. Graduates of the yeshivah formed the entering class of the first advanced-level yeshivah in America, the Rabbi Isaac Elchanan Theological Seminary, incorporated in 1897. The schools merged in 1915 with Rabbi Dr. Bernard Revel as president. The following year, a secular high school program was added, the first to be sponsored by a yeshivah. RIETS became an affiliate of Yeshiva University in 1945.

3277. Catholic seminary under the supervision of the Pope was the Pontifical College Josephinum, Worthington, OH, a Roman Catholic institution immediately subject to the Holy See, established on September 1, 1888. Thirteen students enrolled in the courses in liberal arts and general professional theology.

3278. Catholic seminary for the education of African-American priests was opened by the Missionaries of the Society of the Divine Word at Bay St. Louis, MS, and was dedicated on September 16, 1923.

3279. Greek Orthodox college and orphanage was the Monastery of St. Stephanos in Gastonia, NC, dedicated on September 18, 1932, by Archbishop Athenagaros of the Greek Orthodox Church in North and South America to the "oncoming generations of Greek youth."

EDUCATION—THEOLOGICAL—*continued*

3280. Cantorial school was the Reform movement's Hebrew Union School of Education and Sacred Music, New York City, which opened on October 16, 1948. Cantor-educator diplomas were awarded on June 17, 1951, to the graduating class of 10 men.

EDUCATION—VOCATIONAL

3281. Manual training courses offered in a school were given at the Charity Workers' School, organized in Talbot County, MD, in 1750 by the Reverend Thomas Bacon. It opened on December 1, 1751, with an enrollment of six boys. It was financed through funds from a series of concerts given in Maryland and Virginia.

3282. Industrial school on the Fellenberg plan was established in 1819 in Derby, CT, by Josiah Holbrook. The boys paid a portion of their tuition by laboring on the farm. In 1824, with the cooperation of the Reverend Truman Coe, Holbrook established the Agricultural Seminary. Neither of these enterprises was successful.

3283. Technical institute was the Gardiner Lyceum, Gardiner, ME, founded by Robert Hallowell Gardiner in 1822 "for the purpose of giving to farmers and mechanics such a scientific education as would enable them to become skillful in their professions." Courses were offered in arithmetic, algebra, geometry, trigonometry, mensuration of surfaces and solids, bookkeeping, surveying, navigation, mechanics, hydrostatics, pneumatics, chemistry, natural philosophy, and "the higher branches of mathematics and natural history." The first lecturer was Benjamin Hale.

3284. Printing instruction at a school was given in the community school founded by Robert Owen in his utopian settlement at New Harmony, IN, in 1826. The subjects of study included printing, lithography, and engraving.

3285. Manual training institute was the Fellenberg Manual Labor Institute, opened in 1829 in Greenfield, MA, by James Henry Coffin.

3286. Industrial school for girls was organized in Lancaster, MA, the funds being obtained by subscription undertaken in April 1854. The school was incorporated as a state institution on August 27, 1856, with Bradford K. Pierce as the first superintendent. This school was administered by the Department of Public Welfare.

3287. Railroad apprentice school for railway mechanics was established by the New York Central Railroad at Elkhart, IN, in 1872.

3288. Cooking school was the New York Cooking School, which was opened in November 1876 by Juliet Corson at her residence on St. Mark's Place, New York City. In 1875 she gave cooking instruction in the Ladies' Cooking Class of the free Training School for Women, New York City.

3289. Typing school was opened by D.L. Scott-Browne at 737 Broadway, New York City, in 1878.

3290. Manual training school entirely financed by public taxes was the Baltimore Manual Training School, established in Baltimore, MD, in 1884 under authority of municipal ordinance of October 20, 1883. Instruction and practice were given in carpentry, wood turning, pattern making, chipping and filing, forge work, molding, soldering and brazing, and other crafts.

3291. Trade school for girls was the Manhattan Trade School for Girls, New York City, opened in November 1902. The first director was Professor Mary Schenck Woolman, director of the domestic art department of Teachers College, Columbia University, New York City. Her staff consisted of an executive secretary, six supervisors, six instructors and foremen, six assistants, and four occasional workers. Twenty pupils enrolled the first day for courses in painting, hand sewing, and sewing machine operation. Night classes were begun in 1903.

3292. Automobile school was established in 1903 by the education department of the Young Men's Christian Association, Boston, MA, to train chauffeurs, mechanics, and prospective car owners. The course consisted of lectures on the construction and operation of cars together with laboratory, machine shop, and repair work. Enrollment the first year was approximately 250 students.

3293. Apprentice continuation school funded by a public board of education was established in Cincinnati, OH, on August 30, 1909, to give tool apprentices the opportunity of a technical education along practical lines. Classes were conducted on the third story of a building at 12th and Jackson streets.

3294. Printing lecture course in a college was "an introduction to the technique of printing," offered in February 1911 by the Graduate School of Business Administration, Harvard University, Cambridge, MA. The course was given by Daniel Berkeley Updike.

3295. Vocational guidance chair at a college was established in 1914 at Indiana University, Bloomington, IN. The first professor was Robert Josselyn Leonard, who served from June 1914 to April 1918.

3296. Fisheries school at a college was the College of Fisheries, University of Washington, Seattle, WA, established in March 1919. It offered practical training and a four-year program leading to a Bachelor of Fisheries degree. The first classes had an enrollment of 76 students. The first dean was John Nathan Cobb.

3297. Hotel administration course at a college was offered by Cornell University, Ithaca, NY, in the fall of 1922, and included courses in accounting, administration, economics, engineering, food preparation, housekeeping, and languages. The course required four years and led to a B.S. degree. Professor Howard Bagnall Meek was the first professor of hotel administration.

3298. Modeling school to train young women to be models was officially opened in 1928 in Chicago, IL, and was known as *L'École de Mannequins,* the School of Modeling. Training was based upon the principles of mental control over body movements, a correct understanding of balance, poise, and gracefulness, and personality development.

3299. Farriers' course at a college was presented in 1930 by Jack MacAllan at Michigan State College, East Lansing, MI, as part of a program in horse management. In 1946 a special farriers' course was offered under Jack MacAllan in the winter term to those who wished to train as specialists.

3300. Truck driving school was opened in June 1954 by the Bedford Motor-Transport Drivers Training Program, Bedford, PA. The first class was graduated July 31, 1954.

3301. Circus clown training school was the "clown college" established on September 1, 1968, in Venice, FL, by Irvin Feld, president and producer of the Ringling Brothers and Barnum and Bailey Combined Shows. The eight-week tuition-free course was given during September, October, and November from 9 A.M. to 6 P.M. and included slaps and falls, juggling, stilt-walking, plate-spinning, makeup, mime and pantomine, acrobatics, equilibrium, and elephant riding.

3302. Technical school for Native Americans was the Southwestern Indian Polytechnic Institute, Albuquerque, NM, a coeducational school that opened on September 16, 1971, with 700 Native American students from 64 tribes. It comprised 12 buildings on a 164-acre campus and cost $13 million. John L. Peterson was the first superintendent.

EDUCATION—VOCATIONAL—NAUTICAL

3303. Nautical school was established on May 29, 1827, in Nantucket, MA, and was known as Admiral Sir Isaac Coffin's Lancasterian School. It was conducted by William Coffin, Jr., and Miss A. Meach and was located in a wooden schoolhouse. Courses on shipboard to train sailors had been offered previously.

3304. Nautical school established by a city was the Nautical School of the Port of New York, opened on January 11, 1875, in New York City on board the *St. Mary,* a 150-foot, three-masted, full-rigged vessel known as a sloop of war. It was built in 1844 to chase slavers. The main deck was less than 144 feet above the water line. The commanding officer was Commander Robert Lees Phythian. From July 22 to October 8, 1875, the school conducted a cruise of Long Island Sound. The school was authorized by New York State on April 24, 1873, and was supported by state funds.

3305. Nautical school established by a state was the Massachusetts Nautical Training School, established by Massachusetts on June 11, 1891. On February 17, 1891, the governor was authorized to petition the secretary of the Navy for a suitable vessel, and on October 28, 1892, the steam sloop *Enterprise* was transferred to Massachusetts.

3306. Merchant marine cadet corps was established on March 15, 1938, following the passage of the Merchant Marine Act of June 29, 1936. The first class, started on January 28, 1942, had an enrollment of 74 cadets. The first Bachelor of Science (B.S.) degree was awarded on June 21, 1950, to 220 graduates. Degrees were subsequently awarded retroactively to all classes, beginning with the class of December 1947. Upon completion of three years at the academy and one year at sea, the cadets received a Coast Guard license as Third Assistant Engineer or Third Mate, a B.S. degree, or a commission as ensign in the Naval Reserve, Merchant Marine Academy.

EDUCATION—VOCATIONAL—NAUTI-
CAL—*continued*

3307. Merchant marine academy was the Merchant Marine Academy at Kings Point, NY, dedicated on September 30, 1943, when a message from President Franklin Delano Roosevelt was read to 5,000 guests. The course of instruction was 18 months long. Previously, training had been held aboard ship and in temporary shore establishments.

3308. Merchant Marine Academy cadets who were women were admitted on Acceptance Day, August 31, 1974, after having undergone two weeks of indoctrination and one month of general training at the academy in Kings Point, NY. The class of 1978 consisted of 15 women and 333 men.

3309. Graduate of a four-year maritime school who was a woman was Deborah B. Doane of Essex, CT, who was graduated on May 1, 1976, from the Maine Maritime Academy, Castine, ME.

ELECTIONS

3310. Election held in a colony took place on May 18, 1631, when John Winthrop was elected governor of Massachusetts. It is believed, however, that in 1619 the Virginia Assembly was selected by means of votes.

3311. Election held in defiance of the Royal Courts was held on April 11, 1640, in Wethersfield, CT, when Matthew Mitchell was elected recorder. The King's Court at Hartford refused to recognize the election and penalized Wethersfield £5 and the recorder 40 nobles. The fines were not paid.

3312. Ban on convicts holding public office was passed on March 2, 1642, by Virginia. It stated: "Be it also enacted that no person or persons whatsoever for any offence already committed or to be committed shall be hereafter adjudged to serve the collony."

3313. Corrupt election practices law enacted by a colony was passed on May 22, 1649, by the General Court in Warwick, RI. It provided that "no one should bring in any votes that he did not receive from the voters' own hands, and that all votes should be field by the Recorder in the presence of the Assembly." A committee of four freemen was authorized to determine violations of the law and "to examine parties and present to this court what they find in the case."

3314. Printed ballot was authorized by the "act to regulate the general elections within this commonwealth," enacted on February 15, 1799, by Pennsylvania. The law provided that "every elector may deliver written or printed tickets." The ballots were prepared by political parties and were known as "vest pocket tickets." They contained only the names of the issuing party's candidates.

3315. State nominating convention assembled at Utica, NY, in 1824 for the purpose of nominating candidates for governor and lieutenant governor. The number of delegates corresponded to the number of representatives in the assembly. De Witt Clinton was nominated by the Democratic-Republican Party and was elected on November 3, 1824. He served as governor from January 1, 1825, to his death on February 11, 1828. He had previously served as governor from January 1, 1818, to December 31, 1822.

3316. Corrupt election practices law enacted by a state was passed by the legislature of California and signed by Governor Frederick Low on March 26, 1866. The first state law requiring candidates to file itemized accounts of campaign expenditures, under penalty of imprisonment and loss of office, was passed by New York State and signed by Governor Theodore Roosevelt on April 4, 1890.

3317. Voting machines were authorized for use in New York State on March 15, 1892, by an act "to secure independence of voters at town meetings, secrecy of the ballot and provide for the use of Myers' automatic ballot cabinet." Later legislation extended the use of the machine to cities. The machines were first used on April 12, 1892, at Lockport, NY, where 3,271 votes were cast for the office of mayor and other town offices. The machine was invented by Jacob H. Myers and manufactured by the American Ballot Machine Company, which was later absorbed by the Automatic Voting Machine Corporation of Jamestown, NY.

3318. Primary election law enacted by a state was passed by Minnesota on April 20, 1899. It applied to candidates for city and county offices, judges, and elective members of school, library, and park boards in counties having a population of 200,000 or more. Hennepin County was the only one that had the required population when the law went into effect. In 1903 Wisconsin became the first state to establish statewide primary elections.

3319. Corrupt election practices law enacted by Congress was passed on January 26, 1907. It prohibited corporations from contributing to candidates' campaign funds in presidential and congressional races. An act passed on March 4, 1909, further prohibited national banks and corporations from making financial contributions to campaign funds in connection with any election to any political office.

3320. Election using the preferential ballot system took place in Grand Junction, CO. The charter that contained the preferential ballot provision was adopted on September 14, 1909, and the first election using the system took place on November 2. Opposite the name of each candidate were three columns headed "First Choice," "Second Choice," and "Third Choice." Any person receiving more than half of all the votes cast for first choice was elected; if no one received more than half the first choices, the lowest candidate was dropped and the first and second choices were added together. If any remaining candidate received a majority of the combined votes, he was elected, but if not, then the lowest candidate was again dropped, and all choices for each candidate then added together, and the person receiving the largest total vote was elected. In case of a tie, priority in choice determined election.

3321. Election using proportional representation was held on November 2, 1915, in Ashtabula, OH, to elect seven council members. The votes were counted so that each group consisting of one-seventh of all the voters secured a representative.

3322. Election campaign using radio was undertaken by Senator Harry Stewart New, Republican of Indiana, who waged an unsuccessful campaign for reelection in 1922. He made a number of radio speeches during the campaign, and hired several halls in which the speeches could be heard over loudspeakers. He was defeated by Samuel Moffett Ralston, the Democratic candidate.

3323. Negative election campaign run by media specialists took place during the California governor's race of 1934. The Democratic candidate was the writer and social reformer Upton Beall Sinclair, a Socialist, whose platform was called EPIC ("End Poverty in California"). The Republican Party, for the first time in any major American election, hired outside political consultants and advertising specialists to conduct a wholly negative campaign. It included attack ads on radio and film, thousands of negative cartoons and leaflets comparing Sinclair to Hitler and Stalin, and a secret dirty tricks squad that tapped his phones. The Republican candidate, Frank Merriam, won by more than 250,000 votes.

3324. Governor of Puerto Rico to be elected was Luis Muñoz Marin, journalist and founder of Puerto Rico's Partido Popular Democratico (PPD), the island's ruling party from 1970 to 1977. Muñoz Marin was elected governor in San Juan, PR, in 1948, having previously served as president of the senate since 1942. He was instrumental in securing commonwealth status for Puerto Rico in 1952.

3325. Election in the District of Columbia was the primary election held on Wednesday, May 6, 1964, when the Reverend Edward Franklin Jackson, a Methodist minister who was African-American, defeated Frank Daniel Reeves for the office of Democratic committeeman.

ELECTIONS—CONGRESSIONAL

3326. House of Representatives election that was contested was the race between David Ramsay and William Loughton Smith of South Carolina. Smith took his seat on April 13, 1789. On April 15, 1789, Ramsay presented a petition that Smith be declared ineligible, on the ground that he had not been "seven years a citizen of the United States," as he had studied abroad during that period. The dispute was referred to April 18, 1789, to the Committee on Elections, which ruled that Smith was entitled to his seat.

3327. Senate election that was contested was that of Abraham Alfonse Albert Gallatin of Pennsylvania, who was born in Switzerland and emigrated to the United States in 1780. He was elected to the Senate from Pennsylvania and presented his credentials on February 28, 1793. No action was taken during the Second Congress, which adjourned March 2, but on December 2 a petition was presented alleging that he had not been a citizen of the United States for the nine years required by the Constitution. The trial began on February 20, 1794, and on February 28 the Senate declared his election void. Gallatin was later elected to the House of Representatives, where he served from March 4, 1795, to March 3, 1801. Gallatin's trial was the first occasion on which members of the public were admitted to the Senate. A motion passed on the first day of the trial required that the Senate chamber "be provided with galleries

ELECTIONS—CONGRESSIONAL—*continued*

which shall be permitted to be open every morning so long as the Senate shall be engaged in their legislative capacity, unless in such cases as may in the opinion of the Senate require secrecy."

3328. Voting machines in congressional elections were approved by Congress in a bill signed by President William McKinley on February 14, 1899. It provided that "all votes for representatives in Congress must be by written or printed ballot, or voting machines, the use of which has been duly authorized by the state."

3329. Senator elected by popular vote after the passage of the 17th Amendment to the Constitution was Augustus Octavius Bacon, Democrat of Georgia, who was elected on July 15, 1913, and sworn in on July 28. Section 3, Article 1 of the Constitution provided for the election of senators by the state legislatures. The 17th Amendment, which required senators to be elected by popular vote, was passed in the House of Representatives on April 13, 1912, and by the Senate on June 12, 1912. The 36th state to ratify the amendment was Wisconsin, on May 9, 1913, and the amendment was declared in force May 31, 1913. The first general election in which senators were elected by popular vote took place on November 4, 1913.

3330. Senator unseated after a recount was Smith Wildman Brookhart, Republican of Iowa, the presumed winner of the election of November 4, 1924. He presented his credentials as a senator-elect for the term commencing March 4, 1925, and served until April 12, 1926, when he was ousted by a Senate vote of 45–41. A recount had proved the winner to be Daniel Frederic Steck, the Democrat candidate, who served from April 12, 1926, to March 3, 1931.

3331. Senator elected by a write-in vote was James Strom Thurmond, Democrat of South Carolina, who was elected on November 2, 1954, for the term ending January 3, 1961. Thurmond received 139,106 votes, defeating Edgar Brown, the official candidate of the Democratic Party, who received 80,956 votes.

ELECTIONS—POLITICS

3332. National political platform was adopted on May 11, 1832, by a group of 295 Democratic-Republican delegates from 16 states and the District of Columbia, who assembled in Washington, DC, and drew up a list of resolutions for a platform. At the party's convention, held on December 12, 1831, in Baltimore, MD, Henry Clay was nominated for president and John Sergeant for vice president.

3333. National political convention to adopt the two-thirds rule was the Democratic-Republican convention, held May 21–22, 1832, at the Athenaeum, Baltimore, MD. The rule requires a candidate for nomination to receive two-thirds of the votes of the delegates. Robert Lucas of Ohio was chairman of the convention, which nominated Andrew Jackson for president and Martin Van Buren for vice president.

3334. National political convention to adopt the unit rule was the Whig convention of 1840, held at Harrisburg, PA. The results of the balloting for the presidential nomination were 148 votes for William Henry Harrison of Ohio, 90 votes for Henry Clay, and 16 votes for Winfield Scott. John Tyler of Virginia was nominated for vice president. The unit rule had been adopted on December 4, 1839, when the party instructed each state to select a committee of three delegates who together formed a Committee of the Whole. The state delegates, meeting separately, gave instructions to the members of their committee, who later voted as a unit in the Committee of the Whole.

3335. Delegate to a national political convention who was African-American was Frederick Douglass of Rochester, NY, who attended the National Loyalists' Loyal Union Convention at Philadelphia, PA, on September 6, 1866.

3336. National political convention to be addressed by a woman was the Republican National Convention in Cincinnati, OH, in June 1876. On June 15, Sara Andrews Spencer made a speech against the disfranchisement of women and presented a memorial of the National Woman Suffrage Association stating "that the right to use the ballot inheres in the citizens of the United States."

3337. National political convention of a major party presided over by an African-American met in the Exposition Building, Chicago, IL, on June 3, 1884. John Roy Lynch, an African-American politician who had served three terms as congressman from Mississippi, was nominated for temporary chairman of the Republican Party by Henry Cabot Lodge. The nomination was supported by Theodore Roosevelt and George William Curtis, and was carried by a vote of 424 for Lynch to 384 for Powell Clayton. John Brooks Henderson was the permanent chairman. The convention nominated James Gillespie Blaine for president and General John Alexander Logan for vice president.

3338. Delegates to a national political convention who were women were alternates Therese A. Jenkins of Cheyenne, WY, and Cora G. Carleton of Hilliard, WY, who attended the 10th Republican Party convention at Minneapolis, MN, on June 7–10, 1892.

3339. National political convention at which a woman made a seconding speech was the Democratic National Convention, held at Kansas City, MO, in July 1900. On July 5, delegate Elizabeth Cohn of Utah seconded the nomination of William Jennings Bryan of Nebraska.

3340. Political convention to be broadcast on radio took place on June 10, 1924, when the Republican Convention assembled at Cleveland, OH, to nominate Calvin Coolidge of Massachusetts and Charles Gates Dawes of Illinois for president and vice president. Graham McNamee was the announcer for the program, which was carried by 15 stations of the National Broadcasting Company from Boston, MA, to Kansas City, MO.

3341. State committee chairman of a major political party who was a woman was Mary Teresa Norton, who was elected chairman of the Democratic State Committee of New Jersey at the state convention held in Trenton on May 22, 1934. Mrs. Norton was a member of the House of Representatives from the 13th District, New Jersey.

3342. Political convention to be televised was the 22nd Republican Convention, held on June 24–29, 1940, in Philadelphia, PA, at which Wendell Lewis Willkie of New York and Charles Linza McNary of Oregon were nominated for president and vice president. The telecast was made by station W2XBS of the National Broadcasting Company, New York City. The first to be telecast in color was the 29th Republican Convention, held on August 5–7, 1968, at Miami Beach, FL. The proceedings were broadcast by both the National Broadcasting Company and the Columbia Broadcasting System.

3343. National political convention to propose African-Americans for the offices of president and vice president was the 35th Democratic convention, held on August 26–29, 1968, at Chicago, IL. On August 28, 1968, the Reverend Channing Emery Phillips of Washington, DC, received 67.5 of the 2,622 votes cast for the presidential nomination. On August 29, Julian Bond of Atlanta, GA, was nominated but declined, as he did not fulfill the necessary age requirement.

3344. Chairman of a major political party who was a woman was Frances Jean Miles Westwood of West Jordan, UT, elected chairman on July 14, 1972, at the Democratic National Committee meeting, Miami Beach, FL, which was attended by 303 members from 50 states. The first woman to serve as chairman of the Republican Party's national committee was Mary Louise Smith of Iowa, elected on September 16, 1974, at Washington, DC.

3345. Chairman of a major political party who was African-American was Ronald H. Brown, who was elected chairman of the Democratic Party National Committee on February 10, 1989. Brown later served as secretary of commerce in the cabinet of President William Jefferson Clinton.

ELECTIONS—POLITICS—PARTIES

3346. Quids political faction was organized during the administration of President Thomas Jefferson. Its members took an extreme position in favor of states' rights and were opposed to Jefferson's attempts to acquire West Florida. They were led from 1804 to 1808 by John Randolph of Roanoke, VA. In 1808 they ran James Monroe as a presidential candidate against James Madison. The name is derived from the Latin *tertium quid* ("a third thing"), indicating separation from both existing political parties, or from both administration and opposition forces.

3347. Political machine that was well organized was the Albany Regency, made up of a group of Democrats who, from 1820 to 1854, exercised a controlling influence over the politics of New York State. Their headquarters were in Albany, NY, but their power extended into national politics. Prominent among them were Martin Van Buren, William Learned Marcy, Silas Wright, and John Adams Dix.

3348. Anti-Masonic Party convention to nominate a presidential candidate took place at Baltimore, MD, on September 26, 1831. It was attended by 113 delegates from 13 states. William Wirt of Maryland was nominated for president and Amos Ellmaker of Pennsylvania for vice president. In the 1832 elections Wirt received 7 electoral votes as compared with 219 cast for the Democratic nominee, Andrew Jackson. The party had been formed in 1827 in western New York and held its first national convention in Philadelphia in 1830.

ELECTIONS—POLITICS—PARTIES—*continued*

3349. Democratic Party national convention was held on May 21–23, 1832, in Baltimore, MD, under the name Republican Delegates from the Several States. Delegates from 21 states and the District of Columbia nominated Andrew Jackson for president and Martin Van Buren for vice president. The Democratic party received 687,502 votes in the election of November 6, 1832, and the National Republicans 530,189 votes. The use of the name "Republican" had come down from the time of Jefferson, and the party was popularly known as the Democratic-Republican party. In the party's early national conventions, the names "Democrat" and "Republican" were often used interchangeably. In 1840 the word "Republican" was dropped entirely and the official title of the convention became the Democratic National Convention, although even then speakers employed the name "Republican" when referring to what is now the Democratic party.

3350. Whig Party convention took place in Albany, NY, on February 3, 1836. William Henry Harrison of Ohio was unanimously nominated for president and Francis Granger of New York was nominated for vice president. This was a state convention attended by delegates from 32 of the 52 counties. The Whig Party of Ohio held a state convention in Columbus on February 22–23, 1836. In the election of November 8, Harrison received 73 electoral votes, compared with 170 cast for the winner, the Democratic candidate Martin Van Buren.

3351. Liberty Party convention to nominate presidential candidates took place in Warsaw, NY, on November 13, 1839. James Gillespie Birney of Kentucky was nominated for the presidency and Francis Julius LeMoyne for the vice presidency. The nominations were confirmed despite the unwillingness of the candidates to accept, and in the Harrison-Van Buren election of 1840 they polled 7,069 votes. The Liberty Party was the nation's first antislavery party.

3352. Free Soil Party convention took place in Buffalo, NY, on August 9–10, 1848. In the election of 1848, the party's presidential candidate was Martin Van Buren of New York and the vice presidential candidate Charles Francis Adams of Massachusetts. Van Buren received 291,263 popular votes as compared with 1,360,099 cast for Zachary Taylor, the Whig

candidate. The Free Soil Party was formed by the antislavery element of the Democratic Party and was supported by the Liberty Party. The party's slogan was "Free Soil, Free Speech, Free Labor, Free Men."

3353. Republican Party meeting took place on February 22, 1854, when the antislavery factions of the Whig and Free Democratic parties of Michigan held a preliminary organizational meeting. The new party was organized on February 28 in Ripon, WI, in protest against the Kansas-Nebraska bill, which permitted new territories to introduce slavery. The name Republican was suggested by Alvan Earle Bovay. The first convention formally organized under the name of Republican Party met in Strong, ME, on August 7, 1854. The first national meeting of the party was held in Pittsburgh, PA, on February 22, 1856, and the first national convention took place on June 17 at the Music Fund Hall in Philadelphia, where John Charles Fremont of California was nominated for the presidency, with William Lewis Dayton as his running mate.

3354. Know-Nothing (American) Party convention to nominate a presidential candidate was held on February 18, 1856, in Philadelphia, PA. The party had been founded in 1854 as a secret anti-immigrant organization. Members were required to be American-born and wholly unconnected with the Roman Catholic Church, and were obligated to vote as the society determined. The 1856 convention abolished the secret character of the organization and nominated former president Millard Fillmore of New York for president and Andrew Jackson Donelson of Tennessee for vice president. Fillmore received only eight electoral votes.

3355. Constitutional Union Party convention took place on May 9, 1860, in Baltimore, MD, the occasion on which the party may be said to have been definitely organized. This was the party's first and only convention. The platform declared for "the Constitution of the Country, the Union of the States and the Enforcement of the Laws." The delegates nominated John Bell of Tennessee for president and Edward Everett of Massachusetts for vice president. They received 12 electoral votes in the election of November 6, 1860. Abraham Lincoln, the Republican candidate, received 180.

3356. Prohibition Party convention was the organizational meeting that took place on September 12, 1869, in Chicago, IL, attended by 194 delegates from nine states. The party was organized because neither of the major political parties had put a prohibition plank in its platform. The first national convention met in Columbus, OH, on February 22, 1872, and nominated James Black of Pennsylvania for president and John Russell of Michigan for vice president. The platform advocated prohibition, women's suffrage, a direct popular presidential vote, a sound currency, the encouragement of immigration, and a reduction of transportation rates. Black received 5,608 votes in the 1872 election, as compared with Grant, who received 3,597,132 votes. The organ of the party was *The Voice*, a magazine published in Chicago, the first issue of which appeared on September 25, 1884.

3357. Labor Reform Party national convention took place at Columbus, OH, on February 22, 1872. The presidential candidate was David Davis of Illinois, who received a single electoral vote in the 1872 election. Joel Parker of New Jersey was the vice presidential candidate. Both candidates declined to run, but received popular votes nevertheless. Labor Reform was the first national labor party. The first state labor party was the Workingmen's Party, which was organized in Philadelphia, PA, in July 1828, and held its first convention on August 25, 1828.

3358. Liberal Republican convention was held in Cincinnati, OH, on May 1, 1872, at which meeting the party was formed. Horace Greeley of New York was the presidential candidate and Benjamin Gratz Brown of Missouri the vice presidential candidate. In the election of November 5, 1872, Greeley (who was also the Democratic candidate) received 2,834,079 votes, as compared with 3,597,132 cast for Ulysses Simpson Grant, the Republican candidate.

3359. Greenback Party convention was held in Indianapolis, IN, on May 16–18, 1876. The first presidential candidate was Peter Cooper of New York, who received 81,737 votes in the 1876 election. Samuel Fenton Cary of Ohio was the vice presidential candidate. The party platform advocated the payment of the national debt of the government in greenbacks. The party, also known as the Independent Party, was organized on November 25, 1874, in Indianapolis.

3360. Socialist Labor Party of North America national convention was held in Newark, NJ, on December 26, 1877. The delegates nominated Simon Wing of Boston, MA, and Charles Horatio Matchett of New York City as the party's first presidential and vice presidential candidates. They received 21,512 votes in the election of November 8, 1892, compared to

5.55 million votes cast for Grover Cleveland, the Democratic candidate. The party was formed on July 4, 1874, as the Social Democratic Workmen's Party of North America, and changed its name in December 1877.

3361. Greenback Labor Party convention was held on June 9–11, 1880, in Chicago, IL. James Baird Weaver of Iowa was the nominee for president, Benjamin J. Chambers of Texas for vice president. The party was organized by members of the Labor Reform and Greenback parties on February 22, 1878, in Toledo, OH.

3362. Anti-Monopoly Party convention to nominate a presidential candidate was held in Chicago, IL, on May 14, 1884. The party was officially formed earlier that same day. General Benjamin Franklin Butler of Massachusetts was nominated for the presidency and General Absolom Madden West of Mississippi for the vice presidency; both were also the candidates of the Greenback Labor Party. In the 1884 election, Butler received 175,370 votes, as compared with 4,874,986 cast for Grover Cleveland of New York, the Democratic candidate. The existence of "The Anti-Monopoly Organization of the United States," as it was formally named, was of short duration, and its members joined the People's Party.

3363. Equal Rights Party convention took place in San Francisco, CA, on September 20, 1884, at a convention of the Woman's Rights Party of Female Suffragettes. Belva Ann Bennett Lockwood of the District of Columbia was nominated as the presidential candidate and Marietta Lizzie Bell Stow of California as the vice presidential candidate. The party was formed on May 10, 1872, when 500 delegates from 26 states and four territories seceded from the National Woman Suffrage Association convention in New York City and nominated Victoria Claflin Woodhull of New York for president and Frederick Douglass for vice president under the People's Party ticket.

3364. Union Labor Party convention took place on May 15–17, 1888, in Cincinnati, OH, when 274 delegates from 25 states nominated Alson Jennes Streeter of Illinois for president and Samuel Evans of Texas for vice president. Evans refused the nomination and Charles E. Cunningham of Arkansas was selected instead. They received 146,935 votes in the election of November 6, 1888, which was won by Benjamin Harrison of Indiana, the Republican candidate. The party was formed on February 22, 1887, when 300 delegates, including 10 women, attended the Industrial Labor Conference in Cincinnati. A platform was adopted the following day.

ELECTIONS—POLITICS—PARTIES—*continued*

3365. United Labor Party convention took place on May 15–17, 1888, at the Grand Opera House, Cincinnati, OH. Robert Hall Cowdrey of Illinois was nominated for president and William H.T. Wakefield of Kansas for vice president. In the popular election of November 6, 1888, in which Benjamin Harrison, the Republican candidate, was elected president, Cowdrey received 2,818 votes. The party was formed at Clarendon Hall, New York City, on January 6, 1887.

3366. People's Party national convention was held in Cincinnati, OH, on May 19, 1891, at which time the party was organized and the name adopted. At the second national convention, held on July 2–5, 1892, in Omaha, NE, James Baird Weaver of Iowa was nominated as the presidential candidate, with James Gaven Field of Virginia as his running mate. The People's Party was founded by members of the Farmers' Alliance and other industrial unions and later developed into the Populist Party.

3367. Silverite national convention was held in St. Louis, MO, on July 22, 1896. The delegates, who favored silver as a monetary standard, endorsed the Democratic candidates, William Jennings Bryan and Arthur Sewallt. The temporary chairman of the convention was Francis Griffith Newlands of Nevada, and the permanent chairman was William Pope St. John of New York.

3368. Social Democracy of America Party national convention was held on June 7, 1898, in Chicago, IL. The party was formed by the Brotherhood of the Cooperative Commonwealth, organized by Julius Augustus Wayland and members of the American Railway Union.

3369. Social-Democratic Party of America national convention was held in Rochester, NY, on January 27, 1900. The delegates nominated Eugene Victor Debs for president and Job Harriman for vice president. In the election of November 1900, the party received a popular vote of less than 100,000, compared with 7.2 million cast for the Republican candidate, William McKinley. The party was formed in 1898 by Debs, Victor Louis Berger, and Seymour Stedman, dissenters from the Social Democracy of America Party.

3370. United Christian Party convention took place on May 2, 1900, at which time Silas Comfort Swallow of Pennsylvania was nominated for president and John Granville Woolley of Illinois for vice president. The candidates withdrew, and were replaced by Jonah Fitz

Randolph Leonard of Iowa for president and David H. Martin of Pennsylvania for vice president. The party's popular vote in the election of November 6, 1900, was 1,060, compared with 7.2 million cast for William McKinley, the Republican candidate. The party was organized in Rock Island, IL, and was devoted to the inculcation of religious and moral ideas as controlling forces in politics.

3371. Union Reform Party convention took place in Baltimore, MD, on September 3, 1900. Seth Hockett Ellis of Ohio was nominated for president and Samuel T. Nicholson of Pennsylvania for vice president. They received fewer than 6,000 votes, compared with 7.2 million cast for William McKinley of Ohio, the Republican candidate, in the election of November 6, 1900. The platform had been adopted on March 1, 1899, in Cincinnati, OH.

3372. Socialist Party national convention was held in Indianapolis, IN, on May 1, 1904. The party was formed on March 25, 1900, in Indianapolis, IN, by a group of Socialist Labor Party secessionists led by Morris Hillquit, who united his group with the Social-Democratic Party led by Eugene Victor Debs and Victor Louis Berger.

3373. Progressive Party national convention was held on August 6–7, 1912, at the Coliseum, Chicago, IL. It was attended by 1,800 delegates who nominated Theodore Roosevelt of New York for president and Hiram Warren Johnson of California for vice president. Roosevelt received 4,126,000 popular and 88 electoral votes; William Howard Taft, the Republican candidate, 3,487,922 popular and 8 electoral votes; and Woodrow Wilson, the Democratic candidate, 6,297,099 popular and 435 electoral votes. The Progressive Party was organized on June 19, 1912, by seceding members of the Republican Party, and was nicknamed the Bull Moose Party. Its members reunited with the mainstream Republican Party in 1916.

3374. Communist Labor Party of America convention took place on September 1, 1919, in Chicago, IL. It was attended by 140 delegates representing 58,000 party members. The party had been formed the previous day to advance the principles laid down by the Third Internationale in Moscow. It adopted as its emblem a hammer and sickle surrounded by a wreath of wheat, and the motto "Workers of the world unite." Alfred Wagenknecht was made executive secretary.

3375. Communist Party of America convention took place on September 2, 1919, in Chicago, IL. Members of the party adopted as an emblem the figure of earth with a red flag across the face bearing the inscription "All power to the workers." Their program was the seizure of political power, the overthrow of capitalism, and the destruction of the bourgeois state.

3376. Farmer Labor Party convention took place on June 12, 1920, in Chicago, IL, when the organization was founded. The party was an outgrowth of the National Labor Party, which was formed in 1919. The first presidential candidate was Parley Parker Christensen of Utah and the vice presidential candidate was Maximilian Sebastian Hayes of Ohio. They received approximately 265,000 votes. The party merged with the Democratic Party in 1944.

3377. National Union for Social Justice national convention was held on August 14, 1936, at the Public Auditorium, Cleveland, OH. The delegates voted 8,153–1 to support William Lemke and Thomas Charles O'Brien as candidates for president and vice president of the United States. The group was founded in November 1934 in Royal Oak, MI.

3378. Union Party convention took place on August 15, 1936, in Cleveland, OH. William Lemke was nominated for president and Thomas Charles O'Brien for vice president. The ticket was supported by liberals, the National Union of Social Justice, and Dr. Francis Everett Townsend, the social security insurance advocate, among others. The party was organized on June 18, 1936.

3379. Democratic Party convention between presidential elections was held in Kansas City, MO, on December 6–8, 1974. The party gathered to ratify its first major charter, which required affirmative action in all party affairs, with representation for women and minorities according to their proportion in the American electorate.

ELECTIONS—PRESIDENTIAL

3380. Federal election was authorized on September 13, 1788, by the Constitutional Convention, which "resolved that the first Wednesday in January next be the day for appointing electors in the several states, which, before the said day, shall have ratified the said Constitution; that the first Wednesday in February next be the day for the electors to assemble in their respective states, and vote for a President; and that the first Wednesday in March next be the time, and the present seat of Congress the place

for commencing the proceedings under the said Constitution." Congress was then located in New York City. The presidential election authorized in this resolution took place on February 4, 1789.

3381. President to receive the unanimous vote of the presidential electors was George Washington of Mount Vernon, Virginia, who received all of the 69 votes cast by the electors from the 10 states that voted on February 4, 1789. A nearly unanimous vote took place in November 1816, when James Monroe of Virginia received 231 of the 232 votes cast by the electors from 24 states. The dissenting vote was cast by William Plumer of New Hampshire.

3382. Electoral vote cast contrary to instructions was cast by Samuel Miles, a Pennsylvania Federalist, in the presidential election of 1796. Instead of voting for John Adams, the Federalist candidate, Miles voted for Thomas Jefferson, a Democratic-Republican. The electors were pledged, but not legally bound, to support a candidate belonging to their party. On March 25, 1969, Maine became the first state to require presidential electors to cast their ballots for the presidential and vice presidential candidates of the political party for which they were chosen.

3383. Presidential election in which more than one candidate declared for the presidency was the election of 1797, in which John Adams received 71 electoral votes and was elected president, and Thomas Jefferson received 68 electoral votes and was elected vice president. In the elections of 1789 and 1793, George Washington was the only avowed presidential candidate.

3384. Presidential election in which candidates were nominated for the vice presidency was held on November 6, 1804. Prior to the adoption of the 12th Amendment to the Constitution on September 25, 1804, the candidate for president receiving the highest number of votes became president, and the candidate receiving the second highest number became vice president. Thomas Jefferson and George Clinton were the candidates of the Democratic-Republican Party and Charles Cotesworth Pinckney and Rufus King the candidates of the Federalist Party.

3385. Presidential election in which a loser won took place in November 1824, the first election in which popular votes were counted as well as electoral votes. Andrew Jackson received 153,544 popular and 99 electoral votes, John Quincy Adams received 108,740 popular and 84 electoral votes, and William Harris

ELECTIONS—PRESIDENTIAL—*continued*

Crawford and Henry Clay received 42 and 37 electoral votes respectively. Since no candidate had a majority of the electoral votes, the House of Representatives was called on to exercise its constitutional responsibility to choose from the highest three. In the meantime, Crawford became ill and was practically eliminated, and Clay agreed to use his influence to have Adams elected, provided that Adams promised to appoint him secretary of state. The balloting in the House of Representatives was 13 states for Adams, seven for Jackson, and four for Crawford.

3386. Popular vote in a presidential election took place on November 2, 1824, when 356,038 votes were cast for four candidates. This was also the first election in which the final decision was made by the House of Representatives because none of the candidates won a majority of electoral votes. Although Andrew Jackson received a greater share of both the popular and the electoral vote than the runner-up, John Quincy Adams, a deal was struck to give Adams the electoral votes of Henry Clay, another candidate. Adams thereby acquired enough votes to be declared the winner.

3387. Election day for presidential voting held nationwide was authorized by act of January 23, 1845, "an act to establish a uniform time for holding elections for electors of President and Vice President in all the states of the Union." The day selected for voting was "the Tuesday next after the first Monday in the month of November of the year in which they are to be appointed." The first election under the act was held on November 7, 1848.

3388. Year in which two presidents were elected was 1861, after the formation of the Confederacy as a rival government. Both presidents were from Kentucky. Abraham Lincoln, born on February 12, 1809, in Hardin County, KY, became president of the United States on March 4, 1861. Jefferson Davis, born in Todd County, KY, on June 3, 1808, was chosen president of the Confederacy by the provisional congress on February 18, 1861. He was inaugurated at Richmond, VA, on February 22, 1862, after he was elected by popular vote.

3389. Presidential election in which soldiers in the field were allowed to vote was the election of 1864. Of a total of 150,635 votes cast by the soldiers on November 8, 116,887 were for Abraham Lincoln, Republican, and 33,748 for George Brinton McClellan, Democrat.

3390. Election in which returns were broadcast on radio was the presidential election of November 7, 1916. An experimental station, the De Forest Radio Laboratory in the Highbridge section of the Bronx, New York City, broadcast bulletins from the *New York American* on the results of the presidential race for approximately six hours. The broadcasters signed off about 11 P.M. with the announcement that Charles Evans Hughes had been elected. In fact, Woodrow Wilson was the winner. The first widespread radio broadcast of election results took place on August 31, 1920, when station WWJ of Detroit, MI, broadcast the results of congressional and county primaries. On November 2, 1920, Leo H. Rosenberg of station KDKA of Pittsburgh, PA, broadcast the results of the Harding–Cox presidential election.

3391. Electoral college members invited to a presidential inauguration were the 531 electors who participated in the election of 1932. All but 59 of them were Democrats. The winner, Franklin Delano Roosevelt, officially invited them to attend the inauguration, which took place on March 4, 1933.

3392. Presidential campaign manager who was a woman was Ruth Hanna McCormick Simms, daughter of Republican senator Mark Hanna, who was named one of two managers of Thomas Edmund Dewey's campaign on December 2, 1939. The other manager was J. Russel Sprague, Republican leader of Nassau County, NY.

3393. Presidential election in which a computer was used to predict the outcome was the 1952 presidential race between Dwight David Eisenhower and Adlai Ewing Stevenson. The CBS television network employed the UNIVAC to choose the winner. Only an hour after the polls had closed, when less than 10 percent of the votes had been counted, the computer correctly projected Eisenhower's landslide victory, trumping human experts who had predicted a close race.

3394. Presidential election debates to be shown on television were the debates between Richard Milhous Nixon, the Republican candidate, and John Fitzgerald Kennedy, the Democratic candidate, that took place during the 1960 presidential campaign. The first of four debates was held on September 26 in a Chicago studio; the second on October 7 in a Washington, DC, studio; the third on October 13, with Kennedy in New York City and Nixon in Hollywood, CA; and the fourth on October 21 in a New York City studio.

3395. Presidential election in which votes were tallied electronically was the election of November 3, 1964, when Coleman Vote Tally Systems were used in Hamilton County (Cincinnati), OH; Orange County (Santa Ana-Anaheim), CA; and Contra Costa (Martinez), CA. They counted 600 ballots a minute. Data from each machine and counting center were automatically transmitted by wire to a central computer in the Registrar of Voters office, where countywide returns were made available as fast as the votes were counted.

3396. Electoral vote for a woman was cast by Roger L. McBride of Charlottesville, VA, whose vote for Theodora Nathan of Oregon, vice presidential candidate of the Libertarian Party, was counted on January 6, 1973.

3397. Presidential election debate between an incumbent president and a challenger to be televised was held on September 23, 1976, when three networks pooled their efforts to telecast a debate between President Gerald Rudolph Ford, a Republican, and Jimmy Carter, the Democratic candidate, at the Walnut Street Theatre, Philadelphia, PA. The debate, limited to domestic issues, was sponsored by the League of Women Voters. A second debate took place on October 6, 1976, from the Palace of Fine Arts Theatre, San Francisco, CA. A third debate took place on October 22, 1976, from the stage of Phi Beta Kappa Hall on the campus of the College of William and Mary, Williamsburg, VA. Each confrontation was 90 minutes long.

3398. Debate among party hopefuls for the presidential nomination to be shown on television took place on January 5, 1980, in Des Moines, IA, where six Republican competitors faced each other in a two-hour debate. The six were John Anderson of Illinois, Howard Baker, Jr., of Tennessee, George Herbert Walker Bush of Texas, John Connally of Texas, Philip Crane of Illinois, and Robert Dole of Kansas. Ronald Wilson Reagan was absent. The confrontation was sponsored by the *Des Moines Register and Tribune*.

ELECTIONS—PRESIDENTIAL—CANDIDATES

3399. Presidential candidate nominated at a caucus was Thomas Jefferson of Virginia. The Democratic-Republican Party held a caucus on February 25, 1804, in Washington, DC, at which Jefferson was unanimously nominated for president and George Clinton of New York for vice president. This was the first nominating caucus attended by leaders of a political party. The Federalists did not hold a caucus, but supported Charles Cotesworth Pinckney of South Carolina for president and Rufus King of New York for vice president. At the election in November 1804, Jefferson received 162 electoral votes and Pinckney 14.

3400. Vice presidential candidate to decline the nomination was John Langdon of New Hampshire, who was nominated in Washington, DC, on May 12, 1812, by the congressional caucus of the Republican Party, which gave him 64 votes to James Madison's 82. Langdon declined to run, and a second caucus was held at which Elbridge Gerry was nominated.

3401. Presidential candidate nominated at a national convention was Andrew Jackson of Tennessee, who was nominated by the Democrats at their national convention in Baltimore, MD, in 1832. Martin Van Buren of New York was nominated as the Democratic candidate for vice president.

3402. Presidential candidate to make a campaign speech was William Henry Harrison, the Whig candidate in the election of 1840, who spoke on June 6, 1840, from the steps of the National Hotel in Columbus, OH. Before that time, candidates gave no speeches themselves, but let others in the party speak on their behalf. Harrison gave 23 stump speeches in all, mostly at rallies held in his home state of Ohio.

3403. President who was a "dark horse" candidate was James Knox Polk. His name appeared for the first time on the eighth ballot at the Democratic convention on May 29, 1844, in Baltimore, MD. On the ninth ballot, amid great confusion, the convention stampeded for him.

3404. Presidential candidate to be assassinated was Joseph Smith of Nauvoo, IL, founder and leader of the Church of Jesus Christ of Latter-day Saints (Mormon Church), whose candidacy was advocated in January 1844 by the church's Council of Twelve. The National Reform Party confirmed the nomination in a state convention at Nauvoo on May 17, with Sidney Rigdon of Pennsylvania as his running mate. Smith was killed on June 27, when a mob shot him after breaking into the jail at Carthage, IL, where he was confined while awaiting trial on charges brought against him by his personal enemies and by seceders from the church.

ELECTIONS—PRESIDENTIAL—CANDI-DATES—*continued*

3405. Presidential candidate who was a woman was Victoria Claflin Woodhull, who was nominated by the National Radical Reformers at a convention held on May 10, 1872, at Apollo Hall, New York City, after the group seceded from the National Woman Suffrage Assocation. She was nominated by Judge Carter of Cincinnati, OH. Frederick Douglass was the vice presidential nominee.

3406. Vice presidential candidate who was African-American was Frederick Douglass, who was nominated on May 10, 1872, by the National Woman Suffrage Association convention, assembled at Apollo Hall, New York City, under the name of the National Radical Reformers. About 500 delegates attended from 26 states and 4 territories. The presidential nominee was Victoria Claflin Woodhull.

3407. Presidential candidate who was Catholic was Charles O'Conor of New York, who was nominated at the Democratic convention at Louisville, KY, on September 3, 1872, by a wing of Democrats who refused to accept the nomination of Horace Greeley that had already been made at Baltimore, MD. O'Conor declined the nomination, but his name nevertheless was listed and he received approximately 30,000 votes from 23 states.

3408. Presidential candidate to make campaign speeches in a foreign language was James Abram Garfield of Ohio, who made several political speeches in German. He was elected in November 1880.

3409. Presidential nominee who was African-American was Frederick Douglass of Rochester, NY, who received one vote on June 23, 1888, on the fourth ballot of the Republican national convention. On June 25, on the eighth ballot, the convention nominated Benjamin Harrison, who was elected as the 23rd president. Douglass was later appointed U.S. minister to Haiti.

3410. Presidential candidate to ride in a car was William Jennings Bryan, who was given a ride in 1896 at Decatur, IL, in an automobile made by the Mueller Manufacturing Company, accompanied by his wife. There were only 10 cars in the United States at that time.

3411. Presidential candidate to appear in movie footage was William Jennings Bryan, who was filmed receiving congratulations at his residence at Fairview, NE, after his nomination on July 10, 1908. The film was shown on July 12, 1908, at Hammerstein's Roof, 42nd Street and Broadway, New York City, having been developed on the train heading east.

3412. Presidential nomination ceremony broadcast on radio was the ceremony held at Leland Stanford Junior University Stadium, Palo Alto, CA, on August 11, 1928, when Herbert Clark Hoover was formally notified of his nomination for the presidency by the Republican Party and accepted. The broadcast was carried by more than 107 stations.

3413. Presidential candidate to accept his party's nomination in person was Franklin Delano Roosevelt, who flew from Albany, NY, to Chicago, IL, on July 2, 1932, to address the Democratic National Convention. He delivered the first acceptance speech by a nominee at a convention.

3414. Presidential candidate who was renominated after a defeat was Thomas Edmund Dewey of New York, who was defeated in the election of November 7, 1944, by the incumbent president, Franklin Delano Roosevelt, and went on to be nominated by the Republican national convention at Philadelphia, PA, on June 24, 1948. He was defeated in the 1948 election by Harry S. Truman.

3415. Vice presidential candidate who was an African-American woman was Charlotta A. Bass, who was nominated on July 5, 1952, by the Progressive Party at its convention in the International Amphitheatre, Chicago, IL.

3416. Presidential campaigner to be assassinated while campaigning for his party's nomination as candidate for president was Senator Robert Francis Kennedy of New York, who was assassinated by Sirhan Bishara Sirhan on June 6, 1968, at the Biltmore Hotel, Los Angeles, CA.

3417. Vice presidential candidate of a major political party to resign before the election was Senator Thomas Francis Eagleton of Missouri, who was nominated on July 13, 1972, at the Democratic National Convention at Miami Beach, FL. He submitted his resignation on August 1, 1972. The National Democratic Committee nominated Robert Sargent Shriver of Maryland in his stead.

3418. Presidential candidate who had been an astronaut was Ohio senator John Herschel Glenn, Jr., the first American to orbit the earth, who sought the Democratic nomination in 1984. Glenn entered the race on April 21, 1983, with a speech in his hometown of New Concord, OH, but failed to generate widespread interest in his campaign, despite the release in 1984 of a Hollywood film, *The Right Stuff,* celebrating his status as an American hero. He tried again, also without success, in 1988.

3419. Vice presidential candidate from a major political party who was a woman was Geraldine Ferraro, congressional representative from New York State. She was chosen by Democratic presidential nominee Walter F. Mondale as his running mate on July 12, 1984, at the Democratic National Convention.

ELECTIONS—VOTING RIGHTS

3420. Woman in America to appeal for the right to vote was Margaret Brent, a niece of Lord Baltimore, the founder of the colony of Maryland. She came to America from England in January 1638 and was the first woman in Maryland to own property in her own name. She became one of the colony's principal landowners and a person of influence, raising a troop of soldiers in 1644. On June 24, 1647, she appealed for the right to vote in the colonial assembly by virtue of her position as secretary to Governor Leonard Calvert, asking for a "place and voyce," but was ejected from the meetings. At the death of Calvert, she became his executor and acting governor, presiding over the General Assembly, but was refused a voice in the affairs of the government as "it would set a bad example to the wives of the colony." She moved to Virginia in 1650.

3421. Woman whose vote was recorded was the widow of Josiah Taft of Uxbridge, MA, who participated in a town referendum in 1756. She was granted this privilege because her son, Bazaleel, was a minor. She voted in favor of levying a town tax.

3422. Election law enacted by a colony granting voting rights to women was passed by New Jersey. Its new constitution, adopted on July 2, 1776, provided "that all the inhabitants of this Colony of full age who are worth 50 Pounds Proclamation money, with clear estate in the same, and have resided within the county in which they claim a vote for twelve months immediately preceding the election" were entitled to vote at the general election. In 1790 this was interpreted to mean both men and women.

It did not, however, apply to married women, but only to spinsters and widows. On November 16, 1807, the General Assembly passed laws providing that only free white male citizens could exercise the franchise.

3423. Election law enacted by a state to grant universal voting rights to freemen without restriction as to property or wealth was Vermont. The state constitution adopted at a general convention held on July 28, 1777, at Windsor, VT, permitted all freemen who were natural-born citizens over 21 years of age to elect officers and to be elected to office.

3424. Voting registration law enacted by a state was enacted by Massachusetts and signed on March 7, 1801, by Governor Caleb Strong.

3425. Voting rights convention organized by women was held in the Wesleyan Chapel, Seneca Falls, NY, on July 19–20, 1848. The convention was assembled through the initiative of the reformers Lucretia Mott and Elizabeth Cady Stanton. A Declaration of Sentiments was read and a series of resolutions adopted, one of which called for woman suffrage. The first national convention of this kind was the National Woman's Rights Convention held at Brinley Hall in Worcester, MA, on October 23–24, 1850, "to consider the question of woman's rights, duties and relations."

3426. Literacy qualification for voting was required by Massachusetts. An amendment was passed on May 1, 1857, by a vote of 23,833 for and 13,746 against, providing that "no person shall have the right to vote, or to be eligible to office under the constitution of this commonwealth, who shall not be able to read the constitution in the English language, and write his name," excepting those unable to qualify because of physical disability or those over 60 years of age.

3427. Voting rights organization (national) advocating universal voting rights was the American Equal Rights Association, organized in 1866 to advocate the extension of the voting rights to all citizens, regardless of race, color, or sex. Lucretia Mott was president and Susan Brownell Anthony secretary. In 1869 the association split over the question of whether to place priority on securing voting rights for women or for African-Americans. The result was the formation of two new organizations, the American Woman Suffrage Association, led by Lucy Stone and Julia Ward Howe, and the National Woman Suffrage Association, led by Elizabeth Cady Stanton and Susan B. Anthony. Some 20 years later, the two were reunited to form the National American Woman Suffrage Association.

ELECTIONS—VOTING RIGHTS—*continued*

3428. Election law granting African-American men the right to vote was the congressional act of January 8, 1867, amending voting practices in Washington, DC. Every male citizen of the city who was 21 years of age or over was given the right to vote, except paupers, those under guardianship, men convicted of infamous crimes, and men who gave voluntary comfort to the rebels during the Civil War. The bill was vetoed by President Andrew Johnson on January 5, 1867. His veto was overridden in the Senate by a vote of 29 to 10 and in the House by a vote of 112 to 38.

3429. African-American to vote under authority of the 15th Amendment to the Constitution was Thomas Peterson-Mundy of Perth Amboy, NJ, who voted in Perth Amboy on March 31, 1870, in a special election for ratification or rejection of a city charter. The charter was adopted and he was appointed to the committee to revise the charter. The 15th Amendment to the Constitution, allowing African-American male citizens to vote, became law on March 30, 1870.

3430. Election law enacted by a state to grant voting rights to women after the adoption of the Constitution was Wyoming, which became a state on July 10, 1890. Women had voted in Wyoming from the beginning of its existence as a territory. The first territorial legislature extended the vote to women on December 10, 1869.

3431. Absentee voting law enacted by a state was enacted by Vermont on November 24, 1896. According to its provisions, a voter could obtain a certificate declaring that he was qualified to vote in the state. He could then vote for state officers at any election booth in the state.

3432. Constitutional amendment proposal guaranteeing women the right to vote was submitted in 1868 and at intervals thereafter without success. The woman suffrage amendment that eventually became law was passed by the House of Representatives on May 21, 1919, and by the Senate on June 4. It was ratified by Illinois, Wisconsin, and Michigan on June 10. Tennessee was the 36th state to ratify, on August 18, 1920, completing the necessary three-quarters of the states to put the amendment into effect. On August 26, 1920, the 19th amendment to the Constitution was proclaimed to be in effect.

3433. Election law lowering the voting age in a state to 18 was enacted on March 3, 1943, as an amendment to the Georgia state constitution. It was approved by popular vote on August 4, 1943, by a 3–1 majority. The first election held under this law took place on November 7, 1944. The national voting age was lowered to 18 in 1971, when the 26th Amendment to the Constitution was ratified by the required number of states. It became law on July 5, 1971.

3434. Year when citizens of the District of Columbia could vote in a presidential election was 1964. Residents of Washington, DC, went to the polls on November 3, 1964, to choose between Democrat Lyndon Baines Johnson and Republican Barry Goldwater. Johnson received 85.6 percent of their votes.

3435. Voting rights in space were authorized by the Texas legislature in July 1997. The law was enacted after astronaut John Blaha, a registered voter in Houston, TX, requested the opportunity to vote in the election of November 1996 while he was millions of miles from home aboard the Russian space station *Mir*. Absentee ballots were not available when his mission began, and existing communications technology did not permit him to cast a secret ballot, as required by law. On August 25, 1997, Texas secretary of state Tony Garza announced a new computer program that would allow NASA to collect coded votes from astronauts in space by e-mail. Soviet cosmonauts had already participated in elections while in space, but their votes were not secret.

ELECTRONICS

3436. Colorscope public demonstration was made in New York City on June 5, 1930. The colorscope, invented by Harold Horton Sheldon of New York University and Dr. Walter Arthur Schneider, was a photoelectric cell that reacted to colored light beams. It gave off infinitesimal electric currents capable of operating relays, which started or stopped machinery, operated graph needles, or performed other laboratory or shop services. It matched colors more exactly than the human eye can do.

3437. Electron tube to enable humans to see in the dark was invented by Dr. Vladimir Kosma Zworykin and Dr. George Arthur Morton and described on January 2, 1936, at a meeting of the American Association for the Advancement of Science in St. Louis, MO. The device was sensitive to ultraviolet and infrared rays, and converted light rays from motion pictures into electrons.

3438. Electronic digital calculator was invented by John Vincent Atanasoff, a professor at Iowa State University, Ames, IA. The device was a digital calculator designed to solve linear equations using vacuum tubes for arithmetic units, condensers for memory, and a punch-card input/output system. Atanasoff began working on the calculator in September 1939 and performed the first calculations with it in October of that year.

3439. Transistor was invented at the Bell Telephone Laboratories, Murray Hill, NJ, by John Bardeen, Walter Houser Brattain, and William Shockley. The first demonstration took place on June 30, 1948. The essential element of the device was a tiny wafer of germanium, a semiconductor. Transistors perform the same functions as vacuum tubes, but occupy a fraction of the space and operate on greatly reduced amounts of power. The three inventors shared the Nobel Prize for physics in 1956.

3440. Phototransistor operated by light rather than electric current was invented by Dr. John Northrup Shive of the Bell Telephone Laboratories, Murray Hill, NJ, and announced on March 30, 1950. It was composed of a midget disk of germanium with only a single collector wire. Light focused on one side of the disk controlled the flow of current to the opposite side, the side to which the wire was attached.

3441. Transistors produced commercially for a specific product were made in October 1951 by the Western Electric Company, Allentown, PA, for long-distance dialing equipment of the Bell Telephone System. Experimental transistors had been manufactured and distributed to military and civilian engineering organizations in 1948 for early circuit development work.

3442. Automaton to operate by long-distance control was a machine nicknamed Yes Man. It was made by the General Electric Company's General Engineering Laboratory, Schenectady, NY, for the Aircraft Nuclear Propulsion Department under contract with the Air Force, and its manufacture was announced on May 23, 1956. It was electronically geared to duplicate simultaneously the exact motions of a master machine at long distances. The machine was designed to perform mechanical jobs in dangerously radioactive areas from any required distance by remote control.

3443. Laser was the invention of Charles Hard Townes of New York City and Arthur Leonard Schawlow of Madison, NJ. In 1951, Townes, a physicist with Columbia University, New York City, first conceived of the maser, a practical device for amplifying the stimulated emission of microwaves, basing his idea on the earlier work of English physicist Paul Dirac and others. Townes and his brother-in-law Schawlow developed the first "optical maser," or laser, in September 1957. They filed for a patent on July 30, 1958, which was granted on March 22, 1960. Gordon Gould, a graduate student at Columbia, independently conceived of the laser in October 1957, but did not apply for a patent until April 1959. The first working laser was demonstrated in public on July 7, 1960, by Theodore Harold Maiman, a researcher at the Hughes Aircraft Company in Malibu, CA. Maiman designed a ruby cylinder with polished ends. It was partially silvered on the outside with a small hole at one end for the beam to exit. When illuminated by a powerful xenon lamp, the ruby emitted a coherent beam of red light. The word "maser" is an acronym for "microwave amplification by stimulated emission of radiation." The word "laser" is an acronym for "light amplification by stimulated emission of radiation."

3444. Integrated circuit was invented independently by Jack Kilby of Texas Instruments, Dallas, TX, and Robert Noyce of Fairchild Semiconductor, Mountain View, CA. On September 12, 1958, Kilby tested a working integrated circuit. Between March and June of 1959, Noyce improved on Kilby's cruder device by designing the first reliable, mass-produceable integrated circuit. Noyce was awarded the patent after a 10-year lawsuit between the two men.

3445. Industrial robot that was practical was the Unimate, developed by physicist Joseph F. Engelberger and engineer George C. Devol. The first unit to be produced was installed in 1961 at a General Motors plant to work with heated die-casting machines. That year, Engelberger and Devol founded Unimation, the first commercial company to make robots, and Devol filed the first American robot patent.

3446. Microprocessor was built in late 1970 by the Intel Corporation, Santa Clara, CA, for the Busicom Corporation of Japan. Designed by a team of Intel engineers including Ted Hoff, Stan Mazor, Masatoshi Shima, and Federico Faggin, the Intel 4004 crammed 2,300 transistors onto one silicon chip smaller than a thumbtack and ran at a clock speed of 750 kilohertz. It was the first general-purpose computing device that was small enough, cheap enough, and powerful enough to be used as the brain of a wide variety of devices, including computers, calculators, cars, and appliances. Intel announced the 4004 to the public on November 15, 1971.

ELECTRONICS—*continued*

3447. Electronic pocket calculator was a battery-powered model introduced on August 20, 1971, by Texas Instruments, Dallas, TX. It weighed about 2.5 pounds and cost $149. It could add, subtract, multiply, and divide, displaying the results in an LED (light-emitting diode) window.

3448. Robot to make pizza was developed in 1990 by K.G. Engelhardt and a team of researchers at Carnegie-Mellon University, Pittsburgh, PA. Dubbed PizzaBot, it was intended to help people with disabilities manage fast-food restaurants. The robot used a simple voice-recognition system to interpret orders called out by the manager.

3449. Robot to perform surgery was Robodoc, the world's first robotic device that actively performed surgical procedures. It was developed by Howard "Hap" Paul, a veterinarian-surgeon at the Sacramento Animal Medical Group in Carmichael, CA, and William Bargar, an orthopedic surgeon at Sutter General Hospital, Sacramento, CA, and was manufactured by Integrated Surgical Systems. Robodoc was capable of cutting bone 40 times more precisely than human doctors. In 1995, the $500,000 robot was authorized by the Food and Drug Administration to perform 300 hip replacement procedures on humans.

ENERGY—ELECTRICITY

3450. Electric cooking experiment was performed by Benjamin Franklin on the banks of the Schuylkill River, Philadelphia, PA, in 1749. In a letter dated April 29, 1749, Franklin wrote: "A turkey is to be killed for our dinner by the electrical shock and roasted by the electrical jack, before a fire kindled by the electrified bottle; when the healths of all the famous electricians in England, Holland, France and Germany are to be drank in electrified bumpers, under the discharge of guns from the electrical battery."

3451. Electromagnet was invented by Joseph Henry, who exhibited one before the Albany Institute, Albany, NY, in June 1828. It was closely wound with silk-covered wire about 0.026 inches in diameter.

3452. Electric bell for electromagnets was invented by Joseph Henry of Albany, NY, in 1831. He was the first to insulate iron for the magnetic coil and the first to work out the differing functions of two entirely different kinds of electromagnets, the one surrounded by numerous coils of no great length, the other surrounded by a continuous coil of very great length. Joseph Henry's invention of 1831 increased the lifting power of the magnet from 9 pounds to 3,500 pounds. Every electrical dynamo or motor uses the electromagnet in practically the same form in which Henry left it.

3453. Electric motor using direct current was invented by Thomas Davenport of Brandon, VT, in July 1834. Davenport, a prosperous blacksmith, had traveled to the Penfield Iron Works in Crown Point, NY, to purchase some iron. He saw one of the first electromagnets there, and was so fascinated that he bought it on the spot. After several months of experiments, he built the first practical electric motor. It consisted of a rotating disk with two electromagnets as the spokes, supported by a spindle rising from a base on which were fixed two other electromagnets. When Davenport rapidly switched the direction of the current back and forth, the disk spun at speeds up to 30 revolutions per second. Davenport obtained a patent on the device in 1835.

3454. Dynamo for a direct-current outdoor lighting system was built in 1875 at Cornell University, Ithaca, NY, by Professor William Arnold Anthony and a graduate student, George Sylvanus Moler. It was exhibited at the Philadelphia Centennial in 1876 and was made from designs of the original Gramme machine. It was used to supply the current to light the Cornell campus in 1875.

3455. Electric company was the Edison Electric Light Company, 65 Fifth Avenue, New York City, incorporated on October 15, 1878. Three thousand shares with a par value of $100 each were issued for the express purpose of financing Thomas Alva Edison's work on the incandescent lamp. The Edison Electric Illuminating Company was incorporated on December 17, 1880, with a capitalization of $1 million for the purpose of furnishing electric light in New York City. The first president of the company was Dr. Norvin Green.

3456. Electricity generated by Niagara Falls waterpower was made in 1879, when 16 arc lights in Prospect Park, Niagara Falls, NY, were lit by a small dynamo powered by the falls. The first large-scale use was made by the Niagara River Hydraulic Tunnel Power and Sewer Company (later the Niagara Falls Power Company), which broke ground on October 4, 1890, for a power plant. On October 24, 1893, a contract was executed with the Westinghouse Electric and Manufacturing Company of Pittsburgh, PA, for three 5,000-horsepower generators delivering two-phase currents at 2,200 volts, 25 cycles. On August 26, 1895, power was first transmitted commercially, the current being employed by the Pittsburgh Reduction Company in the reduction of aluminum ore. The city of Buffalo, NY, received its first power for commercial purposes on November 15, 1896.

3457. Electric company organized to produce and sell electricity was the California Electric Light Company, San Francisco, CA, organized on June 30, 1879. In September 1879, it furnished current from a central generating station for lighting Brush arc light lamps.

3458. Hydroelectric power plant to furnish arc lighting service was the Grand Rapids Electric Light and Power Company, Grand Rapids, MI, organized on March 22, 1880, and placed in operation on July 23, 1880. The first president and organizer was William T. Powers. The first generating equipment was a 16-arc-light Brush generator, driven by a water wheel, which supplied power to the factory of the Wolverine Chair Company. On August 1, 1881, a new building was occupied from which current was generated to supply street lighting. This plant furnished arc lighting service for the first four years of its operations.

3459. Electric power plant operated by a city was purchased in 1882 by Fairfield, IA. It supplied power to 13 streetlights and six Brush arc lamps of 2,000 candlepower that were situated on a 185-foot tower. City operation was supervised by Al Robb and James McQuiston. The illumination cost $70 annually per arc. A windstorm blew the tower down on May 9, 1883.

3460. Dynamo that was successful was Jumbo No. 1, a direct-current steam dynamo, which was built in 1881 at the Edison Machine Works, Goerck Street, New York City. It weighed 27 tons, 6 tons of which was the armature. When the armature was air-cooled, the dynamo's capacity was 700 lamps of 16-candlepower each. The dynamo was put in operation September 4, 1882.

3461. Electric power station with a central source was the Edison Electric Illuminating Company of 257 Pearl Street, New York City, which opened on Saturday evening, September 4, 1882. It had one engine, which generated power for 800 electric light bulbs. Within 14 months, the service had 508 subscribers and 12,732 bulbs.

3462. Hydroelectric power plant to furnish incandescent lighting was opened on September 30, 1882, in Appleton, WI. It consisted of a single dynamo of 180 lights, each of 10 candlepower.

3463. Electric power plant with a three-wire central station was the Edison Electric Illuminating Company, Sunbury, PA, incorporated on April 30, 1883. Operations were begun on July 4, 1883. Two 110-volt direct-current generators were connected in series, raising the distribution voltage to 220 volts. This increase in voltage allowed more current to be transported over a given size of wire for a given distance, or allowed an equal amount of current to be transported over a given size of wire for a greater distance than is possible when lower voltages are used. The station was constructed by Thomas Alva Edison, who served in the triple capacity of chief electrical engineer, mechanical expert, and superintendent of construction.

3464. Power plant using alternating current was placed in operation in Great Barrington, MA, on March 6, 1886. The transformers were built by William Stanley in his Great Barrington laboratory and were successfully operated for a considerable time, but an accident disabled the generators and the plant was discontinued. The first such plant to be commercially successful was built in Buffalo, NY, in November 1886 by the Westinghouse Electric and Manufacturing Company, Pittsburgh, PA. The station, located on Wilkerson Street, Buffalo, was placed in operation on November 30, 1886, by the Brush Electric Light Company.

3465. Electric meter indicating the amount of electrical energy dispensed or applied was invented by Oliver B. Shallenberger of Rochester, PA, who obtained a patent on August 14, 1888. Commercial production of the meters was started in August 1888 by the Westinghouse Electric and Manufacturing Company, Pittsburgh, PA.

3466. Hydroelectric power plant generating alternating current to operate over a long distance was built by the Willamette Falls Electric Company at Willamette Falls, Oregon City, OR. It operated two 300-horsepower Stilwell and Bierce water wheels belted to a single-phase generator rated at 720 kilowatts. On June 2, 1889, it supplied current to Portland, OR, a distance of 13 miles from the plant.

3467. Power transmission installation using alternating current was made in 1890 at Telluride, CO, by the Westinghouse Electric and Manufacturing Company. The generator was a 100-horsepower, 88.33-cycle, single-phase, 3,000-volt unit driven by water power. A three-mile transmission line was erected and a single-

ENERGY—ELECTRICITY—*continued*

phase synchronous motor was installed at the end of the line. The motor lacked a starting torque, and a necessary adjunct was a starting motor to bring the unloaded synchronized motor to its normal speed.

3468. Electrical transmission of three-phase alternating high-frequency current for any considerable distance by a utility company was made in March 1893 from the Rainbow Hydroelectric Station on the Farmington River to the State Street station of the Hartford Electric Light Company, Hartford, CT. The power transmitted was 300 kilowatts, between 4,000 and 5,000 volts.

3469. Electric alternator in parallel successfully operated was installed in 1896 by the Hartford Electric Light Company in its station at Hartford, CT. It was used in connection with a waterpower unit.

3470. Hydroelectric power plant to use a storage battery was installed by the Hartford Electric Light Company, Hartford, CT, in 1896. The storage battery made it possible to supply the company's peak load requirements from water power that would otherwise have gone to waste during the periods of relatively small demand.

3471. Aluminum used commercially in a transmission conductor was employed on November 30, 1899, by the Hartford Electric Light Company of Hartford, CT, on a transmission from its waterpower plant at Tariffville, CT.

3472. Steam turbine operated by a public utility to produce electricity was a 1,500-kilowatt steam turbine installed in April 1901 by the Hartford Electric Light Company, Hartford, CT, at its Pearl Street station. The turbine, manufactured by the Westinghouse Electric and Manufacturing Company, East Pittsburgh, PA, began to generate electricity in October 1901.

3473. Hydroelectric power plant built by the federal government was the Minidoka Dam on the Snake River in Idaho, constructed by the Bureau of Reclamation, Department of the Interior. The first unit of the power plant was started on May 1, 1909, and had a capacity of 1,400 kilovolt amperes.

3474. Electric power substation with a rotary converter completely unattended was the Rowena Substation of the Detroit Edison Company, Detroit, MI, which went into service in April 1914. It consisted of a 500-kilowatt General Electric rotary converter, three 175-kilowatt step-down transformers, and the necessary

equipment for balancing direct-current machine voltage against bus voltage at Rowena. Included also were the typical devices to protect against alternating-current failure, direct-current failure, reverse current, and overspeed. This equipment acted to convert three-phase alternating current at 4,600 volts to direct current at 250 volts. This station was fed and controlled from an attended substation about a mile distant.

3475. Alkaline dry cell battery was developed by Thomas Alva Edison in 1914 at his laboratory in West Orange, NJ. It used an alkaline electrolyte of basic nickel-iron and nickel-cadmium, not an acid electrolyte, as in lead storage-cell batteries. Edison did not commercialize the alkaline cell, and it did not become widely used until the 1970s.

3476. Electric power line commercial carrier was placed in operation on December 6, 1922, by the Utica Gas and Electric Company, Utica, NY. The plant was built by the General Electric Company, Schenectady, NY, and consisted of the transmitters, the power lines, and the associated receivers. The transmission lines carried both voices and power. A single power line could carry several different carrier frequencies simultaneously, making possible distant supervisory control of various types of electric equipment.

3477. Mercury boiler turbine was installed at the Dutch Point Station of the Hartford Electric Light Company, Hartford, CT, and placed in service on September 7, 1923. It generated about 1,500 kilowatts.

3478. Photoelectric cell or tube was publicly demonstrated on October 21, 1925, by the Westinghouse Electric and Manufacturing Company at the Electrical Show at Grand Central Palace in New York City. The photoelectric cell, which is sensitive to light, was used to count objects as they interrupted a light beam in passing, to open doors as a person or car approached, and to perform similar functions.

3479. Hydroelectric power plant to use water pumped into a reservoir was constructed in 1927 by the Connecticut Light and Power Company, Waterbury, CT, at Rocky River, CT. The first pumping commenced in February 1928. Two 8,100-horsepower centrifugal pumps delivered water into a reservoir 10 miles long and 1.75 miles wide at its widest point. The water was stored and then used for generating electricity as needed in a 33,000-horsepower turbine.

3480. Hydroelectric power plant operated by a county was placed in operation by the people of Crisp County, GA, on August 1, 1930. The plant was 14 miles southwest of Cordele on the Flint River and was built under government license. Emmet Stephen Killebrew was the chief engineer. It had a capacity of 14,000 horsepower and produced 47 million kilowatt-hours per year.

3481. Floating electric power plant was the *Jacona,* a 7,000-ton steam-driven cargo vessel, 396 feet long and 53 feet wide, built in 1919 by the Todd Dry Dock and Shipbuilding Company, Tacoma, WA, for the United States Shipping Board and rebuilt in 1930 at the Newport News Shipbuilding and Dry Dock Company, Newport News, VA, which installed two 10,000-kilowatt turbines. The *Jacona* was towed by tug to Bucksport, ME, where it supplied a paper mill with 24,121,000-kilowatt hours of power from November 1930 to March 1931, at which time power was obtained from the Central Maine Power Company's Wyman Dam. The idea for the floating power plant was conceived by Walter Scott Wyman and the design engineering done by Nepsco Services.

3482. Electric power contract between a city and the federal government was signed by J.P. Nanney, mayor of Tupelo, MS, and Arthur Ernest Morgan, chairman of the Tennessee Valley Authority, on November 11, 1933. It went into effect on February 7, 1934. The 20-year contract required the city to purchase electricity from TVA and sell it to its customers at rates agreed upon with the Authority. The electricity cost the city of Tupelo about 5.5 mills per kilowatt hour.

3483. Hydrogen-cooled turbine generator was built by the General Electric Company, Schenectady, NY, and installed in the Millers Ford station of the Dayton Power and Light Company, Dayton, OH. The generator was put into commercial operation on October 12, 1937. It had a capacity of 25,000 kilowatts. The first such generator for outdoor installation was built by General Electric for the city of Glendale, CA, at a cost of $391,669. It went into operation on April 11, 1941. The normal rating of the turbogenerator was 20,000 kilowatts. The generator unit was located on an open deck and served with a traveling gantry crane.

3484. Electric power generated by cosmic rays was used on April 30, 1939, when rays were trapped by a Geiger-Mueller counter at the Hayden Planetarium, New York City, and set up a current of electricity that was carried by wire to the New York World's Fair at Flushing, Queens, New York City. The current actuated relays of local battery circuits, each connected with a switch, which turned on the colored lights at the Lagoon of the Nations.

3485. Hydroelectric power plant to produce a million kilowatts was the Boulder Dam, Boulder City, NV, which reached this production peak in June 1943. The Bureau of Reclamation of the Department of the Interior awarded a contract on March 11, 1931, for a concrete arch-gravity dam. The first of its four generators was placed in operation on October 26, 1936, to serve the Los Angeles area. In 1947 its name was changed to the Hoover Dam.

3486. Mobile electric power plant was delivered on January 10, 1944, by the General Electric Company, Schenectady, NY, to the Navy Bureau of Yards and Docks, Navy Yard, Philadelphia, PA. It consisted of six specially built railway cars housing a complete steam-turbine generating plant as well as the switchgear and transformer apparatus for controlling and distributing the 10,000 kilowatts of electric power it was capable of generating. The boilers were fired by oil. The unit had no motive power of its own but could be hauled over the rails at speeds up to 40 miles an hour and could be placed in operation within 24 hours.

3487. Gas turbine used by an electrical utility company was a General Electric turbine that was placed in service on July 29, 1949, in the Belle Isle station of the Oklahoma Gas and Electric Company, Oklahoma City, OK. The unit attained full capacity in 17 minutes.

3488. Battery to convert radioactive energy into electrical energy was a radioelectric cell invented by Philip Edwin Ohmart of Cincinnati, OH, and announced on December 31, 1951. It consisted of two electrochemically dissimilar electrodes separated by a filling gas that was ionized by exposure to nuclear energy to produce an electrical current.

3489. Electric power using municipal garbage as a boiler fuel was obtained by the Union Electric Company's Meramec Plant, St. Louis, MO, on April 4, 1972. Refuse was shredded and burned with coal to generate electricity. In the first month, 200,000 kilowatt hours of electricity were generated.

ENERGY—ELECTRICITY—ILLUMINATION

3490. Electric light for household illumination was probably used by Professor Moses Gerrish Farmer at 11 Pearl Street, Salem, MA. In July 1859 he arranged a series of lamps in his parlor, the current for which was generated by a galvanic battery of some three dozen six-gallon jars in his cellar. The lamps could be turned on individually. He also invented an incandescent lamp that consisted of a strip of sheet platinum operating in air.

3491. Electric light in a store was installed in the Philadelphia, PA, establishment of John Wanamaker on December 26, 1878, in the Grand Depot. Twenty-eight arc lamps were used, with eight dynamos supplying the current.

3492. Incandescent lamp of practical value was invented on October 21, 1879, by Thomas Alva Edison of Menlo Park, NJ. After 13 months of experimenting, he utilized carbonized cotton filaments and produced a light bulb that would burn 40 hours in a vacuum inside a glass bulb. The Pennsylvania Railroad Company ran special trains to Menlo Park on December 31, 1879, to enable the public to view a public demonstration of the lamp. Patent papers on this invention were granted on January 27, 1880.

3493. Electric lights in a church were installed circa 1880 in St. Edward's Church, Shamokin, PA, by Thomas Alva Edison.

3494. Incandescent lamp factory was the Edison Lamp Works, Menlo Park, NJ, opened on October 1, 1880. More than 130,000 bulbs had been manufactured by April 1, 1882, when the factory moved to Harrison, NJ.

3495. Electric light from a power plant in a residence was generated by an independent plant installed in the home of James Hood Wright in the Fort Washington section of New York City sometime before December 1881. Other New York residences that were equipped with power generators were those of William Henry Vanderbilt and John Pierpont Morgan.

3496. Mercury vapor lamp was invented by Peter Cooper Hewitt of New York City, who received eight patents on September 17, 1901. It consisted of an elongated vacuum glass tube with a mercury electrode at one end and an iron electrode at the other end. The light was obtained from the gas or vapor of the mercury, through which an electric current passed. The lamps lacked red rays. They were manufactured by the Cooper Hewitt Electric Company in New York City beginning in December 1902.

3497. Machine to make glass light bulbs was invented by Benjamin D. Chamberlin of Washington, DC, who received a patent on September 1, 1925, on an "apparatus for gathering glass and the treatment thereof on blowpipes," which was assigned to the Hartford-Empire Company, Hartford, CT. The first commercial machine was the result of several individuals' work and went into regular use about 1914 at the main plant of the Corning Glass Works, Corning, NY.

3498. Electric light bulb frosted on the inside with sufficient strength for commercial handling was invented by Marvin Pipkin of the Incandescent Lamp Department of the General Electric Company at Nela Park, OH. He received a patent for it on October 16, 1928. Inside-frosted bulbs have a number of distinct advantages over outside-frosted bulbs, among which are less absorption of light and less collection of dust. Pipkin found that bulbs frosted by previous methods were weak because the etched surface was made up of minute, sharp-angled pits or depressions, and that he could strengthen the bulb by changing these into rounded pits, either by treating the bulb with a weaker etching solution or by using the strong solution for a shorter period of time.

3499. Sodium vapor lamps were installed on June 13, 1933, on the Balltown Road, near Schenectady, NY, by the General Electric Company and the New York Power and Light Corporation. The lamps were monochromatic and glowed in one color, giving 2.5 times the light output of incandescent lamps of the same wattage. The lamp wattage was about 80 to 90 watts and the light output about 4,000 lumens.

3500. Fluorescent lamp successfully developed was made by Arthur Compton at the General Electric Company, Schenectady, NY, in 1934. His fluorescent bulb sent electric current through an argon-filled glass tube that was coated on the inside with phosphor. Mercury vapor inside the tube emitted ultraviolet waves that were changed by the phosphor into visible light. General Electric displayed the lamps at the 1939 New York World's Fair.

ENERGY—FOSSIL FUELS—COAL

3501. Coal is said to have been discovered by Father Louis Hennepin during a journey of exploration from 1673 to 1680. It is asserted that he noticed coal on the bluffs of the Illinois River not far from the future towns of Ottawa and La Salle, IL.

3502. Anthracite coal was discovered accidentally in 1791 by Philip Ginter, a hunter, near Sharp Mountain, Carbon County, PA. It was regarded as a species of black stone. Its value was not appreciated fully, as the coal was difficult to kindle and produced such a high heat that it endangered the old-time boilers, which were designed principally for burning wood.

3503. Anthracite coal burned experimentally was used by Judge Jesse Fell in his home in Wilkes-Barre, PA, February 11, 1808, much to the surprise of the populace, which regarded the coal as valueless.

3504. Anthracite coal used commercially was successfully burned in 1812 in a heating furnace at White and Hazard's Fairmount Nail and Wire Works near Philadelphia, PA. The coal was supplied by Colonel George Shoemaker of Pottsville, PA, who loaded nine wagons from his mine at Centreville. A second wagonload was sold to Mellon and Bishop of the Delaware County Rolling Mill. The remaining seven loads were given away because no one would buy hard coal.

3505. Coke used successfully as a blast furnace fuel was tested in 1835 by William Firmstone at the Mary Ann Furnace in Huntingdon County, PA.

3506. Coal mine disaster with large loss of life occurred in Avondale, PA, early in the morning of September 6, 1869. A fire broke out in the mineshaft, cutting off the miners' escape route and their only source of air. The trapped miners tried to keep toxic fumes out of the tunnel by building a wall of boxes, barrels, and their own clothing, but the effort was hopeless. The death toll was 110 men and boys.

3507. Steam distribution plant of importance was the New York Steam Corporation, 16 Cortlandt Street, New York City, formed on July 26, 1880. The first boiler plant was erected in the New York City block bounded by Cortlandt, Dey, Greenwich, and Washington streets. It contained 48 coal-burning boilers of 250 horsepower each and a chimney 225 feet high. On September 19, 1881, the company was consolidated with the Steam Heating and Power Company of New York, a smaller organization. The first distribution of steam from a central plant in New York City was made on March 3, 1882, to the United Bank Building, 88–92 Broadway. Within nine months, the service had been extended to 62 customers.

3508. Coal mine to be automated was the Butler Consolidated Coal Company's Wildwood mine, Wildwood, PA, which opened in October 1930. The drilling, crushing, loading, screening of sizes, mechanical cleaning, dumping, and transportation operations were accomplished mechanically. Rubber conveyor belts carried the coal.

3509. Coal pipeline was completed on September 12, 1956, and placed in commercial operation on June 4, 1957. It extended 108 miles from the Georgetown Preparation Plant of the Hanna Coal Company, a division of the Pittsburgh Consolidation Coal Company, near Cadiz, OH, to the Eastlake Power Station of the Cleveland Illuminating Company, Eastlake, OH. The pipeline, 10.75 inches in diameter, was originally designed to move an equal mixture of coal and water at the rate of 150 tons of coal per hour.

3510. Coal miner who was a woman to be killed in a mining accident was Marilyn J. McCusker, killed by falling rocks while working as a roof-bolter on October 2, 1979, in the Rushton Mining Company mine, Coalport, PA.

ENERGY—FOSSIL FUELS—GAS

3511. Natural gas used as an illuminant was tried in Fredonia, NY, on June 4, 1825, at the Taylor House, which was lit up in honor of the arrival of General Lafayette. The general arrived at 2 A.M. and found the house brilliantly illuminated, using about 30 burners of 60 candlepower. This was regarded as a great curiosity. The gas was fed through a pipeline from a 27-foot well that had been dug near a gas spring in 1821. It was later walled up because its odor was offensive.

3512. Gas meter to record the amount of gas used was a "gasometer" patented on October 17, 1834, by James Bogardus of New York City. It operated on the principle of a bellows, alternately being filled with gas and emptied, while the pulsations were counted on a register.

3513. Natural gas corporation was the Fredonia Gas Light and Water Works Company, organized in Fredonia, NY, in 1865.

3514. Natural gas for manufacturing was used in Olean, NY, in 1870. The first use of natural gas in ironworking occurred at the Leechburg, PA, works of the Rogers and Burchfield Iron Mill, where it was extensively used in 1873 in both iron and puddle mill furnaces.

ENERGY—FOSSIL FUELS—GAS—*continued*

3515. Natural gas plant operated by a city was acquired by Wheeling, WV, which appointed a board of trustees on June 23, 1871, to operate the gasworks. It had been incorporated on March 18, 1850, as the Wheeling Gas Company, and had received a city franchise on April 13. The company was organized with a capital stock of $50,000, the city subscribing $15,000. After considerable litigation, the city acquired the gas plant in 1871.

3516. Natural gas pipeline constructed over a long distance was a two-inch pipe five miles in length, extending from Newton Wells to Titusville, PA. It was completed on August 1, 1872.

3517. Water gas plant was built in 1874 in Phoenixville, PA. It was the first apparatus of the superheated generator type and was covered by three patents granted on August 13, 1872 to Thaddeus Sobieski Coulincourt Lowe of Norristown, PA, the inventor and originator of water gas production.

3518. Gas commission established by a state government was established by Massachusetts by a law approved on June 11, 1885. The Department of Public Utilities, later called the Department of Public Works, was established to regulate the industry, to supervise the issue of capital stock, to hear consumer complaints, to reduce the price of gas and electricity to consumers, and to require gas companies to file annual returns with the commission. The department of Public Utilities was quasi-judicial in character.

3519. Gas conservation law enacted by a state was enacted on March 2, 1891, by Indiana, "making it unlawful to burn natural gas in what are known as flambeau lights." Violation was considered a misdemeanor subject to a fine not exceeding $25; a second offense was subject to a fine not exceeding $200.

3520. Waterless natural gas storage tank was completed in early February of 1925 and put into service on February 10 by the Northern Indiana Gas and Electric Company in Michigan City, IN. It was 105 feet in diameter and 160 feet high, with a capacity of 1 million cubic feet of gas. The top section did not slide up and down; instead, a steel piston inside the shell rose and fell as the amount of gas varied. The walls of the holder were made of steel plates 20 feet long and 32 inches wide.

3521. Gas turbine to pump natural gas was installed by the Mississippi River Fuel Corporation of St. Louis, MO, at Wilmar, AR, on May 13, 1949. The unit was later moved to Bonne Terre, MO, and placed in operation on January 19, 1951.

3522. Synthetic fuels plant on a commercial scale was constructed beginning in 1980 at Buelah, ND. It was designed to convert lignite into natural gas. In 1985, with the default of $1.5 billion in federally guaranteed loans, the plant passed into the hands of the Department of Energy, which was unable to find a buyer.

ENERGY—FOSSIL FUELS—OIL

3523. Oil spring of record in America was marked on a map of territory near Cuba, NY, in 1627 by François Dollier de Casson and René de Brehant de Galinée, Catholic missionaries of the Order of St. Sulpice. The map was sent by them to Jean Talon, intendant of Canada. A description of the oil spring is contained in a letter written by the Franciscan missionary Joseph de la Roche d'Allion dated July 18, 1627, reproduced in Gabriel Sagard-Théodat's *Histoire du Canada et Voyages que les Frères Mineurs Recollects y ont Faicts pour la Conversion des Infidelles*, published in 1636.

3524. Oil well was drilled unintentionally in 1818 at the mouth of Troublesome Creek, on the Big South Fork of the Cumberland River 28 miles southeast of Monticello, KY, by Martin Beatty, who was seeking brine. The drillers, Marcus Huling and Andrew Zimmerman, searching for salt, drilled a five-inch hole with pole and auger to a depth of 536 feet. The oil had no known value and sand was thrown down the well to plug it up. The "devil's tar," as Beatty called the oil, was allowed to flow into the Cumberland River and covered its surface for a distance of 35 miles. The oil became ignited and an enormous fire ensued that destroyed trees along the banks of the river, as well as the salt works.

3525. Oil company was the Pennsylvania Rock Oil Company, incorporated on December 30, 1854, in New York City by George Henry Bissell of New Haven, CT, with a capital stock of $250,000.

3526. Oil refinery was started by Dr. Samuel M. Kier, a druggist of Pittsburgh, PA, to refine petroleum. He built a small refinery in 1855, using the oil, which he called Kier's Rock Oil, for medicinal purposes. Eventually he distilled the oil in his drugstore using laboratory equipment, bottled the product, and sold it for 50 cents a half pint. He also discovered that the light fractions from the crude oil would burn, and that the heavy fractions or bottoms were good for cleaning wool.

3527. Kerosene distilled from bituminous shale and cannel coal for illuminating purposes was obtained by Dr. Abraham Gesner, who secured a patent on March 27, 1855, covering his process. The product was manufactured by the North American Kerosene Gaslight Company at Newton Creek, NY. Gesner received patents on June 27, 1854, on a process for obtaining kerosene by heat distillation. The name "kerosene" is derived from *keros*, the Greek word for wax, referring to the use of paraffin in the distillation process.

3528. Oil well that was commercially productive was discovered on August 27, 1859, at Titusville, PA, when E.B. Bowditch and Edwin Laurentine Drake of the Seneca Oil Company bored through rock in a section known as Oil Creek. The well produced about 400 gallons a day from a depth of 69.5 feet. Drake was the first to tap petroleum at its source and to offer proof of the occurrence of oil in reservoirs beneath the earth's surface.

3529. Commercial oil refinery was erected by William Barnsdall and William Hawkins Abbott in Oil Creek Valley, PA, in June 1860. The only product saved was the kerosene. The small amount of gasoline manufactured was run into Oil Creek. The kerosene was sold in competition with whale oil and rock oil for use in lamps. In 1864 the refinery and some property were sold for $50,000 to six men who organized an oil company.

3530. Petroleum exported to Europe was shipped in barrels on the *Elizabeth Watts*, a 224-ton brig captained by Charles Bryant. On November 12, 1861, Messrs. Peter Wright and Sons of Philadelphia, PA, chartered this brig from Messrs. Edmund A. Sander and Company. The shipment was made from Philadelphia, PA, on November 19, 1861, and arrived at the Victoria Docks, London, on January 9, 1862, with 1,329 barrels of oil. It was not easy to recruit a crew, since men would not work above a cargo of oil, so a crew was kidnapped.

3531. Oil pipeline was laid in 1862 by Barrows and Company under the direction of J.L. Hutchins. It ran from the James Tarr farm at Oil Creek, PA, a distance of 2.5 miles to the Humboldt refinery at Plumer, PA, on Cherry Run. The pipeline had lead sockets and a two-inch diameter. It was completed on February 19, 1863, but was abandoned because of leakage.

3532. Oil well drilled by torpedoes as an experiment was the Ladies' Well on Watson Flats near Titusville, PA, on January 21, 1865. The method had been advocated in 1862 by Colonel Edward A.L. Roberts of New York City, who received a patent on April 25, 1865, on "exploding torpedoes in artesian wells."

3533. Oil pipeline of importance to transport crude petroleum successfully was completed on October 9, 1865, by Samuel Van Syckel of Titusville, PA. It was about five miles long and extended from Miller's Farm on Oil Creek to Pithole, PA. Wrought iron pipes two inches in diameter were laid underground in 15-foot sections. Two pumping stations supplied the power.

3534. Oil drill offshore rig was patented by Thomas F. Rowland of Greenpoint, NY, who obtained a patent on May 4, 1869, on a "submarine drilling apparatus."

3535. Oil wells successfully drilled in the ocean were drilled off Summerland, Santa Barbara County, CA, in 1896.

3536. Gasoline obtained from crude petroleum by the cracking process was obtained by William M. Burton of Chicago, IL, the inventor of the process, who received a patent on January 7, 1913, on the "manufacture of gasoline." His method of treating the residue of the paraffin group of petroleum by distillation and condensation of the vapors was used by the Standard Oil Company of Indiana, to whom the patent was assigned.

3537. Oil and gas conservation law enacted by a state was enacted by Oklahoma on May 17, 1913. It provided for a chief deputy inspector of oil and gas wells and pipelines to supervise their use and operation.

3538. Ethyl gasoline to be marketed was sold in Dayton, OH, on February 2, 1923. Tetraethyl lead, made from alcohol and lead, was found to influence the combustion rate of gasoline by Thomas Midgley, Jr., of the General Motors Research Laboratories, Dayton. During seven years of experimenting in the development of ethyl gasoline, at least 33,000 compounds were tested to determine their antiknock effect.

3539. Aviation gasoline obtained by the catalytic cracking method was commercially produced on June 6, 1936, by the Socony-Vacuum Oil Company, Paulsboro, NJ, which used the process invented by Eugene Houdry. The gasoline was 100 octane.

ENERGY—FOSSIL FUELS—OIL—*continued*

3540. Fuel alcohol plant was established by the Bailor Manufacturing Company, Atchison, KS, which began selling fuel alcohol on October 2, 1936. Five percent of the total output was butyl alcohol and acetone, which were blended with ethyl alcohol, which in turn was blended with gasoline. Raw materials used were rye, oats, sweet potatoes, barley, milo, kafir corn, molasses, and rice.

3541. Plastic oil pipeline was placed in service on October 19, 1953, by the C.C. Thomas Company to carry oil from Williston Basin, near Poplar, MT, to a railroad car siding of the Great Northern Railway, a distance of nine miles. Its capacity was 2,500 barrels a day. It was a smooth, flexible three-inch pipe of Tenite butyrate plastic produced by the extrusion process. A 20-foot section of the pipe weighed 13 pounds, compared to 153 pounds of steel pipe. It withstood a pressure of 90 pounds per square inch.

3542. Oil refinery with a carbon monoxide boiler to achieve complete conversion of waste gases into useful power was the Sinclair Oil Corporation's refinery in Houston, TX. The boiler, which was designed and developed by the company, was placed in operation in November 1953. Carbon monoxide was converted into carbon dioxide by injecting a stream of air into the waste gases from the generator. The catalyst was regenerated in the catalytic oil cracking process.

3543. Oil drill seagoing rig for drilling in more than 100 feet of water was built in the Beaumont Yard of the Bethlehem Steel Company, Bethlehem, PA, for the C.G. Glasscock Drilling Company. The rig could drive piles with a force of 827 tons and could pull with the force of 942 tons. It was placed in service March 24, 1955.

3544. Oil spill with disastrous consequences occurred on January 28, 1969, when Offshore Well A-21, owned by the Union Oil Company, burst and began leaking crude oil along a 200-mile stretch of coast centered on Santa Barbara, CA. The leak, which took 11 days to plug, fouled beaches and caused widespread loss of animal life.

ENERGY—NUCLEAR

3545. Nuclear product for peacetime use was developed by Clinton Laboratories, Chicago, IL, which delivered one millicurie of carbon-14 to Barnard Free Skin and Cancer Hospital, St. Louis, MO, on August 2, 1946, for use in medical treatment. The radioactive carbon has a

half-life of 10,000 to 25,000 years and gives off millions of beta particles. It was a white powder, in a quantity too small to be seen by the naked eye, and was placed in aluminum and steel containers.

3546. Electric power from nuclear energy was obtained through the use of Experimental Breeder Reactor I, placed in operation during the summer of 1951 at the National Reactor Testing Station operated by the Atomic Energy Commission near Idaho Falls, ID. EBR-I was a fast breeder reactor—the first practical breeder reactor in the nation—designed and operated by the Argonne National Laboratory, Argonne, IL. The core in use at the time of the first production of electricity enabled the reactor to produce 1,400 thermal kilowatts and 150 electrical kilowatts. On December 20, 1951, the reactor supplied steam to a turbogenerator that produced more than 100,000 watts of electricity. This operated the pumps and other reactor equipment and provided light and electrical facilities for the building in which the reactor was housed.

3547. Electric power generated from nuclear energy to illuminate a town was obtained from the Utah Power and Light Company's station at Arco, ID, on July 17, 1955. At 11:28 P.M., the station released steam from a borax reactor into a turbine that drove a 3,500 kilowatt-capacity generator to supply current for the 1,200 inhabitants of Arco. The power, which lasted only one hour, was the sole source of the town's light. The news was withheld until August 11, 1955, when it was announced at the Atoms for Peace Conference at Geneva, Switzerland.

3548. Electric power generated from nuclear energy to be sold commercially was delivered by the Atomic Energy Commission at West Milton, NY, to the Niagara Mohawk Power Corporation, which supplied power on July 18, 1955, to homes and industry at three mills per kilowatt hour. The power was obtained from a nuclear reactor, the prototype of the reactor used in the submarine *Seawolf.* A capacity of about 10,000 kilowatts was integrated with the regular current.

3549. Nuclear reactor built for private industrial research was a 50,000-watt research reactor designed and built by Atomics International, a division of North American Aviation, which began operating on June 28, 1956. The reactor was located on the campus of the Illinois Institute of Technology, Chicago, IL, and operated by the Armour Research Foundation. It was of the "solution" type, fueled by enriched uranium, with a reactor core surrounded by graphite bars arranged in a stack (8 feet by 5 feet by 5 feet) that acts as a reflector. The rate of fission in the reactor was controlled by four boron bars. The reactor produced neutrons and gamma rays and was not used to generate electrical power. Twenty-four industrial companies contributed about $20,000 each toward the total cost of $700,000. The first director of the project was Dr. Richard Franklin Humphreys.

3550. Sodium reactor was built on an experimental basis by Atomics International, a division of North American Aviation, for the Atomic Energy Commission in the Santa Susana Mountains, about 30 miles northwest of Los Angeles, CA. The atomic power reactor reached criticality on April 25, 1957. It generated about 6,000 kilowatts of electricity.

3551. Nuclear power plant devoted exclusively to peaceful uses was the Shippingport Atomic Power Station, Shippingport, PA, whose reactor attained criticality on December 2, 1957. The plant produced its full rated capacity of 60,000 net kilowatts on December 23. It consisted of a single pressurized water-type reactor and its associated systems, four steam generators heated by the reactor, a single turbine-generator and associated systems, a radioactive waste disposal system, laboratory, shops, and administrative facilities. The station was designed to supply an initial electrical output of 60,000 kilowatts net, enough to provide for the residential needs of a city of 250,000 people. To allow for increased output from future nuclear fuel loadings, the turbine generator was designed with a capacity of 1 million kilowatts. President Dwight David Eisenhower broke ground for the station by remote control from Denver, CO, on September 6, 1954, and formally dedicated the plant by remote control from Washington, DC, on May 26, 1958.

3552. Nuclear reactor operated commercially was the $57 million Yankee Atomic Electric Company's plant at Rowe, MA, on the Deerfield River, which began producing power for distribution on November 10, 1960. A pressurized light water reactor, it produced 135,000 kilowatts of atomic-fueled electricity. The company was formed by 12 New England utility companies, which signed a contract on June 4, 1956, with the Westinghouse Electric Corporation, principal contractor. The reactor became critical on August 19, 1960. It was permanently shut down for safety reasons in 1995.

3553. Deaths in an American nuclear reactor occurred on January 3, 1961, when three workers were killed by high levels of radiation from an experimental reactor at a federal installation near Idaho Falls, ID.

3554. Nuclear reactor fueled by plutonium that produced useful amounts of electricity was installed in the experimental reactor of the Argonne National Laboratory's Idaho division, near Idaho Falls, ID. It was announced on June 30, 1963.

3555. Nuclear commercial power plant licensed operator who was a woman was Roberta A. Kankus, a graduate of Rensselaer Polytechnic Institute, Troy, NY, who was licensed on February 12, 1976, by the Nuclear Regulatory Commission, Washington, DC, after 14 months of on-the-job training at the Philadelphia Electric Company's Peach Bottom atomic power plant, 60 miles southwest of Philadelphia, PA. Her title was engineer in the Generating Division.

3556. Nuclear power plant to sustain a major accident was the Three Mile Island nuclear reactor complex near Middletown, PA. On March 28, 1979, homes in nearby neighborhoods were evacuated after the reactor suffered a loss of coolant and a partial core meltdown caused by a series of equipment failures and human errors.

ENERGY—RENEWABLE

3557. Wind turbine to generate energy for a central power system producing alternating current was placed in service at Grandpa's Knob, VT, on October 19, 1941, when it was phased into the Central Vermont Public Service Corporation's system. Synchronized operation continued for two hours, during which a maximum output of 800 kilowatts was delivered. The wind velocity indicated by the anemometers at this load was 26 miles per hour. Palmer Cosslet Putnam was the inventor.

3558. Solar energy battery to convert the sun's energy into useful amounts of electricity was invented by Gerald Leondus Pearson, Calvin Souther Fuller, and Daryl M. Chapin at the Bell Telephone Laboratories, New York City, and announced on April 25, 1954. Made of specially treated strips of silicon, the battery needed no fuel other than the light of the sun. It had no moving parts, nothing in it was consumed or destroyed, and theoretically it was possible for it to last indefinitely.

ENERGY—RENEWABLE—*continued*

3559. Solar energy battery to be manufactured commercially was made by National Fabricated Products, Chicago, IL, in 1955. It consisted of a disc, the size of a half dollar, which was hermetically sealed. It generated a half volt from its two terminals. The battery was first advertised on May 20, 1955, in *Electronic Design,* and the first shipment was made June 1, 1955.

3560. Power plant using solar cells was dedicated on June 7, 1980, by Governor Scott Matheson at Natural Bridges National Monument, UT. The $3 million photovoltaic system had 266,029 solar cells mounted in 12 long rows. They produced a 100-kilowatt output that supplied current for six staff residences, maintenance facilities, a water sanitation system, and a visitors' center. The plant was a joint venture of the National Park System, the Department of Energy, and the Massachusetts Institute of Technology's Lincoln Laboratory. It was 38 miles from the nearest power line.

ENGINEERING

3561. Mechanical engineering laboratory for research work was established at Stevens Institute of Technology at Hoboken, NJ, in 1874. It was proposed by Robert Henry Thurston, professor of mechanical engineering, who on January 30, 1874, outlined the usefulness of the laboratory to the community in a letter which he sent to the trustees of the school.

ENGINEERING—BRIDGES

3562. Bridge was erected in 1634 over the Neponset River from Milton, MA, to Dorchester, MA, by Israel Stoughton. Authority to build a bridge and mill was extended April 1, 1634, by the Massachusetts General Court.

3563. Toll bridge was erected by Richard Thurlow (variously spelled Thorla, Thorlo, and Thurley) in 1654 over the Newbury River at Rowley, MA. He built the bridge with his own money. On May 3, 1654, the General Court of Massachusetts fixed a rate of toll for animals. Passengers were permitted free passage. The bridge remained a toll bridge until 1680.

3564. Stone arch bridge was the Frankford Avenue bridge over Pennypack Creek, built in 1697–98 at Pennepecka, near Germantown, Philadelphia, PA. William Penn wrote from Pennsburg on June 22, 1700, to "urge the justices about the bridge at Pennepecka and Poquessin forthwith for a carriage or I cannot come down" to attend a local meeting.

3565. Pile bridge was designed and constructed by Major Samuel Sewall and built across the York River at York, ME, in 1761. A 270-foot wooden bridge was erected atop 13 bands of piles, which were hammered upright, with the ends protruding above the water.

3566. Bridge on a large scale was the West Boston Bridge, connecting Boston, MA, and Cambridge, MA, begun on July 15, 1792, and opened for traffic on November 23, 1793. It rested on 180 piers. It was 3,483 feet long with a 3,344-foot causeway, and 40 feet wide with a railing on each side. The cost was $76,000. The toll right was granted to the proprietors for 70 years.

3567. Suspension bridge was erected in 1796 by James Finley across Jacob's Creek, Westmoreland County, PA. It had a 70-foot span and cost $6,000. Finley patented his design in 1801. The bridge was on the turnpike between Uniontown, PA, and Greensburg, PA.

3568. Pontoon bridge was floated into place at Collins' Pond, Lynn, MA, in 1804. The Board of Directors authorized Captain Moses Brown to bridge the pond, which was of great depth and which had a soft, peaty bottom that did not permit the use of supporting piers. The pontoon bridge built by Brown was 511 feet in length and 28 feet wide. It consisted of five layers of pine timber, each at right angles to the one below it. The whole mass was secured together by three-inch dowels. Including the top planking, it was about five feet thick.

3569. Bridge in a Y shape was authorized by the General Assembly of Zanesville, OH, on January 21, 1812. The bridge, in the form of the letter *Y,* spanned the Licking and Muskingum rivers and was opened for traffic in 1814. The present concrete bridge is the fourth structure to occupy the site.

3570. Suspension bridge of iron wire was the Schuylkill River bridge at Philadelphia, PA, designed and constructed by Erskine Hazard and Captain Josiah White. It was 408 feet long, with a board floor 18 inches wide. It had a 33-foot sag and could not support more than six or eight persons at a time. It weighed 4,702 pounds, cost $125, and was opened to traffic June 1816. A toll of one cent per person was charged until the tolls defrayed the cost.

3571. Stone arch railroad bridge in the world was the Carrollton Viaduct of the Baltimore and Ohio Railroad, spanning Gwynn's Falls at Baltimore, MD. It was named after Charles Carroll, who laid the last stone in the bridge several weeks prior to its official opening on

December 21, 1829. It was 300 feet long and 70 feet high and had two arches: a large 80-foot span over the stream and a small arch through which, originally, a wagon road passed. The bridge was built by James Lloyd.

3572. Bridge of cast iron was built in 1835 over Dunlap's Creek at Brownsville, PA, by John Snowdon, from the design of and under the direction of his foreman, John Herbertson. It had five tubular arch ribs of 85-foot span and was 25 feet wide.

3573. Wooden railroad bridge of a purely truss type was built in 1838 by Benjamin Henry Latrobe for the Baltimore and Ohio Railroad Company across the Patapsco River at Elysville (now Alberton), MD. It consisted of two spans, each about 150 feet in length. The bridge was completed in 1839 and the wooden trusses were replaced in 1852 by iron Bollman trusses.

3574. Girder bridge of cast iron was built by Earl Trumbull over the Erie Canal at Frankfort, NY, in 1840. It had a span of 77 feet.

3575. Timber trestle pier of lattice construction was started in June 1840 at the Long Hollow Crossing, Shuman's Station, PA. It was originally part of the Little Schuylkill and Susquehanna Railroad line, later the Catawissa Branch of the Reading Company. The pier was designed by James F. Smith and was 740 feet long and 122 feet high. The timber piers were later replaced with stone masonry; then the trusses were replaced with wooden trestles; then the wooden trestles were replaced with iron and steel viaducts. Finally all were replaced with concrete bridges and fill.

3576. Wire suspension bridge for general traffic was erected over the Schuylkill River at Fairmount, PA, by Charles Ellet. The bridge was opened on January 2, 1842. It had a 358-foot span, was supported by wire cables, five at each side, and had a width of 25 feet. It cost $35,000.

3577. Suspension aqueduct bridge of wire cable was built in Pittsburgh, PA, across the Allegheny River by John Augustus Roebling. There were seven spans of 162 feet each, containing a wooden trunk to hold water and supported by a continuous wire cable on each side, seven inches in diameter. The length of the aqueduct without extensions was 1,140 feet; the cables, 1,175 feet. The total weight of the water in the aqueduct was 2,100 tons. The cost of construction and removal of the old wooden bridge was $62,000. The bridge was completed in May 1845.

3578. Iron truss bridge with parallel chords and open web was designed by Richard Osborne, chief engineer of the Reading Company. Construction of trusses began in January 1845 at Pottstown, PA, and was completed in March. The bridge had a 34.2-foot span, with a four-foot space between tracks, and was erected a half mile east of Flat Rock Tunnel, north of the West Manayunk station. Erection was begun Saturday night, May 3, 1845, and the bridge was finished the next day. It remained on the main line of the Philadelphia and Reading Railroad Company until 1901.

3579. Twin covered bridges were built in 1849 by Peter Ent over Huntington Creek at Village Forks, PA, at a cost of $750. They were the 60-foot-long East Paden Bridge, which used a queen post form of truss, and the 92-foot-long West Paden Bridge, a Theodore Burr design. They were constructed of wood reinforced with iron.

3580. Railroad suspension bridge was the suspension bridge over the gorge at Niagara Falls, NY, which was completed in 1854. It had a span of 825 feet and two decks, the lower one carrying a highway 15 feet wide, partially enclosed at the side by timber stiffening trusses. The upper deck, 24 feet wide and 245 feet above high water, had a single railroad track in the center and was floored over to separate it from the highway below. The bridge was started in 1853 by Charles Ellet, who withdrew from the work. It was completed by John Augustus Roebling. The first train crossed the bridge on March 8, 1855.

3581. Railroad bridge across the Mississippi River was the Rock Island Railroad Bridge between Rock Island, IL, and Davenport, IA. It was built of wood resting on stone piers. The piers were completed June 1854. The bridge was fully completed on April 21, 1856. On April 22, a train consisting of three locomotives and eight passenger cars crossed as a test.

3582. Steel arch bridge was the Eads Bridge, built across the Mississippi River by James Buchanan Eads. It was built from St. Louis, MO, to East St. Louis, IL, at a cost of $6.5 million. Construction started in 1869. The center span was 520 feet, the two side spans 502 feet each. On May 24, 1874, more than 15,000 people paid a toll to walk across; on June 3, the upper roadway was ready for vehicles; and on July 4, President Ulysses Simpson Grant made the formal dedication speech. It was the first bridge construction project to use pneumatic caissons.

ENGINEERING—BRIDGES—*continued*

3583. Cantilever bridge was designed by Charles Shaler Smith for the Cincinnati Southern Railroad to cross the Kentucky River. It was built in 1876–77 near Harrodsburg in Mercer County, KY. A contract for an iron-truss bridge was let to the Baltimore Bridge Company on July 9, 1875, for $377,500. Construction started October 12, 1876, and was completed February 20, 1877. The bridge had three spans, each 375 feet long.

3584. Railroad bridge entirely of steel was the Glasgow Bridge, a 2,700-foot structure built by the Chicago and Alton Railroad Company over the Missouri River at Glasgow, MO. The contract for steel was dated October 12, 1878, and the bridge was placed in service about November 1, 1879.

3585. Hanging railroad bridge was built in 1879 at a location several miles east of Canon City, CO, where the Royal Gorge of the Arkansas River is only 30 feet wide and entirely filled by the river. Sheer rock cliffs rise for more than 1,000 feet on each side. The bridge was built above and parallel to the river, one side embedded in the rock cliff and the other suspended over the stream by means of overhead V-type beams. It was designed by Charles Shaler Smith.

3586. Highway bridge with concrete arches was designed by Carl A. Trik, superintendent of bridges for the Bureau of Highways, Philadelphia, PA, and erected in 1893 to carry Pine Road over Pennypack Creek, Philadelphia. It consisted of two arched spans, each 25 feet 4.75 inches wide, with a rise of 6 feet 6 inches, supported by concrete abutments and a concrete pier, built on a light skew. It was 34 feet wide and carried a 26-foot-wide macadam roadway with two granite-paved gutters on concrete foundations. The entire bridge, including the appurtenances and the thorough renovation of the retaining walls on both approaches, cost $9,288.

3587. Rolling lift bridge was the Van Buren Street bridge, located over the Chicago River, Chicago, IL, and was opened to traffic on February 4, 1895. It consisted of two arms meeting at the center of the river, which when open provided a clear channel 82 feet in width, measured along the line of the stream. Each arm consisted of three trusses that carried two roadways, each 18 feet wide, and two sidewalks, each eight feet wide. The bridge was operated by two 50-horsepower electric motors on each side of the river. The total construction cost was $169,700. The bridge's construction was patented by William Scherzer of Chicago.

3588. Suspension bridge with steel towers instead of masonry towers that was important was the Williamsburg Bridge, connecting the boroughs of Brooklyn and Manhattan in New York City. It was opened on December 19, 1903. The cost was $24 million for land and construction.

3589. Aerial ferry was put in operation on April 9, 1905, over the ship canal from Lake Avenue, Duluth, MN, to Minnesota Point, MN. The car was suspended in the air from a superstructure which had a clear height over Lake Superior of 135 feet. The truss in the center was 51 feet, making a total height at the highest part of the superstructure of 186 feet above water level. The clear span was 393.75 feet in length. The car platform was 34 by 50 feet, with room enough to accommodate six automobiles and two glassed-in cabins for passengers, and with a carrying capacity of 125,000 pounds. The platform was 12 feet above the water line. The round trip could be made in 10 minutes.

3590. Concrete cantilever bridge was erected over Indian Creek at Marion, IA, in 1905 for the Marion Street Railway Company. It had three 50-foot spans with two longitudinal ribs 12 inches wide supported on concrete columns and floor slabs on transverse beams.

3591. Double-deck bridge of importance was the Queensboro Bridge over the East River, New York City, which was opened to traffic on March 30, 1909. The Manhattan Suspension Bridge, also a double-deck bridge over the East River, was opened to traffic on December 31, 1909. The total cost of the land and construction of the Queensboro Bridge was approximately $17 million and of the Manhattan Suspension Bridge about $31 million.

3592. Bridge of flowers was instituted at the suggestion of Mrs. Walter Burnham in 1929, when a 400-foot five-arch concrete-span bridge over the Deerfield River between Shelburne, MA, and Buckland, MA, was abandoned with the passing of the trolley line. The bridge at Shelburne Falls was converted into a walk, both sides of which are annually lined with innumerable species of flowering plants and shrubs.

3593. Bridge with piers sunk in the open sea was the Golden Gate suspension span, San Francisco, CA. Construction was officially started on January 5, 1933. Joseph Baermann Strauss was appointed chief engineer. The length of the main structure of the bridge was 8,940 feet, with towers 746 feet above water and a minimum clearance of 220 feet. The Golden Gate Bridge was the first built across the outer mouth of a major ocean harbor.

3594. Bridge with open-mesh steel flooring was the University Bridge, Seattle, WA, opened for traffic on April 7, 1933. The flooring, 80 percent of which was open, self-cleaning, and self-draining, was originated by Walter Edward Irving of the Irving Subway Grating Company, Long Island City, NY (part of Queens, New York City), who obtained a patent on February 12, 1935.

3595. Pontoon bridge of reinforced concrete was the Lake Washington Floating Bridge, Seattle, WA, begun on December 29, 1938, and dedicated on July 2, 1940. It was composed of 25 pontoons bolted together, each having two or more 65-ton anchors. Its total length was 34,021 feet. It was financed by a Public Works Administration grant of $3.8 million and a bond issue of $5.5 million to be repaid by toll charges.

3596. Highway bridge with welded aluminum girders was a four-span structure, 36 feet wide and 222 feet long, on Clive Road, about one mile north and one mile west of Urbandale, IA, erected for the Iowa State Highway Commission by the Jensen Construction Company and the United Contractors of Des Moines, IA. It was completed on September 24, 1958, at a cost of approximately $125,000.

3597. Bridge designed by computer was the Verrazano-Narrows Bridge, which spanned New York Harbor to connect Brooklyn and Staten Island, two boroughs of New York City. Construction began in 1959 under the supervision of Othmar H. Ammann. The main span, 4,260 feet long, was suspended from two towers 690 feet high. When it was completed in 1964, the bridge became the longest suspension bridge in the world.

3598. Bridge named for a woman was the Betsy Ross Bridge, which spanned three miles across the Delaware River, connecting Philadelphia and Pennsauken, NJ. It was officially opened on April 30, 1976. The construction cost about $105 million.

ENGINEERING—CANALS

3599. Canal for creating water power was dug by English settlers in 1639–40 at Dedham, MA, at Mill Creek, or Mother Brook as it is commonly called, and was used to run a mill. It conveyed water from the Charles River into the Neponset River. The order for the construction of the canal follows: "The 25th of the 1 month, Commonly Called March. 1639.... Ordered that a Ditch shalbe made at a Common Charge through purchased Medowe unto the East Brooke, that may both be a pticon fence in the same; as also may serve for a Course unto a water mill."

3600. Canal for boat transportation was built around the falls of the Connecticut River at South Hadley, MA, in 1793. It was chartered by "the Proprietors of the Upper Locks and Canals on the Connecticut River in the County of Hampshire." The canal was two miles long and was opened to traffic in 1794. Benjamin Prescott was the engineer. Boats were run into movable caissons filled with water and were hauled by cables operated by water power. The canal had two levels connected by an incline, along which boats were raised or lowered in a tank of water and propelled by cables operated by water wheels.

3601. Canal of importance was the Erie Canal, which connected the waters of Lake Erie at Buffalo with the waters of the Hudson River at Albany, NY. Lake Erie lies 550 feet above the level of tide water in the Hudson. The canal was 360 miles in length, 40 feet wide at the top and 28 feet wide at the bottom, and 4 feet deep. The canal was authorized on April 15, 1817, and construction started on July 4. The section between the towns of Rome and Utica carried its first boat on October 22, 1819. The canal, which cost about $9 million, was opened for traffic on October 26, 1825.

3602. Canal made of concrete was built by the federal government for the Illinois and Mississippi Canal (the Hennepin canal), which connected Lake Michigan at Chicago, IL, with the Mississippi River south of Rock Island, IL. Excavation work commenced July 1892 and the first section, the Milan section, was opened to traffic on April 17, 1895.

3603. Canal incorporated into a seaway was the 400-mile waterway between Montreal and Lake Erie, connecting the St. Lawrence River with the Great Lakes. It forms part of the St. Lawrence Seaway, 2,342 miles long, which allows oceangoing ships to travel from the Atlantic Ocean to Duluth, MN. It was opened on April 25, 1959.

ENGINEERING—DAMS

3604. Levees were built along the Mississippi River at New Orleans, LA, in 1724. They extended 18 miles above and 18 miles below New Orleans, but they were rudimentary dikes compared with the present mighty embankments. Sieur le Blond de la Tour, a knight of St. Louis and chief engineer of the colony, began construction of the levee in 1718. It was completed in 1727.

3605. Dam filled with rocks was built at Castlewood, CO, for the Denver Land and Water Company, and opened in November 1890. The upstream and downstream faces of the dam were built of dry or mortar rubble masonry. The core of the dam consisted of loosely dumped rock. The maximum height of the dam above the valley floor was about 70 feet, and the length about 600 feet. There was a spillway, located near the center of the dam, consisting of an opening four feet deep and 100 feet long. The outlets through the structure consisted of eight 12-inch cast-iron pipes, placed in pairs at four different elevations, with valves in a chamber built inside the dam. The reservoir capacity was about 3,400 acre-feet.

3606. Steel dam was the Ash Fork Dam in Johnson Canyon, four miles east of Ashfork, AZ, which was built in 1898 by the Atchison, Topeka and Santa Fe Railway Company. It was built of steel with masonry abutments. The west abutment was 84 feet long, and 16 feet high. The steel portion was 184 feet long. The height of the spillway crest was 30 feet above the reservoir bottom and 46 feet above the lowest bedrock. The width of the canyon at the stream bed was 40 feet. The top of the dam, aside from the spillway, was 300 feet. The capacity of this reservoir at spillway crest was 96.7 acre-feet. The canyon drained about 30 square miles.

3607. Needle dam was constructed in 1900 under the supervision of B.F. Thomas at Louisa, KY. It is located on the Levisa Fork of the Big Sandy River, just below the junction of Tug River. This needle dam was built from the West Virginia side to the Kentucky side and created a pool some 40 miles long.

ENGINEERING—ORGANIZATIONS

3608. Engineering society of importance was the Boston Society of Civil Engineers, organized at an informal meeting on April 26, 1848, at the United States Hotel, Boston, MA. The first regular meeting was held on July 3, 1848. The society was incorporated on April 24, 1851, for the purpose of "promoting science and instruction in the department of civil engineering." The first president was James Fowle Baldwin. Attempts had been made to form engineering societies in 1836 by engineers of the Cincinnati and Charleston Railroad, in 1839 by engineers in Baltimore, MD, and in 1841 in Albany, NY, but these sporadic attempts were not successful.

3609. Civil engineering society (national) was the American Society of Civil Engineers, founded as the American Society of Civil Engineers and Architects on November 5, 1852, in New York City. Its purpose was "the advancement of the sciences of engineering and architecture in their several branches, the professional improvement of its members, the encouragement of intercourse between men of practical science, and the establishment of a central point of reference and union for its members." The first president was James Laurie.

3610. Mechanical engineering society (national) was the American Society of Mechanical Engineers, founded February 16, 1880, by 40 men from eight states who met at the office of the *American Machinist* in New York City. An organizational meeting was held April 7, 1880, at the Assembly Hall of the Stevens Institute of Technology, Hoboken, NJ. The first president was Robert Henry Thurston.

ENGINEERING—TUNNELS

3611. Tunnel was built as part of the Schuylkill Navigation Company's canal above Auburn, PA, at the Orwigsburg landing. Job Samson and Solomon Fudge were the contractors. Construction began in 1818 and the tunnel was opened to traffic in 1821. Cut through red shale, it was 20 feet wide, 18 feet high from the canal bottom, and 450 feet long. It was arched for about 75 feet inward from each portal. It was shortened to half its length in 1834 and was shortened once more in 1845. In 1856 it was again shortened "until nothing remained but air."

3612. Mining tunnel on a large scale was started as early as 1824 by the Lehigh Navigation Company. This was the Hacklebernie anthracite coal mine tunnel near Mauch Chunk, PA. It was driven by hand using black powder. Work stopped in 1827, when 790 feet had been penetrated. The opening was 16 feet wide and eight feet high. In 1846, work was resumed and the length was extended to 2,000 feet.

3613. Railroad tunnel was built in 1831 near Johnstown, PA, by the Allegheny Portage Railroad, the first railroad to go west of the Allegheny Mountains. The tunnel, driven through slate, was 901 feet long, 25 feet wide, and 21 feet high. It was lined throughout with masonry 18 inches thick. Construction began on April 12, 1831, and was completed on March 18, 1834. The segmented tunnel extended from Hollidaysburg to Johnstown, PA, a distance of 36.6 miles. The engineer was Solomon White Roberts.

3614. Underwater highway tunnel was the Washington Street Tunnel beneath the Chicago River, Chicago, IL, authorized on July 17, 1866, by the Board of Public Works. Construction began on November 30, 1866, and ended in 1869. The total length of the tunnel and its approaches was 1,520 feet. The contract price was $328,500, but the final cost was $512,709. The tunnel had two roadways, each 11 feet high and 13 feet wide, and a separate footway 10 feet high and 10 feet wide. It was lowered in 1907 to provide a clear draft of 27 feet in the Chicago River.

3615. Water supply tunnel for a city was the Chicago Lake Tunnel, which extended 10,587 feet under Lake Michigan to an inlet crib. It was five feet in diameter. Ellis Sylvester Chesbrough was the city engineer at the time of construction. The contract was given to Dull and Gowan of Philadelphia, PA, who started work on March 17, 1864. The tunnel was completed on December 6, 1866, at a cost of $380,785, and was put into operation on March 25, 1867. The pumping station at the intersection of Michigan Boulevard and Chicago Avenue escaped the fire of 1871.

3616. Tunnel construction using compressed air took place in 1879. This method was introduced by Dewitt Clinton Haskin and was used in the construction of the famous Hudson River tunnel between Hoboken, NJ, and Morton Street, New York City. The tunnel plans called for two tubes, each 16 feet wide and 18 feet high. During the construction, on July 21, 1880, the compressed air blew a hole through the soft silt of the roof about 360 feet from the Hoboken shaft, flooding the tubes and drowning 20 workmen. Work was discontinued. The tunnel was not opened until February 25, 1908.

3617. Underwater railroad tunnel to a foreign country was the St. Clair Railway tunnel between Port Huron, MI, and Sarnia, Ontario, Canada, which was opened for freight traffic on September 19, 1891, and for passenger traffic on December 7. The tunnel was designed and built under the supervision of Joseph Hobson,

chief engineer of the Grand Trunk Railway (later the Canadian National Railways), at a cost of $2.7 million. Its length from portal to portal was 6,025 feet. The tunnel was equipped with electricity on May 17, 1908.

3618. Underwater highway tunnel with twin tubes was the Holland Tunnel between New York City and Jersey City, NJ, beneath the Hudson River. Construction began on October 12, 1920. The tunnel, which was named for the chief engineer, Clifford Milburn Holland, consisted of two tubes 9,250 feet long, of which 5,480 feet passed under the river, and was designed to accommodate 1,900 motor vehicles an hour. The ventilation system changed the air 42 times an hour, at the rate of 3,761,000 cubic feet per minute. The tunnel was opened on November 12, 1927, by President Calvin Coolidge, who gave the signal from the presidential yacht *Mayflower* anchored in the Potomac River off Washington, DC. In that first hour, 20,000 people walked through the tunnel from shore to shore. Vehicular traffic was allowed through on November 13, 1927. On April 21, 1930, all operation was turned over to the Port of New York Authority as agent for the states of New York and New Jersey.

3619. Vehicular tunnel to a foreign country was the Detroit-Windsor tunnel under the Detroit River between Detroit, MI, and Windsor, Ontario, Canada. It was 50 feet below the river and 5,135 feet from portal to portal, 2,200 feet of which were under water. The formal opening of the tunnel took place on November 1, 1930. It was opened to the public on November 2 and opened for traffic on November 3. The capacity was 1,000 motor cars per hour each way.

ENTERTAINMENT—AMUSEMENT PARKS

3620. Carousel patent was granted on July 25, 1871, to Willhelm Schneider of Davenport, IA. It was a two-story carousel and not very successful or practical.

3621. Roller coaster was invented by Lemarcus Adna Thompson, a former Sunday school teacher, and put in operation in June 1884 by the L.A. Thompson Scenic Railway Company at Coney Island, NY (now part of New York City). It traveled along a wooden and steel track 450 feet long at a speed of six miles per hour. The cars started from a peak and ran downgrade, the momentum carrying the cars up an incline. The passengers got out, the attendants pushed the train over a switch to a higher point on a second track, and the passengers returned. The highest drop was only 30

ENTERTAINMENT—AMUSEMENT PARKS—continued

feet. Thompson obtained a patent on January 20, 1885, on a roller-coasting structure and another patent on December 22, 1885 on a gravity switchback railway. The first high-speed roller coaster was The Cyclone, which opened at Coney Island on June 26, 1927. Its one-and-a-half minute ride hit speeds of up to 60 miles per hour.

3622. Mechanized shooting gallery that was fully automatic was invented in 1890 by Charles Wallace Parker of Abilene, KS, whose first sale was made to Leon Brownie of Houston, TX.

3623. Ferris wheel was invented in 1892 by George Washington Gale Ferris, a railroad and bridge engineer. It was erected on the Midway at the World's Columbian Exposition in Chicago, IL, in 1893. It consisted of 36 cars, each capable of holding 60 passengers. The highest point of the wheel was 264 feet. The total weight of the wheels and cars was 2,100 tons, of the levers and machinery 2,200 tons, and of the passengers per trip 150 tons.

3624. Shoot-the-chutes was built by Captain Paul Boyton and opened on July 6, 1895, at the amusement park at Coney Island, NY (now part of New York City). Each passenger toboggan held 16 persons. The inclined railway was 80 feet high with a 50 percent grade to the surface of a large body of water.

3625. Carousel with a jumping horse mechanism was invented by Charles Wallace Parker of the C.W. Parker Amusement Company, Leavenworth, KS. He started manufacturing it in 1896 and completed it in April 1898 in Abilene, KS. The first one was sold to his brother, William T. Parker. The C.W. Parker Amusement Company also produced a portable carousel, the "Carry-Us-All," manufactured in 1896. It weighed 20 tons and consisted of 16 sections.

3626. Roller coaster with a loop-the-loop was a centrifugal railway invented by Edwin Prescott of Arlington, MA, who received a patent for it on August 16, 1898. It was known as Boyton's Centrifugal Railway and was installed at the amusement park on Coney Island, NY (now part of New York City), in 1900. It had a 75-foot incline and a 20-foot-wide loop.

3627. Skee-ball alley was built in 1914 by the National Skee-Ball Company of Coney Island, New York City, and the first battery was operated by William A. Norwood in April 1914 at the Coney Island amusement park.

ENTERTAINMENT—BEAUTY PAGEANTS

3628. Beauty pageant to be held nationwide was the Miss America Pageant, held on September 7–8, 1921, at a two-day carnival at Keith's Theatre on the Garden Pier, Atlantic City, NJ. The award to the most beautiful contestant was made to Margaret Gorman of Washington, DC, 16 years old. The first Jewish winner of the pageant was Bess Myerson, Miss New York of 1945. The first contestant of Asian descent was Yun Tau, Miss Hawaii of 1948. The first Miss America contestant who was African-American was Cheryl Adrenne Browne of Jamaica, Queens, New York City, a sophomore at Luther College in Decorah, IA, who represented Iowa in the contest at Atlantic City on September 6–12, 1970. Vanessa Williams, who entered the contest as Miss New York, was crowned Miss America on September 17, 1984, becoming the first African-American winner. Williams, born in Millwood, NY, went on to a successful singing and acting career.

3629. Beauty pageant to be shown on television was the Fairest of the Fair contest, held at 7 P.M. on June 22, 1939, on the Wild West Show and Rodeo platform of the New York World's Fair, Flushing, Queens, New York City. The first national contest to be televised was the Miss America Pageant, telecast from Convention Hall, Atlantic City, NJ, on September 11, 1954, by ABC, using six cameras. Bess Myerson and John (Charles) Daly narrated and Bert Parks was master of ceremonies. The winner was Lee Ann Meriwether of San Francisco.

ENTERTAINMENT—DANCING

3630. Dance marathon began on March 31, 1923, at 6:57 P.M., at the Audubon Ballroom, New York City, and continued until April 1 at 9:57 P.M., when the winner, Alma Cummings, concluded 27 hours of continuous dancing to a live band and phonograph music. She danced the fox-trot, one-step, and waltz, and tired out six partners. The first dance marathon to exceed 200 hours took place in St. Louis, MO, later that year. The winner was Bernie Brand of Dallas, TX, who danced continuously for 217 hours, beginning on June 1 and ending on June 10. He outlasted 21 other entrants.

3631. Discotheque was the Whiskey a-Go-Go, opened by club owner Elmer Valentine in Los Angeles, CA, on January 16, 1965. A discotheque is a dance club in which the music is provided by a disk jockey playing recordings, not by a live band. Valentine borrowed the discotheque concept from a club in Paris, which was also called the Whiskey a-Go-Go.

ENTERTAINMENT—GAMBLING

3632. Gambling law for ministers enacted by a colony was passed in 1624 by the Virginia Assembly. It specified that "mynisters shall not give themselves to excesse in drinking or yette spend their tyme idelie by day or by night, playing at dice, cards or any unlawful game."

3633. Gambling law for residents enacted by a colony was passed on March 22, 1630, in Boston, MA: "It is ... ordered that all persons whatsoever that have cards, dice or tables in their houses, shall make away with them before the next court under pain of punishment."

3634. Craps was introduced in New Orleans, LA, about 1813 by Bernard Xavier Philippe de Marigny de Mandeville, who had seen the game played in France as "hazards." As a common nickname for a Creole man was Johnny Crapaud, the game became known as Crapaud's game, which later was abbreviated to "craps." Mandeville lost a fortune at the game. He was obliged to cut a street through his property and to sell lots on both sides to obtain funds to pay his debts. Maps show this street as Craps Street, later changed to Burgundy Street.

3635. Slot machine operated by a pull handle and incorporating three spinning wheels was invented in 1895 by Charles Fey of San Francisco, CA. Early slot machines were installed in drugstores, gas stations, bars, and clubs. Lewis C. Thompson of Washington, DC, was the first person to win more than $1 million from a slot machine. In 1988, after playing just eight quarters, he hit the $1.1 million Quartermania jackpot at the Ramada Express Hotel Casino in Laughlin, NV.

3636. Casino in Las Vegas was the Flamingo Hotel, built in 1946 on a strip of Nevada desert (the future intersection of Las Vegas Boulevard and Flamingo Road) by mobster Benjamin "Bugsy" Siegel. Financing was provided by Murder Incorporated co-founder Meyer Lansky. The property was acquired by the Hilton Hotels Corporation on July 14, 1970. A $140 million expansion begun in 1993 demolished Siegel's former quarters and added such amenities as an outdoor habitat of live Chilean flamingos and African penguins.

3637. Off-track betting operation that was legal was started by New York City on April 8, 1971. Betting parlors were set up in retail store locations throughout the city.

3638. Casino outside the state of Nevada was opened in Atlantic City, NJ, on May 28, 1978, after the state's voters approved legalized casino gambling in 1977. Resorts International opened the casino in a hotel on the Atlantic City boardwalk. The first week's take was $2.6 million.

3639. Slot machine payoff of $275,000 occurred on October 29, 1978, when James Schelich of Washington, MO, lined up five sevens on the bottom row of a dollar progressive jackpot slot machine at the Flamingo Hilton Hotel, Las Vegas, NV.

ENTERTAINMENT—GAMBLING—LOTTERIES

3640. Lottery of importance was held on June 26, 1614, by the Virginia Company. The first Great Prize was 4,500 crowns.

3641. Lottery held by the Continental Congress was held on April 10, 1777, in Philadelphia, PA, for the purpose of raising funds. The lottery was approved on November 1, 1776, and seven managers were appointed to conduct it. Treasury bank notes were awarded as prizes, payable at the end of five years. Funds were obtained by lottery by individual colonies at various times prior to this national lottery.

3642. Federal law hostile to lotteries was the act of Congress of March 2, 1827, which provided "that no postmaster or assistant postmaster shall act as agent for lottery offices or under any color of purchase, or otherwise, send lottery tickets; nor shall any postmaster receive free of postage or frank lottery schemes, circulars or tickets."

3643. Lottery in which the top prize was $1 million was conducted by New York State on October 8, 1970, and was won by George and Genevieve Ashton and their son Glenn, of West Hempstead, NY. The lottery was based on the results of a horse race at the Belmont Track on September 24, 1970. The sale of lottery tickets amounted to $16,724,931.

3644. Daily state lotteries with the same winning daily number occurred on October 3, 1977, when number 92 won top prize in New Jersey's Pick-It Game, which paid $411.50, and in Pennsylvania's lottery, where it paid $250. On October 31, 1979, the New Jersey Pick-It and the Connecticut Daily had the same winning number: 728.

ENTERTAINMENT—HOAXES

3645. Historical hoaxes were perpetrated by the Reverend Sam Peters, Episcopalian rector of Hebron, CT, in the late 1700s. His best-known book, *General history of Connecticut, from its first settlement under George Fenwick to its latest period of amity with Great Britain prior to the Revolution ... by a gentleman of the province,* published in 1781, was filled with deliberate falsehoods that represented the Puritan restrictions on Sabbath activities as even more stringent than they really were. He also described fanciful invasions of giant caterpillars and frogs. Peters's books were widely believed, and became such bestsellers that he was able to live off their royalties for the last two decades of his life.

3646. Quack doctor of note was Dr. Elisha Perkins, born in 1740, who invented Perkins' Patented Metallic Tractor, a contraption of metallic rods intended to "pull" diseases from the body. Among his better-known patients were President George Washington and Supreme Court Chief Justice Oliver Ellsworth. Perkins died in 1799 from yellow fever, four weeks after bringing his Tractor to New York City to cure an epidemic of that disease.

3647. Madstone is supposed to have come from Chicago, IL, in 1804. It was sold by one Dr. Parker to Benjamin Milam of Winona, MS, who used it to perform "miraculous cures." A madstone is a light porous stone of greenish color said to possess the property of drawing poison from the bite of a dog.

3648. Prehistoric hoax was the Cardiff Giant, a sensational stunt perpetrated by George Hull (or Hall), a tobacco farmer from Binghamton, NY. In 1868, Hull arranged for a block of gypsum to be carved in the shape of a 10-foot-tall man. It was buried secretly near Cardiff, NY, on a farm that was owned by William C. Newell, who was in on the hoax. On October 16, 1869, the statue was "discovered" by unsuspecting workmen hired by Newell to dig a well. Hull and Newell spread the rumor that it was a petrified man from biblical times. The figure was exhibited at $1 per viewing to large crowds in Syracuse, Albany, New York City, and Boston before the hoax was exposed by Yale University paleontologist Othniel Charles Marsh, who noted that the statue was "of very recent origin, and a decided humbug." In 1948, the Cardiff Giant was put on display in the Farmers' Museum in Cooperstown, NY.

ENTERTAINMENT—SPECTACLES

3649. Fireworks were used in 1608 by Captain John Smith, who fired a few rockets to entertain the Native Americans living near Jamestown, VA. In 1781, the city of Newport, RI, became the first city to celebrate the Fourth of July with fireworks.

3650. Automaton to be shown in this country was advertised in the *New York Weekly Journal* on July 18, 1743. "To be Seen. At Mr. Pacheco's WareHouse, in Marketfield Street, commonly known by the Name of Petticoat Lane, opposite the Cross Guns, near the Fort. A Curious Musical machine, arriv'd from England, the third Day of May last, which performs several strange and diverting Motions to the Admiration of the Spectators, viz. The Doors fly open of their own accord, and there appear six Ringers in white Shirts all busy pulling the Bell-Ropes, and playing several Tunes, Chimes and Changes: They first appear with black Caps and black Beards, at one Corner there is a Barbers Shop and a Barbers Pole hung out, and at the Shop Door stands the Barber's Boy, who, at the Word of Command, gives three Knocks at his Master's Door, out comes the Barber with his Rasor and Baton to shave the Ringers, then the Doors shut themselves whilst the Barber is Shaving them, then the Doors open themselves." Exhibitions were held at 4 P.M. and 7 P.M., admission one shilling one pence.

3651. Saint Patrick's Day parade was held in New York City on March 17, 1762, by the city's Irish population.

3652. Horseriding exhibition was given by John Sharp in 1771. He rode two horses at a time at full speed, standing on the saddles. He also rode three horses, standing with one foot on each of the outside horses. He gave exhibitions in Boston and Salem, MA, and other cities.

3653. Dwarf exhibited as a theatrical attraction was a man, 53 years of age and 22 inches high, who was shown at the house of Widow Bignall, next door to King's Head Tavern, a little above Mr. Hancock's wharf in Boston, MA. Admission was one shilling. His appearance was advertised in the *Massachusetts Spy* on August 22, 1771.

3654. Gaslights for display were introduced in Philadelphia, PA, in August 1796. The inflammable gas was manufactured by Michael Ambroise and Company on Mulberry Street, Philadelphia, between Eighth and Ninth streets. The light showed "a grand fire-work by means of light composed of inflammable air," arranged so as to form an Italian parterre and Masonic figures and emblems. The jets of light were made to issue from orifices in pipes bent into the requisite shapes. The gas was not used for illuminating purposes.

3655. Magician of note was Richard Potter, who was said to have demonstrated "upward of one hundred curious but mysterious experiments with cards, eggs, money, etc." He was also a ventriloquist and performed at the Columbian Museum, Boston, MA, in November 1811.

3656. Sword swallower was Senaa Samma, "an Indian juggler from Madras and late from London," who performed at St. John's Hall, New York City, on November 11, 1817. Admission was $1, children half price. On November 25, 1817, Samma swallowed "a sword manufactured by Mr. William Pyle of New York as a substitute for the one lately stolen from him by some villain."

3657. Tightrope performer who was a woman was Madame Adolphe of Paris, who, accompanied by Monsieur Godau, appeared on June 1, 1819, at the Anthony Street Theatre, New York City.

3658. Giant exhibited as a theatrical attraction was Patrick Magee, "just arrived from Ireland," who went on exhibition on October 6, 1825, at 13 Park, Park Exchange, New York City, from 7 A.M. until 10 P.M. A charge of 25 cents was made to see the giant, "conspicuous for the masculine beauty of his form and his surprising strength."

3659. Parade held by a mystic society was held by the Cowbellian de Rakian Society, organized on December 31, 1830, in Mobile, AL. It started as an impromptu raid on a hardware store staged by a score of young bloods, who were led, according to tradition, by Michael Krafft. The peculiar feature of this society and those which followed later was that absolute secrecy was maintained about their members, who never appeared in public except in costume and mask. Parades by the mystic societies were held annually in Mobile on New Year's Eve until 1867, when the city switched to daylight parades held on Mardi Gras (Shrove Tuesday), the day initiating the penitential Christian season of Lent.

3660. Flea circus was an "Extraordinary Exhibition of the Industrious Fleas" at 187 Broadway, New York City, which opened on January 1835. Admission was 50 cents and performances were given from 11 A.M. to 3 P.M. and from 5 P.M. to 9 P.M. A cold spell forced the exhibit to close to enable the exhibitor "to fill up the vacancies that grim death had made." It was reopened on January 20, 1835, for one week.

3661. Tattooed man exhibited as a theatrical attraction was James F. O'Connell, whose appearance at the Franklin Theatre, Chatham Square, New York City, on October 21, 1849, was advertised as follows in the *New York Herald:* "The manager has at an enormous expense engaged Mr. J.F. O'Connell, the wonderful 'Tattooed Man' who will go through a variety of performances peculiar to himself, and perfectly original."

3662. Parade with float tableaux was held in Mobile, AL, on the evening of Mardi Gras day, February 24, 1868. The Order of Myths produced the first pageant, followed the next day by the Infant Mystics and the Knights of Revelry. These groups were among the original mystic societies of Mobile.

3663. Human cannonball was an American named Eddie Rivers, who in 1871 was fired from a cannon at the Royal Cremorne Music Hall in London. Rivers used the stage name "Lulu."

3664. X-ray machine exhibited in the United States was shown on January 18, 1896, at the Casino Chambers, New York City. Viewers were charged 25 cents to see the "Parisian sensation."

3665. Parade of automobiles was held at Newport, RI, September 7, 1899. Society leaders of Boston, New York, and Philadelphia participated. Nineteen cars were in the line, profusely decorated with flowers and flags. A prize was awarded to Mrs. Hermann Oelrichs, whose automobile, hung with wisteria, appeared to be drawn by a flock of pure white doves perched on the radiator.

3666. Ticker-tape shower for a celebrity occurred on June 18, 1910, in New York City, when former President Theodore Roosevelt returned on the S.S. *Kaiserin Auguste Victoria* from a 15-month hunting trip in Africa. He was greeted at the Battery by Mayor William Jay Gaynor and a delegation of Rough Riders and escorted up Broadway, where he was met by a shower of ticker tape.

ENTERTAINMENT—SPECTACLES—continued

3667. Railroad mystery excursion was run by the Missouri Pacific Railroad on May 21, 1932. The trip was from St. Louis to Arcadia, MO, a distance of 92 miles, but the passengers were not told in advance where they were going. The round trip fare was $2.50, which included a barbecue at Arcadia.

3668. Be-In took place on January 17, 1967, in Golden Gate Park, San Francisco, CA, where as many as 20,000 hippies gathered to make music, dance, and use recreational drugs.

3669. Tightrope walker to span two sky-scrapers was Philippe Petit of Nemours, France, who walked across a tightrope at a height of 1,350 feet between the two towers of the World Trade Center, New York City, on August 7, 1974, at 7:15 A.M. As he arrived at the second tower, he was taken into custody by the police. His sentence was suspended on condition that he give a public demonstration of his skill under controlled conditions in Central Park, New York City.

3670. Parade in which the marching music was supplied by transistor radios was held from 11 A.M. to 12 noon on July 4, 1977, at Streamwood, IL. The marchers carried portable transistor radios that were all tuned to receive music broadcast by radio station WRMN, Elgin, IL. The parade was witnessed by thousands and telecast over channel 2 and channel 5.

3671. Human chain across the United States was attempted on May 21, 1986, when millions of Americans participated in Hands Across America, a fund-raising event sponsored by a consortium of charities and corporations. The chain of hand-holders, which had some gaps, stretched from Battery Park in New York City to Long Beach, CA, a distance of 4,150 miles.

ENTERTAINMENT—SPECTACLES—CIRCUSES

3672. Circus was owned by John Bill Ricketts and known as Ricketts' Circus. A building was erected especially for his use at 12th and Market streets, Philadelphia, PA, where he gave exhibitions as early as 1792. President George Washington attended Ricketts' Circus on April 22, 1793. Ricketts erected a larger building called the Art Pantheon and Amphitheatre, which was opened to the public October 19, 1795. In 1797 he built an Amphitheatre on Greenwich Street in New York City and exhibited in other towns as far north as Albany, NY.

3673. Circus to feature a car as an attraction was Wheeler, Hatch and Hitchcock's Circus and Royal Hippodrome, which toured New York, Massachusetts, Connecticut, and Rhode Island in 1864. It advertised the car as a "tremendous novelty, never seen before, of an ordinary road carriage driven over the common high-ways without the aid of horses or other draught animals, being beyond doubt the most simple, useful and ingenious piece of mechanism ever put into practical use."

3674. Radio broadcast from a circus was made from the menagerie of the Ringling Brothers Barnum and Bailey circus in the basement of Madison Square Garden, New York City, on April 10, 1924. Lew Graham was the circus announcer. The broadcast was transmitted from station WJZ, Aeolian Hall, New York City, to station WGY, Schenectady, NY. The roar of the animals at feeding time and the music of the calliope were broadcast.

3675. Circus to be shown on television was the Ringling Brothers Barnum and Bailey circus, which gave a three-hour show on April 25, 1940, at Madison Square Garden, New York City. It was televised by station W2XBS, New York City, using two cameras.

ENTERTAINMENT—SPECTACLES—DAREDEVILS

3676. Daredevil jumper of note was Sam Patch, a former sailor and mill hand who joined the national jumping craze of the early 19th century. Patch began his public career with a dive from a 90-foot-high bridge spanning the Passaic River in Passaic, NJ, where he worked in the Hamilton Mills. He followed that up with a jump partway down Niagara Falls. A well-publicized jump off the 125-foot-high Genesee Falls in Genesee, NY, in November 1829 turned out to be his last. His body was recovered from Lake Ontario the following spring.

3677. Daredevil to cross Niagara Falls on a tightrope was Jean François Gravelet, a Frenchman better known by his professional name, Émile Blondin, whose first exhibition took place on June 30, 1859, before a crowd of 5,000 people. Wearing pink tights and a spangled tunic of yellow silk, he crossed a cable about two inches in diameter and 1,100 feet long, strung below the suspension bridge with a series of parallel ropes alongside. In 1859 and 1860 Blondin gave a series of "ascensions." They included carrying a man on his back across the cable, trundling a loaded wheelbarrow across, walking across in a sack, and pushing a wheelbarrow while dressed as an ape. He usually carried a long pole that helped him to balance himself and that could also serve as a guard in case he fell, since it would be supported by the parallel ropes and thus prevent him from falling into the river.

3678. Daredevil to jump off the Brooklyn Bridge and survive may have been Stephen Brodie, a 23-year-old unemployed Irish immigrant. On July 23, 1886, Brodie was pulled from the East River, claiming that he had just jumped from the bridge. Although Brodie was unable to produce any objective witnesses to say he had performed the feat—he was accused of having his friends drop a dummy from the bridge while he slipped unnoticed into the water from the riverbank—he became famous anyway. In 1894, he starred in a play called *On the Bowery,* during which he rescued the heroine by jumping off a bridge built onstage.

3679. Daredevil to go over Niagara Falls in a barrel was Anna Edson Taylor, who went over the Horseshoe Falls on the Canadian side on October 24, 1901, in a barrel 4.5 feet high and 3 feet in diameter. A leather harness and cushions were placed inside the barrel to protect her.

3680. Stuntman was Frederick Rodman Law, a steeplejack, who staged a parachute jump from the Statue of Liberty on Bedloe Island in New York Harbor on February 2, 1912, for Pathé News. On April 14, 1912, he jumped from the Brooklyn Bridge, and on November 12, 1912, from a dynamited balloon into the Hudson River.

3681. Daredevil to go over Niagara Falls in a rubber ball was Jean Lussier, who made the descent on July 4, 1928, in a ball of his own construction weighing 750 pounds and costing $1,485. It was equipped with oxygen tanks and reinforced with cushions. It was set adrift from a launch and went over the Horseshoe Falls.

3682. Motorcycle jump across a river canyon was accomplished by stunt rider Robert Craig "Evel" Knievel, who jumped the Snake River Canyon in Twin Falls, ID, on September 8, 1974.

ENTERTAINMENT—SPECTACLES— SHOWS

3683. Puppet show to which admission was charged was held on February 12, 1738, in Mr. Holt's room at Broad and Pearl streets, New York City. The show was entitled *The Adventures of Harlequin and Scaramouche, or The Spaniard Trick'd.* Admission was five shillings. The room was 39 feet long, 19 feet wide, and nine feet high.

3684. Panorama show was *Jerusalem,* exhibited in 1790 at Lawrence Hyer's Tavern, 62 Chatham Street, New York City, "between the Gaol and the Tea Water Pump." It was open from 10 in the morning until 10 at night. According to advertisements in the *Daily Advertiser,* the sight was "most brilliant by candlelight."

3685. Minstrel show troupe was the Virginia Minstrels, organized by Daniel Decatur Emmett, composer of "Dixie." In 1843 they gave performances at the Chatham Theatre, New York City, which was located on Chatham Street between Roosevelt and James streets, and at the Bowery Amphitheatre. Frank Brower played the bones, Richard Pelham the tambourine, Daniel Emmett the violin, and William Whitlock the banjo. They wore white trousers, striped calico shirts, and long blue calico swallowtail coats, and they blackened their faces to give themselves the appearance of African-Americans. Their popular songs included "Old Dan Tucker," "Happy Uncle Tom," and "The Raccoon Hunt."

3686. Peep show machine was patented by Samuel D. Goodale of Cincinnati, OH, who obtained a patent on February 5, 1861, on a stereoscope machine. It was called the Mutoscope and was operated by hand. Pictures were placed on leaves fastened by one edge to an axis in such a way that they stood out like spokes. As the shaft revolved, different images were seen in motion.

3687. Burlesque show of importance was *The Black Crook,* an original magical and spectacular drama in four acts by Charles M. Barras, with the scene laid in and around the Hartz Mountains about the year 1600. The musical show was produced by Barras and William Wheatley and featured 100 scantily clad young women playing a troupe of dancing fairies. It opened on September 12, 1866, at Niblo's Garden, New York City, and ran for an unprecedented 16 months, closing on January 4, 1868, after playing 475 performances and grossing $1.3 million.

3688. Vaudeville show took place in 1883 in Boston, MA, where Benjamin Franklin Keith opened a small museum next to the old Adams House in Washington Street which he called the "Gaiety Museum." One of its principal attractions was "Baby Alice," a midget.

ENTERTAINMENT—SPECTACLES—SHOWS—*continued*

3689. Wild West Show was put together by William Frederick Cody, more familiarly known as "Buffalo Bill," and presented in North Platte, NE, as part of a Fourth of July celebration in 1883. The following year, Cody commercialized the show and took it on tour, starting in Omaha. Exhibitions and contests celebrating frontier life in the West were a frequent feature of local fairs and holidays before the Wild West Show was developed.

3690. Rodeo for roping and tying steers was held on July 4, 1888, at the racetrack at Prescott, AZ, and was won by Juan Leivas. This rodeo developed into an annual competition. Ranchhands working on cattle ranches often took part in impromptu tests of working skills.

3691. Peep show using film in a vending machine or cabinet was exhibited by Andrew M. Holland of the Holland Brothers at 1155 Broadway, New York City, on April 14, 1894. The machine was invented by Thomas Alva Edison, who utilized film prepared by George Eastman. The films were made in the Edison laboratories. The pictures were viewed directly, rather than reflected, and were visible to only one person at a time. Annie Oakley, Sandow, Buffalo Bill, Ruth St. Denis, and other celebrities were shown.

3692. Magic lantern feature show was *Miss Jerry,* previewed October 9, 1894, at the Carbon Studio, New York City. Alexander Black was the author, scenario writer, director, camera man, and titler. The leads were taken by Blanche Bayliss, who played Jerry, William Courtenay as the hero, and Ernest Hastings as the villain. Slides were shown at the rate of five a second.

ENTERTAINMENT—THEATERS

3693. Theater was built in 1718 by William Levingston at Williamsburg, VA. He acquired the lots from the Trustees of Williamsburg on November 5, 1716 and began making plans for the construction of a playhouse where comedies, drolls, and stage plays would be presented. He contracted with Charles Stagg, a dancing master, and Mary Stagg, his wife, to put on plays and teach acting. The finished theater was 86.5 feet long and 30 feet wide. Governor Alexander Spotswood entertained a number of guests at the theater in 1718.

3694. Publicist for a theater company was Robert Upton, who left London in October 1750 for New York City to publicize an upcoming tour by the Hallam Company. Instead, he joined the theater company of Walter Murray and Thomas Kean, which was performing in New York City.

3695. Theater building of brick construction was the Southwark Theatre, on South Street above 4th, Philadelphia, PA, built by David Douglass. It opened on November 21, 1766, with Lewis Hallam of the American Company in *The Gamester.* The walls and the first story were built of brick. The building was used as a hospital in the Revolutionary War and was partly destroyed by fire on May 9, 1821.

3696. Showboat theater was a keel boat converted by Noah Miller Ludlow in 1817 at a cost of $200. It left Nashville, TN, on October 20, 1817, to travel on the Cumberland, Ohio, and Mississippi rivers. The first plays presented were David Garrick's *The Honeymoon* and *The Lying Valet,* which were performed on November 15, 1817. The first showboat of importance was *The Floating Palace,* a flat scow with a superstructure, which plied the Mississippi River in 1852. It was operated by Spalding and Rogers. The dress circle had 1,100 cane-bottom chairs, the family circle 500 cushioned settees, and the gallery 900 seats. It was heated by steam.

3697. Theater lighted by gas was the Chatham Garden and Theatre, New York City. Gas lighting had been used previously in theaters, but as a novelty rather than as illumination. The *New York Post and Mirror* on May 9, 1825, stated that the whole theater was lighted by gas, "which sheds a clear soft light over the audience and stage." The illumination "elicited the loudest plaudits from all present."

3698. Theater ticket scalpers began plying their trade in New York City prior to the first appearance of the Swedish singer and celebrity Jenny Lind at Castle Garden on September 11, 1850. The seats were auctioned by Phineas Taylor Barnum, who charged 25 cents admission to the auction. The first ticket was sold to John Nicholas Genin for $225. One thousand tickets sold for a total of $10,141. Some ticket holders resold their tickets at high premiums. Gross receipts for the performance were $17,864. Jenny Lind donated her share of the gross to New York charities.

3699. Chinese theater was the theater of "Celestial John," on Telegraph Hill, fronting Dupont Street, San Francisco, CA, which opened on December 23, 1852. It consisted of one vast pit or parquet and had a seating capacity of 1,400. There were no tiers of boxes. No scenery was used.

3700. Theater ticket agency was an office at Macoy and Herwig, Stationers, 112–114 Broadway, New York City, which was open from 8 A.M. to 4 P.M. The agency advertised in the *New York Times* on September 9, 1866, that patrons could obtain reserved seats for theaters in New York and Brooklyn, and choice seats and tickets at all times and in advance, when required.

3701. Theater lighted by electricity was the Bijou Theatre, 545 Washington Street, Boston, MA, which was lighted by an Edison isolated plant on December 11, 1882. Six hundred and fifty lamps were used. The proscenium was surrounded by 192 lights, and 140 were used in the borders. The first performance in the theater was Gilbert and Sullivan's *Iolanthe,* presented by Colliers' Standard Opera Company.

3702. Theater to employ women as ushers was the Third Avenue Theatre, New York City, which opened on August 30, 1884, with *49,* starring Mr. and Mrs. McKee Rankin. The young women wore white caps and aprons.

3703. Theater operated by a city was the Academy of Music of Northampton, MA, which was accepted by the City of Northampton as a gift from Edward Hutchinson Robbins Lyman on February 9, 1893. Visiting companies and traveling troupes performed there. The first stock company was that of Jessie Bonstelle and Bertram Harrison, who played from 1912 to 1917.

3704. Theater to show movies was the Electric Theater, 262 South Main Street, Los Angeles, CA, a circus front tent-show called a "black top," which was opened on April 2, 1902, by Thomas Lincoln Tally. Among the first pictures shown were *The Capture of the Biddle Brothers* and *New York in a Blizzard.* The show lasted about one hour; the admission was 10 cents.

3705. Movie theater was the Nickelodeon, which was opened on June 19, 1905, by Harry Davis in an empty store at 433–435 Smithfield Street, Pittsburgh, PA. It had 96 seats taken from Davis's other theaters. Among the first films shown were *Poor But Honest* and *The Baffled Burglar.* A profit of over $1,000 was netted the first week. John Paul Harris was general manager and Isaac Lisbon manager.

3706. Theater built and named for a living actress was the Ethel Barrymore Theatre, New York City, which opened on December 20, 1928, with a performance of *The Kingdom of God,* a translation of a Spanish play by Gregorio Martinez Sierra entitled *Reino de Dios.* Barrymore played Sister Gracia, the lead.

3707. Newsreel theater was the Embassy, on Broadway and 46th Street, New York City, which opened on November 2, 1929.

3708. Theater designed and built for the rear projection of movies was the Trans-Lux Theatre at 58th Street and Madison Avenue, New York City, which was opened on March 14, 1931. The first rear-projection screen of theater size had been installed on March 11, 1927, for the opening night of the Roxy Theatre, New York City. It was a Trans-Lux screen 18 by 22 feet which at first was used only for silhouette work, because the lens of the projector was imperfect.

3709. Drive-in movie theater was opened on June 6, 1933, on a 10-acre plot on Admiral Wilson Boulevard, Camden, NJ, by Richard Milton Hollingshead, Jr., and Willis Warren Smith of Riverton, NJ. Two shows were presented nightly on a screen 40 by 50 feet. Nine rows of inclined planes with aisles 45 feet deep accommodated 500 cars. The sound equipment was supplied by the RCA-Victor Company, Camden, NJ.

3710. Theater operated as part of a state school system was the Washington State Theatre, authorized on April 15, 1936, and sponsored by the state Department of Public Instruction in connection with the Seattle Repertory Playhouse, Seattle, WA. The first play presented was William Shakespeare's *The Comedy of Errors,* produced on November 2, 1936. Traveling troupes from the theater visited schools, performing Shakespearian, classic, and significant modern plays. The first director of the theater was Burton Wakeley James.

ENVIRONMENT

3711. Environmental protection law enacted by a state in connection with advertising was passed by New York on March 28, 1865, amending an 1853 law entitled "an act for the more effectual prevention of wanton and malicious mischief and to prevent the defacement of natural scenery." The amendment declared that painting and printing upon stones, rocks, or trees and the defacement of natural scenery in certain localities constituted a misdemeanor punishable by a fine not exceeding $250, or six months' imprisonment, or both.

ENVIRONMENT—*continued*

3712. Conservationist of note was the naturalist John Muir, born in 1838 in Scotland. Muir came to the United States in 1849 and spent many years traveling through the interior as a botanist. He founded the Sierra Club and campaigned successfully for the establishment of protected national parks and forests, including Yosemite National Park in California, which was formed by act of Congress in 1890. Muir Woods National Monument in California and Alaska's Muir Glacier were named for him.

3713. Garbage incinerator that was successful was established in 1897 in St. Louis, MO, by a private contractor who had a contract with the city for the collection and disposal of garbage. The Merz process was used. The water was drained off, cans, bottles, and rags were taken out, and grease was extracted by means of naphtha.

3714. Public service symbol of the federal government was Smokey Bear. During World War II, the Forest Service sought advertising help to educate the public about the danger of forest fires. On August 9, 1944, Albert Staehle, an illustrator of animals, came up with the image of a fire-fighting bear. The slogan "Only you can prevent forest fires" was coined by a Los Angeles ad agency in 1947. Smokey Bear appeared on posters and comic books distributed to schoolchildren and on television commercials. In 1950, a bear cub rescued from a forest fire in New Mexico was dubbed "Smokey Bear." He was exhibited in the National Zoo in Washington, DC, and died in 1976.

3715. Deaths from smog occurred in October 1947 in Donora, PA. A thermal inversion trapped pollutants over the heavily industrialized town, which is set in a natural basin. The inversion ended four days later, leaving 20 people dead and 6,000 in need of medical treatment.

3716. Water pollution law enacted by Congress was the Water Pollution Control Act, which took effect on June 30, 1948. It provided funds for sewage treatment systems and pollution research and empowered the Justice Department to file suit against polluters.

3717. Smog chamber for air pollution research built by an industrial organization was placed in operation in July 1962 by General Motors Research Laboratories, Warren, MI. The cylindrical chamber contained 300 cubic feet of space irradiated by 247 fluorescent lamps that simulated noonday sunlight.

3718. Air pollution law of importance enacted by Congress was the Clean Air Act of 1963, signed into law on December 17, 1963. It authorized $93 million in matching grants for state-funded air pollution prevention and control programs. The Clean Air Act of 1970, signed into law on December 31, 1970, was the first to set national standards for air polluting emissions from motor vehicles.

3719. Endangered species list issued by the federal government was issued by the Department of the Interior in 1966. It listed 78 species of rare and endangered plants, reptiles, birds, and mammals.

3720. Litter law enacted by a state affecting containers of soft drinks and beer was enacted by Oregon on July 2, 1971. The bill outlawed pull-tab cans and nonreturnable bottles.

3721. Noise-control law enacted by a state was New Jersey's Noise Control Act of 1971, signed on January 24, 1972, by Governor William Thomas Cahill. The act empowered the state Department of Environmental Protection to promulgate codes, rules, and regulations to lessen noise pollution, created a Noise Control Council, and made a $100,000 appropriation.

ENVIRONMENT—FORESTS

3722. Forestry law enacted by a colony was the act of March 29, 1626, passed by the Plymouth Colony, which required the approval of the governor and the council to sell or transport lumber out of the colony.

3723. Community forest was established in 1710 in Newington, NH. An area of 110 acres of pine trees was set aside as a "town forest."

3724. Forest reserve established by a state was the New York State Forest Preserve, designated on May 15, 1885. Legislation prohibiting the sale of state lands in certain counties in the Adirondack Mountains area was passed on February 6, 1883. This forest reserve functioned as a state park, where logging and other commercial forms of exploitation were prohibited.

3725. Forest management on a professional scale was begun in 1891 in Asheville, NC, on the Biltmore estate of George Washington Vanderbilt.

3726. Forest planting by the federal government was begun in 1891 in the sand hills of Nebraska in cooperation with private individuals. A small plantation of jack and Norway pines was established four miles west of Swan, NE, for the purpose of forming shelter belts to hold the sand in place. The land was acquired under authority of the act of March 3, 1891, "an act to repeal timber culture laws, and for other purposes."

3727. National forest was the Shoshone National Forest in Wyoming, established by President Benjamin Harrison on March 30, 1891, by presidential proclamation.

3728. National forest reserve was the Yellowstone Park Timberland Reserve, which was so designated by an act of Congress passed on March 30, 1891, and signed by President Benjamin Harrison. It was placed under the administration of the Land Office of the Department of the Interior.

3729. Forest fire lookout tower was a log cabin with a flat roof erected by the M.G. Shaw Lumber Company, Greenville, ME, on Squaw Mountain, southwest of Moosehead Lake. The first watchman was William Hilton of Bangor, ME, whose service started on June 10, 1905.

3730. Forest Service aerial patrol was established by the Department of Agriculture on June 1, 1919. Two patrols a day were operated out of March Field, Riverside, CA. Five routes were covered, for each of which there was one airplane. The expense was borne mainly by the Army. From June 1 to October 30, the airplanes flew 2,457 hours and covered 202,009 miles. The patrol was discontinued on October 31, 1919.

3731. Dutch elm disease breakout was observed in 1930 in Cleveland and Cincinnati, OH, where it began killing American elm trees, *Ulmus americanus.* The blight, caused by the Asiatic fungus *Ceratocystis ulmi,* was imported to the United States in elm logs shipped from Europe. It spread rapidly, decimating the North American elm population and changing the appearance of many American cities.

3732. Forest fire drenched by artificial rain produced by seeding cumulus clouds with dry ice was attacked on October 29, 1947, at Concord, NH. Seeders from the General Electric Company, Schenectady, NY, flew over the burning area in "rain-making" planes and caused rain to fall. The experiment was Project Cirrus, a joint weather research program of the Army Signal Corps and the Office of Naval Research. General rain caused by natural conditions followed, so it was impossible to determine the extent of artificial rainfall.

ENVIRONMENT—PARKS

3733. Parkland purchased by a city was Elm Park, containing 27 acres, which was sold to Worcester, MA, on March 17 and March 20, 1854, by Levi Lincoln and John Hammond.

3734. State park was the Yosemite Valley park in California, an area embracing the valley itself and the Mariposa Grove of Big Trees some miles south of it. It was granted to the state of California by act of Congress of June 30, 1864, but actual control of the area and its development were delayed some 10 years by the adverse claims of settlers in the area. The Yosemite National Park was created in 1890, and in 1905 the California State Legislature passed an act of retrocession by which the valley and grove were returned to the federal government to be included in the national park.

3735. National park was the Yellowstone National Park in Wyoming, authorized on March 1, 1872, by "an act to set aside a certain tract of land (2,142,720 acres) lying near the headwaters of the Yellowstone River as a public park." The first superintendent was Nathaniel Pitt Langford. The first ranger, hired in 1880, was Harry Yount, a Civil War veteran. Additional grants of land to Yellowstone Park were later made in Wyoming, Montana, and Idaho. Hot Springs National Park in Arkansas, consisting of 911 acres with 46 hot springs, was established as a reservation by an act of Congress on April 20, 1832, but was not designated as a national park until March 4, 1921.

3736. National park east of the Mississippi River and the first located on an ocean is the Acadia National Park, on the island of Mount Desert about a mile south of Bar Harbor, ME. It was established by President Woodrow Wilson on July 8, 1916, as the Sieur de Monts National Monument and became the Lafayette National Park on February 26, 1919. The name was changed on January 19, 1929, to Acadia National Park. It contains 27,871 acres.

3737. National park to contain an active volcano was the Lassen Volcanic National Park in the Sierra Nevada in California, a tract of 104,526 acres. It was established by an act of Congress approved August 9, 1916. Lassen Peak, 10,457 feet high, at the southern end of the Cascade mountain range, erupted in 1914–16 and is the only active volcano in the 48 contiguous states.

ENVIRONMENT—PARKS—*continued*

3738. National seashore was Cape Hatteras National Seashore, an area of 30,319 acres along the coast of North Carolina. Set aside by Congress in 1937, it was one of the longest stretches of undeveloped shoreline on the Atlantic seaboard.

3739. Undersea park established by the federal government was the Key Largo Coral Reef Preserve, an area 21 miles long and 3.5 miles wide in the Atlantic Ocean off Key Largo, FL, which was established on March 15, 1960, by presidential proclamation of President Dwight David Eisenhower. This wildlife refuge contains 40 of the 52 known coral species. Previously, it had been the John Pennekamp Coral Reef State Park, the title to which had been obtained on December 3, 1959, by the Florida Board of Parks and Historic Monuments.

ENVIRONMENT—WILDLIFE

3740. Furs exported were shipped to England on the S.S. *Fortune* on December 13, 1621, under the charge of Robert Cushman, one of the Plymouth colonists. The cargo, valued at $2,450, consisted of furs, sassafras, clapboards, and wainscot. The boat was captured by the French and the cargo seized.

3741. Hunting law enacted by a colony was passed on March 24, 1629, by Virginia and provided that "no ... hides or skins whatever be sent or carried out of this colony upon forfeiture of thrice the value, whereof the half to the informer and the other half to public use."

3742. Fish protection law enacted by a city was an act for "preserving fish in fresh water ponds," enacted on May 28, 1734, by New York City. Fishing by hoop-net, draw-net, purse-net, catching-net, cod-net, bley-net or with any other engine, machine, arts, or ways and means whatsoever, other than by angling with angle-rod, hook, and line, was subject to a fine of 20 shillings.

3743. Bird refuge established by a state was established at Lake Merritt, Oakland, CA, by authority of a law enacted on February 14, 1872.

3744. Game warden to be paid a salary was William Alden Smith of Grand Rapids, MI, appointed for a four-year term at $1,200 annually plus expenses under a state law approved March 15, 1887, "an act to provide for the appointment of a game and fish warden and to prescribe his powers and duties to enforce the statutes of this state for the preservation of

moose, wapiti, deer, birds and fish." Wisconsin approved a similar law on April 12, 1887, authorizing appointment of four game wardens for two-year terms at an annual salary of $600 with a maximum of $250 for expenses.

3745. Bird reservation established by the federal government was established by executive order of President Theodore Roosevelt on March 14, 1903, at Pelican Island, situated in the Indian River near Sebastian, FL. Its goal was to protect a nesting colony of pelicans and herons. This wildlife refuge was enlarged in 1909 to include adjacent mangrove islands and swamps.

3746. Extinction by humans of a native American animal in modern times was that of the the American passenger pigeon *(Ectopistes migratorius)*. Until the mid-1800s the most numerous bird on earth, the passenger pigeon was hunted extensively for meat and vanished from the wild by 1890. The last known specimen, named Martha, died on September 1, 1914, in the Cincinnati Zoo, Cincinnati, OH.

3747. Bird protection international treaty was the Migratory Bird Treaty for the protection of migratory birds in the United States and Canada, signed on August 16, 1916, by the United States and Great Britain at Washington, DC. It was signed by President Woodrow Wilson on September 1, 1916, ratified by Great Britain on October 20, and proclaimed on December 8.

3748. Raptor sanctuary was Hawk Mountain Sanctuary, founded in 1934 on the Kittatinny Ridge near Harrisburg, PA. It was the first bird sanctuary in the world to protect migrating hawks and eagles.

3749. Game preserve appropriation by the federal government to assist state wildlife restoration projects was passed on September 2, 1937. A million dollars was appropriated on June 16, 1938. The federal government paid 75 percent of the costs of such projects and the state 25 percent. The first project was the Utah Fish and Game Commission's plan to stabilize the water levels on some 2,000 acres of land bordering Great Salt Lake, approved on July 23, 1938, by the Fish and Wildlife Service.

3750. Wolf to be reintroduced into the wild was the red wolf *(Canis rufus)*, believed to be the only species of wolf that evolved completely in North America. Once common in the southwestern United States, the red wolf had been extinct in the wild since the 1970s. The only surviving individuals were maintained in captive breeding programs. In 1987, four breeding pairs and their pups were released in the Alligator River National Wildlife Refuge, NC, by the Fish and Wildlife Service.

F

FINANCE

3751. Financial "corner" took place in New Amsterdam (the future New York City) in 1666. Frederick Phillipse cornered the market in wampum by creating a shortage. He buried several hogsheads of it in order to force those who had to use this medium of exchange to purchase wampum from him at a higher price.

3752. Year in which the federal budget exceeded $1 trillion was fiscal year 1988. The budget submitted to Congress on January 5, 1987, by President Ronald Wilson Reagan totaled $1,024.3 billion, or $1.024 trillion, which included revenues of $916.6 billion and a projected deficit of $107.8 billion.

FINANCE—ACCOUNTING

3753. Accounting society was the Institute of Accountants and Bookkeepers, organized on July 28, 1882, in New York City.

3754. Accounting society (national) was the American Association of Public Accountants, formed in New York City on December 22, 1886. The first president was James Yalden.

3755. Certified public accountant was Frank Broaker of New York City, who received certificate No. 1 on December 1, 1896, from the New York State Board of Certified Public Accountant Examiners.

3756. Accounting society (state) was the New York State Society of Certified Public Accountants, which was organized in New York City on March 30, 1897, following the passage of the New York State Certified Public Account Law of April 17, 1896. Charles Waldo Haskins, president of the state's CPA board of examiners, was the first president.

FINANCE—BANKING

3757. Bank chartered by Congress was the Bank of North America in Philadelphia, PA, which was organized on November 1, 1781. It began business on January 7, 1782, with a total capital of $400,000, of which the government subscribed $250,000. Thomas Willing was elected president, and Tench Francis cashier. Later the bank entered the National Banking System.

3758. Bank of the United States was sponsored by the Federalist Party and was chartered in Philadelphia, PA, on February 25, 1791, by "an act to incorporate the subscribers to the Bank of the United States." Although the charter made no specific provision for the deposit of government funds, the secretary of the treasury, Alexander Hamilton, used the bank as a fiscal agent. The charter expired in 1811 and was not renewed by Congress because of the opposition of the Democratic-Republicans. The closing of the bank was partly responsible for the panic of 1814. The second Bank of the United States was authorized on April 10, 1816, and was opened on January 7, 1817. It ceased functioning as a national institution in March 1836.

3759. Savings bank was the Bank for Savings in the City of New York, which was conceived on November 29, 1816, but for which the charter was not granted until March 26, 1819. The bank opened for business on July 3, 1819. The deposits on the first day, received from 80 depositors, amounted to $2,807. The statement for the first six months showed a loss of $27 suffered as a result of the bank's accepting counterfeit money and a short change loss of $23.92.

3760. Savings bank to receive money on deposit was the Philadelphia Saving Fund Society, Philadelphia, PA, which opened for business on December 2, 1816, in the office of George Billington, the secretary-treasurer, on the west side of Sixth Street. Billington received a salary of $250 a year. The affairs of the bank were conducted by 12 managers. Andrew Bayard was the first president. The bank was chartered February 25, 1819.

3761. Trust company permitted to do a trust business was the Farmer's Fire Insurance and Loan Company of New York City, which was incorporated on February 28, 1822. The first company to use "Trust Company" as part of its title was the New York Life Insurance and Trust Company of New York City, which was

FINANCE—BANKING—*continued*

chartered on March 9, 1830, with an authorized capital of $1 million. The first company organized to do a trust business exclusively was the United States Trust Company of New York, which was incorporated on April 12, 1853.

3762. Bank deposit insurance law enacted by a state was the Safety Fund Banking Law of New York, "an act to create a fund for the benefit of the creditors of certain monied corporations," enacted on April 2, 1829. Banking organizations were assessed one-half of 1 percent of the capital stock, until 3 percent was set aside for a bank fund. Three commissioners, known as Bank Commissioners of the State of New York, were appointed for two-year terms at an annual salary of $1,500. Banks, their officers, and their servants were required to be examined under oath at least once every four months.

3763. Building and loan association was the Oxford Provident Building Association, which was organized on January 3, 1831, in Thomas Sidebotham's Tavern, 4219 Frankford Avenue, Frankford, PA. The organizers were Jesse Castor, secretary, Samuel Pilling, treasurer, and Jeremiah Horrocks. The company was succeeded by the Decatur Building Association. The first loan was $500, made on April 11, 1831, to Comly Rich, a lamplighter from Philadelphia, PA.

3764. Bank clearinghouse was the New York Clearing House, organized on August 23, 1853, by representatives of 38 banks, who met at the Merchants Bank, New York City. The exchange was opened on October 11 at 14 Wall Street. Total clearings the first day exceeded $22 million, and the balances exceeded $1.3 million. Clearings for the year ending September 30, 1854, were $5.7 billion; for the same period, ending in 1980, they were $38 trillion.

3765. National bank under the national banking law of February 25, 1863, an "act to provide a national currency," was the First National Bank of Davenport, IA, later called the Union Savings Bank and Trust Company. Subscription books were opened on May 25, and in three days the capital stock of $100,000 had been subscribed. The bank was opened on June 29. The first president was Austin Corbin. For two days the bank was the only national bank in operation under the new act.

3766. Bank for freed African-American slaves was the Freedman's Savings and Trust Company, for the Negro, chartered by Congress on March 3, 1865. A central bank was established in Washington, DC, with branches in 34 cities. The bank was in operation about eight years, during which time it received deposits amounting to $57 million. The depreciation in security values due to the panic of 1873 caused the trustees to vote to close the bank, the affairs of which were placed in the hands of three commissioners.

3767. National bank to fail was the First National Bank of Attica, NY, placed in receivership on April 14, 1865. The failure was due to injudicious banking and failure of large debtors. The receivership was terminated on January 2, 1867.

3768. Banking association (national) was the American Bankers Association, which was organized on May 24, 1875. The first national convention was held at Saratoga, NY, on July 20–22, 1875, at which time Charles Bingley Hall was elected president. The objects of the association were self-protection against frauds, standardization of rules, and bettering of conditions between the banks and their clients.

3769. Savings group for children to teach them to save their money in a methodical manner was started on March 16, 1885, by Professor John Henry Thiry of Long Island City, NY (now part of Queens, New York City), who established a system of fund collections in schools and a school savings bank.

3770. Banking association (state) was the Texas Bankers' Association, which was organized on July 23, 1885, at Lampasas, TX, with an initial membership of 31. The first president was James Francis Miller.

3771. Bank for African-Americans operated by African-Americans was the savings bank of the Grand Fountain of the United Order of True Reformers, a group founded by William W. Browne, which was incorporated in 1881 in Richmond, VA. The bank was chartered on March 2, 1888, and began operations on April 3, with a paid-up capital of $4,000. The first day's deposits were $1,268.69. The board of directors was elected by the society.

3772. Bank president who was a woman was Maggie Lena Walker, the daughter of an African-American slave, who founded the Saint Luke Penny Savings Bank, Richmond, VA, incorporated on July 28, 1903. It had a paid-in capital of $25,000. The first day's deposits exceeded $8,000. The bank later became the Consolidated Bank and Trust Company.

3773. Credit union was founded by Alphonse Desjardins in Manchester, NH, on December 16, 1908. It was known as "La Caisse Populaire Ste. Marie" and was chartered April 6, 1909. Ninety-nine percent of the depositors were French Canadians.

3774. Credit union law enacted by a state was sponsored by Pierre Jay, the first bank commissioner of Massachusetts, and was passed by the Massachusetts legislature. It was approved on May 21, 1909, by Governor Eben Sumner Draper.

3775. Postal savings bank was authorized by President William Howard Taft on June 25, 1910, when he signed the "act to establish postal savings depositories for depositing savings at interest," introduced by Senator Thomas Henry Carter of Montana on January 26, 1910. Postal savings service was established initially at 48 second-class post offices on January 3, 1911. The service was gradually extended to other post offices. In 11 months, deposits reached a total of $11 million, which was distributed among 2,710 national and state banks. The idea of postal savings had been introduced by Postmaster General John Angel James Creswell in 1871, but no action was taken for years, despite the fact that 80 such bills were introduced into Congress between 1873 and 1910.

3776. Bank to establish a branch in a foreign country was the National City Bank of New York, which opened a branch in Buenos Aires, Argentina, on November 10, 1914. The Federal Reserve Act, approved December 23, 1913, permitted American banks to establish branches abroad.

3777. Federal reserve banks were formally opened on November 16, 1914, inaugurating the federal reserve system. The Federal Reserve Act, approved on December 23, 1913, was an "act to provide for the establishment of Federal Reserve Banks, to furnish an elastic currency ... to establish a more effective supervision of banking in the United States." The 12 regional district banks were under the supervision of a seven-member Board of Governors.

3778. Joint stock land bank chartered was the Iowa Joint Stock Land Bank of Sioux City, IA. It was chartered on April 24, 1917, and authorized to do business in the states of Iowa and South Dakota. The charter was granted under the Federal Farm Loan Act of July 17, 1916.

3779. Bank wholly owned and operated by a state was the Bank of North Dakota, Bismarck, ND, established by special referendum election on June 26, 1919, under jurisdiction of the federal Industrial Commission, and opened on July 28. It was the only legal depository of all state funds and those of state institutions.

3780. Bank with resources exceeding $1 billion was the National City Bank (later Citibank), New York City, whose assets on November 17, 1919, were $1,027,938,114.31.

3781. Savings bank with a deposit of half a billion dollars was the Bowery Savings Bank of New York, which, according to its statement of March 31, 1932, had more than $502 million, owned by 378,000 depositors.

3782. Bank deposit insurance law enacted by Congress was the Glass-Steagall Act, known as the Banking Act of 1933, which was passed by Congress on June 16, 1933, "to provide for the safer and more effective use of the assets of banks, to regulate interbank control, and to prevent the undue diversion of funds into speculative operation." It insured deposits up to $2,500 each in all Federal Reserve banks. Deposits in approved banks were insured on a sliding scale: 100 percent up to $10,000; 75 percent from $10,000 to $50,000; and 50 percent over $50,000. A later law, entitled "an act to provide for the sound, effective and uninterrupted operation of the banking system, and for other purposes," approved on August 23, 1935, limited the insurance to $5,000 for any one depositor.

3783. Savings and loan association established by the federal government was the First Federal Savings and Loan Association of Miami, FL, which was chartered on August 8, 1933. The creation of savings and loan institutions had been authorized by the Home Owners Loan Act of June 13, 1933, to provide a convenient place for the investment of small and large sums and to lend money to local applicants for first mortgages.

3784. Payment by the Federal Deposit Insurance Corporation to depositors of a closed insured bank was a payment of $125,000 to 1,789 depositors of the Fond du Lac State Bank of East Peoria, IL, which suspended business on May 28, 1934, and went into receivership on June 25, 1935. The first depositor to receive her share of the payment was a widow, Lydia Lobsiger, whose check arrived on July 3, 1934. The corporation had been created by the Banking Act of 1933.

FINANCE—BANKING—*continued*

3785. Federal credit union chartered under the Federal Credit Union Act approved on June 26, 1934, was the Morris Shepard Federal Credit Union in Texarkana, TX, named in honor of the law's sponsor, which held its organizational meeting on October 1, 1934. The purpose of the law was "to establish a further market for securities of the United States and to make more available to people of small means credit for provident purposes through a national system of cooperative credit, thereby helping to stabilize the credit structure of the United States."

3786. Bank president of a national bank who was a woman was Frances Estelle Mason Moulton, who was elected on January 11, 1938, as president of the Limerick National Bank, Limerick, ME, to fill the vacancy caused by the death of her father, Jeremiah Miller Mason.

3787. World bank was the International Bank for Reconstruction and Development, which entered into force on December 27, 1945, when it was subscribed to by 21 countries, whose subscription amounted to $7,173 million. The United States subscription was $3,175 million. The first loan was made on May 9, 1947, to France—a 30-year loan of $250 million at 3.25 percent and of $150 million at 3 percent.

3788. Bank to open a branch in a trailer was the Meadow Brook National Bank, West Hempstead, NY, which opened a branch at Locust Grove, NY, on May 26, 1956, in a 46-foot air-conditioned trailer. It had four tellers' windows opening out on one side of the trailer. Over $100,000 was received in deposits on the first day. The trailer was used while a permanent structure was built.

3789. Federally chartered bank owned and managed by women was the Women's National Bank of Washington, DC, founded in 1977. Barbara Davis Blum was the first chief executive officer. The bank's name was changed to the Abigail Adams National Bank in 1986, following the incorporation of its holding company, the Abigail Adams National Bancorp, in Delaware on July 22, 1981. The name change was a move to alter the public perception that the bank existed exclusively to serve the banking needs of women.

FINANCE—BANKING—SERVICES

3790. Check protectors were manufactured in 1870 and consisted of punches that perforated figure holes in paper to help protect against forgeries. In June 1899 Libanus McLouth Todd completed the model of a different kind of check protector in a woodshed at 384 Gregory Street, Rochester, NY. The machine forced ink into the paper under pressure, making it part of the fiber of the document. The machine, called the Protectograph, went on the market in the fall of that year. Todd obtained a patent on August 9, 1904.

3791. Traveler's checks were devised in 1891 by Marcellus Fleming Berry, who was then general agent of the American Express Company. In the first year, 248 checks amounting to $9,120 were sold.

3792. Bank open day and night was the Night and Day Bank, New York City, opened on May 1, 1906, with a capital of $200,000, a surplus of $200,000, and a reserve of $100,000. Oakleigh Thorne was the first president. The idea was originated by Thomas Benedict Clarke.

3793. Christmas savings club at a bank was started by the Carlisle Trust Company, Carlisle, PA, in 1909. The idea originated with Merkel Landis, the bank's treasurer. The first payment was received December 1, 1909.

3794. Transatlantic radio fax of a check was transmitted on April 20, 1926. It was drawn by General James Guthrie Harbord in London against the Bankers Trust Company of New York City in the amount of $1,000, payable to the Radio Corporation of America.

3795. Check photographing device was the Checkograph, a microfilm device invented by George Lewis McCarthy, who received a patent for it on February 25, 1930. Commercial manufacture was undertaken on May 1, 1927, by the Eastman Kodak Company, Rochester, NY, which marketed the device as the Recordak and made the first installation on May 1, 1928, at the Empire Trust Company, New York City. The machine photographed checks on 16mm motion picture film. The first application of the machine other than by banking institutions was made in 1929 by the Treasury. The first application in libraries was made in 1935, when the *New York Times* and the New York Public Library cooperated in photographing copies of the *Times* from the World War I period on microfilm.

3796. Drive-in banking service was instituted on November 12, 1946, by the Exchange National Bank of Chicago, IL. Ten tellers' windows protected by heavy bulletproof glass and impregnable corrugated steel were equipped with automatic slideout drawers to enable motorists to transact business without leaving their cars.

3797. Bank to operate a window in a subway station for the convenience of subway riders was the Bowery Savings Bank, New York City, which opened two tellers' windows in a glass-enclosed cubicle in the Grand Central station of the Interborough Rapid Transit subway on September 26, 1955. The windows had bullet-resistant glass. They were equipped with special receptacles for passing money and bankbooks that permitted only one side to be open at a time.

3798. Bank of importance to lease personal property was the Bank of America, San Francisco, CA, which instituted the service on July 22, 1963, under the direction of Robert D'Oyly Syer. James Joseph Saxon, comptroller of the currency, advised national banks on March 18, 1963, that they were permitted to lease personal property, buying equipment and leasing it directly to customers.

3799. Bank to install an automatic teller was the Chemical Bank, New York City, which placed its first machine in operation at Rockville Center, Long Island, NY, on January 1969. A coded card inserted in an opening dispensed a package envelope containing a set sum of cash.

3800. Bank to be automated was the Civic Center branch of the Surety National Bank, Los Angeles, CA, which opened April 27, 1970. It contained six telestations equipped with closed-circuit television and monitored by a teller. A "validator" provided instant validation of checks by code rather than by signature. A money machine dispensed cash in an envelope.

3801. Bank to provide movies for customers waiting in line was the Chemical Bank, New York City. On December 22, 1972, movies were projected on 4-by-5-foot screens at three different branches: 2681 Broadway, 86th Street and Lexington Avenue, and 67 Broad Street.

FINANCE—LOANS AND CREDIT

3802. Loan by a colony was authorized on December 10, 1690, by the Massachusetts Bay Colony, which issued tax anticipation certificates that did not have a maturity date or bear interest. They were not redeemable in metal and were not considered legal tender.

3803. Loan for war purposes by a central governmental agency was negotiated with France by the Continental Congress. A resolution of December 23, 1776, authorized the loan of $181,500 (1 million livres), which was used for the purchasing of supplies and construction of cruisers. The length of the loan was indefi-

nite. Bonds were sold at par. The rate of interest was 5 percent, payable annually. The loan was received on June 4, 1777. The final redemption was made on December 31, 1793, when the balance due was merged into the general account of the French debt.

3804. Loan to the United States was negotiated by Alexander Hamilton. Between September 13, 1789, and February 17, 1790, he obtained from the Bank of New York and the Bank of North America a total of $191,609. It was known as the Temporary Loan of 1789 and was obtained without authority of law. The money was used to pay salaries of the president, senators, representatives, and officers of the first Congress during the first session under the Constitution. The interest rate was 6 percent. The final redemption of the loan was made on June 8, 1790.

3805. Installment finance company to purchase installment contracts from retail dealers was the Fidelity Contract Company, Rochester, NY, which held its first directors' meeting on April 7, 1904. The company, organized by Lee Richmond, Frederick Zoller, and George Gale Foster, became the Bankers Commercial Corporation of New York City.

3806. Car finance company was the Bankers Commercial Corporation, New York City, organized on February 1915, an affiliate of the Commercial Security Company of Chicago.

3807. Loan made by the federal Government to a war ally was a loan of $200 million at 3.5 percent made to Great Britain on April 25, 1917.

3808. Liberty loan subscriptions were taken on May 2, 1917, and continued through June 15, 1917, during which time approximately 4 million people subscribed for $3,035 million in bonds to yield 3.5 percent. The first loan was authorized by act of April 24, 1917, "an act to authorize an issue of bonds to meet expenditure for the national security and defense, and for the purpose of assisting in the prosecution of the war, to extend credit to foreign governments and for other purposes." A subscription of $2 billion was required.

3809. Credit card to be nationally accepted was the Diners Club card, originated in 1950 by Frank X. McNamara, a credit specialist for a credit company in New York City, and Ralph Scheider, an attorney. Previous credit cards had been limited in use to one retail establishment or chain, such as a gas station or department store. Owners of the Diners Club card could use the card at a variety of restaurants and retail outlets.

FINANCE—LOANS AND CREDIT—*continued*

3810. Bank to issue a credit card was the Franklin National Bank, Franklin Square, NY, which did so on April 15, 1952. Purchases were charged to the bank, which made the payments and then billed the card holders. The service was extended to its branches. The first bank credit card to gain national acceptance was the BankAmericard (later called Visa), issued by the Bank of America, San Francisco, CA, in 1959. There was no membership fee or service charge. Full-scale services were offered to cardholders and merchants. Mastercard, originally called Master Charge, was founded by a consortium of 77 western banks led by the Wells Fargo Bank.

FINANCE—STOCKS AND BONDS

3811. Bonds issued by the federal government were interest-bearing obligations that were authorized by the congressional act of August 4, 1790, for the refunding of the domestic debt and for that part of the state debt which was assumed by the federal government. The total issue amounted to $64,456,963.90, of which $30,088,397.75 drew interest at 6 percent, $19,719,237.39 at 3 percent, and $14,649,328.76 at 6 percent after 1800. Practically the entire issue was retired by 1836.

3812. Stock exchange was the New York Stock Exchange, the outgrowth of an agreement signed on May 17, 1792, by 24 brokers to fix the rates of commission on stocks and bonds. The first meeting was held at the Merchants Coffee House, Second and Gold streets, New York City. The first president was Matthew McConnell. This protective league existed until March 8, 1817, when the New York Stock and Exchange Board adopted its constitution, organized on its present lines. On January 29, 1863, the name was changed to the New York Stock Exchange. A securities exchange was informally organized in Philadelphia in 1791.

3813. War bond issued by the federal government aside from the refunding of the Revolutionary War debts was authorized on March 14, 1812, for the purchase of weapons and equipment and the enlargement of the Army in preparation for the impending War of 1812 against Britain. The amount authorized was $11 million. Bonds were issued to the amount of $8,134,700 and sold exclusively in the United States.

3814. Treasury notes bearing interest were authorized by an act of Congress of June 30, 1812. The president was authorized to issue treasury notes to an amount not exceeding $5 million. The interest was fixed at "five and two-fifths per centum a year."

3815. Commercial rating agency was established in New York City on August 1, 1841, as the Mercantile Agency, by Lewis Tappan, who had founded the *Journal of Commerce* in 1828. The first place of business of the agency was at the corner of Hanover Street and Exchange Place. Branch houses were later opened, the first in Boston, MA, in February 1843. On May 1, 1859, the firm was taken over by R.G. Dun and Company.

3816. Stock exchange to specialize in mining securities was the San Francisco Stock and Exchange Board, later known as the San Francisco Stock Exchange and then the San Francisco Mining Exchange. It was organized on September 11, 1862, by a group of 37 independent brokers determined to establish fixed positive prices for shares of the Comstock mining companies. The Comstock Lode in Nevada in 1859 produced $680 million, enough to pay the entire cost of the Civil War. The companies issued shares that were widely traded at prices ranging from $1,000 to $2,000 each.

3817. Stock brokerage concern to use a telegraph ticker was David Groesbeck and Company, a member of the New York Stock Exchange. The ticker was installed on December 29, 1867, by the Gold and Stock Telegraph Company, New York City. A rental of $6 a week was charged for the service, which was operated by Daniel Drew.

3818. Brokerage office owned by women was Woodhull, Claflin and Company, New York City, opened in 1869 by the sisters and social reformers Victoria Claflin Woodhull and Tennessee Celeste Claflin. The company showed a net profit of $750,000 for the first six weeks. A contemporary newspaper cartoon depicted them driving a chariot drawn by bulls and bears with human heads—the heads of the largest financiers of the time—while other financiers were crushed under the wheels.

3819. Clearinghouse for stocks and bonds was the Philadelphia Clearing House, which was organized in Philadelphia, PA, in August 1870 as an adjunct of the Board of Brokers of the Philadelphia stock exchange.

3820. Stock exchange at which more than a million shares were traded in one day was the New York Stock Exchange, New York City, whose transactions on December 15, 1886, totaled 1,096,509 shares.

3821. Stock quotation boards were made of slate and were manufactured by Mount and Robertson of New York City in 1889.

3822. Investment trust is claimed to have been the New York Stock Trust, New York City, a general portfolio statutory trust, formed on April 1, 1889, with 50,000 shares at $10 a share.

3823. Bonds payable specifically in United States gold coins were issued under authority of a financial bill enacted on March 14, 1900, an "act to define and fix the standard of value, to maintain the parity of all forms of money issued or coined by the United States, to refund the public debt."

3824. Automatic electric stock quotation board was manufactured in 1929 by the Teleregister Corporation (later the Bunker-Ramo Corporation), Stamford, CT, and placed in operation on May 21, 1929, in the brokerage office of Sutro Brothers and Company, New York City. The board automatically shifted figures as changes were made. It showed open, high, low, and last prices of each stock listed.

3825. Curb exchange to transact more business in a day than the New York Stock Exchange was the New York Curb Exchange. On June 15, 1929, the volume for the Curb was 1,287,900 shares, compared with 1,260,400 for the Stock Exchange.

3826. Stock order from a zeppelin was radioed on August 8, 1930, from the *Graf Zeppelin*. The radio message was picked up at Tuckerton, NJ, and the order sent to Portland, ME, by telegraph. The order was sent by Alexander Godfrey of Boston, MA.

3827. Commodity exchange member who was a woman was Gretchen B. Schoenleber of the Ambrosia Chocolate Company, Milwaukee, WI, who was admitted September 3, 1935, to membership in the New York Cocoa Exchange, New York City.

3828. Woman to sell securities on the floor of the New York Curb Exchange in New York City was motion picture actress Linda Darnell, who occupied Post 29 on November 19, 1941, to sell U.S. Defense Bonds and stamps.

3829. Visitor to open the New York Stock Exchange was Leonard Ross, a 10-year-old boy from California, who was introduced on April 24, 1956, by Keith Funston, president of the exchange, and who pressed the button that activated the opening gong. Ross had won $100,000 on the television show "The Big Surprise."

3830. Stock brokerage concern of importance whose president was a woman was A.M. Kidder and Company, New York City. Josephine Perfect Bay became chairman and president of the company on December 1, 1956.

3831. Stock exchange director who was a woman was Mary Gindhart Roebling of the Trenton Trust Company, Trenton, NJ. On October 28, 1958, she became one of the 32 governors of the American Stock Exchange, New York City, which entitled her to go on the floor of the exchange. She was one of the three so-called "public" members, not connected with the Wall Street community. The first women to become official members of the American Stock Exchange were Julia Montgomery Walsh, general partner of Ferris and Company, Washington, DC, and Phyllis Kathryn Smith Peterson, general partner of Sade and Company, Washington, DC, both of whom were elected on November 18, 1965.

3832. Stockholder meetings televised coast-to-coast simultaneously were meetings of General Mills stockholders that took place on October 29, 1959, in New York City, Minneapolis, Chicago, Los Angeles, San Francisco, Boston, and Buffalo, NY. By means of a closed-circuit television system, stockholders in each city were able to ask questions of Gerald S. Kennedy, chairman of the company, who presided at the New York meeting, and Charles Heffelfinger Bell, the company's president, who presided at the meeting in Minneapolis.

3833. New York Stock Exchange seat owner who was a woman was Muriel Siebert, who paid $445,000 plus a $7,515 initiation fee on November 18, 1967. She was admitted on December 28, 1967, as a full member with privilege to handle customers' orders on the floor. The first woman to serve as a director of the New York Stock Exchange was Dr. Juanita Morris Kreps, professor of economics and dean of the Women's College, Duke University, Durham, NC, who was nominated on June 6, 1972, and elected on July 5.

FINANCE—STOCKS AND BONDS—*continued*

3834. New York Stock Exchange member who was African-American was Joseph Louis Searles III, a partner in the brokerage firm of Newburger, Loeb and Company, New York City, whose admission was approved by the board of governors on February 13, 1969. The first African-American director of the New York Stock Exchange was Dr. Jerome Heartwell Holland, retired U.S. ambassador to Sweden and one of the 10 public nominees on the 21-member board, who was nominated on June 6, 1972, and elected on July 5.

3835. Brokerage firm whose shares were traded by a major stock exchange was Merrill Lynch, Pierce, Fenner and Smith. The stock opened on the New York Stock Exchange on July 27, 1971, at 38.25, and closed at 37. There were 47,500 shares traded the first day. Previous transactions had been made over the counter.

3836. Dow Jones Industrial Average to exceed 1,000 points occurred on November 14, 1972, when the Dow closed at 1003.16. It first exceeded 2,000 points on January 8, 1987, when it finished at 2002.25 after climbing more than 100 points the previous week. This record was successively topped for the next 13 days in some of the most frenzied trading in New York Stock Exchange history. The Dow topped the 3,000 mark on July 16, 1990, during the course of the day's trading. The closing average was 2999.75.

3837. New York Stock Exchange seat owner of Chinese ancestry was Whalen Lou, who paid $205,000 for his seat. He became a member in September 1979.

3838. Dow Jones Industrial Average to exceed 7,000 points occurred on February 13, 1997. On that day, the Dow climbed 60.81 points to close at 7,022.44. It was the fastest 1,000-point rise ever to occur on Wall Street. The Dow had reached the 6,000-point level just 82 days earlier.

FOOD

3839. Genetically engineered product to appear in food that was widely consumed in the United States was bovine growth hormone (BGH), also called bovine somatotropin, produced from gene-altered bacteria by the Monsanto Company, St. Louis, MO, in the early 1990s. It was added to cattle feed to increase the milk production of cows by up to 25 percent. Milk from cows that had ingested BGH went on sale across the United States in February 1994 after approval by the Food and Drug Administration, but was shunned by many consumers.

3840. Genetically altered food was the Flavr Savr tomato, developed by Calgene, Davis, CA. The tomato contained a gene that caused it to ripen quickly on the vine. The company also claimed an improvement in the flavor. On May 18, 1994, the tomato was approved for sale by the Food and Drug Administration. It began appearing in stores about two weeks later.

FOOD—BEVERAGES

3841. Cider mill was patented by Isaac Quintard of Stanfield, CT, who obtained a patent on April 5, 1806, on a cider and bark mill.

3842. Mineral water bottler was Elie Magloire Durand, who also invented a machine for bottling mineral water under pressure. Durand opened a drugstore in 1825 at the corner of Sixth and Chestnut streets, Philadelphia, PA.

FOOD—BEVERAGES—CARBONATED

3843. Soda water was prepared by Townsend Speakman of Philadelphia, PA, who was hired by the eminent surgeon Dr. Philip Syng Physick to make carbonated water as a medicinal treatment for his patients. In 1807, Speakman added fruit juices to make the drink more palatable. The soda water was dispensed regularly to patients from fountains. The cost was $1.50 a month for one glass a day.

3844. Soda water machine was manufactured by John Matthews, who opened a factory in New York City in 1834 exclusively for the manufacture of soda water apparatus. Various types of machines for making carbonated beverages had been made previously, however.

3845. Soda water commercially bottled was a carbonated water prepared in 1835 by Elias Durand at Philadelphia, PA.

3846. Root beer was manufactured in 1866 by Charles Elmer Hires, a student at the Jefferson Medical College, Philadelphia, PA, in cooperation with Dr. William Simpson and Dr. Henry Leffman. In 1869, Hires opened a drugstore in Philadelphia and placed a sign over his soda fountain offering a glass of root beer for five cents. In 1876, he started a national business selling root beer.

3847. Sugar-free soft drinks were introduced in 1952. They were NoCal, introduced in 1952 by Hyman Kirsch of Kirsch Beverages, College Point, NY, and Diet-Rite Cola, introduced nationwide by Royal Crown Cola.

3848. Official use of the "Coke" trademark by the Coca-Cola Company, Atlanta, GA, was in 1955, 10 years after it registered the name "Coke" as a trademark.

FOOD—BEVERAGES—COFFEE AND TEA

3849. Coffee mill was patented on April 3, 1829, by James Carrington of Wallingford, CT.

3850. Coffee percolator was patented by James H. Nason of Franklin, MA, on December 26, 1865.

3851. Coffee in a can was a roasted blend packed in a sealed tin by the Chase and Sanborn Company of Boston, MA, in 1878.

3852. Instant tea was White Rose Redi-Tea. The powdered beverage was marketed by Seeman Brothers of New York City beginning in 1953.

3853. Freeze-dried coffee was marketed in 1964 and made available nationally in 1968 by General Foods, White Plains, NY. This coffee was percolated and frozen at temperatures below zero. By sublimation, water passed under high vacuum directly from its solid icy state to vapor, bypassing entirely the liquid form.

FOOD—DAIRY

3854. Creamery for commercial production was established by Alanson Slaughter at Wallkill, NY, in 1861.

3855. Centrifugal cream separator was made in 1879 by David M. Weston and Edward Burnett of Boston, MA, and was used on the Deerfoot Farm, Southborough, MA. It made 1,600 revolutions a minute and had a 26-inch bowl. The machine had to be stopped to draw off the cream and skim milk after separation. Two years earlier, on September 25, 1877, an American patent was granted to Wilhelm C. L. Lefeldt and Carl G. O. Lentsch of Schoeningen, Germany, on an "improvement in centrifugal machines for creaming milk." It consisted of an electric rotator that forced the heavy milk to the base of the pan. A centrifugal cream separator with a continuous flow was invented by Carl Gustaf Patrik de Laval of Stockholm, Sweden, who received an American patent for it on October 4, 1881. The first machine of this type used in the United States was put in operation in 1881 by Theodore Augustus Havemeyer, sugar refiner and Jersey stock breeder, on his farm at Mahwah, NJ.

3856. Yogurt dairy was the Colombo Dairy, Methuen, MA, established in 1929 by Sarkis Colombosian. The first year, about 4,000 quarts of yogurt were produced. At that time it was called *madzoon,* the Armenian name for yogurt.

FOOD—DAIRY—CHEESE

3857. Cheese factory cooperative was established by farmers of Cheshire, MA, in 1801. On July 20, 1801, a cheese was pressed at the farm of Elisha Brown, Jr., which on August 20 weighed 1,235 pounds. It was placed on a wagon drawn by six horses and on January 1, 1802, was presented to President Thomas Jefferson at the White House.

3858. Pineapple cheese was made in 1808 by Lewis Mills Norton of Troy, PA. On April 17, 1810, he obtained a patent on a "vat for forming pineapple cheese."

3859. Cheese factory of consequence was established in Rome, NY, by Jesse Williams in 1851. It is referred to as the first permanent system of associated dairying in the United States. The first shipment of milk was received May 10, 1851.

3860. Liederkranz cheese of American origin was made in 1892 by Emil Frey in Monroe, NY. He was a cheesemaker for the Monroe Cheese Company, which was acquired in 1929 by the Borden Company. The cheese was named for the Liederkranz Club, New York City.

FOOD—DAIRY—ICE CREAM

3861. Ice cream to be made commercially was sold by Mr. Hall of 76 Chatham Street (now Park Row), New York City, who advertised it on June 8, 1786.

3862. Ice cream freezer was patented by William G. Young of Baltimore, MD, who received a patent on May 30, 1848, on an "improvement in ice cream freezers." A record of a purchase for "a cream machine for ice" is contained in George Washington's expense ledger under date of May 17, 1784.

3863. Ice cream wholesale dealer was Jacob Fussel, a milk dealer in Baltimore, MD. In 1851, as a means of using up his surplus cream, he started manufacturing ice cream, which sold at 60 cents a quart.

3864. Ice cream soda is supposed to have been introduced by Robert M. Green, the founder of Robert M. Green and Sons, manufacturers of soda fountains in Philadelphia, PA, who added ice cream to plain soda water. The first demonstration of the new beverage was made at the Semi-Centennial Celebration at Franklin Institute, Philadelphia, in the summer of 1874.

FOOD—DAIRY—ICE CREAM—*continued*

3865. Ice cream sundae is said to have originated about 1897 in the Red Cross Pharmacy, State Street, Ithaca, NY, directly opposite the barroom of the Ithaca Hotel. As the barroom was closed on Sunday, thirsty patrons went to the drugstore, where a distinctive drink was sold as a sundae.

3866. Ice cream cone is said to have originated at the Louisiana Purchase Exposition in St. Louis, MO, in 1904. Charles E. Menches, a young ice cream salesman, gave an ice cream sandwich, as well as flowers, to the young lady he was escorting. Lacking a vase for the flowers, she took one of the layers of the sandwich and rolled it in the form of a cone to act as a vase. The remaining layer was similarly rolled to hold the ice cream, resulting in the invention of the ice cream cone. Similar claims have been made by other concessionaires.

3867. Eskimo pie was invented by Christian K. Nelson of Onawa, IA, who obtained a patent on January 24, 1922. The pie was an ice cream confection containing a normally liquid material frozen to a substantially hard state and encased in a chocolate covering to maintain its original form during handling.

3868. Ice cream cone rolling machine was invented by Carl Rutherford Taylor of Cleveland, OH, who obtained a patent on January 29, 1924, on a "machine for spinning or turning a waffle."

FOOD—DAIRY—MILK

3869. Condensed milk was commercially produced in 1851 by Gail Borden of Norwich, NY, who received a patent on August 19, 1856, on an "improvement in concentration of milk," although the patent office doubted the value of the invention. The first condensery was established at Wolcottville, CT, in 1856. It was not successful, and another attempt was made at Burrville, CT, in May 1857, but that was also a failure. A third attempt was made with an enlarged factory at Wassaic, NY, in June 1861. This venture was successful and later developed into the Borden Company, with factories throughout the country.

3870. Dried milk patent was obtained by Samuel R. Percy of New York City, who obtained a patent on April 9, 1872, on a "process for the simultaneous atomizing and desiccating of fluids and solid substances," involving spray-drying of various liquid products. It was never used commercially in its original form.

3871. Milk delivery in glass bottles was made in 1878 in Brooklyn, NY (now part of New York City), by Alexander Campbell.

3872. Malted milk was invented in 1882 or 1883 by William Horlick of Racine, WI, who coined the name in 1886. It was originally known as Diastoid. He dried whole milk and combined it with extract of wheat and malted barley in powder or tablet form. This was the first whole dried milk that would keep.

3873. Evaporated milk was produced by John B. Meyenberg of St. Louis, MO, who received a patent on November 25, 1884, for an "apparatus for preserving milk." On February 14, 1885, Meyenberg formed the Helvetia Milk Condensing Company of Highland, IL. Evaporated milk is milk from which approximately 60 percent of the water has been removed by evaporation.

3874. Milk butterfat tester of value for determining the percentage of butterfat in milk and cream was invented on May 15, 1890, by Stephen Moulton Babcock, professor of agricultural chemistry, University of Wisconsin, Madison, WI. He did not apply for a patent. Prior to this invention, the amount of butterfat in milk and cream was determined by a method that could be used only in a chemical laboratory and was entirely unsuitable for use in a creamery or milk plant.

3875. Milk pasteurized commercially was processed in Bloomville, NY, in 1895 by the Sheffield Farms Company of New York City. The company used flash pasteurization, a very slow process and quite expensive due to the large quantity of ice used. Lewis Benjamin Halsey used two Champion coolers, one for the heating medium and the other for the cooling.

3876. Acidophilus milk was devised early in 1920 by Dr. Leo Frederick Rettger and Harry Cheplin at Yale University, New Haven, CT. Commercial production was undertaken by the Fairlea Farms Company, Orange, CT, in February 1922 under the supervision of Dr. Rettger.

3877. Concentrated milk was Sealtest, which was first sold on November 30, 1950, by the Clover Dairy Company, Wilmington, DE, as a test. Two parts of water were added to one part fluid milk. The Clover Dairy Company was a division of the National Dairy Products Corporation.

FOOD—DISHES

3878. Recipes using standard measurements were invented in the 1880s by Fannie Merritt Farmer, a young woman who was working as a mother's helper in Boston, MA. The little girl in her care wanted to learn how to cook, but the process was slow, since most cooking directions referred only to such vague amounts as a pinch, a dash, a handful, or a spoonful. Farmer converted these measurements to standardized forms, so that all cooks could duplicate the ingredients of a dish in the right proportions. Her cookbook, *The Boston Cooking School Cook Book,* published in 1896, was the first to include standardized recipes.

3879. Chop suey was concocted in New York City on August 29, 1896, by the chef of Chinese Ambassador Li Hung-chang, who devised the dish to appeal to both American and Asian tastes. Chop suey was unknown in China at the time.

3880. Vichyssoise was served by Chef Louis Diat at the Ritz Carlton Hotel in New York City in 1910. Diat adapted his mother's recipe for a hot soup of leeks and potatoes, but offered it cold as a summer treat. The name is derived from Diat's birthplace in Vichy, France.

FOOD—FATS AND OILS

3881. Cottonseed oil was produced in 1768 through the efforts of Dr. Otto, a Moravian, of Bethlehem, PA. He was able to get nine pints of oil from a bushel and a half of cotton seed. The first mill for producing cottonseed oil was established in Petersburg, VA, in 1829 by Francis Follet.

3882. Margarine manufacturer who was successful was Alfred Paraf of New York City, who organized the Oleo-Margarine Manufacturing Company in 1871. On April 8, 1873, he obtained a patent on his process for purifying and separating fats. A previous patent had been granted on January 3, 1871, to Henry W. Bradley of Binghamton, NY, on a "compound for culinary use," composed of lard, vegetable butter, or shortening.

3883. Margarine law enacted by a state was "an act for the protection of dairymen and to prevent deception in sales of butter," passed on June 5, 1877, by New York.

3884. Margarine law enacted by Congress was "an act defining butter, also imposing a tax upon and regulating the manufacture, sale, importing and exporting of oleomargarine," passed on August 2, 1886. It placed a $600 tax on manufacturers, $400 on wholesalers, and $48 on retailers, and levied a manufacturing stamp tax of two cents a pound.

3885. Hydrogenated vegetable shortening was introduced as Crisco by the Procter and Gamble Company, Cincinnati, OH, on August 15, 1911. It was a creamy-white all-vegetable shortening, odorless and tasteless, made from cottonseed oil.

3886. Fat substitute in prepared foods was Simplesse, a low-calorie fat substitute developed by the Nutrasweet Company. Simplesse was made of proteins derived from egg whites and milk. It was approved by the Food and Drug Administration on February 22, 1990.

FOOD—FISH

3887. Salmon cannery was erected in 1864 at Washington, CA, on the banks of the Sacramento River, by Hapgood, Hume and Company. The firm consisted of Andrew S. Hapgood, George W. Hume, and William Hume. About 2,000 cases of salmon were canned the first year. Half of the first production spoiled because the cans were not hermetically sealed.

3888. Sardine cannery that was successful was established in 1876 in Eastport, ME, by Julius Wolff of Wolff and Reesing, New York City. The cans were made of three pieces, top, bottom, and side, which were soldered together.

3889. Canned tuna was packed in 1907 by a small cannery owned by A.P. Halfhill in San Pedro, CA, center of the American tuna industry. Canned tuna did not catch on as a staple of the American diet until 1926, when Van Camp Sea Food of San Pedro began packing yellow-fin tuna in cans and lowered the price. Yellow-fin was a more economical and easier-to-catch fish than the white-fleshed albacore that canneries had packed until then.

FOOD—FRUITS AND VEGETABLES

3890. Potato is believed by some authorities to have been imported from Bermuda by Virginia colonists in December 1621 or January 1622. The first potatoes are said to have been used for food rather than for planting.

3891. Pear and peach trees were brought to America by Walloon settlers from Belgium in the early 17th century. They were first cultivated in what is now New Jersey and New York.

3892. Apples were imported from England in 1629 by John Winthrop, colonial governor of Massachusetts. The first apples grown by colonists were probably obtained from trees planted in Boston, MA, from which "ten fair pippins" were plucked on October 10, 1639.

3893. Rice to be imported was brought to America by Sir William Berkeley, governor of Virginia, in 1647. He directed that a half bushel of seeds be planted. The yield was 16 bushels.

3894. Potatoes to be cultivated were planted in 1719 at Londonderry Common Field (now Derry), NH, by Scotch-Irish immigrants.

FOOD—FRUITS AND VEGETABLES—
continued

3895. Tomatoes eaten in America were given public approval as an edible food by Dr. John Siccary, a Portuguese Jewish physician who came to Virginia in 1745. Until he recognized their nutritional value, tomatoes were thought by the American colonists to be poisonous. The leaves are indeed toxic, though not the fruit. Siccary's fellow Virginian, Thomas Jefferson, grew tomatoes on his estate and helped to publicize their safety.

3896. Sugar cane to be imported was brought to Louisiana by Jesuit priests in 1751 from the island of Hispaniola (present-day Santo Domingo). It was used for making taffia, a kind of rum. The sugar industry started with the work of Étienne de Boré, who planted sugar cane in 1794 and in 1795 harvested a crop of sugar that sold for $12,000. At his death, his wealth was estimated at $300,000, all from sugar.

3897. Rhubarb was shipped by Benjamin Franklin from London, England, to John Bartram in Philadelphia, PA, on January 11, 1770.

3898. Bananas to be imported are recorded as having arrived in 1804, when the schooner *Reynard* brought 30 bundles of bananas from Cuba.

3899. Melons and cantaloupes were grown in Germantown, PA, at the residence of E.B. Gardette on Wissahickon Avenue. The seed was brought over from Tripoli by Commodore James Barron in 1818.

3900. Cranberry cultivation was attempted about 1820 by Captain Henry Hall of Dennis, Cape Cod, MA. Cranberries grow wild on Cape Cod and were probably eaten by the Pilgrims.

3901. Sugar beets were grown about 1830 at Ensfield, PA, by the Beet Sugar Society of Philadelphia, of which James Donaldson was president.

3902. Avocado was imported by Henry Perrine in 1833 and planted at Santa Barbara, CA.

3903. Oranges of the seedless navel variety grown in the United States were grown from a dozen budded saplings brought from Bahia, Brazil, in 1871 by William Saunders, horticulturist of the Department of Agriculture. Two of the trees, which were obtained by Jonathan and Eliza C. Tibbets in 1873, started the industry in Riverside, CA. Other types of oranges, however, had been grown earlier in Florida.

3904. Loganberry was introduced in 1881 by Judge James Harvey Logan in Santa Cruz, CA, and given to the public in 1893 by the University of California. The loganberry is a cross between a California wild blackberry and a red raspberry.

3905. Citrons grown commercially in any large quantity were raised by Edwin Giles Hart, who planted 6,000 trees at La Habra, CA, in 1925.

3906. Tomatoes from space were grown from 6,000 tomato seeds that orbited the earth for nearly six years aboard NASA's Long-Duration Exposure Facility, which was recovered by the space shuttle in January 1990. The space-exposed seeds were distributed to 64,000 teachers and 3.3 million students in the United States and abroad. Compared to Earth-bound control seeds, the space-exposed seeds germinated slightly faster. The resulting plants grew faster for the first few weeks, exhibited premature chlorophyll development, and had greater levels of chlorophyll.

FOOD—GRAIN

3907. Maize to be produced in quantity by English colonists was grown on a 40-acre tract planted in Jamestown, VA, in 1609. It had been grown by Native American peoples for many thousands of years. Maize is indigenous to America, and records of its growth and use were made by the explorers Christopher Columbus and Giovanni da Verrazano in the late 15th and early 16th centuries.

3908. Corn found by English settlers was discovered on November 16, 1620, on the future site of Provincetown, MA, by 16 Pilgrims led by Myles Standish, William Bradford, Stephen Hopkins, and Edward Tilley at a place they named Corn Hill.

3909. Windmill for grinding grain was erected in 1632 in Cambridge, MA. As "it would not grind but with a westerly wind," it was moved in August 1632 to Copp's Hill (Boston Neck), Boston, MA.

3910. Cornmeal machine for grinding maize was invented in 1712 by Sybilla Righton Masters, a Quaker woman from West New Jersey, and installed at Governor's Mill in Philadelphia, PA. Masters took out an English patent on it in 1715 in the name of her husband, Thomas. The machine, which could be run either by horsepower or waterpower, used a set of wooden cogwheels to stamp maize into powder, which Masters called "Tuscarora rice."

3911. Flour mill equipped with elevators conveyors, drills, and a "hopper boy" was designed by Oliver Evans in 1789. With this equipment, the mill could be operated by one man instead of the four who were needed in the old-fashioned mills. The mill had an endless belt conveyor with buckets spaced a foot apart, each bucket holding a quart of grain.

3912. Cornstarch made commercially from maize was made by Thomas Kingsford, who produced a small quantity in 1842 in Jersey City, NJ. He and his son, Thomas, Jr., erected a small cornstarch plant in Bergen, NJ, in 1846 and a larger one in Oswego, NY, in 1848.

3913. Macaroni factory was established by Antoine Zerega in Brooklyn, NY (now part of New York City), in 1848. It consisted of a small mill with crude mechanical equipment for grinding raw materials.

3914. Oat-crushing machine was patented on November 30, 1875, by Asmus J. Ehrrichson of Akron, OH, who obtained a patent on "an improvement in oatmeal machines." A hopper with a perforated bottom and a series of horizontal knives were the basis of his invention, which converted hulled kernels of oats into a cereal meal. The machine superseded the old method of crushing grain with burrs or millstones, which produced a product of inferior quality and reduced the grain to a fine flour of less value than the coarse meal.

3915. Flour rolling mill was invented by John Stevens of Neenah, WI, who was granted a patent on a "grain crushing mill" on March 23, 1880. His method increased production 70 percent and produced a superior flour that sold for $2 more a barrel.

3916. Cereal sold as a breakfast food was Granose, introduced in February 1895 by John Harvey Kellogg and his brother Will Keith Kellogg of Battle Creek, MI. They boiled wheat, pressed it in a machine for rolling out dough, baked it into a thin film, cut it up, and sold the pieces as flakes in 10-ounce packages. John Harvey Kellogg, a champion of vegetarianism and a follower of Dr. Sylvester Graham, developed many other vegetarian foods, including the first granola, which he made in 1877 by grinding up cakes of wheat, oatmeal, and cornmeal, and the first cornflakes, introduced unsuccessfully in 1898. Kellogg's chief rival was Charles William Post, who produced Grape Nuts in 1897, Post Toasties in 1915, and Post's Bran in 1922.

FOOD—GRAIN—BAKED GOODS

3917. Cracker bakery was that of Theodore Pearson of Newburyport, MA, which started in 1792. His products appealed chiefly because they kept better than bread.

3918. Hard water crackers were made by hand in 1801 by Josiah Bent in his home in Milton, MA. They were made from winter wheat and cold water and were baked in ovens heated by bundles of hardwood sticks. Bent peddled them around the country and in 1827 sold his business, which became Bent and Company.

3919. Whole-wheat bread made at home from coarsely ground flour was the subject of a public campaign by the Reverend Sylvester Graham of Northampton, MA, whose book *Treatise on Bread and Bread-Making* was published in 1837. Graham accused the bakers of the era of adulterating the bread they sold and harming the public's health. At one of his lectures, delivered in Boston in 1847, the audience had to defend him from an assault by a mob of enraged bakers. He was also the inventor of Graham crackers.

3920. Meat biscuit was invented by Gail Borden of Norwich, NY, who baked flat, brittle cakes from concentrated meat extract combined with vegetable flour or meal. To make soup, the consumer added hot water and seasoning to the biscuit. Borden obtained a patent on July 30, 1850, on a "preparation of portable soup bread."

3921. Matzah made by machine for the Jewish holiday of Pesach (Passover) was introduced by Moses S. Cohen, a New York City baker, in 1852 or 1853, in his bakery on Front Street. Matzah is traditionally made by hand. Rabbinical approval for machine-made matzah was obtained from the Chief Rabbi of London. The first matzah factory to package the product for widespread distribution was opened by Rabbi Dov Ber Manischewitz in Cincinnati, OH, in 1881.

3922. Pretzel bakery was founded by baker Julius Sturgis in Lititz, PA, in 1861.

3923. Sweet crackers of American manufacture were introduced to the public in 1865 by Belcher and Larrabee of Albany, NY, in competition with English crackers, which were imported in increasing quantities. Soda crackers and salt crackers had been made previously.

FOOD—GRAIN—BAKED GOODS—*continued*

3924. Biscuits of shredded wheat were made by Henry D. Perky and William H. Ford of Watertown, NY, who obtained a patent on August 1, 1893, on a machine for making shreds or filaments of wheat. The Cereal Machine Company, Denver, CO, was formed in 1893 to manufacture them.

3925. Bread factory that was completely automatic was opened on July 1, 1910, by the Ward Baking Company, Chicago, IL. The dough was not touched nor the bread handled except when it was placed on the wrapping machine.

3926. White bread packaged for distribution to stores was Mary Maid, a one-pound loaf made by the Taggart Baking Company of Indianapolis, IN, in 1917.

3927. Bagel bakery that was commercially successful was Lender's Bakery, which opened in 1927 in West Haven, CT. The owner was Harry Lender, who had just arrived from Lublin, Poland. Lender's introduced the first frozen bagels in 1963.

3928. Chocolate chip cookies were concocted by accident in 1933 by Ruth Graves Wakefield, the proprietor of an inn in Whitman, MA, who chopped chocolate squares into small pieces and mixed them into a batter for butter cookies, expecting them to melt. The finished cookies, with their unmelted chocolate chunks, proved popular with customers. Whitman named them Toll House cookies after her inn, which was originally a tollgate on the road to Boston. Packaged chocolate chips were introduced in 1939 by the Nestlé candy company.

3929. Frozen bread was offered to stores on November 3, 1952, by Arnold Bakers, Port Chester, NY.

FOOD—ICE AND SALT

3930. Salt works was established in America in 1630 by Governor John Harvey of Virginia, who designed and established a factory for obtaining salt by evaporation of seawater. The factory was erected at Accomack, VA, on the eastern shore of Chesapeake Bay.

3931. Ice shipped commercially was was cut on Canal Street, New York City, in 1799, and shipped to Charleston, SC.

3932. Ice exported was shipped in August 1805 by Frederick Tudor, who sent 130 tons on the brig *Favorite* from Boston, MA, to the island of Martinique in the West Indies. His business increased, and in 1833 he commenced making shipments to the cities of Madras, Bombay, and Calcutta in India.

3933. Salt well drilled west of the Alleghenies was bored, tubed, rigged, and operated by David Ruffner and his brother Joseph in 1808 at the Great Buffalo Lick, six miles above Charleston, WV, on the Big Kanawha River. They started drilling on November 1, 1807, and on January 15, 1808, had an ample flow of brine. They bored through 40 feet of rock with the most primitive instruments before they were successful.

FOOD—LEAVENING AGENTS

3934. Baking soda commercial production was undertaken in 1846 by John Dwight and Dr. Austin Church in New York City. In 1847 they organized John Dwight and Company.

3935. Compressed fresh yeast was introduced in 1868 by Charles Fleischmann, whose firm, Gaff, Fleischmann and Company, manufactured it in Riverside, near Cincinnati, OH.

3936. Baking powder manufacturer was Benjamin Talbert Babbitt, whose Star Yeast Powder was introduced to the public in 1870.

FOOD—MEAT

3937. Meat packer was William Pynchon, who established a warehouse at Warehouse Point, Springfield, MA, in 1636. He dealt in mutton, tallow, and wool, but his chief business was pork packing. He also sold beaver skins. Competition was keen and "merchants encreased so many that it became little worth, by reason of their out-buying one another, which caused them to live on husbandry."

3938. Beef export was made from Savannah, GA, in 1755, when 40 barrels of beef were shipped out.

3939. Hot dog was introduced to the United States by immigrants from Frankfurt, Germany, where local butchers had created the frankfurter, a thin variation of the traditional sausage, in 1852. One immigrant, Charles Feltman, settled in Coney Island, NY (now part of New York City), where he sold pies from a pushcart. In the 1890s he switched to selling boiled frankfurters on rolls topped with mustard and sauerkraut, which proved highly popular. The first entrepreneur to sell frankfurters at ball games was Harry Stevens, at New York City's Polo Grounds, where they were called dachshund sausages. A sketch by a newspaper cartoonist, Tad Dorgan, of a frankfurter in the shape of a dachshund gave rise to the term "hot dog."

3940. Hamburger evolved from the chopped-beef Hamburg steak of German invention, but the identity of the inventor of the American-style hamburger on a bun is uncertain. Hamburgers on buns, possibly with ketchup or mustard, may first have been served by German-born street vendors at the 1904 International Exposition in St. Louis, MO. Other claimants are Louis Lassen, the owner of the Louis Lunch diner in New Haven, CT, who began serving a broiled Hamburg steak sandwich on toasted bread in 1900, and Billy Ingram, who sold flattened meatballs for five cents each in Wichita, KS, in 1921, and eventually founded the White Castle chain of burger joints.

3941. Canned ham was marketed in 1926 under the name "Hormel Flavor-Sealed Ham" by George A. Hormel and Company of Austin, MN. In 1937, Hormel introduced Spam, the world's most popular canned meat. The name refers to the product's chief ingredients, pork shoulder and ham.

3942. Rattlesnake meat in cans was packed in March 1931 by George Kenneth End of Arcadia, FL. Canned rattlesnake meat was served at an American Legionnaires dinner at the Hillsboro Hotel, Tampa, FL, on April 9. End founded the Floridian Products Corporation, which made its first sale of canned rattlesnake on May 22, 1931.

FOOD—PREPARED FOODS

3943. Mustard was manufactured by Benjamin Jackson, who established the Globe Mills on Germantown Road, Philadelphia, PA, and sold his product in glass bottles with his label on them. He advertised in the *Pennsylvania Chronicle* of February 15, 1768, that he was "the original establisher of the mustard manufactory in America, and ... at present the only mustard manufacturer on the continent. I brought the art with me into the country."

3944. Canning of food was introduced in 1819 by Ezra Daggett and his nephew, Thomas Kensett, who canned salmon, oysters, and lobsters in New York City. On January 19, 1825, they obtained a patent to "preserve animal substances in tin." The vacuum canning process was invented in 1872 by writer and spiritualist

Amanda Jones of Buffalo, NY, who received nine patents on it. Her company, the U.S. Women's Pure Food Vacuum Preserving Company, founded in 1890, produced canned pudding and lunch meat.

3945. Prepared-food producer to achieve great commercial success was Henry John Heinz, a chef of German descent, who in 1869 opened a factory at Sharpsburg, PA. His first product was grated horseradish, but his real breakthrough in the marketplace was bottled ketchup, which he introduced in 1876. The company, known since 1888 as the H.J. Heinz Company, eventually became a major firm that manufactured several hundred varieties of products.

3946. Soup company to market canned, precooked liquid soups was the Franco-American Food Company of New York City, which was organized in November 1886 by Alphonse Biardot and his sons, Ernest and Octave.

3947. Ready-mix food to be sold commercially was Aunt Jemima Pancake Flour, invented at St. Joseph, MO, in 1889 by Chris L. Rutt and Charles G. Underwood. The original recipe consisted of hard wheat flour, corn flour, phosphate of lime, baking soda, and a pinch of salt. It was labeled "Self-Rising Pancake Flour" and sold in one-pound paper sacks. The name was changed to "Aunt Jemima" after Rutt saw a tune of the same name performed by two entertainers at a local minstrel show.

3948. Condensed soup for the consumer market was invented in 1897 by 24-year-old chemist John T. Dorrance of the Joseph Campbell Preserve Company, a cannery in Camden, NJ. His double-strength condensed soups had the advantage of being cheaper to distribute and sell because water, the weightiest part of the formula, was added by the consumer. The low-priced canned soups first appeared on the market in 1898, already sporting the company's characteristic red and white labels. In 1914, Dorrance became president of the company, which changed its name to the Campbell's Soup Company in 1924.

3949. Frozen food for the mass market was developed by Clarence Birdseye, a biologist from Brooklyn, New York City. In 1916, Birdseye began to experiment with methods of retaining the flavor and nutrition of cabbage and fish over long periods by quick-freezing them in brine. In 1924, in Gloucester, MA, he perfected the belt-freezer, a device that subjected food to quick-freezing by pressing it between refrigerated plates. He received a patent

FOOD—PREPARED FOODS—*continued*

for his invention on August 12, 1930. Frozen foods with the Birdseye trademark were first marketed in Springfield, MA, in 1930. Birdseye sold his trademark in 1929 to the Postum Company, later the General Foods Corporation, for $22 million.

3950. Hydrogenated peanut butter was developed in 1928 by the E.K. Pond division of the Swift Packing Company under the brand name Peter Pan Peanut Butter. The hydrogenation process, invented in 1923 by J.L. Rosefield of Alameda, CA, and licensed exclusively to Swift, made the peanut butter smoother and prevented it from becoming rancid. The peanut butter was also homogenized, so that the peanut oil would not separate and rise to the top. In 1932, Rosefield canceled his agreement and began marketing his own brand of peanut butter, Skippy.

3951. Monosodium glutamate commercial production began in 1934. Previously, American consumers used MSG from Japan, where the flavor-enhancing substance was first isolated from seaweed in 1908. MSG was first marketed commercially in 1947 under the Accent brand name.

3952. Paprika mill was the Carolina Paprika Mills, Dillon, SC, incorporated March 25, 1941. The president was Robert Robich.

3953. Food in an aerosol can that was nationally distributed was Reddi-Wip, introduced in 1947 by the Reddi-Wip company, owned by Marcus Lipsky. The product was a brand of sweetened whipped cream aerated and stored in pressurized cans. By pressing on a nozzle, the consumer could release the internal pressure and spray the cream.

FOOD—SNACKS AND SWEETS

3954. Popcorn was introduced to the English colonists at their first Thanksgiving dinner in 1621 by Quadequina, brother of Massasoit. As his contribution to the dinner, he offered a deerskin bag containing several bushels of the "popped" corn.

3955. Chocolate mill was erected beside the Neponset River at Dorchester, MA, in 1765 and was operated by John Hannan. In 1780 Dr. James Baker purchased the mill, originating the chocolate maker Walter Baker and Company.

3956. Sugar refinery that was practical was opened in New Orleans, LA, in 1791 by Antonio Méndez. Attempts had been made in 1759, 1764, 1765, and 1766, but because the exact crystallization point and the proper use of lime were not then known, the mills were unsuccessful and were abandoned. The first commercial mill began operation in New Orleans in 1795.

3957. Glucose from potato starch was obtained in 1831 by Samuel Guthrie in a refinery at Sackets Harbor, NY.

3958. Sugar beet mill belonged to the Northampton Beet Sugar Company and was erected by David Lee Child in Northampton, MA, in 1838. In 1839, the mill produced 1,300 pounds of sugar from beets low in sucrose content. That year, the company received a $100 premium from the Massachusetts Agricultural Society and a silver medal at the exhibition of the Massachusetts Charitable Mechanics Association. The factory did not operate after 1840.

3959. Chewing gum was the "State of Maine Pure Spruce Gum," manufactured in Bangor, ME, in 1848 by John Curtis and his brother on a Franklin stove. In 1850 they moved to Portland, ME, where they made paraffin gums under the brand names Licorice Lulu, Four-in-Hand, Sugar Cream, Biggest and Best, White Mountain, and spruce gums under the names Yankee Spruce, American Flag, Trunk Spruce, and 200 Lump Spruce.

3960. Potato chips are the subject of competing claims. According to some accounts, they were introduced in 1853 by George Crum, a Native American chef at Moon Lake Lodge, Saratoga Springs, NY, and were known as Saratoga Chips. According to others, they were first made by an African-American chef about 1865. The first plant constructed for the exclusive manufacture of potato chips was erected in Albany, NY, in 1925 by A.A. Walter and Company.

3961. Sugar and glucose from cornstarch were manufactured by the Union Sugar Company, New York City. The process was based on a patent, dated May 10, 1864, for a "sugar produced from corn and beets." The patent was granted to Frederick W. Gossling and assigned to Gossling, Henry F. Briggs, and Leman Bradley of Buffalo, NY. Gossling also received a patent on December 20, 1864, for a new and improved compound sugar made by a combination of cane sugar or cane syrup and corn syrup.

3962. Popcorn snack that was successful was Cracker Jack, invented by street vendor Frederick William Rueckheim in 1871. His confection of popcorn, peanuts, and molasses was marketed nationally after Rueckheim scored a success with it at the World's Columbian Exposition of 1893 in Chicago, IL. In 1912, Rueckheim started putting a prize—a miniature toy or book—into each box. The sailor boy on each Cracker Jack box was modeled after his grandson Robert, who died of pneumonia at the age of eight.

3963. Candy packaged in a factory was Smith Brothers Cough Drops, a medicinal candy made by William and Andrew Smith from a recipe handed down by their father James, a restaurant owner and candymaker in Poughkeepsie, NY. They began selling the cough drops locally in 1852. The product was so popular that in 1872 they began packaging it in small boxes for shipment. Until that time, storekeepers kept candies on their countertops in glass containers, from which customers made their selection.

3964. Sugar substitute was saccharine, discovered by Constantine Fahlberg, who was working under the direction of Professor Ira Remsen at Johns Hopkins University, Baltimore, MD. Fahlberg described the discovery in an article entitled "On the Liquid Toluenesulphochloride," which he submitted to the *American Chemical Journal* on February 27, 1879. Saccharine is an edible substance 550 times sweeter than table sugar, but not absorbed by the body.

3965. Chocolate bars manufactured in the United States were produced in 1894 by candymaker Milton Snavely Hershey, using several German chocolate-making machines he purchased at the 1893 World's Columbian Exposition in Chicago. Hershey installed them in his caramel factory in Lancaster, PA. By 1900 he had given up on caramels to focus exclusively on chocolate bars, chocolate kisses, and chocolate cigars. Chocolate bars were originally manufactured on a large scale in Switzerland in 1819.

3966. Gelatin dessert packaged for commercial distribution was Jell-O, a powdered mixture of gelatin and fruit flavoring. It was created in 1897 by Pearle B. Wait, a carpenter in Le Roy, NY. The formula was purchased in 1899 by a marketing expert, orator Frank Woodward, who turned Jell-O into a nationally distributed product.

3967. Bubble gum was invented by Frank Henry Fleer, founder of the Frank H. Fleer Corporation of Philadelphia, PA. In 1906 he developing a chewing gum called Blibber-Blubber. The recipe was perfected in 1928 by company employee Walter Diemer, who called his product Dubble Bubble for its ability to make large bubbles. Successful market testing began in Philadelphia on December 26, 1928.

3968. Confectionary machine for making candy "suckers," more familiarly known by the trade name "lollipops," was manufactured by the Racine Confectioners' Machinery Company, Racine, WI, in 1908. Its capacity at that time was 40 lollipops a minute, a rate that candy makers felt would produce more suckers in a week than they could sell in a year. The term "lollipops" was formerly an exclusive name used for candy produced by the Bradley-Smith Company of New Haven, CT, but it has since passed into the language as a generic term.

3969. Milky Way candy bar was introduced in 1923 by candymaker Frank C. Mars of Minneapolis, MN. The nougat bar was a mixture of milk chocolate, corn syrup, sugar, milk, hydrogenated vegetable oil, cocoa, butter, salt, malt, egg whites, and other ingredients, and was an immediate success. In 1930, Mars's company, Mars, Incorporated, began marketing the Snickers bar, which added peanuts to the Milky Way formula. In 1937, it introduced the five-cent Three Musketeers bar, which contained three bars in one wrapper, each with a different flavor of nougat.

3970. M&M candies were developed in 1940 for the armed forces by Forrest E. Mars and Bruce E. Murrie, whose initials supplied the candy with its name. M&M candies had a candy coating that kept the chocolate inside from melting in warm conditions.

FOOD—VITAMINS

3971. Vitamin to be commercially synthesized and manufactured was vitamin D, which was manufactured by Mead, Johnson and Company, Evansville, IN, beginning in 1927 and was marketed in the spring of 1928. It was made by exposing a solution of ergosterol to ultraviolet light.

3972. Vitamin E reduction to alpha tocopherol was accomplished by Dr. Herbert McLean Evans, Dr. Oliver Hudleston Emerson, and Gladys Anderson Emerson of the Institute for Experimental Biology of the University of California, Berkeley. Announcement of the process was made at the American Chemical Society meeting at San Francisco, CA, on August 20,

FOOD—VITAMINS—*continued*

1935, and published as "The Isolation from Wheat Germ Oil of an Alcohol, Alpha Tocopherol, Having the Properties of Vitamin E," in the *Journal of Biological Chemistry* of February 1936. Vitamin E was first recognized by Dr. Evans and Dr. Katherine Cott Bishop in 1922.

3973. Vitamin K to be synthesized was made by Dr. Louis Frederick Fieser of the Harvard University Department of Chemistry, Cambridge, MA, on August 1, 1939. A report of the achievement was submitted to the meeting of the American Chemical Society in Boston, MA, on September 10, 1939.

FOREIGN RELATIONS

3974. Foreign service committee was formed on November 29, 1775, when the Continental Congress voted "that a committee of five be appointed for the sole purpose of corresponding with our friends in Great Britain, Ireland and other parts of the world." The members of this secret Committee of Correspondence were William Samuel Johnson of Connecticut, John Jay of New York, John Dickinson of Pennsylvania, Benjamin Harrison of Virginia, and Benjamin Franklin of Pennsylvania, who was the chairman.

3975. Foreign nation to recognize the independence of the United States was France. Treaties of amity and alliance between the United States and France were drafted in Paris on February 6, 1778.

3976. Salute fired by Great Britain in honor of an officer of the United States was fired on May 8, 1783, when General George Washington and Governor George Clinton arrived at the British ship *Ceres,* commanded by Sir Guy Carleton, in New York Harbor to arrange for the British evacuation. When they departed, 17 guns were fired in honor of Washington's rank. New York was evacuated by the British on November 25, 1783.

3977. Neutrality proclamation by the federal government was made by President George Washington on April 22, 1793: "Whereas it appears that a state of war exists between Austria, Prussia, Sardinia, Great Britain and the United Netherlands on the one part and France on the other," citizens of the United States will be "liable to punishment or forfeiture under the law of nations by committing, aiding or abetting hostilities against any of the said powers."

3978. Neutrality regulation enacted by Congress that governed the actions of citizens was passed by act of Congress on June 5, 1794. The act provided that any citizen who "accepts and exercises a commission to serve a foreign prince, state, colony, district or people, with whom the United States are at peace shall be fined not more than $2,000 and imprisoned not more than three years." The first conviction was that of Isaac Williams of Norwich, CT, who accepted a commission in a French armed vessel and served against Great Britain. He was tried in September 1799 at Hartford, CT, in U.S. Circuit Court, found guilty under two counts, and sentenced on each count to a fine of $1,000 and imprisonment for four months.

3979. Conference of American republics was the General Congress of South American States, assembled on March 14, 1826, at Panama. Convoked by Simon Bolivar, who sent invitations in December 1824, it was attended by delegates from Mexico, Colombia, Peru, and Central America. Richard Clough Anderson and John Sargeant were appointed delegates from the United States in July 1825, but their appointment was not confirmed until December 6, 1825, and the conference adjourned before they reached it. The first such conference initiated by the United States was the First International Conference of American States, which opened in Washington, DC on October 2, 1889, at the invitation of Secretary of State James Gillespie Blaine. Ten participating nations signed an arbitration treaty.

3980. Conference of great powers to be held on American soil and affecting American interests was the Conference on the Limitation of Armaments, which assembled at Memorial Continental Hall in Washington, DC, from November 12, 1921, to February 6, 1922. Nine nations took part in the conference: the United States, Great Britain, France, Italy, Japan, China, Holland, Belgium, and Portugal. The American delegation was headed by Secretary of State Charles Evans Hughes.

3981. United Nations Security Council resolution vetoed by the United States was a resolution to condemn Great Britain for not using force to overthrow the white minority government of Rhodesia. The veto was cast on March 17, 1970, by Ambassador Charles Woodruff Yost. Great Britain also rejected the resolution. The Security Council met at the United Nations headquarters in New York City.

3982. Hostage crisis in which a large number of American citizens were held prisoner by representatives of a foreign government in peacetime began on November 4, 1979, when the U.S. embassy in Teheran, Iran, was occupied by Islamic revolutionary troops. The occupiers, acting on behalf of Iran's dictator, Ayatollah Ruhollah Khomeini, demanded the forced return of the Shah of Iran, Mohammed Reza Pahlavi, whose regime had been overthrown in January. Pahlavi was in the United States undergoing treatment for cancer. President Jimmy Carter imposed economic sanctions on Iran and ordered a military rescue effort that failed. The 52 hostages were released on January 21, 1981.

FOREIGN RELATIONS—DIPLOMATS

3983. Representative of a foreign country to the United States was Conrad Alexandre Gérard of France, who arrived in July 1778. He was styled minister plenipotentiary and also bore a commission as consul general.

3984. Minister plenipotentiary was Benjamin Franklin of Philadelphia, PA, who was elected by the Continental Congress on September 14, 1778, to represent the United States in the court of France. Thomas Jefferson was the first minister plenipotentiary after the Revolutionary War. He was appointed on March 10, 1785, and served in Paris until October 1789.

3985. Minister to Great Britain was John Adams of Quincy, MA, who on June 1, 1785, was introduced by the Marquis of Carmarthen to the King of Great Britain as ambassador extraordinary from the United States of America to the Court of London. The first minister plenipotentiary to Great Britain was Thomas Pinckney of South Carolina, who was appointed on January 12, 1792.

3986. Consul was Major Samuel Shaw of Massachusetts, who was appointed consul to Canton, China, on January 1, 1786, prior to the ratification of the Constitution, and confirmed on February 10, 1790.

3987. Consul to California (which was not admitted to the Union until 1850) was Thomas Oliver Larkin, who was appointed consul to Monterey, CA, on May 1, 1843, and special agent on October 17, 1845.

3988. Consul who was African-American was Ebenezer Don Carlos Bassett, consul general to Haiti, where he served from April 16, 1869, to November 27, 1877.

3989. Ambassador who was Jewish was Oscar Solomon Straus of New York City, who was appointed envoy extraordinary and minister plenipotentiary to Turkey on March 24, 1887, and served again during crises in 1890, 1897, and 1909. The first Jew to represent the United States in a high diplomatic post was Mordecai Manuel Noah, who served from 1813 to 1816 as consul to Tunis, where he negotiated the release of American sailors held prisoner by Barbary pirates.

3990. Ambassador to the United States who was a woman was Her Excellency Shrimati Vijaya Lakshmi Pandit, ambassador of India, who presented her letter of credence to President Harry S. Truman on May 12, 1949.

3991. Ambassador from the United States who was a woman was Eugenie Moore Anderson of Red Wing, MN, who was sworn in on October 28, 1949, in Washington, DC, as ambassador to Denmark.

3992. United Nations delegate who was African-American was Edith Spurlock Sampson, who was appointed alternate delegate to the fifth General Assembly on August 24, 1950. Her first assignment, on September 28, 1950, was to the Social, Humanitarian and Cultural Committee.

3993. United Nations permanent ambassador who was a woman was Marietta Peabody Tree, who was sworn in on October 28, 1964, to the Trusteeship Council of the United Nations. She had served since 1961 as a United Nations delegate.

3994. Ambassador who was an African-American woman was Patricia Roberts Harris, who was sworn in on July 9, 1965, in Washington, DC, as ambassador to Luxembourg.

3995. Ambassador assassinated in office was John Gordon Mein, ambassador to Guatemala, who was attacked and killed in his automobile on August 27, 1968, about 10 blocks away from the American embassy in the downtown section of Guatemala City, Guatemala.

3996. Ambassador to the United Nations who was a woman was political scientist Jeanne Duane Jordan Kirkpatrick, born in 1926 in Duncan, OK. In 1981, she was chosen by President Ronald Wilson Reagan to be the U.S. representative to the United Nations. She returned to her academic position at Georgetown University, Washington, DC, in 1985.

FOREIGN RELATIONS—DIPLOMATS—
continued

3997. Ambassador to Vietnam after the end of the Vietnam War was Peter Peterson, who presented his portfolio in Hanoi on May 9, 1997. Peterson, a former Air Force captain, had been held as a prisoner of war in Vietnam for 6.5 years after his bomber was shot down near Hanoi in 1966. He was released in March 1973. The United States had not maintained formal diplomatic relations with Vietnam since its previous ambassador, Graham Martin, left Saigon by helicopter in 1975 as the city fell to North Vietnamese forces.

FOREIGN RELATIONS—TREATIES

3998. Treaties entered into by the federal government were a Treaty of Amity and Commerce and a Treaty of Alliance, signed by the United States and France in Paris on February 6, 1778. Benjamin Franklin, Silas Deane, and Arthur Lee represented the United States, and Conrad Alexandre Gérard, first secretary to France's foreign minister, signed for France. These pacts were the first treaties made by the federal government with a foreign power. The treaty was ratified by the Second Continental Congress at York, PA, on May 4, 1778, and by France on July 16, 1778. Ratifications were exchanged in Paris on July 17, 1778, and the treaty was declared in force. The treaty was abrogated on July 7, 1798, when Congress passed an act "to declare the treaties heretofore concluded with France no longer obligatory on the United States."

3999. Treaty between the federal government and a nation with which it had been at war was the armistice with Great Britain that ended the Revolutionary War. Preliminary articles of peace were signed on November 30, 1782, in Paris. Hostilities ceased on January 20, 1783. The treaty was proclaimed by the Continental Congress on April 11, 1783. The definite treaty of peace was signed in Paris on September 3, 1783, by David Hartley, plenipotentiary of Great Britain, and Benjamin Franklin and John Adams of the United States. The treaty was ratified and proclaimed on January 14, 1784. It set the borders of the United States as Canada in the north, Spanish Florida in the south, and the Mississippi River in the west. It also granted the Americans fishing rights off the Newfoundland coast.

4000. Treaty entered into by the federal government after independence was concluded with Prussia and signed at the Hague on September 10, 1785, by Benjamin Franklin, John Adams, and Thomas Jefferson, representing the United States. The treaty was ratified by Congress on May 17, 1786, and the ratifications were exchanged in October 1786.

4001. Extradition treaty with a foreign country was the Treaty of Amity, Commerce and Navigation, popularly known as the Jay Treaty, between the United States and Great Britain, which was signed in London on November 19, 1794. Article XXVII provided for the apprehension and delivery of persons charged with certain crimes. The signatory for the United States was John Jay, and for Great Britain, William Wyndham Grenville, Baron Grenville of Wotton, one of His Majesty's Privy Council and His Majesty's Principal Secretary of State for Foreign Affairs. The treaty was ratified by the Senate on June 24, 1795, and signed by President George Washington on October 28, 1795. The ratification was proclaimed on February 29, 1796.

4002. Treaty between the federal government and a South American nation was the General Convention of Peace, Amity, Navigation and Commerce between the United States and the Republic of Colombia, which was signed at Bogotá, Colombia, on October 3, 1824. The Republic of Colombia then included Venezuela and Ecuador. The treaty was submitted to the Senate on February 22, 1825, and ratified on March 7. It was ratified by Colombia on March 26, 1825. The treaty was proclaimed on May 31, 1825. The plenipotentiaries who signed the treaty were Richard Clough Anderson, minister plenipotentiary of the United States to the Republic of Colombia, and Pedro Gual, secretary of state and foreign relations of Colombia.

4003. Federal treaty rejected by the Senate was a pact with Colombia for suppressing the African slave trade, which was rejected on February 22, 1825, by a vote of 40–0.

4004. Treaty between the federal government and a foreign nation to provide for mutual reduction of import duties was the Convention with France, Regarding Claims and Regarding Duties on Wines and Cottons, signed in Paris on July 4, 1831. The ratifications were exchanged on February 2, 1832, and the treaty was proclaimed on July 13.

4005. Treaty between the federal government and an Asian nation was the Treaty of Amity and Commerce with Siam (now called Thailand), concluded on March 20, 1833, the last day of the fourth month of the Siamese year 1194, called Pi-Marông-chat-tava-sôk, or the year of the Dragon. One copy of the treaty was in Siamese and one in English, with a Portuguese and a Chinese translation annexed. Edmund Roberts was the envoy of the United States. Ratifications were exchanged on April 14, 1836, in the royal city of Bangkok, and the treaty was proclaimed on June 24, 1837, by President Martin Van Buren.

4006. Federal treaty signed by a woman was the Charter of the United Nations, signed on June 26, 1945, at San Francisco, CA, by Virginia Crocheron Gildersleeve, a delegate to the United Nations Conference on International Organization.

4007. Treaty to reduce the number of nuclear missiles in the United States and the Soviet Union was signed by President Ronald Wilson Reagan and Mikhail S. Gorbachev, secretary general of the Soviet Union, on December 8, 1987, in Washington, DC. The agreement required the two nations to destroy 2,611 short-range and medium-range missiles based in Europe and to allow inspection and verification of the destruction.

G

GAMES

4008. Game played in the English colonies in America that was recorded was "bowles," an early form of bowling, which was played by the settlers of Jamestown, VA, in May 1611, and observed by Sir Thomas Dale.

4009. Game manufacturing company to make games and children's books was the McLoughlin Company, organized in New York City in 1828 by John McLoughlin. In 1850 his sons, John and Edmund, were taken into partnership and the firm name became McLoughlin Brothers. In 1920 the company confined its activities to manufacturing books and moved to Springfield, MA.

4010. Crossword puzzle was prepared by Arthur Wynne and was published in the Sunday supplement of the *New York World* of December 21, 1913.

4011. Checkers champion of renown was Marion Tinsley of Tallahassee, FL, widely regarded as the best checkers player in history. A mathematics professor at Florida State University, Tinsley lost only nine games after winning his first world championship in 1955. In the final years of his career, there was no human opponent in his class. His last titles were won against checkers-playing computers.

4012. Computer game was SPACEWAR, invented by Steve Russell, a graduate student at the Masschusetts Institute of Technology, Cambridge, MA, and first demonstrated publicly in 1962 at the university's Spring Open House. The game was based on the science-fiction stories of E.E. "Doc" Smith. Players used joysticks to control a computer graphics display showing two spaceships shooting at each other. The processing was done by a Digital Equipment Corporation PDP-1 minicomputer.

4013. Video game that was commercially successful was the arcade game Pong, an electronic version of ping-pong created by 29-year-old computer engineer Nolan K. Bushnell. Pong was introduced in 1972 by Bushnell's company, Atari Corporation. Bushnell placed the first unit in Andy Capp's Tavern in Sunnyvale, CA, where it was an instant hit. Pong became a national craze, making Bushnell a multimillionaire and inaugurating the video game industry. An early, noncommercial version of Pong was invented in 1958 by William Higinbotham, head of instrumentation design at the Brookhaven National Laboratory, Upton, NY. It was not patented.

4014. Role-playing game was Dungeons and Dragons, invented by traveling salesman Gary Gygax and his friend Dave Arneson in 1973. To play the game, which required only a pair of dice and a rule book, players took on the roles of characters in a sword-and-sorcery fantasy and kept score according to elaborate rules of interaction. Many of the ideas in Dungeons and Dragons were based on *The Lord of the Rings* and other books by the English writer J.R.R. Tolkien. Gygax and Lorraine Williams formed a company, Tactical Studies Rules Hobbies, better known as TSR, to market the game.

GAMES—BILLIARDS

4015. Billiards were brought to America by the Spaniards who settled in St. Augustine, FL, in 1565.

GAMES—BILLIARDS—*continued*

4016. Billiard match of importance was played on May 13, 1854, for a $200 stake at Malcolm Hall, Syracuse, NY, by Joseph N. White of New York City and George Smith of Watertown, NY. It was a four-ball carom game, 500 points up, on a 6-by-12-foot, four-pocket table. White won by a score of 500–484. The score of runs and averages was not kept.

4017. Billiard match to attain international fame was played in Detroit, MI, on April 12, 1859, between Michael Phelan of New York City and John Seereiter of Detroit for the championship of the world and a $15,000 purse. Phelan, known as the "father of billiards," won the championship by a score of 2,000 against his competitor's 1,904. The best run made by Phelan was 129 points. The game was played on a 6-by-12 four-pocket table with four balls. Pushing and crotching were allowed.

4018. Intercollegiate billiard match was played on July 25, 1860, in Worcester, MA, when freshmen of Harvard and Yale engaged in a "grand trial of skill." A six-pocket, 6-by-12-foot table was used. Four balls, white, spotted, light red, and dark red, were used. Pushing and crotching were allowed. Benjamin Thompson Frothingham and William Stackpole of Harvard won with 800 points against 720 for George St. John Sheffield and Theodore C. Bacon of Yale. The best run was 45, made by Bacon.

4019. Billiard ball of composition material resembling ivory was invented by John Wesley Hyatt, the winner of a $10,000 prize offered by Phelan and Collender of New York City for the best substitute for an ivory ball. Hyatt obtained patents on October 10, 1865, on a billiard ball; on April 14, 1868, on a compound for billiard balls; on April 6, 1869, on a method of coating and painting; and on July 12, 1870, on celluloid.

4020. Billiard player to win a match in the first inning was Willie Mosconi of Philadelphia, PA, who ran 150 balls on April 17, 1956, at Kinston, NC, following the break by Jimmy Moore of Albuquerque, NM, who played a safety shot. Mosconi won each of his 14 matches and scored a 150–0 victory in the final match of the world pocket billiards tournament.

GAMES—BRIDGE AND WHIST

4021. Whist organization of importance was the American Whist League, which convened at the Athenaeum, Milwaukee, WI, on April 14–17, 1891, in response to a call made by Cassius M. Paine, president of the Milwaukee Whist Club. The meeting was attended by 83 delegates representing 36 clubs. They standardized the rules and adopted a 61-section code. The first president was Eugene S. Elliott of the Milwaukee Whist Club.

4022. Duplicate whist tournament was held on April 15, 1891, in Milwaukee, WI, by the American Whist League. Forty-eight delegates participated. Twelve tables were arranged in pairs, each with two teams of two players each. The eight players of each pair of tables changed positions after every deal. The medal winner was E. Price Townsend of the Hamilton Club, Philadelphia, PA. The rules were substantially those of used in English whist, with a few slight modifications to suit the American game.

4023. Auction duplicate bridge championship was held on July 9, 1914, at the Lake Placid Club, Lake Placid, NY. The four-man team of the New York Bridge Whist Club defeated the team of the Knickerbocker Whist Club of New York City by seven tricks on 48 boards to win the American Whist League's Hamilton Trophy, symbolic of the whist championship of the United States and Canada.

4024. Bridge table to shuffle and deal cards by electricity was patented on November 29, 1932, by Laurens Hammond of Chicago, IL, who obtained a patent for a "card table with an automatic dealing device." The unshuffled cards were placed in a sliding drawer that started the mechanism and delivered 13 cards to each player. The entire mechanism was concealed in the table. The table was manufactured by the Hammond Clock Company Chicago, IL, which marketed it in 1932.

4025. Bridge hand in which each player was dealt a perfect hand of 13 cards of the same suit occurred on March 12, 1954, at Cranston, RI. Irene Motta bid seven hearts and won the bid.

4026. Father and son team to win the national contract bridge championship was Oswald Jacoby of Dallas, TX, and James Jacoby, 26 years old, at the 29th annual American Contract Bridge League tournament at the Empress Hotel in Miami Beach, FL, on December 1, 1955. About 1,500 contestants participated in the open team-of-four contest.

4027. Bridge player to win more than 1,000 master points in one year was Oswald Jacoby of Dallas, TX, who passed the 1,000 mark on November 15, 1963, in a tournament held at Edgewater Park, MS. His total points for 1963 were 1,034.

GAMES—CHESS

4028. Chess tournament of importance was held from October 6 to November 10, 1857, by the American Chess Congress in New York City under the sponsorship of the New York Chess Club. The victor of the Grand Tournament was Paul Charles Morphy, who received the first prize, a silver service consisting of a pitcher, four goblets, and a salver.

4029. International chess champion from the United States was Paul Charles Morphy, 20 years old, of New Orleans, LA, who won first place at the chess tournament organized by the American Chess Congress, held in New York City from October 6 to November 10, 1857. In the years 1857–59, he played 95 games, including 68 victories, 14 draws, and 13 losses. He won the Grand Tournament of the First National Chess Association in England and France, held from July 19 to August 22, 1858. Technically, however, the world chess championship did not formally exist at that time. The first player to hold that title was Wilhelm Steinitz, in 1866.

4030. Intercollegiate transatlantic chess match by cable was played on April 21–22, 1899, when six players from Columbia, Harvard, Princeton, and Yale universities, sitting at tables at the Knickerbocker Athletic Club in New York City, competed against six from Cambridge, Oxford, and London universities, who were sitting at the British Chess Club in London. The moves were cabled, 20 per hour. The prize, a $1,000 trophy presented by Isaac L. Rice, was won by the British team.

4031. Chess match between players on different ships at sea was played on June 11, 1902, by passengers on the American liner *Philadelphia* and the Cunard liner *Campania*, about 70 miles apart. The moves were broadcast by wireless operators aboard the ships. About 100 moves were made. The match was not concluded, since radios were required for navigational use.

4032. Chess champion to play more than 100 games simultaneously was Frank James Marshall of New York City, who met 105 local players at the National Press Club, Washington, DC, on March 21, 1916. He won a total of 82 games, lost 8, and drew 15.

4033. World chess champion from the United States was Robert James "Bobby" Fischer, born in Chicago, IL, in 1943. In 1972, Fischer captured the world championship title from Soviet grandmaster Boris Spassky at Reykjavik, Iceland. The score was 12.5 games to 8.5. Fischer won a record purse of $250,000. In 1992, Fischer defeated Spassky for a second time in an exhibition match held in Yugoslavia.

4034. Chess computer to beat the world chess champion was Deep Blue, developed by a team of International Business Machines researchers based in Yorktown Heights, NY. Deep Blue was capable of evaluating 200 million chess moves per second, and could project every possible move within 10 to 15 moves. On February 10, 1996, in Philadelphia, PA, Deep Blue won the first game of a six-game match against Gary Kasparov, the world's ranking grandmaster. It was the first time a machine defeated the top human player under championship conditions. In that match, the computer won one game, lost three, and tied two. On May 11, 1997, Deep Blue won a rematch held at the Equitable Center in New York City. Kasparov, one of the strongest chess players in history, resigned the sixth and final game after just 19 moves. It was the first time that he was defeated in a multi-game match by any opponent, human or machine. The final score was 3.5 to 2.5 games. The match was officiated by the Association for Computing Machinery's chess committee.

GLASS AND CERAMICS

4035. Glass factory was established in Jamestown, VA, in October 1608. Eight German and Polish mechanics were imported to start the new industry. Among the factory's products were glass beads for use in trade with the Native Americans. The factory remained in operation spasmodically for about seven years and was then disbanded, owing chiefly to the fact that the workers found it more profitable to grow tobacco for shipment to England. The London Company later sent Captain William Norton, accompanied by four Italians and two servants, to revive the Jamestown glass factory, which resumed operations on July 25, 1621. The massacre of the colonists by Native Americans in 1622 put an end to it.

4036. Window glass factory of importance was the Boston Crown Glass Company of Boston, MA, chartered in 1787. The manufacture of crown window glass began in 1792. The glass was blown through a pipe into a huge bulb, which was opened, flared out into a disc,

GLASS AND CERAMICS—*continued*

and then cut into panes. The legislature gave this company the sole right to manufacture glass in Massachusetts for a 15-year period and exempted the company from taxes and the workers from military duty.

4037. Flint glass factory that was successful was founded in 1807 by George Robinson and Edward Ensel. It was located on the Monongahela River at the foot of Ross Street, Pittsburgh, PA. The first furnace held six 20-inch pots. The factory was sold to Bakewell and Page in 1808, and the name was later changed to Bakewell, Pears and Company.

4038. Porcelain to be manufactured successfully was made about 1825 by William Ellis Tucker at the American China Manufactory at the southwest corner of Sixth and Chestnut streets, Philadelphia, PA.

4039. Stained-glass window was made in 1844 by William Jay Bolton and John Bolton for Christ Church, Pelham Manor, NY. It depicted the Adoration of the Magi, over which was the legend "Behold the Lamb of God, which taketh away the sins of the world." It was placed in a window above the altar.

4040. Plate glass was manufactured about 1853 by James N. Richmond in the factory that he established in 1850 in Cheshire, MA, for the production of window glass. The plate glass was about half an inch thick and sold for 50 cents a square foot. To make 600 square feet of glass—one day's work—required 2,800 pounds of sand, 500 pounds of soda ash, and 800 pounds of lime. The factory operated about nine months a year until 1856, when it went out of business.

4041. Pottery to make sanitary ware was founded in Trenton, NJ, in 1853 by Milington and Astbury. On April 4, 1873, they consolidated with Thomas Maddock and Sons.

4042. Plate glass produced on a large scale was manufactured in 1883 by the New York City Plate Glass Company in Creighton, PA. The company was capitalized for $600,000 but was refinanced a few months later, when its name was changed to the Pittsburgh Plate Glass Company.

4043. Wire glass was invented by Frank Schuman of Philadelphia, PA, in 1892. He obtained a patent on September 20, 1892. While the glass was still malleable, he pressed a wire netting into it, smoothing the abrased surface. This glass was better able to withstand heat and shattering than was plain glass.

4044. Glass-blowing machine was patented on February 26, 1895, by Michael Joseph Owens of Toledo, OH. It operated five molds that circulated around the machine, each one surrounding the melted glass, which was placed in its proper position on the end of a pipe and simultaneously revolved so as to make a perfect article without seams or roughness.

4045. Sheet-glass drawing machine was invented in 1899 by Irving Wightman Colburn, who obtained a patent on March 25, 1902. It was installed in 1899 in an experimental factory on Frankford Avenue, Philadelphia, PA. The glass was not transparent.

4046. Cut glass made from pressed blanks was manufactured in 1902 by Henry Clay Fry, who organized the H.C. Fry Glass Company, Rochester, PA. The glass was pressed into a mold, the marks of the iron plunger remaining on the inside of the glass. Previously, cut glass had been blown.

4047. Vitrolite was manufactured in 1907 in Parkersburg, WV, by the Meyercord-Carter Company. It was an opaque structural flat glass made originally in white. The first important installation was made in 1907 on the walls of the subway stations of the Interborough Rapid Transit System, New York City. About that time, the company began to make colored designs for brewery signs and similar uses, using colors that were fired onto the vitrolite. In 1922, colors were added to the vitrolite itself by the introduction of coloring material into the sand, soda ash, lime, and other ingredients. The Meyercord-Carter Company was purchased in 1935 by the Libbey-Owens-Ford Glass Company.

4048. Heat-resistant glass was Pyrex, developed at the Corning Glass Works factory in Corning, NY, by researchers Eugene C. Sullivan and William C. Taylor. Boric acid added to the glass formula made it more resistant to thermal shock than ordinary glass. Pyrex was patented by Corning in 1915. It was used in laboratory glassware, cookware, and chemical manufacturing.

4049. Glass that was nonreflecting was developed by Katherine Burr Blodgett, a researcher at the General Electric laboratory in Schenectady, NY. Blodgett discovered that transparent glass coated with a gelatinous film one molecule thick would not reflect light and was therefore virtually invisible. She also invented a gauge that used gelatin-film technology to measure extremely thin substances with a precision of less than 0.000001 inches. Although

Blodgett had developed the technology in 1933, the discovery was not announced by GE until December 1938, a few days before a similar discovery was announced by the Masschusetts Institute of Technology in Cambridge, MA.

4050. Invisible-glass installation was made in September 1935 at Marcus and Company, New York City. The glass window was bent at several different radius points. Mirrors flanked the window opening. The glass was covered by a patent granted on May 30, 1933, to Gerald Brown of London on a "means for nullifying or reducing window reflections," and another granted on June 4, 1935, to Gerald Brown and Edward Pollard of London on a "display window."

4051. Photosensitive glass was made in November 1937 by the Corning Glass Works, Corning, NY, and announced publicly 10 years later, on June 1, 1947. It was a crystal-clear glass in which submicroscopic metallic particles could be formed by exposure to ultraviolet light and subsequent heat treatment. Exposure through photographic negatives permitted development of positive images within the glass in a variety of colors, forming an image as permanent as the glass itself.

4052. Fiberglass and the machinery for its manufacture was invented by James Slayter and John H. Thomas of Newark, OH, who obtained four patents on October 11, 1938. On November 1, 1938, the Owens-Corning Fiberglas Corporation was founded by the Owens-Illinois Glass Company and the Corning Glass Works to market the product, used extensively for industrial equipment and building insulation. Fiberglass is also known as glass wool and spun glass.

GROOMING AND HYGIENE

4053. Tattoo shop was opened in 1846 by Martin Hildebrandt on Oak Street between Oliver and James streets, New York City.

4054. Electric tattoo machine was employed by Samuel F. O'Reilly in 1875 in his tattoo shop in Chatham Square on the Bowery, New York City. O'Reilly modified Thomas Edison's electric engraving pen to produce what he called "tattaugraphs."

4055. Floating soap was made in 1878 by two cousins, Harley Procter and James Gamble, founders of the Procter and Gamble Company, Cincinnati, OH. It was invented by accident, when a factory worker forgot to turn off a mixing machine. The extra air that was whipped into the solution made the soap buoyant. It was

known as White Soap until October 1879, when it was renamed Ivory Soap. A trademark was obtained for it on July 18, 1879. The advertising slogan "99 and 44-hundredths percent pure" was introduced on December 21, 1882.

4056. Safety razor was the Star Safety Razor, made by Kampfe Brothers, New York City, in 1880, and consisted of a short portion of a hand-forged blade of a barber's straight razor inserted in a frame with full safety features. The first safety razor to be successfully marketed was invented by King Camp Gillette of Brookline, MA, in 1895 with the help of William Nickerson, a professor at the Massachusetts Institute of Technology, and manufactured by the Gillette Safety Razor Company. It was equipped with a flexible and movable blade that was punched out of thin steel and could be thrown away. The razors cost five dollars each when they went on sale in 1903. Consumers bought 300,000 of them in 1906.

4057. Avon Lady to sell cosmetics products door-to-door was Mrs. P.F.E. Albee of Winchester, NH. The founder of the company, David McConnell, was a door-to-door book salesman from Suffern, NY, who mixed his own perfume to give away as a premium to housewives. In 1886 he switched from selling books to selling the perfume and began hiring women to make sales in rural areas.

4058. False eyelashes used in modern times were invented by the film director D.W. Griffith. In 1916, while filming *Intolerance,* Griffith wanted larger lashes for the actress Seena Owen, to make her eyes appear larger on film. The false eyelashes were constructed of human hair woven into fine gauze, which was then attached to the actress's eyelids with gum arabic.

4059. Sanitary napkin that was disposable was invented by army nurses during World War I. They adapted it from a crepe-cellulose surgical dressing made from wood pulp. The company that manufactured the dressing, the Kimberly and Clark Company (later called Kimberly-Clark, Dallas, TX), began marketing Kotex pads in 1920.

4060. Electric shaver was invented by Colonel Jacob Schick, who recognized that soldiers in the field needed a razor that did not require soap or hot water. He patented a tiny electric motor in 1923 and received patents on his "shaving implement" on November 6, 1928. The first razors manufactured by the Schick company of Stamford, CT, were delivered on March 18, 1931. The dual-headed electric shaver was introduced by Remington in 1940.

GROOMING AND HYGIENE—*continued*

4061. Tampon to be mass-produced was the Tampax, patented in 1930 by Earl C. Haas, a gynecologist in Denver, CO. His design used a compressed cotton roll inside a cardboard applicator tube. Both the tube and the cotton were disposable. Tampons in various forms have been used since ancient times.

4062. Deodorant soap was Dial Soap, produced by Armour and Company, Chicago, IL, in 1948. The white soap incorporated a bactericidal substance, hexachlorophene, that was developed during World War II for use in field hospitals.

4063. Anti-aging skin cream proven effective in a double-blind scientific trial was Retin-A, a retinoic acid derivative of vitamin A. It was first formulated by Albert Kligman, professor of dermatology at the University of Pennsylvania School of Medicine, Philadelphia, PA, and approved as a prescription acne medication in 1968. The first clear evidence of Retin-A's antiaging effects were reported in the January 22, 1988, issue of the *Journal of the American Medical Association* by John Voorhees and colleagues at the University of Michigan Medical Center. In the double-blind trial of 30 subjects, skin treated with Retin-A cream showed fewer wrinkles and sun spots than skin treated with a control cream.

4064. Horse grooming products sold for human use were marketed beginning in 1993 by Straight Arrow of Bethlehem, PA, owned by Roger Dunavant. Previously available only in feed and pet stores, the products, including Straight Arrow hoof strengthener and Mane 'n Tail shampoo, were made available in beauty salons, supermarkets, and drugstores. Dunavant thought of the idea when he learned that grooms were using the products on their own nails and hair.

GROOMING AND HYGIENE—HAIR

4065. Comb factory on a commercial scale was undertaken by Enoch Noyes of West Newbury, MA, in 1759. His combs were made from flattened animal horns, with their original color untouched.

4066. Comb made of ivory was made at Centerbrook, CT, by Andrew Lord in 1789. He cut the plates and teeth with a handsaw.

4067. Comb-cutting machine was invented by Phineas Pratt of Connecticut, who received a patent for it on April 12, 1799. Phineas Pratt and Abel Pratt cut the plates with handsaws and the teeth with circular saws operated by a water-powered windmill at Ivoryton, CT.

4068. Hair clipper was manufactured by George Henry Coates of Worcester, MA, in 1876. His product was so superior to those imported from England and France that he received an initial manufacturing order for 5,000 clippers.

4069. Shampoo commercially produced was made by John Breck, a fire chief who had begun to lose his hair at the age of 25. In 1908 he opened a scalp-treatment center in Springfield, MA, where he began selling his own shampoos and massage oils. His products were receiving nationwide distribution by 1940.

4070. Blow dryer for hair was developed simultaneously by two Wisconsin companies, the Racine Universal Motor Company and Hamilton Beach, in 1920. Both companies were working on developing electric blenders, and both were aware that women were already using home vacuum cleaners to dry their hair. Combining these two technologies, plus a heating coil, yielded the earliest blow driers. The first widely successful model was introduced in the Sears-Roebuck Fall-Winter 1951 catalog. It featured a nozzle attached to a pink plastic bonnet that fit over the head.

GROOMING AND HYGIENE—TEETH

4071. Toothpick manufacturing machine was developed by Charles Forster in Boston, MA. In 1869, while working for a shoe-peg manufacturer, he built a device to cut toothpicks from Maine white birch. A similar machine was patented on February 20, 1872, by Silas Noble and James P. Cooley of Granville, MA. The machine made it possible for "a block of wood, with little waste, at one operation, [to] be cut up into toothpicks ready for use."

4072. Antibacterial mouthwash to be widely used was Listerine, the invention of Dr. Joseph Lawrence of St. Louis, MO. Lawrence was inspired by the work of Sir Joseph Lister, the British pioneer in medical hygiene. He concocted an alcohol-based yellow mouth rinse and marketed it beginning in 1880 through the Lambert Pharmacal Company, St. Louis.

4073. Toothpaste tube was the invention of a dentist, Dr. Washington Wentworth Sheffield of New London, CT, who was seeking a method of packaging toothpaste that was more hygienic than the porcelain jars then in use. In 1892, he introduced a flexible, collapsible metal tube.

4074. Toothbrush with synthetic bristles was Dr. West's Miracle Tuft Toothbrush, made by the E.I. du Pont de Nemours and Company·of Wilmington, DE, and first introduced to the retail trade in September 1938. The bristles were made from nylon, but were stiff enough to hurt the gums. Du Pont introduced a soft-bristle brush in the 1950s. Until the invention of nylon, people cleaned their teeth with hog-bristle brushes or with toothpicks.

4075. Toothpaste with fluoride was Crest, introduced by Procter and Gamble of Cincinnati, OH, in 1952. It contained stannous fluoride, a substance that research had shown to be effective in preventing tooth decay.

4076. Electric toothbrush was the Broxodent, made by the Squibb Company. It went on sale in 1961. A cordless electric toothbrush made by General Electric came on the market the following year.

H

HEADS OF STATE

4077. President of the Republic of Texas was Sam Houston, who was elected on September 5, 1836, and who took the oath of office on October 22, 1836 in Columbia, TX. He served until December 10, 1838, and was succeeded by Mirabeau Buonaparte Lamar. Houston was reelected and served from December 14, 1841, to December 9, 1844. Upon the admission of Texas on December 29, 1845, as the 28th state of the United States, Houston was elected as a Democrat to the Senate, where he served from February 21, 1846, to March 3, 1859.

4078. Prince of Wales to visit the United States was Albert Edward, Prince of Wales (later King Edward VII), who left Plymouth, England, on July 10, 1860, and arrived in Detroit, MI, on September 20 from Hamilton, Ontario, Canada. He was received by Moses Wisner, governor of Michigan, and Mayor Christian Buhl of Detroit. After touring the United States, he sailed from Portland, ME, on October 20. He used the name Baron Renfrew during his travels.

4079. Queen to visit the United States was Queen Emma, widow of King Kamehameha IV of the Sandwich Islands (Hawaii), who arrived in New York City from England on August 8, 1866, on the Cunard liner *Java*. She was received on August 14, 1866, by President Andrew Johnson and introduced to his family.

4080. Queen to visit the United States during her reign was Queen Marie of Rumania, who arrived in New York City on October 18, 1926, on the *Leviathan* and received a 21-gun salute from the fort at Governors Island. She was accompanied by Prince Nicholas and Princess Ileana. They returned on November 24 on the *Berengaria*.

4081. Pope to visit the United States before his election was Eugenio Pacelli, the future Pope Pius XII, who visited America from October 8 to November 7, 1936, while serving as papal secretary of state. His headquarters were at Inisfada, the Long Island mansion of the Papal Duchess Genevieve Garvan Brady.

4082. President of a black African country to visit the United States was President Edwin James Barclay of the Republic of Liberia, who addressed the Senate on May 27, 1943, the day following his arrival. He was accompanied by the vice president, William Vacanarat Shadrach Tubman, who was also the president-elect. They were welcomed by President Franklin Delano Roosevelt.

4083. Pope to visit the United States was Pope Paul VI, who arrived at Kennedy International Airport, New York City, on October 4, 1965, at 9:27 A.M. He went to Saint Patrick's Cathedral and Cardinal Spellman's residence at 11:44 A.M., conferred with President Lyndon Baines Johnson at the Waldorf-Astoria Hotel at 1:40 P.M., addressed the General Assembly of the United Nations in French at 3:30 P.M., attended a public Mass at Yankee Stadium at 8:20 P.M., visited the Vatican Pavilion at the New York World's Fair at 10:25 P.M., and returned to Rome the same day at 11 P.M. on an Alitalia jet liner. He was seen by about 1 million persons and by 100 million on television.

4084. Pope to visit the White House in Washington, DC, was Pope John Paul II, who flew across the Atlantic in the *Shepherd 1*, landing in Boston, MA, on October 1, 1979. In six days, he visited Boston, New York, Philadelphia, Urbandale, IA, Chicago, and Washington. He returned to Rome from Andrews Air Force Base, near Washington, on October 6.

4085. Principal chief of the Cherokee Nation who was a woman was Wilma P. Mankiller, born in Tahlequah, OK. She was elected principal chief of the Cherokee Nation of Oklahoma, the second largest Native American tribe in the United States, in July 1987.

HEALTH AND SAFETY

4086. Food stamps were introduced in May 1939 by the Department of Agriculture as a pilot program for the hungry in Rochester, NY. The program continued until 1943. On May 29, 1961, as part of a national test program, food stamps were distributed in Welch, WV. The first recipients were Chloe and Alderson Muncy, who accepted $95 worth of food stamps from Secretary of Agriculture Orville Freeman. The Muncys immediately used their stamps at a local grocery store.

4087. Emergency 911 telephone system was instituted in New York City in 1968. Dialing 911 summoned emergency police, fire, or medical assistance. Most municipalities in the United States adopted the system within 10 years.

HEALTH AND SAFETY—CIVIL DEFENSE

4088. Air raid shelter was built by Howard Moyer Gounder at Fleetwood, PA, and completed on November 1, 1940. Stone walls 18 inches thick and set in concrete, with 18-inch retaining walls built alongside a mountain boulder, supported an eight-inch reinforced concrete roof, weather-conditioned with asphalt tar. Movable bunks on one wall accommodated six people. The floors were made of cement. Heavy double doors, one opening inward, the other outward, contained small windows. Electric wiring encased in iron pipes supplied illumination. A stove provided heating and cooking facilities, while ventilation was afforded by a protected chimney in the rear.

4089. Civil defense test held nationwide was held on June 14, 1954, in the continental United States, 10 provinces of Canada, Alaska, Hawaii, Puerto Rico, and the Virgin Islands from 10 to 10:10 A.M., when the all-clear signal was given.

4090. Air raid shelter for a community was the Highlands Community Shelter, Boise, ID, which was completed on July 1, 1961. It was designed to accommodate 1,000 people. Family membership cost $100. The shelter cost $142,000, of which $122,000 was government research funds obtained from the Office of Civil Defense.

HEALTH AND SAFETY—FIREFIGHTING

4091. Fire prevention law enacted by a colony was enacted on March 17, 1631, by Cambridge (then called Newtowne), MA, as the result of a fire the previous day in Boston that had spread to an adjoining house. The legislation provided that "no man there shall build his chimney with wood, nor cover his house with thatch."

4092. Fire engine made in America was built in 1654 by Joseph Jencks, an iron maker of Lynn, MA. He made a contract with the selectmen of Boston for an "Ingine" to carry water in case of fire. It was a clumsy pump worked by relays of men at the handles. Its cistern was supplied with water by lines of bucket passers.

4093. Fire department established by a city was organized in 1659 by Peter Stuyvesant, governor of New Amsterdam (later New York City). He distributed 250 leather buckets and a supply of ladders and hooks that he had imported from Holland. A tax of one guilder for every chimney was imposed for the maintenance of this equipment. The fire alarm was given by the twirling of a rattle, with the result that the firemen became known as the Rattle Watch.

4094. Fire chief was the "brent-master," appointed in 1669 to lead the firemen of New Amsterdam (later New York City).

4095. Fire department to be paid was authorized in 1697 by New York City. Two fire wardens were authorized for every ward. A penalty of three shillings was imposed upon owners for neglecting to remedy defective flues and hearths. If a fire resulted after warning, the fine was 40 shillings, half of which went to the wardens and half to the city.

4096. Lightning rod was invented in 1749 by Benjamin Franklin, who installed it on his house at 141 Market Street, Philadelphia, PA. He described his experiments in his *Opinions and Conjectures concerning the Properties and Effects of the Electrical Matter, and the means of preserving Buildings, Ships, etc., from Lightning, arising from Experiments and Observations made at Philadelphia, 1749.*

4097. Fireboats were put in service in New York City in 1800. They were flat-bottom boats shaped like a scow, with sharp bows and square sterns. Each boat was powered by 12 rowers and was equipped with a hand-operated pump. Two of these boats were stationed at the foot of Roosevelt Street on the East River and patrolled the docks and waterfront of New York City. They were imported from England at a cost of $4,000 each and arrived in New York City on September 28, 1800.

4098. Fire patrol to protect property during fires was the Philadelphia Society for the Protection of Movable Property in Time of Fire, organized in Philadelphia, PA, in 1819 to prevent theft during fires and to salvage articles. The company had large baskets in which to place the articles saved and had vehicles for carrying the baskets away. The first fire patrol to be paid a salary was organized in New York City in 1835 and consisted of four men, each of whom received $250 a year.

4099. Fire hose of rubber-lined cotton web to replace old-fashioned hoses of riveted leather was invented by James Boyd of Boston, MA, who obtained a patent for it on May 30, 1821. In 1819 he established James Boyd and Sons in Boston, MA, to manufacture Boyd's Patent Double Fire Engine Hose.

4100. Fire engine with a steam boiler was designed and built by Paul Rapsey Hodge and publicly tested on March 27, 1841, at the City Hall, New York City. It was 14 feet long and weighed about 8 tons. It had two small wheels under the boiler in front and two huge wheels at the rear. Two horses were required to draw it on level ground. It was placed in service by the fire company known as Pearl Hose No. 28, but was abandoned because it was too heavy and because sparks poured from its stacks.

4101. Sprinkler system put into use was a perforated pipe system invented by the hydraulic engineer James Bicheno Francis. The first installation was made in 1852 at the plant of the Proprietors of the Locks and Canals on the Merrimack River at Lowell, MA.

4102. Fire engine that was practical was the Uncle Joe Ross, invented by Alexander Bonner Latta and manufactured by Latta, Shawk and Company in 1852 in Cincinnati, OH, in the shops of John H. McGowan. It took nine months to build, cost $10,000, and was tested on January 1, 1853, the date it went into service. It weighed five tons, was drawn by four horses and its own power, and had a square firebox, like that of a locomotive boiler, with a furnace open at the top, upon which the chimney was placed. It ran on three wheels, the front one revolving in the center of the car. It threw from one to six streams of water. In a single stream 1.75 inches in diameter, it threw water a distance of 240 feet.

4103. Fire department to be paid a salary was established by Cincinnati, OH, on April 1, 1853, through the efforts of Miles Greenwood. Members of the company received $60 a year, lieutenants $100, captains $150, pipemen and drivers $365. The chief engineer received $1,000 a year and assistant engineers $300.

4104. Fire alarm system operated by electricity was invented by William Francis Channing of Boston, MA, and Moses Gerrish Farmer of Salem, MA, who on May 19, 1857, received a patent for "a magnetic electric fire-alarm." The first city to adopt this system was Boston, which in June 1851 voted $10,000 to test the device.

4105. Fire escapes for tenements were required by New York State on April 17, 1860. The law was passed in the aftermath of a serious fire in Elm Street, New York City, on February 2, 1860, in which 20 persons were suffocated or burned to death.

4106. Boiler inspection law enacted by a state was approved on July 9, 1864, by Connecticut. It authorized the governor to appoint an Inspector of Boilers to check every steam boiler used for manufacturing or mechanical purposes.

4107. Sprinkler system patent was granted to Philip W. Pratt of Abington, MA, on September 17, 1872. The system operated by means of a valve to which cords and fuses were attached. When the cords and fuses melted, the valve opened, releasing a stream of water.

4108. Sprinkler head was invented by Henry S. Parmelee of New Haven, CT, who obtained a patent on August 11, 1874. It consisted of a perforated head containing a valve that was held closed against water pressure by a heavy spring made of low fusing material.

4109. Firehouse pole was installed on April 21, 1878, by Captain David B. Kenyon of Engine Company No. 21, New York City. A hole was cut in an upper floor to accommodate a greased pole three inches wide that extended between the two storeys, to enable the firemen to slide down the pole instead of using the stairs.

4110. Fire extinguisher using vaporized chemicals was manufactured by the Pyrene Manufacturing Company, Newark, NJ, and introduced in 1905. The first model had a single-action pump, which had to be tilted down after each stroke in order to suck up liquid for the next discharge stroke.

HEALTH AND SAFETY—FIREFIGHTING
—continued

4111. Fireworks law enacted by a city was passed by Cleveland, OH, on July 18, 1908. It provided that "no person, firm or corporation shall within the city, sell, offer for sale or have in his or its possession or custody any toy pistol, squib, rocket, cracker, Roman candle or fire balloon or other combustibles, or fireworks," under penalty of a $100 fine or 30 days' imprisonment or both. The Board of Public Service was permitted to give pyrotechnic displays when directed by the Council.

4112. Fireboat with two-way radio equipment was placed in service in 1925 by Boston, MA. Bids on four transmitting and receiving radio stations, one on land and three on boats, were opened on August 29, 1923. The boats were licensed on March 17, 1924, and assigned the call letters WEY.

4113. Fireworks law enacted by a state was passed on March 29, 1929, by Michigan. It prohibited the use of fireworks by the general public but allowed displays by approved or licensed operators. Other states had partially restrictive laws.

4114. Fire department composed entirely of women was the Ashville Fire Department, Ashville, NY. In February 1943, 13 women replaced the department's male firefighters, who were serving in the armed forces or were working elsewhere. They served without pay. They operated a 500-gallon-per-minute pumper and were proficient in rescue work and other fire department procedures.

4115. Smoke detector for residential use was the BRK SS68H, a battery-operated model that went on the market in 1968. It contained a photoelectric cell that set off an alarm if its voltage was raised by the presence of smoke particles. Heat detectors made by the Electric Heat Alarm Company were manufactured as far back as the 1890s.

HEALTH AND SAFETY—LIFESAVING

4116. Lifesaving service for distressed mariners was established in 1787 by the Humane Society of the Commonwealth of Massachusetts. Huts were erected at a cost of $40 each at Scituate Beach, Nantucket, MA, and at the west end of Lovell's Island, MA.

4117. Emergency first aid organization was the Humane Society of Philadelphia, PA, which was organized in 1780. The society was incorporated on January 23, 1793. Its object, according to the charter, was the "recovery of drowned persons, and of those whose animation may be suspended from other causes, as breathing air contaminated by burning charcoal, hanging, exposure to the choke-damp of wells, drinking cold water while warm in summer, strokes of the sun, lightning, swallowing laudanum, etc."

4118. Lifeboat was built in Nantucket, MA, by William Raymond under the supervision of Captain Gideon Gardner and was completed in 1807. It was built for the Humane Society of the Commonwealth of Massachusetts and cost $1,433. An additional $160 was used for a shed in Cohasset, MA, where the lifeboat remained until 1813.

4119. Life preserver of cork was invented by Napoleon E. Guerin of New York City, who obtained a patent on November 16, 1841, on "an improvement in buoyant dresses or life-preservers." It was a jacket or waistcoat containing 18 to 20 quarts of rasped or grated cork. The Neversink Cork Jacket, formed of granulated cork compressed under pressure, was invented by David Kahnweiler of New York City, tested in 1872 in the Potomac River, and patented on July 10, 1877. Life preservers of this type saved the lives of 287 persons when the S.S. *San Francisco* of the Pacific Mail Steamship Company was wrecked in the Pacific Ocean in 1877.

4120. Lifeboat of corrugated iron was patented by Joseph Francis of New York City, who obtained a patent on March 26, 1845, on "making boats and other vessels of sheet iron and other materials." His "life car," built in 1850 by Stillman, Allen and Company, New York City, was 33 feet long and made of four sheets of hard-rolled copper pressed into shape. It was used on January 12, 1850, to rescue 201 persons from the British ship *Ayreshire,* wrecked off Squan Beach, Monmouth County, NJ.

4121. Lifesaving service established by the federal government was introduced in 1871 by Sumner Increase Kimball. An act of Congress of June 18, 1878, formally authorized the Life Saving Service as a separate and distinct service in the Treasury Department. This service and the Revenue Cutter Service were merged on January 28, 1915, to form the Coast Guard.

4122. First aid instruction was given at the annual encampment of the New York State militia at Peekskill, NY, in 1885. The idea was proposed by George Ryerson Fowler.

HEALTH AND SAFETY—LIGHTHOUSES

4123. Lighthouse was a conical masonry tower erected by the Province of Massachusetts in 1716 on Little Brewster Island at the entrance to Boston Harbor, at a cost of £2,285, 17 shillings, and 8.5 pence. The lighthouse was authorized by act of July 23, 1715, and the light was first kindled by keeper George Worthylake on September 14, 1716. It had 16 spermaceti oil lamps in groups of four. To support its upkeep, a levy of a penny per ton was placed on all incoming and outgoing vessels except those engaged in coastal service. The lighthouse was rebuilt in 1783.

4124. Lighthouse built after American independence was located at Cape Henry, VA, at the entrance of Chesapeake Bay. On August 7, 1789, an act was passed "for the establishment and support of lighthouses, beacons, buoys and public piers." On March 31, 1791, a contract for the erection of the Cape Henry Lighthouse was made with John McComb, Jr. It was finished in 1792. The first lighthouse keeper was Laban Goffigan. The original fuel for illumination was fish oil, followed later by whale oil, colza oil, lard oil, kerosene, gas, and finally, electricity.

4125. Lightship was placed in the Elizabeth River off Craney Island, VA, on July 14, 1820. The displacement was 70 tons. The ship was built at a cost of $6,000.

4126. Lighthouse fueled by natural gas was the 35-foot stone lighthouse at Barcelona Harbor, NY, on Lake Erie, 17 miles southwest of Fredonia, NY, which was in operation from 1830 to 1859. It had 11 burners. The gas was transported 0.75 miles through a log pipeline from a gas spring on nearby Tupper Creek.

4127. Iron pile lighthouse was built between 1847 and 1849 at Minot's Ledge, MA, by William Henry Swift. The lamp was first lit on January 1, 1850, by Isaac Dunham, the keeper. The lighthouse was swept away in the gale of April 16, 1851, and two keepers were lost at sea. A lightship was placed in service in 1854. Construction of the stonework for a new lighthouse started on July 1, 1855. It was completed on June 29, 1860, and the light was placed in operation on November 15.

4128. Lighthouse on the Pacific Coast was the Spanish lighthouse erected in 1855 at Ballast Point on Point Loma, San Diego, CA.

4129. Atomic-powered lighthouse was the Baltimore Light in Chesapeake Bay, Baltimore Harbor, MD, which went into operation on May 20, 1964. A 60-watt radioisotope nuclear generator, 34.5 inches high and 22 inches in diameter, weighing 4,600 pounds (including shielding), was developed and produced by the Martin Company's Nuclear Division, Baltimore, MD, a division of the Martin Marietta Corporation, to supply a continuous flow of electricity for 10 years without refueling. It used 120 pairs of lead telluride thermo couples to convert heat from radioactive strontium titanate, a form of strontium-90, into electricity.

HEALTH AND SAFETY—POLICE

4130. Extradition of criminals among colonies was established by the New England Confederation of 1643, which provided for extradition among the provinces of Massachusetts, Connecticut, Plymouth, and New Haven.

4131. Police force consisted of eight men employed by New Amsterdam (now New York City) in 1658.

4132. Police uniforms were authorized on July 8, 1693, by the Common Council of New York, which ordered that the mayor should provide the police "with a coat of the citty livery, with a badge of the city arms, shoes and stockings, and charge it to the account of the city."

4133. Interstate anticrime pact was effected between New York and New Jersey and signed on September 16, 1833, in New York City by Benjamin Franklin Butler, Peter Augustus Jay, Henry Seymour, Theodore Frelinghuysen, James Parker, and Lucius Quintius Cincinnatus Elmer. The pact was ratified by act of Congress of June 28, 1834.

4134. State police were the Texas Rangers, who were authorized by the General Council of the Provisional Government of Texas to organize three Ranger companies in 1835. On November 9, 1835, G.W. Davis was commissioned to raise 20 more men for this new service. Texas was a province of Mexico at the time. It was admitted to the Union in 1845. The first African-American officer to serve as a Texas Ranger was Lee Roy Young, who joined the force in 1988.

4135. Traffic police squad was the old "Broadway Squad" of New York City, organized in 1860. This was the first unit of the Police Department to have special functions in the field of traffic regulation. The members of the squad were stationed on the sidewalks along Broadway from Bowling Green to 59th Street,

HEALTH AND SAFETY—POLICE—_continued_

at the intersections of the cross streets. It was their job to stop traffic and escort pedestrians across the street. The pavement of Broadway was made of cobblestones and most of the traffic consisted of horse-drawn vehicles.

4136. Police officer who was a woman was Marie Owen, a patrolman's widow. In 1893 she was appointed to the Detroit Bureau of Police, Detroit, MI, by Morgan A. Collins, superintendent of police. The first policewoman under civil service was Alice Stebbins Wells, who was appointed by the Department of Police, Los Angeles, CA, on September 2, 1910.

4137. Police patrol wagon was designed by Frank Fowler Loomis of Akron, OH, and was placed in service by the Akron Police Department in June 1899. It had three speeds and could go 16 miles per hour. It was operated by electric power and weighed 5,500 pounds, including the batteries.

4138. Printed traffic regulations were _Rules For Driving,_ a four-page pamphlet about 3 by 6 inches in size. The regulations described in it were put into effect on October 30, 1903, by the New York City Police Department.

4139. Motorcycle police were Anthony L. Howe and Eugene Case of the New York Police Department, New York City, who were assigned to the police headquarters in the Bronx and Manhattan, respectively. They received official status on December 10, 1904.

4140. Detective who was a woman was Isabella Goodwin, who was appointed as acting detective sergeant, first grade, on March 1, 1912, by the Police Department of New York City. She had served as a police matron since May 15, 1896.

4141. Director of the Federal Bureau of Investigation was Alexander Bruce Bialaski, a Polish immigrant of Lithuanian extraction. He served from 1912 to 1919. The FBI was founded in 1908 as the Bureau of Investigation, a division of the Department of Justice, and was renamed the Federal Bureau of Investigation in 1935.

4142. Police chief who was a woman was Dolly Spencer, who was appointed in 1914 by the mayor of Milford, OH.

4143. Teletypewriter system employed by a police department was opened by Governor John Stuchell Fisher of Pennsylvania and placed in service on December 23, 1929, at central headquarters, Harrisburgh, PA. It was connected to 95 cities and boroughs by 3,400 miles of telephone wires.

4144. State police officers who were women were appointed by the Division of State Police, Department of Public Safety, MA, on April 18, 1930. They were Lotta Caldwell, who served until April 13, 1940, and Mary Ramsdell, who served until April 18, 1950.

4145. Police bureau of criminal alien investigation was started by the New York Police Department, New York City, on December 23, 1930. The purpose was to bring to the attention of federal immigration authorities undesirable aliens who were subject to deportation under the Immigration Law, because of either their criminal records or their illegal entry into the United States.

4146. Police radio system connecting headquarters to patrol cars, patrol cars to headquarters, and the patrol cars to one another, was installed in Eastchester Township, NY, by Radio Engineering Laboratories, Long Island City, NY (part of Queens, New York City), in 1933. The company contracted with the township on May 8, 1933, to install one transmitter and receiver for police headquarters (20 watts, W2XCT) and two for police cars (4.5 volts, W2XCS and W2XEL). The cars were placed in operation on July 10 and were under the direction of Sergeant William E. Robinson.

4147. National conference on crime was held on October 11–12, 1935, in Trenton, NJ, with a roster of delegates from 41 states and from the federal government. Its purpose was to curb crime throughout the country by developing reciprocal legislation and interstate cooperation agreements.

4148. Police appeal for missing persons to be shown on television was made on October 3, 1943, by the Missing Persons Bureau of the Police Department of the City of New York on W2XWV, the DuMont station in New York City.

4149. Parking meter enforcement division of a police department was appointed on June 1, 1960, by Mayor Robert Ferdinand Wagner of New York City. The "meter maids" underwent about two weeks of training and received salaries ranging from $3,150 to $4,830 a year. The first summons was issued on June 6, 1960.

4150. Sky marshals were appointed in accordance with President Richard Milhous Nixon's presidential directive of October 28, 1970, to deal with the proliferation of hijackings of commercial airplanes. The Treasury Law Enforcement Officers Training School graduated 46 marshals on December 23, 1970, and 81 marshals, including four women, on April 9, 1971.

4151. Federal marshals who were women were Jacqueline P. Balley, of Washington, DC, and Joanne Neely, of Oxon Hill, MD, sworn in on November 21, 1973, at Washington, DC.

4152. Police officer who was a woman to be killed in the line of duty was Gail A. Cobb of the Metropolitan Police Force, Washington, DC, murdered on September 20, 1974, in an underground garage at 20th and L Streets in Washington by a robbery suspect.

4153. State police class in which women completed training was a class of 104 students, including 30 women, who underwent a 20-week training course and were graduated on June 27, 1980, at Sea Girt, NJ. They became members of the New Jersey State Police at a salary of $14,932 a year. They were assigned to 17 different barracks in the state.

4154. Police chief who was both African-American and Jewish was Reuben Morris Greenberg, who became chief of the police force of Charleston, SC, in 1982.

4155. Ban on cheap handguns enacted by a state was enacted in Maryland on May 23, 1988, effective January 1, 1990. The law banned the manufacture and sale of pistols that were unsafe or easy to conceal.

4156. Sheriff who was an African-American woman was Michelle B. Mitchell, elected sheriff in Richmond, VA, in November 1993. Mitchell ran unopposed for the post following a primary election in which she received 59 percent of the vote.

4157. Police officer who was a Chassidic Jew was Rabbi Shlomo Koenig, a member of the Vizhnitzer Chassidic group, who joined the sheriff's office in Rockland County, NY, as a part-time police officer in September 1996. His responsibilities included overseeing the safety of the growing Chassidic community in the town of Monsey and surrounding areas. In keeping with Jewish tradition, Koenig wore a beard and *payos,* or earlocks. The Chassidic movement originated in the Ukraine in the 18th century.

HEALTH AND SAFETY—POLICE—IDENTIFICATION

4158. Police bureau of identification was established by Captain Michael Patrick Evans on January 1, 1884, for the Chicago Police Department, Chicago, IL. At its inception, only photographs were used. On June 1, 1887, the Alphonse Bertillon system of anthropometric identification was adopted, and on November 1, 1904, the Sir E.R. Henry system of fingerprinting was added. Evans was in charge of the Bureau of Identification from the time of its organization until the time of his death, October 6, 1931.

4159. State prison to take fingerprints of its prisoners was Sing Sing Prison, Ossining, NY, which commenced taking impressions on March 3, 1903.

4160. Police department to adopt the fingerprinting system was the St. Louis Metropolitan Police Department, St. Louis, MO, which on October 28, 1904, adopted the Sir E.R. Henry method to fingerprint persons arrested on serious charges. John M. Shea of the department was the first to qualify as a fingerprint expert connected with any police service.

4161. Fingerprinting in federal penitentiaries was undertaken on November 2, 1904, by the Bureau of Criminal Identification at the United States Penitentiary at Leavenworth, KS. This work was carried on until October 1, 1924, when it was taken over by the Federal Bureau of Investigation.

4162. International exchange of fingerprints between the United States and Europe was made on July 6, 1905, when the St. Louis Metropolitan Police Department, St. Louis, MO, obtained the fingerprints of John Walker, alias Captain John Pearson, a frequent offender, from New Scotland Yard, London. The prints were later forwarded to New Orleans, LA, and introduced as part of his criminal record.

4163. Fingerprint conviction in a crime was recorded on February 1, 1911, in the Criminal Court of Cook County, IL, when Thomas Jennings was found guilty and sentenced to death for the murder of Clarence B. Hiller on September 19, 1910. The conviction was upheld by the Illinois Supreme Court on December 21, 1911, when the court ruled that fingerprint evidence was admissible. Jennings was hanged in the Cook County jail on February 16, 1912.

HEALTH AND SAFETY—POLICE—IDEN-
TIFICATION—*continued*

4164. Community to fingerprint its citizens
was Oskaloosa, IA, which acted upon the suggestion made by Police Chief Howard Ray
Allgood on May 21, 1934. Although registration was not compulsory, a Personal Identification Bureau was established through which
most of the town's residents had their fingerprints recorded.

**4165. Identification of human beings from
the pattern formed by the blood vessels of
the retina** was devised by Dr. Isidore
Goldstein, ophthalmic surgeon of Mount Sinai
Hospital, New York City, in collaboration with
Dr. Carleton Simon, former deputy police commissioner of New York. The system was presented before the annual convention of the International Association of Chiefs of Police on
July 7, 1935, in Atlantic City, NJ.

4166. High school to fingerprint its students
was the Watertown Senior High School, Watertown, SD. The fingerprinting was started on
October 19, 1936, as an outgrowth of a talk by
a member of the Federal Bureau of Investigation.

**4167. Criminal convicted on the evidence of
DNA matching** was Timothy W. Spencer, who
died in the electric chair in the Greensville
Correctional Center, Greensville, VA, on April
27, 1994. Spencer was convicted of murdering
four women in Richmond, VA, in 1987. DNA
from his cells was matched with DNA found in
evidence at the scene of the crime, a process
also known as genetic fingerprinting.

HEALTH AND SAFETY—POLICE—SE-
CRET SERVICE

4168. Secret service established in a colony
was the Headquarters Secret Service, organized
by Aaron Burr and Major Benjamin Tallmadge
in June 1778. On July 4, 1778, General George
Washington issued a special order making Burr
head of the Department for Detecting and Defeating Conspiracies and ordered him "to proceed to Elizabeth Town to procure information
of movements of the enemy's shipping about
New York." This was the first official intelli-
gence-gathering government service in the united colonies. Previously, information about the
activities of the British had been gathered secretly by individuals and informal groups.

**4169. Secret service established by the feder-
al government** under the Treasury Department
was created by act of June 23, 1860, to suppress the counterfeiting of U.S. coins, and, by
later legislation, of paper money and securities.
After the assassination of President Abraham
Lincoln, the Secret Service was given the duty
of guarding the president. Special agents are
charged with protecting the president and his
immediate family, the vice president, the president-elect, the vice president-elect, former presidents and their wives, the widows of former
presidents unless they remarry, minor children
of former presidents until they reach 16, major
presidential and vice presidential candidates,
visiting heads of foreign governments, and official government representatives performing special missions abroad. The Federal Bureau of Investigation was created in 1908 under the Department of Justice to supplement the work of
the Secret Service.

4170. Secret Service agents who were women
were Laurie B. Anderson, Sue A. Baker,
Kathryn I. Clark, Holly A. Hufschmidt, and
Phyllis Frances Shantz, former agents of the
Executive Protective Service, who were sworn
in as special agents on December 15, 1971, in
Washington, DC. The first female agent to be
killed in the line of duty was Julie Yvonne
Cross, who was involved in surveillance of a
counterfeiting operation when she was fatally
wounded on June 4, 1980, in Los Angeles, CA.

HEALTH AND SAFETY—PUBLIC HEALTH

**4171. Colonial law for the maintenance of an
insane patient** is found in the records of the
Upland Court, Delaware County, PA, dated
1676. The act reads: "Jan Cornelissen of
Amesland, Complayning to the Court that his
son Erick is bereft of his naturall Senses and is
turned quyt madd and that; he being a poore
man is not able to maintaine him; Ordered: that
three or four persons bee hired to build a little
blockhouse at Amesland for to put in the said
madman, and at the next Court, order will be
taken that; a small Levy be Laid for to pay for
the building of the house and the maintaining
of the said madman according to the laws of
the Government."

4172. Health board established by a city was
appointed by Governor Thomas Sim Lee in
1792 for Baltimore, MD. Dr. John Ross was
appointed quarantine physician for land and Dr.
John Worthington for sea. On September 12
and 17, 1793, a quarantine was proclaimed

against Philadelphia, PA, which had a yellow fever epidemic, and Governor Lee forbade all direct commerce. Beginning on April 24, 1795, the Board of Health was elected instead of appointed.

4173. Epidemiologist was Noah Webster, who is better known as the compiler of a famous dictionary. His *A Collection of Papers on the Subject of Bilious Fevers, Prevalent in the United States for a Few Years Past,* was printed in New York City by Hopkins, Webb and Company in 1797. A two-volume work, *A Brief History of Epidemics and Pestilential Diseases; with the Principal Phenomena of the Physical World, which Precede and Accompany Them, and Observations Deduced from the Facts Stated,* was published by Hudson and Goodwin, Hartford, CT, in 1799.

4174. Health service established by the federal government was the Marine Hospital Service, established by congressional act of July 16, 1798. The law provided that the master of every American merchant ship arriving from a foreign port should pay to the collector of customs the sum of 20 cents a month for each seaman, which he was authorized to deduct from the seamen's wages. The money was spent for health services in the district in which it was collected. The service was reorganized as a national hospital system, the Public Health Service, on June 29, 1870.

4175. Pure food and drug law established by Congress to prevent the importation of adulterated drugs was passed on June 26, 1848. It was enforced by the Treasury Department through the Customs Service.

4176. Health board with emergency powers established by a city was the Metropolitan Board of Health, established in New York City by act of New York State Legislature passed on February 26, 1866, "an act to create a Metropolitan Sanitary District and Board of Health for the preservation of life and health therein, and to prevent the spread of disease therefrom." The first meeting of the board was held on March 5, 1866, and was presided over by Jackson Smith Schultz.

4177. Health board established by a state government was the Massachusetts State Board of Health and Vital Statistics, established on June 21, 1869. The first chairman was Henry Ingersoll Bowditch.

4178. Pure food and drug law enacted by a state was "an act to prevent the adulteration of food or drugs," passed on May 28, 1881, by New York. Violators were guilty of a misdemeanor, subject to a fine up to $50 for the first offense and not exceeding $100 for each subsequent offense. Laws prohibiting the adulteration of specific products had been passed earlier.

4179. Meat inspection law enacted by Congress was approved on August 30, 1890. It provided for the inspection of salted pork and bacon intended for export, as well as the inspection of export swine, cattle, sheep, and other ruminants.

4180. Medical inspection of schoolchildren was established by the Board of Health, Boston, MA, in 1894. Eighty inspectors examined pupils sent to them by teachers and advised with regard to medical and surgical treatment. They also provided for exclusion and isolation in cases of contagious disease and imposed the conditions of readmission to school. This work was transferred to the School Committee in June 1915.

4181. Health ordinance prohibiting spitting on the sidewalks or in other public places was passed on May 12, 1896, by the New York City Department of Health, as a way of preventing the spread of tuberculosis and other contagious diseases.

4182. Hygiene department in a public school district to aid in instructing children in the fundamental laws of health and generally to improve health conditions was established in Boston, MA, in 1907. The department was in charge of physical training and athletics, as well as the newly organized nursing program.

4183. Rat extermination throughout an entire city was accomplished in San Francisco, CA, in 1907–08 by the Public Health Service, which saved the city and perhaps the nation by destroying the rats and ground squirrels that carried plague-bearing fleas.

4184. Safety congress was held on January 28, 1907, under the auspices of the American Institute of Social Science at the American Museum of Natural History, New York City. It included a public exhibition of safety appliances.

4185. Health department of a county organized on a full-time basis was established January 7, 1908, in Jefferson County, KY. The first full-time county health officer was Dr. Benjamin Wilson J. Smock, who received $150 a month.

HEALTH AND SAFETY—PUBLIC HEALTH
—continued

4186. Child hygiene bureau was established in August 1908 in New York City with Dr. Sara Josephine Baker as director. It was the first time a municipal health department undertook to deal with the health of children from birth to legal working age. Dr. Baker's programs included nutrition and health education for residents of slum neighborhoods, health checks for schoolchildren, and licensing of midwives. The result was a drop in the infant mortality rate in poor neighborhoods from 1,500 deaths a week to 300.

4187. Safety association (national) grew out of the Cooperative Safety Congress, which was held from September 30 to October 5, 1912, in Milwaukee, WI. At the second congress, held on September 23–25, 1913, in New York City, the name was changed to the National Council for Industrial Safety, and the following year to the National Safety Council.

4188. Blood testing laws enacted by a state were passed by New York in 1935. Three bills to empower courts to order blood tests were introduced by Assemblyman Charles H. Breitbart on January 9, 1935. They were amendments to the civil practice act, the inferior criminal courts act, and the domestic relations law. They were signed by Governor Herbert Henry Lehman on March 22, 1935.

4189. Blood tests for pregnant women to be required by a state were mandated by the Twomey-Newell bill, signed by Governor Herbert Henry Lehman on March 18, 1938.

4190. Blood tests for marriage license applicants to be required by a state were mandated by New York's Demond-Breitbart Law, signed on April 12, 1938, by Governor Herbert Henry Lehman. The blood tests, along with other medical tests, were intended to prevent the spread of syphilis.

4191. School completely irradiated with germicidal lamps was the Cato-Meridian Central School, Cato, NY. The lamps, made of special glass to permit ultraviolet bactericidal wavelengths to pass through, were made by the General Electric Company, Schenectady, NY, and were installed on January 3, 1945.

4192. AIDS policy coordinator for the federal government was Dr. Kristine Gebbie, appointed by President William Jefferson Clinton on June 25, 1993, in Washington, DC. Gebbie had previously chaired the committee on HIV infection of the Centers for Disease Control and Prevention.

HEALTH AND SAFETY—PUBLIC HEALTH —BATHHOUSES

4193. Public bathhouse and washhouse was opened on January 1, 1852, by the New York Association for Improving the Condition of the Poor in Mott Street, New York City, later known as the Community Service Society. The first year, 80,375 bathers and 10,038 washers availed themselves of the facilities. On August 17, 1891, the association opened the People's Bath, the first bathhouse to offer showers. The building cost $25,922. There was a charge of five cents for the use of a shower, including soap and towel. During the first 13 months there were 69,944 bathers.

4194. Turkish bath was opened on October 6, 1863, by Dr. Charles H. Shepard at 81 Columbia Heights, Brooklyn, NY (now part of New York City). It was known as "The Hammam," the name used in Turkey. Admission was a dollar. Only one bather came the first day. Fifty came the first month.

4195. Bathhouses owned and operated by a city were the L Street baths of Boston, MA, built in 1865. They were first opened to the general public in 1866 and were under the supervision of the Board of Bath Commissioners, which had charge of all baths and gymnasiums up to 1913.

4196. Bathhouses mandated by a state were required by New York in a law passed on April 18, 1895. The law provided for the establishment of free public baths in cities, villages, and towns of 50,000 or over, in such number as determined necessary by local health boards. It required the baths to be kept open not less than 14 hours a day and to be provided with hot and cold water. An earlier law, passed in 1892, had permitted cities to erect free public baths if they desired to do so.

HEALTH AND SAFETY—PUBLIC HEALTH —LABORATORIES

4197. Health laboratory established by a city was established on January 1, 1888, in Providence, RI. Dr. Charles Value Chapin was in charge. Dr. Gardner Taber Swarts was the medical inspector.

4198. Bacteriology diagnostic laboratory in a city health department was the Division of Pathology, Bacteriology and Disinfection, established by the Department of Health of New York City in 1892. The first director of the laboratory was Dr. Hermann Michael Biggs, who served from September 14, 1892, to February 3, 1902.

4199. Tuberculosis laboratory established by a city was authorized on December 13, 1893, and opened by the New York City Department of Health under the direction of Dr. Hermann Michael Biggs. The laboratory conducted diagnostic sputum examinations. It also administered reporting and registration procedures (compulsory for institutions, voluntary for physicians), official supervision of isolation, terminal disinfection, provision of hospital facilities, and public education.

4200. Antitoxin laboratory established by a public health department was established in September 1894 by the New York City Department of Health. Dr. William Hallock Park was in charge. This was the first antitoxin laboratory in the world to be run by a public health organization and the first to provide for the free distribution of antitoxin to the poor.

4201. Health laboratory established by a state to diagnose diseases by the examination of sputum was established on September 1, 1894, in Providence, RI, by the Rhode Island Department of Public Health. The laboratory was supervised by Drs. Gardner Taber Swarts and Jay Perkings. During the first six months, 115 tests were made.

HEALTH AND SAFETY—PUBLIC HEALTH —MILK

4202. Milk purity law enacted by a state was "an act to punish fraud by the sale of adulterated milk," enacted by Massachusetts and signed on May 30, 1856, by Governor Henry Joseph Gardner.

4203. Milk inspection law enacted by a state was enacted by Massachusetts on April 6, 1859. An Inspector of Milk was appointed on August 10, 1859, by Boston, MA, "to prosecute before the proper tribunal all such violations as shall come to his knowledge."

4204. Milk pasteurizing stations were private laboratories set up in New York City in 1892 by the merchant and philanthropist Nathan Straus to kill bacteria in raw milk. He also started the Straus Milk Fund to distribute pasteurized milk to poor families. Some 34,000 bottles were distributed in the first year. The laboratories remained open until pasteurization and inspection of milk became required by law two decades later.

4205. Milk sale regulations enacted by a city were passed by the New York City Department of Health in 1896. The sale of milk without a permit was prohibited. This regulation has since been generally adopted by health authorities. The department of health was also the first to organize a group of milk inspectors to undertake the inspection of dairies located beyond the political boundaries of the city that offered milk for sale in the city, beginning in June 1906.

4206. Milk station operated by a city government to ensure clean, raw, tuberculin-tested milk for children during July and August and to raise the standard of the milk supply was established in 1897 in Rochester, NY, through the efforts of Dr. George Washington Goler.

HEALTH AND SAFETY—PUBLIC HEALTH —QUARANTINES

4207. Quarantine law enacted by a colony was passed by the General Court of Massachusetts in March 1647 to protect against an epidemic that was raging in Barbados and the other islands of the West Indies and that took more than 6,000 lives. The court published an order that all ships coming from the West Indies should stay at the Castle at the entrance to the harbor and not land any passengers or goods without a license from three of the council, under a severe penalty. A like penalty was imposed upon any person visiting such quarantined vessel without permission. The act was repealed on May 2, 1649.

4208. Quarantine law enacted by Congress was passed on February 25, 1799. It required federal officers to aid and assist the enforcement of state and municipal regulations.

4209. Quarantine board established by a state was a joint city and state board of health authorized by Louisiana and approved on March 15, 1855, by Governor Paul Octave Hebert. The board consisted of nine "competent citizens," six appointed by the governor with the consent of the senate and three elected by the council of New Orleans. The first president of the health board was Dr. A. Forster Axson.

4210. Ban by Congress on importation of diseased cattle from foreign countries was enacted on December 18, 1865. The first application of the law took place on July 31, 1875, when meat, cattle, and hides from Spain were excluded on account of the presence of foot-and-mouth disease in that country.

HEALTH AND SAFETY—PUBLIC HEALTH —QUARANTINES—*continued*

4211. Quarantine law for plants enacted by a state was passed by California on March 4, 1881. Quarantine rules for the protection of fruit and fruit trees, covering both intrastate and interstate shipments, were issued on November 12, 1881. The quarantine was particularly designed against an insect known as *Phylloxera vastatrix,* which in 1873 had attacked the cultivated grapevines in the Sonoma Valley, and against the San Jose scale and codling moth, which in 1875 had caused serious damage to tree fruits.

4212. Quarantine law for plants enacted by Congress was the act of August 20, 1912, directed against dangerous plant diseases and injurious insect pests "new to or not theretofore widely prevalent or distributed within and throughout the United States." Plants that could transmit white-pine blister rust or potato wart, and plants that might harbor the Mediterranean fruit fly, were immediately affected. The first quarantine under the authority of this act was issued on September 16, 1912.

HEALTH AND SAFETY—PUBLIC HEALTH —SURGEON GENERAL

4213. Surgeon general was John Maynard Woodworth, appointed Supervising Surgeon of the Marine Hospital Service in April 1871. In 1870, Congress reorganized the MHS, previously a loose network of local hospitals, into a centrally controlled national health agency based in Washington, DC, under the administration of the Treasury Department. Woodworth, formerly the sanitary inspector for the Chicago Board of Health, had distinguished himself during the Civil War as army physician in charge of the ambulance train during General William Tecumseh Sherman's march through Georgia. Woodworth served in the new post until his death in March 1879. The title was changed to Supervising Surgeon General in 1875 and to Surgeon General in 1902.

4214. Surgeon general who was a woman was Dr. Antonia C. Novello, appointed by President George Herbert Walker Bush in October 1989. A native of Fajardo, Puerto Rico, she was also the first Latina to hold the post of surgeon general. Novello was previously a professor of pediatrics at Georgetown University Medical Center in Washington, DC, and deputy director of the National Institute of Child Health and Human Development.

4215. Surgeon general who was African-American was Dr. Joycelyn Elders, born in 1933 in Schaal, AR. Elders, the former health director of the state of Arkansas, was confirmed by a Senate vote of 65 to 34 on September 7, 1993.

HEALTH AND SAFETY—TRANSPORTA-TION

4216. Traffic law enacted by a colony was passed on June 27, 1652, by New Amsterdam (the future New York City): "The Director General and Council of New Netherland in order to prevent accidents do hereby ordain that no Wagons, Carts or Sleighs shall be run, rode or driven at a gallop within this city of New Amsterdam, that the drivers and conductors of all Wagons, Carts and Sleighs within this city (the Broad Highway alone excepted) shall walk by the Wagons, Carts or Sleighs and so take and lead the horses, on the penalty of two pounds Flemish for the first time, and for the second time double, and for the third time to be arbitrarily corrected therefor and in addition to be responsible for all damages which may arise therefrom."

4217. Steamboat inspection service established by Congress was authorized on July 7, 1838, for the "better security of the lives of passengers on board of vessels propelled in whole or in part by steam." Inspectors were appointed by federal district judges and received $5 for each inspection. They gave the owners a certificate stating the age of the boat and the soundness of the vessel. An annual inspection was required.

4218. Railroad safety law enacted by a state was passed by Georgia on March 5, 1856. The law, which made railroad companies liable for injuries to employees and passengers caused by negligence, was "an act to define the liability of the several railroad companies of this state for injuries to persons or property, to prescribe in what counties they may be sued, and how served with process."

4219. Railroad safety law enacted by Congress was the Safety Appliance Act, passed on March 2, 1893, "an act to promote the safety of employees and travelers upon railroads by compelling common carriers engaged in interstate commerce to equip their cars with automatic couplers and continuous brakes and their locomotives with driving wheel brakes, and for other purposes."

4220. License plates for vehicles were required by New York State under a law that took effect on April 25, 1901. Owners of automobiles were obliged to register their names and addresses and a description of their machines with the office of the secretary of state. Each owner received a small license plate, at least three inches high, which bore the owner's initials. The registration fee was one dollar. In 1901 fees totaling $954 were received, and in 1902, $1,082.

4221. Speeding driver law enacted by a state was passed by the General Assembly of Connecticut on May 21, 1901. The bill, which was introduced by State Representative Robert Woodruff of Orange, CT, provided that the speed of all motor vehicles should not exceed 12 miles per hour on country highways and eight miles per hour on highways within city limits.

4222. Federal law requiring radios on ships was the Wireless Ship Act of June 24, 1910, which required wireless equipment on all passenger vessels carrying 50 or more persons as passengers or crew.

4223. Traffic lanes designated by painted lines were the invention of Edward Norris Hines, road commissioner for Wayne County, MI, who called his idea a "center line safety stripe." The lines were painted in white on River Road, near Trenton, MI, in the fall of 1911. A machine was later developed that painted the stripes at a reduced cost.

4224. Electric traffic signal lights were installed on August 5, 1914, at Euclid Avenue and East 105th Street, Cleveland, OH, by the American Traffic Signal Company under the direction of Safety Director Alfred A. Benesch. Cross arms were installed 15 feet above the ground and equipped with red and green lights and buzzers. Two buzzes signalled Euclid Avenue traffic to proceed, and one buzz signalled the traffic on 105th Street.

4225. Automatic traffic light was developed by inventor Garrett A. Morgan, an African-American, in Cleveland, OH, in 1923. Morgan later sold the patent rights to the General Electric Corporation for $40,000. Among Morgan's other inventions were the gas mask used by American troops in World War I and a smoke inhalator that saved the lives of workers trapped in a tunnel under Lake Erie in 1916.

4226. License plates for vehicles were issued by Connecticut and became effective on March 1, 1937. The plates, of plain aluminum, had black letters. A changeable colored insert designated the year.

4227. Automatic headlight control was the "Autronic-Eye," developed by the Guide Lamp Division of General Motors Corporation, Anderson, IN, and offered to the public on January 25, 1952. Headlights automatically dimmed at the approach of an oncoming car and then flashed back to bright.

4228. Seat belt law enacted by a state requiring automobiles to be equipped with frame holes to which seat belts could be fastened was enacted by Illinois on June 27, 1955, and signed by Governor William Grant Stratton on July 6, 1955. The law provided that on or after July 1, 1956, no new motor vehicle could be registered unless equipped with seat belt attachments conforming to the specifications of the Society of Automotive Engineers.

4229. Seat belts in cars were installed by Nash Motors in its 1949 models after their value was demonstrated by Cornell University's Crash Injury Research Program, but they were discontinued after customers complained about them. The first cars to have seat belts installed as standard equipment were the 1964 models manufactured by Studebaker-Packard, South Bend, IN. Three-point lap-and-shoulder belts were introduced by the Ford Motor Company in 1970 and were required by federal law in all American-made cars beginning with the 1974 models.

4230. Speed limit for highway traffic established by Congress was enacted in 1974 in an effort to conserve fuel during the energy crisis of the 1970s. The speed limit was set at 55 miles per hour. The law was repealed on November 28, 1995, after which most states proceeded to raise their speed limits to 65 miles per hour or higher, despite ample evidence that the lower speed limit resulted in fewer deaths in traffic accidents.

4231. Air bag requirement by the federal government took effect on September 1, 1989, when all newly manufactured cars were required to have air bags installed on the driver's side.

HOLIDAYS

4232. Independence Day to be observed as a state holiday was celebrated by Massachusetts on July 4, 1781.

4233. Columbus Day was celebrated on October 12, 1792, to mark the tricentennial of Christopher Columbus's first landing in the New World. The second Columbus Day was celebrated a century later, in 1892. Annual celebrations began in 1893 during the World's Columbian Exposition in Chicago, IL.

HOLIDAYS—*continued*

4234. Mardi Gras celebration in New Orleans, LA, had its inception in 1827 when a group of young men returned from a trip to Paris and introduced the French carnival idea. Mardi Gras is always on the Tuesday before Ash Wednesday, the day that marks the beginning of the Lenten season. "Mardi Gras" means "Fat Tuesday." The term was first used in America in 1699 by the French explorer Pierre le Moyne, Sieur d'Iberville, who gave the name Pointe du Mardi Gras to a spot on the Mississippi River, to commemorate the traditional pre-Lenten observance in France.

4235. Valentines commercially produced were manufactured in 1834 by Robert H. Elton, an engraver, who opened Elton and Company in New York City, specializing in printing and publishing. Previously, valentines were handmade.

4236. Decoration Day was officially observed on May 30, 1868. It originated in Columbus, MS, on April 26, 1866, a year after the end of the Civil War, when the women of the town strewed flowers on the graves of Confederate and Union soldiers at Friendship Cemetery. In May 1868, Adjutant General Norton Parker Chipman suggested to National Commander John Alexander Logan of the Grand Army of the Republic that this organization inaugurate the custom of spreading flowers on the graves of Union soldiers at periodic intervals. General Logan appointed May 30, 1868, as the date "for the purpose of strewing with flowers or otherwise decorating the graves of comrades who died in defense of their country during the late rebellion and with the hope that it will be kept up from year to year." On August 1, 1888, an act of Congress proclaimed Decoration Day a holiday in the District of Columbia.

4237. Labor Day was inaugurated on December 28, 1869, by the Knights of Labor, a workers' organization formed in Philadelphia, PA. The first states to declare Labor Day a state holiday were Oregon, in February 1887; Colorado, in March 1887; and New York, in May 1887. The annual nationwide observance of Labor Day was sponsored by the American Federation of Labor, which resolved in convention at Chicago, IL, on October 7, 1884, "that the first Monday in September be set aside as a laborer's national holiday." On June 28, 1894, Congress designated the first Monday in September a legal holiday for federal employees and for the District of Columbia. The first Labor Day parade was held in New York City on September 5, 1882, under the auspices of the Central Labor Union. It featured musical bands and 10,000 marchers who carried placards reading "Less Work and More Pay," "Less Hours More Pay," "Labor Pays All Taxes," "Labor Creates All Wealth," "To the Workers Should Belong the Wealth," and "The Laborer Must Receive and Enjoy the Full Fruit of His Labor."

4238. Arbor Day was celebrated on April 10, 1872, in Nebraska. Governor Julius Sterling Morton suggested the holiday and helped celebrate it by having trees planted throughout the state. Arbor Day did not become a legal holiday in Nebraska until April 22, 1885, Morton's birthday.

4239. Easter egg roll was held on April 2, 1877, at the Capitol grounds, Washington, DC, during President Rutherford Hayes's administration. The custom was carried on by later Presidents until it was discontinued by President Franklin Delano Roosevelt in 1942. It was reinstated on April 6, 1953, during the administration of President Dwight David Eisenhower.

4240. Flag Day remembrance took place on June 14, 1877. The Government requested that the flag be flown from all public buildings on that day in commemoration of the 100th anniversary of the adoption of the American flag. The first state to make Flag Day a legal holiday was Pennsylvania, which held its first celebration on June 14, 1937. Flag Day became a national holiday in 1949 after a joint congressional resolution dated August 3, 1949, designated June 14 as an annual day of observance.

4241. National holiday was April 30, 1889, authorized by act of Congress on March 21, 1889, in observance of the centennial of the inauguration of George Washington. The day was "hereby declared to be a national holiday throughout the United States." A committee of five senators and five representatives of the 51st Congress was appointed to arrange an appropriate celebration in Congress on December 11, 1889, at which Chief Justice Melville Weston Fuller was the guest speaker.

4242. Frontier Day celebration was the Cheyenne Frontier Day, held at the Fair Grounds in Cheyenne, WY, on September 23, 1897. From a one-day exhibition, the celebration grew to a six-day spectacle of ranch and range sports, Native American games and dances, military maneuvers, and races requiring the utmost skill in horsemanship. Other cities have similar celebrations under different names.

4243. Mother's Day celebration took place in Philadelphia, PA, on May 10, 1908. The idea was suggested by Anna Jarvis of Philadelphia at a public meeting in 1907. She proposed wearing a carnation in honor of mothers on the second Sunday of May. A joint resolution of Congress on May 8, 1914, established the second Sunday in May as Mother's Day. On May 9, President Woodrow Wilson proclaimed the date as a national holiday, which was held for the first time on May 10.

4244. Father's Day was celebrated on June 19, 1910. The idea originated with Mrs. John Bruce Dodd, and the holiday was launched by the Ministerial Association and the YMCA of Spokane, WA. It is now generally observed on the third Sunday in June.

4245. Indian Day celebration was held on May 13, 1916, sponsored by the Society of American Indians. The purpose was to recognize and honor the Native Americans and to improve their conditions.

4246. Veterans' Day celebrations took place simultaneously in many cities on November 11, 1919, to mark the signing of the armistice that ended World War I. Two California redwood trees were planted in Lafayette Square, opposite the White House, Washington, DC, in the presence of cabinet officers, General John Joseph Pershing, and other military and federal officials. Until 1954, the annual commemoration was known as Armistice Day. It was made a legal holiday on May 13, 1938.

4247. Navy Day was celebrated on October 27, 1922, the anniversary of the birth of President Theodore Roosevelt. Celebrations were held in various parts of the United States. The idea was suggested by Mrs. William Hamilton to the Secretary of the Navy.

4248. Maritime Day took place on May 22, 1933. It was established by joint resolution of Congress on May 20, 1933. The resolution authorized and requested the President "annually to issue a proclamation calling upon the people of the United States to observe National Maritime Day by displaying the flag." The designated day was the anniversary of the sailing of the steamship *Savannah* from Savannah, GA, on May 22, 1819.

4249. Kwanzaa celebration was held on December 26, 1966, in California. It was the invention of Ron Karenga, one of the founders of the Black Studies movement on American campuses. Karenga drew upon various African agricultural festivals to create a cultural festival for African-Americans. The name is a Swahili word meaning "first fruit of the harvest." Kwanzaa is held annually from December 26 to January 1. Each of the seven days celebrates a separate principle: unity, self-determination, collective work and responsibility, economic cooperation, purpose, creativity, and faith. A candle is lit on each night to represent the principle of the day.

4250. Earth Day to be celebrated nationwide was held on April 22, 1970, to increase public awareness of the world's environmental problems. Twenty million Americans participated in marches, educational programs, and rallies, including the students at some 2,000 colleges and 10,000 high schools. An earlier Earth Day celebration had been organized on March 21, 1970, in San Francisco, California. In subsequent years some groups and officials have selected April 22 for their annual Earth Day celebrations while others have chosen the Vernal Equinox for their festivities.

4251. Martin Luther King Day was officially observed as a national holiday on January 20, 1986.

4252. Native American Day was celebrated in South Dakota in place of Columbus Day on October 8, 1990.

HOLIDAYS—CHRISTMAS

4253. Colonial law banning Christmas was instituted by the Puritan governing council of the Massachusetts Bay Colony in 1659. The law was repealed in 1681, but not because of popular demand. By then, Puritan leaders were confident that no one wanted to celebrate the holiday. The Puritans considered most Christmas celebrations to be of pagan origin, and thought the feasting and revelry associated with Christmas to be impious. Christmas was legalized in Massachusetts in 1856.

4254. Christmas tree of record was mentioned in the diary of Matthew Zahm of Lancaster, PA, on December 20, 1821. Zahm and other German immigrants to Pennsylvania brought the custom of decorated trees from their homeland.

4255. Poinsettia plants were imported from Mexico, where they were known as "the flower of the blessed night." They were brought to the United States by Dr. Joel Roberts Poinsett, the U.S. ambassador to Mexico, in 1828 as presents for his friends.

HOLIDAYS—CHRISTMAS—*continued*

4256. Christmas cards were designed and produced by Richard H. Pease, engraver and lithographer, at Albany, NY, in 1851. They were printed in black on white paper, 4.5 by 6 inches, with the message "A Merry Christmas and Happy New Year." The illustration showed a fanciful structure with a banner reading "Pease's Great Varety Store in the Temple of Fancy." (He misspelled "Variety.") The cards were sent to his customers and friends.

4257. Christmas tree decorated with electric lights was installed in December 1882 in New York City in the house of Edward H. Johnson, an associate of Thomas Alva Edison.

4258. National Christmas tree was the General Grant Tree, in General Grant National Park, CA, which was the site of a ceremony at noon on Christmas Day 1925. On May 1, 1926, Mayor Henry Leonard Suderman of Sanger, CA, officially dedicated it as "the Nation's Christmas Tree." The greatest horizontal diameter of the tree was 40.3 feet at the base. At 200 feet above the ground the diameter was about 12 feet. The tree was 267 feet high and 3,500-4,000 years old.

4259. Santa Claus school to train men to play the part of Santa Claus was a one-week program that opened on September 27, 1937, in Albion, NY, with an enrollment of six students. It was conducted by Charles Willis Howard.

HOLIDAYS—THANKSGIVING

4260. National day of thanksgiving was authorized by the Continental Congress and held on December 18, 1777, to celebrate the surrender of Lieutenant General John Burgoyne on October 17 at Saratoga (now Schuylerville), NY. The first to be designated by presidential proclamation was November 26, 1789, which was appointed by President George Washington as a day of general thanksgiving for the adoption of the Constitution.

4261. Thanksgiving Day was held in November 1863 to commemorate the feast of thanksgiving held by the Pilgrims at Plymouth, MA, in 1621. A proclamation by President Abraham Lincoln set aside the fourth Thursday in November for an annual nationwide observance. The establishment of Thanksgiving Day was the result of a long campaign by Sarah Josepha Hale, the editor of the popular magazine *Godey's Lady's Book*. The holiday was moved forward to the third Thursday in November in 1939 to accommodate merchants who wanted more time for the pre-Christmas shopping rush, but was returned to its traditional spot two years later.

4262. Macy's Thanksgiving Day Parade was held in New York City on November 27, 1924, along a two-mile stretch of Broadway from Central Park West to Herald Square. The event was intended to boost holiday sales and bring customers to R.H. Macy's recently expanded flagship store at Herald Square.

HOUSEWARES AND APPLIANCES—BEDDING

4263. Horse blankets were manufactured by Thomas Goodall at Troy, NH, in 1852. The only horse blankets then in use were imported and were square in shape. Goodall cut them to fit and put on buckles. He sold out his interest in 1865 to a group of financiers from Keene, NH.

4264. Blanket factory was the Burleigh Blanket Mills, established by Captain John H. Burleigh in 1854 on the Piscataqua River in Maine. The factory was located on the site originally used by the explorer Sir Ferdinando Gorges in 1620 for a grist mill, at what is now South Berwick, ME.

4265. Electric blanket was manufactured by the Simmons Company on October 9, 1946, in Petersburg, VA. Temperature was regulated by an "electronic" thermostatic control. It sold for $39.50.

HOUSEWARES AND APPLIANCES—CLEANING

4266. Soap manufacturer to render fats in his plant for soap stock was William Colgate, who opened a factory in 1806 at 6 Dutch Street, New York City. He had learned his trade at 50 Broadway, New York City, in the plant of John Slidell and Company.

4267. Brushes were manufactured at Medfield, MA, in 1808 by Artemas Woodward.

4268. Cakes of soap of uniform weight and individually wrapped were manufactured by Jessie Oakley of Newburgh, NY, about 1830. Cakes of soap were usually sold to grocers in large blocks from which pieces were cut as desired. Oakley prepared one-pound packages.

4269. Soap powder in packages was introduced by Benjamin Talbert Babbitt about 1845. Rather than remelt the waste shavings of soap, he packaged the shavings in two-pound boxes. This innovation met with instant success at laundries and hotels.

4270. Washing machine with rotary motion was made by Hamilton Erastus Smith of Philadelphia, PA, who obtained a patent on October 26, 1858. It was equipped with a crank that was turned by hand, caused a perforated cylinder within a wooden shell to revolve. Smith continued to improve his machine and in 1863 secured patent protection on a self-reversing-motion attachment to the machine.

4271. Soap in liquid form was patented on August 22, 1865, by William Sheppard of New York City. It was made by mixing a pound of common soap with 100 pounds of ammonia solution or spirits of hartshorn. The soap was dissolved in water or by steam to the consistency of molasses.

4272. Vacuum cleaner that used suction was invented by Ives W. McGaffey of Chicago, IL, who obtained a patent on June 8, 1869, on a "sweeping machine," a light hand-powered suction device for surface cleaning.

4273. Carpet sweeper that was practical was invented in 1876 by Melville Reuben Bissell of Grand Rapids, MI, who obtained a patent for it on September 19, 1876. Although the idea had been introduced earlier, none of the early sweepers worked well. Bissell devised the "broom-action" principle, by which the application of variable pressure on the handle made the sweeper responsive to different grades of floor coverings. Bissell organized the Bissell Carpet Sweeper Company in Grand Rapids, MI.

4274. Dishwasher was invented by Josephine Cochrane of Shelbyville, IL, in 1886. Her initial design was a large copper tub outfitted with removable wire dish racks. Hot soapy water was pumped over the dishes by turning a crank. The Cochrane dishwasher was patented in December 1886 and won an award at the 1893 World's Columbian Exposition in Chicago.

4275. Vacuum cleaner driven by a motor was invented by John S. Thurman of the General Compressed Air and Vacuum Machinery Company, St. Louis, MO, who obtained a patent on October 3, 1899, on a "pneumatic carpet renovator."

4276. Electric washing machine was a Thor machine, which was put on the market in 1907 by the Hurley Machine Company of Chicago, IL. A patent was granted on August 9, 1910, to Alva J. Fisher of Chicago, IL, for a "drive mechanism for washing machines."

4277. Laundry detergent packaged in a form that eliminated the need to slice up a bar of laundry soap was Lux Flakes, introduced by Lever Brothers in 1906. The first granulated detergent, Rinso, was introduced by Lever Brothers in 1918.

4278. Clothes dryer was an invention of J. Ross Moore of Devil's Lake, ND. To spare his mother from having to go outside to hang up the laundry in bone-chilling winter weather, he built an oil-heated drum that he set up in a shed next to the house. Beginning in 1930, he worked on a series of crude drying machines. He eventually sold the idea to the Hamilton Manufacturing Company, Two Rivers, WI, which began selling dryers in 1938.

4279. Synthetic laundry detergent whose formula included a surfactant to emulsify dirt was Dreft, first marketed on October 10, 1933, by the Procter and Gamble Company, Cincinnati, OH. It was a sodium alkyl sulfate made from chlorosulfonic acid and a fatty alcohol. The first effective powdered detergent made for use in washing machines, and the first to contain a phosphate compound as a water softener, was Tide, developed by Procter and Gamble in 1946.

4280. Cellulose sponge for household use was made in 1936 by Dr. William Orlin Kenyon of the Tennessee Eastman Company, Kingsport, TN, a division of the Eastman Kodak Company, Rochester, NY.

4281. Automatic washing machine was the Model S, introduced in 1937 at a county fair in Louisiana. The inventor was John Chamberlain, an engineer at Bendix Home Appliances, part of the Bendix Hydraulic Brake Company, South Bend, IN. The Model S required no more effort from the consumer than to load the soap and laundry and to set dials twice during the washing cycle. Bendix introduced a fully automatic model in 1947.

HOUSEWARES AND APPLIANCES— CONTAINERS

4282. Bottle blown in America was made in a factory set up in the woods one mile from Jamestown, VA, in 1608. The common glass bottle bears the distinction of being the first manufactured product exported from this country.

4283. Mason jar for canning was patented in 1858 by metalworker John Landis Mason of New York City. It was a reusable glass container with a wide, threaded mouth that could be tightly sealed with a flexible ring and a zinc lid. The first Mason jars were made by Whitney Glass Works of Glassboro, NJ.

HOUSEWARES AND APPLIANCES— CONTAINERS—*continued*

4284. Tin can with a key opener was invented by J. Osterhoudt of New York City, who obtained a patent on October 2, 1866, for an "improved method of opening tin cans." The can had a projecting lip and key.

4285. Milk bottles were made by Louis Porter Whiteman, owner of the Warren Glass Works, Cumberland, MD, who manufactured a product he called Glass Air Tight Milk Jars in 1879. They were used by the Echo Farms Dairy Company, New York City. To commemorate the event, the Pennsylvania State Agricultural Society presented a plaque to Whiteman.

4286. Bottle cap with a cork crown was invented in 1892 by William Painter, founder of the Crown Cork and Seal Company, Baltimore, MD, who obtained a patent for the product on February 2, 1892. It was a simple bit of tin with a corrugated rim or skirt into which was inserted a disc of natural or composition cork.

4287. Bottle with a screw cap and a pour lip was patented on May 5, 1936, by Edward A. Ravenscroft, Glencoe, IL. The bottles were manufactured by the Abbott Laboratories, North Chicago, IL.

4288. Household product made entirely of plastic was a clear polyethylene water tumbler invented in 1945 by Massachusetts chemist Earl S. Tupper. In 1948 he began marketing Tupperware, a line of resealable, leak-proof polyethylene containers.

4289. Aluminum cans with tab openings for beer and soft drinks were developed by the Aluminum Corporation of America and first marketed in 1962.

HOUSEWARES AND APPLIANCES— COOKING

4290. Cooking pots made in America were cast-iron pots with three legs and a capacity of one quart. They were made in 1643 at the Saugus Iron Works, Lynn, MA.

4291. Tinware manufacturers are said to have been Edward and William Pattison, brothers who settled in Berlin, CT, about 1740 and manufactured kitchen vessels and household articles from sheet tin. They peddled their wares from house to house. The first successful tinware manufacturers were Lalance and Grosjean, who in 1860 established a factory at Woodhaven, NY, for the manufacture of deep tinware, such as milk pans, wash bowls, and dishpans.

4292. Brass kettles were made in 1834 in Wolcottville (now Torrington), CT, by Israel Coe, who organized the Coe Brass Company.

4293. Electric range was invented by George B. Simpson of Washington, DC, who received a patent on September 20, 1859, on an "electrical heating apparatus" that he called an electroheater. The machine generated heat by passing currents of electricity over coils of platina or other metallic wire.

4294. Waffle iron patent was issued on August 24, 1869, to Cornelius Swarthout of Troy, NY.

4295. Doughnut cutter was invented by John F. Blondel of Thomaston, ME, who obtained a patent on July 9, 1872. A spring pushed the dough out of a center tube to make the hole.

4296. Slicing machine was patented on November 4, 1873, by Anthony Iske of Lancaster, PA, who obtained a patent on a "machine for slicing dried beef." It employed an oblique knife in a vertical sliding frame.

4297. Aluminum pots were made possible by Charles Martin Hall of Oberlin, OH, who on February 23, 1886, invented a simplified procedure for producing aluminum. His line of cast aluminum cookware, called Wear-Ever, met with indifference until 1903, when the Wanamaker's department store, in Philadelphia, gave a demonstration in which a chef made apple butter in a a lightweight aluminum pan without needing to stir it. Aluminum pots quickly became standard kitchen equipment.

4298. Electric stove was a one-ring spiral-coiled conductor invented by William S. Hadaway, Jr., of New York City, who obtained a patent on June 30, 1896. It provided a uniform surface distribution of heat.

4299. Toaster with a pop-up action was developed by mechanic Charles Strite of Stillwater, MN. On May 29, 1919, he applied for a patent on a device that could toast and eject bread when positioned over a fire.

4300. Electric blender was invented by Stephen J. Paplawski of Racine, WI. In 1922 he patented an electric blender designed to make milkshakes for the burgeoning soda-fountain industry.

4301. Electric toaster of the household automatic pop-up type was marketed in June 1926 by the McGraw Electric Company, Minneapolis, MN, under the trademark Toastmaster. One lever lowered the bread into the toaster and another wound the timer. It received one slice of toast at a time. The retail price was $13.50.

4302. Microwave oven for commercial food preparation was introduced by the Raytheon Company, Lexington, MA, in 1947. It was based on research into microwave-generating magnetron tubes by Raytheon scientist Percy Spencer. Spencer was standing near a magnetron when he noticed that a candy bar in his pants pocket had melted, although he had felt no heat. The first microwave oven for home use was the Tappan Oven, which was sold beginning in 1952 by the Tappan Corporation, Tappan, NY, for $1,295.

4303. Electronic range for domestic use was introduced at a press conference at the Hotel Pierre, New York City, on October 25, 1955, by the Tappan Stove Company, Mansfield, OH. A 220-volt electric current produced microwaves that cooked eggs in 22 seconds, bacon in 90 seconds, frozen broccoli in 4.5 minutes, and a five-pound roast in 30 minutes. The retail price of the range was $1,200.

4304. Food processor marketed in the United States was the Cuisinart, introduced in January 1973 at the Chicago Housewares Show, Chicago, IL. It was made by Carl Sontheimer, a Connecticut electronics engineer, who borrowed the basic idea from processing machines invented by the French chef Pierre Verdun. The Cuisinart had exchangeable blades that could divide and blend food in a multiplicity of ways, including grinding, chopping, slicing, mincing, mixing, and pureeing.

HOUSEWARES AND APPLIANCES—DECORATION

4305. Wallpaper was manufactured in 1739 by Plunket Fleeson of Philadelphia, PA. The design was stamped with wooden blocks on sheets of paper that were joined together. A paintbrush was used to apply the color. In August 1739, Fleeson advertised in the *Pennsylvania Gazette* the sale of "bedticks, choice live geese feathers, blankets, as well as paperhangings."

4306. Venetian blinds are said to have been installed in 1761 in St. Peter's Church, Third and Pine streets, Philadelphia, PA. The first patent for them was granted to John Hampson of New Orleans, LA, on August 21, 1841, on a "manner of retaining in any desired position the slats of Venetian Blinds."

4307. Decalcomania pictures that could be transferred from paper to other surfaces were imported in 1862 and used as playthings. The first commercial production of decalcomanias for decorating buggies, sleighs, bicycles, sewing machines, and other objects was undertaken in Philadelphia, PA, in 1890 by Thomas Burke, who established the National Decalcomania Company. The company was incorporated in 1922.

HOUSEWARES AND APPLIANCES—DISHES

4308. Pottery made in America by settlers is believed to have been the work of John Pride of Salem, MA, who operated a pottery from 1641 to 1647. He made red earthenware from common brick clay. Another pottery was established by Dr. Daniel Coxe in Burlington, NJ, in 1680. It produced white and "chiney" ware for the local trade and also for export to Jamaica and Barbados. The factory was sold in 1691.

4309. Chinaware for restaurant use was made by the Greenwood Pottery Company of Trenton, NJ, in 1862. It combined the best qualities of both porcelain and earthenware.

4310. Paper cup was developed in 1908 by Hugh Moore, who also invented an early type of water cooler and the Dixie Cup, a paper container for ice cream.

HOUSEWARES AND APPLIANCES—FLOORING

4311. Carpet mill was founded in 1791 by William Peter Sprague on North Second Street, Philadelphia, PA. He manufactured Axminster carpets on handlooms. One of his earliest designs represented the aims and achievements of the new republic of the United States.

4312. Carpet mill to make ingrain carpets was established in 1810 by George M. Conradt in Frederick, MD. The carpets were produced on handlooms on a drum having rows of pegs, and were two- or three-ply, the warp being worsted or cotton with a wool filling.

4313. Carpet power loom was invented by Erastus Brigham Bigelow of West Boylston, MA, who obtained a patent for it on April 20, 1837. It was used by the Lowell Manufacturing Company of Lowell, MA, in the weaving of carpets.

4314. Velvet carpeting and tapestry were manufactured in Newark, NJ, in 1855 by John Johnson.

4315. Linoleum was manufactured in 1873 by the American Linoleum Manufacturing Company, Richmond, Staten Island, NY (now part of New York City). It was a British invention.

HOUSEWARES AND APPLIANCES—FLOORING—*continued*

4316. Dealer in Oriental rugs was Hagop Boghighian, an immigrant from Armenia, who began selling rugs in Boston, MA, in 1885.

4317. Linoleum manufacturing machine for manufacturing straight-line linoleum was installed in 1911 by Congoleum-Nairn at its Kearny, NJ, plant.

4318. Embossed inlaid linoleum was introduced in 1925 by the Armstrong Cork and Insulation Company of Lancaster, PA. The company manufactured the linoleum and then placed it under an embossing press in which parts of the design were compressed, so that the tile blocks or other portions of the pattern stood out in relief.

4319. Carpeting of tufted plastic was manufactured at La Fayette, GA, by the E.T. Barwick Mills and offered for sale on January 4, 1953. The carpeting, made of Saran fibers, was immune to moths, mildew, and fungi and was almost completely resistant to ink and other stains. It would soften, char, and decompose in flame, but would not support combustion.

HOUSEWARES AND APPLIANCES—FURNITURE

4320. Rocking chair is believed to have been invented by Benjamin Franklin of Philadelphia, PA, about 1760. This date is not verified, but no authentic instance of a prior rocker has come to light.

4321. Chair factory was established by Lambert Hitchcock in Hitchcockville (now Riverton), CT, in 1818. The chairs were generally hand-painted on the back. They were shipped disassembled. They sold extensively in the South.

4322. Bedspring manufacturing patent was granted on August 25, 1831, to Josiah French of Ware, MA.

4323. Caster for bedsteads was patented by Philos Blake, Eli Whitney Blake, and John A. Blake, of New Haven, CT, on June 30, 1838.

4324. Reclining chair was patented on May 22, 1841, by Henry Peres Kennedy, a cabinetmaker and upholsterer of Philadelphia, PA. A spiral spring was placed horizontally between the back rail of the seat and the front rail of the chair.

4325. Desk with a roll top was invented about 1850 by Abner Cutler, who formed the Cutler Desk Company of Buffalo, NY. The original patent showed the top very similar to the roll top of today. Flexible wooden curtains had been used previously. Cutler improved upon their manufacture by using a strong fabric held between an outer row of moldings and an inner row of soft wood slats, which made it possible to operate rolls six feet long and four feet wide.

4326. Folding theater chair was invented by Aaron H. Allen of Boston, MA, who obtained a patent on December 5, 1854, on an "improvement in seats for public buildings."

4327. Box spring was imported from France in 1857 by James Boyle, Chatham Square, New York City, a manufacturer of bedding. Made to be reversible, it was about 12 inches deep. The frame was made of boards joined together with strips of ticking.

4328. Folding bed was successfully built in 1875–76 at Sixth and Filbert streets, Philadelphia, PA, by the Hale and Kilburn Manufacturing Company. The folding bed was invented by a man in the company's employ named Everett and was improved upon by H.S. Hale. The bed was designed because apartment houses were becoming more popular and there was a need for economy in space. The beds were equipped with a flexible spring. They later used a "sectional spring bed," or the ordinary bedspring divided into three sections lengthwise, each of which was filled with springs and enclosed in a canvas covering. This spring developed into the box spring now in use.

4329. Deck chair for steamer passengers was introduced in 1891 by Heinrich Conried, impresario of the Metropolitan Opera House, New York City. He built 500 chairs and formed the Ocean Comfort Company to distribute and rent them. At one time 5,000 chairs were on rental to steamship companies. The first rental contract was signed with Albert Ballin, general director of the Hamburg-American lines.

4330. Bed that could be hidden was manufactured by the Murphy Door Bed Company in San Francisco, CA, in 1909. The beds, known as In-a-Door Beds, operated on a pivot and could be swung out of sight behind doors or in closets.

HOUSEWARES AND APPLIANCES— HEATING AND COOLING

4331. Heating stove was the Pennsylvania fireplace, invented by Benjamin Franklin in 1742 and now called the Franklin stove. It was a wood-burning open box of cast-iron that stood out from the chimney and caused heat from its back and sides to be thrown into the room. Smoke escaped over the top of a flat chamber behind the fire, and passed downward between it and the real back of the stove, then into the chimney. Franklin refused to patent his invention. The stoves were manufactured by Robert Grace, the master of the Warwick furnace in Chester County, PA.

4332. Electric fan was invented by Dr. Schuyler Skaats Wheeler, who in 1882 placed a fan or propeller on the shaft of an electric motor. In 1904, the Franklin Institute awarded him the John Scott medal for this invention.

4333. Air conditioner for home use was designed in 1927 by Willis Haviland Carrier of Buffalo, NY. Carrier, an engineer, received a patent in 1906 for air-conditioning machinery.

HOUSEWARES AND APPLIANCES— HOUSEHOLD GOODS

4334. Friction matches were made in Springfield, MA, in 1834 in a small establishment in the "L" of the Frederick Chapin house on Chicopee Street, Chicopee (then a part of Springfield), by Daniel M. Chapin and Alonzo Dwight Phillips. On October 24, 1836, Phillips received a patent for the product. The constituents of the match head were chalk, phosphorus, glue, and brimstone.The business was sold to Byam and Carlton of Boston, MA, and the product was thereafter known as the Boston Match. Before 1834, the only match in use had been a slender sulfur splint which was ignited by being drawn quickly through a double fold of sandpaper. Nontoxic friction matches, made with sesquisulfide of phosphorus rather than pure phosphorus, which is poisonous, were introduced by the Diamond Match Company in 1911.

4335. Cotton twine factory was established in 1839 by Jacob Sloat of Sloatsburg, NY, at a mill where cotton cloth had been produced since 1815. During the factory's first year of operation it produced as much as 6,000 pounds of cotton twine each week.

4336. Safety pin was invented by Walter Hunt of New York City, who obtained a patent on April 10, 1849. Within the space of three hours, he conceived the idea, made a model, and sold his patent rights for $100. The pins were manufactured in New York City.

4337. Matchbooks were made by the Diamond Match Company at its Barberton, OH, factory in 1896 under a patent granted on September 27, 1892, to Joshua Pusey, an attorney from Lima, PA. Although the patented design had the striking surface on the inside cover, the manufacturer moved it to the outside to prevent fires.

4338. Cellophane was made in the early part of 1924 by the Du Pont Cellophane Company at its plant in Buffalo, NY, with machinery manufactured in its own shops. Cellophane originally sold for $2.65 a pound.

4339. Cellophane transparent tape was invented by Richard Gurley Drew of St. Paul, MN, who obtained a patent on May 27, 1930, on "adhesive tape." The patent was assigned to the Minnesota Mining and Manufacturing Company of St. Paul, MN, better known as 3M. The tape was introduced to the market on September 8, 1930. The tape was developed from an earlier invention of Drew's, pressure-sensitive masking tape for use by car body shops.

4340. Aluminum foil was developed by R.S. Reynolds of Louisville, KY, the founder of Reynolds Metals. In 1947, Reynolds developed a thin foil of aluminum 12 inches wide and 0.0007 inches thick. He sold it on a roll for home use as a protective wrap for cooking and storage.

HOUSEWARES AND APPLIANCES— LAMPS

4341. Candle factory for making spermaceti candles was established by Benjamin Crabb in Newport, RI, in 1748. It was destroyed by fire in 1750, after which the candles were manufactured in Newport by Jacob Rodriguez Rivera. Spermaceti candles, made from the oil obtained from the heads of sperm whales, burned better than the tallow candles then in general use. Rivera and other Sephardic Jewish immigrants made Newport the center of production of candles, soap, and other whale oil products.

4342. Glass crystal chandelier consisted of "six lights and shower upon shower of rainbow casting prisms." It was cut by William Peter Eichbaum at Bakewell's, Pittsburgh, PA, in 1810 and made in a 10-pot furnace. It sold for $300 to a Mr. Kerr, who hung it in his hostelry.

4343. Oil lamp for burning kerosene was developed in 1857 by A.C. Ferris and Company, later the Tarentum Oil, Salt and Coal Company.

HOUSEWARES AND APPLIANCES—LAMPS—*continued*

4344. Electric socket operated by a pull chain was patented on August 11, 1896, by Harvey Hubbell of Bridgeport, CT, who manufactured the sockets in Bridgeport.

HOUSEWARES AND APPLIANCES—REFRIGERATORS AND FREEZERS

4345. Refrigerator was invented in 1803 by Thomas Moore of Baltimore, MD. It consisted of two boxes, one inside the other, separated by insulating material. Ice and food were stored in the inner box. Moore granted manufacturing licenses for his invention, but gave poor people permission to copy it free of charge. The invention was described in a 28-page pamphlet, "An essay on the most eligible construction of ice houses, also, a description of the newly invented machine, called the Refrigerator."

4346. Ice-making machine of the vapor compression type to be made in commercial quantities was invented in 1834 by Jacob Perkins, an American living in London. He obtained a British patent on August 14, 1834, for an "apparatus for producing ice and cooling liquids." Perkins showed that vapors or gases that do not ordinarily exist in liquid state may be liquefied upon being subjected to high pressure.

4347. Mechanical freezer patent was granted Dr. John Gorrie of Apalachicola, FL, on May 6, 1851, on an "improvement in the process for the artificial production of ice." At a dinner on July 14, 1850, at the Mansion House, Apalachicola, Gorrie produced blocks of ice the size of bricks. He installed his system in the U.S. Marine Hospital in Apalachicola.

4348. Gas refrigerator to be successfully introduced into the American market was the Electrolux, which was sponsored in 1926 by the Electrolux Refrigerator Sales Company of Evansville, IN. A tiny gas flame and a tiny flow of water in the refrigerator took the place of all moving parts, circulating a liquid refrigerant that was hermetically sealed in rigid steel. The first patent issued to the Electrolux Servel Corporation on an absorption refrigerating apparatus was granted on December 7, 1926, to Baltzar Carl von Platen and Georg Munters of Stockholm, Sweden.

HOUSEWARES AND APPLIANCES—SEWING

4349. Lock-stitch sewing machine was made in 1832–34 by Walter Hunt of New York, whose machine used two threads, one below the cloth and the other coming down through the cloth, thus interlocking with each other. He made no attempt to patent his machine until June 27, 1854, and his original application was refused on the ground of abandonment. Elias Howe obtained a patent on a lock-stitch machine on September 10, 1846.

4350. Machine for manufacturing pins that was practical was invented by John Ireland Howe of Derby, CT, who obtained a patent for it on June 22, 1832. The machine was exhibited at the American Institute Fair in New York City, and Howe received a silver medal for his contribution to manufacturing. In December 1835, he formed the Howe Manufacturing Company, New York City. He obtained a second patent on March 24, 1841, for an improved model.

4351. Pins manufactured with a solid head were made in 1838 by Samuel Slocum of Rhode Island, who invented the machine to manufacture them. He did not obtain a patent on it. One man tending two machines could produce 100,000 pins in 11 hours. He formed the firm of Slocum, Jilson and Company, Poughkeepsie, NY, in 1839. His products were known as "Poughkeepsie pins."

4352. Sewing machine manufacturer who was successful was Isaac Merritt Singer, who began business at 19 Harvard Place, Boston, MA, in 1851, with a capital of $40 supplied by George B. Zieber. His first machine was made in 11 days in the machine shop owned by Orson C. Phelps. He organized I.M. Singer and Company in 1851 and over the next 12 years patented a series of improvements that made his machine the most popular on the market.

4353. Sewing machine equipped with a rocking treadle or double treadle was invented by Isaac Merritt Singer of New York City, who obtained a patent on August 12, 1851. He used a treadle similar to that employed in old spinning wheels and attached it by means of a pitman to the handle on the driving gear of the machine.

4354. Sewing machine to stitch buttonholes was patented by Charles Miller of St. Louis, MO, on March 7, 1854.

4355. Sewing machine to sew curving seams was patented by Allen Benjamin Wilson of Watertown, CT, on December 19, 1854. The machine operated with four-motion feed, which made it possible to sew a curved seam. Wilson received his first patent on a sewing machine on November 12, 1850.

4356. Chain-stitch single-thread sewing machine that was practical was invented by James Edward Allen Gibbs of Mill Point, VA, who received a patent on June 2, 1857.

4357. Paper sewing patterns using standardized sizes were invented by William and Ellen Curtis Demorest of New York City circa 1858. They cut apart stylish dresses and recreated them in tissue-paper versions packaged in large envelopes, which they sold mainly by mail order. A free pattern was included with each issue of their popular magazine, *Mme. Demorest's Mirror of Fashion.* Their company was notable in its time for being run jointly by a married couple and for employing African-Americans and whites equally. The business was eventually eclipsed by E. Butterick and Company, a New York City firm founded in 1867 by Ebenezer and Eleanor Butterick of Sterling, MA, who had received a patent for paper sewing patterns in 1863.

4358. Sewing needles made by machine were manufactured by the Excelsior Needle Company of Wolcottville, CT, which was organized on March 2, 1866, with $20,000 capital. By means of the cold swaging process, needles of a uniform size and shape were made at a cost very much lower than that of the crude needles previously made.

4359. Sewing machine lamp holder was introduced by the Singer Sewing Machine Company in 1876. It "quite obviated the difficulty experienced by operators when sewing at night" because the lamp would not "jar off the table or upset" and it could "be moved without soiling the fingers." It was patented by Ludwig Martin Nicolaus Wolf of Avon, CT, who obtained a patent on May 13, 1873, on a "lamp bracket for sewing."

4360. Electric sewing machine was manufactured by the Singer Manufacturing Company in 1889 at its factory in Elizabethport, NJ.

HOUSEWARES AND APPLIANCES— SEWING—THREAD

4361. Cotton thread was made in Pawtucket, RI, in 1793 by Hannah Wilkinson Slater, who conceived the idea of twisting fine Surinam cotton yarn on spinning wheels. She manufactured No. 20 two-ply thread, which proved superior to the linen thread then in common use.

4362. Silk thread was manufactured in 1819 at Mansfield, CT, by Rodney Hanks and Horatio Hanks. It was sold in skeins. Silk thread on spools was first produced in 1849 by General Merritt Heminway at Bishop and Heminway, a factory in Watertown, CT, that had opened in 1822. The spools at first contained 12 yards of thread, and later 50 and 100 yards.

4363. Linen thread factory was established in Paterson, NJ, in 1865 by William Barbour and Sons of Lisburn, Ireland. The mill was driven by waterpower. The thread was used principally by shoe manufacturers and harness makers.

4364. Nontwisted sewing thread was made commercially available in February 1946 by Belding Hemingway Corticelli, Putnam, CT. It was sold under the names Monocord and Nymo. It was the first nontwisted sewing thread made of nylon.

HOUSEWARES AND APPLIANCES— UTENSILS

4365. Fork brought to America was in a leather case with a bodkin and knife. Governor John Winthrop of Massachusetts introduced it into this country about 1630, following the style of eating which Queen Elizabeth of England had introduced despite the flaming denunciations of many eminent clergymen.

4366. Sieve was produced in 1768 in Philadelphia, PA, by John Sellers. His sieves were used principally by millers.

4367. Apple parer was invented on February 14, 1803, by Moses Coats, a mechanic of Downington, PA.

4368. Cutlery shears were made in Elizabethport, NJ, in 1825 by Rochus Heinisch.

4369. Cutlery factory of importance was the Green River Works of John Russell and Company, Greenfield, MA, established about 1833 for the manufacture of chisels and table cutlery. It developed into the J. Russell Cutlery Company and had a branch office in New York City in 1840. A factory for making pocket cutlery was started at Lakeville, CT, by the Holley Manufacturing Company in 1845.

4370. Wire sieves were manufactured commercially in 1834 by Edwin Gilbert of Gilbert, Bennett and Company at Georgetown, CT.

4371. Spoons of nickel silver were manufactured by Robert Wallace of Wallingford, CT, in 1835. Earlier spoons were made of silver or pewter. Nickel silver, or German silver, consisted of two parts copper, one part nickel, and one part zinc fused together.

HOUSEWARES AND APPLIANCES— UTENSILS—*continued*

4372. Can opener of practical value was invented by Ezra J. Warner of Waterbury, CT, in 1858. It was essentially a hook and a short blade attached to a handle. The user pierced the top of a sealed can with the hook and then ripped a hole with the blade, repeating the action all around the rim. Previously, people had used everything from knives to bayonets to a hammer and chisel to open cans. Warner's design was adopted by the army and used by soldiers in the Civil War. The first can opener of the modern type with a cutting wheel was patented by William W. Lyman in 1870. Electric can openers appeared in December 1931.

4373. Corkscrew patent was granted on March 27, 1860, to M.L. Byrn of New York City. It covered a gimlet screw with a "T" handle.

4374. Drinking straws were made in 1886 by Marvin Chester Stone of Washington, DC, from paraffined manila paper rolled by hand. He obtained a patent on January 3, 1888. Rye straws had been used previously, but they proved unsatisfactory as they were generally unclean and cracked. Paper drinking straws were made by hand until 1905, when the first machine to manufacture them successfully was made by the Marvin C. Stone Estate.

4375. Stainless steel flatware were knives manufactured by the Silver Company, Meriden, CT, in 1921. Most flatware up to that time was made of carbon steel or silver, which required frequent polishing.

I

INDUSTRY

4376. National manufacturing assocation representing members of diversified industries was the National Association of Manufacturers of the United States, organized on January 22, 1895, at a convention held in Cincinnati, OH. The first president elected was Thomas P. Dolan.

4377. Industrial research laboratory was the General Electric Research Laboratory, Schenectady, NY, opened in September 1900. It was supervised by Dr. Willis Rodney Whitney, former instructor at the Massachusetts Institute of Technology.

4378. Conviction under a National Industrial Recovery Code was obtained on December 2, 1933, against the Hercules Gasoline Filling Stations, Brooklyn, New York City. The defendants pleaded guilty in U.S. District Court to working their employees in excess of the hours allowed by the Petroleum Code and failing to display their gasoline prices properly. They were fined $400. Since the defendants had not signed the Petroleum Code, the decision demonstrated that a code was binding on all members of an industry. Industry codes had been established by the Industrial Recovery Act of 1933, whose goals included fostering fair competition. The act was declared unconstitutional on May 27, 1935, by the Supreme Court, which held that its code-making provisions constituted an invalid delegation by Congress of its legislative authority.

INDUSTRY—FACTORIES

4379. Utilization of Niagara Falls waterpower for industrial purposes was made in 1757 by Chabert Joncaire, who dug a ditch so that the water would operate an overshot waterwheel to drive a crude sawmill.

4380. Industrial park was a planned industrial complex of 700 acres near the 70-foot waterfalls above and below the Great Falls of the Passaic River, Paterson, NJ. It opened in 1792. It was sponsored by Alexander Hamilton, who formed the Society for Establishing Useful Manufactures in 1791.

4381. Factory standardization to federal government specification was required on April 16, 1813, when a contract specifying interchangeable parts was drawn up between Callender Irvine, commissary general of the United States, and Colonel Simeon North of Berlin, CT, in Middletown, CT. The contract was for 20,000 pistols at $7 each to be produced within five years. It stipulated that "component parts of the pistols are to correspond so exactly that any limb or part of one pistol may be fitted to any other pistol of the 20,000." Colonel North established his pistol factory in 1810 in Staddle Hill, a suburb of Middletown. The factory produced about 10,000 pistols a year.

4382. Factory heated by steam was the Burlington Woolen Company at the Winooski River, Burlington, VT, built in 1846. The factory, sold at auction on October 20, 1852, was described in an advertisement in the *Burlington Free Press* as follows: "The factory building and dye houses were heated by steam conducted through iron pipes in the most modern and approved manner."

4383. Factory inspection law enacted by a state was passed on April 30, 1879, by Massachusetts. It provided that the governor appoint two or more of the district police to act as inspectors of factories and public buildings.

4384. Factory with temperature and humidity control was the plant of the Sackett-Wilhelms Lithographing and Publishing Company, Brooklyn, New York City, which in 1902 installed a 30-ton fan-cooled dehumidifying unit designed by Willis Haviland Carrier. Its primary purpose was to stop the expansion and contraction of paper caused by varying weather conditions.

4385. Factory cooled by air conditioning was the Gray Manufacturing Company's Gastonia, NC, plant, erected in 1905 with an air-conditioning system manufactured by Stuart W. Cramer of Charlotte, NC. This equipment drew in fresh air from outdoors, filtered and washed it, heated or cooled it, and corrected any variation in humidity. It completely changed the air in the factory about five times an hour.

4386. Factory without windows was erected in Fitchburg, MA, in 1930. The plant, one story high and consisting of one room, was illuminated by hundreds of 1,000-watt electric lamps containing a small percentage of ultraviolet rays, which were considered healthful. The walls and ceilings were painted orange, blue, green, and white to increase visibility, and the floors were jet black. The building also lacked skylights. It was ventilated by a system that circulated 10 million cubic feet of washed, heated, and humidifed air every 10 minutes. The walls were soundproofed by cork pads. The building was constructed by the Austin Company of Cleveland, OH, for the Simonds Saw and Steel Company at a cost of $1.5 million.

4387. Factories operated by the federal government in peacetime were part of a relief effort during the Great Depression. The factories, both located in Millville, MA, were a jersey cloth mill formerly operated by the Famb Knitting Company and a large hall known as Forester's Hall, in which the Massachusetts branch of the Federal Emergency Relief Administration established sewing and stock rooms. The project was started on June 4, 1934, by authority of Joseph P. Carney, emergency relief administrator of Massachusetts, who detailed Thomas E. Wye as factory supervisor to organize and start the project. The products were not sold but were distributed to different welfare divisions of the cities and towns in Massachusetts.

INDUSTRY—INDUSTRIAL EQUIPMENT

4388. Steam engine for industrial use was imported from England by the pioneer steam engineer Josiah Hornblower. Hornblower left London on the S.S. *Irene* on June 6, 1753, and arrived in New York City on September 9. The engine was delivered to the copper mine of Colonel John Schuyler in New Barbadoes Neck (now North Arlington), NJ, on September 25, 1753. It was assembled, installed, and placed in service on March 12, 1755, to pump water from the mine.

4389. Pile driver was patented on March 10, 1791, by John Stone of Concord, MA, who obtained his patent on "driving pile for bridges."

4390. Belt conveyor system was described by Oliver Evans in his book *The Young Millwright and Millers Guide,* published in Philadelphia, PA, in 1795. Evans illustrated a flat belt receiving material on its upper run and discharging it over the end, on a broad endless strap of thin pliant leather or canvas revolving over two pulleys in a case or trough.

4391. Steam engine for industrial use that was practical was manufactured by Oliver Evans of Philadelphia in 1795. In 1799, he introduced a high-pressure engine that was light and cheap, and thus was ideally suited to the needs of the simple colonial industries.

4392. Belting sold to manufacturers is recorded in the account books of Pliny Jewell, a leather dealer of Hartford, CT. There is an entry in 1826 recording the sale of a leather belt three inches wide. Manufacturers who required belting usually bought skins, cut them to the desired thickness, and stretched them taut by nailing the ends of the pieces to the floor when wet and driving wedges between the leather and floor halfway between the ends.

4393. Belts of leather for transmitting power from shaft to shaft were devised by Paul Moody, who used them in the Appleton cotton mill in Lowell, MA, in 1828. Up to this time all transmissions had been by means of iron gears. Belting, however, had previously been used in some mills to carry power from shafts that in turn were driven by gears from a water wheel.

4394. Sandpaper patent was granted to Isaac Fischer, Jr., of Springfield, VT, on June 14, 1834. His invention was covered by four different patents, all issued on the same date.

4395. Bellows for smiths and furnace fires was invented by John R. Morrison of Springfield, OH, who was granted a patent on December 23, 1834.

INDUSTRY—INDUSTRIAL EQUIPMENT
—continued

4396. Steam shovel was invented in 1838 by William S. Otis of Philadelphia, PA, who obtained a patent on February 24, 1839, on a crane for excavating and removing earth. It was first used on the Western Railroad in Massachusetts.

4397. Independent single direct-acting steam power pump was invented in 1840 by Henry Rossiter Worthington of New York City, who obtained a patent on July 24, 1844, on a steam engine auxiliary for the purpose of supplying a steam boiler with water. The following year, with William H. Baker as partner, he started the firm of Worthington and Baker at Brooklyn, NY. The company later became the Worthington Pump and Machinery Corporation of Harrison, NJ.

4398. Wire rope factory was erected in Saxonburg, PA, in 1841 by John Augustus Roebling, who also created the machinery. The wire was spliced and wound onto reels. Seven separate strands were then drawn together and twisted into one large rope. The twisting machine was out in the open and operated by hand power. The wire rope was used in the construction of suspension bridges, including several for which Roebling served as designer and engineer.

4399. Turbine successfully operated by waterpower was invented in 1844 by Uriah Atherton Boyden and was installed in the cotton mills of the Appleton Company at Lowell, MA. It was an improvement on the turbine waterwheel invented by the French engineer Benoit Fourneyron and utilized approximately 80 percent of the power expended.

4400. Spring manufacturer was Edward Lucian Dunbar, whose factory in Bristol, CT, opened in 1845. He specialized in coiled clock springs, which were tempered by a process invented by Silas Burnham Terry. At the time, weights were generally used in large clocks and imported springs in smaller clocks.

4401. Percussion rock drill was patented on March 27, 1849, by Joseph James Couch. The drill was driven by steam power and was independent of gravity. The machine was stationary and the drill was thrown against the rock, the tool being seized at the end of the blow by means of friction-grips.

4402. Gas mask resembling the modern type was patented by Lewis Phectic Haslett of Louisville, KY, who received a patent on June 12, 1849, on an "inhaler or lung protector." It had a filter of woolen fabric or other porous substance to purify the air and remove dust. A gas mask with a self-contained breathing apparatus was patented on July 2, 1850, by Benjamin J. Lane of Cambridge, MA.

4403. Machine for cutting and straightening wire was invented in 1866 by John Adt, who established a small plant in Wolcottville, CT. Before this invention, wire had been straightened by drawing it between two corrugated wooden blocks or through holes in several wooden blocks. The cutting was done by hand. Adt's machine did the work mechanically. His company was absorbed in 1895 by the F.B. Shuster Company of New Haven, CT.

4404. Sawmill to use a band saw was operated in 1867 by the Hoffman Brothers of Fort Wayne, IN. The band saw was 40 feet in length, and the ends were joined so that it revolved continuously. The saw blades, from four to five inches wide, were obtained from Sweden. The design was patented by Jacob Rosecrans Hoffman of Fort Wayne on July 6, 1869.

4405. Paper bag machine that produced brown paper sacks with flat bottoms was patented in 1870 by Margaret Knight of New Hampshire.

4406. Barbed wire commercial production was begun on November 1, 1873, in De Kalb, IL, by Joseph Farwell Glidden, who obtained a patent for his invention on November 24, 1874. The barbs were cut from sheet metal and were inserted between two twisted wires.

4407. Cold storage plant operated by mechanical refrigeration was opened in 1881 by the Mechanical Refrigerating Company at Boston, MA.

4408. Crane was manufactured in 1883 by the Yale and Towne Manufacturing Company, Stamford, CT, for the Pittsburgh Bessemer Steel Company. This two-ton machine was a full-revolving, self-propelling steam crane mounted on a four-wheel standard-gauge truck.

4409. Wrecking crane was built by the Industrial Brownhoist Corporation, Bay City, MI, in 1883. It had a capacity of 20 tons and was mounted on a nonpropelling car that operated on a standard-gauge track. In 1886 an adaptation of the revolving crane was developed. This was a 15-ton steam-railway-type crane in which the crane was mounted at one end of the car and the boiler at the other.

4410. Gasoline pump was the "Self-measuring Gasoline Storage Pump" made by Sylvanus F. Bowser of Fort Wayne, IN, in 1905. The design, which was based on Bowser's earlier design for a kerosene pump, consisted of a ventilated wooden box containing a 50-gallon metal tank. The gasoline was suction-pumped by hand through a hose.

4411. Spring winding machine in which the size of the spring helix was determined solely by the angle at which the wire was forced between guides was developed and built in 1892 by Clinton S. Marshall of the Washburn and Moen Manufacturing Company, Worcester, MA.

4412. Sawmill driven by electricity that operated successfully was designed and operated in 1896 by the Allis-Chalmers Manufacturing Company for the American River Land and Lumber Company, Folsom, CA.

4413. Air conditioner patent was obtained on January 2, 1906, by Willis Haviland Carrier, a mechanical engineer with the Buffalo Forge Company, Buffalo, NY. Carrier had done earlier research on the effect of humidity on heat absorption by air, and he developed the first machinery that was able to both cool the air and control humidity. Carrier designed the first climate-control systems beginning in 1908, and the first home air-conditioning units in 1927.

4414. Steam-operated pressing machine was invented by Adon J. Hoffman, who received a patent on July 13, 1909. The machine was equipped with a "buck," or lower pressing surface, and a "head," or upper pressing surface, which was heated by gas. It was necessary to lay a damp cloth over the goods, as when pressing with a hand iron. The machine was first marketed in 1907 by the United States Hoffman Company of Seattle, WA.

4415. Ice-loading machinery for icing refrigerator railway cars was operated in May 1917 by the William Metz Ice Company of Pittsburgh, PA. The machines were manufactured by the Thomas Wright Company of Jersey City, NJ. Wright obtained a patent on April 22, 1913, on a "body elevating mechanism." It consisted of a truck with an extension top adjustable to any position to enable ice to be placed in the uppermost section of the car, making it possible for one man to do all the loading without the help of assistants.

4416. Wrecking crane operated from a car was devised in 1917 by Robert E. Manley. The car had a tilting beam that permitted adjustment of height and overhang to suit various conditions and a swivel nose that permitted direct pull from any angle. The crane had six leverages and speeds and two sets of controls so that it could be operated from either side of the car. Manley later formed the Manley Manufacturing Company, York, PA, which in 1928 was absorbed by the American Chain and Cable Company.

4417. Computerized pump was marketed by the Wayne Company, Fort Wayne, IN, on November 1, 1932. The pump was invented by Robert Joseph Jauch, Ivan Richard Farnham, and Ross Harper Arnold, who received a patent on November 22, 1932, on a "liquid dispensing apparatus." The pump accurately computed and indicated the exact quantity delivered in gallons and the price in dollars and cents as delivery was made. Total gallons dispensed and cash received were recorded by two totalizers.

4418. Gasoline pump with price and gallon displays was introduced in 1933 by the Wayne Oil Tank and Pump Company of Fort Wayne, IN. The pump was equipped with a mechanical calculator that the company dubbed a "variator." It had two sets of revolving numbers that showed the number of gallons dispensed and the amount of sale.

4419. Belt conveyor more than four miles long was manufactured by the Goodyear Tire and Rubber Company, Akron, OH, for the National Mines Corporation, to convey coal 10,900 feet from a West Virginia mine to the Monongahela River. The conveyor was installed in 1949. It was a single loop of belting more than four miles in total circumference. It traveled at a speed of 300 feet a minute to deliver 300 tons of coal an hour.

4420. Welding machine for aluminum pipes was a MIG (metal inert-gas) welder jointly developed by the Reynolds Metal Company and the Air Reduction Company. A finished model was tested in 1957 at Corpus Christi, TX. It welded 2,880 feet of four-inch pipe in a four-hour period with no supplemental hand-welding needed at any point. A unit mounted on a tractor rotated around the pipe carrying a shielded electric arc. Inert gas was released to blanket the area being welded.

INDUSTRY—INDUSTRIAL EQUIPMENT
—*continued*

4421. Computer-aided manufacturing system was developed in 1959 by researchers in the Servomechanics Laboratory at the Massachusetts Institute of Technology, Cambridge, MA. In the first public demonstration, a computer issued instructions in a custom programming language to an automated milling machine, which turned out a batch of aluminum ashtrays.

INDUSTRY—INDUSTRIAL EQUIPMENT —EXPLOSIVES

4422. Safety fuse was manufactured in 1836 by the firm of Bacon, Bickford, Eales and Company, Simsbury, CT, on a spinning bench machine with traveling jennies that drew and twisted the yarn. Powder was fed to the center of the twisting strands and the resulting fuse lengths were afterwards "countered" and coated with waterproof compounds. The machine was imported from England.

4423. Dynamite was manufactured in 1866 in San Francisco, CA, on a site that is now in Golden Gate Park, by Julius Bandmann, using the patents granted to the inventor of dynamite, Alfred Nobel. The company, known as Bandmann Neilson and Company, became the Giant Powder Company in 1867.

4424. Detonating fuse of the Cordeau-Bickford type was introduced in 1913 by the Ensign-Bickford Company, Simsbury, CT, which started to manufacture it in 1915. It consisted of a lead tube carefully drawn to a uniform size, filled with trinitrotoluene (TNT). It functioned at a speed of 17,000 feet per second.

4425. Explosion of Thermit to break up ice jams was effected on February 24, 1925, when a 250,000-ton ice jam in the St. Lawrence River at Waddington, NY, was moved in a few hours after the reaction of three thermit charges of 90 pounds each. Thermit is a mixture of finely powdered aluminum metal and oxide of iron. When properly ignited, it reacts vigorously, generating very high temperatures and producing extremely hot liquid iron. This method of using Thermit in ice-breaking work was first applied by Howard Turner Barnes, professor of physics at McGill University, Montreal, Canada.

4426. Textile-wrapped detonating fuse was manufactured in 1936 by the Ensign-Bickford Company, Simsbury, CT. It was known as Primacord and consisted of a core of pentaerythrite tetranitrate enclosed in textile wrappings suitably protected by waterproof coverings. It had a velocity of detonation of approximately 20,000 feet per second.

INDUSTRY—INDUSTRIAL PROCESSES

4427. Sulfuric acid was produced by John Harrison in 1793 in a little shop at Third and Green streets, Philadelphia, PA. At first the acid was concentrated in fragile glass retorts. Later, platinum containers were used instead. The business founded by Harrison, known as Harrison Brothers and Company, was purchased in 1917 by the E.I. du Pont de Nemours and Company of Wilmington, DE.

4428. Glue factory to produce glue from animal parts was established in 1807 at Boston, MA, by Roger Upton. It was absorbed by the American Glue Company of Boston, MA, and later taken over by the Peter Cooper Corporation, Gowanda, NY.

4429. Varnish manufacturer to produce varnish exclusively was Christian Schrack, a carriage maker, who opened a shop in 1815 in Philadelphia, PA. Furniture had previously been finished with shellac or oil.

4430. Boiler plates were made between 1816 and 1825 by Dr. Charles Lukens's mill, the Brandywine Mill at Coatesville, PA. The mill was originally started at Rokeby, PA, by Isaac Pennock in 1790 as the Federal Slitting Mill. Iron slabs were heated in an open charcoal fire, rolled out into plates, and then slit up into rods for general use by blacksmiths. In 1810, Pennock purchased a sawmill at Brandywine, which he converted into the Brandywine Iron Mill. The organization remained in the hands of Lukens's descendants and became known as the Lukens Steel Company, one of the world's largest plate mills.

4431. Coal oil factory to manufacture coal oil from coal tar was started in 1853 by the U.S. Chemical Manufacturing Company in Waltham, MA. The light fractions from this coal oil distillation were called coal oil, and used for illuminating purposes. The oil made in connection with picric acid, benzol, and other products from coal tar was named Coup Oil by Luther Atwood, the inventor. When Edwin Drake demonstrated, in 1859, that petroleum could be secured by drilling, the coal oil industry died a natural death.

4432. Artificial-ice manufacturing plant was the Louisiana Ice Manufacturing Company, built in 1868 on Delachaise Street and the Mississippi River, in New Orleans, LA. The process was kept secret and the factory was guarded.

4433. Dye plant was the Albany Aniline and Chemical Company, Albany, NY, which opened in 1868. It later moved to Rensselaer, NY, and was acquired by the General Aniline and Film Corporation.

4434. Sandblasting process for cleaning, engraving, cutting, and boring glass, stone, metal, and other hard substances was invented by Benjamin Chew Tilghman of Philadelphia, PA, who received a patent on October 18, 1870, for "cutting and engraving stone, metal, glass, etc." with "sand used as a projectile."

4435. Welding by the electric process was invented by Professor Elihu Thomson of Lynn, MA, who obtained a patent on August 10, 1886, on "an apparatus for electric welding." His electric welder was widely used in the auto, shipbuilding, construction, and consumer appliance industries as a substitute for riveting.

4436. Centralized refrigeration service that was successful was put into operation in March 1889 by the Colorado Automatic Refrigerating Company of Denver, CO. A 30-ton ice machine and a 50,000-foot cold storage warehouse supplied refrigeration to local businesses via two miles of street mains. The refrigerant was liquid ammonia.

4437. Acetylene gas was made on May 4, 1892, by Thomas Leopold Wilson of the Wilson Aluminum Company in Spray, NC. He was trying to produce metallic calcium by fusing lime and coal tar in an electric furnace. The experiment was unsuccessful. When the molten slaglike mass was dumped into a nearby stream, a gas was liberated which was recognized as acetylene. The manufacturing of acetylene on a commercial scale was begun afterward.

4438. Carbide factory to manufacture commercial quantities of carbide was established in 1894 by Thomas Leopold Willson in Spray, NC. He obtained two patents on June 18, 1895, on calcium carbide, a compound of calcium and carbide. He produced it by fusing calcium or lime with coke at a very high temperature.

4439. Carbon tetrachloride was manufactured by Charles Ernest Acker, who introduced his process in 1908. He also invented the Acker process of manufacturing caustic soda by the electrolysis of molten salt in 1896, for which he received the Elliott Cresson Gold Medal of the Franklin Institute in 1902. He was also the first to produce carbon and tin tetrachloride on a commercial scale.

4440. Thermosetting resin was patented by the Belgian-American chemist Leo Hendrik Baekeland on December 7, 1909. Working in his private laboratory in Yonkers, NY, Baekeland invented a method of controlling the reaction of phenol and formaldehyde to produce a soft resin that hardened permanently with the application of heat. The commercial product, called Bakelite, found many industrial and consumer uses.

4441. Dry ice manufactured commercially was made by the Prest-Air Devices Company of Long Island City, NY (part of Queens, New York City), in 1925, through the efforts of Thomas Benton Slate. Dry ice is solid carbon dioxide. When compressed and cooled, gaseous carbon dioxide changes to a liquid, then to a solid. Its temperature is 109 degrees below zero. It does not melt but instead turns to gas. Dry ice was first used by Schrafft's, 181 Broadway, New York City, in July 1925 to keep ice cream from melting. The first large sale of dry ice was made later in the year to the Breyer Ice Cream Company of New York City.

4442. Abrasive for commercial use to perform work that previously was possible only with diamond dust was boron carbide. It is lighter than aluminum and its density is 2.52 grams per cubic centimeter. It was produced by the research laboratories of the Norton Company, Worcester, MA, and introduced to the world through a technical paper read before the Electrochemical Society in New York City on September 27, 1934.

4443. Casein fiber was produced in December 1935 by Earle Ovando Whittier and Stephen Philip Gould of Washington, DC, who obtained a patent on December 13, 1938, and dedicated it "to the free use of the people of the United States of America." Casein is a derivative of milk protein used to make plastics and adhesives.

4444. Coal hydrogenation plant designed specifically for converting coal into chemicals was opened on May 8, 1952, in Institute, WV, by the Carbide and Carbon Chemicals Company. Coal was pulverized and mixed with oil to form a paste, then converted under heat and

INDUSTRY—INDUSTRIAL PROCESSES—
continued

pressure in combination with hydrogen gas into liquid chemical intermediate products. The $11 million plant had a production capacity of 300 tons of coal a day. Some of the principal products were cresols, higher phenols, naphthalene, and aromatic hydrocarbon.

INDUSTRY—INDUSTRIAL PROCESSES—IRON

4445. Ironworks was erected at Falling Creek, VA, near Richmond, in 1619 by the Virginia Company. It operated only a short time, however, because of the colony's troubles with the local Native American tribes, and its charter was revoked in 1624. John Berkeley was in charge of operations.

4446. Ironworks that was successful was constructed in 1643 by John Winthrop, Jr., and 10 others who were known as the Company of Undertakers for the Iron Works. The operation was established near the Saugus River, near Lynn, MA. It produced eight tons of iron per week from the neighboring bog ore. It was managed by Captain Robert Bridges and Thomas Dextor. A forge was later installed.

4447. Iron exportation was made in 1650, when Samuel Hutchinson, a Massachusetts merchant, shipped 172 bars of iron to London on the *Charles*. This iron was probably made in Lynn, MA.

4448. Iron casting is credited to Joseph Mallinson of Dusboro, PA, who introduced it in 1739 and received a grant of 200 acres of unimproved land in recognition of his services.

4449. Iron rolling mill was the Sarum ironworks, established in 1746 by John Taylor in Chester, PA. Three stacks worked full blast.

4450. Iron mill to puddle and roll iron was the Plumstock Rolling Mill on Redstone Creek between Connellsville and Brownsville, PA, in Fayette County, put into operation on September 15, 1817, by Isaac Meason. It was wrecked by floods in 1824 and was not rebuilt.

4451. Malleable iron castings were produced in Newark, NJ, on July 4, 1826, by Seth Boyden. At first the iron was melted in crucibles, with lime used as a flux and heated in charcoal or hard coal fires.

4452. Iron blast furnace to use anthracite coal in smelting was a furnace operated by the Lehigh Coal and Navigation Company at Mauch Chunk, PA, in 1837. The anthracite coal used was approximately 80 percent of the fuel consumed. On August 27, 1838, another blast furnace was erected in which anthracite was used exclusively.

4453. Iron blast furnace to use anthracite coal successfully was the Pioneer furnace in Pottsville, PA, which was blown on October 19, 1839, by Benjamin Perry. About 28 tons of foundry iron were produced a week. The furnace was built by William Lyman of Boston, MA.

4454. Hammered iron was made in 1842 at the Weymouth Iron Works, founded in 1754 on New Jersey's Great Egg Harbor River. The iron was hammered at the forge by two great trip hammers operated by waterpower. Stephen Colwell received a medal from the Academy of Natural Sciences for developing the machinery used in this plant.

INDUSTRY—INDUSTRIAL PROCESSES—LEATHER

4455. Leather tanning in America is credited to the Native Americans. The first of the known tanners of European ancestry was Experience Miller, who came to Plymouth, MA, on the *Ann* in 1623.

4456. Leather-splitting machine to split leather to any thickness was invented by Samuel Parker of Billerica, MA, who received patents on July 9, 1808, and April 26, 1809, on "currying and finishing leather." This invention doubled the use of leather.

4457. Leather tanning by the oil tan method of preparing buckskin and other leathers was originated by Talmadge Edwards in Johnstown, NY, in 1810.

4458. Patent leather was tanned in 1819 in Newark, NJ, by Seth Boyden at the tannery that he had established in 1813. At first the varnish was dried in the sun, but later it was dried in a warm room. In 1820, Boyden made an oven to hold 16 skins.

4459. Chrome tanning process for tanning hides and skins through the action of a metallic salt was invented by Augustus Schultz of New York City, who was granted two patents on January 8, 1884. His process enabled leather to be tanned thinner and stronger than was possible by vegetable tanning.

4460. Chrome-tanned leather successfully marketed was produced in 1890 by Robert Herman Foerderer of Philadelphia, PA, who devised a method by which the fibrous and gelatinous matter in animal skin could be prepared to receive tanning agents and a second method to overcome the brittle effect.

INDUSTRY—INDUSTRIAL PROCESSES—METALS

4461. Manufacturer of metal goods was Joseph Jencks, who made the first kitchen utensils, metal tools, and machines in the New World. He opened a brass and iron foundry, the Iron Works, in Lynn, MA, in 1645.

4462. White lead manufacturer was Samuel Wetherill of Philadelphia, PA, who began production in 1789. White lead was used primarily in paint and to some extent for medicinal purposes.

4463. Brass was rolled in 1802 by Abel Porter and Company of Waterbury, CT. The factory was owned by Abel and Levi Porter, who were also the first to make brass by the direct fusion of copper and zinc.

4464. Copper rolling mill was the Soho Copper-Rolling Mill, built in 1812 in Belleville, NJ. The founder, Harmon Hendricks, was the grandson of a Sephardic Jewish immigrant from Amsterdam who started a metal business in New York. The mill made copper sheeting and other products. The company remained in business until 1939.

4465. Brass wire and tubing were manufactured in 1831 on machinery imported from England by Israel Holmes for his firm, Holmes and Hotchkiss, of Waterbury, CT. The first company to manufacture brass wire successfully was the Wolcottville Brass Company, founded in 1841 with a capital investment of $56,000.

4466. Silver plating factory to be successful was Rogers Brothers, Hartford, CT, established in 1847 by three brothers, William, Asa, and Simeon S. Rogers. In 1862, the factory was moved to Meriden, CT, and they associated themselves with the Meriden Britannia Company, which in 1898 was succeeded by the International Silver Company. Silver plate consists of a hard metal that is plated or coated with silver. The base metal is usually nickel-silver, a combination of copper, zinc, and nickel. Prior to the introduction of silver-plated ware, silverware was made from coin silver.

4467. Brass and copper seamless tubes were manufactured in 1851 by the American Tube Works at Somerville, MA. The process was introduced by Joseph Fox. Previously, strips of rounded metal with brazed edges had been used.

4468. Brass spinning was invented by Hiram Washington Hayden of Waterbury, CT, who obtained a patent on December 16, 1851, on machinery for making kettles and articles of like character from discs of metal. A disc was mounted in a chuck that was rotated at a uniform speed. A tool was then pressed against the metal, which was thus shaped to the die. The process was first attempted at Wolcottville (now Torrington), CT, and was later sold to the Waterbury Brass Company.

4469. Silver mill to treat silver ore successfully, as well as the first reducing mill to treat ore-bearing quartz, was established by the Washoe Gold and Silver Mining Company, No. 1, near Virginia City, NV. The mill, operated by waterpower, was built by Almarin B. Paul, who began the construction work on May 25, 1860, and completed it on August 9, 1860. It consisted of 24 stamps that began to crush ore on August 11, 1860.

4470. Zinc sheet mill was erected in Bethlehem, PA. Production began in March 1865.

4471. Nickel plating was invented by William H. Remington of Boston, MA, who obtained a patent on October 6, 1868, on a "process of electroplating with nickel." He used a solution prepared by dissolving refined nickel in nitric acid, then precipitating the nickel by the addition of carbonate of potash, washing the precipitate with water, dissolving it in a solution of salammoniac, and filtering it.

4472. Brass rod was drawn in 1873 by the Coe Brass Company of Torrington, CT.

4473. Tin factory for the manufacture of black plate, as well as tin and terne plate, was established in 1874 by Rogers and Burchheld in Leechburg, PA.

4474. Copper refinery furnace to operate by the use of gaseous fuel was constructed in 1878 by William Franklin Durfee for the Wheeler and Wilson Company in Ansonia, CT.

4475. Aluminum in metallic form produced in commercial quantities was made in November 1888 by the Pittsburgh Reduction Company, Pittsburgh, PA, which later developed into the Aluminum Company of America. It was based upon Charles Martin Hall's invention, in February 1886, of a method of reducing aluminum

INDUSTRY—INDUSTRIAL PROCESSES—
METALS—*continued*

by electrolysis. Hall produced aluminum electrically instead of chemically, greatly reducing its cost. He dissolved alumina in a bath of molten cryolite (the double fluoride of aluminum and sodium) and passed an electric current through the solution.

4476. Chromium plating process for commercial use was invented in 1924 at Columbia University, New York City, by Dr. Colin Garfield Fink, who obtained a patent for it on April 20, 1926. He also received a patent on April 28, 1931, on a process of electro-depositing chromium, which he assigned to the Chemical Treatment Company.

4477. Titanium plant fully self-contained and fully integrated was opened on June 1, 1951, in Henderson, NV, by the Titanium Metals Corporation of America. Titanium ore was converted at the plant to titanium sponge, which was melted and cast into ingots of titanium metal.

4478. Titanium mill for rolling and forging titanium was opened on November 2, 1957, in Toronto, OH, by the Titanium Metals Corporation of America, owned by the National Lead Company and the Allegheny Ludlum Steel Corporation.

4479. Molybdenum centrifugal casting was made on November 4, 1958, when a hollow molybdenum cylinder 4.5 inches wide and 8 inches long was cast at the Albany Metallurgy Research Center of the Bureau of Mines, Albany, OR. The cast metal weighed about 10 pounds. Although molybdenum had previously been arc-melted in water-cooled copper crucibles to form cylindrical ingots, this was the first reported production of a shaped casting obtained from poured metal.

INDUSTRY—INDUSTRIAL PROCESSES—
PLASTICS

4480. Celluloid was invented by John Wesley Hyatt of Albany, NY, and Isaiah Smith Hyatt of Rockford, IL, who obtained a patent for it on June 15, 1869. This invention won a $10,000 prize offered by Phelan and Collender of New York City for a substitute for ivory in billiard balls. The inventors dissolved pyroxyline and camphor in alcohol, then subjected the mixture to heat and pressure in molds. They began manufacturing it in 1872, organized the Newark Celluloid Manufacturing Company, and obtained a trademark registration on the word "celluloid," a word they coined to mean "cellulose-like."

4481. Lucite commercially manufactured was made by E.I. du Pont de Nemours and Company, Wilmington, DE, beginning on May 21, 1936. Lucite, or polymethyl methacrylate, is a plastic that is low in moisture absorption, highly nonconducting, and crystal clear, and that possesses the interesting property of bending light rays as they pass through it.

4482. Teflon created in a laboratory was discovered by chemical engineer Roy J. Plunkett in 1938 at E.I. du Pont de Nemours and Company, Wilmington, DE. Teflon's chemical name is polymer of tetralourethylene, or PTFE. It is a plastic with a nonstick surface that can be sprayed onto utensils or formed into machinery components. It was first used in commercial products in 1954.

4483. Polystyrene was commercially produced by the Koppers Company, Kobuta, PA, in 1954. Polystyrene is produced in small beads. When placed in molds and heated, the beads expand and take the shape of the enclosure.

INDUSTRY—INDUSTRIAL PROCESSES—
RUBBER

4484. Rubber company was the Roxbury India Rubber Company of Roxbury, MA, which began manufacturing various rubber products in 1832. It was incorporated on February 11, 1833, by Lemuel Blake, Luke Baldwin, Edwin M. Chaffee, and Charles Davis, Jr. The rubber was affected by heat and cold and had a disagreeable odor, and the company was unable to find a market for its products.

4485. Gutta-percha was imported from Calcutta in 1840 by William Bartlett, supercargo of the *Mary Parker*. Bartlett presented a whip made of gutta-percha to William Rider of New York City, who subsequently organized William Rider and Brothers to handle the new commodity. On June 1, 1852, John Rider obtained a patent on "vulcanized rubber," and in 1855 the North American Gutta Percha Company, New York City, was formed by the Rider brothers with a capitalization of $500,000.

4486. Vulcanized rubber was successfully produced by Charles Goodyear of New York City, who obtained a patent on June 15, 1844, on an "improvement in India-rubber fabrics." He had received a previous patent on June 17, 1837, for a method of destroying the adhesive properties of rubber by applying bismuth, nitric acid with copper, or other materials.

4487. Pressure-sensitive adhesive was a combination of ingredients that included India rubber, pine gum, and spirits of turpentine. It was patented by Dr. Henry Day in 1845.

4488. Synthetic rubber was made by Lucas Petrou Kyrides and Dr. Richard Blair Earle in 1913 for the Hood Rubber Company, East Watertown, MA. They prepared a number of polymerized hydrocarbons having rubberlike qualities, of which dimethyl butadiene had the most promising commercial possibilities.

4489. Synthetic rubber for manufacture was isolated on April 10, 1930, by Dr. Arnold M. Collins, who isolated a chemical called chloroprene and observed its polymerization. It was synthesized by the E.I. Du Pont de Nemours and Company, Wilmington, DE, after chemists working under Dr. Elmer K. Bolton discovered that chloroprene could be produced by treating vinylacetylene with other substances. Du Pont began manufacturing a synthetic rubber called Du Prene on November 2, 1931, at its plant in Deepwater, NJ. The first commercial production of various articles from Du Prene began in May 1932, when the Manhattan Rubber Manufacturing Division of Raybestos-Manhattan, of Passaic, NJ, made oil hose from Du Prene and offered it for sale to oil companies. Experimental tires were made of this material in February 1934 by the Dayton Rubber Manufacturing Company of Dayton, OH.

INDUSTRY—INDUSTRIAL PROCESSES—STEEL

4490. Steel was manufactured in May 1728 by Samuel Higley of Simsbury, CT, and Joseph Dewey of Hebron, CT. Higley employed three workmen in a "curious art, by which to convert, change and transmute common iron into good steel, sufficient for any use."

4491. Cast steel for plows was made by William Woods at the steel works of Jones and Quigg, Pittsburgh, PA, in 1846. The plows were made by John Deere at Moline, IL.

4492. Bessemer steel converter used commercially was erected by the Eureka Iron and Steel Works in 1864 in Wyandotte, MI, on the future site of the public library. The steel was made in a 2.5-ton experimental converter by William Franklin Durfee by means of the Kelly pneumatic process.

4493. Open-hearth furnace for the manufacture of steel by the Siemens-Martin process was built in 1868 by Frederick J. Slade for Cooper Hewitt and Company, owners of the New Jersey Steel and Iron Company, Trenton, NJ. The furnace was ready for operation in December 1868.

4494. Steel mill to install an electrical machine was the Edgar Thomson Works of the Carnegie Steel Company, Braddock, PA. A two-light arc machine, operated by belt drive from a line shaft, was installed in the blast furnace machine shop in 1882. (Other claims to primacy were made by the Carnegie Steel Company's Homestead Works and other plants in the East.) The first installation of rolls driven by electric motor was made in the No. 3 mill of the Edgar Thomson Works in October 1905.

4495. Manganese steel was manufactured in 1892 by the Taylor Iron and Steel Company in High Bridge, NJ.

4496. Manganese steel for railroad tracks was first manufactured on August 28, 1894, by William Wharton, Jr. and Company, in High Bridge, NJ. The first rail frog with a cast manganese steel plate was installed at Fulton Street and Boerum Place, Brooklyn, NY.

4497. Steel mill to produce continuous sheets was designed by John Butler Tytus and built by the American Rolling Mill Company, Ashland, KY, in 1922. The plant consisted of an arrangement of machines that passed sheet steel through a series of mills in a tandem train at a high speed. The process replaced much slower methods. Operations began in 1924.

4498. Vacuum-cast steel was poured on July 2, 1957, by the Bethlehem Steel Corporation, Bethlehem, PA, in the form of a 93,900-pound ingot 78 inches in diameter. Vacuum-cast steel was melted in either an electric or an open-hearth furnace and poured into ingots. The gases were entrapped by vacuum-stream degassing with equipment designed by the F.J. Stokes Corporation, Philadelphia, PA.

INSURANCE

4499. Insurance regulation enacted by a state was enacted by Massachusetts on February 13, 1799, pursuant to a law establishing the Massachusetts Fire Insurance Company. It required that the company "shall, when and as often required by the legislature of the Commonwealth, lay before them such a statement of their affairs as the said legislature may deem it expedient to require, and submit to an examination hereon under oath."

4500. Insurance agency was opened by Israel Whelan in New York City in 1804. He was a representative of the Phoenix Fire Office of London.

INSURANCE—*continued*

4501. Insurance company owned by African-Americans was the African Insurance Company of Philadelphia, PA, organized in 1810 with a capital stock of $5,000 in $50 shares. It specialized in insuring African-Americans. Joseph Randolph was the first president. The company was not incorporated but was a voluntary association.

4502. Marine insurance law enacted by a state was approved by Massachusetts on February 16, 1818. An act was passed defining the powers, duties, and restrictions of insurance companies. It applied only to companies writing marine insurance and provided for annual publication by the president and directors of the amount of their stock, the risks against which they meant to insure, and the amounts of the single risks. They were also required to report to the legislature whenever so directed and were forbidden to write in any risk a sum exceeding 10 percent of the capital stock of the company.

4503. Insurance board established by a state government was the New Hampshire Insurance Department, established on July 1, 1851, which authorized the governor to appoint three suitable residents of the state to examine personally each year the affairs of all insurance companies and report to the legislature. Each member was appointed to a one-year term. The first board consisted of Albert S. Scott, Jacob E. Ela, and Timo Hoskins.

4504. Accident insurance company was the Travelers Insurance Company of Hartford, CT, chartered June 17, 1863, through the efforts of James Goodwin Batterson. The charter provided for the issuance of accident insurance to cover travel accidents only. In 1864 this was amended to include accidents of every description. The first policy was issued to James Bolter of Hartford for $1,000 in 1864 and covered only the period he spent walking from the post office to his home on Buckingham Street. The premium was two cents. The agreement was oral.

4505. Boiler insurance company was the Hartford Steam Boiler Inspection and Insurance Company of Hartford, CT, chartered in June 1866. The first president of the company was Enoch Roberts. The first policy was issued on February 14, 1867.

4506. Insurance rate standardization was effected on July 18, 1866, in New York City by the National Board of Fire Underwriters, an organization of 75 fire insurance companies. The first annual meeting was held on February 20, 1867, in New York City, and the first president was James McLean.

4507. Plate-glass insurance was written by the United States Plate Glass Insurance Company of Philadelphia, PA, incorporated on April 12, 1867, with an original capital of $20,000. The first president was John Van Dusen.

4508. Fraternal group insurance of consequence was issued in 1869 by the Metropolitan Life Insurance Company, New York City, to the Hildise Bund, an organization of German-American wage earners, which collected weekly premiums from its members. The premiums are said to have amounted at one time to about $7,500 a week.

4509. Title guaranty insurance company was the Real Estate Title Insurance and Trust Company, organized in Philadelphia, PA, on March 31, 1876. It offered security against errors in titles. The original capital was $250,000, half of which was paid in. The first president was Joshua H. Morris.

4510. Hail insurance on tobacco crops was written in 1880 by the Tobacco Growers' Mutual Insurance Company of North Canaan, CT, incorporated on March 24, 1880. This company went out of business in 1887.

4511. Bonding company was the American Surety Company, New York City, incorporated on December 7, 1881. It began business on April 15, 1884.

4512. Credit insurance was briefly attempted in New York State in 1887. The first company that operated for any length of time was the U.S. Credit System Company of New York, organized in 1889.

4513. Mutual liability insurance company was the American Mutual Liability Insurance Company, Boston, MA, incorporated on March 30, 1887, and opened for business on October 1, when 22 policies were written covering liability of employers to injured workers. The rate was 30 cents per $100 of payroll. The first president was William Croad Lovering.

4514. Numerical system of insurance rating was originated by the New York Life Insurance Company of New York City about 1903. Values were assigned to various factors affecting the insurability of an applicant, to aid a company in determining under its rules whether the applicant was insurable, and if so, at what rates of premium.

4515. Hail insurance law enacted by a state was enacted by the legislature of North Dakota and approved on March 18, 1911. The number of policies issued the first year was 1,011, representing risks of about $1 million. The losses during the first year exceeded the premiums by nearly 18 percent, and the losses, as adjusted, had to be prorated at 70 percent.

4516. Aircraft liability and property damage insurance was issued by the Travelers Insurance Company of Hartford, CT, to a New York manufacturer in 1919.

4517. Insurance company to insure the lives of animals exclusively was the Animal Insurance Company of America, New York City, founded on August 1, 1957, by Milton M. Weiss. Coverage was extended only to pedigreed dogs and cats until May 1958, at which time the company added insurance for livestock classes of horses and cattle. Policies on animals were previously written by general insurance companies.

4518. Crime insurance policy authorized by a state was issued on August 2, 1971, by George Romney, secretary of housing and urban development; George Kaskel Bernstein, federal insurance administrator; and James McKinley Rose, Jr., assistant administrator for crime insurance. The policy was issued to William Early, proprietor of Aida TV Sales and Service, Washington, DC. The premium was $50 for $1,000, $60 for $2,000, $70 for $3,000, and $80 for $5,000. It posited a deductible of $100 or 5 percent, whichever was greater.

INSURANCE—CAR

4519. Car insurance policy was issued by the Travelers Insurance Company of Hartford, CT, on February 1, 1898, to Dr. Truman J. Martin of Buffalo, NY. The premium was $11.25, covering $5,000 to $10,000 liability.

4520. Car insurance law enacted by a state was "an act requiring owners of certain motor vehicles and trailers to furnish security for their civil liability on account of personal injury caused by their motor vehicles and trailers," approved on May 1, 1925, by Massachusetts. Automobiles were required to carry $5,000 to $10,000 liability.

4521. No-fault car insurance law enacted by a state was enacted by Massachusetts, "an act providing for compulsory personal injury protection for all registered motor vehicles, defining such protection, restricting the right to claim damages for pain and suffering in certain actions of tort, regulating further the premium

charges for compulsory automobile insurance and amending certain laws relating thereto." The act was approved by Governor Francis Williams Sargent on August 13, 1970. It permitted policyholders to collect up to $2,000 for medical expenses and out-of-pocket costs including wages, to be paid directly by the insurance company, irrespective of fault. A similar law had been enacted previously by Puerto Rico.

INSURANCE—EMPLOYMENT

4522. Workers' compensation insurance law enacted by a state was enacted by Maryland in 1902, followed by Montana in 1909 and New York in 1910, but all three were declared unconstitutional. The first law to remain on the books was approved by Washington on March 14, 1911, but it did not go into effect until October 1. Meantime, Wisconsin passed a law on May 3, 1911, that went into effect the same day. New Jersey's law was approved on April 4, 1911, and went into effect on July 4.

4523. Workers' compensation insurance law enacted by Congress was approved on May 30, 1908. It was applicable to the following classes of federal employees: artisans or laborers in any manufacturing establishment, arsenal, or navy yard; employees in the construction of river and harbor fortifications; employees in hazardous employment on construction work in the reclamation of arid lands; and employees in hazardous employment under the Isthmian Canal Commission in Panama.

4524. Bonding law enacted by a state for the bonding of all officers, deputies, and state employees was enacted by North Dakota on March 1, 1913, but was declared unconstitutional in 1914. Another law was approved on March 5, 1919. The premiums were 25 cents a year for each $100 of the required bond. A state bonding fund was created which in the first year showed a net income of $63,172. The first claim was filed on August 4, 1919, by Riggin Township, Benson County, for $1,000 for misappropriations of funds. It was paid on February 4, 1920.

4525. Unemployment insurance act passed by a state was enacted by Wisconsin on January 28, 1932, and signed by Governor Philip La Follette. Every employer of 10 or more was required to put 2 percent of the payroll aside until a fund accrued equaling $75 per eligible worker. An employee who lost his or her job

INSURANCE—EMPLOYMENT—*continued*

could draw on the fund at the rate of $10 a week for a maximum of 10 weeks. The first payment was made on August 17, 1936. The chairman of the Industrial Commission, which regulated the department, was Voyta Wrabetz.

4526. Social security monthly payment was made to Ida May Fuller of Ludlow, VT, who received check No. 00-000-001 for $22.54, dated January 31, 1940. By 1975, when she died at the age of 100, Fuller had received more than $20,000 in benefits. The Social Security Act was approved by President Franklin Delano Roosevelt on August 14, 1935. It authorized the appointment of a three-member board to administer a federal system of old-age insurance benefits, to approve state unemployment compensation laws, and to administer grants-in-aid to the states to help the needy aged, the blind, and dependent children. These programs, and others added later, were funded by mandatory contributions by workers, employers, and the self-employed, and provided coverage to people with a documented history of employment. Several groups of unemployment insurance cards were issued simultaneously, so that the recipient of the first social security card is not known.

4527. Babysitters' insurance policy was issued on January 26, 1950, by the American Associated Insurance Companies, St. Louis, MO. It covered sitters available through the Missouri State Employment Service, who were bonded up to $2,500 each for fraud and dishonesty.

INSURANCE—FIRE

4528. Fire insurance agent is said to have been John Copson of High Street, Philadelphia, PA, who inserted an advertisement on May 25, 1721, in the *American Weekly Mercury* announcing that he would open an office for insurance on "vessels, goods and merchandise."

4529. Fire insurance company was organized in 1735 in Charleston, SC, as the Friendly Society for the Mutual Insurance of Houses Against Fire, and received subscriptions beginning on January 1, 1735. This company issued policies and conducted business over a period of about six years, as evidenced by advertisements and notices in the *South Carolina Gazette* from November 15, 1735, to February 19, 1741. On November 18, 1740, there was a conflagration that consumed half the town and probably ruined the society, as the last advertisement stated that "the bonds given by the members will be put in suit unless paid."

4530. Fire insurance company to receive a charter was the Philadelphia Contributionship for the Insurance of Houses from Loss by Fire, Philadelphia, PA, which was organized on April 13, 1752, when 12 directors and a treasurer were elected. Its first fire insurance policy was issued on June 1 to John Smith of Philadelphia, the company's treasurer, who for £1 insured his house, valued at £1,000. A charter was granted by the lieutenant governor and proprietaries of the province of Pennsylvania on February 20, 1768, and was subsequently confirmed by King George III of Great Britain upon the advice of his privy council. The first name subscribed to the Articles of Association was that of Lieutenant Governor James Hamilton; the first private name was that of Benjamin Franklin. Each insured house displayed a wooden shield showing the company's seal, "four Hands united."

4531. Fire insurance joint-stock company was the American Fire Insurance Company, organized on February 28, 1810, in Philadelphia, PA. The first president was Captain William Jones, who later became secretary of the navy under President James Madison.

4532. Mutual fire insurance company for insuring factories was the Manufacturers' Mutual Fire Insurance Company of Rhode Island, located in Providence, RI, and incorporated on October 31, 1835. The first policy was issued on December 3, 1835, to Zachariah Allen for $2,500 at a cash premium deposit rate of 60 cents per year. At the expiration of the policy, a 51 percent dividend was declared, resulting in an insurance cost of 29.4 cents per $100 for the year.

4533. Fire and tornado insurance fund enacted by a state was established by North Dakota and began to function on July 1, 1919. For the first five months, the gross income was $28,909 and the losses paid were $3,773. The net income, after expenses were paid, amounted to $24,144. The first loss was $1,500, paid on October 23, 1919, to Conway, SD, to compensate for damage caused by an overheated furnace. The law provided that no policy over $100,000 could be written. When necessary, additional insurance was obtained from private companies.

INSURANCE—HEALTH

4534. Health insurance company was the Massachusetts Health Insurance Company of Boston, MA, organized on April 21, 1847. The company existed for a very short period.

4535. Hospital insurance group plan was effected by Baylor University Hospital, Dallas, TX, on December 21, 1929. The plan was inaugurated by Dr. Justin Ford Kimball, executive vice president of Baylor University. The first group insured were the Dallas public school teachers, who paid 50 cents per month for 21 days of hospital treatment.

4536. Blue Cross and Blue Shield plans were distinguished from other group health insurance plans because they were nonprofit plans and their membership was not restricted to a particular organization or occupation. The Blue Cross symbol was first used by E.A. van Steenwyk, an executive of the Hospital Service Assocation of Minnesota, in 1934. The Blue Shield symbol was adopted by a health plan in Buffalo, NY, in 1939.

4537. Medical insurance group policy for college students covering medical, surgical, and hospital expenses was issued February 1, 1936, by the Ocean Accident and Guarantee Corporation to Vassar College, Poughkeepsie, NY. The plan was sponsored by the college for voluntary participation, and 565 students were included at a premium of $12 each for the year. Known as the Students' Reimbursement Plan, it was organized and managed by the A.W.G. Dewar Company of Boston, MA, whose Tuition Refund Plan in 1929 had first introduced the insurance of school fees in American private schools.

4538. Health insurance clause in a labor contract was put into effect on August 25, 1941, by the International Ladies Garment Workers Union in a contract with the Waist and Dress Manufacturers Association of Philadelphia, PA. The clause set aside 2.5 percent of the payroll to establish a system of weekly sick benefits and a medical clinic to supervise the health of the workers. About 10,000 cotton-dress and -blouse workers in Philadelphia were covered.

4539. Health insurance law enacted by a state was the Rhode Island Cash Sickness Compensation act, approved on April 29, 1942. It required employers to collect 1 percent from employees after June 1, 1942, on salaries up to $3,000 paid in any calendar year, and granted benefits ranging from $6.75 to $18 a week.

4540. Health maintenance organization in which members prepaid for comprehensive medical services was the Kaiser-Permanente Medical Care Program, begun in 1942 by Henry J. Kaiser and Dr. Sidney R. Garfield. The first two programs, in the Pacific Northwest and California, were administered by Kaiser's Permanente Foundations. They were originally intended for groups of employees. Enrollment was opened to the public in 1945.

4541. Health insurance plan enacted by Congress was Medicare, enacted on July 30, 1965, as part of the federal Social Security system, to help pay the cost of medical care for people aged 65 and over. Payments are made from a fund made up of mandatory contributions from employers, employees, and the self-employed, as well as contributions from the general revenue of the federal government. The first payments were made on July 1, 1966. The first payments for skilled nursing facilities, made under the extended care benefit provision of the statute, were made on January 2, 1967. The first Medicare identification cards were presented to former President Harry S. Truman and his wife, Bess Wallace Truman, by President Lyndon Baines Johnson at the Truman Library, Independence, MO, on January 20, 1966.

INSURANCE—LIFE

4542. Life insurance company was the Corporation for the Relief of Poor and Distressed Presbyterian Ministers and of the Poor and Distressed Widows and Children of Presbyterian Ministers, incorporated on January 11, 1759, in Philadelphia, PA. The Reverend Robert Cross was the first president. The first policy was issued on May 22, 1761, to Francis Alison. Survivor annuities were granted at the death of the policyholder, the beneficiary receiving £10 to £35 for the duration of his or her life. The annual premium required was one-fifth of the annuity. The first commercial company specializing in life insurance was the Pennsylvania Company for Insurance on Lives and Granting Annuities, incorporated in Philadelphia in 1812.

4543. Life insurance offered by a general insurance company was offered by the Insurance Company of North America, organized in Philadelphia, PA, on December 10, 1792, with a capital of $600,000, and chartered on April 14, 1794. The first policy was issued on December 15, 1792. Only six policies were written in five years, and in 1804 the life insurance feature was discontinued. The first president was John Maxwell Nesbitt.

INSURANCE—LIFE—*continued*

4544. Mutual life insurance company was the Mutual Life Insurance Company of New York City, which was chartered on April 12, 1842. The first policy was issued on February 1, 1843, to Thomas N. Ayres. The first president was Morris Robinson. Policyholders were entitled to a share in the management through the election of directors. All profits belonged to the policyholders. The New England Mutual Life Insurance Company of Boston, MA, was chartered earlier, on April 1, 1835, but did not do business until December 1, 1843, and issued its first policy on February 1, 1844.

4545. Life insurance nonforfeiture law enacted by a state was approved by Massachusetts on April 10, 1861. It was sponsored by Commissioner Elizur Wright. This law required domestic companies to use four-fifths of the reserve to continue a policy as extended term insurance beyond the date of lapse. In the event of death during the term period, the company had the right to deduct from the claim the premiums that would have been paid had the policy continued in force, plus interest. The first nonforfeiture policy actually written was issued by the New York Life Insurance Company of New York City, on August 13, 1860, about eight months prior to the enactment of the Massachusetts law.

4546. Life insurance policy rated substandard was issued on July 1, 1896, by the New York Life Insurance Company of New York City. A substandard policy is one issued on a life that because of a medical impairment, hazardous occupation, or some other reason is "substandard" and therefore not insurable at "standard," or normal, rates of premium.

4547. Savings bank life insurance was launched by act of the Massachusetts legislature dated June 26, 1907. The plan was originated by Louis Dembitz Brandeis, then a Boston lawyer, and later associate justice of the Supreme Court. The first savings bank to establish an insurance department was the Whitman Savings Bank in Whitman, MA. The department was established on June 18, 1908, and the first policy written on June 22. Savings bank life insurance is legal reserve insurance that is sold "over the counter" by certain mutual savings banks. No solicitors are employed.

4548. Life insurance group policy was written by William J. Graham of the Equitable Life Assurance Society of the United States on June 1, 1911, under one blanket contract. Without medical examination, 121 employees of the Pantasote Leather Company of Passaic, NJ, were insured as a group for $87,030. Each employee was given insurance protection amounting to a year's salary and a funeral benefit of $100.

4549. Life insurance group contract of importance was made on July 1, 1912, between Montgomery Ward and Company of Chicago, IL, and the Equitable Life Assurance Society of the United States, whereby 3,000 persons were insured as a group for approximately $6 million without medical examination.

L

LABOR

4550. Workers' compensation agreement was made on January 26, 1695, by Captain William Kidd of New York City, commander of the *Adventure Galley* of 787 tons burden. He promised to distribute to the crew one-fourth of all booty captured on privateering expeditions. According to the agreement, "If any man should Loose a Leg or Arm in the said service, he should have six hundred pieces of Eight, or six able slaves; if any man should loose a joynt on the said service, he should have a hundred pieces of eight."

4551. Anarchist was Josiah Warren, who was known as the "father of anarchy." He was of the intellectual type and was not an advocate of violence. He was a veteran of the short-lived utopian colony in New Harmony, IN, whose failure convinced him that communistic social arrangements suppress individual initiative and responsibility. In May 1827 he opened his Equity Store in Cincinnati, OH, to vindicate his theory of "labor for labor," in which all labor is held to be equally valuable. The store sold merchandise at cost, plus seven percent for handling and the clerk's hire. Instead of money, the store also accepted "labor notes," in which the customer agreed to provide a specified amount of time and labor (for example, washing or carpentry) in exchange for merchandise. Warren also advocated the transference of government activities to private persons.

4552. Workers' compensation lawsuit involving the rights of an injured servant against his master was the case of *James Murray v. South Carolina Railroad Company,* which was tried before Judge Belton O'Neall at the July Extra Term, 1838, of Barnwell County, SC. The trial resulted in a verdict of $1,500 in favor of the plaintiff. The defendant appealed. The case was heard in February 1841 by the Court of Errors of South Carolina in Charleston, which reversed the decision and granted a new trial. The decision was written by Judge Josiah James Evans.

4553. National labor congress was the First Industrial Congress of the United States, which convened in New York City on October 12, 1845. William E. Wait of Illinois was elected president. Annual meetings were held regularly until 1856.

4554. Workday of 10 hours to be mandated by a state was required by New Hampshire in a law dated July 9, 1847. It stated that "in all contracts relating to labor, ten hours actual labor shall be taken to be a day's work unless otherwise agreed by the parties." As a result of the bargaining provision, the law was ineffective.

4555. Working hours of women to be regulated by a state were set forth in a law enacted by Ohio on March 29, 1852. This law fixed 10 hours per day as the maximum number of working hours for manual labor by children under 18 and women. It was repealed in 1887, when a new code was adopted.

4556. Workday of eight hours to be authorized by Congress was authorized for government laborers in a law dated June 25, 1868, and signed by President Andrew Johnson. It provided, among other things, that "eight hours shall constitute a day's work for all laborers, workmen, and mechanics who may be employed by or on behalf of the Government of the United States." The eight-hour workday had been advocated by a variety of local unions since 1860, and the first unified proposal was made on August 20, 1866, in Baltimore, MD, by the National Labor Union at its first congress, which was attended by 77 delegates from 13 states.

4557. Labor bureau established by a state was the Massachusetts Bureau of Statistics of Labor, established by legislation approved on June 23, 1869, by Governor William Claflin. The duties of the bureau, under a chief and deputy, were "to collect, assort, systematize and

present in annual reports to the legislature ... statistical details relating to all departments of labor in the Commonwealth." Henry Kemble Oliver was appointed chief on July 31, 1869, at a salary of $2,500 a year.

4558. Half holiday on Saturday for factory workers was inaugurated by George Westinghouse, the inventor and manufacturer of the air brake, who established the custom in his factory in Pittsburgh, PA, in June 1871.

4559. Ban enacted by a state on the employment of women in an occupation was "an act providing for the health and safety of persons employed in coal mines," passed and approved by Illinois on May 28, 1879. It prohibited the employment of women in mines in Illinois.

4560. Labor organization (national) of importance was the American Federation of Labor, which was organized in Pittsburgh, PA, in 1881 as the Federation of Organized Trades and Labor Unions. It adopted the new title on December 8, 1886, in Columbus, OH, at a meeting attended by 25 officers of national craft unions representing over 300,000 members. The first woman to serve as a labor delegate to a national convention of the American Federation of Labor was Mary Burke, who represented the Retail Clerks' Union of Findlay, OH, at the convention held in Detroit, MI, December 8–13, 1890.

4561. Labor mediation and arbitration board established by a state was the New York Board of Mediation and Arbitration, organized on June 1, 1886, under authority of an act of May 18, 1886. On June 2, 1886, Massachusetts authorized a state arbitration board "for the settlement of differences between employers and their employees."

4562. Sick-leave benefit funds for teachers were established in 1887 in both New York City and Brooklyn, which was then a separate city. The two organizations were the New York City Teachers Mutual Benefit Association and the Brooklyn Aid Association. The funds were built up from dues imposed on teachers' salaries.

4563. Accident reports by employers concerning personal injuries suffered by employees in their service were required by Massachusetts under the Employers' Liability Act, passed on May 14, 1887.

4564. Labor activists to be executed were four men accused of participating in the Haymarket Riot that occurred on May 4, 1886, in Chicago, IL. A labor rally had been called in Haymarket Square to protest the shooting of several strikers by Chicago police the previous

LABOR—*continued*

day. Anarchist and communist speakers were addressing a crowd of several hundred mostly German-born workers when a squad of 180 police officers arrived to break up the rally. A bomb, thrown by a person who was never positively identified, fatally injured 7 officers and wounded 70. Police fired into the crowd, killing one worker and injuring more than a dozen. A grand jury indicted 31 suspected labor radicals in connection with the bombing. Eight men were tried for murder; seven were convicted. On November 11, 1887, four men—August Spies, Samuel Fielden, Adolph Fischer, and Albert Parsons—were executed by hanging. The other three were pardoned in 1893 by Illinois governor John Peter Altgeld.

4565. Employment service established by a state was created on April 28, 1890, by Ohio. Authorization was given to establish public employment offices in cities of the first and second class, including Cincinnati, Cleveland, Columbus, Dayton, and Toledo. The first office was opened June 4, 1890, in Toledo, with Charles W. Murphy as superintendent. The Commissioner of Labor Statistics, under whom the system of five offices was set up during the year 1890, was John McBride.

4566. Employment office established by a city was authorized by Seattle, WA, on March 5, 1894, by a vote of 2,058–523. John Lamb, the city's first labor commissioner, opened an office on April 1, 1894, in a rough board shanty containing one small room. The following year, the office moved to larger quarters in City Hall.

4567. Work week of 40 hours to be required by Congress was required by the Public Contract Act of 1936 "to provide conditions for the purchase of supplies and the making of contracts by the United States," approved on June 30, 1936. Workers on government contracts over $10,000 were required to receive overtime compensation at the rate of not less than time and a half for hours worked in excess of 40 a week or eight hours in any one day (if such compensation yielded a greater amount than on the weekly 40-hour basis). Workers were not to be paid less than the prevailing minimum wage of industry and locality. The act was known as the Walsh-Healy Act.

4568. Labor antidiscrimination commission of a state government was the New York State Commission Against Discrimination, appointed on July 1, 1945, "to formulate policies to eliminate and prevent discrimination in employment because of race, creed, color or national origin, either by employers, labor organizations, employment agencies or other persons." It consisted of five commissioners at $10,000 a year whose terms ranged from one to five years. The first chairman was Henry C. Turner.

4569. Labor dispute in which the Taft-Hartley Act was invoked took place in 1948 between the American Federation of Labor Atomic Trades and Labor Council and the Oak Ridge National Laboratory, Oak Ridge, TN. The Taft-Hartley Act, also known as the Labor-Management Relations Act of 1947, gave the president power to seek an 80-day injunction against strikes in cases of national emergency. On March 19, 1948, at Knoxville, TN, Federal Judge George Caldwell Taylor, responding to a request from President Harry S. Truman, issued an injunction to the Justice Department that restrained 900 members of the union from leaving their jobs on a walkout for an 80-day period, thus averting a strike by seven hours.

4570. Guaranteed 52-week wage in a major industry was signed into a contract between the American Can and Continental Can companies and the United Steel Workers union on August 13, 1955.

4571. Parental leave law enacted by a state that applied to both mothers and fathers was passed by the Minnesota legislature in 1987. It allowed parents up to six weeks of unpaid leave from work.

LABOR—CHILD

4572. Child labor in a factory on record took place at the cotton mill of Almy, Brown, and Slater in Pawtucket, RI, in 1793. Samuel Slater, the mill's founder, hired children because their small hands could do finer work.

4573. Child labor law enacted by a state that included an education requirement was passed by Massachusetts on April 16, 1836. It required all children to attend school at least three months of the year until they reached the age of 15. Manufacturers were not allowed to hire children to work in their mills for more than nine months a year, but the children were conveniently transferred from mill to mill so that this legislation was not effective.

4574. Child labor law enacted by a state that regulated hours of employment was approved by Massachusetts Governor John Davis on March 3, 1842. Massachusetts prohibited children under 12 years of age from working more than 10 hours a day. Connecticut enacted a similar law, which prohibited children under 14 years of age from working more than 10 hours a day.

4575. Child labor law enacted by a state that restricted the age of the worker was approved on March 28, 1848, by Governor Francis Rawn Shunk of Pennsylvania. The law prohibited children under 12 years of age from engaging in commercial labor. In 1849 the age limit was raised to 13 years. Similar legislation was enacted in 1853 by Rhode Island, in 1855 by Connecticut, and in 1866 by Massachusetts, with age limits of 12, 9, and 10 years, respectively.

4576. Child labor law enacted by Congress was passed on September 1, 1916, "an act to prevent interstate commerce in the products of child labor," the provisions of which were to be administered by the Children's Bureau. The government did not have the constitutional power to regulate labor directly, so the attempt was made to deal with the problem of child labor through the government's constitutional power to regulate interstate commerce. The act became effective on September 1, 1917, but on June 3, 1918, it was declared unconstitutional by the Supreme Court as an invasion of states' rights.

LABOR—MINIMUM WAGE

4577. Minimum wage law enacted by a state was enacted by Massachusetts on June 4, 1912. It established a three-member Minimum Wage Commission to be appointed by the governor with the advice of the Council. The act did not go into effect until July 1, 1913. Oregon, in advance of all other states, set up an administrative body to carry out the provisions of an act of February 17, 1913, which provided for the appointment, within 30 days, of a Welfare Commission to consist of three members, one representing the employer, one the employee, and one the public.

4578. Minimum wage law enacted by Congress was one of the provisions of the Fair Labor Standards Act of 1938, "an act to provide for the establishment of fair labor standards in employment in and affecting interstate commerce," enacted on June 25, 1938.

4579. Minimum hourly wage of one dollar was set by the federal government on August 12, 1955. Since then, the minimum hourly wage has undergone a series of raises. It was set at $3.10 effective January 1, 1980, and at $4.25 effective April 1991.

4580. Minimum wage law established by a city for public contract work was the City Contracts Minimum Wage law, approved by Mayor Robert Ferdinand Wagner of New York City on December 29, 1961. It applied to "every contract for or on behalf of the city for the manufacture, furnishing or purchase of supplies, material or equipment, or for the furnishing of work, labor or services, and entered into by public letting founded in sealed bids."

LABOR—PENSIONS

4581. Pension law enacted by a colony was enacted by the Plymouth Colony in 1636. The legislation provided that "if any [man] shalbee sent forth as a souldier and shall returne maimed, hee shalbee maintained competently by the Collonie of New Plymouth during his life." The act applied particularly to the soldiers engaged in the Pequot Indian War, which concluded on November 20, 1637.

4582. Pension law enacted by Congress was passed by the Continental Congress on August 26, 1776. It provided "that every commissioned officer, non-commissioned officer, and private soldier who shall have lost a limb in any engagement, or be so disabled in the service of the United States of America as to render him incapable afterwards of getting a livelihood, shall receive, during his life or the continuance of such disability, one half of his monthly pay from and after the time that his pay as an officer or soldier ceases." As the resources of the Continental Congress were meager, the states were asked to furnish the payments.

4583. Pensions paid by the federal government were those paid under the act of September 29, 1789, which took up the obligation of paying the pensions granted by the Continental Congress and appropriated money for payments to invalids who were wounded and disabled in the Revolutionary War for one year from March 4, 1789. The act of July 16, 1790, continued the payment of pensions for another year. The act of April 30, 1790, provided for pensions to those wounded or disabled in the line of duty, and the act of March 23, 1792, provided for pensions of those suffering wounds or disabilities known to be of service origin.

4584. Pension granted to the widow of a president was authorized by an "act granting a pension to Mary Lincoln," approved on July 14, 1870. She received $3,000 a year. A congressional act of February 2, 1882, increased the annual pensions to $5,000 for the three widows then living and made a special grant of $15,000 to Mary Lincoln.

LABOR—PENSIONS—*continued*

4585. Pension fund for teachers was set up in New York City under a state law passed on April 14, 1894, which provided for a retirement fund for public school teachers. Contributions to the fund were not drawn from teachers' regular salaries, but from deductions to their salaries on days when they were absent from work.

4586. Pension plan was offered to some 20,000 employees of the American Telephone and Telegraph Company and put into effect on January 1, 1913. The plan included coverage of employees 60 years of age with more than 20 years of employment, accident and disability benefits with full pay for 13 weeks or half-pay up to 6 years, sickness disability (for those employed more than 10 years) paying full pay for 13 weeks or half-pay for 39 years, and a life insurance policy with a maximum value of $5,000.

4587. Pension laws enacted by a state were enacted on March 5, 1923, by Montana and Nevada, whose respective governors signed their pension measures at the same hour on the same day. Montana instituted the first statewide mandatory system. It granted pensions of $25 a month to people who were over 70 years of age and who had been citizens and residents of the state for the previous 15 years. The funds were derived from the counties.

4588. Pensions paid by the federal government to workers in private industry were inaugurated on July 13, 1936, when checks totaling $901.56 were mailed to 18 retired railroad employees. This was done in accordance with the Railroad Retirement Act of August 29, 1935, which appropriated $46.7 million "to establish a retirement system for employees of carriers subject to the Interstate Commerce Act, and for other purposes."

LABOR—STRIKES

4589. Strike by workers took place in New York City in 1741, when the master bakers protested against municipal regulation of the price of bread. They were tried and convicted of unlawfully combining, but no sentence was passed.

4590. Strike benefit by a union was authorized on May 31, 1786, at the home of Henry Myers, Philadelphia, PA, when 26 members of the Typographical Society met to plan a protest against a reduction in wages. They agreed "that we will support such of our brethren as shall be thrown out of employment on account of their refusing to work for less than $6 per week." They won their demands.

4591. Strike in which women participated took place in the textile mills in Pawtucket, RI, in 1824, when female weavers went on strike along with the male workers.

4592. Strike by women occurred at the Dover Manufacturing Company, Dover, NH, in 1828, when about 400 women went on strike against a wage cut and a 10-hour day in the needlework trades.

4593. Strike in which a militia was called out occurred in Paterson, NJ, on July 21, 1828, when the Godwin Guards of the national militia were ordered to keep peace during a strike brought about by the changing of the factory lunch hour from noon to one o'clock. The strikers were defeated, but the noon lunch hour was afterwards restored.

4594. Strike suppressed by federal troops in peacetime was an action by railroad employees that began on July 16, 1877. In response to requests for aid from the governors of West Virginia, Maryland, Pennsylvania, and other states, President Rutherford Birchard Hayes called out federal troops. Earlier, on January 29, 1834, President Andrew Jackson ordered federal troops to put down a "riotous assembly" among laborers on the Chesapeake and Ohio Canal.

4595. Baseball strike took place on May 18, 1912, at Shibe Park, Philadelphia, PA, when 19 players of the Detroit Tigers refused to play the Athletics in sympathy for Ty Cobb, their outfielder, who had been suspended by Ban Johnson, president of the American League, because he mauled a spectator who had cursed him. The strikers were fined $50 a day, $100 for 48 hours. Hugh A. Jennings, the Detroit manager, recruited a scrub team that was defeated 24–2. There was not a regular Detroit player on the team.

4596. Strike settlement mediated by the federal Department of Labor was a dispute by the railway clerks of the New York, New Haven and Hartford Railroad. Commissioners of conciliation had not yet been appointed by the board, but the secretary of labor assigned the dispute to Glossbrenner Wallace William Hanger, chief statistician of the Bureau of Labor Statistics, who entered the case on May 24, 1913, and effected a settlement on June 2.

4597. Massacre of strikebreakers by union members began on June 21, 1922, at the Southern Illinois Coal Company's strip mine near Herrin, IL. During a nationwide strike by the United Mine Workers (UMW), a group of recruited strikebreakers arrived at the mine. Fighting broke out, and one striker and two strikebreakers were killed. The mine was quickly surrounded by armed UMW members. On June 22, approximately 60 strikebreakers inside the mine surrendered to union members, who marched them to a barbed wire fence and gunned them down. A few who managed to escape were hunted down and slain in a nearby cemetery. Twenty-one strikebreakers and one mine official were killed, and most of the rest were severely wounded.

4598. Sit-down strike occurred in the packing plant of George A. Hormel and Company, Austin, MN, on November 13, 1933, when striking employees seized control of the plant. The Industrial Commission of Minnesota, of which Niels Henriksen Debel was chairman, held mediation hearings on November 16–18, 1933, and rendered a decision on December 8 affecting the specific issues involved. Various forms of stay-in strikes, slowdown strikes, and refusal-to-work strikes had been attempted previously in a variety of industries.

4599. Sit-down strikes to be outlawed by a state were banned on April 9, 1937, by Vermont in an act "prohibiting the conspiring of three or more persons unlawfully to occupy, hold and possess certain buildings against the will and without the consent of the lessee thereof." The bill was introduced by Senator Ernest Walter Dunklee of Windham, VT, and provided for penalties of not more than two years' imprisonment or a $1,000 fine.

4600. Strike to last longer than a year started on December 26, 1945, when Local 180 of the United Automobile Workers of America struck the J.I. Case Manufacturing Company, Racine, WI, a manufacturer of farm implements. On March 9, 1947, the workers voted 927–448 in favor of accepting the company offer of an increase in wages from 25 cents to 26 cents an hour.

4601. Strike of postal employees was a wildcat strike of locals of the National Association of Letter Carriers that began in New York City on March 18, 1970, and spread to parts of New York, New Jersey, and Connecticut. On March 23, President Richard Milhous Nixon declared a state of national emergency and called out 30,000 troops to move the mail. The troops included 15,000 army, navy, and marine reservists from the New York City area; 12,000 members of the Army and Air National Guard in New York; and 2,500 men on active duty in New York. The strike ended on March 24.

4602. Strike by physicians against long working hours in hospitals began at 7 A.M. on March 17, 1975, when 21 of New York City's 91 voluntary and municipal hospitals were struck by interns and resident physicians demanding a reduction in work hours, not to exceed 40 hours.

LABOR—UNIONS

4603. Craft union was authorized on October 18, 1648, when the "shoomakers of Boston" were permitted "to assemble and meete together in Boston, at such time and times as they shall appoynt, who being so assembled, they, or the greatest number of them, shall have powre to chuse a master and two wardens, with fowre or six associats, a clarke, a sealer, a searcher, and a beadle...." Similar permission was also extended to coopers.

4604. Labor union to nominate its own political candidates was the Mechanics Union, which nominated candidates for the New York State Assembly in 1784. The first labor union whose candidates won an election was the New York Working Men's Party, whose candidate, Ebenezer Ford, president of the Carpenter's Union, was elected to the New York State Assembly on the Mechanic and Working Men's Ticket on November 7, 1829. Ford polled 6,166 votes.

4605. Craft union contract between employers and organized labor was effected in 1799 by the Federal Society of Journeymen Cordwainers (shoemakers) of Philadelphia, PA, after a strike of 10 weeks. The union was formed in 1794 after an unsuccessful attempt in 1792. In 1806 the members were put on trial for conspiracy.

4606. Labor union for women was the United Tailoresses Society of New York, a protective association formed by tailors in 1825 in New York City. In June 1831 they went on strike for an increase in wages. About 600 women remained on strike for four or five weeks.

4607. Trade union organization established in a city was the Mechanics Union of Trade Associations, which was organized in Philadelphia, PA, in 1827. Invitations to join were sent to "those trades who are as yet destitute of trade societies." They were also urged to "organize and send delegates as soon as possible."

LABOR—UNIONS—*continued*

4608. Railroad union was formed in 1855 when 68 engineers from 45 different railroads in 13 states met in Baltimore, MD, from November 6 to 10 and organized the National Protective Association of the Brotherhood of Locomotive Engineers of the United States "to protect ourselves, the traveling public and our employers from the injurious effects resulting from persons of inferior qualifications being employed as locomotive engineers."

4609. Labor cooperatives to be authorized by a state were authorized in Michigan on March 20, 1865. The act allowed the incorporation of "any ten or more persons, who shall be desirous of uniting as mechanics and laboring men, in any cooperative association."

4610. National union for women was the Daughters of St. Crispin, an organization of shoe operators. Their first convention was held at Lynn, MA, on July 28, 1869. The first president was Carrie Wilson of Lynn. Lynn had been the scene of a strike in March 1860, when 5,000 male shoe operators went on strike and were joined by 1,000 women.

4611. Labor union to admit workers other than craft workers was the Noble Order of the Knights of Labor, a secret society founded in Philadelphia, PA, on December 9, 1869, by six men. One of the founders, Uriah Smith Stevens, a tailor, became its first Master Workman. Membership was originally restricted to garment cutters. "Sojourners" were admitted for the first time on October 20, 1870. By January 5, 1871, there were 69 members.

4612. Labor union label was adopted by the Cigar Makers' International Union and first came into use in San Francisco, CA, in 1874. The label was adopted to protect organized workers from employers who were importing Chinese laborers to do the same work at lower wages. The blue label of the Cigar Makers' International Union was adopted in 1880 at the 13th convention of the organization held in Chicago, IL, and was issued free of charge to all manufacturers who operated strictly union factories. In 1869 the Carpenters' Eight Hour League of San Francisco stamped the lumber produced by planing mills with an eight-hour workday to differentiate it from lumber produced by 10-hour mills.

4613. Labor unions to be legalized by a state were legalized in New Jersey in "an act relative to persons combining and encouraging other persons to combine," approved on February 14, 1883. It provided that combinations organized to persuade workers to enter or leave employment were not unlawful.

4614. Labor union discrimination law enacted by a state prohibiting employers from discriminating in matters of employment against members of trade unions was "an act in relation to the employment of labor by corporations," approved on May 15, 1894, by New Jersey. Violation was subject to a fine not to exceed $500 or three months' imprisonment.

4615. Actors' union was the Actors' National Protective Union, New York City, chartered by the American Federation of Labor on January 4, 1896. In August 1919 it combined with two other unions, the White Rats and the Actors' Equity Association, to form the Associated Actors and Artists of America. A strike was called on August 7, 1919, in 13 theaters in New York City and spread to other cities. The dispute was settled in the union's favor on September 6, 1919.

4616. Laborsaving machine approved by a labor union was the Autoplate stereotype platemaking machine, invented by Henry Alexander Wise Wood, which was approved in 1900 by the Stereotypers' Union. The machine enabled workers to avoid handling large quantities of molten metal type containing poisonous antimony and lead.

4617. Librarians' union affiliated with the American Federation of Labor was the Library Employes' Union No. 15,590 of New York City, chartered on May 15, 1917. The first president was Tilloah Squires. The union was suspended on November 20, 1929.

4618. Housing cooperative sponsored by a labor union was the Amalgamated Houses, originally called the Amalgamated Cooperative Apartments, built by the Amalgamated Housing Corporation, which opened two buildings on November 1, 1927, in the Bronx, New York City. After additional buildings were erected, the project accommodated 1,495 families. The housing project was organized by Abraham Eli Kazan for the Amalgamated Clothing Workers of America.

LAW

4619. Shorthand account of a trial was made in Maryland by John Llywellin, clerk of the Council, who was instructed by Lord Baltimore to record the proceedings held in the Provinciall Court, St. Johns, MD, on November 15, 1681. The Justices Tailoor, Stevens, and Diggens found Josias Fendall guilty of mutiny on March 26, 1681, and sentenced him to pay "40,000 pounds of Tobacco for a fine, Be kept in safe custody at your own proper costes and charges until you shall have paid the same and after the same is paid to be for ever banished out of this Province."

4620. Laws of entail and primogeniture to be abolished by a state were abolished by Georgia, whose constitution of February 5, 1777, abrogated those two bulwarks of legal tradition. Entail is a means of willing property to a specified and unchangeable hierarchy of inheritors. Primogeniture is the right of the eldest child in a family, usually the eldest son, to inherit his parents' entire estate.

4621. Law code adopted by a state was the Louisiana Code of 1825, *A System of Penal Law, Divided into Code of Crimes and Punishments, Code of Procedure, Code of Evidence, Code of Reform and Prison Discipline, Beside a Book of Definitions*. On March 14, 1822, the legislature appointed L. Moreau Lislet, Edward Livingston, and Pierre Derbigny to remodel the colonial code of 1808. The code was approved on April 12, 1824 and promulgated on June 13, 1825.

4622. Temporary insanity defense in a criminal case was used by Daniel Sickles, a congressman from New York. On February 25, 1859, Sickles shot and killed Philip Barton Key, the son of Francis Scott Key, author of "The Star-Spangled Banner," after he learned that the younger Key was having an affair with his wife. His lawyer, James T. Brady, offered the defense of "temporary insanity." Sickles was acquitted. He eventually became a general in the Civil War, in which he lost a leg, and served as minister to Spain.

4623. Lie detector used as evidence in a court of law for consideration by a jury was the Keeler Polygraph, invented by Leonarde Keeler of the Scientific Crime Detection Laboratory, Northwestern University School of Law, Chicago, IL. Keeler conducted a test on February 2, 1935, in Portage, WI, and produced graphs of the test in the case of *Wisconsin State v. Cecil Loniello and Tony Grignano* that was being heard in the Circuit Court of Columbia County, WI. Both defendants were found guilty of assault. Tests of a similar nature had been used in minor civil and criminal cases as early as 1924, when blood pressure readings were made with a Tycos sphygmomanometer.

4624. Murder trial to be televised was the trial of Harry Washburn, held on December 5–9, 1955, in the District Court, Waco, TX, with Judge Drummond William Bartlett presiding. The defendant was accused of killing his former mother-in-law, Helen Harris Weaver, with a car bomb at San Angelo, TX. The defense and prosecution agreed to allow one camera to be placed on a balcony. The entire 25-hour proceedings were televised by KWTX-TV, Waco, TX, as a public service to the community. Washburn was convicted on December 10 and sentenced to life imprisonment.

4625. Trial in which lawyers appeared on a Picturephone took place in the Federal Court of Claims, Washington, DC. On October 16, 1975, a three-judge court, composed of Byron Skelton, Robert Kuntzig, and Philip Nichols, Jr., heard a claim for damages that had been in litigation for 15 years, involving $270,000. The lawyers, Rex E. Lee, assistant attorney general, and Bruce Mayor, counsel for the Merritt-Chapmann and Scott Company, presented their arguments before a Picturephone located in the Bell Telephone Picturephone Service, 393 Seventh Avenue, New York City.

LAW—COPYRIGHT

4626. Colonial copyright law securing benefit of copyright was passed on May 15, 1672, by the General Court of Massachusetts assembled in Boston, MA, which granted John Usher, a bookseller, the privilege of publishing on his own account a revised edition of *The General Laws and Liberties of the Massachusetts Colony*. It was ordered "that for at least seven years, unless he shall have sold them all before that time, there shall be no other or further impression made by any person thereof in this jurisdiction." The penalty for violation of the copyright was treble the whole charges of printing and paper.

4627. Copyright law enacted by a state was "an act for the encouragement of literature and genius," passed during the session of the General Court of Assembly of the Governor and Company of the State of Connecticut, held in Hartford, CT, from January 8 to February 7, 1783. The law gave authors sole right of publi-

LAW—COPYRIGHT—*continued*

cation for 14 years with power of renewal. Massachusetts passed a copyright law on March 17, 1783, for a 21-year period. Both laws extended rights only to other states having reciprocal legislation.

4628. Copyright law enacted by Congress was an act "for the encouragement of learning by securing the copies of maps, charts and books to the authors and proprietors of such copies during the times therein mentioned." The bill was signed by the speaker and the president of the Senate on May 25, 1790, laid before President George Washington on May 27, and signed on May 31. Rights were granted only to citizens of the United States, a policy which continued until 1891. Protection was extended over a 14-year period, renewal rights being granted only if the author was still alive.

4629. Book entered for copyright was *The Philadelphia Spelling Book arranged upon a plan entirely new, adapted to the capacities of children and designed as an immediate improvement in spelling and reading the English language,* which was registered in the clerk's office of the first district of Pennsylvania on June 9, 1790, by John Barry, the author. It was printed in Philadelphia, PA, in 1790 by Carey, Stewart and Company. It was also issued as *The American Spelling Book.*

4630. Copyright law on photographs enacted by Congress was enacted on March 2, 1861, and signed the next day by President James Buchanan.

4631. International copyright agreement was the Platt-Simonds Copyright Act, passed on March 4, 1891. The act enabled citizens of Switzerland, France, Belgium, and Great Britain to obtain copyright protection in the United States. The United States had been represented by Boyd Winchester at the Bern International Copyright Convention in 1886, but had not become a signatory to the convention.

LAW—LAWYERS

4632. Lawyer disbarred was Thomas Lechford, who was engaged by William and Elizabeth Cole in the summer of 1639 for the prosecution of an action against Mrs. Cole's brother, Francis Doughty of Taunton, MA. In a Quarter Court held in Boston on September 3, 1639, Lechford was disbarred by the General Court of Massachusetts because he spoke privately with members of the jury. The records state that "M. Thomas Lechford, for going to the Jewry, pleading with them out of Court, is

debarred from pleading any man's cause thereafter, unless his owne, and admonished not to presume to meddle beyond what hee shalbee called to by the Courts." Lechford was pardoned, but a year later was again disbarred for the same offense, and again pardoned.

4633. Lawyers admitted to practice before the Supreme Court were Elias Boudinot of New Jersey, Thomas Hartly of Pennsylvania, and Richard Harrison of New York, who were admitted on February 5, 1790. The requirements for admittance were "membership for three years past in the Supreme Court of the State in which they respectively belong, and that their private and professional character shall appear to be fair."

4634. Lawyer formally admitted to the bar who was African-American was Macon B. Allen, who passed his legal examination in Worcester, MA, and was admitted on May 3, 1845. He had practiced for two years previously in Maine, where no license was required.

4635. Lawyer admitted to practice before the Supreme Court who was African-American was John S. Rock, who was admitted on February 1, 1865. His admittance was moved by Senator Charles Sumner of Massachusetts. Chief Justice Salmon Portland Chase presided. The first African-American female lawyer admitted was Violette Neatly Anderson of Chicago, IL, who was admitted on January 29, 1926.

4636. Lawyer who was a woman was Arabella A. Mansfield of Mount Pleasant, IA, who was admitted to practice law in June 1869. She had studied in a law office and at home. Previously, women were considered ineligible for admission to the bar because the Iowa Code of 1851 allowed admission to "any white male person." That clause was repealed by an act approved on January 5, 1853, which held that "the affirmative declaration that male persons may be admitted is not an implied denial to the right of females." Mrs. Mansfield was admitted to practice and on March 8, 1870, the words "white male" were omitted from the statute.

4637. Lawyer who was an African-American woman was Charlotte E. Ray, who received an LL.B. degree from the School of Law, Howard University, Washington, DC, on February 27, 1872. On April 23, 1872, she was admitted to the Supreme Court of the District of Columbia, the first African-American woman to be admitted to the Washington bar.

4638. Lawyer who was a woman to be admitted to practice before the Supreme Court was Belva Ann Bennett Lockwood, who was admitted on March 3, 1879. The bill admitting women passed the House of Representatives on February 21, 1878, and the Senate on February 7, 1879. It was titled an "act to relieve certain legal disabilities of women" and was signed on February 15, 1879, by President Rutherford Birchard Hayes. It provided that any female member of the bar of good moral character who had practiced for three years before a state supreme court was eligible for admittance to practice before the Supreme Court of the United States.

4639. County public defender was Walton J. Wood, who assumed his duties on January 7, 1914. The office of public defender had been established by Los Angeles County, CA, on June 13, 1913. Wood's salary was $200 a month. He had three deputies, one secretary, and one assistant secretary.

4640. American Bar Association member who was a woman was Mary Florence Lathrop, who was admitted in 1917. She received her LL.B. degree from the University of Denver, Denver, CO.

4641. Family of lawyers admitted simultaneously to practice before the Supreme Court were William Henry Faust, Mrs. William Henry Faust, and William Henry Faust, Jr., of Indianapolis, IN, who were admitted on March 1, 1940.

4642. Public defender hired by a state was Peter Murray, appointed director of the Office of State Public Defender by Governor Richard Joseph Hughes of New Jersey on June 20, 1967, for a five-year term. A deputy public defender was appointed for each of New Jersey's 21 counties.

LAW—ORGANIZATIONS

4643. Lawyers' society (state) was the New York Bar Association, New York City, which operated from 1747 to 1770. Its purpose was to develop collective opinion on the economic issues prior to the Revolutionary War and to control admission to practice.

4644. Lawyers' society (national) was the American Bar Association, organized on August 21, 1878, at an informal meeting in Saratoga, NY, at the suggestion of Judge Simeon Eben Baldwin. At the close of the meeting, the membership consisted of 291 lawyers from 29 states. The first president was James Overton Broadhead of St. Louis, MO.

4645. Arbitration organization (national) devoted exclusively to advancing principle and practice in this field was the Arbitration Society of America, formed in New York City on May 15, 1922. On January 29, 1926, this group merged with two others to form the American Arbitration Association, whose first president was Anson W. Burchard.

LAW—PATENTS

4646. Patent granted by a colony was awarded to Samuel Winslow in 1641 by Massachusetts for a new method of extracting salt: "Whereas Samuel Winslow hath made a proposition to this Court to furnish the contrey with salt at more easy rates then otherwise can bee had, & to make it by a meanes & way which hitherto hath not bene discovered, it is therefore ordered, that if the said Samuel shall, within the space of one yeare, set upon the said worke, hee shall enjoy the same, to him & his associates, for the space of ten yeares, so as it shall not bee lawfull to any other pson to make salt after the same way during the said yeares; pvided, nevthelesse, that it shall bee lawfull for any pson to bring in any salt, or to make salt after any othrway, dureing the said tearme."

4647. English patent granted to a resident of America was issued on November 25, 1715, to "Thomas Masters, Planter of Pennsylvania, for an invention found out by Sibylla his wife for cleaning and curing the Indian Corn growing in several colonies in America."

4648. Patent granted by the federal government was issued to Samuel Hopkins of Vermont on July 31, 1790, for a process of making potash and pearl ashes. The document bore the signatures of George Washington, president; Thomas Jefferson, secretary of state; and Edmund Randolph, attorney general. Under an act approved on April 10, 1790, "to promote the progress of useful arts," the holders of these three offices constituted a patent commission empowered to issue patents. Only three patents were issued that first year. In May 1802 the Patent Office was organized with Dr. William Thornton as superintendent. In 1833, after 9,000 patents had been issued, the head of the Patent Office said that he wanted to resign because "everything seems to have been done."

4649. Patent recipient to obtain more than one patent was Samuel Mulliken of Philadelphia, PA, who was granted four patents on March 11, 1791. They were on a "machine for threshing grain and corn," a "machine for breaking and swingling hemp," a "machine for cutting and polishing marble," and a "machine for raising a nap on cloths."

317

LAW—PATENTS—*continued*

4650. Patent granted jointly to a father and son was awarded on August 2, 1791, to Samuel Briggs, Sr. and Jr., of Philadelphia, PA, on a machine for making nails.

4651. Patent granted to an inventor who was a woman was granted in 1793 to Hannah Wilkinson Slater of Pawtucket, RI, on a method of spinning cotton thread on spinning wheels. Her husband, Samuel Slater, operated a cotton mill on the Blackstone River.

4652. Patent granted to an African-American inventor was awarded to Henry Blair of Glenross, MD, on October 14, 1834, for a corn planter. Two years later, on August 31, 1836, he obtained a patent on a cotton seed planter.

4653. Numbering system for patents was introduced on July 13, 1836. Prior to that time, 9,957 unnumbered patents had been issued. Patent No. 1 under the consecutive numbering system was issued on July 13, 1836, to John Ruggles of Thomaston, ME, for "traction wheels for locomotive steam-engine for rail and other roads." Ruggles was chairman of the Senate Committee on Patents.

4654. Design patent was issued on November 9, 1842, to George Bruce of New York City for a typeface.

4655. Patent issued by the Confederate States of America was issued on August 1, 1861, to James J. Van Houten of Savannah, GA, on a breech-loading gun.

4656. Patent examiner who was a woman was Anna R.G. Nichols of Melrose, MA, a clerk in the Patent Office, who took office on July 1, 1873, as an assistant examiner. On August 24, 1971, Brereton Sturtevant, of Wilmington, DE, became the first woman to hold the position of examiner-in-chief of the Patent Office.

4657. Label patent was issued on August 1, 1874, to the Baltimore Pearl Hominy Company of Baltimore, MD, for a label to be attached to the sack, barrel, or box in which the firm's breakfast hominy was sold.

4658. Print patent was issued on March 7, 1893, to the H.J. Heinz Company of Pittsburgh, PA, for the phrase "Heinz's Preserves, Celery Sauce, Ketchup" in the shape of a pickle with three designs in circles. A patented print can be used in advertisements but cannot be used as a trademark.

LIBRARIES

4659. Library was established in Charleston, SC, in 1698 through the efforts of Thomas Bray (later the representative in Maryland of the Bishop of London), who in 1696 forwarded religious books to the clergy. On November 16, 1700, Charleston passed an act "for securing the Provincial Library of Charlestown, by which commissioners and trustees were appointed for its preservation." The act authorized any inhabitants to "have liberty to borrow any book out of the said provincial library, giving a receipt."

4660. Library catalog in book form was compiled in Latin by Joshua Gee, librarian of Harvard College, Cambridge, MA, and published in 1723 at Boston by Bartholomew Green. It was entitled *Catalogus Librorum Bibliothecae Collegij Harvardini Quod Est Cantabrigiae in Nova Anglia*. Only 300 copies were printed. It contained 106 pages and listed books according to size (folio, quarto, octavo, duodecimo, and so on), then alphabetically through the first letter of the entry word.

4661. Circulating library was set up by the Library Company of Philadelphia, organized on July 1, 1731 by Benjamin Franklin through his society, the Junto. The first meeting was held November 8, 1731, at the house of Nicholas Scull. Fifty persons contributed 40 shillings each for purchasing the first parcel of books plus a fee of 10 shillings per year. The first books were ordered on March 31, 1732. An agreement to hire Louis Timothee as librarian was made on November 14, 1732. Timothee, a young French immigrant, worked every Wednesday from two to three o'clock and every Saturday from 10 to four. His salary was £3 sterling every trimester.

4662. Library building used exclusively as a library was a frame house erected by James Logan in 1725 on the west side of Sixth Street, between Chestnut and Walnut streets, in Philadelphia, PA. Logan made this house available to the public as a reading room. On March 8, 1745, he turned over the property and 2,000 books to the city, but the library did not start to function as a public library until November 8, 1760. It was known as the Loganian Library, and William Logan, his son, was the first librarian. The library was closed after William Logan's death and on March 31, 1792, was incorporated into the Library Company of Philadelphia.

4663. Librarian of Congress was John James Beckley of Virginia, clerk of the House of Representatives, who was appointed on January 29, 1802, and served until his death on April 8, 1807. The Library of Congress was established by authority of the act of April 24, 1800, appropriating $5,000 "for the purchase of such books as may be necessary for the use of Congress at the said city of Washington and for fitting up a suitable apartment for containing them and for placing them therein." The first library catalog, dated April 1802, listed 964 volumes and nine maps. Until 1815, when George Watterston was appointed, the librarians were the clerks of the House of Representatives.

4664. Children's library was established in January 1803 in Salisbury, CT, through the generosity of Caleb Bingham of Boston, a native of Salisbury. He donated 150 volumes, the nucleus of the Bingham Library for Youth.

4665. Workers' library was opened in New York City in 1820 by the General Society of Mechanics and Tradesmen of the City of New York and was known as the Apprentice's Library. The name was changed in 1898 to the Free Library of the General Society of Mechanics and Tradesmen. Another library for apprentices was opened at Carpenters' Hall in Philadelphia, PA, by the Free Quakers on June 3, 1820. Horace Binney was the first president.

4666. Mercantile library was the Mercantile Library Association of the City of New York, organized at 49 Fulton Street, New York City, on November 9, 1820, with 150 sponsors in attendance. The library was founded to allow clerks and others engaged in mercantile business to enjoy the use of reading facilities. It opened on February 12, 1821. The first president was Lucius Bull.

4667. Library for seamen was inaugurated in March 1829 by the American Seamen's Friend Society of New York City, which was organized on May 5, 1828, to supply traveling libraries to ships. Smith Thomson was the first president. Loan libraries were placed on board American ships and on Coast Guard and naval vessels, as well as in Coast Guard lifesaving stations.

4668. Free public library established by a city was established in Peterborough, NH, on April 9, 1833. The funds for its creation came from state monies that had originally been appropriated for a state university and were then distributed to towns to use for educational purposes. The library was maintained by a public tax, controlled and managed by town vote, and open to all community members without restriction. An earlier but unsuccessful attempt to establish a free public library was made in New Orleans, LA, by the philanthropist Judah Touro, who founded the Touro Free Library Society in 1824.

4669. Library building at a university was the library of the University of South Carolina, Columbia, SC, completed on May 6, 1840. The university's first librarian was Elisha Hammond, who began to serve in 1805. The first librarian in the separate building was Dr. Thomas Park.

4670. Free public libraries authorized by a state were authorized by a New Hampshire bill approved on July 7, 1849. It provided that "the inhabitants of any school district in any city or town, and of any city or town not divided into school districts, in this Commonwealth, may, at any meeting called for that purpose, raise money for the purchase of libraries, in the same manner as school districts may raise money for erecting and repairing school houses in their respective districts ... and that every public library established under provision of this act shall be open to the free use of every inhabitant of this town."

4671. Library newspaper room was opened on November 7, 1859, in the reading room in the great hall on the third floor of Cooper Union for the Advancement of Science and Art, Astor Place, New York City. It contained 12 New York dailies and 16 other dailies. The section was 125 feet long, 82 feet wide, and 32 feet high and was open from 8 A.M. to 10 P.M., free to all persons of good moral character for the use and instruction of the working classes. The attendance was about 3,000 people a week, a tenth of whom were women.

4672. Children's department in a library is said to be that of the Minneapolis Public Library, which separated children's books from the rest of the collection in December 1889. A room was set aside for children in 1892, and in the fall of 1893 a whole corridor was equipped for their use.

4673. County library successfully conducted was the Brumback Library of Van Wert County, Van Wert, OH, which was organized in 1898 and which opened a new building in 1901. Funds were secured from the County Commissioners through a tax levy.

LIBRARIES—*continued*

4674. Librarian who was African-American who was professionally trained was Edward Christopher Williams, who attended New York State Library School in 1899-1900, before library schools were officially closed to African-American students. The first African-American woman to train as a librarian was Virginia Proctor Powell Florence, who attended Pittsburgh Carnegie Library School in 1922-23.

4675. Business library supported by taxes was a branch of the Newark Public Library that was opened on October 1, 1904, at 16 Academy Street, Newark, NJ. The first librarian was Sarah B. Ball. The budget for the year 1904 was approximately $1,500.

4676. Bookwagon traveling library was started at the Washington County Free Library, Hagerstown, MD, in April 1905. A wagon that had previously been used for gathering eggs, butter, and produce was outfitted with shelves to carry books and was driven through the county three times a week by Mr. Thomas, the library's janitor.

4677. Archivist of the United States was Robert Digges Wimberley Connor, appointed on October 10, 1934. The position was created by an act of Congress that established the Archives Bureau. Connor served until September 15, 1941. The archivist has an official seal and is chairman of a national publications committee.

4678. Federal aid to libraries was authorized by the Library Services Act of June 19, 1956, "to promote the further development of public library service in rural areas." It authorized the appropriation for the fiscal year ending June 30, 1957, and for each of the four succeeding fiscal years, of the sum of $7.5 million, to be used for making payments to states.

4679. State library to publish a master catalog of a major part of its holdings was the Oregon State Library, Salem, OR, which in 1974 published a 25-volume master catalog, with two-column pages measuring 8.5 by 11 inches. It contained the entries from over 3,500 catalog drawers of the Oregon State Library's adult nonfiction holdings, 190,000 separate titles in all, classified by author, title, and subject.

4680. Library to possess 100 million items was the Library of Congress, Washington, DC, which acquired its 100 millionth item in 1992. In 1996, its collections included 15 million books, 39 million manuscripts, 13 million photographs, 4 million maps, more than 3.5 million pieces of music, more than half a million motion pictures, and millions of other documents.

LIBRARIES—INFORMATION STORAGE

4681. Microfilm reading device was invented by Bradley Allen Fiske of Washington, DC, who received a patent on March 28, 1922, on a "reading machine." It was known as a Fiskeoscope and could be carried in the pocket. A 2.5-inch newspaper column was reduced to 0.25 inches and 100,000 words were contained on a 40-inch tape.

4682. Newspaper to store issues on microfilm was the *New York Times,* which in November 1935 microfilmed its issues from the years 1914 to 1927, in cooperation with the New York Public Library. The first newspaper to microfilm its current issues was the *New York Herald Tribune,* which began the service with the issue of January 1, 1936.

4683. Book series microfilmed was *A Short Title Catalogue of Books Printed in England, Scotland and Ireland and of English Books Printed Abroad 1475–1640,* compiled by Alfred William Pollard and Gilbert Richard Redgrave, 609 pages, published in London in 1926. It was microfilmed by University Microfilms, Ann Arbor, MI, in 1935 from negatives made by the British Museum.

4684. Book issued on microcards was Fremont Rider's *The Scholar and the Future of the Research Library,* put on microcards by the Microcard Corporation, La Crosse, WI, in the fall of 1947. The 236-page book was reproduced on 3-by-5-inch cards containing about 80 pages to a card. These cards were not offered for sale but were given away to various individuals and institutions.

4685. Magazine on microfilm offered to subscribers was *Newsweek,* published in New York City, which offered a microfilm and microcard service to subscribers on June 1, 1949, for $15 a year. The microcard editions were printed on 3-by-5-inch cards. The microfilm editions were on 35mm reels in 100-foot lengths, 26 issues to a roll. Both editions were available in March and September of each year.

4686. Microfilm editions of federal publications and documents were offered as a regular service by University Microfilms, Ann Arbor, MI, in April 1952. The price was $900 for *Hearings, Reports, Committee Prints for the 82nd Congress.*

4687. Book collection of importance on ultra-microfiche was *The Library of American Civilization,* prepared by Library Resources, a subsidiary of Encyclopaedia Britannica, Chicago, IL. Costing more than $5 million to produce, it consisted of more than 19,000 bibliographic volumes, or 6,500,000 pages, covering the

American experience up to 1914. Ultramicrofiche forms are 3 by 5 inches in size and contain up to 1,000 pages reduced from 55 to 90 times, depending on the size of the original material. They were first delivered to subscribers in July 1971.

LIBRARIES—ORGANIZATIONS

4688. Library association (national) was the American Library Association, organized on October 6, 1876, at a meeting in Philadelphia, PA, attended by 103 librarians. The association was incorporated on December 10, 1879, under the laws of Massachusetts. The first president was Dr. Justin Winsor, and the first secretary was Melvil Dewey.

4689. Library society (local) was the New York Library Club, formed on June 18, 1885, at a meeting held at Columbia University, New York City, "to promote acquaintance and fraternal relations among librarians and those interested in library work and advance the interests of the libraries of New York and its vicinity." Richard Rogers Bowker was the first president.

4690. Library society (state) was the New York Library Association, organized "to promote library interests of the state of New York" by 43 persons on July 11, 1890, at the New York State Library, Albany, NY. The first president was Melvil Dewey.

4691. Bibliography organization (national) was the Bibliographical Society of America, organized on October 18, 1904, in St. Louis, MO, "to promote bibliographical research and to issue bibliographical publications." The first president was William Coolidge Lane.

M

MAGAZINES AND JOURNALS

4692. Magazine published in America was *The American Magazine, or a Monthly View of the Political State of the British Colonies,* edited by John Webbe and published by Andrew Bradford in Philadelphia, PA. It was published monthly for three months in the spring of 1741. On the title page was an illustration of the Philadelphia waterfront. The first issue appeared in the middle of February, about three days prior to Benjamin Franklin's *General Magazine and Historical Chronicle for All the British Plantations in America,* which was also published in Philadelphia.

4693. Religious magazine was *The Christian History,* published weekly in Boston, MA, from March 5, 1743, to February 23, 1745, "containing accounts of the revival and propagation of religion in Great Britain and America." The editor was Thomas Prince, Jr. It was eight pages long and was printed by Samuel Kneeland and Bartholomew Green.

4694. Music magazine was the *American Musical Magazine,* which was published in May 1786 in New Haven, CT. It was issued regularly and was a collection of tunes and hymns. It was published and sold by Amos Doolittle and Daniel Read. The first issue, six pages long, contained the selection "The Seasons Moralized."

4695. Children's magazine was published in Hartford, CT, by Barzillai Hudson and George Goodwin. It was called the *Children's Magazine: Calculated for the Use of Families and Schools.* Four issues were printed from January to April 1789, each containing 48 pages, and presenting an "abridgement of geography, essays on morality, religion, manners, etc., familiar letters, dialogues and select pieces of poetry."

4696. Senate journal was the *Journal of the First Session of the Senate of the United States. Begun and Held at the City of New York, March 4, 1789,* published in 1789 in New York City.

4697. Catholic magazine was the weekly journal *Courier de Boston,* which appeared on April 23, 1789, and continued publication weekly for six months. It was published in French in Boston, MA, and was edited by Paul Joseph Guérard de Nancrède, instructor in French at Harvard University.

4698. Comic magazine was *The Wasp,* edited by Robert Rusticoat, Esq. (also known as "Rusty-Turncoat"), and printed by Harry Crosswell, Hudson, NY. The first issue, dated July 7, 1802, consisted of four pages and lampooned politics and politicans.

4699. College magazine was the *Literary Cabinet,* published on November 15, 1806, at Yale University in New Haven, CT. It was an eight-page biweekly and was edited by three college seniors. It sold for $1 a year. It folded after one year.

4700. Law magazine was the *American Law Journal,* which was published in Baltimore, MD, from 1808 to 1817. It was edited by John Elihu Hall.

MAGAZINES AND JOURNALS—*continued*

4701. Magazine containing a fashion plate was *The Port Folio,* published by Bradford and Inskeep, Philadelphia, PA, and Inskeep and Bradford, New York City. The June 1809 issue contained two engravings, one page showing a full dress and one showing the front and back views of "Fontarabian robes of Saragossa brown net."

4702. Catholic magazine in English was the *Michigan Essay or Impartial Observer,* a weekly, which was issued on August 31, 1809. It was printed and published in Detroit, MI, by James M. Miller and was only semi-Catholic in scope. The idea was advocated by the Reverend Gabriel Richard of Detroit. The weekly consisted of four pages, of which a small part was printed in French. The rates were $5 a year for subscribers living in the city, $4.50 in upper Canada, and $4 elsewhere.

4703. Agricultural journal was the *Agricultural Museum,* a 16-page octavo first issued on July 4, 1810, under the sponsorship of the Columbia Agricultural Society. It was edited by the Reverend David Wiley and printed by W.A. Rind at Georgetown, DC (now part of Washington, DC). Beginning with Volume 2, it was issued monthly. Subscription was $2.50 for 24 numbers. Publication ceased in May 1812. The first agricultural journal to attain prominence was the *American Farmer,* an eight-page quarto-size weekly, which was founded in Baltimore, MD, on April 2, 1819, by John Stuart Skinner. It flourished under various names until 1897.

4704. Quarterly magazine was *The American Review of History and Politics and General Repository of Literature and State Papers,* edited by Robert Walsh and published in Philadelphia, PA. The first issue, dated January 1811, contained 200 pages and a 60-page appendix. Subscription was $6 a year. The last issue was published in October 1812.

4705. Masonic magazine was *Free-Masons Magazine and General Miscellany,* a monthly, published in April 1811 by Levis and Weaver, Philadelphia, PA. It was edited by George Richards.

4706. Educational magazine that was successful was the *Academician,* a 16-page semimonthly, published from February 7, 1818, to January 29, 1820, in New York City. It was edited by Albert Picket and John W. Picket, president and corresponding secretary, respectively, of the Incorporated Society of Teachers, which published the magazine. It offered advice and comments on teaching, and cost $3 a year. The Pickets had previously published an unsuccessful magazine, the *Juvenile Mirror or Educational Magazine,* which made its first appearance in August 1811 but lasted less than a year.

4707. Antislavery magazine was *The Emancipator,* issued monthly from April 30 to October 31, 1820. It was edited and published by Elihu Embree and cost $1 a year.

4708. Children's magazine with literary merit was *The Juvenile Miscellany,* founded by Lydia Maria Frances Child in 1826. It was a bimonthly and appeared from September 1826 to January 1829. It was published by Putnam and Hunt in Boston, MA. The first issue contained 108 pages.

4709. Magazine for women to continue publication for more than five years was the *Ladies' Magazine,* which was founded in Boston, MA, in 1828 by Sarah Josepha Hale, who became its editor. In 1837, the magazine merged with *Godey's Lady's Book,* which Mrs. Hale continued to edit in Philadelphia until 1877.

4710. Trade journal was the *Rail-road Advocate,* published biweekly from July 4, 1831, to June 14, 1832, in Rogersville, TN, by "an association of gentlemen." The first issue contained eight pages measuring 12.5 by 9.75 inches. Its main objects were "to advocate railroads and other internal improvements that would connect East Tennessee with markets for its surplus produce" and "end its isolation from the rest of the country," and to collect and publish "all the information that can be collected on this interesting subject."

4711. Horticultural magazine was the *Floral Magazine and Botanical Repository,* published in May 1832 in Philadelphia, PA, by David and Cuthbert Landreth, nurserymen and seedsmen. Publication ceased after 80 pages and 31 colored lithograph prints had been issued.

4712. Book trade magazine was the *Bookseller's Advertiser & Monthly Chronicle of Literary Enterprises,* also known as the *Bookseller's Advertiser & Monthly Register of New Publications,* which appeared on January 1, 1834. It was published by West and Trow, New York City, and contained eight printed quarto pages. Subscription was $1 yearly. It listed 275 original American works published in 1833 and American reprints of foreign works.

4713. Magazine for blind readers was the *Student's Magazine, a Periodical for the Blind,* published in January 1837 by the Pennsylvania Institution for the Instruction of the Blind, Philadelphia, PA. Embossed raised capital letters were used. It was a monthly and cost $3 a year.

4714. Factory workers' magazine was *The Lowell Offering,* "a repository of original articles on various subjects, wholly written, edited and published by female operatives employed in the mills." It was published bimonthly and cost six and a quarter cents a copy. The first issue was published in October 1840 by Powers and Bagley.

4715. Illustrated weekly magazine was *Brother Jonathan, a Weekly Compend of Belles Lettres and the Fine Arts, Standard Literature and General Intelligence,* first issued on January 1, 1842. It consisted of 28 pages plus a 32-page supplement containing the first installment of "Adventures of Tom Stapleton," by John M. Moore. It was founded by Benjamin Henry Day and Nathaniel Parker Willis and was published by Wilson and Company, New York City. It was not the first magazine to contain illustrations, but the first to make them a fundamental part of the presentation.

4716. Magazine for patients with mental illness was the *Illuminator,* written and published in 1843 by patients in Pennsylvania Hospital, Philadelphia, PA. The first issue appeared on April 1, 1843, and contained 24 three-column pages, each in Spencerian handwriting.

4717. Comic weekly was *The John Donkey,* 16 pages, published by G.B. Zieber and Company of Philadelphia, PA, from January 1 to October 21, 1848. It cost six cents a copy or $3 a year. It was edited by Thomas Dunn English and George G. Foster and was illustrated by Felix Octavius Carr Darley and Henry Louis Stephens.

4718. Shorthand journal was the *American Phonographic Journal,* 16 pages, edited and published by Dyer and Webster, Philadelphia, PA, which first appeared in July 1848. It sold for 10 cents an issue or $1 a year. The journal suspended publication after the issue of October 1848 and resumed publication in March 1849 with E. Webster as the publisher.

4719. Photography magazine was the *Daguerreian Journal; devoted to the Daguerreian and Photogenic Arts, also embracing the Sciences, Arts and Literature,* a 32-page octavo fortnightly that was first published on November 1, 1850, in New York City. It sold for 25 cents a copy or $3 a year. S.D. Humphrey was the editor and publisher and William S. Dorr the printer.

4720. Magazine for and by deaf students was the *Deaf Mute Casket,* a four-page monthly edited by William D. Cooke. It was published in 1851 by the State School for the Blind and the Deaf in Raleigh, NC.

4721. Insurance journal was *Tuckett's Monthly Insurance Journal,* published in 1852 in Philadelphia, PA.

4722. Art magazine of merit was *The Illustrated Magazine of Art,* which contained "selections from the various departments of painting, sculpture, architecture, history, biography, art-industry, manufactures, scientific inventions and discoveries, local and domestic scenes, ornamental works, etc." It was published by Alexander Montgomery in New York City from January 1853 to December 4, 1854. The first issue contained 60 pages.

4723. Magazine for professional printers was the *Typographic Advertiser,* a quarterly published by L. Johnson and Company, Philadelphia, PA, which appeared in April 1855.

4724. Book trade magazine that was successful was the *American Publishers' Circular and Literary Gazette,* a weekly for booksellers and libraries, first issued on September 1, 1855, by the New York Book Publishers' Association, of which William Henry Appleton was president. It was later absorbed by *Publishers Weekly.*

4725. Bibliophile magazine was *The Philobiblion, a Monthly Biographical and Literary Journal Containing Critical Notices of and Extracts from Rare, Curious and Valuable Old Books,* published on India paper by J.W. Bouton, New York City. The first issue was dated December 1861. George Philip Philes was the editor.

4726. Advertising magazine was the *Advertising Agency Circular,* a monthly founded by George Presbury Rowell and published by George P. Rowell and Company, New York City. It was issued from 1865 until December 1866, when the name was changed to the *Advertiser's Gazette.* It became a weekly on Thursday, April 1, 1875.

MAGAZINES AND JOURNALS—*continued*

4727. Stamp collection magazine was the *Stamp Collector's Record,* which consisted of four pages, 5.5 by 8.25 inches, two columns to a page, first published on December 15, 1864, at Albany, NY, by Samuel Allan Taylor. It was issued on the 15th of every month and sold for 50 cents a year. The rate for advertising was 15 cents a line.

4728. Fashion magazine was *Harper's Bazaar,* "a Repository of Fashion, Pleasure and Instruction," whose first issue, 16 pages long, was published on November 2, 1867, by Harper and Brothers in New York City. It cost 10 cents a week or $4 a year. Potential readers were invited to write to the publishers to receive free copies of the first six issues. The magazine was edited by Mary Louise Booth and appeared as a weekly from November 1867 to April 1901, when it changed to a monthly. Within 10 years it had a circulation of 80,000.

4729. Library journal was *Library Journal,* the monthly journal of the American Library Association, published by F. Leypoldt, New York City. The managing editor was Melvil Dewey and the general editor was Richard Rogers Bowker. The subscription price was 50 cents an issue, $5 a year. The first issue, dated September 30, 1876, contained 42 pages.

4730. Phonograph trade magazine was *The Phonogram,* "official organ of the phonograph companies of the United States," edited by V.H. McRae. It was published monthly in New York City from January 1891 to January 1893. The first issue contained an article by Thomas Alva Edison entitled "How Sound Is Reproduced."

4731. All-fiction pulp magazine was the October 1896 issue of *Argosy,* 192 pages, 7 by 10 inches. It was an outgrowth of an eight-page illustrated weekly for boys and girls edited by Frank Andrew Munsey entitled *The Golden Argosy,* which first appeared on December 9, 1882. It was published in New York City.

4732. Science fiction magazine was *Amazing Stories,* published by radio and television pioneer and science proselytizer Hugo Gernsback, who is credited with coining the term "science fiction." The first issue was dated April 1926 and was published from the New York City offices of Gernsback's Experimenter Publishing Company. It billed itself as the first "Magazine of Scientifiction," a blend of "charming romance intermingled with scientific fact and prophetic vision." Early issues of *Amazing Stories* depended heavily on reprints. Later issues con-

tained original tales by Gernsback and others that were noted for their technological prescience, if not for their sophisticated prose. *Amazing Stories* continued publication under various names until 1994.

4733. Music magazine published in Braille was *The Musical Review for the Blind,* the first issue of which appeared in January 1930. It was published by the American Braille Press for War and Civilian Blind.

4734. Religion magazine printed in rotogravure was *Catholic Missions,* issued on October 1, 1934, by the Society for the Propagation of the Faith, New York City. It was issued quarterly and sold for a penny a copy. Its editor was the Right Reverend Monsignor William Quinn.

4735. Magazine of the federal government was the daily *Federal Register,* first issued on March 14, 1936. The masthead was decorated with the eagle shield and the Latin motto *Littera scripta manet* ("the written word endures"). It was published in Washington, DC, by the National Archives under the Federal Register Act approved on July 26, 1935, and contained 16 two-column pages containing federal laws, orders, and reports.

4736. News magazine featuring photographs was *Life,* the weekly magazine founded by Henry Luce and published by Time, Incorporated, in New York City. Luce had conceived of a new kind of magazine in which "the cream of the world's pictures" would be edited into a coherent story. The first issue went on sale on November 19, 1936, with a cover by photojournalist Margaret Bourke-White depicting Montana's Fort Peck Dam. The first printing of 200,000 copies sold out by the end of the day. This magazine had no connection to an earlier publication called *Life,* a magazine of satire and humor published in 1883 in New York City by John Mitchell.

4737. Comics studio for the mass production of comics was started in 1936 by Will Eisner in New York City. Eisner, the creator of "The Spirit," mentored other comic-book artists such as satirist Jules Feiffer, Bob Kane, the creator of "Batman," and Art Spiegelman, the author of *Maus.* In 1978, Eisner wrote the first graphic novel, *A Contract with God,* published by Kitchen Sink Press.

4738. Magazine to contain a phonograph record was the November 1955 issue of *Pageant,* published in New York City, which went on sale on October 10, 1955. It contained a 78-r.p.m. acetate recording of "If You Don't Want My Love," sung by Jaye P. Morgan to the accompaniment of Hugo Winterhalter's orchestra. Approximately 1.1 million copies were issued.

4739. Underground comic book of note was the Apex Novelty Company's *Zap,* which appeared on newsstands in San Francisco, CA, beginning on October 3, 1967, and ran for several issues. It featured sexually frank, politically radical drawings and stories by Robert Crumb, Gilbert Shelton, S. Clay Wilson, Spain, and other artists. One issue was impounded for obscenity in Berkeley, CA, by the police.

4740. Magazine about recreational drugs was *High Times,* published and edited by Thomas Forcade of New York City in August 1974. Its stories described the risks and rewards of using marijuana, hashish, and psychedelic drugs.

MAGAZINES AND JOURNALS—ETHNIC

4741. German magazine was the *Geistliches Magazien,* published in undated numbers between 1764 and 1770 in Germantown, PA, by Christopher Sower. It contained religious observations, essays, sermons, poetry, and simple catechisms designed for family reading, and was given away, not sold.

4742. Irish magazine was *The Shamrock or Hibernian Chronicle,* first published on December 15, 1810, in New York City, and edited by Edward Gillespy.

4743. Welsh magazine was *Cymro Americaidd,* a semimonthly first published in 1832 in Welsh in New York City. J.A. Williams was the editor. An English section was added later.

4744. Magazine in a Native American language was the *Siwinowe Kesibwi* ("The Shawnee Sun"), a monthly, first printed on February 24, 1835, on the press of Jotham Meeker, a missionary at the Shawnee Baptist Mission in Kansas. Johnston Lykins, a Baptist missionary, was editor.

4745. African-American magazine was *The Mirror of Liberty,* a quarterly of 16 pages, edited and published in New York City by David Ruggles. The first issue was dated July 1838.

4746. Jewish magazine that was successful was *The Occident and American Jewish Advocate,* a monthly periodical devoted to the diffusion of knowledge on Jewish literature and religion, edited by Isaac Leeser and published at Philadelphia, PA. The first issue, 60 pages, was dated April 1843 (Nissan 5603). The first Jewish magazine in German was the short-lived *Israels Herold,* eight pages, first published in New York City on March 30, 1849. It was printed every Friday and sold for $1.50 semiannually and 75 cents quarterly. It ceased publication on June 15. Isidor Busch was editor.

4747. Swedish magazine was *Skandinavia,* first published on January 15, 1847, in New York City. Eight issues of the magazine were published.

4748. Arabic magazine was *Kowkab America* ("The Star of America"), a weekly, edited by Abraham Mitrie Rihbany. It was published in New York City in 1892.

4749. Esperanto magazine was *L'Amerika Esperantisto,* "a monthly journal of Esperanto, the international language," published in October 1906 in Oklahoma City, OK. It contained 16 pages and a cover. Subscription was $1 a year.

MAGAZINES AND JOURNALS—MEDICINE

4750. Medical journal was published in New York City on August 8, 1797, and was called *The Medical Repository,* a "depository of facts and reasonings relative to Natural History, Agriculture and Medicine." Printed by T. and J. Swords, printers to The Faculty of Physicians of Columbia College, it was published quarterly and appeared until 1824. It was also the first scientific periodical published in the United States. The first editor was Dr. Samuel Latham Mitchill, who continued in this capacity for 16 years. Drs. Edward Miller and Elihu Hubbard Smith were also active in the founding of this journal.

4751. Pharmacy journal was *The Journal of the Philadelphia College of Pharmacy,* which appeared in December 1825. Its first editor was Daniel B. Smith. The magazine contained 32 pages of "original and selected papers on subjects connected with pharmacy and chemistry," and sold for 25 cents.

4752. Homeopathy journal was the *American Journal of Homeopathia,* 48 pages, issued in February 1835. It was edited by Drs. John F. Gray and Amos Gerald Hull and published by Moore and Payne, New York City. Subscription was $4 a year. Only four issues were printed: February, April, June, and August, 1835.

MAGAZINES AND JOURNALS—MEDICINE—*continued*

4753. Phrenology journal was published by Nathan Allen in October 1838 in Philadelphia, PA. It was entitled the *American Phrenological Journal and Miscellany* and enjoyed a good circulation until its discontinuance in January 1911.

4754. Dental journal was *The American Journal of Dental Science*, 24 pages long, which made its appearance in July 1839. Dr. Chapin Aaron Harris was the first editor. It was published in New York City.

4755. Health journal to advocate water cures was the *Water Cure Journal*, devoted to the "proper explanation of hydropathy, or water cure, including bathing in its various forms, attention to diet, drink, air, exercise, cleanliness, and clothing, as affecting bodily and mental health." Edited by Joel Shew, M.D., and T.D. Pierson, M.D., this 16-page semimonthly was first published in New York City on December 1, 1845, at $1 a copy.

4756. Pediatrics journal was the *American Journal of Obstetrics and Diseases of Women and Children*, a quarterly, started in May 1868 in New York City. It was edited by Dr. Emil Jacob Noeggerath and Dr. Benjamin Frederick Dawson. The first issue contained 96 pages, including an article by Dr. Abraham Jacobi on "The Pathology and Treatment of the Different Forms of Croup."

4757. Laryngology journal was the *Archives of Laryngology*, a 108-page quarterly, published in New York City in March 1880. It was edited by Dr. Louis Elsberg of New York City, Dr. George Morewood Lefferts of New York City, Dr. Jacob Solis-Cohen of Philadelphia, PA, and Dr. Frederick Irving Knight of Boston, MA.

4758. Nursing magazine was *The Nightingale*, "a paper in the interests of the methodical nursing of the sick," which appeared on March 6, 1886, in New York City. The first issue consisted of four pages. It was a monthly, edited by Sarah E. Post of the Graduate Training School for Nurses, Bellevue Hospital, New York City. The subscription price was $2 a year.

4759. Psychology journal was the *American Journal of Psychology*, a quarterly first published in Baltimore, MD, in November 1887 under the editorship of Granville Stanley Hall. The subscription price was $3 a year.

4760. Opticians' journal was *The Optician*, a 16-page monthly, edited and published by Frederick Boger, New York City, beginning in January 1891. The subscription price was 50 cents a year. In May 1892 the name was changed to *The Optician and Allied Interests* and in October 1892 to *The Optician and Jeweler*.

4761. Medical journal published by an African-American was the *Medical and Surgical Observer*, 32 pages, published in Jackson, TN, in December 1892. It appeared regularly for 18 months. The first editor was Vandahurst Lynk, M.D.

4762. Osteopathy journal was the *Journal of Osteopathy*, which was started in May 1894 by the American School of Osteopathy in Kirksville, MO. The first editor was Dr. Jenette Hubbard Bolles.

4763. Orthodontia journal was the *International Journal of Orthodontia*, edited by Dr. Martin Dewey. The first issue was published in January 1915 in St. Louis, MO, and contained 44 pages. The title was changed to the *American Journal of Orthodontics and Oral Surgery* in January 1938.

4764. Allergy journal was the *Journal of Allergy*, published in November 1929 in St. Louis, MO. It was edited by Dr. Harry Louis Alexander. The first issue contained 112 pages.

MAGAZINES AND JOURNALS—SCIENCE AND TECHNOLOGY

4765. Mineralogy journal was the *American Mineralogical Journal*, founded by Archibald Bruce. The first number was printed in New York City in January 1810. This was followed by three other issues, the last of which appeared in 1814. These four numbers, comprising 270 pages, constitute the first and only volume that was published.

4766. Chemistry magazine was the *Memories of the Columbian Chemical Society of Philadelphia*, which was printed by Isaac Peirce, 3 South Fourth Street, Philadelphia, PA, in 1813–14. The first volume consisted of 221 pages. The society was founded in 1811.

4767. Science journal was the *American Journal of Science and Art*, printed in New York City and first issued in July 1818. It was edited by Benjamin Silliman. The first volume of four numbers contained 448 pages.

4768. Magazine for mechanics was *The American Mechanics' Magazine*, "containing useful original matter, on subjects connected with manufactures, the arts, and sciences; as well as selections from the most approved domestic and foreign journals," first published in

New York City by J.V. Seaman on February 5, 1825. From 1826 to 1828 its title was *The Franklin Journal and American Mechanics' Magazine,* and afterwards *The Journal of the Franklin Institute.*

4769. Electricity journal was *The Electro-Magnetic and Mechanics Intelligencer,* which appeared on January 18, 1840. It was printed in New York City on a press "propelled by electro-magnetism." The editor of the magazine and the inventor of the electrical printing press was Thomas Davenport.

4770. Astronomy magazine presenting a popular exposition of astronomy was *The Sidereal Messenger,* published by Ormsby MacKnight Mitchel, editor and director of the Cincinnati Observatory. It cost $3 a year. The first issue was published in July 1846 by Derby Bradley and Company, Cincinnati, OH, and consisted of eight pages. Publication ceased in October 1848.

4771. Gas journal was the *American Gas-Light Journal,* a monthly devoted to light, water supply, and sewerage, published by John B. Murray and Company, New York City, at $3 a year. The first issue, dated July 1, 1859, contained 16 pages. It listed 183 gaslight companies in the United States and 5 in Canada. The second issue, dated August 1, 1859, was larger in size and was described as the "Representative of Light, Water, and the Public Health." In 1917 the name was changed to *American Gas Engineering Journal* and in 1921 to *American Gas Journal.*

4772. Entomology journal devoted to applied entomology was the *Practical Entomologist,* the first issue of which was published in Philadelphia, PA, in October 1865 by the Entomological Society of Philadelphia (later known as the American Entomological Society). The original editors were Ezra Townsend Cresson, Augustus Radcliffe Grote, and James W. McAllister. The journal ceased publication after two years.

4773. Popular science magazine to report news of laboratory and workshop developments in popular terms was *Popular Science Monthly,* published by D. Appleton and Company, New York City, and first issued in May 1872. The first editor was Edward Livingston Youmans. The monthly contained 128 pages and sold for 50 cents. Some of the articles in the first issue were "Early Superstitions of Medicine," "The Study of Sociology," "The Causes of Dyspepsia," "Disinfection and Disinfectants," and "Science and Immortality."

4774. Economics journal was the *Quarterly Journal of Economics,* published in Boston, MA, for Harvard University. The first number appeared in October 1886.

4775. Geography magazine was *National Geographic,* founded in October 1888 by the National Geographic Society, Washington, DC. Alexander Graham Bell, an early editor of the magazine, originated the idea of paying famous explorers to write personal accounts of their exploits.

4776. Aviation magazine was *Aeronautics,* published from October 1893 to September 1894 by the *American Engineer and Railroad Journal,* New York City. It was edited by Matthias Nace Forney, and featured reports and articles about airplanes, gliders, and balloons. It contained 16 pages and sold for 10 cents a copy or $1 a year.

4777. Physiology journal was *The American Journal of Physiology,* 144 pages, the first issue of which was dated February 1898. It was published by Ginn and Company, Boston, MA.

4778. Oil journal was the *Oil Investors' Journal,* a semimonthly whose first issue was published on May 24, 1902, at Beaumont, TX. Holland S. Reavis was the founder and editor. The first issue contained 16 pages. The subscription price was $1 a year. In 1910, it became the *Oil and Gas Journal.*

4779. Radio magazine was *Modern Electrics,* first published in April 1908 by Hugo Gernsback in New York City. The first issue contained 36 pages. The subscription price was $1 a year.

4780. Aviation magazine devoted primarily to airplanes was *Fly,* first published in November 1908 in Philadelphia, PA, by Lawson and Kelley. It contained 20 pages and sold for 10 cents a copy or $1 a year. The magazine's first cover showed a girl seated on the back of an American eagle beckoning to two pilots.

4781. Television magazine was *Television, America's First Television Journal,* first published in June 1928 by the Television Publishing Company, New York City. It contained 32 pages plus cover and sold for 35 cents a copy.

MAGAZINES AND JOURNALS—SPORTS AND GAMES

4782. Horse racing magazine was the *American Turf Register and Sporting Magazine,* published in Baltimore, MD, by John Stuart Skinner. The first issue appeared in September 1829 and contained 56 pages. Its purpose was "to serve as an authentic record of the performances and pedigrees of the bred horse."

MAGAZINES AND JOURNALS—SPORTS AND GAMES—*continued*

4783. Cricket magazine was *The American Cricketer, a Journal Devoted to the Noble Game of Cricket,* four pages long, which was first published on June 28, 1877, at Philadelphia, PA. It was published weekly from May to November and monthly from November to May. The subscription price was $3 a year for 33 issues.

4784. Bicycle magazine was *The American Bicycling Journal,* published December 22, 1877, in Boston, MA. It contained 16 pages and cost 10 cents a copy. It appeared every other Saturday. Frank William Weston was the editor and proprietor. It was eventually absorbed by *Bicycling World and Motor Cycle Review.*

4785. Fishing magazine was the *American Angler,* a monthly magazine published in Philadelphia, PA, and edited by William Charles Harris. The first issue was published on October 15, 1881. On January 28, 1882, it became a weekly.

4786. Bowling magazine was *Gut Holz,* first issued on August 9, 1893, in New York City. It was originally printed in German. On May 19, 1894, it became the *Bowlers' Journal.*

4787. Golf magazine was *Golfing,* a weekly that was introduced in 1894 in New York City by William L. Dudley, editor and publisher. It contained 32 pages and sold for 10 cents a copy or $4 a year.

4788. Car magazine was *The Horseless Age,* first published in November 1895 in New York City by Edward P. Ingersoll.

4789. Motorboat magazine was *Motor Boat,* published by The Motor Boat Publishing Company, New York City. It covered all types of power craft. The first issue was dated April 10, 1904. It contained 40 pages and sold for 10 cents a copy.

MAPS AND CHARTS

4790. Map of a city within the present limits of the United States known to historians appeared in *Expeditis Francisco Draki Eqvitis Angli in Indias Occidentalis—1588,* an account of Sir Francis Drake's explorations. It was a line engraving depicting St. Augustine, FL.

4791. Native American map of record was a pen-and-ink drawing showing the location of rivers, roads, and pueblos in New Mexico. It was made in Mexico City in 1602 by a Native American man known to the Spanish as Miguel. He drew it during an inquiry by the Viceroy of New Spain into the results of Don Juan de Onate's expedition into territories north of New Mexico. Miguel had been captured at a Wichita Indian village on the Arkansas River, in present-day Kansas, after it was sacked by Escanxaque Indians who were serving as the expedition's guides. The place names on the map were written in by a notary. A copy of the map was forwarded to Spain, where it was preserved.

4792. Map made in America to be published in a book appeared in the Reverend William Hubbard's *The Present State of New England, being a narrative of the troubles with the Indians in New England, from the first planting thereof in the year 1607 to 1677,* published by John Foster, Boston, MA, in 1677. It was a topographical woodcut folding map and was known as the Wine Hills Map, since the English edition had "Wine Hills" instead of the "White Hills" of New Hampshire. It bore the inscription "Being the first that ever was here cut, and done by the best Pattern that could be had, which being in some places defective, it made the other less exact, yet doth it sufficiently shew the Scituation of the Countrey and conveniently well the distance of places." The name of the cartographer is unknown.

4793. Road map for public use was printed in *Tulley's Almanac* of 1698, published in Boston, MA, by John Tulley. The almanac showed a list of towns, roads, and distances from Boston. Later editions gave the names of the tavern keepers.

4794. War map was published in the December 24, 1733, issue of John Peter Zenger's *New York Weekly Journal.* It was a map of the harbor and fortifications of Louisburg, Nova Scotia.

4795. Map of the United States engraved in America was a wall map, 41 by 46.5 inches, made by Abel Buell in New Haven, CT, in 1783, after the Treaty of Paris. It was a line engraving, and was advertised for sale in the *Connecticut Journal* of March 31, 1784: "As this Map is the effect of the compiler's long and unwearied application, diligence and industry, and as perfection has been the great object of his labors, and it being the first ever compiled, engraved, and finished by any one man, and an American, he flatters himself, that every patriotic gentleman, and lover of geographical knowledge, will not hesitate to encourage the improvement of his country. Every favour will be most gratefully acknowledged, by the public's most obedient and very humble servant."

4796. Book of road maps was *A Survey of the Roads of the United States of America,* published in 1789 in New York City by Christopher Colles. It contained 86 plates and detailed the routes near the city.

4797. Cryptography chart was P.R. Wouves's *A Syllabical and Steganographical Table,* a chart 27 by 19.25 inches, with a list of syllables and words in English and French intended for secret correspondence. It contained 62 alphabetical columns of 6,138 two-letter combinations, numbered from 1 to 99 so that words could be converted into numerical figures. It had two title pages, one in English and one in French, and was published in 1797 by Benjamin Franklin Bache in Philadelphia, PA.

4798. Globe factory to produce terrestrial and celestial globes was started in 1813 by James Wilson in Bradford, VT. A large globe had been made in 1811 by Ira H. Hill of St. Albans, VT, for the Fairfield Academy of St. Albans.

4799. Atlas issued by a state was *The Atlas of the State of South Carolina, made under the authority of the Legislature; prefaced with a geographical statistical and historical map of the state.* It was prepared under the direction of Robert Mills and printed for the state in 1825 by John D. Toy, Baltimore, MD. It contained a map of the state of South Carolina and 28 district maps scaled 21 miles to the inch, which were engraved by H.S. Tanner and assistants. The atlas was 18 inches by 24 inches and included the location of the roads, rivers, bridges, ferries, factories, taverns, and many of the plantations.

4800. Relief map was made in 1871 by Edwin Eugene Howell and showed the island of San Domingo. In 1876, he made a relief map of the Grand Canyon of the Colorado as part of the Government Exhibit at the Philadelphia Centennial Exposition, Philadelphia, PA.

4801. Road map for motorists was produced by George Walker of Boston, MA, in 1900. His well-designed pocket maps for motorists were printed in color and were easy to fold. The first widely distributed road maps were published and distributed in 1914 by the Gulf Oil Company, Pittsburgh, PA. William B. Akin conceived the idea. The company distributed 10,000 maps showing roads and routes in Allegheny County, PA.

4802. Satellite composite map of the United States was the Earth Resources Technology photomosaic of the contiguous 48 states, constructed from 595 photographs taken from a 560-mile altitude by the *Landsat* satellite launched on July 23, 1972. It measured 10 feet by 16 feet and was assembled in November 1974 by the Department of Agriculture's Soil Cartographic Unit, Hyattsville, MD.

4803. High-resolution maps of the ocean floor were released in July 1995, when the Navy declassified satellite data from *Geosat,* an American satellite launched in 1985, and from the European Space Agency's *ERS-1* satellite. The data provided the first consistent and highly detailed view of the world's ocean basins, with information on many previously unknown submarine features.

MARRIAGES

4804. Breach-of-promise suit was instituted on June 14, 1623, in the Virginia Council of State, Charles City County, VA. The Reverend Greville Pooley brought suit against Cicely Jordan, the widow of Captain Samuel Jordan, who had jilted him in favor of William Ferrar. The penalty for a third offense was either corporal punishment, a fine, or another punishment ordered by the court.

4805. Annulment of a marriage by court decree was passed on December 3, 1639, in Boston, MA, when "James Luxford, being presented for haveing two wifes, his last marriage was declared voyde, or a nullity thereof and to bee divorced, not to come to the sight of her whom hee last tooke, and hee to be sent away to England by the first opportunity; all that hee hath is appointed to her whom hee last married for here and her children; he is also fined 100 t. and to bee set in the stocks an houre upon a market day after the lecture, the next lecture day if the weather permit, or else the next lecture day after (3rd of the 10th month 1639)."

4806. Divorce was granted at a Quarter Court at Boston, MA, on the fifth day of the first month in the year 1643. "Anne Clarke, beeing deserted by Denis Clarke hir husband, and hee refusing to accompany with hir, she is graunted to bee divorced, his refusall was under his hand, and seale, which hee gave before Mr. John Winthrop, Junr. Mr. Emanuel Downing, Mr. Nehemiah Bo'ne [Bourne] and Richard Babington, alsoe hee confesseth hee liveth in adultery with one, by whom he hath had 2 and refuseth hir which hee had two children by."

MARRIAGES—*continued*

4807. Polygamy ban enacted by Congress was enacted on July 1, 1862, "an act to punish and prevent the practice of polygamy in the territories of the United States and other places, and disapproving and annulling certain acts of the legislative assembly of the territory of Utah." Most of the settlers in Utah belonged to the Mormon Church (Church of Jesus Christ of Latter-day Saints), which encouraged men to marry multiple wives. Little effort was made to enforce this law. The first anti-polygamy law with teeth was the act of March 22, 1882, known as the Edmunds law, which defined simultaneous marriages as bigamy and prescribed loss of citizenship as a penalty. It legitimized children born in polygamy before January 1, 1883.

4808. Balloon honeymoon began on June 20, 1909, when Roger Noble Burnham of Brookline, MA, married Eleanor Howard Waring at Woods Hole, Cape Cod, MA. They ascended at 12:40 P.M. in the *Pittsfield,* a balloon piloted by William Van Sleet, and were obliged to land at 4:30 P.M. at Ralph Gilkey's orchard at Holbrook, MA, 14 miles from Boston Common.

4809. Elopement by airplane occurred on October 26, 1912, when 19-year-old Arthur Smith and Aimée Cour left Fort Wayne, IN, in a biplane and flew to Hillsdale, MI, where they landed on the campus of Hillsdale College. They flew 75 miles with one stop for gasoline.

4810. No-fault divorce law enacted by a state was enacted by California on July 6, 1970. It allowed divorces in cases of incurable insanity and irreconcilable differences.

4811. Divorce rate of more than 1 million a year was reached in 1975, when 1,036,000 divorces were granted.

MARRIAGES—WEDDINGS

4812. Wedding of colonists in Virginia was that of Anne Burras, maid of Mistress Forrest, to John Laydon in 1609. The maid and her mistress had arrived in Jamestown, VA, in 1608 as the first female colonists in America. No women came over with the original Jamestown settlers in 1607. The first wedding of African-Americans took place in Virginia in the early 1620s with the marriage of Antoney and Isabell, slaves (with the status of indentured servants) who had arrived in Jamestown in 1619.

4813. Wedding of colonists in New England was that of Edward Winslow and Susanna White, who were married on May 12, 1621 (new style May 22, 1621). Both were Pilgrims and members of the colony in Plymouth, MA, of which Winslow was the governor. His first wife, Elizabeth Barker, whom he had married in Holland in 1618, had died on March 24, 1621. Susanna White's first husband, William White, had died on February 21, 1621. Edward and Susanna Winslow had a son, Josiah Winslow, who became governor of New Plymouth Colony in 1673 and was thus the first American-born governor.

4814. Wedding in a balloon took place on October 19, 1874, in the 62,000-cubic-foot balloon *P.T. Barnum,* more than a mile above Cincinnati, OH. The Reverend Howard B. Jeffries of the Church of Christ (Swedenborgian) presided at the wedding of Mary Elizabeth Walsh and Charles M. Colton. Washington Harrison Donaldson was the balloonist. About 50,000 people assembled in Cincinnati's Lincoln Park to witness the ascent. The wedding was conceived as a publicity stunt for P.T. Barnum's Great Roman Hippodrome circus, which opened at the baseball grounds on October 13, 1874. The bride worked for Barnum as a horseback rider.

4815. Wedding of a president in the White House was Grover Cleveland's marriage to his ward, Frances Folsom, on June 2, 1886, during his first administration. Cleveland served as president from March 4, 1885, to March 4, 1889, and again from March 4, 1893, to March 4, 1897.

4816. Wedding by telegraph took place at noon on April 12, 1900, in Kansas City, MO, when the Reverend Albert H. Linder performed a 25-minute long-distance ceremony for Andrew M. Candell of Washington, DC, who was in Kansas City with two friends, and Penelope Cundiff of Perkins, OK, who was in Mulhall, OK, with her mother and sister. A direct wire conveyed the ceremony a distance of about 200 miles.

4817. Wedding abroad of a soldier in the American Expeditionary Force took place on July 14, 1917, in London. The groom was William Lewis; his wife's name was Kate.

4818. Wedding in an airplane took place on May 31, 1919, in a Handley-Paige bomber with two 12-cylinder motors that was flying about 2,000 feet over Ellington Field, Houston, TX, at the Flying Frolic air show, in front of about 10,000 spectators. The bride was Marjorie Dumont of Yorkville, IN, and the groom was Lieutenant R.W. Meade of Cincinnati, OH. They were married by Lieutenant J.E. Reese, chaplain, of Nevan, OH. The pilot of the bomber was Lieutenant E.W. Kilgore.

4819. Wedding broadcast over the radio was performed on June 15, 1920, in the First Presbyterian Church, Detroit, MI, by the Reverend C.E. Mieras, who received $10 for his services. The bride was Mabelle E. Ebert. The groom, Seaman John R. Wichman, was aboard the U.S.S. *Birmingham* in the Pacific Ocean. A friend stood in as proxy for him at the wedding. The ceremony was telephoned to the telegraph office, wired to the Great Lakes Naval Training Station near Chicago, and sent by radio to the *Birmingham*.

4820. Wedding on television took place on October 14, 1928, in the radio studio at Des Plaines, IL, where Cora Dennison and James Fowlkes of Kansas City, MO, were married by the Reverend Gustave A. Klenle of St. Luke's Evangelical Church. The ceremony was telecast.

4821. Wedding by transatlantic telephone took place on December 2, 1933, when Bertil Hjalmar Clason and Sigrid Sophis Margarete Carlson were married by Judge John Dennis Watts of the Wayne County Common Pleas Court in Detroit, MI. The groom was in Detroit and the bride was in Stockholm, Sweden. The ceremony was relayed from Detroit through New York to a Maine radio station, which sent it to Scotland to be relayed through London to Stockholm.

4822. Wedding during a parachute jump was performed on August 25, 1940, at the World's Fair amusement area, Flushing, Queens, New York City. The Reverend Homer Tomlinson of the Church of God, Jamaica, Queens, performed the wedding ceremony for Arno Rudolphi and Ann Hayward. The minister, the bride and groom, the best man, the maid of honor, and four musicians were all suspended by parachutes about 50 feet in the air.

MEDICINE—AMBULANCES

4823. Ambulance service for hospitals was introduced by the Commercial Hospital (now the General Hospital), Cincinnati, OH, prior to 1865. The list of employees for the year ending February 28, 1866, names James A. Jackson, employee No. 27, as "driver of ambulance" at an annual salary of $360. A similar service was started in June 1869 by Bellevue Hospital, New York City.

4824. Ambulance air service to transport sick people by airplane to hospitals was organized on October 21, 1929, by the Colonial Flying Service and the Scully Walton Ambulance Company of New York City.

4825. Ambulance service with an incubator for the transportation of premature infants was instituted by the city of Chicago, IL. The ambulance was ordered on February 26, 1935, and made its first run on March 21, 1935.

4826. Ambulance equipped for mobile coronary care was ordered by St. Vincent's Hospital and Medical Center of New York City and went into operation in October 1968. It brought doctors, nurses, and paramedics along with defibrillator, respirator, and electrocardiograph equipment to the patient's side within moments after a heart attack. The concept of on-site treatment of cardiac cases was created by Dr. William Joseph Grace.

4827. Ambulance ship for first aid to boaters and pleasure craft was the *Star of Life No. 1,* a 31-foot Uniflite cruiser owned by Fairfield Medical Products Corporation of Stamford, CT, and launched on April 2, 1976. Its equipment consisted of a Fairfield Heart Defibrillator, a coronary surveillance unit, and resuscitator (oxygen and aspirator) vacuum systems. The onboard equipment was equal to that of a typical hospital emergency room. The boat was made of fire-retardant fiberglass and was capable of a top speed exceeding 35 miles per hour. It was used in patrol and rescue duty on Long Island Sound between Greenwich and Norwalk, CT, and Glen Cove and Port Jefferson, NY, covering more than 150 square miles.

MEDICINE—ANESTHESIA

4828. General anesthetic was sulfuric ether, used by Dr. Crawford Williamson Long of Jefferson, GA, in December 1841. On March 30, 1842, he removed a cystic tumor about half an inch in diameter from the back of the neck of James M. Venable, applying ether under a towel. His bill for the operation amounted to $2.25: for sulfuric ether 25 cents and for excising the tumor $2. The discovery was not reported, however, until 1852, when the Georgia State Medical Society was notified.

MEDICINE—ANESTHESIA—*continued*

4829. Anesthetic in dentistry was used by Dr. Horace Wells, a dentist of Hartford, CT, who discovered the anesthetic property of nitrous oxide (laughing) gas. On December 11, 1844, while under the influence of gas, he had one of his teeth extracted by Dr. John M. Riggs. The use of the gas was not successful, as he did not know that it had to be combined with oxygen, a discovery that was not made until 24 years later.

4830. Anesthetic administered in childbirth was ether, employed on December 27, 1845, by Dr. Crawford Williamson Long during the delivery of his second child, Fanny, at Jefferson, GA.

4831. Painless surgery demonstration was given on October 16, 1846, at the Massachusetts General Hospital, Boston, MA. Dr. John Collins Warren operated on Gilbert Abbott, who had a swelling on the right side of his jaw, and removed a tumor, using a drug supplied by William Thomas Green Morton, a dentist of Charleston, MA. Morton was refused admission to hospitals until he divulged the name of the secret drug, which was sulfuric ether. Although he is credited with the discovery of anesthetics, 8 or 10 others have also claimed the honor.

4832. Local anesthetic was pioneered in 1885 by Dr. William Stewart Halsted of Baltimore, MD. Experimenting with the technique of conduction, or block, anesthesia (the production of insensibility in a part of the body by interrupting the conduction of a sensory nerve leading to it), he injected a preparation made from the leaves of the coca plant into a nerve trunk in his own arm. As a result of his experiments, Halsted became addicted to cocaine and morphine.

MEDICINE—BLOOD AND TISSUE

4833. Blood serum made of dried human blood was prepared by Dr. Earl William Flosdorf and Dr. Stuart Mudd of the School of Medicine, University of Pennsylvania, Philadelphia, PA, on December 21, 1933, with glass apparatus made by them. The powdered dried blood serum was used successfully in transfusions for the prevention and treatment of children's diseases at a hospital at Philadelphia, PA. The method was first described at a meeting of the American Chemical Society at St. Petersburg, FL, in April 1934.

4834. Blood bank to preserve blood by refrigeration for future use in transfusions was established on March 15, 1937, by the Cook County Hospital, Chicago, IL.

4835. Rh factor discovery was made in 1940 by Karl Landsteiner and Alexander S. Wiener at the Rockefeller Institute for Medical Research in New York City. Rh factor is a protein substance found on red blood cells that can produce a severe antibody reaction in babies during gestation. It was named after the rhesus monkeys used in the research. Landsteiner, while still working in his native Austria, had established the existence of different blood types in 1909.

4836. Eye bank was opened on May 9, 1944, at New York Hospital, New York City, through the efforts of Dr. Richard Townley Paton of Manhattan Eye, Ear and Throat Hospital and Dr. John McLean of New York Hospital. Twenty-one hospitals in the metropolitan area offered cooperation in obtaining eyes and sending them to the bank.

4837. Bone bank was established in April 1946 by Dr. Leonard Franklin Bush and Dr. Clarence Zent Garber at the New York Orthopaedic Hospital and Dispensary, New York City, and by Dr. Philip Duncan Wilson at the Hospital for Special Surgery, New York City.

4838. Tissue bank to apply the freeze-drying principle to the storage of human tissue grafts was undertaken in 1954 at the Naval Medical School, National Naval Center, Bethesda, MD. Tissues were procured for storage in a centralized unit. The bank was under the supervision of Lieutenant Commander George William Hyatt.

4839. National bone bank to acquire temporal bones for ear research was established in January 1961 at the Department of Otolaryngology, University of Chicago, Chicago, IL.

4840. Transfusion of artificial blood took place at the University of Minnesota Hospital, Minneapolis, MN, on November 20, 1979. The patient was a Jehovah's Witness who on religious grounds refused a transfusion of real blood. Dr. Robert Anderson injected the patient with Fluosol, an artificial blood substitute developed in Japan.

MEDICINE—CLINICS

4841. Pediatric clinic was established in 1862 at the College of Physicians and Surgeons (now part of Columbia University), New York City, by Dr. Abraham Jacobi, a member of the faculty.

4842. Laryngology clinic was established in March 1863 by the Medical Faculty of the University of the City of New York under the supervision of Dr. Louis Elsberg.

4843. General medical clinic of importance was opened by the Johns Hopkins Medical School, Baltimore, MD, in October 1889, five months after the opening of the Johns Hopkins Hospital. The first director was Sir William Osler, Regius Professor of Medicine at Oxford University, who also served as physician in chief of the hospital and professor of medicine at the medical school.

4844. Birth control clinic was opened on October 16, 1916, at 46 Amboy Street, in the Brownsville section of Brooklyn, New York City, by Fania Mindell, Ethel Byrne, and Margaret Sanger. The handbill announcing its opening was printed in English, Yiddish, and Italian. Sanger was jailed for operating the clinic. The first birth-control clinic staffed entirely by doctors opened in 1923.

4845. Flying medical clinic left the United States in January 1930 to attend the Pan American Medical Association convention in Panama City, Panama. It was composed of physicians who demonstrated the latest methods in surgery and medicine in local hospitals in Guatemala, Nicaragua, Panama, Colombia, Venezuela, and other Latin American countries. The first demonstration of an operation was made on January 25, 1930, by Dr. Fred Houdlett Albee.

4846. Ophthalmology clinic was opened by the Fifth Avenue Hospital, New York City, in September 1932. The clinic was devoted to the treatment of ocular muscle imbalances, including some types of strabismus (cross-eye). The clinic was under the direction of Le Grand Haven Hardy, M.D., director of the Eye Service.

4847. Birth control clinic run by a state government was opened on March 15, 1937, in Raleigh, NC, when the North Carolina State Board of Health officially introduced a program setting up contraceptive clinics for poor married women in local maternity and child health services. The first director was Dr. George Marion Cooper of the Division of Preventive Medicine. Roberta Pratt, a Raleigh nurse, was hired to work with the health officers.

4848. Genetics clinic was opened on November 12, 1941, by the Department of Human Heredity, a research unit of the Laboratory of Vertebrate Genetics, University of Michigan, Ann Arbor, MI, under the direction of Dr. Lee Raymond Dice. It secured data on the role that heredity plays and furnished advice to families about matters in which heredity is a factor.

4849. Traveling cancer clinic was established on February 14, 1946, by the Oklahoma Division of the American Cancer Society, Oklahoma City, OK. A school bus was remodeled to convey equipment and instruments for four examination rooms, which were presided over by an internist, a dermatologist, a gynecologist, and a surgeon. All services were rendered free of charge, and the physicians and nurses serving on the staff donated their time and expenses. Clinics were usually set up in church classrooms. The first clinic was set up in Tonkawa, Kay County, OK.

4850. Cancer prevention clinic for children was the Kate Depew Strang Foundation Prevention Clinic, opened on January 3, 1947, in the Prevention Clinic of Memorial Hospital, New York City.

4851. Vasectomy outpatient service was opened on October 3, 1969, by the Margaret Sanger Research Bureau, New York City, under the direction of the bureau's director, Dr. Aquiles Jose Sobrero. The clinical director was Dr. Joseph Edward Davis.

4852. Acupuncture treatment center was the Acupuncture Center of New York, which opened on July 12, 1972, and was quickly closed as a result of legal complications. It reopened on December 27, 1972, as the Acupuncture Center of Washington, Washington, DC.

4853. Natural medicine clinic subsidized by a government was established in Seattle, WA, by the Kings County Council in 1995. Patients at the clinic were treated according to the principles of naturopathy, which seeks to strengthen the body's own immune system rather than eradicate symptoms. Treatments included diet, exercise, and acupuncture.

MEDICINE—DENTISTRY

4854. Dentist who was born in the United States was Josiah Foster Flagg, who started practicing dentistry in Boston, MA, in 1782, at the age of 18. In 1785 he advertised as follows: "Dr. Flagg transplants teeth, cures ulcers and eases them from pain without drawing; fastens those that are loose; mends teeth with foil or gold to be as lasting and useful as the sound teeth ... sells, by wholesale and retail, dentifrices, tinctures, chew-sticks, mastics, teeth and gum brushes, suitable for every age, complaint and climate, with directions for their use."

MEDICINE—DENTISTRY—*continued*

4855. Porcelain teeth were introduced about 1785, owing principally to the efforts of Dr. John Greenwood of New York City. He advertised "artificial teeth set in so firm (without drawing stumps or causing the least pain) as to eat with them, and so exact as not to be distinguished from natural." Greenwood also invented the foot-powered drill. One of his patients was George Washington.

4856. Dental drill was invented in 1790 by John Greenwood of New York City. It was adapted from the spinning wheel. Power was obtained by means of a foot treadle.

4857. Dental dispensary was the City Dispensary for the Medical Relief of the Poor, New York City, which opened on February 1, 1791. Isaac Roosevelt was the first president. From February 1 to November 23, 1791, 310 patients were admitted. The fee for extracting teeth and for filling cavities with silver or lead foil was 50 cents; the fee for filling cavities with gold or for a good set of front teeth was $1.

4858. Dental amalgam for filling teeth was introduced by Messrs. Crawcour and Sons, who advertised it in the *New York Commercial Advertiser* of August 12, 1834, as "Royal Mineral Succedaneum for filling decayed teeth without the slightest pain, heat or pressure." They paid little attention to caries and filled all cavities without first removing decay. Their work was unsatisfactory and they were obliged to flee the country.

4859. Dental chair that provided such necessary conveniences as a headrest and adjustments in height and position was designed by M. Waldo Hanchett of Syracuse, NY, who received a patent on it on August 15, 1848.

4860. Dental filling made of gold was advocated by Dr. Robert Arthur. In 1855 he discovered the cohesive property of annealed gold foil, a discovery that revolutionized the dental profession. He described it in an 86-page book, *A Treatise on the Use of Adhesive Gold Foil,* published in 1857 in Philadelphia, PA.

4861. Dentist who was a woman to maintain a dental office independently was Dr. Emeline Roberts Jones, who began practice in Danielsonville (now Danielson), CT, in May 1855 as an assistant to her husband, Dr. Daniel Albion Jones. In 1859 she became his partner and after he died in 1864 she carried on the practice alone.

4862. Dentist who was a woman to obtain a D.D.S. degree from a dental college was Lucy B. Hobbs, who was graduated on February 21, 1866, from the Ohio College of Dental Surgery, Cincinnati, OH. She became the first female member of a dental society when she was elected a member of the Iowa State Dental Society in July 1865.

4863. Dental crown made of gold was made by Dr. William Newton Morrison, corresponding secretary of the Missouri State Dental Association, who described his process in the May 1869 issue of the *Missouri Dental Journal.* The first patent for such a crown was granted on November 4, 1873, to Dr. John B. Beers of San Francisco, CA.

4864. Dental drill powered by electricity was invented by George F. Green of Kalamazoo, MI, who obtained a patent on January 26, 1875, on "electro-magnetic dental tools" used for sawing, filing, dressing, and polishing teeth. The patent was assigned to Samuel S. White of Philadelphia, PA. The engines were too heavy and the batteries too expensive for general use.

4865. Dental mallet was invented by Dr. William Gibson Arlington Bonwill of Philadelphia, PA, who obtained a patent on November 16, 1875, on "electro-magnetic dental pluggers" used to impact gold into cavities. He conceived the idea of a vibrating mallet on February 27, 1867, while watching the "sounder" of a telegraph key in operation at the Continental Hotel in Philadelphia.

4866. Dental inlay made of gold was described by William H. Taggart, a Chicago dentist, before the New York Odontological Society on January 15, 1907. He invented the method of casting gold inlays by the inverted pattern procedure, using the ancient principle of the "disappearing core."

4867. Tooth-wear gauge was invented in 1990 by Mark F. Teaford of Johns Hopkins University, Baltimore, MD. The gauge directly measured daily or weekly rates of tooth wear by using a scanning electron microscope to examine casts of teeth. The examination detected minute scratches and pits in the tooth enamel caused by chewing.

MEDICINE—HOSPITALS

4868. Hospital was the Pennsylvania Hospital, opened in Philadelphia, PA, through the efforts of Benjamin Franklin and Dr. Thomas Bond. A temporary hospital was erected in 1751 in a private house on High (now Market) Street before the permanent building opened on February 11, 1752. This was the first hospital to give free treatment to the poor and to offer humane treatment to the insane. The care of the sick, however, had been undertaken earlier by both secular and religious agencies. In 1565, the Spanish settlement at St. Augustine, FL, set aside six beds in a home for the poor; on December 20, 1656, the Dutch West India Company appointed Master Jacob Hendrickszen Varrevanger surgeon in New Amsterdam to look after the sick; and on July 17, 1734, the Ursulines of New Orleans, LA, opened an infirmary without restrictions, under the supervision of Sister Xavier Herbert.

4869. Hospital to treat poor patients at no charge was the Pennsylvania Hospital in Philadelphia, PA, which did so as early as December 13, 1752. The first independent dispensary to furnish free medicine to the needy, the Philadelphia Dispensary, was established in the same city on April 12, 1786, by Bishop William White. The Philadelphia Dispensary affiliated with the Pennsylvania Hospital in 1922.

4870. Marine hospital established by Congress was authorized by an act dated July 16, 1798, which empowered the President to appoint medical officers at ports and elsewhere to give medical treatment to disabled seamen. Funds were obtained by a tax of 20 cents a month deducted from the pay of those employed on American vessels. On April 20, 1801, Governor James Monroe of Virginia deeded the Norfolk Naval Hospital, Norfolk, VA, to the United States for this purpose.

4871. Eye infirmary was established in New London, CT, in 1817 by Elisha North, a medical student.

4872. Eye hospital was the New York Eye Infirmary, a two-room hospital on the second floor at 45 Chatham Street, New York City, which was opened on August 14, 1820. The chief surgeons were Dr. Edward Delafield and Dr. John Kearney Rodgers. William Few was the first president. By January 1, 1822, the infirmary had treated 1,120 cases and cured 801. On April 30, 1864, the name was changed to the New York Eye and Ear Infirmary.

4873. Hospital for treatment of the mentally ill established by a state was the Worcester Hospital, Worcester, MA, authorized by the Massachusetts legislature on March 10, 1830. The act appropriated $30,000 and approved the appointment of three commissioners to build and supervise an asylum for "one hundred and twenty lunatics or persons furiously mad." The chief advocate of the project was Horace Mann

of Boston, who sought to ensure humane treatment for people who were incapacitated by mental illness. The hospital was declared open on January 10, 1833, when it began receiving patients who had previously been confined in prisons.

4874. Hospital and asylum for African-Americans founded by whites was chartered on December 24, 1832, in Savannah, GA, as the Georgia Infirmary for the Relief and Protection of Aged and Afflicted Negroes. The organizational meeting was held at the Exchange on January 15, 1833, and the first president was Richard F. Williams.

4875. Homeopathic hospital was the Homeopathic Hospital of Pennsylvania, Philadelphia, PA, incorporated on September 20, 1850. It was opened for service in 1852 with 30 beds. Vincent L. Bradford was the first president.

4876. Hospital under Jewish auspices was Mount Sinai Hospital in New York, organized and incorporated on January 15, 1852, as the Jews' Hospital in New York City for "benevolent, charitable and scientific purposes." The founder and first president was Sampson Simson, a lawyer, who held the distinction of being the first Jew to be graduated from Columbia College and the first to pass the New York bar examination. The first patients were received on June 8, 1855, in the hospital's first building, a four-story brownstone on West 28th Street, New York City. Julius Raymond was the superintendent. Dr. Mark Blumenthal was the attending and resident physician. Operating expenses during the first year totalled $5,494, and 225 patients were treated. The hospital moved uptown in 1872 and became nonsectarian in 1886.

4877. Infirmary for women staffed by physicians who were women was the New York Infirmary for Women and Children, New York City, incorporated on December 13, 1853, "to provide for poor women the medical advice of competent physicians of their own sex." A one-room infirmary was opened in Tompkins Square. On May 12, 1857, a hospital was opened. The physicians were the sisters Dr. Elizabeth Blackwell and Dr. Emily Blackwell, and Dr. Marie Elizabeth Zakrzewska.

4878. Children's hospital was established in 1854 in New York City and was known as the Nursery and Child's Hospital. It originated from a society founded by Sarah Platt Doremus and Mrs. Cornelius Du Bois "for the maintenance and care of the children of wet-nurses, and the daily charge of infants whose parents labor away from home."

MEDICINE—HOSPITALS—*continued*

4879. Alcoholics' asylum was the United States Inebriate Asylum "for the reformation of the poor and destitute inebriates," incorporated on April 15, 1854, and organized on May 15, 1854, in Binghamton, NY, by Dr. James Edward Turner. In 1857 the name was changed to the New York State Inebriate Asylum. John D. Wright was the first president of the corporation.

4880. Women's hospital in the world, that was founded by women for the exclusive use of women was the Woman's Hospital of New York City. On February 10, 1855, a constitution was adopted by 30 women who formed the Woman's Hospital Association. The Woman's Hospital was opened with 40 beds on May 4, 1855, in a hired building at Madison Avenue and 29th Street, with Dr. James Marion Sims as resident surgeon. A permanent building on West 110th Street was opened on December 5, 1906.

4881. Orthopedic hospital was the Hospital for the Ruptured and Crippled, opened on May 1, 1863, in New York City by the New York Society for the Relief of the Ruptured and Crippled. Dr. James Knight was the resident physician and surgeon. During the first year, treatment was given to 828 patients. The hospital's name was changed in 1940 to the Hospital for Special Surgery.

4882. Hospital record system was introduced at the Bellevue Training School for Nurses, New York City, in 1874 by the head nurse, Linda Ann Judson Richards. Record was made of symptoms, diagnosis, medication, temperature, and pulse rate for all patients in the hospital.

4883. Floating hospital was the *Emma Abbott,* which made her trial trip on July 19, 1875. The ship cost $20,000, was 215 feet long with a 40-foot breadth of beam, and had three decks, one of which served as a dining room. It was known as the "poor children's yacht" and was operated by St. John's Guild, New York City. The ship served until 1902, when it was replaced with a more modern ship. The idea for the hospital originated in the summer of 1873, when the guild hired a barge and gave two excursions for sick children. The following summer it gave 18 excursions to 15,202 sick children and their mothers. The health benefits were so obvious that the guild decided to operate its own floating hospitals.

4884. Hospital designed exclusively for infants was the Babies Hospital of the City of New York, which was chartered on June 23, 1887. The hospital opened in a house at 161 East 36th Street, New York City, with eight beds.

4885. Cancer hospital was the New York Cancer Hospital, 106th Street and Central Park West, New York City. The hospital had its beginning at a meeting held on February 7, 1884, at the residence of Mrs. Elizabeth Hamilton Cullum. It was opened for patients on December 7, 1887. In 1916 its name was changed to the Memorial Hospital for the Treatment of Cancer and Allied Diseases. The first attending surgeons were Dr. James Bradbridge Hunter, Dr. Clement Cleveland, and Dr. William Tillinghast Bull. The first president was John E. Parsons. The hospital later affiliated with Memorial Sloan-Kettering Cancer Center.

4886. Hospital open to all races as a matter of policy was the Provident Hospital, Chicago, IL, opened on May 4, 1891. Although primarily for African-Americans, there was no racial barrier to the admission of patients or staff appointments of physicians. Dr. Frank Billings was chief consulting physician; Dr. Christian Fenger, chief consulting surgeon; and Drs. Ralph N. Isham and Daniel Hale Williams, attending surgeons. A nursing school, the Provident Hospital Training School Association, was connected with the hospital.

4887. Leprosy hospital was the Louisiana Leper Home, Carville, LA, founded in 1894 by an act of the Louisiana legislature. It consisted of a plantation of about 200 acres on which were seven cottages, an elevated pavilion, dining hall, kitchen, and quarters for the Sisters of Charity of the order of St. Vincent de Paul, four of whom took care of the patients. The home accommodated 25 patients and was controlled by a Board of Officers. The first president was M.D. Lagan and the first resident physician was Dr. Elihu Morgan Hooper. The home was purchased by the federal government from the state of Louisiana on January 3, 1921, to be operated as a 300-bed hospital by the Public Health Service, with nursing care supplied by the Sisters of Charity.

4888. Hospice for incurable cancer patients operated free of charge was established in a room in an apartment on Scammel Street, New York City, on September 15, 1896, by Rose Hawthorne Lathrop (later Sister Mary Alphonsa, O.D.), who was afterward assisted by Alice Huber (later Sister Mary Rose, O.D.). They organized the Servants of Relief for Incurable Cancer. On May 1, 1899, they opened St. Rose's Free Home for Incurable Cancer in New York City, with accommodations for 15 patients. On June 1, 1901, a building in the country was acquired to carry on the work under the name of Rosary Hill Home at Sherman Park (now Hawthorne), NY.

4889. Hospital for disabled children established by a state was the Gillette State Hospital for Crippled Children, St. Paul, MN, authorized on April 23, 1897, with an appropriation of $5,000. The hospital was named in honor of Dr. Arthur Jay Gillette.

4890. Cancer hospital established by a city was the New York City Cancer Institute on Welfare Island (now Roosevelt Island), New York City, dedicated on August 1, 1923. The first patient was admitted on August 23. Dr. Isaac Levin was the first director.

4891. Hospital for patients of Chinese ancestry was the Chinese Hospital, Jackson Street, San Francisco, CA, opened on April 18, 1925. The first president was B.S. Seid.

4892. Community hospital was the Community Hospital, Elk City, OK, established by Dr. Michael Abraham Shadid. The organizational meeting was held on October 20, 1929. The hospital was dedicated on August 13, 1931.

4893. Children's hospital for research and treatment of catastrophic childhood diseases was St. Jude Children's Research Hospital, Memphis, TN, which opened on February 4, 1962. It was founded by actor Danny Thomas, its first president. There were no charges to patients for treatment, hospitalization, or consultation.

MEDICINE—HOSPITALS—MENTAL ILLNESS

4894. Insane patients' home was built by the Religious Society of Friends (the Quakers), who established it in 1709 in Philadelphia, PA.

4895. Hospital for insane patients established by a colony was the Publick Hospital for Persons of Insane and Disordered Minds, incorporated in Williamsburg, VA, in 1768. It was opened on October 12, 1773, and received as its first patient Zachariah Mallory of Hanover County, VA. The hospital was maintained by the colony from the beginning and later became known as the Eastern State Hospital.

4896. Hospital for insane patients operated privately was founded by the Religious Society of Friends (Quakers) in Philadelphia, PA, on April 14, 1813, as The Asylum for the Relief of Persons Deprived of the Use of Their Reason. The grounds were located 5 miles from Philadelphia and 1 mile west of Frankford and covered 52 acres, 30 of which were cultivated, the balance in woodland. No manacles, handcuffs, iron grates, or bars were used. The name was changed in 1888 to the Friends Asylum for the Insane, and in 1914 to Friends Hospital.

MEDICINE—HOSPITALS—TUBERCULOSIS

4897. Tuberculosis patients' home was the Channing Home, Boston, MA, opened on May 1857 through the benevolence of Harriet Ryan. The home accommodated 12 patients and was not a sanatorium. It also accommodated patients with other chronic diseases.

4898. Tuberculosis sanatorium privately operated was the Mountain Sanatorium for Pulmonary Diseases, opened in 1875 in Asheville, NC, by Dr. William Gleitsmann.

4899. Tuberculosis sanatorium using modern treatment methods was the Trudeau Sanatorium, sometimes called the Adirondack Cottage Sanatorium, a one-room cottage 14 by 18 feet with two cot beds and heated by a wood stove, built at Saranac Lake, NY, for Dr. Edward Livingston Trudeau at a cost of $400. It was opened on February 1, 1885.

4900. Tuberculosis hospital for the poor established by a city was the Branch Hospital of the Cincinnati Hospital (later Cincinnati General Hospital), which opened on July 8, 1897, in Cincinnati, OH, with a capacity of 20 beds. John Fehrenbach was the superintendent and Dr. Benjamin Lyle the chief physician. The name was later changed to the Hamilton County Tuberculosis Hospital.

4901. Tuberculosis sanatorium established by a state was the Massachusetts Hospital for Consumptives and Tuberculosis Patients, Rutland, MA, completed on September 23, 1898. It received its first patient on October 3, 1898. Dr. Walter John Marcley was the first medical director.

4902. Tuberculosis hospital established by Congress was opened at Fort Stanton, NM, on April 27, 1899. The first patient was received on November 18. The hospital was suggested and founded by Walter Wyman. It was not exclusively for men in military service but afforded care and treatment to all beneficiaries of the Public Health Service, most of whom at that time were seamen.

MEDICINE— HOSPITALS— TUBERCULO-
SIS—*continued*

4903. Tuberculosis hospital for needy patients to provide medical and surgical care on a free, nationwide, nonsectarian basis was the National Jewish Hospital, Denver, CO, which opened on December 10, 1899, with 58 beds, under the auspices of the B'nai B'rith organization. An earlier attempt, in 1892, by the Jewish Hospital Association of Colorado to establish such a hospital had failed for lack of funds.

MEDICINE—IMAGING

4904. X-ray photograph was made on January 12, 1896, by Dr. Henry Louis Smith, professor of physics and astronomy, Davidson College, Davidson, NC. Smith obtained the hand of a corpse, fired a bullet into it, and then took a 15-minute exposure which, when developed, revealed the exact location of the bullet.

4905. X-ray of the entire body of a living person made in a single exposure was taken by Dr. William James Morton of New York City in April 1897. The film was a coated single sheet three feet by six feet, made by the Eastman Kodak Company of Rochester, NY. The apparatus employed was a 12-inch induction coil that used the 117-volt Edison current. At each revolution of the break wheel, which made 5,000 revolutions per minute, the coil afforded a free discharge of sparks across a five-inch air gap. The distance of the tube from the film was 4 feet 6 inches. The tube was run steadily for the first 10 minutes; then the current was turned off several times a minute to allow it to cool. The total time consumed, including stoppages, was 30 minutes. The heavier regions of the body, such as the pelvis, spine, and thighs, were underexposed, while the thinner portions, such as the hands, were overexposed.

4906. X-ray photograph of the entire body of a living person taken in a one-second exposure under ordinary clinical conditions available to the average hospital or average radiographer, and the first in which a selective filter was used, was a full-length, full-size, one-piece radiograph taken on July 1, 1934, by Arthur Wolfram Fuchs of the Eastman Kodak Company, Rochester, NY. The size of the film was 32 by 72 inches. The radiograph was exhibited by the Chicago Roentgen Society at the Century of Progress Exposition, Chicago, IL.

4907. X-ray photograph showing the complete arterial circulation in an adult human was completed on July 16, 1936, in Rochester, NY, by Dr. Edmond John Faris of the Wistar Institute of Anatomy and Biology, Philadelphia, PA, and Arthur Wolfram Fuchs of the Medical Division, Eastman Kodak Company, Rochester, NY. A radio-opaque medium was injected into the arteries of a cadaver by Faris. Fuchs made several full-body radiographs on film 32 by 72 inches, employing 30 seconds of exposure at a distance of 12 feet. Ultra-high-speed X-ray intensifying screens were also used in a large cassette made to accommodate the film and screen.

4908. X-ray movies of human organs in action were made by Drs. William Holmes Stewart, William Joseph Hoffman, and Francis Henshall Ghiselin, all of New York City, who set a movie camera in front of a fluoroscopic screen. The pictures showed the motion of the heart, stomach, diaphragm, lungs, and other organs and structures. They were exhibited on October 2, 1937, in New York City, at a convention of the American Roentgen Ray Society.

4909. Photograph of genes was taken by Dr. Daniel Chapin Pease and Dr. Richard Freligh Baker at the University of Southern California, Los Angeles, CA, and announced on January 7, 1949. The tissue sections in the photograph were magnified 120,000 times. Genes are the particles that carry DNA, transmitting physical characteristics from one generation to another.

4910. Movie showing the inside of a living heart was made at Montefiore Hospital, New York City, by Dr. Elliott Samuel Hurwitt, Dr. Adrian Kantrowitz, and Anatol Herskovitz, the photographer. The movie showed the opening and closing of the mitral valve of a dog. The official title of the 9.5-minute color film was *A Cinematographic Study of the Function of the Mitral Valve in Situ*. It was first shown on October 16, 1951, at the clinical session of the New York Academy of Medicine Post Graduate Fortnightly held at Montefiore Hospital.

4911. X-ray three-dimensional stereo fluoroscopic system was installed at the University of Oregon Medical Center, Portland, OR, by Richard J. Kuhn on April 15, 1966. The development engineer was Joseph Quinn. The $30,000 device was primarily intended to be used in heart catherization. It was exhibited on September 27, 1966, at the American Roentgen Ray Society at San Francisco, CA, by the X-ray Department of the General Electric Company, Milwaukee, WI. The "stereo fluoricon" consisted of a single anode dual cathode X-ray tube, an image intensifier with polarizers, and a synchronized analyzer. The 3D image was observed through a viewing mirror without the use of special glasses.

4912. Magnetic resonance image of a human body was made on July 3, 1977, by Dr. Raymond Damadian, founder of the FONAR Corporation in Melville, NY. Working independently, Damadian and Paul C. Lauterbur of the University of Illinois at Urbana-Champaign, IL, developed the application of magnetic resonance imaging (MRI) technology to noninvasive medical diagnosis. MRI scanners produce detailed images of soft tissues, including blood vessels, blood flow, cartilage, bone marrow, muscles, ligaments, the spinal cord, and fluids in the brain and spine, that do not show up well on X-rays.

4913. Comprehensive digital atlas of the human body was the Visible Human Project, led by Victor Spitzer and David Whitlock of the University of Colorado Health Sciences Center in Denver, CO. The body of an executed murderer, 39-year-old Joseph Paul Jernigan, was sliced into ultrathin cross-sections. Detailed views of these cross-sections were made by photography, magnetic resonance imaging, and computer tomography. These views were made available to medical schools, hospitals, and researchers on CD-ROMs and specialized computer networks. (A woman's body was incorporated into the atlas at a later date.) A CD-ROM entitled *Body Voyage* was released to the public in 1997. The program was financed by the National Library of Medicine, a unit of the National Institutes of Health.

MEDICINE—IMMUNIZATIONS

4914. Inoculation against smallpox using material from human smallpox pustules was introduced into America by Dr. Zabdiel Boylston of Boston, MA. On June 26, 1721, Boylston inoculated his six-year-old son, Thomas, and two African-American servants. In 1721 and 1722, Boylston inoculated 247 individuals. The public acceptance of inoculation was due in large measure to the efforts of Cotton Mather, the Boston minister and scientist, who persistently advocated it.

4915. Vaccination against smallpox using cowpox as originated in England by Dr. Edward Jenner was introduced by Dr. Benjamin Waterhouse of Cambridge, MA, professor of the theory and practice of medicine at Harvard, who inoculated his son, Daniel Oliver Waterhouse, and three children and three servants on July 8, 1800.

4916. Smallpox vaccine clinic for research into the smallpox virus and free distribution of the vaccine to the poor was opened by Dr. James Smith in Baltimore, MD, on March 25, 1802.

4917. Vaccination program offered by a city was conducted by the Massachusetts towns of Milton and Bedford, which offered free inoculations against smallpox. A committee chosen on July 8, 1809, authorized Dr. Amos Holbrook to charge a 25-cent fee for his services. He inoculated the entire population of Milton, 337 individuals, and pledged that the people "are for ever secure against Small Pox."

4918. Vaccination law enacted by a state was "an act to diffuse the benefits of inoculation for the Cow-Pox," enacted on March 6, 1810, by Massachusetts, which required every town, district, and plantation to guard against smallpox by choosing "three or more suitable persons, whose duty it shall be to superintend the inoculation of the inhabitants ... with the cowpox."

4919. Vaccination law enacted by Congress was the act of February 27, 1813, to encourage vaccination against smallpox. It authorized the president to appoint a vaccine agent to furnish vaccine through the Post Office to any citizen of the United States who might apply for it. The act was repealed on May 4, 1822.

4920. Vaccination program by the federal government to protect Native Americans against smallpox was authorized by congressional act of May 5, 1832, "an act to provide the means of extending the benefits of vaccination, as a preventive of the smallpox, to the Native American tribes, and thereby, as far as possible, to save them from the destructive ravages of that disease." An appropriation of $12,000 was made. Physicians were paid $6 a day for their services.

4921. Tuberculosis vaccine produced in the United States that was effective was developed in 1928 by Dr. William Hallock Park, director of the research laboratory of the New York City Health Department and professor of preventive medicine at New York University. The vaccine was manufactured at the research laboratories of the Department of Health and was first used in January 1928.

4922. Yellow fever vaccine for human immunization was developed by Drs. Wilbur Augustus Sawyer, Wray Devere Marr Lloyd, and Stuart Fordyce Kitchen and publicly announced on April 28, 1932, at a meeting of the American Societies for Experimental Biology, Philadelphia, PA. The work was sponsored by the Rockefeller Foundation. The first test vaccinations were made in May 1931.

MEDICINE—IMMUNIZATIONS—continued

4923. Poliomyelitis vaccine was produced by Dr. Maurice Brodie of New York City in February 1933. It was obtained from the spinal cords of rare Indian monkeys that had been infected with poliomyelitis. The spinal cords were excised and made into an emulsion that was treated with formalin to kill the virus. The first widely used polio vaccine was developed in 1952 by Jonas Edward Salk, director of the Virus Research Laboratory at the University of Pittsburgh's School of Medicine, who employed a method of virus culture developed by bacteriologists John Franklin Enders, Frederick Chapman Robbins, and Thomas Huckle Weller. For their work, the four shared the 1954 Nobel Prize in physiology or medicine. The first mass poliomyelitis immunization shots were administered on February 23, 1954, to schoolchildren in Pittsburgh, PA. The vaccine was licensed for public use on April 12, 1955.

4924. Anthrax vaccine for human immunization was developed in 1948 by Dr. George Green Wright of the Biological Laboratory of the Army Chemical Laboratory. Anthrax is a rare bacterial disease that infects both humans and animals.

4925. Chicken pox vaccine was approved for public use by the Food and Drug Administration on March 17, 1995. Marketed by Merck and Company, Whitehouse Station, NJ, under the trade name Varivax, the vaccine was believed to be 70 to 90 percent effective.

MEDICINE—LABORATORIES

4926. Physiology laboratory was established in the Sheffield Scientific School at Yale University, New Haven, CT, in 1874 under the direction of Russell Henry Chittenden.

4927. Psychology laboratory was established at Johns Hopkins University, Baltimore, MD, in 1881 by Granville Stanley Hall. It was discontinued in 1888 when Dr. Hall was appointed president of Clark University. A larger laboratory was established at Johns Hopkins in 1904 by Professor George Malcolm Stratton.

4928. Bacteriology laboratory was the Hoagland Laboratory, 335 Henry Street, Brooklyn, NY (now part of New York City), incorporated on February 21, 1887, and opened for experimentation in February 1889. The first director was Dr. George Miller Sternberg, who demonstrated the microbe of pneumonia in saliva. A privately endowed institution, the laboratory later became affiliated with the Long Island College of Medicine in Brooklyn. This was the first bacteriology laboratory run by an institution; private laboratories had been established earlier by individual physicians.

4929. Tuberculosis research laboratory was the Saranac Laboratory, established in 1894 by Dr. Edward Livingston Trudeau in a room in his home at Saranac Lake, NY.

4930. Cancer laboratory exclusively for the study of cancer was the New York State Pathological Laboratory for the Study of Cancer, established in May 1898 at the University of Buffalo under a $10,000 appropriation made by the New York State legislature on April 29. Dr. Roswell Park was the first director.

4931. Laboratory for the study of human parasites was the Hygienic Laboratory, Washington, DC (later incorporated into the National Institutes of Health). It was established on August 16, 1902, by the Public Health Service. Dr. Charles Wardell Stiles was chief of the division of zoology.

4932. Microbiology laboratory was the Institute of Microbiology, Rutgers University, New Brunswick, NJ, dedicated on June 7, 1954. The cost of the building was approximately $3,050,000 and that of the equipment $450,000. Classroom and seminar instruction was offered to graduate students. The first director was Dr. Selman Abraham Waksman.

MEDICINE—LICENSING AND REGULATION

4933. Medical regulations enacted by a colony were passed by Virginia on October 21, 1639, in an "act to compel physicians and surgeons to declare on oath the value of their medicines." Another law, enacted May 3, 1649, in Massachusetts, was directed to "physicians, chirurgians, midwives or others" and forbade them "to exercise or put forth any act contrary to the known rules of art, nor exercise any force, violence, or cruelty upon or towards the bodies of any, whether young or old." The act was "not intended to discourage the lawful use of their skill but to encourage and direct them in the right use thereof and to inhibit and restrain the presumptious arrogance of such as ... exercise violence upon ... bodies."

4934. Medical licensing law enacted by a city that was actually enforced was an "act to regulate the practice of Physick and Surgery in the City of New York," passed on June 10, 1760. It provided that "no person whatsoever shall practice as a physician or surgeon ... before he shall first have been examined in physick or surgery and approved of and admitted by one of His Majesty's Council, the Judges of the Supreme Court, the King's Attorney General and the Mayor of the City of New York for the time being or by any three or more of them." Violators were subject to a penalty of £5, half of which went to the informer and the remainder to the funds for the poor.

4935. Medical licensing law enacted by a colony was New Jersey's law of September 26, 1772. The act was effective for a five-year period. It authorized a licensing board consisting of two judges of the Supreme Court of New Jersey and a third individual appointed by them, and forbade the practice of medicine without a license. Very severe fines were imposed upon violators, but the law did not apply to those who drew teeth, bled patients, or gave medical assistance for which they received no fee or compensation.

4936. Dental surgeons to be licensed by a state were those of Alabama, under a law passed on December 31, 1841. It provided for the establishment of "medical boards of the state to examine and to issue a license to applicants to practice dental surgery under the same rules and regulations, and subject to the same restrictions as those who apply for license to practice medicine."

4937. Chiropodists to be regulated by a city were those of New York City, which enacted a law in 1895 requiring chiropodists to pass an examination. The law did not demand a prescribed course of study. Many prospective applicants for licenses were trained by individual chiropodists rather than by schools, and those schools that did exist taught the theory of chiropody as a sideline of beauty culture.

4938. Nurses to be registered by a state were those of North Carolina, under a law ratified on March 3, 1903. It provided for voluntary registration with the county clerk of the Superior Court of any licensed trained nurse and for an examining and licensing board composed of two physicians and three registered nurses.

4939. Pharmacists to be regulated by a state were those of New York. A law enacted on May 3, 1904, required pharmacists to have two years of training and four years of practical experience.

4940. Chiropractic regulation law enacted by a state was passed on March 18, 1913, by Kansas. It regulated the practice of chiropractic, provided for licensing and examination of chiropractors, and created a three-member board for examination and regulation. Applicants were required to be graduates of a chartered chiropractic school or college having a course of three years, with actual attendance of more than six months each year.

4941. Dental hygienists to be licensed by a state were those of Connecticut, which passed a licensing law during the January 1915 session. It was approved on May 19, 1915. The first examination for dental hygienists was given by the State Board in June 1918, since no hygienists applied for a license prior to that date.

MEDICINE—MEDICAL EQUIPMENT

4942. Adhesive and medicated plaster used in the treatment of fractures was reported in *Anatomy, Physiology and Diseases of the Bones and Joints* by Samuel David Gross, published in 1830 in Philadelphia, PA. The first patent for such a plaster was issued on March 26, 1845, to Dr. Horace Harrel Day of Jersey City, NJ, and Dr. William H. Shecut. They dissolved rubber in a solvent, such as benzine, turpentine, and bisulphide of carbon, which they spread with a brush on fabric. They sold the process to Dr. Thomas Allcock, who introduced Allcock's Porous Plaster.

4943. Incubator for premature babies was constructed by Dr. William Champion Deming, in charge of the maternity ward of the State Emigrant Hospital, Ward's Island, New York City, in 1888, by order of Dr. Allan M. Thomas. It was called a "hatching cradle" and was 3 feet square and 4 feet high and built in two sections, one of which contained 15 gallons of water. The first child placed in it was Edith Eleanor McLean, who weighed 2 pounds 7 ounces when she was born on September 7, 1888.

4944. Electric heating pad was patented by S.I. Russell in 1912. It was intended for use in tuberculosis sanatariums, to keep the patients' chests warm.

4945. Bandage with built-in adhesive was the Band-Aid, the invention of Earle Dickson, of the Johnson and Johnson Company, New Brunswick, NJ. In 1921, while preparing a dressing for his accident-prone wife, Dickson came up with the idea of a small, ready-to-apply bandage made of a wad of sterile gauze backed by a strip of surgical adhesive.

MEDICINE—MEDICAL EQUIPMENT—
continued

Dickson's key innovation was the use of a removable nonstick material to protect the sticky side of the adhesive tape. Another Johnson and Johnson employee, W. Johnson Kenyon, suggested the name "Band-Aid."

4946. Portable electric stethoscope to amplify the sounds of the human body was demonstrated to 500 doctors by the Western Electric Company of New York City on June 10, 1924, at the Municipal Pier, Chicago, IL. It was developed by Western Electric in cooperation with Bell System engineers and Dr. Horatio Burt Williams, professor of physiology, Columbia University, New York City. The stethoscope was first marketed in October 1925.

4947. Respirator known as the iron lung was invented by Professor Philip Drinker and Louis Agassiz Shaw, who made the original model in April 1927. It consisted of a cheap galvanized iron box with a bed made from "garage creepers" and two household vacuum cleaners with hand-operated valves as the source of alternate positive and negative pressure. The Consolidated Gas Company of New York donated $7,000 to Harvard University, Cambridge, MA, to produce a second model, which was first used on October 12, 1928, at the Children's Hospital, Boston, MA, to help a little girl suffering from respiratory failure caused by poliomyelitis. The machine was manufactured by Warren E. Collins, Boston, MA.

4948. Diathermy machine for medical use that was practical was constructed by Dr. Willis Rodney Whitney, director of research for the General Electric Company, Schenectady, NY, in December 1928. Albert B. Page first used the set on February 19, 1929, at the Ellis Hospital, Schenectady, NY, and the first patient was treated on February 23 by Dr. Charles Milton Carpenter.

4949. Electrobasograph was invented by Dr. Russell Plato Schwartz of the University of Rochester Medical School, Rochester, NY, who exhibited it on June 12, 1933, at the American Medical Association convention, Milwaukee, WI. It was designed "to record the walking gait of individuals, to distinguish between actual and spurious limps in damage claims for injuries."

4950. Electric sterilamp was introduced in March 1938 by the Lamp Division of the Westinghouse Electric and Manufacturing Company, Bloomfield, NJ. It was designed to reduce the germ population of the air by bactericidal ultraviolet radiation.

4951. Cellulose sponge for medical and surgical use was marketed by Parke Davis and Company, Detroit, MI, under the trademark Oxycel, on June 5, 1946. It was a hemostatic material used as a surgical dressing, which converted to an absorbable form when left in contact with incised body tissues.

4952. Pacemaker was invented in 1952 by Paul M. Zoll, a cardiologist at Beth Israel Hospital in Boston, MA. He was seeking a way to aid cardiac patients suffering from Stokes-Adams attacks, also called complete heart block, a breakdown of the heart's ability to beat regularly. Zoll inserted a bare wire into the recipient's heart to convey electrical pulses provided by an external pulse generator. Since the generator had to be plugged into an electrical outlet, the patient's mobility was severely limited. The first battery-powered external pulse generator was developed in 1958 by electrical engineer Earl Bakken at the request of C. Walton Lillehei, an open-heart surgeon at the University of Minnesota medical school. It was the size of a transistor radio and ran on flashlight batteries.

4953. Pacemaker to be implanted in a patient's body was invented by Dr. William M. Chardack and engineer Wilson Greatbatch, both of Buffalo, NY. On April 18, 1960, Chardack inserted a wire implant into the heart of Frank Henefelt, a cardiac patient, to test the pacemaker's reliability. The battery-powered pulse generator unit tested successfully and was implanted into Henefelt's abdomen on June 6. He lived for 2.5 years with the device. Swedish doctors first implanted a similar device in 1958.

4954. Home screening kit for HIV infection was approved on May 14, 1996, by the Food and Drug Administration. The kit, sold under the name Confide, was developed by Direct Access Diagnostics, a subsidiary of Johnson and Johnson, New Brunswick, NJ. Users pricked their fingers to get a drop of blood and sent the sample to a laboratory, then called a week later for the results and counseling. HIV (Human Immunodeficiency Virus) is the retrovirus that causes AIDS.

MEDICINE—MEDICAL EQUIPMENT— SUTURES

4955. Silver wire suture in place of silk thread was used by Dr. James Marion Sims of Montgomery, AL, who reported his experiments in an article, "On the Treatment of Vesico-vaginal Fistula," in the *American Journal of the Medical Sciences* of January 1852. Sims had begun his experiments on December 9, 1845. He performed a vesico-vaginal fistula operation on June 21, 1849. The suture was removed on the eighth day after the operation.

4956. Silk sutures and ligatures used instead of catgut in operations were used in 1882 by Dr. William Stewart Halsted of Baltimore, MD. He advocated black silk, which he introduced in 1889 at the Johns Hopkins Hospital, Baltimore.

4957. Fiberglass sutures were used by Dr. Roy Philip Scholz of St. Louis, MO, on July 19, 1939, in a mastoid operation. The caliber of the suture was that of #00 silk. It had a carrying strength of 7.4 pounds.

4958. Catgut substitute for medical use was Dexon, a polyglycolic acid suture, a virtually nonirritating synthetic absorbable, produced in April 1966 by the Davis and Geck department of Lederle Laboratories, Pearl River, NY, a division of the American Cyanamid Company. Work began in January 1962 at Cyanamid's Central Research Laboratory in Stamford, CT.

MEDICINE—MEDICAL PRACTITIONERS

4959. Physician in the colony of Virginia was Lawrence Bohune, who arrived in the first half of 1610. He was the first physician of the London Company. He was killed on March 19, 1622, on board the *Margaret and John* when the vessel was attacked by Spanish ships.

4960. Physician in the New England colonies was Dr. Samuel Fuller, who arrived on board the *Mayflower* on December 21, 1620, and was one of the signers of the Mayflower Compact. For some time he was the sole physician in Massachusetts. In a letter dated June 28, 1630, written at Salem, MA, to Governor William Bradford of Plymouth, he described one of the customary treatments, in which he "let some twenty of these people blood."

4961. Midwife to practice professionally was Tryn Jonas, an immigrant from Norway. She was employed by the Dutch West India Company circa 1625 as a midwife for the colony of New Amsterdam (now New York City).

4962. Physician who was Jewish was Jacob Lumbrozo, who settled in Maryland on January 24, 1656. He was a native of Lisbon, Portugal. He died in May 1666. The first Jewish physician to head an asylum for the mentally ill was Dr. John de Sequeyra, a Portugese physician educated in Holland, who was appointed in 1770 at Williamsburg, VA.

4963. Pharmacist who was a woman was Elizabeth Marshall, daughter of Charles Marshall, the president of the Philadelphia College of Pharmacy. She became manager of the apothecary originally established by her grandfather, Christopher Marshall, in 1729 in Philadelphia, PA. She served from 1804 until 1825, when the store was sold.

4964. Physician born in America who was graduated from a foreign medical school was Dr. William Bull of Charleston, SC. He received his degree from Leyden University, Leyden, the Netherlands, on August 18, 1734. The title of his thesis was "Colica pictonum."

4965. Druggist to fill prescriptions other than his own was Jonathan Roberts, who served from May 1754 to May 1755 as apothecary in the Pennsylvania Hospital, Philadelphia, PA. Previously, each apothecary had prepared remedies to use in his own practice.

4966. Physician who was African-American was James Derham of Philadelphia, PA, who settled in New Orleans, LA, before 1790. The prominent physician Dr. Benjamin Rush said of him: "I thought I could give him information concerning the treatment of diseases, but I learned more from him than he could expect from me." The first African-American doctor to become a member of a medical association was Dr. John Vancerlle De Grasse, who was admitted to the Massachusetts Medical Society in 1854. He was graduated from Bowdoin College and the Hampton Medical College, and practiced in New York City.

4967. Physiologist of note was Dr. William Beaumont, a surgeon in the Army, whose book *Experiments and Observations on the Gastric Juice and the Physiology of Digestion* was published in 1833 in Plattsburgh, NY. He achieved fame by his treatment of Alexis St. Martin (also called Samata or San Maten), who was shot in the stomach on June 6, 1822, at the Fort Mackinac trading post. Dr. Beaumont was able to watch the digestive process through the opening in the patient's stomach wall and to find by experiment the effect of different foods

MEDICINE—MEDICAL PRACTITION-ERS—*continued*

and medicines. He found that gastric juices were secreted only when there was food in the stomach and that simple irritation of the mucous membrane would not initiate a flow of gastric juices.

4968. Homeopathy practitioner was Dr. Hans Birch Gram, a Dutch homeopathy doctor who emigrated to New York City in 1825. In 1828, Gram was elected a member of the New York Medical and Philosophical Society, and in 1829 he became its president.

4969. Phrenologist of importance to visit the United States was Johann Gaspar Spurzheim, an associate of Dr. Franz Joseph Gall, the German physician who originated the now-discredited theory of phrenology, which posited that an individual's character and personality could be determined from the shape of the skull. Spurzheim arrived in New York City on August 6, 1832, and gave a series of lectures in Boston and Cambridge, MA. He died on November 10. His funeral was attended by the Boston Medical Association as a group.

4970. Chiropodist was Nehemiah Kenison, who, together with his brother and a cousin, opened an office in 1840 directly opposite the Old South Church on Washington Street, Boston, MA. They developed instruments and protective dressings to aid in the relief of the pain caused by corns and other foot conditions.

4971. Physician who was a woman was Dr. Elizabeth Blackwell, a native of Bristol, England, who came to the United States in her youth and received her M.D. degree from the Geneva Medical College (later known as Hobart College), Geneva, NY, on January 23, 1849, receiving the highest grades in her class. She opened a private dispensary in New York City in 1853 and afterwards became professor of gynecology at the London School of Medicine for Women.

4972. Ophthalmologist of note was Dr. Edward Delafield. In 1818 he formulated a plan to establish the New York Eye Infirmary, which opened in 1820 in two rooms at 45 Chatham Street, treating 436 patients in the first seven months. In 1864, he became the first president of the American Ophthalmological Society.

4973. Physician who was an African-American woman was Rebecca Lee Crumpler, who received an M.D. degree on March 1, 1864, from the New England Female Medical College, Boston, MA.

4974. Surgeon who was a woman was Dr. Mary Harris Thompson, who received her M.D. degree in 1863 from the New England Medical College, Boston, MA. In May 1865 she founded the Mary Thompson Hospital in Chicago, IL, to care for widows and children of the poor, to sustain a free dispensary, and to train competent nurses. The hospital had 14 beds. It was destroyed by fire on October 9, 1871, but the patients were removed to another location and operation resumed the same day. The hospital is now the Women's and Children's Hospital, Chicago, IL.

4975. Osteopathic physician was Dr. Andrew Taylor Still of Macon, MO, who cured a case of "flux" on June 22, 1874. He was instrumental in founding both a college and a magazine devoted to osteopathy.

4976. Osteopathic physicians who were women were Jenette Hubbard Bolles, Mamie B. Carter and Lou J. Kern, who were graduated on March 1, 1894, from the American School of Osteopathy, Kirksville, MO.

4977. Chiropractor was Daniel David Palmer, who gave the first adjustment treatment of vertebrae to Harvey Lillard in Davenport, IA, on September 18, 1895.

4978. Physician who was a Chinese woman was Dr. Mary Stone (Shih Mai-yu), who was graduated from the Medical School of the University of Michigan, Ann Arbor, MI, on June 22, 1896. She founded the Women's Hospital at Kiukiang, China, under the auspices of the Methodist Foreign Mission and served as its head for 25 years.

4979. Physician with a mobile medical office for his private patients was Dr. Huerta Cortez Neals, cardiovascular specialist of the Jersey City Medical Center, who placed a motor home in service on June 23, 1970, in Jersey City, NJ, equipped with a bathroom, refrigerator, heating unit, air conditioner, 30-gallon water tank, electrocardiograph, blood-pressure apparatus, scale, blood Auto-Analyzer, and other instruments.

MEDICINE—MEDICINES

4980. Cod-liver oil was described in Thomas Morton's *New English Canaan*, published in 1637, an account of the author's adventures in what is now Quincy, MA. A "great store of traine oyle is mayd of the livers of the Codd, and is a commodity that without question will enrich the inhabitants of New England quicly and is therefore a principall commodity."

4981. Patented pills were introduced in 1796 by Samuel Lee, Jr., of Connecticut, and were known as Lee's Windham Pills and Lee's New London Bilious Pills. On April 30, 1796, he obtained a patent on a "composition of bilious pills."

4982. Drug mill was established in 1812 in Philadelphia, PA, by Charles V. Hagner, who used waterpower for grinding. He was able to perform in one day work that previously would have required months of hand powdering in mortars. His first task of importance was the grinding of several tons of cream of tartar, for which Dr. Haral, a druggist, paid him three cents a pound.

4983. Quinine was manufactured in 1822 by John Farr and Abraham Kunzi in Philadelphia, PA.

4984. Quinine sulfate was manufactured commercially in 1823 by Powers and Weightman of New York City.

4985. Chloroform was distilled in 1831 by Dr. Samuel Guthrie in Sackets Harbor, NY. He called it "chloric ether," and obtained it by distilling chloride of lime with alcohol in a copper still. He described it in "A New Mode of Preparing a Spirituous Solution of Chloric Ether." It is a colorless liquid known chemically as trichloromethane.

4986. Homeopathic pharmacy was established by J.G. Wesselhoeft at 9 Broad Street, Philadelphia, PA, in 1834. In 1835 he opened a branch at 498 Greenwich Street, New York City, which was purchased by William Radde, his clerk. Dr. Francis E. Boericke acquired the business and in 1869 formed a partnership with Adolph J. Tafel as Boericke and Tafel.

4987. Compressed pills or tablets to be commercially manufactured were made in 1863–64 by Jacob Dunton, a wholesale druggist of Philadelphia, PA, who employed a machine in their manufacture. The formulas that were sold in tablet form consisted principally of simple chemicals such as potassium chlorate and ammonium chloride. Dunton sold his products to dispensing druggists and did not attempt to market them under his own name until 1869. His entire production from 1869 to 1876 was less than that now made daily in the laboratories of this country.

4988. Petroleum jelly or petrolatum, a semisolid gel derived from petroleum and used as a lubricant and skin emollient, was developed in 1870 by Robert Augustus Chesebrough, a chemist from Brooklyn, NY (now part of New York City), after a trip to the Pennsylvania oil fields, where he was shown a gummy waste product that was thought to heal wounds. He coined the word Vaseline for his gel and registered it on May 14, 1878, as a trademark. On May 10, 1880, he organized the Chesebrough Manufacturing Company, New York City, which he headed until 1909.

4989. Patent medicine to achieve nationwide popularity was Lydia E. Pinkham's Vegetable Compound, a bottled elixir of herbal extracts, preserved in 19 percent alcohol, that attracted thousands of customers. The ingredients included black cohosh, fenugreek, and unicorn root. The formula, which, despite its name, was never patented, was a household remedy used by a Massachusetts mother, Lydia Estes Pinkham, to cure the ailments of her own four children. Pinkham began selling the compound by mail order in 1876, when she placed her first advertisement in the *Boston Herald.*

4990. Eye wash commercially manufactured was Murine, a solution of muriate of berberine. It was packaged in 1891 by Drs. James and George McFatrich, two brothers who were both ophthalmologists, and Otis Hall, a banker from Spokane, WA. Hall had used the solution at the suggestion of the doctors to heal an eye wound caused by a blow from a horse's tail.

4991. Laxative in candy form was Ex-Lax, invented in 1905 in New York City by Max Kiss, a Hungarian-born pharmacist. He combined chocolate with phenolphthalein, a chemical with a relaxing effect on the intestines. The name is a contraction of "Excellent Laxative."

4992. Peritonitis preventive that was successful was amniotic fluid, first used to prevent postoperative peritonitis and adhesions in 1922 by Dr. Herbert Lester Johnson of Boston, MA. The first fluid was of human origin, from cesarean operations, but the widespread use of this new principle of preventive medicine resulted in the development of a commercial preparation known as Amniotic Fluid Concentrate, made from bovine amniotic fluid.

4993. Sulfanilamide production took place in December 1930 at the Jackson Laboratory of E.I. du Pont de Nemours and Company, Wilmington, DE, for use in dyeing cellulose acetate fibers. Sulfanilamide was not used in medicine until 1935, when Dr. Ashley Weech of Babies Hospital, New York City, used it as a treatment for streptococcic infections, but without formally reporting it. Dr. Perrin Hamilton Long of Johns Hopkins Hospital, Baltimore, MD, obtained a one-pound vial from the Du Pont company on November 9, 1936, and to-

MEDICINE—MEDICINES—*continued*

gether with Eleanor Bliss used it to treat a seven-year-old child with erysipelas. They reported their use of the drug to the Southern Medical Association, Baltimore, MD, on November 17, 1936.

4994. Fizzing cold remedy was Alka-Seltzer. In 1931, Hubert Beardsley, president of Dr. Miles Laboratories, Elkhart, IN, was told about a local cold remedy combining aspirin and baking soda. He asked Miles's chief chemist, Maurice Treneer, to develop an analgesic tablet that would fizz when dropped in water. It went on sale that year as Alka-Seltzer. The original formula contained baking soda, monocalcium phosphate (an antacid), aspirin, and citric acid. Alka-Seltzer achieved nationwide popularity at the end of Prohibition as a cure for hangovers.

4995. Radioactive isotope medicine was phosphorus 32, artificially produced in a 37-inch cyclotron. It was administered on December 24, 1936, to a 28-year-old woman with chronic leukemia by Dr. John Hunsdale Lawrence, director of the Donner Laboratory at the University of California at Berkeley.

4996. Pituitary hormone isolated in chemically pure crystalline form was announced on July 23, 1937, in *Science* by Drs. Abraham White, Hubert Ralph Catchpole, and Cyril Norman Hugh Long of the Laboratories of Physiological Chemistry and Physiology, Yale University School of Medicine, New Haven, CT.

4997. Chlorophyll was patented by Dr. Benjamin Gruskin of Philadelphia, PA, who obtained a patent on June 14, 1938, on a "therapeutic agent for use in the treatment of infection." Chlorophyll was first synthesized on June 27, 1960, by Professor Robert Burns Woodward at the Converse Memorial Laboratory, Harvard University, Cambridge, MA. The chlorophyll molecule is composed of 55 atoms of carbon, 72 atoms of hydrogen, 5 atoms of oxygen, 4 atoms of nitrogen, and 1 atom of magnesium.

4998. Antibiotic discovered in America was streptomycin, isolated from a culture of a soil microbe known as *Streptomyces griseus* by Dr. Selman Abraham Waksman and four students—Albert Schatz, Elizabeth Bugie, Doris Jones, and H. Christine Reilly—at the New Jersey Agricultural Experiment Station, Rutgers University, New Brunswick, NJ, in January 1944. It was first manufactured commercially by Merck and Company, Rahway, NJ, in September 1944. This antibiotic is active against both gram-positive and gram-negative bacteria as well as

upon acidfast bacteria, of which the most important is the organism that causes tuberculosis. Waksman, a Jewish immigrant from the Ukraine, won the Nobel Prize in physiology and medicine in 1952.

4999. Synthetic quinine was produced on April 10, 1944, by Dr. Robert Burns Woodward and Dr. William von Eggers Doering at the Converse Memorial Laboratory, Harvard University, Cambridge, MA. It consists of 20 atoms of carbon, 24 atoms of hydrogen, 2 atoms of oxygen, and 2 atoms of nitrogen.

5000. Broad-spectrum antibiotic was aureomycin chlortetracycline, released to American physicians in November 1948. It was developed and produced by Lederle Laboratories, a division of the American Cyanamid Company, Pearl River, NY. Discovered by Dr. Benjamin Minge Duggar, the antibiotic is a yellow crystalline substance obtained from a mold named *Streptomyces aureofaciens*.

5001. Fungicide used medicinally was nystatin, discovered in 1948 by microbiologists Elizabeth Hazen and Rachel Brown in soil from a Virginia farm. Nystatin proved to have applications in medicine, agriculture, and even art restoration (it was used in 1966 to protect artworks damaged by flooding in Florence, Italy).

5002. Antibiotic synthetically manufactured for commercial production was chloromycetin. A laboratory to produce chloromycetin by chemical means was opened on March 13, 1952, by Parke Davis and Company, Holland, MI. The main processing building was longer than a football field and had a 40-foot ceiling.

5003. Polypeptide hormone synthesized was oxytocin, a proteinlike compound made up of eight amino acids that stimulates uterine contractions in a mother giving birth and starts the flow of her milk. Dr. Vincent du Vigneaud, biochemist of Cornell University Medical College, New York City, and his co-workers isolated oxytocin and synthetically reproduced the hormone. The announcement of the synthesis was made in the fall of 1953. On November 2, 1955, Dr. du Vigneaud was awarded the Nobel Prize in chemistry for this and other work on the chemistry and metabolism of sulfur compounds.

5004. Medicine produced using recombinant DNA was human insulin, produced in 1978 by the City of Hope Medical Center, Duarte, CA, in a joint venture with the biotechnology firm Genentech. The insulin was created using bacteria that had been implanted with human DNA. The Food and Drug Administration did not approve use of the bioengineered insulin until 1982.

5005. Human antibodies produced artificially were announced by Dr. Henry Kaplan and Dr. Lennart Olson on July 29, 1980, at the Stanford University Medical School, Stanford, CA. Kaplan and Olson, seeking a method of manufacturing pure human antibodies to help diagnose and treat disease, created a line of antibody-producing hybrid cells by fusing bone-marrow cancer cells with human spleen cells.

5006. Drug for treating AIDS to win the approval of the Food and Drug Administration was AZT (azidothymidine). Approval was given on March 20, 1987. The drug was made by Burroughs Wellcome and initially cost more than $10,000 a year for each patient.

MEDICINE—MILITARY

5007. Naval hospital established by Congress was authorized on February 26, 1811, with an appropriation of $50,000. On April 2, 1827, the cornerstone was laid at Portsmouth, VA. One wing was ready for occupancy in July 1830, and the building was completed and dedicated in 1833.

5008. Army medical corps is generally claimed to have been established by the Reorganization Act of April 14, 1818. From 1789 to 1798, individual medical officers were appointed for regiments as they were authorized by Congress, beginning with Richard Allison of Pennsylvania, who was appointed surgeon of a corps of 700 rank and file which the first Congress authorized in September 1789.

5009. Navy bureau of medicine and surgery was authorized by act of Congress on August 31, 1842. It was organized in 1842 by Dr. William Paul Crillon Barton, who served as its first chief.

5010. Army field hospital was a tent hospital established by Brigadier General Bernard John Dowling Irwin of the Army Medical Corps at Shiloh, TN, prior to the Civil War battle of April 6–7, 1862, when the Union army suffered more than 13,000 casualties.

5011. Army ambulance corps was established on August 2, 1862, by Major General George Brinton McClellan, who issued General Order No. 147 authorizing one captain to each army corps as the commandant of the Ambulance Corps, a first lieutenant for a division, a second lieutenant for a brigade, and a sergeant for each regiment. The members of the corps wore a green band on the cap and a green half chevron two inches broad on each arm above the elbow. On March 11, 1864, Congress approved a law providing each army corps with two-horse ambulances in accordance with its strength. Infantry regiments of 200 to 500 men were entitled to two ambulances, those of more than 500 men to three; cavalry regiments with fewer than 500 men were entitled to one ambulance, those of more than 500 to two.

5012. Hospital ship operated by the Navy was the U.S.S. *Red Rover,* which was captured from the Confederate forces on September 20, 1862. On December 26, 1862, it was converted into a hospital ship. It remained in service until August 12, 1865.

5013. Military hospital was the Army and Navy Hospital, Hot Springs, AR, which opened for the reception of patients on January 17, 1887. The appropriation was authorized by act of Congress of June 30, 1882. The hospital had five separate buildings, which were connected by verandas.

5014. Dentist officially employed in the Army was Dr. W.H. Ware, an enlisted man in the Medical Department, who served as a dental surgeon in the army in the Philippine Islands in 1898.

5015. Ambulance ship operated by the Navy was the U.S.S. *Solace,* of 5,700 tons, placed in service on April 14, 1898, and used in naval warfare in the Spanish-American War. Formerly the S.S. *Creole,* it was purchased on April 7, 1898. The *Solace* was the creation of Admiral William Knickerbocker Van Reypen. It was fitted out under the terms of the Geneva Convention and was the first designated ambulance ship, used for transporting as well as caring for the sick and wounded, and the first to carry the Geneva Cross flag at the fore. It was removed from the Navy list on August 6, 1930, and sold on November 6, 1930.

5016. Army dental corps was authorized by the Army Reorganization Act of February 2, 1901, "an act to increase the efficiency of the permanent military establishments of the United States." It authorized the employment of contract dental surgeons "not to exceed one to ev-

MEDICINE—MILITARY—*continued*

ery 30,000 of said army, and not to exceed 30 in all." The first three contract dental surgeons were Drs. John Sayre Marshall, Robert T. Oliver, and Robert W. Morgan. Commissions in the Army Dental Corps were authorized by act of Congress on March 3, 1911.

5017. Army nurse corps for women was established as a permanent organization of the Army on February 2, 1901. Two years earlier, Anita Newcomb McGee, acting assistant surgeon of the Army, had organized the nurses who remained with the Army after the Spanish-American War into a corps under the surgeon general. The 1901 law provided for one superintendent who would receive annual compensation of $1,800 and nurses and reserve nurses who would receive $40 a month within the continental limits of the United States and $50 a month when on foreign service. Quarters, subsistence, and medical attendance were also provided. The first superintendent was Mrs. Dita H. Kinney.

5018. Navy nurses' corps was established on May 13, 1908, in the Navy Medical Department. Navy nurses received the same pay allowances, emoluments, and privileges as the nurse corps of the Army. The first superintendent was Esther Voorhees Hasson. Women had been serving as contract nurses aboard American naval vessels as early as the War of 1812.

5019. Navy dental corps was authorized by act of Congress of August 22, 1912, which provided for not more than 30 dental surgeons to be part of the medical department of the Navy and to provide professional services for navy personnel. They received the rank of lieutenant, junior grade.

5020. Dentist in the Navy to serve aboard a naval ship was Dr. Harry Edward Harvey, who was assigned to the hospital ship U.S.S. *Solace* on March 5, 1913. He served until October 1915.

5021. Army veterinary corps was established as part of the Medical Department of the Army by the National Defense Act of 1916, enacted on June 3, 1916. The legislation authorized two officers for each regiment of cavalry, one for every three batteries of field artillery, and one for each mounted battalion of engineers.

5022. Ambulance ship designed and built by the Navy as a hospital for the transportation of sick and wounded naval men was the U.S.S. *Relief*. Congress authorized the construction of the *Relief* on August 29, 1916. The keel was laid on July 4, 1917. The vessel was launched on December 23, 1919, and delivered to the Navy on December 28, 1920. The overall length of the *Relief* was 484 feet and it had a displacement of 9,750 tons and a speed of 16 knots. The hospital capacity was 515 beds in 14 wards and 15 officers' rooms.

MEDICINE—NURSING

5023. Nurse to receive formal training was Linda Ann Judson Richards, first in a class of five to register as a student nurse at the Training School of the New England Hospital for Women and Children, Roxbury, MA, on September 1, 1872. The school offered a one-year program in medical, surgical, and obstetric nursing. After graduation, Richards served as night superintendent at Bellevue Hospital, New York City, and as superintendent of the Training School of the Massachusetts General Hospital, Boston, MA. The first trained nurse who was African-American was Mary Eliza Mahoney, who graduated in 1879 from the same program.

5024. District nurse was employed by the Woman's Branch of the New York City Mission Society, New York City, in 1877.

5025. Visiting nurses were organized by Lillian Wald in 1892 to help the poor in New York City's Lower East Side tenement district. The service, later known as the Visiting Nurses' Service, eventually operated out of Wald's Henry Street Settlement.

5026. Company nurse hired by a firm to attend to the health of its employees was Ada Stewart, who was employed by the Vermont Marble Company of Proctor, VT, in 1896.

5027. School nurses in public schools were employed in November 1902 by the New York City Department of Health.

5028. Nurse appointed to a college professorship was Mary Adelaide Nutting, who was appointed professor of household administration at Teachers College, Columbia University, New York City, in 1906. From 1910 to 1923 she served as professor of nursing education, and from 1923 to 1925 as professor of nursing education at the Helen Hartley Foundation.

MEDICINE—ORGANIZATIONS

5029. Medical society was founded in Boston, MA, prior to 1735, and functioned until 1741. It was not very effective and was only local in character.

5030. Medical society (state) of consequence was the Massachusetts Medical Society, which was incorporated in Boston, MA, on November 1, 1781. Membership was limited to 70 fellows. The first president was Dr. Edward Augustus Holyoke. The charter was signed by Samuel Adams as president of the Senate, and by John Hancock as governor of the Commonwealth.

5031. Homeopathic medical society was the Hahnemann Society, organized on April 10, 1833, in Philadelphia, PA, by Drs. Carl Ihm, George H. Bute, Charles F. Matlack, Constantine Hering, and William Wesselhoeft.

5032. Dental society of a city was the Society of Surgeon-Dentists of the City and State of New York, which was formed on December 3, 1834, with Dr. Eleazar Parmly as the first president and Dr. Solyman Brown as the first corresponding secretary. Both men were also on the publishing committee of the first dental journal, the *American Journal of Dental Science.*

5033. Physiology society was the American Physiological Society, organized on February 11, 1837, in Boston, MA, by 124 men and 39 women who signed the constitution. The object was to acquire and diffuse a knowledge of the laws of life and of the means of promoting human health and longevity. Dues were $1 per year. The first monthly meeting was held on March 7, 1837. The first president was William Andrus Alcott.

5034. Dental society (national) was the American Society of Dental Surgeons, organized on August 18, 1840, at a meeting held at the American Hotel, New York City. Dr. Horace Henry Hayden of Baltimore, MD, was the first president. The society disbanded in 1856.

5035. Psychiatry association (national) was the Association of Medical Superintendents of American Institutions for the Insane, formed on October 16, 1844, in Philadelphia, PA, by 13 members. The first president was Samuel B. Woodward. The name of the association was changed in 1892 to the American Medico-Psychological Association and in 1921 to the American Psychiatric Association.

5036. Medical society (national) was the National Medical Association, which was organized on May 5, 1846, with Dr. Jonathan Knight as the first president. Two hundred and fifty delegates attended, representing 22 states, 28 medical schools, and 40 medical societies.

The American Medical Association was founded the following year, on May 5, 1847, in Philadelphia, PA, as an outgrowth of the National Medical Association. The first female member of the AMA was Dr. Sarah Hackett Stevenson, who was graduated from the Woman's Medical College of Chicago in 1874 and was elected to membership in the AMA in 1876 as a delegate from the Illinois State Medical Society.

5037. Medical society for women was the American Medical Educational Society of Boston, MA, organized by Samuel Gregory on November 23, 1848, with six members "to provide and promote the education of midwives, nurses and woman physicians, and to diffuse among women generally a knowledge of physiology and the principles and means of preserving and restoring health." Timothy Gilbert was president. Membership was not confined to the professions.

5038. Pharmacy society (national) was the American Pharmaceutical Association, organized on October 6, 1852, in Philadelphia, PA, with Daniel B. Smith as the first president. The first annual meeting was held in Boston, MA, on August 24, 1853.

5039. Medical society for African-Americans was the Medico-Chirurgical Society of the District of Columbia, organized on April 24, 1884, at the office of Dr. Robert Reyburn, Washington, DC. Reyburn was the first president. The society was revived and incorporated on January 15, 1895. Three of the eight incorporators were white.

5040. Nursing society was the Philomena Society, organized on November 24, 1885, in New York City. It disbanded in 1887.

5041. Physiology society (national) was the American Physiological Society, organized in New York City on December 30, 1887, with Silas Weir Mitchell of Philadelphia as president and Henry Newell Martin, professor of biology at Johns Hopkins University, as secretary. Their proceedings, the *American Journal of Physiology,* were first published on January 3, 1898. This society was unrelated to the local society of the same name that was founded in Boston in 1837.

5042. Tuberculosis research and prevention society was the Pennsylvania Society for the Prevention of Tuberculosis, founded on April 10, 1892, in Philadelphia, PA, by Lawrence Francis Flick.

MEDICINE—ORGANIZATIONS—continued

5043. Psychology society (national) was the American Psychological Association, organized on July 8, 1892, at Clark University, Worcester, MA, to advance psychology as a science. Professor Granville Stanley Hall was the first president. The first scientific meeting was held on December 27, 1892, at the University of Pennsylvania, Philadelphia, PA.

5044. Optometry society (national) was the American Association of Opticians, organized on October 10, 1898, by 183 charter members from 31 states and Canada in the Broadway Central Hotel, New York City. Charles Lembke of New York City was the first president. The name was changed in 1910 to the American Optical Association and in 1919 to the American Optometric Association.

5045. Orthodontists' society was the American Society of Orthodontists, founded in June 1900 in St. Louis, MO. The first president was Dr. Edward Hartley Angle of St. Louis. The society was incorporated on February 23, 1917, in Pennsylvania, and the name changed on April 21, 1937, to the American Association of Orthodontists.

5046. Disease research and treatment organization composed of physicians and laymen was the National Tuberculosis Association, organized on June 6, 1904, in Atlantic City, NJ. It had about 400 members. The first annual meeting was held on May 18–19, 1905, in Washington, DC. The first president was Dr. Edward Livingston Trudeau.

5047. Surgery society (national) was the American College of Surgeons, incorporated on November 25, 1912, in Springfield, IL, and organized in Washington, DC, on May 5, 1913, "to elevate the standard of surgery, to establish a standard of competency and of character for practitioners of surgery, and to educate the public and the profession to understand that the practice of surgery calls for special training." Dr. John Miller Turpin Finney of Baltimore, MD, was the first president. The first annual convocation for the admission of fellows took place in Chicago, IL, on November 13, 1913. An African-American surgeon, Dr. Daniel Hale Williams, was in the first group of fellows admitted. The first female surgeons to become fellows were Dr. Alice Gertrude Bryant and Dr. Florence West Duckering, both of Boston, MA, who were admitted along with 1,093 other candidates on June 22, 1914.

5048. Immunology society was the American Association of Immunologists, organized in Minneapolis, MN, on June 19, 1913, with Dr. Gerald Bertram Webb as temporary chairman. The first annual meeting was held on June 22, 1914, in Atlantic City, NJ. The original goal of the society was to bring together vaccine therapists, but in 1915 it developed into a scientific organization covering the whole field of immunology. Its purpose was to study problems of immunology and its application to clinical medicine.

5049. President of a major medical society who was a woman was Dr. Emma Sadler Moss of the Charity Hospital, New Orleans, LA, who was installed as president of the American Society of Clinical Pathologists on October 13, 1955, at the 34th annual meeting.

MEDICINE—PROSTHETIC DEVICES

5050. Artificial leg patent was granted to Benjamin F. Palmer of Meredith, NH, on November 4, 1846. The leg had a pliable joint that worked noiselessly and preserved its contour in all positions. Artificial legs had been made previously. Howland and Company, of Brookfield, MA, exhibited one in 1837 at the Massachusetts Charitable Mechanics Association.

5051. Artificial eyes were manufactured by Pierre Gougelman in 1851 at Van Dam Street, New York City, from glass imported from France. The business was later known as Mager and Gougelman.

5052. Artificial lens for cataract patients was fitted on March 18, 1952, at Wills Eye Hospital, Philadelphia, PA, by Dr. Warren Snyder Reese. He performed the Ridley operation, developed by Frederick Thomas Ridley, which involved the insertion of a plastic lens approximately eight millimeters in diameter into the eye of a patient whose diseased lens had been removed.

5053. Artificial aortic valve was made by Dr. Charles Anthony Hufnagel of the Georgetown University Medical Center, Washington, DC, and successfully fitted on a 30-year-old patient on September 11, 1952. It was made of Flexiglas and contained a float 0.75 inches in diameter. When blood was forced into the aorta during the upbeat of the heart's pumping cycle, the float rose and slipped into one of three sockets in the side of the valve sleeve.

MEDICINE—RESEARCH

5054. Dissection of a living animal to demonstrate anatomy and physiology was performed about 1855 by Dr. John Call Dalton, who introduced the methods of vivisection in classroom demonstrations. In 1859 he published his *Treatise on Human Physiology,* and in 1860 he became professor of physiology and microscopic anatomy at the Long Island College Hospital, NY.

5055. Anatomy research institute was the Wistar Institute of Anatomy and Biology, which was established in Philadelphia, PA, on July 20, 1891, with a $20,000 gift from General Isaac Jones Wistar. The first building was dedicated on May 21, 1894.

5056. Cancer research fund was the Collis P. Huntington Fund for cancer research, established in 1902 by Mrs. Collis Potter Huntington. The fund, amounting to $100,000, was used by the New York Cancer Hospital, New York City. It enabled the hospital to administer X-ray treatments and install new equipment.

5057. Neurological disease research institute was the Neurological Institute of New York, incorporated on April 5, 1909, which opened its hospital on October 1, 1909, in New York City. The first superintendent was Alexander H. Candlish.

5058. Pellagra experiment of note was made by Dr. Joseph Goldberger of the U.S. Public Health Service at the Mississippi State Penitentiary, eight miles east of Jackson, MS. Twelve convicts agreed to submit to a restricted-diet test in exchange for an offer of pardon made by Governor Earl LeRoy Brewer. The test was held from February 4, 1915, to April 19, 1915. Six of the 11 convicts (one was excused) developed pellagra, confirming suspicions that pellagra is caused by a deficiency of the B vitamin niacin.

5059. Virus obtained in crystalline form was a plant virus, the tobacco mosaic virus, which was crystallized by Dr. Wendell Meredith Stanley at the Rockefeller Institute for Medical Research, Princeton, NJ. The research was reported in *Science* magazine on June 28, 1935. The first human virus to be crystallized was the poliomyelitis virus, which was crystallized by Dr. Carlton Everett Schwerdt of the Virus Laboratory, University of California, Berkeley. The achievement was announced on November 3, 1955, at the meeting of the National Academy of Sciences held at the California Institute of Technology, Pasadena, CA.

5060. Heart pump was a spirally coiled glass tube and pump invented in 1935 by Dr. Alexis Carrel, assisted by Colonel Charles Augustus Lindbergh. The apparatus consisted of a culture chamber and the electrically operated glass pump. A surgically removed heart was suspended in the culture chamber and the main artery and vein were connected with the glass tubes of the pump, which circulated a nutritive fluid through the organ and kept it alive. The experiments were carried on in the Rockefeller Institute in New York City.

5061. Nuclear reactor used in medical therapy was the Atomic Energy Commission's Brookhaven National Laboratory unit in Upton, near Brookhaven, NY, placed in operation on February 15, 1951.

5062. Virus separated into component parts which on reconstruction yielded a material as effective as it was in its original form was the tobacco virus, which causes a disease in tobacco and many other plants. The research was performed by Drs. Heinz Ludwig Fraenkel-Conrat and Robley Cook Williams of the Virus Laboratory of the University of California at Berkeley early in 1955. It was reported on June 10, 1955.

5063. Artificial gene was produced in 1973 by Har Gobind Khorana at the Massachusetts Institute of Technology, Cambridge, MA. The gene, created in a series of replications using transfer-ribonucleic acid, was a 207-base-pair chain identical to a virus gene.

5064. Identification of the AIDS virus was announced by two scientific teams in March 1983. The human immune deficiency virus (HIV), the retrovirus that causes AIDS, was isolated and reported by Dr. Robert Gallo of the National Cancer Institute in Bethesda, MD, and by Dr. Luc Montagnier at the Institute Pasteur in Paris. AIDS stands for acquired immunodeficiency syndrome.

5065. DNA chain polymerization was invented in 1983 by Kary B. Mullis, a staff chemist for the Cetus Corporation in Emeryville, CA. The DNA polymerase chain reaction enabled Mullis to replicate an entire chain of deoxyribonucleic acid (DNA) as many times as needed from a single original DNA strand. The technique had many practical applications in genetic engineering, human genome mapping, DNA fingerprinting, evolutionary science, and genetic diagnosis. Mullis won the 1993 Nobel Prize in chemistry for his work.

MEDICINE—RESEARCH—*continued*

5066. Genetically altered virus approved for use in a vaccine was approved by the Department of Agriculture on April 22, 1986. The virus was used in veterinary medicine to fight a form of swine herpes.

5067. Alternative medicine department in a federal research institution was the Office of Alternative Medicine, established in 1992 by the National Institutes of Health, Bethesda, MD. Joe Jacobs, a pediatrician, was the first director. Among the healing therapies studied by the department were acupuncture, acupressure, herbal medicine, chiropractic, massage, aromatherapy, Tai Chi, meditation, and prayer.

5068. Human stem cells to be cultured in a laboratory were grown by Dr. John D. Gearhart and a team of researchers at the Johns Hopkins University, Baltimore, MD, using tissue taken from aborted human embryos. Stem cells are the basic, unspecialized cells from which all other cells in the body develop during the growth of a baby in the womb. The announcement of the discovery was made on July 25, 1997.

MEDICINE—SENSORY AIDS—HEARING

5069. Hearing aid other than ear trumpets was the Audiphone, a fanlike device held against the teeth, patented on September 23, 1879, by Richard S. Rhodes of River Park, IL.

5070. Electrical hearing aid produced commercially was the Acousticon, invented by Miller Reese Hutchinson of New York City in 1901. On April 27, 1880, Francis D. Clarke and M.G. Foster had secured a patent on a "device for aiding the deaf to hear" that made its own electricity and operated by bone conduction.

5071. Hearing aid using transistors was manufactured by the Sonotone Corporation, Elmsford, NY, and offered for sale on December 29, 1952. It weighted 3.5 ounces and was three inches long.

MEDICINE—SENSORY AIDS—VISION

5072. Bifocal eyeglasses were invented by Benjamin Franklin of Philadelphia, PA, who was annoyed at having to carry two pairs of glasses. He took a frame and equipped it with lenses that consisted of two parts with different focusing powers. On May 23, 1785, from Passy, France, he wrote to George Whatley, "I have only to move my eyes up and down as I want to see distinctly far or near." Inasmuch as ordinary spectacles in the colonies cost as much as $100 each, his invention did not receive a ready popular response. Eyeglass frames were invented by a London optician in 1727.

5073. Contact lenses were imported for commercial purposes in New York City in 1924 from Jena, Germany, where they were manufactured by Carl Zeiss. The lenses were ground rather than blown. They were thin saucershaped shells of optical glass that were worn under the eyelid in direct contact with the eye itself.

5074. Bifocal contact lenses was developed by Newton K. Wesley, O.D., of the Eye Research Foundation and the Plastic Contact Lens Company, Chicago, IL. They were officially introduced in May 1958. Prescriptions for distant vision were ground in the center of the lens, and reading prescriptions were ground on the outer circle. The cost of a pair ranged from $200 to $400.

MEDICINE—SURGERY

5075. Cesarean operation that was successful was performed by Dr. Jessee Bennett on his wife, Elizabeth Hog Bennett, on January 14, 1794, in Edom, VA. Bennett had asked Dr. Alexander Humphreys of Staunton, VA, to assist in performing the operation, but because of the low chance of success, Humphreys had declined. Dr. Bennett performed the operation with the assistance of two slaves, who held the patient. She was placed on a table made of two planks laid on a couple of barrels and was given laudanum in lieu of an anesthetic.

5076. Abdominal operation other than a cesarean section was an ovariotomy, the surgical removal of an ovarian tumor. It was performed by Dr. Ephraim McDowell on December 13, 1809, at Danville, KY. The operation was performed without anesthetic. The patient, Jane Todd Crawford, sang hymns to distract her mind. She was 45 years of age at the time of the operation, and lived to be 78.

5077. Skin grafting was suggested in 1847 by Dr. Frank Hastings Hamilton of Buffalo, NY. In 1854 he reported a case in which he had succesfully grafted skin on a large raw surface of a man's leg that had been injured by a heavy stone.

5078. Mastoid operation to relieve infected ears was performed on June 15, 1859, at the Brooklyn City Hospital, Brooklyn, NY (now part of New York City), by Dr. Joseph Chrisman Hutchison, and was described by him at the April 1865 meeting of the Medical Society of Kings County, Brooklyn. His report, entitled "Otitis; Perforating of Mastoid Process with a Trephine," appeared in the *Transactions of the Medical Society of Kings County* in April 1865 and in the *Buffalo Medical and Surgical Journal* in October 1865.

5079. Gallstone operation was performed on June 15, 1867, by Dr. John Stough Bobbs, known as "the father of cholecystotomy," in Indianapolis, IN, and was reported to the Indiana Medical Society on May 19–20, 1868. The patient was Mary E. Wiggins of McCordsville, IN,

5080. Appendectomy to remove a perforated appendix was performed in Davenport, IA, on January 4, 1885, by Dr. William West Grant. The patient was Mary Gartside, age 22. The patient lived until 1919, when she died of a quite different illness.

5081. Lung removal was performed on April 5, 1933, at the Barnes Hospital, St. Louis, MO, by Dr. Evarts Ambrose Graham of St. Louis, who removed the left lung of Dr. Robert Gilmore, a Pittsburgh obstetrician. Seven ribs were also removed for the purpose of allowing the soft tissues of the chest wall to collapse against the bronchial stump and therefore to obliterate as much as possible of the pleural cavity.

5082. Surgical elevation of the skull to treat epilepsy was demonstrated on November 2, 1933, at the Flower Hospital, New York City, by Dr. Karl Winfield Ney, professor of neurosurgery at the New York Medical College and Flower Hospital in New York City, before the members of the Eastern Homeopathic Medical Association and Clinical Congress. The top of the patient's skull was cut through almost all the way around, lifted slightly, and then replaced.

5083. Surgical operation televised on a closed circuit was a half-hour hernia operation that took place on March 21, 1939, at the Israel Zion Hospital, Brooklyn, New York City. It was filmed by the American Television Corporation using a television camera and a microphone suspended above the operating table and was transmitted to medical students 500 feet away in another building of the hospital. The first closed-circuit telecast of surgery that was viewed by physicians, rather than by students, was shown on February 27, 1947, at a meeting of the Johns Hopkins Medical and Surgical Association held at the Johns Hopkins Hospital, Baltimore, MD. There were four heart operations and one on the spinal vertebra. The images were transmitted to 10 receivers in four classrooms.

5084. Surgical operation shown on a local television program for the general public was performed by Dr. Isador Schwaner Ravdin at the University of Pennsylvania Hospital, Philadelphia, PA, on March 16, 1952. It was a peptic ulcer operation that lasted 2.5 hours. Ten minutes of the operation were shown by WPTZ, Philadelphia.

5085. Surgical operation televised coast-to-coast was transmitted on June 10, 1952, from the Wesley Memorial Hospital, Chicago, IL, in connection with the 101st annual meeting of the American Medical Association at the Palmer House, Chicago, IL. The program showed an eight-minute portion of a 3.5-hour duodenal ulcer operation performed on a 60-year-old man by Dr. Samuel Julian Fogelson. The program was sponsored by Smith, Kline and French Laboratories, and presented by the National Broadcasting Company.

5086. Lung tumor operation in which the patient was under hypnosis was performed at Cedars of Lebanon Hospital, Los Angeles, CA, in January 1955. The hypnosis was performed by Dr. Milton Jacob Marmer, an anesthesiologist of Beverly Hills, CA. The patient was a 25-year-old woman. The operation was reported at the 105th annual meeting of the American Medical Association at Chicago, IL, on June 12, 1956.

5087. Prefrontal lobotomy was performed by Dr. James Winston Watts and Dr. Walter Freeman on September 14, 1956, at George Washington University Hospital, Washington, DC. The patient was a 63-year-old woman. The operation involved the cutting of nerve pathways in the frontal lobe of the brain to relieve symptoms of mental illness.

5088. Limb reattachment that was successful was performed on May 23, 1962, by surgeons Donald A. Malt and J. McKhann of Massachusetts General Hospital, Boston, MA. They reattached the severed right arm of a 12-year-old boy.

5089. Surgical facility outside a hospital run independently and intended for minor surgical procedures on ambulatory patients was Surgicenter, Phoenix, AZ, opened on February 12, 1970, by John Laurence Ford, M.D., and Wallace Allison Reed, M.D. The surgeons performed various kinds of procedures in the categories of orthopedic, urological, gynecological, ophthalmological, otolaryngological, and other surgical specialties.

MEDICINE—SURGERY—HEART

5090. Suture of the human heart that was successful was accomplished on July 9, 1893, at the Provident Hospital, Chicago, IL. The patient was James Cornish, whose internal mammary artery had been damaged by a knife wound. Dr. Daniel Hale Williams sutured the pericardium. The operation, which was witnessed by six doctors, was described in March 27, 1897, in the *Medical Record*.

5091. Heart operation for the relief of angina pectoris was performed on February 13, 1935, by Dr. Claude Schaeffer Beck, associate professor of surgery at Western Reserve University, on a patient at the Lakeside Hospital, Cleveland, OH. Dr. Beck resected one of the pectoral muscles in the chest and fastened the cut end to the heart wall, to provide an additional source of blood for the heart.

5092. Mitral valve corrective surgery was carried out on July 3, 1952, by Dr. Forest Dewey Dodrill at the Harper Hospital, Detroit, MI. The patient was a 41-year-old man. The Michigan Heart was used as a substitute for the lower left ventricle during the operation, which was the first to involve prolonged exposure of the mitral valve.

5093. Heart operation in which the deep-freezing technique was employed was a 58-minute operation performed on September 2, 1952, by Dr. Floyd John Lewis, associate professor of surgery at the Medical School of the University of Minnesota, Minneapolis, MN. The patient was a five-year-old girl. During the operation, her body temperature was reduced to 79 degrees F, except in her head. She recovered and left the hospital 11 days after the operation.

5094. Heart operation in which the elective cardiac arrest technique was employed was performed in May 1956 on a 17-month-old boy at the Cleveland Clinic, Cleveland, OH, by Dr. Donald Brian Effler and a task force of 15 doctors and nurses. The boy's heartbeat was temporarily stopped by an application of potassium citrate.

MEDICINE—SURGERY—TRANSPLANTS

5095. Kidney transplant from one human to another was performed by Dr. Richard Harold Lawler of the Little Company of Mary Hospital, Chicago, IL, on June 17, 1950, in a 45-minute operation witnessed by 40 visiting surgeons and doctors. A healthy kidney was removed by Dr. James Ward West from the body of a woman who had died. Dr. Lawler transplanted the kidney into the renal pedicle of a patient from whom a polycystic left kidney had been removed.

5096. Organ transplant that was successful was performed at the Peter Brent Brigham Hospital, Boston, MA, on December 23, 1954. The surgery was conducted by Joseph E. Murray of Harvard University, who transplanted a kidney from one identical twin to another. The recipient lived for seven years. For his work in transplantation, Murray was awarded the Nobel Prize in physiology or medicine on December 10, 1990. He was the first graduate of a Jesuit college to receive the prize.

5097. Liver transplant was performed as an experimental procedure on March 1, 1963, by a team led by surgeon Thomas Earl Starzl at the University of Colorado Health Sciences Center, Denver, CO. Starzl went on to perform scores of hepatic transplants, including the first baboon-to-human liver transplant. He was the author of *Experience in Hepatic Transplantation* (1969), the first full published account of liver grafting.

5098. Lung transplant in the United States was performed on June 11, 1963, at the University of Mississippi Medical Center in Jackson, MS. In a three-hour operation, a team of doctors headed by Dr. James D. Hardy replaced the left lung of John Richard Russell. He survived for 18 days.

5099. Transplant of an animal organ into a human being took place at the University of Mississippi Medical Center in Jackson, MS, on January 23, 1964, when a team of 12 doctors headed by Dr. James D. Hardy transplanted the heart of a chimpanzee into the body of a 64-year-old patient. The patient, whose name was not made public, died 90 minutes later.

5100. Heart transplant in the United States was performed at Maimonides Hospital in Brooklyn, New York City, on December 6, 1967. The surgeon was Dr. Adrian Kantrowitz, and the patient was a two-week-old baby boy, who lived for 6.5 hours after the operation. The transplant took place three days after Dr. Christiaan Barnard performed the first heart transplant in history in Cape Town, South Africa. The first heart transplant performed on an adult in the United States took place on January 6, 1968, at the Stanford Medical Center, Palo Alto, CA. The patient was Mike Kasperak and the surgeon was Dr. Norman Shumway.

5101. Heart transplant using an artificial heart took place at St. Luke's Episcopal Hospital in Houston, TX, on April 4, 1969. Dr. Denton A. Cooley implanted the world's first entirely artificial heart into Haskell Karp, age 47, from Skokie, IL. The prosthetic heart was made of Dacron and plastic. Karp lived with the heart for three days, when it was replaced by a transplanted human heart. He died on April 8.

5102. Transplant of artificial skin took place at Massachusetts General Hospital, Boston, MA, on April 23, 1981. Doctors reported that an artificial skin composed of cowhide, shark cartilage, and plastic was applied with successful results to 10 burn patients, 3 of whom would have died without the treatment. The artificial skin was developed by Ioannis V. Yannas and a team of researchers at the Massachusetts Institute of Technology, Cambridge, MA.

5103. Heart transplant using an artificial heart that was intended to be permanent was performed on December 2, 1982, when a team of doctors at the University of Utah Medical Center, Salt Lake City, UT, headed by Dr. William C. DeVries, implanted a mechanical heart into Barney B. Clark, 61, a retired dentist from Des Moines, IA. The device, called the Jarvik-7, was designed by Dr. Robert K. Jarvik. Clark survived for nearly four months before dying of vascular collapse on March 23, 1983.

5104. Heart transplant using a baboon heart was performed by Dr. Leonard L. Bailey at the Loma Linda University Medical Center, Loma Linda, CA, on October 16, 1984. The patient was a 15-day-old baby girl known to the public as "Baby Fae." Her body rejected the transplant and she died on November 15.

5105. Liver transplant from a live donor was performed at the University of Chicago Medical Center, Chicago, IL, in October 1989. The patient was Alyssa Leanne Smith, who had been diagnosed as having biliary atresia, a fatal liver disease. In a 14-hour transplant, Alyssa's diseased liver was removed and replaced with a section of liver donated by her mother, Teri Smith of Schertz, TX. This was the first mother-to-daughter liver transplant in the United States.

5106. Liver transplant using a baboon liver took place at the University of Pittsburgh Medical Center, Pittsburgh, PA, in July 1992. A team of surgeons led by Thomas Earl Starzl transplanted the liver of a baboon into a 35-year-old patient infected with human immune deficiency virus (HIV) whose liver had been destroyed by hepatitis B. A human liver could not be used because it too would have been destroyed by the hepatitis. The patient died two months later, apparently of unrelated causes.

5107. Transplant of a major organ into a person with mental retardation took place on January 23, 1996, at the Sutter General Hospital in Sacramento, CA. The patient was Sandra Jensen of Sacramento, who was born with Down syndrome. She received a heart-lung transplant to treat a congenital heart ailment. Doctors had initially refused her the operation because of her low IQ. Jensen died on May 23, 1997.

5108. Transplant of human embryo tissue to be done in the United States took place at the University of Florida's Brain Institute at Shands Hospital in Gainesville, FL, on July 11, 1997. Neurosurgeon Richard Fessler injected spinal cord cells from a human embryo into a patient suffering from syringomyelia, a paralytic spinal disease. It was hoped that the graft of embryo spinal tissue would eventually replace the diseased tissue. Doctors in Russia were the first to perform transplant operations involving human embryo tissue.

MEDICINE—TREATMENTS

5109. Spa at a mineral spring opened to the public was deeded to the colony of Virginia in 1756 by Thomas Fairfax, sixth Baron Fairfax, "to be forever free to the publick for the welfare of suffering humanity." The spa was located in Bath, Berkeley County, VA (now Berkeley Springs, Morgan County, WV), and was chartered in October 1776. George Washington had visited the mineral springs on March 18, 1748.

5110. Steam baths for curing disease were advocated by Samuel Thomson, who in 1796 experimented with steam in the treatment of his daughter, whom physicians were unable to cure. He traveled on horseback through New Hampshire, Maine, Vermont, and Massachusetts, advocating treatment by steam as well as by the use of herbs.

MEDICINE—TREATMENTS—*continued*

5111. Stomach washing with a tube or syringe was accomplished by Dr. Philip Syng Physick in 1800 in Philadelphia, PA. His procedure is described in his article "Account of a New Mode of Extracting Poisonous Substances from the Stomach," which appeared in the *Eclectic Report and Analytic Review* in 1813.

5112. Water cures were advocated by David Campbell, originator of the *Water Cure Journal,* who opened a water-cure resort in 1843 at 63 Barclay Street, New York City. Joel Shew, M.D., was the physician. The therapeutic use of baths was popular at the time.

5113. Artificial insemination of a woman resulting in conception was made in 1866 by Dr. James Marion Sims, gynecologist and chief of the Woman's Hospital, New York City. Sims gave 54 other injections in 1866 and 1867.

5114. Occupational therapy treatment was given by Susan Edith Tracy, author of *Studies in Invalid Occupation,* at the Training School for Nurses of the Adams Nervine Asylum, Jamaica Plain, Boston, MA. The school had been established under the will of Seth Adams, who died on December 7, 1873, and was incorporated on March 16, 1877. The first patients were admitted in April 1880.

5115. Radium treatment for cancer instead of surgery was advocated by Dr. Robert Abbe, who published his conclusions in the June 1904 *Yale Medical Journal.* He held professorships of surgery in the Women's Medical College and the New York Post Graduate School of New York City.

5116. Psychodrama treatment for psychiatric patients was instituted by Dr. Jacob L. Moreno in Beacon, NY, in 1937. The treatment was designed to enable the psychiatric worker to achieve a clearer understanding of the patient's mental processes. None but interested participants and doctors were privileged to see the reenactment of cases.

5117. Artificial insemination for women to be permitted by a state was allowed under legislation enacted by Oklahoma and signed on May 18, 1967, by Governor Dewey Follett Bartlett.

5118. Gene therapy was conducted on September 14, 1990, by W. French Anderson, chief of the Molecular Hematology Branch of the National Heart, Lung, and Blood Institute in Bethesda, MD, and Drs. Kenneth Culver and Michael Blaese. The gene procedure was intended to correct a genetic immunodeficiency disease, adenosine deaminase deficiency, inherited by a four-year-old girl. Samples of her white blood cells were cultured and exposed to an engineered retrovirus that carried a healthy version of the gene that produces adenosine deaminase. The virus transferred the gene to her cells, which were then reinjected into her.

MEDICINE—VETERINARY

5119. Veterinary hospital was opened by Charles C. Grice in 1830 on Pearl Street, New York City. In later years, he moved it to White Street and then to Macdougal Street. Grice was graduated from the Royal Veterinary College of England in 1826 and came to America in 1830. He was the first veterinary graduate to practice his profession in the United States.

5120. Laboratory for the study of parasites in livestock was opened on August 1, 1886, in Washington, DC, in the Bureau of Animal Industry of the Department of Agriculture, with Dr. Cooper Curtice in charge. Dr. Charles Wardell Stiles took over the supervision in 1891, when the laboratory was designated a "zoological laboratory."

5121. Cattle tuberculosis test was made on March 3, 1892, on a herd of cattle belonging to Dr. J.E. Gillingham, Claremont Farms, Villa Nova, PA. The herd was tested with tuberculin brought from Europe by Dr. Leonard Pearson, dean of the Veterinary Department of the University of Pennsylvania, Philadelphia.

5122. Animal disease of American origin was tularemia, an epizootic of wild rabbits and other animals, which was recognized in 1910 in ground squirrels of Tulare County, CA, by Dr. George Walter McCoy. He and Dr. Charles Willard Chapin named the organism *Bacterium tularense.* The disease was named by Dr. Edward Francis of the Public Health Service, who was awarded a gold medal by the American Medical Association for his research into it.

5123. Surrogate birth experiment with an animal resulted from experiments by Dr. Gregory Pincus of Clark University, Worcester, MA, conducted at Harvard University, Cambridge, MA, in November 1939 under the auspices of the Dazian and Josiah Macy, Jr., Foundation. Pincus removed an egg from the ovary of a female rabbit, fertilized it with a salt solution, and transferred it to the uterus of a second rabbit that acted as an "incubator." The second rabbit gave birth in October 1939. Pincus exhibited the baby rabbit on November 1, 1939, at the 12th annual Graduate Fortnight at the New York Academy of Medicine.

5124. Surgical operation on a bull to correct a sperm block was performed on July 25, 1965, by Dr. James Hicks and Dr. Donald F. Walker at the Auburn University School of Veterinary Medicine, Auburn, AL, on Linderis Evulse, a $176,000 Aberdeen-Angus bull. The bull, owned by the Black Watch Farms, Wappinger Falls, NY, was strapped on a hydraulic operating table for the operation.

5125. Veterinary hospital established by a city was the Spay and Neuter Clinic of the Los Angeles City Department of Animal Regulation, Los Angeles, CA, which opened on February 17, 1971. The cost for spaying was $17.50 and for neutering $11.50. The first head of the hospital was Walter E. Ziegler, D.V.M., chief of veterinary services. The general manager was Robert I. Rush.

MILITARY

5126. Arsenal of the federal government was the Springfield Armory, Springfield, MA, founded in April 1778 as a laboratory for the preparation of all kinds of ammunition and established on April 2, 1794, as a national armory for the manufacture of small arms. The first superintendent was David Ames and the master armorer was Robert Orr. It took a month to complete the first 20 muskets. Two hundred and forty-five muskets were made the first year.

5127. State law prohibiting discrimination against soldiers was passed on May 5, 1908, by Rhode Island. The bill, sponsored by Theodore Francis Green, imposed a penalty for excluding soldiers in uniform from public places.

5128. Military think tank was the RAND Corporation, founded on October 1, 1946, at Hamilton Field, San Francisco, CA, by a group of scientists and researchers associated with the Army Air Force under the direction of General Henry Harley "Hap" Arnold. Arnold appropriated $10 million from leftover wartime research funds to establish a semi-independent organization devoted to the scientific study of national security issues. The acronym RAND stood for "research and development." Frank Collbohm was RAND's first president. In May 1948, RAND became an independent nonprofit enterprise.

5129. Chairman of the Joint Chiefs of Staff who was African-American was Army General Colin Luther Powell, appointed by President George Herbert Walker Bush on August 9, 1989. Powell, born in New York City in 1937, served from 1987 to 1989 as national security advisor to President Ronald Wilson Reagan. In 1989, he was promoted to four-star general, thus becoming the highest-ranking African-American officer up to that time. During his service as chairman he oversaw the 1991 Gulf War military campaign. He resigned in 1993.

MILITARY—AIR FORCE

5130. Air service of the Army was established on July 18, 1914, when an aviation section was created within the Signal Corps with an allotted strength of 60 officers and 260 men. The entire equipment consisted of six planes. A provisional aero squadron with 20 officers and 90 enlisted men had been prescribed in December 1913 by War Department General Order No. 75.

5131. Air service under one command was effected on September 3, 1917, when Brigadier General William Lacy Kenly was made chief of the Air Service of the American Expeditionary Force in France. He served until February 1918.

5132. Aviation unit of the military trained for overseas duty was the Marine Aeronautic Company, comprising 12 officers and 133 enlisted men, which sailed on January 9, 1918, from Cape May, NJ, and landed on January 21, 1918, at Ponta Delgada, Azores.

5133. Air force branch of the military was the Army Air Corps, established by congressional act of July 2, 1926, which authorized a Chief of the Air Corps (major general), 3 assistants (brigadier generals), 1,514 officers (from second lieutenants to colonels), and 16,000 enlisted men.

5134. Air defense military organization was the Air Defense Command, created on February 26, 1940, with headquarters at Mitchel Field, Long Island, NY, pursuant to War Department Orders dated February 26, 1940, for defense against air attack through the practical application of the coordinated effort of aviation, antiaircraft artillery, and aircraft warning agencies, including fixed military and civilian installations. It was charged with the development of a system for unified air defense of an area and the determination of tasks within the capabilities of the various combinations of tactical units that might be assembled for the air defense of cities, continental bases, manufacturing and industrial areas, or of armies in the field. The first commander was Brigadier General James Eugene Chaney.

MILITARY—AIR FORCE—OFFICERS

5135. Air Force general who was African-American was Benjamin Oliver Davis, Jr., of Washington, DC, director of operations and training of the Far East Air Force, who was named brigadier general on October 27, 1954. He was the son of Brigadier General Benjamin Oliver Davis of the Army.

5136. Air Force chairman of the Joint Chiefs of Staff was General Nathan Farragut Twining, who was sworn in on August 15, 1957, in Washington, DC, by President Dwight David Eisenhower. On September 29, 1960, the day before Twining retired as chief of staff, President Eisenhower decorated him with the Distinguished Service Medal.

5137. Air Force chief master sergeant who was African-American was Thomas N. Barnes of Chester, PA, who entered the Air Force in April 1949. He became a master sergeant on December 1, 1969, and chief master sergeant of the Air Force on October 1, 1973, for a two-year term.

5138. Air Force Reserve officer who was a nun was Sister Nancy Ann Eagan, a nurse, who became a lieutenant on May 5, 1970. She was assigned to the 932d Aeromedical Airlift Group, Scott Air Force Base, IL.

5139. Air Force military engineer who was a woman was Second Lieutenant Susanne M. Ocobock, who served from April 8, 1971, to August 15, 1972, as an industrial civil engineer at Kelly Air Force Base, TX.

5140. Air Force general who was a woman was Brigadier General Jeanne Marjorie Holm of Portland, OR, nominated on December 12, 1970, by President John Fitzgerald Kennedy. She received her silver stars at the Pentagon, Washington, DC, on July 16, 1971. Holm had served since 1965 as Director of Women in the Air Force.

5141. Air Force general who was an African-American woman was Marcelite Jordan Harris, who attained the rank of general in 1991. In 1995 she was promoted to major general, with overall responsibility for maintenance on every USAF base. She thus became the first African-American woman to attain the rank of major general in any of the nation's armed forces. In 1969, Harris had served with the 36th Tactical Wing at Bitburg Air Base, West Germany, where she became the first female aircraft maintenance officer in the air force.

MILITARY—ARMY

5142. Army uniform was standardized by order of the Continental Army in October 1779, when George Washington, as the commander in chief, prescribed a uniform through a general order. The coat was blue. The facings for the infantry were varied—white, buff, red, and blue; the artillery and artificers' coats were faced with scarlet and had scarlet linings; and the light dragoons' coats were faced with white and had white buttons and linings.

5143. Army organization under the Constitution was enacted on April 30, 1789. It provided for one regiment of infantry to consist of three battalions of four companies each, one battalion of artillery with four companies, and a total strength not to exceed 1,216 noncommissioned officers, privates, and musicians. The monthly authorized pay was $60 for the lieutenant colonel commandant, majors $40, captains $30, lieutenants $22, corporals $4, privates $3, and musicians $3.

5144. Battle fought by federal troops after the formation of the Union was the Miami Expedition. On October 19, 1790, Colonel John Hardin, under Brigadier General Josiah Harmar, led 400 troops against 150 Native Americans in the Great Lakes region northwest of Ohio, but because of poor leadership, insufficient training, and unworkable guns, the attack ended in a retreat.

5145. Military service by African-Americans to be authorized by Congress was authorized by an act introduced on July 16, 1862, by Senator Henry Wilson of Massachusetts and signed on July 17, 1862, by President Abraham Lincoln. It empowered the president to accept "persons of African descent, for the purpose of constructing intrenchments or performing camp competent."

MILITARY—ARMY—GENERALS

5146. General of the Continental Army was George Washington, who was appointed commander of all continental armies on June 15, 1775, by the Second Continental Congress assembled at the State House, Philadelphia, PA. Congress resolved "that five hundred dollars per month be allowed for the pay and expenses of the general." Washington took command the following month at Cambridge, MA, and led the American forces for six years during the Revolutionary War. After forcing Britain's Lord Cornwallis to surrender in October 1781, he served until December 23, 1783, when he resigned his commission.

5147. Commander-in-chief of the U.S. Army was Josiah Harmar, who served from September 29, 1789, to March 4, 1791, with the rating of lieutenant colonel of infantry. He had been brevetted brigadier general in 1787. He was succeeded by Arthur St. Clair, Anthony Wayne, James Wilkinson, and George Washington, the fifth commander-in-chief, who served from July 3, 1798, to December 14, 1799, as lieutenant general and general.

5148. Army lieutenant general was George Washington of Mount Vernon, VA, appointed on July 11, 1798, by President John Adams, under authorization of the act of May 28, 1798, as lieutenant-general and commander in chief of all the armies raised for the service of the United States. He was authorized to receive a salary of $250 monthly, $50 monthly allowance for forage, and 40 rations per day, or money in lieu thereof at the current price. He served from July 3, 1798, to December 14, 1799, when he died.

5149. Army general who was a Russian immigrant was John Basil Turchin (formerly Ivan Vasilevitch Turchininoff), who emigrated in 1856 after serving in Russia's Imperial Guards during the Crimean War. He joined the Union Army when the Civil War broke out and developed a successful plan for the capture of Huntsville, AL, for which he was made a brigadier general.

5150. Army general to become an admiral in the Navy was Samuel Powhatan Carter, who served in the Navy from 1840 to 1862. In 1861, during the Civil War, he organized the Tennessee Brigade militia. He became Army brigadier general of volunteers on May 1, 1862, and was breveted major general in March 1865 for gallantry and meritorious service as a cavalry commander. He returned to the Navy and was appointed lieutenant commander in charge of the gunboat *Monocacy* on the Asiatic station. He was appointed rear admiral on May 16, 1882, and retired on August 6, 1882.

5151. General of the U.S. Army was Ulysses Simpson Grant, commander of the Union forces during the Civil War, who was appointed on July 25, 1866. He served until March 4, 1869, when he was inaugurated as President of the United States.

5152. General of the Armies of the United States was General John Joseph Pershing, commander in chief of the American expeditionary forces during World War I, whose appointment was unanimously confirmed by the Senate on September 4, 1919.

5153. Army officer to occupy both the nation's highest military post and the highest nonelective civilian post was General George Catlett Marshall of Pennsylvania. He was the Army's chief of staff with rank of major general from September 1, 1939, to November 20, 1945; secretary of state from January 21, 1947, to January 20, 1949; and secretary of defense from September 21, 1950, to September 12, 1951.

5154. Army general who was African-American was Benjamin Oliver Davis, commanding officer of Harlem's 369th Coast Artillery (National Guard), who was appointed on October 25, 1940, to command a brigade in the 2nd Cavalry Division at Fort Riley, KS, with the rank of brigadier general.

5155. Army general who rose from draftee was Keith L. Ware, who was drafted on November 23, 1940. He attended Officer's Candidate School, Fort Benning, GA, and rose to commander of the 1st Infantry Division in Vietnam, becoming brigadier general on November 28, 1967. He, his staff of three, and four helicopter crewmen were killed on September 13, 1968, when his helicopter was shot down about 60 miles north of Saigon during the battle of Locninh. He was the fourth general killed in the Vietnam War.

5156. Army general appointed from civilian rank was William Signius Knudsen, director general of Office of Priority Management, appointed a lieutenant general on January 16, 1942, by President Franklin Delano Roosevelt.

5157. Army generals to wear the five-star insignia were Henry Harley "Hap" Arnold, Dwight David Eisenhower, Douglas MacArthur, and George Catlett Marshall, whose appointments were ratified on December 15, 1944, by the Senate. The grade of General of the Army was established by act of Congress on December 14, 1944.

5158. Army general to be consecrated a bishop was Major General William Richard Arnold, former chief of chaplains of the Army, who was in active service as a major general in the inspector general's office when he was consecrated titular bishop of Phocaea on October 11, 1945, in St. Patrick's Cathedral, New York City, by Archbishop Francis Joseph Spellman of the Roman Catholic Church.

MILITARY—ARMY—GENERALS—continued

5159. Army general who was African-American to lead an infantry brigade in combat was Major General Frederic Ellis Davison, who led the 199th Light Infantry brigade in the Tet offensive at Long Binh, Vietnam, in February 1968. Fourteen Americans and about 900 attacking troops were killed.

5160. Army generals who were brother and sister were Perry Milo Hoisington, who was made a brigadier general in March 1958, and his sister, Elizabeth Paschel Hoisington of Newton, KS, who was sworn in on June 11, 1970, as a brigadier general. Their two brothers and their father were also officers.

5161. General of the Armies of the United States with the rank of six stars was George Washington, whose posthumous promotion to General of the Armies was signed by President Gerald Rudolph Ford on October 19, 1976. The appointment was authorized by a joint congressional resolution enacted on October 11, 1976, to take effect on July 4, 1976.

5162. Army general who was an African-American woman was Hazel Winifred Johnson, who was promoted to the rank of brigadier general in 1979. Johnson was also the first African-American to head the Army Nurse Corps. The first African-American woman to become a brigadier general by rising through the ranks of the regular Army was Sherian Grace Cadoria, who received her promotion in 1985.

MILITARY—ARMY—OFFICERS

5163. Army chief engineer of the Continental Army was Colonel Richard Gridley, who served from June 17, 1775, to August 5, 1776. On June 16, 1775, the Continental Congress authorized one chief engineer at $60 a month, and two assistants at $20.

5164. Paymaster general of the Continental Army was James Warren of Massachusetts, appointed on June 27, 1775. On June 16, 1775, the Continental Congress established a separate department in the Army to take care of payments to troops. The department consisted of the paymaster general, who received $100 a month, and a deputy at $50 a month. Warren resigned on April 19, 1776.

5165. Surgeon general of the Continental Army was Benjamin Church, who served from July 27 to October 16, 1775. He held the position of director general and chief physician and received compensation of four dollars a day. On November 1, 1775, he was jailed for treason. The first surgeon general of the Army to

whom the title was officially applied was James Tilton of Delaware, the author of *Economical Observations on Military Hospitals,* who served from June 11, 1813, until June 15, 1815. The first medical officer to serve as surgeon general under the Reorganization Act of 1818 was Joseph Lovell, who served from April 18, 1818, until his death on October 17, 1836. His yearly salary was $2,500.

5166. Quartermaster of the Continental Army was Major Thomas Mifflin, who served from August 14, 1775, to November 7, 1777.

5167. Brevet commission in the Army was authorized by the Continental Congress on July 20, 1776, for Jacques Antoine de Franchessin, a Knight of the Order of St. Louis, an experienced officer in the service of France, who received a brevet commission of lieutenant colonel.

5168. Brevet conferred by the Army on an American was authorized on November 19, 1777, by the Continental Congress, which granted the rank of lieutenant colonel and a sword valued at $100 to Major Walter Stewart.

5169. Army major who was African-American was Martin Robinson Delany, who received his commission on February 8, 1865. On April 5, 1865, he was ordered to report to Charleston, SC.

5170. Army officer who was a woman was Florence Aby Blanchfield, who on July 9, 1947, was appointed lieutenant colonel in the Army with permanent rank under authority of the Army Nurses Law of April 16, 1947. The ceremony was held at the Pentagon, Washington, DC. General Dwight David Eisenhower, Chief of Staff, presented her with her commission. On June 1, 1943, she had been appointed superintendent of army nurses. The first nonmedical female army officer to be sworn into the regular Army was Colonel Mary Agnes Hallaren, who took the oath of office on December 3, 1948. She became director of the Women's Army Corps, Regular Army.

5171. Women's Army Corps member to be part of the Regular Army was Technician 3rd Grade Vietta M. Bates of Camden, NJ, who was sworn in on July 8, 1948, in Washington, DC, by General Omar Nelson Bradley, army chief of staff. The ceremony was televised.

5172. Doctor commissioned in the regular Army who was a woman was First Lieutenant Fae Margaret Adams of San Jose, CA, sworn in on March 11, 1953, in Washington, DC. Previously, she had been a WAC reserve medical officer. She obtained her degree under the GI Bill of Rights.

5173. Army nurse in modern times who was a man was Second Lieutenant Edward L.T. Lyon of Kings Park, NY, who was sworn in on October 6, 1955, in the chapel of St. Cornelius the Centurion on Governors Island, NY. Nurses' commissions were extended to men on August 9, 1955, by the Bolton Amendment to the Army–Navy Nurses Act of 1947.

5174. Sergeant major of the Army was William O. Wooldridge, a native of Shawnee, OK, who served in the Army starting in 1940, fought in World War II, in Korea, and in Vietnam, and was sworn in on July 11, 1966, to present the enlisted man's point of view to the army chief of staff, General Harold Keith Johnson.

5175. Mother and son to enlist simultaneously in the Army were Michael Fleming, age 17, and his mother, Ethel Fleming, 34, who enlisted on October 15, 1975, in Merced, CA, as transportation specialists.

5176. Army officer who was a woman to lead troops in combat was Captain Linda L. Bray, a military police officer. During the invasion of Panama in 1989, she led a platoon that captured an attack-dog compound near Panama City after a firefight with Panamanian soldiers.

MILITARY—ARMY—UNITS

5177. Army engineering department was authorized by the Continental Congress on June 16, 1775. It established a separate engineering department in the Continental Army, composed of a chief engineer, who received $60 a month, and two assistant engineers at $20 a month. The first chief engineer was Colonel Richard Gridley. A formal Corps of Engineers was established on March 11, 1779, but was disbanded on November 3, 1783, upon the dissolution of the Revolutionary Army.

5178. Army engineer corps was established by Act of March 16, 1802, "fixing the military peace establishments of the United States." The corps consisted of one engineer (major), two assistant engineers (captains), two other assistants (second lieutenants), and 10 cadets. The first engineer in charge was Major Jonathan Williams, appointed on April 13, 1802.

5179. Army cavalry unit to be formally established was the Regiment of Dragoons, later known as the 1st Regiment of Dragoons, organized at Jefferson Barracks, MO, in August 1833, with Colonel Henry Dodge in command. The designation of this organization was changed to the 1st Cavalry by act of Congress of August 3, 1861. Earlier, in March 1792, Congress had given the president power to raise a squadron of cavalry at his direction to serve for three years.

5180. Army signal corps was established under act of June 1, 1860, which appropriated $2,000 "for the manufacture or purchase of apparatus and equipment for field signals" and the appointment of one signal officer. On June 27, 1860, Assistant Surgeon Albert James Myer was appointed signal officer, with the rank of major. The corps became a separate branch of the Army by act of Congress of March 3, 1863.

5181. Army secret service bureau was inaugurated in 1861 by President Abraham Lincoln, who appointed the prominent detective Allan Pinkerton to be in charge. The identity of Pinkerton was not revealed, and he served as "Major Allan." He was attached to the staff of General George Brinton McClellan.

5182. Army balloon corps was the Balloon (Aeronautic) Corps of five balloons and 50 men under the command of Thaddeus Sobieski Coulincourt Lowe, chief aeronaut of the Army of the Potomac, formed on October 1, 1861, during the Civil War. Four balloons were ready for service on November 10, 1861, and were used for reconnaissance and for directing artillery fire via telegraph in Virginia.

5183. Army Reserve Officers Training Corps units were infantry units formed under authority of War Department Bulletin No. 44, dated October 21, 1916, at six locations: the University of Arkansas, Fayetteville, AR; the University of Maine, Orono, ME; St. John's College, Annapolis, MD; the Agricultural and Mechanical College of Texas, College Station, TX; the College of St. Thomas, St. Paul, MN; and the Citadel, Charleston, SC. The Reserve Officers Training Corps had been established by the National Defense Act of June 3, 1916, for the purpose of training men during peacetime so that they could take the place of officers in time of war.

5184. Army training camp for African-American officers was established on June 15, 1917, at Fort Des Moines, Des Moines, IA, and was known as the 17th Provisional Training Regiment. On October 15, 1917, the first commissions were granted, with 106 African-Americans commissioned as second lieutenants.

MILITARY—ARMY—UNITS—*continued*

5185. Volunteer unit made up of college women to serve overseas was the Smith College Relief Unit, which sailed on August 12, 1917, on the S.S. *Rochambeau.* The unit, which was under the direction of Harriet Boyd Hawes, consisted of 18 members, 17 of whom were graduates from the classes of 1888 to 1914 of Smith College, Northampton, MA.

5186. Army gas regiment was authorized on August 15, 1917, by General Order No. 108, and was organized by Colonel Earl James Atkisson. The first year it was known as the 30th Engineers; afterwards, as the 1st Gas Regiment. The first battalion was organized on October 16, 1917. Its first independent action took place on June 18, 1918, against Germans in the Toul sector, France, during World War I.

5187. Army armored car unit was Troop A, 1st Armored Car Squadron, which was organized at Fort Meade, MD, in 1928. It was commanded by Captain Harold G. Holt.

5188. Army parachute battalion was the 501st, organized on October 1, 1940, at Fort Benning, GA, under the command of Major William Maynadier Miley.

5189. Army corps for women was the Women's Army Auxiliary Corps, authorized on May 14, 1942, to allow women to serve in the Army. The first director was Oveta Culp Hobby. The first training course took place at Fort Des Moines, Des Moines, IA, from July 20 to August 29, 1942, when 346 women were commissioned third officers. The corps was renamed the Women's Army Corps on September 30, 1943.

5190. Army specialist corps for women was the Women's Army Medical Specialist Corps, authorized under the Army–Navy Nurses Act of 1947, dated April 16, 1947, which established a dietitians' section, a physical therapists' section, and an occupational therapists' section to consist of 24 majors and 385 captains and first and second lieutenants.

5191. Army helicopter battalion to be activated was the 8th Transportation Battalion, consisting of three helicopter companies and one maintenance company, formed on April 1, 1954, at Fort Bragg, NC, under command of Major Robert Kolb.

5192. Army ballistic missile operational unit was the 259th Field Artillery Missile Battalion, which completed training in November 1954 at Fort Bliss, TX. The unit was deployed to Europe in February 1955 to provide guided missile support for units in the Seventh Army.

5193. Armored division transported by airplanes to a foreign country was the 2nd Armored Division, commanded by Major General Edwin Hess Hurba, who took off with 62 men of his staff on October 22, 1963, in a C-135 Stratolifter from the Bergstrom Air Force Base, near Austin, TX, for the Rhein-Main Air Base in West Germany as part of Operation Big Lift. In 63 hours and 20 minutes, 196 airplanes, including 23 jets, transported 15,268 combat-ready troops in 235 missions. The division returned to Texas from November 12 to 21, 1963. Major General Archie J. Old, Jr., of the 15th Air Force was the overall commander of the flight.

MILITARY—CHAPLAINS

5194. Army chaplain who was Catholic was the Reverend Louis Eustace Lotbinière, appointed on January 26, 1776, by General Benedict Arnold to act as chaplain to the regiment of Colonel James Livingston in the Continental Army. The first Catholic army chaplain in the Army was the Reverend Samuel H. Milley, who served as post chaplain at Monterey, CA, from September 1849 to February 1850.

5195. Army chaplain killed in action was John Rosbrugh of Allen Township, PA, who served as chaplain of Northampton County. He was commissioned on December 26, 1776, and was killed at the battle of Assunpink, or the Second Battle of Trenton, on January 2, 1777.

5196. Navy chaplain in the Continental Navy known to have served was the Reverend Benjamin Parks, a Congregationalist minister, appointed on October 28, 1788, with the relative rank of lieutenant. It is possible that others preceded him, but if so, their identities are unknown.

5197. Chaplain of the U.S. Army was the Reverend John Hurt, who was appointed on March 4, 1791, and resigned on April 30, 1794. He had served during the Revolution as chaplain of the 6th Virginia Infantry, beginning on October 1, 1776. He became brigade chaplain on August 18, 1778, and served as such to the close of the war.

5198. Navy chaplain was William Balch, a Congregationalist. He received his commission from President John Adams on October 30, 1799, and served until May 10, 1801.

5199. Navy chaplain killed in action was Chaplain John L. Lenhart, who was commissioned chaplain on February 27, 1847. At that time chaplains did not hold naval rank and were known simply as chaplains. On March 8, 1862, the Confederate ironclad *Merrimac* encountered the Union frigate *Cumberland* off Hampton Roads, VA. The *Merrimac* crushed the *Cumberland* by driving her iron prow through the side of the *Cumberland,* at the same time pouring in a fire of shells. Chaplain Lenhart died with his sinking ship.

5200. Army chaplain who was Jewish was Rabbi Jacob Frankel of Philadelphia, PA, who was appointed on September 10, 1862, four months after Congress amended its law of 1861 requiring chaplains to be Christians. Frankel served from 1863 through 1865 at the United States Hospital in Philadelphia. Rabbi Ferdinand Sarner of Rochester, NY, served as chaplain in the 44th New York Regiment and was wounded at the Battle of Gettysburg. The first rabbi to serve officially as a regimental chaplain was Elkan Cohen Voorsanger, commissioned as chaplain first lieutenant on November 24, 1917, in Paris while serving with the American Expeditionary Forces. In the spring of 1918, during Passover, he became the first U.S. officer to preside over the observance of a Jewish holiday. He was promoted to captain on February 22, 1919.

5201. Army chaplain who was African-American was Henry McNeal Turner, pastor of the Israel African Methodist Episcopal Church, Washington, DC. He was commissioned chaplain of the United States Colored Troops by President Abraham Lincoln in 1863. Turner enlisted in the 1st U.S. Colored Infantry, otherwise known as the 1st District Regiment of Columbia, and was present and active in all its military engagements. He was mustered out of service in September 1865 and was appointed a chaplain in the regular Army by President Andrew Johnson.

5202. Navy chaplain who was Catholic was the Reverend Charles Henry Parks, who was commissioned on April 30, 1888, with the relative rank of lieutenant. He was advanced to the rank of lieutenant commander on March 3, 1899, and resigned on January 25, 1900. (Actual rank was not given to chaplains until March 3, 1899.)

5203. Navy chaplain who was Jewish was Rabbi David Goldberg of Corsicana, TX, who was appointed with the rank of lieutenant (j.g.) on October 30, 1917. He was advanced to lieutenant commander on January 1, 1938, and retired on March 1, 1941. The first Jewish district chaplain was Captain Joshua L. Goldberg of the 3rd Naval District, who served in both world wars.

5204. Army chaplain of Japanese ancestry was First Lieutenant Masao Yamada, a Congregational minister, assigned on June 9, 1943, to Camp Shelby, MS, to preach to soldiers of Japanese ancestry.

5205. Navy chaplain who was a woman was Lieutenant Florence Dianna Pohlman of La Jolla, CA, a Presbyterian, who was sworn in on July 2, 1973, at Newport, RI, and later assigned to the Naval Training Center, Orlando, FL.

5206. Navy chaplain who was an African-American woman was Lieutenant (j.g.) Vivian McFadden, a Methodist, of John's Island, SC, who was sworn in on September 8, 1974, at the Naval Air Station, Atlanta, GA.

5207. Navy chaplain who was a Muslim was Lieutenant (j.g.) Monje Malak Abd al-Muta Ali Noel, Jr. Noel, who was commissioned in 1994, was the second Muslim chaplain to serve in the armed forces.

MILITARY—COAST GUARD

5208. Coast guard service was the Revenue Cutter Service, organized by an act of Congress of August 4, 1790, "an act to provide more effectually for the collection of the duties imposed by law on goods, wares and merchandise imported into the United States and on the tonnage of ships and vessels." The Life Saving Service was authorized by an act of June 18, 1878. The two services were combined on January 28, 1915, into the Coast Guard. The motto of the Coast Guard is *Semper paratus* ("always ready"). The first commandant was Alexander V. Fraser.

5209. Coast Guard serviceman who was African-American was Michael A. Healy of Georgia, who was appointed on March 7, 1865, to the Revenue Cutter Service, the predecessor of the Coast Guard. He was appointed second lieutenant on June 6, 1866, first lieutenant on July 20, 1870, and captain on March 3, 1883. He was commanding officer of the *Bear* from 1886 to 1895. He retired on September 22, 1903.

5210. Coast Guard inland station was opened on November 3, 1881, when four surfmen were employed on Station No. 10 of the 9th Life Saving District, embracing Lake Erie and Lake Ontario, at Louisville, KY, near the falls of the Ohio River. The station was commanded by Captain William M. Devan. The first rescue was made on November 7, four days after the station opened, when the 1,603-ton steamer

MILITARY—COAST GUARD—*continued*

City of Baton Rouge of St. Louis, MO, valued at $125,000, with 26 persons on board, was stranded on the left-hand reef of the falls. The vessel was finally floated off the rocks on November 24.

5211. Coast Guard aviation unit was formed under an act of Congress of August 29, 1916, which authorized the secretary of the treasury "to establish, equip, and maintain aviation stations, not exceeding ten in number, for the purpose of saving life and property along the coasts of the United States and at sea contiguous thereto."

5212. Coast Guard unit for women was the Coast Guard Women's Reserve, called SPARS, from the initials of the Coast Guard motto *Semper paratus* ("always ready"). It was authorized on November 23, 1942, and placed under the command of Lieutenant Commander Dorothy Constance Stratton. The first recruit was Dorothy Edith Lorne Tuttle, who enlisted on December 7, 1942, as a yeoman third class.

5213. Coast Guard airplane pilot who was a woman was Ensign Janna Lambine, who was graduated on March 4, 1977, from the Naval Air Station, Whiting Field, Milton, FL.

5214. Coast Guard officers who were women who served aboard ships other than hospital ships were Ensign Beverly Gwin Kelley of Bonita Springs, FL, assigned to the seagoing cutter *Morgenthau,* and Petty Officer Third Class Debra Lee Wilson of San Jose, CA, assigned to the seagoing cutter *Gallatin,* on June 22, 1977.

5215. Coast Guard ship commander who was a woman was Lieutenant (j.g.) Beverly Gwin Kelley, who was appointed on April 16, 1979, to command the 95-foot cutter *Cape Newagen,* with a crew of 14, based in Maalaea, Maui, HI. Her assignment included search missions, boating safety, antipollution patrols, and law enforcement. The first woman to command a Coast Guard ship on regular patrol was Lieutenant (j.g.) Susan Ingalls Moritz, who assumed command of the U.S.S. *Cape Current* on June 8, 1979. The ship operated in the Straits of Florida, where smuggling of drugs and immigrants was a constant problem.

MILITARY—DRAFT

5216. Draft law enacted by a colony was enacted on April 18, 1637, in Boston, MA, by the Massachusetts Bay Colony legislature, which provided "there shalbee 160 men pvided to be chosen out of the severall townes according to the portion underwritten," to serve in the conflict known as the Pequot War. The conscription call was as follows: Boston 26, Salem 18, Ipswich 17, Saugus 16, Watertown 14, Dorchester 13, Charlestown 12, Roxbury 10, Cambridge 9, Newbury 8, Hingham 6, Weymouth 5, Medford 3, and Marblehead 3.

5217. Conscientious objectors who refused for religious reasons to participate in war were the Shakers, members of a pacifist Christian sect that had originated in England. The group's formal title was "The United Society of Believers in Christ's Second Appearing." A group of Shakers, led by their founder, Ann Lee, had emigrated from England in 1774 and settled in Watervliet, NY. They refused to aid the colonies in the Revolutionary War, with the result that they were accused of treason and imprisoned without trial in the old fort in Albany, NY. On December 20, 1780, they were all released from prison with the exception of Ann Lee, who was transferred to the jail at Poughkeepsie, NY. She was released soon thereafter.

5218. Draft of civilians by Congress was authorized by the act of May 8, 1792, "effectually to provide for the National Defense by establishing a uniform militia throughout the United States." Every free able-bodied white male citizen between the ages of 18 and 45 was required to be enrolled in the militia of the United States and to supply himself with a gun and no fewer than 24 cartridges suited to the bore of his musket. There was no penalty for noncompliance. This law left the militia under the command of the states.

5219. Draft law enacted by Congress during wartime was passed on March 3, 1863, "an act for enrolling and calling out the national forces, and for other purposes." It required men 20 to 45 years of age to be enrolled on April 1, 1863, by provost marshals. Exemptions could be bought for $300. The first draft call was made on July 7, 1863. Earlier draft bills had been passed by the House and Senate during the War of 1812, but the need to produce a compromise bill ended with the signing of a peace treaty on December 24, 1814.

5220. Draft law enacted by Congress during peactime was passed on September 14, 1940, by a vote of 47–35 in the Senate and 232–124 in the House. It called for a total of 900,000 men to be trained in any given year. Registration was required of all men who had attained the age of 21 and who had not reached the age of 36 on October 16, 1940. Each registrant was assigned a number, so that quotas of soldiers could be filled by lottery. The first drawing of numbers was made on October 29, 1940, in

Washington, DC. The first number to come up, No. 158, was drawn by Secretary of War Henry Lewis Stimson. On November 15, the government issued a call for 75,000 men. The director of the draft was Dr. Clarence Addison Dykstra.

5221. Camp for conscientious objectors was the Patapsco Civilian Public Service Camp, Relay Post Office, MD, opened on May 15, 1941, to house 26 men of various faiths and beliefs who chose to do public service rather than participate in war. The director was Dr. Ernest Atkins Wildman, professor of chemistry, Earlham College, Richmond, IN. Inmates worked in the neighboring Patapsco State Park and in the State Forestry Nursery. Similar camps were later opened by the National Service Board for Religious Objectors.

MILITARY—INSIGNIA

5222. Insignia to designate state army regiments was instituted by the Massachusetts Provincial Congress on July 5, 1775, which "resolved that thirteen thousand coats be provided ... and one thereof given to each noncommissioned officer and soldier in the Massachusetts Forces ... and that the Committee of Supplies ... are to cause all the coats to be buttoned with pewter buttons, and that the coats for each regiment, respectively, have buttons of the same number stamped on the face of them."

5223. Chevrons for noncommissioned army officers were authorized in 1847 by the General Regulations for the Army of the United States, which provided three bars and an arc for sergeant major, three bars and a tie for quartermaster sergeant, three bars and a lozenge for first sergeant, three bars for sergeant, and two bars for corporal.

5224. Corps badges systematically assigned to an entire army were adopted in March 1863 by the Army of the Potomac during the Civil War. The I Corps was assigned a circle, the II Corps a trefoil, the III Corps a diamond, the IV Corps a triangle with two equal sides inside a larger triangle, the V Corps a cross pattée, and so on.

5225. Wound chevron issued by the Army was authorized, pursuant to General Order No. 6, War Department, on January 2, 1918. It was a gold chevron, identical to that of war service, worn on the left sleeve.

5226. Service number issued by the Army to an enlisted man, also known as the GI serial number, was number ASN-1, which was assigned to Master Sergeant Arthur B. Crean on February 28, 1918, during World War I. The first service number issued to an officer was

No. 0–1, which was assigned to General John Joseph Pershing, army chief of staff, in June 1921. Social Security numbers replaced all service numbers on dogtags on July 1, 1969. By 1972, a similar numbering system covered the Air Force, Navy, and Marine Corps.

5227. Shoulder sleeve insignia issued by the Army and known as a shoulder patch depicted a wildcat in a circle and was authorized on October 19, 1918, for the 81st Division, variously nicknamed the Stonewall Jackson Division, the Bobcat Division, and the Wildcat Division.

MILITARY—MARINE CORPS

5228. British marine corps of American colonists was organized in 1740 when three regiments of American colonists were recruited in New York to serve under the British flag. They wore green swallowtail coats faced with red, white waistcoats, buff trousers, crossed white belts, and three-cornered hats.

5229. Marines were organized in two battalions on November 10, 1775, under authority of the Continental Congress. They were called the 1st and 2nd Battalions of American Marines, and were commanded by a colonel, two lieutenant colonels, and two majors. The first marine officer was Samuel Nicholas, a Philadelphia Quaker, commissioned captain on November 28, 1775, at $32 a month. The Marines were under the jurisdiction of the War Department until April 30, 1798, when Congress created the Navy Department. The present Marine Corps was created by act of July 11, 1798, which authorized a major, 4 captains, 16 first lieutenants, 12 second lieutenants, 48 sergeants, 48 corporals, 32 drums and fifes, and 720 privates, including enlisted men. The first major was William Ward Burrows of South Carolina, who was appointed July 12, 1798, and served nearly 6 years.

5230. Marine band was authorized by act of Congress of July 11, 1798, which allowed the appointment of a drum major, a fife major, and 32 drummers and fifers. William Farr was leader of the Marine band from January 21, 1799, to November 22, 1804. The first president to review the band from his residence was John Adams on January 1, 1801.

MILITARY—MARINE CORPS—*continued*

5231. Marine Corps commando raid was made on February 16, 1804, in North Africa by Lieutenent Stephen Decatur, who led 74 volunteers, including 8 Marines under Sergeant Solomon Wren, in a 20-minute raid to burn the U.S.S. *Philadelphia,* which had been captured by the Tripolitans and was lying under the protection of their shore guns. The raiders killed or captured all the enemy but two and set the *Philadelphia* afire.

5232. Marine who was a woman was Lucy Brewer, alias George Baker and Louisa Baker, who concealed her sex and served on board the *Constitution* in its battle with the *Guerrière* on August 19, 1812.

5233. Marine reserve member who was a woman was Mrs. Opha May Johnson, who enrolled on August 13, 1918, as a private and was assigned to duty as a clerk at the headquarters of the Marine Corps Quartermaster Corps, Washington, DC, following an order from the secretary of the navy allowing women to enroll in the Marine Corps Reserve for clerical duty. She was appointed sergeant on September 11, 1918, and was honorably discharged on February 28, 1919.

MILITARY—MARINE CORPS—OFFICERS

5234. Marine officer killed in service was John Fitzpatrick, a second lieutenant in the Continental Marines, who was killed on April 6, 1777, when the *Alfred,* a 24-gun frigate under command of Captain Samuel Nicholas, was attacked off Block Island, RI, by the 20-gun H.M.S. *Glasgow.*

5235. Marine pilot was Lieutenant Alfred Austell Cunningham, assigned for training and instruction to the Navy Aviation Camp, Annapolis, MD, on July 9, 1912. He made his first solo flight on August 1, 1912, received seaplane license certificate No. 2, and became naval aviator No. 5. From November 17, 1919, to December 12, 1920, he served as director of Marine Corps Aviation.

5236. Marine pilot to fly over Antarctica was Captain Alton U. Parker of the Marine Corps Reserve. He was the pilot on the *Floyd Bennett,* the airplane of the First Byrd Antarctic Expedition, which took off from Little America, Byrd's Antarctic base, on December 5, 1929.

5237. Marine general to wear four stars was Major General Thomas Holcomb, commandant of the Marine Corps, who was advanced to lieutenant general on January 20, 1942. On January 1, 1944, he was placed on the retired list and his rank was raised to that of full general. The first four-star general in active service was Lieutenant General Alexander Archer Vandegrift, appointed on April 4, 1945, with date of rank from March 21, 1945.

5238. Marine officer of Chinese descent was Wilbur Carl Sze, commissioned a second lieutenant on December 15, 1943. He was born in Washington, DC, and at the age of five went to China, where he remained for 11 years before returning to the United States.

5239. Commissioned officer in the Marine Corps who was African-American was John Earl Rudder, a midshipman in the regular Naval Reserve Officers' Training Corps at Purdue University, Lafayette, IN, who was commissioned on June 8, 1948, as a second lieutenant. He had served as an enlisted man in the Marine Corps Reserve from July 24, 1943, to June 26, 1946.

5240. Marine general who was a woman was Brigadier General Margaret Ann Brewer, nominated on April 6, 1978, by President Jimmy Carter and sworn in on May 11, 1978, as director of the division of information.

5241. Marine general who was African-American was Brigadier General Frank E. Petersen, Jr., of Topeka, KS, nominated on February 23, 1979, by President Jimmy Carter. He was the 30th African-American to achieve the rank of general or admiral.

MILITARY—MILITARY EQUIPMENT

5242. Signal flares for communication between ships over long distances were developed in the late 1850s by Martha Hunt Coston of Washington, DC, widow of inventor Benjamin Coston, who came up with the original idea. Her Coston Telegraphic Signals, in white, red, and green, were used by the Union navy during the Civil War.

5243. Army field telegraph used in warfare was employed on May 24, 1862, in the Peninsula campaign during the Civil War. A wire several miles long extended from the headquarters of General George Brinton McClellan near Williamsport, VA, to an advance guard at Mechanicsville, VA, commanded by General George Stoneman, chief of cavalry in the Army of the Potomac.

5244. Periscope was invented by Thomas Doughty, acting chief engineer of the Navy, in 1864. During Nathaniel Prentiss Banks's Red River expedition, Doughty was on the turreted monitor *Osage*. Annoyed by bushwhackers and snipers who could not be seen yet did deadly work, Doughty rigged up a sheet-iron tube extending from a few feet above the deck to the engine room below, with an internal arrangement of mirrors that allowed him to see the shore. When attacked, he would signal the gunners to fire. Admiral David Dixon Porter officially thanked him for his invention.

5245. Army field range drawn by horses, known as a "moving kitchen," was introduced by Captain Daniel Frank Craig of the Army's 4th Field Artillery on a 21-day march in May 1908, while he was serving on the staff of Colonel Alexander Brydie Dyer at Vancouver, WA. It was mounted on a two-wheeled truck or trailer and was drawn behind a rations wagon. Though extensively used, it was never officially adopted by the War Department.

5246. Radio car for military use was designed in 1911 by Colonel Royal Page Davidson at Lake Geneva, WI, and was equipped with telescopic masts for radio broadcasting. Current for the operation of the radio was generated by the automobile motor. The car was also equipped with rapid-fire machine guns and two powerful electric searchlights with helix shutters for flashlight signaling.

5247. Smokescreen for concealing the movement of troops and ships was invented in 1923 by Thomas Buck Hine. It was first demonstrated publicly on September 5, 1923, during naval bombing tests off Cape Hatteras, NC.

5248. General purpose military vehicle was the jeep, designed in 1940 by Karl K. Pabst, consulting engineer to the American Bantam Company, Butler, PA. That summer, the army had asked for prototypes of a "low-silhouette scout car" that was powerful, light, rugged, and easy to service. The Bantam prototype featured a four-cylinder Continental engine, four-wheel drive, and a fold-down windshield. Similar models were manufactured by Willys-Overland and the Ford Motor Company. Almost 650,000 jeeps were manufactured by the end of World War II. The basic jeep design was abandoned by the military in the 1970s but persisted in consumer vehicles. The name jeep derived from the initials of "General Purpose."

5249. Laryngophone throat microphone commercially manufactured was made by the Western Electric Company, New York City, in 1941. Sales were confined exclusively to the armed forces of democratic powers.

5250. Wire recorder for sound recording was invented in the late 1930s by Marvin Camras, a student at the Armour Institute of Technology, Chicago, IL, who patented it on June 13, 1944. The recorder was used experimentally in 1939 and in 1940. In 1941, several models were used by the Navy.

MILITARY—MILITIAS

5251. Military leader of the English settlers was Myles Standish, one of the Mayflower Pilgrims, who in 1621 was unanimously chosen military captain of the colony.

5252. Militia was established by the Court of Assistants of the Massachusetts Bay Colony, Boston, MA, which ordered on April 12, 1631, "that there shall be a watch of 4 kept [every] night att Dorchester and another of 4 att Waterton, the watches to begin att sunset."

5253. Military organization established by a colony was the Ancient and Honorable Artillery Company, chartered in Boston, MA, on March 13, 1638. At the first elections, in June 1638, Captain Robert Keayne was elected commander; Daniel Haugh (Howe), lieutenant; and Joseph Weld, ensign.

5254. Military organization to oppose the British was the Light Horse of the City of Philadelphia, PA, organized on November 17, 1774, by 28 gentlemen, three of whom were members of the Committee of Correspondence of the first Congress of America, to resist the aggressions of the British crown.

5255. Naval militia established by a state was the Massachusetts Naval Battalion, organized under executive order of March 18, 1890, authorizing the formation of four companies. The companies were formed on March 25, 1890, with Thomas A. DeBlois, William M. Paul, William M. Wood, and John W. Weeks, all of Boston, commanding companies A, B, C, and D, respectively. On May 7, 1890, John Codman Soley, a graduate of the U.S. Naval Academy, was commissioned lieutenant commander of the naval battalion.

5256. Naval militia of a state to have a hydroplane was the Illinois Naval Reserve. Stewart MacDonald and Commodore A.M. Andrews presented the group with the *Alice*, a Curtiss flying boat with a 100-horsepower engine that developed a speed of 70 miles per hour. It was launched on May 22, 1915, at ceremonies in government hangars at the foot of Washington Street, Chicago IL.

MILITARY—NAVY

5257. Navy fleet was authorized on October 13, 1775, when the Continental Congress appointed a marine committee consisting of John Adams, John Langdon, and Silas Deane to be in complete control of naval affairs. Although open hostilities against the British began on April 19, 1775, little consideration was given to protection by sea until October 5, when the Congress received news that a British naval fleet was on its way. The Continental Navy was organized on December 22, 1775, and consisted of two 24-gun frigates, the *Alfred* and the *Columbus,* as well as two 14-gun brigs, the *Andrea Doria* and the *Cabot,* and the schooners *Hornet, Wasp* and *Fly.* Esek Hopkins was commissioned commander of the fleet and his pay was set at $125 a month. Sailors received $8 a month.

5258. Navy uniforms to be standardized were adopted by the Marine Committee on September 5, 1776. The uniform of captains in the Navy consisted of a coat of blue with red lapels, slashed cuffs, a stand-up collar, flat yellow buttons, blue breeches, and a red waistcoat with yellow lace. The sailors or mariners were to have green coats faced with white, round cuffs, slashed sleeves and pockets, with buttons around the cuff, a silver epaulet on the right shoulder, shirt collars turned back, buttons to match the facings, white waistcoats and breeches edged with green, black gaiters, and garters. The men were also to have green shirts, "if they can be procured."

5259. Naval protection was afforded by the Revenue Cutter Service, which was organized on August 4, 1790, under an act of Congress approved by President George Washington. It operated under the general direction of the secretary of the treasury. Commissions were granted on March 21, 1791, to captains to command "a cutter in the Service of the United States of America." For nearly seven years, the revenue cutters formed the only armed force of the United States afloat. The service was later merged with the Coast Guard.

5260. Warship builder was Joshua Humphreys, "father of the American Navy," who was appointed master builder on June 28, 1794, at an annual salary of $2,000. On March 27, 1794, Congress passed an "act to provide a naval armament," which authorized four ships of 44 guns and two of 36 guns. Humphreys constructed *Constitution, Constellation, Chesapeake, President, United States,* and numerous other ships. He served until October 26, 1801.

5261. Navy yard acquired after the establishment of the Navy Department on April 30, 1798, was the Portsmouth Navy Yard, Portsmouth, NH, which was purchased on June 12, 1800, from William Dennet and his wife for $5,500. It embraced 58.18 acres and had previously been used for building man-of-war ships.

5262. Prize money awarded by the Navy was granted to the U.S.S. *Delaware,* commanded by Captain Stephen Decatur, Sr., which captured the French schooner *Croyable* in June 1798 off the Delaware Capes during the undeclared naval war with France (1798–1801). By act of Congress on June 28, 1798, cases involving captured ships were tried in federal district courts. The act provided that after the condemnation of a captured ship, the part accruing to the United States was to be paid into the public treasury, and the amount due the officers and crews was to be distributed among them in the proportions which the president should direct. Prize money had been awarded as early as the Revolution to men on the vessels of the Continental and state navies and privateers.

5263. Shipbuilding law enacted by Congress was the shipbuilding act of February 25, 1799, which authorized the president to direct a sum "not exceeding $200,000 to be laid out in the purchase of growing or other timber, or of lands on which timber was growing, suitable for the navy." On December 19, 1799, a tract of 350 acres on Grover's Island, GA, was purchased for $7,500.

5264. Standardization of nomenclature for naval vessels was mandated by a congressional resolution passed on March 3, 1819, which provided that "the Secretary of the Navy shall name ships of the first class for states, of the second class for rivers, and of the third class for cities and towns."

5265. Navy contract for armor plate was awarded to the Bethlehem Iron Company, South Bethlehem, PA, on June 1, 1887. A total of 6,700 tons was ordered at $536 a ton for the battleships *Maine* and *Texas* and the monitors *Puritan, Amphitrite, Monadnock,* and *Terror.*

5266. Navy personnel in the regular Navy who were women took their oaths of office on July 7, 1948, in Washington, DC. They were Frances Teresa Devaney, Ruth Flora, Kay Louise Langdon, Wilma Juanita Marchal, Doris Roberta Robertson, and Edna Earle Young, all of whom were transferred from the Naval Reserve.

5267. Sailor to reenlist in the Navy while under the North Pole was James Robert Sordelet of Fort Wayne, IN, electrician's mate first class on the submarine *Nautilus,* who reenlisted on August 3, 1958.

5268. Navy divers to submerge for 10 days were Lieutenant Commander Robert E. Thompson of the Medical Corps, Gunners Mate First Class Lester E. Anderson, Chief Quartermaster Robert A. Barth, and Chief Hospital Corpsman Sanders W. Manning, who descended in *Sealab 1* to a depth of 192 feet, 30 miles off Hamilton, Bermuda, on July 22, 1964. *Sealab 1* was a 40-foot compartment nine feet in diameter. The divers breathed air that was a mixture of 80 percent helium, 4 percent oxygen, and 16 percent nitrogen at 86 pounds of pressure. They surfaced on July 31, 1964.

5269. Sailors assigned to regular Navy shipboard duty who were women were Ensign Rosemary Elaine Nelson, assistant supply officer, and Lieutenant (j.g.) Ann Kerr, personnel officer, who were respectively assigned on August 11 and October 25, 1972, to the hospital ship U.S.S. *Sanctuary.*

MILITARY—NAVY—ADMIRALS

5270. Navy officer to become an admiral was David Glasgow Farragut, who received his appointment on July 25, 1866. On July 16, 1862, Farragut had been given the rank of rear admiral, with rank comparable to that of major general in the Army, at a compensation of $5,000 a year at sea, $4,000 on shore duty and leave of absence, or $3,000 awaiting orders. On December 13, 1864, he had received the title of vice admiral, for which the pay was $7,000 at sea, $6,000 on shore duty, and $5,000 when awaiting orders. On July 25, 1866, the Navy was authorized by Congress to have 10 rear admirals, a vice admiral, and an admiral.

5271. Admiral of the Navy was Admiral George Dewey, who served from March 3, 1899, until his death on January 16, 1917. The rank was conferred by act of Congress, passed on March 2, 1899.

5272. Navy admiral who was Jewish was Rear Admiral Adolph Marix, who was advanced to the rank of rear admiral on July 4, 1908. He had entered the service as a midshipman on September 26, 1864.

5273. Navy admirals to wear the five-star insignia as Admirals of the Fleet were Ernest Joseph King, William Daniel Leahy, and Chester William Nimitz, whose appointments were ratified on December 15, 1944, by the Senate. The grade of fleet admiral of the Navy was established by act of Congress on December 14, 1944.

5274. Navy admiral who was African-American was Samuel Lee Gravely, Jr., of Richmond, VA, whose date of rank was July 1, 1972.

5275. Sailor to become a four-star admiral was Jeremy M. "Mike" Boorda, the only man in the Navy's history to rise from the lowest rank of sailor to the highest rank of admiral. Boorda, who was born in 1938, became chief of naval operations in April 1994.

MILITARY—NAVY—OFFICERS

5276. Navy doctor was Dr. Joseph Harrison, appointed in 1775 in Philadelphia, PA, to serve on the *Alfred.*

5277. Commander-in-chief of the Continental Navy was Esek Hopkins of Rhode Island, who served from December 22, 1775, to January 2, 1778.

5278. Navy officer commissioned was Captain Hopley Yeaton of New Hampshire, appointed on March 21, 1791, by George Washington to command "a cutter in the service of the United States of America." He was assigned to the *Scammel,* built at Portsmouth, NH.

5279. Commodore in the Navy was John Barry, senior officer in the Navy, who was appointed in 1794 after the Navy was reorganized.

5280. Navy surgeon was Dr. George Balfour, who was ordered to Norfolk, VA, in 1801 to take charge of the first marine hospital. He had entered the Army on April 11, 1792, and was transferred to the Navy on March 9, 1798. He resigned on April 12, 1804, to enter private practice.

5281. Navy officer to abolish corporal punishment on his ship was Uriah Phillips Levy, the son of a prominent Sephardic Jewish family of Philadelphia, PA. He joined the service as a sailing master on October 21, 1812, during the War of 1812. As captain of the U.S.S. *Vandalia,* he proved that it was possible to maintain discipline on a ship without flogging. He captured 21 British merchant ships before

MILITARY—NAVY—OFFICERS—*continued*

being taken prisoner and continued his naval career when the war ended. In 1860, after becoming the nation's first Jewish commodore, he persuaded the Navy to abolish corporal punishment throughout the service.

5282. Navy officer to become an engineer was Charles Haynes Haswell. He was commissioned on February 19, 1836, by Secretary of the Navy Mahlon Dickerson, and was appointed to design steam-power equipment. He was made chief engineer on July 12, 1836, and engineer-in-chief on October 3, 1844.

5283. Navy officer condemned for mutiny was Midshipman Philip Spencer, son of the Secretary of War, who was hanged on December 1, 1842, from the yardarm of the U.S.S. *Somers,* a brig of war, while at sea in West Indian waters. Boatswain Samuel Cromwell and Seaman Elisha Small were hanged at the same time. They were convicted, at a court-martial held on shipboard, of conspiring to organize a mutiny, murder the officers, and turn the ship into a pirate cruiser. The commander of the *Somers* was Alexander Slidell Mackenzie, who was exonerated by a court of inquiry.

5284. Judge advocate of the Navy was William Eaton Chandler of New Hampshire, who on March 6, 1865, was appointed by President Abraham Lincoln to be solicitor and naval judge advocate general under act of March 2, 1865. His salary was $3,500 a year.

5285. Naval attaché was Lieutenant Commander French Ensor Chadwick. He was sent to London on November 15, 1882, and remained there until April 3, 1889.

5286. Navy petty officer who was a woman was Loretta Walsh, age 18, of Philadelphia, PA, who was sworn in as chief yeoman on March 21, 1917. She assumed office on March 22, 1917, and was in charge of recruiting for the Naval Coast Defense Reserve.

5287. Navy officer commissioned in the U.S. Naval Reserve who was a woman was Mildred Helen McAfee, who was appointed lieutenant commander on August 3, 1942, to serve as director of the Women's Reserve, U.S. Naval Reserve. Members of this unit were nicknamed WAVES (Women Accepted for Volunteer Emergency Service). On November 13, 1943, McAfee became the first woman in the Navy to hold the rank of captain as a line officer.

5288. Navy captain who was a woman was Captain Sue Sophia Dauser, superintendent of the Navy's Nurse Corps, who received the rank of captain on February 26, 1944. Previously, she had held the relative rank of captain as authorized by the Pay Bill, effective December 22, 1942. She had entered the service on September 15, 1917, when she was appointed a naval reserve nurse. On December 14, 1945, she became the first Navy nurse to receive the Distinguished Service Medal.

5289. Naval Reserve Nurse Corps nurse who was African-American was Phyllis Mae Daley, a registered nurse of New York City, who was sworn in on March 8, 1945, as an ensign at the office of the Naval Officer Procurement, New York City.

5290. Navy commissioned officer who was African-American was Ensign John W. Lee of Indianapolis, IN, who was commissioned on March 15, 1947, and assigned to the U.S.S. *Kearsarge.* The first African-American commissioned officer in the Naval Reserve was Bernard Whitfield Robinson, a medical student at Harvard University, Cambridge, MA, who was commissioned ensign on June 18, 1942.

5291. Doctor in the regular Navy who was a woman was Dr. Frances Lois Willoughby of Pitman, NJ, appointed a lieutenant commander on October 15, 1948. During World War II, women were accepted in the Medical Corps of the Naval Reserve on a temporary basis.

5292. Medical officer assigned to a naval vessel who was a woman was Lieutenant Commander Bernice Rosenthal Walters of New York, an officer in the Medical Corps, Naval Reserve, who was assigned on March 8, 1950, to the Hospital Ship U.S.S. *Consolation* and reported for duty on July 13, 1950. She had served during World War II at the Naval Shipyards in Boston, MA; the Naval Air Station in Weymouth, MA; and the Naval Hospital in Bainbridge, MD.

5293. Navy chairman of the Joint Chiefs of Staff was Admiral Arthur William Radford, who served from August 15, 1953, to August 15, 1957.

5294. Navy admirals who were brothers were Rear Admirals Augustus Joseph Wellings, Naval Academy graduate No. 5370, who retired on July 1, 1954; Timothy Francis Wellings, graduate No. 5851, who retired on July 1, 1952; and Joseph Harold Wellings, graduate No. 7948, who retired on August 1, 1963.

5295. Commander of a combat ship who was African-American was Lieutenant Commander Samuel Lee Gravely, Jr., of Richmond, VA, who on January 31, 1961, assumed command of the destroyer escort U.S.S. *Falgout,* one of the vessels of Escort Squadron 5 on duty with the barrier Pacific force. The ship had a crew of 150 and 13 officers.

5296. Navy captain who was African-American was Thomas David Parham, Jr., of Newport News, VA, a Presbyterian chaplain, whose rank was raised from commander to captain on February 1, 1966.

5297. Navy officer who was a woman to hold a major command was Captain Robin Lindsay Quigley, who assumed command on May 17, 1973, of the Navy Service School, San Diego, CA, supervising 30,000 students.

5298. Member of the Navy's Hurricane Hunters who was a woman was Lieutenant Judith Ann Neuffer, who flew a four-engine P-3 Orion into Hurricane Carmen in the Caribbean on September 1, 1974, encountering 120-knot winds.

5299. Navy officer who was a woman to command a ship at sea was Lieutenant Commander Darlene Iskra, who took command of the U.S.S. *Opportune* in 1991.

5300. Executive officer of a man-of-war who was a woman was Lieutenant Commander Claire V. Bloom, who served as the executive officer of the frigate U.S.S. *Constitution,* the flagship of the Navy, during its 200th-anniversary voyage that began on July 21, 1997, in Marblehead, MA.

MILITARY—NAVY—UNITS

5301. Naval radio station was established in 1903 at the Highlands, Navesink, NJ. Chief Radioman Jack Scanlin was in charge.

5302. Navy task force assembled for foreign service was Task Force 19, consisting of 25 ships commanded by Rear Admiral David McDougal Le Breton. Formed at Argentina, it sailed on July 1, 1941. It included the battleships *Arkansas* and *New York,* the light cruisers *Brooklyn* and *Nashville,* and destroyers.

5303. Navy jet airplane squadron was Fighter Squadron 17-A, which received its first jet airplane, a McDonnell FH-1 Phantom, at the Naval Air Station, Quonset Point, RI, on July 23, 1947. On May 5, 1948, at the close of three days of operations aboard the U.S.S. *Saipan,* the squadron became the first Navy jet squadron to qualify aboard a carrier.

5304. Seagoing radio broadcasting station was the 5,800-ton, 338-foot Coast Guard cutter *Courier,* commissioned on February 15, 1952, at Hoboken, NJ, and dedicated on March 4, 1952, by President Harry S. Truman at a pier on the Potomac River, Washington, DC. The ship had a 150,000-watt mediumwave transmitter and two 35,000-watt shortwave transmitters. It was used to broadcast the Department of State's "Voice of America" program to Eurasian areas. The first official test was made on April 2, 1952, off the coast of Colombia, South America. The first broadcast from European waters was made on September 7, 1952, off the island of Rhodes, Greece. The *Courier* was a 1945 Navy cargo ship converted and equipped at a cost of over $2 million. The first captain was Oscar Cottman Buckingham Wev.

5305. Navy task force to fight undersea craft was Task Force Alfa, which consisted of an aircraft carrier with a group of antisubmarine aircraft, a helicopter squadron, destroyers, shore-based patrol planes, and submarines. The task force was created on March 24, 1958, under the command of Rear Admiral John Smith Thach and placed in operation in April 1958.

5306. Navy nuclear submarine division was Atomic Submarine Division 102, formed on March 31, 1958, at New London, CT, under command of Commander Robert Glennwood Black. The division consisted of the atomic submarines *Nautilus, Sea Wolf,* and *Skate,* and the conventional submarines *Hardhead, Bang,* and *Half-break.*

5307. Navy nuclear task force to circumnavigate the globe without refueling or other logistic support was Task Force One, consisting of the attack carrier U.S.S. *Enterprise,* the guided missile cruiser U.S.S. *Long Beach,* and the guided missile frigate U.S.S. *Bainbridge.* The task force left Norfolk, VA, on July 31, 1964, and returned on October 3, completing Operation Sea Orbit, a 30,000-knot trip that included 18 cities in 10 countries by way of the Cape of Good Hope and Cape Horn. The crew of 6,000 men was under the command of Rear Admiral Bernard Max Strean.

MILITARY—VETERANS

5308. Revolutionary War national veterans' organization was the Society of the Cincinnati, founded on May 13, 1783, at the Verplanck house, near Fishkill, NY. The first general meeting was held on May 7, 1784, in Philadelphia. Membership was limited to officers who had served three years in the Continental army or who had been honorably discharged for dis-

MILITARY—VETERANS—*continued*

ability. George Washington was elected the first president general in 1783; he remained in office until his death and was succeeded by Major General Alexander Hamilton. The first state branches were established in New York and Massachusetts on June 9, 1783. The French branch was organized on January 7, 1784, in Paris. The name was derived from Lucius Quinctius Cincinnatus, the distinguished Roman who, called from the plow, "left all to save the republic."

5309. Soldiers' homes established by Congress for disabled veterans were authorized by act of Congress of March 21, 1866, an "act to incorporate a national military and naval asylum for the relief of the totally disabled officers and men of the volunteer forces of the United States." The first homes, which began operating in 1867, were the Eastern Home, Togus, ME; the Central Home, Dayton, OH; and the Northwestern Home, Milwaukee, WI. The first female resident of such a home was Private First Class Regina C. Jones of the Women's Army Corps, who was admitted to the Soldiers' and Airmen's Home, Washington, DC, on September 2, 1955.

5310. Grand Army of the Republic post for veterans of the Civil War was established in Decatur, IL, on April 6, 1866. The organization was founded principally through the efforts of Dr. Benjamin Franklin Stephenson, surgeon, and the Reverend William J. Rutledge, chaplain, both of the 14th Illinois Infantry. The first state convention was held on July 12, 1866, in Springfield, IL. Stephen Augustus Hurlbut was elected the first national commander in chief.

5311. Veterans of Foreign Wars of the United States meeting took place on August 18–20, 1913, in Denver, CO, where the organization was founded. It was composed of Army, Navy, and Marine Corps veterans who served in time of war in theaters of operation. Rice W. Means was the first commander in chief. The VFW was an amalgamation of three separate groups: the American Veterans of Foreign Service, organized in September 1899; the Army of the Philippines, organized in December 1899; and the American Veterans of Foreign Service, organized on September 10–12, 1903, which was itself a combination of the Philippine War Veterans, organized in October 1901, and the American Veterans of the Philippines and China Wars, organized in July 1902.

5312. American Legion convention of veterans of World War I was held in Minneapolis, MN, on November 10–12, 1919. The group had been organized in Paris on February 15–16, 1919. It was incorporated by act of Congress of September 16, 1919, "to uphold and defend the Constitution of the United States; to maintain law and order; to foster and perpetuate one hundred per cent Americanism; to preserve our memories of incidents in the Great War; to inculcate a sense of individual obligation to the community, state and nation; to safeguard and transmit to posterity the principles of justice, freedom and democracy; to consecrate and sanctify our comradeship by our devotion to mutual helpfulness."

5313. World War II veterans' society officially recognized by Congress was the American Veterans of World War II, which was founded on December 12, 1944, in Kansas City, MO, as an amalgamation of 11 groups with a membership of about 1,700. The first national commander was Elmo Woodrow Keel. The organization was chartered by Congress on July 23, 1947.

MINING AND MINERALS

5314. Lead was mined and smelted in 1620 near Falling Creek, VA, to supply the local demand for bullets and shot at the Jamestown colony. Mining operations ceased after John Berkeley and 20 workmen were killed by Native Americans in May 1622.

5315. Lime was manufactured on January 27, 1662, in Providence, RI. Thomas Hackelton was granted liberty by the town to burn lime at a certain place on the commons. On October 27, 1665, the town ordered that the lime rocks about the limekiln should remain in common ownership.

5316. Copper mine known to have been worked was the Simsbury mine at Granby, CT, with a history dating back to 1705. A company to mine the ore was formed in 1709 by John Winthrop and was the first mining company chartered in America. The mine was also known as the Granby mine and was worked for several years by convicts in the Newgate prison established there. In 1737 the copper obtained from this mine was used in the manufacture of the "Granby coppers," among the earliest colonial coins minted. The mine was worked at intervals until 1773.

5317. Gem-cutting machine was invented by Abel Buell of Killingworth, CT, in 1766. He claimed that his "method of grinding and polishing crystals and other stones of great value, all the growth of the Colony" would effect a great saving in money. The machine was called a lapidary.

5318. Marble quarry was operated in 1785 by Isaac Underhill on land owned by Reuben Bloomer in Dorset, VT. The quarry was first worked for stone for fire jambs, chimney backs, hearths, and lintels. A quarry was also opened in Rutland, VT, in 1785. Marble used before 1785 was obtained from exposed marble ledges.

5319. Jewelers' supply house of importance was established in 1794 by Nehemiah Dodge, silversmith, goldsmith, and watch repairer, in a shop on North Main Street, Providence, RI. In addition to his retail business, he sold gold plate made of a thin sheet of gold united with a thicker sheet of copper to manufacturing jewelers.

5320. Gold nugget was found in the Reed Mine, Cabarrus County, North Carolina, in 1799. For several years its nature was not known. The nugget was the size of a "small smoothing iron." Later another was found there that weighed 28 pounds. Gold in limited quantities had been discovered elsewhere, however. In 1782, Thomas Jefferson described a lump of ore of about four pounds, found four miles below the falls on the north side of the Rappahannock River in Virginia, that yielded 17 pennyweight of gold.

5321. Mica was obtained from the Ruggles mine, Isinglass Mountain, Grafton, NH, in 1803.

5322. Tungsten and tellurium were found in 1819 in a bismuth mine in Huntington, CT. The mine was owned by Ephraim Lane. Tungsten, a ferruginous metal known to mineralogists as wolfram, was found in the state of yellow oxide. Tellurium was found in the metallic state.

5323. Granite was quarried in Quincy, MA, in 1820 for the Bunker Hill Monument in Boston. About 9,000 tons in blocks 2.5 inches square and 12 feet long were transported by the Granite Railway Company from the Quincy quarry to the wharf at Charlestown, MA.

5324. Stone breaking machine was patented on April 13, 1831, by Benjamin F. Lodge and Ezekial T. Cox of Zanesville, OH.

5325. Zinc was produced in 1835–36 by John Hitz in the Arsenal at Washington, DC.

5326. Fluorspar commercial mining was attempted in 1837 at Trumbull, CT. It was used with magnetic iron pyrite in the smelting of copper ores and sold for $60 a ton.

5327. Silver mine was the Silver Hill Mine, discovered in 1838 about 10 miles from Lexington, NC. The company was incorporated on January 7, 1839, for $500,000.

5328. Graphite was produced commercially in 1840 at Ticonderoga, NY, which became the center of the graphite industry of the United States. Graphite occurs in association with igneous and metamorphic rocks.

5329. Gold discovered in California was found near the San Fernando Mission in 1842, but no importance was attached to it. On January 24, 1848, James Wilson Marshall found a nugget on property owned by John Augustus Sutter in a millrace on a branch of the Sacramento River near Coloma, CA. This was the discovery that started the gold rush of the Forty-Niners to California.

5330. Zinc commercial production was undertaken at the Pennsylvania and Lehigh Zinc Company Mill, which was opened in Bethlehem, PA, on October 13, 1853, by Samuel Wetherill. The zinc was obtained from calamine ores. Wetherill received patents on February 20, 1855, for an apparatus for separating zinc white; on November 13, 1855, for the process of making zinc white; on September 30, 1856, for a zinc white furnace; on January 6, 1857, for a process of reducing zinc ore; and on January 7, 1868, for the process of manufacturing white oxide of zinc.

5331. Borax was discovered by Dr. John A. Veatch, January 8, 1856, in mineral water from Tuscan Springs, Tehama County, CA. Commercial production began at Borax Lake, Lake County, CA, in 1864, when pure crystals were refined by immersion in solution and permitted to crystallize out again, thus disposing of an apparently very minute amount of impurities. This deposit supplied the United States until 1868, when larger deposits were found in Nevada.

5332. Stone crusher of value was built by Eli Whitney Blake of New Haven, CT, who obtained a patent on June 15, 1858, on an "improvement in machines for crushing stones." Blake's stone crusher had upright convergent jaws, one fixed and one movable. The stones descended by gravity into pits and were sorted by screens. The device was first used in 1859 in Hartford, CT, on a road construction job.

MINING AND MINERALS—*continued*

5333. Sulfur deposit was discovered in 1869 in a salt dome in Calcasieu Parish, LA. It was later developed as the Sulphur Dome of the Union Sulphur Company. Sulfur was first extracted from a well in the dome in October 1895 by Herman Frasch of Cleveland, OH. On October 20, 1891, he received two patents on "mining sulphur" and a third on "an apparatus for mining sulphur." Sulfur was melted in the ground and pumped to the surface in a liquid state to congeal in bins or blocks.

5334. Fuller's earth was imported in 1878 and used for refining edible oils and petroleum. A deposit of fuller's earth (also called bentonite) was discovered by John Olson in 1891 in Benton, AR. A claylike substance, it was used in cleansing (fulling) cloth, wool, and fur, and later in the bleaching, clarifying, and filtering of fats, greases, and oils.

5335. Mineral segregation by oil flotation was patented in 1886 by Carrie J. Everson, a Colorado schoolteacher. Her method, which was adopted by miners throughout the West, separated precious metals from rocky ore by running them through a bath of oily water. The particles of dross floated, but the particles of gold, silver, and copper sank.

5336. Bauxite was discovered in 1887 at a point a few miles northeast of Rome, Floyd County, GA. A few fragments of the unknown mineral were picked up on the Holland lot two miles north of the Ridge Valley Iron Company's furnace at Hermitage, GA. Bauxite mining began in April 1888, when the deposits on the Holland property were first opened and worked. The first shipments of the ore were made in May 1888 to the Pennsylvania Salt Company, Natrona, PA, and to Greenwich Point, PA. This ore is said to have been used for the manufacture of both alum and metallic aluminum.

5337. Carborundum was invented by Edward Goodrich Acheson in 1891 in Monongahela City, PA, as an abrasive to be used in place of emery, corundum, and other similar materials. By running a current of electricity through a mixture of silica and carbon, Acheson obtained a material hard enough for rough-polishing diamonds, rubies, sapphires, and other precious and semiprecious stones. He obtained a patent on February 28, 1893, on the production of artificial crystalline carbonaceous materials. The first sale of this material was 10 carats at the rate of 40 cents a carat or $880 a pound.

5338. Diamonds in a meteorite were found in June 1891 by Dr. George Augustus Koenig, professor of mineralogy and geology at the University of Pennsylvania, Philadelphia, PA, while cutting a meteorite found at Canon Diablo, AZ. In various cavities he found small black diamonds of little commercial value which cut through polished corundum.

5339. Gold leaf in roll form was patented on April 5, 1892, by Walter Hamilton Coe of Providence, RI. It was made by the W.H. Coe Manufacturing Company of Providence in rolls 67 feet in length and 0.00250 inches thick, varying in width from 0.06 inches to 3.75 inches.

5340. Diamonds in actual rock were found in peridotite on August 1, 1906, by John W. Huddleson at Murfreesboro, Pike County, AR. He found two diamonds, each weighing about three carats.

5341. Ductile tungsten was produced in 1908 by Dr. William David Coolidge of the General Electric Company, Schenectady, NY, who used high temperatures to draw the tungsten into fine filaments for incandescent lamps. Coolidge reported his findings in the issue of May 17, 1910, of the *Journal of the American Institute of Electrical Engineers* and obtained a patent on December 30, 1913, on "tungsten and method of making the same, for use as filaments of incandescent electric lamps."

5342. Taconite production was undertaken in November 1919 by the Mesabi Iron Company, Babbitt, MN. The first cargo, of 5,076 tons, was shipped on October 1 to the Ford Motor Company, River Rouge, MI. Taconite is a hard ferruginous rock containing 25 percent to 30 percent iron. The first large-scale commercial production was begun on September 13, 1956, by the E.W. Davis Works at Silver Bay, MN, built by the Reserve Mining Company, Duluth, MN, and owned jointly by the Armco Steel Corporation and the Republic Steel Corporation. Its capacity was rated at 3.75 million tons of iron ore pellets annually. The rock was crushed, ground, and processed by magnetic separation, producing small pellets containing 62.5 percent iron.

5343. Underground mill for the separation of zinc and lead by the flotation process was completed in 1929 at the New Jersey Zinc Company's mine under Battle Mountain at Gilman, CO. The mine was air-conditioned and fireproof and had its own water system, elevator, and 100 miles of steel track. Ore was hauled to a central point at the 450-foot level, where it was ground into small particles to enable the flotation milling process to separate the ore into zinc and lead concentrates.

5344. Magnesium commercially produced from seawater was extracted on January 21, 1941, by the Dow Chemical Company, Freeport, TX. It sold for approximately 23 cents a pound.

5345. Synthetic mica was produced commercially by the Synthetic Mica Corporation, Caldwell Township, NJ, and offered for sale on May 17, 1956, under the trade name of Synthamica. It was a chemically pure synthetic fluorphlogopite mica capable of withstanding sustained temperatures as high as 2000 degrees F without physical or electrical failure. Research on synthetic mica was begun in 1947 by the Bureau of Mines in Norris, TN.

5346. Sulfur mine offshore was the Grand Isle offshore mine, 2,000 feet beneath the bottom of the Gulf of Mexico, about seven miles off the Louisiana coast. The mine was operated by means of a steel structure equipped with boilers, generators, and drilling rigs and situated in 50 feet of water. The deposit was discovered by the Humble Oil and Refining Company and the mine was built and operated by the Freeport Sulphur Company. The first sulfur was obtained on March 14, 1960.

MONEY

5347. Continental money was an issue of $3 million, of which $2 million was issued on June 22, 1775, and $1 million on July 25, 1775. A second issue of $3 million was authorized on November 29, 1775. The largest share of the original issue, $434,244, was given to Massachusetts, and the next largest share was the $372,208 awarded to Pennsylvania. Only 12 states were granted money. Georgia was not included, as it was not represented in the Congress.

5348. Decimal system of money with the dollar as a unit was adopted on July 6, 1785, by the Continental Congress, which established "that the money unit of the United States of America be one dollar; that the smallest coin be of copper, of which two hundred shall pass

for one dollar; that the several pieces shall increase in a decimal ratio." On August 8, 1786, it was voted "that the standard of the United States of America for gold and silver, shall be eleven parts fine and one part alloy."

5349. Gold price fixed by Congress was $19.39 an ounce, authorized on April 2, 1792. Except for the period between August 1814 and February 1817, this value remained firm until June 28, 1834, when the value of an ounce of gold was raised to $20.67. This price remained firm until May 29, 1933, except during the panics of 1837 and 1857 and from February 25, 1862, to January 1, 1879.

5350. Mint of the United States was located at Philadelphia, PA. Robert Morris, as head of the Finance Department of the federal government, laid a plan for American money coinage before Congress on January 15, 1782. Through his efforts and the cooperation of Thomas Jefferson and Alexander Hamilton, an act "establishing a mint and regulating the coins of the United States" was approved by both houses and signed by George Washington on April 2, 1792. The cornerstone was laid on July 31, 1792, and construction was completed on September 7. The first director was David Rittenhouse. The first woman to serve as director was Nellie Tayloe Ross, who assumed office on May 3, 1933.

5351. Federal government employees who were women were Sarah Waldrake and Rachael Summers, who were employed in 1795 by the Mint in Philadelphia, PA, as adjusters to weigh gold coins. Their pay was 50 cents a day.

5352. Private mint authorized by the federal government was the Moffat Assay Office, Mount Ophir, Mariposa County, CA, built in 1850 by John L. Moffat. The mint manufactured $50 hexagonal gold ingots used as legal tender to replace gold dust and nuggets. Beginning on February 20, 1851, the ingots were made under the supervision of the United States Assayer, and on July 3, 1852, Congress passed an "act to establish a branch of the mint of the United States in California." Augustus Humbert of New York was appointed United States Assayer to place the government stamp upon the ingots produced by Moffat and Company. In 1852 the mint became the United States Assay Office.

MONEY—COINS

5353. Coinage dies made in America were made in 1652 by Joseph Jencks at the Iron Works of Lynn, MA, for the General Court of Massachusetts, which established a mint house in Boston on May 27, 1652. The dies were for silver coins worth 3, 6, and 12 pence, "forme flatt," with "N.E. Anno 1652" and a Roman numeral denoting the value on the obverse side. On the reverse were "Massachusetts" and a pine tree. The date was not changed annually. John Hull was the mint master.

5354. Copper coins were made from copper obtained from the Simsbury mine in Granby, CT, by John Higley in 1737. They were stamped upon planchets of the pure copper, and in consequence were in demand by goldsmiths for alloy. The obverse side showed a standing deer, facing left, occupying the whole field, with the legend, "Value me as you please." The reverse side showed three hammers, each bearing a crown upon the head with the legend "I am good copper—1737."

5355. Copper cents minted by a state were issued by Vermont. On June 15, 1785, the state granted authority to Reuben Harmon, Jr., to make these coins for two years, beginning on July 1, 1785. The copper coins were to be one-third of an ounce each, troy weight. Harmon established a mint at Rupert, VT, where he lived. In October 1785, Connecticut authorized the coinage of 10,000 pounds of copper cents at the mint at New Haven, which was operated by Samuel Bishop and John Goodrich of New Haven and Joseph Hopkins of Waterbury, CT.

5356. Coin to use *E pluribus unum* **as a motto** was the cent issued by New Jersey in 1786, the obverse of which showed a horse's head above a plow with the date of coinage and the name of the state in Latin, *Nova Caesarea*. The reverse showed a heart-shaped shield of the United States and the national motto *E pluribus unum* ("from many, one"). The first United States coin bearing the motto was the half eagle, authorized by act of Congress of April 2, 1792, and coined in 1795. The obverse showed the draped bust of Liberty facing right, with long, loose hair, and a liberty cap; above, "Liberty" and 15 stars; below, "1795." The reverse displayed an eagle, bearing the shield of the United States on its breast, with arrows in right claw and olive branch in left; in its beak, a scroll inscribed *E pluribus unum*; above the head, 16 stars; beneath, an arch of clouds. The coin had a reeded edge and weighed 135 grains.

5357. Continental coin was the copper Fugio or Franklin cent, designed by Benjamin Franklin and authorized on July 6, 1787. One side showed 13 circles linked together to form a circle around the edge; a small circle in the middle bore the words "United States" around it, with the words "We are one" in the center. The other side showed a dial with hours on the face and a meridian sun above; on the left was the word *Fugio* ("I fly"), and on the right, "1787"; below the dial were the words "Mind Your Business." A contract for the manufacture of 300 tons of the coins was awarded to James Jarvis, who manufactured them in New Haven, CT. The dies were made by Abel Buell, also of New Haven.

5358. Trade tokens were issued in 1789 by William and John Mott, manufacturers and dealers in watches and jewelry, Water Street, New York City. They were smaller in size than the ordinary copper cent and beautifully engraved. On the obverse was a regulator supported by two columns and surmounted by a small eagle. The inscription read "Motts, NY. Importers, Dealers, Manufacturers of Gold and Silver Ware." On the reverse was an eagle with expanded wings, facing to the left, holding an olive branch in one talon and three barbed arrows in the other, the shield of the United States upon its breast. The date "1789" was above the eagle, while below was the inscription "Watches, Jewelry, Silver Ware, Chronometers, Clocks."

5359. Copper coins made by the U.S. Mint were one-cent and half-cent issues, of which there were four designs, the "chain cent," the "wreath cent," the "flowing hair," and the "liberty cap," which were authorized by congressional act "establishing a mint regulating the coins of the United States," approved on April 2, 1792. The cent equaled the hundredth part of a dollar and contained 11 pennyweights of copper, while the half cent contained 5 pennyweights of copper. This issue was discontinued by act of February 21, 1857.

5360. Gold coinage was authorized by Congress on April 2, 1792, when eagles ($10), half eagles ($5), and quarter eagles ($2.50) were authorized. On March 3, 1849, the coinage of double eagles ($20) and one-dollar gold pieces was authorized, and on February 21, 1853, three-dollar gold pieces were authorized. The minting of the one-dollar and three-dollar gold pieces was discontinued on September 26, 1890. All gold coins were discontinued by the Gold Reserve Act of January 30, 1934, which stated that "no gold shall hereafter be coined."

On April 5, 1933, President Franklin Delano Roosevelt issued an order forbidding the hoarding of gold, and on June 5 he signed a bill making it illegal to require repayment of financial obligations in gold.

5361. Half cent was authorized by act of Congress of April 2, 1792. It was designed by the engraver Robert Scot. The obverse depicted "Liberty" facing left, over the date 1793. The reverse bore the inscription "United States of America" and a wreath of olive branches enclosing the words "half cent." On the edge appeared the words "Two hundred for a dollar." It was size 14 and weighed 132 grains. Coinage was discontinued by act of February 21, 1857.

5362. Silver coins were the half dollar, quarter dollar, dime, and half dime authorized under the congressional act of April 2, 1792. Under this act, all gold and silver coins struck at the Mint in Philadelphia, PA, were full tender. President George Washington, in his address to Congress of November 6, 1792, reported: "There has been a small beginning in the coinage of silver half dimes; the want of small coins in circulation calling the first attention to them." Silver dollars, which were also authorized by the same act, were coined at the Mint in 1794. They continued in use until February 12, 1873, when Congress passed an act, known as "the Crime of '73," that made gold the sole monetary standard.

5363. Metal purchased for coinage was six pounds of old copper at one shilling and three pence per pound, which was coined and delivered to the Treasurer in 1793.

5364. Silver deposit for coinage was made by the Bank of Maryland on July 18, 1794. It consisted of coins of France worth $80,716 as silver bullion. The first return of American silver coins to the Treasury was made on October 15, 1794.

5365. Gold bullion deposit for coinage was made by Moses Brown, a merchant of Boston, MA, on February 12, 1795. It was of gold ingots worth $2,276.72, which were paid for in silver coins.

5366. Coins produced by steam power were coined in 1836 in Philadephia, PA, on a machine invented by M. Thonnelier of France in 1833. Previously, all the work at the Mint had been done by hand or horsepower.

5367. Fifty-dollar gold pieces were manufactured on February 20, 1851, by the Moffat Assay Office, Mount Ophir, Mariposa County, CA. They were octagonal. On the obverse was an eagle surrounded by the words "United States of America." Above it was the legend "887 thous," indicating the fineness of the gold, and at the bottom, "50 D C." On the reverse, a number of radii extended from a center in which was stamped in small figures "50." Around the edge was the phrase "The United States Assayer."

5368. Confederate coin was a silver half dollar produced at the mint in New Orleans, LA, in 1861. Only four pieces were minted. On the obverse was the Confederate shield with a liberty cap and a wreath of sugar cane and cotton branches. On the reverse side was the regular United States die.

5369. Coin to use the motto "In God We Trust" was the two-cent piece of 1864. Salmon Portland Chase, secretary of the treasury, addressed a letter to the director of the Mint at Philadelphia, PA, stating that American coinage should bear a motto expressing in the fewest words possible that no nation can be strong except in the strength of God. Congress established the motto by act of April 22, 1864, which authorized the director of the Mint to fix the shape, mottoes, and devices to be used. On July 11, 1955, Congress enacted a law to provide that "all United States currency (and coins) shall bear the inscription 'In God We Trust.'" The phrase was made the national motto of the United States on July 30, 1956, when President Dwight David Eisenhower signed a joint resolution of Congress.

5370. Nickel five-cent piece was authorized on May 16, 1866. It weighed 77.16 grains and was composed of 75 percent copper and 25 percent nickel. The obverse showed a United States shield surmounted by a cross, an olive branch pendant at each side; in back of the base of the shield were two arrows, only the heads and feathers visible; beneath, "1866"; above in the field, "In God We Trust." The reverse showed the figure "5" within a circle of 13 stars and rays, and the words "United States of America."

5371. Trade dollars were authorized by act of Congress of February 12, 1873, and were not intended for circulation in the United States, but for export to China. Each dollar weighed 420 grains, 900 fine. When its coinage was authorized it was inadvertently made legal tender in the amount of five dollars, but this was repealed on July 22, 1876. The trade dollar was discontinued on March 3, 1887.

MONEY—COINS—*continued*

5372. Coins manufactured for a foreign government were made for Venezuela in 1876 by the Mint in Philadelphia, PA. They comprised 10 million pieces of *un centavo* of the nominal value of $100,000 and 2 million pieces of *dos y medio centavos* of the nominal value of $50,000. The coins were composed of copper, nickel, and zinc and had a diameter of 23 millimeters and 19 millimeters respectively. The charge for the manufacture was equal to the expense, including labor and use of machinery. The production was authorized on January 29, 1874, by an act providing for coinage to be executed for foreign countries at the mints of the United States and stipulating that such production was not to interfere with the required coinage for the United States.

5373. Commemorative coin was the Columbus silver half dollar authorized by the congressional act of August 5, 1892, for the World's Columbian Exposition, held in Chicago, IL. It was first issued in November 1892. The Isabella silver quarter, issued for the same exposition, was authorized by act of March 3, 1893. Charles E. Barber designed the obverse; George T. Morgan, the reverse.

5374. Coin bearing the likeness of a foreign monarch was the Isabella silver quarter issued for the World's Columbian Exposition in Chicago, IL. The coin was authorized on March 3, 1893, and issued in June 1893. It bore on its obverse a crowned bust of Queen Isabella, facing left, with "1893" to the right in the field. About the center design was the inscription "United States of America." On the reverse, a spinner was pictured kneeling to the left, holding a distaff in her left hand and a spindle in her right. Below was the inscription "Columbian Quar. Dol."

5375. Coin bearing the likeness of a president was the 1909 Lincoln penny, a copper cent, designed by Victor David Brenner and based on a photograph of President Abraham Lincoln taken in 1864 by Mathew B. Brady. The design was adopted in April 1909 and in May 1909 coinage began at the Mint in Philadelphia, PA. The first delivery of the coins was made on June 30, 1909, to the Cashier of the Mint, and distribution began on August 2. The reverse was redesigned in 1959 to show the Lincoln Memorial. The first coin to bear the likeness of a living President was the 1926 Sesquicentennial half dollar, the obverse of which

bore the heads of Presidents George Washington and Calvin Coolidge. The reverse depicted the original Liberty Bell. The net coinage was 141,120 pieces, struck at the Mint at Philadelphia, PA.

5376. Fifty-dollar gold pieces minted by the federal government were coined on June 15, 1915, at the mint at San Francisco, CA, for the Panama Pacific International Exposition. They were designed by Robert Aitken. About 3,000 were produced. Half were octagonal and half were round. The main design was a bust of Minerva with crested helmet.

5377. Coin bearing the likeness of a living person was the 1921 Alabama Centennial commemorative half dollar, of which 70,000 were struck at the Mint at Philadelphia, PA. The obverse showed the heads of William Wyatt Bibb, the first governor of Alabama, and Thomas Erby Kilby, governor in office at the time of the centennial. The reverse depicted an American eagle.

5378. Wooden money was issued at Tenino, WA, in February 1932. When the Citizens Bank of Tenino closed its doors on December 5, 1931, during the Depression, the town was without ready cash to do business. The Tenino Chamber of Commerce, through three trustees and the State Supervisor of Banking, devised the assignment of scrip. By this plan a depositor could assign to the Chamber a certain amount of his own proven deposit in exchange for a similar amount of scrip, which the Chamber guaranteed to redeem when the liquidation of the bank paid them the necessary funds. The first scrip was printed on lithographed sheets by the *Thurston County Independent* in December 1931. In February 1932, wooden money in denominations of 25 cents, 50 cents, and $1 was printed on three-ply sitka spruce wood. Red cedar and Port Orford cedar were used afterward.

5379. Coin bearing the likeness of an African-American was the 50-cent silver commemorative honoring Booker Taliaferro Washington, the founder of Tuskegee Institute. It was authorized on August 7, 1946. The first coin was presented to President Harry S. Truman on December 17, 1946. The obverse showed the head of Washington and the reverse a stylized Hall of Fame, under which were the words "From Slave Cabin to Hall of Fame." Centered under this wording was a slave cabin, to the left of which was the inscription "In God We Trust," and to the right, "Franklin County, Va." Around the rim was the inscription "Booker T. Washington Birthplace Memorial—Liberty." The coin was designed by Isaac Scott Hathaway.

5380. Coins bearing dates other than the year of issue were authorized by Congress on July 23, 1965. The statute provided that "any coins minted after the enactment of the Coinage Act of 1965 from .900 fine coin silver shall be inscribed with the year 1964." The first of these coins were issued on November 1, 1965, at the Mint in Philadelphia, PA.

5381. Coin bearing the likeness of an American woman was a copper- and nickel-clad dollar coin depicting Susan Brownell Anthony, founder of the National Woman Suffrage Association. The coin was authorized by act of Congress of October 10, 1978, and was issued on December 13, 1978, at the Mint in Philadelphia, PA. The coin, which was round, featured an 11-sided frame on both sides. A profile of Anthony was depicted within the frame on the obverse. The reverse showed an eagle symbolizing the Apollo 11 spacecraft (dubbed *The Eagle*) landing on the moon. The weight was 0.3 ounce, the diameter 1.04 inches. The coin was also produced at the Denver and San Francisco mints. It was placed in circulation on July 1, 1979, but was withdrawn after some years because its small size made it easy to confuse with quarters.

MONEY—PAPER

5382. Paper money was issued in the colonies. On February 3, 1690, Massachusetts established a provincial bank and issued money in denominations from two shillings to £5 to pay the soldiers who served in the war with Quebec. Other colonies and states also issued paper money without any basis, so that in 1780 the ratio of paper to silver was 40 to 1.

5383. Paper money issued by the Native Americans is believed to have been issued about 1840 or 1850 by the Arapahos in Oregon. A later specimen bears the following inscription: "Office of Discount at Arrapahos Way in the Far West. The President and Directors of the Oregon State Bank promise to pay five dollars on demand." The Cherokee Nation in Oklahoma also issued paper money. The only known specimen is a one-dollar note, on which was inscribed, in ink, the date June 18, 1862, and the number 592. It bore the legend "Lewis Ross—Cherokee Nation" and was payable "in notes of the Confederated States at Tahlequah." It also bore numerous Cherokee symbols.

5384. Confederate paper money was issued under the Confederate States Act of March 9, 1861, at Mobile, AL, authorizing $1 million in treasury notes in denominations of $50, $100, $500, and $1,000. The $50 note featured three African-American slaves in a field, two of them hoeing; the $100 note, a train of cars at a depot, at the right, and Liberty standing, at the left; the $500 note, a rural scene with cattle wading in a brook; and the $1,000 note, busts of Andrew Jackson and John Caldwell Calhoun.

5385. Paper money issued by the federal government was authorized by acts of Congress of July 17, 1861, and August 5, 1861, in the amount of $50 million. The notes were first issued on March 10, 1862. The denominations were $5 (Hamilton), $10 (Lincoln), and $20 (Liberty). They were called "demand notes" because they were payable on demand at certain designated subtreasuries. They were not legal tender when first issued but were made so by act of March 17, 1862.

5386. Legal tender was authorized by act of Congress of February 25, 1862, "an act to authorize the issue of United States notes and for the redemption or funding thereof, and for funding the floating debt of the United States." This was known as the Legal Tender Act and authorized the issuance of greenbacks up to $150 million.

5387. Bill bearing the likeness of a president was the $10 bill issued on March 10, 1862, which bore a portrait of Abraham Lincoln.

5388. Paper money fractional currency was issued from August 21, 1862, to May 27, 1863, in denominations of 5 cents, 10 cents, 25 cents, and 50 cents. The bills were originally issued with perforated edges, but later were cut plain. They were also known as "postage currency," as they depicted postage stamps. They were receivable in payment for all dues to the United States less than $5 and were exchangeable for United States notes by any assistant treasurer or designated U.S. Depository in sums not less than $5.

5389. Gold certificates were authorized by act of Congress of March 3, 1863. Gold certificates of one- and two-year notes, and of compound interest notes, and certificates under the fifth section of the act were used for clearing-house purposes soon after the passage of the national bank act. They were issued on November 13, 1865, and were authorized to be received at par in payment of duties.

MONEY—PAPER—*continued*

5390. Notes wholly engraved and printed at the Bureau of Engraving and Printing in Washington, DC, were those of the fractional currency authorized by act of Congress of March 3, 1863. Over 3 million sheets of this currency, with a monetary value of more than $13 million, had been printed by November 26, 1864.

5391. Bill bearing the likeness of a woman was the one-dollar silver certificate, series of 1886, delivered by the Bureau of Engraving and Printing to the Department of the Treasury in September 1886. It had a portrait of Martha Washington. The reverse was in green, covered with ornamental lathe work.

5392. Bill depicting a battleship was the two-dollar note issued by the Federal Reserve Bank of Boston in 1918. The reverse side showed the head of Thomas Jefferson.

5393. Paper money of the present small size was issued on July 10, 1929. At that time there was outstanding a total of $4,997 million in the older large-size currency, about 823 million pieces.

5394. Bill of $100,000 denomination was the gold certificate bearing the portrait of President Woodrow Wilson and delivered by the Bureau of Engraving and Printing in January 1935 to the Department of the Treasury. These bills were not issued for general circulation but were used within the Federal Reserve System.

5395. Bill to depict both sides of the Great Seal of the United States was the one-dollar silver certificate, series of 1935, issued on December 18, 1935. The steel plates from which the bills were printed did not carry the signature of the Secretary of the Treasury or the Treasurer. The signatures were printed in a blank space on the face of bills at the same time that the bills were numbered and sealed.

MONUMENTS

5396. Monument to Christopher Columbus was the Columbus Monument, dedicated on October 12, 1792, in Baltimore, MD, 300 years after his first journey to this continent.

5397. Monument to George Washington was the Washington monument of Baltimore, MD, the cornerstone of which was laid on July 4, 1815, with Masonic ceremony. The monument was not completed until October 19, 1829. The Baltimore monument has a shaft 180 feet high and is surmounted by a 16-foot statue of George Washington. The site was donated by

General John Eager Howard and the funds were raised by lottery. Another monument, begun later but completed earlier, was finished by Isaac C. Lutz in Boonsboro, MD, on July 4, 1827. It was a cairnlike structure, 54 feet in circumference at its base and 15 feet high. The wall of the monument was composed of huge stones, many weighing upward of a ton. A flight of steps ran to the top, which was also used as an observation tower.

5398. Bronze statue of full length was executed by Ball Hughes in 1847 and placed in the cemetery at Mount Auburn, Cambridge, MA. It represented the astronomer Nathaniel Bowditch, seated and holding a copy of his translated work, La Place's *Mécanique Céleste,* with a globe and a quadrant beside him. The statue was imperfect and was recast by Gruet Jne. Fondeur of Paris in 1886.

5399. Bronze equestrian statue was Clark Mills's statue of General Andrew Jackson, unveiled on January 8, 1853, in Lafayette Park, Washington, DC. It was cast from cannons captured by Jackson in the War of 1812.

5400. Monument to commemorate the Civil War was a plain brownstone shaft designed by Nelson Augustus Moore and dedicated in Kensington, CT, on July 25, 1863, two years before the end of the war, at a cost of $350. It was "erected to commemorate the death of those who perished in suppressing the Southern Rebellion," and eventually carried the names of 16 men.

5401. Monument ordered by the federal government from a sculptor who was a woman was a life-size model of Abraham Lincoln. An act of Congress of July 28, 1866, authorized the secretary of the interior to enter into contract with the sculptor Vinnie Ream. A contract was signed on August 30, 1866, to pay her $10,000, half upon presentation of the model in plaster and the balance upon completion of the marble statue. The statue was unveiled on January 25, 1871, in the Rotunda of the Capitol.

5402. Monument to an American poet was a full-length bronze statue of Fitz-Greene Halleck. It was the work of Wilson MacDonald and was presented to New York City by a committee of private citizens. It was unveiled in Central Park on May 15, 1877, 10 years after the death of Halleck, by President Rutherford Birchard Hayes.

5403. Obelisk to be brought to the United States was loaded in Alexandria, Egypt, on June 12, 1880, and arrived in New York City on July 20 on the U.S.S. *Dessoug* under Commander Henry Honeychurch Gorringe. A hole was cut in the starboard bow of the ship to accommodate the massive object. William Henry Vanderbilt paid the expenses of its removal. The obelisk was 90 feet high and weighed 443,000 pounds. It was built in Heliopolis, Egypt, between 1591 and 1565 B.C.E. and was removed about 22 B.C.E. to Alexandria, where it stood until it was brought to the United States as a present from the Khedive of Egypt. The cornerstone was laid with Masonic services on October 9, 1880, and the obelisk was erected on its pedestal in Central Park, New York City, on January 22, 1881. It is popularly known as "Cleopatra's Needle."

5404. Statue cast by the federal government was a bronze statue of Admiral David Glasgow Farragut. On January 28, 1875, George Maxwell Robeson, secretary of the Navy, awarded a $20,000 contract to the sculptor Vinnie Ream. It was cast at the Washington Navy Yard, Washington, DC, and the mechanical work was performed by artisans employed by the government. It was accepted on April 25, 1881, by President James Abram Garfield. The base of the monument is formed of three tiers of uncut granite, the lower tier measuring 20 feet. The figure is of heroic size, standing in an easy position with one foot resting upon a pulley block around which a cable is coiled. In the hands is a telescope. The statue is located at Farragut Square, Washington, DC.

5405. Statue presented to the United States by a foreign country was Liberty Enlightening the World, popularly called the Statue of Liberty, which stands on Liberty Island (formerly Bedloe Island) in New York Harbor, New York City. The statue, designed by the French sculptor Frédéric Auguste Bartholdi, was a gift of the people of France in commemoration of the hundredth anniversary of American independence. The right hand and torch of the statue were exhibited at the Centennial Exhibition in Philadelphia in 1876. The statue was put in place in 1885 and unveiled on October 28, 1886. It is 151 feet high and stands on a granite pedestal 155 feet high that was provided by popular subscription in the United States.

5406. Monument to a woman financed by women was dedicated on May 10, 1894, to "Mary, the Mother of Washington," over the grave of Mary Ball Washington, mother of President George Washington, in Fredericksburg, VA. The original monument had been raised in 1833 but had been neglected and had fallen into disrepair. The National Mary Washington Memorial Association, chartered on February 22, 1890, raised a fund of $11,500 to replace it. The new monument, a 40-foot monolith on bases and plinth 10 feet high, was designed and built by a Mr. Crawford. The cornerstone was laid on October 21, 1893.

5407. Statue officially sanctioned by the Pope was the figure of Our Lady of Prompt Succor, the Patroness of Louisiana, which was blessed by Archbishop Janssens in the name of Pope Leo XIII on November 10, 1895, at the Ursulines Convent, New Orleans, LA.

5408. Monument to commemorate the Spanish-American War was unveiled in Monroeville, OH, on Thursday, September 29, 1904.

5409. Statue of a woman installed in the Capitol's National Statuary Hall in Washington, DC, was the figure of Frances Elizabeth Willard, educator, editor, and temperance reformer, erected by Illinois and dedicated on February 17, 1905.

5410. National monument designated by the federal government was the Devils Tower, a massive fluted column of volcanic rock 865 feet tall in the Black Hills at Belle Fourche River, WY. The base of this gray igneous rock is 1,700 feet in diameter. President Theodore Roosevelt signed a bill on September 24, 1906, establishing 1,153 acres as a national monument.

5411. Monument to a bird was unveiled on October 1, 1913, at Salt Lake City, UT. It was designed by Mahonri Young, a grandson of Brigham Young, to commemorate the sea gulls from the Great Salt Lake that attacked a devouring horde of black crickets, or grasshoppers, that were destroying the wheat fields of the Mormon settlers in May 1848.

5412. Monument to an insect was dedicated on December 11, 1919, at Enterprise, AL. It was erected by the citizens of Enterprise, Coffee County, AL, "in profound appreciation of the Boll Weevil and what it has done as the herald of prosperity." The deadly destruction of cotton crops by the weevil had caused the farmers to diversify their crops, with the result that their income shortly jumped to triple the amount received in the best cotton years.

MONUMENTS—*continued*

5413. Statue to commemorate literary characters was the Tom Sawyer and Huck Finn statue, a bronze group by Frederick Cleveland Hibbard, donated by Mr. and Mrs. George Addison Mahan and their son, Daniel Dulany Mahan. It was erected on a base of red granite on May 27, 1926, at Hannibal, MO.

5414. Monument to the American flag was dedicated at Schenley Park, Pittsburgh, PA, on June 14, 1927, on the 150th anniversary of the adoption of the Stars and Stripes as the national banner. It was designed by Harvey A. Schwab, dedicated by William T. Kerr, founder of the American Flag Day Association, and unveiled by Florence Bent of Pittsburgh's Bellefield High School.

5415. Monument to a comic-strip character was the Popeye statue in Popeye Park, Crystal City, TX, unveiled on March 26, 1937, during the Second Annual Spinach Festival. It was six feet tall, made of concrete, and colored to represent Elzie Crisler Segar's cartoon character "Popeye."

5416. National monument dedicated to an African-American was the George Washington Carver National Monument, authorized on July 14, 1943, officially established on June 14, 1951, and dedicated on July 14, 1953. It consists of 210 acres about 2.5 miles southwest of Diamond in Newton County, MO. It is administered by the National Park Service.

5417. Monument to a Native American was carved out of a granite mountain north of Custer, SD. The world's largest sculpture, it was a 563-foot-high, 600-foot-long monument to Crazy Horse, the Lakota chief who led the victory over Custer's forces at the Little Big Horn in 1876. In 1939, sculptor Korczak Ziolkowski, an assistant on the construction of the Mount Rushmore presidential monument, was asked by Lakota chief Henry Standing Bear to "caress a mountain so that the white man will know that the red man had heroes, too." Ziolkowski started work in 1948 and removed some 7 million tons of granite. He died in 1982, leaving the monument unfinished.

MOTOR VEHICLES—BUSES

5418. Sightseeing bus was the Motor Tally-Ho, built by the Mack Motor Truck Corporation, Brooklyn, New York City, in 1900 and sold for approximately $3,000 to Isaac Harris, who used it to take visitors on tours of Brooklyn's Prospect Park. It carried 19 passengers and the driver. It ran on gasoline and had a 60-horsepower engine.

5419. Double-deck bus was imported from France and introduced on Fifth Avenue, New York City, by the Fifth Avenue Coach Company in 1906. The company began manufacturing its own double-deck buses in 1915.

5420. Bus with cross seats was introduced by the Fifth Avenue Coach Company in New York City. The company's double-deck buses were fitted with cross seats on March 17, 1914, and single-deck buses on August 27, 1915. All seats had been longitudinal before that. The single-deck buses seated 16 people; the double-deck, 44.

5421. Transcontinental bus service was offered by the Yelloway Bus Line, which began service on September 11, 1928, from Los Angeles, CA, to New York City. Three 26-passenger buses departed daily from each terminal, covering 3,433 miles in 5 days and 14 hours.

5422. Night coach was built by the Pickwick Corporation in Los Angeles, CA, and placed in service in July 1929 between Los Angeles and San Francisco, CA. The car was of metal construction, chiefly of Duralumin, and provided sleeping and seating accommodation for 26 people. The bus had two lavatories, a kitchen, and a pantry, and carried a crew of three: pilot, steward, and porter.

5423. Transcontinental express bus service was instituted on September 8, 1953, by Continental Trailways, which started its through service at 9 P.M. from the Port Authority Bus Terminal, New York City, to San Francisco, CA. The fare for the 3,154-mile trip was $56.70. The trip took 88 hours 50 minutes, of which 77 hours 19 minutes was actual riding time.

5424. Gas-turbine bus was the GM Turbocruiser, a modified coach built by the research staff of the General Motors Corporation, Detroit, MI, and publicly announced on June 10, 1954, after it had already logged more than 2,000 miles. The engine used a single burner and two turbine wheels, one to drive the centrifugal compressor, the other to drive a transmission that was connected to the rear wheels of the bus.

MOTOR VEHICLES—CARS

5425. Steam car was invented in 1866 by Henry Alonzo House. It was driven through the streets of Bridgeport, CT, and surrounding towns for several months. On October 6, 1866, House and his brother and co-inventor, James A. House, drove the car to Stratford, CT, taking a party of men to a vessel launching.

5426. Car with an electric storage battery was designed by William Morrison and built by Morrison and Schmidt, Des Moines, IA, in the summer of 1891. It was powered by 24 storage battery cells placed under the seats and could run continuously for 13 hours. The battery cells took 10 hours to charge. The car carried 12 people, had a four-horsepower motor, and was capable of a speed of 14 miles per hour. It was sold to J.B. McDonald, president of the American Battery Company of Chicago, in 1892.

5427. Foreign car exhibited was displayed at the World's Columbian Exposition in Chicago, IL, in 1893 by Karl Benz of Germany. It was built by Gottlieb Daimler of Germany and was named after his daughter, Mercedes.

5428. Car patent was filed on May 8, 1879, by George Baldwin Selden, an attorney of Rochester, NY. It was granted to him on November 5, 1895, and embodied his claims to the original application of the internal-combustion hydrocarbon motor to a road vehicle. His design resembled a horse-drawn carriage, with high wheels and a buckboard.

5429. Car produced for commercial sale was manufactured by Charles Edgar Duryea, America's pioneer automobile manufacturer. Duryea began building his first automobile in August 1891. It was completed at his shop in Springfield, MA, and was successfully operated on April 19, 1892. In 1895 he organized the Duryea Motor Wagon Company in Springfield to produce cars for sale. The first was sold in 1896.

5430. Electric taxicabs were introduced in New York City in the spring of 1897 by the Electric Vehicle Company, whose office and garage were located at 1684 Broadway, New York City.

5431. Car exported from the United States was a steam-powered tricycle built in 1886 in Lansing, MI, by Ransom Eli Olds, the founder of Oldsmobile. After adding a fourth wheel to it, he sold it in 1898 to a buyer in Bombay, India.

5432. Armored car was designed by Colonel Royal Page Davidson in May 1898. A Colt automatic machine gun was mounted on the car, which was intended for military use. The automobile was manufactured by the Duryea Automobile Company of Peoria, IL, and was used by the Northwestern Military and Naval Academy of Lake Geneva, WI.

5433. Car factory was an Oldsmobile factory, built in 1899 by Ransom Eli Olds in Detroit, MI. It manufactured 433 vehicles in 1901, 2,500 cars in 1902, and 5,508 cars in 1904.

5434. Car show was held at Madison Square Garden, New York City, on November 3–10, 1900, under the auspices of the Automobile Club of America. There were 51 exhibitors, of whom 31 showed cars, and the others showed accessories. A ramp was built to demonstrate the hill-climbing ability of the cars, and barrels were placed on the floor to demonstrate their steering. Braking contests and starting contests were held. Admission to the "horseless horse show" was 50 cents.

5435. Shaft-driven car was constructed in 1901 by the Autocar Company of Ardmore, PA. It was driven in 6 hours 15 minutes from Ardmore to Madison Square Garden, New York City, where it was exhibited in the New York Automobile Show of December 1901. The first 800 cars were equipped with steering levers, but the later ones were equipped with steering wheels.

5436. Car to exceed the speed of a mile a minute was driven on November 16, 1901, by A.C. Bostwick on a straightaway course at Ocean Parkway, Brooklyn, New York City, in a race sponsored by the Long Island Automobile Club. He covered the distance in 56.4 seconds.

5437. Car with a circulating lubrication system was the Autocar model of 1904, manufactured at Ardmore, PA.

5438. Car with the steering wheel on the left side was the Northern four-cylinder car of 1907, manufactured by the Northern Motor Car Company of Detroit, MI. The automobile was also equipped with air brakes. The designer of these improvements was Charles Brady King, one of America's pioneer automobile inventors.

5439. Brake for four-wheeled cars was invented by Otto Zachow and William Besserdich of Clintonville, WI, who obtained a patent on December 29, 1908, on a "power applying mechanism."

5440. Year in which more than 100,000 passenger cars were produced was 1909, when 123,990 cars were manufactured. More than 1 million cars (1,525,578) were manufactured in 1916; more than 5 million cars (5,119,466) in 1949; more than 7 million cars (7,920,186) in 1955.

5441. Electric-gasoline combination car was placed in service about 1910. It was equipped with the Owen magnetic drive and a generator in a combined unit.

MOTOR VEHICLES—CARS—*continued*

5442. Electric self-starter used in cars was offered to the public in May 1911 by the Cadillac Motor Car Company of Detroit, MI. It was patented by Charles Franklin Kettering. The electric self-starter had been invented by Clyde Jay Coleman of New York City in 1899, but his invention was impractical.

5443. Sedan car was the 1913 Hudson Sedan, manufactured by the Hudson Motor Car Company, Detroit, MI. It was officially shown on January 11, 1913, at the 13th National Automobile Show, New York City. It carried all accessories as standard equipment.

5444. Armored car in commercial use was employed by Brink's Incorporated, Chicago, IL, in 1918. It had one thickness of armor-plate steel, but was not of all-steel construction throughout. The first armored car that was completely protected was put in service on February 1, 1920, by Michael Francis Sweeney of the Sweeney Detective Bureau, St. Paul, MN. Construction was started in March 1919 by the Boyd Auto Shops, Minneapolis, MN. The side walls and roof were steel, with welded-steel construction; no wooden walls or roof supports were used. The glass was "polished plate wired glass." The windshield and windows could be covered by hinged steel plates that fell into place when a catch was tripped.

5445. Car to exceed the speed of 200 miles per hour was a 1,000-horsepower *Mystery Sunbeam* driven by Major Henry O'Neil de Hane Segrave on March 29, 1927, at Daytona Beach, FL, at an average speed of 203.79 miles per hour both ways.

5446. Automatic parking meter was the Park-O-Meter, devised by Carlton Cole Magee, which was installed in Oklahoma City, OK, on July 16, 1935, by the Dual Parking Meter Company of Oklahoma City. Twenty-foot spaces were painted on the pavement and a parking meter that accepted nickels was installed at the head of each space. The city paid for the meters with funds collected from them.

5447. Car-airplane combination was the Arrowbile, built by the Waterman Arrowplane Corporation, Santa Monica, CA, and completed for testing on February 20, 1937. Delivery of five Arrowbiles was made on August 15, 1937, to the Studebaker Corporation, South Bend, IN. In the air, the Arrowbile's top speed was 120 miles per hour and its cruising speed was 105 miles per hour. It had a 6-cylinder, 100-horsepower Studebaker engine.

5448. Miniature car was offered for sale on April 28, 1939, by the Crosley Corporation of Cincinnati, OH. It had an 80-inch wheelbase and was 10 feet long from bumper to bumper. It had two cylinders, three forward speeds and a reverse, four-wheel mechanical brakes, a four-gallon capacity tank, and safety glass. The two-passenger convertible coupe and the four-passenger convertible sedan sold for $325 and $350. On June 19, 1939, the Crosley cars were put on sale in R.H. Macy's basement in New York City.

5449. Air-conditioned car was manufactured by the Packard Motor Car Company, Detroit, MI, and publicly exhibited on November 4–12, 1939, at the 40th Automobile Show, Chicago, IL. Air in the car was cooled to the temperature desired, dehumidified, filtered, and circulated. The refrigerating coils were located behind the rear seat in an air duct, with heating coils in another compartment of the same duct. The capacity of the unit was equivalent to 1.5 tons of ice in 24 hours when the car was driven at 60 miles per hour, or 2 tons at 80 miles per hour.

5450. Car with an automatic transmission was the Oldsmobile model of 1940, for which the Hydramatic automatic transmission, made by General Motors of Detroit, MI, was available as an option. An infinitely variable transmission, an earlier version of automatic transmission, had been offered on a few Austin cars between 1934 and 1936.

5451. Plastic car was manufactured by the Ford Motor Company, Dearborn, MI, in August 1941. Fourteen plastic panels were mounted on a tubular welded frame. Windows and windshield were of acrylic sheets, which resulted in an approximately 30 percent decrease in weight. On January 13, 1942, a patent was obtained by Henry Ford on the automoile body construction, an auto body chassis frame made from steel tubes or pipes designed for use with automobiles made from plastics.

5452. Subcompact car designed to be fuel-efficient was the Volkswagen Beetle, imported from Germany beginning in 1949. The Beetle, famous for its unglamorous look and its rear-mounted, air-cooled engine, had been designed by Ferdinand Porsche in 1935.

5453. Year in which more than 1 million passenger cars of one make were produced was 1949, when 1,109,958 Chevrolets were manufactured by the General Motors Corporation, Detroit, MI.

5454. Mail delivery car with the steering wheel on the right was a Crosley, placed in service in Cincinnati, OH, on December 27, 1951. It is possible that prior to this date some mail delivery had been made using old automobiles manufactured with right-side drives.

5455. Sports car with a plastic laminated fiberglass body was the Chevrolet Corvette, produced on June 30, 1953, at Flint, MI, by the Chevrolet Motor Division of the General Motors Corporation. The list price was $3,250, including a 1953 powerglide automatic transmission as standard equipment. The car was only 33 inches at the door (body height), 70 inches wide, and 167 inches long on a 102-inch wheelbase. Its curb weight was approximately 2,900 pounds.

5456. Gas-turbine car was the XP-21 Firebird, built by the General Motors Corporation and tested by Mauri Rose in October 1953 at the GM Proving Ground, near Milford, MI. Its first public appearance took place on January 21–26, 1954, at the GM Motorama, Waldorf-Astoria Hotel, New York City. A 370-horsepower Whirlfire turbojet was installed in the rear of the car. The total weight of the engine unit, including the gasifier and the power sections, was 775 pounds, the overall weight of the entire car being 2,500 pounds. It had a plastic body and accommodated only the driver. Its speed was 150 miles per hour, but it was believed capable of 235 miles per hour. Since it consumed fuel faster than conventional cars, it was not commercially produced.

5457. Solar-powered car was a 15-inch sunmobile built by William G. Cobb of the General Motors Corporation and publicly demonstrated on August 31, 1955, at the General Motors Powerama, Chicago, IL. It had 12 photoelectric cells made of selenium which converted light into electric current. The current powered a tiny electric motor with a driveshaft connected to the rear axle by a pulley.

5458. Free-piston car was the XP-500, an advanced-design experimental model built by the research staff of the General Motors Corporation, Detroit, MI. The first public display took place on May 16, 1956, at the dedication of the GM Technical Center. The engine had two horizontal cylinders, each containing two opposed pistons. These cylinders and pistons served to produce hot gases which turned a turbine wheel geared to the rear wheels of the car. The engine generated 250 horsepower.

5459. Car with front-wheel drive to be mass-produced as a full-size vehicle by a domestic manufacturer was the 1966 Oldsmobile Toronado, built by General Motors, Detroit, MI. The enormous front end, including V-8 engine, power train, drive train, and automatic transmission, weighed about 2,750 pounds. The two-door Toronado was also the first car with a single large window pane on each side, instead of a split window with a quarter vent in the front.

5460. Diesel cars to be mass-produced were the Oldsmobile 88 and 98 diesel-engine models introduced by General Motors, Detroit, MI, on September 13, 1977.

5461. Rocket-powered car to break the sound barrier on land was the *Budweiser Rocket*, a three-wheeled, rocket-powered vehicle driven by stunt rider Stan Barrett. On December 16, 1979, Barrett clocked an unofficial speed of 739.666 mph, or Mach 1.01, on the dry lake bed at Edwards Air Force Base, Muroc, CA. The car, which cost about $800,000, was powered by a 48,000-horsepower rocket engine boosted by a 12,000-horsepower Sidewinder missile. It was brought to a stop by drag parachutes.

5462. Subcompact car with front wheel drive was the World Car, built by the Ford Motor Company's plant in Fort Wayne, MI. The first car off the assembly line was driven on August 11, 1980, by John Barson, president of the United Auto Workers Local 900.

5463. Car fueled by methanol was the Chevrolet Lumina Variable Fuel Vehicle, introduced by General Motors, Detroit, MI, in June 1992. The car could be powered by unleaded gas, by methanol (a fuel derived from plant fermentation that is similar to alcohol), or by any combination of the two. The first production model was delivered to Governor Tommy G. Thompson of Wisconsin.

5464. Electric car to be mass-produced using modern technology was the Electric Vehicle One, or EV1, marketed by General Motors, Detroit, MI, beginning on December 4, 1996. The first models were leased to customers in Los Angeles, CA, at a price tag of $34,000. The two-seater coupe was powered by a 137-horsepower, three-phase induction motor that ran on stored energy in a lead-acid battery pack. The EV1 could travel 70 to 90 miles between chargings, which took 3 to 12 hours.

MOTOR VEHICLES—CARS—DRIVERS

5465. Automobile club was the American Motor League, which held its preliminary meeting on November 1, 1895, in Chicago, IL, with 60 members. The first slate of officers included Charles Edgar Duryea, the car manufacturer, and Hiram Percy Maxim, car designer and inventor, as two of the four vice presidents, and the inventor Charles Brady King as treasurer.

5466. Car accident occurred in New York City on May 30, 1896, when Henry Wells of Springfield, MA, driving a Duryea Motor Wagon, collided with Evylyn Thomas, a bicycle rider, who was taken to the Manhattan Hospital with a fractured leg. Wells spent the night in jail.

5467. Car driver who was a woman was Genevra Delphine Mudge, who drove a Waverly Electric in 1898 in New York City. On December 31, 1899, she participated in an automobile race in New York City, driving a Locomobile that skidded on the snow and knocked five spectators down.

5468. Driver arrested for speeding was Jacob German, operator of a taxicab for the Electric Vehicle Company, who was arrested on May 20, 1899, by Bicycle Roundsman Schuessler for driving at a "breakneck speed" of 12 miles per hour on Lexington Avenue, New York City. German was booked and jailed in the East 22nd Street station house.

5469. Driver license board was the Board of Examiners of Operators of Automobiles, authorized on July 6, 1899, by the city of Chicago, IL, to ascertain the qualifications of persons seeking licenses. It included the city electrician, the city engineer, and the commissioner of health.

5470. Car accident fatality was Henry H. Bliss, a real estate broker, 68 years old, who was knocked down and run over as he was alighting from a southbound streetcar at Central Park West and 74th Street, New York City, on September 13, 1899. He was taken to Roosevelt Hospital, where he died. Arthur Smith, the driver, was arrested and held on $1,000 bail.

MOTOR VEHICLES—CARS—JOURNEYS

5471. Transcontinental car trip by a nonprofessional driver in his own car was made by Dr. Horatio Nelson Jackson of Burlington, VT, a physician, with Sewell K. Crocker of Seattle, WA, as his mechanic. The car was a 20-horsepower $2,500 Winton, manufactured by the Winton Motor Carriage Company of Cleveland, OH. Jackson and Crocker left San Francisco, CA, on May 23, 1903, and arrived in New York City on July 26. The average daily run was 125 miles. The trip lasted 63 days, of which 44 were spent traveling and 19 awaiting supplies.

5472. Transcontinental car trip by women was made by Alice Huyler Ramsey of Hackensack, NJ, and Nettie R. Powell, Margaret Atwood, and Hermine Jahns, who left New York City on June 9, 1909, in a 30-horsepower Maxwell-Briscoe open car and arrived at San Francisco, CA, on August 6. Mrs. Ramsey was president of the Women's Motoring Club of New York.

5473. Transcontinental group tour by car was begun on June 26, 1911, when 10 Premier automobiles with 40 occupants, accompanied by a pilot car and a truck, left Atlantic City, NJ, on an "ocean to ocean" tour. They arrived at Los Angeles, CA, on August 10 and concluded the trip on August 13 at Venice, CA, having covered 4,617.6 miles.

5474. Car trip made with a diesel engine was made by Clessie Lyle Cummins of the Cummins Engine Company, Columbus, IN, with a stock model engine weighing 1,200 pounds, delivering 50 horsepower at 1,000 revolutions per minute with four cylinders of 4.5-by-6-inch bore, installed in a seven-passenger Packard sedan. He left Indianapolis, IN, on January 3, 1930, and arrived in New York City on January 6, covering 792 miles at a total fuel cost of $1.38.

5475. Transcontinental car trip driven entirely in reverse was achieved by Charles Creighton and James Hargis, both of Maplewood, NJ. Between July 23 and August 13, 1930, they backed up a 1929 Ford Model A roadster from New York City to Los Angeles, CA, a distance of 3,340 miles, without once stopping the engine.

5476. Transcontinental trip in a gas-turbine car took place in 1956. The Turbine Special, a 1956 stock four-door Plymouth sedan, left New York City on March 26, 1956, and arrived in Los Angeles, CA, on March 30, covering 3,020 miles in 95 hours 15 minutes, including 74 hours 19 minutes of driving time. It was driven by two-man teams of turbine research engineers under the direction of George John Huebner, Jr., executive engineer in charge of research for the Chrysler Corporation.

MOTOR VEHICLES—ENGINES

5477. Internal-combustion engine was invented by Captain Samuel Morey of Orford, NH, who received a patent on April 1, 1826, "on a gas or vapor engine." His engine had two cylinders, 180-degree cranks, poppet valves, a carburetor, an electric spark, and a water cooling device. He employed the vapor of spirits of turpentine and common air. A small tin dish contained the spirits, and the only heat he used was from a common table lamp. A rotary movement was obtained by means of a crank and flywheel, as in a steam engine.

5478. Gas engine was invented by Stuart Perry of New York City, who received a patent for it on May 25, 1844. He invented both air- and water-cooled types and used turpentine gases as fuel.

5479. Diesel engine built for commercial service was a two-cylinder 60-horsepower unit built in September 1898 in the plant of the St. Louis Iron and Marine Works, St. Louis, MO. The engine, which drove a direct-current generator, was erected and operated in the Second Street plant of the Anheuser Busch brewery and was the first diesel engine in the world to be placed in commercial service. Adolphus Busch bought Dr. Rudolf Diesel's American patent rights in 1897 for a sum of approximately $250,000. The next engines were built for the Diesel Motor Company of America, which was formed by Busch. These engines were built in the plant of the Hewes and Philips Iron Works, Newark, NJ, circa 1900, and were of one size. They had 11-by-20-inch cylinders that were designed to develop 20 horsepower when running at 200 revolutions per minute.

5480. Electric motor using single-phase alternating current of variable speed was first used in 1901 in interurban service. In 1907 the first steam railroad adopted it.

5481. Electric motor using interpole direct current was invented by Mathias Pfatischer of Philadelphia, PA, who obtained a patent on November 22, 1904, on a "variable speed motor."

5482. Diesel engine speed record that was official was made on March 20, 1930, by Clessie Lyle Cummins of the Cummins Engine Company, Columbus, IN, in a Packard roadster chassis equipped with a four-cylinder marine-type diesel engine with a bore and stroke of 4.5 by 6 inches and piston displacement of 381.5 cubic inches. The car was stripped of fenders, windshield, and spare tires and fitted with a fabric cover over the driver's compartment. Cummins averaged 80.398 miles per hour in the test at Daytona Beach, FL.

MOTOR VEHICLES—GARAGES

5483. Public garage was established in Boston, MA, on May 24, 1899, by W.T. McCullough as the Back Bay Cycle and Motor Company. He advertised its opening as a "stable for renting, sale, storage and repair of motor vehicles."

5484. City parking garage was designed by Hassel T. Hicks and opened on September 1, 1941, in Welch, WV. It accommodated 232 cars and showed a profit the first year.

5485. Parking garage that was completely automated was the Park-O-Mat Garage, opened on December 5, 1951, in Washington, DC, by the Parking Services company. A car could be parked or returned in 50 seconds. The garage was an open building with 16 floors and 2 basement levels. Two elevators parked 72 cars on a lot 25 by 40 feet. There were no ramps, no aisles, no lanes, and only one attendant, who used push-button controls and did not enter the cars. The "vehicle parking apparatus" was patented on October 14, 1947, by Richard L. Sinclair of Los Angeles, CA.

5486. Hydraulic-lift parking garage device was the Sky-Park, manufactured by Simmons Industries, Albany, NY. The first unit was installed in October 1954 in Washington, DC. A rigid central column with two hydraulically powered platforms operated by push-button controls raised automobiles, singly or doubly, thus providing double the parking space.

MOTOR VEHICLES—MOTORCYCLES

5487. Steam-driven motorcycle was a two-wheeled vehicle invented by William A. Austin of Winthrop, MA, in 1868. The steam boiler was suspended amidships. The vehicle had a very limited traveling radius because of the small amount of steam generated.

5488. Motorcycle that was practical was manufactured by the E.R. Thomas Motor Company of Buffalo, NY, in 1900. A single-cylinder gasoline engine was attached to the transverse bar of an ordinary bicycle and a flat belt ran to a concentric pulley on the rear wheel.

5489. Motorcycle with a built-in gasoline engine was manufactured in Springfield, MA, by George M. Hendee, who formed the Hendee Manufacturing Company, which began to market the Indian motorcycle in 1901. Previously, motorcycles had been ordinary bicycles to which motors were attached. Three motorcycles were built in 1901. The following year, production was increased to 143. The motors were

MOTOR VEHICLES—MOTORCYCLES—
continued
made by the Aurora Machine Company, Aurora, IL, and were mounted to the motorcycle frames in Springfield. The machines were first publicly demonstrated on June 1, 1901, in a hill-climbing exhibition.

5490. Twin-cycle motorcycle was an Indian, made in 1905 in Springfield, MA, by the Hendee Manufacturing Company. It had a spring-front fork, battery ignition, and a gravity-feed oiling system. The machine was started by pedaling. The gas tank was mounted on the rear fender.

5491. Motorcycle to exceed 200 miles per hour was ridden by Wilhelm Herz, who rode a measured mile over the salt flats at Wendover, UT, on August 4, 1956, at a speed of 210 miles per hour.

MOTOR VEHICLES—MOTORCYCLES—
JOURNEYS

5492. Transcontinental motorcycle trip was made by George A. Wyman of San Francisco, CA, on a Yale-California motorcycle built by L.W. Leavitt and Company, San Francisco. Wyman left San Francisco on May 16, 1903, and arrived in New York City on July 6. The motorcycle was a 3.5-horsepower single-cylinder machine with a belt drive.

5493. Transcontinental motorcycle trip by women was made by Adelina and Augusta Van Buren, who left New York City on July 5, 1916, and arrived in San Diego, CA, on September 12, traveling through Buffalo, Chicago, Omaha, Denver, and Salt Lake City.

5494. Motorcycle trip from the United States to Tierra del Fuego by a woman was made by Catharine Rambeau, a 54-year-old grandmother from Michigan. On December 11, 1988, she began a 373-day motorcycle journey from Lantana, FL, to the town of Ushuaia in Argentina, at the southern tip of South America, a trip of of 14,312 miles.

MOTOR VEHICLES—TIRES

5495. Pneumatic tires were made in 1895 by the Hartford Rubber Works, Hartford, CT, owned by the Pope Manufacturing Company. They were used in March 1895 on the Duryea automobile that later won the first car race in the United States, the *Times-Herald* race in Chicago on Thanksgiving Day, 1895.

5496. Clincher tire was manufactured in 1899 by the B.F. Goodrich Company of Akron, OH, in sizes ranging from 28 by 2.5 inches to 36 by 3 inches. The tire was of 19-ply construction.

5497. Tire chains were invented by Harry D. Weed of Canastota, NY, who obtained a patent on August 23, 1904, on a "griptread for pneumatic tires." Weed licensed manufacture to the Weed Chain Tire Grip Company, which later was acquired by the American Chain and Cable Company.

5498. Cord tires for commercial use were manufactured in 1910 by the B.F. Goodrich Company of Akron, OH.

5499. Demountable tire-carrying rim was invented by Louis Henry Perlman of New York City, who applied for a patent on May 21, 1906, and received it on February 4, 1913.

5500. Nonskid tires of the modern type were patented by Stacy G. Carkhuff of the Firestone Tire and Rubber Company, Akron, OH. The patent was applied for on September 4, 1908, and granted on April 14, 1914. The angle formation of the edges of the raised portions molded on the tire provided against skidding in all directions.

5501. Balloon tire production on a regular basis was introduced on April 5, 1923, by the Firestone Tire and Rubber Company of Akron, OH. On several previous occasions, large-section, thin-walled tires with small bead diameters were used experimentally or for special purposes, but no commercial use was made of them.

5502. Synthetic rubber tires were commercially marketed by the B.F. Goodrich Company, Akron, OH. On June 5, 1940, the company exhibited passenger car tires made of butadiene, synthesized from soap, gas, petroleum, and air. These tires were trademarked Ameripol.

5503. Tubeless car tires were manufactured by the B.F. Goodrich Company, Akron, OH, which announced the manufacture on May 11, 1947. The tires automatically sealed themselves when punctured. They were marketed in Indiana, Kentucky, Ohio, and West Virginia before being offered for national distribution.

MOTOR VEHICLES—TRUCKS

5504. Truck was designed and built in Pittsburgh, PA, in 1898-99 by Louis Semple Clarke and his associates. They were organized as the Pittsburgh Motor Vehicle Company and later incorporated as the Autocar Company. The first truck was pictured and described in Autocar's 1899 catalog as "a delivery wagon which can be made of any size or design, that will be fitted with five to eight horsepower motors. Complete with motors it will weigh from 900 to 1400 pounds—so simple in construction that any driver of ordinary intelligence can operate it with more safety than he could drive a horse."

5505. Mobile home was designed in 1929 by aviation pioneer Glenn Hammond Curtiss. The streamlined, wheeled trailer was built by the Hudson Motor Car Company, Detroit, MI, and was put on display in dealer showrooms in New York City.

5506. Truck completely streamlined from the ground up was introduced by the White Motor Company, Cleveland, OH, on September 4, 1935.

5507. Refrigeration system for trucks was patented in 1949 by Fred Jones, an African-American inventor. His roof-mounted cooling device enabled trucks to carry perishable goods over long distances.

5508. Motor vehicles powered by natural gas were light utility trucks purchased by the Southern California Gas Company beginning on September 2, 1992. Fifty of the trucks, which were powered by liquid natural gas, were put into service by the company under a California law promoting the commercialization of vehicles using alternative fuels.

MOVIES

5509. Movie exhibition was held on May 9, 1893, before 400 people at the Department of Physics, Brooklyn Institute, Brooklyn, NY (now part of New York City). Thomas Alva Edison's Kinetograph was used. An optical lantern projector showed moving images of a blacksmith and his two helpers passing a bottle and forging a piece of iron. Each filmstrip had 700 images, each of which appeared for about 0.01 seconds. The equipment that was to have provided sound accompaniment failed to operate at this showing.

5510. Movie recorded on film to be shown on a screen was exhibited by Woodville Latham, who demonstrated his Pantoptikon at 35 Frankfort Street, New York City, on April 21, 1895. A continuous roll of film, with hole perforations on the sides for spokes of the sprocket, was reeled in front of an electric light contained in a projector of the magic lantern type. On May 5, 1895, Latham filmed a staged bout of four minutes' duration between Young Griffo and Battling Charles Barnett on the roof of Madison Square Garden, New York City. The film was exhibited on May 20 at 153 Broadway, New York City, after which it was shown in a tent on Surf Avenue on Coney Island for the rest of the summer.

5511. Movie exhibition in a theater to a paying audience was held on April 23, 1896, in Koster and Bial's Music Hall, 34th Street, New York City. Thomas Alva Edison's Vitascope depicted a series of short scenes, including a ballet scene, a burlesque boxing match, surf breaking on the shore, and a comic allegory entitled *The Monroe Doctrine*. The images were about half life size and were shown in conjunction with other acts. The audience called for Edison, but he did not appear and refused to take a bow.

5512. Foreign feature film exhibited was *Queen Elizabeth,* shown to an invited audience on July 12, 1912, at the Lyceum Theatre, New York City, and commercially exhibited on August 12, 1912, at the Powers Theater, Chicago, IL. It was a four-reel feature made in France that starred Sarah Bernhardt as Queen Elizabeth and Lou Tellegen as Robert Devereux, Earl of Essex. It was released by Famous Players Film Company, of which Adolph Zukor was president and Daniel Frohman managing director.

5513. Movie to gross $50 million was *The Clansman, or The Birth of a Nation,* 12 reels, produced by D.W. Griffith and starring Henry Walthall and Lillian Gish, with a cast of 18,000 people and 3,000 horses. It was based on *The Clansman* by Thomas Dixon and premiered on February 8, 1915, at Clune's Auditorium, Los Angeles, CA. Two performances were presented daily. There was a matinee at 2:30 P.M., admission 25 cents and 50 cents, and an evening show at 8 P.M., admission 25 cents, 50 cents, and 75 cents.

5514. Movie entertainment shown on an airplane was a newsreel and two cartoon comedies. They were shown on October 8, 1929, by the Transcontinental Air Transport company in a Ford transport plane 5,000 feet in the air. The projector was installed by J. Frankenberg, its originator. It weighed about eight pounds; the entire apparatus together with batteries weighed less than 34 pounds. It utilized a delicate filament lamp, specially designed to operate on low voltage, which was unaffected by the vibration of the engines. Regular in-flight movie service began on July 19, 1961, on a Trans World Airlines flight between New York City and Los Angeles. The movie was *By Love Possessed.*

MOVIES—*continued*

5515. Movie to earn $1 billion was Walt Disney's animated film *Snow White and the Seven Dwarfs,* first exhibited on December 21, 1937, in Los Angeles, CA. In its nine theatrical releases it earned approximately $1 billion in 1994 U.S. dollars. The home video version of *Snow White* was officially released on October 28, 1994, after receiving about 27 million retail orders, making it the top-selling video up to that time.

5516. Movie to be shown on a television screen was Alexander Korda's *The Return of the Scarlet Pimpernel,* a 1.5-hour film shown by NBC on May 31, 1938. The image was 7 by 10 inches. Preceding the film, five actors produced a 20-minute play for children entitled *Sauce for the Gander.*

5517. Movie premiere festivities to be shown on television were presented on December 19, 1939, on station W2XBS of the National Broadcasting Company on the occasion of the New York opening of *Gone With the Wind.* Two cameras, one on the sidewalk outside the Capitol Theatre, New York City, and the other in the lobby, recorded interviews with celebrities. Ben Grauer was the master of ceremonies. The film, based on Margaret Mitchell's novel, was produced by David Oliver Selznick and starred Clark Gable and Vivien Leigh.

5518. Movie to premiere on television was a two-reel short, *Patrolling the Ether,* that was televised on April 10, 1944, simultaneously by WNBT of New York City, WRGB of Schenectady, NY, and WPTZ of Philadelphia. The film depicted the wartime activities of the radio intelligence division of the Federal Communications Commission in tracing illegal and espionage radio transmitters. It was produced by Metro-Goldwyn-Mayer and released to theaters on April 22, 1944, 12 days after its premiere on television. The first full-length American film to receive its premiere on television was *The Constant Husband,* directed by Sir Alexander Korda and starring Rex Harrison and Margaret Leighton, which was shown coast-to-coast by the National Broadcasting Company from WNBT-TV, New York City, on November 6, 1955.

5519. Movie to be shown simultaneously on pay television and in movie theaters was Paramount's *Forever Female,* directed by Pat Duggan and starring William Holden, Ginger Rogers, and Paul Douglas. It was transmitted on November 28, 1953, to 70 Telemeter receiving sets in Palm Springs, CA. At the same time, it was shown at the Plaza Theatre in Palm Springs. The telecast fee, $1.35, was placed in a coinbox attached to each set.

5520. Movie premiered simultaneously in major cities throughout the world was *On the Beach,* an adaptation of the novel by Nevil Shute, which had its premiere on December 17, 1959, at New York City's Astor Theatre and in 17 other cities. The 134-minute film was produced by Stanley Kramer and written by John Paxton. It starred Gregory Peck, Ava Gardner, Fred Astaire, and Anthony Perkins.

5521. Movie broadcast on the Internet was *Wax: Or the Discovery of Television Among the Bees,* a cult science-fiction film by director David Blair. Blair uploaded the film in digital video format on May 22, 1993, for viewing worldwide.

5522. Movie that cost more than $100 million to make was *True Lies,* a 20th Century–Fox action-adventure film directed by James Cameron and starring Arnold Schwarzenegger. It opened nationwide on July 15, 1994. Though exact figures were not released by the studio, the film was estimated to have cost $115 million.

5523. Movie to earn more than $400 million in the United States market was *Star Wars,* a 1977 science-fiction film directed by George Lucas for 20th Century–Fox. It reached the $400 million mark after it was re-released in February 1997 in a 20th-anniversary edition with enhanced special effects.

MOVIES—ACTORS

5524. Actor to have an exclusive movie contract for a single appearance in a movie was the prizefighter James John Corbett, engaged by the Kinetoscope Exhibition Company to appear in a six-round fight, one minute each round, with Pete Courtney of Trenton, NJ, in August 1894.

5525. Movie star was Max Aronson, known as Bronco Billy, Max Anderson, and Gilbert M. Anderson. His first film appearance was in 1903 in *The Great Train Robbery,* in which he played the roles of the bandit, the brakeman, and the passenger who was shot. His first starring role was in *The Messenger Boy's Mistake,* for which he was paid 50 cents an hour.

5526. Movie star who was a woman was Florence Lawrence, whose first performance in films was in 1907 for the Edison company. She then worked for the Vitagraph Company. In 1909 she went to the Biograph Company and was featured as "The Biograph Girl." Later she became known as "The IMP Girl," working for the Independent Moving Picture Company.

5527. Movie star who was a weapons inventor was Hedy Lamarr, born Hedwig Eva Maria Kiesler in Vienna about 1914. While under contract with the MGM studio in Hollywood, CA, she developed the concept of "frequency hopping" as a means of controlling torpedoes by radio. The method was highly resistant to jamming and eavesdropping because it utilized quick and unpredictable changes in the frequency of the controlling radio transmission. Co-inventor George Antheil, an avant-garde composer born in New Jersey, came up with the idea of using punched paper rolls like those in player pianos to synchronize the frequency changes between transmitter and receiver. They received a patent for the system on August 11, 1942. Although it was not used during World War II, the technique of frequency hopping later became a standard feature of military wireless remote-control systems.

MOVIES—ANIMATIONS

5528. Animated picture machine was the Zoetrope, the Wheel of Life, patented on April 23, 1867, by William E. Lincoln of Providence, RI, who assigned it to Milton Bradley and Company, Springfield, MA. It consisted of a horizontal wheel with a series of animated drawings showing successive steps at right angles to the circumference. The drawings were viewed through a slit and, when the wheel revolved, appeared to show animation.

5529. Animated photograph projection before a theater audience was shown on February 5, 1870, at the Academy of Music, Philadelphia, PA, at the Ninth Annual Entertainment of the Young Men's Society of St. Mark's Evangelical Lutheran Church of Philadelphia, by Henry Renno Heyl. Heyl used his Phasmatrope, a converted projecting lantern in front of which was a revolving disc containing 16 openings near the edge on which photographic plates were placed. The first plate showed dancers who appeared to move as the revolving wheel showed successive motions. The pictures were continuous and did not change.

5530. Flicker animation was patented by Henry Van Hoevenbergh of Elizabeth, NJ, who obtained a patent on May 16, 1882, on an "optical toy." The flicker was a series of successive drawings bound together in book form that, when riffled front-to-back, appeared to show animation. On June 20, 1882, Van Hoevenbergh obtained a patent on an improvement combining two or more series of superposed leaves. Alternate leaves were indented and cut.

5531. Animated cartoon was James Stuart Blackton's *Humorous Phases of Funny Faces,* containing about 8,000 drawings showing a man rolling his eyes and blowing smoke at a girl, a dog jumping over a hoop, and similar scenes. The final scene was a chalk-type drawing that the artist started as a sketch of one object, but that ended as a sketch of another. The film was released by Vitagraph in 1906.

5532. Animated cartoon made with cel animation using clear sheets of celluloid or acetate was *The Artist's Dream,* also known as *The Dachshund,* released on June 12, 1913, by Pathé Frères. It was produced by John Randolph Bray of New York City, who received a patent for the technique on August 11, 1914. The cartoon showed Bray drawing a dachshund that ate sausages until he exploded.

5533. Animated cartoon in color was *The Debut of Thomas Kat,* the story of a kitten taught by his mother to catch mice who confidently and tragically tackled a rat. The cartoon was produced by the Bray Pictures Corporation, New York City, and was released in 1916 by Paramount. The drawings were made on transparent celluloid, with the colors painted on the reverse side, and were photographed with a regular color camera. The Brewster color process was used.

5534. Animation for technical purposes was produced in 1916 by the Bray Pictures Corporation of New York City. Animated sequences permitted the visualization of "unseeable" phenomena such as the flow of invisible gases and radio waves.

5535. Animated cartoon with sound was Walt Disney's *Steamboat Willie,* produced in Hollywood, CA, depicting the antics of Mickey Mouse. It was shown on September 19, 1928, at the Colony Theatre, New York City.

5536. Animated feature-length cartoon in Technicolor was Walt Disney's *Snow White and the Seven Dwarfs,* based on the fairy tale. It was first exhibited on December 21, 1937, at the Carthay Circle Theatre, Los Angeles, CA. The running time was 75 minutes.

MOVIES—ANIMATIONS—*continued*

5537. Animated three-dimensional cartoon in Technicolor was Walt Disney's *Melody,* distributed by RKO Radio Pictures. Its world premiere took place on May 28, 1953, at the Hollywood Theatre and the Downtown Paramount Theatre, Los Angeles, CA.

5538. Animated film inducted into the National Film Registry was "What's Opera, Doc?," an animated short directed by Chuck Jones in 1957 for the Warner Brothers animation studio. It featured a Siegfried-like Elmer Fudd invoking the elements against Bugs Bunny in a parody of Wagnerian opera. On December 4, 1992, the short was inducted into the National Film Registry in Washington, DC, for being "among the most culturally, historically or aesthetically significant films of our time," an honor bestowed on only 100 films up to that time.

5539. Movie that was entirely computer-animated was *Toy Story,* 81 minutes long, released on November 21, 1995, by Walt Disney Pictures, Burbank, CA. It was produced at Pixar Corporation and directed by former Disney animator John Lasseter. The plot involves the adventures of two dolls, a cowboy and a space hero, who are rivals for the attention of a young boy. *Toy Story* was one of the year's top-grossing films, earning close to $300 million worldwide in its first 12 months of release.

MOVIES—CENSORSHIP

5540. Movie censorship board at the national level was the National Board of Censorship of Motion Pictures, organized in March 1909 by the People's Institute of New York City, which had been founded on May 15, 1897. Producing companies agreed to prorate a review charge among their member companies based on a fee of $3.50 for each negative reel of 1,000 feet. The fund was applied to the office expenses of the board. In 1916 the name was changed to the National Board of Review of Motion Pictures.

5541. Movie censorship board established by a state was the State Board of Censors, created in Pennsylvania by act of June 19, 1911. No appropriation was made until April 4, 1913, when $7,500 was provided. Censors were appointed on February 1, 1914. Ohio approved an act on May 3, 1913, providing for a three-member censorship board. Kansas approved an act on March 13, 1913, but no provisions to enforce it were made until 1915. The Supreme Court in February 1915 held the Ohio and Kansas censorship laws unconstitutional.

5542. Movie censorship law enacted by Congress was the act of July 31, 1912, "to prohibit the importation and the interstate transportation of films or other pictorial representations of prize fights." The penalty for violation was not more than $1,000, or one year at hard labor, or both.

MOVIES—PRODUCTIONS

5543. Movie studio was a frame cabin covered with black roofing paper, built on Thomas Alva Edison's property in West Orange, NJ, in 1892. The structure was built so that it could be pivoted to enable the stage to secure the maximum sunlight. It was called a "revolving photographic building" and was completed on February 1, 1893, at a cost of $638. It was nicknamed Black Maria.

5544. Movie to be copyrighted consisted of 47 successive frames showing Fred Ott sneezing. The images had been filmed on February 2, 1893, at the Edison studio, West Orange, NJ, by William Kennedy Laurie Dickson. The copyright was recorded as follows: "Edison Kinetoscopic Record of a Sneeze, January 7, 1894. Entered in the name of W.K.L. Dickson, under No. 2,887, January 9, 1894." This was also the first movie closeup. Earlier, on August 28, 1882, a series of photographs showing sequential motion had been copyrighted by Eadweard Muybridge. They could not be projected, but could be arranged to simulate movement when viewed in an electrical tachyscope.

5545. Movies with color were exhibited in September 1895 by Thomas Alva Edison at the Cotton States Exposition, Atlanta, GA. One of them was *Annabelle, the Dancer.* The film was hand-colored at Edison's studios in West Orange, NJ, in 1894. The first movies to use a color-sensitive film process were exhibited on December 11, 1909, at the Madison Square Garden Concert Hall, New York City. They were run through red and green screens at about twice the present speed and were very hard on the eyes. The presentation was about 10 minutes long and was composed of short subjects and views. The pictures used the Kinemacolor film invented by Charles Urban and G. Albert Smith of England and licensed to Gilbert Henry Aymer and James Klein Bowen of Allentown, PA.

5546. Movie of a heavyweight championship boxing fight was taken on March 17, 1897, at Carson City, NV, by a 38-millimeter Veriscope. It showed Robert L. Fitzsimmons, 167 pounds, knocking out James John Corbett, 183 pounds, in one minute 45 seconds of the 14th round to win a purse of $15,000. A movie of a staged prizefight had been made by Thomas Alva Edison's Kinetoscope Exhibition Company in West Orange, NJ, in July 1894, and showed Michael Leonard defeating Jack Cushing. The pictures were shown in six peep machines, each showing one round of the fight, at 83 Nassau Street, New York City.

5547. Movie with a plot was *The Great Train Robbery,* produced by the Edison Company in the fall of 1903. It was staged and directed by Edwin Stanton Porter. The scenes were filmed in New Jersey. The cast included George Barnes, Max Aronson (also known variously as Bronco Billy, Max Anderson, and Gilbert M. Anderson), Marie Murray, and A.C. Abadie. The film was printed on celluloid tinted different shades for different scenes—for example, yellow for the dance hall, bluish green for the woods.

5548. Movie photographed from an airplane was shot on February 16, 1912, by Frank Trenholm Coffin in a hydroplane flying over lower Manhattan and New York Harbor. Still photographs from the movie were shown on a full page of the *New York Times* issue of February 18, 1912.

5549. Movie version of a Shakespeare play to be made in the United States was *Richard III,* produced in 1912. The movie was the second feature-length American film. It starred English actor Frederick Warde and cost $30,000, a huge budget for the time. A print of the long-lost film was donated to the American Film Institute, Los Angeles, CA, on September 17, 1996, by William Buffum, a 77-year-old former projectionist living in Portland, OR.

5550. Serial movie with installments longer than one reel was *The Adventures of Kathlyn,* issued by Selig's Polyscope Company, Chicago, IL, on December 29, 1913. The first installment was a two-part drama, "The Unwelcome Throne," in three reels, featuring Kathlyn Williams, Tom Santochi, Charles Clary, William Carpenter, and Goldie Caldwell. Twelve other installments of two reels each followed. F.J. Grandon was the director. The film was adapted by Gilson Willets from a story by Harold MacGrath that appeared in the Hearst newspapers in 1913 and that was published in book form by the Bobbs-Merrill Company, Indianapolis, IN, in 1914.

5551. Movie of feature length made in Hollywood was *The Squaw Man,* shot in 1913 in a rented stable when Hollywood was still a quiet village. Dustin Farnum played the lead, and Cecil B. De Mille directed. The movie was the first to be produced by Samuel Goldfish, later known as Samuel Goldwyn.

5552. Movie comedy of feature length was *Tillie's Punctured Romance,* released on December 21, 1914, by the Alco Film Corporation. It took four weeks to produce. The director was Mack Sennett and the stars were Marie Dressler, Mabel Normand, Charles Chaplin, and Mack Swain.

5553. Movie sex shocker was *A Daughter of the Gods,* directed by Herbert Brenon, with music by Robert Hood Bowers, which was shown at the Lyric Theatre, New York City, on October 17, 1916. It featured Annette Kellerman, about whom a reviewer wrote that she "wanders disconsolately ... through the film, all undressed and nowhere to go."

5554. Movie featuring an African-American actor was *Natural Born Gambler,* produced by Biograph in 1916. It starred Bert Williams, leading comedian of the Ziegfeld Follies from 1909 to 1919. The first movie with sound to feature African-American entertainers was *Snappy Tunes,* featuring Noble Sissle and Eubie Blake, which was released in 1923. It used the Phonofilm system invented by Dr. Lee De Forest.

5555. Movie in Technicolor that was really successful was *The Toll of the Sea,* released on December 3, 1922, at the Rialto Theatre, New York City. The process was developed by Dr. Herbert Thomas Kalmus, president and general manager of Technicolor Motion Picture Corporation from its inception until 1959.

5556. Movie with sound recorded on the film was Dr. Lee De Forest's Phonofilm, demonstrated on March 12, 1923, for the press and on April 4, 1923, before the New York Electrical Society in New York City. Pictures were shown with music, but no voices were heard. The pictures were shown on April 15 to an invited audience at the Rivoli Theatre, New York City. Presented on the film were "The Gavotte" (a man and woman dancing to old-time music); "The Serenade" (four musicians playing on wind, percussion, and string instruments); and an Egyptian dancer. The sound occupied a narrow margin of the film on which the pictures appeared.

5557. Movie with sound to be released as a feature or "talking picture" was presented on August 5, 1926, at an invitation performance at the Warner Theatre, New York City. On August 6, a gala premiere was held at which seats sold for $10. The show used the Vitaphone system, meaning that the film did not carry a sound recording but was synchronized with disc phonograph records of the musical score. The

MOVIES—PRODUCTIONS—*continued*

main feature was *Don Juan,* directed by Alan Crosland, which starred John Barrymore, Mary Astor, Warner Oland, Estelle Taylor, and Myrna Loy. The musical score was played by the New York Philharmonic Orchestra. It was preceded by a number of short features showing performances by Mischa Elman, Efrem Zimbalist, a marimba band, and other musicians.

5558. Movie of feature length made outdoors was *In Old Arizona,* a film version of O. Henry's "The Caballero's Way," a Fox Movietone with sound recorded on the film. It was released on January 20, 1929. Most of the production was shot on location in Zion National Park and Bryce Canyon, Utah; in California's Mojave desert; and at the old San Fernando mission in California. It was directed by Raoul Walsh and Irving Cummings and featured Edmund Lowe, Warner Baxter, and Dorothy Burgess.

5559. Movie by a major company for an African-American audience was the William Fox Movietone feature *Hearts in Dixie,* a musical comedy drama of the South featuring 200 entertainers, which was first shown on February 27, 1929, at the Gaiety Theatre, New York City. It was a Paul Sloane production, written and directed by Eugene Walter, with story and dialogue by Walter Weems. The featured actor was Stephen "Stepin'" Fetchit. The entire cast, with one exception, was African-American.

5560. Movie with both sound and color was Warner Brothers' Vitaphone Technicolor film *On with the Show,* exhibited on May 28, 1929, at the Winter Garden, New York City. The cast included Betty Compson, Joe E. Brown, and Ethel Waters. It was directed by Alan Crosland and was based on a story by Humphrey Pearson.

5561. Movie in Esperanto was a four-minute film made on July 13, 1929, in the Paramount studio, New York City. The actors were Germaine Chomette and Henry W. Hetzel. Donald E. Parrish, secretary for the United States section of the Universal Esperanto Association, delivered an address and salutation to accompany the film at the 22nd annual convention of the Esperanto Society of North America. The film was exported to 16 countries.

5562. Movie in Cinemascope was Henry Koster's *The Robe,* a biblical epic released in 1953 and starring Richard Burton, Jean Simmons, and Victor Mature. The Cinemascope screen was wider than conventional screens, providing viewers with a greater sense of immersion in the movie. However, production was more costly than for traditional films, and relatively few Cinemascope theaters were built. Cinemascope was eventually abandoned by Hollywood when it failed to lure viewers away from the newer medium of television.

5563. Three-dimensional feature movie was *Bwana Devil,* produced, directed, and written by Arch Oboler of Arch Oboler Productions and released by United Artists in 1953. It was a Natural Vision-Magnetic Sound Track picture requiring Polaroid viewers. It opened on February 18, 1953, at Loew's State Theatre, New York City. It was the story of a British engineer who tracked two man-eating lions that were disrupting the construction of the first railroad in East Africa at the turn of the century. The cast included Robert Stack, Barbara Britton, Nigel Bruce, and Ramsay Hill.

5564. Three-dimensional feature movie in color produced by a major studio was *The House of Wax,* starring Vincent Price, first exhibited on April 10, 1953, at the Paramount Theatre, New York City. It was a remake of the 1933 movie *Mystery of the Wax Museum. The House of Wax* was in Warnercolor and was seen through Polaroid viewers.

5565. Phase-contrast cinemicrography film to be shown on television was a presentation of *The Birth of a Plant,* about plant reproduction, shown on February 28, 1954, by KPIX-TV, San Francisco, CA. The film process, which utilized a system of optics that permits ordinarily invisible objects to be seen, was the invention of Colonel Arthur T. Brice of Ross, CA, who produced the film under the supervision of Dr. Ralph Emerson, professor of botany at the University of California, Berkeley, CA.

5566. Movie with scent was *Behind the Great Wall,* a travelog of modern China, presented on December 8, 1959, at the De Mille Theatre, New York City. The film depicted a tiger hunt, fishing with cormorants, a May Day parade in Beijing, and other scenes. The scent was forced through ceiling vents by the Aromarama process.

5567. Movie directed by an African-American director to be released in the United States was *Story of a Three Day Pass,* directed by Melvin Van Peebles, which opened on July 8, 1968. Van Peebles's story of an African-American serviceman on leave in France, based on his book of the same name, led to his being signed by Columbia Pictures to make more films for African-American audiences.

5568. Movie for which one woman served as producer, director, and star was *Yentl,* a 1983 movie by Barbra Streisand. It was based on a story by the Yiddish-language writer Isaac Bashevis Singer.

MOVIES—TECHNOLOGY

5569. Photographic attempt to show motion was made by Dr. Coleman Sellers of Philadelphia, PA, who obtained a patent on February 5, 1861, on the Kinematoscope, an "improvement in exhibiting stereoscopic pictures of moving objects." A series of still pictures with successive stages of action was mounted on blades of a paddle and viewed through slits passed under the lens of a stereoscope revolved at right angles. The pictures were not reflected on a screen, and were visible only in the cabinet. The whole of the picture was not seen at once, but only by degrees as the cylinder revolved.

5570. Movie projector patent was awarded to O.B. Brown of Malden, MA, on August 10, 1869, for an "optical instrument." It combined the principles of the phenakistoscope and the magic lantern.

5571. Movie film was manufactured beginning on March 26, 1885, by the Eastman Dry Plate and Film Company of Rochester, NY, which was also the first to produce, manufacture, and market films in continuous strips on reels.

5572. Klieg light unit for movie production was invented by John Hugh Kliegl and Anton Tiberius Kliegl and placed in use in 1911. The unit used two 35-ampere arcs operating in series and equipped with an automatic arc-feed arrangement, using white flame carbons. It gave four times as much light as other available sources. The lights were first used by the Carlton Motion Picture Laboratory, Coney Island, New York City; the Lubin Manufacturing Company, Philadelphia, PA; and Thomas Alva Edison's Decatur Avenue Studio, New York City. The name was not adopted until later.

5573. Portable movie projector was invented by Dr. Herman Adolf De Vry and produced in 1913 in Chicago, IL. It weighed approximately 26 pounds, cost $200, and was known as "the projector in a suitcase."

5574. Portable movie camera was the Victor Cine Camera, manufactured by the Victor Animatograph Company, Davenport, IA, in 1923. It was 3 by 6 by 8 inches, weighed 5 pounds, and cost $55. It was advertised on August 12, 1923.

MUSEUMS

5575. Waxworks museum was opened by James Wyatt in New York City in June 1749. The figures were imported from England and exhibited from June to December 1749 at "the Sign of the Dolphin, Privateer, near the Work-House." Effigies were shown of King George II and Frederick, Prince of Wales, "both dressed in Royal Robes ... as when sitting in the Parliament House," the Duke of Cumberland "in his Regimentals," the "famous present actress" Miss Peggy Woffington, nuns, friars, British and Hungarian-Bohemian royal personages, and several others.

5576. Public museum in America was the Charleston Museum of Charleston, SC. It was organized on January 12, 1773, at the annual anniversary meeting of the Charleston Library Society. The first curators of the museum were the diplomat Charles Cotesworth Pinckney, the politician Thomas Heyward, and two physicians, Alexander Baron and Peter Fayssoux. Eventually the building was torn down, and the collection was moved to the College of Charleston. On August 29, 1850, the city council ratified an ordinance "to provide for the appointment of a Curator for the Museum of the College of Charleston." Francis Simmons Holmes was elected to the post on November 25, 1850, and was appointed professor of geology and paleontology at the college on December 28.

5577. Museum especially constructed as a museum and art gallery was Peale's Baltimore Museum and Gallery of the Fine Arts, operated by Rembrandt Peale. It was a three-story building at 225 North Holliday Street, Baltimore, MD, and was designed by Robert Cary Long, Sr. The opening was advertised for August 15, 1814. The building was sold in 1830 to the City of Baltimore, which used it as its first City Hall.

5578. Egyptian antiquities collection was imported in 1835 by Colonel Mendes I. Cohen of Baltimore, MD. It was not publicly displayed until 1884, when it was bequeathed to Johns Hopkins University, Baltimore.

5579. National hall of fame was National Statuary Hall, formerly the Hall of the United States House of Representatives in the Capitol at Washington, DC, which was established by act of Congress of July 2, 1864. Each state was invited to contribute marble or bronze statues of its most distinguished citizens.

MUSEUMS—*continued*

5580. Commercial museum was the Philadelphia Commercial Museum, organized by city ordinance approved on June 15, 1894. It was developed by Dr. William Powell Wilson, who conceived the idea of the institution and who served as its director and executive head from 1894 to 1927. The Philadelphia Commercial Museum comprised the museum proper, the Department of Visual Education, the Foreign Trade Bureau, the Library, and the Exhibition Hall with its convention hall.

5581. Children's museum was the Brooklyn Children's Museum, Brooklyn Avenue and Park Place, New York City, in the Brower Park Building in the Crown Heights neighborhood. It opened on December 16, 1899.

5582. Academic hall of fame was the Hall of Fame, which was dedicated on May 30, 1901, on the University Heights campus of New York University, New York City. Twenty-nine tablets were unveiled. The oration was delivered by Senator Chauncey Mitchell Depew. The idea originated with Dr. Henry Mitchell MacCracken, chancellor of the university, who was aided in the project by a $250,000 endowment from Helen Miller Gould.

5583. Semitic museum was the Harvard University Semitic Museum, Cambridge, MA, which was formally opened on February 5, 1903, in the Peabody Museum of Archeology and Ethnology, though it had been opened to students and the public on May 13, 1891. It was founded by a donation from Jacob Henry Schiff. The collection included Syrian, Arabic, and Hebrew manuscripts.

5584. Industrial museum was established by the Association for the Establishment and Maintenance for the People of the City of New York of a Museum of Peaceful Arts. It was incorporated on February 26, 1914. The name was changed in 1931 to the New York Museum of Science and Industry.

5585. Outdoor museum with nature trails was established in 1925 by Dr. Frank Eugene Lutz at the Station for the Study of Insects, located in the Ramapo Mountains in Tuxedo Park, NY. The nature trails were developed under the auspices of the American Museum of Natural History, New York City, with the cooperation of the Palisades Interstate Park Commission. There were two trails, the Training Trail and the Testing Trail, each half a mile long, which were posted with signs describing the trees, shrubs, flowering plants, and insects.

5586. Museum to install refrigerated vaults with automatic temperature control for the preservation of valuable specimens of furs and similar articles was the University of California Museum of Vertebrate Zoology, Berkeley, CA. The equipment was installed sometime before March 1930.

5587. Maritime museum worldwide in scope was the Mariners' Museum, Newport News, VA, established on June 2, 1930, by Archer Milton Huntington.

5588. Costume museum was the Museum of Costume Arts, New York City, incorporated on April 28, 1937, to develop "cultural education in connection with those arts and industries which function in conjunction with design in form of apparel and accessories by applying to this field the ways and means now commonly used or applied by fine arts and industrial museum associations and foundations and musical societies of various kinds in their respective fields."

5589. Museum devoted exclusively to papermaking was the Dard Hunter Paper Museum of the Massachusetts Institute of Technology, Cambridge, MA, which opened on June 5, 1939. The curator was Dr. Dard Hunter, who personally collected material in every papermaking country of the world over a period of about 40 years.

5590. Health museum not connected with another institution was the Cleveland Health Museum, Cleveland, OH, opened on November 12, 1940, to give an accurate understanding of the body and knowledge of how it functions and how to care for it. The first director was Dr. Bruno Gebhard.

5591. Museum devoted exclusively to nuclear energy was the American Museum of Atomic Energy, Oak Ridge, TN, opened to the public on March 19, 1949, the anniversary of the removal of the security fence from the city of Oak Ridge. During World War II, Oak Ridge was the site of a secret military installation where research into nuclear weapons was conducted. The museum was operated for the Atomic Energy Commission as a service to the public by the Oak Ridge Institute of Nuclear Studies, a nonprofit educational organization.

5592. Museum commemorating the Holocaust was the U.S. Holocaust Memorial Museum, opened to the public on April 22, 1993, in Washington, DC. The museum combined innovative multimedia displays with one of the nation's largest repositories of documentary information about the Holocaust.

MUSEUMS—ART

5593. Art museum of importance was the Pennsylvania Academy of Fine Arts, which was established in Philadelphia, PA, on December 26, 1805, "to promote the cultivation of the Fine Arts in the United States of America, by introducing correct and elegant copies from works of the first masters in sculpture and painting." The first president of the Academy was George Clymer.

5594. College art museum was the Yale University Art Gallery at 1111 Chapel Street, New Haven, CT, founded in 1832. It was known as the Trumbull Art Gallery of Yale University.

5595. Free public art museum in continuous existence is the Wadsworth Athenaeum, located in Hartford, CT. It was founded by Daniel Wadsworth in 1842 to house his extensive collection of historical paintings, portraits, and American landscapes by John Trumbull, Frederic Edwin Church, Thomas Cole, and others. The Colt Memorial Wing, donated by Elizabeth Hart Jarvis Colt in 1907, was the first museum wing in the United States named for a woman.

5596. Art museum to sell reproductions of items in its collection was the Metropolitan Museum of Art in New York City. In 1871, the museum's trustees commissioned an engraver to make etchings of 10 recently acquired Old Master paintings. They were sold on consignment to raise money for the museum, which did not yet have a permanent home. Half a century later, in the 1920s, the museum, now well established in its Fifth Avenue location, began selling reproductions in its gift shop and through mail-order catalogs. During the 1980s and 1990s, it established retail stores in cities throughout the United States and other countries. In 1997, merchandising revenues for the Met reached $79 million.

5597. Modern art museum was the Phillips Collection in Washington, DC. Duncan Phillips, whose collection of modern works formed the basis for the museum's permanent collection, directed the institution from its opening in 1921 until his death in 1966.

5598. Artmobile was conceived and designed by the Virginia Museum of Fine Arts, Richmond, VA, and began its tours on October 13, 1953, at Fredericksburg, VA, with an exhibition of art objects. It was an all-aluminum trailer weighing over five tons, measuring 34 feet in length and 7 feet 10 inches in height on the inside. When set up for exhibitions, it required a space 60 by 35 feet.

5599. Art museum devoted to work by women was the National Museum of Women in the Arts, Washington, DC, founded in December 1981, by Wilhelmina Cole Holladay, who became its first president. The museum was formally opened on April 7, 1987, with a collection of 500 works from the Renaissance to the modern era.

5600. Art museum of importance devoted to the work of an individual woman was the Georgia O'Keeffe Museum, which opened on July 17, 1997, in Santa Fe, NM. It housed major works by O'Keeffe, whose paintings of desert scenes and flowers made her the best-known 20th-century artist of the American Southwest. The museum, which contained 116 paintings and one sculpture, was housed in a sprawling adobe building renovated and expanded by architect Richard Gluckman. Peter H. Hassrick was the first director.

N

NEWS

5601. Opinion poll was published in the *Harrisburg Pennsylvanian* on July 24, 1824. Local voters were asked their preference in the presidential contest between Andrew Jackson and John Quincy Adams. Jackson was preferred by a wide majority. Adams won the election.

5602. News dispatch by telegraph was sent from Washington, DC, to the offices of the *Baltimore Patriot* on May 25, 1844. The message read: "One o'clock. There has just been made a motion in the House to go into committee of the whole on the Oregon question. Rejected. Ayes 79—Nays 86."

5603. News dispatch by commercial telegraph was received on August 26, 1858, and was published in the *New York Sun* on August 27. It stated that a treaty of peace had been concluded by China in which Britain and France obtained all their demands, including the establishment of embassies at Peking and indemnification for military expenses.

5604. Press censorship by military authorities occurred shortly after the beginning of the Civil War. Worried that press accounts of activities in Washington, DC, might prove helpful to the enemy, Winfield Scott, general in chief of the Union army, announced on July 8, 1861, that the Washington telegraph office would no longer carry "dispatches concerning the operations of the Army not permitted by the commanding general."

NEWS—*continued*

5605. News dispatch by telephone was sent from Salem, MA, on February 12, 1877, to the *Boston Globe,* Boston, MA, using equipment provided by Alexander Graham Bell. The *Globe* reported: "This special dispatch to the *Globe* has been transmitted by telephone in the presence of twenty people who have thus been witnesses to a feat never before attempted—the sending of news over the space of 16 miles by the human voice."

5606. Airplane used for newspaper reporting was a Canadian Curtiss biplane, piloted by Lieutenant William D. Tipton, which was placed in service by the *Evening Sun* of Baltimore, MD, on September 1, 1920, when it reported a railroad wreck at Back River. Two days later it flew out to sea and located the submarine *S-5,* in trouble off the Delaware Capes.

5607. Unscheduled event to be televised as it occurred was an outdoor scene of firemen answering an alarm on April 24, 1936, in Camden, NJ. It was shown in green tint, 5 by 7 inches, 24 pictures per second, on a 343-line screen. The pictures were taken by engineers from the RCA-Victor Company, Camden.

5608. Space-to-ground news conference telecast took place at 7:30 P.M. on November 23, 1969, when *Apollo 12* was 108,000 miles from earth, traveling earthward at 3,670 miles per hour. Commanders Charles Conrad, Jr., Alan La Vern Bean, and Richard Francis Gordon, Jr., answered questions submitted in writing by reporters at the Manned Spacecraft Center, Houston, TX, to Lieutenant Colonel Gerald P. Carr, who read them to the astronauts. *Apollo 12* took off on November 14, 1969, and splashed down on November 24.

NEWS—JOURNALISTS

5609. Newspaper publisher was Benjamin Harris, "the father of American newspapers." His paper, *Publick Occurrances, Both Foreign and Domestic,* issued from the London Coffee House, Boston, MA, was printed by R. Pierce on September 25, 1690. It was promptly suppressed because of certain "reflexions" distasteful to Governor Simon Bradstreet of Massachusetts. Harris had intended to issue it monthly "or if any Glut of Occurrances happen, oftener," but only the one issue appeared. It was a one-sheet paper folded to present four pages, containing news in double columns. The last page was blank. There were no advertisements.

5610. Newspaper editor who was a woman was Ann Franklin, Benjamin Franklin's sister-in-law, who became editor of the *Newport Mercury* of Newport, RI, after the death of her son, James Franklin, Jr., on August 22, 1762. She edited the paper until her death on April 16, 1763.

5611. Washington news correspondent of importance was James Gordon Bennett (the elder), whose articles first appeared on January 2, 1828, in the *New York Enquirer,* later known as the *Courier and Enquirer.*

5612. Sportswriter was Henry William Herbert, who used the nom de plume Frank Forester, and who acquired fame in 1834 as an authority on outdoor sports.

5613. Book review editor was the author and literary critic Margaret Fuller, formerly the editor of the Transcendentalist magazine *Dial,* who was hired in December 1844 by Horace Greeley for his *New York Tribune.* Fuller served until 1846. She was killed in 1850 in the wreck of a ship off Fire Island, NY, together with her husband and child.

5614. News reporter at a political convention who was a woman was Mary Ashton Rice Livermore, one of the editors of the *New Covenant,* who covered the Republican National Convention, May 12-18, 1860, at the Chicago Wigwam, Chicago, IL, which nominated Abraham Lincoln.

5615. News reporter tried as a spy was Thomas Wallace Knox, staff war correspondent of the *New York Herald,* who was tried on February 5, 1863, at Young's Point, LA, before a military court composed of a brigadier general, four colonels, and a major. He was charged with giving information to the enemy, being a spy, and disobeying orders. The trial lasted 14 days. Knox was found guilty on the first two charges and not guilty on the third, and was banished from General Grant's and General Sherman's theater of war. The sentence was revoked by President Abraham Lincoln.

5616. News correspondent accredited to the White House was Emily Edson Briggs, correspondent for the *Philadelphia Press* of Philadelphia, PA, who wrote a series of letters that were published between January 1866 and January 1882, during the administrations of Presidents Johnson, Grant, Hayes, and Garfield. She wrote under the pseudonym "Olivia."

5617. Newspaper association was the American Newspaper Publishers Association, organized on November 17, 1886, in Detroit, MI. The call was made by William Henry Brearley of the *Detroit News.* The first convention was held on February 16–17, 1887, in Rochester, NY, and was attended by 51 delegates.

5618. Photojournalist was Jacob Riis, a Danish-born reporter for the *New York Tribune* and *New York Evening Sun,* who wrote articles about the living conditions in New York City's slum neighborhoods and documented his observations with photographs. His 1890 book *How the Other Half Lives* helped persuade reformers and legislators to aid the city's poor.

5619. News correspondent who was African-American was Joel Augustus Rogers, who was sent to Addis Ababa, Ethiopia, by the *Pittsburgh Courier* of Pittsburgh, PA, in October 1935. He returned on April 21, 1936. The first African-American correspondent accredited to the White House was Harry McAlpin, representing the *Daily World* of Atlanta, GA, and the press service of the Negro Newspaper Publishers Association, who attended his first White House press conference on February 8, 1944. The first to be admitted to the congressional press gallery was Percival L. Prattis, representative of *Our World,* New York City, who was accredited on February 3, 1947.

5620. Television news commentator who was African-American was Malvin Russell "Mel" Goode of Pittsburgh, PA, who was assigned on August 29, 1962, by WABC-TV to the United Nations staff, New York City.

5621. Television network evening news program anchor who was a woman was Barbara Walters, who co-hosted the "ABC Evening News" with Harry Reasoner beginning in 1976. Her $1 million salary was at that time the largest ever paid to any broadcast journalist.

5622. Editor of a major daily newspaper who was a woman was Mary Anne Dolan, who edited the *Los Angeles Herald Examiner,* Los Angeles, CA, from 1981 to 1989, when the paper ceased publication.

NEWS—NEWS AGENCIES

5623. News agency for gathering news was established in Boston, MA, in 1814, when Samuel Topliff became the owner of the Merchant's Reading Room (formerly Gilbert's Coffee House and Marine Diary), one of several Boston coffeehouses where customers read local weekly newspapers and discussed current news.

Topliff maintained a correspondence with associates in foreign countries who supplied him with news. He kept a record of their reports for his own patrons and also distributed their reports to the newspapers for publication.

5624. Financial news agency was the Kiernan Financial News Agency, established in 1869 by John James Kiernan at 21 Wall Street, New York City. In 1882, the service was extended to include results of athletic contests, arrivals of steamships, commodity quotations abroad, and similar items.

5625. Newspaper clipping bureau was opened at 60 Ann Street, New York City, on April 15, 1884, by Samuel Leavitt. The business was absorbed by Henry Romeike, who had established a similar service in June 1881 in London. It was known as Henry Romeike's Press Cuttings.

5626. Newspaper syndicate to supply articles and stories was started on November 8, 1884, by Samuel Sidney McClure of New York City, who organized the McClure Syndicate. The syndicate paid writers directly and distributed their articles to its membership of daily newspapers throughout the country. The first attempt at syndication took place in 1841, when Moses Yale Beach of New York City printed up President John Tyler's December 7 message to the second session of the 27th Congress. He sold the sheets to the *Advertiser* of Albany, NY, the *Whig* of Troy, NY, the *Gazette* of Salem, MA, the *Times* of Boston, MA, and other papers. Each newspaper printed its own name in the blank space provided for that purpose.

5627. Fax transmission by a press syndicate direct to newspaper offices was an 8-by-10-inch aerial view of an American Airlines Curtiss Condor transport plane that had crashed in the Adirondack mountains 10 miles from Newhouseville, NY, on a flight from Cleveland, OH, to Boston, MA. The facsimile was transmitted simultaneously to eight newspapers in 24 cities by the Wirephoto service of the Associated Press on January 1, 1935.

5628. Teletypesetter circuit operated by a news agency was established on April 23, 1951, in Charlotte, NC, by the Associated Press. The first message was: "Greetings. This is the opening of the first teletypesetter circuit." Messages were sent by means of tape, which was perforated by machine and fed into a transmitter. At the receiving stations, a reperforating machine fed the tape into a monitor printer, which prepared the type for publication.

NEWS—NEWSPAPERS

5629. Newspapers published in America were broadsides, single sheets printed on one side with announcements of news. One of the earliest broadsides, and in some ways the most important, was *The Present State of the New English Affairs*. It was published by Samuel Green in Cambridge, MA, in 1689 "to prevent false reports." It consisted of a sheet of folio size, 8 by 14.5 inches, printed in two columns.

5630. Newspaper that was successful was the *Boston News-Letter,* the first issue of which was dated April 17–24, 1704. The editor was John Campbell, a New England postmaster, who earned the distinction of being America's first vendor of news. It was printed by Bartholomew Green in a back room of his home in Boston, MA. The page size was 7.5 by 12.5 inches. The text was set in small pica type. The paper was without competition for 15 years and reached a circulation of 300 copies.

5631. Editorial apology for false news to appear in a newspaper appeared in the Philadelphia, PA, *American Weekly Mercury* of April 20, 1721. It stated: "N.B. In our last week's *Mercury* No. 70, there is an account inserted from a private Letter sent to Boston, dated the 20th of September last, That the Government of Pennsilvania is Surrendered to the Crown, etc. These are to give Notice that we have now Letters from London, of a later Date, by which we find that the said Report concerning the Province of Pennsilvania is false and groundless and therefore was both by them and us too rashly inserted."

5632. Political newspaper the *New York Weekly Journal,* established on November 5, 1733, by John Peter Zenger as a political organ to expose Governor William Cosby's corruption. Zenger was arrested on November 17, 1734, and charged with seditious libel. His acquittal was seen as a vindication of the right of free speech. The first political newspaper of national importance was the *Gazette of the United States,* the political organ of Alexander Hamilton, edited by John Fenno. The first issue appeared in New York City on April 15, 1789. The newspaper moved to Philadelphia when the government moved its headquarters there in 1790.

5633. Trial in which freedom of the press was upheld took place in New York City in 1735. John Peter Zenger, the German-born editor of the *New York Weekly Journal,* had reported that Governor William Cosby of New York had attempted to rig an election in Eastchester, PA, in 1733. Cosby brought suit against Zenger, charging him with seditious libel. Zenger was defended by lawyer Andrew Hamilton of Philadelphia, who convinced the jury that printing the truth does not constitute libel. Zenger's acquittal establishing a legal precedent for freedom of the press.

5634. Daily newspaper is claimed to have been the *Pennsylvania Evening Post and Daily Advertiser* of Philadelphia, PA, originally known as the *Pennsylvania Evening Post and Public Advertiser,* which started out as a triweekly in June 1775, became a semiweekly in January 1779, and switched to a daily in 1783. Benjamin Towne was editor and publisher. The claim of being the first daily newspaper is also made for the *Pennsylvania Packet and Daily Advertiser,* published by David C. Claypoole and John Dunlap in Philadelphia, PA, which appeared on September 21, 1784, and sold for fourpence a copy. It was founded in 1771 as a weekly, the *Pennsylvania Packet and General Advertiser.*

5635. Sunday newspaper was the *Sunday Monitor* of Baltimore, MD, published by Philip Edwards, which appeared on December 18, 1796. It consisted of four pages, 10.25 by 17 inches.

5636. Religious weekly newspaper was *The Religious Remembrancer,* first issued in Philadelphia, PA, on September 4, 1813, by John Welwood Scott. In 1840 the name was changed to *The Christian Observer.* In 1869 the offices were moved to Louisville, KY.

5637. Abolition newspaper was the *Philanthropist,* published and edited by Charles Osborn, which appeared in Mount Pleasant, OH, on August 29, 1817. It published "An Appeal to Philanthropists" by Benjamin Lundy, which is said by some to be the most powerful abolition appeal ever made.

5638. Penny daily newspaper was *The Cent,* which was published in Philadelphia, PA, in 1830 by Dr. Christopher Columbus Conwell. The first successful penny paper was the *New York Sun,* published by Benjamin Henry Day, which appeared on September 3, 1833.

5639. Labor newspaper was *The Working Man's Advocate,* first published in New York City on February 18, 1834, by George Henry Evans. He advocated free homesteads, equal rights for women, and abolition of all laws governing collection of debts and imprisonment for debt. An earlier newspaper, the *Daily Sentinel,* first published on February 15, 1830, in New York City, was sympathetic to labor.

5640. Newspaper published on the Pacific Coast was the *Oregon Spectator,* a semimonthly issued in Oregon City, OR, beginning on February 5, 1846. Its slogan was "Westward the star of empire takes its way." The newspaper was published by the Oregon Printing Association and was nonpolitical. The first editor was Colonel William G. T'Vault. The first California newspaper was the *Californian,* published on August 15, 1846, in Monterey, CA, by Robert Semple and the Reverend Walter Colton.

5641. Newspaper published by soldiers in the field was the *United States American Volunteer,* which first appeared on May 21, 1861, at De Soto, MO. It was published by members of Company A, 5th Regiment, Missouri Volunteers, commanded by Captain Nelson Cole. The issue consisted of a single page. It was printed on the back of a sheet of the *Jefferson County Herald.*

5642. Newspaper published at sea was the illustrated *Atlantic Telegraph,* printed on board the cablelaying *Great Eastern,* captained by James Anderson. It sold for five shillings for the series. Issues were published on July 29, August 5, and August 12, 1865. The first to use a radio news service was the *Transatlantic Times,* a four-page paper issued on November 15, 1899, on board the American ocean liner *St. Paul* by Guglielmo Marconi and two engineers. It sold for $1 a copy, with proceeds donated to the Seaman's Fund. The news was obtained by wireless from the Needles Station, Isle of Wight. The first daily paper published at sea to carry world news was the *Cunard Daily Bulletin,* inaugurated by Marconi in October 1902 on the liners S.S. *Campania* and the S.S. *Lucania.* The news was obtained from the wireless stations at Poldhu, Cornwall, England, and Glace Bay, Canada.

5643. Newspaper index separately published was *The Index to the New York Times for 1865,* published in 1866 by Henry J. Raymond and Company, New York City. It contained 182 pages. Earlier indexes had been printed primarily for staff use.

5644. Livestock market paper was the *Drover's Journal,* published by Harvey L. Goodall at the Chicago Union Stock Yards, Chicago, IL. The first issue was dated January 11, 1873. On January 19, 1877, it became a daily.

5645. Illustrated daily newspaper was the *New York Daily Graphic,* an illustrated evening newspaper that sold for five cents a copy. It was issued on March 4, 1873, from 41 Park Place, New York City, and consisted of eight pages printed by chromolithography using zinc plates.

5646. College daily newspaper was the *Yale News,* which was first published in New Haven, CT, on January 28, 1878.

5647. Newspaper delivery train was operated by the International Great Northern Railroad over the Galveston, Houston and Henderson Railroad, in 1883 to deliver the *Galveston News* to subscribers located between Galveston and Houston, TX. The *News* paid $500 a month for the exclusive lease of the train.

5648. Newsboy was Barney Flaherty, a 10-year-old who answered the advertisement, "To the Unemployed—A number of steady men can find employment by vending this paper. A liberal discount is allowed to those who buy to sell again," inserted in the *New York Sun,* New York City, on September 4, 1833, by Benjamin Day, the publisher.

5649. European edition of an American newspaper was the Paris edition of the *New York Herald,* first published on October 4, 1887. It consisted of four six-column pages, of which the last page was devoted to advertisements.

5650. Book review newspaper supplement was the Book Review Supplement of the *New York Times,* first issued on Saturday, October 10, 1896. It contained eight pages of four columns each. The first editor was Francis Whiting Halsey. On January 29, 1911, it began appearing on Sunday as a 16-page supplement.

5651. Newspaper with an aviation section was the *Philadelphia Inquirer* of Philadelphia, PA, whose issue of June 7, 1908, devoted five columns on page 2A to "News from the Aeronautic Sphere."

5652. Newspaper circulation audit was made by a group of advertisers who organized the Association of American Advertisers to verify circulation figures. On August 21, 1914, the Audit Bureau of Circulations was formed in Chicago, IL, as a cooperative nonprofit organization. Membership was composed of advertisers, advertising agencies, and publishers. Of the 25 directors, 4 were from daily newspapers, 2 from magazines, 2 from business papers, 2 from farm papers, 2 from advertising agencies, and 13 from various advertisers.

NEWS—NEWSPAPERS—*continued*

5653. Illustrated tabloid was the *Illustrated Daily News* of New York City, which appeared on June 26, 1919. It was published by Robert Rutherford McCormick and Joseph Medill Patterson.

5654. Mimeographed daily newspaper was the *Kellogg Daily Reminder,* published on July 25, 1923, by Eaton's Letter Shop, Kellogg, ID. The founder and first editor was Marson M. Eaton, Jr. The first issue consisted of one sheet printed on both sides.

5655. Combined newspaper was issued in September 1923 during a citywide newspaper strike and bore on its masthead the names *New York American, New York Herald, The Journal of Commerce, The Daily News, The Morning Telegraph, The New York Times, The New York Tribune, The World, The New York Staats-Zeitung, Il Progresso Italo-Americano,* and *Americand.*

5656. Radio facsimile newspaper was transmitted by KSTP, St. Paul, MN, on December 17, 1937. It consisted of a roll of sensitized paper nearly five inches wide, with perforations at the sides, that issued from a receiving set.

5657. Transoceanic newspaper was the *Daily Mail,* a weekly digest of the *Daily Mail* of London, which first appeared on January 5, 1944. It was made up and edited in London, microfilmed, and flown to New York City, where it was enlarged and printed. It contained 12 pages, 9 by 12 inches, four columns wide.

5658. Newspaper reproduced commercially and regularly by radio facsimile was the San Francisco edition of *The Wall Street Journal,* which was prepared by conventional methods until the spring of 1962. Experimental editions, not distributed to the public, first appeared on April 10, and regular daily fax operations began on May 28. Page proofs were telecast by coaxial cable through microwave circuits to Riverside, CA, where they were reproduced by photoetching, using zinc plates.

5659. Large-type weekly newspaper for persons with impaired vision was the *New York Times Large Type Weekly,* 28 pages long, first published on March 6, 1967. It was printed in New York City in 18-point type and was priced at $29 a year.

5660. Newspaper whose contents were transmitted by a communications satellite was the *Wall Street Journal,* set in type at Chicopee, MA, and sent to Orlando, FL, via the *Westar* communications satellite at 3.5 minutes per page. Dedication ceremonies for the new system were held on November 20, 1978.

NEWS—NEWSPAPERS—ETHNIC

5661. German newspaper was published on May 6, 1732, by Benjamin Franklin in Philadelphia, PA, and was entitled *Philadelphische Zeitung.* It was a small four-page sheet, with the text set in double columns and in roman type. Christopher Sower's newspaper *Der Hoch-Deutsch Pennsylvanische Geschichts-Schreiber, oder Sammlung wichtiger Nachrichten aus dem Naturund-Kirchen-Reich* ("The High German Pennsylvania Recorder of Events or Collection of Important News from the Kingdom of Nature and of the Church"), first published on August 20, 1739, in Germantown, PA, is usually considered the first German newspaper. The first daily was the *New Yorker Staats-Zeitung,* introduced in New York City on January 26, 1850. It had begun publication on December 24, 1834, as a weekly. The first editor was Gustav Adolf Neumann.

5662. French newspaper was the *Courier de l'Amérique* of Philadelphia, PA, published from July 27, 1784, to October 26, 1784. The first French newspaper to be published daily was the *Courrier Français* of Philadelphia, PA, established on April 15, 1794, which was published triweekly between August 24 and October 26, 1795, and was discontinued on July 3, 1798. The first successful French daily was the *Courrier des États Unis,* which appeared on June 10, 1851, in New York City, with Paul Arpin as editor. It was started as a weekly on March 1, 1828, by E. William Hoskin, the founder and first editor.

5663. Newspaper for Jewish readers was *The Jew,* published monthly in New York City from March 1823 to March 1825. Solomon Henry Jackson, the first Jewish printer in New York, was the editor. Subscriptions cost $1.50 per year. Editorials in the paper were intended to counteract the activities of the American Society for Meliorating the Condition of the Jews, a missionary group. The first Jewish weekly in English was *The Asmonean,* which called itself "a family journal of commerce, politics, religion, and literature." It was first issued on October 26, 1849, in New York City. It was published by Robert Lyon and sold for $3 a year. It was eight pages long, with three columns on a page.

5664. Newspaper for African-American readers edited by African-Americans was *Freedom's Journal,* a four-page weekly published in New York City from March 16, 1827, to March 28, 1829, and edited by John Brown Russwurm and Samuel E. Cornish. The first African-American daily newspaper was the *New Orleans Tribune,* which appeared on October 14, 1864, in New Orleans, LA. It was printed in both French and English.

5665. Spanish newspaper was *El Redactor,* first published on July 1, 1827, in New York City. The first editor was Juan José de Lerena.

5666. Native American newspaper was the *Cherokee Phoenix,* a weekly newspaper in English and Cherokee, published from February 21, 1828, to October 1835 in New Echota, GA, the capital of the Cherokee nation. The paper was edited by Elias Boudinot, a Cherokee who had been educated at the foreign mission school in Cornwall, CT, with the help of a philanthropist whose name he adopted. It was printed in the Cherokee writing symbols invented by Sikwayi (Sequoyah), a silversmith, painter, and soldier.

5667. Norwegian newspaper was *Nordlyset* ("The Northern Light"), first published on July 29, 1847, in Muskego, WI. James De Noon Reymert was the first editor.

5668. Chinese newspaper was *Kim Shan Jit San Luk* ("San Francisco Golden Hills News"), published in San Francisco, CA, beginning in 1854. The bilingual *China World,* in Chinese and English, appeared in San Francisco in 1891. The first daily Chinese newspaper was San Francisco's *Chung Sai Yat Po* ("The Chinese Western Daily Paper"), whose first issue appeared on February 16, 1900. It was 15 by 22 inches and consisted of four pages. The founder of the paper was Ng Poon Chew, who served as the president and managing editor until his death in 1931.

5669. Czech newspaper was *Slovan Amerikansky,* a small folio weekly sheet edited by Frank Korizek. It was first issued on January 1, 1860, in Racine, WI.

5670. Yiddish newspaper was the weekly *Yiddisher Zeitung* "Jewish Times"), founded in New York City in 1870 by J.K. Buchner. The first daily newspaper in Yiddish was the *Yiddishes Tageblatt* ("Jewish Daily News"), published in New York City beginning in 1885 by Kasriel Hersch Sarasohn. It merged with the *Yiddishe Morgen Zhurnal* ("Jewish Morning Journal") in 1928 and continued publication until 1952.

5671. Hebrew newspaper was *Ha-Tzofeh be-Eretz ha-Chadash* ("The New World Scout"), edited by Hirsch Bernstein and published in New York City from 1871 to 1876. It was eight pages long and cost 10 cents.

5672. Danish newspaper was *Den Danske Pioneer,* first published in 1872.

5673. Lithuanian newspaper was *Lietuwiszka Gazieta,* published in 1874 in Shamokin, PA.

5674. Italian newspaper was *Il Progresso Italo-Americano,* first issued in New York City in September 1880. The first owner and editor was Charles Barsotti.

5675. Armenian newspaper was *Arekag* ("The Sun"), published in Jersey City, NJ. The first issue appeared in May 1888.

5676. Greek newspaper was the *Atlantis,* first issued on March 3, 1894, from 2 Stone Street, New York City, as a four-page weekly of tabloid size. On January 3, 1905, it became a full-sized four-page daily. It was the first Greek publication in America and the first publication in the world to use typesetting machinery for the Greek alphabet. Its founder and first editor was Solon John Vlasto.

5677. Latvian newspaper was *Amerikas Vestnesis,* published in Boston, MA, in 1896.

5678. Arabic daily newspaper was *Al-Hoda,* founded as a weekly on February 22, 1898, in Philadelphia, PA, by Naoum Anthony Mokarzel. On August 25, 1902, it started publication as a daily in New York City. Mokarzel was the owner and editor-in-chief until his death in 1932.

5679. Hungarian daily newspaper was the *Amerikai Magyar Népszava,* first published on October 18, 1904, in New York City. Its founder and editor in chief was Geza David Berko. It was originally established in March 1899 as a weekly.

5680. Flemish newspaper was *De Gazette van Moline,* which appeared in 1907 in Moline, IL. Flemish is one of the languages spoken in Belgium.

5681. Russian newspaper was *Novoye Russkoye Slovo,* which began publication in New York City in 1910. A biweekly newspaper in Russian and English was circulated in San Francisco in 1868.

NEWS—NEWSPAPERS—ETHNIC—*continued*

5682. Japanese newspaper in continuous publication was the *Utah Nippo,* founded in Salt Lake City, UT, in 1914 by Kuniko Terasawa, who served as its publisher, editor, reporter, typesetter, and proofreader. By the 1990s, it was the only remaining Japanese-language newspaper in the United States that had once been read by the early immigrants from Japan. It continued to be published in old-style, pre-World War II characters no longer used by most Japanese.

5683. Ukrainian daily newspaper was the *Ukrainian Daily News,* established on January 31, 1920, in New York City. The first editor was M. Tkach.

NEWS—NEWSPAPERS—ILLUSTRATIONS

5684. Newspaper cartoon was "Join or Die," designed by Benjamin Franklin and published in Philadelphia, PA, in his newspaper, the *Pennsylvania Gazette,* on May 9, 1754. It was printed in the first column of the second page. It depicted a snake cut up into segments representing South Carolina, North Carolina, Virginia, Maryland, Pennsylvania, New Jersey, New York, and New England.

5685. Line drawing to illustrate a newspaper article appeared on January 15, 1840, in the *New York Sun* of New York City. A four-page supplement showed a drawing under the five-column headline "Steamboat Lexington Burnt!! One Hundred and Fifty Lives Lost."

5686. Newspaper with a full page of woodcut engravings was the *Weekly Herald* of New York City, whose edition of June 28, 1845, printed six woodcuts depicting the grand funeral procession of Andrew Jackson.

5687. Comic strip in a newspaper was published on September 11, 1875, in the *New York Daily Graphic,* New York City, and showed 17 successive pictures on one full page. It was entitled "Professor Tigwissel's Burglar Alarm."

5688. Sunday comics section in a newspaper was published in 1893 by the *New York World,* New York City. The drawings were made by Richard Felton Outcault and depicted a humorous set of characters under the title of "Hogan's Alley." On November 18, 1894, the newspaper published the first of his six-box cartoon series "The Origin of a New Species." This was the first successful colored newspaper section.

5689. Newspaper with a color page was in the *New York Recorder,* whose issue of Sunday, April 2, 1893, carried on page 13 a full-page advertisement for R.H. Macy, 14th Street and 6th Avenue, New York City, showing a large star printed in red. The first illustrated color page in a newspaper appeared in the *New York World* of Sunday, May 21, 1893. One large sheet, printed in color and folded once, made up four pages. Page 29 showed a Walt McDougall cartoon in color, "Broadway Cable Car Possibilities." Page 32 was a full-page color reproduction of a painting of the Spanish ship *The Santa Maria.*

5690. Newspaper colored supplement was issued by the *New York World* on Sunday, November 19, 1893, and consisted of a four-page section, the outside pages of which were printed in five colors. Two half-page drawings in color featured "A Scene in Atlantic Gardens, Saturday Night," and "The Cathedral at Eleven O'Clock Mass." The inside pages were printed in black.

5691. Comic strip in continuous newspaper publication was "The Katzenjammer Kids," created by Rudolph Dirks. The strip first appeared in the *New York Journal* on December 12, 1897, and was still in syndication in 1996.

5692. Newspaper rotogravure sections were simultaneously instituted by seven newspapers on March 29, 1914, when an eight-page supplement showing 13 masterpieces of the Altman Collection in the Metropolitan Museum of Art, New York City, was included with the *New York Times,* the *Boston Sun-Herald,* the *Philadelphia Public Ledger,* the *Chicago Tribune,* the *Cleveland Plain Dealer,* the *St. Louis Post-Dispatch,* and the *Kansas City Star.*

5693. Composograph photograph in a newspaper was published on November 25, 1925, in the *Evening Graphic,* New York City. It purported to depict a scene in the private chambers of Justice Morschauser in White Plains, NY, showing Alice Jones and her husband, Leonard Kip Rhinelander. A model was used and the photograph was pasted in true perspective to form a composite layout.

5694. Transatlantic radio fax of a drawing was a sketch of Ambassador Alanson Bigelow Houghton, drawn on April 30, 1926, by Augustus John, which was transmitted in 58 minutes from London to the offices of the *New York Times* in New York City on May 2, 1926.

5695. Color news photograph transmitted by radio fax for publication was a photograph of President Harry S. Truman, Soviet leader Josef Stalin, and British Prime Minister Clement Richard Attlee, taken at the Potsdam Conference in Germany and transmitted on August 3, 1945, to Washington, DC. A one-shot camera exposed three negatives simultaneously. From the negatives, three black and white prints were made, and each was placed on a cylinder representing one of the three primary colors, red, blue, and yellow.

5696. Photoengraving high-speed process for making halftones, line plates, and combination plates was developed by the Dow Chemical Company of Freeport, TX, in cooperation with the American Newspaper Publishers Association Research Institute, Easton, PA. By means of this process, a machine could produce zinc or magnesium plates in about one-fifth the conventional time. The first commercial machine was placed in operation in February 1954 by the *Patriot-Ledger* of Quincy, MA.

NEWS—NEWSREELS

5697. Newsreel was the Pathé Weekly, later known as Pathé News, which was first shown in November 1910. Herbert Case Hoagland was the editor. Moving pictures of historic events had, however, been taken earlier, including films of the McKinley inaugural parade of 1896, the funeral procession in Colón, Cuba, of the *Maine* victims in 1898, and the embarkation of Theodore Roosevelt's Rough Riders.

5698. Newsreels showing presidential candidates were filmed on August 11, 1924, by Theodore W. Case and Lee De Forest. They showed the Republican incumbent, President Calvin Coolidge, on the grounds of the White House in Washington, DC, and his Progressive opponent, Senator Robert Marion La Follette, on the steps of the Capitol. The Democratic candidate, John William Davis, was photographed at Locust Valley, NY. The newsreel was shown in various theaters in September 1924.

5699. Newsreel in color was a Warner Brothers-Pathé newsreel taken on January 1, 1948, of the Tournament of Roses and the Rose Bowl Game, Pasadena, CA. It was made by Cinecolor process and released on January 5, 1948.

5700. Newsreel telecast presented daily was the 20th Century–Fox Movietone News telecast, first presented on February 16, 1948, over the National Broadcasting Company's East Coast network. The program was sponsored by the R.J. Reynolds Tobacco Company.

NEWS—POLITICAL CARTOONS

5701. Cartoon showing Uncle Sam appeared in the New York *Lantern,* a comic weekly, on March 13, 1852. It was called "Raising the Wind" and depicted the struggle between an American shipowner and the Cunard Company, with John Bull, symbol of Great Britain, actively helping his line while Uncle Sam, symbol of the United States, was an onlooker. The cartoonist was Frank Henry Temple Bellew.

5702. Cartoon showing the Democratic Party as a donkey was drawn by Thomas Nast and appeared in *Harper's Weekly,* New York City, on January 15, 1870. It was entitled "A Live Jackass Kicking a Dead Lion." The jackass was tagged "Copperhead papers" and the dead lion represented Edwin McMasters Stanton, Lincoln's secretary of war. The background showed an eagle perched on a rock and in the far background was the Capitol.

5703. Cartoon showing the Republican Party as an elephant was drawn by Thomas Nast and appeared in *Harper's Weekly,* New York City, on November 7, 1874. It was entitled "The Third-Term Panic" and referred to the possibility that President Ulysses S. Grant might seek a third term. It depicted an ass labeled "N.Y. Herald" in a lion's skin labeled "Caesarism," frightening numerous timid animals labeled "N.Y. Times," "N.Y. Trib.," etc., while a berserk elephant, labeled "Republican vote," about to fall into "Chaos," tossed platform planks to right and left. The quotation accompanying the title read: "An Ass having put on the Lion's skin, roamed about the Forest, and amused himself by frightening all the foolish Animals he met with in his wanderings."

NEWS—RADIO AND TELEVISION

5704. News program on radio was an announcement of local election returns, broadcast on August 31, 1920, by station 8MK (later WWJ), Detroit, MI.

5705. Daily news program on radio began broadcasting on September 1, 1922, by station WBAY, American Telegraph and Telephone Company, New York City, between 4:30 P.M. and 5:30 P.M. It was known as "The Radio Digest" and was edited by George F. Thompson. Questions and answers concerning radio were also broadcast.

NEWS—RADIO AND TELEVISION—*continued*

5706. Coast-to-coast radio news broadcast to be recorded was made on May 6, 1937, by Herbert Morrison, who described the explosion of the dirigible *Hindenburg* at Lakehurst, NJ. The recording was flown to New York City and was broadcast over both networks, the Red and the Blue, of the National Broadcasting Company.

5707. Editorial to be broadcast over radio and television was made from 8 P.M. to 8:15 P.M. on August 26, 1954, over the Columbia Broadcasting System network. Dr. Frank Stanton, the network's president, protested the Senate's decision to bar radio and television coverage of its hearings into the conduct of Senator Joseph Raymond McCarthy, Republican of Wisconsin.

5708. Television newsmagazine was "60 Minutes," produced for the CBS television network by Don Hewitt. The biweekly program premiered on September 24, 1968, with hosts Mike Wallace and Harry Reasoner. The first interview was with Attorney General Ramsey Clark.

O

ORGANIZATIONS—CULTURAL AND HISTORICAL

5709. Arts and sciences organization (national) was the American Academy of Arts and Sciences, founded in Boston, MA, and chartered on May 4, 1780, "to cultivate every art and science which may tend to advance the interest, dignity, honor and happiness of a free, independent and virtuous people." The first president was James Bowdoin, who served from 1780 to 1790. The first female member was Maria Mitchell, elected unanimously on May 30, 1848. On October 1, 1847, at Nantucket, MA, she had discovered a telescopic comet, for which King Frederick VI of Denmark presented her with a gold medal.

5710. Historical society (state) was the Massachusetts Historical Society, organized on August 26, 1790, in Boston, MA, by five persons under the leadership of the Reverend Jeremy Belknap. The main purpose of the society was to gather manuscript material to be preserved and published for general use and to establish a library that would carry on the founders' plan.

5711. Historical society (national) was the American Antiquarian Society, founded in Worcester, MA, by Isaiah Thomas, the first printer of Worcester. Incorporated on October 24, 1812, it had the first great American historical collection. The first meeting was held on November 19, 1812, at the Exchange Coffee House, Boston, MA.

5712. Young Men's Christian Association in the United States was organized on December 29, 1851, in Boston, MA. It was patterned after a similar organization started in London on June 6, 1844. The first gymnasium was opened in New York City in 1869, and in the same year the first separate boys' department was opened in Salem, MA. The first YMCA branch for African-American members was organized in Washington, DC, in 1853 by Anthony Bowen and Jerome Johnson, who served respectively as president and secretary.

5713. Young Women's Christian Association was a local organization founded in Boston, MA, in 1866. In 1858 an organization called the Ladies Christian Association was formed in New York City, and a branch of this group later took the name of Young Women's Christian Association. In 1871 the local eastern associations met in national convention in Hartford, CT, and in 1886 a central group met in Lake Geneva, WI. These two national organizations came together as the YWCA of the United States of America. The first president of the national organization was Grace Hoadley Dodge of New York City.

5714. Young Men's Hebrew Association originated in the 1840s as the Young Men's Hebrew Literary Association. The first YMHA opened in Baltimore, MD, in 1854, but was unsuccessful. The first permanent YMHA was founded on March 22, 1874, by a group of German-Jewish businessmen and professionals headed by Dr. Simeon Newton Leo. The first president was Lewis May. A second club was started in Philadelphia in 1875.

5715. Young Women's Hebrew Association was organized on February 6, 1902, in New York City. Mrs. Bella Unterberg was the founder and the first president. The first building used by the organization was at 1584 Lexington Avenue, New York City.

5716. Arts and letters organization (national) was the National Institute of Arts and Letters, founded in September 1898. The first female member was Julia Ward Howe, author of "The Battle Hymn of the Republic," who was elected in January 1907. The first African-American member, elected in December 1943, was William Edward Burghardt Du Bois, head of the Department of Sociology of Atlanta University, and one of the founders of the National Association for the Advancement of Colored People. An important subsidiary organization, the American Academy of Arts and Letters, was founded in New York City on April 23, 1904, and counted among its original members William Dean Howells, Augustus Saint-Gaudens, Edmund Clarence Stedman, John La Farge, Mark Twain, John Hay, and Edward MacDowell.

5717. Esperanto club was the Esperanto Association, organized on February 16, 1905, at Boston, MA. John Fogg Twombly was the first secretary. A national club, the Esperanto Assocation of North America, was organized on September 7, 1908, at Chautauqua Lake, NY, with George Brinton McClellan Harvey as the first president. Esperanto is an artificial language created in 1887 by Dr. Lazarus Ludwig Zamenhof, a Russian-Jewish physician, to be a common, universal language.

5718. Daughters of the American Revolution member who was African-American was Karen Batchelor Farmer of Detroit, MI, who became the 623,128th member of the Daughters of the American Revolution in October 1977. She traced her ancestry to William Hood, who served in the militia of Lancaster, PA, during the Revolutionary War.

ORGANIZATIONS—FRATERNAL AND SOCIAL

5719. Odd Fellows lodge was Washington Lodge No. 1, established on April 26, 1819, in Baltimore, MD. It was organized by Thomas Wildey and acted under a charter obtained from the Duke of York Lodge of England. In 1821, Wildey organized the Grand Lodge of Maryland, of which he became grand master, and the Grand Lodge of the United States, of which he became grand sire.

5720. Fraternal society for Jews was B'nai B'rith (Sons of the Covenant), founded on October 13, 1843, in New York City by Henry Jones and 11 others. The first lodge was formed on November 12, 1843, at which time Isaac Dittenhoefer was elected president. The first national organization of Jewish women was the National Council of Jewish Women, founded in Chicago, IL, in January 1894, with Hannah Greenebaum Solomon as president.

5721. Knights of Pythias meeting took place on February 19, 1864, in Washington, DC, when the organization was formed as a fraternal assocation by Justus Henry Rathbone and 12 associates. It was based on the Greek myth of Damon and Pythias and advocated toleration in religion, obedience to law, and loyalty to government. Washington Lodge No. 1 was the first lodge organized. The Supreme Lodge of the Knights of Pythias of the World was convened on August 11, 1868, in Washington, DC.

5722. Elks meeting that organized the Benevolent and Protective Order of Elks took place on February 16, 1868, in New York City. It derived from an older social and benevolent organization, the Jolly Corks. The first Exalted Ruler was George W. Thompson. The Grand Lodge was incorporated on March 10, 1871, in New York and the first Grand Exalted Ruler was George J. Green.

5723. Women's professional club was Sorosis, founded in New York City on March 21, 1868, by Jane Cunningham Croly and Ellen Curtis Demorest. The first president was Alice Carey.

5724. Knights of Columbus meeting took place at St. Mary's Roman Catholic Church in New Haven, CT, on January 16, 1882, when the organization was founded as a fraternal benefit association for Catholic men by the Reverend Michael Joseph McGivney and nine parishioners.

5725. Social organization for the hard of hearing (national) was the American Association for the Hard of Hearing, formed on February 27, 1919, in New York City. The first annual meeting was held in New York City on March 12, 1920. The name was changed to the American Society for the Hard of Hearing on June 5, 1935, at a meeting held in Cincinnati, OH.

5726. Chinese-American women's organization to be incorporated was the Chinese Women's Association, organized in New York City on March 29, 1932, and incorporated on June 10, 1936. The first president was Theodora Chan Wang.

ORGANIZATIONS—FRATERNAL AND SOCIAL—FREEMASONS

5727. Mason known to arrive in America was John Skene (or Skeen), member of a lodge in Aberdeen, Scotland. He came to New Jersey in 1682, settling in Burlington, and later became deputy governor of West Jersey. The first Mason born in America was Jonathan Belcher, a

ORGANIZATIONS—FRATERNAL AND SOCIAL—FREEMASONS—*continued*

citizen of Boston, MA, who was made a Mason in England in 1704. Belcher served as royal governor of the Colony of Massachusetts Bay from 1730 to 1741 and royal governor of New Jersey from 1746 to 1757.

5728. Masonic lodge was St. John's Lodge, Philadelphia, PA, for which there are records dating back to 1730. The first lodge to receive a regular charter was St. John's Lodge of Boston, MA, organized by Henry Price and established on July 30, 1733. The first military lodge was formed at Crown Point, NY, under authority granted on April 13, 1759, by Provincial Grand Master Jeremy Gridley of Massachusetts. The first grand lodge was organized at Williamsburg, VA, on October 13, 1778, when the Grand Lodge of Virginia was established with Right Worshipful John Blair, past-master of Williamsburg Lodge No. 6, as the first grand master.

5729. Mason who was African-American was Prince Hall, initiated on March 6, 1775, in an army lodge that was stationed at Castle William under General Thomas Gage in or near Boston, MA. It operated under Irish constitutions. When the British evacuated Boston, Hall and his fellow members were given a permit to form African Lodge No. 1, which they did on July 3, 1776. On June 30, 1784, after the Revolution, Hall and others applied to the Grand Lodge of England for a warrant, which was issued on September 29, 1784, to African Lodge No. 459, with Prince Hall as Master. The first meeting under the charter was held on May 6, 1787, in Boston, MA. The lodge was not recognized by American masonry. The first African-American lodge to be recognized was the Alpha Lodge of New Jersey, No. 116 Free and Accepted Masons, the warrant for which was granted at the Annual Communication of the Grand Lodge in Trenton, NJ, on January 19, 1871.

ORGANIZATIONS—HUMANITARIAN AND CHARITABLE

5730. Interfaith charity organization was the Union Society, a cooperative effort of Protestants, Catholics, and Jews, formed in Savannah, GA, in 1776. Its purpose was to assist needy widows and orphans. The founder was Mordecai Sheftall, a Jewish businessman. Sheftall, who served as commissary general of the Georgia state militia during the Revolutionary War, was captured by the British during their attack on Savannah, but continued to hold meetings of the society as a prisoner of war.

5731. Endowment for social service purposes was the White-Williams Foundation, established in February 1800 as the Magdalen Society, a Home for Girls, for the purpose of "providing more normal opportunities of development and inculcating good habits and to ameliorate the distressed condition of those unhappy females who have been seduced from the paths of virtue, and are desirous of returning to a life of rectitude."

5732. Women's club was the Female Charitable Society of Wiscasset, ME, which held its first meeting on November 18, 1805, at the home of Tempe Lee, wife of Judge Silas Lee, a member of Congress. Thirty women were present. A total of $78 was subscribed. The first president was Sally Sayward Wood, Maine's first female novelist.

5733. Peace society was the New York Peace Society, which was organized on August 16, 1815. David Low Dodge was its first president. Similar societies were formed elsewhere. On May 8, 1828, the New York Peace Society became a member of a national organization called the American Peace Society, which held its first annual meeting on May 13, 1829, in New York City.

5734. Fund-raising organization to sell stamps was a group of women in Cleveland, OH, who came up with the idea of holding fairs where they would sell stamps as a way of raising money to aid soldiers wounded in the Civil War. They first met on April 20, 1861, eight days after the first gun was fired on Fort Sumter. Five days later, another group formed in New York City. Fairs were also held in Chicago, Albany, Boston, Stamford, and other cities, and special offices were established to sell the stamps, which were known as Sanitary Fair Stamps.

5735. Animal humane society was the American Society for the Prevention of Cruelty to Animals, founded in New York City by Henry Bergh, formerly of the American Legation at St. Petersburg, Russia, who was appalled by the beatings which droshky drivers in Russia administered to their horses. When he returned to the United States he organized the A.S.P.C.A., incorporated April 10, 1866, and patterned after the Royal S.P.C.A. of London.

5736. Free lunches for the poor and sick were offered by the New York Diet Kitchen Association. On April 24, 1873, the association opened a kitchen at 410 East 23rd Street, New York City, for the relief of the destitute sick. Beef tea, soup, milk-cooked rice, eggs, and oatmeal were served. The first president was Mrs. A.H. Gibbons.

5737. Child abuse prevention organization was the New York Society for the Prevention of Cruelty to Children, founded in New York City on December 15, 1874, by Henry Bergh, Elbridge Gerry, and James Wright. In its charter, the society's founding members pledged to shield "the unprotected children of this city and state from the cruelty and demoralization which neglect and abandonment engender." Initial funding was provided by Cornelius Vanderbilt. Bergh founded the American Society for the Prevention of Cruelty to Animals in 1866.

5738. Animal humane society (national) was the American Humane Association, which was organized on October 9, 1877, in Cleveland, OH, and was incorporated under the laws of the District of Columbia on November 12, 1903, as a federation of societies for the prevention of cruelty to animals, with the primary purpose of preventing cruelty in the transportation of livestock. The first president was Edwin Lee Brown of Chicago, IL.

5739. Red Cross meeting took place on May 21, 1881, at the home of Adolphus Simeon Solomons in Washington, DC, where he and Clara Barton founded the American Association of the Red Cross as part of an international humanitarian movement to provide help to victims of war and natural disasters. The organization was made a part of the International Red Cross on March 16, 1882.

5740. Animal rights organization (national) was the American Anti-Vivisection Society, organized on February 23, 1883, at Philadelphia, PA. Its object, according to its charter, was "the restriction of the practice of vivisection within proper limits, and the prevention of the injudicious and needless infliction of suffering upon animals under the pretense of medical and scientific research." Vivisection is the practice of cutting open living, and often unanesthetized, animals. The founder of the society was Caroline Earle White. The first president was Dr. Thomas George Morton. The first annual meeting was held on January 30, 1884, in Philadelphia.

5741. Fund-raising organization to sell Christmas seals was the Delaware chapter of the American National Red Cross, which sold them to raise funds to fight tuberculosis. The idea for the seals was proposed in 1907 by Emily Perkins Bissell of Wilmington, DE, who drew the designs and had them lithographed by Theo. Leonhardt and Son, Philadelphia, PA. They were first placed on sale on December 9, 1907, in the Wilmington post office. They were issued in perforated sheets, 228 seals to a sheet, in two types: "Merry Christmas" and "Merry Christmas and a Happy New Year." About $3,000 was realized from the project.

5742. Community trust charity was the Cleveland Foundation, Cleveland, OH, which was established on January 2, 1914, by the board of directors of the Cleveland Trust Company. The idea for a community fund-raising campaign was thought up by Frederick Harris Goff, the company's president. After various surveys of the community were conducted, the first distribution committee was appointed in May 1917, with Dr. James De Long Williamson as chairman. The first director of the Cleveland Foundation was Dr. Raymond Moley.

ORGANIZATIONS—PHILOSOPHICAL

5743. Theosophical society was the American Theosophical Society, founded on November 17, 1875, by Helena Petrovna Blavatsky and Colonel Henry Steele Olcott in New York City. The society later was incorporated in Adyar, Madras, India, the city that became the international headquarters of the society. The American section of the organization had its headquarters in Wheaton, IL. Theosophy is a "synthesis of the principles underlying all religions and science." Its object is to form a nucleus of the "universal brotherhood of humanity," without distinctions of race, creed, sex, caste, or color; to encourage the study of comparative religion, philosophy, and science; and to investigate the unexplained laws of nature and the powers latent in humans.

5744. Ethical culture society was the New York Society for Ethical Culture, founded in New York City in May 1876 by Dr. Felix Adler. Additional groups were formed and in 1886 the American Ethical Union was organized.

5745. Atheist organization of importance was the American Association for the Advancement of Atheism, the first society in the United States to use the word "atheism" or any of its forms as a title. The society was organized in New York City in October 1925, and was incorporated on November 16, 1925, in New York State. The charter was at first denied by the Supreme Court. The first president of the association was Charles Smith.

ORGANIZATIONS— PHILOSOPHICAL—
continued

5746. Humanist association was the Humanist Society, established on January 13, 1929, in Hollywood, CA, "to humanize religion, disseminate science, stimulate thought and promote good will." The first director was the Reverend Theodore Curtis Abell. The first Humanist National Assembly was held in New York City, on October 10–11, 1934.

P

PAPER AND PRINTING—PAPER

5747. Paper mill was built in 1690 by William Rittenhouse, Samuel Carpenter, Robert Turner, Thomas Tresse, and William Bradford in Germantown, PA, on a rivulet called Paper Mill Run, about two miles above the junction of the Wissahickon River with the Schuylkill. The mill was built on 20 acres of land leased from Samuel Carpenter at an annual rental of five shillings. The paper was made by hand from linen rags that were pounded into pulp in stone mortars. Each sheet was made separately. The production rate was about 250 pounds a day.

5748. Watermark in paper was the single word "company," which was formed in the paper manufactured in 1690 by William Rittenhouse in his mill on Paper Mill Run, Germantown, PA. Afterwards he used several other watermarks to distinguish his paper.

5749. Paper made by machine in the United States was produced in Thomas Gilpen's paper mill at Brandywine, DE. Previously, paper had been made by hand in small sizes because of limited facilities and molds. Gilpin's cylinder machine, which he built in August 1817, permitted paper to be made in unlimited lengths and widths.

5750. Fourdrinier papermaking machine capable of making an endless roll of paper in any size was imported from England and set up in Joseph Pickering's shop in North Windham, CT, in January 1828. The first such machine to be manufactured in the United States was built in 1829 in South Windham, CT, by James Phelps and George Spafford, who formed the firm of Phelps and Spafford. Aided by Charles Smith, they produced a machine that was set up in May 1829 in the mill of Amos H. Hubbard of Norwich Falls, CT. The machine had no driers. The paper was run off wet and hung up to dry. The firm name was changed to Smith, Winchester and Company in 1837.

5751. Straw paper was made from straw and grass in 1829 by George Augustus Shryrock of Philadelphia, PA, in the Hollywell mill near Chambersburg, PA. He also invented a machine for producing it.

5752. Manila paper was invented by John Mark and Lyman Hollingsworth of South Braintree, MA, partners under the firm name of J.M. and L. Hollingsworth, who received a patent on December 4, 1843. They manufactured it from hemp sails, canvas, and rope.

5753. Paper for printing made from rags and wood-pulp fiber was manufactured by William Orr at his paper mill in Troy, NY, in 1854. The composition of the paper was three-fourths rag and one-fourth wood fiber.

5754. Paper made from wood pulp was made of basswood by John Beardsley of Buffalo, NY. He exhibited three samples of it on December 26, 1854, to the editor of the *Buffalo Democrat*.

5755. Blotting paper was made in New Haven, CT, by Joseph Parker and Son in 1856 at the West Rock Paper Mill on a Fourdrinier machine. Until this time, only small quantities had been imported from England. Most people used sand to dry their ink.

5756. Toilet paper was unbleached pearl-colored pure manila hemp paper made in 1857 by Joseph C. Gayetty of New York City, whose name was watermarked on each sheet. It sold at 500 sheets for 50 cents and was known as "Gayetty's Medicated Paper—a perfectly pure article for the toilet and for the prevention of piles." It did not catch on with the public. The first toilet paper to be marketed successfully was introduced by Edward and Clarence Scott of Philadelphia, PA, who sold it in small rolls.

5757. Paper bag manufacturing machine was invented by William Goodale of Clinton, MA, who obtained a patent for it on July 12, 1859. A machine to manufacture paper bags with square bottoms was invented by Luther Childs Crowell of Boston, MA, and patented on February 20, 1872. The bags produced by the machine had two longitudinal inward folds.

5758. Perforated wrapping paper was patented on July 25, 1871, by Seth Wheeler of Albany, NY. The paper was wound into rolls and could easily be torn off at the perforations.

5759. Corrugated paper was invented by Albert L. Jones of New York City, who received a patent on December 19, 1871, on an "improvement in paper for packing." His patent covered corrugated sheets only and made no mention of backing or facing sheets. Later a facing sheet was applied to one side, and then to both sides, making single-face and double-face corrugated cardboard. Jones assigned his patent to the Thompson and Norris Company of Brooklyn, NY (now part of New York City), which was the first manufacturer of corrugated paper in the United States. Corrugated paper boxes came into use about 1890.

5760. Crepe paper was manufactured in 1890 by Charles T. Bainbridge's Sons, Brooklyn, NY (now part of New York City). It was made of rag paper with only one ratio of stretch. It was made in a variety of colors and sold to the trade for 50 cents a roll. Each roll was 20 inches wide and 10 feet long.

5761. Paper twine machine was patented on December 17, 1895, by George Loomis Brownell of Worcester, MA. It twisted strips or ribbons of paper into cord that was as strong as any known steel.

PAPER AND PRINTING—PAPER—ENVE-LOPES

5762. Envelope manufacturer was a Mr. Pierson of New York City, who manufactured envelopes in a little store on Fulton Street in 1839. Prior to the manufacture of envelopes, letters were folded and sealed and the name and address written on the blank side.

5763. Envelope folding machine that proved practical commercially was patented on January 21, 1853, by Dr. Russell L. Hawes of Worcester, MA. It was not self-gumming, but nevertheless it enabled three girls to produce the finished product at the rate of about 25,000 envelopes in 10 hours.

5764. Paper folding machine to fold paper for books and newspapers was invented by Cyrus Chambers, Jr., of Kennet Square, PA, who obtained a patent on October 7, 1856. It was for plain three-fold right-angle work and delivered a 16-page folded signature to the packing box. It was installed in the Bible printing house of Jasper Harding and Son, Philadelphia, PA.

5765. Envelope folding and gumming machine was patented on February 8, 1898, by John Ames Sherman of Worcester, MA. It reduced the cost of a completely gummed envelope ready for market from 60 cents to 8 cents per 1,000.

5766. Envelope with a window was patented by Americus F. Callahan of Chicago, IL, on June 10, 1902. It was first manufactured in July 1902 by the U.S. Envelope Company of Springfield, MA, which had leased the patent.

PAPER AND PRINTING—PRESSES

5767. Printing press was imported from England in the summer of 1638 by the Reverend Jesse "Jose" Glover of Sutton, England. Glover hired Stephen Day, a printer skilled in the operation of the press, to sail to Massachusetts in the same ship, together with his wife and children. Glover died on board the ship. The press was set in operation in March 1639 at Cambridge, MA, and Day became the first printer in colonial America.

5768. Printing press invented in the United States was the Columbian Press, an iron hand-printing press that was operated by a combination of compound levers instead of a screw to give the downward pressure. It was invented by George E. Clymer of Philadelphia, PA, in 1816. The first to be successful was the Washington Press, invented in 1827 by Samuel Rust of New York City, and valued for its usefulness in taking fine proofs. Rust obtained patents on May 13, 1821, March 2, 1826, and April 17, 1829. The machine was manufactured by R. Hoe and Company, New York City.

5769. Steam-powered printing press was made by Daniel Treadwell of Boston, MA, in 1822. Only three or four were manufactured.

5770. Printing press for printing wallpaper in color was invented by Peter Force of Washington, DC, who patented it on August 22, 1822.

5771. Power printing press capable of fine book work was the Adams Press, invented by Isaac Adams of Boston, MA, who obtained a patent for it on October 4, 1830. He received an additional patent on improvements to it on March 2, 1836.

5772. Cylinder printing press was made by R. Hoe and Company, New York City, in 1831 and was operated initially by hand power and later by steam. It was used to print the *Temperance Recorder,* a monthly that was first published on March 6, 1832, in Albany, NY.

5773. Embossing press was a standing hand-lever press built in New York City in 1838 by Bernard Sheridan. An object placed between the descending die and the bed was given a raised surface when pressure was applied. The press sold for $200.

PAPER AND PRINTING—PRESSES—*continued*

5774. Electric printing press was invented by Thomas Davenport of Brandon, VT, and used in 1839 in New York City. It was a rotary press operated by an engine weighing less than 100 pounds. Beginning in January 1840, he used it to print the journal *Electro-Magnet and Mechanics Intelligencer*, of which he was the editor. He obtained a patent on February 25, 1837, on an "electrical motor."

5775. Cylinder and flatbed combination printing press was manufactured in 1844 by R. Hoe and Company, New York City. It was invented by Robert Hoe, who obtained a patent on April 17, 1844. The circumference of the cylinder was equivalent to the entire travel of the bed forward and backward. The cylinder made one revolution for each impression in printing without stopping.

5776. Printing press for polychromatic printing was invented by Thomas F. Adams of Philadelphia, PA, who obtained a patent for it on September 17, 1844. Different color rollers, operating in parallel, were used to produce linear work.

5777. Rotary printing press was the double-cylinder machine invented by Richard March Hoe of New York City. It was first used in the office of the *Philadelphia Ledger*, Philadelphia, PA, in 1846. The bed was of such length that the form of type passed backward and forward under both cylinders. The central cylinder was placed in a horizontal position. The output was 2,000 sheets per hour for each of four feeders. A patent was obtained on July 24, 1847.

5778. Printing press to use a continuous web or roll of paper was the Bullock Press, produced by William Bullock of Pittsburgh, PA, in 1865. It was the first machine built especially for curved stereotype plates. It printed both sides of the sheet, and cut it either before or after printing. A patent on the machine was granted on April 14, 1863. The press was first used by the *New York Sun*.

5779. Rotary printing press with a continuous-roll feed to be perfected was produced in 1871 by R. Hoe and Company, New York City, and utilized the first gathering and delivery cylinder patented by Stephen D. Tucker of New York City. The press was installed in the *New York Tribune* plant and produced as many as 18,000 newspapers an hour.

5780. Web-fed four-color rotary printing press was made in 1890 by Walter Scott and Company, Plainfield, NJ, for the *Chicago Inter-Ocean* of Chicago, IL. It was placed in operation in 1892. Curved stereotype plates, cast to fit the cylinders, were used in printing a roll of paper two pages wide.

5781. Rotogravure press was imported in November 1904 by the American Photogravure Company of Philadelphia, PA. It had been built in Ramsbottom, England, by John Wood.

PAPER AND PRINTING—PRINTING

5782. Printer who was a woman was Dinah Nuthead of Annapolis, MD, who successfully petitioned the Assembly on May 5, 1696, for license to print and carry on the printing trade of her late husband, William Nuthead.

5783. Printer's ink was successfully manufactured in America by Charles Eneu Johnson, who began manufacturing inks in Philadelphia, PA, in 1804. His concern later became part of the United Carbon Company.

5784. Mimeograph was invented by Thomas Alva Edison of Menlo Park, NJ, who obtained a patent on August 8, 1876, on a "method of preparing autographic stencils for printing." On February 17, 1880, he obtained a second patent for an improved model.

5785. Halftone printing plate for reproducing photographs in books, magazines, and newspapers was the work of Frederic Eugene Ives, a photographer at Cornell University, Ithaca, NY, who received the first U.S. patent for the halftone printing screen and process on February 8, 1881. Earlier printers had conceived the idea of reproducing photographs by dividing them up into lines that could be transferred to a printer's plate. Ives was the first to devise a consistent method of producing halftones that could be applied to large printing operations. In 1878, he converted a photographic negative into a dot-screen gelatin relief from which he made a printing plate with good fidelity to the original image. The first halftone using the Ives process was printed in the June 1881 issue of the *Philadelphia Photographer*.

5786. Photoengraved magazine was the *Literary Digest*, 80 pages, published in New York City on October 18, 1919. The material was typewritten and photoengraved. A strike of printers at the time made it impossible to issue regularly printed issues of the magazine without great difficulty.

5787. Ink paste was invented by Frank Buckley Cooney of Minneapolis, MN, who obtained a patent on January 1, 1924. The paste, known as Cooney's Ink Paste, was manufactured on February 10, 1923, by the Standard Ink Manufacturing Company, Minneapolis, MN. The inventor sold rights to manufacture to the American Crayon Company.

PAPER AND PRINTING—PRINTING— NEWSPAPERS

5788. Curved stereotype plate was cast by Charles Craske in 1854 in New York City for a Hoe rotary press. It was used by the *New York Tribune.* On August 31, 1861, full pages of the *Tribune* were printed from curved plates.

5789. Newspaper printed on a train was the *Weekly Herald,* a single sheet of approximately seven by eight inches, printed on both sides. It was issued by Thomas Alva Edison and distributed on the train between Port Huron and Detroit, MI. The first known issue was dated Port Huron, MI, February 3, 1862.

5790. Newspaper printed on wood-pulp paper was the *Boston Morning Journal* of Boston, MA, first published on January 15, 1863. It was a four-page, eight-column newspaper and sold for three cents a copy.

5791. High-speed newspaper printing and folding machine utilizing the gathering cylinder with a rotary folding cylinder was installed in 1876 on the presses of the *Philadelphia Times,* Philadelphia, PA. It printed and folded four-page sheets at the rate of 400 a minute. The press was shown in operation at the Philadelphia Centennial Exposition in 1876.

5792. Newspaper printing plant to install electricity was the *New York Times,* which turned on the current on September 4, 1882. Electricity was supplied by the Edison Electric Illuminating Company's central station at 257 Pearl Street, New York City. The editorial room had 27 electric lights, the counting room 25. The composing rooms and the press room were equipped later.

5793. Newspaper page set by linotype was the *New York Daily Tribune,* whose editorial page was set by linotype on July 3, 1886.

5794. Quadruple newspaper press was constructed in 1887 by R. Hoe and Company, New York City, for the *New York World* plant, where it was installed in 1891. It produced newspapers at a running speed of 48,000 per hour for an 8-page newspaper or 24,000 per hour for newspapers of 10, 12, 14, or 16 pages. The papers were cut and folded, ready for delivery.

5795. Sextuple newspaper printing press was constructed by R. Hoe and Company, New York City, and installed in 1891 at the *New York Herald* plant. It took 18 months to construct, weighed 58 tons, and was composed of 16,000 pieces. The form and impression cylinders were placed parallel instead of at right angles. It could print and fold 90,000 four-page newspapers an hour.

5796. Automatic plate-casting and finishing machine for stereotype printing was the Autoplate, invented by Henry Alexander Wise Wood, which greatly increased the speed at which newspapers could be printed. It was adopted by the *New York Herald* in 1900.

5797. Newspaper printed on pine-pulp paper in color was the *Dallas News* of Dallas, TX, a daily, which printed a pine-paper edition on March 31, 1937.

5798. Newspaper printed on bagasse newsprint made from waste fiber left after grinding sugar cane was the *Daily World* of Opelousas, LA, printed on February 11, 1954.

PAPER AND PRINTING—PRINTING— TYPESETTING

5799. Hebrew type was used in the *Bay Psalm Book,* the first book to be published in America, printed by Stephen Day and issued in 1640 by the Cambridge Press, Cambridge, MA.

5800. Stereotype printing was tried in 1745 in Philadelphia, PA, by Benjamin Mecom, a nephew of Benjamin Franklin. He commenced casting plates for the New Testament but never finished the task. The first successful stereotypers were David and George Bruce, who established the firm of D. and G. Bruce in New York City in 1813. They designed machinery and molds patterned after those in use in England and had them cast in New York City. The business remained in the family until 1895, when it was sold.

5801. Type foundry in America belonged to Abel Buell, who cast his first font on April 1, 1769, at Killingworth, CT. It is said that the statue of King George III that was torn down in New York City was brought to Buell's foundry to be cast into type.

5802. Dollar marks to be made in type were cast in 1797 by Archibald Binny and James Ronaldson, type-founders of Philadelphia, PA, who started in business on November 1, 1796.

PAPER AND PRINTING—PRINTING—
TYPESETTING—*continued*

5803. Electrotype was produced in 1839, in New York City, from a wood engraving by Joseph Alexander Adams. The electrotype was made by an impression taken in an alloy of soft metal, of which bismuth was probably the chief ingredient. Electrotypes were first published in 1840 in *Mapes Magazine*.

5804. Typesetting machine that actually operated was invented by Timothy Alden of New York City, who obtained a patent on September 15, 1857. The type was arranged in cells around the circumference of a horizontal wheel. As the wheel revolved, several receivers also started to rotate. The desired type was picked up and dropped in proper order in a line.

5805. Linotype machine was invented by Ottmar Mergenthaler of Baltimore, MD, who obtained a patent on August 26, 1884, on a "matrix making machine." The first Linotype machine to be used commercially was a blower machine installed on July 1, 1886, by the Mergenthaler Linotype Company in the printing plant of the *New York Tribune* and used to cast type for the July 3 issue. The machine had a keyboard assembling mechanism, a mechanism for casting a full line of type in a single bar, and a matrix lifting and distributing device. When the matrix was released from a vertical tube that resembled a pipe of an organ, it was carried by air blast along an inclined chute to its place in the assembling line of matrices.

5806. Monotype machine was invented by Tolbert Lanston of Washington, DC, who received five patents for it on June 7, 1887. The machine cast new type, letter by letter, from matrices that were used over and over.

5807. Teletypesetter was manufactured by the Teletypesetter Corporation, Chicago, IL, and sold in October 1932 to a job printing plant in Detroit, MI. The teletypesetter consisted of two units: a perforator for preparing a paper tape and an operating unit for attachment to either a Linotype or an Intertype machine. As the tape was automatically fed into the operating unit, the keys of the linecasting machine were depressed and lines of type were steadily produced at a speed impossible to match by manual operation.

5808. Typesetting machine to dispense with metal type was the Intertype Fotosetter Photographic Line Composing Machine, manufactured by the Intertype Corporation, Brooklyn, New York City, and installed at the plant of Stecher-Traung Lithograph Corporation, Rochester, NY, in 1949. The machine was exhibited at the 6th Educational Graphic Arts Exposition, held at the International Amphitheater, Chicago, on September 11, 1950.

5809. Photographic type-composing machine was the Photon (Higonnet-Moyroud) machine, which was manufactured by Photon beginning in April 1953 under license from the Graphic Arts Research Foundation. The machine, operated from a standard typewriter keyboard at full electric-typewriter speed, delivered film negatives instead of type. The first book set by the Photon process was *The Wonderful World of Insects,* by Albro Tilton Gaul, offered for sale to the public on February 26, 1953, by Rinehart and Company, New York City. The first copy was presented to Dr. Karl Taylor Compton, chairman of the corporation of the Massachusetts Institute of Technology, on February 5, 1953, by Dr. Vannevar Bush, a director of the Graphic Arts Research Foundation, Boston, MA.

PHOTOGRAPHY

5810. Photographs used in surveying were taken by Edward Anthony of New York City, who used a complete daguerreotype outfit to survey the northeast boundary between the United States and Canada as part of the resolution of a border dispute with Great Britain, to which Canada then belonged. He delivered the photographs in 1839 to Daniel Webster of the Joint Boundary Commission, who submitted them to Alexander Baring, Baron Ashburton. The treaty resolving the dispute was ratified at Washington, DC, on August 20, 1842.

5811. Photograph taken in the United States was a daguerreotype, a form of image recording invented by Louis Jacques Mandé Daguerre of France in 1839. The first published description of the method appeared in the *London Globe*, which arrived in the United States on September 20, 1839, on the *British Queen*. Among those who are credited with taking the first daguerreotype are the inventor and artist Samuel Finley Breese Morse, Amasa Holcomb, a Philadelphia lamp maker named Robert Cornelius, and Joseph Saxton, a balance maker at the Philadelphia mint. A picture taken by Dr. John William Draper of his sister Dorothy Catherine Draper in the summer of 1840, using a six-minute sunlight exposure, is believed to be the first daguerreotype portrait.

5812. Commercial photography studio was opened on March 4, 1840, in New York City by Alexander S. Wolcott and John Johnson. On May 8, 1840, Wolcott received the first photography patent, for "a method of taking likenesses by means of a concave reflector and plates so prepared that luminous or other rays will act thereon." The photographs, 1.75 by 2.5 inches, were not reversed, as were daguerreotypes with refracting lenses.

5813. Class photograph was taken by Professor Samuel Finley Breese Morse on August 18, 1840. It showed the Yale College class of 1810 at their 30th reunion in New Haven, CT. He made 35 daguerreotypes, each a half-inch square.

5814. Photograph to gain world fame was a daguerreotype panorama of Niagara Falls, NY, taken in July 1845 by William and Frederick Langenheim of the Philadelphia Daguerrotype Establishment, Philadelphia, PA, from a site near the Clifton House on the Canadian side of the falls. Sets were made and presented to Louis Mandé Daguerre, President James Knox Polk, Queen Victoria, the kings of Prussia, Saxony, and Wurtemberg, and the duke of Brunswick.

5815. Aerial photograph was entitled "Boston as the Eagle and the Wild Goose See It," taken on October 13, 1860, by James Wallace Black of Boston, MA, from a balloon navigated by Samuel Archer King of Providence, RI. The balloon, *The Queen of the Air,* was held by a cable 1,200 feet above the city. Eight pictures were taken, only one of which was good. It showed an area bounded by Brattle Street on the north, the harbor on the east, Sumner Street on the south, and Park Street on the west. Wet plates were used, which were prepared in the balloon before each exposure.

5816. Photographs of combat were two pictures taken during the siege of Charleston, SC, in the summer of 1863 by Southern photographer G.S. Cook. One photograph, taken from the parapet of Fort Moultrie, shows Union gunboats in the act of shelling the fort. The other depicts a shell bursting inside Fort Sumter. No known Civil War photograph shows men in combat.

5817. News photographs of distinction were made during the Civil War by Mathew B. Brady of New York City who, with the permission of President Abraham Lincoln and the Secret Service, followed the Union Army and photographed it in action. He took more than 7,000 pictures, 2,000 of which were purchased by the Government for $25,000. Many of these photographs appeared in a book, *Brady's National Photographic Collection,* in 1870. Brady studied photography with Samuel Finley Breese Morse and had a studio, Brady's Daguerrian Miniature Gallery, at Broadway and Fulton Street in New York City.

5818. Photographs showing action were taken by Eadweard Muybridge in 1872 on a stock farm owned by Leland Stanford at Palo Alto, CA. He used a series of 12 clocks for breaking electric circuits connected with camera shutters. This enabled him to take a series of photographs at regular intervals, in rapid succession, of a racehorse in action.

5819. Photograph taken by incandescent electric light was a portrait of Charles Batchelor made in December 1879 in Menlo Park, NJ.

5820. Photograph taken from an airplane was taken by Major H.A. "Jimmie" Erickson on January 10, 1911, in a Curtiss biplane piloted by Charles Hamilton over San Diego, CA.

5821. Photographs taken under the sea that were successful were obtained by John Ernest Williamson at Chesapeake Bay, VA, in 1913 with the use of the Williamson Submarine Tube and Photosphere.

5822. Photograph showing air in motion across airplane wings was taken by Colonel Rutherford B. Harts during the winter of 1918–19 at Bolling Field, Washington, DC, under the auspices of the Division of Military Aeronautics and the invention secretary of the army general staff. The three miles of film shot by Harts showed that no flying power whatever is exerted on the wings of an aircraft by the air flow produced by the air screws for about 30 percent of a flight, and that rarefication, which produces the lifting power of an airplane, is not continuous but is exerted in intermittent or pulsating air waves.

5823. Demonstration of rapid aerial photography was made on September 5, 1925, before the U.S. General Staff and Command School at Leavenworth, KS. Lieutenant George Goddard, director of photography of the Army Air Corps Technical School, took photographs of the Fort Leavenworth area in the "Flying Laboratory." They were developed, finished, and dropped to the ground within eight minutes from the time of exposure. A photographic transmitting set sent the picture to Governors Island in New York Harbor, where it was in the hands of General Charles Pelot Summerall within 27

PHOTOGRAPHY—*continued*

minutes after it had been taken in Kansas, 1,700 miles away. Copies were also sent to General William Sidney Graves in Chicago, IL, and General Charles Thomas Menoher in San Francisco, CA.

5824. Photograph taken from an airplane at night was taken on November 20, 1925, over Rochester, NY, by Lieutenant George Goddard in cooperation with the Eastman Kodak Company, which supplied a photometer by which the intensity of light was measured. The photographs were taken from a 3,000-foot altitude and showed about three square miles of the city's area. A light bomb was dropped that made a flash lasting 0.05 seconds.

5825. Photographs taken under the sea in natural colors were made for the magazine *National Geographic* off the Tortugas of the Florida Keys on July 16, 1926, and were published in the January 1927 issue. The work was carried out by Dr. William Harding Longley of Goucher College and Charles Martin, chief of the National Geographic Society's photographic laboratory. The camera used in making these autochromes was enclosed in a brass case with a plate-glass window in front of the lens. A supplementary hood was fitted above the regulation reflector. The photographer was able to focus his instrument by means of an acute-angle mirror.

5826. Aerial photograph in natural colors was made in July 1930 by Melville Bell Grosvenor, assistant chief of illustrations of *National Geographic* magazine, and published in the September 1930 issue.

5827. Infrared photograph taken in the dark with a short exposure was made in the Eastman Kodak Research Laboratories in Rochester, NY, on October 7, 1931. A photograph was taken with a one-second exposure, in apparently total darkness, of a group of 50 visitors to the laboratories. The room was flooded with invisible infrared rays, and a new photographic emulsion sensitive to infrared was used.

5828. Aerial photograph showing the lateral curvature of the horizon and the beginning of the stratosphere was taken by Captain Albert William Stevens from the gondola of the stratosphere balloon *Explorer 11,* which was sent up on November 11, 1935, by the National Geographic Society and the Army Air Corps. The photograph was made from an altitude of 72,395 feet, or 13.71 miles, above sea level. It was the first photograph of the horizon taken from such a great altitude; the first photograph

for which the line of sight was entirely in the stratosphere; and the first photograph showing the extreme top of the "dust sphere" that marks the dividing line between the lower atmosphere with its clouds and dust and the stratosphere, which is clear. The balloon took off from Rapid City, SD, and landed 8 hours 13 minutes later at White Lake, SD.

5829. Photograph of a beam of 1-billion-volt x-rays was made by William Morris and Hubert Luckett in October 1946. It showed the rays emanating from the betatron of the General Electric Company, Schenectady, NY. The beam did not cause a glowing of the air through which it passed, but was made visible to the camera by the placement of a fluorescent screen in its path. The camera exposure was made through a three-foot concrete wall in which an opening was made for the lens.

5830. Photograph bounced off the moon was transmitted by the Navy from Hawaii and received on January 28, 1960, at Washington, DC.

5831. Photograph bounced off a satellite was a photograph of President Dwight David Eisenhower. On August 18, 1960, it was beamed 1,000 miles up to the satellite *Echo 1* from a dish antenna by the Collins Radio Company, Cedar Rapids, IA. It was received on standard Associated Press Wirephoto equipment by the Alpha Corporation near Dallas, TX.

PHOTOGRAPHY—CAMERAS AND FILM

5832. Camera exposure scale was prepared by D.W. Seager and published in the March 1840 issue of the *American Repertory of Arts, Sciences, and Manufactures.* The shortest tabulated exposure was five minutes at noon on a very brilliant and clear day; the longest was 50–70 minutes at 3 P.M. on a cloudy day.

5833. Achromatic lenses were made in 1844 in Cambridgeport, MA, by Alvan Clark.

5834. Tintype camera was patented by Professor Hamilton Lamphere Smith, professor of natural sciences, Kenyon College, Gambier, OH, who obtained a patent on February 19, 1856, on "photographic pictures on japanned surfaces." The photographs were collodion positives on black or chocolate-colored iron plates.

5835. Film rolls for cameras were patented by David Henderson Houston of Cambria, WI, who obtained a patent on October 11, 1881, for a "photographic apparatus." He had a camera with a receptacle or box at its inner end containing a "roll of sensitized paper or any other suitable tissue, such as gelatine or any more durable material that may be discovered, and an empty reel, upon which the sensitized band is wound as rapidly as it has been acted upon by the light." The purpose of the camera was "to facilitate taking a number of photographic views successively in a short time."

5836. Transparent paper-strip photographic film was invented in February 1884 by George Eastman of Rochester, NY, who obtained a patent for it on October 14, 1884. The film consisted of paper coated with an insoluble sensitive gelatin emulsion.

5837. Camera to use film rolls was Kodak No. 1, a fixed-focus box camera, announced in June 1888 by George Eastman of Rochester, NY. It weighed 22 ounces and had a lens fast enough to make instantaneous exposures. It used a roll of film of 100 exposures and took a round picture 2.5 inches in diameter. It did not require a table or tripod for support. The camera was covered by a patent dated September 4, 1888, and the name Kodak was registered on the same date.

5838. Celluloid photographic film and the process for producing it were invented by the Reverend Hannibal Williston Goodwin of Newark, NJ, who received a patent on September 13, 1898, on "nitro cellulose transparent flexible photographic film pellicles." He received an order from Thomas Alva Edison for one roll at $2.50 on September 2, 1889.

5839. Filmpack camera was the Premo Film Camera, a box camera introduced in 1903 by the Rochester Optical and Camera Company, Rochester, NY. It cost $4. In 1905 the Premo Folding Film bellows camera was offered at $10.

5840. Film-developing machine that was fully automatic was the Photomaton, invented by Anatol M. Josepho, who constructed the first model in a loft building on 125th Street, New York City. He received a patent on January 17, 1928, on an apparatus for developing photographic film strips. The first Photomaton studio was opened to the public at 1659 Broadway, New York City, in September 1926.

5841. Stroboscopic lamp for high-speed photography was invented in 1927 by Harold Eugene "Doc" Edgerton, a graduate student at the Massachusetts Institute of Technology in Cambridge, MA. Edgerton's stroboscope, or strobe, emitted a bright light for a tiny fraction of a second. Previous researchers had conceived of a fast-flashing light, but Edgerton was the first to synchronize a strobe light to the shutter of a camera and develop the techniques of high-

speed photography. His stop-action photographs of the splash of a single milk droplet, a bullet in mid-flight, and other previously invisible events revealed a world of unknown natural phenomena. The holder of 47 patents, Edgerton also invented specialized sonar, underwater cameras, and high-intensity lamps.

5842. Photographic flashbulbs that were fireless, smokeless, odorless, and noiseless, similar to incandescent lamp bulbs, were made by the General Electric Company of Schenectady, NY, on August 1, 1930, under a patent awarded on September 23, 1930, to Johannes Ostermeier of Althegnenberg, Germany. A small filament in the bulb, when connected to a source of electricity, became heated and ignited the foil and oxygen, causing a flash of light of high intensity and short duration. The bulb was the size of a 150-watt incandescent bulb.

5843. Camera exposure meter was invented in 1931 by William Nelson Goodwin, Jr., of the Weston Electrical Instrument Corporation, Newark, NJ, who obtained a patent on February 21, 1932, on a thermal ammeter. The first one, manufactured in February 1932, was called the photronic photoelectric cell, popularly known as a camera exposure meter. It contained a dial calculating device for translating brightness values into camera aperture settings. It required no battery for its operation, as it changed light energy directly into electrical energy.

5844. Color film that was commercially successful was Kodachrome, developed by Leopold Godowsky, Jr., and Leopold Damrosch Mannes at the Kodak Research Laboratories in Rochester, NY. Godowsky and Mannes improved on earlier color film products by developing a reversal-process color film with three emulsion layers that was simpler and less expensive to process while yielding good color fidelity. Kodak released Kodachrome 16mm movie film in April 1935 and 35mm still film in August 1936.

5845. Aerial camera with nine lenses for large-scale mapping was designed by personnel of the Coast and Geodetic Survey in 1934 under the direction of Lieutenant Oliver Scott Reading and built under contract by the Fairchild Aerial Camera and Instrument Company, Jamaica, Queens, New York City, in 1935. It was placed in operation in 1936. It was 29 inches wide, 27 inches fore and aft, and 31 inches high, and weighed 306 pounds net. Gross weight with all equipment for photography was 750 pounds. The nine lenses photographed the terrain simultaneously on one piece of film. The camera was loaded with a strip of

PHOTOGRAPHY—CAMERAS AND FILM
—*continued*

film 23 inches wide and 200 feet long, and could take 100 exposures without reloading. When flown at a height of 13,750 feet, the camera photographed 121 square miles at one exposure at a scale of 1 inch to 1,667 feet.

5846. Instant camera was the Polaroid camera, invented by Edwin Herbert Land and demonstrated on February 21, 1947, at a meeting of the Optical Society of America at the Hotel Pennsylvania, New York City. The camera contained a specially prepared photographic paper with "pods" of developer and hypo sandwiched with the film. The turning of a knob squeezed open one of the pods, which developed the negative and made the print. The picture was produced in about one minute.

5847. Flashbulb device with multiple flashbulbs was made by the Sylvania Electric Company, Montoursville, PA, and introduced on July 8, 1965, at a press conference at the Waldorf-Astoria Hotel, New York City. It was known as the Flashcube and contained four flash bulbs set in a single socket. A sleeve of three cubes retailed for $1.95. The cubes were presented jointly by Sylvania Electric Products and the Eastman Kodak Company.

POPULATION

5848. Census of the United States was authorized by act of Congress of March 1, 1790, "providing for the enumeration of the inhabitants of the United States." The census compilation cost $44,377 and utilized the services of 17 marshals and 650 assistants. Marshals received from $100 to $500 and assistants received $1 for every 150 persons in county districts and $3 for every 300 in cities and towns. The enumeration, as of August 1, 1790, showed a population of 3,939,326 located in 16 states and the Ohio territory. Virginia, with 747,610, was the most populous state; Rhode Island, with 68,825, the least. New York City had a population of 33,131, Philadelphia had a population of 28,522, and Boston had a population of 18,320.

5849. States with populations of more than 1 million were New York, with 1,372,812; Virginia, with 1,065,366; and Pennsylvania, with 1,049,456, according to the census of 1820. The first state to exceed 5 million in population was New York, which reached 5,082,871 in the census of 1880. It was also the first state to exceed the 10 million mark, which it reached in the 1920 census, when it had a population of 10,385,227.

5850. Census in which the national population exceeded 10 million was the fifth census, the census of 1830, which showed a population of 12,866,620. The first census to show a population of more than 50 million was the 10th census, the census of 1880, which listed the population as 50,155,783. The first census over 100 million was the census of 1920, which showed a population of 105,710,620. The first census over 150 million was that of 1950, which showed a population of 150,697,361. The first census over 200 million was that of 1970, which showed a population of 203,184,772, later revised to 203,211,926. A public ceremony was held on November 20, 1967, at the Department of Commerce, Washington, DC, when the nation's population reached 200 million persons.

5851. Census that included deaf, mute, and blind people was taken in 1830. Previously, people with these disabilities were not enumerated at all.

5852. City with a population of more than 1 million was New York City, whose population according to the census of 1880 was 1,206,299. This number was for Manhattan alone. Brooklyn was then an independent city. Brooklyn and three other areas (the Bronx, Queens, and Staten Island) were combined with Manhattan in 1898 to form the five boroughs of New York City. The population of the city in 1920 was 5,620,048, making it the first city with a population exceeding 5 million.

5853. Census compiled by machines was the 1890 census, which recorded a population of 62,979,766 on June 1, 1890.

5854. Census compiled in part from statistics obtained by mail was the 19th decennial census, mailed on April 1, 1970.

5855. Birth rate below the rate necessary to maintain the population occurred in the first quarter of 1972. Among the causes cited by demographers were easy access to contraception and abortion and the entry of more women into the workforce.

5856. Census based on a sample of the population was the census for the year 2000. On February 28, 1996, the Census Bureau, Washington, DC, announced that for the upcoming census it would no longer use a direct head count, as had been done in all previous censuses, but would count 90 percent of the population and use statistical sampling methods to project the characteristics of the remaining 10 percent.

POPULATION—IMMIGRATION AND CITIZENSHIP

5857. Deportation took place in 1628, when Thomas Morton was sent back to England by the Plymouth Colony for being a troublemaker. Morton, an Englishman who had emigrated in 1624, had built a house at Merry Mount, in what is now Quincy, MA, where he hosted wild parties, earned a reputation as "the lord of misrule," and taunted the Pilgrims, calling Myles Standish "Captain Shrimp." In 1627, the Pilgrims cut down a Maypole he erected "upon the festival day of Philip and Jacob" when he regaled some Native Americans with a "barrel of excellent beer." He was also accused of supplying them with guns. He was deported to England on June 9, 1628, came back and was again deported, came back a third time and was jailed in Boston. His book *New English Canaan,* containing satirical remarks about the colonies, was published in England in 1637.

5858. Jew to win full citizenship was Asser Levy of New Amsterdam (later New York City). After the first Jews arrived in the city in 1654, the Council of New Amsterdam passed a law denying them the privilege of standing guard and keeping watch, compulsory for all other citizens, and taxed them for the exemption. Asser Levy and Jacob Barsimson objected to the discrimination and a decision was rendered against them. Levy appealed the decision after doing guard duty voluntarily and on April 20, 1657, was admitted to the status of a burgher, or town citizen. He became a prosperous trader, the first Jew to own land in America and the first to serve on a jury (in 1671, after the colony had been taken over by the English).

5859. Naturalization act in the American colonies was provided for on March 12, 1664, in the letters patent of King Charles II of England to James, the Duke of York, who was permitted to bring in subjects of the realm as well as "any other subjects who would become subjects."

5860. Public official of Italian ancestry was Onorio Razzolini, who was appointed Maryland's armorer and keeper of stores in 1736.

5861. Citizenship conferred by special grant was awarded to the Marquis de Lafayette, Washington's French ally in the Revolutionary War, by the General Assembly of Maryland at the session held on November 1, 1784, to January 22, 1785, at Annapolis, MD. It provided that "the Marquis de Lafayette and his heirs male for ever, shall be, and they and each of them are hereby deemed, adjudged, and taken to be, natural born citizens of this state, and shall henceforth be entitled to all the immunities, rights and privileges, of natural born citizens thereof."

5862. Naturalization act enacted by Congress was passed on March 26, 1790. It authorized courts of record to "entertain the applications" of alien free white persons who had resided in the United States for two years or more, one year of which should be in a particular state, on proof of good character and on their taking an oath or affirmation to support the Constitution.

5863. Immigration law enacted by Congress requiring the recording of data pertaining to the arrival of aliens in the United States was the act of June 25, 1798, which required the master or commander of a vessel to make a written report to the customs officer in charge of the port of entry, giving the names of all arriving aliens and other prescribed data pertaining to them.

5864. Deportation of aliens authorized by Congress was authorized by the act passed on July 6, 1798, which required that aliens above the age of 14 who were "not actually naturalized shall be liable to be apprehended, restrained, rescued and removed as alien enemies."

5865. Chinese labor immigration was arranged through the efforts of William Kelly of Pittsburgh, PA, who in 1854 induced 12 Chinese laborers to work in his foundries for extremely low wages.

5866. Restrictions by Congress on immigration of Chinese laborers were passed on May 6, 1882, suspending Chinese immigration for a 10-year period and forbidding naturalization. According to the provisions of a treaty between China and the United States, signed on May 9, 1881, by President Chester Alan Arthur and proclaimed on October 5, it was agreed that the United States could "regulate, limit or suspend" the immigration of Chinese labor, but not prohibit it altogether. The Chinese exclusion acts were repealed on December 17, 1943.

5867. Immigration ban enacted by Congress was passed on August 3, 1882. The law denied entry to convicts, paupers, and people with physical or mental defects, and required each immigrant to pay a tax of 50 cents. In 1903 the fee was $2; in 1907, $4; and in 1918, $8.

POPULATION—IMMIGRATION AND CITIZENSHIP—*continued*

5868. Border patrol officer was Jefferson Davis Milton of the Immigration and Naturalization Service, who served from April 13, 1904, to June 30, 1932. He was appointed under authority of annual appropriation acts before the border patrol was formally established by act of Congress on May 28, 1924. His job was to prevent the smuggling of illegal Asian immigrants across the Mexican border.

5869. Immigration quota enacted by Congress was the act of May 19, 1921, which limited immigration to 3 percent of the number of foreign-born persons of any given nationality in the United States as shown in the 1910 census. Not more than 20 percent of any country's quota was permitted to arrive in one month.

5870. State law to establish English as an official language was the Illinois law enacted on June 19, 1923, which stated that "the official language of the State of Illinois shall be known hereafter as the 'American' language."

5871. Citizenship statute for Native Americans was enacted on June 2, 1924. It provided that "all non-citizen Indians born within the territorial limits of the United States be, and they are hereby declared to be, citizens of the United States."

5872. Registration of aliens by the federal government was authorized by Congress under the Alien Registration Act of 1940, approved on June 28, 1940, "to amend certain provisions of law with respect to the admission and deportation of aliens; to require the fingerprinting and registration of aliens." The registration was conducted by the Alien Registration Division of the Immigration and Naturalization Service. Earl Grant Harrison was the director in charge of registration. During the period from August 27, 1940, to December 26, 1940, the number of noncitizens who registered was 4,741,971.

5873. Citizenship granted on foreign soil was conferred on December 4, 1942, in the Panama Canal Zone by Thomas Buckman Shoemaker, assistant commissioner of the Immigration and Naturalization Service, on Private James Alexander Finnell Hoey, who had been born in Ireland. The Second War Powers Act of March 27, 1942, authorized the commissioner of Immigration and Naturalization to designate a representative who shall have power to naturalize "any person entitled to naturalization, who while serving honorably in the military or naval forces of the United States is not within the jurisdiction of any court authorized to naturalize aliens."

5874. Chinese person granted citizenship after the repeal of the Chinese exclusion act was Edward Bing Kan of Chicago, IL, an interpreter for the Immigration and Naturalization Service, who filed his application on December 18, 1943, and was naturalized on January 18, 1944, in Chicago. On December 17, 1943, President Franklin Delano Roosevelt signed the Chinese Act, which made Chinese residents eligible for naturalization and permitted the annual immigration of a quota of 105 Chinese nationals.

5875. Nazi collaborator to be deported by the Immigration and Naturalization Service was Ferenc Vajta, a Hungarian newspaper editor who had helped to plan the arrangements by which more than half a million Hungarian Jews were sent to Nazi death camps and forced labor camps during the Holocaust. After World War II he did espionage work for the United States and was allowed to enter the country. He was arrested in 1948 and was deported to Colombia in February 1950.

5876. Japanese person to receive an immigration visa was Sozaburo Kujiraoka of Tokyo, Japan, who was given a visa on February 22, 1953. The McCarran-Walter Immigration and Nationality Act of June 27, 1952, allowed an annual quota of 100 immigrants from Japan.

5877. Refugee to arrive under the Refugee Relief Act of 1953 was Stamatoula Roumanis, a 12-year-old Greek girl, who arrived at Idlewild International Airport, New York City, on January 1, 1954. The law had been enacted by Congress on August 7, 1953, "for the relief of certain refugees and orphans, and for other purposes."

5878. Honorary citizenship authorized by Congress was conferred on Sir Winston Churchill, the former prime minister of Great Britain, by proclamation of April 9, 1963, by President John Fitzgerald Kennedy.

5879. Naturalization ceremony in the White House was held on November 23, 1968, when 54 immigrants from 26 nations became citizens. The youngest was an 8-year-old Filipino girl and the oldest was a 72-year-old Chinese laundry worker.

5880. Nazi death camp guard to be deported by the Immigration and Naturalization Service was Hermine Braunsteiner Ryan of New York City. During the Holocaust, she worked as a guard at Nazi concentration camps in Poland, where she tortured and murdered prisoners with extreme cruelty. She became a naturalized American citizen in 1963. After her crimes were made public by the Nazi-hunter Simon

Wiesenthal, she became the subject of an INS investigation and gave up her citizenship. She was deported in August 1973 to Germany, where she stood trial along with 14 other defendants. She was convicted of murder in 1981 and received a life prison term.

5881. Cuban boatlift began on April 21, 1980, when the Carter Administration agreed to accept into the United States a large number of refugees seeking political asylum from Cuba's communist regime. Most of the 125,262 immigrants traveled in small boats to Key West, FL, from the Cuban port of Mariel. The boatlift lasted until September 26, when Mariel was closed by Cuban authorities to further emigration.

5882. Political asylum granted on grounds of sexual orientation was given to Jose Garcia (a pseudonym), a Mexican citizen, who was granted asylum by the Immigration and Naturalization Service on March 25, 1994. Garcia was a homosexual who said that he had been harassed and raped by Mexican police.

5883. Political asylum granted to avoid genital mutilation was given on June 13, 1996, to Fauziya Kasinga, 19, a citizen of the West African country of Togo. Kasinga was kept in immigration detention centers for more than a year before the Immigration Service's Board of Immigration Appeals decided that fear of genital mutilation represented a legitimate ground for asylum. Mutilation of the genitals of girls and young women for religious and cultural reasons is a common practice in many parts of Africa.

POPULATION—IMMIGRATION AND CITIZENSHIP—PASSPORTS

5884. Passport recorded in the Passport Division of the State Department is dated July 8, 1796. The passport was issued to Francis Maria Barrere, "a citizen of the United States having occasion to pass into foreign countries about his lawful affairs," and was signed by Thomas Pickering, secretary of state.

5885. Passport fee was levied under the Internal Revenue Act of July 1, 1862, "to provide internal revenue to support the government and to pay interest on the public debt." It fixed a fee of $3 for "every passport issued in the office of the Secretary of State." Prior to this time, consuls in foreign countries charged a fee not exceeding $1 for passports they issued, but passports issued in the United States were free.

5886. Passport photographs were required by a regulation effective on November 20, 1914.

POPULATION—SETTLEMENT

5887. Humans in America crossed the Bering Strait from Siberia about 30 millennia ago. The earliest evidence of human occupation in the New World, derived from analysis of the mitochondrial DNA of Central American indigenous peoples, has been dated at circa 29,000 B.C.E. The earliest definitively dated human group in the area that is now the United States is the Clovis culture of circa 10,000 B.C.E., named for Clovis, NM, where sharp, fluted projectile points of chalcedony or obsidian and other artifacts were first unearthed in the early 1930s.

5888. Human construction in North America known to archeologists was built more than nine millennia ago, beginning approximately in the year 7000 B.C.E., at Watson Brake, LA, on the flood plain of the Ouachita River. The structure, which covered an area about 900 feet in diameter, consisted of 11 mounds of earth connected by low earthen ridges. A team of scientists led by Dr. Joe W. Saunders, professor of geosciences at Northeast Louisiana University, Monroe, LA, opened the site and found plant seeds, fish bones, and animal bones. Their findings were announced on September 20, 1997. The mounds were not used for habitation and their purpose could not be identified. They were some 1,500 years older than other early Native American sites.

5889. European to sight America was probably Bjarni Herjolffson, a trader from Iceland who was on his way to Greenland about the year 986 when his ship was blown off course by a storm. He and his men found themselves near an unknown tree-covered land, which they did not stop to investigate. His account of this adventure inspired Leif Eriksson to undertake a voyage of exploration some years later.

5890. European settlement in America was Vinland, founded by the Icelandic Viking explorer Leif Eriksson circa 1000 somewhere on the northeastern coast of North America, with guesses ranging from as far south as Virginia and as far north as Newfoundland. It was, according to the account given in an Icelandic saga, a land with hardwood forests, ample pastureland, and wild grapes. Leif and his crew wintered there and returned to Greenland in the spring with a cargo of timber. A group of colonists led by Leif's sister Freydis Erikssdottir returned to the area in 1004 and again circa 1007. The settlement was abandoned by 1015.

POPULATION—SETTLEMENT—*continued*

5891. Settlement in America in continuous habitation is the mountain village of Acoma, NM. First settled in the 11th century by Indians from nearby Enchanted Mesa, Acoma still has a few dozen permanent residents.

5892. Jews to arrive in America were Marranos, Spanish Jews who had converted to Christianity in order to escape torture and death under the Inquisition. Marranos were part of Columbus's voyage of discovery in 1492 and of Spanish explorations and settlements in the 16th century. A handful of Jews came to the English colonies in Virginia and Massachusetts in the first half of the 17th century, but most historians consider the first permanent Jewish settler in America to have been Jacob Barsimson of Holland, who landed at the Dutch colony of New Amsterdam (the future New York City) on August 22, 1654. A month later, a group of 23 Jews from Recife, Brazil, arrived in New Amsterdam seeking refuge from Portuguese persecution. Against the wishes of the colony's governor, Peter Stuyvesant, the Dutch West India Company allowed them to stay, provided "the poor among them should not become a burden to the Company or the community, but be supported by their own nation."

5893. European to set foot on the North American continent after the Vikings was John Cabot (also spelled Caboto, Cabotto, Caboote, Gabote, Calbot, or Talbot), a mariner who was probably born in Genoa, Italy. In 1496, King Henry VII of England granted Cabot a charter to sail west to Asia and set up a spice-trade monopoly. Cabot's ship, a 70-foot caravel called the *Mathew,* embarked from Bristol, England, on May 20, 1497, and arrived on the coast of Newfoundland—or possibly Maine—on June 24. After planting the English and Venetian flags, Cabot and his men spent a few hours exploring the landing site, then returned to their ship.

5894. Battle between Native Americans and European soldiers occurred in May 1539 in Clarke County, AL, when Hernando de Soto's Spanish forces killed several thousand Native Americans, members of a war party under Chief Tuscaloosa, in nine hours of fighting at the Battle of Mauvilla. The Spanish loss was 70 killed and 900 wounded, including de Soto.

5895. Exploration of the Mississippi River by a European was made by Hernando de Soto, the Spanish explorer. On May 21, 1541, he and his crew arrived at a village called Chisca, where they erected a huge cross. Shortly afterward de Soto died near what is now Ferriday, LA, and was buried in the "Father of Waters,"

the first European to be buried in the Mississippi. In 1519 Alonso Alvarez de Piñeda, who was sent out by Francisco de Garay, governor of Jamaica, entered the mouth of the river, which he called the Rio de Espiritu Santo.

5896. Exploration of land on the Pacific coast by a European who made actual contact with it was made by Juan Rodríguez Cabrillo, who left Navidad, Mexico, on June 27, 1542, and landed on September 28 at what is now known as Ballast Point, San Diego, CA. Other Europeans had encountered the Pacific Ocean previously, including Vasco Nuñez de Balboa, who had laid eyes on the Pacific in 1513, and Ferdinand Magellan, who had sailed across the Pacific in 1520–21 during the first circumnavigation of the world.

5897. League of Native American nations was the Iroquois Confederacy, located in what is now New York State and the surrounding area. According to tradition, the Confederacy was formed in about the year 1550 by Hiawatha (Haio-hwat'ha), a Mohawk Indian, and his mentor, Dekanawida, a Huron. It included the Cayuga, Mohawk, and Oneida tribes, which were later joined by the Seneca and the Onondaga. The Tuscarora joined the Confederacy in 1715. The league was formed on cooperative principles, with each tribe represented at a policy-making council.

5898. French to arrive in America were explorers and traders who came in the 16th century. The first French settlement, located on Parris Island, SC, was established in 1562 by Huguenots (Protestants) seeking refuge from France's religious wars. It lasted two years. Another Huguenot settlement, at Fort Caroline, FL, founded in 1564, was attacked and destroyed by the Spanish the following year and its inhabitants massacred.

5899. European settlement in America that was permanent was St. Augustine, FL, founded on September 8, 1565, by the sea captain Pedro Menéndez de Avilés. He left Cadiz, Spain, on July 28, 1565, on a mission to stop the settlement activities of the French Huguenots. He sighted land off the Florida coast on August 28, the feast day of St. Augustine of Hippo, for whom he named the garrison that he built nearby. The city of St. Augustine is the oldest colonial site to be continuously inhabited and the first permanent site of Catholic settlement.

5900. Colonial warfare between European powers in America took place in 1565 between Spain and France. Pedro Menéndez de Avilés and 400 Spaniards arrived on the northeastern coast of Florida from Cadiz, Spain, on August 28, 1565, and proceeded overland to the St. Johns River, where they surprised and captured the French Huguenot settlement at Fort Caroline (near the present site of Jacksonville) on September 20. The French, commanded by René Goulaine de Laudonnière, lost 140 men in the attack. The Spanish lost none.

5901. Truce violation occurred on September 20, 1565, when Pedro Menéndez de Avilés, the Spanish navigator, captured the French Huguenot colony at Fort Caroline, near present-day Jacksonville, FL. The French surrendered under the terms of a truce that guaranteed them amnesty, but Menéndez hanged them, putting a sign over the bodies that read: "I do this not to Frenchmen but to Lutherans." In 1568, the fort was recaptured by a Huguenot corsair, Dominique de Gourges, who took his revenge by killing all his prisoners. His sign read: "I do this not to Spaniards...but as to traitors, robbers, and murderers."

5902. Surveyor in America was the English mathematician Thomas Harriot (or Hariot), surveyor and historian of Sir Walter Raleigh's first colony at Roanoke, who arrived in 1585. He remained a year and returned to England in July 1586 with the fleet commanded by Sir Richard Grenville. He published his observations in London in 1588 as *A Briefe and True Report of the New Found Land of Virginia, of the Commodities There Found and to be Raysed, As Well Merchantable, As Others for Victuall, Building and Other Necessarie Uses For Those That Are and Shalbe the Planters There....*

5903. Exploration of the New England region by an Englishman was made by Captain Bartholomew Gosnold, who left Falmouth, England, on March 26, 1602, in the *Concord* with a crew of 31. On May 15, 1602, he landed on the southern Maine coast near what is now Cape Porpoise.

5904. European settlement in the northeast after the Vikings was on Neutral Island at Calais, ME, on the St. Croix River at the head of Passamaquoddy Bay. It was founded in 1604 by Pierre du Guast, Sieur de Monts, the French explorer.

5905. Rebellion in the English colonies was attempted in 1607 at the colony in Jamestown, VA. George Kendall, one of the original first councilors appointed in England, "was put off from being of the Council, and committed to prison; for that it did manyfestly appear he did practize to sew discord between the President and Council." He was shot to death for mutiny.

5906. Colonial council was held in Jamestown, VA, on May 13, 1607. Its members were Bartholomew Gosnold, Edward Maria Wingfield, Christopher Newport, John Smith, John Ratcliffe, John Martin, and George Kendall. They had been selected for the council by King James I, who had placed their names in a sealed box that was not to be opened until the colonists sponsored by the London Company arrived in America. The council elected Wingfield as the first president.

5907. English settlement in America that was permanent was established at Jamestown, VA, on May 13, 1607, with the arrival of the colonists who had been sent out by the London Company from Blackwell, England, on December 19, 1606. A total of 105 colonists arrived on the *Susan Constant,* 100 tons, under Captain Christopher Newport; the *Godspeed,* 40 tons, under Captain Bartholomew Gosnold; and the *Discovery,* 20 tons, under Captain John Ratcliffe.

5908. Battle between English colonists and Native Americans took place on May 27, 1607, when the English settlers of Jamestown, VA, repulsed an attack by 200 Native American warriors. It is recorded that the English leader, Captain Edward Maria Wingfield, "was shot clean through his beard."

5909. Polish settlers in America were artisans recruited by the sponsors of the English colony in Jamestown, VA, to produce items for export. Their number included glassblowers, soap makers, and pitch makers. They arrived on the *Mary and Margaret* in 1609.

5910. Naval expedition mounted by an English colony was undertaken in 1613 against a French settlement in Nova Scotia. It consisted of 11 vessels carrying a total of 14 light guns, and was commanded by Samuel Argall of Virginia. The expedition captured Mount Desert, St. Croix, and Port Royal, Nova Scotia.

5911. Colonial warfare between England and France in America occurred in 1613 at Mount Desert, ME, where Father Pierre Biard, superior of Saint Sauveur, had established a settlement of French Jesuits. The settlement was attacked by an English expedition under the command of Captain Samuel Argall. His aim was to sup-

POPULATION—SETTLEMENT—*continued*

press piracy and to defend England's claim to the country, which was based on explorations made by John and Sebastian Cabot in the 15th and 16th centuries. A brief description of the conflict records that an English "vessel and forty soldiers landed at a place called Mount Desert in Nova Scotia, near St. John's River, or Tweed, possessed by the French; they killed some French, took away their guns and dismantled the Fort."

5912. Dutch settlement in America was a trading post set up in 1614 at what is now Albany, NY, following the explorations of the Dutch explorer Henry Hudson in 1609. The Dutch West India Company established Fort Orange at Albany in 1624. The entire colony, stretching along the Hudson River, was called New Netherland and had its capital at New Amsterdam, on Manhattan Island. Lack of interest by Dutch people in emigrating to New Netherland forced the company to recruit volunteers from France, Belgium, Sweden, and other Western European countries. The first director general of the colony was Peter Minuit.

5913. Waterpower development grant to a colonist was part of a charter obtained from the English crown in 1620 by the English mariner Sir Ferdinando Gorges, who planned to start new fiefdoms and noble estates in New England. The charter gave him the right to develop the territory lying between the 40th and 48th parallels, north latitude, from sea to sea, and required him to develop waterpower. Gorges constructed a log dam at the future site of South Berwick, ME, on that part of the Piscataqua River known as the Newwichawanick River. He erected a grist mill and sent some of the meal to England as proof that he was conforming to the agreement. The establishment of the colonies of Plymouth and Massachusetts ruined his plans, though he retained his claim to Maine.

5914. Greeting addressed to the Pilgrims by a Native American was a phrase in the English language: "Welcome, Englishmen." It was spoken by Samoset, an Abenaki Indian, on March 16, 1621, when he entered the Pilgrim settlement at what is now Plymouth, MA. Samoset was a sagamore of the Pemaquid tribe who had learned some English from the fishermen who harvested cod off the coast of Maine. He was in Massachusetts as a guest of the Wampanoag chief Massasoit, whose territories included Plymouth. Samoset introduced the Pilgrims to Massasoit and to Tisquantum (also known as Squanto), the English-speaking Patuxet Indian who instructed the settlers in agriculture.

5915. Colonial treaty with the Native Americans was a defensive alliance made on April 1, 1621, on Strawberry Hill, Plymouth, MA, between Massasoit, chief of the Wampanoags, and the Plymouth colonists, acting in behalf of King James I. They promised not to "doe hurt" to one another. If a Wampanoag broke the law, he was sent to Plymouth for punishment; if a colonist was the offender, he was sent to the Wampanoags. The agreement in all its parts was kept by both parties for more than half a century.

5916. Massacre of settlers by Native Americans took place at Jamestown, VA, on March 22, 1622, when 347 colonists out of a population of 1,240 were slain.

5917. Belgian immigrants were Walloons, led by Jesse de Forest, who came to New Amsterdam (later New York City) in 1624 aboard the ship *New Netherland.* They settled in New Amsterdam, Brooklyn, Albany, and in Gloucester, NJ, becoming the first European residents in what is now the Middle Atlantic region.

5918. Land sale by Native Americans to Europeans known to have taken place occurred in July 1625, when John Brown of New Harbor, ME, purchased 12,000 acres of Pemaquid land in Maine. The deed was signed by two leaders of the Pemaquid, Samoset and Unungoit.

5919. Land sale swindle was the sale of Manhattan Island to Dutch colonists under Peter Minuit in 1626. The Canarsie chiefs who accepted 60 guilders' worth of trinkets for the island (a sum worth several thousand dollars, not $24 as is often reported) had no claim to it. They hailed from the area that is now called Brooklyn. The future site of New York City belonged to the Manhattans (also called the Manados), and Minuit had to pay them separately.

5920. Fur trading post was established by the Pilgrims of Plymouth Colony in Augusta, ME, in 1628. Trade was carried on with the Norridgewock tribe of Native Americans. Most of the pelts were exported to England.

5921. Czech settler in America may have been Augustine Herrmann, who disembarked in New Amsterdam (the future New York City) in 1633 and eventually made his home in Maryland.

5922. Naval battle between colonists took place on April 23, 1635, when *The Cockatrice,* a pinnace commanded by Lieutenant Ratcliff Warren, attacked two pinnaces commanded by Captain Thomas Cornwallis, the *St. Helen* and the *St. Margaret,* in the Little Pocomoke or Wicomoco River at St. Mary's, on the eastern shore of Maryland.

5923. Religious refuge for people of all faiths to be founded anywhere in the world was Providence, RI, established in 1636 by Roger Williams. Williams, an English-born minister, emigrated to Massachusetts Bay Colony in 1630 and served briefly as pastor of Plymouth and then of Salem. He was banished from Massachusetts in 1635 for holding dissident religious and political opinions. With the help of the Narragansett tribe of Native Americans, he founded the town of Providence and the colony of Rhode Island as a refuge "for such as were destitute for conscience' sake." Among those who found a haven there were Anne Hutchinson, who was exiled from Massachusetts for theological reasons; some of the first families of Jews to settle in North America; and the Quakers, who were a persecuted sect in Massachusetts.

5924. Swedes to arrive in America landed in 1638. The Dutch colonial administrator Peter Minuit led an expedition that sailed from Gothenburg, Sweden, on November 20, 1637, in two Dutch vessels, *Kalmar Nyckel* and *Vogel Grip,* with Jan Hendricksen van de Waeter as skipper. The expedition landed in March 1638 at "The Rocks" on the Christina River (the future site of Wilmington, DE). Fort Christina, built nearby, was named in honor of the Swedish queen. Another settlement, New Sweden, was built on the Delaware River, near the present site of Trenton, NJ.

5925. Danish settlers in America arrived early in the 17th century. One of the first was Jonas Bronck, who settled in 1641 in the area north of Manhattan Island. It is now known as the Bronx and is one of New York City's five boroughs.

5926. Colonial government federation was the United Colonies of New England, organized on May 10, 1643, in Boston, MA, by the colonies of Connecticut, Massachusetts, New Haven, and Plymouth as "a firm and perpetual league of friendship and amity for offence and defence, mutual advice and succor, upon all occasions, both for preserving and propagating the truth and liberties of the gospel, and for their own mutual safety and welfare." A board of eight commissioners, two from each colony, formed

the "consociation." Issues could be referred to the general courts for appeal if not approved by six votes. John Winthrop of Massachusetts was the first president. Massachusetts, the largest colony, gradually withdrew because it did not have proportional representation.

5927. Expedition of Englishmen to cross the Allegheny Mountains began on August 27, 1650, at Fort Henry, at the falls of the Appomattox River, VA, and returned on September 4. The party consisted of Captain Abraham Wood and his servant Henry Newcombe; Edward Bland, merchant, and his servant Robert Farmer; Elias Pennant and Sackford Brewster; and two guides, Oyeocker, a Nottaway chief, and Pyancha, an Appamattuck war captain.

5928. Landowner of substance who was African-American in the English colonies was probably Anthony Johnson, one of the first 20 Africans to arrive in Jamestown, VA, in 1619. Johnson earned his freedom from indentured servitude, married a white Englishwoman, Mary Johnson, and on July 24, 1651, was granted 250 acres of farmland in Northampton County, VA. Johnson imported five servants, some of whom were white, to work the land.

5929. Colonial badges issued to "friendly" Native Americans were authorized in Virginia by the Act of 1661, which authorized "silver and plated placques to be worn by the Indians when visiting the settlements." One of these has a crude representation of a tobacco plant and scrolls, above which is "The King Of" on the obverse, while on the reverse is a similarly engraved plant and the word "Patomeck" with the *e* overlined. The surface edges were engraved to represent scrolls and foldings, while the medal was holed for suspension. On December 2, 1662, an act "prohibiting the entertainment of Indians without badges" was passed by the Assembly at James City, VA.

5930. Rebellion by colonists against an English governor took place in Delaware against Governor Francis Lovelace and was led by Marcus Jacobson, "The Long Finne," who claimed to be the son of the Swedish general Hans Christoph Konigsmark. He was trapped and turned over to the English commandant. On December 20, 1669, he was condemned for insurrection in the first trial by jury in Delaware. He was lashed in public, branded with the letter *R,* and sold in chains as a slave in Barbados.

5931. Swiss settlement in America was established in 1670 near Charleston, SC. A Swiss mercenary, Diebold von Erlach, who was employed by Spain, had arrived in Florida more than a century earlier, in 1562.

POPULATION—SETTLEMENT—*continued*

5932. Irish to arrive in America were explorers and settlers: William Ayers, from Galway, who was a sailor in Columbus's crew in 1492; Francis Maguire, who was a member of the colony in Jamestown, VA, in 1607; and John Coleman, who sailed with Henry Hudson in 1609. The first community of Irish settlers to arrive, in 1678, were a group of 100 families who had been working as laborers in Barbados after the English government forced them off their land. They became indentured servants in Virginia and the Carolinas.

5933. Settler heroine publicly rewarded was Hannah Duston, who was captured in a Native American attack on Haverhill, MA, on March 16, 1697, in which 40 settlers were murdered or taken prisoner. The attackers killed Duston's week-old baby by dashing it against a tree. On April 29, she escaped from a guarded campsite after killing 10 Native Americans with a tomahawk, scalping them as proof of her deed. The Great and General Court of Massachusetts on June 8, 1697, voted to pay her a reward of £25. Smaller rewards were given to two people who helped her: Mary Neff, the baby's nurse, who had been captured at the same time, and Samuel Leonardson, a young boy from Worcester, MA, who had been held prisoner for two years.

5934. Mass scalping of Native Americans by colonists took place on February 20, 1725. A posse of New Hampshire volunteers ran across a band of 10 sleeping Native Americans and scalped them all. The posse entered Dover in triumph with the 10 scalps stretched on hoops and elevated on poles. A bounty of £100 for each scalp was paid in Boston out of the public treasury. Individual scalps had been brought in earlier.

5935. Colonial settlement west of the Allegheny Mountains other than military forts and outposts was established by the Loyal Land Company of Virginia in 1750. On March 6, a group of six men in the employ of the company, led by Dr. Thomas Walker, a physician, started out from Charlottesville, VA. They reached the future site of Barbourville, KY, on April 23, and built a house that was completed on April 30.

5936. Conestoga wagon was manufactured in 1753 by German immigrants in Lancaster, PA, near Conestoga Creek. A century later, the canvas-roofed wagons became popular with settlers of the American West.

5937. Reservation for Native Americans established by a state was set aside on August 29, 1758, when the New Jersey Legislature appropriated 1,600 acres of a tract of 3,044 acres in the township of Evesham, Burlington County, NJ, to be used as a reservation for the Native Americans of New Jersey. Governor Francis Bernard named the tract Brotherton. About 200 Native Americans, probably Lenapes and Unamis, were settled on it. In 1801, the land was sold and the Native Americans moved to the Lake Oneida Reservation.

5938. Greek settlement was New Smyrna, FL, founded in 1767 by some 1,400 Greek and Italian farmers led by Andrew Turnbull. The colony was named for Smyrna, Greece, the birthplace of Turnbull's wife.

5939. Independent civil government in America was the Watauga Commonwealth, an independent civil government. By the treaty of Fort Stanwix in 1768, the Six Nations confederacy of Native American tribes agreed to surrender all the lands between the Ohio and Tennessee rivers to the British. Inasmuch as there was some misunderstanding because the Iroquois had ceded land to which they had no legal right, the settlers organized a civil government of their own in May 1772 and drew up the "Articles of the Watauga Association," the first written constitution ever adopted by a community of American-born freemen. The settlers elected a representative assembly of 13 men, which in turn elected a committee of 5—John Sevier, James Robertson, Charles Robertson, Zachariah Isbell, and John Carter—who were vested with judicial and executive authority. This was the first free and independent community established on the American continent. The area was in North Carolina and the mountains of Tennessee.

5940. Independent government in an American colony was formed in March 1776 in Charleston, SC. John Rutledge was elected president, Henry Laurens vice president, and William Henry Drayton chief justice. An army and navy were created, a privy council and an assembly were elected, and the issue of $600,000 of paper money was authorized, as well as the issue of coin.

5941. Treaty entered into by the federal government with Native American tribes was a treaty with the Delaware Nation, signed on September 17, 1778. The signers were Andrew and Thomas Lewis, commissioners for the United States, and Captain White Eyes, Captain Pipe, and Captain John Kill Buck on behalf of the Delawares. This treaty, agreed upon at Fort

Pitt, PA (now Pittsburgh), contained the following provisions: all offenses were to be mutually forgiven; peace and friendship were to be perpetual; in case of war, each party was to assist the other; the United States was to have free passage to forts and towns of former enemies, and such warriors as could be spared were to join the troops of the United States; neither party was to inflict punishment without an impartial trial; an agent was to be appointed by the United States to trade with the Delaware Nation; the United States was to guarantee all territorial rights granted by former treaties and to allow a Delaware representative in Congress under certain conditions.

5942. Territory owned by the federal government was the Northwest Territory, also known as the Old Northwest, an area of land about 248,000 square miles around the Great Lakes and the Mississippi River, which was acquired by the United States in the Treaty of Paris of 1783 that ended the Revolutionary War. Between 1781 and 1802, pieces of the territory claimed by New York, Virginia, Massachusetts, Connecticut, and other states were ceded to the federal government. Arthur St. Clair was appointed the first governor of the Northwest Territory in October 1787. The first territorial legislature assembled on September 24, 1799. A separate entity, the Indiana Territory, was formed from part of it in 1800. The area was divided into states beginning with Ohio in 1803, followed by Indiana, Illinois, Michigan, Wisconsin, and Minnesota.

5943. Russian settlement was Three Saints Bay on Kodiak Island, AK, founded by Grigori Shelikhov, a fur trader, in 1784, before Alaska was claimed by Russia. Shelikhov lived there with his wife, Natalia, and 190 men. The first Russian settlement in what would be the continental United States was established on March 15, 1812, at Cazadero, 18 miles north of Bodega Bay on the Russian River in California. The party consisted of 95 Russians and 80 Aleut hunters from Sitka, AK, under the command of Ivan Alexandrovich Kuskof. They built Fort Rumiantzof, a compound of nine buildings surrounded by a 12-foot spiked stockade, as well as 50 buildings outside the stockade. The fort was dedicated on September 11, 1812. On April 15, 1839, the Russians decided to abandon it, and it was sold to the German-American pioneer John Augustus Sutter for $30,000. The Russians evacuated the fort in December and sailed from San Francisco on January 1, 1842. The Spaniards called the settlement Fuerto de los Rusos, the Americans, Fort Ross. Sutter built a trading post there called Sutter's Mill, the site of the 1849 Gold Rush.

5944. Sale of federal land authorized by Congress was authorized by a law enacted on May 20, 1785. It provided for the sale of land in the Northwest Territory.

5945. Survey of public lands was authorized by the Ordinance of 1785, which was passed by the Continental Congress on May 20, 1785. The first surveys were made in the Seven Ranges in the Western Reserve. The Ordinance of 1785 provided for the division of all public lands into townships six miles square, numbered east and west from primary meridians and north and south from base lines. This rectangular system of surveying prevails throughout the United States except in the original 13 states and in Maine, Vermont, Kentucky, Tennessee, and West Virginia.

5946. Reservation for Native Americans established by the federal government was set aside in 1786. The first official notice of the removal of Native Americans residing east of the Mississippi River to reservations west of the river was contained in the act of March 26, 1804. Reservations established by executive order without an act of Congress were not held to be permanent before the general allotment act of February 8, 1887, an "act to provide for the allotment of lands ... severally to Indians on the various reservations, and to extend the protection of the laws of the United States and the territories over the Indians."

5947. Rebellion against the federal government took place in Massachusetts in 1786, when Daniel Shays of Pelham, MA, organized a group of malcontents into an armed force that overthrew courts and committed other acts of violence. They were protesting the depreciation of paper money, the insistence of creditors on being paid in silver money, and the imprisonment of debtors. On December 5, 1786, the rebels seized Worcester. By February 1787, however, they were completely routed.

5948. Land office was established in 1789 by Oliver Phelps and Nathaniel Gorham, who purchased 2,600,000 acres in the "Great American Wilderness" at Canandaigua, NY, for resale to settlers. William Walker was the agent.

POPULATION—SETTLEMENT—*continued*

5949. Exploration by ship of the mouth of the Columbia River in Oregon took place on May 11, 1792, when Robert Gray, a fur trader on his second commercial voyage to the northwest coast of America, rounded Cape Disappointment and sailed the *Columbia Rediviva* 22 miles up the river. Earlier explorers had passed the Columbia's mouth but had not recognized it as such.

5950. Sale of federal land to an individual was authorized by act of Congress of May 17, 1796, "an act providing for the sale of the lands of the United States in the territory northwest of the River Ohio, and above the mouth of the Kentucky River." Congress granted Ebenezer Zane three tracts of land in Ohio, each one mile square, for the purpose of operating ferries: one on the Muskingum River, one on the Sciota, and one on the Hockhocking. These grants were confirmed and patented to Zane on February 14, 1800, in return for his activities in opening Zane's "trail" or "trace" in 1797. The trail, about 200 miles long, led from Wheeling, WV, through Ohio to Limestone (now Maysville), KY.

5951. Protection of Native American hunting grounds authorized by Congress was included in an act approved on May 19, 1796, "to regulate the trade and intercourse with the Native American tribes and to preserve peace on the frontiers." The penalty for crossing the line to hunt or destroy game within Native American territory was a fine of $100 and six months in jail. A later treaty with the Native Americans signed in 1832 is generally regarded as the first national hunting law.

5952. Tax rebellion occurred in February 1799, when John Fries raised an armed force in Northampton, Bucks, and Montgomery counties, PA, to protest a direct federal property tax that had been passed by Congress in July 1798 to raise funds for an expected war with France. Federal troops were called out by President John Adams to suppress the uprising. Fries was arrested in Bethlehem, PA, after resisting a federal marshal. He was convicted of treason and sentenced to death by Supreme Court Justice Samuel Chase. Adams pardoned Fries in 1800.

5953. District land office opened on July 2, 1800, in Steubenville, OH, with David Hoge as the first registrar. It was established under the act of May 10, 1800, which also authorized district land offices in Ohio in Cincinnati, Chillicothe, and Marietta.

5954. Grant of federal land to a foreigner was enacted by Congress on March 3, 1803. The act authorized the secretary of war to issue land warrants to the Marquis de Lafayette (Major General Marie Joseph Paul Yves Roch Gilbert du Motier) for 11,520 acres, which at his option were to be located, surveyed, and patented in conformity with the provisions of the act regulating the grants of land appropriated for military services.

5955. Territory annexed by the federal government was the Louisiana Purchase, a tract of land bought from France on April 30, 1803, for $15 million. It covered 1,171,931 square miles and included the entire Mississippi Valley from the Mississippi River to the Rocky Mountains and from the Gulf of Mexico to Canada. This territory included the present states of Louisiana, Arkansas, Missouri, Iowa, North and South Dakota, Nebraska, Kansas, and Oklahoma, part of Colorado and Wyoming, and most of Montana and Minnesota. The treaty was arranged by Robert R. Livingston, minister at Paris, and James Monroe, who had been sent by President Thomas Jefferson as a special envoy to assist Livingston. The tract was also claimed by Spain, which ceded it to France on November 30, 1803. On December 20, France formally delivered the colony to the American representatives.

5956. Coast survey was authorized by act of Congress of February 10, 1807, "an act to provide for surveying the coasts of the United States," which appropriated a sum not exceeding $50,000. The first superintendent of the survey was Ferdinand Rudolph Hassler, who was appointed on August 3, 1816. Hassler received $3,000 a year and $2,000 for personal expenses in the field.

5957. Settlers to reach the Pacific coast left New York City on September 6, 1810, on the S.S. *Tonquin,* a 290-ton vessel captained by Jonathan Thorn. They rounded Cape Horn on December 25, 1810, landing on April 12, 1811, at Cape Disappointment, WA, a promontory at the mouth of the Columbia River. The enterprise was sponsored by John Jacob Astor.

5958. Land office established by Congress was established in the Department of the Treasury by act of April 25, 1812. The salary of the commissioner was $2,250 a year.

5959. Native American language to be given a written form was the Cherokee language. The inventor of its written form was Sikwayi (also called Sequoyah), a Cherokee silversmith born circa 1776 in the East Tennessee settlement of Tuskegee. His father was Nathaniel Gist, a French trader. Sikwayi, though illiterate, was fascinated by books, and understood the immense advantage that a system of writing gave to European settlers. Over many years, he developed a syllabary in which 85 characters derived from English, Hebrew, and Greek were assigned to serve as symbols for Cherokee sounds, allowing the Cherokee to write in their own language for the first time. Although his writing was at first considered witchcraft, the syllabary was adopted by the Tribal Council in 1821 and was used to produce the first Native American newspaper in 1828. Specimens of Sikwayi's writings are preserved in the Sequoyah Birthplace Museum near Vonore, TN.

5960. Settlers to cross the continent who were women were Narcissa Prentiss Whitman and Eliza Hart Spalding, who crossed the Continental Divide at South Pass, WY, on July 4, 1836. They reached Fort Walla Walla, WA, on September 1, 1836. They were accompanied by their husbands, Marcus Whitman, M.D., and the Reverend Henry Harmon Spalding, Presbyterian missionaries sent by the American Board of Commissioners for Foreign Missions. The Whitmans and 12 others were murdered by the Cayuse in 1847.

5961. Japanese to enter the United States was Manjiro Nakahama, a 15-year-old boy who was one of five Japanese shipwrecked in 1841 and rescued by American sailors. After the other four were landed at Honolulu, HI, Nakaham was brought to Fairhaven, MA, where he attended school for six years. He returned to Japan and was beaten for having left his country. When Commodore Matthew Calbraith Perry went to Japan on a diplomatic mission in 1853, Nakahama acted as interpreter. The first naturalized citizen of Japanese birth was another castaway, Hikozo Hamada, who became an American citizen in 1850.

5962. Wagon train to California left Sapling Grove in what is now Kansas in the spring of 1841 and arrived at Mount Diablo, 50 miles from San Francisco, on November 4, 1841. The party of settlers was led by John Batleson and Paul Geddes and traveled part of the way with Father Pierre-Jean De Smet, the Jesuit missionary, and the mountain man Thomas Fitzpatrick.

5963. Government on the Pacific Coast was authorized by the people of Willamette Valley at Champoeg, OR, on May 2, 1843, when American and Canadian residents met in a field to consider the report of an organizational committee that had been appointed the previous month. A committee of nine was chosen on

July 5, 1843, to devise a plan of civil government. The first governor was George Abernethy, who served from June 12, 1845, to March 3, 1849, when the United States took over jurisdiction of the Oregon territory.

5964. Chinese immigrants to America were two men and a woman who arrived in San Francisco, CA, in 1848, on the brig *Eagle*. According to some historians, there were Chinese shipbuilders on the West Coast as early as 1571, and Chinese laborers there toward the end of the 18th century.

5965. Community leader to exercise the authority of king and high priest was James J. Strang, an expelled Mormon elder who organized a dissident sect of 5,000 Mormons. In 1847 the group settled on Big Beaver Island, MI, where Strang crowned himself King James I in 1850. He was elected to the Michigan legislature in 1852. Strang was assassinated by two of his followers on June 16, 1856.

5966. Traveler's aid program was instituted in 1851, when Bryan Mullanphy of St. Louis, MO, willed approximately one-third of his fortune of more than $1 million to a trust fund to be administered by the City Council for the purpose of assisting those who were "traveling to the west." St. Louis was the usual starting point for westward-bound settlers. In 1885, William Collins and Edward Prior, of the Society of Friends (the Quakers), paid the salary of the first employed worker among travelers.

5967. Homestead law enacted by Congress was the Homestead Act, "an act to secure homesteads to actual settlers on the public domain," passed by both houses of Congress on May 19, 1862, and approved on May 20, 1862, by President Abraham Lincoln. Under this law, any man or woman of 21 years or older could secure title to 160 acres of public land by living on it for five years, making certain improvements, and paying fees of approximately $18. The first homestead granted under the act was taken by Daniel Freeman, a Union soldier, on January 1, 1863, near Beatrice, NE.

5968. Territory annexed by the federal government that was noncontiguous was Alaska, which was purchased from Russia on June 20, 1867, for $7.2 million. General Lovell Harrison Rousseau, the first military governor of the territory, took formal possession of Alaska in October 1867.

POPULATION—SETTLEMENT—*continued*

5969. Territory annexed by the federal government beyond the nation's continental limits was Midway Island in the North Pacific Ocean, claimed on August 28, 1867, by Captain William Reynolds of the Navy for the United States.

5970. Native American to win territorial concessions from the federal government was Red Cloud, a chief of the Oglala Sioux. After years of leading successful assaults against U.S. forts in the Powder River area of Montana, Red Cloud signed a treaty at Fort Laramie on November 6, 1868. The treaty provided for the abandonment of Forts Reno, Kearney, and C.F. Smith.

5971. Lithuanian settlement was founded by four Lithuanian immigrants in Danville, PA, in 1869.

5972. Indian Affairs Commissioner who was Native American was Brigadier General Ely Samuel Parker (Donehogawa), a prominent civil engineer and chief of the Tonawanda Seneca who had served as military secretary to General Ulysses S. Grant during the Civil War. As President, Grant appointed Parker to the post of commissioner of Indian affairs on April 21, 1869. He served until December 1871. The first Native American superintendent of an agency of the Bureau of Indian Affairs was Shirley Plume, an Oglala Sioux, who was designated as acting superintendent of the Standing Rock Agency at Fort Yates, ND, on August 20, 1973. She was appointed superintendent on January 24, 1974.

5973. County created by federal law was Latah County in Idaho, authorized by Congress in a bill enacted on May 14, 1888. The bill set aside a portion of Nez Perce County in Idaho to become Latah County, with the county seat at Moscow.

5974. Island territory annexed by the federal government was the Hawaiian Islands, which were formally annexed on August 12, 1898. The treaty was signed on June 16, 1897, by John Sherman, secretary of state. A joint congressional resolution to provide for the annexation was passed on July 7, 1898.

5975. Old age home for pioneers was the Home for Aged and Infirm Arizona Pioneers, Prescott, AZ, authorized by the legislative assembly of the Territory of Arizona on March 10, 1909. Applicants for admission were required to be residents of Arizona not less than 35 years or over 60 years of age who were citizens of the United States for at least 5 years prior to the date of application, who were active in the development in Arizona, and who were unable to provide themselves with the necessities and comforts of life because of adverse circumstances or failing health. The home was opened for guests on February 6, 1911. The first superintendent was Major A.J. Doran.

5976. Commonwealth of the United States was Puerto Rico, which ratified its status as a commonwealth in a constitution adopted on July 25, 1952. Residents of Puerto Rico possess all the rights of U.S. citizens except that of voting in federal elections.

5977. Occupation of federal territory by Native American protesters in the modern era lasted for four hours on March 9, 1964, when five Sioux led by Richard McKenzie took over Alcatraz Island in San Francisco Bay, off San Francisco, CA, demanding the establishment of a cultural center and university on the island. On November 20, 1969, these demands were raised again by Richard Oakes and a group of about 100 Native Americans, mostly college students, who began an organized occupation of Alcatraz that lasted 19 months.

5978. Armed occupation by Native American protesters in the modern era began on February 27, 1973, when 200 members of the American Indian Movement, led by Russell Means and Dennis Banks, occupied Wounded Knee, SD, a town on the Pine Ridge Indian Reservation. Their demands included a review of treaties between the federal government and indigenous peoples, a Senate investigation into the treatment of Native Americans, and free elections of tribal leaders. The occupation ended on May 8 when the group surrendered to federal marshals. Gunfights during the siege killed one marshal and two protesters. Wounded Knee was the site of a massacre in December 1890 when Army troops machine-gunned 200 Sioux men, women, and children.

5979. African-American history trail was the Black History Trail, dedicated in Washington, DC, in 1988. The seven-and-a-half-mile trail visited important sites in African-American history. It was the brainchild of Willard Andre Hutt, who came up with the idea in 1978, when he was a 17-year-old Boy Scout.

POSTAL SERVICE

5980. Postal route between cities was the route between New York City and Boston, MA. On December 10, 1672, Governor Francis Lovelace of New York announced that monthly service would be inaugurated on January 1, 1673. The first post rider left New York City on January 22, 1673, and arrived in Boston three weeks later.

5981. Parliamentary act to establish a colonial post office in the American colonies was passed in April 1692. A royal patent had been granted to Thomas Neale on February 17, 1691, by the English sovereigns William and Mary, with "full power and authority to erect, settle and establish within the chief parts of their Majesties' colonies and plantations in America, an office or offices for the receiving and dispatching of letters and pacquets, and to receive, send and deliver the same under such rates and sums of money as the planters shall agree to give, and to hold and enjoy the same for the term of 21 years." Neale did not come to America but named Andrew Hamilton as postmaster general, an appointment that was confirmed on April 4, 1692, by the English postmaster general.

5982. Postmaster who was a woman was Mary Katherine Goddard, appointed postmaster at Baltimore, MD, in 1775. She served until November 14, 1789. The first woman to be appointed postmaster after the adoption of the Constitution was Sarah De Crow, who was made postmaster at Hertford, NC, on September 27, 1792. She was the only woman among 195 postmasters.

5983. Postmaster general under the Continental Congress was Benjamin Franklin, who was appointed on July 26, 1775, by the Second Continental Congress at a salary of $1,000 a year and who served until November 7, 1776. He had served the crown as deputy postmaster at Philadelphia, PA, from 1737 to 1753, and as deputy postmaster general for the colonies from 1753 to 1774.

5984. Mail franking privilege allowing free use of the mail was granted to members of Congress and private soldiers in service on November 8, 1775. Regulations of January 9, 1776, provided that soldiers' mail was to be franked by the officer in charge. On April 3, 1800, free franking of mail during her natural life was granted to Martha Washington.

5985. Postmaster general of the United States was Samuel Osgood, who was appointed by President George Washington and who served from September 26, 1789, to August 19, 1791. His office was authorized by act of Congress of September 22, 1789, which gave the general supervision of the post office to a postmaster general under the direction of the President. Other postmasters under Washington's administration were Timothy Pickering, appointed in 1791, and Joseph Habersham, in 1797.

5986. Postal service law enacted by Congress was signed by President George Washington on February 20, 1792. This act set the rates at 6 cents for letters to be carried not more than 30 miles, 8 cents between 30 and 60 miles, 10 cents between 60 and 100 miles, and 12.5 cents between 100 and 150 miles.

5987. Mailbox see-through locker was invented in 1810 by Thomas Brown, who was governor of Florida from 1849 to 1853. His mailboxes consisted of a series of numbered pigeonholes with glass fronts. People who owned or rented boxes were thus able to see whether there was any mail waiting for them without having to open the box.

5988. Mail delivery by steamboat was authorized by act of Congress of February 27, 1813. The postmaster general was granted the power to transport mail in steamboats as long as the expense was not more, "taking into consideration distance, expedition and frequency, than is paid for carrying the mail by stages on the post road, or roads, adjacent to the course of such steamboats."

5989. Dead letter office of the Post Office Department was organized in 1825 in Washington, DC. A dead letter is a letter that is unclaimed and undeliverable.

5990. Ocean mail contracts were authorized by act of Congress of March 3, 1845, "to provide for the transportation of the mail between the United States and foreign countries." The first contract was made in 1847 with the Ocean Navigation Company, which agreed to transport United States mail once a month between the ports of New York City; Southampton, England; and Bremen, Germany. Compensation was $16,666 for each round trip. The *Washington*, pioneer of American ocean steamers, started this service on June 1, 1847. The contract expired on June 1, 1857.

5991. Registered mail was authorized by act of Congress of March 3, 1855. The system was placed in operation on July 1, 1855. The fee was five cents.

POSTAL SERVICE—*continued*

5992. Street letter box was invented by Albert Potts of Philadelphia, PA, who obtained a patent on March 9, 1858, on "a mode of attaching metallic letter-boxes." The box had a center hole through which the shaft of an ordinary cast-iron lamppost was placed. Boxes were erected on August 2, 1858, in Boston and New York City.

5993. Overland mail service to the Pacific Coast was begun on September 15, 1858, by the Overland Mail coaches, the old John Butterfield stage line. Stages left Tipton, MO, and San Francisco, CA, simultaneously every Monday and Thursday. The route was operated under government contract, authorized by act of Congress of March 3, 1857. The contract was signed on September 16, 1857, and specified payment of $600,000 a year for six years, for semiweekly trips in both directions, in "good fourhorse post coaches or spring wagons suitable for the convenience of passengers as well as safety and security of the mails." The specified running time for the 2,800 miles was a maximum of 25 days. The first trips were made in a little less than 24 days.

5994. Pony Express mail left St. Joseph, MO, and Sacramento, CA, simultaneously on April 3, 1860, carried by Henry Wallace riding west and John Roff riding east. The westbound packet was delivered in 10 days, the eastbound in 12. (According to some accounts, the first rider westward was William Richardson or John Frey, and the first rider eastward was Samuel Hamilton, who rode 20 miles in 59 minutes.) The route went through Fort Kearney, Fort Laramie, Fort Bridger, Salt Lake City, Camp Floyd, Carson City, Washoe Silver Mines, and Placerville. Until the service was discontinued on October 24, 1861, riders left St. Joseph every day at noon and Sacramento every day at 8 A.M. except on Sundays. It was a private enterprise under a charter granted by the state of Kansas to the Central Overland and Pike's Peak Express Company. The charge was $5 a half ounce.

5995. Newspaper wrappers for mailing newspapers were issued in October 1861 under act of Congress of February 27, 1861. They were manila and buff, and bore a one-cent blue stamp with the head of Benjamin Franklin. In 1863, a two-cent wrapper was added, bearing a black stamp with the head of Andrew Jackson.

5996. Free mail delivery in cities was authorized by congressional act of March 3, 1863. City delivery service was placed in operation on July 1, 1863, in 49 major cities, using 440 carriers at an annual cost of $300,000. On January 3, 1887, free delivery service was extended to cities with populations of 50,000 or more and was permitted in places having a population of at least 10,000 and postal receipts of $10,000.

5997. Money order system was established on November 1, 1864, in order to promote public convenience and ensure safety in the transfer by mail of small sums of money. Foreign service was authorized on July 27, 1868. The first agreement was made with Switzerland, effective September 1, 1869. Service was extended to Great Britain in October 1871 and to Germany in October 1872.

5998. Uniforms for mail carriers were authorized by Congress on July 27, 1868, by an act that authorized the postmaster general "to prescribe a uniform dress to be worn by the letter-carriers." A standard uniform was approved on October 31, 1868.

5999. Mail fraud law enacted by Congress was enacted on June 8, 1872. It outlawed any "fraudulent lottery, gift enterprise, or scheme for the distribution of money, or of any real or personal property, by lot, chance, or drawing of any kind, or in conducting any other scheme or device for obtaining money through the mails by means of false or fraudulent pretenses, representations, or promises." The postmaster general was authorized to stamp mail, registered mail, and money orders "fraudulent" and return them to the sender instead of making the delivery to the addressee.

6000. Mail chute for dropping mail from the upper stories of office buildings, hotels, apartment houses, and other tall structures was installed in 1883 in the Elwood Building, Rochester, NY, following plans prepared by James Goold Cutler, the architect of the building, who received a patent for a mail chute on September 11, 1883. The device was later developed and suited to the requirements of the Post Office and public use by Joseph Warren Cutler under a series of about 30 patents issued to him.

6001. Special delivery mail service was authorized by congressional act of March 3, 1885. The service was established on October 1, 1885, and at first was restricted to free delivery offices in towns of 4,000 or more inhabitants. An additional charge of 10 cents a letter was made for this service, and a blue special delivery stamp was required. On August 4, 1886, the service was extended to all free delivery offices.

6002. Rural free mail delivery was established on October 1, 1896, when three routes were designated in West Virginia: one from Charles Town, one from Uvilla, and one from Halltown.

6003. Mail truck built especially for mail collection was constructed by the Winton Motor Vehicle Company of Cleveland, OH, in 1899. A test was made in Cleveland over a 22-mile route, when mail was collected from 120 boxes. Although the test was made in a severe snowstorm under adverse conditions, the trip took only 2 hours 27 minutes. A horse and wagon took six hours to make the same trip.

6004. Bulk mail was authorized by Congress on April 28, 1904, and went into use on October 1, 1904. It permitted 2,000 or more identical pieces of third-class or fourth-class mail to be mailed without stamps affixed, in exchange for a fee. The denomination of the postage, the place of mailing, and the permit issued by the post office for the mailing was printed in place of the stamp.

6005. Navy mail service was established on May 27, 1908, when an appropriation was made for the year ending June 30, 1909, to designate enlisted men of the Navy as naval mail clerks for an extra $500 in pay and assistant naval mail clerks for an extra $300. The U.S.S. *Illinois, Prairie,* and *Rhode Island* were the first vessels equipped with postal facilities, beginning on August 15, 1908.

6006. Parcel post service was authorized on August 24, 1912, when appropriations were made for the service that started on January 1, 1913. Previously the weight limit of mail had been four pounds. The rates of the parcel post service depended upon the weight of the package and the distance carried.

6007. Mail collection and delivery in cars owned by the federal government took place on October 19, 1914, in Washington, DC.

6008. Postage meter was officially set at Stamford, CT, by the Pitney-Bowes Postage Meter Company on November 16, 1920. Although the idea of metered mail originated in 1900, when the American Postage Meter Company was organized in Chicago, it was not until September 1, 1920, that the Post Office Department approved it. About $2 million was spent on research and development of the machine.

6009. Drive-up mailbox enabling motorists to mail letters without moving from the seats of their cars was installed in July 1927 at Houston, TX. The box had metal handles 8 to 10 inches long and was tilted 4 inches. The boxes were known as "courtesy collection boxes."

6010. International dogsled mail left Lewiston, ME, on December 20, 1928, with Alden William Pulsifer, postmaster of Minot, ME, in charge, and arrived on January 14, 1929, at Montreal, Canada. The mail traveled in a regular eight-foot mushing sled weighing 200 pounds, pulled by six blackhead Eskimo dogs. They averaged nine miles an hour (seven to eight on bare ground) and covered from 40 to 60 miles a day. The mail pouch contained 385 letters in government-stamped canceled envelopes. The trip was not an official one. The sled returned to Lewiston on February 2, 1929, having passed through 118 cities and covered 600 miles, of which 90 percent was bare of snow.

6011. Coin-operated mailbox was the Mailomat, combining a postage meter with a U.S. letter box. Manufactured by the Pitney-Bowes Postage Meter Company, Stamford, CT, the first machine was installed at the General Post Office, New York City, on May 17, 1939. It was covered by a patent granted on July 28, 1942, to Linden A. Thatcher of Stamford, CT. Coins were dropped in slots, the desired stamp denomination was dialed, and the letter was inserted in a letter slot. The machine did the rest automatically, printing a meter stamp with postmark and date of mailing and holding the letter for scheduled collection. It provided postage from 1 cent to 33 cents, including airmail, special delivery, and other services. It obviated the need for ordinary adhesive stamps, operated day or night, and speeded mail delivery because metered mail needs no post office "facing," canceling, or postmarking.

6012. V-mail film was dispatched overseas from New York City to London on June 22, 1942. It consisted of a partial roll of film on which there were 212 individual letters. A complete roll of film contained 1,600 letters.

POSTAL SERVICE—*continued*

6013. Zip codes to speed mail delivery were inaugurated in July 1963. The system assigned five-digit codes to each location in the United States, with the first digit indicating the region. The word "zip" stands for "Zone Improvement Plan." It was preceded by a two-digit system that was put into use by the Post Office Department on May 1, 1943, at Pittsburgh, PA, and later in 125 of its large-volume offices.

POSTAL SERVICE—AIRMAIL

6014. Airmail dispatched from a post office in a balloon and bearing postage stamps was sent in the *Jupiter,* piloted by John Wise. On July 1, 1859, Wise endeavored to fly mail from St. Louis, MO, to New York City, but he jettisoned it in a storm over Lake Ontario. On August 17, he left Lafayette, IN, carrying 123 letters and 23 circulars in a pouch. His destination was New York City, but instead he landed at Crawfordsville, IN, about 27 miles south of the takeoff point.

6015. Airmail pilot was Earl Lewis Ovington, who was sworn in on September 23, 1911, at Garden City, Long Island, NY, as "air mail pilot number one." In his Blériot monoplane, *Dragonfly,* he delivered airmail from Postmaster General Frank Harris Hitchcock in Garden City to postmaster William McCarthy in Mineola, NY, a distance of six miles, inaugurating the first official airmail service authorized by the Post Office Department. The first mail consisted of 640 letters and 1,280 postcards that bore the cancellation "Aeroplane No. 1, Garden City Estates, NY."

6016. Airmail regular service was established on August 12, 1918, by the Post Office Department between New York City and Washington, DC. Ben B. Lipsner was the first superintendent of airmail. The pilots were Edward V. Gardner, Maurice Newton, Max Miller, and Robert F. Shank.

6017. International airmail was inaugurated on March 3, 1919, between Seattle, WA, and Victoria, British Columbia, Canada, a distance of 74 miles, by Edward Hubbard of the Hubbard Air Service, who piloted a Boeing Type C open cockpit biplane with pontoons. William Edward Boeing was a passenger on the flight. Regular service under contract began on October 14, 1920, and continued under successive contracts until June 30, 1937.

6018. Transcontinental airmail flight was from San Francisco, CA, to New York City. The plane left San Francisco at 4:30 A.M. on February 22, 1921, and arrived at Hazelhurst Field, Long Island, NY, at 4:50 P.M. on February 23, 33 hours 20 minutes later. The actual flying time was 25 hours 16 minutes; the average speed for the 2,629 miles was 104 miles per hour.

6019. Transcontinental regular airmail service was established between New York City and San Francisco, CA on July 1, 1924, when the airmail-railroad service was discontinued. The first westward flight of this service was made by Wesley Leland Smith, who flew from New York City to Cleveland, OH, and the first eastward flight by Claire K. Vance, who flew from San Francisco, CA, to Reno, NE. The service was daily including Sunday, with 14 stops en route.

6020. Airmail long-distance night service was established on July 1, 1925, from New York City to Chicago, IL, over a 774-mile course. The first plane, from Hadley Field, New Brunswick, NJ (in the metropolitan New York area), was piloted by Dean C. Smith. It was followed by a second plane piloted by J.D. Hill. The first plane eastward was simultaneously dispatched from Chicago, piloted by Shirley Short, and was likewise followed by a second plane carrying the surplus mail.

6021. Airmail contractor was the Varney Air Line, which operated a single-engine Swallow biplane on April 6, 1926, between Pasco, WA, and Elko, NV, where connections were made with the Post Office Department's transcontinental line. Chief pilot Leon Cuddeback took off from Pasco. Franklin Rose, who took off from Elko, crashed in the desert.

6022. Airmail service from ship to shore was inaugurated on August 13, 1928, by the Trans-Atlantic Aerial Company when an amphibian was launched from the *Ile de France,* 400 miles at sea. Three sacks of mail, including two packages of films, were delivered to New York City 15 hours before the ship docked. Service was discontinued on September 28, 1928.

6023. Airmail letter sheet depicted an airplane in blue on white stock and was placed on sale on January 12, 1929. The stamped sheet, issued by the Post Office Department, was designed to be folded and serve as an envelope. It cost five cents.

6024. Airmail pickup by an airplane without landing in which sacks of mail were snatched into the plane from the ground was demonstrated on October 1, 1929, by Pennsylvania-Central Airlines at Washington, DC. Despite rain, 253 successful pickups were made in 255 attempts. The pickup device was authorized by the Post Office Department for use on PCA, later known as Capital Airlines, and was used on regular schedules at Beaver Falls, PA, Newcastle, PA, and Youngstown, OH, on the Pittsburgh-Cleveland route.

6025. Transpacific airmail flight and the first air crossing from California to the Philippines was made by the *China Clipper* of Pan American Airways, commanded by Edwin Charles Musick. The plane left San Francisco, CA, on November 22, 1935, at 3:46 A.M. and made stops at Honolulu, Midway, Wake, and Guam, landing at Manila, Philippine Islands, on November 28 at 11:31 P.M., having covered 8,210 miles in 59 hours 48 minutes. It carried 58 sacks of mail containing 110,865 letters. The return trip started on December 1, 1935, from Manila and was completed on December 6 at 10:37 A.M. at San Francisco, CA. The eastbound flight was made in 63 hours 24 minutes. The total flying time was 123 hours 12 minutes.

6026. Airmail flight by rocket was made on February 23, 1936, at Greenwood Lake, NY, in the *Gloria,* an 11-foot rocket with a 15-foot wing spread. The fuel was liquid oxygen and alcohol. The inventors of the rocket were Willy Ley, Louis Goodman, and Hugh Franklin Pierce. The flight was sponsored by Frido W. Kessler. The rocket carried 4,323 letters and 1,826 postcards. Each cover was franked with special rocket stamps in addition to the regular postage stamps.

6027. Letter to circumnavigate the world by commercial airmail was dispatched from New York City on April 19, 1937. It was routed via San Francisco, Hong Kong, Penang, Amsterdam, and Brazil and was returned to New York on May 25, 1937.

6028. Transatlantic airmail service was inaugurated by Pan American Airways on May 20, 1939, when the *Yankee Clipper,* a four-engine, 41.5-ton flying boat, took off from Manhasset Bay, Port Washington, NY, at 9:07 P.M. It made one stop at Horta, in the Azores, and arrived at Lisbon, Portugal, on May 21 at 8:42 P.M. The elapsed time was 26.5 hours, the flying time 20 hours 16 minutes. It was commanded by Captain Arthur Earl La Porte and carried a crew of 14, 3 airline employees, and 1,680 pounds of mail.

6029. Airmail regular delivery service by autogiro began on July 6, 1939, when Captain John MacDonald Miller flew an Eastern Air Line autogiro from the roof of the Philadelphia Post Office to the Central Airport, Camden, NJ, six miles away, in six minutes. The autogiro made the round trip to its starting place in 14 minutes.

6030. Jet airplane to transport mail was a P-80 Shooting Star that on June 22, 1946, carried a letter addressed to President Harry S. Truman. It was piloted by Captain Robert Atkinson Baird III of Clarksdale, MS, who left the Schenectady County Airport, Schenectady, NY, and arrived at the National Airport, Washington, DC, a distance of 370 miles, in 49 minutes. Another jet-propelled P-80, piloted by Major Kenneth Oscar Chilstrom of Elmhurst, IL, left for Dayton, OH, with a letter for Orville Wright and, after a stopover at Wright Field, arrived at Chicago, IL, in 2 hours 2 minutes.

6031. Airmail and express service by helicopter was inaugurated in a Sikorski S-51 on October 1, 1947, by Los Angeles Airways, Los Angeles, CA, to serve the San Fernando Valley area. On May 20, 1947, the company received the first Civil Aeronautics Board certificate, which covered a three-year period. Service was extended on October 15, 1947, and January 8, 1948, to serve 42 communities. During the first three-year period, 200,000 flights were made and 13 million pounds of mail carried. Pilots on the first flight were Boyd Kesselering and John De Blauw.

6032. Parcel post international air service was inaugurated on March 15, 1948, between the United States and 21 countries in Europe and Africa. Service to South America was instituted on September 4, 1948, and to the Pacific area on September 11.

6033. Parcel post domestic air service was authorized on June 29, 1948, and began on September 1, 1948. Overnight delivery of packages was planned. The country was divided into eight postal zones, with a maximum rate of 80 cents for the first pound and 65 cents for each additional pound or fraction thereof.

6034. Airmail by missile to be officially dispatched was sent from the submarine U.S.S. *Barbero,* about 100 miles at sea off the Atlantic coast, to the Mayport Naval Auxiliary Station near Jacksonville, FL, on June 8, 1959. Bearing four-cent postage rather than seven-cent airmail stamps, 3,000 letters were shot in a 36-foot Regulus 1 winged missile at about 600 miles

POSTAL SERVICE—AIRMAIL—continued

per hour. The missile landed 22 minutes after being launched. The letters, signed by Postmaster General Arthur Ellsworth Summerfield, were addressed to President Dwight David Eisenhower and to other government officials and important personages. The project was under the supervision of Captain Arnold Schade.

POSTAL SERVICE—POST OFFICES

6035. Post office in a colony for the collection of mail was established by order of the General Court of Massachusetts on November 5, 1639, in Boston, MA, at the house of Richard Fairbanks for "all letters which are brought from beyond the seas, or are to be sent thither." He was allowed a penny for the transmission of each letter and was accountable to the authorities in charge of the colony.

6036. Post office building built for that purpose was the Custom House and Post Office in Newport, RI, built in 1829 and occupied in 1830. An act of Congress approved on May 24, 1828, authorized the erection of the building. The title to the site was vested in the government on November 12, 1828.

6037. Railroad post office was placed in operation on July 28, 1862, on Missouri's Hannibal and St. Joseph Railroad during the administration of Postmaster General Montgomery Blair. The idea was originated by William Augustine Davis and the mail was car built at Hannibal, MO.

6038. Post office aboard a naval vessel was established on August 20, 1908, on the U.S.S. *Nebraska*.

6039. Open-air post office was opened on October 1, 1917, in St. Petersburg, FL. It had a roof, but no sides or enclosing walls. A lobby 18 feet wide extended around three sides of the building. The floor was made of pink stone resembling sandstone.

6040. Post office in an airplane was Flagship Station 1, which was open during National Air Mail Week in 1938, beginning on May 15, 1938. It was an American Airlines sleeper plane with its wings removed, set up as a special post office on Pennsylvania Avenue, Washington, DC. Stamps were to have been sold in the plane, but this was found impractical and a station was set up in an adjoining building. The plane was exhibited and viewed by 78,636 people during the week it was open.

6041. Highway post office service was approved on July 11, 1940. The first route was established on February 10, 1941, between Washington, DC, and Harrisonburg, VA. Mail was transported in large bus-like vehicles equipped with facilities for sorting, handling, and dispatch of mail.

6042. Post office fully mechanized was opened on October 20, 1960, in Providence, RI. A $20 million experimental installation designated Project Turnkey and built by Intelex Systems, a subsidiary of the International Telephone and Telegraph Corporation, was leased to the Post Office Department for 20 years. Letters were electronically faced and canceled and automatically transported to 300 destination bins at the rate of 18,000 per hour.

6043. Self-service post office was an unattended unit installed in the Wheaton Plaza Regional Shopping Center at Wheaton, MD, on October 17, 1964. Located on a concrete island in the parking area, it dispensed stamps, envelopes, and postal cards at the same price as at stamp windows. It had a machine to make change for coins and bills, a scale for weighing letters and parcels up to 50 pounds, and a zone map for calculating parcel postage.

POSTAL SERVICE—POSTCARDS

6044. Postal card was issued on May 1, 1873, under act of Congress of June 8, 1872. A one-cent stamp printed on the upper right-hand corner showed a profile of the Goddess of Liberty looking to the left and surrounded by a lathework border with the words "U.S. Postage" inserted above, and the words "One Cent" below. The body of the card was light buff, the printing velvet brown. The size of the card was 3 by 5.125 inches. The cards were made by the Morgan Envelope Company, Springfield, MA. The first known cancelation was May 12, 1873.

6045. Reply-paid card was the one-cent black on buff reply card attached to a one-cent black on buff message card issued on October 25, 1892, as a souvenir of the World's Columbian Exposition held in Chicago, IL. It showed a likeness of President Ulysses Simpson Grant. It was sold as two unsevered cards, one for the message and one for the reply. The message card had originally been issued as a single card on December 16, 1891.

6046. Postcard privately printed and mailed was authorized on May 19, 1898. The regulation allowed the use of private mailing cards of the same form, quality, and weight as postal cards printed by the government. Postcards, unlike postal cards, required a one-cent stamp.

6047. Airmail postal card was the four-cent card issued on January 10, 1949. It depicted an eagle in flight, printed in orange-red on buff stock.

6048. Commemorative postal card depicted the uplifted arm of the Statue of Liberty holding a flaming torch. It was issued on May 4, 1956, at New York City to commemorate the Fifth International Philatelic Exhibit, held at the Coliseum, New York City, from April 28 to May 6, 1956. It was a two-cent deep carmine and dark blue triangular design on buff stock.

6049. International postal card was the 7-cent single and identical 14-cent reply-paid postal card designed by Suren H. Ermoyan and placed on sale at New York City on August 30, 1963. It depicted a map of North America, highlighting Alaska and the continental United States, and was printed on white stock by offset. It bore the slogan "World vacationland, USA" against a bright blue background to publicize the Visit USA program.

6050. Pictorial postal cards printed by the Government Printing Office, Washington, DC, were issued on June 29, 1972, at Boston, MA, in observance of Tourism Year of the Americas. There were five pictorial cards, each 6 by 4.25 inches, printed in black and dull orange on beige stock: three 6-cent cards for regular domestic surface mail; a 9-cent airpost card for domestic airmail, including Canada and Mexico; and a 15-cent card for international airmail beyond Canada and Mexico. Each featured four outstanding tourist attractions on the reverse side.

POSTAL SERVICE—STAMPS

6051. Adhesive postage stamps were used by the City Despatch Post, established on February 15, 1842, by Alexander M. Greig, with its principal office at 46 William Street, New York City. They were engraved by Rawdon, Wright and Hatch, New York City, and printed in sheets of 42. They were a three-cent denomination and sold for $2.50 for a hundred stamps.

6052. Postage stamps issued by the Post Office Department were authorized by act of Congress of March 3, 1847, and were placed on sale in New York City on July 1, 1847. The issue consisted of two stamps, a 5-cent red-brown stamp depicting Benjamin Franklin and a 10-cent black stamp bearing the likeness of George Washington. These were the first stamps that bore the likeness of a president. They were printed by Rawdon, Wright, Hatch and Edson of New York City. They were withdrawn from use on June 30, 1851. The issue

consisted of 3,712,200 of the 5-cent denomination and 891,000 of the 10-cent denomination. The first stamps printed by the Bureau of Engraving and Printing were the 1894 issue of the "triangle" design stamps.

6053. Stamped envelopes were issued in June 1853 under congressional act of August 31, 1852, and were manufactured by George F. Nesbitt and Company of New York City under a contract dated October 25, 1852. They showed the profile of George Washington in an oval, the value above, and "cents" below. They were printed on white and buff paper. The first series included a 3-cent red, a 6-cent red and green, and a 10-cent green.

6054. Postage stamp issued with perforations was the one-cent blue Benjamin Franklin, issued on February 24, 1857. Originally issued in sheets on July 1, 1851, the stamp bore the inscriptions "U.S. Postage" and "One Cent." The picture on the stamp was modeled after the bust of Franklin by Jean Jacques Caffieri. All U.S. postage stamps issued previously were imperforate, as were many after 1857.

6055. Encased postage stamps were introduced by John Gault of Boston, MA, who obtained a patent for them on August 12, 1862. He inserted an unused postage stamp in a circular brass disc faced on one side by a transparent sheet of mica that allowed the value to be seen. The denominations of the stamps were 1-cent and 30-cent Franklin, 5-cent Jefferson, and 3-cent, 12-cent, 24-cent, and 90-cent Washington. On the reverse side was an advertisement by the issuing firm. Due to the scarcity of coins, these discs became popular and served in place of coins. They were sold to stores and bars at up to 20 percent above face value. They were produced by the Scovill Button Works, Waterbury, CT.

6056. Stamp collection society was the New York Philatelic Society, organized on March 21, 1867, in New York City, by eight collectors of postage stamps. The first president was the Reverend J.A. Morley, D.D., LL.D.

6057. Stamp auction was held on the evening of May 28, 1870, at the Clinton Hall Book Sales Rooms and Art Galleries, New York City, by Leavitt, Streibeigh and Company, auctioneers. About 14,000 stamps in 269 lots were offered for sale. The highest price for a single lot was $38 for 1,800 stamps. The highest price for a single stamp was $11, the lowest 35 cents. The bid for the first lot, 100 foreign stamps, started at 25 cents and closed at 60 cents. The total receipts for the day were approximately $500.

POSTAL SERVICE—STAMPS—*continued*

6058. Public exhibition of postage stamps was held from May 10 to November 10, 1876, in the United States Building at the Centennial Exhibition at Fairmount Park, Philadelphia, PA. It was arranged by John Walter Scott. The first important exhibit by collectors opened on March 11, 1889, at the Eden Musée, New York City, where 31 exhibitors showed 272 sheets of stamps from 161 countries, valued in excess of $200,000.

6059. Postage stamp for balloon mail was engraved by Mrs. J.H. Snively and privately issued by John F.B. Lillard for use on mail carried on June 18, 1877, on the balloon *Buffalo* from Nashville to Gallatin, TN. Only 23 of the 300 stamps were used. They sold for five cents each.

6060. Postage stamp with valuation of one dollar was the salmon-colored $1 stamp issued from January 2, 1893, to April 12, 1894. It depicted the legend of Queen Isabella of Spain pledging her jewels to finance the first voyage of Columbus, after a painting by Antonio Muñoz Degrain.

6061. Books of postage stamps were issued on April 16, 1900. They contained two-cent stamps. Books containing 12 stamps cost 25 cents each; books containing 24 stamps cost 49 cents; and books containing 48 stamps cost 97 cents.

6062. Postage stamps in coils were issued on February 18, 1908. They were coarsely perforated, 8.5 holes to two centimeters, and were printed by the Bureau of Engraving and Printing, Washington, DC, for the Post Office Department. The first coils prepared from sheets had appeared in 1902. They were made from sheets of 400 stamps cut into strips of 20 and spliced together into rolls to be used in vending and affixing machines by commercial organizations.

6063. Airmail stamps were issued on May 13, 1918, and consisted of three denominations: 6-cent orange, 16-cent green, and 24-cent carmine, rose, and blue, all with airplanes depicted on them. The 24-cent stamp was placed on sale on May 13, the 16-cent on July 11, and the 6-cent on December 6.

6064. Precanceled stamps printed on rotary presses at the Bureau of Engraving and Printing, Washington, DC, were issued on April 21, 1923. This initial order embraced one-cent stamps of the 1923 series. One-cent precanceled stamps in coils were first issued on January 7, 1924. Prior to the addition of precanceling devices to rotary presses, the Bureau of Engraving and Printing precanceled one-cent stamps in sheets for a limited number of post offices with electrotype plates containing 400 stamps each. The records indicate that Bureau-precanceled stamps of this style were first issued to the post offices in New Orleans, LA, Augusta, ME, and Springfield, MA, in January 1917.

6065. Sheet of souvenir postage stamps was the White Plains Commemorative, issued to commemorate the 150th anniversary of the Battle of White Plains. The sheet consisted of 25 two-cent horizontal rectangle stamps printed in red ink. The margins of each sheet bore the inscription "International Philatelic Exhibition, October 16 to 23, 1926, New York, NY, U.S.A." The sheets were placed on sale on October 18, 1926, and were not issued to postmasters for sale to the general public. They were printed in sheets of 100 subjects in four panes of 25 two-cent stamps, each separated by one-inch gutters with central guidelines. The regular sheets containing 100 stamps were also placed on sale on the same date.

6066. Dual-purpose postage stamp was the Air Post Special Delivery 16-cent stamp, which was used for prepayment of the 6-cent air postage and the 10-cent special delivery fee. It bore a reproduction of the great seal of the United States and was printed in blue ink. It was offered for sale on August 30, 1934, at the American Air Mail Society Convention Station, Chicago, IL.

6067. First-day special cancellation of a postage stamp was prepared for the Virginia Dare commemorative stamp, released on August 18, 1937, at Manteo, NC. The one-inch-square blue five-cent stamp commemorated the 350th anniversary of her birth. Virginia Dare, the child of English settlers in Sir Walter Raleigh's Roanoke colony, was the first English child born in America.

6068. United Nations postage stamps in U.S. denominations were placed on sale on October 24, 1951, on United Nations Day in New York City. Six stamps were issued on that date: 1-cent magenta, 1.5-cent blue green, 3-cent magenta and blue, 5-cent blue, 25-cent olive gray and blue, and $1 red. Five stamps were issued on November 16, 1951: 2-cent purple, 10-cent chocolate, 15-cent violet and blue, 20-cent dark brown, and 50-cent indigo. The stamps were only valid for use from United Nations headquarters.

6069. Postage stamp issued jointly by two countries was the four-cent green and rose Mexican Independence stamp commemorating the 150th anniversary of Mexican independence, issued by the United States and Mexico on September 16, 1960, in Los Angeles, CA. It was designed by Leon Helguera and Charles Chickering. The first holiday stamp jointly issued by the United States and another country was the USPS/Israeli Holiday Celebration Series Chanukah stamp, simultaneously issued in Washington, DC, and Jerusalem on October 23, 1996. The stamp art, identical in its American and Israeli versions, portrayed a Chanukah menorah.

6070. Postage stamp issued on the date of the event it commemorated was the Project Mercury commemorative of 1962, placed on sale throughout the nation on February 20, 1962. This four-cent dark blue and yellow stamp showed the spaceship in which Colonel John Herschel Glenn, Jr., orbited the earth. Three million covers were canceled the first day at Cape Canaveral, FL.

6071. Postage stamp with fluorescent tagging was the eight-cent fire-red stamp issued on August 1, 1963, at Dayton, OH. It depicted a jet airplane soaring past the dome of the Capitol. Under fluorescent light, the stamp glowed an orange red. The stamp was the regular airmail stamp issued on December 5, 1962, at Washington, DC, to meet new postal rates that would take effect on January 7, 1963.

6072. Postage stamp issued in the United States and canceled by a foreign country was the five-cent multicolored postage stamp commemorating the 100th anniversary of Canada's achievement of federation, issued on May 25, 1967, at the United States Pavillion at Expo 67, Montreal, Canada. The date of issue and cancelation coincided with President Lyndon Baines Johnson's visit to Ottawa and Montreal. The stamp was designed by Ivan Chermayeff of New York City and showed a symbolic depiction of the scenic grandeur of Canada.

6073. Twin postage stamps were issued on September 29, 1967, and were first placed on sale at the Kennedy Space Center, at a branch of the Orlando, FL, post office. A single horizontal design picture was perforated through the center. Each half was of the five-cent denomination and could be used separately. The pair could also be used as a 10-cent stamp. The stamp on the left depicted an astronaut in space

and the stamp on the right showed the Gemini spaceship with the earth in the background. It was designed by Paul Calle of Stamford, CT. Each sheet contained 200 subjects in four panes of 50 each.

6074. Gravure-printed postage stamp was a horizontal five-cent stamp printed by the Bureau of Engraving and Printing, Washington, DC, and issued on November 2, 1967, at Washington, DC. It was printed with red, yellow, blue, and black inks and featured a photographic reproduction of Thomas Eakins's oil painting *The Biglin Brothers Racing* surrounded by a gold frame. The original picture, which depicts a sculling scene on the Schuylkill River near Philadelphia, PA, hangs in the National Gallery of Art, Washington, DC.

6075. Books of postage stamps with humidity-resistant adhesive that eliminated the need for tissue paper between the leaves were booklets of one-cent and six-cent stamps issued on March 1, 1971, at Washington, DC. The adhesive gum had a dull finish instead of the conventional glossy finish. The booklet cost $2 each and contained four panes of eight 6-cent stamps and one pane of eight 1-cent stamps. The first production order was for 2 million booklets.

6076. Pressure-sensitive adhesive postage stamp was the 10-cent Dove of Peace precanceled Christmas stamp issued on November 15, 1974, at New York City. It depicted a dove weather vane.

6077. Postage stamps without a denomination were the Christmas stamps printed in plates of 200 subjects in four panes of 50 each and issued on October 14, 1975, in Washington, DC. The stamps sold for 10 cents each and were printed before the postage rate was increased to 13 cents. One was based on a painting by Domenico Ghirlandaio in the National Gallery of Art, Washington, DC, the other on a Christmas greeting card produced by Louis Prang in Boston in 1878.

POSTAL SERVICE—STAMPS—DESIGNS

6078. Postage stamps depicting a president were a 5-cent red-brown stamp bearing a likeness of Benjamin Franklin and a 10-cent black stamps bearing a likeness of George Washington. They were authorized by act of Congress on March 3, 1847, and were placed on sale in New York City on July 1. They were printed by Rawdon, Wright, Hatch and Edson of New York City.

6079. Postage stamps depicting the American eagle were the one-cent carrier's stamps in blue, issued on November 17, 1851.

POSTAL SERVICE—STAMPS—DESIGNS
—*continued*

6080. Mourning postage stamp was the 15-cent black postage stamp depicting the assassinated President Abraham Lincoln, issued on June 17, 1866. A 10-cent and a 12-cent black stamp showing portraits of George Washington had been issued on July 1, 1847, and July 1, 1851, but these were not mourning stamps.

6081. Postage stamps depicting scenes were the series of 1869, issued from March 1, 1869, to April 9, 1870. The designs were furnished by the National Bank Note Company of New York City, which received a contract on December 12, 1868, for furnishing the stamps. There were 10 denominations. The 2-cent stamp depicted a post horse and rider, the 3-cent brown a locomotive, the 12-cent ultramarine blue and green a steamboat, the 15-cent Prussian blue the landing of Columbus, and the 24-cent light green the signing of the Declaration of Independence. The 1-cent ocher, 6-cent ultramarine blue, and 90-cent black and carmine stamps carried portraits of Franklin, Washington, and Lincoln, respectively. The 10-cent orange and 30-cent carmine and blue stamps pictured an eagle resting on a shield.

6082. Postage stamp depicting the American flag was the 30-cent blue and carmine stamp issued on May 15, 1869. It depicted an eagle with outstretched wings, facing to the left, resting on a shield with flags grouped on either side.

6083. Commemorative stamped envelopes were the three-cent green stamped envelopes printed on a Hartford press that was set up in the Post Office Department in the Government Building at the Centennial Exposition in Philadelphia, PA, between May 10 and November 10, 1876. A shield design showed the initials "U.S.," a man on horseback above a locomotive pulling cars, the dates 1776 and 1876, and the words "three cents."

6084. Commemorative postage stamps issued by the Post Office Department were the Columbian series of 1893, which depicted incidents in the discovery of America by Christopher Columbus. The stamps were of 16 denominations and ranged in value from one cent to $5. They were issued on January 2, 1893, with the exception of the eight-cent stamp, which was issued on March 3. The World's Columbian Exposition at Chicago, IL, was held from May 1 to October 30, 1893, to celebrate the 400th anniversary of Columbus's voyage of discovery.

6085. Postage stamps depicting a woman were the Columbus commemorative stamps of 1893. Queen Isabella was depicted on three varieties that were placed on sale on January 2, 1893. The 5-cent stamp (35,248,250 issued) was in chocolate brown and depicted "Columbus Soliciting the Aid of Isabella"; the $1 stamp (55,050 issued) was in rose salmon and showed "Isabella Pledging Her Jewels"; and the $4 stamp (26,350 issued) was in carmine, with portraits of Columbus and Isabella. Women were also shown as characters in group scenes in this set, but their identity was not given.

6086. Postage stamps to feature paintings were placed on sale on January 2, 1893. They were the 2-cent brown violet stamp showing the painting *Landing of Columbus* by John Vanderlyn, which hung in the rotunda of the Capitol, Washington, DC, and the 15-cent dark green stamp showing the painting *Columbus Announcing His Discovery,* by R. Balaca.

6087. Postage stamp depicting an American woman was a violet-black eight-cent stamp, issued on December 6, 1902, that showed the likeness of Martha Washington. The portrait was based on a painting by Gilbert Stuart.

6088. Postage stamp depicting a Native American was the five-cent Jamestown Commemorative issued on May 7, 1907, to honor the first permanent English settlement in America, at Jamestown, VA, in 1607. It showed a likeness of Pocahontas, who is said to have saved the life of Captain John Smith when he was captured by warriors of the Powhatan Confederacy, ruled by her father, Chief Powhatan. She later married the colonist John Rolfe and visited England, where she was received with royal honors and where she died in 1617 at the age of about 22.

6089. Memorial postage stamp was the Lincoln two-cent memorial issue, commemorating the 100th anniversary of the birth of Abraham Lincoln, that was placed on sale on February 12, 1909. This stamp was red, the size and shape of the regular issue of postage stamps. It depicted a profile of the head of Lincoln from Saint-Gaudens's statue in an oval with the words "1809 Feb. 12 1909" on a ribbon below.

6090. Postage stamp depicting an African-American showed the educator Booker Taliaferro Washington, whose likeness was on the 10-cent brown stamp first placed on sale on April 7, 1940, at Tuskegee Institute, AL. The stamp was one of the Famous American Commemorative series issue of 1940. A three-cent deep blue stamp depicting the log cabin in which Washington lived had been issued on April 5, 1936.

6091. Postage stamp depicting a Jew was the three-cent bright red-violet postage stamp issued on January 27, 1950, at Washington, DC, to commemorate the centenary of the birth of labor leader Samuel Gompers, one of the founders of the American Federation of Labor. The stamps were printed by rotary press, 70 stamps to the pane.

6092. Postage stamp having the same design as that of another country was issued on June 26, 1959. The inscriptions, denominations, and sizes differed, however. The denomination of the United States stamp was four cents, that of the Canadian stamp five cents. The design featured two interlocking links superimposed on a map of the Great Lakes with the St. Lawrence Seaway leading from them toward the sea. Within the left link was a maple leaf, Canada's emblem, and within the right link was a bald eagle, the emblem of the United States. The stamps commemorated the opening of the seaway.

6093. Postage stamp featuring a work of art in true color was the four-cent stamp placed on sale on October 4, 1961, at Washington, DC, to commemorate the 100th anniversary of the birth of Frederic Remington, artist of the West. Shown on the stamp is a portion of Remington's oil painting *The Smoke Signal,* from the Amon Carter Museum of Western Art, Fort Worth, TX. The stamp was printed on Giori presses in gradations of red, blue, and yellow on white paper.

6094. Christmas postage stamp regular issue was placed on sale on November 1, 1962, at Pittsburgh, PA. It was a four-cent red and green stamp, showing burning candles and an evergreen wreath with a red bow and the inscription "Christmas 1962." It was designed by Jim Crawford and printed by the Giori press, 400 subjects to a sheet, in four panes of 100 each. The first Christmas stamp series to depict both a religious and a nonreligious subject was the eight-cent series issued on November 10, 1971, at Washington, DC. The religious stamp, multicolored with gold, was an adaptation of Giorgione's *Adoration of the Shepherds,* designed by Bradbury Thompson. The nonreligious stamp was dark green, red, and multicolored, designed by Jamie Wyeth and printed by rotogravure on the Andreotti rotary press. It was entitled *A Partridge in a Pear Tree.*

6095. Commemorative postage stamp depicting a president's wife was the five-cent light purple stamp issued on October 11, 1963, at Washington, DC, on the anniversary of the birthday of Eleanor Roosevelt, the wife of Franklin Delano Roosevelt.

6096. Postage stamps of four different designs sold as a single sheet of regular size was the 1964 Christmas issue of five-cent green and carmine postage stamps, depicting holly, mistletoe, poinsettia, and a sprig of conifer. Each pane of 100 contained 25 blocks of four different stamps. They were placed on sale at Bethlehem, PA, on November 9, 1964.

6097. Postage stamp depicting a living American was the multicolored 10-cent airmail stamp, 1.05 by 1.8 inches, issued on September 9, 1969, to commemorate the moon landing of *Apollo 11* on July 20, 1969. It showed astronaut Neil Alden Armstrong stepping onto the moon from the *Eagle.* The stamp was printed in sheets of 128 and panes of 32 stamps, instead of the usual sheets of 200 and panes of 50, and was a horizontal stamp. The plates used for printing the stamp were made from a master steel die that had been on board the *Apollo 11* landing module and had made the round-trip journey to the moon.

6098. Postage stamps of 50 different designs sold as a single sheet were part of the American Bicentennial Issue, displaying 50 state flags in varied colors, issued on February 23, 1976. They were sold in plates of 200 in four panes of 50 each. The designer was Walt Reed.

6099. Postage stamp depicting a nurse was a 13-cent stamp issued on August 18, 1976, at Belleville, NJ, commemorating Clara Maass. It was printed on the gravure press of the Bureau of Engraving and Printing in colors of yellow, magenta, cyan, black, blue line, and black line.

6100. Postage stamp depicting an African-American woman was issued on February 1, 1978, at Washington, DC. It showed the likeness of Harriet Tubman, the escaped slave and abolitionist who led more than 300 slaves to freedom along the Underground Railroad.

6101. Postage stamp whose design was decided by popular vote was the Elvis Presley stamp, issued in 1992. The Postal Service solicited votes on which of two portraits of the singer would be used: one of Presley as a young man, or one of him as a mature entertainer. On June 4, 1992, the results were announced: 1.1 million voters picked the younger Presley by a margin of three to one.

PRESIDENCY—CABINET

6102. Cabinet was appointed by President George Washington during his first term, April 30, 1789, to March 3, 1793. Members of the Cabinet were Thomas Jefferson of Virginia, secretary of state; Alexander Hamilton of New York, secretary of the treasury; Henry Knox of

PRESIDENCY—CABINET—*continued*

Massachusetts, secretary of war; Samuel Osgood of Massachusetts, postmaster general; and Edmund Jennings Randolph of Virginia, attorney general. The seat of the federal government at that time was New York City.

6103. Secretary of the treasury was Alexander Hamilton of New York City, who was appointed by President George Washington on September 11, 1789, and who served until February 1, 1795.

6104. Secretary of state was Thomas Jefferson, who was appointed by President George Washington. John Jay, who served as secretary for foreign affairs for the Continental Congress from December 21, 1784, was held over without appointment or commission and continued, though not officially, to superintend the department under the Constitution until Jefferson took office as secretary of state on March 22, 1790.

6105. Cabinet member who was Catholic was Roger Brooke Taney of Maryland, attorney general in President Andrew Jackson's cabinet from July 20, 1831, until September 23, 1833, and secretary of the treasury from September 23, 1833, until June 25, 1834.

6106. Cabinet appointee rejected by the Senate was Roger Brooke Taney of Maryland, appointed secretary of the treasury by President Andrew Jackson on September 23, 1833. This was a recess appointment, since Congress was not in session. Jackson submitted Taney's name on June 23, 1834, and it was rejected by a vote of 28 to 18 on September 24.

6107. Cabinet member who had served as a Confederate officer was David McKendree Key, a senator from Tennessee, who served from March 12, 1877, to August 24, 1880, as postmaster general in the cabinet of President Rutherford Birchard Hayes. He had been a lieutenant colonel in the 43rd Regiment of Tennessee and had been wounded and captured at Vicksburg.

6108. Cabinet member who was Jewish was Oscar Solomon Straus of New York, who was secretary of commerce and labor during President Theodore Roosevelt's second administration. He was appointed on December 12, 1906, and served from December 17, 1906, to March 3, 1909.

6109. Father and son to occupy the same Cabinet post were Henry Cantwell Wallace, secretary of agriculture under Presidents Warren Gamaliel Harding and Calvin Coolidge from March 5, 1921, to October 25, 1924, and Henry Agard Wallace, secretary of agriculture under President Franklin Delano Roosevelt from March 4, 1933, to August 26, 1940.

6110. Cabinet member convicted of a crime committed during his tenure was Albert Bacon Fall, secretary of the interior in President Warren Gamaliel Harding's cabinet, who was tried in the District of Columbia Supreme Court in 1929. He was charged with accepting a bribe of $100,000 from Edward Laurence Doheny of the Pan-American Petroleum and Transport Company, who wanted Fall to grant his firm valuable oil leases in the Elk Hills Naval Oil Reserve in California. Fall was found guilty by Justice William Hitz on October 25, 1929. On November 1, he was sentenced to one year in prison and was fined $100,000.

6111. Cabinet in which all members were sworn in at the same time and place by the same official took office on March 4, 1933, when Justice Benjamin Nathan Cardozo of the Supreme Court swore in nine men and one woman as President Franklin Delano Roosevelt's cabinet in the library on the second floor of the White House.

6112. Cabinet member who was a woman was Frances Perkins, appointed secretary of labor by President Franklin Delano Roosevelt. She served from March 4, 1933, to June 30, 1945, the only cabinet member who served throughout all four terms of Roosevelt's administration. She had been state industrial commissioner for New York prior to this appointment.

6113. Cabinet member to address a joint session of Congress was Secretary of State Cordell Hull, who reported on November 18, 1943, that the tripartite conference at Moscow pointed toward the maintenance of peace and security in the postwar world. The two houses, being in recess, assembled to hear him, but technically it was not a "joint session."

6114. Cabinet conference to be telecast was presented on June 3, 1953, from the White House, Washington, DC. President Dwight David Eisenhower conferred for half an hour with Oveta Culp Hobby, secretary of health, education, and welfare; George Magoffin Humphrey, secretary of the treasury; Ezra Taft Benson, secretary of agriculture; and Herbert Brownell, attorney general. The telecast was carried by four networks.

6115. Cabinet session to be telecast and broadcast was recorded at the White House, Washington, DC, on October 25, 1954. The telecast showed a special meeting to hear the report of Secretary of State John Foster Dulles on agreements in regard to West Germany signed in Paris on October 23, 1954. All the members of President Dwight David Eisenhower's Cabinet were present, with the exception of Vice President Richard Milhous Nixon. The report was broadcast and telecast over the ABC, NBC, and CBS radio and television networks.

6116. Cabinet session held at a place other than the seat of the federal government was held on November 22, 1955, at President Dwight David Eisenhower's farm at Gettysburg, PA. It was attended by the President, the vice president, the 10 cabinet officers, and 4 other government officials.

6117. Cabinet member who was the brother of the president was Robert Francis Kennedy, who took office as attorney general in the cabinet of President John Fitzgerald Kennedy on January 21, 1961, in Washington, DC.

6118. Cabinet meeting attended by a foreign national was held on April 20, 1965, at Washington, DC. At the invitation of President Lyndon Baines Johnson, the meeting was attended by Aldo Moro, the visiting Italian premier; Amintore Fanfani, the Italian foreign minister; and Dr. Sergio Fenoaltea, the Italian ambassador to the United States.

6119. Cabinet member who was African-American was Robert Clifton Weaver of Washington, DC, nominated on January 13, 1966, by President Lyndon Baines Johnson and sworn in on January 18, 1966, as secretary of housing and urban development.

6120. Cabinet member to serve in four different capacities was Elliott Lee Richardson of Massachusetts, who was sworn in on June 24, 1970, as secretary of health, education and welfare; February 2, 1973, as secretary of defense; May 25, 1973, as attorney general; and February 2, 1976, as secretary of commerce. The first three posts were in the cabinet of President Richard Milhous Nixon, the fourth in the cabinet of President Gerald Rudolph Ford.

6121. Cabinet member who was an African-American woman was Patricia Roberts Harris, appointed secretary of housing and urban development by President Jimmy Carter in 1977. In 1979, she left HUD to become secretary of health, education, and welfare, a position she held until 1982. Harris had served as ambassador to Luxembourg from 1965 to 1967.

6122. Cabinet member indicted while in office was Raymond L. Donovan, secretary of labor under President Ronald Wilson Reagan from 1981 to 1985. Facing a trial for larceny and fraud in New York, Donovan resigned on March 15, 1985. He was acquitted of all charges on May 25, 1987, after an eight-month trial in New York City.

6123. Secretary of state who was a woman was Madeleine Korbel Albright, born in Prague, Czechoslovakia, in 1937. Albright served as ambassador to the United Nations during the first administration of President William Jefferson Clinton. After a 99–0 vote of confirmation by the Senate, she was sworn into office by Vice President Albert Gore on January 23, 1997, at the White House, Washington, DC.

PRESIDENCY—CABINET—ATTORNEY GENERAL

6124. Attorney general of the United States was Edmund Jennings Randolph, who was appointed by President George Washington on September 26, 1789, entered on his duties on February 2, 1790, and served until January 1, 1794. The office was created by act of Congress of September 24, 1789, an "act to establish the Judicial Courts of the United States." His salary was $1,500 a year. He was required to provide his own quarters, law books, fuel, furniture, and stationery, and to pay a law clerk. The office of attorney general was made a part of the President's cabinet in 1814.

6125. Attorney general whose father also served as attorney general was William Ramsey Clark of Texas, sworn in on March 10, 1967, at Washington, DC. His father, Thomas Campbell Clark of Texas, who had served from June 30, 1945, to August 22, 1949, administered the oath to his son.

6126. Attorney general to plead guilty to a criminal offense was Richard Gordon Kleindienst of Arizona, who served in the administration of President Richard Milhous Nixon from June 12, 1972, to April 30, 1973, when he resigned, along with two other close associates of the president, as a result of the Watergate scandal. On May 18, 1974, in Federal District Court, Washington, DC, he pleaded guilty to charges that he had given inaccurate testimony before the Senate Judiciary Committee in March– April 1972, during its investigation into an antitrust settlement involving the International Telephone and Telegraph Corporation. He was convicted of a criminal misdemeanor.

PRESIDENCY—CABINET—ATTORNEY GENERAL—*continued*

6127. Attorney general to be incarcerated was John Newton Mitchell, attorney general during President Richard Milhous Nixon's first term in office, who was convicted on January 1, 1975, of perjury, conspiracy, and obstruction of justice in connection with the Watergate burglary and cover-up. He entered the federal minimum security prison at Maxwell Air Force Base, near Montgomery, AL, on June 21, 1977. He was the 25th person convicted of crimes in connection with the Watergate scandal, which had forced the resignation of President Nixon in 1974.

6128. Attorney general who was a woman was Janet Reno of Miami, FL. She took the oath of office on March 12, 1993, after quick confirmation by the Senate on March 11. Reno had earned a law degree from Harvard University in 1963 and had been elected state attorney for Dade County, FL, in 1979.

PRESIDENCY—FIRST LADIES

6129. First Lady who was not born in the United States was Louisa Catherine Johnson, who married John Quincy Adams. She was born on February 12, 1775, in London. Her father was Joshua Johnson of Maryland, the first American consul in London. The wedding took place on July 26, 1797, at the Church of the Parish of All Hallows, Barking, England. At the time, Adams was serving as U.S. minister to Holland.

6130. First Lady to receive free mail franking privileges was Martha Washington of Mount Vernon, VA. On April 3, 1800, an "act to extend the privilege of franking letters and packages to Martha Washington" was passed. This privilege was granted her "for and during her life."

6131. First Lady to travel in an airplane to a foreign country was Eleanor Roosevelt, who left Miami, FL, in a commercial airplane on March 6, 1934, and visited Puerto Rico, the Virgin Islands, Port au Prince in Haiti, and Nuevitas in Cuba in the course of a trip of 2,836 air miles. She returned to the United States on March 16.

6132. First Lady to pilot an airship was Rosalynn Smith Carter, who was a passenger on the Goodyear airship *America* on her 51st birthday, August 18, 1978. The airship left Dulles Airport, Washington, DC, under the command of Captain Larry Chambers, who invited Mrs. Carter to pilot the ship as it cruised over northern Virginia.

6133. First Lady who was also a federal official was Hillary Rodham Clinton, wife of President William Jefferson Clinton. On June 22, 1993, the U.S. Appeals Court in Washington, DC, ruled that Mrs. Clinton was a "de facto" federal official. The issue arose in the wake of controversy surrounding her chairmanship of a closed-door task force to revise the national health care system.

6134. First Lady to be depicted on a monument to a president was Eleanor Roosevelt, the wife of Franklin Delano Roosevelt. The Franklin Delano Roosevelt Monument in Washington, DC, was dedicated on May 2, 1997. Eleanor Roosevelt was depicted in a sculpture in the fourth room of the monument, with the symbol of the United Nations in the background. The statue was sculpted by Neil Estern. The memorial was designed by Lawrence Halprin and occupied 7.5 acres between the Tidal Basin and the Potomac River.

PRESIDENCY—PRESIDENTS

6135. President elected under the Constitution was George Washington, who was inaugurated in the Federal Building on Wall Street in New York City and served from April 30, 1789, to March 4, 1797. He was not, however, the first person to be known as the president of the United States. After the adoption of the Articles of Confederation in 1781, the presidents of the sessions of the Continental Congress signed themselves "President of the United States in Congress Assembled." The first to do so was Thomas McKean of Delaware.

6136. Presidential inauguration took place on Thursday, April 30, 1789, in New York City, on the balcony of the Senate Chamber at Federal Hall, at the corner of Wall and Nassau streets. Robert R. Livingston, Chancellor of New York State, administered the oath of office to George Washington, whose right hand rested on a Bible borrowed from St. John's Lodge, Free and Accepted Masons. The Bible was opened to the first verse of Psalm 127. Washington, who wore a suit of homespun cloth, then delivered his inaugural address in the Senate Chamber. He had traveled to his inauguration from Elizabeth Town, NJ, on a barge rowed by 13 sailors.

6137. Inaugural ball was held on May 7, 1789, at the Assembly Rooms, on the east side of Broadway, a little way north of Wall Street, New York City. A medallion portrait of President George Washington in profile on a fan was presented as a souvenir to the ladies.

6138. Presidential appointment was made by George Washington in June 1789, when he nominated William Short for the diplomatic post of *chargé d'affaires* for France. The first presidential appointment to be rejected was that of Benjamin Fishbourn, nominated to be naval officer of the port of Savannah, GA. Congress refused to accept the nomination because Washington had failed to consult with Georgia's senators on the matter.

6139. President who had been a senator was James Monroe, who served as senator from Virginia from November 9, 1790, to May 27, 1794, filling the vacancy caused by the death of William Grayson on March 12, 1790.

6140. Presidential proclamation concerned the surveying of future site of the nation's capital, and was made in New York City on January 24, 1791, by George Washington. The proclamation directed surveyors "to survey and limit a part of the territory of ten miles square on both sides of the river Potomac, so as to comprehend Georgetown, in Maryland, and extend to the Eastern Branch."

6141. Presidential veto of a congressional bill was exercised by President George Washington on April 5, 1792, when he vetoed a bill for the apportionment of representation. The House of Representatives sustained the veto on April 6, 1792, by a vote of 33 to 22. A two-thirds vote of both houses is necessary to override a veto.

6142. Presidential commission was appointed by President George Washington to deal with the Whiskey Rebellion of 1794, in which the farmers of Washington and Allegheny counties, PA, attacked federal officers who were trying to collect an excise tax on whiskey. In sixth annual address, on November 19, 1794, he declared: "The report of the commissioners marks their firmness and abilities, and must unite all virtuous men, by shewing that the means of conciliation have been exhausted." The rebellion was then put down by an army of 13,000 militiamen.

6143. Presidential amnesty issued to rebellious citizens was issued by President George Washington on July 10, 1795, when he extended a full pardon to participants in the Whiskey Rebellion who were willing to sign an oath of allegiance to the United States. The first amnesty granted during the Civil War was issued by President Abraham Lincoln on December 8, 1863. He issued another on March 26, 1864. President Andrew Johnson issued supplementary proclamations on May 29, 1865; September 7, 1867; July 4, 1868; and December 25, 1868.

6144. President to reside in Washington was John Adams. On June 3, 1800, he took up residence at the Union Tavern, Georgetown, DC (now part of Washington, DC). In November 1800, he moved into the President's House, the Executive Mansion. George Washington was the only President who did not live in Washington, DC, as the Executive Mansion was not completed during his administration. In 1798 he did purchase two lots near the Capitol for $963, on the condition than he build two brick houses there. The houses were never built.

6145. President elected by the House of Representatives was Thomas Jefferson. After the election of 1800, the electoral vote stood as follows: Thomas Jefferson 73, Aaron Burr 73, John Adams 65, Charles Cotesworth Pinckney 64, and John Jay 1. The House of Representatives assembled on February 11, 1801, and on the 36th ballot elected Jefferson. Delaware and South Carolina cast blank ballots, with the result that the vote was 10 states for Jefferson and 4 for Burr.

6146. President inaugurated in the city of Washington was Thomas Jefferson, who was inaugurated on March 4, 1801. Jefferson walked from his boarding house to the unfinished Capitol building, where he was greeted with an artillery salute. He took the oath of office in the Senate chamber with the help of Chief Justice John Marshall. He then delivered his first inaugural address, in a voice so quiet that few in the audience could hear him.

6147. President to review the military forces at his residence was Thomas Jefferson. On July 4, 1801, he reviewed the Marines, led by the Marine Band, on the White House grounds.

6148. President to face enemy gunfire while in office and the first president actively to use his authority as commander-in-chief was James Madison. On August 25, 1814, he assumed command of Commodore Joshua Barney's battery, stationed a half mile north of Bladensburg, MD.

6149. Former president who was elected to the House of Representatives was John Quincy Adams, who served as president from March 4, 1825, to March 3, 1829. He represented the Plymouth, MA, district in Congress as a Whig for 17 years, from March 4, 1831, to February 23, 1848, when he died.

PRESIDENCY—PRESIDENTS—*continued*

6150. Spoils system of presidential patronage was introduced by President Andrew Jackson as a reward to Simon Cameron of Pennsylvania and other supporters for their political assistance. The system allowed the president to appoint his supporters to public offices. Jackson served as president from March 4, 1829, to March 3, 1837.

6151. President to be censured by Congress was Andrew Jackson, who had incurred displeasure by his handling of the Bank of the United States matter. On March 28, 1834, by a vote of 26–20, the Senate passed a resolution declaring that President Jackson "in the last executive proceedings in relation to the public revenue, has assumed upon himself authority and power not conferred by the constitution and laws, but in derogation of both."

6152. Presidential protest was signed on April 15, 1834, by Andrew Jackson. He protested against the Senate resolution censuring him for his course in the bank controversy.

6153. Photograph of a former president was taken by the Southworth and Hawes Studio, Tremont Street, Boston, MA. It was a photograph of John Quincy Adams taken in 1843 at his home in the town of Braintree (now Quincy), MA. In 1845, Mathew B. Brady photographed Andrew Jackson at the Hermitage, Nashville, TN.

6154. Presidential veto to be overridden by Congress concerned "an act relating to revenue cutters and steamers," which provided that no revenue cutter could be built without prior appropriation. President John Tyler vetoed the bill on February 20, 1845, arguing that contracts for two revenue cutters had already been arranged, one with a firm in Richmond, VA, and another with a contractor in Pittsburgh, PA. The bill was reconsidered by the Senate and House on March 3, 1845. The Senate overrode the veto without debate by a vote of 41–1, and the House by a vote of 127–30.

6155. Photograph of a president in office was a picture of President James Knox Polk, made on February 14, 1849, in New York City by Mathew B. Brady.

6156. President who had received a patent was Abraham Lincoln. On March 10, 1849, in Springfield, IL, he applied for a patent on a device for "buoying vessels over shoals" by means of inflated cylinders. His application was granted on May 22, 1849.

6157. Portrait of Abraham Lincoln known to historians and accepted as authentic was painted in 1856 by Philip O. Jenkins, an itinerant physician and artist, before Lincoln became a national figure. It was discovered hanging in the Illinois home of one of Jenkins's descendants in 1988. The earliest known photograph of Lincoln is thought to be a daguerrotype taken in 1843.

6158. Former president to serve as an official of an enemy government was John Tyler of Virginia, president of the United States from 1841 to 1845. On August 1, 1861, he became a delegate to the Provisional Congress of the Confederate States. He was elected a member of the House of Representatives of the permanent Confederate Congress on November 7, 1861, but died on January 18, 1862, before taking his seat.

6159. President to be impeached was Andrew Johnson, the 17th President. The House of Representatives on February 24, 1868, voted to impeach him because he had dismissed Edwin McMasters Stanton, the secretary of war, and had declared several laws unconstitutional. The charges were usurpation of the law, corrupt use of the veto power, interference at elections, and misdemeanors. The trial was held in the Senate from March 13 to May 16, 1868, with Chief Justice Salmon Portland Chase presiding. Fifty-four senators took oaths as jurors. The vote was 35–19 against Johnson, but since this was one vote short of the two-thirds necessary for a conviction, he was acquitted. An earlier but unsuccessful attempt to bring impeachment proceedings against a president had been made on January 10, 1843, in the House of Representatives by John Minor Botts of Virginia, who introduced a resolution charging "John Tyler, Vice President acting as President" of corruption, malconduct in office, high crimes and misdemeanors. The nine charges were rejected and the resolution was not accepted by a vote of 83 ayes, 127 nays.

6160. Former president to become a senator was Andrew Johnson of Tennessee. Johnson was an unsuccessful candidate for election to the Senate in 1869 and to the House of Representatives in 1872. He was elected to the Senate from Tennessee in 1875 and served from March 4, 1875, until his death on July 31, 1875.

6161. President to use a telephone was James Abram Garfield, who first used a telephone while he was a member of Congress in 1878.

6162. President elected for two nonconsecutive terms was Grover Cleveland, who served as the 22nd president (1885–89) and the 24th president (1893–97).

6163. President to pitch a ball to open the baseball season was William Howard Taft. On April 14, 1910, he threw the baseball that opened the American League's Washington–Philadelphia game, which Washington won 3–0. The crowd, which included 12,226 paying spectators, broke all previous baseball attendance records.

6164. Former president to become chief justice of the Supreme Court was William Howard Taft, who was appointed chief justice on June 30, 1921. He resigned on February 3, 1930, a few weeks before his death.

6165. President to invite the president-elect to discuss government problems was Herbert Clark Hoover. On November 12, 1932, Hoover invited president-elect Franklin Delano Roosevelt to confer with him regarding the request made by Great Britain for suspension of payments of its war debt. An installment of $95 million was due on December 15, 1932. Roosevelt, then governor of New York, called on President Hoover on November 22, 1932.

6166. President to conduct religious services as commander-in-chief of the Navy was Franklin Delano Roosevelt, who read from the *Book of Common Prayer* of the Episcopal Church on Easter Sunday, April 1, 1934, while on the quarterdeck of Vincent Astor's yacht *Nourmahal* east of Key West, FL. The services were attended by the crew of the *Nourmahal* and the U.S.S. *Ellis,* a destroyer.

6167. President to go through the Panama Canal while in office was Franklin Delano Roosevelt. He passed through the canal on July 11, 1934, on the U.S.S. *Houston* on his way to Hawaii. He was greeted at Balboa, Panama, by President Harmodio Arias of Panama.

6168. President to read a veto message to Congress was Franklin Delano Roosevelt, who appeared before a joint session of Congress at Washington, DC, on May 22, 1935, to read his veto of the Patman Bonus Bill. The bill, introduced by Representative Wright Patman of Texas, provided for the immediate payment to veterans of the 1945 face value of their adjusted service certificates. Within an hour after the veto, the House voted to override it by a vote of 322–98 (the original vote on the measure had been 318–90). The following day, the Senate voted 54–40 to override the veto (the original vote had been 55–33).

6169. President inaugurated on January 20 in accordance with the 20th Amendment to the Constitution was Franklin Delano Roosevelt. The amendment was ratified on February 6, 1933, and President Roosevelt was inaugurated for his second term on January 20, 1937, in Washington, DC. Previously, presidents had been inaugurated in March.

6170. President elected for third and fourth terms was Franklin Delano Roosevelt. In the election of November 1940, when he was running for a third term, he received 27,241,939 popular votes, against Wendell Lewis Willkie's 22,304,755. In November 1944 he received 25,603,152 votes against Thomas Edmund Dewey's 22,006,616. He served only a few months of his fourth term, from January 20, 1945, until his death on April 12, 1945, when he was succeeded by his vice president, Harry S. Truman.

6171. Presidential library was the Franklin Delano Roosevelt Presidential Library, which opened in June 1941 at the Roosevelt family estate in Hyde Park, NY. Roosevelt had announced on December 10, 1938, that he would donate his papers to a library that would be open to the public. Previously, presidential papers had remained the private property of each chief executive's estate.

6172. Pension for presidents and their widows was enacted by Congress on August 25, 1958. The act provided a pension of $25,000 for former presidents and $10,000 to their widows.

6173. Presidential hot line was installed on August 30, 1962, between the White House, Washington, DC, and the Kremlin, Moscow, during the administration of President John Fitzgerald Kennedy.

6174. President to witness the firing of a Polaris missile was John Fitzgerald Kennedy. On November 16, 1963, while aboard the U.S.S. *Observation Island* 32 miles off Cape Canaveral, FL, Kennedy watched the submerged nuclear submarine U.S.S. *Andrew Jackson* fire a Polaris A-2 missile, which broke through the surface of the water and headed on a 1,500-mile flight into the Caribbean.

6175. Former president to address the Senate was Harry S. Truman, who had served as a senator from Missouri (1935–45) and as the 33rd president (1945–53). On May 8, 1964, his 80th birthday, he was present in the Senate chamber in Washington, DC. His presence was formally acknowledged, and he responded with a 68-word speech.

PRESIDENCY—PRESIDENTS—continued

6176. President to attend the launching of a manned space flight was Richard Milhous Nixon, who viewed the launching of *Apollo 12* at 11:22 A.M. on November 14, 1969, from Pad A at Cape Canaveral, FL.

6177. President to resign was Richard Milhous Nixon, who submitted his resignation to Secretary of State Henry Alfred Kissinger on August 8, 1974, and announced at 9:04 P.M., via radio and television, his intention to resign at noon on August 9, an intention that he carried out. He had been named an unindicted co-conspirator in the Watergate corruption case and was at risk of being impeached.

6178. President who came to the office through appointment rather than election was Gerald Rudolph Ford. Ford had been a longtime member of the House of Representatives when he was appointed by President Richard Milhous Nixon on October 12, 1973, to succeed Spiro T. Agnew, the vice president, who had resigned after he was charged with taking bribes. The president himself resigned on August 8, 1974, after he was named as an unindicted co-conspirator in the Watergate political burglary case. He was succeeded by Ford, who took the oath of office at noon on August 9 in the Oval Office of the White House, Washington, DC, as the 38th president.

6179. President to receive a presidential pardon was Richard Milhous Nixon, who accepted a pardon from his successor, Gerald Rudolph Ford, on September 8, 1974, exactly a month after Nixon resigned from the presidency in the wake of the Watergate scandal. Ford unconditionally pardoned Nixon for all federal offenses that the former president "committed or may have committed or taken part in" while in office.

6180. President to take the oath of office using a nickname was Jimmy Carter, who was sworn into office in Washington, DC, on January 20, 1977, by Chief Justice Warren E. Burger. Instead of his formal name, James Earl Carter, Jr., he used his nickname, Jimmy.

6181. President to use the line-item veto was William Jefferson Clinton, who used it on August 11, 1997, to eliminate three provisions from legislation that had been passed by Congress. One provision, deleted from a bipartisan bill to balance the federal budget, would have allowed the state of New York to tax Medicaid funding received by health-care providers. Two other provisions, deleted from a tax-cutting measure, would have allowed special tax deferrals for food-processing plants and financial service companies. The line-item veto, a power sought by presidents since Ulysses S. Grant, enables presidents to strike particular items from newly enacted federal laws without having to veto the entire bill. Congress passed the line-item veto in 1996.

PRESIDENCY—PRESIDENTS—LIVES AND DEATHS

6182. President born after the death of his father was Andrew Jackson. He was born on March 15, 1767, in Union County, NC, a few days after the death of his father.

6183. President born an American citizen was Martin Van Buren. He was born on December 5, 1782, in Kinderhook, NY.

6184. President whose son became president was John Adams, the second president, who was inaugurated on March 4, 1797. He was the father of John Quincy Adams, the sixth president, inaugurated on March 4, 1825.

6185. Congressional eulogy for a president was delivered by Representative Henry Lee of Virginia on December 26, 1799, before both houses of Congress, in honor of George Washington. This was the speech in which Washington was called "first in war, first in peace and first in the hearts of his countrymen."

6186. President born beyond the boundaries of the original 13 states was Abraham Lincoln. He was born near Hodgenville, KY, on February 12, 1809.

6187. President whose assassination was attempted was Andrew Jackson. On January 30, 1835, Richard Lawrence fired two pistols at President Jackson as he attended the funeral of Representative Warren Ransom Davis of South Carolina at the Capitol in Washington, DC. Both weapons misfired.

6188. President whose grandson became president was William Henry Harrison, the ninth president (1841). His grandson, Benjamin Harrison, was the 23rd president (1888–93).

6189. President to die in Washington was William Henry Harrison, who died in the White House on April 4, 1841. He had caught pneumonia a month earlier at his inauguration on March 4, 1841.

6190. President married while in office was John Tyler. He married Julia Gardiner, daughter of a New York State senator, on June 25, 1844, at the Church of the Ascension, New York City. His first wife, Letitia Christian Polk, whom he had married on March 29, 1813, had died on September 10, 1842, in the White House.

6191. President to celebrate his silver wedding anniversary at the White House was Rutherford Birchard Hayes. The Reverend Dr. Lorenzo Dow McCabe of Ohio Wesleyan University, who had united him in marriage with Lucy Webb on December 30, 1852, performed the ceremony on December 31, 1877. Mrs. Hayes wore her wedding gown of white flowered satin.

6192. President who was a bachelor was James Buchanan, the 15th president. Buchanan was elected in 1856 and served as president until 1861.

6193. President to be assassinated was Abraham Lincoln. On April 14, 1865, a few days after the Civil War came to an end with the surrender of Confederate General Robert E. Lee, Lincoln attended a performance of *Our American Cousin* at Ford's Theatre, Washington, DC, where he was shot by the actor and Confederate sympathizer John Wilkes Booth. He died the following day, April 15, 1865.

6194. Body of a president to lie in state in the Capitol rotunda was that of Abraham Lincoln, who died from an assassin's bullet on April 15, 1865. His body was removed to the White House, where it remained until April 18, after which it was removed to the Capitol rotunda, where it lay in state on a catafalque on April 19 and 20. On April 21 it was taken to the railroad station and put aboard a train that conveyed it to Springfield, IL. Lincoln was buried on May 4, 1865, in Oak Ridge Cemetery, near Springfield.

6195. President whose mother lived at the White House was James Abram Garfield, who was elected in November 1880. His mother, Eliza Ballou Garfield, lived in the Executive Mansion with her son. Garfield died from an assassin's bullet in September 1881.

6196. President and First Lady to die during the term for which he had been elected were Warren Gamaliel Harding, who died on August 2, 1923, in San Francisco, CA, and Florence Kling De Wolfe Harding, who died on November 21, 1924, in Marion, OH. The term for which Harding had been elected was March 4, 1921–March 3, 1925.

6197. President buried in Washington was Woodrow Wilson. He was buried on February 5, 1924, in the National Cathedral, the Protestant Episcopal Cathedral of Sts. Peter and Paul, in Washington, DC.

6198. President to be born in a hospital was Jimmy Carter, the 39th President. The son of Lilian Gordy Carter and James Earl Carter, Sr., he was born on October 1, 1924, in Wise Sanitarium in the town of Plains, GA.

6199. President buried in the National Cemetery at Arlington, VA, was William Howard Taft. He was buried on March 11, 1930.

6200. President to become a godfather to a member of the British royal family was Franklin Delano Roosevelt. On August 4, 1942, the Duke of Kent, youngest brother of King George VI, served as proxy for President Roosevelt at the christening of his son, Michael George Charles Franklin, Prince George of Kent, who was born on July 4, 1942.

6201. Presidential pet to star in a movie was Fala, the black Scottie owned by President Franklin Delano Roosevelt. In 1943, the Metro-Goldwyn-Mayer movie studio made a short film about Fala's typical day at the White House, starting with the dog's morning biscuit, delivered to him on the presidential breakfast tray.

6202. President who had been divorced was Ronald Wilson Reagan, who was elected in November 1980. He had married his first wife, actress Jane Wyman, on January 24, 1940, when Reagan was a successful movie actor. They were divorced on July 19, 1949. They had two children, Michael and Maureen. Reagan married his second wife, Nancy Davis, on March 4, 1952.

6203. President who was Catholic was John Fitzgerald Kennedy, who was inaugurated on January 20, 1961, in Washington, DC, as the 35th president.

6204. Presidential physician who was a woman was Dr. Janet Graeme Travell of New York City, whose appointment was announced on January 25, 1961, by President John Fitzgerald Kennedy. She was the first woman to serve as a president's personal physician, but earlier presidents had received treatment from female medical practitioners. One of these was Dr. Susan Ann Edson, who was graduated from the Cleveland Homeopathic Medical College, Cleveland, OH, in 1854, treated President James Abram Garfield from July 2, 1881, the day he was shot by an assassin, to September 19, 1881, when he died.

6205. President with a brother in the Senate was John Fitzgerald Kennedy, whose brother Edward Moore Kennedy was elected on November 6, 1962, to fill his unexpired term as senator from Massachusetts after he was elected president.

PRESIDENCY—PRESIDENTS—LIVES AND DEATHS—*continued*

6206. President who was a Rhodes Scholar was William Jefferson Clinton, a graduate of Georgetown University, Washington, DC, who attended University College, Oxford University, in Oxford, England, from 1968 to 1970 on a Rhodes Scholarship. He studied politics. The scholarship program, founded by bequest of the British colonial administrator and financier Cecil Rhodes, allows outstanding students from the British colonies, the United States, and Germany to study at Oxford. Oxford awarded Clinton an honorary doctorate in civil law in 1994.

6207. President to be wounded in an unsuccessful assassination attempt while in office was Ronald Wilson Reagan. On March 30, 1981, President Reagan was shot in the chest by a lone gunman, John Warnock Hinckley, Jr., as he was walking to his limousine from the Washington Hilton Hotel in Washington, DC. The president was rushed to nearby George Washington University Hospital, where a bullet was removed from his left lung. Three other people were wounded in the attack, including President Reagan's press secretary, James Brady, who was left paralyzed from the waist down.

6208. President whose body was exhumed was Zachary Taylor, the 12th president. Taylor died suddenly of acute gastrointestinal illness on July 9, 1850. Some historians suggested that he might have been poisoned. To test this theory, his remains were exhumed from a cemetery in Louisville, KY, on June 17, 1991. A coroner's report dated June 26 found no evidence of foul play.

PRESIDENCY—PRESIDENTS—MASS MEDIA

6209. President to use a radio was Warren Gamaliel Harding, who had a vacuum-tube detector and two-stage amplifier receiving set installed in a bookcase in his study on the second floor of the White House, Washington, DC, on February 8, 1922.

6210. President to make a radio broadcast was Warren Gamaliel Harding. His speech at the dedication of the Francis Scott Key Memorial at Fort McHenry, Baltimore, MD, on June 14, 1922, was broadcast by WEAR, Baltimore, MD. His voice was carried over telephone lines to the studio and broadcast from there. On November 5, 1921, a message from President Harding had been broadcast from Washington, DC, to 28 countries. It was sent in code over the 25,000-volt RCA station at Rocky Point (near Port Jefferson), NY.

6211. Presidential message to Congress that was broadcast on radio was heard on December 6, 1923, when President Calvin Coolidge delivered his message to a joint session of Congress held in the House of Representatives, Washington, DC. It was broadcast by KSD, St. Louis, MO; WCAP, Washington, DC; WDAF, Kansas City, MO; WEAF, New York City; WFAA, Dallas, TX; and WJAR, Providence, RI. His voice was transmitted over telephone wires.

6212. President to make a radio broadcast from the White House was Calvin Coolidge, who delivered a speech from his study in the White House, Washington, DC, on February 22, 1924, on the occasion of George Washington's birthday. The speech was heard on 42 stations from coast to coast.

6213. Presidential inauguration to be broadcast on radio took place on March 4, 1925, when 24 stations broadcast the ceremony in which Calvin Coolidge and his vice president, Charles Gates Dawes, took the oath of office in Washington, DC. In the previous inauguration, on March 4, 1921, radio listeners heard Harold W. Arlin of station KDKA, Pittsburgh, PA, read a copy of President Warren Gamaliel Harding's 41-minute inaugural address at the same time that Harding was reading it. Arlin's reading was carried by 24 stations and heard by an audience estimated at 22.8 million.

6214. President to make a radio broadcast from a foreign country was Franklin Delano Roosevelt, whose speech at Cartagena, Colombia, on July 10, 1934, was relayed to New York and transmitted over the combined WEAF, WJZ, and WABC networks.

6215. President to appear on television was Franklin Delano Roosevelt, who spoke at the Federal Building on the exposition grounds overlooking the Court of Peace at the opening session of the New York World's Fair, Flushing, Queens, New York City, on April 30, 1939, over WNBT-TV of the National Broadcasting Company, New York City. Two NBC mobile vans were used, one containing a transmitter and the other handling the pickup. Burke Crotty was the producer of the show, which lasted 3.5 hours. It began with a view of the World's Fair Trylon and the Perisphere. The first president to appear on color television was Dwight David Eisenhower, who addressed the 40th reunion of the U.S. Military Academy class of 1915 at West Point, NY, on June 6, 1955. The telecast was aired on June 7, 1955, from 11 A.M. to noon on the *Home Show* on NBC-TV.

6216. President to make a radio broadcast in a foreign language was Franklin Delano Roosevelt. He addressed the French people on November 7, 1942, from Washington, DC, at the same time that the American army was taking part in the invasion of French territorial possessions in Africa.

6217. Presidential address televised from the White House was a speech by President Harry S. Truman about food conservation and the world food crisis, delivered on October 5, 1947. The telecast was relayed from Washington, DC, to New York City, Philadelphia, and Schenectady. The president proposed meatless Tuesdays and eggless and poultryless Thursdays.

6218. Presidential press conference recorded on tape was held on January 25, 1951, at the White House, Washington, DC. Portions were released by consent of President Harry S. Truman. It was recorded for the White House archives by the Army Signal Corps unit that handled White House communications.

6219. Presidential news conference filmed for television and newsreels was held on January 19, 1955, in the treaty room of the State Department building, Washington, DC, where President Dwight David Eisenhower held a 33-minute conference. The film was cut to 28 minutes 25 seconds, plus introductory and closing remarks. The television film was recorded by the National Broadcasting Company on a pooled basis with the Columbia Broadcasting System, the American Broadcasting System, and the DuMont Network. The cost was prorated.

6220. Presidential news conference to be televised live was held on January 25, 1961, in the auditorium of the State Department building, Washington, DC. President John Fitzgerald Kennedy answered 31 questions in 38 minutes. The conference was also broadcast on radio.

6221. Radio broadcast in which citizens telephoned the president was the "Ask President Carter" show, in which President Jimmy Carter, sitting in the Oval Office in the White House, Washington, DC, replied to 42 listeners from 26 states who phoned in questions on the nationwide radio broadcast. The program was presented on March 5, 1977, on the CBS network. Walter Cronkite served as the moderator.

PRESIDENCY—PRESIDENTS—TRANSPORTATION

6222. President to ride on a railroad train while in office was Andrew Jackson, who on June 6, 1833, took the stagecoach to Ellicott's Mills, where he boarded the Baltimore and Ohio train for Baltimore, MD, on a pleasure trip. John Quincy Adams had made a trip on the same line a few months earlier, after he had left the presidency.

6223. President to ride in a car was Theodore Roosevelt, who rode in a purple-lined Columbia Electric Victoria on August 22, 1902, at Hartford, CT. He was accompanied by Colonel Jacob Lyman Greene. Twenty carriages followed the presidential car during the tour of the city.

6224. President to hold an airplane pilot's license was Dwight David Eisenhower. He was issued pilot's license No. 93,258 on November 30, 1939, by the Civil Aeronautics Administration. He learned to fly in 1939 when he was a lieutenant colonel on General Douglas MacArthur's staff in the Philippines.

6225. Presidential railroad car was U.S. Car No. 1, formerly known as the *Ferdinand Magellan,* built in 1942 by the Association of American Railroads. It was purchased for a nominal fee by the government and assigned to the White House. It weighed 285,000 pounds, was built on extra heavy trucks, and was sheathed throughout with armor plate 0.625 inches thick. It had bulletproof glass three inches thick in all of the windows and doors. The car had a lounge-observation compartment, a dining room seating 12 persons, a kitchen, and four bedrooms. It carried no identification marks other than the presidential seal on the brass-railed rear platform. A private railroad car had been built for Abraham Lincoln, but it was never accepted by him or assigned to the White House. It was used to bear his remains from Washington, DC, to Springfield, IL.

6226. President to fly in an airplane while in office was Franklin Delano Roosevelt, who in January 1943 flew 5,000 miles in a four-engine Boeing Flying Boat from Miami, FL, to the west coast of French Morocco to participate in the Casablanca Conference with British Prime Minister Winston Churchill. The first president, in or out of office, to fly in any kind of aircraft was Theodore Roosevelt. He was a passenger in a Wright biplane piloted by Archibald Hoxsey at the St. Louis Aviation Field, St. Louis, MO, on October 11, 1910, more than a year after he had left office. The flight lasted four minutes.

6227. Presidential airplane was the *Sacred Cow,* a four-engine Skymaster C-54 built at the Douglas Aircraft Company's plant in Santa Monica, CA, and delivered on June 1944 to the Air Transport Command. Its first mission outside the United States was to fly Henry Lewis Stimson, the secretary of war, from Washington, DC, to Naples, Italy, a distance of 4,200 miles, in 24 hours.

6228. President to travel underwater in a captured enemy submarine was Harry S. Truman. On November 21, 1946, he embarked at Key West, FL, in the *U-2513,* a captured German submarine. At sea off Key West, the vessel engaged in exercises during which it submerged.

6229. President to fly in a helicopter was Dwight David Eisenhower. On July 12, 1957, he flew in a three-seat Bell Ranger H-47J piloted by Major Joseph E. Barrett from the White House to an undisclosed site chosen for relocation of the White House during an atomic attack drill. He had previously flown in a helicopter while he was supreme Allied commander of the North Atlantic Treaty Organization.

PRESIDENCY—PRESIDENTS—VISITS

6230. President to tour the country was George Washington, who traveled through the New England states from October 15 to November 13, 1789. He traveled in a hired coach accompanied by Major William Jackson, his aide-de-camp, and Tobias Lear, his private secretary, along with six servants, nine horses, and a luggage wagon. He went as far north as Kittery, ME (then part of Massachusetts). As Rhode Island and Vermont had not yet joined the new government, he did not visit those states. Washington's first tour of the southern states was made from April 7 to June 12, 1791, during which time he made a 1,887-mile trip from his estate in Mount Vernon, VA, through Philadelphia, south through Virginia and the Carolinas into Georgia, and back to Mount Vernon.

6231. President to visit a foreign country while in office was Theodore Roosevelt, who sailed to Panama on the U.S.S. *Louisiana* in 1906. He remained in Panama from November 14 to 17, after which he went to Puerto Rico.

6232. President to receive a passport while in office was Woodrow Wilson, whose passport was made out on November 27, 1918. He left the United States on December 5, 1918, on the transport *George Washington* and arrived at Brest, France, on December 13.

6233. President to visit Europe was Woodrow Wilson. He left Washington, DC, on December 4, 1918, on the S.S. *George Washington* and arrived at Brest, France, on December 13, returning to Boston, MA, on February 24, 1919. A few months later, Wilson made a second trip, leaving Hoboken, NJ, on March 5 and arriving at Brest on March 13, 1919. He returned to Hoboken on July 8.

6234. President to visit Alaska and Canada while in office was Warren Gamaliel Harding, who visited Metlakahtla, AK, on July 8, 1923, and Vancouver, British Columbia, Canada, on July 26, 1923. He sailed on the U.S. naval transport *Henderson.* Alaska was then a territory of the United States.

6235. President to visit South America while in office was Franklin Delano Roosevelt. He stopped off at Cartagena, Colombia, on July 10, 1934, to return the visit of President Enrique Olaya Herrera of Colombia, who had paid a formal visit to Roosevelt on board the cruiser U.S.S. *Houston.*

6236. President to visit Hawaii while in office was Franklin Delano Roosevelt, who landed on July 25, 1934, at Hilo, HI. He was officially welcomed by Governor Joseph Poindexter on board the cruiser U.S.S. *Houston.* Hawaii was then a territory of the United States.

6237. President to visit a foreign country in wartime was Franklin Delano Roosevelt, who flew from Miami, FL, to Trinidad, British West Indies, on January 10, 1943. From Trinidad, he continued on to Belém, Brazil; Bathurst, Gambia; and Casablanca, Morocco, where he arrived on January 14. He returned to Miami by plane via South Africa and Trinidad, and arrived in Washington, DC, by train on January 31.

6238. President to visit a nation not recognized by the federal government was Richard Milhous Nixon, who visited the People's Republic of China in 1972. This was also the first trip to China, the world's most populous nation, by any American president. Accompanied by a small army of journalists, Nixon left the United States on February 17, 1972. He arrived in Beijing on February 21 for talks with Chairman Mao Zedong and Premier Zhou Enlai. Later that year, Nixon became the first president to visit the Soviet Union when he arrived in Moscow on May 22 for a summit with Soviet leaders. Among the agreements that were reached during the visit was the Strategic Arms Limitation Treaty, signed by President Nixon and the Soviet leader Leonid I. Brezhnev on May 26, which limited both nations to 200 antiballistic missiles each, divided between two defensive systems.

PRESIDENCY—VICE PRESIDENTS

6239. Vice president who had served in the House of Representatives was Elbridge Gerry of Massachusetts, who served as a representative from March 4, 1789, to March 3, 1793, and as vice president from March 4, 1813, to November 23, 1814, when he died.

6240. Vice president who was nominated specifically for that office was George Clinton, Governor of New York, who ran with Thomas Jefferson in the 1804 election. He served under Jefferson from 1805 to 1809, and again under James Madison from 1809 to 1812. Prior to the ratification of the 12th Amendment to the Constitution on September 24, 1804, the presidential candidate receiving the second highest number of votes became vice president. Clinton was also the first vice president to serve under two presidents.

6241. Former vice president to be arrested was Aaron Burr, who served under Thomas Jefferson from 1801 to 1805. In 1807, he was accused of organizing an expedition to invade Mexico and set up a separate republic in the Southwest. He was arrested on February 19, 1807, in Wakefield, AL, by Captain Edmund P. Gaines and taken to Richmond, VA, where he was brought before Chief Justice John Marshall of the U.S. Circuit Court on March 30. On June 24, he was indicted for treason. The trial began on August 3 and ended in an acquittal on September 1.

6242. Vice president to die in office was George Clinton, who served under President Thomas Jefferson from March 4, 1805, to March 4, 1809, and under President James Madison from March 4, 1809, to April 20, 1812, when he died in Washington, DC. William Harris Crawford acted as president pro tempore of the Senate for the unexpired portion of Clinton's term.

6243. Vice president to resign before the expiration of his term of office was John Caldwell Calhoun, who served as vice president under President John Quincy Adams from March 4, 1825, to March 4, 1829, and under President Andrew Jackson from March 4, 1829 to December 28, 1832. He resigned to fill the vacancy in the Senate caused by the resignation of Robert Young Hayne, senator from South Carolina. Calhoun was elected to fill the vacancy on December 12, 1832.

6244. Vice president elected by the Senate was Richard Mentor Johnson, who was chosen by the Senate on February 8, 1837, because no candidate had received a majority of the electoral votes. He served from March 4, 1837, to March 4, 1841, under President Martin Van Buren.

6245. Vice president to succeed to the presidency after the death of a president was John Tyler, the 10th president. Tyler succeeded William Henry Harrison, who died on April 4, 1841, a few weeks after his inauguration. Harrison served from March 4, 1841, to April 4, 1841, and Tyler from April 4, 1841, to March 4, 1845.

6246. Vice president sworn in on foreign soil was William Rufus de Vane King, a Democrat, the running mate of Franklin Pierce in the 1852 election. King took the oath of office on March 4, 1853, in Havana, Cuba, where he had gone for his health. The oath was administered by William L. Sharkey, the American consul in Havana. The privilege was extended to King by a special act of Congress. King's term of office was of short duration. He died on April 17, 1853, in Cahawba, AL.

6247. Vice president's widow to receive a pension was Lois I. Kimsey Marshall, widow of Thomas Riley Marshall, who died on June 1, 1925. A congressional act of January 25, 1929, awarded her an annual allowance of $3,000 and instructed the secretary of the interior to place her name on the pension roll.

6248. Vice president who was Native American was Charles Curtis of Kansas, who served under President Herbert Clark Hoover from March 4, 1929, to March 4, 1933.

6249. Vice president chosen under the 25th Amendment to the Constitution was Gerald Rudolph Ford, sworn into office as President Richard Milhous Nixon's vice president on December 6, 1973. The 25th Amendment, ratified on February 10, 1967, enables the president to appoint a vice president in the event that the office becomes vacant. On October 10, 1973, Vice President Spiro T. Agnew resigned to face charges of income tax evasion, leaving the vice presidency open for the first time since the passage of the amendment.

PRESIDENCY—WHITE HOUSE

6250. Presidential mansion was No. 1 Cherry Street, the Franklin House, at the corner of Franklin and Cherry streets (now Franklin Square), New York City. It was occupied by President and Mrs. George Washington from April 23, 1789, to February 23, 1790. It was originally the home of Samuel Osgood, the first commissioner of the treasury and later the first postmaster general.

6251. Child born in the White House was James Madison Randolph, born on January 17, 1806 in Washington, DC. He was the son of Thomas Mann Randolph and Martha (Jefferson) Randolph, the daughter of President Thomas Jefferson.

6252. Wedding in the White House took place on March 29, 1812, when Lucy Payne Washington was married to Thomas Todd, associate justice of the Supreme Court. Mrs. Washington was the widow of George Steptoe Washington, a nephew of George Washington. Her sister was Dolly Madison, the wife of James Madison, who was president at the time of the wedding.

6253. Gaslight in the White House in Washington, DC, was turned on on December 29, 1848, during the administration of President James Knox Polk.

6254. Child born in the White House who was the offspring of a president was Esther Cleveland, born on September 9, 1893 in Washington, DC. She was the second child of President Grover Cleveland and Frances Folsom Cleveland.

6255. Airplane to land on the White House lawn was the *Moth,* piloted by Harry Nelson Atwood, who landed on July 14, 1911, about 3 P.M., and was presented by President William Howard Taft with the gold medal of the Aero Club of Washington. Atwood circled the Capitol and the Library of Congress and flew down Pennsylvania Avenue and over the Washington Monument and the Executive Mansion.

6256. Dish set made in America for the White House was ordered by President Woodrow Wilson and delivered on July 31, 1918. The set, consisting of 1,700 pieces bearing the seal of the President of the United States, was manufactured by Walter Scott Lenox of Lenox Incorporated, Trenton, NJ.

6257. Swimming pool in the White House was built by popular subscription. It was located in the west terrace of the mansion and was 50 feet long and 15 feet wide, with a depth ranging from 4 to 8 feet. The pool was lined with aquamarine terra-cotta and a six-foot wainscot of pale green terra-cotta. The water was both filtered and sterilized. The pool was built under the direction of Lieutenant Colonel Ulysses Simpson Grant III, Director of Public Buildings, and was formally accepted by President Franklin Delano Roosevelt on June 2, 1933.

6258. State dinner televised from the White House took place at the Rose Garden of the White House, Washington, DC, on July 7, 1976. The dinner was held in honor of Queen Elizabeth II of England and Prince Philip, and was attended by 224 guests.

R

RADIO

6259. Radio society was the Wireless Association of America, formed in New York City in November 1908, with Dr. Lee De Forest as president and Hugo Gernsback as chairman and business manager. There were no dues and no obligations. Within a few months, more than 3,000 members were enrolled.

6260. Radio contest was held by the United Wireless Telegraph Company in Philadelphia, PA, on February 23, 1910. Contestants demonstrated their speed and accuracy in receiving and transmitting signals in Morse telegraphic code. The winner was Robert F. Miller of the United Wireless Company. Harvey Williams of Western Union was the runner-up.

6261. Radio receiving contest was held on October 8, 1921, at the New York Electrical Show, 71st Regiment Armory, New York City. The open championship was won by B.G. Seutter, wireless operator of the transatlantic receiving division of the *New York Times,* who received from Major Andrew White the National Amateur Wireless Association award cup donated by the New York Edison Company. Seutter received code at 44.3 words per minute with no mistakes. The first radio receiver to record a speed of more than 50 words per minute was Theodore R. McElroy, telegraph operator for the *Boston Herald.* On May 7, 1922, at the Boston Radio Show, he typed for three minutes at a speed of 51.5 words per minute without making a mistake. On May 24 he was a contestant at the New York Radio Show at the 71st Regiment Armory, where he typed perfect copy for two minutes at 50.5 words per minute. He won a silver cup inscribed "Presented to the Champion Radio Code Operator of the World."

RADIO—BROADCASTING

6262. Radio broadcast demonstration was made by Nathan B. Stubblefield of Murray, KY, in 1892. He was the first person to transmit a voice by air without the aid of wires. He gave a public exhibition of his invention on January 1, 1902. At another exhibition on May 30, 1902, in Fairmont Park, Philadelphia, PA, his voice was heard a mile away from the transmitter. He obtained a patent on May 12, 1908, but he was something of an eccentric and did not permit knowledge of his invention to be spread abroad.

6263. Transatlantic radio broadcast was sent in code on January 19, 1903, between Cape Cod, MA, and Cornwall, England. Greetings were exchanged between King Edward VII and President Theodore Roosevelt. Experimental broadcasts had been made earlier. The first transatlantic broadcast in which a voice was transmitted took place on December 31, 1923, when station KDKA of Pittsburgh, PA, broadcast the voice of Dr. Harry Phillips Davis, vice president of the Westinghouse Electric and Manufacturing Company, via short wave. It was received by 2AZ, a station operated by the Metropolitan Vickers Company, Manchester, England, and rebroadcast to London.

6264. Radio program broadcast was sent by Professor Reginald Aubrey Fessenden on December 24, 1906, from Brant Rock, MA. The general call "CQ" was heard, followed by a song, a poetry reading, a violin solo, a speech, and an invitation to listeners to report on the reception. Fessenden used a 40-horsepower steam engine driving a 35-kilowatt, 125-cycle alternator, with rotary spark at a frequency of 250 per second. The antenna consisted of a single straight tube, 36 inches in outside diameter and 429 feet high, in eight-foot sections bolted together.

6265. Transatlantic radio message of the regular westward service was sent in code by Privy Councillor Lord Avebury, formerly Sir John Lubbock, to the *New York Times* from Clifden, Ireland, via Glace Bay, Nova Scotia, on October 17, 1907, on regular Marconi transatlantic service. The message included the statement: "Trust introduction wireless more closely unite people States Great Britain who seem form one Nation though under two Governments and whose interests are really identical." This occurred six years after the first transatlantic radio signal, consisting of the letter *S* in Morse code, was sent by Guglielmo Marconi from Poldhu, Cornwall, to St. Johns, Newfoundland, in December 1901.

6266. Radio broadcast sent from an airplane was dispatched on August 27, 1910, by James A. Macready from an airplane above the racetrack in Sheepshead Bay, NY. The message was "Another chapter in aerial achievement is hereby written in the receiving of this first message ever recorded from an airplane in flight."

6267. Transpacific radio conversation was transmitted on October 6, 1911, from the steamer *Chive Maru* to the wireless station on Hokkaido Island in the northern part of Japan and thence to the Hillcrest station, San Francisco, CA, approximately 6,000 miles away. The operators exchanged messages.

6268. Radio broadcast from a submerged submarine was made on October 5, 1919, from the U.S.S. *Nautilus* while it was submerged in the Hudson River. The demonstration was conducted by Lieutenant C. Clark Withers. Communication could be received within 50 miles.

6269. Radio broadcast of a debate was made on May 23, 1922, over station WJH of the White and Boyer Company, Washington, DC. Both sides were argued by students of the National University Law School, Washington, DC. The affirmative, "Resolved, That daylight saving is an advantage," was taken by Calvin Ira Kephart, representing the Miller Debating Society, and the negative by Thomas E. Rhodes, representing the Alvey Debating Society. The audience was requested to act as judge.

6270. Chain radio broadcast was accomplished on October 7, 1922, when station WJZ and station WGY transmitted a World Series baseball game from the Polo Grounds, New York City, where the New York Giants were playing the New York Yankees. Ordinary telegraph lines from Newark, NJ, and Schenectady, NY, were connected with the field, where they picked up sounds through a microphone. It was not possible to transmit the highest and lowest frequencies. Graham McNamee was the announcer.

6271. Transatlantic radio program received from Great Britain was transmitted from eight stations in Bournemouth, Cardiff, Glasgow, Birmingham, Newcastle, Manchester, Aberdeen, and Liverpool, and rebroadcast from London. It consisted of the words "Hello America" and piano selections. The program was received from 10 to 10:30 P.M. on November 25, 1923, at Garden City, NY, Chatham, MA, Quincy, MA, and Tarrytown, NY. All radio stations in the United States went off the air during this period to enable the broadcast to be heard.

RADIO—BROADCASTING—*continued*

6272. Coast-to-coast radio hookup took place on February 8, 1924, when General John Joseph Carty, vice president and chief of research of the Bell Telephone system, spoke from the meeting of the Bond Men's Club at the Congress Hotel, Chicago, IL. The speech was broadcast by WJAR, Providence, RI; WEAF, New York City; WCAP, Washington, DC; WMAQ, Chicago, IL; KLX, Oakland, CA; and KTO, San Francisco, CA. It was heard by some 50 million people.

6273. Radio two-way broadcast from an airplane was accomplished on August 14, 1924, in New York City by station WJZ. A conversation was broadcast between Major William Nicholas Hensley, commandant of Mitchel Field, who was aloft in a plane, and Major Lester Durand Gardner, who was on the ground in Central Park, New York City.

6274. Radio network broadcast received on the Pacific Coast was the speech of President Calvin Coolidge on October 23, 1924, at the dedication of the Chamber of Commerce of the United States building, Washington, DC. The 45-minute speech was broadcast by 23 stations, including stations in Los Angeles, CA; Portland, OR; and Seattle, WA.

6275. Round-the-world radio broadcast was accomplished in 0.125 seconds on June 30, 1930, by a series of radio relays. Clyde Decker Wagoner spoke into a short-wave microphone from station W2XAD, Schenectady, NY. His voice was relayed to Holland, to Java, to Australia, across the Pacific Ocean to North America, and back to Schenectady.

6276. Radio broadcast from a moving train of a regular program on a national network was made by station WABC at 9 P.M., March 27, 1932, from a train on the Baltimore and Ohio Railroad. Pickup points were at Beltsville, MD, and Laurel, MD. The transmitter was operated on a frequency of 1542 kilocycles, employing high-percentage modulation and running on 50 watts of power. Belle Baker and Jack Denny's orchestra were featured on the program.

6277. Radio broadcast heard in both the Arctic and the Antarctic regions was made on September 23, 1934, by W2XAF, the short-wave station of the General Electric Company, Schenectady, NY. The program, broadcast by the New York Coffee House, was sent to the American artist Rockwell Kent, who was near Labrador. It was also heard by Admiral Richard Evelyn Byrd, who was with his second Antarctic expedition at Little America.

6278. Simultaneous radio broadcast on all three major networks was made from Radio City Music Hall, New York City, from midnight to 2 A.M. on February 11, 1937, for the benefit of the flood relief fund of the American National Red Cross. The master of ceremonies was Major Edward Bowes, assisted by Noel Coward and others. The three networks were CBS, NBC, and Mutual.

6279. Radio broadcast from a tape recording was made by WQXR, the station of the Interstate Broadcasting Company, New York City, on August 26, 1938, from 6:30 P.M. to 7 P.M. A sapphire stylus engraved a 15-minute program on 1,000 feet of tape. The recording used Millertape, the invention of James Arthur Miller of the Miller Broadcasting System, New York City, which allowed editing and cutting.

6280. Radio program simultaneously transmitted over 24 AM and FM stations, and telecast over five, was presented on March 20, 1948, when a sustaining feature, the NBC Symphony, was broadcast. The first commercial program similarly aired was "The Voice of Firestone" on March 22, 1948. The New York City outlet was WNBC.

6281. Radio broadcast using an orbiting satellite was made on December 19, 1958, when a tape recording of the voice of President Dwight David Eisenhower delivering Christmas greetings was broadcast on frequencies of 107.97 and 107.94 megacycles from a rocket revolving around the earth.

6282. Coast-to-coast solar-powered two-way radio conversation was accomplished on June 23, 1960, by the Army Signal Corps, when Colonel Leon J.D. Rouge at Fort Monmouth, NJ, conversed with Sheldon Stern, who was manning the transmitter on the roof of the Hoffman Electronics plant at El Monte, CA. Each terminal station had a 20-foot square panel with 7,800 individual solar cells.

6283. Transatlantic undersea radio conversation took place on October 2, 1965, between aquanauts in *Sealab 2,* at a depth of 205 feet in the Pacific Ocean off La Jolla, CA, and French divers in *Conshelf 3,* at a depth of 330 feet in the Mediterranean Sea off Cape Ferrat, France.

6284. Auction of radio spectrum for satellite services took place on January 24, 1996. The Federal Communications Commission solicited bids for rights to two of the eight orbital slots given to the United States by international agreement for direct broadcast satellite services in the 12.2–12.7 GHz range. One of the slots sold was the last unused slot that could provide satellites with a view of the whole continental United States.

RADIO—DISTRESS SIGNAL

6285. Radio distress signal from an American ship was sent on December 7, 1903, by Ludwig Arnson from the *Kroonland* of the Red Star line, bound from Antwerp, Belgium, to New York City. Heavy seas struck the rudder and broke the tiller on which the steering engine was mounted, leaving the ship out of control. The call, sent out 130 miles west of Fastnet on the Irish coast, was received by the British H.M.S. *Kent,* which arrived about two hours later and towed the disabled ship to Queenstown, Ireland.

6286. Radio distress signal officially established was the CQD signal, established on January 7, 1904, by the Marconi Company, effective February 1. "CQ" was the general signal for "Stop sending and listen." The popular interpretation of the call was "Come quick—danger." The SOS distress signal was adopted on November 22, 1906, at the International Radio Telegraphic Convention in Berlin, Germany, and superseded the CQD call in July 1908.

6287. Radio SOS call from an American ship was transmitted by Theodore D. Haubner, operator of the Clyde liner *Arapahoe,* a single-screw freight and passenger steamer of some 3,000 tons, bound for Charleston, SC, and Jacksonville, FL, from New York City. Its engines were disabled 21 miles southeast of Diamond Shoals, off Cape Hatteras, at 3:45 P.M. on August 11, 1909. Both the SOS and the CQD signals were sent. The SOS was first heard and acknowledged by R.J. Vosburg, wireless operator at station HA in Cape Hatteras, NC. Foreign registry ships had used SOS signals earlier.

6288. Radio distress signal resulting in an airship rescue was sent by Jack K. Irwin, wireless operator of the Wellman airship *America.* The Royal Mail steamship *Trent* responded at 7 A.M. on October 18, 1910, and rescued the crew of six in a lifeboat about 400 miles off Cape Hatteras, NC. The radio equipment was designed by Archie Frederick Collins. The *America* had taken off from Atlantic City, NJ, on October 15, bound for Europe.

RADIO—PRODUCTIONS

6289. Radio program theme song was sung on October 21, 1921, by Billy Jones and Ernie Hare to introduce their program "The Happiness Boys," sponsored by Happiness Candy. The first line was: "How do you do, everybody, how do you do?"

6290. Radio show with a plot and with repeating characters who had different adventures each week was "Amos 'n' Andy," a comedy show in which two white actors, Freeman Gosden and Charles Correll, played the parts of two African-American taxi drivers. The show originated in 1926 on WMAQ, Chicago, IL, as "Sam 'n' Henry." It moved to WGN in March 1928 in search of a wider audience and premiered on the NBC Blue network in August 1929 after the manufacturers of Pepsodent toothpaste agreed to sponsor it. Previously, all radio programs were either variety shows or broadcasts of events like ball games and church services.

6291. Radio variety show with a live studio audience who interacted with the host and laughed audibly at his jokes was "The Chase and Sanborn Hour," which aired on the NBC network starting in 1931 with the vaudeville comedian Eddie Cantor as the host. Cantor also introduced scripted jokes in place of off-the-cuff banter.

6292. Soap opera on radio was "Ma Perkins," a weekly show that ran from 1933 to 1956. It featured melodramatic stories interspersed with commercials for Oxydol laundry detergent. For years, soap operas were aired on Monday, the traditional laundry day of a homemaker's week.

RADIO—STATIONS

6293. Radio license granted to an individual was given to George Hill Lewis of Cincinnati, OH, in 1911.

6294. Commercial radio station licensed was station 8MK, which instituted daily service in Detroit, MI, on August 20, 1920, with the program "Tonight's Dinner." The station was owned by the *Detroit News,* the first newspaper to operate a radio station. The call letters were changed later to WWJ. Station KDKA, Pittsburgh, PA, was licensed on October 27, 1920, and began offering a semiweekly broadcast on November 2, 1920.

6295. College radio station was WRUC, Union College, Schenectady, NY, which went on the air on October 14, 1920, playing weekly music programs from phonograph records. The programs were broadcast from 8 P.M. to 8:30 P.M. with a three-minute interval. They were ini-

RADIO—STATIONS—*continued*

tially heard within a 50-mile radius, which increased under favorable weather conditions. The station used a U-tube transmitter with five 50-watt tubes. Frederic L. Ganter was president of the Radio Club of Union College, Wendell W. King the chief engineer, and Francis J. Campbell the chief operator. The station was owned by the trustees of the college.

6296. City radio station was WRR, Dallas, TX (50 watts), established in 1920 to broadcast fire alarms. The station played phonograph records so that owners of radio receivers could check to determine whether they were tuned in. In 1925 the station began selling time to sponsors.

6297. International radio broadcasting license issued by the Federal Communications Commission was granted on October 15, 1927, to the Experimenter Publishing Company, New York City. The frequency was 9,700 kilocycles and the power 500 watts. The station was taken over in 1929 and subsequently moved to Boston, MA, where it was operated as W1XAL by the World Wide Broadcasting Corporation.

6298. School radio station on ultrahigh frequency to receive a license from the Federal Communications Commission was station WBOE, Cleveland, OH, which was licensed as an ultrahigh-frequency station on November 21, 1938. It operated at 500 watts, 41,500 kilocycles. Regular classroom lessons and music were broadcast Monday through Friday from 8:30 A.M. to 4:30 P.M. The station became an FM station in February 1941.

6299. FM radio transmitter to receive a commercial license was station W47NV, Nashville, TN, which operated on a frequency of 44,700 kilocycles with a power of 20,000 watts. It was licensed to cover a 16,000-square-mile radius. It began operations on March 1, 1941, when it presented a commercial for the Standard Candy Company, Nashville.

6300. Radio station owned and operated by African-Americans was WERD, Atlanta, GA (1,000 watts), which opened on October 3, 1949. It was owned by Radio Atlanta, of which Jesse Bee Blayton was president. It became WXAT in 1972.

6301. Local radio network was formed on May 15, 1950, by five local stations: WARL, Arlington, VA, 1,000 watts; WGAY, Silver Spring, MD, 1,000 watts; WPIK, Alexandria, VA, 1,000 watts; WBCC, Bethesda, MD, 250 watts; and WFAX, Falls Church, VA, 250 watts. Time on all five stations was offered at $300 an hour.

6302. Radio network for African-Americans was the National Negro Network, formed on January 20, 1954. The first program was "The Story of Ruby Valentine," starring Juanita Hall, which was broadcast on January 25 on 40 stations. It was sponsored five days a week alternately by Philip Morris and Company and the Pet Milk Company. The New York outlet was WOV.

6303. All-news radio station was WINS in New York City, which began broadcasting news 24 hours a day at the 1010 AM frequency on April 19, 1965. Previously, it had broadcast rock and roll. The news-only format was quickly copied by WCBS, another New York station, and then by AM stations throughout the country.

RADIO—TECHNOLOGY

6304. Radio impulse transmission was accomplished by Joseph Henry in Princeton, NJ, in December 1840. Current obtained from a group of Leyden jars was passed through a wire which, by means of a magnetized needle, produced a vibration on another line about 100 feet away. The lines were not connected with each other; the transmission was the result of induction.

6305. Radio patent of importance was granted on December 29, 1891, to Thomas Alva Edison of Menlo Park, NJ, for a "means for transmitting signals electrically." In the patent, he stated that "signalling between distant points can be carried on by induction without the use of wires connecting such distant points."

6306. Radio receiver advertised was the Telimco, a $7.50 outfit announced in a one-inch advertisement in the January 13, 1906, issue of the *Scientific American*. The receiver was made by Hugo Gernsback's Electro Importing Company of New York. The advertisement offered a "complete outfit comprising one inch spark coil, balls, key, coherer with auto decoherer and sounder, 50 ohm relay, 4 cell dry battery, send and catch wires and connections with instructions and diagrams. Will work up to one mile. Unprecedented introduction prices. Agents wanted. Illustrated pamphlet."

6307. Triode for radios was announced to the public by Dr. Lee De Forest of New York City at a meeting of the American Institute of Electrical Engineers held in New York City on October 20, 1906. A triode is a vacuum tube with three elements: a filament and two plate electrodes. The first such tube was patented by Dr. De Forest on January 15, 1907, as a "device for amplifying feeble electrical currents." The first public description of the grid electrode tube was contained in another one of his patents, dated February 18, 1908. The name "audion" was given to the tube by Clifford D. Babcock.

6308. Carbon microphone used in radio broadcasting was employed by Dr. Lee De Forest in 1907 in his laboratory at the Parker Building, 19th Street and Fourth Avenue, New York City. It was of the ordinary telephone variety.

6309. Car radio was invented in 1929 by Paul Vincent Galvin, 34, an engineer, in a garage in Chicago, IL. The radio was roughly the size of a large toolbox and had a speaker that was installed under the car's floorboards. It had poor sound but was a commercial success. Galvin went on to found the Motorola Company.

6310. FM radio was the invention of Edwin Howard Armstrong, an electrical engineer and researcher at Columbia University in New York City. In 1933, he devised a method of transmitting static-free radio signals using frequency modulation (FM), a system superior to the older amplitude modulation (AM) method. He received patents for this technology on December 26, 1933. Armstrong had previously received important patents for other radio devices, including the feedback receiver and the superheterodyne receiver.

6311. Radio tube made of metal was announced on April 1, 1935, by the General Electric Company, Schenectady, NY. Metal tubes are smaller and sturdier than conventional glass tubes and provide their own shielding. They are particularly advantageous in the field of shortwave reception because the metal shell is a better heat conductor and radiator than glass.

6312. Transistor radio receiver to be mass-produced was the Regency Radio, manufactured by the Regency Division of Industrial Development Engineering Associates, Indianapolis, IN. The first shipments to dealers were made in October 1954. The receiver was 3 by 5 by 1.25 inches and weighed 12 ounces. It had no tubes but instead contained four transistors. It was powered entirely by a 22.5-volt B battery.

6313. Radio receiver with an auxiliary solar-cell power unit to convert solar rays into electrical power was the Sun Power Pak, made by the Admiral Corporation, Chicago, IL, which was first developed in October 1955 and offered for sale on April 16, 1956. The radio weighed 5.25 pounds and contained six transistors in place of vacuum tubes. It was 2.875 inches thick, 8.75 inches high, and 10.375 inch-

es long and cost $59.95. It was operated by six ordinary flashlight batteries lasting from 700 to 1,000 hours. The auxiliary Sun Power Pak, which converted solar energy into power, cost $185. It had a silicon "solar cell element" to pick up rays from the sun or from an incandescent bulb.

6314. Master skyscraper antenna was erected in 1965 on the 102nd floor of the Empire State Building in New York City, at the 1,250-foot level. The antenna was built at an estimated cost of $30,000 by the Alfred Manufacturing Company of Boston. It enabled 17 frequency modulation stations to broadcast simultaneously. The first were WQXR-FM, WHOM-FM, WLIB-FM, and WNCM-FM. Transmissions were made beginning in mid-October 1965. The transmitters were located on the 81st floor.

RAILROADS

6315. Inclined railroad was erected in 1764 at Lewiston, NY, by British soldiers under the command of Captain John Montresor, for transporting supplies between the Niagara portage and the lower Niagara River 300 feet below. The road consisted of two sets of parallel logs laid up the banks on stone piers from the ship wharf below to the portage above. The logs were deeply grooved to receive the wheels of two cradle cars. The cars were joined by heavy ropes passed around a revolving drum to provide balance when one car was at the bottom and the other at the top. Originally, the road was used solely for military purposes by the troops, but later it was used for transporting merchandise.

6316. Railroad for freight transportation was a tramroad built in 1809 by John Thompson for Thomas Leiper so that he could carry stone from his quarries on Crum Creek to Ridley Creek, PA, a distance of about 0.75 miles. It had wooden rails that rested on sleepers eight feet apart. The cars had grooved wheels and were pulled by horses. The service was in operation for 19 years.

6317. Railroad charter granted by a state was granted on February 6, 1815, by New Jersey, which passed "an act to incorporate a company to erect a rail-road from the river Delaware, near Trenton, to the river Raritan, at or near New Brunswick." The railroad, advocated by John Stevens of Hoboken, NJ, was not completed.

RAILROADS—*continued*

6318. Railroad with iron-plated wooden rails was constructed by Gridley Bryant of the Granite Railway Company between April and October 1826. It was used to carry heavy blocks of granite from the quarries at Quincy, MA, to the docks about three miles away in Milton, where they were shipped to Boston to be used in the building of the Bunker Hill Monument. The tracks were five-foot gauge, and the rails were pine, a foot deep and covered with oak plate and then with flat bars of iron. The cost of construction was about $50,000. Horses and oxen supplied the power.

6319. Railroad owned by a state was the Philadelphia and Columbia Railway, constructed under a Pennsylvania act dated March 24, 1828, which required the state's canal commissioners to build a railroad from Philadelphia to Columbia by way of Lancaster and extending to the west end of York. The first locomotive trip was made on April 2, 1834, from Lancaster to Columbia. This line was completed in 1834 from Philadelphia to Pittsburgh, in four divisions, the first of which was the Columbia Railroad. The construction and regulation of this road was the responsibility of the Pennsylvania Board of Canal Commissioners until August 1, 1857, when the Pennsylvania Railroad purchased it from the state and the road came under private management and control.

6320. Railroad station for both passengers and freight was the Baltimore and Ohio Railroad depot on Poppleton Street, south of Pratt Street, Baltimore, MD. The original two-story building, erected in 1830, was later converted to a museum.

6321. Railroad for commercial transportation of passengers and freight was the Baltimore and Ohio Railroad Company, incorporated in Maryland and Virginia in 1827. Construction began at Baltimore, MD, on July 4, 1828, and the first passenger revenue was obtained on January 7, 1830. Tickets were 9 cents each, or three for 25 cents, for a ride from Pratt Street in Baltimore to the Carrollton Viaduct. At first, passengers rode primarily for the novel experience.

6322. Interstate railroad was the Petersburg Railroad, chartered by special act of the General Assembly of Virginia on February 10, 1830, and by special act of the North Carolina Legislature on January 1, 1831. It was opened in 1833 on a route along the north bank of the Roanoke River from Petersburg, VA, to Blakely, NC, a distance of 59 miles. On November 21, 1898, it became part of the Atlantic Coast Line Railroad Company system.

6323. Railroad timetable advertised in a newspaper appeared in the *Baltimore American* of Baltimore, MD, on May 20, 1830, by the Baltimore and Ohio Railroad Company. The advertisement announced that on May 24, 1830, passenger transportation would be effected between Baltimore and Ellicott's Mills, MD, and that a brigade of train coaches would leave the company's depot on Pratt Street, Baltimore, at 7 A.M., 11 A.M., and 4 P.M. and would return from Ellicott's Mills at 9 A.M., 1 P.M., and 6 P.M. The price for the 26-mile trip was 75 cents. Because of a shortage of cars, passengers were obliged to return in the same coach and had to book passage for the whole trip. When additional cars were available, passengers could use any car and could engage passage for a shorter distance, if desired.

6324. Railroad to carry troops was the Baltimore and Ohio Railroad Company. On June 30, 1831, the railroad transported Brigadier General George H. Steuart, 1st Division Maryland Guards, and about 100 volunteer troops to Sykes Mills (now Sykesville), MD, where they quelled a riot of railroad workers who were striking for back pay due them. The troops arrested about 50 workers.

6325. Railroad accident occurred on July 25, 1832, on the Granite Railway, Quincy, MA. Four visitors, after seeing the process of transporting large and weighty loads of stone, were invited to ascend the inclined plane in one of the vacant returning cars. The cable chain snapped and they were precipitated over a cliff, a distance of 30 to 40 feet. One man was killed and the others seriously injured.

6326. State aid to railroads was granted by Illinois, which was empowered by Congress on March 2, 1833, to sell land it had acquired from the federal government and to use the proceeds to aid in the construction of railroads. This grant did not become effective and was not used by the state.

6327. Railroad to run trains to Washington was the Baltimore and Ohio Railroad, which made its first trial run from Baltimore, MD, to Washington, DC, on July 1, 1835.

6328. Railroad to run west out of Chicago was the Galena and Chicago Union Railroad, a constituent company of the Chicago and North Western Railway. Its first train was hauled by *The Pioneer*, a 10-ton wood-burning locomotive, which left Chicago, IL, on October 25, 1848, for Oak Park, five miles away. The North Western rails reached the Missouri River at Council Bluffs, IA, in 1867. The first railroad to run west of the Mississippi River was the Pacific Railway of Missouri (later known as the Missouri Pacific), which began passenger service from St. Louis on December 23, 1852.

6329. Railroad excursion rates originated in 1849, during an exhibition in Boston, MA, of a panorama of the Saguenay, St. Lawrence, and Niagara Falls. Josiah Perham of Boston persuaded railroads to grant a one-day low excursion rate to visitors from outside the city who wanted to see the panorama.

6330. Railroad land grant of importance was authorized by act of September 20, 1850, "an act granting the right of way and making a grant of land to the states of Illinois, Mississippi and Alabama in aid of the construction of a railroad from Chicago to Mobile." Illinois received 2,595,133 acres of land and transferred them to the Illinois Central Railroad Company, which broke ground on December 23, 1851. The first 60-mile section of the railroad, from La Salle to Bloomington, IL, was completed on May 16, 1853.

6331. Railroad merger of importance was the agreement of May 17, 1853, in which 10 companies consolidated under the title of New York Central Railroad Company with an aggregate capital of $23.1 million. On April 2, 1853, an act was passed by the New York legislature "to authorize the consolidation of certain railroad companies." The equipment consisted of 187 first-class passenger coaches, 55 second-class coaches, 65 baggage, mail, and express cars, and 1,702 freight cars. There were 298 miles of main line, 236 miles of branch line, and 29 miles of leased road.

6332. Union passenger station used by several railroad companies was the Union Station in Indianapolis, IN, opened on September 20, 1853, for the trains of five railroad companies. The depot was 100 feet wide and 420 feet long, and contained five tracks inside and through the depot, and two tracks outside and north of the depot. The constructing engineer was Colonel T.A. Morris. Edwards and Copeland were the general contractors. The depot was owned and operated by the Indianapolis Union Railway Company, which ran the station, the tracks, and the Indianapolis Belt Railroad.

6333. Cog railroad in the world was the Mount Washington Cog Railway, which ran to the summit of Mount Washington, NH. The railway was invented by Sylvester Marsh of Littleton, NH. Work was begun in May 1866. The first public demonstration was made at the base of the mountain on August 29, 1866, on a half-mile section of track. The railway was completed in July 1869 at a cost of $139,500.

6334. Elevated railroad was opened for traffic on July 2, 1867, in New York City. Charles T. Harvey built the first half-mile test section on single columns along the curb line of Greenwich Street, between Battery Place and Dey Street. The speed of the cars was from 12 to 15 miles per hour. The line was unsuccessful and was sold at a sheriff's sale. It was reorganized February 14, 1870, and placed in operation with steam power. Service was extended as far north as the New York Central Railroad Passenger station at 29th Street and Ninth Avenue.

6335. Railroad owned by a city was authorized by the Ohio legislature on May 4, 1869, with an "act to authorize cities of the first class to build railroads and to lease or operate the same." The first city to construct a railroad was Cincinnati. The Cincinnati Southern Railway started regular passenger service to Ludlow and Somerset, KY, on July 23, 1877. Freight service started on August 13. Freight service to Chattanooga, TN, was inaugurated on February 21, 1880, and through passenger trains on March 5. The railroad was leased on October 12, 1881, to the Cincinnati, New Orleans and Texas Pacific Railway Company for five five-year periods.

6336. Transcontinental railroad service became possible on May 10, 1869, when Senator Leland Stanford drove the last spike into the the Union Pacific's rails at Promontory, UT, completing a rail network that stretched across the country and that was made up of numerous railroad companies.

6337. Electric elevated railroad was operated at the Chicago Railway Exposition in June 1883 by the Electric Railway Company of the United States. The *Judge*, a 15-horsepower electric locomotive, hauled the trains on a three-foot-gauge track around the outer edge of a gallery of the main exhibition building, curving sharply at either end on a radius of 56 feet. The total length of the track was 1,553 feet. The trial trip was made on June 2, 1883, but the line was not permitted to operate until June 9. It ceased operating on June 23, having run 118.75 hours. It made 1,588 trips, carried 26,805 passengers, and ran 446.24 miles. It was

RAILROADS—*continued*

the first commercial electric line to operate. The first permanent electric elevated railroad was the Metropolitan West Side Elevated Railway in Chicago, which opened on May 17, 1895. It ran from Franklin Street to Logan Square, a distance of five miles.

6338. Piggyback railroad operation began on January 5, 1885, on the Long Island Rail Road in New York State. A produce train, consisting of eight flatcars for carrying farmers' wagons, eight cars to carry their horses, and a coach for teamsters, left Albertson's Station, a railroad station on Long Island. It arrived at 6:30 A.M. at Long Island City, where a ferry carried the wagons across the East River to New York City.

6339. Transcontinental daily railroad service was established in 1887. Passengers changed trains at Omaha, NE. On November 17, 1889, direct service was inaugurated between Chicago, IL, and Portland, OR, and between Chicago and San Francisco, CA, by the Union Pacific Railroad Company. This train was the *Overland Limited.*

6340. Railroad to use an electric engine for a short distance in place of a steam engine was the Baltimore and Ohio, Baltimore, MD, which ran its first train with an electric engine through the Baltimore tunnel for a distance of 3.6 miles. The regular use of electric engines for freight trains for this distance was begun on August 4, 1894, and for passenger trains on May 1, 1895.

6341. Railroad operated by an electric third-rail system was the Lackawanna and Wyoming Valley Railroad Company (Laurel Company), which commenced operations in Scranton, PA, on May 25, 1903. After the system had been tried out successfully in Scranton, the elevated railway in New York City was electrified with a third rail.

6342. All-electric railroad was the Long Island Rail Road, which in 1905 installed a low-voltage third rail system on all its lines, eliminating the need for steam locomotion.

6343. Railroad operated by the federal government was the Alaska Railroad, acquired under the Alaska Railroad Enabling Act of March 12, 1914, from various private railroad companies. The golden spike marking the completion of the rail network was driven by President Warren Gamaliel Harding at Nenana, AK, on July 15, 1923. The railroad, which operated 478 miles of track, was under the control of the Federal Railroad Administration within the Department of Transportation.

6344. Railroad to be completely equipped with diesel-electric engines was the New York, Susquehanna and Western Railroad. The first diesel unit was placed in service on December 27, 1941. By May 25, 1945, all 16 engines in the fleet were diesel-electrics. They were built by the American Locomotive Company, New York City, and the General Electric Company, Schenectady, NY.

6345. Transcontinental Pullman sleeping car daily service requiring no change of cars was inaugurated on March 30, 1946, between New York City and Los Angeles, CA. The "Imperial Forest," a sleeping car of the *Twentieth Century Limited,* left New York City at 5:30 P.M. and arrived at Los Angeles on April 3, 1946, at 11:50 A.M., attached to the *Santa Fe Chief.* The hookup and transfer were made at Chicago. Eastward service ran from Los Angeles to New York. This service was discontinued in April 1958.

6346. Railroad freight yard that was fully automatic was the Elgin, Joliet and Eastern Railway Company's Kirk Yard at Gary, IN, which began operating under manual control on January 25, 1952, and changed to fully automatic operation on December 17, 1954. Radar and electronic brain circuits were used to sort out and assemble freight cars by destination, weigh them automatically, and couple them into trains. The equipment was installed by the General Railway Signal Company, Rochester, NY.

RAILROADS—LOCOMOTIVES

6347. Locomotive to pull a train on a track was a steam locomotive that was designed and built by John Stevens in 1824, when he was 76 years old. The locomotive could pull a 1,000-pound load at 12 miles per hour. It was operated on a circular track 220 feet in circumference on Stevens's estate at Hoboken, NJ. It moved by means of a large gear wheel engaging a toothed rack placed on the ties between the rails. The wheels had no flanges, so to keep the train from running off the track, Stevens affixed little horizontal friction rollers on the underside chassis that pressed and rolled along the inner vertical face of the wooden beams used for rails. The locomotive was completed on October 23, 1824.

6348. Locomotive for railroad use was the *Stourbridge Lion,* built by Foster, Rastrick and Company of Stourbridge, England. The diameter of the driving wheel was 48 inches. The gauge was 4 feet 3 inches. Horatio Allen was sent to England by the Delaware and Hudson

Railroad Company to purchase it. The engine weighed seven tons and traveled at the speed of 10 miles per hour. Its first run in the United States took place on August 9, 1829, on the tracks of the Delaware and Hudson in Pennsylvania between Carbondale, a coal mining center, and Honesdale, the canal terminus. The locomotive was too heavy for the track.

6349. Passenger locomotive built in the United States was the *Tom Thumb,* designed and built by Peter Cooper in Baltimore, MD. It weighed six tons and had a 30-inch driving wheel. Its gauge was 4 feet 8.5 inches. On August 28, 1830, it carried 26 passengers a distance of 13 miles over the tracks of the Baltimore and Ohio Railroad in 1 hour 15 minutes. It returned with 30 passengers in 61 minutes, including a four-minute stop to take on water. Another American locomotive, the *Best Friend,* built at the West Point Foundry for use on the Charleston and Hamburg Railroad, made its initial trip on November 2, 1830, but it was derailed.

6350. Locomotive illumination was devised by Horatio Allen for the Charleston and Hamburg Railroad in 1831. He placed a little square flat car, about five feet long, in front of the locomotive and spread a layer of sand several inches deep, on top of which he built a fire of pinewood knots. The device was impractical because sparks from the fire blew into the cars when the train was in motion and caused frequent fires.

6351. Locomotive bid was solicited by the Baltimore and Ohio Railroad Company, Baltimore, MD, in a series of advertisements that first appeared on January 4, 1831, in the *Baltimore American.* The sum of $4,000 was offered for the most approved engine of American manufacture, and $3,500 for the next best. The winner was the *York,* built by Phineas Davis of York, PA.

6352. Locomotive to burn coal was the *York,* invented by Phineas Davis, a watchmaker, and built at York, PA. Its first trial took place on February 19, 1831. It was the first locomotive that had coupled wheels and a double instead of a single pair of drivers. It weighed 3.5 tons and attained velocity by gearing, using a spur wheel and pinion on one of the axles of the wheels. The only accident in which it was involved occurred on September 27, 1835, as the result of a defective track. The accident killed Phineas Davis, who was riding on the locomotive.

6353. Locomotive with six or eight driving wheels attached to parallel axles was patented by Ross Winans on October 1, 1834. Winans was also the first to introduce eight-wheel cars in railroading. The first car was the *Columbus,* which was put into use by the Baltimore and Ohio Railroad Company, Baltimore, MD, on July 4, 1831.

6354. Locomotive with a cab for the engineer and crew was the *Samuel D. Ingham,* built in 1835–36 in Philadelphia, PA, for the Beaver Meadow Railroad (later the Lehigh Valley Railroad). It was of the eight-wheel type and had a peculiar valve motion, the reversing being done by a block sliding on the valve seats. It was designed by Andrew Eastwick. Abner Houston was the engineer, and Stephen Maxwell and "Squire Longshore" were the spragmen who pressed the brake blocks against the wheels to lessen the speed.

6355. Locomotive steam whistle was made by the Rogers Locomotive and Machine Works, Paterson, NJ, and used on October 6, 1837, by the Paterson and Hudson River Railroad on *The Sandusky,* a locomotive with a four-wheeled truck under the forward part of the engine. The whistle was so overworked on the locomotive's run from Paterson to New Brunswick, NJ, that the supply of steam was affected. The locomotive was sold to the Mad River and Lake Erie Railroad Company for $6,750 and on October 14, 1837, was packed in boxes and shipped by schooner.

6356. Electric locomotive made a trial round trip on April 29, 1851, on the Washington branch of the Baltimore and Ohio Railroad from Washington, DC, to Bladensburg, MD, five miles each way. It was designed by Charles Grafton Page of Salem, MA. It was 15 feet long and 6 feet wide, and had a platform truck of four wheels under the forward end and two 5-foot driving wheels under the rear end. It attained a speed of 19 miles per hour. It was operated by galvanized storage batteries, but was not practical, as it did not run any appreciable distance. The first electric freight locomotive was built by the Pullman Car Company at Pullman, IL, in 1888 for the Ansonia, Derby and Birmingham Electric Line, which later became part of the Connecticut Company and thus a part of Conrail (New Haven Division). It weighed 17.5 tons and was capable of hauling a train weighing about 35 tons at less than 10 miles per hour. The first trial took place on May 1, 1888.

RAILROADS—LOCOMOTIVES—*continued*

6357. Narrow-gauge locomotive was constructed in Philadelphia, PA, by the Baldwin Locomotive Works. It was known as Engine No. 1, the *Montezuma,* and was first used by the Denver and Rio Grande Western Railroad Company on July 3, 1871. It had a 3-foot gauge, a length of 30 feet, and a total weight of 25,000 pounds.

6358. Locomotive to use oil for fuel was the *Young America,* an eight-wheeled wood-burning locomotive that was equipped with an oil burner from a San Francisco steamboat in 1879 by the Central Pacific Railroad. The fuel supply consisted of one barrel of crude oil mounted on a tender and connected to the burner with five hose lines.

6359. Locomotive to attain a speed of one mile in less than a minute was a No. 10 locomotive, built at Altoona, PA. During a 34-mile run from Huntingdon to Harrisburg, PA, on March 17, 1881, it covered one mile in 58 seconds and another mile in 59 seconds.

6360. Locomotive owned by an industrial company was ordered in June 1890 by the Whitin Machine Works, Whitinsville, MA, from the Thomson-Houston Electric Company, Lynn, MA, and placed in service on May 11, 1892, hauling freight cars to the plant. It could haul 60 tons at a speed of seven miles per hour.

6361. Locomotive to attain a proven speed of 112.5 miles per hour was the New York Central's famous Locomotive 999, the *Empire State Express,* built at the West Albany shops of the New York Central and Hudson River Railroad. The coupled wheels were 7 feet 2 inches in diameter. The time was clocked on May 10, 1893.

6362. Duplex compound locomotive was built in 1904 at the Schenectady, NY, plant of the American Locomotive Company for the Baltimore and Ohio Railroad. The engine, No. 2400, burned bituminous coal and had a driving-wheel diameter of 56 inches. Its weight on drivers was 334,500 pounds.

6363. Diesel-electric locomotive was No. 1000, a 300-horsepower locomotive placed in service on December 17, 1924, by the Central Railroad of New Jersey at the Bronx terminal, New York City. The diesel engine was built by the Ingersoll-Rand Company, Phillipsburg, NJ, the electrical components by the General Electric Company, Elmira, NY, and the locomotive structure by the American Locomotive Compa-

ny, Schenectady, NY. The locomotive remained in service until June 13, 1957. The first diesel-electric freight locomotive was constructed by the New York Central Lines in January 1928 and placed in operation in June 1928.

6364. Streamlined steam locomotive was introduced by the New York Central Lines on December 14, 1934, between Albany and Karner, NY. Built in West Albany, NY, it was named the *Commodore Vanderbilt* after the founder of the New York Central Lines. It was 96 feet long, weighed 228 tons, and developed 4,075 horsepower.

6365. Streamlined electric locomotive was No. 4800, type GG1, placed in service by the Pennsylvania Railroad Company on January 28, 1935, in a test run between Washington, DC, and Philadelphia, PA. The engine was 79.5 feet long, of all-steel construction, and weighed 230 tons. It operated on an 11,000-volt, 25-cycle, single-phase system, the current fed by overhead wires through a pantograph. The electric engine was placed in passenger service on February 10, 1935.

6366. Rack-rail diesel-electric locomotive was built by the General Electric Company, Schenectady, NY, for the Manitou and Pikes Peak Railway, Colorado Springs, CO, the highest cog railroad in the world, and placed in service on July 16, 1939. It pushed the 50-passenger car up the 16 percent grade, and on the downward trip backed down the grade in front of the car. Dynamic braking assisted in holding the car at a safe speed in descending the steep slopes.

6367. Super-giant locomotive to carry the weight of 1 million pounds on drivers was the Class EL-2B No. 125, a 6,800-horsepower electric locomotive built by the General Electric Company, Erie, PA, and placed in operation on January 27, 1948, by the Virginia Railway Company, Norfolk, VA, between Roanoke, VA, and Mullens, WV. It had 16 driving axles and an overall length of 150 feet 8 inches.

6368. Gas-turbine-electric locomotive was track-tested on November 15, 1948, at Erie, PA. It was built by the American Locomotive Company for the Union Pacific Railroad Company and publicly demonstrated on June 16, 1949. The locomotive was 83 feet 7.5 inches long, weighed 500,000 pounds, and had a continuous tractive effort of 68,500 pounds at 20.4 miles per hour. Power from the generator was supplied to eight traction motors, each of which drove an axle. It was geared for 79 miles per hour, the locomotive carrying enough fuel for 12 hours of operation at 4,500 horsepower. The gas turbine power was rated at 4,800 horsepower.

6369. Gas-turbine propane-fueled locomotive was placed in service on June 8, 1953, by the Union Pacific Railroad to haul freight between Los Angeles, CA, and Las Vegas, NV. It delivered 4,800 horsepower, more than three diesel units operated together. The locomotive was built by the General Electric Company. Propane burns without leaving carbonlike deposits on the turbine blades.

RAILROADS—RAILROAD CARS

6370. Double-deck railroad coaches were built by Richard Imlay in August 1830 and used on the Baltimore and Ohio Railroad between Baltimore, MD, and Ellicott's Mill, MD. They were called "Improved Passenger Cars." Each coach accommodated 12 passengers on the lower deck. An additional six people, including the driver, occupied outside seats at the end of the deck. The upper deck of each carriages was furnished with a double sofa that accommodated 12 more passengers, who were shaded by an awning stretched over an iron frame.

6371. Railroad car with a center aisle was the *Columbus,* introduced on July 4, 1831, by the Baltimore and Ohio Railroad Company, despite fears that the aisle would become one long spittoon. The car was designed by Ross Winans and built at Baltimore, MD.

6372. Railroad sleeping car was *The Chambersburg,* used in 1836 by the Cumberland Valley Railroad between Harrisburg and Chambersburg, PA. It included four sleeping sections, each of which had three bunks. No bedding was provided. It was common for persons traveling to sleep fully clothed and to cover themselves with shawls, which they carried with them for the purpose.

6373. Railroad coach modeled after English coaches was built at the Old Colony South Boston shops in Boston, MA, for the Fall River Line, and placed in service on May 19, 1847.

6374. Private railroad car was outfitted for the singer Jenny Lind, the "Swedish Nightingale," who made her first American appearance on September 11, 1850, at Castle Garden, New York City. The car was used on her tour of the country.

6375. Pullman sleeping car was "Old No. 9," built by Ben Field and George Mortimer Pullman in 1859 in Chicago, IL, and placed in service on September 1, 1859, on the Chicago and Alton Railroad between Bloomington and Chicago. It was a reconstructed day coach, little more than half the length of present coaches. Except for the wheels and axles, it was constructed almost entirely of wood. The roof was flat and low. The seats were adamantine. Two small woodburning stoves furnished heat. The illumination was furnished by candles. There was a small lavatory at each end. The drinking faucet supplied water to a nonenclosed washbasin. There were 10 upper and 10 lower berths with mattresses and blankets but no sheets. The upper berth was suspended about halfway between the floor and ceiling at night, and by day was drawn up to the ceiling by pulleys.

6376. Oil tank railroad cars were introduced by Charles P. Hatch of the Empire Transportation Company, Philadelphia, PA, in 1864–65 and used on the Oil Creek Railroad, the Warren and Franklin Railroad, and other lines. Cars with three wooden tanks containing 3,500 gallons were used, but rain dissolved the glue coating and caused leakage. Later, riveted iron tanks mounted horizontally were used. On September 1, 1865, Amos Densmore mounted two wooden tanks over the trucks of a flatcar and used them to ship oil from Miller's Farm to New York City over the Atlantic and Great Western Railroad. The shipment consisted of two cars, each with two tanks, and each tank containing about 40 barrels.

6377. Pullman sleeping car that was comfortable was *The Pioneer,* built by George Mortimer Pullman in 1865 in Chicago, IL, at a cost of $18,000. It rested on 16 wheels (a later version of the car had 12 wheels). The car was longer, higher, and wider than its predecessors and had the first raised upper deck and folding upper berth. It was heated by hot air furnaces under the floor, lighted with candles, and ventilated through deck windows. It was fully carpeted, and the seats were covered with French plush upholstery.

6378. Refrigerated railroad car was patented by J.B. Sutherland of Detroit, MI, on November 26, 1867. He received a patent on an insulated car constructed with ice bunkers in each end. Air came in at the top, was passed through the ice chambers, and circulated through the car by means of gravity, controlled by the use of hanging flaps that created differences in air temperature. The first refrigerated railroad car to carry a load of fresh fruit was constructed in

RAILROADS—RAILROAD CARS—*continued*

1866 by Parker Earle of Cobden, IL, who built and shipped chests of strawberries on the Illinois Central Railroad. The chests had three layers of board and were airtight and watertight. They held 100 pounds of ice and 200 quarts of strawberries, which brought $2 a quart. In 1872, Earle shipped a full carload from Anna, IL, to Chicago.

6379. Railroad dining car ever operated in the world was the *Delmonico,* built in 1868 by the Pullman Palace Car Company, Pullman, IL, and placed in service between Chicago, IL, and St. Louis, MO, by the Chicago and Alton Railroad Company. It had tables and chairs and was serviced by a kitchen. Passengers on the Philadelphia–Baltimore run of the Philadelphia, Wilmington and Baltimore Railroad in 1863 were able to buy food at a 50-foot-long refreshment car fitted with an eating bar and steam box, where food prepared at the terminals was heated and sold.

6380. Railroad parlor car was the *Maritana,* built by George Mortimer Pullman and placed in operation in 1875. The chairs in the car were richly upholstered, with adjustable backs, and revolved on swivels.

6381. Railroad chapel car was the *Evangel,* dedicated on May 23, 1891, in Cincinnati, OH. The dedication address was delivered by Dr. Wayland Hoyt. The car was fitted out for religious services and was used on the Northern Pacific Railroad's tracks. Experimental services were held in St. Paul and Minneapolis, MN. The car was committed for the winter to the Reverend and Mrs. E.G. Wheeler, who conducted services in it on the Pacific Coast.

6382. Steel railroad passenger coach was built in 1902–03 by the Pennsylvania Railroad Company in its shop at Altoona, PA. It had a steel underframe and superstructure, a composite roof, and wooden window frames and sills. The first all-steel passenger coach was completed on December 23, 1907.

6383. Steel railroad mail car was built by the Standard Steel Car Company, Pittsburgh, PA, and exhibited on May 4–13, 1905, at the International Railway Congress, Washington, DC, before being placed in service on June 7 by the New York, Salamanca and Chicago Railroad Company. The car was lighted with acetylene gas and lined with fireproof composite board. The inside length was 65 feet 2 inches. It was framed with steel posts and girders, covered with steel plates, and insulated with hair felt.

6384. Pullman sleeping car made entirely of steel was manufactured in 1907 to comply with the regulations of the Hudson and Manhattan Railroad System, New York City, which specified that no combustible equipment be used in the Hudson River tubes. The 74-foot-long car, which was manufactured in Pullman, IL, had a steel-sheeted exterior and a low-pressure vapor heat system. Electric light was obtained from an axle device.

6385. Railroad tank car lined with glass for transporting milk was built in 1910 by the Pflaudler Company, Rochester, NY, for the Whiting Milk Company, Boston, MA. It was used on the Boston and Maine Railroad to collect milk from the country for city consumption.

6386. Air-conditioned railroad cars were installed by the Atchison, Topeka and Santa Fe Railway Company in 1914, when 15 new dining cars were put in service on the *California Limited* between Chicago, IL, and Los Angeles, CA. The system was known as the Duntley Air Washer and consisted of a motor-driven spray wheel partially submerged in ice water. Fresh air was drawn through the spray and delivered into the car by means of a fan and air ducts. This system lowered the temperature a few degrees, but the capacity was inadequate. An air-conditioning experiment was tried in 1854 by the New York and Erie Railroad, using a device that caught air through a funnel and passed it through a water tank underneath the car on its way to the car's interior. In winter, the air was heated by a stove. An opening in the rear of the car enabled the air to escape.

6387. Gasoline-mechanical railroad cars installed in regular service were ordered by the Pennsylvania Railroad Company, which placed them in operation in February 1923 on the Berwick, Flemington and Bustleton branches in the Philadelphia district. These cars superseded local passenger trains whose operation was unprofitable. They were replaced in 1926 by gasoline-electric cars.

6388. Railroad car with an observation dome was placed in service on July 23, 1945, by the Chicago, Burlington and Quincy Railroad. It was a standard Budd stainless-steel coach equipped with three decks. A section of the top deck had a curved double glass roof called a VistaDome. The section was 19.5 feet long, extended the full width of the car, and seated 24 passengers. The first superdome observation cars were built by the Pullman-Standard Car Manufacturing Company and placed in service on January 1, 1953, by the Chicago, Milwaukee, St. Paul and Pacific Railroad. They were 85 feet long, 10 feet wide, and 15 feet 6 inches from top to rail. The dome section contained 625 square feet of curved safety glass in sections 3 feet wide and 5 feet high. The laminated glass consisted of polished plate glass and layers of plastic.

6389. Railroad dining car powered by electricity was the *Cafe St. Louis,* built in Chicago, IL, and placed in service on March 9, 1949, between Chicago and St. Louis, MO, by the Illinois Central Railroad. It had a self-contained electric power unit that developed approximately 50,000 watts, supplying the power for two broilers, two ranges, a hot food table, a coffee urn, plate and cup warmers, a deep-fry kettle, a dishwasher, a glass washer, mixers and fruit juice extractors, refrigerators, and a garbage disposal system.

6390. Railroad freight cars with compartments were developed jointly by the Western Pacific Railroad Company and the Pullman Standard Car Company and placed in service on September 12, 1952, between Chicago, IL, and San Francisco, CA. Four gates were installed in each car to separate the contents into sections and to prevent shifting and crushing.

6391. Remote-controlled railroad passenger car was put in operation on December 1, 1955, between New Rochelle, NY, and Rye, NY, on 7.5 miles of the New York, New Haven and Hartford system. The car was operated from a control panel at Larchmont, NY, which started it, stopped it, and increased its speed up to 70 miles per hour. The tests were conducted by the Union Switch and Signal Division of the Westinghouse Air Brake Company.

6392. Adaptable railroad freight car was built by the American Car and Foundry Division of ACF Industries at Berwick, PA, and was placed in service on July 24, 1956, by the Chicago, Rock Island and Pacific Railroad Company between St. Louis, MO, and Wichita, KS. It was called an Adapto Car. Sections of various shapes and sizes were made to fit above the chassis of a flatcar. The sections could be removed along with their contents to allow reuse of the car without unloading.

RAILROADS—STREETCARS

6393. Streetcar company was the New York and Harlem Railway, New York City, incorporated on April 25, 1831, "to construct a single or double railroad." It was capitalized for $350,000 and received a 30-year franchise on December 22, 1831, from the Common Council. The first secretary was John Mason, who later became president.

6394. Streetcar was the *John Mason,* a horse-drawn conveyance designed and constructed by John Stephenson in Philadelphia, PA, and placed in service in New York City by the New York and Harlem Railway on November 26, 1832. Named for the prominent New York banker who organized the railway company, the *John Mason* was equipped with iron wheels and was drawn over iron rails laid in the center of the pavement. Lank O'Dell was the first driver. The car was divided into three nonconnecting compartments with 10 seats in each. The first of the three doors bore on its panel the name *New York,* the second *Yorkville,* and the third *Harlaem.* The fare was 12.5 cents. Tracks for the streetcar were laid along Fourth Avenue from Prince Street to 14th Street. In November 1835, a double track running north to Yorkville was completed.

6395. Cable car was invented by Eleazer A. Gardner of Philadelphia, PA, who obtained a patent on March 23, 1858, on an "improvement in tracks for city railways." The cable was housed in an underground tunnel with a series of pulleys inside.

6396. Coin box for streetcars was invented about 1870 in Louisville, KY, by Thomas Loftin Johnson, who rose from clerk to owner of a street railway in Indianapolis and became a large stockholder in railroad companies in New York City, Cleveland, and Detroit.

6397. Gas-powered streetcar was operated in 1873 in Providence, RI, from the car barns to Olneyville Square. Henry Thompson was the conductor. It had a gas and air engine, compressed by separate pumps. The engine was patented on April 2, 1872, by its designer, George B. Brayton of Boston, MA.

6398. Cable car put into service began operation on August 1, 1873, on Clay Street Hill, San Francisco, CA. The ride cost five cents. This was the first cable car put into service anywhere in the world. It was invented by Andrew Smith Hallidie, who obtained a patent on January 17, 1871, on an "endless-wire rope way."

6399. Electric streetcar run with current generated by a stationary dynamo was invented by Stephen Dudley Field of New York City in 1874. In this system, the current was carried by one of the rails to a wheel of the car and thence to the motor. It flowed back through another wheel, which was insulated from the first one, to the second rail, which returned it to the dynamo. Field obtained a patent on July 13,

RAILROADS—STREETCARS—*continued*

1880, on a method of "propelling railway cars by electro-magnetism." It covered his claim for an electric tramway motor for which the current was supplied to the rails by a stationary source of power.

6400. Electric streetcars commercially operated were those of the Baltimore and Hampden Line, a third-rail system that began operation on one line only on August 10, 1885, in Baltimore, MD. The line continued in service for more than a year. The first cars traveled on the Hampden Branch of the Baltimore Union Passenger Railway Company, which later became a part of the United Railways and Electric Company of Baltimore, MD.

6401. Double-deck streetcar was operated on July 4, 1892, on a trial trip in San Diego, CA. The upper deck was on the roof, with longitudinal seats facing outward that accommodated 12 people on each side. It was reached by a winding stairway at each end of the car, and shaded by a canopy. There were no sides or enclosures on the upper deck other than a railing.

6402. Printed streetcar transfers were invented by John Harry Stedman of Rochester, NY, who patented them on August 23, 1892. They were 1.875 by 2.5 inches and were first used on October 31, 1892, in Rochester.

6403. Interurban streetcar line was the Union Traction Company, established by Charles Lewis Henry. The company ran its first car on June 1, 1898, between Anderson and Alexandria, IN. The first conductor was Hadley Clifford.

6404. Trackless trolley system was built by Charles Mann and placed in operation on September 11, 1910, between "Bungalow Land" in Laurel Canyon, CA, and the terminal point of the Los Angeles Pacific Electric Railway Company in Los Angeles, a distance of 1.5 miles. Two automobile buses were used. On top of the buses were trolley poles making contact with overhead wires.

6405. Municipal streetcars were put into service on December 28, 1912, in San Francisco, CA. The Municipal Railway, an overhead trolley system, began operation with 10 cars on Geary Street, from Kearney Street to 33rd Avenue and Park. Thomas A. Cashin was superintendent. Mayor James Rolph, Jr., acted as motorman on the first car.

6406. Lightweight solo streetcar was designed by Charles O. Birney and built by the American Car Company of St. Louis, MO. The first one-man Birney cars were placed in operation in Fort Worth, TX, in November 1916. The safety features included a single front door for both entrance and exit and a controller that shut down the power, applied sand to the tracks, and set the brakes when the operator failed to keep his hand in place. The door could not be opened or the step lowered until the brakes were set.

6407. Aluminum streetcar in which aluminum was used for the truck as well as for the body and underframe was placed in service on December 2, 1926, by the Cleveland Railway Company. The total weight of the car was 30,300 pounds, of which 6,647 pounds were aluminum.

6408. Tieless streetcar tracks that were soundless and shockless were laid in New Orleans, LA. The roadway was paved with eight inches of concrete base and three inches of wearing surface, of which the top half was the finest oil asphalt. The line was officially completed on February 4, 1930.

RAILROADS—SUBWAYS

6409. Subway was the pneumatic subway invented by Alfred Ely Beach and was known as the Beach Pneumatic Underground Railway of New York City. The company was incorporated for freight traffic on June 1, 1868, and for passenger traffic on May 3, 1869, with a capital stock of $5 million. The system was opened to the public on February 26, 1870. The tunnel was 312 feet long and ran from the west curb line of Broadway at Warren Street down the middle of Broadway to a point south of Murray Street. It consisted of a circular tube nine feet in diameter. The straightaways were built of brick masonry, and the curves were built of iron plate. The cars, which were well upholstered, carried 22 persons each. They were propelled by a rotary blower that drove a blast of air through the tunnel against the rear of the car, carrying it along "like a sailboat before the wind."

6410. Municipal subway was the Tremont Street Subway, Boston, MA, construction of which was begun on March 28, 1895. The section between the Public Garden and Park Street was opened for traffic on September 1, 1897, and the section to North Station on September 3, 1898. The subway was built by the City of Boston at a cost of $4,369,000 and leased to the Boston Elevated Railway at an annual rental of 4.5 percent of construction cost. This was also the first time that a subway was built with a shallow tunnel instead of a deep tunnel.

6411. Rapid-transit subway was the Interborough Rapid Transit subway in New York City. The route ran north from City Hall (Brooklyn Bridge) under Lafayette Street and Park Avenue to Grand Central Station, west along 42nd Street to Times Square, then north on Broadway to 145th Street. The line was opened on October 27, 1904. At 7 P.M., 111,881 passengers paid a nickel each to ride for 26 minutes on the express train or 46 minutes on the local. The IRT's 300 subway motor cars and trailers were the first to have finish work, moldings, window panels, and other parts made of aluminum.

6412. Subway car with side doors was placed in service on February 16, 1909, when eight cars of the Interborough Rapid Transit of New York City left Lenox Avenue and 148th Street going south. The side doors, four feet from each end of the car, were opened and closed by a pneumatic-lever system. The cars cost $12,000 each. The doors were the invention of James McElroy of the Consolidated Car Heating Company.

6413. Subway train to run automatically without conductors or motormen was placed in operation in New York City on January 4, 1962, between Grand Central Station and Times Square. The train carried a motorman who stood by without performing any duties. This was a safety measure demanded by the transport workers' union, which was involved in a labor dispute with the New York City Transit Authority.

6414. Subway service in Los Angeles began on January 30, 1993. It consisted of a single route, a 4.4-mile, five-station track connecting Union Station with MacArthur Park. An expanded system with 22 miles of track and 20 stations was planned for the year 2001.

RAILROADS—TRACKS AND EQUIPMENT

6415. Railroad track that was practical was laid in Philadelphia, PA, in 1809. It was made of wood laid on a steep grade of 1.5 inches to the yard and was 180 feet in length. On July 31, a carriage weighing 10,696 pounds with four grooved wheels was placed on the track at the lower end and a single horse walking on the loose dirt between the tracks pulled it up the slope.

6416. Railroad rails of T shape were invented in 1830 by Robert Livingston Stevens, president and engineer of the Camden and Amboy Railroad. They were made of malleable iron and weighed 36 pounds a yard. Their adoption was very slow, as the type of rail then preferred was the flat rail that was nailed to the ties.

6417. Locomotive cowcatcher was invented by Isaac Dripps and used in 1833 on the Camden and Amboy Railroad between Bordentown and Hightstown, NJ. It consisted originally of a small attachment on two wheels with projecting points, but since the prongs impaled animals, it was replaced by a heavy bar set at right angles to the rails.

6418. Railroad rails of iron were rolled in 1844 at the Mount Savage Rolling Mill, Mount Savage, MD, and weighed 42 pounds a yard. Five hundred tons of the inverted U-type rails were rolled in 1845. They were laid between Mount Savage and Cumberland, MD, a distance of approximately nine miles. This rolling mill also produced T rails, which weighed 50 pounds a yard.

6419. Railroad rails of steel were used by the Pennsylvania Railroad. They weighed 56 pounds a yard and were placed in service in 1864 between Altoona and Pittsburgh, PA. The first rails of Bessemer steel were rolled at the North Chicago rolling mill, Chicago, IL, on May 24, 1865, from ingots made at the experimental steel works at Wyandotte, MI. Their manufacture was witnessed by members of the American Iron and Steel Association, who were assembled in conference at Chicago.

6420. Air brake was invented by George Westinghouse, Jr., of Schenectady, NY, who received a patent on April 13, 1869, on a "steam power brake." It was used on an experimental train carrying officials of the Panhandle Railroad. It immediately demonstrated its value. But inasmuch as it took longer for the air to reach the last cars of a train, each car stopped at a different time. A "triple air brake" that corrected this fault was patented by Westinghouse on March 5, 1872. He invented an automatic brake 15 years later.

6421. Railroad to install track water tanks to allow trains to take water on the run was the Pennsylvania Railroad, which placed a track tank in the northbound track at Sang Hollow on the Pittsburgh division during the early months of 1870, followed by a 1,200-foot tank in the southbound track at the same location. In the same year, the New York Central installed track tanks between Montrose and Albany.

RAILROADS—TRACKS AND EQUIPMENT—*continued*

6422. Railroad signal system with automatic electric block was invented by Thomas S. Hall of Stamford, CT, in 1867 and was installed on the New York and Harlem Railroad. Hall obtained a patent on June 7, 1870, for his electromagnetic railway signal apparatus. The wheels of the locomotive struck a lever fastened to the rail and this in turn set the signal at danger until the train was out of the block. The first signal system with a manual block had been installed in 1863 between Philadelphia, PA, and Trenton, NJ, on the Philadelphia and Trenton Railroad.

6423. Railroad coupler with which every railroad car in the United States, Canada, and Mexico was equipped was invented by Eli Hamilton Janney of Alexandria, VA, who obtained a patent on an "improvement in car-couplings" on April 29, 1873.

6424. Railroad interlocking signal machine was placed in service at Spuyten Duyvil, the Bronx, NY (now part of New York City), in 1874 by the New York Central and Hudson River Railroad. Levers operated from a central location controlled an arrangement of switch and signal appliances, providing a safe path for the movement of trains through switches, junctions, grade crossings, and terminal stations, and over drawbridges.

6425. Electric locomotive headlight was patented by Leonidas G. Woolley of Mendon, MI, on May 3, 1881. It was a polygonal lamp frame suspended in position by a series of opposing springs that neutralized the engine's jarring.

6426. Railroad signal system of continuous cab signals was used by the Pennsylvania Railroad. On July 11, 1923, cab signals were installed experimentally in locomotives hauling trains between Lewiston Junction and Sunbury, PA. These cab signals, located on the locomotives where the engineman and fireman could readily see them, were actuated by electric currents in track circuits of the track on which the locomotive was located. This was accomplished by coding the electric circuits to reflect the conditions on the track ahead of the locomotive.

6427. Locomotive communications headlight was installed on November 6, 1934, on a Union Pacific six-car streamlined train, and was demonstrated the following day at the railway station in Schenectady, NY. The operator on the train aimed the beacon of his projector at a concave mirror mounted on the platform. Persons aboard the train were able to speak over the beam of light to others on the platform. The installation was made by the General Electric Company of Schenectady.

RAILROADS—TRAINS

6428. Streamlined railroad train was invented by the Reverend Samuel R. Calthorp of Roxbury, MA, who obtained a patent on August 8, 1865, on an "air resister train." He gave "to the exterior surface of a railway train a form tapering from the center of the train toward either end, for the purpose of diminishing the atmosphere resistance." The front and rear ends of the train were pointed, and the wheels were enclosed in casing. The only projection was the smokestack. The tender was attached to the locomotive by an accordion hood.

6429. Train with electric lighting was the *Pennsylvania Limited* of the Pennsylvania Railroad Company, placed in service in June 1887 between Chicago, IL, and New York City. Steam from the engine was carried to a turbine in the forward compartment of the baggage car, where it drove an electric generator supplying current to the entire train.

6430. Air-conditioned train was installed by the Baltimore and Ohio Railroad Company. Air-conditioned service began on May 24, 1931, on the Washington–New York route, in both directions. The westbound train left New York City at 3:57 P.M. and the eastbound train left Washington, DC, at 4 P.M. Each train was made up of the following cars, all of which were air-conditioned and air-cooled: smoking car, coach, lounge car, colonial dining car, Pullman parlor car, and observation sunroom parlor car. The train was drawn by one of the President series of locomotives.

6431. Streamlined lightweight high-speed three-car passenger train was first operated by the Union Pacific System on March 2, 1934, westward from Omaha, NE. It was developed by E.E. Adams, the company's vice president. The train was constructed of aluminum alloys that had three times the strength of steel and therefore required only one-third of the material to obtain equivalent strength. The train was tubular in shape. The equipment was designed for a maximum speed of 110 miles per hour, with a sustained speed on straight and level track of 90 miles per hour. The train of three cars weighed 80 tons, the weight of one old-style Pullman sleeping car. The train was fully air-conditioned. Windows were sealed and forced ventilation was used to heat the train in winter, to cool it in summer, and to filter dirt and dust from the air as it was brought into the train.

6432. Train to run 1,000 miles nonstop was the Chicago, Burlington and Quincy's stream-lined train *Zephyr,* powered by a 660-horsepower diesel engine. The *Zephyr* left Union Station, Denver, CO, at 6:04 A.M. on May 26, 1934, and arrived at the Halsted Street station, Chicago, IL, in 13 hours 5 minutes 44 seconds. The trip covered a distance of 1,015 miles. The average speed was 77.6 miles per hour and the top speed 112 miles per hour. There were 65 persons aboard.

6433. Streamlined all-steel diesel-motor train was the *Zephyr,* 196 feet long and 208,061 pounds in weight, built by the Edward G. Budd Manufacturing Company of Philadelphia, PA, for the Chicago, Burlington and Quincy Rail-road for service between Kansas City, MO, and Lincoln, NE. It was driven by a Winton 660-horsepower high-compression two-cycle eight-in-line diesel-electric motor. The first trip, on November 11, 1934, was a run from Lincoln to Kansas City via Omaha and back the same day.

6434. Train with fluorescent lights was the *General Pershing Zephyr,* a stainless-steel streamlined train operated by the Chicago, Bur-lington and Quincy Railroad. Its first run, on April 30, 1939, was between St. Louis and Kansas City, MO. Coaches, parlor lounge, din-ing car, rear car, dressing rooms, and lavatories were all equipped with fluorescent lights.

6435. Train to transport passengers and their cars was the Auto-Train, which began daily service on December 6, 1971, between Lorton, VA, outside Washington, DC, and Sanford, FL, a town north of Orlando. At full complement, it consisted of 13 vehicle carriers, 2 buffet-movie cars, 5 coaches, 4 bedroom cars, 2 locomotives, a steam-generator car, and a kitchen car. Automobiles were loaded on two-level enclosed piggyback cars. Passengers rode in bilevel domed coaches and could have bed-room accommodations at an extra charge. One-way fare was $190 for an automobile and up to four people, with a charge of $15 for each ad-ditional passenger up to the legal maximum of the shipped auto's capacity. A buffet dinner, late-evening snacks, a continental breakfast, and movies were included in the charge. The train could transport 100 cars and 400 people.

6436. Train operated exclusively by women was placed in service on June 6, 1979, by the Long Island Rail Road. It started from Port Washington, NY, at 4:35 P.M. and arrived at Pennsylvania Station, New York City, at 5:07 P.M. The train's conductor was Deirdre Hickey, the first woman to qualify in yard, freight, and passenger service. Doreen Boyle was the fare collector; Beverly Terrillion and Eileen Denn, the brakemen.

RELIGION

6437. Universal chapel embracing eight faiths was dedicated on April 8, 1956, in the Universalist Church of the Divine Paternity, New York City. On its altar was a globe of the earth representing "human unity" and the sym-bols of eight religions—Buddhism, Christianity, Confucianism, Hinduism, Judaism, Shinto, Tao-ism, and Zoroastrianism.

RELIGION—BUDDHIST

6438. Buddhist temple on the American main-land was established on July 15, 1904, in Los Angeles, CA, in a meeting room. The chief priest was Rinban Izumeda. Most of the con-gregation belonged to the Shinshu sect of Bud-dhism, a branch of the Hompa Hongwanji Bud-dhist Temple. Japanese immigrants had earlier established Buddhist temples in Hawaii, which became an American territory in 1899.

6439. Zen Buddhist monastery was Tassajara, also called Zenshinji or Zen Mountain Center, officially opened in July 1967 at Tassajara Springs, CA. The first abbot was Shunryu Suzuki and the first director was Richard Ba-ker.

6440. American to be recognized by Tibetan Buddhists as a reincarnated lama was Catharine Burroughs of Poolesville, MD, who was formally recognized in September 1988 as the reincarnation of Ahkon Lhamo, a Tibetan Buddhist saint of the 17th century. Her divinity was announced in 1987 by His Holiness the Third Drubwang Padma Norbu Rinpoche, the supreme head of the Palyul lineage of Nyingmapa Tibetan Buddhism. She was the first Western woman to be so honored in the religion's 1,200-year history.

RELIGION—CATHOLIC

6441. Christian in America was Leif Eriksson, who founded the Icelandic settlement of Vin-land on the North American coast about the year 1000. Leif was born into a Viking family that adhered to the pagan Norse religion and was converted to Christianity on a visit to Nor-way shortly before his journey.

RELIGION—CATHOLIC—*continued*

6442. Baptism in America was performed in March 1540 by Spanish priests who were part of the expedition of Hernando de Soto. Two Native American guides were baptized in the Ocmulgee River near Macon, GA, and given the names Peter and Mark.

6443. Christian martyr on American soil was Fray Juan de Padilla, a Spanish Franciscan missionary accompanying the expedition of Francis Vasquez Coronado. He was murdered by the Kansas tribe of Native Americans in 1542 near what is now Lyon, KS.

6444. Catholic mass to take place in what is now the continental United States was celebrated on August 28, 1565, the feast day of St. Augustine of Hippo, by priests who accompanied the expedition of Pedro Menéndez de Avilés to Florida. The garrison built by Menéndez de Avilés was given the name St. Augustine.

6445. Catholic parish was the parish of St. Augustine, FL, founded on September 8, 1565, on the day of the Feast of the Nativity of the Blessed Virgin, by Pedro Menéndez de Avilés. The first parish register is also owned by this church and consists of 15 volumes beginning January 1, 1594, and continuing down to the time of the British occupation of Florida in 1763. The first parish priest was Martin Francisco López de Mendozo Grajales.

6446. Catholic bishop to exercise episcopal functions was Fray Juan Cabezas de Altamirano, son of Juan Cabezas and Doña Ana Calzado, appointed Bishop of Santiago de Cuba in 1603. He visited the Provinces of Florida in 1607 and at St. Augustine administered the sacrament of confirmation to many Spaniards and converted Native Americans.

6447. Catholics to settle in the English colonies in America arrived in Maryland in March 1634 on the ships *Ark* and *Dove*. They established St. Mary's Village, the first colonial settlement in Maryland. Their leader was Leonard Calvert. His brother, Cecil Calvert, Lord Baltimore, had founded Maryland in 1632 as a haven for Roman Catholics, who were unwelcome in England. The colony allowed freedom of religion for Christians of any denomination that accepted the doctrine of the Trinity.

6448. Catholic priest born in America was Father Francisco de Florencia, who joined the Jesuit order in 1643. He was born in St. Augustine, FL, in 1620.

6449. Ban on Jesuits to be enacted by a colony was passed in Puritan Massachusetts on May 26, 1647. It provided that "no Jesuit or eclesiasticl person ordayned by the authoritie of the pope shall henceforth come within our jurisdiction" excepting survivors of shipwrecks and traders who "behave themselves inoffencively during their abode here." A second offense was punishable by death.

6450. Catholic holy orders were conferred by Gabriel Diaz Vara Calderón, Bishop of Santiago de Cuba, on a visit to St. Augustine, FL, on August 24, 1675. Minor orders were conferred on seven candidates.

6451. Catholic convent permanently established was in New Orleans, LA, in a two-story frame building with six apartments on each floor. It was occupied on August 6, 1727, by the Ursulines. On August 9, Mass was offered there for the first time. The superioress was Mother Marie (Tranchepain) of St. Augustine, FL.

6452. Catholic nun who professed her vows in the United States was Sister St. Stanislas Hachard of the Ursuline Convent, New Orleans, LA, who took her vows on March 15, 1729. The first nun born in the United States was Mary Turpin of Illinois, born in 1731, who entered the Ursuline Convent in 1748. She began her novitiate on July 2, 1749, and made her profession of faith on January 31, 1752. She died on November 20, 1761, at the age of 30.

6453. Catholic church in the English colonies to be used for public worship was St. Joseph's Church, founded in Philadelphia, PA, in 1733.

6454. Catholic mission in California was dedicated and blessed by Father Junipero Serra on July 16, 1769. After high mass, the royal standard of Spain was unfurled over the mission, which was named in honor of San Diego de Alcala. The mission, located in what is now San Diego, CA, was the first of a chain of 21 that were erected.

6455. Catholic funeral attended by the Continental Congress was that of Philippe Charles Jean Baptiste Tronson du Coudray, a French officer who was serving as inspector general of the American army. On September 15, 1777, while crossing the Schuylkill River in Pennsylvania on a ferry to join Washington's army, his horse became frightened and plunged overboard, and Tronson du Coudray was drowned. Congress resolved that he should be buried with military honors and that the members of Congress should attend his funeral, which was held in Philadelphia, PA, on September 17.

6456. Catholic diocese and archdiocese was the diocese of Baltimore, MD, established on April 6, 1789, and raised to the dignity of the first archdiocese in the United States on April 8, 1808. By a decree of the Sacred Congregation of the Propaganda, approved by Pope Pius IX on July 5, 1858, prerogative of place was conferred on the archdiocese of Baltimore, so that it is known as the Premier See of the country.

6457. Catholic bishop appointed to serve in the United States was the Right Reverend John Carroll of Maryland. A petition for appointment of an American bishop was sent to Pope Pius VI on March 12, 1788, and was voted upon favorably. The result was confirmed by the Pope on November 6, 1789. The Right Reverend Charles Walmesley consecrated Carroll bishop of Baltimore, MD, on August 15, 1790, in the chapel of Lulworth Castle, Dorset, England. On April 8, 1808, he became an archbishop.

6458. Catholic African-Americans were French-speaking Catholics from Haiti, who came to Baltimore, MD, in 1793 as refugees from Haiti's revolution.

6459. Catholic priest ordained in the United States was Father Stephen Theodore Badin, ordained on May 25, 1793, by Bishop John Carroll in Baltimore, MD. He was appointed to the mission of Kentucky and held his first mass there on the first Sunday of Advent, 1793, in the house of Dennis McCarthy in Lexington, KY. The first priest to receive his full theological training in the United States was Demetrius Augustine Gallitzin (Dimitri Augustin Golitzyn), who was ordained a bishop by Bishop Carroll on March 18, 1795, in Baltimore.

6460. Catholic bishop consecrated in the United States was Leonard Neale, who was consecrated bishop of Gortyna, Crete, in the procathedral of St. Peter's in Baltimore, MD, on December 7, 1800.

6461. Cathedral was the Cathedral of the Assumption of the Blessed Virgin Mary, in Baltimore, MD, a primatial see of the Catholic Church. The cornerstone was laid July 7, 1806, and the building was dedicated on May 31, 1821, by Archbishop Ambrose Marechal. It was completed in 1851. In 1936, the Baltimore Cathedral was raised to the rank of a minor basilica by Pope Pius XI.

6462. Catholic community of African-American nuns was the Oblate Sisters of Providence, founded by Jacques Hector Nicholas Joubert de la Muraille on July 2, 1829, in Baltimore, MD. Pope Gregory XVI approved the order on October 2, 1831. The nuns were members of Baltimore's Haitian community. The first convent to admit African-American women as sisters was the Sisters of Loretto, Loretto, KY. The Reverend Charles Nerinck in May 1824 admitted to the novitiate five African-American women who followed the same community exercises as the other sisters but lived apart from them.

6463. Bohemian church was St. John Nepomuk Church, St. Louis, MO, opened on April 20, 1855, by the first pastor, the Reverend Henry Lipowsky, a former lieutenant in the Austrian Army. The first solemn high mass was sung by Father Pierre-Jean De Smet, the famous Jesuit missionary among the Native Americans, on May 16, 1855, the patronal feast day.

6464. Catholic parish church for African-Americans was St. Francis Xavier's Church, Baltimore, MD, purchased on October 10, 1863, and dedicated on February 21, 1864.

6465. Catholic priest from the United States to be made a cardinal was John McCloskey, who was made a cardinal under the title of Santa Maria supra Minervam by Pope Pius IX. The investiture was made in the cathedral on Mott Street, New York City, on April 27, 1875.

6466. Catholic hillside shrine similar to those in European Catholic countries was "The Way of the Cross," built in New Ulm, MN, in 1884. Connected with the shrine were the Loretto Hospital and the St. Alexander Home for the Aged.

6467. Catholic priest who was African-American and assigned to work in the United States was the Reverend Augustus Tolton. He was ordained at the College of Propaganda, Rome, Italy, on April 24, 1886, and opened a mission in Quincy, IL, in the diocese of Springfield, IL. The first African-American priest to be ordained in the United States was Charles Randolph Uncles, who was ordained in the Baltimore Cathedral, Baltimore, MD, on December 19, 1891, by Cardinal Gibbons.

6468. Lithuanian church was St. Casimir's Lithuanian Church, Plymouth, PA, organized on October 27, 1889. The first pastor was the Reverend Alexander Burba.

RELIGION—CATHOLIC—*continued*

6469. Catholic mass for night workers was held on May 5, 1901, at the Church of St. Andrew, New York City. Father Luke J. Evers obtained special permission from the Pope to institute this service, as church law did not permit mass before sunrise.

6470. Catholic nuns in a cloistered community were the Magdalen Sisters at the Convent of the Good Shepherd, Baltimore, MD, founded on April 24, 1922.

6471. Catholic church to become a basilica was the Sanctuary of Our Lady of Victory, Lackawanna, in the diocese of Buffalo, NY. It was dedicated and consecrated on May 25, 1926, as Our Lady of Victory Shrine, and on July 28, by apostolic decree of Pope Pius XI, it was dignified with the title of "Basilica of Our Blessed Lady of Victory."

6472. Catholic saints who were active in North America were canonized in a three-day celebration commencing on June 30, 1930. Each of those canonized was credited with having performed two miracles and having met a heroic death. Among them were two laymen, René Goupil and John Lalande, and six Jesuit priests: Isaac Jogues, John De Brébeuf, Noel Chabanel, Anthony Daniel, Gabriel Lalemant, and Charles Garnier. The Pontifical Mass was celebrated at the Vatican by Archbishop Forbes of Ottawa, Canada.

6473. Catholic mass in an airship over the ocean conducted by an American priest was conducted in the zeppelin *Hindenburg* on August 6, 1936, by Father James Renshaw Cox of St. Patrick's Church, Pittsburgh, PA.

6474. Catholic beatification of a Native American took place on May 9, 1939, when the Cardinals of the Congregation of Rites in Rome, Italy, recommended the beatification of Kateri Tekakwitha, the "lily of the Mohawks." Their decision was sanctioned by Pope Pius XII on May 19, 1939. Kateri Tekakwitha was born in 1656 at Ossernenon, near the future Auriesville, NY.

6475. Catholic saint who was an American citizen was Frances Xavier Cabrini, known as Mother Cabrini, founder of the Institute of the Missionary Sisters of the Sacred Heart. Born Maria Francesca Cabrini on July 15, 1850, in Italy, she came to the United States in 1889 and became a citizen in 1909. She was responsible for establishing hospitals, schools, and orphanages throughout the United States and South America. She died on December 22,

1917. She was declared venerable in November 1937, was beatified on November 13, 1938 (the first beatification of an American citizen), and was canonized a saint on July 7, 1946, by Pope Pius XII in Rome.

6476. Catholic midnight mass to be televised was transmitted on December 24, 1948, from St. Patrick's Cathedral, New York City, by stations WNBT-TV, WJZ-TV, and WCBS-TV.

6477. Catholic cardinal whose see was west of the Rockies was James Francis Cardinal McIntyre, Archbishop of Los Angeles, CA, who was elevated to the Sacred College of Cardinals on January 12, 1953, by Pope Pius XII.

6478. Catholic prelate named to the Roman Curia who was American-born was Samuel Alphonsus Cardinal Stritch, archbishop of Chicago, IL, nominated on March 1, 1958, by Pope Pius XII to head one of the 12 departments of the Church's central administration, the Sacred Congregation for the Propagation of the Faith. He arrived in Rome on April 25, 1958, and on April 26 was admitted to the Sanatrix Clinic, where he died on May 27 before he could take up his post.

6479. Catholic mass in English was celebrated on August 24, 1964, in Kiel Auditorium, St. Louis, MO, by the Reverend Frederick Richard McManus of the Catholic University of America. The Gloria, most of the responses, the Creed, and the Agnus Dei (Lamb of God) prayer were in English. Joseph Elmer Cardinal Ritter, the archbishop of St. Louis, authorized the celebration to mark the 25th annual Liturgical Week, attended by about 11,000 bishops, priests, nuns, and laymen.

6480. Catholic bishop who was an American-born African-American was the Very Reverend Bishop Harold Robert Perry of Lake Charles, LA, named auxiliary bishop of the Archdiocese of New Orleans on October 2, 1965, by Pope Paul VI. He was consecrated in the Basilica of St. Louis, New Orleans, LA, on January 6, 1966, and was the pastor of the New Orleans Parish of St. Theresa of the Child of Jesus, Society of the Divine Word. The first bishop of African-American descent was James Augustine Healy, the son of a mulatto slave and an Irish immigrant, who was consecrated on June 21, 1875, as bishop of Portland, ME. The first African-American archbishop was Eugene Antonio Marino, appointed archbishop of Atlanta, GA, on March 15, 1988, by Pope John Paul II.

6481. Catholic saint who was born in America was Elizabeth Ann Bayley Seton, who was born into an Episcopalian family in New York City on August 28, 1774. The mother of five children, she founded the Society for the Relief of Poor Widows with Small Children in 1797. She converted to Roman Catholicism in New York City in 1805 and founded an order of nuns, the Sisters of Charity of St. Joseph. She died on January 4, 1821, in Emmitsburg, MD, was beatified on March 17, 1963, at the Vatican, Rome, by Pope John XXIII, and was canonized on September 14, 1975.

6482. Catholic saint who was a male American citizen was John Nepomucene Neumann, born in Bohemia on March 28, 1811, who arrived in New York City in January 1836 and was ordained in St. Patrick's Cathedral, Mott Street, New York City. In 1848 he became an American citizen. From 1852 until his death in 1860 he served as the fourth bishop of Philadelphia. He was responsible for organizing the first diocesan school system in America and for building schools, churches, and asylums. He was declared venerable in 1896. In 1963 he became the first male American citizen to be beatified, and on June 19, 1977, he was canonized in Rome by Pope Paul VI.

RELIGION—JEWISH

6483. Jewish congregation was Congregation Shearith Israel ("Remnant of Israel"), established in 1655 in New Amsterdam (later New York City) by Sephardic Jews seeking refuge from persecution in Portuguese Brazil. It was formed despite a law prohibiting all religious assemblies except those of the Dutch Reformed Church. The first Ashkenazic congregation was Congregation Rodeph Shalom ("Seeker of Peace") of Philadelphia, PA, founded on October 10, 1802. Sephardic Jews, whose name derives from *Sfard*, the Hebrew word for Spain, are those whose families originated in Spain and Portugal. Ashkenazic Jews, from *Ashkenaz*, the Hebrew word for Germany, are those whose families originated in Central and Eastern Europe.

6484. Jewish synagogue was a one-room house in New York City, on Beaver Street, that was rented by Congregation Shearith Israel in 1682 after the repeal of a law forbidding public worship by anyone except members of the Dutch Reformed Church. The first permanent Jewish house of worship in America was a small stone building built by the congregation on Mill Street (now South William Street) and

completed on April 8, 1730. Saul Pardo, the first prayer leader, received a salary of £50, six cords of wood, and a supply of unleavened bread for Passover. The congregation's present synagogue is located at Central Park West and 70th Street.

6485. Jewish religious school for children was Yeshivat Minhat Areb, founded in 1728 by New York City's Congregation Shearith Israel, the first Jewish congregation in North America. Its successor, the Shearith Israel Congregation School, opened in 1755 with a curriculum combining religious and secular studies (arithmetic, Spanish, and English). The first Jewish Sunday school, held for 50 pupils, was the Hebrew Sunday School of Philadelphia, PA, organized on March 4, 1838, by Rebecca Gratz for "the religious instruction and general improvement of children of the Jewish faith." (The much-admired and famously beautiful Gratz was the model for the character Rebecca in Sir Walter Scott's novel *Ivanhoe*.) Philadelphia's Gratz College was the first to offer training for teachers in Jewish schools, beginning in 1897.

6486. Jewish congregation in the Reform movement was the Reform Society of Israelites, organized on November 21, 1824, by dissident members of Congregation Beth Elohim of Charleston, SC, an Orthodox synagogue that had been founded by Sephardic Jews in 1750. The group was formed after the trustees of the synagogue refused a request to modernize the prayer service. Its leader was Isaac Harby, a teacher and journalist. The society disbanded in 1833, but many of its members rejoined the synagogue after the arrival of Rabbi Gustav Poznanski, who approved radical alterations in the service.

6487. Zionist organization (national) was the United American Zionists, formed on October 22, 1897, in New York City by 10 local societies. The first convention was held on July 4, 1898, in New York City. Local Zionist societies, known as Chovevei Tzion or Chibat Tzion ("Lovers of Zion"), had been formed as early as 1882 to advocate the return of the Jewish people to their homeland.

6488. Orthodox rabbi born in America to be ordained was Sol B. Friedman, who received rabbinical ordination in New York City on March 23, 1919, along with four other graduates of the Rabbi Isaac Elchanan Theological Seminary.

RELIGION—JEWISH—*continued*

6489. Passover seder to be shown on television took place on April 25, 1940, in New York City, in the studio of the National Broadcasting Company, which had been set up as a dining room. Rabbi Saul Bezalel Applebaum of Central Synagogue, New York City, led seven participants in the seder; Lazar Weiner directed the music and the Central Synagogue choir. The program was produced with the cooperation of the United Jewish Layman's Committee.

6490. Rabbi in the Reform movement who was a woman was Paula Ackerman of Meridian, MS, who was appointed on January 26, 1951, to serve in the place of her late husband as rabbi of Temple Beth Israel. The first woman to receive ordination as a Reform rabbi was Sally Jane Priesand, who was ordained on June 3, 1972, in the Isaac M. Wise Temple, Cincinnati, OH. The Conservative movement ordained its first female rabbi, Amy Eilberg, on May 12, 1985, at the Jewish Theological Seminary in New York City. The first woman to serve as a cantor in a Reform temple was Betty Robbins of Massapequa, NY, whose sang on September 15, 1955, the eve of Rosh Hashanah, the Jewish New Year, at Temple Avodah, Oceanside, NY.

6491. Jewish mobile synagogue was the Circuit Riding Rabbi Bus, dedicated on March 27, 1955, at the Amity Country Club, Charlotte, NC. It was the project of the North Carolina Association of Jewish Men. The first rabbi was Harold A. Friedman. The bus was equipped with desks, blackboards, maps, a projection machine, a record player, and a library.

RELIGION—MORMON CHURCH

6492. Mormon Church meeting took place on April 6, 1830, in Fayette, NY, in the home of Peter Whitmer. Joseph Smith, the founder of the church, declared that an angel of God had shown him gold plates on which was engraved a divine scripture, *The Book of Mormon,* which he had translated. The official title of the Mormon Church is the Church of Jesus Christ of Latter-day Saints.

6493. Mormon temple was built in Kirtland, OH, by Joseph Smith, the founder of the Church of Jesus Christ of Latter-Day Saints (or Mormon Church), who had moved to Ohio from New York with about 50 families. The temple's cornerstone was laid on July 23, 1833, and it was dedicated on March 27, 1836. It measured 59 by 79 feet and was 50 feet high. It had a tower 110 feet high.

6494. Mormon man ordained to the priesthood who was African-American was Joseph Freeman, Jr., who was ordained on June 11, 1978, in Salt Lake City, UT. He was a lay minister, a regular member of his congregation, not a pastor.

RELIGION—ORTHODOX

6495. Russian Orthodox mission was founded in 1794 at Kodiak Island in southeastern Alaska, the capital of Russian America. In 1808 the capital was moved to Novoarkhangelsk (Sitka), where the Cathedral of St. Michael was built in 1848. Novoarkhangelsk was the seat of the Bishop of Kamchatka, Alaska, and the Kurile and Aleutian Islands, an expanse of more than 1 million square miles.

6496. Greek Orthodox church was the Holy Trinity Church, 1222 North Dorgenois Street, New Orleans, LA, founded in 1867. The first pastor was Paisios Ferentinos.

6497. Serbian Orthodox cathedral was the Cathedral of St. Sava, New York City, which was elevated on June 11, 1944, from a procathedral. On the same day, Bishop Dionisije Milivojevich conferred the Gold Cross and the title Stravrophor on Rector Doushan Jefta Shoukletovich and elevated him to dean. The cathedral was the diocesan headquarters of the Serbian Orthodox Church in Canada and the United States.

6498. Russian Orthodox saint canonized in the United States was the Reverend John Sergiev, known as Father John of Cronstadt, who was canonized on November 1, 1964, in a ceremony in the Cathedral of Our Lady of the Sign, New York City. The canonization ceremony was presided over by Metropolitan Philaret, primate of the Russian Orthodox Church Outside of Russia. Father John died in 1909 at the age of 80.

6499. Armenian Orthodox cathedral was the Armenian Cathedral of St. Vartan, New York City, consecrated on April 28, 1968, by His Holiness Vasken I, Supreme Patriarch and Catholicos of All Armenians. The Most Reverend Torkom Manoogian was the first upon whom the Catholicos personally bestowed the rank of archbishop in the United States.

6500. Coptic Orthodox Church bishop was Bishop Serapion, appointed by the Patriarch of the Coptic Orthodox Church in Egypt to become the first Coptic Orthodox bishop in North America. On December 30, 1995, he was welcomed by the congregation of the Coptic Orthodox Church in Los Angeles, CA.

RELIGION—PROTESTANT

6501. Christian religious service in English on the Pacific Coast was the Holy Communion service conducted on June 24, 1579, at San Francisco Bay, CA, by the Reverend Francis Fletcher, who read from the *Book of Common Prayer* of the Church of England. Fletcher was chaplain on Sir Francis Drake's ship, the *Golden Hind,* during its voyage of circumnavigation from 1577 to 1580. Drake named the place Nova Albion, Latin for New England. A 57-foot marble cross commemorates the event in Golden Gate Park, San Francisco, CA.

6502. Native American to become a Protestant was Manteo, chief of the Hatteras, who was baptized into the Christian faith as a member of the Church of England on August 13, 1587. He was invested by Sir Walter Raleigh with the power of Lord of Roanoke and of Dasamonguepeuk. There were earlier baptisms of Native Americans by Roman Catholic priests in Florida.

6503. Thanksgiving worship service was held on August 9, 1607, at Phippsburg, ME, by colonists on *The Gift of God* and the *Mary and John,* who landed at "St. Georges Illand" under the leadership of George Popham. Services were held by the Reverend Richard Seymour, "gyvinge God thanks for our happy metinge & saffe aryval into the country."

6504. Sabbath law enacted by a colony was enacted by the first legislative body assembled in America, the Virginia House of Burgesses, at its first session in 1619. The law provided that "all persons whatsoever upon the Sabbath days shall frequent divine service and sermons, both forenoon and afternoon." The Anglican Church was made the sole legal religion, and the creed of the church was the rule of the colony.

6505. Congregational church was founded at Plymouth Colony (the future Plymouth, MA) in 1620 by 102 English Separatists under the leadership of William Brewster, William Bradford, and Edward Winslow, upon their arrival at Plymouth. Ralph Smith was the first pastor. The Separatists, who had withdrawn from the established Church of England for theological reasons, made up the greater part of the group of settlers known as the Pilgrims.

6506. Dutch Reformed church was established by Jonas Michaëlius in 1628 in New Amsterdam (now New York City). It was a Calvinist Presbyterian group under the authority of the Church of Holland.

6507. Religious leader in the American colonies who was a woman was Anne Hutchinson, born Anne Marbury in England. She and her family arrived in the Massachusetts Bay Colony on September 18, 1634. She organized groups of women who met at her house and led them in the discussion of secular and theological questions. She taught that each person could attain understanding in matters of faith and therefore owed no obedience to church law. Her influence became so great that in November 1637 she was brought to trial in Cambridge for undermining the authority of the colony's Puritan ministers. Banished from the colony, she was given a safe haven in Roger Williams's settlement (the future Providence, RI) along with 70 followers. In 1642 she moved to the wilderness near what is now Pelham Bay, NY, where she and her family were killed by Native Americans.

6508. Synod held in America met at Mr. Shepard's church, Cambridge (then Newtowne), MA, on August 30, 1637, to condemn the preachings of Anne Hutchinson, the first female religious leader in the American colonies. Eighty-two errors in her teachings were enumerated and condemned. The synod adjourned on September 22, 1637. Hutchinson was brought to trial on the strength of this condemnation and was exiled from the Massachusetts Bay Colony.

6509. Sabbath laws published by a colony were first published in New Haven, CT, in 1638. They established Sunday as the day of rest and restricted various activities on that day in accordance with biblical teachings. The commonly used term "blue laws" derives from the blue paper with which the printed laws were bound.

6510. Ecumenical synod was held at Cambridge, MA, in 1646, and protracted its sessions by adjournments until 1648, when the Cambridge Platform was adopted. It was a platform of church discipline recommended to the General Court and to the churches. The synod was attended by 25 churchmen who discussed 80 subjects in an effort to reconcile Presbyterianism and Congregationalism.

6511. Religious toleration law enacted by a colony was the Tolerance Act, enacted by Maryland in April 1649. It ordered toleration for all who professed faith in Jesus Christ and subscribed to the orthodox interpretation of the Trinity, but prescribed the death penalty for Arian heretics, atheists, and Jews. It stated that "whatsoever person or persons within this province and the islands thereunto belonging shall

RELIGION—PROTESTANT—*continued*

from henceforth blaspheme God or deny our Saviour Jesus Christ to be the Son of God, or shall deny the Holy Trinity, the Father, Son and Holy Ghost, or the Godhead of any of these said persons of the Trinity, or the unity of the Godhead, shall be punished with death and forfeiture of all his or her lands and goods to the Lord Proprietary." The Arians were Christians who did not believe that Jesus was of the same substance as God.

6512. Church for Native Americans in New England was established in Natick, MA, by John Eliot in 1660. Six other "praying towns" were established before 1674.

6513. Native American preacher of Christianity was Hiacoomes, who was taught to read and write by Thomas Mayhew. He was ordained on August 22, 1670, by John Eliot and John Cotton, and preached to his countrymen in a small church in Martha's Vineyard, MA.

6514. Labadist community was established at Bohemia Manor, MD, in 1683, by followers of the French religious reformer Jean de Labadie, a former Jesuit priest who called for a return to the original forms of Christianity. The first Labadists were P. Vorstman and J. Shilders, who arrived on September 23, 1679, in New Netherlands on the *Charles.*

6515. Christian worship services organized by African-American slaves took place in Massachusetts in 1693, when the Puritan minister Cotton Mather wrote his "Rules for the Society of Negroes" at the request of a group of slaves who wanted to adopt Christian practices and hold their own prayer meetings. The rules stipulated that religious meetings would be held on Sabbath evenings between the hours of seven and nine, at a convenient time for the slaves' masters. Mather wrote a treatise on the subject, *The Negro Christianized,* that was published in 1701. Many slaveowners opposed missionary efforts to the slaves for fear that baptized slaves would someday be freed by law.

6516. Reformed Church meeting took place in Falkner Swamp, Montgomery County, PA, on October 15, 1725, when the new denomination was organized by John Philip Boehm.

6517. Great Awakening of religious revival began in Northampton, MA, in 1734, when pastor Jonathan Edwards began preaching sermons on the transforming action of divine grace on the human spirit. It was brought to a fever pitch by the the preaching tour of English

minister George Whitefield, who arrived in Georgia in 1739. His oratory, as he traveled throughout Britain's American colonies, produced thousands of conversions and helped create an atmosphere of ferment that gave rise to several new religions and denominations.

6518. Protestant Sunday school was opened in Christ Church, Savannah, GA, in 1736 by John Wesley and was under the leadership of Charles Delamotte. Before the Sunday evening services, Wesley instructed between 30 and 40 children and heard them recite their catechism. Prior to this, religious instruction had been given to children individually and in small unorganized groups.

6519. Protestant church west of the Alleghenies was built in 1772 at Schoenbrunn, OH, by Moravian missionaries. The first communion service was held on June 9, 1772, although the church was not finished until September 19. A larger church was dedicated on October 24, 1773. The same missionaries built the first schoolhouse west of the Alleghenies, completing it on July 29, 1773. The Reverend David Zeisberger was the church's first preacher and the school's first teacher.

6520. Universalist church services were held in 1774. The church was formally organized on January 1, 1779, when the articles of association were signed by 31 men and 30 women led by the Reverend John Murray, who was made the first minister. A church built in Winthrop Sargent's garden, Water Street, Gloucester, MA, was dedicated on December 25, 1780. It contained 30 box pews.

6521. Shaker religious community was founded in Watervliet, NY, in 1776 by Ann Lee of Manchester, England, and eight others who left Liverpool on the *Mariah* and arrived in New York City on August 6, 1774. The group's full name was "The United Society of Believers in Christ's Second Appearing." Its followers believed in pacifist principles and a celibate communal life. The rules of the Society stated that "the head of the Shaker Order is Christ, Represented in a Dual Order of Leaders, Ministry, Elders and Trustees." Women and men had different responsibilities but were treated as equals. Shaker communities were founded in New Hampshire, Ohio, and in other locations in New York. They began to decline after the Civil War.

6522. Congregational Church minister who was African-American was the Reverend Lemuel Haynes, who was ordained in 1785. Until 1833, he served as pastor to several congregations in New York, Connecticut, and Vermont. Most of the members of these congregations were white.

6523. Unitarian church was King's Chapel, Boston, MA, originally founded in 1686 as the first Church of England (Episcopalian) church organized in Puritan New England. In 1785 the congregation abandoned the Anglican ritual in favor of Unitarian principles and reordained its minister, James Freeman. The first Unitarian church to be identified as such in its name was the Society of Unitarian Christians, organized in Philadelphia on June 12, 1796, under the leadership of Joseph Priestley. An organized movement of Unitarians was founded by William Ellery Channing in 1819. The first woman ordained as a Unitarian minister was Celia C. Burleigh, who was given a parish in Brooklyn, CT, on October 5, 1871.

6524. Swedenborgian or New Church temple was erected at the southwest corner of Exeter and Baltimore streets, Baltimore, MD, in 1799. The brick structure was built with funds supplied by citizens of the community. The first church service was held on Sunday, January 5, 1800. The New Church group in Baltimore was led by Robert Carter, a member of the Virginia Colonial Council, which began meeting in 1792. The first New Church ministers ordained in America were the Reverend Ralph Mather, formerly of England, and the Reverend John Hargrove, a former preacher of the Methodist Episcopal Church who was also the Baltimore City registrar. Hargrove became the first pastor. The first General Convention met in 1817 in Philadelphia, PA, where Hargrove was chosen as the first president.

6525. Camp meeting was held in 1803 by James M'Geary, William McGee (a Presbyterian), and John McGee (a Methodist) in a little log church on the Gaspar River in Logan County, KY.

6526. Evangelical Church conference took place on November 15, 1807, at the house of Samuel Becker in Muhlbach, PA (now Kleinfeltersville). It was attended by church officials, five itinerant ministers, three local preachers, and 20 class leaders and exhorters. Jacob Albright, who had founded the group in 1800, was elected bishop. The first church building was the Evangelical Church, a structure 34 by 38 feet, erected in 1816 in New Berlin, PA. The Reverend John Dreisbach

preached the sermon at the dedication on March 2, 1817. The denomination changed its name to the Evangelical Association at its general conference in October 1816, in Buffalo Valley, PA.

6527. Disciples of Christ meeting was held on August 17, 1809, in Washington, PA, when a group of Presbyterians headed by Thomas Campbell formed themselves into the Christian Association of Washington. On May 4, 1811, a church was established in Brush Run, PA, with Thomas Campbell as elder and Alexander Campbell, his son, as preacher. No attempt at forming a separate and distinct denomination was made until 1823, when Alexander Campbell and several members of the Brush Run Church founded a church in Wellsburg, WV.

6528. Prayers in sign language were offered by the Reverend Thomas Hopkins Gallaudet, a Congregational minister and teacher of the deaf, in 1817 at the American Institution for the Deaf, Hartford, CT. His son, the Reverend Thomas Gallaudet, an Episcopal priest, held the first church service for deaf worshippers on October 3, 1852, in the small chapel of New York University, New York City. He held spoken worship services in the morning, services using American Sign Language in the afternoon. The first church whose purpose was to serve deaf people was St. Ann's Church for Deaf-Mutes, which held its first services on August 7, 1859. The first ordained clergyman who was deaf was the Reverend Henry Winter Syle, who became a deacon in 1876 and a priest in 1883. He founded All Souls' Church for the Deaf, Philadelphia, PA, in 1885.

6529. Adventist church to accept Saturday as the Sabbath was the Adventist church in Washington Center, NH, which began to keep the seventh day as the Sabbath in the spring of 1844 under the influence of its minister, Frederick Wheeler. The first general conference of Seventh-Day Adventists was organized on May 21, 1863.

6530. Minister who was a woman was the Reverend Antoinette Brown Blackwell, who was ordained on September 15, 1853, at the Congregational Church, South Butler, NY.

6531. Salvation Army services took place at Castle Garden, New York City, on March 10, 1880, after Commissioner George Scott Railton and seven women arrived on the *Australia* at the Battery in lower Manhattan. Early services were held at street meetings and between per-

RELIGION—PROTESTANT—*continued*

formances of *Uncle Tom's Cabin* at Harry Hill's Gentleman's Sporting Theatre. The Salvation Army is a missionary group founded by William Booth in London in 1865 under the name of the East London Mission.

6532. Portable church was the Chapel of the Transfiguration, which was consecrated on June 3, 1899, at Conanicut Island, RI. An Episcopal church, it was 27 feet long and 18 feet wide and contained 14 benches, 20 chairs, a platform, and an altar. The interior, including the pews, prayer desk, and altar, was made of oak. The church was built on a wooden chassis with four wheels and was drawn from place to place by horses. The first preacher was the Reverend Charles E. Preston of St. Matthew's Church. The first service was held on April 23, 1899.

6533. Protestant church for lepers was the Community Church, dedicated at Carville, LA, on June 14, 1915. The sermon was "A merry heart doeth good like a medicine." The church was served by visiting ministers from Baton Rouge and New Orleans. There was no settled pastor until the summer of 1922, when the Reverend Henry Thomas Cousins was called.

6534. Trailer church was St. Paul's Wayside Cathedral, which was placed in operation on October 1, 1937, by the Diocese of Southern Ohio Protestant Episcopal Church under the direction of Bishop Henry Wise Hobson. It was designed by Norman R. Sturgis and built by the Aerocar Company, Detroit, MI. The exterior was of sheet metal with a backing of Masonite painted gunmetal gray. The roof was covered with a silver-finish fabric. The church was equipped with a removable altar, an organ, an amplification unit, and a movie projector. It seated about 25 people.

6535. Children's church that was built to scale and intended to be operated by children was the Children's Church, Milton, MA, dedicated on November 14, 1937, by the Reverend Vivian Towse Pomeroy, pastor of the First Parish Unitarian Church, Milton, MA. The miniature church was 18 feet by 32 feet, complete with steeple, belfry, organ, spire, and pews 2 feet 8 inches in height. It cost in excess of $5,000. The first pastor was the Reverend Mrs. Dorothy Pomeroy.

6536. United Church of Christ ordination of a woman in which all the principal roles were filled by women was held on September 17, 1972, at the United Church of Christ, Northfield, CT, when Davida Foy Crabtree was ordained. The sermon was preached by Dr. Nelle Morton, professor emeritus at Drew Theological Seminary; the charge was given by the Reverend Emily Preston, minister of the Community Church in Deerfield Center, NH; the scriptures were read by Dr. Phyllis Trible, associate professor of Old Testament at Andover Newton Theological Seminary; and the ordination prayer was offered by the Reverend Barbara W. McCall, special assistant to the president of the United Church of Christ.

RELIGION—PROTESTANT—ANABAPTIST

6537. Mennonites to arrive in America were 13 German and Dutch families from Krefeld, Germany, led by Francis Daniel Pastorius, who disembarked on October 6, 1683, from the *Concord*. They were induced to come to America through the generosity of William Penn, who offered them 5,000 acres of land in Pennsylvania and freedom from religious persecution. Their settlement, called Germantown, is now a neighborhood in Philadelphia.

6538. Mennonite meetinghouse was built in 1708 on the east side of Germantown Avenue, above Herman Street, Germantown, PA. It was succeeded in 1770 by a stone building. The first minister was William Rittenhouse (Rittinghuysen), who served for two years.

6539. Schwenkfelder to arrive in America was George Schultz, who arrived at Philadelphia, PA, in 1731. He was followed three years later by 180 Schwenkfelders who had been exiled from Silesia. They formally organized a church in 1782. The Schwenkfelders were followers of Kaspar Schwenkfeld von Ossig, a 16th-century nobleman and mystic.

6540. Moravian settlement in America began with the arrival of George Boehnischt in Pennsylvania on September 22, 1734. The following year, a group of Moravians led by Augustus Gottlieb Spangenberg came to Georgia for the purpose of converting Native Americans. Their first church was built in 1735 in Savannah, GA, where General James Edward Oglethorpe had given 600 acres of land for a colony. Bishop David Nitschmann arrived from Germany in 1736 and ordained Anton Sieffert as pastor, the first ordination by a Protestant bishop in America. The group soon relocated to Pennsylvania and built a settlement in Bethlehem, PA, in

1741. Spangenberg became the Moravians' first American bishop in 1744. Moravians are followers of Jan Hus, the 15th-century Bohemian religious reformer, and call themselves the Church of the Brethren, or Unitas Fratrum.

6541. United Brethren in Christ meeting took place on May 18, 1766, in Isaac Long's barn in Lancaster, PA. The church was founded by the Reverend Martin Boehm and the Reverend Philip William Otterbein, who were elected bishops in September 1800.

6542. Hutterites arrived in New York City from Europe in 1874 and went on to found the Bonhomme community in Yankton, SD. They went on to found some 200 additional communities in North and South Dakota, Minnesota, Montana, Washington, and Canada. The Hutterites are a separatist Anabaptist sect who live in farming communes, where they hold all property in common. They follow the teachings of Jakob Hutter, who was martyred in 1536.

RELIGION—PROTESTANT—BAPTIST

6543. Baptist church in the American colonies was probably established in 1639 in Providence, RI, by Roger Williams, "the Apostle of Religious Liberty," who had already been banned from the Massachusetts Bay Colony for his dissident religious and political views. The first church to identify itself by name as Baptist was the Baptist Church of Newport, RI, founded by Dr. John Clarke, its first pastor, in 1644, although the congregation may have originated in 1638.

6544. Seventh Day Baptist Church was organized at Newport, RI, in 1671 by Stephen Mumford, an English Sabbatarian Baptist. The first deacon was William Weeden.

6545. Brethren (also known as Dunkards, Dunkers, Tunkers, and German Baptists) arrived in America in 1719 and settled in the area of Germantown, PA. They held their first immersion on December 25, 1723, at Wissahickon Creek in Germantown. The first chosen elder was Peter Becker. The first congregation was the Coventry Congregation, which met on September 7, 1724. The group originated in Schwarzenau, Germany, in 1708. The official name Church of the Brethren was adopted in 1908.

6546. Baptist churches for African-Americans were part of the Separatist (or New Light) Baptist movement, which emphasized independent congregations. The earliest congregation for African-Americans in the South was established in 1756 on a plantation at Lunenburg, VA. The first to have a major influence was the plantation congregation founded in 1773 at Silver Bluff, SC, from which came a number of "exhorters," or African-American preachers, who went on to found Baptist churches in other locations, including Jamaica and the African nation of Sierre Leone.

RELIGION—PROTESTANT—EPISCOPAL

6547. Episcopal church service in an English colony took place at Cape Henry, near Jamestown, VA, on May 9, 1607, when the Reverend Robert Hunt celebrated the Eucharist. The event was reported as follows: "We did hang an awning (which is an old saile) to three or four trees, to shadow us from the sunne, our walles were railes of wood, our seats unhewed trees till we cut plankes; our Pulpit a bar of wood nailed to two neighboring trees." The founding of the Episcopal Church in America dates from April 29, 1607, when Captain Gabriel Archer, Christopher Newport, George Percy, Bartholomew Gosnold, Edward Maria Wingfield, and 25 other English colonists set up a cross at Cape Henry. The first parish was started at Jamestown on June 21. The Episcopal Church originated in the Church of England, also known as the Anglican Church.

6548. Episcopal church organized in New England was King's Chapel, at the corner of Tremont and School Streets, Boston, MA, built in 1686.

6549. Episcopal bishop was Samuel Seabury, consecrated on November 14, 1784, at Aberdeen, Scotland, by the Scottish bishops Robert Kilgour, Arthur Petrie, and John Skinner. He was rector of St. James Church, New London, CT, and bishop of Rhode Island and Connecticut from that date until his death on February 25, 1796. The first to be consecrated in the United States was the Reverend Thomas John Claggett, founder of the Trinity Episcopal Church, Upper Marlboro, MD. He was consecrated on September 17, 1792, at Trinity Church, New York City, by Bishops Seabury, White, Provoost, and Madison.

6550. Episcopal cathedral was the Cathedral of Our Merciful Saviour, Faribault, MN, built by the Right Reverend Henry Benjamin Whipple, First Bishop of Minnesota, as his own church. The cathedral was begun in 1862 and completed in 1869 at a cost of $100,000. A tower was added in 1902.

RELIGION— PROTESTANT— EPISCO-PAL—continued

6551. Episcopal bishop who was African-American was the Reverend Samuel David Ferguson, who was elected to the House of Bishops of the Protestant Episcopal Church in 1884. He was consecrated on June 24, 1885, at Grace Church, New York City, as the successor of the Missionary Bishop of Liberia.

6552. Episcopal bishop deposed for heresy in the United States was William Montgomery Brown, Protestant Episcopal Bishop of Arkansas and the author of *Communism and Christianity*, who was deposed for heresy at New Orleans, LA, on October 12, 1925. The deposition was imposed by the Right Reverend Ethelbert Talbot, presiding officer of the House of Bishops of the Protestant Episcopal Church. The Secretary of the House, Dr. Charles Laban Pardee, drew a line through Brown's name on the record. He was not excommunicated.

6553. Episcopal priest who was a woman was Jacqueline Means, who received her ordination on January 1, 1977, three years after an irregular ordination of 11 women in Philadelphia, PA, that was not recognized by the church's House of Bishops. The first female Episcopal bishop was Barbara C. Harris, who was elected suffragan bishop of the Diocese of Massachusetts on September 24, 1988.

RELIGION—PROTESTANT—LUTHERAN

6554. Lutheran pastor was Reorus Torkillus from Mölndal, Sweden, who came over on the *Kalmar Nyckel* with Governor Peter Hollander Ridder, landing on April 17, 1640, at Fort Christina, DE. He died of the plague in 1643. The first Lutheran pastor ordained in America was Justus Falckner, ordained in Gloria Dei Church at Wicaco, Philadelphia, PA, on November 24, 1703, with Andrew Rudman, Erick Biörck, and Andrew Sandel as officiating clergymen.

6555. Lutheran church was dedicated by the Reverend Johannes Campanius at Christina (Tinicum Island), near the present site of Essington, PA, on September 4, 1645. Before the church was built, Campanius had conducted services in a small blockhouse at Fort Göteborg.

6556. Lutheran services in English were held in 1694 in Germantown and Philadelphia, PA, by Heinrich Bernhard Koester.

RELIGION—PROTESTANT—METHODIST

6557. Methodist preacher was Philip Embury, who arrived on August 11, 1760, in New York City on the *Perry,* which carried 70 passengers, half of whom were Methodists. With the assistance of Barbara Heck, he organized the first Methodist Society in America in 1776.

6558. Methodist meetinghouse was the Wesley Chapel, 42 John Street, New York City, also known as the John Street Church, built by a group of Irish Methodists and dedicated by Philip Embury, the first minister, on October 30, 1768. It was a small frame house, 42 by 60 feet and one and a half stories high, built in antique Dutch style. It accommodated 700 people.

6559. Methodist minister who was African-American was Richard Allen, who was accepted as a minister by Bishop Francis Asbury in 1784 at the first general conference of American Methodists, held in Baltimore, MD. He was ordained a deacon in 1799 and eventually became an elder. In 1816 he became the founder and first bishop of the African Methodist Episcopal Church. An earlier African-American preacher, Harry Hosier, traveled with Francis Asbury, the bishop who carried Methodism throughout the English colonies in the late 18th century. The first African-American minister of an all-white Methodist congregation was the Reverend Simon Peter Montgomery of Pineville, SC, who assumed the pulpit of the Old Mystic Methodist Church, Old Mystic, CT, on October 2, 1955.

6560. Methodist bishop was Francis Asbury, who was appointed in 1784 by Thomas Coke, to whom the title really belonged. They were known as the joint bishops of the Church in North America. Bishop Asbury was elected by the first General Conference, called the Christmas Conference, which met on December 24, 1784, in the Light Street Church, Baltimore, MD.

6561. Methodist churches for African-Americans were founded in Baltimore, MD, after the formation of the Colored Methodist Society in 1787. The congregants were former members of the city's Methodist meeting houses who objected to segregated seating and insulting treatment. The first Methodist church in the North to be organized by African-Americans, and for the same reasons, was the Mother Bethel Church, founded in August 1794 by Richard Allen, a former slave, at Sixth and Lombard streets, Philadelphia, PA.

6562. Methodist bishop who was a woman was the Reverend Marjorie Swank Matthews of Traverse City, MI, elected bishop of the United Methodist Church on July 17, 1980, at Dayton, OH. She was consecrated on July 18, 1980, at Selinsgrove, PA. The first Methodist bishop who was an African-American woman was Leontine T.C. Kelly, elected by the United Methodist Church in 1984. She served a San Francisco–area diocese of nearly 400 churches and 100,000 members.

RELIGION—PROTESTANT—METHODIST EPISCOPAL

6563. African Methodist Episcopal church convention took place on April 9–11, 1816, in Philadelphia, PA, when 16 delegates from five independent churches met to form an African-American denomination based on the principles of Methodism. The earliest African-American Methodist organization, the African Union Methodist Church, was founded in 1813 by the Reverend Peter Spencer in Wilmington, DE.

6564. African Methodist Episcopal bishop was Richard Allen, who was elected on April 11, 1816, at the church's founding convention in Philadelphia, PA. Allen had been born into slavery in 1760, when his family was owned by the chief justice of Pennsylvania, and had purchased his freedom in 1786 after converting his current owner to Methodism. He became a licensed exhorter, or traveling preacher, and was accepted as a minister in 1784. Ten years later, he established an independent congregation of African-Americans, which led to the founding in 1816 of the African Methodist Episcopal denomination.

6565. African Methodist Episcopal preacher who was a woman was Jarena Lee of Bethel Church, Philadelphia, PA. In 1809, having felt a call to preach, she asked permission from Bishop Richard Allen, who responded that he had no authority to allow it. Eight years later, in 1817, she was moved to stand up in church and speak. Allen then gave her an informal license to travel as a missionary, preaching to camp meetings and churches.

6566. Scandinavian Methodist Episcopal church was organized in Cambridge, WI, in April 1851 by the Reverend Christian B. Willerup with an initial membership of 52. The denomination was incorporated on May 3, 1851, and a stone building costing $4,000 was dedicated in the summer of 1852. This church is the oldest Methodist Episcopal church built by Scandinavians in this or any other country.

RELIGION—PROTESTANT—MISSIONARIES

6567. Missionary society established for the English colonies was the New England Protestant Missionary Society, chartered in July 1649 by Parliament to propagate the gospel. Missionary work among the Native Americans had been carried on earlier by John Eliot, John Cotton, Henry Dunster, and others.

6568. Missionary society organized in the English colonies was the Society for the Propagation of Christian Knowledge Among the Indians of North America, which was founded in 1762 in the Massachusetts Bay Colony. The Archbishop of Canterbury persuaded King George III to cancel the charter, fearing it might become a channel of influence for churches that did not adhere to Church of England teachings.

6569. Missionary to the Native Americans who was African-American was John Marrant of New York, ordained on May 15, 1785, as a Methodist minister in London. Among his converts were the chief of the Cherokees and his daughter.

6570. Religious tract society was the Massachusetts Society for Promoting Christian Knowledge, instituted in Boston, MA, on September 1, 1803, at the suggestion of Samuel Phillips and Professor D. Tappan.

6571. Bible society was the Bible Society of Philadelphia, organized on December 12, 1808, at Philadelphia, PA. The name was changed to the Pennsylvania Bible Society in 1840. The Reverend William White was the first president and B.B. Hopkins the first secretary. The initiation fee was $5 and the dues $2 a year. Life membership was $50.

6572. Foreign missionary society was the American Board of Commissioners for Foreign Missions, organized on June 29, 1810, by the General Association of Massachusetts at its annual meeting in Bradford, MA. The board received its charter in 1812 from Massachusetts.

6573. Bible society (national) was the American Bible Society, formed by delegates from 35 Bible societies for the purpose of increasing the circulation of the Holy Scriptures. The delegates met on May 8, 1816, in New York City, and organized the society on May 11, 1816. The first president was Elias Boudinot, who served from 1816 to 1821. In the first year, 6,140 Bibles were distributed.

RELIGION—PROTESTANT—MISSIONARIES—*continued*

6574. Methodist missionary was Ebenezer Brown, sent out by the Methodist Missionary Society. In 1819 he was assigned a residence in New Orleans, LA, to preach to the French people of Louisiana.

6575. Mariners' church was built on June 4, 1820, by the New York Port Society, as a nonsectarian, interdenominational church. The society was organized in May 1818 and was chartered on April 13, 1819, as the Society for Promoting the Gospel Among Seamen in the Port of New York. The first pastor was the Reverend Ward Stafford, who preached from 1818 to 1821.

6576. Religious tract society (national) was the American Tract Society, organized on May 11, 1825, in New York City. It was formed from a combination of about 50 large and small tract societies. The society was organized to minister to all classes and conditions of people, in many languages, through the medium of the printed page. The first president was Sampson Vryling Stoddard and the first secretary the Reverend William Allen Hallock.

6577. Floating church was the Floating Church of Our Saviour, constructed in 1843 and moored in the East River at the foot of Pike Street, New York City. The church was organized by the Young Men's Church Missionary Society, an auxiliary of the City Mission Society. The society dissolved in 1844 and deeded the church to the Protestant Episcopal Church Missionary Society for Seamen in the City and Port of New York, an organization that emanated from the original group.

6578. Foreign missionary society organized by women to send unmarried missionaries to Asia was the Woman's Union Missionary Society of America for Heathen Lands, organized in November 1860 in Boston, MA, by Mrs. Ellen H.B. Mason and nine other women. In May 1861, a similar society was formed in Philadelphia, PA, which united with the Boston group to form the Woman's Union Missionary Society for Heathen Lands. The first president was Mrs. Sarah B. Doremus. The first missionary was Sarah H. Marston, who sailed in November 1861 for Tounghoo, Burma.

6579. Bibles in hotel rooms were placed in the Superior Hotel, Iron Mountain (now Superior), MT, in October 1908, by the Gideons, the Christian Commercial Traveling Men's Association. The organization was founded in 1899 at Boscobel, WI. The first president was Samuel Eugene Hill. The work was extended to include distribution to hotels, hospitals, penal institutions, and public schools.

RELIGION—PROTESTANT—PRESBYTERIAN

6580. Presbyterian church was established in 1611 in Virginia. The Reverend Alexander Whitaker was installed as pastor of the church, which was governed by him and a few of the most religious men of the colony.

6581. Presbyterian presbytery met in Philadelphia, PA, in 1705 and was composed of 7 ministers—Francis Makemie, John Hampton, George McNish, Samuel Davis, Nathaniel Taylor, John Wilson, and Jedidiah Andrews—and 34 others. The first known ordination, which took place in 1706, was that of John Boyd, who settled in Freehold, NJ.

6582. Communion cups for individuals were introduced in May 1894 by the Central Presbyterian Church, Rochester, NY. One of the elders, Dr. Charles Forbes, urged the adoption of individual cups to replace the traditional single chalice that was shared by the worshippers.

6583. Presbyterian elder who was a woman was Sarah E. Dickson of the Wauwatosa Presbyterian Church of Milwaukee, WI, who was elected on June 2, 1930, and served until January 1, 1934. Her election was permitted by the church's General Assembly in its meeting at Cincinnati, OH, on May 31, 1930.

6584. Presbyterian minister who was a woman was the Reverend Margaret Ellen Towner, ordained on October 24, 1956, in her home church in Syracuse, NY. She was appointed minister of Christian education of the First Presbytery Church, Allentown, PA. She had received a Bachelor of Divinity degree from Union Theological Seminary, New York City, in 1954.

RELIGION—PROTESTANT—SOCIETY OF FRIENDS

6585. Quakers to arrive in America were two Englishwomen, Ann Austin and Mary Fisher, who landed at Boston, MA, on July 11, 1656. They had come from Barbados, where the Quakers had established a center for missionary work. After five weeks' imprisonment, they were deported to Barbados. The Quakers were followers of George Fox, who preached reliance on the "inner light" over the authority of the church.

6586. Ban on Quakers enacted by a colony was passed by the General Court of the Massachusetts Bay Colony on October 14, 1656, at the urging of Governor John Endecott. The law provided for a fine of £100 for any ship captain who delivered Quakers "or any other blasphemous heretics" to the colony. Possessing Quaker books and coming to the defense of Quakers was also outlawed and punished with fines, whipping, and jailing. Subsequent anti-Quaker laws included the penalties of having the ears cut off and the tongue bored through with a hot iron.

6587. Quakers executed for their religious beliefs were William Robinson and Marmaduke Stevenson, English Quakers who had come to America in 1656. They were hanged from an elm tree on Boston Common, Boston, MA, on October 27, 1659. They were condemned by the Massachusetts General Court under a law passed on October 19, 1658, that banished Quakers from the colony under pain of death. Also condemned, but reprieved at the last moment, was Mary Dyer, who returned to Boston the following year and was hanged on June 1, 1660.

6588. Quaker annual meeting was held in Scituate, MA, in 1660. The first monthly meeting is believed to have been held in Sandwich, MA, on June 25, 1672. It is possible that earlier meetings were held, but no records of them have been preserved.

RELIGION—RADIO AND TELEVISION

6589. Religious service broadcast on radio took place on January 2, 1921, when the Calvary Episcopal Church of Pittsburgh, PA, broadcast its services through station KDKA. The preacher was the Reverend Edwin Jan Van Etten.

6590. Radio church was established on November 27, 1921, when services of the Radio Church of America were broadcast by Walter J. Garvey from his home at 2000 University Avenue, the Bronx, New York City. Hospitals, military installations, and radio operators were alerted to the program. The sermon was preached by Richard Jay Ward, assisted by Dr. M.H. Leventhal. Solos were sung by Clara Brookhurst and Adele Lauriat Barrow.

6591. Sermon preached from an airplane by radio was delivered on Sunday, April 16, 1922, by Belvin W. Maynard, the "Flying Parson," an ordained Baptist minister, who broadcast a sermon from his Fokker airplane by radio. Listeners were asked to donate to the Veterans Mountain Camp, Tupper Lake, NY.

6592. Religious services to be shown on television were produced on March 24, 1940, by station W2XBS of the National Broadcasting Company, New York City. At 11:30 A.M., the station aired a Protestant Easter service led by the Reverend Dr. Samuel McCrea Cavert of the Federal Council of the Churches of Christ in America, with music provided by the Westminster Choir, directed by Dr. John Finley Williamson. At 12:30, the station aired a Roman Catholic Easter service led by the Right Reverend Monsignor Fulton John Sheen of the Catholic University of America, Washington, DC, with music provided by the Paulist Choristers under the direction of Father William Joseph Finn, C.S.P., in cooperation with the National Council of Catholic Men. Other Easter services were televised from the Hollywood Bowl, Hollywood, CA, and from Central Park, New York City.

6593. Religious service to be televised from a church was the candlelight service on December 24, 1946, at Grace Episcopal Church, Broadway at 10th Street, New York City, which was telecast at 8:30 P.M. by WABD on the New York–Philadelphia–Washington network. The service was led by the Reverend Louis W. Pitt. The choir of 50 men and boys was led by the organist, Ernest Mitchell.

6594. Church service in sign language to be televised was conducted by the Reverend Floyd F. Possehl, who read the Scriptures and preached a sermon in sign language from St. Matthew's Lutheran Church for the Deaf, Jamaica, Queens, New York City, on December 5, 1948, over WPIX-TV, New York City.

RELIGION—RADIO AND TELEVISION—
continued

6595. Jewish prayer services to be televised in their entirety were shown on November 4, 1951, by WPIX-TV, New York City. The services were held at Temple Israel in New York City, a Reform synagogue. Rabbi William Franklin Rosenblum preached the sermon. Cantor Harold Orbach of Temple Israel, New Rochelle, NY, conducted the musical portions. This service, as well as three others on successive Saturdays, was arranged by the Radio and Television Division of the American Jewish Committee.

6596. Religious radio program broadcast by a husband and wife was conducted by Dr. Norman Vincent Peale, minister of the Marble Collegiate Church, New York City, and Mrs. Ruth Peale. On October 1, 1952, they began a television series entitled "What's Your Trouble?" The program was produced by the Broadcasting and Film Commission of the National Council of the Churches of Christ in the United States and presented on the Columbia Broadcasting System.

6597. Television station owned by a religious organization was WYAR-TV, Channel 27, Portsmouth, VA, a nonprofit station that began operating on October 1, 1961. It was founded by M.G. Robertson as the Christian Broadcasting Network. The station was on the air on Sundays from 1 to 6 P.M. and on weekdays, except Mondays, from 7 to 10 P.M.

RELIGION—VARIOUS

6598. Rosicrucian Order lodge as well as temple and laboratories were erected in 1694 in what is now Fairmount Park, Philadelphia, PA, by Magister Kelpius. The order, also known as the Ancient Mystical Order of the Rosy Cross, originated in Europe and promotes esoteric teachings which it claims to have derived from ancient sources. The national headquarters of the Grand Lodge of the Rosicrucian Order of the North and South Jurisdiction is located at Rosicrucian Park, San Jose, CA. Each jurisdiction is under the direction of an imperator who has a Supreme Council as an advisory board that charters lodges and chapters.

6599. Spiritualist was John D. Fox of Hydeville, Wayne County, NY. In 1848, his house attracted hordes of the curious who wanted to hear spirit knockings and rappings. Fox's daughters, Margaret and Catherine, continued his work and acted as mediums.

6600. Christian Science church was founded by Mary Baker Eddy in Boston, MA, in 1879, following her founding of Christian Science as a religion and her publication of its textbook, *Science and Health, with Key to the Scriptures,* in 1875.

6601. Vedanta Center for spreading the teachings of the Vedanta movement, a form of the Hindu religion, was founded in 1894 in New York City by Swami Vivekananda. He became the first Hindu spiritual leader to visit America when he came to Chicago in 1893 to attend the World's Parliament of Religions at the Columbian Exposition.

6602. Church without theology, creed, or dogma was organized by Richard Wolfe of Denver, CO, in 1912. The First Liberal Church of Denver, the first of the new sect, was organized in 1922. Wolfe became the first bishop of the Liberal Church of America.

6603. Church organized by Native Americans was the First American Church, incorporated on October 10, 1918, with its principal seat of government and place of business at El Reno, Canadian County, OK. The organizers, all residents of the state of Oklahoma, were Mack Haag and Sidney White Crane of the Cheyenne; Charles W. Dailey, George Pipestem and Charles N. Moore of the Oto; Frank Eagle of the Ponca; William Peawa and Manwat of the Comanche; Kiowa Charlie of the Kiowa; and Apache Ben of the Apache.

6604. Baha'i house of worship was opened at Wilmette, IL, for public lectures and guided tours on May 1, 1931. The site had been blessed on May 1, 1912, by Abdu'l-Baha, the son of Baha'u'llah, founder of the Baha'i religion.

6605. Mosque of importance was the Islamic Center, Washington, DC, whose cornerstone was laid on January 11, 1949. It had a minaret 160 feet above street level from which calls to prayer were announced through a loudspeaker. A colonnade cloister joined the mosque to two wings that housed an institute containing a library, a museum, classrooms, and administrative offices. An auditorium in the basement of the mosque was designed to accommodate 300 people. The first director was Dr. Mahmoud Hoballah.

ROADS AND STREETS

6606. Road pavement was laid at Pemaquid, ME, in 1625. It was 33 feet wide and consisted of stones, rocks, and cobblestones.

6607. Road construction law enacted by a colony was passed by the Virginia legislature on September 4, 1632, at James City. It provided that "highways shall be layd out in such convenient places as are requisite accordinge as the Governor and Counsell or the Commissioners for the monthlie corts shall appoynt, or accordinge as the parishoners of every parish shall agree."

6608. Stone pavement was laid in New York City in 1657 on Brouwere (Brewer Street), the location of many breweries. On January 24, 1658, Isaaq de Foreest and Jieronimus Ebbingh were authorized to contract for paving stones and to assess payment from each house in the street. Cobblestones were used and the street was consequently known as Stone Street.

6609. Hard-surfaced road extended about 100 miles from the Pahaquarry Mines, NJ, to Kingston, NY, through Warren and Sussex counties in New Jersey It was completed by the Dutch in 1663.

6610. Toll road was the Little River Turnpike in Virginia, which led from Alexandria to Snicker's Gap (or Snigger's Gap), a pass through the Blue Ridge Mountains leading into the Shenandoah Valley in the northwest part of the state. The General Assembly in October 1785 appointed nine commissioners to erect a chain of toll gates on the turnpike. The receipts were to be applied to clearing and repairing this road and the road between Alexandria and Georgetown. The road was not surfaced and by 1795 was completely worn out.

6611. One-way street appears to have been arranged temporarily in New York City on December 17, 1791, when the audience at a performance at the John Street Theatre received the following request: "Ladies and Gentlemen will order their Coachmen to take up and set down with their Horse Heads to the East River, to avoid Confusion."

6612. Road authorization by a state was made by Kentucky on December 14, 1793, when Daniel Weisiger, Bennett Pemberton, and Nathaniel Sanders were appointed "commissioners to receive subscriptions in money, labor or property, to raise a fund for clearing a wagon road from Frankfort, Kentucky, to Cincinnati, Ohio."

6613. Macadam road was the Lancaster Turnpike, 62 miles long, connecting Philadelphia and Lancaster, PA. Work was begun in February 1793 by the Philadelphia and Lancaster Turnpike Railroad Company, of which William Bingham was the first president. The road was completed in December 1795 at an approximate cost of $7,500 a mile, a total of $465,000, which was provided by individual investors. The first two miles of the road were surfaced with coarse gravel. The remainder was surfaced with "pounded" or broken stone. It was 24 feet in width, 18 inches deep in the center, and 12 inches deep at the edge. Since the angular crushed stone was hard on the feet of horses, a dirt road 13 feet wide was built alongside the main road, to be used in good weather.

6614. Road appropriation of a specific sum by a state was made by Kentucky on December 19, 1795, when $2,000 was appropriated for the purpose of opening a wagon road from Crab Orchard to Cumberland Gap.

6615. Land subsidy by Congress for road improvements was authorized on April 30, 1802, by "an act to enable the people of the eastern division of the territory northwest of the river Ohio to form a constitution and state government, and for the admission of such state into the union on an equal footing with the original states." It authorized Ohio to appropriate a twentieth of the net proceeds of the funds received from the sale of public lands to the laying out and construction of public roads.

6616. Highway built by the federal government with funds from the national treasury was the Great National Pike, also known as the Cumberland Road, built in sections from 1806 to 1840 between Cumberland, MD, and Vandalia, IL. The first appropriation, of $30,000, was made by congressional act of March 29, 1806, and the last was made on May 25, 1838. The total appropriation was $6,821,246. In 1856 the road was turned over to the states through which it passed. Some of the money obtained from the sale of public lands was appropriated for state road work.

6617. Overland wagon road across the Rocky Mountains to the Pacific Coast was the Oregon Trail. It followed Native American and buffalo trails and was blazed by many, but it may be considered to date from 1842, when John Charles Fremont made a survey of it for the government prior to the great covered-wagon expeditions. The Oregon Trail began in Independence, MO, on the Missouri River, followed the Sante Fe trail for a short distance, then extended for some 2,000 miles across Missouri, Kansas, Nebraska, Wyoming, Idaho, and Oregon to Vancouver on the north side of the Columbia River, in what is now the state of Washington.

ROADS AND STREETS—*continued*

6618. Plank road was completed on July 18, 1846, by the Salina and Central Square Plank Road Company between Syracuse and Central Square, NY. Trenches were dug slightly below the level of the road and a single track of hemlock planks about four inches thick and eight feet long was placed at right angles to the road. The track was covered with dirt as protection against horses' hoofs.

6619. Divided road was Savery's Avenue, a half-mile dirt road in Carver, MA, which was built in 1861–62 and presented to the public by William Savery. Trees were left standing between the roads "for shade and ornament for man and beast." Both roads were paved with macadam in 1907.

6620. Brick pavement on a city street was laid in Charleston, WV, in 1870 by a private citizen at his own expense. In 1873, the city extended the paving to include several streets.

6621. Road pavement of sheet asphalt was laid on William Street, Newark, NJ, on July 29, 1870, by Professor Edward Joseph De Smedt of the American Asphalt Pavement Company, New York City. It was known as French asphalt pavement. On May 31, 1870, De Smedt obtained two patents, which he assigned to the New York Improved Anthracite Coal Company.

6622. Concrete road was built in Bellefontaine, OH, in 1892 on the west side of Main Street. A strip 10 feet wide and 220 feet long was put down. In 1893–94 the remainder of Main Street was paved, together with Columbus, Opera, and Court streets, which together formed the four sides of the public square.

6623. Brick pavement on a rural road was begun in 1893 on 7.93 miles of the Wooster Pike, now U.S. Route 42, leading out of Cleveland, OH. An eight-foot brick pavement was laid on a six-inch base of broken stones and was edged with stone curbs. Completed in 1895, it extended from the York Road to the Lunn Road, then in the countryside outside the city.

6624. Concrete rural road was laid in Wayne County, MI, in July 1909. One mile of concrete pavement 18 feet wide and 6.5 inches deep was laid on Woodward Road between Six Mile and Seven Mile roads near Detroit, at a cost of $13,535.

6625. Coast-to-coast paved road was the Lincoln Highway, a 3,300-mile highway stretching from New York City to San Francisco, CA, opened on September 10, 1913. It was originally proposed by Carl Graham Fisher. The highway traversed 13 states—New York, New Jersey, Pennsylvania, Ohio, Indiana, Illinois, Iowa, Nebraska, Colorado, Wyoming, Utah, Nevada, and California—and cost about $10 million. The first complete coast-to-coast run over the official route was made by Neil Patterson.

6626. Grant-in-aid enacted by Congress to help the states build roads was the Federal Aid Road Act, "to provide that the United States shall aid the states in the construction of rural post roads, and for other purposes," passed on July 11, 1916. For the fiscal year ending June 30, 1917, $5 million was appropriated, an amount that was increased by $5 million every year until 1921, when the appropriation was $25 million. The first project was in Contra Costa County, CA, for 2.55 miles between the Alameda-Contra Costa boundary and the city limits of Richmond, CA. The contract was awarded on July 10, 1916. The work cost $53,938, of which $24,247 came from the federal appropriation.

6627. Nationwide highway numbering system was adopted on March 2, 1925, by Joint Board of State and Federal Highway officials appointed by the secretary of agriculture. To eliminate confusion caused by the motley array of signs in various localities, the board adopted the familiar shield-shaped numbered marker.

6628. Road with a depressed trough was constructed on the Meridian Highway No. 2 between Temple and Belton, TX, at a cost of approximately $50,000 a mile. It was opened to traffic on December 15, 1925, but did not prove satisfactory.

6629. Cotton fabric used on a road was placed on a short stretch of experimental bituminous double-surface pavement on Route 2 between Chapin and Prosperity, Newberry County, SC, in 1926. The fabric, classed as cider duck, was laid on the road in longitudinal strips overlapping each other by two or three inches, atop a coat of tar prime. Hot asphalt was then applied and was covered with coarse sand and crushed rock.

6630. Mosaic pavement similar to the mosaics of the ancient world was laid on Canal Street, New Orleans, LA. The mosaic effect was secured by mixing chipped metronite, crown point spar, and mica with the cement, then pouring the mixture into diamond-shaped brass-stripped forms, sanding it down, and polishing it. The work was completed on February 4, 1930, and was part of the project referred to as the "Beautification of Canal Street."

6631. Nationwide highway planning surveys authorized by Congress were included in the Hayden-Cartwright Act, approved on June 18, 1934. The surveys were designed to obtain traffic volume, load weight, and other information needed for the rational planning of a nationwide system of interstate highways. They were made by the Bureau of Public Roads of the Department of Agriculture, in cooperation with state highway departments.

6632. Electronic road system to guide and control cars was conceived by Dr. Vladimir Kosma Zworykin at the RCA Laboratories, David Sarnoff Research Center, Princeton, NJ. Demonstrations were given in June 1953 with a controlled miniature car and on June 3, 1960, with a standard automobile. Wire cables buried under the pavement conveyed impulses to electronic circles in the automobiles in order to reduce speed automatically and thus prevent collisions.

6633. Highway interchange structure with four levels was built in Los Angeles, CA, and connected the Hollywood, Harbor, Santa Ana, and Arroyo Seco (now Pasadena) freeways. All sections were opened and in operation on September 22, 1953.

6634. Toll collection machine was placed in service on November 19, 1954, at the Union Toll Plaza on the Garden State Parkway of New Jersey, in the Newark-Irvington-Union area. Motorists paid the 25-cent toll by depositing coins in a wire mesh hopper. A green light flashed when the money was received, and an audible alarm sounded if the motorist failed to pay. A machine that could provide correct change went into operation at the extreme right lane of each direction of traffic.

6635. Road paved with glasphalt was completed on August 6, 1971, on 15th Street in Omaha, NE, from Dodge Street to Capitol Avenue. The work was done by the J.J. Parks Company of Omaha at a cost of $13 a ton. Glasphalt, a combination of crushed waste glass and a paving material, is 0.75 inches thick.

6636. Metric distance markers on a state highway were put up by the Ohio Department of Transportation, which began the erection of four signs on February 12, 1973, on Interstate 71 between Cincinnati and Columbus and between Columbus and Cleveland. The signs showed the distance in both miles and kilometers.

6637. Border-to-border national highway was Interstate 75, which extended 1,564 miles from Canada to the Gulf of Mexico. The final section was dedicated on December 22, 1977.

ROADS AND STREETS—MOVING SIDEWALKS

6638. Moving sidewalk was installed at the World's Columbian Exposition in Chicago, IL, in 1893 to convey passengers from one part of the fairgrounds to the other. It traveled at two speeds, three and six miles per hour, and accommodated 5,610 persons.

6639. Moving sidewalk in a railroad station was placed in operation on May 24, 1954, by the Hudson and Manhattan Railroad Company at its Erie station in Jersey City, NJ. It cost $75,000. Made of rubber and canvas, it was 227 feet long and 5.5 feet wide, and traveled up a 10 percent grade at 1.5 miles per hour.

6640. Two-way moving sidewalk was placed in service on January 30, 1958, at Love Field Air Terminal, Dallas, TX. It consisted of three loops totaling 1,435 feet of moving walkway. In each loop a continuous rubber carpet was attached to an endless train of wheeled pallets, flexibly interconnected so that they could follow vertical or horizontal curves as required. The walk was also known as a passenger conveyor.

ROYALTY AND NOBILITY

6641. Knighthood conferred on a person born in America was awarded at Windsor Castle, England, on June 28, 1687, by King James II to William Phips [Phipps] for his fair distribution of 34 tons of silver, gold, and jewels valued at $1,350,000 that he salvaged from a sunken Spanish ship that had lain in the sea near the Bahama Islands for 44 years. Phips's share amounted to $72,000. He was born on February 2, 1651, at Pemaquid (now Bristol), ME.

6642. Knighthood conferred on a soldier born in America was awarded on September 23, 1745, to General William Pepperell, who was born in Kittery, ME. He was made a baronet by Great Britain because of his military exploit on April 29, 1745, when he undertook the siege and reduction of Louisburg, a French fortress on the island of Cape Breton, Nova Scotia, built at a cost of $6 million. The siege, a joint American and British campaign, lasted 49 days. The fortress capitulated on June 16, 1745.

6643. Knighthood conferred on American soil was awarded to Major General Jeffery Amherst for his campaign against the French and for his capture of Montreal on September 8, 1760. He was awarded the thanks of Parliament, and on May 26, 1761, King George III made him a knight of the Bath, with Sir

ROYALTY AND NOBILITY—*continued*

Charles Cotterel-Dormer serving as his proxy. Major Robert Monckton, governor of New York, conferred the award in a special ceremony on October 25, 1761, at Staten Island, NY (now part of New York City). Amherst served as commander in chief of the British army from 1772 to 1795.

6644. American woman to become a countess was Sarah Thompson, who became the Countess of Rumford when her father, Benjamin Thompson, an American physicist born in North Woburn, MA, was knighted as Count Rumford on February 23, 1784, by King George III of England. He was also created a count of the Holy Roman Empire in 1791 by Charles Philip Frederick, Duke of Bavaria. The Countess of Rumford had the privilege of residing in any country she chose and receiving half of her father's pension of 2,000 florins.

6645. Reigning king to visit the United States was David Kalakaua, King of the Sandwich Islands (Hawaii), who was elected king on February 12, 1874, by a vote of 39–6. He embarked on the U.S.S. *Benicia* on November 17, 1874, and was received at the White House, Washington, DC, by President Ulysses Simpson Grant on December 15. Congress tendered him a reception on December 18. He arranged for a treaty of reciprocity, which was concluded on January 30, 1875. He returned to his country on February 15 on the U.S.S. *Pensacola.*

6646. Coronation on territory that would later become part of the United States took place on February 12, 1883, when King Kalakaua and Queen Kapiolani were crowned king and queen of the Hawaiian Islands at Iolani Palace, Honolulu.

6647. American woman of European descent to be made a Native American chief was Harriet Maxwell Converse, who was made a chief of the Six Nations on September 18, 1891, at the Tonawanda Reservation, NY, in a ceremony known as the Condolence. In recognition of her services to the Native Americans, she was given the name Gaiswanoh, meaning "the watcher." In 1884, Mrs. Converse had been adopted as a member of the Seneca in appreciation of her efforts on their behalf.

6648. American woman to become a member of the British Parliament was Lady Astor, born Nancy Witcher Langhorne in Danville, VA. She succeeded her second husband, Waldorf Astor, in the House of Commons when he moved to the House of Lords in 1919 after becoming Viscount Astor of Hever on the death of his father. She was elected to represent the Plymouth constituency and took her oath of office on December 1, 1919. She was not only the first American-born woman to sit in Parliament, but the first woman of any nationality.

6649. King born in the United States was Bhumibol Adulyadej (Phumiphon Aduldet), king of Thailand, who was born on December 5, 1927, at Mount Auburn Hospital, Cambridge, MA. He was crowned on May 5, 1950, as King Rama IX. He was the son of Prince Mahidol.

6650. Absolute monarch to visit the United States was King Prajadhipok of Siam, who crossed from Canada to Portal, ND, on April 29, 1931, accompanied by his wife, Queen Rambai Barni, and the royal entourage. President Herbert Clark Hoover received him on April 29, 1931. The king had visited the United States in 1924, when he was a prince.

6651. Woman of American ancestry to become a queen was Countess Geraldine Apponyi of Hungary, who married King Zog of Albania on April 27, 1938, at the Royal Palace, Tirana, Albania. The marriage was proclaimed by Heqmet Delvina, vice president of the Albanian Parliament. The countess was the daughter of Count Julius Apponyi, a Hungarian nobleman, and Virginia Gladys Stewart, his American-born wife.

6652. King of Great Britain to visit the United States were King George VI and his wife, Elizabeth, who crossed the international border from Canada at 10:39 P.M. on June 7, 1939, at the Suspension Bridge Station, Niagara Falls, NY. They visited New York City and Washington, DC, and recrossed the border at 5:22 A.M. on June 12. They sailed from Halifax, Nova Scotia, on June 15.

6653. King and queen to be shown on television were King George VI and Queen Elizabeth of Great Britain, who visited the New York World's Fair, New York City, on June 10, 1939, during "British Week." They were pictured visiting the exhibits.

6654. European king buried in the United States was King Peter II of Yugoslavia, who died on November 4, 1970, in the Colorado General Hospital, Denver, CO, and was buried at the Liberty Eastern Serbian Orthodox Monastery, Liberty, IL. His Serbian name was Petar Karadjordjević. He became king on October 11, 1934. He left Yugoslavia in 1941 after it was invaded by Germany, and headed the exiled Yugoslav government during World War II. After 1945, when Yugoslavia became a republic, he lived in New York City.

6655. Emperor of Japan to visit the United States was Emperor Hirohito of Japan, who landed at Patrick Henry Airport, Williamsburg, VA, on September 30, 1975, accompanied by his wife. In 1971, he had stopped briefly at Alaska on his way to Europe.

6656. American to hug the Queen of England was an African-American woman named Alice Frazier. She affectionately wrapped her arms around Queen Elizabeth II of Great Britain when the queen visited Frazier's new government-subsidized home on Drake's Place in Washington, DC, in 1991. Under British protocol, people are restricted from touching the queen, though they may shake her hand if she extends it. The event attracted so much international media attention that neighborhood officials decided to rename the street "Queen's Stroll" to commemorate the event.

S

SCIENCE—ASTRONOMY

6657. Astronomer to acquire international fame was David Rittenhouse, born near Philadelphia, PA, in 1732. Trained as a clockmaker, Rittenhouse crafted precise scientific instruments, including compass verniers, surveying devices, and orreries. He observed the transit of Venus in 1769, charted the position of Uranus after its discovery in 1781, and invented the first light diffraction grating. Rittenhouse also served as a member of Pennsylvania's constitutional convention, the treasurer of Pennsylvania, the first director of the United States Mint, and the president of the American Philosophical Society.

6658. Planetarium to show mechanically the movement of celestial bodies within the solar system was imported from England in 1732 and was presented by Thomas Hollis to Harvard College, Cambridge, MA. It was built by Joseph Page and was "a very costly orrery, an instrument that this, or any other part of America, as far as we can learn, has never before been favored with."

6659. Astronomer of note was John Winthrop of Cambridge, MA, a professor at Harvard College, who made sunspot observations on April 19, 20, and 22, 1739. No observations were made on April 21, as it was cloudy. The observations consist of one-page reports in the University Archives, Harvard University Library,

and have never been published. Winthrop observed the transits of Mercury in 1740, 1743, and 1769 and of Venus in 1761 and 1769. In 1746 he established the first laboratory of experimental physics in America.

6660. Planetarium built in America was constructed in 1743 by Thomas Clap, president of Yale College, New Haven, CT. In the center was a globe three inches in diameter, from which extended 12 wooden arms about seven feet long. The sun, planets, satellites, and other celestial bodies were represented. The orrery had no gear work and was operated by hand.

6661. Scientific expedition sponsored by a colony was outfitted by the Commonwealth of Massachusetts in 1761. John Winthrop, the Harvard College astronomer and physicist, went to Newfoundland in a vessel in the Provincial Service to make astronomical observations. His expenses were defrayed by the colonial government.

6662. Astronomical expedition to record an eclipse of the sun consisted of Professors Samuel Williams, Stephen Sewall, James Winthrop, Fortesque Vernon, and six students, who were sent on October 9, 1780, from Harvard College, Cambridge, MA, to Penobscot Bay (then in Massachusetts, now in Maine). The Commonwealth of Massachusetts supplied a boat. Although the country was at war with Britain, the British officer in command at Penobscot Bay permitted the expedition to land and observe the eclipse of October 27, 1780, which lasted from 11:11 A.M. to 1:50 P.M.

6663. Reflecting telescope was manufactured by Amasa Holcomb of Southwick, MA, about 1826. The first one, made to order for John A. Fulton of Chillicothe, OH, was 14 feet long, with a 10-inch aperture and six eyepieces that magnified from 90 to 960 times. Telescopes were later made in four standard sizes. The reflecting telescope was invented by Isaac Newton.

6664. Observatory operated by a college was built in 1830 by Joseph Caldwell, president of the University of North Carolina, Chapel Hill, NC. It contained a meridian transit telescope, a zenith telescope, a refracting telescope, an astronomical clock, a sextant, a reflecting circle, and a Hadley's quadrant. The observatory was completed in 1831, having been built with Caldwell's own funds at a cost of $430. Caldwell was eventually reimbursed by the trustees of the college.

SCIENCE—ASTRONOMY—*continued*

6665. Observatory established by the federal government was established by the Navy on December 6, 1830, in Washington, DC. The first instrument installed was a 30-inch portable transit telescope, which was made by Richard Patten of New York. Lieutenant Louis Malesherbes Goldsborough was appointed the first officer in charge of the observatory and served until 1833.

6666. Observatory on a mountaintop was the Lick Observatory on Mount Hamilton in California. Founded by wealthy financier and philanthropist James Lick in 1876 and completed in 1888, it was the world's first mountaintop modern astronomical observatory and housed what was then the world's largest telescope, a 36-inch refractor. Lick, who died in 1876, was buried in a tomb directly under the telescope.

6667. Astronomer employed in the Naval Observatory who was a woman was Eleanor Annie Lamson, a graduate of George Washington University, Washington, DC, who was hired on July 20, 1900, and who served until her death on July 27, 1932. She computed all the results for gravity determination from observations made by Dr. Felix Andries Vening-Meinesz on a submarine cruise to the West Indies and was working on the reports of his second expedition, an East Indian cruise, at the time of her death.

6668. Astronomer to measure the size of a fixed star was Dr. Francis Gladheim Pease, who on December 13, 1920, at Mount Wilson Observatory, Mount Wilson, CA, measured Betelgeuse, the bright red star in the right shoulder of Orion, by means of an inferometer designed by Professor Albert Abraham Michelson. He found the star to be 260 million miles in diameter.

6669. Planetarium open to the public was the Adler Planetarium and Astronomical Museum, presented to the city of Chicago, IL, by Max Adler, a local businessman. The dome was 68 feet in diameter and seated 450 people. It was under the direction of Professor Philip Fox and was opened to the public on May 10, 1930. The projector was manufactured by Carl Zeiss of Jena, Germany. It was the first modern planetarium in the western hemisphere.

6670. Radio astronomer was radio engineer Grote Reber, born in 1911, who in 1937 built the world's first radio telescope in his backyard in Wheaton, IL. With the scope, a bowl-shaped antenna 31 feet in diameter, he discovered the first point radio sources in the sky. He worked virtually alone in the field until after World War II, when radiotelescopy became a valuable and widespread tool for astronomers.

6671. Telescope lens 200 inches in diameter was installed in a telescope at the Mount Palomar Observatory on Palomar Mountain, San Diego County, CA, in 1947. The lens was molded by the Corning Glass Works, Corning, NY. On December 2, 1934, molten glass at 2,700 degrees F was poured into a ceramic mold that had taken several months to construct. The temperature of 20-ton disc was lowered gradually over a period of 11 months. It was ground and polished at the California Institute of Technology over a period of 11 years and was completed on October 3, 1947. The telescope and observatory were dedicated on June 3, 1948, at which time the instrument was named the Hale telescope in memory of Dr. George Ellery Hale, who had conceived and promoted it. The telescope was first used on February 1, 1949, to observe the constellation of Coma Berenices, near the north pole of the Milky Way, and objects 6 sextillion (6 billion trillion) miles away.

6672. Scientific program to search for extraterrestrial life was SETI (Search for Extraterrestrial Intelligence), conducted over a three-month period in 1960 at the National Radio Astronomy Observatory in Green Bank, WV. Astronomer Frank Drake was the lead researcher. Two nearby stars, Tau Ceti and Epsilon Eridani, were scanned on radio bands for signals indicating intelligent life, but none were discovered.

6673. Orbiting observatory of importance was the Hubble Space Telescope, named after American astronomer Edwin Powell Hubble. The $1.5 billion orbiting optical observatory was launched from Space Shuttle *Discovery* on April 15, 1990, in an orbit 381 miles above the earth. Fourteen feet wide and 43 feet long, the Hubble contained a 94.5-inch primary mirror and five main instrument packages, plus additional cameras sensitive to various parts of the electromagnetic spectrum. Early technical problems, including a flaw in the primary mirror, were repaired in December 1993 by a team of astronauts on Space Shuttle *Endeavor*.

6674. Telescope of importance with a compound objective mirror was the William M. Keck I telescope on Mauna Kea, HI. It had a 394-inch main objective mirror of 36 hexagonal segments that could be precisely positioned by computer. An interferometer combined the light from the 36 segments into a single focused image. The first astronomical image from the Keck was produced on November 24, 1990, when nine of the segments were in place.

SCIENCE—ASTRONOMY—DISCOVERIES

6675. Comet recorded was seen in November 1618. Edward Johnson, in his *Johnson's Wonder-working Providence,* described it as "that perspicuous bright blazing comet; anon after Sun set it appeared as they say in the Southwest, about three houres, continuing in her horizon for the space of thirty sleepes."

6676. Meteor shower on record was observed by Andrew Ellicott on November 12, 1799, off the Florida Keys. In his journal, Ellicott wrote that the "whole heaven appeared as if illuminated with sky rockets, flying in an infinity of directions, and I was in constant expectation of some of them falling on the vessel. They continued until put out by the light of the sun after day break."

6677. Meteorite whose landing was recorded fell at 6:30 A.M. on December 14, 1807, at Weston (now Easton), CT, making a hole 5 feet long and 4.5 feet wide.

6678. Asteroid named for an American president was Hooveria. It was discovered in March 1920 by Professor Johann Palisan of the University of Vienna, Austria, and named for Herbert Clark Hoover, who at that time was engaged in feeding the distressed European peoples.

6679. Cosmic ray to be discovered was detected in 1925 by Robert Andrews Millikan at the California Institute of Technology, Pasadena, CA. The formal announcement of the discovery was made on November 11, 1925, before the National Academy of Sciences assembled in convention at Madison, WI.

6680. Planet found beyond Neptune was Pluto, discovered at the Lowell Observatory, Flagstaff, AZ, on February 18, 1930, by Clyde William Tombaugh, on photographic plates made as part of a long-term systematic search begun under the direction of the late Dr. Percival Lowell. Lowell had mathematically predicted the location of the planet many years before, almost exactly in the position where it was ultimately found. Even after the planet had been observed many times, the announcement of its discovery was withheld until March 13, 1930, the anniversary of Lowell's birth (and of William Herschel's discovery of Uranus).

6681. Radio waves from space to be observed were discovered in 1931 by Karl Guthe Jansky, a physicist at the Bell Telephone Laboratories in Holmdel, NJ. Asked to identify and classify sources of radio interference, Jansky found one source of static that moved across the sky each day. He eventually found that this source emanated from the center of the galaxy in the constellation of Sagittarius. Jansky moved on to other work when Bell Telephone rejected his proposal for a 100-foot-wide dish-shaped radiotelescope.

6682. Meteorite known to have struck a person crashed through the roof of a house at Sylacauga, AL, on November 30, 1954, bounced off a radio, and struck Mrs. Elizabeth Hodges on the hip. She was not permanently injured. The space rock was a sulfide meteorite weighing 8.5 pounds and measuring seven inches long. It was put on display in the University of Alabama Museum of Natural History, Moundville, AL.

6683. Quasar to be observed was discovered by Allan Rex Sandage, an astronomer with the Mount Wilson and Palomar Observatories, Palomar, CA. In 1961, Sandage and radio astronomer Thomas A. Matthews recorded signals from an extremely distant starlike object that was a strong emitter of radio waves, and located it with a large optical telescope. To describe the new object, Sandage coined the term "quasar," short for "quasi-stellar radio source."

6684. Moon of Pluto to be observed was discovered by astronomer James Christy of the Naval Observatory in Flagstaff, AZ. On July 2, 1978, Christy obtained a photograph of Pluto that showed the orb to be distinctly elongated, indicating the existence of a satellite. The moon, which was given the name Charon, is 750 miles across, orbits at 12,000 miles from Pluto, and has an orbital period of 6.4 days. This is also the approximate duration of its day and of Pluto's day, meaning that Charon and Pluto always show the same face to each other.

6685. Brown dwarf star to be discovered was detected in the constellation of the Pleiades by Gibor Basri and James R. Graham of the University of California, Berkeley, CA, and Geoffrey W. Marcy of San Francisco State University. At a meeting of the American Astronomical Society held in Pittsburgh, PA, on June 13,

SCIENCE— ASTRONOMY— DISCOVERIES—continued

1995, the team presented evidence for the existence of a brown dwarf, a substellar object midway between a large planet and a small star. The object was the first major discovery by the Keck Observatory on Mauna Kea in Hawaii.

SCIENCE—ASTRONOMY—MOVIES AND VIDEO

6686. Movie of a solar eclipse taken from an airship was photographed from the Navy dirigible *Los Angeles* on January 24, 1925, when it was about 4,500 feet in the air about 18.75 miles east of Montauk Point, NY. The total eclipse of the sun, which lasted 2 minutes 4.6 seconds, was recorded by four astronomical cameras, two moving picture cameras, and one spectrograph.

6687. Movie showing another planet was made in October 1926 by William Hammond Wright at the Lick Observatory, Mount Hamilton, CA, with the aid of the Crossley telescope, and showed the planet Mars. Another was made in September 1927 of Jupiter. Exposures were made every three minutes, so that at the rate of 32 frames a minute, the movement of the planet took as many seconds on the screen as it did hours in the sky. The photographs were taken in several colors, ranging from ultraviolet to infrared, and illustrated alterations in the appearance of the planets.

6688. Movie of a solar eclipse taken from an airplane was made on April 28, 1930, by Lieutenant Leslie Edward Gehres and Chief Photographer J.M.F. Haase of the Navy, flying approximately 18,000 feet over Honey Lake, CA. The flight was sponsored by the U.S. Naval Observatory. The totality of the eclipse was 1.5 seconds. An attempt to take similar pictures had been made on September 10, 1923, at Santa Catalina, CA, by Captain Albert Ware Marshall, Lieutenant Ben Harrison Wyatt, and Chief Photographer Haase, but the weather was cloudy and the pictures were of little value.

6689. Movie of the sun when not in eclipse was taken by Robert Raynolds McMath at the McMath-Hulbert Observatory of the University of Michigan at Lake Angelus, Pontiac, MI, on June 19, 1934, with the Spectroheliokinematograph. The pictures, which showed solar prominences or sunspots in motion as well as activity in connection with sunspot groups, were first shown publicly before the American Astronomical Society on September 10, 1934, at Connecticut College, New London, CT.

6690. Telecast from space showing the earth was transmitted on August 14, 1959, when the cameras in the paddlewheel satellite *Explorer 6* sent back pictures showing a 20,000-square-mile area of the earth. The satellite was launched on August 7 and had a total weight of 142 pounds.

6691. Live telecast from space was made on October 14, 1968, during the flight of *Apollo 7*, which had been launched on October 11 from the Kennedy Space Center at Cape Canaveral, FL. The astronauts, Captain Walter Marty Schirra, Jr., Major Donn Fulton Eisele, and Major Ronnie Walter Cunningham, showed views of the inside of the capsule and views through the windows.

SCIENCE—ASTRONOMY—PHOTOGRAPHS

6692. Astronomy photograph was a daguerreotype of the moon taken on December 18, 1839, by John William Draper, professor of chemistry at New York University, New York City. He exposed the plate for 20 minutes. The image was one inch in diameter. He presented the photographs on March 23, 1840, to the Lyceum of Natural History of New York City.

6693. Photograph of a star other than the sun was a picture of Vega, Alpha Lyrae, made at the Harvard College Observatory, Cambridge, MA, on July 17, 1850, by Whipple, a professional photographer, under the direction of William Cranch Bond, the first director of the observatory. A 15-inch telescope was used as a camera lens and the daguerreotype plate was set up at the eye end.

6694. Photograph of a solar eclipse was made on March 25, 1857, by Frederick Langenheim of Philadelphia, PA, who took eight pictures in sequence. The first photograph of a total solar eclipse was taken on August 7, 1869, by Professor Edward Charles Pickering at Mount Pleasant, IA. Using a portrait lens, he made the first successful photographs of the corona. The eclipse crossed America diagonally from Alaska to North Carolina.

6695. Photograph of a stellar spectrum showing the dark lines was one of Vega, Alpha Lyrae, made in 1872 by Dr. Henry Draper at Hastings-on-Hudson, NY.

6696. Photograph of a lightning flash was taken by W.C. Gurley of the Marietta observatory in Marietta, OH, on the evening of May 4, 1884. The lightning was about three miles away.

6697. Photograph of a meteor taken in the United States was made on August 10, 1889, by the Harvard College Observatory, Harvard University, Cambridge, MA. The meteor appeared as a straight dense line. The exposure, 13 hours 50 minutes long, was taken by a Gundlach camera strapped to an 11-inch telescope.

6698. Ultraviolet pictures of the sun were taken on March 13, 1959, from an Aerobee-Hi research rocket at an altitude of 123 miles over the White Sands Proving Ground, NM, under the direction of the Naval Research Laboratory. A camera with spectroscopic mirrors reflected out the visible light of the sun, leaving only the Lyman-Alpha radiation to fall on the special film.

6699. Astronomy photographs in color to be published in a magazine appeared in the May 1959 issue of *National Geographic,* Washington, DC, and showed the Great Nebula in Orion, the Crab Nebula, and the Veil Nebula in Cygnus. They were taken by William C. Miller, research photographer of the Mount Wilson and Palomar Observatories in California, using Super Anscochrome film and the 200-inch Hale telescope on Palomar Mountain.

6700. Color photograph of the earth taken from space was taken on December 1, 1959, from the nose cone of a Thor missile launched from Cape Canaveral, FL. The camera was found on February 16, 1960, in the data capsule on the beach of Mayaguana Island, Bahama Islands, approximately 1,700 miles from the takeoff point.

6701. Photographs of the moon in close-up were taken on July 31, 1964, by six RCA-TV cameras aboard the Ranger 7 rocket, which was launched on July 28, 1964, from Cape Canaveral, FL. The pictures were received by the National Aeronautics and Space Administration's receiving station in the Mojave Desert, CA. The cameras took 4,316 close-up still pictures over the course of 17 minutes before Ranger 7 crashed in the area northwest of the Sea of Clouds.

6702. Photograph of the earth taken from the moon was made by a camera aboard the space probe *Lunar Orbiter 1,* which was launched on August 10, 1966. On August 14, the day it achieved lunar orbit (the first American probe to do so), it photographed nine possible landing sites on the back side of the moon. On August 23 it relayed 207 sets of photographs to earth. *Lunar Orbiter 1* was crashed into the moon's far side on October 29, to make way for the next launch.

6703. Photograph of a solar eclipse taken from the atmosphere was made on November 12, 1966, when *Gemini 12* was in direct line with the solar eclipse at 7:49 P.M. E.S.T. for seven seconds. *Gemini 12* took off at 2:08 P.M. on November 11, 1966, from Cape Canaveral, FL. The astronauts were Captain James Arthur Lovell, Jr., and Major Edwin E. "Buzz" Aldrin, Jr., who circled the earth 59 times in a flight of 94 hours 34 minutes 31 seconds.

6704. Photograph of a comet taken from space was made of the comet Kohoutek on December 29, 1973, by Dr. Edward George Gibson and Lieutenant Colonel Gerald Paul Carr from the space station *Skylab 3.*

6705. Photograph taken on Mars was a 340-degree panorama taken by the two cameras aboard the 1,300-pound, 10-foot *Viking 1* lander, which was launched on August 20, 1975, and landed on Chryse Planitia (the Plain of Gold) on Mars on July 20, 1976. The pictures, taken on July 20, were transmitted to the *Viking* mother ship in orbit around Mars, which sent them to the Jet Propulsion Laboratory in Pasadena, CA, via a radio telescope in Spain.

6706. Photograph taken close up of an asteroid in space was taken on October 29, 1991, by the American space probe *Galileo,* and showed the asteroid Gaspara. The *Galileo* was launched from Space Shuttle *Atlantis* on October 18, 1989, on a multi-year mission to Jupiter.

SCIENCE—EARTH SCIENCES

6707. Geographer of the United States was Thomas Hutchins, appointed under an ordinance of May 20, 1785. He was the first and only incumbent of this office. He was in charge of surveys of land in the public domain.

6708. Geological survey for a state government was undertaken by Edward Hitchcock for Massachusetts from 1830 to 1833.

6709. Diving suit that was practical was invented by Leonard Norcross of Dixfield, ME, who obtained a patent on June 14, 1834, on a "water-dress." It consisted of an airtight rubber garment to which was attached a brass cap or helmet that rested on the shoulders. The cap was connected to an air pump on the boat by means of a rubber hose. The feet were weighted with heavy lead shot.

SCIENCE—EARTH SCIENCES—continued

6710. Geological survey authorized by Congress was authorized on June 28, 1834, when Congress appropriated $5,000 to be applied to geological and mineralogical survey and research. The funds were used in making a geological survey of the country between the Missouri and the Red rivers. George William Featherstonhaugh was in charge of the survey.

6711. Geodetic survey was undertaken by Simeon Borden and completed by him in 1841. In 1830 he made an apparatus for measuring the base line for the trigonometrical survey required by Massachusetts. The apparatus was 50 feet long and was enclosed in a tube. It was also fitted with four compound microscopes, everything being adjustable to permit movement in any direction.

6712. Seismograph was installed at the Lick Observatory, University of California, Mount Hamilton, CA, and exhibited at the formal opening of the building on June 1, 1888. The equipment consisted of a three-component Ewing seismograph, a Gray seismograph, and a Duplex seismograph.

6713. Oceanography institution was the Scripps Institution of Oceanography of the University of California, located at La Jolla, CA. It developed from the Scripps Institution for Biological Research of the University of California, which was established in 1912. Its investigations covered the circulation of the waters in the ocean, the interrelation of the sea and the atmosphere, the chemistry of ocean water, the sediments on the sea floor, and the life of marine organisms.

6714. Fathometer to measure the depth of water was invented by Herbert Grove Dorsey of the U.S. Coast and Geodetic Survey, who received a patent on April 24, 1928. The device measured depth by means of a series of electrical sounds and light signals.

6715. Fluorescent mineral exhibit was opened on April 26, 1929, at the Academy of Natural Sciences of Philadelphia, PA. Carbon arc lamps with Corning filters were used by Samuel George Gordon, associate professor of minerals, to activate a display of minerals.

6716. Snow cruiser for Antarctic research was designed by the staff of the Research Foundation of the Armour Institute of Technology, Chicago, IL, under the direction of Dr. Thomas Charles Poulter. Built at a cost of $150,000, it was 55 feet 8 inches long and 19 feet 10.5 inches wide and contained living quarters, a combination galley and darkroom, a two-way radio station, an engine room, a scientific laboratory, a machine shop, and a control room. It was powered by an engine and could be driven like a truck. It moved for the first time under its own power on October 22, 1939, in Chicago. On October 24, the Snow Cruiser was driven to Boston, MA, where it sailed on November 15 on the *North Star* for the Antarctic.

6717. Ship with a floating scientific instrument platform was developed by the Navy and the Marine Physical Laboratory of the Scripps Institution of Oceanography, University of California, San Diego, CA, with financial support from the Office of Naval Research, and was built at the Gunderson Brothers Engineering Corporation yard in Portland, OR. It was called a FLIP ship, for "floating instrument platform." It was launched on June 22, 1962. The ship towed like a log and could turn on end with only 55 of its 355-foot length above water. It weighed about 750 tons and cost less than $600,000. It was placed in service in September 1962. Commander Earl D. Bronson supervised the construction and developed operating techniques.

6718. Geologist to reach the moon was Dr. Harrison Hagan Schmitt, who accompanied Captain Eugene A. Cernan and Commander Ronald E. Evans, both of the Navy, in Apollo 17, which was launched on December 7, 1972, at 12:33 A.M. at Cape Canaveral, FL. Schmitt stepped out onto the surface of the moon from the lunar landing module Challenger on December 11. He and Cernan spent three days on the surface of the moon gathering scientific data.

6719. Oceanographer of distinction who was a woman was marine biologist and environmentalist Sylvia A. Earle. In 1991 and 1992, she served as the first female chief scientist of the National Oceanographic and Atmospheric Administration (NOAA), Washington, DC. In 1979, Earle made the world's deepest untethered dive when she walked along the ocean floor off Oahu, HI, for 2.5 hours at a depth of 1,250 feet.

SCIENCE—EXPLORATION

6720. Arctic expedition to seek the Northwest Passage for the £20,000 reward offered by Parliament for proof of its existence sailed in March 1753 from Philadelphia, PA. Captain Charles Swaine made the voyage in the *Argo,* a 60-ton schooner. Swaine encountered ice off Cape Farewell and entered Hudson Strait in the latter part of June 1753. He returned to Philadelphia in November 1753, and made a second voyage the following year.

6721. Transcontinental expedition to the Pacific coast was undertaken by Captains Meriwether Lewis and William Clark, who left St. Louis, MO, on May 14, 1804, reached the mouth of the Columbia River on November 8, 1805, and returned to St. Louis on September 23, 1806. The expedition consisted of 9 Kentucky men, 14 army men, 2 French voyageurs, an African-American servant, and a Shoshone guide, Sacagawea, who was married to one of the voyageurs.

6722. Discovery of Antarctica by an American was made on November 18, 1820, by Captain Nathaniel Brown Palmer in the *Hero,* a sloop of 44 tons, with a crew of six men including the captain and the mate. He sailed from Stonington, CT, on July 25, 1820, and returned on May 8, 1821. His discovery of the Antarctic peninsula now called Palmer's Peninsula was made at a point near latitude 64 degrees S and longitude 60 degrees W. Palmer did not realize he had seen a continent. The first American to set foot on Antarctica was probably John Davis, a seal hunter, who went ashore at Hughes Bay on February 7, 1821. Antarctica had already been seen from a distance by the English explorer James Cook and the crew of his ship, the *Endeavour,* which circumnavigated the continent between 1773 and 1775.

6723. Scientific expedition fitted out by the federal government was authorized by Congress on May 14, 1836. An appropriation of $150,000 was made for a surveying and exploring expedition to the Pacific Ocean and the South Seas. Instructions were received on August 11, 1838. The expedition left Hampton Roads, VA, on August 18, with Lieutenant Charles Wilkes in command, explored the South Seas, and returned to New York City on June 10, 1842. The explorers saw the Antarctic continent on January 16, 1840.

6724. Arctic expedition by an American explorer was made by Elisha Kent Kane and his crew, who left New York City on May 31, 1853, in the *Advance.* They arrived at Cape Constitution, where they remained for 21 months while their ship remained frozen in the ice pack. After disease broke out on board, the crew made a 1,000-mile trek to the nearest Eskimo village.

6725. Exploration of the Grand Canyon of the Colorado by a white man was made by Major John Wesley Powell, who left Green River City, above the head of the Colorado River, on May 24, 1869, and emerged from the lower end of the Grand Canyon on August 29, 1869, with five of the nine men who had started with him. The following year he was appointed chief of the Topographical and Geological Survey of the Colorado River of the West. The Grand Canyon had been observed by Spanish explorers in 1540 and described by the Sitgreaves expedition in 1851. A War Department team had explored navigable waters from the south in 1858, but had stopped at the foot of the canyon.

6726. Polar expedition of which a woman was a member was the Peary Expedition, led by Robert Edwin Peary, who sailed in the *Kite* on June 6, 1891, from New York City, with his wife, Josephine Peary, among the crew. This expedition did not reach the Pole.

6727. Discovery of the North Pole was long thought to have been made on April 6, 1909, by a dogsled expedition led by Robert Edwin Peary, who was accompanied by his African-American assistant, Matthew Alexander Henson, and four Eskimos. This claim was disputed by Frederick A. Cook, who maintained that he had reached the Pole by dogsled on April 21, 1908. Both claims were ruled incorrect in 1997 by historian Robert M. Bryce, who said that neither explorer succeeded in reaching 90 latitude N. The first person known to have set foot on the Pole was Lieutenant Colonel Joseph Otis Fletcher of Shawnee, OK, who arrived by plane on May 3, 1952.

6728. Airplane flight over the North Pole was claimed to have been made by Navy Lieutenant Commander Richard Evelyn Byrd and his pilot, aviator Floyd Bennett, on May 9, 1926. In the *Josephine Ford,* a triple-engine Fokker monoplane, they flew from King's Bay, Spitzbergen, to the Pole and back, without stopping, covering 1,545 miles in 15 hours 30 minutes. Both received the Medal of Honor. However, Byrd's diary, analyzed in 1996, indicated that he turned back 150 miles short of the Pole.

SCIENCE—EXPLORATION—*continued*

If so, Italy's Umberto Nobile and his co-adventurers, Norwegian explorer Roald Amundsen and U.S. coal-mining heir Lincoln Ellsworth, would receive the credit for their flight over the North Pole on May 12, 1926.

6729. Airplane flight over the South Pole was made in a Ford tri-motor airplane on November 28, 1929, by Navy Lieutenant Commander Richard Evelyn Byrd, who took off from Little America, his base in the Antarctic, at 10:29 P.M. E.S.T. The crew consisted of Bernt Balchen, pilot, Harold I. June, radio operator, and Captain Ashley C. McKinley, photographer. They reported that they reached the Pole about 8:55 A.M. on November 29 and dropped an American flag there, returning at 5:10 P.M.

6730. American base in Antarctica that was permanent was East Base, built in 1940 on Stonington Island, Antarctica, and used for exploration, mapping, and scientific research. The two expeditions that used the camp were led by Richard Black and Finn Ronne. By the time of the explorers' final departure in 1948, they had carried out epic dogsled journeys as well as dangerous airplane expeditions to map some of the last unknown areas of the continent. The first women in Antarctica were Edith "Jackie" Ronne, Finn Ronne's wife, and Jennie Darlington, the wife of pilot Harry Darlington, who were part of a private 23-person expedition assembled in 1947 that spent a year on East Base.

6731. Airplane flight to land at the North Pole was made by a ski-wheeled Air Force C-47, which landed on May 3, 1952. It took off from Fletcher's Ice Island, about 115 miles from the Pole, carrying 10 air force officials and scientists. It was piloted by Lieutenant Colonel William Pershing Benedict of San Rafael, CA, and copilot Lieutenant Colonel Joseph Otis Fletcher of Shawnee, OK. In 1997, historian Robert M. Bryce published the results of research indicating that no previous explorer succeeded in reaching the Pole, despite two long-standing claims, and that Fletcher was the first human known to set foot on it.

6732. Explorer to set foot on both the North and South Poles was Dr. Albert Paddock Crary. On May 3, 1952, he visited the North Pole by aircraft. On Febrary 12, 1961, he reached the South Pole by tracked vehicle as part of a scientific expedition.

6733. Airplane flight to land at the South Pole landed on October 31, 1956, at 8:30 A.M. Greenwich time. Rear Admiral George John Dufek and six officers landed in the *Que Sera Sera,* a twin-engine Douglas R4D Skytrain transport plane. The flight was part of Operation Deepfreeze, commanded by Admiral Richard Evelyn Byrd and undertaken in connection with the International Geophysical Year 1957–58. Dufek, commander of the Naval Support Force, was in charge of logistic support for the scientific body of the expedition. He became the first American to set foot on the South Pole.

6734. Charting of the Northwest Passage between the Atlantic and the Pacific oceans was accomplished in the period from June to September 1957 by three Coast Guard cutters, the *Bramble,* the *Spar,* and the *Storis,* which were led by the *Labrador,* a Canadian ice patrol ship, through Beloit Strait between Boothia Peninsula and Somerset Island. The commanding officer was Commander Harold L. Wood.

SCIENCE—LIFE SCIENCES

6735. Botanical report on plant hybridization was authored by the minister and scientist Cotton Mather of Boston, MA, and published on September 24, 1716. He described the hybridization of Indian corn and squash.

6736. Botanical garden was planned and made by John Bartram, who laid out five or six acres with his own hands in 1728. The garden was located at 43rd and Eastwick streets, Philadelphia, PA, on the banks of the Schuylkill River. Bartram at one time acted as botanist to King George III of England.

6737. Botanist of note who was a woman was Jane Colden, daughter of Cadwallader Colden, the lieutenant governor of New York and an accomplished botanist. She manifested her interest in botany in 1728, at the age of four. By the time she was 34, in 1758, she had described 400 plants according to the Linnaean method, using English terms (since her father had prevented her from learning Latin). She was the first to identify and name the gardenia.

6738. Botanic expedition to study and classify botanical species was made in the New England area by Manasseh Cutler, who set out from Ipswich, MA, on July 19, 1784. At Mount Washington, NH, he examined 350 species and classified them according to the Linnaean method.

6739. Dinosaur fossils found in the United States were three-toed footprints discovered in 1802 in sandstone near the town of South Hadley, MA, in the Connecticut River valley. A boy named Pliny Moody found the tracks, which were so much like those of birds that local people believed them to be the footprints of Noah's raven. Edward Hitchcock, a professor at Amherst College, Amherst, MA, believed the tracks were left by large, flightless birds. His analysis, *Ichnology of New England: A Report on the Sandstone of the Connecticut Valley, Especially its Fossil Footprints,* published in 1858, was the first scholarly work on fossil footprints.

6740. Bird banding was done in 1803 at Mill Grove Farm, Montgomery County, 24 miles northwest of Philadelphia, PA, by John James Audubon, who used silver wire to band a brood of phoebes and was fortunate in obtaining two returns.

6741. Botanist to become a prominent landscape gardener was Andrew Jackson Downing of Newburgh, NY. In 1841 he wrote *A Treatise on the Theory and Practice of Landscape Gardening Adapted to North America,* the first serious discussion of the subject.

6742. Entomologist hired by a state was Asa Fitch. The New York State Legislature on April 15, 1854, made an appropriation of $1,000 to pay for an examination and description of the insects of New York State, particularly those harmful to plants. The executive committee of the New York State Agricultural Society, meeting at the Astor House, New York City, on May 4, 1854, appointed Asa Fitch to do this work. His report appeared in the Agricultural Society's report for 1855.

6743. Entomologist hired by the federal government was Townend Glover, who was commissioned on June 14, 1854. He was the "expert for collecting statistics and other information on seeds, fruits and insects of the United States." His first report, which appeared under the imprint of the Patent Office, was *Insects Injurious and Beneficial to Vegetation,* printed in 1854.

6744. Dinosaur skeleton found in the United States was that of a hadrosaur, a duck-billed dinosaur of the Cretaceous period. The skeleton consisted of most of the animal's left side plus 28 vertebrae and nine teeth. The bones were unearthed in 1858 by William Parker Foulke, a member of the Academy of Natural Sciences in Philadelphia, PA, on the farm of John Hopkins in Haddonfield, NJ. They were first described by Joseph Leidy, professor of anatomy at the University of Pennsylvania, who gave the animal the name *Hadrosaurus foulkii* in honor of Foulke, and who connected this discovery with the dinosaur skeleton that had been found earlier in Britain. The hadrosaur skeleton was assembled for display at the academy by Benjamin Waterhouse Hawkins. The missing bones were sculpted in plaster.

6745. Biological study of camouflage in nature was undertaken by the painter Abbott Handerson Thayer. His treatise on the subject, "The Law Which Underlies Protective Coloration," appeared in the April 1896 issue of *The Auk,* an ornithological journal published in New York City.

6746. Taxidermy method of stuffing animals was devised by Carl Ethan Akeley in 1902. He mounted skins on specially constructed forms, lifelike and true in all details to the living animals. His first important work, "The Four Seasons," representing four groups of Virginia deer and their appropriate surroundings in spring, summer, autumn, and winter, was prepared for the Field Museum of Natural History, Chicago, IL.

6747. Bird banding by federal authorities was done by the United States Biological Survey. Bands were attached to different species of ducks and other water birds during the summer of 1914 by Dr. Alexander Wetmore, who was making investigations of the duck sickness at the Bear River marshes in Utah.

6748. Anthropology laboratory was the Laboratory of Anthropology, formally opened to the public on September 1, 1931, at Santa Fe, NM. Jesse Logan Nusbaum was in charge.

6749. Flea laboratory was opened on January 1, 1939, at the University of California's Hooper Foundation for Medical Research, San Francisco, CA. It was a flea-tight, rodent-tight, two-story concrete building, air-conditioned at a constant temperature. The first director was Dr. Karl Friedrich Meyer.

6750. Acoustic microscope was announced by its inventor, Professor Calvin Quate of Stanford University, Stanford, CA, on August 23, 1980. Quate's acoustic microscope used very short sound waves rather than light waves or electron beams to examine living cells and other materials, creating images based on the sound-absorbing properties of the objects being observed.

SCIENCE—LIFE SCIENCES—*continued*

6751. Patent on an animal was awarded to Harvard University, Cambridge, MA, in April 1988. Developed by geneticists Philip Leder and Timothy A. Stewart, the animal was a genetically engineered "oncomouse" that was highly susceptible to breast cancer. The use of oncomice in testing anticancer therapies was intended to reduce the number of animals used in medical experimentation and to improve the accuracy of experimental results. E.I. du Pont de Nemours and Company, Wilmington, DE, had commercial rights to the animals and initially sold them for $50 each. Patents on nonhuman animals created by reproductive technologies were authorized by the federal government on April 16, 1987, making the United States the first nation in the world to allow applications for such patents.

6752. Bacterium to be discovered that was visible to the naked eye was found by scientists at the University of Indiana, Bloomington, IN. The organism, *Epulopiscium fishelsoni*, which lives in the gut of surgeonfish, was first identified in 1985 as a protozoan. Some of these organisms can grow to visible size. In a paper published in the March 18, 1993, issue of the journal *Nature*, Norman R. Pace and Esther R. Angert analyzed the creature's genetic material and proved it to be a bacterium of unprecented size—.015 inches across, or about the size of a period in a small-print book.

6753. Forest canopy crane to be used in North America was erected in the Wind River Experimental Forest, part of the Gifford Pinchot National Forest in Washington State's southern Cascade Range, in 1995. The 285-foot-tall crane, the largest of the world's three canopy cranes, raised researchers to the canopy of an old-growth conifer forest that was impossible to reach by climbing. It was the first time such a crane was used to study a temperate forest canopy.

6754. Cloning of a primate from an embryo was announced on March 2, 1997, by M. Susan Smith and Donald Wolf of the Oregon Regional Primate Research Center, Beaverton, OR. Two rhesus monkeys were cloned by the process known as nuclear transfer, which produced two genetically identical monkeys from chromosomes extracted from a single monkey embryo.

6755. Ban on federal funding for human cloning research was imposed on March 4, 1997, by President William Jefferson Clinton. The ban followed the successful cloning of a sheep in Scotland and two rhesus monkeys in Oregon.

6756. Commercial DNA bank was founded in 1996 by GeneLink, Margate, NJ, a company owned by John R. DePhillipo and Dr. Richard Ricciardi, a microbiologist. GeneLink maintained a long-term repository at the University of North Texas Health Science Center in Fort Worth, TX, where DNA samples swabbed from the cheeks of recently deceased people were kept on ice at a cost of $175 to $295.

6757. Complete DNA sequencing of a free-living organism was achieved by a team led by J. Craig Venter of the Institute for Genomic Research in Gaithersburg, MD, and Hamilton O. Smith of the Johns Hopkins University School of Medicine, Baltimore, MD. In May 1997, the researchers announced that they had determined the complete genetic blueprint of *Hemophilus influenzae*, a bacterium that can cause human infections, including a form of meningitis. The organism's DNA was comprised of 1,830,137 base pairs, containing the coded instructions for 1,743 genes.

SCIENCE—MATHEMATICS

6758. Mathematical theory of economic decisionmaking was the theory of games, described in 1944 by the Hungarian-American mathematician John von Neumann (born Janos von Neumann) of the Institute for Advance Study, Princeton, NJ, and the German-American economist Oskar Morgenstern in their book *Theory of Games and Economic Behavior*. Games theory provided a theoretical framework for applying statistical logic to the choice of strategies in any competitive situation, including the marketplace.

6759. Quantum theory of electromagnetic radiation that was successful was quantum electrodynamics, developed in 1948 by two American physicists, Richard Phillips Feynman of Cornell University, Ithaca, NY, and Julian Seymour Schwinger of Harvard University, Cambridge, MA, together with a Japanese physicist, Tomonaga Shinichiro. They shared the 1965 Nobel Prize in physics for their work. Quantum electrodynamics describes the quantum properties of electromagnetic radiation, especially light, and its interaction with electrically charged particles.

6760. Factoring of a 100-digit number was accomplished on October 11, 1988, when Mark Manasse of the Systems Research Center of the Digital Equipment Corporation in Palo Alto, CA, and Arjen Lenstra of the University of Chicago announced that they had succeeded in fully factoring a huge number, 11 to the 104th power plus 1. They used the "quadratic sieve" factoring method invented by Carl Pomerance of the University of Georgia at Athens. The work was calculated by a network of hundreds of computers in the United States, Europe, and Australia.

6761. Mathematical proof of Fermat's last theorem was announced in June 1993 by mathematician Andrew Wiles of Princeton University, Princeton, NJ, at the Isaac Newton Institute in Cambridge, England. Fermat's last theorem, proposed in 1637 by Pierre Fermat, is an extension of the Pythagorean theorem. It states that no number raised to any power higher than two can be the sum of two other numbers raised to like powers. Mathematicians seeking to prove the deceptively simple theorem, the most famous unsolved problem in mathematics, had been frustrated for centuries. Wiles's 200-page proof was so specialized that only a few dozen mathematicians in the world could understand it. It was published in the May 1994 issue of *Annals of Mathematics*.

6762. Theory of fair division was published by political scientist Steven Brams of New York University, New York City, and mathematician Alan Taylor of Union College, Schenectady, NY, in the January 1995 issue of *American Mathematical Monthly*. Their technique made it possible to fairly divide anything—from cakes to war reparations—even among parties that strongly disagree.

6763. Encyclopedia of integer sequences was published in 1995 by Neil J.A. Sloane of AT&T Bell Laboratories in Murray Hill, NJ, and Simon Plouffe of the University of Quebec in Montreal. Each entry in the encyclopedia gave the first dozen or more numbers from a particular sequence, the sequence's name, a mathematical formula showing how to obtain successive terms, and citations indicating where the sequence had appeared in the mathematical or scientific literature.

6764. Patent on a number was granted by the Patent Office to mathematician Roger Schlafly of Real Software, Soquel, CA, in 1995. The number was nearly 150 digits long. It was useful in speeding up mathematical calculations performed within the Diffie-Hellman public-key data encryption system.

SCIENCE—METEOROLOGY

6765. Aurora borealis display recorded in America took place in New England on December 11, 1719. A contemporary account in the collection of the Massachusetts Historical Society contained this description: "This evening, about eight o'clock, there arose a bright and red light in the E.N.E. like the light which arises from an house when on fire (as I am told by several credible persons who saw it, when it first arose) which soon spread itself through the heavens from east to west, reaching about 43 or 44 degrees in height, and was equally broad."

6766. Weather observations to be systematically recorded were made by Dr. John Lining, a physician of Charleston, SC, who took daily observations at 6:30 A.M., 3 P.M., and 10 P.M. in January 1738. He recorded temperature, rainfall, atmospheric pressure, humidity, wind direction and force, and the state of the weather, as well as the effect of the weather on the human body, communicating his reports to the Royal Society of London.

6767. Lightning demonstration showing the relationship between lightning and electricity was made on June 15, 1752, in Philadelphia, PA, by Benjamin Franklin. His letter to Peter Collison, dated October 19, 1752, describing his experiments was read before the Royal Society of London in December 1752.

6768. Weather report delivered to the Army was submitted by Benjamin Waterhouse of Cambridge, MA, in response to Surgeon General James Tilton's general order of May 2, 1814, for army surgeons to maintain a weather diary. Waterhouse filed weather reports for March through June 1816. They were published as *Topographico-Medical Remarks, Together with Meteorological Tables, or Diary of the Weather, Made near the Headquarters of the 2nd Military Department, by Benj. Waterhouse, Hos. Surg. & Director, July 1816*. Some historians suggest that the observations attributed to Waterhouse may have been made by Professor John Farrar and appended to Waterhouse's report.

6769. Weather forecast broadcast on radio was made on January 3, 1921, by station 9XM of the University of Wisconsin, Madison, WI. The first radio weather forecasts made for the federal government were broadcast on April 26, 1921, by station WEW, St. Louis, MO.

6770. Artificial lightning demonstration was conducted on June 10, 1932, in Pittsfield, MA, by the General Electric Company, using 10 million volts of artificial lightning. Five million volts had been the previous maximum voltage attained in the laboratory.

SCIENCE—METEOROLOGY—continued

6771. Lightning observatory was erected during the summer of 1935 on top of the Pittsfield Works, the General Electric Company's building in Pittsfield, MA. It was built almost entirely of metal and enclosed a circular area 14 feet in diameter. Within was a lightproof room seven feet square that contained a periscope with a brilliantly silvered area reflecting lightning flashes from any direction and sending their images to a mirror set at an angle of 45 degrees. A 12-lens motor-operated high-speed camera recorded on a moving strip of film any flash of lightning within range.

6772. Weather forecasting service by telephone was inaugurated on April 8, 1939, at New York City. A steel tape recorder, developed by the Bell Telephone Laboratories, was equipped to answer 30,000 inquiries a day. The forecasts were based on reports obtained from the New York City Weather Bureau.

6773. Lightning bolt to be scientifically measured was trapped by engineers of the Westinghouse Company in Pittsburgh, PA, during an electrical storm on September 15, 1939. The bolt contained enough electrical energy to power 40,000 light bulbs of 100 watts.

6774. Artificial snow from a natural cloud was produced on November 13, 1946, by Vincent Joseph Schaefer of the General Electric Company, who flew in an airplane over Mount Greylock, MA. He dispensed small dry-ice pellets over a tract of cloud about three miles long from a height of about 14,000 feet. The cloud produced snow, which fell for an estimated distance of 3,000 feet, but the dryness of the atmosphere beneath the cloud caused the snow to evaporate before it reached the ground. Schaefer had already succeeded in producing snow in a cold chamber, on July 12, 1946.

6775. Ship outfitted for hurricane research was the *Crawford,* a 125-foot converted cutter, which was placed in service on July 3, 1956, by the Oceanographic Institution, Woods Hole, MA, to study how hurricanes originate. It carried a crew of 14 and 8 scientists. The first captain was David Casiles.

SCIENCE—ORGANIZATIONS

6776. Science society was the Boston Philosophical Society, which was founded by Increase Mather in 1683 in Boston, MA. He wrote that it was "a philosophical society of agreeable gentlemen who met once a fortnight for a conference upon improvements in philosophy and additions to the stores of natural history." The first one of importance was the American Philosophical Society, organized in 1743 in Philadelphia, PA, by Benjamin Franklin. On May 14, 1743, he issued a broadside, "A Proposal for Promoting Useful Knowledge Among the British Plantations in America," as a prospectus. The organization was an outgrowth of the Junto, a Philadelphia society that he had organized in 1727.

6777. Chemistry society in the world was the Chemical Society of Philadelphia, founded in Philadelphia, PA, in 1792 by James Woodhouse.

6778. Geology society (national) was the American Geological Society, founded in 1819 at Yale College, New Haven, CT. The society functioned until 1828. The first president was William Maclure.

6779. Statistical society of importance was the American Statistical Association, organized on November 27, 1839, in Boston, MA, "to collect, preserve and diffuse statistical information in the different departments of human knowledge." The first president was Richard Fletcher.

6780. Science society (national) was the American Association for the Advancement of Science, organized on September 20, 1848, in Philadelphia, PA, for the purpose of advancing science in every way. The first president was William Charles Redfield.

6781. National science institute was the National Academy of Sciences, incorporated by act of Congress and approved by President Abraham Lincoln on March 3, 1863, with the stipulation that "the Academy shall, whenever called upon by any department of the Government, investigate, examine, experiment, and report upon any subject of science or art, the actual expense of such investigations, examinations, experiments, and reports to be paid from appropriations which may be made for the purpose, but the Academy shall receive no compensation whatever for any services to the Government of the United States." The Academy's first president was Alexander Dallas Bache. The first woman elected to the Academy was Dr. Florence Rena Sabin, elected on April 29, 1925. At the time she was professor of histology at Johns Hopkins University, Baltimore, MD.

6782. Social science society (national) was the American Social Science Association, founded in 1865 and incorporated by act of Congress on January 28, 1899. One of its departments, organized in 1912, was the National Institute of Social Sciences, whose first president was Hamilton Wright Mabie. Since 1926, when the federal charter was amended, the National Institute of Social Sciences has operated as the main organization.

6783. Philology society (national) was the American Philological Association, organized in New York City on November 13, 1868, to promote the advancement and diffusion of philological knowledge. The first convention was held on July 27, 1869, in Poughkeepsie, NY, and the first president was William Dwight Whitney.

6784. Forestry association (national) was the American Forestry Association, organized on September 10, 1875, in Chicago, IL. The American Forestry Congress merged with the association in 1882.

6785. Forestry association (state) was the Minnesota Forestry Association, organized on January 12, 1876, in St. Paul, MN, to promote the planting of forest trees. E.R. Drake was the first president. On March 2, 1876, the state appropriated $2,500 to carry on the work.

6786. Chemistry organization (national) was the American Chemical Society, organized in New York City on April 20, 1876. The first president was John William Draper.

6787. Archeology organization (national) was the Archaeological Institute of America, which was founded on May 10, 1879, at Boston, MA, to promote and direct archeological research. The first president was Charles Eliot Norton.

6788. Economics association was the American Economic Association, founded on September 9, 1885, in Saratoga, NY. The purpose of the association was to encourage "economic research and freedom of economic discussion." The first president was Francis Amasa Walker.

6789. Physics association (national) was the American Physical Society for the advancement and diffusion of the knowledge of physics, formed on May 20, 1899, at Columbia University, New York City, by physicists from 17 institutions. The first president was Henry Augustus Rowland. The society admitted 59 fellows the first year.

6790. Political science association (national) was the American Political Science Association, founded in New Orleans, LA, on December 30, 1903, for the encouragement of the scientific study of politics, public law, administration, and diplomacy. The first president was Professor Frank Johnson Goodnow.

6791. Sociology society (national) was the American Sociological Society, organized in Baltimore, MD, in December 1905, for the "encouragement of sociological research and discussion, and the promotion of intercourse between persons engaged in the scientific study of society." The first president was Lester Frank Ward. The first annual meeting was held in Providence, RI, on December 27–29, 1906.

6792. Bird banding association (national) was the American Bird Banding Association, formed in New York City by 30 charter members on December 8, 1909. The society was dissolved in 1920, when records and effects were turned over to the Bureau of Biological Survey of the Department of Agriculture, Washington, DC.

6793. Research society (national) was the National Research Council, established in 1916 by the National Academy of Sciences at the request of President Woodrow Wilson "to bring into co-operation existing governmental, educational, industrial and other research organizations, with the object of encouraging the investigation of natural phenomena, the increased use of scientific research in the development of American industries, the employment of scientific methods in strengthening the national defense, and such other applications of science as will promote the national security and welfare." The original membership numbered 44, including 10 officers of the federal government assigned by President Wilson. The council held its first meeting on September 20, 1916, in New York City.

6794. Society of Automotive Engineers member who was a woman was Marie Luhring, draftsman for the International Motor Company, who was elected an associate member of the society on April 9, 1920. She received the Master of Engineering degree from Cooper Union, New York City, on June 5, 1922.

6795. History of science society (national) was organized in Boston, MA, on January 12, 1924, "to encourage and maintain active interest in the history of science and the various sciences in particular." The first president was Lawrence Joseph Henderson.

SCIENCE—PHYSICAL SCIENCES

6796. Blowpipe was invented in 1801 by Professor Robert Hare of Philadelphia, PA, who called it a "hydrostatic blowpipe." He reported his discovery to the Chemical Society of Philadelphia in *A Memoir of the Supply and Application of the Blow-Pipe, Containing an Account of the new method of supplying the Blow-Pipe either with common air or oxygen gas; and also of the effects of the intense heat produced by the combustion of the hydrogen and oxygen gases.*

6797. Helium plant was the United States Production Plant, Fort Worth, TX, completed in April 1921 under the cognizance of the Navy Department. It was operated by the Linde Air Products Company using its own process. The Bureau of Mines assumed the supervision of this plant on July 1, 1925, and operated it until 1929, when it was closed on account of insufficient gas supply.

6798. Cyclotron spiral atom smasher was developed by Professor Ernest Orlando Lawrence at the University of California, Berkeley, CA, in 1934 to study the nuclear structure of the atom. A magnetic whirling machine using an 80-ton magnet produced 10-million- to 15-million-volt rays and sent a stream of high-energy bullets from the nuclei of helium gas atoms or alpha particles in the form of a beam of light a foot from the machine.

6799. Spectrophotometer was invented by Professor Arthur Cobb Hardy of Wellesley, MA, who received a patent on January 8, 1935, on a "photometric apparatus." This electronic device detected 2 million different shades of color and produced for permanent records a chart of each color. The patent was assigned to the General Electric Company, Schenectady, NY, which sold the first machine on May 24, 1935.

6800. Electron microscope was invented by Dr. Vladimir Kosma Zworykin of the RCA Laboratory, Camden, NJ, and was first publicly demonstrated by Dr. Ladislaus Morton on April 20, 1940, at the American Philosophical Society convention in Philadelphia, PA. The instrument was 10 feet high, weighed about 1,000 pounds, and magnified up to 100,000 diameters.

6801. Betatron was built at the University of Illinois, Urbana, IL, by Professor Donald William Kerst and placed in operation on July 15, 1940. It had an output energy of 2.3 million electron volts. The betatron is a machine to accelerate electrons by the use of a magnetic field and can produce either a sharp beam of high-energy X rays or a free beam of high-energy electrons.

6802. Synchrotron was constructed by the General Electric Research Laboratory, Schenectady, NY, by Dr. Herbert Chermside Pollock and Willem Fredrik Westendorp, and installed at the Radiation Laboratory, University of California, Berkeley, CA, where it released its full energy on January 17, 1949. It was invented by Edwin Mattison McMillan of the university. It weighed about eight tons and had a betatron-type magnet and accelerated electrons that had negative charges.

6803. Microscope with a radiation block to use with radioactive specimens was built by the American Optical Company, Buffalo, NY, and installed in September 1951 at the Knolls Atomic Power Laboratory, Schenectady, NY, operated by the General Electric Company for the Atomic Energy Commission. The microscope included a camera, periscopes, and an illuminating system to permit light to get in and out through the thick walls of the test chamber.

6804. Nuclear reactor privately operated was the Raleigh Research Reactor, Raleigh, NC, placed in operation on September 5, 1953, by the North Carolina State College of Agriculture and Engineering and the University of North Carolina. Completely independent of the Atomic Energy Commission and other federal government financial support, the reactor was free of secret or classified data and was available without restriction to the general public for observation and to students and staff for study and research.

6805. Bevatron was built for the Radiation Laboratory of the University of California at Berkeley and placed in operation on February 15, 1954. It had a maximum beam energy of 6.25 billion volts. It was housed in a circular building 220 feet in diameter and 69 feet high.

6806. Nuclear reactor patent was granted on May 17, 1955, to Enrico Fermi of Santa Fe, NM, and Leo Szilard of Chicago, IL, assigned to the United States of America as represented by the Atomic Energy Commission.

6807. Instrument for observing radiation in total darkness that was nonelectronic was the Evaporograph, built by Baird Associates, Cambridge, MA, an affiliate of the American Research and Development Corporation, and announced to the public on February 15, 1956. It cost $9,500 and was housed in a cabinet 18 by 14 by 11 inches. It was designed to observe radiation differences corresponding to temperature variations of one to several thousand degrees Fahrenheit.

6808. Stroboradiograph was made in 1956 by General Electric's General Engineering Laboratory, Schenectady, NY, in cooperation with the Detroit Arsenal, Center Line, MI, and the General Electric X-ray Department, Milwaukee, WI. It was announced on August 14, 1956. Used with the X-ray betatron, operating at 5 million to 15 million volts, it could take still photographs of the inside of an engine operating at normal speed under load conditions. These photographs were spliced at graduated intervals to produce X-ray motion pictures of the complete cycle of an engine.

6809. Nuclear reactor for research and development was part of the Plutonium Recycle Program conducted by the General Electric Company for the Atomic Energy Commission at the Hanford Atomic Products Operation, Richland, WA. It reached criticality on November 25, 1960. It was designed to determine the feasibility of plutonium-containing fuels for power reactors. The use of plutonium-239 as an enrichment material instead of uranium-235 was intended to permit the operation of enriched-fuel reactors without dependence on expensive uranium isotope separation facilities, to increase the amount of energy recovered from a given amount of raw uranium, and to provide a way of utilizing for peaceful purposes plutonium not needed for weapons use.

6810. Superconducting motor using high-temperature superconductors was developed by Reliance Electric of Cleveland, OH, and American Superconductor of Watertown, MA, and was first demonstrated in 1991. Reliance built the motor with coils of flexible wire that American Superconductor fashioned from a superconducting bismuth compound. The prototype produced 25 watts of power.

6811. Molecular measuring machine was announced in 1995 by physicist Clayton Teague of the National Institute of Standards and Technology in Gaithersburg, MD. The machine could measure distances as large as a millimeter or as small as the width of a few atoms. It combined a scanning tunneling microscope with a laser interferometer that allowed researchers to track the position of the microscope tip with extreme accuracy to within 20 to 40 nanometers (billionths of a meter).

SCIENCE—PHYSICAL SCIENCES—DISCOVERIES

6812. Universal constant in physics to be measured by American scientists was C, the speed of light, 186,282 miles per second, which was calculated with high precision in 1881 by physicists Albert Abraham Michelson and Edward W. Morley of the Case Institute of Technology in Cleveland, OH. The "Michelson-Morley experiment," one of the most famous in the history of physics, used an optical interferometer invented by Michelson to detect the existence of the "luminiferous ether," a hypothetical universal medium that was thought to be necessary for the transmission of light waves. No ether was detected, but the experiment did determine the speed of light with unprecedented accuracy. It was Albert Einstein's determination in 1905 that the speed of light is a universal constant.

6813. Helium in natural gas was discovered in 1905 by Professor Hamilton Perkins Cady and Dr. David Ford McFarland of the University of Kansas. They tested the residuum from a gas well at Dexter, KS, and found that it had a 1.84 percent helium content.

6814. Heavy water to be identified was discovered by Harold Clayton Urey in the autumn of 1931 and subsequently named deuterium. The first public scientific announcement of the discovery was made at a meeting of the American Association for the Advancement of Science in New Orleans, LA, on December 29, 1931. Heavy water is a water molecule that contains a hydrogen atom with an extra neutron in its nucleus.

6815. Antimatter to be observed was discovered in 1934 by Dr. Carl David Anderson at the California Institute of Technology, Pasadena, CA. While working with cosmic rays, he noticed a line that curved in the wrong direction, a trailing vapor in a "cloud expansion chamber." He identified it as a positively charged particle with the same mass and energy as the electron, which has a negative charge, and gave it the name "positron." Anderson, who received a Nobel Prize in physics in 1936, was also the co-discoverer in 1936 of the meson, a particle intermediate in mass between the proton and electron.

SCIENCE—PHYSICAL SCIENCES—DISCOVERIES—*continued*

6816. Radioactive substance produced synthetically was radium E, made by Dr. John Jacob Livingood of the University of California, Berkeley, CA, on February 4, 1936. Radium E is one of the intermediary products in the slow deterioration of radium. Synthetic radium E was obtained through the bombardment of common inert bismuth with deuterons at an energy of approximately 5.5 million volts. Radiobismuth made synthetically is theoretically identical with natural radium E.

6817. Neptunium (Element 93, symbol Np, atomic weight 237) was created at the University of California at Berkeley, CA, by Edwin Mattison McMillan and Philip Hauge Abelson. Their announcement was made on June 8, 1940. Neptunium was the first element created that was heavier than uranium, the heaviest naturally occurring element.

6818.. Plutonium (Element 94, symbol Pu, atomic weight 242) was discovered in 1940 at the University of California at Berkeley, CA, by Dr. Glenn Theodore Seaborg and Dr. Edwin Mattison McMillan. They received the 1951 Nobel Prize in chemistry for their discovery.

6819. Self-sustaining nuclear chain reaction demonstration was made on December 2, 1942, by Enrico Fermi and his staff at the Metallurgical Laboratory of the University of Chicago, Chicago, IL, before approximately 40 persons. Atomic particles known as neutrons, spontaneously released by atoms of metallic uranium or uranium oxide, embedded in a suitable pattern throughout a block of graphite, were permitted to collide with neighboring atoms of uranium or uranium oxide, causing these neighboring atoms to split. The split atoms released additional neutrons, which caused further reactions with still other uranium atoms, and so on at a rapidly increasing rate.

6820. Radioactive isotopes exported were produced from phosphorus 31 at the Oak Ridge National Laboratory, Oak Ridge, TN, and flown by way of San Francisco, CA, to Canberra, Australia, where they arrived on September 11, 1947. They were a by-product of a chain-reacting uranium pile and were used in the Australian commonwealth's X-ray and medical laboratory. The Oak Ridge National Laboratory was operated by the Union Carbide Corporation for the United States Atomic Energy Commission.

6821. Quark to be observed was discovered by Jerome Friedman and Henry Kendall of the Massachusetts Institute of Technology, Cambridge, MA, and Richard Taylor of the Stanford Linear Accelerator Center (SLAC), Stanford, CA, during experiments performed at the SLAC between 1967 and 1973. They found unexpectedly large numbers of electrons being scattered at large angles—clear evidence for hard subparticles, called quarks, within protons. The existence of quarks, the building blocks of subatomic particles, was first proposed in the early 1960s by Murray Gell-Mann of the California Institute of Technology, Pasadena, CA, who took the name from James Joyce's linguistically playful novel *Finnegans Wake*. Friedman, Kendall, and Taylor received the 1990 Nobel Prize in physics for their work.

6822. Fullerenes to be observed were identified by the American chemists Richard E. Smalley and Robert F. Curl, Jr., of Rice University, Houston, TX, in 1985. They are carbon molecules in the shape of closed spheres or cylinders. The first to be discovered was a large molecule of 60 carbon atoms in the shape of a truncated icosahedron, the basic shape of a geodesic sphere. It was produced as a byproduct of experiments in which graphite was vaporized using a laser. Smalley and Curl gave the molecule the name "buckminsterfullerene" (usually shortened to "fullerene") in honor of Buckminster Fuller, the inventor of the geodesic dome. Fullerenes are produced in nature as a result of lightning strikes. Scientists refer to the spherical type as "buckyballs" and to the cylindrical type as "buckytubes."

6823. Superconducting material that operated at relatively high temperatures was developed in February 1987 by research teams under Paul Chu of the University of Houston, Houston, TX, and Maw-Kuen Wu at the University of Alabama, Huntsville, AL. Previously, the operation of superconductors required frigid temperatures near absolute zero that were hard to reach and maintain. Searching for superconductors that could perform at higher temperatures, the researchers mixed yttrium, barium, copper, and oxygen to form a compound that lost its electrical resistance at 90 degrees K (-297 degrees F), an unprecedentedly high temperature. The discovery was officially reported in the March 2, 1988, issue of *Physical Review Letters*.

6824. Physical manipulation of individual atoms was achieved by Donald M. Eigler and Erhard K. Schweizer of the IBM Almaden Research Center, San Jose, CA. In January 1990, it was announced that the two had used a scanning tunneling microscope to position 35 individual atoms of xenon on a nickel surface to spell the initials "IBM." A photograph of the initials clearly showed "bumps" indicating the presence of individual atoms.

6825. Microscopic cantilever thousands of times thinner than a human hair was developed in March 1997 by a team of researchers at International Business Machines and Stanford University, Stanford, CA, under Daniel Rugar, manager of nanoscale studies for IBM. The tiny device was intended to aid in measuring very small forces, such as the weight of single molecules.

SEX AND GENDER

6826. Prostitute is recorded as "this goodly creature of incontinency" in Thomas Morton's *New English Canaan,* published in England in 1637. Morton had been a colonist in Plymouth, MA, until the leaders of the colony deported him for leading a licentious life.

6827. Cross-dresser of note was Edward Hyde, Viscount Cornbury, the royal governor of the colonies of New York and New Jersey from 1702 to 1708. Cornbury was often seen parading about town in elegant women's dresses, gifts of his patron, Queen Anne of England.

6828. Ban on sex discrimination in employment enacted by a state was passed by Illinois and approved by Governor John McAuley Palmer on March 22, 1872. The act provided that "no person shall be precluded or debarred from any occupation or employment (except military) on account of sex; Provided that this act shall not be construed to affect the eligibility of any person to an elective office. Nothing in this act shall be construed as requiring any female to work on streets or roads, or serve on juries. All laws inconsistent with this act are hereby repealed."

6829. Sterilization of humans by a state government as a matter of public policy was approved by Indiana on March 9, 1907. The law, which allowed sterilization for eugenic, punitive, and therapeutic reasons, was entitled "an act to prevent the procreation of criminals, idiots, imbeciles and rapists." One hundred and twenty operations were performed under the law. The constitutionality of the law was challenged, and on May 11, 1921, the Supreme Court of Indiana, in the case of *Williams v.*

Smith, held it unconstitutional because it denied the appellee due process of law. A sterilization bill had been passed by the Pennsylvania legislature on March 21, 1905, but was vetoed by Governor Samuel Whitaker Pennypacker.

6830. Constitutional amendment proposal mandating equal legal rights for women and men was submitted to Congress in 1923. The author was Alice Paul. The amendment was reintroduced at every subsequent session of Congress without success until March 22, 1972, when the Senate passed the Equal Rights Amendment by a vote of 84N8. The first state to ratify the amendment was Hawaii, which did so later the same day. Ratification by three-fourths of the 50 states, or 38 states, was required for adoption. Although the deadline for ratification of the ERA was extended in 1978 to June 30, 1982, it fell short by three states.

6831. Scientific survey of sexual behavior among Americans was conducted by Alfred Charles Kinsey, a biologist at the University of Indiana. He described his results in *Sexual Behavior in the Human Male,* published in 1948, and *Sexual Behavior in the Human Female,* published in 1953. The reports presented data on human sexual behavior gathered nationwide through interviews with 18,500 men and women. Funding was provided by the National Research Council and the Rockefeller Foundation. The studies were considered highly flawed by many observers, in part because the respondents were mainly students and convicts. In 1942 Kinsey founded the University of Indiana's Institute for Sex Research, the first of its kind.

6832. Sex-change operation performed on an American was conducted by Dr. Christian Hamburger at Gentofte Hospital, Copenhagen, Denmark, on September 24, 1951, after a course of hormone treatments. The patient was George Jorgensen of New York City, 25 years old, who later adopted the name Christine Jorgensen. Two additional operations were needed to complete the change. The first hospital to offer sex-change surgery was the Johns Hopkins University, Baltimore, MD, which began performing operations in September 1966. The cost was about $1,500.

6833. Birth-control pill was developed over a five-year period by Gregory Pincus, a biochemist at the Worcester Foundation for Experimental Biology, Shrewsbury, MA, and John Rock, a gynecologist at Harvard Medical School, Cambridge, MA. It used synthetic progesterone and estrogen to repress ovulation in women. Clinical tests were performed in 1954. The

SEX AND GENDER—*continued*

project was initially commissioned and funded by birth-control pioneer Margaret Sanger and heiress Katherine Dexter McCormick. The contraceptive was intended to be "without danger, sure, simple, practical, suitable for all women, and ethically acceptable for the couple." The first brand to be authorized for sale by prescription was Enovid-10, made by the G.D. Searle Company, Chicago, IL, which received approval by the Food and Drug Administration on May 9, 1960.

6834. Ban on sex discrimination in wages enacted by Congress was the Equal Pay Act of 1963, enacted on June 10, 1963, "to prohibit discrimination on account of sex in the payment of wages by employers engaged in commerce or in the production of goods for commerce."

6835. Abortion legalized by a state as a medical procedure was legalized in an act signed on April 25, 1967, by Governor John Arthur Love of Colorado. It permitted therapeutic abortions in cases in which a three-doctor board of an accredited hospital licensed by the Colorado State Department of Health agreed unanimously.

6836. Homosexual rights protest took place on June 27, 1969, outside the Stonewall Inn in New York City's Greenwich Village neighborhood. Gay patrons and local residents rioted after a raid on the bar by Manhattan police. The first large-scale gay and lesbian protest took place in Washington, DC, on April 25, 1993. The march and rally drew an estimated 300,000 to 1 million demonstrators demanding a federal gay rights bill and more federal money to fight AIDS.

6837. Minister who was openly homosexual was the Reverend William Johnson of the United Church of Christ, San Francisco, CA, a graduate of the Pacific School of Religion, Berkeley, CA, who announced his homosexuality in 1972. His ordination was sanctioned on April 30, 1972, by the Golden Gate Association by 62 of 96 votes.

6838. Homosexual rights organization was the National Gay and Lesbian Task Force, founded in New York City in 1973.

6839. Politician who was openly homosexual to win an election at the state level was Elaine Noble, a Democrat, who was elected on November 5, 1974, to the Massachusetts State Legislature from the 6th Suffolk district, the Fenway–Back Bay district of Boston, MA. She received 1,730 of the 2,931 votes cast. The first

declared homosexual to be elected to an important local office was Harvey Milk, who was elected to the board of supervisors of San Francisco in 1977. Milk was assassinated by former city supervisor Dan White in 1978.

6840. Sex discrimination law enacted by a state that affected high school athletic competitions was passed by Pennsylvania. On March 19, 1975, the Pennsylvania Commonwealth Court, by a five-to-three decision, upheld a law opening "interscholastic practice and competition to girls in all high school sports, including football and wrestling," and declaring "unconstitutional the ban against girls competing with boys in the bylaws of the Pennsylvania Interscholastic Athletic Association."

6841. Voluntary sterilization regulation enacted by a state was enacted on April 10, 1976, by the state of Virginia. It barred physicians from performing a vasectomy, salpingectomy, or other surgical sterilization procedure upon any person under the age of 21, or over 21 and legally incompetent.

6842. Homosexual rights march took place on October 14, 1979, in Washington, DC. More than 100,000 marchers participated.

6843. Condom commercials on television to be aired in a large urban market were broadcast on January 16, 1987, by KRON in San Francisco, CA. Stations in Detroit and Indianapolis showed the ads soon after. On February 16, 1987, the commercials were endorsed by Surgeon General C. Everett Koop. They were intended to encourage the use of condoms in preventing AIDS rather than in preventing conception.

6844. Minister who was a transsexual in a mainstream Christian church was Erin Swenson, a Presbyterian minister who had received ordination as Eric Swenson before undergoing a sex-change procedure. On October 22, 1996, the Presbytery of Greater Atlanta, a Georgia branch of the Presbyterian Church (USA), decided by a vote of 186–161 to continue to recognize the ordination.

6845. Television network sitcom to feature a lead character who was homosexual was "Ellen," an ABC network comedy starring Ellen DeGeneres. The series had been on the air for several seasons before the producers decided to air a show in which the character, Ellen Morgan, concluded that she was a lesbian. The show was aired on April 30, 1997. DeGeneres had recently announced that she was a lesbian in real life. The first regularly appearing homosexual character in a television situation comedy was Jodie Dallas, played by comedian Billy Crystal beginning in 1977 on the series "Soap."

SHIPS AND BOATS

6846. Ships built by Europeans in America were crude flatboats constructed by the Spanish expedition led by Pánfilo de Narváez between April 14, 1528, and the following September, near what is now the town of St. Marks, FL. The men reached the western shore of Florida on April 14 and traveled inland, but were unable to return to their supply ship. They spent six weeks building five boats, each 33 feet long. About 250 men embarked on these boats in the hope of finding their way to the Spanish settlement on the Panuco River in Mexico. Only four of them reached civilization.

6847. Ship built in America to cross the Atlantic Ocean was a pinnace, a light sailing ship, built by the Huguenots (French Protestants) of Jean Ribaut's colony at Port Royal, SC, in 1562. In the winter of 1562–63, about 30 of them endeavored to return to France in the pinnace. They ran out of food and water and killed La Chere, one of their crew, who was eaten by the rest. They reached the coast of France, which was hostile to Protestants, but were rescued by an English ship that took them to Queen Elizabeth.

6848. Ship built by English colonists in America was the *Virginia of Sagadahock,* launched in Maine from the banks of the Sagadahoc River (now the Kennebec) in Maine by the colonists of the short-lived Popham settlement in 1607. A ship of 30 tons, it was 30 feet long, had a beam of 13 feet, and drew 8 feet. Moss was used for caulking and shirts were used for its sails.

6849. Prefabricated ship built in America was an open shallop that was assembled by the London Company's Virginia colonists at the entrance to Chesapeake Bay. It was begun on April 17, 1607, and completed and launched on May 18. Captain John Smith, in his account of the colony, wrote that the shallop "had been shipped in portions easy to be fitted together."

6850. Decked ship built in America was built at the southern tip of what is now Manhattan Island, New York City, by the Dutch explorer Adriaen Block in the summer of 1614. He named it the *Onrust* ("Restless"). It was a 16-ton ship, 38 feet on the keel, 44.5 feet overall, and 11 feet in the beam, and was launched in the Hudson River.

6851. Great Lakes vessel was *Le Griffon,* a two-masted armored square-rigger built in 1679 by the explorer Robert Cavelier, Sieur de La Salle, at Cayuga Creek, near the Niagara River in New York. The keel was laid on January 26, 1679, and its first voyage was made on August 7. It was of 60 tons burden and sailed Lake Erie and Lake Michigan. It sank on September 18, 1679, in a gale in Mackinaw Strait and is believed to be resting in Mississagi Strait, Manitoulin Island, Canada.

6852. Schooner built in America was launched at Gloucester, Cape Ann, MA, in 1714. It was built by Henry Robinson.

6853. Steamboat was built by William Henry in 1763. He built an engine and a model stern-wheel boat that was tested unsuccessfully on the Conestoga Creek at Lancaster, PA.

6854. Steamboat to carry a man was built by John Fitch. On August 27, 1787, his boat plied up and down the Delaware River at the speed of three miles per hour. The boat was propelled by 12 large wooden paddles, 6 arranged in tandem along each side of the boat, alternately dipping into and drawing out of the water. The action of the paddles was the same as that used by the Native Americans in paddling a canoe.

6855. Steamboat patent was issued by the state of Georgia to Isaac Briggs and William Longstreet on February 1, 1788, through the General Assembly at Augusta, GA. This was the first and only patent issued by Georgia, authority having been vested by the Articles of Confederation, which were then in effect. The steamboat worked but was not practical. It was equipped with a boiler, two cylinders, and a condenser.

6856. Ship built on the Pacific coast was the *Northwest America,* a schooner of 40 tons, which was begun on June 11, 1788. It was built, launched, and equipped at Friendly Cove in King George's Sound (now Nootka Sound) abreast of the village of Nootka, British Columbia, Canada. Robert Funter was master. The ship was captured on June 9, 1789, by Spain.

6857. Federal revenue cutter was the *Massachusetts,* the keel of which was laid in 1791 in the yard of William Searle and Joseph Tyler at Newburyport, MA. It had one deck and two masts and cost $1,440. It was one of 10 revenue cutters authorized on August 4, 1790, at a cost of $10,000, to be paid out of the duties on goods imported. The master was John Foster Williams and the first mate Hezekiah Welch, both of whom were appointed on March 21, 1791.

SHIPS AND BOATS—*continued*

6858. Ship from the Atlantic coast to anchor in a California port was the *Otter* of Boston, MA, commanded by Captain Ebenezer Dorr. It carried six guns and 26 men and arrived on October 29, 1796, at Monterey, CA, where it remained until November 6, 1796.

6859. Yacht was the *Jefferson,* a 22-ton sloop that was constructed in Salem, MA, in 1801 by Christopher Turner for Captain George Crowninshield. It was 35 feet 10 inches long and 12 feet 4 inches wide, and had a 6-foot depth. It was rigged first as a schooner, afterward as a sloop.

6860. Steamboat with a twin-screw propeller was built by John Stevens at Hoboken, NJ, in 1803. He patented the engine on April 11, 1803, and successfully navigated in New York Harbor in 1804. The boat was 25 feet long and 4 feet wide and had two 5-foot screw propellers with four blades set at an angle of 35 degrees. It was operated by a double direct-acting noncondensing engine with a 4.5-inch cylinder and a 9-inch stroke.

6861. Steamboat to make regular trips was the *Clermont,* designed by Robert Fulton. The hull of the *Clermont* was built under his supervision by Charles Brown, a shipbuilder of New York. A Boulton and Watt engine was installed, and the boat began its trial trip to Albany, NY, on August 7, 1807. It made the 150-mile journey in 32 hours and returned in 30 hours.

6862. Steamboat to make an ocean voyage was the *Phoenix,* 100 feet long, built at Hoboken, NJ, by Robert Livingston Stevens with his father, John Stevens. On June 10, 1809, it went from New York City to Philadelphia, PA, by sea, navigating the Atlantic from Sandy Hook to Cape May, NJ, under the command of Moses Rogers.

6863. Steamboat to sail down the Mississippi was the *New Orleans,* which left Pittsburgh, PA, in September 1811 under the ownership and guidance of Nicholas J. Roosevelt. It arrived at New Orleans, LA, on October 1. The crew consisted of the captain, an engineer, a pilot, six sailors, two servants, a waiter, and a cook. Mr. and Mrs. Roosevelt were the only passengers. The *New Orleans* cost $38,000.

6864. Double-deck steamboat was the stern-wheel Mississippi River flatboat *Washington,* built by Captain Henry Miller Shreve at the mouth of Wheeling Creek, Wheeling, VA (now in West Virginia). Its keel was laid on September 10, 1815, and it was launched on June 4,

1816. It arrived at its first destination, New Orleans, LA, on October 7, 1816. Each of the two side wheels was operated by a high-pressure engine with 24-inch cylinders and 6-foot strokes. They were unconnected, so that the pilot could go forward on one wheel and reverse on the other, thus turning the boat around in its own length of 148 feet. Instead of putting the engines in the hull in an upright position, Shreve placed them on the deck in a horizontal position and added another deck to carry the passengers and the horizontal boilers, thus creating the first double-deck steamboat.

6865. Steamboat on the Great Lakes was the *Frontenac,* built by Teabout and Chapman and launched on September 7, 1816. It plied Lake Ontario. The first steamboat to sail on all the Great Lakes was the *Walk-in-the-Walter,* 135 feet long with 388 tons of gross tonnage, built at Black Rock, Buffalo, NY, for McIntyre and Stewart and launched on April 4, 1818. Its first trip took place on October 10, 1818, when it left Buffalo with 100 passengers, bound for Detroit, MI.

6866. Clipper ship was probably the *Ann McKim,* launched on June 3, 1833, for Isaac McKim by Kennard and Williamson of Fells Point, Baltimore, MD. It was 143 feet long and 31 feet wide and weighed 493 tons. The first master was Joseph Martin. Since definitions vary as to what constitutes a clipper ship, there are many other claims for primacy.

6867. Iron sailing vessel was the *John Randolph,* 122 tons, which was built in 1834 at Savannah, GA, by John Caut for Gazaway Bugg Lamar. The plates were made by John Laird of Birkenhead, England, and shipped in sections to Savannah, where they were riveted together. Two other iron vessels were also built in Savannah of iron manufactured in England: the *Chatham,* 198 tons, built by John Caut in 1836, and the *Lamar,* 196 tons, built by John Wade in 1838.

6868. Steamboat on the Pacific coast was the *Beaver,* tested on May 16, 1836, at Vancouver, WA. On May 31, during its maiden voyage, it entered the Willamette River in Oregon, ran down the river under steam, and entered the lower reaches of the Columbia River near Vancouver. It was 101.4 feet long and 20 feet in the beam, with a depth of 11 feet and a tonnage of 109. The engines were built by Boulton and Watt of England.

6869. Screw-propelled steamboat on the Great Lakes was the *Vandalia,* which was launched on December 1, 1841, at the port of Oswego, NY. The engine was designed by John Ericsson and built by Captain Sylvester Doolittle. It had two vertical cylinders, 14 inches in diameter, the stroke of which was 22 inches. Ericsson had previously built two engines that were installed in British ships. The *Vandalia* was 91 feet long, with a beam of 20 feet 2 inches and a depth of hold of 8 feet 3 inches. Its displacement was 138 tons.

6870. Iron steamship built for transatlantic service was the *Bangor,* constructed by Betts, Harlan and Hollingsworth at Wilmington, DE, for the Bangor Steam Navigation Company and launched in May 1844. It was 120 feet long with a burden of 231 tons. It was schooner-rigged, had three wooden masts, and carried eight sails.

6871. Transpacific sidewheeler steamer was the *Celestial Empire,* built by William Henry Webb for the Pacific Mail Steamship Company. The steamer's keel was laid on January 13, 1866, and the ship was launched on December 8. It made its trial trip on June 4, 1867, and sailed for Panama and San Francisco, CA, on July 1, 1867. The *Celestial Empire* was 360 feet long with a 47.4-foot beam, a depth of 23.3 feet, and a weight of 3,386 tons. It burned 45 tons of coal daily. The name was later changed to the *China.* The ship accommodated 1,200 passengers.

6872. Iron sloop yacht was the *Vindex,* built in 1871 at Chester, PA, by Reany, Son and Company. It was 54 gross tons, 36 net tons, 62.5 feet long, 17.3 feet wide, and had a depth of 7.9 feet and a draft of 8.95 feet. Robert Center was the first owner. It was abandoned on June 30, 1898.

6873. Steamboat to employ electric lights successfully was the *Columbia,* built at Chester, PA, for the Oregon Railway and Navigation Company. Its length was 309 feet, its beam 38 feet 5 inches, its hold 23 feet 3 inches, and its net tonnage 1,746 tons. The *Columbia* plied between San Francisco, CA, and Portland, OR. An "A" type dynamo, placed in operation on May 2, 1880, illuminated the passenger rooms and main salons. It operated successfully for 15 years, until a larger dynamo was installed. An earlier attempt to employ electric lights had been made by the newspaper publisher James Gordon Bennett in his steamboat *Jeannette,* which he donated to the government for use in

an expedition to the Bering Straits. The expedition left San Francisco, CA, on July 8, 1879. The electric system failed to work. On January 19, 1880, the ship sprang a leak from ice pressure. It sank on June 13, 1881.

6874. Steel sailing vessel was the *Dirigo,* built by Arthur Sewall and Company, Bath, ME, and launched on February 3, 1894. George W. Goodwin was the first captain. The *Dirigo* had a gross tonnage of 3,004 tons and a net tonnage of 2,855 tons. Its length was 310 feet, its width 45.15 feet, and its depth 25.6 feet. It had two full decks and carried 13,000 square yards of canvas.

6875. Steel seven-masted schooner was the *Thomas W. Lawson,* built at Quincy, MA, by the Fore River Ship and Engine Company for the Coastwise Transportation Company of Boston, MA. The keel was laid on November 1, 1901, and the ship was launched on July 10, 1902. Its overall length was 403 feet 4 inches, its beam 50 feet, and its depth 35 feet 3 inches. Its sail area was 40,617 square feet. The masts weighed about 17 tons apiece, and the rigging of each weighed three tons. The ship's tonnage was 4,914 net and 5,218 gross, and its carrying capacity was 8,100 tons.

6876. Concrete seagoing ship was the *Faith,* built by the San Francisco Shipbuilding Company at Redwood City, CA, and launched on March 14, 1918, six weeks after the pouring of the concrete had started. It cost $750,000 and was the first concrete ship to cross the Atlantic Ocean. The ship was 8,000 tons burden, 320 feet long, 44.6 feet wide, and 30 feet deep. The builder and owner was W. Leslie Comyn, president of the San Francisco Shipbuilding Company. The engineers were Allan MacDonald and Victor Poss.

6877. Passenger ship with a diesel engine was *The City of New York,* built by the Sun Shipbuilding Company, Chester, PA, under the Merchant Marine Act of May 22, 1928, and tested on January 11, 1930, on the Delaware River. The ship was 470.8 feet long and 61.6 feet in the beam, with a 26-foot draft. It carried 61 first-class passengers and had a 10,000-ton deadweight tonnage. The ship was propelled by Sun-Doxford diesel engines that made 13 knots. The first direct voyage left Brooklyn, New York City, on February 1, 1930, for Capetown, South Africa, for the American South African Line.

SHIPS AND BOATS—*continued*

6878. Ship completed in less than two weeks was the *Joseph N. Teal,* built by Henry John Kaiser's Oregon Shipbuilding Corporation at Portland, OR. It made a trial run on September 27, 1942, and was turned over to the Maritime Commission 13 days 23.5 hours after the laying of the keel. The previous record had been 29 days. Speedy construction of ships was essential to American efforts in World War II.

SHIPS AND BOATS—COMMERCIAL

6879. Trading ship sent to China was the *Empress of China,* a 360-ton privateer commanded by Captain John Green. It left New York City on February 22, 1784, arrived in Canton, China, on August 28, left China on the return voyage on December 28, and returned to New York on May 11, 1785. Its owners made a profit of $30,727 on a $120,000 investment, which was financed by Robert Morris, Peter Whiteside, and William Whiteside.

6880. Tugboat powered by steam was the *Rufus King,* built in 1825 by Smith and Dimon for the New York Dry Dock Company to tow vessels to and from the railway at the foot of East 10th Street, New York City. It was 102 feet long and 19 feet wide and had a square engine with a 34-inch cylinder and a 4-inch stroke.

6881. Transatlantic steamboat service was started by the *Great Western* and the *Sirius,* both of which arrived in New York City on April 23, 1838. The *Sirius* made the trip from London in 19 days and the *Great Western* from Bristol in 15 days. They were built by Isambard Kingdom Brunel, the celebrated English engineer.

6882. Steamship passenger line between American and European ports to fly the American flag was the Ocean Steam and Navigation Company. Service began on June 1, 1847, when the *Washington* sailed from New York City for Bremen, Germany, with 120 passengers. The 1,700-ton *Washington* had four decks, three masts, and a full-length effigy of George Washington as a figurehead. It was 260 feet long and had a 39-foot beam and a hold 31 feet deep. It was launched in 1847 from the East River yard of Wesstervelt and Mackary in New York City. The cost of the ship was $390,000. The *Hermann* was later added to the service.

6883. Steamboat service to California around Cape Horn was established by the Pacific Mail Steamship Company in 1849. The S.S. *California,* 1,050 tons, left New York City on October 6, 1848. It stopped at Rio de Janeiro, Brazil; Valparaiso, Chile; and Callao and Paita, Peru. On February 1, 1849, it arrived at Panama, where it took on 350 passengers. Further stops were made at Acapulco, San Blas, and Mazatlán, Mexico, and at San Diego and Monterey, CA. On February 28, 1849, the ship reached San Francisco, where most of the crew deserted to work in the gold fields. Captain Cleveland Forbes was in command. This trip started a semimonthly mail service between New York and Panama and a monthly service between Panama and Oregon.

6884. Seagoing dredge with a hopper was the *General Moultrie,* a steam dredge built by William Colyer of New York City in 1855. The 365-ton dredge was 150 feet long, 26 feet 8 inches wide, and 10 feet 3 inches deep. Originally a commercial steamer, it was converted into a dredge by the installation of centrifugal dredging pumps, piping, and other equipment, and the construction of bins in the holds. The machinery was furnished by C.H. De Lamater, New York City. The dredge was used in the harbor of Charleston, SC.

6885. Steam whaler was the *Pioneer,* whose first trip was made from April 28 to November 14, 1866, under Captain Ebenezer Morgan. It had been converted in 1865 by Thomas W. Williams of New London, CT, from a government transport. It was crushed in the ice while on a whaling expedition in 1867.

6886. Turbine-propelled oceangoing merchant vessel was the *Governor Cobb,* launched on April 21, 1906, and delivered on October 17 to the Eastern Steamship Line for service between Boston, MA, and St. John, New Brunswick, Canada. It weighed 2,522 gross tons and was 289 feet 1 inch long. The turbine was built by the W.A. Fletcher Company at Hoboken, NJ.

6887. Concrete barge was the *Socony 200,* which was also the first reinforced-steel concrete barge for carrying oil in bulk. It was built to specifications for the Standard Oil Company of New York and was 98 feet long, 31 feet wide, and 9 feet 6 inches deep. The vessel was launched on July 27, 1918, and placed in service on August 12, 1918. It was built by the Fougner Shipbuilding Company, Flushing Bay, New York City.

6888. Round-the-world steamboat passenger service was inaugurated by the S.S. *President Harrison* of the Dollar Steamship Line, which sailed from San Francisco, CA, in February 1924. Previous trips were made irregularly by cruise steamers.

6889. Tugboat with a diesel-electric engine was placed in service in 1929 on the Warrior River, AL, by the Tennessee Coal, Iron and Railroad Company. The power plant included two 550-horsepower diesel engines. Each propeller was driven by a double motor rated at 400 horsepower. The length of the tow was limited to seven barges.

6890. Seatrain was built in 1928 by the Sun Shipbuilding Company of Chester, PA, for the Seatrain Lines, which inaugurated a service on January 12, 1929, between New Orleans, LA, and Havana, Cuba. Loaded freight cars were hoisted from the railroad rails and placed aboard the seatrain, which accommodated 95 railroad cars.

6891. Rivetless cargo vessel was built by the Charleston Dry Dock and Machine Company, Charleston, SC, for the Texas Oil Company and was launched in February 1930. The entire hull was put together by the arc welding process under a new system of dovetailed lock-notched plates. Only 11,000 pounds of welding wire was used, instead of 18,000 pounds of rivets. A 20 percent to 25 percent saving in hull construction cost was effected by the use of the welding process. The ship had a 10-foot draft and a cargo capacity of 120 by 23 feet.

6892. All-welded self-propelled seagoing petroleum carrier ship was the motorship *White Flash,* launched on September 10, 1931, at the Sun Shipbuilding and Dry Dock Company, Chester, PA, and placed in service by the Atlantic Refining Company on September 14, 1931.

6893. Merchant ship formally blessed at a launching ceremony was the *Rio Hudson* of the Moore-McCormack Lines, blessed on November 27, 1940, by the Right Reverend Francis Taitt, bishop of the Pennsylvania Protestant Episcopal Diocese, at the yards of the Sun Shipbuilding and Drydock Company, Chester, PA. It had a 17,500-ton displacement and carried 197 passengers.

6894. Liberty ship built to carry cargo during World War II was the *Patrick Henry,* launched on September 27, 1941. It was built by the Bethlehem-Fairfield Shipbuilding Company, Baltimore, MD, in 244 days and delivered on December 30, 1941, to the U.S. Maritime Com-

mission, which transferred it to the Lykes Brothers Steamship Company of New Orleans, LA. It had an overall length of 441 feet 6 inches, a beam of 57 feet, a depth of 37 feet 4 inches, a total displacement of 14,100 tons, and a general cargo capacity of 9,146 tons. It had single-screw steam reciprocating propulsion and on its first voyage, to Alexandria, Egypt, its average speed was 11.19 knots. The first captain was Richard Gailard Ellis.

6895. Merchant ship commanded by an African-American captain was the *Booker T. Washington,* a Liberty ship launched by the California Shipbuilding Corporation at Wilmington, DE, on September 29, 1942. It was commanded by Captain Hugh Mulzac, the first African-American to hold an unlimited mariner's license. It arrived at its first port, London, on February 12, 1843.

6896. Victory ship launched was the *United Victory,* launched on January 12, 1944, at the yard of Henry J. Kaiser's Oregon Shipbuilding Corporation at Portland, OR. The Victory ships made 15 knots, which was faster than Liberty ships, and had three times as much power.

6897. Carrier for liquid bulk chemicals was the *Marine-Dow Chem,* a 16,500-ton oil tanker, 351 feet long, built by the Bethlehem Steel Company's shipbuilding division for the Marine Transport Lines, New York City, and under charter to the Dow Chemical Company. The ship arrived at New York City on its first run, on April 13, 1954, from Freeport, TX.

6898. Roll-on-roll-off carrier was the *Searoad,* placed in service on September 1, 1955, between Hyannis and Nantucket Island, MA, by the Searoad Transport Company, Hyannis, MA. It was 64 feet long, had a superstructure 14 feet high, and drew only 6.5 feet of water. Its 220-horsepower General Motors diesel engine attained a speed of nine knots. It was built by the Blount Marine Corporation of Warren, RI, and cost $65,000 to build and $25,000 to equip. The first skipper was Morris Johnson.

6899. Liner equipped with a gyrostabilizer was the S.S. *Mariposa* of the Matson Lines, launched on October 16, 1956, in Portland, OR, by Electa Sevier. It sailed on its maiden voyage on October 26, 1956, from Los Angeles, CA, to Australia and the South Seas. Fins made by the Sperry Gyroscope Company were built into the hull, below the surface of the sea, to remove up to 90 percent of the rolling motion.

SHIPS AND BOATS—COMMERCIAL—
continued

6900. Nuclear-powered merchant ship was the N.S. *Savannah,* 595 feet and 21,000 tons. It was built by the New York Shipbuilding Corporation, Camden, NJ, for the U.S. Maritime Commission. The pressurized waterpower reactor was built by the Babcock and Wilcox Company, New York City. The keel was laid on May 22, 1958, and the ship was launched on July 21, 1959.

6901. Cargo ship fully automated and flying the American flag was the 12,000-ton S.S. *Mormacargo,* whose keel was laid on April 22, 1963, at the Ingalls Shipbuilding Corporation, Pascagoula, MS. The ship, which cost in excess of $10 million, was launched on January 25, 1964. Its first run, from Pascagoula to Boston, started on August 28, 1964, and its first transatlantic trip started on September 11, 1964, from New York City. It was 550 feet 9 inches long overall, with a beam of 75 feet and a displacement of 19,800 tons. It had a bridge console with electronic control of speed, boiler temperatures, and reefer temperatures, and other automatic devices. Instead of the usual crew of 49, the crew numbered 32, each with a private room. Kenneth L. Chambers was the first captain.

6902. Automated tanker under the American flag was the *Texaco Rhode Island,* a 25,413-ton tanker built by the Bethlehem Steel Company at Sparrows Point, Baltimore, MD, for Texaco, Wilmington, DE, and launched on July 2, 1964. It was 575 feet long, 68 feet wide, 78 feet deep, and 33 feet 10 inches in draft. It had a centralized engine-room control system. An oil burner fueled the two-cylinder steam turbine.

6903. Commercial crude-oil carrier was the *Brooklyn,* built at the Brooklyn Navy Yard, New York City, by the Seatrain Shipbuilding Corporation and launched on June 30, 1973. The first test trip was made on October 22, 1973, in the East River. The ship was 1,094 feet long with a 226,200-ton displacement and cost $80 million. It could carry 1.5 million barrels of crude oil and could unload in 14 hours.

SHIPS AND BOATS—DRY DOCKS

6904. Dry dock for the repair of ships was constructed by Robert Fulton in 1805 in front of his foundry on the corner of Green and Morgan streets, in Jersey City, NJ. A block of ground was sold to him by the Associates of the Jersey Company for $1,000, allowing him five years on the purchase money without interest. The deed was dated November 3, 1804. An earlier dry dock had been authorized by Charlestown, MA, on October 30, 1677, to be constructed by James Russell, John Heyman, Samuel Ballard, and John Phillips, but it was never built.

6905. Federal dry docks were constructed at Boston, MA, and Norfolk, VA, under authority of act of Congress of March 28, 1827. They were designed by Colonel Loammi Baldwin of Boston, MA, who was hired by Secretary of the Navy Samuel Southard. The dry docks were founded upon piles and were built entirely of stone faced with cut granite. Construction of the Boston dry dock was started on June 1827, the cornerstone laid on May 21, 1829, and the dry dock turned over to the commandant on September 9, 1833. It cost $677,090. The Norfolk dry dock was begun on November 1827 and completed on March 15, 1834. It cost $943,677. Earlier, in February 1799, Congress had approved the construction of federal dry docks, but failed to appropriate sufficient funds.

6906. Timber dry dock was erected at Buffalo, NY, in 1840 for Great Lakes ships. The excavation was lined entirely with wood secured to poles driven in the bottom and upon the slopes of the sides, and faced with longitudinal timbers forming steps or altars upon the sides. The first timber dry dock on the Atlantic coast was erected in 1854 at Boston, MA, by J.E. Simpson and Company. The construction cost for these dry docks was small, but they did not prove practical for long periods as they deteriorated rapidly.

SHIPS AND BOATS—FERRIES

6907. Steam-propelled ferryboat was the *Juliana,* operated on October 11, 1811, by the engineers John Stevens and Robert Livingston Stevens, father and son, between Hoboken, NJ, and New York City.

6908. Steel-hulled ferryboat was the *Lackawanna,* built in 1881 at Newburgh, NY, by Ward Stanton at a cost of $76,000. It weighed 822 gross tons, 645 net tons, and was 200 feet long and 35 feet wide, with a 13-foot draft. The boat plied between Hoboken, NJ, and New York City.

6909. Double-deck ferryboat was the *Bergen,* launched on October 25, 1888, at the Delmater Iron Works, Newburgh, NY. Its route went across the Hudson River from New York City to Hoboken, NJ. It was 203 feet in length and 62 feet wide, with a 10-foot draft, and was first piloted by Captain G. Beckwith.

6910. Municipal ferryboats were placed in operation in New York City on October 25, 1905, between Whitehall Street, Manhattan, and St. George, Staten Island.

6911. Ferryboat built exclusively to transport cars was the *Governor Moore,* a diesel-electric ferry placed in service on November 8, 1926. It was built by the New York Shipbuilding Company of Camden, NJ, from plans conceived by Eads Johnson. Five other boats were built in 1926, each with capacity for 46 automobiles. They were operated by the Electric Ferries company on routes from 23rd Street in New York City to Edgewater, NJ, and Weehawken, NJ.

6912. Streamlined ferryboat was the *Kalakala,* first placed in commercial operation on July 4, 1935, by the Puget Sound Navigation Company, Seattle, WA, between Seattle and Bremerton, WA, on Puget Sound, under the command of Captain Wallace H. Mangan. It was 276 feet long, had a beam of 55 feet 8 inches and a draft of 13 feet, and was designed to carry 2,000 passengers and 110 automobiles. The boat was built at the Lake Washington Shipyards at Houghton, WA, and was 97.75 percent steel in construction. The name Kalakala is a Chinook word meaning "flying bird." The accent is on the second syllable.

SHIPS AND BOATS—MILITARY

6913. Naval ship of the line was the *America,* authorized by the Continental Congress on November 20, 1776. It was designed by Joshua Humphreys and laid down on May 1777 in John Langdon's shipyard in Portsmouth, NH. John Paul Jones was elected commander. On September 3, 1782, the *America* was presented to King Louis XVI of France in appreciation of his country's assistance during the Revolutionary War. It sailed for France on June 24, 1783.

6914. Frigate was the *United States,* which was built by Joshua Humphreys at what was formerly the Association Battery, Philadelphia, PA, and launched on May 10, 1797. President John Adams attended the launching. The vessel weighed 1,576 tons and was first captained by Commodore John Barry. It was scuttled on April 20, 1861, by federal forces abandoning the Norfolk Navy Yard in Norfolk, VA.

6915. Ship constructed by the federal government was the *Chesapeake,* built at the Navy Yard, Gosport, VA, under an act of Congress of of March 27, 1794, "to provide a naval armament." The president was authorized to obtain six ships by purchase or otherwise and to equip and employ four ships of 44 guns each and two ships of 36 guns each to protect commerce. The marine yard was lent to the government by Virginia, and Captain Richard Dale was appointed its superintendent. Construction started in 1794, but as peace was concluded in 1796, the work was discontinued. Work was again undertaken in 1797, after materials on hand had been sold, with Commodore Samuel Barron as superintendent of the yard. The *Chesapeake* was launched on December 2, 1799.

6916. Steam-propelled frigate was the *Demologos,* or *Fulton, the First,* 2,475 tons, built by Robert Fulton for the Navy. Its keel was laid on June 20, 1814, and it was launched on October 29, 1814, without engines, at Brown's Ship Yard, New York City. It was propelled by its own steam and machinery for the first time on June 1, 1815. The vessel cost $320,000. It was made of wood five feet thick and had a center-wheel propulsion. Its length was 156 feet on deck, its breadth of beam was 56 feet, and its depth was 20 feet. It drew eight feet of water. It carried thirty 32-pound carronades and two columbiads, each of which fired a 100-pound red-hot ball. The guns were mounted in a battery protected by massive wooden sides.

6917. Iron vessel built for the Navy was an iron sidewheel steamer, the *Michigan,* built in Erie, PA, under authority of act of Congress of September 9, 1841. Construction began in 1842 with the building of sections in Pittsburgh, PA. These sections were transported to Erie, where the ship was completed. It was launched on December 5, 1843. The cost of the ship was $165,000. Its hull was designed and built by Stockhouse and Tomlinson, Pittsburgh. Its displacement was 685 tons; length, 163 feet 3 inches; breadth, 27 feet 1.5 inches; depth of hold, 13 feet 9 inches. It was renamed the *Wolverine* on June 17, 1905, and loaned to the city of Erie on July 19, 1927, by act of Congress of December 21, 1926. The vessel was stricken from the navy list on March 12, 1927.

6918. Warship with propelling machinery below the waterline and out of reach of hostile shot was the screw-warship *Princeton,* which was designed by John Ericsson in 1841. Its length on deck was 164 feet, its beam 30.5 feet, and its displacement 954 tons. Its wooden hull was built at the Navy Yard in Philadelphia, PA, under the supervision of Captain Robert Field Stockton. The propelling machinery was built by Merrick and Towne, Philadelphia. The *Princeton cost $212,615 to construct and was launched on December 10, 1843. It carried two*

SHIPS AND BOATS—MILITARY—continued

long 225-pound wrought-iron guns and twelve 42-pound carronades. On February 28, 1844, while the ship was on a demonstration run, one of its guns exploded, killing several of the distinguished visitors.

6919. Balloon carrier was the U.S.S. *Fanny,* an armed transport ship which John La Mountain used on August 3, 1861, to transport a balloon that was attached to a windlass at the stern. The balloon floated at a height of 2,000 feet and was used to observe military positions at Fortress Monroe, VA.

6920. Turreted frigate in the Navy was the U.S.S. *Roanoke,* originally a wooden screw steam frigate built at the Norfolk Navy Yard, Norfolk, VA, under authorization of Congress dated April 6, 1854. It was launched on December 13, 1855, and made its trial trip in 1857. It was altered to an ironclad in 1862–63 by the Novelty Iron Works, New York City, and was transferred to the New York Navy Yard on April 16, 1863. The alteration gave the *Roanoke* three revolving turrets of the design pioneered by John Ericsson, two pilothouses, and a battery of two 15-inch, two 11-inch, and two 150-pounder rifle guns. The hull proved to be too weak sustain the weight, and the ship was sold in 1883.

6921. Ironclad naval vessels were the *Benton* and the *Essex,* 1,000 tons each, and seven others of 512 tons each, delivered at St. Louis, MO, where they were accepted for the government by Captain Andrew Hull Foote on January 15, 1862. They were constructed under contract with James Buchanan Eads at Mound City and Cairo, IL, and added to the Western Flotilla, also known as the Gunboat Flotilla on Western Waters, or the Mississippi Squadron, which was organized on October 1, 1862.

6922. Ironclad seagoing naval warship was the *Galena,* built by Cornelius Scranton Bushnell and H.L. Bushnell of New Haven, CT, and launched on February 14, 1862, at the Maxson and Fish Yard, Mystic, CT. The ironclad vessel *Monitor* had been launched earlier, on January 30, 1862, but it was not a seagoing ironclad, merely a floating battery for harbor defense.

6923. Ironclad turreted vessel in the Navy was the U.S.S. *Monitor,* designed and built by John Ericsson, with a gun turret designed by Theodore Ruggles Timby. The terms of the contract, signed on October 4, 1861, provided that the ship was to be completed within 100

days. The keel was laid on October 22, 1861, and the ship was launched at Greenpoint, Brooklyn, NY (now part of New York City), on January 30, 1862. It was completed on February 19, 1862, and delivered to the Navy on February 20. It was 172 feet long and had two 11-inch guns in the turret that fired a solid shot weighing 180 pounds. It left New York City on March 6, 1862, with Lieutenant John Lorimer Worden in command and arrived at Hampton Roads, VA, on March 8. The next day it went into action against the Confederate ironclad ship *Merrimac,* the first battle between ironclad vessels in the Civil War, in which it was the victor.

6924. Torpedo boat worthy of the name was the *Lightning,* built in 1876 at Bristol, RI, by John Brown Herreshoff and Nathanael Greene Herreshoff. It was 58 feet long and had a speed of about 20 knots.

6925. Steel vessels of the Navy were the cruisers *Atlanta, Boston,* and *Chicago* and the dispatch boat *Dolphin,* authorized by Congress on March 3, 1883. The hulls were built by John Roach and Sons, Chester, PA, and the machinery was manufactured at the New York Navy Yard. The *Atlanta* and the *Boston* were 270 feet 3 inches long and 42 feet wide, and had horizontal back-acting engines and cylindrical tubular boilers. The *Chicago* was 325 feet long and 48 feet 2 inches wide. The *Atlanta* was launched on October 9, 1884, and commissioned on July 19, 1886; the *Boston* was launched on December 4, 1884, and commissioned on May 2, 1887.

6926. Battleship of importance was the U.S.S. *Maine,* authorized by act of Congress on August 3, 1886. It was built at the Brooklyn Navy Yard, Brooklyn, NY (now part of New York City). Its keel was laid on October 17, 1888, and it was launched on November 18, 1890, and commissioned on September 17, 1895. Its length was 319 feet, beam 57 feet, mean draft 21 feet 6 inches, displacement 6,682 tons. On the night of February 15, 1898, the *Maine* was mysteriously destroyed by an explosion in the harbor of Havana, Cuba, that killed 260 men of the 354-man crew.

6927. Battleship built on the Pacific coast was the *Nebraska,* 441 feet 3 inches long, extreme beam 76 feet 3 inches, normal displacement 14,948 tons. The ship was authorized on March 3, 1899, and built by the Moran Company, Seattle, WA. Its keel was laid on July 4, 1902. It was commissioned on July 1, 1907, and launched on October 7. The first captain was Reginald Fairfax Nicholson.

6928. Turbine-propelled naval ship was the *Chester,* a scout cruiser, launched on July 26, 1907, and commissioned on April 25, 1908. It was built at the Bath Iron Works Company, Bath, ME. The contract price for the hull and machinery was $1,688,000. The *Chester* was equipped with four Parsons turbines. It had an overall length of 423 feet 1 inch and a displacement of 3,750 tons. Its trial speed was 26.52 knots.

6929. Naval vessel equipped with a gyrostabilizer was the U.S.S. *Worden.* The equipment was installed in April 1913 by the Sperry Gyroscope Company, Brooklyn, New York City. A gyrostabilizer reduces the side-to-side rolling of a vessel.

6930. Electrically propelled naval ship was the U.S.S. *Jupiter,* built as a collier at the Navy Yard, Mare Island, CA. Its keel was laid on October 16, 1911, and it was launched on August 24, 1912, and commissioned on April 7, 1913. Its conversion to an aircraft carrier was authorized on July 11, 1919, when $2.5 million was appropriated. Its name was changed from *Jupiter* to *Langley* on April 21, 1920.

6931. Naval vessel equipped to lay mines was the cruiser *Baltimore,* which was commissioned on January 7, 1890. It was built by William Cramp and Sons, Philadelphia, PA, and its keel was laid on May 5, 1887. It was 252 feet 4 inches long. The captain was Winfield Scott Schley. The *Baltimore* served during the Spanish-American War as a cruiser. It was converted into a minelayer and recommissioned on March 8, 1915. During World War I, it saw considerable service in this assignment. The first naval vessel constructed as a minelayer was the U.S.S. *Terror,* launched on June 6, 1941, at the Philadelphia Navy Yard and commissioned on July 15, 1942. The ship, which had an overall length of 454 feet 10 inches, cruised at 20 knots and mounted four 5-inch .38-caliber dual-purpose guns and two twin 40mm antiaircraft guns. Howard W. Fitch was the commander.

6932. Warship propelled by electricity was the U.S.S. *New Mexico,* which was built at the Brooklyn Navy Yard, New York City. The keel was laid on October 14, 1915. The ship was launched on April 23, 1917, and commissioned on May 20, 1918. The *New Mexico* was 624 feet in length, displaced 30,000 tons, and carried twelve 14-inch guns and twelve 5-inch guns.

6933. Navy destroyer named for a Confederate officer was the *Buchanan,* named for Admiral Franklin Buchanan, ranking officer in the Confederate Navy. The ship was 314 feet 5 inches long, 31 feet 8 inches in breadth. It was launched at the Bath Iron Works, Bath, ME, on January 2, 1919, and commissioned on January 20. Lieutenant Howard Hartwell James Benson was the first in command.

6934. Aircraft carrier wholly designed and built as such was the *Ranger,* constructed by the Newport News Shipbuilding and Drydock Company, Newport News, VA. Its keel was laid on September 26, 1931, and it was launched on February 25, 1933. It was placed in service at Norfolk, VA, on June 4, 1934. The first captain was Arthur Leroy Bristol.

6935. Ship transported overland across the Rocky Mountains was the destroyer escort *Brennan,* which was prefabricated in Denver, CO, and shipped in sections by rail to the Mare Island Naval Shipyard, CA, where it was assembled and launched on August 22, 1942. On January 20, 1943, Lieutenant Commander H.A. Adams, Jr., was placed in temporary command. The *Brennan* was 289 feet 5 inches long with a breadth of 35 feet 1 inch and a displacement of 1,146 tons. The ship's complement was 156.

6936. Naval ship with a plural name was the destroyer *The Sullivans,* launched on April 4, 1943, at San Francisco, CA. It was named for the five Sullivan brothers of Waterloo, IA—George Thomas, Francis Henry, Joseph Eugene, Madison Abel, and Albert Leo—who enlisted on January 3, 1942, and were lost when the cruiser *Juneau* was sunk on November 15, 1942, in a battle off Guadalcanal in the Solomon Islands.

6937. Naval ship with a mixed company of male and female personnel was the U.S.S. *Sanctuary,* a 520-foot hospital ship with a hospital staff and ship's company of 70 officers and 460 enlisted personnel, including 2 female naval officers and 60 enlisted women. The ship was laid down as the U.S.S. *Marine Owl* by the Sun Shipbuilding and Dry Dock Company, Chester, PA, on August 15, 1944. It was converted and commissioned on June 20, 1945. On November 18, 1972, the ship was recommissioned at Hunter's Point Naval Shipyard, San Francisco, CA.

SHIPS AND BOATS—MILITARY—*continued*

6938. Ship from which a long-range rocket was launched was the airplane carrier *Midway.* On September 6, 1947, a captured German V-2 rocket was fired from the flight deck while the ship was several hundred miles off the east coast of the United States. The rocket traveled about six miles. Rear Admiral John Jennings Ballentine commanded the task group of which the U.S.S. *Midway,* commanded by Captain Albert Kellogg Morehouse, was the flagship.

6939. Aircraft carrier with an angle deck was the supercarrier U.S.S. *Forrestal,* authorized in March 1951 and laid down on July 14, 1952. It was launched on December 11, 1954, by the Newport News Shipbuilding and Drydock Company at Newport News, VA, and was placed in service on October 1, 1955. The first captain was Captain Roy Lee Johnson. The carrier cost $198 million, was 1,046 feet long and 252 feet wide, and carried a crew of 3,500, including its own air group. Its height from keel to top of mast was equal to that of a 25-story building, and its flight deck had an area of nearly four acres. The carrier's displacement was 65,000 tons.

6940. Guided missile cruiser was the cruiser *Boston,* 13,600 tons standard, 17,200 tons full load, which was laid down on June 30, 1941, launched on August 26, 1942 at the Bethlehem Steel Company, Quincy, MA, and commissioned on June 30, 1943. It was converted to guided-missile use beginning on November 1, 1955. Its superstructure was entirely remodeled, including the removal of one of its two stacks to accommodate twin launchers capable of firing Terrier missiles. The ship was 673.5 feet long and had a 71-foot beam and a draft of 26 feet. Captain Charles Bowling Martell was the first commanding officer of the converted cruiser.

6941. Nuclear-powered cruiser was the Coast Guard cruiser *Long Beach,* 9,721 feet long, with a beam of 73 feet, a draft of 26 feet, a 14,000-ton standard displacement, and an 18,000-ton full-load displacement. The cost of construction was about $320 million. The keel was laid on December 2, 1957, and the ship launched on July 14, 1959, at the Fore River Shipyard of the Bethlehem Steel Company's shipyard at Quincy, MA. The ship, which had two nuclear reactors, attained a speed of 30 knots.

6942. Nuclear-powered aircraft carrier was the *Enterprise,* ordered on August 16, 1957, laid down on February 4, 1958, launched on September 24, 1960, and completed on December 20, 1961. It was 1,101 feet long and 252 feet wide, with a 133-foot beam, a 75,700-ton standard displacement, an 85,350-ton full-load displacement, and a draft of 37 feet. The carrier, built by the Newport News Shipbuilding and Dry Dock Company, Newport News, VA, had a complement of 440 officers and 4,160 enlisted men. It was equipped with eight pressurized water-cooled nuclear reactors and was capable of steaming for five years without refueling. Its flight deck was large enough to accommodate four football fields, and each of its four propellers was the height of a two-story building.

6943. Amphibious vehicle was the Marsh Screw Amphibian, designed and developed by the Chrysler Corporation's Defense Operations Division for the Navy Bureau of Ships under sponsorship of the Defense Department's Advanced Research Projects Agency. Two rotary aluminum pontoons fitted with spiral blades propel the amphibious craft forward, backward, and even sideways. It weighed 2,330 pounds without cargo or crew and was 13 feet 8 inches long and 8 feet 4 inches wide, with an overall height of 57 inches. It had an operational range of 10 continuous hours at full power and could carry six passengers plus the driver, or a cargo of approximately 1,050 pounds. It was first tested in March 1963 in Louisiana.

6944. Naval ship with a crew of mixed nationalities was the *Claude V. Ricketts,* a 3,370-ton guided-missile armed destroyer, which was named for Admiral Claude Vernon Ricketts. The ship sailed on January 4, 1965, from Norfolk, VA, on a three-week cruise to the Caribbean Sea for the North Atlantic Treaty Organization. The destroyer had a seven-nation crew comprising 336 officers and men, half of them American and half foreign. The ship was laid down by the New York Shipbuilding Corporation on May 18, 1959, launched on June 4, 1960, and completed on August 18, 1962. It was originally named the *William P. Biddle* and was renamed on July 28, 1964.

6945. Rocket-tracking ship was the *Vanguard,* a World War II tanker cut apart and fitted with a new mid-body at the Electric Boat Division of General Dynamics Corporation at the shipyard in Quincy, MA. It was 595 feet long and was used as an Apollo instrumentation ship by the Navy's Military Sea Transportation Service for the National Aeronautics and Space Administration. The ship completed initial trials in the Atlantic Ocean off Boston, MA, on January 31, 1966, and was then placed in service.

6946. Ship with a combined diesel and gas-turbine engine was the Coast Guard's twin-screw 2,800-ton cutter *Alexander Hamilton,* launched on December 18, 1965, at the Avondale Shipyards, New Orleans, LA. The ship's length was 378 feet 3 inches overall, the beam 42 feet, and the draft 20 feet. It had two 35,000-horsepower Fairbanks Morse diesel engines and two 18,000-horsepower Pratt and Whitney gas turbines. The ship cost $14.5 million. It was commissioned on March 18, 1967. The crew consisted of 15 officers and 137 men. The commanding officer was Captain William Francis Adams.

6947. Naval ship to surrender in peacetime without a fight was the U.S.S. *Pueblo,* an electronic intelligence ship. The *Pueblo* had been launched on April 16, 1944, at Kewaunee, WI, by the Kewaunee Shipbuilding and Engineering Corporation. On January 23, 1968, while in North Korean waters, it was surrounded by three 50-knot torpedo boats and two subchasers and was brought into Wonsan, North Korea. Commander Lloyd Mark Bucher and several of the crew were wounded and fireman Duane D. Hodges of Creswell, OR, was killed when one of the subchasers fired 57mm cannons. Commander Bucher and 82 surviving crew members were released on December 22, 1968, but the ship was held.

SHIPS AND BOATS—MOTORBOATS

6948. Motorboat was invented by James Rumsey and exhibited by him in September 1784 on the Potomac River, in the presence of George Washington. It worked against the stream by mechanical means. He subsequently gave his attention to steam as a motive power and in March 1786 propelled a boat on the Potomac by a steam engine that produced motion by a pump at the stern. In December 1787 the experiment was successfully repeated on a larger scale.

6949. Motorboat pleasure craft was produced in 1885 by F.W. Ofeldt and manufactured by the Gas Engine and Power Company, New York City. The boat contained a two-horsepower engine, propelled by naphtha, which developed a speed of five to seven knots. It was 21 feet long and had a 64-inch beam and a draft of 22 inches.

6950. Motorboat with a storage battery was the *Magnet,* which was operated by one motor revolving a two-blade screw 18 inches in diameter. The battery consisted of 56 storage cells. A 10-hour charge ran the boat for 60 to 70 miles at a speed of 10 miles per hour. The *Magnet* was built in Newark, NJ, in 1888 and was owned by Anthony and Frederick Reckenzaun. It was 28 feet long, with a 6-foot beam, and was 3 feet deep amidships.

6951. Outboard motor that was commercially successful was developed in Milwaukee, WI, in 1909 by Ole Evinrude. It was a single-cylinder, two-port, two-cycle, battery-ignited engine, developing 1.5 horsepower at about 1,000 revolutions per minute. It weighed 46 pounds.

6952. Motorboat to travel at a speed of more than 40 miles per hour was the *Furlong,* built and owned by Victor Emerson, Alexandria, VA, which made 42.5 miles per hour on May 27, 1911, on the Potomac River. It was 26 feet long and had a 1,200-pound hull, a 5-foot beam, and a 250-horsepower gasoline engine with two propellers that revolved in opposite directions.

6953. Speedboat to exceed 200 miles per hour was the jet-powered *Bluebird,* piloted by Donald Malcolm Campbell, which averaged 216.2 miles per hour on November 16, 1955, on a measured kilometer course on Lake Mead, NV. The speed for one leg of the course was 239.5 miles per hour.

SHIPS AND BOATS—NAVIGATION

6954. Quadrant that was practical was invented in 1730 by Thomas Godfrey, who called it a "reflecting quadrant." It was used on vessels plying between the West Indies and the colonies in 1731–32. The invention was credited to John Hadley of England, but the Royal Society sent FL200 to Godfrey to make amends. A quadrant is an instrument that measures the altitude of the sun and the stars.

6955. Gyrocompass installed on an American naval vessel was placed on the U.S.S. *Delaware* and tested at sea on August 28, 1911. The installation consisted of a master gyrocompass, employing the meridian-seeking properties of a pendulous gyro. The master compass was designed to be installed in a protected station, with repeaters that followed the movements of the master located suitably for steering and taking bearings.

SHIPS AND BOATS—NAVIGATION—*continued*

6956. Gyroscopic stabilizer was patented by Elmer Ambrose Sperry and Harry Laurence Tanner of Brooklyn, New York City, who obtained a patent on August 14, 1917. The patent was assigned to the Sperry Gyroscope Company of Brooklyn.

6957. Radio navigation beacons were originally known as radio fog signals. The first successful radio beacons, which sent out signals by radio in all directions around the horizon, were established by the U.S. Lighthouse Service at three stations in the approaches to New York Harbor: the Ambrose Channel Lightship, the Fire Island Lightship, and the Sea Girt Lighthouse at Sea Girt, NJ. They were placed in regular operation on May 1, 1921. Tests of radio fog signal transmitting sets leading to the installation of these stations were begun in 1916–17 at Navesink Light Station, Atlantic Highlands, NJ, by the Lighthouse Service and the Bureau of Standards. The tests were interrupted when the United States entered World War I but were resumed in the fall of 1919 and lasted until September 1920.

6958. Automatic steering gear for ships was installed on the *John D. Archibold* of the Standard Oil Company of New Jersey and tested on April 7, 1922. The device was called Gyro-Pilot, or Metalmike.

6959. Radar installation aboard a commercial carrier operated by an American company was installed on April 27, 1946, on the S.S. *African Star* of the American South African Line, and placed in operation on May 1, 1946, at which time the ship made its maiden voyage from New York City. The equipment, supplied by the General Electric Company, Schenectady, NY, was known as the Mariner.

6960. Radio sextant was made by the Collins Radio Company, Cedar Rapids, IA, and announced on July 14, 1954, although it had already been used for two years as a secret device on naval ships. It determined the sun's position automatically and continuously through reception of microwave energy emitted from the sun.

SHIPS AND BOATS—SUBMARINES

6961. Submarine built for use in war was the *American Turtle,* built in 1776 by David Bushnell of Saybrook, CT. The vessel, which was large enough to accommodate one operator, had a 24-inch two-bladed wooden screw propeller, operated by hand, that enabled it to travel forward or in reverse at three knots. A crank operated the rudder aft. Water was admitted for descent and forced out with a hand pump for surfacing. Another screw, on the bottom, moved the submarine vertically. On September 7, 1776, Ezra Lee used the craft to attach a torpedo time bomb to the hull of the British flagship, the 64-gun *Eagle,* in New York Harbor. An explosion resulted, but no serious damage occurred, as the bomb had drifted away from the ship.

6962. Navy submarine contract was awarded to the John P. Holland Torpedo Boat Company of New York City by Navy Secretary Hilary Abner Herbert on March 13, 1895. The contractual amount was $150,000. Construction was started at the Columbian Iron Works, Baltimore, MD. The keel was laid on June 20, 1896, and the submarine was launched on August 7, 1897. It was 85 feet 3 inches in length and 11 feet 6 inches in extreme breadth, with a displacement of 168 tons, and was known as the *Plunger.* The project was abandoned and all expenses and advances returned to the government when the contract was canceled in April 1900. A new contract for another submarine was signed on November 7, 1900.

6963. Submarine fitted with an internal combustion engine was the *Argonaut,* invented by Simon Lake and built by the Columbian Iron Works and Dry Dock Company of Baltimore, MD, in 1897. A working model had been built by Lake in 1894. He patented the engine on April 7, 1896, and the submarine vessel on April 20, 1897. The *Argonaut* was also the first submarine to salvage sunken objects of value. On December 16, 1897, a demonstration was given on the Patapsco River during which 22 newspaper reporters made short descents ranging from 1.5 to 4 hours.

6964. Submarine that was practical and submersible was the *Holland No. 9,* built by the John P. Holland Torpedo Boat Company of New York City. Launched on March 17, 1898, it submerged off Staten Island, remaining under water for 1 hour 40 minutes. Its overall length was 53 feet 11 inches and its diameter 10 feet 3 inches. Its equipment included a dynamite gun and one torpedo tube. The vessel was purchased by the Navy on April 11, 1900, for $150,000 (though the actual cost of construction was greater) and was placed in commission on October 12.

6965. Diesel engine in a submarine was the Vickers air-injection type, a four-cycle, four-cylinder, non-airstarting and nonreversing unit. Two of these engines were placed in Submarines E-1 and E-2, built by the New London Ship and Engine Company of Groton, CT, in 1911.

6966. Submarine disaster occurred on March 25, 1915, when the F-4, commanded by Lieutenant Alfred L. Ede, sank with a loss of 21 men while approximately 1.5 miles out of Honolulu Harbor, HI.

6967. Submarine emergency air supply container was an oxygen bag with a canister of soda lime and tubes similar to those of an army gas mask. The invention, known as the submarine escape lung, was the result of the combined efforts of two naval officers, Lieutenant Charles Bowers Momsen and Chief Gunner Clarence Louis Tibbals, and a civilian, Frank M. Hobson, a civil engineer of the Naval Bureau of Construction and Repairs. Momsen and Tibbals tested the device on May 10, 1929, by using it to escape from depths of water as great as 206 feet. They were rewarded with the Distinguished Service Cross. Hobson received a year's pay for his part in the invention. The Navy tested the device under actual conditions in the Thames River at New London, CT, on August 30, 1929, when 26 officers and men successfully escaped from the after hatch of the submerged submarine S-4.

6968. Streamlined submarine was the U.S.S. *Nautilus,* built at the Navy Yard, Mare Island, Vallejo, CA. The keel was laid on May 10, 1927. The ship was launched on March 15, 1930, and commissioned on July 1. Its length was 371 feet, extreme beam 33 feet 3 inches, mean draft 15 feet 9 inches, and displacement 2,730 tons. It carried two six-inch .53-caliber guns and a complement of 88. (A nuclear submarine with the same name was constructed later.)

6969. Submarine escape training tank was placed in operation on August 15, 1930, at the U.S. Submarine Base, New London, CT. It was a cylindrical "water tower" column 100 feet deep, with a spiral stairway winding around it and an abutting elevator shaft. Candidates entered the tank through locks at various depths, wearing the submarine-escape lung, and climbed up a rope, hand over hand, in order to slow down their ascent sufficiently to let their bodies become gradually adjusted to the decrease in pressure.

6970. Submarine to be refloated was the U.S.S *Squalus,* launched at Portsmouth, NH, on September 14, 1938. It foundered in 240 feet of water off Portsmouth on May 23, 1939, with a loss of 26 men. The ship was completely raised after a 113-day job and was towed back to Portsmouth on September 13, 1939. On May 5, 1940, its name was changed to the U.S.S. *Sailfish.*

6971. Submarine with a pressure hull of high-tensile steel was the U.S.S. *Balao,* authorized on December 23, 1941, laid down on June 26, 1942, launched on October 27, 1942, at the Portsmouth Naval Shipyard, Portsmouth, NH, and commissioned on Feburary 4, 1943. The ship was 311 feet 8 inches long, 273 feet 3 inches wide, and had a 2,424-ton displacement. The first commanding officer was Lieutenant Commander Richard H. Crane.

6972. Leaping submarine was the U.S.S. *Pickerel,* laid down on February 8, 1944, at the Boston Naval Shipyard, Boston, MA, and launched on December 15, 1944. The submarine was commissioned at the Portsmouth Shipyard, Portsmouth, NH, on April 4, 1949. It was 311 feet 8 inches long and 27 feet 3 inches wide, with a 2,015-ton displacement. The submarine's first sea trials took place between April 4 and July 25, 1949. The first commanding officer was Commander Paul Richard Schratz. The *Pickerel* surfaced from a depth of 150 feet with a 48-degree up-angle during a routine training exercise off Oahu, HI. Its bow seemed to leap up out of the water. It set a record for underwater travel in 1950 by snorkeling from Hong Kong to Pearl Harbor, Honolulu, HI, a distance of 5,200 miles, in 21 days, from March 16 to April 5.

6973. Nuclear-powered submarine was the *Nautilus,* built by the Electric Boat Company, a division of the General Dynamics Corporation, Groton, CT, under the supervision of Captain Hyman George Rickover. President Harry S. Truman participated in the keel-laying ceremony on June 14, 1952. The submarine, launched on January 21, 1954, on the Thames River at Groton, was commissioned on September 21, 1954, tested under nuclear power on January 17, 1955, and completed on April 22, 1955. Its crew consisted of 11 officers and 85 enlisted men. The first commander was Eugene Parks Wilkinson. The steam turbines were powered by a liquid-cooled atomic reactor. The *Nautilus* was 323.25 feet overall. Its displacement was 2,975 tons light, 3,200 tons standard, and 3,747 tons submerged. It is now a national landmark, permanently berthed at Groton.

SHIPS AND BOATS—SUBMARINES—continued

6974. Submarine to remain submerged for two weeks was the nuclear submarine *Nautilus,* which left Groton, CT, on August 19, 1957, to participate in NATO exercises in the North Atlantic under Commander William Robert Anderson. It remained under water for 14 days 3.5 hours, traveling 5,007 miles to a location within 180 miles of the North Pole (latitude 87 degrees). It then spent five days submerged under the Arctic ice pack, where it traveled 1,000 miles. The maneuvers ended on September 24, 1957, and the *Nautilus* returned to Groton on October 28.

6975. Submarine expressly designed and built to fire guided missiles was the U.S.S. *Grayback,* ordered on June 19, 1952, laid down on July 1, 1954, launched on July 2, 1957, and commissioned on March 7, 1958, at Mare Island, CA. The *Grayback,* designed to fire Regulus I and Regulus II missiles, carried a crew of 85 officers and men. It was 322.5 feet long and had a displacement of 1,740 tons light, 2,287 tons surface, and 3,638 tons submerged.

6976. Submarine equipped with ballistic missiles was the nuclear-powered *George Washington,* laid down on November 7, 1957, launched on June 9, 1959, and commissioned on December 30, 1959, at Groton, CT, on the Thames River. The cost of construction was approximately $110 million. The first commander was James Butler Osborn. The submarine was 380 feet long and had a displacement of 5,400 tons light, 5,600 tons standard, and 6,700 tons submerged. It went on patrol duty on November 15, 1960, from Charleston, SC, and returned on January 21, 1961, having traveled 67 days underwater. It was equipped with 16 vertical Polaris missile tubes that were fired below the surface.

6977. Submarine to have two complete crews was the U.S.S. *George Washington,* a nuclear submarine that was commissioned on December 30, 1959. The blue crew, under Commander James Butler Osborn, reported at Groton, CT, in June 1959; the gold crew, under Commander John Lawrence From, Jr., reported in September 1959. While one crew was at sea operating the submarine, the other was ashore for recreation and refresher training. The two-crew system enabled the submarine to remain on station for extended periods of time.

6978. Nuclear-powered submarine with turbine-electric drive was the *Tullibee,* 273 feet long, with a displacement of 2,000 tons light and 2,175 tons submerged, whose keel was laid on May 26, 1958. It was launched on April 27, 1960, at the Thames River plant of the General Dynamics Corporation's Electric Boat Company division at Groton, CT. The commanding officer was Commander Richard Edmund Jortberg. The vessel was commissioned at Groton on November 9, 1960. It carried a crew of 60 men and 6 officers. All other submarines utilized reduction gears. The torpedo tubes of the *Tullibee* were located amidships rather than in the bow. The *Tullibee* was also the first submarine equipped with closed-circuit television.

SHIPS AND BOATS—VOYAGES

6979. Transatlantic crossing by an American steamboat was made by the *Savannah,* a 350-ton full-rigged wooden boat designed by Daniel Dod of Elizabeth, NJ. It was built at Corlear's Hook, NY, at the shipyards of Crocker and Fickett, and was launched on August 22, 1818. It had one inclined direct-acting low-pressure engine of 90 horsepower. The trial trip from New York City to Savannah, GA, was made on March 28, 1819. The *Savannah* sailed on May 22, 1819, from Savannah, GA, and arrived at Liverpool, England, on June 20. Steam power was used for only 80 hours during the trip. Moses Rogers was the captain and Steven Rogers the first officer. The ship had 32 staterooms, but no passengers dared to make the trip.

6980. Circumnavigation of the globe by a warship was done by the three-masted U.S.S. *Vincennes,* a 16-gun sloop of war of 700 tons burden, which left New York City on August 31, 1826, under the command of Commander William Bolton Finch (afterward known as William Compton Bolton). It sailed to the Pacific by way of Cape Horn and returned in 1829 by way of the Cape of Good Hope, arriving at New York on June 8, 1830. The ship was 127 feet long and had a beam of 34 feet.

6981. Naval vessel to sail around the Cape of Good Hope to the west coast of the United States was the *Constellation,* which left Boston, MA, in December 1840. Stopping first at Rio de Janeiro, it proceeded to the Cape of Good Hope and thence to China. On the return voyage, it anchored in Monterey Bay, CA, on September 15, 1843.

6982. Circumnavigation of the world by a yacht was accomplished by the *North Star*, about 2,000 tons, owned by Cornelius Vanderbilt, which started its first voyage on May 21, 1853, from New York City. It went on the rocks at Corlears Hook and returned to drydock for minor repairs, after which the trip was resumed. The ship made stops at Southampton, Copenhagen, Le Havre, Malaga, Leghorn, and Rome. It was not allowed to moor at Naples because the authorities did not believe it possible for a single individual to own the ship and feared a sinister design. Further stops were made at Malta, Constantinople, Gibraltar, Tangier, and Madeira. The *North Star* returned to New York City on September 23, 1853, after a trip of more than 15,000 miles. Asa Eldridge was the captain. The only untoward incident on the voyage was the death of the quartermaster, who was accidently knocked overboard and drowned.

6983. World tour by a woman traveling alone was made by the reporter Elizabeth Cochrane, better known as Nellie Bly, who made the tour in 1889–90 as a stunt for the *New York World*, trying to beat the record set by the hero of Jules Verne's novel *Around the World in Eighty Days*. She left New York City on November 14, 1889, sailing from Hoboken, NJ, on the *Augusta Victoria* for Southampton, England, and continued traveling eastward on a variety of conveyances, including boats, rickshaws, and mules. The *World* published daily reports on her progress. Bly returned to New York with much fanfare on January 25, 1890, on a chartered express train. The tour took 72 days 6 hours 11 minutes 14 seconds, of which 56 days 12 hours 41 minutes were spent in actual travel.

6984. Round-the-world solo sailing journey was accomplished by Captain Joshua Slocum, who sailed from Boston, MA, on April 24, 1895, in a little sloop called *The Spray*. It was 36 feet 9 inches long, 14 feet 2 inches wide, and 4 feet 2 inches deep. Its tonnage was nine tons net and its cost was $554. The round trip of 46,000 miles was completed on July 3, 1898, when Captain Slocum sailed into the harbor at Fairhaven, MA, where the ship had been built.

6985. Transatlantic trip by rowboat was accomplished by George Harbo and Frank Samuelson, who left Battery Park, New York City, on June 6, 1896, in a cedar boat 5 feet wide and 18 feet 4 inches long, with air tanks at both ends. It had oak timbers but no masts or sails. Provisions consisted of 60 gallons of water, 100 pounds of bread and canned meat, 6 gallons of oil, 2 gallons of signal oil, and one dozen night signals. Harbo and Samuelson arrived at St. Mary's, the Scilly Isles, off southwest England, on August 1, where they made a two-day stopover. They reached Le Havre, France, on August 7, ending a 3,250-mile voyage.

6986. Circumnavigation of the globe by a fleet of warships began on December 16, 1907, at Hampton Roads, VA, under the command of Rear Admiral Robley Dunglison Evans, who relinquished his command on May 9, 1908, to Rear Admiral Charles Stillman Sperry. The fleet left San Francisco, CA, on July 7, 1908, and returned to Hampton Roads on February 22, 1909, stopping at Honolulu, Auckland, Sydney, Melbourne, Manila, Yokohama, Amoy, Colombo, Suez, and Gibraltar en route. The fleet was made up of the *Connecticut, Vermont, Kansas, Minnesota, Georgia, Nebraska, New Jersey, Rhode Island, Louisiana, Virginia, Missouri, Ohio, Wisconsin, Illinois, Kentucky, Kearsarge*, and several auxiliary vessels.

6987. Battleship to visit an inland city was the U.S.S. *Mississippi* (length, 375 feet; draft, 24.8 feet; extreme breadth, 77 feet; displacement, 13,000 tons), which sailed 300 miles up the Mississippi River to Natchez, MS, on May 20, 1909, and departed for New Orleans on May 24, 1909. It was built by William Cramp and Sons, Philadelphia, PA, and was placed in service on February 1, 1908.

6988. Transatlantic crossing by a submarine under its own power was made by the *E-1*, which was laid down on December 22, 1909 and launched on May 27, 1911, at the Fore River Shipbuilding Company, Quincy, MA. It was commissioned on February 14, 1912, and its first commander was Lieutenant Chester William Nimitz. The ship left Newport, RI, on December 4, 1917, for Ponta Delgada, the Azores, where it was ordered to protect the islands from German attack by submarines. It returned to New London, CT, on September 17, 1918. It was 135 feet 3 inches long and displaced 342 tons.

6989. Circumnavigation of the world by a cruise ship was accomplished by the Cunard liner *Laconia*, which left New York City on November 21, 1922, with 440 passengers and returned on March 30, 1923, after a 130-day cruise.

SHIPS AND BOATS—VOYAGES—*continued*

6990. Transatlantic solo boat journey by a woman was made by Ann Davidson in a 23-foot sailboat, the *Felicity Ann,* which left Plymouth, England, on May 18, 1952, and arrived at Miami, FL, on August 12, 1953. Davidson made stops en route at Douarnenez, France; Vigo, Spain; Gilbraltar; and Dominica, Antigua, Nevis, St. Thomas, and Nassau, British West Indies.

6991. Circumnavigation of the world by a submarine was made by the *Gudgeon,* which sailed from Pearl Harbor, HI, on July 8, 1957, visited Asian, African, and European ports, and returned to Hawaii on February 21, 1958. It traveled approximately 25,000 miles in 228 days. The *Gudgeon* was 269 feet 2 inches long, had a complement of 83 and a 2,050-ton displacement, and was launched on June 11, 1952, at the Portsmouth Naval Shipyard, Portsmouth, NH. It was commissioned on November 21, 1952.

6992. Circumnavigation of the North American continent by a ship was achieved by the Coast Guard cutter *Spar,* of the Military Sea Transport Service task unit, based at Bristol, RI. In 1957 the cutter sailed to Seattle, WA, where it was joined by the *Bramble* and the *Storis,* all of which completed the Northwest Passage on September 7, 1957. They followed the *Labrador,* a Canadian ice-patrol ship that cleared Bellot Strait, the keystone of the Northwest Passage.

6993. Crossing of the North Pole underwater by a submerged submarine was accomplished on August 3, 1958, by the nuclear-powered submarine *Nautilus* under the command of Commander William Robert Anderson. The submarine carried 116 persons, including 14 officers, 98 crewmen, and 4 civilian scientists. It left Pearl Harbor, HI, on July 23, 1958, crossed the Pacific Ocean through the Bering Strait, surfaced, and went under the ice cap at Point Barrow, Alaska, on August 1, 1958, at 11:15 P.M. E.D.T. Traveling 1,830 miles under the ice in 96 hours, it arrived under the North Pole on August 3. The *Nautilus* then continued its voyage, reaching Iceland on August 7. The expedition was designated "Northwest Passage."

6994. Submarine to travel under the North Pole from the east was the U.S.S. *Skate,* built by the Electric Boat Division of the General Dynamics Corporation. The *Skate* took off from New London, CT, on July 30, 1958, under Commander James Francis Calvert of Cleveland, OH, with a crew of 10 officers, 9 scientists and technicians, and 87 enlisted men. It passed between Iceland and Greenland and sent the following message on August 12, 1958: "North Geographic Pole August eleventh—now in Polynya—about forty miles from pole—all well." The submarine logged a total of 12,000 miles, including 10,100 miles submerged. The voyage ended at Boston, MA, on September 22, 1958.

6995. Submarine to surface at the North Pole was the U.S.S. *Skate,* which left New London, CT, on March 4, 1959, traveled under the Arctic ice, and surfaced at the Pole on March 17.

6996. Circumnavigation of the earth by a submerged submarine was accomplished by the U.S.S. *Triton,* which left New London, CT, on February 16, 1960, crossed the equator on February 24, and completed the submerged circumnavigation on April 25, having traveled 41,500 miles in 84 days. It returned to New London on May 11. The hull of the submarine was submerged during the entire trip, but the upper portion broached the surface twice. The nuclear-powered *Triton* was 447 feet long and had a 37-foot beam. Its displacement was 5,650 tons light, 5,900 tons standard, and 7,750 tons submerged. It carried a crew of 13 officers and 135 men and was commanded by Captain Edward Latimer Beach. The *Triton* was laid down on May 21, 1956, launched on August 19, 1958, and commissioned on November 10, 1959.

6997. Submarine to make a submerged passage through the Northwest Passage from the Atlantic to the Pacific by way of the North Pole was the *Seadragon,* commanded by George P. Steele II which sailed from Portsmouth, NH, on August 1, 1960, cleared the ice pack on September 3, and docked at Pearl Harbor, HI, on September 14.

6998. Transatlantic solo trip by rowboat was made by John Fairfax, who left Las Palmas in the Canary Islands, off the coast of Morocco, in the *Britannia,* a 22-foot rowboat, on January 20, 1969. He was swept down to the Cape Verde Islands, crossed the Atlantic, and landed in the surf at Hollywood, FL, at 1:48 P.M. on July 19, after a 180-day voyage.

6999. Transpacific sailboat crossing by a woman was made by Sharon Sites Adams, who sailed from Yokohama, Japan, on May 12, 1969, in a 31-foot fiberglass ketch, the *Sea Sharp.* She arrived at San Diego, CA, on July 25, having covered a distance of approximately 5,620 miles in 74 days 17 hours 15 minutes.

7000. Commercial ship to conquer the Northwest Passage was the ice-breaking oil tanker *Manhattan,* which left Chester, PA, on August 24, 1969, and made a round-trip journey from Halifax, Nova Scotia, between August 29 and November 8, passing through the Prince of Wales Strait to the Amundsen Gulf in the Beaufort Sea on September 14. The captain was Roger Steward. The ship was chartered from Seatrain Lines by the Humble Oil and Refining Company.

7001. Ship to pass both ways through the Northwest Passage was the Coast Guard icebreaker *Northwind,* an escort icebreaker that accompanied the oil tanker *Manhattan* in 1969. Built by the Western Pipe and Steel Company, San Pedro, CA, the icebreaker had been launched on February 25, 1945. It was 250 feet long, with a full load displacement of 6,515 tons.

7002. Round-the-world solo sailing trip by an African-American was achieved by marketing executive and Coast Guard captain William Pinkney in the cutter *Commitment.* The 22-month voyage, across a distance of 32,000 nautical miles, began in Boston, MA, on August 5, 1990. Pinkney sailed south past the coast of South America, across the Atlantic Ocean to Capetown, South Africa, and on to the Australian island of Tasmania. After a nine-month break, he sailed around Cape Horn and back up the coast of South America. The *Commitment* was equipped with a satellite computer system and a shortwave radio that allowed 20,000 schoolchildren in Boston and Chicago to followed Pinkney's progress.

SOUND RECORDING

7003. Compact disc players were introduced in the United States in 1983. They were manufactured by the Japanese firm Sony using technology pioneered in 1979 by the Dutch firm Philips. To make CD recordings, sounds were digitally rendered on magnetic tape as electronic signals in binary form. These signals were encoded as microscopic pits in the reflective surface of a five-inch disc made from plastic and aluminum. The sound was played back by focusing a laser beam on the spinning disc. When the beam encountered the pits, it was reflected back at an angle to a detector that converted it into an analog signal for output to a hi-fi stereo system.

SOUND RECORDING—PHONOGRAPHS

7004. Phonograph was invented by Thomas Alva Edison of Menlo Park, NJ, who secured a patent on February 19, 1878, on a "phonograph or speaking machine." His original idea had been to invent a telegraph repeater, and he had given construction directions to one of his mechanics, John Kreusi, on August 12, 1877. The first cylinder, operated by a hand crank, was wrapped in tin foil, with which two needles fastened to diaphragms made contact. The first verse recorded on the new instrument was "Mary Had a Little Lamb." A clock spring motor and waxlike record were invented some 10 years later.

7005. Phonograph that was practical was the Graphophone, manufactured by the firm of Bell and Tainter, Washington, DC. On May 4, 1886, Chichester Bell and Charles Sumner Tainter received a patent "for recording and reproducing speech and other sounds." Patents on "reproducing sounds from phonograph records" and on "transmitting and recording sounds by radiant energy" were also received on May 4, 1886, jointly with Alexander Graham Bell.

7006. Phonograph record of the modern disk type was invented by Emile Berliner of Washington, DC, and first publicly demonstrated before the Franklin Institute in Philadelpha, PA, on May 16, 1888. Berliner's "Gramophone" record was a flat disk in which the grooves were cut in a lateral spiral, making it much easier to duplicate for the mass market than Edison's recording cylinder.

7007. Jukebox was a coin-operated phonograph player installed in the Palais Royale, San Francisco, CA, on November 23, 1889, by Louis Glas. The first widely successful jukebox manufacturer was the Rudolph Wurlitzer Company of North Tonawanda, NY. The company's most popular model was the Wurlitzer Model 1015, designed in 1946 by Paul Fuller. Among its novel features were curved plastic tubes containing a fluid with a low boiling point. Small heaters kept the fluid bubbling. Wurlitzer sold 56,246 of the Model 1015 at $750 each.

7008. Phonograph record of a stage performance by the original cast was a 10-inch single-face disc record of "Old Folks at Home" ("Swanee River"), sung in Act I of the spectacular military operetta *When Johnny Comes Marching Home,* which was recorded in 1904 and released by the Victor Talking Machine Company, Camden, NJ. The libretto was by Stanislaus Stange, the music by Julian Edwards, and the production by the Whitney Opera Company.

SOUND RECORDING—PHONOGRAPHS
—*continued*

7009. Phonograph with an enclosed horn in the cabinet was the Victor Victrola, first manufactured on August 22, 1906, by the Victor Talking Machine Company, Camden, NJ. It was sold in a mahogany cabinet 4 feet high, 20 inches wide, and 22 inches deep, and cost $200.

7010. Phonograph with an automatic record changer was introduced by the Victor Talking Machine Company, Camden, NJ, in March 1927. It played twelve 10-inch or 12-inch records and stopped automatically after the last record had been played.

7011. Instantaneous phonograph recording was made on October 22, 1934, during a balloon flight made by Professor Jean Picard and his wife. They took off from Ford Airport, Detroit, MI, at 6:58 A.M. and made an eight-hour flight, two hours of which were spent in the stratosphere. The balloon crossed Lake Erie and landed in a treetop at Cadiz, OH.

7012. Long-playing microgroove phonograph records that were successfully manufactured were made by Columbia Records, Bridgeport, CT, a division of the Columbia Broadcasting System, and introduced to the public on June 21, 1948, at the Waldorf-Astoria Hotel, New York City. CBS engineer Peter Goldmark was the inventor of the nonbreakable Vinylite plastic disks, which played at a speed of 33.3 revolutions per minute. One side of a 12-inch "LP" played for 23 minutes, compared to 4 minutes for one side of a standard 78-r.p.m. record; 78s were quickly supplanted by the new technology.

SOUND RECORDING—TAPE RECORDERS

7013. Tape recorders imported into the United States were two Magnetophon recorders that were transported from Occupied Germany in 1945 and rebuilt by an American engineer, John Mullin. They arrived with 50 reels of BASF Luvitherm tape (plastic tape coated with magnetite). Although wire recording was well known in the United States, audio tape-recording technology had not yet been used in any commercial sound-recording equipment. The Magnetophon ran at 30 inches per second and had a frequency response of up to 15 KHz.

7014. Tape recorder built in the United States for commercial use was the Model 200, developed by the Ampex Corporation, Redwood City, CA, in 1948. The Model 200 was invented to make pre-recordings of Bing Crosby's national radio series of 1947–48. The first American-made audio tape was Scotch 111, developed by the 3M Corporation, St. Paul, MN, for use with the Ampex recorder.

7015. Tape-recording machine for mass production of tapes was announced on January 26, 1949, by the Minnesota Mining and Manufacturing Company (3M), St. Paul, MN. The machine taped 48 hours of recorded music in one hour.

7016. Cassette audio tape recorder was the CarryCorder 150, sold in the United States beginning in 1965 by Norelco, the North American division of the Philips Company, a Dutch consumer-products manufacturer. It was battery-powered and was the first machine to use the quarter-inch tape cassette format that later became standard in the consumer audio industry.

SPACE

7017. Rocket flight using liquid fuel was made on March 16, 1926, at Auburn, MA, under the direction of Professor Robert Hutchins Goddard. Pressure was produced internally by an outside pressure tank, and after launching by an alcohol heater on the rocket. The rocket traversed 184 feet in 2.5 seconds, moving along the trajectory at about 60 miles an hour. The flight was reported to the Smithsonian Institution on May 5, 1926. As early as 1920, Goddard, working under a grant from Clark University, Worcester, MA, had demonstrated the lifting force of rockets using liquid oxygen and ether.

7018. Rocket to break the sound barrier was Rocket No. 4, flown on September 9, 1934, at Marine Park, Staten Island, New York City, by the American Rocket Society. It climbed 400 feet and traveled 1,600 feet horizontally, reaching a speed of 700 miles per hour.

7019. Rocket to attain a 100-mile altitude was a captured German V-2 rocket, fired on July 30, 1946, from the White Sands Proving Ground, NM. It descended 69 miles north of the launching platform, having attained an altitude of 104 miles.

7020. Rocket to reach outer space was a two-stage rocket consisting of a Wac Corporal set in the nose of a captured German V-2. It was fired on February 24, 1949, from the White Sands Proving Ground, NM, by a team of scientists under Dr. Wernher von Braun. It reached an altitude of 250 miles.

7021. Rocket-driven sled on rails was tested on March 19, 1954, by Air Force Lieutenant Colonel John Paul Stapp, chief of the Aero Medical Field Laboratory of the Holloman Air Development Center at the Holloman Air Force Base, Alamogordo, NM. It was known as the "abrupt deceleration vehicle." It was designed by Northrop Aircraft to determine the effect upon fliers of bailing out at very high altitudes at supersonic speeds. The sled was propelled by six rockets at 421 miles per hour, which was eventually increased to over 3,000 miles per hour. It moved along heavy rails mounted in concrete and was halted by water scooped in vents in the bottom of the sled. The water trough was 5 feet wide and 18 inches deep.

7022. Space cabin simulator was a hermetically sealed cabin with equipment that supplied oxygen, removed waste products by chemical means, and recirculated body moisture to cool the cabin's temperature. It was used at the Air Force School of Aviation Medicine at Randolph Air Force Base, TX. The cabin simulated the conditions that an astronaut would meet in the sealed cabin of a rocket ship in space. The first person to spend 24 hours in the cabin, living in outer-space conditions, was Dalton F. Smith of New Orleans, LA, an aeromedical technician, who was observed through glass ports from 3 P.M. on March 31, 1956, to 3 P.M. on April 1.

7023. Animals to survive a space flight were Able and Baker, two one-pound female monkeys, one a rhesus, the other a spider monkey, who survived a 15-minute flight in separate containers in the nose cone of a Jupiter rocket launched on May 28, 1959, from Cape Canaveral, FL. The cone was shot 300 miles into space and was recovered about 90 minutes later off the island of Antigua, about 1,500 miles away, by Navy frogmen from the tug *Kiowa*. A previous attempt made on December 13, 1958, had been unsuccessful.

7024. Animal fired into space to orbit the earth was Enos, a 37.5-pound five-year-old male chimpanzee, sent aloft at 1:28 P.M. on November 29, 1961, from Cape Canaveral, FL, in a capsule atop a Mercury–Atlas 5 rocket. The satellite orbited the earth twice at a speed of 17,500 miles per hour in a flight lasting 3

hours 21 minutes. It landed in the ocean near Puerto Rico and was recovered by the U.S.S. *Stormes*. The first animal from any country launched into space was Laika, a dog carried by the Soviet satellite *Sputnik II* in 1957.

7025. Rocket with an electrostatic (ion) engine to produce thrust in space was SERT 1 (Space Electric Rocket Test), 375 pounds, launched on July 20, 1964, from Wallops Island, VA. The rocket climbed 2,500 miles, had a 48-minute suborbital flight, and fell to earth 2,000 miles away from the launch site. The mercury-propelled engine performed in space for 16 minutes, generating 0.0055 pounds of thrust.

7026. Sport played on the moon was golf. On January 31, 1971, astronaut Alan Bartlett Shepard, Jr., commander of *Apollo 14*, used a six-iron to hit a golf ball on the moon. In the low lunar gravity, the ball kept going until it was far out of sight.

7027. Scientific evidence for life on Mars was announced by Daniel Goldin, administrator of the National Aeronautics and Space Administration, on August 6, 1996. The discovery was made by Dr. Roberta Score and a team of American scientists. Using electron microscopes, they examined a 4.5-billion-year-old Martian meteorite that struck Antarctica 13,000 years ago and found fossils of what appeared to be "a primitive form of microscopic life."

SPACE—ASTRONAUTS

7028. Astronauts trained by the United States were chosen by the National Aeronautics and Space Administration for the first manned space program, Project Mercury. They were Air Force Captains Leroy Gordon Cooper of Carbondale, CO, Virgil Ivan Grissom of Mitchell, IN, and Donald Kent Slayton of Sparta, WI; Navy Lieutenants Malcolm Scott Carpenter of Boulder, CO, and Walter Marty Schirra, Jr., of Hackensack, NJ; Navy Lieutenant Commander Alan Bartlett Shepard, Jr., of East Derry, NH; and Lieutenant Colonel of Marines John Herschel Glenn, Jr., of New Concord, OH. The selection of the seven men was announced on April 7, 1959. The group trained at the Langley Research Center, Hampton, VA.

7029. Astronaut to be launched into space was Commander Alan Bartlett Shepard, Jr. His capsule, *Freedom 7*, launched on May 5, 1961, by a Mercury–Redstone 3 rocket from Cape Canaveral, FL, reached a height of 1,165 miles. The capsule, weighing slightly more than 2,000 pounds, made a 302-mile trip at a ground speed of 4,500 miles per hour; it reached an altitude

SPACE—ASTRONAUTS—*continued*

of 115 miles before reentering the earth's atmosphere. Shepard experienced a 5-minute period of weightlessness. The first human to fly in space was the Russian cosmonaut Yury Gagarin, who was launched into orbit on April 12, 1961.

7030. Astronaut to orbit the earth was Lieutenant Colonel John Herschel Glenn, Jr., of New Concord, OH, who was blasted off at 9:48 A.M. on February 20, 1962, from Cape Canaveral, FL, in an Atlas D rocket 93 feet high. The bell-shaped capsule traveled around the earth three times, covering 83,450 miles at an average speed of 17,400 miles per hour. The capsule came down at 2:43 P.M. in the Atlantic Ocean. Two Soviet cosmonauts had orbited the earth previously.

7031. Astronaut to walk in space was Major Edward Higgins White II, who opened the hatch of *Gemini 4* at 3:42 P.M. on June 3, 1965, stepped out into space at a 120-mile altitude at 3:45 P.M., and remained outside for 20 minutes, until 4:05 P.M., attached to the craft by a 25-foot tether. A hand-held 7.5-pound oxygen jet propulsion gun operated by pressure on a trigger gave him control over his movements. Command pilot Major James Alton McDivitt remained inside *Gemini 4*. The spacecraft was launched on June 3, 1965, at 11:16 A.M. from Cape Canaveral, FL, made 62 revolutions in a flight lasting 97 hours and 56 minutes, and touched down on June 7 at 1:14 P.M. in the Atlantic Ocean. The first human to walk in space was cosmonaut Aleksei A. Leonov, who stepped out of his *Voskhod 2* spacecraft on March 18, 1965.

7032. Astronaut to orbit the earth on two trips was Lieutenant Colonel Leroy Gordon Cooper, whose first trip was made from Cape Canaveral, FL, on May 15–16, 1963, in *Faith 7*, when he made 22 orbits in 34 hours 19 minutes 45 seconds. His second flight was made on August 21–29, 1965, when he and Lieutenant Commander Charles Conrad, Jr., made a two-man spaceflight of 120 orbits in 190 hours 55 minutes 14 seconds in *Gemini 5*.

7033. Astronaut to converse with an aquanaut while each performed in his respective field was Lieutenant Colonel Leroy Gordon Cooper, who spoke from spacecraft *Gemini 5* 100 miles above the earth on August 29, 1965, on its 117th orbit. He spoke by radio to Commander Malcolm Scott Carpenter, who was in *Sealab 2*, a 12-by-58-foot steel capsule resting 205 feet beneath the surface of the Pacific Ocean, about 1,000 yards off La Jolla, CA.

7034. Astronauts to rendezvous in space with another spacecraft were Captain Walter Marty Schirra, Jr., and Major Thomas Patten Stafford, who took off on December 15, 1965, at 8:43 A.M. from Cape Canaveral, FL, in *Gemini 6* to meet *Gemini 7*, which was orbiting the earth with Major Frank Borman and Lieutenant Commander James Arthur Lovell, Jr., aboard. The two *Gemini* spacecraft flew in formation within 20 to 100 feet of each other for 5 hours 16 minutes, during which the astronauts photographed each others' crafts, sighted a fire in Madagascar, and conversed. *Gemini 6* reentered the atmosphere and landed in the Atlantic Ocean on December 16 after 25 hours 52 minutes and 16 revolutions.

7035. Astronaut who was a civilian to orbit the earth was Neil Alden Armstrong, who orbited for 10 hours 42 minutes in *Gemini 8*, accompanied by Major David Randolph Scott. The spacecraft was launched at 9 A.M. on March 16, 1966, from Cape Canaveral, FL, achieved the world's first docking in space, and splashed down on March 17.

7036. Astronauts to die in a spacecraft were Lieutenant Colonel Virgil Ivan Grissom, Lieutenant Colonel Edward Higgins White II, and Lieutenant Commander Roger Bruce Chaffee, who died on January 27, 1967, when a flash fire caused by electrical arcing erupted inside the *Apollo 1* spacecraft command module on the ground at the Kennedy Space Center, Cape Canaveral, FL. The astronauts had been participating in a simulation of the *Apollo 1* flight scheduled for February 21.

7037. Astronaut international rescue agreement was the Agreement on the Rescue of Astronauts, the Return of Astronauts and the Return of Objects Launched into Outer Space, signed by Dean Rusk, secretary of state, at a ceremony held on April 22, 1968, and ratified by the Senate on October 8 by a vote of 66 to 0. President Lyndon Baines Johnson announced on December 3, 1968, that it was in force. The signatories were the United States, the United Kingdom, and the Union of Soviet Socialist Republics.

7038. Astronauts to orbit the moon were Colonel Frank Borman, Captain James Arthur Lovell, Jr., and Major William Alison Anders, who made 10 lunar orbits in *Apollo 7*, launched by a three-stage Saturn 5 rocket from Cape Canaveral, FL, at 7:51 A.M. on December 21, 1968. The spacecraft reentered the atmosphere and splashed down in the Pacific Ocean 147 hours 11 seconds later.

7039. Astronauts to transfer from one spacecraft to another while in orbit were Russell Louis Schweickart and Colonel James Alton McDivitt, who made an intravehicular transfer from *Gumdrop*, the *Apollo 9* command ship, to *Spider*, the lunar module, on March 6, 1969, leaving the pilot, Colonel David Randolph Scott, in the command ship. A Saturn 5 rocket launched the satellite at 11 A.M. on March 3, 1969, from Cape Canaveral, FL. It redocked at 2 P.M. It made a 10-day orbit (241 hours 40 minutes 53 seconds) and landed on March 13 in the Atlantic Ocean, 250 miles east southeast of Bermuda.

7040. Astronauts to land on the moon were Neil Alden Armstrong and Lieutenant Colonel Edwin E. "Buzz" Aldrin, Jr., the first human beings to set foot on land beyond the earth. Together with Lieutenant Colonel Michael Collins, they were lifted off in *Apollo 11* at 9:32 A.M. by a Saturn 5 rocket on July 16, 1969, from Kennedy Space Center, Cape Canaveral, FL, with Armstrong as flight commander. The flight reached the moon on Sunday, July 20. Collins remained in orbit as pilot of the command module *Columbia* while the other two, with Aldrin as pilot, descended to the surface of the moon in the lunar module *Eagle*. At 4:17:42 P.M. E.D.T. the *Eagle* touched down on the moon's Sea of Tranquility. At 10:56 P.M. Armstrong came down the ladder, placed his foot on the moon, and said: "That's one small step for a man, one giant leap for mankind." He was joined on the lunar surface by Aldrin at 11:14 P.M. They placed a plaque on the moon and erected an 8-foot aluminum staff with a 3-by-5-foot nylon United States flag. They also set up scientific instruments, collected rocks, and took photographs. At 1:34 P.M. on July 21 the *Eagle* lifted off the lunar surface to rejoin the mother ship. The *Columbia* splashed down at 12:50 P.M. E.D.T. on July 24 in the Pacific Ocean, about 920 miles southwest of Hawaii. The astronauts were taken on board the U.S.S. *Hornet* at 2:12 P.M. and entered a mobile quarantine facility, where they remained until August 11.

7041. Astronauts to retrieve a manmade object from the moon were Commanders Charles Conrad, Jr., mission leader, and Alan La Vern Bean, lunar landing module pilot, who on November 19, 1969, recovered a piece of the unmanned spacecraft *Surveyor 3*, which had landed on the Ocean of Storms of the Moon on April 19, 1967. They were two of the three astronauts on *Apollo 12*, which was launched by a Saturn 5 rocket from Cape Canaveral, FL, at 11:22 A.M. on November 14, 1969. While Commander Richard Francis Gordon, Jr., remained in orbit to pilot the command module, Conrad and Bean descended to the moon's surface in the lunar module *Intrepid* and remained there for one day, the second time that human beings landed on the moon. Splashdown took place on November 24, 1969, 400 miles from Samoa, after a flight of 244 hours 36 minutes 25 seconds.

7042. Astronauts to ride a vehicle on the moon were Colonel David Randolph Scott and Lieutenant Colonel James Benson Irwin, who on July 31, 1971, rode the four-wheeled electric cart Rover, an LRV (Lunar Roving Vehicle), alongside the 1,200-foot-deep canyon Hadley Hills on the moon. With Major Alfred Merrill Worden, they were launched on July 26, 1971, at 9:34 A.M. from Cape Canaveral, FL, in *Apollo 15* and landed on August 7, 1971.

7043. Astronaut to become an admiral was Alan Bartlett Shepard, Jr., of the Navy, the first American astronaut to be launched into space, whose date of rank was December 1, 1971.

7044. Astronaut to become a general was Colonel James Alton McDivitt of the Air Force, who was nominated on December 12, 1970, by President Richard Milhous Nixon and promoted to the temporary grade of brigadier general effective March 1, 1972, with date of rank on February 17, 1972. McDivitt was commander of the *Apollo 9* flight, March 3–13, 1969.

7045. Physician to practice as an astronaut in space was Navy Commander Dr. Joseph Peter Kerwin, who flew aboard *Skylab 2*, which took off from Cape Canaveral, FL, on May 25, 1973, and splashed down on June 22 in the Pacific Ocean. The duration of the flight was 28 days 49 minutes 49 seconds. Kerwin made daily routine medical tests on his fellow astronauts, Charles Conrad, Jr., and Paul Weitz.

7046. Astronauts to participate in an international spaceflight were Thomas Patten Stafford, mission commander, Donald Kent Slayton, pilot of the docking module, and Vance Devoe Brand, pilot of the command module, who participated in the joint Soviet-American Apollo-Soyuz Test Project. They took off from Cape Canaveral, FL on July 15, 1975, and returned on July 24, traveling 217 hours 28 minutes 24 seconds. Their craft, *Apollo 18*, docked with the Soviet spacecraft *Soyuz 19*, manned by Aleksei Arkhipovich Leonov and Valery Nikolayevich Kubasov, on July 17.

SPACE—ASTRONAUTS—*continued*

7047. Astronauts who were women were selected by the National Aeronautics and Space Administration in 1977 and announced on January 16, 1978. They were Anna L. Fisher of Rancho Palos Verdes, CA; Shannon W. Lucid of Oklahoma City, OK; Judith A. Resnik of Akron, OH; Sally K. Ride of Stanford, CA; Margaret R. Seddon of Memphis, TN; and Kathryn D. Sullivan of Paterson, NJ. They were chosen from 3,000 applicants.

7048. Astronaut who was a woman to fly in space was Dr. Sally K. Ride of Stanford, CA, who served as a crew member aboard Space Shuttle *Challenger* when it was launched on June 18, 1983. Ride trained as an astrophysicist and in 1978 joined NASA, where she helped design the robot arm for the space shuttle. She retired from the astronaut corps in 1987. Valentina V. Tereshkova of the Soviet Union, who crewed Vostok 6 on June 16, 1963, was the first woman from any country to fly in space. The first astronaut who was a mother was Dr. Anna L. Fisher, a member of the crew of Space Shuttle *Discovery* mission that lifted off on November 16, 1984, from Cape Canaveral, FL. She participated in the world's first satellite retrieval and repair operation. The first spacewalk by a female astronaut took place on October 11, 1984, when Kathryn D. Sullivan exited Space Shuttle *Challenger* on a tether and flew in space for 3.5 hours.

7049. Astronaut to fly in space who was African-American was Air Force Lieutenant Colonel Guion Bluford, a mission specialist on the third flight of Space Shuttle *Challenger*, launched on August 30, 1983, from Cape Canaveral, FL. The main activity of the mission was to deploy a communications satellite built for India. The first African-American woman to fly in space was Dr. Mae Carol Jemison, a physician who also held degrees in chemical engineering and African-American studies. Jemison, who left private practice to join NASA in 1987, made her first space flight on September 12, 1992, as a payload mission specialist on Space Shuttle *Endeavor*. She performed experiments on space motion sickness and bone cell loss in the space environment.

7050. Astronauts to fly free in space were Navy Captain Bruce McCandless and Army Lieutenant Colonel Robert Stewart. On February 7, 1984, while in orbit over the earth, McCandless exited Space Shuttle *Challenger* and maneuvered freely, without a tether, using a rocket pack of his own design. Stewart also used the rocket pack to fly untethered later that day.

7051. Senator to fly in space was Jake Garn, Republican senator from Utah, who joined the crew of Space Shuttle *Discovery* as a "congressional observer" when the shuttle lifted off from Cape Canaveral, FL, on April 12, 1985. A former Navy pilot, Garn had taken several months of astronaut training. Another senator, John Herschel Glenn, Jr., of Ohio, was an astronaut in the 1960s, before he entered politics.

7052. Husband and wife to fly in space together were Mission Specialist N. Jan Davis, an engineer, and Air Force Lieutenant Colonel Mark C. Lee, who served as crew members aboard the mission of Space Shuttle *Endeavor* that began on September 12, 1992. Although NASA has a rule forbidding married couples to take part in the same mission, the rule was waived for Davis and Lee because they had no children and both had trained as astronauts for several years before they were married.

7053. Astronaut who was a woman to pilot the space shuttle was Lieutenant Colonel Eileen Marie Collins, a 1990 graduate of the Air Force Test Pilot School at Edwards Air Force Base, Muroc, CA, who joined NASA in July 1991. In February 1995 she served as pilot on the shuttle mission STS-63, which docked with the Russian space station *Mir* in the first flight of the joint Russian-American space program. She piloted another space shuttle flight to *Mir* in May 1997.

7054. Astronaut who was a woman to live in a space station was biochemist Dr. Shannon W. Lucid, 53, of Bethany, OK. On March 24, 1996, Lucid transferred from Space Shuttle *Atlantis* to the Russian space station *Mir* for a planned five-month stay. It was the first time the shuttle returned to earth with one less person aboard than had been present at the launch. Lucid remained on the station for 188 days, the longest space sojourn by any American and any woman until that time. Her return was delayed more than six weeks by emergency repairs to the booster rockets of the *Atlantis* and by a hurricane. She came home in the *Atlantis*, which touched down at Edwards Air Force Base, Muroc, CA, on September 26, 1996.

7055. Joint space walk by American and Russian astronauts took place in earth orbit on April 29, 1997, when Dr. Jerry L. Linenger and Vasily Tsibliyev collected cosmic dust samples and installed a radiation meter outside the Russian space station *Mir*.

SPACE—SATELLITES

7056. Satellite placed in orbit by the United States was *Explorer 1*, launched on January 31, 1958, from Cape Canaveral, FL, by a Jupiter C Army missile. It was a bullet-shaped tubular rocket 80 inches long that weighed 30.8 pounds. The weight of the satellite proper was 18.13 pounds; the weight of the final stage of rocket after burnout, 12.67 pounds. The satellite was airborne at 10:48:16 A.M. and went into orbit around the earth at 10:55 A.M., traveling at a speed ranging from 18,000 to 19,000 miles per hour.

7057. Satellite to transmit photographs of the earth was *Explorer 6*, launched on August 7, 1959, from the Atlantic Missile Range, Cape Canaveral, FL. The pictures, received in Hawaii, took 40 minutes to transmit. They were released on September 28, 1959, by the National Aeronautics and Space Administration, and depicted a crescent shape of part of the earth in sunlight. They were taken about 19,500 miles over Mexico from a position facing the Pacific Ocean. The velocity of the satellite at perigee was 23,031 miles per hour. The perigee was 156 miles and the apogee 26,357 miles.

7058. Weather satellite to provide cloud-cover photographs was *Tiros 1* (Television and Infra Red Observatory Satellite), launched by a Thor-Able rocket on April 1, 1960, from Cape Canaveral, FL. It took photographs of the earth's cloud cover from an altitude of 450 miles. The last transmission took place on June 17, 1960.

7059. Navigational satellite was *Transit 1–B*, launched on April 13, 1960, by a Thor-Able-Star rocket from Cape Canaveral, FL. The payload, weighing 265 pounds, included two ultrastable oscillators, two telemetry transmitters and receivers, batteries, and solar cells.

7060. Spy satellite that was successful was *Midas 2*, launched on May 24, 1960, at 12:37 P.M. from Cape Canaveral, FL, by a two-stage Atlas-Agena rocket. *Midas 2* was 122 feet long and 5 feet in diameter and weighed 5,000 pounds. It circled the earth every 94.34 minutes. Its apogee was 292 miles, its perigee 322 miles. It was intended to replace the U-2 reconnaissance aircraft in gathering intelligence on the Soviet Union.

7061. Multisatellite launching of several satellites in one shot was made at 1:54 A.M. on June 22, 1960, from Cape Canaveral, FL, by a Navy Thor-Able-Star rocket. The main satellite, designated *Transit 2-A*, carried two instrumented payload satellites: *Eta 1*, a 36-inch sphere that weighed 223 pounds, and *Eta 2*, a 20-inch sphere that weighed 42 pounds.

7062. Space capsule recovered from an orbiting satellite was located on August 11, 1960, in the Pacific Ocean. It was recovered from *Discoverer 8*, a satellite that had been launched by a Thor-Agena rocket from Vandenberg Air Force Base, CA, on August 10, 1960. The capsule, which measured 27 by 33 inches and weighed 350 pounds, was ejected from the satellite during its 17th polar orbit at a height of 200 miles over latitude 70 degrees N. The descent of the capsule was slowed down by a parachute, which opened at about 50,000 feet. The capsule was recovered by a Navy frogman, Boatswain's Mate Third Class Robert W. Carroll of Keene, NH, who dived from a helicopter that took off from the naval vessel *Haiti Victory*.

7063. Communications satellite was *Echo 1*, a 26.5-inch magnesium sphere launched by a Thor-Delta rocket at 5:39 A.M. on August 12, 1960, from Cape Canaveral, FL. The satellite went into orbit at 7:45 A.M. after the three stages of the rocket had been fired successfully. A taped message was transmitted from Goldstone, CA, bounced off the satellite, and received by the Bell Telephone laboratory at Holmdel, NJ.

7064. Space capsule recovered in midair from an orbiting satellite was a 300-pound capsule ejected from the satellite *Discoverer 14* and retrieved on August 19, 1960. The capsule dropped back to earth by parachute and was snatched at 8,000 feet by an Air Force C-119 airplane piloted by Captain Harold E. Mitchell about 360 miles southwest of Honolulu, HI. *Discoverer 14* was launched by a Thor-Agena rocket on August 18, 1960, from Vandenberg Air Force Base, CA.

7065. Communications satellite with signal reception and transmission equipment was *Courier 1B*, a delayed repeater satellite weighing 500 pounds that was launched at 1:50 P.M. on October 4, 1960, from Cape Canaveral, FL, by a two-stage Thor-Able-Star launch vehicle. On its second orbit, it received and recorded from Fort Monmouth, NJ, a transcribed message by President Dwight David Eisenhower to Secretary of State Christian Archibald Herter at the United Nations in New York City, who de-

SPACE—SATELLITES—*continued*

livered it to Frederick Henry Boland, president of the General Assembly. The first attempt to launch such a satellite had ended in an explosion on August 18, 1960. Early communications satellites were for testing purposes only.

7066. Orbiting solar observatory was *OSO 1,* launched by a Thor-Delta booster on March 7, 1962, at 11:06 A.M. from Cape Canaveral, FL. It was 37 inches tall and weighed 458 pounds. It transmitted data on solar flares and was stabilized and sun-oriented, so that the instruments always pointed toward the sun. Its apogee was 370 miles, its perigee 340 miles.

7067. International satellite was the United States–United Kingdom satellite *Ariel 1,* launched at 1 P.M. on April 26, 1962, from the Atlantic Missile Range, Cape Canaveral, FL, by a Thor-Delta booster. The 132-pound cylinder payload was 23 inches in diameter and less than 11 inches long. It carried six British experiments: three to measure electron density, temperatures, and the composition of positive ions in the ionshere; two to monitor intensity of radiation from the sun; and one to measure cosmic rays. Its apogee was 754.2 miles and its perigee 242.1 miles.

7068. Satellite from the United States to impact the moon was the *Ranger IV,* launched on April 23, 1962, at 3:50 P.M. from the Atlantic Missile Range, Cape Canaveral, FL. It was launched by an Atlas-Agena B, 102 feet high, with a 16-foot base diameter and a liftoff weight of 275,000 pounds. It traveled an estimated 229,541 miles and impacted the moon at 7:49:53 A.M. E.S.T. on April 26, 1962. The velocity at lunar impact was 5,963 miles per hour.

7069. Commercial satellite was *Telstar 1,* an active relay-communications satellite that was designed and built by the Bell Telephone Laboratories for the American Telephone and Telegraph Company. An application permit was filed on October 21, 1960, and an experimental license was granted on January 19, 1961. The satellite was launched on July 10, 1962, at 4:35 A.M. from Cape Canaveral, FL, by the National Aeronautics and Space Administration, using a three-stage Thor-Delta rocket. The satellite payload was a sphere 34.5 inches in diameter that weighed 170 pounds. The perigee was 593 miles and the apogee 3,503 miles. Orbit time was 157.8 minutes.

7070. Geodetic satellite was *Anna 1B,* 350 pounds, launched by a Thor-Able-Star rocket at 3:08 A.M. on October 31, 1962, from Cape Canaveral, FL. It had four flashing lights that gave off five flashes spaced 5.6 seconds apart. It had an apogee of 727 miles and a perigee of 670 miles. Distances on the earth were computed by triangulation. The name Anna is an acronym for Army, Navy, NASA, and Air Force.

7071. Geosynchronous satellite was *Syncom 2,* launched at 10:33 A.M. on July 26, 1963, from the Atlantic Missile Range, Cape Canaveral, FL, by NASA. It was conceived and designed by the Hughes Aircraft Company. The cylinder was 28 inches in diameter and 15.5 inches high and weighed 147 pounds. Its orbital period was 23.9 hours. Its apogee was 22,239 miles and its perigee 22,230 miles, almost equal to the time required for the earth to rotate once on its axis so that it seems to stand still in space.

7072. Weather satellite to provide high-resolution cloud-cover photographs at night was *Nimbus 1,* launched into polar orbit on August 28, 1964, from the Western Test Range, Point Arguello, CA, by a Thor-Agena B rocket. The conical payload was 10 feet tall and 57 inches in diameter and weighed 830 pounds. On its first day in orbit, *Nimbus 1* obtained pictures of Hurricane Cleo. It later obtained pictures of Hurricanes Dora, Ethel, and Florence in the Atlantic, and of Typhoons Ruby and Sally in the Pacific. It viewed Hurricane Dora and Typhoon Ruby in complete darkness. The satellite returned 27,000 photographs and ceased operating on September 23, 1964.

7073. Orbiting geophysical observatory was *OGO 1,* launched on September 4, 1964, at 9:23 P.M. from Cape Canaveral, FL, by an Atlas-Agena B rocket. The payload weighed 1,073 pounds and was 6 feet long and 3 feet wide. The satellite carried 13 protruding appendages and had 32,250 solar cells and two 28-volt nickel cadmium batteries. Its velocity varied from 1,124 miles per hour at the apogee of 92,827 miles to 23,180 miles per hour at the perigee of 175 miles.

7074. Satellite with a nuclear reactor to orbit the earth was *Snapshot I,* a 970-pound satellite, 12 feet long with a base 5 feet in diameter, that was launched by an Atlas-Agena booster from Vandenberg Air Force Base, CA, on April 3, 1965. It contained a System for Nuclear Auxiliary Power reactor (SNAP 10A), 15.5 inches high and 9 inches in diameter, that weighed 250 pounds and generated 500 watts of power after it was in stable orbit. The reactor operated for 43 days, until May 16, 1965, and produced 500,000 watt-hours of electricity. It orbited the earth every 112 minutes at an apogee of 820 miles and a perigee of 788 miles. SNAP 10A was developed by the Atomics International division of North American Aviation at Canoga Park, CA.

7075. Satellite to transmit colored photographs of the full earth face was *Dodge,* a truncated octahedron that was launched from Cape Canaveral, FL, on July 1, 1967, by a Titan 3C rocket. It weighed 430 pounds and had an apogee of 20,925 miles and a perigee of 20,685 miles.

7076. Satellite launched from the earth to orbit another planet was *Mariner 9,* an unmanned American spacecraft that was sent to Mars to photograph the surface and to study the planet's thin atmosphere, clouds, and hazes, surface chemistry, and seasonable changes. The satellite entered Martian orbit at 7:33 P.M. E.S.T. on November 13, 1971. It mapped 70 percent of the planet's surface.

7077. Satellite repair in orbit was performed by the crew of the fifth mission of Space Shuttle *Challenger.* On April 10, 1984, using the shuttle's robot arm, the crew hooked an ailing science satellite, the *Solar Max,* and brought it into the cargo bay. Mission specialists George Nelson and James Van Hoften replaced the satellite's attitude control module, then returned the *Solar Max* to orbit on April 12. The shuttle landed on April 13.

SPACE—SPACECRAFT

7078. Spacecraft placed in solar orbit to investigate interplanetary space between the orbits of Earth and Venus was *Pioneer 5,* launched on March 11, 1960, from Cape Canaveral, FL, by a three-stage Thor-Able IV rocket. The payload was a 26-inch sphere plus four vanes covered by 4,800 solar cells with a total weight of 94.8 pounds, including approximately 40 pounds of instruments. The spacecraft orbited the sun in 311.6 days. Its velocity at the third-stage burnout was 24,689 miles per hour. It was 74.9 million miles from the sun in perigee and 92.3 million miles in apogee. Its last message was received on June 26, 1960, when it was 22.5 million miles from earth and had transmitted data for 138.9 hours.

7079. Spacecraft to transmit data from Venus was *Mariner 2,* a 447-pound spacecraft that was launched on August 27, 1962, at 2:53 A.M. from Cape Canaveral, FL, by an Atlas-Agena B rocket. On December 14, 1962, it passed within approximately 21,600 miles of the planet Venus and measured temperatures and other characteristics of the Venusian surface and its atmosphere.

7080. Spacecraft to transmit close-up photographs of the lunar surface was *Ranger 7,* launched on July 28, 1964, from Cape Canaveral, FL. The payload weighed 806 pounds, measured 8.25 feet high with a 5-foot diameter, and included six RCA-TV cameras. It impacted the moon's surface in the area northwest of the Sea of Clouds at 9:25 A.M. E.D.T. on July 31, after taking 4,316 pictures of the moon's surface. The total elapsed flight time to the moon, 240,000 miles away, was 68 hours 36 minutes.

7081. Spacecraft to transmit close-up photographs of Mars was *Mariner 4,* a 574-pound spacecraft that was launched at 9:22 A.M. on November 28, 1964, from Cape Canaveral, FL, by a two-stage Atlas-Agena D rocket. On July 14, 1965, when the satellite was 134 million miles away from earth and 10,500 miles from Mars, it sent a transmission of photographs consisting of 8.3 dots per second of varying degrees of darkness. The transmission lasted for 8.5 hours and depicted the regions on Mars known as Cebrenia, Arcadia, and Amazonis.

7082. Manned docking of two spacecraft was effected on March 16, 1966, by *Gemini 8,* which made a rendezvous and docking on its fourth orbit, 6.5 hours after launching, with a 26-foot Agena target vehicle launched at 9 A.M. the same day. *Gemini 8* was launched from Cape Canaveral, FL, at 10:41 A.M. by a two-stage Titan II. It made seven orbits in 10 hours 42 minutes, landing in the Pacific Ocean at 10:23 P.M. E.S.T. near Okinawa, where it was picked up 3.5 hours after splashdown and hauled on to the deck of U.S.S. *Leonard F. Mason* at 1:38 A.M. on March 17. Its apogee was 164 miles, its perigee 99 miles. Neil Alden Armstrong was the command pilot and Major David Randolph Scott the pilot.

7083. Spacecraft to transmit photographs from lunar orbit was *Lunar Orbiter 1,* launched by an Atlas-Agena D rocket from Cape Canaveral, FL, on August 10, 1966. Its total weight was 853 pounds. Its apogee was 1,152 miles, its perigee 119 miles. It achieved lunar orbit on August 14, 1966. On October 29, it crashed into the far side of the moon.

SPACE—SPACECRAFT—*continued*

7084. Spacecraft to carry a message intended to be read by living beings elsewhere in the universe was *Pioneer 10,* the planetary probe that was launched from Cape Canaveral, FL, on March 2, 1972, by NASA. Bolted to the probe's exterior wall was a gold-anodized plaque, six by nine inches in area, that carried a number of illustrations: drawings of a human man and woman, a star map marked with the location of the sun, and a second map showing the flight path of *Pioneer 10.* The message was designed by astronomer Carl Sagan.

7085. Space station launched by the United States was *Skylab 2,* which lifted off on May 25, 1973, from Cape Canaveral, FL. Three astronauts, Charles Conrad, Jr., Joseph Peter Kerwin, and Paul J. Weitz, spent nearly a month in the station conducting long-duration flight tests and other scientific experiments. The mission ended successfully on June 22 when the astronauts returned to earth, leaving *Skylab* in orbit. It later disintegrated in the earth's upper atmosphere. The first manned space stations were launched by the Soviet Union beginning in 1971.

7086. Spacecraft to land on Mars was the American planetary probe *Viking 1,* launched on August 20, 1975, from Cape Canaveral, FL. Its sister craft *Viking 2* was launched on September 9, 1975. *Viking 1* touched down on Mars on July 20, 1976, and began sending photographs back to Earth. The probe operated for 6.5 years. *Viking 2* landed on September 3, 1976, and functioned for 3.5 years.

7087. Reusable manned spacecraft was Space Shuttle *Columbia,* piloted by astronauts Robert L. Crippen and John W. Young, which was launched at 7 A.M. on April 12, 1981, from Cape Canaveral, FL. After a 54-hour, 22-minute flight of 36 orbits, the 80-ton shuttle touched down on the dry lake bed at Edwards Air Force Base, Muroc, CA, on April 14, 1981, at 10:21 A.M. Development of the hybrid spacecraft-airplane cost almost $10 billion and took nine years. The first free atmospheric flight by a space shuttle took place on August 12, 1977, when Space Shuttle *Enterprise* was lifted to a height of 25,000 feet by a Boeing 747 airplane and glided back to Edwards Air Force Base, Muroc, CA, piloted by astronauts C. Gordon Fullerton and Fred W. Haise, Jr.

7088. Spacecraft to leave the solar system was the planetary probe *Pioneer 10,* launched on March 2, 1972, from Cape Canaveral, FL. *Pioneer 10* passed Jupiter on December 3, 1973, taking the first close-up pictures of the giant planet. It left the solar system on June 14,

1983, and sent back the first data from interstellar space. The 25th anniversary of the launch took place on March 3, 1997, when *Pioneer 10* became the world's oldest functioning spacecraft. It was also the farthest man-made object from Earth, having traveled a distance of 6 billion miles. NASA officially ended the mission on March 31, 1997, but *Pioneer 10* continued to travel. In the year 34,600, the probe is expected to pass within three light years of the star Ross 246.

7089. Salvage operation in space was performed by astronauts Joseph Allen and Dale Gardner. On November 12, 1984, during the second flight of Space Shuttle *Discovery,* they used the shuttle's robot arm to snare an orbiting satellite and bring it into the cargo bay for repair.

7090. Space shuttle disaster occurred on January 28, 1986, when Space Shuttle *Challenger* exploded off the coast of Florida 74 seconds after liftoff. It was the largest single space disaster in history. All six astronauts on board—Francis R. Scobee, Michael J. Smith, Ronald E. McNair, Ellison S. Onizuka, Judith A. Resnik, and Gregory B. Jarvis—were killed. Also killed was Christa McAuliffe, a New Hampshire elementary school teacher who had won a competition to become the first ordinary civilian to fly in space, and who thus became the first civilian to die in a spacecraft accident. The cause of the explosion was cold weather on the morning of the launch. The icy temperatures had reduced the elasticity of o-ring seals on the shuttle's solid fuel boosters and the seals had cracked, allowing exploding gases to escape. An inquiry revealed that NASA had relaxed its own safety regulations to advance the launch date.

7091. Spacecraft launched by the United States to dock with a Russian space station was Space Shuttle *Atlantis,* commanded by Navy Captain Robert L. Gibson. At 8 A.M. on June 29, 1995, the 122-foot-long shuttle docked with the 112-foot-long Russian space station *Mir* 245 miles above the earth, forming the largest structure ever assembled in space up to that time. The station's two Russian cosmonauts and one American astronaut, combined with the shuttle's five Americans and two Russians, also constituted the largest human population that had ever been in orbit.

7092. Planetary probe to enter the atmosphere of Jupiter was a 746-pound probe carried on the *Galileo* spacecraft, launched in October 1989 from Cape Canaveral, FL. The probe, outfitted with instruments to measure the temperature, pressure, and composition of Jupiter's atmosphere, detached from *Galileo* in July 1995 and entered Jupiter's upper cloud layer on December 5, 1995. It descended by parachute several hundred miles before being crushed and vaporized under intense atmospheric pressure. Analysis of the probe data revealed that Jupiter's composition was closer to the sun's than had been supposed, and that its atmosphere lacked water and complex organic molecules. *Galileo* itself was the first spacecraft to orbit one of the giant outer planets for a long-term survey.

7093. Robot to conduct a roving exploration of the surface of another planet was Sojourner, a 25-pound, six-wheeled robot designed to explore and analyze the surface of Mars. The *Pathfinder* mission, which carried Sojourner into space, was launched from Cape Canaveral, FL, on December 4, 1996. On July 4, 1997, *Pathfinder* landed on the Ares Vallis, an ancient Martian floodplain. Upon landing, the craft was renamed the Sagan Memorial Station, in honor of the late American astronomer Carl Sagan. On July 6, Sojourner rolled away from *Pathfinder* and began conducting an analysis of soil and rocks in the immediate area. The $23 million robot was named for Sojourner Truth, the African-American abolitionist.

SPORTS AND RECREATION

7094. Team sport played in America was lacrosse, a favorite game among Native American tribes. The racquet was a wooden stick with a curve or loop that held a net made of animal skin. The ball was made of animal hide stuffed with hair. Team sizes and rules of play differed from tribe to tribe, with some groups providing extensive training and coaching for their athletes. In 1830, after observing the Seneca of New York State play the game, a white writer, Robert Bently Howe, noted in his description: "The players handled their racquets with great dexterity and out-maneuvered their opponents with such art and adroitness that frequently several minutes passed before the ball flew clear."

SPORTS AND RECREATION—BASEBALL

7095. Baseball rules standardizing the game were adopted in May 1858 in New York City by the National Baseball Association. The rules provided that the bat was not to exceed 2.5 inches in diameter and the ball 10.5 inches in circumference, the latter to weigh 6.5 ounces. The game was to last nine innings or until one team won 21 runs. Previously each team had played under its own set of rules. Three delegates from each of the following clubs attended the meeting: Atlantic, Baltic, Bedford, Continental, Eagle, Empire, Excelsior, Eckford, Gotham, Harmony, Knickerbocker, Nassau, Olympic, Putnam, and Union.

7096. Baseball league of importance was the National Association of Professional Base-Ball Players, organized on March 17, 1871, at Collier's Cafe, New York City. James N. Kerns of Troy, NY, was elected president. The member clubs were the Athletics of Philadelphia, the Mutuals of New York, the Kekiongas of Fort Wayne, the Olympics of Washington, the Haymakers of Troy, the Bostons of Boston, the White Stockings of Chicago, and teams from Cleveland and Rockford. Each club paid an entry fee of $10. The first game was played on May 4, 1871, at Fort Wayne, IN, and the score was Fort Wayne 2, Cleveland 0. The series consisted of three out of five games with the other teams. The champion team was the Athletics, under manager Elias Hicks Hayhurst, who won 22 games and lost seven (.759). Chicago was second, winning 20 games and losing nine (.690). Boston was third, winning 22 games and losing 10 (.688). The National League was started in 1876 and the American League in 1900.

7097. Baseball league for children was the Waynesburg, PA, Juvenile Baseball League, formed in 1908 by three teams—the Colts, the North Side Cubs, and the Times Pirates (the last composed of carrier boys for the *Waynesburg Times*). An admission fee of 10 cents was charged for each game, the seasonal proceeds of $60 being donated to a library fund.

7098. Baseball commissioner was Judge Kenesaw Mountain Landis, elected on November 12, 1920, for a seven-year term from 1921 to 1928. He received a salary of $42,500 a year plus $10,000 for expenses to rule the 16 American and National League baseball clubs. He was re-elected three times and died in office on November 24, 1944.

SPORTS AND RECREATION—BASEBALL—continued

7099. Baseball manager to win pennants in both leagues was Joseph Vincent McCarthy, nonplaying manager of the Chicago National League team, which earned the pennant on October 6, 1929, by winning 98 games and losing 54. As manager of the New York American League team he won the pennant on September 23, 1932, winning 106 games and losing 46 games. New York went on to win the world championship on October 2, defeating Chicago in four straight games.

7100. Sports event to be televised live was a Columbia–Princeton baseball game that was played on May 17, 1939, at Columbia's Baker Field in New York City. An Iconoscope camera mounted near third base fed signals to station W2XBS in the Empire State Building. Commentary was provided by a radio announcer, Bill Stern. The camera was unable to follow the ball with sufficient speed, and the audience—mostly visitors to the New York World's Fair in Flushing, Queens, New York City—saw little more than white dots and streaks on a gray background.

7101. Baseball league for women was the All-American Girls Professional Baseball League, founded in the Chicago, IL, area in 1943, when major-league baseball was feeling the absence of male players who had joined the armed services during World War II. The women's league, which disbanded in 1954, was the subject of Penny Marshall's 1992 film *A League of Their Own*.

7102. Umpire in organized baseball who was African-American was Emmett Littleton Ashford of the Class C Southwestern International League, who was authorized as a substitute umpire on February 20, 1952, by league president Les Powers. Ashford went on to become the first African-American umpire in the major leagues. He was purchased on September 15, 1965, from the Pacific Coast League by the American League. His salary was $7,500 a year plus $27 daily for expenses. He umpired at third base at the opening game of the season at Washington, DC, on April 12, 1966, between the Cleveland Indians and the Washington Senators.

7103. Baseball coach in the major leagues who was African-American was John O'Neil, hired on May 29, 1962, by the Chicago Cubs as one of the team's six coaches. Previously he had served the team in various other capacities. The first African-American manager of a major league team was Frank Robinson, who was hired by the Cleveland Indians as both player and manager on October 3, 1974.

SPORTS AND RECREATION—BASEBALL—EQUIPMENT

7104. Baseball uniforms were worn by the members of the Knickerbocker Club of New York, which adopted a blue and white uniform in 1848.

7105. Baseball glove was worn by Charles Waite, first baseman of Boston, MA, in 1875. It was flesh-color so as not to be conspicuous and had a large round opening at the back for ventilation.

7106. Baseball catchers' chest protector was invented by William Gray of Hartford, CT, and used in 1878. He sold his rights in the 1880s to Albert Goodwill Spalding for $5,000.

7107. Baseball catcher's mask was invented by Frederick Winthrop Thayer of Waverly, MA, captain of the Harvard University Baseball Club, who obtained a patent on February 12, 1878, on a "face guard or safety mask." It was made by a tinsmith in Cambridge, MA, tried out in the gymnasium in the winter of 1876–77, and used by James Alexander Tyng in a game with the Live Oaks at Lynn, MA, April 12, 1877. Louis Trauschke, catcher of the Foster Baseball Club, Lawrence, MA, who had been hurt by a pitched ball, adopted the mask. Eventually it was manufactured by Peck and Snyder, New York City.

7108. Baseball batting and fielding cage was built at Yale University, New Haven, CT, in the fall of 1885 by Captain Philip Battell Stewart. The building was about 70 feet long and 20 feet wide and had skylights protected by wire. It was the forerunner of the expensive cages and field houses now common in American colleges and universities.

7109. Baseball with a cork center was invented by Benjamin F. Shibe of Bala, PA, who obtained a patent for it on June 15, 1909. It was manufactured by A.G. Spalding and Brothers, Chicago, IL, and was used in occasional league games in 1909 and in regular play in 1910. The ball was first used in a World Series game on October 20, 1910, in Chicago, IL.

7110. Baseball dyed yellow was used on April 27, 1938, in the Columbia–Fordham game, New York City. It was a regulation National League ball dyed yellow, with red stitches, and was developed by Frederic Rahr.

SPORTS AND RECREATION—BASE-BALL—GAMES

7111. Baseball game to be played as part of an organized sport took place on June 19, 1846, at Elysian Fields, Hoboken, NJ, when the Knickerbocker Baseball Club of New York, the first organized baseball team, was defeated by an informal team called the New York Nine. The score was 23–1 in four innings. The umpire was Alexander Joy Cartwright, a member of the Knickerbocker team. Cartwright was the author of the first set of formal rules for baseball. He also laid out the sport's diamond-shaped field and established its nine playing positions. The widespread legend that attributes the founding of baseball to Abner Doubleday, a West Point cadet (later a general), at Cooperstown, NY, is false. Early versions of baseball, based on the English games of rounders and cricket, were played in the English colonies of America as far back as the early 1700s.

7112. Baseball game in which spectators were charged admission was the game of July 20, 1858, between two amateur teams at the Fashion Race Course in Long Island, NY, the opening game of the first series ever played. A 50-cent admission fee was charged each of the 1,500 people who attended to cover the cost of renting the racetrack.

7113. Baseball series was played July 20, August 17, and September 10, 1858, at the Fashion Race Course on Long Island, NY, between two amateur teams, the Brooklyn Brooklynites and the New York All Stars. New York won the first game 22–18 and took the series with two out of three games.

7114. Intercollegiate baseball game was played on July 1, 1859, between Amherst College and Williams College, in Pittsfield, MA. Amherst won by a score of 73–32. The game, played on a 60-foot square with the pitcher 35 feet from the batter, began at 11 A.M. and continued for four hours without interruption. Each team had 13 players and the game lasted 26 innings. The captain of Amherst was James Fitzgerald Claffin, the Williams captain Humphrey Stevenson Anderson.

7115. Baseball game in which one team scored more than 100 runs was played on Sunday, October 1, 1865. In a nine-inning game in Philadelphia, PA, the Philadelphia Athletics defeated the Jersey City Nationals 114–2. About 500 women were among the 5,000 spectators.

7116. Baseball game between an all-white team and an all-African-American team was played in Chicago, IL, on July 6, 1871. The African-American Uniques beat the Alerts by a score of 17–16.

7117. Baseball game in which a team made no runs in nine innings was played on May 11, 1875, at Red Stocking Park, St. Louis, MO, between the Chicago White Stockings and the St. Louis Reds of the National Association. The score of the 1-hour 35-minute game was Chicago 1, St. Louis 0. Chicago made six base hits and scored one run; St. Louis made three base hits and did not score. George Zettlein was the Chicago pitcher and Joseph Myles Blong the St. Louis pitcher.

7118. Baseball game in which a team made no hits in nine innings was pitched by Joseph Emley Borden of the National Association's Philadelphia team on July 28, 1875, in Philadelphia, PA, against Chicago. The score was Philadelphia 4, Chicago 0.

7119. Baseball game that was a shutout was the National League's Chicago vs. Louisville game, played on April 25, 1876, at Louisville, KY, before 2,000 spectators. Albert Goodwill Spalding, the Chicago White Stockings pitcher, pitched a seven-hitter and also made three of Chicago's eight hits off James Alexander Devlin. The score was Chicago 4, Louisville 0.

7120. Unassisted triple play in organized baseball took place on May 8, 1878, at Providence, RI, in a game between Providence and Boston. The play was made by Paul Hines, center fielder for the Providence team. Providence won 3–1.

7121. Baseball game at night was played on June 2, 1883, at League Park, Fort Wayne, IN, between a club of boys known as the M.E. College and the Quincy professional team from Adams County, IL. The score was Quincy 19, College 11. The field was illuminated by 17 lights of 4,000 candlepower each. Seven innings were played. The game was witnessed by 2,000 people.

SPORTS AND RECREATION—BASE-BALL—GAMES—*continued*

7122. Baseball championship was played at the Polo Grounds, New York City, in October 1884. The Providence Grays defeated the New York Metropolitans three games to none. Providence won the first game 6–0 in two hours on October 23, the second game 3–1 in 1 hour 35 minutes on October 24, the third game 11–2 in 1 hour 20 minutes on October 25.

7123. World Series baseball game was played on October 1, 1903, at Boston, MA, when the Pittsburgh Pirates defeated the Boston Red Sox 7–3 before a crowd of 16,200 people. James Dennison Sebring of the Pirates hit a home run, the first in the World Series. The Pirates defeated the Boston Red Sox 7–3. Boston came back from a three-game loss and won the series on October 13 with five victories in seven games.

7124. World Series baseball game that was a shutout was played on October 13, 1905, at New York City between the New York Nationals and the Philadelphia Athletics of the American League. It was the fourth game in the 1905 series. Joseph Jerome McGinnity of New York shut out the Philadelphia team 1–0. New York won the series 4–1. A shutout game had been played at an earlier World Series, on October 2, 1903, at Boston, when Samuel W. Leever of the Pittsburgh Nationals shut out the Boston Americans 3–0. This series, however, was not sanctioned by the leagues.

7125. Double-header baseball games that were shutouts were played on September 26, 1908, at Washington Park, Brooklyn, New York City. Edward Marvin Reulbach of the National League Chicago Cubs defeated the Brooklyn Superbas 5–0 and 3–0. He allowed only five singles in the first game, which lasted 1 hour 40 minutes, and 3 singles in the second game, which lasted 1 hour 12 minutes.

7126. Unassisted triple play in a major league baseball game was made by Cornelius Ball, shortstop of the American League's Cleveland team, on July 19, 1909, at Cleveland, OH, in the second inning of the first game of a doubleheader against the American League's Boston team. Ball caught Ambrose Moses McConnell's liner; touched second, retiring Charles F. Wagner, who was on his way to third; and tagged Garland Stahl as he came up to second. When Ball came to bat in the same inning, he hit a home run. Cleveland defeated Boston 6–1 in the first game. Boston defeated Cleveland 8–2 in the second game.

7127. Unassisted triple play in a World Series baseball game was made on October 10, 1920, at Cleveland, OH, in the fifth inning of the fifth game between the Cleveland Indians and the Brooklyn Dodgers. The Indians' second baseman, William Adolph Wambsganss, caught a line drive from Otto Miller's bat, tagged Peter John Kilduff at second base, then ran to first and tagged Clarence Elmer Mitchell. Cleveland defeated Brooklyn 8–1.

7128. Radio broadcast of a baseball game with a play-by-play description took place at Pittsburgh, PA, on August 5, 1921, when the Pittsburgh Corsairs defeated Philadelphia by a score of 8–5 for their third straight victory. The baseball field was connected by wire to the broadcasting station of KDKA, Pittsburgh.

7129. World Series baseball games to gross $1 million were played on October 10–15, 1923, in New York City, between the New York Yankees and the New York Giants. Receipts were $1,063,815, of which the players' share was $368,783.04. The Yankees won 4–2.

7130. All-star major league baseball game was played on July 6, 1933, at Comiskey Park, Chicago, IL. The American League defeated the National League 4–2. The American runs were batted in by Earl Douglas Averill, Vernon Louis Gomez, and George Herman "Babe" Ruth, who hit two runs, one of which was a homer in the third inning. The National runs were made by Johnny Leonard, Roosevelt Martin, and Francis Frisch. The attendance was 49,200; receipts were $56,379.

7131. Baseball game at night by major league teams was played at Crosley Field, Cincinnati, OH, on May 24, 1935, when the Cincinnati Reds defeated the Philadelphia Phillies 2 to 1 before a paid attendance of 20,422. President Franklin Delano Roosevelt, in Washington, DC, pressed a button that turned on 363 lights of 1,000 kilowatts each on eight giant towers for this National League game.

7132. Major league baseball game to be shown on television was a double-header played at Ebbets Field, Brooklyn, New York City, on August 26, 1939, between the Cincinnati Reds and the Brooklyn Dodgers. Both games were televised by station W2XBS, New York City, using two cameras that alternated according to the play. During the intermission, there were appearances by Leo Durocher, manager of the Dodgers, William McKechnie, manager of the Reds, and several players. Walter Lanier "Red" Barber was the announcer. The first major-league baseball game to be shown in color was also a double-header played at Ebbets Field, where the Brooklyn Dodgers played the Boston Braves on August 11, 1951. The games were televised by WCBS-TV of the Columbia Broadcasting System, with Red Barber and Connie Desmond as the announcers.

7133. Major league no-hitter baseball game on opening day was played on April 16, 1940, in Chicago. Robert William Andrew Feller of the American League Cleveland Indians retired 15 men in a row from the fourth inning to the eighth inning against the Chicago White Sox.

7134. Baseball play-off series took place the first week of October 1946 in St. Louis, MO, and Brooklyn, New York City, after the Brooklyn Dodgers and the St. Louis Cardinals had tied on September 29, both teams having won 96 and lost 58 games for a .623 average in the National League. The Cardinals won the first two of the two-out-of-three series by the scores of 4–2 and 8–4, thus earning the National League pennant and the right to play the Boston Red Sox of the American League in the World Series. They beat the Red Sox in four out of seven games.

7135. World Series baseball game to be shown on television was the opening game of the 1947 series, played on September 30, 1947, between the New York Yankees and the Brooklyn Dodgers at Yankee Stadium, New York City. The game was transmitted to three stations (WABD, WCBS, and WNBT) in New York City and to all the television outlets along the Eastern seaboard. The entire series was telecast under the joint sponsorship of the Ford Motor Company and the Gillette Safety Razor Company at a cost of $65,000. The Yankees won the first game 5–3 and the series four games to three. The play-by-play descriptions were given by Bob Edge, Bob Stanton, and Bill Slater.

7136. Major league baseball game in which the majority of the players on one team were African-American was played on July 17, 1954, between the Brooklyn Dodgers and the Milwaukee Braves at Milwaukee, WI. The Braves won 6 to 1. The black players on the Brooklyn team were Donald N. Newcombe, pitcher; Roy Campanella, catcher; James William Gilliam, second base; Jackie Robinson, third base; and Edmundo Isasi Amoros, left field.

7137. World Series disrupted by an earthquake was the third game of the World Series between the San Francisco Giants and the Oakland Athletics on October 17, 1989, at Candlestick Park in San Francisco, CA. Minutes before the start of the game, a massive earthquake hit the San Francisco Bay area, causing scores of deaths and widespread damage. After a 10-day postponement, play resumed. The Athletics won games three and four for the first Series sweep in 13 years.

SPORTS AND RECREATION—BASEBALL—PLAYERS

7138. Baseball pitcher to throw a curve ball is reported to have been William Arthur Cummings, who introduced this innovation in 1866. He played with the Excelsior Junior Nine and the Stars of Brooklyn. Others for whom the claim is made are Fred Goldsmith of the Chicago White Stockings and George McConnell.

7139. Baseball player to play as a professional was Alfred James Reach, outfielder of the Philadelphia Athletics of the National Association from 1871 to 1875. He played in 82 games. In 1874 he received $1,000 for playing 14 games.

7140. Baseball player on a white team who was African-American was John Jackson, who played in 1872 on a white baseball team in New Castle, PA, under the name of John W. "Bud" Fowler. From 1872 to 1899 he usually played second base.

7141. Baseball players to hit home runs were Ross Barnes of the Chicago White Stockings and Charles Wesley "Baby" Jones of the Cincinnati Reds, on May 2, 1876, at Cincinnati, OH. Chicago won 15–9.

7142. Major league baseball player who was African-American was Moses Fleetwood "Fleet" Walker, catcher on the Northwestern League Toledo team, who played with that team from 1883 to 1889. He played in 41 games in 1884 and hit .251. The team entered the American Association in 1884. He was also the first African-American college baseball player, playing for Oberlin College in 1881 and later for the University of Michigan, where he was a law student.

7143. Baseball player who was Native American was Jim Toy of the American Association, who played first base for the Cleveland team in 1887 and catcher for the Brooklyn and Baltimore teams in 1890.

SPORTS AND RECREATION—BASEBALL—PLAYERS—*continued*

7144. Baseball pinch hitter was John Joseph Doyle, a substitute catcher, ordered to bat in the ninth inning by Oliver Wendell Tebeau of the Cleveland Spiders in a game played on June 7, 1892, in Brooklyn, NY (now part of New York City), against the Brooklyn Ward's Wonders. Doyle made a single, advancing John Joseph O'Connor from first to third base. The 1891 rules allowed substitutions anywhere at any time during a game.

7145. Baseball player to catch a ball dropped from the Washington Monument in Washington, DC, from the 500-foot level, was William F. Schriver of the Chicago National League club, who accomplished this feat on August 29, 1892, and again on August 25, 1895. Charles Evard Street, catcher of the Washington club of the American League, caught a baseball dropped from the top of the monument on August 21, 1908.

7146. Baseball "Home Run King" to hit 25 home runs in one season was Bucky Freeman, outfielder of the Washington Club of the National League, who hit 25 home runs and 27 triples in 1899.

7147. Baseball player in the American League who was African-American was Charles Grant, who played second base with the Columbia Giants. In 1901 he was hired by John Joseph McGraw and billed as Charles Tokohama, a full-blooded Cherokee. At that time the American League had not yet been recognized as a major league.

7148. Major league baseball player killed in a game was Raymond Johnson Chapman, shortstop of the Cleveland Indians, who was accidentally hit on the left side of his head by a pitch thrown by Willie Mays of the New York Yankees in a game at the Polo Grounds, New York City, on August 16, 1920.

7149. Baseball pitcher who was a woman was Virne Beatrice "Jackie" Mitchell, who pitched a single game for the Chattanooga Baseball Club of the minor-league Southern Association. In an April 1, 1931, exhibition game against the New York Yankees, the 19-year-old Mitchell struck out Babe Ruth, Lou Gehrig, and Tony Lazzeri. After Mitchell was taken out of the game, Chattanooga lost 14 to 4.

7150. Baseball player to hit a home run in an All-Star game was Babe Ruth of the New York Yankees, who on July 6, 1933, at Comiskey Park, Chicago, IL, hit a home run in the third inning of the first game of the annual series. The run brought in Charles Leonard Gehringer of Detroit. The American League team won 4–2. William Anthony Hallahan of the St. Louis Cardinals was the National League pitcher and James Alger Wilson of the Cardinals was the catcher.

7151. Major league baseball player in the postwar era who was African-American was Jackie Robinson of the Brooklyn Dodgers, who played first base in an exhibition game on April 11, 1947, against the New York Yankees. In the course of the season he hit 12 home runs, stole 29 bases, and was voted Rookie of the Year. He won the Most Valuable Player award in 1949. His success opened the way for the racial integration of other baseball teams.

7152. Baseball player who was African-American to hit a home run in a World Series was Larry Doby of the Cleveland Indians, who hit a 425-foot drive in the third inning into right field on October 9, 1948, at Cleveland, OH. Cleveland defeated the Boston Braves 4–2.

7153. Baseball pitcher to pitch a perfect no-hit, no-run, no-walk World Series game was Donald James Larsen of the New York Yankees, who pitched a perfect game on October 8, 1956, at Yankee Stadium, New York City, in the fifth game of the World Series against the Brooklyn Dodgers. The score was New York 2, Brooklyn 0.

7154. Baseball player to steal more than 100 bases in a season was Maury Wills, shortstop for the Los Angeles Dodgers, who set the record during the 1962 season. He stole his first base on April 13 in Game 4 against Milwaukee and his 100th on September 26 in the third inning against the Houston Colts at Los Angeles, when he and left-fielder Tommy Davis pulled a double steal.

7155. Baseball player to play all nine positions in one game was Bert Campaneris of the Kansas City Athletics, who played all nine positions in a 13-inning night game at Kansas City, MO, on September 8, 1965. The Athletics were defeated by the California Angels 5–3.

7156. Major league baseball player to make seven consecutive hits in seven times at bat in the same game was Cesar Dario Gutierrez, shortshop for the American League Detroit Tigers, who, in the second game of a doubleheader with the Cleveland Indians at Cleveland, OH, on June 21, 1970, hit a single in the first, third, fifth, eighth, tenth, and twelfth innings and a double in the seventh inning. Detroit beat Cleveland 9–8.

7157. Designated hitter in a major league baseball game to bat for the pitcher was first baseman Ron Blomberg of the New York Yankees. On April 6, 1973, at Fenway Park, Boston, MA, he came to bat in the first inning and was walked by Luis Tiant of the Boston Red Sox. The first designated hitter to come to bat in a World Series game was Dan Driessen of the Cincinnati Reds. He stepped up to the plate in the opening game of the 1976 World Series between the Reds and the New York Yankees, but the runner at first base was picked off before a pitch was thrown, ending the inning for the Reds. The first player to serve as designated hitter for all games of a season was Rusty Staub of the Detroit Tigers, who played in all of the Tigers' 162 season games in 1978. The designated hitter rule was adopted on January 11, 1973, by American League club owners, whose teams at that time lagged behind those of the National League in batting prowess. The Triple-A International League had experimented successfully with the concept in 1969.

7158. Free agents in major league baseball were Andy Messersmith of the Los Angeles Dodgers and Dave McNally of the Montreal Expos. On December 23, 1974, a federal arbitrator ruled that the two players, and by extension other major league baseball players not bound to a current contract, were free to sell their services to the team that offered them the most money.

SPORTS AND RECREATION—BASEBALL—TEAMS

7159. Baseball team was the Knickerbocker Club of New York, organized on September 23, 1845, by Alexander Joy Cartwright, the man who laid out the diamond-shaped baseball field and gave the game its modern form. Duncan F. Curry was the club's first president. The club played its first game in June 1846, losing 23–1. A previous team that played an earlier form of baseball was the Olympic Club of Philadelphia, PA, which played "cat ball," also known as

town ball, from July 4, 1833, to the year 1860, when they changed to standard baseball. Town ball, a game similar to the British game of rounders, was the immediate forerunner of regular baseball in the United States.

7160. Baseball team to tour was the Brooklyn Excelsiors, under the management of Captain Joseph B. Leggett, who left on June 30, 1860, for Albany, NY. They played at Troy, Buffalo, and cities in the west and south.

7161. Baseball teams for women were organized in the 1860s. In 1866, college women formed two baseball clubs, the Laurel Base Ball Club and the Abenakis, at Vassar Female College, Poughkeepsie, NY. A non-collegiate team was organized in Peterboro, NH, in 1868. The squad of 50 women wore short blue and white tunics reaching to the knees, white stockings, and straw hats. The captain of the senior team was Nannie Miller, who was also the catcher. Clara Mills was the pitcher; Mary Manning first base; Fran Richardson, second base; Bertha Powell, third base; Jennie Hand, shortstop; Hattie Ferris, left field; Maggie Marshall, right field; and Mary Frothingham, center field.

7162. Baseball team whose players received a regular salary was the Cincinnati Red Stockings, led by Harry and George Wright, who traveled in 1869 to various cities, engaging local teams. Through 1869 and up to June 1870, they played without losing a game. A salary of $1,400 was paid to the shortstop, $1,200 to the center fielder, $1,100 to the pitcher, $1,000 to the third baseman, and $800 each to the first and second basemen, the catcher, the left and right fielders, and the substitute.

7163. Baseball teams to travel abroad were the Boston Red Stockings and the Philadelphia Athletic Blue Stockings, National Association teams that played a series of 15 exhibition games from July 30 to August 27, 1874, in England and Ireland.

7164. Baseball team of African-American players to play professionally was the Cuban Giants, organized in New York City by Frank P. Thompson in 1885. S.K. Govern was manager. The players received expenses and weekly salaries according to positions: pitchers and catchers, $18; infielders, $15; and outfielders, $12. The players also served as waiters during the summer season at the Argyle Hotel, Babylon, NY.

SPORTS AND RECREATION—BASE-BALL—TEAMS—*continued*

7165. Baseball teams to go on a world tour were the Chicago and All America teams. They started their world tour on October 20, 1888, and returned on April 20, 1889. They played 53 games of four innings and over in Australia, Ceylon, Egypt, Italy, France, England, and the United States. Twenty-eight games were won by the All America team, 22 by the Chicago team, and three were tied. Their first game abroad was played on December 10, 1888, in Auckland, New Zealand.

SPORTS AND RECREATION—BASKET-BALL

7166. Basketball game was invented in 1892 by Dr. James Naismith, an instructor at the International Young Men's Christian Association Training School in Springfield, MA. The game was originally played with peach baskets mounted on poles. It was necessary for the players to use a ladder to remove the ball from the basket. The first game was played at the YMCA gymnasium on January 20, 1892. The first public game was played on March 11. The rules were standardized in 1894.

7167. Basketball played at a college was introduced in 1892 by Senda Berenson, director of physical education at Smith College, Northampton, MA. Several intercollegiate games were played against other colleges. The first college to have an official team was Mount Union College, Alliance, OH, in December 1892.

7168. Basketball rules were published in the *Triangle Magazine,* Springfield, MA, on January 15, 1892. The rules were later compiled in more complete form in a book, *Rules for Basketball,* by James Naismith, basketball's inventor. The book was published in 1892 by the Springfield Printing and Binding Company, Springfield, MA.

7169. Intercollegiate basketball game was played in Minnesota on February 9, 1895, when the Minnesota State School of Agriculture defeated Hamline College 9–3. The first intercollegiate basketball game with five-man teams was played on January 16, 1896, in Iowa City, IA. The University of Chicago team defeated the University of Iowa team 15–12. There were no substitutions.

7170. Basketball game at a large commercial sports arena was a benefit performance for the New York Relief Fund, played on January 19, 1931, at Madison Square Garden, New York City. Six college teams played. Columbia University defeated Fordham University 26–18, Manhattan College defeated New York University 16–14, and St John's University defeated City College 17–8. About 15,000 persons attended, and $22,854 was raised.

7171. Basketball game to be shown on television was played on February 28, 1940, at Madison Square Garden and televised by station W2XBS, New York City. Fordham University played the University of Pittsburgh, which won the game by a score of 50–37. That game was followed by another in which New York University beat Georgetown University by a score of 50–27. Both games were televised.

7172. National Basketball Association commissioner was Maurice Podoloff, a lawyer from New Haven, CT. Podoloff had previously served three years as president of the Basketball Association of America, the first professional basketball league. He was chosen as commissioner in 1949 when the BAA merged with the National Basketball League to form the NBA.

7173. Basketball professional player who was African-American was Charles Henry Cooper, all-star player, who was drafted on April 24, 1950, by the Boston Celtics and who played his first game for that team on November 1, 1950, in Fort Wayne, IN.

7174. All-Star Game of the National Basketball Association was played on March 2, 1951, at the Boston Garden, Boston, MA, before a crowd of 10,094 patrons. The East team, coached by Joe Lapchick, defeated the West team, coached by John Kundla, by the score of 111–94.

7175. Basketball collegiate player to score more than 1,000 points in one season was Johnny O'Brien of South Amboy, NJ, scoring champion of the National Collegiate Athletic Association, who scored 1,051 points in 37 games for Seattle University, Seattle, WA, in the 1951–52 season. He achieved his score on February 28, 1952, when he made 30 points in the game against Portland University. Seattle won 79–75.

7176. Basketball team to score more than 10,000 points in one season was the Philadelphia Warriors of the eastern division of the National Basketball Association, who scored 10,035 points in the 1961–62 season. In the 1966–67 season the team scored 10,143 points.

7177. Coach of a professional basketball team who was African-American was Bill Russell, who became coach of the Boston Celtics, Boston, MA, in 1966 and led the team to the National Basketball Association championship the following year.

7178. Basketball leagues for women to attract significant attendance at games were the American Basketball League (ABL), which originated in 1994, and the Women's National Basketball Association (WNBA), established on April 24, 1996, when the National Basketball Association (NBA) Board of Governors approved the concept. The ABL, headquartered in Palo Alto, CA, began its inaugural season on October 18, 1996. The first game of the WNBA, headquartered in New York, NY, was played on June 21, 1997. As of November 1997 the average attendance was 4,227 fans per ABL game (a 19 percent increase over the previous year) and 9,669 at a WNBA game.

SPORTS AND RECREATION—BICYCLING

7179. Bicycles were imported in 1819. The first one in New York City made its appearance on May 21, 1819. The Common Council met on August 19 and passed a law "to prevent the use of velocipedes in the public places and on the sidewalks of the city of New York." In their early years, bicycles were called velocipedes, curricles, or swift walkers.

7180. Bicycle patent was granted to William K. Clarkson, Jr., of New York City on June 26, 1819, for an "improved curricle."

7181. Bicycle with a rotary crank was patented on November 20, 1866, by Pierre Lallemont of Paris. It was known as a "bone shaker." He rode on it from Ansonia, CT, to New Haven, CT. The fore wheel was axled to the jaws of a depending bar, which was pivoted in the frame, and turned by a horizontal lever bar, which was revolved by a treadle crank.

7182. Bicycle school was opened in New York City on December 5, 1868, at 932 Broadway, by Pearsall Brothers.

7183. Bicycle factory was established by Colonel Albert Augustus Pope of Hartford, CT, who saw a bicycle at the 1876 Centennial Exposition in Philadelphia, PA, and commissioned W.S. Atwell of Boston, MA, to build a 70-pound model for him at a cost of $313. In 1878, he arranged with the Weed Sewing Machine Company of Hartford to produce 50 Standard Columbus bicycles, which he sold promptly.

7184. Bicycle club was the Boston Bicycle Club, formed on February 11, 1878, in Boston, MA, by 14 members. George B. Woodward was president and Thatcher Goddard captain. The uniform was a gray jacket, shirt, breeches, and stockings and a blue Glengarry Scotch cap with a small visor in front. The first meet was held on March 9, 1878.

7185. Bicycle organization (national) was the League of American Wheelmen, formed on May 31, 1880, at Newport, RI, by 128 members representing 28 cycling clubs. The first president was Charles Ed Pratt of Boston, MA.

7186. Six-day bicycle race for women was held on February 11–16, 1889, at Madison Square Garden, New York City, under the management of William O'Brien. The week's proceeds amounted to $10,212, of which $4,085 went to the winner, Lottie Stanley. It was later disclosed that a promoter from Troy, NY, had entered 10 salaried riders.

7187. Bicycle with a back-pedal brake was patented on December 24, 1889, by Daniel C. Stover and William A. Hance of Freeport, IL.

7188. Pneumatic bicycle tire was made in the tire factory of the George R. Bidwell Cycle Company of New York City in April 1891 for use on its bicycles.

7189. International six-day bicycle race was held in Madison Square Garden, New York City, from midnight on Sunday, October 18, 1891, to midnight on Saturday, October 24, and was won by William "Plugger Bill" Martin of Detroit, MI, who rode a "high wheeler" bicycle. There were 40 contestants, but only 6 finished, all of whom won prizes. Martin covered 1,466 miles and won a $2,100 prize. The gate receipts were $26,000. The first two-man team event was held from February 12 to February 17, 1899, and was won by Charles Miller and Frank Waller, who rode a combined total of 2,733.4 miles.

7190. Bicycle tire made of cord was invented by John F. Palmer of Chicago, IL. On June 7, 1892, he obtained a patent on a self-healing tire in which the tread portion of the rubber was placed under compression, so that a puncture would tend to close rather than gape open. The tire was manufactured in 1892 by the B.F. Goodrich Company of Akron, OH, and was first exhibited at the Philadelphia Cycle Show in February 1893.

7191. Bicycle track of wood was built by the Bay City Club, San Francisco, CA, and placed in use on July 1, 1893. The outer edges of the track were built on an incline.

SPORTS AND RECREATION—BICY-CLING—*continued*

7192. Intercollegiate bicycle race was held on May 27, 1896, at the Manhattan Beach Track, New York City, under the auspices of the Intercollegiate Association of Amateur Athletes of America. Five races were held—a quarter mile, a half mile, one mile, one mile tandem, and five miles. Contestants scored five points for each first place, two points for each second place, and one point for each third place. The score was Columbia 20, Yale 8, Pennsylvania 5, Columbian University of Washington 5, and Harvard 2.

7193. Bicycle racer to attain the speed of a mile a minute was Charles Minthorn Murphy, known as Mile-A-Minute-Murphy, who on June 30, 1899, rode a mile in 57.8 seconds, riding behind a Long Island Railroad train from Farmingdale, NY, to Maywood, NY, on a three-mile measured track. The train was equipped with an extension top and sides so that Murphy raced in a comparative vacuum.

7194. Bicycle race paced by a motorcycle was a 100-mile race held on July 29, 1899, at the Manhattan Beach Track, Manhattan Beach, New York City, for a $1,000 prize. There were four entries: Harry Elkes, Frank Waller, Charles Miller, and Burns Pierce. Pierce covered the course in 3 hours 27 minutes 5.4 seconds, beating the nearest competitor by 7.3 miles.

7195. Paired six-day bicycle race was held at Madison Square Garden, New York City, on December 9–14, 1901. The winners of the $1,500 team prize were Robert Walthour of Atlanta, GA, and Archie McEachern of Toronto, Canada, who pedaled 2,555 miles. Sixteen professional riders from nine nations competed. Paired races were instituted because the law prohibited one man from being on the track more than 12 hours a day.

7196. Bicycle traffic court was held at Racine, WI, on June 18, 1936, under authority of Grover Cleveland Lutter, chief of police. The judges of the court were Sergeant Wilbur Hansen and Officer Alphonse Costabile of the Racine Police Department. Sessions were held Saturday mornings. A city law passed on May 4, 1937, required all bicycles to be registered with the police department.

7197. Bicycle champion who was a woman to win an event sponsored by the National Amateur Bicycle Association was Doris Kopsky of Belleville, NJ, who covered a mile in 4 minutes 22.4 seconds on September 4, 1937, in Buffalo, NY.

7198. Bicycle race to be shown on television was the six-day bicycle race at Madison Square Garden, New York City, which lasted from May 15 to May 21, 1939. The telecast was shown by W2XBS, National Broadcasting Company, on May 20 from 8:30 P.M. to 9 P.M. and showed 10 teams in action. Only 8 of the 12 teams of riders completed the race. The starting gun was fired by Joe DiMaggio, center fielder for the New York Yankees. Bill Stern was the announcer. The race, 2,388 miles long, was won by William and Doug Peden, who scored 1,498 points in sprints.

7199. Bicyclist from the United States to win the Tour de France was Gregory James LeMond of Los Angeles, CA. LeMond first won the Tour de France, world bicycling's premiere racing event, in 1986. He was seriously wounded in a hunting accident in 1987 but returned to win the tour again in 1989 and 1990. LeMond retired from professional cycling in 1994, suffering from a muscular disorder believed caused by lead pellets in his body.

SPORTS AND RECREATION—BICY-CLING—JOURNEYS

7200. Bicycle trip of 100 miles sponsored by a club took place on September 6, 1882, when the Boston Bicycle Club, Boston, MA, sponsored a trip from Worcester, MA, to Boston. The trip started at 4:38 A.M. and ended at 9:30 P.M., with frequent stopoffs for food, refreshments, and repairs. The elapsed time was 16 hours 52 minutes, of which 12 hours 6 minutes was the actual riding time. Seven men covered the complete 102.5 miles, but many others rode along for varying distances. The route was via South Framingham, Natick, Wellesley, Dedham, Stoughton, Brockton, Randolph, Braintree, Quincy, Mattapan, Waltham, and Newton.

7201. Round-the-world bicycle trip was made by Thomas Stevens, who started from San Francisco, CA, on April 22, 1884, on a 50-inch bicycle (the diameter of the large front wheel was 50 inches). He pedaled across the United States, arriving at Boston, MA, on August 24. He left for Europe by ship and visited England, France, Germany, Austria-Hungary, Serbia, Bulgaria, Turkey, Persia, India, China, and Japan. On December 17, 1886, he landed at Yokohama, Japan, having actually wheeled about 13,500 miles. He left Yokohama on the *City of Peking* and arrived at San Francisco on January 7, 1887.

7202. Round-the-world bicycle trip by a woman was made by Annie Londonberry, who left on June 26, 1894, from the State House, Boston, MA, and ended her trip on September 12, 1895, at Chicago. She returned to Boston on September 24, 1895, to collect a $10,000 bet for completing the trip within 15 months, as well as $5,000 in lecture fees.

7203. Round-the-world bicycle trip by a husband and wife was made by Dr. and Mrs. H. Darwin McIlrath of Chicago, IL, who left Chicago on April 10, 1895. They arrived in San Francisco on June 4, crossed the Pacific by ship to Japan, and continued on to China, Burma, India, Persia, Russia, Austria, Hungary, Germany, France, and Great Britain. They departed from Southampton, England, on the S.S. *Pennland,* arrived in New York City on October 27, 1898, and completed their trip of approximately 28,000 miles at Chicago on December 1. The trip took 3 years 8 months.

7204. Transcontinental bicycle trip made in less than three weeks was made in 1949 by Eugene McPherson, 22 years old, of Ohio State University, who left Santa Monica, CA, on September 1 and arrived at New York City on September 21, covering 3,054 miles in 20 days 4 hours 29 minutes.

SPORTS AND RECREATION—BOATING AND SAILING

7205. Ice yacht was built by Oliver Booth at Poughkeepsie, NY, in 1790 and consisted of a square box mounted on three runners covered with iron, a sail, a rudder post, and a wooden tiller.

7206. Boat club was the Knickerbocker Boat Club of New York, organized in 1811. The club had a white boat with green gunwales and gilt stripes, named the *Knickerbocker,* built by John Baptist. John Palmerton was coxswain. The *Knickerbocker* raced the *Invincible,* built by John and William Chambers, from Harsimus, NJ, to the Battery, New York City. The club disbanded in 1812.

7207. Yacht club was the New York Yacht Club, organized on July 30, 1844, by four yachting enthusiasts in the cabin of John Cox Stevens's schooner *Gimcrack.* Stevens was elected commodore on March 17, 1845, and a clubhouse was opened at Elysian Fields, Hoboken, NJ, in 1846 (it was towed to Glen Cove, NY, in 1904). On August 7, 1848, the secretary of the Navy authorized the club's sloops and schooners to proceed from port to port in the United States without entering or clearing at the Custom House, provided that they did not

transport merchandise for pay. An earlier yacht club, the Boston Yacht Club, founded in 1835 with Captain R.B. Forbes as commodore, was chiefly a fishing organization, and went out of existence in 1837.

7208. Regatta of importance was held by the New York Yacht Club, New York City, on July 16, 1845. The following contestants entered the competition: *Cygnet,* 45 tons; *Sybil,* 42 tons; *Spray,* 37 tons; *Newburg,* 33 tons; *Minra,* 30 tons; *Coquille,* 27 tons; *Gimcrack,* 25 tons; *Lancet,* 20 tons; and *Ada,* 17 tons. The yachts raced in the waters of New York from Robbin's Reef to Bay Ridge, thence to Stapleton, thence to the Southwest Spit buoy, and then back to the starting point.

7209. Yacht from the United States to win an international yacht race was *America,* owned by a syndicate headed by Commodore John Cox Stevens of the New York Yacht Club. It was designed by George Steers and built by William Henry Brown of New York. It was 101 feet 9 inches overall and 90 feet 3 inches at the waterline, with a beam of 23 feet 11 inches. The foremast measured 79 feet 6 inches and the mainmast 81 feet. The race, the first international yacht race ever held, took place in England on August 22, 1851, under the auspices of the Royal Yacht Squadron. The course circled the Isle of Wight, a distance of 53 miles. *America* covered the course in 10 hours 37 minutes, defeating 14 other contestants. It received a trophy valued at £100 sterling and known as the Queen's Cup, in honor of Queen Victoria.

7210. Ice yacht club was the Poughkeepsie Ice Yacht Club of Poughkeepsie, NY, which was organized in 1861. Regattas and races were held on the Hudson River.

7211. Transatlantic yacht race started on December 11, 1866. According to an agreement made on October 27, 1866, each of the three contestants put up $30,000, winner-take-all. The competing yachts were the *Henrietta,* 205 tons, owned by James Gordon Bennett; the *Vesta,* 201 tons, owned by Pierre Lorillard; and the *Fleetwing,* 212 tons, owned by George Osgood. The winner was the *Henrietta,* which made the trip from Sandy Hook, NJ, to Cowes, England, in 13 days 22 hours.

7212. Canoe club was the New York Canoe Club, founded in New York City in 1870. A clubhouse was built in 1879, during which year a regatta was held. The club was dissolved on August 3, 1880.

SPORTS AND RECREATION—BOATING AND SAILING—continued

7213. Catamaran was patented by Nathanael Greene Herreshoff of Providence, RI, who received a patent on April 10, 1877, on two parallel hulls. A catamaran is a jointed boat, used principally by lifeguards at public beaches.

7214. Boat race for fishermen was held on May 1, 1886, over a triangular course. The start was off the Boston Light, Little Brewster Island, Boston, MA, to and around the Davis Ledge buoy off Minot's Ledge, thence to and around Half Way Rock off the Marblehead shore, and back to Boston Light. The *John H. McManus* won the first prize of $1,500, finishing two miles ahead of the *Sarah H. Prior*, which was a few minutes ahead of the *Gertie S. Windsor*. The pilot schooner *Hesper* won the race and the cup, but not the prize money, as it was not truly a fisherman's boat.

7215. Yacht race broadcast on radio took place on October 16, 1899. It was the first of three races held off Sandy Hook, NJ, for the International Yacht Race trophy. The *Columbia*, under Commander John Pierpont Morgan of the New York Yacht Club, defeated the *Shamrock*, under Sir Thomas Lipton of the Royal Ulster Yacht Club. The signal was transmitted to coast stations and relayed by land wires to the Associated Press.

7216. Motorboat race under organized rules was held on June 23–24, 1904, under the jurisdiction of the Columbia Yacht Club, 86th Street and Hudson River, New York City. A 32-mile race was held for the Gold Cup of the Challenge Cup Series, from the clubhouse to a point 16 miles north and back. The trophy was won by C.C. Riotte in the *Standard*, a 100-horsepower motorboat 59 feet long, with an average speed of 22.57 statute miles (19.67 nautical miles) per hour. The contest was decided by a point system. The rules were formulated on April 22, 1903, by the American Power Boat Association, which was organized by seven yacht clubs on January 20, 1903.

7217. International lifeboat race was held on September 7, 1927, from the Statue of Liberty to Pier A, New York City, under the auspices of the Neptune Association. Eleven boats of different sizes, shapes, and weights from seven different nations competed. A prize cup was presented to Captain John F. Milliken of the M.S. *Segundo* of Norway, whose team of eight men covered the course in 15 minutes 27 seconds. Second honors went to the crew of the M.S. *Titania* of Norway and third place to the crew of the *De Grasse* of France. Later races developed uniform conditions.

7218. Motorboat ocean race under the rules of the Union of International Motorboating was the Sam Griffith Memorial Race, 172 miles, from Miami, FL, to Bimini, Bahamas, and back, on February 22, 1966. Although 31 boats started from Biscayne Bay, a 20-knot crosswind prevented 27 of them from reaching Bimini, and only two attempted the return trip. The *Thunderbird*, a 32-foot aluminum boat powered by two 500-horsepower United Aircraft gas turbine engines, with Jim Wynne and Walt Walters as codrivers, made the trip in 4 hours 45 minutes 23 seconds, at an average speed of 37 miles per hour. The *Thunderbird* was declared experimental and thus ineligible for the $3,000 prize. The award was made to Jerry Langer of the *No. 10*, which returned 2.5 hours after the *Thunderbird*.

7219. Human-powered submarine race was the International Submarine Race, which was organized by Henry Perry and took place in West Palm Beach, FL, on June 23–25, 1989. The race was run over a 5,396-foot underwater course and was intended to promote innovative design in submarine technology.

SPORTS AND RECREATION—BOWLING

7220. Bowling match recorded is that of January 1, 1840, played at the Knickerbocker Alleys, New York City.

7221. Bowling rule standardization was undertaken on November 13, 1875, when 27 delegates met at Germania Hall, New York City, and organized the National Bowling Association. The association soon went out of existence, however, as did the American Amateur Bowling Union, which was organized in 1890. The first important bowling convention to standardize rules was held by the American Bowling Congress, when it organized on September 9, 1895, in New York City.

7222. Bowling with duckpins was introduced in the spring of 1900 at the Diamond Bowling Alleys, Howard Street, Baltimore, MD, owned by Wilbert Robinson and John Joseph McGraw. A duckpins match at Schuetzen Park, Union Hill, NJ, on July 18, 1900, was won by Baltimore with 412 pins; the Stuyvesants of Brooklyn were second with 373 pins.

7223. Bowling tournament sponsored by the American Bowling Congress convened in Chicago, IL, on January 8–11, 1901. The participants were 41 five-man teams, 79 two-man teams, and 115 individuals. The prize money was $2,500. The individual winner was Frank "Pop" Breill (or Brill) of Chicago, with a score of 648. A two-man team, J. Voorhies and C.K.

Starr of the Metropolitan Bowling Club of New York, rolled 1,203 points and won $80. The Standard Bowling Club of Chicago rolled 2,720 points, defeating the Crescents of Chicago, who had 2,692 points, and winning $200.

7224. Bowler to make a perfect score of 300 in an American Bowling Congress tournament was William Knox of Philadelphia, PA, who rolled a perfect game on March 10, 1913, in Toledo, OH, in the 13th international bowling tournament. It was the 14th perfect game recognized with a gold medal.

7225. Bowling tournament for women held under the auspices of the Women's International Bowling Congress was held on March 17, 1917, in St. Louis, MO. Eight five-woman teams, 16 two-woman teams, and 24 individuals participated. The individual high score was won by Mrs. M. Koester, with an average of 162. The Women's International Bowling Congress had been organized on November 29, 1916.

7226. Bowler to roll two perfect games in a sanctioned league competition was Frank Caruana of Buffalo, NY, who rolled two perfect games in succession on March 5, 1924, in Buffalo. He had five strikes on a third game, rolling 29 strikes in succession. His score for four games was 1,115 (300, 300, 268, 247).

7227. Bowler who was a woman to obtain a perfect score was Emma Fahning of the Germain Cleaning team, who bowled a perfect game on March 4, 1930, in Buffalo, NY. This was the first perfect score in a sanctioned competition under conditions of the Woman's International Bowling Congress. Rose Jacobs, who rolled a 300 in Schenectady, NY, in 1929, was the first woman of record to achieve that feat in unsanctioned competition.

7228. Bowling match that used white balls on black lanes was held on May 23, 1959, at the Neptune Lanes, Brooklyn, New York City. The lanes were coated with a formula made by the Brunswick-Balke Collender Company. The match was televised on "The Major League Bowling Show."

7229. Bowler to win $10,000 in a tournament was Harry Smith of the St. Louis Falstaff team, who won the 19th annual All-Star match-game bowling championship for men on January 15, 1960, at the Civic Auditorium, Omaha, NE. He scored 13,399 pins in 64 games plus 212 for various winnings.

7230. Bowling automatic scoring machine was the Brunswick Automatic Scorer, installed in September 1967 at Village Lanes, a 16-lane bowling center in Chicago, IL. It could automatically record pinfall, ball by ball, frame by frame; compute and total individual and team scores; and, in a fraction of a second, print scores on a permanent scorecard and project them onto an overhead screen. One console served four lanes. The machine was first used in sanctioned league games on October 10, 1967.

7231. Bowling Triple Crown winner was Billy Hardwick, who won the United States National Championship in 1963, the Firestone Tournament of Champions in 1965, and the United States Open in 1969.

7232. Bowler to earn $100,000 in one year in tournaments was Earl Anthony of Tacoma, WA, who won $8,000 at the Buzz Fazio Open at Battle Creek, MI, on October 27, 1975, bringing his earnings to $100,890. It was his seventh victory in a Professional Bowlers Association tournament.

SPORTS AND RECREATION—BOXING

7233. Heavyweight boxing match to last longer than 100 rounds took place on September 9, 1841, at Caldwell's Landing, NY. Tom Hyer, son of fighter Jacob Hyer, defeated George "Country" McChester in a two-hour 55-minute match that lasted 101 rounds.

7234. Prizefighting ban enacted by a state was passed by Louisiana on May 12, 1890. Although the act defined prizefighting as a crime, it did not "apply to exhibitions and glove contests between human beings, which may take place within the rooms of regularly chartered athletic clubs."

7235. Boxing match timed by automatic timer took place on May 21, 1891, at the California Athletic Club, San Francisco, CA, when Peter Jackson, an Australian, and James John Corbett met in a 61-round fight that ended in a draw. The timer sounded a gong at the expiration of each three-minute round.

7236. Boxing match under the Marquis of Queensberry rules requiring the use of gloves was the heavyweight championship fight between John Lawrence Sullivan and James John Corbett on September 7, 1892, at the New Orleans Olympic Club, New Orleans, LA, for a winner-take-all purse of $25,000 and an outside bet of $10,000. Five-ounce gloves were used. Corbett won in the 21st round. An unofficial match under the rules took place on August 29,

SPORTS AND RECREATION—BOXING—
continued

1885, at Chester Park, Cincinnati, OH, between Sullivan and Dominick F. McCaffery. It was billed as "six rounds to decide the Marquis of Queensberry glove contest for the championship of the world." Sullivan was the winner but "ascribed his failure to knock the youngster out to the latter's get-away tactics and to the restrictions of the Marquis of Queensberry Rules."

7237. Championship heavyweight boxing title won in the first round was won by Jim Jefferies, 250 pounds, who knocked out Jack Finnegan, 180 pounds, in 55 seconds of the first round at Detroit, MI, on April 6, 1900.

7238. Boxing match broadcast on radio was presented on September 6, 1920, by station WWJ, Detroit, MI. The fight took place in Benton Harbor, MI. Jack Dempsey knocked out Billy Miske in the third round of a scheduled 10-round fight.

7239. Boxing match broadcast on radio from ringside was presented on December 22, 1920, from Madison Square Garden, New York City, where Joe Lynch of New York City defended his bantamweight title against Peter Herman of New Orleans in a 15-round fight.

7240. Boxing match to gross $1 million was held on July 2, 1921, at Jersey City, NJ. Approximately 75,000 persons paid $1,626,580 in gate receipts to see Jack Dempsey fight Georges Carpentier in a match that was billed as "the battle of the century." Dempsey won by a knockout in the 57th second of the fourth round. He received $300,000 and Carpentier $200,000 as purses.

7241. Heavyweight championship boxing match broadcast on radio was the Jack Dempsey–Georges Carpentier fight on July 2, 1921 at Boyle's Thirty Acres, Jersey City, NJ, in which Carpentier was knocked down in the fourth round. The fight was broadcast by Major J. Andrew White through station WJY, Hoboken, NJ.

7242. Boxing match to attract 100,000 spectators was the Jack Dempsey–Gene Tunney fight, held on September 23, 1926, at the Sesquicentennial Stadium, Philadelphia, PA. The attendance was 120,757 and the gate receipts were $1,895,733. Tunney defeated Dempsey in a 10-round fight under the point system.

7243. Boxing match to be shown on television was the fight between Lou Nova and Max Baer at Yankee Stadium, New York City, on June 1, 1939, which was televised by WNBT-TV, New York City. Sam Taub was the announcer. Referee Frank Fullam halted the bout in the 11th round and awarded the decision to Nova. About 300 persons saw the telecast in the smoking room of the New Amsterdam Theatre, and about 20,000 saw it in stores and dealer display rooms.

7244. Boxing referee who was a woman was Belle Martell of Van Nuys, CA, who was granted a license on April 30, 1940, by the California State Athletic Commission. She also held an announcer's license and a timekeeper's license. Her first assignment was a complete show of eight bouts in San Bernardino, CA, on May 2, 1940. She retired the following month, on June 24, 1940. The first female referee to judge a heavyweight championship match was Eva Shain, who refereed the 15-round Muhammad Ali–Earnie Shavers prizefight on September 29, 1977, at Madison Square Garden, New York City. She voted nine rounds for Ali, six for Shavers. She had been licensed by the New York State Athletic Commission on January 6, 1975.

7245. Boxing match at which admission tickets sold at $100 was the Joe Louis–Billy Conn world heavyweight championship fight that took place at Yankee Stadium, New York City, on June 19, 1946. It was promoted by the Twentieth Century Sporting Club. Louis won in the eighth round. The attendance was 45,266.

7246. Boxing referee in a heavyweight championship match who was African-American was Zack Clayton of Philadelphia, PA, who refereed the Jersey Joe Walcott–Ezzard Charles fight at Municipal Stadium, Philadelphia, PA, on June 5, 1952. Walcott outpointed Charles in the 15th round and retained his title.

7247. Amateur boxing match for women officially sanctioned by the United States Amateur Boxing Association took place on October 30, 1993, at Edmonds Community College, Lynnwood, WA. Sixteen-year-old Dallas Molloy defeated Heather Poyner, a 20-year-old kick boxer. Each weighed 144 pounds.

SPORTS AND RECREATION—BOXING—BOXERS

7248. Boxer to win distinction in the ring was Bill Richmond, born in Richmond, Staten Island, NY (now part of New York City), on August 5, 1763, the son of a slave owned by the Reverend Charlton. On July 8, 1805, Richmond knocked out Jack Holmes, alias Tom

Tough, in the 26th round at Cricklewood Green, a short distance from Kilburn Wells, England. On October 8, 1805, he was defeated by Tom Cribb at Hailsham, Sussex. He never fought in the United States.

7249. Boxer of fame who was African-American was Tom Molineux, who grew up in slavery, probably on a plantation in Virginia, and who is said to have won his freedom by winning boxing bouts arranged by slaveowners. He had a wide following by the time he left for England in 1810 to fight the English champion Tom Cribb on December 10. Although he knocked Cribb out in the 23rd round, he was falsely accused of using lead weights in his gloves and the fight continued, ending in a victory for Cribb in the 40th round.

7250. Boxer to die from blows inflicted in a fight was Andy Marsden, a British heavyweight, who fought a French heavyweight in New Orleans, LA, in 1834, and died the next morning of a fractured skull. The first known boxing death to take place in the ring occurred in a bareknuckle fight on September 13, 1842, at Hastings, NY. Christopher Lilly, an Englishman, age 23, weighing 140 pounds, fought Thomas McCoy, an Irish-American, age 21, weighing 137, for a purse of $200. The fight lasted 2 hours 41 minutes (120 rounds). McCoy suffered internal wounds and suffocated in his own blood.

7251. Bareknuckle world heavyweight boxing champion from the United States was Paddy Ryan, who won an undisputed title by knocking out Joe Goss of England in the 85th round on June 1, 1880, near Colliers, WV, about 300 yards from the Pennsylvania border. The fight, which lasted 1 hour 27 minutes, was witnessed by 300 spectators. The prize was $2,000.

7252. Heavyweight boxing champion of the world who was African-American was Jack Johnson, who defeated Tommy Burns at Sydney, Australia, on December 26, 1908, in 14 rounds, technically winning the championship. The actual title was earned on July 4, 1910, when he defeated Jim Jefferies in 15 rounds at Reno, NV. Johnson lost his title on April 5, 1915, at Havana, Cuba, to Jess Willard in 26 rounds.

7253. Boxer to hold three titles simultaneously was Henry Jackson Armstrong, who became featherweight champion by defeating Petey Sarron on October 29, 1937, at Madison Square Garden, New York City; welterweight champion by defeating Barney Ross on May 31, 1938, at Madison Square Garden Bowl, Long Island City (part of Queens, New York City); and lightweight champion by defeating Lou Ambers at Madison Square Garden, New York City, on August 17, 1938.

7254. World heavyweight boxing champion to retire undefeated was Rocky Marciano, who won all his 49 professional bouts, notably the heavyweight championship in Philadelphia, PA, on September 23, 1952. Marciano retired following the sixth defense of his heavyweight title, in which he knocked out Archie Moore at Yankee Stadium on September 21, 1955.

7255. World heavyweight boxing champion to regain his crown was Floyd Patterson. The title had been relinquished by the undefeated Rocky Marciano at his retirement. Patterson won it on November 30, 1956, in the Chicago Stadium, Chicago, IL, when he knocked down Archie Moore twice in the fifth round before the referee stopped the fight. He lost the title on June 26, 1959, in Yankee Stadium, New York City, to Ingemar Johansson of Goteborg, Sweden, who won with a technical knockout in the third round after knocking Patterson down seven times. He regained it in a 15-round rematch held on June 20, 1960, at the Polo Grounds, New York City, by knocking out Johansson in 1 minute 51 seconds of the fifth round.

7256. Boxer to win world titles in five weight divisions was Sugar Ray Leonard. He captured his first title, the World Boxing Council's welterweight championship, after knocking out Wilfredo Benitez of Puerto Rico in 1979. The next year he won the junior middleweight division in a victory over Ayub Kalule in Houston, TX. In 1987, he outpointed Marvin Hagler to win the middleweight title. In November 1988, he defeated Donny Lalonde of Canada to take the WBC light heavyweight and super middleweight titles. Leonard also won the gold medal in the light welterweight boxing event in the 1976 Summer Olympic Games in Montreal.

SPORTS AND RECREATION—BOXING—BOXERS—*continued*

7257. Boxer who was a woman to earn national recognition was Christy Martin, who fought Sue Chase in February 1996 in the first women's boxing match to be broadcast live on national television (by the Showtime cable network). In the following month she bested Deirdre Gogarty in front of a pay-per-view cable television audience of 1.1 million people, winning the World Boxing Council's women's championship belt.

SPORTS AND RECREATION—BULL-FIGHTING

7258. Bullfight was held on July 4, 1884, in Dodge City, KS. The first bull put up a good fight but was not killed. The next four bulls showed little inclination to fight and likewise were spared. To appease the crowd, the first bull was returned to the ring and was killed by Captain Gregorio Gallardo. Among the bulls were Ringtailed Snorter, Iron Gall, Sheriff, Rustler, Loco Jim, Ku Klux, and Eat-em-up Richard. Another bullfight was held the following day. Earlier, on July 31, 1880, a steer-baiting contest had been held in New York City before 4,000 spectators, but rubber caps had been placed on the bulls' horns and the matadors were not permitted to kill the bulls. The rosettes were not stuck into the bulls, but glued on.

7259. Bullfighter who was a woman to fight professionally was Patricia McCormick of Big Spring, TX, whose professional debut was made January 20, 1952, in Ciudad Juarez, Mexico. On that occasion she killed two bulls. In her first two years, she killed 80 bulls.

SPORTS AND RECREATION—CAR RACING

7260. Car race was held on Thanksgiving Day, November 28, 1895, over snowy roads from Chicago to Waukegan, IL, a distance of approximately 52 miles. The prize was $2,000, offered by the Chicago *Times-Herald*. Of the 80-odd entries, only 6 were able to start. The winner was James Franklin Duryea, who drove a gasoline-fueled automobile invented by his brother, Charles Edgar Duryea. It had a water-cooled engine with a water pump, a bevel-gear transmission with three speeds forward and reverse, and electric ignition. It was equipped with a rigid front axle with steering knuckles at the ends and was steered by a tiller handle, the

up-and-down motion of which changed the speed. Only one other entry finished, an American-rebuilt Benz electric car, which had to be pushed many miles. The average speed in the race was 7.5 miles per hour.

7261. Car race on a racetrack was held on September 7, 1896, at Narragansett Park, Cranston, RI, as a feature of the Rhode Island State Fair, and was witnessed by 40,000 spectators. Six gasoline and two electric automobiles raced. There were five heats of five miles each on a one-mile dirt track, one heat to be raced each afternoon of the fair week for a prize of $1,000 each day. The winner was a Riker Electric Stanhope made by the Riker Electric Motor Car Company, Brooklyn, NY (now part of New York City), which won in 15 minutes 1.75 seconds with a speed of approximately 24 miles per hour. The driver was A.H. Whiting and the passenger was A.L. Riker, the owner.

7262. Car hill-climbing contest was sponsored by the Automobile Club of America and held on September 9, 1901, at Nelson Hill, just outside Peekskill, NY, as one of the feature events in the 500-mile test run from New York City to Buffalo, NY. The Class A race was won by the Grout brothers, automobile manufacturers of Orange, MA, who entered a steam-propelled open Stanhope automobile of their own manufacture. The car weighed 920 pounds and seated two people, including the driver. The climb took 2 minutes 45 seconds. The hill was 226 feet high and 2,372 feet long, with a slant varying from 12 to 17 degrees.

7263. Long-distance car race was held on September 9–14, 1901, under the auspices of the Automobile Club of America, which sponsored a 500-mile race from its clubhouse at Fifth Avenue and 58th Street, New York City, to Buffalo, NY. The exact mileage was 464.2 miles, divided into day trips, with stops at Poughkeepsie, Albany, Herkimer, Syracuse, Rochester, and Buffalo. There were 87 entries in the race, with 80 starters. The race was not a speed or endurance test but a reliability test. It was won by David Wolfe Bishop, who drove a Panhard automobile manufactured by Panhard-Levassor of Paris. The car carried one passenger and driver and was powered by gasoline. The average speed was 15 miles per hour.

7264. Car race for the Vanderbilt Cup started at Hicksville, NY, on October 8, 1904, on a 10-lap course over a 30-mile circuit. Five Mercedes cars, three Panhards, two Fiats, two Pope-Toledos, and one each by Renault, De Dietrich, Clement-Bayard, Simplex, Packard, and Royal Tourist were entered. The race was concluded when two cars finished. The winner was George Heath in a Panhard, with an average speed of 52.2 miles per hour. The first Vanderbilt Cup race to be won by an American took place on October 24, 1908, at the Motor Parkway, Long Island, NY, over a 23.46-mile circuit for a distance of 11 rounds, or 258.06 miles. George H. Robertson won in a 90-horsepower Locomobile. His average speed was 64.3 miles per hour, his time 4 hours 48.2 seconds.

7265. Car race from New York to Paris via Seattle and Yokohama started on February 12, 1908, from Times Square, New York City. Six automobiles were entered: three French, one Italian, one German, and one American. The race was won by George Schuster, driver, George J. Miller, mechanic, and Montague Roberts, assistant mechanic, in a car made by the E.R. Thomas Motor Company, Buffalo, NY. The elapsed time was 170 days, of which 88 were spent in actual driving. The average daily run was 152 miles, the longest daily run 420 miles. The Thomas car arrived in Paris on August 1 and returned to New York City on the SS *Lorraine,* arriving on August 15. The race was sponsored by the *New York Times* and the Paris newspaper *Le Matin.*

7266. Transcontinental car race started on June 1, 1909, from New York City and ended on June 22 at Seattle, WA, scene of the Alaska-Yukon Pacific Exposition. Mayor George Brinton McClellan fired the starting gun. There were six entrants: an Acme, an Itala, a Shawmut, two Model T Fords, and a Stearns that failed to start. The race was won by Bert W. Scott and C. James Smith, who drove one of the Ford cars. They received a silver prize and a $2,000 award from H. Robert Guggenheim.

7267. Long-distance car race on a racetrack took place on May 30, 1911, at the Indianapolis Speedway, Indianapolis, IN. It was won by Ray Harroun, 29 years old, who drove a 16-cylinder Marmon Wasp over the 2.5-mile oval course for a distance of 500 miles in 6 hours 41 minutes 8 seconds, an average of 74.7 miles per hour. Only 38 of the 44 cars entered completed the race. One contestant was killed in an accident. The race was witnessed by 85,000 spectators.

7268. Race-car driver to win $100,000 was Roger Ward of Indianapolis, IN, who drove a Leader Card Special on May 30, 1959, at an average speed of 185.857 miles per hour for the 500-mile race at the Indianapolis Speedway.

7269. Driver who was a woman to compete in the Indianapolis 500 was Janet Guthrie of Iowa City, IA, who qualified on May 22, 1977, at the Indianapolis Speedway with an average speed of 188.403 miles per hour for four consecutive laps. She drove a Lightning-Offenhauser. In the race, which was held on May 29, she reached a speed of 151.207 miles per hour, but was forced out by mechanical trouble after 27 laps, finishing 29th out of 33 entries. The following year, she qualified again and finished ninth. Guthrie was an aerospace engineer before she started competitive driving in the 1960s.

SPORTS AND RECREATION—CRICKET

7270. Cricket match was held in New York City, on the future site of Fulton Market, on May 1, 1751, between the Londoners and the New Yorkers. The New Yorkers made 80 and 86 and the Londoners 43 and 47. Cricket had been played by local teams on the same site about five years earlier.

7271. Cricket club was the Boston Cricket Club, founded in 1809 in Boston, MA. The first president was Andrew Allen.

7272. Cricket game played by a college team is said to have been played at Haverford College, Haverford, PA. The game was introduced in 1836 by William Carvill, the college gardener. The bats and balls were of home manufacture.

7273. International cricket tournament was held on October 3–5, 1859, at St. George's ground, Hoboken, NJ, between the All-England team, captained by George Parr, and the St. George's Cricket Club of New York, captained by J. Wisden. The American team was weak at bat and the English team won in one inning with a score of England 156, United States 92. A second game was played on October 10, 1859, at Philadelphia, PA, the English winning by seven wickets. The English team played two games in the United States and two in Canada.

7274. College cricket club team to tour England was the Haverford College team, Haverford, PA, captained by John Lester, which competed from July 17 to July 31, 1896, against Harrow School, Eton College, Cambridge University, and others. They won four games, lost four games, and drew seven games. They returned to the United States on the *Belgenland* on August 5, 1896.

SPORTS AND RECREATION—CURLING

7275. Curling club was the Orchard Lake Curling Club, organized in the winter of 1831–32 near the present site of Pontiac, MI. Lacking genuine curling stones, the club improvised wooden blocks sawed from hickory and shaped with ax and chisel.

7276. Indoor curling rink devoted exclusively to curling was opened on December 19, 1920, by the Country Club, Brookline, MA.

7277. National curling championship competition was held on March 28–30, 1957, at the Stadium, Chicago, IL, with 10 teams competing. The winner was the Hibbing Curling Club from Hibbing, MN, which won eight games and lost one.

SPORTS AND RECREATION—DOG RACING

7278. Dog racetrack to use an imitation rabbit was opened on February 22, 1920, at Emeryville, CA. It was designed by R.S. Hawley and built by Owen Patrick Smith. The track was about 300 yards around. A car was run through a housing that covered the trolley and track. The arm carrying the rabbit extended from the car through a slot on the track side.

7279. Greyhound racing association was the International Greyhound Racing Association, formed on March 3, 1926, in Miami, FL, to systematize efforts and to conduct the races on the highest possible standard. The first high commissioner was Owen P. Smith.

7280. Dogsled race on an Olympic demonstration program was held on February 6–7, 1932, when the United States and Canada entered 13 teams. Contestants were required to cover a course of 25.1 miles on two consecutive days. First place was won by Emile St. Goddard of Canada, but the United States teams won 7 of the 12 points. The race was held at Lake Placid, NY.

SPORTS AND RECREATION—FENCING

7281. National fencing league was the Amateur Fencers League of America, organized on May 6, 1891 with Dr. Graeme M. Hammond of New York City as the first president. The first competition was held in 1892. The winners were W. Scott O'Connor of the Fencers Club, men's foils; Dr. B.F. O'Connor of the New York Athletic Club, dueling swords; and R.O. Haubold of the New York Athletic Club, sabers.

7282. Intercollegiate fencing championship competition was held by the International Fencing Association on May 5, 1894, at the Racquet and Tennis Club, New York City. Harvard defeated Columbia five matches to four and won the silver challenge cup. Yale, the only other entry in the competition, withdrew after an accident to one of the team. Fitzhugh Townsend of Columbia had the highest individual score.

7283. International fencing championship competition was held at the Racquet Club, Washington, DC, on November 18–19, 1921. The United States team defeated Great Britain 13–3 the first day. The U.S. team lost 10–4 on the second day. The finals were held on November 21 at the Hotel Astor, New York City, where the final score was 8–8. The United States won 25 of the 46 matches to win the Colonel Robert M. Thompson International Trophy.

SPORTS AND RECREATION—FISHING

7284. Fishing club of more than temporary existence was the Schuylkill Fishing Company, founded in 1732 in Philadelphia, PA, with a limited membership of 25.

7285. Fly casting tournament was held on June 18, 1861, in Utica, NY, by the New York State Sportsmen's Association. The "throwing the fly" competition was won by George Lennebacker of Utica, NY.

7286. Indoor fly casting tournament was held March 15-20, 1897, under the auspices of the Sportsmen's Association at Madison Square Garden, New York City. Competitions were held in casting for distance, casting for accuracy and distance, bass fly casting, and so on. A record for the first cast to exceed 100 feet was made by R.C. Leonard, who cast a distance of 101 feet 6 inches on March 17.

7287. Wooden plug lure for fishing that was patented was invented by James Heddon, a fisherman renowned for his hand-carved lures, including wooden frogs used for bass fishing. Heddon opened a factory in 1896. In 1902, he received a patent for a wooden lure he called "Fish-Bait."

SPORTS AND RECREATION—FLYING

7288. Balloon cup race held in the United States for the James Gordon Bennett Aeronautic Cup took place on October 21, 1907, at St. Louis, MO, with a field of nine entrants. It was won by the German balloon *Pommern*, which flew 880 miles to Asbury Park, NJ, in 39 hours

59 minutes 25 seconds, with Oscar Erbslöh and Henry Holm Clayton as pilots. The previous year's race, which was held in Europe, was the first to be won by an American. It took place on September 30, 1906, with a field of 16 balloons from seven countries. The route was from Paris, France, to Whitby, England, a distance of 410 miles. The winner was Lieutenant Frank Purdy Lahm, pilot of the balloon *United States,* who arrived in 22 hours 17 minutes.

7289. Aviation correspondence school was the International School of Aeronautics, New York City, which opened on January 1, 1908. It offered three courses—in spherical balloons, dirigible balloons, and heavier-than-air machines—for amateurs in aerostatics and aviation. Albert C. Triaca was the founder and director of the school, and Lieutenant Colonel Espitallier of the French army prepared the lessons.

7290. Airplane race won by an American in Europe was the First International Air Race held at Reims, France, during the week of August 22, 1909. The fastest time on the 20-kilometer course was 15 minutes 50.6 seconds. The race was won by Glenn Hammond Curtiss of Hammondsport, NY, in the *Golden Flyer* (length 31 feet 1 inch, wingspan 30 feet, height 11 feet).

7291. Airship race was held at St. Louis, MO, on October 4–9, 1909, when four dirigibles—all the existing dirigibles in the United States—flew from Forest Park and Clayton Road to Kingshighway and Lindell avenues and back. The first prize of $1,000 was won by Lincoln Beachey. Roy Knabenshue and Captain Thomas Scott Baldwin were close runners-up. Cornwall Dixon, using foot power, was carried over the city and landed in East St. Louis. The four dirigibles were housed in improvised tents and were filled with hydrogen produced by a slow process with sulfuric acid and iron filings.

7292. Aviation meet was held on January 10–20, 1910, under the auspices of the Aero Club of California, at Dominguez Field in Los Angeles, where American planes were given an opportunity to prove their power in competition with foreign planes. The foreign exhibits included two Farman biplanes and two Blériot monoplanes. The American exhibits included three Curtiss biplanes, which were piloted by Glenn Hammond Curtiss, Charles Keeney Hamilton, and Charles Foster Willard. Louis Paulhan broke the world altitude record at the meet with a flight to 4,165 feet.

7293. Airplane race between cities was held on August 5, 1911, between New York City and Philadelphia, PA. Three Curtiss machines with Curtiss engines left Governors Island, NY. The race was won by Lincoln Beachey, who covered the 83 miles in 1 hour 50 minutes. Hugh Robinson completed the trip in 2 hours 8 minutes 47 seconds, while Eugene Burton Ely was forced to land at Princeton, NJ.

7294. Airplane flying school operated by a woman was the Stinson School of Flying, Stinson Field, San Antonio, TX, opened in 1914 by Emma Beaver Stinson. In 1916 the school moved to a field of about 200 acres that was leased from the city of San Antonio for $5 a year. The school trained Canadian pilots during World War I. The chief instructors were Mrs. Stinson's daughters, Marjorie and Katherine. Katherine was a famed stunt flyer who, in 1917, became the first female stunt pilot to tour China and Japan. Their brothers, Jack and Eddie, were also pilots and opened an aircraft manufacturing company in 1920.

7295. Transcontinental air race was an aerial derby sponsored by the American Flying Club of New York. It began on October 8, 1919. Fifteen planes left the Presidio, San Francisco, CA, and 48 left Roosevelt Field, Mineola, NY, in a 5,400-mile race across the continent and back. The winner was Lieutenant Belvin W. Maynard, in a de Havilland-4 with a Liberty motor. He left Mineola at 9:24 A.M. on October 8 and reached the Presidio on October 11 with an elapsed time of 3 days 6 hours 4 minutes. On his return trip, he left the Presidio on October 14 at 1:19 P.M. and landed at Roosevelt Field on October 17 with elapsed time of 3 days 21 hours 31 minutes. His actual flying time for the round trip was 24 hours 59 minutes 48.5 seconds. Maynard won by elapsed time, but in his actual flying time he was eclipsed by three others.

7296. Parachute-jumping contest was held on October 12, 1923, at Mitchel Field, NY. Two men on a Martin bomber and two men on a de Havilland jumped from a 4,500-foot height and landed 400 feet from each other, 1.5 minutes apart. The first to land was Staff Sergeant Theodore Schieuming of Brooklyn, New York City. One thousand spectators witnessed the jump.

7297. Transcontinental air derby for women was the Powder Puff Air Derby, which began on August 18, 1929, when 19 pilots took off from Santa Monica, CA, in 10-minute intervals. Overnight stops were made at San Bernardino, CA; Phoenix and Douglas, AZ; Midland and Abilene, TX; Wichita, KS; East St. Louis, IL;

SPORTS AND RECREATION—FLYING—
continued

and Columbus, OH. On August 26, 1929, 15 women completed the trip at Cleveland, a distance of 2,350 miles from the starting point. The winner was Louise McPhetridge Thaden of Pittsburgh, PA, whose time was 20 hours 19 minutes 10 seconds.

7298. Airplane race of importance in which both men and women were contestants was the National Air Race, held on August 30–31, 1931, from Los Angeles, CA, to Cleveland, OH, in which 36 men and 16 women competed. It was a handicap derby scored on the basis of comparative power of motor and speed of plane. It was won by Phoebe Fairgrave Omlie of Memphis, TN. She also won the grand prize and the prize for the women's division.

7299. Round-the-world airplane passenger race started on September 30, 1936, from Lakehurst, NJ. Three reporters, Dorothy Kilgallen, Herbert Roslyn Ekins, and Leo Kiernan, made the trip by three different commercial flying routes as a test. The race was won by Ekins of the *New York World-Telegram,* who returned to Lakehurst on October 19, having covered 25,654 miles in 18 days 11 hours 14 minutes 33 seconds. The average speed was 127 miles per hour. The total flying time was 8 days 10 hours 6 minutes.

7300. Hang-gliding national championships were held on October 25, 1973, at the Angeles National Forest in Sylmar, CA. The distance winner was Chris Wills, a student from Santa Ana, CA.

SPORTS AND RECREATION—FOOT-BALL

7301. Football club was the Oneida Football Club, which was organized in 1862 by Gerrit Smith Miller at Epes Sargent Dixwell's School in Boston, MA. The members played all comers from 1862 to 1865. They were never defeated, nor was their goal line crossed.

7302. Football rules were formulated at a meeting held on October 18, 1873, in New York City and attended by delegates from Columbia, Princeton, Rutgers, and Yale universities.

7303. Intercollegiate football association was the Intercollegiate Football Association, organized at the Massasoit House, Springfield, MA, on November 23, 1876, with Columbia, Harvard, and Princeton as its three charter members (Rutgers and Yale joined later). The association standardized the number of men on each team at 15 and set the area of the field at 140 by 70 yards.

7304. Penalty rule in football was passed in 1885. It required five points to be deducted from a team's score if one of its players crossed the scrimmage line before the ball was snapped. The rule was the invention of Walter Chauncey Camp, the head of football at Yale University, New Haven, CT, who was hoping to discourage the kind of violent play that resulted in numerous deaths among student football players each year.

7305. Professional football association was the American Professional Football Association, formed in Canton, OH, on September 17, 1920, by 11 clubs representing the following cities: Chicago, Decatur, and Rock Island, IL; Hammond and Muncie, IN; Rochester, NY; and Akron, Canton, Cleveland, Dayton, and Masillon, OH.

7306. Big-league football team to travel coast-to-coast was the Chicago Bears, who tied the Chicago Cardinals 0–0 on November 26, 1925, at Chicago, IL. Harold "Red" Grange, known as the "Galloping Ghost," gained a net of 40 yards in 14 plays and added 69 more in running back three points; this was his first professional game. The season concluded in January 1926 with Grange having played at New York, Providence, Pittsburgh, Detroit, Chicago, Tampa, Jacksonville, Maimi, New Orleans, Los Angeles, San Diego, San Francisco, Portland, and Seattle.

7307. College football player to score 50 points in one game was Clark Hinkle of Bucknell University, Lewisburg, PA, who scored 50 points on November 28, 1929 at Lewisburg against Dickinson College, Carlisle, PA. He made eight touchdowns and two extra points. Bucknell won 78–0.

7308. Professional football game to be shown on television took place on October 22, 1939, from Ebbets Field, Brooklyn, New York City, where the Brooklyn Dodgers defeated the Philadelphia Eagles by a score of 23–14. The game was transmitted by station W2XBS of the National Broadcasting Company, New York City. The first telecast of a pro football championship game was the Super Bowl game that took place on January 15, 1967, at Los Angeles, CA, where the Green Bay Packers defeated the Kansas City Chiefs by a score of 35–10. The telecast was pooled and shown by NBC-TV and CBS-TV.

SPORTS AND RECREATION—FOOTBALL—EQUIPMENT

7309. Football goalpost was used in the contest between McGill University and Harvard University that was played at Jarvis Field, Cambridge, MA, on May 14, 1874. The teams played rugby football under Harvard's rules, which stated that every goal constituted a game. McGill arrived with 11 men and Harvard with 15, four of whom were dropped to equalize the teams. Harvard won three games, the first two lasting about five minutes and the third about 12 minutes. As McGill is located in Montreal, Canada, this was the first international rugby football contest to be played, as well as the first instance in which an admission fee was charged at a collegiate sporting event. The proceeds were used for lavishly entertaining the McGill team. A second match was played the following day, and a third match was played in the fall in Montreal.

7310. Football uniforms worn in a game were worn on November 13, 1875, at New Haven, CT, by teams from Yale and Harvard colleges. The Yale team wore dark trousers, blue shirts, and yellow caps, while the Harvard team wore crimson shirts and stockings and knee breeches. Harvard won the game 4–0. The game at that time was closer to rugby than to present-day football. Each team had 15 players.

7311. Football dummy for tackling purposes was improvised by Amos Alonzo Stagg at Yale University, New Haven, CT, in the fall of 1889. He used an old gymnasium mat for the purpose.

7312. Football uniform numerals sewn on the players' uniforms to enable the spectators easily to distinguish the players were used by the University of Pittsburgh, Pittsburgh, PA, on December 5, 1908, for the game against Washington and Jefferson College. The score was 14–0 in favor of Washington and Jefferson.

7313. Football with a rubber covering was made by the W.J. Voit Rubber Corporation, Los Angeles, CA, in March 1936. The ball, which did not soak up water, was otherwise identical to conventional leather-covered footballs. It was also cheaper and longer-lasting.

7314. Football goalposts of collapsible folding metal were manufactured by Fisher Metal Parts Manufacturing Company, New York City, and were installed in June 1936 at Yankee Stadium, New York City.

SPORTS AND RECREATION—FOOTBALL—GAMES

7315. Intercollegiate football contest in the world was played at Rutgers Field, New Brunswick, NJ, on November 6, 1869. Captain William Stryker Gummere '70 of Princeton University (later chief justice of New Jersey) challenged Captain William James Leggett of Rutgers to a friendly game. Each team consisted of 25 men. The rules were that each goal constituted a game and that six games would decide the match, which lasted one hour. The first team to score six goals was Rutgers, while Princeton scored four.

7316. International football game was played on December 6, 1873, at New Haven, CT. The Yale team defeated a team from Eton College, England, with a score of two goals to one.

7317. Intercollegiate football championship was won in the fall of 1876 by Yale University, New Haven, CT, under Captain Eugene Voy Baker '77. Although it was not a member of the Intercollegiate Football Association, Yale played and defeated Columbia, Harvard, and Princeton. The standing of the teams was Yale 2, Princeton 2, Harvard 1, Columbia 0.

7318. Tournament of Roses was held on January 1, 1890, at Pasadena, CA, under the auspices of the Valley Hunt Club. It was originally called the Battle of the Flowers and consisted of amateur sports contests held in the afternoon. The first college football contest at the Tournament, held on January 1, 1902, was a game between the University of Michigan and Stanford University, which was won by Michigan 49–0. Football games have been a regular annual event since January 1, 1916, when Washington State College defeated Brown University 14–0.

7319. Football game played indoors was played by the Young Men's Christian Association of Springfield, MA, against the Yale Consolidated Team of New Haven, CT, a team that had five of the Yale varsity players on it. The game was played as part of a three-day winter carnival at Madison Square Garden, New York City, after the close of the 1891 season. The score was 16–10 in Yale's favor.

SPORTS AND RECREATION—FOOTBALL—GAMES—*continued*

7320. Intercollegiate Army–Navy football game was played on November 29, 1890, at West Point, NY. The Army (U.S. Military Academy) captain was Dennis Michie '92, and the Navy (U.S. Naval Academy) captain was Charles Rulf Emerich '91. The score was Navy 24, Army 0.

7321. Football game at night was played on September 29, 1892, at the Mansfield Fair, Mansfield, PA, between the Mansfield Teachers College and the Wyoming Seminary of Kingston, PA. Twenty electric lights of 2,000 candlepower were used with a Thompson and Huston Dynamo Machine. The game lasted 70 minutes, but only one half was played, neither team scoring.

7322. Professional football game was played on September 3, 1895, at Latrobe, PA, between the Latrobe Young Men's Christian Association and the Jeannette Athletic Club, Jeannette, PA, which Latrobe won 12–0. Latrobe's captain was Harry Ryan and Jeannette's was "Posie" Flowers. Since the regular quarterback was unable to play, John K. Brallier of Indiana, PA, was paid $10 and expenses to fill in. The following year four men were paid, and in 1897 the entire team was paid.

7323. Intercollegiate football game between African-American colleges was played on January 1, 1897, at Brisbine Park, Atlanta, GA, between Atlanta University and Tuskegee Normal and Industrial Institute. Atlanta won 10–0. Atlanta's captain was George F. Porter, and Tuskegee's captain was Clarence Matthews.

7324. Football game to be broadcast on radio with a play-by-play description was presented on November 25, 1920, by station WTAW of College Station, TX. The game was played at College Station on Thanksgiving Day between Texas University and the Agricultural and Mechanical College of Texas. At that time the station was operating under an experimental license and had the call letters 5XB. A spark transmitter was used and the transmission was in code.

7325. Intercollegiate football game to attract 100,000 spectators was played for the Pacific Coast championship at Memorial Stadium, Berkeley, CA, on November 22, 1924, by teams from the University of California and Leland Stanford University, both undefeated. The score was 20 to 20. The stadium accommodated 76,000 spectators, and 24,000 more witnessed the game from "Tight Wad" hill.

7326. World championship professional football game was played on December 17, 1933, at Wrigley Field, Chicago, IL, when the Chicago Bears of the Western Division defeated the New York Giants of the Eastern Division of the National Football League 23–21. The purse was divided, with 60 percent going to the players, 15 percent to each club, and 10 percent to the league. Shares for individual players were $210 for the Bears and $140 for the Giants.

7327. All-star football game was sponsored by Chicago Tribune Charities, a nonprofit organization, and was played on August 31, 1934, at Soldier Field, Chicago, IL. The Chicago Bears, coached by George Halas, played the College All-Stars, coached by Noble Kizer of Purdue, to a 0–0 tie. The players each received $150 and expenses. Attendance was 79,432.

7328. Professional football game in which 10 touchdowns were made took place at Temple Stadium, Philadelphia, PA, on November 6, 1934, when the Philadelphia Eagles defeated the Cincinnati Reds 64–0. Three touchdowns each were made by Homer "Swede" Hanson and Joseph Carter and one each by Edward Matesic, Edward Storm, Marvin Ellstrom, and Roger "Red" Kirkman.

7329. Intercollegiate football game to be shown on television was played at Randall's Island, New York City, on September 30, 1939, between Fordham University and Waynesburg College. It was televised by station W2XBS, New York City. Fordham won 34–7.

7330. Professional football championship game broadcast on radio took place on December 8, 1940, at Griffith Stadium, Washington, DC. The Mutual Broadcasting System paid $25,000 for the rights to the game, which was broadcast by Walter Lanier "Red" Barber. The Chicago Bears defeated the Washington Redskins 73–0 and won the Ed Thorp Memorial Trophy.

7331. Championship game of the American Football League was played on January 1, 1961, at Houston, TX. The Houston Oilers of the Eastern Division defeated the Los Angeles Chargers of the Western Division 24–16. The Oilers received $1,025 per man and the Chargers $718. The attendance was approximately 32,200.

7332. Football game to gross $1 million was played on December 31, 1961, when the Green Bay Packers defeated the New York Giants 37–0 for the National Football League championship at City Stadium, Green Bay, WI. There were 39,029 spectators, and the paid attendance amounted to $1,013,792. Each of the Packers received $5,195 and each of the Giants $3,340. The Packers scored two touchdowns, three field goals, and four conversions.

7333. Super Bowl football game between the National Football League and the American Football League for the world championship was played on January 15, 1967, at the Memorial Coliseum, Los Angeles, CA, before 63,036 spectators. The Green Bay Packers (NFL) defeated the Kansas City Chiefs (AFL) 35–10. The winning Packers received $15,000 each, the Chiefs $7,500 each.

7334. Professional football game in which a woman participated took place on August 15, 1970, at Orlando, FL, when the Orlando Panthers of the Atlantic Coast League played the Bridgeport Jets. Patricia Palinkas, 27 years old, the wife of a player on the Panthers team, held the ball as her husband attempted to kick for the extra point. The 122-pound woman was forced to run with the ball and was brought down within seconds by a 235-pound tackle. The Panthers won 26–7.

7335. Football game to last longer than 80 minutes was the American Football League divisional playoff game on December 25, 1971, at Arrowhead Stadium, Kansas City, MO. The game had three halves (six quarters) and lasted 1 hour 22 minutes 40 seconds. The Miami Dolphins defeated the Kansas City Chiefs 27–24.

7336. Football game in which referees were allowed to check television instant replays was the Hall of Fame game played on July 29, 1978, at Canton, OH, when the Philadelphia Eagles defeated the Miami Dolphins 17–3. The game was telecast on Channel 7.

SPORTS AND RECREATION—GOLF

7337. Golf players' club was formed in Charleston, SC, in 1786.

7338. National championship stroke-play golf match was held on September 3–4, 1894, at the Newport Country Club, Newport, RI. The championship was won by W.G. Lawrence with a score of 188. The runner-up was Charles Blair Macdonald, whose score was 189.

7339. Amateur golf tournament was played on the Grey Oaks course of the St. Andrews Golf Club, Yonkers, NY, on October 13, 1894. Thirty-two contestants played an 18-hole match. The winner was Lawrence B. Stoddard of St. Andrews Golf Club, one up, and the runner-up was Charles Blair Macdonald of Chicago, IL. The first amateur tournament officially held under the rules of the United States Golf Association was played on October 12, 1895, at the Newport Country Club, Newport, RI. There were 32 entries. The winner was Charles Blair Macdonald and the runner-up Charles E. Sands.

7340. Golf association (national) of importance was the United States Golf Association, formed in New York City on December 22, 1894, by the following charter members: Newport Golf Club, Newport, RI; Shinnecock Hills Golf Club, Southampton, NY; the Country Club, Brookline, MA; St. Andrews Golf Club, Mount Hope, NY; and the Chicago Golf Club, Wheaton, IL. The first president was Theodore A. Havemeyer of the Newport Golf Club.

7341. Open golf championship tournament sponsored by the United States Golf Association was held on October 4, 1895, at the New Newport Country Club, Newport, RI. It was won by Horace Rawlins, age 19, of the club. His score was 173 for 36 holes (45–46–41–41). Rawlins defeated 10 professionals and 1 amateur. He won $150 and a gold medal.

7342. Amateur golf championship tournament for women was won by Mrs. Charles R. Brown in November 1895 at the Meadow Brook Golf Club, Westbury, NY. There were 13 entries in the unofficial match. Mrs. Brown scored 132 for 18 holes.

7343. Intercollegiate golf association was formed in January 1897 by representatives from Columbia, Harvard, Princeton, and Yale. The first tournament was held on May 13–14, 1897, at the Ardsley Casino Golf Club, Ardsley-on-Hudson, NY. The team championship was won by Yale; the individual championship was won by Louis Pintard Bayard, Jr., of Princeton's class of 1898.

7344. Professional open golf championship match under the rules of the United States Golf Association was held June 14, 15, and 17, 1901, at the Myopia Hunt Club, Hamilton, MA. Willie Anderson and Alex Smith tied for first place with 331 for 72 holes. An 18-hole playoff was won by Anderson 85–86.

SPORTS AND RECREATION—GOLF—
continued

7345. Professional Golfers Association tournament was held from October 10 to October 14, 1916, at the Siwanoy Golf Club, Mount Vernon, NY, by James "Long Jim" Barnes of the Whitemarsh Country Club, Philadelphia, PA, who defeated runner-up Jock Hutchinson at medal play, one up. Barnes won the Rodman Wanamaker trophy, $500, a diamond-studded gold medal, and custody of a huge silver cup. There were 31 players in the 36-hole tournament.

7346. International golf match for the Walker Cup was held at the National Golf Links of America, Southampton, NY, on August 28–29, 1922. The course was 6,650 yards and 18 holes. The U.S. team, captained by William Clark Fownes, Jr., obtained eight points, five points in the singles and three points in the foursomes, while the team from Great Britain and Ireland, captained by R. Harris, obtained four points, three points in the singles and one point in the foursomes. The cup was presented by George Herbert Walker, president of the United States Golf Association. An informal competition had been held the preceding year.

SPORTS AND RECREATION—GOLF—
COURSES

7347. Golf course with nine holes was completed at Brenton's Point, near Newport, RI, in 1890.

7348. Golf course with 18 holes was designed and constructed by Charles Blair Macdonald for the Chicago Golf Club at Wheaton, IL. It was opened for play in 1893.

7349. Miniature golf course is said to have been built in 1929 by John Garnet Carter near Chattanooga, TN. The greens were made of a compound of cottonseed hulls dyed green. Carter patented the name "Tom Thumb," which was the trade name of a midget golf course system that was leased and sold as an amusement game device. Small golf courses with fewer than nine holes and courses with short holes, however, had been established previously. The Tom Thumb system presented hazards, obstacles, and so on. The game was played exclusively with a putter.

7350. Illuminated nine-hole regulation golf course was the 3,230-yard course of the Tall Pines Golf Club, Sewell, NJ, illuminated on August 23, 1963, by 121 mercury flood lights of 1,000 watts each. It was a private course by day and open to the public at night.

SPORTS AND RECREATION—GOLF—
EQUIPMENT

7351. Golf clubs for hitting balls are mentioned in an account of the estate of William Burnet, governor of New York and Massachusetts, who died in 1729. Among his possessions were "Nine Golf clubs, one iron ditto and seven dozen balls."

7352. Golf tee was invented by George F. Grant of Boston, MA, who obtained a patent on December 12, 1899, on a wooden tee with a tapering base portion and a flexible tubular concave shoulder to hold the golf ball.

7353. Golf club with a steel shaft was invented by Arthur F. Knight of Schenectady, NY, who obtained a patent on November 22, 1910, on a golf club with tapered and tempered steel tubing.

SPORTS AND RECREATION—GOLF—
GOLFERS

7354. Golf mixed foursome was played on March 30, 1889, at the Grey Oaks course of the St. Andrews Golf Club, Yonkers, NY. John B. Upham and Carrie Low played John Reid and Mrs. John G. Reid.

7355. Golf player in an official amateur tournament who was African-American was John M. Shippen, 16 years old, who played in a tournament held on July 18, 1896, at the Shinnecock Hills Golf Club, a 4,423-yard course in Southampton, NY, where he worked as a caddie. His score was 159 (78 and 81). The first prize of $200 was won by James Foulis of Chicago, IL, whose score was 152 (78 and 74).

7356. Golfer to win the United States Women's Amateur Championship was Beatrice Hoyt, who won by seven strokes at the Morris Country Club, Morristown, NJ, on October 7–9, 1896; by six strokes at the Essex Golf Club, Manchester, MA, on August 24–26, 1897; and by eight strokes at the Ardsley Golf Club, Ardsley, NY, on October 11–16, 1898.

7357. Golf champion born in America to win the United States Amateur Golf Championship was Herbert M. Harriman of the Meadow Brook Golf Club, Hempstead, NY, who on July 8, 1899, defeated Findlay S. Douglas, the defending champion, by a score of 3–2. Ninety-eight entrants participated in the tournament, the fifth United States Championship, which was played at the Onwentsia Club, Lake Forest, IL. Harriman's scores were 81 and 82.

7358. Golfer to win both the U.S. Open and the U.S. Amateur in the same year was Charles "Chick" Evans, Jr., who won the national open championship at the Minikahda Country Club, Minneapolis, MN, on June 27th, 29th, and 30th, 1916, with a score of 286 (70, 69, 74, and 73), and the amateur championship at the Merion links, Philadelphia, PA, on September 9, 1916, defeating Bob Gardner 4 up 3 to play in the final round.

7359. Golfer to play 180 holes in one day was Edward Styles, who started the marathon contest at 5:53 A.M. on July 11, 1919, at the Old York Road Country Club, Philadelphia, PA, played 180 holes, 10 rounds of golf, in 796 strokes, and finished playing at 8:32 P.M. The average time per round was 1 hour 19 minutes, the total playing time 13 hours 10 minutes. He walked nearly 40 miles and took time out three times for a change of shoes and for refreshments. His average score was 79.6 strokes per round.

7360. Golf champion to win both the U.S. Open and the Professional tournaments was Gene Sarazen, who won the United States Open Golf Championship on July 15, 1922, at the Skokie Country Club, Glencoe, IL, with a score of 288 for 72 holes, defeating 320 starters. He won the Professional Golfers' Tournament at the Oakmont Country Club, Oakmont, PA, on August 18, 1922, winning a diamond medal and a purse of $500.

7361. Golf champion to hold the four highest golf titles at one time was Bobby Jones of Atlanta, GA, who won the British Open Championship at Hoylake, England, on June 20, 1930; the British Amateur at St. Andrews, Scotland, on May 31, 1930; the United States Open at Minneapolis, MN, on July 12, 1930; and the United States Amateur at Philadelphia, PA, on September 27, 1930.

7362. Holes in one shot by a father and son in the same golf game were shot by Charles H. Calhoun, Sr. and Jr., on August 24, 1932, at the third hole of the Washington Golf Club, Washington, GA, while the two were playing in a foursome.

7363. Golfer born in America to win the British Women's Amateur Golf Tournament was Babe Didrikson Zaharias, who defeated Jacqueline Gordon on June 12, 1947, at Kullane, Scotland, to win the championship.

7364. Golfer to break 60 for 18 holes in a major tournament was Sam Snead, who shot a 59 (31 out, 28 coming home), 11 strokes under par, in the third round of the Sam Snead Festival golf tournament at White Sulphur Springs, WV, on May 16, 1959. He had a score of 196 for 54 holes and won $4,500. The tournament was originally named the Greenbrier Open.

7365. Golfer to play 24 hours continuously on a regulation course was James J. Johnson of Fort Worth, TX, who played 363 holes at the 6,101-yard course of the Abilene Country Club, Abilene, TX, on October 14–15, 1959. The rules enabled him to walk or run.

7366. Golfer to earn over $100,000 in one year in regular tournaments was Arnold Palmer, whose winnings in 1963 were $130,835, of which $128,230 was won in 20 official events and $2,605 in nine unofficial events.

7367. Golfer to earn $100,000 in a contest was Miller Barber of Texas, who won the first prize of $100,000 in 144 strokes in the World Open at Pinehurst, NC, on November 8–17, 1973.

7368. Golfer to break 60 in a Professional Golfers Association tour was Allen L. Geiberger of California, who shot a 59 on June 10, 1977, in the second round of the Danny Thomas Memphis Open at the Colonial Country Club course, Memphis, TN (7,249 feet; par 72). His score was 273 and he won $40,000.

7369. Golfer to shoot below his age on a Professional Golfers Association Tour was Sam Snead, age 67, who shot a 66 on the fourth day of the Quad Cities Open tournament at Coal City, IL, on July 22, 1979. His score was 277 (70, 67, 74, and 66).

7370. Golf champion of African-American and Asian descent was Tiger Woods, 18, who won the U.S. Amateur Golf Championship, held at the Tournament Players Club–Sawgrass Stadium course in Ponte Vedra, FL, on August 28, 1994. He defeated 22-year-old Trip Kuehne to become the youngest winner in the 99-year history of the event. Woods went on to win two more amateur championships before turning professional in 1996. On April 13, 1997, Woods won the Masters Tournament at the Augusta National Golf Club, Augusta, GA, becoming at age 21 the youngest person ever to do so. His final round of 69 gave him a total score of 270, or 18 under par, the lowest in the history of the event. Woods's grandparents were African-American, Chinese, and Thai.

SPORTS AND RECREATION—GYMNAS-TICS

7371. Gymnasium to offer systematic instruction was started by the Round Hill School, Northampton, MA, which was opened on October 1, 1823, by John Green Cogswell and George Bancroft. Charles Beck was the instructor in Latin and gymnastics. Gymnastics was scheduled from 5 P.M. to 7 P.M.

7372. Gymnastics instruction at a college was offered in 1826 at Harvard University, Cambridge, MA. Charles Theodore Christian Follen, professor of German, was appointed superintendent of the gymnasium. He introduced Friedrich Ludwig Jahn's system of gymnastics.

7373. Gymnastics instruction at a college for women was offered in 1862 by Mount Holyoke College, South Hadley, MA. The first teacher of gymnastics was a Miss Evans. During the first year, the course was optional, and the instruction was given "in the long storeroom over the wood and coal shed at the northwest corner of the court." A gymnasium was erected in 1865. Courses in calisthenics had been introduced in 1835, but were replaced by the Dio Lewis system of gymnastics.

7374. Trampoline commercially manufactured was produced in 1937 by the Nissen Trampoline Company, Cedar Rapids, IA, a company founded by George P. and Paul F. Nissen. They were known as bouncing nets, bouncing tables, and rebound tumblers. The name was derived from the Spanish word for diving board.

SPORTS AND RECREATION—HOCKEY

7375. Professional hockey team was the Portage Lake Hockey Club of Houghton, MI, formed in 1896. It became a professional team in 1903 under the leadership of Dr. J.L. Gibson, a dentist. In 1903, the team won 24 of the 26 games it played.

7376. Hockey team from the United States to win the Stanley Cup was the Seattle Metropolitans, Seattle, WA, of the Pacific Coast League of Canada, which defeated the Montreal Canadiens of the National Hockey League on March 21, 24, and 27, 1917, winning three of the four games played to decide the series.

7377. National Hockey League team from the United States was the Boston Bruins, admitted to the NHL in 1924. Previously, only Canadian teams had qualified for the organization.

7378. Hockey game to be shown on television was played on February 25, 1940, at Madison Square Garden, New York City, between the New York Rangers and the Montreal Canadiens. It was televised by station W2XBS, New York City. The Rangers won, 6–2.

7379. Professional hockey player to score 50 goals in one season was Joseph Henri Maurice "Rocket" Richard of the National Hockey League's Montreal Canadiens, who scored his 50th goal on March 18, 1945, in the 17th minute 45th second of the third and last period against the Boston Bruins at the Boston Garden, Boston, MA. He retired in 1960 with 544 goals in 16 regular seasons.

7380. Professional hockey player who was African-American was forward Willie O'Ree of the National Hockey League's Boston Bruins, whose first game was played on January 18, 1958, against the Montreal Canadiens at the Forum, Montreal, Canada. Boston won 3–0. O'Ree participated in two games in 1957–58 and 43 games in 1960–61, when he scored 14 points (4 goals, 10 assists). The first African-American player on an amateur team was Arthur Dorrington, who signed with the Atlantic City Seagulls of the Eastern Amateur League on November 15, 1950, in Atlantic City, NJ, and played for them in 1950 and 1951.

7381. Professional hockey player to reach a score of more than 1,000 points was Gordie Howe of the National Hockey League's Detroit Red Wings, who made two goals on November 27, 1960, at Detroit, MI, in a game against the Toronto Maple Leafs, bringing his score to 1,001 points. He became the first player to score more than 100 points in one season in 1968, when he scored 103 points (44 goals, 59 assists). In his NHL career, Howe scored 786 goals and made 1,023 assists, for a total of 1,809 points.

7382. Goalie in a National Hockey League team to score a goal was Bill Smith of the New York Islanders. On November 28, 1979, in a game against the Colorado Rockies at the Nassau Coliseum in Uniondale, NY, Smith stopped a shot that rebounded and slid all the way down the ice into the opposing team's goal.

7383. Professional hockey player who was a woman was Manon Rheaume, a 20-year-old goalie from Quebec. In September 1992, she became the first woman to play in a National Hockey League game when she minded the net for an American team, the Tampa Bay Lightning, in the first period of an exhibition contest. She gave up two goals and made seven saves.

SPORTS AND RECREATION—HORSE RACING

7384. Horse race run on a regular basis was held on the Newmarket Course, Hempstead Plains, NY, in 1665, when Governor Richard Nicolls, the first English governor of New York, established the course. He issued the order to measure off a mile course on the level prairie near the village and gave a cup to reward the owner of the swiftest-running horse, "not so much for the divertisement of youth as for encouraging the bettering of the breed of horses, which through neglect has been impaired."

7385. Horse racing ban by a colony was enacted on June 4, 1674, by Massachusetts. It provided "that whatsoever p'son shall run a race with any horse in any street or Comon road shall forfeite five shillings in Mony forthwith to be levied by the Constable or set in the stockes one houre if it be not payed."

7386. Horse breeders' society was the Massachusetts Society for Encouraging the Breed of Fine Horses, formed in Boston, MA, in 1810. Annual trials and competitions were held on October 23–25 at Boston's Washington course. The rules provided that "every driver shall be dressed at starting neatly with a jockey cap, silk jacket with sleeves."

7387. Horse race trotting course was established at Jamaica, NY (now part of the borough of Queens, New York City), in 1825 by the New York Trotting Club. On May 16, 1825, the main race was won by Screwdriver.

7388. Race between a locomotive and a horse-drawn vehicle took place on August 25, 1830, between Relay and Baltimore, MD, a distance of nine miles. The locomotive was the *Tom Thumb,* an engine of the Baltimore and Ohio Railroad, driven by Peter Cooper. The *Tom Thumb* was involved in an accident, and the horse won.

7389. Harness horse race at night was held at the Beacon Track, Hoboken, NJ, on October 5, 1843. The winner of the two-mile race for the $300 purse was Dutchman, who won in 5:19. Hiram Woodruff was the driver. Americus (George Spicer, driver) was second and Lady Suffolk (Dave Bryan, driver) was third, having previously run a dead heat.

7390. Futurity horse race was held on October 10, 1843, at Nashville, TN, and known as the Peyton Stakes. Out of 30 nominations, only four faced the starter. Four one-mile heats were held. Glumbalditch, a filly owned by Thomas Kirkham of Nashville, won the third and fourth heats, thereby winning the race and a purse of $35,000. She was later renamed Peytona.

7391. Steeplechase was held on October 26, 1869, at Jerome Park, Westchester County, NY, by the American Jockey Club. Seven horses participated. The race was won by Oysterman, Jr., a five-year-old owned by Colonel D. McDaniel. Between 15,000 and 20,000 spectators witnessed the inaugural race.

7392. Kentucky Derby horse race was run on May 17, 1875, at the Churchill Downs Course at Louisville, KY. There were 15 starters. Aristides won a $2,850 purse covering the mile-and-a-half course in 2 minutes 37.75 seconds. Oliver Lewis was the jockey. Volcano was second, Verdigris third.

7393. American Derby horse race was held at Washington Park Club, Chicago, IL, on June 28, 1884. The race for three-year-olds was won by Modesty, whose time for the 1.5-mile course was 2 minutes 42.75 seconds. He won $10,700 in a field of 12. Isaac Murphy was the jockey.

7394. Coursing club was the American Coursing Club, which was organized at Topeka, KS, on July 9, 1886, with Colonel Taylor of Emporia, KS, as president. There were 38 entries at the first inaugural meeting, which took place from October 10 to October 23, 1886, at Great Bend. The first all-age stake winner was Midnight, owned by Colonel Taylor.

7395. Race between a horse and a bicycle was the Great Velocipede Race of 1888, run over a gravel road between Silver City and Deming, NM, a distance of almost 60 miles. H.J. Kennedy of Denver, CO, rode the bicycle. His competitors were Billy King, a cowboy, who rode a horse named Rattler, and a rider on a pinto horse. The pinto won. King came in second but was so exhausted he collapsed and had to be put to bed. The bicyclist was last.

7396. Horse race of 1,000 miles started at 5:30 P.M. on June 13, 1893, at Chadron, NE. The destination was Chicago, IL, via Long Pine, Oneill, and Wausa, NE; Sioux City, Galva, Fort Dodge, Iowa Falls, Waterloo, Manchester, and Dubuque, IA; and Freeport and De Kalb, IL. Each contestant was allowed two race

SPORTS AND RECREATION—HORSE RACING—continued

horses, one to ride and one to follow. The winner, John Berry, riding Poison, arrived on June 27 at 9:30 P.M., followed on June 28 by Emmet Albright at 11:15 A.M. and Joe Gillespie at 1:31 P.M.

7397. Horse race mutuel ticket to pay more than $1,000 was made on June 17, 1912, at the Latonia track, Covington, KY, when Wishing Ring, a four-year-old colt, paid $1,885.50 to win, $744.40 to place, and $172.40 to show. Only four $2 tickets were sold. The colt was owned by J.S. Respess and won the sixth race; the odds were 900–1.

7398. Hambletonian harness horse race for three-year-olds was won by Guy McKinney, a four-year old, winner of $45,868.42 of the $73,451.32 purse in 2 minutes 5.14 seconds at the initial stake on August 30, 1926, at the New York State Fair, Syracuse, NY. The horse was owned by Henry B. Rea of Pittsburgh, PA, and driven by Nat Ray.

7399. Totalisator to record racetrack bets and odds was invented by Sir George Julius, an Australian engineer, and installed in 1931 by the American Totalisator Company, Baltimore, MD, at the Hialeah Race Track, Miami, FL. It was known as "the totalizer" and "the Julius" and was first used on January 14, 1932. The first totalisator that was fully electronic and capable of data processing was the Westbury Tote, first used on May 15, 1965, at the Roosevelt Raceway, Westbury, NY.

7400. Electric-eye camera installed at a racetrack to measure photo finishes was placed in operation on January 16, 1936, at the Hialeah Race Course, Hialeah, FL. Called the Futurity Foto-Finish Camera, it was invented by G. Harry Adalian, a rug dealer from Boston.

7401. Electric starting gate for horse races was invented by Clay Puett, who installed a two-stall working model on May 8, 1939, at Hollywood Park, Inglewood, CA. The first full-size gate was used at Bay Meadows Race Track, San Francisco, CA, on October 7, 1939. The gates were equipped with a bomb-release type of lock operated by solenoids. The front doors when closed formed a V and opened outward by means of springs.

7402. Horse stakes race ending in a triple dead heat was the 46th running of the Carter Handicap, the sixth race at Belmont Park, NY, on June 10, 1944. It was seven-furlong race (about 0.875 miles) for horses three years old or older. The winning time was 1 minute 23.4 seconds. The $11.700 purse was split equally between Eric Guerin on Joe W. Brown's Brownie, Jimmy Stout on Belair Stud's Bossuet, and G.L. Smith on William Ziegler, Jr.'s Wait-A-Bit.

7403. Perfecta or Exacta horse race in which bettors select the first two horses in the same race paid $30.40 for a $2 winning ticket on Wednesday, June 30, 1965, at Monticello Raceway, Monticello, NY. Bayard was first and Sonny Ardin second. There were 481 winning tickets; $17,242 was bet.

7404. Horse race for a purse of more than $1 million was the All American Futurity for quarter horses held on September 4, 1972, at Ruidoso Downs, Ruidoso, NM. It was won by Possumjet, a chestnut filly two-year-old quarter horse owned by Jack Byers of Blanchard, OK. Pete Herrera was the jockey. Possumjet won $336,629.70 of the $1,035,900 purse and returned $44.60, $16, and $7.20 across the boards. The time for the 400 yards was 20:04 seconds. Attendance was 14,338.

SPORTS AND RECREATION—HORSE RACING—HORSES

7405. Horse bred in the United States to win a major race abroad was Prioress, a four-year-old bay mare, winner of the Cesarewitch Handicap at Newmarket, England, on October 13, 1857. There were 37 starters, of which 3 tied. In the runoff after the regular daily program, Prioress won by a length and a half (4 minutes 15 seconds for the 2-mile 468-yard course). The odds were 100–1. Her owner was Richard Ten Broeck.

7406. Horse whose total purses exceeded $100,000 was Miss Woodford, foaled in 1880. She won 37 of 48 races between 1882 and 1886 for a purse of $118,270.00. The mare was the entry of the brothers Michael and Philip Dwyer.

7407. Horse bred in the United States to win the English Derby was Iroquois, a three-year-old, winner of the Epsom Derby at Epsom Downs, England, on June 1, 1881. There were 14 competitors. Fred Archer was the jockey. The horse was owned by Pierre Lorillard IV, inventor of the tuxedo.

7408. Filly to win the Kentucky Derby horse race at Churchill Downs, Louisville, KY, was Regret, Harry Payne Whitney's chestnut filly. She ran the mile and a quarter in 2 minutes 5.4 seconds on May 8, 1915, to win the 41st Kentucky Derby. There were 16 starters.

7409. Horse to win the Triple Crown for three-year-olds was Sir Barton. In 1919 he won a total of $57,275. He won $20,825 in the Kentucky Derby, Churchill Downs, KY, on May 1; $24,500 in the Preakness, Pimlico, MD, on May 14; and $11,950 in the Belmont Stakes, Elmont Park, NY, on June 11. At Belmont a new track record was set for the mile and three-furlong course. The rider in all three races was J. Loftus, making him the first jockey to win the Triple Crown.

7410. Horse to win a $100,000 purse in one race was Whichone, a two-year-old, son of Chicle and Flying Witch, who won the 40th Belmont Futurity at Belmont Park Race Track, Elmont Park, NY, on September 14, 1929. The time was 1 minute 19.6 seconds for 6.75 furlongs (approximately 0.88 mile). The purse was $105,730. Harry Payne Whitney was the owner and Sonny Workman the jockey. There were 17 starters in the race.

7411. Horse to win $1 million in races was Citation, a six-year-old bay colt born and owned by Calumet Farms, which won the $100,000 Hollywood Gold Cup Handicap at Hollywood Park, Inglewood, CA, on July 14, 1951. His total earnings in 1947–48 and 1950–51 in 45 starts, resulting in 32 firsts, 10 seconds, 2 thirds, and 1 unplaced finish, amounted to $1,085,760.

SPORTS AND RECREATION—HORSE RACING—JOCKEYS

7412. Jockey to win the Triple Crown twice was Eddie Arcaro, who rode Whirlaway in 1941 and Citation in 1948 to win the "Big Three": the Kentucky Derby at Churchill Downs, Louisville, KY, the Preakness at Pimlico, MD, and the Belmont Stakes at Belmont Park, Elmont, NY. The combined purses amounted to $150,410 in 1941 and $324,090 in 1948.

7413. Jockey to win the Kentucky Derby five times at Churchill Downs, Louisville, KY, was Eddie Arcaro. He rode Lawrin on May 7, 1938, to win $47,500; Whirlaway on May 3,1941, to win $61,275; Hoop Jr. on June 9, 1945, to win $64,850; Citation on May 1, 1948, to win $83,400; and Hill Gail on May 3, 1952, to win $96,300.

7414. Jockey to win seven consecutive races in one day was Leroy Moyers, who rode seven straight winners at Suffolk Downs, Boston, MA, on July 4, 1967, including Four Fingers in the $11,525 Mayflower Stakes.

7415. Jockey who was a woman to win on a regular parimutuel flat track was Barbara Jo Rubin of Miami Beach, FL, who rode Cohesian in the ninth race (6.5 furlongs) on February 22, 1969, at the Charles Town Race Track, Charles Town, WV, in 1 minute 20.2 seconds.

7416. Jockey who was a woman to ride two winners in one day was Barbara Jo Rubin of Miami Beach, FL, who won by three lengths in the 5.5-furlong race on Co Zipper in the second race and the 5-furlong race on Cohesian in the 11th race at Waterford Park, Chester, WV, on March 8, 1969. Both horses were owned by D. Forrest Lawson.

7417. Horse race pari-mutuel in which all the jockeys were women was the six-furlong Lady Godiva $10,000 handicap at Suffolk Downs, Boston, MA, on April 19, 1969. The third race, in which $115.044 was wagered, was won by Penny Ann Early on Royal Fillet, which paid $5.40. Second place was won by Diane Crump on Destiny's Twist, third place by Tuesee Testa on Critical.

7418. Jockey who was a woman to ride in the Kentucky Derby was Diane Crump of Oldsman, FL, who rode Fathom on May 2, 1970, in the 1.25-mile 96th Kentucky Derby, Churchill Downs, KY. In the 17-horse race, she finished 15th.

7419. Jockey who was a woman to win a major stakes race was Robyn Smith, who won the six-furlong Paumanauk Handicap ($27,450) on March 1, 1973. She rode North Sea, a four-year-old colt, winning by four lengths at the Aqueduct Race Track, Aqueduct, NY. The horse, owned by Alfred Gwynn Vanderbilt, paid $26.20 on a $2 ticket.

7420. Jockey to win more than $5 million in purses in one year was Steve Cauthen of Kentucky, whose purses on October 24, 1977, amounted to $5,009,692.

7421. Jockey who was a woman to win a Triple Crown race was Julie Krone, who won the 1993 Belmont Stakes in Elmont, NY, riding Colonial Affair.

SPORTS AND RECREATION—HUNTING

7422. Fox hunting club was the Gloucester Fox Hunting Club, composed of residents of Philadelphia, PA, and Gloucester County, NJ. A group of 27 dog owners met on October 29, 1766, in Philadelphia and decided to formulate rules for a club, which began its activities on January 1, 1767. John Massey, huntsman, was appointed to keep the dogs. The club dissolved in 1818.

7423. Game protection society was the New York Sportsmen's Club, founded on May 20, 1844, in New York City. B.J. Meserole was president. On March 10, 1873, it became the New York Association for the Protection of Game.

7424. Game preserve was established by Judge John Dean Caton of Ottawa, IL, about 1860, on his own estate. The preserve was well stocked with all kinds and species of American native game.

7425. Hunting license required by a state was mandated by New York in a law passed on April 30, 1864. Deer hunters in Suffolk County were obliged to pay $10 for a license, the money to be "paid over to the overseers of the poor of such town for the benefit of the poor thereof."

7426. Bird hunting regulation law enacted by Congress was passed by Congress on March 4, 1909. It amplified state protections by prohibiting the interstate transportation of birds, parts, feathers, and so on. The first federal law regulating the shooting of migratory birds, known as the McLean Law, was passed by Congress on March 4, 1913.

SPORTS AND RECREATION—ICE SKATING

7427. Ice skating champion was Charles June of Newburgh, NY, who defeated recognized English contestants in 1849.

7428. Ice skating club was the Skaters' Club of the City and County of Philadelphia, formed on December 21, 1849, at Stigman's Hotel, Philadelphia, PA. The first president was James Page.

7429. Figure skater of note was former ballet master Jackson Haines, known as the "American Ice Master." He was born in New York City and moved to Europe in 1865 after winning the men's ice skating championship. Haines revolutionized the sport of ice skating with balletic turns, glides, and spirals that were unknown to skating at that time. The "Haines Method" is the basis for modern figure skating.

7430. Indoor ice skating rink was built by Thomas L. Rankin at Madison Square Garden, New York City, in 1879. It had 6,000 square feet of surface. On February 12, 1879, a gala carnival was presented.

7431. International championship figure skating tournament was held on March 20, 1914, at the Arena Ice Rink, New Haven, CT, under the rules of the Skating Union of America. The ladies' championship was won by Theresa Weld of the Skating Club of Boston, MA, the men's by Norman Scott of the Winter Club of Montreal, Canada. Other events were pair skating to music and waltzing.

7432. Figure skating champion from the United States to compete in the Olympic Games was Richard Button of Englewood, NJ, who earned the title on February 5, 1948, at the Fifth Winter Olympic Games, St. Moritz, Switzerland.

7433. World figure skating champion from the United States was Tenley Albright of Newton Center, MA, who won the title on February 15, 1953, at Davos, Switzerland. She was 17 years old.

7434. National women's figure skating four-time winner was Carol Elizabeth Heiss of Ozone Park, Queens, New York City, who won her first title on March 15, 1957, at Berkeley, CA; her second and third in 1958 and 1959; and her fourth consecutive title on January 29, 1960, at Seattle, WA.

7435. Artificial ice skating rink of Olympic size was formally opened by Vice President Richard Milhous Nixon on February 18, 1960, at Squaw Valley, CA, for the Eighth Olympic Winter Games. Freezing brine was piped into the rink through 70 miles of steel tubing. It had 300 feet of roof floating on cables suspended from 80-foot steel and concrete pillars.

7436. Ice skater to cover 100 miles in less than six hours was Kirt Barnes, whose time on February 26, 1971, for 100 miles at the Fuller ice skating rink, Ann Arbor, MI, without a pause, was 5 hours 34 minutes 1.45 seconds.

SPORTS AND RECREATION—MOTORCYCLING

7437. Motorcycle endurance run was held July 4–5, 1902, covering a distance of 254 miles from Boston, MA, to New York City, through South Framingham, Worcester, Warren, and Springfield in Massachusetts, and Hartford (where there was an overnight stop), Meriden, New Haven, Bridgeport, and Greenwich in Connecticut. Of the 32 entries, 31 started, 13 finished, and 7 made a perfect score of 1,000 points. The winner was George N. Holly of Bradford, PA, who arrived at 5:18 P.M. on July 5, followed half a minute later by N.P. Bernard of Hartford, CT. The race was sponsored by the Metropole Cycling Club of New York.

7438. Motorcycle hill-climbing contest was staged in Riverdale, NY, on May 30, 1903, and was won by Glenn Hammond Curtiss, who received a gold medal from the New York Motorcycle Club. The race created quite a sensation because it was not believed that a motorcycle had much power.

7439. Motorcycle association was the Federation of American Motorcyclists, organized on September 7, 1903, at Manhattan Beach, NY. The first president was R.G. Betts of the New York Motor Cycle Club. About 200 delegates attended the first meeting.

7440. Motorcycle racer who was a woman and who was licensed by the American Motorcycle Association was Kerry Kleid, 21 years old, of Rye, NY, who received license No. 143B on August 22, 1971. Her debut was made on October 17, 1971, in the Mt. Peter motocross, six miles north of Greenwood Lake, NY.

SPORTS AND RECREATION—OLYMPIC GAMES

7441. Olympic athlete from the United States to win a gold medal was James Brendan Connolly of the Suffolk Athletic Club of South Boston, MA, who represented the United States in the hop, skip, and jump (triple jump) contest on April 6, 1896, at the Olympiad in Athens, Greece, the first Olympic Games held in the modern era. His jump of 45 feet exceeded that of his nearest competitor by 3 feet 3 inches. The American team of 10 men won 9 of the 12 events.

7442. Olympic athlete from the United States to win 10 medals was Ray Ewry of Lafayette, IN, who won the standing high jump and the standing broad jump at the games held in Paris in 1900, in St. Louis in 1904, in Athens in 1906, and in London in 1908. At the Paris and St. Louis Games, he also won the hop, step, and jump (now called the triple jump).

7443. Olympic Games held in the United States was the Third Olympiad, held in St. Louis, MO, from May 14 to August 1, 1904. The games were first awarded to Chicago, IL, but were later given to St. Louis to be staged in connection with the World's Fair. There were few entrants other than Americans in the 14 events. In the field competitions, the American athletes made a clean sweep of all the events with the exception of lifting the bar and throwing the 56-pound weight.

7444. Olympic medalist who was African-American was George C. Poage of the Milwaukee Athletic Club, Milwaukee, WI, who participated in the Third Olympiad at St. Louis, MO, in 1904. He placed third in the 400-meter hurdles on August 31 and third in the 200-meter hurdles on September 1. The first African-American athlete to win an individual event in the Olympic Games was William DeHart Hubbard of the University of Michigan, who won first place in the running long jump competition on July 8, 1924, in the Colombes stadium in Paris.

7445. Olympic gold medalist from the United States who was a woman was Ethelda Bleibtrey, who competed in the Seventh Olympiad, held in Antwerp, Belgium, in 1920. She won the 100-meter free-style swim on August 25 and the 300-meter free-style swim on August 26.

7446. Olympic Games competition to be held in the winter was held at Lake Placid, NY. Governor Franklin Delano Roosevelt of New York opened the games on February 4, 1932. The participants included 307 athletes from 17 nations.

7447. Olympic gold medalist in both the Summer and Winter Olympics was Edward Eagan. He captured the gold medal in the light-heavyweight boxing competition at the 1920 summer games in Antwerp, Belgium, and was also a member of the winning four-man bobsled team in the 1932 winter games, held in Lake Placid, NY.

7448. Olympic athlete from the United States to win four gold medals in one year was Jesse Owens. In the Olympic Games held in Berlin, Germany in 1936, he won the 100-meter run on August 3, the broad jump on August 4, the 200-meter run on August 5, and the 400-meter relay on August 9. The relay team consisted of Owens, Ralph Metcalfe, Foy Draper, and Frank Wykoff. Owens was African-American, and his success was considered a rebuke to the Nazi ideology of the Germans who hosted the games.

SPORTS AND RECREATION—OLYMPIC GAMES—*continued*

7449. Olympic gold medalist who was an African-American woman was Alice Coachman, who set a record in the women's high-jump competition with a jump of 5 feet 6.125 inches at the 1948 Summer Olympic Games in London. She was one of 100 American athletes to be honored at the 1996 Centennial Olympic Games in Atlanta, GA.

7450. Olympic Games boycott took place in 1980, when the United States refused to send its athletes to the Summer Olympic Games in Moscow to protest the Soviet Union's invasion of Afghanistan. On April 22, 1980, at the urging of President Jimmy Carter, the U.S. Olympic Committee voted 1,604 to 797 to boycott the games. The following day, a number of athletes and coaches filed a class-action suit in U.S. District Court in Washington, DC, to block the boycott, but the suit was dismissed on May 16. The Soviet Union retaliated by boycotting the 1984 Summer Olympics in Los Angeles, CA.

SPORTS AND RECREATION—PHYSICAL EDUCATION

7451. Physical education and hygiene professorship at a college was established in 1860 by Amherst College, Amherst, MA.

7452. Physical education department at a college on a par with other departments was established by the University of Chicago, Chicago, IL. Amos Alonzo Stagg was made assistant professor and director of the Department of Physical Culture and Athletics and a regular member of the faculty in 1892. In 1901 he was granted a full professorship. He and other members of the department coached the university athletic teams. Previously, in most colleges, athletics had been under the control of a student athletic association.

SPORTS AND RECREATION—PINBALL

7453. Toy pinball game machine was the Caille Log Tavern, built in 1910 by Adolph Caille of the Caille Brothers Company, Detroit, MI. The machine, which was placed flat on a table, had a slightly inclined board with pins on it. Marbles were shot up the board through an alley to top position, and would then roll down into scoring positions.

7454. Pinball game machine was the Whoopee Game, manufactured in 1930 by the In and Outdoor Games Company, Chicago, IL. It was 24 inches wide and 48 inches long and had adjustable legs. It sold for $175. The fee for playing was five cents for 10 balls. The game was modeled after the children's game known as Bagatelle.

7455. Pinball ban enacted by a city was approved on June 19, 1939, by Atlanta, GA, and was signed by Mayor William Berry Hartsfield. The act provided that any person convicted of a violation of this ordinance be subject to a fine not to exceed $20 and a sentence to the public works of the city for a period of 30 days, at the discretion of the recorder.

SPORTS AND RECREATION—POLO

7456. Polo club was the Westchester Polo Club, organized in New York City in 1876. Matches were played at the Jerome Park racetrack in Westchester County, New York.

7457. Polo mallets and balls were imported from England in 1876 by the newspaper publisher James Gordon Bennett, who introduced polo to the United States. The first games were played in Dickel's Riding Academy, at the northeast corner of Fifth Avenue and 39th Street, New York City. The horses were brought up from Texas by Harry Blassan, a New York riding master.

7458. International polo series was played at Newport, RI, on August 25, 1886, between teams representing England and the United States. England won the series of two games with scores of 10–4 and 14–2. The American team consisted of Captain Thomas Hitchcock, Raymond Belmont, Foxhall P. Keene, and W.K. Thorne.

7459. Polo association (national) was the United States Polo Association, formed on June 6, 1890, in New York City, by the Meadow Brook Club, Westbury, NY; the Philadelphia Country Club, Bala, PA; the Rockaway Hunting Club, Cedarhurst, NY; and the Westchester Polo Club, Newport, RI. The first chairman was H.L. Herbert and the first secretary-treasurer was Douglas Robinson.

7460. Intercollegiate indoor polo championship was won by Princeton University, which defeated Yale University on March 18, 1922, at the Squadron A Armory, New York City. Each team consisted of three players.

7461. Polo game played outdoors at night took place on July 2, 1931, at Homewood Field, Baltimore, MD, between the Maryland Polo Club and the 110th Field Artillery. The first game was played with four men on each side. Homewood Field was amply lighted for the event.

SPORTS AND RECREATION—ROLLER SKATING

7462. Roller skates were invented by Dr. James Leonard Plimpton of Boston, MA, in 1863. Plimpton's patented wooden skates had with four wheels each and were strapped onto ordinary shoes. They earned him more than $2 million in royalties and license fees.

7463. Roller skating rink open to the public was opened at Newport, RI, in 1866 under the auspices of James Leonard Plimpton of Boston, MA, the inventor of the Plimpton skate. The skating rink was located in the Atlantic House, at the corner of Bellevue Avenue and Pelham Street, on the site later occupied by the Elks' Home.

7464. All-metal roller skate was marketed by Everett Hosmer Barney. In 1864 he started a business in Springfield, MA, as Barney and Berry. In 1919 the capital stock was purchased by the Winchester Repeating Arms Company, which in 1922 moved the manufacturing business to its plant in New Haven, CT. Barney was the first to conceive and develop the idea of fastening shoes to skates by means of metal clamps. He obtained a patent covering his invention of a screw-clamp skate on January 16, 1866.

7465. Roller derby was the Transcontinental Roller Derby, which opened on August 13, 1935, at the Coliseum, Chicago, IL, under the direction of Leo A. Seltzer. Fifty contestants, paired two to a team, endeavored to skate a distance equal to the distance from New York to California.

7466. In-line roller skate that was commercially successful was invented by Minnesota students Scott and Brennan Olson in 1980. Rummaging through a sporting goods store, they discovered an old in-line skate and decided that it would make a good off-season hockey training tool. Their design, an ice-hockey boot with three in-line wheels instead of a blade, was called the Rollerblade.

SPORTS AND RECREATION—ROWING

7467. College to feature rowing as a sport was Yale, New Haven, CT, which in 1844 held races between various classes and students.

7468. Intercollegiate rowing race in eight-oared boats took place on August 3, 1852, between Yale and Harvard on a two-mile course on Lake Winnepesaukee, Centre Harbor, NH. Harvard's lone entry, the *Oneida*, a 38-foot boat captained by Joseph Mansfield Brown, won by two lengths over Yale's *Shawmut*, followed by Yale's *Undine* and *Atlanta*.

7469. Racing shell was the *Harvard*, a six-oared 40-foot rudderless round-bottom boat of white pine. It was built in 1857 by James Mackay of Brooklyn, NY (now part of New York City), for the Harvard Boat Club of Harvard College, Cambridge, MA. It was 26 inches wide and weighed 50 pounds.

7470. Intercollegiate regatta was held on July 26, 1859, at Lake Quinsigamond, Worcester, MA. Harvard defeated Yale and Brown over a three-mile course. A regatta had been scheduled for July 23 of the previous year at Springfield, MA, but was postponed because a member of the Yale crew had drowned the day before.

7471. Coxswain of a men's college varsity rowing team who was a woman was Sally Stearns of Rollins College, Winter Park, FL. She led the shell on May 27, 1936, against Marietta College and on June 1, 1936, against Manhattan College. The crew lost to Marietta by four lengths and beat Manhattan by a half length.

SPORTS AND RECREATION—SHOOTING

7472. Rifle society (national) was the National Rifle Association, organized and chartered on November 24, 1871, in New York City with 35 members. Its first shooting meet was held on April 25, 1873, at Creedmoor, NY. The contestants included nine regiments of the New York National Guard, one regiment of the New Jersey National Guard, the U.S. Engineers, and a squad of regular servicemen from Governors Island. The first president of the association was General Ambrose Everett Burnside, who had commanded the Army of the Potomac during the Civil War.

7473. International rifle tournament of consequence was held on September 26, 1874, at Creedmoor, NY, between an American team commanded by Colonel George Wood Wingate and an Irish team commanded by Captain Arthur Blennerhassett Leech. Each team was composed of six men who fired 15 shots each at targets set at distances of 800, 900, and 1,000 yards. The targets had square bull's-eyes and scores were rated at 4, 3, and 2 according to position. The maximum score possible was

SPORTS AND RECREATION—SHOOTING—*continued*

1,080 points. The Americans, represented by the Amateur Rifle Club of New York, used American breechloaders and won the contest by a score of 934–931 points. Captain Leech of the Irish team presented a cup to the National Rifle Association. In 1875 Princess Louise, on behalf of Queen Victoria, presented the association with the Wimbledon Cup, which has been the trophy since that date.

7474. Clay pigeon target for trapshooting was invented by George Ligowsky of Cincinnati, OH, who obtained a patent on September 7, 1880, on a concave slotted "flying target."

7475. Grand American Trapshoot tournament using live birds was held in March 1893 at Dexter Park, Jamaica, Queens, NY (now part of New York City), with 21 entries. The winner was R.A. Welch, who killed 23 out of 25 birds from a distance of 23 yards.

7476. Grand American Trapshoot tournament with clay targets was held at Interstate Park, Queens, New York City, on June 12, 1900, and was won by Rolla O. "Pop" Heikes of Dayton, OH, who scored 91 targets out of a possible 100 from a distance of 22 yards. There were 74 entries. Walter S. Beaver of Berwyn, PA, was the first shooter to win the Grand American from the extreme distance of 25 yards. On August 25, 1933, he broke 99 out of 100 targets.

7477. Revolver shooting tournament was held on June 16, 1900, between teams representing the United States and France. Each contestant had 30 shots at targets placed at 150 feet and 52.5 feet. The American team won by 61 points. Out of a possible score of 6,000 points, the Americans received 4,889 and the Frenchmen 4,828. The contest was held at the shooting range in Armbruster Park, Greenville, NJ, and Gastinne-Renett's pistol range, Paris. The scores were cabled to the opposing teams.

7478. College skeet tournament was held on November 12, 1928, in Princeton, NJ. A five-man team from Yale defeated Princeton 221–202. Bob Rosien of Yale scored a perfect 50.

7479. National skeet tournament sponsored by the National Skeet Association was won by Lovell S. Pratt of Indianapolis, IN, who led a field of 114 in Solon, OH, on August 31, 1935, to win the national all-bore with a score of 244 out of a possible 250. Second place was won by Phip Conway of Green Village, NJ, with 242 points. The women's title was won by Esther Abbie Ingalls of Hot Springs, VA, with a score of 95 out of 100.

SPORTS AND RECREATION—SKIING

7480. Ski club association was the Central Organization, formed by 10 clubs in 1891. The first meeting and tournament were held at Ishpeming, MI, on January 16, 1891. The National Ski Association of America was formed at Ishpeming on February 21, 1904, with Carl Tellefsen of Ishpeming as president.

7481. Steel ski jump was built in November 1908 at Chippewa Falls, WI. It was 98 feet high, with a concrete foundation above the ground that raised it to 100 feet. In 1910, the national ski tournament was held on this jump.

7482. International ski meet of importance was held on February 10–13, 1932, at Lake Placid, NY, during the Olympic Games. Finland and Sweden each won an event and Norway won two events.

7483. Ski tow made of rope was built by Robert Royce and placed in operation on January 28, 1934, at Woodstock, VT. About 900 yards of manila rope 0.875 inches thick was spliced together, passed over pulleys and around a wheel attached to a tractor, and extended up the hill 300 yards.

7484. Ski lift was the Cannon Mountain Tramway at Franconia, NH, a 5,410-foot suspension ride that opened on June 17, 1938. It was suspended by giant cables 40 feet above the trees and ran from the base of Cannon Mountain to one of its peaks. It had two cars, each accommodating 27 persons, which made the trip up or down in eight minutes at the speed of a thousand feet a minute.

7485. Skimobile ski lift was invented in 1937 by George Morton of Goodrich Falls, NH. A 3,000-foot section was placed in operation on December 27, 1938, by Cranmore Skimobiles at North Conway, NH. One hundred and fifty toy cars, each seating one or two persons, were conveyed up a wide wood and steel trestle by a 6,000-foot endless steel cable 0.875 inches in diameter, which was propelled by electric motors. On August 1, 1939, another 2,000-foot unit was added to propel 60 cars from the halfway station to the summit of Cranmore Mountain. The system had a capacity of 1,000 passengers per hour. The vertical lift from bottom to top was 1,367 feet.

7486. Indoor ski school was the Bob Johnson Ski Center, opened on October 16, 1939, in the Wells Memorial Building, Boston, MA. About 300 square feet were covered with a special form of crystal plastic invented by Robert H. Johnson of Boston, MA, who received a patent for it on July 3, 1951. Johnson subsequently opened a larger school of 7,000 square feet at Framingham, MA.

7487. Ski lifts to be regulated by the state were those of New Hampshire, which approved a regulation law on September 17, 1959. It mandated the registration, inspection, and approval of all ski-lift devices and established a tramway safety board consisting of four appointed members and the commissioner of public works and highways.

7488. Indoor ski slope was the Ski-Dek Center, Buffalo, NY, which opened on January 17, 1962, in a former movie theater. It consisted of a huge bank of endlessly moving slopes that were treated to simulate two inches of powdered snow on a firm base. It had nine slopes and could accommodate 144 skiers.

7489. Ski carousel was the Doppelmayr Carousel, placed in service in November 1975 at Stratton Mountain, VT. It consisted of four 20-foot metal arms extending from a revolving hub powered by a small motor. Skiers holding the arms were rotated at various speeds to simulate skiing conditions. The carousel cost about $5,500 and was imported from Austria.

SPORTS AND RECREATION—SNOWMOBILING

7490. Snowmobile patent was obtained by Carl J.E. Eliason of Sayner, WI, who received a patent on November 22, 1927, on a "vehicle for snow travel."

7491. Snowmobile to exceed a speed of 125 miles per hour was a 1972 Ski-Doo Blizzard X2R driven by Yvon Duhamel of Valcourt, Quebec, Canada. On February 11, 1972, he reached a speed of 127.3 miles per hour at the Boonville Airport, Boonville, NY.

SPORTS AND RECREATION—SOCCER

7492. Soccer team entirely made up of Americans is believed to have been the St. Louis Kensingtons, of St. Louis, MO, formed in 1890. Soccer had been played for at least two centuries in the Americas, and an American team from New Jersey was fielded for an international soccer match in 1886, but until 1890 all American teams included foreign players.

7493. Professional soccer organization recognized internationally was the United States Football Association (now known as the United States Soccer Federation), formed on April 5, 1913, in New York City. The first president was G. Randolph Manning, elected in June 1913. Later that year, the association was recognized by the Federation Internationale de Football Associations, the international governing body of soccer.

7494. Soccer player to score 12 points in one game was Giorgio Chinaglia of the New York Cosmos, who scored five goals for two points each and two assists for one point each in a game played on August 10, 1976, at Yankee Stadium, New York City, against the Miami Toros. The final score was Cosmos 8, Toros 2.

7495. Soccer world champion who was a woman was Michelle Akers, who led the U.S. national women's soccer team to its first World Cup title in 1991, the first year the competition was held. It was America's first world championship in soccer since 1862. From the beginning of her career through 1995, she scored 82 goals in 87 international games, a feat unmatched in women's or men's competition.

7496. World Cup soccer tournament held in the United States began on June 17, 1994, with a game at Soldier Field, Chicago, IL. Fourteen nations competed in the marathon tournament, with games held in nine American cities. Brazil won the cup after defeating Italy at the Rose Bowl in Pasadena, CA.

SPORTS AND RECREATION—SOFTBALL

7497. Softball game was played on November 30, 1887, at the Farragut Boat Club, Chicago, IL. The game was invented by George W. Hancock, who devised a set of rules that gradually developed as the game progressed. A broomstick was used for the bat and a boxing glove for the ball. The game was known variously as Diamond Ball, Fast Ball, Kitten Ball, Playground Ball, and Recreation Ball. It was named softball by Walter C. Hakanson.

7498. Softball game of 365 innings was played at Summerville Field, Monticello, NY, on August 14–15, 1976, between teams representing Gager's Diner and the Bend n' Elbow Tavern. The game began at 10 A.M. on Friday and continued until 4 P.M. Saturday, when it was called because of rain and fog. About 70 players, including 20 women, participated. Some $4,000 was raised for the construction of

SPORTS AND RECREATION—SOFT-BALL—*continued*

a new softball field and for the Community General Hospital. The Gagers made 832 hits and scored 491 runs; the Elbows made 738 hits, scoring 467 runs. There were 31 home runs.

SPORTS AND RECREATION—SQUASH

7499. Squash rackets champion to win the U.S.A. Squash Racquets Singles championship was John A. Miskey of the Overbrook Golf Club, Philadelphia, PA, who won the championship in 1907.

7500. Squash tennis organization (national) was the National Squash Tennis Association, formed by 14 charter members on March 20, 1911, at the Harvard Club of New York City. The first president was John W. Prentiss.

7501. Squash tennis tournament sponsored by the National Squash Tennis Association was held at the Harvard Club, New York City, on April 8–10, 1911. Forty entries from 13 clubs played. The champion was Dr. Alfred Stillman II, who defeated John W. Prentiss on April 10 by scores of 15–5 and 17–15.

7502. Squash rackets champion who was a woman was Eleanora R. Sears of the Harvard Club, Boston, MA, who won the U.S.A. Women's Squash Racquets Singles Championship at the Round Hill Club, Greenwich, CT, on January 16–19, 1928, beating her opponent in three of four matches. Forty players entered.

SPORTS AND RECREATION—STADIUMS AND ARENAS

7503. Boxing arena was built near Worcester, MA, for the fight between Tom Springs and Jack Langan, the Irish champion, on January 7, 1824. It had about 4,000 seats and room for 22,000 people to stand. Admission was 10 shillings ($2.50), half of which went to the fighters.

7504. Enclosed baseball park was the Union Grounds, Brooklyn, NY (now part of New York City), which opened on May 15, 1862, on a site at Lee Avenue and Rutledge Street that had been formerly used as a skating rink.

7505. Football stadium was the Harvard Stadium, Cambridge, MA, constructed by the Aberthaw Construction Company. Boston, MA, under the direction of Professor Lewis Jerome Johnson and Joseph Ruggles, from a general architectural design worked out by George Bruns de Gersdorff. It was completed in the spring of 1904. The first stadium built specifically for football, it was also the first stadium built primarily of concrete and the largest steel-reinforced concrete structure in the world at the time of construction. The outer walls measured 527 by 420 feet and were divided into 37 reinforced concrete sections. A colonnade was added in 1910 and steel stands in 1929. The first football game played there was the Harvard–Dartmouth game of November 14, 1903, won by Dartmouth 11–0. The stadium had a seating capacity of 40,000.

7506. Stadium operated by a city was the Golden Gate Park Stadium, San Francisco, CA, completed in 1907. It was oval in shape and covered a 30-acre field. It had two entrances, one on the north and one on the south side, through tunnels 20 feet wide and 10 feet high. A three-quarter-mile trotting track 60 feet wide encircled the stadium. Bicycle races were held on November 29, 1906, before completion.

7507. Fireproof baseball stadium built of concrete and steel was Forbes Field, Pittsburgh, PA. The stadium was named after Brigadier General John Forbes, the British officer who commanded the expeditionary force that captured Fort Duquesne, at what is now Pittsburgh. The first game to be played in the stadium took place on June 30, 1909, when the Pittsburgh Pirates defeated the Chicago Cubs 3–2 before a paying crowd of 30,338 spectators.

7508. Speedway with a board track was the Los Angeles Motordrome, near Playa del Rey, CA, opened on April 7, 1910. It was made of wood, with a circumference of 5,281 feet, and was under the direction of Fred Evans Moskovics.

7509. School stadium was built in Tacoma, WA, and was dedicated on June 10, 1910. It was 250 feet wide at the narrowest point next to the curve and 400 feet wide at the open ends. It cost $150,000, of which $100,000 was paid by the school district and $50,000 was obtained through the sale of five-year passes at $10 each. Frederick Heath was the architect and L.A. Nicholson the engineer.

7510. Asphalt-covered racetrack was opened on September 18, 1915, at the Narragansett Speedway, Cranston, RI, where two world records were broken.

7511. Domed sports stadium that was fully enclosed was the Astrodome, Houston, TX, formally known as the Harris County Domed Stadium. Construction work started on March 18, 1963. The overall cost was $35.5 million. The building had a permanent translucent roof spanning 642 feet and covered with 4,596 plastic skylights. The distance to the top of the dome was 208 feet. The arena could accommodate 66,000 people at conventions and 48,000 at baseball games. The playing field was 466 feet by 288 feet, an area of 405,000 square feet. The first baseball game under the dome was played on April 9, 1965, between the Houston Astros and the New York Yankees, who lost 2–1. The first football game was played on September 11, 1965, when the University of Tulsa defeated the University of Houston 14–0.

7512. Adjustable stadium was the Aloha Stadium, Honolulu, HI, dedicated on September 12, 1975. It had seating accommodations for 50,000 people in six 147-foot-high grandstand sections, of which two were fixed (the north and the south) and four were removable (the east and west). Each section weighed 1,750 tons and was about 14 stories high. Three large compressors forced air into 416 discs, making it possible for hydraulic jacks to move any of the four sections a distance of 180 feet in 25 minutes. The stadium was designed by Charles Luckman Associates, Los Angeles, CA.

SPORTS AND RECREATION—SWIMMING

7513. Swimmer of note was Benjamin Franklin. In 1724, Franklin, then 18 years old, went to London to buy equipment for the printing business he was starting in Philadelphia, PA. His swimming feats on the Thames River astonished Londoners, one of whom offered to open a swimming school with Franklin as teacher. Franklin, who was known in England as "the watery American," was the first American to skin dive, invented a wet suit and webbed sandals made of reeds, and experimented with water skis. He also wrote a book on how to swim.

7514. Swimming school was opened on July 23, 1827, in Boston, MA. A boat beyond the Toll House on the Charles River conveyed the students to the Mill Dam, where the school was located. It was open from 5:30 A.M. to 7 A.M., from 9 A.M. to 1 P.M., and from 4 P.M. to 8 P.M. The method of instruction was described as follows: "A belt is placed about the bodies, under the arms, attached to a rope and pole, by which the head and body are kept in the proper position in the water, while the pupil is learning the use of his limbs."

7515. Amateur open swimming championship meet was held on September 30, 1877, on the Harlem River by the New York Athletic Club, New York City.

7516. Swimmer to cover 100 meters freestyle in less than one minute was Johnny Weissmuller of the Illinois Athletic Club, who swam the course in 58.3 seconds on July 9, 1922, at the Neptune Beach Tank, Alameda, CA. In the 1924 Olympics, he won a gold medal with a time of 59 seconds, and repeated the performance in 1928 for another gold medal with a time of 58.6 seconds.

7517. Swimmer from the United States to swim the English Channel was Henry F. Sullivan of Lowell, MA, who swam from Dover, England, to Cape Gris-Nez, France, a distance of 56 miles, in 27 hours 23 minutes on August 5–6, 1923. Sullivan was the fourth man to swim the Channel.

7518. Swimmer who was an American woman to swim the English Channel from France to England was Gertrude Caroline Ederle, born October 23, 1906, in New York City, who accomplished the feat on August 6, 1926. She swam from Gris-Nez, France, to Kingsdown, Dover, England, in 14 hours 34 minutes, beating the world record by nearly two hours. She suffered permanent hearing loss during the swim.

7519. Swimmer who was a woman to swim the English Channel in both directions was Florence Chadwick of San Diego, CA, who swam from Cape Gris-Nez, France, to Dover, England, in 13 hours 28 minutes on August 8, 1950, and from St. Margaret's Bay near Dover to Sangatte, France, in 16 hours 22 minutes on September 10, 1951.

7520. Swimmer to swim the English Channel underwater was Fred Baldasare of Cocoa Beach, FL, who left Cape Gris-Nez, France, at 1 P.M. on July 10, 1962, and arrived at Pegwell Bay, southwest of Ramsgate, England, about 8:15 A.M. on July 11, a little over 18 hours later. He used aqualung equipment and received tanks of air from his helpers, and was guided by a frame towed beneath the surface. Baldasare, a specialist in underwater long-distance swimming, was also the first to swim underwater across the Messina Strait, the Oresund Strait, the Bosphorus Strait roundtrip, the Hellespont, Algeciras Bay, and the Strait of Gibraltar (all from June to December 1962), and the Laguna del Sol (in June 1964).

SPORTS AND RECREATION—SWIMMING—*continued*

7521. Swimmer from the United States to make a round-trip crossing of the English Channel was Ted Erikson of Chicago, IL, 37 years old, who swam from St. Margaret's Bay, England, to the beach near Calais, France, in 14 hours 15 minutes on September 21, 1965. He stopped for three minutes to receive a fresh coating of grease and returned in 15 hours 48 minutes, taking a total of 30 hours 3 minutes for the round-trip swim.

7522. Swimmer to cross the Bering Strait was 30-year-old Lynne Cox. In August 1987 she swam 2.7 miles across the Bering Strait from Little Diomede Island off the coast of Alaska to Big Diomede Island off the coast of Soviet Siberia. The water temperature was 34 degrees to 39 degrees F, cold enough to send most unprotected swimmers into hypothermia. Cox's thick layer of subcutaneous fat, rapid freestyle crawl rhythm, and outstanding cardiovascular fitness kept her alive. She wore neither wetsuit nor grease. Her swim was the longest intentional cold-water ocean swim on record, and the only one to cross the International Date Line, which runs between the two islands. It was also the first time an American had set foot on the Soviet island of Big Diomede since 1948.

SPORTS AND RECREATION—TENNIS

7523. Lawn tennis was introduced in March 1874 by Mary Ewing Outerbridge, who imported rackets and other equipment from Bermuda. It is said that customs officials were unable to determine under what section of the Tariff Act the equipment belonged, and after a week's indecision permitted it to enter duty-free. A court was laid out in 1874 at the Staten Island Cricket and Baseball Club, New Brighton, NY (now part of New York City), to which Miss Outerbridge's family belonged. The first players were members of the family. Within seven years, tennis had become popular, and on May 21, 1881, Eugenius H. Outerbridge, Mary Outerbridge's brother, organized the United States Lawn Tennis Association, to which 33 tennis clubs sent delegates. General Robert Shaw Oliver of the Albany Tennis Club was elected the first president.

7524. Court tennis was introduced in Boston, MA, in 1876 by Hollis Hunnewell and Nathaniel Thayer, who built a court on Buckingham Street. Ted Hunt, an English professional, was in charge. The game is played with a racket on a court 110 feet long and 38 feet wide, usually enclosed, with an elaborate layout.

7525. Tennis society (national) was the United States Lawn Tennis Association, formed on May 21, 1881, at the Fifth Avenue Hotel, New York City, by 34 clubs. It formulated the rules of play, standardized the height of the net and the size of the ball, and ruled on such matters as the service line and the size of the court. The first president was Robert Shaw Oliver of the Albany Tennis Club. In 1975 the name was changed to United States Tennis Association.

SPORTS AND RECREATION—TENNIS—MATCHES

7526. Tennis tournament of national scope was held on September 1–4, 1880, at Camp Washington of the Staten Island Cricket and Baseball Club, New Brighton, NY (now part of New York City). Twenty-three entrants competed for the first prize, a silver cup valued at about $100, inscribed "The Champion Lawn Tennis Player of America." It was won by O.E. Woodhouse of England.

7527. National tennis championship matches were held at the Newport Casino, Newport, RI, on August 31, 1881, by the United States Lawn Tennis Association, which introduced the first national uniform conditions. The singles match was won by Richard Dudley Sears, who defeated W.E. Glyn 6–0, 6–3, and 6–2. The doubles were won by Clarence Monroe Clark and Frederick W. Taylor.

7528. Intercollegiate lawn tennis match was held on June 7–8, 1883, at Hartford, CT, on the grounds of Trinity College. Joseph Sill Clark of Philadelphia, PA, won the singles. The doubles were won by Clark and Howard Augustus Taylor of New York City. The winners represented Harvard. At a second series, played on September 2, 1883, Howard Augustus Taylor won the singles and teamed with R.E. Presbrey to win the doubles.

7529. National tennis championship match for women run by the United States Lawn Tennis Association was an outdoor singles match held at the Philadelphia Cricket Club, Philadelphia, PA, in 1887. It was won by Ellen F. Hansell, who defeated Laura Knight 6–1 and 6–0. The first women's doubles championship was played in 1890 and won by Ellen C. and Grace W. Roosevelt.

7530. International professional tennis contest was begun at the Newport Casino, Newport, RI, on August 29, 1889. George Kerr, an Irish professional, defeated Thomas Pettit 6–3, 6–1, 6–1. Pettit won 6–4, 2–6, 6–3, 6–4 on September 21, 1889, at Springfield, MA. The third match was held at the Longwood Cricket Club, Brookline, MA, on September 25, 1889, where Kerr won 6–3, 3–6, 6–4.

7531. International tennis matches for the Davis Cup challenge trophy were held at the Longwood Cricket Club, Brookline, MA, on August 8–10, 1900, under the auspices of the United States Lawn Tennis Association. The Davis Cup was first won by an American team consisting of Malcolm Douglass Whitman, Dwight Filley Davis, and Holcombe Ward, all of Harvard, who won three matches to none, 10 sets to one, and 76 games to 50 against England. The tournament called for one doubles match and four singles matches. The United States won the first three matches (rain spoiled the other two) and was declared victorious.

7532. Tennis match broadcast on radio was the Davis Cup match between Australia and Great Britain, broadcast on August 4, 1921, from the Allegheny Country Club, Sewickley, PA, by station KDKA, Pittsburgh, PA.

7533. Tennis tournament to be shown on television was the Eastern Grass Court championship tournament that opened on August 9, 1939, at the Westchester Country Club, Rye, NY. Station W2XBS, New York City, used a telescopic lens in addition to the iconoscope to obtain closeups of important points. The first one to be televised in color was the Davis Cup match between Australia and the United States that was held at the West Side Tennis Club, Forest Hills, Queens, New York City, on August 26, 1955, which was televised by station WNBT-TV of the National Broadcasting Company.

7534. Intercollegiate court tennis match was played on May 4, 1954, at the Racquet and Tennis Club, New York City, between Yale University and Princeton University. James Laughlin of Yale defeated Kenley Webster of Princeton, Charles Watson of Yale defeated Gary Nash of Princeton, and Dozier Gardner of Princeton defeated Robert Easton of Yale. On May 23, at Manhasset, NY, Yale defeated Harvard 4–3 for the challenge bowl donated by James H. Van Alen.

SPORTS AND RECREATION—TENNIS—PLAYERS

7535. Tennis champions who were brothers were Carr Baker Neel and Samuel R. Neel of Chicago, IL. On August 18, 1896, they won the United States Lawn Tennis Association outdoor men's doubles championship at Newport Casino, Newport, RI, defeating Robert D. Wrenn and M.G. Chace 6–3, 1–6, 6–1, 3–6, 6–1.

7536. Tennis champion to win the Grand Slam of four major titles in one year was John Donald Budge of Oakland, CA, who achieved this feat in 1938. He won the Australian title in Adelaide on January 29, the French title in Auteuil on June 11, the British title at Wimbledon, England, on July 1, and the American title at Forest Hills, Queens, New York City, on September 24.

7537. Tennis champion who was a woman to win the Grand Slam of four major titles in one year was Maureen "Little Mo" Connolly of San Diego, CA, who achieved this feat in 1953. She won the Australian title at Melbourne on January 17, the French title in Paris on May 30, the British title at Wimbledon, England, on July 4, and the American title at Forest Hills, Queens, New York City, on September 7.

7538. Tennis champion who was African-American was Althea Gibson, a sharecropper's daughter who grew up in New York City. In 1950, she became the first African-American tennis player to enter the U.S. Open tennis tournament at Forest Hills, Queens, New York City, and a year later, she became the first to play in the Wimbledon tournament in England. She won the women's singles championships at Wimbledon and Forest Hills in 1957 and again in 1958.

7539. Brother and sister to win national tennis singles championships in the same tournament were Clifford and Nancy Richey of San Angelo, TX. On July 16, 1966, at the Town Hall Stadium, Milwaukee, WI, Clifford Richey defeated Frank Froehling of East Orange, NJ, 13–11, 6–1, and 6–3 for the National Clay Courts championship, and Nancy Richey won the women's title by defeating Stephanie De Fina of Hollywood, FL.

7540. Athlete who was a woman to earn more than $100,000 in one season was tennis player Billie Jean King, who earned $117,400 in 1971. That year, she won the U.S. Open women's singles and mixed doubles and the Wimbledon women's doubles and mixed doubles, as well as a number of other tournaments.

SPORTS AND RECREATION—TENNIS—PLAYERS—*continued*

7541. Athlete who was a woman to earn more than $1 million in a year was Czechborn tennis star Martina Navratilova, who passed that landmark in 1982. In 1984 she earned $2,173,556 in prize money, the fourth highest gross for any athlete in any sport that year, and the highest for a woman in any sport up to that time. Her total prize earnings at the time of her retirement from singles tennis in 1994 were more than $20 million.

SPORTS AND RECREATION—TRACK AND FIELD

7542. Athletic club was the New York Athletic Club, which was organized on September 8, 1868, at the Knickerbocker Cottage, Sixth Avenue and 28th Street.

7543. Amateur athletic games held indoors took place on November 11, 1868, at the Empire City Skating Rink at 63rd Street and Third Avenue, New York City, sponsored by the New York Athletic Club. The events included the 75-yard race, the 220-yard race, the 440-yard race, the half-mile race, the one-mile walk, the standing broad jump, the standing high jump, the running broad jump, the running high jump, the shot put, and standing three-jumps. During the intermissions, Dodsworth's Band played. The rink was 350 feet long, 170 feet wide, 70 feet high, and had accommodations for 10,000 spectators.

7544. Amateur athletic games held outdoors were held on October 21, 1871, by the New York Athletic Club on its grounds at 130th Street and the Harlem River. This site was used afterward for the foundations of the Harlem Bridge.

7545. Intercollegiate athletic association of importance was the Intercollegiate Association of Amateur Athletes of America, organized in Saratoga, NY, in June 1876, when a track meet was held. The charter members were Amherst, Bowdoin, Brown, City College of New York, Columbia, Cornell, Dartmouth, Harvard, Pennsylvania, Princeton, Trinity, Union, Wesleyan, Williams, and Yale. The association originated in 1873, when the newspaper publisher James Gordon Bennett offered a cup to the best track athlete among various college rowing crews.

7546. Intercollegiate track meet was held in Saratoga, NY, on July 20–21, 1876, under the auspices of the Intercollegiate Association of Amateur Athletes of America. The participating teams represented Bowdoin, the City College of New York, Columbia, Dartmouth, Pennsylvania, Princeton, Wesleyan, Williams, and Yale. A silver cup was awarded annually to the winning team. The first meet was won by Princeton with four firsts and four seconds. The cup was given permanently to Harvard, which won 8 of the first 14 meets.

7547. Amateur athletic competition was held on September 27, 1879, by the National Association of Amateur Athletes of America at the New York Athletic Club's grounds in Mott Haven, Brooklyn, NY (now part of New York City). Twenty games were on the program.

7548. Sports trainer to work professionally was Bob Rogers, who was engaged by the New York Athletic Club on May 1, 1883. He had previously been a trainer with the London Athletic Club.

7549. Cross-country championships were run on November 6, 1883, under the auspices of the New York Athletic Club.

7550. Relay race in a college track meet was held by the New Jersey Athletic Club at Bayonne, NJ, on May 30, 1893, before 5,000 spectators. The one-mile team race was won by Harvard in 3 minutes 25.4 seconds, three seconds faster than the record. Princeton was second, Yale third. Four men constituted a team, and each team member ran 440 yards.

7551. Discus-throwing competition in modern times took place in 1896 at the Olympic Games in Athens, Greece. Robert Garrett of Princeton University, representing the United States, won with a record throw of 95 feet 7.5 inches.

7552. Marathon race held annually was the American Marathon Race, now called the Boston Marathon. It was first run on April 19, 1897. The course began in Hopkinton, MA, and continued through Ashland, Framingham, Natick, Wellesley, and Newton to Exeter Street, Boston, a distance of 26 miles 385 feet. The winner was John J. McDermott of the Pastime Athletic Club of New York City, whose time was 2 hours 55 minutes 10 seconds.

7553. Olympic athlete from the United States to win the marathon race was John J. Hayes, who won the marathon of the London Olympics on July 26, 1908, with a time of 2 hours 55 minutes 18.4 seconds.

7554. Olympic athlete from the United States to win the pentathlon and decathlon was Jim Thorpe of Prague, OK. Thorpe, of Irish, French, and Native American descent (his mother was the granddaughter of the Sauk chieftain Black Hawk), achieved this feat at the Olympic Games in Stockholm, Sweden, in 1912. His medals were revoked in 1913 on a technicality concerning his amateur status. His winning status was restored in 1982.

7555. Broad jump to reach more than 25 feet was made on July 23, 1921, by Edward O. Gourdin of Harvard College, who jumped 25 feet 3 inches during the International Meet at Harvard Stadium, Cambridge, MA. The participants at the meet represented Harvard, Yale, Oxford, and Cambridge.

7556. Decathlon champion from the United States was Harold M. Osborne of the Illinois Athletic Club, Chicago, IL, who won 7,710.775 points on July 12, 1924, at the Olympic Games in Paris. The 10 events in the decathlon are the 100-meter dash, the 400-meter run, the 1,500-meter run, the 110-meter hurdle, the broad jump, the high jump, the shot put, the discus throw, the pole vault, and the javelin throw.

7557. Transcontinental foot race was the brainchild of promoter C.C. "Cash and Carry" Pyle, who conceived of the ultimate marathon race, a coast-to-coast run that he dubbed the Bunion Derby. The first Bunion Derby started from Ascot Park, Los Angeles, CA, on March 4, 1928, and ended on May 26, on its 84th day, inside Madison Square Garden, New York City, where a final 20-mile contest was held. A field of 275 runners started the race, and 55 runners completed it. The first prize of $25,000 was won by Andrew Payne, a Cherokee of Claremore, OK, whose time for the 3,422.3 miles was 573 hours 4 minutes 34 seconds. The runner-up and winner of the $10,000 prize was Long John Salo of Passaic, NJ, whose time was 588 hours 40 minutes 13 seconds. Philip Granville was third and won $5,000; Mike Joyce, fourth, won $2,500. Six additional prizes of $1,000 each were awarded.

7558. Electrical timing device for foot races was tested on May 14, 1932, at Baker Field, New York City, in three events, when Columbia University defeated Syracuse University in a track meet. The results, however, were not accepted as final.

7559. Intercollegiate track meet to be shown on television was the 19th annual Intercollegiate Association of Amateur Athletes of America track and field championship meet at Madison Square Garden, New York City, televised on March 2, 1940, by station W2XBS. Twenty-three colleges participated in the various events, which included dashes, runs, relays, high hurdles, shot put, pole vault, weight throwing, broad jumps, and high jumps. New York University won, with 27 points.

7560. Pole vaulter to clear the bar at 15 feet was Cornelius Warmerdam of the San Francisco Olympic Club, who established this record on April 13, 1940, at Berkeley, CA, at the triangular meet of Washington State College, the Olympic Club of San Francisco, and the University of California. In 33 meets, 8 indoors and 25 outdoors, he duplicated or bettered this mark 43 times from 1940 through 1944.

7561. High-jump standards using electric eye detectors were constructed by a team headed by Lyle Hudson Bennett Peer of the General Electric Research Laboratory. They were used on May 31, 1941, at the Schenectady Patrolmen's Association interscholastic track meet, Schenectady, NY. A series of four parallel beams of light, one inch apart, recorded the height of each jump.

7562. Shot-put toss over 60 feet was made at Los Angeles on May 8, 1954, when Parry O'Brien, formerly of the University of Southern California, tossed the 16-pound shot 60 feet 5.25 inches at the University of California at Los Angeles—Southern California Pacific Coast Conference dual meet.

7563. High jump over seven feet was made on June 29, 1956, at the Coliseum, Los Angeles, CA, by Charles Dumas, a 19-year-old Compton College freshman, who jumped an official height of 7 feet .5 inch.

7564. Runner from the United States to run a mile in less than four minutes was Don Bowden of the University of California, who ran the mile in 3 minutes 58.7 seconds at the Pacific Amateur Athletic Union Meet at Stockton, CA, on June 1, 1957. He was the 11th man in the world to better the four-minute mile. The first runner to accomplish this feat indoors was James Tully "Jim" Beatty of the Los Angeles Track Club, who ran the mile in 3 minutes 58.9 seconds in the *Los Angeles Times* indoor track and field meet at the Los Angeles Memorial Sports Arena, Los Angeles, CA, on February 10, 1962.

SPORTS AND RECREATION—TRACK AND FIELD—*continued*

7565. Marathon runner from the United States who was a woman was Roberta "Bobbi" Gibb, the first woman to run in the Boston Marathon. Gibb applied to enter the 1966 race but was turned down by the Boston Athletic Association, which cited its rule banning women from competition. Race officials claimed that women were physically unable to run a marathon. On the day of the race, Gibb slipped into the pack at the start and finished in 3 hours 21 minutes 40 seconds. In 1967, she again ran without registering. Another woman, Katherine Switzer, officially entered the marathon that year by inaccurately completing the registration form. She became widely known as the first woman to run the race, although Gibb beat Switzer's time by 59 minutes. Gibb's achievement was acknowledged in 1984, when she was invited to start at the first Women's Olympic Marathon Trials.

7566. New York City Marathon was held on September 23, 1970, in New York City. Queens fireman Gary Muhrcke won the race, which consisted of four laps around Central Park. The course was later changed to run from Staten Island to Central Park.

7567. Olympic athlete to win two consecutive heptathlon events was Jackie Joyner-Kersee, widely regarded as America's greatest female track-and-field athlete. She won her first gold medal in the heptathlon event in the 1988 Summer Olympic Games in Seoul, South Korea, and won the gold again in 1992 at the summer games in Barecelona, Spain.

SPORTS AND RECREATION—VARIOUS

7568. Archery club was the United Bowmen of Philadelphia, founded in 1825 by Franklin Peale, Titian Ramsey Peale, Robert E. Griffith, M.D., Samuel P. Griffith, Jr., Jacob M. Morris, and Thomas Sully. The club was not formally organized until 1828, when membership was limited to 25. Members dressed in frock coats of Lincoln green ornamented with gold braid and wore broad straw hats with three black ostrich plumes. The first national organization was the National Archery Association, formed on January 23, 1879, in Crawfordsville, IN, by representatives of eight archery clubs. The first president was Maurice Thompson. The first grand annual meeting and the first tournament were held on August 12–14 in Chicago, IL, at which 20 women and 69 men competed. High score was made by Will H. Thompson, who won with 172 hits and a score of 624.

7569. Coaching club to encourage four-in-hand driving was the Coaching Club, formed by nine men on December 3, 1875, at the Knickerbocker Club, New York City. William Jay was the first president. The first meet, in which six coaches participated, was held April 22, 1876.

7570. Coach riding as a pastime was brought to the United States in 1875 by Colonel Delancey Astor Kane. A coach called the *Tallyho* was built by Holland and Holland of London and imported to New York City. Its first trip, on May 1, 1876, started from the Hotel Brunswick, Fifth Avenue and 26th Street, New York City, and ended at the Arcubarius Hotel, Pelham, NY. The fare was $1.50 each way. Some coaches had been imported earlier.

7571. Croquet league was the National Croquet League, organized on February 12, 1880, in Philadelphia, PA. The first president was George Washington Johnson of the Lemon Hill Croquet Club. Representatives from 18 clubs attended to standardize the game. Wickets were reduced in size and the balls reduced in diameter.

7572. Intercollegiate lacrosse association was the Intercollegiate Lacrosse Association, organized on March 11, 1882, in Princeton, NJ, with Columbia, Harvard, New York University, and Princeton as charter members. Each college team was scheduled to play one game with every other member. George William Gilmore of Princeton was president.

7573. Pushball was invented by M.G. Crane of Newport, MA, in 1894. It found favor the following year at Harvard, but never became a major sport. It was played with a huge six-foot ball.

7574. Medicine ball was invented by Robert Jeffries Roberts, physical education director of the Boston Young Men's Christian Association, in 1895, and first used in Boston, MA.

7575. Volleyball was developed in 1895 as a game by Physical Director William George Morgan of the Young Men's Christian Association, Holyoke, MA. The game, at first called mintonette, was played with a basketball bladder over a rope. Later, a lightweight leather-covered ball was adopted, and an eight-foot net was substituted for the rope. Rules were adopted locally until 1900, when the Young Men's Christian Association Physical Directors' Association Volley Ball Committee developed standard rules. The first rules were published in the *Physical Education Magazine* in July 1896.

7576. Log-rolling national championship tournament was held on September 9, 1898, on the lagoon at the Trans-Mississippi Exposition, Omaha, NE, on Lumbermen's Day, by the Lumbermen's Association of America. There were six entries. The winner was Tommy Fleming of Eau Claire, WI. Log rolling is also known as birling.

7577. Intercollegiate wrestling association was formed on April 7, 1905, at the University of Pennsylvania, Philadelphia, PA, through the efforts of Leonard Mason, an instructor in gymnastics, who visited other eastern universities in search of members. The first tournament, held on April 7, 1905, in the gymnasium of the University of Pennsylvania, was witnessed by over 1,000 spectators. Yale won, Columbia came in second, Princeton was third, and Pennsylvania was fourth.

7578. International horseshoe pitching contest open to all was held in Bronson, KS, in the summer of 1909. The contest was held on dirt courts. Pegs were 2 inches high and were spaced 38.5 feet apart. Frank Jackson of Blue Mound, KS, was awarded the World's Championship belt with miniature horseshoes attached to it. The first association of horseshoe pitchers was the Grand League of the American Horseshoe Pitchers Association, organized on May 16, 1914, in Kansas City, KS, to standardize the rules. Pegs were raised to 8 inches and spaced 38.5 feet apart. Ringers counted five points and leaners three points. The association's first championship tournament was held on October 23, 1915, in Kellerton, IA, and was won by Frank Jackson with 24 out of 25 games.

7579. Surfer was Duke Kahanomoku, a Hawaiian who introduced the Polynesian sport of surfing to California in 1910 and also formed the first surfing club in Waikiki, HI. He used surfboards made of California redwood. Kahanomoku went on to win gold medals in the 100-meter freestyle swimming competitions in the 1912 and 1920 Olympic Games.

7580. Nudist organization was the American League for Physical Culture, organized by three men on December 5, 1929, in New York City. The first nudist summer camp was opened by the American League in Central Valley, NY, in June 1930. There were approximately 30 participants.

7581. Bobsled run of international specifications was the Mountain Van Hoevenberg run at North Elba, NY, on the highway between Lake Placid and Elizabethtown, NY, designed by Stanislaus Zentzytzki. It was built for the New York State Olympic Winter Games Commis-

sion at a cost of more than $200,000. Work was begun on August 4, 1930, and the run was opened to the public on December 25 . It contained 26 curves and was 1.5 miles long. About 29,000 gallons of water were needed every 24 hours to spray the run. The first two-man competition was held on February 9–10, 1932, at the Olympic Winter Games, with 15 teams from eight nations. First place was won by the United States team of J. Hubert Stevens, driver, and Curtis Stevens, brakeman, in 8 minutes 14.74 seconds for the four heats. The first four-man competition took place at the Games on February 14–15, with 13 teams from six nations competing. First place was won by the United States team of William L. Fiske, driver, and Edward F. Eagan, Clifford B. Gray, and Jay O'Brien, brakemen, in a contest which covered the four heats in a total time of 7 minutes 53.68 seconds.

7582. Shuffleboard championship tournament was won by Carroll L. Bailey of Richmond, VA, who defeated 25 state champions at St. Petersburg, FL, on March 27, 1931, to win the U.S. shuffleboard title.

7583. Soapbox derby was officially held in 1934 in Dayton, OH. It was the first racing event for children. The idea for the derby originated in 1933 when photographer Myron Scott snapped pictures of three Dayton boys racing down a hill on wooden crates with baby buggy wheels. Scott organized larger races that soon attracted hundreds of participants and tens of thousands of spectators. The race was moved to Akron, OH, in 1935, after the *Akron Beacon-Journal* offered to build a permanent track. The derby's first official sponsor was Chevrolet. The first girl to win the derby was Karren Stead, in 1975. The first contestant to win two years in a row was 13-year-old Danielle Del Ferraro, who won the Kit Car division in 1993 and the Masters division in 1994 and won her division's award for best in construction both years.

7584. Badminton championship tournament was sponsored by the United States Badminton Association and played in April 1937 at the Naval Pier in Chicago, IL. A field of 150 entrants competed in singles and doubles matches. Walter R. Kramer won the men's singles title and Del Barkhuff won the women's singles.

7585. Flying disk for use in throwing games was the Frisbee Flying Saucer, invented by Walter Frederick Morrison and sold by the Wham-O Company of San Gabriel, CA, starting on January 13, 1957. Inspired by the UFO craze then sweeping the nation, Morrison devised a lightweight metal throwing disk that

SPORTS AND RECREATION—VARIOUS—continued

looked like a flying saucer. Later versions were made of plastic. The name Frisbee was given to the disks by Wham-O president Richard Knerr. While traveling in New England, he saw college students tossing pie plates with the name "Frisbie" embossed on them. These were manufactured for the Frisbie Pie Company of Bridgeport, CT, founded in the 1870s. Knerr copyrighted an alternative spelling, "Frisbee," and had it embossed on each Wham-O disk.

7586. National wheelchair games were held on June 1, 1957, at Adelphi College, Garden City, NY. The athletes were paraplegics (people paralyzed from the chest down) from Ohio, Pennsylvania, and nearby states, as well as Canada, who competed in team and individual events. Some of the winners were Tony Mucci, Pan American Jets, 60-yard dash; Al Slootsky, Jersey Wheelers, javelin throwing; Sol Welger, Pan American Jets, table tennis (singles); and Pierre Brousseau, Montreal Wheel Chair Wonders, archery. Other events, including shot put, bowling, weight lifting, discus throwing, and adapted swimming, were added in subsequent years.

7587. Weight lifter to lift more than 6,000 pounds was Paul Anderson, age 22. On June 17, 1957, in Toccoa, GA, Anderson backlifted off the ground a table holding heavy automobile parts and a safe full of lead. The total weight was 6,270 pounds.

7588. Ascent of Mount Everest by an American that was successful was made by James W. Whittaker of Redmond, WA. He was a leading member of the first American Mount Everest Expedition, which attempted the summit in the spring of 1963, 10 years after Sir Edmund Hillary and Tenzing Norgay made the first ascent of the 29,028-foot peak. Whittaker and his Sherpa climbing partner Nawang Gombu reached the top of Mount Everest at 1 P.M. on May 1, 1963. The first successful ascent by an American woman was made by Stacy Allison of the Northwest American Everest Expedition, who reached the summit on September 29, 1988. Peggy Luce, who was part of the same expedition, completed her ascent two days later. Both used the South Col route.

SPORTS AND RECREATION—WALKING

7589. Transcontinental journey on foot made entirely in one trip was accomplished by Edward Payson Weston, a professional walker. Payson began his trek in New York City on March 15, 1909. He reached San Francisco, CA, after a 3,795-mile journey that took 104

days 7 hours. The feat was all the more remarkable because Weston was 70 years old at the time. The next year, he walked the return route from Los Angeles, CA, to New York City, completing the trip in 76 days 23 hours.

7590. Round-the-world journey on foot was made by David Kunst, who walked 14,450 miles across four continents between June 20, 1970, and October 5, 1974. Another American, George Matthew Schilling, claimed to have made a round-the-world walk beginning on August 3, 1897, but his achievement has not been verified. A Christian preacher, Arthur Blessitt of North Fort Myers, FL, walked to all seven continents over a period of 25 years beginning on December 25, 1969.

SPORTS AND RECREATION—WATER SKIING

7591. Water skis were the brainchild of Benjamin Franklin, who, in the course of experimenting with kites, theorized that a swimmer wearing barrel staves on his feet could be towed along the surface of the water by a large kite. Franklin never put the idea into practice. The first practical water skis were invented in 1922 by Ralph W. Samuelson, who steam-bent two eight-foot-long pine boards into skis. He took his first ride behind a motorboat on a lake in Lake City, MN.

7592. National water skiing tournament was held at Jones Beach State Park, Long Island, NY, on June 22, 1939. Bruce Parker of Garden City, NY, won the men's championship and Esther Yates of Amityville, NY, the women's championship. The events included the slalom, jumping, and trick riding.

7593. Water skier to jump 100 feet was Warren Witherell of The Weirs, a northern suburb of Laconia, NH, who jumped 106 feet at Laconia on August 15, 1954.

STATES

7594. Treaty between states after the Declaration of Independence was concluded between Georgia and South Carolina on May 20, 1777, at Dewitt's Corner, SC. Under its provisions, the Cherokees were forced to retire behind a line running southwest through Georgia from the straight part of Pickens County on the North to a point just below the mouth of the Tallulah at the western tip the state.

7595. State nullification proceedings to obstruct federal legislation were the Kentucky Resolutions introduced by John Breckinridge. They were adopted by the Lower House of Kentucky on November 10, 1798, and by the Upper House on November 13, and approved by Governor James Garrard on November 16. Objection was taken to the congressional "act concerning aliens" of June 25, 1798, and the "act for the punishment of certain crimes against the United States" of July 14, 1798.

7596. Federal treasury surplus to be returned to the states was authorized by congressional act of June 23, 1836. Twenty-six states received a total of $28,101,645, which was distributed in proportion to their respective representation in the Senate and House and delivered in three installments. This money was supposed to remain on deposit until Congress directed otherwise, but no request for its return was ever made.

7597. State to repudiate a debt was Mississippi, in 1842. The sovereign state of Mississippi sold $5 million worth of bonds in June 1838 to pay for 50,000 shares in the Union Bank of Mississippi. The bank became hopelessly insolvent in 1840, and in 1842 the legislature denied that the state was under legal or moral obligation to pay the bonds in question.

7598. State named for a person born in America was Washington, the 42nd state, admitted into the Union on November 11, 1889. The first governor was Elisha Peyre Ferry, a Republican, who served from 1889 to 1893.

7599. State seal designed by a woman was the Seal of Idaho, designed by Emma Sarah Edwards. The seal was officially adopted on March 14, 1891.

7600. State to have a state sport was Maryland, which established jousting as the official state sport in 1962.

STATES—ADMISSION TO THE UNION

7601. State denied admission into the Union was Franklin, formed on August 23, 1784, when it seceded from North Carolina. It was formed by three counties between the Bald Mountains and the Holston River, an area that is now in eastern Tennessee. Its citizens established a senate and a house of commons at Jonesboro and elected John Sevier as governor for a four-year term with an annual salary of £200 or 1,000 deerskins. Sevier was arrested in 1788 on charges of high treason. After his release, he was elected to the House of Representatives. He served as the first governor of Tennessee after it was admitted to the Union as the 16th state in 1796.

7602. State admitted to the Union after the ratification of the Constitution by the original 13 colonies was Vermont, which was authorized to join the Union by Congress on February 18, 1791, and which formally joined on March 4. Vermont was formed from the New Hampshire Grants, a region that was claimed by Massachusetts, New York, and New Hampshire. In 1777 it declared itself an independent commonwealth, the Republic of Vermont, and elected Thomas Chittenden as the first governor. All claims by other states were withdrawn by 1790. Chittenden went on to become the first state governor, serving to 1797.

7603. State west of the Mississippi River to be admitted to the Union was Missouri, which joined on August 10, 1821. The first governor of the new state was Alexander McNair, a Democrat, who served from 1820 to 1824. (Louisiana, the 18th state, admitted on April 30, 1812, is both east and west of the Mississippi.)

7604. State on the Pacific coast to be admitted to the Union was California, which joined on September 9, 1850. The first state governor was Peter Hardeman Burnett, a Democrat, who served from 1849 to 1851.

7605. State readmitted to the Union after the Civil War was Tennessee, on July 24, 1866. A new constitution was adopted on January 9, 1865, and ratified on February 22.

7606. States admitted to the Union simultaneously were North and South Dakota, which were formed from the Dakota Territory. The act of admission was signed on February 22, 1889, by President Grover Cleveland. Each state held a constitutional convention beginning on July 4, 1889, and both held the ratifying election on October 1, 1889. President Benjamin Harrison signed the proclamations of admission on November 3, 1889, without knowing which was which. The first governors of both states were Republicans: John Miller, in North Dakota; Arthur Calvin Mellette, in South Dakota. Washington and Montana were admitted by the same enabling act, but the proclamations were not signed until a few days later.

7607. State admitted to the Union that had no border with another state was Alaska, which was admitted as the 49th state on January 3, 1959, by proclamation of President Dwight David Eisenhower. Alaska had become a territory on August 24, 1912. A constitution was approved by popular vote on April 24, 1956, and was ratified by Congress on July 7, 1958. Voters approved statehood on August 26, 1958, and the first state election was held on November 25.

STATES—ADMISSION TO THE UNION—
continued

7608. State admitted to the Union that was separated by a substantial body of water from the contiguous United States was Hawaii, 2,090 miles across the Pacific from San Francisco, CA. It was voted into the Union by Congress on March 12, 1959, by a vote of 323–89. Hawaii was admitted as the 50th state by proclamation of President Dwight David Eisenhower on August 21, 1959.

STATES—GOVERNORS

7609. Governor of a colony who was born in America was Josiah Winslow of Plymouth, MA. He was elected governor of New Plymouth Colony in 1673 and served until his death in 1680. In 1675–76 he led the United Colonies forces against the Wampanoags and their allies in the conflict known as King Philip's War. His parents, Edward and Susanna Winslow, were the first English colonists to be married in New England.

7610. Brothers to serve simultaneously as governors of their respective states were Governor Levi Lincoln, Jr., who served as governor of the Commonwealth of Massachusetts from May 27, 1825, until January 21, 1834, and Governor Enoch Lincoln, who served as governor of Maine from January 4, 1827, until his death on October 8, 1829. Both were Whigs.

7611. Governor who was Catholic was Edward Douglass White, who served as governor of Louisiana from 1835 to 1839. Before and after his term, he served in the U.S. House of Representatives.

7612. Governor to be removed from office by a state supreme court was William Augustus Barstow, Democrat of Wisconsin, who served a full term from January 2, 1854, to January 7, 1856. He was installed for a second term on January 7, 1856. On March 20, 1856, the supreme court held that Coles Bashford, a Republican, was entitled to the office because of irregularities in the election. On March 21, Barstow resigned, and the lieutenant governor, Arthur MacArthur, was sworn in. The state assembly recognized Bashford on March 27, 1856.

7613. Governor to be impeached and acquitted was Charles Robinson, the first governor of Kansas (1861–63) and a leader of the Free State antislavery party. He was indicted for treason and conspiracy on a charge brought by the proslavery party. He was acquitted in 1862 by a federal grand jury and completed his term as governor.

7614. Governor of a state who had also been governor of a territory was John White Geary, who served as governor of the Kansas territory from September 9, 1856, to March 4, 1857, and as governor of Pennsylvania from January 15, 1867, to January 21, 1873.

7615. Governor to be impeached and convicted was William Woods Holden, the 39th governor of North Carolina. On December 20, 1870, impeachment proceedings were brought against him in which he was charged with "high crimes and misdemeanors." The trial was conducted by Chief Justice Richmond Mumford Pearson. On March 22, 1871, he was ordered to be removed from office, two-thirds of the state Senate having found him guilty of six of the eight charges brought against him.

7616. Election for governor in which two brothers were the opposing candidates was held on November 2, 1886, in Tennessee. Robert Love Taylor, the Democratic candidate, received 125,151 votes, defeating his brother, Alfred Alexander Taylor, the Republican candidate, who obtained 109,837 votes. Robert Love Taylor served as governor from January 17, 1887, to January 19, 1891, and from January 21, 1897, to January 16, 1899. Alfred Alexander Taylor defeated Albert Houston Roberts on November 2, 1920, and served as governor of Tennessee from January 15, 1921, to January 16, 1923.

7617. Governor who was Jewish was Moses Alexander of Idaho, a Democrat, who served from January 4, 1915, to January 6, 1919. A previous governor of Jewish descent was David Emanuel of Georgia, a convert to Christianity, who served from March 3, 1801, to November 7, 1801, after the resignation of Governor James Jackson. It is not clear whether he became governor by virtue of the fact that he was president of the senate when Governor Jackson resigned, or whether he was regularly elected.

7618. Governor who was a woman was Nellie Tayloe Ross, who was elected governor of Wyoming on November 4, 1924, to fill the unexpired term of her late husband, William Bradford Ross. From 1933 to 1935 she served as director of the Mint, the first woman to do so.

The first woman to be elected state governor in her own right was Ella Grasso, a Democrat, elected on November 5, 1974, as the 83rd governor of Connecticut. She was reelected in November 1978 for a second term, which, because of illness, she did not complete. She resigned on December 31, 1980, and died on February 5, 1981.

7619. Governor to be granted almost dictatorial power was Paul Vories McNutt of Indiana. The Democrat-controlled legislature empowered him in February 1933 to organize the state government, which at that time was spread among 168 boards and commissions, into nine departments: Executive, State, Audit, Treasury, Law, Education, Public Works, Commerce, and Industry. He was authorized to hire and fire all state employees and to raise or lower salaries as he saw fit. His power was limited by legislative appropriations and by the authority of the courts to review and void his decisions.

7620. Governor of Italian ancestry was John Pastore, who was elected chief executive of Rhode Island in 1945. In 1950 he became the first Italian-American to be elected a U.S. senator.

7621. Governor who was African-American was L. Douglas Wilder, who was elected governor of Virginia on November 7, 1989. More than a century earlier, another African-American, Pinckney Benton Stewart Pinchback, the lieutenant governor of Louisiana, served as the state's governor from December 11, 1872, to January 14, 1873, during the impeachment of Governor Henry Clay Warmoth.

STATES—LEGISLATURES

7622. Legislative assembly of a colony met in Jamestown, VA, on July 30, 1619. The location was the Old Church, a wooden structure 50 by 20 feet. The men sat with their hats on. It was decided that the new governor, Sir George Yeardley, was to summon a "General Assembly" elected by the inhabitants, with every free man voting. The assembly was to consist of 22 members, 2 from each borough. The speaker was Master John Pory. The session was opened with prayer by a Mr. Bucke. The first laws enacted were prohibitions against idleness, drunkenness, and gambling.

7623. Legislature of a colony to establish two chambers convened in Massachusetts in 1644. "An Act of the Generall Court at Boston, March 7/17, 1644," established one house for magistrates and another for deputies.

7624. State legislators who were African-American were Edwin Garrison Walker and Charles Lewis Mitchell of Boston, MA, who in 1866 were elected to the Massachusetts House of Representatives.

7625. State legislator who was African-American to represent a constituency with a white majority was Bishop Benjamin William Arnett of the African Methodist Episcopal Church, Greene County, OH, who served in the lower house of the Ohio State Legislature from 1885 to 1887. He served in the 66th session, which convened on January 6, 1885, and adjourned on May 4, 1885, and the 67th, which convened on January 4, 1886, and adjourned on May 19, 1886.

7626. State senator who was a woman was Martha Hughes Cannon, elected to the second session of the Utah senate on November 3, 1896, and reelected to the third. She was a Democrat and represented the 6th Senatorial District, comprising Salt Lake County.

7627. State legislature to use an electric vote recorder was that of Wisconsin. The machine was installed on January 11, 1917, in the Wisconsin Assembly Chamber in Madison. It displayed green and white signal lights opposite the name of each legislator to show how he or she voted. A roll call could be recorded in 11 seconds, at a savings of more than 99 percent of the time previously consumed in roll calls. The acquisition of the vote recorder was approved on July 29, 1915.

7628. State speaker of the House who was a woman was Minnie Davenport Craig of Esmond, ND, a Republican, who was elected speaker on January 3, 1933. She served for one session, until March 31, 1933.

7629. Interstate legislative conference assembled in Washington, DC, on February 3, 1933, under the auspices of the American Legislators' Association. The conference was attended by 100 state legislators and tax experts from 32 states who discussed double taxation, overlapping and conflicting of federal and state taxes, and similar matters. Only the legislators were entitled to vote.

7630. State legislature with a single chamber in the post-Revolutionary era was Nebraska, which adopted a unicameral system by constitutional amendment on November 6, 1934. A single body of 43 members replaced a House of 100 members and a Senate of 33. The first bill, passed on January 21, 1937, appropriated $10,000 for mileage, postage, and incidental expenses for the members. All of the original

STATES—LEGISLATURES—*continued*

states adopted bicameral systems at the formation of the United States, except Pennsylvania, Georgia, and Vermont, which changed to a bicameral system after 4, 12, and 58 years, respectively.

7631. State legislator who was an African-American woman was Crystal Bird Fauset of Philadelphia, PA, elected on November 8, 1938, to the Pennsylvania House of Representatives. Her term of office began on December 1, 1938, and she was sworn in and assumed her seat on January 3, 1939.

7632. Husband and wife to be elected simultaneously to both chambers of a state legislature were Richard Lewis Neuberger, state senator, and Maurine Brown Neuberger, state representative, both Democrats, elected to the Oregon legislature on November 7, 1950. Richard Neuberger had served previously as state senator, having been elected on November 2, 1948, to represent the 13th district.

7633. State legislative hearing to be shown on television was a hearing by the New Jersey senate's Committee on Federal and Interstate Relations that took place on April 11, 1954, and was aired from 7:30 to 8 P.M. on WATV, Newark, NJ. The subject was a proposal by Senator Malcolm Forbes to stop all new projects by the Port of New York Authority (later nown as the Port Authority of New York and New Jersey). The proposal was defeated.

STATES—SECESSION

7634. Secession idea to be mentioned in Congress was mentioned in the House of Representatives on June 4, 1811, during a debate on the proposal to create a state from the Orleans Territory, which entered the Union as Louisiana on April 30, 1812. The debate concerned the extension of slavery to the proposed state. Representative Josiah Quincy of Massachusetts declared: "It will be the right of all and the duty of some [of the states] definitely to prepare for a separation; amicably, if they can; violently, if they must." Representative Poindexter of Mississippi called Quincy to order, as did the speaker of the House. On appeal, the speaker's decision was reversed, and Quincy was sustained by a vote of 53 ayes to 56 nays on the point of order.

7635. Secession convention during the War of 1812 was held on December 15, 1814, at Hartford, CT, by delegates from Connecticut, Massachusetts, New Hampshire, Rhode Island, and Vermont who opposed the War of 1812 and planned secession from the United States.

7636. Secession act at the start of the Civil War was the Ordinance of Secession, passed by the legislature of South Carolina on December 20, 1860.

T

TAXATION

7637. Property tax levied by a colony was passed on May 14, 1634, and signed by Governor William Bradford of the Plymouth colony in Massachusetts: "It is further ordered that in all rates and public charges, the towns shall have respect to levy each man according to his estate, and with consideration of all other his abilities, whatsoever, and not according to the number of persons."

7638. Income tax levied by a colony was levied on the colonists of New Plymouth, MA, in 1643, giving the town the distinction of being the first place in America to impose an income tax.

7639. Tax on Britain's American colonists without their consent was levied in 1672, when the British Parliament passed a law imposing a duty on sugar, tobacco, ginger, coconuts, indigo, logwood fustic, wool, and cotton.

7640. Inheritance tax levied by a colony was levied by Virginia in 1687, when the Colony of Virginia provided that the governor of the colony should collect a fee of a cask and 200 pounds of tobacco for impressing documents with the public seal, without which they were invalid. These documents included probates, letters testamentary, and letters of administration.

7641. Direct tax on Britain's American colonists without their consent was the Stamp Act, enacted on March 22, 1765, by Parliament. It required colonists to buy revenue stamps for every pair of dice, every pack of playing cards, and every newspaper, document, and pamphlet. The purpose of the tax was to raise funds to pay for the upkeep of the British army in America. The first American locality to repudiate the act was Frederick County, MD. On November 23, 1765, 12 judges of the Court of Frederick County declared that "all proceedings shall be valid and effectual without the use of stamps." The act was repealed in March 1766 after the colonists mounted a sustained boycott of British goods.

7642. Internal revenue tax levied by Congress was imposed on March 3, 1791, as part of an act that established 14 revenue districts, one for each state. The law levied a tax on distilled spirits, both domestic and imported, of 11 to 30 cents a gallon, depending on alcoholic content prior to removal from the distillery. Carriages were also taxed. Subsequent early modifications of the act of 1791 imposed taxes on retail dealers in distilled spirits, as well as on refined sugar, snuff, property sold at auction, legal instruments, and bonds. On July 9, 1798, a direct tax was placed on real estate. The receipts for the fiscal year 1792 from internal revenue netted the government $208,943.

7643. Tax levied by Congress directly on the states was a direct pro rata tax upon the 16 states, authorized by act of July 14, 1798. It was levied on dwellings, land, and slaves. The amount to be collected was $2 million, which was apportioned to the states in direct ratio to the population.

7644. Bachelor tax enacted by a state was levied by Missouri, which on December 20, 1820, placed a $1 tax "on every unmarried free white male, above the age of 21 years and under 50 years."

7645. Inheritance tax enacted by a state was passed by Pennsylvania on April 7, 1826, and signed by Governor John Andrew Shulze. It established a 2.5 percent collateral inheritance tax. The surviving spouse, the parents, and the descendants of the decedent were exempted.

7646. Income tax levied by Congress was imposed during the Civil War by act of August 5, 1861, effective January 1, 1862, which imposed a 3 percent tax on incomes exceeding $800 and a 1.5 percent tax on income derived from government securities. The income tax lists were open to public inspection by "all persons who may apply to inspect the same." This was interpreted in such a way as to eliminate idle curiosity seekers. The law was not enforced and was replaced the following year by another. It was rescinded in 1872 along with other Civil War taxes. An income tax law was passed by Congress on August 27, 1894, as part of the tariff act, but it was declared unconstitutional. The 16th Amendment to the Constitution, which was declared ratified on February 25, 1913, gave Congress the power to lay and collect income taxes.

7647. Inheritance tax levied by Congress was a part of the Internal Revenue Law of July 1, 1862, which assessed a tax on legacies and distributive shares of personal property.

7648. Revenue stamps issued by the federal government were issued in 1862 under authority of an act of Congress of July 1, 1862, "to provide Internal Revenue to support the government and to pay interest on the public debt." At first, specific taxes were identified on the stamps, such as bill of lading, foreign exchange, probate of will, warehouse receipt, and so on, but after December 25, 1862, they were used indiscriminately. Revenue stamps were issued in various sizes, in valuations from one cent to $200.

7649. Customs fee stamps were issued by the New York Custom House, New York City, in 1887. There were eight denominations, ranging from 20 cents to 90 cents. All were decorated with a distinctive background and a likeness of Silas Wright, New York State's former senator and governor. Their use was discontinued on February 28, 1918.

7650. Single Tax League national conference assembled on September 1, 1890, in New York City and adopted a platform on September 3. Five hundred delegates from 30 states formed a national organization, the Single Tax League of the United States, with a national committee composed of one member from each state and an executive committee of which William T. Croasdale was the chairman. The first noted proponent of a single tax was the economic reformer Henry George, who advocated the elimination of all government taxes except for the tax on land in order to free industry of restrictive tax burdens and equalize opportunities for individuals.

7651. Single tax adopted by a city for local revenue purposes was adopted by Hyattsville, MD, which operated under this system from July 1892 to March 1893, under laws that were declared unconstitutional. The single tax system eliminates all government taxes except the tax on land.

7652. Tax on aviation levied by a city was enacted in August 1908 by the town of Kissimmee City, FL. The law imposed a tax of $100 on airplanes, $150 on helicopters, $200 on ornithopters, and $300 on all other types of flying machines, plus a tax on their carrying capacity, and authorized the purchase of an "aeroplane of approved modern type" for the marshal to enforce the provisions of the ordinance. No attempt was made to enforce the law.

7653. Corporation tax levied by Congress was passed on August 5, 1909. The act taxed all corporations with an income over $5,000. The law was passed prior to the adoption of the U.S. income tax amendment.

TAXATION—*continued*

7654. Tax levied by Congress on excess profits of corporations was passed on March 3, 1917, an "act to provide increased revenue to defray the expenses of the increased appropriation for the army and navy and the extension of fortifications." The act provided for taxation of the profits of all corporations in excess of 7 to 9 percent of the capital. The rates were progressive: 20 percent on excess profits up to 15 percent; 35 percent on the excess from 15 to 25 percent; 35 percent on the excess from 25 percent to 33 percent; and 60 percent on the excess above 33 percent. The act was repealed by the Revenue Act of 1917, approved on October 3, 1917.

7655. Gasoline tax levied by a state was enacted on February 25, 1919, when Oregon placed a tax of one cent per gallon on all motor fuel. The funds collected were used for road construction and maintenance.

7656. Sales tax enacted by a state was approved on May 3, 1921, by West Virginia, and became effective on July 1. The funds collected were used largely in place of funds from a tax on corporate net income. The rate was one-fifth of 1 percent on the gross income of banks, street railroads, telephones, telegraph, express, and electric light and power retailers, and two-fifths of 1 percent on timber, oil, coal, natural gas, and other minerals. Payments could be made to the state quarterly or annually.

7657. Internal revenue collector for the federal government who was a woman was Mabel Gilmore Reinecke, who served from June 1, 1923, to March 31, 1929, as collector of Internal Revenue for the 1st District of Illinois. She was appointed by President Warren Gamaliel Harding.

7658. Tax on chain stores enacted by a state was levied by Indiana. This statute, commonly referred to as the Indiana Chain Store Tax Law, was signed on March 16, 1929, by Governor Harry Leslie. Under the statute, owners were required to pay an annual license fee of $3 to operate a store in Indiana. For two to five stores under the same management, supervision, or ownership, the tax was $10 for each additional store; for stores in excess of 5 but not in excess of 10, $15 for each additional store; for stores in excess of 10 but not in excess of 20, $20 for each additional store; for all stores in excess of 20, $25 plus a 50-cent filing fee for

each additional store. An amendment to this act was signed on March 11, 1933, by Governor Paul Vories McNutt, requiring owners of stores in excess of 20 to pay $150 for each additional store.

7659. Gasoline tax levied by Congress was the Revenue Act of 1932, enacted on June 6, 1932, which placed a tax of one cent per gallon on gasoline and other motor fuel.

7660. Revenue stamp printed by the Post Office Department was the "Federal duck stamp," a $1 stamp required of all waterfowl hunters over 16 years of age, to be attached to game licenses as required by the Migratory Bird Conservation Act of March 16, 1934. The stamp went on sale on August 14, 1934. It depicted a male and female mallard coming to rest on a marshland and was drawn by Jay Norwood "Ding" Darling, chief of the Bureau of Biological Survey of the Department of Agriculture. Stamps of this class, as well as all other revenue stamps, had previously been issued by the Treasury Department. Although sold through the Post Office Department, the proceeds went to the Department of Agriculture, where 10 percent was used for the expense of printing and selling the stamps and the balance to lease or purchase marsh areas for waterfowl sanctuaries.

7661. Gambling permit stamp issued by the federal government was authorized on October 20, 1951, by the Revenue Act of 1951. The ungummed stamps measured 6.5 by 4 inches and cost $50 per year. In the first six months of issue, 22,401 stamps were purchased, mostly in Nevada.

TAXATION—TARIFFS

7662. Free trade policy by the federal government was in effect from 1775 to 1780, but imports were taxed by the various states. Trade was free in Massachusetts from 1774 to 1781, in South Carolina from 1776 to 1783, in Maryland and Connecticut from 1776 to 1780. Although there were no federal restrictions, the situation was extremely complicated, and taxes were different in practically every state.

7663. Tariff legislation enacted by Congress after the adoption of the Constitution was the Tariff Act of July 4, 1789, an "act for laying a duty on goods, wares and merchandises imported into the United States." The main purpose was the collection of revenue, but protection was also extended to certain industries that the government wished to encourage, such as glass and earthenware. The act was signed by President George Washington and was to continue in force until July 1796. It laid specific duties on some articles and ad valorem duties on others, equivalent to an 8.5 percent ad valorem rate, with drawback, up to 1 percent of the duties on all articles exported within 12 months, except distilled spirits other than brandy and geneva.

7664. Tariff passed by Congress for protection rather than primarily for revenue was the "act to regulate the duties on imports and tonnage," passed on April 27, 1816.

7665. Tariff enacted by Congress to prevent the importation of obscene literature and pictures was the Tariff Act of August 30, 1842, an "act to provide revenue from imports." Section 28 stated: "The importation of all indecent and obscene prints, paintings, lithographs, engravings and transparencies is hereby prohibited ... and all invoices and packages whereof any such article shall compose a part are ... liable ... to be seized and forfeited ... and the said articles shall be forthwith destroyed."

7666. Tariff commission established by Congress was authorized on June 7, 1882. Nine tariff commissioners at $10 a day and expenses were appointed from civil life to investigate tariff questions relating to agriculture, commerce, manufacturing, mining, and mercantile and industrial interests. The first chairman was John Lord.

TELECOMMUNICATIONS—FAXES

7667. Radio fax patents were awarded on March 28, 1905, to Cornelius D. Ehret of Rosemont, PA, for "the art of transmitting intelligence" and "a system of transmitting intelligence."

7668. Transatlantic radio fax transmission of a photograph took place on June 11, 1922, when a photograph of Pope Pius XI was transmitted from Rome by Dr. Arthur Korn, a German physicist. It was published in the *New York World* the same day. The picture, a halftone 7 by 9.5 inches, was received 40 minutes after transmission at Bar Harbor, ME, by Chief Radioman Edmund H. Hansen of the Navy. Light falling on a selenium cell produced a group of shaded dots that formed a halftone.

7669. Transcontinental radio fax transmission of a photograph took place on March 4, 1925, when nine photographs taken in Washington, DC, of the inauguration of President Calvin Coolidge were sent to New York City, Chicago, and San Francisco by the American Telegraph and Telephone Company. One picture was sent every 12 minutes, and each photograph took 7 minutes to travel the distance.

7670. Transpacific radio fax transmission was made on May 6, 1925. It was also the first transcontinental radio fax transmission. Photographs of war games and of a general, an admiral, and a governor were transmitted by Alfred J. Koenig from Honolulu, HI, using a transmitted designed by Captain Richard Howland Ranger. The photographs went to Kahuku, HI, by wire; to Marshall, CA, by radio; to Bolinas, CA, by radio; to Riverhead, NY, by radio; and to New York City by wire. The total distance was 5,136 miles.

7671. Long-distance radio fax transmission of medical information was made on May 28, 1925, when the American Telegraph and Telephone Company transmitted stethogram and electrocardiogram pictures from its New York City office to a physician in Chicago.

7672. Fax transmission of movie film was a two-hour transmission of 10 feet of film showing the actress Vilma Banky, which was sent over telephone wires from Chicago, IL, on April 4, 1928, to the American Telephone and Telegraph Company's New York City studio. The negatives were placed between glass plates, rephotographed, and reassembled. There were only eight telephone fax stations in the United States at the time. The feat had been attempted two years earlier, but the images received were blurred.

7673. Radio fax transmission to a moving train was demonstrated on June 4, 1946, when Postmaster General Robert Emmet Hannegan sent a message from the law library in the Capitol, Washington, DC, to a railroad car moving from Baltimore, MD, to Washington on the Baltimore and Ohio Railroad. It was sent over radio station WCBM, Baltimore, MD. The message, "What hath God wrought," written and signed by Margaret Truman, daughter of President Harry S. Truman, was the same as the telegraph message by Samuel Finley Breese Morse that inaugurated commercial telegraph service in 1844.

7674. High-speed radio fax transmission was demonstrated on October 21, 1948, by the Radio Corporation of America at the Library of Congress, Washington, DC, using Ultrafax, a system capable of transmitting a million words per minute. The first message was handwritten by David Sarnoff, president and chairman of the board of RCA. Margaret Mitchell's *Gone with the Wind*, a novel of 457,000 words and 1,047 pages, was transmitted from station WNBW, Washington, DC, to the Library of Congress, a distance of three miles, in 2 minutes 21 seconds.

TELECOMMUNICATIONS—RADAR

7675. Radar observations were made on September 27, 1922, by Dr. Albert Hoyt Taylor and Leo C. Young of the Naval Aircraft Radio Laboratory, Anacostia, DC (now part of Washington, DC). They reported to the Navy that radio detection equipment placed on any two ships could detect the passage of any vessel between them despite fog, darkness, or smoke screen, and that tall buildings reflect radio signals.

7676. Radar detection of airplanes was accomplished on June 24, 1930, by Dr. Albert Hoyt Taylor and Leo C. Young of the Naval Aircraft Radio Laboratory, Anacostia, DC (now part of Washington, DC), who noted that airplanes reflect radio waves even though they fly above the transmitter and receiver, rather than between them.

7677. Passenger ship equipped with radar was the flagship *New York* of the Hamburg-American Line. Two circular appendages three feet in diameter were installed atop the pilothouse of the ship. The equipment was placed in service on February 26, 1938.

7678. Battleship equipped with radar was the U.S.S. *New York,* which was tested during battle maneuvers at sea in the months of January, February, and March of 1939. This radar set operated on a wavelength of 1.5 meters, detecting destroyers at a distance of approxmiately 8 miles. The first set to be installed on the *New York* was constructed at the Naval Research Laboratory at Washington, DC. The first contract was awarded in October 1939 to the Radio Corporation of America for the manufacture of six sets of aircraft detection equipment.

7679. Radar used to detect enemy airplanes was employed at Pearl Harbor, HI, on December 7, 1941. At 7:20 A.M., Private Joseph L. Lockard of Williamsport, PA, reported to his superiors that he heard the approach of planes. The planes were assumed to be friendly and proper precautions were not taken, with the result that the Japanese succeeded in making a devastating surprise attack on the United States fleet. On February 8, 1942, Lockard received the Distinguished Service Medal and was sent to Officer Training School, Fort Monmouth, NJ.

7680. Radar signal to the moon was beamed by the Army Signal Corps on January 10, 1946, from the Evans Signal Laboratories, Belmar, NJ. The experiment was supervised by Lieutenant Colonel John H. De Witt. An echo was received 2.4 seconds later that consisted of a 180-cycle note of a quarter-second duration.

7681. Radar for commercial and private planes was developed by Howard Robard Hughes and the electronic engineers of the Hughes Aircraft Corporation, Culver City, CA, and was demonstrated on May 1, 1947, at Culver City on a TWA (Transcontinental and Western Air) plane. A brilliant red light on the instrument panel and a horn in the cockpit warned the pilot whenever he came too close to an obstacle.

7682. Offshore radar warning station was built by the Bethlehem Steel Company's shipbuilding division at Fore River, Quincy, MA, for the Continental Air Defense Command. The keel was laid on January 10, 1955, and the station was launched on May 20. Known as a Texas Tower, it was a triangular 6,000-ton platform resting on three legs 87 feet above the water level, and served as a weather collecting and reporting station. It was turned over to the First Naval District of the Navy on December 2, 1955.

7683. Radar signal bounced off the sun was transmitted on April 7, 1959, at Stanford University, Stanford, CA, by Professor Von Russel Eshleman, Lieutenant Colonel Robert Charles Barthle, and Dr. Philip Benjamin Gallagher, who used a 40,000-watt transmitter. The signals reached the sun's corona about a half million miles above the visible part of the sun. They required 1,000 seconds for transmission in both directions. The signals consisted of a series of dots and dashes that were detected by an electronic computer even though they were much weaker than the radio noise from the sun.

TELECOMMUNICATIONS—TELEGRAPH

7684. Semaphore telegraph system was invented in 1799 by Jonathan Grout of Belchertown, MA, who installed a series of towers, each within sight of the next, between Boston and Martha's Vineyard, 90 miles distant. By means of a combination of the semaphore and flag systems, he was able to ask a question and receive an answer within 10 minutes. This system did not involve the use of an electric telegraph line.

7685. Telegraph system was constructed in 1827 by Harrison Gray Dyar, who operated a two-mile telegraph system at the racecourse at Long Island City, NY (now part of Queens, New York City). Iron wire attached to glass insulators on wooden posts enabled the current to produce a red mark on litmus paper at the receiving station. The lapse of time between the sparks indicated the different letters.

7686. Electromagnetic telegraph was invented by Joseph Henry, who exhibited it in 1831 at the Albany Academy, Albany, NY. The device was 14 inches long. At each excitation of the electric magnet, one end of a compass rod or needle remained in contact with a limb of the soft iron core. Near the opposite end of the compass rod was a small stationary office bell. When the current was reversed, the compass rod moved back to the opposite limb of the electromagnet. Signals were transmitted by means of the electromagnet through more than a mile of wire. The invention was not put to practical use; it merely demonstrated the possibility of transmitting signals.

7687. Telegraphic system in which dots and dashes represented letters was invented by Alfred Vail of Morristown, NJ, in September 1837. On January 8, 1838, the message "A patient waiter is no loser" was transmitted. On January 24, in a public demonstration given at New York University, New York City, the message "Attention the Universe. By Kingdom's Right Wheel" was transmitted through a circuit of 10 miles. Previously, words had been assigned numbers, with the marks appearing as acutely angulated lines like the letter V or V in reverse, which appeared on cylinders at the receiving station.

7688. Telegraph cable was an insulated copper wire laid on October 18, 1842, by Samuel Finley Breese Morse in New York Harbor between the Battery and Governors Island. On the following day, while transmitting signals, the cable stopped working because a vessel, in raising its anchor, had caught and wrecked 200 feet of it. Another cable was laid in New York Harbor for commercial use in 1843 by Samuel Colt. It was insulated with cotton yarn, beeswax, and asphaltum encased in a lead pipe, and connected New York City with both Fire Island and Coney Island.

7689. Telegraph appropriation by Congress was made on March 3, 1843. A sum of $30,000 was appropriated "to test the practicability of establishing a system of electromagnetic telegraphs by the United States."

7690. Telegraph station was opened in Washington, DC, in 1844 under the direction of Samuel Finley Breese Morse. The station was located between Seventh and Eighth streets and E and F streets.

7691. Telegraph ticker to print letters of the alphabet was patented by Royal Earl House of New York City, who obtained a patent on April 18, 1846, on a "magnetic letter printing telegraph." It printed 50 words a minute in Roman letters. The ticker was first publicly exhibited in 1844 at the American Institute Fair, New York City. It was extensively used for about 10 years until superseded by new models.

7692. Commercial telegraph service was inaugurated on May 24, 1844, by Professor Samuel Finley Breese Morse, who sent a message from the Supreme Court room in the Capitol, Washington, DC, to Alfred Vail at the Mount Clare station of the Baltimore and Ohio Railroad Company, Baltimore, MD. Vail retransmitted it to Morse. The message, "What hath God wrought," was selected from the 23rd verse of the 23rd chapter of the biblical Book of Numbers by Annie Ellsworth, daughter of the commissioner of patents.

7693. Underwater telegraph cable that was practical was laid by Ezra Cornell, an associate of Samuel Finley Breese Morse. In 1845 he laid 12 miles of cable enclosed in lead pipes across the Hudson River, connecting Fort Lee, NJ, with New York City. This cable was carried away by ice in 1846. Before the cable was installed, messages for Philadelphia, PA, and Washington, DC, were carried across the Hudson by messengers in boats.

7694. Telegrapher who was a woman was Sarah G. Bagley, who was in charge of the Lowell, MA, office of the New York and Boston Magnetic Telegraph Association when the line opened on February 21, 1846, between Boston and Lowell.

7695. Telegraph company was the Magnetic Telegraph Company, incorporated on February 4, 1847, under the laws of Maryland. The first president was Amos Kendall. Offices were rented in New York City at a cost of $250 a year, in Philadelphia for $150, in Baltimore for $150, and in Washington, DC, for $50. At first, messages were sent by pigeons across the Hudson River from Jersey City, NJ, to New York City. Later, a lead pipe enclosing a covered wire saturated with pitch was laid under the river. The rates from Baltimore to Washington were 10 cents for the first 10 words and 1 cent for each additional word. The rates from New York to Washington were 50 cents for the first 10 words and 5 cents for each additional word.

TELECOMMUNICATIONS—TELEGRAPH
—continued

7696. Telegraph used by a railroad was used on September 22, 1851, when Charles Minot, superintendent of the Erie Railroad, telegraphed 14 miles to Goshen, NY, to delay a train so that his own train would not have to wait. Trains were run on the interval system.

7697. Telegraph ticker to print type successfully was invented by David Edward Hughes of Louisville, KY, who received a patent on May 20, 1856. He had sold his rights to the Commercial Company for $100,000 on November 1, 1855.

7698. Transatlantic telegraph cable was completed on August 5, 1858, through the efforts of Cyrus West Field, after two unsuccessful attempts. On July 28, 1858, a splice was made in midocean, and on the following day four ships belonging to Britain and the United States paid out the cable as they sailed for home—the *Agamemnon* and *Valorous,* bound for Valentia, Ireland, and the *Niagara* and *Gorgon,* bound for Trinity Bay, Newfoundland. These destinations were to be the terminals of the cable. The cable was 1,950 statute miles long and more than two-thirds of it was laid more than 2 miles deep. Introductory and complimentary messages were exchanged by President James Buchanan and Queen Victoria on August 16, 1858. The cable was weak and the current insufficient, and service was suspended on September 1, 1858.

7699. Telegram dispatched from an aerial station was sent from the balloon *Enterprise* on June 18, 1861, to President Abraham Lincoln by Professor Thaddeus Sobieski Coulincourt Lowe, who acknowledged his indebtedness "for the opportunity of demonstrating the availability of the science of aeronautics in the military service of the country."

7700. Transcontinental telegraph line was placed in operation on October 24, 1861, when Stephen Johnson Field, chief justice of California, sent a message to President Abraham Lincoln. On October 25, 1861, telegrams were exchanged between Mayor Fernando Wood of New York City and Mayor H.F. Teschemacher of San Francisco, CA. Rates during the first week were $1 a word between San Francisco and the Missouri River. Later the rates were reduced: 10 words from San Francisco to New York City cost $6, and each additional word cost 75 cents.

7701. Telegraph call boxes were installed on June 22, 1872, in Brooklyn, NY (now part of New York City), by the American District Telegraph Company. Each metal box contained "a Seth Thomas clock movement supported upon a circular iron base ... [with] two break wheels ... attached to the clockwork, either of which could be brought into circuit by means of a switch." One wheel was notched for the even number and the other for the odd, the former indicating "messenger" and the latter "fire." The idea was conceived by Edward A. Calahan, who obtained patents on June 11, 1872, and July 16, 1873.

7702. Two-way telegraph that was practical was invented by Thomas Alva Edison of Newark, NJ, who obtained a patent on August 9, 1892, in the United States, after receiving patents in Britain, France, Italy, Austria-Hungary, and Russia. The telegraph enabled "two operators to simultaneously send over one wire in one direction, by reversal of a battery current in one instance and increasing and decreasing the strength of the current in the other instance, and the connections are so arranged that the party at the receiving station can signal to the sender to repeat in case of inaccuracy."

7703. Transpacific telegraph cable was paid out beginning on December 14, 1902, between San Francisco, CA, and Honolulu, HI, a distance of 2,277 nautical miles (2,620 miles), by the cableship *Silverton*. It was landed on the beach near Honolulu on January 1, 1903. The first message was sent at 11:03 P.M. San Francisco time on that day. On January 5, the cable was opened for public use.

7704. Telegraph message sent around the world by commercial telegraph was "This message sent around the world," sent at 7 P.M. on August 20, 1911, from the 17th floor of the New York Times building, New York City, by the *New York Times* and received by the *Times* at 7:16:30 P.M. The message traveled over 28,613 miles and 16 relays by way of the Azores, Gibraltar, Bombay, Philippine Islands, Midway, Guam, Honolulu, and San Francisco.

7705. Permalloy was developed on June 7, 1913, at the Bell Telephone Laboratories, New York City, by Gustaf Waldemar Elmen. Made from an alloy of nickel and iron, it was used in the form of a thin tape, 0.006 inches thick, which was wound around the conductor. Its extraordinarily high magnetic permeability at very low magnetizing forces permitted the high inductance necessary for high-speed transmission. It was first applied commercially in 1924, when it was used in the New York–Azores submarine telegraph cable, increasing the transmission rate from 300 to 2,000 letters per minute.

7706. Coaxial cable was invented by Lloyd Espenschied of Kew Gardens, NY, and Herman A. Affel of Ridgewood, NJ. On May 23, 1929, they applied for a patent on a "concentric conducting system." The patent was granted on December 8, 1931, and was assigned to the American Telegraph and Telephone Company, New York City.

7707. Teletype commercial service was inaugurated on November 20, 1931, by the American Telegraph and Telephone Company. Messages typed on tape were transmitted automatically to a central office and retransmitted to their destinations. The charges were based on the time required to transmit each message, not on the number of words. On December 1, 1931, the teletype systems of the Postal Telegraph Company and the Western Union Telegraph Company cooperated in "Timed Wire Service" so that a patron of one service could transmit to a patron of the other service.

7708. Singing telegram was introduced by the Western Union Telegraph Company, New York City, on July 28, 1933. The innovation, opposed by a company executive, proved popular with customers. Many telegrams were sung by messengers in person, but after 1950 all singing was done by telephone.

7709. Submarine cable plow was patented on January 12, 1937, by Chester S. Lawton of Ridgewood, NJ, and Captain Melville H. Bloomer of Halifax, Nova Scotia, Canada, who assigned it to the Western Union Telegraph Company. The plow dug a trench in the bed of the ocean and simultaneously fed the cable into the furrow. The plow could be used in depths as great as half a mile. The first transatlantic cable of a high-speed permalloy was buried on June 14, 1938.

7710. Telegraph code converter was the Trak Code Converter, made by CGS Laboratories, Stamford, CT, and announced to the public in the October 1954 issue of *Wire and Radio Communications Magazine*. Incoming International Morse Code signals were converted by a teleprinter that recorded at speeds up to 600 words per minute. The converter, which cost $14,850, was housed in a relay rack 19 inches long and 54 inches high.

TELECOMMUNICATIONS—TELEPHONES

7711. Voice synthesizer was demonstrated to the public on December 22, 1845, at the Musical Fund Hall in Philadelphia, PA, by Joseph Faber, an inventor recently arrived from Germany. His device took 17 years to develop. It consisted of a keyboard that by mechanical means operated a series of reeds, bellows, and chambers, designed to work like the human mouth, tongue, teeth, glottis, larynx, and lungs. Passing air through the device produced sixteen basic phonemes, enough to pronounce accurately any word in any European language. The machine's slow, sepulchral voice seemed to emerge from a mechanical head that was fixed to the frame. In 1846, Phineas T. Barnum exhibited Faber's invention, dubbed the Euphonium, in London, where it was viewed by Melville Bell, the father of Alexander Graham Bell, inventor of the telephone.

7712. Telephone for domestic use was installed in April 1877 at the home of Charles Williams, Jr., of Somerville, MA, at the corner of Arlington and Lincoln streets. Williams also had a telephone installed at the same time in his office at 109 Court Street, Boston, MA.

7713. Automatic telephone system was patented on December 5, 1879, by Daniel Connolly of Philadelphia, PA, Thomas A. Connolly of Washington, DC, and Thomas J. McTighe of Pittsburgh, PA. The system employed a single-line wire, a battery of cells located at each telephone, and a dial-switching mechanism for each line. The system could accommodate only a few lines and was not commercially applied. The first successful system was invented by Almon B. Strowger. It was installed at La Porte, IN, where it was formally opened to the public on November 3, 1892. The first exchange equipped with a rotating dial was an interior system in the City Hall of Milwaukee, WI, which was installed in 1896.

7714. Desk telephone was used in 1886. Previous telephones were of the wall box variety.

7715. Pay telephone was invented by William Gray of Hartford, CT, who received a patent on August 13, 1889, on a "coin-controlled apparatus for telephones." The first machine in commercial use was installed in the lobby of the Hartford Bank in 1889 under the supervision of Ellis Benjamin Baker, superintendent of the Southern New England Telephone Company. In 1891, Gray, with Amos Whitney and Francis Pratt, incorporated the Gray Telephone Pay Station Company (later the Gray Manufacturing

TELECOMMUNICATIONS—TELEPHONES
—continued

Company) and installed the telephones in stores on a rental basis. The company rented out pay phones for 25 percent of the take. Ten percent of the take went to the place of business in which the telephones were installed and 65 percent went to the telephone company.

7716. Mobile radio telephone marine demonstration was held on board the steamer *Bartholdi* on the Potomac River on March 20, 1902. The apparatus and equipment were the inventions of Nathan B. Stubblefield of Murray, KY.

7717. Car equipped with a two-way radio was built by the Chalmers-Detroit Company and demonstrated in March 1910 in New York City. Successful demonstrations were made from the moving car as it traveled through Central Park to the Terminal Building, 42nd Street and Park Avenue, at distances varying from one to three miles. The sending set contained two storage cells, a 10-inch spark coil, two Leyden jars, a high and low voltage battery, and a seven-foot aerial.

7718. Transcontinental telephone demonstration took place on January 25, 1915, when Alexander Graham Bell, calling from the offices of the American Telephone and Telegraph Company in New York City and using a model of the first telephone, spoke with his associate, Thomas Augustus Watson, in San Francisco, about 3,000 miles away. Bell repeated the words "Mr. Watson, come here, I want you," the phrase he had spoken 40 years earlier, in March 1876, during the world's first telephone conversation. Later, Mayor John Purroy Mitchel of New York City talked with Mayor James Rolph, Jr., of San Francisco.

7719. Mobile telephone one-way communication was established by Bell System engineers on April 4, 1915, from Montauk Point, NY, to Wilmington, DE, a distance of 250 miles.

7720. Transcontinental commercial telephone service from New York to California was inaugurated on April 7, 1915, at a cost of $20.70 for the first three minutes and $6.75 for each minute thereafter.

7721. Transcontinental demonstration of radio telephone operation was given on September 29, 1915, when speech was transmitted from New York City to Arlington, VA, thence to Mare Island, San Francisco, 2,500 miles away, and on to Honolulu that night.

7722. Walkie-Talkie two-way radio device was built in 1933 at the Signal Corps Engineering Laboratories, Fort Monmouth, NJ. Its official name was the portable superregenerative receiver and transmitter. The personnel principally concerned with this project were John Hessel, radio mechanic; C.W. Hayhurst, mechanical design engineer; and John Reid, shop mechanic. Commercial production was undertaken in 1934 by the Allen D. Cardwell Company, Brooklyn, New York City.

7723. Electronic voice mechanism capable of creating complex sounds of speech in an intelligible manner was Pedro, the Voder, designed by Homer Walter Dudley, Robert Richard Riesz, and Stanley Sylvester Alexander Watkins of the Bell Telephone Laboratories, New York City, and publicly exhibited on June 5, 1938, at the Franklin Institute, Philadelphia, PA.

7724. Telephone recording devices were authorized by the Federal Communications Commission on June 30, 1948. They were required to have a tone-warning device that produced a distinctive "beep" signal at regular intervals, to let those taking part in the conversation know that their voices were being recorded. Recording devices had been used previously by government and business.

7725. Trimline telephone was placed in service by the Michigan Bell Telephone Company, Detroit, MI, at Jackson, MI, on October 21, 1963. The phone became commercially available on an optional basis throughout the company's territory on August 2, 1965, at a monthly charge of $1. The dial was mounted in the receiver midway between the mouth and the ear pieces, eliminating the need to reach for the base when dialing.

7726. Telephone with push buttons instead of a rotary dial was the Touch-Tone Telephone with 10 push buttons, manufactured by the Western Electric Manufacturing and Supply Unit of the Bell System and placed in commercial service in Carnegie and Greensburg, PA, on November 18, 1963, following marketing trials in Ohio and Pennsylvania. Touch-Tone service was offered at an extra charge on an optional basis.

7727. Cellular telephone system began operation in Chicago, IL, in 1983. It was a microwave-based radiotelephone system in which the service area was divided into geographic "cells," each of which was assigned a transmission frequency. The first such system in the world was put into service in Tokyo in 1979.

TELECOMMUNICATIONS—TELEPHONES —COMMERCIAL SERVICE

7728. Telephone switchboard or exchange was put in operation on May 17, 1877. It was located at 342 Washington Street, Boston, MA, where Edwin Thomas Holmes was operating an electrical burglar alarm business. Holmes's office was connected by wire to a number of banks and similar institutions, and the telephones were placed in the offices of six of his subscribers and connected to these wires. The system served as a telephone system by day and as a burglar alarm system at night. The telephones were connected only in the daytime.

7729. Telephone operator who was a woman was Emma M. Nutt, who went to work for the Telephone Despatch Company, Boston, MA, on September 1, 1878. Previously, all operators had been men.

7730. Commercial telephone service using toll lines was instituted on April 2, 1879, between Springfield and Holyoke, MA, by the District Telephone Company of New Haven, CT. The distance was about eight miles.

7731. Pay station telephone service began on June 1, 1880, in the office of the Connecticut Telephone Company, Yale Bank Building, State and Chapel streets, New Haven, CT. The toll was given to an attendant.

7732. International commercial telephone service was begun on July 1, 1881, when service was inaugurated by the National Bell Telephone Company of the State of Maine between Calais, ME, and St. Stephen, New Brunswick, Canada, two points separated by the St. Croix River, the international boundary line between the United States and Canada.

7733. Telephone exchange for Chinese-American subscribers was established in 1894 by Loo Kum Shu in the Chinatown district of San Francisco, CA. It was operated by three Chinese-American men who handled all the calls. The exchange later became the "China" central office of the Pacific Telephone and Telegraph Company and was located on Washington Street, east of Grant Avenue, San Francisco. The original number of subscribers was 100, a total that had increased by 1946 to more than 2,000. At first all calls were made by name, but later the number system was adopted.

7734. Multiple common battery telephone switchboard was put in service in the fall of 1897 by the Ohio Valley Telephone Company in Louisville, KY.

7735. Mobile telephone commercial service was inaugurated on July 16, 1920, between Los Angeles and Santa Catalina Island, CA. A radio link connected the town of Avalon on the island to telephone lines in Long Beach, CA. The service was maintained by the Bell Telephone System for three years. It was replaced by cable because "speech-scrambling" devices had not yet been developed and messages sent over the radio could be picked up by anyone capable of tuning a receiving set.

7736. Telephone cable deep-sea service was established on April 11, 1921, between Key West, FL, and Havana, Cuba. It was officially opened by President Warren Gamaliel Harding, who placed the first call from the Pan American Building, Washington, DC, to Cuba's President Mario García Menocal at Havana.

7737. Transatlantic commercial telephone service was established between New York City and London. It was inaugurated on January 7, 1927, when Walter Sherman Gifford, president of the American Telephone and Telegraph Company, who was in New York, talked to Sir George Evelyn Pemberton Murray, secretary of the British Post Office, who was in London. Thirty-one commercial calls were made the first day. The charge was $75 for a three-minute conversation. The first private conversation was made by Adolph Simon Ochs, publisher of the *New York Times,* to Geoffrey Dawson, editor of the *Times* of London. The messages were transmitted from Rocky Point, NY.

7738. Telephone switchboard with Braille markings and devices to enable a blind person to operate it by touch and sound was designed by the Western Electric Company and installed by the New York Telephone Company on April 1, 1928, in the New York Institute for the Education of the Blind, the Bronx, New York City. The first operator was Frances Sievert, who held the position for more than 25 years.

7739. Ship-to-shore mobile telephone commercial service was inaugurated on December 8, 1929, when Walter Sherman Gifford, president of the American Telephone and Telegraph Company, lifted a receiver in New York City and spoke to Commodore Harold A. Cunningham of the S.S. *Leviathan*. The first personal call was made by William Hector Rankin, a New York advertising man, to Sir Thomas Lipton, who was a passenger aboard the liner. The rate varied from $7 to $11 a minute, depending upon the zone.

TELECOMMUNICATIONS—TELEPHONES —COMMERCIAL SERVICE—*continued*

7740. Mobile telephone commercial service was inaugurated on June 17, 1946, by the Southwestern Bell Telephone Company, St. Louis, MO. Installations were completed in the automobiles of two subscribers, the Monsanto Chemical Company and Henry L. Perkinson, a contractor. Conversation was possible with any Bell Telephone System or connecting company telephone.

7741. Commercial telephone service on railroad trains for passengers was placed in operation on August 15, 1947, on the Baltimore and Ohio Railroad Company's *Royal Blue* and the Pennsylvania Railroad Company's *Congressional Limited* between New York City and Washington, DC. Two-way radio telephone conversations could be carried on in the same way as ordinary telephone calls.

7742. Long-distance dial telephone service began on October 17, 1949, when Mark Sullivan, president of the Pacific Telephone and Telegraph Company, dialed Oakland, CA, from New York City. He spoke to Dr. Oliver E. Buckley, president of the Bell Telephone Laboratories, and Keith S. McHugh, president of the New York Telephone Company. It took less than one minute to complete the call.

7743. Radio paging service was instituted on October 15, 1950, in the New York City area by Aircall. The first call was for a doctor who was on a golf course 25 miles away. Subscribers equipped with six-ounce Aircall pocket radio receivers could hear their call numbers repeated in numerical sequence on the air at least once per minute within a 30-mile area.

7744. Telephone company answering service was provided by the Ohio Bell Telephone Company, which marketed a recording machine and offered service at $12.50 a month, plus a $15 installment fee. As many as twenty 30-second messages could be recorded on a cylinder, which could then be cleaned and used again. The service was offered to the public in March 1951.

7745. Transcontinental dial telephone service without the aid of operators was commercially inaugurated on November 10, 1951, with a conversation between Mayor M. Leslie Denning of Englewood, NJ, and Mayor Frank P. Osborn of Alameda, CA. Conversation was initiated 18 seconds after dialing. Raymond J. Neiligan was the manager of the Englewood exchange.

7746. Telephone call on a commercial line using solar energy took place on October 4, 1955, at Americus, GA, over the lines of the Southern Bell Telephone and Telegraph Company. The current was supplied by a solar battery developed by the Bell Telephone Laboratories. The aluminum housing of the battery, less than a yard square, contained 432 silicon cells cushioned in oil and covered with glass. The first call, over a distance of about 14 miles, was made to Gene Summerford by George Mathews, who said, "Hello, Gene. This is George Mathews. How many bales of cotton do I have in your warehouse?"

7747. Transatlantic telephone service using the transoceanic cable began with a conversation between Samuel H. Berlin of New York City and John Blackburn Batley of England. The rate was $12 for a three-minute call. The transatlantic cable, which ran for a distance of about 2,250 miles between Clarenville, Newfoundland, Canada, and Oban, Scotland, was laid by the *Monarch* from June 22 to September 26, 1955.

7748. Air-to-ground public telephone service began on September 15, 1957, in the Chicago–Detroit area, when about 20 airplanes were equipped for the two-way service. The rates varied from $1.50 to $4.25 for a three-minute call, depending on the location of the airplane and of the telephone on the ground.

7749. Transpacific telephone service using the transoceanic cable began on June 18, 1964, when President Lyndon Baines Johnson in Washington, DC, spoke to Premier Hayato Ikeda in Tokyo, Japan. The cable, with a capacity of 138 voice channels, stretched 5,300 nautical miles from Oahu, Hawaii, to Japan via Midway, Wake, and Guam, and joined existing cables to the United States mainland, Canada, and Australia. Partners in the $80-million cable project were the American Telephone and Telegraph Company, Kokusai Denshin Denwa Company of Japan, the Hawaiian Telephone Company, and RCA Communications.

7750. Picturephone commercial service was inaugurated on June 24, 1964, in New York City, Chicago, and Washington, DC, when Lady Bird Johnson, wife of President Lyndon Baines Johnson, spoke in Washington, DC, to Dr. Elizabeth A. Wood of the Bell Laboratories in New York City. The picturephone had three parts: a chassis containing the camera, loudspeaker, and screen, which was 4.375 inches wide and 5.75 inches high; a control unit; and the power supply. It was possible to both hear and see the person talking. Service for the general public opened on June 25, 1964. Rates for calls were $16 for the initial three-minute period between New York and Washington, $21 between Washington and Chicago, and $27 between Chicago and New York.

TELECOMMUNICATIONS—TELEPHONES —PHONE CALLS

7751. Telephone message that was distinguishable was "Mr. Watson, come here, I want you," spoken into the telephone on March 10, 1876, by Alexander Graham Bell and received by his associate Thomas Augustus Watson on another floor in Bell's home at 5 Exeter Place, Boston, MA. This was the world's first telephone conversation. Three days earlier, on March 7, Bell had received the first telephone patent, for an "improvement in telegraphy."

7752. Telephone conversation over outdoor wires took place on October 9, 1876, between Alexander Graham Bell in Boston, MA, and Thomas Augustus Watson in Cambridge. The sound traveled over the private telegraph wire of the Walworth Manufacturing Company from Boston to Cambridgeport, a distance of two miles. Parallel accounts of the conversation, as recorded separately by both Bell and Watson, were published in the *Boston Advertiser* on October 19, 1876, in answer to the skeptics who did not believe that the telephone was as reliable as the telegraph.

7753. Interstate telephone call took place on May 17, 1877, when a call was made from New Brunswick, NJ, to Dr. Alexander Graham Bell at Chickering Hall, New York City.

7754. Long-distance telephone call was made on March 27, 1884, by branch managers of the American Bell Telephone Company in Boston, MA, and New York City. Said a contemporary account: "The words were heard as perfectly as though the speakers were standing close by, while no extra effort was needed at the other end of the line to accomplish the result."

7755. Radio telephone message from a submerged submarine to shore was sent on January 6, 1898, by Simon Lake, submerged at the bottom of the Patapsco River in Maryland in the submarine he invented. Lake telephoned William Talbot Malster, the mayor of Baltimore, MD, at his office in the City Hall, and then called people in Washington, DC, and New York City.

7756. Long-distance telephone call over underground cables took place on February 26, 1914, between Boston, MA, and Washington, DC.

7757. Transatlantic message over radio telephone was transmitted on October 21, 1915, from Arlington, VA, to Paris. The voice of B.B. Webb was heard by Herbert E. Shreeve and Austen M. Custis of the American Telephone and Telegraph Company and by Lieutenant Colonel Ferrie of the French government at the receiving station installed in the Eiffel Tower by Bell System engineers.

7758. Ship-to-shore conversation over radio telephone took place on May 6, 1916, over the regular telephone network to demonstrate a way of mobilizing the telephone and telegraph in case of war. Captain Lloyd Horwitz Chandler of the battleship *New Hampshire,* while at sea off Hampton Roads, VA, reported to, and received orders from, Secretary of the Navy Josephus Daniels and Admiral William Shepherd Benson, who were in Washington, DC.

7759. Radio telephone communication from an airplane took place on July 2, 1917, at Langley Field, VA, where speech of good volume and quality was received from a transmitting plane two miles away. On July 4, speech from the ground was received by L.M. Clement of the Western Electric Company in a plane several miles away. On August 18, the first two-way communication was established between a plane and the ground, and on August 20, 1917, between two planes. Both events took place at Langley Field.

7760. Two-way radio conversation between a submerged submarine and another vessel took place on October 5, 1919, between the U.S. submarine *H-2,* commanded by Lieutenant Commander Clark Withers, and the destroyer *Blakey.* The submarine was submerged in the Hudson River off 96th Street, New York City.

7761. Mobile telephone conversation between the ground and an airship took place on May 16, 1925, when Arthur Atwater Kent, on board the dirigible *Los Angeles,* conversed with his wife, Mabel Lucas Kent, who was in a car in Philadelphia, PA. A single wire 300 feet long trailed from the airship.

7762. Round-the-world telephone conversation was held on April 25, 1935, between Walter Sherman Gifford, president of the American Telephone Company, in his office in New York City, and T.G. Miller, a company vice president, who was in an office about 50 feet away. The call was routed over 23,000 miles of telephone wire as well as by radio through San Francisco, Java, Amsterdam, and London and back to New York.

TELECOMMUNICATIONS—TELEPHONES —PHONE CALLS—*continued*

7763. Mobile overseas telephone call from a moving vehicle was made on July 16, 1946, by Roger Pierce from St. Louis, MO, to Honolulu, HI.

7764. Long-distance car-to-car telephone conversation was made on September 11, 1946, when a reporter with the *Houston Post* of Houston, TX, telephoned a reporter with the *St. Louis Globe Democrat* of St. Louis, MO.

7765. Transatlantic mobile telephone call between two cars was made on June 26, 1947, by U.S. Ambassador James Clement Dunn from Milan, Italy, to Vincent R. Impellitteri, president of the New York City Council, on the occasion of Marconi Day at the Milan Fair.

7766. Mobile telephone call between an airplane in flight and a moving car made with commercial equipment over commercial communication lines was accomplished on October 9, 1947, by executives of the Hercules Power Company, Wilmington, DE, from an airplane 2,000 feet in the air to an automobile about 5 miles west of Wilmington, on the Lancaster Pike (Route 41).

7767. Transatlantic telephone call carried by the transoceanic telephone cable took place on September 25, 1956, when Cleo Frank Craig, chairman of the board of the American Telegraph and Telephone Company, who was in New York City, spoke to Dr. Charles Hill, the British postmaster general, who was at Lancaster House, London. The cable, designed to carry 36 conversations at the same time, was the joint undertaking of the Bell System, the British Post Office (operator of the telephone service in Great Britain), and the Canadian Overseas Telecommunications Corporation.

7768. Telephone call conveyed by a privately owned satellite was made on July 10, 1962, at 7:28 P.M. by Frederick Russell Kappel, board chairman of the American Telephone and Telegraph Company, to Vice President Lyndon Baines Johnson in Washington, DC, on the sixth orbit of the satellite *Telstar 1*. Kappel's voice went from Andover, ME, to the satellite, bounced back to Andover, and then was carried by land line to Washington, DC. Johnson's voice was carried by land line to Andover.

7769. Transcontinental Picturephone call was made on April 20, 1964, when William Leonard Laurence, science consultant to the New York World's Fair, New York City, spoke to Donald Shaffer, managing editor of the *Anaheim Bulletin,* at Disneyland, Anaheim, CA. The set was about 12 inches across, 7 inches high, and 13 inches deep.

7770. Mobile telephone call to the moon was made by President Richard Milhous Nixon on July 20, 1969, to astronauts Neil Alden Armstrong and Edwin E. "Buzz" Aldrin, Jr., aboard *Apollo 11* during the first moon-landing mission.

TELEVISION

7771. Television was invented by several people, including the Russian-American electrical engineer Vladimir Kosma Zworykin, who received the two essential television patents on December 20, 1938. One patent was for the iconoscope, a cathode-ray transmitting tube that was the heart of all television cameras until the late 1980s. The second patent was for the kinescope, or cathode-ray receiving tube, the device that displays the image on all televisions and most computer monitors.

7772. Year in which television industry profits exceeded those of radio was 1953. According to the Federal Communications Commission, profits for that year were $68 million for television and $55 million for radio.

7773. Year in which color television sets outsold black and white sets was 1968, when 11.4 million sets were sold, 5.8 color and 5.5 million black and white.

TELEVISION—PRODUCTIONS

7774. Television programs to be shown regularly began appearing on May 11, 1928, from the General Electric Station, WGY, at Schenectady, NY. The programs were shown three times a week. The image consisted of 24 scanning lines repeated 20 times a second.

7775. Television theater to be licensed was the Massachusetts Television Institute, Boston, MA. It opened on July 13, 1938, with a 45-minute show witnessed by 200 people who had paid a 25-cent admission fee. The show consisted of vocal, instrumental, and dance numbers. They were performed in a room above the auditorium and transmitted by a wire to a 9-by-12-inch screen on which black and white images appeared, accompanied by sound.

7776. Television variety talent show series was telecast by WNBT-TV, New York City, for Standard Brands on Thursday nights from May 9, 1946, until March 6, 1947. The first episode, "The Hour Glass," starred Edgar Bergen, Paul Douglas, Joe Besser, and Evelyn Knight. The first variety talent show series with an African-American cast was "Happy Pappy," which was first televised on April 1, 1949, over WENR-TV, Chicago, IL. The program featured Ray Grant as master of ceremonies, the Four Vagabonds, and Modern Modes, and guests.

7777. Commercial program telecast on a network was "Geographically Speaking," sponsored by the Bristol-Myers Company and first broadcast on October 27, 1946, on WNBT, New York, and WPTZ, Philadelphia, PA.

7778. Television drama program regularly scheduled was "Kraft Television Theater," telecast on the National Broadcasting Company's network from May 7, 1947, to October 1, 1958, from 7:30 to 8:30 P.M. The program ran for 11 years, during which time it presented 650 plays that required 5,236 sets and the participation of 3,955 actors. The first drama was *Double Door*, starring John Baragrey.

7779. Western series on television was "Hopalong Cassidy," which first aired on November 28, 1948, on NBC-TV. Actor Bill Boyd, 53, starred in the title role.

7780. Sitcom television show was "The Goldbergs," which debuted on January 17, 1949, and aired weekly until June 1951. It was derived from the radio show of the same name. The star was Molly Berg. The term "sitcom" is short for "situation comedy."

7781. Soap opera on daytime television was "These Are My Children," by Irna Phillips, which was aired between 5 and 5:15 P.M. every weekday from January 31 to February 25, 1949, by NBC from Chicago, IL.

7782. Animated cartoon made for television was "Crusader Rabbit," which premiered in 1949. It was the creation of animator Jay Ward, who with writer Bill Scott also produced "Rocky and His Friends" for the ABC network in 1959.

7783. Television series in which an African-American performer had a starring role was the 1950 sitcom "Beulah," which starred Ethel Waters.

7784. Television program in color to be presented daily was Ivan T. Sanderson's "The World Is Yours," first seen on the CBS network over Channel 2 (W2CBS) on June 26, 1951, from 4:30 to 5 P.M. It depicted the earth's natural treasures. The first regular prime-time series broadcast in color was "Bonanza," which aired on NBC from 1959 to 1973.

7785. Pay television presentation of a sporting event was the closed-circuit coast-to-coast telecast of the Jersey Joe Walcott–Rocky Marciano fight at the Municipal Stadium, Philadelphia, PA, on September 23, 1952. Marciano won the heavyweight title by a knockout 43 seconds into the 13th round. The telecast was viewed by 40,379 persons in 49 theaters located in 31 cities. Ticket sales totaled $504,645.

7786. Animated cartoon series on prime-time television was "The Flintstones," which debuted on September 30, 1960, on the ABC television network. The half-hour show, produced by William Hanna and Joseph Barbera, featured the antics of two prehistoric families.

7787. Pay television dramatic program was shown on June 29, 1962, by WHCT-TV, Channel 18, Hartford, CT, on ultrahigh frequency. The program consisted of a play, *Sunrise at Campobello*, starring Ralph Bellamy as President Franklin Delano Roosevelt, plus a Czechoslovakian presentation of William Shakespeare's *Midsummer Night's Dream*. No commercials were shown. Subscribers, who had decoders installed on their sets, paid a $1 fee. The station operated under a test license granted on February 24, 1961, for three years by the Federal Communications Commission, effective when 2,000 paying customers signed up.

7788. Soap opera on prime-time television was "Peyton Place," which first aired on the CBS network on September 15, 1964, and continued to run for five years. The series was based on the 1956 novel by Grace Metalious, which also spawned a popular 1957 Hollywood film. It detailed the steamy doings in a small New England town.

7789. Made-for-TV movie was *See How They Run*, which starred John Forsythe and Jane Wyman. It aired on the NBC network on October 7, 1964. The joint NBC–Universal Studios production was not a ratings success.

7790. Television dramatic series in which an African-American performer had a starring role was "I Spy," which starred Bill Cosby as secret agent Alexander Scott. The show premiered on the NBC network on September 15, 1965 and ran until September 2, 1968.

TELEVISION—PRODUCTIONS—*continued*

7791. British-made television series to be shown coast-to-coast on an American network in prime time as part of the regular weekly schedule, rather than as a replacement for a canceled series, was "The Avengers," starring Patrick Macnee and Diana Rigg. It was aired by ABC beginning in 1967. The show, which had been on the air in Britain since 1961, already had an audience of more than 30 million viewers in 40 countries. The first 13 episodes shown in the United States were filmed in black and white, the remaining episodes in color.

7792. Episode of "Sesame Street" to be shown on television aired on November 10, 1969, on the Public Television System. The show was produced by the Children's Television Workshop. It used techniques borrowed from commercial television to teach letters and numbers to preschoolers.

7793. Movie shown on a television network without interruption by commercials was *Schindler's List,* Steven Spielberg's 1993 film about the Holocaust. It was broadcast by the NBC network on Sunday, February 23, 1997. The sponsor, Ford Motor Company, presented one commercial before the film and one afterward, but none during the telecast. This was also the first broadcast rated TV-M (for "mature" audiences) under the television ratings system implemented by broadcasters in late 1996.

TELEVISION—STATIONS

7794. Television license was issued on February 25, 1928, by the Federal Radio Commission to the Charles Francis Jenkins Laboratories for the operation of a television broadcast station at 1519 Connecticut Avenue, NW, Washington, DC, using the call letters W3XK. In 1929, the station was authorized to move its transmitter to a location between Silver Spring and Wheaton, MD. The station ceased to operate on October 31, 1932.

7795. Standard broadcast station to transmit a television image was Hugo Gernsback's station WRNY, Coytesville, NJ, which transmitted a 1.5-inch square image of the face of Mrs. John Geloso on August 13, 1928. The image was viewed at Philosophy Hall, New York University, New York City, by 500 persons. It was magnified by a lens to twice the size.

7796. Commercial television licenses were granted to 10 stations on May 2, 1941, by the Federal Communications Commission, with permission to begin operations on July 1, 1941. The first license, No. 1, was issued to W2XBS, NBC, which telecast from the Empire State Building using Channel 1. The station had four sponsors: Lever Brothers, for Spry; Proctor and Gamble, for Ivory Soap; the Sun Oil Company; and the Bulova Watch Company.

7797. Commercial television station west of the Mississippi River was KTLA-TV, Hollywood, Los Angeles, CA, which began operations on January 22, 1947, at 8:30 P.M., from a converted garage. Dick Lane was the announcer.

7798. Illegal television station closed by the Federal Communications Commission was operated by the Tube Division of Sylvania Electric Products at Emporium, PA. It was shut down on October 19, 1950. The station, which used a 90-foot transmission tower on top of Whittemore Mountain, had televised programs from WJAC-TV, Johnstown, PA, without authorization.

7799. Pay television system was Phonovision, first demonstrated on January 1, 1951, by station KS2KSBS of the Zenith Radio Corporation, Chicago, IL, under authority of the Federal Communications Commission. The station transmitted a scrambled radio signal that could be received only by customers whose home television sets were activated by a "key signal" sent by a telephone circuit. The demonstration consisted of three movies: *April Showers,* with Jack Carson, shown at 4 P.M.; *Welcome Stranger,* with Bing Crosby, at 7 P.M.; and *Homecoming,* with Clark Gable and Lana Turner, at 9 P.M. A charge of $1 was made for each full-length feature program. During the first four weeks, 2,561 sales were made. The test was limited to 300 families chosen from 51,000 applicants by the National Opinion Research Council of the University of Chicago.

7800. Commercial television station on ultrahigh frequency was KPTV, Channel 27, Portland, OR, owned by the Empire Coil Company, which went on the air with its test pattern on September 18, 1952. Commercial service began on October 1.

7801. Educational television station was KUHT, University of Houston, Houston, TX, which broadcast test patterns on May 12, 1953. Programming began on May 25, 1953, from 5 to 9 P.M. five days a week over Channel 8, on the very-high-frequency band. The station was licensed jointly by the University of Houston and the Houston public school system on April 14, 1952. John Schwarzwalder was director.

7802. Television stations to share the same frequency were KSBW-TV, Salinas, CA, and KMBY-TV, Monterey, CA. On February 19, 1953, both stations were granted licenses on the same frequency. A protest was filed, but the licenses were declared valid on June 26, 1953, and both stations began telecasting officially on September 11, 1953, from the same transmitter atop Mount Toro, CA. The hours were divided equally on alternate nights, each station transmitting alone on alternate Sundays.

7803. Educational television station sponsored by a city was WQED, Channel 13, Pittsburgh, PA, which received its license on May 13, 1953, and went on the air on April 1, 1954. A second education channel, WQEX, Channel 16, was granted a license on July 16, 1958, making Pittsburgh the first city with two educational television stations.

7804. Microwave television station was KTRE-TV, Lufkin, TX, owned by the Forest Capital Broadcasting Company, which began operations on August 31, 1955, on Channel 9, on the very-high-frequency band. Signals from KPRC-TV, Houston, TX, on Channel 2, were deflected to booster equipment at the bottom of a tower at Coldspring, 60 miles away. There the signals were amplified and sent to the next relay tower, at Carmona, 30 miles away, where they were again amplified and sent to Lufkin, another 30 miles away. Richman Lewin was general manager of KTRE-TV.

7805. All-color television station to televise live local programs was WNBQ-TV, Channel 5, Chicago, IL, which began operations in color on April 15, 1956. Three color studios were equipped with five color cameras and two color-film projector chains for 16mm and 35mm films. The station had started showing black and white telecasts on January 7, 1949, and had begun the conversion to color on November 3, 1955.

7806. Educational television network that was statewide and state-supported was officially opened by Governor James Elisha Folsom of Alabama on August 9, 1956, when WAIQ, Channel 2, Andalusia, AL, was joined to WBIQ, Channel 10, Birmingham, and WTIQ, Channel 7, Munford. The network reached 90 percent of the state of Alabama. Programs were supplied by the University of Alabama, Alabama Polytechnic Institute, and the Greater Birmingham Area Educational Television Association.

7807. Educational television network operated as a nonprofit corporation was National Educational Television (NET), New York City, which started in 1952 as a nonprofit Illinois corporation, the Educational Television and Radio Center. On January 10, 1967, NET interconnected 70 of its 100 independent affiliated educational stations for a live broadcast and analysis of President Lyndon Baines Johnson's State of the Union message. Regularly scheduled noncommercial network broadcasting began on November 5, 1967, with the premiere of the Public Broadcast Laboratory over the NET network.

7808. Television station to regularly broadcast high-definition television was WRAL, a CBS affiliate in Raleigh, NC. On July 23, 1996, WRAL-HD, an experimental station, began broadcasting high-definition digital television data from a spectrum analyzer. WHD-TV, an experimental station at NBC affiliate WRC-TV in Washington, DC, broadcast the first full high-definition television pictures a week later. A high-definition version of the long-running news show "Meet the Press" was broadcast by WHD-TV beginning in February 1997.

TELEVISION—TECHNOLOGY

7809. Miniature television tube was the "peanut tube," an N-type tube, 2 inches high and 0.625 inches in diameter, operated on a single dry cell. The tube was created by Howard W. Weinhart of Elizabeth, NJ, who obtained a patent on August 25, 1925, on an "electric discharge device." The patent was assigned to the Western Electric Company, New York City.

7810. Television sets to be installed in homes on an experimental basis were installed in Schenectady, NY, on January 13, 1928, by the Radio Corporation of America and the General Electric Company. Three sets were installed. The images were transmitted over a wavelength of 37.8 meters and the sound sent simultaneously over a wavelength of 379.5 meters. The picture was 1.5 inches square. The television receiver's elements were a light source, a scanning device, and a synchronizing system.

TELEVISION—TECHNOLOGY—*continued*

7811. Public demonstration of color television was given on June 27, 1929, in the Bell Telephone Laboratories, New York City. Some of the objects shown in color were an American flag, a watermelon, and a bunch of roses. The images were of low definition and were mechanically scanned. The equipment demonstrated utilized three complete systems of photoelectric cells, amplifiers, and glow tubes. Each system had a red, blue, or green screen. A system of mirrors superposed the three monochromatic images to make one combined picture in color.

7812. Demonstration of home reception of television was given in New York City on August 20, 1930, when a half-hour program broadcast from two stations was received on screens placed in a store in the Hotel Ansonia at Broadway and 73d Street, in the Hearst Building at Eighth Avenue and 57th Street, and in a residence at 98 Riverside Drive. On these screens appeared the images of performers talking and singing in the studios of the Jenkins W2XCR television station at Jersey City, NJ, and the De Forest W2XCD station at Passaic, NJ. The distance, approximately six miles, was the greatest over which pictures had yet been transmitted by television. The cartoonist Harry Hirschfeld was master of ceremonies.

7813. Mobile television unit for outdoor events consisted of two large motor vans containing television control apparatus and a microwave transmitter. The unit was completed by the RCA Manufacturing Company, Camden, NJ, and turned over to station W2XBT of the National Broadcasting Company, New York City, on December 12, 1937. The telecasts were relayed by microwave to a tower transmitter in the Empire State Building, New York City, and rebroadcast from there. The first mobile color units were placed in operation on January 1, 1954, by the National Broadcasting Company's station WNBT, New York City, and consisted of two three-color mobile units with complete audio-video control, housed in a van 35 feet long, 8 feet wide, and 10 feet 7 inches high.

7814. Coin-operated television receiver was the Tradio-Vision, manufactured by Tradio, Asbury Park, NJ, and publicly exhibited on November 7, 1946, in New York City. The receiver, housed in a metal cabinet 16 inches high, 8 inches deep, and 9 inches wide, contained 20 tubes and a 5-inch cathode tube that reflected a 500-line image on a mirror on the lid. The apparatus was designed to operate after a 25-cent coin was inserted.

7815. Television camera lens to provide zoom effects without requiring the camera to be moved toward or away from the televised object was the Zoomar lens, invented by Dr. Frank Gerard Back of New York City, who received a patent on November 23, 1948, on a "varifocal lens for cameras" adjustable for closeups or long-distance shots. It was demonstrated on April 16, 1947, by the National Broadcasting Company in New York City.

7816. Television image using a split screen was exhibited on December 8, 1948, by the NBC at the Television Broadcasters Association Clinic held at the Waldorf-Astoria Hotel, New York City. The technique presented two pictures from different points of origin side by side on the same kinescope picture tube. The telecast showed John Cameron Swayze, in New York City, interviewing Representative Karl Earl Mundt of South Dakota, who was in Washington, DC.

7817. Rectangular television tube that was practical was announced to the trade on July 10, 1949, by the Kimble Glass Company, a subsidiary of Owens-Illinois in Toledo, OH. The bulb faces of the tube were approximately 12 by 16 inches. The tube sold for approximately $12. The first deliveries were made on October 1, 1949.

7818. Video recording on high-definition magnetic tape was made on October 3, 1952, when the electronics division of Bing Crosby Enterprises, Los Angeles, CA, recorded images on magnetic tape, rewound the tape, and immediately reproduced the picture through a standard television monitor tube. A one-inch tape with 12 tracks, 1 for sound and 11 for pictures, was used. The cost was one-third that of photographic processes.

7819. Television receiver that showed two programs simultaneously was the Duoscopic, publicly demonstrated on January 7, 1954, in New York City and Chicago, IL, by the Allen B. Du Mont Laboratories. Two superimposed images were projected onto the screen by two cathode ray tubes set at right angles. The images were viewed through polaroid glasses. Contrast controls were separate, and two separate systems were used to carry sounds through personalized earpieces. Each speaker could be turned off independently. The viewer could choose to watch only one image, as in standard sets, or to watch one picture on the screen and listen to the other through the earpiece. The system was announced for sale in a full-page advertisement that ran on January 21, 1954, in the *New York Times*.

7820. Television receivers to project large images up to 9 by 12 feet were installed in April 1955 in seven Sheraton Hotels. The receivers, built by the Fleetwood Corporation, Toledo, OH, were 4 feet high, 2 feet wide, and 3 feet deep and weighed 400 pounds. They were mounted on rubber-tired casters so that they could be moved easily. They were designed to show closed-circuit programs in ballrooms, conference rooms, and places of assembly.

7821. Video tape recorder for sounds and pictures was manufactured by the Ampex Corporation, Redwood City, CA, and demonstrated simultaneously in Redwood City and Chicago, IL, on April 14, 1956. The tape, 2 inches wide, moved at a speed of 15 inches per second. A single 14-inch reel accommodated a 65-minute recording. The developers were Charles P. Ginsberg, Charles E. Anderson, and Ray Dolby. The Columbia Broadcasting System purchased three of the video tape recorders at $75,000 each in 1956.

7822. Television receiver and transmitter operated by laser beam was demonstrated on February 20, 1963, by the General Telephone and Electronics Corporation, Bayside, NY, where it was developed by Samuel M. Stone and Louis Richard Bloom. A laser device produces a narrow highly-intense beam of light that can be focused and directed over long distances. The first network television show to be transmitted by laser was the Columbia Broadcasting System show "I've Got A Secret," telecast on May 14, 1963, from New York City. An electronic signal from a studio television camera was fed into a laser transmitter, carried across a two-foot space on a light beam, picked up by a laser receiver, and transmitted via the studio control room over the national television network.

7823. Video cassette recorder for home use was the Betamax, which was sold in the United States by the Sony Corporation of Japan beginning in November 1975. It was built into a console that also contained a Sony color television set. The tape was contained in a plastic cassette to make it easy to handle. Sony had marketed the first open-reel video tape recorder for home use, the TCV-2010, beginning in 1966. The device required a separate camera set up on a tripod, as well as a separate microphone to record sound.

7824. Satellite dish for personal use was designed by electronics engineer Taylor Howard in 1976. The dish enabled the user to receive broadcast signals directly from communications satellites.

TELEVISION—TELECASTS

7825. Telecast of an object in motion was sent on June 13, 1925, from radio station NOF, Bellevue, DC (now part of Washington, DC), and was received at the laboratory of Charles Francis Jenkins, 1519 Connecticut Avenue, Washington. The apparatus used was Vision-by-Radio, invented by Jenkins. The image showed a small model windmill with its blades in motion.

7826. Weather map to be telecast from a land sending station to a land receiving station was sent on August 18, 1926, from radio station NAA, Arlington, VA, and received at the Weather Bureau Office, Washington, DC. The demonstration was arranged by the Jenkins Laboratory, Washington, DC. The first weather map to be telecast to a transatlantic steamer was sent by the Radiomarine Corporation station, New York City, on June 20, 1930, to the S.S. *America,* nearly 3,000 miles distant.

7827. Telecast of image and sound transmitted over any considerable distance was demonstrated on April 7, 1927, when Secretary of Commerce Herbert Clark Hoover, at 1208 H Street, Washington, DC, read a speech into a telephone and was both seen and heard by a large group gathered in the auditorium of the Bell Telephone Laboratories, New York City. The picture was 2 by 3 inches and was transmitted at the rate of 18 images per second.

7828. Transoceanic radio signal conveying a television image was received on February 8, 1928, at Hartsdale, NY, by Robert M. Hart, owner of shortwave station W2CVJ. The sound vision, a picture of Mrs. Mia Howe, was sent across the ocean from 2 KZ, Purley, England, a station with two kilowatts of power, by John Logie Baird of the Baird Television Development Company of London, using short radio waves.

7829. Outdoor scenes to be televised were viewed in the offices of the Bell Telephone Laboratories, New York City, on July 12, 1928. Scenes enacted in the open air were almost as clear as those taken in specially designed studios.

7830. Remote television pickup took place on August 22, 1928, from the New York State Assembly chamber at Albany, NY, where the presidential candidate of the Democratic Party, Alfred Emanuel Smith, was notified of his nomination. Television images of his acceptance were transmitted from Schenectady, NY, and relayed by short wave over 2XAF and 2XAD by the General Electric Company. It was the first televised news broadcast.

TELEVISION—TELECASTS—*continued*

7831. Speaker to address an organization by television was Dr. Peter Irving Wold, president of the Fortnightly Club, Schenectady, NY, who conducted a meeting of the club from the television station at the General Electric Laboratory on April 1, 1930. The members were assembled at the home of Dr. Ernst Fredrik Werner Alexanderson in Schenectady.

7832. Telecast images received in an airplane were sent on May 21, 1932, to a Western Air Express trimotor airplane in flight over Los Angeles, CA. The images, which originated about 10 miles away, were transmitted by station W6XAO of the Don Lee Broadcasting System, Los Angeles, under the direction of Harry R. Lubcke, director of television. A 150-watt transmitter on an ultrahigh frequency of 44.500 kilocycles transmitted at the rate of 15 pictures per second with an 80-line screen. The telecast was shown for five minutes on a screen eight inches in diameter. The first long-distance telecast received in an airplane took place on October 17, 1939, when a plane flying high above Washington, DC, intercepted ultrashort waves that came in a straight line from station W2XBS in New York City.

7833. Telecast using coaxial cable was sent on June 10, 1936, from the Radio City complex, New York City, to the transmitter atop the Empire State Building, a distance of approximately 1.5 miles.

7834. High-definition telecast was made on June 29, 1936, by station W2XBS from the Empire State Building, New York City, at the rate of 30 pictures per second with a 343-line screen. On July 7, 1936, David Sarnoff, president of the Radio Corporation of America, and Major General James Guthrie Harbord, chairman of the board of RCA, opened for invited guests a program in which Henry Hull, Graham McNamee, Ed Wynn, and members of the Water Lily Ensemble appeared as performers. A fashion show and a film were also presented.

7835. Public telecast made over telephone wires took place on May 20, 1939, when the National Broadcasting Company televised bicycle races at Madison Square Garden, New York City. The images were transmitted from Madison Square Garden to the NBC studio at the Radio City complex in New York City via the Circle telephone exchange at Ninth Avenue and 50th Street. When the images were received at the studio over telephone wire, they were conveyed over a coaxial cable to the transmitter in the tower of the Empire State Building, from which they were telecast.

7836. Ship-to-shore telecast took place on May 11, 1940, when passengers on S.S. *President Roosevelt,* operated by the United States Lines, watched the opening day ceremonies of the New York World's Fair as they were telecast by station W2XBS of the National Broadcasting Company from the Empire State Building, New York City. The transmission was viewed while the liner was 102 miles away, en route to Bermuda. On May 15, 1940, a distance record of 234 miles was established. The first oceangoing vessel in which television receivers were permanently installed was the pilot boat *New Jersey.* The installation was made on November 20, 1947, by the Radio Corporation of America. The ship picked up good signals from all three New York television stations while sailing near the Ambrose Light, 20 miles from New York City.

7837. Telecommunication by deaf people that was both visual and oral was accomplished on October 13, 1940, when Bertha O'Donnell and Adele Costa conversed in sign language through two-way television sets at W2USA, the amateur television booth at the New York World's Fair, and W2HID, 220 East 42nd Street, New York City, eight miles away.

7838. Telecast from a submerged submarine was made on April 10, 1947, from the U.S.S. *Trumpetfish* at the Brooklyn Navy Yard, New York City, by WNBT, New York City. It was relayed by coaxial cable to WTTG, Washington, DC, WPTZ, Philadelphia, and WRGB, Schenectady, NY. Three cameras were installed in the submarine. Another camera, on the dock, filmed the submarine as it submerged, conducted a simulated torpedo attack, and finally surfaced after 15 minutes. Ray Forrest and Bob Stanton were the announcers.

7839. Stratovision flight by an airplane during which a television signal was transmitted took place on April 30, 1948, and consisted of the test pattern of WMAR-TV, Baltimore, MD. The first public demonstration of stratovision was made on June 23, 1948, at 8:55 P.M., when an airplane flying 25,000 feet in the air over Pittsburgh, PA, received a telecast of the Republican National Convention meeting at Philadelphia from WMAR and rebroadcast it. It was received in nine states over an area 525 miles in diameter.

7840. Transcontinental telecast received on the East Coast was transmitted from the War Memorial Opera House, San Francisco, CA, on September 4, 1951, at 10:30 P.M. by a pool of the four networks to 94 of the 107 television stations then in operation. The telecast was transmitted by microwave relays to Omaha,

NE, and then by coaxial cables to stations in the east, north, and south. Secretary of State Dean Acheson introduced President Harry S. Truman, who made an address from the Opera House in conjunction with the signing of the Japanese peace treaty.

7841. Transcontinental telecast received on the West Coast was the Columbia Broadcasting System program "Crusade for Freedom," transmitted from WCBS-TV, New York City, on September 23, 1951. General Lucius DuBignon Clay was chairman of the program.

7842. Telecast from a foreign country took place on October 15, 1951, from 10:45 to 11:15 A.M., when WWJ-TV, Detroit, MI, had its mobile unit cover the informal reception given to Princess Elizabeth of Great Britain and Philip, Duke of Edinburgh, on Government Dock, Windsor, Canada. Budd Lynch was the announcer. The program was carried by the National Broadcasting Company and the American Broadcasting Company on Channel 4 and Channel 7. The first live telecast from a noncontiguous foreign country was transmitted on November 13, 1955, by CMQ, Havana, Cuba. A five-minute aerial view of Havana was televised from an airplane to CMQ and relayed by airplanes to WIOD, Miami, FL, for telecasting on Dave Garroway's show "Wide Wide World" on the National Broadcasting System network.

7843. Telecast transmitted to Canada was conveyed on January 20, 1953, over a 66-mile microwave link between Buffalo, NY, and Toronto, Ontario. The lines of the American Telegraph and Telephone Company were linked with those of the Bell Telephone Company of Canada. The first live show, a "Studio One" play, was televised on station CBLT, Toronto, by the Canadian Broadcasting System.

7844. Three-dimensional telecast was presented on April 29, 1953, from KECA-TV, Los Angeles, CA, by American Broadcasting–Paramount Theatres. The audience was 70 newspaper and trade publishers attending the 31st annual convention of the National Association of Radio and Television Broadcasters at the Biltmore Hotel, Los Angeles, where special receivers had been installed. The one-hour telecast included a live performance of "Space Patrol" and Lloyd Nolan's prologue to the motion picture *Bwana Devil*. The three-dimension effect was achieved by showing two offscreen images simultaneously. The images appeared blurred unless viewed through polaroid lenses.

7845. Coast-to-coast live telecast in color was transmitted on November 3, 1953, from the Colonial Theatre, New York City, by WNBT-TV, New York City. The program, which starred Nanette Fabray, was sent in compatible color over the radio relay circuit system of the Bell Telephone Company and was received by 14-inch receivers at Burbank, CA.

7846. Telecast originating live in three countries was presented on June 27, 1955, on NBC's network program "Wide Wide World" under the sponsorship of the Ford Motor Company and RCA. Pictures were shown of a fiesta-time bullfight in Tijuana, Mexico; the opening night of the Shakespeare Festival at Stratford, Ontario, Canada; and events in Washington, DC, Denver, San Francisco, and New York City.

7847. Video recording on magnetic tape televised coast-to-coast was "The Jonathan Winters Show," televised from 7:30 to 7:45 P.M. on October 23, 1956, by WRCA-TV, New York City. The process was developed by RCA for NBC. Instead of film, the system utilized instantaneous tape with pictures that could be played back immediately after recording. The telecast was shown in full compatible color and also in black-and-white.

7848. Public telecast over telephone wires using the narrow-band system was demonstrated on March 20, 1957, by C. Raymond Kraus, general staff transmission engineer of the Bell Telephone Company of Pennsylvania at the Franklin Institute, Philadelphia, PA. A 128-line picture, approximately 5 by 7 inches, was received over 3.2 miles of cable from the Franklin Institute, and was routed through two telephone central offices back to the Franklin Institute. This system enabled transmission on practically all pairs in a cable of over 1,000 pairs of conductors. The band width was 5 to 8 kc.

7849. Telecast from the stratosphere was made on July 26, 1958, from the 17-story Navy plastic balloon *Strato-Lab High III* at an altitude of 60,000 feet over Minnesota. The images were transmitted by Commander Malcolm Ross and Commander Morton Lee Lewis and received by KSTP-TV, St. Paul, MN. The balloon took off from an open-pit mine at Crosby, MN, soared to 82,000 feet, and remained aloft for 34 hours 29 minutes, establishing an endurance record, before landing at Jamestown, ND.

7850. Video recording on magnetic tape televised in color was "The Betty Feezor Show," recorded from 11 to 11:30 P.M. and shown from 1 to 1:30 P.M. on September 5, 1958, by WBTV, Charlotte, NC.

TELEVISION—TELECASTS—*continued*

7851. Telecast received from England was transmitted via cable on June 18, 1959, from London to Montreal, Canada, and relayed by the Canadian Broadcasting Company to the National Broadcasting Company in New York City, which sent it out over the entire NBC network. The film showed the departure from London of Queen Elizabeth and Prince Philip, who were on their way to attend the opening ceremonies for the St. Lawrence Seaway. The Motion Picture Facsimile process used in the telecast was developed by the BBC. Each frame required eight seconds for transmission. The film was seen 2 hours and 21 minutes after the recording was made.

7852. Coast-to-coast telecast by satellite was accomplished on April 24, 1962, when the Massachusetts Institute of Technology's Lincoln Laboratory field station at Camp Parks, CA, transmitted airwaves to the two-year-old orbiting balloon *Echo I*, which bounced them back to earth. They were received at Millstone Hill, Westford, MA. The pictures were of poor quality but were recognizable.

7853. Transoceanic telecast by satellite was transmitted on July 10, 1962, from Andover, ME. It was bounced off the 170-pound orbiting relay communications satellite *Telstar 1* and was received at various stations in Europe and the United States. The following day, a telecast from Pleumeur-Bodou, France, was received at Andover received by means of the 380-ton horn-shaped antenna. The satellite was launched on July 10 from Cape Canaveral, FL.

7854. Live telecast to Europe by satellite was transmitted by the American Broadcasting System, the National Broadcasting System, and the Columbia Broadcasting System by *Telstar 1* on July 23, 1962, to the Eurovision network of 18 nations. The program was narrated in seven languages and showed sequences picturing the Statue of Liberty, buffalo on the western plains, the Phillies–Cubs baseball game at Chicago, President John Fitzgerald Kennedy's news conference, the Abraham Lincoln carving at Mount Rushmore, the Mormon Tabernacle Choir, astronaut Lieutenant Commander Walter Marty Schirra, a small boy admiring a Native American chief, and similar scenes. Three hours later, a 20-minute telecast was received from Europe, showing Big Ben and the House of Commons, reindeer in the Arctic Circle, Swiss guards at the Sistine Chapel, the entrance to the Louvre, the Colosseum in Rome, a painting in the National Museum of Belgrade, and fishermen in Sicily.

7855. Telecast transmitted by satellite to Japan was a 15-minute news program beamed at 7 P.M. on November 22, 1963, from the U.S. ground station in the Mojave Desert. It was relayed by the communications satellite *Relay 1* and received by the Space Communications Laboratory north of Tokyo, Japan, from 5:16 to 5:46 A.M. on November 23. ABC and NBC shared in producing the program. Japanese viewers saw scenic and cultural sequences and heard taped messages from Ryuji Takeuchi, the Japanese ambassador, and James Edwin Webb, director of the National Aeronautics and Space Administration. The first telecast transmitted by satellite from Japan to the United States was beamed over the satellite *Relay 2* and viewed simultaneously on three national networks. It was rebroadcast on the "Today Show" on March 25, 1964, from 7:32 to 7:40 A.M. The telecast showed Prime Minister Hayato Ikeda.

7856. Worldwide live television program was "Our World," shown in 26 countries on June 25, 1967, via four satellites. The two-hour production involved 10,000 technicians and 300 cameras in 14 countries on five continents. It opened with glimpses of births in Mexico, Canada, Denmark, and Japan. The rest of the program featured clips of Leonard Bernstein and Van Cliburn rehearsing a Rachmaninoff concerto at New York City's Lincoln Center, the Beatles recording a song in London, a rehearsal of *Lohengrin* in Bayreuth, Germany, the making of a movie in Italy, and other presentations. The American outlet was the National Educational Television network. The program cost about $5 million.

7857. Stereo telecast was a double-channel telecast made on December 28, 1972, from 11:30 P.M. to midnight over WNEW-TV (Channel 5) and WNET (Channel 13), New York City. The program was entitled "Two's Better Than One" and featured four playlets: *Boxes, Are You There?, What A Life,* and *The Yin and Yang of It.* The hosts were Bob Elliott on Channel 5, where half the action took place, and Ray Goulding on Channel 13, for the other half.

TEXTILES

7858. Cloth mill was built in 1638 by John Pearson in Rowley, MA. According to Captain Edward Johnson's book, *Wonder-Working Providences of Sion's Savior in New England,* published in London in 1654, "the Lord brought over the zealous affected and judicious servant of His, Master Ezekiel Rogers, who with an holy and humble people, made his progress to the northeastward and erected a town about six miles from Ipswich, called Rowley—they were the first people that set upon making cloth in this western world."

7859. Calico printery was established in Boston, MA, by George Leason and Thomas Webber, who advertised in the *Boston News Letter*, April 21–28, 1712, that they had "set up a Callender-Mill and Dye House in Cambridge Street, Boston, near the Bowling Green where all gentlemen, Merchants, and others may have all sorts of Linnens, callicoes, stuffs or Silks Callendered: Prints all sorts of Linnens."

7860. Fustians, everlastings, and coating were made commercially by Samuel Wetherill, Jr., of Philadelphia, PA. Prior to April 3, 1782, his products were sold at his dwelling house and factory on what was then South Alley, between Market and Arch streets.

7861. Textile machine that could spin, card, and rope was manufactured in 1786 by Hugh Orr with the help of Robert and Alexander Barr in their workshop in Bridgewater, MA. On November 16, 1786, the Senate granted them £200 for their ingenuity, and afterward granted them a further compensation of six tickets in the land lottery of that period.

7862. Sailcloth factory was the Boston Sail Cloth Factory, Boston, MA, established in 1788. It was two stories high and 180 feet long. In 1789, 30 women and girls working 26 looms turned out 40 yards each a week.

7863. Broadcloth was produced in Pittsfield, MA, in 1793, from fleeces of the merino sheep of Arthur and John Scholfield.

7864. Oiled silk patent was granted on February 1, 1793, to Ralph Hodgson, Lansingburg, NY, on "manufacturing oiled silk and linen."

7865. Textile machinery patent was a patent for a carding and spinning machine, granted on February 14, 1794, to James Davenport, who established the Globe Mills, Philadelphia, PA.

7866. Haircloth was manufactured at Rahway, NJ, in 1813. The process was covered by patents granted to William Shotwell and Arthur Kinder of New York City on July 23, 1813. It was called Taurine cloth and was a coarse fabric made from the hair of cattle with a mixture of wool.

7867. Felt manufacturing mechanical process was invented by Thomas Robinson Williams of Newport, RI, in 1820. The wool was carded and placed in layers until the desired thickness was obtained, the outside rolls being the finest in texture. The mass was then placed between rollers and partly immersed in water while it was beaten, pressed, and oscillated. Dyeing and finishing completed the process.

7868. Bunting manufacture was undertaken in 1838 by Michael Hodge Simpson at the New England Worsted Company, Saxonville, MA.

7869. Elastic webbing was produced by power machinery in the plant of the Russell Manufacturing Company of Middletown, CT, in 1841, through the efforts of Henry Griswold Hubbard. The concern was incorporated in 1834 with a capital stock of $40,000, nine-tenths of which was owned by Samuel Russell and Samuel D. Hubbard. Originally the company manufactured nonelastic webbing, a venture which was not profitable. The elastic webbing, however, proved very successful.

7870. Oilcloth factory that was successful was erected in 1845 in Winthrop, ME, by Ezekiel Bailey. It was known as C.M. Bailey Sons and Company. Within 10 years, it was doing an annual business of $200,000.

7871. Gingham factory was opened in Clinton, MA, by Erastus Brigham Bigelow in 1846. It was named Lancaster Mills and was capitalized at $500,000. On April 10, 1845, Bigelow received a patent for his invention of gingham manufacturing machinery. Previously, all gingham had been made by hand at home.

7872. Mohair from Angora goats was commercially manufactured by the Arlington Mills, Lawrence, MA, in 1872.

7873. Kapok was commercially introduced by the Netherlands on May 1, 1893, at the formal opening of the World's Columbian Exposition, Chicago, IL.

7874. Rayon made from cellulose was commercially produced by the American Viscose Company in Marcus Hook, PA, on December 19, 1910. Production in 1911 amounted to 362,000 pounds. The patents were acquired from the General Artificial Silk Company, Lansdowne, PA, which started in 1901. The term "rayon" was adopted in 1924 to replace "artificial silk" and similar names.

7875. Crepe was produced in France in 1912 and was introduced into New York City in the same year by the firm of Haas Brothers, who registered the name "crepe georgette" at the patent office on December 30, 1913, and commenced production in the United States.

TEXTILES—*continued*

7876. Synthetic fiber produced entirely from chemicals was nylon, invented by Dr. Wallace Hume Carothers, a chemist at E.I. du Pont de Nemours and Company, Wilmington, DE, who obtained a patent for it on February 16, 1937. The patent covered synthetic linear condensation polymers capable of being drawn into strong, pliable fibers, as well as the process for making them.

7877. Nylon was introduced to the public by its manufacturer, the E.I. du Pont de Nemours Company, at the Golden Gate International Exposition held in San Francisco, CA, in 1939.

7878. Artificial leather was Corfam, a durable and permeable poromeric material that looked and felt like leather. It was introduced to the press by E.I. du Pont de Nemours and Company, Wilmington, DE, on October 2, 1963, and to stores in 20 cities on January 27, 1964. It was used mainly for shoe uppers.

7879. Synthetic fabric that was waterproof and breathable was Gore-Tex, a fabric developed by Wilbert L. Gore and his son Robert Gore in 1969. Derived from polymer of tetrafluorethylene (PTFE, also called Teflon), which Wilbert Gore had helped develop at E.I. du Pont de Nemours and Company, Wilmington, DE. Gore-Tex was a laminated fabric that allowed water vapor to pass through while completely blocking water droplets. Gore-Tex was used in sports clothing, shoes, electronics, and medical applications.

7880. Thread as strong as steel was Kevlar aramid fiber, invented in 1976 by Dr. Stephanie L. Kwolek, a chemist at E.I. Du Pont de Nemours and Company, Wilmington, DE. Kevlar was used in bulletproof vests, radial tires, structural composites for aircraft and space vehicles, and other products that required extremely high strength and low weight. For her work, Kwolek received the American Chemical Society Award for creative invention in 1980.

TEXTILES—COTTON

7881. Spinning jenny for cotton was put into operation by Daniel Jackson, a coppersmith of Providence, RI, in 1786. At first it was set up in a private house, but it was afterward removed to the upper room in the Market House.

7882. Cotton mill was established in Beverly, MA, sometime in 1788 by a company of proprietors known as the Beverly Cotton Manufactory. The company was incorporated on February 3, 1789, and was visited on October 30, 1789, by President George Washington. The spinning jenny spun 60 threads at one time and the carding machine carded 40 pounds of cotton a day. The mill's products were the first cotton goods to be trademarked. On June 6, 1788, it was enacted "that all goods which may be manufactured by the said corporation, shall have a label of lead affixed to one end thereof, which shall have the same impression as the seal of the corporation, and that if any person shall knowingly use a like seal or label with that used by said corporation, by annexing same to any cotton or cotton and linen goods, not manufactured by said corporation with a view of vending or distributing thereof, as the proper manufacture of said corporation, every person so offending shall forfeit and pay treble the value of said goods to be sued for and recovered for the use of said corporation, by action of debt, in any court of record proper to try the same."

7883. Cotton mill to spin cotton yarn successfully was started on December 20, 1790, by Samuel Slater in Pawtucket, RI. It was 40 feet long, 26 feet wide, and two stories high, with an attic. Power was obtained from the old fulling mill water wheel in Ezekiel Carpenter's clothier's shop on the east bank of the Blackstone River. Secretary of the Treasury Alexander Hamilton, in his report of December 5, 1791, said, "The manufactory at Providence has the merit of being the first in introducing into the United States the celebrated cotton mill, which not only furnishes materials for the manufactory itself but for the supply of private families, for household manufacturing."

7884. Cotton mill entirely powered by water was established in 1813 by the Boston Manufacturing Company in Waltham, MA. This was the first cotton mill in the world in which the entire process of cotton manufacturing, from spinning to weaving, was carried on by water power under a single management. The mill workers were organized into departments and paid a fixed wage. Nathan Appleton, Francis Cabot Lowell, and Patrick Tracy Jackson were the main sponsors of this organization. The machinery was constructed by Paul Moody.

TEXTILES—SILK

7885. Silk culture was started about 1623 in Virginia, where the Colonial Assembly directed the planting of mulberry trees. In 1656, an act was passed in which silk was described as the most profitable commodity for the country. It imposed "a penalty of ten pounds of tobacco ... upon every planter who should fail to plant at least ten mulberry trees for every hundred acres of land in his possession."

7886. Silk export took place in 1735 when a shipment of raw silk weighing eight pounds was exported from Savannah, GA, to England. The Trustees of Georgia reported in 1736: "The raw silk from Georgia, organized by Sir Thomas Lombe, was made into a piece of silk and presented to the queen." This entry appears in the manuscript book of the trustees. It is possible that some silk may have been sent previously from Virginia, where silk cultivation was first introduced.

7887. Silk mill was erected in 1810 for the Mansfield Silk Company by Rodney and Horatio Hanks in Mansfield, CT, in a building 12 by 12 feet.

7888. Silk dyers to achieve success were Edward Vallentine and Lewis Leigh, who emigrated from England in 1838. They began business at Gurleyville, CT, and achieved fame by producing silk dyed permanently black.

7889. Silk power loom with the figure or pattern of the cloth made on a chain was invented by William Crompton of Taunton, MA, who obtained a patent on November 25, 1837, on a figure power loom.

7890. Silk loom of importance was the Gem Silk Loom, built in 1887 by the Knowles Loom Works, Worcester, MA. On April 23, 1887, three 40-inch, four-by-four box loom machines were ordered by the Empire Silk Company, Paterson, NJ. Crepes, chiffons, and fancy pattern material requiring up to 20 harnesses could be woven on this loom.

TEXTILES—WOOL

7891. Fulling mill for making wool cloth was established by John Pearson in Rowley, MA, in 1643. It cleaned, felted, and shrank the cloth until the desired consistency was obtained. The mill was operated by emigrants from Yorkshire, England.

7892. Worsted mill for making wool yarn was established in 1695 in Boston, MA, by John Cornish. The mill cleaned the wool and removed the noil, or short fibers. The spinning of the yarn was done by local farmers. An appraisal of Cornish's estate revealed "two pairs of combs, four looms and tackling, and two dye furnaces."

7893. Worsted mill operated by waterpower and the first operated on a strictly commercial basis was the Hartford Woolen Manufactory, Hartford, CT, which was organized on April 15, 1788. A capital of 1,250 pounds was raised by subscription in nearby towns. The largest contributor was Jeremiah Wadsworth. A bounty of one penny per pound was given for all yarn spun in the factory before June 1, 1789, as a means of encouraging the new industry. Waterpower had previously been used to power fulling mills.

7894. Wool carding machine was built by John and Arthur Scholfield in Newburyport, MA, and installed in a mill in Byfield, MA, in 1793. It was 25 inches wide and had a single cylinder 33 inches in diameter. It carried two workers and strippers, a fancy, and a 14-inch doffer cover with card clothing sheets. A fluted cylinder of 13 inches was arranged behind the doffer.

TIME

7895. Standard time program went into effect in the United States at noon on November 18, 1883, when the Naval Observatory at Washington, DC, changed its daily telegraph signals to conform to the new system. The first standard time proposal, which was unsuccessful, was made by Charles Ferdinand Dowd of Saratoga Springs, NY, in 1870. It was raised again in 1879, and was finally adopted in 1883 on the initiative of the American Railway Association. The Uniform Time Act of 1966, enacted on April 13 and effective April 1, 1967, divided the United States into eight time zones: Eastern, Central, Mountain, Pacific, Yukon, Alaska, Hawaii, and Bering.

7896. Daylight saving time program was put into operation in the United States on March 31, 1918, when clocks were set one hour ahead. The idea was sponsored by the National Daylight Saving Association. A bill to adjust the time in order to save daylight was introduced by Senator William Musgrave Calder of New York on April 17, 1917, but was defeated. It was passed without a roll call on June 27, 1917.

TIME—CLOCKS

7897. Clock to strike the hours was constructed in 1754 by Benjamin Banneker at Elkridge Landing, near Baltimore, MD. At the age of 23, without any tools except a jackknife, and without ever having seen anything similar but a sundial and a watch, Banneker constructed a wooden clock that kept time for more than 20 years. Banneker, an African-American, later became distinguished as a mathematician and astronomer.

7898. Alarm clock was made by Levi Hutchins of Concord, NH, in 1787. It was 29 inches high and 14 inches wide and had a pine case with a mirror in the door. The alarm rang at a specified time and could not be set or altered.

TIME—CLOCKS—*continued*

7899. Watchmaker was Luther Goddard, who in 1809 opened a shop in Shrewsbury, MA, his birthplace. He was aided by a law that forbade the importation of clocks and watches, and so was able to develop a small business. In reality, he assembled more watches from imported parts than he actually constructed. The real beginning of the watch industry came in 1849, when the American Horologe Company was formed in Roxbury, MA, by three men: Aaron L. Dennison of Boston, who was an experienced watchmaker; Edward Howard of Bingham, MA, who was skilled in making machinery for watches; and Samuel Curtis, who financed the enterprise, which later became the Waltham Watch Company.

7900. Brass clock works were invented in 1837 by Chauncey Jerome of the Jerome Clock Company, Bristol, CT, later known as the New Haven Clock Company. Jerome's production of standardized parts of pierced brass plates from steel dies enabled him to sell an eight-day metal clock for $4, cheaper than one-day wooden clocks that sold for $12.

7901. Watch made by machinery was placed on the market in 1838 by James and Henry Pitkin of Hartford, CT, the manufacturers. The factory was moved to New York, but in 1841 it was closed down, being unable to meet the competition of the imported Swiss watches.

7902. Clock movement to be electrically wound and synchronized was made by H. Chester Pond in Chicago, IL, in the fall of 1885. In the summer of 1886, 50 of these movements were made and set up in New York City as a system. A high-grade master clock transmitted an hourly signal to the various self-winding or "subsidiary" clocks, correcting them hourly, and thereby maintaining in each clock location the same high degree of time accuracy that was inherent in the master clock.

7903. Clock to operate by nuclear power was the Atomicron, made by the National Company, Malden, MA, and exhibited on October 2, 1956, at the Overseas Press Club, New York City. It was 84 inches high, 22 inches wide, and 18 inches deep, and was priced at $50,000. Its "pendulum" was the cesium atom, which oscillates at a never-changing frequency of 9,192,631,830 megacycles a second.

7904. Electric watch was made by the Hamilton Watch Company, Lancaster, PA, and introduced to the public on January 3, 1957. The movement was powered by a small energy cell guaranteed to operate the watch for a year. It had no mainspring and had 35 percent fewer parts than an automatic or self-winding watch.

7905. Electronic watch was produced by the Bulova Watch Company in its plant at Jackson Heights, NY, and placed on sale October 25, 1960. In place of mainspring, hairspring, and related gears, the watch had a precision tuning fork that vibrated exactly 360 times per second, transistorized electronic circuitry, and a miniature power cell to move the hands and maintain timekeeping accuracy (less than one minute per month was lost or gained). The watch was called the Accutron.

TOOLS AND HARDWARE

7906. Steel shovel was manufactured in 1774 by Captain John Ames in West Bridgewater, MA.

7907. Nails were cold-cut in 1777 and were manufactured by Jeremiah Wilkinson of Cumberland, RI. The first nails were cut from an old chest lock with a pair of shears and were headed in a smith's vice. Later, Wilkinson began cutting small nails from sheet iron.

7908. Nail cutting and heading machine was patented on December 12, 1796, by George Chandler of Maryland.

7909. Ax factory was erected in 1800 at Johnstown, NY, by William Mann. The business was continued by his family at various locations and was sold in 1890 to the American Axe and Tool Company.

7910. Whips commercially manufactured were made in 1801 by Titus Pease and Thomas Rose in Westfield, MA. In 1808, Joseph Jokes of Westfield developed a new style of whip using hickory wood shafts, with a strip of horsehide fastened to the stock by a "keeper."

7911. Screw auger was manufactured in 1810 by Walter French in Seymour, CT. He was also the first to put a screw point on augers. Previously, only pod augers without screws had been used, and a gouge was required to start the hole before an auger could be made to work.

7912. Screw factory was established in 1810 by Aborn and Jackson at Bellefonte, RI. Screw manufacturing was a complicated matter. A blank was forged and the head of the screw was pinched between dies while hot, after which the threads were made by filing.

7913. Circular saw is supposed to have been produced by Benjamin Cummins in Bentonsville, NY, about 1814. His saws were originally used for cutting the teeth of clock wheels, and were later used for cutting wood.

7914. Lathe used for fashioning irregular forms was a profile lathe, patented by Thomas Blanchard of Middlebury, CT, on September 6, 1819, as a "machine for manufacturing gun stocks." The lathe did the work of 13 operators and made possible a great reduction in woodworking prices.

7915. File factory to manufacture files was started by Broadmeadow and Company in Pittsburgh, PA, in 1829. The files were made by hand. The first factory where files were successfully made by machine was the Nicholson File Company, organized in Providence, RI, in 1864. This company used a machine patented by William Nicholson of Providence on April 5, 1864. A file-making machine had been invented by Morris B. Belknap in 1812 in Greenfield, MA, but as far as is known, the machine was not a success.

7916. Wrench patent was obtained on August 17, 1835, by Solyman Merrick of Springfield, MA.

7917. Tool factory devoted exclusively to the manufacture of machinists' tools was established in 1838 by John H. Gage in the Water Street shop of the Nashua Manufacturing Company, Nashua, NH.

7918. Nuts and bolts factory was established by Micah Rugg and Martin Barnes in Marion, CT, in 1840, although they began making bolts and nuts for the market in 1838 in Rugg's blacksmith shop. Their factory was a one-story wooden building, 30 feet by 20 feet. They employed six operators, and the capacity production was 500 bolts a day. Prior to 1838, when they started making bolts commercially, these articles were hammered out and hand-finished by blacksmiths. Rugg invented a machine to trim the heads of nuts and bolts and obtained a patent for it on August 31, 1842. An earlier but impractical machine had been patented by David Wilkinson of Rhode Island.

7919. Collapsible tube was invented by John Rand, who received a patent on September 11, 1841, on a "mode of preserving paints, and other fluids, by confining them in close metallic vessels so constructed as to collapse with slight pressure, and thus force out the paint or fluid confined therein through proper openings for that purpose." The tubes, molded of lead and used to hold oil colors, were provided with caps to keep them airtight.

7920. Wire gauge for standardizing the sizes of drawn wire was a "V"-type gauge developed in 1849 by Ichabod Washburn of Worcester, MA. It was used by the Washburn and Moen Manufacturing Company (afterward part of the American Steel and Wire Company) and was the foundation for the steel wire gauge.

7921. Nail machine for making nails from wire was built under the supervision of Major Thomas Norton by Adolph and Felix Brown of New York City and was used in 1851 by William Hassall of New York City.

7922. Steel animal traps commercially manufactured were made in 1855 by Sewell Newhouse of the Oneida Community, Oneida, NY. He made them in eight different sizes, to trap animals ranging from the house rat to the grizzly bear, and sold them principally to Native Americans. Various types of traps had been made earlier by Newhouse and by others, but they had been devised for individual use and were not marketed. Newhouse was the author of *The Trapper's Guide: A Manual of Instructions for Capturing All Kinds of Fur-Bearing Animals and Curing Their Skins.*

7923. Screw machine to make pointed screws was devised by Cullen Whipple of Providence, RI, who obtained a patent on June 3, 1856. Prior to this invention, screws were blunt on their threaded ends, and it was necessary to bore a hole in order to insert them.

7924. Fishing line factory was established in 1859 in Harlem, New York City, by Henry Hall, who manufactured linen and silk lines. The company moved to Astoria, NY (now part of Queens, New York City), and later operated under the trade name Henry Hall and Sons.

7925. Paint ready-mixed was manufactured by the Averill Paint Company of New York City, using as a basis a patent granted on July 16, 1867, to D.R. Averill of Newburg, OH. The concern went out of business about 1900. It was unable to maintain a consistent standard of paint. The first manufacturer to do so was Henry Alden Sherwin, founder of the Sherwin-Williams Company, Cleveland, OH, which began producing paint in 1880.

7926. Tape measure was patented by Alvin J. Fellows of New Haven, CT, on July 14, 1868. The tape measure was enclosed in a circular case with a spring click lock to hold the tape at any desired point.

TOOLS AND HARDWARE—*continued*

7927. Collapsible tube machine was built in 1873 at Philadelphia, PA, under the direction of August Herman Wirz. Wirz had seen tube-making machines in operation when he was U.S. Commissioner at the Industrial Exposition in Vienna, and had brought over the plans. The first machine-made tubes produced in the United States were used for cucumber jelly.

7928. Screw caliper was constructed by John Edson Sweet in 1874 in the shops of Sibley College, Cornell University, Ithaca, NY. The screw of the machine had 16 threads per inch and its divided circle had 625 readings, the calibration reading to 0.0001 inches. The machine stood on three legs.

7929. Pipe or screw wrench that was practical was the Stillson wrench, invented by Daniel C. Stillson of Somerville, MA, who obtained a patent on December 5, 1876. Stillson whittled the first model out of wood in 1869.

7930. Paint prepared from standard formulas for floors, woodwork, furniture, walls, and so on was manufactured by the Sherwin-Williams Company of Cleveland, OH, in 1880. Stains, enamels, varnishes, and varnish stains were later produced under uniform production methods.

7931. Steel-cut nails were manufactured in 1883 by the Riverside Iron Works of Wheeling, WV.

7932. Fishing rod of telescoping steel tubes was made by Everett Horton of Bristol, CT, who obtained a patent on March 8, 1887, on a fishing rod in "tubular metallic sections."

7933. Lawn mower that was practical was invented by Elwood McGuire of Richmond, IN, in the 1890s. He attached a set of sharp blades to a rotating reel with a cutting bed at the center. The grass was clipped off as it came between the bed and the blades. The first power mower was the Moto-Mower, a gasoline-powered machine invented by Edward George in 1919.

7934. Pneumatic hammer was invented by Charles Brady King of Detroit, MI, in 1890. Brady received a patent for it on January 30, 1894. The hammer was exhibited at the World's Columbian Exposition in Chicago, IL, in 1893.

7935. Flashlight was manufactured by the American Electric and Novelty Manufacturing Company of New York City, which started in business in 1896. The first flashlight was produced about 1898. The model consisted of a paper tube with metal fittings, a rough brass stamping used for a reflector, without any lens, and a spring contact switch. The lamp was handmade, as was the battery. The company later changed its name to the American Eveready Company and subsequently became a part of the National Carbon Company.

7936. Paint-spraying device commercially manufactured was made in 1909 by the De Vilbiss Company of Toledo, OH, using the same principle used in the De Vilbiss medical atomizer combined with compressed air.

7937. Electric hand drill was invented in 1914 by S. Duncan Black and Alonzo G. Decker, founders of the Black and Decker Corporation of Towson, MD. The bulky but portable drill weighed 24 pounds and had a pistol grip and trigger switch. Black and Decker introduced the world's first portable half-inch electric drill in 1916 and the world's first cordless electric drill, powered by self-contained nickel-cadmium cells, in 1961. In 1968 it developed the Apollo Lunar Surface Drill, the first cordless drill used on the moon. The power head for the drill was designed to remove core samples from the lunar surface.

7938. Fluorescent paint was invented in 1934 by two brothers, Robert and Joseph Switzer, who were students at the University of California, Berkeley, CA. They collected chemicals from their father's drugstore and checked them under ultraviolet light to identify naturally fluorescent organic compounds, which they mixed with shellac. During World War II the American military found many uses for their fluorescent paints and inks. Aircraft carrier runways were marked with fluorescent stripes, enabling American fighter planes to make night landings, and ground troops carried fluorescent signals that could be identified from the air by Allied dive bombers. Products made by the Day-Glo Color Corporation, which the Switzer brothers founded in Cleveland, OH, after the war, came to be used in hundreds of products, including toys, packaging, bathing suits, and traffic cones.

7939. Spray can was invented by Julian Seth Kahn of New York City, who received a patent on August 22, 1939, for an "apparatus for mixing a liquid with gas." It was equipped with an inexpensive disposable valve mechanism. Under controlled pressure, it dispensed such items as whipped cream, paints, pharmaceuticals, and insecticides.

7940. Two-handed shovel was used on May 16, 1940, at the bridge dedication ceremonies at Niagara Falls. Mayor Ernst W. Mirrington, Jr., of Niagara Falls, NY, and Mayor George B. Ingles of Niagara Falls, Ontario, Canada, each held one of the handles.

7941. Soldering gun was invented by Carl E. Weller of Easton, PA, who received a patent on August 13, 1946, on an "electrical heating apparatus." The patent was assigned to the Weller Manufacturing Company, Easton, PA. Other electrically heated soldering irons were on the market at that time.

7942. Latex paint was Spred Satin, made by the Glidden Company in 1948. It was formulated with latex paint resin that had been developed by the Dow Chemical Company, Freeport, TX. The latex was a styrene-butadiene polymer suspended in a water-based solution. Latex paints were easier to apply than oil-based paints, dried faster, and did not emit strong solvent fumes. The first acrylic latex paint resin, which produced weather-resistant paints suitable for exterior walls, was made by the Rohm and Haas Company in 1953.

7943. Electric spinning reel was made by Old Pal, a subsidiary of Woodstream Corporation, Lititz, PA. It was introduced at the American Fishing Tackle Manufacturer's Show at Chicago, IL, on August 15, 1967. It weighed 26.5 ounces, had three lure-retrieve speeds, and retailed for about $150. Enough power was supplied by two rechargeable nickel-cadmium energy cells to last a whole day.

W

WARS—CIVIL WAR

7944. Confederate cruiser to raid Union commerce was the *Sumter,* commanded by Captain Raphael Semmes. The *Sumter* was a merchantman that had been fitted out in 1861 at New Orleans, LA, with five small guns. The *Sumter* captured 18 vessels, of which 8 were burned.

7945. State to secede from the Union was South Carolina. On December 20, 1860, the state legislature passed the Ordinance of Secession, declaring: "We, the people of the State of South Carolina, in convention assembled, do declare and ordain, that the ordinance adopted by us in convention on the 23d day of May, in the year of our Lord 1788, whereby the Consti-

tution of the United States was ratified, and also all acts and parts of the General Assembly of this State ratifying amendments of the said Constitution, are hereby repealed; and that the Union now subsisting between South Carolina and other States, under the name of the United States of America, is hereby dissolved." On December 24, the South Carolina delegation in Congress offered its resignation, but it was not accepted by the speaker of the House. A new state constitution was ratified on April 3, 1861, by a vote of 114–6.

7946. Act inaugurating the Civil War took place on January 9, 1861, when a detachment of Confederate forces at Morris Island, in Charleston Harbor, Charleston, SC, fired upon the *Star of the West,* a merchant steam vessel. The vessel had been chartered by the federal government to convey supplies and men to reinforce Major Robert Anderson at Fort Sumter, Charleston Harbor, although the announced destinations were Savannah, GA, and New Orleans, LA. It left New York harbor January 5, 1861, and was fired on within two miles of Forts Sumter and Moultrie. Its captain, John McGowan, retired from the scene after 17 shots had been fired at his ship. The first shot was fired by Cadet George E. Haynesworth of Sumter, SC, who was ordered to fire by Major P.F. Stevens.

7947. Confederate congressional session took place in Montgomery, AL, from February 4, 1861, to March 16, 1861. Its official title was Congress of the Confederate States. The president of the Senate was Alexander Hamilton Stephens of Georgia, the president pro tempore was Robert Mercer Taliaferro Hunter of Virginia, and the secretary of the Senate was James H. Nash of South Carolina. The House of Representatives under the permanent constitution met in Richmond, VA, on February 18, 1861. Emmet Dixon of Georgia was elected clerk and Thomas Salem Bocock of Virginia was elected speaker. The session adjourned on April 21, 1862.

7948. Confederate government bond was authorized by act of February 28, 1861, "to raise money for the support of the government and to provide for the defense of the Confederate States of America." The bond issue limit was $15 million.

7949. Civil War attack was made on Fort Sumter, SC. The first gun was fired on the morning of April 12, 1861, by Edmund Ruffin, a 67-year-old Virginian. There were no casualties.

WARS—CIVIL WAR—continued

7950. Naval skirmish in the Civil War took place on April 12, 1861, off Charleston, SC, when the side-wheeler *Harriet Lane* fired a shot across the bow of the merchantman steamer *Nashville* to force it to show its colors. The *Nashville* hoisted a U.S. ensign and was allowed to proceed, even though it was a Confederate ship. The *Harriet Lane,* 270 feet long with a 22-foot beam, had been built by William Henry Webb in 1857 as a Treasury Department revenue cutter and was transferred to the Navy in 1858. It was named after a niece of President James Buchanan and was the first federal steamer named for a woman. On January 1, 1863, the *Harriet Lane* was captured by Confederate forces in Galveston Bay after desperately resisting boarding parties from four rebel ships.

7951. Civil War call for volunteers was made by President Abraham Lincoln on April 15, 1861, the day after the surrender of Fort Sumter, SC. His call was for 75,000 volunteers. The first regiment to respond to the call was the Ringgold Light Artillery of Reading, PA, known as the First Defenders, commanded by Dr. John Keys. They reported to Governor Eli Slifer at Harrisburg, PA, on April 16. Their first engagement took place on September 24, 1861, at Hanging Rocks, WV. They and the other Pennsylvania regiments were the first state militias to arrive at Washington, DC.

7952. Civil War bloodshed occurred on April 19, 1861, near Baltimore, MD. When President Abraham Lincoln issued his proclamation on April 15, 1861, declaring a state of insurrection and calling for volunteers, Governor John Albion Andrew of Massachusetts sent five regiments of infantry, a battalion of riflemen, and a battery of artillery to Washington, DC. While they were passing through Baltimore, a mob attacked them, killing 4 soldiers and injuring 20. Nine casualties were reported among the mob.

7953. Confederate general killed in the Civil War was Robert Selden Garnett, a graduate of the United States Military Academy at West Point, who resigned from the Army on April 30, 1861, and was appointed a brigadier general of the Confederate States on June 6, 1861. He was killed July 13, 1861, at the battle of Carrick's Ford, VA (now near Parsons, WV).

7954. Union soldier killed by enemy action in the Civil War was Bailey Thornsberry Brown, Company B, 2nd West Virginia Volunteer Infantry. On May 22, 1861, while engaged in obtaining recruits, he was shot by Confederate pickets at Fetterman, near Grafton, WV. He was given a military funeral and buried in a temporary cemetery on upper Maple Avenue in Fetterman. In 1900, Reno Post No. 7 of the Grand Army of the Republic, a veterans' organization, erected a shaft to Brown's memory on Pearl Street in Grafton, and in 1928 the Betsy Ross Tent Daughters of the Union Veterans erected a monument in Fetterman on the spot where Brown fell.

7955. Confederate officer killed in the Civil War was Captain John Quincy Marr of Warrenton, VA, commander of the Warrenton Rifle Guards (designated Company K of the 17th Virginia Infantry Regiment), who was killed on June 1, 1861, in a skirmish at Fairfax Court House, VA. Marr was actually a lieutenant colonel, having been commissioned on May 2, 1861, but his letter of commission from Governor John Letcher had not been delivered to him.

7956. Union naval officer killed in the Civil War was Captain James Harmon Ward of the *Thomas Freeborn,* who landed at Mathias Point, VA, on the Potomac River about 50 miles south of Washington, DC, on June 27, 1861, with about 35 men and 250 sandbags to erect breastworks to unload a cannon. They were surprised by 1,500 infantrymen who attacked them and drove them off. Ward was hit in the breast by a Minié ball and died from an internal hemorrhage. He had been appointed on May 16, 1861, to command the Potomac flotilla.

7957. Civil War battle took place on Bull Run Creek, VA, on July 21, 1861. The Confederate forces under General Joseph Eccleston Johnston defeated the Union forces under General Irvin McDowell.

7958. Confederate forts to surrender in the Civil War were Fort Clark and Fort Hatteras on Hatteras Island, NC, guarding Pamlico Sound. They surrendered on August 29, 1861, to Flag Officer Silas H. Stringham and General Benjamin Franklin Butler, who had captured the garrison with 715 men, 31 heavy guns, and 1,000 stands of arms.

7959. Naval battle in the Civil War took place on September 14, 1861, at Pensacola, FL. Lieutenant John Henry Russell, leading a detachment of the crew of the U.S.S. *Colorado,* descended upon the Confederate navy yard at Pensacola at 2 A.M. They burned the five-gun steamer *Judah,* lying at anchor, and spiked the only gun in the yard. There were no Confederate casualties. Three of the Union troops were killed and four wounded.

7960. Union ship captured in the Civil War was the U.S.S. *Fanny,* an Army steam tug that grounded on a shoal on October 1, 1861, in Pamlico Sound, NC, while it was en route to Chicomacomica, the encampment of the 20th Indiana Regiment. The pilot and deckhand escaped by swimming ashore, but the ship was captured by Confederate naval forces. Also captured were the *Raleigh,* a small iron-hull propeller-driven towing steamer; the *Junaluska,* a vessel of 79 tons; and the *Culew,* 260 tons.

7961. Naval battle between ironclad vessels in the Civil War was fought between the *Monitor* and the *Merrimac* at Hampton Roads, VA, on March 9, 1862. The *Monitor* was a 172-foot Union ship with a crew of 58 under the command of Lieutenant John Lorimer Worden, who was partially blinded by a shot while observing action and was superseded by Lieutenant S. Dana Greene. It had been designed by John Ericsson and had a revolving gun turret. The *Merrimac* was a 275-foot Confederate ship with a crew of 300 under the command of Captain Franklin Buchanan, who was wounded and superseded by Lieutenant Catesby ap Roger Jones. It was a scuttled Union steam frigate that had been salvaged and armored by the Confederates and renamed the *Virginia.* The battle ended with the sinking of the *Merrimac.*

7962. Confederate cruiser built in England was the *Oneto,* which sailed from Liverpool, England, on March 22, 1862, bound for the Bahamas. The ship was transferred to Captain John Newland Maffitt of the Confederate Navy, who took rank as commodore. The guns and stores were sent in another ship that followed.

7963. Confederate ship surrendered to the Union was the *Planter,* a 313-ton side-wheel steamer serving as an armed dispatch boat. It was surrendered on May 12, 1862, off the harbor in Charleston, SC, by Robert Smalls, an African-American slave who was its pilot. He and the African-American crew took charge of the ship while the captain was ashore. Flying the Confederate flag, they saluted the forts on their voyage northward. When out of reach of ammunition, Smalls hoisted a white flag of truce and turned over the ship to the U.S.S. *Onward.* In appreciation, a special act of Congress was passed on May 30, 1862, awarding Smalls and his partners one-half the value of the *Planter* and its cargo.

7964. Balloonist to direct artillery fire was Professor Thaddeus Sobieski Coulincourt Lowe, who communicated with Union artillery units by telegraph on May 24, 1862, during the Civil War. Lowe made his first official ascent on July 24, 1861, and saw the movements of the Confederate troops after the battle of Manassas, VA. He also detected a Confederate maneuver to attack the troops of General Heintzelman, who was separated from the main force at Fair Oaks.

7965. Warship sunk by an underwater torpedo mine was sunk during the Civil War. The target was the ironclad Union gunboat *Cairo,* built by James Eads and Company, Mound City, IL, and commissioned on January 25, 1862. It was 175 feet long with a beam of 51 feet 2 inches, had a 512-ton displacement, and carried a crew of 251 officers and men. While clearing mines from the Yazoo River, near Vicksburg, MS, on December 12, 1862, the ship struck a bottle containing cannon powder that was floating beneath the surface. It sank in 30 feet of water within 12 minutes. The crew was rescued by the gunboat *Queen of the West.* An earlier but unsuccessful attack had been made on July 7, 1861, at Acquia Creek on the Potomac River, when Confederate forces attempted to destroy the Union ship *Pawnee* by floating a torpedo mine down the river on pieces of cork. The first Confederate vessel lost to a torpedo mine was a torpedo boat that was destroyed on February 17, 1864, off Charleston, SC.

7966. Union regiment in the Civil War made up of African-American soldiers was the 1st Regiment, South Carolina Volunteers, organized in the summer of 1862 by Major General David Hunter. Since there was no authority at that time for its muster into federal service, it was disbanded, then reorganized in October 1862 and mustered into federal service at Buford, SC, on January 31, 1863. Its designation was changed on February 8, 1864, to the 33rd U.S. Colored Infantry.

7967. Civil War bloodshed north of the Mason-Dixon Line was a battle that took place on June 30, 1863, between Brigadier General Judson Kilpatrick's 3rd Cavalry Division, Army of the Potomac, and Major General James Ewell Brown Stuart's Cavalry Division, Army of Northern Virginia, at Hanover, PA. About 11,000 troops were in this cavalry and artillery engagement, which resulted in more than 300 casualties. This battle was one of the determining factors that enabled the North to win the battle at Gettysburg, PA, in July 1863.

WARS—CIVIL WAR—*continued*

7968. Submarine built in the United States to sink an enemy warship in actual warfare was the Confederate submarine *Hunley,* named after its designer, Horace L. Hunley, and built by the firm of Hunley, McClintock and Watson in the shops of Parks and Lyons, Mobile, AL, in 1863. The interior height of the vessel was five feet, its breadth was four feet, and its maximum speed was four knots. Its propeller was operated by eight men using hand power. There were no provisions for storage of air. On the night of February 17, 1864, the *Hunley,* under the command of Lieutenant George Dixon, succeeded in approaching the U.S.S. *Housatonic,* a new ship of 1,400 tons displacement, which was awash off Charleston, SC, and sank it by exploding a torpedo under its bottom. The wave thrown up by the explosion swamped the submarine, whose forward hatch was open, and killed its crew. The wreck of the *Hunley* was found off the coast of Charleston in 1995.

7969. Trial of a war criminal by the federal government was held in Washington, DC, from August 23 to November 4, 1865. The defendant was Captain Henry Wirz, superintendent of the Confederate prison at Andersonville, GA, who was accused of conspiring to torture, injure, and murder Union prisoners. He was tried under 13 separate specifications by a military commission presided over by General Lewis Wallace, U.S. Volunteers. Wirz was convicted and sentenced to death by hanging. He was executed on November 10, 1865, and buried in Mount Olivet Cemetery, Washington, DC.

WARS—FRENCH AND INDIAN WAR

7970. Bloodshed in the French and Indian War occurred on May 28, 1754, on an isolated mountainside a few miles east of Uniontown, PA. Lieutenant Colonel George Washington, at the head of several companies of Virginia militia, reached the Monongahela River and overtook a French reconnoitering party from Fort Duquesne (the future site of Pittsburgh). Jumonville, the French commander, was slain and his force captured.

7971. Battle in the French and Indian War took place on the Great Meadows in southwestern Pennsylvania, near the present site of Uniontown, where Lieutenant Colonel George Washington, commanding 400 Virginia and South Carolina provincial troops, had built a small entrenchment known as Fort Necessity.

On July 3, 1754, the fort was attacked by the French commander Coulon de Villiers and his army of 1,600 French regulars, French Canadian militia, and Native Americans. Washington surrendered on July 4.

WARS—GULF WAR

7972. War that was predicted by pizza orders was Operation Desert Storm, which was launched on Wednesday, January 16, 1991, by a United Nations coalition led by the United States. At 5 A.M. that morning, the Domino's Pizza fast-food chain put out a warning to its franchisees that war was likely later that day, based on record orders of pizza the previous night from the Pentagon. The Pentagon is the headquarters of the Department of Defense in Washington, DC.

7973. Pilot to destroy an enemy airplane in the Gulf War was F-15C pilot Jon Kelk, who shot down an Iraqi Soviet-built MIG fighter over southern Iraq on January 16, 1991. Flying combat air patrol with three other F-15Cs, Kelk spotted an unidentified aircraft on radar and fired a radar-guided missile that brought the craft down before it could return fire.

7974. Serviceman killed in the Gulf War was Navy pilot Scott Speicher. His F-18 Hornet fighter was shot down over Iraq by antiaircraft fire on January 17, 1991.

WARS—KOREAN WAR

7975. Pilot to destroy an enemy airplane in the Korean War was First Lieutenant William G. Hudson of the 68th Fighter Squadron, who shot down a YAK-9 on June 26, 1950, while flying an F-82 airplane over Kimpo to provide cover for its evacuation. The war began on June 25, when South Korea was invaded by Communist forces from North Korea. The defense of South Korea was assisted by the United States as part of a United Nations effort.

7976. Korean War combat mission involving an exchange of fire occurred on June 27, 1950, between Communist forces and an F-80C airplane from the 8th Fighter-Bomber Group, 5th Air Force, which was based at Itazuke Air Base in southern Japan.

7977. Soldier killed in action in the Korean War was Private Kenneth Shadrick, 19, of Skin Fork, WV, a member of a bazooka squad, who was killed on July 5, 1950, near Sojong, Korea, by a bullet fired from an enemy tank.

7978. Officer killed in action in the Korean War was Colonel Robert R. Martin of Toledo, OH, who was killed on July 8, 1950, while leading a rocket and grenade attack against an enemy tank. He was awarded the first Distinguished Service Cross of the Korean War, posthumously presented to his son, Robert, a cadet at the U.S. Military Academy.

7979. Helicopter rescue of an American pilot behind enemy lines was effected in Korea on September 4, 1950, by First Lieutenant Paul Van Boven of San Mateo, CA, and hospital corpsman Corporal John Fuentz of Kansas City, MO, who rescued Captain Robert Earl Wayne of Garden City, NY, shot down on his 95th mission.

7980. Tank crew to cross the 38th parallel in the Korean War was a patrol of the 1st Cavalry Division that crossed into the Kaesong Area, about 85 miles south of the Communist capital of Pyongsang, at 3:14 P.M. on October 7, 1950. The crew members were Sergeant Homer Lee of Evansville, IN, Private First Class James Emerich of Sutton, WV, Sergeant Walter Hill of Fairmont, ND, Sergeant Charles Gissendanner of Autaughville, AL, and Corporal Clarence Johnson of Taylorsville, NC. The 38th parallel was the line of latitude that had divided North Korea from South Korea since the end of World War II.

7981. Pilot of a jet fighter to win a dogfight in the Korean War was First Lieutenant Russell John Brown of Pasadena, CA, the pilot of an Air Force F-80, who destroyed a MiG-15 over North Korea in jet-versus-jet combat on November 8, 1950.

WARS—PEACEKEEPING MISSIONS

7982. Serviceman to die in Somalia was Private First Class Domingo Arroyo, a 21-year-old Marine from Elizabeth, NJ. He was shot by an unknown gunman while on night patrol at the airport near the Somali capital of Mogadishu in January 1993.

7983. Serviceman killed during the Bosnia conflict was Sergeant First Class Donald Allen Dugan of Ridgeway, OH, a member of the peacekeeping force organized by the North Atlantic Treaty Organization that entered Bosnia-Hercegovina in December 1995. Dugan was killed in an explosion in Sarajevo, Bosnia, on February 3, 1996. The cause of the explosion was not determined.

WARS—REVOLUTIONARY WAR

7984. Attack on British soldiers by civilians in the Revolution was made in New York City on January 18, 1770, by the Sons of Liberty, a crowd of Americans who attacked a group of 40 to 50 soldiers because they had cut down the liberty poles that the Americans had erected. The soldiers used their bayonets and dispersed them. No one was killed, but several persons on both sides were seriously injured. The mob fight has been termed the Battle of Golden Hill.

7985. Child to be killed in the Revolution was Christopher Snider, an 11-year-old boy who was killed on February 22, 1770, in Boston, MA. A man named Theophilus Lille had violated the merchants' agreement against importing and his house had been marked as a punishment. These marks were removed by another man, Ebenezer Richardson. A mob gathered to attack Richardson's house and Richardson fired into it, killing the boy and wounding another person. Shops and schools were closed on the day of the funeral. Richardson was convicted of murder and sentenced to two years in prison.

7986. Americans killed by British soldiers in the Revolution were shot on March 5, 1770, at Boston, MA, when British soldiers of the 29th Regiment of Foot fired at a taunting crowd, killing Crispus Attucks, James Caldwell, Patrick Carr, Samuel Gray, and Samuel Maverick. The incident became known as the Boston Massacre. The soldiers were tried for murder and were defended by John Adams and Josiah Quincy, Jr. Two soldiers were found guilty, branded on the hand, and discharged. Six other soldiers and an officer were acquitted.

7987. Naval attack in the Revolutionary War was made on June 9, 1772, against the British revenue cutter *Gaspee*, commanded by Lieutenant William Duddingston, which ran aground while chasing the packet *Hanna* off Namquit Point, Providence, RI, in Narragansett Bay. During the night, merchant John Brown and a number of others rowed out in eight longboats captained by Abraham Whipple, boarded the *Gaspee*, and set it on fire.

7988. Revolutionary War incident occurred on December 13, 1774, when Major John Sullivan of the Granite State Volunteers, later a major general in the Continental Army, and 400 patriots attacked Fort William and Mary at New Castle, NH, in Portsmouth harbor. They

WARS—REVOLUTIONARY WAR—_continued_

bound the commander of the fort and frightened the soldiers away, capturing 100 casks of powder and small arms. This attack took place some four months before the battle of Lexington.

7989. Revolutionary War armed conflict was the Battle of Lexington, a skirmish at Lexington, MA, on April 19, 1775, between 70 Minutemen volunteers under Captain John Parker and about 700 British Regulars under Major John Pitcairn, who were on their way to destroy illegal military stores at nearby Concord. The Americans were ordered to disperse. As they were doing so, one of them fired a shot. The British returned fire, killing 8 Minutemen and wounding 10.

7990. Revolutionary War military action occurred on May 10, 1775, when Ethan Allen and 83 men who called themselves the Green Mountain Boys crossed Lake Champlain from Vermont in scows, entered Fort Ticonderoga, NY, through the south gate, and swarmed into the barracks while the soldiers were asleep. Allen demanded the surrender of the fort "in the name of the Great Jehovah and the Continental Congress." The fort, commanded by Captain William Delaplace and Lieutenant Jocelyn Feltham, was captured with 78 guns, 6 mortars, 3 howitzers, thousands of cannon balls, 30,000 flints, and other supplies.

7991. Naval battle in the Revolutionary War took place on June 12, 1775, when Captain James Moore of the British schooner _Margaretta_ arrived in the harbor of Machias, ME, and ordered the inhabitants to take down a liberty pole they had erected. The townspeople, led by Jeremiah and John O'Brien, set out in a confiscated sloop, the _Unity,_ and in a hand-to-hand encounter captured the _Margaretta_ and confiscated her cannons. The captured crew was marched overland to Cambridge, MA, where they were turned over to General George Washington. The American loss was four killed and eight wounded.

7992. Revolutionary War volunteer detachment to arrive in Cambridge, MA, to fight the British was the Reading Riflemen of Reading, PA, which arrived on July 18, 1775. The Riflemen of York, PA, arrived on July 25.

7993. Warship to receive definite orders to attack the enemy was the 78-ton schooner _Hannah,_ commanded by Captain Nicholson Broughton of Marblehead, MA. His order was dated September 2, 1775. The crew consisted of a detachment of soldiers from the Essex County Regiment of Marblehead. They sailed on September 5, 1775, from Beverly, MA, and on September 6 they captured the 260-ton British ship _Unity_ en route from Portsmouth to Boston.

7994. Marine engagement in battle took place on March 4, 1776, during the Revolutionary War, when Captain Samuel Nicholas and approximately 200 marines captured Fort Nassau in the Bahamas. Nicholas was assisted by 50 sailors under Lieutenant Thomas Weaver of the _Cabot._ The assault was a surprise attack and the fort surrendered without conflict. The Americans captured large military stores, including about 100 cannon, 15 mortars, 5,400 shells, and 11,000 rounds of ammunition, and brought them back to New London, CT, on April 8. This naval expedition, which left the Delaware Capes on February 17, 1776, was under the command of Esek Hopkins of the _Alfred._

7995. Capture of an enemy warship by a commissioned American naval officer took place on April 17, 1776, when the brig _Lexington_ under Captain John Barry met the British warship _Edward_ off the Virginia coast, captured it, and conveyed it to Philadelphia, PA. The _Lexington_ had been purchased by the federal government in February 1776.

7996. Soldier killed in the Revolutionary War who was Jewish was Francis Salvador, known as the Southern Paul Revere for having warned of the approach of the British fleet at Charleston, SC. On August 1, 1776, while he was leading the militia under the command of Major Andrew Wilkinson, his group was ambushed by Native Americans and loyalists near Esseneka (Seneca). Salvador was shot through the body and the left leg and was scalped by a group of Cherokees who sided with the British.

7997. Land grant to deserters from the British Army during the Revolutionary War was authorized by the act of the Continental Congress of August 14, 1776. The act offered American citizenship to British and Hessian deserters from the British Army and gave each deserter or his heirs 50 acres of unappropriated land in certain states. On August 27, 1776, a similar act was passed to encourage officers in the British forces to desert.

7998. Traitor to the American cause during the Revolutionary War was William Demont (or Dement), a member of the 5th Pennsylvania Battalion, who was appointed adjutant in Colonel Robert Magraw's battalion on February 29, 1776. He deserted on November 2, 1776, and notified the British of the position of Fort Washington (now a neighborhood in New York City). Demont's act enabled the British general Sir William Howe to conquer the fort with a force of 8,900 men on November 16, 1776. They captured 2,818 American officers and men, 43 guns, and 2,800 muskets.

7999. Capture of an enemy ship in enemy waters was accomplished by the 16-gun brig *Reprisal,* which sailed for France on December 4, 1776, under the command of Captain Lambert Wickes. One of the passengers was Benjamin Franklin, who was traveling incognito to Auray, France, to obtain French assistance. On the way over, the *Reprisal* captured two British vessels. It captured two others in the Bay of Biscay, one of which was the King's packet plying between Falmouth and Lisbon. This was the first time an American warship entered enemy waters and the first attempt to block and destroy British commerce at the source.

8000. Warship captured overseas was the *Lexington,* which had made the first American capture of an enemy warship in April 1776. The ship was 86 feet long and 24 feet 6 inches wide, and carried a 16 guns and a complement of 110. On September 20, 1777, the ship was becalmed in the English Channel. Captain Henry Johnson, who was out of ammunition, surrendered the ship to the British cutter H.M.S. *Alert,* commanded by Lieutenant John Bazely.

8001. Blockade of enemy ships that was effective was completed on April 30, 1778, stretching from West Point, NY, to Constitution Island, NY. A huge chain was forged at the Sterling Iron Works in Orange County, NY, from ore mined in the same county and was carried in sections to West Point, where it was joined and stretched across the Hudson River to prevent British ships from passing. The chain weighed 180 tons and was 1,700 feet long; each link was 2.5 inches wide and 30 inches long. It was placed in position on April 16 and on April 30 was secured at both ends. Earlier in the war, in the summer of 1776, a chain of chevaux-de-frise and sunken ships had been extended between Fort Washington, NY, and Fort Lee, NJ, to serve as a blockade, but the British passed it on October 9, 1776, without firing a gun.

8002. Revolutionary War conflict in which American and British troops met on equal terms was the Battle of Monmouth Courthouse, Freehold, NJ, on June 28, 1778. The Americans under General George Washington lost 69 killed and 160 wounded; the British under Sir Henry Clinton lost 300 killed and 100 wounded or captured.

8003. Revolutionary War bayonet charge occurred on July 16, 1779, when General Anthony Wayne, known as "Mad Anthony," charged the British garrison at Stony Point, NY, with 1,200 men and forced it to surrender. He was slightly wounded. The British loss was 63 killed and 553 wounded; the American loss, 15 killed and 83 wounded.

8004. American imprisoned as an enemy agent in the Tower of London was Henry Laurens of Charlestown, SC, president of the Continental Congress from 1777 to 1778. On August 13, 1780, Laurens sailed from Philadelphia, PA, on the brigantine *Mercury* en route to Holland, where he was to negotiate a loan and treaty. Three weeks later, he was captured by the British off Newfoundland. He threw his papers overboard, but they were recovered and led to the British declaration of war against Holland. From October 6, 1780, to December 31, 1781, he was imprisoned in the Tower on suspicion of high treason, and was forced to pay for his room, board, and guard. He was released in exchange for the British army leader Lord Cornwallis, who had surrendered to General George Washington at Yorktown, VA. Laurens, with Benjamin Franklin and John Jay, drew up the preliminary treaty of peace with Great Britain on November 30, 1782, to terminate the Revolutionary War.

8005. Warship to capture an enemy ship after the Revolution was the U.S.S. *Constellation,* a 36-gun frigate of 1,265 tons, authorized by Congress on March 27, 1794, and launched on September 7, 1797, at the Sterrett Shipyard, Baltimore, MD. The ship was 164 feet long, 40.5 feet in the beam, and 13.5 feet deep in the hold. On February 9, 1799, off the island of Nevis, West Indies, the 36-gun *Constellation,* under the command of Commodore Thomas Truxton, met and captured the 40-gun French frigate *Insurgente,* inflicting 70 casualties at the cost of only 4 American casualties.

WARS—REVOLUTIONARY WAR—*continued*

8006. Centennial celebration of the Revolution was held at Lexington and Concord, MA, on April 19, 1875, to commemorate the 100th birthday of American liberty. The participants included President Ulysses Simpson Grant, three cabinet secretaries, and many state governors.

WARS—SPANISH-AMERICAN WAR

8007. Capture of a ship in the Spanish-American War was made by the American gunboat *Nashville,* which took the Spanish ship *Buena Ventura* on April 22, 1898. On April 24, Spain declared that a state of war existed with the United States. The following day, Congress declared that a state of war had existed since April 21.

8008. Navy officer killed in action in the Spanish-American War was Ensign Worth Bagley, executive officer of the torpedo boat U.S.S. *Winslow,* who was killed on May 11, 1898. The *Winslow* had been sent to the wharves at Cardenas, Cuba, for a closer inspection of the docks, and was fired upon simultaneously by a shore battery and a Spanish gunboat. Also killed was a sailor, George Burton Meek, to whose memory a monument was erected in the McPherson Cemetery, Clyde, OH.

8009. Military expeditionary force to be sent beyond the Western Hemisphere sailed on May 25, 1898, from San Francisco, CA, on the *Australia, City of Pekin,* and *City of Sydney,* bound for Manila, Philippines, a distance of 6,220 miles. The expeditionary force consisted of 115 officers and 2,386 enlisted men commanded by General Wesley Merritt. They arrived off Manila on June 30 and landed on July 1. Admiral George Dewey and General Merritt demanded the surrender of Manila on August 7. The city complied on August 13.

8010. Army officer killed in battle in the Spanish-American War was Captain Allen Kissam Capron, who was killed in action on June 24, 1898, at Las Guásimas, Cuba.

8011. Land battle in the Spanish-American War took place on June 24, 1898, at Las Guásimas, Cuba. The 1st Cavalry, the 10th Cavalry, and the Rough Riders, all unmounted, took part. Juragua was captured and 11 Spanish dead were left on the field. Sixteen Americans were killed and 52 wounded.

8012. Balloon destroyed by enemy gunfire was shot down by the Spanish on July 1, 1898, at Santiago, Cuba. It was piloted by Colonel George Derby of the Army Engineer Department, who reported on the enemy's movements as he floated above the American troops. The soldiers were glad that it was brought down, as it had been drawing fire in their direction.

WARS—VIETNAM WAR

8013. Pilot wounded in Vietnam who was a civilian was Paul Robert Holden of Greenleaf, KS, who was wounded in the right thigh and arm by 37mm antiaircraft shells over Dien Bien Phu on April 24, 1954. Holden was flying a C-119 Flying Boxcar for the Civil Air Transport, delivering supplies to the French. His copilot, Wallace Abbott Buford, of Kansas City, KS, managed to land the plane safely in French territory. Buford was killed on May 7, 1954, near Dien Bien Phu.

8014. Troops sent to Vietnam were 425 helicopter crewmen sent by President John Fitzgerald Kennedy on December 11, 1961, to provide support and training for South Vietnamese forces.

8015. Navy pilot shot down and captured in North Vietnam was Lieutenant (j.g.) Everett Alvarez, Jr., 26, of San Jose, CA, aviator on the U.S.S. *Constellation,* who was shot down on August 5, 1964, and parachuted into the ocean. He was rescued by the crew of a small Vietnamese boat, to whom he surrendered. He was confined in the Hon Gay naval base and later in the Hoa Lo prison. He was returned to the United States on February 13, 1973.

8016. Ground troops sent to Vietnam were 3,500 Marines who landed at the port of Da Nang in South Vietnam on March 8, 1965. The Marines' mission was to guard the air base there. They raised the total U.S. troop strength in Vietnam to 27,000.

8017. Demonstration in Washington against the Vietnam War took place in April 1965, when 20,000 protesters organized by the radical group Students for a Democratic Society picketed the White House and marched from the Washington Monument to the steps of the Capitol building. The first campus teach-in was also held that month, at the University of Michigan at Ann Arbor.

8018. General killed in Vietnam by enemy fire was Major General Bruno Arthur Hochmuth, commander of the 3rd Marine Division, killed on November 14, 1967, at Hué, Vietnam, when ground fire downed the helicopter in which he was a passenger. Two American pilots, an American crew chief, and a Vietnamese interpreter were also killed in the crash.

8019. Vietnam War Moratorium Day demonstration took place on October 15, 1969. Millions of antiwar protesters wearing black armbands marched in major cities across the country. The largest protest was in Washington, DC, where 250,000 demonstrators gathered and were led in a candlelight march past the White House by Coretta Scott King, the widow of Martin Luther King, Jr.

WARS—WAR OF 1812

8020. Naval battle in the War of 1812 took place before war was declared, on May 16, 1811, in the Atlantic Ocean about 40 miles off Cape Cod, MA. The 18-gun British sloop *Little Belt* under Captain A.B. Bingham attacked the 44-gun American frigate *President* under Commodore John Rodgers, striking the mainmast and the foremast and wounding one man. The *President* returned fire, killing or wounding 20 of the crew of the *Little Belt.* The first naval battle after the United States declaration of war of June 18, 1812, took place in the Atlantic on June 23 between the *President* and the *Belvidera* under Captain Richard Byron. The *President* closed in for the telling shot, but one of its guns exploded, killing or wounding 22 men. The *Belvidera* escaped in the confusion.

8021. Naval action of importance in the War of 1812 took place in the Atlantic Ocean about 750 miles east of Boston, MA, on August 19, 1812, when the *Constitution,* commanded by Captain Isaac Hull, met the British 38-gun frigate *Guerrière,* commanded by Captain James Richard Dacres. The *Constitution,* built in Boston in 1797, was rated as a frigate of 1,576 tons, with an armament of 44 guns. Within a quarter of an hour the mizzenmast of the *Guerrière* had been shot away, and its spars, sails, and rigging torn to shreds. The American loss was 14 killed or wounded; the British, 79 killed or wounded. On March 3, 1813, Congress awarded $50,000 to Hull and the crew for the victory over the *Guerrière.*

8022. Prisoners captured in the War of 1812 were taken by Lieutenant William Learned Marcy, who captured a corps of Canadian militia at St. Regis, NY, on October 22–23, 1812.

8023. Capture of a British frigate in the War of 1812 was accomplished by the frigate *United States,* 44 guns, under Captain Stephen Decatur, which captured the *Macedonian,* 38 guns, under Captain John Surnam Garden, near the Madeira Islands, off the Moroccan coast, on October 25, 1812. The *Macedonian* sustained a loss of 36 killed and 68 wounded, of whom 53 later died of wounds. The *United States* suffered six killed and seven wounded. The captured *Macedonian* was taken into the harbor of New London, CT, on December 4, 1812, and was later brought to the East River, New York City.

8024. Defeat of a British naval squadron in the War of 1812 and in all of British history was the Battle of Lake Erie, which took place on September 10, 1813. The American naval officer Oliver Hazard Perry left Erie, PA, with a fleet of nine ships and encountered a squadron of six British warships off Put-in-Bay, OH. Perry's attack was hampered by his short-range guns, and his ship was battered to a hulk with only a handful of capable men left. He renewed the fight from a sister ship, the *Niagara,* and had the satisfaction of seeing the British strike their colors. His message of victory contained the famous phrase, "We have met the enemy and they are ours."

WARS—WORLD WAR I

8025. American to sail to Europe to fight in World War I was Denis Patrick Dowd, Jr., of Sea Cliff, NY, who enlisted on August 6, 1914. He fought with the French Foreign Legion, was transferred to a line regiment when the battered legion was withdrawn, was wounded, and upon recovery was transferred to the Lafayette Escadrille, the squadron of American volunteer airmen attached to the French air force. He died on August 11, 1916, when his plane crashed in a nose dive at Buc, near Paris, the day before he was to fly to the front. He was buried in the Memorial Cemetery of the Lafayette Escadrille in the Parc du Villeneuve l'Étang near St. Cloud, France.

8026. Ship from the United States lost in World War I was the *William P. Frye,* a steel sailing vessel of 3,374 gross tons, built in 1901 and owned by Arthur Sewall and Company of Maine. The ship left Seattle, WA, on November 4, 1914, bound for England, with a cargo of 186,950 bushels of wheat. It was sunk on January 28, 1915, by the German cruiser *Prinz Eitel Friedrich.*

WARS—WORLD WAR I—*continued*

8027. American combatant to die in World War I was Edward Mandell Stone of Chicago, IL, an expatriate living in Paris who enlisted in the French Foreign Legion and was assigned to the second regiment. He served at Champagne and in the Aisne, where he was mortally wounded on February 17, 1915. He died on February 27. He was posthumously awarded the Croix de Guerre and the Military Medal.

8028. Cargo ship from the United States attacked by a German submarine in World War I was the *Nantucket Chief* from Port Arthur, TX, a 5,189-ton tanker 360 feet long with a net tonnage of 3,262 tons. It was carrying a cargo of oil bound for Rouen, France, when it was torpedoed by the German submarine *U-30* off the Scilly Isles, England, on May 1, 1915. The first to be sunk by a submerged German submarine was the S.S. *Frederick R. Kellogg*, 7,127 tons, owned by the Pan-American Petroleum and Transportation Company, which was sunk 12 miles north of Barnegat Light, NJ, on August 13, 1918, when a torpedo struck the engine room. The ship sank in 15 seconds.

8029. Pilot from the United States shot down in World War I was H. Clyde Balsley of the Lafayette Escadrille volunteer air unit, who was attacked by a German squadron at a height of 10,000 feet above Verdun, France, on June 18, 1916. Although wounded, he managed to land his airplane within the Allied lines. He received the Military Medal and the War Cross for his bravery.

8030. Pilot from the United States killed in World War I while serving in the Lafayette Escadrille was Victor Emmanuel Chapman, who was shot down on June 23, 1916, northeast of Douamont, France, in the Verdun sector. He had served for a year in the Foreign Legion before joining the Lafayette Escadrille.

8031. Shot fired by the Navy in World War I was fired on April 7, 1917, at Guam Island. Commander William Alden Hall, in command of a prize crew, left the U.S.S. *Supply* and proceeded to the port town of Piti with orders to follow the governor's aide, who had boarded the interned German cruiser *Cormorant* in Apra harbor under a flag of truce to demand its surrender. The Americans sighted a German launch with a cutter in tow and fired two warning shots across her bow, both of which were disregarded. After several shots, the launch hove to and was ordered to Piti to surrender to the authorities there. The Germans refused and blew up their ship. Seven crew members were killed and the rest were captured and sent as prisoners to an army camp in Utah.

8032. Army general to fly over enemy lines was Brigadier General William Lendrum Mitchell, who took off at 5:30 P.M. from La Cheppe, France, on April 24, 1917, in an airplane piloted by Lieutenant Franҫois Lafont and flew over the German lines at an altitude of 6,000 feet, returning at 7 P.M.

8033. Troops from the United States to sail to Europe in World War I were members of the American Expeditionary Force under General John Joseph Pershing. The group included 40 regular army officers, 17 reserve officers, 2 Marine Corps officers, 67 enlisted men, 36 field clerks, 20 civilians, 3 interpreters, and 3 news correspondents. They left New York City on May 28, 1917, on the *Baltic,* docked at Liverpool, England, on June 8, and reached Paris on June 13. The United States had been in a state of war with Germany since April 6, 1917, when it became the 13th nation to declare war against the Central Powers.

8034. Marine regiment to land in Europe in World War I was the 5th Regiment of Marines, commanded by Colonel Charles A. Doyen, which sailed from New York City on board the *Henderson, De Kalb,* and *Hancock* on June 14, 1917. By July 2, 1917, the entire regiment had arrived at St. Nazaire, France. The regiment was detached for service in France by executive order of May 25, 1917.

8035. Navy enlisted man killed in World War I action was Gunners Mate First Class Osmond Kelly Ingram of Pratt City, AL, a member of the crew of the destroyer U.S.S. *Cassin,* which was on patrol duty. On October 16, 1917, Ingram was blown overboard by a torpedo fired by a German submarine from a distance of five miles, which hit the stern of the *Cassin,* knocked out the engine, and wounded five other sailors. A destroyer, the *Osmond Ingram,* was named in his honor. It was laid down on October 15, 1918, by the Bethlehem Shipbuilding Company, Quincy, MA, launched on February 23, 1919, and commissioned on June 28, 1919, at Boston. It was the first naval ship to be named for an enlisted man.

8036. Army division to go into battle in World War I was the 1st Division, which entered the trenches on October 21, 1917, in the Lunéville sector, near Nancy, France. Each unit was attached to a corresponding French unit.

8037. Shot fired by American infantry in World War I was fired at 6:05 A.M. on October 23, 1917, by Battery C of the 6th Field Artillery under the command of Sergeant Alexander L. Arch of South Bend, IN. Corporal Robert E. Bralet is credited with having jerked the lanyard on a French 75mm gun to send the first shot into a German trench half a mile away.

8038. Soldiers in the American army killed in combat in World War I were Corporal James B. Gresham of Evansville, IN, and Privates Thomas F. Enright of Pittsburgh, PA, and Merle D. Hay of Glidden, IA, members of Company F, 16th Infantry, 1st Division. They met death when the Germans raided the 16th Infantry's trenches near Bathelémont, France, on the night of November 2–3, 1917. On November 3, General Bordeaux of the French Army commended their heroism and sacrifice. Earlier, on September 4, 1917, a group of American soldiers assigned to a field hospital operated by the British Expeditionary Force at Dannes-Camiers, France, had been killed when the hospital was bombed by a German airplane. They were First Lieutenant William Thomas Fitzsimons of Kansas City, MO, and enlisted men Rudolph Rubino, Jr., of the Bronx, New York City, Oscar Le Tugo of Boston, MA, and Leslie G. Woods of Streator, IL.

8039. Naval vessels to sink an enemy submarine in the Atlantic were the U.S.S. *Fanning* and the U.S.S. *Nicholson*. On November 17, 1917, at 4:10 P.M., in latitude 57 degrees 37 minutes N, longitude 8 degrees 12 minutes W, the *Fanning*, while in convoy, sighted the periscope of a submarine. The *Fanning* headed for the spot and dropped depth charges. The *Nicholson*, one of the vessels of the convoy, speeded to the spot and also dropped depth charges. The German submarine *U-58* came to the surface. The *Nicholson* fired three shots from her stern while the *Fanning* headed for the submarine and fired its bow gun. After three shots, the crew of the submarine came on deck and surrendered. The submarine sank shortly afterward. The commanding officer of the *Fanning* was Lieutenant Commander Arthur Schuyler Carpenter, and the commanding officer of the *Nicholson* was Lieutenant Commander Frank Dunn Berrien.

8040. Troop ship from the United States torpedoed by a German submarine in World War I was the S.S. *Tuscania*, carrying 119 officers and 2,037 men. It was torpedoed and sunk by the submarine *U-77* on February 15, 1918, off the north coast of Ireland, with a loss of 183 men.

8041. Air squadron of the Army in World War I was Squadron No. 1, also known as the 1st Aero Squadron, assigned to the front on April 8, 1918, for observation duty. The first combat action took place on April 12, 1918, when the squadron was attacked while on a reconnaissance mission.

8042. Combat mission of American pilots ordered to battle in World War I by an American squadron commander was the 94th Aero Pursuit Squadron, the "Hat-in-the-Ring Squadron." On April 13, 1918, Major John Huffer ordered Captain David Peterson, Lieutenant Reed Chambers, and Lieutenant Edward Vernon Rickenbacker to make a two-hour patrol from Pont-à-Mousson to St. Mihiel, France, at 6 A.M. the following day.

8043. Pilots in American units to participate in air combat in World War I were Alan Francis Winslow and Douglas Campbell, who shot down two German single-seaters almost directly over the Squadron Aerodrome at Toul, France, on April 14, 1918.

8044. Airplane bombing raid by an American air unit was made by six airplanes of the Army's 96th Aero Squadron. The unit left the airdrome at Amanty, France, in Breguet airplanes on June 12, 1918. Five airplanes dropped 80 bombs on a railroad junction at Dommary-Baroncourt, about 40 miles inside enemy territory. Lieutenant Howard Grant Rath was the lead observer.

8045. Shots fired by German forces to land on American soil in World War I were fired on July 21, 1918, by the German submarine *U-156*. The target was the tugboat *Perth Amboy* and four barges loaded with stone off Nauset Bluffs, Orleans, MA. About 70 or 80 shots were fired three miles offshore. A few shots landed on shore at Meeting House Pond.

8046. Night-flying scout group was the 185th Pursuit Squadron, which went to the front on October 5, 1918, assigned to the Meuse-Argonne sector in France.

8047. American division to cross the Rhine River in World War I was the 1st Division, which passed over the pontoon bridge at Coblentz on the morning of December 13, 1918, led by Company M, 18th Infantry, commanded by Lieutenant Donald McClure.

WARS—WORLD WAR II—EUROPE

8048. Ship from the United States sunk by a German submarine in World War II was the *Robin Moor,* 4,985 tons, operated by the Robin Line of New York, which sailed on May 6, 1941, from New York City for Cape Town, South Africa, with 8 passengers and a crew of 38 under Captain Edward Myers. It was sunk on May 21 in the South Atlantic, 400 miles south of the Cape Verde Islands and 900 miles due west of Monrovia, Liberia.

8049. Capture of a German ship by an American ship in World War II was accomplished by the Coast Guard cutter *Northland,* captained by Commander Carl Christian von Paulsen, which captured the 60-ton trawler *Busko* at Mackenzie Bay, Greenland, on September 12, 1941. The *Busko* had entered U.S. waters without proper documentation and had radioed weather reports and other information to Germany. The captured ship was sent under the escort of the Navy-manned U.S.S. *Bear* under Lieutenant Commander Joseph Gainard to Commonwealth Pier, Boston, MA, where its crew of 20 men and 1 woman was held without bail.

8050. Warship convoy across the Atlantic Ocean in World War II was convoy HX-150, consisting of the destroyers *Dallas, Eberle, Ellis, Ericsson,* and *Upshur,* commanded by Captain Morton L. Deyo. On September 17, 1941, the warships assumed charge of 50 merchant ships that had left Nova Scotia, Canada, the previous day.

8051. Destroyer from the United States torpedoed in World War II was the *Kearny,* commanded by Lieutenant Commander Anthony Leo Danis, which was attacked on October 17, 1941, 350 miles southwest of Iceland. Eleven of the crew were killed, two were seriously wounded, and eight sustained minor wounds, but the *Kearny* remained afloat and arrived at Iceland on October 19. The first American destroyer torpedoed and sunk while on convoy duty was the *Reuben James,* commanded by Lieutenant Commander Heywood Lane Edwards, which was attacked on October 30, 1941, off the western coast of Ireland by the German submarine *U-562.* The torpedo hit a magazine on the port side and exploded, sinking the destroyer with the loss of 115 of the crew of 160.

8052. American expeditionary force to land in Europe in World War II arrived in Ireland on January 26, 1942, and was greeted by Sir Archibald Sinclair, the British air minister. The first officer to land was Major General Russell Peter Hartle. The first enlisted man to land was Private Milburn Henke of Hutchinson, MN.

8053. Pilot from the United States to sink a German submarine was Ensign William Tepuni, Naval Reserve, who was flying a Lockhead-Hudson airplane of Squadron VP-82 when he attacked and sank the German submarine *U-656* off Cape Race, Newfoundland, Canada, on March 1, 1942.

8054. Naval vessel from the United States to sink a German submarine in World War II was the destroyer *Roper,* captained by Lieutenant Commander Hamilton Wilcox Howe, which sank the German submarine *U-85* on April 13–14, 1942, off Wimble Shoal, near Hatteras, NC.

8055. American expeditionary force to land in Africa in World War II was the 41st Engineers General Service Regiment, which landed on June 17, 1942, at Port Takoradi, Gold Coast, Africa. The first man to land was Private Napoleon Edward Taylor of Baltimore, MD, orderly of Major Charles S. Ward.

8056. Bombing mission by American forces over enemy-occupied territory in Europe in World War II took place on July 4, 1942, when a Royal Air Force group of twelve A-20 Boston bombers, six manned by British crews and six by American crews, made a daylight attack against three German airfields in the Netherlands.

8057. Capture of an American ship captain by a German submarine in World War II took place on July 9, 1942, when the Grace Line's *Santa Rita* was sunk by a U-boat torpedo about 500 miles south of Bermuda. The captain, Henry Stephenson of Larchmont, NY, was removed from a lifeboat as it pulled away from the sinking ship. He was taken prisoner and interned until February 1945, when he was repatriated. He was then 69 years old.

8058. Enemy saboteurs executed in the United States were six Germans who were electrocuted on August 8, 1942, in a jail in Washington, DC. They were part of a group of eight who were tried by a military commission of seven generals. One saboteur, George John Dasch, was sentenced to 30 years in prison, and another, Ernest Peter Burger, received a life sentence. All eight were found guilty of landing in rubber boats from enemy submarines, carrying explosives, incendiaries, fuses, detonators, timing devices, acids, and similar materials. Four of them landed on June 13, 1942, at Amagansett, NY, on Long Island, and were discovered by Seaman Second Class John C. Cullen of the Amagansett Coast Guard Station. Four others landed on June 17, 1942, at Ponte Vedra Beach near Jacksonville, FL.

8059. Pilot from the United States to shoot down a German fighter plane in World War II was Second Lieutenant Sam F. Junkin of Natchez, MS, who shot down a Focke-Wulf-190 plane over Dieppe, France, in a Commando-Ranger raid on August 19, 1942. Junkin was wounded and jumped from his disabled plane. He was picked up by a returning Commando barge. On the same date, a similar plane was shot down by Frank A. Hill of the 31st Fighter Group, but it was listed as "probably destroyed," since observers did not see the plane hit the ground or explode in the air, or see the pilot bail out.

8060. Soldier from the United States to land on French soil in World War II was Corporal Franklin M. Koons of Iowa, one of the Rangers who accompanied Lieutenant Colonel Lord Lovat's Commandos in a raid on Dieppe on August 19, 1942. Koons destroyed a German 155mm gun and was awarded the British Military Medal for "conspicuous gallantry and admirable leadership" on October 2, 1942.

8061. Air attack on Germany by the Army Air Force in World War II was made on January 27, 1943, by the 8th Air Force led by Brigadier General Haywood Shepherd Hansell III from bases in England. The targets were naval bases and docks at Wilhelmshaven and factories in Emden in northwest Germany. The Americans lost three planes on the mission, two Liberators and one Flying Fortress. The German loss was 22 fighter airplanes and 3 bombers.

8062. American land victory without infantry in World War II was won on June 11, 1943, when the Italian fortress on the island of Pantelleria in the Mediterranean Sea, about 70 miles southwest of Sicily, surrendered to the Northwest African Air Forces of the Anglo-American Air Command, which had dropped 6,200 tons of bombs in more than 5,000 sorties. The island was occupied 22 minutes after landing. Lieutenant General Carl Andrew Spaatz commanded the operation.

8063. Army pilot who was African-American to shoot down an Axis airplane in World War II was First Lieutenant Charles Hall of Brazil, IN, who shot down a German Focke-Wulf 190 over Sicily on July 2, 1943. He was flying a Warhawk as part of a fighter squadron escorting bombers. The squadron commander was Lieutenant Colonel Benjamin Oliver Davis, Jr., who later became the first African-American general of the Air Force.

8064. Airship from the United States lost to enemy action in World War II was the K-74, a nonrigid blimp on patrol over the East Coast that attacked a German submarine submerged in the Caribbean on July 18, 1943. The airship was destroyed by gunfire and was forced to alight on the water. All of the 11-man crew was saved with the exception of Isadore Stessel of Brooklyn, New York City, Aviation Machinist First Class.

8065. Capture and boarding of an enemy submarine on the high seas by American forces took place on June 4, 1944, when the 740-ton German submarine *U-505* was attacked and captured by airplanes and ships under the command of Captain Daniel Vincent Gallery of the aircraft carrier U.S.S. *Guadalcanal* off Cape Blanco on the west coast of Africa, between Cape Verde and the Canary Islands. The submarine was boarded by Lieutenant (j.g.) Albert Leroy David and eight crewmen from the destroyer U.S.S. *Pillsbury*, commanded by George W. Cassleman. The *Guadalcanal* towed the *U-505* more than 1,700 miles across the Atlantic Ocean to Port Royal Bay, Bermuda, where it arrived on June 19, 1944.

WARS—WORLD WAR II—PACIFIC

8066. Submarine from the United States destroyed in World War II was the *Sealion*, launched on May 25, 1939, at the Electric Boat Division of General Dynamics at Groton, CT, and commissioned on November 27, 1939. The ship, 311 feet long with a 2,350-ton displacement, was docked at Machina Wharf at the Navy Yard at Cavite, Philippine Islands, on December 10, 1941, when a group of 54 Japanese airplanes dropped bombs on it. Four men were lost and the ship was badly damaged. Since the closest repair facilities were at Pearl Harbor, Honolulu, HI, the *Sealion* was towed out to sea, where it was exploded on December 25 by three depth charges placed inside. Lieutenant Commander Richard G. Voge was the commanding officer.

WARS—WORLD WAR II—PACIFIC—*continued*

8067. American losses in the Pacific in World War II took place on December 7, 1941, when Japan carried out a surprise attack against the American fleet at Pearl Harbor, HI. The United States lost five battleships, three destroyers, a minelayer, and a target vessel. Many other ships were damaged and about 400 airplanes were destroyed. American casualties totaled 2,117 killed, 1,272 wounded, and 960 missing.

8068. Navy admiral killed in action in World War II was Rear Admiral Isaac Campbell Kidd, staff aide to Admiral Husband Edward Kimmel, commander in chief of the United States Fleet. Kidd was killed on December 7, 1941, when the U.S.S. *Arizona* blew up during the Japanese attack on Pearl Harbor, HI.

8069. Ship from the United States to sink a Japanese submarine in World War II was the U.S.S. *Ward,* which hit the Japanese submarine *I-170* with fire from a four-inch gun on December 7, 1941, during the Japanese attack on Pearl Harbor, HI.

8070. Ship from the United States to surrender to the Japanese in World War II was the 370-ton shallow-draft river gunboat *Wake,* which carried two three-inch pieces. The ship was the target of a surprise assault on December 8, 1941, at Shanghai. The crew attempted in vain to scuttle the ship before surrendering. The captured ship, renamed *Tataru* by the Japanese, was turned over in 1945 to the United States, which gave it to the navy of the Republic of China, which in turn renamed it *Tai Yuan.* During the civil war in China it fell into the hands of the Chinese Communists and was added to their navy.

8071. Bombing mission by American forces in Asia in World War II took place on December 9, 1941, two days after the Japanese attack on Pearl Harbor, when B-17 airplanes of the 19th Bombardment Group attacked Japanese ships off the east coast of Vigan, Luzon, Philippine Islands.

8072. Fighter plane from the United States to destroy a Japanese airplane in World War II was a Grumman F4-F Wildcat fighter of the Marines, which downed a twin-engine bomber on December 9, 1941, off Wake Island.

8073. General of the American armed forces killed in World War II was Major General Herbert Arthur Dargue, who was killed on December 12, 1941, in an airplane that crashed en route to the Pacific area.

8074. Submarine from the United States to sink a Japanese ship in World War II was the U.S.S. *Swordfish,* commanded by Lieutenant Chester Carl Smith, which torpedoed the 8,662-ton Japanese freighter *Atsutusan Maru* on December 16, 1941, off the coast of Indochina. The *Swordfish* was 311 feet long and displaced 2,350 tons. It was launched on April 1, 1939, and commissioned on July 22. The ship was destroyed by a mine on its 13th patrol in January 1945, near Okinawa, with the loss of all aboard.

8075. Bombing raid on the continental United States in World War II was made on February 23, 1942, at about 7 P.M. P.S.T., while President Franklin Delano Roosevelt was delivering his weekly "fireside chat" by radio to the American public. The Japanese submarine *I-17,* captained by Captain Kozo Nishino, fired 12 to 15 shots during the space of 20 minutes at the Barnsdall Oil Refinery in Ellwood, CA, about 12 miles west of Santa Barbara. The submarine was about half a mile offshore. One shell made a direct hit on the rigging and pumping equipment of an oil well, causing damage of about $500. Other shells made crater holes, one of which was about five feet deep. No one was injured.

8076. Naval counterattack by American forces against the Japanese in World War II was a surface engagement known as the Battle of Balikpapan, or the Battle of the Makassar Strait, which took place on February 23–24, 1942, in the harbor of Balikpapan, East Borneo. The U.S. destroyers *John D. Ford, Parrott, Pope,* and *Paul Jones,* under the command of Lieutenant Commander Paul H. Talbot, came in at night at high speed and sank a patrol craft and the transports *Tatsukami Maru* (7,064 tons), *Tsuruga Maru* (6,988 tons), *Kuretake Maru* (5,175 tons), and *Somanouri Maru* (3,519 tons).

8077. Air attack against the Japanese homeland in World War II was made on April 18, 1942, by 16 B-25 airplanes of the 17th Bombardment Group, 8th Air Force. The bombers, led by Colonel James Harold Doolittle, took off from the U.S. *Hornet.* Traveling low over the water, they dropped bombs on the cities of Tokyo, Kobe, and Nagoya, then continued straight on until they ran out of fuel and crash-landed in the Chinese countryside. The raid took the Japanese military establishment by surprise and demonstrated for the first time the vulnerability of the Japanese home islands.

8078. Sea battle in World War II fought solely by air power was the Battle of the Coral Sea, which took place on May 4–8, 1942, between Navy Task Force 17 and Vice Admiral Takeo Takagi's Japanese Carrier Striking Force. American planes took off from carriers 180 miles away from each other. The Japanese lost 39 ships. The United States lost the aircraft carrier *Lexington*. The attack was planned by Admiral Chester W. Nimitz.

8079. Aircraft carrier from the United States sunk in World War II was the 33,000-ton *Lexington,* commanded by Rear Admiral Frederick Carl Sherman, which was hit on May 8, 1942, in the Coral Sea by two bombs and two aircraft torpedoes launched from Japanese aircraft. Some 150 men were killed.

8080. American territory occupied by the Japanese in World War II was the undefended island of Attu and the island of Kiska in the Western Aleutians, which were captured on June 7, 1942. The capture was announced by the Navy on June 13. The islands were retaken by American forces in May 1943 in the only battle fought on U.S. soil during World War II.

8081. American offensive in the Pacific in World War II was undertaken on August 7, 1942, at Guadalcanal, Solomon Islands, by the Marines under Lieutenant General Alexander Archer Vandergrift. The Marines landed at Floria, Gavutu, Guadalcanal, Tanambogo, and Tulagi. The overall commander was Vice Admiral Robert Lee Ghormley, South Pacific commander.

8082. Coded military radio transmissions using a Native American language began in 1942, when the Allied and Axis powers were competing to devise communications codes that could not be deciphered by the enemy. Philip Johnston, a missionary's son who had grown up on the Navajo reservation, proposed the idea of using the Navajo language, a complicated system in which the meaning of a word is often determined by expression and pronunciation. Marine Major General Clayton B. Vogel approved the plan and recruited 420 Navajo "code talkers" to handle coded radio communications in the Pacific theater. The codes combined everyday Navajo words with about 400 special terms made up by the code talkers. Members of other tribes were employed as well. The Japanese were aware of the Navajo codes, but never broke them. They were kept top secret until 1968. The first National Navajo Code Talkers Day was held on August 14, 1982.

8083. Submarine from the United States sunk by an enemy submarine was the *Corvina,* of Task Force 72. Its length was 311 feet 9 inches, its breadth 27 feet 3 inches, its draft 15 feet 3 inches, and its displacement 2,424 tons. It was launched on May 9, 1943, at the Electric Boat Company, Groton, CT, and commissioned on August 6. It left Pearl Harbor, HI, on its first war patrol on November 4, 1943, and was torpedoed south of the Truk Islands on November 16 by Japanese submarine *I-176,* which fired three torpedoes, two of which hit. The ship, with a crew of 82, was officially presumed lost as of December 23, 1943, and the loss was announced on March 14, 1944. Commander Roderick Shanahan Rooney was in command.

8084. American civilians killed in the continental United States in World War II were Elsie Mitchell and five neighborhood children of Lakeview, OR, who tried to drag a Japanese balloon out of the woods on May 5, 1945. The balloon was armed and it exploded, killing all six. On June 7, 1949, Congress awarded $5,000 to Elsie Mitchell's husband as compensation for his loss, and $3,000 to the parents of each of the children: Edward Milian Engen, Jay Gifford, Ethel Jean Patzke, Richard Joe Patzke, and Sherman Shoemaker.

8085. Naval bombardment of the Japanese homeland in World War II was made on July 14, 1945, by the U.S. Pacific Fleet under the immediate tactical command of Rear Admiral John Franklin Shafroth. The battleships *Massachusetts, Indiana,* and *South Dakota,* the heavy cruisers *Chicago* and *Quincy,* and nine destroyers bombed the iron works in the coastal city of Kamaishi, Honshu, 275 miles northeast of Tokyo. Damage was inflicted on 342 airplanes, 4 ships, and 15 airfields.

8086. Atomic bomb explosion over enemy territory took place on August 6, 1945, over Hiroshima, Japan, from the *Enola Gay,* a B-29 airplane. The pilot was Colonel Paul Warfield Tibbets, Jr., of Miami, FL, and the bombardier was Major Thomas W. Ferebee of Mocksville, NC.

8087. Compensation of Japanese-Americans interned during World War II was enacted by Congress and signed into law on August 10, 1988. The bill provided for a payment of $20,000 to each surviving internee and a formal apology from the federal government. More than 110,000 men, women, and children of Japanese descent, including both American citizens and aliens, were rounded up from their homes in California, Arizona, Oregon, and Washington

WARS—WORLD WAR II—PACIFIC—*continued*

in the spring of 1942 and confined in rural internment camps until the end of the war, on suspicion that they might collaborate with Japan. The evacuation was carried out by executive order of President Franklin Delano Roosevelt.

WEAPONS

8088. Gunpowder mill was operated by Edward Rawson, to whom the General Court of Massachusetts granted 500 acres of land at Pecoit, MA, on June 6, 1639, on which to erect it.

8089. Germ warfare was suggested in July 1763 by Major General Jeffery Amherst, commander of the British army in North America, after a series of Native American uprisings in the Great Lakes area. Amherst suggested to Colonel Henry Bouquet that he distribute to the tribes blankets that had been used by smallpox victims. "Could it not be contrived to send the Small Pox among these disaffected tribes of Indians?" he wrote to Bouquet, who responded on July 13, 1763, "I will try to inoculate [them] with Some Blankets that may fall into their Hands." It is not known whether this stratagem was carried out. Another British officer, Captain Ecuyer, the commander of Fort Pitt (now Pittsburgh, PA), claimed to have given two infected blankets to hostile chiefs during the summer of 1763.

8090. Mine barrage was the invention of David Bushnell, who conceived the idea of floating kegs containing explosives and equipped with a gunlock and hammer that would ignite upon contact with ships. In August 1777 he attached a series of mines together in Black Point Bay, near New London, CT. Members of the crew of the British frigate *Cerberus,* commanded by Captain J. Symons, noticed a rope alongside their ship. They hauled it in, not realizing that a mine was attached to the other end. They hoisted the mine on board and it exploded, killing three of the crew and blowing a fourth into the water.

8091. Muskets produced at a government arsenal were made in 1795 at the Springfield Armory, Springfield, MA, under the direction of David Ames, the first superintendant, and Robert Orr, a master armorer. The first gunlock was filed by Alexander Crawford after a struggle of three days and was hand-stocked by Richard Beebe. In the first year, the armory produced 245 muskets.

8092. Government contract authorized by Congress for pistols was authorized on May 4, 1798, when Congress appropriated $800,000 for guns, pistols, and other weapons. The first contract was made on March 9, 1799, with Simeon North of Berlin, CT, for 500 horse pistols at $6.50 each. A second contract for 1,500 additional pistols of the same type was signed on February 6, 1880.

8093. Revolving gun was made by John Gill of Newberne, NC, in 1829. It had 14 chambers and was a percussion gun. It was never patented. The first patent for this type of gun was granted to David G. Colburn of Canton Canal, NY, on June 29, 1833.

8094. Rifled gun was made in 1834 by Cyrus Alger, who had made the first perfect bronze cannon for the Ordnance Department in 1827 at the foundry of the South Boston Iron Company.

8095. Bowie knife was invented by Colonel James Bowie in Texas about 1835. It is variously claimed that he made a weapon out of a file; that the knife was originally used by the Mexicans; and that in an encounter with Mexicans his original sword broke to within 20 inches of the hilt, leaving a shortened blade that was easier to handle. The knife had one edge and a curved point, which necessitated its being carried in a sheath.

8096. Revolver pistol with a revolving cylinder was invented in 1830 by Samuel Colt while he was traveling on the S.S. *Corlo.* With a pocket knife he whittled a wood model. He obtained a patent from England in 1835 and another from the United States on February 25, 1836, on "an improvement in revolving fire-arms." He formed the Patent Arms Manufacturing Company of Paterson, NJ, capitalized at $230,000, to manufacture them. The first revolvers produced by the factory were .34-caliber models.

8097. Land mines were invented by Captain Gabriel Jones Rains and were used against the Seminole peoples in Florida in 1840. They were later employed in the retreat from Yorktown, VA, on May 3, 1862, by Rains's Brigade under Major General John Bankhead "Jeb" Magruder during the Civil War. They were also known as booby traps and land torpedoes. They were not considered a proper or effective method of war and were outlawed, except at river defenses.

8098. Underwater torpedo operated by electric current was invented by Samuel Colt of Hartford, CT, who informed President John Tyler in a letter dated June 19, 1841, that he could sink ships by mines. He sank the gunboat *Boxer* in New York Harbor on July 4, 1842, and the 300-ton brig *Volta* on October 18, 1842. On April 13, 1843, in the presence of President Tyler, his Cabinet, General Winfield Scott, and other officials, Colt blew up a schooner on the Potomac River by an electric mine from a distance of five miles. His invention was a combination of Robert Fulton's stationary torpedo and Professor Robert Hare's galvanic current.

8099. Breech-loading cannon was invented by Benjamin Chambers, Sr., who obtained a patent on July 31, 1849, on "an improvement in movable breeches for fire-arms and the locks and appurtenances of the same." His wooden model was discovered in an old smithy and became part of the collection of the Virginia Historical Society.

8100. Airship bombing plan was a scheme to capture the Mexican port of Veracruz that was thought up by balloonist John Wise of Lancaster, PA, the first American aeronaut. He proposed to send out a ship that would serve as the launch site for a tethered balloon from which bombs could be dropped on the city. Wise petitioned Congress in 1851 for funds with which to carry out the plan, but was turned down.

8101. Rifled breech-loading steel cannon was made in 1854 by James Richards Haskell. He sold 25 to the Mexican government.

8102. Seacoast gun carriage made of wrought iron was constructed in 1855 by James Gilchrist Benton, instructor in ordnance and gunnery at the U.S. Military Academy, West Point, NY. It was immediately adopted by the federal government.

8103. Revolver that was self-cocking was the Rider model, invented by John Rider and manufactured in 1856 by E. Remington and Sons of Ilion, NY.

8104. Machine gun was invented by Charles E. Barnes of Lowell, MA, who obtained a patent on July 8, 1856, on an "improved automatic cannon." It was operated by a crank, the speed of firing depending upon the speed with which the crank was turned.

8105. Metal gun cartridge successfully produced was made by Daniel Baird Wesson of the Smith and Wesson Company, Springfield, MA, in 1857, based upon a patent granted to him on August 8, 1854. In 1860, additional patents were granted on a cartridge in which the fulminate was enclosed in the hollow annular projecting case. Metal cartridges revolutionized the firearms industry and made the breech-loading rifle possible.

8106. Revolving gun turret for ships was invented by Theodore Ruggles Timby of Brooklyn, NY (now part of New York City), who was also the first to advocate the use of iron in the construction of ships. He showed the War Department an ivory model of a revolving battery in April 1841 and filed a caveat in 1843 for "a revolving tower for offensive and defensive warfare to be used on land and water." The design was adapted from the shape of Castle Williams in New York. Twenty years elapsed before the War Department adopted the idea for use during the Civil War. Timby's revolving gun turret was installed on the Union ship *Monitor,* which defeated the Confederate ship *Merrimac* on March 9, 1862, at Hampton Roads, VA, in the first Civil War battle between ironclad ships.

8107. Rapid-fire machine gun was the Gatling gun, invented by Richard Jordan Gatling of Indianapolis, IN, who obtained a patent on November 4, 1862, on "an improvement in revolving battery guns." The first gun, which fired 250 shots a minute, was made in Indianapolis.

8108. Cartridge belt patent was granted on August 20, 1867, to Anson Mills, brevet lieutenant colonel in the Army, Fort Bridger, UT. Moisture had previously affected cartridge belts. Mills invented a woven cartridge belt, and the machinery for making it, which was adopted by both the Army and Navy.

8109. Torpedo manufacturing station was established in September 1869 on Goat Island, in the harbor of Newport, RI, under the supervision of Commander Edmund O. Matthews of the Bureau of Ordnance of the Navy Department. The purpose of the station was to instruct naval officers in the manufacture of torpedoes.

8110. Cartridge-loading machinery was invented by G. Moore Peters of Xenia, OH, who received two patents on July 7, 1885, for a round-table loading machine. One was installed at his factory, the Peters Cartridge Company, in King Mills, OH.

WEAPONS—*continued*

8111. Air gun was the "Chicago," a wooden gun marketed in March 1886 by the Markham Manufacturing Company, Plymouth, MI. It fired a size "BB" shot. In 1888 a metal gun was manufactured and on January 16, 1889, sales rights were granted to the Plymouth Iron Windmill Company.

8112. Shot tower used by an American manufacturer of ammunition was erected in 1895 by the Peters Cartridge Company at Kings Mills, OH. The factory was organized by G. Moore Peters and was incorporated on January 24, 1887.

8113. Airplane bombing experiment was made over Lake Keuka, Hammondsport, NY, on June 30, 1910, by Glenn Hammond Curtiss under the auspices of the *New York World*. Curtiss released lead missiles attached to colored streamers from a height of 50 feet toward a target 500 feet by 90 feet. He scored 10 hits and 4 misses. The tests were witnessed by Admiral William Wirt Kimball.

8114. Airplane torpedo was invented by Bradley Allen Fiske of the Navy, who obtained a patent on July 16, 1912, on a "method of and apparatus for delivering submarine torpedoes from airships." The torpedo, held rigidly in place with its bow pointing in the same direction as the airplane, was dropped under its own power.

8115. Submachine gun was the .45-caliber Thompson submachine gun, known as the "Tommy gun." It was invented by Brigadier General John Taliaferro Thompson, who organized the Auto-Ordnance Company in 1915 to build lightweight semiautomatic infantry shoulder rifles. The first model was proof-fired at the Warner and Swasey Company, Cleveland, OH, where the first gun was built. The gun weighed approximately 10 pounds and had a cyclic rate of fire of between 600 and 800 shots a minute.

8116. Tank operated by Army troops was the French-built Renault tank used in the Battle of St. Mihiel on September 12, 1918. The first chief of the Tank Corps was Brigadier General Samuel Dickerson Rockenbach, appointed in June 1919. No American-built tanks were used in World War I.

8117. Airplane bombing experiment to sink a battleship took place on July 21, 1921, near Hampton Roads, VA, in an Army bombing demonstration conducted by General William Mitchell. The target was the *Ostfriesland*, a former German battleship. Martin bombers dropped seven 2,000-pound bombs on the battleship and nearby, causing it to turn on its port side and sink stern first within 21 minutes. This was the first of several demonstrations by Mitchell with the goal of persuading military leaders to strengthen the air power of the armed forces.

8118. Semiautomatic rifle adopted as standard by the Army was the U.S. Rifle Caliber .30, M1, known as the Garand Semi-Automatic Shoulder Rifle. It was invented by John C. Garand of Somerset, MD, who obtained a patent on October 19, 1926, on an "automatic gun." It was adopted by the Army on January 9, 1936.

8119. Automatic aircraft cannon of 20 millimeters was manufactured by the Eclipse Machine Division of the Bendix Aviation Corporation, Elmira, NY, and was delivered to the Army on May 16, 1941.

8120. Heavy tank built in the United States for the Army was constructed by the Baldwin Locomotive Works, Eddystone, PA, and presented by William Henry Harman, vice president of the company, to Brigadier General Gladeon Marcus Barnes of the Army Ordnance Department on December 8, 1941. It weighed 60 tons and had a 75-millimeter (three-inch) cannon in the turret.

8121. Ship motion simulator to aid in the development of ballistic missiles fired from shipboard was built and installed in 1958 at the Cape Canaveral Missile Testing Center, Cocoa Beach, FL. It could simulate three important sea movements: roll, pitch, and vertical undulation or heave. It was designed by Loewy-Hydropress, later a division of the Baldwin-Lima-Hamilton Corporation.

8122. Tank with a turbine engine was the XM-1, known as the Abrams tank. It was powered by an AVCO Lycoming rotary diesel-fuel turbine engine that was rolled out on February 29, 1980, at the Chrysler Corporation's factory in Lima, OH. The tank had Chobham-type armor and a laser range-finder on its main gun, could attain 20 miles per hour in six seconds, and could cruise at 45 miles per hour. It cost $1.5 million. The first unit recipient was H Company, 2nd Squadron, 6th Armored Cavalry Lightning Brigade.

WEAPONS—NUCLEAR

8123. Atomic bomb explosion occurred on July 16, 1945, in a desert area at Alamogordo Air Base, 120 miles southeast of Albuquerque, NM. The shot, designated "Trinity," was part of Operation Trinity. It was a tower shot with a 100-foot height of burst.

8124. Atomic bomb dropped from an airplane over water was released from *Dave's Dream,* an Air Force B-29 Superfortress, on June 30, 1946 (21:01 Greenwich Civil Time), over the Bikini Lagoon in the Pacific Ocean. The shot, designated "Able," was part of Operation Crossroads. It had a 520-foot height of burst and caused the sinking of two transports (the *Gilliam* and the *Carlisle*) and damage to 18 other ships that were among a group of 73 vessels used as a target.

8125. Atomic bomb underwater explosion took place on July 24, 1946, in the Pacific Ocean, three miles off Bikini. The bomb was dropped from an airplane at a height of 7,000 feet and exploded 90 feet underwater. The shot, designated "Baker," was part of Operation Crossroads. It resulted in the sinking of 10 vessels (including the battleship *Arkansas*) that were set up as a target.

8126. Atomic bomb explosion to be shown on television took place on February 1, 1951, at Frenchman Flat, NV. It was the third blast set off by the Atomic Energy Commission. A camera on Mount Wilson, 300 miles away, telecast the explosion for station KTLA, Los Angeles, CA. It was shown on Channel 4 of the NBC network.

8127. Atomic bomb underground explosion was detonated on November 29, 1951, at Frenchman Flat, NV, and witnessed by a group consisting of some members of Congress and some military officers headed by Chief of Staff General Joseph Lawton Collins. The explosion, which produced a hole about 800 feet in diameter and 100 feet deep, was designated as "Uncle," a part of Operation Buster-Jangle.

8128. Hydrogen bomb was detonated on October 31, 1952, and designated as "Mike," part of Operation Ivy. It was a tower shot with a burst of 20 feet at the Elugelab Atoll at the Eniwetok Proving Ground, Marshall Islands.

8129. Nuclear cannon was a 40-foot, 85-ton cannon known as Atomic Annie or Amazon Annie, which was electronically fired at 8:30 A.M. on May 25, 1953, at Frenchman Flat, NV. A 280-millimeter projectile, 11 inches by 3 feet, was loaded by a crew of nine from the 52nd Field Artillery Group, Fort Sill, OK, and aimed at a target seven miles away. The shot produced an eight-second fireball visible for a distance of 65 miles despite the bright sunshine. The charge was touched off by scientists of the Atomic Energy Commission from a site 10 miles away. The explosion was witnessed from points three to seven miles from the target area by the secretary of defense and other executives and by 100 members of Congress.

8130. Hydrogen bomb dropped from an airplane exploded on May 20, 1956, over Namu Atoll at the northwest edge of the Bikini Atoll. It was designated as "Cherokee," a part of Operation Redwing. It created a fireball four miles in diameter.

8131. Nuclear warhead mounted on a rocket was installed on an MB-I, known as the Genie, that was fired on July 19, 1957, at Yucca Flat, NV. It was an air-to-air rocket and contained a built-in guidance mechanism. It was made by the Douglas Aircraft Company, Santa Monica, CA, and was fired from an F89 Scorpion jet.

8132. Nuclear warhead fired from a Polaris submarine was fired on May 6, 1962, from the U.S.S. *Ethan Allen,* submerged off Christmas Island in the Pacific test area. The missile sped skyward in a parabolic trajectory and then exploded. It carried a force estimated at 500,000 tons of TNT.

WEAPONS—ROCKETS AND MISSILES

8133. Handheld rocket launcher was developed by Capt. L.A. Skinner and C.N. Hickman and produced on June 14, 1942, by the General Electric Company, Bridgeport, CT. Dubbed the "bazooka," after a crude wind instrument made of pipes invented by American comedian Bob Burns, it weighed 12 pounds and was operated by a two-man team. It consisted of a smoothbore steel tube about 50 inches long and 2.5 inches in diameter, open at both ends. Attached to the tube were a shoulder stock and front and rear grips for the gunner, together with sights and an electric battery that set off the rocket-propelled charge when the launcher trigger was squeezed. The rocket was nearly two feet long. It fired about 300 yards. The first 5,000 bazookas were completed within 30 days and were used in the field mainly against tanks and armored vehicles.

8134. Ballistic missile was a Corporal, fired on May 22, 1947, at the White Sands Proving Ground, NM. It responded accurately to guidance commands and reached a range of 63 miles.

8135. Air-to-air rocket was the Mighty Mouse, created by the Navy's Bureau of Ordnance for use by interceptor planes to destroy bombers. The rocket, which was placed in production in October 1951, was 4 feet long, weighed 18 pounds, and had a diameter of 2.75 inches. The rockets could be fired one at a time or in salvos of 6, 12, 18, or 24.

WEAPONS—ROCKETS AND MISSILES—
continued

8136. Rocket to intercept an airplane was a Nike, fired on November 27, 1951, at the White Sands Proving Ground, NM, at an aerial target. The missile detonated about 25 feet from the target, which was flying at a range of about 15 miles at an altitude of 33,000 feet and a speed of 300 miles per hour.

8137. Jet drone target missile was a Ryan Firebee pilotless jet plane made by the Ryan Aeronautical Company, San Diego, CA, and first flown on April 23, 1954, at the Holloman Air Development Center, Alamogordo, NM. It was powered by a 1,000-pound-thrust jet engine and was able to fly at a speed of more than 600 miles per hour at altitudes up to 42,500 feet. It was air- or ground-launched, pilotless, and flown by electronic remote control from a ground station. It was 17 feet 3 inches long and 5 feet 10 inches high, had a wingspan of 11 feet 2 inches, and weighed 1,848 pounds gross.

8138. Intermediate-range ballistic missile was a Jupiter, fired on May 31, 1957, from the Atlantic Missile Range, Cape Canaveral, FL. The firing was conducted by the Jet Propulsion Laboratories and the Army Ballistic Missile Agency.

8139. Rocket to intercept a supersonic target missile was a Nike Hercules missile, fired in November 1958, that destroyed a supersonic target missile traveling faster than 1,500 miles per hour at an altitude greater than 60,000 feet.

8140. Ship to fire a Polaris missile was the *Observation Island,* commissioned on December 5, 1958. It was 563 feet long overall and had a beam of 76 feet, a full load displacement of 16,100 tons, a draft of 24 feet, and a speed of 20 knots. It was commanded by Captain Leslie Slack. Formerly, it had been the S.S. *Empire State Mariner,* a merchant cargo ship that had been launched on August 15, 1953, by the New York Shipbuilding Corporation, Camden, NJ, and transferred to the Navy on September 10, 1956. On August 27, 1959, a Polaris missile was launched from the *Observation Island* seven miles off Cape Canaveral, FL. The missile, fired by compressed air, ignited successfully at 70 feet and sped 700 miles to the target area. It was a solid-propellant two-stage missile, 28 feet long and 4 feet 6 inches in diameter.

8141. Guided missile launched from a nuclear submarine was a Regulus I, launched on March 25, 1960, from the *Halibut* off Oahu, HI. The missile was guided over its simulated target on Lehua Island, 120 miles away, before landing, about 15 minutes after launching, at Bonham Air Force Base, Kauai, HI, 20 miles beyond the target.

8142. Submerged submarine to fire a Polaris missile was the U.S.S. *George Washington,* commanded by Commander James Butler Osborn, which submerged to a depth of 90 feet about 30 miles off Cape Canaveral, FL, on July 20, 1960, and fired a 28,500-pound Polaris missile at 1:39 P.M. The 28-foot two-stage rocket traveled 1,150 statute miles eastward in less than 14 minutes. A second missile was fired at 4:32 P.M. News of the firing was sent to President Dwight David Eisenhower: "Polaris ... from out of the deep to target. Perfect."

8143. Launching silos for Atlas F missiles were built by General Dynamics–Astronautics and turned over to the Strategic Air Command on September 13, 1962. Twelve underground silos, 175 feet deep, were built around Salina, KS. The complex cost about $150 million. The missiles had a range of 6,000 miles.

8144. MX intercontinental ballistic missile base was built in 1986 at Warren Air Force Base, WY. The MX were multiple-warhead nuclear missiles capable of being transported underground by rail to any of thousands of secret launch sites. The MX system was designed to survive an enemy's nuclear first strike and to give the United States a first-strike capability of its own. The $30 billion system, approved on June 7, 1979, by President Jimmy Carter, was only partially completed.

8145. Cruise missiles used in war were launched on January 16, 1991, the first day of the Gulf War, when approximately 100 Tomahawk cruise missiles were fired from American ships in the Persian Gulf. They struck targets in Baghdad, Iraq.

8146. Destruction of an attacking missile by a defensive missile in combat occurred on January 18, 1991, when a SCUD missile launched from Iraq during the Gulf War was blown out of the sky over northern Saudi Arabia by an American-made Patriot antimissile missile.

WRITING IMPLEMENTS

8147. Invisible ink used in diplomatic correspondence was employed by Silas Deane in 1776. As a member of the Committee of Secret Correspondence, organized on November 29, 1775, "for the sole purpose of corresponding with our friends in Great Britain, Ireland, and other parts of the world," he left Philadelphia, PA, on March 5, 1776, and arrived in France on May 4 on a mission to purchase military supplies on credit. From France, he sent letters to John Jay, member of the Continental Congress, that were interlined with invisible ink, which was invented by Sir James Jay in 1776. Using this method, Deane sent the first authentic account that Congress received of the determination of the British to reduce the colonies to unconditional surrender. The writing was done with a solution of tannic acid. To make the ink visible, the paper was sponged with ferrous sulfate, which combined with the tannic acid to form a dark compound.

8148. Pencil factory was established by William Monroe of Concord, MA, in June 1812. He manufactured about 30 lead pencils of unfinished cedar, unpolished, very thin, with square leads, which he sold to Benjamin Adams, a hardware dealer of Union Street, Boston, MA. Adams then contracted to purchase all the pencils Monroe could produce.

8149. Ink was manufactured by the Thaddeus Davids Ink Company, established by Thaddeus Davids in New York City in 1825. The ink was bottled in various sizes and sold at retail. The first year, a few hundred bottles were manufactured.

8150. Steel pens commercially produced were manufactured by Richard Esterbrook, who founded the Esterbrook Steel Pen Manufacturing Company and established a factory in Camden, NJ, in 1858.

8151. Pencil with an attached eraser was patented by Hyman L. Lipman of Philadelphia, PA, who received a patent on March 30, 1858. The pencil had a groove into which was "secured a piece of prepared rubber, glued in at one end."

8152. Indelible pencil was invented by Edson P. Clark of Northampton, MA, who obtained a patent on July 10, 1866. It had a "filling composed of silver, black lead, calcined gypsum and lamp-black or asphaltum" that was shellacked to the groove in the wood.

8153. Fountain pen that was practical was invented by Lewis Edson Waterman and was manufactured in 1884 by the L.E. Waterman Company in New York City. The first year, about 200 fountain pens were manufactured. They were originally manufactured by hand. Waterman also invented the machinery to produce fountain pens in commercial quantities.

8154. Ball-point pen was patented on October 30, 1888, by John J. Loud of Weymouth, MA. The patent was on a pen having a spheroidal marking point capable of revolving in all directions.

8155. Pen with truly erasable ink was the Eraser Mate pen, which went on the market in April 1979. It was a refillable ball-point pen, a product of the Paper Mate Division of the Gillette Company, Boston, MA. The ink was 1 million times thicker than water. The pen was made under a patent issued on June 27, 1978, to Frank Andrew Miller of West Los Angeles and Henry Peper, Jr., of Pacific Palisades, CA, for "ball-point instruments writing with improved transitorially erasable trace and ink compositions therefor." The pen was produced in Santa Monica, CA.

Subject Index

Each entry in the main body of the text begins with a boldface head. The Subject Index is an alphabetical listing of these headings. Also included are heads representing "internal" firsts that appear as part of larger entries. Cross-references are given for various populations; they are introduced by the key word followed by a colon (for example, Native American: School for Native Americans to be permanently established). To find an entry in the text, please go to the italicized number.

A

Abdominal operation other than a cesarean section, *5076*

Abolition newspaper, *5637*

Abolition organization, *2243*

Abortion legalized by a state as a medical procedure, *6835*

Abrasive for commercial use, *4442*

Absentee voting law enacted by a state, *3431*

Absolute monarch to visit the United States, *6650*

Abstract paintings, *1217*

Academic costume standardization for colleges, *2957*

Academic hall of fame, *5582*

Academy, *2929*

Accident insurance company, *4504*

Accident reports by employers, *4563*

Accounting society, *3753*

Accounting society (national), *3754*

Accounting society (state), *3756*

Ace in World War II, *1616*

Ace of Aces from the United States, *1611*

Ace to fly a jet, *1620*

Ace to fly under American colors, *1612*

Acetylene gas, *4437*

Achromatic lenses, *5833*

Acidophilus milk, *3876*

Acoustic microscope, *6750*

Act inaugurating the Civil War, *7946*

Actor of American birth, *1273*

Actor to appear abroad, *1276*

Actor to have an exclusive movie contract, *5524*

Actor to receive curtain applause, *1275*

Actors' home, *1277*

Actors' union, *4615*

Acupuncture treatment center, *4852*

Adaptable railroad freight car, *6392*

Adding machine absolutely accurate at all times, *2377*

Adding machine successfully marketed, *2378*

Adding machine to employ depressible keys, *2375*

Adding machine to print totals and subtotals, *2376*

Addressograph, *2365*

Adhesive and medicated plaster, *4942*

Adhesive postage stamps, *6051*

Adjustable stadium, *7512*

Admiral of the Navy, *5271*

Admission fee charged at a collegiate sporting event, *7309*

Adventist church to accept Saturday as the Sabbath, *6529*

Advertisement on a space vehicle, *2348*

Advertising agency, *2322*

Advertising association to combat business abuses, *2452*

Advertising magazine, *4726*

Advertising school, *2921*

Advertising show to be held annually, *2412*

Aerial camera with nine lenses for large-scale mapping, *5845*

Aerial ferry, *3589*

Aerial photograph, *5815*

Aerial photograph in natural colors, *5826*

Aerial photograph showing the lateral curvature of the horizon and the beginning of the stratosphere, *5828*

Aerocycle, *1570*

Aeronautical engineering course at a college, *3244*

African-American: Abolition organization, *2243*

African-American: Air Force Academy graduates who were African-American, *3192*

African-American: Air Force chief master sergeant who was African-American, *5137*

African-American: Air Force general who was African-American, *5135*

African-American: Air Force general who was an African-American woman, *5141*

African-American: Airline flight attendant who was an African-American woman, *1412*

African-American: Ambassador who was an African-American woman, *3994*

African-American: American College of Surgeons member who was African-American, *5047*

African-American: Antislavery book, *2023*

African-American: Antislavery magazine, *4707*

African-American: Army chaplain who was African-American, *5201*

African-American: Army general who was African-American, *5154*

African-American: Army general who was African-American to lead an infantry brigade in combat, *5159*

African-American: Army general who was an African-American woman, *5162*

African-American: Army major who was African-American, *5169*

African-American: Army pilot who was African-American to shoot down an Axis airplane in World War II, *8063*

African-American: Army training camp for African-American officers, *5184*

African-American: Art exhibition of importance by an African-American artist, *1209*

African-American: Artist of renown who was African-American, *1209*

African-American: Astronaut to fly in space who was African-American, *7049*

African-American: Astronaut to fly in space who was an African-American woman, *7049*

African-American: Athlete who was African-American to win the James E. Sullivan Memorial Trophy, *1720*

African-American: Athlete who was an African-American woman to win the James E. Sullivan Memorial Trophy, *1721*

African-American: Aviator who was African-American, *1609*

African-American: Bank for African-Americans operated by African-Americans, *3771*

African-American: Bank for freed African-American slaves, *3766*

African-American: Baptist churches for African-Americans, *6546*

African-American: Baseball coach in the major leagues who was African-American, *7103*

African-American: Baseball game between an all-white team and an all-African-American team, *7116*

African-American: Baseball player in the American League who was African-American, *7147*

African-American: Baseball player on a white team who was African-American, *7140*

African-American: Baseball player who was African-American to hit a home run in a World Series, *7152*

African-American: Baseball player who was African-American to win the Most Valuable Player award, *1723*

African-American: Baseball team of African-American players to play professionally, *7164*

African-American: Basketball professional player who was African-American, *7173*

African-American: Black Power advocate, *2262*

African-American: Boxer of fame who was African-American, *7249*

African-American: Boxing referee in a heavyweight championship match who was African-American, *7246*

African-American: Business organization for African-Americans (national), *2450*

African-American: Cabinet member who was African-American, *6119*

African-American: Cabinet member who was an African-American woman, *6121*

African-American: Catholic African-Americans, *6458*

African-American: Catholic archbishop who was an African-American, *6480*

African-American: Catholic bishop who was an American-born African-American, *6480*

African-American: Catholic community of African-American nuns, *6462*

African-American: Catholic parish church for African-Americans, *6464*

African-American: Catholic priest who was African-American, *6467*

African-American: Catholic seminary for the education of African-American priests, *3278*

African-American: Chairman of a major political party who was African-American, *3345*

African-American: Chairman of the Joint Chiefs of Staff who was African-American, *5129*

African-American: Chief justice of a state supreme court who was African-American, *2720*

African-American: Christian worship services organized by African-American slaves, *6515*

African-American: City founded by an African-American pioneer, *2187*

African-American: Civil rights law enacted by Congress, *2254*

African-American: Civil rights sit-in, *2260*

African-American: Coach of a professional basketball team who was African-American, *7177*

African-American: Coast Guard Academy graduate who was African-American, *3210*

African-American: Coast Guard serviceman who was African-American, *5209*

African-American: Coin bearing the likeness of an African-American, *5379*

African-American: College baseball player who was African-American, *7142*

African-American: College for African-American students, *2949*

African-American: College graduate who was African-American, *3009*

African-American: College graduate who was an African-American woman, *3010*

African-American: College to enroll African-American and white students on equal terms, *2943*

African-American: Commander of a combat ship who was African-American, *5295*

African-American: Commissioned officer in the Marine Corps who was African-American, *5239*

African-American: Congregational Church minister who was African-American, *6522*

African-American: Congressional page who was African-American, *2592*

African-American: Congressional representative who was African-American, *2603*

African-American: Congressional representative who was an African-American woman, *2617*

African-American: Congressional standing committee headed by an African-American, *2591*

African-American: Consul who was African-American, *3988*

African-American: Cosmetics company that catered exclusively to African-American customers, *2444*

African-American: Croix de Guerre awarded to an African-American, *1648*

African-American: Daughters of the American Revolution member who was African-American, *5718*

African-American: Delegate to a national political convention who was African-American, *3335*

African-American: District attorney who was African-American, *2716*

African-American: Doctor of Philosophy degree awarded to an African-American scholar, *2978*

African-American doctor to become a member of a medical association, *4966*

African-American: Election law granting African-American men the right to vote, *3428*

African-American: Emancipation proclamation, *2252*

African-American: Episcopal bishop who was African-American, *6551*

African-American: Execution for slave trading carried out by the federal government, *2797*

African-American: Federal administrator who was an African-American woman, *2257*

African-American: Football player who was African-American to win the Heisman Memorial Trophy, *1726*

African-American: Fugitive slave law enacted by Congress, *2247*

African-American: Golf champion of African-American and Asian descent, *7370*

African-American: Golf player in an official amateur tournament who was African-American, *7355*

African-American: Governor who was African-American, *7621*

African-American: Heavyweight boxing champion of the world who was African-American, *7252*

African-American: History of African-Americans, *1871*

African-American history trail, *5979*

African-American: Hockey player on an amateur team who was African-American, *7380*

African-American: Hospital and asylum for African-Americans, *4874*

African-American: Hymnbook compiled by an African-American editor, *1973*

African-American: Insurance company owned by African-Americans, *4501*

African-American: Intercollegiate football game between African-American colleges, *7323*

African-American: Jim Crow law, *2255*

African-American: Judge of a federal district court who was African-American, *2729*

African-American: Judge of a federal district court who was an African-American woman, *2729*

African-American: Judge of the U.S. Court of Appeals who was an African-American woman, *2732*

African-American: Judge on the federal bench who was African-American, *2727*

African-American: Judge who was an African-American woman, *2726*

African-American: Justice of a state supreme court who was African-American, *2720*

African-American: Land grant college for African-American students, *2895*

African-American: Senator elected on an anti-slavery ticket, *2250*

African-American: Senator who was African-American, *2649*

African-American: Senator who was African-American to be elected by popular vote, *2658*

African-American: Senator who was an African-American woman, *2661*

African-American: Sheriff who was an African-American woman, *4156*

African-American: Slave importation ban enacted by a colony, *2242*

African-American: Slave rebellion after the Revolution, *2249*

African-American: Slave to be emancipated, *2245*

African-American: Slavery ban enacted for a territory of the United States, *2246*

African-American: Slavery emancipation law enacted by a colony, *2239*

African-American: Slavery emancipation law enacted by a state, *2244*

African-American: Sorority for African-American students at a college, *2988*

African-American speaker to deliver the keynote speech at a Democratic National Convention, *2617*

African-American: State law to end de facto segregation in schools, *2261*

African-American: State legislator who was African-American to represent a constituency with a white majority, *7625*

African-American: State legislator who was an African-American woman, *7631*

African-American: State legislators who were African-American, *7624*

African-American student elected to Phi Beta Kappa, *2978*

African-American: Supreme Court justice who was African-American, *2763*

African-American: Surgeon general who was African-American, *4215*

African-American: Symphony on an African-American folk theme, *1297*

African-American: Tap dancer of renown, *1233*

African-American: Television dramatic series in which an African-American performer had a starring role, *7790*

African-American: Television news commentator who was African-American, *5620*

African-American: Television series in which an African-American performer had a starring role, *7783*

African-American: Television variety talent show series with an African-American cast, *7776*

African-American: Tennis champion who was African-American, *7538*

African-American: Texas Ranger who was African-American, *4134*

African-American: Theology school graduate who was African-American, *3270*

African-American to vote under authority of the 15th Amendment, *3429*

African-American: Town built by free African-Americans, *2183*

African-American town in continuous existence, *2193*

African-American: Transcontinental flight made by African-Americans in their own airplane, *1458*

African-American: Umpire in organized baseball who was African-American, *7102*

African-American: Union regiment in the Civil War made up of African-American soldiers, *7966*

African-American: United Nations delegate who was African-American, *3992*

African-American: University for African-American students, *2951*

African-American: University for African-American students founded as a Catholic institution, *2964*

African-American: Vice presidential candidate who was African-American, *3406*

African-American: Vice presidential candidate who was an African-American woman, *3415*

African-American: Wedding of African-Americans, *4812*

African-American: West Point graduate who was African-American, *3199*

African-American: Year in which there were no reported lynchings of African-Americans, *2258*

African-American: Young Men's Christian Association branch for African-Americans, *5712*

African Methodist Episcopal bishop, *6564*

African Methodist Episcopal church convention, *6563*

African Methodist Episcopal preacher who was a woman, *6565*

African slaves in America, *2238*

Agricultural book, *1757*

Agricultural book distinctly American, *1758*

Agricultural college to be chartered by a state, *2891*

Agricultural dictionary, *1799*

Agricultural encyclopedia, *1831*

Agricultural experiment farm, *1002*

Agricultural experiment station operated by a state, *1003*

Agricultural fair held annually, *1001*

Agricultural journal, *4703*

Agricultural seed distribution on a national scale, *1015*

Agriculture bureau scientific publication, *1763*

Agriculture organization (national), *1089*

Agriculture professor at a college, *2890*

Agriculture society, *1087*

AIDS epidemic, *2878*

AIDS policy coordinator for the federal government, *4192*

Air attack against the Japanese homeland in World War II, *8077*

Air attack on Germany by the Army Air Force in World War II, *8061*

Air bag requirement by the federal government, *4231*

Air brake, *6420*

Air-conditioned car, *5449*

Air-conditioned office building, *2065*

Air-conditioned public elementary school, *2120*

Air-conditioned railroad cars, *6386*

Air-conditioned train, *6430*

Air conditioner for home use, *4333*

Air conditioner patent, *4413*

Air defense military organization, *5134*

Air Force academy, *3190*

Air Force Academy cadets who were women, *3193*

Air Force Academy graduate who was Native American, *3191*

Air Force Academy graduates who were African-American, *3192*

Air Force ace in Vietnam, *1624*

Air force branch of the military, *5133*

Air Force chairman of the Joint Chiefs of Staff, *5136*

Air Force chief master sergeant who was African-American, *5137*

Air Force general who was a woman, *5140*

Air Force general who was African-American, *5135*

Air Force general who was an African-American woman, *5141*

Air Force Medal of Honor for action in the Korean War, *1667*

Air Force military engineer who was a woman, *5139*

Air Force Reserve officer who was a nun, *5138*

Air gun, *8111*

Air hero in World War II, *1615*

Air Mail Flyer's Medal of Honor, *1642*

Air piracy law, *2784*

Air pollution law of importance enacted by Congress, *3718*

Air raid shelter, *4088*

Air raid shelter for a community, *4090*

Air rights lease, *2064*

Air service of the Army, *5130*

Air service under one command, *5131*

Air squadron of the Army in World War I, *8041*

Air-to-air rocket, *8135*

Air-to-ground public telephone service, *7748*

Airborne express delivery service, *2489*

Aircraft carrier, *6934*

Aircraft carrier from the United States sunk in World War II, *8079*

Aircraft carrier with an angle deck, *6939*

Aircraft liability and property damage insurance, *4516*

Airline flight attendant who was a woman, *1412*

Airline flight attendant who was an African-American woman, *1412*

Airline to carry 100 million passengers, *1423*

Airline to install rear-facing passenger seats, *1419*

Airmail and express service by helicopter, *6031*

Airmail by missile, *6034*

Airmail contractor, *6021*

Airmail dispatched from a post office in a balloon, *6014*

Airmail flight by rocket, *6026*

Airmail letter sheet, *6023*

Airmail long-distance night service, *6020*

Airmail pickup by an airplane without landing, *6024*

Airmail pilot, *6015*

Airmail postal card, *6047*

Airmail regular delivery service by autogiro, *6029*

Airmail regular service, *6016*

Airmail service from ship to shore, *6022*

Airmail stamps, *6063*

Airplane accident in a solo military airplane that was fatal, *1392*

Airplane accident involving a woman that was fatal, *1393*

Airplane accident that was fatal, *1387*

Airplane bombing experiment, *8113*

Airplane bombing experiment to sink a battleship, *8117*

Airplane bombing raid by a mercenary soldier, *2781*

Airplane bombing raid by an American air unit, *8044*

Airplane bombing raid by criminals, *2778*

Airplane catapulted from an airship, *1452*

Airplane diesel engine, *1498*

Airplane disaster involving more than 100 persons, *1404*

Airplane endurance flight exceeding one hour, *1427*

Airplane flight, *1426*

Airplane flight between New York and Alaska, *1446*

Airplane flight from a ship, *1433*

Airplane flight longer than 500 miles, *1444*

Airplane flight over the North Pole, *6728*

Airplane flight over the South Pole, *6729*

Airplane flight over water, *1432*

Airplane flight to land at the North Pole, *6731*

Airplane flight to land at the South Pole, *6733*

Airplane flight to the deck of a carrier, *1434*

Airplane flight under a bridge, *1437*

Airplane flying school, *3188*

Airplane flying school operated by a woman, *7294*

Airplane human pickup, *1463*

Airplane in actual military operation, *1485*

Airplane instructor's license, *1601*

Airplane loop-the-loop, *1443*

Airplane model to make a sustained flight under its own power, *1425*

Airplane outfitted with a machine gun, *1484*

Airplane propeller blade of hollow steel, *1502*

Airplane purchased by the federal government, *1389*

Airplane race between cities, *7293*

Airplane race of importance in which both men and women were contestants, *7298*

Airplane race won by an American in Europe, *7290*

Airplane refueling attempt in midair, *1496*

Airplane rescue at sea, *1435*

Airplane rescue at sea by another airplane, *1438*

Airplane round trip, *1430*

Airplane round-trip flight over water, *1441*

Airplane scheduled passenger flight at night, *1410*

Airplane sea flight out of sight of land, *1435*

Airplane sleeping berths, *1413*

Airplane sold commercially, *1388*

Airplane solo flight by an American woman, *1596*

Airplane takeoff from a hotel roof, *1442*

Airplane to fly faster than 200 miles per hour, *1448*

Airplane to fly faster than the speed of sound, *1468*

Airplane to fly higher than a mile in altitude, *1431*

Airplane to fly with a load of 100,000 pounds, *1471*

Airplane to land on the White House lawn, *6255*

Airplane torpedo, *8114*

Airplane used for newspaper reporting, *5606*

Airplane with a delta wing, *1402*

Airplane with a fuselage of molded plywood, *1395*

Airplane with ailerons, *1394*

Airport baggage scanning system, *1511*

Airport fog disposal unit, *1509*

Airport manager who was a woman, *1507*

Airport owned by a city, *1503*

Airport owned by a county, *1505*

Airport runway illumination, *1504*

Airship, *1512*

Airship bombing plan, *8100*

Airship disaster, *1513*

Airship filled with helium gas, *1519*

Airship for private commercial operation, *1526*

Airship from the United States lost to enemy action in World War II, *8064*

Airship made completely of metal, *1524*

Airship ordered by the federal government, *1514*

Airship passenger transfer to an airplane, *1525*

Airship race, *7291*

Airship that was certified by the Federal Aviation Administration, *1528*

Airship to land and take off from an oceangoing steamship, *1527*

Airship to land on a roof, *1517*

Airship transfer of mail to a train, *1523*

Airship with an enclosed cabin, *1522*

Alarm clock, *7898*

Albert Medal presented to a person born in America, *1647*

Alcohol abuse programs required in schools by the federal government, *2679*

Alcohol prohibition enforcement officers, *2672*

Alcohol prohibition law enacted by a state, *2676*

Alcohol prohibition law enacted by Congress, *2684*

Alcohol prohibition vote taken in Congress, *2682*

Alcohol temperance law enacted by a colony, 2674

Alcoholics' asylum, 4879

Alfalfa, 1012

Algebra book, 1883

Algebra book by an American-born author, 1885

Alkaline dry cell battery, 3475

All-blind airplane flight, 1451

All-color television station to televise live local programs, 7805

All-electric railroad, 6342

All-fiction pulp magazine, 4731

All-glass windowless structure, 2089

All-male dance company in the United States, 2908

All-metal roller skate, 7464

All-news radio station, 6303

All-star football game, 7327

All-Star Game of the National Basketball Association, 7174

All-star major league baseball game, 7130

All-welded self-propelled seagoing petroleum carrier ship, 6892

Allergy book, 1916

Allergy journal, 4764

Alligator farm, 1072

Almanac, 1764

Almanac with a continuous existence, 1766

Alternative medicine department in a federal research institution, 5067

Aluminum cans with tab openings, 4289

Aluminum-faced building, 2091

Aluminum foil, 4340

Aluminum in metallic form, 4475

Aluminum pots, 4297

Aluminum streetcar, 6407

Aluminum used commercially in a transmission conductor, 3471

Amateur athletic competition, 7547

Amateur athletic games held indoors, 7543

Amateur athletic games held outdoors, 7544

Amateur boxing match for women, 7247

Amateur golf championship tournament for women, 7342

Amateur golf tournament, 7339

Amateur open swimming championship meet, 7515

Ambassador assassinated in office, 3995

Ambassador from the United States who was a woman, 3991

Ambassador to the United Nations who was a woman, 3996

Ambassador to the United States who was a woman, 3990

Ambassador to Vietnam after the end of the Vietnam War, 3997

Ambassador who was an African-American woman, 3994

Ambassador who was Jewish, 3989

Ambulance air service, 4824

Ambulance equipped for mobile coronary care, 4826

Ambulance service for hospitals, 4823

Ambulance service with an incubator, 4825

Ambulance ship designed and built by the Navy as a hospital, 5022

Ambulance ship for first aid to boaters and pleasure craft, 4827

Ambulance ship operated by the Navy, 5015

American Bar Association member who was a woman, 4640

American base in Antarctica that was permanent, 6730

American civilians killed in the continental United States in World War II, 8084

American College of Surgeons member who was African-American, 5047

American College of Surgeons members who were women, 5047

American combatant to die in World War I, 8027

American Derby horse race, 7393

American division to cross the Rhine River in World War I, 8047

American elected to the Royal Society of London, 1974

American expeditionary force to land in Africa in World War II, 8055

American expeditionary force to land in Europe in World War II, 8052

American flag displayed from the right hand of the Statue of Liberty, 1130

American flag displayed on a man-of-war, 1119

American flag flown in battle, 1120

American flag flown over a fortress of the Old World, 1125

American flag flown over a schoolhouse, 1126

American flag made of American bunting to fly over the Capitol, 1129

American flag on the high seas, 1121

American flag saluted by a foreign nation, 1122

American flag saluted by a foreigner, 1117

American flag to orbit the earth, 1131

American flag to represent the United States, 1118

American gazetteer, 1814

American history book of importance whose author was a woman, *1865*

American history chair at a college, *3096*

American imprisoned as an enemy agent in the Tower of London, *8004*

American land victory without infantry in World War II, *8062*

American Legion convention of veterans of World War I, *5312*

American losses in the Pacific in World War II, *8067*

American offensive in the Pacific in World War II, *8081*

American "Robin Hood", *2769*

American Stock Exchange members who were women, *3831*

American territory occupied by the Japanese in World War II, *8080*

American to be recognized by Tibetan Buddhists as a reincarnated lama, *6440*

American to hug the Queen of England, *6656*

American to sail to Europe to fight in World War I, *8025*

American to set foot on Antarctica, *6722*

American woman of European descent to be made a Native American chief, *6647*

American woman to become a countess, *6644*

American woman to become a member of the British Parliament, *6648*

Americans killed by British soldiers in the Revolution, *7986*

Amphibious seaplane glider, *1554*

Amphibious vehicle, *6943*

Analytical chemistry course requirement for pharmacy students, *3146*

Anarchist, *4551*

Anatomy book, *1896*

Anatomy lectures, *3129*

Anatomy research institute, *5055*

Ancient and modern history chair at a college, *3095*

Anesthesiology professor at a college, *3158*

Anesthetic administered in childbirth, *4830*

Anesthetic in dentistry, *4829*

Angle iron, *2040*

Animal disease of American origin, *5122*

Animal fired into space to orbit the earth, *7024*

Animal humane society, *5735*

Animal humane society (national), *5738*

Animal husbandry professor at a college, *2896*

Animal rights organization (national), *5740*

Animals to survive a space flight, *7023*

Animated cartoon, *5531*

Animated cartoon in color, *5533*

Animated cartoon made for television, *7782*

Animated cartoon made with cel animation, *5532*

Animated cartoon series on prime-time television, *7786*

Animated cartoon with sound, *5535*

Animated feature-length cartoon in Technicolor, *5536*

Animated film inducted into the National Film Registry, *5538*

Animated photograph projection before a theater audience, *5529*

Animated picture machine, *5528*

Animated three-dimensional cartoon in Technicolor, *5537*

Animation for technical purposes, *5534*

Annulment of a marriage by court decree, *4805*

Annunciator, *2358*

Anthology of American literature, *1740*

Anthracite coal, *3502*

Anthracite coal burned experimentally, *3503*

Anthracite coal used commercially, *3504*

Anthrax vaccine for human immunization, *4924*

Anthropology laboratory, *6748*

Anti-aging skin cream, *4063*

Anti-Masonic Party convention, *3348*

Anti-Monopoly Party convention, *3362*

Anti-saloon organization, *2680*

Antibacterial mouthwash, *4072*

Antibiotic, *4998*

Antibiotic synthetically manufactured, *5002*

Antimatter to be observed, *6815*

Antiquarian bookseller, *1784*

Antislavery book, *2023*

Antislavery magazine, *4707*

Antislavery party, *3351*

Antismoking law enacted by a colony, *2696*

Antitoxin laboratory established by a public health department, *4200*

Antitrust law enacted by a state, *2520*

Antitrust law enacted by Congress, *2521*

Apartment house cooperative, *2126*

Apartment house to occupy a square city block, *2127*

Apartment house with a modern layout, *2125*

Appendectomy, *5080*

Apple parer, *4367*

Apples, *3892*

Applied chemistry professor at a college, *3234*

Apprentice continuation school, *3293*

Aquarium for large marine animals, *1190*

Aquarium with an inland saltwater environment, *1187*

Army Reserve Officers Training Corps units, *5183*

Army school for chaplains, *3202*

Army secret service bureau, *5181*

Army signal corps, *5180*

Army specialist corps for women, *5190*

Army training camp for African-American officers, *5184*

Army uniform, *5142*

Army veterinary corps, *5021*

Army war college, *3200*

Army War College graduates who were women, *3206*

Arsenal of the federal government, *5126*

Art auction televised on a coast-to-coast circuit, *1230*

Art exhibition of importance by an African-American artist, *1209*

Art magazine, *4722*

Art museum, *5593*

Art museum devoted to work by women, *5599*

Art museum of importance devoted to the work of an individual woman, *5600*

Art museum to sell reproductions, *5596*

Articles of Confederation, *1102*

Artificial animal breeding cooperative organization, *1083*

Artificial aortic valve, *5053*

Artificial eyes, *5051*

Artificial gene, *5063*

Artificial-ice manufacturing plant, *4432*

Artificial ice skating rink of Olympic size, *7435*

Artificial insemination for women to be permitted by a state, *5117*

Artificial insemination of a woman resulting in conception, *5113*

Artificial leather, *7878*

Artificial leg patent, *5050*

Artificial lens for cataract patients, *5052*

Artificial lightning demonstration, *6770*

Artificial snow from a natural cloud, *6774*

Artist in the English colonies, *1196*

Artist of American birth to head the Royal Academy of London, *1202*

Artist of importance to be born in America, *1200*

Artist of renown who was African-American, *1209*

Artist to come to America, *1195*

Artists' organization (national), *1205*

Artmobile, *5598*

Arts and letters organization (national), *5716*

Arts and sciences national organization member who was a woman, *5709*

Arts and sciences organization (national), *5709*

Artwork to incorporate lightning, *1220*

Ascent of Mount Everest by an American, *7588*

Ascent of Mount Everest by an American woman, *7588*

Asian: Miss America contestant of Asian descent, *3628*

Asphalt-covered racetrack, *7510*

Asteroid named for an American president, *6678*

Astronaut international rescue agreement, *7037*

Astronaut to be launched into space, *7029*

Astronaut to become a general, *7044*

Astronaut to become an admiral, *7043*

Astronaut to converse with an aquanaut, *7033*

Astronaut to fly in space who was African-American, *7049*

Astronaut to fly in space who was an African-American woman, *7049*

Astronaut to orbit the earth, *7030*

Astronaut to orbit the earth on two trips, *7032*

Astronaut to walk in space, *7031*

Astronaut who was a civilian to orbit the earth, *7035*

Astronaut who was a mother, *7048*

Astronaut who was a woman to fly in space, *7048*

Astronaut who was a woman to live in a space station, *7054*

Astronaut who was a woman to pilot the space shuttle, *7053*

Astronauts to die in a spacecraft, *7036*

Astronauts to fly free in space, *7050*

Astronauts to land on the moon, *7040*

Astronauts to orbit the moon, *7038*

Astronauts to participate in an international spaceflight, *7046*

Astronauts to rendezvous in space with another spacecraft, *7034*

Astronauts to retrieve a manmade object from the moon, *7041*

Astronauts to ride a vehicle on the moon, *7042*

Astronauts to transfer from one spacecraft to another while in orbit, *7039*

Astronauts trained by the United States, *7028*

Astronauts who were women, *7047*

Astronomer employed in the Naval Observatory who was a woman, *6667*

Astronomer of note, *6659*

Astronomer to acquire international fame, *6657*

Astronomer to measure the size of a fixed star, *6668*

Astronomical expedition to record an eclipse of the sun, *6662*

Astronomical observations book, *1985*

Astronomy magazine, *4770*

Astronomy photograph, *6692*

Astronomy photographs in color to be published in a magazine, *6699*

Atheist organization, *5745*

Athlete to win the James E. Sullivan Memorial Trophy, *1719*

Athlete who was a woman to earn more than $1 million in a year, *7541*

Athlete who was a woman to earn more than $100,000 in one season, *7540*

Athlete who was African-American to win the James E. Sullivan Memorial Trophy, *1720*

Athlete who was an African-American woman to win the James E. Sullivan Memorial Trophy, *1721*

Athletic club, *7542*

Atlas issued by a state, *4799*

Atomic bomb dropped from an airplane over water, *8124*

Atomic bomb explosion, *8123*

Atomic bomb explosion over enemy territory, *8086*

Atomic bomb explosion to be shown on television, *8126*

Atomic bomb underground explosion, *8127*

Atomic bomb underwater explosion, *8125*

Atomic-powered lighthouse, *4129*

Attack on British soldiers by civilians in the Revolution, *7984*

Attorney general of the United States, *6124*

Attorney general to be incarcerated, *6127*

Attorney general to plead guilty to a criminal offense, *6126*

Attorney general who was a woman, *6128*

Attorney general whose father also served as attorney general, *6125*

Attorney of the United States, *2711*

Auction duplicate bridge championship, *4023*

Auction of radio spectrum for satellite services, *6284*

Audio tape made in the United States, *7014*

Aurora borealis display, *6765*

Autogiro flown in America, *1529*

Autogiro licensed for commercial use, *1530*

Autogiro owned by the federal government, *1533*

Autogiro to land and take off from a ship, *1534*

Automated tanker under the American flag, *6902*

Automatic aircraft cannon, *8119*

Automatic computing pendulum scale, *2380*

Automatic electric stock quotation board, *3824*

Automatic headlight control, *4227*

Automatic parking meter, *5446*

Automatic pilot on an airplane, *1499*

Automatic plate-casting and finishing machine for stereotype printing, *5796*

Automatic steering gear for ships, *6958*

Automatic streetlight system, *2217*

Automatic swinging doors operated by a photo-electric cell, *2087*

Automatic telephone system, *7713*

Automatic traffic light, *4225*

Automatic washing machine, *4281*

Automaton, *3650*

Automaton to operate by long-distance control, *3442*

Automobile club, *5465*

Automobile school, *3292*

Autopsy, *2847*

Autopsy officially recorded, *2848*

Autopsy performed by a woman physician on a male corpse, *2850*

Autopsy with verdict of a coroner's jury, *2849*

Aviation book, *1987*

Aviation correspondence school, *7289*

Aviation course in a high school, *3089*

Aviation department of a state government, *1385*

Aviation gasoline obtained by the catalytic cracking method, *3539*

Aviation law enacted by a state, *1384*

Aviation magazine, *4776*

Aviation magazine devoted primarily to airplanes, *4780*

Aviation medicine book, *1921*

Aviation meet, *7292*

Aviation trophy, *1641*

Aviation unit of the military trained for overseas duty, *5132*

Aviator who was African-American, *1609*

Avocado, *3902*

Avon Lady, *4057*

Ax factory, *7909*

B

Baby carriage, *2140*

Baby carriage factory, *2140*

Baby carrier, *2154*

Baby show, *2141*

Babysitters' insurance policy, *4527*

Bachelor of Arts degree, *2976*

Bachelor tax enacted by a state, *7644*

Bacteriology courses at a college, *3149*

Bacteriology diagnostic laboratory in a city health department, *4198*

Bacteriology laboratory, *4928*

Bacteriology textbook, *1918*

Bacterium to be discovered that was visible to the naked eye, *6752*

Badge of honor for enlisted men and noncommissioned officers, *1656*

Badminton championship tournament, *7584*

Bagel bakery, *3927*

Baha'i house of worship, *6604*

Baking powder manufacturer, *3936*

Baking soda commercial production, *3934*

Ball bearing commercial installation, *2038*

Ball-point pen, *8154*

Ballet, *1232*

Ballet choreographer of international renown, *1235*

Ballet on an American theme by an American choreographer, *1236*

Ballet technique course at a college, *2915*

Ballet transmitted by satellite, *1238*

Ballistic missile, *8134*

Balloon carrier, *6919*

Balloon cup race, *7288*

Balloon destroyed by enemy gunfire, *8012*

Balloon flight, *1535*

Balloon flight by an aeronaut born in America, *1537*

Balloon flight in which a presidential order was carried, *1536*

Balloon flight powered by solar energy, *1542*

Balloon flight to rise higher than 100,000 feet, *1541*

Balloon honeymoon, *4808*

Balloon pilot who was a woman, *1539*

Balloon tire production, *5501*

Balloon to land on a building, *1540*

Balloon to land on board a ship, *1537*

Balloonist to direct artillery fire, *7964*

Ban by Congress on importation of diseased cattle, *4210*

Ban enacted by a state on the employment of women in an occupation, *4559*

Ban on cheap handguns enacted by a state, *4155*

Ban on convicts holding public office, *3312*

Ban on federal funding for human cloning research, *6755*

Ban on Jesuits to be enacted by a colony, *6449*

Ban on Quakers enacted by a colony, *6586*

Ban on sex discrimination in employment enacted by a state, *6828*

Ban on sex discrimination in wages enacted by Congress, *6834*

Ban on surrogate motherhood enacted by a state, *2168*

Bananas to be imported, *3898*

Bandage with built-in adhesive, *4945*

Bandwagon, *2326*

Bank and train robbery gang, *2775*

Bank chartered by Congress, *3757*

Bank clearinghouse, *3764*

Bank deposit insurance law enacted by a state, *3762*

Bank deposit insurance law enacted by Congress, *3782*

Bank for African-Americans operated by African-Americans, *3771*

Bank for freed African-American slaves, *3766*

Bank holdup, *2775*

Bank of importance to lease personal property, *3798*

Bank of the United States, *3758*

Bank open day and night, *3792*

Bank president of a national bank who was a woman, *3786*

Bank president who was a woman, *3772*

Bank robbery, *2773*

Bank to be automated, *3800*

Bank to establish a branch in a foreign country, *3776*

Bank to install an automatic teller, *3799*

Bank to issue a credit card, *3810*

Bank to open a branch in a trailer, *3788*

Bank to operate a window in a subway station, *3797*

Bank to provide movies for customers waiting in line, *3801*

Bank wholly owned and operated by a state, *3779*

Bank with resources exceeding $1 billion, *3780*

Banking association (national), *3768*

Banking association (state), *3770*

Bankruptcy act, *2308*

Baptism in America, *6442*

Baptist church, *6543*

Baptist churches for African-Americans, *6546*

Bar code scanner, *2373*

Barbed wire commercial production, *4406*

Barbie doll, *2152*

Bareknuckle world heavyweight boxing champion, *7251*

Bas relief of stainless steel in large size, *1219*

Baseball batting and fielding cage, *7108*

Bauxite, *5336*

Be-In, *3668*

Beauty pageant to be held nationwide, *3628*

Beauty pageant to be shown on television, *3629*

Bed that could be hidden, *4330*

Bedspring manufacturing patent, *4322*

Beef export, *3938*

Beehive with removable frames, *1050*

Beer, *2663*

Beer in cans, *2671*

Belgian immigrants, *5917*

Bellows, *4395*

Belly-dancing course at a college, *2916*

Belt conveyor more than four miles long, *4419*

Belt conveyor system, *4390*

Belting, *4392*

Belts of leather for transmitting power, *4393*

Benefit performance of a play, *1244*

Bessemer steel converter, *4492*

Betatron, *6801*

Bevatron, *6805*

Bible concordance, *1960*

Bible for the blind in embossed form, *1968*

Bible in folio size to be illustrated, *1964*

Bible in Hebrew, *1967*

Bible printed in English, *1962*

Bible printed in German, *1961*

Bible society, *6571*

Bible society (national), *6573*

Bible translated into a Native American language, *1959*

Bible translated into English, *1966*

Bible translation by a woman, *1970*

Bibles in hotel rooms, *6579*

Bibliography course at a college, *3098*

Bibliography of Americana in English, *1739*

Bibliography organization (national), *4691*

Bibliophile magazine, *4725*

Bicycle champion who was a woman, *7197*

Bicycle club, *7184*

Bicycle corps of cadets, *3187*

Bicycle factory, *7183*

Bicycle magazine, *4784*

Bicycle organization (national), *7185*

Bicycle patent, *7180*

Bicycle race paced by a motorcycle, *7194*

Bicycle race to be shown on television, *7198*

Bicycle racer to attain the speed of a mile a minute, *7193*

Bicycle school, *7182*

Bicycle tire made of cord, *7190*

Bicycle track of wood, *7191*

Bicycle traffic court, *7196*

Bicycle trip of 100 miles sponsored by a club, *7200*

Bicycle with a back-pedal brake, *7187*

Bicycle with a rotary crank, *7181*

Bicycles, *7179*

Bicyclist from the United States to win the Tour de France, *7199*

Bifocal contact lenses, *5074*

Bifocal eyeglasses, *5072*

Big-league football team to travel coast-to-coast, *7306*

Bilingual report of a congressional committee, *2595*

Bill bearing the likeness of a president, *5387*

Bill bearing the likeness of a woman, *5391*

Bill depicting a battleship, *5392*

Bill of $100,000 denomination, *5394*

Bill to depict both sides of the Great Seal of the United States, *5395*

Billiard ball of composition material resembling ivory, *4019*

Billiard match, *4016*

Billiard match to attain international fame, *4017*

Billiard player to win a match in the first inning, *4020*

Billiards, *4015*

Billiards book, *2000*

Billionaire, *2445*

Biological study of camouflage in nature, *6745*

Biology course offered at a college, *3240*

Bird banding, *6740*

Bird banding association (national), *6792*

Bird banding by federal authorities, *6747*

Bird for which a definite crossing of the Atlantic was recorded, *1165*

Bird hunting regulation law enacted by Congress, *7426*

Bird protection international treaty, *3747*

Bird refuge established by a state, *3743*

Bird reservation established by the federal government, *3745*

Birth control clinic, *4844*

Birth control clinic run by a state government, *4847*

Birth-control pill, *6833*

Birth rate below the rate necessary to maintain the population, *5855*

Birth registration law enacted by a state, *2159*

Birth registration uniform numbering system, *2162*

Birth to be shown on closed-circuit television, *2163*

Book showing photographs of movements in sequence, *1750*

Book trade magazine, *4712 4724*

Book with color plates, *1741*

Book written for publication as a paperback, *1791*

Book written in America, *1727*

Bookbinder, *1731*

Books of postage stamps, *6061*

Books of postage stamps with humidity-resistant adhesive, *6075*

Bookseller, *1777*

Bookseller's guide, *1787*

Booksellers' organization, *1782*

Bookwagon traveling library, *4676*

Borax, *5331*

Border patrol officer, *5868*

Border-to-border national highway, *6637*

Botanic expedition, *6738*

Botanical garden, *6736*

Botanical report on plant hybridization, *6735*

Botanist of note who was a woman, *6737*

Botanist to become a prominent landscape gardener, *6741*

Botany book by an American-born author, *1979*

Botany professor at a college, *3229*

Bottle, *4282*

Bottle cap with a cork crown, *4286*

Bottle with a screw cap, *4287*

Bourbon whiskey, *2666*

Bowie knife, *8095*

Bowler to earn $100,000 in one year in tournaments, *7232*

Bowler to make a perfect score of 300, *7224*

Bowler to roll two perfect games, *7226*

Bowler to win $10,000 in a tournament, *7229*

Bowler who was a woman to obtain a perfect score, *7227*

Bowling automatic scoring machine, *7230*

Bowling magazine, *4786*

Bowling match, *7220*

Bowling match that used white balls on black lanes, *7228*

Bowling rule standardization, *7221*

Bowling tournament for women, *7225*

Bowling tournament sponsored by the American Bowling Congress, *7223*

Bowling Triple Crown winner, *7231*

Bowling with duckpins, *7222*

Box spring, *4327*

Boxer of fame who was African-American, *7249*

Boxer to die from blows inflicted in a fight, *7250*

Boxer to hold three titles simultaneously, *7253*

Boxer to win distinction in the ring, *7248*

Boxer to win world titles in five weight divisions, *7256*

Boxer who was a woman to earn national recognition, *7257*

Boxing arena, *7503*

Boxing match at which admission tickets sold at $100, *7245*

Boxing match broadcast on radio, *7238*

Boxing match broadcast on radio from ringside, *7239*

Boxing match timed by automatic timer, *7235*

Boxing match to attract 100,000 spectators, *7242*

Boxing match to be shown on television, *7243*

Boxing match to gross $1 million, *7240*

Boxing match under the Marquis of Queensberry rules, *7236*

Boxing referee in a.heavyweight championship match who was African-American, *7246*

Boxing referee who was a woman, *7244*

Boy Scouts of America uniformed troop, *2149*

Boycott law enacted by a state, *2310*

Braille encyclopedia, *1834*

Brake for four-wheeled cars, *5439*

Branding law enacted by a colony, *1065*

Branding punishment by a federal court, *2818*

Brass, *4463*

Brass and copper seamless tubes, *4467*

Brass clock works, *7900*

Brass kettles, *4292*

Brass rod, *4472*

Brass spinning, *4468*

Brass wire and tubing, *4465*

Brassiere patent, *2276*

Brawl in the House of Representatives, *2583*

Breach-of-promise suit, *4804*

Bread factory that was completely automatic, *3925*

Breech-loading cannon, *8099*

Breeder reactor, *3546*

Brethren, *6545*

Brevet commission in the Army, *5167*

Brevet conferred by the Army on an American, *5168*

Brewery to remain in business for 200 years, *2664*

Brick building, *2068*

Brick kiln, *2053*

Brick machine, *2057*

Brick pavement on a city street, *6620*

Brick pavement on a rural road, *6623*

Brick roofing tile, *2036*

Bridge, *3562*

Bridge designed by computer, *3597*

Bridge hand in which each player was dealt a perfect hand, *4025*

Bridge in a Y shape, *3569*

Bridge named for a woman, *3598*

Bridge of cast iron, *3572*

Bridge of flowers, *3592*

Bridge on a large scale, *3566*

Bridge player to win more than 1,000 master points in one year, *4027*

Bridge table to shuffle and deal cards by electricity, *4024*

Bridge with open-mesh steel flooring, *3594*

Bridge with piers sunk in the open sea, *3593*

British-made television series, *7791*

British marine corps of American colonists, *5228*

Broad jump to reach more than 25 feet, *7555*

Broad-spectrum antibiotic, *5000*

Broadcloth, *7863*

Broadway play shown in a color television version with its original cast, *1266*

Broadway play shown in a television version with its original cast, *1266*

Brokerage firm whose shares were traded by a major stock exchange, *3835*

Brokerage office owned by women, *3818*

Bronchitis treatise, *1911*

Bronze equestrian statue, *5399*

Bronze statue of full length, *5398*

Brother and sister to win national tennis singles championships in the same tournament, *7539*

Brothers to serve as representatives in Congress simultaneously, *2602*

Brothers to serve simultaneously as governors of their respective states, *7610*

Brown dwarf star to be discovered, *6685*

Brushes, *4267*

Bubble gum, *3967*

Buddhist: American to be recognized by Tibetan Buddhists as a reincarnated lama, *6440*

Buddhist temple, *6438*

Buddhist: Zen Buddhist monastery, *6439*

Building and loan association, *3763*

Building built completely inside a factory, *2090*

Building built to serve as a hotel, *2421*

Building constructed wholly of cast iron, *2076*

Building containing 6.5 million square feet of usable space, *2118*

Building designed to be used by artists, *2062*

Building erected in the United States for public use, *2115*

Building erected in Washington, DC, by the federal government, *2116*

Building floated across a river, *2090*

Building heated by steam, *2074*

Building in all-Gothic architecture, *2071*

Building in which wrought-iron beams were used, *2077*

Building in which wrought-iron window sashes were installed, *2052*

Building known as a Quonset hut, *2117*

Building of fireproof construction, *2072*

Building of large size with a retractable roof, *2095*

Building of pressed structural steel, *2086*

Building shaped like an elephant, *2079*

Building with a high steeple, *2097*

Building with a large-scale clear-span dome, *2085*

Building with an all-marble dome, *2084*

Building with caisson foundations, *2083*

Building with its roof supported by cables, *2092*

Building with prefabricated walls of mosaic concrete, *2088*

Bulk mail, *6004*

Bullfight, *7258*

Bullfighter who was a woman to fight professionally, *7259*

Bunting manufacture, *7868*

Burglar alarm, *2132*

Burglar alarm operated by ultrasonic or radio waves, *2136*

Burglar alarm system, *2134*

Burial at the Tomb of the Unknown Soldier, *2854*

Burlesque show, *3687*

Bus with cross seats, *5420*

Business economics course at a college, *2918*

Business high school, *3084*

Business history chair at a college, *2922*

Business library supported by taxes, *4675*

Business manual, *1793*

Business organization for African-Americans (national), *2450*

Business school, *2917*

Business school at a college, *2919*

Bustle, *2269*

Buttons of freshwater pearl, *2290*

Buttons of pewter or block tin, *2286*

C

Cabinet, *6102*

Cabinet appointee rejected by the Senate, *6106*

Cabinet conference to be telecast, *6114*

Cabinet in which all members were sworn in at the same time and place, *6111*

Cabinet meeting attended by a foreign national, *6118*

Cabinet member convicted of a crime, *6110*

Cabinet member indicted while in office, *6122*

Cabinet member to address a joint session of Congress, *6113*

Cabinet member to serve in four different capacities, *6120*

Cabinet member who had served as a Confederate officer, *6107*

Cabinet member who was a woman, *6112*

Cabinet member who was African-American, *6119*

Cabinet member who was an African-American woman, *6121*

Cabinet member who was Catholic, *6105*

Cabinet member who was Jewish, *6108*

Cabinet member who was the brother of the president, *6117*

Cabinet session held at a place other than the seat of the federal government, *6116*

Cabinet session to be telecast and broadcast, *6115*

Cable car, *6395*

Cable car put into service, *6398*

Cafeteria, *2459*

Cakes of soap of uniform weight and individually wrapped, *4268*

Calico printery, *7859*

Calliope, *1311*

Camel, *1137*

Camel race, *1146*

Camels imported for military purposes, *1145*

Camera exposure meter, *5843*

Camera exposure scale, *5832*

Camera to use film rolls, *5837*

Camp for boys, *2143*

Camp for conscientious objectors, *5221*

Camp meeting, *6525*

Campus takeover by student protesters, *3015*

Can opener, *4372*

Canal for boat transportation, *3600*

Canal for creating water power, *3599*

Canal incorporated into a seaway, *3603*

Canal made of concrete, *3602*

Canal of importance, *3601*

Cancer hospital, *4885*

Cancer hospital established by a city, *4890*

Cancer laboratory, *4930*

Cancer prevention clinic for children, *4850*

Cancer research fund, *5056*

Candle factory for making spermaceti candles, *4341*

Candy packaged in a factory, *3963*

Canned ham, *3941*

Canned tuna, *3889*

Cannibal, *2838*

Canning book, *1849*

Canning of food, *3944*

Canoe club, *7212*

Cantilever bridge, *3583*

Cantor in the Reform movement who was a woman, *6490*

Cantorial school, *3280*

Capture and boarding of an enemy submarine on the high seas by American forces, *8065*

Capture of a British frigate in the War of 1812, *8023*

Capture of a German ship by an American ship in World War II, *8049*

Capture of a ship in the Spanish-American War, *8007*

Capture of an American ship captain by a German submarine in World War II, *8057*

Capture of an enemy ship in enemy waters, *7999*

Capture of an enemy warship by a commissioned American naval officer, *7995*

Car accident, *5466*

Car accident fatality, *5470*

Car advertisement in a national magazine, *2332*

Car advertisement in a specialty magazine, *2331*

Car-airplane combination, *5447*

Car driver who was a woman, *5467*

Car equipped with a two-way radio, *7717*

Car exported from the United States, *5431*

Car factory, *5433*

Car finance company, *3806*

Car fueled by methanol, *5463*

Car hill-climbing contest, *7262*

Car insurance law enacted by a state, *4520*

Car insurance policy, *4519*

Car magazine, *4788*

Car patent, *5428*

Car produced for commercial sale, *5429*

Car race, *7260*

Car race for the Vanderbilt Cup, *7264*

Car race from New York to Paris, *7265*

Car race on a racetrack, *7261*

Car radio, *6309*

Car show, *5434*

Car to exceed the speed of 200 miles per hour, *5445*

Car to exceed the speed of a mile a minute, *5436*

Car trip made with a diesel engine, *5474*

Car with a circulating lubrication system, *5437*

Car with an automatic transmission, *5450*

Car with an electric storage battery, *5426*

Car with front-wheel drive, *5459*

Car with the steering wheel on the left side, *5438*

Carbide factory, *4438*

Carbon microphone used in radio broadcasting, *6308*

Carbon tetrachloride, *4439*

Carborundum, *5337*

Card time recorder, *2383*

Cargo airlines licensed by the Civil Aeronautics Board, *1417*

Cargo ship from the United States attacked by a German submarine in World War I, *8028*

Cargo ship fully automated and flying the American flag, *6901*

Caricature, *1213*

Carillon, *1305*

Carnegie Hero Fund Commission award granted to a woman, *1639*

Carousel patent, *3620*

Carousel with a jumping horse mechanism, *3625*

Carpet mill, *4311*

Carpet mill to make ingrain carpets, *4312*

Carpet power loom, *4313*

Carpet sweeper, *4273*

Carpeting of tufted plastic, *4319*

Carrier for liquid bulk chemicals, *6897*

Cartel of corporations, *2524*

Cartoon showing the Democratic Party as a donkey, *5702*

Cartoon showing the Republican Party as an elephant, *5703*

Cartoon showing Uncle Sam, *5701*

Cartooning school, *2911*

Cartridge belt patent, *8108*

Cartridge-loading machinery, *8110*

Casein fiber, *4443*

Cash carrier system, *2360*

Cash register, *2363*

Casino in Las Vegas, *3636*

Casino outside the state of Nevada, *3638*

Cassette audio tape recorder, *7016*

Cast-iron plow, *1041*

Cast steel for plows, *4491*

Caster for bedsteads, *4323*

Cat domestically bred in America, *1134*

Cat show, *1147*

Catalog of first American editions of American authors, *1773*

Catalog of government publications, *1772*

Catalog of recordings on disk, *1940*

Catalog of the Library of Congress, *1768*

Catalog of theological and biblical literature, *1952*

Catamaran, *7213*

Caterpillar Club member, *1584*

Caterpillar Club member who was a woman, *1586*

Caterpillar Club members who were father and son, *1587*

Catgut substitute, *4958*

Cathedral, *6461*

Catholic African-Americans, *6458*

Catholic archbishop who was an African-American, *6480*

Catholic: Army chaplain who was Catholic, *5194*

Catholic: Ban on Jesuits to be enacted by a colony, *6449*

Catholic: Baptism in America, *6442*

Catholic beatification of a Native American, *6474*

Catholic Bible in English, *1963*

Catholic bishop appointed to serve in the United States, *6457*

Catholic bishop consecrated in the United States, *6460*

Catholic bishop to exercise episcopal functions, *6446*

Catholic bishop who was an American-born African-American, *6480*

Catholic: Bohemian church, *6463*

Catholic: Cabinet member who was Catholic, *6105*

Catholic cardinal whose see was west of the Rockies, *6477*

Catholic: Cathedral, *6461*

Catholic church in the English colonies, *6453*

Catholic church to become a basilica, *6471*

Catholic: College for women founded as a Catholic institution, *2958*

Catholic: College founded as a Catholic institution, *2938*

Catholic community of African-American nuns, *6462*

Catholic: Congressional chaplain who was Catholic, *2585*

Catholic: Congressional representative who was a Catholic priest, *2601*

Catholic: Congressional representative who was Catholic, *2597*

Catholic convent, *6451*

Catholic diocese and archdiocese, *6456*

Catholic funeral attended by the Continental Congress, *6455*

Catholic: Governor who was Catholic, *7611*

Catholic hillside shrine, *6466*

Catholic holy orders, *6450*

Catholic: Lithuanian church, *6468*

Catholic magazine, *4697*

Catholic magazine in English, *4702*

Catholic mass, *6444*

Catholic mass for night workers, *6469*

Catholic mass in an airship over the ocean, *6473*

Catholic mass in English, *6479*

Catholic midnight mass to be televised, *6476*

Catholic mission in California, *6454*

Catholic: Navy chaplain who was Catholic, *5202*

Catholic nun, *6452*

Catholic nuns in a cloistered community, *6470*

Catholic parish, *6445*

Catholic parish church for African-Americans, *6464*

Catholic: Parish priest, *6445*

Catholic prelate named to the Roman Curia who was American-born, *6478*

Catholic: President who was Catholic, *6203*

Catholic: Presidential candidate who was Catholic, *3407*

Catholic priest, *6459*

Catholic priest born in America, *6448*

Catholic priest from the United States to be made a cardinal, *6465*

Catholic priest who was African-American, *6467*

Catholic saint who was a male American citizen, *6482*

Catholic saint who was an American citizen, *6475*

Catholic saint who was born in America, *6481*

Catholic saints who were active in North America, *6472*

Catholic school, *3042*

Catholic school for Native Americans, *3053*

Catholic: School run by missionaries in America, *3037*

Catholic seminary, *3268*

Catholic seminary for the education of African-American priests, *3278*

Catholic seminary under the supervision of the Pope, *3277*

Catholic: Senator who was Catholic, *2638*

Catholic settlement that was permanent, *5899*

Catholic: Supreme Court chief justice who was Catholic, *2759*

Catholic: University for African-American students founded as a Catholic institution, *2964*

Catholics to settle in the English colonies in America, *6447*

Cattle club to promote Guernsey cattle, *1092*

Cattle club to promote Jersey cattle, *1090*

Cattle fair, *1078*

Cattle of the Aberdeen-Angus breed, *1081*

Cattle of the Afrikaaner breed, *1082*

Cattle of the Guernsey breed, *1079*

Cattle that were purebred shorthorns, *1080*

Cattle to be exported, *1077*

Cattle to be imported, *1076*

Cattle tuberculosis test, *5121*

Cave paintings, *1210*

Cellophane, *4338*

Cellophane transparent tape, *4339*

Cellular telephone system, *7727*

Celluloid, *4480*

Celluloid photographic film, *5838*

Cellulose sponge for household use, *4280*

Cellulose sponge for medical and surgical use, *4951*

Cement, *2044*

Census based on a sample of the population, *5856*

Census compiled by machines, *5853*

Census compiled in part from statistics obtained by mail, *5854*

Census in which the national population exceeded 10 million, *5850*

Census in which the national population exceeded 100 million, *5850*

Census in which the national population exceeded 200 million, *5850*

Census in which the national population exceeded 50 million, *5850*

Census of the United States, *5848*

Census that included deaf, mute, and blind people, *5851*

Centennial celebration of the Revolution, *8006*

Centennial exhibition, *2410*

Centralized refrigeration service, *4436*

Centrifugal cream separator, *3855*

Ceramics school, *2906*

Cereal sold as a breakfast food, *3916*

Certified public accountant, *3755*

Cesarean operation, *5075*

Chain radio broadcast, *6270*

Chain-stitch single-thread sewing machine, *4356*

Chain store organization, *2493*

Chair factory, *4321*

Chairman of a major political party who was a woman, *3344*

Chairman of a major political party who was African-American, *3345*

Chairman of the Joint Chiefs of Staff who was African-American, *5129*

Chamber music ensemble, *1359*

Chamber of Commerce, *2446*

Chamber of commerce established by a state, *2448*

Championship game of the American Football League, *7331*

Championship heavyweight boxing title won in the first round, *7237*

Changes in the American flag to be authorized by Congress, *1124*

Chaplain of the U.S. Army, *5197*

Charles Stark Draper Prize for engineering and technology, *1645*

Charting of the Northwest Passage, *6734*

Chautauqua organization meeting, *2885*

Check photographing device, *3795*

Check protectors, *3790*

Checkers champion of renown, *4011*

Cheese factory cooperative, *3857*

Cheese factory of consequence, *3859*

Chemical laboratory at a college, *3235*

Chemistry laboratory manual, *1980*

Chemistry magazine, *4766*

Chemistry organization (national), *6786*

Chemistry professor at a college, *3230*

Chemistry society, *6777*

Chemistry textbook, *1976*

Chess book, *1995*

Chess champion to play more than 100 games simultaneously, *4032*

Chess computer to beat the world chess champion, *4034*

Chess match between players on different ships at sea, *4031*

Chess tournament, *4028*

Chevrons for noncommissioned army officers, *5223*

Chewing gum, *3959*

Chicken pox vaccine, *4925*

Chief justice of a state supreme court who was African-American, *2720*

Child abuse prevention organization, *5737*

Child born in an airplane, *2160*

Child born in the United States through in vitro fertilization, *2166*

Child born in the White House, *6251*

Child born in the White House who was the offspring of a president, *6254*

Child born of African-American parents in America, *2158*

Child born of English parents in America, *2156*

Child born of English parents in New England, *2157*

Child born of European parents on American soil, *2155*

Child delinquency law enacted by a state, *2147*

Child hygiene bureau, *4186*

Child labor in a factory, *4572*

Child labor law enacted by a state that included an education requirement, *4573*

Child labor law enacted by a state that regulated hours of employment, *4574*

Child labor law enacted by a state that restricted the age of the worker, *4575*

Child labor law enacted by Congress, *4576*

Child to be killed in the Revolution, *7985*

Child welfare congress, *2146*

Children: Racing event for children, *7583*

Children's book, *1729*

Children's church, *6535*

Children's department in a library, *4672*

Children's hospital, *4878*

Children's hospital for research and treatment of catastrophic childhood diseases, *4893*

Children's library, *4664*

Children's magazine, *4695*

Children's magazine with literary merit, *4708*

Children's museum, *5581*

Chimes and bells, *1302*

Chinaware for restaurant use, *4309*

Chinchilla farm, *1074*

Chinese-American women's organization to be incorporated, *5726*

Chinese embassy, *3011*

Chinese graduate of an American college, *3011*

Chinese: Hospital for patients of Chinese ancestry, *4891*

Chinese immigrants to America, *5964*

Chinese: Judge of Chinese ancestry, *2728*

Chinese labor immigration, *5865*

Chinese language and literature lectureship at a college, *3116*

Chinese laundry, *2439*

Chinese: Marine officer of Chinese descent, *5238*

Chinese: New York Stock Exchange seat owner of Chinese ancestry, *3837*

Chinese newspaper, *5668*

Chinese person granted citizenship, *5874*

Chinese: Physician who was a Chinese woman, *4978*

Chinese: Public school for Chinese-American children, *3062*

Chinese restaurant, *2455*

Chinese: Restrictions by Congress on immigration of Chinese laborers, *5866*

Chinese: Senator of Chinese ancestry, *2657*

Chinese students in the United States, *3011*

Chinese: Telephone exchange for Chinese-American subscribers, *7733*

Chinese theater, *3699*

Chinese theatrical performance, *1250*

Chinese: West Point graduates who were Chinese nationals, *3201*

Chiropodist, *4970*

Chiropodists to be regulated by a city, *4937*

Chiropody book, *1913*

Chiropody school at a college, *3175*

Chiropody school of note, *3174*

Chiropractic regulation law enacted by a state, *4940*

Chiropractic school, *3172*

Chiropractor, *4977*

Chloroform, *4985*

Chlorophyll, *4997*

Chocolate bars, *3965*

Chocolate chip cookies, *3928*

Chocolate mill, *3955*

Cholera epidemic, *2876*

Chop suey, *3879*

Christian in America, *6441*

Christian martyr on American soil, *6443*

Christian religious service in English on the Pacific Coast, *6501*

Christian Science church, *6600*

Christian worship services organized by African-American slaves, *6515*

Christian: Young Men's Christian Association branch for African-Americans, *5712*

Christian: Young Women's Christian Association, *5713*

Christmas cards, *4256*

Christmas postage stamp regular issue, *6094*

Christmas savings club at a bank, *3793*

Christmas tree, *4254*

Christmas tree decorated with electric lights, *4257*

Chrome-tanned leather successfully marketed, *4460*

Chrome tanning process, *4459*

Chromium plating process, *4476*

Chromolithograph, *1216*

Church for Native Americans in New England, *6512*

Church organized by Native Americans, *6603*

Church service in sign language to be televised, *6594*

Church without theology, creed, or dogma, *6602*

Cider mill, *3841*

Cigar bands of special interest, *2703*

Cigar factory, *2702*

Cigar-rolling machine, *2706*

Cigarette-manufacturing machine, *2705*

Cigarette tax, *2698*

Cigarette tax enacted by a state, *2699*

Circular office building, *2066*

Circular saw, *7913*

Circular school building, *2121*

Circulating library, *4661*

Circumnavigation of the earth by a submerged submarine, *6996*

Circumnavigation of the globe by a fleet of warships, *6986*

Circumnavigation of the globe by a warship, *6980*

Circumnavigation of the North American continent by a ship, *6992*

Circumnavigation of the world by a cruise ship, *6989*

Circumnavigation of the world by a submarine, *6991*

Circumnavigation of the world by a yacht, *6982*

Circus, *3672*

Circus clown training school, *3301*

Circus tights, *2265*

Circus to be shown on television, *3675*

Circus to feature a car as an attraction, *3673*

Citizen of the United States to be hanged for treason, *2835*

Citizenship and public affairs school at a college, *3255*

Citizenship conferred by special grant, *5861*

Citizenship granted on foreign soil, *5873*

Citizenship statute for Native Americans, *5871*

Citrons, *3905*

City carriage service, *2190*

City college, *2936*

City directory, *1813*

City founded by an African-American pioneer, *2187*

City government using the commission plan, *2202*

City government using the manager plan, *2204*

City in miniature, *2197*

City incorporated in the colonies, *2181*

City law requiring reporting of premature births, *2161*

City manager, *2203*

City mayor elected by popular vote, *2206*

City orchestra supported by taxes, *1362*

City parking garage, *5484*

City radio station, *6296*

City to celebrate the Fourth of July with fireworks, *3649*

City with a population of more than 1 million, *5852*

Civic center with an aluminum geodesic dome, *2093*

Civic design chair at a college, *3254*

Civil defense test held nationwide, *4089*

Civil engineering course at a college, *3232*

Civil engineering society (national), *3609*

Civil rights anthem to achieve fame, *1383*

Civil rights chair at a college, *3128*

Civil rights law enacted by Congress, *2254*

Civil rights sit-in, *2260*

Civil War amnesty issued by the president to rebellious citizens, *6143*

Civil War attack, *7949*

Civil War battle, *7957*

Civil War bloodshed, *7952*

Civil War bloodshed north of the Mason-Dixon Line, *7967*

Civil War call for volunteers, *7951*

Civil War: Union vessel to fire a shot in the Civil War, *7950*

Civilian airport owned and operated by the federal government, *1508*

Civilian to die in a spacecraft accident, *7090*

Claims court established by the federal government, *2712*

Clarinet made exclusively of metal, *1319*

Class photograph, *5813*

Clay pigeon target for trapshooting, *7474*

Clearinghouse for stocks and bonds, *3819*

Clerk of the House of Representatives, *2577*

Climatology professor at a college, *3242*

Clincher tire, *5496*

Clinic for teaching medical students, *3138*

Clinical instruction and bedside demonstration, *3135*

Clipper ship, *6866*

Clock movement to be electrically wound, *7902*

Clock to operate by nuclear power, *7903*

Clock to strike the hours, *7897*

Cloning of a primate from an embryo, *6754*

Close-up photographs of Jupiter, *7088*

Cloth-covered buttons, *2288*

Cloth mill, *7858*

Clothes dryer, *4278*

Clothing designer of international renown, *2280*

Coach of a professional basketball team who was African-American, *7177*

Coach riding, *7570*

Coaching club, *7569*

Coal, *3501*

Coal hydrogenation plant, *4444*

Coal mine disaster, *3506*

Coal mine to be automated, *3508*

Coal miner who was a woman to be killed in a mining accident, *3510*

Coal oil factory, *4431*

Coal pipeline, *3509*

Coast Guard Academy graduate who was African-American, *3210*

Coast Guard Academy graduates who were women, *3211*

Coast Guard airplane pilot who was a woman, *5213*

Coast Guard aviation unit, *5211*

Coast Guard inland station, *5210*

Coast Guard officers' training school, *3209*

Coast Guard officers who were women who served aboard ships, *5214*

Coast guard service, *5208*

Coast Guard serviceman who was African-American, *5209*

Coast Guard ship commander who was a woman, *5215*

Coast Guard unit for women, *5212*

Coast survey, *5956*

Coast survey book, *2014*

Coast-to-coast live telecast in color, *7845*

Coast-to-coast paved road, *6625*

Coast-to-coast radio hookup, *6272*

Coast-to-coast radio news broadcast to be recorded, *5706*

Coast-to-coast solar-powered two-way radio conversation, *6282*

Coast-to-coast telecast by satellite, *7852*

Coastal shipping service, *2478*

Coaxial cable, *7706*

Cocktail, *2665*

Cod-liver oil, *4980*

Coded military radio transmissions using a Native American language, *8082*

Coffee in a can, *3851*

Coffee mill, *3849*

Coffee percolator, *3850*

Cog railroad, *6333*

Coin bearing the likeness of a foreign monarch, *5374*

Coin bearing the likeness of a living person, *5377*

Coin bearing the likeness of a president, *5375*

Coin bearing the likeness of an African-American, *5379*

Coin bearing the likeness of an American woman, *5381*

Coin box for streetcars, *6396*

Coin-operated locker, *2369*

Coin-operated mailbox, *6011*

Coin-operated television receiver, *7814*

Coin to use *E pluribus unum* as a motto, *5356*

Coin to use the motto "In God We Trust", *5369*

Coinage dies, *5353*

Coins bearing dates other than the year of issue, *5380*

Coins manufactured for a foreign government, *5372*

Coins produced by steam power, *5366*

Coke used successfully as a blast furnace fuel, *3505*

Cold storage plant, *4407*

Collapsible tube, *7919*

Collapsible tube machine, *7927*

Collar factory, *2284*

Collar manufacturer, *2283*

College alumni association, *2991*

College art museum, *5594*

College baseball player who was African-American, *7142*

College charter granted by a governor, *2928*

College charter granted by the Crown, *2926*

College classes intended to combat the influence of communism, *3002*

College commencement exercises in a prison, *2982*

College comprehensive senior examination program, *3000*

College course in the contemporary novel, *3101*

College course without Greek or Latin, *2992*

College cricket club team to tour England, *7274*

College daily newspaper, *5646*

College degree awarded to a ventriloquist's dummy, *2981*

College diploma made of silver, *2980*

College entrance plan using certified schools, *2994*

College entrance requirement other than Greek, Latin, and arithmetic, *2941*

College extension courses, *2997*

College football player to score 50 points in one game, *7307*

College for African-American students, *2949*

College for deaf students, *3033*

College for women, *2944*

College for women founded as a Catholic institution, *2958*

College for women founded as a Jewish institution, *2968*

College for women to affiliate with a university, *2956*

College foreign-language house, *2999*

College founded as a Catholic institution, *2938*

College founded as a Methodist institution, *2937*

College founded as a Quaker institution, *2942*

College founded in America, *2925*

College graduate in geology who was a woman, *3241*

College graduate who was African-American, *3009*

College graduate who was an African-American woman, *3010*

College graduate who was Jewish, *3008*

College graduate who was Native American, *3006*

College literary society, *2990*

College magazine, *4699*

College named after George Washington, *2934*

College of liberal arts and sciences founded as a Jewish institution, *2965*

College on a Native American reservation, *2969*

College orchestra, *1357*

College president who was a woman, *2971*

College principally for war veterans, *2967*

College professor who was a woman, *2947*

College program of study abroad, *2995*

College proposed in America, *2924*

College radio station, *6295*

College secret society for women, *2986*

College skeet tournament, *7478*

College student to receive assistance from the federal government as the child of a deceased veteran, *3014*

College student to work his way through college, *3005*

College summer school, *2993*

College that was nondenominational, *2939*

College to confer medals as prizes, *2930*

College to dispense with credits, hours, points, and grades, *3001*

College to enroll African-American and white students on equal terms, *2943*

College to enroll women and men on equal terms, *2943*

College to feature rowing as a sport, *7467*

College to have a full faculty, *2927*

College to offer athletic scholarships to women, *3004*

College to offer courses to railroad commuters, *3003*

College to prohibit discrimination because of race, religion, or color, *2946*

College to sponsor an endowed lecture series, *2950*

College to use the honor system during examinations, *2931*

College to use the unit-cost plan, *2966*

College under Jewish auspices that was nonsectarian, *2963*

College varsity sports program, *2998*

College whose tuition fees were based on family income, *2970*

College with an elective system of study, *2932*

Colonial badges issued to "friendly" Native Americans, *5929*

Colonial congress, *2572*

Colonial copyright law, *4626*

Colonial council, *5906*

Colonial government federation, *5926*

Colonial law banning Christmas, *4253*

Colonial law for the maintenance of an insane patient, *4171*

Colonial law requiring towns to hire teachers and construct schools, *3045*

Colonial settlement west of the Allegheny Mountains, *5935*

Colonial treaty with the Native Americans, *5915*

Colonial warfare between England and France in America, *5911*

Colonial warfare between European powers in America, *5900*

Colonist hanged for treason, *2834*

Colonists in America who were women, *4812*

Color film, *5844*

Color news photograph transmitted by radio fax for publication, *5695*

Color photograph of the earth taken from space, *6700*

Colorscope public demonstration, *3436*

Columbus Day, *4233*

Comb-cutting machine, *4067*

Comb factory, *4065*

Comb made of ivory, *4066*

Combat mission of American pilots ordered to battle in World War I, *8042*

Combined newspaper, *5655*

Comet recorded, *6675*

Comic book containing original material, *2028*

Comic book starring a superhero, *2028*

Comic book versions of literary works, *2030*

Comic books, *2028*

Comic history of the United States, *1867*

Comic magazine, *4698*

Comic opera written for the American stage, *1343*

Comic strip in a newspaper, *5687*

Comic strip in continuous newspaper publication, *5691*

Comic weekly, *4717*

Comics studio, *4737*

Commander-in-chief of the Continental Navy, *5277*

Commander-in-chief of the U.S. Army, *5147*

Commander of a combat ship who was African-American, *5295*

Commemorative coin, *5373*

Commemorative postage stamp depicting a president's wife, *6095*

Commemorative postage stamps, *6084*

Commemorative postal card, *6048*

Commemorative stamped envelopes, *6083*

Commerce court established by the federal government, *2713*

Commercial advertising agent, *2322*

Commercial artist, *1201*

Commercial building with solar heating, *2067*

Commercial corporation, *2402*

Commercial crude-oil carrier, *6903*

Commercial DNA bank, *6756*

Commercial fishery, *2416*

Commercial high school, *3083*

Commercial hydroponicum, *1039*

Commercial museum, *5580*

Commercial oil refinery, *3529*

Commercial photography studio, *5812*

Commercial power laundry, *2440*

Commercial production of plants in water, *1038*

Commercial program telecast on a network, *7777*

Commercial radio station licensed, *6294*

Commercial rating agency, *3815*

Commercial satellite, *7069*

Commercial ship to conquer the Northwest Passage, *7000*

Commercial software for personal computers, *2552*

Commercial telegraph service, *7692*

Commercial telephone service on railroad trains for passengers, *7741*

Commercial telephone service using toll lines, *7730*

Commercial television licenses, *7796*

Commercial television station on ultrahigh frequency, *7800*

Commercial television station west of the Mississippi River, *7797*

Commissioned officer in the Marine Corps who was African-American, *5239*

Commodity exchange member who was a woman, *3827*

Commodore in the Navy, *5279*

Commonwealth of the United States, *5976*

Communications satellite, *7063*

Communications satellite with signal reception and transmission equipment, *7065*

Communion cups for individuals, *6582*

Communist Labor Party of America convention, *3374*

Communist Party of America convention, *3375*

Communistic settlement that was not religious, *2189*

Communistic settlement with a religious basis, *2182*

Community chorus, *1361*

Community forest, *3723*

Community hospital, *4892*

Community leader to exercise the authority of king and high priest, *5965*

Community to fingerprint its citizens, *4164*

Community trust charity, *5742*

Compact disc players, *7003*

Company nurse, *5026*

Company to pay a fine of $100 million for a price-fixing scheme, *2525*

Comparative philology chair at a college, *3115*

Compensation of Japanese-Americans interned during World War II, *8087*

Compiler programming language, *1655*

Complete DNA sequencing of a free-living organism, *6757*

Composer born in America, *1327*

Composer born in America to win an international reputation, *1329*

Composer of gospel music, *1332*

Composer of jazz music, *1331*

Composograph photograph in a newspaper, *5693*

Comprehensive digital atlas of the human body, *4913*

Compressed fresh yeast, *3935*

Compressed pills or tablets, *4987*

Compulsory education law enacted by a state, *3059*

Compulsory education law in a colony, *3043*

Computer-aided design (CAD) software, *2549*

Computer-aided manufacturing system, *4421*

Computer bug, *2527*

Computer: Chess computer to beat the world chess champion, *4034*

Computer: Compiler programming language, *1655*

Computer game, *4012*

Computer graphics software, *2548*

Computer hacker to be convicted, *2789*

Computer modem that was practical, *2534*

Computer mouse, *2535*

Computer operating system for multiple users, *2545*

Computer programming language for business, *1655*

Computer programming language for children, *2551*

Computer software application on Digital Video Disc, *2555*

Computer: Video game, *4013*

Computerized pump, *4417*

Computing device with electronic components, *2526*

Concentrated milk, *3877*

Concert with documentation, *1287*

Concrete, *2041*

Concrete barge, *6887*

Concrete cantilever bridge, *3590*

Concrete road, *6622*

Concrete rural road, *6624*

Concrete seagoing ship, *6876*

Condensed milk, *3869*

Condensed soup, *3948*

Condom commercials on television, *6843*

Conestoga wagon, *5936*

Confectionary machine, *3968*

Confederate coin, *5368*

Confederate congressional session, *7947*

Confederate cruiser built in England, *7962*

Confederate cruiser to raid Union commerce, *7944*

Confederate forts to surrender in the Civil War, *7958*

Confederate general killed in the Civil War, *7953*

Confederate government bond, *7948*

Confederate officer killed in the Civil War, *7955*

Confederate paper money, *5384*

Confederate ship surrendered to the Union, *7963*

Conference of American republics, *3979*

Conference of great powers, *3980*

Congregational church, *6505*

Consul who was African-American, *3988*

Consumer protection law enacted by Congress, *2311*

Consumer protection medical alert, *2312*

Contact lenses, *5073*

Containerized shipping, *2487*

Containership, *2487*

Containership facility, *2487*

Continental coin, *5357*

Continental Congress assembly to be opened with prayer, *2575*

Continental Congress session, *2573*

Continental money, *5347*

Continuation school for adults established by a state government, *2889*

Conviction under a National Industrial Recovery Code, *4378*

Cookbook, *1846*

Cookbook by an American author, *1847*

Cooking pots made in America, *4290*

Cooking school, *3288*

Cooperative store at a college, *2497*

Cooperative store for consumers, *2490*

Cooperative store operated by women, *2503*

Copley Medal awarded to an American, *1646*

Copper cents minted by a state, *5355*

Copper coins, *5354*

Copper coins made by the U.S. Mint, *5359*

Copper mine, *5316*

Copper refinery furnace, *4474*

Copper rolling mill, *4464*

Coptic Orthodox Church bishop, *6500*

Copy machine, *2374*

Copy made by xerography, *2372*

Copyright law enacted by a state, *4627*

Copyright law enacted by Congress, *4628*

Copyright law on photographs enacted by Congress, *4630*

Copyright registered for a choreographic score, *1237*

Cord tires, *5498*

Cordless drill used on the moon, *7937*

Cork for covering steam pipes, *2046*

Cork manufacturer, *2043*

Corkboard patent, *2045*

Corkscrew patent, *4373*

Corn found by English settlers, *3908*

Corn-husking championship, *1025*

Corncob pipe commercial manufacture, *2704*

Cornflakes, *3916*

Cornmeal machine for grinding maize, *3910*

Cornstarch made commercially from maize, *3912*

Cornstone, *2051*

Coronation, *6646*

Corporate body chartered by a special act of Congress, *2403*

Corporation tax levied by Congress, *7653*

Corporation to own its own airplane, *1396*

Corporation with a capitalization of $1 billion, *2405*

Corporation with a net income of more than $1 billion in one year, *2406*

Corps badges systematically assigned to an entire army, *5224*

Correction fluid for typewriters, *2389*

Correspondence course of a serious nature, *2886*

Correspondence school for workers, *2888*

Correspondence school to offer instruction in Braille, *3029*

Corrugated paper, *5759*

Corrupt election practices law enacted by a colony, *3313*

Corrupt election practices law enacted by a state, *3316*

Corrupt election practices law enacted by Congress, *3319*

Corset, *2271*

Cosmetics company that catered exclusively to African-American customers, *2444*

Cosmic ray to be discovered, *6679*

Costume museum, *5588*

Cotton acreage reduction payment, *1034*

Cotton boll weevil, *1032*

Cotton crop commercially produced entirely by machinery, *1035*

Cotton crop exported, *1029*

Cotton fabric used on a road, *6629*

Cotton gin, *1030*

Cotton goods to be trademarked, *7882*

Cotton mill, *7882*

Cotton mill entirely powered by water, *7884*

Cotton mill to spin cotton yarn successfully, *7883*

Cotton thread, *4361*

Cotton twine factory, *4335*

Cottonseed hulling machine, *1031*

Cottonseed oil, *3881*

Country day school, *3066*

County created by federal law, *5973*

County high school, *3085*

County library, *4673*

County public defender, *4639*

Coursing club, *7394*

Court-martial at which the judges included enlisted men, *2740*

Court-martial by the Army, *2739*

Court-martial in a colony, *2738*

Court-martial of an officer for collaborating with his captors, *2741*

Court tennis, *7524*

Courtroom verdict to be televised, *2717*

Cover of the *Saturday Evening Post* by Norman Rockwell, *1218*

Cow flown in an airplane, *1153*

Cow town, *2192*

Cowboy hat, *2297*

Coxswain of a men's college varsity rowing team who was a woman, *7471*

Cracker bakery, *3917*

Craft union, *4603*

Craft union contract, *4605*

Cranberry cultivation, *3900*

Cranberry treatise, *1762*

Crane, *4408*

Cranioscopy book, *1909*

Craps, *3634*

Creamery for commercial production, *3854*

Credit card to be nationally accepted, *3809*

Credit insurance, *4512*

Credit protection group, *2447*

Credit report book, *1795*

Credit union, *3773*

Credit union law enacted by a state, *3774*

Cremation, *2856*

Crematory, *2857*

Crematory established by a state government, *2858*

Crepe, *7875*

Crepe paper, *5760*

Cricket club, *7271*

Cricket game played by a college team, *7272*

Cricket magazine, *4783*

Cricket match, *7270*

Crime insurance policy authorized by a state, *4518*

Criminal convicted on the evidence of DNA matching, *4167*

Croix de Guerre awarded to an African-American, *1648*

Crop limitation law enacted by a colony, *1007*

Crop surplus destruction ordered by a government, *1008*

Croquet league, *7571*

Cross-country championships, *7549*

Cross-dresser of note, *6827*

Crossing of the North Pole underwater by a submerged submarine, *6993*

Crossword puzzle, *4010*

Crossword puzzle book, *2004*

Croup report, *1894*

Cruise missiles used in war, *8145*

Cryptography book, *2017*

Cryptography chart, *4797*

Cuban boatlift, *5881*

Curb exchange to transact more business in a day than the New York Stock Exchange, *3825*

Curfew bell, *2180*

Curling club, *7275*

Curved stereotype plate, *5788*

Customhouse, *2469*

Customs fee stamps, *7649*

Cut glass, *4046*

Cutlery factory, *4369*

Cutlery shears, *4368*

Cyber cafe, *2467*

Cyclone of record, *2862*

Cyclotron, *6798*

Cylinder and flatbed combination printing press, *5775*

Cylinder printing press, *5772*

Czech newspaper, *5669*

Czech settler in America, *5921*

D

Daguerreotype, *5811*

Daily news program on radio, *5705*

Daily newspaper, *5634*

Daily state lotteries with the same winning daily number, *3644*

Dairy association (state), *1091*

Dairy school at a college, *2897*

Dam disaster of great consequence, *2868*

Dam filled with rocks, *3605*

Dance major at a college, *2909*

Dance marathon, *3630*

Danish newspaper, *5672*

Danish settlers in America, *5925*

Daredevil jumper of note, *3676*

Daredevil to cross Niagara Falls on a tightrope, *3677*

Daredevil to go over Niagara Falls in a barrel, *3679*

Daredevil to go over Niagara Falls in a rubber ball, *3681*

Daredevil to jump off the Brooklyn Bridge and survive, *3678*

Data from interstellar space, *7088*

Daughters of the American Revolution member who was African-American, *5718*

Daylight saving time program, *7896*

Dead letter office, *5989*

Dealer in Oriental rugs, *4316*

Dean of a university graduate school who was a woman, *2974*

Dean of students at a college, *2973*

Dean of the faculty at a college, *2972*

Death by suicide machine, *2845*

Death penalty authorized by federal law, *2802*

Death penalty ban by a state, *2796*

Deaths from smog, *3715*

Deaths in an American nuclear reactor, *3553*

Debate among party hopefuls for the presidential nomination to be shown on television, *3398*

Decalcomania pictures, *4307*

Decathlon champion from the United States, *7556*

Decimal system of money, *5348*

Deck chair for steamer passengers, *4329*

Decked ship built in America, *6850*

Declaration of independence by a colonial government, *1112*

Declaration of independence by citizens of an American colony, *1110*

Declaration of rights, *1111*

Decoration Day, *4236*

Deep-dish pizza, *2462*

Defeat of a British naval squadron in the War of 1812, *8024*

Delegate to a national political convention who was African-American, *3335*

Delegates to a national political convention who were women, *3338*

Democratic Party convention between presidential elections, *3379*

Democratic Party national convention, *3349*

Demonstration in Washington against the Vietnam War, *8017*

Demonstration of home reception of television, *7812*

Demonstration of rapid aerial photography, *5823*

Demountable tire-carrying rim, *5499*

Dental amalgam for filling teeth, *4858*

Dental chair, *4859*

Dental college, *3162*

Dental crown made of gold, *4863*

Dental dispensary, *4857*

Dental drill, *4856*

Dental drill powered by electricity, *4864*

Dental filling made of gold, *4860*

Dental hygienists' book, *1925*

Dental hygienists to be licensed by a state, *4941*

Dental inlay made of gold, *4866*

Dental journal, *4754*

Dental mallet, *4865*

Dental school to be associated with a medical school, *3167*

Dental society member who was a woman, *4862*

Dental society (national), *5034*

Dental society of a city, *5032*

Dental surgeons to be licensed by a state, *4936*

Dental surgery textbook, *1923*

Dentist, *4854*

Dentist in the Navy to serve aboard a naval ship, *5020*

Dentist officially employed in the Army, *5014*

Dentist who was a woman, *4861*

Dentist who was a woman to obtain a D.D.S. degree, *4862*

Dentistry book, *1922*

Deodorant soap, *4062*

Department store, *2491*

Department store sales demonstrations using television, *2342*

Department store to hold a public art auction, *2507*

Department store to occupy a city block, *2492*

Department store to sell apartments, *2510*

Department store to sell insurance, *2511*

Deportation, *5857*

Deportation of aliens authorized by Congress, *5864*

Derby hat, *2295*

Dermatology chair at a college, *3144*

Dermatology treatise, *1917*

Description of hydroponic agriculture, *1036*

Design for the Great Seal of the United States, *1132*

Design patent, *4654*

Designated hitter in a major league baseball game, *7157*

Designated hitter rule, *7157*

Designated hitter to come to bat in a World Series game, *7157*

Desk telephone, *7714*

Desk with a roll top, *4325*

Destroyer from the United States torpedoed in World War II, *8051*

Destruction of an attacking missile by a defensive missile in combat, *8146*

Detachable collar, *2282*

Detective story, *1844*

Detective who was a woman, *4140*

Detonating fuse of the Cordeau-Bickford type, *4424*

Dial combination bank lock, *2133*

Dial time recorder, *2382*

Diamonds in a meteorite, *5338*

Diamonds in actual rock, *5340*

Diapers that were disposable, *2151*

Diathermy machine, *4948*

Dictionary compiled by a woman, *1808*

Dictionary of American law, *1805*

Dictionary of the English language compiled by an American, *1800*

Dictionary published in the United States, *1797*

Diesel cars to be mass-produced, *5460*

Diesel-electric locomotive, *6363*

Diesel engine built for commercial service, *5479*

Diesel engine in a submarine, *6965*

Diesel engine speed record, *5482*

Diesel-powered tractor, *1057*

Digest of American law, *1878*

Dinosaur fossils, *6739*

Dinosaur skeleton found in the United States, *6744*

Direct tax on Britain's American colonists without their consent, *7641*

Director of the Federal Bureau of Investigation, *4141*

Director of the Mint of the United States, *5350*

Director of the Mint of the United States who was a woman, *5350*

Disciples of Christ meeting, *6527*

Discotheque, *3631*

Discount clothing store, *2498*

Discovery of Antarctica by an American, *6722*

Discovery of the North Pole, *6727*

Discus-throwing competition, *7551*

Disease research and treatment organization, *5046*

Dish set made in America for the White House, *6256*

Dishwasher, *4274*

Dissection of a living animal to demonstrate anatomy and physiology, *5054*

Dissection report, *1890*

Distilling book, *1848*

Distinguished Service Cross awarded in enemy-occupied territory, *1660*

Distinguished Service Cross awarded to an animal, *1664*

Distinguished Service Cross of the Korean War, *7978*

Distinguished Service Medal awarded to a Navy nurse, *5288*

District attorney who was a woman, *2714*

District attorney who was African-American, *2716*

District land office, *5953*

District nurse, *5024*

Divided road, *6619*

Diving suit, *6709*

Divinity professor at a college, *3266*

Divorce, *4806*

Divorce rate of more than 1 million a year, *4811*

DNA chain polymerization, *5065*

Docks owned by a state, *2481*

Doctor commissioned in the regular Army who was a woman, *5172*

Doctor in the regular Navy who was a woman, *5291*

Doctor of Philosophy degree, *2977*

Doctor of Philosophy degree awarded to a woman, *2979*

Doctor of Philosophy degree awarded to an African-American scholar, *2978*

Document known to have been printed in America, *1096*

Dog domestically bred, *1170*

Dog hotel, *2436*

Dog license law enacted by a state, *1172*

Dog racetrack to use an imitation rabbit, *7278*

Dog show, *1171*

Dogs trained to guide the blind, *1173*

Dogsled race on an Olympic demonstration program, *7280*

Doll marketed for boys, *2153*

Dollar marks, *5802*

Domed sports stadium, *7511*

Domestic relations court, *2709*

Double-deck bridge, *3591*

Double-deck bus, *5419*

Double-deck elevator, *2112*

Double-deck ferryboat, *6909*

Double-deck railroad coaches, *6370*

Double-deck steamboat, *6864*

Double-deck streetcar, *6401*

Double-header baseball games that were shut-outs, *7125*

Doughnut cutter, *4295*

Dow Jones Industrial Average to exceed 1,000 points, *3836*

Dow Jones Industrial Average to exceed 7,000 points, *3838*

Draft law enacted by a colony, *5216*

Draft law enacted by Congress during peactime, *5220*

Draft law enacted by Congress during wartime, *5219*

Draft of civilians by Congress, *5218*

Drama broadcast on radio, *1257*

Drama broadcast on radio from a regular stage, *1262*

Drama broadcast on radio from a ship at sea, *1261*

Drama school, *2905*

Drama school at a college, *2910*

Drawback legislation enacted by Congress, *2471*

Dress made of spun glass, *2274*

Dried milk patent, *3870*

Drinking straws, *4374*

Drinking water conduit to be built underwater, *2227*

Drinking water supply to be chemically treated with chlorine compounds, *2235*

Drive-in banking service, *3796*

Drive-in gas station, *2499*

Drive-in movie theater, *3709*

Drive-up mailbox, *6009*

Driver arrested for speeding, *5468*

Driver license board, *5469*

Driver who was a woman to compete in the Indianapolis 500, *7269*

Driving course in a high school, *3090*

Drought of record, *2865*

Drug control chief appointed by the federal government, *2693*

Drug control law enacted by Congress, *2687*

Drug for treating AIDS, *5006*

Drug mill, *4982*

Drug treatment center for addicts established by Congress, *2688*

Drug treatment center for minors, *2690*

Druggist, *4965*

Dry dock, *6904*

Dry ice manufactured commercially, *4441*

Dual-purpose postage stamp, *6066*

Dual sewer system for sewage and storm water, *2229*

Ductile tungsten, *5341*

Duel, *2807*

Duel between representatives in Congress, *2810*

Duel in which a future president of the United States participated, *2809*

Dueling law enacted by a state, *2808*

Dugong, *1158*

Duplex compound locomotive, *6362*

Duplicate whist tournament, *4022*

Dutch elm disease breakout, *3731*

Dutch Reformed church, *6506*

Dutch: School for colonial children in America, *3038*

Dutch settlement in America, *5912*

Dwarf exhibited as a theatrical attraction, *3653*

Dye plant, *4433*

Dynamite, *4423*

Dynamo for a direct-current outdoor lighting system, *3454*

Dynamo that was successful, *3460*

E

Eagle Scout, *2149*

Earmuffs, *2270*

Earth Day to be celebrated nationwide, *4250*

Earthquake description, *2861*

Earthquake of consequence to be recorded, *2867*

Easter egg roll, *4239*

Ecology book, *1991*

Economics association, *6788*

Economics journal, *4774*

Ecumenical synod, *6510*

Editor in chief of a law review who was a woman, *3127*

Editor of a major daily newspaper who was a woman, *5622*

Editorial apology for false news to appear in a newspaper, *5631*

Editorial to be broadcast over radio and television, *5707*

Education association, *3223*

Education book, *1827*

Education department at a college, *3265*

Educational association (national), *3224*

Educational computer programming language, *2550*

Educational magazine, *4706*

Educational multimedia CD-ROM, *2554*

Educational television network operated as a nonprofit corporation, *7807*

Educational television network that was statewide and state-supported, *7806*

Educational television station, *7801*

Educational television station sponsored by a city, *7803*

Egg incubator, *1068*

Egyptian antiquities collection, *5578*

Elastic webbing, *7869*

Election campaign using radio, *3322*

Electric watch, *7904*

Electrical engineering school at a college, *3239*

Electrical hearing aid, *5070*

Electrical show, *2411*

Electrical timing device for foot races, *7558*

Electrical transmission of three-phase alternating high-frequency current, *3468*

Electrically propelled naval ship, *6930*

Electricity generated by Niagara Falls waterpower, *3456*

Electricity journal, *4769*

Electrobasograph, *4949*

Electrocution experiment, *2794*

Electromagnet, *3451*

Electromagnetic telegraph, *7686*

Electron microscope, *6800*

Electron tube, *3437*

Electronic computer, *2528*

Electronic computer for commercial use, *2529*

Electronic computer with solid-state components, *2530*

Electronic digital calculator, *3438*

Electronic pocket calculator, *3447*

Electronic range for domestic use, *4303*

Electronic road system, *6632*

Electronic voice mechanism, *7723*

Electronic watch, *7905*

Electrotherapy book, *1914*

Electrotype, *5803*

Element heavier than uranium, *6817*

Elementary schools to use closed-circuit televisions in teaching, *3069*

Elephant, *1142*

Elevated railroad, *6334*

Elevator, *2103*

Elevator in a hotel, *2107*

Elevator in an office building, *2108*

Elevator with a completely enclosed car, *2105*

Elevator with electronic signal controls, *2113*

Elevator with safety devices, *2104*

Elevator with two cars, *2111*

Elks meeting, *5722*

Elliptical office building, *2096*

Elopement by airplane, *4809*

Emancipation proclamation, *2252*

Embalming book, *1910*

Embargo act enacted by Congress, *2475*

Embargo act of the Continental Congress, *2470*

Embossed inlaid linoleum, *4318*

Embossing press, *5773*

Emergency 911 telephone system, *4087*

Emergency first aid organization, *4117*

Emmy awards for excellence in television, *1628*

Emperor of Japan to visit the United States, *6655*

Employment office established by a city, *4566*

Employment service established by a state, *4565*

Encased postage stamps, *6055*

Enclave, *2195*

Enclosed baseball park, *7504*

Enclosed climate-controlled suburban shopping mall, *2512*

Encyclopedia compiled by American editors, *1832*

Encyclopedia of integer sequences, *6763*

Encyclopedia printed in the United States, *1830*

Endangered species list issued by the federal government, *3719*

Endowment for social service purposes, *5731*

Enemy saboteurs executed in the United States, *8058*

Engineering book, *1977*

Engineering college, *3233*

Engineering society, *3608*

English actor of note to perform in America, *1274*

English: Battle between English colonists and Native Americans, *5908*

English charter for a city in America, *2181*

English: Child born of English parents in America, *2156*

English: Child born of English parents in New England, *2157*

English: Colonial council, *5906*

English: Colonial government federation, *5926*

English: Colonial warfare between England and France in America, *5911*

English: Expedition of Englishmen to cross the Allegheny Mountains, *5927*

English: Exploration of the New England region by an Englishman, *5903*

English grammar by an American, *1853*

English grammar by an American published in America, *1856*

English grammar instruction at a college, *3113*

English: Letters written in English in America, *1095*

English: Military leader of the English settlers, *5251*

English: Naval battle between colonists, *5922*

English: Naval expedition mounted by an English colony, *5910*

English patent granted to a resident of America, *4647*

English: Rebellion by colonists against an English governor, *5930*

English: Rebellion in the English colonies, *5905*

English: School for colonial children in America, *3038*

English settlement in America that was permanent, *5907*

English: Ship built by English colonists in America, *6848*

English: State law to establish English as an official language, *5870*

English: Surveyor in America, *5902*

Engraving of any artistic merit, *1223*

Engraving to achieve popularity, *1225*

Entomologist hired by a state, *6742*

Entomologist hired by the federal government, *6743*

Entomology book, *1984*

Entomology journal, *4772*

Entomology professor at a college, *3238*

Envelope folding and gumming machine, *5765*

Envelope folding machine, *5763*

Envelope manufacturer, *5762*

Envelope with a window, *5766*

Environmental protection law enacted by a state in connection with advertising, *3711*

Epidemiologist, *4173*

Epidemiology report, *1888*

Episcopal bishop, *6549*

Episcopal bishop consecrated in the United States, *6549*

Episcopal bishop deposed for heresy in the United States, *6552*

Episcopal bishop who was a woman, *6553*

Episcopal bishop who was African-American, *6551*

Episcopal catechism, *1955*

Episcopal cathedral, *6550*

Episcopal church organized in New England, *6548*

Episcopal church service in an English colony, *6547*

Episcopal priest who was a woman, *6553*

Episode of "Sesame Street" to be shown on television, *7792*

Equal Rights Party convention, *3363*

Escalator of the modern type, *2110*

Escalator patent, *2106*

Eskimo pie, *3867*

Esperanto club, *5717*

Esperanto course at a college, *3117*

Esperanto magazine, *4749*

Etcher, *1206*

Ethical culture society, *5744*

Ethyl gasoline to be marketed, *3538*

European edition of an American newspaper, *5649*

European king buried in the United States, *6654*

European settlement in America, *5890*

European settlement in America that was permanent, *5899*

European settlement in the northeast after the Vikings, *5904*

European to set foot on the North American continent after the Vikings, *5893*

European to sight America, *5889*

Evangelical Church conference, *6526*

Evaporated milk, *3873*

Evening school for working children, *3046*

Execution by electrocution, *2799*

Execution by lethal gas, *2800*

Execution by lethal injection, *2806*

Execution by the Army, *2795*

Execution carried out by the federal government for the killing of an FBI agent, *2804*

Execution for kidnapping, *2801*

Execution for slave trading carried out by the federal government, *2797*

Execution for witchcraft, *2793*

Execution in America, *2792*

Execution of a woman by electrocution, *2799*

Execution of a woman by hanging by the federal government, *2798*

Execution of an organized crime leader in the electric chair, *2803*

Executive officer of a man-of-war who was a woman, *5300*

Exhibition of the *Mona Lisa* in the United States, *1231*

Expedition of Englishmen to cross the Allegheny Mountains, *5927*

Exploration by ship of the mouth of the Columbia River, *5949*

Exploration of land on the Pacific coast by a European, *5896*

Exploration of the Grand Canyon of the Colorado, *6725*

Exploration of the Mississippi River by a European, *5895*

Exploration of the New England region by an Englishman, *5903*

Explorer to set foot on both the North and South Poles, *6732*

Explosion of Thermit to break up ice jams, *4425*

Export report by the federal government, *2473*

Express delivery service, *2479*

Extinction by humans of a native American animal, *3746*

Extradition of criminals among colonies, *4130*

Extradition treaty with a foreign country, *4001*

Eye bank, *4836*

Eye conservation class, *3028*

Eye hospital, *4872*

Eye infirmary, *4871*

Eye wash commercially manufactured, *4990*

F

Factories operated by the federal government in peacetime, *4387*

Factoring of a 100-digit number, *6760*

Factory cooled by air conditioning, *4385*

Factory heated by steam, *4382*

Factory inspection law enacted by a state, *4383*

Factory standardization to federal government specification, *4381*

Factory with temperature and humidity control, *4384*

Factory without windows, *4386*

Factory workers' magazine, *4714*

False eyelashes, *4058*

Family of lawyers admitted simultaneously to practice before the Supreme Court, *4641*

Farm bureau, *1004*

Farmer Labor Party convention, *3376*

Farmers' institute sponsored by a college, *2894*

Farmers' institute sponsored by a state, *2893*

Farriers' course at a college, *3299*

Fashion magazine, *4728*

Fashion show to be shown on television, *2414*

Fat substitute in prepared foods, *3886*

Father and son team to win the national contract bridge championship, *4026*

Father and son to become commercial airline pilots, *1602*

Father and son to occupy the same Cabinet post, *6109*

Father and son who were senators at the same session, *2644*

Father's Day, *4244*

Fathometer, *6714*

Fax transmission by a press syndicate direct to newspaper offices, *5627*

Fax transmission of movie film, *7672*

Federal administrator who was an African-American woman, *2257*

Federal aid program for primary and secondary schools, *3070*

Federal aid to libraries, *4678*

Federal cemetery to contain graves of both Union and Confederate soldiers, *2853*

Federal credit union, *3785*

Federal dry docks, *6905*

Federal election, *3380*

Federal government building built to withstand a nuclear attack, *2119*

Federal government employees who were women, *5351*

Federal judge to be impeached, *2719*

Federal law exempting debtors from prison, *2814*

Federal law hostile to lotteries, *3642*

Federal law requiring radios on ships, *4222*

Federal marshals who were women, *4151*

Federal reserve banks, *3777*

Federal revenue cutter, *6857*

Federal treasury surplus to be returned to the states, *7596*

Federal treaty rejected by the Senate, *4003*

Federal treaty signed by a woman, *4006*

Federally chartered bank owned and managed by women, *3789*

Felt hats for women, *2296*

Felt manufacturing mechanical process, *7867*

Fence made of woven wire, *1052*

Fencing book, *1992*

Ferris wheel, *3623*

Ferryboat built exclusively to transport cars, *6911*

Fiberglass, *4052*

Fiberglass sutures, *4957*

Fiction best seller, *1781*

Fiction writer to win the Pulitzer Prize twice, *1709*

Fifty-dollar gold pieces, *5367*

Fifty-dollar gold pieces minted by the federal government, *5376*

Fighter plane, *1486*

Fighter plane equipped with a cannon, *1487*

Fighter plane from the United States to destroy a Japanese airplane in World War II, *8072*

Figure skater of note, *7429*

Figure skating champion from the United States to compete in the Olympic Games, *7432*

File factory, *7915*

Filly to win the Kentucky Derby horse race, *7408*

Film-developing machine, *5840*

Film professorship at a college, *2914*

Film rolls for cameras, *5835*

Filmpack camera, *5839*

Financial "corner", *3751*

Financial news agency, *5624*

Fine arts department in a college, *2902*

Fingerprint conviction in a crime, *4163*

Fingerprinting expert, *4160*

Fingerprinting in federal penitentiaries, *4161*

Finnish college, *2959*

Fire alarm system operated by electricity, *4104*

Fire and tornado insurance fund enacted by a state, *4533*

Fire brick, *2054*

Fire brick to withstand high heat, *2055*

Fire chief, *4094*

Fire department composed entirely of women, *4114*

Fire department established by a city, *4093*

Fire department to be paid, *4095*

Fire department to be paid a salary, *4103*

Fire engine, *4092*

Fire engine that was practical, *4102*

Fire engine with a steam boiler, *4100*

Fire escapes for tenements, *4105*

Fire extinguisher using vaporized chemicals, *4110*

Fire hose of rubber-lined cotton web, *4099*

Fire in a mine, *2880*

Fire in an oil well, *2882*

Fire insurance agent, *4528*

Fire insurance company, *4529*

Fire insurance company to receive a charter, *4530*

Fire insurance joint-stock company, *4531*

Fire of great destructive force, *2881*

Fire of serious consequence, *2879*

Fire patrol to protect property during fires, *4098*

Fire prevention law enacted by a colony, *4091*

Fireboat with two-way radio equipment, *4112*

Fireboats, *4097*

Firehouse pole, *4109*

Fireproof baseball stadium, *7507*

Fireproof safe, *2357*

Fireworks, *3649*

Fireworks book, *2021*

Fireworks law enacted by a city, *4111*

Fireworks law enacted by a state, *4113*

First aid instruction, *4122*

First-day special cancellation of a postage stamp, *6067*

First Lady to be depicted on a monument to a president, *6134*

First Lady to pilot an airship, *6132*

First Lady to receive free mail franking privileges, *6130*

First Lady to travel in an airplane to a foreign country, *6131*

First Lady who was also a federal official, *6133*

First Lady who was not born in the United States, *6129*

Fish hatchery, *1059*

Fish hatchery run by the federal government, *1060*

Fish protection law enacted by a city, *3742*

Fisheries school at a college, *3296*

Fishing club, *7284*

Fishing line factory, *7924*

Fishing magazine, *4785*

Fishing rod of telescoping steel tubes, *7932*

Fishing treatise, *1993*

Five-cent store, *2496*

Fizzing cold remedy, *4994*

Flag Day, *4240*

Flashbulb device with multiple flashbulbs, *5847*

Flashlight, *7935*

Flea circus, *3660*

Flea laboratory, *6749*

Flemish newspaper, *5680*

Flicker animation, *5530*

Flight trainer for airplane pilots, *1500*

Flint glass factory, *4037*

Floating church, *6577*

Floating electric power plant, *3481*

Floating hospital, *4883*

Floating soap, *4055*

Flood of which there is any known record, *2859*

Floppy disk, *2536*

Flour mill, *3911*

Flour rolling mill, *3915*

Fluorescent electric lighting to be installed on every street of a city, *2218*

Fluorescent lamp, *3500*

Fluorescent mineral exhibit, *6715*

Fluorescent paint, *7938*

Fluorspar, *5326*

Fly casting tournament, *7285*

Flying disk for use in throwing games, *7585*

Flying medical clinic, *4845*

FM radio, *6310*

FM radio transmitter to receive a commercial license, *6299*

Folding bed, *4328*

Folding theater chair, *4326*

Food in an aerosol can, *3953*

Food-O-Mat, *2509*

Food processor, *4304*

Food stamps, *4086*

Football book, *2002*

Football club, *7301*

Football dummy, *7311*

Football game at night, *7321*

Football game in which referees were allowed to check television instant replays, *7336*

Football game played indoors, *7319*

Football game to be broadcast on radio with a play-by-play description, *7324*

Football game to gross $1 million, *7332*

Football game to last longer than 80 minutes, *7335*

Football goalpost, *7309*

Football goalposts of collapsible folding metal, *7314*

Football player to win the Heisman Trophy for excellence in college football, *1725*

Football player who was African-American to win the Heisman Memorial Trophy, *1726*

Football rules, *7302*

Football stadium, *7505*

Football uniform numerals, *7312*

Football uniforms worn in a game, *7310*

Football with a rubber covering, *7313*

Foreign car exhibited, *5427*

Foreign feature film exhibited, *5512*

Foreign language course broadcast on radio, *3118*

Foreign missionary society, *6572*

Foreign missionary society organized by women, *6578*

Foreign nation to recognize the independence of the United States, *3975*

Foreign service committee, *3974*

Foreign service school in a college, *3126*

Foreign servicewomen interred in the Arlington National Cemetery, *2855*

Forest canopy crane to be used in North America, *6753*

Forest fire drenched by artificial rain, *3732*

Forest fire lookout tower, *3729*

Forest fire of consequence, *2883*

Forest horse, *1184*

Forest management on a professional scale, *3725*

Forest planting by the federal government, *3726*

Forest reserve established by a state, *3724*

Forest Service aerial patrol, *3730*

Forestry association (national), *6784*

Forestry association (state), *6785*

Forestry book, *1990*

Forestry course established by a state, *3076*

Forestry law enacted by a colony, *3722*

Forestry school at a college, *3076*

Forestry school operated privately, *3077*

Fork, *4365*

Former president to address the Senate, *6175*

Former president to become a senator, *6160*

Former president to become chief justice of the Supreme Court, *6164*

Former president to serve as an official of an enemy government, *6158*

Former president who was elected to the House of Representatives, *6149*

Former vice president to be arrested, *6241*

Fortune 1000 company to be owned and chaired by a woman, *2407*

Fountain pen, *8153*

Fourdrinier papermaking machine, *5750*

Fox hunting club, *7422*

Franchise chain, *2463*

Frankfurter, *3939*

Fraternal group insurance, *4508*

Fraternal society for Jews, *5720*

Fraternity house at a college, *2985*

Free agents in major league baseball, *7158*

Free kindergarten, *3075*

Free lunches for the poor and sick, *5736*

Free mail delivery in cities, *5996*

Free-piston car, *5458*

Free port, *2486*

Free public art museum in continuous existence, *5595*

Free public libraries authorized by a state, *4670*

Free public library established by a city, *4668*

Free school funded by an endowment, *3039*

Free Soil Party convention, *3352*

Free trade policy by the federal government, *7662*

Freeze-dried coffee, *3853*

Freezing of a corpse for future resuscitation, *2841*

French: Colonial warfare between England and France in America, *5911*

French: Colonial warfare between European powers in America, *5900*

French: European settlement in the northeast after the Vikings, *5904*

French grammar, *1857*

French instruction at a college, *3110*

French newspaper, *5662*

French: Painting of an American scene by a European painter, *1211*

French to arrive in America, *5898*

French: Truce violation, *5901*

Friction matches, *4334*

Frigate, *6914*

Frog-jumping jubilee, *1151*

Frontier Day, *4242*

Frozen bread, *3929*

Frozen food for the mass market, *3949*

Fruit culture treatise, *1759*

Fruit spraying, *1019*

Fruit tree patent, *1026*

Fuel alcohol plant, *3540*

Fugitive slave law enacted by Congress, *2247*

Full-page magazine advertisement for a food product, *2329*

Full-scale wind tunnel for testing airplanes, *1501*

Fullerenes to be observed, *6822*

Fuller's earth, *5334*

Fulling mill for making wool cloth, *7891*

Fund-raising organization to sell Christmas seals, *5741*

Fund-raising organization to sell stamps, *5734*

Funeral home operated on the cooperative plan, *2839*

Fungicide used medicinally, *5001*

Fur-bearing animals raised commercially, *1070*

Fur trading post, *5920*

Furs exported, *3740*

Fustians, everlastings, and coating, *7860*

Futurity horse race, *7390*

G

Gag rule in the House of Representatives, *2586*

Gallstone operation, *5079*

Gambling law for ministers enacted by a colony, *3632*

Gambling law for residents enacted by a colony, *3633*

Gambling permit stamp issued by the federal government, *7661*

Game management chair at a college, *3078*

Game manufacturing company, *4009*

Game played in the English colonies in America, *4008*

Game preserve, *7424*

Game preserve appropriation by the federal government, *3749*

Game protection society, *7423*

Game warden to be paid a salary, *3744*

Garbage incinerator, *3713*

Gardener's manual, *1760*

Gas commission established by a state government, *3518*

Gas conservation law enacted by a state, *3519*

Gas engine, *5478*

Gas journal, *4771*

Gas mask, *4402*

Gas meter, *3512*

Gas-powered streetcar, *6397*

Gas refrigerator, *4348*

Gas streetlights, *2213*

Gas streetlights throughout a city, *2214*

Gas-turbine bus, *5424*

Gas-turbine car, *5456*

Gas-turbine-electric locomotive, *6368*

Gas-turbine helicopter, *1566*

Gas-turbine propane-fueled locomotive, *6369*

Gas-turbine propeller-driven airplane, *1400*

Gas turbine to pump natural gas, *3521*

Gas turbine used by an electrical utility company, *3487*

Gaslight in the White House, *6253*

Gaslights for display, *3654*

Gasoline-mechanical railroad cars, *6387*

Gasoline obtained from crude petroleum by the cracking process, *3536*

Gasoline pump, *4410*

Gasoline pump with price and gallon displays, *4418*

Gasoline tax levied by a state, *7655*

Gasoline tax levied by Congress, *7659*

Gasoline tractor, *1055*

Gastroenterology treatise, *1898*

Gazetteer of the world, *1815*

Gelatin dessert, *3966*

Gem-cutting machine, *5317*

Gene therapy, *5118*

Genealogical collective work, *1869*

Genealogy of an American family, *1864*

General anesthetic, *4828*

General killed in Vietnam by enemy fire, *8018*

General medical clinic, *4843*

General of the American armed forces killed in World War II, *8073*

General of the Armies of the United States, *5152*

General of the Armies of the United States with the rank of six stars, *5161*

General of the Continental Army, *5146*

General of the U.S. Army, *5151*

General pharmacopoeia, *1930*

General-purpose computer network, *2544*

General purpose military vehicle, *5248*

Genetically altered food, *3840*

Genetically altered plants, *1028*

Genetically altered virus approved for use in a vaccine, *5066*

Genetically engineered product to appear in food, *3839*

Genetics clinic, *4848*

Geodesic dome of substantial size, *2094*

Geodetic satellite, *7070*

Geodetic survey, *6711*

Geographer of the United States, *6707*

Geography book, *1978*

Geography magazine, *4775*

Geography school at a college, *3245*

Geological map of the United States, *1981*

Geological survey authorized by Congress, *6710*

Geological survey for a state government, *6708*

Geologist of note, *1981*

Geologist to reach the moon, *6718*

Geology book, *1981*

Geology society (national), *6778*

Geology textbook, *1983*

Georgia patent, *6855*

Geosynchronous satellite, *7071*

Gerenuk, *1160*

Germ warfare, *8089*

German bible, *1961*

German book printed in America, *1953*

German instruction at a college, *3111*

German magazine, *4741*

German newspaper, *5661*

Giant exhibited as a theatrical attraction, *3658*

Giant panda, *1154*

Gilt buttons, *2287*

Gingham factory, *7871*

Girder bridge of cast iron, *3574*

Girl to win the Soapbox derby, *7583*

Glass-blowing machine, *4044*

Glass crystal chandelier, *4342*

Glass factory, *4035*

Glass that was nonreflecting, *4049*

Glider commercial freight service, *1555*

Glider entirely built of plywood and plastic, *1553*

Glider flight, *1546*

Glider flight indoors, *1549*

Glider license awarded to a woman, *1599*

Glider pilot's license, *1598*

Glider released from an airship, *1548*

Glider with cambered wings, *1547*

Globe factory, *4798*

Gloves, *2264*

Glucose from potato starch, *3957*

Glue factory, *4428*

Goalie in a National Hockey League team to score a goal, *7382*

Goat show, *1073*

Gold bullion deposit for coinage, *5365*

Gold certificates, *5389*

Gold coinage, *5360*

Gold discovered in California, *5329*

Gold leaf, *5339*

Gold nugget, *5320*

Gold price fixed by Congress, *5349*

Goldfish hatchery, *1061*

Golf association (national), *7340*

Golf book, *2003*

Golf champion born in America, *7357*

Golf champion of African-American and Asian descent, *7370*

Golf champion to hold the four highest golf titles, *7361*

Golf champion to win both the U.S. Open and the Professional tournaments, *7360*

Golf club with a steel shaft, *7353*

Golf clubs for hitting balls, *7351*

Golf course with 18 holes, *7348*

Golf course with nine holes, *7347*

Golf magazine, *4787*

Golf mixed foursome, *7354*

Golf player in an official amateur tournament who was African-American, *7355*

Golf players' club, *7337*

Golf tee, *7352*

Golfer born in America to win the British Women's Amateur Golf Tournament, *7363*

Golfer to break 60 for 18 holes in a major tournament, *7364*

Golfer to break 60 in a Professional Golfers Association tour, *7368*

Golfer to earn $100,000 in a contest, *7367*

Golfer to earn over $100,000 in one year, *7366*

Golfer to play 180 holes in one day, *7359*

Golfer to play 24 hours continuously on a regulation course, *7365*

Golfer to shoot below his age, *7369*

Golfer to win both the U.S. Open and the U.S. Amateur in the same year, *7358*

Golfer to win the United States Women's Amateur Championship, *7356*

Gorilla, *1159*

Gospel singer, *1337*

Gospel song, *1332*

Gourmet restaurant, *2454*

Government contract authorized by Congress for pistols, *8092*

Government on the Pacific Coast, *5963*

H

Hard-surfaced road, *6609*
Hard water crackers, *3918*
Harness horse race at night, *7389*
Harpsichord, *1307*
Hat factory, *2293*
Health board established by a city, *4172*
Health board established by a state government, *4177*
Health board with emergency powers established by a city, *4176*
Health department of a county organized on a full-time basis, *4185*
Health insurance clause in a labor contract, *4538*
Health insurance company, *4534*
Health insurance law enacted by a state, *4539*
Health insurance plan enacted by Congress, *4541*
Health journal to advocate water cures, *4755*
Health laboratory established by a city, *4197*
Health laboratory established by a state to diagnose diseases by the examination of sputum, *4201*
Health maintenance organization, *4540*
Health museum, *5590*
Health ordinance prohibiting spitting, *4181*
Health service established by the federal government, *4174*
Hearing aid, *5069*
Hearing aid using transistors, *5071*
Heart operation for the relief of angina pectoris, *5091*
Heart operation in which the deep-freezing technique was employed, *5093*
Heart operation in which the elective cardiac arrest technique was employed, *5094*
Heart pump, *5060*
Heart transplant, *5100*
Heart transplant using a baboon heart, *5104*
Heart transplant using an artificial heart, *5101*
Heart transplant using an artificial heart that was intended to be permanent, *5103*
Heat-resistant glass, *4048*
Heating stove, *4331*
Heating system to heat buildings from a central station, *2078*
Heavy tank, *8120*
Heavy water to be identified, *6814*
Heavyweight boxing champion of the world who was African-American, *7252*
Heavyweight boxing match to last longer than 100 rounds, *7233*
Heavyweight championship boxing match broadcast on radio, *7241*

Hebrew book other than the Bible, *1958*
Hebrew dictionary, *1801*
Hebrew grammar, *1854*
Hebrew instruction at a college, *3109*
Hebrew newspaper, *5671*
Hebrew spelling book, *1858*
Hebrew type, *5799*
Helicopter, *1557*
Helicopter commercially designed, *1558*
Helicopter flight, *1572*
Helicopter flight from water, *1574*
Helicopter flight of one-hour duration, *1573*
Helicopter fully operated by remote control, *1567*
Helicopter hoist rescue, *1563*
Helicopter licensed for commercial use, *1560*
Helicopter passenger service, *1568*
Helicopter refueling flight, *1577*
Helicopter rescue of an American pilot behind enemy lines, *7979*
Helicopter to deliver material across a picket line, *1562*
Helicopter with a fully servo-controlled intermeshing rotor, *1561*
Helicopter with a twin engine, *1559*
Heliport commercial base, *1565*
Helium in natural gas, *6813*
Helium plant, *6797*
Hemophilia treatise, *1899*
Hemp to be exported, *1010*
Herbal book, *1927*
Herd book for livestock, *1761*
High-definition telecast, *7834*
High jump over seven feet, *7563*
High-jump standards using electric eye detectors, *7561*
High-resolution maps of the ocean floor, *4803*
High school, *3080*
High school chapter of Alcoholics Anonymous, *2662*
High school for girls, *3081*
High school for pregnant teenage girls, *3092*
High school night classes, *3082*
High school to fingerprint its students, *4166*
High-speed newspaper printing and folding machine, *5791*
High-speed radio fax transmission, *7674*
Highway bridge with concrete arches, *3586*
Highway bridge with welded aluminum girders, *3596*
Highway built by the federal government, *6616*
Highway interchange structure with four levels, *6633*

Highway post office service, *6041*

Hindu spiritual leader to visit America, *6601*

Historical hoaxes, *3645*

Historical novel, *1841*

Historical print engraved in America, *1224*

Historical society (national), *5711*

Historical society (state), *5710*

History book by a Jewish author of ancient times, *1862*

History book of the colonial era, *1859*

History of African-Americans, *1871*

History of medicine, *1863*

History of medicine department at a college, *3157*

History of New England, *1860*

History of New England to be published in New England, *1860*

History of printing, *1866*

History of science society (national), *6795*

Hockey game to be shown on television, *7378*

Hockey player on an amateur team who was African-American, *7380*

Hockey team from the United States to win the Stanley Cup, *7376*

Holding companies authorized by a state, *2404*

Holes in one shot by a father and son in the same golf game, *7362*

Holiday Inn, *2432*

Holiday stamp jointly issued by the United States and another country, *6069*

Holographic data storage system, *2540*

Home screening kit for HIV infection, *4954*

Homeopathic hospital, *4875*

Homeopathic medical society, *5031*

Homeopathic pharmacy, *4986*

Homeopathic treatise, *1906*

Homeopathy college, *3163*

Homeopathy journal, *4752*

Homeopathy practitioner, *4968*

Homeopathy school, *3161*

Homestead law enacted by Congress, *5967*

Homosexual character in a television sitcom, *6845*

Homosexual: Political asylum granted on grounds of sexual orientation, *5882*

Homosexual rights march, *6842*

Homosexual rights organization, *6838*

Homosexual rights protest, *6836*

Honorary citizenship authorized by Congress, *5878*

Honors program offered by a university, *2996*

Hooks and eyes, *2289*

Horse blankets, *4263*

Horse bred in the United States to win a major race abroad, *7405*

Horse bred in the United States to win the English Derby, *7407*

Horse breeders' society, *7386*

Horse farm operated by the federal government, *1182*

Horse grooming products sold for human use, *4064*

Horse motel, *2435*

Horse race for a purse of more than $1 million, *7404*

Horse race mutuel ticket to pay more than $1,000, *7397*

Horse race of 1,000 miles, *7396*

Horse race pacing register, *1997*

Horse race pari-mutuel in which all the jockeys were women, *7417*

Horse race run on a regular basis, *7384*

Horse race trotting course, *7387*

Horse race trotting register, *2001*

Horse racing ban by a colony, *7385*

Horse racing magazine, *4782*

Horse show, *1180*

Horse show of national scope, *1181*

Horse stakes race ending in a triple dead heat, *7402*

Horse that was a thoroughbred, *1175*

Horse to win $1 million in races, *7411*

Horse to win a $100,000 purse in one race, *7410*

Horse to win the Triple Crown, *7409*

Horse whose total purses exceeded $100,000, *7406*

Horseriding exhibition, *3652*

Horses, *1174*

Horseshoe manufacturing machine, *1178*

Horticultural magazine, *4711*

Horticultural society, *1088*

Hospice for incurable cancer patients, *4888*

Hospital, *4868*

Hospital and asylum for African-Americans, *4874*

Hospital designed exclusively for infants, *4884*

Hospital for disabled children established by a state, *4889*

Hospital for insane patients established by a colony, *4895*

Hospital for insane patients operated privately, *4896*

Hospital for patients of Chinese ancestry, *4891*

Hospital for treatment of the mentally ill established by a state, *4873*

Hospital insurance group plan, *4535*

Hospital open to all races as a matter of policy, *4886*

Hospital record system, *4882*

Hospital ship operated by the Navy, *5012*

Hospital to treat poor patients at no charge, *4869*

Hospital under Jewish auspices, *4876*

Hostage crisis, *3982*

Hot dog, *3939*

Hotel administration course at a college, *3297*

Hotel at an airport, *2431*

Hotel built over a pier, *2434*

Hotel for women, *2425*

Hotel recognized as a modern first-class hotel, *2422*

Hotel that was fireproof, *2424*

Hotel to establish a heliport, *2433*

Hotel to install electric lights, *2426*

Hotel to install radio reception, *2430*

Hotel transported from one location to another, *2427*

Hotel with individually controlled air conditioning and heating in every room, *2428*

Hotel with plumbing, *2422*

Hotel with safe deposit boxes, *2423*

House completely heated by solar energy, *2128*

House of Representatives election that was contested, *3326*

House of Representatives filibuster, *2581*

House with a built-in nuclear bomb shelter, *2130*

House with solar heating and radiation cooling, *2129*

Household product made entirely of plastic, *4288*

Housing cooperative sponsored by a labor union, *4618*

Human antibodies produced artificially, *5005*

Human beings to set foot on land beyond the earth, *7040*

Human cannonball, *3663*

Human chain across the United States, *3671*

Human construction in North America, *5888*

Human-powered aircraft, *1406*

Human-powered aircraft to cross the English Channel, *1406*

Human-powered helicopter, *1571*

Human-powered submarine race, *7219*

Human stem cells to be cultured in a laboratory, *5068*

Humanist association, *5746*

Humans in America, *5887*

Humor writer who was a woman, *2033*

Hungarian daily newspaper, *5679*

Hunting law enacted by a colony, *3741*

Hunting law (national), *5951*

Hunting license required by a state, *7425*

Hurricane of record, *2860*

Husband and wife to be elected simultaneously to both chambers of a state legislature, *7632*

Husband and wife to fly in space together, *7052*

Hutterites, *6542*

Hybrid seed corn shipment, *1022*

Hydraulic-lift parking garage device, *5486*

Hydroelectric power plant built by the federal government, *3473*

Hydroelectric power plant generating alternating current to operate over a long distance, *3466*

Hydroelectric power plant operated by a county, *3480*

Hydroelectric power plant to furnish arc lighting service, *3458*

Hydroelectric power plant to furnish incandescent lighting, *3462*

Hydroelectric power plant to produce a million kilowatts, *3485*

Hydroelectric power plant to use a storage battery, *3470*

Hydroelectric power plant to use water pumped into a reservoir, *3479*

Hydrogen bomb, *8128*

Hydrogen bomb dropped from an airplane, *8130*

Hydrogen-cooled turbine generator, *3483*

Hydrogenated peanut butter, *3950*

Hydrogenated vegetable shortening, *3885*

Hydrophobia book, *1902*

Hydroplane, *1391*

Hydroplane flight to and from a ship, *1436*

Hydroplane international service, *1409*

Hydroplane service, *1408*

Hydrotherapy book, *1887*

Hydrotherapy chair at a college, *3152*

Hygiene and public health school at a college, *3177*

Hygiene department in a public school district, *4182*

Hygiene lectures at a college, *3136*

Hymnbook compiled by an African-American editor, *1973*

Hymnbook published in America, *1931*

Hymnbook with music, *1972*

I

Ice cream cone, *3866*

Ice cream cone rolling machine, *3868*

Ice cream freezer, *3862*

Ice cream soda, *3864*

Ice cream sundae, *3865*

Ice cream to be made commercially, *3861*

Ice cream wholesale dealer, *3863*

Ice exported, *3932*

Ice-loading machinery, *4415*

Ice-making machine, *4346*

Ice shipped commercially, *3931*

Ice skater to cover 100 miles in less than six hours, *7436*

Ice skating champion, *7427*

Ice skating club, *7428*

Ice yacht, *7205*

Ice yacht club, *7210*

Identification of human beings from the pattern formed by the blood vessels of the retina, *4165*

Identification of the AIDS virus, *5064*

Illegal television station, *7798*

Illuminated nine-hole regulation golf course, *7350*

Illustrated daily newspaper, *5645*

Illustrated tabloid, *5653*

Illustrated weekly magazine, *4715*

Immigration ban enacted by Congress, *5867*

Immigration law enacted by Congress, *5863*

Immigration quota enacted by Congress, *5869*

Immunology society, *5048*

Impregnated corkboard, *2048*

Impression made by the Great Seal of the United States, *1133*

In-line roller skate that was commercially successful, *7466*

Inaugural ball, *6137*

Incandescent lamp, *3492*

Incandescent lamp factory, *3494*

Inclined railroad, *6315*

Income tax levied by a colony, *7638*

Income tax levied by Congress, *7646*

Incubator for premature babies, *4943*

Indelible pencil, *8152*

Independence Day, *4232*

Independent civil government in America, *5939*

Independent government in an American colony, *5940*

Independent single direct-acting steam power pump, *4397*

Index to books, *1770*

Indian Affairs Commissioner who was Native American, *5972*

Indian Day, *4245*

Indigo crop, *1009*

Indoor curling rink, *7276*

Indoor fly casting tournament, *7286*

Indoor ice skating rink, *7430*

Indoor ski school, *7486*

Indoor ski slope, *7488*

Industrial and labor relations school at a college, *3257*

Industrial corporation course at a college, *2920*

Industrial museum, *5584*

Industrial park, *4380*

Industrial research laboratory, *4377*

Industrial robot that was practical, *3445*

Industrial school, *3282*

Industrial school for girls, *3286*

Infirmary for women staffed by physicians who were women, *4877*

Influenza epidemic, *2874*

Infrared photograph, *5827*

Inheritance tax enacted by a state, *7645*

Inheritance tax levied by a colony, *7640*

Inheritance tax levied by Congress, *7647*

Ink, *8149*

Ink paste, *5787*

Inoculation against smallpox using material from human smallpox pustules, *4914*

Insane patients' home, *4894*

Insignia to designate state army regiments, *5222*

Installment finance company, *3805*

Installment sales law enacted by a state, *2314*

Instant book, *1791*

Instant camera, *5846*

Instant tea, *3852*

Instantaneous phonograph recording, *7011*

Institute for research into sexual behavior, *6831*

Instruction for deaf students, *3030*

Instrument for observing radiation in total darkness, *6807*

Insulating brick, *2059*

Insurance agency, *4500*

Insurance board established by a state government, *4503*

Insurance book, *1794*

Insurance company owned by African-Americans, *4501*

Insurance company to insure the lives of animals exclusively, *4517*

Insurance journal, *4721*

Insurance law treatise, *1873*

Insurance rate standardization, *4506*

Insurance regulation enacted by a state, *4499*

Integrated circuit, *3444*

Intelligence test in a school for children with mental retardation, *3021*

Interactive multimedia authoring program, *2553*

Intercity airplane flight by a U.S. military officer, *1428*

Intercity stagecoach service, *2184*

Intercity trucking service, *2484*

Intercollegiate Army–Navy football game, *7320*

Intercollegiate athletic association, *7545*

Intercollegiate baseball game, *7114*

Intercollegiate basketball game, *7169*

Intercollegiate bicycle race, *7192*

Intercollegiate billiard match, *4018*

Intercollegiate court tennis match, *7534*

Intercollegiate fencing championship competition, *7282*

Intercollegiate football association, *7303*

Intercollegiate football championship, *7317*

Intercollegiate football contest, *7315*

Intercollegiate football game between African-American colleges, *7323*

Intercollegiate football game to attract 100,000 spectators, *7325*

Intercollegiate football game to be shown on television, *7329*

Intercollegiate golf association, *7343*

Intercollegiate indoor polo championship, *7460*

Intercollegiate lacrosse association, *7572*

Intercollegiate lawn tennis match, *7528*

Intercollegiate regatta, *7470*

Intercollegiate rowing race, *7468*

Intercollegiate track meet, *7546*

Intercollegiate track meet to be shown on television, *7559*

Intercollegiate transatlantic chess match by cable, *4030*

Intercollegiate wrestling association, *7577*

Interfaith charity organization, *5730*

Intermediate-range ballistic missile, *8138*

Internal-combustion engine, *5477*

Internal revenue collector for the federal government who was a woman, *7657*

Internal revenue tax levied by Congress, *7642*

International airmail, *6017*

International airplane passenger station, *1506*

International championship figure skating tournament, *7431*

International chess champion from the United States, *4029*

International commercial telephone service, *7732*

International copyright agreement, *4631*

International cricket tournament, *7273*

International dogsled mail, *6010*

International exchange of fingerprints, *4162*

International federation of students, *3228*

International fencing championship competition, *7283*

International football game, *7316*

International golf match, *7346*

International horseshoe pitching contest, *7578*

International lifeboat race, *7217*

International polo series, *7458*

International postal card, *6049*

International professional tennis contest, *7530*

International radio broadcasting license, *6297*

International rifle tournament of consequence, *7473*

International satellite, *7067*

International six-day bicycle race, *7189*

International ski meet, *7482*

International tennis matches for the Davis Cup challenge trophy, *7531*

Interracial jury, *2735*

Interstate anticrime pact, *4133*

Interstate commerce act enacted by Congress, *2483*

Interstate Commerce Commission Medal of Honor, *1654*

Interstate legislative conference, *7629*

Interstate railroad, *6322*

Interstate telephone call, *7753*

Interurban streetcar line, *6403*

Investment trust, *3822*

Invisible-glass installation, *4050*

Invisible ink, *8147*

Irish magazine, *4742*

Irish to arrive in America, *5932*

Iron blast furnace to use anthracite coal in smelting, *4452*

Iron blast furnace to use anthracite coal successfully, *4453*

Iron casting, *4448*

Iron exportation, *4447*

Iron mill to puddle and roll iron, *4450*

Iron piano frame, *1308*

Iron pile lighthouse, *4127*

Iron rolling mill, *4449*

Iron sailing vessel, *6867*

Iron sloop yacht, *6872*

Iron steamship built for transatlantic service, *6870*

Iron truss bridge, *3578*

Iron vessel built for the Navy, *6917*

Ironclad naval vessels, *6921*

Ironclad seagoing naval warship, *6922*

Ironclad turreted vessel in the Navy, *6923*

Ironworks, *4445*

Ironworks that was successful, *4446*

Irrigation law enacted by Congress, *1017*

Island territory annexed by the federal government, *5974*

Italian: Congressional representative of Italian ancestry, *2605*

Italian: European to set foot on the North American continent after the Vikings, *5893*

Italian instruction at a college, *3114*

Italian newspaper, *5674*

Italian opera, *1346*

Italian: Public official of Italian ancestry, *5860*

Italian: Senator of Italian ancestry, *7620*

Italian: State governor of Italian ancestry, *7620*

J

Japanese: Army chaplain of Japanese ancestry, *5204*

Japanese beetle, *1023*

Japanese cherry trees, *1062*

Japanese: Compensation of Japanese-Americans interned during World War II, *8087*

Japanese: Congressional representative of Japanese ancestry, *2616*

Japanese: Congressional representative of Japanese ancestry who was a woman, *2616*

Japanese high school in the United States, *3093*

Japanese: Medal of Honor awarded to a soldier of Japanese ancestry, *1683*

Japanese: Naval Academy graduate who was Japanese, *3214*

Japanese newspaper in continuous publication, *5682*

Japanese person to receive an immigration visa, *5876*

Japanese: Senator of Japanese ancestry, *2616*

Japanese to become an American citizen, *5961*

Japanese to enter the United States, *5961*

Jazz composition to appear on the Top 40 charts, *1301*

Jazz concert at Carnegie Hall, *1298*

Jazz record, *1294*

Jet airplane, *1399*

Jet airplane passenger trip, *1474*

Jet airplane to land on a ship, *1466*

Jet airplane to transport mail, *6030*

Jet airplane used for commercial transport, *1403*

Jet drone target missile, *8137*

Jet-propelled fighter plane, *1489*

Jet-propelled landing on an aircraft carrier, *1464*

Jetway, *1510*

Jew to own land in America, *5858*

Jew to serve on a jury, *5858*

Jew to win full citizenship, *5858*

Jewelers' supply house, *5319*

Jewish: Ambassador who was Jewish, *3989*

Jewish: Army chaplain who was Jewish, *5200*

Jewish: Cabinet member who was Jewish, *6108*

Jewish: Cantor in the Reform movement who was a woman, *6490*

Jewish: Cantorial school, *3280*

Jewish cemetery, *2851*

Jewish: College for women founded as a Jewish institution, *2968*

Jewish: College graduate who was Jewish, *3008*

Jewish: College of liberal arts and sciences founded as a Jewish institution, *2965*

Jewish: College under Jewish auspices that was nonsectarian, *2963*

Jewish congregation, *6483*

Jewish congregation in the Reform movement, *6486*

Jewish: Congressional representative who was Jewish, *2598*

Jewish: Fraternal society for Jews, *5720*

Jewish: Governor who was Jewish, *7617*

Jewish high school in a yeshivah, *3276*

Jewish: History book by a Jewish author of ancient times, *1862*

Jewish: Hospital under Jewish auspices, *4876*

Jewish: Kosher cyber cafe, *2467*

Jewish magazine, *4746*

Jewish: Medal of Honor awarded to a Jewish soldier, *1675*

Jewish: Medical college founded as a Jewish institution, *3179*

Jewish: Miss America who was Jewish, *3628*

Jewish mobile synagogue, *6491*

Jewish: Navy admiral who was Jewish, *5272*

Jewish: Navy chaplain who was Jewish, *5203*

Jewish: Navy commodore who was Jewish, *5281*

Jewish: Newspaper for Jewish readers, *5663*

Jewish: Organization (national) of Jewish women, *5720*

Jewish: Orthodox rabbi born in America to be ordained, *6488*

Jewish: Physician who was Jewish, *4962*

Jewish: Play presented by a Jewish professional acting troupe, *1253*

Jewish: Police chief who was both African-American and Jewish, *4154*

Jewish: Police officer who was a Chassidic Jew, *4157*

Jewish: Postage stamp depicting a Jew, *6091*

Jewish prayer book, *1954*

Jewish prayer services to be televised in their entirety, *6595*

Jewish: Rabbi in the Conservative movement who was a woman, *6490*

Jewish: Rabbi in the Reform movement who was a woman, *6490*

Jewish: Rabbi to open the House of Representatives with prayer, *2587*

Jewish: Rabbinical college for the Reform Jewish movement, *3274*

Jewish religious school for children, *6485*

Jewish: Senator who was Jewish, *2647*

Jewish settler in America, *5892*

Jewish: Soldier killed in the Revolutionary War who was Jewish, *7996*

Jewish: Supreme Court justice who was Jewish, *2762*

Jewish synagogue, *6484*

Jewish: Theological college for Jews, *3272*

Jewish: U.S. officer to preside over the observance of a Jewish holiday, *5200*

Jewish: West Point graduate who was a Jewish woman, *3195*

Jewish: West Point graduate who was Jewish, *3195*

Jewish: Yeshivah for Jewish religious study, *3276*

Jewish: Yiddish newspaper, *5670*

Jewish: Yiddish professorship at a college, *3119*

Jewish: Yiddish theater performance, *1255*

Jewish: Young Men's Hebrew Association, *5714*

Jews to arrive in America, *5892*

Jim Crow law, *2255*

Jockey to win more than $5 million in purses in one year, *7420*

Jockey to win seven consecutive races in one day, *7414*

Jockey to win the Kentucky Derby five times, *7413*

Jockey to win the Triple Crown, *7409*

Jockey to win the Triple Crown twice, *7412*

Jockey who was a woman to ride in the Kentucky Derby, *7418*

Jockey who was a woman to ride two winners in one day, *7416*

Jockey who was a woman to win a major stakes race, *7419*

Jockey who was a woman to win a Triple Crown race, *7421*

Jockey who was a woman to win on a regular parimutuel flat track, *7415*

Joint meeting of the Senate and the House of Representatives, *2557*

Joint space walk by American and Russian astronauts, *7055*

Joint stock land bank, *3778*

Journalism course at a college, *3097*

Journalism school at a college, *3102*

Judge advocate of the Navy, *5284*

Judge of a federal district court who was African-American, *2729*

Judge of a federal district court who was an African-American woman, *2729*

Judge of Chinese ancestry, *2728*

Judge of the U.S. Court of Appeals who was an African-American woman, *2732*

Judge on the federal bench who was African-American, *2727*

Judge to be impeached, *2718*

Judge to impose the death penalty who was a woman, *2722*

Judge who had served time in prison, *2731*

Judge who was an African-American woman, *2726*

Jukebox, *7007*

Jumbo jet, *1405*

Junior chamber of commerce, *2453*

Junior high school, *3087*

Jury composed of women, *2734*

Jury school, *2736*

Justice of a state supreme court who was African-American, *2720*

Justice of the peace who was a woman, *2721*

Justice on the federal bench who was a woman, *2725*

Jute culture, *1018*

Juvenile court, *2707*

K

Kapok, *7873*

Keedoozle store, *2506*

Kenaf fiber, *1027*

Kentucky Derby horse race, *7392*

Kerosene, *3527*

Ketchup in bottles, *3945*

Key time recorder, *2381*

Kidnapping, *2766*

Kidney transplant, *5095*

Killer bees, *1163*

Kindergarten, *3073*

Kindergarten for blind children, *3027*

Kindergarten for children with disabilities, *3018*

Kindergarten manual, *1828*

King and queen to be shown on television, *6653*

King born in the United States, *6649*

King cobra snakes, *1157*

King of Great Britain to visit the United States, *6652*

Klieg light unit for movie production, *5572*

Knighthood conferred on a person born in America, *6641*

Knighthood conferred on a soldier born in America, *6642*

Knighthood conferred on American soil, *6643*

Knights of Columbus meeting, *5724*

Knights of Pythias meeting, *5721*

Know-Nothing (American) Party convention, *3354*

Korean War combat mission, *7976*

Kosher cyber cafe, *2467*

Ku Klux Klan meeting, *2253*

Kwanzaa celebration, *4249*

L

Labadist community, *6514*

Label patent, *4657*

Labor activists to be executed, *4564*

Labor antidiscrimination commission of a state government, *4568*

Labor bureau established by a state, *4557*

Labor cooperatives to be authorized by a state, *4609*

Labor Day, *4237*

Labor delegate to a national convention of the American Federation of Labor who was a woman, *4560*

Labor dispute in which the Taft-Hartley Act was invoked, *4569*

Labor mediation and arbitration board established by a state, *4561*

Labor newspaper, *5639*

Labor organization (national), *4560*

Labor party, *3357*

Labor Reform Party national convention, *3357*

Labor union discrimination law enacted by a state, *4614*

Labor union for women, *4606*

Labor union label, *4612*

Labor union to admit workers other than craft workers, *4611*

Labor union to nominate its own political candidates, *4604*

Labor unions to be legalized by a state, *4613*

Laboratory for the study of human parasites, *4931*

Laboratory for the study of parasites in livestock, *5120*

Laboratory of experimental physics in America, *6659*

Laborsaving machine approved by a labor union, *4616*

Lager beer, *2667*

Land battle in the Spanish-American War, *8011*

Land grant college for African-American students, *2895*

Land grant for an agricultural college, *2892*

Land grant to deserters from the British Army during the Revolutionary War, *7997*

Land grant university, *2940*

Land mines, *8097*

Land office, *5948*

Land office established by Congress, *5958*

Land sale by Native Americans to Europeans, *5918*

Land sale swindle, *5919*

Land set-aside for schools authorized by the Continental Congress, *3051*

Land subsidy by Congress for road improvements, *6615*

Landowner of substance who was African-American, *5928*

Landscape architect, *1192*

Landscape painter, *1203*

Large commercial computer network, *2543*

Large-type weekly newspaper, *5659*

Laryngology clinic, *4842*

Laryngology instruction at a college, *3142*

Laryngology journal, *4757*

Laryngophone, *5249*

Laser, *3443*

Latex paint, *7942*

Lathe, *7914*

Latin book written in New England, *1949*

Latin grammar textbook, *1852*

Latino: Bilingual report of a congressional committee, *2595*

Latino: Congressional representative of Puerto Rican ancestry, *2618*

Latino: Governor of Puerto Rico to be elected, *3324*

Latino: Mayor of a major city who was of Mexican descent, *2211*

Latino: Senator who was a Latino, *2652*

Latino: Surgeon general who was a woman, *4214*

Latvian newspaper, *5677*

Launching silos for Atlas F missiles, *8143*

Laundromat, *2442*

Laundry, *2438*

Laundry detergent, *4277*

Law book containing laws enacted by more than one session of Congress, *1875*

Law book of colonial laws, *1872*

Law book of federal laws, *1876*

Law book of federal laws then in force, *1880*

Law code adopted by a state, *4621*

Law history book, *1861*

Law instruction at a college, *3120*

Law magazine, *4700*

Law report, *1874*

Law school at a college, *3121*

Law school at a university to admit women, *3123*

Law school graduate who was a woman, *3124*

Law school operated privately, *3122*

Law school where the entire faculty was 65 years of age or over, *3125*

Law text, *1877*

Lawn mower, *7933*

Lawn tennis, *7523*

Laws of entail and primogeniture to be abolished by a state, *4620*

Lawyer admitted to practice before the Supreme Court who was African-American, *4635*

Lawyer admitted to practice before the Supreme Court who was an African-American woman, *4635*

Lawyer disbarred, *4632*

Lawyer formally admitted to the bar who was African-American, *4634*

Lawyer who was a woman, *4636*

Lawyer who was a woman to be admitted to practice before the Supreme Court, *4638*

Lawyer who was an African-American woman, *4637*

Lawyers admitted to practice before the Supreme Court, *4633*

Lawyers' society (national), *4644*

Lawyers' society (state), *4643*

Laxative in candy form, *4991*

Lead, *5314*

Lead coffins, *2837*

League of Native American nations, *5897*

Leaping submarine, *6972*

Leather-splitting machine, *4456*

Leather tanning, *4455*

Leather tanning by the oil tan method, *4457*

Legal tender, *5386*

Legislative assembly of a colony, *7622*

Legislature of a colony to establish two chambers, *7623*

Leopard, *1143*

Leprosy hospital, *4887*

Lethal injection as a method of execution, *2805*

Letter containing a description of America, *1093*

Letter to circumnavigate the world by commercial airmail, *6027*

Letter written on a typewriter, *2384*

Letters written in English in America, *1095*

Levees, *3604*

Liberal Republican convention, *3358*

Liberty loan subscriptions, *3808*

Liberty Party convention, *3351*

Liberty ship, *6894*

Librarian of Congress, *4663*

Librarian who was African-American, *4674*

Librarian who was an African-American woman, *4674*

Librarians' union, *4617*

Library, *4659*

Library association (national), *4688*

Library building, *4662*

Library building at a university, *4669*

Library catalog in book form, *4660*

Library for seamen, *4667*

Library journal, *4729*

Library newspaper room, *4671*

Library school at a college, *3099*

Library society (local), *4689*

Library society (state), *4690*

Library to possess 100 million items, *4680*

License plates for vehicles, *4220 4226*

Lie detector, *4623*

Liederkranz cheese, *3860*

Life insurance company, *4542*

Life insurance group contract, *4549*

Life insurance group policy, *4548*

Life insurance nonforfeiture law enacted by a state, *4545*

Life insurance offered by a general insurance company, *4543*

Life insurance policy rated substandard, *4546*

Life preserver of cork, *4119*

Lifeboat, *4118*

Lifeboat of corrugated iron, *4120*

Lifesaving medal awarded by the Treasury Department, *1653*

M

M&M candies, *3970*

Macadam road, *6613*

Macaroni factory, *3913*

Machine for cutting and straightening wire, *4403*

Machine for manufacturing pins, *4350*

Machine gun, *8104*

Machine to make glass light bulbs, *3497*

Macy's Thanksgiving Day Parade, *4262*

Made-for-TV movie, *7789*

Madstone, *3647*

Magazine about recreational drugs, *4740*

Magazine containing a fashion plate, *4701*

Magazine for and by deaf students, *4720*

Magazine for blind readers, *4713*

Magazine for mechanics, *4768*

Magazine for patients with mental illness, *4716*

Magazine for professional printers, *4723*

Magazine for women, *4709*

Magazine in a Native American language, *4744*

Magazine of the federal government, *4735*

Magazine on microfilm offered to subscribers, *4685*

Magazine published in America, *4692*

Magazine to contain a phonograph record, *4738*

Magic lantern book, *2018*

Magic lantern feature show, *3692*

Magician of note, *3655*

Magician's advertisement, *2319*

Magnesium commercially produced from seawater, *5344*

Magnetic resonance image of a human body, *4912*

Mail chute, *6000*

Mail collection and delivery in cars, *6007*

Mail delivery by steamboat, *5988*

Mail delivery car with the steering wheel on the right, *5454*

Mail franking privilege, *5984*

Mail fraud law enacted by Congress, *5999*

Mail-order business, *2494*

Mail-order catalog, *2494*

Mail truck, *6003*

Mailbox see-through locker, *5987*

Maize, *3907*

Major league baseball game in which the majority of the players on one team were African-American, *7136*

Major league baseball game to be shown on television, *7132*

Major league baseball player in the postwar era who was African-American, *7151*

Major league baseball player killed in a game, *7148*

Major league baseball player to make seven consecutive hits in seven times at bat in the same game, *7156*

Major league baseball player who was African-American, *7142*

Major league no-hitter baseball game on opening day, *7133*

Malleable iron castings, *4451*

Malted milk, *3872*

Manganese steel, *4495*

Manganese steel for railroad tracks, *4496*

Manila paper, *5752*

Manned docking of two spacecraft, *7082*

Manual training courses offered in a school, *3281*

Manual training institute, *3285*

Manual training school entirely financed by public taxes, *3290*

Manufactured product exported from America, *4282*

Manufacturer of metal goods, *4461*

Manufacturers' fair, *2408*

Map made in America to be published in a book, *4792*

Map of a city within the present limits of the United States, *4790*

Map of the United States, *4795*

Marathon race held annually, *7552*

Marathon runner from the United States who was a woman, *7565*

Marble building, *2070*

Marble quarry, *5318*

Marble statuary group, *1215*

Mardi Gras, *4234*

Margarine law enacted by a state, *3883*

Margarine law enacted by Congress, *3884*

Margarine manufacturer, *3882*

Marijuana ban enacted by Congress, *2689*

Marine band, *5230*

Marine Corps commando raid, *5231*

Marine Corps jet ace in Korea, *1619*

Marine engagement in battle, *7994*

Marine general, *5237*

Marine general who was a woman, *5240*

Marine general who was African-American, *5241*

Marine hospital established by Congress, *4870*

Marine insurance law enacted by a state, *4502*

Marine officer, *5229*

Marine officer killed in service, *5234*

Medals of Honor awarded to African-American servicemen for service in World War II, *1689*

Medical book by a navy medical officer, *1901*

Medical center devoted to teaching, treatment, and research, *3178*

Medical chemistry course at a college, *3145*

Medical college, *3159*

Medical college founded as a Jewish institution, *3179*

Medical college on the Pacific Coast, *3165*

Medical dictionary, *1804*

Medical education book, *1891*

Medical encyclopedia, *1833*

Medical ethics book, *1892*

Medical inspection of schoolchildren, *4180*

Medical insurance group policy for college students, *4537*

Medical journal, *4750*

Medical journal published by an African-American, *4761*

Medical jurisprudence course at a college, *3134*

Medical jurisprudence treatise, *1879*

Medical licensing law enacted by a city, *4934*

Medical licensing law enacted by a colony, *4935*

Medical officer assigned to a naval vessel who was a woman, *5292*

Medical pamphlet, *1886*

Medical record of an epidemic, *2875*

Medical regulations enacted by a colony, *4933*

Medical research chair at a college, *3154*

Medical school for women, *3164*

Medical school that was coeducational, *3164*

Medical slang dictionary, *1810*

Medical society, *5029*

Medical society for African-Americans, *5039*

Medical society for women, *5037*

Medical society (national), *5036*

Medical society (state), *5030*

Medicare identification cards, *4541*

Medicine advertisement in booklet form, *2318*

Medicine ball, *7574*

Medicine produced using recombinant DNA, *5004*

Melodeon patent, *1309*

Melons and cantaloupes, *3899*

Member of the Navy's Hurricane Hunters who was a woman, *5298*

Memorial postage stamp, *6089*

Mennonite meetinghouse, *6538*

Mennonites to arrive in America, *6537*

Mercantile library, *4666*

Merchant marine academy, *3307*

Merchant Marine Academy cadets who were women, *3308*

Merchant marine cadet corps, *3306*

Merchant ship commanded by an African-American captain, *6895*

Merchant ship formally blessed at a launching ceremony, *6893*

Mercury boiler turbine, *3477*

Mercury vapor lamp, *3496*

Metal gun cartridge, *8105*

Metal purchased for coinage, *5363*

Meteor shower on record, *6676*

Meteorite known to have struck a person, *6682*

Meteorite whose landing was recorded, *6677*

Methadone program, *2692*

Methodist bishop, *6560*

Methodist bishop who was a woman, *6562*

Methodist bishop who was an African-American woman, *6562*

Methodist churches for African-Americans, *6561*

Methodist meetinghouse, *6558*

Methodist minister who was African-American, *6559*

Methodist missionary, *6574*

Methodist preacher, *6557*

Metric distance markers on a state highway, *6636*

Metric system usage to be approved by Congress, *2309*

Metropolitan Opera orchestra conductor who was a woman, *1340*

Metropolitan Opera orchestra conductor who was African-American, *1339*

Metropolitan Opera singer who was African-American, *1338*

Mexican: Mayor of a major city who was of Mexican descent, *2211*

Mezzotint engraving, *1199*

Mica, *5321*

Microbiology laboratory, *4932*

Microfilm editions of federal publications and documents, *4686*

Microfilm reading device, *4681*

Micropaleontology course at a college, *3247*

Microprocessor, *3446*

Microscope with a radiation block, *6803*

Microscopic cantilever, *6825*

Microwave oven, *4302*

Microwave television station, *7804*

Midwife to practice professionally, *4961*

Midwifery professor at a college, *3130*

Milestones between cities, *2185*

Military campaign medal, *1657*

Military computer network, *2542*

Military dictionary, *1802*

Military drill manual, *2011*

Military expeditionary force to be sent beyond the Western Hemisphere, *8009*

Military field strategy manual, *2010*

Military heliport, *1569*

Military hospital, *5013*

Military leader of the English settlers, *5251*

Military organization established by a colony, *5253*

Military organization to oppose the British, *5254*

Military prison on an island, *2821*

Military school, *3184*

Military school established by a state, *3185*

Military school operated by a church, *3186*

Military service academies' enrollment of women, *3189*

Military service by African-Americans to be authorized by Congress, *5145*

Military think tank, *5128*

Militia, *5252*

Milk bottles, *4285*

Milk butterfat tester, *3874*

Milk delivery in glass bottles, *3871*

Milk inspection law enacted by a state, *4203*

Milk pasteurized commercially, *3875*

Milk pasteurizing stations, *4204*

Milk purity law enacted by a state, *4202*

Milk sale regulations enacted by a city, *4205*

Milk station operated by a city government, *4206*

Milky Way candy bar, *3969*

Millionaire who was an African-American woman, *2444*

Millionaire with a fortune greater than $100 million, *2443*

Mimeograph, *5784*

Mimeographed daily newspaper, *5654*

Mine barrage, *8090*

Mineral segregation by oil flotation, *5335*

Mineral water bottler, *3842*

Mineralogy instruction at a college, *3231*

Mineralogy journal, *4765*

Mineralogy textbook, *1982*

Mines school at a college, *3236*

Miniature book, *1733*

Miniature car, *5448*

Miniature golf course, *7349*

Miniature television tube, *7809*

Minicomputer, *2533*

Minimum hourly wage of one dollar, *4579*

Minimum wage law enacted by a state, *4577*

Minimum wage law enacted by Congress, *4578*

Minimum wage law established by a city for public contract work, *4580*

Mining company chartered, *5316*

Mining tunnel on a large scale, *3612*

Minister plenipotentiary, *3984*

Minister to Great Britain, *3985*

Minister who was a transsexual, *6844*

Minister who was a woman, *6530*

Minister who was openly homosexual, *6837*

Minstrel show troupe, *3685*

Mint of the United States, *5350*

Miss America, *3628*

Miss America contestant of Asian descent, *3628*

Miss America who was African-American, *3628*

Miss America who was Jewish, *3628*

Missionary society established for the English colonies, *6567*

Missionary society organized in the English colonies, *6568*

Missionary to the Native Americans who was African-American, *6569*

Missionary training school, *3275*

Mitral valve corrective surgery, *5092*

Mobile computer center, *2531*

Mobile electric power plant, *3486*

Mobile home, *5505*

Mobile overseas telephone call from a moving vehicle, *7763*

Mobile radio telephone marine demonstration, *7716*

Mobile telephone call between an airplane in flight and a moving car, *7766*

Mobile telephone call to the moon, *7770*

Mobile telephone commercial service, *7735 7740*

Mobile telephone conversation between the ground and an airship, *7761*

Mobile telephone one-way communication, *7719*

Mobile television unit, *7813*

Mobster convicted for tax evasion, *2782*

Model laboratory school at a college, *3259*

Modeling school, *3298*

Modern art exhibition, *1228*

Modern art museum, *5597*

Modern carillon, *1323*

Modern dancer, *1234*

Mohair, *7872*

Molecular measuring machine, *6811*

Molybdenum centrifugal casting, *4479*

Money order system, *5997*

Mongolian dictionary, *1809*

Monkey trained to perform, *1139*

Monolithic concrete building, *2075*

Monoplane, *1390*

Monosodium glutamate commercial production, *3951*

Monotype machine, *5806*

Monthly cumulative index of books, *1774*

Monument ordered by the federal government from a sculptor who was a woman, *5401*

Monument to a bird, *5411*

Monument to a comic-strip character, *5415*

Monument to a Native American, *5417*

Monument to a woman financed by women, *5406*

Monument to an American poet, *5402*

Monument to an insect, *5412*

Monument to Christopher Columbus, *5396*

Monument to commemorate the Civil War, *5400*

Monument to commemorate the Spanish-American War, *5408*

Monument to George Washington, *5397*

Monument to the American flag, *5414*

Moon of Pluto to be observed, *6684*

Moravian settlement in America, *6540*

Morgan horse, *1176*

Mormon Church meeting, *6492*

Mormon man ordained to the priesthood who was African-American, *6494*

Mormon temple, *6493*

Mortised lock, *2131*

Mosaic pavement, *6630*

Mosque, *6605*

Motel, *2429*

Mother and son simultaneously elected to Congress, *2613*

Mother and son to enlist simultaneously in the Army, *5175*

Mother's Day, *4243*

Motor vehicles powered by natural gas, *5508*

Motorboat, *6948*

Motorboat magazine, *4789*

Motorboat ocean race, *7218*

Motorboat pleasure craft, *6949*

Motorboat race under organized rules, *7216*

Motorboat to travel at a speed of more than 40 miles per hour, *6952*

Motorboat with a storage battery, *6950*

Motorcycle association, *7439*

Motorcycle endurance run, *7437*

Motorcycle hill-climbing contest, *7438*

Motorcycle jump across a river canyon, *3682*

Motorcycle police, *4139*

Motorcycle racer who was a woman, *7440*

Motorcycle that was practical, *5488*

Motorcycle to exceed 200 miles per hour, *5491*

Motorcycle trip from the United States to Tierra del Fuego by a woman, *5494*

Motorcycle with a built-in gasoline engine, *5489*

Mountain climbing: Ascent of Mount Everest by an American, *7588*

Mountain climbing: Ascent of Mount Everest by an American woman, *7588*

Mourning postage stamp, *6080*

Mouse: Computer mouse, *2535*

Movie broadcast on the Internet, *5521*

Movie by a major company for an African-American audience, *5559*

Movie censorship board at the national level, *5540*

Movie censorship board established by a state, *5541*

Movie censorship law enacted by Congress, *5542*

Movie comedy of feature length, *5552*

Movie directed by an African-American director, *5567*

Movie entertainment shown on an airplane, *5514*

Movie exhibition, *5509*

Movie exhibition in a theater to a paying audience, *5511*

Movie featuring an African-American actor, *5554*

Movie film, *5571*

Movie for training soldiers, *3203*

Movie for which one woman served as producer, director, and star, *5568*

Movie in Cinemascope, *5562*

Movie in Esperanto, *5561*

Movie in Technicolor, *5555*

Movie of a heavyweight championship boxing fight, *5546*

Movie of a solar eclipse taken from an airplane, *6688*

Movie of a solar eclipse taken from an airship, *6686*

Movie of feature length made in Hollywood, *5551*

Movie of feature length made outdoors, *5558*

Movie of the sun, *6689*

Movie photographed from an airplane, *5548*

Movie premiere festivities to be shown on television, *5517*

Movie premiered simultaneously in major cities throughout the world, *5520*

Movie projector patent, *5570*

Movie recorded on film to be shown on a screen, *5510*

Movie sex shocker, *5553*

Movie showing another planet, *6687*

Movie showing the inside of a living heart, *4910*

Movie shown on a television network without interruption by commercials, *7793*

Movie star, *5525*

Movie star who was a weapons inventor, *5527*

Movie star who was a woman, *5526*

Movie studio, *5543*

Movie that cost more than $100 million to make, *5522*

Movie that was entirely computer-animated, *5539*

Movie theater, *3705*

Movie to be copyrighted, *5544*

Movie to be shown on a television screen, *5516*

Movie to be shown simultaneously on pay television and in movie theaters, *5519*

Movie to earn $1 billion, *5515*

Movie to earn more than $400 million in the United States market, *5523*

Movie to gross $50 million, *5513*

Movie to premiere on television, *5518*

Movie trailer to be shown on television, *2343*

Movie version of a Shakespeare play to be made in the United States, *5549*

Movie with a plot, *5547*

Movie with both sound and color, *5560*

Movie with scent, *5566*

Movie with sound recorded on the film, *5556*

Movie with sound to be released as a feature, *5557*

Movies with color, *5545*

Moving sidewalk, *6638*

Moving sidewalk in a railroad station, *6639*

Mule born in the United States, *1141*

Multigraph, *2367*

Multiple common battery telephone switchboard, *7734*

Multisatellite launching, *7061*

Municipal ferryboats, *6910*

Municipal streetcars, *6405*

Municipal subway, *6410*

Murder to be shown live on television, *2786*

Murder trial to be televised, *4624*

Museum commemorating the Holocaust, *5592*

Museum devoted exclusively to nuclear energy, *5591*

Museum devoted exclusively to papermaking, *5589*

Museum especially constructed as a museum and art gallery, *5577*

Museum show of Native American art, *1229*

Museum to install refrigerated vaults, *5586*

Museum wing in the United States named for a woman, *5595*

Music book by an author born in America, *1934*

Music book for children, *1939*

Music book printed from type, *1935*

Music book printed with bars, *1932*

Music by Native Americans to be recorded, *1284*

Music chair at a college, *2904*

Music convention of singing teachers, *2901*

Music distributed by electronic equipment, *1321*

Music festival, *1283*

Music instruction in a public school, *2900*

Music magazine, *4694*

Music magazine published in Braille, *4733*

Music printed in a magazine, *1280*

Music publishers, *1281*

Music school authorized to confer degrees, *2899*

Music society, *1278*

Music society for the protection of composers and song writers, *1286*

Music synthesizer powered by electricity, *1321*

Musical comedy broadcast on radio, *1264*

Musical comedy to be shown on television, *1268*

Musical comedy written by African-Americans for African-American performers, *1256*

Musical comedy written for television, *1269*

Musical composition consisting entirely of silence, *1300*

Musical instrument capable of making any audible sound, *1326*

Musical instrument dealer, *1279*

Musical to run for more than 3,000 performances, *1271*

Musical with an American theme and original score, *1252*

Musician born in America to achieve fame in Europe, *1328*

Musk ox, *1150*

Muskets, *8091*

Mustard, *3943*

Mutual fire insurance company, *4532*

Mutual liability insurance company, *4513*

Mutual life insurance company, *4544*

MX intercontinental ballistic missile base, *8144*

N

Nail cutting and heading machine, *7908*

Nail machine, *7921*

Nails, *7907*

Narcotics ban enacted by a state, *2691*

Narcotics ban enacted by Congress, *2686*

Narcotics tariff enacted by Congress, *2685*

Narrow-gauge locomotive, *6357*

National Academy of Sciences member who was a woman, *6781*

National anti-saloon league, *2681*

National bank, *3765*

National bank to fail, *3767*

National Basketball Association commissioner, *7172*

National bone bank to acquire temporal bones for ear research, *4839*

National cemetery, *2852*

National championship stroke-play golf match, *7338*

National Christmas tree, *4258*

National college fraternity for African-American men, *2989*

National conference on crime, *4147*

National convention of African-Americans, *2248*

National curling championship, *7277*

National day of thanksgiving, *4260*

National fencing league, *7281*

National forest, *3727*

National forest reserve, *3728*

National Geographic Society gold medal, *1640*

National hall of fame, *5579*

National Hockey League team from the United States, *7377*

National holiday, *4241*

National Institute of Arts and Letters member who was a woman, *5716*

National Institute of Arts and Letters member who was African-American, *5716*

National labor congress, *4553*

National manufacturing assocation, *4376*

National monument dedicated to an African-American, *5416*

National monument designated by the federal government, *5410*

National Navajo Code Talkers Day, *8082*

National park, *3735*

National park east of the Mississippi River, *3736*

National park ranger, *3735*

National park to contain an active volcano, *3737*

National political convention at which a woman made a seconding speech, *3339*

National political convention of a major party presided over by an African-American, *3337*

National political convention to adopt the two-thirds rule, *3333*

National political convention to adopt the unit rule, *3334*

National political convention to be addressed by a woman, *3336*

National political convention to propose African-Americans for the offices of president and vice president, *3343*

National political platform, *3332*

National science institute, *6781*

National seashore, *3738*

National skeet tournament, *7479*

National tennis championship match for women, *7529*

National tennis championship matches, *7527*

National Union for Social Justice national convention, *3377*

National union for women, *4610*

National water skiing tournament, *7592*

National wheelchair games, *7586*

National women's figure skating four-time winner, *7434*

Nationwide highway numbering system, *6627*

Nationwide highway planning surveys authorized by Congress, *6631*

Native American: Air Force Academy graduate who was Native American, *3191*

Native American: American woman of European descent to be made a Native American chief, *6647*

Native American: Armed occupation by Native American activists in the modern era, *5978*

Native American art exhibition, *1229*

Native American: Baseball player who was Native American, *7143*

Native American: Battle between English colonists and Native Americans, *5908*

Native American: Battle between Native Americans and European soldiers, *5894*

Native American: Bible translated into a Native American language, *1959*

Native American: Boarding school on a Native American reservation, *3063*

Native American: Catholic beatification of a Native American, *6474*

Native American: Catholic school for Native Americans, *3053*

Native American: Church for Native Americans in New England, *6512*

Native American: Church organized by Native Americans, *6603*

Native American: Citizenship statute for Native Americans, *5871*

Native American: Coded military radio transmissions using a Native American language, *8082*

Native American: College graduate who was Native American, *3006*

Native American: College on a Native American reservation, *2969*

Native American: Colonial badges issue to friendly Native Americans, *5929*

Native American: Colonial treaty with the Native Americans, *5915*

Native American Day, *4252*

Native American dictionary, *1796*

Native American grammar, *1850*

Native American: Greeting addressed to the Pilgrims by a Native American, *5914*

Native American: Human construction in North America, *5888*

Native American: Humans in America, *5887*

Native American: Indian Affairs Commissioner who was Native American, *5972*

Native American: Land sale by Native Americans to Europeans, *5918*

Native American language to be given a written form, *5959*

Native American: League of Native American nations, *5897*

Native American: Magazine in a Native American language, *4744*

Native American map of record, *4791*

Native American: Mass scalping of Native Americans by colonists, *5934*

Native American: Massacre of settlers by Native Americans, *5916*

Native American: Missionary to the Native Americans who was African-American, *6569*

Native American: Monument to a Native American, *5417*

Native American: Museum show of Native American art, *1229*

Native American: Music by Native Americans to be recorded, *1284*

Native American: National Navajo Code Talkers Day, *8082*

Native American newspaper, *5666*

Native American: Novel by an American to depict Native Americans in a realistic manner, *1843*

Native American: Occupation of federal territory by Native American protesters in the modern era, *5977*

Native American: Paper money issued by the Native Americans, *5383*

Native American: Play about a Native American, *1247*

Native American: Postage stamp depicting a Native American, *6088*

Native American preacher of Christianity, *6513*

Native American: Primer in a Native American dialect, *1851*

Native American: Protection of Native American hunting grounds authorized by Congress, *5951*

Native American: Reservation for Native Americans established by a state, *5937*

Native American: Reservation for Native Americans established by the federal government, *5946*

Native American: School for Native Americans to be permanently established, *3049*

Native American: School of prominence for Native American children, *3065*

Native American: Senator who was Native American, *2650*

Native American: Settlement in America in continuous habitation, *5891*

Native American superintendent of an agency of the Bureau of Indian Affairs, *5972*

Native American: Team sport played in America, *7094*

Native American: Technical school for Native Americans, *3302*

Native American to become a Protestant, *6502*

Native American to win territorial concessions from the federal government, *5970*

Native American: Treaty entered into by the federal government with Native American tribes, *5941*

Native American: Vaccination program by the federal government to protect Native Americans against smallpox, *4920*

Native American: Vice president who was Native American, *6248*

Native American: West Point graduate who was Native American, *3198*

Natural cement rock, *2039*

Natural gas corporation, *3513*

Natural gas for manufacturing, *3514*

Natural gas pipeline constructed over a long distance, *3516*

Natural gas plant operated by a city, *3515*

Natural gas used as an illuminant, *3511*

Natural medicine clinic subsidized by a government, *4853*

Naturalization act enacted by Congress, *5862*

Naturalization act in the American colonies, *5859*

Naturalization ceremony in the White House, *5879*

Nautical almanac, *1765*

Nautical school, *3303*

Nautical school established by a city, *3304*

Nautical school established by a state, *3305*

Naval academy, *3213*

Naval Academy graduate to attain the rank of rear admiral, *3215*

Naval Academy graduate who was African-American, *3219*

Naval Academy graduate who was Japanese, *3214*

Naval Academy midshipman who was African-American, *3219*

Naval Academy students who were women, *3221*

Naval action of importance in the War of 1812, *8021*

Naval air training school, *3217*

Naval airplane, *1483*

Naval attaché, *5285*

Naval attack in the Revolutionary War, *7987*

Naval battle between colonists, *5922*

Naval battle between ironclad vessels in the Civil War, *7961*

Naval battle in the Civil War, *7959*

Naval battle in the Revolutionary War, *7991*

Naval battle in the War of 1812, *8020*

Naval bombardment of the Japanese homeland in World War II, *8085*

Naval counterattack by American forces against the Japanese in World War II, *8076*

Naval expedition mounted by an English colony, *5910*

Naval hospital established by Congress, *5007*

Naval militia established by a state, *5255*

Naval militia of a state to have a hydroplane, *5256*

Naval officers' training school, *3212*

Naval patrol bomber, *1488*

Naval pilots, *1483*

Naval protection, *5259*

Naval radio station, *5301*

Naval Reserve flier who was African-American, *1618*

Naval Reserve Nurse Corps nurse who was African-American, *5289*

Naval ship named for an African-American naval officer, *1618*

Naval ship named for an enlisted man, *8035*

Naval ship of the line, *6913*

Naval ship to surrender in peacetime without a fight, *6947*

Naval ship with a crew of mixed nationalities, *6944*

Naval ship with a mixed company of male and female personnel, *6937*

Naval ship with a plural name, *6936*

Naval skirmish in the Civil War, *7950*

Naval vessel equipped to lay mines, *6931*

Naval vessel equipped with a gyrostabilizer, *6929*

Naval vessel from the United States to sink a German submarine in World War II, *8054*

Naval vessel to display the American flag around Cape Horn, *1127*

Naval vessel to sail around the Cape of Good Hope, *6981*

Naval vessels to sink an enemy submarine in the Atlantic, *8039*

Naval war college, *3216*

Naval War College president who was a former prisoner of war, *3222*

Naval War College students who were African-American, *3220*

Navigation act enacted by Congress, *2472*

Navigational satellite, *7059*

Navy ace in Korea, *1622*

Navy ace in World War I, *1613*

Navy ace in World War II, *1617*

Navy admiral killed in action in World War II, *8068*

Navy admiral who was African-American, *5274*

Navy admiral who was Jewish, *5272*

Navy admirals to wear the five-star insignia, *5273*

Navy admirals who were brothers, *5294*

Navy airship, *1516*

Navy bureau of medicine and surgery, *5009*

Navy captain who was a woman, *5288*

Navy captain who was African-American, *5296*

Navy chairman of the Joint Chiefs of Staff, *5293*

Navy chaplain, *5198*

Navy chaplain in the Continental Navy, *5196*

Navy chaplain killed in action, *5199*

Navy chaplain who was a Muslim, *5207*

Navy chaplain who was a woman, *5205*

Navy chaplain who was an African-American woman, *5206*

Navy chaplain who was Catholic, *5202*

Navy chaplain who was Jewish, *5203*

Navy commissioned officer who was African-American, *5290*

Nuclear-powered aircraft carrier, *6942*

Nuclear-powered cruiser, *6941*

Nuclear-powered merchant ship, *6900*

Nuclear-powered submarine, *6973*

Nuclear-powered submarine with turbine-electric drive, *6978*

Nuclear product for peacetime use, *3545*

Nuclear reactor built for private industrial research, *3549*

Nuclear reactor for research and development, *6809*

Nuclear reactor fueled by plutonium, *3554*

Nuclear reactor operated commercially, *3552*

Nuclear reactor patent, *6806*

Nuclear reactor privately operated, *6804*

Nuclear reactor used in medical therapy, *5061*

Nuclear warhead fired from a Polaris submarine, *8132*

Nuclear warhead mounted on a rocket, *8131*

Nudist organization, *7580*

Numbering system for patents, *4653*

Numerical system of insurance rating, *4514*

Nurse appointed to a college professorship, *5028*

Nurse to receive formal training, *5023*

Nurse who was African-American to receive formal training, *5023*

Nursery school, *3072*

Nurses to be registered by a state, *4938*

Nurses' training, *3133*

Nursing magazine, *4758*

Nursing school at a college, *3173*

Nursing school for African-American students, *3169*

Nursing school to award a diploma, *3166*

Nursing society, *5040*

Nuts and bolts factory, *7918*

Nylon, *7877*

Nylon stockings, *2278*

O

Oat-crushing machine, *3914*

Obelisk to be brought to the United States, *5403*

Observatory established by the federal government, *6665*

Observatory on a mountaintop, *6666*

Observatory operated by a college, *6664*

Obstetrics book, *1900*

Occupation of federal territory by Native American protesters in the modern era, *5977*

Occupational therapy course at a college, *3155*

Occupational therapy treatment, *5114*

Ocean mail contracts, *5990*

Oceanographer of distinction who was a woman, *6719*

Oceanography institution, *6713*

Odd Fellows lodge, *5719*

Off-track betting operation, *3637*

Officer killed in action in the Korean War, *7978*

Officer to preside over both of the branches of Congress, *2565*

Official use of the "Coke" trademark, *3848*

Offshore radar warning station, *7682*

Oil and gas conservation law enacted by a state, *3537*

Oil and gas production course at a college, *3243*

Oil company, *3525*

Oil drill offshore rig, *3534*

Oil drill seagoing rig, *3543*

Oil journal, *4778*

Oil lamp, *4343*

Oil pipeline, *3531*

Oil pipeline of importance, *3533*

Oil refinery, *3526*

Oil refinery with a carbon monoxide boiler, *3542*

Oil spill with disastrous consequences, *3544*

Oil spring, *3523*

Oil tank railroad cars, *6376*

Oil well, *3524*

Oil well drilled by torpedoes, *3532*

Oil well that was commercially productive, *3528*

Oil wells successfully drilled in the ocean, *3535*

Oilcloth factory, *7870*

Oiled silk patent, *7864*

Okapi, *1155*

Old age home for pioneers, *5975*

Olympic athlete from the United States to win 10 medals, *7442*

Olympic athlete from the United States to win a gold medal, *7441*

Olympic athlete from the United States to win four gold medals in one year, *7448*

Olympic athlete from the United States to win the marathon race, *7553*

Olympic athlete from the United States to win the pentathlon and decathlon, *7554*

Olympic athlete to win two consecutive heptathlon events, *7567*

Olympic Games boycott, *7450*

Olympic Games competition to be held in the winter, *7446*

Olympic Games held in the United States, *7443*

Olympic gold medalist from the United States who was a woman, *7445*

Olympic gold medalist in both the Summer and Winter Olympics, *7447*

Olympic gold medalist who was an African-American woman, *7449*

Olympic medalist who was African-American, *7444*

One-way street, *6611*

Open-air post office, *6039*

Open golf championship tournament, *7341*

Open-hearth furnace for the manufacture of steel, *4493*

Opera broadcast over the radio in its entirety, *1350*

Opera by an American composer, *1345*

Opera by an American composer to be performed at the Metropolitan Opera House, *1349*

Opera composed by a woman to be performed at the Metropolitan Opera House, *1348*

Opera composer who was a woman, *1334*

Opera house established by a city, *1351*

Opera libretto published, *1343*

Opera of a serious nature, *1344*

Opera performed by a professional visiting troupe, *1342*

Opera performed in America, *1341*

Opera prima donna who was African-American, *1333*

Opera produced at the Metropolitan Opera House, *1347*

Opera singer who was African-American to sing a white role, *1336*

Opera to be televised from the Metropolitan Opera House, *1353*

Opera to be televised in its entirety, *1352*

Opera written for television, *1354*

Ophthalmologist of note, *4972*

Ophthalmology book, *1905*

Ophthalmology clinic, *4846*

Ophthalmology course at a college, *3137*

Opinion poll, *5601*

Optical computer, *2539*

Opticians' journal, *4760*

Optometry courses at a college, *3153*

Optometry school, *3168*

Optometry society (national), *5044*

Oral school for deaf students, *3031*

Oranges of the seedless navel variety, *3903*

Oratorio by an American, *1289*

Oratorio performance, *1288*

Orbiting geophysical observatory, *7073*

Orbiting observatory, *6673*

Orbiting solar observatory, *7066*

Orca, *1161*

Orchestra, *1355*

Orchestra from the United States to make a European tour, *1363*

Orchestra in a theater, *1356*

Orchestra of international stature, *1358*

Orchestral song to be printed, *1378*

Organ built in the United States, *1304*

Organ school, *2907*

Organ transplant that was successful, *5096*

Organ with color display, *1315*

Organists' society (national), *1285*

Organization (national) of Jewish women, *5720*

Organized crime massacre, *2780*

Organs, *1303*

Ornamented soda fountain for restaurants, *2456*

Ornithopter that succeeded in flying, *1407*

Orphanage, *2137*

Orthodontia journal, *4763*

Orthodontia treatise, *1924*

Orthodontists' society, *5045*

Orthodox rabbi born in America to be ordained, *6488*

Orthopedic hospital, *4881*

Orthopedics chair at a college, *3143*

Oscar awarded to a performer who was African-American, *1633*

Oscar for best actor awarded to a performer who was African-American, *1633*

Oscar for best picture, *1630*

Oscar for best picture awarded to a movie that was independently produced, *1637*

Oscar for best picture awarded to an X-rated movie, *1638*

Oscar movie awards ceremony to be telecast, *1636*

Oscar winners who were father and son, *1634*

Oscar winners who were husband and wife, *1635*

Oscars for best acting, *1631*

Oscars for best movie director, *1632*

Osteopathic physician, *4975*

Osteopathic physicians who were women, *4976*

Osteopathy journal, *4762*

Osteopathy school, *3170*

Ostrich farm, *1071*

Outboard motor, *6951*

Outdoor museum with nature trails, *5585*

Outdoor scenes to be televised, *7829*

Outdoor school for children with tuberculosis, 3020

Overland mail service, 5993

Overland wagon road across the Rocky Mountains, 6617

Oyster cocktail, 2669

Oyster propagation, 1058

P

Pacemaker, 4952

Pacemaker to be implanted in a patient's body, 4953

Painless surgery demonstration, 4831

Paint prepared from standard formulas, 7930

Paint ready-mixed, 7925

Paint-spraying device, 7936

Painter to obtain a public commission, 1198

Painting by an African-American artist to hang in the White House, 1221

Painting movement, 1204

Painting of an American scene by a European painter, 1211

Paired six-day bicycle race, 7195

Paleontological report on fossil footprints, 6739

Paleontology chair at a college, 3237

Paleontology report, 1974

Pamphlet produced from a steel plate engraving, 1744

Panorama show, 3684

Paper bag machine, 4405

Paper bag manufacturing machine, 5757

Paper collar, 2285

Paper cup, 4310

Paper folding machine, 5764

Paper for printing made from rags and wood-pulp fiber, 5753

Paper made by machine, 5749

Paper made from wood pulp, 5754

Paper mill, 5747

Paper money, 5382

Paper money fractional currency, 5388

Paper money issued by the federal government, 5385

Paper money issued by the Native Americans, 5383

Paper money of the present small size, 5393

Paper sewing patterns, 4357

Paper twine machine, 5761

Paperback publisher, 1790

Paprika mill, 3952

Parachute fatality in the Army, 1590

Parachute jump from a balloon, 1580

Parachute jump from an airplane, 1581

Parachute jump from an airplane by a woman, 1582

Parachute jump from an autogiro, 1588

Parachute jump using a nylon parachute, 1591

Parachute jumper snagged by airplane in midair, 1593

Parachute-jumping contest, 7296

Parachute known as the "free parachute", 1583

Parachute tower for training jumpers, 1589

Parade held by a mystic society, 3659

Parade in which the marching music was supplied by transistor radios, 3670

Parade of automobiles, 3665

Parade with float tableaux, 3662

Parcel post domestic air service, 6033

Parcel post international air service, 6032

Parcel post service, 6006

Parent-teacher assocation, 3226

Parent-teacher association (national), 3227

Parental leave law enacted by a state that applied to both mothers and fathers, 4571

Parish priest, 6445

Parking garage that was completely automated, 5485

Parking meter enforcement division of a police department, 4149

Parkland purchased by a city, 3733

Parliamentary act to establish a colonial post office, 5981

Partridge propagation, 1067

Passenger locomotive, 6349

Passenger ship equipped with radar, 7677

Passenger ship with a diesel engine, 6877

Passenger to circle the world on commercial airlines in less than 100 hours, 1477

Passover seder to be shown on television, 6489

Passport, 5884

Passport fee, 5885

Passport photographs, 5886

Pastelist, 1197

Patent examiner who was a woman, 4656

Patent granted by a colony, 4646

Patent granted by the federal government, 4648

Patent granted jointly to a father and son, 4650

Patent granted to an African-American inventor, 4652

Patent granted to an inventor who was a woman, 4651

Patent issued by the Confederate States of America, 4655

Patent leather, 4458

Patent list, 2027

Patent medicine advertisement, *2316*

Patent medicine to achieve nationwide popularity, *4989*

Patent on a number, *6764*

Patent on an animal, *6751*

Patent recipient to obtain more than one patent, *4649*

Patented pills, *4981*

Pathology chair at a college, *3139*

Pathology textbook, *1907*

Patriotic song by an American, *1376*

Patriotic song to achieve national popularity, *1374*

Pay station telephone service, *7731*

Pay telephone, *7715*

Pay television dramatic program, *7787*

Pay television presentation of a sporting event, *7785*

Pay television system, *7799*

Paymaster general of the Continental Army, *5164*

Payment by the Federal Crop Insurance Corporation, *1006*

Payment by the Federal Deposit Insurance Corporation, *3784*

Peace society, *5733*

Peacetime death sentence for espionage, *2836*

Pear and peach trees, *3891*

Pedestrian shopping mall, *2513*

Pediatric clinic, *4841*

Pediatrics book, *1920*

Pediatrics journal, *4756*

Pediatrics monograph, *1897*

Pediatrics professor at a college, *3141*

Peep show machine, *3686*

Peep show using film in a vending machine, *3691*

Pellagra experiment of note, *5058*

Pen with truly erasable ink, *8155*

Penalty rule in football, *7304*

Pencil factory, *8148*

Pencil with an attached eraser, *8151*

Penitentiary building opened by the federal government, *2826*

Penny daily newspaper, *5638*

Penny restaurant, *2460*

Pension for presidents and their widows, *6172*

Pension fund for teachers, *4585*

Pension granted to the widow of a president, *4584*

Pension law enacted by a colony, *4581*

Pension law enacted by Congress, *4582*

Pension laws enacted by a state, *4587*

Pension plan, *4586*

Pensions paid by the federal government, *4583*

Pensions paid by the federal government to workers in private industry, *4588*

People's Party national convention, *3366*

Percheron horse importation, *1179*

Percussion rock drill, *4401*

Perfecta or Exacta horse race, *7403*

Perforated wrapping paper, *5758*

Performance by a British rock group, *1370*

Performance of "America the Beautiful", *1380*

Performance of *The Stars and Stripes Forever*, *1292*

Periodical index, *1771*

Periscope, *5244*

Peritonitis preventive, *4992*

Permalloy, *7705*

Person to apply the term "capitol" to a government building, *2114*

Personal computer, *2537*

Personal computer operating system, *2546*

Personal computer software company, *2552*

Petroleum exported to Europe, *3530*

Petroleum jelly, *4988*

Petroleum refining course at a college, *3246*

Pharmaceuticals book, *1929*

Pharmacist who was a woman, *4963*

Pharmacist who was a woman to receive a degree from a pharmacy college, *3147*

Pharmacists to be regulated by a state, *4939*

Pharmacopoeia, *1926*

Pharmacopoeia prepared by a medical association, *1928*

Pharmacy college, *3160*

Pharmacy journal, *4751*

Pharmacy professorship at a college, *3132*

Pharmacy society (national), *5038*

Phase-contrast cinemicrography film to be shown on television, *5565*

Philology society (national), *6783*

Philosophy book printed in America, *2008*

Phonetic Bible, *1969*

Phonetic dictionary, *1806*

Phonograph, *7004*

Phonograph record, *7006*

Phonograph record of a stage performance by the original cast, *7008*

Phonograph that was practical, *7005*

Phonograph trade magazine, *4730*

Phonograph with an automatic record changer, *7010*

Phonograph with an enclosed horn in the cabinet, *7009*

Photoelectric cell, *3478*

Pilot of a jet fighter to win a dogfight in the Korean War, *7981*

Pilot of an airplane to qualify as an astronaut by attaining a 50-mile altitude, *1623*

Pilot on a regularly scheduled major airline who was a woman, *1606*

Pilot on a scheduled passenger line who was African-American, *1604*

Pilot to bail out of a disabled airplane, *1585*

Pilot to bail out of an airplane flying at supersonic speed, *1592*

Pilot to circumnavigate the world twice, *1457*

Pilot to destroy an enemy airplane in the Gulf War, *7973*

Pilot to destroy an enemy airplane in the Korean War, *7975*

Pilot to die because of a lack of oxygen, *1614*

Pilot to fire a gun from an airplane, *1608*

Pilot to fly a million miles in a jet airplane, *1605*

Pilot to fly a regularly scheduled airmail transport who was a woman, *1600*

Pilot to receive the Congressional Medal of Honor, *1658*

Pilot who was a woman to be inducted into the Army Aviation Hall of Fame, *1625*

Pilot who was a woman to cross the English Channel in a plane, *1596*

Pilot who was a woman to die in a combat zone, *1625*

Pilot who was an African-American woman, *1597*

Pilot wounded in Vietnam who was a civilian, *8013*

Pilots in American units to participate in air combat in World War I, *8043*

Pin-tumbler cylinder lock, *2133*

Pinball ban enacted by a city, *7455*

Pinball game machine, *7454*

Pineapple cheese, *3858*

Pins manufactured with a solid head, *4351*

Pipe or screw wrench, *7929*

Pipeless organ, *1324*

Piracy law enacted by Congress, *2772*

Pirate on the Atlantic seaboard, *2768*

Pituitary hormone, *4996*

Pizzeria, *2462*

Planet found beyond Neptune, *6680*

Planetarium, *6658*

Planetarium built in America, *6660*

Planetarium in the western hemisphere, *6669*

Planetarium open to the public, *6669*

Planetary probe to enter the atmosphere of Jupiter, *7092*

Plank road, *6618*

Planned suburban development, *2199*

Plant patent, *1063*

Plastic bonded airplane, *1398*

Plastic car, *5451*

Plastic oil pipeline, *3541*

Plastic surgery professor at a college, *3156*

Plate glass, *4040*

Plate-glass insurance, *4507*

Plate glass produced on a large scale, *4042*

Platform scale, *2379*

Platypus, *1149*

Play about a Native American, *1247*

Play by an African-American woman to appear on Broadway, *1270*

Play by an American writer to be successfully presented by an established company, *1246*

Play-by-play broadcast of a football game, *7324*

Play by William Shakespeare produced in America, *1243*

Play in which a horse race was run on stage, *1251*

Play of full length by an African-American writer to be performed in New York City, *1258*

Play of note written by an American, *1240*

Play on Broadway in which an African-American actress had a starring role, *1267*

Play performed 1,000 times, *1248*

Play presented by a Jewish professional acting troupe, *1253*

Play presented by professional players, *1242*

Play to be shown on television, *1260*

Play written in America that was printed, *1241*

Player piano, *1316*

Player piano that was completely automatic, *1317*

Playground, *2144*

Playwright to write professionally, *1245*

Pleurisy book, *1889*

Plow for pulverizing the soil, *1049*

Plow patent, *1041*

Plow with interchangeable parts, *1042*

Plumbing law enacted by a state, *2231*

Plutonium, *6818*

Plywood, *2049*

Pneumatic bicycle tire, *7188*

Pneumatic hammer, *7934*

Pneumatic piano player, *1320*

Pneumatic tires, *5495*

Pocket dictionary, *1798*

Poem to be printed in a newspaper, *1945*

Poem to win national acclaim, *1947*

Poet laureate of the United States, *2034*

Poet laureate who was a woman, *2034*

Poet laureate who was African-American, *2034*

Poet to win a Pulitzer Prize four times, *1713*

Poet who was an African-American woman, *1946*

Poet who was an African-American woman to win the Pulitzer Prize, *1715*

Poetry collection by an African-American woman, *1946*

Poetry collection by an American poet, *1943*

Poetry collection by an American poet who was a man, *1944*

Poetry translation prepared in America, *1942*

Poinsettia plants, *4255*

Poisoning of store merchandise, *2788*

Polar bear, *1138*

Polar expedition of which a woman was a member, *6726*

Pole vaulter to clear the bar at 15 feet, *7560*

Police appeal for missing persons to be shown on television, *4148*

Police bureau of criminal alien investigation, *4145*

Police bureau of identification, *4158*

Police chief who was a woman, *4142*

Police chief who was both African-American and Jewish, *4154*

Police department to adopt the fingerprinting system, *4160*

Police force, *4131*

Police officer who was a Chassidic Jew, *4157*

Police officer who was a woman, *4136*

Police officer who was a woman to be killed in the line of duty, *4152*

Police patrol wagon, *4137*

Police radio system, *4146*

Police uniforms, *4132*

Poliomyelitis epidemic, *2877*

Poliomyelitis vaccine, *4923*

Polish settlers in America, *5909*

Political asylum granted on grounds of sexual orientation, *5882*

Political asylum granted to avoid genital mutilation, *5883*

Political convention to be broadcast on radio, *3340*

Political convention to be televised, *3342*

Political economy chair at a college, *3251*

Political economy course at a college, *3250*

Political history book, *1868*

Political machine, *3347*

Political newspaper, *5632*

Political science association (national), *6790*

Politician who was openly homosexual to win an election, *6839*

Polo association (national), *7459*

Polo club, *7456*

Polo game played outdoors at night, *7461*

Polo mallets and balls, *7457*

Polygamy ban enacted by Congress, *4807*

Polypeptide hormone synthesized, *5003*

Polystyrene, *4483*

Pontoon bridge, *3568*

Pontoon bridge of reinforced concrete, *3595*

Pony Express mail, *5994*

Popcorn, *3954*

Popcorn snack, *3962*

Pope to visit the United States, *4083*

Pope to visit the United States before his election, *4081*

Pope to visit the White House, *4084*

Popular science magazine, *4773*

Popular vote in a presidential election, *3386*

Porcelain, *4038*

Porcelain teeth, *4855*

Porpoise, *1156*

Portable church, *6532*

Portable electric stethoscope, *4946*

Portable movie camera, *5574*

Portable movie projector, *5573*

Portable typewriter, *2387*

Portrait of Abraham Lincoln, *6157*

Post office aboard a naval vessel, *6038*

Post office building, *6036*

Post office fully mechanized, *6042*

Post office in a colony, *6035*

Post office in an airplane, *6040*

Postage meter, *6008*

Postage stamp catalog, *2026*

Postage stamp depicting a Jew, *6091*

Postage stamp depicting a living American, *6097*

Postage stamp depicting a Native American, *6088*

Postage stamp depicting a nurse, *6099*

Postage stamp depicting a president, *6052*

Postage stamp depicting an African-American, *6090*

Postage stamp depicting an African-American woman, *6100*

Postage stamp depicting an American woman, *6087*

Postage stamp depicting the American flag, *6082*

Postage stamp featuring a work of art in true color, *6093*

Postage stamp for balloon mail, *6059*

Postage stamp having the same design as that of another country, *6092*

Postage stamp issued in the United States and canceled by a foreign country, *6072*

Postage stamp issued jointly by two countries, *6069*

Postage stamp issued on the date of the event it commemorated, *6070*

Postage stamp issued with perforations, *6054*

Postage stamp whose design was decided by popular vote, *6101*

Postage stamp with fluorescent tagging, *6071*

Postage stamp with valuation of one dollar, *6060*

Postage stamps depicting a president, *6078*

Postage stamps depicting a woman, *6085*

Postage stamps depicting scenes, *6081*

Postage stamps depicting the American eagle, *6079*

Postage stamps in coils, *6062*

Postage stamps issued by the Post Office Department, *6052*

Postage stamps of 50 different designs sold as a single sheet, *6098*

Postage stamps of four different designs sold as a single sheet, *6096*

Postage stamps to feature paintings, *6086*

Postage stamps without a denomination, *6077*

Postal card, *6044*

Postal directory, *1816*

Postal route between cities, *5980*

Postal savings bank, *3775*

Postal service law enacted by Congress, *5986*

Postcard, *6046*

Postmaster general of the United States, *5985*

Postmaster general under the Continental Congress, *5983*

Postmaster who was a woman, *5982*

Potato, *3890*

Potato chips, *3960*

Potatoes to be cultivated, *3894*

Pottery, *4308*

Pottery to make sanitary ware, *4041*

Poultry show, *1069*

Pounds for stray livestock, *1066*

Power mower, *7933*

Power plant using alternating current, *3464*

Power plant using solar cells, *3560*

Power printing press capable of fine book work, *5771*

Power transmission installation using alternating current, *3467*

Powered soaring glider commercially licensed, *1556*

Prayers in sign language, *6528*

Precanceled stamps printed on rotary presses, *6064*

Prefabricated ship built in America, *6849*

Prefrontal lobotomy, *5087*

Prehistoric hoax, *3648*

Premiums given away with merchandise, *2323*

Prepared-food producer, *3945*

Presbyterian church, *6580*

Presbyterian elder who was a woman, *6583*

Presbyterian minister who was a woman, *6584*

Presbyterian presbytery, *6581*

President and First Lady to die during the term for which he had been elected, *6196*

President born after the death of his father, *6182*

President born an American citizen, *6183*

President born beyond the boundaries of the original 13 states, *6186*

President buried in the National Cemetery, *6199*

President buried in Washington, *6197*

President elected by the House of Representatives, *6145*

President elected for third and fourth terms, *6170*

President elected for two nonconsecutive terms, *6162*

President elected under the Constitution, *6135*

President inaugurated in the city of Washington, *6146*

President inaugurated on January 20, *6169*

President married while in office, *6190*

President of a black African country to visit the United States, *4082*

President of a major medical society who was a woman, *5049*

President of a major university who was African-American, *2975*

President of the Continental Congress, *2574*

President of the Republic of Texas, *4077*

President of the United States in Congress assembled, *6135*

President to appear on color television, *6215*

President to appear on television, *6215*

President to attend the launching of a manned space flight, *6176*

President to be assassinated, *6193*

President to be born in a hospital, *6198*

President to be censured by Congress, *6151*

President to be impeached, *6159*

President to be wounded in an unsuccessful assassination attempt while in office, *6207*

President to become a godfather to a member of the British royal family, *6200*

President to celebrate his silver wedding anniversary at the White House, *6191*

President to conduct religious services as commander-in-chief of the Navy, *6166*

President to die in Washington, *6189*

President to face enemy gunfire while in office, *6148*

President to fly in a helicopter, *6229*

President to fly in an airplane, *6226*

President to go through the Panama Canal while in office, *6167*

President to hold an airplane pilot's license, *6224*

President to invite the president-elect, *6165*

President to make a radio broadcast, *6210*

President to make a radio broadcast from a foreign country, *6214*

President to make a radio broadcast from the White House, *6212*

President to make a radio broadcast in a foreign language, *6216*

President to pitch a ball to open the baseball season, *6163*

President to read a veto message to Congress, *6168*

President to receive a passport while in office, *6232*

President to receive a presidential pardon, *6179*

President to receive the unanimous vote of the presidential electors, *3381*

President to reside in Washington, *6144*

President to resign, *6177*

President to review the military forces, *6147*

President to ride in a car, *6223*

President to ride on a railroad train, *6222*

President to take the oath of office using a nickname, *6180*

President to tour the country, *6230*

President to travel underwater in a captured enemy submarine, *6228*

President to use a radio, *6209*

President to use a telephone, *6161*

President to use the line-item veto, *6181*

President to visit a foreign country in wartime, *6237*

President to visit a foreign country while in office, *6231*

President to visit a nation not recognized by the federal government, *6238*

President to visit Alaska and Canada while in office, *6234*

President to visit China, *6238*

President to visit Europe, *6233*

President to visit Hawaii while in office, *6236*

President to visit South America while in office, *6235*

President to visit the Soviet Union, *6238*

President to witness the firing of a Polaris missile, *6174*

President who came to the office through appointment rather than election, *6178*

President who had been a senator, *6139*

President who had been divorced, *6202*

President who had received a patent, *6156*

President who was a bachelor, *6192*

President who was a "dark horse" candidate, *3403*

President who was a Rhodes Scholar, *6206*

President who was Catholic, *6203*

President whose assassination was attempted, *6187*

President whose body was exhumed, *6208*

President whose grandson became president, *6188*

President whose mother lived at the White House, *6195*

President whose son became president, *6184*

President with a brother in the Senate, *6205*

Presidential address televised from the White House, *6217*

Presidential airplane, *6227*

Presidential amnesty issued to rebellious citizens, *6143*

Presidential appointment, *6138*

Presidential campaign manager who was a woman, *3392*

Presidential campaigner to be assassinated, *3416*

Presidential candidate nominated at a caucus, *3399*

Presidential candidate nominated at a national convention, *3401*

Presidential candidate to accept his party's nomination in person, *3413*

Presidential candidate to appear in movie footage, *3411*

Presidential candidate to be assassinated, *3404*

Presidential candidate to make a campaign speech, *3402*

Presidential candidate to make an acceptance speech at a nominating convention, *3413*

Presidential candidate to make campaign speeches in a foreign language, *3408*

Presidential candidate to ride in a car, *3410*

Presidential candidate who had been an astronaut, *3418*

Presidential candidate who was a woman, *3405*

Presidential candidate who was Catholic, *3407*

Presidential candidate who was renominated after a defeat, *3414*

Presidential citation to an entire division, *1666*

Presidential Citizen Medal, *1644*

Presidential commission, *6142*

Presidential election debate between an incumbent president and a challenger to be televised, *3397*

Presidential election debates to be shown on television, *3394*

Presidential election in which a computer was used to predict the outcome, *3393*

Presidential election in which a loser won, *3385*

Presidential election in which candidates were nominated for the vice presidency, *3384*

Presidential election in which more than one candidate declared for the presidency, *3383*

Presidential election in which soldiers in the field were allowed to vote, *3389*

Presidential election in which votes were tallied electronically, *3395*

Presidential hot line, *6173*

Presidential inauguration, *6136*

Presidential inauguration to be broadcast on radio, *6213*

Presidential library, *6171*

Presidential mansion, *6250*

Presidential message to Congress that was broadcast on radio, *6211*

Presidential news conference filmed for television and newsreels, *6219*

Presidential news conference to be televised live, *6220*

Presidential nomination ceremony broadcast on radio, *3412*

Presidential nominee who was African-American, *3409*

Presidential pet to star in a movie, *6201*

Presidential physician who was a woman, *6204*

Presidential press conference recorded on tape, *6218*

Presidential proclamation, *6140*

Presidential protest, *6152*

Presidential railroad car, *6225*

Presidential Unit Citation award in peacetime, *1643*

Presidential veto of a congressional bill, *6141*

Presidential veto to be overridden by Congress, *6154*

Press censorship by military authorities, *5604*

Pressure-sensitive adhesive, *4487*

Pressure-sensitive adhesive postage stamp, *6076*

Pressure suit, *1386*

Pretzel bakery, *3922*

Price regulation agreement by colonists, *2516*

Price regulation law enacted by a colony, *2517*

Price regulation law enacted by a state, *2522*

Price sheet for commodities, *2321*

Primary election law enacted by a state, *3318*

Primer in a Native American dialect, *1851*

Prince of Wales to visit the United States, *4078*

Principal chief of the Cherokee Nation who was a woman, *4085*

Print patent, *4658*

Printed ballot, *3314*

Printed copies of the Constitution, *1103*

Printed streetcar transfers, *6402*

Printed traffic regulations, *4138*

Printer, *5767*

Printer who was a woman, *5782*

Printer's ink, *5783*

Printing instruction at a school, *3284*

Printing lecture course in a college, *3294*

Printing of the Declaration of Independence, *1114*

Printing press, *5767*

Printing press for polychromatic printing, *5776*

Printing press for printing wallpaper in color, *5770*

Printing press invented in the United States, *5768*

Printing press to use a continuous web or roll of paper, *5778*

Prison, *2811*

Prison built for women and managed by women, *2823*

Prison commissioner who was a woman, *2830*

Prison established by the federal government for women, *2829*

Prison guard who was a woman to serve in a maximum security prison for men, *2831*

Prison matrons for guarding women prisoners, *2819*

Prison organized into community groups, *2827*

Prison reform society, *2812*

Prison to have individual cells for prisoners, *2813*

Prison treadmill, *2816*

Prisoners captured in the War of 1812, *8022*

Prisoners in a federal penitentiary to be employed in industry, *2828*

Private housing development designed as a complete community, *2200*

Private hydroponic garden, *1037*

Private mint authorized by the federal government, *5352*

Private railroad car, *6374*

Private school for children with disabilities, *3017*

Prize money awarded by the Navy, *5262*

Prizefighting ban enacted by a state, *7234*

Probate delay law enacted by a state, *2842*

Probation officer for juvenile delinquents to be hired by a state, *2822*

Probation system for criminals of all ages, *2825*

Product liability lawsuit to result in a criminal trial, *2315*

Professional aeronaut, *1537*

Professional football association, *7305*

Professional football championship game broadcast on radio, *7330*

Professional football game, *7322*

Professional football game in which 10 touchdowns were made, *7328*

Professional football game in which a woman participated, *7334*

Professional football game to be shown on television, *7308*

Professional fraternity at a college, *2987*

Professional Golfers Association tournament, *7345*

Professional hockey player to reach a score of more than 1,000 points, *7381*

Professional hockey player to score 50 goals in one season, *7379*

Professional hockey player who was a woman, *7383*

Professional hockey player who was African-American, *7380*

Professional hockey team, *7375*

Professional open golf championship match, *7344*

Professional soccer organization recognized internationally, *7493*

Professor at a first-class medical school who was a woman, *3151*

Progressive Party national convention, *3373*

Prohibition Party convention, *3356*

Pronghorn antelope, *1148*

Propaganda course at a college, *3256*

Property tax established by a colony to support public schools, *3041*

Property tax levied by a colony, *7637*

Prostitute, *6826*

Protection of Native American hunting grounds authorized by Congress, *5951*

Protest against slavery, *2240*

Protest by college students, *3007*

Protestant: Adventist church to accept Saturday as the Sabbath, *6529*

Protestant: African Methodist Episcopal bishop, *6564*

Protestant: African Methodist Episcopal church convention, *6563*

Protestant: African Methodist Episcopal preacher who was a woman, *6565*

Protestant: Ban on Quakers enacted by a colony, *6586*

Protestant: Baptist church, *6543*

Protestant: Baptist churches for African-Americans, *6546*

Protestant: Bible society, *6571*

Protestant: Bible society (national), *6573*

Protestant: Bibles in hotel rooms, *6579*

Protestant: Brethren, *6545*

Protestant: Camp meeting, *6525*

Protestant: Children's church, *6535*

Protestant: Christian religious service in English on the Pacific Coast, *6501*

Protestant: Christian worship services organized by African-American slaves, *6515*

Protestant church for lepers, *6533*

Protestant: Church for Native Americans in New England, *6512*

Protestant church west of the Alleghenies, *6519*

Protestant: College founded as a Methodist institution, *2937*

Protestant: College founded as a Quaker institution, *2942*

Protestant: Communion cups for individuals, *6582*

Protestant: Congregational church, *6505*

Protestant: Congregational Church minister who was African-American, *6522*

Protestant: Disciples of Christ meeting, *6527*

Protestant: Divinity professor at a college, *3266*

Protestant: Dutch Reformed church, *6506*

Protestant: Ecumenical synod, *6510*

Protestant: Episcopal bishop, *6549*

Protestant: Episcopal bishop deposed for heresy in the United States, *6552*

Protestant: Episcopal bishop who was African-American, *6551*

Protestant: Episcopal cathedral, *6550*

Protestant: Episcopal church organized in New England, *6548*

Protestant: Episcopal church service in an English colony, *6547*

Protestant: Episcopal priest who was a woman, *6553*

Protestant: Evangelical Church conference, *6526*

Protestant: Floating church, *6577*

Protestant: Foreign missionary society, *6572*

Protestant: Foreign missionary society organized by women, *6578*

Protestant: French to arrive in America, *5898*

Protestant: Great Awakening of religious revival, *6517*

Protestant: Hutterites, *6542*

Protestant: Labadist community, *6514*

Protestant: Lutheran church, *6555*

Protestant: Lutheran pastor, *6554*

Protestant: Lutheran services in English, *6556*

Protestant: Mariners' church, *6575*

Protestant: Mennonite meetinghouse, *6538*

Protestant: Mennonites to arrive in America, *6537*

Protestant: Methodist bishop, *6560*

Protestant: Methodist bishop who was a woman, *6562*

Protestant: Methodist churches for African-Americans, *6561*

Protestant: Methodist meetinghouse, *6558*

Protestant: Methodist minister who was African-American, *6559*

Protestant: Methodist missionary, *6574*

Protestant: Methodist preacher, *6557*

Protestant: Military school operated by a church, *3186*

Protestant: Minister who was a woman, *6530*

Protestant: Missionary society established for the English colonies, *6567*

Protestant: Missionary society organized in the English colonies, *6568*

Protestant: Missionary to the Native Americans who was African-American, *6569*

Protestant: Missionary training school, *3275*

Protestant: Moravian settlement in America, *6540*

Protestant: Native American preacher of Christianity, *6513*

Protestant: Native American to become a Protestant, *6502*

Protestant: Portable church, *6532*

Protestant: Prayers in sign language, *6528*

Protestant: Presbyterian church, *6580*

Protestant: Presbyterian elder who was a woman, *6583*

Protestant: Presbyterian minister who was a woman, *6584*

Protestant: Presbyterian presbytery, *6581*

Protestant: Quaker annual meeting, *6588*

Protestant: Quakers executed for their religious beliefs, *6587*

Protestant: Quakers to arrive in America, *6585*

Protestant: Reformed Church meeting, *6516*

Protestant: Religious leader in the American colonies who was a woman, *6507*

Protestant: Religious toleration law enacted by a colony, *6511*

Protestant: Religious tract society, *6570*

Protestant: Religious tract society (national), *6576*

Protestant: Sabbath law enacted by a colony, *6504*

Protestant: Sabbath laws published by a colony, *6509*

Protestant: Salvation Army services, *6531*

Protestant: Scandinavian Methodist Episcopal church, *6566*

Protestant: School for colonial children in America, *3038*

Protestant: School for Protestant girls, *3050*

Protestant: Schwenkfelder to arrive in America, *6539*

Protestant: Seventh Day Baptist Church, *6544*

Protestant: Shaker religious community, *6521*

Protestant Sunday school, *6518*

Protestant: Swedenborgian or New Church temple, *6524*

Protestant: Synod held in America, *6508*

Protestant: Thanksgiving worship service, *6503*

Protestant: Theology school, *3267*

Protestant: Trailer church, *6534*

Protestant: Unitarian church, *6523*

Protestant: United Brethren in Christ meeting, *6541*

Protestant: United Church of Christ ordination of a woman in which all the principal roles were filled by women, *6536*

Protestant: Universalist church services, *6520*

Psychiatric institute, *3150*

Psychiatry association (national), *5035*

Psychiatry book, *1903*

Psychiatry textbook, *1912*

Psychodrama treatment for psychiatric patients, *5116*

Psychology journal, *4759*

Psychology laboratory, *4927*

Psychology professor at a college, *3148*

Psychology society (national), *5043*

Ptarmigan, *1166*

Public bathhouse and washhouse, *4193*

Public defender hired by a state, *4642*

Public demonstration of color television, *7811*

Public exhibition of postage stamps, *6058*

Public garage, *5483*

Public high school to specialize in the performing arts, *3091*

Public locker plant, *2366*

Public museum, *5576*

Public official of Italian ancestry, *5860*

Public reading of the Declaration of Independence, *1116*

Public school classes for children with epilepsy, *3022*

Public school for children with disabilities, *3019*

Public school for Chinese-American children, *3062*

Public school kindergarten, *3074*

Public school with a continuous existence, *3040*

Public service symbol of the federal government, *3714*

Public speaking department at a college, *3100*

Public telecast made over telephone wires, *7835*

Public telecast over telephone wires using the narrow-band system, *7848*

Publicist for a theater company, *3694*

Publisher of denominational religious books, *1957*

Publishing society, *1785*

Puerto Rican: Congressional representative of Puerto Rican ancestry, *2618*

Puetro Rico: Governor of Puerto Rico to be elected, *3324*

Pulitzer Prize awarded to a comic book, *1717*

Pulitzer Prize awarded to a musical, *1712*

Pulitzer Prize awarded to a newspaper, *1707*

Pulitzer Prize awarded to a newspaper reporter, *1704*

Pulitzer prize awarded to a science book, *1718*

Pulitzer Prize for a newspaper editorial, *1705*

Pulitzer Prize for a novel written by a woman, *1711*

Pulitzer Prize for an editorial cartoon, *1710*

Pulitzer Prize for drama, *1708*

Pulitzer Prize for fiction, *1706*

Pullman sleeping car, *6375*

Pullman sleeping car made entirely of steel, *6384*

Pullman sleeping car that was comfortable, *6377*

Punchboards, *2368*

Puppet show, *3683*

Puppet show to be televised, *1259*

Pure food and drug law enacted by a state, *4178*

Pure food and drug law established by Congress, *4175*

Purple Heart, *1656*

Pushball, *7573*

Q

Quack doctor of note, *3646*

Quadrant, *6954*

Quadruple newspaper press, *5794*

Quadruplets delivered by cesarean operation, *2174*

Quadruplets to graduate from college, *2173*

Quaker annual meeting, *6588*

Quakers executed for their religious beliefs, *6587*

Quakers to arrive in America, *6585*

Quantum theory of electromagnetic radiation, *6759*

Quarantine board established by a state, *4209*

Quarantine law enacted by a colony, *4207*

Quarantine law enacted by Congress, *4208*

Quarantine law for plants enacted by a state, *4211*

Quarantine law for plants enacted by Congress, *4212*

Quark to be observed, *6821*

Quarterly magazine, *4704*

Quartermaster of the Continental Army, *5166*

Quasar to be observed, *6683*

Queen to visit the United States, *4079*

Queen to visit the United States during her reign, *4080*

Quetzal bird, *1168*

Quids political faction, *3346*

Quinine, *4983*

Quinine sulfate, *4984*

Quintuplets, *2172*

Quintuplets to live more than five years, *2176*

Quintuplets to survive infancy who were African-American, *2177*

Quorum of the House of Representatives, *2556*

Quorum of the Senate, *2556*

R

Rabbi in the Conservative movement who was a woman, *6490*

Rabbi in the Reform movement who was a woman, *6490*

Rabbi: Orthodox rabbi born in America to be ordained, *6488*

Rabbi to open the House of Representatives with prayer, *2587*

Rabbinical college for the Reform Jewish movement, *3274*

Race between a horse and a bicycle, *7395*

Race between a locomotive and a horse-drawn vehicle, *7388*

Race-car driver to win $100,000, *7268*

Racing event for children, *7583*

Racing shell, *7469*

Rack-rail diesel-electric locomotive, *6366*

Radar detection of airplanes, *7676*

Radar for commercial and private planes, *7681*

Radar installation aboard a commercial carrier, *6959*

Radar observations, *7675*

Radar signal bounced off the sun, *7683*

Radar signal to the moon, *7680*

Radar used to detect enemy airplanes, *7679*

Radio advertising contract for FM broadcasts, *2340*

Radio advertising course at a college, *2923*

Radio: All-news radio station, *6303*

Radio astronomer, *6670*

Radio: Auction of radio spectrum for satellite services, *6284*

Radio: Battery to convert radioactive energy into electrical energy, *3488*

Radio: Boxing match broadcast on radio, *7238*

Radio: Boxing match broadcast on radio from ringside, *7239*

Radio braodcast of election results, *3390*

Radio broadcast demonstration, *6262*

Radio broadcast from a circus, *3674*

Radio broadcast from a moving train, *6276*

Radio broadcast from a submerged submarine, *6268*

Radio broadcast from a tape recording, *6279*

Radio broadcast from a zoo, *1189*

Radio broadcast from the Senate chamber, *2631*

Radio broadcast heard in both the Arctic and the Antarctic regions, *6277*

Radio broadcast in which citizens telephoned the president, *6221*

Radio broadcast of a baseball game with a play-by-play description, *7128*

Radio broadcast of a concert from an airplane, *1295*

Radio broadcast of a debate, *6269*

Radio broadcast of a livestock auction, *1075*

Radio broadcast of an open session of Congress, *2567*

Radio broadcast sent from an airplane, *6266*

Radio broadcast using an orbiting satellite, *6281*

Radio: Burglar alarm operated by ultrasonic or radio waves, *2136*

Radio: Car equipped with a two-way radio, *7717*

Radio car for military use, *5246*

Radio: Car radio, *6309*

Radio: Carbon microphone used in radio broadcasting, *6308*

Radio: Chain radio broadcast, *6270*

Radio church, *6590*

Radio: City radio station, *6296*

Radio: Coast-to-coast radio hookup, *6272*

Radio: Coast-to-coast radio news broadcast to be recorded, *5706*

Radio: Coast-to-coast solar-powered two-way radio conversation, *6282*

Radio: Coded military radio transmissions using a Native American language, *8082*

Radio: College radio station, *6295*

Radio: Color news photograph transmitted by radio fax for publication, *5695*

Radio commercial, *2333*

Radio: Commercial radio station licensed, *6294*

Radio compass on a naval airplane, *1495*

Radio contest, *6260*

Radio: Daily news program on radio, *5705*

Radio distress signal from an American ship, *6285*

Radio distress signal officially established, *6286*

Radio distress signal resulting in an airship rescue, *6288*

Radio: Drama broadcast on radio, *1257*

Radio: Drama broadcast on radio from a regular stage, *1262*

Radio: Drama broadcast on radio from a ship at sea, *1261*

Radio: Editorial to be broadcast over radio and television, *5707*

Radio: Election campaign using radio, *3322*

Radio: Election in which returns were broadcast on radio, *3390*

Radio facsimile newspaper, *5656*

Radio fax patents, *7667*

Radio fax transmission to a moving train, *7673*

Radio: Federal law requiring radios on ships, *4222*

Radio: Fireboat with two-way radio equipment, *4112*

Radio: FM radio, *6310*

Radio: FM radio transmitter to receive a commercial license, *6299*

Radio: Football game to be broadcast on radio with a play-by-play description, *7324*

Radio: Foreign language course broadcast on radio, *3118*

Radio: Heavyweight championship boxing match broadcast on radio, *7241*

Radio: Transatlantic undersea radio conversation, *6283*

Radio: Transcontinental demonstration of radio telephone operation, *7721*

Radio: Transcontinental radio fax transmission of a photograph, *7669*

Radio: Transistor radio receiver to be mass-produced, *6312*

Radio: Transoceanic radio signal conveying a television image, *7828*

Radio: Transpacific radio conversation, *6267*

Radio: Transpacific radio fax transmission, *7670*

Radio: Triode for radios, *6307*

Radio tube made of metal, *6311*

Radio two-way broadcast from an airplane, *6273*

Radio: Two-way radio conversation between a submerged submarine and another vessel, *7760*

Radio variety show with a live studio audience, *6291*

Radio: Volcanic eruption to be broadcast on radio, *2870*

Radio: Walkie-Talkie two-way radio device, *7722*

Radio waves from space to be observed, *6681*

Radio: Weather forecast broadcast on radio, *6769*

Radio: Wedding broadcast over the radio, *4819*

Radio: Yacht race broadcast on radio, *7215*

Radio: Year in which television industry profits exceeded those of radio, *7772*

Radioactive isotope medicine, *4995*

Radioactive isotopes exported, *6820*

Radioactive substance produced synthetically, *6816*

Radium treatment for cancer, *5115*

Ragtime instruction book, *1941*

Railroad accident, *6325*

Railroad apprentice school, *3287*

Railroad bridge across the Mississippi River, *3581*

Railroad bridge entirely of steel, *3584*

Railroad car with a center aisle, *6371*

Railroad car with an observation dome, *6388*

Railroad chapel car, *6381*

Railroad charter granted by a state, *6317*

Railroad coach modeled after English coaches, *6373*

Railroad coupler, *6423*

Railroad dining car, *6379*

Railroad dining car powered by electricity, *6389*

Railroad excursion rates, *6329*

Railroad for commercial transportation of passengers and freight, *6321*

Railroad for freight transportation, *6316*

Railroad freight cars with compartments, *6390*

Railroad freight yard that was fully automatic, *6346*

Railroad interlocking signal machine, *6424*

Railroad land grant, *6330*

Railroad merger, *6331*

Railroad mystery excursion, *3667*

Railroad operated by an electric third-rail system, *6341*

Railroad operated by the federal government, *6343*

Railroad owned by a city, *6335*

Railroad owned by a state, *6319*

Railroad parlor car, *6380*

Railroad post office, *6037*

Railroad rails of iron, *6418*

Railroad rails of steel, *6419*

Railroad rails of T shape, *6416*

Railroad safety law enacted by a state, *4218*

Railroad safety law enacted by Congress, *4219*

Railroad signal system of continuous cab signals, *6426*

Railroad signal system with automatic electric block, *6422*

Railroad sleeping car, *6372*

Railroad station for both passengers and freight, *6320*

Railroad suspension bridge, *3580*

Railroad tank car lined with glass, *6385*

Railroad timetable advertised in a newspaper, *6323*

Railroad to be completely equipped with diesel-electric engines, *6344*

Railroad to carry troops, *6324*

Railroad to install track water tanks, *6421*

Railroad to run trains to Washington, *6327*

Railroad to run west of the Mississippi River, *6328*

Railroad to run west out of Chicago, *6328*

Railroad to use an electric engine, *6340*

Railroad track that was practical, *6415*

Railroad treatise, *2020*

Railroad tunnel, *3613*

Railroad union, *4608*

Railroad with iron-plated wooden rails, *6318*

Ramjet helicopter, *1564*

Rap album to attract a mass audience, *1373*

Rapid-fire machine gun, *8107*

Rapid-transit subway, *6411*

Raptor sanctuary, *3748*

Rat extermination throughout an entire city, *4183*

Rat of record, *1140*

Rattlesnake meat in cans, *3942*

Rayon, *7874*

Ready-made clothing for children, *2273*

Ready-mix food, *3947*

Reaper machine that was practical, *1044*

Reaper machine that worked, *1043*

Rebellion against the federal government, *5947*

Rebellion by colonists against an English governor, *5930*

Rebellion in the English colonies, *5905*

Rebellion of African-American slaves in a colony, *2241*

Recipes using standard measurements, *3878*

Reclining chair, *4324*

Record album to hit No. 1 in the pop charts, *1367*

Rectangular television tube, *7817*

Red Cross meeting, *5739*

Reflecting telescope, *6663*

Reformatory for boys established by a state, *2820*

Reformatory for juvenile deliquents, *2817*

Reformatory for women established by a state, *2824*

Reformed Church meeting, *6516*

Refrigerated railroad car, *6378*

Refrigeration system for trucks, *5507*

Refrigerator, *4345*

Refugee to arrive under the Refugee Relief Act of 1953, *5877*

Regatta, *7208*

Registered mail, *5991*

Registration of aliens by the federal government, *5872*

Reigning king to visit the United States, *6645*

Reindeer, *1152*

Relay race in a college track meet, *7550*

Relief map, *4800*

Religion magazine printed in rotogravure, *4734*

Religious leader in the American colonies who was a woman, *6507*

Religious magazine, *4693*

Religious radio program broadcast by a husband and wife, *6596*

Religious refuge for people of all faiths, *5923*

Religious service broadcast on radio, *6589*

Religious service to be televised from a church, *6593*

Religious services to be shown on television, *6592*

Religious toleration law enacted by a colony, *6511*

Religious tract society, *6570*

Religious tract society (national), *6576*

Religious weekly newspaper, *5636*

Remote-controlled railroad passenger car, *6391*

Remote television pickup, *7830*

Reply-paid card, *6045*

Representative of a foreign country to the United States, *3983*

Republican Party meeting, *3353*

Resale price maintenance law enacted by a state, *2313*

Research society (national), *6793*

Reservation for Native Americans established by a state, *5937*

Reservation for Native Americans established by the federal government, *5946*

Respirator known as the iron lung, *4947*

Restaurant with an automatic arrangement for vending food, *2461*

Restrictions by Congress on immigration of Chinese laborers, *5866*

Retail store whose sales in one day exceeded $1 million, *2508*

Retirement colony, *2198*

Reusable manned spacecraft, *7087*

Revenue stamp printed by the Post Office Department, *7660*

Revenue stamps issued by the federal government, *7648*

Revolutionary War armed conflict, *7989*

Revolutionary War bayonet charge, *8003*

Revolutionary War conflict in which American and British troops met on equal terms, *8002*

Revolutionary War incident, *7988*

Revolutionary War military action, *7990*

Revolutionary War national veterans' organization, *5308*

Revolutionary War volunteer detachment, *7992*

Revolver pistol, *8096*

Revolver shooting tournament, *7477*

Revolver that was self-cocking, *8103*

Revolving door, *2081*

Revolving gun, *8093*

Revolving gun turret for ships, *8106*

Revolving restaurant, *2465*

Rh factor discovery, *4835*

Rhinoceros, *1144*

Rhodes Scholar who was African-American, *2961*

Rhodes Scholars, *2961*

Rhubarb, *3897*

Rhyming dictionary, *1803*

Rice to be imported, *3893*
Rifle society (national), *7472*
Rifled breech-loading steel cannon, *8101*
Rifled gun, *8094*
Right-to-die law enacted by a state, *2843*
Right-to-die society, *2840*
Rigid airship, *1521*
Rivet production, *2037*
Rivetless cargo vessel, *6891*
Road appropriation of a specific sum by a state, *6614*
Road authorization by a state, *6612*
Road construction law enacted by a colony, *6607*
Road map for motorists, *4801*
Road map for public use, *4793*
Road paved with glasphalt, *6635*
Road pavement, *6606*
Road pavement of sheet asphalt, *6621*
Road with a depressed trough, *6628*
Robot manufacturing company, *3445*
Robot patent, *3445*
Robot to conduct a roving exploration of the surface of another planet, *7093*
Robot to make pizza, *3448*
Robot to perform surgery, *3449*
Rock and roll broadcast on FM radio, *1371*
Rock and roll song, *1368*
Rock and roll song to hit No. 1 in the pop charts, *1369*
Rock music festival, *1372*
Rock musical, *1272*
Rock wool insulation factory, *2047*
Rocket airplane for military use, *1490*
Rocket-driven sled on rails, *7021*
Rocket flight using liquid fuel, *7017*
Rocket glider flight, *1552*
Rocket plane for manned supersonic flight, *1492*
Rocket-powered car to break the sound barrier on land, *5461*
Rocket to attain a 100-mile altitude, *7019*
Rocket to break the sound barrier, *7018*
Rocket to intercept a supersonic target missile, *8139*
Rocket to intercept an airplane, *8136*
Rocket to reach outer space, *7020*
Rocket-tracking ship, *6945*
Rocket with an electrostatic (ion) engine, *7025*
Rocking chair, *4320*
Rodeo for roping and tying steers, *3690*
Role-playing game, *4014*
Roll-on-roll-off carrier, *6898*

Roller coaster, *3621*
Roller coaster with a loop-the-loop, *3626*
Roller derby, *7465*
Roller skates, *7462*
Roller skating rink open to the public, *7463*
Rolling lift bridge, *3587*
Root beer, *3846*
Rosicrucian Order lodge, *6598*
Rotary Club meeting, *2451*
Rotary printing press, *5777*
Rotary printing press with a continuous-roll feed, *5779*
Rotating milking platform, *1056*
Rotogravure press, *5781*
Rough-dry laundry service, *2441*
Round-the-world airplane passenger race, *7299*
Round-the-world bicycle trip, *7201*
Round-the-world bicycle trip by a husband and wife, *7203*
Round-the-world bicycle trip by a woman, *7202*
Round-the-world commercial airplane service, *1416*
Round-the-world flight by a commercial airplane, *1462*
Round-the-world flight over the North Pole on a regularly scheduled air route, *1479*
Round-the-world helicopter flight, *1579*
Round-the-world journey on foot, *7590*
Round-the-world nonstop airplane flight without refueling, *1482*
Round-the-world nonstop flight by a jet airplane, *1480*
Round-the-world nonstop flight by an airplane, *1470*
Round-the-world radio broadcast, *6275*
Round-the-world solo airplane flight, *1457*
Round-the-world solo sailing journey, *6984*
Round-the-world solo sailing trip by an African-American, *7002*
Round-the-world steamboat passenger service, *6888*
Round-the-world telephone conversation, *7762*
Royal navigation act affecting the American colonies, *2468*
Rubber company, *4484*
Rubber shoe heel, *2305*
Rubber shoe manufacturer, *2301*
Rugby: International rugby football contest, *7309*
Runner from the United States to run a mile in less than four minutes, *7564*
Running shoes, *2306*
Rural free mail delivery, *6002*

Russian: Army general who was a Russian immigrant, *5149*

Russian newspaper, *5681*

Russian Orthodox mission, *6495*

Russian Orthodox saint canonized in the United States, *6498*

Russian settlement, *5943*

S

Sabbath law enacted by a colony, *6504*

Sabbath laws published by a colony, *6509*

Safe deposit vault, *2359*

Safety association (national), *4187*

Safety congress, *4184*

Safety fuse, *4422*

Safety pin, *4336*

Safety razor, *4056*

Sailcloth factory, *7862*

Sailor to become a four-star admiral, *5275*

Sailor to reenlist in the Navy while under the North Pole, *5267*

Sailors assigned to regular Navy shipboard duty who were women, *5269*

Saint Patrick's Day parade, *3651*

Sale of federal land authorized by Congress, *5944*

Sale of federal land to an individual, *5950*

Sales tax enacted by a state, *7656*

Salmon cannery, *3887*

Salt well drilled west of the Alleghenies, *3933*

Salt works, *3930*

Salute fired by Great Britain in honor of an officer of the United States, *3976*

Salvage operation in space, *7089*

Salvation Army services, *6531*

Sandblasting process, *4434*

Sandpaper patent, *4394*

Sanitary napkin, *4059*

Santa Claus school, *4259*

Sardine cannery, *3888*

Satellite composite map of the United States, *4802*

Satellite dish for personal use, *7824*

Satellite from the United States to impact the moon, *7068*

Satellite launched from the earth to orbit another planet, *7076*

Satellite placed in orbit by the United States, *7056*

Satellite repair in orbit, *7077*

Satellite to transmit colored photographs of the full earth face, *7075*

Satellite to transmit photographs of the earth, *7057*

Satellite with a nuclear reactor to orbit the earth, *7074*

Savings and loan association established by the federal government, *3783*

Savings bank, *3759*

Savings bank life insurance, *4547*

Savings bank to receive money on deposit, *3760*

Savings bank with a deposit of half a billion dollars, *3781*

Savings group for children, *3769*

Sawmill driven by electricity, *4412*

Sawmill to use a band saw, *4404*

Saxophone production, *1318*

Scandinavian Methodist Episcopal church, *6566*

Scholastic fraternity at a college, *2983*

Scholastic fraternity at an African-American college, *2983*

School band, *1360*

School committee, *3044*

School completely irradiated with germicidal lamps, *4191*

School for African-American children established by a state, *3064*

School for blind African-American students, *3026*

School for blind students, *3023*

School for blind students to adopt the Braille system, *3025*

School for children with mental disabilities, *3016*

School for colonial children in America, *3038*

School for deaf students, *3032*

School for freed slaves, *2251*

School for music teachers, *2898*

School for Native Americans to be permanently established, *3049*

School for Protestant girls, *3050*

School for the higher education of women, *3079*

School nurses in public schools, *5027*

School of modern dance, *2908*

School of modern history at a college, *3094*

School of modern languages at a college, *3112*

School of prominence for Native American children, *3065*

School radio station on ultrahigh frequency, *6298*

School run by missionaries in America, *3037*

School stadium, *7509*

School to provide separate classrooms for each class, *3058*

School to use platoon organization, *3067*

Schoolbook, *1823*

Schoolhouse west of the Alleghenies, *6519*

Schools to specialize in business communications, *3057*

Schooner built in America, *6852*

Schwenkfelder to arrive in America, *6539*

Science fiction course at a college, *3108*

Science fiction magazine, *4732*

Science journal, *4767*

Science society, *6776*

Science society (national), *6780*

Scientific evidence for life on Mars, *7027*

Scientific expedition fitted out by the federal government, *6723*

Scientific expedition sponsored by a colony, *6661*

Scientific journal, *4750*

Scientific program to search for extraterrestrial life, *6672*

Scientific survey of sexual behavior among Americans, *6831*

Scientist to win two Pulitzer prizes, *1718*

Scouting organization for girls, *2148*

Screw auger, *7911*

Screw caliper, *7928*

Screw factory, *7912*

Screw machine to make pointed screws, *7923*

Screw-propelled steamboat on the Great Lakes, *6869*

Sculptor of renown, *1208*

Sculptor to obtain a federal commission, *1207*

Sea battle in World War II fought solely by air power, *8078*

Seacoast gun carriage, *8102*

Seagoing dredge with a hopper, *6884*

Seagoing radio broadcasting station, *5304*

Seaplane glider, *1550*

Seat belt law enacted by a state, *4228*

Seat belts in cars, *4229*

Seatrain, *6890*

Seawater conversion plant, *2237*

Secession act at the start of the Civil War, *7636*

Secession convention during the War of 1812, *7635*

Secession idea to be mentioned in Congress, *7634*

Secret Service agents who were women, *4170*

Secret service established by the federal government, *4169*

Secret service established in a colony, *4168*

Secretary of state, *6104*

Secretary of state who was a woman, *6123*

Secretary of the treasury, *6103*

Secular song by a composer born in America, *1375*

Secular song hit, *1379*

Sedan car, *5443*

Seed business, *1011*

Seeding machine, *1047*

Seeing Eye dog, *1173*

Seismograph, *6712*

Self-portrait, *1212*

Self-service grocery store, *2500*

Self-service post office, *6043*

Self-service restaurant, *2458*

Self-service supermarket, *2504*

Self-sustaining nuclear chain reaction demonstration, *6819*

Self-winding clock, *1302*

Semaphore telegraph system, *7684*

Semiautomatic rifle, *8118*

Semitic museum, *5583*

Senate election in which neither candidate was seated after a recount, *2630*

Senate election race in which both candidates were women, *2634*

Senate election that was contested, *3327*

Senate filibuster, *2627*

Senate filibuster to last for more than 24 hours, *2633*

Senate hearing witness who was a woman, *2628*

Senate journal, *4696*

Senate page who was African-American, *2636*

Senate parliamentarian, *2632*

Senate president pro tempore, *2625*

Senate proceeding to be shown on television, *2637*

Senate session open to the public, *3327*

Senate whip, *2629*

Senator appointed by a governor, *2639*

Senator elected by a write-in vote, *3331*

Senator elected by popular vote, *3329*

Senator elected on an antislavery ticket, *2250*

Senator of Chinese ancestry, *2657*

Senator of Italian ancestry, *7620*

Senator of Japanese ancestry, *2616*

Senator to act in the movies, *2659*

Senator to address the Senate in military uniform, *2648*

Senator to be censured, *2643*

Senator to be impeached, *2641*

Senator to fly in space, *7051*

Senator to serve in contravention to the age limit, *2642*

Senator to serve three states, *2645*

Senator to win a seat that had been occupied by his father and his mother, *2654*

Senator unseated after a recount, *3330*

Senator who had been a newspaper reporter, *2655*

Senator who had been an astronaut, *2660*

Senator who was a Latino, *2652*

Senator who was a woman, *2651*

Senator who was a woman who had previously served in the House of Representatives, *2653*

Senator who was African-American, *2649*

Senator who was African-American to be elected by popular vote, *2658*

Senator who was an African-American woman, *2661*

Senator who was Catholic, *2638*

Senator who was Jewish, *2647*

Senator who was Native American, *2650*

Senator who was returned to the Senate after being defeated for the presidency, *2646*

Senators elected but not seated, *2640*

Septuplets, *2178*

Serbian: European king buried in the United States, *6654*

Serbian Orthodox cathedral, *6497*

Sergeant major of the Army, *5174*

Serial movie with installments longer than one reel, *5550*

Sermon preached from an airplane by radio, *6591*

Sermon to be printed, *1948*

Service number issued by the Army, *5226*

Serviceman killed during the Bosnia conflict, *7983*

Serviceman killed in the Gulf War, *7974*

Serviceman to die in Somalia, *7982*

Session of Congress, *2556*

Session of the House of Representatives, *2576*

Session of the Senate, *2624*

Settlement house in a poor city neighborhood, *2194*

Settlement in America in continuous habitation, *5891*

Settler heroine publicly rewarded, *5933*

Settlers to cross the continent who were women, *5960*

Settlers to reach the Pacific coast, *5957*

Seventh Day Baptist Church, *6544*

Sewage disposal by chemical precipitation, *2233*

Sewage-disposal system separate from the city water system, *2230*

Sewer district established by a city, *2232*

Sewing machine equipped with a rocking treadle or double treadle, *4353*

Sewing machine lamp holder, *4359*

Sewing machine manufacturer, *4352*

Sewing machine to sew curving seams, *4355*

Sewing machine to stitch buttonholes, *4354*

Sewing needles made by machine, *4358*

Sex-change operation, *6832*

Sex discrimination law enacted by a state that affected high school athletic competitions, *6840*

Sex education program for high schools, *3088*

Sextuple newspaper printing press, *5795*

Sextuplets, *2171*

Shaft-driven car, *5435*

Shaker religious community, *6521*

Shampoo commercially produced, *4069*

Sheep, *1084*

Sheep of the Karakul breed, *1086*

Sheep of the Merino breed, *1085*

Sheet-glass drawing machine, *4045*

Sheet music to sell millions of copies, *1293*

Sheet of souvenir postage stamps, *6065*

Sheriff who was an African-American woman, *4156*

Ship built by English colonists in America, *6848*

Ship built in America to cross the Atlantic Ocean, *6847*

Ship built on the Pacific coast, *6856*

Ship completed in less than two weeks, *6878*

Ship constructed by the federal government, *6915*

Ship from the Atlantic coast to anchor in a California port, *6858*

Ship from the United States lost in World War I, *8026*

Ship from the United States sunk by a German submarine in World War II, *8048*

Ship from the United States to sink a Japanese submarine in World War II, *8069*

Ship from the United States to surrender to the Japanese in World War II, *8070*

Ship from which a long-range rocket was launched, *6938*

Ship motion simulator to aid in the development of ballistic missiles fired from shipboard, *8121*

Ship outfitted for hurricane research, *6775*

Ship sunk by a whale, *2420*

Ship to carry the American flag around the world, *1123*

Ship to fire a Polaris missile, *8140*

Ship to pass both ways through the Northwest Passage, *7001*

Ship-to-shore conversation over radio telephone, 7758

Ship-to-shore mobile telephone commercial service, 7739

Ship-to-shore telecast, 7836

Ship to transport fresh orange juice in stainless-steel tanks, 2488

Ship transported overland across the Rocky Mountains, 6935

Ship with a combined diesel and gas-turbine engine, 6946

Ship with a floating scientific instrument platform, 6717

Shipbuilding law enacted by Congress, 5263

Shipment of merchandise by airplane, 2485

Ships built by Europeans in America, 6846

Shirt factory, 2266

Shoe manufacturing machine, 2303

Shoe measuring stick, 2299

Shoe peg, 2300

Shoe pegging machine, 2302

Shoes to be manufactured, 2298

Shoot-the-chutes, 3624

Shopping cart, 2371

Shopping center in a suburban business area, 2501

Shopping mall, 2502

Shorthand account of a trial, 4619

Shorthand book, 1735

Shorthand journal, 4718

Shot fired by American infantry in World War I, 8037

Shot fired by the Navy in World War I, 8031

Shot-put toss over 60 feet, 7562

Shot tower, 8112

Shots fired by German forces to land on American soil in World War I, 8045

Shoulder sleeve insignia issued by the Army, 5227

Showboat theater, 3696

Shuffleboard championship tournament, 7582

Siamese twins, 2170

Siamese twins separated successfully by surgery, 2175

Sick-leave benefit funds for teachers, 4562

Sieve, 4366

Sightseeing bus, 5418

Signal flares, 5242

Signer of the Declaration of Independence, 1113

Silk culture, 7885

Silk dyers, 7888

Silk export, 7886

Silk loom, 7890

Silk mill, 7887

Silk power loom, 7889

Silk sutures and ligatures, 4956

Silk thread, 4362

Silo, 1051

Silver coins, 5362

Silver deposit for coinage, 5364

Silver mill, 4469

Silver mine, 5327

Silver plating factory, 4466

Silver Star Medal awarded to a civilian, 1662

Silver Star Medal awarded to a navy chaplain, 1669

Silver wire suture, 4955

Silverite national convention, 3367

Simultaneous radio broadcast on all three major networks, 6278

Singer whose voice was broadcast over radio, 1330

Singing contest, 1282

Singing telegram, 7708

Single tax adopted by a city for local revenue purposes, 7651

Single Tax League national conference, 7650

Singles bar, 2466

Sit-down strike, 4598

Sit-down strikes to be outlawed by a state, 4599

Sitcom television show, 7780

Six-day bicycle race for women, 7186

Skee-ball alley, 3627

Ski carousel, 7489

Ski club association, 7480

Ski lift, 7484

Ski lifts to be regulated by the state, 7487

Ski tow made of rope, 7483

Skimobile ski lift, 7485

Skin diver, 7513

Skin grafting, 5077

Sky marshals, 4150

Skyjacking in which the skyjacker disappeared, 2787

Skyjacking law enacted by Congress, 2785

Skyjacking of a commercial American airplane, 2784

Skyscraper, 2098

Skyscraper higher than 1,250 feet, 2100

Skyscraper higher than 1,400 feet in height, 2102

Skyscraper higher than 750 feet in height, 2099

Skyscraper of bronze and glass, 2101

Skywriting advertisement exhibition, 2334

Skywriting advertisement written at night, 2337

Space cabin simulator, *7022*

Space capsule recovered from an orbiting satellite, *7062*

Space capsule recovered in midair from an orbiting satellite, *7064*

Space shuttle disaster, *7090*

Space station launched by the United States, *7085*

Space-to-ground news conference telecast, *5608*

Spacecraft launched by the United States to dock with a Russian space station, *7091*

Spacecraft placed in solar orbit, *7078*

Spacecraft to carry a message intended to be read by living beings elsewhere in the universe, *7084*

Spacecraft to land on Mars, *7086*

Spacecraft to leave the solar system, *7088*

Spacecraft to transmit close-up photographs of Mars, *7081*

Spacecraft to transmit close-up photographs of the lunar surface, *7080*

Spacecraft to transmit data from Venus, *7079*

Spacecraft to transmit photographs from lunar orbit, *7083*

Spacewalk by an astronaut who was a woman, *7048*

Spanish: Battle between Native Americans and European soldiers, *5894*

Spanish: Catholic settlement that was permanent, *5899*

Spanish: Colonial warfare between European powers in America, *5900*

Spanish: European settlement in America that was permanent, *5899*

Spanish: European to be buried in the Mississippi, *5895*

Spanish: Exploration of land on the Pacific coast by a European, *5896*

Spanish: Exploration of the Mississippi River by a European, *5895*

Spanish grammar, *1855*

Spanish newspaper, *5665*

Spanish: School run by missionaries in America, *3037*

Spanish: Truce violation, *5901*

Sparrows, *1164*

Speaker of the House, *2578*

Speaker to address an organization by television, *7831*

Special delivery mail service, *6001*

Special session of Congress, *2561*

Special session of the Senate, *2626*

Spectrophotometer, *6799*

Speed limit for highway traffic established by Congress, *4230*

Speedboat to exceed 200 miles per hour, *6953*

Speeding driver law enacted by a state, *4221*

Speedway with a board track, *7508*

Spelling book, *1822*

Sperm whale captured at sea, *2418*

Spinning jenny for cotton, *7881*

Spiritualist, *6599*

Split-level buildings, *2073*

Spoils system of presidential patronage, *6150*

Spoons of nickel silver, *4371*

Sport played on the moon, *7026*

Sports book, *1994*

Sports bra, *2281*

Sports car with a plastic laminated fiberglass body, *5455*

Sports event to be televised live, *7100*

Sports trainer to work professionally, *7548*

Sportswriter, *5612*

Spray can, *7939*

Spring manufacturer, *4400*

Spring winding machine, *4411*

Sprinkler head, *4108*

Sprinkler system, *4101*

Sprinkler system patent, *4107*

Spy satellite, *7060*

Squash rackets champion, *7499*

Squash rackets champion who was a woman, *7502*

Squash tennis organization (national), *7500*

Squash tennis tournament, *7501*

Stabilized airplane in commercial use, *1397*

Stadium built primarily of concrete, *7505*

Stadium operated by a city, *7506*

Stained-glass window, *4039*

Stainless steel flatware, *4375*

Stamp auction, *6057*

Stamp collection magazine, *4727*

Stamp collection society, *6056*

Stamped envelopes, *6053*

Standard broadcast station to transmit a television image, *7795*

Standard time program, *7895*

Standardization of nomenclature for naval vessels, *5264*

Standardization of weights and measures for customs, *2474*

State admitted to the Union after the ratification of the Constitution, *7602*

State admitted to the Union that had no border with another state, *7607*

State admitted to the Union that was separated by a substantial body of water, *7608*

State aid to railroads, *6326*

State college for women, *2954*

State committee chairman of a major political party who was a woman, *3341*

State denied admission into the Union, *7601*

State dinner televised from the White House, *6258*

State governor, *1106*

State law abolishing imprisonment for debt, *2815*

State law prohibiting discrimination against soldiers, *5127*

State law to end de facto segregation in schools, *2261*

State law to establish English as an official language, *5870*

State legislative hearing to be shown on television, *7633*

State legislator who was African-American to represent a constituency with a white majority, *7625*

State legislator who was an African-American woman, *7631*

State legislators who were African-American, *7624*

State legislature to use an electric vote recorder, *7627*

State legislature with a single chamber in the post-Revolutionary era, *7630*

State library to publish a master catalog, *4679*

State named for a person born in America, *7598*

State nominating convention, *3315*

State nullification proceedings to obstruct federal legislation, *7595*

State on the Pacific coast to be admitted to the Union, *7604*

State park, *3734*

State police, *4134*

State police class in which women completed training, *4153*

State police officers who were women, *4144*

State prison to take fingerprints, *4159*

State readmitted to the Union after the Civil War, *7605*

State school for blind students, *3024*

State seal designed by a woman, *7599*

State senator who was a woman, *7626*

State speaker of the House who was a woman, *7628*

State supreme court chief justice who was a woman, *2730*

State supreme court in which all the judges were women, *2724*

State supreme court justice who was a woman, *2723*

State to have a state sport, *7600*

State to ratify the federal Constitution, *1106*

State to ratify the Prohibition Amendment to the Constitution, *2683*

State to repudiate a debt, *7597*

State to secede from the Union, *7945*

State university, *2935*

State university supported by a direct property tax, *2952*

State university to grant equal privileges to women, *2953*

State west of the Mississippi River to be admitted to the Union, *7603*

Statehouse, *2114*

States admitted to the Union simultaneously, *7606*

States with populations of more than 1 million, *5849*

Statistical society, *6779*

Statue cast by the federal government, *5404*

Statue of a woman installed in the Capitol's National Statuary Hall, *5409*

Statue officially sanctioned by the Pope, *5407*

Statue presented to the United States by a foreign country, *5405*

Statue to commemorate literary characters, *5413*

Stealth aircraft, *1493*

Steam baths for curing disease, *5110*

Steam car, *5425*

Steam distribution plant, *3507*

Steam-driven motorcycle, *5487*

Steam engine for industrial use, *4388*

Steam engine for industrial use that was practical, *4391*

Steam-operated pressing machine, *4414*

Steam-powered printing press, *5769*

Steam-propelled ferryboat, *6907*

Steam-propelled frigate, *6916*

Steam shovel, *4396*

Steam tractor, *1054*

Steam turbine operated by a public utility to produce electricity, *3472*

Steam whaler, *6885*

Steamboat, *6853*

Steamboat inspection service established by Congress, *4217*

Steamboat on the Great Lakes, *6865*

Steamboat on the Pacific coast, *6868*

Steamboat patent, *6855*

Steamboat service to California around Cape Horn, *6883*

Steamboat to carry a man, *6854*

Steamboat to employ electric lights successfully, *6873*

Steamboat to make an ocean voyage, *6862*

Steamboat to make regular trips, *6861*

Steamboat to sail down the Mississippi, *6863*

Steamboat with a twin-screw propeller, *6860*

Steamship passenger line between American and European ports, *6882*

Steel, *4490*

Steel animal traps commercially manufactured, *7922*

Steel arch bridge, *3582*

Steel-cut nails, *7931*

Steel dam, *3606*

Steel-frame building, *2080*

Steel-frame residence, *2082*

Steel-hulled ferryboat, *6908*

Steel mill to install an electrical machine, *4494*

Steel mill to produce continuous sheets, *4497*

Steel pens, *8150*

Steel plow with a steel moldboard, *1045*

Steel railroad mail car, *6383*

Steel railroad passenger coach, *6382*

Steel sailing vessel, *6874*

Steel seven-masted schooner, *6875*

Steel shovel, *7906*

Steel ski jump, *7481*

Steel vessels of the Navy, *6925*

Steeplechase, *7391*

Stenotype device, *2361*

Stereo telecast, *7857*

Stereotype printing, *5800*

Stereotyped book, *1743*

Sterilization of humans by a state government as a matter of public policy, *6829*

Stock brokerage concern of importance whose president was a woman, *3830*

Stock brokerage concern to use a telegraph ticker, *3817*

Stock exchange, *3812*

Stock exchange at which more than a million shares were traded in one day, *3820*

Stock exchange director who was a woman, *3831*

Stock exchange to specialize in mining securities, *3816*

Stock order from a zeppelin, *3826*

Stock quotation boards, *3821*

Stockholder meetings televised coast-to-coast simultaneously, *3832*

Stomach washing with a tube or syringe, *5111*

Stone arch bridge, *3564*

Stone arch railroad bridge, *3571*

Stone breaking machine, *5324*

Stone crusher, *5332*

Stone pavement, *6608*

Store with fixed prices, *2495*

Story serialized in a newspaper, *1835*

Stowaway on an aircraft, *1518*

Stratovision flight by an airplane during which a television signal was transmitted, *7839*

Straw hats, *2294*

Straw paper, *5751*

Streamlined all-steel diesel-motor train, *6433*

Streamlined electric locomotive, *6365*

Streamlined ferryboat, *6912*

Streamlined lightweight high-speed three-car passenger train, *6431*

Streamlined railroad train, *6428*

Streamlined steam locomotive, *6364*

Streamlined submarine, *6968*

Street-cleaning machine, *2220*

Street gangs, *2770*

Street letter box, *5992*

Street-sweeping service, *2219*

Streetcar, *6394*

Streetcar company, *6393*

Strike benefit by a union, *4590*

Strike by physicians against long working hours in hospitals, *4602*

Strike by women, *4592*

Strike by workers, *4589*

Strike in which a militia was called out, *4593*

Strike in which women participated, *4591*

Strike of postal employees, *4601*

Strike settlement mediated by the federal Department of Labor, *4596*

Strike suppressed by federal troops in peacetime, *4594*

Strike to last longer than a year, *4600*

Stroboradiograph, *6808*

Stroboscopic lamp for high-speed photography, *5841*

Student government at a college, *3013*

Stuntman, *3680*

Subcompact car designed to be fuel-efficient, *5452*

Subcompact car with front wheel drive, *5462*

Submachine gun, *8115*

Submarine built for use in war, *6961*

Submarine built in the United States to sink an enemy warship in actual warfare, *7968*

Submarine cable plow, *7709*

Submarine disaster, *6966*

Submarine emergency air supply container, *6967*

Submarine equipped with ballistic missiles, *6976*

Surgeon who was a woman, *4974*

Surgery manual, *1893*

Surgery society (national), *5047*

Surgical elevation of the skull to treat epilepsy, *5082*

Surgical facility outside a hospital, *5089*

Surgical operation on a bull to correct a sperm block, *5124*

Surgical operation shown on a local television program, *5084*

Surgical operation televised coast-to-coast, *5085*

Surgical operation televised on a closed circuit, *5083*

Surrogate birth experiment with an animal, *5123*

Survey of public lands, *5945*

Surveyor in America, *5902*

Suspension aqueduct bridge of wire cable, *3577*

Suspension bridge, *3567*

Suspension bridge of iron wire, *3570*

Suspension bridge with steel towers, *3588*

Suture of the human heart, *5090*

Swedenborgian or New Church temple, *6524*

Swedes to arrive in America, *5924*

Swedish magazine, *4747*

Sweet crackers, *3923*

Sweet potato, *1020*

Swimmer from the United States to make a round-trip crossing of the English Channel, *7521*

Swimmer from the United States to swim the English Channel, *7517*

Swimmer of note, *7513*

Swimmer to cover 100 meters freestyle in less than one minute, *7516*

Swimmer to cross the Bering Strait, *7522*

Swimmer to swim the English Channel underwater, *7520*

Swimmer who was a woman to swim the English Channel in both directions, *7519*

Swimmer who was an American woman to swim the English Channel, *7518*

Swimming pool in the White House, *6257*

Swimming school, *7514*

Swimsuit, *2277*

Swiss settlement in America, *5931*

Sword swallower, *3656*

Symphonic concert to be shown on television, *1299*

Symphonic work by an American composer, *1290*

Symphonic work to require an airplane propeller, *1296*

Symphony on an African-American folk theme, *1297*

Symphony orchestra devoted exclusively to radio broadcasting, *1365*

Synchrotron, *6802*

Synod held in America, *6508*

Synthetic fabric that was waterproof and breathable, *7879*

Synthetic fabric used for clothing, *2278*

Synthetic fertilizer, *1016*

Synthetic fiber, *7876*

Synthetic fuels plant, *3522*

Synthetic laundry detergent, *4279*

Synthetic mica, *5345*

Synthetic quinine, *4999*

Synthetic rubber, *4488*

Synthetic rubber for manufacture, *4489*

Synthetic rubber tires, *5502*

T

Taconite production, *5342*

Talking book for blind listeners, *2029*

Tampon to be mass-produced, *4061*

Tank crew to cross the 38th parallel in the Korean War, *7980*

Tank operated by Army troops, *8116*

Tank with a turbine engine, *8122*

Tap dancer of renown, *1233*

Tape measure, *7926*

Tape recorder built in the United States for commercial use, *7014*

Tape recorders, *7013*

Tape-recording machine for mass production of tapes, *7015*

Taps, *1382*

Tariff commission established by Congress, *7666*

Tariff enacted by Congress to prevent the importation of obscene literature and pictures, *7665*

Tariff legislation enacted by Congress, *7663*

Tariff passed by Congress for protection, *7664*

Tattoo shop, *4053*

Tattooed man exhibited as a theatrical attraction, *3661*

Tax enacted by a state to support public schools, *3054*

Tax levied by Congress directly on the states, *7643*

Tax levied by Congress on excess profits of corporations, *7654*

Television: Basketball game to be shown on television, 7171

Television: Beauty pageant to be shown on television, 3629

Television: Bicycle race to be shown on television, 7198

Television: Birth to be shown on closed-circuit television, 2163

Television: Birth to be televised for the public, 2164

Television: Boxing match to be shown on television, 7243

Television: British-made television series, 7791

Television: Broadway play shown in a television version with its original cast, 1266

Television: Cabinet conference to be telecast, 6114

Television: Cabinet session to be telecast and broadcast, 6115

Television camera lens to provide zoom effects, 7815

Television: Catholic midnight mass to be televised, 6476

Television: Church service in sign language to be televised, 6594

Television: Circus to be shown on television, 3675

Television: Coast-to-coast live telecast in color, 7845

Television: Coast-to-coast telecast by satellite, 7852

Television: Coin-operated television receiver, 7814

Television commercial, 2341

Television commercial in color to appear on a local show, 2346

Television: Commercial program telecast on a network, 7777

Television: Commercial television licenses, 7796

Television: Commercial television station on ultrahigh frequency, 7800

Television: Commercial television station west of the Mississippi River, 7797

Television: Condom commercials on television, 6843

Television: Congressional opening session to be televised, 2571

Television: Courtroom verdict to be televised, 2717

Television: Debate among party hopefuls for the presidential nomination to be shown on television, 3398

Television: Demonstration of home reception of television, 7812

Television: Department store sales demonstrations using television, 2342

Television drama program regularly scheduled, 7778

Television dramatic series in which an African-American performer had a starring role, 7790

Television: Editorial to be broadcast over radio and television, 5707

Television: Educational television network operated as a nonprofit corporation, 7807

Television: Educational television network that was statewide and state-supported, 7806

Television: Educational television station, 7801

Television: Educational television station sponsored by a city, 7803

Television: Elementary schools to use closed-circuit televisions in teaching, 3069

Television: Emmy awards for excellence in television, 1628

Television: Episode of "Sesame Street" to be shown on television, 7792

Television eyewitness allowed to testify in a federal court, 2715

Television: Fashion show to be shown on television, 2414

Television: Football game in which referees were allowed to check television instant replays, 7336

Television: High-definition telecast, 7834

Television: Hockey game to be shown on television, 7378

Television: Illegal television station, 7798

Television image using a split screen, 7816

Television: Intercollegiate football game to be shown on television, 7329

Television: Intercollegiate track meet to be shown on television, 7559

Television: Jewish prayer services to be televised in their entirety, 6595

Television: King and queen to be shown on television, 6653

Television license, 7794

Television: Live telecast from space, 6691

Television: Live telecast to Europe by satellite, 7854

Television: Made-for-TV movie, 7789

Television magazine, 4781

Television: Major league baseball game to be shown on television, 7132

Television: Microwave television station, 7804

Television: Miniature television tube, 7809

Television: Mobile television unit, 7813

Television: Movie premiere festivities to be shown on television, 5517

Television: State dinner televised from the White House, *6258*

Television: State legislative hearing to be shown on television, *7633*

Television station owned by a religious organization, *6597*

Television station to regularly broadcast high-definition television, *7808*

Television stations to share the same frequency, *7802*

Television: Stereo telecast, *7857*

Television: Stockholder meetings televised coast-to-coast simultaneously, *3832*

Television: Stratovision flight by an airplane during which a television signal was transmitted, *7839*

Television: Supreme Court justice to participate in a television program, *2764*

Television: Surgical operation shown on a local television program, *5084*

Television: Surgical operation televised coast-to-coast, *5085*

Television: Surgical operation televised on a closed circuit, *5083*

Television: Symphonic concert to be shown on television, *1299*

Television: Telecast from a foreign country, *7842*

Television: Telecast from a submerged submarine, *7838*

Television: Telecast from space showing the earth, *6690*

Television: Telecast from the stratosphere, *7849*

Television: Telecast images received in an airplane, *7832*

Television: Telecast of an object in motion, *7825*

Television: Telecast of image and sound, *7827*

Television: Telecast originating live in three countries, *7846*

Television: Telecast received from England, *7851*

Television: Telecast transmitted by satellite to Japan, *7855*

Television: Telecast transmitted to Canada, *7843*

Television: Telecast using coaxial cable, *7833*

Television: Tennis tournament to be shown on television, *7533*

Television theater to be licensed, *7775*

Television: Three-dimensional telecast, *7844*

Television: Transcontinental telecast received on the East Coast, *7840*

Television: Transcontinental telecast received on the West Coast, *7841*

Television: Transoceanic radio signal conveying a television image, *7828*

Television: Transoceanic telecast by satellite, *7853*

Television: Unscheduled event to be televised as it occurred, *5607*

Television variety talent show series, *7776*

Television variety talent show series with an African-American cast, *7776*

Television: Video recording on magnetic tape televised coast-to-coast, *7847*

Television: Video recording on magnetic tape televised in color, *7850*

Television: Weather map to be telecast, *7826*

Television: Wedding on television, *4820*

Television: Western series on television, *7779*

Television: World Series baseball game to be shown on television, *7135*

Television: Worldwide live television program, *7856*

Television: Year in which color television sets outsold black and white sets, *7773*

Television: Year in which television industry profits exceeded those of radio, *7772*

Temperance organization, *2675*

Temperance society for women (national), *2678*

Temperance society for women (state), *2677*

Temporary insanity defense in a criminal case, *4622*

Ten Most Wanted list, *2783*

Tenement house, *2124*

Tennis champion to win the Grand Slam, *7536*

Tennis champion who was a woman to win the Grand Slam, *7537*

Tennis champion who was African-American, *7538*

Tennis champions who were brothers, *7535*

Tennis match broadcast on radio, *7532*

Tennis society (national), *7525*

Tennis tournament of national scope, *7526*

Tennis tournament to be shown on television, *7533*

Teraflop computer, *2541*

Terra cotta, *2056*

Terra cotta factory, *2058*

Territory annexed by the federal government, *5955*

Territory annexed by the federal government beyond the nation's continental limits, *5969*

Territory annexed by the federal government that was noncontiguous, *5968*

Territory owned by the federal government, *5942*

Test for newborn health, *2165*

Test pilot who was a woman, *1603*

Toy pinball game machine, 7453

Trackless trolley system, 6404

Tract housing development, 2196

Tractor with an endless chain, 1053

Trade association, 2519

Trade directory, 1812

Trade dollars, 5371

Trade journal, 4710

Trade monopoly, 2515

Trade school for girls, 3291

Trade tokens, 5358

Trade union organization established in a city, 4607

Trademark character, 2328

Trademark for food, 2324

Trading ship sent to China, 6879

Trading stamp, 2327

Traffic lanes designated by painted lines, 4223

Traffic law enacted by a colony, 4216

Traffic police squad, 4135

Trailer church, 6534

Train of airplanes, 1459

Train operated exclusively by women, 6436

Train robbery of a disabled train, 2774

Train robbery of a train in motion, 2776

Train to run 1,000 miles nonstop, 6432

Train to transport passengers and their cars, 6435

Train with electric lighting, 6429

Train with fluorescent lights, 6434

Traitor to the American cause during the Revolutionary War, 7998

Trampoline commercially manufactured, 7374

Transatlantic airmail service, 6028

Transatlantic airplane flight carrying 100 people, 1472

Transatlantic airship flight, 1515

Transatlantic balloon flight, 1543

Transatlantic commercial airplane service, 1415

Transatlantic commercial telephone service, 7737

Transatlantic crossing attempted by a balloon, 1538

Transatlantic crossing by a submarine under its own power, 6988

Transatlantic crossing by an American steamboat, 6979

Transatlantic eastward flight by jet airplane, 1469

Transatlantic flight by a robot airplane, 1467

Transatlantic helicopter flight, 1576

Transatlantic hydroplane flight made in stages, 1445

Transatlantic message over radio telephone, 7757

Transatlantic mobile telephone call between two cars, 7765

Transatlantic nonstop jet airplane eastward flight, 1476

Transatlantic nonstop jet airplane flight, 1473

Transatlantic nonstop solo flight westbound by a woman, 1453

Transatlantic passenger line, 2477

Transatlantic radio broadcast, 6263

Transatlantic radio fax of a check, 3794

Transatlantic radio fax of a drawing, 5694

Transatlantic radio fax transmission of a photograph, 7668

Transatlantic radio message of the regular westward service, 6265

Transatlantic radio program received from Great Britain, 6271

Transatlantic round-trip airplane flight from the United States, 1461

Transatlantic solo airplane flight, 1450

Transatlantic solo airplane flight by a woman, 1455

Transatlantic solo balloon flight, 1545

Transatlantic solo boat journey by a woman, 6990

Transatlantic solo trip by rowboat, 6998

Transatlantic steamboat service, 6881

Transatlantic supersonic jet service, 1424

Transatlantic telegraph cable, 7698

Transatlantic telephone call carried by the transoceanic telephone cable, 7767

Transatlantic telephone service using the transoceanic cable, 7747

Transatlantic trip by rowboat, 6985

Transatlantic undersea radio conversation, 6283

Transatlantic yacht race, 7211

Transcontinental air derby for women, 7297

Transcontinental air race, 7295

Transcontinental airmail flight, 6018

Transcontinental airplane flight made in stages, 1439

Transcontinental airplane flight made within 24 hours, 1447

Transcontinental airship flight, 1520

Transcontinental autogiro flight, 1531

Transcontinental autogiro flight by a woman, 1532

Transcontinental bicycle trip made in less than three weeks, 7204

Transcontinental bus service, 5421

Transcontinental car race, 7266

Transcontinental car trip, 5471

Treaty between the federal government and a nation with which it had been at war, *3999*

Treaty between the federal government and a South American nation, *4002*

Treaty between the federal government and an Asian nation, *4005*

Treaty entered into by the federal government after independence, *4000*

Treaty entered into by the federal government with Native American tribes, *5941*

Treaty to reduce the number of nuclear missiles, *4007*

Trial in which freedom of the press was upheld, *5633*

Trial in which lawyers appeared on a Picturephone, *4625*

Trial of a surrogate mother for refusing to give up her baby, *2167*

Trial of a teacher for violating a state ban on teaching the theory of evolution, *3068*

Trial of a war criminal by the federal government, *7969*

Trimline telephone, *7725*

Triode for radios, *6307*

Triple jet ace, *1621*

Triplets born several weeks apart, *2179*

Trombone, *1306*

Troop ship from the United States torpedoed by a German submarine in World War I, *8040*

Troops from the United States to sail to Europe in World War I, *8033*

Troops sent to Vietnam, *8014*

Trotting horse, *1177*

Truancy law enacted by a state, *3061*

Truce violation, *5901*

Truck, *5504*

Truck completely streamlined, *5506*

Truck driving school, *3300*

Trust, *2518*

Trust company, *3761*

Truth-in-advertising law enacted by a state, *2330*

Tubeless car tires, *5503*

Tuberculosis hospital established by Congress, *4902*

Tuberculosis hospital for needy patients, *4903*

Tuberculosis hospital for the poor established by a city, *4900*

Tuberculosis laboratory established by a city, *4199*

Tuberculosis patients' home, *4897*

Tuberculosis research and prevention society, *5042*

Tuberculosis research laboratory, *4929*

Tuberculosis sanatorium, *4898*

Tuberculosis sanatorium established by a state, *4901*

Tuberculosis sanatorium using modern treatment methods, *4899*

Tuberculosis vaccine, *4921*

Tugboat powered by steam, *6880*

Tugboat with a diesel-electric engine, *6889*

Tung trees, *1021*

Tungsten and tellurium, *5322*

Tunnel, *3611*

Tunnel construction using compressed air, *3616*

Turbine-propelled naval ship, *6928*

Turbine-propelled oceangoing merchant vessel, *6886*

Turbine successfully operated by waterpower, *4399*

Turkish bath, *4194*

Turreted frigate in the Navy, *6920*

Tuxedo coat, *2272*

Twelve-step rehabilitation program, *2662*

Twin covered bridges, *3579*

Twin-cycle motorcycle, *5490*

Twin-engine pressurized airplane, *1401*

Twin postage stamps, *6073*

Two-handed shovel, *7940*

Two-way moving sidewalk, *6640*

Two-way radio conversation between a submerged submarine and another vessel, *7760*

Two-way telegraph, *7702*

Type foundry, *5801*

Type specimen book from an American type foundry, *1742*

Typesetting machine, *5804*

Typesetting machine to dispense with metal type, *5808*

Typewriter, *2384*

Typewriter ribbon, *2386*

Typewriter that could retype text automatically, *2392*

Typewriter that was practical, *2385*

Typewriter to produce a line of writing visible as it was being typed, *2388*

Typewriter without type arms, *2391*

Typewriting primer, *1829*

Typing school, *3289*

U

U.S. officer to preside over the observance of a Jewish holiday, *5200*

Ukrainian daily newspaper, *5683*

Ultraviolet pictures of the sun, *6698*

Umbrella, *2263*

Umpire in organized baseball who was African-American, *7102*

Unassisted triple play in a major league baseball game, *7126*

Unassisted triple play in a World Series baseball game, *7127*

Unassisted triple play in organized baseball, *7120*

Underground burial of electric wires to be required by a state, *2222*

Underground city sewer system, *2228*

Underground comic book of note, *4739*

Underground mill for the separation of zinc and lead, *5343*

Underground school, *2122*

Undersea hotel, *2437*

Undersea park established by the federal government, *3739*

Underwater highway tunnel, *3614*

Underwater highway tunnel with twin tubes, *3618*

Underwater railroad tunnel to a foreign country, *3617*

Underwater telegraph cable that was practical, *7693*

Underwater torpedo operated by electric current, *8098*

Unemployment insurance act, *4525*

Uniforms for mail carriers, *5998*

Uniforms for working women, *2275*

Union catalog of books in a state library, *1776*

Union catalog of books in American libraries, *1775*

Union Labor Party convention, *3364*

Union naval officer killed in the Civil War, *7956*

Union Party convention, *3378*

Union passenger station used by several railroad companies, *6332*

Union Reform Party convention, *3371*

Union regiment in the Civil War made up of African-American soldiers, *7966*

Union ship captured in the Civil War, *7960*

Union soldier killed by enemy action in the Civil War, *7954*

Unitarian church, *6523*

Unitarian minister who was a woman, *6523*

Unitarian prayer book, *1956*

United Brethren in Christ meeting, *6541*

United Christian Party convention, *3370*

United Church of Christ ordination of a woman in which all the principal roles were filled by women, *6536*

United Labor Party convention, *3365*

United Nations delegate who was African-American, *3992*

United Nations permanent ambassador who was a woman, *3993*

United Nations postage stamps in U.S. denominations, *6068*

United Nations Security Council resolution vetoed by the United States, *3981*

Universal chapel embracing eight faiths, *6437*

Universal constant in physics to be measured by American scientists, *6812*

Universalist church services, *6520*

University for African-American students, *2951*

University for African-American students founded as a Catholic institution, *2964*

University legally designated as such, *2933*

University on the Pacific Coast, *2948*

University president who was a woman, *2971*

University press, *2960*

Unscheduled event to be televised as it occurred, *5607*

Urban planning instruction at a college, *3253*

Use of "America" as a geographical designation, *1094*

Use of "American" as an adjective, *1098*

Use of the name United States instead of United Colonies, *1097*

Utilization of Niagara Falls waterpower for industrial purposes, *4379*

V

V-mail film, *6012*

Vacation fund to send poor children to the country, *2139*

Vaccination against smallpox using cowpox, *4915*

Vaccination law enacted by a state, *4918*

Vaccination law enacted by Congress, *4919*

Vaccination program by the federal government to protect Native Americans against smallpox, *4920*

Vaccination program offered by a city, *4917*

Vacuum-cast steel, *4498*

Vacuum cleaner driven by a motor, *4275*

Vacuum cleaner that used suction, *4272*

Valentines commercially produced, *4235*

Valeteria, *2398*

Varnish manufacturer, *4429*

Vasectomy outpatient service, *4851*

Vaudeville show, *3688*

Vedanta Center, *6601*

Vehicular tunnel to a foreign country, *3619*

Voting rights organization (national) advocating universal voting rights, *3427*

Vulcanized rubber, *4486*

W

Waffle iron patent, *4294*

Wagon train to California, *5962*

Wal-Mart store, *2514*

Walkie-Talkie two-way radio device, *7722*

Wall and floor tiles, *2042*

Wallpaper, *4305*

War bond issued by the federal government, *3813*

War map, *4794*

War song, *1377*

War that was predicted by pizza orders, *7972*

Warehouse legislation enacted by Congress, *2480*

Warship builder, *5260*

Warship captured overseas, *8000*

Warship convoy across the Atlantic Ocean in World War II, *8050*

Warship propelled by electricity, *6932*

Warship sunk by an underwater torpedo mine, *7965*

Warship to capture an enemy ship after the Revolution, *8005*

Warship to enter enemy waters, *7999*

Warship to receive definite orders to attack the enemy, *7993*

Warship with propelling machinery below the waterline, *6918*

Washing machine, *4270*

Washington news correspondent, *5611*

Watch made by machinery, *7901*

Watchmaker, *7899*

Water cures, *5112*

Water filtration system for bacterial purification of a city water supply, *2234*

Water gas plant, *3517*

Water pollution law enacted by Congress, *3716*

Water pumping plant, *2225*

Water skier to jump 100 feet, *7593*

Water skis, *7591*

Water supply system built for a city, *2224*

Water supply to be fluoridated, *2236*

Water supply tunnel for a city, *3615*

Waterless natural gas storage tank, *3520*

Watermark in paper, *5748*

Waterpower development grant to a colonist, *5913*

Waterworks system to use cast-iron pipes, *2226*

Waxworks museum, *5575*

Weather forecast broadcast on radio, *6769*

Weather forecasting service by telephone, *6772*

Weather map to be telecast, *7826*

Weather observations to be systematically recorded, *6766*

Weather report delivered to the Army, *6768*

Weather satellite to provide cloud-cover photographs, *7058*

Weather satellite to provide high-resolution cloud-cover photographs at night, *7072*

Web-fed four-color rotary printing press, *5780*

Wedding abroad of a soldier in the American Expeditionary Force, *4817*

Wedding broadcast over the radio, *4819*

Wedding by telegraph, *4816*

Wedding by transatlantic telephone, *4821*

Wedding during a parachute jump, *4822*

Wedding in a balloon, *4814*

Wedding in an airplane, *4818*

Wedding in the White House, *6252*

Wedding of a president in the White House, *4815*

Wedding of African-Americans, *4812*

Wedding of colonists in New England, *4813*

Wedding of colonists in Virginia, *4812*

Wedding on television, *4820*

Weight lifter to lift more than 6,000 pounds, *7587*

Welding by the electric process, *4435*

Welding machine for aluminum pipes, *4420*

Welsh magazine, *4743*

West Point cadet who was a woman to graduate at the top of her class, *3208*

West Point cadets who were women, *3207*

West Point graduate killed in action, *3197*

West Point graduate who was a Jewish woman, *3195*

West Point graduate who was African-American, *3199*

West Point graduate who was Jewish, *3195*

West Point graduate who was Native American, *3198*

West Point graduates, *3196*

West Point graduates who were Chinese nationals, *3201*

West Point instructor who was a woman, *3205*

Western series on television, *7779*

Whaling expedition, *2419*

Whaling industry established by a city, *2417*

Whig Party convention, *3350*

Whips commercially manufactured, *7910*

Whist organization, *4021*

Whist rule book, *1999*
White bread, *3926*
White lead manufacturer, *4462*
Whole-wheat bread, *3919*
Whooping crane, *1169*
Wild West Show, *3689*
Wind tunnel for testing airplane parts, *1497*
Wind turbine, *3557*
Windmill for grinding grain, *3909*
Window glass factory, *4036*
Wire gauge, *7920*
Wire glass, *4043*
Wire recorder for sound recording, *5250*
Wire rope factory, *4398*
Wire sieves, *4370*
Wire suspension bridge for general traffic, *3576*
Wolf bounty, *1135*
Wolf to be reintroduced into the wild, *3750*
Woman: African Methodist Episcopal preacher who was a woman, *6565*
Woman: Air Force general who was a woman, *5140*
Woman: Air Force general who was an African-American woman, *5141*
Woman: Air Force military engineer who was a woman, *5139*
Woman: Airline flight attendant who was a woman, *1412*
Woman: Airline flight attendant who was an African-American woman, *1412*
Woman: Airplane accident involving a woman that was fatal, *1393*
Woman: Airplane flying school operated by a woman, *7294*
Woman: Airplane instructor's license received by a woman, *1601*
Woman: Airplane solo flight by an American woman, *1596*
Woman: Airport manager who was a woman, *1507*
Woman: Ambassador from the United States who was a woman, *3991*
Woman: Ambassador to the United Nations who was a woman, *3996*
Woman: Ambassador to the United States who was a woman, *3990*
Woman: Ambassador who was an African-American woman, *3994*
Woman: American Bar Association member who was a woman, *4640*
Woman: American history book of importance whose author was a woman, *1865*
Woman: American Medical Association member who was a woman, *5036*

Woman: American woman of European descent to be made a Native American chief, *6647*
Woman: American woman to become a countess, *6644*
Woman: American woman to become a member of the British Parliament, *6648*
Woman: Architect who was a woman, *1194*
Woman: Architectural patent received by a woman, *1194*
Woman: Army general who was an African-American woman, *5162*
Woman: Army officer who was a woman, *5170*
Woman: Army officer who was a woman to lead troops in combat, *5176*
Woman: Art museum of importance devoted to the work of an individual woman, *5600*
Woman: Artificial insemination of a woman resulting in conception, *5113*
Woman: Arts and sciences national organization member who was a woman, *5709*
Woman: Ascent of Mount Everest by an American woman, *7588*
Woman: Astronaut to fly in space who was an African-American woman, *7049*
Woman: Astronaut who was a mother, *7048*
Woman: Astronaut who was a woman to fly in space, *7048*
Woman: Astronaut who was a woman to live in a space station, *7054*
Woman: Astronomer employed in the Naval Observatory who was a woman, *6667*
Woman: Athlete who was a woman to earn more than $1 million in a year, *7541*
Woman: Athlete who was a woman to earn more than $100,000 in one season, *7540*
Woman: Athlete who was an African-American woman to win the James E. Sullivan Memorial Trophy, *1721*
Woman: Attorney general who was a woman, *6128*
Woman: Autopsy performed by a woman physician on a male corpse, *2850*
Woman: Balloon pilot who was a woman, *1539*
Woman: Bank president of a national bank who was a woman, *3786*
Woman: Bank president who was a woman, *3772*
Woman: Baseball pitcher who was a woman, *7149*
Woman: Bible translation by a woman, *1970*
Woman: Bicycle champion who was a woman, *7197*
Woman: Bill bearing the likeness of a woman, *5391*
Woman: Botanist of note who was a woman, *6737*

Woman: Bowler who was a woman to obtain a perfect score, *7227*

Woman: Boxer who was a woman to earn national recognition, *7257*

Woman: Boxing referee who was a woman, *7244*

Woman: Bridge named for a woman, *3598*

Woman: Bullfighter who was a woman to fight professionally, *7259*

Woman: Cabinet member who was a woman, *6112*

Woman: Cabinet member who was an African-American woman, *6121*

Woman: Cantor in the Reform movement who was a woman, *6490*

Woman: Car driver who was a woman, *5467*

Woman: Carnegie Hero Fund Commission award granted to a woman, *1639*

Woman: Caterpillar Club member who was a woman, *1586*

Woman: Catholic saint who was an American citizen, *6475*

Woman: Chairman of a major political party who was a woman, *3344*

Woman: Coal miner who was a woman to be killed in a mining accident, *3510*

Woman: Coast Guard airplane pilot who was a woman, *5213*

Woman: Coast Guard ship commander who was a woman, *5215*

Woman: Coin bearing the likeness of an American woman, *5381*

Woman: College graduate in geology who was a woman, *3241*

Woman: College graduate who was an African-American woman, *3010*

Woman: College president who was a woman, *2971*

Woman: College professor who was a woman, *2947*

Woman: Commodity exchange member who was a woman, *3827*

Woman: Congressional committee headed by a woman, *2589*

Woman: Congressional lobbyist who was a woman, *2563*

Woman: Congressional representative of Japanese ancestry who was a woman, *2616*

Woman: Congressional representative to serve 18 terms who was a woman, *2611*

Woman: Congressional representative who was a woman, *2609*

Woman: Congressional representative who was an African-American woman, *2617*

Woman: Coxswain of a men's college varsity rowing team who was a woman, *7471*

Woman: Dean of a university graduate school who was a woman, *2974*

Woman: Dentist who was a woman, *4861*

Woman: Dentist who was a woman to obtain a D.D.S. degree, *4862*

Woman: Detective who was a woman, *4140*

Woman: Dictionary compiled by a woman, *1808*

Woman: Director of the Mint of the United States who was a woman, *5350*

Woman: Distinguished Service Medal awarded to a Navy nurse, *5288*

Woman: District attorney who was a woman, *2714*

Woman: Doctor commissioned in the regular Army who was a woman, *5172*

Woman: Doctor in the regular Navy who was a woman, *5291*

Woman: Doctor of Philosophy degree awarded to a woman, *2979*

Woman: Driver who was a woman to compete in the Indianapolis 500, *7269*

Woman: Editor in chief of a law review who was a woman, *3127*

Woman: Editor of a major daily newspaper who was a woman, *5622*

Woman: Electoral vote for a woman, *3396*

Woman: Episcopal bishop who was a woman, *6553*

Woman: Episcopal priest who was a woman, *6553*

Woman: Execution of a woman by electrocution, *2799*

Woman: Execution of a woman by hanging by the federal government, *2798*

Woman: Executive officer of a man-of-war who was a woman, *5300*

Woman: Federal administrator who was an African-American woman, *2257*

Woman: Federal treaty signed by a woman, *4006*

Woman: Fortune 1000 company to be owned and chaired by a woman, *2407*

Woman: Glider license awarded to a woman, *1599*

Woman: Governor who was a woman, *7618*

Woman: Graduate of a four-year maritime school who was a woman, *3309*

Woman: Graduate student who was a woman to receive a university fellowship, *3012*

Woman: Grand jury foreman who was a woman, *2737*

Woman: Humor writer who was a woman, *2033*

Woman in America to appeal for the right to vote, *3420*

Woman: Internal revenue collector for the federal government who was a woman, *7657*

Woman: Jockey who was a woman to ride in the Kentucky Derby, *7418*

Woman: Jockey who was a woman to ride two winners in one day, *7416*

Woman: Jockey who was a woman to win a major stakes race, *7419*

Woman: Jockey who was a woman to win a Triple Crown race, *7421*

Woman: Jockey who was a woman to win on a regular parimutuel flat track, *7415*

Woman: Judge of a federal district court who was an African-American woman, *2729*

Woman: Judge of the U.S. Court of Appeals who was an African-American woman, *2732*

Woman: Judge to impose the death penalty who was a woman, *2722*

Woman: Judge who was an African-American woman, *2726*

Woman: Justice of the peace who was a woman, *2721*

Woman: Justice on the federal bench who was a woman, *2725*

Woman: Labor delegate to a national convention of the American Federation of Labor who was a woman, *4560*

Woman: Law school graduate who was a woman, *3124*

Woman: Lawyer admitted to practice before the Supreme Court who was an African-American woman, *4635*

Woman: Lawyer who was a woman, *4636*

Woman: Lawyer who was a woman to be admitted to practice before the Supreme Court, *4638*

Woman: Lawyer who was an African-American woman, *4637*

Woman: Librarian who was an African-American woman, *4674*

Woman: Marathon runner from the United States who was a woman, *7565*

Woman: Marine general who was a woman, *5240*

Woman: Marine reserve member who was a woman, *5233*

Woman: Marine who was a woman, *5232*

Woman: Mayor of a major city who was a woman, *2210*

Woman: Mayor who was a woman, *2207*

Woman: Medal of Technology awarded to a woman, *1655*

Woman: Medical officer assigned to a naval vessel who was a woman, *5292*

Woman: Member of the Navy's Hurricane Hunters who was a woman, *5298*

Woman: Methodist bishop who was a woman, *6562*

Woman: Methodist bishop who was an African-American woman, *6562*

Woman: Metropolitan Opera orchestra conductor who was a woman, *1340*

Woman: Millionaire who was an African-American woman, *2444*

Woman: Minister who was a woman, *6530*

Woman: Monument ordered by the federal government from a sculptor who was a woman, *5401*

Woman: Monument to a woman financed by women, *5406*

Woman: Motorcycle racer who was a woman, *7440*

Woman: Motorcycle trip from the United States to Tierra del Fuego by a woman, *5494*

Woman: Movie for which one woman served as producer, director, and star, *5568*

Woman: Movie star who was a woman, *5526*

Woman: Museum wing in the United States named for a woman, *5595*

Woman: National Academy of Sciences member who was a woman, *6781*

Woman: National Institute of Arts and Letters member who was a woman, *5716*

Woman: National political convention at which a woman made a seconding speech, *3339*

Woman: National political convention to be addressed by a woman, *3336*

Woman: National women's figure skating four-time winner, *7434*

Woman: Navy captain who was a woman, *5288*

Woman: Navy chaplain who was a woman, *5205*

Woman: Navy chaplain who was an African-American woman, *5206*

Woman: Navy–Marine Corps Medal for Heroism awarded to a woman, *1668*

Woman: Navy officer commissioned in the U.S. Naval Reserve who was a woman, *5287*

Woman: Navy officer who was a woman to command a ship at sea, *5299*

Woman: Navy officer who was a woman to hold a major command, *5297*

Woman: Navy petty officer who was a woman, *5286*

Woman: New York Stock Exchange director who was a woman, *3833*

Woman: New York Stock Exchange seat owner who was a woman, *3833*

Woman: News reporter at a political convention who was a woman, *5614*

Woman: Newspaper editor who was a woman, *5610*

Woman: Nobel Peace Prize awarded to an American woman, *1695*

Woman: Nobel Prize in literature awarded to an American woman, *1694*

Woman: Nuclear commercial power plant licensed operator who was a woman, *3555*

Woman: Oceanographer of distinction who was a woman, *6719*

Woman of American ancestry to become a queen, *6651*

Woman: Olympic gold medalist from the United States who was a woman, *7445*

Woman: Olympic gold medalist who was an African-American woman, *7449*

Woman: Opera composed by a woman to be performed at the Metropolitan Opera House, *1348*

Woman: Opera composer who was a woman, *1334*

Woman: Osteopathic physician who was a woman, *4976*

Woman: Parachute jump from an airplane by a woman, *1582*

Woman: Patent examiner who was a woman, *4656*

Woman: Patent granted to an inventor who was a woman, *4651*

Woman: Pharmacist who was a woman, *4963*

Woman: Pharmacist who was a woman to receive a degree from a pharmacy college, *3147*

Woman: Physician who was a Chinese woman, *4978*

Woman: Physician who was a woman, *4971*

Woman: Physician who was an African-American woman, *4973*

Woman: Pilot licensed by the Aero Club of America who was a woman, *1596*

Woman: Pilot of a B-52 bomber who was a woman, *1626*

Woman: Pilot on a regularly scheduled major airline who was a woman, *1606*

Woman: Pilot to break the sound barrier who was a woman, *1468*

Woman: Pilot to fly a regularly scheduled airmail transport who was a woman, *1600*

Woman: Pilot who was a woman to be inducted into the Army Aviation Hall of Fame, *1625*

Woman: Pilot who was a woman to cross the English Channel in a plane, *1596*

Woman: Pilot who was a woman to die in a combat zone, *1625*

Woman: Pilot who was an African-American woman, *1597*

Woman: Play by an African-American woman to appear on Broadway, *1270*

Woman: Poet laureate who was a woman, *2034*

Woman: Poet who was an African-American woman, *1946*

Woman: Poet who was an African-American woman to win the Pulitzer Prize, *1715*

Woman: Poetry collection by an African-American woman, *1946*

Woman: Polar expedition of which a woman was a member, *6726*

Woman: Police chief who was a woman, *4142*

Woman: Police officer who was a woman, *4136*

Woman: Police officer who was a woman to be killed in the line of duty, *4152*

Woman: Political asylum granted to avoid genital mutilation, *5883*

Woman: Postage stamp depicting an African-American woman, *6100*

Woman: Postage stamp depicting an American woman, *6087*

Woman: Postage stamps depicting a woman, *6085*

Woman: Postmaster who was a woman, *5982*

Woman: Presbyterian elder who was a woman, *6583*

Woman: Presbyterian minister who was a woman, *6584*

Woman: President of a major medical society who was a woman, *5049*

Woman: Presidential campaign manager who was a woman, *3392*

Woman: Presidential candidate who was a woman, *3405*

Woman: Presidential physician who was a woman, *6204*

Woman: Principal chief of the Cherokee Nation who was a woman, *4085*

Woman: Printer who was a woman, *5782*

Woman: Prison commissioner who was a woman, *2830*

Woman: Prison guard who was a woman to serve in a maximum security prison for men, *2831*

Woman: Professional football game in which a woman participated, *7334*

Woman: Professional hockey player who was a woman, *7383*

Woman: Professor at a first-class medical school who was a woman, *3151*

Woman: Pulitzer Prize for a novel written by a woman, *1711*

Woman: Rabbi in the Conservative movement who was a woman, *6490*

Woman: Rabbi in the Reform movement who was a woman, *6490*

Woman: Religious leader in the American colonies who was a woman, *6507*

Woman: Round-the-world bicycle trip by a woman, *7202*

Woman: Secretary of state who was a woman, *6123*

Woman: Senate hearing witness who was a woman, *2628*

Woman: Senator who was a woman, *2651*

Woman: Senator who was a woman who had previously served in the House of Representatives, *2653*

Woman: Senator who was an African-American woman, *2661*

Woman: Sheriff who was an African-American woman, *4156*

Woman: Soccer world champion who was a woman, *7495*

Woman: Society of Automotive Engineers member who was a woman, *6794*

Woman: Soldier's Medal awarded to a woman, *1663*

Woman: Spacewalk by an astronaut who was a woman, *7048*

Woman: Squash rackets champion who was a woman, *7502*

Woman: State committee chairman of a major political party who was a woman, *3341*

Woman: State legislator who was an African-American woman, *7631*

Woman: State seal designed by a woman, *7599*

Woman: State senator who was a woman, *7626*

Woman: State speaker of the House who was a woman, *7628*

Woman: State supreme court chief justice who was a woman, *2730*

Woman: State supreme court justice who was a woman, *2723*

Woman: Statue of a woman installed in the Capitol's National Statuary Hall, *5409*

Woman: Stock brokerage concern of importance whose president was a woman, *3830*

Woman: Stock exchange director who was a woman, *3831*

Woman: Supreme Court justice who was a Jewish woman, *2762*

Woman: Supreme Court justice who was a woman, *2765*

Woman: Surgeon general who was a woman, *4214*

Woman: Surgeon who was a woman, *4974*

Woman: Swimmer who was a woman to swim the English Channel in both directions, *7519*

Woman: Swimmer who was an American woman to swim the English Channel, *7518*

Woman: Teacher training school principal who was a woman, *3264*

Woman: Telegrapher who was a woman, *7694*

Woman: Telephone operator who was a woman, *7729*

Woman: Television network evening news program anchor who was a woman, *5621*

Woman: Tennis champion who was a woman to win the Grand Slam, *7537*

Woman: Tennis champion who was African-American, *7538*

Woman: Test pilot who was a woman, *1603*

Woman: Tightrope performer who was a woman, *3657*

Woman to sell securities on the floor of the New York Curb Exchange, *3828*

Woman: Town founded by a woman, *2188*

Woman: Transatlantic nonstop solo flight westbound by a woman, *1453*

Woman: Transatlantic solo airplane flight by a woman, *1455*

Woman: Transatlantic solo boat journey by a woman, *6990*

Woman: Transcontinental autogiro flight by a woman, *1532*

Woman: Transcontinental nonstop airplane flight by a woman, *1456*

Woman: Transcontinental solo airplane flight by a woman, *1453*

Woman: Transcontinental solo trip on horseback by a woman, *1183*

Woman: Transpacific sailboat crossing by a woman, *6999*

Woman: Transpacific solo airplane flight by a woman, *1460*

Woman: Unitarian minister who was a woman, *6523*

Woman: United Church of Christ ordination of a woman in which all the principal roles were filled by women, *6536*

Woman: United Nations delegate who was African-American, *3992*

Woman: United Nations permanent ambassador who was a woman, *3993*

Woman: University president who was a woman, *2971*

Woman: Vice presidential candidate from a major political party who was a woman, *3419*

Woman: Vice presidential candidate who was an African-American woman, *3415*

Woman: West Point cadet who was a woman to graduate at the top of her class, *3208*

Woman: West Point graduate who was a Jewish woman, *3195*

Women: Hotel for women, *2425*

Women in Antartica, *6730*

Women: Infirmary for women staffed by physicians who were women, *4877*

Women: Jury composed of women, *2734*

Women: Labor union for women, *4606*

Women: Law school at a university to admit women, *3123*

Women: Magazine for women, *4709*

Women: Medical school for women, *3164*

Women: Medical society for women, *5037*

Women: Merchant Marine Academy cadets who were women, *3308*

Women: Military service academies' enrollment of women, *3189*

Women: National tennis championship match for women, *7529*

Women: National union for women, *4610*

Women: Naval Academy students who were women, *3221*

Women: Navy personnel in the regular Navy who were women, *5266*

Women: Organization (national) of Jewish women, *5720*

Women: Prison built for women and managed by women, *2823*

Women: Prison established by the federal government for women, *2829*

Women: Prison matrons for guarding women prisoners, *2819*

Women: Reformatory for women established by a state, *2824*

Women: Sailors assigned to regular Navy shipboard duty who were women, *5269*

Women: School for the higher education of women, *3079*

Women: Secret Service agents who were women, *4170*

Women: Senate election race in which both candidates were women, *2634*

Women: Settlers to cross the continent who were women, *5960*

Women: Six-day bicycle race for women, *7186*

Women: State college for women, *2954*

Women: State police class in which women completed training, *4153*

Women: State police officers who were women, *4144*

Women: State supreme court in which all the judges were women, *2724*

Women: State university to grant equal privileges to women, *2953*

Women: Strike by women, *4592*

Women: Strike in which women participated, *4591*

Women: Technical college for women, *2962*

Women: Temperance society for women (national), *2678*

Women: Temperance society for women (state), *2677*

Women: Theater to employ women as ushers, *3702*

Women: Theological school to admit women as students, *3273*

Women: Train operated exclusively by women, *6436*

Women: Transcontinental air derby for women, *7297*

Women: Transcontinental car trip by women, *5472*

Women: Transcontinental motorcycle trip by women, *5493*

Women: Uniforms for working women, *2275*

Women: Volunteer unit made up of college women to serve overseas, *5185*

Women: Voting rights convention organized by women, *3425*

Women: West Point cadets who were women, *3207*

Women: Women's club, *5732*

Women: Women's hospital, *4880*

Women: Women's professional club, *5723*

Women: Women's World Fair, *2413*

Women: Working hours of women to be regulated by a state, *4555*

Women: Young Women's Christian Association, *5713*

Women: Young Women's Hebrew Association, *5715*

Women's Army Corps member to be part of the Regular Army, *5171*

Women's club, *5732*

Women's hospital, *4880*

Women's professional club, *5723*

Women's World Fair, *2413*

Wood engraving made with an engraving tool, *1226*

Woodcut, *1222*

Wooden money, *5378*

Wooden plug lure for fishing, *7287*

Wooden railroad bridge of a purely truss type, *3573*

Wool carding machine, *7894*

Word processor, *2392*

Work of satirical fiction, *1837*

Work week of 40 hours to be required by Congress, *4567*

Workday of 10 hours to be mandated by a state, *4554*

X

Y

Year when half of the nation's agricultural counties were designated disaster areas, *2872*

Yellow fever vaccine for human immunization, *4922*

Yellow pages telephone directory, *1819*

Yeshivah for Jewish religious study, *3276*

Yiddish newspaper, *5670*

Yiddish professorship at a college, *3119*

Yiddish theater performance, *1255*

Yogurt dairy, *3856*

Young Men's Christian Association, *5712*

Young Men's Christian Association branch for African-Americans, *5712*

Young Men's Hebrew Association, *5714*

Young Women's Christian Association, *5713*

Young Women's Hebrew Association, *5715*

Youth hostel, *2150*

Z

Zebra mussels, *1162*

Zen Buddhist monastery, *6439*

Zinc, *5325*

Zinc commercial production, *5330*

Zinc sheet mill, *4470*

Zionist organization (national), *6487*

Zip codes, *6013*

Zipper, *2292*

Zither factory, *1313*

Zoning ordinance, *2205*

Zoo, *1186*

Zoo habitat constructed of simulated rock formations without bars, *1188*

Zoo with twilight conditions, *1191*

Index by Years

The following is a chronological listing of entries, arranged by year. To find an entry in the main body of the text, please go to the italicized number.

1579

Christian religious service in English on the Pacific Coast, *6501*

1581

African slaves in America, *2238*

1585

Artist in the English colonies, *1196*
Letters written in English in America, *1095*
Surveyor in America, *5902*

1587

Beer, *2663*
Child born of English parents in America, *2156*
Native American to become a Protestant, *6502*

1588

Map of a city within the present limits of the United States, *4790*

1602

Exploration of the New England region by an Englishman, *5903*
Native American map of record, *4791*

1603

Catholic bishop to exercise episcopal functions, *6446*

1604

European settlement in the northeast after the Vikings, *5904*

1606

School run by missionaries in America, *3037*

1607

Battle between English colonists and Native Americans, *5908*
Colonial council, *5906*
English settlement in America that was permanent, *5907*
Episcopal church service in an English colony, *6547*
Prefabricated ship built in America, *6849*
Rebellion in the English colonies, *5905*
Ship built by English colonists in America, *6848*
Slander proceedings, *2767*
Thanksgiving worship service, *6503*
Tobacco cultivation, *2694*

1608

Book written in America, *1727*

Bottle, *4282*
Colonists in America who were women, *4812*
Fireworks, *3649*
Glass factory, *4035*
History book of the colonial era, *1859*

1609

Maize, *3907*
Polish settlers in America, *5909*
Sheep, *1084*
Trade monopoly, *2515*
Wedding of colonists in Virginia, *4812*

1610

Physician in the colony of Virginia, *4959*

1611

Game played in the English colonies in America, *4008*
Presbyterian church, *6580*

1613

Colonial warfare between England and France in America, *5911*
Naval expedition mounted by an English colony, *5910*

1614

Decked ship built in America, *6850*
Dutch settlement in America, *5912*
Lottery, *3640*

1616

Smallpox epidemic, *2873*

1617

College proposed in America, *2924*

1618

Comet recorded, *6675*

1619

Ironworks, *4445*
Legislative assembly of a colony, *7622*
Sabbath law enacted by a colony, *6504*

1620

Child born of English parents in New England, *2157*
Congregational church, *6505*
Corn found by English settlers, *3908*
Lead, *5314*
Physician in the New England colonies, *4960*
Waterpower development grant to a colonist, *5913*

1621

Colonial treaty with the Native Americans, *5915*

1638—*continued*

Cloth mill, *7858*

Curfew bell, *2180*

Earthquake description, *2861*

Log cabins, *2069*

Military organization established by a colony, *5253*

Sabbath laws published by a colony, *6509*

Swedes to arrive in America, *5924*

1639

Annulment of a marriage by court decree, *4805*

Autopsy officially recorded, *2848*

Baptist church, *6543*

Bookseller, *1777*

Canal for creating water power, *3599*

Constitution to declare that "the foundation of authority is in the free consent of the people", *1099*

Crop surplus destruction ordered by a government, *1008*

Document known to have been printed in America, *1096*

Gunpowder mill, *8088*

Lawyer disbarred, *4632*

Medical regulations enacted by a colony, *4933*

Post office in a colony, *6035*

Printing press, *5767*

Property tax established by a colony to support public schools, *3041*

1640

Book published in America, *1728*

Catholic school, *3042*

Election held in defiance of the Royal Courts, *3311*

Hebrew type, *5799*

Hymnbook published in America, *1931*

Lutheran pastor, *6554*

Poetry collection by an American poet, *1943*

1641

Agricultural fair held annually, *1001*

Danish settlers in America, *5925*

Patent granted by a colony, *4646*

Pottery, *4308*

1642

Bachelor of Arts degree, *2976*

Ban on convicts holding public office, *3312*

City incorporated in the colonies, *2181*

Compulsory education law in a colony, *3043*

Thesis directory, *1811*

1643

Catholic priest born in America, *6448*

Colonial government federation, *5926*

Cooking pots made in America, *4290*

Divorce, *4806*

Extradition of criminals among colonies, *4130*

Fulling mill for making wool cloth, *7891*

Income tax levied by a colony, *7638*

Ironworks that was successful, *4446*

Native American dictionary, *1796*

Spelling book, *1822*

1644

Branding law enacted by a colony, *1065*

Legislature of a colony to establish two chambers, *7623*

Whaling industry established by a city, *2417*

1645

Lutheran church, *6555*

Manufacturer of metal goods, *4461*

School committee, *3044*

1646

Children's book, *1729*

Ecumenical synod, *6510*

Wolf bounty, *1135*

1647

Ban on Jesuits to be enacted by a colony, *6449*

Colonial law requiring towns to hire teachers and construct schools, *3045*

Execution for witchcraft, *2793*

Quarantine law enacted by a colony, *4207*

Rice to be imported, *3893*

Woman in America to appeal for the right to vote, *3420*

1648

Craft union, *4603*

Latin book written in New England, *1949*

Law book of colonial laws, *1872*

1649

Corrupt election practices law enacted by a colony, *3313*

Missionary society established for the English colonies, *6567*

Religious toleration law enacted by a colony, *6511*

1650

Dog domestically bred, *1170*

Expedition of Englishmen to cross the Allegheny Mountains, *5927*

Iron exportation, *4447*

Lead coffins, *2837*

Pounds for stray livestock, *1066*

1651

Landowner of substance who was African-American, *5928*

Royal navigation act affecting the American colonies, *2468*

1652

Coinage dies, *5353*
Slavery emancipation law enacted by a colony, *2239*
Traffic law enacted by a colony, *4216*
Water supply system built for a city, *2224*

1654

Fire engine, *4092*
History of New England, *1860*
Jewish settler in America, *5892*
Orphanage, *2137*
Toll bridge, *3563*

1655

Jewish congregation, *6483*

1656

Ban on Quakers enacted by a colony, *6586*
Book intended for circulation in the English colonies, *1730*
Jewish cemetery, *2851*
Jury composed of women, *2734*
Physician who was Jewish, *4962*
Quakers to arrive in America, *6585*

1657

Autopsy with verdict of a coroner's jury, *2849*
College student to work his way through college, *3005*
Jew to win full citizenship, *5858*
Shoe measuring stick, *2299*
Stone pavement, *6608*

1658

Police force, *4131*

1659

Colonial law banning Christmas, *4253*
Fire department established by a city, *4093*
Quakers executed for their religious beliefs, *6587*

1660

Church for Native Americans in New England, *6512*
Quaker annual meeting, *6588*

1661

Bible translated into a Native American language, *1959*
Evening school for working children, *3046*

1662

Book auction, *1778*

Colonial badges issued to "friendly" Native Americans, *5929*
Lime, *5315*

1663

Hard-surfaced road, *6609*

1664

Bookbinder, *1731*
Naturalization act in the American colonies, *5859*

1665

Book privately printed, *1732*
College graduate who was Native American, *3006*
Horse race run on a regular basis, *7384*
Theatrical performance, *1239*

1666

Financial "corner", *3751*
Native American grammar, *1850*

1667

Cyclone of record, *2862*

1669

Fire chief, *4094*
History of New England to be published in New England, *1860*
Primer in a Native American dialect, *1851*
Rebellion by colonists against an English governor, *5930*
Woodcut, *1222*

1670

Native American preacher of Christianity, *6513*
Self-portrait, *1212*
Swiss settlement in America, *5931*

1671

Jew to serve on a jury, *5858*
Seventh Day Baptist Church, *6544*

1672

Colonial copyright law, *4626*
Postal route between cities, *5980*
Tax on Britain's American colonists without their consent, *7639*

1673

Coal, *3501*
Governor of a colony who was born in America, *7609*

1674

Horse racing ban by a colony, *7385*

1675

Catholic holy orders, *6450*
Commercial corporation, *2402*

1676

Colonial law for the maintenance of an insane patient, *4171*
Court-martial in a colony, *2738*
Fire of serious consequence, *2879*
Poetry collection by an American poet who was a man, *1944*
Prison, *2811*

1677

Map made in America to be published in a book, *4792*
Medical pamphlet, *1886*

1678

Irish to arrive in America, *5932*

1679

Great Lakes vessel, *6851*
Labadist community, *6514*
Price regulation agreement by colonists, *2516*

1681

Shorthand account of a trial, *4619*

1682

Jewish synagogue, *6484*
Mason, *5727*
Tornado of record, *2863*
Town trust fund for education, *3047*

1683

Bible concordance, *1960*
Landscape architect, *1192*
Mennonites to arrive in America, *6537*
Science society, *6776*

1685

Judge to be impeached, *2718*

1686

Episcopal church organized in New England, *6548*

1687

Brewery to remain in business for 200 years, *2664*
Inheritance tax levied by a colony, *7640*
Knighthood conferred on a person born in America, *6641*
Law history book, *1861*

1688

Protest against slavery, *2240*

1689

Newspapers, *5629*
Schoolbook, *1823*

1690

Indigo crop, *1009*
Loan by a colony, *3802*
Newspaper publisher, *5609*
Paper mill, *5747*
Paper money, *5382*
Play of note written by an American, *1240*
Theological treatise, *1950*
Watermark in paper, *5748*

1691

Colonist hanged for treason, *2834*

1692

Parliamentary act to establish a colonial post office, *5981*
Patent medicine advertisement, *2316*

1693

Christian worship services organized by African-American slaves, *6515*
College charter granted by the Crown, *2926*
Police uniforms, *4132*

1694

Lutheran services in English, *6556*
Rosicrucian Order lodge, *6598*
Volcanic eruption for which a date can be estimated, *2864*

1695

Workers' compensation agreement, *4550*
Worsted mill for making wool yarn, *7892*

1696

Printer who was a woman, *5782*

1697

Book catalog of a college, *1767*
Fire department to be paid, *4095*
Settler heroine publicly rewarded, *5933*
Stone arch bridge, *3564*

1698

Library, *4659*
Road map for public use, *4793*
Statehouse, *2114*

1699

Chimes and bells, *1302*

1700

Organs, *1303*

1701

Engraving of any artistic merit, *1223*

1702

Cross-dresser of note, *6827*

1703

Business manual, *1793*

1704

Newspaper advertisement, *2317*
Newspaper that was successful, *5630*

1705

Copper mine, *5316*
Miniature book, *1733*
Poem to be printed in a newspaper, *1945*
Presbyterian presbytery, *6581*

1706

Customhouse, *2469*

1707

Pastelist, *1197*

1708

Mennonite meetinghouse, *6538*

1709

Insane patients' home, *4894*
Latin grammar textbook, *1852*

1710

Agricultural book, *1757*
Community forest, *3723*

1711

Sperm whale captured at sea, *2418*

1712

Calico printery, *7859*
Cornmeal machine for grinding maize, *3910*
Rebellion of African-American slaves in a colony, *2241*

1713

Book auction catalog, *1779*
Paleontology report, *1974*

1714

Blackboards for use in schools, *3048*

Play written in America that was printed, *1241*
Schooner built in America, *6852*

1715

Book of Common Prayer in the Mohawk language, *1951*
English patent granted to a resident of America, *4647*
Whaling expedition, *2419*

1716

Botanical report on plant hybridization, *6735*
Lighthouse, *4123*
Lion, *1136*

1717

Book auction printed catalog, *1780*

1718

Theater, *3693*

1719

Arithmetic book printed in America, *1881*
Aurora borealis display, *6765*
History book by a Jewish author of ancient times, *1862*
Potatoes to be cultivated, *3894*

1720

School for Native Americans to be permanently established, *3049*

1721

Camel, *1137*
Editorial apology for false news to appear in a newspaper, *5631*
Fire insurance agent, *4528*
Inoculation against smallpox using material from human smallpox pustules, *4914*
Music book printed with bars, *1932*
Painter to obtain a public commission, *1198*
Vocal instruction book, *1933*

1722

Divinity professor at a college, *3266*

1723

Brethren, *6545*
Hydrotherapy book, *1887*
Library catalog in book form, *4660*

1724

English grammar by an American, *1853*
Levees, *3604*
Swimmer of note, *7513*

1725

Insurance book, *1794*

1725—*continued*

Mass scalping of Native Americans by colonists, *5934*

Reformed Church meeting, *6516*

1726

Book of folio size, *1734*

Catalog of theological and biblical literature, *1952*

1727

Catholic convent, *6451*

Drought of record, *2865*

Mezzotint engraving, *1199*

1728

Botanical garden, *6736*

German book printed in America, *1953*

Jewish religious school for children, *6485*

Shorthand book, *1735*

Steel, *4490*

1729

Arithmetic book by an American-born author, *1882*

Catholic nun, *6452*

College to have a full faculty, *2927*

Golf clubs for hitting balls, *7351*

Pharmacist who was a woman, *4963*

Story serialized in a newspaper, *1835*

1730

Algebra book, *1883*

Hemp to be exported, *1010*

Horse that was a thoroughbred, *1175*

Masonic lodge, *5728*

Quadrant, *6954*

1731

Circulating library, *4661*

Concert with documentation, *1287*

Medicine advertisement in booklet form, *2318*

Schwenkfelder to arrive in America, *6539*

1732

Astronomer to acquire international fame, *6657*

Fishing club, *7284*

German newspaper, *5661*

Planetarium, *6658*

Play presented by professional players, *1242*

1733

Catholic church in the English colonies, *6453*

Communistic settlement with a religious basis, *2182*

French instruction at a college, *3110*

Influenza epidemic, *2874*

Polar bear, *1138*

Political newspaper, *5632*

War map, *4794*

1734

Fencing book, *1992*

Fish protection law enacted by a city, *3742*

Great Awakening of religious revival, *6517*

Magician's advertisement, *2319*

Masonic book, *2007*

Moravian settlement in America, *6540*

Physician born in America who was graduated from a foreign medical school, *4964*

Slate used for roofing material, *2035*

1735

Agricultural experiment farm, *1002*

Brick roofing tile, *2036*

Fire insurance company, *4529*

Hebrew grammar, *1854*

Logic book, *1975*

Medical society, *5029*

Opera performed in America, *1341*

Silk export, *7886*

Translation of a classic, *1736*

Trial in which freedom of the press was upheld, *5633*

1736

Epidemiology report, *1888*

Pleurisy book, *1889*

Protestant Sunday school, *6518*

Public official of Italian ancestry, *5860*

1737

Copper coins, *5354*

Music society, *1278*

1738

Artist of importance to be born in America, *1200*

Puppet show, *3683*

Town built by free African-Americans, *2183*

Weather observations to be systematically recorded, *6766*

1739

Astronomer of note, *6659*

Fishing treatise, *1993*

Iron casting, *4448*

Wallpaper, *4305*

1740

Book plate, *1737*

British marine corps of American colonists, *5228*

1757

Street-sweeping service, 2219
Utilization of Niagara Falls waterpower for industrial purposes, 4379

1758

Botanist of note who was a woman, 6737
Reservation for Native Americans established by a state, 5937

1759

Comb factory, 4065
Composer born in America, 1327
Life insurance company, 4542
Musical instrument dealer, 1279
Secular song by a composer born in America, 1375

1760

Agricultural book distinctly American, 1758
Knighthood conferred on American soil, 6643
Library building, 4662
Medical licensing law enacted by a city, 4934
Methodist preacher, 6557
Rocking chair, 4320

1761

Milestones between cities, 2185
Music book by an author born in America, 1934
Pile bridge, 3565
Scientific expedition sponsored by a colony, 6661
Slide rule book, 1884
Venetian blinds, 4306

1762

Anatomy lectures, 3129
Caricature, 1213
Missionary society organized in the English colonies, 6568
Newspaper editor who was a woman, 5610
Saint Patrick's Day parade, 3651

1763

Germ warfare, 8089
Steamboat, 6853

1764

Cotton crop exported, 1029
German magazine, 4741
Greenhouse, 1040
Inclined railroad, 6315

1765

Chocolate mill, 3955

College literary society, 2990
Direct tax on Britain's American colonists without their consent, 7641
English grammar by an American published in America, 1856
Fire in a mine, 2880
Medical college, 3159
Medical education book, 1891

1766

Fox hunting club, 7422
Gem-cutting machine, 5317
Jewish prayer book, 1954
Protest by college students, 3007
Theater building of brick construction, 3695
United Brethren in Christ meeting, 6541

1767

Comic opera written for the American stage, 1343
Greek settlement, 5938
Midwifery professor at a college, 3130
Music book printed from type, 1935
Opera libretto published, 1343
President born after the death of his father, 6182

1768

Arbitration tribunal, 2354
Book advocating spelling reform, 1826
Botany professor at a college, 3229
Commercial artist, 1201
Cottonseed oil, 3881
Fire insurance company to receive a charter, 4530
Independent civil government in America, 5939
Methodist meetinghouse, 6558
Mustard, 3943
Patriotic song by an American, 1376
Physician to receive a Bachelor of Medicine degree, 3131
Sieve, 4366

1769

Catholic mission in California, 6454
Chemistry professor at a college, 3230
Harpsichord, 1307
History of medicine, 1863
Medical ethics book, 1892
Summer home, 2123
Type foundry, 5801

1770

Americans killed by British soldiers in the Revolution, 7986
Attack on British soldiers by civilians in the Revolution, 7984
Book of music by a composer born in America, 1936

Nautical almanac, *1765*
President born an American citizen, *6183*

1783

College named after George Washington, *2934*
Copyright law enacted by a state, *4627*
Daily newspaper, *5634*
Map of the United States, *4795*
Purple Heart, *1656*
Revolutionary War national veterans' organization, *5308*
Salute fired by Great Britain in honor of an officer of the United States, *3976*
Sports book, *1994*
Territory owned by the federal government, *5942*
Treaty between the federal government and a nation with which it had been at war, *3999*

1784

American woman to become a countess, *6644*
Balloon flight, *1535*
Botanic expedition, *6738*
Citizenship conferred by special grant, *5861*
Episcopal bishop, *6549*
French grammar, *1857*
French newspaper, *5662*
Geography book, *1978*
Hailstone shower of record that was fatal, *2866*
Labor union to nominate its own political candidates, *4604*
Law school operated privately, *3122*
Methodist bishop, *6560*
Methodist minister who was African-American, *6559*
Motorboat, *6948*
Political economy course at a college, *3250*
Russian settlement, *5943*
Seed business, *1011*
State denied admission into the Union, *7601*
Theology school, *3267*
Trading ship sent to China, *6879*
Writer to work professionally who was a woman, *2031*

1785

Agriculture society, *1087*
Bifocal eyeglasses, *5072*
Botany book by an American-born author, *1979*
City college, *2936*
City directory, *1813*
College founded as a Methodist institution, *2937*
Congregational Church minister who was African-American, *6522*
Copper cents minted by a state, *5355*
Decimal system of money, *5348*
Episcopal catechism, *1955*
Geographer of the United States, *6707*

Land set-aside for schools authorized by the Continental Congress, *3051*
Marble quarry, *5318*
Minister to Great Britain, *3985*
Missionary to the Native Americans who was African-American, *6569*
Mule born in the United States, *1141*
Porcelain teeth, *4855*
Sale of federal land authorized by Congress, *5944*
State university, *2935*
Street gangs, *2770*
Survey of public lands, *5945*
Toll road, *6610*
Treaty entered into by the federal government after independence, *4000*
Unitarian church, *6523*
Unitarian prayer book, *1956*

1786

Coin to use *E pluribus unum* as a motto, *5356*
Consul, *3986*
Golf players' club, *7337*
Ice cream to be made commercially, *3861*
Mineralogy instruction at a college, *3231*
Music magazine, *4694*
Rebellion against the federal government, *5947*
Reservation for Native Americans established by the federal government, *5946*
Spinning jenny for cotton, *7881*
Strike benefit by a union, *4590*
Textile machine, *7861*

1787

Alarm clock, *7898*
Constitution of the United States, *1104*
Continental coin, *5357*
Lifesaving service for distressed mariners, *4116*
Masonic lodge for African-Americans, *5729*
Methodist churches for African-Americans, *6561*
Newspaper to publish the Constitution, *1105*
Play by an American writer to be successfully presented by an established company, *1246*
Playwright to write professionally, *1245*
Printed copies of the Constitution, *1103*
Prison reform society, *2812*
Ship to carry the American flag around the world, *1123*
Slavery ban enacted for a territory of the United States, *2246*
Songbook of secular songs, *1937*
State to ratify the federal Constitution, *1106*
Steamboat to carry a man, *6854*
Window glass factory, *4036*

1788

Algebra book by an American-born author, *1885*

1788—*continued*

Book of secular songs by an American-born composer, *1327*

Cotton goods to be trademarked, *7882*

Cotton mill, *7882*

Dictionary published in the United States, *1797*

Federal election, *3380*

Navy chaplain in the Continental Navy, *5196*

Pocket dictionary, *1798*

Sailcloth factory, *7862*

Ship built on the Pacific coast, *6856*

Songbook of secular songs by a composer born in America, *1938*

Steamboat patent, *6855*

Worsted mill operated by waterpower, *7893*

1789

Army organization under the Constitution, *5143*

Attorney general of the United States, *6124*

Attorney of the United States, *2711*

Bibliography of Americana in English, *1739*

Book of road maps, *4796*

Bourbon whiskey, *2666*

Cabinet, *6102*

Catholic Bible in English, *1963*

Catholic diocese and archdiocese, *6456*

Catholic magazine, *4697*

Children's magazine, *4695*

Clerk of the House of Representatives, *2577*

College founded as a Catholic institution, *2938*

Comb made of ivory, *4066*

Commander-in-chief of the U.S. Army, *5147*

Congressional act, *2558*

Congressional act declared unconstitutional by the Supreme Court, *2559*

Congressional chaplain, *2580*

Congressional committee, *2579*

Congressional representative appointed to a presidential cabinet, *2596*

Congressional representative who was Catholic, *2597*

Drawback legislation enacted by Congress, *2471*

Flour mill, *3911*

House of Representatives election that was contested, *3326*

Inaugural ball, *6137*

Insurance law treatise, *1873*

Joint meeting of the Senate and the House of Representatives, *2557*

Land office, *5948*

Law report, *1874*

Lighthouse built after American independence, *4124*

Loan to the United States, *3804*

Morgan horse, *1176*

Navigation act enacted by Congress, *2472*

Novel by an American writer to be published in America, *1839*

Pensions paid by the federal government, *4583*

Pharmacy professorship at a college, *3132*

Postmaster general of the United States, *5985*

President elected under the Constitution, *6135*

President to receive the unanimous vote of the presidential electors, *3381*

President to tour the country, *6230*

Presidential appointment, *6138*

Presidential inauguration, *6136*

Presidential mansion, *6250*

Publisher of denominational religious books, *1957*

Secretary of the treasury, *6103*

Senate journal, *4696*

Senate president pro tempore, *2625*

Senator who was Catholic, *2638*

Session of Congress, *2556*

Session of the House of Representatives, *2576*

Session of the Senate, *2624*

Speaker of the House, *2578*

Supreme Court chief justice, *2752*

Tariff legislation enacted by Congress, *7663*

Temperance organization, *2675*

Trade tokens, *5358*

Vice president who had served in the House of Representatives, *6239*

White lead manufacturer, *4462*

1790

Actor of American birth, *1273*

Agricultural dictionary, *1799*

Army medical book, *1895*

Battle fought by federal troops after the formation of the Union, *5144*

Bonds issued by the federal government, *3811*

Book entered for copyright, *4629*

Buttons of pewter or block tin, *2286*

Catholic bishop appointed to serve in the United States, *6457*

Census of the United States, *5848*

Coast guard service, *5208*

Copyright law enacted by Congress, *4628*

Cotton mill to spin cotton yarn successfully, *7883*

Dental drill, *4856*

Historical society (state), *5710*

House of Representatives filibuster, *2581*

Ice yacht, *7205*

Lawyers admitted to practice before the Supreme Court, *4633*

Music publishers, *1281*

Naturalization act enacted by Congress, *5862*

Naval protection, *5259*

Panorama show, *3684*

Partridge propagation, *1067*

Patent granted by the federal government, *4648*

Physician who was African-American, *4966*

President who had been a senator, *6139*

Prison to have individual cells for prisoners, *2813*

Secretary of state, *6104*

Senator appointed by a governor, 2639
Singing contest, 1282
Supreme Court clerk, 2743
Supreme Court of the United States, 2742

1791

Anthracite coal, 3502
Bank of the United States, 3758
Bible in folio size to be illustrated, 1964
Carpet mill, 4311
Catholic seminary, 3268
Chaplain of the U.S. Army, 5197
Congressional representative who was Jewish, 2598
Constitutional amendments, 1107
Corporate body chartered by a special act of Congress, 2403
Dental dispensary, 4857
Export report by the federal government, 2473
Federal revenue cutter, 6857
Internal revenue tax levied by Congress, 7642
Law book containing laws enacted by more than one session of Congress, 1875
Law book of federal laws, 1876
Marble building, 2070
Navy officer commissioned, 5278
One-way street, 6611
Orchestral song to be printed, 1378
Patent granted jointly to a father and son, 4650
Patent recipient to obtain more than one patent, 4649
Pile driver, 4389
Presidential proclamation, 6140
Special session of the Senate, 2626
State admitted to the Union after the ratification of the Constitution, 7602
Sugar refinery, 3956
Supreme Court decision, 2744

1792

Agriculture professor at a college, 2890
Almanac with a continuous existence, 1766
Anatomy book, 1896
Artist of American birth to head the Royal Academy of London, 1202
Book advocating voting rights for women, 2012
Bridge on a large scale, 3566
Building erected in the United States for public use, 2115
Building erected in Washington, DC, by the federal government, 2116
Chemistry society, 6777
Circus, 3672
Columbus Day, 4233
Congressional apportionment of representatives, 2582
Congressional investigation, 2560
Copper coins made by the U.S. Mint, 5359
Cotton gin, 1030
Cracker bakery, 3917

Cremation, 2856
Draft of civilians by Congress, 5218
Exploration by ship of the mouth of the Columbia River, 5949
Gold coinage, 5360
Gold price fixed by Congress, 5349
Half cent, 5361
Industrial park, 4380
Life insurance offered by a general insurance company, 4543
Maternity book, 2013
Mint of the United States, 5350
Monument to Christopher Columbus, 5396
Postal service law enacted by Congress, 5986
Presidential veto of a congressional bill, 6141
Silver coins, 5362
Stock exchange, 3812

1793

Alfalfa, 1012
Anthology of American literature, 1740
Balloon flight in which a presidential order was carried, 1536
Broadcloth, 7863
Canal for boat transportation, 3600
Catholic African-Americans, 6458
Catholic priest, 6459
Child labor in a factory, 4572
Cotton thread, 4361
Emergency first aid organization, 4117
Fugitive slave law enacted by Congress, 2247
Metal purchased for coinage, 5363
Neutrality proclamation by the federal government, 3977
Oiled silk patent, 7864
Patent granted to an inventor who was a woman, 4651
Road authorization by a state, 6612
Senate election that was contested, 3327
Sulfuric acid, 4427
Supreme Court nominee who was rejected by the Senate, 2753
Wood engraving made with an engraving tool, 1226
Wool carding machine, 7894

1794

Arsenal of the federal government, 5126
Ball bearing commercial installation, 2038
Building built to serve as a hotel, 2421
Cesarean operation, 5075
Changes in the American flag to be authorized by Congress, 1124
College that was nondenominational, 2939
Commodore in the Navy, 5279
Death penalty ban by a state, 2796
Dentistry book, 1922
Extradition treaty with a foreign country, 4001
Fiction best seller, 1781
Jewelers' supply house, 5319

1794—*continued*

Medical record of an epidemic, *2875*
Neutrality regulation enacted by Congress that governed the actions of citizens, *3978*
Opera of a serious nature, *1344*
Presidential commission, *6142*
Rivet production, *2037*
Russian Orthodox mission, *6495*
Silver deposit for coinage, *5364*
Textile machinery patent, *7865*
Tobacco tax enacted by Congress, *2697*
Warship builder, *5260*

1795

American gazetteer, *1814*
Belt conveyor system, *4390*
English grammar instruction at a college, *3113*
Federal government employees who were women, *5351*
Gold bullion deposit for coinage, *5365*
Health board established by a city, *4172*
Lutheran hymnbook, *1971*
Macadam road, *6613*
Muskets, *8091*
Presidential amnesty issued to rebellious citizens, *6143*
Road appropriation of a specific sum by a state, *6614*
Steam engine for industrial use that was practical, *4391*
Supreme Court chief justice whose nomination was not confirmed, *2754*

1796

Architect and engineer who worked professionally, *1193*
Coast survey book, *2014*
Cookbook by an American author, *1847*
Dollar marks, *5802*
Electoral vote cast contrary to instructions, *3382*
Elephant, *1142*
Federal law exempting debtors from prison, *2814*
Gaslights for display, *3654*
Nail cutting and heading machine, *7908*
Opera by an American composer, *1345*
Passport, *5884*
Patented pills, *4981*
Pediatrics monograph, *1897*
Protection of Native American hunting grounds authorized by Congress, *5951*
Sale of federal land to an individual, *5950*
Senators elected but not seated, *2640*
Ship from the Atlantic coast to anchor in a California port, *6858*
Steam baths for curing disease, *5110*
Sunday newspaper, *5635*
Suspension bridge, *3567*

1797

Architecture book distinctly American, *2015*
Chemistry laboratory manual, *1980*
Congressional representative to serve before his 25th birthday, *2599*
Cryptography chart, *4797*
Epidemiologist, *4173*
Frigate, *6914*
Medical journal, *4750*
Novel published in America to be republished in England, *1840*
Plow patent, *1041*
President whose son became president, *6184*
Presidential election in which more than one candidate declared for the presidency, *3383*
Special session of Congress, *2561*

1798

Army lieutenant general, *5148*
Brawl in the House of Representatives, *2583*
Deportation of aliens authorized by Congress, *5864*
Encyclopedia printed in the United States, *1830*
Health service established by the federal government, *4174*
Hymnbook with music, *1972*
Immigration law enacted by Congress, *5863*
Marine band, *5230*
Navy surgeon, *5280*
Navy yard, *5261*
Novel in the Gothic horror genre, *2032*
Nurses' training, *3133*
Prize money awarded by the Navy, *5262*
State nullification proceedings to obstruct federal legislation, *7595*
Straw hats, *2294*
Tax levied by Congress directly on the states, *7643*
Vineyard, *1013*
Writer whose livelihood was obtained exclusively by writing, *2032*

1799

Comb-cutting machine, *4067*
Congressional eulogy for a president, *6185*
Craft union contract, *4605*
Education association, *3223*
Gold nugget, *5320*
Government contract authorized by Congress for pistols, *8092*
Ice shipped commercially, *3931*
Insurance regulation enacted by a state, *4499*
Italian instruction at a college, *3114*
Meteor shower on record, *6676*
Navy chaplain, *5198*
Printed ballot, *3314*
Quack doctor of note, *3646*
Quarantine law enacted by Congress, *4208*
Semaphore telegraph system, *7684*

Senator to be impeached, *2641*
Ship constructed by the federal government, *6915*
Shipbuilding law enacted by Congress, *5263*
Standardization of weights and measures for customs, *2474*
Supreme Court chief justice who had been a congressional representative, *2755*
Supreme Court decision in a matter between states, *2745*
Swedenborgian or New Church temple, *6524*
Tax rebellion, *5952*
Warship to capture an enemy ship after the Revolution, *8005*

1800

Ax factory, *7909*
Bankruptcy act, *2308*
Book with color plates, *1741*
Catholic bishop consecrated in the United States, *6460*
Congressional caucus, *2584*
District land office, *5953*
Endowment for social service purposes, *5731*
Fireboats, *4097*
First Lady to receive free mail franking privileges, *6130*
Greek Testament, *1965*
President to reside in Washington, *6144*
Stomach washing with a tube or syringe, *5111*
Vaccination against smallpox using cowpox, *4915*

1801

Blowpipe, *6796*
Booksellers' organization, *1782*
Cheese factory cooperative, *3857*
Dueling law enacted by a state, *2808*
Guide to parliamentary rules of order, *2016*
Hard water crackers, *3918*
Herbal book, *1927*
Hymnbook compiled by an African-American editor, *1973*
Landscape painter, *1203*
Marine hospital established by Congress, *4870*
President elected by the House of Representatives, *6145*
President inaugurated in the city of Washington, *6146*
President to review the military forces, *6147*
Supreme Court chief justice to serve in a presidential cabinet, *2756*
Voting registration law enacted by a state, *3424*
Whips commercially manufactured, *7910*
Yacht, *6859*

1802

Army academy, *3194*
Army engineer corps, *5178*

Book fair, *1783*
Brass, *4463*
Catalog of the Library of Congress, *1768*
Chess book, *1995*
Comic magazine, *4698*
Dinosaur fossils, *6739*
Fruit culture treatise, *1759*
Gilt buttons, *2287*
Gymnastics book, *1996*
Land subsidy by Congress for road improvements, *6615*
Law text, *1877*
Leopard, *1143*
Librarian of Congress, *4663*
Sheep of the Merino breed, *1085*
Smallpox vaccine clinic, *4916*
West Point graduate who was Jewish, *3195*
West Point graduates, *3196*

1803

Apple parer, *4367*
Bird banding, *6740*
Camp meeting, *6525*
Children's library, *4664*
Digest of American law, *1878*
Federal judge to be impeached, *2719*
Gastroenterology treatise, *1898*
Grant of federal land to a foreigner, *5954*
Hemophilia treatise, *1899*
Mica, *5321*
Refrigerator, *4345*
Religious tract society, *6570*
School of modern history at a college, *3094*
Supreme Court decision voiding an act of Congress, *2746*
Territory annexed by the federal government, *5955*

1804

Agricultural encyclopedia, *1831*
Bananas to be imported, *3898*
Book publishers' catalog, *1769*
Distilling book, *1848*
Insurance agency, *4500*
Land grant university, *2940*
Madstone, *3647*
Marine Corps commando raid, *5231*
Pontoon bridge, *3568*
Presidential candidate nominated at a caucus, *3399*
Presidential election in which candidates were nominated for the vice presidency, *3384*
Printer's ink, *5783*
Quids political faction, *3346*
Steamboat with a twin-screw propeller, *6860*
Supreme Court justice to be impeached, *2757*
Transcontinental expedition to the Pacific coast, *6721*
Vice president who was nominated specifically for that office, *6240*

1805

American flag flown over a fortress of the Old World, *1125*
American history book of importance whose author was a woman, *1865*
Art museum, *5593*
Boxer to win distinction in the ring, *7248*
Cryptography book, *2017*
Dry dock, *6904*
Ice exported, *3932*
Magic lantern book, *2018*
Pharmacopoeia prepared by a medical association, *1928*
Women's club, *5732*

1806

Child born in the White House, *6251*
Cider mill, *3841*
College magazine, *4699*
Dictionary of the English language compiled by an American, *1800*
Duel in which a future president of the United States participated, *2809*
Highway built by the federal government, *6616*
Pharmaceuticals book, *1929*
Senator to serve in contravention to the age limit, *2642*
Soap manufacturer to render fats in his plant, *4266*
Town founded by a woman, *2188*

1807

Coast survey, *5956*
College entrance requirement other than Greek, Latin, and arithmetic, *2941*
Embargo act enacted by Congress, *2475*
Evangelical Church conference, *6526*
Flint glass factory, *4037*
Former vice president to be arrested, *6241*
Glue factory, *4428*
Instruction for deaf students, *3030*
Lifeboat, *4118*
Meteorite whose landing was recorded, *6677*
Obstetrics book, *1900*
Salt well drilled west of the Alleghenies, *3933*
Soda water, *3843*
Steamboat to make regular trips, *6861*

1808

Anthracite coal burned experimentally, *3503*
Bible society, *6571*
Bible translated into English, *1966*
Brushes, *4267*
College orchestra, *1357*
Duel between representatives in Congress, *2810*
Law magazine, *4700*
Leather-splitting machine, *4456*
Medical book by a navy medical officer, *1901*
Pineapple cheese, *3858*

Play about a Native American, *1247*
Trotting horse, *1177*

1809

Abdominal operation other than a cesarean section, *5076*
Catholic magazine in English, *4702*
Cricket club, *7271*
Disciples of Christ meeting, *6527*
Geology book, *1981*
Gloves, *2264*
Hebrew dictionary, *1801*
Magazine containing a fashion plate, *4701*
President born beyond the boundaries of the original 13 states, *6186*
Railroad for freight transportation, *6316*
Railroad track that was practical, *6415*
Steamboat to make an ocean voyage, *6862*
Supreme Court decision establishing the power of the federal government, *2747*
Type specimen book from an American type foundry, *1742*
Vaccination program offered by a city, *4917*
Watchmaker, *7899*

1810

Agricultural journal, *4703*
Book on child-rearing, *2019*
Boxer of fame who was African-American, *7249*
Carpet mill to make ingrain carpets, *4312*
Cattle fair, *1078*
Cigar factory, *2702*
English actor of note to perform in America, *1274*
Fire insurance joint-stock company, *4531*
Foreign missionary society, *6572*
Glass crystal chandelier, *4342*
History of printing, *1866*
Horse breeders' society, *7386*
Insurance company owned by African-Americans, *4501*
Irish magazine, *4742*
Leather tanning by the oil tan method, *4457*
Mailbox see-through locker, *5987*
Military dictionary, *1802*
Mineralogy journal, *4765*
Screw auger, *7911*
Screw factory, *7912*
Silk mill, *7887*
Supreme Court decision declaring a state law unconstitutional, *2748*
Vaccination law enacted by a state, *4918*

1811

Boat club, *7206*
Conscience fund, *2771*
Magician of note, *3655*
Masonic magazine, *4705*

Naval battle in the War of 1812, *8020*
Naval hospital established by Congress, *5007*
Quarterly magazine, *4704*
Secession idea to be mentioned in Congress, *7634*
Senate filibuster, *2627*
Senator to be censured, *2643*
Settlers to reach the Pacific coast, *5957*
Steam-propelled ferryboat, *6907*
Steamboat to sail down the Mississippi, *6863*
Year in which exports exceeded imports, *2476*

1812

American flag flown over a schoolhouse, *1126*
Anthracite coal used commercially, *3504*
Bridge in a Y shape, *3569*
Canning book, *1849*
Capture of a British frigate in the War of 1812, *8023*
Comic history of the United States, *1867*
Copper rolling mill, *4464*
Drug mill, *4982*
Historical society (national), *5711*
Hydrophobia book, *1902*
Land office established by Congress, *5958*
Marine who was a woman, *5232*
Naval action of importance in the War of 1812, *8021*
Naval vessel to display the American flag around Cape Horn, *1127*
Navy officer to abolish corporal punishment on his ship, *5281*
Pencil factory, *8148*
Prisoners captured in the War of 1812, *8022*
Psychiatry book, *1903*
Railroad treatise, *2020*
Supreme Court justice who had been a representative in Congress, *2758*
Treasury notes bearing interest, *3814*
Vice president to die in office, *6242*
Vice presidential candidate to decline the nomination, *3400*
War bond issued by the federal government, *3813*
Wedding in the White House, *6252*
West Point graduate killed in action, *3197*

1813

Chemistry magazine, *4766*
Cotton mill entirely powered by water, *7884*
Craps, *3634*
Defeat of a British naval squadron in the War of 1812, *8024*
Factory standardization to federal government specification, *4381*
Gas streetlights, *2213*
Globe factory, *4798*
Haircloth, *7866*
Hospital for insane patients operated privately, *4896*

Mail delivery by steamboat, *5988*
Medical jurisprudence course at a college, *3134*
Religious weekly newspaper, *5636*
Stereotyped book, *1743*
Superintendent of schools hired by a state, *3052*
Supreme Court decision reversing the ruling of a state supreme court, *2749*
Vaccination law enacted by Congress, *4919*

1814

Bible in Hebrew, *1967*
Building in all-Gothic architecture, *2071*
Circular saw, *7913*
Cottonseed hulling machine, *1031*
Museum especially constructed as a museum and art gallery, *5577*
News agency, *5623*
President to face enemy gunfire while in office, *6148*
School for the higher education of women, *3079*
Secession convention during the War of 1812, *7635*

1815

Music festival, *1283*
Naval officers' training school, *3212*
Oral school for deaf students, *3031*
Pamphlet produced from a steel plate engraving, *1744*
Peace society, *5733*
Railroad charter granted by a state, *6317*
Steam-propelled frigate, *6916*
Varnish manufacturer, *4429*

1816

African Methodist Episcopal bishop, *6564*
African Methodist Episcopal church convention, *6563*
Bible society (national), *6573*
Boiler plates, *4430*
Book on Americanisms, *1745*
Double-deck steamboat, *6864*
Mineralogy textbook, *1982*
National cemetery, *2852*
Printing press invented in the United States, *5768*
Savings bank, *3759*
Savings bank to receive money on deposit, *3760*
Steamboat on the Great Lakes, *6865*
Suspension bridge of iron wire, *3570*
Tariff passed by Congress for protection, *7664*
Theology school that was nonsectarian, *3269*
Transatlantic passenger line, *2477*
Weather report delivered to the Army, *6768*

1817

Abolition newspaper, *5637*

1817—*continued*

African Methodist Episcopal preacher who was a woman, *6565*

Canal of importance, *3601*

Eye infirmary, *4871*

Gas streetlights throughout a city, *2214*

Geological map of the United States, *1981*

Iron mill to puddle and roll iron, *4450*

Paper made by machine, *5749*

Prayers in sign language, *6528*

School for deaf students, *3032*

Showboat theater, *3696*

Sword swallower, *3656*

Therapeutics book, *1904*

Trust, *2518*

Waterworks system to use cast-iron pipes, *2226*

1818

Army medical corps, *5008*

Chair factory, *4321*

Clinical instruction and bedside demonstration, *3135*

Educational magazine, *4706*

Geology textbook, *1983*

Horticultural society, *1088*

Hygiene lectures at a college, *3136*

Marine insurance law enacted by a state, *4502*

Melons and cantaloupes, *3899*

Natural cement rock, *2039*

Oil well, *3524*

Oratorio performance, *1288*

Science journal, *4767*

Shoe peg, *2300*

Theology school graduate who was African-American, *3270*

1819

Angle iron, *2040*

Bicycle patent, *7180*

Bicycles, *7179*

Canning of food, *3944*

Civil engineering course at a college, *3232*

Fire patrol to protect property during fires, *4098*

Geology society (national), *6778*

Industrial school, *3282*

Lathe, *7914*

Lithograph, *1214*

Methodist missionary, *6574*

Military school, *3184*

Odd Fellows lodge, *5719*

Parachute jump from a balloon, *1580*

Patent leather, *4458*

Piracy law enacted by Congress, *2772*

Plow with interchangeable parts, *1042*

Silk thread, *4362*

Standardization of nomenclature for naval vessels, *5264*

Tightrope performer who was a woman, *3657*

Transatlantic crossing by an American steamboat, *6979*

Tungsten and tellurium, *5322*

1820

Antislavery magazine, *4707*

Bachelor tax enacted by a state, *7644*

Concrete, *2041*

Cranberry cultivation, *3900*

Discovery of Antarctica by an American, *6722*

Eye hospital, *4872*

Felt manufacturing mechanical process, *7867*

General pharmacopoeia, *1930*

Granite, *5323*

High school, *3080*

Lightship, *4125*

Mariners' church, *6575*

Mercantile library, *4666*

Political machine, *3347*

Ship sunk by a whale, *2420*

States with populations of more than 1 million, *5849*

Workers' library, *4665*

1821

Actor to receive curtain applause, *1275*

American to set foot on Antarctica, *6722*

Cathedral, *6461*

Christmas tree, *4254*

College alumni association, *2991*

Fire hose of rubber-lined cotton web, *4099*

Historical novel, *1841*

Pharmacy college, *3160*

State law abolishing imprisonment for debt, *2815*

State west of the Mississippi River to be admitted to the Union, *7603*

Tunnel, *3611*

1822

Building of fireproof construction, *2072*

Physiologist of note, *4967*

Printing press for printing wallpaper in color, *5770*

Prison treadmill, *2816*

Quinine, *4983*

Steam-powered printing press, *5769*

Technical institute, *3283*

Trust company, *3761*

West Point graduate who was Native American, *3198*

1823

Ancient and modern history chair at a college, *3095*

Birth registration law enacted by a state, *2159*

Congressional representative to be refused a seat, *2600*

Congressional representative who was a Catholic priest, *2601*

Gymnasium to offer systematic instruction, *7371*
Medical jurisprudence treatise, *1879*
Newspaper for Jewish readers, *5663*
Ophthalmology book, *1905*
Ophthalmology course at a college, *3137*
Quinine sulfate, *4984*
Rhyming dictionary, *1803*
Teacher training school, *3258*

1824

Boxing arena, *7503*
Catholic school for Native Americans, *3053*
College course without Greek or Latin, *2992*
Engineering college, *3233*
Entomology book, *1984*
Jewish congregation in the Reform movement, *6486*
Locomotive to pull a train on a track, *6347*
Mining tunnel on a large scale, *3612*
Opinion poll, *5601*
Popular vote in a presidential election, *3386*
Presidential election in which a loser won, *3385*
State nominating convention, *3315*
Strike in which women participated, *4591*
Supreme Court decision in a commerce case, *2750*
Treaty between the federal government and a South American nation, *4002*

1825

Archery club, *7568*
Artists' organization (national), *1205*
Atlas issued by a state, *4799*
Brothers to serve simultaneously as governors of their respective states, *7610*
Communistic settlement that was not religious, *2189*
Cutlery shears, *4368*
Dead letter office, *5989*
Detachable collar, *2282*
Federal treaty rejected by the Senate, *4003*
Fire brick, *2054*
Fireworks book, *2021*
Former president who was elected to the House of Representatives, *6149*
Giant exhibited as a theatrical attraction, *3658*
Homeopathic treatise, *1906*
Homeopathy practitioner, *4968*
Horse race trotting course, *7387*
Ink, *8149*
Italian opera, *1346*
Labor union for women, *4606*
Law code adopted by a state, *4621*
Magazine for mechanics, *4768*
Mineral water bottler, *3842*
Natural gas used as an illuminant, *3511*
Painting movement, *1204*
Pharmacy journal, *4751*

Porcelain, *4038*
Reformatory for juvenile deliquents, *2817*
Religious tract society (national), *6576*
Secular song hit, *1379*
Social fraternity at a college, *2984*
Tax enacted by a state to support public schools, *3054*
Theater lighted by gas, *3697*
Tugboat powered by steam, *6880*

1826

Arcade, *2061*
Belting, *4392*
Children's magazine with literary merit, *4708*
Circumnavigation of the globe by a warship, *6980*
Cloth-covered buttons, *2288*
College graduate who was African-American, *3009*
Conference of American republics, *3979*
Gymnastics instruction at a college, *7372*
High school for girls, *3081*
Inheritance tax enacted by a state, *7645*
Internal-combustion engine, *5477*
Lyceum for adult education, *2884*
Malleable iron castings, *4451*
Printing instruction at a school, *3284*
Railroad with iron-plated wooden rails, *6318*
Reaper machine that worked, *1043*
Reflecting telescope, *6663*
Rhinoceros, *1144*
Transportation report, *2022*

1827

Actor to appear abroad, *1276*
Anarchist, *4551*
Ballet, *1232*
Book commercially bound in cloth, *1746*
Federal dry docks, *6905*
Federal law hostile to lotteries, *3642*
Gourmet restaurant, *2454*
Mardi Gras, *4234*
Nautical school, *3303*
Newspaper for African-American readers, *5664*
Nursery school, *3072*
Spanish newspaper, *5665*
Swimming school, *7514*
Telegraph system, *7685*
Trade union organization established in a city, *4607*

1828

Belts of leather for transmitting power, *4393*
Circus tights, *2265*
Electromagnet, *3451*
Fourdrinier papermaking machine, *5750*
Game manufacturing company, *4009*
Magazine for women, *4709*
Manufacturers' fair, *2408*

1828—_continued_
Native American language to be given a written form, *5959*
Native American newspaper, *5666*
Native American newspaper, *5959*
Poinsettia plants, *4255*
Political history book, *1868*
Railroad owned by a state, *6319*
Strike by women, *4592*
Strike in which a militia was called out, *4593*
Washington news correspondent, *5611*

1829

Bank deposit insurance law enacted by a state, *3762*
Catholic community of African-American nuns, *6462*
City carriage service, *2190*
Coffee mill, *3849*
Collar manufacturer, *2283*
Daredevil jumper of note, *3676*
Dental surgery textbook, *1923*
Education book, *1827*
Encyclopedia compiled by American editors, *1832*
File factory, *7915*
Genealogical collective work, *1869*
High school night classes, *3082*
Horse racing magazine, *4782*
Hotel recognized as a modern first-class hotel, *2422*
Letter written on a typewriter, *2384*
Library for seamen, *4667*
Locomotive for railroad use, *6348*
Manual training institute, *3285*
Monument to George Washington, *5397*
Pathology textbook, *1907*
Post office building, *6036*
Revolving gun, *8093*
School for blind students, *3023*
Siamese twins, *2170*
Spoils system of presidential patronage, *6150*
Stone arch railroad bridge, *3571*
Straw paper, *5751*
Typewriter, *2384*

1830

Adhesive and medicated plaster, *4942*
Antiquarian bookseller, *1784*
Balloon flight by an aeronaut born in America, *1537*
Cakes of soap of uniform weight and individually wrapped, *4268*
Census in which the national population exceeded 10 million, *5850*
Census that included deaf, mute, and blind people, *5851*
Cooperative store for consumers, *2490*
Double-deck railroad coaches, *6370*
Educational association (national), *3224*

Etcher, *1206*
Geological survey for a state government, *6708*
Hospital for treatment of the mentally ill established by a state, *4873*
Interstate railroad, *6322*
Lighthouse fueled by natural gas, *4126*
Marble statuary group, *1215*
Mormon Church meeting, *6492*
National convention of African-Americans, *2248*
Observatory established by the federal government, *6665*
Observatory operated by a college, *6664*
Parade held by a mystic society, *3659*
Passenger locomotive, *6349*
Penny daily newspaper, *5638*
Platform scale, *2379*
Power printing press capable of fine book work, *5771*
Race between a locomotive and a horse-drawn vehicle, *7388*
Railroad for commercial transportation of passengers and freight, *6321*
Railroad rails of T shape, *6416*
Railroad station for both passengers and freight, *6320*
Railroad timetable advertised in a newspaper, *6323*
Split-level buildings, *2073*
Sugar beets, *3901*
Team sport played in America, *7094*
Veterinary hospital, *5119*

1831

Anti-Masonic Party convention, *3348*
Bank robbery, *2773*
Bedspring manufacturing patent, *4322*
Brass wire and tubing, *4465*
Building and loan association, *3763*
Cabinet member who was Catholic, *6105*
Cattle of the Guernsey breed, *1079*
Chloroform, *4985*
Coastal shipping service, *2478*
Congress in which 1,000 bills were introduced, *2562*
Congressional chaplain who was Catholic, *2585*
Curling club, *7275*
Cylinder printing press, *5772*
Electric bell for electromagnets, *3452*
Electromagnetic telegraph, *7686*
Glucose from potato starch, *3957*
Locomotive bid, *6351*
Locomotive illumination, *6350*
Locomotive to burn coal, *6352*
Music book for children, *1939*
Play performed 1,000 times, *1248*
Railroad car with a center aisle, *6371*
Railroad to carry troops, *6324*
Railroad tunnel, *3613*
Reaper machine that was practical, *1044*

Sculptor to obtain a federal commission, *1207*
Slave rebellion after the Revolution, *2249*
Stone breaking machine, *5324*
Streetcar company, *6393*
Trade journal, *4710*
Treaty between the federal government and a foreign nation to provide for mutual reduction of import duties, *4004*

1832

Cholera epidemic, *2876*
College art museum, *5594*
Democratic Party national convention, *3349*
Guano for use as a soil fertilizer, *1014*
Horticultural magazine, *4711*
Hospital and asylum for African-Americans, *4874*
Hunting law (national), *5951*
Lock-stitch sewing machine, *4349*
Machine for manufacturing pins, *4350*
National political convention to adopt the two-thirds rule, *3333*
National political platform, *3332*
Performance of "America the Beautiful", *1380*
Phrenologist, *4969*
Phrenology book, *1908*
Presidential candidate nominated at a national convention, *3401*
Railroad accident, *6325*
Rubber company, *4484*
Streetcar, *6394*
Theater history, *1870*
Toy distribution center, *2138*
Vaccination program by the federal government to protect Native Americans against small-pox, *4920*
Vice president to resign, *6243*
Welsh magazine, *4743*

1833

Annunciator, *2358*
Antislavery book, *2023*
Army cavalry unit, *5179*
Avocado, *3902*
Book for the blind, *1747*
Book jacket, *1748*
Cabinet appointee rejected by the Senate, *6106*
Clipper ship, *6866*
Collar factory, *2284*
College founded as a Quaker institution, *2942*
College to enroll women and men on equal terms, *2943*
Cutlery factory, *4369*
Fireproof safe, *2357*
Free public library established by a city, *4668*
Homeopathic medical society, *5031*
Horse race pacing register, *1997*
Interstate anticrime pact, *4133*
Locomotive cowcatcher, *6417*
Medical dictionary, *1804*

President to ride on a railroad train, *6222*
School for music teachers, *2898*
State aid to railroads, *6326*
Tenement house, *2124*
Treaty between the federal government and an Asian nation, *4005*

1834

Baseball book, *1998*
Bellows, *4395*
Book trade magazine, *4712*
Boxer to die from blows inflicted in a fight, *7250*
Brass kettles, *4292*
Cattle that were purebred shorthorns, *1080*
City mayor elected by popular vote, *2206*
Dental amalgam for filling teeth, *4858*
Dental society of a city, *5032*
Diving suit, *6709*
Electric motor using direct current, *3453*
Friction matches, *4334*
Gas meter, *3512*
Geological survey authorized by Congress, *6710*
Homeopathic pharmacy, *4986*
Ice-making machine, *4346*
Iron sailing vessel, *6867*
Labor newspaper, *5639*
Locomotive with six or eight driving wheels, *6353*
Novel about whaling, *1842*
Patent granted to an African-American inventor, *4652*
President to be censured by Congress, *6151*
Presidential protest, *6152*
Rifled gun, *8094*
Sandpaper patent, *4394*
Soda water machine, *3844*
Sportswriter, *5612*
Valentines commercially produced, *4235*
Wire sieves, *4370*

1835

Bible for the blind in embossed form, *1968*
Bowie knife, *8095*
Bridge of cast iron, *3572*
Coke used successfully as a blast furnace fuel, *3505*
Egyptian antiquities collection, *5578*
Fire of great destructive force, *2881*
Flea circus, *3660*
Gardener's manual, *1760*
Governor who was Catholic, *7611*
Homeopathy journal, *4752*
Homeopathy school, *3161*
Horseshoe manufacturing machine, *1178*
Laundry, *2438*
Locomotive with a cab, *6354*
Magazine in a Native American language, *4744*
Mortised lock, *2131*

765

1835—continued

Music school authorized to confer degrees, *2899*
Mutual fire insurance company, *4532*
Novel by an American to depict Native Americans in a realistic manner, *1843*
President whose assassination was attempted, *6187*
Railroad to run trains to Washington, *6327*
Sculptor of renown, *1208*
Soda water, *3845*
Spoons of nickel silver, *4371*
State police, *4134*
Wrench patent, *7916*
Zinc, *5325*

1836

Agricultural seed distribution on a national scale, *1015*
Child labor law enacted by a state that included an education requirement, *4573*
Coins produced by steam power, *5366*
College for women, *2944*
Cricket game played by a college team, *7272*
Federal treasury surplus to be returned to the states, *7596*
Gag rule in the House of Representatives, *2586*
Hooks and eyes, *2289*
Medical encyclopedia, *1833*
Mormon temple, *6493*
Navy officer to become an engineer, *5282*
Numbering system for patents, *4653*
President of the Republic of Texas, *4077*
Railroad sleeping car, *6372*
Revolver pistol, *8096*
Safety fuse, *4422*
Scientific expedition fitted out by the federal government, *6723*
Settlers to cross the continent who were women, *5960*
Steamboat on the Pacific coast, *6868*
Superintendent of schools hired by a city, *3055*
Supreme Court chief justice who was Catholic, *2759*
Tourist guide for train travelers, *2024*
Whig Party convention, *3350*

1837

Board of education established by a state, *3056*
Brass clock works, *7900*
Carpet power loom, *4313*
Fluorspar, *5326*
Iron blast furnace to use anthracite coal in smelting, *4452*
Iron piano frame, *1308*
Locomotive steam whistle, *6355*
Magazine for blind readers, *4713*
Music instruction in a public school, *2900*
Physiology society, *5033*
Silk power loom, *7889*

State school for blind students, *3024*
Steel plow with a steel moldboard, *1045*
Threshing machine to employ steam, *1046*
Vice president elected by the Senate, *6244*
Whole-wheat bread, *3919*

1838

African-American magazine, *4745*
Alcohol prohibition law enacted by a state, *2676*
Astronomical observations book, *1985*
Bunting manufacture, *7868*
Caster for bedsteads, *4323*
Embossing press, *5773*
Hebrew spelling book, *1858*
Model laboratory school at a college, *3259*
Music convention of singing teachers, *2901*
Phrenology journal, *4753*
Pins manufactured with a solid head, *4351*
Silk dyers, *7888*
Silver mine, *5327*
Steam shovel, *4396*
Steamboat inspection service established by Congress, *4217*
Sugar beet mill, *3958*
Telegraphic system in which dots and dashes represented letters, *7687*
Tool factory, *7917*
Transatlantic steamboat service, *6881*
Watch made by machinery, *7901*
Wooden railroad bridge of a purely truss type, *3573*
Workers' compensation lawsuit involving the rights of an injured servant against his master, *4552*

1839

Astronomy photograph, *6692*
Building with a high steeple, *2097*
Cotton twine factory, *4335*
Cranioscopy book, *1909*
Dental journal, *4754*
Dictionary of American law, *1805*
Electrotype, *5803*
Envelope manufacturer, *5762*
Express delivery service, *2479*
Fraternity house at a college, *2985*
Iron blast furnace to use anthracite coal successfully, *4453*
Liberty Party convention, *3351*
Military school established by a state, *3185*
National political convention to adopt the unit rule, *3334*
Percheron horse importation, *1179*
Photographs used in surveying, *5810*
Statistical society, *6779*
Teacher training school established by a state, *3260*
Teachers' institute, *3261*

1840

Aquatic play, *1249*
Bowling match, *7220*
Camera exposure scale, *5832*
Cannibal, *2838*
Chiropodist, *4970*
Class photograph, *5813*
Clinic for teaching medical students, *3138*
Commercial photography studio, *5812*
Dental college, *3162*
Dental society (national), *5034*
Electric printing press, *5774*
Electricity journal, *4769*
Embalming book, *1910*
Factory workers' magazine, *4714*
Girder bridge of cast iron, *3574*
Graphite, *5328*
Gutta-percha, *4485*
Independent single direct-acting steam power pump, *4397*
Lager beer, *2667*
Land mines, *8097*
Library building at a university, *4669*
Line drawing to illustrate a newspaper article, *5685*
Naval vessel to sail around the Cape of Good Hope, *6981*
Nuts and bolts factory, *7918*
Photograph taken in the United States, *5811*
Presidential candidate to make a campaign speech, *3402*
Radio impulse transmission, *6304*
Seeding machine, *1047*
Tap dancer of renown, *1233*
Timber dry dock, *6906*
Timber trestle pier of lattice construction, *3575*

1841

Advertising agency, *2322*
Botanist to become a prominent landscape gardener, *6741*
Collapsible tube, *7919*
Commercial rating agency, *3815*
Dental surgeons to be licensed by a state, *4936*
Detective story, *1844*
Elastic webbing, *7869*
Fire brick to withstand high heat, *2055*
Fire engine with a steam boiler, *4100*
General anesthetic, *4828*
Geodetic survey, *6711*
Heavyweight boxing match to last longer than 100 rounds, *7233*
Japanese to enter the United States, *5961*
Life preserver of cork, *4119*
Orthodontia treatise, *1924*
President to die in Washington, *6189*
President whose grandson became president, *6188*
Reclining chair, *4324*

Screw-propelled steamboat on the Great Lakes, *6869*
Teaching methodology course at a college, *3262*
Underwater torpedo operated by electric current, *8098*
Vice president to succeed to the presidency after the death of a president, *6245*
Wagon train to California, *5962*
Wire rope factory, *4398*

1842

Adhesive postage stamps, *6051*
Business school, *2917*
Child labor law enacted by a state that regulated hours of employment, *4574*
Cornstarch made commercially from maize, *3912*
Credit protection group, *2447*
Department store, *2491*
Design patent, *4654*
Free public art museum in continuous existence, *5595*
Hammered iron, *4454*
Illustrated weekly magazine, *4715*
Mutual life insurance company, *4544*
Narcotics tariff enacted by Congress, *2685*
Navy bureau of medicine and surgery, *5009*
Navy officer condemned for mutiny, *5283*
Orchestra of international stature, *1358*
Overland wagon road across the Rocky Mountains, *6617*
Rubber shoe manufacturer, *2301*
State to repudiate a debt, *7597*
Tariff enacted by Congress to prevent the importation of obscene literature and pictures, *7665*
Telegraph cable, *7688*
Wire suspension bridge for general traffic, *3576*

1843

Consul to California, *3987*
Egg incubator, *1068*
Floating church, *6577*
Fraternal society for Jews, *5720*
Futurity horse race, *7390*
Government on the Pacific Coast, *5963*
Grain elevator operated by steam, *1048*
Harness horse race at night, *7389*
Index to books, *1770*
Iron vessel built for the Navy, *6917*
Jewish magazine, *4746*
Magazine for patients with mental illness, *4716*
Manila paper, *5752*
Minstrel show troupe, *3685*
Photograph of a former president, *6153*
Stained-glass window, *4039*
Telegraph appropriation by Congress, *7689*
Warship with propelling machinery below the waterline, *6918*

1843—*continued*
Water cures, *5112*

1844

Achromatic lenses, *5833*
Adventist church to accept Saturday as the Sabbath, *6529*
Anesthetic in dentistry, *4829*
Book review editor, *5613*
Branding punishment by a federal court, *2818*
College to feature rowing as a sport, *7467*
Commercial telegraph service, *7692*
Credit report book, *1795*
Cylinder and flatbed combination printing press, *5775*
Game protection society, *7423*
Gas engine, *5478*
Iron steamship built for transatlantic service, *6870*
Masonic college, *2945*
News dispatch by telegraph, *5602*
President married while in office, *6190*
President who was a "dark horse" candidate, *3403*
Presidential candidate to be assassinated, *3404*
Printing press for polychromatic printing, *5776*
Psychiatry association (national), *5035*
Railroad rails of iron, *6418*
Telegraph station, *7690*
Telegraph ticker to print letters of the alphabet, *7691*
Turbine successfully operated by waterpower, *4399*
Vulcanized rubber, *4486*
Whist rule book, *1999*
Yacht club, *7207*

1845

Anesthetic administered in childbirth, *4830*
Baseball team, *7159*
Building heated by steam, *2074*
Health journal to advocate water cures, *4755*
Iron truss bridge, *3578*
Law book of federal laws then in force, *1880*
Lawyer formally admitted to the bar who was African-American, *4634*
Lifeboat of corrugated iron, *4120*
Military school operated by a church, *3186*
Monolithic concrete building, *2075*
National labor congress, *4553*
Naval academy, *3213*
Newspaper with a full page of woodcut engravings, *5686*
Ocean mail contracts, *5990*
Oilcloth factory, *7870*
Photograph to gain world fame, *5814*
Presidential veto to be overridden by Congress, *6154*
Pressure-sensitive adhesive, *4487*

Prison matrons for guarding women prisoners, *2819*
Regatta, *7208*
Silver wire suture, *4955*
Soap powder in packages, *4269*
Spring manufacturer, *4400*
Suspension aqueduct bridge of wire cable, *3577*
Underwater telegraph cable that was practical, *7693*
Voice synthesizer, *7711*
Wall and floor tiles, *2042*

1846

Applied chemistry professor at a college, *3234*
Artificial leg patent, *5050*
Astronomy magazine, *4770*
Baking soda commercial production, *3934*
Baseball game, *7111*
Bronchitis treatise, *1911*
Cast steel for plows, *4491*
Factory heated by steam, *4382*
Gingham factory, *7871*
Handwriting teaching system widely used in schools, *3057*
Herd book for livestock, *1761*
Humor writer who was a woman, *2033*
Newspaper published on the Pacific Coast, *5640*
Painless surgery demonstration, *4831*
Plank road, *6618*
Rotary printing press, *5777*
School to provide separate classrooms for each class, *3058*
Senator elected on an antislavery ticket, *2250*
Supreme Court decision in a state boundary case, *2751*
Tattoo shop, *4053*
Telegrapher who was a woman, *7694*
Warehouse legislation enacted by Congress, *2480*

1847

Bronze statue of full length, *5398*
Chevrons for noncommissioned army officers, *5223*
Health insurance company, *4534*
Medical society (national), *5036*
Navy chaplain killed in action, *5199*
Norwegian newspaper, *5667*
Pathology chair at a college, *3139*
Plow for pulverizing the soil, *1049*
Postage stamps depicting a president, *6078*
Postage stamps issued by the Post Office Department, *6052*
Railroad coach modeled after English coaches, *6373*
Reformatory for boys established by a state, *2820*
Silver plating factory, *4466*
Skin grafting, *5077*

Steamship passenger line between American and European ports, *6882*
Swedish magazine, *4747*
Synthetic fertilizer, *1016*
Telegraph company, *7695*
Tourist guide with train schedules, *2025*
Vacation fund to send poor children to the country, *2139*
Workday of 10 hours to be mandated by a state, *4554*

1848

Arts and sciences national organization member who was a woman, *5709*
Baby carriage, *2140*
Baseball uniforms, *7104*
Bloomers, *2267*
Building constructed wholly of cast iron, *2076*
Chewing gum, *3959*
Child labor law enacted by a state that restricted the age of the worker, *4575*
Chinese immigrants to America, *5964*
Comic weekly, *4717*
Congressional lobbyist who was a woman, *2563*
Dental chair, *4859*
Drinking water conduit to be built underwater, *2227*
Election day for presidential voting held nationwide, *3387*
Engineering society, *3608*
Father and son who were senators at the same session, *2644*
Free Soil Party convention, *3352*
Gaslight in the White House, *6253*
Gold discovered in California, *5329*
Homeopathy college, *3163*
Ice cream freezer, *3862*
Macaroni factory, *3913*
Medical school for women, *3164*
Medical society for women, *5037*
Periodical index, *1771*
Phonetic Bible, *1969*
Pure food and drug law established by Congress, *4175*
Railroad to run west out of Chicago, *6328*
School for children with mental disabilities, *3016*
Science society (national), *6780*
Shirt factory, *2266*
Shorthand journal, *4718*
Spiritualist, *6599*
Steamboat service to California around Cape Horn, *6883*
Voting rights convention organized by women, *3425*

1849

Breech-loading cannon, *8099*
Business economics course at a college, *2918*

Chamber music ensemble, *1359*
Chinese restaurant, *2455*
Free public libraries authorized by a state, *4670*
Gas mask, *4402*
Ice skating champion, *7427*
Ice skating club, *7428*
Melodeon patent, *1309*
Percussion rock drill, *4401*
Photograph of a president in office, *6155*
Photography book, *1986*
Physician who was a woman, *4971*
Poultry show, *1069*
President who had received a patent, *6156*
Railroad excursion rates, *6329*
Safety pin, *4336*
Senator to serve three states, *2645*
Senator who was returned to the Senate after being defeated for the presidency, *2646*
Tattooed man exhibited as a theatrical attraction, *3661*
Twin covered bridges, *3579*
Wire gauge, *7920*

1850

Adding machine to employ depressible keys, *2375*
American history chair at a college, *3096*
Aviation book, *1987*
Billiards book, *2000*
College graduate who was an African-American woman, *3010*
Community leader to exercise the authority of king and high priest, *5965*
Cork manufacturer, *2043*
Derby hat, *2295*
Desk with a roll top, *4325*
Elevator, *2103*
Homeopathic hospital, *4875*
Iron pile lighthouse, *4127*
Japanese to become an American citizen, *5961*
Meat biscuit, *3920*
Paper money issued by the Native Americans, *5383*
Photograph of a star other than the sun, *6693*
Photography magazine, *4719*
Piano wire, *1310*
Private railroad car, *6374*
Railroad land grant, *6330*
Sparrows, *1164*
State on the Pacific coast to be admitted to the Union, *7604*
Theater ticket scalpers, *3698*

1851

Airship bombing plan, *8100*
Artificial eyes, *5051*
Brass and copper seamless tubes, *4467*
Brass spinning, *4468*
Brothers to serve as representatives in Congress simultaneously, *2602*

1851—*continued*

Cheese factory of consequence, *3859*
Chinese laundry, *2439*
Christmas cards, *4256*
College secret society for women, *2986*
College to prohibit discrimination because of race, religion, or color, *2946*
Commercial power laundry, *2440*
Condensed milk, *3869*
Electric locomotive, *6356*
Felt hats for women, *2296*
Fifty-dollar gold pieces, *5367*
Ice cream wholesale dealer, *3863*
Insurance board established by a state government, *4503*
Magazine for and by deaf students, *4720*
Mechanical freezer patent, *4347*
Medal awarded to an American food producer, *1651*
Nail machine, *7921*
Postage stamps depicting the American eagle, *6079*
Private mint authorized by the federal government, *5352*
Scandinavian Methodist Episcopal church, *6566*
Sewing machine equipped with a rocking treadle or double treadle, *4353*
Sewing machine manufacturer, *4352*
Telegraph used by a railroad, *7696*
Traveler's aid program, *5966*
Yacht from the United States to win an international yacht race, *7209*
Young Men's Christian Association, *5712*

1852

Beehive with removable frames, *1050*
Body to lie in state in the Capitol rotunda, *2564*
Cartoon showing Uncle Sam, *5701*
Chinese theater, *3699*
Chinese theatrical performance, *1250*
Civil engineering society (national), *3609*
College professor who was a woman, *2947*
Compulsory education law enacted by a state, *3059*
Horse blankets, *4263*
Hospital under Jewish auspices, *4876*
Insurance journal, *4721*
Intercollegiate rowing race, *7468*
Matzah made by machine, *3921*
Musician born in America to achieve fame in Europe, *1328*
Pharmacy society (national), *5038*
President to celebrate his silver wedding anniversary at the White House, *6191*
Public bathhouse and washhouse, *4193*
Railroad to run west of the Mississippi River, *6328*
Senator who was Jewish, *2647*
Shoe pegging machine, *2302*

Sprinkler system, *4101*
Temperance society for women (state), *2677*
Working hours of women to be regulated by a state, *4555*

1853

Arctic expedition by an American explorer, *6724*
Art magazine, *4722*
Bank clearinghouse, *3764*
Blue jeans, *2268*
Bronze equestrian statue, *5399*
Circumnavigation of the world by a yacht, *6982*
Coal oil factory, *4431*
Elevator with safety devices, *2104*
Envelope folding machine, *5763*
Fire department to be paid a salary, *4103*
Fire engine that was practical, *4102*
Horse show, *1180*
Infirmary for women staffed by physicians who were women, *4877*
Mechanics textbook, *1988*
Minister who was a woman, *6530*
Novel by an African-American writer, *1845*
Physical education classes in elementary schools, *3060*
Physiology and hygiene courses at a liberal arts college, *3140*
Plate glass, *4040*
Potato chips, *3960*
Pottery to make sanitary ware, *4041*
Railroad merger, *6331*
Stamped envelopes, *6053*
Terra cotta, *2056*
Trade association, *2519*
Truancy law enacted by a state, *3061*
Union passenger station used by several railroad companies, *6332*
University on the Pacific Coast, *2948*
Vice president sworn in on foreign soil, *6246*
Village improvement society, *2191*
World's fair, *2409*
Young Men's Christian Association branch for African-Americans, *5712*
Zinc commercial production, *5330*

1854

Alcoholics' asylum, *4879*
Baby show, *2141*
Billiard match, *4016*
Blanket factory, *4264*
Building in which wrought-iron beams were used, *2077*
Children's hospital, *4878*
Chinese graduate of an American college, *3011*
Chinese labor immigration, *5865*
Chinese newspaper, *5668*
College for African-American students, *2949*
Curved stereotype plate, *5788*

1858—*continued*

Burglar alarm, *2132*
Cable car, *6395*
Can opener, *4372*
Chemical laboratory at a college, *3235*
Cigar bands of special interest, *2703*
Congressional medal awarded to a physician, *1652*
Dinosaur skeleton found in the United States, *6744*
Mason jar, *4283*
Medical college on the Pacific Coast, *3165*
News dispatch by commercial telegraph, *5603*
Ornamented soda fountain for restaurants, *2456*
Overland mail service, *5993*
Pencil with an attached eraser, *8151*
Psychiatry textbook, *1912*
Shoe manufacturing machine, *2303*
Steel pens, *8150*
Stone crusher, *5332*
Street letter box, *5992*
Transatlantic telegraph cable, *7698*
Washing machine, *4270*

1859

Agricultural college to be chartered by a state, *2891*
Airmail dispatched from a post office in a balloon, *6014*
Billiard match to attain international fame, *4017*
Daredevil to cross Niagara Falls on a tightrope, *3677*
Electric light for household illumination, *3490*
Electric range, *4293*
Elevator in a hotel, *2107*
Escalator patent, *2106*
Fishing line factory, *7924*
Gas journal, *4771*
Grand piano with a cast-metal plate, *1312*
Intercollegiate baseball game, *7114*
Intercollegiate regatta, *7470*
International cricket tournament, *7273*
Library newspaper room, *4671*
Mastoid operation, *5078*
Milk inspection law enacted by a state, *4203*
Oil well that was commercially productive, *3528*
Paper bag manufacturing machine, *5757*
Public school for Chinese-American children, *3062*
Pullman sleeping car, *6375*
School for blind students to adopt the Braille system, *3025*
Song popular in the Confederate States, *1381*
Temporary insanity defense in a criminal case, *4622*

1860

Aerial photograph, *5815*

Army signal corps, *5180*
Baseball team to tour, *7160*
Boarding school on a Native American reservation, *3063*
Chiropody book, *1913*
Commercial oil refinery, *3529*
Constitutional Union Party convention, *3355*
Corkscrew patent, *4373*
Cowboy hat, *2297*
Czech newspaper, *5669*
Department store to occupy a city block, *2492*
Doctor of Philosophy degree, *2977*
Electrotherapy book, *1914*
Fire escapes for tenements, *4105*
Foreign missionary society organized by women, *6578*
Game preserve, *7424*
Hebrew book other than the Bible, *1958*
Intercollegiate billiard match, *4018*
Mass-market paperback book, *1786*
Navy commodore who was Jewish, *5281*
News reporter at a political convention who was a woman, *5614*
Physical education and hygiene professorship at a college, *7451*
Pony Express mail, *5994*
Prince of Wales to visit the United States, *4078*
Rabbi to open the House of Representatives with prayer, *2587*
Secession act at the start of the Civil War, *7636*
Secret service established by the federal government, *4169*
Signal flares, *5242*
Silver mill, *4469*
State to secede from the Union, *7945*
Traffic police squad, *4135*

1861

Act inaugurating the Civil War, *7946*
Army balloon corps, *5182*
Army secret service bureau, *5181*
Balloon carrier, *6919*
Battle flag, *1128*
Bibliophile magazine, *4725*
Camp for boys, *2143*
Chromolithograph, *1216*
Civil War attack, *7949*
Civil War battle, *7957*
Civil War bloodshed, *7952*
Civil War call for volunteers, *7951*
Composer born in America to win an international reputation, *1329*
Confederate coin, *5368*
Confederate congressional session, *7947*
Confederate cruiser to raid Union commerce, *7944*
Confederate forts to surrender in the Civil War, *7958*

Confederate general killed in the Civil War, *7953*

Confederate government bond, *7948*

Confederate officer killed in the Civil War, *7955*

Confederate paper money, *5384*

Constitutional amendment proposal to bear the signature of a president, *1108*

Copyright law on photographs enacted by Congress, *4630*

Creamery for commercial production, *3854*

Divided road, *6619*

Fire in an oil well, *2882*

Fly casting tournament, *7285*

Former president to serve as an official of an enemy government, *6158*

Fund-raising organization to sell stamps, *5734*

Ice yacht club, *7210*

Income tax levied by Congress, *7646*

Laryngology instruction at a college, *3142*

Life insurance nonforfeiture law enacted by a state, *4545*

Medal of Honor action, *1670*

Medal of Honor awarded to a member of the Naval Service, *1671*

Military prison on an island, *2821*

Naval battle in the Civil War, *7959*

Naval skirmish in the Civil War, *7950*

Newspaper published by soldiers in the field, *5641*

Newspaper wrappers for mailing newspapers, *5995*

Nursing school to award a diploma, *3166*

Orthopedics chair at a college, *3143*

Paper money issued by the federal government, *5385*

Patent issued by the Confederate States of America, *4655*

Peep show machine, *3686*

Petroleum exported to Europe, *3530*

Photographic attempt to show motion, *5569*

Pin-tumbler cylinder lock, *2133*

Press censorship by military authorities, *5604*

Pretzel bakery, *3922*

School for freed slaves, *2251*

Senator to address the Senate in military uniform, *2648*

Teacher training school at which students conducted practice classes, *3263*

Telegram dispatched from an aerial station, *7699*

Transcontinental telegraph line, *7700*

Union naval officer killed in the Civil War, *7956*

Union ship captured in the Civil War, *7960*

Union soldier killed by enemy action in the Civil War, *7954*

Year in which two presidents were elected, *3388*

1862

Agriculture bureau scientific publication, *1763*

Army ambulance corps, *5011*

Army chaplain who was Jewish, *5200*

Army field hospital, *5010*

Army field telegraph used in warfare, *5243*

Army general to become an admiral in the Navy, *5150*

Balloonist to direct artillery fire, *7964*

Bill bearing the likeness of a president, *5387*

Chinaware for restaurant use, *4309*

Citizen of the United States to be hanged for treason, *2835*

Confederate cruiser built in England, *7962*

Confederate ship surrendered to the Union, *7963*

Decalcomania pictures, *4307*

Emancipation proclamation, *2252*

Encased postage stamps, *6055*

Enclosed baseball park, *7504*

Episcopal cathedral, *6550*

Execution for slave trading carried out by the federal government, *2797*

Football club, *7301*

Governor to be impeached and acquitted, *7613*

Gymnastics instruction at a college for women, *7373*

Homestead law enacted by Congress, *5967*

Hospital ship operated by the Navy, *5012*

Inheritance tax levied by Congress, *7647*

Ironclad naval vessels, *6921*

Ironclad seagoing naval warship, *6922*

Ironclad turreted vessel in the Navy, *6923*

Land grant for an agricultural college, *2892*

Legal tender, *5386*

Medal of Honor awarded to a Marine in the Civil War, *1672*

Medal of Honor of the Army, *1673*

Military service by African-Americans to be authorized by Congress, *5145*

Naval battle between ironclad vessels in the Civil War, *7961*

Newspaper printed on a train, *5789*

Oil pipeline, *3531*

Paper money fractional currency, *5388*

Passport fee, *5885*

Pediatric clinic, *4841*

Polygamy ban enacted by Congress, *4807*

Postage stamp catalog, *2026*

Railroad post office, *6037*

Rapid-fire machine gun, *8107*

Revenue stamps issued by the federal government, *7648*

Revolving gun turret for ships, *8106*

Snowshoe production, *2304*

Stock exchange to specialize in mining securities, *3816*

Taps, *1382*

Turreted frigate in the Navy, *6920*

1862—*continued*

Warship sunk by an underwater torpedo mine, *7965*

1863

Accident insurance company, *4504*
Army chaplain who was African-American, *5201*
Book on vellum, *1749*
Catholic parish church for African-Americans, *6464*
Civil War amnesty issued by the president to rebellious citizens, *6143*
Civil War bloodshed north of the Mason-Dixon Line, *7967*
Compressed pills or tablets, *4987*
Corps badges systematically assigned to an entire army, *5224*
Docks owned by a state, *2481*
Draft law enacted by Congress during wartime, *5219*
Farmers' institute sponsored by a state, *2893*
Free mail delivery in cities, *5996*
Gold certificates, *5389*
Laryngology clinic, *4842*
Monument to commemorate the Civil War, *5400*
National bank, *3765*
National science institute, *6781*
News reporter tried as a spy, *5615*
Newspaper printed on wood-pulp paper, *5790*
Notes wholly engraved and printed at the Bureau of Engraving and Printing, *5390*
Officer to preside over both of the branches of Congress, *2565*
Orthopedic hospital, *4881*
Paper sewing patterns, *4357*
Photographs of combat, *5816*
Printing press to use a continuous web or roll of paper, *5778*
Private school for children with disabilities, *3017*
Roller skates, *7462*
Teacher training school principal who was a woman, *3264*
Thanksgiving Day, *4261*
Turkish bath, *4194*
Union regiment in the Civil War made up of African-American soldiers, *7966*

1864

Bessemer steel converter, *4492*
Boiler inspection law enacted by a state, *4106*
Camel race, *1146*
Cigarette tax, *2698*
Circus to feature a car as an attraction, *3673*
Coin to use the motto "In God We Trust", *5369*
Fine arts department in a college, *2902*
Fish hatchery, *1059*

Hunting license required by a state, *7425*
Knights of Pythias meeting, *5721*
Mines school at a college, *3236*
Money order system, *5997*
National hall of fame, *5579*
News photographs of distinction, *5817*
Oil tank railroad cars, *6376*
Ophthalmologist of note, *4972*
Periscope, *5244*
Physician who was an African-American woman, *4973*
Presidential election in which soldiers in the field were allowed to vote, *3389*
Professional fraternity at a college, *2987*
Railroad rails of steel, *6419*
Salmon cannery, *3887*
Stamp collection magazine, *4727*
State park, *3734*
Submarine built in the United States to sink an enemy warship in actual warfare, *7968*
Sugar and glucose from cornstarch, *3961*

1865

Advertising magazine, *4726*
African-American preacher to deliver a sermon in the House of Representatives, *2588*
Architecture department at a college, *2903*
Army major who was African-American, *5169*
Ban by Congress on importation of diseased cattle, *4210*
Bank for freed African-American slaves, *3766*
Baseball game in which one team scored more than 100 runs, *7115*
Bathhouses owned and operated by a city, *4195*
Billiard ball of composition material resembling ivory, *4019*
Body of a president to lie in state in the Capitol rotunda, *6194*
Coast Guard serviceman who was African-American, *5209*
Coffee percolator, *3850*
College to sponsor an endowed lecture series, *2950*
Congressional directory, *1817*
Dental society member who was a woman, *4862*
Entomology journal, *4772*
Environmental protection law enacted by a state in connection with advertising, *3711*
Execution of a woman by hanging by the federal government, *2798*
Figure skater of note, *7429*
Judge advocate of the Navy, *5284*
Ku Klux Klan meeting, *2253*
Labor cooperatives to be authorized by a state, *4609*
Lawyer admitted to practice before the Supreme Court who was African-American, *4635*
Linen thread factory, *4363*

Medal of Honor winner to receive two awards, *1674*

National bank to fail, *3767*

Natural gas corporation, *3513*

Newspaper published at sea, *5642*

Oil pipeline of importance, *3533*

Oil well drilled by torpedoes, *3532*

Premiums given away with merchandise, *2323*

President to be assassinated, *6193*

Pullman sleeping car that was comfortable, *6377*

Safe deposit vault, *2359*

Soap in liquid form, *4271*

Social science society (national), *6782*

Streamlined railroad train, *6428*

Sweet crackers, *3923*

Train robbery of a disabled train, *2774*

Trial of a war criminal by the federal government, *7969*

Zinc sheet mill, *4470*

1866

All-metal roller skate, *7464*

Ambulance service for hospitals, *4823*

American flag made of American bunting to fly over the Capitol, *1129*

Animal humane society, *5735*

Artificial insemination of a woman resulting in conception, *5113*

Bank and train robbery gang, *2775*

Baseball pitcher to throw a curve ball, *7138*

Baseball teams for women, *7161*

Bicycle with a rotary crank, *7181*

Boiler insurance company, *4505*

Burlesque show, *3687*

Civil rights law enacted by Congress, *2254*

Cog railroad, *6333*

Corrupt election practices law enacted by a state, *3316*

Delegate to a national political convention who was African-American, *3335*

Dentist who was a woman to obtain a D.D.S. degree, *4862*

Dynamite, *4423*

Fur-bearing animals raised commercially, *1070*

General of the U.S. Army, *5151*

Grand Army of the Republic post for veterans of the Civil War, *5310*

Health board with emergency powers established by a city, *4176*

Hotel with safe deposit boxes, *2423*

Indelible pencil, *8152*

Insurance rate standardization, *4506*

Interracial jury, *2735*

Irrigation law enacted by Congress, *1017*

Machine for cutting and straightening wire, *4403*

Metric system usage to be approved by Congress, *2309*

Monument ordered by the federal government from a sculptor who was a woman, *5401*

Mourning postage stamp, *6080*

Navy officer to become an admiral, *5270*

News correspondent accredited to the White House, *5616*

Newspaper index separately published, *5643*

Nickel five-cent piece, *5370*

Oyster cocktail, *2669*

Paleontology chair at a college, *3237*

Queen to visit the United States, *4079*

Roller skating rink open to the public, *7463*

Root beer, *3846*

Sewing needles made by machine, *4358*

Sextuplets, *2171*

Soldiers' homes established by Congress, *5309*

State legislators who were African-American, *7624*

State readmitted to the Union after the Civil War, *7605*

Steam car, *5425*

Steam whaler, *6885*

Theater ticket agency, *3700*

Tin can with a key opener, *4284*

Train robbery of a train in motion, *2776*

Transatlantic yacht race, *7211*

Underwater highway tunnel, *3614*

University for African-American students, *2951*

Voting rights organization (national) advocating universal voting rights, *3427*

Young Women's Christian Association, *5713*

Zither factory, *1313*

1867

Agriculture organization (national), *1089*

Animated picture machine, *5528*

Cartridge belt patent, *8108*

Cow town, *2192*

Dental school to be associated with a medical school, *3167*

Election law granting African-American men the right to vote, *3428*

Elevated railroad, *6334*

Fashion magazine, *4728*

Gallstone operation, *5079*

Governor of a state who had also been governor of a territory, *7614*

Greek Orthodox church, *6496*

Paint ready-mixed, *7925*

Plate-glass insurance, *4507*

Refrigerated railroad car, *6378*

Stamp collection society, *6056*

State university supported by a direct property tax, *2952*

Stock brokerage concern to use a telegraph ticker, *3817*

Terra cotta factory, *2058*

Territory annexed by the federal government beyond the nation's continental limits, *5969*

1867—*continued*

Territory annexed by the federal government that was noncontiguous, *5968*
Theological college for Jews, *3272*
Theological school that was multisectarian, *3271*
Trademark for food, *2324*
Transpacific sidewheeler steamer, *6871*
Typewriter that was practical, *2385*
Water supply tunnel for a city, *3615*

1868

Amateur athletic games held indoors, *7543*
Artificial-ice manufacturing plant, *4432*
Athletic club, *7542*
Bicycle school, *7182*
Cattle club to promote Jersey cattle, *1090*
Chamber of commerce established by a state, *2448*
Commercial high school, *3083*
Compressed fresh yeast, *3935*
Decoration Day, *4236*
Dye plant, *4433*
Elevator in an office building, *2108*
Elks meeting, *5722*
Farmers' institute sponsored by a college, *2894*
Horse race trotting register, *2001*
Kindergarten, *3073*
Native American to win territorial concessions from the federal government, *5970*
Nickel plating, *4471*
Open-hearth furnace for the manufacture of steel, *4493*
Parade with float tableaux, *3662*
Pediatrics journal, *4756*
Philology society (national), *6783*
President to be impeached, *6159*
Railroad dining car, *6379*
Steam-driven motorcycle, *5487*
Tape measure, *7926*
Uniforms for mail carriers, *5998*
Veterinary department at a college, *3182*
Women's professional club, *5723*
Workday of eight hours to be authorized by Congress, *4556*

1869

Air brake, *6420*
Apartment house with a modern layout, *2125*
Architectural patent received by a woman, *1194*
Baseball team whose players received a regular salary, *7162*
Bookseller's guide, *1787*
Brokerage office owned by women, *3818*
Celluloid, *4480*
Chain store organization, *2493*
Coal mine disaster, *3506*
Consul who was African-American, *3988*
Corncob pipe commercial manufacture, *2704*
Dairy association (state), *1091*

Dental crown made of gold, *4863*
Exploration of the Grand Canyon of the Colorado, *6725*
Financial news agency, *5624*
Fraternal group insurance, *4508*
Health board established by a state government, *4177*
Indian Affairs Commissioner who was Native American, *5972*
Intercollegiate football contest, *7315*
Journalism course at a college, *3097*
Jute culture, *1018*
Kindergarten manual, *1828*
Labor bureau established by a state, *4557*
Labor Day, *4237*
Labor union to admit workers other than craft workers, *4611*
Law school at a university to admit women, *3123*
Lawyer who was a woman, *4636*
Lithuanian settlement, *5971*
Movie projector patent, *5570*
National union for women, *4610*
Naval Academy graduate who was Japanese, *3214*
Oil drill offshore rig, *3534*
Postage stamp depicting the American flag, *6082*
Postage stamps depicting scenes, *6081*
Prehistoric hoax, *3648*
Prepared-food producer, *3945*
Probation officer for juvenile delinquents to be hired by a state, *2822*
Prohibition Party convention, *3356*
Railroad owned by a city, *6335*
Sawmill to use a band saw, *4404*
School for blind African-American students, *3026*
Senate hearing witness who was a woman, *2628*
Snow-melting apparatus, *2221*
State university to grant equal privileges to women, *2953*
Steeplechase, *7391*
Sulfur deposit, *5333*
Supreme Court nominee to die before taking office, *2760*
Toothpick manufacturing machine, *4071*
Torpedo manufacturing station, *8109*
Transcontinental railroad service, *6336*
Vacuum cleaner that used suction, *4272*
Waffle iron patent, *4294*

1870

African-American to vote under authority of the 15th Amendment, *3429*
Animated photograph projection before a theater audience, *5529*
Autopsy performed by a woman physician on a male corpse, *2850*

Baking powder manufacturer, *3936*
Boardwalk, *2063*
Brick pavement on a city street, *6620*
Canoe club, *7212*
Cartoon showing the Democratic Party as a donkey, *5702*
Check protectors, *3790*
Clearinghouse for stocks and bonds, *3819*
Coin box for streetcars, *6396*
College summer school, *2993*
Congressional representative who was African-American, *2603*
Entomology professor at a college, *3238*
Governor to be impeached and convicted, *7615*
Justice of a state supreme court who was African-American, *2720*
Justice of the peace who was a woman, *2721*
Law school graduate who was a woman, *3124*
Medal of Honor awarded to a Jewish soldier, *1675*
Natural gas for manufacturing, *3514*
Newspaper premiums, *2325*
Paper bag machine, *4405*
Pension granted to the widow of a president, *4584*
Petroleum jelly, *4988*
Railroad signal system with automatic electric block, *6422*
Railroad to install track water tanks, *6421*
Road pavement of sheet asphalt, *6621*
Sandblasting process, *4434*
School for African-American children established by a state, *3064*
Senator who was African-American, *2649*
Sorority at a college, *2988*
Stamp auction, *6057*
Subway, *6409*
Tong organized crime gang, *2777*
Yiddish newspaper, *5670*

1871

Amateur athletic games held outdoors, *7544*
Art museum to sell reproductions, *5596*
Bandwagon, *2326*
Baseball game between an all-white team and an all-African-American team, *7116*
Baseball league, *7096*
Baseball player to play as a professional, *7139*
Carousel patent, *3620*
Cement, *2044*
College entrance plan using certified schools, *2994*
Corrugated paper, *5759*
Dermatology chair at a college, *3144*
Forest fire of consequence, *2883*
Half holiday on Saturday for factory workers, *4558*
Hebrew newspaper, *5671*
Human cannonball, *3663*
Iron sloop yacht, *6872*

Land grant college for African-American students, *2895*
Lifesaving service established by the federal government, *4121*
Medical chemistry course at a college, *3145*
Narrow-gauge locomotive, *6357*
Natural gas plant operated by a city, *3515*
Neurology textbook, *1915*
Oranges of the seedless navel variety, *3903*
Perforated wrapping paper, *5758*
Political economy chair at a college, *3251*
Popcorn snack, *3962*
Relief map, *4800*
Rifle society (national), *7472*
Rotary printing press with a continuous-roll feed, *5779*
Surgeon general, *4213*
Surgeon who was a woman, *4974*
Theological school to admit women as students, *3273*
Unitarian minister who was a woman, *6523*
Visible speech method of instruction for deaf students, *3034*

1872

Adding machine to print totals and subtotals, *2376*
Allergy book, *1916*
Analytical chemistry course requirement for pharmacy students, *3146*
Arbor Day, *4238*
Ban on sex discrimination in employment enacted by a state, *6828*
Baseball player on a white team who was African-American, *7140*
Bird refuge established by a state, *3743*
Book showing photographs of movements in sequence, *1750*
Burglar alarm system, *2134*
Candy packaged in a factory, *3963*
Cigarette-manufacturing machine, *2705*
Congressional representative to serve a single day, *2604*
Danish newspaper, *5672*
Doughnut cutter, *4295*
Dried milk patent, *3870*
Fish hatchery run by the federal government, *1060*
Labor Reform Party national convention, *3357*
Lawyer who was an African-American woman, *4637*
Liberal Republican convention, *3358*
Lunch wagon, *2457*
Mail fraud law enacted by Congress, *5999*
Mail-order business, *2494*
Mail-order catalog, *2494*
Mohair, *7872*
National park, *3735*
Natural gas pipeline constructed over a long distance, *3516*

1872—*continued*

Naval Academy midshipman who was African-American, *3219*
Nurse to receive formal training, *5023*
Optometry school, *3168*
Patent list, *2027*
Photograph of a stellar spectrum showing the dark lines, *6695*
Photographs showing action, *5818*
Popular science magazine, *4773*
Presidential candidate who was a woman, *3405*
Presidential candidate who was Catholic, *3407*
Railroad apprentice school, *3287*
Sprinkler system patent, *4107*
Telegraph call boxes, *7701*
Vice presidential candidate who was African-American, *3406*

1873

Barbed wire commercial production, *4406*
Brass rod, *4472*
Cable car put into service, *6398*
Cattle of the Aberdeen-Angus breed, *1081*
Collapsible tube machine, *7927*
College president who was a woman, *2971*
Earmuffs, *2270*
Education department at a college, *3265*
Football rules, *7302*
Free lunches for the poor and sick, *5736*
Gas-powered streetcar, *6397*
Hotel that was fireproof, *2424*
Illustrated daily newspaper, *5645*
International football game, *7316*
Linoleum, *4315*
Livestock market paper, *5644*
Margarine manufacturer, *3882*
Measurement organization (national), *2449*
Occupational therapy treatment, *5114*
Oratorio by an American, *1289*
Patent examiner who was a woman, *4656*
Postal card, *6044*
Prison built for women and managed by women, *2823*
Public school kindergarten, *3074*
Railroad coupler, *6423*
Sewing machine lamp holder, *4359*
Silo, *1051*
Slicing machine, *4296*
Tong war, *2777*
Trade dollars, *5371*
Transatlantic crossing attempted by a balloon, *1538*

1874

Baseball teams to travel abroad, *7163*
Cartoon showing the Republican Party as an elephant, *5703*
Chautauqua organization meeting, *2885*
Child abuse prevention organization, *5737*

Coins manufactured for a foreign government, *5372*
Corset, *2271*
Electric streetcar run with current generated by a stationary dynamo, *6399*
Football goalpost, *7309*
Hospital record system, *4882*
Hutterites, *6542*
Ice cream soda, *3864*
International rifle tournament of consequence, *7473*
Label patent, *4657*
Labor union label, *4612*
Lawn tennis, *7523*
Lithuanian newspaper, *5673*
Mechanical engineering laboratory, *3561*
Medical school that was coeducational, *3164*
Musical with an American theme and original score, *1252*
Osteopathic physician, *4975*
Physiology laboratory, *4926*
Railroad interlocking signal machine, *6424*
Reigning king to visit the United States, *6645*
Screw caliper, *7928*
Sprinkler head, *4108*
Steel arch bridge, *3582*
Store with fixed prices, *2495*
Temperance society for women (national), *2678*
Tin factory, *4473*
Water gas plant, *3517*
Wedding in a balloon, *4814*
Young Men's Hebrew Association, *5714*
Zoo, *1186*

1875

Agricultural experiment station operated by a state, *1003*
Banking association (national), *3768*
Baseball game in which a team made no hits in nine innings, *7118*
Baseball game in which a team made no runs in nine innings, *7117*
Baseball glove, *7105*
Book manuscript that was typewritten, *1751*
Bowling rule standardization, *7221*
Cantilever bridge, *3583*
Cash carrier system, *2360*
Catholic priest from the United States to be made a cardinal, *6465*
Centennial celebration of the Revolution, *8006*
Coaching club, *7569*
College program of study abroad, *2995*
Comic strip in a newspaper, *5687*
Dental drill powered by electricity, *4864*
Dental mallet, *4865*
Dynamo for a direct-current outdoor lighting system, *3454*
Electric tattoo machine, *4054*
Floating hospital, *4883*
Folding bed, *4328*

Football uniforms worn in a game, *7310*
Forestry association (national), *6784*
Former president to become a senator, *6160*
Jim Crow law, *2255*
Kentucky Derby horse race, *7392*
Music chair at a college, *2904*
Nautical school established by a city, *3304*
Oat-crushing machine, *3914*
Quintuplets, *2172*
Rabbinical college for the Reform Jewish movement, *3274*
Railroad parlor car, *6380*
Theosophical society, *5743*
Time lock, *2135*
Tuberculosis sanatorium, *4898*

1876

Actors' home, *1277*
Baseball game that was a shutout, *7119*
Baseball players to hit home runs, *7141*
Bible translation by a woman, *1970*
Bicycle factory, *7183*
Bohemian dictionary, *1807*
Carpet sweeper, *4273*
Cattle club to promote Guernsey cattle, *1092*
Centennial exhibition, *2410*
Chemistry organization (national), *6786*
Coach riding, *7570*
Coast Guard officers' training school, *3209*
Commemorative stamped envelopes, *6083*
Cooking school, *3288*
Court tennis, *7524*
Crematory, *2857*
Dermatology treatise, *1917*
Doctor of Philosophy degree awarded to an African-American scholar, *2978*
Electric organ, *1314*
Electric turnstile with a rachet, *2362*
Ethical culture society, *5744*
Forestry association (state), *6785*
Free kindergarten, *3075*
Greenback Party convention, *3359*
Hair clipper, *4068*
High-speed newspaper printing and folding machine, *5791*
Intercollegiate athletic association, *7545*
Intercollegiate football association, *7303*
Intercollegiate football championship, *7317*
Intercollegiate track meet, *7546*
Ketchup in bottles, *3945*
Library association (national), *4688*
Library journal, *4729*
Lifesaving medal awarded by the Treasury Department, *1653*
Mimeograph, *5784*
National political convention to be addressed by a woman, *3336*
Patent medicine to achieve nationwide popularity, *4989*
Pipe or screw wrench, *7929*

Polo club, *7456*
Polo mallets and balls, *7457*
Public exhibition of postage stamps, *6058*
Sardine cannery, *3888*
Stenotype device, *2361*
Symphonic work by an American composer, *1290*
Telephone conversation over outdoor wires, *7752*
Telephone message, *7751*
Title guaranty insurance company, *4509*
Torpedo boat, *6924*

1877

African-American town in continuous existence, *2193*
Amateur open swimming championship meet, *7515*
Animal humane society (national), *5738*
Bicycle magazine, *4784*
Cabinet member who had served as a Confederate officer, *6107*
Catamaran, *7213*
Chinese language and literature lectureship at a college, *3116*
Cricket magazine, *4783*
District nurse, *5024*
Doctor of Philosophy degree awarded to a woman, *2979*
Dog show, *1171*
Easter egg roll, *4239*
Flag Day, *4240*
Granola, *3916*
Heating system to heat buildings from a central station, *2078*
Interstate telephone call, *7753*
Margarine law enacted by a state, *3883*
Millionaire with a fortune greater than $100 million, *2443*
Monument to an American poet, *5402*
News dispatch by telephone, *5605*
Organ with color display, *1315*
Postage stamp for balloon mail, *6059*
Reformatory for women established by a state, *2824*
Socialist Labor Party of North America national convention, *3360*
Strike suppressed by federal troops in peacetime, *4594*
Telephone concert held long-distance, *1291*
Telephone for domestic use, *7712*
Telephone switchboard or exchange, *7728*
West Point graduate who was African-American, *3199*
Year-round railroad shipments of dressed beef, *2482*

1878

Airship, *1512*
Baseball catchers' chest protector, *7106*

1878—*continued*
Baseball catcher's mask, *7107*
Bibliography course at a college, *3098*
Bicycle club, *7184*
Chinese embassy, *3011*
Coffee in a can, *3851*
College daily newspaper, *5646*
Copper refinery furnace, *4474*
Correspondence course of a serious nature, *2886*
Electric company, *3455*
Electric light in a store, *3491*
Firehouse pole, *4109*
Floating soap, *4055*
Fruit spraying, *1019*
Fuller's earth, *5334*
Hotel for women, *2425*
Law school where the entire faculty was 65 years of age or over, *3125*
Lawyers' society (national), *4644*
Milk delivery in glass bottles, *3871*
Modern dancer, *1234*
Phonograph, *7004*
President to use a telephone, *6161*
Probation system for criminals of all ages, *2825*
Railroad bridge entirely of steel, *3584*
Telephone directory, *1818*
Telephone operator who was a woman, *7729*
Typing school, *3289*
Unassisted triple play in organized baseball, *7120*

1879

Amateur athletic competition, *7547*
Archeology organization (national), *6787*
Automatic telephone system, *7713*
Ban enacted by a state on the employment of women in an occupation, *4559*
Cash register, *2363*
Centrifugal cream separator, *3855*
Christian Science church, *6600*
Commercial telephone service using toll lines, *7730*
Electric arc streetlights, *2215*
Electric company organized to produce and sell electricity, *3457*
Electricity generated by Niagara Falls water-power, *3456*
Factory inspection law enacted by a state, *4383*
Five-cent store, *2496*
Hanging railroad bridge, *3585*
Hearing aid, *5069*
Incandescent lamp, *3492*
Indoor ice skating rink, *7430*
Lawyer who was a woman to be admitted to practice before the Supreme Court, *4638*
Locomotive to use oil for fuel, *6358*
Milk bottles, *4285*
Nurse who was African-American to receiving formal training, *5023*

Photograph taken by incandescent electric light, *5819*
School of prominence for Native American children, *3065*
Sugar substitute, *3964*
Veterinary school established by a state, *3183*

1880

Antibacterial mouthwash, *4072*
Bacteriology textbook, *1918*
Balloon pilot who was a woman, *1539*
Bareknuckle world heavyweight boxing champion, *7251*
Bicycle organization (national), *7185*
City with a population of more than 1 million, *5852*
Clay pigeon target for trapshooting, *7474*
Croquet league, *7571*
Electric lights in a church, *3493*
Electric streetlight installed in a city, *2216*
Electrical hearing aid, *5070*
Flour rolling mill, *3915*
Greenback Labor Party convention, *3361*
Hail insurance, *4510*
Halftone engraving, *1227*
Horse whose total purses exceeded $100,000, *7406*
Hydroelectric power plant to furnish arc lighting service, *3458*
Incandescent lamp factory, *3494*
Italian newspaper, *5674*
Laryngology journal, *4757*
Mechanical engineering society (national), *3610*
National park ranger, *3735*
Neurasthenia book, *1919*
Obelisk to be brought to the United States, *5403*
Paint prepared from standard formulas, *7930*
Pay station telephone service, *7731*
Play presented by a Jewish professional acting troupe, *1253*
Safety razor, *4056*
Salvation Army services, *6531*
Sewage-disposal system separate from the city water system, *2230*
Steam distribution plant, *3507*
Steamboat to employ electric lights successfully, *6873*
Tennis tournament of national scope, *7526*
Tunnel construction using compressed air, *3616*

1881

Architect who was a woman, *1194*
Bonding company, *4511*
Business school at a college, *2919*
Coast Guard inland station, *5210*
Cold storage plant, *4407*
College baseball player who was African-American, *7142*

Electric light from a power plant in a residence, *3495*
Electric locomotive headlight, *6425*
Film rolls for cameras, *5835*
Fishing magazine, *4785*
Greek play, *1254*
Halftone printing plate, *5785*
Horse bred in the United States to win the English Derby, *7407*
International commercial telephone service, *7732*
Labor organization (national), *4560*
Locomotive to attain a speed of one mile in less than a minute, *6359*
Loganberry, *3904*
National tennis championship matches, *7527*
Nursing school for African-American students, *3169*
Player piano, *1316*
Player piano that was completely automatic, *1317*
Plumbing law enacted by a state, *2231*
President whose mother lived at the White House, *6195*
Presidential candidate to make campaign speeches in a foreign language, *3408*
Psychology laboratory, *4927*
Pure food and drug law enacted by a state, *4178*
Quarantine law for plants enacted by a state, *4211*
Red Cross meeting, *5739*
Statue cast by the federal government, *5404*
Steel-hulled ferryboat, *6908*
Tennis society (national), *7525*
Universal constant in physics to be measured by American scientists, *6812*

1882

Accounting society, *3753*
Alcohol abuse programs required in schools by the federal government, *2679*
Bicycle trip of 100 miles sponsored by a club, *7200*
Building shaped like an elephant, *2079*
Christmas tree decorated with electric lights, *4257*
Cooperative store at a college, *2497*
Dynamo that was successful, *3460*
Electric fan, *4332*
Electric power plant operated by a city, *3459*
Electric power station with a central source, *3461*
Flicker animation, *5530*
Forestry book, *1990*
Honors program offered by a university, *2996*
Hotel to install electric lights, *2426*
Hydroelectric power plant to furnish incandescent lighting, *3462*
Immigration ban enacted by Congress, *5867*

Intercollegiate lacrosse association, *7572*
Knights of Columbus meeting, *5724*
Lipreading instruction for deaf people, *3035*
Malted milk, *3872*
Naval attaché, *5285*
Newspaper printing plant to install electricity, *5792*
Restrictions by Congress on immigration of Chinese laborers, *5866*
Silk sutures and ligatures, *4956*
Steel mill to install an electrical machine, *4494*
Tariff commission established by Congress, *7666*
Theater lighted by electricity, *3701*
Yiddish theater performance, *1255*

1883

Animal rights organization (national), *5740*
Antitrust law enacted by a state, *2520*
Apartment house cooperative, *2126*
Baseball game at night, *7121*
Catalog of government publications, *1772*
Cigar-rolling machine, *2706*
Coronation, *6646*
Crane, *4408*
Cross-country championships, *7549*
Electric elevated railroad, *6337*
Electric power plant with a three-wire central station, *3463*
Electrical engineering school at a college, *3239*
Fence made of woven wire, *1052*
History of African-Americans, *1871*
Horse show of national scope, *1181*
Intercollegiate lawn tennis match, *7528*
Labor unions to be legalized by a state, *4613*
Mail chute, *6000*
Major league baseball player who was African-American, *7142*
Missionary training school, *3275*
Newsboy, *5648*
Newspaper delivery train, *5647*
Opera produced at the Metropolitan Opera House, *1347*
Pharmacist who was a woman to receive a degree from a pharmacy college, *3147*
Plate glass produced on a large scale, *4042*
Sports trainer to work professionally, *7548*
Standard time program, *7895*
Steel-cut nails, *7931*
Vaudeville show, *3688*
Wild West Show, *3689*
Wrecking crane, *4409*
Yellow pages telephone directory, *1819*

1884

Adding machine absolutely accurate at all times, *2377*
Albert Medal presented to a person born in America, *1647*
American Derby horse race, *7393*

1884—*continued*
Anti-Monopoly Party convention, *3362*
Baseball championship, *7122*
Bullfight, *7258*
Catholic hillside shrine, *6466*
Chrome tanning process, *4459*
Dean of the faculty at a college, *2972*
Drama school, *2905*
Electrical show, *2411*
Equal Rights Party convention, *3363*
Evaporated milk, *3873*
Fountain pen, *8153*
Glider flight, *1546*
Graduate student who was a woman to receive a university fellowship, *3012*
Linotype machine, *5805*
Long-distance telephone call, *7754*
Manual training school entirely financed by public taxes, *3290*
Martini, *2670*
Medical society for African-Americans, *5039*
National political convention of a major party presided over by an African-American, *3337*
Naval Academy graduate to attain the rank of rear admiral, *3215*
Newspaper clipping bureau, *5625*
Newspaper syndicate, *5626*
Parent-teacher assocation, *3226*
Photograph of a lightning flash, *6696*
Police bureau of identification, *4158*
Roller coaster, *3621*
Round-the-world bicycle trip, *7201*
Skyscraper, *2098*
State college for women, *2954*
Theater to employ women as ushers, *3702*
Transparent paper-strip photographic film, *5836*
Underground burial of electric wires to be required by a state, *2222*
Vending machine that dispensed liquid automatically, *2393*

1885

Appendectomy, *5080*
Banking association (state), *3770*
Baseball batting and fielding cage, *7108*
Baseball team of African-American players to play professionally, *7164*
Biology course offered at a college, *3240*
Cartridge-loading machinery, *8110*
Catalog of first American editions of American authors, *1773*
Clock movement to be electrically wound, *7902*
Dealer in Oriental rugs, *4316*
Economics association, *6788*
Electric streetcars commercially operated, *6400*
Episcopal bishop who was African-American, *6551*
First aid instruction, *4122*
Forest reserve established by a state, *3724*

Gas commission established by a state government, *3518*
Gasoline pump, *4410*
Graduate school for women, *2955*
Library society (local), *4689*
Local anesthetic, *4832*
Motorboat pleasure craft, *6949*
Movie film, *5571*
Naval war college, *3216*
Nursing society, *5040*
Penalty rule in football, *7304*
Piggyback railroad operation, *6338*
President elected for two nonconsecutive terms, *6162*
Savings group for children, *3769*
Self-service restaurant, *2458*
Special delivery mail service, *6001*
State legislator who was African-American to represent a constituency with a white majority, *7625*
Tuberculosis sanatorium using modern treatment methods, *4899*

1886

Accounting society (national), *3754*
Adding machine successfully marketed, *2378*
Air gun, *8111*
Aluminum pots, *4297*
Avon Lady, *4057*
Bill bearing the likeness of a woman, *5391*
Boat race for fishermen, *7214*
Catholic priest who was African-American, *6467*
College for women to affiliate with a university, *2956*
Coursing club, *7394*
Daredevil to jump off the Brooklyn Bridge and survive, *3678*
Desk telephone, *7714*
Dishwasher, *4274*
Drinking straws, *4374*
Earthquake of consequence to be recorded, *2867*
Economics journal, *4774*
Election for governor in which two brothers were the opposing candidates, *7616*
International polo series, *7458*
Labor mediation and arbitration board established by a state, *4561*
Laboratory for the study of parasites in livestock, *5120*
Margarine law enacted by Congress, *3884*
Mineral segregation by oil flotation, *5335*
Newspaper association, *5617*
Newspaper page set by linotype, *5793*
Nursing magazine, *4758*
Ostrich farm, *1071*
Phonograph that was practical, *7005*
Playground, *2144*
Power plant using alternating current, *3464*

Settlement house in a poor city neighborhood, *2194*

Social register published, *1820*

Soup company, *3946*

Statue presented to the United States by a foreign country, *5405*

Steel vessels of the Navy, *6925*

Stock exchange at which more than a million shares were traded in one day, *3820*

Tractor with an endless chain, *1053*

Tuxedo coat, *2272*

Typewriter ribbon, *2386*

Wedding of a president in the White House, *4815*

Welding by the electric process, *4435*

Yeshivah for Jewish religious study, *3276*

1887

Accident reports by employers, *4563*

Ambassador who was Jewish, *3989*

Bacteriology laboratory, *4928*

Baseball player who was Native American, *7143*

Bauxite, *5336*

Book set by linotype, *1752*

Cancer hospital, *4885*

Congressional representative of Italian ancestry, *2605*

Credit insurance, *4512*

Customs fee stamps, *7649*

European edition of an American newspaper, *5649*

Fishing rod of telescoping steel tubes, *7932*

Game warden to be paid a salary, *3744*

Hospital designed exclusively for infants, *4884*

Interstate commerce act enacted by Congress, *2483*

Kindergarten for blind children, *3027*

Labor activists to be executed, *4564*

Library school at a college, *3099*

Mayor who was a woman, *2207*

Military hospital, *5013*

Monotype machine, *5806*

Mutual liability insurance company, *4513*

National tennis championship match for women, *7529*

Navy contract for armor plate, *5265*

Physiology society (national), *5041*

Psychology journal, *4759*

Shot tower, *8112*

Sick-leave benefit funds for teachers, *4562*

Silk loom, *7890*

Softball game, *7497*

Steel-frame building, *2080*

Train with electric lighting, *6429*

1888

Aluminum in metallic form, *4475*

Armenian newspaper, *5675*

Ball-point pen, *8154*

Bank for African-Americans operated by African-Americans, *3771*

Baseball teams to go on a world tour, *7165*

Camera to use film rolls, *5837*

Catholic seminary under the supervision of the Pope, *3277*

County created by federal law, *5973*

Crematory established by a state government, *2858*

Double-deck ferryboat, *6909*

Electric meter, *3465*

Geography magazine, *4775*

Health laboratory established by a city, *4197*

Holding companies authorized by a state, *2404*

Hotel transported from one location to another, *2427*

Incubator for premature babies, *4943*

Industrial corporation course at a college, *2920*

Key time recorder, *2381*

Motorboat with a storage battery, *6950*

Navy chaplain who was Catholic, *5202*

Observatory on a mountaintop, *6666*

Phonograph record, *7006*

Presidential nominee who was African-American, *3409*

Psychology professor at a college, *3148*

Race between a horse and a bicycle, *7395*

Revolving door, *2081*

Rodeo for roping and tying steers, *3690*

Saxophone production, *1318*

Seismograph, *6712*

Sweet potato, *1020*

Union Labor Party convention, *3364*

United Labor Party convention, *3365*

1889

Bacteriology courses at a college, *3149*

Bicycle with a back-pedal brake, *7187*

Business high school, *3084*

Centralized refrigeration service, *4436*

Children's department in a library, *4672*

Clarinet made exclusively of metal, *1319*

County high school, *3085*

Dam disaster of great consequence, *2868*

Dial time recorder, *2382*

Electric elevator successfully operated, *2109*

Electric sewing machine, *4360*

Electric tabulating machine, *2364*

Football dummy, *7311*

General medical clinic, *4843*

Golf mixed foursome, *7354*

Hydroelectric power plant generating alternating current to operate over a long distance, *3466*

International professional tennis contest, *7530*

Investment trust, *3822*

Jukebox, *7007*

Lithuanian church, *6468*

National holiday, *4241*

Night school for immigrants, *2887*

Pay telephone, *7715*

1889—*continued*

Photograph of a meteor, *6697*
Ready-made clothing for children, *2273*
Ready-mix food, *3947*
Sewer district established by a city, *2232*
Six-day bicycle race for women, *7186*
State named for a person born in America, *7598*
States admitted to the Union simultaneously, *7606*
Steam tractor, *1054*
Stock quotation boards, *3821*
Transcontinental daily railroad service, *6339*
World tour by a woman traveling alone, *6983*

1890

Animal husbandry professor at a college, *2896*
Antitrust law enacted by Congress, *2521*
Buttons of freshwater pearl, *2290*
Census compiled by machines, *5853*
Chrome-tanned leather successfully marketed, *4460*
Conservationist of note, *3712*
Crepe paper, *5760*
Dairy school at a college, *2897*
Dam filled with rocks, *3605*
Election law enacted by a state to grant voting rights to women after the adoption of the Constitution, *3430*
Employment service established by a state, *4565*
Execution by electrocution, *2799*
Golf course with nine holes, *7347*
Hot dog, *3939*
Intercollegiate Army–Navy football game, *7320*
Lawn mower, *7933*
Library society (state), *4690*
Meat inspection law enacted by Congress, *4179*
Mechanized shooting gallery, *3622*
Milk butterfat tester, *3874*
Naval militia established by a state, *5255*
Photojournalist, *5618*
Pneumatic hammer, *7934*
Polo association (national), *7459*
Power transmission installation using alternating current, *3467*
Prizefighting ban enacted by a state, *7234*
Sewage disposal by chemical precipitation, *2233*
Single Tax League national conference, *7650*
Soccer team entirely made up of Americans, *7492*
Steel-frame residence, *2082*
Tournament of Roses, *7318*
Web-fed four-color rotary printing press, *5780*

1891

American woman of European descent to be made a Native American chief, *6647*
Anatomy research institute, *5055*

Boxing match timed by automatic timer, *7235*
Car with an electric storage battery, *5426*
Carborundum, *5337*
Congress to appropriate $1 billion, *2566*
Congressional representative elected by prohibitionists, *2606*
Corkboard patent, *2045*
Correspondence school for workers, *2888*
Deck chair for steamer passengers, *4329*
Diamonds in a meteorite, *5338*
Duplicate whist tournament, *4022*
Eye wash commercially manufactured, *4990*
Football book, *2002*
Football game played indoors, *7319*
Forest management on a professional scale, *3725*
Forest planting by the federal government, *3726*
Gas conservation law enacted by a state, *3519*
Hospital open to all races as a matter of policy, *4886*
International copyright agreement, *4631*
International six-day bicycle race, *7189*
National fencing league, *7281*
National forest, *3727*
National forest reserve, *3728*
Nautical school established by a state, *3305*
Opticians' journal, *4760*
People's Party national convention, *3366*
Phonograph trade magazine, *4730*
Pneumatic bicycle tire, *7188*
Polar expedition of which a woman was a member, *6726*
Quadruple newspaper press, *5794*
Radio patent, *6305*
Railroad chapel car, *6381*
Sextuple newspaper printing press, *5795*
Ski club association, *7480*
State seal designed by a woman, *7599*
Trading stamp, *2327*
Traveler's checks, *3791*
Underwater railroad tunnel to a foreign country, *3617*
Whist organization, *4021*

1892

Acetylene gas, *4437*
Alligator farm, *1072*
Arabic magazine, *4748*
Bacteriology diagnostic laboratory in a city health department, *4198*
Baseball pinch hitter, *7144*
Baseball player to catch a ball dropped from the Washington Monument, *7145*
Basketball game, *7166*
Basketball played at a college, *7167*
Basketball rules, *7168*
Bicycle tire made of cord, *7190*
Bottle cap with a cork crown, *4286*

Boxing match under the Marquis of Queensberry rules, 7236
Cattle tuberculosis test, 5121
Commemorative coin, 5373
Concrete road, 6622
Cotton boll weevil, 1032
Delegates to a national political convention who were women, 3338
Double-deck streetcar, 6401
Electric sign of large dimensions, 2349
Ferris wheel, 3623
Football game at night, 7321
Gasoline tractor, 1055
Gold leaf, 5339
Liederkranz cheese, 3860
Locomotive owned by an industrial company, 6360
Manganese steel, 4495
Medical journal published by an African-American, 4761
Milk pasteurizing stations, 4204
Osteopathy school, 3170
Physical education department at a college, 7452
Portable typewriter, 2387
Printed streetcar transfers, 6402
Psychology society (national), 5043
Public speaking department at a college, 3100
Reply-paid card, 6045
Rough-dry laundry service, 2441
Single tax adopted by a city for local revenue purposes, 7651
Sociology professor at a college, 3252
Spring winding machine, 4411
Student government at a college, 3013
Toothpaste tube, 4073
Tuberculosis research and prevention society, 5042
Two-way telegraph, 7702
Vending machine to dispense postage stamps, 2394
Voting machines, 3317
Wire glass, 4043

1893

Addressograph, 2365
Anti-saloon organization, 2680
Aquarium with an inland saltwater environment, 1187
Aviation magazine, 4776
Bicycle track of wood, 7191
Biscuits of shredded wheat, 3924
Bowling magazine, 4786
Brick pavement on a rural road, 6623
Child born in the White House who was the offspring of a president, 6254
Coin bearing the likeness of a foreign monarch, 5374
College extension courses, 2997
Commemorative postage stamps, 6084

Dress made of spun glass, 2274
Electrical transmission of three-phase alternating high-frequency current, 3468
Foreign car exhibited, 5427
Golf course with 18 holes, 7348
Grand American Trapshoot tournament using live birds, 7475
Highway bridge with concrete arches, 3586
Hindu spiritual leader to visit America, 6601
Horse race of 1,000 miles, 7396
Kapok, 7873
Locomotive to attain a proven speed of 112.5 miles per hour, 6361
Lynching ban enacted by a state, 2256
Movie exhibition, 5509
Movie studio, 5543
Moving sidewalk, 6638
Navy medical school, 3171
Newspaper colored supplement, 5690
Newspaper with a color page, 5689
Police officer who was a woman, 4136
Postage stamp with valuation of one dollar, 6060
Postage stamps depicting a woman, 6085
Postage stamps to feature paintings, 6086
Print patent, 4658
Railroad safety law enacted by Congress, 4219
Relay race in a college track meet, 7550
Slide fastener, 2291
Sunday comics section in a newspaper, 5688
Suture of the human heart, 5090
Theater operated by a city, 3703
Trademark character, 2328
Tuberculosis laboratory established by a city, 4199
Typewriter to produce a line of writing visible as it was being typed, 2388
Visiting nurses, 5025
Water filtration system for bacterial purification of a city water supply, 2234

1894

Actor to have an exclusive movie contract, 5524
Amateur golf tournament, 7339
Antitoxin laboratory established by a public health department, 4200
Bicycle corps of cadets, 3187
Building with caisson foundations, 2083
Card time recorder, 2383
Catalog of recordings on disk, 1940
Ceramics school, 2906
Chocolate bars, 3965
Commercial museum, 5580
Communion cups for individuals, 6582
Cork for covering steam pipes, 2046
Dog license law enacted by a state, 1172
Employment office established by a city, 4566
Full-page magazine advertisement for a food product, 2329

1894—*continued*

Golf association (national), *7340*
Golf magazine, *4787*
Greek newspaper, *5676*
Health laboratory established by a state to diagnose diseases by the examination of sputum, *4201*
Intercollegiate fencing championship competition, *7282*
Labor union discrimination law enacted by a state, *4614*
Leprosy hospital, *4887*
Magic lantern feature show, *3692*
Manganese steel for railroad tracks, *4496*
Medical inspection of schoolchildren, *4180*
Monument to a woman financed by women, *5406*
Movie to be copyrighted, *5544*
Music by Native Americans to be recorded, *1284*
National championship stroke-play golf match, *7338*
Organization (national) of Jewish women, *5720*
Osteopathic physicians who were women, *4976*
Osteopathy journal, *4762*
Pediatrics book, *1920*
Peep show using film in a vending machine, *3691*
Pension fund for teachers, *4585*
Poliomyelitis epidemic, *2877*
Pushball, *7573*
Railroad to use an electric engine, *6340*
Round-the-world bicycle trip by a woman, *7202*
Steel sailing vessel, *6874*
Telephone exchange for Chinese-American subscribers, *7733*
Tuberculosis research laboratory, *4929*
Vedanta Center, *6601*

1895

Academic costume standardization for colleges, *2957*
Amateur golf championship tournament for women, *7342*
Automobile club, *5465*
Bathhouses mandated by a state, *4196*
Battleship, *6926*
Cafeteria, *2459*
Canal made of concrete, *3602*
Car magazine, *4788*
Car patent, *5428*
Car race, *7260*
Carbide factory, *4438*
Cat show, *1147*
Cereal sold as a breakfast food, *3916*
Chiropodists to be regulated by a city, *4937*
Chiropractor, *4977*
College course in the contemporary novel, *3101*

College for women founded as a Catholic institution, *2958*
Enclave, *2195*
Glass-blowing machine, *4044*
Glider with cambered wings, *1547*
Golf book, *2003*
Intercollegiate basketball game, *7169*
Medicine ball, *7574*
Milk pasteurized commercially, *3875*
Movie recorded on film to be shown on a screen, *5510*
Movies with color, *5545*
National anti-saloon league, *2681*
National manufacturing assocation, *4376*
Navy submarine contract, *6962*
Open golf championship tournament, *7341*
Paper twine machine, *5761*
Pneumatic tires, *5495*
Professional football game, *7322*
Rolling lift bridge, *3587*
Round-the-world bicycle trip by a husband and wife, *7203*
Round-the-world solo sailing journey, *6984*
Shoot-the-chutes, *3624*
Slot machine, *3635*
Statue officially sanctioned by the Pope, *5407*
Volleyball, *7575*

1896

Absentee voting law enacted by a state, *3431*
Actors' union, *4615*
Airplane model to make a sustained flight under its own power, *1425*
All-fiction pulp magazine, *4731*
Biological study of camouflage in nature, *6745*
Book review newspaper supplement, *5650*
Car accident, *5466*
Car produced for commercial sale, *5429*
Car race on a racetrack, *7261*
Carousel with a jumping horse mechanism, *3625*
Certified public accountant, *3755*
Chop suey, *3879*
College cricket club team to tour England, *7274*
Company nurse, *5026*
Discus-throwing competition, *7551*
Electric alternator, *3469*
Electric socket operated by a pull chain, *4344*
Electric stove, *4298*
Finnish college, *2959*
Flashlight, *7935*
Golf player in an official amateur tournament who was African-American, *7355*
Golfer to win the United States Women's Amateur Championship, *7356*
Health ordinance prohibiting spitting, *4181*
Hospice for incurable cancer patients, *4888*
Hydroelectric power plant to use a storage battery, *3470*

Intercollegiate bicycle race, *7192*
Latvian newspaper, *5677*
Life insurance policy rated substandard, *4546*
Matchbooks, *4337*
Milk sale regulations enacted by a city, *4205*
Movie exhibition in a theater to a paying audience, *5511*
Nonfiction best seller, *1788*
Oil wells successfully drilled in the ocean, *3535*
Olympic athlete from the United States to win a gold medal, *7441*
Organists' society (national), *1285*
Physician who was a Chinese woman, *4978*
Pneumatic piano player, *1320*
Presidential candidate to ride in a car, *3410*
Psychiatric institute, *3150*
Recipes using standard measurements, *3878*
Rural free mail delivery, *6002*
Sawmill driven by electricity, *4412*
Silverite national convention, *3367*
State senator who was a woman, *7626*
Tennis champions who were brothers, *7535*
Transatlantic trip by rowboat, *6985*
Uniforms for working women, *2275*
X-ray machine exhibited in the United States, *3664*
X-ray photograph, *4904*

1897

Accounting society (state), *3756*
Comic strip in continuous newspaper publication, *5691*
Condensed soup, *3948*
Country day school, *3066*
Electric taxicabs, *5430*
Frontier Day, *4242*
Garbage incinerator, *3713*
Gelatin dessert, *3966*
Hospital for disabled children established by a state, *4889*
Ice cream sundae, *3865*
Indoor fly casting tournament, *7286*
Intercollegiate football game between African-American colleges, *7323*
Intercollegiate golf association, *7343*
Marathon race held annually, *7552*
Milk station operated by a city government, *4206*
Movie of a heavyweight championship boxing fight, *5546*
Multiple common battery telephone switchboard, *7734*
Municipal subway, *6410*
Parent-teacher association (national), *3227*
Performance of *The Stars and Stripes Forever*, *1292*
Ragtime instruction book, *1941*
Rock wool insulation factory, *2047*

Submarine fitted with an internal combustion engine, *6963*
Tuberculosis hospital for the poor established by a city, *4900*
Vending machine to operate automatically, *2395*
Vending machine to sell food from bulk, *2396*
X-ray of the entire body of a living person made in a single exposure, *4905*
Zionist organization (national), *6487*

1898

Ambulance ship operated by the Navy, *5015*
Arabic daily newspaper, *5678*
Armored car, *5432*
Army officer killed in battle in the Spanish-American War, *8010*
Balloon destroyed by enemy gunfire, *8012*
Cancer laboratory, *4930*
Capture of a ship in the Spanish-American War, *8007*
Car advertisement in a specialty magazine, *2331*
Car driver who was a woman, *5467*
Car exported from the United States, *5431*
Car insurance policy, *4519*
Celluloid photographic film, *5838*
College graduate in geology who was a woman, *3241*
County library, *4673*
Dentist officially employed in the Army, *5014*
Diesel engine built for commercial service, *5479*
Envelope folding and gumming machine, *5765*
Foreign service school in a college, *3126*
Forestry school at a college, *3076*
Interurban streetcar line, *6403*
Island territory annexed by the federal government, *5974*
Land battle in the Spanish-American War, *8011*
Log-rolling national championship tournament, *7576*
Military campaign medal, *1657*
Military expeditionary force to be sent beyond the Western Hemisphere, *8009*
Monthly cumulative index of books, *1774*
Musical comedy written by African-Americans for African-American performers, *1256*
Navy officer killed in action in the Spanish-American War, *8008*
Optometry society (national), *5044*
Physiology journal, *4777*
Postcard, *6046*
Radio telephone message from a submerged submarine to shore, *7755*
Roller coaster with a loop-the-loop, *3626*
Social Democracy of America Party national convention, *3368*
Steel dam, *3606*

1898—*continued*

Submarine that was practical and submersible, *6964*

Truck, *5504*

Truth-in-advertising law enacted by a state, *2330*

Tuberculosis sanatorium established by a state, *4901*

Vending machine law enacted by a city, *2397*

1899

Admiral of the Navy, *5271*

Aluminum used commercially in a transmission conductor, *3471*

Baseball "Home Run King", *7146*

Bicycle race paced by a motorcycle, *7194*

Bicycle racer to attain the speed of a mile a minute, *7193*

Car accident fatality, *5470*

Car factory, *5433*

Children's museum, *5581*

Clincher tire, *5496*

Driver arrested for speeding, *5468*

Driver license board, *5469*

Execution of a woman by electrocution, *2799*

Goldfish hatchery, *1061*

Golf champion born in America, *7357*

Golf tee, *7352*

Intercollegiate transatlantic chess match by cable, *4030*

Juvenile court, *2707*

Librarian who was African-American, *4674*

Mail truck, *6003*

Medal of Honor awarded to an African-American soldier in the Spanish-American War, *1676*

Organ school, *2907*

Parade of automobiles, *3665*

Physics association (national), *6789*

Police patrol wagon, *4137*

Portable church, *6532*

Primary election law enacted by a state, *3318*

Public garage, *5483*

Rhodes Scholars, *2961*

Rubber shoe heel, *2305*

School to use platoon organization, *3067*

Sheet-glass drawing machine, *4045*

Sheet music to sell millions of copies, *1293*

Tuberculosis hospital established by Congress, *4902*

Tuberculosis hospital for needy patients, *4903*

University press, *2960*

Vacuum cleaner driven by a motor, *4275*

Voting machines in congressional elections, *3328*

Yacht race broadcast on radio, *7215*

1900

Astronomer employed in the Naval Observatory who was a woman, *6667*

Automatic computing pendulum scale, *2380*

Automatic plate-casting and finishing machine for stereotype printing, *5796*

Bonds payable specifically in United States gold coins, *3823*

Books of postage stamps, *6061*

Bowling with duckpins, *7222*

Business organization for African-Americans (national), *2450*

Car advertisement in a national magazine, *2332*

Car show, *5434*

Championship heavyweight boxing title won in the first round, *7237*

Chiropractic school, *3172*

Grand American Trapshoot tournament with clay targets, *7476*

Hamburger, *3940*

Impregnated corkboard, *2048*

Industrial research laboratory, *4377*

International tennis matches for the Davis Cup challenge trophy, *7531*

Kindergarten for children with disabilities, *3018*

Laborsaving machine approved by a labor union, *4616*

Medal of Honor awarded to an African-American soldier in the Civil War, *1677*

Motorcycle that was practical, *5488*

National political convention at which a woman made a seconding speech, *3339*

Needle dam, *3607*

Olympic athlete from the United States to win 10 medals, *7442*

Orthodontists' society, *5045*

Penny restaurant, *2460*

Public school for children with disabilities, *3019*

Revolver shooting tournament, *7477*

Road map for motorists, *4801*

Sightseeing bus, *5418*

Social-Democratic Party of America national convention, *3369*

Union Reform Party convention, *3371*

United Christian Party convention, *3370*

Wedding by telegraph, *4816*

1901

Academic hall of fame, *5582*

Army dental corps, *5016*

Army nurse corps for women, *5017*

Army war college, *3200*

Baseball player in the American League who was African-American, *7147*

Bowling tournament sponsored by the American Bowling Congress, *7223*

Building with an all-marble dome, *2084*

Car hill-climbing contest, *7262*

Car to exceed the speed of a mile a minute, *5436*

Catholic mass for night workers, *6469*

City government using the commission plan, *2202*

Corporation with a capitalization of $1 billion, *2405*

Daredevil to go over Niagara Falls in a barrel, *3679*

Dean of students at a college, *2973*

Electric motor using single-phase alternating current, *5480*

Escalator of the modern type, *2110*

License plates for vehicles, *4220*

Long-distance car race, *7263*

Mercury vapor lamp, *3496*

Motorcycle with a built-in gasoline engine, *5489*

Paired six-day bicycle race, *7195*

Professional open golf championship match, *7344*

Professor at a first-class medical school who was a woman, *3151*

Shaft-driven car, *5435*

Speeding driver law enacted by a state, *4221*

Steam turbine operated by a public utility to produce electricity, *3472*

Union catalog of books in American libraries, *1775*

1902

Building with a large-scale clear-span dome, *2085*

Cancer research fund, *5056*

Chess match between players on different ships at sea, *4031*

Cut glass, *4046*

Envelope with a window, *5766*

Factory with temperature and humidity control, *4384*

Laboratory for the study of human parasites, *4931*

Mobile radio telephone marine demonstration, *7716*

Motorcycle endurance run, *7437*

Oil journal, *4778*

Penitentiary building opened by the federal government, *2826*

Postage stamp depicting an American woman, *6087*

President to ride in a car, *6223*

Radio broadcast demonstration, *6262*

Restaurant with an automatic arrangement for vending food, *2461*

School nurses in public schools, *5027*

Steel railroad passenger coach, *6382*

Steel seven-masted schooner, *6875*

Taxidermy method of stuffing animals, *6746*

Technical college for women, *2962*

Teddy bear, *2145*

Theater to show movies, *3704*

Trade school for girls, *3291*

Transpacific telegraph cable, *7703*

Wooden plug lure for fishing, *7287*

Workers' compensation insurance law enacted by a state, *4522*

Young Women's Hebrew Association, *5715*

1903

Airplane flight, *1426*

Automobile school, *3292*

Bank president who was a woman, *3772*

Bird reservation established by the federal government, *3745*

Boycott law enacted by a state, *2310*

Filmpack camera, *5839*

Football stadium, *7505*

Motorcycle association, *7439*

Motorcycle hill-climbing contest, *7438*

Movie star, *5525*

Movie with a plot, *5547*

Multigraph, *2367*

Naval radio station, *5301*

Numerical system of insurance rating, *4514*

Nurses to be registered by a state, *4938*

Opera composed by a woman to be performed at the Metropolitan Opera House, *1348*

Political science association (national), *6790*

Printed traffic regulations, *4138*

Professional hockey team, *7375*

Pronghorn antelope, *1148*

Public locker plant, *2366*

Radio distress signal from an American ship, *6285*

Railroad operated by an electric third-rail system, *6341*

Semitic museum, *5583*

State prison to take fingerprints, *4159*

Suspension bridge with steel towers, *3588*

Transatlantic radio broadcast, *6263*

Transcontinental car trip, *5471*

Transcontinental motorcycle trip, *5492*

World Series baseball game, *7123*

1904

Arts and letters organization (national), *5716*

Bibliography organization (national), *4691*

Border patrol officer, *5868*

Buddhist temple, *6438*

Bulk mail, *6004*

Business library supported by taxes, *4675*

Car race for the Vanderbilt Cup, *7264*

Car with a circulating lubrication system, *5437*

Carnegie Hero Fund Commission award granted to a woman, *1639*

College varsity sports program, *2998*

Comic books, *2028*

Disease research and treatment organization, *5046*

Duplex compound locomotive, *6362*

Electric motor using interpole direct current, *5481*

Fingerprinting in federal penitentiaries, *4161*

1904—*continued*

Hotel with individually controlled air conditioning and heating in every room, *2428*
Hungarian daily newspaper, *5679*
Ice cream cone, *3866*
Installment finance company, *3805*
Intercity trucking service, *2484*
Monument to commemorate the Spanish-American War, *5408*
Motorboat magazine, *4789*
Motorboat race under organized rules, *7216*
Motorcycle police, *4139*
Olympic Games held in the United States, *7443*
Olympic medalist who was African-American, *7444*
Pharmacists to be regulated by a state, *4939*
Phonograph record of a stage performance by the original cast, *7008*
Police department to adopt the fingerprinting system, *4160*
Radio distress signal officially established, *6286*
Radium treatment for cancer, *5115*
Rapid-transit subway, *6411*
Rotogravure press, *5781*
Socialist Party national convention, *3372*
Tire chains, *5497*
Use of "American" as an adjective, *1098*
Vocational high school for girls, *3086*

1905

Aerial ferry, *3589*
All-electric railroad, *6342*
Balloon to land on a building, *1540*
Bookwagon traveling library, *4676*
Concrete cantilever bridge, *3590*
Esperanto club, *5717*
Factory cooled by air conditioning, *4385*
Fire extinguisher using vaporized chemicals, *4110*
Forest fire lookout tower, *3729*
Helium in natural gas, *6813*
Intercollegiate wrestling association, *7577*
International exchange of fingerprints, *4162*
Interstate Commerce Commission Medal of Honor, *1654*
Laxative in candy form, *4991*
Movie theater, *3705*
Municipal ferryboats, *6910*
Pizzeria, *2462*
Plywood, *2049*
Punchboards, *2368*
Radio fax patents, *7667*
Rotary Club meeting, *2451*
Sociology society (national), *6791*
Statue of a woman installed in the Capitol's National Statuary Hall, *5409*
Steel railroad mail car, *6383*
Tung trees, *1021*
Twin-cycle motorcycle, *5490*

West Point graduates who were Chinese nationals, *3201*
World Series baseball game that was a shutout, *7124*

1906

Advertising show to be held annually, *2412*
Air conditioner patent, *4413*
Animated cartoon, *5531*
Balloon cup race, *7288*
Bank open day and night, *3792*
Bubble gum, *3967*
Cabinet member who was Jewish, *6108*
Consumer protection law enacted by Congress, *2311*
Diamonds in actual rock, *5340*
Double-deck bus, *5419*
Esperanto magazine, *4749*
Music synthesizer powered by electricity, *1321*
National college fraternity for African-American men, *2989*
National Geographic Society gold medal, *1640*
National monument designated by the federal government, *5410*
Nobel Prize awarded to an American, *1690*
Nurse appointed to a college professorship, *5028*
Phonograph with an enclosed horn in the cabinet, *7009*
President to visit a foreign country while in office, *6231*
Radio program broadcast, *6264*
Radio receiver advertised, *6306*
Stadium operated by a city, *7506*
Turbine-propelled oceangoing merchant vessel, *6886*

1907

Battleship built on the Pacific coast, *6927*
Building of pressed structural steel, *2086*
Canned tuna, *3889*
Car with the steering wheel on the left side, *5438*
Carbon microphone used in radio broadcasting, *6308*
Circumnavigation of the globe by a fleet of warships, *6986*
College under Jewish auspices that was nonsectarian, *2963*
Corrupt election practices law enacted by Congress, *3319*
Dental inlay made of gold, *4866*
Electric washing machine, *4276*
Flemish newspaper, *5680*
Fund-raising organization to sell Christmas seals, *5741*
Horse farm operated by the federal government, *1182*
Hydrotherapy chair at a college, *3152*

Hygiene department in a public school district, 4182

Movie star who was a woman, 5526

Museum wing in the United States named for a woman, 5595

Night court, 2708

Nobel Prize for physics awarded to an American, 1691

Postage stamp depicting a Native American, 6088

Pullman sleeping car made entirely of steel, 6384

Rat extermination throughout an entire city, 4183

Safety congress, 4184

Savings bank life insurance, 4547

Senator who was Native American, 2650

Singer whose voice was broadcast over radio, 1330

Squash rackets champion, 7499

Steam-operated pressing machine, 4414

Sterilization of humans by a state government as a matter of public policy, 6829

Transatlantic radio message of the regular westward service, 6265

Triode for radios, 6307

Vitrolite, 4047

1908

Airplane accident that was fatal, 1387

Airplane endurance flight exceeding one hour, 1427

Airship disaster, 1513

Airship ordered by the federal government, 1514

Army field range, 5245

Arts and letters organization member who was a woman, 5716

Aviation correspondence school, 7289

Aviation magazine devoted primarily to airplanes, 4780

Aviation trophy, 1641

Baseball league for children, 7097

Bibles in hotel rooms, 6579

Brake for four-wheeled cars, 5439

Car race from New York to Paris, 7265

Carbon tetrachloride, 4439

Child hygiene bureau, 4186

Child welfare congress, 2146

City manager, 2203

Confectionary machine, 3968

Credit union, 3773

Double-header baseball games that were shut-outs, 7125

Drinking water supply to be chemically treated with chlorine compounds, 2235

Ductile tungsten, 5341

Esperanto course at a college, 3117

Fireworks law enacted by a city, 4111

Football uniform numerals, 7312

Health department of a county organized on a full-time basis, 4185

Heavyweight boxing champion of the world who was African-American, 7252

Intelligence test in a school for children with mental retardation, 3021

Journalism school at a college, 3102

Mother's Day, 4243

Navy admiral who was Jewish, 5272

Navy mail service, 6005

Navy nurses' corps, 5018

Newspaper with an aviation section, 5651

Nursing school at a college, 3173

Olympic athlete from the United States to win the marathon race, 7553

Outdoor school for children with tuberculosis, 3020

Paper cup, 4310

Post office aboard a naval vessel, 6038

Postage stamps in coils, 6062

Presidential candidate to appear in movie footage, 3411

Price regulation law enacted by a state, 2522

Radio magazine, 4779

Radio society, 6259

Shampoo commercially produced, 4069

Sheep of the Karakul breed, 1086

Sorority for African-American students at a college, 2988

Sousaphone, 1322

State law prohibiting discrimination against soldiers, 5127

Steel ski jump, 7481

Tax on aviation levied by a city, 7652

Turbine-propelled naval ship, 6928

Workers' compensation insurance law enacted by Congress, 4523

1909

Airplane purchased by the federal government, 1389

Airplane race won by an American in Europe, 7290

Airplane sold commercially, 1388

Airship race, 7291

Apartment house to occupy a square city block, 2127

Apprentice continuation school, 3293

Army pilot to fly solo in an airplane, 1607

Balloon honeymoon, 4808

Baseball with a cork center, 7109

Battleship to visit an inland city, 6987

Bed that could be hidden, 4330

Bird banding association (national), 6792

Bird hunting regulation law enacted by Congress, 7426

Child delinquency law enacted by a state, 2147

Christmas savings club at a bank, 3793

Coin bearing the likeness of a president, 5375

Concrete rural road, 6624

1909—*continued*

Corporation tax levied by Congress, *7653*
Credit union law enacted by a state, *3774*
Discount clothing store, *2498*
Discovery of the North Pole, *6727*
Domestic relations court, *2709*
Double-deck bridge, *3591*
Election using the preferential ballot system, *3320*
Fireproof baseball stadium, *7507*
Forestry school operated privately, *3077*
Hydroelectric power plant built by the federal government, *3473*
Intercity airplane flight by a U.S. military officer, *1428*
International horseshoe pitching contest, *7578*
Japanese cherry trees, *1062*
Junior high school, *3087*
Memorial postage stamp, *6089*
Monoplane, *1390*
Movie censorship board at the national level, *5540*
Narcotics ban enacted by Congress, *2686*
Neurological disease research institute, *5057*
Old age home for pioneers, *5975*
Outboard motor, *6951*
Paint-spraying device, *7936*
Radio SOS call from an American ship, *6287*
Subway car with side doors, *6412*
Thermosetting resin, *4440*
Transcontinental car race, *7266*
Transcontinental car trip by women, *5472*
Transcontinental journey on foot, *7589*
Unassisted triple play in a major league baseball game, *7126*
Union catalog of books in a state library, *1776*
Urban planning instruction at a college, *3253*
Year in which more than 100,000 passenger cars were produced, *5440*

1910

Abstract paintings, *1217*
Air rights lease, *2064*
Airplane bombing experiment, *8113*
Airplane flight from a ship, *1433*
Airplane flight over water, *1432*
Airplane flying school, *3188*
Airplane round trip, *1430*
Airplane solo flight by an American woman, *1596*
Airplane to fly higher than a mile in altitude, *1431*
Animal disease of American origin, *5122*
Aviation meet, *7292*
Bread factory that was completely automatic, *3925*
Car equipped with a two-way radio, *7717*
Chiropody school of note, *3174*
Climatology professor at a college, *3242*

Commerce court established by the federal government, *2713*
Cord tires, *5498*
Electric-gasoline combination car, *5441*
Father's Day, *4244*
Federal law requiring radios on ships, *4222*
Golf club with a steel shaft, *7353*
Mayor of a major city who was a Socialist, *2208*
Medical research chair at a college, *3154*
Millionaire who was an African-American woman, *2444*
Newsreel, *5697*
Night flight in an airplane, *1429*
Opera by an American composer to be performed at the Metropolitan Opera House, *1349*
Optometry courses at a college, *3153*
Photographic copying machine, *2370*
Pilot from the United States to establish an airplane altitude record, *1594*
Pilot to fire a gun from an airplane, *1608*
Postal savings bank, *3775*
President to pitch a ball to open the baseball season, *6163*
Radio broadcast sent from an airplane, *6266*
Radio contest, *6260*
Radio distress signal resulting in an airship rescue, *6288*
Railroad tank car lined with glass, *6385*
Rayon, *7874*
Russian newspaper, *5681*
School stadium, *7509*
Shipment of merchandise by airplane, *2485*
Speedway with a board track, *7508*
Supreme Court justice to be appointed chief justice, *2761*
Surfer, *7579*
Ticker-tape shower for a celebrity, *3666*
Toy pinball game machine, *7453*
Trackless trolley system, *6404*
Transatlantic airship flight, *1515*
Transcontinental solo trip on horseback by a woman, *1183*
Vichyssoise, *3880*

1911

Advertising association to combat business abuses, *2452*
Airmail pilot, *6015*
Airplane accident in a solo military airplane that was fatal, *1392*
Airplane flight to the deck of a carrier, *1434*
Airplane flight under a bridge, *1437*
Airplane race between cities, *7293*
Airplane rescue at sea, *1435*
Airplane rescue at sea by another airplane, *1438*
Airplane sea flight out of sight of land, *1435*

Airplane to land on the White House lawn, 6255

Aviation law enacted by a state, 1384

Baseball players to win the Most Valuable Player award, 1722

Billionaire, 2445

Blue-sky laws enacted by a state, 2523

Boy Scouts of America uniformed troop, 2149

Coin-operated locker, 2369

College foreign-language house, 2999

Composer of jazz music, 1331

Congressional representative to attend college after his term of service, 2608

Congressional representative who was a Socialist, 2607

Continuation school for adults established by a state government, 2889

Diesel engine in a submarine, 6965

Electric self-starter used in cars, 5442

Farm bureau, 1004

Federal cemetery to contain graves of both Union and Confederate soldiers, 2853

Fingerprint conviction in a crime, 4163

Gyrocompass installed on an American naval vessel, 6955

Hail insurance law enacted by a state, 4515

Hydrogenated vegetable shortening, 3885

Hydroplane, 1391

Hydroplane flight to and from a ship, 1436

Klieg light unit for movie production, 5572

Life insurance group policy, 4548

Linoleum manufacturing machine, 4317

Long-distance car race on a racetrack, 7267

Motorboat to travel at a speed of more than 40 miles per hour, 6952

Movie censorship board established by a state, 5541

Naval airplane, 1483

Photograph taken from an airplane, 5820

Pilot licensed by the Aero Club of America, 1595

Pilot licensed by the Aero Club of America who was a woman, 1596

Printing lecture course in a college, 3294

Radio car for military use, 5246

Radio license, 6293

Squash tennis organization (national), 7500

Squash tennis tournament, 7501

Telegraph message sent around the world by commercial telegraph, 7704

Traffic lanes designated by painted lines, 4223

Transcontinental airplane flight made in stages, 1439

Transcontinental eastbound airplane flight made in stages, 1440

Transcontinental group tour by car, 5473

Transpacific radio conversation, 6267

1912

Airplane accident involving a woman that was fatal, 1393

Airplane outfitted with a machine gun, 1484

Airplane round-trip flight over water, 1441

Airplane takeoff from a hotel roof, 1442

Airplane torpedo, 8114

Baseball strike, 4595

Brassiere patent, 2276

Church without theology, creed, or dogma, 6602

City government using the manager plan, 2204

Community chorus, 1361

Detective who was a woman, 4140

Director of the Federal Bureau of Investigation, 4141

Eagle Scout, 2149

Electric heating pad, 4944

Elopement by airplane, 4809

Foreign feature film exhibited, 5512

Horse race mutuel ticket to pay more than $1,000, 7397

Life insurance group contract, 4549

Marine pilot, 5235

Minimum wage law enacted by a state, 4577

Movie censorship law enacted by Congress, 5542

Movie photographed from an airplane, 5548

Movie version of a Shakespeare play to be made in the United States, 5549

Municipal streetcars, 6405

Navy dental corps, 5019

Oceanography institution, 6713

Oil and gas production course at a college, 3243

Olympic athlete from the United States to win the pentathlon and decathlon, 7554

Parachute jump from an airplane, 1581

Parcel post service, 6006

Progressive Party national convention, 3373

Quarantine law for plants enacted by Congress, 4212

Safety association (national), 4187

Scouting organization for girls, 2148

Stuntman, 3680

Surgery society (national), 5047

1913

Aeronautical engineering course at a college, 3244

Airplane loop-the-loop, 1443

Animated cartoon made with cel animation, 5532

Bird for which a definite crossing of the Atlantic was recorded, 1165

Bonding law enacted by a state, 4524

Bowler to make a perfect score of 300, 7224

Chiropractic regulation law enacted by a state, 4940

Civic design chair at a college, 3254

1913—*continued*

Coast-to-coast paved road, *6625*

College comprehensive senior examination program, *3000*

County public defender, *4639*

Crepe, *7875*

Crossword puzzle, *4010*

Demountable tire-carrying rim, *5499*

Dentist in the Navy to serve aboard a naval ship, *5020*

Detonating fuse of the Cordeau-Bickford type, *4424*

Drive-in gas station, *2499*

Electrically propelled naval ship, *6930*

Eye conservation class, *3028*

Gasoline obtained from crude petroleum by the cracking process, *3536*

Goat show, *1073*

Gyroscope, *1494*

Ice-loading machinery, *4415*

Immunology society, *5048*

Insulating brick, *2059*

Modern art exhibition, *1228*

Monument to a bird, *5411*

Movie of feature length made in Hollywood, *5551*

Naval vessel equipped with a gyrostabilizer, *6929*

Occupational therapy course at a college, *3155*

Oil and gas conservation law enacted by a state, *3537*

Parachute jump from an airplane by a woman, *1582*

Pension plan, *4586*

Permalloy, *7705*

Photographs taken under the sea, *5821*

Portable movie projector, *5573*

Professional soccer organization recognized internationally, *7493*

Sedan car, *5443*

Senate whip, *2629*

Senator elected by popular vote, *3329*

Serial movie with installments longer than one reel, *5550*

Sex education program for high schools, *3088*

Skyscraper higher than 750 feet in height, *2099*

Small claims court, *2710*

Strike settlement mediated by the federal Department of Labor, *4596*

Synthetic rubber, *4488*

Tract housing development, *2196*

Veterans of Foreign Wars of the United States meeting, *5311*

Zipper, *2292*

1914

Air-conditioned railroad cars, *6386*

Air service of the Army, *5130*

Airplane flying school operated by a woman, *7294*

Airplane with ailerons, *1394*

Alcohol prohibition vote taken in Congress, *2682*

Alkaline dry cell battery, *3475*

American to sail to Europe to fight in World War I, *8025*

Auction duplicate bridge championship, *4023*

Bank to establish a branch in a foreign country, *3776*

Bird banding by federal authorities, *6747*

Bus with cross seats, *5420*

Community trust charity, *5742*

Drug control law enacted by Congress, *2687*

Electric hand drill, *7937*

Electric power substation with a rotary converter completely unattended, *3474*

Electric traffic signal lights, *4224*

Extinction by humans of a native American animal, *3746*

Federal reserve banks, *3777*

Hydroplane service, *1408*

Industrial museum, *5584*

International championship figure skating tournament, *7431*

Japanese newspaper in continuous publication, *5682*

Long-distance telephone call over underground cables, *7756*

Mail collection and delivery in cars, *6007*

Movie comedy of feature length, *5552*

Music society for the protection of composers and song writers, *1286*

Naval air training school, *3217*

Newspaper circulation audit, *5652*

Newspaper rotogravure sections, *5692*

Nobel Prize for chemistry awarded to an American, *1692*

Nonskid tires, *5500*

Passport photographs, *5886*

Police chief who was a woman, *4142*

Prison organized into community groups, *2827*

Railroad operated by the federal government, *6343*

Skee-ball alley, *3627*

Vocational guidance chair at a college, *3295*

1915

American combatant to die in World War I, *8027*

Asphalt-covered racetrack, *7510*

Car finance company, *3806*

Cargo ship from the United States attacked by a German submarine in World War I, *8028*

Chiropody school at a college, *3175*

City orchestra supported by taxes, *1362*

Dental hygienists to be licensed by a state, *4941*

Election using proportional representation, *3321*

Fifty-dollar gold pieces minted by the federal government, *5376*

1917—*continued*

Radio telephone communication from an airplane, *7759*

Shot fired by American infantry in World War I, *8037*

Shot fired by the Navy in World War I, *8031*

Soil conference, *1005*

Soldiers in the American army killed in combat in World War I, *8038*

State legislature to use an electric vote recorder, *7627*

Tax levied by Congress on excess profits of corporations, *7654*

Transatlantic crossing by a submarine under its own power, *6988*

Troops from the United States to sail to Europe in World War I, *8033*

Volunteer unit made up of college women to serve overseas, *5185*

Wedding abroad of a soldier in the American Expeditionary Force, *4817*

White bread, *3926*

Wrecking crane operated from a car, *4416*

1918

Ace of Aces from the United States, *1611*

Ace to fly under American colors, *1612*

Air squadron of the Army in World War I, *8041*

Airmail regular service, *6016*

Airmail stamps, *6063*

Airplane bombing raid by an American air unit, *8044*

Airplane with a fuselage of molded plywood, *1395*

Alcohol prohibition law enacted by Congress, *2684*

American division to cross the Rhine River in World War I, *8047*

Armored car in commercial use, *5444*

Army nursing school, *3176*

Army pilot to win a victory over an enemy airplane, *1610*

Army school for chaplains, *3202*

Aviation unit of the military trained for overseas duty, *5132*

Bill depicting a battleship, *5392*

Church organized by Native Americans, *6603*

Combat mission of American pilots ordered to battle in World War I, *8042*

Concrete barge, *6887*

Concrete seagoing ship, *6876*

Croix de Guerre awarded to an African-American, *1648*

Daylight saving time program, *7896*

Dish set made in America for the White House, *6256*

District attorney who was a woman, *2714*

Fiction writer to win the Pulitzer Prize twice, *1709*

Fighter plane, *1486*

Hygiene and public health school at a college, *3177*

Laundry detergent, *4277*

Marine reserve member who was a woman, *5233*

Night-flying scout group, *8046*

Photograph showing air in motion across airplane wings, *5822*

Pilots in American units to participate in air combat in World War I, *8043*

President to receive a passport while in office, *6232*

President to visit Europe, *6233*

Pulitzer Prize awarded to a newspaper, *1707*

Pulitzer Prize for drama, *1708*

Service number issued by the Army, *5226*

Shots fired by German forces to land on American soil in World War I, *8045*

Shoulder sleeve insignia issued by the Army, *5227*

State to ratify the Prohibition Amendment to the Constitution, *2683*

Tank operated by Army troops, *8116*

Troop ship from the United States torpedoed by a German submarine in World War I, *8040*

Warship propelled by electricity, *6932*

Wound chevron issued by the Army, *5225*

Zoo habitat constructed of simulated rock formations without bars, *1188*

1919

Aircraft liability and property damage insurance, *4516*

Airport owned by a city, *1503*

Airship to land on a roof, *1517*

American Legion convention of veterans of World War I, *5312*

American woman to become a member of the British Parliament, *6648*

Bank wholly owned and operated by a state, *3779*

Bank with resources exceeding $1 billion, *3780*

Book series of small-size paperbacks, *1753*

Caterpillar Club member, *1584*

Communist Labor Party of America convention, *3374*

Communist Party of America convention, *3375*

Editor in chief of a law review who was a woman, *3127*

Fire and tornado insurance fund enacted by a state, *4533*

Fisheries school at a college, *3296*

Forest Service aerial patrol, *3730*

Gasoline tax levied by a state, *7655*

General of the Armies of the United States, *5152*

Golfer to play 180 holes in one day, *7359*

Horse to win the Triple Crown, *7409*

Illustrated tabloid, *5653*

1921—*continued*

Radio broadcast of a baseball game with a play-by-play description, *7128*
Radio church, *6590*
Radio navigation beacons, *6957*
Radio program theme song, *6289*
Radio receiving contest, *6261*
Religious service broadcast on radio, *6589*
Sales tax enacted by a state, *7656*
Stainless steel flatware, *4375*
Telephone cable deep-sea service, *7736*
Tennis match broadcast on radio, *7532*
Transcontinental airmail flight, *6018*
Transcontinental airplane flight made within 24 hours, *1447*
Weather forecast broadcast on radio, *6769*

1922

Airplane to fly faster than 200 miles per hour, *1448*
Arbitration organization (national), *4645*
Automatic steering gear for ships, *6958*
Catholic nuns in a cloistered community, *6470*
Chain radio broadcast, *6270*
Circumnavigation of the world by a cruise ship, *6989*
Congressional representative who was a mother, *2610*
Cornstone, *2051*
Daily news program on radio, *5705*
Drama broadcast on radio, *1257*
Election campaign using radio, *3322*
Electric blender, *4300*
Electric power line commercial carrier, *3476*
Eskimo pie, *3867*
Golf champion to win both the U.S. Open and the Professional tournaments, *7360*
Helicopter flight, *1572*
Hotel administration course at a college, *3297*
Intercollegiate indoor polo championship, *7460*
International golf match, *7346*
Librarian who was an African-American woman, *4674*
Massacre of strikebreakers by union members, *4597*
Microfilm reading device, *4681*
Modern carillon, *1323*
Movie in Technicolor, *5555*
Navy Day, *4247*
Peritonitis preventive, *4992*
Petroleum refining course at a college, *3246*
Pilot to bail out of a disabled airplane, *1585*
Pilot who was an African-American woman, *1597*
Platypus, *1149*
President to make a radio broadcast, *6210*
President to use a radio, *6209*
Radar observations, *7675*
Radio broadcast of a concert from an airplane, *1295*

Radio broadcast of a debate, *6269*
Radio commercial, *2333*
Radio orchestra, *1364*
Senator who was a woman, *2651*
Sermon preached from an airplane by radio, *6591*
Shopping mall, *2502*
Skywriting advertisement exhibition, *2334*
Soybean processing plant, *1024*
State supreme court justice who was a woman, *2723*
Steel mill to produce continuous sheets, *4497*
Swimmer to cover 100 meters freestyle in less than one minute, *7516*
Taconite production, *5342*
Transatlantic radio fax transmission of a photograph, *7668*
Transcontinental airship flight, *1520*
Water skis, *7591*

1923

Airplane refueling attempt in midair, *1496*
Airport runway illumination, *1504*
Automatic traffic light, *4225*
Balloon tire production, *5501*
Book completed entirely by one man, *1754*
Business history chair at a college, *2922*
Cancer hospital established by a city, *4890*
Catholic seminary for the education of African-American priests, *3278*
Chinchilla farm, *1074*
Combined newspaper, *5655*
Constitutional amendment proposal mandating equal legal rights for women and men, *6830*
Dance marathon, *3630*
Ethyl gasoline to be marketed, *3538*
Fireboat with two-way radio equipment, *4112*
Gasoline-mechanical railroad cars, *6387*
Internal revenue collector for the federal government who was a woman, *7657*
Mercury boiler turbine, *3477*
Milky Way candy bar, *3969*
Mimeographed daily newspaper, *5654*
Movie with sound recorded on the film, *5556*
Neon advertising sign, *2350*
Parachute-jumping contest, *7296*
Pension laws enacted by a state, *4587*
Portable movie camera, *5574*
Precanceled stamps printed on rotary presses, *6064*
President and First Lady to die during the term for which he had been elected, *6196*
President to visit Alaska and Canada while in office, *6234*
Presidential message to Congress that was broadcast on radio, *6211*
Radio broadcast of an open session of Congress, *2567*
Railroad signal system of continuous cab signals, *6426*

Rigid airship, *1521*

Shopping center in a suburban business area, *2501*

Smokescreen for concealing the movement of troops and ships, *5247*

State law to establish English as an official language, *5870*

Swimmer from the United States to swim the English Channel, *7517*

Transatlantic radio program received from Great Britain, *6271*

Transcontinental nonstop airplane flight, *1449*

World Series baseball games to gross $1 million, *7129*

1924

Bowler to roll two perfect games, *7226*

Cellophane, *4338*

Chromium plating process, *4476*

Citizenship and public affairs school at a college, *3255*

Citizenship statute for Native Americans, *5871*

Coast-to-coast radio hookup, *6272*

Contact lenses, *5073*

Corn-husking championship, *1025*

Crossword puzzle book, *2004*

Decathlon champion from the United States, *7556*

Diesel-electric locomotive, *6363*

Execution by lethal gas, *2800*

Foreign language course broadcast on radio, *3118*

Frozen food for the mass market, *3949*

Governor who was a woman, *7618*

History of science society (national), *6795*

Ice cream cone rolling machine, *3868*

Ink paste, *5787*

Intercollegiate football game to attract 100,000 spectators, *7325*

Macy's Thanksgiving Day Parade, *4262*

Marriage course at a college, *3103*

Micropaleontology course at a college, *3247*

National Hockey League team from the United States, *7377*

Newsreels showing presidential candidates, *5698*

Political convention to be broadcast on radio, *3340*

Portable electric stethoscope, *4946*

President buried in Washington, *6197*

President to be born in a hospital, *6198*

President to make a radio broadcast from the White House, *6212*

Radio broadcast from a circus, *3674*

Radio broadcast of a livestock auction, *1075*

Radio network broadcast received on the Pacific Coast, *6274*

Radio network program sponsored by commercial advertising, *2335*

Radio two-way broadcast from an airplane, *6273*

Round-the-world steamboat passenger service, *6888*

Transcontinental flight by a dirigible, *1521*

Transcontinental regular airmail service, *6019*

1925

Airmail long-distance night service, *6020*

Airport owned by a county, *1505*

Airship with an enclosed cabin, *1522*

Arbitration law enacted by Congress, *2356*

Atheist organization, *5745*

Big-league football team to travel coast-to-coast, *7306*

Car insurance law enacted by a state, *4520*

Caterpillar Club member who was a woman, *1586*

Citrons, *3905*

City in miniature, *2197*

Composograph photograph in a newspaper, *5693*

Congressional representative to serve 18 terms who was a woman, *2611*

Cosmic ray to be discovered, *6679*

Demonstration of rapid aerial photography, *5823*

Dry ice manufactured commercially, *4441*

Embossed inlaid linoleum, *4318*

Episcopal bishop deposed for heresy in the United States, *6552*

Explosion of Thermit to break up ice jams, *4425*

Hospital for patients of Chinese ancestry, *4891*

Long-distance radio fax transmission of medical information, *7671*

Machine to make glass light bulbs, *3497*

Miniature television tube, *7809*

Mobile telephone conversation between the ground and an airship, *7761*

Motel, *2429*

Movie of a solar eclipse taken from an airship, *6686*

Musk ox, *1150*

National Academy of Sciences member who was a woman, *6781*

Nationwide highway numbering system, *6627*

Outdoor museum with nature trails, *5585*

Photoelectric cell, *3478*

Photograph taken from an airplane at night, *5824*

Play of full length by an African-American writer to be performed in New York City, *1258*

Presidential inauguration to be broadcast on radio, *6213*

Road with a depressed trough, *6628*

State supreme court in which all the judges were women, *2724*

Telecast of an object in motion, *7825*

1925—continued

Tornado disaster on a large scale, *2869*

Transcontinental radio fax transmission of a photograph, *7669*

Transpacific radio fax transmission, *7670*

Trial of a teacher for violating a state ban on teaching the theory of evolution, *3068*

Waterless natural gas storage tank, *3520*

Women's World Fair, *2413*

1926

Air force branch of the military, *5133*

Airmail contractor, *6021*

Airplane bombing raid by criminals, *2778*

Airplane flight over the North Pole, *6728*

Aluminum streetcar, *6407*

Aviation medicine book, *1921*

Book course at a college, *3104*

Book-of-the-Month Club selection, *1789*

Boxing match to attract 100,000 spectators, *7242*

Canned ham, *3941*

Catholic church to become a basilica, *6471*

Composer of gospel music, *1332*

Cotton fabric used on a road, *6629*

Dance major at a college, *2909*

Electric toaster, *4301*

Ferryboat built exclusively to transport cars, *6911*

Film-developing machine, *5840*

Gas refrigerator, *4348*

Gospel song, *1332*

Greyhound racing association, *7279*

Hambletonian harness horse race for three-year-olds, *7398*

Lawyer admitted to practice before the Supreme Court who was an African-American woman, *4635*

Lipreading tournament held nationally, *3036*

Movie showing another planet, *6687*

Movie with sound to be released as a feature, *5557*

National Christmas tree, *4258*

Photographs taken under the sea in natural colors, *5825*

Plastic surgery professor at a college, *3156*

Prison established by the federal government for women, *2829*

Queen to visit the United States during her reign, *4080*

Radio show with a plot, *6290*

Rocket flight using liquid fuel, *7017*

Science fiction magazine, *4732*

Semiautomatic rifle, *8118*

Senate election in which neither candidate was seated after a recount, *2630*

Senator unseated after a recount, *3330*

Sheet of souvenir postage stamps, *6065*

Statue to commemorate literary characters, *5413*

Swimmer who was an American woman to swim the English Channel, *7518*

Transatlantic radio fax of a check, *3794*

Transatlantic radio fax of a drawing, *5694*

Weather map to be telecast, *7826*

1927

Air conditioner for home use, *4333*

Airplane scheduled passenger flight at night, *1410*

American flag displayed from the right hand of the Statue of Liberty, *1130*

Armored truck holdup, *2779*

Aviation department of a state government, *1385*

Bagel bakery, *3927*

Book on the game of bridge, *2005*

Car to exceed the speed of 200 miles per hour, *5445*

Congress to enact more than 1,000 laws, *2568*

Corporation to own its own airplane, *1396*

Drive-up mailbox, *6009*

Hotel to install radio reception, *2430*

Housing cooperative sponsored by a labor union, *4618*

International airplane passenger station, *1506*

International lifeboat race, *7217*

International radio broadcasting license, *6297*

King born in the United States, *6649*

Lightweight brick, *2060*

Monument to the American flag, *5414*

Phonograph with an automatic record changer, *7010*

Pilot to die because of a lack of oxygen, *1614*

Propaganda course at a college, *3256*

Respirator known as the iron lung, *4947*

Snowmobile patent, *7490*

Stroboscopic lamp for high-speed photography, *5841*

Symphonic work to require an airplane propeller, *1296*

Telecast of image and sound, *7827*

Transatlantic commercial telephone service, *7737*

Transatlantic solo airplane flight, *1450*

Underwater highway tunnel with twin tubes, *3618*

Vitamin to be commercially synthesized and manufactured, *3971*

Wind tunnel for testing airplane parts, *1497*

1928

Air-conditioned office building, *2065*

Airmail service from ship to shore, *6022*

Airplane diesel engine, *1498*

Airship transfer of mail to a train, *1523*

Animated cartoon with sound, *5535*

Army armored car unit, *5187*

Autogiro flown in America, *1529*

Caterpillar Club members who were father and son, *1587*

College of liberal arts and sciences founded as a Jewish institution, *2965*

College skeet tournament, *7478*

Daredevil to go over Niagara Falls in a rubber ball, *3681*

Dogs trained to guide the blind, *1173*

Electric flashing sign, *2351*

Electric light bulb frosted on the inside, *3498*

Fathometer, *6714*

Fax transmission of movie film, *7672*

Frog-jumping jubilee, *1151*

Hydroelectric power plant to use water pumped into a reservoir, *3479*

Hydrogenated peanut butter, *3950*

International dogsled mail, *6010*

Justice on the federal bench who was a woman, *2725*

Mechanical cotton picker, *1033*

Medical center devoted to teaching, treatment, and research, *3178*

Modeling school, *3298*

Outdoor scenes to be televised, *7829*

Physician to Congress, *2569*

Play to be shown on television, *1260*

Presidential nomination ceremony broadcast on radio, *3412*

Puppet show to be televised, *1259*

Remote television pickup, *7830*

Seeing Eye dog, *1173*

Squash rackets champion who was a woman, *7502*

Standard broadcast station to transmit a television image, *7795*

Telephone switchboard with Braille markings, *7738*

Television license, *7794*

Television magazine, *4781*

Television programs to be shown regularly, *7774*

Television sets to be installed in homes on an experimental basis, *7810*

Theater built and named for a living actress, *3706*

Transcontinental bus service, *5421*

Transcontinental foot race, *7557*

Transoceanic radio signal conveying a television image, *7828*

Tuberculosis vaccine, *4921*

Wedding on television, *4820*

1929

Airmail letter sheet, *6023*

Airmail pickup by an airplane without landing, *6024*

Airplane bombing raid by a mercenary soldier, *2781*

Airplane flight over the South Pole, *6729*

Airship made completely of metal, *1524*

Airship passenger transfer to an airplane, *1525*

All-blind airplane flight, *1451*

Allergy journal, *4764*

Ambulance air service, *4824*

Automatic electric stock quotation board, *3824*

Automatic pilot on an airplane, *1499*

Aviation course in a high school, *3089*

Baseball manager to win pennants in both leagues, *7099*

Bridge of flowers, *3592*

Building in which wrought-iron window sashes were installed, *2052*

Cabinet member convicted of a crime, *6110*

Car radio, *6309*

Child born in an airplane, *2160*

Coaxial cable, *7706*

College football player to score 50 points in one game, *7307*

Community hospital, *4892*

Curb exchange to transact more business in a day than the New York Stock Exchange, *3825*

Description of hydroponic agriculture, *1036*

Diathermy machine, *4948*

Fireworks law enacted by a state, *4113*

Flight trainer for airplane pilots, *1500*

Fluorescent mineral exhibit, *6715*

History of medicine department at a college, *3157*

Horse to win a $100,000 purse in one race, *7410*

Hospital insurance group plan, *4535*

Hotel at an airport, *2431*

Humanist association, *5746*

Marine pilot to fly over Antarctica, *5236*

Miniature golf course, *7349*

Mobile home, *5505*

Movie by a major company for an African-American audience, *5559*

Movie entertainment shown on an airplane, *5514*

Movie in Esperanto, *5561*

Movie of feature length made outdoors, *5558*

Movie with both sound and color, *5560*

Newsreel theater, *3707*

Night coach, *5422*

Nudist organization, *7580*

Organized crime massacre, *2780*

Oscar for best picture, *1630*

Oscars for best acting, *1631*

Oscars for best movie director, *1632*

Paper money of the present small size, *5393*

Public demonstration of color television, *7811*

Radio broadcast from the Senate chamber, *2631*

Reindeer, *1152*

Seatrain, *6890*

Ship-to-shore mobile telephone commercial service, *7739*

Submarine emergency air supply container, *6967*

1929—*continued*

Tax on chain stores enacted by a state, *7658*

Teletypewriter system employed by a police department, *4143*

Transcontinental air derby for women, *7297*

Transcontinental daily air-rail passenger service, *1411*

Tugboat with a diesel-electric engine, *6889*

Underground mill for the separation of zinc and lead, *5343*

Vice president who was Native American, *6248*

Vice president's widow to receive a pension, *6247*

Yogurt dairy, *3856*

1930

Aerial photograph in natural colors, *5826*

Airline flight attendant who was a woman, *1412*

Airplane catapulted from an airship, *1452*

Airship for private commercial operation, *1526*

Airship to land and take off from an oceangoing steamship, *1527*

Athlete to win the James E. Sullivan Memorial Trophy, *1719*

Bobsled run, *7581*

Bowler who was a woman to obtain a perfect score, *7227*

Car trip made with a diesel engine, *5474*

Catholic saints who were active in North America, *6472*

Cellophane transparent tape, *4339*

Check photographing device, *3795*

Clothes dryer, *4278*

Coal mine to be automated, *3508*

Colorscope public demonstration, *3436*

Computing device with electronic components, *2526*

Consumer protection medical alert, *2312*

Cow flown in an airplane, *1153*

Demonstration of home reception of television, *7812*

Diesel engine speed record, *5482*

Dutch elm disease breakout, *3731*

Factory without windows, *4386*

Farriers' course at a college, *3299*

Floating electric power plant, *3481*

Flying medical clinic, *4845*

Funeral home operated on the cooperative plan, *2839*

Glider flight indoors, *1549*

Glider pilot's license, *1598*

Glider released from an airship, *1548*

Golf champion to hold the four highest golf titles, *7361*

Hydroelectric power plant operated by a county, *3480*

Maritime museum, *5587*

Mosaic pavement, *6630*

Movie of a solar eclipse taken from an airplane, *6688*

Museum to install refrigerated vaults, *5586*

Music magazine published in Braille, *4733*

Nobel Prize for literature awarded to an American, *1694*

Nobel Prize for physiology or medicine awarded to an American citizen, *1693*

Passenger ship with a diesel engine, *6877*

Photographic flashbulbs, *5842*

Pinball game machine, *7454*

Planet found beyond Neptune, *6680*

Planetarium open to the public, *6669*

Police bureau of criminal alien investigation, *4145*

Presbyterian elder who was a woman, *6583*

President buried in the National Cemetery, *6199*

Radar detection of airplanes, *7676*

Radio advertising course at a college, *2923*

Radio broadcast from a zoo, *1189*

Rivetless cargo vessel, *6891*

Rotating milking platform, *1056*

Round-the-world radio broadcast, *6275*

Seaplane glider, *1550*

Speaker to address an organization by television, *7831*

State police officers who were women, *4144*

Stock order from a zeppelin, *3826*

Streamlined submarine, *6968*

Submarine escape training tank, *6969*

Sulfanilamide production, *4993*

Synthetic rubber for manufacture, *4489*

Tampon to be mass-produced, *4061*

Tieless streetcar tracks that were soundless and shockless, *6408*

Transcontinental car trip driven entirely in reverse, *5475*

Transcontinental glider tow, *1551*

Transcontinental solo airplane flight by a woman, *1453*

Vehicular tunnel to a foreign country, *3619*

1931

Absolute monarch to visit the United States, *6650*

Air-conditioned train, *6430*

Airplane race of importance in which both men and women were contestants, *7298*

All-welded self-propelled seagoing petroleum carrier ship, *6892*

Anthropology laboratory, *6748*

Autogiro licensed for commercial use, *1530*

Autogiro owned by the federal government, *1533*

Autogiro to land and take off from a ship, *1534*

Automatic swinging doors operated by a photoelectric cell, *2087*

Baha'i house of worship, *6604*

Baseball pitcher who was a woman, *7149*

Basketball game at a large commercial sports arena, *7170*
Cattle of the Afrikaaner breed, *1082*
Congressional committee headed by a woman, *2589*
Diesel-powered tractor, *1057*
Electric shaver, *4060*
Elevator with two cars, *2111*
Fizzing cold remedy, *4994*
Full-scale wind tunnel for testing airplanes, *1501*
Glider license awarded to a woman, *1599*
Heavy water to be identified, *6814*
Infrared photograph, *5827*
Mobster convicted for tax evasion, *2782*
Native American art exhibition, *1229*
Nobel Peace Prize awarded to an American woman, *1695*
Parachute jump from an autogiro, *1588*
Plant patent, *1063*
Polo game played outdoors at night, *7461*
Private hydroponic garden, *1037*
Radio variety show with a live studio audience, *6291*
Radio waves from space to be observed, *6681*
Rattlesnake meat in cans, *3942*
Resale price maintenance law enacted by a state, *2313*
Rocket glider flight, *1552*
Shuffleboard championship tournament, *7582*
Skyscraper higher than 1,250 feet, *2100*
Stabilized airplane in commercial use, *1397*
Teletype commercial service, *7707*
Theater designed and built for the rear projection of movies, *3708*
Transcontinental autogiro flight, *1531*
Transcontinental autogiro flight by a woman, *1532*
Transpacific nonstop airplane flight, *1454*
Volcanic eruption to be broadcast on radio, *2870*

1932

Airport manager who was a woman, *1507*
Artificial lightning demonstration, *6770*
Bridge table to shuffle and deal cards by electricity, *4024*
Camera exposure meter, *5843*
Computerized pump, *4417*
Cooperative store operated by women, *2503*
Dogsled race on an Olympic demonstration program, *7280*
Double-deck elevator, *2112*
Electrical timing device for foot races, *7558*
Franchise chain, *2463*
Fruit tree patent, *1026*
Gasoline tax levied by Congress, *7659*
Greek Orthodox college and orphanage, *3279*
Holes in one shot by a father and son in the same golf game, *7362*

International ski meet, *7482*
Olympic Games competition to be held in the winter, *7446*
Olympic gold medalist in both the Summer and Winter Olympics, *7447*
Opera house established by a city, *1351*
Ophthalmology clinic, *4846*
President to invite the president-elect, *6165*
Presidential candidate to accept his party's nomination in person, *3413*
Pulitzer Prize awarded to a musical, *1712*
Radio broadcast from a moving train, *6276*
Railroad mystery excursion, *3667*
Savings bank with a deposit of half a billion dollars, *3781*
Self-service supermarket, *2504*
Telecast images received in an airplane, *7832*
Teletypesetter, *5807*
Totalisator to record racetrack bets and odds, *7399*
Transatlantic solo airplane flight by a woman, *1455*
Transcontinental nonstop airplane flight by a woman, *1456*
Unemployment insurance act, *4525*
Wooden money, *5378*
Yellow fever vaccine for human immunization, *4922*

1933

Air Mail Flyer's Medal of Honor, *1642*
Airplane sleeping berths, *1413*
All-star major league baseball game, *7130*
Ballet choreographer of international renown, *1235*
Bank deposit insurance law enacted by Congress, *3782*
Baseball player to hit a home run in an All-Star game, *7150*
Blood serum made of dried human blood, *4833*
Bridge with open-mesh steel flooring, *3594*
Bridge with piers sunk in the open sea, *3593*
Cabinet in which all members were sworn in at the same time and place, *6111*
Cabinet member who was a woman, *6112*
Chocolate chip cookies, *3928*
College to use the unit-cost plan, *2966*
Conviction under a National Industrial Recovery Code, *4378*
Cotton acreage reduction payment, *1034*
Director of the Mint of the United States who was a woman, *5350*
Drama broadcast on radio from a regular stage, *1262*
Drama broadcast on radio from a ship at sea, *1261*
Drive-in movie theater, *3709*
Electoral college members invited to a presidential inauguration, *3391*

1933—*continued*

Electric power contract between a city and the federal government, *3482*
Electrobasograph, *4949*
Execution for kidnapping, *2801*
FM radio, *6310*
Game management chair at a college, *3078*
Gasoline pump with price and gallon displays, *4418*
Glass that was nonreflecting, *4049*
Governor to be granted almost dictatorial power, *7619*
Interstate legislative conference, *7629*
Lung removal, *5081*
Maritime Day, *4248*
Opera prima donna who was African-American, *1333*
Police radio system, *4146*
Poliomyelitis vaccine, *4923*
Round-the-world solo airplane flight, *1457*
Savings and loan association established by the federal government, *3783*
Singing telegram, *7708*
Sit-down strike, *4598*
Soap opera on radio, *6292*
Sodium vapor lamps, *3499*
State speaker of the House who was a woman, *7628*
Surgical elevation of the skull to treat epilepsy, *5082*
Swimming pool in the White House, *6257*
Synthetic laundry detergent, *4279*
Transcontinental flight made by African-Americans in their own airplane, *1458*
Typewriting primer, *1829*
Walkie-Talkie two-way radio device, *7722*
Wedding by transatlantic telephone, *4821*
World championship professional football game, *7326*

1934

Abrasive for commercial use, *4442*
Aerial camera with nine lenses for large-scale mapping, *5845*
Aircraft carrier, *6934*
All-star football game, *7327*
Antimatter to be observed, *6815*
Archivist of the United States, *4677*
Blue Cross and Blue Shield plans, *4536*
Book bound with preprinted offset cloth, *1755*
Cartel of corporations, *2524*
College diploma made of silver, *2980*
College to dispense with credits, hours, points, and grades, *3001*
Commercial production of plants in water, *1038*
Community to fingerprint its citizens, *4164*
Cyclotron, *6798*
Death penalty authorized by federal law, *2802*
Driving course in a high school, *3090*
Dual-purpose postage stamp, *6066*

Factories operated by the federal government in peacetime, *4387*
Federal credit union, *3785*
First Lady to travel in an airplane to a foreign country, *6131*
Fluorescent lamp, *3500*
Fluorescent paint, *7938*
Instantaneous phonograph recording, *7011*
Laundromat, *2442*
Liquor stores run by a state government, *2505*
Locomotive communications headlight, *6427*
Monosodium glutamate commercial production, *3951*
Movie of the sun, *6689*
Musical comedy broadcast on radio, *1264*
Nationwide highway planning surveys authorized by Congress, *6631*
Negative election campaign run by media specialists, *3323*
Payment by the Federal Deposit Insurance Corporation, *3784*
Pilot to fly a regularly scheduled airmail transport who was a woman, *1600*
Pipeless organ, *1324*
President to conduct religious services as commander-in-chief of the Navy, *6166*
President to go through the Panama Canal while in office, *6167*
President to make a radio broadcast from a foreign country, *6214*
President to visit Hawaii while in office, *6236*
President to visit South America while in office, *6235*
Pressure suit, *1386*
Professional football game in which 10 touchdowns were made, *7328*
Ptarmigan, *1166*
Radio broadcast heard in both the Arctic and the Antarctic regions, *6277*
Raptor sanctuary, *3748*
Religion magazine printed in rotogravure, *4734*
Revenue stamp printed by the Post Office Department, *7660*
Rocket to break the sound barrier, *7018*
Ski tow made of rope, *7483*
Snow goose, *1167*
Soapbox derby, *7583*
State committee chairman of a major political party who was a woman, *3341*
State legislature with a single chamber in the post-Revolutionary era, *7630*
Streamlined all-steel diesel-motor train, *6433*
Streamlined lightweight high-speed three-car passenger train, *6431*
Streamlined steam locomotive, *6364*
Symphony on an African-American folk theme, *1297*
Talking book for blind listeners, *2029*
Theater and dramatic criticism course at a college, *3105*

Theatrical presentation sponsored by the federal government, *1263*

Train of airplanes, *1459*

Train to run 1,000 miles nonstop, *6432*

X-ray photograph of the entire body of a living person taken in a one-second exposure, *4906*

Youth hostel, *2150*

1935

Aerial photograph showing the lateral curvature of the horizon and the beginning of the stratosphere, *5828*

Ambulance service with an incubator, *4825*

Automatic parking meter, *5446*

Baseball game at night by major league teams, *7131*

Beer in cans, *2671*

Bill of $100,000 denomination, *5394*

Bill to depict both sides of the Great Seal of the United States, *5395*

Blood testing laws enacted by a state, *4188*

Book on the game of bridge by a championship team, *2006*

Book series microfilmed, *4683*

Building with prefabricated walls of mosaic concrete, *2088*

Casein fiber, *4443*

City law requiring reporting of premature births, *2161*

College classes intended to combat the influence of communism, *3002*

Color film, *5844*

Commercial hydroponicum, *1039*

Commodity exchange member who was a woman, *3827*

Drama school at a college, *2910*

Drug treatment center for addicts established by Congress, *2688*

Electric guitar, *1325*

Fax transmission by a press syndicate direct to newspaper offices, *5627*

Football player to win the Heisman Trophy for excellence in college football, *1725*

Heart operation for the relief of angina pectoris, *5091*

Heart pump, *5060*

Identification of human beings from the pattern formed by the blood vessels of the retina, *4165*

Invisible-glass installation, *4050*

Lie detector, *4623*

Lightning observatory, *6771*

Medical college founded as a Jewish institution, *3179*

National conference on crime, *4147*

National skeet tournament, *7479*

News correspondent who was African-American, *5619*

Newspaper to store issues on microfilm, *4682*

Opera composer who was a woman, *1334*

Paperback publisher, *1790*

Parachute tower for training jumpers, *1589*

President to read a veto message to Congress, *6168*

Public school classes for children with epilepsy, *3022*

Radio tube made of metal, *6311*

Roller derby, *7465*

Round-the-world telephone conversation, *7762*

Senator who was a Latino, *2652*

Spectrophotometer, *6799*

Streamlined electric locomotive, *6365*

Streamlined ferryboat, *6912*

Transatlantic nonstop solo flight westbound by a woman, *1453*

Transpacific airmail flight, *6025*

Transpacific solo airplane flight by a woman, *1460*

Transport airplane designed for transoceanic service, *1414*

Truck completely streamlined, *5506*

Twelve-step rehabilitation program, *2662*

Virus obtained in crystalline form, *5059*

Vitamin E reduction to alpha tocopherol, *3972*

1936

Airmail flight by rocket, *6026*

All-glass windowless structure, *2089*

Aviation gasoline obtained by the catalytic cracking method, *3539*

Bicycle traffic court, *7196*

Bottle with a screw cap, *4287*

Catholic mass in an airship over the ocean, *6473*

Cellulose sponge for household use, *4280*

Chinese-American women's organization to be incorporated, *5726*

Comics studio, *4737*

Coxswain of a men's college varsity rowing team who was a woman, *7471*

Electric-eye camera installed at a racetrack, *7400*

Electron tube, *3437*

Federal administrator who was an African-American woman, *2257*

Football goalposts of collapsible folding metal, *7314*

Football with a rubber covering, *7313*

Fuel alcohol plant, *3540*

Giant panda, *1154*

High-definition telecast, *7834*

High school to fingerprint its students, *4166*

Lucite commercially manufactured, *4481*

Magazine of the federal government, *4735*

Medical insurance group policy for college students, *4537*

National Union for Social Justice national convention, *3377*

News magazine featuring photographs, *4736*

1936—*continued*

Olympic athlete from the United States to win four gold medals in one year, *7448*

Pensions paid by the federal government to workers in private industry, *4588*

Pope to visit the United States before his election, *4081*

Radioactive isotope medicine, *4995*

Radioactive substance produced synthetically, *6816*

Round-the-world airplane passenger race, *7299*

Telecast using coaxial cable, *7833*

Textile-wrapped detonating fuse, *4426*

Theater operated as part of a state school system, *3710*

Transatlantic round-trip airplane flight from the United States, *1461*

Union Party convention, *3378*

Unscheduled event to be televised as it occurred, *5607*

Work week of 40 hours to be required by Congress, *4567*

X-ray photograph showing the complete arterial circulation in an adult human, *4907*

1937

Animated feature-length cartoon in Technicolor, *5536*

Automatic washing machine, *4281*

Badminton championship tournament, *7584*

Bicycle champion who was a woman, *7197*

Birth control clinic run by a state government, *4847*

Blood bank, *4834*

Boxer to hold three titles simultaneously, *7253*

Car-airplane combination, *5447*

Children's church, *6535*

Coast-to-coast radio news broadcast to be recorded, *5706*

Costume museum, *5588*

Electric sign showing an animated cartoon, *2352*

First-day special cancellation of a postage stamp, *6067*

Free port, *2486*

Game preserve appropriation by the federal government, *3749*

Grand jury foreman who was a woman, *2737*

Hydrogen-cooled turbine generator, *3483*

Jury school, *2736*

Keedoozle store, *2506*

Letter to circumnavigate the world by commercial airmail, *6027*

License plates for vehicles, *4226*

Lighting designer for the stage, *1265*

Marijuana ban enacted by Congress, *2689*

Mobile television unit, *7813*

Monument to a comic-strip character, *5415*

Movie to earn $1 billion, *5515*

National seashore, *3738*

Newspaper advertisement scented with perfume, *2336*

Newspaper printed on pine-pulp paper in color, *5797*

Okapi, *1155*

Photographer to receive the John Simon Guggenheim Memorial Foundation award, *1627*

Photosensitive glass, *4051*

Pituitary hormone, *4996*

President inaugurated on January 20, *6169*

Psychodrama treatment for psychiatric patients, *5116*

Quadruplets to graduate from college, *2173*

Radio astronomer, *6670*

Radio facsimile newspaper, *5656*

Radio news program sponsored by a cooperative of commercial advertisers, *2339*

Radio show sponsored by a cooperative of commercial advertisers, *2338*

Retirement colony, *2198*

Santa Claus school, *4259*

Senate parliamentarian, *2632*

Shopping cart, *2371*

Simultaneous radio broadcast on all three major networks, *6278*

Sit-down strikes to be outlawed by a state, *4599*

Ski lift, *7484*

Skywriting advertisement written at night, *2337*

Submarine cable plow, *7709*

Symphony orchestra devoted exclusively to radio broadcasting, *1365*

Synthetic fiber, *7876*

Trailer church, *6534*

Trampoline commercially manufactured, *7374*

X-ray movies of human organs in action, *4908*

1938

Airplane instructor's license, *1601*

Aquarium for large marine animals, *1190*

Archival course at a college, *3106*

Artificial animal breeding cooperative organization, *1083*

Ballet on an American theme by an American choreographer, *1236*

Bank president of a national bank who was a woman, *3786*

Baseball dyed yellow, *7110*

Blood tests for marriage license applicants to be required by a state, *4190*

Blood tests for pregnant women to be required by a state, *4189*

Broadway play shown in a television version with its original cast, *1266*

Building built completely inside a factory, *2090*

Building floated across a river, *2090*

Cartooning school, *2911*

Chlorophyll, *4997*

College degree awarded to a ventriloquist's dummy, *2981*
Comic book starring a superhero, *2028*
Copy made by xerography, *2372*
Electric sterilamp, *4950*
Electronic voice mechanism, *7723*
Fiberglass, *4052*
Fighter plane equipped with a cannon, *1487*
Jazz concert at Carnegie Hall, *1298*
Merchant marine cadet corps, *3306*
Minimum wage law enacted by Congress, *4578*
Movie to be shown on a television screen, *5516*
Nobel Prize in literature awarded to an American woman, *1694*
Passenger ship equipped with radar, *7677*
Pontoon bridge of reinforced concrete, *3595*
Post office in an airplane, *6040*
Radio broadcast from a tape recording, *6279*
Right-to-die society, *2840*
School radio station on ultrahigh frequency, *6298*
Skimobile ski lift, *7485*
State legislator who was an African-American woman, *7631*
Teflon created in a laboratory, *4482*
Television, *7771*
Television theater to be licensed, *7775*
Tennis champion to win the Grand Slam, *7536*
Toothbrush with synthetic bristles, *4074*
Woman of American ancestry to become a queen, *6651*

1939

Air-conditioned car, *5449*
Airmail regular delivery service by autogiro, *6029*
Army officer to occupy both the nation's highest military post and the highest nonelective civilian post, *5153*
Battleship equipped with radar, *7678*
Beauty pageant to be shown on television, *3629*
Bicycle race to be shown on television, *7198*
Bluegrass musician of renown, *1335*
Boxing match to be shown on television, *7243*
Catholic beatification of a Native American, *6474*
Coin-operated mailbox, *6011*
Congressional page who was female, *2590*
Dean of a university graduate school who was a woman, *2974*
Electric power generated by cosmic rays, *3484*
Electric starting gate for horse races, *7401*
Electronic digital calculator, *3438*
Fashion show to be shown on television, *2414*
Fiberglass sutures, *4957*
Flea laboratory, *6749*
Food stamps, *4086*
Indoor ski school, *7486*
Intercollegiate football game to be shown on television, *7329*

Judge who was an African-American woman, *2726*
King and queen to be shown on television, *6653*
King of Great Britain to visit the United States, *6652*
Lightning bolt to be scientifically measured, *6773*
Major league baseball game to be shown on television, *7132*
Miniature car, *5448*
Movie premiere festivities to be shown on television, *5517*
Museum devoted exclusively to papermaking, *5589*
Musical comedy to be shown on television, *1268*
National water skiing tournament, *7592*
Nylon, *7877*
Payment by the Federal Crop Insurance Corporation, *1006*
Pinball ban enacted by a city, *7455*
Play on Broadway in which an African-American actress had a starring role, *1267*
President to appear on television, *6215*
President to hold an airplane pilot's license, *6224*
Presidential campaign manager who was a woman, *3392*
Professional football game to be shown on television, *7308*
Public telecast made over telephone wires, *7835*
Rack-rail diesel-electric locomotive, *6366*
Radio production course at a college, *2912*
Snow cruiser for Antarctic research, *6716*
Sports event to be televised live, *7100*
Spray can, *7939*
Submarine from the United States destroyed in World War II, *8066*
Submarine to be refloated, *6970*
Surgical operation televised on a closed circuit, *5083*
Surrogate birth experiment with an animal, *5123*
Tennis tournament to be shown on television, *7533*
Train with fluorescent lights, *6434*
Transatlantic airmail service, *6028*
Transatlantic commercial airplane service, *1415*
Vitamin K to be synthesized, *3973*
Weather forecasting service by telephone, *6772*

1940

Air defense military organization, *5134*
Air raid shelter, *4088*
American base in Antarctica that was permanent, *6730*
Archivist training program at a college, *3107*
Army general who rose from draftee, *5155*

1940—*continued*

Army general who was African-American, *5154*
Army parachute battalion, *5188*
Bas relief of stainless steel in large size, *1219*
Basketball game to be shown on television, *7171*
Betatron, *6801*
Boxing referee who was a woman, *7244*
Car with an automatic transmission, *5450*
Circus to be shown on television, *3675*
Comic book versions of literary works, *2030*
Congress in session a full year, *2570*
Dictionary compiled by a woman, *1808*
Draft law enacted by Congress during peacetime, *5220*
Electron microscope, *6800*
Family of lawyers admitted simultaneously to practice before the Supreme Court, *4641*
General purpose military vehicle, *5248*
Health museum, *5590*
Helicopter, *1557*
Hockey game to be shown on television, *7378*
Intercollegiate track meet to be shown on television, *7559*
M&M candies, *3970*
Major league no-hitter baseball game on opening day, *7133*
Merchant ship formally blessed at a launching ceremony, *6893*
Neptunium, *6817*
Nylon stockings, *2278*
Oscar awarded to a performer who was African-American, *1633*
Passover seder to be shown on television, *6489*
Plutonium, *6818*
Pole vaulter to clear the bar at 15 feet, *7560*
Political convention to be televised, *3342*
Porpoise, *1156*
Postage stamp depicting an African-American, *6090*
President elected for third and fourth terms, *6170*
Professional football championship game broadcast on radio, *7330*
Quetzal bird, *1168*
Radio advertising contract for FM broadcasts, *2340*
Registration of aliens by the federal government, *5872*
Religious services to be shown on television, *6592*
Rh factor discovery, *4835*
Senator who was a woman who had previously served in the House of Representatives, *2653*
Ship-to-shore telecast, *7836*
Social security monthly payment, *4526*
Song to hit No. 1 in the pop charts, *1366*
Synthetic rubber tires, *5502*
Telecommunication by deaf people that was both visual and oral, *7837*

Television production course at a college, *2913*
Tetraploid flower, *1064*
Two-handed shovel, *7940*
Wedding during a parachute jump, *4822*

1941

Ace in World War II, *1616*
Air hero in World War II, *1615*
American losses in the Pacific in World War II, *8067*
Army language school, *3204*
Automatic aircraft cannon, *8119*
Bombing mission by American forces in Asia in World War II, *8071*
Building known as a Quonset hut, *2117*
Camp for conscientious objectors, *5221*
Capture of a German ship by an American ship in World War II, *8049*
City parking garage, *5484*
Civilian airport owned and operated by the federal government, *1508*
Commercial television licenses, *7796*
Department store to hold a public art auction, *2507*
Destroyer from the United States torpedoed in World War II, *8051*
Father and son to become commercial airline pilots, *1602*
Fighter plane from the United States to destroy a Japanese airplane in World War II, *8072*
Film professorship at a college, *2914*
FM radio transmitter to receive a commercial license, *6299*
General of the American armed forces killed in World War II, *8073*
Genetics clinic, *4848*
Glider entirely built of plywood and plastic, *1553*
Health insurance clause in a labor contract, *4538*
Heavy tank, *8120*
Helicopter flight from water, *1574*
Helicopter flight of one-hour duration, *1573*
High-jump standards using electric eye detectors, *7561*
Highway post office service, *6041*
Laryngophone, *5249*
Liberty ship, *6894*
Magnesium commercially produced from seawater, *5344*
Naval patrol bomber, *1488*
Navy admiral killed in action in World War II, *8068*
Navy task force assembled for foreign service, *5302*
Paprika mill, *3952*
Parachute fatality in the Army, *1590*
Plastic bonded airplane, *1398*
Plastic car, *5451*
Presidential library, *6171*

Radar used to detect enemy airplanes, *7679*

Railroad to be completely equipped with diesel-electric engines, *6344*

Round-the-world flight by a commercial airplane, *1462*

Ship from the United States sunk by a German submarine in World War II, *8048*

Ship from the United States to sink a Japanese submarine in World War II, *8069*

Ship from the United States to surrender to the Japanese in World War II, *8070*

Submarine from the United States to sink a Japanese ship in World War II, *8074*

Television commercial, *2341*

Test pilot who was a woman, *1603*

Warship convoy across the Atlantic Ocean in World War II, *8050*

Wind turbine, *3557*

Woman to sell securities on the floor of the New York Curb Exchange, *3828*

1942

Air attack against the Japanese homeland in World War II, *8077*

Aircraft carrier from the United States sunk in World War II, *8079*

Airplane propeller blade of hollow steel, *1502*

American expeditionary force to land in Africa in World War II, *8055*

American expeditionary force to land in Europe in World War II, *8052*

American offensive in the Pacific in World War II, *8081*

American territory occupied by the Japanese in World War II, *8080*

Army corps for women, *5189*

Army general appointed from civilian rank, *5156*

Bombing mission by American forces over enemy-occupied territory in Europe in World War II, *8056*

Bombing raid on the continental United States in World War II, *8075*

Capture of an American ship captain by a German submarine in World War II, *8057*

Citizenship granted on foreign soil, *5873*

Coast Guard unit for women, *5212*

Coded military radio transmissions using a Native American language, *8082*

Distinguished Service Cross awarded in enemy-occupied territory, *1660*

Enemy saboteurs executed in the United States, *8058*

Foreign servicewomen interred in the Arlington National Cemetery, *2855*

Handheld rocket launcher, *8133*

Health insurance law enacted by a state, *4539*

Health maintenance organization, *4540*

Jet airplane, *1399*

Long-distance helicopter flight, *1575*

Marine general, *5237*

Medal of Honor awarded in World War II, *1679*

Medal of Honor awarded to a Marine in World War II, *1679*

Merchant ship commanded by an African-American captain, *6895*

Movie star who was a weapons inventor, *5527*

Naval counterattack by American forces against the Japanese in World War II, *8076*

Naval vessel from the United States to sink a German submarine in World War II, *8054*

Navy ace in World War II, *1617*

Navy Cross awarded to a Coast Guard officer in World War II, *1659*

Navy–Marine Corps Medals for Heroism awarded to Marines, *1661*

Navy officer commissioned in the U.S. Naval Reserve who was a woman, *5287*

Navy school for chaplains, *3218*

Parachute jump using a nylon parachute, *1591*

Pilot from the United States to shoot down a German fighter plane in World War II, *8059*

Pilot from the United States to sink a German submarine, *8053*

President to become a godfather to a member of the British royal family, *6200*

President to make a radio broadcast in a foreign language, *6216*

Presidential railroad car, *6225*

Sea battle in World War II fought solely by air power, *8078*

Self-sustaining nuclear chain reaction demonstration, *6819*

Sexual behavior research institute, *6831*

Ship completed in less than two weeks, *6878*

Ship transported overland across the Rocky Mountains, *6935*

Silver Star Medal awarded to a civilian, *1662*

Soldier from the United States to land on French soil in World War II, *8060*

V-mail film, *6012*

1943

Air attack on Germany by the Army Air Force in World War II, *8061*

Airplane human pickup, *1463*

Airship from the United States lost to enemy action in World War II, *8064*

American land victory without infantry in World War II, *8062*

Amphibious seaplane glider, *1554*

Army chaplain of Japanese ancestry, *5204*

Army pilot who was African-American to shoot down an Axis airplane in World War II, *8063*

Baseball league for women, *7101*

Building containing 6.5 million square feet of usable space, *2118*

1943—*continued*

Cabinet member to address a joint session of Congress, *6113*

Deep-dish pizza, *2462*

Distinguished Service Cross awarded to an animal, *1664*

Election law lowering the voting age in a state to 18, *3433*

Fire department composed entirely of women, *4114*

Hydroelectric power plant to produce a million kilowatts, *3485*

Marine officer of Chinese descent, *5238*

Medal of Honor awarded posthumously to a Coastguardsman killed in action in World War II, *1680*

Merchant marine academy, *3307*

National monument dedicated to an African-American, *5416*

Naval ship with a plural name, *6936*

Opera to be televised in its entirety, *1352*

Poet to win a Pulitzer Prize four times, *1713*

Police appeal for missing persons to be shown on television, *4148*

President of a black African country to visit the United States, *4082*

President to fly in an airplane, *6226*

President to visit a foreign country in wartime, *6237*

Presidential pet to star in a movie, *6201*

Soldier's Medal awarded to a woman, *1663*

Submarine from the United States sunk by an enemy submarine, *8083*

Submarine with a pressure hull of high-tensile steel, *6971*

1944

Antibiotic, *4998*

Army generals to wear the five-star insignia, *5157*

Army officer to receive the three highest decorations, *1665*

Capture and boarding of an enemy submarine on the high seas by American forces, *8065*

Chinese person granted citizenship, *5874*

Cotton crop commercially produced entirely by machinery, *1035*

Execution of an organized crime leader in the electric chair, *2803*

Eye bank, *4836*

Horse stakes race ending in a triple dead heat, *7402*

Jet-propelled fighter plane, *1489*

Mathematical theory of economic decision-making, *6758*

Mobile electric power plant, *3486*

Movie to premiere on television, *5518*

Musical comedy written for television, *1269*

Navy admirals to wear the five-star insignia, *5273*

Navy captain who was a woman, *5288*

Presidential airplane, *6227*

Public service symbol of the federal government, *3714*

Quadruplets delivered by cesarean operation, *2174*

Retail store whose sales in one day exceeded $1 million, *2508*

Rocket airplane for military use, *1490*

Serbian Orthodox cathedral, *6497*

Synthetic quinine, *4999*

Transoceanic newspaper, *5657*

Victory ship launched, *6896*

Wire recorder for sound recording, *5250*

World War II veterans' society officially recognized by Congress, *5313*

1945

American civilians killed in the continental United States in World War II, *8084*

Army general to be consecrated a bishop, *5158*

Atomic bomb explosion, *8123*

Atomic bomb explosion over enemy territory, *8086*

Book written for publication as a paperback, *1791*

Color news photograph transmitted by radio fax for publication, *5695*

Computer bug, *2527*

Congressional representative who had been an actress, *2612*

Department store sales demonstrations using television, *2342*

Distinguished Service Medal awarded to a Navy nurse, *5288*

Federal treaty signed by a woman, *4006*

Food-O-Mat, *2509*

Gas-turbine propeller-driven airplane, *1400*

Governor of Italian ancestry, *7620*

Household product made entirely of plastic, *4288*

Industrial and labor relations school at a college, *3257*

Instant book, *1791*

Jet-propelled landing on an aircraft carrier, *1464*

Judge on the federal bench who was African-American, *2727*

Labor antidiscrimination commission of a state government, *4568*

Medal of Honor awarded to a conscientious objector, *1681*

Naval bombardment of the Japanese homeland in World War II, *8085*

Naval Reserve Nurse Corps nurse who was African-American, *5289*

Naval ship with a mixed company of male and female personnel, *6937*

Opera singer who was African-American to sing a white role, *1336*

Presidential citation to an entire division, *1666*
Professional hockey player to score 50 goals in one season, *7379*
Railroad car with an observation dome, *6388*
Record album to hit No. 1 in the pop charts, *1367*
School completely irradiated with germicidal lamps, *4191*
Strike to last longer than a year, *4600*
Tape recorders, *7013*
Water supply to be fluoridated, *2236*
World bank, *3787*

1946

Artificial snow from a natural cloud, *6774*
Atomic bomb dropped from an airplane over water, *8124*
Atomic bomb underwater explosion, *8125*
Baseball play-off series, *7134*
Bomber plane with the Flying Wing design, *1491*
Bone bank, *4837*
Boxing match at which admission tickets sold at $100, *7245*
Casino in Las Vegas, *3636*
Catholic saint who was an American citizen, *6475*
Cellulose sponge for medical and surgical use, *4951*
Coin bearing the likeness of an African-American, *5379*
Coin-operated television receiver, *7814*
College principally for war veterans, *2967*
Commercial program telecast on a network, *7777*
Drive-in banking service, *3796*
Electric blanket, *4265*
Electronic computer, *2528*
Glider commercial freight service, *1555*
Gospel singer, *1337*
Helicopter commercially designed, *1558*
Helicopter hoist rescue, *1563*
Helicopter licensed for commercial use, *1560*
Helicopter with a twin engine, *1559*
Jet airplane to land on a ship, *1466*
Jet airplane to transport mail, *6030*
Long-distance car-to-car telephone conversation, *7764*
Medal of Honor awarded to a chaplain, *1682*
Medal of Honor awarded to a soldier of Japanese ancestry, *1683*
Military think tank, *5128*
Mobile overseas telephone call from a moving vehicle, *7763*
Mobile telephone commercial service, *7740*
Movie trailer to be shown on television, *2343*
Nontwisted sewing thread, *4364*
Nuclear product for peacetime use, *3545*
Photograph of a beam of 1-billion-volt x-rays, *5829*

Powered soaring glider commercially licensed, *1556*
President to travel underwater in a captured enemy submarine, *6228*
Radar installation aboard a commercial carrier, *6959*
Radar signal to the moon, *7680*
Radio fax transmission to a moving train, *7673*
Religious service to be televised from a church, *6593*
Rocket plane for manned supersonic flight, *1492*
Rocket to attain a 100-mile altitude, *7019*
Snow-melting apparatus using pipes embedded in the sidewalk, *2223*
Soldering gun, *7941*
Television show to be sponsored by a commercial advertiser, *2344*
Television variety talent show series, *7776*
Transcontinental Pullman sleeping car daily service, *6345*
Transcontinental round-trip airplane flight made within 24 hours, *1465*
Traveling cancer clinic, *4849*

1947

Airmail and express service by helicopter, *6031*
Airplane to fly faster than the speed of sound, *1468*
Aluminum foil, *4340*
Army officer who was a woman, *5170*
Army specialist corps for women, *5190*
Ballistic missile, *8134*
Book issued on microcards, *4684*
Cancer prevention clinic for children, *4850*
Commercial telephone service on railroad trains for passengers, *7741*
Commercial television station west of the Mississippi River, *7797*
Congressional opening session to be televised, *2571*
Deaths from smog, *3715*
Food in an aerosol can, *3953*
Forest fire drenched by artificial rain, *3732*
Golfer born in America to win the British Women's Amateur Golf Tournament, *7363*
Helicopter to deliver material across a picket line, *1562*
Helicopter with a fully servo-controlled intermeshing rotor, *1561*
Horse to win $1 million in races, *7411*
Instant camera, *5846*
Major league baseball player in the postwar era who was African-American, *7151*
Microwave oven, *4302*
Mobile telephone call between an airplane in flight and a moving car, *7766*
Navy commissioned officer who was African-American, *5290*
Navy jet airplane squadron, *5303*

1947—*continued*

Nobel Prize shared by an American husband and wife, *1696*

Planned suburban development, *2199*

Presidential address televised from the White House, *6217*

Radar for commercial and private planes, *7681*

Radioactive isotopes exported, *6820*

Ramjet helicopter, *1564*

Round-the-world commercial airplane service, *1416*

Ship from which a long-range rocket was launched, *6938*

Telecast from a submerged submarine, *7838*

Television drama program regularly scheduled, *7778*

Transatlantic flight by a robot airplane, *1467*

Transatlantic mobile telephone call between two cars, *7765*

Tubeless car tires, *5503*

Twin-engine pressurized airplane, *1401*

Women in Antarctica, *6730*

World Series baseball game to be shown on television, *7135*

Writer to win the Pulitzer Prize in both fiction and poetry, *1714*

1948

Airplane with a delta wing, *1402*

Anthrax vaccine for human immunization, *4924*

Baseball player who was African-American to hit a home run in a World Series, *7152*

Birth registration uniform numbering system, *2162*

Broad-spectrum antibiotic, *5000*

Cantorial school, *3280*

Catholic midnight mass to be televised, *6476*

Church service in sign language to be televised, *6594*

Commissioned officer in the Marine Corps who was African-American, *5239*

Deodorant soap, *4062*

Doctor in the regular Navy who was a woman, *5291*

Elevator with electronic signal controls, *2113*

Figure skating champion from the United States to compete in the Olympic Games, *7432*

Fungicide used medicinally, *5001*

Gas-turbine-electric locomotive, *6368*

Governor of Puerto Rico to be elected, *3324*

High-speed radio fax transmission, *7674*

House completely heated by solar energy, *2128*

Jockey to win the Triple Crown twice, *7412*

Labor dispute in which the Taft-Hartley Act was invoked, *4569*

Latex paint, *7942*

Long-playing microgroove phonograph records, *7012*

Monument to a Native American, *5417*

Navy personnel in the regular Navy who were women, *5266*

Newsreel in color, *5699*

Newsreel telecast presented daily, *5700*

Olympic gold medalist who was an African-American woman, *7449*

Opera to be televised from the Metropolitan Opera House, *1353*

Parcel post domestic air service, *6033*

Parcel post international air service, *6032*

Presidential candidate who was renominated after a defeat, *3414*

Public high school to specialize in the performing arts, *3091*

Quantum theory of electromagnetic radiation, *6759*

Radio program simultaneously transmitted, *6280*

Scientific survey of sexual behavior among Americans, *6831*

Senator to win a seat that had been occupied by his father and his mother, *2654*

Stratovision flight by an airplane during which a television signal was transmitted, *7839*

Super-giant locomotive, *6367*

Symphonic concert to be shown on television, *1299*

Tape recorder built in the United States for commercial use, *7014*

Telephone recording devices, *7724*

Television camera lens to provide zoom effects, *7815*

Television image using a split screen, *7816*

Transatlantic eastward flight by jet airplane, *1469*

Transistor, *3439*

Water pollution law enacted by Congress, *3716*

Western series on television, *7779*

Women's Army Corps member to be part of the Regular Army, *5171*

1949

Airmail postal card, *6047*

Airplane to fly with a load of 100,000 pounds, *1471*

Airport fog disposal unit, *1509*

Ambassador from the United States who was a woman, *3991*

Ambassador to the United States who was a woman, *3990*

Anesthesiology professor at a college, *3158*

Animated cartoon made for television, *7782*

Automatic streetlight system, *2217*

Ballet technique course at a college, *2915*

Bar code scanner, *2373*

Baseball player who was African-American to win the Most Valuable Player award, *1723*

Belt conveyor more than four miles long, *4419*

Cargo airlines licensed by the Civil Aeronautics Board, *1417*

Congressional standing committee headed by an African-American, *2591*
Court-martial at which the judges included enlisted men, *2740*
Emmy awards for excellence in television, *1628*
Gas turbine to pump natural gas, *3521*
Gas turbine used by an electrical utility company, *3487*
Heliport commercial base, *1565*
Leaping submarine, *6972*
Long-distance dial telephone service, *7742*
Magazine on microfilm offered to subscribers, *4685*
Mosque, *6605*
Museum devoted exclusively to nuclear energy, *5591*
National Basketball Association commissioner, *7172*
Naval Academy graduate who was African-American, *3219*
Naval Reserve flier who was African-American, *1618*
Oscar winners who were father and son, *1634*
Oscar winners who were husband and wife, *1635*
Photograph of genes, *4909*
President who had been divorced, *6202*
Radio station owned and operated by African-Americans, *6300*
Railroad dining car powered by electricity, *6389*
Rectangular television tube, *7817*
Refrigeration system for trucks, *5507*
Rocket to reach outer space, *7020*
Round-the-world nonstop flight by an airplane, *1470*
Sitcom television show, *7780*
Soap opera on daytime television, *7781*
Subcompact car designed to be fuel-efficient, *5452*
Synchrotron, *6802*
Tape-recording machine for mass production of tapes, *7015*
Telescope lens 200 inches in diameter, *6671*
Television variety talent show series with an African-American cast, *7776*
Transatlantic airplane flight carrying 100 people, *1472*
Transcontinental bicycle trip made in less than three weeks, *7204*
Typesetting machine to dispense with metal type, *5808*
Year in which more than 1 million passenger cars of one make were produced, *5453*

1950

Babysitters' insurance policy, *4527*
Basketball professional player who was African-American, *7173*

Burglar alarm operated by ultrasonic or radio waves, *2136*
Concentrated milk, *3877*
Copy machine, *2374*
Credit card to be nationally accepted, *3809*
Diapers that were disposable, *2151*
Helicopter rescue of an American pilot behind enemy lines, *7979*
Hockey player on an amateur team who was African-American, *7380*
Husband and wife to be elected simultaneously to both chambers of a state legislature, *7632*
Illegal television station, *7798*
Kidney transplant, *5095*
Korean War combat mission, *7976*
Local radio network, *6301*
Marine Corps jet ace in Korea, *1619*
Medal of Honor awarded in the Korean War, *1684*
Medical officer assigned to a naval vessel who was a woman, *5292*
Nazi collaborator to be deported, *5875*
Nobel Peace Prize awarded to an African-American, *1697*
Nuclear engineering course at a college, *3248*
Officer killed in action in the Korean War, *7978*
Phototransistor, *3440*
Pilot of a jet fighter to win a dogfight in the Korean War, *7981*
Pilot to destroy an enemy airplane in the Korean War, *7975*
Poet who was an African-American woman to win the Pulitzer Prize, *1715*
Postage stamp depicting a Jew, *6091*
Radio paging service, *7743*
Soldier killed in action in the Korean War, *7977*
Swimmer who was a woman to swim the English Channel in both directions, *7519*
Tank crew to cross the 38th parallel in the Korean War, *7980*
Television series in which an African-American performer had a starring role, *7783*
Ten Most Wanted list, *2783*
Transatlantic nonstop jet airplane flight, *1473*
United Nations delegate who was African-American, *3992*

1951

Ace to fly a jet, *1620*
Air Force Medal of Honor for action in the Korean War, *1667*
Air-to-air rocket, *8135*
All-Star Game of the National Basketball Association, *7174*
Atomic bomb explosion to be shown on television, *8126*
Atomic bomb underground explosion, *8127*

1951—*continued*

Battery to convert radioactive energy into electrical energy, *3488*

Birth to be shown on closed-circuit television, *2163*

Correction fluid for typewriters, *2389*

Electric power from nuclear energy, *3546*

Electronic computer for commercial use, *2529*

Gambling permit stamp issued by the federal government, *7661*

Gas-turbine helicopter, *1566*

Jet airplane passenger trip, *1474*

Jewish prayer services to be televised in their entirety, *6595*

Kenaf fiber, *1027*

Mail delivery car with the steering wheel on the right, *5454*

Medal of Honor awarded to a Marine in the Korean War, *1684*

Microscope with a radiation block, *6803*

Movie showing the inside of a living heart, *4910*

Nuclear reactor used in medical therapy, *5061*

Opera written for television, *1354*

Parking garage that was completely automated, *5485*

Pay television system, *7799*

Peacetime death sentence for espionage, *2836*

Presidential press conference recorded on tape, *6218*

Rabbi in the Reform movement who was a woman, *6490*

Rock and roll song, *1368*

Rocket to intercept an airplane, *8136*

Senator who had been a newspaper reporter, *2655*

Sex-change operation, *6832*

Suits for men made of Dacron, *2279*

Telecast from a foreign country, *7842*

Telephone company answering service, *7744*

Teletypesetter circuit operated by a news agency, *5628*

Television eyewitness allowed to testify in a federal court, *2715*

Television program in color, *7784*

Titanium plant fully self-contained and fully integrated, *4477*

Transcontinental dial telephone service without the aid of operators, *7745*

Transcontinental telecast received on the East Coast, *7840*

Transcontinental telecast received on the West Coast, *7841*

Transistors produced commercially for a specific product, *3441*

United Nations postage stamps in U.S. denominations, *6068*

Valeteria, *2398*

Year in which air traffic volume exceeded first-class rail traffic volume, *1418*

1952

Airplane flight to land at the North Pole, *6731*

Antibiotic synthetically manufactured, *5002*

Artificial aortic valve, *5053*

Artificial lens for cataract patients, *5052*

Automatic headlight control, *4227*

Bank to issue a credit card, *3810*

Basketball collegiate player to score more than 1,000 points in one season, *7175*

Birth to be televised for the public, *2164*

Boxing referee in a heavyweight championship match who was African-American, *7246*

Bullfighter who was a woman to fight professionally, *7259*

Coal hydrogenation plant, *4444*

Commercial television station on ultrahigh frequency, *7800*

Commonwealth of the United States, *5976*

Copyright registered for a choreographic score, *1237*

Drug treatment center for minors, *2690*

Explorer to set foot on both the North and South Poles, *6732*

Frozen bread, *3929*

Hearing aid using transistors, *5071*

Heart operation in which the deep-freezing technique was employed, *5093*

Holiday Inn, *2432*

Hydrogen bomb, *8128*

Jockey to win the Kentucky Derby five times, *7413*

Microfilm editions of federal publications and documents, *4686*

Mitral valve corrective surgery, *5092*

Mother and son simultaneously elected to Congress, *2613*

Musical composition consisting entirely of silence, *1300*

Pacemaker, *4952*

Pay television presentation of a sporting event, *7785*

Presidential election in which a computer was used to predict the outcome, *3393*

Railroad freight cars with compartments, *6390*

Religious radio program broadcast by a husband and wife, *6596*

Seagoing radio broadcasting station, *5304*

Sugar-free soft drinks, *3847*

Surgical operation shown on a local television program, *5084*

Surgical operation televised coast-to-coast, *5085*

Test for newborn health, *2165*

Toothpaste with fluoride, *4075*

Transatlantic helicopter flight, *1576*

Transpacific nonstop jet airplane flight, *1475*

Umpire in organized baseball who was African-American, *7102*

Vice presidential candidate who was an African-American woman, *3415*

Video recording on high-definition magnetic tape, *7818*
World heavyweight boxing champion to retire undefeated, *7254*
Year in which there were no reported lynchings of African-Americans, *2258*
Yiddish professorship at a college, *3119*

1953

Airline to install rear-facing passenger seats, *1419*
Aluminum-faced building, *2091*
Animated three-dimensional cartoon in Technicolor, *5537*
Artmobile, *5598*
Book censorship board established by a state, *1792*
Building with its roof supported by cables, *2092*
Cabinet conference to be telecast, *6114*
Carpeting of tufted plastic, *4319*
Catholic cardinal whose see was west of the Rockies, *6477*
Coast-to-coast live telecast in color, *7845*
Department store to sell apartments, *2510*
Department store to sell insurance, *2511*
Doctor commissioned in the regular Army who was a woman, *5172*
Educational television station, *7801*
Electronic road system, *6632*
Fluorescent electric lighting to be installed on every street of a city, *2218*
Gas-turbine propane-fueled locomotive, *6369*
Helicopter fully operated by remote control, *1567*
Helicopter passenger service, *1568*
Highway interchange structure with four levels, *6633*
Hotel to establish a heliport, *2433*
Instant tea, *3852*
Japanese person to receive an immigration visa, *5876*
Mongolian dictionary, *1809*
Movie in Cinemascope, *5562*
Movie to be shown simultaneously on pay television and in movie theaters, *5519*
Navy ace in Korea, *1622*
Navy chairman of the Joint Chiefs of Staff, *5293*
Navy–Marine Corps Medal for Heroism awarded to a woman, *1668*
Newspaper advertisement that looked three-dimensional, *2345*
Nobel Peace Prize awarded to a professional soldier, *1698*
Nuclear cannon, *8129*
Nuclear reactor privately operated, *6804*
Oil refinery with a carbon monoxide boiler, *3542*

Oscar movie awards ceremony to be telecast, *1636*
Passenger to circle the world on commercial airlines in less than 100 hours, *1477*
Photographic type-composing machine, *5809*
Plastic oil pipeline, *3541*
Polypeptide hormone synthesized, *5003*
Scholastic fraternity at an African-American college, *2983*
Science fiction course at a college, *3108*
Siamese twins separated successfully by surgery, *2175*
Sports car with a plastic laminated fiberglass body, *5455*
Telecast transmitted to Canada, *7843*
Television stations to share the same frequency, *7802*
Tennis champion who was a woman to win the Grand Slam, *7537*
Three brothers from one family to serve in the Senate, *2656*
Three-dimensional feature movie, *5563*
Three-dimensional feature movie in color, *5564*
Three-dimensional telecast, *7844*
Transatlantic nonstop jet airplane eastward flight, *1476*
Transatlantic solo boat journey by a woman, *6990*
Transcontinental express bus service, *5423*
Transcontinental nonstop eastbound airplane service, *1420*
Transcontinental nonstop two-way airplane service, *1421*
Transcontinental round-trip solo flight between sunrise and sunset, *1478*
Triple jet ace, *1621*
World figure skating champion from the United States, *7433*
Year in which television industry profits exceeded those of radio, *7772*

1954

Air Force general who was African-American, *5135*
Army ballistic missile operational unit, *5192*
Army helicopter battalion, *5191*
Athlete who was African-American to win the James E. Sullivan Memorial Trophy, *1720*
Bevatron, *6805*
Birth-control pill, *6833*
Bridge hand in which each player was dealt a perfect hand, *4025*
Cabinet session to be telecast and broadcast, *6115*
Carrier for liquid bulk chemicals, *6897*
Civil defense test held nationwide, *4089*
College for women founded as a Jewish institution, *2968*
Court-martial of an officer for collaborating with his captors, *2741*

1954—*continued*

Editorial to be broadcast over radio and television, *5707*

Educational television station sponsored by a city, *7803*

Execution carried out by the federal government for the killing of an FBI agent, *2804*

Gas-turbine bus, *5424*

Gas-turbine car, *5456*

Hydraulic-lift parking garage device, *5486*

Intercollegiate court tennis match, *7534*

Jet airplane used for commercial transport, *1403*

Jet drone target missile, *8137*

Major league baseball game in which the majority of the players on one team were African-American, *7136*

Meteorite known to have struck a person, *6682*

Microbiology laboratory, *4932*

Military heliport, *1569*

Moving sidewalk in a railroad station, *6639*

Navy admirals who were brothers, *5294*

Newspaper printed on bagasse newsprint, *5798*

Newspaper vending machine to deliver a single copy, *2399*

Nobel Prize winner to receive awards in two different categories, *1699*

Organ transplant that was successful, *5096*

Phase-contrast cinemicrography film to be shown on television, *5565*

Photoengraving high-speed process, *5696*

Pilot wounded in Vietnam who was a civilian, *8013*

Polystyrene, *4483*

Prison commissioner who was a woman, *2830*

Radio network for African-Americans, *6302*

Radio sextant, *6960*

Railroad freight yard that was fully automatic, *6346*

Refugee to arrive under the Refugee Relief Act of 1953, *5877*

Rocket-driven sled on rails, *7021*

Round-the-world flight over the North Pole on a regularly scheduled air route, *1479*

Senator elected by a write-in vote, *3331*

Shot-put toss over 60 feet, *7562*

Solar energy battery, *3558*

State legislative hearing to be shown on television, *7633*

Telegraph code converter, *7710*

Television commercial in color to appear on a local show, *2346*

Television receiver that showed two programs simultaneously, *7819*

Tissue bank, *4838*

Toll collection machine, *6634*

Transistor radio receiver to be mass-produced, *6312*

Truck driving school, *3300*

Water skier to jump 100 feet, *7593*

1955

Aerocycle, *1570*

Air-conditioned public elementary school, *2120*

Aircraft carrier with an angle deck, *6939*

Army nurse in modern times who was a man, *5173*

Bank to operate a window in a subway station, *3797*

Broadway play shown in a color television version with its original cast, *1266*

Cabinet session held at a place other than the seat of the federal government, *6116*

Checkers champion of renown, *4011*

Compiler programming language, *1655*

Corporation with a net income of more than $1 billion in one year, *2406*

Dugong, *1158*

Electric power generated from nuclear energy to be sold commercially, *3548*

Electric power generated from nuclear energy to illuminate a town, *3547*

Electronic range for domestic use, *4303*

Father and son team to win the national contract bridge championship, *4026*

Federal government building built to withstand a nuclear attack, *2119*

Guaranteed 52-week wage in a major industry, *4570*

Guided missile cruiser, *6940*

House with solar heating and radiation cooling, *2129*

Jewish mobile synagogue, *6491*

King cobra snakes, *1157*

Lung tumor operation in which the patient was under hypnosis, *5086*

Magazine to contain a phonograph record, *4738*

Mass boycott by civil rights protesters, *2259*

McDonald's restaurant, *2464*

Medal of Honor awarded to a helicopter pilot, *1685*

Metropolitan Opera singer who was African-American, *1338*

Microwave television station, *7804*

Minimum hourly wage of one dollar, *4579*

Murder trial to be televised, *4624*

Musical instrument capable of making any audible sound, *1326*

Nuclear-powered submarine, *6973*

Nuclear reactor patent, *6806*

Official use of the "Coke" trademark, *3848*

Offshore radar warning station, *7682*

Oil drill seagoing rig, *3543*

Pilot to bail out of an airplane flying at supersonic speed, *1592*

President of a major medical society who was a woman, *5049*

President to appear on color television, *6215*

Presidential news conference filmed for television and newsreels, *6219*

Remote-controlled railroad passenger car, *6391*

Rock and roll song to hit No. 1 in the pop charts, *1369*

Roll-on-roll-off carrier, *6898*

Seat belt law enacted by a state, *4228*

Solar energy battery to be manufactured commercially, *3559*

Solar-powered car, *5457*

Speedboat to exceed 200 miles per hour, *6953*

Telecast originating live in three countries, *7846*

Telephone call on a commercial line using solar energy, *7746*

Television receivers to project large images, *7820*

Transatlantic telephone service using the transoceanic cable, *7747*

Virus separated into component parts, *5062*

1956

Adaptable railroad freight car, *6392*

Airplane disaster involving more than 100 persons, *1404*

Airplane flight to land at the South Pole, *6733*

All-color television station to televise live local programs, *7805*

Automaton to operate by long-distance control, *3442*

Bank to open a branch in a trailer, *3788*

Baseball pitcher to pitch a perfect no-hit, no-run, no-walk World Series game, *7153*

Billiard player to win a match in the first inning, *4020*

Circular office building, *2066*

Circular school building, *2121*

Clock to operate by nuclear power, *7903*

Coal pipeline, *3509*

College student to receive assistance from the federal government as the child of a deceased veteran, *3014*

Commemorative postal card, *6048*

Congressional representative of Indian ancestry, *2614*

Congressional representative reelected after serving a prison term, *2615*

Containerized shipping, *2487*

Containership, *2487*

Educational television network that was statewide and state-supported, *7806*

Electric portable typewriter, *2390*

Elementary schools to use closed-circuit televisions in teaching, *3069*

Enclosed climate-controlled suburban shopping mall, *2512*

Federal aid to libraries, *4678*

Forest horse, *1184*

Free-piston car, *5458*

Gorilla, *1159*

Heart operation in which the elective cardiac arrest technique was employed, *5094*

Helicopter refueling flight, *1577*

High jump over seven feet, *7563*

Hydrogen bomb dropped from an airplane, *8130*

Instrument for observing radiation in total darkness, *6807*

Liner equipped with a gyrostabilizer, *6899*

Motorcycle to exceed 200 miles per hour, *5491*

Nobel Prize winner to win twice in the same field, *1701*

Nuclear reactor built for private industrial research, *3549*

Oscar for best picture awarded to a movie that was independently produced, *1637*

Pilot on a scheduled passenger line who was African-American, *1604*

Prefrontal lobotomy, *5087*

Presbyterian minister who was a woman, *6584*

Radio receiver with an auxiliary solar-cell power unit, *6313*

Ship outfitted for hurricane research, *6775*

Skyscraper of bronze and glass, *2101*

Space cabin simulator, *7022*

Stock brokerage concern of importance whose president was a woman, *3830*

Stroboradiograph, *6808*

Synthetic mica, *5345*

Transatlantic telephone call carried by the transoceanic telephone cable, *7767*

Transcontinental nonstop helicopter flight, *1578*

Transcontinental trip in a gas-turbine car, *5476*

Universal chapel embracing eight faiths, *6437*

Video recording on magnetic tape televised coast-to-coast, *7847*

Video tape recorder for sounds and pictures, *7821*

Visitor to open the New York Stock Exchange, *3829*

1957

Air Force chairman of the Joint Chiefs of Staff, *5136*

Air-to-ground public telephone service, *7748*

Balloon flight to rise higher than 100,000 feet, *1541*

Charting of the Northwest Passage, *6734*

Circumnavigation of the North American continent by a ship, *6992*

Circumnavigation of the world by a submarine, *6991*

Civic center with an aluminum geodesic dome, *2093*

Commercial building with solar heating, *2067*

Electric watch, *7904*

Flying disk for use in throwing games, *7585*

Installment sales law enacted by a state, *2314*

Insurance company to insure the lives of animals exclusively, *4517*

Intermediate-range ballistic missile, *8138*

Laser, *3443*

National curling championship, *7277*

1957—*continued*

National wheelchair games, *7586*

National women's figure skating four-time winner, *7434*

Nuclear power plant devoted exclusively to peaceful uses, *3551*

Nuclear warhead mounted on a rocket, *8131*

President to fly in a helicopter, *6229*

Public telecast over telephone wires using the narrow-band system, *7848*

Round-the-world nonstop flight by a jet airplane, *1480*

Runner from the United States to run a mile in less than four minutes, *7564*

Senate filibuster to last for more than 24 hours, *2633*

Ship to transport fresh orange juice in stainless-steel tanks, *2488*

Sodium reactor, *3550*

Submarine to remain submerged for two weeks, *6974*

Tennis champion who was African-American, *7538*

Titanium mill, *4478*

Vacuum-cast steel, *4498*

Weight lifter to lift more than 6,000 pounds, *7587*

Welding machine for aluminum pipes, *4420*

Writer to win a Pulitzer Prize four times for drama, *1716*

1958

Air Force academy, *3190*

Airline flight attendant who was an African-American woman, *1412*

Bifocal contact lenses, *5074*

Catholic prelate named to the Roman Curia who was American-born, *6478*

Crossing of the North Pole underwater by a submerged submarine, *6993*

Electronic computer with solid-state components, *2530*

Grammy awards for musical recordings, *1629*

Haflinger horse, *1185*

Highway bridge with welded aluminum girders, *3596*

Integrated circuit, *3444*

Military computer network, *2542*

Molybdenum centrifugal casting, *4479*

Navy nuclear submarine division, *5306*

Navy task force to fight undersea craft, *5305*

Newspaper advertisement printed on aluminum foil, *2347*

Pension for presidents and their widows, *6172*

Presidential Unit Citation award in peacetime, *1643*

Professional hockey player who was African-American, *7380*

Radio broadcast using an orbiting satellite, *6281*

Rocket to intercept a supersonic target missile, *8139*

Sailor to reenlist in the Navy while under the North Pole, *5267*

Satellite placed in orbit by the United States, *7056*

Ship motion simulator to aid in the development of ballistic missiles fired from shipboard, *8121*

Stock exchange director who was a woman, *3831*

Submarine expressly designed and built to fire guided missiles, *6975*

Submarine to travel under the North Pole from the east, *6994*

Telecast from the stratosphere, *7849*

Two-way moving sidewalk, *6640*

Video recording on magnetic tape televised in color, *7850*

1959

Airmail by missile, *6034*

Animals to survive a space flight, *7023*

Astronauts trained by the United States, *7028*

Astronomy photographs in color to be published in a magazine, *6699*

Barbie doll, *2152*

Bowling match that used white balls on black lanes, *7228*

Braille encyclopedia, *1834*

Canal incorporated into a seaway, *3603*

Color photograph of the earth taken from space, *6700*

Computer-aided manufacturing system, *4421*

Congressional representative of Japanese ancestry, *2616*

Golfer to break 60 for 18 holes in a major tournament, *7364*

Golfer to play 24 hours continuously on a regulation course, *7365*

House with a built-in nuclear bomb shelter, *2130*

Jetway, *1510*

Judge of Chinese ancestry, *2728*

Medical slang dictionary, *1810*

Movie premiered simultaneously in major cities throughout the world, *5520*

Movie with scent, *5566*

Nuclear-powered cruiser, *6941*

Nuclear-powered merchant ship, *6900*

Pedestrian shopping mall, *2513*

Pilot to fly a million miles in a jet airplane, *1605*

Play by an African-American woman to appear on Broadway, *1270*

Postage stamp having the same design as that of another country, *6092*

Race-car driver to win $100,000, *7268*

Radar signal bounced off the sun, *7683*

Satellite to transmit photographs of the earth, *7057*

Senator of Chinese ancestry, *2657*

Ship to fire a Polaris missile, *8140*

Ski lifts to be regulated by the state, *7487*

State admitted to the Union that had no border with another state, *7607*

State admitted to the Union that was separated by a substantial body of water, *7608*

Stockholder meetings televised coast-to-coast simultaneously, *3832*

Submarine equipped with ballistic missiles, *6976*

Submarine to have two complete crews, *6977*

Submarine to surface at the North Pole, *6995*

Telecast from space showing the earth, *6690*

Telecast received from England, *7851*

Transcontinental jet airplane passenger service, *1422*

Ultraviolet pictures of the sun, *6698*

1960

American flag to orbit the earth, *1131*

Animated cartoon series on prime-time television, *7786*

Art auction televised on a coast-to-coast circuit, *1230*

Artificial ice skating rink of Olympic size, *7435*

Birth-control pill, *6833*

Bowler to win $10,000 in a tournament, *7229*

Circumnavigation of the earth by a submerged submarine, *6996*

Civil rights anthem to achieve fame, *1383*

Civil rights sit-in, *2260*

Coast-to-coast solar-powered two-way radio conversation, *6282*

Communications satellite, *7063*

Communications satellite with signal reception and transmission equipment, *7065*

Electronic watch, *7905*

Geodesic dome of substantial size, *2094*

Guided missile launched from a nuclear submarine, *8141*

Multisatellite launching, *7061*

Navigational satellite, *7059*

Nuclear-powered submarine with turbine-electric drive, *6978*

Nuclear reactor for research and development, *6809*

Nuclear reactor operated commercially, *3552*

Pacemaker to be implanted in a patient's body, *4953*

Parking meter enforcement division of a police department, *4149*

Photograph bounced off a satellite, *5831*

Photograph bounced off the moon, *5830*

Post office fully mechanized, *6042*

Postage stamp issued jointly by two countries, *6069*

Presidential election debates to be shown on television, *3394*

Professional hockey player to reach a score of more than 1,000 points, *7381*

Scientific program to search for extraterrestrial life, *6672*

Senate election race in which both candidates were women, *2634*

Space capsule recovered from an orbiting satellite, *7062*

Space capsule recovered in midair from an orbiting satellite, *7064*

Spacecraft placed in solar orbit, *7078*

Spy satellite, *7060*

Submarine to make a submerged passage through the Northwest Passage, *6997*

Submerged submarine to fire a Polaris missile, *8142*

Sulfur mine offshore, *5346*

Undersea park established by the federal government, *3739*

Weather satellite to provide cloud-cover photographs, *7058*

World heavyweight boxing champion to regain his crown, *7255*

1961

Air piracy law, *2784*

Air raid shelter for a community, *4090*

Airline to carry 100 million passengers, *1423*

Animal fired into space to orbit the earth, *7024*

Astronaut to be launched into space, *7029*

Baseball player to win Most Valuable Player award in both major leagues, *1724*

Basketball team to score more than 10,000 points, *7176*

Building of large size with a retractable roof, *2095*

Cabinet member who was the brother of the president, *6117*

Championship game of the American Football League, *7331*

Commander of a combat ship who was African-American, *5295*

Deaths in an American nuclear reactor, *3553*

District attorney who was African-American, *2716*

Electric toothbrush, *4076*

Football game to gross $1 million, *7332*

Football player who was African-American to win the Heisman Memorial Trophy, *1726*

Industrial robot that was practical, *3445*

Jazz composition to appear on the Top 40 charts, *1301*

Judge of a federal district court who was African-American, *2729*

Minimum wage law established by a city for public contract work, *4580*

Mobile computer center, *2531*

1961—*continued*

National bone bank to acquire temporal bones for ear research, *4839*

Nuclear-powered aircraft carrier, *6942*

Postage stamp featuring a work of art in true color, *6093*

President who was Catholic, *6203*

Presidential news conference to be televised live, *6220*

Presidential physician who was a woman, *6204*

Private housing development designed as a complete community, *2200*

Quasar to be observed, *6683*

Revolving restaurant, *2465*

Seawater conversion plant, *2237*

Skyjacking law enacted by Congress, *2785*

Skyjacking of a commercial American airplane, *2784*

Television station owned by a religious organization, *6597*

Troops sent to Vietnam, *8014*

Typewriter without type arms, *2391*

Vending machine to dispense fresh flowers, *2400*

1962

Air Force Academy graduate who was Native American, *3191*

Aluminum cans with tab openings, *4289*

Astronaut to orbit the earth, *7030*

Athlete who was an African-American woman to win the James E. Sullivan Memorial Trophy, *1721*

Baseball coach in the major leagues who was African-American, *7103*

Baseball player to steal more than 100 bases in a season, *7154*

Children's hospital for research and treatment of catastrophic childhood diseases, *4893*

Christmas postage stamp regular issue, *6094*

Coast-to-coast telecast by satellite, *7852*

Commercial satellite, *7069*

Computer game, *4012*

Ecology book, *1991*

Exhibition of the *Mona Lisa* in the United States, *1231*

Geodetic satellite, *7070*

Indoor ski slope, *7488*

International satellite, *7067*

Launching silos for Atlas F missiles, *8143*

Limb reattachment, *5088*

Live telecast to Europe by satellite, *7854*

Newspaper reproduced commercially and regularly by radio facsimile, *5658*

Nobel Prize winner to receive awards in two different categories, *1699*

Nuclear warhead fired from a Polaris submarine, *8132*

Orbiting solar observatory, *7066*

Pay television dramatic program, *7787*

Pilot of an airplane to qualify as an astronaut by attaining a 50-mile altitude, *1623*

Postage stamp issued on the date of the event it commemorated, *6070*

President with a brother in the Senate, *6205*

Presidential hot line, *6173*

Running shoes, *2306*

Satellite from the United States to impact the moon, *7068*

Senator of Japanese ancestry, *2616*

Ship with a floating scientific instrument platform, *6717*

Smog chamber for air pollution research, *3717*

Spacecraft to transmit data from Venus, *7079*

State to have a state sport, *7600*

Subway train to run automatically without conductors or motormen, *6413*

Swimmer to swim the English Channel underwater, *7520*

Telephone call conveyed by a privately owned satellite, *7768*

Television news commentator who was African-American, *5620*

Transoceanic telecast by satellite, *7853*

Wal-Mart store, *2514*

World's Fair that was financially successful, *2415*

1963

Air Force Academy graduates who were African-American, *3192*

Air pollution law of importance enacted by Congress, *3718*

Amphibious vehicle, *6943*

Armored division transported by airplanes to a foreign country, *5193*

Artificial leather, *7878*

Ascent of Mount Everest by an American, *7588*

Ban on sex discrimination in wages enacted by Congress, *6834*

Bank of importance to lease personal property, *3798*

Bridge player to win more than 1,000 master points in one year, *4027*

Commemorative postage stamp depicting a president's wife, *6095*

Computer graphics software, *2548*

Domed sports stadium, *7511*

Elliptical office building, *2096*

Geosynchronous satellite, *7071*

Gerenuk, *1160*

Golfer to earn over $100,000 in one year, *7366*

Honorary citizenship authorized by Congress, *5878*

Illuminated nine-hole regulation golf course, *7350*

International postal card, *6049*

Liver transplant, *5097*

Lung transplant, *5098*

Murder to be shown live on television, *2786*

Naval War College students who were African-American, *3220*
Nuclear reactor fueled by plutonium, *3554*
Photograph of the Senate in session, *2635*
Postage stamp with fluorescent tagging, *6071*
President to witness the firing of a Polaris missile, *6174*
Quintuplets to live more than five years, *2176*
Supercomputer, *2532*
Telecast transmitted by satellite to Japan, *7855*
Telephone with push buttons, *7726*
Television receiver and transmitter operated by laser beam, *7822*
Trimline telephone, *7725*
Zip codes, *6013*

1964

Atomic-powered lighthouse, *4129*
Automated tanker under the American flag, *6902*
Bridge designed by computer, *3597*
Campus takeover by student protesters, *3015*
Cargo ship fully automated and flying the American flag, *6901*
Catholic mass in English, *6479*
Computer-aided design (CAD) software, *2549*
Courtroom verdict to be televised, *2717*
Election in the District of Columbia, *3325*
Former president to address the Senate, *6175*
Freeze-dried coffee, *3853*
Large commercial computer network, *2543*
Made-for-TV movie, *7789*
Medal of Honor awarded in the Vietnam war, *1686*
Methadone program, *2692*
Musical to run for more than 3,000 performances, *1271*
Navy divers to submerge for 10 days, *5268*
Navy nuclear task force to circumnavigate the globe without refueling, *5307*
Navy pilot shot down and captured in North Vietnam, *8015*
Occupation of federal territory by Native American protesters in the modern era, *5977*
Orbiting geophysical observatory, *7073*
Oscar for best actor awarded to a performer who was African-American, *1633*
Performance by a British rock group, *1370*
Photographs of the moon in close-up, *6701*
Picturephone commercial service, *7750*
Postage stamps of four different designs sold as a single sheet, *6096*
Presidential election in which votes were tallied electronically, *3395*
Rocket with an electrostatic (ion) engine, *7025*
Russian Orthodox saint canonized in the United States, *6498*
Seat belts in cars, *4229*
Self-service post office, *6043*
Soap opera on prime-time television, *7788*

Spacecraft to transmit close-up photographs of the lunar surface, *7080*
Toy action figure, *2153*
Transcontinental Picturephone call, *7769*
Transpacific telephone service using the transoceanic cable, *7749*
Transplant of an animal organ into a human being, *5099*
Typewriter that could retype text automatically, *2392*
United Nations permanent ambassador who was a woman, *3993*
Weather satellite to provide high-resolution cloud-cover photographs at night, *7072*
Word processor, *2392*
Year when citizens of the District of Columbia could vote in a presidential election, *3434*

1965

All-news radio station, *6303*
Ambassador who was an African-American woman, *3994*
American Stock Exchange members who were women, *3831*
Astronaut to converse with an aquanaut, *7033*
Astronaut to orbit the earth on two trips, *7032*
Astronaut to walk in space, *7031*
Astronauts to rendezvous in space with another spacecraft, *7034*
Baseball player to play all nine positions in one game, *7155*
Cabinet meeting attended by a foreign national, *6118*
Cassette audio tape recorder, *7016*
Catholic bishop who was an American-born African-American, *6480*
Coins bearing dates other than the year of issue, *5380*
Congressional page who was African-American, *2592*
Demonstration in Washington against the Vietnam War, *8017*
Discotheque, *3631*
Educational computer programming language, *2550*
Federal aid program for primary and secondary schools, *3070*
Flashbulb device with multiple flashbulbs, *5847*
Ground troops sent to Vietnam, *8016*
Health insurance plan enacted by Congress, *4541*
Hotel built over a pier, *2434*
Master skyscraper antenna, *6314*
Minicomputer, *2533*
Narcotics ban enacted by a state, *2691*
Naval ship with a crew of mixed nationalities, *6944*
Perfecta or Exacta horse race, *7403*
Pope to visit the United States, *4083*

1965—*continued*

Satellite with a nuclear reactor to orbit the earth, *7074*

Senate page who was African-American, *2636*

Singles bar, *2466*

Spacecraft to transmit close-up photographs of Mars, *7081*

State law to end de facto segregation in schools, *2261*

State supreme court chief justice who was a woman, *2730*

Surgical operation on a bull to correct a sperm block, *5124*

Swimmer from the United States to make a round-trip crossing of the English Channel, *7521*

Teach-in against the Vietnam War, *8017*

Television dramatic series in which an African-American performer had a starring role, *7790*

Transatlantic undersea radio conversation, *6283*

1966

Astronaut who was a civilian to orbit the earth, *7035*

Black Power advocate, *2262*

Brother and sister to win national tennis singles championships in the same tournament, *7539*

Cabinet member who was African-American, *6119*

Car with front-wheel drive, *5459*

Catgut substitute, *4958*

Coach of a professional basketball team who was African-American, *7177*

Coast Guard Academy graduate who was African-American, *3210*

Computer modem that was practical, *2534*

Endangered species list issued by the federal government, *3719*

Judge of a federal district court who was an African-American woman, *2729*

Kwanzaa celebration, *4249*

Manned docking of two spacecraft, *7082*

Marathon runner from the United States who was a woman, *7565*

Medal of Honor awarded posthumously in the Vietnam War to an African-American soldier, *1687*

Medal of Honor awarded to a Seabee, *1688*

Medicare identification cards, *4541*

Motorboat ocean race, *7218*

Navy captain who was African-American, *5296*

Parachute jumper snagged by airplane in midair, *1593*

Photograph of a solar eclipse taken from the atmosphere, *6703*

Photograph of the earth taken from the moon, *6702*

Rocket-tracking ship, *6945*

Senator who was African-American to be elected by popular vote, *2658*

Sergeant major of the Army, *5174*

Spacecraft to transmit photographs from lunar orbit, *7083*

Video tape recorder for home use, *7823*

X-ray three-dimensional stereo fluoroscopic system, *4911*

1967

Abortion legalized by a state as a medical procedure, *6835*

Artificial insemination for women to be permitted by a state, *5117*

Astronauts to die in a spacecraft, *7036*

Attorney general whose father also served as attorney general, *6125*

Be-In, *3668*

Bowling automatic scoring machine, *7230*

British-made television series, *7791*

Computer programming language for children, *2551*

Educational television network operated as a nonprofit corporation, *7807*

Electric spinning reel, *7943*

Freezing of a corpse for future resuscitation, *2841*

General killed in Vietnam by enemy fire, *8018*

Gravure-printed postage stamp, *6074*

Heart transplant, *5100*

High school for pregnant teenage girls, *3092*

Horse motel, *2435*

Jockey to win seven consecutive races in one day, *7414*

Large-type weekly newspaper, *5659*

Mayor of a major city who was African-American, *2209*

New York Stock Exchange seat owner who was a woman, *3833*

Postage stamp issued in the United States and canceled by a foreign country, *6072*

Public defender hired by a state, *4642*

Quark to be observed, *6821*

Rock and roll broadcast on FM radio, *1371*

Rock music festival, *1372*

Rock musical, *1272*

Satellite to transmit colored photographs of the full earth face, *7075*

Ship with a combined diesel and gas-turbine engine, *6946*

Super Bowl football game, *7333*

Supreme Court justice who was African-American, *2763*

Twin postage stamps, *6073*

Underground comic book of note, *4739*

Worldwide live television program, *7856*

Zen Buddhist monastery, *6439*

1968

Ambassador assassinated in office, *3995*

Ambulance equipped for mobile coronary care, *4826*

1970—*continued*

Physician with a mobile medical office, *4979*

President of a major university who was African-American, *2975*

Professional football game in which a woman participated, *7334*

Sky marshals, *4150*

Sneakers, *2307*

Strike of postal employees, *4601*

Surgical facility outside a hospital, *5089*

United Nations Security Council resolution vetoed by the United States, *3981*

1971

Air Force general who was a woman, *5140*

Air Force military engineer who was a woman, *5139*

Airport baggage scanning system, *1511*

Astronaut to become an admiral, *7043*

Astronauts to ride a vehicle on the moon, *7042*

Athlete who was a woman to earn more than $100,000 in one season, *7540*

Book collection of importance on ultramicrofiche, *4687*

Books of postage stamps with humidity-resistant adhesive, *6075*

Brokerage firm whose shares were traded by a major stock exchange, *3835*

College to offer courses to railroad commuters, *3003*

College whose tuition fees were based on family income, *2970*

Crime insurance policy authorized by a state, *4518*

Electronic pocket calculator, *3447*

Floppy disk, *2536*

Football game to last longer than 80 minutes, *7335*

Ice skater to cover 100 miles in less than six hours, *7436*

Litter law enacted by a state, *3720*

Mayor of a major city who was a woman, *2210*

Motorcycle racer who was a woman, *7440*

Off-track betting operation, *3637*

Road paved with glasphalt, *6635*

Satellite launched from the earth to orbit another planet, *7076*

Secret Service agents who were women, *4170*

Skyjacking in which the skyjacker disappeared, *2787*

Sport played on the moon, *7026*

Technical school for Native Americans, *3302*

Train to transport passengers and their cars, *6435*

Veterinary hospital established by a city, *5125*

Vote in the House of Representatives to be tallied by machine, *2593*

1972

Acupuncture treatment center, *4852*

Air Force ace in Vietnam, *1624*

Astronaut to become a general, *7044*

Attorney general to plead guilty to a criminal offense, *6126*

Bank to provide movies for customers waiting in line, *3801*

Birth rate below the rate necessary to maintain the population, *5855*

Chairman of a major political party who was a woman, *3344*

Congressional candidate elected while missing, *2619*

Dow Jones Industrial Average to exceed 1,000 points, *3836*

Electric power using municipal garbage as a boiler fuel, *3489*

Geologist to reach the moon, *6718*

Horse race for a purse of more than $1 million, *7404*

Metropolitan Opera orchestra conductor who was African-American, *1339*

Minister who was openly homosexual, *6837*

Naval ship named for an African-American naval officer, *1618*

Navy admiral who was African-American, *5274*

New York Stock Exchange director who was African-American, *3834*

New York Stock Exchange governor who was a woman, *3833*

Nobel Prize winner to win twice in the same field, *1701*

Noise-control law enacted by a state, *3721*

Pictorial postal cards, *6050*

President to visit a nation not recognized by the federal government, *6238*

President to visit the Soviet Union, *6238*

Sailors assigned to regular Navy shipboard duty who were women, *5269*

Satellite composite map of the United States, *4802*

Snowmobile to exceed a speed of 125 miles per hour, *7491*

Spacecraft to carry a message intended to be read by living beings elsewhere in the universe, *7084*

Stereo telecast, *7857*

United Church of Christ ordination of a woman in which all the principal roles were filled by women, *6536*

Vice presidential candidate of a major political party to resign before the election, *3417*

Video game, *4013*

World chess champion from the United States, *4033*

1973

Airborne express delivery service, *2489*

Armed occupation by Native American protesters in the modern era, *5978*

Artificial gene, *5063*

Balloon flight powered by solar energy, *1542*
Belly-dancing course at a college, *2916*
College to offer athletic scholarships to women, *3004*
Commercial crude-oil carrier, *6903*
Congressional representative to give birth while holding office, *2620*
Designated hitter in a major league baseball game, *7157*
Designated hitter rule, *7157*
Electoral vote for a woman, *3396*
Federal marshals who were women, *4151*
Food processor, *4304*
Golfer to earn $100,000 in a contest, *7367*
Hang-gliding national championships, *7300*
Homosexual rights organization, *6838*
Jockey who was a woman to win a major stakes race, *7419*
Metric distance markers on a state highway, *6636*
Native American superintendent of an agency of the Bureau of Indian Affairs, *5972*
Navy chaplain who was a woman, *5205*
Navy officer who was a woman to hold a major command, *5297*
Nazi death camp guard to be deported, *5880*
Photograph of a comet taken from space, *6704*
Physician to practice as an astronaut in space, *7045*
Pilot on a regularly scheduled major airline who was a woman, *1606*
Presidential Citizen Medal, *1644*
Prison guard who was a woman to serve in a maximum security prison for men, *2831*
Probate delay law enacted by a state, *2842*
Role-playing game, *4014*
Skyscraper higher than 1,400 feet in height, *2102*
Space station launched by the United States, *7085*
Vice president chosen under the 25th Amendment, *6249*
Vote in the House of Representatives to be recorded electronically, *2594*
Zoo with twilight conditions, *1191*

1974

Congressional representative who was a grandmother, *2621*
Democratic Party convention between presidential elections, *3379*
Free agents in major league baseball, *7158*
Magazine about recreational drugs, *4740*
Member of the Navy's Hurricane Hunters who was a woman, *5298*
Merchant Marine Academy cadets who were women, *3308*
Motorcycle jump across a river canyon, *3682*
Navy chaplain who was an African-American woman, *5206*

Personal computer, *2537*
Personal computer operating system, *2546*
Police officer who was a woman to be killed in the line of duty, *4152*
Politician who was openly homosexual to win an election, *6839*
President to receive a presidential pardon, *6179*
President to resign, *6177*
President who came to the office through appointment rather than election, *6178*
Pressure-sensitive adhesive postage stamp, *6076*
Round-the-world journey on foot, *7590*
Senate proceeding to be shown on television, *2637*
Senator who had been an astronaut, *2660*
Speed limit for highway traffic established by Congress, *4230*
State library to publish a master catalog, *4679*
Tightrope walker to span two skyscrapers, *3669*

1975

Adjustable stadium, *7512*
Astronauts to participate in an international spaceflight, *7046*
Bowler to earn $100,000 in one year in tournaments, *7232*
Catholic saint who was born in America, *6481*
Chief justice of a state supreme court who was African-American, *2720*
College commencement exercises in a prison, *2982*
Commercial software for personal computers, *2552*
Divorce rate of more than 1 million a year, *4811*
Dog hotel, *2436*
Emperor of Japan to visit the United States, *6655*
Military service academies' enrollment of women, *3189*
Mother and son to enlist simultaneously in the Army, *5175*
Postage stamps without a denomination, *6077*
Sex discrimination law enacted by a state that affected high school athletic competitions, *6840*
Ski carousel, *7489*
Soapbox derby winner who was a girl, *7583*
Spacecraft to land on Mars, *7086*
Strike by physicians against long working hours in hospitals, *4602*
Trial in which lawyers appeared on a Picturephone, *4625*
Video cassette recorder for home use, *7823*
Whooping crane, *1169*

1976

Air Force Academy cadets who were women, *3193*

1976—*continued*

Ambulance ship for first aid to boaters and pleasure craft, *4827*

Bridge named for a woman, *3598*

Congressional representative of Polish ancestry, *2623*

Congressional representatives to marry each other, *2622*

General of the Armies of the United States with the rank of six stars, *5161*

Graduate of a four-year maritime school who was a woman, *3309*

Metropolitan Opera orchestra conductor who was a woman, *1340*

Naval Academy students who were women, *3221*

Nuclear commercial power plant licensed operator who was a woman, *3555*

Photograph taken on Mars, *6705*

Postage stamp depicting a nurse, *6099*

Postage stamps of 50 different designs sold as a single sheet, *6098*

Presidential election debate between an incumbent president and a challenger to be televised, *3397*

Right-to-die law enacted by a state, *2843*

Satellite dish for personal use, *7824*

Soccer player to score 12 points in one game, *7494*

Softball game of 365 innings, *7498*

Speaker to deliver the keynote speech at a Democratic National Convention who was African-American, *2617*

State dinner televised from the White House, *6258*

Television network evening news program anchor who was a woman, *5621*

Thread as strong as steel, *7880*

Transatlantic supersonic jet service, *1424*

Underground school, *2122*

Voice reader, *2538*

Voluntary sterilization regulation enacted by a state, *6841*

West Point cadets who were women, *3207*

Year in which Nobel Prizes were won by Americans in five of six categories, *1702*

1977

Artwork to incorporate lightning, *1220*

Attorney general to be incarcerated, *6127*

Baby carrier, *2154*

Border-to-border national highway, *6637*

Cabinet member who was an African-American woman, *6121*

Catholic saint who was a male American citizen, *6482*

Coast Guard airplane pilot who was a woman, *5213*

Coast Guard officers who were women who served aboard ships, *5214*

Daily state lotteries with the same winning daily number, *3644*

Daughters of the American Revolution member who was African-American, *5718*

Diesel cars to be mass-produced, *5460*

Driver who was a woman to compete in the Indianapolis 500, *7269*

Episcopal priest who was a woman, *6553*

Federally chartered bank owned and managed by women, *3789*

Golfer to break 60 in a Professional Golfers Association tour, *7368*

Homosexual character in a television sitcom, *6845*

Human-powered aircraft, *1406*

Jockey to win more than $5 million in purses in one year, *7420*

Judge who had served time in prison, *2731*

Lethal injection as a method of execution, *2805*

Magnetic resonance image of a human body, *4912*

Naval War College president who was a former prisoner of war, *3222*

Orca, *1161*

Parade in which the marching music was supplied by transistor radios, *3670*

President to take the oath of office using a nickname, *6180*

Radio broadcast in which citizens telephoned the president, *6221*

Suicidal person to jump off the Empire State Building and live, *2844*

1978

Astronauts who were women, *7047*

Ballet transmitted by satellite, *1238*

Bilingual report of a congressional committee, *2595*

Casino outside the state of Nevada, *3638*

Coin bearing the likeness of an American woman, *5381*

First Lady to pilot an airship, *6132*

Football game in which referees were allowed to check television instant replays, *7336*

Graphic novel, *4737*

Marine general who was a woman, *5240*

Medicine produced using recombinant DNA, *5004*

Moon of Pluto to be observed, *6684*

Mormon man ordained to the priesthood who was African-American, *6494*

Newspaper whose contents were transmitted by a communications satellite, *5660*

Postage stamp depicting an African-American woman, *6100*

Slot machine payoff of $275,000, *3639*

Sports bra, *2281*

Transatlantic balloon flight, *1543*

University president who was a woman, *2971*

1979

Army general who was an African-American woman, *5162*

Boxer to win world titles in five weight divisions, *7256*

Coal miner who was a woman to be killed in a mining accident, *3510*

Coast Guard ship commander who was a woman, *5215*

Goalie in a National Hockey League team to score a goal, *7382*

Golfer to shoot below his age, *7369*

Homosexual rights march, *6842*

Hostage crisis, *3982*

Human-powered aircraft to cross the English Channel, *1406*

Judge of the U.S. Court of Appeals who was an African-American woman, *2732*

Marine general who was African-American, *5241*

New York Stock Exchange seat owner of Chinese ancestry, *3837*

Nuclear power plant to sustain a major accident, *3556*

Oceanographer of distinction who was a woman, *6719*

Pen with truly erasable ink, *8155*

Pope to visit the White House, *4084*

Rocket-powered car to break the sound barrier on land, *5461*

Solar-powered long-distance airplane flight, *1481*

Train operated exclusively by women, *6436*

Transfusion of artificial blood, *4840*

1980

Acoustic microscope, *6750*

Coast Guard Academy graduates who were women, *3211*

Cuban boatlift, *5881*

Debate among party hopefuls for the presidential nomination to be shown on television, *3398*

Human antibodies produced artificially, *5005*

In-line roller skate that was commercially successful, *7466*

Methodist bishop who was a woman, *6562*

Olympic Games boycott, *7450*

Power plant using solar cells, *3560*

Solar-powered airplane to cross the English Channel, *1481*

State police class in which women completed training, *4153*

Subcompact car with front wheel drive, *5462*

Synthetic fuels plant, *3522*

Tank with a turbine engine, *8122*

Transcontinental nonstop balloon flight, *1544*

Volcano known to claim human life, *2871*

West Point graduate who was a Jewish woman, *3195*

1981

AIDS epidemic, *2878*

Ambassador to the United Nations who was a woman, *3996*

Child born in the United States through in vitro fertilization, *2166*

Editor of a major daily newspaper who was a woman, *5622*

Graphical user interface for a commercial computer, *2547*

Mayor of a major city who was of Mexican descent, *2211*

President to be wounded in an unsuccessful assassination attempt while in office, *6207*

Product liability lawsuit to result in a criminal trial, *2315*

Reusable manned spacecraft, *7087*

Supreme Court justice who was a woman, *2765*

Transplant of artificial skin, *5102*

1982

Athlete who was a woman to earn more than $1 million in a year, *7541*

Heart transplant using an artificial heart that was intended to be permanent, *5103*

National Navajo Code Talkers Day, *8082*

Poisoning of store merchandise, *2788*

Police chief who was both African-American and Jewish, *4154*

Round-the-world helicopter flight, *1579*

1983

Astronaut to fly in space who was African-American, *7049*

Astronaut who was a woman to fly in space, *7048*

Cellular telephone system, *7727*

Compact disc players, *7003*

Data from interstellar space, *7088*

DNA chain polymerization, *5065*

Execution by lethal injection, *2806*

Identification of the AIDS virus, *5064*

Movie for which one woman served as producer, director, and star, *5568*

Presidential candidate who had been an astronaut, *3418*

Quintuplets to survive infancy who were African-American, *2177*

Spacecraft to leave the solar system, *7088*

Teacher testing requirement to be enacted by a state, *3071*

1984

Astronaut who was a mother, *7048*

Astronauts to fly free in space, *7050*

Heart transplant using a baboon heart, *5104*

Methodist bishop who was an African-American woman, *6562*

Miss America who was African-American, *3628*

1984—*continued*

Rap album to attract a mass audience, *1373*

Salvage operation in space, *7089*

Satellite repair in orbit, *7077*

Transatlantic solo balloon flight, *1545*

Vice presidential candidate from a major political party who was a woman, *3419*

Year in which the average price of a new house topped $100,000, *2201*

1985

Cabinet member indicted while in office, *6122*

Fullerenes to be observed, *6822*

Rabbi in the Conservative movement who was a woman, *6490*

Senator to fly in space, *7051*

Septuplets, *2178*

Vending machine for art, *2401*

1986

Bicyclist from the United States to win the Tour de France, *7199*

Fortune 1000 company to be owned and chaired by a woman, *2407*

Genetically altered plants, *1028*

Genetically altered virus approved for use in a vaccine, *5066*

Human chain across the United States, *3671*

Martin Luther King Day, *4251*

MX intercontinental ballistic missile base, *8144*

Poet laureate of the United States, *2034*

Round-the-world nonstop airplane flight without refueling, *1482*

Space shuttle disaster, *7090*

1987

Art museum devoted to work by women, *5599*

Condom commercials on television, *6843*

Drug for treating AIDS, *5006*

Interactive multimedia authoring program, *2553*

Parental leave law enacted by a state that applied to both mothers and fathers, *4571*

Principal chief of the Cherokee Nation who was a woman, *4085*

Superconducting material that operated at relatively high temperatures, *6823*

Swimmer to cross the Bering Strait, *7522*

Treaty to reduce the number of nuclear missiles, *4007*

Trial of a surrogate mother for refusing to give up her baby, *2167*

Undersea hotel, *2437*

Wolf to be reintroduced into the wild, *3750*

Year in which the federal budget exceeded $1 trillion, *3752*

1988

African-American history trail, *5979*

American to be recognized by Tibetan Buddhists as a reincarnated lama, *6440*

Anti-aging skin cream, *4063*

Ascent of Mount Everest by an American woman, *7588*

Ban on cheap handguns enacted by a state, *4155*

Ban on surrogate motherhood enacted by a state, *2168*

Compensation of Japanese-Americans interned during World War II, *8087*

Computer hacker to be convicted, *2789*

Cyber cafe, *2467*

Episcopal bishop who was a woman, *6553*

Factoring of a 100-digit number, *6760*

High school chapter of Alcoholics Anonymous, *2662*

Motorcycle trip from the United States to Tierra del Fuego by a woman, *5494*

Patent on an animal, *6751*

Smoking ban on airplane flights, *2700*

Texas Ranger who was African-American, *4134*

Year when half of the nation's agricultural counties were designated disaster areas, *2872*

Zebra mussels, *1162*

1989

Air bag requirement by the federal government, *4231*

Airship that was certified by the Federal Aviation Administration, *1528*

Army officer who was a woman to lead troops in combat, *5176*

Chairman of a major political party who was African-American, *3345*

Chairman of the Joint Chiefs of Staff who was African-American, *5129*

Drug control chief appointed by the federal government, *2693*

Governor who was African-American, *7621*

Human-powered helicopter, *1571*

Human-powered submarine race, *7219*

Japanese high school in the United States, *3093*

Liver transplant from a live donor, *5105*

Mayor of New York City who was African-American, *2212*

Stealth aircraft, *1493*

Surgeon general who was a woman, *4214*

World Series disrupted by an earthquake, *7137*

1990

Charles Stark Draper Prize for engineering and technology, *1645*

Death by suicide machine, *2845*

Fat substitute in prepared foods, *3886*

Gene therapy, *5118*

Killer bees, *1163*

Native American Day, *4252*

Orbiting observatory, *6673*

Physical manipulation of individual atoms, *6824*
Pulitzer Prize awarded to a comic book, *1717*
Pulitzer prize awarded to a science book, *1718*
Robot to make pizza, *3448*
Round-the-world solo sailing trip by an African-American, *7002*
Telescope of importance with a compound objective mirror, *6674*
Tomatoes from space, *3906*
Tooth-wear gauge, *4867*

1991

Air Force general who was an African-American woman, *5141*
American to hug the Queen of England, *6656*
Cruise missiles used in war, *8145*
Destruction of an attacking missile by a defensive missile in combat, *8146*
Educational multimedia CD-ROM, *2554*
Grandmother to give birth to her own grandchild, *2169*
Medal of Technology awarded to a woman, *1655*
Navy officer who was a woman to command a ship at sea, *5299*
Ornithopter that succeeded in flying, *1407*
Photograph taken close up of an asteroid in space, *6706*
Pilot to destroy an enemy airplane in the Gulf War, *7973*
Pilot who was a woman to die in a combat zone, *1625*
President whose body was exhumed, *6208*
Serviceman killed in the Gulf War, *7974*
Soccer world champion who was a woman, *7495*
Superconducting motor, *6810*
War that was predicted by pizza orders, *7972*

1992

Alternative medicine department in a federal research institution, *5067*
Animated film inducted into the National Film Registry, *5538*
Astronaut to fly in space who was an African-American woman, *7049*
Car fueled by methanol, *5463*
Husband and wife to fly in space together, *7052*
Library to possess 100 million items, *4680*
Liver transplant using a baboon liver, *5106*
Motor vehicles powered by natural gas, *5508*
Olympic athlete to win two consecutive heptathlon events, *7567*
Pilot who was a woman to be inducted into the Army Aviation Hall of Fame, *1625*
Poet laureate who was a woman, *2034*
Postage stamp whose design was decided by popular vote, *6101*

Professional hockey player who was a woman, *7383*
Senator who was an African-American woman, *2661*

1993

Advertisement on a space vehicle, *2348*
AIDS policy coordinator for the federal government, *4192*
Amateur boxing match for women, *7247*
Attorney general who was a woman, *6128*
Bacterium to be discovered that was visible to the naked eye, *6752*
Bombing of a skyscraper by foreign terrorists, *2790*
First Lady who was also a federal official, *6133*
Horse grooming products sold for human use, *4064*
Jockey who was a woman to win a Triple Crown race, *7421*
Mathematical proof of Fermat's last theorem, *6761*
Movie broadcast on the Internet, *5521*
Museum commemorating the Holocaust, *5592*
Nobel Prize for literature awarded to an African-American writer, *1703*
Optical computer, *2539*
Serviceman to die in Somalia, *7982*
Sheriff who was an African-American woman, *4156*
Subway service in Los Angeles, *6414*
Supreme Court justice who was a Jewish woman, *2762*
Surgeon general who was African-American, *4215*

1994

Basketball leagues for women to attract significant attendance at games, *7178*
Criminal convicted on the evidence of DNA matching, *4167*
Genetically altered food, *3840*
Genetically engineered product to appear in food, *3839*
Golf champion of African-American and Asian descent, *7370*
Holographic data storage system, *2540*
Movie that cost more than $100 million to make, *5522*
Navy chaplain who was a Muslim, *5207*
Political asylum granted on grounds of sexual orientation, *5882*
Sailor to become a four-star admiral, *5275*
Team to achieve a perfect score in the International Mathematical Olympiad, *3249*
World Cup soccer tournament held in the United States, *7496*
Year in which the prison population exceeded 1 million, *2832*

1995

Bombing by domestic terrorists resulting in large loss of life, *2791*
Brown dwarf star to be discovered, *6685*
Chicken pox vaccine, *4925*
Coptic Orthodox Church bishop, *6500*
Encyclopedia of integer sequences, *6763*
Forest canopy crane to be used in North America, *6753*
High-resolution maps of the ocean floor, *4803*
Molecular measuring machine, *6811*
Movie that was entirely computer-animated, *5539*
Natural medicine clinic subsidized by a government, *4853*
Patent on a number, *6764*
Planetary probe to enter the atmosphere of Jupiter, *7092*
Robot to perform surgery, *3449*
Spacecraft launched by the United States to dock with a Russian space station, *7091*
Theory of fair division, *6762*
Triplets born several weeks apart, *2179*
West Point cadet who was a woman to graduate at the top of her class, *3208*

1996

Astronaut who was a woman to live in a space station, *7054*
Astronaut who was a woman to pilot the space shuttle, *7053*
Auction of radio spectrum for satellite services, *6284*
Boxer who was a woman to earn national recognition, *7257*
Census based on a sample of the population, *5856*
Chess computer to beat the world chess champion, *4034*
Commercial DNA bank, *6756*
Company to pay a fine of $100 million for a price-fixing scheme, *2525*
Computer software application on Digital Video Disc, *2555*
Electric car to be mass-produced, *5464*
Holiday stamp jointly issued by the United States and another country, *6069*
Home screening kit for HIV infection, *4954*
Medals of Honor awarded to African-American servicemen for service in World War II, *1689*
Minister who was a transsexual, *6844*
Painting by an African-American artist to hang in the White House, *1221*
Pilot of a B-52 bomber who was a woman, *1626*

Police officer who was a Chassidic Jew, *4157*
Political asylum granted to avoid genital mutilation, *5883*
Scientific evidence for life on Mars, *7027*
Serviceman killed during the Bosnia conflict, *7983*
Television station to regularly broadcast high-definition television, *7808*
Transplant of a major organ into a person with mental retardation, *5107*
Women's boxing match to be broadcast live on national television, *7257*

1997

Ambassador to Vietnam after the end of the Vietnam War, *3997*
Art museum of importance devoted to the work of an individual woman, *5600*
Ban on federal funding for human cloning research, *6755*
Cloning of a primate from an embryo, *6754*
Complete DNA sequencing of a free-living organism, *6757*
Comprehensive digital atlas of the human body, *4913*
Dow Jones Industrial Average to exceed 7,000 points, *3838*
Executive officer of a man-of-war who was a woman, *5300*
First Lady to be depicted on a monument to a president, *6134*
Human stem cells to be cultured in a laboratory, *5068*
Joint space walk by American and Russian astronauts, *7055*
Kosher cyber cafe, *2467*
Microscopic cantilever, *6825*
Movie shown on a television network without interruption by commercials, *7793*
Movie to earn more than $400 million in the United States market, *5523*
President to use the line-item veto, *6181*
Robot to conduct a roving exploration of the surface of another planet, *7093*
Secretary of state who was a woman, *6123*
Space burial, *2846*
Telephone directory with internet addresses, *1821*
Television network sitcom to feature a lead character who was homosexual, *6845*
Teraflop computer, *2541*
Tobacco sales to minors to be restricted by federal regulations, *2701*
Transplant of human embryo tissue, *5108*
Voting rights in space, *3435*

Index by Days

The following is a chronological listing of entries, arranged by month and day. To find an entry in the main body of text, please go to the italicized number.

January 1—*continued*
1977 Episcopal priest who was a woman, *6553*

January 2

1777 Army chaplain killed in action, *5195*
1811 Senator to be censured, *2643*
1828 Washington news correspondent, *5611*
1842 Wire suspension bridge for general traffic, *3576*
1854 Governor to be removed from office by a state supreme court, *7612*
1893 Commemorative postage stamps, *6084*
Postage stamp with valuation of one dollar, *6060*
Postage stamps depicting a woman, *6085*
Postage stamps to feature paintings, *6086*
1906 Air conditioner patent, *4413*
1914 Community trust charity, *5742*
1918 Wound chevron issued by the Army, *5225*
1919 Navy destroyer named for a Confederate officer, *6933*
1921 Religious service broadcast on radio, *6589*
1934 Liquor stores run by a state government, *2505*
1936 Electron tube, *3437*
1970 President of a major university who was African-American, *2975*

January 3

1831 Building and loan association, *3763*
1872 Patent list, *2027*
1876 Free kindergarten, *3075*
1890 Dairy school at a college, *2897*
1921 Weather forecast broadcast on radio, *6769*
1930 Car trip made with a diesel engine, *5474*
1933 State speaker of the House who was a woman, *7628*
1939 Congressional page who was female, *2590*
1940 Congress in session a full year, *2570*
1945 Congressional representative who had been an actress, *2612*
School completely irradiated with germicidal lamps, *4191*
1947 Cancer prevention clinic for children, *4850*
Congressional opening session to be televised, *2571*
1953 Three brothers from one family to serve in the Senate, *2656*
1957 Electric watch, *7904*
1959 State admitted to the Union that had no border with another state, *7607*
1961 Deaths in an American nuclear reactor, *3553*
1976 Congressional representatives to marry each other, *2622*

1977 Judge who had served time in prison, *2731*

January 4

1831 Locomotive bid, *6351*
1869 School for blind African-American students, *3026*
1885 Appendectomy, *5080*
1896 Actors' union, *4615*
1915 Governor who was Jewish, *7617*
1939 Dean of a university graduate school who was a woman, *2974*
1953 Carpeting of tufted plastic, *4319*
1962 Subway train to run automatically without conductors or motormen, *6413*
1965 Naval ship with a crew of mixed nationalities, *6944*

January 5

1643 Divorce, *4806*
1863 Teacher training school principal who was a woman, *3264*
1885 Piggyback railroad operation, *6338*
1887 Library school at a college, *3099*
1895 Enclave, *2195*
1933 Bridge with piers sunk in the open sea, *3593*
1944 Transoceanic newspaper, *5657*
1980 Debate among party hopefuls for the presidential nomination to be shown on television, *3398*
1987 Year in which the federal budget exceeded $1 trillion, *3752*

January 6

1639 Crop surplus destruction ordered by a government, *1008*
1885 State legislator who was African-American to represent a constituency with a white majority, *7625*
1898 Radio telephone message from a submerged submarine to shore, *7755*
1973 Electoral vote for a woman, *3396*

January 7

1751 Benefit performance of a play, *1244*
1784 Seed business, *1011*
1824 Boxing arena, *7503*
1830 Railroad for commercial transportation of passengers and freight, *6321*
1869 Bookseller's guide, *1787*
1904 Radio distress signal officially established, *6286*
1908 Health department of a county organized on a full-time basis, *4185*
1913 Gasoline obtained from crude petroleum by the cracking process, *3536*
1927 Transatlantic commercial telephone service, *7737*

1949 Photograph of genes, *4909*
1954 Television receiver that showed two programs simultaneously, *7819*
1955 Metropolitan Opera singer who was African-American, *1338*

January 8

1675 Commercial corporation, *2402*
1783 Copyright law enacted by a state, *4627*
1833 School for music teachers, *2898*
1838 Telegraphic system in which dots and dashes represented letters, *7687*
1853 Bronze equestrian statue, *5399*
1856 Borax, *5331*
1867 Election law granting African-American men the right to vote, *3428*
1884 Chrome tanning process, *4459*
1889 Electric tabulating machine, *2364*
1901 Bowling tournament sponsored by the American Bowling Congress, *7223*
1918 State to ratify the Prohibition Amendment to the Constitution, *2683*
1925 State supreme court in which all the judges were women, *2724*
1935 Spectrophotometer, *6799*
1962 Exhibition of the *Mona Lisa* in the United States, *1231*
1965 State supreme court chief justice who was a woman, *2730*

January 9

1793 Balloon flight in which a presidential order was carried, *1536*
1861 Act inaugurating the Civil War, *7946*
1894 Movie to be copyrighted, *5544*
1918 Aviation unit of the military trained for overseas duty, *5132*
1935 Blood testing laws enacted by a state, *4188*

January 10

1910 Aviation meet, *7292*
1911 Photograph taken from an airplane, *5820*
1943 President to visit a foreign country in wartime, *6237*
1944 Mobile electric power plant, *3486*
1946 Radar signal to the moon, *7680*
1949 Airmail postal card, *6047*
1951 Jet airplane passenger trip, *1474*
1967 Educational television network operated as a nonprofit corporation, *7807*

January 11

1759 Life insurance company, *4542*
1770 Rhubarb, *3897*
1873 Livestock market paper, *5644*
1875 Nautical school established by a city, *3304*

1913 Sedan car, *5443*
1917 State legislature to use an electric vote recorder, *7627*
1935 Transpacific solo airplane flight by a woman, *1460*
1938 Bank president of a national bank who was a woman, *3786*
1949 Mosque, *6605*
1973 Designated hitter rule, *7157*

January 12

1773 Public museum, *5576*
1853 University on the Pacific Coast, *2948*
1876 Forestry association (state), *6785*
1896 X-ray photograph, *4904*
1910 Pilot from the United States to establish an airplane altitude record, *1594*
1924 History of science society (national), *6795*
1929 Airmail letter sheet, *6023*
Seatrain, *6890*
1937 Submarine cable plow, *7709*
1944 Victory ship launched, *6896*
1953 Catholic cardinal whose see was west of the Rockies, *6477*

January 13

1794 Changes in the American flag to be authorized by Congress, *1124*
1906 Radio receiver advertised, *6306*
1928 Television sets to be installed in homes on an experimental basis, *7810*
1929 Humanist association, *5746*
1931 Elevator with two cars, *2111*
1953 Department store to sell apartments, *2510*
1957 Flying disk for use in throwing games, *7585*
1976 Metropolitan Opera orchestra conductor who was a woman, *1340*
Voice reader, *2538*
1996 Medals of Honor awarded to African-American servicemen for service in World War II, *1689*

January 14

1639 Constitution to declare that "the foundation of authority is in the free consent of the people", *1099*
1794 Cesarean operation, *5075*
1799 Senator to be impeached, *2641*
1813 Superintendent of schools hired by a state, *3052*
1932 Totalisator to record racetrack bets and odds, *7399*
1938 Right-to-die society, *2840*

January 15

1825 Tax enacted by a state to support public schools, *3054*

January 15—*continued*

1840 Line drawing to illustrate a newspaper article, *5685*

1847 Swedish magazine, *4747*

1852 Hospital under Jewish auspices, *4876*

1862 Ironclad naval vessels, *6921*

1863 Newspaper printed on wood-pulp paper, *5790*

1867 Governor of a state who had also been governor of a territory, *7614*

1870 Cartoon showing the Democratic Party as a donkey, *5702*

1892 Basketball rules, *7168*

1907 Dental inlay made of gold, *4866*
Triode for radios, *6307*

1908 Sorority for African-American students at a college, *2988*

1936 All-glass windowless structure, *2089*

1943 Building containing 6.5 million square feet of usable space, *2118*

1955 House with solar heating and radiation cooling, *2129*

1960 Bowler to win $10,000 in a tournament, *7229*

1967 Super Bowl football game, *7333*

1991 War that was predicted by pizza orders, *7972*

January 16

1866 All-metal roller skate, *7464*

1877 Organ with color display, *1315*

1882 Knights of Columbus meeting, *5724*

1891 Ski club association, *7480*

1920 Constitutional amendment submitted to the states for repeal, *1109*

1928 Squash rackets champion who was a woman, *7502*

1936 Electric-eye camera installed at a racetrack, *7400*

1937 Jury school, *2736*

1942 Army general appointed from civilian rank, *5156*

1943 Amphibious seaplane glider, *1554*

1957 Round-the-world nonstop flight by a jet airplane, *1480*

1965 Discotheque, *3631*

1978 Astronauts who were women, *7047*

1987 Condom commercials on television, *6843*

1991 Cruise missiles used in war, *8145*
Pilot to destroy an enemy airplane in the Gulf War, *7973*

January 17

1806 Child born in the White House, *6251*

1887 Military hospital, *5013*

1905 Punchboards, *2368*

1938 Jazz concert at Carnegie Hall, *1298*

1949 Sitcom television show, *7780*
Synchrotron, *6802*

1962 Indoor ski slope, *7488*

1967 Be-In, *3668*

1991 Serviceman killed in the Gulf War, *7974*

January 18

1733 Polar bear, *1138*

1770 Attack on British soldiers by civilians in the Revolution, *7984*

1840 Electricity journal, *4769*

1896 X-ray machine exhibited in the United States, *3664*

1911 Airplane flight to the deck of a carrier, *1434*

1944 Chinese person granted citizenship, *5874*

1949 Congressional standing committee headed by an African-American, *2591*

1958 Professional hockey player who was African-American, *7380*

1966 Cabinet member who was African-American, *6119*

1991 Destruction of an attacking missile by a defensive missile in combat, *8146*

1996 Computer software application on Digital Video Disc, *2555*

January 19

1861 Military prison on an island, *2821*

1903 Transatlantic radio broadcast, *6263*

1931 Basketball game at a large commercial sports arena, *7170*

1955 Presidential news conference filmed for television and newsreels, *6219*

January 20

1778 Court-martial by the Army, *2739*

1809 Geology book, *1981*

1869 Senate hearing witness who was a woman, *2628*

1870 Senator who was African-American, *2649*

1929 Movie of feature length made outdoors, *5558*

1937 President inaugurated on January 20, *6169*

1942 Marine general, *5237*

1952 Bullfighter who was a woman to fight professionally, *7259*

1953 Telecast transmitted to Canada, *7843*

1954 Radio network for African-Americans, *6302*

1961 President who was Catholic, *6203*

1966 Medicare identification cards, *4541*

1969 Transatlantic solo trip by rowboat, *6998*

1975 College commencement exercises in a prison, *2982*

1977 President to take the oath of office using a nickname, *6180*

1986 Martin Luther King Day, *4251*

January 21

1677 Medical pamphlet, *1886*
1789 Novel by an American writer to be published in America, *1839*
1812 Bridge in a Y shape, *3569*
1853 Envelope folding machine, *5763*
1865 Oil well drilled by torpedoes, *3532*
1880 Sewage-disposal system separate from the city water system, *2230*
1941 Magnesium commercially produced from seawater, *5344*
1954 Gas-turbine car, *5456*
1961 Cabinet member who was the brother of the president, *6117*
1970 Jumbo jet, *1405*

January 22

1895 National manufacturing assocation, *4376*
1947 Commercial television station west of the Mississippi River, *7797*
1988 Anti-aging skin cream, *4063*

January 23

1789 College founded as a Catholic institution, *2938*
1793 Emergency first aid organization, *4117*
1849 Physician who was a woman, *4971*
1907 Senator who was Native American, *2650*
1946 Medal of Honor awarded to a chaplain, *1682*
1964 Transplant of an animal organ into a human being, *5099*
1968 Naval ship to surrender in peacetime without a fight, *6947*
1973 Vote in the House of Representatives to be recorded electronically, *2594*
1996 Transplant of a major organ into a person with mental retardation, *5107*
1997 Secretary of state who was a woman, *6123*

January 24

1656 Physician who was Jewish, *4962*
1722 Divinity professor at a college, *3266*
1791 Presidential proclamation, *6140*
1848 Gold discovered in California, *5329*
1887 Shot tower, *8112*
1899 Rubber shoe heel, *2305*
1922 Eskimo pie, *3867*
1925 Movie of a solar eclipse taken from an airship, *6686*
1935 Beer in cans, *2671*
1972 Noise-control law enacted by a state, *3721*
1996 Auction of radio spectrum for satellite services, *6284*

January 25

1915 Transcontinental telephone demonstration, *7718*
1929 Vice president's widow to receive a pension, *6247*
1945 Water supply to be fluoridated, *2236*
1949 Emmy awards for excellence in television, *1628*
1951 Presidential press conference recorded on tape, *6218*
1952 Automatic headlight control, *4227*
1959 Transcontinental jet airplane passenger service, *1422*
1961 Presidential news conference to be televised live, *6220*
    Presidential physician who was a woman, *6204*
1964 Cargo ship fully automated and flying the American flag, *6901*

January 26

1695 Workers' compensation agreement, *4550*
1776 Army chaplain who was Catholic, *5194*
1838 Alcohol prohibition law enacted by a state, *2676*
1875 Dental drill powered by electricity, *4864*
1907 Corrupt election practices law enacted by Congress, *3319*
1911 Hydroplane, *1391*
1942 American expeditionary force to land in Europe in World War II, *8052*
1949 Tape-recording machine for mass production of tapes, *7015*
1950 Babysitters' insurance policy, *4527*
1951 Rabbi in the Reform movement who was a woman, *6490*

January 27

1662 Lime, *5315*
1785 State university, *2935*
1870 Sorority at a college, *2988*
1900 Social-Democratic Party of America national convention, *3369*
1908 Outdoor school for children with tuberculosis, *3020*
1943 Air attack on Germany by the Army Air Force in World War II, *8061*
1948 Super-giant locomotive, *6367*
1950 Postage stamp depicting a Jew, *6091*
1967 Astronauts to die in a spacecraft, *7036*

January 28

1808 Trotting horse, *1177*
1878 College daily newspaper, *5646*
1907 Safety congress, *4184*
1915 Ship from the United States lost in World War I, *8026*
1932 Unemployment insurance act, *4525*

January 28—*continued*

1934 Ski tow made of rope, *7483*
1935 Streamlined electric locomotive, *6365*
1960 Photograph bounced off the moon, *5830*
1969 Oil spill with disastrous consequences, *3544*
1986 Space shuttle disaster, *7090*

January 29

1802 Librarian of Congress, *4663*
1861 Pin-tumbler cylinder lock, *2133*
1874 Coins manufactured for a foreign government, *5372*
1904 College varsity sports program, *2998*
1924 Ice cream cone rolling machine, *3868*
1926 Lawyer admitted to practice before the Supreme Court who was an African-American woman, *4635*
1940 Tetraploid flower, *1064*
1951 Television eyewitness allowed to testify in a federal court, *2715*
1973 Pilot on a regularly scheduled major airline who was a woman, *1606*

January 30

1798 Brawl in the House of Representatives, *2583*
1835 President whose assassination was attempted, *6187*
1874 Mechanical engineering laboratory, *3561*
1911 Airplane rescue at sea, *1435*
Airplane sea flight out of sight of land, *1435*
1934 Theatrical presentation sponsored by the federal government, *1263*
1958 Two-way moving sidewalk, *6640*
1993 Subway service in Los Angeles, *6414*

January 31

1863 Union regiment in the Civil War made up of African-American soldiers, *7966*
1920 Ukrainian daily newspaper, *5683*
1930 Glider released from an airship, *1548*
1940 Social security monthly payment, *4526*
1949 Soap opera on daytime television, *7781*
1958 Satellite placed in orbit by the United States, *7056*
1961 Commander of a combat ship who was African-American, *5295*
1966 Rocket-tracking ship, *6945*
1971 Sport played on the moon, *7026*

February

1799 Tax rebellion, *5952*
1800 Endowment for social service purposes, *5731*
1824 Supreme Court decision in a commerce case, *2750*

1835 Homeopathy journal, *4752*
1853 Trade association, *2519*
1884 Transparent paper-strip photographic film, *5836*
1895 Cereal sold as a breakfast food, *3916*
1898 Monthly cumulative index of books, *1774*
Physiology journal, *4777*
1910 Air rights lease, *2064*
1911 Printing lecture course in a college, *3294*
1915 Car finance company, *3806*
1917 Jazz record, *1294*
1921 Civil rights chair at a college, *3128*
1923 Gasoline-mechanical railroad cars, *6387*
1924 Round-the-world steamboat passenger service, *6888*
1928 Hydroelectric power plant to use water pumped into a reservoir, *3479*
1930 Rivetless cargo vessel, *6891*
1932 Wooden money, *5378*
1933 Governor to be granted almost dictatorial power, *7619*
Poliomyelitis vaccine, *4923*
1934 Commercial production of plants in water, *1038*
1935 Building with prefabricated walls of mosaic concrete, *2088*
1938 Cartooning school, *2911*
1943 Fire department composed entirely of women, *4114*
1946 Nontwisted sewing thread, *4364*
1950 Nazi collaborator to be deported, *5875*
1954 Photoengraving high-speed process, *5696*
1964 Toy action figure, *2153*
1968 Army general who was African-American to lead an infantry brigade in combat, *5159*
1987 Superconducting material that operated at relatively high temperatures, *6823*
1990 Charles Stark Draper Prize for engineering and technology, *1645*
1994 Genetically engineered product to appear in food, *3839*
1996 Astronaut who was a woman to pilot the space shuttle, *7053*
Boxer who was a woman to earn national recognition, *7257*
Women's boxing match to be broadcast live on national television, *7257*
1997 Movie to earn more than $400 million in the United States market, *5523*
Telephone directory with internet addresses, *1821*

February 1

1788 Steamboat patent, *6855*
1790 Supreme Court of the United States, *2742*
1791 Dental dispensary, *4857*
1793 Oiled silk patent, *7864*
1831 Music book for children, *1939*

1860 Rabbi to open the House of Representatives with prayer, *2587*

1865 Lawyer admitted to practice before the Supreme Court who was African-American, *4635*

1885 Tuberculosis sanatorium using modern treatment methods, *4899*

1893 Movie studio, *5543*

1898 Car insurance policy, *4519*

1907 Horse farm operated by the federal government, *1182*

1911 Fingerprint conviction in a crime, *4163*

1930 Passenger ship with a diesel engine, *6877*

1936 Medical insurance group policy for college students, *4537*

1937 Free port, *2486*

1949 Court-martial at which the judges included enlisted men, *2740*

Telescope lens 200 inches in diameter, *6671*

1951 Atomic bomb explosion to be shown on television, *8126*

1960 Civil rights sit-in, *2260*

1966 Navy captain who was African-American, *5296*

1968 West Point instructor who was a woman, *3205*

1973 Prison guard who was a woman to serve in a maximum security prison for men, *2831*

1978 Postage stamp depicting an African-American woman, *6100*

February 2

1802 Leopard, *1143*

1870 Justice of a state supreme court who was African-American, *2720*

1880 Electric streetlight installed in a city, *2216*

1892 Bottle cap with a cork crown, *4286*

1901 Army dental corps, *5016*

Army nurse corps for women, *5017*

1912 Stuntman, *3680*

1923 Ethyl gasoline to be marketed, *3538*

1935 Lie detector, *4623*

1940 Dictionary compiled by a woman, *1808*

February 3

1690 Paper money, *5382*

1790 Supreme Court clerk, *2743*

1803 Supreme Court decision voiding an act of Congress, *2746*

1812 Supreme Court justice who had been a representative in Congress, *2758*

1836 Whig Party convention, *3350*

1862 Newspaper printed on a train, *5789*

1894 Steel sailing vessel, *6874*

1933 Interstate legislative conference, *7629*

1996 Serviceman killed during the Bosnia conflict, *7983*

February 4

1789 President to receive the unanimous vote of the presidential electors, *3381*

1801 Supreme Court chief justice to serve in a presidential cabinet, *2756*

1847 Telegraph company, *7695*

1861 Confederate congressional session, *7947*

1887 Interstate commerce act enacted by Congress, *2483*

1895 Rolling lift bridge, *3587*

1913 Demountable tire-carrying rim, *5499*

1915 Pellagra experiment of note, *5058*

1930 Mosaic pavement, *6630*

Tieless streetcar tracks that were soundless and shockless, *6408*

1932 Olympic Games competition to be held in the winter, *7446*

1936 Radioactive substance produced synthetically, *6816*

1943 Submarine with a pressure hull of high-tensile steel, *6971*

1962 Children's hospital for research and treatment of catastrophic childhood diseases, *4893*

February 5

1644 Branding law enacted by a colony, *1065*

1777 Laws of entail and primogeniture to be abolished by a state, *4620*

1790 Lawyers admitted to practice before the Supreme Court, *4633*

1825 Magazine for mechanics, *4768*

1846 Newspaper published on the Pacific Coast, *5640*

1850 Adding machine to employ depressible keys, *2375*

1861 Peep show machine, *3686*

Photographic attempt to show motion, *5569*

1863 News reporter tried as a spy, *5615*

1870 Animated photograph projection before a theater audience, *5529*

1903 Semitic museum, *5583*

1918 Army pilot to win a victory over an enemy airplane, *1610*

1924 President buried in Washington, *6197*

1931 Glider license awarded to a woman, *1599*

1948 Figure skating champion from the United States to compete in the Olympic Games, *7432*

February 6

1778 Foreign nation to recognize the independence of the United States, *3975*

Treaties entered into by the federal government, *3998*

1815 Railroad charter granted by a state, *6317*

1902 Young Women's Hebrew Association, *5715*

February 6—*continued*

1932 Dogsled race on an Olympic demonstration program, *7280*

1956 Circular school building, *2121*

February 7

1818 Educational magazine, *4706*

1821 American to set foot on Antarctica, *6722*

1827 Ballet, *1232*

1964 Performance by a British rock group, *1370*

1984 Astronauts to fly free in space, *7050*

February 8

1693 College charter granted by the Crown, *2926*

1837 Vice president elected by the Senate, *6244*

1865 Army major who was African-American, *5169*

1881 Halftone printing plate, *5785*

1889 Steam tractor, *1054*

1898 Envelope folding and gumming machine, *5765*

1915 Movie to gross $50 million, *5513*

1922 President to use a radio, *6209*

1924 Coast-to-coast radio hookup, *6272*
Execution by lethal gas, *2800*

1928 Transoceanic radio signal conveying a television image, *7828*

February 9

1799 Warship to capture an enemy ship after the Revolution, *8005*

1893 Theater operated by a city, *3703*

1895 Intercollegiate basketball game, *7169*

1909 Forestry school operated privately, *3077*
Narcotics ban enacted by Congress, *2686*

1918 Army school for chaplains, *3202*

February 10

1807 Coast survey, *5956*

1830 Interstate railroad, *6322*

1925 Waterless natural gas storage tank, *3520*

1932 International ski meet, *7482*

1941 Highway post office service, *6041*

1942 Medal of Honor awarded in World War II, *1679*

1989 Chairman of a major political party who was African-American, *3345*

1996 Chess computer to beat the world chess champion, *4034*

February 11

1752 Hospital, *4868*

1801 President elected by the House of Representatives, *6145*

1808 Anthracite coal burned experimentally, *3503*

1811 Senate filibuster, *2627*

1836 College for women, *2944*

1837 Physiology society, *5033*

1875 College program of study abroad, *2995*

1878 Bicycle club, *7184*

1889 Six-day bicycle race for women, *7186*

1937 Simultaneous radio broadcast on all three major networks, *6278*

1945 Gas-turbine propeller-driven airplane, *1400*

1952 Yiddish professorship at a college, *3119*

1954 Newspaper printed on bagasse newsprint, *5798*

1958 Airline flight attendant who was an African-American woman, *1412*

1972 Snowmobile to exceed a speed of 125 miles per hour, *7491*

February 12

1738 Puppet show, *3683*

1775 First Lady who was not born in the United States, *6129*

1793 Fugitive slave law enacted by Congress, *2247*

1795 Gold bullion deposit for coinage, *5365*

1809 President born beyond the boundaries of the original 13 states, *6186*

1865 African-American preacher to deliver a sermon in the House of Representatives, *2588*

1873 Trade dollars, *5371*

1877 News dispatch by telephone, *5605*

1878 Baseball catcher's mask, *7107*

1879 Indoor ice skating rink, *7430*

1880 Croquet league, *7571*

1883 Coronation, *6646*

1908 Car race from New York to Paris, *7265*

1909 Memorial postage stamp, *6089*

1924 Radio network program sponsored by commercial advertising, *2335*

1925 Arbitration law enacted by Congress, *2356*

1970 Surgical facility outside a hospital, *5089*

1973 Metric distance markers on a state highway, *6636*

1976 Nuclear commercial power plant licensed operator who was a woman, *3555*

February 13

1635 Public school with a continuous existence, *3040*

1799 Insurance regulation enacted by a state, *4499*

1861 Medal of Honor action, *1670*

1866 Bank and train robbery gang, *2775*

1875 Quintuplets, *2172*

1914 Music society for the protection of composers and song writers, *1286*

1935 Heart operation for the relief of angina pectoris, *5091*
1969 New York Stock Exchange member who was African-American, *3834*
1997 Dow Jones Industrial Average to exceed 7,000 points, *3838*

February 14

1794 Textile machinery patent, *7865*
1803 Apple parer, *4367*
1849 Photograph of a president in office, *6155*
1862 Ironclad seagoing naval warship, *6922*
1865 Congressional directory, *1817*
1872 Bird refuge established by a state, *3743*
1883 Labor unions to be legalized by a state, *4613*
1899 Voting machines in congressional elections, *3328*
1929 Organized crime massacre, *2780*
1940 Porpoise, *1156*
1946 Electronic computer, *2528*
Traveling cancer clinic, *4849*

February 15

1768 Mustard, *3943*
1799 Printed ballot, *3314*
1842 Adhesive postage stamps, *6051*
1918 Troop ship from the United States torpedoed by a German submarine in World War I, *8040*
1951 Nuclear reactor used in medical therapy, *5061*
1953 World figure skating champion from the United States, *7433*
1954 Bevatron, *6805*
1956 Instrument for observing radiation in total darkness, *6807*

February 16

1804 Marine Corps commando raid, *5231*
1815 Music festival, *1283*
1818 Marine insurance law enacted by a state, *4502*
1857 College for deaf students, *3033*
1859 Agricultural college to be chartered by a state, *2891*
1868 Elks meeting, *5722*
1880 Mechanical engineering society (national), *3610*
1905 Esperanto club, *5717*
1909 Subway car with side doors, *6412*
1912 Movie photographed from an airplane, *5548*
1932 Fruit tree patent, *1026*
1937 Synthetic fiber, *7876*
1946 Helicopter commercially designed, *1558*
1948 Newsreel telecast presented daily, *5700*
1957 Ship to transport fresh orange juice in stainless-steel tanks, *2488*

1960 Circumnavigation of the earth by a submerged submarine, *6996*

February 17

1761 Milestones between cities, *2185*
1817 Gas streetlights throughout a city, *2214*
1864 Submarine built in the United States to sink an enemy warship in actual warfare, *7968*
1870 Justice of the peace who was a woman, *2721*
1897 Parent-teacher association (national), *3227*
1905 Statue of a woman installed in the Capitol's National Statuary Hall, *5409*
1911 Hydroplane flight to and from a ship, *1436*
1913 Modern art exhibition, *1228*
1934 Driving course in a high school, *3090*
1971 Veterinary hospital established by a city, *5125*
1972 Astronaut to become a general, *7044*
President to visit a nation not recognized by the federal government, *6238*

February 18

1688 Protest against slavery, *2240*
1735 Opera performed in America, *1341*
1804 Land grant university, *2940*
1834 Labor newspaper, *5639*
1856 Know-Nothing (American) Party convention, *3354*
Play in which a horse race was run on stage, *1251*
1908 Postage stamps in coils, *6062*
1930 Cow flown in an airplane, *1153*
Planet found beyond Neptune, *6680*
1953 Three-dimensional feature movie, *5563*
1960 Artificial ice skating rink of Olympic size, *7435*

February 19

1807 Former vice president to be arrested, *6241*
1831 Locomotive to burn coal, *6352*
1836 Navy officer to become an engineer, *5282*
1856 Tintype camera, *5834*
1864 Knights of Pythias meeting, *5721*
1878 Phonograph, *7004*
1929 Diathermy machine, *4948*
1953 Book censorship board established by a state, *1792*

February 20

1725 Mass scalping of Native Americans by colonists, *5934*
1768 Fire insurance company to receive a charter, *4530*

February 20—*continued*

1792 Postal service law enacted by Congress, *5986*

1809 Supreme Court decision establishing the power of the federal government, *2747*

1851 Fifty-dollar gold pieces, *5367*
Private mint authorized by the federal government, *5352*

1865 Architecture department at a college, *2903*

1937 Car-airplane combination, *5447*

1942 Navy ace in World War II, *1617*

1952 Umpire in organized baseball who was African-American, *7102*

1962 Astronaut to orbit the earth, *7030*
Postage stamp issued on the date of the event it commemorated, *6070*

1963 Television receiver and transmitter operated by laser beam, *7822*

February 21

1828 Native American newspaper, *5666*

1846 Telegrapher who was a woman, *7694*

1858 Burglar alarm, *2132*

1862 Execution for slave trading carried out by the federal government, *2797*

1866 Dentist who was a woman to obtain a D.D.S. degree, *4862*

1878 Telephone directory, *1818*

1887 Bacteriology laboratory, *4928*

1921 Transcontinental airplane flight made within 24 hours, *1447*

1932 Camera exposure meter, *5843*

1947 Instant camera, *5846*

February 22

1656 Jewish cemetery, *2851*

1770 Child to be killed in the Revolution, *7985*

1784 Trading ship sent to China, *6879*

1825 Federal treaty rejected by the Senate, *4003*

1854 Republican Party meeting, *3353*

1872 Labor Reform Party national convention, *3357*

1879 Five-cent store, *2496*

1889 States admitted to the Union simultaneously, *7606*

1898 Arabic daily newspaper, *5678*

1920 Dog racetrack to use an imitation rabbit, *7278*

1921 Transcontinental airmail flight, *6018*

1923 Chinchilla farm, *1074*

1924 President to make a radio broadcast from the White House, *6212*

1953 Japanese person to receive an immigration visa, *5876*

1966 Motorboat ocean race, *7218*

1969 Jockey who was a woman to win on a regular parimutuel flat track, *7415*

1990 Fat substitute in prepared foods, *3886*

February 23

1784 American woman to become a countess, *6644*

1821 Pharmacy college, *3160*

1839 Express delivery service, *2479*

1883 Animal rights organization (national), *5740*
Antitrust law enacted by a state, *2520*

1886 Aluminum pots, *4297*

1892 Student government at a college, *3013*

1905 Rotary Club meeting, *2451*

1910 Radio contest, *6260*

1936 Airmail flight by rocket, *6026*

1942 Bombing raid on the continental United States in World War II, *8075*
Naval counterattack by American forces against the Japanese in World War II, *8076*
Navy school for chaplains, *3218*

1962 Athlete who was an African-American woman to win the James E. Sullivan Memorial Trophy, *1721*

1976 Postage stamps of 50 different designs sold as a single sheet, *6098*

1979 Marine general who was African-American, *5241*

1997 Movie shown on a television network without interruption by commercials, *7793*

February 24

1835 Magazine in a Native American language, *4744*

1855 Claims court established by the federal government, *2712*

1857 Postage stamp issued with perforations, *6054*

1866 American flag made of American bunting to fly over the Capitol, *1129*

1868 Parade with float tableaux, *3662*
President to be impeached, *6159*

1925 Explosion of Thermit to break up ice jams, *4425*

1949 Rocket to reach outer space, *7020*

February 25

1751 Monkey trained to perform, *1139*

1791 Bank of the United States, *3758*
Corporate body chartered by a special act of Congress, *2403*

1799 Quarantine law enacted by Congress, *4208*
Shipbuilding law enacted by Congress, *5263*

1804 Presidential candidate nominated at a caucus, *3399*

1836 Revolver pistol, *8096*

1859 Temporary insanity defense in a criminal case, *4622*
1862 Legal tender, *5386*
1863 National bank, *3765*
1901 Corporation with a capitalization of $1 billion, *2405*
1919 Gasoline tax levied by a state, *7655*
1928 Television license, *7794*
1930 Check photographing device, *3795*
1940 Hockey game to be shown on television, *7378*
1952 Copyright registered for a choreographic score, *1237*

February 26

1811 Naval hospital established by Congress, *5007*
1866 Health board with emergency powers established by a city, *4176*
1870 Subway, *6409*
1895 Glass-blowing machine, *4044*
1914 Industrial museum, *5584*
Long-distance telephone call over underground cables, *7756*
1935 Ambulance service with an incubator, *4825*
1938 Passenger ship equipped with radar, *7677*
1940 Air defense military organization, *5134*
1944 Navy captain who was a woman, *5288*
1949 Round-the-world nonstop flight by an airplane, *1470*
1953 Photographic type-composing machine, *5809*
1955 Pilot to bail out of an airplane flying at supersonic speed, *1592*
1971 Ice skater to cover 100 miles in less than six hours, *7436*
1986 Poet laureate of the United States, *2034*
1993 Bombing of a skyscraper by foreign terrorists, *2790*

February 27

1729 College to have a full faculty, *2927*
1793 Supreme Court nominee who was rejected by the Senate, *2753*
1813 Mail delivery by steamboat, *5988*
Vaccination law enacted by Congress, *4919*
1847 Navy chaplain killed in action, *5199*
1879 Sugar substitute, *3964*
1883 Cigar-rolling machine, *2706*
1915 American combatant to die in World War I, *8027*
1919 Social organization for the hard of hearing (national), *5725*
1929 Movie by a major company for an African-American audience, *5559*
1973 Armed occupation by Native American protesters in the modern era, *5978*

February 28

1793 Senate election that was contested, *3327*
1810 Fire insurance joint-stock company, *4531*
1822 Trust company, *3761*
1861 Confederate government bond, *7948*
1866 Ambulance service for hospitals, *4823*
1882 Cooperative store at a college, *2497*
1918 Service number issued by the Army, *5226*
1940 Basketball game to be shown on television, *7171*
1952 Basketball collegiate player to score more than 1,000 points in one season, *7175*
1954 Phase-contrast cinemicrography film to be shown on television, *5565*
1977 Orca, *1161*
1996 Census based on a sample of the population, *5856*
1997 Tobacco sales to minors to be restricted by federal regulations, *2701*

February 29

1940 Oscar awarded to a performer who was African-American, *1633*
1980 Tank with a turbine engine, *8122*

March

1540 Baptism in America, *6442*
1624 Cattle to be imported, *1076*
1634 Catholics to settle in the English colonies in America, *6447*
1638 Swedes to arrive in America, *5924*
1639 Document known to have been printed in America, *1096*
Printing press, *5767*
1647 Quarantine law enacted by a colony, *4207*
1753 Arctic expedition to seek the Northwest Passage, *6720*
1776 Independent government in an American colony, *5940*
1791 Orchestral song to be printed, *1378*
1796 Coast survey book, *2014*
1816 Weather report delivered to the Army, *6768*
1823 Newspaper for Jewish readers, *5663*
1829 Library for seamen, *4667*
1840 Camera exposure scale, *5832*
1863 Corps badges systematically assigned to an entire army, *5224*
Laryngology clinic, *4842*
1865 Zinc sheet mill, *4470*
1874 Lawn tennis, *7523*
1886 Air gun, *8111*
1889 Centralized refrigeration service, *4436*
1893 Electrical transmission of three-phase alternating high-frequency current, *3468*
Grand American Trapshoot tournament using live birds, *7475*

March—*continued*

1895 Pneumatic tires, *5495*
1909 Movie censorship board at the national level, *5540*
1910 Car equipped with a two-way radio, *7717*
1916 Airplane in actual military operation, *1485*
1919 Fisheries school at a college, *3296*
1920 Asteroid named for an American president, *6678*
1923 Shopping center in a suburban business area, *2501*
1927 Phonograph with an automatic record changer, *7010*
1930 Museum to install refrigerated vaults, *5586*
1931 Rattlesnake meat in cans, *3942*
1933 Airplane sleeping berths, *1413*
1936 Football with a rubber covering, *7313*
1938 Electric sterilamp, *4950*
1946 Helicopter with a twin engine, *1559*
1950 Ten Most Wanted list, *2783*
1951 Telephone company answering service, *7744*
1983 Identification of the AIDS virus, *5064*
1997 Microscopic cantilever, *6825*

March 1

1642 City incorporated in the colonies, *2181*
1785 Agriculture society, *1087*
1864 Physician who was an African-American woman, *4973*
1869 Postage stamps depicting scenes, *6081*
1872 National park, *3735*
1876 Cattle club to promote Guernsey cattle, *1092*
1883 Catalog of government publications, *1772*
1894 Osteopathic physicians who were women, *4976*
1912 Detective who was a woman, *4140*
     Parachute jump from an airplane, *1581*
1913 Bonding law enacted by a state, *4524*
1934 Cartel of corporations, *2524*
1937 License plates for vehicles, *4226*
1940 Family of lawyers admitted simultaneously to practice before the Supreme Court, *4641*
1941 FM radio transmitter to receive a commercial license, *6299*
1942 Pilot from the United States to sink a German submarine, *8053*
1958 Catholic prelate named to the Roman Curia who was American-born, *6478*
1963 Liver transplant, *5097*
1971 Books of postage stamps with humidity-resistant adhesive, *6075*
1973 Jockey who was a woman to win a major stakes race, *7419*
1991 Pilot who was a woman to die in a combat zone, *1625*

March 2

1642 Ban on convicts holding public office, *3312*
1799 Standardization of weights and measures for customs, *2474*
1827 Federal law hostile to lotteries, *3642*
1829 School for blind students, *3023*
1831 Sculptor to obtain a federal commission, *1207*
1833 State aid to railroads, *6326*
1861 Constitutional amendment proposal to bear the signature of a president, *1108*
     Copyright law on photographs enacted by Congress, *4630*
1866 Sewing needles made by machine, *4358*
1888 Bank for African-Americans operated by African-Americans, *3771*
1891 Gas conservation law enacted by a state, *3519*
1893 Railroad safety law enacted by Congress, *4219*
1925 Nationwide highway numbering system, *6627*
1930 Glider flight indoors, *1549*
1934 Streamlined lightweight high-speed three-car passenger train, *6431*
1940 Intercollegiate track meet to be shown on television, *7559*
1949 Automatic streetlight system, *2217*
1951 All-Star Game of the National Basketball Association, *7174*
1972 Spacecraft to carry a message intended to be read by living beings elsewhere in the universe, *7084*
1997 Cloning of a primate from an embryo, *6754*

March 3

1791 Internal revenue tax levied by Congress, *7642*
1794 Opera of a serious nature, *1344*
1803 Federal judge to be impeached, *2719*
     Grant of federal land to a foreigner, *5954*
1819 Piracy law enacted by Congress, *2772*
     Standardization of nomenclature for naval vessels, *5264*
1842 Child labor law enacted by a state that regulated hours of employment, *4574*
1843 Telegraph appropriation by Congress, *7689*
1845 Law book of federal laws then in force, *1880*
     Ocean mail contracts, *5990*
     Presidential veto to be overridden by Congress, *6154*
1863 Draft law enacted by Congress during wartime, *5219*
     Gold certificates, *5389*
     National science institute, *6781*

Notes wholly engraved and printed at the Bureau of Engraving and Printing, *5390*

1865 Bank for freed African-American slaves, *3766*

1879 Lawyer who was a woman to be admitted to practice before the Supreme Court, *4638*

1891 Forest planting by the federal government, *3726*

1892 Cattle tuberculosis test, *5121*

1893 Coin bearing the likeness of a foreign monarch, *5374*

1894 Greek newspaper, *5676*

1899 Admiral of the Navy, *5271*

1903 Nurses to be registered by a state, *4938*
State prison to take fingerprints, *4159*

1911 Federal cemetery to contain graves of both Union and Confederate soldiers, *2853*

1917 Tax levied by Congress on excess profits of corporations, *7654*

1919 International airmail, *6017*

1926 Greyhound racing association, *7279*

1943 Election law lowering the voting age in a state to 18, *3433*

1971 Vote in the House of Representatives to be tallied by machine, *2593*

March 4

1776 Marine engagement in battle, *7994*

1789 Congressional representative appointed to a presidential cabinet, *2596*
Congressional representative who was Catholic, *2597*
Senate journal, *4696*
Senator who was Catholic, *2638*
Session of Congress, *2556*
Session of the House of Representatives, *2576*
Session of the Senate, *2624*
Vice president who had served in the House of Representatives, *6239*

1791 Chaplain of the U.S. Army, *5197*
Congressional representative who was Jewish, *2598*
Special session of the Senate, *2626*
State admitted to the Union after the ratification of the Constitution, *7602*

1797 Congressional representative to serve before his 25th birthday, *2599*
President whose son became president, *6184*

1799 Supreme Court chief justice who had been a congressional representative, *2755*

1801 President inaugurated in the city of Washington, *6146*

1823 Congressional representative who was a Catholic priest, *2601*

1825 Former president who was elected to the House of Representatives, *6149*

1829 Spoils system of presidential patronage, *6150*

1831 Congressional chaplain who was Catholic, *2585*

1840 Commercial photography studio, *5812*

1849 Senator to serve three states, *2645*
Senator who was returned to the Senate after being defeated for the presidency, *2646*

1851 Brothers to serve as representatives in Congress simultaneously, *2602*

1853 Vice president sworn in on foreign soil, *6246*

1861 Battle flag, *1128*

1863 Officer to preside over both of the branches of Congress, *2565*

1873 Illustrated daily newspaper, *5645*

1875 Former president to become a senator, *6160*

1880 Halftone engraving, *1227*

1881 President whose mother lived at the White House, *6195*
Quarantine law for plants enacted by a state, *4211*

1887 Congressional representative of Italian ancestry, *2605*

1891 Congress to appropriate $1 billion, *2566*
Congressional representative elected by prohibitionists, *2606*
International copyright agreement, *4631*

1909 Bird hunting regulation law enacted by Congress, *7426*

1911 Congressional representative who was a Socialist, *2607*

1917 Congressional representative who was a woman, *2609*

1925 Presidential inauguration to be broadcast on radio, *6213*
Transcontinental radio fax transmission of a photograph, *7669*

1927 Congress to enact more than 1,000 laws, *2568*

1928 Transcontinental foot race, *7557*

1929 Radio broadcast from the Senate chamber, *2631*
Vice president who was Native American, *6248*

1930 Bowler who was a woman to obtain a perfect score, *7227*

1933 Cabinet in which all members were sworn in at the same time and place, *6111*
Cabinet member who was a woman, *6112*
Electoral college members invited to a presidential inauguration, *3391*

1944 Execution of an organized crime leader in the electric chair, *2803*

March 4—*continued*

1977 Coast Guard airplane pilot who was a woman, *5213*

1997 Ban on federal funding for human cloning research, *6755*

March 5

1623 Alcohol temperance law enacted by a colony, *2674*

1743 Religious magazine, *4693*

1750 Play by William Shakespeare produced in America, *1243*

1770 Americans killed by British soldiers in the Revolution, *7986*

Engraving to achieve popularity, *1225*

1856 Railroad safety law enacted by a state, *4218*

1894 Employment office established by a city, *4566*

1913 Dentist in the Navy to serve aboard a naval ship, *5020*

1921 Father and son to occupy the same Cabinet post, *6109*

1923 Pension laws enacted by a state, *4587*

1924 Bowler to roll two perfect games, *7226*

1935 City law requiring reporting of premature births, *2161*

1977 Radio broadcast in which citizens telephoned the president, *6221*

March 6

1775 Mason who was African-American, *5729*

1808 College orchestra, *1357*

1810 Vaccination law enacted by a state, *4918*

1862 Ironclad turreted vessel in the Navy, *6923*

1865 Judge advocate of the Navy, *5284*

1886 Nursing magazine, *4758*

Power plant using alternating current, *3464*

1928 Medical center devoted to teaching, treatment, and research, *3178*

1934 First Lady to travel in an airplane to a foreign country, *6131*

1941 Parachute fatality in the Army, *1590*

1967 Large-type weekly newspaper, *5659*

1969 Astronauts to transfer from one spacecraft to another while in orbit, *7039*

March 7

1644 Legislature of a colony to establish two chambers, *7623*

Whaling industry established by a city, *2417*

1801 Voting registration law enacted by a state, *3424*

1854 Sewing machine to stitch buttonholes, *4354*

1865 Coast Guard serviceman who was African-American, *5209*

1893 Print patent, *4658*

1911 Coin-operated locker, *2369*

1955 Broadway play shown in a color television version with its original cast, *1266*

1958 Submarine expressly designed and built to fire guided missiles, *6975*

1959 Pilot to fly a million miles in a jet airplane, *1605*

1962 Orbiting solar observatory, *7066*

March 8

1855 Railroad suspension bridge, *3580*

1887 Fishing rod of telescoping steel tubes, *7932*

1894 Dog license law enacted by a state, *1172*

1915 Naval vessel equipped to lay mines, *6931*

1945 Naval Reserve Nurse Corps nurse who was African-American, *5289*

1946 Helicopter licensed for commercial use, *1560*

1950 Medical officer assigned to a naval vessel who was a woman, *5292*

1965 Ground troops sent to Vietnam, *8016*

1969 Jockey who was a woman to ride two winners in one day, *7416*

March 9

1798 Navy surgeon, *5280*

1799 Government contract authorized by Congress for pistols, *8092*

1858 Street letter box, *5992*

1861 Confederate paper money, *5384*

1862 Naval battle between ironclad vessels in the Civil War, *7961*

1907 Sterilization of humans by a state government as a matter of public policy, *6829*

1947 Helicopter to deliver material across a picket line, *1562*

1949 Railroad dining car powered by electricity, *6389*

1964 Occupation of federal territory by Native American protesters in the modern era, *5977*

March 10

1791 Pile driver, *4389*

1830 Hospital for treatment of the mentally ill established by a state, *4873*

1849 President who had received a patent, *6156*

1862 Bill bearing the likeness of a president, *5387*

1876 Telephone message, *7751*

1880 Salvation Army services, *6531*

1903 Multigraph, *2367*

1908 Child welfare congress, *2146*

1909 Old age home for pioneers, *5975*

1911 Blue-sky laws enacted by a state, *2523*
1913 Bowler to make a perfect score of 300, *7224*
1967 Attorney general whose father also served as attorney general, *6125*

March 11

1791 Patent recipient to obtain more than one patent, *4649*
1823 Teacher training school, *3258*
1882 Intercollegiate lacrosse association, *7572*
1903 Opera composed by a woman to be performed at the Metropolitan Opera House, *1348*
1927 Armored truck holdup, *2779*
1930 President buried in the National Cemetery, *6199*
1953 Doctor commissioned in the regular Army who was a woman, *5172*
1959 Play by an African-American woman to appear on Broadway, *1270*
1960 Spacecraft placed in solar orbit, *7078*

March 12

1613 Colonial warfare between England and France in America, *5911*
1664 Naturalization act in the American colonies, *5859*
1755 Steam engine for industrial use, *4388*
1804 Supreme Court justice to be impeached, *2757*
1877 Cabinet member who had served as a Confederate officer, *6107*
1884 State college for women, *2954*
1912 Scouting organization for girls, *2148*
1914 Railroad operated by the federal government, *6343*
1923 Movie with sound recorded on the film, *5556*
1954 Bridge hand in which each player was dealt a perfect hand, *4025*
1993 Attorney general who was a woman, *6128*

March 13

1638 Military organization established by a colony, *5253*
1770 Chamber of Commerce, *2446*
1790 Actor of American birth, *1273*
1852 Cartoon showing Uncle Sam, *5701*
1895 Navy submarine contract, *6962*
1946 Medal of Honor awarded to a soldier of Japanese ancestry, *1683*
1952 Antibiotic synthetically manufactured, *5002*
1955 Federal government building built to withstand a nuclear attack, *2119*
1959 Ultraviolet pictures of the sun, *6698*
1981 Product liability lawsuit to result in a criminal trial, *2315*

March 14

1812 War bond issued by the federal government, *3813*
1826 Conference of American republics, *3979*
1891 State seal designed by a woman, *7599*
1900 Bonds payable specifically in United States gold coins, *3823*
1903 Bird reservation established by the federal government, *3745*
1918 Concrete seagoing ship, *6876*
1931 Theater designed and built for the rear projection of movies, *3708*
1936 Magazine of the federal government, *4735*
1942 Medal of Honor awarded to a Marine in World War II, *1679*
1960 Sulfur mine offshore, *5346*
1964 Courtroom verdict to be televised, *2717*

March 15

1729 Catholic nun, *6452*
1767 President born after the death of his father, *6182*
1830 Educational association (national), *3224*
1855 Quarantine board established by a state, *4209*
1867 State university supported by a direct property tax, *2952*
1887 Game warden to be paid a salary, *3744*
Kindergarten for blind children, *3027*
1892 Voting machines, *3317*
1897 Indoor fly casting tournament, *7286*
1909 Transcontinental journey on foot, *7589*
1913 Small claims court, *2710*
1930 Seaplane glider, *1550*
1937 Birth control clinic run by a state government, *4847*
Blood bank, *4834*
1938 Merchant marine cadet corps, *3306*
1945 Presidential citation to an entire division, *1666*
1947 Navy commissioned officer who was African-American, *5290*
1948 Parcel post international air service, *6032*
1957 National women's figure skating four-time winner, *7434*
1960 Undersea park established by the federal government, *3739*
1985 Cabinet member indicted while in office, *6122*

March 16

1621 Greeting addressed to the Pilgrims by a Native American, *5914*
1802 Army academy, *3194*
Army engineer corps, *5178*
1810 Supreme Court decision declaring a state law unconstitutional, *2748*

845

March 16—*continued*

1827 Newspaper for African-American readers, *5664*

1829 High school night classes, *3082*

1883 Pharmacist who was a woman to receive a degree from a pharmacy college, *3147*

1885 Savings group for children, *3769*

1926 Rocket flight using liquid fuel, *7017*

1929 Tax on chain stores enacted by a state, *7658*

1947 Twin-engine pressurized airplane, *1401*

1952 Surgical operation shown on a local television program, *5084*

1966 Astronaut who was a civilian to orbit the earth, *7035*

Manned docking of two spacecraft, *7082*

March 17

1631 Fire prevention law enacted by a colony, *4091*

1762 Saint Patrick's Day parade, *3651*

1776 Medal awarded by the Continental Congress, *1649*

1854 Parkland purchased by a city, *3733*

1871 Baseball league, *7096*

1881 Locomotive to attain a speed of one mile in less than a minute, *6359*

1884 Glider flight, *1546*

1897 Movie of a heavyweight championship boxing fight, *5546*

1898 Submarine that was practical and submersible, *6964*

1914 Bus with cross seats, *5420*

1917 Bowling tournament for women, *7225*

1959 Submarine to surface at the North Pole, *6995*

1970 United Nations Security Council resolution vetoed by the United States, *3981*

1975 Strike by physicians against long working hours in hospitals, *4602*

1995 Chicken pox vaccine, *4925*

March 18

1543 Flood of which there is any known record, *2859*

1734 Magician's advertisement, *2319*

1748 Spa at a mineral spring, *5109*

1813 Gas streetlights, *2213*

1890 Naval militia established by a state, *5255*

1910 Opera by an American composer to be performed at the Metropolitan Opera House, *1349*

1911 Hail insurance law enacted by a state, *4515*

1913 Chiropractic regulation law enacted by a state, *4940*

1922 Intercollegiate indoor polo championship, *7460*

1925 Tornado disaster on a large scale, *2869*

1931 Electric shaver, *4060*

1938 Blood tests for pregnant women to be required by a state, *4189*

1945 Professional hockey player to score 50 goals in one season, *7379*

1948 Birth registration uniform numbering system, *2162*

1952 Artificial lens for cataract patients, *5052*

1958 Newspaper advertisement printed on aluminum foil, *2347*

1963 Domed sports stadium, *7511*

1967 Ship with a combined diesel and gas-turbine engine, *6946*

1970 Strike of postal employees, *4601*

1972 Naval ship named for an African-American naval officer, *1618*

1993 Bacterium to be discovered that was visible to the naked eye, *6752*

March 19

1785 City college, *2936*

1831 Bank robbery, *2773*

1948 Labor dispute in which the Taft-Hartley Act was invoked, *4569*

1949 Museum devoted exclusively to nuclear energy, *5591*

1953 Oscar movie awards ceremony to be telecast, *1636*

1954 Rocket-driven sled on rails, *7021*

1965 Narcotics ban enacted by a state, *2691*

1975 Sex discrimination law enacted by a state that affected high school athletic competitions, *6840*

March 20

1833 Treaty between the federal government and an Asian nation, *4005*

1865 Labor cooperatives to be authorized by a state, *4609*

1872 Analytical chemistry course requirement for pharmacy students, *3146*

1899 Execution of a woman by electrocution, *2799*

1902 Mobile radio telephone marine demonstration, *7716*

1911 Farm bureau, *1004*

Squash tennis organization (national), *7500*

1914 International championship figure skating tournament, *7431*

1930 Diesel engine speed record, *5482*

1948 Radio program simultaneously transmitted, *6280*

Symphonic concert to be shown on television, *1299*

1954 Newspaper vending machine to deliver a single copy, *2399*

1957 Public telecast over telephone wires using the narrow-band system, *7848*

March 28—*continued*

1865 Environmental protection law enacted by a state in connection with advertising, *3711*

1905 Radio fax patents, *7667*

1922 Microfilm reading device, *4681*

1937 Photographer to receive the John Simon Guggenheim Memorial Foundation award, *1627*

1957 National curling championship, *7277*

1978 Bilingual report of a congressional committee, *2595*

1979 Nuclear power plant to sustain a major accident, *3556*

March 29

1626 Forestry law enacted by a colony, *3722*

1806 Highway built by the federal government, *6616*

1812 Wedding in the White House, *6252*

1839 Military school established by a state, *3185*

1852 Working hours of women to be regulated by a state, *4555*

1914 Newspaper rotogravure sections, *5692*

1927 Car to exceed the speed of 200 miles per hour, *5445*

1928 College of liberal arts and sciences founded as a Jewish institution, *2965*

1929 Fireworks law enacted by a state, *4113*

1949 Airport fog disposal unit, *1509*

March 30

1843 Egg incubator, *1068*

1858 Pencil with an attached eraser, *8151*

1871 Theological school to admit women as students, *3273*

1887 Mutual liability insurance company, *4513*

1889 Golf mixed foursome, *7354*

1891 National forest, *3727*
National forest reserve, *3728*

1897 Accounting society (state), *3756*

1909 Double-deck bridge, *3591*

1930 Transcontinental glider tow, *1551*

1946 Transcontinental Pullman sleeping car daily service, *6345*

1950 Phototransistor, *3440*

1981 President to be wounded in an unsuccessful assassination attempt while in office, *6207*

March 31

1790 Senator appointed by a governor, *2639*

1814 Cottonseed hulling machine, *1031*

1870 African-American to vote under authority of the 15th Amendment, *3429*

1876 Title guaranty insurance company, *4509*

1877 Telephone concert held long-distance, *1291*

1900 Car advertisement in a national magazine, *2332*

1918 Daylight saving time program, *7896*

1923 Dance marathon, *3630*

1932 Savings bank with a deposit of half a billion dollars, *3781*

1937 Newspaper printed on pine-pulp paper in color, *5797*

1956 Space cabin simulator, *7022*

1958 Navy nuclear submarine division, *5306*

1987 Trial of a surrogate mother for refusing to give up her baby, *2167*

April

1629 Horses, *1174*

1649 Religious toleration law enacted by a colony, *6511*

1669 Woodcut, *1222*

1692 Parliamentary act to establish a colonial post office, *5981*

1774 Music printed in a magazine, *1280*

1811 Masonic magazine, *4705*

1826 Railroad with iron-plated wooden rails, *6318*

1841 Detective story, *1844*

1843 Jewish magazine, *4746*

1855 Magazine for professional printers, *4723*

1871 Surgeon general, *4213*

1877 Telephone for domestic use, *7712*

1891 Pneumatic bicycle tire, *7188*

1896 Biological study of camouflage in nature, *6745*

1897 X-ray of the entire body of a living person made in a single exposure, *4905*

1901 Steam turbine operated by a public utility to produce electricity, *3472*

1905 Bookwagon traveling library, *4676*

1908 Radio magazine, *4779*

1910 Mayor of a major city who was a Socialist, *2208*

1913 Naval vessel equipped with a gyrostabilizer, *6929*

1914 Electric power substation with a rotary converter completely unattended, *3474*

1917 Navy airship, *1516*

1921 Helium plant, *6797*

1926 Science fiction magazine, *4732*

1927 Respirator known as the iron lung, *4947*

1935 Color film, *5844*
Parachute tower for training jumpers, *1589*

1937 Badminton championship tournament, *7584*

1945 Instant book, *1791*

1946 Bone bank, *4837*

1948 Elevator with electronic signal controls, *2113*

1952 Microfilm editions of federal publications and documents, *4686*

1955 Television receivers to project large images, *7820*

1965 Demonstration in Washington against the Vietnam War, *8017*

Teach-in against the Vietnam War, *8017*

1966 Catgut substitute, *4958*

1968 Book set into type completely by electronic composition, *1756*

1969 Computer operating system for multiple users, *2545*

1973 Airborne express delivery service, *2489*

1979 Pen with truly erasable ink, *8155*

1988 Patent on an animal, *6751*

1994 Sailor to become a four-star admiral, *5275*

April 1

1621 Colonial treaty with the Native Americans, *5915*

1634 Bridge, *3562*

1769 Type foundry, *5801*

1789 Clerk of the House of Representatives, *2577*

Speaker of the House, *2578*

1826 Internal-combustion engine, *5477*

1843 Magazine for patients with mental illness, *4716*

1853 Fire department to be paid a salary, *4103*

1889 Investment trust, *3822*

1927 Airplane scheduled passenger flight at night, *1410*

1928 Telephone switchboard with Braille markings, *7738*

1930 Speaker to address an organization by television, *7831*

1931 Baseball pitcher who was a woman, *7149*

1934 President to conduct religious services as commander-in-chief of the Navy, *6166*

1935 Radio tube made of metal, *6311*

1949 Television variety talent show series with an African-American cast, *7776*

1954 Army helicopter battalion, *5191*

Educational television station sponsored by a city, *7803*

1960 Weather satellite to provide cloud-cover photographs, *7058*

1970 Census compiled in part from statistics obtained by mail, *5854*

April 2

1789 Congressional committee, *2579*

1792 Building erected in the United States for public use, *2115*

Copper coins made by the U.S. Mint, *5359*

Gold coinage, *5360*

Gold price fixed by Congress, *5349*

Half cent, *5361*

Mint of the United States, *5350*

Silver coins, *5362*

1794 Arsenal of the federal government, *5126*

1829 Bank deposit insurance law enacted by a state, *3762*

1877 Easter egg roll, *4239*

1878 Hotel for women, *2425*

1879 Commercial telephone service using toll lines, *7730*

1893 Newspaper with a color page, *5689*

1902 Theater to show movies, *3704*

1908 City manager, *2203*

1931 Autogiro licensed for commercial use, *1530*

1952 Seagoing radio broadcasting station, *5304*

1976 Ambulance ship for first aid to boaters and pleasure craft, *4827*

April 3

1782 Fustians, everlastings, and coating, *7860*

1800 First Lady to receive free mail franking privileges, *6130*

1829 Coffee mill, *3849*

1837 State school for blind students, *3024*

1860 Pony Express mail, *5994*

1888 Hotel transported from one location to another, *2427*

1913 Eye conservation class, *3028*

1965 Satellite with a nuclear reactor to orbit the earth, *7074*

1973 Zoo with twilight conditions, *1191*

April 4

1800 Bankruptcy act, *2308*

1841 President to die in Washington, *6189*

Vice president to succeed to the presidency after the death of a president, *6245*

1859 Song popular in the Confederate States, *1381*

1887 Mayor who was a woman, *2207*

1888 Holding companies authorized by a state, *2404*

1898 Musical comedy written by African-Americans for African-American performers, *1256*

1915 Mobile telephone one-way communication, *7719*

1928 Fax transmission of movie film, *7672*

1943 Naval ship with a plural name, *6936*

1949 Leaping submarine, *6972*

1953 Scholastic fraternity at an African-American college, *2983*

1969 Heart transplant using an artificial heart, *5101*

1972 Electric power using municipal garbage as a boiler fuel, *3489*

1981 Mayor of a major city who was of Mexican descent, *2211*

April 5

1792 Presidential veto of a congressional bill, *6141*
1806 Cider mill, *3841*
1827 Actor to appear abroad, *1276*
1868 Chamber of commerce established by a state, *2448*
1892 Gold leaf, *5339*
1909 Neurological disease research institute, *5057*
1913 Professional soccer organization recognized internationally, *7493*
1923 Balloon tire production, *5501*
1933 Lung removal, *5081*
1941 Plastic bonded airplane, *1398*
1951 Peacetime death sentence for espionage, *2836*

April 6

1712 Rebellion of African-American slaves in a colony, *2241*
1777 Marine officer killed in service, *5234*
1789 Catholic diocese and archdiocese, *6456*
Joint meeting of the Senate and the House of Representatives, *2557*
Senate president pro tempore, *2625*
1808 Play about a Native American, *1247*
1830 Mormon Church meeting, *6492*
1857 Veterinary college of importance, *3181*
1859 Milk inspection law enacted by a state, *4203*
1862 Army field hospital, *5010*
1866 Grand Army of the Republic post for veterans of the Civil War, *5310*
1869 Snow-melting apparatus, *2221*
1896 Olympic athlete from the United States to win a gold medal, *7441*
1900 Championship heavyweight boxing title won in the first round, *7237*
1909 Discovery of the North Pole, *6727*
1926 Airmail contractor, *6021*
1937 Grand jury foreman who was a woman, *2737*
1938 Fighter plane equipped with a cannon, *1487*
1956 Circular office building, *2066*
1973 Designated hitter in a major league baseball game, *7157*
1978 Marine general who was a woman, *5240*

April 7

1826 Inheritance tax enacted by a state, *7645*
1864 Camel race, *1146*
1904 Installment finance company, *3805*
1905 Intercollegiate wrestling association, *7577*
1910 Speedway with a board track, *7508*
1913 Electrically propelled naval ship, *6930*
1915 Transcontinental commercial telephone service, *7720*

1917 Shot fired by the Navy in World War I, *8031*
1922 Automatic steering gear for ships, *6958*
1927 Telecast of image and sound, *7827*
1933 Bridge with open-mesh steel flooring, *3594*
1940 Postage stamp depicting an African-American, *6090*
1953 Transatlantic nonstop jet airplane eastward flight, *1476*
1959 Astronauts trained by the United States, *7028*
Radar signal bounced off the sun, *7683*
1967 Rock and roll broadcast on FM radio, *1371*

April 8

1834 City mayor elected by popular vote, *2206*
1848 Homeopathy college, *3163*
1873 Margarine manufacturer, *3882*
1911 Squash tennis tournament, *7501*
1918 Air squadron of the Army in World War I, *8041*
1939 Weather forecasting service by telephone, *6772*
1955 Medal of Honor awarded to a helicopter pilot, *1685*
1956 Universal chapel embracing eight faiths, *6437*
1971 Air Force military engineer who was a woman, *5139*
Off-track betting operation, *3637*

April 9

1816 African Methodist Episcopal church convention, *6563*
1833 Free public library established by a city, *4668*
1847 Reformatory for boys established by a state, *2820*
1866 Civil rights law enacted by Congress, *2254*
1872 Dried milk patent, *3870*
1905 Aerial ferry, *3589*
1920 Society of Automotive Engineers member who was a woman, *6794*
1937 Sit-down strikes to be outlawed by a state, *4599*
1963 Honorary citizenship authorized by Congress, *5878*

April 10

1777 Lottery held by the Continental Congress, *3641*
1833 Homeopathic medical society, *5031*
1835 Homeopathy school, *3161*
1846 Gingham factory, *7871*
1849 Safety pin, *4336*
1861 Life insurance nonforfeiture law enacted by a state, *4545*

April 14—*continued*

1922 Radio broadcast of a concert from an airplane, *1295*

1939 Payment by the Federal Crop Insurance Corporation, *1006*

1956 Video tape recorder for sounds and pictures, *7821*

April 15

1788 Worsted mill operated by waterpower, *7893*

1817 Canal of importance, *3601*
School for deaf students, *3032*

1834 Presidential protest, *6152*

1854 Alcoholics' asylum, *4879*

1861 Civil War call for volunteers, *7951*

1884 Newspaper clipping bureau, *5625*

1891 Duplicate whist tournament, *4022*

1936 Theater operated as part of a state school system, *3710*

1941 Helicopter flight of one-hour duration, *1573*

1949 Airplane to fly with a load of 100,000 pounds, *1471*
Naval Reserve flier who was African-American, *1618*

1952 Bank to issue a credit card, *3810*

1955 McDonald's restaurant, *2464*

1956 All-color television station to televise live local programs, *7805*

1966 X-ray three-dimensional stereo fluoroscopic system, *4911*

1990 Orbiting observatory, *6673*

April 16

1787 Play by an American writer to be successfully presented by an established company, *1246*

1813 Factory standardization to federal government specification, *4381*

1836 Child labor law enacted by a state that included an education requirement, *4573*

1869 Consul who was African-American, *3988*

1900 Books of postage stamps, *6061*

1922 Sermon preached from an airplane by radio, *6591*

1926 Book-of-the-Month Club selection, *1789*

1935 Transport airplane designed for transoceanic service, *1414*

1940 Major league no-hitter baseball game on opening day, *7133*

1947 Army specialist corps for women, *5190*

1956 Radio receiver with an auxiliary solar-cell power unit, *6313*

1979 Coast Guard ship commander who was a woman, *5215*

April 17

1629 Commercial fishery, *2416*

1640 Lutheran pastor, *6554*

1704 Newspaper that was successful, *5630*

1776 Capture of an enemy warship by a commissioned American naval officer, *7995*

1844 Cylinder and flatbed combination printing press, *5775*

1860 Fire escapes for tenements, *4105*

1861 Fire in an oil well, *2882*

1895 Canal made of concrete, *3602*

1941 Helicopter flight from water, *1574*

1956 Billiard player to win a match in the first inning, *4020*

1957 Installment sales law enacted by a state, *2314*

April 18

1637 Draft law enacted by a colony, *5216*

1662 Book auction, *1778*

1796 Opera by an American composer, *1345*

1895 Bathhouses mandated by a state, *4196*

1910 Night flight in an airplane, *1429*

1924 Crossword puzzle book, *2004*

1925 Hospital for patients of Chinese ancestry, *4891*
Women's World Fair, *2413*

1930 State police officers who were women, *4144*

1934 Laundromat, *2442*

1942 Air attack against the Japanese homeland in World War II, *8077*

1960 Pacemaker to be implanted in a patient's body, *4953*

1968 Silver Star Medal awarded to a navy chaplain, *1669*

1975 Chief justice of a state supreme court who was African-American, *2720*

April 19

1739 Astronomer of note, *6659*

1775 Revolutionary War armed conflict, *7989*

1861 Civil War bloodshed, *7952*

1865 Body of a president to lie in state in the Capitol rotunda, *6194*

1875 Centennial celebration of the Revolution, *8006*

1897 Marathon race held annually, *7552*

1901 City government using the commission plan, *2202*

1937 Letter to circumnavigate the world by commercial airmail, *6027*

1965 All-news radio station, *6303*

1969 Horse race pari-mutuel in which all the jockeys were women, *7417*

1995 Bombing by domestic terrorists resulting in large loss of life, *2791*

April 20

1564 Artist to come to America, *1195*

1657 Jew to win full citizenship, *5858*

1721 Editorial apology for false news to appear in a newspaper, *5631*

1767 Comic opera written for the American stage, *1343*

1801 Marine hospital established by Congress, *4870*

1812 Vice president to die in office, *6242*

1837 Carpet power loom, *4313*

1852 Temperance society for women (state), *2677*

1855 Bohemian church, *6463*

1861 Fund-raising organization to sell stamps, *5734*

1876 Chemistry organization (national), *6786*

1899 Primary election law enacted by a state, *3318*

1926 Transatlantic radio fax of a check, *3794*

1940 Electron microscope, *6800*

1964 Transcontinental Picturephone call, *7769*

1965 Cabinet meeting attended by a foreign national, *6118*

April 21

1712 Calico printery, *7859*

1847 Health insurance company, *4534*

1856 Railroad bridge across the Mississippi River, *3581*

1857 Bustle, *2269*

1869 Indian Affairs Commissioner who was Native American, *5972*

1878 Firehouse pole, *4109*

1895 Movie recorded on film to be shown on a screen, *5510*

1899 Intercollegiate transatlantic chess match by cable, *4030*

Juvenile court, *2707*

1923 Precanceled stamps printed on rotary presses, *6064*

1930 Radio broadcast from a zoo, *1189*

1962 World's Fair that was financially successful, *2415*

1966 Medal of Honor awarded posthumously in the Vietnam War to an African-American soldier, *1687*

1980 Cuban boatlift, *5881*

1983 Presidential candidate who had been an astronaut, *3418*

1997 Space burial, *2846*

April 22

1793 Neutrality proclamation by the federal government, *3977*

1794 Death penalty ban by a state, *2796*

1864 Coin to use the motto "In God We Trust", *5369*

1884 Round-the-world bicycle trip, *7201*

1898 Capture of a ship in the Spanish-American War, *8007*

1913 Ice-loading machinery, *4415*

1920 Orchestra from the United States to make a European tour, *1363*

1955 Nuclear-powered submarine, *6973*

1970 Earth Day to be celebrated nationwide, *4250*

1980 Olympic Games boycott, *7450*

1986 Genetically altered virus approved for use in a vaccine, *5066*

1993 Museum commemorating the Holocaust, *5592*

April 23

1635 Naval battle between colonists, *5922*

1750 Colonial settlement west of the Allegheny Mountains, *5935*

1789 Catholic magazine, *4697*

Presidential mansion, *6250*

1838 Transatlantic steamboat service, *6881*

1867 Animated picture machine, *5528*

1872 Lawyer who was an African-American woman, *4637*

1896 Movie exhibition in a theater to a paying audience, *5511*

1897 Hospital for disabled children established by a state, *4889*

1904 Arts and letters organization (national), *5716*

1951 Senator who had been a newspaper reporter, *2655*

Teletypesetter circuit operated by a news agency, *5628*

1954 Jet drone target missile, *8137*

1981 Transplant of artificial skin, *5102*

1988 Smoking ban on airplane flights, *2700*

April 24

1783 College named after George Washington, *2934*

1795 Health board established by a city, *4172*

1863 Docks owned by a state, *2481*

1873 Free lunches for the poor and sick, *5736*

1884 Medical society for African-Americans, *5039*

1886 Catholic priest who was African-American, *6467*

1895 Round-the-world solo sailing journey, *6984*

1913 Skyscraper higher than 750 feet in height, *2099*

1917 Army general to fly over enemy lines, *8032*

Joint stock land bank, *3778*

1922 Catholic nuns in a cloistered community, *6470*

1928 Fathometer, *6714*

1934 Pipeless organ, *1324*

April 24—*continued*

1936 Unscheduled event to be televised as it occurred, *5607*
1946 Glider commercial freight service, *1555*
1950 Basketball professional player who was African-American, *7173*
1954 Pilot wounded in Vietnam who was a civilian, *8013*
1956 Visitor to open the New York Stock Exchange, *3829*
1962 Coast-to-coast telecast by satellite, *7852*

April 25

1812 Land office established by Congress, *5958*
1831 Streetcar company, *6393*
1876 Baseball game that was a shutout, *7119*
1881 Statue cast by the federal government, *5404*
1901 License plates for vehicles, *4220*
1908 Turbine-propelled naval ship, *6928*
1917 Loan made by the federal Government to a war ally, *3807*
1935 Round-the-world telephone conversation, *7762*
1940 Circus to be shown on television, *3675*
Passover seder to be shown on television, *6489*
1954 Solar energy battery, *3558*
1956 Containerized shipping, *2487*
Containership, *2487*
1957 Sodium reactor, *3550*
1959 Canal incorporated into a seaway, *3603*
1967 Abortion legalized by a state as a medical procedure, *6835*

April 26

1819 Odd Fellows lodge, *5719*
1848 Engineering society, *3608*
1929 Fluorescent mineral exhibit, *6715*
1962 International satellite, *7067*
1962. Satellite from the United States to impact the moon, *7068*

April 27

1805 American flag flown over a fortress of the Old World, *1125*
1816 Tariff passed by Congress for protection, *7664*
1875 Catholic priest from the United States to be made a cardinal, *6465*
1880 Electrical hearing aid, *5070*
1899 Tuberculosis hospital established by Congress, *4902*
1938 Baseball dyed yellow, *7110*
Woman of American ancestry to become a queen, *6651*
1960 Art auction televised on a coast-to-coast circuit, *1230*

1970 Bank to be automated, *3800*
1994 Criminal convicted on the evidence of DNA matching, *4167*

April 28

1798 Writer whose livelihood was obtained exclusively by writing, *2032*
1855 Veterinary college, *3180*
1866 Steam whaler, *6885*
1890 Employment service established by a state, *4565*
1909 Child delinquency law enacted by a state, *2147*
1919 Parachute known as the "free parachute", *1583*
1930 Movie of a solar eclipse taken from an airplane, *6688*
1932 Yellow fever vaccine for human immunization, *4922*
1937 Costume museum, *5588*
Electric sign showing an animated cartoon, *2352*
1939 Miniature car, *5448*
1968 Armenian Orthodox cathedral, *6499*

April 29

1749 Electric cooking experiment, *3450*
1851 College to prohibit discrimination because of race, religion, or color, *2946*
Electric locomotive, *6356*
1854 College for African-American students, *2949*
1864 Professional fraternity at a college, *2987*
1873 Railroad coupler, *6423*
1879 Electric arc streetlights, *2215*
1898 Cancer laboratory, *4930*
1913 Zipper, *2292*
1918 Ace of Aces from the United States, *1611*
1925 National Academy of Sciences member who was a woman, *6781*
1931 Absolute monarch to visit the United States, *6650*
1940 Bas relief of stainless steel in large size, *1219*
1942 Health insurance law enacted by a state, *4539*
1949 Cargo airlines licensed by the Civil Aeronautics Board, *1417*
1953 Three-dimensional telecast, *7844*
1997 Joint space walk by American and Russian astronauts, *7055*

April 30

1778 Blockade of enemy ships, *8001*
1789 Army organization under the Constitution, *5143*
Cabinet, *6102*
President elected under the Constitution, *6135*

Presidential inauguration, *6136*
1796 Patented pills, *4981*
1798 Navy yard, *5261*
1802 Land subsidy by Congress for road improvements, *6615*
1803 Territory annexed by the federal government, *5955*
1820 Antislavery magazine, *4707*
1837 Board of education established by a state, *3056*
1861 Confederate general killed in the Civil War, *7953*
1864 Hunting license required by a state, *7425*
1870 Medal of Honor awarded to a Jewish soldier, *1675*
1879 Factory inspection law enacted by a state, *4383*
1883 Electric power plant with a three-wire central station, *3463*
1888 Navy chaplain who was Catholic, *5202*
1889 National holiday, *4241*
1898 Truth-in-advertising law enacted by a state, *2330*
1939 Electric power generated by cosmic rays, *3484*
President to appear on television, *6215*
Train with fluorescent lights, *6434*
1948 Stratovision flight by an airplane during which a television signal was transmitted, *7839*
1972 Attorney general to plead guilty to a criminal offense, *6126*
Minister who was openly homosexual, *6837*
1976 Bridge named for a woman, *3598*
1997 Television network sitcom to feature a lead character who was homosexual, *6845*

May

1541 Exploration of the Mississippi River by a European, *5895*
1611 Game played in the English colonies in America, *4008*
1650 Pounds for stray livestock, *1066*
1728 Steel, *4490*
1740 Organ built in the United States, *1304*
1754 Druggist, *4965*
1772 Written constitution adopted by a community of American-born freemen, *1100*
1786 Music magazine, *4694*
1789 Publisher of denominational religious books, *1957*
1799 Education association, *3223*
1812 American flag flown over a schoolhouse, *1126*
1820 High school, *3080*
1827 Anarchist, *4551*
1832 Horticultural magazine, *4711*

1844 Iron steamship built for transatlantic service, *6870*
1845 Suspension aqueduct bridge of wire cable, *3577*
1848 Building constructed wholly of cast iron, *2076*
1857 Tuberculosis patients' home, *4897*
1858 Baseball rules standardizing the game, *7095*
1868 Pediatrics journal, *4756*
1872 Popular science magazine, *4773*
1876 Ethical culture society, *5744*
1881 Greek play, *1254*
1888 Armenian newspaper, *5675*
1894 Communion cups for individuals, *6582*
Osteopathy journal, *4762*
1898 Armored car, *5432*
1908 Army field range, *5245*
1911 Electric self-starter used in cars, *5442*
1930 Airline flight attendant who was a woman, *1412*
1939 Food stamps, *4086*
1956 Heart operation in which the elective cardiac arrest technique was employed, *5094*
1959 Astronomy photographs in color to be published in a magazine, *6699*
1984 Year in which the average price of a new house topped $100,000, *2201*
1989 Japanese high school in the United States, *3093*
1997 Complete DNA sequencing of a free-living organism, *6757*

May 1

1704 Newspaper advertisement, *2317*
1751 Cricket match, *7270*
1789 Congressional chaplain, *2580*
1843 Consul to California, *3987*
1857 Literacy qualification for voting, *3426*
1861 Teacher training school at which students conducted practice classes, *3263*
1862 Army general to become an admiral in the Navy, *5150*
1863 Orthopedic hospital, *4881*
Private school for children with disabilities, *3017*
1872 Liberal Republican convention, *3358*
1873 Postal card, *6044*
1876 Coach riding, *7570*
1883 Sports trainer to work professionally, *7548*
1884 Skyscraper, *2098*
1886 Boat race for fishermen, *7214*
1893 Kapok, *7873*
1894 Building with caisson foundations, *2083*
1904 Socialist Party national convention, *3372*
1906 Bank open day and night, *3792*
1909 Hydroelectric power plant built by the federal government, *3473*

May 1—*continued*

1915 Cargo ship from the United States attacked by a German submarine in World War I, *8028*

1921 Radio navigation beacons, *6957*

1925 Car insurance law enacted by a state, *4520*

1926 National Christmas tree, *4258*

1931 Baha'i house of worship, *6604*
Skyscraper higher than 1,250 feet, *2100*

1946 Radar installation aboard a commercial carrier, *6959*

1947 Radar for commercial and private planes, *7681*

1950 Poet who was an African-American woman to win the Pulitzer Prize, *1715*

1961 Skyjacking of a commercial American airplane, *2784*

1963 Ascent of Mount Everest by an American, *7588*

1976 Graduate of a four-year maritime school who was a woman, *3309*

May 2

1843 Government on the Pacific Coast, *5963*

1876 Baseball players to hit home runs, *7141*

1880 Steamboat to employ electric lights successfully, *6873*

1900 United Christian Party convention, *3370*

1917 Liberty loan subscriptions, *3808*

1923 Transcontinental nonstop airplane flight, *1449*

1926 Transatlantic radio fax of a drawing, *5694*

1932 Pulitzer Prize awarded to a musical, *1712*

1940 Boxing referee who was a woman, *7244*

1941 Commercial television licenses, *7796*

1970 Jockey who was a woman to ride in the Kentucky Derby, *7418*

1997 First Lady to be depicted on a monument to a president, *6134*

May 3

1654 Toll bridge, *3563*

1765 Medical college, *3159*

1768 Arbitration tribunal, *2354*

1826 Arcade, *2061*

1845 Lawyer formally admitted to the bar who was African-American, *4634*

1851 Scandinavian Methodist Episcopal church, *6566*

1865 Medal of Honor winner to receive two awards, *1674*

1881 Electric locomotive headlight, *6425*

1902 Workers' compensation insurance law enacted by a state, *4522*

1904 Pharmacists to be regulated by a state, *4939*

1906 Advertising show to be held annually, *2412*

1933 Director of the Mint of the United States who was a woman, *5350*

1943 Poet to win a Pulitzer Prize four times, *1713*

1952 Airplane flight to land at the North Pole, *6731*
Explorer to set foot on both the North and South Poles, *6732*
Jockey to win the Kentucky Derby five times, *7413*

May 4

1780 Arts and sciences organization (national), *5709*

1845 Iron truss bridge, *3578*

1854 Entomologist hired by a state, *6742*

1855 Women's hospital, *4880*

1869 Oil drill offshore rig, *3534*
Railroad owned by a city, *6335*

1884 Photograph of a lightning flash, *6696*

1886 Phonograph that was practical, *7005*

1891 Hospital open to all races as a matter of policy, *4886*

1892 Acetylene gas, *4437*

1905 Steel railroad mail car, *6383*

1928 Justice on the federal bench who was a woman, *2725*

1942 Sea battle in World War II fought solely by air power, *8078*

1954 Intercollegiate court tennis match, *7534*

1956 Commemorative postal card, *6048*

1973 Skyscraper higher than 1,400 feet in height, *2102*

May 5

1696 Printer who was a woman, *5782*

1832 Vaccination program by the federal government to protect Native Americans against smallpox, *4920*

1847 Medical society (national), *5036*

1865 Train robbery of a disabled train, *2774*

1894 Intercollegiate fencing championship competition, *7282*

1901 Catholic mass for night workers, *6469*

1908 State law prohibiting discrimination against soldiers, *5127*

1914 Airplane with ailerons, *1394*

1936 Bottle with a screw cap, *4287*

1945 American civilians killed in the continental United States in World War II, *8084*

1947 Ramjet helicopter, *1564*

1961 Astronaut to be launched into space, *7029*

1970 Air Force Reserve officer who was a nun, *5138*

1973 College to offer athletic scholarships to women, *3004*

May 6

1732 German newspaper, *5661*
1787 Masonic lodge for African-Americans, *5729*
1840 Library building at a university, *4669*
1851 Mechanical freezer patent, *4347*
1882 Restrictions by Congress on immigration of Chinese laborers, *5866*
1891 National fencing league, *7281*
1896 Airplane model to make a sustained flight under its own power, *1425*
1916 Ship-to-shore conversation over radio telephone, *7758*
1925 Transpacific radio fax transmission, *7670*
1937 Coast-to-coast radio news broadcast to be recorded, *5706*
1941 Ship from the United States sunk by a German submarine in World War II, *8048*
1957 Writer to win a Pulitzer Prize four times for drama, *1716*
1962 Nuclear warhead fired from a Polaris submarine, *8132*
1964 Election in the District of Columbia, *3325*

May 7

1634 Treason trial by a colony, *2833*
1789 Inaugural ball, *6137*
1907 Postage stamp depicting a Native American, *6088*
1912 Airplane outfitted with a machine gun, *1484*
1947 Television drama program regularly scheduled, *7778*

May 8

1783 Salute fired by Great Britain in honor of an officer of the United States, *3976*
1784 Hailstone shower of record that was fatal, *2866*
1787 Prison reform society, *2812*
1792 Draft of civilians by Congress, *5218*
1816 Bible society (national), *6573*
1866 Interracial jury, *2735*
1877 Dog show, *1171*
1878 Unassisted triple play in organized baseball, *7120*
1895 Cat show, *1147*
1915 Filly to win the Kentucky Derby horse race, *7408*
1919 Transatlantic hydroplane flight made in stages, *1445*
1931 Resale price maintenance law enacted by a state, *2313*
1939 Electric starting gate for horse races, *7401*
1942 Aircraft carrier from the United States sunk in World War II, *8079*

1951 Suits for men made of Dacron, *2279*
1952 Coal hydrogenation plant, *4444*
1954 Shot-put toss over 60 feet, *7562*
1961 Seawater conversion plant, *2237*
1964 Former president to address the Senate, *6175*
1980 Transcontinental nonstop balloon flight, *1544*

May 9

1607 Episcopal church service in an English colony, *6547*
1754 Newspaper cartoon, *5684*
1783 Purple Heart, *1656*
1796 Senators elected but not seated, *2640*
1825 Theater lighted by gas, *3697*
1860 Constitutional Union Party convention, *3355*
1893 Movie exhibition, *5509*
1926 Airplane flight over the North Pole, *6728*
1939 Catholic beatification of a Native American, *6474*
1944 Eye bank, *4836*
1946 Television variety talent show series, *7776*
1960 Birth-control pill, *6833*
1989 Airship that was certified by the Federal Aviation Administration, *1528*
1997 Ambassador to Vietnam after the end of the Vietnam War, *3997*

May 10

1643 Colonial government federation, *5926*
1775 Revolutionary War military action, *7990*
1797 Frigate, *6914*
1851 Cheese factory of consequence, *3859*
1864 Sugar and glucose from cornstarch, *3961*
1869 Transcontinental railroad service, *6336*
1872 Presidential candidate who was a woman, *3405*
 Vice presidential candidate who was African-American, *3406*
1876 Centennial exhibition, *2410*
 Commemorative stamped envelopes, *6083*
 Electric turnstile with a rachet, *2362*
 Public exhibition of postage stamps, *6058*
1879 Archeology organization (national), *6787*
1892 Osteopathy school, *3170*
1893 Locomotive to attain a proven speed of 112.5 miles per hour, *6361*
1894 Monument to a woman financed by women, *5406*
1898 Vending machine law enacted by a city, *2397*
1908 Mother's Day, *4243*
1911 Airplane accident in a solo military airplane that was fatal, *1392*
1912 Airplane round-trip flight over water, *1441*

May 10—*continued*

1927 Aviation department of a state government, *1385*

Hotel to install radio reception, *2430*

1930 Planetarium open to the public, *6669*

1977 Lethal injection as a method of execution, *2805*

May 11

1792 Exploration by ship of the mouth of the Columbia River, *5949*

1824 Catholic school for Native Americans, *3053*

1825 Religious tract society (national), *6576*

1832 National political platform, *3332*

1858 Congressional medal awarded to a physician, *1652*

1875 Baseball game in which a team made no runs in nine innings, *7117*

1892 Locomotive owned by an industrial company, *6360*

1898 Navy officer killed in action in the Spanish-American War, *8008*

1928 Television programs to be shown regularly, *7774*

1940 Ship-to-shore telecast, *7836*

1947 Tubeless car tires, *5503*

May 12

1812 Vice presidential candidate to decline the nomination, *3400*

1844 Masonic college, *2945*

1860 News reporter at a political convention who was a woman, *5614*

1862 Confederate ship surrendered to the Union, *7963*

1890 Prizefighting ban enacted by a state, *7234*

1896 Health ordinance prohibiting spitting, *4181*

Psychiatric institute, *3150*

1949 Ambassador to the United States who was a woman, *3990*

1969 Transpacific sailboat crossing by a woman, *6999*

1985 Rabbi in the Conservative movement who was a woman, *6490*

May 13

1607 Colonial council, *5906*

English settlement in America that was permanent, *5907*

Tobacco cultivation, *2694*

1854 Billiard match, *4016*

1873 Sewing machine lamp holder, *4359*

1908 Navy nurses' corps, *5018*

1916 Indian Day, *4245*

1918 Airmail stamps, *6063*

1942 Long-distance helicopter flight, *1575*

1949 Gas turbine to pump natural gas, *3521*

May 14

1634 Property tax levied by a colony, *7637*

1804 Transcontinental expedition to the Pacific coast, *6721*

1836 Scientific expedition fitted out by the federal government, *6723*

1856 Camels imported for military purposes, *1145*

1874 Football goalpost, *7309*

1884 Anti-Monopoly Party convention, *3362*

1887 Accident reports by employers, *4563*

1888 County created by federal law, *5973*

1897 Performance of *The Stars and Stripes Forever*, *1292*

1904 Olympic Games held in the United States, *7443*

1921 Judge to impose the death penalty who was a woman, *2722*

1931 Transcontinental autogiro flight, *1531*

1932 Electrical timing device for foot races, *7558*

1942 Army corps for women, *5189*

1973 Presidential Citizen Medal, *1644*

1996 Home screening kit for HIV infection, *4954*

May 15

1602 Exploration of the New England region by an Englishman, *5903*

1672 Colonial copyright law, *4626*

1685 Judge to be impeached, *2718*

1785 Missionary to the Native Americans who was African-American, *6569*

1797 Special session of Congress, *2561*

1851 College secret society for women, *2986*

1862 Enclosed baseball park, *7504*

1869 Postage stamp depicting the American flag, *6082*

1877 Monument to an American poet, *5402*

1885 Forest reserve established by a state, *3724*

1888 Union Labor Party convention, *3364*

United Labor Party convention, *3365*

1890 Milk butterfat tester, *3874*

1894 Labor union discrimination law enacted by a state, *4614*

1917 Librarians' union, *4617*

1922 Arbitration organization (national), *4645*

1937 Keedoozle store, *2506*

1938 Post office in an airplane, *6040*

1939 Bicycle race to be shown on television, *7198*

1940 Nylon stockings, *2278*

1941 Camp for conscientious objectors, *5221*

1950 Local radio network, *6301*

1957 Civic center with an aluminum geodesic dome, *2093*

May 16

1691 Colonist hanged for treason, *2834*
1775 Constitution adopted by a state, *1101*
1811 Naval battle in the War of 1812, *8020*
1825 Horse race trotting course, *7387*
1836 Steamboat on the Pacific coast, *6868*
1866 Nickel five-cent piece, *5370*
1876 Greenback Party convention, *3359*
1882 Flicker animation, *5530*
1888 Phonograph record, *7006*
1893 Typewriter to produce a line of writing visible as it was being typed, *2388*
1895 Academic costume standardization for colleges, *2957*
1903 Transcontinental motorcycle trip, *5492*
1925 Mobile telephone conversation between the ground and an airship, *7761*
1929 Oscar for best picture, *1630*
Oscars for best acting, *1631*
Oscars for best movie director, *1632*
1938 Artificial animal breeding cooperative organization, *1083*
1940 Two-handed shovel, *7940*
1941 Automatic aircraft cannon, *8119*
1956 Free-piston car, *5458*
1959 Golfer to break 60 for 18 holes in a major tournament, *7364*
1973 Balloon flight powered by solar energy, *1542*

May 17

1792 Stock exchange, *3812*
1796 Pediatrics monograph, *1897*
Sale of federal land to an individual, *5950*
1853 Railroad merger, *6331*
1875 Kentucky Derby horse race, *7392*
1877 Interstate telephone call, *7753*
Telephone switchboard or exchange, *7728*
1913 Oil and gas conservation law enacted by a state, *3537*
1939 Coin-operated mailbox, *6011*
Fashion show to be shown on television, *2414*
Sports event to be televised live, *7100*
1955 Nuclear reactor patent, *6806*
1956 Synthetic mica, *5345*
1973 Navy officer who was a woman to hold a major command, *5297*

May 18

1607 Prefabricated ship built in America, *6849*
1631 Election held in a colony, *3310*
1652 Slavery emancipation law enacted by a colony, *2239*
1713 Book auction catalog, *1779*
1766 United Brethren in Christ meeting, *6541*
1852 Compulsory education law enacted by a state, *3059*

1912 Baseball strike, *4595*
1934 College diploma made of silver, *2980*
Death penalty authorized by federal law, *2802*
1949 Heliport commercial base, *1565*
1953 Triple jet ace, *1621*
1956 Forest horse, *1184*
1967 Artificial insemination for women to be permitted by a state, *5117*
1980 Volcano known to claim human life, *2871*
1994 Genetically altered food, *3840*

May 19

1796 Protection of Native American hunting grounds authorized by Congress, *5951*
1847 Railroad coach modeled after English coaches, *6373*
1857 Fire alarm system operated by electricity, *4104*
1862 Homestead law enacted by Congress, *5967*
1891 People's Party national convention, *3366*
1898 Postcard, *6046*
1915 Dental hygienists to be licensed by a state, *4941*
1921 Immigration quota enacted by Congress, *5869*
Opera broadcast over the radio in its entirety, *1350*
1928 Frog-jumping jubilee, *1151*
1941 Father and son to become commercial airline pilots, *1602*

May 20

1639 Property tax established by a colony to support public schools, *3041*
1777 Treaty between states after the Declaration of Independence, *7594*
1785 Geographer of the United States, *6707*
Land set-aside for schools authorized by the Continental Congress, *3051*
Sale of federal land authorized by Congress, *5944*
Survey of public lands, *5945*
1830 Railroad timetable advertised in a newspaper, *6323*
1844 Game protection society, *7423*
1856 Telegraph ticker to print type successfully, *7697*
1865 College to sponsor an endowed lecture series, *2950*
1899 Driver arrested for speeding, *5468*
Physics association (national), *6789*
1909 Battleship to visit an inland city, *6987*
1916 Cover of the *Saturday Evening Post* by Norman Rockwell, *1218*
1918 Warship propelled by electricity, *6932*
1927 Transatlantic solo airplane flight, *1450*

May 20—*continued*

1930 Airplane catapulted from an airship, *1452*

1932 Transatlantic solo airplane flight by a woman, *1455*

1939 Public telecast made over telephone wires, *7835*

Transatlantic airmail service, *6028*

1951 Ace to fly a jet, *1620*

1953 Hotel to establish a heliport, *2433*

1955 Offshore radar warning station, *7682*

Solar energy battery to be manufactured commercially, *3559*

1956 Hydrogen bomb dropped from an airplane, *8130*

1964 Atomic-powered lighthouse, *4129*

May 21

1819 Bicycles, *7179*

1832 Democratic Party national convention, *3349*

National political convention to adopt the two-thirds rule, *3333*

1853 Circumnavigation of the world by a yacht, *6982*

1861 Newspaper published by soldiers in the field, *5641*

1881 Red Cross meeting, *5739*

Tennis society (national), *7525*

1888 Crematory established by a state government, *2858*

1891 Boxing match timed by automatic timer, *7235*

1901 Speeding driver law enacted by a state, *4221*

1909 Credit union law enacted by a state, *3774*

1919 Medal of Honor awarded in World War I, *1678*

1927 Corporation to own its own airplane, *1396*

1929 Automatic electric stock quotation board, *3824*

1932 Railroad mystery excursion, *3667*

Telecast images received in an airplane, *7832*

1934 Community to fingerprint its citizens, *4164*

1936 Lucite commercially manufactured, *4481*

1980 Coast Guard Academy graduates who were women, *3211*

1985 Septuplets, *2178*

1986 Human chain across the United States, *3671*

May 22

1621 Wedding of colonists in New England, *4813*

1649 Corrupt election practices law enacted by a colony, *3313*

1819 Transatlantic crossing by an American steamboat, *6979*

1841 Reclining chair, *4324*

1861 Union soldier killed by enemy action in the Civil War, *7954*

1900 Automatic computing pendulum scale, *2380*

1915 Naval militia of a state to have a hydroplane, *5256*

1930 Airship for private commercial operation, *1526*

1933 Maritime Day, *4248*

1934 State committee chairman of a major political party who was a woman, *3341*

1935 President to read a veto message to Congress, *6168*

1947 Ballistic missile, *8134*

1961 Revolving restaurant, *2465*

1972 President to visit the Soviet Union, *6238*

1993 Movie broadcast on the Internet, *5521*

May 23

1785 Bifocal eyeglasses, *5072*

1879 Veterinary school established by a state, *3183*

1891 Railroad chapel car, *6381*

1900 Medal of Honor awarded to an African-American soldier in the Civil War, *1677*

1903 Transcontinental car trip, *5471*

1908 Airship disaster, *1513*

1919 Airship to land on a roof, *1517*

1922 Radio broadcast of a debate, *6269*

1929 Coaxial cable, *7706*

1956 Automaton to operate by long-distance control, *3442*

1959 Bowling match that used white balls on black lanes, *7228*

1962 Limb reattachment, *5088*

1988 Ban on cheap handguns enacted by a state, *4155*

May 24

1844 Commercial telegraph service, *7692*

1862 Army field telegraph used in warfare, *5243*

Balloonist to direct artillery fire, *7964*

1869 Exploration of the Grand Canyon of the Colorado, *6725*

1874 Steel arch bridge, *3582*

1875 Banking association (national), *3768*

1893 Anti-saloon organization, *2680*

1899 Public garage, *5483*

1902 Oil journal, *4778*

1913 Strike settlement mediated by the federal Department of Labor, *4596*

1918 Croix de Guerre awarded to an African-American, *1648*

1931 Air-conditioned train, *6430*

1935 Baseball game at night by major league teams, *7131*

1945 Food-O-Mat, *2509*
1954 Moving sidewalk in a railroad station, *6639*
1959 House with a built-in nuclear bomb shelter, *2130*
1960 Spy satellite, *7060*
1976 Transatlantic supersonic jet service, *1424*

May 25

1721 Fire insurance agent, *4528*
1790 Copyright law enacted by Congress, *4628*
1793 Catholic priest, *6459*
1829 Letter written on a typewriter, *2384*
1844 Gas engine, *5478*
News dispatch by telegraph, *5602*
1895 Golf book, *2003*
1898 Military expeditionary force to be sent beyond the Western Hemisphere, *8009*
1903 Railroad operated by an electric third-rail system, *6341*
1918 Army nursing school, *3176*
1926 Catholic church to become a basilica, *6471*
1953 Educational television station, *7801*
Nuclear cannon, *8129*
1967 Postage stamp issued in the United States and canceled by a foreign country, *6072*
1973 Physician to practice as an astronaut in space, *7045*
Space station launched by the United States, *7085*

May 26

1647 Ban on Jesuits to be enacted by a colony, *6449*
1836 Gag rule in the House of Representatives, *2586*
1913 College comprehensive senior examination program, *3000*
1934 Train to run 1,000 miles nonstop, *6432*
1941 Film professorship at a college, *2914*
1956 Bank to open a branch in a trailer, *3788*

May 27

1607 Battle between English colonists and Native Americans, *5908*
1647 Execution for witchcraft, *2793*
1652 Coinage dies, *5353*
1755 Water pumping plant, *2225*
1825 Brothers to serve simultaneously as governors of their respective states, *7610*
1896 Intercollegiate bicycle race, *7192*
1911 Motorboat to travel at a speed of more than 40 miles per hour, *6952*
1926 Statue to commemorate literary characters, *5413*
1930 Cellophane transparent tape, *4339*
1931 Full-scale wind tunnel for testing airplanes, *1501*

1936 Coxswain of a men's college varsity rowing team who was a woman, *7471*
1943 Medal of Honor awarded posthumously to a Coastguardsman killed in action in World War II, *1680*
President of a black African country to visit the United States, *4082*

May 28

1734 Fish protection law enacted by a city, *3742*
1754 Bloodshed in the French and Indian War, *7970*
1796 Federal law exempting debtors from prison, *2814*
1870 Stamp auction, *6057*
1879 Ban enacted by a state on the employment of women in an occupation, *4559*
1881 Pure food and drug law enacted by a state, *4178*
1913 Senate whip, *2629*
1917 Troops from the United States to sail to Europe in World War I, *8033*
1922 Radio orchestra, *1364*
1925 Long-distance radio fax transmission of medical information, *7671*
1929 Movie with both sound and color, *5560*
1932 Airport manager who was a woman, *1507*
1953 Animated three-dimensional cartoon in Technicolor, *5537*
1959 Animals to survive a space flight, *7023*
1975 Whooping crane, *1169*
1978 Casino outside the state of Nevada, *3638*

May 29

1827 Nautical school, *3303*
1844 President who was a "dark horse" candidate, *3403*
1909 Domestic relations court, *2709*
1919 Toaster, *4299*
1931 Transcontinental autogiro flight by a woman, *1532*
1935 Drug treatment center for addicts established by Congress, *2688*
1962 Baseball coach in the major leagues who was African-American, *7103*
1977 Driver who was a woman to compete in the Indianapolis 500, *7269*

May 30

1734 Masonic book, *2007*
1806 Duel in which a future president of the United States participated, *2809*
1821 Fire hose of rubber-lined cotton web, *4099*
1848 Arts and sciences national organization member who was a woman, *5709*
Ice cream freezer, *3862*

May 30—*continued*

1856 Milk purity law enacted by a state, *4202*
1868 Decoration Day, *4236*
1881 Plumbing law enacted by a state, *2231*
1893 Relay race in a college track meet, *7550*
1896 Car accident, *5466*
1901 Academic hall of fame, *5582*
1903 Motorcycle hill-climbing contest, *7438*
1908 Workers' compensation insurance law enacted by Congress, *4523*
1911 Long-distance car race on a racetrack, *7267*
1959 Race-car driver to win $100,000, *7268*

May 31

1786 Strike benefit by a union, *4590*
1821 Cathedral, *6461*
1853 Arctic expedition by an American explorer, *6724*
1880 Bicycle organization (national), *7185*
1889 Dam disaster of great consequence, *2868*
1918 Ace to fly under American colors, *1612*
1919 Wedding in an airplane, *4818*
1929 Reindeer, *1152*
1937 Quadruplets to graduate from college, *2173*
1938 Movie to be shown on a television screen, *5516*
1941 High-jump standards using electric eye detectors, *7561*
1957 Intermediate-range ballistic missile, *8138*

June

1654 Orphanage, *2137*
1749 Waxworks museum, *5575*
1779 Oyster propagation, *1058*
1789 Presidential appointment, *6138*
1793 Wood engraving made with an engraving tool, *1226*
1798 Straw hats, *2294*
1809 Magazine containing a fashion plate, *4701*
1812 Pencil factory, *8148*
1813 Stereotyped book, *1743*
1828 Electromagnet, *3451*
1834 Cattle that were purebred shorthorns, *1080*
1853 Stamped envelopes, *6053*
1857 Gyroscopes for use as toys, *2142*
1860 Commercial oil refinery, *3529*
1866 Boiler insurance company, *4505*
1869 Lawyer who was a woman, *4636*
1870 College summer school, *2993*
1871 Half holiday on Saturday for factory workers, *4558*
1876 Intercollegiate athletic association, *7545*
1884 Roller coaster, *3621*
1887 Train with electric lighting, *6429*
1891 Diamonds in a meteorite, *5338*

1892 Electric sign of large dimensions, *2349*
1899 Police patrol wagon, *4137*
1900 Orthodontists' society, *5045*
1904 Radium treatment for cancer, *5115*
1907 Building of pressed structural steel, *2086*
1912 City government using the manager plan, *2204*
1913 Insulating brick, *2059*
1926 Electric toaster, *4301*
1928 Seeing Eye dog, *1173*
Television magazine, *4781*
1936 Football goalposts of collapsible folding metal, *7314*
1937 Shopping cart, *2371*
1938 Comic book starring a superhero, *2028*
1941 Presidential library, *6171*
1942 Airplane propeller blade of hollow steel, *1502*
1943 Hydroelectric power plant to produce a million kilowatts, *3485*
1944 Presidential airplane, *6227*
1950 Burglar alarm operated by ultrasonic or radio waves, *2136*
1953 Electronic road system, *6632*
1954 Truck driving school, *3300*
1957 Charting of the Northwest Passage, *6734*
1966 Black Power advocate, *2262*
1992 Car fueled by methanol, *5463*
1993 Mathematical proof of Fermat's last theorem, *6761*

June 1

1638 Earthquake description, *2861*
1785 Minister to Great Britain, *3985*
1789 Congressional act, *2558*
1802 Book fair, *1783*
1815 Steam-propelled frigate, *6916*
1819 Tightrope performer who was a woman, *3657*
1840 Gutta-percha, *4485*
1847 Steamship passenger line between American and European ports, *6882*
1860 Army signal corps, *5180*
1861 Confederate officer killed in the Civil War, *7955*
1880 Bareknuckle world heavyweight boxing champion, *7251*
Pay station telephone service, *7731*
1881 Horse bred in the United States to win the English Derby, *7407*
1886 Labor mediation and arbitration board established by a state, *4561*
1887 Navy contract for armor plate, *5265*
1888 Seismograph, *6712*
1890 Census compiled by machines, *5853*
1897 Rock wool insulation factory, *2047*
1898 Interurban streetcar line, *6403*
1901 Motorcycle with a built-in gasoline engine, *5489*
1909 Transcontinental car race, *7266*

1911 Life insurance group policy, *4548*
1919 Forest Service aerial patrol, *3730*
1923 Internal revenue collector for the federal government who was a woman, *7657*
1931 Autogiro owned by the federal government, *1533*
1939 Boxing match to be shown on television, *7243*
1949 Magazine on microfilm offered to subscribers, *4685*
1951 Titanium plant fully self-contained and fully integrated, *4477*
1953 Airline to install rear-facing passenger seats, *1419*
1957 National wheelchair games, *7586*
Runner from the United States to run a mile in less than four minutes, *7564*
1960 Parking meter enforcement division of a police department, *4149*

June 2

1857 Chain-stitch single-thread sewing machine, *4356*
1883 Baseball game at night, *7121*
Electric elevated railroad, *6337*
1886 Wedding of a president in the White House, *4815*
1889 Hydroelectric power plant generating alternating current to operate over a long distance, *3466*
1924 Citizenship statute for Native Americans, *5871*
1930 Maritime museum, *5587*
Presbyterian elder who was a woman, *6583*
1933 Swimming pool in the White House, *6257*

June 3

1800 President to reside in Washington, *6144*
1833 Clipper ship, *6866*
1856 Screw machine to make pointed screws, *7923*
1873 Oratorio by an American, *1289*
1884 National political convention of a major party presided over by an African-American, *3337*
1898 Military campaign medal, *1657*
1899 Portable church, *6532*
1916 Army veterinary corps, *5021*
Supreme Court justice who was Jewish, *2762*
1925 Airship with an enclosed cabin, *1522*
1940 Senator who was a woman who had previously served in the House of Representatives, *2653*
1949 Naval Academy graduate who was African-American, *3219*
1953 Cabinet conference to be telecast, *6114*

1965 Astronaut to walk in space, *7031*
1995 West Point cadet who was a woman to graduate at the top of her class, *3208*

June 4

1674 Horse racing ban by a colony, *7385*
1811 Secession idea to be mentioned in Congress, *7634*
1816 Double-deck steamboat, *6864*
1820 Mariners' church, *6575*
1825 Natural gas used as an illuminant, *3511*
1912 Minimum wage law enacted by a state, *4577*
1917 Pulitzer Prize awarded to a newspaper reporter, *1704*
Pulitzer Prize for a newspaper editorial, *1705*
Pulitzer Prize for fiction, *1706*
1931 Rocket glider flight, *1552*
1934 Aircraft carrier, *6934*
Factories operated by the federal government in peacetime, *4387*
1942 Navy Cross awarded to a Coast Guard officer in World War II, *1659*
1944 Capture and boarding of an enemy submarine on the high seas by American forces, *8065*
1946 Radio fax transmission to a moving train, *7673*
1980 West Point graduate who was a Jewish woman, *3195*
1990 Death by suicide machine, *2845*
1992 Postage stamp whose design was decided by popular vote, *6101*

June 5

1785 College founded as a Methodist institution, *2937*
1794 Neutrality regulation enacted by Congress that governed the actions of citizens, *3978*
1865 Safe deposit vault, *2359*
1877 Margarine law enacted by a state, *3883*
1918 Pulitzer Prize awarded to a newspaper, *1707*
Pulitzer Prize for drama, *1708*
1930 Colorscope public demonstration, *3436*
1938 Electronic voice mechanism, *7723*
1939 Museum devoted exclusively to papermaking, *5589*
1940 Synthetic rubber tires, *5502*
1946 Cellulose sponge for medical and surgical use, *4951*
1952 Boxing referee in a heavyweight championship match who was African-American, *7246*
1963 Air Force Academy graduates who were African-American, *3192*

June 6

1639 Gunpowder mill, *8088*
1822 Physiologist of note, *4967*
1833 President to ride on a railroad train, *6222*
1840 Presidential candidate to make a campaign speech, *3402*
1877 Doctor of Philosophy degree awarded to a woman, *2979*
1890 Polo association (national), *7459*
1891 Polar expedition of which a woman was a member, *6726*
1896 Transatlantic trip by rowboat, *6985*
1904 Disease research and treatment organization, *5046*
1907 College under Jewish auspices that was nonsectarian, *2963*
1925 City in miniature, *2197*
1932 Gasoline tax levied by Congress, *7659*
1933 Drive-in movie theater, *3709*
1936 Aviation gasoline obtained by the catalytic cracking method, *3539*
1942 Parachute jump using a nylon parachute, *1591*
1962 Air Force Academy graduate who was Native American, *3191*
1968 Presidential campaigner to be assassinated, *3416*
1979 Train operated exclusively by women, *6436*

June 7

1801 Booksellers' organization, *1782*
1860 Mass-market paperback book, *1786*
1862 Citizen of the United States to be hanged for treason, *2835*
1870 Railroad signal system with automatic electric block, *6422*
1882 Tariff commission established by Congress, *7666*
1883 Intercollegiate lawn tennis match, *7528*
1887 Monotype machine, *5806*
1892 Baseball pinch hitter, *7144*
   Bicycle tire made of cord, *7190*
   Delegates to a national political convention who were women, *3338*
1898 Social Democracy of America Party national convention, *3368*
1908 Newspaper with an aviation section, *5651*
1913 Permalloy, *7705*
1938 Broadway play shown in a television version with its original cast, *1266*
1939 King of Great Britain to visit the United States, *6652*
1942 American territory occupied by the Japanese in World War II, *8080*
1954 Microbiology laboratory, *4932*
1955 President to appear on color television, *6215*
1980 Power plant using solar cells, *3560*

June 8

1697 Settler heroine publicly rewarded, *5933*
1786 Ice cream to be made commercially, *3861*
1869 Vacuum cleaner that used suction, *4272*
1872 Mail fraud law enacted by Congress, *5999*
1911 Aviation law enacted by a state, *1384*
   Pilot licensed by the Aero Club of America, *1595*
1940 Neptunium, *6817*
1948 Commissioned officer in the Marine Corps who was African-American, *5239*
1953 Gas-turbine propane-fueled locomotive, *6369*
1959 Airmail by missile, *6034*
1966 Coast Guard Academy graduate who was African-American, *3210*

June 9

1628 Deportation, *5857*
1772 Naval attack in the Revolutionary War, *7987*
   Protestant church west of the Alleghenies, *6519*
1783 Revolutionary War national veterans' organization, *5308*
1790 Book entered for copyright, *4629*
1846 Senator elected on an antislavery ticket, *2250*
1880 Greenback Labor Party convention, *3361*
1902 Restaurant with an automatic arrangement for vending food, *2461*
1909 Transcontinental car trip by women, *5472*
1943 Army chaplain of Japanese ancestry, *5204*

June 10

1682 Tornado of record, *2863*
1760 Medical licensing law enacted by a city, *4934*
1809 Steamboat to make an ocean voyage, *6862*
1884 Albert Medal presented to a person born in America, *1647*
1902 Envelope with a window, *5766*
1905 Forest fire lookout tower, *3729*
1910 School stadium, *7509*
1924 Political convention to be broadcast on radio, *3340*
   Portable electric stethoscope, *4946*
1932 Artificial lightning demonstration, *6770*
1935 Twelve-step rehabilitation program, *2662*
1936 Chinese-American women's organization to be incorporated, *5726*
   Telecast using coaxial cable, *7833*
1939 King and queen to be shown on television, *6653*

1944 Horse stakes race ending in a triple dead heat, *7402*
1952 Surgical operation televised coast-to-coast, *5085*
1954 Gas-turbine bus, *5424*
1955 Virus separated into component parts, *5062*
1963 Ban on sex discrimination in wages enacted by Congress, *6834*
1967 Horse motel, *2435*
1977 Golfer to break 60 in a Professional Golfers Association tour, *7368*

June 11

1788 Ship built on the Pacific coast, *6856*
1790 House of Representatives filibuster, *2581*
1885 Gas commission established by a state government, *3518*
1889 Business high school, *3084*
1891 Nautical school established by a state, *3305*
1902 Chess match between players on different ships at sea, *4031*
1912 Airplane takeoff from a hotel roof, *1442*
1919 Horse to win the Triple Crown, *7409*
1922 Transatlantic radio fax transmission of a photograph, *7668*
1943 American land victory without infantry in World War II, *8062*
1944 Serbian Orthodox cathedral, *6497*
1963 Lung transplant, *5098*
1970 Army generals who were brother and sister, *5160*
1978 Mormon man ordained to the priesthood who was African-American, *6494*

June 12

1775 Naval battle in the Revolutionary War, *7991*
1849 Gas mask, *4402*
1880 Obelisk to be brought to the United States, *5403*
1900 Grand American Trapshoot tournament with clay targets, *7476*
1913 Animated cartoon made with cel animation, *5532*
1918 Airplane bombing raid by an American air unit, *8044*
1920 Farmer Labor Party convention, *3376*
1933 Electrobasograph, *4949*
1946 Transcontinental round-trip airplane flight made within 24 hours, *1465*
1947 Golfer born in America to win the British Women's Amateur Golf Tournament, *7363*
1950 Nuclear engineering course at a college, *3248*
1953 Newspaper advertisement that looked three-dimensional, *2345*

1979 Human-powered aircraft to cross the English Channel, *1406*

June 13

1774 Slave importation ban enacted by a colony, *2242*
1825 Law code adopted by a state, *4621*
1854 Chinese graduate of an American college, *3011*
1893 Horse race of 1,000 miles, *7396*
1906 Consumer protection law enacted by Congress, *2311*
1910 Airplane round trip, *1430*
1913 County public defender, *4639*
1917 Soil conference, *1005*
1925 Telecast of an object in motion, *7825*
1927 American flag displayed from the right hand of the Statue of Liberty, *1130*
1933 Sodium vapor lamps, *3499*
1944 Wire recorder for sound recording, *5250*
1967 Supreme Court justice who was African-American, *2763*
1995 Brown dwarf star to be discovered, *6685*
1996 Political asylum granted to avoid genital mutilation, *5883*

June 14

1623 Breach-of-promise suit, *4804*
1642 Compulsory education law in a colony, *3043*
1777 American flag to represent the United States, *1118*
1834 Diving suit, *6709*
　　　Sandpaper patent, *4394*
1854 Entomologist hired by the federal government, *6743*
1877 Flag Day, *4240*
　　　West Point graduate who was African-American, *3199*
1881 Player piano, *1316*
1884 Underground burial of electric wires to be required by a state, *2222*
1901 Professional open golf championship match, *7344*
1915 Protestant church for lepers, *6533*
1917 Marine regiment to land in Europe in World War I, *8034*
1922 President to make a radio broadcast, *6210*
1927 Monument to the American flag, *5414*
1929 Transcontinental daily air-rail passenger service, *1411*
1938 Chlorophyll, *4997*
1942 Handheld rocket launcher, *8133*
1951 Birth to be shown on closed-circuit television, *2163*
　　　Electronic computer for commercial use, *2529*
1954 Civil defense test held nationwide, *4089*
1983 Data from interstellar space, *7088*

June 14—*continued*

Spacecraft to leave the solar system, *7088*

1993 Supreme Court justice who was a Jewish woman, *2762*

June 15

1752 Lightning demonstration, *6767*
1775 General of the Continental Army, *5146*
1844 Vulcanized rubber, *4486*
1858 Stone crusher, *5332*
1859 Mastoid operation, *5078*
1867 Gallstone operation, *5079*
1869 Celluloid, *4480*
1876 National political convention to be addressed by a woman, *3336*
1894 Commercial museum, *5580*
1905 West Point graduates who were Chinese nationals, *3201*
1909 Baseball with a cork center, *7109*
1915 Fifty-dollar gold pieces minted by the federal government, *5376*
1917 Army training camp for African-American officers, *5184*
1920 Wedding broadcast over the radio, *4819*
1928 Airship transfer of mail to a train, *1523*
1929 Curb exchange to transact more business in a day than the New York Stock Exchange, *3825*
1967 Rock music festival, *1372*

June 16

1775 Army engineering department, *5177*
1900 Revolver shooting tournament, *7477*
1909 Airplane sold commercially, *1388*
1922 Helicopter flight, *1572*
1933 Bank deposit insurance law enacted by Congress, *3782*
1941 Civilian airport owned and operated by the federal government, *1508*
1969 Army War College graduates who were women, *3206*

June 17

1775 Army chief engineer, *5163*
1863 Accident insurance company, *4504*
1866 Mourning postage stamp, *6080*
1894 Poliomyelitis epidemic, *2877*
1912 Airplane accident involving a woman that was fatal, *1393*

Horse race mutuel ticket to pay more than $1,000, *7397*

1937 Ski lift, *7484*
1942 American expeditionary force to land in Africa in World War II, *8055*
1946 Mobile telephone commercial service, *7740*
1947 Round-the-world commercial airplane service, *1416*

1950 Kidney transplant, *5095*
1957 Weight lifter to lift more than 6,000 pounds, *7587*
1991 President whose body was exhumed, *6208*
1994 World Cup soccer tournament held in the United States, *7496*

June 18

1621 Duel, *2807*
1861 Fly casting tournament, *7285*

Telegram dispatched from an aerial station, *7699*

1877 Postage stamp for balloon mail, *6059*
1885 Library society (local), *4689*
1895 Carbide factory, *4438*
1910 Commerce court established by the federal government, *2713*

Ticker-tape shower for a celebrity, *3666*

1916 Pilot from the United States shot down in World War I, *8029*
1934 Nationwide highway planning surveys authorized by Congress, *6631*
1936 Bicycle traffic court, *7196*
1959 Telecast received from England, *7851*
1964 Transpacific telephone service using the transoceanic cable, *7749*
1983 Astronaut who was a woman to fly in space, *7048*

June 19

1754 Colonial congress, *2572*
1841 Underwater torpedo operated by electric current, *8098*
1846 Baseball game, *7111*
1849 Melodeon patent, *1309*
1876 Lifesaving medal awarded by the Treasury Department, *1653*
1884 Graduate student who was a woman to receive a university fellowship, *3012*
1905 Movie theater, *3705*
1910 Father's Day, *4244*
1911 Movie censorship board established by a state, *5541*
1913 Immunology society, *5048*
1923 State law to establish English as an official language, *5870*
1931 Automatic swinging doors operated by a photoelectric cell, *2087*
1934 Movie of the sun, *6689*
1939 Pinball ban enacted by a city, *7455*
1946 Boxing match at which admission tickets sold at $100, *7245*
1956 Federal aid to libraries, *4678*
1977 Catholic saint who was a male American citizen, *6482*

June 20

1867 Territory annexed by the federal government that was noncontiguous, *5968*

1909 Balloon honeymoon, *4808*
1945 Naval ship with a mixed company of male and female personnel, *6937*
1960 World heavyweight boxing champion to regain his crown, *7255*
1967 Public defender hired by a state, *4642*

June 21

1622 Alcohol prohibition enforcement officers, *2672*
1768 Physician to receive a Bachelor of Medicine degree, *3131*
1869 Health board established by a state government, *4177*
1913 Parachute jump from an airplane by a woman, *1582*
1922 Massacre of strikebreakers by union members, *4597*
Taconite production, *5342*
1943 Soldier's Medal awarded to a woman, *1663*
1948 Long-playing microgroove phonograph records, *7012*
1970 Major league baseball player to make seven consecutive hits in seven times at bat in the same game, *7156*
1977 Attorney general to be incarcerated, *6127*

June 22

1775 Continental money, *5347*
1832 Machine for manufacturing pins, *4350*
1843 Grain elevator operated by steam, *1048*
1872 Telegraph call boxes, *7701*
1874 Osteopathic physician, *4975*
1896 Physician who was a Chinese woman, *4978*
1939 Beauty pageant to be shown on television, *3629*
National water skiing tournament, *7592*
1942 V-mail film, *6012*
1946 Jet airplane to transport mail, *6030*
1960 Multisatellite launching, *7061*
1973 Probate delay law enacted by a state, *2842*
1977 Coast Guard officers who were women who served aboard ships, *5214*
1993 First Lady who was also a federal official, *6133*

June 23

1775 Book made with American paper, ink, and type, *1738*
1836 Federal treasury surplus to be returned to the states, *7596*
1844 Branding punishment by a federal court, *2818*
1848 Congressional lobbyist who was a woman, *2563*
1860 Secret service established by the federal government, *4169*

1869 Labor bureau established by a state, *4557*
Probation officer for juvenile delinquents to be hired by a state, *2822*
1871 Natural gas plant operated by a city, *3515*
1887 Hospital designed exclusively for infants, *4884*
1888 Presidential nominee who was African-American, *3409*
1899 Medal of Honor awarded to an African-American soldier in the Spanish-American War, *1676*
1904 Motorboat race under organized rules, *7216*
1916 Pilot from the United States killed in World War I, *8030*
1926 Lipreading tournament held nationally, *3036*
1938 Airplane instructor's license, *1601*
Aquarium for large marine animals, *1190*
1960 Coast-to-coast solar-powered two-way radio conversation, *6282*
1967 High school for pregnant teenage girls, *3092*
1970 Physician with a mobile medical office, *4979*
1989 Human-powered submarine race, *7219*

June 24

1497 European to set foot on the North American continent after the Vikings, *5893*
1579 Christian religious service in English on the Pacific Coast, *6501*
1647 Woman in America to appeal for the right to vote, *3420*
1784 Balloon flight, *1535*
1885 Episcopal bishop who was African-American, *6551*
1898 Army officer killed in battle in the Spanish-American War, *8010*
Land battle in the Spanish-American War, *8011*
1910 Federal law requiring radios on ships, *4222*
1930 Radar detection of airplanes, *7676*
1936 Federal administrator who was an African-American woman, *2257*
1940 Political convention to be televised, *3342*
1948 Presidential candidate who was renominated after a defeat, *3414*
1964 Picturephone commercial service, *7750*
1970 Cabinet member to serve in four different capacities, *6120*

June 25

1798 Immigration law enacted by Congress, *5863*
1844 President married while in office, *6190*

June 25—*continued*

1868 Workday of eight hours to be authorized by Congress, *4556*

1873 College president who was a woman, *2971*

1910 Postal savings bank, *3775*

1938 Minimum wage law enacted by Congress, *4578*

1946 Bomber plane with the Flying Wing design, *1491*

1953 Passenger to circle the world on commercial airlines in less than 100 hours, *1477*

1967 Worldwide live television program, *7856*

1993 AIDS policy coordinator for the federal government, *4192*

June 26

1614 Lottery, *3640*

1721 Inoculation against smallpox using material from human smallpox pustules, *4914*

1797 Plow patent, *1041*

1819 Bicycle patent, *7180*

1848 Pure food and drug law established by Congress, *4175*

1870 Boardwalk, *2063*

1894 Round-the-world bicycle trip by a woman, *7202*

1907 Savings bank life insurance, *4547*

1911 Transcontinental group tour by car, *5473*

1919 Bank wholly owned and operated by a state, *3779*

Illustrated tabloid, *5653*

1945 Federal treaty signed by a woman, *4006*

1947 Transatlantic mobile telephone call between two cars, *7765*

1950 Pilot to destroy an enemy airplane in the Korean War, *7975*

1951 Television program in color, *7784*

1959 Postage stamp having the same design as that of another country, *6092*

June 27

1564 Painting of an American scene by a European painter, *1211*

1652 Traffic law enacted by a colony, *4216*

1775 Paymaster general of the Continental Army, *5164*

1776 Execution by the Army, *2795*

1844 Presidential candidate to be assassinated, *3404*

1861 Union naval officer killed in the Civil War, *7956*

1911 Airplane flight under a bridge, *1437*

1923 Airplane refueling attempt in midair, *1496*

1929 Public demonstration of color television, *7811*

1950 Korean War combat mission, *7976*

1955 Telecast originating live in three countries, *7846*

1969 Homosexual rights protest, *6836*

1979 Judge of the U.S. Court of Appeals who was an African-American woman, *2732*

1980 State police class in which women completed training, *4153*

1988 Ban on surrogate motherhood enacted by a state, *2168*

June 28

1687 Knighthood conferred on a person born in America, *6641*

1778 Revolutionary War conflict in which American and British troops met on equal terms, *8002*

1794 Warship builder, *5260*

1798 Prize money awarded by the Navy, *5262*

1832 Cholera epidemic, *2876*

1834 Geological survey authorized by Congress, *6710*

1845 Newspaper with a full page of woodcut engravings, *5686*

1877 Cricket magazine, *4783*

1884 American Derby horse race, *7393*

1919 Naval vessel named for an enlisted man, *8035*

1925 Caterpillar Club member who was a woman, *1586*

1935 Virus obtained in crystalline form, *5059*

1939 Transatlantic commercial airplane service, *1415*

1940 Registration of aliens by the federal government, *5872*

1956 Nuclear reactor built for private industrial research, *3549*

1976 Air Force Academy cadets who were women, *3193*

June 29

1810 Foreign missionary society, *6572*

1936 High-definition telecast, *7834*

1948 Parcel post domestic air service, *6033*

1955 Rock and roll song to hit No. 1 in the pop charts, *1369*

1956 College student to receive assistance from the federal government as the child of a deceased veteran, *3014*

High jump over seven feet, *7563*

1962 Pay television dramatic program, *7787*

1972 Pictorial postal cards, *6050*

1995 Spacecraft launched by the United States to dock with a Russian space station, *7091*

June 30

1812 Treasury notes bearing interest, *3814*

1831 Railroad to carry troops, *6324*
1838 Caster for bedsteads, *4323*
1859 Daredevil to cross Niagara Falls on a tightrope, *3677*
1860 Baseball team to tour, *7160*
1863 Civil War bloodshed north of the Mason-Dixon Line, *7967*
1864 Cigarette tax, *2698*
State park, *3734*
1870 Law school graduate who was a woman, *3124*
1879 Electric company organized to produce and sell electricity, *3457*
1896 Electric stove, *4298*
1899 Bicycle racer to attain the speed of a mile a minute, *7193*
1905 Balloon to land on a building, *1540*
1909 Coin bearing the likeness of a president, *5375*
Fireproof baseball stadium, *7507*
1910 Airplane bombing experiment, *8113*
1921 Former president to become chief justice of the Supreme Court, *6164*
1930 Catholic saints who were active in North America, *6472*
Round-the-world radio broadcast, *6275*
1936 Work week of 40 hours to be required by Congress, *4567*
1946 Atomic bomb dropped from an airplane over water, *8124*
1948 Telephone recording devices, *7724*
Transistor, *3439*
Water pollution law enacted by Congress, *3716*
1953 Sports car with a plastic laminated fiber-glass body, *5455*
1956 Airplane disaster involving more than 100 persons, *1404*
1963 Nuclear reactor fueled by plutonium, *3554*
1965 Hotel built over a pier, *2434*
Perfecta or Exacta horse race, *7403*

July

1625 Land sale by Native Americans to Europeans, *5918*
1640 Book published in America, *1728*
Hymnbook published in America, *1931*
1649 Missionary society established for the English colonies, *6567*
1778 Representative of a foreign country to the United States, *3983*
1818 Science journal, *4767*
1819 Lithograph, *1214*
1834 Electric motor using direct current, *3453*
1838 African-American magazine, *4745*
Workers' compensation lawsuit involving the rights of an injured servant against his master, *4552*
1839 Dental journal, *4754*

1845 Photograph to gain world fame, *5814*
1846 Astronomy magazine, *4770*
1848 Shorthand journal, *4718*
1855 Postal directory, *1816*
1859 Electric light for household illumination, *3490*
1862 Taps, *1382*
1865 Dental society member who was a woman, *4862*
1868 Cattle club to promote Jersey cattle, *1090*
1874 Corset, *2271*
1892 Single tax adopted by a city for local revenue purposes, *7651*
1904 Vocational high school for girls, *3086*
1909 Concrete rural road, *6624*
1911 Naval airplane, *1483*
1923 Neon advertising sign, *2350*
1925 Dry ice manufactured commercially, *4441*
1927 Drive-up mailbox, *6009*
1929 Night coach, *5422*
1930 Aerial photograph in natural colors, *5826*
1934 Talking book for blind listeners, *2029*
1951 Kenaf fiber, *1027*
1953 Helicopter fully operated by remote control, *1567*
1962 Smog chamber for air pollution research, *3717*
1963 Zip codes, *6013*
1967 Zen Buddhist monastery, *6439*
1971 Book collection of importance on ultra-microfiche, *4687*
1987 Principal chief of the Cherokee Nation who was a woman, *4085*
1992 Liver transplant using a baboon liver, *5106*
1994 Team to achieve a perfect score in the International Mathematical Olympiad, *3249*
1995 High-resolution maps of the ocean floor, *4803*
1997 Teraflop computer, *2541*

July 1

1731 Circulating library, *4661*
1785 Copper cents minted by a state, *5355*
1795 Supreme Court chief justice whose nomination was not confirmed, *2754*
1827 Spanish newspaper, *5665*
1835 Railroad to run trains to Washington, *6327*
1847 Postage stamps depicting a president, *6078*
Postage stamps issued by the Post Office Department, *6052*
1851 Insurance board established by a state government, *4503*
1852 Body to lie in state in the Capitol rotunda, *2564*
1855 Registered mail, *5991*
1859 Gas journal, *4771*

July 1—*continued*

Intercollegiate baseball game, *7114*
1862 Inheritance tax levied by Congress, *7647*
  Passport fee, *5885*
  Polygamy ban enacted by Congress, *4807*
  Revenue stamps issued by the federal government, *7648*
1863 Free mail delivery in cities, *5996*
1867 Transpacific sidewheeler steamer, *6871*
1873 Patent examiner who was a woman, *4656*
1874 Zoo, *1186*
1881 International commercial telephone service, *7732*
1893 Bicycle track of wood, *7191*
1896 Life insurance policy rated substandard, *4546*
1898 Balloon destroyed by enemy gunfire, *8012*
1899 Rhodes Scholars, *2961*
1910 Bread factory that was completely automatic, *3925*
1912 Life insurance group contract, *4549*
1919 Fire and tornado insurance fund enacted by a state, *4533*
1921 Sales tax enacted by a state, *7656*
1924 Transcontinental regular airmail service, *6019*
1925 Airmail long-distance night service, *6020*
1930 Streamlined submarine, *6968*
1933 Drama broadcast on radio from a ship at sea, *1261*
1934 X-ray photograph of the entire body of a living person taken in a one-second exposure, *4906*
1937 Senate parliamentarian, *2632*
1941 Navy task force assembled for foreign service, *5302*
  Television commercial, *2341*
1945 Labor antidiscrimination commission of a state government, *4568*
1952 Drug treatment center for minors, *2690*
1954 Navy admirals who were brothers, *5294*
1961 Air raid shelter for a community, *4090*
1967 Satellite to transmit colored photographs of the full earth face, *7075*
1972 Navy admiral who was African-American, *5274*

July 2

1717 Book auction printed catalog, *1780*
1776 Election law enacted by a colony granting voting rights to women, *3422*
1777 Slavery emancipation law enacted by a state, *2244*
1800 District land office, *5953*
1829 Catholic community of African-American nuns, *6462*
1862 Land grant for an agricultural college, *2892*
1864 National hall of fame, *5579*

1867 Elevated railroad, *6334*
1890 Antitrust law enacted by Congress, *2521*
1908 Price regulation law enacted by a state, *2522*
1917 Radio telephone communication from an airplane, *7759*
1919 Stowaway on an aircraft, *1518*
1921 Boxing match to gross $1 million, *7240*
  Heavyweight championship boxing match broadcast on radio, *7241*
1922 Modern carillon, *1323*
1926 Air force branch of the military, *5133*
1931 Polo game played outdoors at night, *7461*
1932 Presidential candidate to accept his party's nomination in person, *3413*
1935 Drama school at a college, *2910*
1943 Army pilot who was African-American to shoot down an Axis airplane in World War II, *8063*
1957 Vacuum-cast steel, *4498*
1964 Automated tanker under the American flag, *6902*
1971 Litter law enacted by a state, *3720*
1973 Navy chaplain who was a woman, *5205*
1978 Moon of Pluto to be observed, *6684*

July 3

1754 Battle in the French and Indian War, *7971*
1839 Teacher training school established by a state, *3260*
1871 Narrow-gauge locomotive, *6357*
1878 Airship, *1512*
1886 Newspaper page set by linotype, *5793*
1913 Bird for which a definite crossing of the Atlantic was recorded, *1165*
1934 Payment by the Federal Deposit Insurance Corporation, *3784*
1952 Mitral valve corrective surgery, *5092*
1956 Ship outfitted for hurricane research, *6775*
1977 Magnetic resonance image of a human body, *4912*

July 4

1776 Signer of the Declaration of Independence, *1113*
1777 American flag displayed on a man-of-war, *1119*
1778 Secret service established in a colony, *4168*
1781 Independence Day, *4232*
1789 Drawback legislation enacted by Congress, *2471*
  Tariff legislation enacted by Congress, *7663*
1801 President to review the military forces, *6147*
1810 Agricultural journal, *4703*

1826 Malleable iron castings, *4451*
1831 Railroad car with a center aisle, *6371*
Trade journal, *4710*
Treaty between the federal government and a foreign nation to provide for mutual reduction of import duties, *4004*
1832 Performance of "America the Beautiful", *1380*
1836 Settlers to cross the continent who were women, *5960*
1840 Aquatic play, *1249*
1883 Wild West Show, *3689*
1884 Bullfight, *7258*
1888 Rodeo for roping and tying steers, *3690*
1892 Double-deck streetcar, *6401*
1902 Motorcycle endurance run, *7437*
1908 Aviation trophy, *1641*
Navy admiral who was Jewish, *5272*
1928 Daredevil to go over Niagara Falls in a rubber ball, *3681*
1935 Streamlined ferryboat, *6912*
1942 Bombing mission by American forces over enemy-occupied territory in Europe in World War II, *8056*
1955 King cobra snakes, *1157*
1967 Jockey to win seven consecutive races in one day, *7414*
1976 General of the Armies of the United States with the rank of six stars, *5161*
1977 Parade in which the marching music was supplied by transistor radios, *3670*

July 5

1775 Insignia to designate state army regiments, *5222*
1776 Printing of the Declaration of Independence, *1114*
1900 National political convention at which a woman made a seconding speech, *3339*
1916 Transcontinental motorcycle trip by women, *5493*
1944 Rocket airplane for military use, *1490*
1950 Soldier killed in action in the Korean War, *7977*
1952 Vice presidential candidate who was an African-American woman, *3415*
1972 New York Stock Exchange director who was African-American, *3834*
New York Stock Exchange governor who was a woman, *3833*

July 6

1776 Newspaper to publish the Declaration of Independence, *1115*
1785 Decimal system of money, *5348*
1787 Continental coin, *5357*
1798 Deportation of aliens authorized by Congress, *5864*
1858 Shoe manufacturing machine, *2303*

1869 Sawmill to use a band saw, *4404*
1871 Baseball game between an all-white team and an all-African-American team, *7116*
1895 Shoot-the-chutes, *3624*
1899 Driver license board, *5469*
1905 International exchange of fingerprints, *4162*
1933 All-star major league baseball game, *7130*
Baseball player to hit a home run in an All-Star game, *7150*
1939 Airmail regular delivery service by autogiro, *6029*
1955 Seat belt law enacted by a state, *4228*
1961 District attorney who was African-American, *2716*
1970 No-fault divorce law enacted by a state, *4810*
1976 Naval Academy students who were women, *3221*
1997 Robot to conduct a roving exploration of the surface of another planet, *7093*

July 7

1802 Comic magazine, *4698*
1838 Steamboat inspection service established by Congress, *4217*
1849 Free public libraries authorized by a state, *4670*
1885 Cartridge-loading machinery, *8110*
1920 Radio compass on a naval airplane, *1495*
1935 Identification of human beings from the pattern formed by the blood vessels of the retina, *4165*
1946 Catholic saint who was an American citizen, *6475*
1948 Navy personnel in the regular Navy who were women, *5266*
1976 State dinner televised from the White House, *6258*
West Point cadets who were women, *3207*
1980 Solar-powered airplane to cross the English Channel, *1481*

July 8

1524 Kidnapping, *2766*
1693 Police uniforms, *4132*
1776 Public reading of the Declaration of Independence, *1116*
1796 Passport, *5884*
1800 Vaccination against smallpox using cowpox, *4915*
1805 Boxer to win distinction in the ring, *7248*
1809 Vaccination program offered by a city, *4917*
1856 Machine gun, *8104*
1861 Press censorship by military authorities, *5604*

July 8—*continued*
1862 Revolving gun turret for ships, *8106*
1892 Psychology society (national), *5043*
1897 Tuberculosis hospital for the poor established by a city, *4900*
1899 Golf champion born in America, *7357*
1916 National park east of the Mississippi River, *3736*
1923 President to visit Alaska and Canada while in office, *6234*
1948 Women's Army Corps member to be part of the Regular Army, *5171*
1950 Officer killed in action in the Korean War, *7978*
1957 Circumnavigation of the world by a submarine, *6991*
1965 Flashbulb device with multiple flashbulbs, *5847*
1968 Movie directed by an African-American director, *5567*

July 9

1792 Agriculture professor at a college, *2890*
1808 Leather-splitting machine, *4456*
1847 Workday of 10 hours to be mandated by a state, *4554*
1864 Boiler inspection law enacted by a state, *4106*
1872 Doughnut cutter, *4295*
1875 Cantilever bridge, *3583*
1886 Coursing club, *7394*
1893 Suture of the human heart, *5090*
1910 Airplane to fly higher than a mile in altitude, *1431*
1914 Auction duplicate bridge championship, *4023*
1922 Swimmer to cover 100 meters freestyle in less than one minute, *7516*
1942 Capture of an American ship captain by a German submarine in World War II, *8057*
1947 Army officer who was a woman, *5170*
1953 Helicopter passenger service, *1568*
1965 Ambassador who was an African-American woman, *3994*

July 10

1791 Catholic seminary, *3268*
1795 Presidential amnesty issued to rebellious citizens, *6143*
1830 Antiquarian bookseller, *1784*
1862 Medal of Honor awarded to a Marine in the Civil War, *1672*
1866 Indelible pencil, *8152*
1890 Election law enacted by a state to grant voting rights to women after the adoption of the Constitution, *3430*
1902 Steel seven-masted schooner, *6875*
1908 Presidential candidate to appear in movie footage, *3411*

1929 Paper money of the present small size, *5393*
1933 Police radio system, *4146*
1934 President to make a radio broadcast from a foreign country, *6214*
President to visit South America while in office, *6235*
1935 Transatlantic nonstop solo flight westbound by a woman, *1453*
1949 Rectangular television tube, *7817*
1962 Commercial satellite, *7069*
Swimmer to swim the English Channel underwater, *7520*
Telephone call conveyed by a privately owned satellite, *7768*
Transoceanic telecast by satellite, *7853*

July 11

1656 Quakers to arrive in America, *6585*
1798 Army lieutenant general, *5148*
Marine band, *5230*
1870 School for African-American children established by a state, *3064*
1890 Library society (state), *4690*
1916 Grant-in-aid enacted by Congress to help the states build roads, *6626*
1919 Golfer to play 180 holes in one day, *7359*
Prisoners in a federal penitentiary to be employed in industry, *2828*
1923 Railroad signal system of continuous cab signals, *6426*
1934 President to go through the Panama Canal while in office, *6167*
1942 Distinguished Service Cross awarded in enemy-occupied territory, *1660*
1966 Sergeant major of the Army, *5174*
1997 Transplant of human embryo tissue, *5108*

July 12

1774 Declaration of independence by citizens of an American colony, *1110*
1859 Paper bag manufacturing machine, *5757*
1862 Medal of Honor of the Army, *1673*
1912 Foreign feature film exhibited, *5512*
1924 Decathlon champion from the United States, *7556*
1928 Outdoor scenes to be televised, *7829*
1957 President to fly in a helicopter, *6229*
1972 Acupuncture treatment center, *4852*
1984 Vice presidential candidate from a major political party who was a woman, *3419*

July 13

1763 Germ warfare, *8089*
1787 Slavery ban enacted for a territory of the United States, *2246*
1836 Numbering system for patents, *4653*
1875 Cash carrier system, *2360*

1915 City orchestra supported by taxes, *1362*
1929 Movie in Esperanto, *5561*
1936 Pensions paid by the federal government to workers in private industry, *4588*
1938 Television theater to be licensed, *7775*

July 14

1798 Tax levied by Congress directly on the states, *7643*
1820 Lightship, *4125*
1853 World's fair, *2409*
1868 Tape measure, *7926*
1870 Pension granted to the widow of a president, *4584*
1891 Corkboard patent, *2045*
1911 Airplane to land on the White House lawn, *6255*
1917 Wedding abroad of a soldier in the American Expeditionary Force, *4817*
1943 National monument dedicated to an African-American, *5416*
1945 Naval bombardment of the Japanese homeland in World War II, *8085*
1954 Radio sextant, *6960*
1959 Nuclear-powered cruiser, *6941*
1965 Spacecraft to transmit close-up photographs of Mars, *7081*
1972 Chairman of a major political party who was a woman, *3344*

July 15

1779 Medal awarded by the Continental Congress to a foreigner, *1650*
1792 Bridge on a large scale, *3566*
1904 Buddhist temple, *6438*
1913 Senator elected by popular vote, *3329*
1920 Airplane flight between New York and Alaska, *1446*
1922 Platypus, *1149*
1929 Hotel at an airport, *2431*
1933 Round-the-world solo airplane flight, *1457*
1940 Betatron, *6801*
1952 Transatlantic helicopter flight, *1576*
1954 Jet airplane used for commercial transport, *1403*
1975 Astronauts to participate in an international spaceflight, *7046*
1994 Movie that cost more than $100 million to make, *5522*

July 16

1769 Catholic mission in California, *6454*
1779 Revolutionary War bayonet charge, *8003*
1798 Health service established by the federal government, *4174*
1845 Regatta, *7208*
1867 Paint ready-mixed, *7925*
1877 Strike suppressed by federal troops in peacetime, *4594*

1912 Airplane torpedo, *8114*
1920 Mobile telephone commercial service, *7735*
1926 Photographs taken under the sea in natural colors, *5825*
1935 Automatic parking meter, *5446*
1936 X-ray photograph showing the complete arterial circulation in an adult human, *4907*
1939 Rack-rail diesel-electric locomotive, *6366*
1945 Atomic bomb explosion, *8123*
1946 Mobile overseas telephone call from a moving vehicle, *7763*
1966 Brother and sister to win national tennis singles championships in the same tournament, *7539*
1969 Astronauts to land on the moon, *7040*
1971 Air Force general who was a woman, *5140*

July 17

1850 Photograph of a star other than the sun, *6693*
1861 Paper money issued by the federal government, *5385*
1862 Military service by African-Americans to be authorized by Congress, *5145*
1867 Dental school to be associated with a medical school, *3167*
1896 College cricket club team to tour England, *7274*
1933 Transcontinental flight made by African-Americans in their own airplane, *1458*
1953 Navy ace in Korea, *1622*
1954 Major league baseball game in which the majority of the players on one team were African-American, *7136*
1955 Electric power generated from nuclear energy to illuminate a town, *3547*
1962 Pilot of an airplane to qualify as an astronaut by attaining a 50-mile altitude, *1623*
1997 Art museum of importance devoted to the work of an individual woman, *5600*

July 18

1627 Oil spring, *3523*
1743 Automaton, *3650*
Newspaper advertisement across two columns, *2320*
1768 Patriotic song by an American, *1376*
1775 Revolutionary War volunteer detachment, *7992*
1794 Silver deposit for coinage, *5364*
1846 Plank road, *6618*
1866 Insurance rate standardization, *4506*
1896 Golf player in an official amateur tournament who was African-American, *7355*
1908 Fireworks law enacted by a city, *4111*

July 18—*continued*

1914 Air service of the Army, *5130*

1940 Helicopter, *1557*

1943 Airship from the United States lost to enemy action in World War II, *8064*

1955 Electric power generated from nuclear energy to be sold commercially, *3548*

1980 Methodist bishop who was a woman, *6562*

July 19

1784 Botanic expedition, *6738*

1848 Bloomers, *2267*

Voting rights convention organized by women, *3425*

1875 Floating hospital, *4883*

1886 Steel vessels of the Navy, *6925*

1909 Unassisted triple play in a major league baseball game, *7126*

1939 Fiberglass sutures, *4957*

1949 President who had been divorced, *6202*

1957 Nuclear warhead mounted on a rocket, *8131*

July 20

1776 Brevet commission in the Army, *5167*

1789 Navigation act enacted by Congress, *2472*

1801 Cheese factory cooperative, *3857*

1831 Cabinet member who was Catholic, *6105*

1858 Baseball game in which spectators were charged admission, *7112*

Baseball series, *7113*

1875 Agricultural experiment station operated by a state, *1003*

Time lock, *2135*

1876 Intercollegiate track meet, *7546*

1891 Anatomy research institute, *5055*

1900 Astronomer employed in the Naval Observatory who was a woman, *6667*

1940 Song to hit No. 1 in the pop charts, *1366*

1948 Transatlantic eastward flight by jet airplane, *1469*

1960 Submerged submarine to fire a Polaris missile, *8142*

1964 Rocket with an electrostatic (ion) engine, *7025*

1969 Mobile telephone call to the moon, *7770*

1976 Photograph taken on Mars, *6705*

July 21

1828 Strike in which a militia was called out, *4593*

1861 Civil War battle, *7957*

1880 Tunnel construction using compressed air, *3616*

1918 Shots fired by German forces to land on American soil in World War I, *8045*

1919 Caterpillar Club member, *1584*

1921 Airplane bombing experiment to sink a battleship, *8117*

1946 Jet airplane to land on a ship, *1466*

1959 Nuclear-powered merchant ship, *6900*

1997 Executive officer of a man-of-war who was a woman, *5300*

July 22

1896 Silverite national convention, *3367*

1933 Opera prima donna who was African-American, *1333*

1939 Judge who was an African-American woman, *2726*

1963 Bank of importance to lease personal property, *3798*

1964 Navy divers to submerge for 10 days, *5268*

1978 Ballet transmitted by satellite, *1238*

1979 Golfer to shoot below his age, *7369*

July 23

1813 Haircloth, *7866*

1827 Swimming school, *7514*

1829 Typewriter, *2384*

1885 Banking association (state), *3770*

1886 Daredevil to jump off the Brooklyn Bridge and survive, *3678*

1921 Broad jump to reach more than 25 feet, *7555*

1930 Transcontinental car trip driven entirely in reverse, *5475*

1937 Pituitary hormone, *4996*

1945 Railroad car with an observation dome, *6388*

1947 Navy jet airplane squadron, *5303*

1953 Transcontinental round-trip solo flight between sunrise and sunset, *1478*

1962 Live telecast to Europe by satellite, *7854*

1965 Coins bearing dates other than the year of issue, *5380*

1972 Satellite composite map of the United States, *4802*

1996 Television station to regularly broadcast high-definition television, *7808*

July 24

1651 Landowner of substance who was African-American, *5928*

1824 Opinion poll, *5601*

1860 Doctor of Philosophy degree, *2977*

1866 State readmitted to the Union after the Civil War, *7605*

1934 Ptarmigan, *1166*

1946 Atomic bomb underwater explosion, *8125*

1956 Adaptable railroad freight car, *6392*

July 25

1832 Railroad accident, *6325*

1854 Paper collar, *2285*
1860 Intercollegiate billiard match, *4018*
1863 Monument to commemorate the Civil War, *5400*
1866 General of the U.S. Army, *5151*
Navy officer to become an admiral, *5270*
1871 Carousel patent, *3620*
Perforated wrapping paper, *5758*
1916 Zoning ordinance, *2205*
1918 District attorney who was a woman, *2714*
1923 Mimeographed daily newspaper, *5654*
1934 President to visit Hawaii while in office, *6236*
1939 Musical comedy to be shown on television, *1268*
1952 Commonwealth of the United States, *5976*
1965 Surgical operation on a bull to correct a sperm block, *5124*
1997 Human stem cells to be cultured in a laboratory, *5068*

July 26

1775 Postmaster general under the Continental Congress, *5983*
1859 Intercollegiate regatta, *7470*
1866 Irrigation law enacted by Congress, *1017*
1880 Steam distribution plant, *3507*
1893 Addressograph, *2365*
1908 Olympic athlete from the United States to win the marathon race, *7553*
1958 Telecast from the stratosphere, *7849*
1963 Geosynchronous satellite, *7071*

July 27

1775 Surgeon general of the Continental Army, *5165*
1784 French newspaper, *5662*
1868 Uniforms for mail carriers, *5998*
1874 Musical with an American theme and original score, *1252*
1933 Execution for kidnapping, *2801*
1971 Brokerage firm whose shares were traded by a major stock exchange, *3835*

July 28

1777 Election law enacted by a state to grant universal voting rights to freemen, *3423*
1862 Railroad post office, *6037*
1866 Metric system usage to be approved by Congress, *2309*
Monument ordered by the federal government from a sculptor who was a woman, *5401*
1869 National union for women, *4610*
1875 Baseball game in which a team made no hits in nine innings, *7118*
1882 Accounting society, *3753*

1903 Bank president who was a woman, *3772*
1933 Cotton acreage reduction payment, *1034*
Singing telegram, *7708*
1959 Congressional representative of Japanese ancestry, *2616*

July 29

1773 Schoolhouse west of the Alleghenies, *6519*
1847 Norwegian newspaper, *5667*
1865 Newspaper published at sea, *5642*
1870 Road pavement of sheet asphalt, *6621*
1899 Bicycle race paced by a motorcycle, *7194*
1949 Gas turbine used by an electrical utility company, *3487*
1952 Transpacific nonstop jet airplane flight, *1475*
1959 Jetway, *1510*
1978 Football game in which referees were allowed to check television instant replays, *7336*
1980 Human antibodies produced artificially, *5005*

July 30

1619 Legislative assembly of a colony, *7622*
1774 Price sheet for commodities, *2321*
1844 Yacht club, *7207*
1850 Meat biscuit, *3920*
1874 Baseball teams to travel abroad, *7163*
1898 Car advertisement in a specialty magazine, *2331*
1909 Airplane purchased by the federal government, *1389*
Intercity airplane flight by a U.S. military officer, *1428*
1946 Rocket to attain a 100-mile altitude, *7019*
1965 Health insurance plan enacted by Congress, *4541*

July 31

1790 Patent granted by the federal government, *4648*
1809 Railroad track that was practical, *6415*
1849 Breech-loading cannon, *8099*
1876 Coast Guard officers' training school, *3209*
1912 Movie censorship law enacted by Congress, *5542*
1918 Dish set made in America for the White House, *6256*
1930 Airship to land and take off from an oceangoing steamship, *1527*
1964 Navy nuclear task force to circumnavigate the globe without refueling, *5307*
Photographs of the moon in close-up, *6701*
Spacecraft to transmit close-up photographs of the lunar surface, *7080*

July 31—*continued*
1971 Astronauts to ride a vehicle on the moon, *7042*

August

1746 Poet who was an African-American woman, *1946*
Poetry collection by an African-American woman, *1946*
1777 Mine barrage, *8090*
1787 Songbook of secular songs, *1937*
1788 Cotton mill, *7882*
1791 Supreme Court decision, *2744*
1796 Gaslights for display, *3654*
1805 Ice exported, *3932*
1817 Paper made by machine, *5749*
1830 Double-deck railroad coaches, *6370*
1833 Army cavalry unit, *5179*
1861 Camp for boys, *2143*
1870 Clearinghouse for stocks and bonds, *3819*
1894 Actor to have an exclusive movie contract, *5524*
1908 Child hygiene bureau, *4186*
Intelligence test in a school for children with mental retardation, *3021*
Tax on aviation levied by a city, *7652*
1913 Gyroscope, *1494*
1921 Correspondence school to offer instruction in Braille, *3029*
1932 Cooperative store operated by women, *2503*
1933 Game management chair at a college, *3078*
1934 Pressure suit, *1386*
1941 Plastic car, *5451*
1963 Supercomputer, *2532*
1973 Belly-dancing course at a college, *2916*
Nazi death camp guard to be deported, *5880*
1974 Magazine about recreational drugs, *4740*
1987 Swimmer to cross the Bering Strait, *7522*

August 1

1776 Soldier killed in the Revolutionary War who was Jewish, *7996*
1787 Printed copies of the Constitution, *1103*
1790 Census of the United States, *5848*
1841 Commercial rating agency, *3815*
1861 Former president to serve as an official of an enemy government, *6158*
Patent issued by the Confederate States of America, *4655*
1872 Natural gas pipeline constructed over a long distance, *3516*
1873 Cable car put into service, *6398*
1874 Label patent, *4657*
1886 Laboratory for the study of parasites in livestock, *5120*
1893 Biscuits of shredded wheat, *3924*

Navy medical school, *3171*
1906 Diamonds in actual rock, *5340*
1911 Pilot licensed by the Aero Club of America who was a woman, *1596*
1912 Marine pilot, *5235*
1923 Cancer hospital established by a city, *4890*
1930 Hydroelectric power plant operated by a county, *3480*
Photographic flashbulbs, *5842*
1939 Vitamin K to be synthesized, *3973*
1951 Medal of Honor awarded to a Marine in the Korean War, *1684*
1953 Aluminum-faced building, *2091*
1957 Commercial building with solar heating, *2067*
Insurance company to insure the lives of animals exclusively, *4517*
1960 Submarine to make a submerged passage through the Northwest Passage, *6997*
1963 Postage stamp with fluorescent tagging, *6071*
1972 Vice presidential candidate of a major political party to resign before the election, *3417*

August 2

1791 Patent granted jointly to a father and son, *4650*
1819 Parachute jump from a balloon, *1580*
1862 Army ambulance corps, *5011*
1886 Margarine law enacted by Congress, *3884*
1923 President and First Lady to die during the term for which he had been elected, *6196*
1934 Train of airplanes, *1459*
1937 Marijuana ban enacted by Congress, *2689*
1946 Nuclear product for peacetime use, *3545*
1971 Crime insurance policy authorized by a state, *4518*

August 3

1492 Letter containing a description of America, *1093*
1750 Teaching methodology book, *1825*
1852 Intercollegiate rowing race, *7468*
1861 Balloon carrier, *6919*
1882 Immigration ban enacted by Congress, *5867*
1904 Use of "American" as an adjective, *1098*
1922 Drama broadcast on radio, *1257*
1942 Navy officer commissioned in the U.S. Naval Reserve who was a woman, *5287*
1945 Color news photograph transmitted by radio fax for publication, *5695*
1958 Crossing of the North Pole underwater by a submerged submarine, *6993*
Sailor to reenlist in the Navy while under the North Pole, *5267*

August 4

1790 Bonds issued by the federal government, *3811*

Coast guard service, *5208*

Naval protection, *5259*

1874 Chautauqua organization meeting, *2885*

1894 Railroad to use an electric engine, *6340*

1921 Tennis match broadcast on radio, *7532*

1930 Bobsled run, *7581*

1937 Okapi, *1155*

1942 President to become a godfather to a member of the British royal family, *6200*

1956 Motorcycle to exceed 200 miles per hour, *5491*

August 5

1799 Supreme Court decision in a matter between states, *2745*

1858 Transatlantic telegraph cable, *7698*

1861 Income tax levied by Congress, *7646*

1892 Commemorative coin, *5373*

1909 Corporation tax levied by Congress, *7653*

1911 Airplane race between cities, *7293*

1914 Electric traffic signal lights, *4224*

1921 Pulitzer Prize for an editorial cartoon, *1710*

Radio broadcast of a baseball game with a play-by-play description, *7128*

1923 Swimmer from the United States to swim the English Channel, *7517*

1926 Movie with sound to be released as a feature, *5557*

1964 Navy pilot shot down and captured in North Vietnam, *8015*

1990 Round-the-world solo sailing trip by an African-American, *7002*

August 6

1727 Catholic convent, *6451*

1776 Shaker religious community, *6521*

1819 Military school, *3184*

1832 Phrenologist, *4969*

1846 Warehouse legislation enacted by Congress, *2480*

1890 Execution by electrocution, *2799*

1912 Progressive Party national convention, *3373*

1914 American to sail to Europe to fight in World War I, *8025*

1926 Swimmer who was an American woman to swim the English Channel, *7518*

1936 Catholic mass in an airship over the ocean, *6473*

1945 Atomic bomb explosion over enemy territory, *8086*

1954 Television commercial in color to appear on a local show, *2346*

1971 Road paved with glasphalt, *6635*

1996 Scientific evidence for life on Mars, *7027*

August 7

1679 Great Lakes vessel, *6851*

1782 Badge of honor for enlisted men and noncommissioned officers, *1656*

1789 Lighthouse built after American independence, *4124*

1794 Presidential commission, *6142*

1807 Steamboat to make regular trips, *6861*

1847 Plow for pulverizing the soil, *1049*

1888 Revolving door, *2081*

1942 American offensive in the Pacific in World War II, *8081*

1953 Navy–Marine Corps Medal for Heroism awarded to a woman, *1668*

1959 Satellite to transmit photographs of the earth, *7057*

1974 Tightrope walker to span two skyscrapers, *3669*

August 8

1797 Medical journal, *4750*

1865 Streamlined railroad train, *6428*

1866 Queen to visit the United States, *4079*

1876 Mimeograph, *5784*

1900 International tennis matches for the Davis Cup challenge trophy, *7531*

1930 Stock order from a zeppelin, *3826*

1933 Savings and loan association established by the federal government, *3783*

1942 Enemy saboteurs executed in the United States, *8058*

1950 Swimmer who was a woman to swim the English Channel in both directions, *7519*

1958 Presidential Unit Citation award in peacetime, *1643*

August 9

1607 Thanksgiving worship service, *6503*

1829 Locomotive for railroad use, *6348*

1848 Free Soil Party convention, *3352*

1859 Escalator patent, *2106*

1892 Two-way telegraph, *7702*

1893 Bowling magazine, *4786*

1916 National park to contain an active volcano, *3737*

1939 Tennis tournament to be shown on television, *7533*

1944 Public service symbol of the federal government, *3714*

1956 Educational television network that was statewide and state-supported, *7806*

1971 Airport baggage scanning system, *1511*

1974 President to resign, *6177*

President who came to the office through appointment rather than election, *6178*

1989 Chairman of the Joint Chiefs of Staff who was African-American, *5129*

August 10

1821 State west of the Mississippi River to be admitted to the Union, *7603*
1869 Movie projector patent, *5570*
1878 Correspondence course of a serious nature, *2886*
1885 Electric streetcars commercially operated, *6400*
1886 Welding by the electric process, *4435*
1889 Photograph of a meteor, *6697*
1960 American flag to orbit the earth, *1131*
1976 Soccer player to score 12 points in one game, *7494*
1988 Compensation of Japanese-Americans interned during World War II, *8087*

August 11

1760 Methodist preacher, *6557*
1860 Silver mill, *4469*
1861 Senator to address the Senate in military uniform, *2648*
1874 Sprinkler head, *4108*
1896 Electric socket operated by a pull chain, *4344*
1909 Radio SOS call from an American ship, *6287*
1924 Newsreels showing presidential candidates, *5698*
1928 Presidential nomination ceremony broadcast on radio, *3412*
1942 Movie star who was a weapons inventor, *5527*
1960 Space capsule recovered from an orbiting satellite, *7062*
1972 Sailors assigned to regular Navy shipboard duty who were women, *5269*
1980 Subcompact car with front wheel drive, *5462*
1997 President to use the line-item veto, *6181*

August 12

1585 Letters written in English in America, *1095*
1834 Dental amalgam for filling teeth, *4858*
1851 Sewing machine equipped with a rocking treadle or double treadle, *4353*
1862 Encased postage stamps, *6055*
1898 Island territory annexed by the federal government, *5974*
1917 Volunteer unit made up of college women to serve overseas, *5185*
1918 Airmail regular service, *6016*
Concrete barge, *6887*
1923 Portable movie camera, *5574*
1953 Transatlantic solo boat journey by a woman, *6990*
1954 Execution carried out by the federal government for the killing of an FBI agent, *2804*

1955 Minimum hourly wage of one dollar, *4579*
1958 Submarine to travel under the North Pole from the east, *6994*
1960 Communications satellite, *7063*

August 13

1587 Native American to become a Protestant, *6502*
1751 Academy, *2929*
1838 Astronomical observations book, *1985*
1889 Pay telephone, *7715*
1918 Marine reserve member who was a woman, *5233*
1928 Airmail service from ship to shore, *6022*
Standard broadcast station to transmit a television image, *7795*
1935 Roller derby, *7465*
1946 Soldering gun, *7941*
1955 Guaranteed 52-week wage in a major industry, *4570*
1970 No-fault car insurance law enacted by a state, *4521*

August 14

1775 Quartermaster of the Continental Army, *5166*
1776 Land grant to deserters from the British Army during the Revolutionary War, *7997*
1820 Eye hospital, *4872*
1834 Ice-making machine, *4346*
1888 Electric meter, *3465*
1911 Airplane rescue at sea by another airplane, *1438*
1917 Gyroscopic stabilizer, *6956*
1924 Radio two-way broadcast from an airplane, *6273*
1934 Revenue stamp printed by the Post Office Department, *7660*
1936 National Union for Social Justice national convention, *3377*
1956 Helicopter refueling flight, *1577*
Stroboradiograph, *6808*
1959 Telecast from space showing the earth, *6690*
1965 Congressional page who was African-American, *2592*
1966 Photograph of the earth taken from the moon, *6702*
Spacecraft to transmit photographs from lunar orbit, *7083*
1976 Softball game of 365 innings, *7498*
1982 National Navajo Code Talkers Day, *8082*

August 15

1635 Hurricane of record, *2860*
1790 Catholic bishop appointed to serve in the United States, *6457*

August 21—*continued*

1923 Airport runway illumination, *1504*
1928 Puppet show to be televised, *1259*
1959 State admitted to the Union that was separated by a substantial body of water, *7608*
1965 Astronaut to orbit the earth on two trips, *7032*

August 22

1654 Jewish settler in America, *5892*
1670 Native American preacher of Christianity, *6513*
1762 Newspaper editor who was a woman, *5610*
1771 Dwarf exhibited as a theatrical attraction, *3653*
1822 Printing press for printing wallpaper in color, *5770*
1851 Yacht from the United States to win an international yacht race, *7209*
1865 Soap in liquid form, *4271*
1902 President to ride in a car, *6223*
1904 Carnegie Hero Fund Commission award granted to a woman, *1639*
1906 Phonograph with an enclosed horn in the cabinet, *7009*
1909 Airplane race won by an American in Europe, *7290*
1912 Navy dental corps, *5019*
1928 Remote television pickup, *7830*
1939 Spray can, *7939*
1942 Ship transported overland across the Rocky Mountains, *6935*

August 23

1784 State denied admission into the Union, *7601*
1853 Bank clearinghouse, *3764*
1859 Elevator in a hotel, *2107*
1865 Trial of a war criminal by the federal government, *7969*
1892 Printed streetcar transfers, *6402*
1900 Business organization for African-Americans (national), *2450*
1904 Tire chains, *5497*
1956 Transcontinental nonstop helicopter flight, *1578*
1963 Illuminated nine-hole regulation golf course, *7350*
1977 Human-powered aircraft, *1406*
1980 Acoustic microscope, *6750*

August 24

1675 Catholic holy orders, *6450*
1676 Court-martial in a colony, *2738*
1853 Village improvement society, *2191*
1869 Waffle iron patent, *4294*

1912 Parcel post service, *6006*
1932 Holes in one shot by a father and son in the same golf game, *7362*
Transcontinental nonstop airplane flight by a woman, *1456*
1950 United Nations delegate who was African-American, *3992*
1951 Air Force Medal of Honor for action in the Korean War, *1667*
1959 Senator of Chinese ancestry, *2657*
1964 Catholic mass in English, *6479*
1969 Commercial ship to conquer the Northwest Passage, *7000*

August 25

1814 President to face enemy gunfire while in office, *6148*
1830 Race between a locomotive and a horse-drawn vehicle, *7388*
1831 Bedspring manufacturing patent, *4322*
1840 Seeding machine, *1047*
1886 International polo series, *7458*
1920 Olympic gold medalist from the United States who was a woman, *7445*
1925 Miniature television tube, *7809*
1940 Wedding during a parachute jump, *4822*
1941 Health insurance clause in a labor contract, *4538*
1958 Pension for presidents and their widows, *6172*
1997 Voting rights in space, *3435*

August 26

1776 Pension law enacted by Congress, *4582*
1790 Historical society (state), *5710*
1857 Teachers' organization (national), *3225*
1858 News dispatch by commercial telegraph, *5603*
1873 Public school kindergarten, *3074*
1884 Linotype machine, *5805*
1920 Constitutional amendment proposal guaranteeing women the right to vote, *3432*
1938 Radio broadcast from a tape recording, *6279*
1939 Major league baseball game to be shown on television, *7132*
1954 Editorial to be broadcast over radio and television, *5707*
1968 National political convention to propose African-Americans for the offices of president and vice president, *3343*

August 27

1650 Expedition of Englishmen to cross the Allegheny Mountains, *5927*
1665 Theatrical performance, *1239*
1667 Cyclone of record, *2862*
1787 Steamboat to carry a man, *6854*
1856 Industrial school for girls, *3286*

1859 Oil well that was commercially productive, *3528*
1889 Clarinet made exclusively of metal, *1319*
1910 Radio broadcast sent from an airplane, *6266*
1959 Ship to fire a Polaris missile, *8140*
1968 Ambassador assassinated in office, *3995*

August 28

1798 Vineyard, *1013*
1830 Passenger locomotive, *6349*
1867 Territory annexed by the federal government beyond the nation's continental limits, *5969*
1894 Manganese steel for railroad tracks, *4496*
1911 Gyrocompass installed on an American naval vessel, *6955*
1922 International golf match, *7346*
Radio commercial, *2333*
1938 College degree awarded to a ventriloquist's dummy, *2981*
1957 Senate filibuster to last for more than 24 hours, *2633*
1964 Weather satellite to provide high-resolution cloud-cover photographs at night, *7072*
1972 Air Force ace in Vietnam, *1624*
1994 Golf champion of African-American and Asian descent, *7370*

August 29

1758 Reservation for Native Americans established by a state, *5937*
1817 Abolition newspaper, *5637*
1861 Confederate forts to surrender in the Civil War, *7958*
1866 Cog railroad, *6333*
1889 International professional tennis contest, *7530*
1892 Baseball player to catch a ball dropped from the Washington Monument, *7145*
1893 Slide fastener, *2291*
1896 Chop suey, *3879*
1916 Coast Guard aviation unit, *5211*
1923 Fireboat with two-way radio equipment, *4112*
1929 Airship passenger transfer to an airplane, *1525*
1958 Air Force academy, *3190*
1962 Television news commentator who was African-American, *5620*
1965 Astronaut to converse with an aquanaut, *7033*
1966 Parachute jumper snagged by airplane in midair, *1593*

August 30

1637 Synod held in America, *6508*
1664 Bookbinder, *1731*

1842 Narcotics tariff enacted by Congress, *2685*
Tariff enacted by Congress to prevent the importation of obscene literature and pictures, *7665*
1875 Music chair at a college, *2904*
1884 Theater to employ women as ushers, *3702*
1890 Meat inspection law enacted by Congress, *4179*
1909 Apprentice continuation school, *3293*
1926 Hambletonian harness horse race for three-year-olds, *7398*
1929 Submarine emergency air supply container, *6967*
1931 Airplane race of importance in which both men and women were contestants, *7298*
1934 Dual-purpose postage stamp, *6066*
1962 Presidential hot line, *6173*
1963 International postal card, *6049*
1983 Astronaut to fly in space who was African-American, *7049*

August 31

1809 Catholic magazine in English, *4702*
1826 Circumnavigation of the globe by a warship, *6980*
1842 Navy bureau of medicine and surgery, *5009*
1881 National tennis championship matches, *7527*
1886 Earthquake of consequence to be recorded, *2867*
1904 Olympic medalist who was African-American, *7444*
1910 Airplane flight over water, *1432*
1920 News program on radio, *5704*
1934 All-star football game, *7327*
1935 National skeet tournament, *7479*
1955 Microwave television station, *7804*
Solar-powered car, *5457*
1974 Merchant Marine Academy cadets who were women, *3308*

September

1639 Autopsy officially recorded, *2848*
1784 Motorboat, *6948*
1811 Steamboat to sail down the Mississippi, *6863*
1821 College alumni association, *2991*
1826 Children's magazine with literary merit, *4708*
1829 Horse racing magazine, *4782*
1847 Tourist guide with train schedules, *2025*
1852 College professor who was a woman, *2947*
1859 Public school for Chinese-American children, *3062*

September—*continued*

1867 Theological school that was multisectarian, *3271*

1869 Torpedo manufacturing station, *8109*

1871 College entrance plan using certified schools, *2994*

1880 Italian newspaper, *5674*

1882 Honors program offered by a university, *2996*

1883 Apartment house cooperative, *2126*

1889 County high school, *3085*

1893 Water filtration system for bacterial purification of a city water supply, *2234*

1894 Antitoxin laboratory established by a public health department, *4200*

1895 Movies with color, *5545*

1897 Country day school, *3066*

1898 Diesel engine built for commercial service, *5479*

1899 School to use platoon organization, *3067*

1910 Airplane flying school, *3188*

1923 Combined newspaper, *5655*

1926 Film-developing machine, *5840*

1929 Aviation course in a high school, *3089*

1932 Ophthalmology clinic, *4846*

1935 Invisible-glass installation, *4050*

1938 Toothbrush with synthetic bristles, *4074*

1939 Radio production course at a college, *2912*

1941 Building known as a Quonset hut, *2117*

1951 Microscope with a radiation block, *6803*

1956 Elementary schools to use closed-circuit televisions in teaching, *3069*

1957 Laser, *3443*

1961 Air piracy law, *2784*

1962 Ship with a floating scientific instrument platform, *6717*

1964 Campus takeover by student protesters, *3015*

1979 New York Stock Exchange seat owner of Chinese ancestry, *3837*

1987 Interactive multimedia authoring program, *2553*

1988 American to be recognized by Tibetan Buddhists as a reincarnated lama, *6440*
Computer hacker to be convicted, *2789*

1992 Professional hockey player who was a woman, *7383*

1996 Police officer who was a Chassidic Jew, *4157*

September 1

1635 Grand jury, *2733*

1803 Religious tract society, *6570*

1819 Plow with interchangeable parts, *1042*

1855 Book trade magazine, *4724*

1859 Pullman sleeping car, *6375*

1872 Nurse to receive formal training, *5023*

1878 Telephone operator who was a woman, *7729*

1880 Tennis tournament of national scope, *7526*

1888 Catholic seminary under the supervision of the Pope, *3277*

1890 Single Tax League national conference, *7650*

1894 Health laboratory established by a state to diagnose diseases by the examination of sputum, *4201*

1897 Municipal subway, *6410*

1902 Building with a large-scale clear-span dome, *2085*

1907 Night court, *2708*

1910 Transcontinental solo trip on horseback by a woman, *1183*

1913 Civic design chair at a college, *3254*

1914 Extinction by humans of a native American animal, *3746*

1916 Child labor law enacted by Congress, *4576*

1919 Communist Labor Party of America convention, *3374*

1920 Airplane used for newspaper reporting, *5606*

1922 Daily news program on radio, *5705*

1925 Machine to make glass light bulbs, *3497*

1931 Anthropology laboratory, *6748*

1939 Army officer to occupy both the nation's highest military post and the highest nonelective civilian post, *5153*

1941 City parking garage, *5484*

1949 Transcontinental bicycle trip made in less than three weeks, *7204*

1955 Roll-on-roll-off carrier, *6898*

1968 Circus clown training school, *3301*

1974 Member of the Navy's Hurricane Hunters who was a woman, *5298*

1989 Air bag requirement by the federal government, *4231*

September 2

1775 Warship to receive definite orders to attack the enemy, *7993*

1858 Cigar bands of special interest, *2703*

1895 College for women founded as a Catholic institution, *2958*

1910 Airplane solo flight by an American woman, *1596*

1919 Communist Party of America convention, *3375*

1936 Transatlantic round-trip airplane flight from the United States, *1461*

1937 Game preserve appropriation by the federal government, *3749*

1952 Heart operation in which the deep-freezing technique was employed, *5093*

1992 Motor vehicles powered by natural gas, *5508*

September 8—*continued*

1868 Athletic club, *7542*

1896 Finnish college, *2959*

1917 Aviator who was African-American, *1609*

1953 Transcontinental express bus service, *5423*

1965 Baseball player to play all nine positions in one game, *7155*

1974 Motorcycle jump across a river canyon, *3682*

Navy chaplain who was an African-American woman, *5206*

President to receive a presidential pardon, *6179*

September 9

1776 Use of the name United States instead of United Colonies, *1097*

1830 Balloon flight by an aeronaut born in America, *1537*

1841 Heavyweight boxing match to last longer than 100 rounds, *7233*

1850 State on the Pacific coast to be admitted to the Union, *7604*

1866 Theater ticket agency, *3700*

1885 Economics association, *6788*

1893 Child born in the White House who was the offspring of a president, *6254*

1898 Log-rolling national championship tournament, *7576*

1901 Car hill-climbing contest, *7262*

Long-distance car race, *7263*

1908 Airplane endurance flight exceeding one hour, *1427*

1934 Rocket to break the sound barrier, *7018*

1945 Computer bug, *2527*

1966 Judge of a federal district court who was an African-American woman, *2729*

1969 Postage stamp depicting a living American, *6097*

September 10

1785 Treaty entered into by the federal government after independence, *4000*

1794 College that was nondenominational, *2939*

1813 Defeat of a British naval squadron in the War of 1812, *8024*

1862 Army chaplain who was Jewish, *5200*

1875 Forestry association (national), *6784*

1913 Coast-to-coast paved road, *6625*

September 11

1789 Secretary of the treasury, *6103*

1841 Collapsible tube, *7919*

1850 Private railroad car, *6374*

Theater ticket scalpers, *3698*

1862 Stock exchange to specialize in mining securities, *3816*

1875 Comic strip in a newspaper, *5687*

1883 Mail chute, *6000*

1910 Trackless trolley system, *6404*

1928 Play to be shown on television, *1260*

Transcontinental bus service, *5421*

1946 Long-distance car-to-car telephone conversation, *7764*

1947 Radioactive isotopes exported, *6820*

1952 Artificial aortic valve, *5053*

1953 Television stations to share the same frequency, *7802*

September 12

1808 Bible translated into English, *1966*

1866 Burlesque show, *3687*

1869 Prohibition Party convention, *3356*

1918 Tank operated by Army troops, *8116*

1935 Medical college founded as a Jewish institution, *3179*

1941 Capture of a German ship by an American ship in World War II, *8049*

1952 Railroad freight cars with compartments, *6390*

1956 Coal pipeline, *3509*

1958 Integrated circuit, *3444*

1975 Adjustable stadium, *7512*

1992 Astronaut to fly in space who was an African-American woman, *7049*

Husband and wife to fly in space together, *7052*

September 13

1788 Federal election, *3380*

1789 Loan to the United States, *3804*

1790 Agricultural dictionary, *1799*

1826 Rhinoceros, *1144*

1898 Celluloid photographic film, *5838*

1899 Car accident fatality, *5470*

1939 Submarine to be refloated, *6970*

1948 Public high school to specialize in the performing arts, *3091*

1954 College for women founded as a Jewish institution, *2968*

1962 Launching silos for Atlas F missiles, *8143*

1966 Medal of Honor awarded to a Seabee, *1688*

1977 Diesel cars to be mass-produced, *5460*

September 14

1716 Lighthouse, *4123*

1778 Minister plenipotentiary, *3984*

1861 Naval battle in the Civil War, *7959*

1886 Typewriter ribbon, *2386*

1892 Bacteriology diagnostic laboratory in a city health department, *4198*

1908 Journalism school at a college, *3102*

1909 Election using the preferential ballot system, *3320*

1915 Sound-absorbing material made of rigid insulating board, *2050*
1922 Transcontinental airship flight, *1520*
1929 Horse to win a $100,000 purse in one race, *7410*
1931 All-welded self-propelled seagoing petroleum carrier ship, *6892*
1940 Draft law enacted by Congress during peacetime, *5220*
1956 Prefrontal lobotomy, *5087*
1963 Quintuplets to live more than five years, *2176*
1975 Catholic saint who was born in America, *6481*
1990 Gene therapy, *5118*

September 15

1817 Iron mill to puddle and roll iron, *4450*
1830 National convention of African-Americans, *2248*
1853 Minister who was a woman, *6530*
1857 Typesetting machine, *5804*
1858 Overland mail service, *5993*
1896 Hospice for incurable cancer patients, *4888*
1913 Goat show, *1073*
1927 Book on the game of bridge, *2005*
1930 Funeral home operated on the cooperative plan, *2839*
1934 Musical comedy broadcast on radio, *1264*
1939 Lightning bolt to be scientifically measured, *6773*
1957 Air-to-ground public telephone service, *7748*
1964 Soap opera on prime-time television, *7788*
1965 Television dramatic series in which an African-American performer had a starring role, *7790*

September 16

1782 Impression made by the Great Seal of the United States, *1133*
1833 Interstate anticrime pact, *4133*
1908 Esperanto course at a college, *3117*
1923 Catholic seminary for the education of African-American priests, *3278*
1946 College principally for war veterans, *2967*
1960 Postage stamp issued jointly by two countries, *6069*
1971 Technical school for Native Americans, *3302*

September 17

1607 Slander proceedings, *2767*
1777 Catholic funeral attended by the Continental Congress, *6455*

1778 Treaty entered into by the federal government with Native American tribes, *5941*
1787 Constitution of the United States, *1104*
1844 Printing press for polychromatic printing, *5776*
1861 School for freed slaves, *2251*
1872 Sprinkler system patent, *4107*
1895 Battleship, *6926*
1901 Mercury vapor lamp, *3496*
1908 Airplane accident that was fatal, *1387*
1911 Transcontinental airplane flight made in stages, *1439*
1920 Professional football association, *7305*
1938 Building built completely inside a factory, *2090*
     Building floated across a river, *2090*
1941 Warship convoy across the Atlantic Ocean in World War II, *8050*
1953 Siamese twins separated successfully by surgery, *2175*
1959 Ski lifts to be regulated by the state, *7487*
1961 Building of large size with a retractable roof, *2095*
1972 United Church of Christ ordination of a woman in which all the principal roles were filled by women, *6536*
1984 Miss America who was African-American, *3628*

September 18

1634 Religious leader in the American colonies who was a woman, *6507*
1769 Harpsichord, *1307*
1891 American woman of European descent to be made a Native American chief, *6647*
1895 Chiropractor, *4977*
1915 Asphalt-covered racetrack, *7510*
1932 Greek Orthodox college and orphanage, *3279*
1937 Skywriting advertisement written at night, *2337*
1948 Airplane with a delta wing, *1402*
1952 Commercial television station on ultrahigh frequency, *7800*
1984 Transatlantic solo balloon flight, *1545*

September 19

1787 Newspaper to publish the Constitution, *1105*
1876 Carpet sweeper, *4273*
1891 Underwater railroad tunnel to a foreign country, *3617*
1898 Forestry school at a college, *3076*
1928 Airplane diesel engine, *1498*
     Animated cartoon with sound, *5535*
1951 Valeteria, *2398*

September 20

1565 Colonial warfare between European powers in America, *5900*
1777 Warship captured overseas, *8000*
1848 Science society (national), *6780*
1850 Homeopathic hospital, *4875*
Railroad land grant, *6330*
1853 Elevator with safety devices, *2104*
Union passenger station used by several railroad companies, *6332*
1859 Electric range, *4293*
1860 Prince of Wales to visit the United States, *4078*
1862 Hospital ship operated by the Navy, *5012*
1884 Equal Rights Party convention, *3363*
1892 Wire glass, *4043*
1915 Chiropody school at a college, *3175*
1916 Research society (national), *6793*
1946 Movie trailer to be shown on television, *2343*
1974 Police officer who was a woman to be killed in the line of duty, *4152*

September 21

1782 Bible printed in English, *1962*
1872 Naval Academy midshipman who was African-American, *3219*
1883 Electrical engineering school at a college, *3239*
1942 Navy–Marine Corps Medals for Heroism awarded to Marines, *1661*
1965 Swimmer from the United States to make a round-trip crossing of the English Channel, *7521*

September 22

1656 Jury composed of women, *2734*
1734 Moravian settlement in America, *6540*
1851 Telegraph used by a railroad, *7696*
1862 Emancipation proclamation, *2252*
1926 Book course at a college, *3104*
1947 Transatlantic flight by a robot airplane, *1467*
1950 Transatlantic nonstop jet airplane flight, *1473*
1953 Highway interchange structure with four levels, *6633*
1961 Judge of a federal district court who was African-American, *2729*
1964 Musical to run for more than 3,000 performances, *1271*

September 23

1642 Bachelor of Arts degree, *2976*
1679 Labadist community, *6514*
1745 Knighthood conferred on a soldier born in America, *6642*
1833 Cabinet appointee rejected by the Senate, *6106*

1845 Baseball team, *7159*
1879 Hearing aid, *5069*
1885 Biology course offered at a college, *3240*
1897 Frontier Day, *4242*
1898 Tuberculosis sanatorium established by a state, *4901*
1911 Airmail pilot, *6015*
1926 Boxing match to attract 100,000 spectators, *7242*
1931 Autogiro to land and take off from a ship, *1534*
1934 Radio broadcast heard in both the Arctic and the Antarctic regions, *6277*
1951 Transcontinental telecast received on the West Coast, *7841*
1952 Pay television presentation of a sporting event, *7785*
World heavyweight boxing champion to retire undefeated, *7254*
1954 Court-martial of an officer for collaborating with his captors, *2741*
1970 New York City Marathon, *7566*
1976 Presidential election debate between an incumbent president and a challenger to be televised, *3397*

September 24

1657 Autopsy with verdict of a coroner's jury, *2849*
1716 Botanical report on plant hybridization, *6735*
1789 Congressional act declared unconstitutional by the Supreme Court, *2559*
Supreme Court chief justice, *2752*
1832 Toy distribution center, *2138*
1889 Dial time recorder, *2382*
1906 National monument designated by the federal government, *5410*
1929 All-blind airplane flight, *1451*
1933 Drama broadcast on radio from a regular stage, *1262*
1934 Theater and dramatic criticism course at a college, *3105*
1951 Sex-change operation, *6832*
1958 Highway bridge with welded aluminum girders, *3596*
1963 Photograph of the Senate in session, *2635*
1968 Television newsmagazine, *5708*
1988 Episcopal bishop who was a woman, *6553*

September 25

1690 Newspaper publisher, *5609*
1880 Play presented by a Jewish professional acting troupe, *1253*
1924 Micropaleontology course at a college, *3247*
1940 Archivist training program at a college, *3107*

1956 Transatlantic telephone call carried by the transoceanic telephone cable, *7767*
1981 Supreme Court justice who was a woman, *2765*

September 26

1772 Medical licensing law enacted by a colony, *4935*
1789 Attorney general of the United States, *6124*
Attorney of the United States, *2711*
Postmaster general of the United States, *5985*
1831 Anti-Masonic Party convention, *3348*
Play performed 1,000 times, *1248*
1871 Cement, *2044*
1874 International rifle tournament of consequence, *7473*
1903 Boycott law enacted by a state, *2310*
1908 Double-header baseball games that were shutouts, *7125*
1940 Television production course at a college, *2913*
1955 Bank to operate a window in a subway station, *3797*
1960 Presidential election debates to be shown on television, *3394*

September 27

1879 Amateur athletic competition, *7547*
1915 University for African-American students founded as a Catholic institution, *2964*
1922 Radar observations, *7675*
1934 Abrasive for commercial use, *4442*
1937 Santa Claus school, *4259*
1941 Liberty ship, *6894*
1942 Ship completed in less than two weeks, *6878*

September 28

1542 Exploration of land on the Pacific coast by a European, *5896*
1800 Fireboats, *4097*
1910 Optometry courses at a college, *3153*
1930 Radio advertising course at a college, *2923*
1944 Musical comedy written for television, *1269*
1945 Opera singer who was African-American to sing a white role, *1336*

September 29

1789 Commander-in-chief of the U.S. Army, *5147*
Pensions paid by the federal government, *4583*
1892 Football game at night, *7321*
1904 Monument to commemorate the Spanish-American War, *5408*

1915 Transcontinental demonstration of radio telephone operation, *7721*
1938 Archival course at a college, *3106*
1942 Merchant ship commanded by an African-American captain, *6895*
1953 Department store to sell insurance, *2511*
1967 Twin postage stamps, *6073*
1982 Poisoning of store merchandise, *2788*
1988 Ascent of Mount Everest by an American woman, *7588*

September 30

1630 Execution in America, *2792*
1641 Agricultural fair held annually, *1001*
1787 Ship to carry the American flag around the world, *1123*
1791 Export report by the federal government, *2473*
1811 Year in which exports exceeded imports, *2476*
1876 Library journal, *4729*
1877 Amateur open swimming championship meet, *7515*
1882 Hydroelectric power plant to furnish incandescent lighting, *3462*
1906 Balloon cup race, *7288*
1912 Safety association (national), *4187*
1936 Round-the-world airplane passenger race, *7299*
1939 Intercollegiate football game to be shown on television, *7329*
1943 Merchant marine academy, *3307*
1947 World Series baseball game to be shown on television, *7135*
1950 Medal of Honor awarded in the Korean War, *1684*
1960 Animated cartoon series on prime-time television, *7786*
1963 Gerenuk, *1160*
1975 Emperor of Japan to visit the United States, *6655*
1976 Right-to-die law enacted by a state, *2843*
1982 Round-the-world helicopter flight, *1579*

October

1608 Glass factory, *4035*
1750 Publicist for a theater company, *3694*
1779 Army uniform, *5142*
1826 Lyceum for adult education, *2884*
1838 Phrenology journal, *4753*
1839 Teachers' institute, *3261*
1840 Factory workers' magazine, *4714*
1861 Newspaper wrappers for mailing newspapers, *5995*
1865 Entomology journal, *4772*
1884 Baseball championship, *7122*
1888 Geography magazine, *4775*
1889 General medical clinic, *4843*
1893 Aviation magazine, *4776*

October—*continued*

1896 All-fiction pulp magazine, *4731*
1899 Yacht race broadcast on radio, *7215*
1906 Esperanto magazine, *4749*
1925 Atheist organization, *5745*
1926 Movie showing another planet, *6687*
1930 Coal mine to be automated, *3508*
1931 Diesel-powered tractor, *1057*
1932 Teletypesetter, *5807*
1935 News correspondent who was African-American, *5619*
1939 Electronic digital calculator, *3438*
1946 Baseball play-off series, *7134*
Photograph of a beam of 1-billion-volt x-rays, *5829*
1947 Deaths from smog, *3715*
1951 Air-to-air rocket, *8135*
Transistors produced commercially for a specific product, *3441*
1954 Telegraph code converter, *7710*
Transistor radio receiver to be mass-produced, *6312*
1955 Air-conditioned public elementary school, *2120*
1968 Ambulance equipped for mobile coronary care, *4826*
1977 Daughters of the American Revolution member who was African-American, *5718*
1989 Liver transplant from a live donor, *5105*
Surgeon general who was a woman, *4214*
1990 Killer bees, *1163*

October 1

1785 City directory, *1813*
1810 Cattle fair, *1078*
1823 Gymnasium to offer systematic instruction, *7371*
1834 Locomotive with six or eight driving wheels, *6353*
1848 School for children with mental disabilities, *3016*
1861 Army balloon corps, *5182*
Union ship captured in the Civil War, *7960*
1865 Baseball game in which one team scored more than 100 runs, *7115*
1880 Incandescent lamp factory, *3494*
1883 Missionary training school, *3275*
1884 Drama school, *2905*
1885 Special delivery mail service, *6001*
1892 Sociology professor at a college, *3252*
1896 Rural free mail delivery, *6002*
1903 World Series baseball game, *7123*
1904 Bulk mail, *6004*
Business library supported by taxes, *4675*
1908 Nursing school at a college, *3173*
1913 Monument to a bird, *5411*
1917 Open-air post office, *6039*

1918 Hygiene and public health school at a college, *3177*
1924 President to be born in a hospital, *6198*
1929 Airmail pickup by an airplane without landing, *6024*
1934 College to dispense with credits, hours, points, and grades, *3001*
Federal credit union, *3785*
Religion magazine printed in rotogravure, *4734*
1937 Trailer church, *6534*
1940 Army parachute battalion, *5188*
1942 Jet airplane, *1399*
1946 Military think tank, *5128*
1947 Airmail and express service by helicopter, *6031*
1952 Religious radio program broadcast by a husband and wife, *6596*
1955 Aircraft carrier with an angle deck, *6939*
1961 Television station owned by a religious organization, *6597*
1979 Pope to visit the White House, *4084*

October 2

1721 Camel, *1137*
1866 Tin can with a key opener, *4284*
1876 Actors' home, *1277*
1936 Fuel alcohol plant, *3540*
1937 X-ray movies of human organs in action, *4908*
1956 Clock to operate by nuclear power, *7903*
1963 Artificial leather, *7878*
1965 Catholic bishop who was an American-born African-American, *6480*
Transatlantic undersea radio conversation, *6283*
1979 Coal miner who was a woman to be killed in a mining accident, *3510*

October 3

1632 Tobacco tax enacted by a colony, *2695*
1805 Pharmacopoeia prepared by a medical association, *1928*
1824 Treaty between the federal government and a South American nation, *4002*
1859 International cricket tournament, *7273*
1875 Rabbinical college for the Reform Jewish movement, *3274*
1899 Vacuum cleaner driven by a motor, *4275*
1922 Senator who was a woman, *2651*
1924 Citizenship and public affairs school at a college, *3255*
1942 Silver Star Medal awarded to a civilian, *1662*
1943 Police appeal for missing persons to be shown on television, *4148*
1949 Radio station owned and operated by African-Americans, *6300*
1952 Video recording on high-definition magnetic tape, *7818*

1967 Underground comic book of note, *4739*
1969 Vasectomy outpatient service, *4851*
1977 Daily state lotteries with the same winning daily number, *3644*

October 4

1830 Power printing press capable of fine book work, *5771*
1881 Player piano that was completely automatic, *1317*
1887 European edition of an American newspaper, *5649*
1895 Open golf championship tournament, *7341*
1909 Airship race, *7291*
1940 Quetzal bird, *1168*
1955 Telephone call on a commercial line using solar energy, *7746*
1960 Communications satellite with signal reception and transmission equipment, *7065*
1961 Postage stamp featuring a work of art in true color, *6093*
1965 Pope to visit the United States, *4083*

October 5

1646 Wolf bounty, *1135*
1843 Harness horse race at night, *7389*
1852 Beehive with removable frames, *1050*
1853 Physiology and hygiene courses at a liberal arts college, *3140*
1854 Baby show, *2141*
1871 Unitarian minister who was a woman, *6523*
1918 Night-flying scout group, *8046*
1919 Radio broadcast from a submerged submarine, *6268*
Two-way radio conversation between a submerged submarine and another vessel, *7760*
1930 Transcontinental solo airplane flight by a woman, *1453*
1931 Transpacific nonstop airplane flight, *1454*
1947 Presidential address televised from the White House, *6217*
1974 Round-the-world journey on foot, *7590*

October 6

1683 Mennonites to arrive in America, *6537*
1780 American imprisoned as an enemy agent in the Tower of London, *8004*
1825 Giant exhibited as a theatrical attraction, *3658*
1837 Locomotive steam whistle, *6355*
1848 Steamboat service to California around Cape Horn, *6883*
1852 Pharmacy society (national), *5038*
1857 Chess tournament, *4028*
International chess champion from the United States, *4029*

1863 Turkish bath, *4194*
1866 Steam car, *5425*
Train robbery of a train in motion, *2776*
1868 Nickel plating, *4471*
1873 Transatlantic crossing attempted by a balloon, *1538*
1876 Library association (national), *4688*
1911 Transpacific radio conversation, *6267*
1929 Baseball manager to win pennants in both leagues, *7099*
1955 Army nurse in modern times who was a man, *5173*
1978 University president who was a woman, *2971*

October 7

1856 Paper folding machine, *5764*
1868 Veterinary department at a college, *3182*
1896 Golfer to win the United States Women's Amateur Championship, *7356*
1907 Battleship built on the Pacific coast, *6927*
1922 Chain radio broadcast, *6270*
1930 Glider pilot's license, *1598*
1931 Infrared photograph, *5827*
1950 Tank crew to cross the 38th parallel in the Korean War, *7980*
1964 Made-for-TV movie, *7789*
1975 Military service academies' enrollment of women, *3189*

October 8

1818 Hygiene lectures at a college, *3136*
1871 Forest fire of consequence, *2883*
1873 Prison built for women and managed by women, *2823*
1904 Car race for the Vanderbilt Cup, *7264*
1919 Transcontinental air race, *7295*
1921 Radio receiving contest, *6261*
1929 Automatic pilot on an airplane, *1499*
Movie entertainment shown on an airplane, *5514*
1936 Pope to visit the United States before his election, *4081*
1956 Baseball pitcher to pitch a perfect no-hit, no-run, no-walk World Series game, *7153*
1968 Astronaut international rescue agreement, *7037*
1970 Lottery in which the top prize was $1 million, *3643*
1990 Native American Day, *4252*

October 9

1780 Astronomical expedition to record an eclipse of the sun, *6662*
1855 Calliope, *1311*
1865 Oil pipeline of importance, *3533*
1871 Surgeon who was a woman, *4974*
1876 Telephone conversation over outdoor wires, *7752*

October 9—*continued*

1877 Animal humane society (national), *5738*
1894 Magic lantern feature show, *3692*
1946 Electric blanket, *4265*
1947 Mobile telephone call between an airplane in flight and a moving car, *7766*
1948 Baseball player who was African-American to hit a home run in a World Series, *7152*
1956 Electric portable typewriter, *2390*
1969 Senator to act in the movies, *2659*

October 10

1843 Futurity horse race, *7390*
1845 Naval academy, *3213*
1863 Catholic parish church for African-Americans, *6464*
1865 Billiard ball of composition material resembling ivory, *4019*
1886 Tuxedo coat, *2272*
1896 Book review newspaper supplement, *5650*
1898 Optometry society (national), *5044*
1916 Professional Golfers Association tournament, *7345*
1918 Church organized by Native Americans, *6603*
1920 Unassisted triple play in a World Series baseball game, *7127*
1923 World Series baseball games to gross $1 million, *7129*
1933 Synthetic laundry detergent, *4279*
1934 Archivist of the United States, *4677*
1937 Radio show sponsored by a cooperative of commercial advertisers, *2338*
1955 Magazine to contain a phonograph record, *4738*
1967 Bowling automatic scoring machine, *7230*

October 11

1753 Arbitration law enacted by a colony, *2353*
1811 Steam-propelled ferryboat, *6907*
1881 Film rolls for cameras, *5835*
1884 Electrical show, *2411*
1886 College for women to affiliate with a university, *2956*
1924 Transcontinental flight by a dirigible, *1521*
1935 National conference on crime, *4147*
1938 Fiberglass, *4052*
1945 Army general to be consecrated a bishop, *5158*
1963 Commemorative postage stamp depicting a president's wife, *6095*
1971 College whose tuition fees were based on family income, *2970*
1988 Factoring of a 100-digit number, *6760*

October 12

1773 Hospital for insane patients established by a colony, *4895*
1792 Columbus Day, *4233*
Monument to Christopher Columbus, *5396*
1802 West Point graduate who was Jewish, *3195*
West Point graduates, *3196*
1845 National labor congress, *4553*
1878 Railroad bridge entirely of steel, *3584*
1882 Hotel to install electric lights, *2426*
1923 Parachute-jumping contest, *7296*
1925 Episcopal bishop deposed for heresy in the United States, *6552*
1937 Hydrogen-cooled turbine generator, *3483*
1945 Medal of Honor awarded to a conscientious objector, *1681*
1991 Grandmother to give birth to her own grandchild, *2169*

October 13

1775 Navy fleet, *5257*
1792 Building erected in Washington, DC, by the federal government, *2116*
1843 Fraternal society for Jews, *5720*
1853 Zinc commercial production, *5330*
1857 Horse bred in the United States to win a major race abroad, *7405*
1860 Aerial photograph, *5815*
1894 Amateur golf tournament, *7339*
1905 World Series baseball game that was a shutout, *7124*
1915 Junior chamber of commerce, *2453*
1925 Play of full length by an African-American writer to be performed in New York City, *1258*
1940 Telecommunication by deaf people that was both visual and oral, *7837*
1953 Artmobile, *5598*
1955 President of a major medical society who was a woman, *5049*
1977 Naval War College president who was a former prisoner of war, *3222*

October 14

1656 Ban on Quakers enacted by a colony, *6586*
1774 Declaration of rights, *1111*
Embargo act of the Continental Congress, *2470*
1834 Patent granted to an African-American inventor, *4652*
1920 College radio station, *6295*
1922 Airplane to fly faster than 200 miles per hour, *1448*
1928 Wedding on television, *4820*
1947 Airplane to fly faster than the speed of sound, *1468*

October 20

1817 Showboat theater, *3696*
1888 Baseball teams to go on a world tour, *7165*
1922 Pilot to bail out of a disabled airplane, *1585*
1929 Community hospital, *4892*
1951 Gambling permit stamp issued by the federal government, *7661*
1960 Post office fully mechanized, *6042*
1961 Vending machine to dispense fresh flowers, *2400*

October 21

1639 Medical regulations enacted by a colony, *4933*
1849 Tattooed man exhibited as a theatrical attraction, *3661*
1871 Amateur athletic games held outdoors, *7544*
1879 Incandescent lamp, *3492*
1915 Transatlantic message over radio telephone, *7757*
1916 Army Reserve Officers Training Corps units, *5183*
1917 Army division to go into battle in World War I, *8036*
1921 Radio program theme song, *6289*
1925 Photoelectric cell, *3478*
1929 Ambulance air service, *4824*
1948 High-speed radio fax transmission, *7674*
1963 Trimline telephone, *7725*

October 22

1746 College charter granted by a governor, *2928*
1812 Prisoners captured in the War of 1812, *8022*
1883 Horse show of national scope, *1181*
Opera produced at the Metropolitan Opera House, *1347*
1897 Zionist organization (national), *6487*
1934 Instantaneous phonograph recording, *7011*
1938 Copy made by xerography, *2372*
1939 Professional football game to be shown on television, *7308*
Snow cruiser for Antarctic research, *6716*
1963 Armored division transported by airplanes to a foreign country, *5193*
1973 Commercial crude-oil carrier, *6903*
1996 Minister who was a transsexual, *6844*

October 23

1824 Locomotive to pull a train on a track, *6347*
1885 Graduate school for women, *2955*
1917 Shot fired by American infantry in World War I, *8037*

1924 Radio network broadcast received on the Pacific Coast, *6274*
1947 Nobel Prize shared by an American husband and wife, *1696*
1956 Video recording on magnetic tape televised coast-to-coast, *7847*
1961 Jazz composition to appear on the Top 40 charts, *1301*
1996 Holiday stamp jointly issued by the United States and another country, *6069*

October 24

1812 Historical society (national), *5711*
1828 Manufacturers' fair, *2408*
1861 Transcontinental telegraph line, *7700*
1901 Daredevil to go over Niagara Falls in a barrel, *3679*
1931 Mobster convicted for tax evasion, *2782*
1943 Distinguished Service Cross awarded to an animal, *1664*
1945 Department store sales demonstrations using television, *2342*
1951 United Nations postage stamps in U.S. denominations, *6068*
1956 Presbyterian minister who was a woman, *6584*
1977 Jockey to win more than $5 million in purses in one year, *7420*

October 25

1812 Capture of a British frigate in the War of 1812, *8023*
1848 Railroad to run west out of Chicago, *6328*
1888 Double-deck ferryboat, *6909*
1892 Reply-paid card, *6045*
1905 Municipal ferryboats, *6910*
1929 Cabinet member convicted of a crime, *6110*
1940 Army general who was African-American, *5154*
1954 Cabinet session to be telecast and broadcast, *6115*
1955 Electronic range for domestic use, *4303*
1960 Electronic watch, *7905*
1973 Hang-gliding national championships, *7300*

October 26

1785 Mule born in the United States, *1141*
1858 Washing machine, *4270*
1869 Steeplechase, *7391*
1909 Army pilot to fly solo in an airplane, *1607*
1912 Elopement by airplane, *4809*

October 27

1659 Quakers executed for their religious beliefs, *6587*

1812 Naval vessel to display the American flag around Cape Horn, *1127*
1867 Theological college for Jews, *3272*
1869 Dairy association (state), *1091*
1889 Lithuanian church, *6468*
1904 Rapid-transit subway, *6411*
1922 Navy Day, *4247*
1946 Commercial program telecast on a network, *7777*
Television show to be sponsored by a commercial advertiser, *2344*
1954 Air Force general who was African-American, *5135*
1975 Bowler to earn $100,000 in one year in tournaments, *7232*
1994 Year in which the prison population exceeded 1 million, *2832*

October 28

1788 Navy chaplain in the Continental Navy, *5196*
1833 College founded as a Quaker institution, *2942*
1886 Statue presented to the United States by a foreign country, *5405*
1904 Police department to adopt the fingerprinting system, *4160*
1927 International airplane passenger station, *1506*
1929 Child born in an airplane, *2160*
1949 Ambassador from the United States who was a woman, *3991*
1958 Stock exchange director who was a woman, *3831*
1964 United Nations permanent ambassador who was a woman, *3993*
1970 Sky marshals, *4150*

October 29

1766 Fox hunting club, *7422*
1796 Ship from the Atlantic coast to anchor in a California port, *6858*
1904 Intercity trucking service, *2484*
1937 Boxer to hold three titles simultaneously, *7253*
1947 Forest fire drenched by artificial rain, *3732*
1959 Stockholder meetings televised coast-to-coast simultaneously, *3832*
1967 Rock musical, *1272*
1978 Slot machine payoff of $275,000, *3639*
1991 Photograph taken close up of an asteroid in space, *6706*

October 30

1768 Methodist meetinghouse, *6558*
1794 Ball bearing commercial installation, *2038*
1799 Navy chaplain, *5198*

1888 Ball-point pen, *8154*
1894 Card time recorder, *2383*
1903 Printed traffic regulations, *4138*
1917 Navy chaplain who was Jewish, *5203*
1993 Amateur boxing match for women, *7247*

October 31

1835 Mutual fire insurance company, *4532*
1838 Model laboratory school at a college, *3259*
1952 Hydrogen bomb, *8128*
1956 Airplane flight to land at the South Pole, *6733*
1962 Geodetic satellite, *7070*

November

1618 Comet recorded, *6675*
1811 Magician of note, *3655*
1824 Presidential election in which a loser won, *3385*
1829 Daredevil jumper of note, *3676*
1837 Music instruction in a public school, *2900*
1860 Boarding school on a Native American reservation, *3063*
Foreign missionary society organized by women, *6578*
1863 Thanksgiving Day, *4261*
1873 Hotel that was fireproof, *2424*
1876 Cooking school, *3288*
1881 Presidential candidate to make campaign speeches in a foreign language, *3408*
1884 Adding machine absolutely accurate at all times, *2377*
1887 Psychology journal, *4759*
1888 Aluminum in metallic form, *4475*
1890 Dam filled with rocks, *3605*
1895 Amateur golf championship tournament for women, *7342*
Car magazine, *4788*
1902 School nurses in public schools, *5027*
Trade school for girls, *3291*
1904 Rotogravure press, *5781*
1908 Aviation magazine devoted primarily to airplanes, *4780*
Radio society, *6259*
Steel ski jump, *7481*
1910 Newsreel, *5697*
1916 Lightweight solo streetcar, *6406*
1919 Editor in chief of a law review who was a woman, *3127*
1929 Allergy journal, *4764*
1930 Floating electric power plant, *3481*
1933 Typewriting primer, *1829*
1935 Newspaper to store issues on microfilm, *4682*
1937 Photosensitive glass, *4051*
Radio news program sponsored by a cooperative of commercial advertisers, *2339*

November—*continued*

1940 President elected for third and fourth terms, *6170*
1948 Broad-spectrum antibiotic, *5000*
1953 Oil refinery with a carbon monoxide boiler, *3542*
1958 Rocket to intercept a supersonic target missile, *8139*
1963 Elliptical office building, *2096*
1975 Ski carousel, *7489*
Video cassette recorder for home use, *7823*
1993 Sheriff who was an African-American woman, *4156*

November 1

1777 American flag saluted by a foreign nation, *1122*
1781 Bank chartered by Congress, *3757*
Medical society (state), *5030*
1784 Citizenship conferred by special grant, *5861*
1796 Dollar marks, *5802*
1807 Salt well drilled west of the Alleghenies, *3933*
1848 Medical school for women, *3164*
1850 Photography magazine, *4719*
1864 Money order system, *5997*
1873 Barbed wire commercial production, *4406*
1879 School of prominence for Native American children, *3065*
1894 Catalog of recordings on disk, *1940*
Music by Native Americans to be recorded, *1284*
1895 Automobile club, *5465*
1920 Hydroplane international service, *1409*
1927 Housing cooperative sponsored by a labor union, *4618*
1930 Vehicular tunnel to a foreign country, *3619*
1932 Computerized pump, *4417*
1939 Surrogate birth experiment with an animal, *5123*
1940 Air raid shelter, *4088*
1941 Army language school, *3204*
1944 Quadruplets delivered by cesarean operation, *2174*
1955 Guided missile cruiser, *6940*
1962 Christmas postage stamp regular issue, *6094*
1964 Russian Orthodox saint canonized in the United States, *6498*

November 2

1776 Traitor to the American cause during the Revolutionary War, *7998*
1824 Popular vote in a presidential election, *3386*
1867 Fashion magazine, *4728*

1886 Election for governor in which two brothers were the opposing candidates, *7616*
Tractor with an endless chain, *1053*
1904 Fingerprinting in federal penitentiaries, *4161*
1915 Election using proportional representation, *3321*
1917 Soldiers in the American army killed in combat in World War I, *8038*
1926 Senate election in which neither candidate was seated after a recount, *2630*
1929 Newsreel theater, *3707*
1933 Surgical elevation of the skull to treat epilepsy, *5082*
1945 Industrial and labor relations school at a college, *3257*
1954 Senator elected by a write-in vote, *3331*
1957 Titanium mill, *4478*
1967 Gravure-printed postage stamp, *6074*
1976 Congressional representative of Polish ancestry, *2623*

November 3

1824 State nominating convention, *3315*
1840 Dental college, *3162*
1881 Coast Guard inland station, *5210*
1896 State senator who was a woman, *7626*
1900 Car show, *5434*
1911 Continuation school for adults established by a state government, *2889*
1945 Judge on the federal bench who was African-American, *2727*
1952 Frozen bread, *3929*
1953 Coast-to-coast live telecast in color, *7845*
1964 Presidential election in which votes were tallied electronically, *3395*
Year when citizens of the District of Columbia could vote in a presidential election, *3434*
1970 Congressional representative of Puerto Rican ancestry, *2618*
1992 Senator who was an African-American woman, *2661*

November 4

1661 Evening school for working children, *3046*
1846 Artificial leg patent, *5050*
1862 Rapid-fire machine gun, *8107*
1873 Slicing machine, *4296*
1924 Governor who was a woman, *7618*
1927 Pilot to die because of a lack of oxygen, *1614*
1939 Air-conditioned car, *5449*
1951 Jewish prayer services to be televised in their entirety, *6595*
1952 Mother and son simultaneously elected to Congress, *2613*
Presidential election in which a computer was used to predict the outcome, *3393*

1958 Molybdenum centrifugal casting, *4479*
1970 European king buried in the United States, *6654*
1979 Hostage crisis, *3982*

November 5

1639 Post office in a colony, *6035*
1733 Political newspaper, *5632*
1824 Engineering college, *3233*
1852 Civil engineering society (national), *3609*
1872 Congressional representative to serve a single day, *2604*
1889 Sewer district established by a city, *2232*
1895 Car patent, *5428*
1968 Congressional representative who was an African-American woman, *2617*
1974 Congressional representative who was a grandmother, *2621*
Politician who was openly homosexual to win an election, *6839*
Senator who had been an astronaut, *2660*

November 6

1804 Presidential election in which candidates were nominated for the vice presidency, *3384*
1855 Railroad union, *4608*
1868 Native American to win territorial concessions from the federal government, *5970*
1869 Intercollegiate football contest, *7315*
1883 Cross-country championships, *7549*
1928 Electric flashing sign, *2351*
1934 Locomotive communications headlight, *6427*
Professional football game in which 10 touchdowns were made, *7328*
State legislature with a single chamber in the post-Revolutionary era, *7630*
1945 Jet-propelled landing on an aircraft carrier, *1464*
1956 Congressional representative of Indian ancestry, *2614*
Congressional representative reelected after serving a prison term, *2615*
1962 President with a brother in the Senate, *6205*

November 7

1848 Election day for presidential voting held nationwide, *3387*
1859 Library newspaper room, *4671*
1874 Cartoon showing the Republican Party as an elephant, *5703*
1877 Reformatory for women established by a state, *2824*
1910 Shipment of merchandise by airplane, *2485*
1916 Election in which returns were broadcast on radio, *3390*

1922 Congressional representative who was a mother, *2610*
1934 Book bound with preprinted offset cloth, *1755*
1942 President to make a radio broadcast in a foreign language, *6216*
1946 Coin-operated television receiver, *7814*
1950 Husband and wife to be elected simultaneously to both chambers of a state legislature, *7632*
1967 Mayor of a major city who was African-American, *2209*
1972 Congressional candidate elected while missing, *2619*
1989 Governor who was African-American, *7621*
Mayor of New York City who was African-American, *2212*

November 8

1760 Library building, *4662*
1775 Mail franking privilege, *5984*
1825 Artists' organization (national), *1205*
1864 Presidential election in which soldiers in the field were allowed to vote, *3389*
1884 Newspaper syndicate, *5626*
1926 Ferryboat built exclusively to transport cars, *6911*
1938 State legislator who was an African-American woman, *7631*
1941 Naval patrol bomber, *1488*
1950 Pilot of a jet fighter to win a dogfight in the Korean War, *7981*
1960 Senate election race in which both candidates were women, *2634*
1966 Senator who was African-American to be elected by popular vote, *2658*
1973 Golfer to earn $100,000 in a contest, *7367*

November 9

1756 Intercity stagecoach service, *2184*
1790 President who had been a senator, *6139*
1820 Mercantile library, *4666*
1835 State police, *4134*
1842 Design patent, *4654*
1960 Nuclear-powered submarine with turbine-electric drive, *6978*
1964 Postage stamps of four different designs sold as a single sheet, *6096*

November 10

1775 Marines, *5229*
1798 State nullification proceedings to obstruct federal legislation, *7595*
1801 Dueling law enacted by a state, *2808*
1817 Trust, *2518*
1855 Poem to win national acclaim, *1947*
1895 Statue officially sanctioned by the Pope, *5407*

November 10—*continued*

1914 Bank to establish a branch in a foreign country, *3776*

1919 American Legion convention of veterans of World War I, *5312*

1951 Transcontinental dial telephone service without the aid of operators, *7745*

1960 Nuclear reactor operated commercially, *3552*

1969 Episode of "Sesame Street" to be shown on television, *7792*

November 11

1647 Colonial law requiring towns to hire teachers and construct schools, *3045*

1817 Sword swallower, *3656*

1868 Amateur athletic games held indoors, *7543*

1887 Labor activists to be executed, *4564*

1889 State named for a person born in America, *7598*

1919 Veterans' Day, *4246*

1920 Navy ace in World War I, *1613*

1921 Burial at the Tomb of the Unknown Soldier, *2854*

1925 Cosmic ray to be discovered, *6679*

1926 Dance major at a college, *2909*

1933 Electric power contract between a city and the federal government, *3482*

1934 Streamlined all-steel diesel-motor train, *6433*

1935 Aerial photograph showing the lateral curvature of the horizon and the beginning of the stratosphere, *5828*

November 12

1799 Meteor shower on record, *6676*

1861 Petroleum exported to Europe, *3530*

1920 Baseball commissioner, *7098*

1921 Conference of great powers, *3980*

1926 Airplane bombing raid by criminals, *2778*

1927 Underwater highway tunnel with twin tubes, *3618*

1928 College skeet tournament, *7478*

1932 President to invite the president-elect, *6165*

1940 Health museum, *5590*

1941 Genetics clinic, *4848*
Test pilot who was a woman, *1603*

1946 Drive-in banking service, *3796*

1966 Photograph of a solar eclipse taken from the atmosphere, *6703*

1975 Dog hotel, *2436*

1984 Salvage operation in space, *7089*

November 13

1789 President to tour the country, *6230*

1839 Liberty Party convention, *3351*

1868 Philology society (national), *6783*

1875 Bowling rule standardization, *7221*
Football uniforms worn in a game, *7310*

1930 Rotating milking platform, *1056*

1933 Sit-down strike, *4598*

1937 Symphony orchestra devoted exclusively to radio broadcasting, *1365*

1946 Artificial snow from a natural cloud, *6774*

1971 Satellite launched from the earth to orbit another planet, *7076*

November 14

1784 Episcopal bishop, *6549*

1868 Farmers' institute sponsored by a college, *2894*

1889 World tour by a woman traveling alone, *6983*

1903 Football stadium, *7505*

1906 President to visit a foreign country while in office, *6231*

1910 Airplane flight from a ship, *1433*

1934 Symphony on an African-American folk theme, *1297*

1937 Children's church, *6535*

1941 Department store to hold a public art auction, *2507*

1967 General killed in Vietnam by enemy fire, *8018*

1969 President to attend the launching of a manned space flight, *6176*

1972 Dow Jones Industrial Average to exceed 1,000 points, *3836*

November 15

1681 Shorthand account of a trial, *4619*

1754 Trombone, *1306*

1777 Articles of Confederation, *1102*

1806 College magazine, *4699*

1807 Evangelical Church conference, *6526*

1849 Poultry show, *1069*

1864 Mines school at a college, *3236*

1882 Naval attaché, *5285*

1898 Foreign service school in a college, *3126*

1931 Parachute jump from an autogiro, *1588*

1948 Gas-turbine-electric locomotive, *6368*

1950 Hockey player on an amateur team who was African-American, *7380*

1954 Round-the-world flight over the North Pole on a regularly scheduled air route, *1479*

1963 Bridge player to win more than 1,000 master points in one year, *4027*

1974 Pressure-sensitive adhesive postage stamp, *6076*

November 16

1620 Corn found by English settlers, *3908*

1676 Prison, *2811*

1776 American flag saluted by a foreigner, *1117*
1841 Life preserver of cork, *4119*
1875 Dental mallet, *4865*
1901 Car to exceed the speed of a mile a minute, *5436*
1914 Federal reserve banks, *3777*
1920 Postage meter, *6008*
1943 Submarine from the United States sunk by an enemy submarine, *8083*
1955 Dugong, *1158*
    Speedboat to exceed 200 miles per hour, *6953*
1963 President to witness the firing of a Polaris missile, *6174*
1984 Astronaut who was a mother, *7048*

November 17

1774 Military organization to oppose the British, *5254*
1851 Postage stamps depicting the American eagle, *6079*
1875 Theosophical society, *5743*
1886 Newspaper association, *5617*
1889 Transcontinental daily railroad service, *6339*
1917 Naval vessels to sink an enemy submarine in the Atlantic, *8039*
1919 Bank with resources exceeding $1 billion, *3780*
1949 Transatlantic airplane flight carrying 100 people, *1472*

November 18

1805 Women's club, *5732*
1820 Discovery of Antarctica by an American, *6722*
1874 Temperance society for women (national), *2678*
1883 Standard time program, *7895*
1913 Airplane loop-the-loop, *1443*
1921 International fencing championship competition, *7283*
1943 Cabinet member to address a joint session of Congress, *6113*
1949 Baseball player who was African-American to win the Most Valuable Player award, *1723*
1950 Marine Corps jet ace in Korea, *1619*
1963 Telephone with push buttons, *7726*
1965 American Stock Exchange members who were women, *3831*
1967 New York Stock Exchange seat owner who was a woman, *3833*

November 19

1777 Brevet conferred by the Army on an American, *5168*
1794 Extradition treaty with a foreign country, *4001*

1806 Senator to serve in contravention to the age limit, *2642*
1893 Newspaper colored supplement, *5690*
1916 Airplane flight longer than 500 miles, *1444*
1928 Caterpillar Club members who were father and son, *1587*
1936 News magazine featuring photographs, *4736*
1941 Woman to sell securities on the floor of the New York Curb Exchange, *3828*
1942 Foreign servicewomen interred in the Arlington National Cemetery, *2855*
1954 Toll collection machine, *6634*
1969 Astronauts to retrieve a manmade object from the moon, *7041*

November 20

1620 Child born of English parents in New England, *2157*
1771 Town named for George Washington, *2186*
1776 Naval ship of the line, *6913*
1820 Ship sunk by a whale, *2420*
1866 Bicycle with a rotary crank, *7181*
    University for African-American students, *2951*
1888 Key time recorder, *2381*
1914 Passport photographs, *5886*
1919 Airport owned by a city, *1503*
1925 Photograph taken from an airplane at night, *5824*
1931 Teletype commercial service, *7707*
1978 Newspaper whose contents were transmitted by a communications satellite, *5660*
1979 Transfusion of artificial blood, *4840*

November 21

1766 Theater building of brick construction, *3695*
1810 English actor of note to perform in America, *1274*
1824 Jewish congregation in the Reform movement, *6486*
1918 Alcohol prohibition law enacted by Congress, *2684*
1922 Circumnavigation of the world by a cruise ship, *6989*
1938 School radio station on ultrahigh frequency, *6298*
1946 President to travel underwater in a captured enemy submarine, *6228*
1969 General-purpose computer network, *2544*
1973 Federal marshals who were women, *4151*
1995 Movie that was entirely computer-animated, *5539*

November 22

1904 Electric motor using interpole direct current, *5481*

November 22—*continued*
1910 Golf club with a steel shaft, *7353*
1924 Intercollegiate football game to attract 100,000 spectators, *7325*
1927 Snowmobile patent, *7490*
1935 Transpacific airmail flight, *6025*
1955 Cabinet session held at a place other than the seat of the federal government, *6116*
1961 Baseball player to win Most Valuable Player award in both major leagues, *1724*
1963 Telecast transmitted by satellite to Japan, *7855*

November 23

1835 Horseshoe manufacturing machine, *1178*
1848 Medical society for women, *5037*
1876 Intercollegiate football association, *7303*
1889 Jukebox, *7007*
1935 Opera composer who was a woman, *1334*
1940 Army general who rose from draftee, *5155*
1942 Coast Guard unit for women, *5212*
1948 Television camera lens to provide zoom effects, *7815*
1968 Naturalization ceremony in the White House, *5879*
1969 Space-to-ground news conference telecast, *5608*
1973 Congressional representative to give birth while holding office, *2620*
1995 Triplets born several weeks apart, *2179*

November 24

1871 Rifle society (national), *7472*
1885 Nursing society, *5040*
1896 Absentee voting law enacted by a state, *3431*
1924 Corn-husking championship, *1025*
1963 Murder to be shown live on television, *2786*
1971 Skyjacking in which the skyjacker disappeared, *2787*
1990 Telescope of importance with a compound objective mirror, *6674*

November 25

1715 English patent granted to a resident of America, *4647*
1837 Silk power loom, *7889*
1884 Evaporated milk, *3873*
1912 Surgery society (national), *5047*
1920 Football game to be broadcast on radio with a play-by-play description, *7324*
1923 Transatlantic radio program received from Great Britain, *6271*
1925 Composograph photograph in a newspaper, *5693*

1960 Nuclear reactor for research and development, *6809*

November 26

1716 Lion, *1136*
1825 Social fraternity at a college, *2984*
1832 Streetcar, *6394*
1867 Refrigerated railroad car, *6378*
1925 Big-league football team to travel coast-to-coast, *7306*

November 27

1676 Fire of serious consequence, *2879*
1779 University legally designated as such, *2933*
1839 Statistical society, *6779*
1901 Army war college, *3200*
1918 President to receive a passport while in office, *6232*
1921 Radio church, *6590*
1924 Macy's Thanksgiving Day Parade, *4262*
1939 Submarine from the United States destroyed in World War II, *8066*
1940 Merchant ship formally blessed at a launching ceremony, *6893*
1951 Rocket to intercept an airplane, *8136*
1960 Professional hockey player to reach a score of more than 1,000 points, *7381*

November 28

1775 Marine officer, *5229*
1895 Car race, *7260*
1922 Skywriting advertisement exhibition, *2334*
1929 Airplane flight over the South Pole, *6729*
     College football player to score 50 points in one game, *7307*
1948 Western series on television, *7779*
1953 Movie to be shown simultaneously on pay television and in movie theaters, *5519*
1961 Football player who was African-American to win the Heisman Memorial Trophy, *1726*
1979 Goalie in a National Hockey League team to score a goal, *7382*

November 29

1775 Foreign service committee, *3974*
1816 Savings bank, *3759*
1825 Italian opera, *1346*
1890 Intercollegiate Army–Navy football game, *7320*
1906 Stadium operated by a city, *7506*
1932 Bridge table to shuffle and deal cards by electricity, *4024*
1948 Opera to be televised from the Metropolitan Opera House, *1353*

1951 Atomic bomb underground explosion, *8127*
1953 Transcontinental nonstop two-way airplane service, *1421*
1961 Animal fired into space to orbit the earth, *7024*

November 30

1866 Underwater highway tunnel, *3614*
1875 Oat-crushing machine, *3914*
1887 Softball game, *7497*
1899 Aluminum used commercially in a transmission conductor, *3471*
1939 President to hold an airplane pilot's license, *6224*
1950 Concentrated milk, *3877*
1954 Meteorite known to have struck a person, *6682*

December

1621 Potato, *3890*
1795 Macadam road, *6613*
1825 Pharmacy journal, *4751*
1840 Naval vessel to sail around the Cape of Good Hope, *6981*
Radio impulse transmission, *6304*
1841 General anesthetic, *4828*
1844 Book review editor, *5613*
1861 Bibliophile magazine, *4725*
1879 Photograph taken by incandescent electric light, *5819*
1881 Electric light from a power plant in a residence, *3495*
1882 Christmas tree decorated with electric lights, *4257*
1889 Children's department in a library, *4672*
1892 Medical journal published by an African-American, *4761*
Public speaking department at a college, *3100*
1905 Sociology society (national), *6791*
1911 Advertising association to combat business abuses, *2452*
1929 Description of hydroponic agriculture, *1036*
1930 Sulfanilamide production, *4993*
1935 Casein fiber, *4443*

December 1

1751 Manual training courses offered in a school, *3281*
1841 Screw-propelled steamboat on the Great Lakes, *6869*
Teaching methodology course at a college, *3262*
1842 Navy officer condemned for mutiny, *5283*
1845 Health journal to advocate water cures, *4755*

1896 Certified public accountant, *3755*
1909 Christmas savings club at a bank, *3793*
1913 Drive-in gas station, *2499*
1914 Naval air training school, *3217*
1919 American woman to become a member of the British Parliament, *6648*
1921 Airship filled with helium gas, *1519*
1941 Glider entirely built of plywood and plastic, *1553*
1955 Father and son team to win the national contract bridge championship, *4026*
Mass boycott by civil rights protesters, *2259*
Remote-controlled railroad passenger car, *6391*
1956 Stock brokerage concern of importance whose president was a woman, *3830*
1959 Color photograph of the earth taken from space, *6700*
1969 Air Force chief master sergeant who was African-American, *5137*
1971 Astronaut to become an admiral, *7043*

December 2

1662 Colonial badges issued to "friendly" Native Americans, *5929*
1799 Ship constructed by the federal government, *6915*
1816 Savings bank to receive money on deposit, *3760*
1926 Aluminum streetcar, *6407*
1933 Conviction under a National Industrial Recovery Code, *4378*
Wedding by transatlantic telephone, *4821*
1939 Presidential campaign manager who was a woman, *3392*
1941 Round-the-world flight by a commercial airplane, *1462*
1942 Self-sustaining nuclear chain reaction demonstration, *6819*
1952 Birth to be televised for the public, *2164*
1957 Nuclear power plant devoted exclusively to peaceful uses, *3551*
1982 Heart transplant using an artificial heart that was intended to be permanent, *5103*

December 3

1639 Annulment of a marriage by court decree, *4805*
1750 Opera performed by a professional visiting troupe, *1342*
1833 College to enroll women and men on equal terms, *2943*
1834 Dental society of a city, *5032*
1875 Coaching club, *7569*
1922 Movie in Technicolor, *5555*
1923 Radio broadcast of an open session of Congress, *2567*

December 3—*continued*

1968 Supreme Court justice to participate in a television program, *2764*

1979 Solar-powered long-distance airplane flight, *1481*

December 4

1776 Capture of an enemy ship in enemy waters, *7999*

1779 Law school at a college, *3121*

1839 National political convention to adopt the unit rule, *3334*

1843 Manila paper, *5752*

1867 Agriculture organization (national), *1089*

1906 National college fraternity for African-American men, *2989*

1917 Transatlantic crossing by a submarine under its own power, *6988*

1918 President to visit Europe, *6233*

1935 College classes intended to combat the influence of communism, *3002*

1942 Citizenship granted on foreign soil, *5873*

1992 Animated film inducted into the National Film Registry, *5538*

1996 Electric car to be mass-produced, *5464*

December 5

1776 Scholastic fraternity at a college, *2983*

1782 President born an American citizen, *6183*

1786 Rebellion against the federal government, *5947*

1831 Congress in which 1,000 bills were introduced, *2562*

1843 Iron vessel built for the Navy, *6917*

1851 Felt hats for women, *2296*

1854 Folding theater chair, *4326*

1868 Bicycle school, *7182*

1876 Pipe or screw wrench, *7929*

1879 Automatic telephone system, *7713*

1905 Interstate Commerce Commission Medal of Honor, *1654*

1908 Football uniform numerals, *7312*

1927 King born in the United States, *6649*

1929 Marine pilot to fly over Antarctica, *5236*
Nudist organization, *7580*

1935 Commercial hydroponicum, *1039*

1948 Church service in sign language to be televised, *6594*

1951 Parking garage that was completely automated, *5485*

1955 Murder trial to be televised, *4624*

1964 Medal of Honor awarded in the Vietnam war, *1686*

1995 Planetary probe to enter the atmosphere of Jupiter, *7092*

December 6

1732 Play presented by professional players, *1242*

1787 State to ratify the federal Constitution, *1106*

1830 Observatory established by the federal government, *6665*

1873 International football game, *7316*

1876 Crematory, *2857*

1902 Postage stamp depicting an American woman, *6087*

1922 Electric power line commercial carrier, *3476*

1923 Presidential message to Congress that was broadcast on radio, *6211*

1967 Heart transplant, *5100*

1971 Train to transport passengers and their cars, *6435*

1973 Vice president chosen under the 25th Amendment, *6249*

1974 Democratic Party convention between presidential elections, *3379*

December 7

1800 Catholic bishop consecrated in the United States, *6460*

1842 Orchestra of international stature, *1358*

1848 Father and son who were senators at the same session, *2644*

1873 Occupational therapy treatment, *5114*

1881 Bonding company, *4511*

1887 Cancer hospital, *4885*

1903 Radio distress signal from an American ship, *6285*

1909 Thermosetting resin, *4440*

1925 Congressional representative to serve 18 terms who was a woman, *2611*

1926 Gas refrigerator, *4348*

1941 Air hero in World War II, *1615*
American losses in the Pacific in World War II, *8067*
Navy admiral killed in action in World War II, *8068*
Radar used to detect enemy airplanes, *7679*
Ship from the United States to sink a Japanese submarine in World War II, *8069*

1944 Army officer to receive the three highest decorations, *1665*
Retail store whose sales in one day exceeded $1 million, *2508*

1954 Military heliport, *1569*

1983 Execution by lethal injection, *2806*

December 8

1792 Cremation, *2856*

1850 College graduate who was an African-American woman, *3010*

1863 Civil War amnesty issued by the president to rebellious citizens, *6143*
Farmers' institute sponsored by a state, *2893*

1869 Naval Academy graduate who was Japanese, *3214*
1909 Bird banding association (national), *6792*
1928 Physician to Congress, *2569*
1929 Ship-to-shore mobile telephone commercial service, *7739*
1940 Professional football championship game broadcast on radio, *7330*
1941 Heavy tank, *8120*
Ship from the United States to surrender to the Japanese in World War II, *8070*
1946 Snow-melting apparatus using pipes embedded in the sidewalk, *2223*
1948 Television image using a split screen, *7816*
1959 Movie with scent, *5566*
1987 Treaty to reduce the number of nuclear missiles, *4007*

December 9

1621 Sermon to be printed, *1948*
1845 Silver wire suture, *4955*
1869 Labor union to admit workers other than craft workers, *4611*
1901 Paired six-day bicycle race, *7195*
1907 Fund-raising organization to sell Christmas seals, *5741*
1909 Monoplane, *1390*
1940 Radio advertising contract for FM broadcasts, *2340*
1941 Bombing mission by American forces in Asia in World War II, *8071*
Fighter plane from the United States to destroy a Japanese airplane in World War II, *8072*
1946 Rocket plane for manned supersonic flight, *1492*

December 10

1672 Postal route between cities, *5980*
1690 Loan by a colony, *3802*
1810 Boxer of fame who was African-American, *7249*
1815 Naval officers' training school, *3212*
1843 Warship with propelling machinery below the waterline, *6918*
1899 Tuberculosis hospital for needy patients, *4903*
1904 Motorcycle police, *4139*
1931 Nobel Peace Prize awarded to an American woman, *1695*
1938 Nobel Prize in literature awarded to an American woman, *1694*
1950 Nobel Peace Prize awarded to an African-American, *1697*
1951 Gas-turbine helicopter, *1566*
1953 Nobel Peace Prize awarded to a professional soldier, *1698*

1976 Year in which Nobel Prizes were won by Americans in five of six categories, *1702*
1989 Human-powered helicopter, *1571*

December 11

1719 Aurora borealis display, *6765*
1735 Translation of a classic, *1736*
1844 Anesthetic in dentistry, *4829*
1866 Transatlantic yacht race, *7211*
1882 Theater lighted by electricity, *3701*
1919 Monument to an insect, *5412*
1931 Cattle of the Afrikaaner breed, *1082*
1961 Troops sent to Vietnam, *8014*
1972 Geologist to reach the moon, *6718*
1988 Motorcycle trip from the United States to Tierra del Fuego by a woman, *5494*

December 12

1789 Catholic Bible in English, *1963*
1796 Nail cutting and heading machine, *7908*
1808 Bible society, *6571*
1862 Warship sunk by an underwater torpedo mine, *7965*
1870 Congressional representative who was African-American, *2603*
1897 Comic strip in continuous newspaper publication, *5691*
1899 Golf tee, *7352*
1906 Cabinet member who was Jewish, *6108*
1910 Supreme Court justice to be appointed chief justice, *2761*
1925 Motel, *2429*
1937 Mobile television unit, *7813*
1941 General of the American armed forces killed in World War II, *8073*
1944 World War II veterans' society officially recognized by Congress, *5313*

December 13

1621 Furs exported, *3740*
1752 Hospital to treat poor patients at no charge, *4869*
1759 Musical instrument dealer, *1279*
1774 Revolutionary War incident, *7988*
1809 Abdominal operation other than a cesarean section, *5076*
1853 Infirmary for women staffed by physicians who were women, *4877*
1893 Tuberculosis laboratory established by a city, *4199*
1918 American division to cross the Rhine River in World War I, *8047*
1920 Astronomer to measure the size of a fixed star, *6668*
1933 Air Mail Flyer's Medal of Honor, *1642*
1941 Ace in World War II, *1616*
1978 Coin bearing the likeness of an American woman, *5381*

December 14

1793 Road authorization by a state, *6612*
1807 Meteorite whose landing was recorded, *6677*
1849 Chamber music ensemble, *1359*
1902 Transpacific telegraph cable, *7703*
1934 Streamlined steam locomotive, *6364*
1945 Distinguished Service Medal awarded to a Navy nurse, *5288*
1962 Spacecraft to transmit data from Venus, *7079*

December 15

1778 Arbitration law enacted by a state, *2355*
1791 Constitutional amendments, *1107*
1792 Life insurance offered by a general insurance company, *4543*
1810 Irish magazine, *4742*
1814 Secession convention during the War of 1812, *7635*
1820 General pharmacopoeia, *1930*
1854 Street-cleaning machine, *2220*
1864 Stamp collection magazine, *4727*
1874 Child abuse prevention organization, *5737*

Reigning king to visit the United States, *6645*
1886 Stock exchange at which more than a million shares were traded in one day, *3820*
1906 National Geographic Society gold medal, *1640*
1925 Road with a depressed trough, *6628*
1931 Congressional committee headed by a woman, *2589*
1943 Marine officer of Chinese descent, *5238*
1944 Army generals to wear the five-star insignia, *5157*

Navy admirals to wear the five-star insignia, *5273*
1965 Astronauts to rendezvous in space with another spacecraft, *7034*
1971 Secret Service agents who were women, *4170*

December 16

1835 Fire of great destructive force, *2881*
1851 Brass spinning, *4468*
1884 Vending machine that dispensed liquid automatically, *2393*
1897 Submarine fitted with an internal combustion engine, *6963*
1899 Children's museum, *5581*
1907 Circumnavigation of the globe by a fleet of warships, *6986*

Singer whose voice was broadcast over radio, *1330*
1908 Credit union, *3773*

1922 State supreme court justice who was a woman, *2723*
1930 Athlete to win the James E. Sullivan Memorial Trophy, *1719*
1941 Submarine from the United States to sink a Japanese ship in World War II, *8074*
1979 Rocket-powered car to break the sound barrier on land, *5461*

December 17

1679 Price regulation agreement by colonists, *2516*
1791 One-way street, *6611*
1821 State law abolishing imprisonment for debt, *2815*
1895 National anti-saloon league, *2681*
Paper twine machine, *5761*
1903 Airplane flight, *1426*
1924 Diesel-electric locomotive, *6363*
1933 World championship professional football game, *7326*
1937 Radio facsimile newspaper, *5656*
1946 Coin bearing the likeness of an African-American, *5379*
1954 Railroad freight yard that was fully automatic, *6346*
1956 Pilot on a scheduled passenger line who was African-American, *1604*
Skyscraper of bronze and glass, *2101*
1959 Movie premiered simultaneously in major cities throughout the world, *5520*
1963 Air pollution law of importance enacted by Congress, *3718*
1984 Rap album to attract a mass audience, *1373*

December 18

1777 National day of thanksgiving, *4260*
1796 Sunday newspaper, *5635*
1839 Astronomy photograph, *6692*
1865 Ban by Congress on importation of diseased cattle, *4210*
1924 Radio broadcast of a livestock auction, *1075*
1935 Bill to depict both sides of the Great Seal of the United States, *5395*
1936 Giant panda, *1154*

December 19

1683 Landscape architect, *1192*
1795 Road appropriation of a specific sum by a state, *6614*
1823 Birth registration law enacted by a state, *2159*
1854 Sewing machine to sew curving seams, *4355*
1871 Corrugated paper, *5759*
1903 Suspension bridge with steel towers, *3588*
1910 Rayon, *7874*

December 26—*continued*

1865 Coffee percolator, *3850*
1877 Socialist Labor Party of North America national convention, *3360*
1878 Electric light in a store, *3491*
1908 Heavyweight boxing champion of the world who was African-American, *7252*
1933 FM radio, *6310*
1945 Strike to last longer than a year, *4600*
1966 Kwanzaa celebration, *4249*

December 27

1845 Anesthetic administered in childbirth, *4830*
1934 Youth hostel, *2150*
1938 Skimobile ski lift, *7485*
1941 Railroad to be completely equipped with diesel-electric engines, *6344*
1945 World bank, *3787*
1951 Mail delivery car with the steering wheel on the right, *5454*

December 28

1832 Vice president to resign, *6243*
1869 Labor Day, *4237*
1912 Municipal streetcars, *6405*
1920 Ambulance ship designed and built by the Navy as a hospital, *5022*
1931 Volcanic eruption to be broadcast on radio, *2870*
1961 Airline to carry 100 million passengers, *1423*
1972 Stereo telecast, *7857*
1981 Child born in the United States through in vitro fertilization, *2166*

December 29

1782 Nautical almanac, *1765*
1837 Threshing machine to employ steam, *1046*
1848 Gaslight in the White House, *6253*
1851 Young Men's Christian Association, *5712*
1867 Stock brokerage concern to use a telegraph ticker, *3817*
1891 Radio patent, *6305*

1908 Brake for four-wheeled cars, *5439*
1913 Serial movie with installments longer than one reel, *5550*
1938 Pontoon bridge of reinforced concrete, *3595*
1952 Hearing aid using transistors, *5071*
1955 Aerocycle, *1570*
1961 Minimum wage law established by a city for public contract work, *4580*
1973 Photograph of a comet taken from space, *6704*

December 30

1731 Concert with documentation, *1287*
1852 President to celebrate his silver wedding anniversary at the White House, *6191*
1854 Oil company, *3525*
1873 Measurement organization (national), *2449*
1887 Physiology society (national), *5041*
1903 Political science association (national), *6790*
1913 Crepe, *7875*
1954 Athlete who was African-American to win the James E. Sullivan Memorial Trophy, *1720*
1959 Submarine equipped with ballistic missiles, *6976*
Submarine to have two complete crews, *6977*
1995 Coptic Orthodox Church bishop, *6500*

December 31

1776 Price regulation law enacted by a colony, *2517*
1800 Book with color plates, *1741*
1830 Parade held by a mystic society, *3659*
1841 Dental surgeons to be licensed by a state, *4936*
1934 Pilot to fly a regularly scheduled airmail transport who was a woman, *1600*
1948 Senator to win a seat that had been occupied by his father and his mother, *2654*
1951 Battery to convert radioactive energy into electrical energy, *3488*
1961 Football game to gross $1 million, *7332*

Index to Personal Names

The following is a listing of key personal names in the main body of the text, arranged alphabetically by last name. To find an entry in the main body of the text, please go to the italicized number.

A

Abbe, Robert: Radium treatment for cancer, *5115*

Abbott, William Hawkins: Commercial oil refinery, *3529*

Abdu'l-Baha: Baha'i house of worship, *6604*

Abel, Thomas: Slide rule book, *1884*

Abell, Theodore Curtis: Humanist association, *5746*

Abelson, Philip Hauge: Neptunium, *6817*

Abernethy, George: Government on the Pacific Coast, *5963*

Abrahams, Isaac: College graduate who was Jewish, *3008*

Abramovitz, Max: Elliptical office building, *2096*

Abruzzo, Ben: Transatlantic balloon flight, *1543*

Acheson, Dean: Transcontinental telecast received on the East Coast, *7840*

Acheson, Edward Goodrich: Carborundum, *5337*

Acker, Charles Ernest: Carbon tetrachloride, *4439*

Ackerman, Paula: Rabbi in the Reform movement who was a woman, *6490*

Adalian, G. Harry: Electric-eye camera installed at a racetrack, *7400*

Adams, Alva Blanchard: Radio broadcast of an open session of Congress, *2567*

Adams, Annette Abbott: District attorney who was a woman, *2714*

Adams, Benjamin: Pencil factory, *8148*

Adams, E.E.: Streamlined lightweight highspeed three-car passenger train, *6431*

Adams, Fae Margaret: Doctor commissioned in the regular Army who was a woman, *5172*

Adams, H.A., Jr.: Ship transported overland across the Rocky Mountains, *6935*

Adams, Hannah: Writer to work professionally who was a woman, *2031*

Adams, Isaac: Power printing press capable of fine book work, *5771*

Adams, John: Army lieutenant general, *5148*
Building erected in Washington, DC, by the federal government, *2116*
Congressional caucus, *2584*

Design for the Great Seal of the United States, *1132*
Marine band, *5230*
Minister to Great Britain, *3985*
Navy fleet, *5257*
President to reside in Washington, *6144*
President whose son became president, *6184*
Presidential election in which more than one candidate declared for the presidency, *3383*
Senate president pro tempore, *2625*
Special session of Congress, *2561*
Supreme Court chief justice to serve in a presidential cabinet, *2756*
Supreme Court decision voiding an act of Congress, *2746*
Tax rebellion, *5952*
Treaty between the federal government and a nation with which it had been at war, *3999*
Treaty entered into by the federal government after independence, *4000*

Adams, John Quincy: First Lady who was not born in the United States, *6129*
Former president who was elected to the House of Representatives, *6149*
Opinion poll, *5601*
Photograph of a former president, *6153*
President whose son became president, *6184*
Presidential election in which a loser won, *3385*

Adams, Joseph Alexander: Electrotype, *5803*

Adams, Julius: Dual sewer system for sewage and storm water, *2229*

Adams, Sharon Sites: Transpacific sailboat crossing by a woman, *6999*

Adams, Thomas F.: Printing press for polychromatic printing, *5776*

Adams, William Francis: Ship with a combined diesel and gas-turbine engine, *6946*

Addams, Jane: Nobel Peace Prize awarded to an American woman, *1695*

Adkins, Janet: Death by suicide machine, *2845*

Adler, Cyrus: College under Jewish auspices that was nonsectarian, *2963*

Adler, Felix: Ethical culture society, *5744*

Adler, Max: Planetarium open to the public, *6669*

Adolphe, Madame: Tightrope performer who was a woman, *3657*

Adt, John: Machine for cutting and straightening wire, *4403*

Adulyadej, Bhumibol: King born in the United States, *6649*

Affel, Herman A.: Coaxial cable, *7706*

Agnew, Spiro T.: President who came to the office through appointment rather than election, *6178*

Agronsky, Martin: Supreme Court justice to participate in a television program, *2764*

Aitken, Jane: Bible translated into English, *1966*

Aitken, Robert: Bible printed in English, *1962*
Engineering book, *1977*
Fifty-dollar gold pieces minted by the federal government, *5376*
Trade directory, *1812*

Akeley, Carl Ethan: Taxidermy method of stuffing animals, *6746*

Akers, Michelle: Soccer world champion who was a woman, *7495*

Akin, William B.: Road map for motorists, *4801*

Albee, Fred Houdlett: Flying medical clinic, *4845*

Albert Edward, Prince of Wales: Prince of Wales to visit the United States, *4078*

Albright, Harrison: Building with a large-scale clear-span dome, *2085*

Albright, Jacob: Evangelical Church conference, *6526*

Albright, Madeleine Korbel: Secretary of state who was a woman, *6123*

Albright, Tenley: World figure skating champion from the United States, *7433*

Alcott, William Andrus: Physiology society, *5033*

Alden, Timothy: Typesetting machine, *5804*

Aldrin, Edwin E. "Buzz," Jr.: Astronauts to land on the moon, *7040*
Mobile telephone call to the moon, *7770*
Photograph of a solar eclipse taken from the atmosphere, *6703*

Aleichem, Sholem: Musical to run for more than 3,000 performances, *1271*

Alen, James H. Van: Intercollegiate court tennis match, *7534*

Alexander, Charles M.: Parachute jumper snagged by airplane in midair, *1593*

Alexander, Harry Louis: Allergy journal, *4764*

Alexander, Moses: Governor who was Jewish, *7617*

Alexanderson, Ernst Fredrik Werner: Speaker to address an organization by television, *7831*

Alger, Cyrus: Rifled gun, *8094*

Alison, Francis: Life insurance company, *4542*

Allen, Aaron H.: Folding theater chair, *4326*

Allen, Andrew: Cricket club, *7271*

Allen, Arthur Augustus: Ptarmigan, *1166*

Allen, Bryan: Human-powered aircraft, *1406*

Allen, Chet: Opera written for television, *1354*

Allen, Ethan: Revolutionary War military action, *7990*

Allen, Florence Ellinwood: Judge to impose the death penalty who was a woman, *2722*
Justice on the federal bench who was a woman, *2725*
State supreme court justice who was a woman, *2723*

Allen, George: Book on vellum, *1749*

Allen, Horatio: Locomotive for railroad use, *6348*
Locomotive illumination, *6350*

Allen, J.: Hymnbook with music, *1972*

Allen, John: Agricultural book, *1757*
Book catalog of a college, *1767*

Allen, Joseph: Salvage operation in space, *7089*

Allen, Lewis Falley: Herd book for livestock, *1761*

Allen, Macon B.: Lawyer formally admitted to the bar who was African-American, *4634*

Allen, Nathan: Phrenology journal, *4753*

Allen, Paul Gardner: Commercial software for personal computers, *2552*

Allen, Richard: African Methodist Episcopal bishop, *6564*
African Methodist Episcopal preacher who was a woman, *6565*
Hymnbook compiled by an African-American editor, *1973*
Methodist churches for African-Americans, *6561*
Methodist minister who was African-American, *6559*
National convention of African-Americans, *2248*

Allen, Zachariah: Mutual fire insurance company, *4532*

Allgood, Howard Ray: Community to fingerprint its citizens, *4164*

Allison, Richard: Army medical corps, *5008*

Allison, Stacy: Ascent of Mount Everest by an American, *7588*

Altgeld, John Peter: Labor activists to be executed, *4564*

Alvarez, Everett, Jr.: Navy pilot shot down and captured in North Vietnam, *8015*

Ambler, Richard: Customhouse, *2469*

Ames, David: Arsenal of the federal government, *5126*
Muskets, *8091*

Ames, John: Steel shovel, *7906*

Ames, Nathan: Escalator patent, *2106*

Amherst, Jeffery: Germ warfare, *8089*
Knighthood conferred on American soil, *6643*

Ammann, Othmar H.: Bridge designed by computer, *3597*

Amme, Daniel: Goldfish hatchery, *1061*

Amundsen, Roald: Airplane flight over the North Pole, *6728*

Anagnos, Michael: Kindergarten for blind children, *3027*

Anders, William Alison: Astronauts to orbit the moon, *7038*

Anderson, Alexander: Wood engraving made with an engraving tool, *1226*

Anderson, Carl David: Antimatter to be observed, *6815*

Anderson, Charles Alfred: Transcontinental flight made by African-Americans in their own airplane, *1458*

Anderson, Charles E.: Video tape recorder for sounds and pictures, *7821*

Anderson, Eugenie Moore: Ambassador from the United States who was a woman, *3991*

Anderson, Garland: Play of full length by an African-American writer to be performed in New York City, *1258*

Anderson, George K.: Typewriter ribbon, *2386*

Anderson, Humphrey Stevenson: Intercollegiate baseball game, *7114*

Anderson, James: Newspaper published at sea, *5642*

Anderson, John: Debate among party hopefuls for the presidential nomination to be shown on television, *3398*

Anderson, Kris: Transcontinental nonstop balloon flight, *1544*

Anderson, Laurie B.: Secret Service agents who were women, *4170*

Anderson, Louis Francis: Dean of students at a college, *2973*

Anderson, Marian: Metropolitan Opera singer who was African-American, *1338*

Anderson, Maxie: Transatlantic balloon flight, *1543*

Anderson, Maxie Leroy: Transcontinental nonstop balloon flight, *1544*

Anderson, Paul: Weight lifter to lift more than 6,000 pounds, *7587*

Anderson, Richard Clough: Conference of American republics, *3979*

Treaty between the federal government and a South American nation, *4002*

Anderson, Robert (doctor): Transfusion of artificial blood, *4840*

Anderson, Robert (soldier): Act inaugurating the Civil War, *7946*

Anderson, Violette Neatly: Lawyer admitted to practice before the Supreme Court who was African-American, *4635*

Anderson, W. French: Gene therapy, *5118*

Anderson, William Robert: Crossing of the North Pole underwater by a submerged submarine, *6993*

Submarine to remain submerged for two weeks, *6974*

Anderson, Willie: Professional open golf championship match, *7344*

Andrew, John Albion: Civil War bloodshed, *7952*

Andrews, A.M.: Naval militia of a state to have a hydroplane, *5256*

Andrews, Ebenezer T.: American gazetteer, *1814*

Angert, Esther R.: Bacterium to be discovered that was visible to the naked eye, *6752*

Angle, Edward Hartley: Orthodontists' society, *5045*

Antheil, George: Movie star who was a weapons inventor, *5527*

Symphonic work to require an airplane propeller, *1296*

Anthony, Earl: Bowler to earn $100,000 in one year in tournaments, *7232*

Anthony, Edward: Photographs used in surveying, *5810*

Anthony, Susan Brownell: Coin bearing the likeness of an American woman, *5381*

Temperance society for women (state), *2677*

Voting rights organization (national) advocating universal voting rights, *3427*

Anthony, William Arnold: Dynamo for a direct-current outdoor lighting system, *3454*

Antoney: Wedding of colonists in Virginia, *4812*

Apgar, Virginia: Anesthesiology professor at a college, *3158*

Test for newborn health, *2165*

Applebaum, Saul Bezalel: Passover seder to be shown on television, *6489*

Appleton, William Henry: Book trade magazine, *4724*

Apponyi, Geraldine: Woman of American ancestry to become a queen, *6651*

Arcaro, Eddie: Jockey to win the Kentucky Derby five times, *7413*

Jockey to win the Triple Crown twice, *7412*

Arch, Alexander L.: Shot fired by American infantry in World War I, *8037*

Archer, Fred: Horse bred in the United States to win the English Derby, *7407*

Archer, Gabriel: Episcopal church service in an English colony, *6547*

Archer, John: Physician to receive a Bachelor of Medicine degree, *3131*

Argall, Samuel: Colonial warfare between England and France in America, *5911*

Naval expedition mounted by an English colony, *5910*

Aristides: Kentucky Derby horse race, *7392*

Arlin, Harold W.: Presidential inauguration to be broadcast on radio, *6213*

Armstrong, Edwin Howard: FM radio, *6310*

Armstrong, Henry Jackson: Boxer to hold three titles simultaneously, *7253*

Armstrong, Neil Alden: Astronaut who was a civilian to orbit the earth, *7035*
Astronauts to land on the moon, *7040*
Manned docking of two spacecraft, *7082*
Mobile telephone call to the moon, *7770*
Postage stamp depicting a living American, *6097*

Arneson, Dave: Role-playing game, *4014*

Arnett, Benjamin William: State legislator who was African-American to represent a constituency with a white majority, *7625*

Arnheim, William: Aviation course in a high school, *3089*

Arnold, Benedict: Army chaplain who was Catholic, *5194*

Arnold, Charles: Journalism school at a college, *3102*

Arnold, Frank Atkinson: Radio advertising course at a college, *2923*

Arnold, Henry Harley "Hap": Army generals to wear the five-star insignia, *5157*
Military think tank, *5128*

Arnold, Lewis Golding: Military prison on an island, *2821*

Arnold, Ross Harper: Computerized pump, *4417*

Arnold, William Richard: Army general to be consecrated a bishop, *5158*

Arnson, Ludwig: Radio distress signal from an American ship, *6285*

Aronson, Max: Movie star, *5525*
Movie with a plot, *5547*

Arpin, Paul: French newspaper, *5662*

Arroyo, Domingo: Serviceman to die in Somalia, *7982*

Arthur, Chester Alan: Restrictions by Congress on immigration of Chinese laborers, *5866*

Arthur, Robert: Dental filling made of gold, *4860*

Asbury, Francis: Methodist bishop, *6560*
Methodist minister who was African-American, *6559*

Ashburner, Charles Edward: City manager, *2203*

Ashford, Emmett Littleton: Umpire in organized baseball who was African-American, *7102*

Ashley, Hannah Hogeboom: Slave to be emancipated, *2245*

Ashmun, Jehudi: College for African-American students, *2949*

Ashton, Genevieve: Lottery in which the top prize was $1 million, *3643*

Ashton, George: Lottery in which the top prize was $1 million, *3643*

Asing, Norman: Chinese restaurant, *2455*

Aspinwall, Nan Jane: Transcontinental solo trip on horseback by a woman, *1183*

Assing, Norman: Chinese theatrical performance, *1250*

Astor, John Jacob: Settlers to reach the Pacific coast, *5957*

Astor, Mary: Movie with sound to be released as a feature, *5557*

Astor, Nancy Witcher Langhorne: American woman to become a member of the British Parliament, *6648*

Atanasoff, John Vincent: Electronic digital calculator, *3438*

Athenagaros, Archbishop: Greek Orthodox college and orphanage, *3279*

Atkins, Captain: Polar bear, *1138*

Atkins, Charles Grandison: Fish hatchery run by the federal government, *1060*

Atkinson, Eudora Clark: Reformatory for women established by a state, *2824*

Atkinson, William: Interactive multimedia authoring program, *2553*

Atkisson, Earl James: Army gas regiment, *5186*

Attucks, Crispus: Americans killed by British soldiers in the Revolution, *7986*

Attwater, Henry Smith: College course without Greek or Latin, *2992*

Atwater, Robert: Seaplane glider, *1550*

Atwater, Wilbur Olin: Agricultural experiment station operated by a state, *1003*

Atwell, W.S.: Bicycle factory, *7183*

Atwood, Ernestine F.: Carnegie Hero Fund Commission award granted to a woman, *1639*

Atwood, Harry Nelson: Airplane to land on the White House lawn, *6255*

Atwood, Luther: Coal oil factory, *4431*

Atwood, Wallace Walter: Geography school at a college, *3245*

Audubon, John James: Bird banding, *6740*

Austin, Ann: Quakers to arrive in America, *6585*

Austin, C.: Melodeon patent, *1309*

Austin, William A.: Steam-driven motorcycle, *5487*

Averill, D.R.: Paint ready-mixed, *7925*

Avila, John B.: Sweet potato, *1020*

Axson, A. Forster: Quarantine board established by a state, *4209*

Axtater, Karl S.: Airship transfer of mail to a train, *1523*

Ayers, William: Irish to arrive in America, *5932*

Ayres, Thomas N.: Mutual life insurance company, *4544*

B

Babbitt, Benjamin Talbert: Baking powder manufacturer, 3936
Bandwagon, 2326
Premiums given away with merchandise, 2323
Soap powder in packages, 4269
Babcock, Stephen Moulton: Milk butterfat tester, 3874
Baby Fae: Heart transplant using a baboon heart, 5104
Bache, Alexander Dallas: National science institute, 6781
Bache, Benjamin Franklin: Cryptography chart, 4797
Bache, Franklin: Pharmaceuticals book, 1929
Bache, Richard: Partridge propagation, 1067
Back, Frank Gerard: Television camera lens to provide zoom effects, 7815
Bacon, Augustus Octavius: Senator elected by popular vote, 3329
Bacon, Thomas: Manual training courses offered in a school, 3281
Badillo, Herman: Congressional representative of Puerto Rican ancestry, 2618
Badin, Stephen Theodore: Catholic priest, 6459
Baekeland, Leo Hendrik: Thermosetting resin, 4440
Baer, Max: Boxing match to be shown on television, 7243
Bagley, Sarah G.: Telegrapher who was a woman, 7694
Bagley, Worth: Navy officer killed in action in the Spanish-American War, 8008
Bagno, Samuel: Burglar alarm operated by ultrasonic or radio waves, 2136
Bailey, Carroll L.: Shuffleboard championship tournament, 7582
Bailey, Ezekiel: Oilcloth factory, 7870
Bailey, Francis: City directory, 1813
Bailey, John: Congressional representative to be refused a seat, 2600
Bailey, Leonard L.: Heart transplant using a baboon heart, 5104
Bailey, Theodorus: Citizen of the United States to be hanged for treason, 2835
Bainbridge, William: Naval officers' training school, 3212
Baine, John: Catholic Bible in English, 1963
Baird, Robert Atkinson, III: Jet airplane to transport mail, 6030
Baker, Belle: Radio broadcast from a moving train, 6276
Baker, Edward Dickinson: Senator to address the Senate in military uniform, 2648
Baker, Ellis Benjamin: Pay telephone, 7715

Baker, Eugene Voy: Intercollegiate football championship, 7317
Baker, Howard, Jr.: Debate among party hopefuls for the presidential nomination to be shown on television, 3398
Baker, James: Chocolate mill, 3955
Baker, Newton Diehl: Army nursing school, 3176
Baker, Richard: Zen Buddhist monastery, 6439
Baker, Richard Freligh: Photograph of genes, 4909
Baker, Sara Josephine: Child hygiene bureau, 4186
Baker, Sue A.: Secret Service agents who were women, 4170
Baker, Vernon: Medals of Honor awarded to African-American servicemen for service in World War II, 1689
Bakken, Earl: Pacemaker, 4952
Balaca, R.: Postage stamps to feature paintings, 6086
Balanchine, George: Ballet choreographer of international renown, 1235
Balch, William: Navy chaplain, 5198
Balcom, Homer Gage: Skyscraper higher than 1,250 feet, 2100
Baldasare, Fred: Swimmer to swim the English Channel underwater, 7520
Baldwin, James Fowle: Engineering society, 3608
Baldwin, John: Abolition organization, 2243
Baldwin, Loammi: Federal dry docks, 6905
Baldwin, Luke: Rubber company, 4484
Baldwin, Simeon Eben: Lawyers' society (national), 4644
Baldwin, Thomas Scott: Airship ordered by the federal government, 1514
Airship race, 7291
Balfour, George: Navy surgeon, 5280
Ball, Cornelius: Unassisted triple play in a major league baseball game, 7126
Ball, Sarah B.: Business library supported by taxes, 4675
Ballantyne, William: Stowaway on an aircraft, 1518
Ballentine, John Jennings: Ship from which a long-range rocket was launched, 6938
Balley, Jacqueline P.: Federal marshals who were women, 4151
Balsley, H. Clyde: Pilot from the United States shot down in World War I, 8029
Baltimore, Lord: Catholics to settle in the English colonies in America, 6447
Horse that was a thoroughbred, 1175
Shorthand account of a trial, 4619
Baltzell, Robert C.: Death penalty authorized by federal law, 2802
Bancroft, George: Gymnasium to offer systematic instruction, 7371

Bandmann, Julius: Dynamite, *4423*

Banks, Arthur J.: Airplane instructor's license, *1601*

Banks, Dennis: Armed occupation by Native American protesters in the modern era, *5978*

Banky, Vilma: Fax transmission of movie film, *7672*

Banneker, Benjamin: Clock to strike the hours, *7897*

Banvard, John: Chromolithograph, *1216*

Baptist, John: Boat club, *7206*

Baragrey, John: Television drama program regularly scheduled, *7778*

Barber, Charles E.: Commemorative coin, *5373*

Barber, Miller: Golfer to earn $100,000 in a contest, *7367*

Barber, Walter Lanier "Red": Major league baseball game to be shown on television, *7132*
Professional football championship game broadcast on radio, *7330*

Barbera, Joseph: Animated cartoon series on prime-time television, *7786*

Barbour, Edmund D.: Adding machine to print totals and subtotals, *2376*

Barbour, William: Linen thread factory, *4363*

Barclay, Edwin James: President of a black African country to visit the United States, *4082*

Bard, John: Dissection report, *1890*

Bard, Samuel: Medical ethics book, *1892*
Obstetrics book, *1900*

Bardeen, John: Nobel Prize winner to win twice in the same field, *1701*
Transistor, *3439*

Bargar, William: Robot to perform surgery, *3449*

Barker, James Nelson: Play about a Native American, *1247*

Barkhuff, Del: Badminton championship tournament, *7584*

Barnaby, Ralph Stanton: Amphibious seaplane glider, *1554*
Glider released from an airship, *1548*

Barnard, Frederick Augustus Porter: Measurement organization (national), *2449*

Barnard, Henry: Teachers' institute, *3261*

Barnes, Charles E.: Machine gun, *8104*

Barnes, Gladeon Marcus: Heavy tank, *8120*

Barnes, Howard Turner: Explosion of Thermit to break up ice jams, *4425*

Barnes, James "Long Jim": Professional Golfers Association tournament, *7345*

Barnes, Kirt: Ice skater to cover 100 miles in less than six hours, *7436*

Barnes, Martin: Nuts and bolts factory, *7918*

Barnes, Ross: Baseball players to hit home runs, *7141*

Barnes, Thomas N.: Air Force chief master sergeant who was African-American, *5137*

Barnes, Tracy: Balloon flight powered by solar energy, *1542*

Barnes, W.M.: Rough-dry laundry service, *2441*

Barney, Everett Hosmer: All-metal roller skate, *7464*

Barney, Joshua: President to face enemy gunfire while in office, *6148*

Barnhart, Harry: Community chorus, *1361*

Barnsdall, William: Commercial oil refinery, *3529*

Barnwell, Barbara Olive: Navy–Marine Corps Medal for Heroism awarded to a woman, *1668*

Baron, Alexander: Public museum, *5576*

Barr, Asa: Music convention of singing teachers, *2901*

Barr, Robert and Alexander: Textile machine, *7861*

Barras, Charles M.: Burlesque show, *3687*

Barrere, Francis Maria: Passport, *5884*

Barrett, George W.: Death penalty authorized by federal law, *2802*

Barrett, Joseph E.: President to fly in a helicopter, *6229*

Barrett, Stan: Rocket-powered car to break the sound barrier on land, *5461*

Barrie, James Matthew: Broadway play shown in a television version with its original cast, *1266*

Barron, James: Melons and cantaloupes, *3899*

Barron, John H.: Farm bureau, *1004*

Barron, Samuel: Ship constructed by the federal government, *6915*

Barry, John: Book entered for copyright, *4629*
Capture of an enemy warship by a commissioned American naval officer, *7995*
Commodore in the Navy, *5279*

Barrymore, Ethel: Theater built and named for a living actress, *3706*

Barrymore, John: Movie with sound to be released as a feature, *5557*

Barsimson, Jacob: Jew to win full citizenship, *5858*
Jews to arrive in America, *5892*

Barson, John: Subcompact car with front wheel drive, *5462*

Barsotti, Charles: Italian newspaper, *5674*

Barstow, William Augustus: Governor to be removed from office by a state supreme court, *7612*

Bartelme, Mary Margaret: Juvenile court, *2707*

Barthle, Robert Charles: Radar signal bounced off the sun, *7683*

Bartholdi, Frédéric Auguste: Statue presented to the United States by a foreign country, *5405*

Bartlett, Drummond William: Murder trial to be televised, *4624*

Bartlett, George Arthur: Congressional representative to attend college after his term of service, *2608*

Bartlett, William: Gutta-percha, *4485*

Bartlett, William Holmes Chambers: Mechanics textbook, *1988*

Barton, Andrew: Comic opera written for the American stage, *1343*

Barton, Clara: Red Cross meeting, *5739*

Barton, George Edward: Opera by an American composer to be performed at the Metropolitan Opera House, *1349*

Barton, William: Design for the Great Seal of the United States, *1132*

Barton, William Paul Crillon: Navy bureau of medicine and surgery, *5009*

Bartram, John: Botanical garden, *6736*
Rhubarb, *3897*

Baruch, Simon: Hydrotherapy chair at a college, *3152*

Bashaw, Matthew: Holographic data storage system, *2540*

Bashford, Coles: Governor to be removed from office by a state supreme court, *7612*

Basie, Count: Jazz concert at Carnegie Hall, *1298*

Basri, Gibor: Brown dwarf star to be discovered, *6685*

Bass, Charlotta A.: Vice presidential candidate who was an African-American woman, *3415*

Bassett, Ebenezer Don Carlos: Consul who was African-American, *3988*

Batchelor, Charles: Photograph taken by incandescent electric light, *5819*

Bates, Vietta M.: Women's Army Corps member to be part of the Regular Army, *5171*

Batleson, John: Wagon train to California, *5962*

Battell, Joseph: Horse farm operated by the federal government, *1182*

Batterson, James Goodwin: Accident insurance company, *4504*

Bauer, Louis Hopewell: Aviation medicine book, *1921*

Baxter, Warner: Movie of feature length made outdoors, *5558*

Bay, Josephine Perfect: Stock brokerage concern of importance whose president was a woman, *3830*

Bayard, Andrew: Savings bank to receive money on deposit, *3760*

Bayard, Louis Pintard, Jr.: Intercollegiate golf association, *7343*

Bayley, Richard: Croup report, *1894*

Beach, Alfred Ely: Subway, *6409*

Beach, Edward Latimer: Circumnavigation of the earth by a submerged submarine, *6996*

Beach, Moses Yale: Newspaper syndicate, *5626*

Beachey, Lincoln: Airplane flight under a bridge, *1437*
Airplane loop-the-loop, *1443*
Airplane race between cities, *7293*
Airship race, *7291*

Bean, Alan La Vern: Astronauts to retrieve a manmade object from the moon, *7041*
Space-to-ground news conference telecast, *5608*

Beard, Floyd S.: Parachute fatality in the Army, *1590*

Beard, George Miller: Neurasthenia book, *1919*

Beard, Richard Olding: Nursing school at a college, *3173*

Beard, Thomas: Shoes to be manufactured, *2298*

Beardsley, Hubert: Fizzing cold remedy, *4994*

Beardsley, John: Paper made from wood pulp, *5754*

Beatles, The: Performance by a British rock group, *1370*

Beatty, Charles: Fire in a mine, *2880*

Beatty, James Tully "Jim": Runner from the United States to run a mile in less than four minutes, *7564*

Beatty, Martin: Oil well, *3524*

Beauchamp, George: Electric guitar, *1325*

Beaumont, William: Physiologist of note, *4967*

Beaver, Walter S.: Grand American Trapshoot tournament with clay targets, *7476*

Beck, Claude Schaeffer: Heart operation for the relief of angina pectoris, *5091*

Beck, Clifford Keith: Nuclear engineering course at a college, *3248*

Beck, Paul N.: Airplane flying school, *3188*

Becker, Peter: Brethren, *6545*

Becket, Welton: Circular office building, *2066*

Beckley, John James: Clerk of the House of Representatives, *2577*
Librarian of Congress, *4663*

Beck's, Theodoric Romeyn: Medical jurisprudence treatise, *1879*

Beckwith, G.: Double-deck ferryboat, *6909*

Bedford, James H.: Freezing of a corpse for future resuscitation, *2841*

Beebe, Richard: Muskets, *8091*

Beecher, Henry Ward: Newspaper premiums, *2325*

Beekman, James: Greenhouse, *1040*

Beighle, Jackson: Helicopter hoist rescue, *1563*

Beissel, Johann Conrad: Communistic settlement with a religious basis, *2182*
German book printed in America, *1953*

Belcher, Jonathan: Mason, *5727*

Belkin, Samuel: College for women founded as a Jewish institution, *2968*

Belknap, Jeremy: Historical society (state), *5710*

Belknap, Morris B.: File factory, *7915*

Bell, Alexander Graham: Geography magazine, *4775*

Interstate telephone call, *7753*

News dispatch by telephone, *5605*

Telephone conversation over outdoor wires, *7752*

Telephone message, *7751*

Transcontinental telephone demonstration, *7718*

Bell, Alexander Melville: Visible speech method of instruction for deaf students, *3034*

Bell, Charles Heffelfinger: Stockholder meetings televised coast-to-coast simultaneously, *3832*

Bell, Chichester: Phonograph that was practical, *7005*

Bell, John: Constitutional Union Party convention, *3355*

Hydrotherapy book, *1887*

Bell, Melville: Voice synthesizer, *7711*

Bell, Robert Mowry: Esperanto course at a college, *3117*

Bellamy, Ralph: Pay television dramatic program, *7787*

Bellew, Frank Henry Temple: Cartoon showing Uncle Sam, *5701*

Bellinger, Patrick Nelson Lynch: Gyroscope, *1494*

Bellini, Carlo: Italian instruction at a college, *3114*

Bellow, Saul: Year in which Nobel Prizes were won by Americans in five of six categories, *1702*

Benedict, William Pershing: Airplane flight to land at the North Pole, *6731*

Benedict, Zadoc: Hat factory, *2293*

Benesch, Alfred A.: Electric traffic signal lights, *4224*

Benjamin, Asher: Architecture book distinctly American, *2015*

Benjamin, Judah Philip: Senator who was Jewish, *2647*

Bennett, Elizabeth Hog: Cesarean operation, *5075*

Bennett, Floyd: Airplane flight over the North Pole, *6728*

Bennett, James Gordon: Balloon cup race, *7288*

Intercollegiate athletic association, *7545*

Polo mallets and balls, *7457*

Steamboat to employ electric lights successfully, *6873*

Transatlantic yacht race, *7211*

Washington news correspondent, *5611*

Bennett, Jessee: Cesarean operation, *5075*

Bennett, John James: Heliport commercial base, *1565*

Bennett, William J.: Drug control chief appointed by the federal government, *2693*

Benson, Howard Hartwell James: Navy destroyer named for a Confederate officer, *6933*

Bent, Josiah: Hard water crackers, *3918*

Benton, James Gilchrist: Seacoast gun carriage, *8102*

Benz, Karl: Foreign car exhibited, *5427*

Berenson, Senda: Basketball played at a college, *7167*

Berg, Molly: Sitcom television show, *7780*

Bergen, Edgar: College degree awarded to a ventriloquist's dummy, *2981*

Television variety talent show series, *7776*

Berger, Victor Louis: Congressional representative who was a Socialist, *2607*

Socialist Party national convention, *3372*

Bergh, Henry: Animal humane society, *5735*

Child abuse prevention organization, *5737*

Bergstrom, George Edwin: Building containing 6.5 million square feet of usable space, *2118*

Berkeley, John: Ironworks, *4445*

Lead, *5314*

Berkeley, William: Rice to be imported, *3893*

Wolf bounty, *1135*

Berko, Geza David: Hungarian daily newspaper, *5679*

Berlin, Samuel H.: Transatlantic telephone service using the transoceanic cable, *7747*

Berliner, Emile: Catalog of recordings on disk, *1940*

Phonograph record, *7006*

Berliner, Henry Adler: Helicopter flight, *1572*

Berman, Peter: College to offer courses to railroad commuters, *3003*

Bernhardt, Sarah: Foreign feature film exhibited, *5512*

Bernstein, Hirsch: Hebrew newspaper, *5671*

Bernstein, Leonard: Worldwide live television program, *7856*

Berrien, Frank Dunn: Naval vessels to sink an enemy submarine in the Atlantic, *8039*

Berry, Albert: Parachute jump from an airplane, *1581*

Berry, John: Horse race of 1,000 miles, *7396*

Berry, Marcellus Fleming: Traveler's checks, *3791*

Berwanger, John J. "Jay": Football player to win the Heisman Trophy for excellence in college football, *1725*

Besserdich, William: Brake for four-wheeled cars, *5439*

Best, Daniel: Steam tractor, *1054*

Bethune, Joanna: Nursery school, *3072*

Bethune, Louise Blanchard: Architect who was a woman, *1194*

Bethune, Mary Jane McLeod: Federal administrator who was an African-American woman, *2257*

Betts, R.G.: Motorcycle association, *7439*

Bevan, Thomas: Hygiene lectures at a college, *3136*

Bialaski, Alexander Bruce: Director of the Federal Bureau of Investigation, *4141*

Biard, Pierre: Colonial warfare between England and France in America, *5911*

Biardot, Alphonse: Soup company, *3946*

Biardot, Ernest and Octave: Soup company, *3946*

Bibb, William Wyatt: Coin bearing the likeness of a living person, *5377*

Biddle, Nicholas: American flag saluted by a foreigner, *1117*

Bidwell, George R.: Pneumatic bicycle tire, *7188*

Bierstadt, Albert: Building designed to be used by artists, *2062*
Painting movement, *1204*

Bigelow, Charles D.: Shoe pegging machine, *2302*

Bigelow, Erastus Brigham: Carpet power loom, *4313*
Gingham factory, *7871*

Biggs, Hermann Michael: Bacteriology diagnostic laboratory in a city health department, *4198*
Tuberculosis laboratory established by a city, *4199*

Biggs, John F.: Payment by the Federal Crop Insurance Corporation, *1006*

Biggs, Wayne: Horse motel, *2435*

Bignall, Widow: Dwarf exhibited as a theatrical attraction, *3653*

Billings, Frank: Hospital open to all races as a matter of policy, *4886*

Billings, William: Book of music by a composer born in America, *1936*
War song, *1377*

Billington, George: Savings bank to receive money on deposit, *3760*

Billington, John: Execution in America, *2792*

Bingham, Caleb: Children's library, *4664*

Bingham, William: Macadam road, *6613*

Binney, Horace: Workers' library, *4665*

Binny, Archibald: Dollar marks, *5802*
Type specimen book from an American type foundry, *1742*

Bird, Robert Montgomery: Play performed 1,000 times, *1248*

Birdseye, Clarence: Frozen food for the mass market, *3949*

Birger, Charles: Airplane bombing raid by criminals, *2778*

Birney, Alice McLellan: Parent-teacher association (national), *3227*

Birney, Charles O.: Lightweight solo streetcar, *6406*

Birney, James Gillespie: Liberty Party convention, *3351*

Bishop, Bainbridge: Organ with color display, *1315*

Bishop, David Wolfe: Long-distance car race, *7263*

Bissell, Daniel: Purple Heart, *1656*

Bissell, Emily Perkins: Fund-raising organization to sell Christmas seals, *5741*

Bissell, George Henry: Oil company, *3525*

Bissell, Melville Reuben: Carpet sweeper, *4273*

Black, Alexander: Magic lantern feature show, *3692*

Black, Hugo Lafayette: Supreme Court justice to participate in a television program, *2764*

Black, James: Prohibition Party convention, *3356*

Black, James Wallace: Aerial photograph, *5815*

Black, Richard: American base in Antarctica that was permanent, *6730*

Black, Robert Glennwood: Navy nuclear submarine division, *5306*

Black, S. Duncan: Electric hand drill, *7937*

Black, William Henry: Cattle of the Afrikaaner breed, *1082*

Blackford, Isaac: Claims court established by the federal government, *2712*

Blackton, James Stuart: Animated cartoon, *5531*

Blackwell, Antoinette Brown: Minister who was a woman, *6530*

Blackwell, Edward: Fencing book, *1992*

Blackwell, Elizabeth: Infirmary for women staffed by physicians who were women, *4877*
Physician who was a woman, *4971*

Blackwell, Emily: Infirmary for women staffed by physicians who were women, *4877*

Blackwell, H.M.: Radio commercial, *2333*

Blaese, Michael: Gene therapy, *5118*

Blaha, John: Voting rights in space, *3435*

Blaine, James Gillespie: Conference of American republics, *3979*

Blair, David: Movie broadcast on the Internet, *5521*

Blair, Henry: Patent granted to an African-American inventor, *4652*

Blair, Izell: Civil rights sit-in, *2260*

Blair, John: Supreme Court of the United States, *2742*

Blair, Joseph Cullen: Civic design chair at a college, *3254*

Blair, William Reid: Okapi, *1155*

Blake, Alexander Vietts: Book publishers' catalog, *1769*

Blake, Eli Whitney: Caster for bedsteads, *4323*
Mortised lock, *2131*
Stone crusher, *5332*
Blake, Eubie: Movie featuring an African-American actor, *5554*
Blake, John A.: Caster for bedsteads, *4323*
Blake, Lemuel: Rubber company, *4484*
Blake, Lyman Reed: Shoe manufacturing machine, *2303*
Blake, Philos: Caster for bedsteads, *4323*
Mortised lock, *2131*
Blanchard, Jean Pierre: Balloon flight in which a presidential order was carried, *1536*
Blanchard, Thomas: Lathe, *7914*
Blanchfield, Florence Aby: Army officer who was a woman, *5170*
Blavatsky, Helena Petrovna: Theosophical society, *5743*
Blayton, Jesse Bee: Radio station owned and operated by African-Americans, *6300*
Bleibtrey, Ethelda: Olympic gold medalist from the United States who was a woman, *7445*
Blessitt, Arthur: Round-the-world journey on foot, *7590*
Blickensderfer, George C.: Portable typewriter, *2387*
Bliss, Eleanor: Sulfanilamide production, *4993*
Bliss, Henry H.: Car accident fatality, *5470*
Bliss, Raymond Whitcomb: House with solar heating and radiation cooling, *2129*
Block, Adriaen: Decked ship built in America, *6850*
Blodget, Samuel: Historical print engraved in America, *1224*
Marble building, *2070*
Blodgett, Katherine Burr: Glass that was nonreflecting, *4049*
Blomberg, Ron: Designated hitter in a major league baseball game, *7157*
Blondel, John F.: Doughnut cutter, *4295*
Blondin, Émile: Daredevil to cross Niagara Falls on a tightrope, *3677*
Blong, Joseph Myles: Baseball game in which a team made no runs in nine innings, *7117*
Bloom, Claire V.: Executive officer of a man-of-war who was a woman, *5300*
Bloom, Louis Richard: Television receiver and transmitter operated by laser beam, *7822*
Bloomer, Amelia Jenks: Bloomers, *2267*
Blount, William: Senator to be impeached, *2641*
Senators elected but not seated, *2640*
Blow, Susan Elizabeth: Public school kindergarten, *3074*
Bluford, Guion: Astronaut to fly in space who was African-American, *7049*

Blum, Barbara Davis: Federally chartered bank owned and managed by women, *3789*
Blumberg, Baruch Samuel: Year in which Nobel Prizes were won by Americans in five of six categories, *1702*
Blumenthal, Mark: Hospital under Jewish auspices, *4876*
Bly, Nellie: World tour by a woman traveling alone, *6983*
Boardman, Alexander: Boardwalk, *2063*
Bobbs, John Stough: Gallstone operation, *5079*
Bock, Jerry: Musical to run for more than 3,000 performances, *1271*
Bocock, Thomas Salem: Confederate congressional session, *7947*
Boehm, John Philip: Reformed Church meeting, *6516*
Boehm, Martin: United Brethren in Christ meeting, *6541*
Boehnisch, George: Moravian settlement in America, *6540*
Boepple, John F.: Buttons of freshwater pearl, *2290*
Boericke, Francis E.: Homeopathic pharmacy, *4986*
Boettner, John: Caterpillar Club member, *1584*
Bogardus, James: Building constructed wholly of cast iron, *2076*
Gas meter, *3512*
Boger, Frederick: Opticians' journal, *4760*
Boggs, Thomas Hale: Congressional candidate elected while missing, *2619*
Boghighian, Hagop: Dealer in Oriental rugs, *4316*
Bohune, Lawrence: Physician in the colony of Virginia, *4959*
Boldin, Bernard: Triplets born several weeks apart, *2179*
Boldin, Delvonda: Triplets born several weeks apart, *2179*
Bolin, Jane Matilda: Judge who was an African-American woman, *2726*
Bolles, Frank: Cooperative store at a college, *2497*
Bolles, Jenette Hubbard: Osteopathic physicians who were women, *4976*
Osteopathy journal, *4762*
Bolling, William: Oral school for deaf students, *3031*
Bolster, Calvin: Airship passenger transfer to an airplane, *1525*
Bolt, John F.: Marine Corps jet ace in Korea, *1619*
Bolton, Elmer K.: Synthetic rubber for manufacture, *4489*
Bolton, Frances Payne: Mother and son simultaneously elected to Congress, *2613*

Bolton, John: Stained-glass window, *4039*

Bolton, Oliver Payne: Mother and son simultaneously elected to Congress, *2613*

Bolton, William Compton: Circumnavigation of the globe by a warship, *6980*

Bolton, William Jay: Stained-glass window, *4039*

Bonaparte, Charles Joseph: College for women founded as a Catholic institution, *2958*

Bond, Julian: National political convention to propose African-Americans for the offices of president and vice president, *3343*

Bond, Thomas: Hospital, *4868*

Bond, William Cranch: Photograph of a star other than the sun, *6693*

Bonner, James: Town named for George Washington, *2186*

Bonstelle, Jessie: Theater operated by a city, *3703*

Bonwill, William Gibson Arlington: Dental mallet, *4865*

Boone, Nicholas: Engraving of any artistic merit, *1223*

Boorda, Jeremy M. "Mike": Sailor to become a four-star admiral, *5275*

Booth, John Wilkes: Execution of a woman by hanging by the federal government, *2798*

President to be assassinated, *6193*

Booth, Mary Louise: Fashion magazine, *4728*

Booth, Oliver: Ice yacht, *7205*

Booth, Shirley: Oscar movie awards ceremony to be telecast, *1636*

Borcherdt, Victor: Zoo habitat constructed of simulated rock formations without bars, *1188*

Bordelon, Guy: Navy ace in Korea, *1622*

Borden, Gail: Condensed milk, *3869*

Meat biscuit, *3920*

Borden, Gail, Jr.: Medal awarded to an American food producer, *1651*

Borden, Joseph Emley: Baseball game in which a team made no hits in nine innings, *7118*

Borden, Simeon: Geodetic survey, *6711*

Boren, Horace C.: Passenger to circle the world on commercial airlines in less than 100 hours, *1477*

Borgenicht, Louis: Ready-made clothing for children, *2273*

Borgfeldt, Nicholas H.: Snow-melting apparatus, *2221*

Borman, Frank: Astronauts to orbit the moon, *7038*

Astronauts to rendezvous in space with another spacecraft, *7034*

Borzage, Frank: Oscars for best movie director, *1632*

Bosenberg, Henry F.: Plant patent, *1063*

Bostwick, A.C.: Car to exceed the speed of a mile a minute, *5436*

Botetourt, Lord: College to confer medals as prizes, *2930*

Bouchet, Edward Alexander: Doctor of Philosophy degree awarded to an African-American scholar, *2978*

Boudinot, Elias: Bible society (national), *6573*

Lawyers admitted to practice before the Supreme Court, *4633*

Native American newspaper, *5666*

Bouquet, Henry: Germ warfare, *8089*

Bourke-White, Margaret: News magazine featuring photographs, *4736*

Bouton, J. W.: Bibliophile magazine, *4725*

Bouvier, John: Dictionary of American law, *1805*

Bovay, Alvan Earle: Republican Party meeting, *3353*

Bowden, Don: Runner from the United States to run a mile in less than four minutes, *7564*

Bowditch, E. B.: Oil well that was commercially productive, *3528*

Bowditch, Henry Ingersoll: Health board established by a state government, *4177*

Bowdoin, James: Arts and sciences organization (national), *5709*

Bowen, Anthony: Young Men's Christian Association, *5712*

Bowers, Robert Hood: Movie sex shocker, *5553*

Bowes, Edward: Simultaneous radio broadcast on all three major networks, *6278*

Bowie, James: Bowie knife, *8095*

Bowker, Richard Rogers: Library society (local), *4689*

Bowlus, William Hawley: Powered soaring glider commercially licensed, *1556*

Bowser, Augustus: Gasoline pump, *4410*

Bowser, Sylvanus F.: Gasoline pump, *4410*

Boyd, Bill: Western series on television, *7779*

Boyd, James: Fire hose of rubber-lined cotton web, *4099*

Boyd, John: Presbyterian presbytery, *6581*

Boyden, Seth: Malleable iron castings, *4451*

Patent leather, *4458*

Boyden, Uriah Atherton: Turbine successfully operated by waterpower, *4399*

Boyle, Doreen: Train operated exclusively by women, *6436*

Boyle, James: Box spring, *4327*

Boyle, Robert: School for Native Americans to be permanently established, *3049*

Boylston, Zabdiel: Inoculation against smallpox using material from human smallpox pustules, *4914*

Boynton, Charles Brandon: University for African-American students, *2951*

Boyton, Paul: Shoot-the-chutes, *3624*

Brackett, Anna Callender: Teacher training school principal who was a woman, *3264*

Bradford, Andrew: German book printed in America, *1953*
Magazine published in America, *4692*

Bradford, Lawrence Wallace, Jr.: Senate page who was African-American, *2636*

Bradford, Vincent L.: Homeopathic hospital, *4875*

Bradford, William: City directory, *1813*
Corn found by English settlers, *3908*
Earthquake description, *2861*
Law history book, *1861*
Medical education book, *1891*
Paper mill, *5747*
Play written in America that was printed, *1241*
Property tax levied by a colony, *7637*

Bradley, Henry W.: Margarine manufacturer, *3882*

Bradstreet, Anne Dudley: Poetry collection by an American poet, *1943*

Brady, Genevieve Garvan: Pope to visit the United States before his election, *4081*

Brady, James T.: Temporary insanity defense in a criminal case, *4622*

Brady, Mathew B.: Coin bearing the likeness of a president, *5375*
News photographs of distinction, *5817*
Photograph of a president in office, *6155*

Braidwood, John: Oral school for deaf students, *3031*

Bralet, Robert E.: Shot fired by American infantry in World War I, *8037*

Brams, Steven: Theory of fair division, *6762*

Brand, Bernie: Dance marathon, *3630*

Brand, Vance Devoe: Astronauts to participate in an international spaceflight, *7046*

Brandeis, Louis Dembitz: Savings bank life insurance, *4547*
Supreme Court justice who was Jewish, *2762*

Brantley, William Theophilus: City college, *2936*

Brattain, Walter Houser: Transistor, *3439*

Brattle, William: Logic book, *1975*

Braun, Carol Mosely: Senator who was an African-American woman, *2661*

Braunsteiner Ryan, Hermine: Nazi death camp guard to be deported, *5880*

Bray, John Randolph: Animated cartoon made with cel animation, *5532*

Bray, Linda: Army officer who was a woman to lead troops in combat, *5176*

Bray, Thomas: Library, *4659*

Brayton, George B.: Gas-powered streetcar, *6397*

Brazzil, Ruth: State supreme court in which all the judges were women, *2724*

Brearley, William Henry: Newspaper association, *5617*

Breck, John: Shampoo commercially produced, *4069*

Breckinridge, John: Senator to address the Senate in military uniform, *2648*
State nullification proceedings to obstruct federal legislation, *7595*

Breedlove, Sarah: Millionaire who was an African-American woman, *2444*

Breill, Frank "Pop": Bowling tournament sponsored by the American Bowling Congress, *7223*

Breitbart, Charles H.: Blood testing laws enacted by a state, *4188*

Brenner, Victor David: Coin bearing the likeness of a president, *5375*

Brenon, Herbert: Movie sex shocker, *5553*

Brenston, Jackie: Rock and roll song, *1368*

Brent, Margaret: Woman in America to appeal for the right to vote, *3420*

Brewer, Charles A.: Punchboards, *2368*

Brewer, Joseph: College to dispense with credits, hours, points, and grades, *3001*

Brewer, Lucy: Marine who was a woman, *5232*

Brewer, Margaret Ann: Marine general who was a woman, *5240*

Brice, Arthur T.: Phase-contrast cinemicrography film to be shown on television, *5565*

Bridgeman, Thomas: Gardener's manual, *1760*

Bridgers, Frank Hillman: Commercial building with solar heating, *2067*

Bridges, Robert: Ironworks that was successful, *4446*

Brigden, Zechariah: College student to work his way through college, *3005*

Briggs, Emily Edson: News correspondent accredited to the White House, *5616*

Briggs, Enos: Naval vessel to display the American flag around Cape Horn, *1127*

Briggs, Isaac: Steamboat patent, *6855*

Briggs, Samuel, Sr. and Jr.: Patent granted jointly to a father and son, *4650*

Bristol, Arthur Leroy: Aircraft carrier, *6934*

Britt, Maurice L.: Army officer to receive the three highest decorations, *1665*

Broadhead, James Overton: Lawyers' society (national), *4644*

Broadwick, Georgia: Parachute jump from an airplane by a woman, *1582*

Broaker, Frank: Certified public accountant, *3755*

Brodie, Maurice: Poliomyelitis vaccine, *4923*

Brodie, Stephen: Daredevil to jump off the Brooklyn Bridge and survive, *3678*

Bronck, Jonas: Danish settlers in America, *5925*

Bronson, Earl D.: Ship with a floating scientific instrument platform, *6717*

Brooke, Edward William: Senator who was African-American to be elected by popular vote, *2658*

Brooke, Robert: Dog domestically bred, *1170*

Brookhart, Smith Wildman: Senator unseated after a recount, *3330*

Brookins, Walter Richard: Airplane to fly higher than a mile in altitude, *1431*
Night flight in an airplane, *1429*

Brooks, Charles, Jr.: Execution by lethal injection, *2806*

Brooks, Gwendolyn: Poet who was an African-American woman to win the Pulitzer Prize, *1715*

Broome, Joseph: Magician's advertisement, *2319*

Broughton, Nicholson: Warship to receive definite orders to attack the enemy, *7993*

Brow, John: Land sale by Native Americans to Europeans, *5918*

Brower, A.: City carriage service, *2190*

Brown, Bailey Thornsberry: Union soldier killed by enemy action in the Civil War, *7954*

Brown, Benjamin Harrison: Dean of students at a college, *2973*

Brown, Charles: Steamboat to make regular trips, *6861*

Brown, Charles Brockden: Writer whose livelihood was obtained exclusively by writing, *2032*

Brown, David: Cash carrier system, *2360*

Brown, Ebenezer: Collar manufacturer, *2283*
Methodist missionary, *6574*

Brown, Edgar: Senator elected by a write-in vote, *3331*

Brown, Edward Fisher: Consumer protection medical alert, *2312*

Brown, Edwin Lee: Animal humane society (national), *5738*

Brown, Elisha, Jr.: Cheese factory cooperative, *3857*

Brown, Gerald: Invisible-glass installation, *4050*

Brown, Germaine: Belly-dancing course at a college, *2916*

Brown, James: Law book of federal laws then in force, *1880*

Brown, Janice: Solar-powered long-distance airplane flight, *1481*

Brown, Jesse Leroy: Naval Reserve flier who was African-American, *1618*

Brown, Joe E.: Movie with both sound and color, *5560*

Brown, Joseph Brantley: Courtroom verdict to be televised, *2717*

Brown, Joseph Mansfield: Intercollegiate rowing race, *7468*

Brown, Moses: Gold bullion deposit for coinage, *5365*

Pontoon bridge, *3568*

Brown, Mrs. Charles R.: Amateur golf championship tournament for women, *7342*

Brown, O. B.: Movie projector patent, *5570*

Brown, Rachel: Fungicide used medicinally, *5001*

Brown, Ronald H.: Chairman of a major political party who was African-American, *3345*

Brown, Russell John: Pilot of a jet fighter to win a dogfight in the Korean War, *7981*

Brown, Samuel Robbins: Chinese graduate of an American college, *3011*

Brown, Solyman: Orthodontia treatise, *1924*

Brown, Thomas: Mailbox see-through locker, *5987*

Brown, Wesley Anthony: Naval Academy graduate who was African-American, *3219*

Brown, William: Pharmacopoeia, *1926*
Purple Heart, *1656*

Brown, William Henry: Yacht from the United States to win an international yacht race, *7209*

Brown, William Hill: Novel by an American writer to be published in America, *1839*

Brown, William Montgomery: Episcopal bishop deposed for heresy in the United States, *6552*

Brown, William Wells: Novel by an African-American writer, *1845*

Browne, Cheryl Adrenne: Beauty pageant to be held nationwide, *3628*

Browne, Joseph: Army medical book, *1895*

Browne, William W.: Bank for African-Americans operated by African-Americans, *3771*

Brownell, George Loomis: Paper twine machine, *5761*

Brubeck, Dave: Jazz composition to appear on the Top 40 charts, *1301*

Bruce, Archibald: Mineralogy journal, *4765*

Bruce, Blanche Kelso: Senator who was African-American, *2649*

Bruce, David and George: Stereotype printing, *5800*

Bruce, George: Design patent, *4654*

Bruce, Philip Alexander: Theatrical performance, *1239*

Brundin, Ernest Walfrid: Commercial hydroponicum, *1039*

Brunel, Isambard Kingdom: Transatlantic steamboat service, *6881*

Brunner, Edward: University for African-American students founded as a Catholic institution, *2964*

Brush, Charles Francis: Electric arc streetlights, *2215*

Bryan, William: Cooperative store for consumers, *2490*

Bryan, William Jennings: Presidential candidate to appear in movie footage, *3411*
Presidential candidate to ride in a car, *3410*
Silverite national convention, *3367*
Trial of a teacher for violating a state ban on teaching the theory of evolution, *3068*
Bryant, Alice Gertrude: Surgery society (national), *5047*
Bryant, Charles: Petroleum exported to Europe, *3530*
Bryant, Gridley: Railroad with iron-plated wooden rails, *6318*
Buchalter, Louis: Execution of an organized crime leader in the electric chair, *2803*
Buchanan, Franklin: Naval academy, *3213*
Naval battle between ironclad vessels in the Civil War, *7961*
Navy destroyer named for a Confederate officer, *6933*
Buchanan, James: Copyright law on photographs enacted by Congress, *4630*
President who was a bachelor, *6192*
Steel arch bridge, *3582*
Bucher, Lloyd Mark: Naval ship to surrender in peacetime without a fight, *6947*
Buck, Pearl Sydenstricker: Nobel Prize for literature awarded to an American, *1694*
Buck, Solon Justus: Archival course at a college, *3106*
Buckley, Oliver E.: Long-distance dial telephone service, *7742*
Bucknill, John Charles: Psychiatry textbook, *1912*
Budge, John Donald: Tennis champion to win the Grand Slam, *7536*
Buell, Abel: Continental coin, *5357*
Gem-cutting machine, *5317*
Map of the United States, *4795*
Type foundry, *5801*
Buffum, William: Movie version of a Shakespeare play to be made in the United States, *5549*
Bugie, Elizabeth: Antibiotic, *4998*
Bull, Dixie: Pirate on the Atlantic seaboard, *2768*
Bull, Lucius: Mercantile library, *4666*
Bull, William: Physician born in America who was graduated from a foreign medical school, *4964*
Bullard, Eugene: Aviator who was African-American, *1609*
Bullock, William: Printing press to use a continuous web or roll of paper, *5778*
Bunche, Ralph Johnson: Nobel Peace Prize awarded to an African-American, *1697*
Bundy, Willard L.: Key time recorder, *2381*
Bunker, William: Prison, *2811*
Buranelli, Prosper: Crossword puzzle book, *2004*
Burba, Alexander: Lithuanian church, *6468*

Burbank, Asa: College alumni association, *2991*
Burchard, Anson W.: Arbitration organization (national), *4645*
Burden, Henry: Horseshoe manufacturing machine, *1178*
Buren, Martin Van: Democratic Party national convention, *3349*
Political machine, *3347*
Typewriter, *2384*
Vice president elected by the Senate, *6244*
Burgess, Charles Frederick: Lightweight brick, *2060*
Burgess, Dorothy: Movie of feature length made outdoors, *5558*
Burgoyne, John: National day of thanksgiving, *4260*
Burke, Thomas: Decalcomania pictures, *4307*
Burke, Yvonne Braithwaite: Congressional representative to give birth while holding office, *2620*
Burleigh, John H.: Blanket factory, *4264*
Burleson, Donald: Computer hacker to be convicted, *2789*
Burnet, William: Golf clubs for hitting balls, *7351*
Burnett, Edward: Centrifugal cream separator, *3855*
Burnett, Peter Hardeman: State on the Pacific coast to be admitted to the Union, *7604*
Burnham, Mrs. Walter: Bridge of flowers, *3592*
Burnham, Roger Noble: Balloon honeymoon, *4808*
Burnside, Ambrose Everett: Rifle society (national), *7472*
Burpee, David: Tetraploid flower, *1064*
Burr, Aaron: Former vice president to be arrested, *6241*
Secret service established in a colony, *4168*
Burras, Anne: Wedding of colonists in Virginia, *4812*
Burroughs, Catharine: American to be recognized by Tibetan Buddhists as a reincarnated lama, *6440*
Burroughs, William Seward: Adding machine successfully marketed, *2378*
Burrows, William Ward: Marines, *5229*
Burt, William Austin: Typewriter, *2384*
Burton, Charles: Baby carriage, *2140*
Burton, Richard: Movie in Cinemascope, *5562*
Burton, William M.: Gasoline obtained from crude petroleum by the cracking process, *3536*
Busch, Adolphus: Diesel engine built for commercial service, *5479*
Busch, Fritz: Opera to be televised from the Metropolitan Opera House, *1353*

Bush, Charles Vernon: Air Force Academy graduates who were African-American, *3192*

Bush, George Herbt Walker: Debate among party hopefuls for the presidential nomination to be shown on television, *3398*

Bush, Leonard Franklin: Bone bank, *4837*

Bush, Vannevar: Computing device with electronic components, *2526*
Photographic type-composing machine, *5809*

Bushnell, Cornelius Scranton: Ironclad seagoing naval warship, *6922*

Bushnell, David: Mine barrage, *8090*
Submarine built for use in war, *6961*

Bushnell, H.L.: Ironclad seagoing naval warship, *6922*

Bushnell, James: Sextuplets, *2171*

Bushnell, Jennie A. Lewis: Sextuplets, *2171*

Bushnell, Nolan K.: Video game, *4013*

Bute, George H.: Homeopathic medical society, *5031*

Butler, Benjamin Franklin: Anti-Monopoly Party convention, *3362*
Citizen of the United States to be hanged for treason, *2835*
Confederate forts to surrender in the Civil War, *7958*

Butler, Jean Marie: Coast Guard Academy graduates who were women, *3211*

Butler, John: Intercity stagecoach service, *2184*

Butterfield, Daniel: Taps, *1382*

Butterick, Ebenezer: Paper sewing patterns, *4357*

Butterick, Eleanor: Paper sewing patterns, *4357*

Buttolph, Nicholas: History book by a Jewish author of ancient times, *1862*

Byers, Jack: Horse race for a purse of more than $1 million, *7404*

Byrd, Andrew D.: Court-martial at which the judges included enlisted men, *2740*

Byrd, Richard Evelyn: Airplane flight over the North Pole, *6728*
Airplane flight over the South Pole, *6729*
Airplane flight to land at the South Pole, *6733*
Radio broadcast heard in both the Arctic and the Antarctic regions, *6277*

Byrn, M.L.: Corkscrew patent, *4373*

Byrne, Ethel: Birth control clinic, *4844*

Byron, O.H.: Martini, *2670*

C

Cabezas de Altamirano, Juan: Catholic bishop to exercise episcopal functions, *6446*

Cabot, John: European to set foot on the North American continent after the Vikings, *5893*

Cabrillo, Juan Rodríguez: Exploration of land on the Pacific coast by a European, *5896*

Cabrini, Frances Xavier: Catholic saint who was an American citizen, *6475*

Cadoria, Sherian Grace: Army general who was an African-American woman, *5162*

Cady, Hamilton Perkins: Helium in natural gas, *6813*

Caffieri, Jean Jacques: Postage stamp issued with perforations, *6054*

Cage, John: Musical composition consisting entirely of silence, *1300*

Cahill, Thaddeus: Music synthesizer powered by electricity, *1321*

Caille, Adolph: Toy pinball game machine, *7453*

Caines, George: Law text, *1877*

Calahan, Edward A.: Telegraph call boxes, *7701*

Calder, William Musgrave: Daylight saving time program, *7896*

Calderón, Gabriel Dıaz Vara: Catholic holy orders, *6450*

Caldwell, Charles: Pediatrics monograph, *1897*

Caldwell, James: Americans killed by British soldiers in the Revolution, *7986*

Caldwell, Joseph: Observatory operated by a college, *6664*

Caldwell, Lotta: State police officers who were women, *4144*

Caldwell, Sarah: Metropolitan Opera orchestra conductor who was a woman, *1340*

Calhoun, Charles H., Jr.: Holes in one shot by a father and son in the same golf game, *7362*

Calhoun, Charles H., Sr.: Holes in one shot by a father and son in the same golf game, *7362*

Calhoun, John Caldwell: Vice president to resign, *6243*

Callahan, Americus F.: Envelope with a window, *5766*

Callahan, George: Heliport commercial base, *1565*

Calle, Paul: Twin postage stamps, *6073*

Calthorp, Samuel R.: Streamlined railroad train, *6428*

Calver, George Wehnes: Physician to Congress, *2569*

Calvert, Cecil: Catholics to settle in the English colonies in America, *6447*

Calvert, James Francis: Submarine to travel under the North Pole from the east, *6994*

Calvert, Leonard: Catholics to settle in the English colonies in America, *6447*

Cameron, James: Movie that cost more than $100 million to make, *5522*

Cameron, Simon: Spoils system of presidential patronage, *6150*

Camp, Walter Chauncey: Football book, *2002*
Penalty rule in football, *7304*

Campanella, Roy: Major league baseball game in which the majority of the players on one team were African-American, *7136*

Campaneris, Bert: Baseball player to play all nine positions in one game, *7155*

Campanius, Johannes: Book intended for circulation in the English colonies, *1730*
Lutheran church, *6555*

Campbell, Alexander: Disciples of Christ meeting, *6527*
Milk delivery in glass bottles, *3871*

Campbell, David: Water cures, *5112*

Campbell, Donald Malcolm: Speedboat to exceed 200 miles per hour, *6953*

Campbell, Douglas: Ace to fly under American colors, *1612*
Pilots in American units to participate in air combat in World War I, *8043*

Campbell, George Washington: Duel between representatives in Congress, *2810*

Campbell, James: Apartment house cooperative, *2126*

Campbell, John: Newspaper that was successful, *5630*

Campbell, Thomas: Disciples of Christ meeting, *6527*

Camras, Marvin: Wire recorder for sound recording, *5250*

Canaday, Rudd: Computer operating system for multiple users, *2545*

Candee, Leverett: Rubber shoe manufacturer, *2301*

Candell, Andrew M.: Wedding by telegraph, *4816*

Candlish, Alexander H.: Neurological disease research institute, *5057*

Cannon, George "Ham" Hammon: Medal of Honor awarded in World War II, *1679*

Cannon, Martha Hughes: State senator who was a woman, *7626*

Cantor, Eddie: Radio show sponsored by a cooperative of commercial advertisers, *2338*
Radio variety show with a live studio audience, *6291*

Cantrell, J.F.: Laundromat, *2442*

Capone, Alphonse: Mobster convicted for tax evasion, *2782*
Organized crime massacre, *2780*

Capron, Allen Kissam: Army officer killed in battle in the Spanish-American War, *8010*

Capron, Henri: Music publishers, *1281*

Caraway, Hattie Ophelia Wyatt: Senator who was a woman, *2651*

Cardinal McIntyre, James Francis: Catholic cardinal whose see was west of the Rockies, *6477*

Cardinal Stritch, Samuel Alphonsus: Catholic prelate named to the Roman Curia who was American-born, *6478*

Cardozo, Benjamin Nathan: Cabinet in which all members were sworn in at the same time and place, *6111*

Carey, Alice: Women's professional club, *5723*

Carey, Mathew: Booksellers' organization, *1782*
Maternity book, *2013*

Carkhuff, Stacy G.: Nonskid tires, *5500*

Carl, William Crane: Organ school, *2907*

Carleton, Cora G.: Delegates to a national political convention who were women, *3338*

Carlisle, David: Herbal book, *1927*

Carlson, Chester Floyd: Copy made by xerography, *2372*

Carlson, Sigrid Sophis Margarete: Wedding by transatlantic telephone, *4821*

Carmichael, Stokely: Black Power advocate, *2262*

Carnes, Peter: Balloon flight, *1535*

Carney, Joseph P.: Factories operated by the federal government in peacetime, *4387*

Carney, William Harvey: Medal of Honor awarded to an African-American soldier in the Civil War, *1677*

Carothers, Wallace Hume: Synthetic fiber, *7876*

Carpenter, Arthur Schuyler: Naval vessels to sink an enemy submarine in the Atlantic, *8039*

Carpenter, Charles Milton: Diathermy machine, *4948*

Carpenter, Malcolm Scott: Astronaut to converse with an aquanaut, *7033*
Astronauts trained by the United States, *7028*

Carpentier, Georges: Boxing match to gross $1 million, *7240*
Heavyweight championship boxing match broadcast on radio, *7241*

Carr, Benjamin: Opera by an American composer, *1345*

Carr, Elizabeth Jordan: Child born in the United States through in vitro fertilization, *2166*

Carr, Gerald Paul: Photograph of a comet taken from space, *6704*

Carr, Patrick: Americans killed by British soldiers in the Revolution, *7986*

Carrel, Alexis: Heart pump, *5060*

Carrick, Samuel: College that was nondenominational, *2939*

Carrier, Willis Haviland: Air conditioner for home use, *4333*
Air conditioner patent, *4413*
Factory with temperature and humidity control, *4384*

Carrington, James: Coffee mill, *3849*

Channing, William Ellery: Unitarian church, 6523

Channing, William Francis: Fire alarm system operated by electricity, 4104

Chanute, Octave: Glider with cambered wings, 1547

Chapin, Charles Value: Health laboratory established by a city, 4197

Chapin, Charles Willard: Animal disease of American origin, 5122

Chapin, Daniel M.: Friction matches, 4334

Chapin, Daryl M.: Solar energy battery, 3558

Chapin, William: State school for blind students, 3024

Chaplin, Charles: Movie comedy of feature length, 5552

Chapman, Mathias Farrell: Chinchilla farm, 1074

Chapman, Nathaniel: Therapeutics book, 1904

Chapman, Raymond Johnson: Major league baseball player killed in a game, 7148

Chapman, Victor Emmanuel: Pilot from the United States killed in World War I, 8030

Chardack, William M.: Pacemaker to be implanted in a patient's body, 4953

Charles III of Spain, King: Mule born in the United States, 1141

Chase, Owen: Ship sunk by a whale, 2420

Chase, Salmon Portland: Coin to use the motto "In God We Trust", 5369
Interracial jury, 2735

Chase, Samuel: Supreme Court justice to be impeached, 2757
Tax rebellion, 5952

Chase, William Merritt: Building designed to be used by artists, 2062

Chavez, Dennis: Senator who was a Latino, 2652

Chayefsky, Paddy: Oscar for best picture awarded to a movie that was independently produced, 1637

Cheeshahteaumuck, Caleb: College graduate who was Native American, 3006

Cheever, Ezekiel: Latin grammar textbook, 1852

Chenoweth, William B.: Intercity trucking service, 2484

Chermayeff, Ivan: Postage stamp issued in the United States and canceled by a foreign country, 6072

Chesbrough, Ellis Sylvester: Water supply tunnel for a city, 3615

Chesebrough, Robert Augustus: Petroleum jelly, 4988

Chew, Ng Poon: Chinese newspaper, 5668

Chick, Tong: Chinese theatrical performance, 1250

Chickering, Charles: Postage stamp issued jointly by two countries, 6069

Chickering, Jonas: Iron piano frame, 1308

Child, David Lee: Sugar beet mill, 3958

Child, Lydia Maria Frances: Children's magazine with literary merit, 4708

Child, Lydia Maria Francis: Antislavery book, 2023

Childs, Francis: Law book containing laws enacted by more than one session of Congress, 1875

Chilstrom, Kenneth Oscar: Jet airplane to transport mail, 6030

Chinaglia, Giorgio: Soccer player to score 12 points in one game, 7494

Chisholm, Shirley Anita St. Hill: Congressional representative who was an African-American woman, 2617

Chittenden, Russell Henry: Physiology laboratory, 4926

Chittenden, Thomas: State admitted to the Union after the ratification of the Constitution, 7602

Chomette, Germaine: Movie in Esperanto, 5561

Christensen, Parley Parker: Farmer Labor Party convention, 3376

Christiansen, Hans Christopher: Water pumping plant, 2225

Christmas, William Whitney: Airplane with ailerons, 1394

Christoferson, Silas: Airplane takeoff from a hotel roof, 1442

Christy, James: Moon of Pluto to be observed, 6684

Chu, Paul: Superconducting material that operated at relatively high temperatures, 6823

Church, Austin: Baking soda commercial production, 3934

Church, Benjamin: Surgeon general of the Continental Army, 5165

Church, Ellen: Airline flight attendant who was a woman, 1412

Church, Frederick Edwin: Building designed to be used by artists, 2062
Painting movement, 1204

Church, Sheldon P.: Credit protection group, 2447
Credit report book, 1795

Churchill, Elijah: Purple Heart, 1656

Churchill, Winston: Honorary citizenship authorized by Congress, 5878

Cibber, Colley: Opera performed in America, 1341
Play by William Shakespeare produced in America, 1243

Ciceri, Charles: Opera of a serious nature, 1344

Cierva, Juan de la: Autogiro flown in America, 1529

Cirminello, Joseph: Quadruplets delivered by cesarean operation, 2174

Cisneros, Henry Gabriel: Mayor of a major city who was of Mexican descent, *2211*

Claesse, Lawrence: Book of Common Prayer in the Mohawk language, *1951*

Claffin, James Fitzgerald: Intercollegiate baseball game, *7114*

Claflin, Tennessee Celeste: Brokerage office owned by women, *3818*

Claggett, Thomas John: Episcopal bishop, *6549*

Claiborne, William Charles Cole: Congressional representative to serve before his 25th birthday, *2599*

Clair, Arthur St.: Congressional investigation, *2560*

Clap, Thomas: Planetarium built in America, *6660*

Clark, Alvan: Achromatic lenses, *5833*

Clark, Barney B.: Heart transplant using an artificial heart that was intended to be permanent, *5103*

Clark, Clarence Monroe: National tennis championship matches, *7527*

Clark, Edson P.: Indelible pencil, *8152*

Clark, Joseph Sill: Intercollegiate lawn tennis match, *7528*

Clark, Julia: Airplane accident involving a woman that was fatal, *1393*

Clark, Kathryn I.: Secret Service agents who were women, *4170*

Clark, Ramsey: Television newsmagazine, *5708*

Clark, Thomas Campbell: Attorney general whose father also served as attorney general, *6125*

Clark, William: Grand jury foreman who was a woman, *2737*
Jury school, *2736*
Transcontinental expedition to the Pacific coast, *6721*

Clark, William Ramsey: Attorney general whose father also served as attorney general, *6125*

Clarke, Anne: Divorce, *4806*

Clarke, Denis: Divorce, *4806*

Clarke, Francis D.: Electrical hearing aid, *5070*

Clarke, Louis Semple: Truck, *5504*

Clarke, Walter: Court-martial in a colony, *2738*

Clarkson, William K.: Bicycle patent, *7180*

Clason, Bertil Hjalmar: Wedding by transatlantic telephone, *4821*

Claude, George: Neon advertising sign, *2350*

Clay, Henry: Body to lie in state in the Capitol rotunda, *2564*
National political platform, *3332*
Senator to serve in contravention to the age limit, *2642*

Senator who was returned to the Senate after being defeated for the presidency, *2646*

Clay, Lucius DuBignon: Transcontinental telecast received on the West Coast, *7841*

Claypoole, David C.: Daily newspaper, *5634*
Newspaper to publish the Constitution, *1105*

Clayton, Henry Holm: Balloon cup race, *7288*

Clayton, Zack: Boxing referee in a heavyweight championship match who was African-American, *7246*

Cleaveland, Parker: Mineralogy textbook, *1982*

Clement, L.M.: Radio telephone communication from an airplane, *7759*

Clemente, Roberto Walker: Presidential Citizen Medal, *1644*

Clemons, Lucian M.: Lifesaving medal awarded by the Treasury Department, *1653*

Cleveland, Esther: Child born in the White House who was the offspring of a president, *6254*

Cleveland, Grover: President elected for two nonconsecutive terms, *6162*
Wedding of a president in the White House, *4815*

Cliburn, Van: Worldwide live television program, *7856*

Clifford, Hadley: Interurban streetcar line, *6403*

Cline, Genevieve Rose: Justice on the federal bench who was a woman, *2725*

Clinton, De Witt: State nominating convention, *3315*

Clinton, George: Salute fired by Great Britain in honor of an officer of the United States, *3976*
Vice president to die in office, *6242*
Vice president who was nominated specifically for that office, *6240*

Clinton, Hillary Rodham: First Lady who was also a federal official, *6133*

Clinton, William Jefferson: Ban on federal funding for human cloning research, *6755*
Medals of Honor awarded to African-American servicemen for service in World War II, *1689*
President to use the line-item veto, *6181*
President who was a Rhodes Scholar, *6206*

Clymer, George: Art museum, *5593*

Clymer, George E.: Printing press invented in the United States, *5768*

Coachman, Alice: Olympic gold medalist who was an African-American woman, *7449*

Coates, George Henry: Hair clipper, *4068*

Coats, Moses: Apple parer, *4367*

Cobb, Gail A.: Police officer who was a woman to be killed in the line of duty, *4152*

Cobb, John Nathan: Fisheries school at a college, *3296*

Cobb, Ty: Baseball players to win the Most Valuable Player award, *1722*
Baseball strike, *4595*
Cobb, William G.: Solar-powered car, *5457*
Cobbett, William: Fruit culture treatise, *1759*
Coburn, Jay: Round-the-world helicopter flight, *1579*
Cochran, Jacqueline: Airplane to fly faster than the speed of sound, *1468*
Cochrane, Elizabeth: World tour by a woman traveling alone, *6983*
Cochrane, Josephine: Dishwasher, *4274*
Cocke, William: Senators elected but not seated, *2640*
Cody, William Frederick (Buffalo Bill): Wild West Show, *3689*
Coe, Israel: Brass kettles, *4292*
Brass rod, *4472*
Coe, Walter Hamilton: Gold leaf, *5339*
Coffin, Frank Trenholm: Movie photographed from an airplane, *5548*
Coffin, James Henry: Manual training institute, *3285*
Coffin, William, Jr.: Nautical school, *3303*
Cogswell, John Green: Gymnasium to offer systematic instruction, *7371*
Cogswell, Mason Fitch: School for deaf students, *3032*
Cohen, Mendes I.: Egyptian antiquities collection, *5578*
Cohen, Moses S.: Matzah made by machine, *3921*
Cohn, Elizabeth: National political convention at which a woman made a seconding speech, *3339*
Coit, Stanton: Settlement house in a poor city neighborhood, *2194*
Coke, Thomas: College founded as a Methodist institution, *2937*
Methodist bishop, *6560*
Colburn, David G.: Revolving gun, *8093*
Colburn, Irving Wightman: Sheet-glass drawing machine, *4045*
Colden, Cadwallader David: Reformatory for juvenile delinquents, *2817*
Colden, Jane: Botanist of note who was a woman, *6737*
Cole, Bob: Musical comedy written by African-Americans for African-American performers, *1256*
Cole, Nat King: Record album to hit No. 1 in the pop charts, *1367*
Cole, Nelson: Newspaper published by soldiers in the field, *5641*
Cole, Thomas: Landscape painter, *1203*
Painting movement, *1204*
Coleman, Bessie: Pilot who was an African-American woman, *1597*
Coleman, Clyde Jay: Electric self-starter used in cars, *5442*

Coleman, Edward: Street gangs, *2770*
Coleman, John: Irish to arrive in America, *5932*
Coleman, Nancy: Broadway play shown in a television version with its original cast, *1266*
Colfax, Schuyler: Officer to preside over both of the branches of Congress, *2565*
Colgate, William: Soap manufacturer to render fats in his plant, *4266*
Collbohm, Frank: Military think tank, *5128*
Colles, Christopher: Book of road maps, *4796*
Colley, Russell: Pressure suit, *1386*
Collins, Arnold M.: Synthetic rubber for manufacture, *4489*
Collins, Eileen Marie: Astronaut who was a woman to pilot the space shuttle, *7053*
Collins, Isaac: Prison treadmill, *2816*
Collins, Joseph Lawton: Atomic bomb underground explosion, *8127*
Collins, Michael: Astronauts to land on the moon, *7040*
Collins, Paul Fisk: Caterpillar Club members who were father and son, *1587*
Collins, Paul Liske: Caterpillar Club members who were father and son, *1587*
Collins, Thomas: State to ratify the federal Constitution, *1106*
Collins, Warren E.: Respirator known as the iron lung, *4947*
Collins, William: Traveler's aid program, *5966*
Collison, Peter: Lightning demonstration, *6767*
Colman, Benjamin: Play of note written by an American, *1240*
Colombosian, Sarkis: Yogurt dairy, *3856*
Colt, Elizabeth Hart Jarvis: Free public art museum in continuous existence, *5595*
Colt, Samuel: Revolver pistol, *8096*
Telegraph cable, *7688*
Underwater torpedo operated by electric current, *8098*
Colton, Charles M.: Wedding in a balloon, *4814*
Colton, Walter: Newspaper published on the Pacific Coast, *5640*
Columbus, Christopher: Columbus Day, *4233*
Commemorative postage stamps, *6084*
Letter containing a description of America, *1093*
Colwell, Stephen: Hammered iron, *4454*
Colyer, William: Seagoing dredge with a hopper, *6884*
Compson, Betty: Movie with both sound and color, *5560*
Compton, Arthur: Fluorescent lamp, *3500*
Compton, Karl Taylor: Photographic type-composing machine, *5809*
Comstock, Andrew: Phonetic Bible, *1969*
Comyn, W. Leslie: Concrete seagoing ship, *6876*

Corbett, James John —*continued*

Boxing match timed by automatic timer, *7235*

Boxing match under the Marquis of Queensberry rules, *7236*

Movie of a heavyweight championship boxing fight, *5546*

Corbin, Austin: National bank, *3765*

Cori, Carl Ferdinand: Nobel Prize shared by an American husband and wife, *1696*

Cori, Gerty Theresa: Nobel Prize shared by an American husband and wife, *1696*

Cormier, Lucia Marie: Senate election race in which both candidates were women, *2634*

Cornbury, Viscount: Cross-dresser of note, *6827*

Cornelia, Miss: Private school for children with disabilities, *3017*

Cornelissen, Jan: Colonial law for the maintenance of an insane patient, *4171*

Cornelius, Robert: Photograph taken in the United States, *5811*

Cornell, Ezra: Underwater telegraph cable that was practical, *7693*

Cornish, James: Suture of the human heart, *5090*

Cornish, John: Worsted mill for making wool yarn, *7892*

Cornish, Samuel E.: Newspaper for African-American readers, *5664*

Cornwallis, Charles: American flag flown in battle, *1120*

Cornwallis, Lord: General of the Continental Army, *5146*

Cornwallis, Thomas: Naval battle between colonists, *5922*

Coronado, Francis Vasquez: Christian martyr on American soil, *6443*

Correll, Charles: Radio show with a plot, *6290*

Corson, Juliet: Cooking school, *3288*

Cosby, Bill: Television dramatic series in which an African-American performer had a starring role, *7790*

Cosby, William: Trial in which freedom of the press was upheld, *5633*

Costa, Adele: Telecommunication by deaf people that was both visual and oral, *7837*

Coston, Martha Hunt: Signal flares, *5242*

Cotton, John: Children's book, *1729*

Missionary society established for the English colonies, *6567*

Native American preacher of Christianity, *6513*

Couch, Joseph James: Percussion rock drill, *4401*

Courtney, Pete: Actor to have an exclusive movie contract, *5524*

Cousins, Henry Thomas: Protestant church for lepers, *6533*

Couzins, Phoebe W.: Law school at a university to admit women, *3123*

Coward, Noel: Simultaneous radio broadcast on all three major networks, *6278*

Cowdrey, Robert Hall: United Labor Party convention, *3365*

Cox, Ezekial T.: Stone breaking machine, *5324*

Cox, Gene: Congressional page who was female, *2590*

Cox, James Renshaw: Catholic mass in an airship over the ocean, *6473*

Cox, Lynne: Swimmer to cross the Bering Strait, *7522*

Coxe, Daniel: Pottery, *4308*

Coxe, John Redman: Pharmaceuticals book, *1929*

Crabb, Benjamin: Candle factory for making spermaceti candles, *4341*

Crabtree, Davida Foy: United Church of Christ ordination of a woman in which all the principal roles were filled by women, *6536*

Cradock, Matthewe: Horses, *1174*

Craig, Cleo Frank: Transatlantic telephone call carried by the transoceanic telephone cable, *7767*

Craig, Daniel Frank: Army field range, *5245*

Craig, Elijah: Bourbon whiskey, *2666*

Craig, John Alexander: Animal husbandry professor at a college, *2896*

Craig, Minnie Davenport: State speaker of the House who was a woman, *7628*

Cramer, Stuart W.: Factory cooled by air conditioning, *4385*

Crane, M.G.: Pushball, *7573*

Crane, Philip: Debate among party hopefuls for the presidential nomination to be shown on television, *3398*

Crane, Richard H.: Submarine with a pressure hull of high-tensile steel, *6971*

Crary, Albert Paddock: Explorer to set foot on both the North and South Poles, *6732*

Craske, Charles: Curved stereotype plate, *5788*

Crawford, Alexander: Muskets, *8091*

Crawford, Jane Todd: Abdominal operation other than a cesarean section, *5076*

Crawford, Jim: Christmas postage stamp regular issue, *6094*

Cray, Seymour R.: Supercomputer, *2532*

Crazy Horse: Monument to a Native American, *5417*

Creamer, William: German instruction at a college, *3111*

Crean, Arthur B.: Service number issued by the Army, *5226*

Creighton, Charles: Transcontinental car trip driven entirely in reverse, *5475*

Cresson, Ezra Townsend: Entomology journal, 4772

Crippen, Robert L.: Reusable manned spacecraft, 7087

Croasdale, William T.: Single Tax League national conference, 7650

Crocker, Sewell K.: Transcontinental car trip, 5471

Croezens, Anna Claas: Book auction, 1778

Croly, Jane Cunningham: Women's professional club, 5723

Crompton, William: Silk power loom, 7889

Cronkite, Walter: Radio broadcast in which citizens telephoned the president, 6221

Crosby, Bing: Video recording on high-definition magnetic tape, 7818

Crosby, Caresse: Brassiere patent, 2276

Crosby, Harry: Rocket airplane for military use, 1490

Crosland, Alan: Movie with both sound and color, 5560
Movie with sound to be released as a feature, 5557

Cross, Andrew Jay: Optometry courses at a college, 3153

Cross, Julie Yvonne: Secret Service agents who were women, 4170

Cross, Robert: Life insurance company, 4542

Cross, Thaddeus M.B.: Neurology textbook, 1915

Crosswell, Harry: Comic magazine, 4698

Crothers, Rachel: Broadway play shown in a television version with its original cast, 1266

Crotty, Burke: President to appear on television, 6215

Crowell, Luther Childs: Paper bag manufacturing machine, 5757

Crowninshield, George: Yacht, 6859

Crowninshield, Jacob: Elephant, 1142

Cruger, John: Chamber of commerce established by a state, 2448

Crukshank, Joseph: Botany book by an American-born author, 1979

Crum, George: Potato chips, 3960

Crumb, Robert: Underground comic book of note, 4739

Crump, Diane: Jockey who was a woman to ride in the Kentucky Derby, 7418

Crumpler, Rebecca Lee: Physician who was an African-American woman, 4973

Cuddeback, Leon: Airmail contractor, 6021

Cullen, John C.: Enemy saboteurs executed in the United States, 8058

Cullum, Elizabeth Hamilton: Cancer hospital, 4885

Culver, Kenneth: Gene therapy, 5118

Cummings, Alma: Dance marathon, 3630

Cummings, Irving: Movie of feature length made outdoors, 5558

Cummings, William Arthur: Baseball pitcher to throw a curve ball, 7138

Cummins, Benjamin: Circular saw, 7913

Cummins, Clessie Lyle: Car trip made with a diesel engine, 5474
Diesel engine speed record, 5482

Cundiff, Penelope: Wedding by telegraph, 4816

Cunningham, Alfred Austell: Marine pilot, 5235

Cunningham, Charles E.: Union Labor Party convention, 3364

Cunningham, Harold A.: Ship-to-shore mobile telephone commercial service, 7739

Cunningham, Ronnie Walter: Live telecast from space, 6691

Curl, Robert F., Jr.: Fullerenes to be observed, 6822

Curtice, Cooper: Laboratory for the study of parasites in livestock, 5120

Curtis, Charles: Senator who was Native American, 2650
Vice president who was Native American, 6248

Curtis, Glenn Hammond: Airship ordered by the federal government, 1514

Curtis, John: Chewing gum, 3959

Curtiss, Glenn Hammond: Airplane bombing experiment, 8113
Airplane flight over water, 1432
Airplane flying school, 3188
Airplane race won by an American in Europe, 7290
Airplane sold commercially, 1388
Aviation meet, 7292
Aviation trophy, 1641
Hydroplane, 1391
Hydroplane flight to and from a ship, 1436
Mobile home, 5505
Motorcycle hill-climbing contest, 7438
Pilot licensed by the Aero Club of America, 1595
Pilot licensed by the Aero Club of America who was a woman, 1596

Cushing, William: Supreme Court of the United States, 2742

Cushman, Robert: Furs exported, 3740
Sermon to be printed, 1948

Custer, Thomas W.: Medal of Honor winner to receive two awards, 1674

Custis, Austen M.: Transatlantic message over radio telephone, 7757

Cutbush, Edward: Medical book by a navy medical officer, 1901

Cutbush, James: Fireworks book, 2021

Cutler, Abner: Desk with a roll top, 4325

Cutler, James Goold: Mail chute, 6000

Cutler, Manasseh: Botanic expedition, 6738

D

Daggett, Ezra: Canning of food, *3944*

Daimler, Gottlieb: Foreign car exhibited, *5427*

Dale, Porter Hinman: Radio broadcast of an open session of Congress, *2567*

Dale, Richard: Ship constructed by the federal government, *6915*

Dale, Thomas: Game played in the English colonies in America, *4008*

Daley, Phyllis Mae: Naval Reserve Nurse Corps nurse who was African-American, *5289*

Dalton, John Call: Dissection of a living animal to demonstrate anatomy and physiology, *5054*

Daly, John (Charles): Beauty pageant to be shown on television, *3629*

Damadian, Raymond: Magnetic resonance image of a human body, *4912*

Damrosch, Walter Johannes: Orchestra from the United States to make a European tour, *1363*

Dane, Nathan: Slavery ban enacted for a territory of the United States, *2246*

Danis, Anthony Leo: Destroyer from the United States torpedoed in World War II, *8051*

Darby, William: Theatrical performance, *1239*

Dare, Virginia: Child born of English parents in America, *2156*
First-day special cancellation of a postage stamp, *6067*

Dargue, Herbert Arthur: General of the American armed forces killed in World War II, *8073*

Darley, Felix Octavius Carr: Comic weekly, *4717*

Darling, Jay Norwood "Ding": Revenue stamp printed by the Post Office Department, *7660*

Darlington, Harry: American base in Antarctica that was permanent, *6730*

Darlington, Jennie: American base in Antarctica that was permanent, *6730*

Darnell, Linda: Woman to sell securities on the floor of the New York Curb Exchange, *3828*

Darrow, Clarence: Trial of a teacher for violating a state ban on teaching the theory of evolution, *3068*

Dart, Joseph: Grain elevator operated by steam, *1048*

Dasch, George John: Enemy saboteurs executed in the United States, *8058*

Dauser, Sue Sophia: Navy captain who was a woman, *5288*

Davenport, James: Textile machinery patent, *7865*

Davenport, Thomas: Electric motor using direct current, *3453*
Electric printing press, *5774*
Electricity journal, *4769*

Daventry, Monica M.: Foreign servicewomen interred in the Arlington National Cemetery, *2855*

Davey, John: Forestry school operated privately, *3077*

David, Albert Leroy: Capture and boarding of an enemy submarine on the high seas by American forces, *8065*

Davids, Thaddeus: Ink, *8149*

Davidson, Ann: Transatlantic solo boat journey by a woman, *6990*

Davidson, Royal Page: Armored car, *5432*
Bicycle corps of cadets, *3187*
Radio car for military use, *5246*

Davies, Arthur Bowen: Modern art exhibition, *1228*

Davies, Charles: Teachers' institute, *3261*

Davies, Ralph Kenneth: Cartel of corporations, *2524*

Davis, Allan: Business high school, *3084*

Davis, Benjamin Oliver: Army general who was African-American, *5154*

Davis, Benjamin Oliver, Jr.: Air Force general who was African-American, *5135*

Davis, Charles, Jr.: Rubber company, *4484*

Davis, David: Labor Reform Party national convention, *3357*

Davis, Dwight Filley: International tennis matches for the Davis Cup challenge trophy, *7531*

Davis, Ernie: Football player who was African-American to win the Heisman Memorial Trophy, *1726*

Davis, G.W.: State police, *4134*

Davis, Harry: Movie theater, *3705*

Davis, Harry Phillips: Transatlantic radio broadcast, *6263*

Davis, Jacob: Blue jeans, *2268*

Davis, Jefferson: Interracial jury, *2735*
Song popular in the Confederate States, *1381*
Year in which two presidents were elected, *3388*

Davis, John: Child labor law enacted by a state that regulated hours of employment, *4574*
Discovery of Antarctica by an American, *6722*

Davis, John William: Newsreels showing presidential candidates, *5698*

Davis, Joseph Edward: Vasectomy outpatient service, *4851*

Davis, Miles Lewis: Crematory established by a state government, *2858*

Davis, N. Jan: Husband and wife to fly in space together, *7052*

Davis, Phineas: Locomotive bid, *6351*
Locomotive to burn coal, *6352*
Davis, Raymond Cazallis: Bibliography course at a college, *3098*
Davis, William Augustine: Railroad post office, *6037*
Davison, Frederic Ellis: Army general who was African-American to lead an infantry brigade in combat, *5159*
Davison, James J.: Jet airplane to land on a ship, *1466*
Dawson, Benjamin Frederick: Pediatrics journal, *4756*
Dawson, Roy O.: Self-service supermarket, *2504*
Dawson-Scott, Catharine Amy: Opera composer who was a woman, *1334*
Dawson, William Levi: Congressional standing committee headed by an African-American, *2591*
Symphony on an African-American folk theme, *1297*
Day, Benjamin: Newsboy, *5648*
Day, Benjamin Henry: Illustrated weekly magazine, *4715*
Penny daily newspaper, *5638*
Day, Henry: Pressure-sensitive adhesive, *4487*
Day, Stephen: Almanac, *1764*
Book published in America, *1728*
Children's book, *1729*
Document known to have been printed in America, *1096*
Hebrew type, *5799*
Hymnbook published in America, *1931*
Printing press, *5767*
Spelling book, *1822*
Thesis directory, *1811*
De Blauw, John: Airmail and express service by helicopter, *6031*
de Bore, Étienne: Sugar cane to be imported, *3896*
De Bow, James Dunwoody Brownson: Business economics course at a college, *2918*
de Brehant de Galinée, René: Oil spring, *3523*
de Cass, François Dollier: Oil spring, *3523*
De Crow, Sarah: Postmaster who was a woman, *5982*
de Fleury, François Louis Teisseidre: Medal awarded by the Continental Congress to a foreigner, *1650*
de Florencia, Francisco: Catholic priest born in America, *6448*
de Foreest, Isaac: Stone pavement, *6608*
de Forest, Jesse: Belgian immigrants, *5917*
De Forest, Lee: Carbon microphone used in radio broadcasting, *6308*
Movie featuring an African-American actor, *5554*
Movie with sound recorded on the film, *5556*

Newsreels showing presidential candidates, *5698*
Radio society, *6259*
Singer whose voice was broadcast over radio, *1330*
Triode for radios, *6307*
de Franchessin, Jacques Antoine: Brevet commission in the Army, *5167*
de Gersdorff, George Bruns: Football stadium, *7505*
de Graeff, Johannes: American flag saluted by a foreigner, *1117*
de Graff, Robert: Paperback publisher, *1790*
De Grasse, John Vancerlle: Physician who was African-American, *4966*
de La Salle, Robert Cavelier, Sieur: Great Lakes vessel, *6851*
de la Tour, Sieur Le Blond: Levees, *3604*
de Lerena, Juan José: Spanish newspaper, *5665*
De Luce, Nathaniel: Italian opera, *1346*
de Mandeville, Bernard Xavier Philippe De Marigny: Craps, *3634*
de Maria, Walter: Artwork to incorporate lightning, *1220*
De Mille, Cecil B.: Movie of feature length made in Hollywood, *5551*
de Moksa, Agoston Haraszthy: Grape vines planted in California for wine-making, *2668*
de Nancrède, Paul Joseph Guérard: Catholic magazine, *4697*
de Narváez, Pánfilo: Ships built by Europeans in America, *6846*
de Padilla, Juan: Christian martyr on American soil, *6443*
de Palm, Joseph Henry Louis: Crematory, *2857*
De Priest, Oscar Stanton: Congressional representative who was African-American, *2603*
de Rojamón, Felipe: Autopsy, *2847*
de Sequeyra, John: Physician who was Jewish, *4962*
De Smedt, Edward Joseph: Road pavement of sheet asphalt, *6621*
De Smet, Pierre-Jean: Bohemian church, *6463*
Wagon train to California, *5962*
de Soto, Hernando: Baptism in America, *6442*
Battle between Native Americans and European soldiers, *5894*
Exploration of the Mississippi River by a European, *5895*
Flood of which there is any known record, *2859*
De Vilbiss, Allen, Jr.: Automatic computing pendulum scale, *2380*
De Vry, Herman Adolf: Portable movie projector, *5573*

De Witt, John H.: Radar signal to the moon, *7680*

Deane, Charles: Book on vellum, *1749*

Deane, Samuel: Agricultural dictionary, *1799*

Deane, Silas: Invisible ink, *8147*
Navy fleet, *5257*
Treaties entered into by the federal government, *3998*

Debel, Niels Henriksen: Sit-down strike, *4598*

DeBlois, Thomas A.: Naval militia established by a state, *5255*

Debrett, J.: Bibliography of Americana in English, *1739*

Debs, Eugene Victor: Social-Democratic Party of America national convention, *3369*
Socialist Party national convention, *3372*

Decatur, Stephen: Capture of a British frigate in the War of 1812, *8023*
Marine Corps commando raid, *5231*

Decatur, Stephen, Sr.: Prize money awarded by the Navy, *5262*

Decker, Alonzo G.: Electric hand drill, *7937*

Decker, John Wright: Dairy school at a college, *2897*

Dee, Ruby: Play by an African-American woman to appear on Broadway, *1270*

Deere, John: Cast steel for plows, *4491*
Steel plow with a steel moldboard, *1045*

Defoe, Daniel: Story serialized in a newspaper, *1835*

DeGeneres, Ellen: Television network sitcom to feature a lead character who was homosexual, *6845*

Dekanawida: League of Native American nations, *5897*

Del Ferraro, Danielle: Soapbox derby, *7583*

Del-Monico, Giovanni: Gourmet restaurant, *2454*

Del-Monico, Pietro: Gourmet restaurant, *2454*

Delafield, Edward: Eye hospital, *4872*
Ophthalmologist of note, *4972*

Delamotte, Charles: Protestant Sunday school, *6518*

Delany, Martin Robinson: Army major who was African-American, *5169*

Delaplace, William: Revolutionary War military action, *7990*

DeLaurier, James: Ornithopter that succeeded in flying, *1407*

Delk, Edward Buehler: Shopping center in a suburban business area, *2501*

Delmonico, Lorenzo: Gourmet restaurant, *2454*

Deming, William Champion: Incubator for premature babies, *4943*

Demont, William: Traitor to the American cause during the Revolutionary War, *7998*

Demorest, Ellen Curtis: Paper sewing patterns, *4357*
Women's professional club, *5723*

Demorest, William: Paper sewing patterns, *4357*

Dempsey, Jack: Boxing match broadcast on radio, *7238*
Boxing match to attract 100,000 spectators, *7242*
Boxing match to gross $1 million, *7240*
Heavyweight championship boxing match broadcast on radio, *7241*

Denman, James: Public school for Chinese-American children, *3062*

Denn, Eileen: Train operated exclusively by women, *6436*

Dennet, William: Navy yard, *5261*

Denning, M. Leslie: Transcontinental dial telephone service without the aid of operators, *7745*

Dennison, Cora: Wedding on television, *4820*

Denny, Jack: Radio broadcast from a moving train, *6276*

Densmore, Amos: Oil tank railroad cars, *6376*

DePhillipo, John R.: Commercial DNA bank, *6756*

Derbigny, Pierre: Law code adopted by a state, *4621*

Derby, George: Balloon destroyed by enemy gunfire, *8012*

Derham, James: Physician who was African-American, *4966*

Dering, Thomas: Book plate, *1737*

Desjardins, Alphonse: Credit union, *3773*

Devan, William M.: Coast Guard inland station, *5210*

Devaney, Frances Teresa: Navy personnel in the regular Navy who were women, *5266*

Devol, George C.: Industrial robot that was practical, *3445*

DeVries, William C.: Heart transplant using an artificial heart that was intended to be permanent, *5103*

Dewey, George: Admiral of the Navy, *5271*
Military campaign medal, *1657*
Military expeditionary force to be sent beyond the Western Hemisphere, *8009*

Dewey, Joseph: Steel, *4490*

Dewey, Martin: Orthodontia journal, *4763*

Dewey, Melvil: Library school at a college, *3099*
Library society (state), *4690*

Dewey, Thomas Edmund: Presidential campaign manager who was a woman, *3392*
Presidential candidate who was renominated after a defeat, *3414*

Dexter, Gregory: Native American dictionary, *1796*

Dextor, Thomas: Ironworks that was successful, *4446*

Dey, Alexander: Dial time recorder, *2382*

Deyo, Morton L.: Warship convoy across the Atlantic Ocean in World War II, *8050*

Diat, Louis: Vichyssoise, *3880*

Dice, Lee Raymond: Genetics clinic, *4848*

Dickins, John: Publisher of denominational religious books, *1957*

Dickinson, Charles: Duel in which a future president of the United States participated, *2809*

Dickinson, John: Patriotic song by an American, *1376*

Dickinson, Jonathan: College charter granted by a governor, *2928*

Dickinson, Thomas Herbert: Drama school at a college, *2910*

Dickson, Earle: Bandage with built-in adhesive, *4945*

Dickson, Sarah E.: Presbyterian elder who was a woman, *6583*

Dickson, William Kennedy Laurie: Movie to be copyrighted, *5544*

Diemer, Walter: Bubble gum, *3967*

Dietz, Howard: Musical comedy broadcast on radio, *1264*

Digges, Thomas Atwood: Novel by an American writer to be translated into a foreign language, *1838*

Dinkins, David N.: Mayor of New York City who was African-American, *2212*

Dinsmoor, Charles: Tractor with an endless chain, *1053*

Dirks, Rudolph: Comic books, *2028*

Comic strip in continuous newspaper publication, *5691*

Dirksen, Everett McKinley: Senator to act in the movies, *2659*

Disney, Walt: Animated cartoon with sound, *5535*

Animated feature-length cartoon in Technicolor, *5536*

Animated three-dimensional cartoon in Technicolor, *5537*

Movie to earn $1 billion, *5515*

Disturnell, J.: Tourist guide for train travelers, *2024*

Dittenhoefer, Isaac: Fraternal society for Jews, *5720*

Dix, Dorothea Lynde: Congressional lobbyist who was a woman, *2563*

Dix, Henry A.: Uniforms for working women, *2275*

Dix, John Adams: Political machine, *3347*

Dixon, Cornwall: Airship race, *7291*

Dixon, George: Submarine built in the United States to sink an enemy warship in actual warfare, *7968*

Dixon, Thomas: Movie to gross $50 million, *5513*

Doak, Samuel: College named after George Washington, *2934*

Doane, Deborah B.: Graduate of a four-year maritime school who was a woman, *3309*

Dobson, Judah: Embalming book, *1910*

Dobson, Thomas: Anatomy book, *1896*

Bible in Hebrew, *1967*

Encyclopedia printed in the United States, *1830*

Medical record of an epidemic, *2875*

Doby, Larry: Baseball player who was African-American to hit a home run in a World Series, *7152*

Dock, Christopher: Blackboards for use in schools, *3048*

Teaching methodology book, *1825*

Dod, Daniel: Transatlantic crossing by an American steamboat, *6979*

Dodd, Mrs. John Bruce: Father's Day, *4244*

Dodge, Augustus Caesar: Father and son who were senators at the same session, *2644*

Dodge, David Low: Peace society, *5733*

Dodge, Grace Hoadley: Young Women's Christian Association, *5713*

Dodge, Henry: Army cavalry unit, *5179*

Father and son who were senators at the same session, *2644*

Dodge, Nehemiah: Jewelers' supply house, *5319*

Dodrill, Forest Dewey: Mitral valve corrective surgery, *5092*

Doering, William von Eggers: Synthetic quinine, *4999*

Doggett, John, Jr.: Tourist guide with train schedules, *2025*

Dolan, Mary Anne: Editor of a major daily newspaper who was a woman, *5622*

Dolan, Thomas P.: National manufacturing assocation, *4376*

Dolby, Ray: Video tape recorder for sounds and pictures, *7821*

Dole, Robert: Debate among party hopefuls for the presidential nomination to be shown on television, *3398*

Dole, Vincent P.: Methadone program, *2692*

Dollenberg, Fred Paul: Glider commercial freight service, *1555*

Dolph, William B.: Radio news program sponsored by a cooperative of commercial advertisers, *2339*

Donahue, Tom: Rock and roll broadcast on FM radio, *1371*

Donaldson, James: Sugar beets, *3901*

Donaldson, Washington Harrison: Transatlantic crossing attempted by a balloon, *1538*

Donehogawa: Indian Affairs Commissioner who was Native American, *5972*

Donlon, Mary Honor: Editor in chief of a law review who was a woman, *3127*

Donlon, Roger Hugh: Medal of Honor awarded in the Vietnam war, *1686*

Donovan, Marion: Diapers that were disposable, *2151*

Donovan, Raymond L.: Cabinet member indicted while in office, 6122

Doolittle, Amos: Music magazine, 4694

Doolittle, James Harold: Air attack against the Japanese homeland in World War II, 8077
Airline to carry 100 million passengers, 1423
All-blind airplane flight, 1451

Doolittle, Sylvester: Screw-propelled steamboat on the Great Lakes, 6869

Doran, A.J.: Old age home for pioneers, 5975

Doremus, Sarah B.: Foreign missionary society organized by women, 6578

Doremus, Sarah Platt: Children's hospital, 4878

Dorr, Ebenezer: Ship from the Atlantic coast to anchor in a California port, 6858

Dorrance, John T.: Condensed soup, 3948

Dorrington, Arthur: Professional hockey player who was African-American, 7380

Dorsey, Herbert Grove: Fathometer, 6714

Dorsey, Thomas Andrew: Composer of gospel music, 1332

Dorsey, Tommy: Song to hit No. 1 in the pop charts, 1366

Dorton, J.S.: Building with its roof supported by cables, 2092

Doss, Desmond T.: Medal of Honor awarded to a conscientious objector, 1681

Doster, Alexis: Airplane human pickup, 1463

Dotey, Edward: Duel, 2807

Doughty, Thomas: Periscope, 5244

Douglas, Alexander: Bustle, 2269

Douglas, Findlay S.: Golf champion born in America, 7357

Douglas, Helen Gahagan: Congressional representative who had been an actress, 2612

Douglas, Paul: Movie to be shown simultaneously on pay television and in movie theaters, 5519

Douglass, David: Theater building of brick construction, 3695

Douglass, Frederick: Delegate to a national political convention who was African-American, 3335
Presidential nominee who was African-American, 3409
Vice presidential candidate who was African-American, 3406

Douglass, William: Epidemiology report, 1888

Dove, Arthur: Abstract paintings, 1217

Dove, Rita: Poet laureate of the United States, 2034

Dowd, Charles Ferdinand: Standard time program, 7895

Dowd, Denis Patrick, Jr.: American to sail to Europe to fight in World War I, 8025

Downing, Andrew Jackson: Botanist to become a prominent landscape gardener, 6741

Dows, Gustavus D.: Ornamented soda fountain for restaurants, 2456

Doyen, Charles A.: Marine regiment to land in Europe in World War I, 8034

Doyle, John Joseph: Baseball pinch hitter, 7144

Drake, E.R.: Forestry association (state), 6785

Drake, Edwin Laurentine: Oil well that was commercially productive, 3528

Drake, Francis: Christian religious service in English on the Pacific Coast, 6501
Map of a city within the present limits of the United States, 4790

Drake, Frank: Scientific program to search for extraterrestrial life, 6672

Drake, Samuel Gardner: Antiquarian bookseller, 1784

Draper, Henry: Photograph of a stellar spectrum showing the dark lines, 6695

Draper, John William: Astronomy photograph, 6692
Chemistry organization (national), 6786
Photograph taken in the United States, 5811

Draper, Richard: Historical print engraved in America, 1224

Dressler, Marie: Movie comedy of feature length, 5552

Drew, Daniel: Stock brokerage concern to use a telegraph ticker, 3817

Drew, Richard Gurley: Cellophane transparent tape, 4339

Driessen, Dan: Designated hitter in a major league baseball game, 7157

Drinker, Philip: Respirator known as the iron lung, 4947

Dripps, Isaac: Locomotive cowcatcher, 6417

Dropsie, Moses Aaron: College under Jewish auspices that was nonsectarian, 2963

Du Bois, Mrs. Cornelius: Children's hospital, 4878

Du Bois, William Edward Burghardt: Arts and letters organization (national), 5716

du Guast, Pierre: European settlement in the northeast after the Vikings, 5904

du Vigneaud, Vincent: Polypeptide hormone synthesized, 5003

Duane, William: Catalog of the Library of Congress, 1768
Gymnastics book, 1996
Military dictionary, 1802

Duchamp, Marcel: Modern art exhibition, 1228

Duche, Jacob: Continental Congress assembly to be opened with prayer, 2575

Duckering, Florence West: Surgery society (national), 5047

Duddingston, William: Naval attack in the Revolutionary War, 7987

Dudley, Homer Walter: Electronic voice mechanism, 7723

Dudley, William L.: Golf magazine, *4787*

Dufek, George John: Airplane flight to land at the South Pole, *6733*

Duffield, Howard: Organ school, *2907*

Dufour, John James: Vineyard, *1013*

Dugan, Donald Allen: Serviceman killed during the Bosnia conflict, *7983*

Duggan, Pat: Movie to be shown simultaneously on pay television and in movie theaters, *5519*

Duggar, Benjamin Minge: Broad-spectrum antibiotic, *5000*

Duhamel, Yvon: Snowmobile to exceed a speed of 125 miles per hour, *7491*

Duhring, Louis Adolphus: Dermatology treatise, *1917*

Dulany, Richard Hunter: Horse show, *1180*

Dumas, Charles: High jump over seven feet, *7563*

Dumont, Marjorie: Wedding in an airplane, *4818*

Dunavant, Roger: Horse grooming products sold for human use, *4064*

Dunbar, Asa: Protest by college students, *3007*

Dunbar, Charles Franklin: Political economy chair at a college, *3251*

Dunbar, Edward Lucian: Spring manufacturer, *4400*

Duncan, Isadora: Modern dancer, *1234*

Duncan, Joseph Smith: Addressograph, *2365*

Duncan, Robert Todd: Opera singer who was African-American to sing a white role, *1336*

Dunglison, Robley: Circumnavigation of the globe by a fleet of warships, *6986*
Medical dictionary, *1804*

Dunham, Alanson Millen, Jr.: Snowshoe production, *2304*

Dunham, Isaac: Iron pile lighthouse, *4127*

Dunham, Otis Emerson: Reindeer, *1152*

Dunklee, Ernest Walter: Sit-down strikes to be outlawed by a state, *4599*

Dunlap, John: Daily newspaper, *5634*
Newspaper to publish the Constitution, *1105*

Dunlap, Maxine: Glider license awarded to a woman, *1599*

Dunlap, William: Etcher, *1206*
Opera by an American composer, *1345*
Playwright to write professionally, *1245*
Theater history, *1870*

Dunlop, John: Printing of the Declaration of Independence, *1114*

Dunlop, W.: Composer born in America, *1327*

Dunn, James Clement: Transatlantic mobile telephone call between two cars, *7765*

Dunster, Henry: College founded in America, *2925*
Missionary society established for the English colonies, *6567*

Dunton, Jacob: Compressed pills or tablets, *4987*

Durand, Asher Brown: Painting movement, *1204*

Durand, Elias: Soda water, *3845*

Durand, Elie Magloire: Mineral water bottler, *3842*

Durant, Charles Ferson: Balloon flight by an aeronaut born in America, *1537*

Durant, Howard M.: Hotel to install electric lights, *2426*

Durfee, William Franklin: Bessemer steel converter, *4492*
Copper refinery furnace, *4474*

Durocher, Leo: Major league baseball game to be shown on television, *7132*

Duryea, Charles Edgar: Automobile club, *5465*
Car produced for commercial sale, *5429*
Car race, *7260*

Duryea, James Franklin: Car race, *7260*

Duston, Hannah: Settler heroine publicly rewarded, *5933*

Duvall, Gabriel: Supreme Court justice who had been a representative in Congress, *2758*

Duyn, Mona Van: Poet laureate of the United States, *2034*

Dwight, Edmund: Teacher training school established by a state, *3260*

Dwight, John: Baking soda commercial production, *3934*

Dwyer, Michael and Philip: Horse whose total purses exceeded $100,000, *7406*

Dyar, Harrison Gray: Telegraph system, *7685*

Dyer, Mary: Quakers executed for their religious beliefs, *6587*

Dykstra, Clarence Addison: Draft law enacted by Congress during peacetime, *5220*

E

Eads, James Buchanan: Albert Medal presented to a person born in America, *1647*
Ironclad naval vessels, *6921*

Eagan, Edward: Olympic gold medalist in both the Summer and Winter Olympics, *7447*

Eagan, Sister Nancy Ann: Air Force Reserve officer who was a nun, *5138*

Eagleton, Thomas Francis: Vice presidential candidate of a major political party to resign before the election, *3417*

Eakins, Thomas: Gravure-printed postage stamp, *6074*

Eames, A. G.: Public locker plant, *2366*

Earhart, Amelia: Transatlantic solo airplane flight by a woman, *1455*

Presidential citation to an entire division, *1666*

Presidential election in which a computer was used to predict the outcome, *3393*

Presidential news conference filmed for television and newsreels, *6219*

Presidential Unit Citation award in peacetime, *1643*

Radio broadcast using an orbiting satellite, *6281*

State admitted to the Union that had no border with another state, *7607*

State admitted to the Union that was separated by a substantial body of water, *7608*

Undersea park established by the federal government, *3739*

Eisner, Will: Comics studio, *4737*

Ekin, Herbert Roslyn: Round-the-world airplane passenger race, *7299*

Ela, Jacob E.: Insurance board established by a state government, *4503*

Elders, Joycelyn: Surgeon general who was African-American, *4215*

Eldred, Arthur Rose: Boy Scouts of America uniformed troop, *2149*

Eldridge, Asa: Circumnavigation of the world by a yacht, *6982*

Eliason, Carl J.E.: Snowmobile patent, *7490*

Eliot, Jared: Agricultural book distinctly American, *1758*

Eliot, John: Bible translated into a Native American language, *1959*

Book privately printed, *1732*

Bookbinder, *1731*

Church for Native Americans in New England, *6512*

Missionary society established for the English colonies, *6567*

Native American grammar, *1850*

Native American preacher of Christianity, *6513*

Primer in a Native American dialect, *1851*

Eliot, Samuel Atkins: School for music teachers, *2898*

Elkes, Harry: Bicycle race paced by a motorcycle, *7194*

Ellet, Charles: Railroad suspension bridge, *3580*

Wire suspension bridge for general traffic, *3576*

Ellicott, Andrew: Meteor shower on record, *6676*

Elliott, Bob: Stereo telecast, *7857*

Elliott, Eugene S.: Whist organization, *4021*

Ellis, Richard Gailard: Liberty ship, *6894*

Ellis, Seth Hockett: Union Reform Party convention, *3371*

Ellsworth, Henry Leavitt: Agricultural seed distribution on a national scale, *1015*

Ellsworth, Lincoln: Airplane flight over the North Pole, *6728*

Ellsworth, Oliver: Quack doctor of note, *3646*

Supreme Court decision in a matter between states, *2745*

Ellyson, Theodore Gordon: Naval airplane, *1483*

Elmen, Gustaf Waldemar: Permalloy, *7705*

Elsberg, Louis: Laryngology clinic, *4842*

Laryngology instruction at a college, *3142*

Laryngology journal, *4757*

Elton, Robert H.: Valentines commercially produced, *4235*

Ely, Eugene Burton: Airplane flight from a ship, *1433*

Airplane flight to the deck of a carrier, *1434*

Airplane race between cities, *7293*

Emanuel, David: Governor who was Jewish, *7617*

Embree, Elihu: Antislavery magazine, *4707*

Embury, Philip: Methodist meetinghouse, *6558*

Methodist preacher, *6557*

Emerich, Charles Rulf: Intercollegiate Army–Navy football game, *7320*

Emerich, James: Tank crew to cross the 38th parallel in the Korean War, *7980*

Emerson, Gladys Anderson: Vitamin E reduction to alpha tocopherol, *3972*

Emerson, Oliver Hudleston: Vitamin E reduction to alpha tocopherol, *3972*

Emerson, Victor: Motorboat to travel at a speed of more than 40 miles per hour, *6952*

Emmes, Thomas: Engraving of any artistic merit, *1223*

Emmett, Daniel Decatur: Minstrel show troupe, *3685*

Song popular in the Confederate States, *1381*

End, George Kenneth: Rattlesnake meat in cans, *3942*

Endecott, John: Ban on Quakers enacted by a colony, *6586*

Enders, John Franklin: Poliomyelitis vaccine, *4923*

Engelbart, Douglas: Computer mouse, *2535*

Engelberger, Joseph F.: Industrial robot that was practical, *3445*

Engelhardt, K.G.: Robot to make pizza, *3448*

Engen, Edward Milian: American civilians killed in the continental United States in World War II, *8084*

English, Thomas Dunn: Comic weekly, *4717*

Enos, John L.: Teachers' organization (national), *3225*

Enright, Thomas F.: Soldiers in the American army killed in combat in World War I, *8038*

Ensel, Edward: Flint glass factory, *4037*

Ent, Peter: Twin covered bridges, *3579*

Erbslöh, Oscar: Balloon cup race, *7288*

Erdmann, Bertha: Nursing school at a college, *3173*

Erickson, B. A.: Airplane to fly with a load of 100,000 pounds, *1471*

Erickson, H.A. "Jimmie": Photograph taken from an airplane, *5820*

Ericsson, John: Ironclad turreted vessel in the Navy, *6923*

Screw-propelled steamboat on the Great Lakes, *6869*

Warship with propelling machinery below the waterline, *6918*

Erikson, Ted: Swimmer from the United States to make a round-trip crossing of the English Channel, *7521*

Erikssdottir, Freydis: European settlement in America, *5890*

Eriksson, Leif: Child born of European parents on American soil, *2155*

Christian in America, *6441*

European settlement in America, *5890*

European to sight America, *5889*

Ermoyan, Suren H.: International postal card, *6049*

Ernst, Harold Clarence: Bacteriology courses at a college, *3149*

Eshleman, Von Russel: Radar signal bounced off the sun, *7683*

Espenschied, Lloyd: Coaxial cable, *7706*

Esterbrook, Richard: Steel pens, *8150*

Estern, Neil: First Lady to be depicted on a monument to a president, *6134*

Eustis, Mrs. Harrison: Dogs trained to guide the blind, *1173*

Evans, Charles "Chick", Jr.: Golfer to win both the U.S. Open and the U.S. Amateur in the same year, *7358*

Evans, George Henry: Labor newspaper, *5639*

Evans, Herbert Mclean: Vitamin E reduction to alpha tocopherol, *3972*

Evans, Michael Patrick: Police bureau of identification, *4158*

Evans, Oliver: Belt conveyor system, *4390*

Flour mill, *3911*

Steam engine for industrial use that was practical, *4391*

Evans, Robley Dunglison: Singer whose voice was broadcast over radio, *1330*

Evans, T.W.: Child born in an airplane, *2160*

Everett, Edward: Constitutional Union Party convention, *3355*

Evers, Luke J.: Catholic mass for night workers, *6469*

Everson, Carrie J.: Mineral segregation by oil flotation, *5335*

Evinrude, Ole: Outboard motor, *6951*

Ewry, Ray: Olympic athlete from the United States to win 10 medals, *7442*

F

Faber, Joseph: Voice synthesizer, *7711*

Fabray, Nanette: Coast-to-coast live telecast in color, *7845*

Faggin, Federico: Microprocessor, *3446*

Fahlberg, Constantine: Sugar substitute, *3964*

Fahning, Emma: Bowler who was a woman to obtain a perfect score, *7227*

Fairbanks, Erastus and Thaddeus: Platform scale, *2379*

Fairbanks, Richard: Post office in a colony, *6035*

Fairchild, David: Tung trees, *1021*

Fairfax, John: Transatlantic solo trip by rowboat, *6998*

Fairfax, Thomas: Spa at a mineral spring, *5109*

Supreme Court decision reversing the ruling of a state supreme court, *2749*

Fairman, Gideon: Pamphlet produced from a steel plate engraving, *1744*

Falckner, Justus: Lutheran pastor, *6554*

Falk, Joshua Ben Mordecai ha-Cohen: Hebrew book other than the Bible, *1958*

Fall, Albert Bacon: Cabinet member convicted of a crime, *6110*

Faneuil, Andrew: Greenhouse, *1040*

Faragher, Warren Fred: Petroleum refining course at a college, *3246*

Faris, Edmond John: X-ray photograph showing the complete arterial circulation in an adult human, *4907*

Farmer, Fannie Merritt: Recipes using standard measurements, *3878*

Farmer, John: Genealogical collective work, *1869*

Farmer, Karen Batchelor: Daughters of the American Revolution member who was African-American, *5718*

Farmer, Moses Gerrish: Electric light for household illumination, *3490*

Fire alarm system operated by electricity, *4104*

Farnham, Ivan Richard: Computerized pump, *4417*

Farnsworth, Willis S.: Coin-operated locker, *2369*

Farnum, Dustin: Movie of feature length made in Hollywood, *5551*

Farquhar, George: Play presented by professional players, *1242*

Farr, John: Quinine, *4983*

Farr, William: Marine band, *5230*

Farragut, David Glasgow: Citizen of the United States to be hanged for treason, *2835*

Navy officer to become an admiral, *5270*

Statue cast by the federal government, *5404*

Farrar, Eugenia H.: Singer whose voice was broadcast over radio, *1330*

Farrar, John: Weather report delivered to the Army, *6768*

Fauset, Crystal Bird: State legislator who was an African-American woman, *7631*

Faust, Mrs. William Henry: Family of lawyers admitted simultaneously to practice before the Supreme Court, *4641*

Faust, William Henry: Family of lawyers admitted simultaneously to practice before the Supreme Court, *4641*

Faust, William Henry, Jr.: Family of lawyers admitted simultaneously to practice before the Supreme Court, *4641*

Fayssoux, Peter: Public museum, *5576*

Featherstonhaugh, George William: Geological survey authorized by Congress, *6710*

Feezor, Betty: Video recording on magnetic tape televised in color, *7850*

Fehrenbach, John: Tuberculosis hospital for the poor established by a city, *4900*

Feld, Irvin: Circus clown training school, *3301*

Felker, Alfred Charles: Military heliport, *1569*

Fell, Jesse: Anthracite coal burned experimentally, *3503*

Feller, Robert William Andrew: Major league no-hitter baseball game on opening day, *7133*

Fellowes, Cornelius: Horse show of national scope, *1181*

Fellows, Alvin J.: Tape measure, *7926*

Felt, Dorr Eugene: Adding machine absolutely accurate at all times, *2377*

Feltham, Jocelyn: Revolutionary War military action, *7990*

Feltman, Charles: Hot dog, *3939*

Felton, Rebecca Latimer: Senator who was a woman, *2651*

Fendall, Josias: Shorthand account of a trial, *4619*

Fenno, John: Political newspaper, *5632*

Fenwick, Millicent Hammond: Congressional representative who was a grandmother, *2621*

Ferebee, Thomas W.: Atomic bomb explosion over enemy territory, *8086*

Ferentinos, Paisios: Greek Orthodox church, *6496*

Ferguson, Samuel David: Episcopal bishop who was African-American, *6551*

Fermi, Enrico: Nuclear reactor patent, *6806*
Self-sustaining nuclear chain reaction demonstration, *6819*

Fernald, Walter Elmore: School for children with mental disabilities, *3016*

Fernow, Bernhard Eduard: Forestry school at a college, *3076*

Ferraro, Geraldine: Vice presidential candidate from a major political party who was a woman, *3419*

Ferris, George Washington Gale: Ferris wheel, *3623*

Ferry, Elisha Peyre: State named for a person born in America, *7598*

Fessenden, Reginald Aubrey: Radio program broadcast, *6264*

Fessler, Richard: Transplant of human embryo tissue, *5108*

Fetchit, Stephen "Stepin": Movie by a major company for an African-American audience, *5559*

Fey, Charles: Slot machine, *3635*

Feynman, Richard Phillips: Quantum theory of electromagnetic radiation, *6759*

Fickel, Jacob Earl: Pilot to fire a gun from an airplane, *1608*

Field, Ben: Pullman sleeping car, *6375*

Field, Cyrus West: Cigar bands of special interest, *2703*
Transatlantic telegraph cable, *7698*

Field, Stephen Dudley: Electric streetcar run with current generated by a stationary dynamo, *6399*

Field, Stephen Johnson: Transcontinental telegraph line, *7700*

Fielden, Samuel: Labor activists to be executed, *4564*

Fieser, Louis Frederick: Vitamin K to be synthesized, *3973*

Filene, Abraham Lincoln: Discount clothing store, *2498*

Filene, Edward P.: Discount clothing store, *2498*

Filene, William: Discount clothing store, *2498*

Fillmore, Millard: Know-Nothing (American) Party convention, *3354*

Finch, William Bolton: Circumnavigation of the globe by a warship, *6980*

Findley, Paul: Congressional page who was African-American, *2592*

Fink, Colin Garfield: Chromium plating process, *4476*

Finley, James: Suspension bridge, *3567*

Finnegan, Jack: Championship heavyweight boxing title won in the first round, *7237*

Finney, John Miller Turpin: Surgery society (national), *5047*

Firmstone, William: Coke used successfully as a blast furnace fuel, *3505*

Firzer, Arthur: Play presented by a Jewish professional acting troupe, *1253*

Fischer, Adolph: Labor activists to be executed, *4564*

Fischer, Andrew J.: Quintuplets to live more than five years, *2176*

Fischer, Isaac, Jr.: Sandpaper patent, *4394*

Fischer, Louis R.: Frog-jumping jubilee, *1151*

Fischer, Robert James "Bobby": World chess champion from the United States, *4033*

Fishbourn, Benjamin: Presidential appointment, *6138*

Fisher, Alva J.: Electric washing machine, *4276*

Fisher, Anna L.: Astronaut who was a woman to fly in space, *7048*
Astronauts who were women, *7047*

Fisher, Carl Graham: Coast-to-coast paved road, *6625*

Fisher, John Dix: School for blind students, *3023*

Fisher, John Stuchell: Teletypewriter system employed by a police department, *4143*

Fisher, Mary: Quakers to arrive in America, *6585*

Fiske, Bradley Allen: Airplane torpedo, *8114*
Microfilm reading device, *4681*

Fiske, Willard: Journalism course at a college, *3097*

Fitch, Asa: Entomologist hired by a state, *6742*

Fitch, Howard W.: Naval vessel equipped to lay mines, *6931*

Fitch, John: Steamboat to carry a man, *6854*

Fitch, Samuel Sheldon: Dental surgery textbook, *1923*

Fitzgerald, Eugenia Tucker: College secret society for women, *2986*

Fitzpatrick, John: Marine officer killed in service, *5234*

Fitzpatrick, Thomas: Wagon train to California, *5962*

Fitzsimmons, Robert: Movie of a heavyweight championship boxing fight, *5546*

Fitzsimons, Thomas: Congressional investigation, *2560*
Congressional representative who was Catholic, *2597*

Fitzsimons, William Thomas: Soldiers in the American army killed in combat in World War I, *8038*

Flagg, Josiah Foster: Dentist, *4854*
Dentistry book, *1922*

Flaherty, Barney: Newsboy, *5648*

Flanagan, Betsy: Cocktail, *2665*

Fleer, Frank Henry: Bubble gum, *3967*

Fleeson, Plunket: Wallpaper, *4305*

Fleischmann, Charles: Compressed fresh yeast, *3935*

Fleming, Ethel: Mother and son to enlist simultaneously in the Army, *5175*

Fleming, Harry: Court-martial of an officer for collaborating with his captors, *2741*

Fleming, John: Patriotic song by an American, *1376*

Fleming, Michael: Mother and son to enlist simultaneously in the Army, *5175*

Fleming, Tommy: Log-rolling national championship tournament, *7576*

Fletcher, Francis: Christian religious service in English on the Pacific Coast, *6501*

Fletcher, Joseph Otis: Airplane flight to land at the North Pole, *6731*
Discovery of the North Pole, *6727*

Fletcher, Richard: Statistical society, *6779*

Fletcher, Robert: Supreme Court decision declaring a state law unconstitutional, *2748*

Flick, Lawrence Francis: Tuberculosis research and prevention society, *5042*

Flinn, Kelly Jean: Pilot of a B-52 bomber who was a woman, *1626*

Flipper, Henry Ossian: West Point graduate who was African-American, *3199*

Flora, Ruth: Navy personnel in the regular Navy who were women, *5266*

Florence, Virginia Proctor Powell: Librarian who was African-American, *4674*

Flosdorf, Earl William: Blood serum made of dried human blood, *4833*

Flowers, "Posie": Professional football game, *7322*

Foerderer, Robert Herman: Chrome-tanned leather successfully marketed, *4460*

Fogelson, Samuel Julian: Surgical operation televised coast-to-coast, *5085*

Follen, Charles Theodore Christian: Gymnastics instruction at a college, *7372*

Folsom, Frances: Wedding of a president in the White House, *4815*

Fones, Alfred Civilion: Dental hygienists' book, *1925*

Fong, Hiram Leong: Senator of Chinese ancestry, *2657*

Foote, Andrew Hull: Ironclad naval vessels, *6921*

Forbes, Charles: Communion cups for individuals, *6582*

Forbes, Cleveland: Steamboat service to California around Cape Horn, *6883*

Forbes, John: Fireproof baseball stadium, *7507*

Forbes, Malcolm: State legislative hearing to be shown on television, *7633*

Forbes, R.B.: Yacht club, *7207*

Forcade, Thomas: Magazine about recreational drugs, *4740*

Force, Peter: Printing press for printing wallpaper in color, *5770*

Ford, Alfred: Transatlantic crossing attempted by a balloon, *1538*

Ford, Ebenezer: Labor union to nominate its own political candidates, *4604*

Ford, Gerald Rudolph: Cabinet member to serve in four different capacities, *6120*
General of the Armies of the United States with the rank of six stars, *5161*
President to receive a presidential pardon, *6179*
President who came to the office through appointment rather than election, *6178*

Presidential election debate between an incumbent president and a challenger to be televised, *3397*

Vice president chosen under the 25th Amendment, *6249*

Ford, Henry: Plastic car, *5451*

Ford, John Laurence: Surgical facility outside a hospital, *5089*

Ford, Robert: Round-the-world flight by a commercial airplane, *1462*

Ford, William H.: Biscuits of shredded wheat, *3924*

Forester, Frank: Sportswriter, *5612*

Forney, Matthias Nace: Aviation magazine, *4776*

Forrest, Edwin: Play performed 1,000 times, *1248*

Forrest, Nathan Bedford: Ku Klux Klan meeting, *2253*

Forrest, Ray: Telecast from a submerged submarine, *7838*

Forster, Charles: Toothpick manufacturing machine, *4071*

Forsyth, William: Fruit culture treatise, *1759*

Forsythe, Albert Ernest: Transcontinental flight made by African-Americans in their own airplane, *1458*

Forsythe, John: Made-for-TV movie, *7789*

Fortesque, George K.: Musical with an American theme and original score, *1252*

Foster Dulles, John: Cabinet session to be telecast and broadcast, *6115*

Foster, George G.: Comic weekly, *4717*

Foster, George Gale: Installment finance company, *3805*

Foster, John: Federal revenue cutter, *6857*
Map made in America to be published in a book, *4792*
Woodcut, *1222*

Foster, M.G.: Electrical hearing aid, *5070*

Foster, Thomas Jefferson: Correspondence school for workers, *2888*

Foulis, James: Golf player in an official amateur tournament who was African-American, *7355*

Foulke, William Parker: Dinosaur skeleton found in the United States, *6744*

Foulois, Benjamin Delahauf: Intercity airplane flight by a U.S. military officer, *1428*

Fowler, George Ryerson: First aid instruction, *4122*

Fowler, John W. "Bud": Baseball player on a white team who was African-American, *7140*

Fowler, Robert Grant: Transcontinental eastbound airplane flight made in stages, *1440*

Fowlkes, James: Wedding on television, *4820*

Fownes, William Clark, Jr.: International golf match, *7346*

Fox, Chastity: Belly-dancing course at a college, *2916*

Fox, John D.: Spiritualist, *6599*

Fox, John R.: Medals of Honor awarded to African-American servicemen for service in World War II, *1689*

Fox, Joseph: Brass and copper seamless tubes, *4467*

Fox, Philip: Planetarium open to the public, *6669*

Fox, William: Movie by a major company for an African-American audience, *5559*

Fraenkel-Conrat, Heinz Ludwig: Virus separated into component parts, *5062*

Frances, Mary: University for African-American students founded as a Catholic institution, *2964*

Francis, Edward: Animal disease of American origin, *5122*

Francis, James Bichens: Sprinkler system, *4101*

Francis, Joseph: Lifeboat of corrugated iron, *4120*

Frank, Morris S.: Dogs trained to guide the blind, *1173*

Frankau, Gilbert: Zipper, *2292*

Frankel, Jacob: Army chaplain who was Jewish, *5200*

Frankenberg, J.: Movie entertainment shown on an airplane, *5514*

Franklin, Ann: Newspaper editor who was a woman, *5610*

Franklin, Benjamin: Academy, *2929*
Bifocal eyeglasses, *5072*
Book advocating spelling reform, *1826*
Capture of an enemy ship in enemy waters, *7999*
Circulating library, *4661*
Continental coin, *5357*
Copley Medal awarded to an American, *1646*
Design for the Great Seal of the United States, *1132*
Electric cooking experiment, *3450*
Electrocution experiment, *2794*
Fire insurance company to receive a charter, *4530*
German newspaper, *5661*
Heating stove, *4331*
Hospital, *4868*
Lightning demonstration, *6767*
Lightning rod, *4096*
Masonic book, *2007*
Minister plenipotentiary, *3984*
Newspaper cartoon, *5684*
Philosophy book printed in America, *2008*
Postage stamp issued with perforations, *6054*
Postage stamps depicting a president, *6078*
Postage stamps issued by the Post Office Department, *6052*

Franklin, Benjamin —*continued*
Postmaster general under the Continental Congress, *5983*
Rhubarb, *3897*
Rocking chair, *4320*
Science society, *6776*
Street-sweeping service, *2219*
Swimmer of note, *7513*
Textbook printed in America, *1824*
Translation of a classic, *1736*
Treaties entered into by the federal government, *3998*
Treaty between the federal government and a nation with which it had been at war, *3999*
Treaty entered into by the federal government after independence, *4000*
Water skis, *7591*
Franklin, Roswell Earl: Train of airplanes, *1459*
Transcontinental glider tow, *1551*
Frasch, Herman: Sulfur deposit, *5333*
Fraser, Alexander V.: Coast guard service, *5208*
Frazee, John: Sculptor to obtain a federal commission, *1207*
Frazier, Alice: American to hug the Queen of England, *6656*
Freeburg, Mal Bryan: Air Mail Flyer's Medal of Honor, *1642*
Freeman, Bucky: Baseball "Home Run King", *7146*
Freeman, Daniel: Homestead law enacted by Congress, *5967*
Freeman, Elizabeth (Mum Bett): Slave to be emancipated, *2245*
Freeman, James: Unitarian prayer book, *1956*
Freeman, Joseph, Jr.: Mormon man ordained to the priesthood who was African-American, *6494*
Freeman, Orville: Food stamps, *4086*
Freeman, Walter: Prefrontal lobotomy, *5087*
Fremont, John Charles: Overland wagon road across the Rocky Mountains, *6617*
Republican Party meeting, *3353*
French, Josiah: Bedspring manufacturing patent, *4322*
French, Walter: Screw auger, *7911*
Frey, Emil: Liederkranz cheese, *3860*
Frick, George: Ophthalmology book, *1905*
Friedman, Harold A.: Jewish mobile synagogue, *6491*
Friedman, Jerome: Quark to be observed, *6821*
Friedman, Milton: Year in which Nobel Prizes were won by Americans in five of six categories, *1702*
Friedman, Sol B.: Orthodox rabbi born in America to be ordained, *6488*
Fries, John: Tax rebellion, *5952*

Frieze, Henry Simmons: College entrance plan using certified schools, *2994*
Froebel, Friedrich Wilhelm August: Parent-teacher assocation, *3226*
Froelich, John: Gasoline tractor, *1055*
From, John Lawrence, Jr.: Submarine to have two complete crews, *6977*
Frost, Robert: Poet to win a Pulitzer Prize four times, *1713*
Frothingham, Benjamin Thompson: Intercollegiate billiard match, *4018*
Frowick, Roy Halston: Clothing designer of international renown, *2280*
Fruen, William Henry: Vending machine that dispensed liquid automatically, *2393*
Frustaci, Patti: Septuplets, *2178*
Fry, Henry Clay: Cut glass, *4046*
Fry, Joseph Reese: Opera by an American composer, *1345*
Fry, William Henry: Opera by an American composer, *1345*
Fuchs, Arthur Wolfram: X-ray photograph of the entire body of a living person taken in a one-second exposure, *4906*
X-ray photograph showing the complete arterial circulation in an adult human, *4907*
Fudge, Solomon: Tunnel, *3611*
Fuentz, John: Helicopter rescue of an American pilot behind enemy lines, *7979*
Fuller, Buckminster: Fullerenes to be observed, *6822*
Fuller, Calvin Souther: Solar energy battery, *3558*
Fuller, George Allon: Steel-frame building, *2080*
Fuller, Ida May: Social security monthly payment, *4526*
Fuller, Margaret: Book review editor, *5613*
Fuller, Richard Buckminster: Geodesic dome of substantial size, *2094*
Fuller, Samuel: Physician in the New England colonies, *4960*
Fuller, Seth: Annunciator, *2358*
Fullerton, C. Gordon: Reusable manned spacecraft, *7087*
Fulton, John A.: Reflecting telescope, *6663*
Fulton, Robert: Dry dock, *6904*
Steam-propelled frigate, *6916*
Steamboat to make regular trips, *6861*
Funter, Robert: Ship built on the Pacific coast, *6856*
Furlong, Lawrence: Coast survey book, *2014*
Fussel, Jacob: Ice cream wholesale dealer, *3863*

G

Gaddis, Hugh: Transcontinental nonstop helicopter flight, *1578*

Gage, John H.: Tool factory, *7917*

Gaine, Hugh: History of medicine, *1863*

Gaines, Edmund P.: Former vice president to be arrested, *6241*

Gaines, Hugh: Book fair, *1783*

Gaither, Sidney: Quintuplets to survive infancy who were African-American, *2177*

Gaither, Suzanne: Quintuplets to survive infancy who were African-American, *2177*

Gajdusek, Daniel Carleton: Year in which Nobel Prizes were won by Americans in five of six categories, *1702*

Gallagher, Jack S.: Helicopter passenger service, *1568*

Gallagher, James: Round-the-world nonstop flight by an airplane, *1470*

Gallagher, Michael: Birth to be shown on closed-circuit television, *2163*

Gallagher, Philip Benjamin: Radar signal bounced off the sun, *7683*

Gallardo, Gregorio: Bullfight, *7258*

Gallatin, Abraham Alfonse Albert: Senate election that was contested, *3327*

Gallaudet, Edward Miner: College for deaf students, *3033*

Gallaudet, Thomas: Prayers in sign language, *6528*

Gallaudet, Thomas Hopkins: College for deaf students, *3033*
Prayers in sign language, *6528*
School for deaf students, *3032*
Teachers' institute, *3261*

Gallery, Daniel Vincent: Capture and boarding of an enemy submarine on the high seas by American forces, *8065*

Gallitzin, Demetrius Augustine: Catholic priest, *6459*

Gallo, Robert: Identification of the AIDS virus, *5064*

Galloway, Jesse James: Micropaleontology course at a college, *3247*

Galloway, Kit: Cyber cafe, *2467*

Galvin, Paul Vincent: Car radio, *6309*

Gamble, James: Floating soap, *4055*

Gammeter, Harry Christian: Multigraph, *2367*

Gannal, Jean Nicolas: Embalming book, *1910*

Gannon, Oscar B.: Court-martial at which the judges included enlisted men, *2740*

Ganter, Frederic L.: College radio station, *6295*

Garand, John C.: Semiautomatic rifle, *8118*

Garber, Clarence Zent: Bone bank, *4837*

Garcia, Jose: Political asylum granted on grounds of sexual orientation, *5882*

Garden, John Surnam: Capture of a British frigate in the War of 1812, *8023*

Gardenier, Barent: Duel between representatives in Congress, *2810*

Gardette, E. B.: Melons and cantaloupes, *3899*

Gardiner, Julia: President married while in office, *6190*

Gardiner, Robert Hallowell: Technical institute, *3283*

Gardner, Dale: Salvage operation in space, *7089*

Gardner, Dozier: Intercollegiate court tennis match, *7534*

Gardner, Eleazer A.: Cable car, *6395*

Gardner, Gideon: Lifeboat, *4118*

Gardner, Lester Durand: Radio two-way broadcast from an airplane, *6273*

Garfield, Eliza Ballou: President whose mother lived at the White House, *6195*

Garfield, James Abram: President to use a telephone, *6161*
President whose mother lived at the White House, *6195*
Presidential candidate to make campaign speeches in a foreign language, *3408*

Garfield, Sidney R.: Health maintenance organization, *4540*

Garlow, Melvin C.: Pilot to fly a million miles in a jet airplane, *1605*

Garn, Jake: Senator to fly in space, *7051*

Garnet, Henry Highland: African-American preacher to deliver a sermon in the House of Representatives, *2588*

Garnett, Robert Selden: Confederate general killed in the Civil War, *7953*

Garratt, Alfred Charles: Electrotherapy book, *1914*

Garrett, Robert: Discus-throwing competition, *7551*

Garroway, Dave: Telecast from a foreign country, *7842*

Gartside, Mary: Appendectomy, *5080*

Garve, Andrew: Book set into type completely by electronic composition, *1756*

Garvey, Walter J.: Radio church, *6590*

Garza, Tony: Voting rights in space, *3435*

Gaston, William: College founded as a Catholic institution, *2938*

Gates, William Henry, III: Commercial software for personal computers, *2552*

Gatling, Richard Jordan: Rapid-fire machine gun, *8107*

Gauguin, Paul: Modern art exhibition, *1228*

Gaul, Albro Tilton: Photographic type-composing machine, *5809*

Gault, John: Encased postage stamps, *6055*

Gay, John: Opera performed by a professional visiting troupe, *1342*

Gayetty, Joseph C.: Toilet paper, *5756*

Gayler, Charles A.: Fireproof safe, *2357*

Gaynor, Janet: Oscars for best acting, *1631*

Gaynor, William Jay: Ticker-tape shower for a celebrity, *3666*

Gearhart, John D.: Human stem cells to be cultured in a laboratory, *5068*

Geary, John White: Governor of a state who had also been governor of a territory, *7614*

Gebbie, Kristine: AIDS policy coordinator for the federal government, *4192*

Gebhard, Bruno: Health museum, *5590*

Geddes, Paul: Wagon train to California, *5962*

Gee Jon: Execution by lethal gas, *2800*

Gee, Joshua: Library catalog in book form, *4660*

Geen, John van: Computer modem that was practical, *2534*

Gehres, Leslie Edward: Movie of a solar eclipse taken from an airplane, *6688*

Geiberger, Allen L.: Golfer to break 60 in a Professional Golfers Association tour, *7368*

Gell-Mann, Murray: Quark to be observed, *6821*

Geloso, Mrs. John: Standard broadcast station to transmit a television image, *7795*

Genin, John Nicholas: Felt hats for women, *2296*

George, Edward: Lawn mower, *7933*

George, Henry: Single Tax League national conference, *7650*

Gérard, Conrad Alexandre: Representative of a foreign country to the United States, *3983*

Gerberg, Gary: Undersea hotel, *2437*

Gericke, William Frederick: Description of hydroponic agriculture, *1036*

Private hydroponic garden, *1037*

German, Jacob: Driver arrested for speeding, *5468*

Gernsback, Hugo: Radio magazine, *4779*

Radio receiver advertised, *6306*

Science fiction magazine, *4732*

Standard broadcast station to transmit a television image, *7795*

Gerrish, Samuel: Book auction printed catalog, *1780*

Gerry, Elbridge: Child abuse prevention organization, *5737*

House of Representatives filibuster, *2581*

Vice president who had served in the House of Representatives, *6239*

Gershwin, George: Pulitzer Prize awarded to a musical, *1712*

Gershwin, Ira: Pulitzer Prize awarded to a musical, *1712*

Gesner, Abraham: Kerosene, *3527*

Gessner, Robert: Film professorship at a college, *2914*

Ghiselin, Francis Henshall: X-ray movies of human organs in action, *4908*

Ghormley, Robert Lee: American offensive in the Pacific in World War II, *8081*

Gibb, Roberta "Bobbi": Marathon runner from the United States who was a woman, *7565*

Gibbons, Herbert Adams: Civil rights chair at a college, *3128*

Gibbons, Joseph: Seeding machine, *1047*

Gibbons, Mrs. A. H.: Free lunches for the poor and sick, *5736*

Gibbons, William: Book advocating voting rights for women, *2012*

Gibbs, James Edward Allen: Chain-stitch single-thread sewing machine, *4356*

Gibbs, Wolcott: Measurement organization (national), *2449*

Gibson, Althea: Tennis champion who was African-American, *7538*

Gibson, Edward George: Photograph of a comet taken from space, *6704*

Gibson, J.L.: Professional hockey team, *7375*

Gibson, Robert L.: Spacecraft launched by the United States to dock with a Russian space station, *7091*

Giddings, Franklin Henry: Sociology professor at a college, *3252*

Giessenbier, Henry, Jr.: Junior chamber of commerce, *2453*

Gifford, Jay: American civilians killed in the continental United States in World War II, *8084*

Gifford, Sanford: Building designed to be used by artists, *2062*

Gifford, Walter Sherman: Round-the-world telephone conversation, *7762*

Ship-to-shore mobile telephone commercial service, *7739*

Transatlantic commercial telephone service, *7737*

Gilbert, Cass: Skyscraper higher than 750 feet in height, *2099*

Gilbert, Edwin: Wire sieves, *4370*

Gilbert, Timothy: Medical society for women, *5037*

Gilchrist, John James: Claims court established by the federal government, *2712*

Gildersleeve, Virginia Crocheron: Federal treaty signed by a woman, *4006*

Giles, Harriet E.: Nursing school for African-American students, *3169*

Gill, John: Revolving gun, *8093*

Gillespie, James Milligan: Transatlantic flight by a robot airplane, *1467*

Gillespy, Edward: Irish magazine, *4742*

Gillette, Arthur Jay: Hospital for disabled children established by a state, *4889*

Gillette, King Camp: Safety razor, *4056*

Gillingham, J. E.: Cattle tuberculosis test, *5121*

Gillis, James Melville: Astronomical observations book, *1985*

Gilmore, George William: Intercollegiate lacrosse association, *7572*

Gilmore, Robert: Lung removal, *5081*

Gilpen, Thomas: Paper made by machine, *5749*

Gimbel, Adam: Department store, *2491*

Ginsberg, Charles P.: Video tape recorder for sounds and pictures, *7821*

Ginsburg, Ruth Bader: Supreme Court justice who was Jewish, *2762*

Ginter, Philip: Anthracite coal, *3502*

Gish, Lillian: Movie to gross $50 million, *5513*

Gissendanner, Charles: Tank crew to cross the 38th parallel in the Korean War, *7980*

Gist, George: Native American language to be given a written form, *5959*

Gleason, Kate: Tract housing development, *2196*

Gleitsmann, William: Tuberculosis sanatorium, *4898*

Glenn, John Herschel, Jr.: Astronaut to orbit the earth, *7030*
Astronauts trained by the United States, *7028*
Postage stamp issued on the date of the event it commemorated, *6070*
Presidential candidate who had been an astronaut, *3418*
Senator to fly in space, *7051*
Senator who had been an astronaut, *2660*

Glidden, Joseph Farwell: Barbed wire commercial production, *4406*

Glover, J. N.: Terra cotta factory, *2058*

Glover, Jesse "Jose": Printing press, *5767*

Glover, Townend: Entomologist hired by the federal government, *6743*

Gluckman, Richard: Art museum of importance devoted to the work of an individual woman, *5600*

Goddard, George: Demonstration of rapid aerial photography, *5823*
Photograph taken from an airplane at night, *5824*

Goddard, Henry Herbert: Intelligence test in a school for children with mental retardation, *3021*

Goddard, Luther: Watchmaker, *7899*

Goddard, Mary Katherine: Postmaster who was a woman, *5982*

Goddard, Robert Hutchins: Rocket flight using liquid fuel, *7017*

Godfrey, Alexander: Stock order from a zeppelin, *3826*

Godfrey, Thomas: Quadrant, *6954*

Godowsky, Leopold, Jr.: Color film, *5844*

Gof, Frederick Harris: Community trust charity, *5742*

Goffigan, Laban: Lighthouse built after American independence, *4124*

Goldberg, David: Navy chaplain who was Jewish, *5203*

Goldberg, Joshua L.: Navy chaplain who was Jewish, *5203*

Goldberger, Joseph: Pellagra experiment of note, *5058*

Golden, John: Broadway play shown in a television version with its original cast, *1266*

Goldfaden, Abraham: Yiddish theater performance, *1255*

Goldin, Daniel: Scientific evidence for life on Mars, *7027*

Goldman, Sylvan N.: Shopping cart, *2371*

Goldmark, Peter: Long-playing microgroove phonograph records, *7012*

Goldsborough, Louis Malesherbes: Observatory established by the federal government, *6665*

Goldstein, Isidore: Identification of human beings from the pattern formed by the blood vessels of the retina, *4165*

Goldwyn, Samuel: Movie of feature length made in Hollywood, *5551*

Goler, George Washington: Milk station operated by a city government, *4206*

Golitzyn, Dimitri Augustin: Catholic priest, *6459*

Golubok, Leon: Play presented by a Jewish professional acting troupe, *1253*

Gompers, Samuel: Postage stamp depicting a Jew, *6091*

Goodale, Samuel D.: Peep show machine, *3686*

Goodale, William: Paper bag manufacturing machine, *5757*

Goodall, Harvey L.: Livestock market paper, *5644*

Goodall, Thomas: Horse blankets, *4263*

Goode, Malvin Russell "Mel": Television news commentator who was African-American, *5620*

Goodlin, Chalmers: Rocket plane for manned supersonic flight, *1492*

Goodman, Benny: Jazz concert at Carnegie Hall, *1298*

Goodman, Louis: Airmail flight by rocket, *6026*

Goodnow, Frank Johnson: Political science association (national), *6790*

Goodrich, Annie Warburton: Army nursing school, *3176*

Goodrich, Joseph: Monolithic concrete building, *2075*

Goodwin, George: Children's magazine, *4695*

Goodwin, George W.: Steel sailing vessel, *6874*

Goodwin, Hannibal Williston: Celluloid photographic film, *5838*

Goodwin, Isabella: Detective who was a woman, *4140*

Goodwin, J. Cheever: Musical with an American theme and original score, *1252*

Goodwin, William Nelson, Jr.: Camera exposure meter, *5843*

Goodyear, Charles: Sneakers, *2307*
Vulcanized rubber, *4486*

Gorbachev, Mikhail S.: Treaty to reduce the number of nuclear missiles, *4007*

Gordon, Daisy: Scouting organization for girls, *2148*

Gordon, Hugh: Round-the-world commercial airplane service, *1416*

Gordon, Jacqueline: Golfer born in America to win the British Women's Amateur Golf Tournament, *7363*

Gordon, Nathaniel: Execution for slave trading carried out by the federal government, *2797*

Gordon, Richard Francis, Jr.: Space-to-ground news conference telecast, *5608*

Gordon, Samuel George: Fluorescent mineral exhibit, *6715*

Gore, Robert: Synthetic fabric that was waterproof and breathable, *7879*

Gore, Wilbert L.: Synthetic fabric that was waterproof and breathable, *7879*

Gorges, Ferdinando: City incorporated in the colonies, *2181*
Waterpower development grant to a colonist, *5913*

Gorham, Nathaniel: Land office, *5948*

Gorman, Margaret: Beauty pageant to be held nationwide, *3628*

Gorrie, John: Mechanical freezer patent, *4347*

Gorringe, Henry Honeychurch: Obelisk to be brought to the United States, *5403*

Gorton, Adolphus W.: Airship passenger transfer to an airplane, *1525*

Gosden, Freeman: Radio show with a plot, *6290*

Gosnold, Bartholomew: English settlement in America that was permanent, *5907*
Episcopal church service in an English colony, *6547*
Exploration of the New England region by an Englishman, *5903*

Gossling, Frederick W.: Sugar and glucose from cornstarch, *3961*

Gottschalk, Louis Moreau: Musician born in America to achieve fame in Europe, *1328*

Gougelman, Pierre: Artificial eyes, *5051*

Gould, Gordon: Laser, *3443*

Gould, Stephen Philip: Casein fiber, *4443*

Goulding, Ray: Stereo telecast, *7857*

Gounder, Howard Moyer: Air raid shelter, *4088*

Gounod, Charles François: Opera produced at the Metropolitan Opera House, *1347*

Goupil, René: Catholic saints who were active in North America, *6472*

Gourdin, Edward O.: Broad jump to reach more than 25 feet, *7555*

Grace, Robert: Heating stove, *4331*

Grace, William Joseph: Ambulance equipped for mobile coronary care, *4826*

Graham, Bette Nesmith: Correction fluid for typewriters, *2389*

Graham, Evarts Ambrose: Lung removal, *5081*

Graham, James R.: Brown dwarf star to be discovered, *6685*

Graham, John: Revolving restaurant, *2465*

Graham, Lew: Radio broadcast from a circus, *3674*

Graham, Sylvester: Whole-wheat bread, *3919*

Graham, William J.: Life insurance group policy, *4548*

Gram, Hans: Orchestral song to be printed, *1378*

Gram, Hans Birch: Homeopathic treatise, *1906*
Homeopathy practitioner, *4968*

Grandon, F.J.: Serial movie with installments longer than one reel, *5550*

Grange, Harold "Red": Big-league football team to travel coast-to-coast, *7306*

Granger, Austin: Collar factory, *2284*

Grant, Charles: Baseball player in the American League who was African-American, *7147*

Grant, George: Cattle of the Aberdeen-Angus breed, *1081*

Grant, George F.: Golf tee, *7352*

Grant, Ray: Television variety talent show series, *7776*

Grant, Ulysses Simpson: Centennial celebration of the Revolution, *8006*
General of the U.S. Army, *5151*
Reigning king to visit the United States, *6645*
Reply-paid card, *6045*

Grant, Ulysses Simpson, III: Swimming pool in the White House, *6257*

Grant, William West: Appendectomy, *5080*

Gras, Norman Scott Brien: Business history chair at a college, *2922*

Grasso, Ella: Governor who was a woman, *7618*

Gratz, Rebecca: Jewish religious school for children, *6485*

Grauer, Ben: Movie premiere festivities to be shown on television, *5517*

Graupner, Johann Christian Gottlieb: Orchestra, *1355*

Gravelet, Jean François: Daredevil to cross Niagara Falls on a tightrope, *3677*

944

Groves, Ernest Rutherford: Marriage course at a college, *3103*

Groves, John: Civilian airport owned and operated by the federal government, *1508*

Gruen, Victor: Enclosed climate-controlled suburban shopping mall, *2512*
Pedestrian shopping mall, *2513*

Grundy, Joseph Ridgway: Senate election in which neither candidate was seated after a recount, *2630*

Gruskin, Benjamin: Chlorophyll, *4997*

Guerin, Eric: Horse stakes race ending in a triple dead heat, *7402*

Guerin, Napoleon E.: Egg incubator, *1068*
Life preserver of cork, *4119*

Guille, Charles: Parachute jump from a balloon, *1580*

Gulick, Mrs. Luther Halsey: Scouting organization for girls, *2148*

Gummere, William Stryker: Intercollegiate football contest, *7315*

Gunn, Frederick William: Camp for boys, *2143*

Gunnells, Leonard Blake: Birth registration uniform numbering system, *2162*

Gunther, Thomas: Carillon, *1305*

Gurley, W.C.: Photograph of a lightning flash, *6696*

Guthrie, Janet: Driver who was a woman to compete in the Indianapolis 500, *7269*

Guthrie, Samuel: Chloroform, *4985*
Glucose from potato starch, *3957*

Gutierrez, Cesar Dario: Major league baseball player to make seven consecutive hits in seven times at bat in the same game, *7156*

Guyot, Arnold: College to sponsor an endowed lecture series, *2950*

Gygax, Gary: Role-playing game, *4014*

H

Haas, Earl C.: Tampon to be mass-produced, *4061*

Haase, J.M.F.: Movie of a solar eclipse taken from an airplane, *6688*

Hachard, Sister St. Stanislas: Catholic nun, *6452*

Hackelton, Thomas: Lime, *5315*

Hackett, James Henry: Actor to appear abroad, *1276*

Hadaway, William S., Jr.: Electric stove, *4298*

Hadley, William Aaron: Correspondence school to offer instruction in Braille, *3029*

Haefner, Ralph: Typewriting primer, *1829*

Hagen, Hermann August: Entomology professor at a college, *3238*

Hagner, Charles V.: Drug mill, *4982*

Haines, Jackson: Figure skater of note, *7429*

Haio-hwat'ha: League of Native American nations, *5897*

Haise, Fred W., Jr.: Reusable manned spacecraft, *7087*

Hakanson, Walter C.: Softball game, *7497*

Halas, George: All-star football game, *7327*

Hale, Benjamin: Technical institute, *3283*

Hale, George Ellery: Telescope lens 200 inches in diameter, *6671*

Hale, H.S.: Folding bed, *4328*

Hale, John Parker: Senator elected on an antislavery ticket, *2250*

Hale, Mrs. Stephen: American flag flown over a schoolhouse, *1126*

Hale, Sarah Josepha: Magazine for women, *4709*

Haley, Bill: Rock and roll song to hit No. 1 in the pop charts, *1369*

Halfhill, A.P.: Canned tuna, *3889*

Hall, Charles: Army pilot who was African-American to shoot down an Axis airplane in World War II, *8063*

Hall, Charles Bingley: Banking association (national), *3768*

Hall, Charles Corydon: Rock wool insulation factory, *2047*

Hall, Charles Martin: Aluminum in metallic form, *4475*
Aluminum pots, *4297*

Hall, Granville Stanley: Psychology journal, *4759*
Psychology laboratory, *4927*
Psychology society (national), *5043*

Hall, Henry: Book set by linotype, *1752*
Cranberry cultivation, *3900*
Fishing line factory, *7924*

Hall, John Elihu: Law magazine, *4700*

Hall, Juanita: Radio network for African-Americans, *6302*

Hall, Otis: Eye wash commercially manufactured, *4990*

Hall, Prince: Mason who was African-American, *5729*

Hall, Samuel Read: Education book, *1827*
Teacher training school, *3258*

Hall, Thomas S.: Railroad signal system with automatic electric block, *6422*

Hall, William Alden: Shot fired by the Navy in World War I, *8031*

Hallam, Lewis: Play by an American writer to be successfully presented by an established company, *1246*

Hallaren, Mary Agnes: Army officer who was a woman, *5170*

Halleck, Fitz-Greene: Monument to an American poet, *5402*

Hallidie, Andrew Smith: Cable car put into service, *6398*

Hallock, William: Tuberculosis vaccine, *4921*

Halprin, Lawrence: First Lady to be depicted on a monument to a president, *6134*

Halsey, Francis Whiting: Book review newspaper supplement, *5650*

Halsey, Lewis Benjamin: Milk pasteurized commercially, *3875*

Halsted, William Stewart: Local anesthetic, *4832*

Silk sutures and ligatures, *4956*

Halston: Clothing designer of international renown, *2280*

Halvorson, Kittel: Congressional representative elected by prohibitionists, *2606*

Hamada, Hikozo: Japanese to enter the United States, *5961*

Hamburger, Christian: Sex-change operation, *6832*

Hamilton, Alexander: Bank of the United States, *3758*

Congressional caucus, *2584*

Industrial park, *4380*

Loan to the United States, *3804*

Political newspaper, *5632*

Revolutionary War national veterans' organization, *5308*

Secretary of the treasury, *6103*

Hamilton, Andrew: Parliamentary act to establish a colonial post office, *5981*

Trial in which freedom of the press was upheld, *5633*

Hamilton, Charles Keeney: Airplane round trip, *1430*

Aviation meet, *7292*

Hamilton, Frank Hastings: Skin grafting, *5077*

Hamilton, James: Fire insurance company to receive a charter, *4530*

Hamilton, John: College charter granted by a governor, *2928*

Hamilton, Mrs. William: Navy Day, *4247*

Hamilton, Perrin: Sulfanilamide production, *4993*

Hammerstein, Oscar: Cigar-rolling machine, *2706*

Hammond, Elisha: Library building at a university, *4669*

Hammond, Frankie: Parachute jump from an autogiro, *1588*

Hammond, Graeme M.: National fencing league, *7281*

Hammond, John: Parkland purchased by a city, *3733*

Hammond, Laurens: Bridge table to shuffle and deal cards by electricity, *4024*

Pipeless organ, *1324*

Hammond, William Alexander: Neurology textbook, *1915*

Hampson, John: Venetian blinds, *4306*

Hance, William A.: Bicycle with a back-pedal brake, *7187*

Hanchett, M. Waldo: Dental chair, *4859*

Hancock, George W.: Softball game, *7497*

Hancock, John: Constitution adopted by a state, *1101*

Signer of the Declaration of Independence, *1113*

Hancock, Thomas: Catalog of theological and biblical literature, *1952*

Handel, George Frideric: Oratorio performance, *1288*

Handler, Ruth and Eliot: Barbie doll, *2152*

Handy, William Christopher "W.C.": Composer of jazz music, *1331*

Hanger, Glossbrenner Wallace William: Strike settlement mediated by the federal Department of Labor, *4596*

Hanks, Benjamin: Chimes and bells, *1302*

Hanks, Horatio: Silk thread, *4362*

Hanks, Rodney: Silk thread, *4362*

Hanks, Rodney and Horatio: Silk mill, *7887*

Hanna, William: Animated cartoon series on prime-time television, *7786*

Hannan, John: Chocolate mill, *3955*

Hannegan, Robert Emmet: Radio fax transmission to a moving train, *7673*

Hansberry, Lorraine: Play by an African-American woman to appear on Broadway, *1270*

Hansell, Ellen F.: National tennis championship match for women, *7529*

Hansell, Haywood Shepherd: Air attack on Germany by the Army Air Force in World War II, *8061*

Hansen, Edmund H.: Transatlantic radio fax transmission of a photograph, *7668*

Hanson, John: Impression made by the Great Seal of the United States, *1133*

Hapgood, Andrew S.: Salmon cannery, *3887*

Harbo, George: Transatlantic trip by rowboat, *6985*

Harbord, James Guthrie: High-definition telecast, *7834*

Transatlantic radio fax of a check, *3794*

Harby, Isaac: Jewish congregation in the Reform movement, *6486*

Hardin, John: Battle fought by federal troops after the formation of the Union, *5144*

Harding, Florence Kling De Wolfe: President and First Lady to die during the term for which he had been elected, *6196*

Harding, Warren Gamaliel: Burial at the Tomb of the Unknown Soldier, *2854*

Cabinet member convicted of a crime, *6110*

President and First Lady to die during the term for which he had been elected, *6196*

President to make a radio broadcast, *6210*

President to use a radio, *6209*

President to visit Alaska and Canada while in office, *6234*

Harding, Warren Gamaliel —*continued*
Presidential inauguration to be broadcast on radio, *6213*
Railroad operated by the federal government, *6343*
Telephone cable deep-sea service, *7736*
Hardwick, Billy: Bowling Triple Crown winner, *7231*
Hardy, Arthur Cobb: Spectrophotometer, *6799*
Hardy, James D.: Lung transplant, *5098*
Transplant of an animal organ into a human being, *5099*
Hardy, Le Grand Haven: Ophthalmology clinic, *4846*
Hare, Ernie: Radio program theme song, *6289*
Hare, Robert: Blowpipe, *6796*
Hargis, James: Transcontinental car trip driven entirely in reverse, *5475*
Hargrove, John: Swedenborgian or New Church temple, *6524*
Harkness, Mrs. William H., Jr.: Giant panda, *1154*
Harlan, Richard: Embalming book, *1910*
Harman, William Henry: Heavy tank, *8120*
Harmar, Josiah: Commander-in-chief of the U.S. Army, *5147*
Harmon, Hubert Reilly: Air Force academy, *3190*
Harmon, Reuben: Copper cents minted by a state, *5355*
Harnden, William Frederick: Express delivery service, *2479*
Harney, Ben: Ragtime instruction book, *1941*
Harnick, Sheldon: Musical to run for more than 3,000 performances, *1271*
Harriman, Herbert M.: Golf champion born in America, *7357*
Harriot, Thomas: Surveyor in America, *5902*
Harris, Barbara C.: Episcopal priest who was a woman, *6553*
Harris, Benjamin: Newspaper publisher, *5609*
Patent medicine advertisement, *2316*
Schoolbook, *1823*
Harris, Chapin Aaron: Dental college, *3162*
Dental journal, *4754*
Harris, Charles Nathan: Night court, *2708*
Harris, Edward: Percheron horse importation, *1179*
Harris, Harold R.: Pilot to bail out of a disabled airplane, *1585*
Harris, Isaac: Sightseeing bus, *5418*
Harris, Jeremy: Ornithopter that succeeded in flying, *1407*
Harris, John: Harpsichord, *1307*
Harris, Marcelite Jordan: Air Force general who was an African-American woman, *5141*
Harris, Mary Belle: Prison established by the federal government for women, *2829*

Harris, Patricia Roberts: Ambassador who was an African-American woman, *3994*
Cabinet member who was an African-American woman, *6121*
Harris, Paul Percy: Rotary Club meeting, *2451*
Harris, Thomas: Navy medical school, *3171*
Harris, William Charles: Fishing magazine, *4785*
Harris, William Torrey: Public school kindergarten, *3074*
Harrison, Benjamin: National forest reserve, *3728*
President whose grandson became president, *6188*
Harrison, Bertram: Theater operated by a city, *3703*
Harrison, Earl Grant: Registration of aliens by the federal government, *5872*
Harrison, Francis Burton: Drug control law enacted by Congress, *2687*
Harrison, John: Sulfuric acid, *4427*
Harrison, Joseph: Navy doctor, *5276*
Harrison, Richard: Lawyers admitted to practice before the Supreme Court, *4633*
Harrison, Robert Hanson: Supreme Court of the United States, *2742*
Harrison, Wallace Kirkman: Elliptical office building, *2096*
Harrison, William Henry: National political convention to adopt the unit rule, *3334*
President to die in Washington, *6189*
President whose grandson became president, *6188*
Presidential candidate to make a campaign speech, *3402*
Vice president to succeed to the presidency after the death of a president, *6245*
Whig Party convention, *3350*
Harroun, Ray: Long-distance car race on a racetrack, *7267*
Hart, Edwin Giles: Citrons, *3905*
Hart, Joseph C.: Novel about whaling, *1842*
Hart, Robert M.: Transoceanic radio signal conveying a television image, *7828*
Hartford, George Huntington: Chain store organization, *2493*
Hartle, Russell Peter: American expeditionary force to land in Europe in World War II, *8052*
Hartly, Thomas: Lawyers admitted to practice before the Supreme Court, *4633*
Harts, Rutherford B.: Photograph showing air in motion across airplane wings, *5822*
Hartsfield, William Berry: Pinball ban enacted by a city, *7455*
Harvard, John: College founded in America, *2925*
Harvey, Charles T.: Elevated railroad, *6334*

Harvey, George Brinton McClellan: Esperanto club, 5717

Harvey, Harry Edward: Dentist in the Navy to serve aboard a naval ship, 5020

Harvey, John: Salt works, 3930
Treason trial by a colony, 2833

Haskell, Emma: Public school for children with disabilities, 3019

Haskell, James Richards: Rifled breechloading steel cannon, 8101

Haskin, Dewitt Clinton: Tunnel construction using compressed air, 3616

Haskins, Charles Waldo: Accounting society (state), 3756

Haskins, Roswell Willson: Superintendent of schools hired by a city, 3055

Haslett, Lewis Phectic: Gas mask, 4402

Hassall, William: Nail machine, 7921

Hassler, Ferdinand Rudolph: Coast survey, 5956

Hasson, Esther Voorhees: Navy nurses' corps, 5018

Hassrick, Peter H.: Art museum of importance devoted to the work of an individual woman, 5600

Haswell, Charles Haynes: Navy officer to become an engineer, 5282

Hatch, Charles P.: Oil tank railroad cars, 6376

Hatch, Fred L.: Silo, 1051

Hathaway, Isaac Scott: Coin bearing the likeness of an African-American, 5379

Hatswick, F. Gregory: Crossword puzzle book, 2004

Hatton, Anne Julia Kemble: Opera of a serious nature, 1344

Haubner, Theodore D.: Radio SOS call from an American ship, 6287

Haughwout, E.V.: Elevator with a completely enclosed car, 2105

Haugland, Vern: Silver Star Medal awarded to a civilian, 1662

Havemeyer, Theodore A.: Golf association (national), 7340

Haviland, John: Arcade, 2061

Hawes, Harriet Boyd: Volunteer unit made up of college women to serve overseas, 5185

Hawes, Russell L.: Envelope folding machine, 5763

Hawkins, Benjamin Waterhouse: Dinosaur skeleton found in the United States, 6744

Hawks, Frank Monroe: Seaplane glider, 1550
Transcontinental glider tow, 1551

Hawley, Gideon: Superintendent of schools hired by a state, 3052

Hawley, R.S.: Dog racetrack to use an imitation rabbit, 7278

Hay, John: Arts and letters organization (national), 5716
Use of "American" as an adjective, 1098

Hay, Merle D.: Soldiers in the American army killed in combat in World War I, 8038

Hayden, Hiram Washington: Brass spinning, 4468

Hayden, Horace Henry: Dental society (national), 5034

Hayes, Janet Gray: Mayor of a major city who was a woman, 2210

Hayes, John J.: Olympic athlete from the United States to win the marathon race, 7553

Hayes, Lucy Webb: President to celebrate his silver wedding anniversary at the White House, 6191

Hayes, Rutherford Birchard: Cabinet member who had served as a Confederate officer, 6107
President to celebrate his silver wedding anniversary at the White House, 6191
Strike suppressed by federal troops in peacetime, 4594

Hayhurst, C.W.: Walkie-Talkie two-way radio device, 7722

Hayhurst, Susan: Pharmacist who was a woman to receive a degree from a pharmacy college, 3147

Haynes, Lemuel: Congregational Church minister who was African-American, 6522

Haynesworth, George E.: Act inaugurating the Civil War, 7946

Hays, Isaac: Medical encyclopedia, 1833

Hayward, Ann: Wedding during a parachute jump, 4822

Hazard, Erskine: Suspension bridge of iron wire, 3570

Hazen, Elizabeth: Fungicide used medicinally, 5001

H'Doubler, Margaret Newell: Dance major at a college, 2909

Heady, Thomas: Play presented by professional players, 1242

Healy, James Augustine: Catholic bishop who was an American-born African-American, 6480

Healy, Michael A.: Coast Guard serviceman who was African-American, 5209

Heanue, John: Holographic data storage system, 2540

Hearst, Phoebe Apperson: Parent-teacher association (national), 3227

Heath, Frederick: School stadium, 7509

Heath, George: Car race for the Vanderbilt Cup, 7264

Hecht, Harold: Oscar for best picture awarded to a movie that was independently produced, 1637

Heck, Barbara: Methodist preacher, 6557

Heddon, James: Wooden plug lure for fishing, 7287

Hefflinger, William Walter: Football game played indoors, *7319*

Heflin, Alma: Test pilot who was a woman, *1603*

Heineman, Arthur S.: Motel, *2429*

Heinisch, Rochus: Cutlery shears, *4368*

Heinz, Henry John: Prepared-food producer, *3945*

Heinze, Shirley Rowell: Army War College graduates who were women, *3206*

Heisman, John: Football player to win the Heisman Trophy for excellence in college football, *1725*

Heiss, Carol Elizabeth: National women's figure skating four-time winner, *7434*

Helguera, Leon: Postage stamp issued jointly by two countries, *6069*

Helms, Thomas: Suicidal person to jump off the Empire State Building and live, *2844*

Hendee, George M.: Motorcycle with a built-in gasoline engine, *5489*

Henderson, George: College extension courses, *2997*

Henderson, James Arnold: Artificial animal breeding cooperative organization, *1083*

Henderson, Lawrence Joseph: History of science society (national), *6795*

Hendricks, Gerhard: Protest against slavery, *2240*

Hendricks, Harmon: Copper rolling mill, *4464*

Henefelt, Frank: Pacemaker to be implanted in a patient's body, *4953*

Henenberg, Hattie L.: State supreme court in which all the judges were women, *2724*

Henke, Milburn: American expeditionary force to land in Europe in World War II, *8052*

Henley, David: Court-martial by the Army, *2739*

Hennepin, Louis: Coal, *3501*

Henriques, J. A.: Coast Guard officers' training school, *3209*

Henry, Charles Lewis: Interurban streetcar line, *6403*

Henry, John: Play by an American writer to be successfully presented by an established company, *1246*

Henry, Joseph: Electric bell for electromagnets, *3452*
Electromagnet, *3451*
Electromagnetic telegraph, *7686*
Radio impulse transmission, *6304*

Henry, William: Steamboat, *6853*

Hensley, William Nicholas: Radio two-way broadcast from an airplane, *6273*

Henson, Matthew Alexander: Discovery of the North Pole, *6727*

Herbert, H.L.: Polo association (national), *7459*

Herbert, Henry William: Sportswriter, *5612*

Herbert, Sister Xavier: Hospital, *4868*

Hering, Constantine: Homeopathic medical society, *5031*
Homeopathy school, *3161*

Herjolffson, Bjarni: European to sight America, *5889*

Herman, Peter: Boxing match broadcast on radio from ringside, *7239*

Herndon, Hugh, Jr.: Transpacific nonstop airplane flight, *1454*

Herrera, Pete: Horse race for a purse of more than $1 million, *7404*

Herreshoff, John Brown and Nathanael Greene: Torpedo boat, *6924*

Herreshoff, Nathanael Greene: Catamaran, *7213*

Herrmann, Augustine: Czech settler in America, *5921*

Hershey, Milton Snavely: Chocolate bars, *3965*

Herskovitz, Anatol: Movie showing the inside of a living heart, *4910*

Herter, Christian Archibald: Communications satellite with signal reception and transmission equipment, *7065*

Hertz, Alfred: Opera composed by a woman to be performed at the Metropolitan Opera House, *1348*

Herz, Wilhelm: Motorcycle to exceed 200 miles per hour, *5491*

Hessel, John: Walkie-Talkie two-way radio device, *7722*

Hesselink, Lambertus: Holographic data storage system, *2540*

Hesselius, Gustavus: Painter to obtain a public commission, *1198*

Hetzel, Henry W.: Movie in Esperanto, *5561*

Heuring, Vincent P.: Optical computer, *2539*

Hewitt, Don: Television newsmagazine, *5708*

Hewitt, James: Opera of a serious nature, *1344*

Hewitt, John Hill: Secular song hit, *1379*

Heyl, Henry Renno: Animated photograph projection before a theater audience, *5529*

Heyward, Dorothy and DuBose: Play on Broadway in which an African-American actress had a starring role, *1267*

Heyward, Thomas: Public museum, *5576*

Hiacoomes: Native American preacher of Christianity, *6513*

Hiawatha: League of Native American nations, *5897*

Hibbard, Frederick Cleveland: Statue to commemorate literary characters, *5413*

Hickey, Deirdre: Train operated exclusively by women, *6436*

Hickey, Thomas: Execution by the Army, *2795*

Hickman, C.N.: Handheld rocket launcher, *8133*

Hicks, Hassel T.: City parking garage, *5484*

Hicks, James: Surgical operation on a bull to correct a sperm block, *5124*

Higgins, Thomas Joseph: College classes intended to combat the influence of communism, *3002*

Higinbotham, William: Video game, *4013*

Higley, John: Copper coins, *5354*

Higley, Samuel: Steel, *4490*

Hildebrandt, Martin: Tattoo shop, *4053*

Hill, Alfred: Pronghorn antelope, *1148*

Hill, Frank A.: Pilot from the United States to shoot down a German fighter plane in World War II, *8059*

Hill, Ira H.: Globe factory, *4798*

Hill, John: Business manual, *1793*

Hill, Samuel Eugene: Bibles in hotel rooms, *6579*

Hill, Samuel Lapham: Free kindergarten, *3075*

Hill, Ureli Corelli: Orchestra of international stature, *1358*

Hill, Walter: Tank crew to cross the 38th parallel in the Korean War, *7980*

Hillegas, Michael: Musical instrument dealer, *1279*

Hiller, Clarence B.: Fingerprint conviction in a crime, *4163*

Hilles, Samuel: College founded as a Quaker institution, *2942*

Hillquit, Morris: Socialist Party national convention, *3372*

Hilton, William: Forest fire lookout tower, *3729*

Hinckley, John Warnock, Jr.: President to be wounded in an unsuccessful assassination attempt while in office, *6207*

Hine, Thomas Buck: Smokescreen for concealing the movement of troops and ships, *5247*

Hines, Edward Norris: Traffic lanes designated by painted lines, *4223*

Hines, Paul: Unassisted triple play in organized baseball, *7120*

Hinkle, Clark: College football player to score 50 points in one game, *7307*

Hires, Charles Elmer: Root beer, *3846*

Hirohito: Emperor of Japan to visit the United States, *6655*

Hirschfeld, Harry: Demonstration of home reception of television, *7812*

Hiss, Philip: Apartment house to occupy a square city block, *2127*

Hitchcock, Edward: Dinosaur fossils, *6739*
Geological survey for a state government, *6708*

Hitchcock, Lambert: Chair factory, *4321*

Hitchcock, Thomas: International polo series, *7458*

Hitz, John: Zinc, *5325*

Hitz, William: Cabinet member convicted of a crime, *6110*

Hoagland, Herbert Case: Newsreel, *5697*

Hoballah, Mahmoud: Mosque, *6605*

Hoban, James: Building erected in Washington, DC, by the federal government, *2116*

Hobbs, Lucy B.: Dentist who was a woman to obtain a D.D.S. degree, *4862*

Hobby, Oveta Culp: Army corps for women, *5189*

Hobson, Frank M.: Submarine emergency air supply container, *6967*

Hobson, Henry Wise: Trailer church, *6534*

Hobson, Joseph: Underwater railroad tunnel to a foreign country, *3617*

Hobson, Richmond Pearson: Alcohol prohibition vote taken in Congress, *2682*

Hochmuth, Bruno Arthur: General killed in Vietnam by enemy fire, *8018*

Hodder, James: Arithmetic book printed in America, *1881*

Hodge, Paul Rapsey: Fire engine with a steam boiler, *4100*

Hodges, Duane D.: Naval ship to surrender in peacetime without a fight, *6947*

Hodges, Elizabeth: Meteorite known to have struck a person, *6682*

Hodgson, Ralph: Oiled silk patent, *7864*

Hoe, Richard March: Rotary printing press, *5777*

Hoe, Robert: Cylinder and flatbed combination printing press, *5775*

Hoevenbergh, Henry Van: Flicker animation, *5530*

Hoff, Ted: Microprocessor, *3446*

Hoffman, Adon J.: Steam-operated pressing machine, *4414*

Hoffman, Dustin: Oscar for best picture awarded to an X-rated movie, *1638*

Hoffman, Edward L.: Parachute known as the "free parachute", *1583*

Hoffman, Jacob Rosecrans: Sawmill to use a band saw, *4404*

Hoffman, William Joseph: X-ray movies of human organs in action, *4908*

Hoften, James Van: Satellite repair in orbit, *7077*

Hoge, David: District land office, *5953*

Hoisington, Elizabeth Paschel: Army generals who were brother and sister, *5160*

Hoisington, Perry Milo: Army generals who were brother and sister, *5160*

Holbrook, Amos: Vaccination program offered by a city, *4917*

Holbrook, Josiah: Industrial school, *3282*
Lyceum for adult education, *2884*

Holcomb, Amasa: Photograph taken in the United States, *5811*
Reflecting telescope, *6663*

Holcomb, Thomas: Marine general, *5237*

Holden, Paul Robert: Pilot wounded in Vietnam who was a civilian, *8013*

Holden, William: Movie to be shown simultaneously on pay television and in movie theaters, *5519*

Holden, William Woods: Governor to be impeached and convicted, *7615*

Holderied, Kristine: Naval Academy students who were women, *3221*

Holladay, Wilhemina Cole: Art museum devoted to work by women, *5599*

Holland, Andrew M.: Peep show using film in a vending machine, *3691*

Holland, Clifford Milburn: Underwater highway tunnel with twin tubes, *3618*

Holland, Jerome Heartwell: New York Stock Exchange member who was African-American, *3834*

Holland, John P.: Submarine that was practical and submersible, *6964*

Holldobler, Bert: Pulitzer prize awarded to a science book, *1718*

Hollerith, Herman: Electric tabulating machine, *2364*

Hollingshead, Richard Milton, Jr.: Drive-in movie theater, *3709*

Hollingsworth, Lyman: Manila paper, *5752*

Hollis, Thomas: Planetarium, *6658*

Holly, Birdsall: Heating system to heat buildings from a central station, *2078*

Holly, George N.: Motorcycle endurance run, *7437*

Holm, Hanya: Copyright registered for a choreographic score, *1237*

Holm, Jeanne Marjorie: Air Force general who was a woman, *5140*

Holman, Francis: Intercity stagecoach service, *2184*

Holmes, Edwin Thomas: Burglar alarm, *2132*
Telephone switchboard or exchange, *7728*

Holmes, Francis Simmons: Public museum, *5576*

Holmes, Israel: Brass wire and tubing, *4465*

Holt, Benjamin: Oratorio performance, *1288*
Tractor with an endless chain, *1053*

Holt, Hamilton: College to use the unit-cost plan, *2966*

Holt, Harold G.: Army armored car unit, *5187*

Holt, John: Jewish prayer book, *1954*

Holt, Luther Emmett: Pediatrics book, *1920*

Holyoke, Edward Augustus: Medical society (state), *5030*

Homer, Winslow: Building designed to be used by artists, *2062*

Hook, Albert H.: Cigarette-manufacturing machine, *2705*

Hooker, Thomas: Constitution to declare that "the foundation of authority is in the free consent of the people", *1099*

Hooper, Elihu Morgan: Leprosy hospital, *4887*

Hoover, Herbert Clark: Absolute monarch to visit the United States, *6650*
Asteroid named for an American president, *6678*
President to invite the president-elect, *6165*
Presidential nomination ceremony broadcast on radio, *3412*
Radio broadcast from the Senate chamber, *2631*
Skyscraper higher than 1,250 feet, *2100*
Telecast of image and sound, *7827*

Hoover, J. Edgar: Execution of an organized crime leader in the electric chair, *2803*

Hoover, Lou Henry: College graduate in geology who was a woman, *3241*

Hopkins, Esek: Commander-in-chief of the Continental Navy, *5277*
Navy fleet, *5257*

Hopkins, John: Dinosaur skeleton found in the United States, *6744*

Hopkins, Mary Gross: Village improvement society, *2191*

Hopkins, Samuel: Patent granted by the federal government, *4648*

Hopkins, Stephen: Corn found by English settlers, *3908*
Duel, *2807*

Hopkinson, Francis: Composer born in America, *1327*
Music book printed from type, *1935*
Secular song by a composer born in America, *1375*
Songbook of secular songs by a composer born in America, *1938*
Work of satirical fiction, *1837*

Hopper, Edward: Modern art exhibition, *1228*

Hopper, Grace Murray: Computer bug, *2527*
Medal of Technology awarded to a woman, *1655*

Horgan, Stephen Henry: Halftone engraving, *1227*

Horlick, William: Malted milk, *3872*

Hormel, George A.: Canned ham, *3941*

Hornblower, Josiah: Steam engine for industrial use, *4388*

Horner, William Edmonds: Pathology textbook, *1907*

Horrocks, Jeremiah: Building and loan association, *3763*

Horton, Everett: Fishing rod of telescoping steel tubes, *7932*

Hosier, Harry: Methodist minister who was African-American, *6559*

Hoskin, E. William: French newspaper, *5662*

Hoskins, Timo: Insurance board established by a state government, *4503*

Hosmer, Bradley Clark: Air Force academy, *3190*

Houdry, Eugene: Aviation gasoline obtained by the catalytic cracking method, *3539*

Hough, Franklin Benjamin: Forestry book, *1990*

Houghton, Alanson Bigelow: Transatlantic radio fax of a drawing, *5694*

House, Henry Alonzo: Steam car, *5425*

House, James A.: Steam car, *5425*

House, Royal Earl: Telegraph ticker to print letters of the alphabet, *7691*

Houston, David Henderson: Film rolls for cameras, *5835*

Houston, Sam: President of the Republic of Texas, *4077*

Howard, Charles Willis: Santa Claus school, *4259*

Howard, Philip: Theatrical performance, *1239*

Howard, Taylor: Satellite dish for personal use, *7824*

Howe, Anthony L.: Motorcycle police, *4139*

Howe, Elias: Lock-stitch sewing machine, *4349*

Howe, Gordie: Professional hockey player to reach a score of more than 1,000 points, *7381*

Howe, Hamilton Wilcox: Naval vessel from the United States to sink a German submarine in World War II, *8054*

Howe, John Ireland: Machine for manufacturing pins, *4350*

Howe, Julia Ward: Arts and letters organization (national), *5716*

Howe, Mia: Transoceanic radio signal conveying a television image, *7828*

Howe, Richard: American flag flown in battle, *1120*

Howe, Samuel Gridley: School for blind students, *3023*
School for children with mental disabilities, *3016*

Howell, Edwin Eugene: Relief map, *4800*

Howells, William Dean: Arts and letters organization (national), *5716*

Hower, Nelson: Circus tights, *2265*

Hoyt, Beatrice: Golfer to win the United States Women's Amateur Championship, *7356*

Hoyt, John Wesley: Physiology and hygiene courses at a liberal arts college, *3140*

Hoyt, Wayland: Railroad chapel car, *6381*

Hubbard, Edward: International airmail, *6017*

Hubbard, Henry Griswold: Elastic webbing, *7869*

Hubbard, William: Map made in America to be published in a book, *4792*

Hubbard, William DeHart: Olympic medalist who was African-American, *7444*

Hubbell, Harvey: Electric socket operated by a pull chain, *4344*

Hubble, Edwin Powell: Orbiting observatory, *6673*

Huber, Alice: Hospice for incurable cancer patients, *4888*

Huber, Frederick R.: City orchestra supported by taxes, *1362*

Huck, Winnifred Sprague Mason: Congressional representative who was a mother, *2610*

Huddleson, John W.: Diamonds in actual rock, *5340*

Hudson, Barzillai: Children's magazine, *4695*

Hudson, Seth: Caricature, *1213*

Hudson, William G.: Pilot to destroy an enemy airplane in the Korean War, *7975*

Huebner, George John, Jr.: Transcontinental trip in a gas-turbine car, *5476*

Huffer, John: Combat mission of American pilots ordered to battle in World War I, *8042*

Hufnagel, Charles Anthony: Artificial aortic valve, *5053*

Hufschmidt, Holly A.: Secret Service agents who were women, *4170*

Hughes, Ball: Bronze statue of full length, *5398*

Hughes, Charles Evans: Conference of great powers, *3980*

Hughes, David Edward: Telegraph ticker to print type successfully, *7697*

Hughes, Henry: Sociology treatise, *1989*

Hughes, Howard Robard: Radar for commercial and private planes, *7681*

Hull, Amos Gerald: Homeopathy journal, *4752*

Hull, Cordell: Cabinet member to address a joint session of Congress, *6113*

Hull, George: Prehistoric hoax, *3648*

Hull, Isaac: Naval action of importance in the War of 1812, *8021*

Hume, George W.: Salmon cannery, *3887*

Hume, William: Salmon cannery, *3887*

Humperdinck, Engelbert: Opera broadcast over the radio in its entirety, *1350*
Opera to be televised in its entirety, *1352*

Humphrey, S.D.: Photography magazine, *4719*

Humphreys, David: Sheep of the Merino breed, *1085*

Humphreys, Frederic Erastus: Army pilot to fly solo in an airplane, *1607*

Humphreys, James: Chess book, *1995*

Humphreys, Joshua: Frigate, *6914*
Naval ship of the line, *6913*
Warship builder, *5260*

Humphreys, Richard Franklin: Nuclear reactor built for private industrial research, *3549*

Hunley, Horace L.: Submarine built in the United States to sink an enemy warship in actual warfare, *7968*

Hunnewell, Hollis: Court tennis, *7524*

Hunt, Richard Morris: Apartment house with a modern layout, *2125*
Building designed to be used by artists, *2062*
Hunt, Walter: Lock-stitch sewing machine, *4349*
Paper collar, *2285*
Safety pin, *4336*
Hunter, Dard: Book completed entirely by one man, *1754*
Museum devoted exclusively to papermaking, *5589*
Hunter, David: Execution of a woman by hanging by the federal government, *2798*
Union regiment in the Civil War made up of African-American soldiers, *7966*
Hunter, Robert: Play written in America that was printed, *1241*
Siamese twins, *2170*
Hunter, William: Croup report, *1894*
Huntington, Archer Milton: Maritime museum, *5587*
Huntington, Collis Potter: Cancer research fund, *5056*
Hurba, Edwin Hess: Armored division transported by airplanes to a foreign country, *5193*
Hurd, Nathaniel: Book plate, *1737*
Caricature, *1213*
Hurlbut, Stephen Augustus: Grand Army of the Republic post for veterans of the Civil War, *5310*
Hurt, John: Chaplain of the U.S. Army, *5197*
Hurwitt, Elliott Samuel: Movie showing the inside of a living heart, *4910*
Hüster: Brick roofing tile, *2036*
Huston, John: Oscar winners who were father and son, *1634*
Huston, Walter: Oscar winners who were father and son, *1634*
Hutchins, J.L.: Oil pipeline, *3531*
Hutchins, Levi: Alarm clock, *7898*
Hutchins, Thomas: Geographer of the United States, *6707*
Hutchinson, Anne: Religious leader in the American colonies who was a woman, *6507*
Synod held in America, *6508*
Hutchinson, Miller Reese: Electrical hearing aid, *5070*
Hutchinson, Samuel: Iron exportation, *4447*
Hutchinson, Thomas H.: Television production course at a college, *2913*
Hutchison, Joseph Chrisman: Mastoid operation, *5078*
Hutin, Francisquy: Ballet, *1232*
Hutt, Willard Andre: African-American history trail, *5979*
Hyatt, George William: Tissue bank, *4838*
Hyatt, Isaiah Smith: Celluloid, *4480*

Hyatt, John Wesley: Billiard ball of composition material resembling ivory, *4019*
Celluloid, *4480*
Hyde, Edward: Cross-dresser of note, *6827*
Hyer, Tom: Heavyweight boxing match to last longer than 100 rounds, *7233*

I

Ihm, Carl: Homeopathic medical society, *5031*
Imlay, Richard: Double-deck railroad coaches, *6370*
Impellitteri, Vincent R.: Transatlantic mobile telephone call between two cars, *7765*
Ingalls, David Sinton: Navy ace in World War I, *1613*
Ingalls, Esther Abbie: National skeet tournament, *7479*
Ingalls, Laura: Transcontinental solo airplane flight by a woman, *1453*
Ingersoll, Edward P.: Car magazine, *4788*
Ingles, George B.: Two-handed shovel, *7940*
Ingram, Osmond Kelly: Navy enlisted man killed in World War I action, *8035*
Inouye, Daniel Ken: Congressional representative of Japanese ancestry, *2616*
Irvin, Leslie Le Roy: Parachute known as the "free parachute", *1583*
Irvine, Callender: Factory standardization to federal government specification, *4381*
Irving, Walter Edward: Bridge with open-mesh steel flooring, *3594*
Irwin, Bernard John Dowling: Army field hospital, *5010*
Medal of Honor action, *1670*
Irwin, Harriet Morrison: Architect who was a woman, *1194*
Irwin, Jack K.: Radio distress signal resulting in an airship rescue, *6288*
Irwin, James Benson: Astronauts to ride a vehicle on the moon, *7042*
Isabell: Wedding of colonists in Virginia, *4812*
Isbell, Zachariah: Independent civil government in America, *5939*
Iske, Anthony: Slicing machine, *4296*
Iskra, Darlene: Navy officer who was a woman to command a ship at sea, *5299*
Ives, Frederic Eugene: Halftone printing plate, *5785*
Ives, Irving McNeil: Industrial and labor relations school at a college, *3257*
Izumeda, Rinban: Buddhist temple, *6438*

J

Jabara, James: Ace to fly a jet, *1620*

Jay, William: Coaching club, *7569*
Jefferies, Jim: Championship heavyweight boxing title won in the first round, *7237*
Jeffers, Henry W.: Rotating milking platform, *1056*
Jefferson, Thomas: Bill depicting a battleship, *5392*
Cheese factory cooperative, *3857*
Child born in the White House, *6251*
Congressional caucus, *2584*
Design for the Great Seal of the United States, *1132*
Embargo act enacted by Congress, *2475*
Former vice president to be arrested, *6241*
Gold nugget, *5320*
Guide to parliamentary rules of order, *2016*
President elected by the House of Representatives, *6145*
President inaugurated in the city of Washington, *6146*
President to review the military forces, *6147*
Presidential candidate nominated at a caucus, *3399*
Presidential election in which candidates were nominated for the vice presidency, *3384*
Presidential election in which more than one candidate declared for the presidency, *3383*
Secretary of state, *6104*
Supreme Court decision voiding an act of Congress, *2746*
Territory annexed by the federal government, *5955*
Treaty entered into by the federal government after independence, *4000*
Vice president who was nominated specifically for that office, *6240*
Jeffries, John: Anatomy lectures, *3129*
Jemison, Mae Carol: Astronaut to fly in space who was African-American, *7049*
Jencks, Joseph: Coinage dies, *5353*
Fire engine, *4092*
Manufacturer of metal goods, *4461*
Jenkins, Charles Francis: Telecast of an object in motion, *7825*
Jenkins, Philip O.: Portrait of Abraham Lincoln, *6157*
Jenkins, Therese A.: Delegates to a national political convention who were women, *3338*
Jenney, William Le Baron: Skyscraper, *2098*
Jennings, Hugh A.: Baseball strike, *4595*
Jennings, Thomas: Fingerprint conviction in a crime, *4163*
Jensen, Sandra: Transplant of a major organ into a person with mental retardation, *5107*
Jernigan, Joseph Paul: Comprehensive digital atlas of the human body, *4913*
Jerom, Chauncey: Brass clock works, *7900*

Jessel, George: Radio show sponsored by a co-operative of commercial advertisers, *2338*
Jester, Maurice D.: Navy Cross awarded to a Coast Guard officer in World War II, *1659*
Jewell, Pliny: Belting, *4392*
Jobs, Steven: Personal computer, *2537*
John, Augustus: Transatlantic radio fax of a drawing, *5694*
Johnso, Samuel: Novel by a writer born in America, *1836*
Johnson, Andrew: Election law granting African-American men the right to vote, *3428*
Former president to become a senator, *6160*
President to be impeached, *6159*
Presidential amnesty issued to rebellious citizens, *6143*
Workday of eight hours to be authorized by Congress, *4556*
Johnson, Anthony: Landowner of substance who was African-American, *5928*
Johnson, Ban: Baseball strike, *4595*
Johnson, Billy: Musical comedy written by African-Americans for African-American performers, *1256*
Johnson, Charles Eneu: Printer's ink, *5783*
Johnson, Clarence: Tank crew to cross the 38th parallel in the Korean War, *7980*
Johnson, Clarence L.: Jet-propelled fighter plane, *1489*
Johnson, Eads: Ferryboat built exclusively to transport cars, *6911*
Johnson, Edward: Comet recorded, *6675*
History of New England, *1860*
Johnson, Edward H.: Christmas tree decorated with electric lights, *4257*
Johnson, Frank: Quintuplets to survive infancy who were African-American, *2177*
Johnson, George Arthur: Drinking water supply to be chemically treated with chlorine compounds, *2235*
Johnson, George Washington: Croquet league, *7571*
Johnson, Hazel Winifred: Army general who was an African-American woman, *5162*
Johnson, Henry: Croix de Guerre awarded to an African-American, *1648*
Martini, *2670*
Warship captured overseas, *8000*
Johnson, Herbert Lester: Peritonitis preventive, *4992*
Johnson, Howard Dearing: Franchise chain, *2463*
Johnson, Jack: Heavyweight boxing champion of the world who was African-American, *7252*
Johnson, James B.: Fish hatchery, *1059*
Johnson, James J.: Golfer to play 24 hours continuously on a regulation course, *7365*

Jorgensen, George: Sex-change operation, *6832*

Jortberg, Richard Edmund: Nuclear-powered submarine with turbine-electric drive, *6978*

Josepho, Anatol M.: Film-developing machine, *5840*

Josephus, Flavius: History book by a Jewish author of ancient times, *1862*

Joubert de la Muraille, Jacques Hector Nicholas: Catholic community of African-American nuns, *6462*

Joyner-Kersee, Jackie: Olympic athlete to win two consecutive heptathlon events, *7567*

Judd, Orange: Agricultural experiment station operated by a state, *1003*

Judson, Whitcomb L.: Slide fastener, *2291*

Julius, George: Totalisator to record racetrack bets and odds, *7399*

June, Charles: Ice skating champion, *7427*

Junkin, George: Model laboratory school at a college, *3259*

Junkin, Sam F.: Pilot from the United States to shoot down a German fighter plane in World War II, *8059*

K

Kahanomoku, Duke: Surfer, *7579*

Kahn, Julian Seth: Spray can, *7939*

Kahn, Robert E.: General-purpose computer network, *2544*

Kahnweiler, David: Life preserver of cork, *4119*

Kaiser, Henry J.: Health maintenance organization, *4540*
Victory ship launched, *6896*

Kaiser, Henry John: Ship completed in less than two weeks, *6878*

Kalakaua, David: Reigning king to visit the United States, *6645*

Kalakaua, King: Coronation, *6646*

Kalmus, Herbert Thomas: Movie in Technicolor, *5555*

Kan, Edward Bing: Chinese person granted citizenship, *5874*

Kane, Delancey Astor: Coach riding, *7570*

Kane, Elisha Kent: Arctic expedition by an American explorer, *6724*

Kankus, Roberta A.: Nuclear commercial power plant licensed operator who was a woman, *3555*

Kanouse, Edna Beecham: Quintuplets, *2172*

Kanter, Albert: Comic book versions of literary works, *2030*

Kantrowitz, Adrian: Heart transplant, *5100*
Movie showing the inside of a living heart, *4910*

Kapiolani, Queen: Coronation, *6646*

Kaplan, Henry: Human antibodies produced artificially, *5005*

Kappel, Frederick Russell: Telephone call conveyed by a privately owned satellite, *7768*

Karenga, Ron: Kwanzaa celebration, *4249*

Karp, Haskell: Heart transplant using an artificial heart, *5101*

Karpeles, Leopold: Medal of Honor awarded to a Jewish soldier, *1675*

Kasinga, Fauziya: Political asylum granted to avoid genital mutilation, *5883*

Kasparov, Gary: Chess computer to beat the world chess champion, *4034*

Kasperak, Mike: Heart transplant, *5100*

Kauffman, Doc: Electric guitar, *1325*

Kaufman, George Simon: Pulitzer Prize awarded to a musical, *1712*

Kaufman, Irving Robert: Peacetime death sentence for espionage, *2836*
Television eyewitness allowed to testify in a federal court, *2715*

Kazan, Abraham Eli: Housing cooperative sponsored by a labor union, *4618*

Kean, Edmund: Actor to receive curtain applause, *1275*

Kean, Murray and Thomas: Publicist for a theater company, *3694*

Kean, Thomas: Play by William Shakespeare produced in America, *1243*

Kearse, Amalya Lyle: Judge of the U.S. Court of Appeals who was an African-American woman, *2732*

Keayne, Robert: Military organization established by a colony, *5253*

Keck, William M.: Telescope of importance with a compound objective mirror, *6674*

Keel, Elmo Woodrow: World War II veterans' society officially recognized by Congress, *5313*

Keeler, Leonarde: Lie detector, *4623*

Keeler, Sarah Warren: Lipreading instruction for deaf people, *3035*

Keep, John: Book jacket, *1748*

Keep, Nathan Cooley: Dental school to be associated with a medical school, *3167*

Kegelman, Charles C.: Distinguished Service Cross awarded in enemy-occupied territory, *1660*

Keim, Elwood: Train of airplanes, *1459*

Keim, Jacob: Boardwalk, *2063*

Keimer, S.: Insurance book, *1794*
Shorthand book, *1735*

Keimer, Samuel: Hydrotherapy book, *1887*
Story serialized in a newspaper, *1835*

Keith, Benjamin Franklin: Vaudeville show, *3688*

Kelk, Jon: Pilot to destroy an enemy airplane in the Gulf War, *7973*

Keller, Franklin J.: Public high school to specialize in the performing arts, *3091*

Kellerman, Annette: Movie sex shocker, *5553*

Kelley, Beverly Gwin: Coast Guard officers who were women who served aboard ships, *5214*

Coast Guard ship commander who was a woman, *5215*

Kelley, George B.: National college fraternity for African-American men, *2989*

Kelley, Oliver Hudson: Agriculture organization (national), *1089*

Kellogg, John Harvey: Cereal sold as a breakfast food, *3916*

Kellogg, Will Keith: Cereal sold as a breakfast food, *3916*

Kelly, Gene: Ballet transmitted by satellite, *1238*

Kelly, George E. Maurice: Airplane accident in a solo military airplane that was fatal, *1392*

Kelly, John M.: Transatlantic airplane flight carrying 100 people, *1472*

Kelly, Leontine T.C.: Methodist bishop who was a woman, *6562*

Kelly, Oakley G.: Transcontinental nonstop airplane flight, *1449*

Kelly, William: Chinese labor immigration, *5865*

Kelpius, Magister: Rosicrucian Order lodge, *6598*

Kemeny, John: Educational computer programming language, *2550*

Kemmler, William: Execution by electrocution, *2799*

Kemper, W.H.: Small claims court, *2710*

Kendall, Amos: Telegraph company, *7695*

Kendall, George: Colonial council, *5906*

Rebellion in the English colonies, *5905*

Kendall, Henry: Quark to be observed, *6821*

Kendrick, Captain: Ship to carry the American flag around the world, *1123*

Kenison, Nehemiah: Chiropodist, *4970*

Kenly, William Lacy: Air service under one command, *5131*

Kennedy, Edward Moore: President with a brother in the Senate, *6205*

Three brothers from one family to serve in the Senate, *2656*

Kennedy, Gerald S.: Stockholder meetings televised coast-to-coast simultaneously, *3832*

Kennedy, H.J.: Race between a horse and a bicycle, *7395*

Kennedy, Henry Peres: Reclining chair, *4324*

Kennedy, Jacqueline: Exhibition of the *Mona Lisa* in the United States, *1231*

Kennedy, John Fitzgerald: Cabinet member who was the brother of the president, *6117*

President to witness the firing of a Polaris missile, *6174*

President who was Catholic, *6203*

President with a brother in the Senate, *6205*

Presidential election debates to be shown on television, *3394*

Presidential news conference to be televised live, *6220*

Seawater conversion plant, *2237*

Skyjacking law enacted by Congress, *2785*

Three brothers from one family to serve in the Senate, *2656*

Troops sent to Vietnam, *8014*

World's Fair that was financially successful, *2415*

Kennedy, Robert Francis: Cabinet member who was the brother of the president, *6117*

Presidential campaigner to be assassinated, *3416*

Three brothers from one family to serve in the Senate, *2656*

Kensett, Thomas: Canning of food, *3944*

Kent, Arthur Atwater: Mobile telephone conversation between the ground and an airship, *7761*

Kent, Mabel Lucas: Mobile telephone conversation between the ground and an airship, *7761*

Kent, Rockwell: Radio broadcast heard in both the Arctic and the Antarctic regions, *6277*

Kenyon, David B.: Firehouse pole, *4109*

Kenyon, W. Johnson: Bandage with built-in adhesive, *4945*

Kenyon, William Orlin: Cellulose sponge for household use, *4280*

Kephart, Calvin Ira: Radio broadcast of a debate, *6269*

Kepley, Ada H.: Law school graduate who was a woman, *3124*

Kepner, William E.: Airship made completely of metal, *1524*

Kern, Lou J.: Osteopathic physicians who were women, *4976*

Kernodle, George Riley: Theater and dramatic criticism course at a college, *3105*

Kerns, James N.: Baseball league, *7096*

Kerr, Ann: Sailors assigned to regular Navy shipboard duty who were women, *5269*

Kerr, George: International professional tennis contest, *7530*

Kerr, Gordon Campbell: Birth to be televised for the public, *2164*

Kerst, Donald William: Betatron, *6801*

Kerwin, Joseph Peter: Physician to practice as an astronaut in space, *7045*

Space station launched by the United States, *7085*

Kesselering, Boyd: Airmail and express service by helicopter, *6031*

Kettering, Charles Franklin: Electric self-starter used in cars, *5442*

Kevorkian, Jack: Death by suicide machine, *2845*

Key, David McKendree: Cabinet member who had served as a Confederate officer, *6107*

Key, Philip Barton: Temporary insanity defense in a criminal case, *4622*

Keys, John: Civil War call for volunteers, *7951*

Keys, Martha Elizabeth: Congressional representatives to marry each other, *2622*

Keys Sisters: Quadruplets to graduate from college, *2173*

Khomeini, Ruhollah: Hostage crisis, *3982*

Khorana, Har Gobind: Artificial gene, *5063*

Kidd, Isaac Campbell: Navy admiral killed in action in World War II, *8068*

Kidd, William: Workers' compensation agreement, *4550*

Kieft, Wilhelm: Curfew bell, *2180*

Kieft, Willem: Antismoking law enacted by a colony, *2696*

Kier, Samuel M.: Oil refinery, *3526*

Kiernan, John James: Financial news agency, *5624*

Kiernan, Leo: Round-the-world airplane passenger race, *7299*

Kilby, Jack: Integrated circuit, *3444*

Kilby, Jack S.: Charles Stark Draper Prize for engineering and technology, *1645*

Kilby, Thomas Erby: Coin bearing the likeness of a living person, *5377*

Kildall, Gary: Personal computer operating system, *2546*

Kilgallen, Dorothy: Round-the-world airplane passenger race, *7299*

Kilgore, Evelyn Pinckert: Airplane instructor's license, *1601*

Kill Buck, Captain John: Treaty entered into by the federal government with Native American tribes, *5941*

Killebrew, Emmet Stephen: Hydroelectric power plant operated by a county, *3480*

Kilpatrick, Judson: Civil War bloodshed north of the Mason-Dixon Line, *7967*

Kimball, Ernest: Cafeteria, *2459*

Kimball, Francis Henry: Building with caisson foundations, *2083*

Kimball, Justin Ford: Hospital insurance group plan, *4535*

Kimball, Sumner Increase: Lifesaving service established by the federal government, *4121*

Kinder, Arthur: Haircloth, *7866*

King, Billie Jean: Athlete who was a woman to earn more than $100,000 in one season, *7540*

King, Billy: Race between a horse and a bicycle, *7395*

King, Charles Brady: Automobile club, *5465*
Car with the steering wheel on the left side, *5438*
Pneumatic hammer, *7934*

King Charles II: Naturalization act in the American colonies, *5859*

King, Coretta Scott: Vietnam War Moratorium Day demonstration, *8019*

King, Ernest Joseph: Navy admirals to wear the five-star insignia, *5273*

King George VI: King and queen to be shown on television, *6653*
King of Great Britain to visit the United States, *6652*

King, Martin Luther, Jr: Mass boycott by civil rights protesters, *2259*

King, Martin Luther, Jr.: Martin Luther King Day, *4251*

King Peter II (Petar Karadjordjević): European king buried in the United States, *6654*

King, Samuel Archer: Aerial photograph, *5815*

King, William: Cork manufacturer, *2043*

King, William Rufus De Vane: Vice president sworn in on foreign soil, *6246*

Kingsford, Thomas: Cornstarch made commercially from maize, *3912*

Kinney, Dita H.: Army nurse corps for women, *5017*

Kinsey, Alfred Charles: Scientific survey of sexual behavior among Americans, *6831*

Kip, Charles Hayden: Cooperative store at a college, *2497*

Kirby, Ephraim: Law report, *1874*

Kirby, Fred Morgan: Civil rights chair at a college, *3128*

Kirby, Rollin: Pulitzer Prize for an editorial cartoon, *1710*

Kirkbride, Raymond Watson: College program of study abroad, *2995*

Kirkham, Charles: Airplane with a fuselage of molded plywood, *1395*
Fighter plane, *1486*

Kirkham, Thomas: Futurity horse race, *7390*

Kirkpatrick, Jeanne Duane Jordan: Ambassador to the United Nations who was a woman, *3996*

Kirsch, Hyman: Sugar-free soft drinks, *3847*

Kirstein, Lincoln: Ballet on an American theme by an American choreographer, *1236*

Kiss, Max: Laxative in candy form, *4991*

Kitchen, Stuart Fordyce: Yellow fever vaccine for human immunization, *4922*

Kittinger, Joe: Transatlantic solo balloon flight, *1545*

Kizer, Noble: All-star football game, *7327*

Kleid, Kerry: Motorcycle racer who was a woman, *7440*

Klein, Nelson Bernard: Death penalty authorized by federal law, *2802*

Kleindienst, Richard Gordon: Attorney general to plead guilty to a criminal offense, *6126*

Klemm, Johann Gottlob: Organ built in the United States, *1304*

Kliegl, Anton Tiberius: Klieg light unit for movie production, *5572*

Kliegl, John Hugh: Klieg light unit for movie production, *5572*

Kligman, Albert: Anti-aging skin cream, *4063*

Kline, A. C.: Postage stamp catalog, *2026*

Knabenshue, A. Roy: Balloon to land on a building, *1540*

Knabenshue, Roy: Airship race, *7291*

Knapp, James Henry: Derby hat, *2295*

Kneeland, Samuel: History book by a Jewish author of ancient times, *1862*
Religious magazine, *4693*

Knerr, Richard: Flying disk for use in throwing games, *7585*

Knievel, Robert Craig "Evel": Motorcycle jump across a river canyon, *3682*

Knight, Arthur F.: Golf club with a steel shaft, *7353*

Knight, Frederick Irving: Laryngology journal, *4757*

Knight, James: Orthopedic hospital, *4881*
Private school for children with disabilities, *3017*

Knight, Jonathan: Medical society (national), *5036*

Knight, Margaret: Paper bag machine, *4405*

Knowles, Asa Smallidge: College principally for war veterans, *2967*

Knox, Thomas Wallace: News reporter tried as a spy, *5615*

Knox, William: Bowler to make a perfect score of 300, *7224*

Knudsen, William Signius: Army general appointed from civilian rank, *5156*

Koelsch, John Kelvin: Medal of Honor awarded to a helicopter pilot, *1685*

Koenig, Alfred J.: Transpacific radio fax transmission, *7670*

Koenig, George Augustus: Diamonds in a meteorite, *5338*

Koenig, Shlomo: Police officer who was a Chassidic Jew, *4157*

Koester, Heinrich Bernhard: Lutheran services in English, *6556*

Koester, M.: Bowling tournament for women, *7225*

Kogel, Marcus David: Medical college founded as a Jewish institution, *3179*

Kolb, Lawrence: Drug treatment center for addicts established by Congress, *2688*

Kolb, Robert: Army helicopter battalion, *5191*

Koons, Franklin M.: Soldier from the United States to land on French soil in World War II, *8060*

Kopsky, Doris: Bicycle champion who was a woman, *7197*

Korizek, Frank: Czech newspaper, *5669*

Koster, Henry: Movie in Cinemascope, *5562*

Krafft, Michael: Parade held by a mystic society, *3659*

Krafft, Michael August: Distilling book, *1848*

Kramer, Stanley: Movie premiered simultaneously in major cities throughout the world, *5520*

Kramer, Walter R.: Badminton championship tournament, *7584*

Kraus, C. Raymond: Public telecast over telephone wires using the narrow-band system, *7848*

Kreps, Juanita Morris: New York Stock Exchange seat owner who was a woman, *3833*

Kreusi, John: Phonograph, *7004*

Kroc, Ray: McDonald's restaurant, *2464*

Krone, Julie: Jockey who was a woman to win a Triple Crown race, *7421*

Kross, Anna Moscowitz: Prison commissioner who was a woman, *2830*

Krueger, Otto: Radio orchestra, *1364*

Kuchins, Harry: Glider flight indoors, *1549*

Kuhn, Adam: Botany professor at a college, *3229*

Kuhn, Richard J.: X-ray three-dimensional stereo fluoroscopic system, *4911*

Kujiraoka, Sozaburo: Japanese person to receive an immigration visa, *5876*

Kunst, David: Round-the-world journey on foot, *7590*

Kunze, Johann Christoff: Lutheran hymnbook, *1971*

Kunzi, Abraham: Quinine, *4983*

Kurtz, Thomas: Educational computer programming language, *2550*

Kurzweil, Raymond: Voice reader, *2538*

Kuskof, Ivan Alexandrovich: Russian settlement, *5943*

Kwolek, Stephanie L.: Thread as strong as steel, *7880*

Kyrides, Lucas Petrou: Synthetic rubber, *4488*

L

La Farge, John: Arts and letters organization (national), *5716*

La Farge, Oliver: Native American art exhibition, *1229*

La Follette, Philip: Unemployment insurance act, *4525*

La Follette, Robert Marion: Newsreels showing presidential candidates, *5698*

La Mountain, John: Balloon carrier, *6919*

La Porte, Arthur Earl: Transatlantic airmail service, *6028*

La Rocca, Nick: Jazz record, *1294*

Labadie, Jean de: Labadist community, *6514*

Laban, Rudolf: Copyright registered for a choreographic score, *1237*

Lafayette, Marquis de: Citizenship conferred by special grant, *5861*

Grant of federal land to a foreigner, *5954*

Lafferty, James V.: Building shaped like an elephant, *2079*

Lagan, M.D.: Leprosy hospital, *4887*

Lahm, Frank Purdy: Airplane purchased by the federal government, *1389*

Balloon cup race, *7288*

Lake, Simon: Radio telephone message from a submerged submarine to shore, *7755*

Submarine fitted with an internal combustion engine, *6963*

Lalande, John: Catholic saints who were active in North America, *6472*

Lallemont, Pierre: Bicycle with a rotary crank, *7181*

Lamarr, Hedy: Movie star who was a weapons inventor, *5527*

Lamb, John: Employment office established by a city, *4566*

Lamb, William Frederick: Skyscraper higher than 1,250 feet, *2100*

Lambine, Janna: Coast Guard airplane pilot who was a woman, *5213*

Lamson, Eleanor Annie: Astronomer employed in the Naval Observatory who was a woman, *6667*

Lancaster, Burt: Oscar for best picture awarded to a movie that was independently produced, *1637*

Land, Edwin Herbert: Instant camera, *5846*

Landis, Kenesaw Mountain: Baseball commissioner, *7098*

Landis, Merkel: Christmas savings club at a bank, *3793*

Landreth, Cuthbert: Horticultural magazine, *4711*

Landreth, David: Horticultural magazine, *4711*

Seed business, *1011*

Landsteiner, Karl: Nobel Prize for physiology or medicine awarded to an American citizen, *1693*

Rh factor discovery, *4835*

Lane, Dick: Commercial television station west of the Mississippi River, *7797*

Lane, Ephraim: Tungsten and tellurium, *5322*

Lane, Ralph: Letters written in English in America, *1095*

Lane, Thomas Joseph: Congressional representative reelected after serving a prison term, *2615*

Lane, William Coolidge: Bibliography organization (national), *4691*

Lane, William Henry: Tap dancer of renown, *1233*

Langan, Jack: Boxing arena, *7503*

Langdon, John: Navy fleet, *5257*

Senate president pro tempore, *2625*

Session of the Senate, *2624*

Vice presidential candidate to decline the nomination, *3400*

Langdon, Kay Louise: Navy personnel in the regular Navy who were women, *5266*

Langenheim, Frederick: Photograph of a solar eclipse, *6694*

Langenheim, William and Frederick: Photograph to gain world fame, *5814*

Langer, Jerry: Motorboat ocean race, *7218*

Langford, Nathaniel Pitt: National park, *3735*

Langley, Samuel Pierpont: Airplane model to make a sustained flight under its own power, *1425*

Langloiserie, Louis: French instruction at a college, *3110*

Langstroth, Lorenzo Lorraine: Beehive with removable frames, *1050*

Lansdowne, Zachary: Rigid airship, *1521*

Lansky, Meyer: Casino in Las Vegas, *3636*

Lanston, Tolbert: Monotype machine, *5806*

Lapchick, Joe: All-Star Game of the National Basketball Association, *7174*

Larkin, Thomas Oliver: Consul to California, *3987*

Larsen, Donald James: Baseball pitcher to pitch a perfect no-hit, no-run, no-walk World Series game, *7153*

Lassen, Louis: Hamburger, *3940*

Lasseter, John: Movie that was entirely computer-animated, *5539*

Lasswell, Harold Dwight: Propaganda course at a college, *3256*

Latham, Woodville: Movie recorded on film to be shown on a screen, *5510*

Lathrop, Mary Florence: American Bar Association member who was a woman, *4640*

Lathrop, Rose Hawthorne: Hospice for incurable cancer patients, *4888*

Latrobe, Benjamin Henry: Architect and engineer who worked professionally, *1193*

Wooden railroad bridge of a purely truss type, *3573*

Latta, Alexander Bonner: Fire engine that was practical, *4102*

Latting, Patience Sewell: Mayor of a major city who was a woman, *2210*

Laudonnière, René Goulaine de: Artist to come to America, *1195*

Colonial warfare between European powers in America, *5900*

Painting of an American scene by a European painter, *1211*

Laughlin, James: Intercollegiate court tennis match, *7534*

Laurence, William Leonard: Transcontinental Picturephone call, *7769*

Laurens, Henry: American imprisoned as an enemy agent in the Tower of London, *8004*

Cremation, *2856*

Laurie, James: Civil engineering society (national), *3609*

Lauterbur, Paul C.: Magnetic resonance image of a human body, *4912*

Law, Frederick Rodman: Stuntman, *3680*

Law, James: Veterinary department at a college, *3182*

Law, Ruth: Airplane flight longer than 500 miles, *1444*

Lawler, Richard Harold: Kidney transplant, *5095*

Lawrence, Cornelius Van Wyck: City mayor elected by popular vote, *2206*

Lawrence, Ernest Orlando: Cyclotron, *6798*

Lawrence, Florence: Movie star who was a woman, *5526*

Lawrence, Gertrude: Broadway play shown in a television version with its original cast, *1266*

Lawrence, John Hunsdale: Radioactive isotope medicine, *4995*

Lawrence, Joseph: Antibacterial mouthwash, *4072*

Lawrence, Richard: President whose assassination was attempted, *6187*

Lawrence, W.G.: National championship stroke-play golf match, *7338*

Lawson, D. Forrest: Jockey who was a woman to ride two winners in one day, *7416*

Lawson, Michael F.: Advertisement on a space vehicle, *2348*

Lawton, Chester S.: Submarine cable plow, *7709*

Laydon, John: Wedding of colonists in Virginia, *4812*

Le Breton, David McDougal: Navy task force assembled for foreign service, *5302*

Le Moyne de Morgues, Jacques: Artist to come to America, *1195*

Painting of an American scene by a European painter, *1211*

le Moyne, Pierre: Mardi Gras, *4234*

Le, Simeon Newton: Young Men's Hebrew Association, *5714*

Leahy, William Daniel: Navy admirals to wear the five-star insignia, *5273*

Leary, Timothy: Space burial, *2846*

Leason, George: Calico printery, *7859*

Leavitt, Samuel: Newspaper clipping bureau, *5625*

Lechford, Thomas: Lawyer disbarred, *4632*

Leder, Philip: Patent on an animal, *6751*

Lee, Ann: Conscientious objectors, *5217*

Shaker religious community, *6521*

Lee, Arthur: Treaties entered into by the federal government, *3998*

Lee, E. Hamilton: Father and son to become commercial airline pilots, *1602*

Lee, Ezra: Submarine built for use in war, *6961*

Lee, Henry: Congressional eulogy for a president, *6185*

Lee, Homer: Tank crew to cross the 38th parallel in the Korean War, *7980*

Lee, James Parrish: Golf book, *2003*

Lee, Jarena: African Methodist Episcopal preacher who was a woman, *6565*

Lee, John W.: Navy commissioned officer who was African-American, *5290*

Lee, Mark C.: Husband and wife to fly in space together, *7052*

Lee, Rex E.: Trial in which lawyers appeared on a Picturephone, *4625*

Lee, Robert E.: Father and son to become commercial airline pilots, *1602*

Lee, Robert Edward: Journalism course at a college, *3097*

Lee, Samuel, Jr.: Patented pills, *4981*

Lee, Tempe: Women's club, *5732*

Lee, Thomas Sim: Health board established by a city, *4172*

Leech, Daniel Tompkins: Postal directory, *1816*

Leeser, Isaac: Hebrew spelling book, *1858*

Jewish magazine, *4746*

Theological college for Jews, *3272*

Lefavour, Henry: Technical college for women, *2962*

Lefferts, George Morewood: Laryngology journal, *4757*

LeFrak, Samuel Jayson: Private housing development designed as a complete community, *2200*

Leggett, Joseph B.: Baseball team to tour, *7160*

Leggett, William James: Intercollegiate football contest, *7315*

Legins, Ethel: Opera composer who was a woman, *1334*

Leginska, Ethel: Opera composer who was a woman, *1334*

Leidy, Joseph: Dinosaur skeleton found in the United States, *6744*

Leigh, Douglas: Electric sign showing an animated cartoon, *2352*

Leigh, Lewis: Silk dyers, *7888*

Leigh, Vivien: Oscar winners who were husband and wife, *1635*

Leisler, Jacob: Colonist hanged for treason, *2834*

Leister, Claude Willard: Radio broadcast from a zoo, *1189*

Leister, Edward: Duel, *2807*

Leivas, Juan: Rodeo for roping and tying steers, *3690*

Lembke, Charles: Optometry society (national), *5044*

Lemke, William: National Union for Social Justice national convention, *3377*
Union Party convention, *3378*

LeMond, Greg: Bicyclist from the United States to win the Tour de France, *7199*

LeMoyne, Francis Julius: Crematory, *2857*

Lender, Harry: Bagel bakery, *3927*

Lenhart, John L.: Navy chaplain killed in action, *5199*

Lennebacker, George: Fly casting tournament, *7285*

Lennox, Charlotte Ramsay: Novel by a writer born in America, *1836*

Lenox, Walter Scott: Dish set made in America for the White House, *6256*

Lenstra, Arjen: Factoring of a 100-digit number, *6760*

Leon, Jerome Louis: Drug treatment center for minors, *2690*

Leonard, Gardner Cotrell: Academic costume standardization for colleges, *2957*

Leonard, Jonah Fitz Randolph: United Christian Party convention, *3370*

Leonard, R.C.: Indoor fly casting tournament, *7286*

Leonard, Robert Josselyn: Vocational guidance chair at a college, *3295*

Leonard, Samuel: Angle iron, *2040*

Leonard, Sugar Ray: Boxer to win world titles in five weight divisions, *7256*

Leoncavallo, Ruggiero: Opera to be televised from the Metropolitan Opera House, *1353*

Leopold, Aldo: Game management chair at a college, *3078*

Lepke, Louis: Execution of an organized crime leader in the electric chair, *2803*

Lester, John: College cricket club team to tour England, *7274*

Leveaux, Edward H.: Player piano that was completely automatic, *1317*

Levin, Isaac: Cancer hospital established by a city, *4890*

Levin, Lewis Charles: Congressional representative who was Jewish, *2598*

Levingston, William: Theater, *3693*

Levitt, William Jaird: Planned suburban development, *2199*

Levy, Asser: Jew to win full citizenship, *5858*

Levy, Simon Magruder: West Point graduate who was Jewish, *3195*
West Point graduates, *3196*

Levy, Uriah Phillips: Navy officer to abolish corporal punishment on his ship, *5281*

Lewi, Maurice J.: Chiropody school of note, *3174*

Lewin, Richman: Microwave television station, *7804*

Lewis, Andrew and Thomas: Treaty entered into by the federal government with Native American tribes, *5941*

Lewis, Colby: Television production course at a college, *2913*

Lewis, Elizabeth Matthew: West Point instructor who was a woman, *3205*

Lewis, Floyd John: Heart operation in which the deep-freezing technique was employed, *5093*

Lewis, Fulton, Jr.: Radio news program sponsored by a cooperative of commercial advertisers, *2339*

Lewis, George Hill: Radio license, *6293*

Lewis, Henry: Metropolitan Opera orchestra conductor who was African-American, *1339*

Lewis, James Hamilton: Senate whip, *2629*

Lewis, Meriwether: Transcontinental expedition to the Pacific coast, *6721*

Lewis, Morton Lee: Telecast from the stratosphere, *7849*

Lewis, Oliver: Kentucky Derby horse race, *7392*

Lewis, Sinclair: Nobel Prize for literature awarded to an American, *1694*

Lewis, William and Kate: Wedding abroad of a soldier in the American Expeditionary Force, *4817*

Ley, Willy: Airmail flight by rocket, *6026*

Leypoldt, F.: Library journal, *4729*

Li Hung-chang: Chop suey, *3879*

Lick, James: Observatory on a mountaintop, *6666*

Licklider, J.C.R.: General-purpose computer network, *2544*

Lieber, Francis: Encyclopedia compiled by American editors, *1832*

Ligowsky, George: Clay pigeon target for trapshooting, *7474*

Likeoon, Mr.: Chinese theatrical performance, *1250*

Lillard, Harvey: Chiropractor, *4977*

Lillard, John F.B.: Postage stamp for balloon mail, *6059*

Lillehei, C. Walton: Pacemaker, *4952*

Lincoln, Abraham: African-American preacher to deliver a sermon in the House of Representatives, *2588*
Army secret service bureau, *5181*
Bill bearing the likeness of a president, *5387*
Body of a president to lie in state in the Capitol rotunda, *6194*
Civil War bloodshed, *7952*

Civil War call for volunteers, *7951*

Coin bearing the likeness of a president, *5375*

Constitutional amendment proposal to bear the signature of a president, *1108*

Emancipation proclamation, *2252*

Execution of a woman by hanging by the federal government, *2798*

Homestead law enacted by Congress, *5967*

Memorial postage stamp, *6089*

Military service by African-Americans to be authorized by Congress, *5145*

Monument ordered by the federal government from a sculptor who was a woman, *5401*

Mourning postage stamp, *6080*

Portrait of Abraham Lincoln, *6157*

President born beyond the boundaries of the original 13 states, *6186*

President to be assassinated, *6193*

President who received a patent, *6156*

Presidential amnesty issued to rebellious citizens, *6143*

Presidential election in which soldiers in the field were allowed to vote, *3389*

Presidential railroad car, *6225*

Telegram dispatched from an aerial station, *7699*

Thanksgiving Day, *4261*

Transcontinental telegraph line, *7700*

Year in which two presidents were elected, *3388*

Lincoln, Charles: Dog show, *1171*

Lincoln, Enoch: Brothers to serve simultaneously as governors of their respective states, *7610*

Lincoln, Levi: Parkland purchased by a city, *3733*

Lincoln, Levi, Jr.: Brothers to serve simultaneously as governors of their respective states, *7610*

Lincoln, Mary: Pension granted to the widow of a president, *4584*

Lincoln, William E.: Animated picture machine, *5528*

Lind, Jenny: Private railroad car, *6374*

Theater ticket scalpers, *3698*

Lindbergh, Anne Morrow: National Geographic Society gold medal, *1640*

Lindbergh, Charles Augustus: American flag displayed from the right hand of the Statue of Liberty, *1130*

Heart pump, *5060*

Transatlantic solo airplane flight, *1450*

Lindley, Jacob: Land grant university, *2940*

Lineback, John: Cottonseed hulling machine, *1031*

Lineger, Jerry L.: Joint space walk by American and Russian astronauts, *7055*

Lining, John: Weather observations to be systematically recorded, *6766*

Link, Edwin Albert: Flight trainer for airplane pilots, *1500*

Linn, William: Congressional chaplain, *2580*

Linquist, Ona: Vending machine for art, *2401*

Lipman, Hyman L.: Pencil with an attached eraser, *8151*

Lipowsky, Henry: Bohemian church, *6463*

Lipscomb, William Nunn, Jr.: Year in which Nobel Prizes were won by Americans in five of six categories, *1702*

Lipsky, Marcus: Food in an aerosol can, *3953*

Lipsner, Ben B.: Airmail regular service, *6016*

Lipton, Thomas: Ship-to-shore mobile telephone commercial service, *7739*

Lislet, L. Moreau: Law code adopted by a state, *4621*

Litchfield, Paul Weeks: Airship to land and take off from an oceangoing steamship, *1527*

Little, Charles C.: Law book of federal laws then in force, *1880*

Livermore, Mary Ashton Rice: News reporter at a political convention who was a woman, *5614*

Livingood, John Jacob: Radioactive substance produced synthetically, *6816*

Livingston, Edward: Law code adopted by a state, *4621*

Livingston, John Henry: Theology school, *3267*

Livingston, Robert R.: Presidential inauguration, *6136*

Territory annexed by the federal government, *5955*

Lloyd, Wray Devere Marr: Yellow fever vaccine for human immunization, *4922*

Llywellin, John: Shorthand account of a trial, *4619*

Loar, Lloyd: Electric guitar, *1325*

Lobsiger, Lydia: Payment by the Federal Deposit Insurance Corporation, *3784*

Lockard, Joseph L.: Radar used to detect enemy airplanes, *7679*

Locke, Alain Le Roy: Rhodes Scholars, *2961*

Lockwood, Belva Ann Bennett: Equal Rights Party convention, *3363*

Lawyer who was a woman to be admitted to practice before the Supreme Court, *4638*

Lockwood, Lorna Elizabeth: State supreme court chief justice who was a woman, *2730*

Lodge, Benjamin F.: Stone breaking machine, *5324*

Loftus, J.: Horse to win the Triple Crown, *7409*

Logan, James: Library building, *4662*

Translation of a classic, *1736*

Logan, James Harvey: Loganberry, *3904*

Logan, William: Library building, *4662*

Lombardi, G.: Pizzeria, *2462*

Londonberry, Annie: Round-the-world bicycle trip by a woman, *7202*

Long, Crawford Williamson: Anesthetic administered in childbirth, *4830*
General anesthetic, *4828*

Long, Cyril Norman Hugh: Pituitary hormone, *4996*

Long, Robert Cary, Sr.: Museum especially constructed as a museum and art gallery, *5577*

Long, Russell: Senator to win a seat that had been occupied by his father and his mother, *2654*

Longfellow, Henry Wadsworth: Musical with an American theme and original score, *1252*
Poem to win national acclaim, *1947*

Longley, William Harding: Photographs taken under the sea in natural colors, *5825*

Longstreet, William: Steamboat patent, *6855*

Longworth, David: Canning book, *1849*

Loomis, Frank Fowler: Police patrol wagon, *4137*

López de Mendozo Grajales, Martin Francisco: Catholic parish, *6445*

Lord, Andrew: Comb made of ivory, *4066*

Lord, John: Tariff commission established by Congress, *7666*

Lorillard, Griswold: Tuxedo coat, *2272*

Lorillard, Pierre: Horse bred in the United States to win the English Derby, *7407*
Tuxedo coat, *2272*

Loring, Eugene: Ballet on an American theme by an American choreographer, *1236*

Lotbinière, Louis Eustace: Army chaplain who was Catholic, *5194*

Lou, Whalen: New York Stock Exchange seat owner of Chinese ancestry, *3837*

Loud, John J.: Ball-point pen, *8154*

Louis, Joe: Boxing match at which admission tickets sold at $100, *7245*

Lovelace, Francis: Postal route between cities, *5980*

Lovell, James Arthur, Jr.: Astronauts to orbit the moon, *7038*
Astronauts to rendezvous in space with another spacecraft, *7034*
Photograph of a solar eclipse taken from the atmosphere, *6703*

Lovell, Joseph: Surgeon general of the Continental Army, *5165*

Lovering, William Croad: Mutual liability insurance company, *4513*

Low, Carrie: Golf mixed foursome, *7354*

Low, Juliette Gordon: Scouting organization for girls, *2148*

Low Sing: Tong organized crime gang, *2777*

Lowe, Edmund: Movie of feature length made outdoors, *5558*

Lowe, Thaddeus Sobieski Coulincourt: Army balloon corps, *5182*
Balloonist to direct artillery fire, *7964*
Telegram dispatched from an aerial station, *7699*
Water gas plant, *3517*

Lowell, Percival: Planet found beyond Neptune, *6680*

Lowman, Mary D.: Mayor who was a woman, *2207*

Lubcke, Harry R.: Telecast images received in an airplane, *7832*

Lubin, David: Store with fixed prices, *2495*

Lucas, George: Movie to earn more than $400 million in the United States market, *5523*

Lucas, Robert: National political convention to adopt the two-thirds rule, *3333*

Luce, Henry: News magazine featuring photographs, *4736*

Luce, Peggy: Ascent of Mount Everest by an American, *7588*

Luce, Stephen Bleecker: Naval war college, *3216*

Lucid, Shannon W.: Astronaut who was a woman to live in a space station, *7054*
Astronauts who were women, *7047*

Luckett, Hubert: Photograph of a beam of 1-billion-volt x-rays, *5829*

Luckman, Charles: Adjustable stadium, *7512*

Ludlow, Noah Miller: Showboat theater, *3696*

Ludlow, Roger: Constitution to declare that "the foundation of authority is in the free consent of the people", *1099*

Luhring, Marie: Society of Automotive Engineers member who was a woman, *6794*

Luke, Frank: Pilot to receive the Congressional Medal of Honor, *1658*

Lukens, Charles: Boiler plates, *4430*

Lumbrozo, Jacob: Physician who was Jewish, *4962*

Lundy, Benjamin: Abolition newspaper, *5637*

Lunt, George Ashton: Transatlantic crossing attempted by a balloon, *1538*

Lussier, Jean: Daredevil to go over Niagara Falls in a rubber ball, *3681*

Lutter, Grover Cleveland: Bicycle traffic court, *7196*

Lutz, Frank Eugene: Outdoor museum with nature trails, *5585*

Lutz, Isaac C.: Monument to George Washington, *5397*

Luxford, James: Annulment of a marriage by court decree, *4805*

Lykins, Johnston: Magazine in a Native American language, *4744*

Lyle, Benjamin: Tuberculosis hospital for the poor established by a city, *4900*

Lyle, Ethel Hedgeman: Sorority at a college, *2988*

Lyman, Edward Hutchinson Robbins: Theater operated by a city, *3703*

Lyman, William: Iron blast furnace to use anthracite coal successfully, *4453*

Lyman, William W.: Can opener, *4372*

Lynch, Budd: Telecast from a foreign country, *7842*

Lynch, Joe: Boxing match broadcast on radio from ringside, *7239*

Lynch, John Roy: National political convention of a major party presided over by an African-American, *3337*

Lynk, Vandahurst: Medical journal published by an African-American, *4761*

Lyon, Edward L.T.: Army nurse in modern times who was a man, *5173*

Lyon, Frank Farrington: Commercial hydroponicum, *1039*

Lyon, James: Music book by an author born in America, *1934*

Lyon, Mary: College for women, *2944*

Lyon, Matthew: Brawl in the House of Representatives, *2583*

Lyons, Richard M.: Silver Star Medal awarded to a navy chaplain, *1669*

M

Maass, Clara: Postage stamp depicting a nurse, *6099*

Mabie, Hamilton Wright: Social science society (national), *6782*

MacAllan, Jack: Farriers' course at a college, *3299*

MacArthur, Douglas: Army generals to wear the five-star insignia, *5157*
Silver Star Medal awarded to a civilian, *1662*

Macatee, Charles: Transcontinental jet airplane passenger service, *1422*

MacAuliffe, Christa: Space shuttle disaster, *7090*

MacCracken, Henry Mitchell: Academic hall of fame, *5582*

MacCready, Paul: Human-powered aircraft, *1406*

MacDermott, Galt: Rock musical, *1272*

Macdonald, Charles Blair: Amateur golf tournament, *7339*
Golf course with 18 holes, *7348*

MacDonald, Stewart: Naval militia of a state to have a hydroplane, *5256*

MacDonald, Wilson: Monument to an American poet, *5402*

MacDowell, Edward: Arts and letters organization (national), *5716*

MacDowell, Edward Alexander: Composer born in America to win an international reputation, *1329*

Macfadden, Bernarr Adolphus: Penny restaurant, *2460*

Mackay, James: Racing shell, *7469*

Mackenzie, Alexander Slidell: Navy officer condemned for mutiny, *5283*

Mackie, John Freeman: Medal of Honor awarded to a Marine in the Civil War, *1672*

Mackle, Barbara Jane: Ten Most Wanted list, *2783*

Maclure, William: Geology book, *1981*
Geology society (national), *6778*

Macnee, Patrick: British-made television series, *7791*

Macpherson, John: City directory, *1813*

Macready, James A.: Radio broadcast sent from an airplane, *6266*

Macready, John A.: Transcontinental nonstop airplane flight, *1449*

Macready, Renee: Fashion show to be shown on television, *2414*

Macy, R.H.: Macy's Thanksgiving Day Parade, *4262*
Retail store whose sales in one day exceeded $1 million, *2508*

Madison, James: Congressional representative appointed to a presidential cabinet, *2596*
Conscience fund, *2771*
Constitutional amendments, *1107*
President to face enemy gunfire while in office, *6148*

Maffitt, John Newland: Confederate cruiser built in England, *7962*

Magee, Carlton Cole: Automatic parking meter, *5446*

Magee, Patrick: Giant exhibited as a theatrical attraction, *3658*

Magill, Helen: Doctor of Philosophy degree awarded to a woman, *2979*

Magruder, John Bankhead "Jeb": Land mines, *8097*

Maguire, Francis: Irish to arrive in America, *5932*

Mahan, George Addison: Statue to commemorate literary characters, *5413*

Mahoney, Mary Eliza: Nurse to receive formal training, *5023*

Mai-yu, Shih: Physician who was a Chinese woman, *4978*

Maiman, Theodore Harold: Laser, *3443*

Maitland, Lester James: Airplane to fly faster than 200 miles per hour, *1448*

Maller, Donna: West Point graduate who was Jewish, *3195*

Mallinson, Joseph: Iron casting, *4448*

Mallory, Zachariah: Hospital for insane patients established by a colony, *4895*

Maloney, Margaret Helen: Soldier's Medal awarded to a woman, *1663*

Malraux, André: Exhibition of the *Mona Lisa* in the United States, *1231*

Malster, William Talbot: Radio telephone message from a submerged submarine to shore, *7755*

Malt, Donald A.: Limb reattachment, *5088*

Manasse, Mark: Factoring of a 100-digit number, *6760*

Mancini, Henry: Grammy awards for musical recordings, *1629*

Mangan, Wallace H.: Streamlined ferryboat, *6912*

Manischewitz, Dov Ber: Matzah made by machine, *3921*

Mankiller, Wilma P.: Principal chief of the Cherokee Nation who was a woman, *4085*

Manley, Robert E.: Wrecking crane operated from a car, *4416*

Mann, Charles: Trackless trolley system, *6404*

Mann, Horace: Board of education established by a state, *3056*

Hospital for treatment of the mentally ill established by a state, *4873*

Visible speech method of instruction for deaf students, *3034*

Mann, William: Ax factory, *7909*

Manners, J. Hartley: Play to be shown on television, *1260*

Mannes, Leopold Damrosch: Color film, *5844*

Manning, G. Randolph: Professional soccer organization recognized internationally, *7493*

Mansfield, Arabella A.: Lawyer who was a woman, *4636*

Manteo: Native American to become a Protestant, *6502*

Mapes, James Jay: Synthetic fertilizer, *1016*

Marbury, William: Supreme Court decision voiding an act of Congress, *2746*

March, Francis Andrew: Comparative philology chair at a college, *3115*

Marchal, Wilma Juanita: Navy personnel in the regular Navy who were women, *5266*

Marciano, Rocky: Pay television presentation of a sporting event, *7785*

World heavyweight boxing champion to retire undefeated, *7254*

Marcley, Walter John: Tuberculosis sanatorium established by a state, *4901*

Marconi, Guglielmo: Newspaper published at sea, *5642*

Marcy, Geoffrey W.: Brown dwarf star to be discovered, *6685*

Marcy, William Learned: Political machine, *3347*

Prisoners captured in the War of 1812, *8022*

Marechal, Ambrose: Cathedral, *6461*

Marie (Tranchepain), Mother: Catholic convent, *6451*

Marier, Rebecca: West Point cadet who was a woman to graduate at the top of her class, *3208*

Marin, John: Modern art exhibition, *1228*

Marino, Eugene Antonio: Catholic bishop who was an American-born African-American, *6480*

Marix, Adolph: Navy admiral who was Jewish, *5272*

Mark, John: Manila paper, *5752*

Markham, James E.: Fruit tree patent, *1026*

Marmer, Milton Jacob: Lung tumor operation in which the patient was under hypnosis, *5086*

Marr, John Quincy: Confederate officer killed in the Civil War, *7955*

Marrant, John: Missionary to the Native Americans who was African-American, *6569*

Mars, Forrest E.: M&M candies, *3970*

Mars, Frank C.: Milky Way candy bar, *3969*

Marsden, Andy: Boxer to die from blows inflicted in a fight, *7250*

Marsh, Othniel Charles: Paleontology chair at a college, *3237*

Prehistoric hoax, *3648*

Marsh, Sylvester: Cog railroad, *6333*

Marshall, Charles: Pharmacy college, *3160*

Marshall, Clinton S.: Spring winding machine, *4411*

Marshall, Elizabeth: Pharmacist who was a woman, *4963*

Marshall, Florence M.: Vocational high school for girls, *3086*

Marshall, Frank James: Chess champion to play more than 100 games simultaneously, *4032*

Marshall, George Catlett: Army generals to wear the five-star insignia, *5157*

Army officer to occupy both the nation's highest military post and the highest nonelective civilian post, *5153*

Nobel Peace Prize awarded to a professional soldier, *1698*

Marshall, Humphry: Botany book by an American-born author, *1979*

Marshall, James Wilson: Gold discovered in California, *5329*

Marshall, John: Former vice president to be arrested, *6241*

Supreme Court chief justice to serve in a presidential cabinet, *2756*

Supreme Court chief justice who had been a congressional representative, *2755*

Supreme Court decision establishing the power of the federal government, *2747*

Supreme Court decision in a commerce case, *2750*

Marshall, John Sayre: Army dental corps, *5016*

Marshall, Lois I. Kimsey: Vice president's widow to receive a pension, *6247*

Marshall, Penny: Baseball league for women, *7101*

Marshall, Thurgood: Supreme Court justice who was African-American, *2763*

Marston, Sarah H.: Foreign missionary society organized by women, *6578*

Martell, Belle: Boxing referee who was a woman, *7244*

Martell, Charles Bowling: Guided missile cruiser, *6940*

Martin, Christy: Boxer who was a woman to earn national recognition, *7257*

Martin, Edward: Theatrical performance, *1239*

Martin, Glenn Luther: Airplane round-trip flight over water, *1441*

Martin, Graham: Ambassador to Vietnam after the end of the Vietnam War, *3997*

Martin, Henry: Brick machine, *2057*

Martin, John: Actor of American birth, *1273*
Colonial council, *5906*

Martin, Joseph: Clipper ship, *6866*

Martin, Mary: Broadway play shown in a television version with its original cast, *1266*

Martin, Robert R.: Officer killed in action in the Korean War, *7978*

Martin, Truman J.: Car insurance policy, *4519*

Martin, William "Plugger Bill": International six-day bicycle race, *7189*

Mary Alphonsa, Sister: Hospice for incurable cancer patients, *4888*

Mary, John: French grammar, *1857*

Mary Rose, Sister: Hospice for incurable cancer patients, *4888*

Mason, Eben: Veterinary college of importance, *3181*

Mason, Ellen H.B.: Foreign missionary society organized by women, *6578*

Mason, John: Streetcar company, *6393*

Mason, John Landis: Mason jar, *4283*

Mason, Leonard: Intercollegiate wrestling association, *7577*

Mason, Lowell: Music book for children, *1939*
Music instruction in a public school, *2900*

Massasoit: Colonial treaty with the Native Americans, *5915*
Greeting addressed to the Pilgrims by a Native American, *5914*
Intercollegiate football association, *7303*

Massey, John: Fox hunting club, *7422*

Masters, Sybilla Righton: Cornmeal machine for grinding maize, *3910*

Matesic, Edward: Professional football game in which 10 touchdowns were made, *7328*

Mather, Cotton: Botanical report on plant hybridization, *6735*
Christian worship services organized by African-American slaves, *6515*
Inoculation against smallpox using material from human smallpox pustules, *4914*
Mezzotint engraving, *1199*
Paleontology report, *1974*

Mather, Increase: Engraving of any artistic merit, *1223*
Science society, *6776*

Mather, Ralph: Swedenborgian or New Church temple, *6524*

Mather, Richard: Woodcut, *1222*

Mathews, George: Telephone call on a commercial line using solar energy, *7746*

Matisse, Henri: Modern art exhibition, *1228*

Matlack, Charles F.: Homeopathic medical society, *5031*

Matthews, Clarence: Intercollegiate football game between African-American colleges, *7323*

Matthews, Edmund O.: Torpedo manufacturing station, *8109*

Matthews, John: Soda water machine, *3844*

Matthews, Marjorie Swank: Methodist bishop who was a woman, *6562*

Matthews, Thomas: Whist rule book, *1999*

Matthews, Thomas A.: Quasar to be observed, *6683*

Mature, Victor: Movie in Cinemascope, *5562*

Matzmulla, Zun Zow: Naval Academy graduate who was Japanese, *3214*

Mauchly, John W.: Electronic computer, *2528*

Maverick, Samuel: Americans killed by British soldiers in the Revolution, *7986*

Maxim, Hiram Percy: Automobile club, *5465*

Maxwell, George: Music society for the protection of composers and song writers, *1286*

Maxwell, George Holmes: Citizenship and public affairs school at a college, *3255*

Maxwell, William: American flag flown in battle, *1120*

May, Lewis: Young Men's Hebrew Association, *5714*

Maynard, Belvin W.: Radio broadcast of a concert from an airplane, *1295*
Sermon preached from an airplane by radio, *6591*
Transcontinental air race, *7295*

Maynard, Lambert: Hotel with safe deposit boxes, *2423*

Mayor, Bruce: Trial in which lawyers appeared on a Picturephone, *4625*

Mays, Willie: Major league baseball player killed in a game, *7148*

Mazor, Stan: Microprocessor, *3446*

McAfee, Mildred Helen: Navy officer commissioned in the U.S. Naval Reserve who was a woman, *5287*

McAllister, James W.: Entomology journal, *4772*

McAlpin, Harry: News correspondent who was African-American, *5619*

McArdle, Joseph: Actors' home, *1277*

McBride, John: Employment service established by a state, *4565*

McBride, Roger L.: Electoral vote for a woman, *3396*

McCaffery, Dominick F.: Boxing match under the Marquis of Queensberry rules, *7236*

McCain, Franklin: Civil rights sit-in, *2260*

McCall, Barbara W.: United Church of Christ ordination of a woman in which all the principal roles were filled by women, *6536*

McCandless, Bruce: Astronauts to fly free in space, *7050*

McCarthy, Charlie: College degree awarded to a ventriloquist's dummy, *2981*

McCarthy, George Lewis: Check photographing device, *3795*

McCarthy, Joseph Vincent: Baseball manager to win pennants in both leagues, *7099*

McChester, George "Country": Heavyweight boxing match to last longer than 100 rounds, *7233*

McClellan, George Brinton: Army ambulance corps, *5011*
Army field telegraph used in warfare, *5243*
Presidential election in which soldiers in the field were allowed to vote, *3389*

McCloskey, John: Catholic priest from the United States to be made a cardinal, *6465*

McClure, Donald: American division to cross the Rhine River in World War I, *8047*

McClure, Samuel Sidney: Newspaper syndicate, *5626*

McComb, John, Jr.: Lighthouse built after American independence, *4124*

McConnell, Joseph Christopher: Triple jet ace, *1621*

McConnell, Matthew: Stock exchange, *3812*

McCormick, Cyrus Hall: Reaper machine that was practical, *1044*

McCormick, Katherine Dexter: Birth-control pill, *6833*

McCormick, Patricia: Bullfighter who was a woman to fight professionally, *7259*

McCormick, Robert Rutherford: Illustrated tabloid, *5653*

McCoy, George Walter: Animal disease of American origin, *5122*

McCoy, Joseph Geating: Cow town, *2192*

McCoy, Michael Norman Wright: Transatlantic nonstop jet airplane eastward flight, *1476*

McCoy, Thomas: Boxer to die from blows inflicted in a fight, *7250*

McCullough, W.T.: Public garage, *5483*

McCurdy, John Alexander Douglas: Airplane rescue at sea, *1435*

McCusker, Marilyn J.: Coal miner who was a woman to be killed in a mining accident, *3510*

McDaniel, Colonel D.: Steeplechase, *7391*

McDaniel, Hattie: Oscar awarded to a performer who was African-American, *1633*

McDaniels, "MC" Darryl "D": Rap album to attract a mass audience, *1373*

McDermott, John J.: Marathon race held annually, *7552*

McDivitt, James Alton: Astronaut to become a general, *7044*
Astronaut to walk in space, *7031*
Astronauts to transfer from one spacecraft to another while in orbit, *7039*

McDonald, Marshall: Aquarium with an inland saltwater environment, *1187*

McDonald, Maurice: McDonald's restaurant, *2464*

McDonald, Richard: McDonald's restaurant, *2464*

McDowell, Ephraim: Abdominal operation other than a cesarean section, *5076*

McDowell, Irvin: Civil War battle, *7957*

McDowell, John Huber: Theater and dramatic criticism course at a college, *3105*

McEachern, Archie: Paired six-day bicycle race, *7195*

McElroy, James: Subway car with side doors, *6412*

McElroy, Theodore R.: Radio receiving contest, *6261*

McEntire, George W.: Transcontinental airship flight, *1520*

McFadden, Vivian: Navy chaplain who was an African-American woman, *5206*

McFarland, David Ford: Helium in natural gas, *6813*

McFarland, Irene: Caterpillar Club member who was a woman, *1586*

McFatrich, George W.: Optometry school, *3168*

McFatrich, James and George: Eye wash commercially manufactured, *4990*

McGaffey, Ives W.: Vacuum cleaner that used suction, *4272*

McGee, John: Camp meeting, *6525*

McGee, Walter H.: Execution for kidnapping, *2801*

McGee, William: Camp meeting, *6525*

McGinnity, Joseph Jerome: World Series baseball game that was a shutout, *7124*

McGivney, Michael Joseph: Knights of Columbus meeting, *5724*

McGovern, Vincent Howard: Transatlantic helicopter flight, *1576*

McGowan, John: Act inaugurating the Civil War, *7946*

McGrath, Paul: Broadway play shown in a television version with its original cast, *1266*

McGraw, John Joseph: Bowling with duckpins, *7222*

McGuire, Elwood: Lawn mower, *7933*

McHugh, Keith S.: Long-distance dial telephone service, *7742*

Mcilrath, H. Darwin: Round-the-world bicycle trip by a husband and wife, *7203*

McKean, Thomas: President elected under the Constitution, *6135*

McKechnie, William: Major league baseball game to be shown on television, *7132*

McKenzie, John: Free port, *2486*

McKenzie, Richard: Occupation of federal territory by Native American protesters in the modern era, *5977*

McKhann, J.: Limb reattachment, *5088*

McKim, Isaac: Clipper ship, *6866*

McLaughlin, Frank: Drive-in gas station, *2499*

McLean, Edith Eleanor: Incubator for premature babies, *4943*

McLean, James: Insurance rate standardization, *4506*

McLean, John: Ancient and modern history chair at a college, *3095*
Eye bank, *4836*

McLoughlin, John: Game manufacturing company, *4009*

McManus, Frederick Richard: Catholic mass in English, *6479*

McMath, Robert Raynolds: Movie of the sun, *6689*

McMillan, Edwin Mattison: Neptunium, *6817*
Plutonium, *6818*
Synchrotron, *6802*

McNair, Alexander: State west of the Mississippi River to be admitted to the Union, *7603*

McNair, Ronald E.: Space shuttle disaster, *7090*

McNally, Dave: Free agents in major league baseball, *7158*

McNamara, Frank X.: Credit card to be nationally accepted, *3809*

McNamee, Graham: Chain radio broadcast, *6270*
Political convention to be broadcast on radio, *3340*

McNeil, Claudia: Play by an African-American woman to appear on Broadway, *1270*

McNeil, Joseph: Civil rights sit-in, *2260*

McNutt, Paul Vories: Governor to be granted almost dictatorial power, *7619*

Mcpherson, Eugene: Transcontinental bicycle trip made in less than three weeks, *7204*

McQuiston, James: Electric power plant operated by a city, *3459*

McRae, V.H.: Phonograph trade magazine, *4730*

McTammany, John, Jr.: Player piano, *1316*

McTighe, Thomas J.: Automatic telephone system, *7713*

McVeigh, Timothy: Bombing by domestic terrorists resulting in large loss of life, *2791*

McVickar, John: Political economy chair at a college, *3251*

Meach, A.: Nautical school, *3303*

Meade, R.W.: Wedding in an airplane, *4818*

Means, Jacqueline: Episcopal priest who was a woman, *6553*

Means, Rice W.: Veterans of Foreign Wars of the United States meeting, *5311*

Means, Russell: Armed occupation by Native American protesters in the modern era, *5978*

Meason, Isaac: Iron mill to puddle and roll iron, *4450*

Mecom, Benjamin: Stereotype printing, *5800*

Meek, George Burton: Navy officer killed in action in the Spanish-American War, *8008*

Meek, Howard Bagnall: Hotel administration course at a college, *3297*

Meeker, Jotham: Magazine in a Native American language, *4744*

Mein, John: Patriotic song by an American, *1376*

Mein, John Gordon: Ambassador assassinated in office, *3995*

Mellette, Arthur Calvin: States admitted to the Union simultaneously, *7606*

Melville, David: Gas streetlights, *2213*

Melville, Herman: Ship sunk by a whale, *2420*

Menches, Charles E.: Ice cream cone, *3866*

Méndez, Antonio: Sugar refinery, *3956*

Menéndez de Avilés, Pedro: Catholic mass, *6444*
Catholic parish, *6445*
Colonial warfare between European powers in America, *5900*
European settlement in America that was permanent, *5899*
Truce violation, *5901*

Menotti, Gian-Carlo: Opera written for television, *1354*

Mergenthaler, Ottmar: Linotype machine, *5805*

Meriwether, Lee Ann: Beauty pageant to be shown on television, *3629*

Merriam, Frank: Negative election campaign run by media specialists, *3323*

Merrick, Solyman: Wrench patent, *7916*

Merrill, Richard: Transatlantic round-trip airplane flight from the United States, *1461*

Merritt, Wesley: Military expeditionary force to be sent beyond the Western Hemisphere, *8009*

Meserole, B.J.: Game protection society, *7423*

Messersmith, Andy: Free agents in major league baseball, *7158*

Metalious, Grace: Soap opera on prime-time television, *7788*

Metcalf, Betsey: Straw hats, *2294*

Meyenberg, John B.: Evaporated milk, *3873*

Meyer, Karl Friedrich: Flea laboratory, *6749*

M'Geary, James: Camp meeting, *6525*

Michaëlius, Jonas: Dutch Reformed church, *6506*

Michelson, Albert Abraham: Nobel Prize for physics awarded to an American, *1691*
Universal constant in physics to be measured by American scientists, *6812*

Michie, Dennis: Intercollegiate Army–Navy football game, *7320*

Michtom, Morris: Teddy bear, *2145*

Middleton, Henry: President of the Continental Congress, *2574*

Middleton, Peter: Dissection report, *1890*
History of medicine, *1863*

Midgley, Thomas, Jr.: Ethyl gasoline to be marketed, *3538*

Mientka, Walter: Team to achieve a perfect score in the International Mathematical Olympiad, *3249*

Mifflin, Thomas: Quartermaster of the Continental Army, *5166*

Miguel: Native American map of record, *4791*

Mikulski, Barbara Ann: Congressional representative of Polish ancestry, *2623*

Milam, Benjamin: Madstone, *3647*

Miles, Samuel: Electoral vote cast contrary to instructions, *3382*

Milestone, Lewis: Oscars for best movie director, *1632*

Miley, William Maynadier: Army parachute battalion, *5188*

Milk, Harvey: Politician who was openly homosexual to win an election, *6839*

Miller, Abraham: Wall and floor tiles, *2042*

Miller, Charles: Bicycle race paced by a motorcycle, *7194*
International six-day bicycle race, *7189*
Sewing machine to stitch buttonholes, *4354*

Miller, Elizabeth Smith: Bloomers, *2267*

Miller, Experience: Leather tanning, *4455*

Miller, Frank Andrew: Pen with truly erasable ink, *8155*

Miller, Gerrit Smith: Football club, *7301*

Miller, Gordon: Navy–Marine Corps Medals for Heroism awarded to Marines, *1661*

Miller, Hinda: Sports bra, *2281*

Miller, James Arthur: Radio broadcast from a tape recording, *6279*

Miller, James Francis: Banking association (state), *3770*

Miller, James M.: Catholic magazine in English, *4702*

Miller, John: States admitted to the Union simultaneously, *7606*

Miller, John MacDonald: Airmail regular delivery service by autogiro, *6029*
Transcontinental autogiro flight, *1531*

Miller, Lewis: Chautauqua organization meeting, *2885*
College summer school, *2993*

Miller, Nannie: Baseball teams for women, *7161*

Miller, Phineas: Cotton gin, *1030*

Miller, Robert F.: Radio contest, *6260*

Miller, T.G.: Round-the-world telephone conversation, *7762*

Miller, William C.: Astronomy photographs in color to be published in a magazine, *6699*

Milley, Samuel H.: Army chaplain who was Catholic, *5194*

Millikan, Robert Andrews: Cosmic ray to be discovered, *6679*

Milliken, John F.: International lifeboat race, *7217*

Milling, Thomas de Witt: Airplane outfitted with a machine gun, *1484*

Mills, Anson: Cartridge belt patent, *8108*

Mills, Clark: Bronze equestrian statue, *5399*

Mills, Hiram Francis: Water filtration system for bacterial purification of a city water supply, *2234*

Mills, Robert: Atlas issued by a state, *4799*
Building of fireproof construction, *2072*

Milton, Jefferson Davis: Border patrol officer, *5868*

Mindell, Fania: Birth control clinic, *4844*

Ming Long: Tong organized crime gang, *2777*

Minot, Charles: Telegraph used by a railroad, *7696*

Minuit, Peter: Dutch settlement in America, *5912*
Land sale swindle, *5919*
Swedes to arrive in America, *5924*

Mirrington, Ernst W., Jr.: Two-handed shovel, *7940*

Miske, Billy: Boxing match broadcast on radio, *7238*

Miskey, John A.: Squash rackets champion, *7499*

Mitchel, Ormsby MacKnight: Astronomy magazine, *4770*

Mitchell, Arthur Wergs: Congressional representative who was African-American, *2603*

Mitchell, Charles Lewis: State legislators who were African-American, *7624*

Mitchell, Elsie: American civilians killed in the continental United States in World War II, *8084*

Mitchell, Frank: Congressional page who was African-American, *2592*

Mitchell, Harold E.: Space capsule recovered in midair from an orbiting satellite, *7064*

Mitchell, John: News magazine featuring photographs, *4736*

Mitchell, John Newton: Attorney general to be incarcerated, *6127*

Mitchell, Margaret: High-speed radio fax transmission, *7674*

Mitchell, Matthew: Election held in defiance of the Royal Courts, *3311*

Mitchell, Michelle B.: Sheriff who was an African-American woman, *4156*

Mitchell, Samuel Augustus: Entomology book, *1984*

Mitchell, Silas Weir: Physiology society (national), *5041*

Mitchell, Virne Beatrice "Jackie": Baseball pitcher who was a woman, *7149*

Mitchell, William: Airplane bombing experiment to sink a battleship, *8117*

Mitchell, William Lendrum: Army general to fly over enemy lines, *8032*

Mitchill, Samuel Latham: Agriculture professor at a college, *2890*
Medical journal, *4750*

Mixon, Rhoda Holly Singleton: Town founded by a woman, *2188*

Mizell, "Jam Master" Jason: Rap album to attract a mass audience, *1373*

Modugno, Domenico: Grammy awards for musical recordings, *1629*

Moffat, John L.: Private mint authorized by the federal government, *5352*

Moisant, Matilde: Pilot licensed by the Aero Club of America who was a woman, *1596*

Mokarzel, Naoum Anthony: Arabic daily newspaper, *5678*

Moley, Raymond: Community trust charity, *5742*

Molineux, Tom: Boxer of fame who was African-American, *7249*

Moller, John C.: Music publishers, *1281*

Mollison, Irvin Charles: Judge on the federal bench who was African-American, *2727*

Molloy, Dallas: Amateur boxing match for women, *7247*

Momsen, Charles Bowers: Submarine emergency air supply container, *6967*

Mondale, Walter F.: Vice presidential candidate from a major political party who was a woman, *3419*

Moniac, David: West Point graduate who was Native American, *3198*

Monis, Judah: College graduate who was Jewish, *3008*
Hebrew grammar, *1854*

Monroe, James: Marine hospital established by Congress, *4870*

President to receive the unanimous vote of the presidential electors, *3381*
President who had been a senator, *6139*
Territory annexed by the federal government, *5955*

Monroe, William: Pencil factory, *8148*

Monroe, William Smith "Bill": Bluegrass musician of renown, *1335*

Montagnier, Luc: Identification of the AIDS virus, *5064*

Montague, Hannah Lord: Detachable collar, *2282*

Montague, Orlando: Collar factory, *2284*

Montgomery, Alexander: Art magazine, *4722*

Montgomery, John: Declaration of independence by citizens of an American colony, *1110*

Montgomery, John Joseph: Glider flight, *1546*

Montgomery, Simon Peter: Methodist minister who was African-American, *6559*

Montresor, John: Inclined railroad, *6315*

Moody, Blair: Senator who had been a newspaper reporter, *2655*

Moody, Paul: Belts of leather for transmitting power, *4393*
Cotton mill entirely powered by water, *7884*

Moody, Pliny: Dinosaur fossils, *6739*

Moore, Ann: Baby carrier, *2154*

Moore, Clement Clarke: Hebrew dictionary, *1801*

Moore, Hugh: Paper cup, *4310*

Moore, J. Ross: Clothes dryer, *4278*

Moore, James: Naval battle in the Revolutionary War, *7991*

Moore, John M.: Illustrated weekly magazine, *4715*

Moore, Nelson Augustus: Monument to commemorate the Civil War, *5400*

Moore, Thomas: Refrigerator, *4345*

Moores, Frank Edward: Vending machine law enacted by a city, *2397*

Moran, George "Bugs": Organized crime massacre, *2780*

More, Nicolas: Judge to be impeached, *2718*

Morehouse, Albert Kellogg: Ship from which a long-range rocket was launched, *6938*

Moreno, Jacob L.: Psychodrama treatment for psychiatric patients, *5116*

Morey, Samuel: Internal-combustion engine, *5477*

Morgan, Arthur Ernest: Electric power contract between a city and the federal government, *3482*

Morgan, Ebenezer: Steam whaler, *6885*

Morgan, Garrett A.: Automatic traffic light, *4225*

Morgan, George T.: Commemorative coin, *5373*

Morgan, Jaye P.: Magazine to contain a phonograph record, *4738*

Morgan, John: Medical education book, *1891*

Morgan, John Pierpont: Electric light from a power plant in a residence, *3495*
Yacht race broadcast on radio, *7215*

Morgan, Justin: Morgan horse, *1176*

Morgan, Robert W.: Army dental corps, *5016*

Morgan, William George: Volleyball, *7575*

Morgenstern, Oskar: Mathematical theory of economic decisionmaking, *6758*

Moritz, Susan Ingalls: Coast Guard ship commander who was a woman, *5215*

Morley, Edward W.: Universal constant in physics to be measured by American scientists, *6812*

Morley, J A.: Stamp collection society, *6056*

Moro, Aldo: Cabinet meeting attended by a foreign national, *6118*

Morphy, Paul Charles: Chess tournament, *4028*
International chess champion from the United States, *4029*

Morrell, John A.: Airship disaster, *1513*

Morrill, Justin Smith: Land grant for an agricultural college, *2892*

Morris, Anthony: Brewery to remain in business for 200 years, *2664*

Morris, Charles Lester: Long-distance helicopter flight, *1575*

Morris, Esther Hobart: Justice of the peace who was a woman, *2721*

Morris, Jacob M.: Archery club, *7568*

Morris, Joshua H.: Title guaranty insurance company, *4509*

Morris, Kenneth: Civil rights anthem to achieve fame, *1383*

Morris, Robert: American flag to represent the United States, *1118*
Mint of the United States, *5350*

Morris, T.A.: Union passenger station used by several railroad companies, *6332*

Morris, William: Photograph of a beam of 1-billion-volt x-rays, *5829*

Morris, William E.: Cotton acreage reduction payment, *1034*

Morrison, Effie: Retirement colony, *2198*

Morrison, Herbert: Coast-to-coast radio news broadcast to be recorded, *5706*

Morrison, John R.: Bellows, *4395*

Morrison, Sarah Parke: State university to grant equal privileges to women, *2953*

Morrison, Toni: Nobel Prize for literature awarded to an African-American writer, *1703*

Morrison, Walter Frederick: Flying disk for use in throwing games, *7585*

Morrison, William: Car with an electric storage battery, *5426*

Morrison, William Newton: Dental crown made of gold, *4863*

Morse, Jedidiah: American gazetteer, *1814*
Geography book, *1978*

Morse, Samuel Finley Breese: Artists' organization (national), *1205*
Class photograph, *5813*
College to sponsor an endowed lecture series, *2950*
Commercial telegraph service, *7692*
Painting movement, *1204*
Photograph taken in the United States, *5811*
Telegraph cable, *7688*
Telegraph station, *7690*

Mortimore, Alice: Public school classes for children with epilepsy, *3022*

Morton, George: Skimobile ski lift, *7485*

Morton, George Arthur: Electron tube, *3437*

Morton, Julius Sterling: Arbor Day, *4238*

Morton, Ladislaus: Electron microscope, *6800*

Morton, Nathaniel: History of New England, *1860*

Morton, Nelle: United Church of Christ ordination of a woman in which all the principal roles were filled by women, *6536*

Morton, Samuel George: Cranioscopy book, *1909*

Morton, Sarah Wentworth Apthorp: Novel by an American writer to be published in America, *1839*
Orchestral song to be printed, *1378*

Morton, Thomas: Cod-liver oil, *4980*
Deportation, *5857*

Morton, Thomas George: Animal rights organization (national), *5740*

Morton, William James: X-ray of the entire body of a living person made in a single exposure, *4905*

Morton, William Thomas Green: Painless surgery demonstration, *4831*

Mosconi, Willie: Billiard player to win a match in the first inning, *4020*

Mosher, Eliza Maria: Reformatory for women established by a state, *2824*

Mosher, William Eugene: Citizenship and public affairs school at a college, *3255*

Moskovics, Fred Evans: Speedway with a board track, *7508*

Moskowitz, Samuel: Science fiction course at a college, *3108*

Moss, Emma Sadler: President of a major medical society who was a woman, *5049*

Motley, Constance Baker: Judge of a federal district court who was African-American, *2729*

Mott, John: Trade tokens, *5358*

Mott, Lucretia: Voting rights convention organized by women, *3425*
Voting rights organization (national) advocating universal voting rights, *3427*

Mott, William: Trade tokens, *5358*

Motta, Irene: Bridge hand in which each player was dealt a perfect hand, *4025*

Moulton, Frances Estelle Mason: Bank president of a national bank who was a woman, *3786*

Mouton, Carolyn Anne: Siamese twins separated successfully by surgery, *2175*

Mouton, Catherine Anne: Siamese twins separated successfully by surgery, *2175*

Moyers, Leroy: Jockey to win seven consecutive races in one day, *7414*

Mucci, Tony: National wheelchair games, *7586*

Mudd, Stuart: Blood serum made of dried human blood, *4833*

Mudge, Genevra Delphine: Car driver who was a woman, *5467*

Muench, Carl Gebhard: Sound-absorbing material made of rigid insulating board, *2050*

Muhlenberg, Frederick Augustus Conrad: Speaker of the House, *2578*

Muhlenberg, William Augustus: Vacation fund to send poor children to the country, *2139*

Muhrcke, Gary: New York City Marathon, *7566*

Muir, John: Conservationist of note, *3712*

Mullanphy, Bryan: Traveler's aid program, *5966*

Mulliken, Samuel: Patent recipient to obtain more than one patent, *4649*

Mullin, John: Tape recorders, *7013*

Mullis, Kary B.: DNA chain polymerization, *5065*

Mulzac, Hugh: Merchant ship commanded by an African-American captain, *6895*

Mumford, Stephen: Seventh Day Baptist Church, *6544*

Mumford, William Bruce: Citizen of the United States to be hanged for treason, *2835*

Muncy, Alderson: Food stamps, *4086*

Muncy, Chloe: Food stamps, *4086*

Mundt, Karl Earl: Television image using a split screen, *7816*

Munemori, Sadao S.: Medal of Honor awarded to a soldier of Japanese ancestry, *1683*

Muñoz Marin, Luis: Governor of Puerto Rico to be elected, *3324*

Munro, Douglas Albert: Medal of Honor awarded posthumously to a Coastguardsman killed in action in World War II, *1680*

Munsey, Frank Andrew: All-fiction pulp magazine, *4731*

Munters, Georg: Gas refrigerator, *4348*

Murphy, Charles Minthorn: Bicycle racer to attain the speed of a mile a minute, *7193*

Murphy, Charles W.: Employment service established by a state, *4565*

Murphy, Isaac: American Derby horse race, *7393*

Murphy, Patrick: Airplane bombing raid by a mercenary soldier, *2781*

Murphy, Ward E.: Prison commissioner who was a woman, *2830*

Murray, John: Universalist church services, *6520*

Murray, Joseph E.: Organ transplant that was successful, *5096*

Murray, Peter: Public defender hired by a state, *4642*

Murray, Walter: Benefit performance of a play, *1244*

Play by William Shakespeare produced in America, *1243*

Murrie, Bruce E.: M&M candies, *3970*

Musick, Edwin Charles: Transpacific airmail flight, *6025*

Transport airplane designed for transoceanic service, *1414*

Musser, John Herr: Medical research chair at a college, *3154*

Mustin, Henry Croskey: Naval air training school, *3217*

Muths, Johann Christoph Friedrich Guts: Gymnastics book, *1996*

Muybridge, Eadweard: Book showing photographs of movements in sequence, *1750*

Movie to be copyrighted, *5544*

Photographs showing action, *5818*

Mycall, John: Algebra book by an American-born author, *1885*

Myer, Albert James: Army signal corps, *5180*

Myerhofer, "Swede": Airport owned by a city, *1503*

Myers, Edward: Ship from the United States sunk by a German submarine in World War II, *8048*

Myers, Henry: Strike benefit by a union, *4590*

Myers, Jacob H.: Voting machines, *3317*

Myers, Mary H.: Balloon pilot who was a woman, *1539*

Myerson, Bess: Beauty pageant to be held nationwide, *3628*

Beauty pageant to be shown on television, *3629*

N

Nagel, Charles: Chamber of Commerce, *2446*

Nagot, Francis Charles: Catholic seminary, *3268*

Naismith, James: Basketball game, *7166*

Basketball rules, *7168*

Nakahama, Manjiro: Japanese to enter the United States, *5961*

Nanney, J.P.: Electric power contract between a city and the federal government, *3482*

Nash, Gary: Intercollegiate court tennis match, *7534*

Nash, Simon Augustine: Domestic relations court, *2709*

Nason, James H.: Coffee percolator, *3850*

Nason, Joseph: Building heated by steam, *2074*

Nast, Thomas: Cartoon showing the Democratic Party as a donkey, *5702*
Cartoon showing the Republican Party as an elephant, *5703*

Nathan, Theodora: Electoral vote for a woman, *3396*

Naugle, Harry Merrill: Building of pressed structural steel, *2086*

Navratilova, Martina: Athlete who was a woman to earn more than $1 million in a year, *7541*

Neale, Leonard: Catholic bishop consecrated in the United States, *6460*

Neale, Thomas: Parliamentary act to establish a colonial post office, *5981*

Neals, Huerta Cortez: Physician with a mobile medical office, *4979*

Needles, William B.: Optometry school, *3168*

Neel, Carr Baker: Tennis champions who were brothers, *7535*

Neel, Samuel R.: Tennis champions who were brothers, *7535*

Neely, Joanne: Federal marshals who were women, *4151*

Neff, Pat Morris: State supreme court in which all the judges were women, *2724*

Neilson, Martha: High school for pregnant teenage girls, *3092*

Nelson, Christian K.: Eskimo pie, *3867*

Nelson, George: Satellite repair in orbit, *7077*

Nelson, Murray: Sewer district established by a city, *2232*

Nelson, Ray: Musical comedy written for television, *1269*

Nelson, Robert F.: Freezing of a corpse for future resuscitation, *2841*

Nelson, Rosemary Elaine: Sailors assigned to regular Navy shipboard duty who were women, *5269*

Nesbitt, John Maxwell: Life insurance offered by a general insurance company, *4543*

Neuberger, Maurine Brown: Husband and wife to be elected simultaneously to both chambers of a state legislature, *7632*

Neuberger, Richard Lewis: Husband and wife to be elected simultaneously to both chambers of a state legislature, *7632*

Neuffer, Judith Ann: Member of the Navy's Hurricane Hunters who was a woman, *5298*

Neumann, Gustav Adolf: German newspaper, *5661*

Neumann, John Nepomucene: Catholic saint who was a male American citizen, *6482*

New, Harry Stewart: Election campaign using radio, *3322*

Newbold, Charles: Plow patent, *1041*

Newell, William C.: Prehistoric hoax, *3648*

Newhouse, Benjamin: Elevator with safety devices, *2104*

Newhouse, Sewell: Steel animal traps commercially manufactured, *7922*

Newman, Larry: Transatlantic balloon flight, *1543*

Newman, Samuel: Bible concordance, *1960*

Newman, William: Shoe measuring stick, *2299*

Newport, Christopher: Colonial council, *5906*
English settlement in America that was permanent, *5907*
Episcopal church service in an English colony, *6547*

Newton, Hubert Anson: Measurement organization (national), *2449*

Ney, Karl Winfield: Surgical elevation of the skull to treat epilepsy, *5082*

Neyhart, Amos Earl: Driving course in a high school, *3090*

Nicholas, Samuel: Marine engagement in battle, *7994*
Marines, *5229*

Nichols, Anna R.G.: Patent examiner who was a woman, *4656*

Nichols, J.C.: Shopping mall, *2502*

Nichols, Jesse Clyde: Shopping center in a suburban business area, *2501*

Nichols, Terry: Bombing by domestic terrorists resulting in large loss of life, *2791*

Nichols, William: Lion, *1136*

Nicholson, Charles Ambrose: Airplane catapulted from an airship, *1452*

Nicholson, Francis: Colonist hanged for treason, *2834*
Statehouse, *2114*

Nicholson, L.A.: School stadium, *7509*

Nicholson, Reginald Fairfax: Battleship built on the Pacific coast, *6927*

Nicholson, William: File factory, *7915*

Nicola, Lewis: Engineering book, *1977*

Nicoll, Allardyce: Theater and dramatic criticism course at a college, *3105*

Nicolls, Richard: Horse race run on a regular basis, *7384*

Nikander, Juho Kustra: Finnish college, *2959*

Nimitz, Chester William: Navy admirals to wear the five-star insignia, *5273*
Transatlantic crossing by a submarine under its own power, *6988*

Nininger, Alexander Ramsey "Sandy", Jr.: Medal of Honor awarded in World War II, *1679*

Nishino, Kozo: Bombing raid on the continental United States in World War II, *8075*

Nissen, George P. and Paul F.: Trampoline commercially manufactured, *7374*

Nixon, John: Public reading of the Declaration of Independence, *1116*

Nixon, Richard Milhous: Artificial ice skating rink of Olympic size, *7435*

Cabinet member to serve in four different capacities, *6120*

Mobile telephone call to the moon, *7770*

President to attend the launching of a manned space flight, *6176*

President to receive a presidential pardon, *6179*

President to resign, *6177*

President to visit a nation not recognized by the federal government, *6238*

President who came to the office through appointment rather than election, *6178*

Presidential Citizen Medal, *1644*

Presidential election debates to be shown on television, *3394*

Strike of postal employees, *4601*

Vice president chosen under the 25th Amendment, *6249*

Noah, Mordecai Manuel: Ambassador who was Jewish, *3989*

Nobile, Umberto: Airplane flight over the North Pole, *6728*

Noble, Elaine: Politician who was openly homosexual to win an election, *6839*

Noble, Silas: Toothpick manufacturing machine, *4071*

Noeggerath, Emil Jacob: Pediatrics journal, *4756*

Noel, Garrat: Spanish grammar, *1855*

Noel, Monje Malak Abd al-Muta Ali, Jr.: Navy chaplain who was a Muslim, *5207*

Noguchi, Isamu: Bas relief of stainless steel in large size, *1219*

Nolan, Lloyd: Three-dimensional telecast, *7844*

Norcross, Leonard: Diving suit, *6709*

Norman, John: French grammar, *1857*

North, Elisha: Eye hospital, *4872*

Eye infirmary, *4871*

North, Simeon: Factory standardization to federal government specification, *4381*

Government contract authorized by Congress for pistols, *8092*

Norton, Charles Eliot: Archeology organization (national), *6787*

Norton, John: Latin book written in New England, *1949*

Norton, Lewis Mills: Pineapple cheese, *3858*

Norton, Mary Teresa: State committee chairman of a major political party who was a woman, *3341*

Norton, Mary Teresa Hopkins: Congressional committee headed by a woman, *2589*

Norton, Oliver Willcox: Taps, *1382*

Norton, Thomas: Nail machine, *7921*

Norton, William: Glass factory, *4035*

Norwood, William A.: Skee-ball alley, *3627*

Nova, Lou: Boxing match to be shown on television, *7243*

Novello, Antonia C.: Surgeon general who was a woman, *4214*

Novy, Frederick George: Bacteriology courses at a college, *3149*

Noyce, Robert: Integrated circuit, *3444*

Noyce, Robert N.: Charles Stark Draper Prize for engineering and technology, *1645*

Noyes, Eliot Fette: Typewriter without type arms, *2391*

Noyes, Enoch: Comb factory, *4065*

Nusbaum, Jesse Logan: Anthropology laboratory, *6748*

Nuthead, Dinah: Printer who was a woman, *5782*

Nutt, Emma M.: Telephone operator who was a woman, *7729*

Nutting, Mary Adelaide: Nurse appointed to a college professorship, *5028*

Nyswander, Marie: Methadone program, *2692*

O

Oakley, Jessie: Cakes of soap of uniform weight and individually wrapped, *4268*

O'Bannon, Presley Neville: American flag flown over a fortress of the Old World, *1125*

Oboler, Arch: Three-dimensional feature movie, *5563*

O'Brien, Jeremiah and John: Naval battle in the Revolutionary War, *7991*

O'Brien, Johnny: Basketball collegiate player to score more than 1,000 points in one season, *7175*

O'Brien, Parry: Shot-put toss over 60 feet, *7562*

O'Brien, Thomas Charles: National Union for Social Justice national convention, *3377*

O'Callahan, Timothy: Medal of Honor awarded to a chaplain, *1682*

Ochs, Adolph Simon: Transatlantic commercial telephone service, *7737*

Ocobock, Susanne M.: Air Force military engineer who was a woman, *5139*

O'Connell, James F.: Tattooed man exhibited as a theatrical attraction, *3661*

O'Connor, Donald: Television show to be sponsored by a commercial advertiser, *2344*

O'Connor, Sandra Day: Supreme Court justice who was a woman, *2765*

O'Conor, Charles: Presidential candidate who was Catholic, *3407*

O'Dell, Lank: Streetcar, *6394*

O'Donnell, Bertha: Telecommunication by deaf people that was both visual and oral, *7837*

Oelrichs, Mrs. Hermann: Parade of automobiles, *3665*

Ofeldt, F.W.: Motorboat pleasure craft, *6949*

Ogden, Aaron: Supreme Court decision in a commerce case, *2750*

Ogle, Henry: Reaper machine that worked, *1043*

Ogle, Samuel: Horse that was a thoroughbred, *1175*

O'Hare, Edward Henry: Navy ace in World War II, *1617*

Ohmart, Philip Edwin: Battery to convert radioactive energy into electrical energy, *3488*

O'Keefe, Walter: Emmy awards for excellence in television, *1628*

O'Keeffe, Georgia: Art museum of importance devoted to the work of an individual woman, *5600*

Olcott, Henry Steele: Theosophical society, *5743*

Old, Archie J., Jr.: Armored division transported by airplanes to a foreign country, *5193*

Round-the-world nonstop flight by a jet airplane, *1480*

Olds, Ransom Eli: Car exported from the United States, *5431*

Car factory, *5433*

Olds, Robin: Transcontinental round-trip airplane flight made within 24 hours, *1465*

Olive, Milton Lee, III: Medal of Honor awarded posthumously in the Vietnam War to an African-American soldier, *1687*

Oliver, Anna: Theological school to admit women as students, *3273*

Oliver, Henry Kemble: Labor bureau established by a state, *4557*

Oliver, Robert Shaw: Lawn tennis, *7523*

Tennis society (national), *7525*

Oliver, Robert T.: Army dental corps, *5016*

Olivier, Laurence: Oscar winners who were husband and wife, *1635*

Olson, John: Fuller's earth, *5334*

Olson, Lennart: Human antibodies produced artificially, *5005*

Olson, Scott and Brennan: In-line roller skate that was commercially successful, *7466*

O'Meara, Jack: Train of airplanes, *1459*

Omlie, Phoebe Fairgrave: Airplane race of importance in which both men and women were contestants, *7298*

Onate, Juan de: Native American map of record, *4791*

O'Neall, Belton: Workers' compensation lawsuit involving the rights of an injured servant against his master, *4552*

O'Neil, John: Baseball coach in the major leagues who was African-American, *7103*

O'Neill, Eugene Gladstone: Writer to win a Pulitzer Prize four times for drama, *1716*

Onizuka, Ellison S.: Space shuttle disaster, *7090*

op den Graeff, Abraham: Protest against slavery, *2240*

op den Graeff, Dirck: Protest against slavery, *2240*

Opper, Frederick Burr: Comic books, *2028*

O'Ree, Willie: Professional hockey player who was African-American, *7380*

O'Reilly, Samuel F.: Electric tattoo machine, *4054*

Ormandy, Eugene: Symphonic concert to be shown on television, *1299*

Orr, Hugh: Textile machine, *7861*

Orr, Robert: Arsenal of the federal government, *5126*

Muskets, *8091*

Orr, William: Paper for printing made from rags and wood-pulp fiber, *5753*

Ortiz, Antillo: Skyjacking of a commercial American airplane, *2784*

Orton, Edward: Ceramics school, *2906*

Osborn, Charles: Abolition newspaper, *5637*

Osborn, Frank P.: Transcontinental dial telephone service without the aid of operators, *7745*

Osborn, James Butler: Submarine equipped with ballistic missiles, *6976*

Submarine to have two complete crews, *6977*

Submerged submarine to fire a Polaris missile, *8142*

Osborne, Harold M.: Decathlon champion from the United States, *7556*

Osborne, Richard: Iron truss bridge, *3578*

Osgood, Samuel: Postmaster general of the United States, *5985*

Presidential mansion, *6250*

Osler, William: General medical clinic, *4843*

Osterhoudt, J.: Tin can with a key opener, *4284*

Ostermeier, Johannes: Photographic flashbulbs, *5842*

O'Sullivan, Humphrey: Rubber shoe heel, *2305*

Oswald, Lee Harvey: Murder to be shown live on television, *2786*

Otis, Bass: Lithograph, *1214*

Otis, Elisha Graves: Elevator with a completely enclosed car, *2105*

Elevator with safety devices, *2104*

Otis, Robert M.: Self-service supermarket, *2504*

Otis, William S.: Steam shovel, *4396*

Ott, Fred: Movie to be copyrighted, *5544*

Otterbein, Philip William: United Brethren in Christ meeting, *6541*

Otto, Dr.: Cottonseed oil, *3881*

Otto, John Conrad: Hemophilia treatise, *1899*

Outcault, Richard Felton: Sunday comics section in a newspaper, *5688*

Outerbridge, Eugenius H.: Lawn tennis, *7523*

Outerbridge, Mary Ewing: Lawn tennis, *7523*

Ovington, Earl Lewis: Airmail pilot, *6015*

Owen, Marie: Police officer who was a woman, *4136*

Owen, Robert: Communistic settlement that was not religious, *2189*

Printing instruction at a school, *3284*

Owens-Adair, Bethenia: Autopsy performed by a woman physician on a male corpse, *2850*

Owens, Jesse: Olympic athlete from the United States to win four gold medals in one year, *7448*

Owens, Michael Joseph: Glass-blowing machine, *4044*

P

Pabst, Karl K.: General purpose military vehicle, *5248*

Pace, Norman R.: Bacterium to be discovered that was visible to the naked eye, *6752*

Packard, Sophia Booker: Nursing school for African-American students, *3169*

Page, Albert B.: Diathermy machine, *4948*

Page, Charles Grafton: Electric locomotive, *6356*

Page, George: Plow for pulverizing the soil, *1049*

Page, James: Ice skating club, *7428*

Page, John Wallace: Fence made of woven wire, *1052*

Pahlavi, Mohammed Reza: Hostage crisis, *3982*

Paine, Cassius M.: Whist organization, *4021*

Paine, John Knowles: Music chair at a college, *2904*

Oratorio by an American, *1289*

Symphonic work by an American composer, *1290*

Painter, William: Bottle cap with a cork crown, *4286*

Palinkas, Patricia: Professional football game in which a woman participated, *7334*

Palisan, Johann: Asteroid named for an American president, *6678*

Palmer, Arnold: Golfer to earn over $100,000 in one year, *7366*

Palmer, Benjamin F.: Artificial leg patent, *5050*

Palmer, Daniel David: Chiropractic school, *3172*

Chiropractor, *4977*

Palmer, John F.: Bicycle tire made of cord, *7190*

Palmer, Nathaniel Brown: Discovery of Antarctica by an American, *6722*

Palmer, Potter: Hotel that was fireproof, *2424*

Palmer, Volney B.: Advertising agency, *2322*

Palmerton, John: Boat club, *7206*

Pandit, Shrimati Vijaya Lakshmi: Ambassador to the United States who was a woman, *3990*

Pangborn, Clyde: Transpacific nonstop airplane flight, *1454*

Papert, Seymour: Computer programming language for children, *2551*

Paplawski, Stephen J.: Electric blender, *4300*

Paraf, Alfred: Margarine manufacturer, *3882*

Pardo, Saul: Jewish synagogue, *6484*

Parham, Thomas David, Jr.: Navy captain who was African-American, *5296*

Pariser, Alan: Rock music festival, *1372*

Park, James Alan: Insurance law treatise, *1873*

Park, Roswell: Cancer laboratory, *4930*

Park, Thomas: Library building at a university, *4669*

Park, William Hallock: Antitoxin laboratory established by a public health department, *4200*

Parker, Alton U.: Marine pilot to fly over Antarctica, *5236*

Parker, Bruce: National water skiing tournament, *7592*

Parker, Charles Wallace: Carousel with a jumping horse mechanism, *3625*

Mechanized shooting gallery, *3622*

Parker, Dr.: Madstone, *3647*

Parker, Ely Samuel: Indian Affairs Commissioner who was Native American, *5972*

Parker, James: Music book printed from type, *1935*

Spanish grammar, *1855*

Parker, John: Revolutionary War armed conflict, *7989*

Parker, Joseph: Blotting paper, *5755*

Parker, Samuel: Leather-splitting machine, *4456*

Parker, Willard: Clinic for teaching medical students, *3138*

Parks, Benjamin: Navy chaplain in the Continental Navy, *5196*

Parks, Bert: Beauty pageant to be shown on television, *3629*

Parks, Charles Henry: Navy chaplain who was Catholic, *5202*

Parks, Rosa: Mass boycott by civil rights protesters, *2259*

Parks, William: Cookbook, *1846*
Fencing book, *1992*
Parmelee, Du Bois D.: Adding machine to employ depressible keys, *2375*
Parmelee, Henry S.: Sprinkler head, *4108*
Parmelee, Philip: Shipment of merchandise by airplane, *2485*
Parmly, Eleazar: Dental society of a city, *5032*
Parsons, Albert: Labor activists to be executed, *4564*
Parsons, James Benton: Judge of a federal district court who was African-American, *2729*
Parsons, John E.: Cancer hospital, *4885*
Partridge, Alden: Civil engineering course at a college, *3232*
Military school, *3184*
Pastore, John: Governor of Italian ancestry, *7620*
Pastorius, Francis Daniel: Mennonites to arrive in America, *6537*
Protest against slavery, *2240*
Theological treatise, *1950*
Patch, Sam: Daredevil jumper of note, *3676*
Paterson, William: Supreme Court nominee who was rejected by the Senate, *2753*
Paton, Richard Townley: Eye bank, *4836*
Patten, Richard: Observatory established by the federal government, *6665*
Patterson, Floyd: World heavyweight boxing champion to regain his crown, *7255*
Patterson, Joseph Medill: Illustrated tabloid, *5653*
Patterson, Neil: Coast-to-coast paved road, *6625*
Pattison, Edward: Tinware manufacturers, *4291*
Pattison, William: Tinware manufacturers, *4291*
Patzke, Ethel Jean: American civilians killed in the continental United States in World War II, *8084*
Patzke, Richard Joe: American civilians killed in the continental United States in World War II, *8084*
Paul, Alice: Constitutional amendment proposal mandating equal legal rights for women and men, *6830*
Paul, Almarin B.: Silver mill, *4469*
Paul, Howard "Hap": Robot to perform surgery, *3449*
Paul, Les: Electric guitar, *1325*
Paul, William M.: Naval militia established by a state, *5255*
Paulding, James Kirke: Comic history of the United States, *1867*
Paulhan, Louis: Aviation meet, *7292*
Pilot from the United States to establish an airplane altitude record, *1594*

Pauling, Linus Carl: Nobel Prize winner to receive awards in two different categories, *1699*
Paulsen, Carl Christian Von: Capture of a German ship by an American ship in World War II, *8049*
Paxton, Donald: Commercial building with solar heating, *2067*
Payne, Andrew: Transcontinental foot race, *7557*
Payne, Isaac Sanders, IV: Air Force Academy graduates who were African-American, *3192*
Peabody, Amelia: House completely heated by solar energy, *2128*
Peabody, Elizabeth Palmer: Kindergarten, *3073*
Peake, Mary S.: School for freed slaves, *2251*
Peale, Franklin: Archery club, *7568*
Peale, Norman Vincent: Religious radio program broadcast by a husband and wife, *6596*
Peale, Rembrandt: Museum especially constructed as a museum and art gallery, *5577*
Peale, Ruth: Religious radio program broadcast by a husband and wife, *6596*
Peale, Titian Ramsey: Archery club, *7568*
Pearce, Richard Mills: Medical research chair at a college, *3154*
Pearson, Gerald Leondus: Solar energy battery, *3558*
Pearson, John: Cloth mill, *7858*
Fulling mill for making wool cloth, *7891*
Pearson, Norman C.S.: Navy–Marine Corps Medals for Heroism awarded to Marines, *1661*
Pearson, Richmond Mumford: Governor to be impeached and convicted, *7615*
Pearson, Theodore: Cracker bakery, *3917*
Peary, Josephine: Polar expedition of which a woman was a member, *6726*
Peary, Robert Edwin: Discovery of the North Pole, *6727*
Pease, Daniel Chapin: Photograph of genes, *4909*
Pease, Francis Gladheim: Astronomer to measure the size of a fixed star, *6668*
Pease, Richard H.: Christmas cards, *4256*
Pease, Titus: Whips commercially manufactured, *7910*
Peck, John: Supreme Court decision declaring a state law unconstitutional, *2748*
Peden, William and Doug: Bicycle race to be shown on television, *7198*
Peebles, Melvin Van: Movie directed by an African-American director, *5567*
Peer, Lyle Hudson Bennett: High-jump standards using electric eye detectors, *7561*
Peirce, Isaac: Chemistry magazine, *4766*
Peirce, William: Almanac, *1764*

Pelham, Peter: Concert with documentation, *1287*
Mezzotint engraving, *1199*

Pemberton, Bennett: Road authorization by a state, *6612*

Pemberton, Ebenezer: Book auction printed catalog, *1780*

Penn, William: Law history book, *1861*
Mennonites to arrive in America, *6537*
Stone arch bridge, *3564*

Pennell, Rebecca Mann: College professor who was a woman, *2947*
Physiology and hygiene courses at a liberal arts college, *3140*

Penniman, Anson W.: State school for blind students, *3024*

Pennock, Cyril: Military school, *3184*

Pennypacker, Samuel Whitaker: Sterilization of humans by a state government as a matter of public policy, *6829*

Peper, Henry, Jr.: Pen with truly erasable ink, *8155*

Pepperell, William: Knighthood conferred on a soldier born in America, *6642*

Percy, George: Episcopal church service in an English colony, *6547*

Percy, Samuel R.: Dried milk patent, *3870*

Perham, Josiah: Railroad excursion rates, *6329*

Perkings, Jay: Health laboratory established by a state to diagnose diseases by the examination of sputum, *4201*

Perkins, Elisha: Quack doctor of note, *3646*

Perkins, Frances: Cabinet member who was a woman, *6112*

Perkins, Jacob: Ice-making machine, *4346*
Pamphlet produced from a steel plate engraving, *1744*

Perkinson, Henry L.: Mobile telephone commercial service, *7740*

Perky, Henry D.: Biscuits of shredded wheat, *3924*

Perlman, Louis Henry: Demountable tire-carrying rim, *5499*

Perot, Ross, Jr.: Round-the-world helicopter flight, *1579*

Perrine, Henry: Avocado, *3902*

Perry, Benjamin: Iron blast furnace to use anthracite coal successfully, *4453*

Perry, Harold Robert: Catholic bishop who was an American-born African-American, *6480*

Perry, Henry: Human-powered submarine race, *7219*

Perry, Marmaduke: Autopsy officially recorded, *2848*

Perry, Matthew Calbraith: Japanese to enter the United States, *5961*

Perry, Michael: Hymnbook with music, *1972*

Perry, Oliver Hazard: Defeat of a British naval squadron in the War of 1812, *8024*

Perry, Stuart: Gas engine, *5478*

Perry, William: Dictionary published in the United States, *1797-*
Pocket dictionary, *1798*

Pershing, John Joseph: Airplane in actual military operation, *1485*
General of the Armies of the United States, *5152*
Service number issued by the Army, *5226*
Troops from the United States to sail to Europe in World War I, *8033*
Veterans' Day, *4246*

Peters, G. Moore: Cartridge-loading machinery, *8110*
Shot tower, *8112*

Peters, Richard: Law book of federal laws then in force, *1880*

Peters, Sam: Historical hoaxes, *3645*

Petersen, Frank E., Jr.: Marine general who was African-American, *5241*

Peterson, David: Combat mission of American pilots ordered to battle in World War I, *8042*

Peterson, John L.: Technical school for Native Americans, *3302*

Peterson-Mundy, Thomas: African-American to vote under authority of the 15th Amendment, *3429*

Peterson, Peter: Ambassador to Vietnam after the end of the Vietnam War, *3997*

Peterson, Phyllis Kathryn Smith: Stock exchange director who was a woman, *3831*

Petherbridge, Margaret: Crossword puzzle book, *2004*

Petit, Philippe: Tightrope walker to span two skyscrapers, *3669*

Pfatischer, Mathias: Electric motor using interpole direct current, *5481*

Phelan, Michael: Billiard match to attain international fame, *4017*
Billiards book, *2000*

Phelps, James: Fourdrinier papermaking machine, *5750*

Phelps, Oliver: Land office, *5948*

Phelps, Orson C.: Sewing machine manufacturer, *4352*

Phelps, William Lyon: College course in the contemporary novel, *3101*

Phiel, Abram Cump: Hydroplane service, *1408*

Philaret, Metropolitan: Russian Orthodox saint canonized in the United States, *6498*

Phillips, Alonzo Dwight: Friction matches, *4334*

Phillips, Channing Emery: National political convention to propose African-Americans for the offices of president and vice president, *3343*

Phillips, Duncan: Modern art museum, *5597*

Phillips, Eleazar: Agricultural book, *1757*

Phillips, Harriet N.: Nursing school to award a diploma, *3166*

Phillips, Irna: Soap opera on daytime television, *7781*

Phillips, Samuel: Religious tract society, *6570*

Phillipse, Frederick: Financial "corner", *3751*

Phips, William: Knighthood conferred on a person born in America, *6641*

Physick, Philip Syng: Soda water, *3843*
Stomach washing with a tube or syringe, *5111*

Phythian, Robert Lees: Nautical school established by a city, *3304*

Picard, Jean: Instantaneous phonograph recording, *7011*

Picken, Mary Brooks: Dictionary compiled by a woman, *1808*

Pickering, Edward Charles: Photograph of a solar eclipse, *6694*

Pickering, John: Book on Americanisms, *1745*
Federal judge to be impeached, *2719*

Pickering, Joseph: Fourdrinier papermaking machine, *5750*

Pickering, Thomas: Passport, *5884*

Pickering, Timothy: Senator to be censured, *2643*

Picket, Albert: Educational magazine, *4706*

Picket, John W.: Educational magazine, *4706*

Pierce, Bradford K.: Industrial school for girls, *3286*

Pierce, Burns: Bicycle race paced by a motorcycle, *7194*

Pierce, Cyrus: Teacher training school established by a state, *3260*

Pierce, Franklin: Claims court established by the federal government, *2712*
World's fair, *2409*

Pierce, Hugh Franklin: Airmail flight by rocket, *6026*

Pierce, Roger: Mobile overseas telephone call from a moving vehicle, *7763*

Pierson, Josiah Gilbert: Rivet production, *2037*

Pierson, Mr.: Envelope manufacturer, *5762*

Pierson, T.D.: Health journal to advocate water cures, *4755*

Pike, Nicholas: Sparrows, *1164*

Pilling, Samuel: Building and loan association, *3763*

Pillsbury, Moody Adams: Cattle of the Guernsey breed, *1079*

Pinchback, Pinckney Benton Stewart: Congressional representative to serve a single day, *2604*
Governor who was African-American, *7621*

Pinchbeck, William Frederick: Magic lantern book, *2018*

Pinckney, Charles Cotesworth: Presidential election in which candidates were nominated for the vice presidency, *3384*
Public museum, *5576*

Pinckney, Elizabeth Lucas: Indigo crop, *1009*

Pinckney, Thomas: Minister to Great Britain, *3985*

Pincus, Gregory: Birth-control pill, *6833*
Surrogate birth experiment with an animal, *5123*

Piñeda, Alonso Alvarez de: Exploration of the Mississippi River by a European, *5895*

Pinkerton, Allan: Army secret service bureau, *5181*

Pinkham, Lydia Estes: Patent medicine to achieve nationwide popularity, *4989*

Pinkney, William: Round-the-world solo sailing trip by an African-American, *7002*

Pinto, Isaac: Jewish prayer book, *1954*

Pipe, Captain: Treaty entered into by the federal government with Native American tribes, *5941*

Pipkin, Marvin: Electric light bulb frosted on the inside, *3498*

Pise, Charles Constantine: Congressional chaplain who was Catholic, *2585*

Pitcairn, Harold Frederick: Autogiro flown in America, *1529*

Pitcairn, John: Revolutionary War armed conflict, *7989*

Pitkin, Henry: Watch made by machinery, *7901*

Pitkin, James: Watch made by machinery, *7901*

Pitkin, Timothy: Political history book, *1868*

Pitt, Louis W.: Religious service to be televised from a church, *6593*

Pitts, Hiram Abial: Threshing machine to employ steam, *1046*

Pitts, John A.: Threshing machine to employ steam, *1046*

Pius IX, Pope: Catholic diocese and archdiocese, *6456*

Pius XI, Pope: Catholic church to become a basilica, *6471*
Transatlantic radio fax transmission of a photograph, *7668*

Place, Ira A.: Air rights lease, *2064*

Place, Martha M.: Execution by electrocution, *2799*

Plimpton, James Leonard: Roller skates, *7462*
Roller skating rink open to the public, *7463*

Plouffe, Simon: Encyclopedia of integer sequences, *6763*

Plume, Shirley: Indian Affairs Commissioner who was Native American, *5972*

Plunkett, Roy J.: Teflon created in a laboratory, *4482*

Poage, George C.: Olympic medalist who was African-American, *7444*

Pocahontas: Play about a Native American, *1247*
Postage stamp depicting a Native American, *6088*

Podoloff, Maurice: National Basketball Association commissioner, *7172*

Poe, Edgar Allan: Detective story, *1844*

Poell, George H.: Interstate Commerce Commission Medal of Honor, *1654*

Pohlman, Florence Dianna: Navy chaplain who was a woman, *5205*

Poinsett, Joel Roberts: Poinsettia plants, *4255*

Point du Sable, Jean Baptiste: City founded by an African-American pioneer, *2187*

Poitier, Sidney: Oscar awarded to a performer who was African-American, *1633*
Play by an African-American woman to appear on Broadway, *1270*

Polacco, Giorgio: Opera broadcast over the radio in its entirety, *1350*

Polk, James Knox: Gaslight in the White House, *6253*
Photograph of a president in office, *6155*
President who was a "dark horse" candidate, *3403*

Pollak, Simon: School for blind students to adopt the Braille system, *3025*

Pollard, Alfred William: Book series microfilmed, *4683*

Pollard, Othello: Leopard, *1143*

Pollock, Herbert Chermside: Synchrotron, *6802*

Pomerance, Carl: Factoring of a 100-digit number, *6760*

Pomeroy, Dorothy: Children's church, *6535*

Pomeroy, Vivian Towse: Children's church, *6535*

Pond, H. Chester: Clock movement to be electrically wound, *7902*

Poole, Cecil Francis: District attorney who was African-American, *2716*

Poole, Ernest: Pulitzer Prize for fiction, *1706*

Poole, William Frederick: Periodical index, *1771*

Pooley, Greville: Breach-of-promise suit, *4804*

Poore, Benjamin Perley: Catalog of government publications, *1772*
Congressional directory, *1817*

Pope, Albert Augustus: Bicycle factory, *7183*

Pope John Paul II: Pope to visit the White House, *4084*

Pope Leo XIII: Statue officially sanctioned by the Pope, *5407*

Pope Paul VI: Pope to visit the United States, *4083*

Pope Pius XII (Eugenio Pacelli): Pope to visit the United States before his election, *4081*

Popham, George: Thanksgiving worship service, *6503*

Pormort, Philemon: Public school with a continuous existence, *3040*

Porsche, Ferdinand: Subcompact car designed to be fuel-efficient, *5452*

Porter, Abel: Brass, *4463*
Gilt buttons, *2287*

Porter, Cole: Copyright registered for a choreographic score, *1237*

Porter, David: Naval vessel to display the American flag around Cape Horn, *1127*

Porter, David Dixon: Camels imported for military purposes, *1145*

Porter, Edwin Stanton: Movie with a plot, *5547*

Porter, George F.: Intercollegiate football game between African-American colleges, *7323*

Pory, John: Legislative assembly of a colony, *7622*

Possehl, Floyd F.: Church service in sign language to be televised, *6594*

Post, Charles William: Cereal sold as a breakfast food, *3916*

Post, Wiley Hardeman: Pressure suit, *1386*
Round-the-world solo airplane flight, *1457*

Potter, Charles Francis: Right-to-die society, *2840*

Potter, Richard: Magician of note, *3655*

Potts, Albert: Street letter box, *5992*

Poulson, Niels: Steel-frame residence, *2082*

Poulter, Thomas Charles: Snow cruiser for Antarctic research, *6716*

Powell, Colin Luther: Chairman of the Joint Chiefs of Staff who was African-American, *5129*

Powell, John Wesley: Exploration of the Grand Canyon of the Colorado, *6725*

Powell, William Frank: School for African-American children established by a state, *3064*

Powers, Hiram: Sculptor of renown, *1208*

Powers, Marie E.: Outdoor school for children with tuberculosis, *3020*

Powers, William T.: Hydroelectric power plant to furnish arc lighting service, *3458*

Poyner, Heather: Amateur boxing match for women, *7247*

Poznanski, Gustav: Jewish congregation in the Reform movement, *6486*

Prajadhipok, King: Absolute monarch to visit the United States, *6650*

Pratt, Abel: Comb-cutting machine, *4067*

Pratt, Charles Ed: Bicycle organization (national), *7185*

Pratt, Lewellyn E.: Advertising association to combat business abuses, *2452*

Pratt, Lovell S.: National skeet tournament, *7479*

Pratt, Matthew: Commercial artist, *1201*

Pratt, Philip W.: Sprinkler system patent, *4107*

Pratt, Phineas: Comb-cutting machine, *4067*

Pratt, Richard Henry: School of prominence for Native American children, *3065*

Pratt, Roberta: Birth control clinic run by a state government, *4847*

Prattis, Percival L.: News correspondent who was African-American, *5619*

Pray, James Sturgis: Urban planning instruction at a college, *3253*

Prentiss, John W.: Squash tennis organization (national), *7500*

Prescott, Benjamin: Canal for boat transportation, *3600*

Prescott, Edwin: Roller coaster with a loop-the-loop, *3626*

Presley, Elvis: Postage stamp whose design was decided by popular vote, *6101*

Preston, Charles E.: Portable church, *6532*

Preston, David: Ballet technique course at a college, *2915*

Preston, Emily: United Church of Christ ordination of a woman in which all the principal roles were filled by women, *6536*

Price, Henry: Masonic lodge, *5728*

Price, Hiram: National anti-saloon league, *2681*

Price, Vincent: Three-dimensional feature movie in color, *5564*

Pride, Alfred Melville: Autogiro to land and take off from a ship, *1534*

Pride, John: Pottery, *4308*

Priesand, Sally: Rabbi in the Reform movement who was a woman, *6490*

Priestley, Joseph: Unitarian church, *6523*

Prince, Harold: Musical to run for more than 3,000 performances, *1271*

Prince, Lucy Terry: Poetry collection by an African-American woman, *1946*

Prince, Thomas, Jr.: Religious magazine, *4693*

Prior, Edward: Traveler's aid program, *5966*

Pritchard, Benjamin Dudley: Interracial jury, *2735*

Procter, Harley: Floating soap, *4055*

Ptacek, Stephen R.: Solar-powered long-distance airplane flight, *1481*

Puccini, Giacomo: Metropolitan Opera orchestra conductor who was African-American, *1339*

Puett, Clay: Electric starting gate for horse races, *7401*

Puff, Gerhard: Execution carried out by the federal government for the killing of an FBI agent, *2804*

Pugh, David: Gas streetlights throughout a city, *2214*

Pullman, George Mortimer: Pullman sleeping car, *6375*

Pullman sleeping car that was comfortable, *6377*

Railroad parlor car, *6380*

Pulsifer, Alden William: International dogsled mail, *6010*

Pusey, Joshua: Matchbooks, *4337*

Putnam, Amelia Earhart: Transpacific solo airplane flight by a woman, *1460*

Putnam, Palmer Cosslet: Wind turbine, *3557*

Pyle, C.C.: Transcontinental foot race, *7557*

Pynchon, William: Meat packer, *3937*

Q

Quadequina: Popcorn, *3954*

Quanpen: Court-martial in a colony, *2738*

Quate, Calvin: Acoustic microscope, *6750*

Queen Emma: Queen to visit the United States, *4079*

Queen Marie of Rumania: Queen to visit the United States during her reign, *4080*

Quigley, Robin Lindsay: Navy officer who was a woman to hold a major command, *5297*

Quimby, Harriet: Pilot licensed by the Aero Club of America who was a woman, *1596*

Quincy, Josiah: Secession idea to be mentioned in Congress, *7634*

Quinn, Joseph: X-ray three-dimensional stereo fluoroscopic system, *4911*

Quinn, William: Religion magazine printed in rotogravure, *4734*

Quintard, Isaac: Cider mill, *3841*

R

Rabinowitz, Sherrie: Cyber cafe, *2467*

Radford, Arthur William: Navy chairman of the Joint Chiefs of Staff, *5293*

Rahman, Omar Abdel: Bombing of a skyscraper by foreign terrorists, *2790*

Rahr, Frederic: Baseball dyed yellow, *7110*

Railton, George Scott: Salvation Army services, *6531*

Rainey, Joseph Hayne: Congressional representative who was African-American, *2603*

Rains, Gabriel Jones: Land mines, *8097*

Raleigh, Walter: Artist in the English colonies, *1196*

Beer, *2663*

Native American to become a Protestant, *6502*

Ralston, Samuel Moffett: Election campaign using radio, *3322*

Reese, William and James: Slate used for roofing material, *2035*

Reeve, Tapping: Law school operated privately, *3122*

Reeves, Frank Daniel: Election in the District of Columbia, *3325*

Reid, John: Golf mixed foursome, *7354*
Landscape architect, *1192*
Walkie-Talkie two-way radio device, *7722*

Reid, Mrs. John G.: Golf mixed foursome, *7354*

Reilly, H. Christine: Antibiotic, *4998*

Reinagle, Alexander: Songbook of secular songs, *1937*

Reinecke, Mabel Gilmore: Internal revenue collector for the federal government who was a woman, *7657*

Remington, Frederic: Postage stamp featuring a work of art in true color, *6093*

Remington, William H.: Nickel plating, *4471*

Renick, Felix: Cattle that were purebred shorthorns, *1080*

Reno, Janet: Attorney general who was a woman, *6128*

Reno, Jesse W.: Escalator patent, *2106*

Reno, John: Train robbery of a train in motion, *2776*

Reno, Simeon: Train robbery of a train in motion, *2776*

Renwick, James: Terra cotta, *2056*

Resnik, Judith A.: Astronauts who were women, *7047*
Space shuttle disaster, *7090*

Respess, J.S.: Horse race mutuel ticket to pay more than $1,000, *7397*

Ressegue, H.: Fur-bearing animals raised commercially, *1070*

Rettger, Leo Frederick: Acidophilus milk, *3876*

Reulbach, Edward Marvin: Double-header baseball games that were shutouts, *7125*

Revel, Bernard: College of liberal arts and sciences founded as a Jewish institution, *2965*
Yeshivah for Jewish religious study, *3276*

Revels, Hiram Rhodes: Senator who was African-American, *2649*

Revere, Paul: Engraving to achieve popularity, *1225*

Reyburn, Robert: Medical society for African-Americans, *5039*

Reymert, James De Noon: Norwegian newspaper, *5667*

Reynolds, R.S.: Aluminum foil, *4340*

Reynolds, William: Territory annexed by the federal government beyond the nation's continental limits, *5969*

Rheaume, Manon: Professional hockey player who was a woman, *7383*

Rhinelander, Leonard Kip: Composograph photograph in a newspaper, *5693*

Rhodes, Cecil: Rhodes Scholars, *2961*

Rhodes, Richard S.: Hearing aid, *5069*

Rhodes, Thomas E.: Radio broadcast of a debate, *6269*

Ribaut, Jean: Ship built in America to cross the Atlantic Ocean, *6847*

Riccardo, Ric: Pizzeria, *2462*

Ricciardi, Richard: Commercial DNA bank, *6756*

Rice, Isaac L.: Intercollegiate transatlantic chess match by cable, *4030*

Rich, Comly: Building and loan association, *3763*

Richard, Gabriel: Congressional representative who was a Catholic priest, *2601*

Richard, Joseph Henri Maurice "Rocket": Professional hockey player to score 50 goals in one season, *7379*

Richards, George: Masonic magazine, *4705*

Richards, Linda Ann Judson: Hospital record system, *4882*
Nurse to receive formal training, *5023*

Richards, Theodore William: Nobel Prize for chemistry awarded to an American, *1692*

Richardson, Ebenezer: Child to be killed in the Revolution, *7985*

Richardson, Elliott Lee: Cabinet member to serve in four different capacities, *6120*

Richardson, Jack: Transcontinental round-trip airplane flight made within 24 hours, *1465*

Richey, Clifford and Nancy: Brother and sister to win national tennis singles championships in the same tournament, *7539*

Richey, Helen: Pilot to fly a regularly scheduled airmail transport who was a woman, *1600*

Richman, Harry: Transatlantic round-trip airplane flight from the United States, *1461*

Richmond, Bill: Boxer to win distinction in the ring, *7248*

Richmond, David: Civil rights sit-in, *2260*

Richmond, James N.: Plate glass, *4040*

Richmond, Lee: Installment finance company, *3805*

Richter, Burton: Year in which Nobel Prizes were won by Americans in five of six categories, *1702*

Rickenbacker, Adolph: Electric guitar, *1325*

Rickenbacker, Edward Vernon: Ace of Aces from the United States, *1611*
Airplane sleeping berths, *1413*
Combat mission of American pilots ordered to battle in World War I, *8042*

Ricketts, Claude Vernon: Naval ship with a crew of mixed nationalities, *6944*

Ricketts, John Bill: Circus, *3672*

Rickover, Hyman George: Nuclear-powered submarine, *6973*

Rockefeller, Nelson Aldrich: Senate proceeding to be shown on television, *2637*

Rockenbach, Samuel Dickerson: Tank operated by Army troops, *8116*

Rockwell, Alphonse David: Execution by electrocution, *2799*

Rockwell, Norman: Cover of the *Saturday Evening Post* by Norman Rockwell, *1218*

Roddenberry, Gene: Space burial, *2846*

Rodgers, Calbraith Perry: Transcontinental airplane flight made in stages, *1439*

Rodgers, hn: Naval battle in the War of 1812, *8020*

Rodgers, John Kearney: Eye hospital, *4872*

Roebling, John Augustus: Railroad suspension bridge, *3580*

Suspension aqueduct bridge of wire cable, *3577*

Wire rope factory, *4398*

Roebling, Mary Gindhart: Stock exchange director who was a woman, *3831*

Roediger, Virginia More: Theater and dramatic criticism course at a college, *3105*

Roelantsen, Adam: School for colonial children in America, *3038*

Roff, John: Pony Express mail, *5994*

Rogers, Asa: Silver plating factory, *4466*

Rogers, Bob: Sports trainer to work professionally, *7548*

Rogers, Donald Howard: Jet airplane passenger trip, *1474*

Rogers, Edith Frances Nourse: Congressional representative to serve 18 terms who was a woman, *2611*

Rogers, Ginger: Movie to be shown simultaneously on pay television and in movie theaters, *5519*

Rogers, Harriet: Oral school for deaf students, *3031*

Rogers, Joel Augustus: News correspondent who was African-American, *5619*

Rogers, Moses: Steamboat to make an ocean voyage, *6862*

Transatlantic crossing by an American steamboat, *6979*

Rogers, Simeon S.: Silver plating factory, *4466*

Rogers, William: Silver plating factory, *4466*

Rolando, Henry: Medal of Honor awarded to a Marine in the Civil War, *1672*

Rolfe, John: Tobacco cultivation, *2694*

Rolph, James, Jr.: Municipal streetcars, *6405*

Ronaldson, James: Dollar marks, *5802*

Type specimen book from an American type foundry, *1742*

Ronan, George: West Point graduate killed in action, *3197*

Ronemus, William: Baby show, *2141*

Ronne, Edith "Jackie": American base in Antarctica that was permanent, *6730*

Ronne, Finn: American base in Antarctica that was permanent, *6730*

Rooney, Roderick Shanahan: Submarine from the United States sunk by an enemy submarine, *8083*

Roosevelt, Eleanor: Commemorative postage stamp depicting a president's wife, *6095*

First Lady to be depicted on a monument to a president, *6134*

First Lady to travel in an airplane to a foreign country, *6131*

Roosevelt, Ellen C. and Grace W.: National tennis championship match for women, *7529*

Roosevelt, Franklin Delano: Baseball game at night by major league teams, *7131*

Cabinet in which all members were sworn in at the same time and place, *6111*

Cabinet member who was a woman, *6112*

Civilian airport owned and operated by the federal government, *1508*

Compensation of Japanese-Americans interned during World War II, *8087*

Easter egg roll, *4239*

Electoral college members invited to a presidential inauguration, *3391*

First Lady to be depicted on a monument to a president, *6134*

Olympic Games competition to be held in the winter, *7446*

President elected for third and fourth terms, *6170*

President inaugurated on January 20, *6169*

President to appear on television, *6215*

President to become a godfather to a member of the British royal family, *6200*

President to conduct religious services as commander-in-chief of the Navy, *6166*

President to fly in an airplane, *6226*

President to go through the Panama Canal while in office, *6167*

President to invite the president-elect, *6165*

President to make a radio broadcast from a foreign country, *6214*

President to make a radio broadcast in a foreign language, *6216*

President to read a veto message to Congress, *6168*

President to visit a foreign country in wartime, *6237*

President to visit Hawaii while in office, *6236*

President to visit South America while in office, *6235*

Presidential candidate to accept his party's nomination in person, *3413*

Presidential library, *6171*

Presidential pet to star in a movie, *6201*

Social security monthly payment, *4526*

Rush, Robert I.: Veterinary hospital established by a city, *5125*

Rusk, Dean: Astronaut international rescue agreement, *7037*

Russell, Bill: Coach of a professional basketball team who was African-American, *7177*

Russell, Howard Hyde: Anti-saloon organization, *2680*

Russell, John: Cutlery factory, *4369*

Russell, John Henry: Naval battle in the Civil War, *7959*

Russell, John Richard: Lung transplant, *5098*

Russell, S.I.: Electric heating pad, *4944*

Russell, Steve: Computer game, *4012*

Russwurm, John Brown: Newspaper for African-American readers, *5664*

Rust, John Daniel: Mechanical cotton picker, *1033*

Rust, Samuel: Printing press invented in the United States, *5768*

Rusticoat, Robert: Comic magazine, *4698*

Rutan, Richard: Round-the-world nonstop airplane flight without refueling, *1482*

Ruth, Babe: Baseball player to hit a home run in an All-Star game, *7150*

Ruth, George Herman: All-star major league baseball game, *7130*

Rutledge, John: Independent government in an American colony, *5940*

Supreme Court chief justice whose nomination was not confirmed, *2754*

Supreme Court justice to be appointed chief justice, *2761*

Supreme Court of the United States, *2742*

Rutledge, William J.: Grand Army of the Republic post for veterans of the Civil War, *5310*

Rutt, Chris L.: Ready-mix food, *3947*

Ryan, Frank B.: Vote in the House of Representatives to be recorded electronically, *2594*

Ryan, Harriet: Tuberculosis patients' home, *4897*

Ryan, Harry: Professional football game, *7322*

Ryan, Paddy: Bareknuckle world heavyweight boxing champion, *7251*

Ryskind, Morrie: Pulitzer Prize awarded to a musical, *1712*

S

Sabin, Florence Rena: National science institute, *6781*

Professor at a first-class medical school who was a woman, *3151*

Sacagawea: Transcontinental expedition to the Pacific coast, *6721*

Sagan, Carl: Robot to conduct a roving exploration of the surface of another planet, *7093*

Spacecraft to carry a message intended to be read by living beings elsewhere in the universe, *7084*

Sager, Lester W.: Play of full length by an African-American writer to be performed in New York City, *1258*

Saint-Gaudens, Augustus: Arts and letters organization (national), *5716*

Saint-Saëns, Camille: Opera broadcast over the radio in its entirety, *1350*

Salk, Jonas Edward: Poliomyelitis vaccine, *4923*

Salmaggi, Alfredo: Opera prima donna who was African-American, *1333*

Salter, Susanna Medora: Mayor who was a woman, *2207*

Salvador, Francis: Soldier killed in the Revolutionary War who was Jewish, *7996*

Samma, Senaa: Sword swallower, *3656*

Samoset: Greeting addressed to the Pilgrims by a Native American, *5914*

Land sale by Native Americans to Europeans, *5918*

Sampson, Edith Spurlock: Judge who was an African-American woman, *2726*

United Nations delegate who was African-American, *3992*

Samson, Job: Tunnel, *3611*

Samuelson, Frank: Transatlantic trip by rowboat, *6985*

Samuelson, Paul Anthony: Nobel Prize in economic sciences, *1700*

Samuelson, Ralph W.: Water skis, *7591*

Sanchez, Raphael: Letter containing a description of America, *1093*

Sandage, Allan Rex: Quasar to be observed, *6683*

Sanders, Nathaniel: Road authorization by a state, *6612*

Sanderson, Ivan T.: Television program in color, *7784*

Sandys, George: Poetry translation prepared in America, *1942*

Sanger, Margaret: Birth control clinic, *4844*

Birth-control pill, *6833*

Vasectomy outpatient service, *4851*

Santangel, Luis de: Letter containing a description of America, *1093*

Sarasohn, Kasriel Hersch: Yiddish newspaper, *5670*

Sarazen, Gene: Golf champion to win both the U.S. Open and the Professional tournaments, *7360*

Sargent, Edith: Public school classes for children with epilepsy, *3022*

Sargent, Franklin Haven: Drama school, *2905*

Sargent, James: Time lock, *2135*

Schweickart, Russell Louis: Astronauts to transfer from one spacecraft to another while in orbit, *7039*

Schweitzer, Arlette: Grandmother to give birth to her own grandchild, *2169*

Schweizer, Erhard K.: Physical manipulation of individual atoms, *6824*

Schwerdt, Carlton Everett: Virus obtained in crystalline form, *5059*

Schwinger, Julian Seymour: Quantum theory of electromagnetic radiation, *6759*

Scobee, Francis R.: Space shuttle disaster, *7090*

Scopes, John Thomas: Trial of a teacher for violating a state ban on teaching the theory of evolution, *3068*

Score, Roberta: Scientific evidence for life on Mars, *7027*

Scot, Robert: Half cent, *5361*

Scott, Albert S.: Insurance board established by a state government, *4503*

Scott, Bert W.: Transcontinental car race, *7266*

Scott, Bill: Animated cartoon made for television, *7782*

Scott, Blanche: Pilot licensed by the Aero Club of America who was a woman, *1596*

Scott-Browne, D.L.: Typing school, *3289*

Scott, David Randolph: Astronaut who was a civilian to orbit the earth, *7035*
Astronauts to ride a vehicle on the moon, *7042*

Scott, Edward and Clarence: Toilet paper, *5756*

Scott, John Walter: Public exhibition of postage stamps, *6058*

Scott, John Welwood: Religious weekly newspaper, *5636*

Scott, Myron: Soapbox derby, *7583*

Scott, Norman: International championship figure skating tournament, *7431*

Scott, Walter: Lunch wagon, *2457*
Web-fed four-color rotary printing press, *5780*

Scott, Winfield: Press censorship by military authorities, *5604*

Scull, Nicholas: Circulating library, *4661*

Seaborg, Glenn Theodore: Plutonium, *6818*

Seabury, Samuel: Episcopal bishop, *6549*

Seager, D.W: Camera exposure scale, *5832*

Seaman, J.V.: Magazine for mechanics, *4768*

Seaman, Valentine: Nurses' training, *3133*

Searles, Joseph Louis, III: New York Stock Exchange member who was African-American, *3834*

Sears, Eleanora R.: Squash rackets champion who was a woman, *7502*

Sears, Richard Dudley: National tennis championship matches, *7527*

Sebille, Elizabeth J.: Air Force Medal of Honor for action in the Korean War, *1667*

Sebille, Louis J.: Air Force Medal of Honor for action in the Korean War, *1667*

Sebree, Trow: Automatic pilot on an airplane, *1499*

Sebring, James Dennison: World Series baseball game, *7123*

Seccombe, Joseph: Fishing treatise, *1993*

Secker, William: Miniature book, *1733*

Seddon, Margaret R.: Astronauts who were women, *7047*

Sedgwick, Theodore: Slave to be emancipated, *2245*
Theology school graduate who was African-American, *3270*

Seereiter, John: Billiard match to attain international fame, *4017*

Segar, Elzie Crisler: Monument to a comic-strip character, *5415*

Segrave, Henry O'Neil de Hane: Car to exceed the speed of 200 miles per hour, *5445*

Seid, B.S.: Hospital for patients of Chinese ancestry, *4891*

Seidel, Emil: Mayor of a major city who was a Socialist, *2208*

Selden, George Baldwin: Car patent, *5428*

Selfridge, Thomas Etholen: Airplane accident that was fatal, *1387*

Sellers, Coleman: Photographic attempt to show motion, *5569*

Sellers, John: Sieve, *4366*

Seltzer, Leo A.: Roller derby, *7465*

Semmes, Raphael: Confederate cruiser to raid Union commerce, *7944*

Semple, Robert: Newspaper published on the Pacific Coast, *5640*

Sennett, Mack: Movie comedy of feature length, *5552*

Sequoyah: Native American language to be given a written form, *5959*

Serapion, Bishop: Coptic Orthodox Church bishop, *6500*

Sergiev, John: Russian Orthodox saint canonized in the United States, *6498*

Serra, Junipero: Catholic mission in California, *6454*

Servoss, Thomas Lowery: Coastal shipping service, *2478*

Seton, Elizabeth Ann Bayley: Catholic saint who was born in America, *6481*
Catholic school, *3042*

Seutter, B.G.: Radio receiving contest, *6261*

Sevareid, Eric: Supreme Court justice to participate in a television program, *2764*

Sevier, Electa: Liner equipped with a gyrostabilizer, *6899*

Sevier, John: Independent civil government in America, *5939*
State denied admission into the Union, *7601*

Sewall, Arthur: Steel sailing vessel, *6874*

Shotwell, William: Haircloth, *7866*

Shoukletovich, Doushan Jefta: Serbian Orthodox cathedral, *6497*

Shreeve, Herbert E.: Transatlantic message over radio telephone, *7757*

Shreve, Henry Miller: Double-deck steamboat, *6864*

Shryrock, George Augustus: Straw paper, *5751*

Shu, Loo Kum: Telephone exchange for Chinese-American subscribers, *7733*

Shuckburgh, Richard: Patriotic song to achieve national popularity, *1374*

Shugart, Alan: Floppy disk, *2536*

Shumway, Norman: Heart transplant, *5100*

Shunk, Francis Rawn: Child labor law enacted by a state that restricted the age of the worker, *4575*

Shuster, Joe: Comic books, *2028*

Shute, Nevil: Movie premiered simultaneously in major cities throughout the world, *5520*

Siccary, John: Tomatoes eaten in America, *3895*

Sickles, Daniel: Temporary insanity defense in a criminal case, *4622*

Siebert, Muriel: New York Stock Exchange seat owner who was a woman, *3833*

Siegel, Benjamin "Bugsy": Casino in Las Vegas, *3636*

Siegel, Jerry: Comic books, *2028*

Sievert, Frances: Telephone switchboard with Braille markings, *7738*

Sikorsky, Igor Ivan: Helicopter, *1557*
Helicopter flight from water, *1574*
Helicopter flight of one-hour duration, *1573*
Long-distance helicopter flight, *1575*

Sikwayi: Native American language to be given a written form, *5959*

Silliman, Benjamin: Science journal, *4767*

Silliman, Benjamin, Jr.: Applied chemistry professor at a college, *3234*

Sills, Beverly: Metropolitan Opera orchestra conductor who was a woman, *1340*

Silver, Bernard: Bar code scanner, *2373*

Simmons, Amelia: Cookbook by an American author, *1847*

Simmons, Jean: Movie in Cinemascope, *5562*

Simmons, John: Technical college for women, *2962*

Simmons, Joseph "Run": Rap album to attract a mass audience, *1373*

Simms, Ruth Hanna McCormick: Presidential campaign manager who was a woman, *3392*

Simms, William Gilmore: Novel by an American to depict Native Americans in a realistic manner, *1843*

Simon, Carleton: Identification of human beings from the pattern formed by the blood vessels of the retina, *4165*

Simon, Rene: Airplane rescue at sea by another airplane, *1438*

Simon, William: Analytical chemistry course requirement for pharmacy students, *3146*

Simonds, Frank Herbert: Pulitzer Prize for a newspaper editorial, *1705*

Simons, David Goodman: Balloon flight to rise higher than 100,000 feet, *1541*

Simpson, Albert Benjamin: Missionary training school, *3275*

Simpson, Edward: Naval Academy graduate to attain the rank of rear admiral, *3215*

Simpson, George B.: Electric range, *4293*

Simpson, Michael Hodge: Bunting manufacture, *7868*

Sims, James Marion: Artificial insemination of a woman resulting in conception, *5113*
Silver wire suture, *4955*
Women's hospital, *4880*

Sims, Julia Isabelle: Grand jury foreman who was a woman, *2737*

Sims, Roger Bernard: Air Force Academy graduates who were African-American, *3192*

Simson, Sampson: Hospital under Jewish auspices, *4876*

Sinatra, Frank: Song to hit No. 1 in the pop charts, *1366*

Sinclair, Lee: Building with a large-scale clear-span dome, *2085*

Sinclair, Richard L.: Parking garage that was completely automated, *5485*

Sinclair, Upton Beall: Negative election campaign run by media specialists, *3323*

Singer, Isaac Bashevis: Movie for which one woman served as producer, director, and star, *5568*

Singer, Isaac Merritt: Sewing machine equipped with a rocking treadle or double treadle, *4353*
Sewing machine manufacturer, *4352*

Sirhan, Sirhan Bishara: Presidential campaigner to be assassinated, *3416*

Sissle, Noble: Movie featuring an African-American actor, *5554*

Skene, John: Mason, *5727*

Skinner, John Stuart: Horse racing magazine, *4782*

Skinner, L.A.: Handheld rocket launcher, *8133*

Skinner, Richard Cort: Dentistry book, *1922*

Slack, Leslie: Ship to fire a Polaris missile, *8140*

Slade, Daniel Denison: Veterinary college, *3180*

Slade, Frederick J.: Open-hearth furnace for the manufacture of steel, *4493*

Slate, Thomas Benton: Dry ice manufactured commercially, *4441*

Slater, Bill: World Series baseball game to be shown on television, *7135*

Smith, Mary Louise: Chairman of a major political party who was a woman, *3344*

Smith, Merle James, Jr.: Coast Guard Academy graduate who was African-American, *3210*

Smith, Michael J.: Space shuttle disaster, *7090*

Smith, Owen P.: Greyhound racing association, *7279*

Smith, Owen Patrick: Dog racetrack to use an imitation rabbit, *7278*

Smith, Ralph: Congregational church, *6505*

Smith, Robert: City college, *2936*

Smith, Robert H.: Twelve-step rehabilitation program, *2662*

Smith, Robyn: Jockey who was a woman to win a major stakes race, *7419*

Smith, Samuel Francis: Performance of "America the Beautiful", *1380*

Smith, Samuel Harrison: Guide to parliamentary rules of order, *2016*

Smith, Sarah J.: Prison built for women and managed by women, *2823*

Smith, Stanley: Train of airplanes, *1459*

Smith, Tempel: Haflinger horse, *1185*

Smith, Teri: Liver transplant from a live donor, *5105*

Smith, Thomas: Self-portrait, *1212*

Smith, Wesley Leland: Transcontinental regular airmail service, *6019*

Smith, William: Osteopathy school, *3170*

Smith, William Alden: Game warden to be paid a salary, *3744*

Smith, William and Andrew: Candy packaged in a factory, *3963*

Smith, William Loughton: House of Representatives election that was contested, *3326*

House of Representatives filibuster, *2581*

Smith, Willis Warren: Drive-in movie theater, *3709*

Smock, Benjamin Wilson J.: Health department of a county organized on a full-time basis, *4185*

Smyth, Ethel Mary: Opera composed by a woman to be performed at the Metropolitan Opera House, *1348*

Snead, Sam: Golfer to break 60 for 18 holes in a major tournament, *7364*

Golfer to shoot below his age, *7369*

Snelling, Henry Hunt: Photography book, *1986*

Snider, Christopher: Child to be killed in the Revolution, *7985*

Snider, Jacob, Jr.: Book for the blind, *1747*

Snively, Mrs. J.H.: Postage stamp for balloon mail, *6059*

Snorri: Child born of European parents on American soil, *2155*

Snowdon, John: Bridge of cast iron, *3572*

Sobrero, Aquiles Jose: Vasectomy outpatient service, *4851*

Soley, John Codman: Naval militia established by a state, *5255*

Solis-Cohen, Jacob: Laryngology journal, *4757*

Solomon, Hannah Greenebaum: Fraternal society for Jews, *5720*

Solomons, Adolphus Simeon: Red Cross meeting, *5739*

Sontheimer, Carl: Food processor, *4304*

Sordelet, James Robert: Sailor to reenlist in the Navy while under the North Pole, *5267*

Sothell, Seth: Indigo crop, *1009*

Sousa, John Philip: Performance of *The Stars and Stripes Forever*, *1292*

Sousaphone, *1322*

Sowagonish: Court-martial in a colony, *2738*

Sower, Christopher: Bible printed in German, *1961*

German magazine, *4741*

German newspaper, *5661*

Spaatz, Carl Andrew: American land victory without infantry in World War II, *8062*

Spafford, George: Fourdrinier papermaking machine, *5750*

Spain: Underground comic book of note, *4739*

Spalding, Albert Goodwill: Baseball game that was a shutout, *7119*

Spalding, Eliza Hart: Settlers to cross the continent who were women, *5960*

Spalding, Lyman: General pharmacopoeia, *1930*

Spangenberg, Augustus Gottlieb: Moravian settlement in America, *6540*

Sparks, Frank: Train robbery of a train in motion, *2776*

Sparks, Jared: Ancient and modern history chair at a college, *3095*

Speakman, Townsend: Soda water, *3843*

Speicher, Scott: Serviceman killed in the Gulf War, *7974*

Spencer, Dolly: Police chief who was a woman, *4142*

Spencer, Percy: Microwave oven, *4302*

Spencer, Peter: African Methodist Episcopal church convention, *6563*

Spencer, Philip: Navy officer condemned for mutiny, *5283*

Spencer, Platt Rogers: Handwriting teaching system widely used in schools, *3057*

Spencer, Sara Andrews: National political convention to be addressed by a woman, *3336*

Spencer, Timothy W.: Criminal convicted on the evidence of DNA matching, *4167*

Sperry, Charles Stillman: Circumnavigation of the globe by a fleet of warships, *6986*

Sperry, Elmer Ambrose: Gyroscopic stabilizer, *6956*

Steinweg, Henry Engelhard: Grand piano with a cast-metal plate, *1312*

Stephens, Alexander Hamilton: Confederate congressional session, *7947*

Stephens, Ann S.: Mass-market paperback book, *1786*

Stephens, Henry Louis: Comic weekly, *4717*

Stephenson, Benjamin Franklin: Grand Army of the Republic post for veterans of the Civil War, *5310*

Stephenson, Henry: Capture of an American ship captain by a German submarine in World War II, *8057*

Stephenson, John: Streetcar, *6394*

Sterbini, Cesare: Italian opera, *1346*

Stern, Bill: Bicycle race to be shown on television, *7198*

Stern, Sheldon: Coast-to-coast solar-powered two-way radio conversation, *6282*

Stern, William and Elizabeth: Trial of a surrogate mother for refusing to give up her baby, *2167*

Sternberg, George Miller: Bacteriology laboratory, *4928*
Bacteriology textbook, *1918*

Stessel, Isadore: Airship from the United States lost to enemy action in World War II, *8064*

Stetson, John B.: Cowboy hat, *2297*

Steuart, George H.: Railroad to carry troops, *6324*

Steuben, Baron von: Military drill manual, *2011*

Stevens, Albert William: Aerial photograph showing the lateral curvature of the horizon and the beginning of the stratosphere, *5828*

Stevens, Alexander Hodgdon: Clinical instruction and bedside demonstration, *3135*

Stevens, George B.: Modern carillon, *1323*

Stevens, John: Flour rolling mill, *3915*
Locomotive to pull a train on a track, *6347*
Railroad charter granted by a state, *6317*
Railroad treatise, *2020*
Steam-propelled ferryboat, *6907*
Steamboat to make an ocean voyage, *6862*
Steamboat with a twin-screw propeller, *6860*

Stevens, John Cox: Yacht club, *7207*
Yacht from the United States to win an international yacht race, *7209*

Stevens, Robert Livingston: Railroad rails of T shape, *6416*
Steam-propelled ferryboat, *6907*
Steamboat to make an ocean voyage, *6862*

Stevens, Thomas: Round-the-world bicycle trip, *7201*

Stevens, Uriah Smith: Labor union to admit workers other than craft workers, *4611*

Stevenson, Adlai Ewing: Presidential election in which a computer was used to predict the outcome, *3393*

Stevenson, Marmaduke: Quakers executed for their religious beliefs, *6587*

Stevenson, Roger: Military field strategy manual, *2010*

Stevenson, Sarah Hackett: Medical society (national), *5036*

Steward, Roger: Commercial ship to conquer the Northwest Passage, *7000*

Stewart, Ada: Company nurse, *5026*

Stewart, Alexander Turney: Hotel for women, *2425*

Stewart, David: Pharmacy professorship at a college, *3132*

Stewart, Joan Wyatt: Prison guard who was a woman to serve in a maximum security prison for men, *2831*

Stewart, Mortimer: Play to be shown on television, *1260*

Stewart, Philip Battell: Baseball batting and fielding cage, *7108*

Stewart, Robert: Astronauts to fly free in space, *7050*

Stewart, Timothy A.: Patent on an animal, *6751*

Stewart, Virginia Gladys: Woman of American ancestry to become a queen, *6651*

Stewart, Walter: Brevet conferred by the Army on an American, *5168*

Stewart, William Holmes: X-ray movies of human organs in action, *4908*

Stiles, Charles Wardell: Laboratory for the study of human parasites, *4931*
Laboratory for the study of parasites in livestock, *5120*

Still, Andrew Taylor: Osteopathic physician, *4975*
Osteopathy school, *3170*

Stillman, Alan: Singles bar, *2466*

Stillman, Alfred: Squash tennis tournament, *7501*

Stillson, Daniel C.: Pipe or screw wrench, *7929*

Stimson, Henry Lewis: Presidential airplane, *6227*

Stinis, Andy: Skywriting advertisement written at night, *2337*

Stinson, Emma Beaver: Airplane flying school operated by a woman, *7294*

Stockdale, James Bond: Naval War College president who was a former prisoner of war, *3222*

Stoddard, Joshua C.: Calliope, *1311*

Stoddard, Lawrence B.: Amateur golf tournament, *7339*

Stoddard, Sampson Vryling: Religious tract society (national), *6576*

Sutherland, J.B.: Refrigerated railroad car, *6378*

Sutter, John Augustus: Russian settlement, *5943*

Suzuki, Shunryu: Zen Buddhist monastery, *6439*

Swaine, Charles: Arctic expedition to seek the Northwest Passage, *6720*

Swaine, John: Law book containing laws enacted by more than one session of Congress, *1875*

Swallow, Silas Comfort: United Christian Party convention, *3370*

Swan, Abraham: Architecture book printed in America, *2009*

Swan, William G.: Rocket glider flight, *1552*

Swarthout, Cornelius: Waffle iron patent, *4294*

Swarts, Gardner Taber: Health laboratory established by a city, *4197*
Health laboratory established by a state to diagnose diseases by the examination of sputum, *4201*

Swayze, John Cameron: Television image using a split screen, *7816*

Sweeney, Michael Francis: Armored car in commercial use, *5444*

Sweet, John Edson: Screw caliper, *7928*

Swenson, Erin: Minister who was a transsexual, *6844*

Swift, Gustavus Franklin: Year-round railroad shipments of dressed beef, *2482*

Swift, Joseph Gardner: West Point graduates, *3196*

Swift, William Henry: Iron pile lighthouse, *4127*

Swinnerton, James: Comic books, *2028*

Switzer, Robert and Joseph: Fluorescent paint, *7938*

Swope, Herbert Bayard: Pulitzer Prize awarded to a newspaper reporter, *1704*

Syer, Robert D'oyly: Bank of importance to lease personal property, *3798*

Syle, Henry Winter: Prayers in sign language, *6528*

Syms, Benjamin: Free school funded by an endowment, *3039*

Sze, Wilbur Carl: Marine officer of Chinese descent, *5238*

Szilard, Leo: Nuclear reactor patent, *6806*

Szold, Henrietta: Night school for immigrants, *2887*

T

Tafel, Adolph J.: Homeopathic pharmacy, *4986*

Taft, Mrs. Josiah: Woman whose vote was recorded, *3421*

Taft, William Howard: Airplane to land on the White House lawn, *6255*
Chamber of Commerce, *2446*
Commerce court established by the federal government, *2713*
Former president to become chief justice of the Supreme Court, *6164*
Postal savings bank, *3775*
President buried in the National Cemetery, *6199*
President to pitch a ball to open the baseball season, *6163*

Taggart, William H.: Dental inlay made of gold, *4866*

Tainter, Charles Sumner: Phonograph that was practical, *7005*

Taitt, Francis: Merchant ship formally blessed at a launching ceremony, *6893*

Talbot, Paul H.: Naval counterattack by American forces against the Japanese in World War II, *8076*

Tallmadge, Benjamin: Secret service established in a colony, *4168*

Tally, Thomas Lincoln: Theater to show movies, *3704*

Talmadge, Norma: Radio show sponsored by a cooperative of commercial advertisers, *2338*

Taney, Roger Brooke: Cabinet appointee rejected by the Senate, *6106*
Cabinet member who was Catholic, *6105*
Supreme Court chief justice who was Catholic, *2759*
Supreme Court decision in a state boundary case, *2751*

Tanner, Harry Laurence: Gyroscopic stabilizer, *6956*

Tanner, Henry Ossawa: Artist of renown who was African-American, *1209*
Painting by an African-American artist to hang in the White House, *1221*

Tappan, D.: Religious tract society, *6570*

Tappan, Lewis: Commercial rating agency, *3815*

Tarkington, Booth: Fiction writer to win the Pulitzer Prize twice, *1709*

Tau, Yun: Beauty pageant to be held nationwide, *3628*

Taub, Sam: Boxing match to be shown on television, *7243*

Taylor, Alan: Theory of fair division, *6762*

Taylor, Albert Hoyt: Radar detection of airplanes, *7676*
Radar observations, *7675*

Taylor, Alfred Alexander: Election for governor in which two brothers were the opposing candidates, *7616*

Taylor, Anna Edson: Daredevil to go over Niagara Falls in a barrel, *3679*

Taylor, Carl Rutherford: Ice cream cone rolling machine, *3868*

Taylor, Colonel: Coursing club, *7394*

Taylor, Frederick W.: National tennis championship matches, *7527*

Taylor, George Caldwell: Labor dispute in which the Taft-Hartley Act was invoked, *4569*

Taylor, Howard Augustus: Intercollegiate lawn tennis match, *7528*

Taylor, Jimmy: Fighter plane equipped with a cannon, *1487*

Taylor, John: Iron rolling mill, *4449*

Taylor, Napoleon Edward: American expeditionary force to land in Africa in World War II, *8055*

Taylor, Richard: Quark to be observed, *6821*

Taylor, Robert: General-purpose computer network, *2544*

Taylor, Robert Love: Election for governor in which two brothers were the opposing candidates, *7616*

Taylor, Samuel Allan: Stamp collection magazine, *4727*

Taylor, William C.: Heat-resistant glass, *4048*

Taylor, Zachary: Free Soil Party convention, *3352*

President whose body was exhumed, *6208*

Teaford, Mark F.: Tooth-wear gauge, *4867*

Teague, Clayton: Molecular measuring machine, *6811*

Tekakwitha, Kateri: Catholic beatification of a Native American, *6474*

Telkes, Maria: House completely heated by solar energy, *2128*

Tellefsen, Carl: Ski club association, *7480*

Ten Broeck, Richard: Horse bred in the United States to win a major race abroad, *7405*

Tennent, John: Pleurisy book, *1889*

Tennent, John Van Brugh: Midwifery professor at a college, *3130*

Tepuni, William: Pilot from the United States to sink a German submarine, *8053*

Terasawa, Kuniko: Japanese newspaper in continuous publication, *5682*

Terrillion, Beverly: Train operated exclusively by women, *6436*

Thach, John Smith: Navy task force to fight undersea craft, *5305*

Thacher, Thomas: Medical pamphlet, *1886*

Thacher's, James: Hydrophobia book, *1902*

Thaden, Louise McPhetridge: Transcontinental air derby for women, *7297*

Thatcher, Linden A.: Coin-operated mailbox, *6011*

Thayer, Abbott Handerson: Biological study of camouflage in nature, *6745*

Thayer, Frederick Winthrop: Baseball catcher's mask, *7107*

Thayer, Nathaniel: Court tennis, *7524*

Thiry, John Henry: Savings group for children, *3769*

Thomas, Allan M.: Incubator for premature babies, *4943*

Thomas, B.F.: Needle dam, *3607*

Thomas, Charles L.: Medals of Honor awarded to African-American servicemen for service in World War II, *1689*

Thomas, Danny: Children's hospital for research and treatment of catastrophic childhood diseases, *4893*

Thomas, Evylyn: Car accident, *5466*

Thomas, Isaiah: Agricultural dictionary, *1799*

American gazetteer, *1814*

Bible in folio size to be illustrated, *1964*

Dictionary published in the United States, *1797*

Greek Testament, *1965*

Historical society (national), *5711*

History of printing, *1866*

Music printed in a magazine, *1280*

Pocket dictionary, *1798*

Thomas, John H.: Fiberglass, *4052*

Thomas, Martha Carey: Dean of the faculty at a college, *2972*

Thomas, Mr.: Bookwagon traveling library, *4676*

Thomas, Robert Bailey: Almanac with a continuous existence, *1766*

Thomas, Theodore: Symphonic work by an American composer, *1290*

Thomashefsky, Boris: Yiddish theater performance, *1255*

Thompson, Bradbury: Christmas postage stamp regular issue, *6094*

Thompson, Frank Adoniram: Chiropody school at a college, *3175*

Thompson, Frank P.: Baseball team of African-American players to play professionally, *7164*

Thompson, George F.: Daily news program on radio, *5705*

Thompson, George Irwin: Naval War College students who were African-American, *3220*

Thompson, George Kramer: Building with caisson foundations, *2083*

Thompson, George W.: Elks meeting, *5722*

Thompson, Henry: Gas-powered streetcar, *6397*

Thompson, John: Intercity stagecoach service, *2184*

Railroad for freight transportation, *6316*

Thompson, John Taliaferro: Submachine gun, *8115*

Thompson, Ken: Computer operating system for multiple users, *2545*

Thompson, Lemarcus Adna: Roller coaster, *3621*

Thompson, Lewis C.: Slot machine, *3635*

Thompson, Mary Harris: Surgeon who was a woman, *4974*

Thompson, Maurice: Archery club, *7568*

Thompson, Robert E.: Navy divers to submerge for 10 days, *5268*

Thompson, Sarah: American woman to become a countess, *6644*

Thompson, Stephen W.: Army pilot to win a victory over an enemy airplane, *1610*

Thompson, Thomas: American flag on the high seas, *1121*

Thompson, Will H.: Archery club, *7568*

Thomson, Charles: Bible translated into English, *1966*

Impression made by the Great Seal of the United States, *1133*

Signer of the Declaration of Independence, *1113*

Thomson, Elihu: Welding by the electric process, *4435*

Thomson, Samuel: Steam baths for curing disease, *5110*

Thomson, Smith: Library for seamen, *4667*

Thoreau, Henry David: Protest by college students, *3007*

Thorn, Jonathan: Settlers to reach the Pacific coast, *5957*

Thorne, Oakleigh: Bank open day and night, *3792*

Thornton, William: Patent granted by the federal government, *4648*

Thorpe, Jim: Olympic athlete from the United States to win the pentathlon and decathlon, *7554*

Thurlow, Richard: Toll bridge, *3563*

Thurman, John S.: Vacuum cleaner driven by a motor, *4275*

Thurmond, James Strom: Senate filibuster to last for more than 24 hours, *2633*

Senator elected by a write-in vote, *3331*

Thurston, Robert Henry: Mechanical engineering laboratory, *3561*

Mechanical engineering society (national), *3610*

Tiant, Luis: Designated hitter in a major league baseball game, *7157*

Tibbals, Clarence Louis: Submarine emergency air supply container, *6967*

Tibbe, Anton A.: Corncob pipe commercial manufacture, *2704*

Tibbe, Henry: Corncob pipe commercial manufacture, *2704*

Tibbet, Jonathan: Oranges of the seedless navel variety, *3903*

Tibbets, Eliza C.: Oranges of the seedless navel variety, *3903*

Tibbets, Paul Warfield, Jr.: Atomic bomb explosion over enemy territory, *8086*

Tilghman, Benjamin Chew: Sandblasting process, *4434*

Tilley, Edward: Corn found by English settlers, *3908*

Tilton, James: Surgeon general of the Continental Army, *5165*

Timby, Theodore Ruggles: Ironclad turreted vessel in the Navy, *6923*

Revolving gun turret for ships, *8106*

Timms, Ross L.: Valeteria, *2398*

Timothee, Louis: Circulating library, *4661*

Ting Chia Chen: West Point graduates who were Chinese nationals, *3201*

Ting, Samuel Chao Chung: Year in which Nobel Prizes were won by Americans in five of six categories, *1702*

Tinsley, Marion: Checkers champion of renown, *4011*

Tipton, William D.: Airplane used for newspaper reporting, *5606*

Tisquantum: Greeting addressed to the Pilgrims by a Native American, *5914*

Tkach, M.: Ukrainian daily newspaper, *5683*

Todd, Libanus Mclouth: Check protectors, *3790*

Todd, Thomas: Wedding in the White House, *6252*

Tokohama, Charles: Baseball player in the American League who was African-American, *7147*

Tolton, Augustus: Catholic priest who was African-American, *6467*

Tombaugh, Clyde William: Planet found beyond Neptune, *6680*

Tombs, Rudolph, Jr.: College foreign-language house, *2999*

Tompson, Benjamin: Poetry collection by an American poet who was a man, *1944*

Topliff, Samuel: News agency, *5623*

Torkillus, Reorus: Lutheran pastor, *6554*

Toscanini, Arturo: Orchestra from the United States to make a European tour, *1363*

Symphonic concert to be shown on television, *1299*

Symphony orchestra devoted exclusively to radio broadcasting, *1365*

Towers, John Henry: Naval airplane, *1483*

Town, Ithiel: Building in all-Gothic architecture, *2071*

Towne, Benjamin: Daily newspaper, *5634*

Towner, Margaret Ellen: Presbyterian minister who was a woman, *6584*

Townes, Charles Hard: Laser, *3443*

Townsend, E. Price: Duplicate whist tournament, *4022*

Townsend, Fitzhugh: Intercollegiate fencing championship competition, *7282*

Townsend, Francis Everett: Union Party convention, *3378*

Toy, Jim: Baseball player who was Native American, *7143*

Tracy, Susan Edith: Occupational therapy treatment, *5114*

Travell, Janet Graeme: Presidential physician who was a woman, *6204*

Treadwell, Daniel: Steam-powered printing press, *5769*

Tree, Marietta Peabody: United Nations permanent ambassador who was a woman, *3993*

Treneer, Maurice: Fizzing cold remedy, *4994*

Tresse, Thomas: Paper mill, *5747*

Triaca, Albert C.: Aviation correspondence school, *7289*

Trible, Phyllis: United Church of Christ ordination of a woman in which all the principal roles were filled by women, *6536*

Trik, Carl A.: Highway bridge with concrete arches, *3586*

Tronson du Coudray, Philippe Charles Jean Baptiste: Catholic funeral attended by the Continental Congress, *6455*

Troost, Gerardt: Pharmacy college, *3160*

Troxel, Dorothy A.: Mongolian dictionary, *1809*

Trudeau, Edward Livingston: Disease research and treatment organization, *5046*
Tuberculosis research laboratory, *4929*
Tuberculosis sanatorium using modern treatment methods, *4899*

Trueblood, Thomas Clarkson: Public speaking department at a college, *3100*

Truman, Bess Wallace: Health insurance plan enacted by Congress, *4541*

Truman, Harry S.: Ambassador to the United States who was a woman, *3990*
Color news photograph transmitted by radio fax for publication, *5695*
Former president to address the Senate, *6175*
Health insurance plan enacted by Congress, *4541*
Labor dispute in which the Taft-Hartley Act was invoked, *4569*
Medal of Honor awarded in the Korean War, *1684*
President to travel underwater in a captured enemy submarine, *6228*
Presidential address televised from the White House, *6217*
Presidential press conference recorded on tape, *6218*
Transcontinental telecast received on the East Coast, *7840*

Truman, Margaret: Radio fax transmission to a moving train, *7673*

Trumbull, Earl: Girder bridge of cast iron, *3574*

Truscott, Lucian: Distinguished Service Cross awarded to an animal, *1664*

Truth, Sojourner: Robot to conduct a roving exploration of the surface of another planet, *7093*

Truxton, Thomas: Warship to capture an enemy ship after the Revolution, *8005*

Tsibliyev, Vasily: Joint space walk by American and Russian astronauts, *7055*

Tubman, Harriet: Postage stamp depicting an African-American woman, *6100*

Tucker, John: Supreme Court clerk, *2743*

Tucker, Stephen D.: Rotary printing press with a continuous-roll feed, *5779*

Tucker, Tommy: Radio show sponsored by a cooperative of commercial advertisers, *2338*

Tucker, William: Child born of African-American parents in America, *2158*

Tucker, William Ellis: Porcelain, *4038*

Tudor, Frederick: Ice exported, *3932*

Tufts, John: Vocal instruction book, *1933*

Tugo, Oscar Le: Soldiers in the American army killed in combat in World War I, *8038*

Tuke, Daniel Hack: Psychiatry textbook, *1912*

Tulley, John: Road map for public use, *4793*

Tunney, Gene: Boxing match to attract 100,000 spectators, *7242*

Tunnicliffe, George: Hotel to install electric lights, *2426*

Tupper, Earl S.: Household product made entirely of plastic, *4288*

Turchin, John Basil: Army general who was a Russian immigrant, *5149*

Turnbull, Andrew: Greek settlement, *5938*

Turner, Christopher: Yacht, *6859*

Turner, Cyril: Skywriting advertisement exhibition, *2334*

Turner, George A.: College student to receive assistance from the federal government as the child of a deceased veteran, *3014*

Turner, Henry C.: Labor antidiscrimination commission of a state government, *4568*

Turner, Henry McNeal: Army chaplain who was African-American, *5201*

Turner, James Edward: Alcoholics' asylum, *4879*

Turner, Nat: Slave rebellion after the Revolution, *2249*

Turner, Robert: Paper mill, *5747*

Turner, William G.: College student to receive assistance from the federal government as the child of a deceased veteran, *3014*

Turpin, Mary: Catholic nun, *6452*

Tuscaloosa, Chief: Battle between Native Americans and European soldiers, *5894*

Tuthill, Richard Stanley: Juvenile court, *2707*

Tuttle, Dorothy Edith Lorne: Coast Guard unit for women, *5212*

T'Vault, William G.: Newspaper published on the Pacific Coast, *5640*

Twain, Mark: Book manuscript that was typewritten, *1751*
Frog-jumping jubilee, *1151*

Twain, Mark (Samuel Langhorn Clemens): Arts and letters organization (national), *5716*

Twigg, Atrong: Civil rights anthem to achieve fame, *1383*

Twilight, Alexander Lucius: College graduate who was African-American, *3009*

Twining, Nathan Farragut: Air Force chairman of the Joint Chiefs of Staff, *5136*

Twombly, John Fogg: Esperanto club, *5717*

Tyler, John: Former president to serve as an official of an enemy government, *6158*
President married while in office, *6190*
Presidential veto to be overridden by Congress, *6154*
Vice president to succeed to the presidency after the death of a president, *6245*

Tyler, Royall: Novel published in America to be republished in England, *1840*
Play by an American writer to be successfully presented by an established company, *1246*

Tyng, James Alexander: Baseball catcher's mask, *7107*

Tytus, John Butler: Steel mill to produce continuous sheets, *4497*

U

Uchytil, Christa: Grandmother to give birth to her own grandchild, *2169*

Uncles, Charles Randolph: Catholic priest who was African-American, *6467*

Underhill, Isaac: Marble quarry, *5318*

Underwood, Charles G.: Ready-mix food, *3947*

Underwood, John Curtiss: Interracial jury, *2735*

Unterberg, Mrs. Israel: Young Women's Hebrew Association, *5715*

Unungoit: Land sale by Native Americans to Europeans, *5918*

Updike, Daniel Berkeley: Printing lecture course in a college, *3294*

Upham, John B.: Golf mixed foursome, *7354*

Upson, Ralph Hazlett: Airship to land on a roof, *1517*

Upton, Robert: Publicist for a theater company, *3694*

Upton, Roger: Glue factory, *4428*

Urey, Harold Clayton: Heavy water to be identified, *6814*

Usher, Hezekiah: Bookseller, *1777*
Law book of colonial laws, *1872*

Usher, John: Colonial copyright law, *4626*

V

Vail, Alfred: Telegraphic system in which dots and dashes represented letters, *7687*

Vajta, Ferenc: Nazi collaborator to be deported, *5875*

Valentine, Elmer: Discotheque, *3631*

Vallentine, Edward: Silk dyers, *7888*

Van Bokkelen, Libertius: Military school operated by a church, *3186*

Van Boven, Paul: Helicopter rescue of an American pilot behind enemy lines, *7979*

Van Buren, Adelina: Transcontinental motorcycle trip by women, *5493*

Van Buren, Augusta: Transcontinental motorcycle trip by women, *5493*

Van Buren, Martin: Free Soil Party convention, *3352*
Political machine, *3347*
President born an American citizen, *6183*

van der Rohe, Mies: Skyscraper of bronze and glass, *2101*

Van Dusen, John: Plate-glass insurance, *4507*

Van Etten, Edwin Jan: Religious service broadcast on radio, *6589*

Van Gieson, Ira: Psychiatric institute, *3150*

van Gogh, Vincent: Modern art exhibition, *1228*

Van Houten, James J.: Patent issued by the Confederate States of America, *4655*

Van Kannel, Theophilus: Revolving door, *2081*

Van Quickenborne, Father: Catholic school for Native Americans, *3053*

Van Reypen, William Knickerbocker: Ambulance ship operated by the Navy, *5015*

van Steenwyk, E.A: Blue Cross and Blue Shield plans, *4536*

Van Syckel, Samuel: Oil pipeline of importance, *3533*

Van Twiller, Wouter: Brick building, *2068*

Vance, Claire K.: Transcontinental regular airmail service, *6019*

Vandegrift, Alexander Archer: Marine general, *5237*

Vanderbilt, Alfred Gwynn: Jockey who was a woman to win a major stakes race, *7419*

Vanderbilt, Cornelius: Child abuse prevention organization, *5737*
Circumnavigation of the world by a yacht, *6982*

Millionaire with a fortune greater than $100 million, 2443

Vanderbilt, George Washington: Forest management on a professional scale, 3725

Vanderbilt, Harold Stirling: Book on the game of bridge, 2005

Book on the game of bridge by a championship team, 2006

Vanderbilt, William Henry: Electric light from a power plant in a residence, 3495

Obelisk to be brought to the United States, 5403

Vandergrift, Alexander Archer: American offensive in the Pacific in World War II, 8081

Vanderlyn, John: Postage stamps to feature paintings, 6086

Vare, William Scott: Senate election in which neither candidate was seated after a recount, 2630

Varrevanger, Jacob Hendrickszen: Hospital, 4868

Vasken I, Supreme Patriarch: Armenian Orthodox cathedral, 6499

Vaughan, Victor Clarence: Bacteriology courses at a college, 3149

Veatch, John A.: Borax, 5331

Venable, James M.: General anesthetic, 4828

Venema, Pieter: Algebra book, 1883

Venter, J. Craig: Complete DNA sequencing of a free-living organism, 6757

Verdi, Giuseppe: Metropolitan Opera singer who was African-American, 1338

Opera prima donna who was African-American, 1333

Opera to be televised from the Metropolitan Opera House, 1353

Verdi, Giuseppi: Metropolitan Opera orchestra conductor who was a woman, 1340

Verdun, Pierre: Food processor, 4304

Vernon, Fortesque: Astronomical expedition to record an eclipse of the sun, 6662

Verplanck, Gulian Crommelin: City mayor elected by popular vote, 2206

Verrazano, Giovanni da: Kidnapping, 2766

Vespucci, Amerigo: Use of "America" as a geographical designation, 1094

Vianesi, Augusto: Opera produced at the Metropolitan Opera House, 1347

Viets, Simeon: Cigar factory, 2702

Vincent, Ambrose: Book auction catalog, 1779

Vincent, John Heyl: Chautauqua organization meeting, 2885

Viner, Jimmy: Helicopter hoist rescue, 1563

Vlasto, Solon John: Greek newspaper, 5676

Voge, Richard G.: Submarine from the United States destroyed in World War II, 8066

Vogel, Clayton B.: Coded military radio transmissions using a Native American language, 8082

Voight, Jon: Oscar for best picture awarded to an X-rated movie, 1638

Voit, W.J.: Football with a rubber covering, 7313

Von Braun, Wernher: Rocket to reach outer space, 7020

von Erlach, Diebold: Swiss settlement in America, 5931

Von Hagen, Victor Wolfgang: Quetzal bird, 1168

von Knyphausen, Wilhelm: American flag flown in battle, 1120

von Neumann, John: Mathematical theory of economic decisionmaking, 6758

von Platen, Baltzar Carl: Gas refrigerator, 4348

Voorsanger, Elkan Cohen: Army chaplain who was Jewish, 5200

Vorstman, P.: Labadist community, 6514

Votey, Edwin S.: Pneumatic piano player, 1320

Vreeland, Jeanette: Radio broadcast of a concert from an airplane, 1295

W

Wachner, Linda: Fortune 1000 company to be owned and chaired by a woman, 2407

Wade, John: Iron sailing vessel, 6867

Wadsworth, Daniel: Free public art museum in continuous existence, 5595

Wadsworth, James Wolcott: Senate whip, 2629

Wadsworth, Jeremiah: Worsted mill operated by waterpower, 7893

Wagenknecht, Alfred: Communist Labor Party of America convention, 3374

Wagner, Boyd David: Ace in World War II, 1616

Wagner, Herman L.: Typewriter to produce a line of writing visible as it was being typed, 2388

Wagner, John: Lager beer, 2667

Wagner, Robert Ferdinand: Minimum wage law established by a city for public contract work, 4580

Parking meter enforcement division of a police department, 4149

Wagoner, Clyde Decker: Round-the-world radio broadcast, 6275

Wait, Pearle B.: Gelatin dessert, 3966

Wait, William E.: National labor congress, 4553

Waite, Charles: Baseball glove, 7105

Wakefield, Ruth Graves: Chocolate chip cookies, 3928

Waksman, Selman Abraham: Antibiotic, 4998

Waksman, Selman Abraham —*continued*
Microbiology laboratory, *4932*

Walcott, Jersey Joe: Pay television presentation of a sporting event, *7785*

Wald, Lillian: Visiting nurses, *5025*

Walden, Henry W.: Monoplane, *1390*

Waldrake, Sarah: Federal government employees who were women, *5351*

Waldseemüller, Martin H.: Use of "America" as a geographical designation, *1094*

Walker, Donald F.: Surgical operation on a bull to correct a sperm block, *5124*

Walker, Edwin Garrison: State legislators who were African-American, *7624*

Walker, Francis Amasa: Economics association, *6788*

Walker, George: Road map for motorists, *4801*

Walker, James John: Transcontinental daily air-rail passenger service, *1411*

Walker, John: International exchange of fingerprints, *4162*
Rhyming dictionary, *1803*
Senator appointed by a governor, *2639*

Walker, Jonathan: Branding punishment by a federal court, *2818*

Walker, Joseph: Shoe peg, *2300*

Walker, Madame C.J.: Millionaire who was an African-American woman, *2444*

Walker, Maggie Lena: Bank president who was a woman, *3772*

Walker, Moses Fleetwood "Fleet": Major league baseball player who was African-American, *7142*

Walker, Samuel Hamilton: Anti-saloon organization, *2680*

Walker, Thomas: Colonial settlement west of the Allegheny Mountains, *5935*

Walker, William: Land office, *5948*

Wallace, Henry: Pony Express mail, *5994*

Wallace, Henry Agard: Father and son to occupy the same Cabinet post, *6109*

Wallace, Henry Cantwell: Father and son to occupy the same Cabinet post, *6109*

Wallace, James: Medicine advertisement in booklet form, *2318*

Wallace, John Hankins: Horse race trotting register, *2001*

Wallace, Lewis: Trial of a war criminal by the federal government, *7969*

Wallace, Mike: Television newsmagazine, *5708*

Wallace, Robert: Spoons of nickel silver, *4371*

Waller, Frank: Bicycle race paced by a motorcycle, *7194*
International six-day bicycle race, *7189*

Waller, William: Intercity stagecoach service, *2184*

Walsh, Julia Montgomery: Stock exchange director who was a woman, *3831*

Walsh, Loretta: Navy petty officer who was a woman, *5286*

Walsh, Mary Elizabeth: Wedding in a balloon, *4814*

Walsh, Raoul: Movie of feature length made outdoors, *5558*

Walsh, Robert: Quarterly magazine, *4704*

Walter, Eugene: Drama broadcast on radio, *1257*
Movie by a major company for an African-American audience, *5559*

Walter, Thomas: Music book printed with bars, *1932*

Walters, Barbara: Television network evening news program anchor who was a woman, *5621*

Walters, Bernice Rosenthal: Medical officer assigned to a naval vessel who was a woman, *5292*

Walters, Walt: Motorboat ocean race, *7218*

Walthall, Henry: Movie to gross $50 million, *5513*

Walthour, Robert: Paired six-day bicycle race, *7195*

Walton, Samuel Moore: Wal-Mart store, *2514*

Walworth, James Jones: Building heated by steam, *2074*

Wambsganss, William Adolph: Unassisted triple play in a World Series baseball game, *7127*

Wanamaker, John: Electric light in a store, *3491*

Wang, Theodora Chan: Chinese-American women's organization to be incorporated, *5726*

Wanton, George Henry: Medal of Honor awarded to an African-American soldier in the Spanish-American War, *1676*

Ward, Aaron Montgomery: Mail-order business, *2494*

Ward, Augustus: Cattle club to promote Guernsey cattle, *1092*

Ward, Holcombe: International tennis matches for the Davis Cup challenge trophy, *7531*

Ward, Hortense: State supreme court in which all the judges were women, *2724*

Ward, James Harmon: Union naval officer killed in the Civil War, *7956*

Ward, Jay: Animated cartoon made for television, *7782*

Ward, Lester Frank: Sociology society (national), *6791*

Ward, Robert De Courcy: Climatology professor at a college, *3242*

Ward, Roger: Race-car driver to win $100,000, *7268*

Ware, Keith L.: Army general who rose from draftee, *5155*

Ware, W.H.: Dentist officially employed in the Army, *5014*

Ware, William Robert: Architecture department at a college, *2903*

Waring, Eleanor Howard: Balloon honeymoon, *4808*

Waring, George Edwin: Sewage-disposal system separate from the city water system, *2230*

Warmerdam, Cornelius: Pole vaulter to clear the bar at 15 feet, *7560*

Warner, Amos Griswold: Industrial corporation course at a college, *2920*

Warner, Emily H.: Pilot on a regularly scheduled major airline who was a woman, *1606*

Warner, Ezra J.: Can opener, *4372*

Warner, Ira Dever: Corset, *2271*

Warner, Lucien Calvin: Corset, *2271*

Warner, Sylvia Townsend: Book-of-the-Month Club selection, *1789*

Warren, Edward: Balloon flight, *1535*

Warren, James: Paymaster general of the Continental Army, *5164*

Warren, John Collins: Painless surgery demonstration, *4831*

Pharmacopoeia prepared by a medical association, *1928*

Warren, Josiah: Anarchist, *4551*

Warren, Mercy Otis: American history book of importance whose author was a woman, *1865*

Warren, Ratcliff: Naval battle between colonists, *5922*

Warren, Robert Penn: Poet laureate of the United States, *2034*

Writer to win the Pulitzer Prize in both fiction and poetry, *1714*

Washburn, Cadwallader Colden: Brothers to serve as representatives in Congress simultaneously, *2602*

Washburn, Harry: Murder trial to be televised, *4624*

Washburn, Ichabod: Piano wire, *1310*

Wire gauge, *7920*

Washburn, Israel, Jr.: Brothers to serve as representatives in Congress simultaneously, *2602*

Washburn, William Drew: Brothers to serve as representatives in Congress simultaneously, *2602*

Washburne, Elihu Benjamin: Brothers to serve as representatives in Congress simultaneously, *2602*

Washington, Booker T.: Business organization for African-Americans (national), *2450*

Washington, Booker Taliaferro: Coin bearing the likeness of an African-American, *5379*

Postage stamp depicting an African-American, *6090*

Washington, George: American flag to represent the United States, *1118*

Army lieutenant general, *5148*

Army uniform, *5142*

Balloon flight in which a presidential order was carried, *1536*

Battle in the French and Indian War, *7971*

Bloodshed in the French and Indian War, *7970*

Cabinet, *6102*

Circus, *3672*

Coin bearing the likeness of a president, *5375*

Congressional act, *2558*

Congressional eulogy for a president, *6185*

Copyright law enacted by Congress, *4628*

Execution by the Army, *2795*

General of the Armies of the United States with the rank of six stars, *5161*

General of the Continental Army, *5146*

Impression made by the Great Seal of the United States, *1133*

Inaugural ball, *6137*

Joint meeting of the Senate and the House of Representatives, *2557*

Medal awarded by the Continental Congress, *1649*

Monument to George Washington, *5397*

Mule born in the United States, *1141*

National day of thanksgiving, *4260*

National holiday, *4241*

Naval battle in the Revolutionary War, *7991*

Naval protection, *5259*

Neutrality proclamation by the federal government, *3977*

Partridge propagation, *1067*

Postage stamps depicting a president, *6078*

Postage stamps issued by the Post Office Department, *6052*

President elected under the Constitution, *6135*

President to receive the unanimous vote of the presidential electors, *3381*

President to tour the country, *6230*

Presidential amnesty issued to rebellious citizens, *6143*

Presidential appointment, *6138*

Presidential commission, *6142*

Presidential inauguration, *6136*

Presidential mansion, *6250*

Presidential proclamation, *6140*

Presidential veto of a congressional bill, *6141*

Purple Heart, *1656*

Quack doctor of note, *3646*

Revolutionary War conflict in which American and British troops met on equal terms, *8002*

Revolutionary War national veterans' organization, *5308*

Salute fired by Great Britain in honor of an officer of the United States, *3976*

Hygiene and public health school at a college, *3177*

Pathology chair at a college, *3139*

Weld, Theresa: International championship figure skating tournament, *7431*

Welger, Sol: National wheelchair games, *7586*

Weller, Carl E.: Soldering gun, *7941*

Weller, Thomas Huckle: Poliomyelitis vaccine, *4923*

Wellings, Augustus Joseph: Navy admirals who were brothers, *5294*

Wellings, Joseph Harold: Navy admirals who were brothers, *5294*

Wellings, Timothy Francis: Navy admirals who were brothers, *5294*

Wellman, Walter: Transatlantic airship flight, *1515*

Wellman, William A.: Oscar for best picture, *1630*

Wells, Alice Stebbins: Police officer who was a woman, *4136*

Wells, Henry: Car accident, *5466*

Wells, Henry M.: Navy medical school, *3171*

Wells, Horace: Anesthetic in dentistry, *4829*

Wentworth, John: Summer home, *2123*

Wesberry, James: Book censorship board established by a state, *1792*

Wesley, John: Protestant Sunday school, *6518*

Wesley, Newton K.: Bifocal contact lenses, *5074*

Wesselhoeft, J.G.: Homeopathic pharmacy, *4986*

Wesselhoeft, William: Homeopathic medical society, *5031*

Wesson, Daniel Baird: Metal gun cartridge, *8105*

West, Benjamin: Artist of American birth to head the Royal Academy of London, *1202*

West, Jake C.: Jet-propelled landing on an aircraft carrier, *1464*

West, James Ward: Kidney transplant, *5095*

West, John: Treason trial by a colony, *2833*

Westcott, Oliver J.: Building with a large-scale clear-span dome, *2085*

Westendorp, Willem Fredrik: Synchrotron, *6802*

Westinghouse, George: Half holiday on Saturday for factory workers, *4558*

Westinghouse, George, Jr.: Air brake, *6420*

Weston, David M.: Centrifugal cream separator, *3855*

Weston, Edward: Photographer to receive the John Simon Guggenheim Memorial Foundation award, *1627*

Weston, Edward Payson: Transcontinental journey on foot, *7589*

Weston, Frank William: Bicycle magazine, *4784*

Westwood, Frances Jean Miles: Chairman of a major political party who was a woman, *3344*

Wetherill, Charles Mayer: Agriculture bureau scientific publication, *1763*

Wetherill, Samuel: White lead manufacturer, *4462*

Zinc commercial production, *5330*

Wetherill, Samuel, Jr.: Fustians, everlastings, and coating, *7860*

Wetmore, Alexander: Bird banding by federal authorities, *6747*

Wev, Oscar Cottman Buckingham: Seagoing radio broadcasting station, *5304*

Wharton, Clifton Reginald, Jr.: President of a major university who was African-American, *2975*

Wharton, Edith Newbold Jones: Pulitzer Prize for a novel written by a woman, *1711*

Wharton, Joseph: Business school at a college, *2919*

Whatley, George: Bifocal eyeglasses, *5072*

Wheatcraft, T.S.: Vending machine to sell food from bulk, *2396*

Wheatley, Phillis: Poetry collection by an African-American woman, *1946*

Wheeler, Frederick: Adventist church to accept Saturday as the Sabbath, *6529*

Wheeler, Schuyler Skaats: Electric fan, *4332*

Wheeler, Seth: Perforated wrapping paper, *5758*

Whelan, Israel: Insurance agency, *4500*

Whipple: Photograph of a star other than the sun, *6693*

Whipple, Abraham: Naval attack in the Revolutionary War, *7987*

Whipple, Charles: Pamphlet produced from a steel plate engraving, *1744*

Whipple, Cullen: Screw machine to make pointed screws, *7923*

Whipple, Henry Benjamin: Episcopal cathedral, *6550*

Whisler, George H., Jr.: Transcontinental round-trip solo flight between sunrise and sunset, *1478*

Whitaker, Alexander: Presbyterian church, *6580*

Whitcher, Frances Miriam Berry: Humor writer who was a woman, *2033*

White, Abraham: Pituitary hormone, *4996*

White, Andrew: Electrical engineering school at a college, *3239*

White, Canvass: Concrete, *2041*

Natural cement rock, *2039*

White, Caroline Earle: Animal rights organization (national), *5740*

White, David: Social fraternity at a college, *2984*

White, Edward Douglass: Governor who was Catholic, *7611*
Supreme Court justice to be appointed chief justice, *2761*
White, Edward H.: Airship transfer of mail to a train, *1523*
White, Edward Higgins, II: Astronaut to walk in space, *7031*
Astronauts to die in a spacecraft, *7036*
White Eyes, Captain: Treaty entered into by the federal government with Native American tribes, *5941*
White, Goodrich Cook: Scholastic fraternity at a college, *2983*
White, J. Andrew: Heavyweight championship boxing match broadcast on radio, *7241*
White, James Clarke: Dermatology chair at a college, *3144*
White, John: Artist in the English colonies, *1196*
White, Joseph N.: Billiard match, *4016*
White, Josiah: Suspension bridge of iron wire, *3570*
White, Peregrine: Child born of English parents in New England, *2157*
White, Robert Michael: Pilot of an airplane to qualify as an astronaut by attaining a 50-mile altitude, *1623*
White, Samuel S.: Dental drill powered by electricity, *4864*
White, Susanna: Wedding of colonists in New England, *4813*
White, William: Bible society, *6571*
Hospital to treat poor patients at no charge, *4869*
Prison reform society, *2812*
Whitefield, George: Great Awakening of religious revival, *6517*
Whitehead, Gustave: Airplane flight, *1426*
Whitehead, Mary Beth: Trial of a surrogate mother for refusing to give up her baby, *2167*
Whiteman, Louis Porter: Milk bottles, *4285*
Whitfield, Malvin Greston: Athlete who was African-American to win the James E. Sullivan Memorial Trophy, *1720*
Whiting, A.H.: Car race on a racetrack, *7261*
Whitlock, David: Comprehensive digital atlas of the human body, *4913*
Whitman, Malcolm Douglass: International tennis matches for the Davis Cup challenge trophy, *7531*
Whitman, Narcissa Prentiss: Settlers to cross the continent who were women, *5960*
Whitney, Eli: Cotton gin, *1030*
Whitney, Harry Payne: Filly to win the Kentucky Derby horse race, *7408*
Horse to win a $100,000 purse in one race, *7410*

Whitney, William Dwight: Philology society (national), *6783*
Whitney, Willis Rodney: Diathermy machine, *4948*
Industrial research laboratory, *4377*
Whiton, James Morris: Doctor of Philosophy degree, *2977*
Whittaker, James W.: Ascent of Mount Everest by an American, *7588*
Whittier, Earle Ovando: Casein fiber, *4443*
Whittlesey, Oramel: Music school authorized to confer degrees, *2899*
Wichman, John R.: Wedding broadcast over the radio, *4819*
Wickes, Lambert: Capture of an enemy ship in enemy waters, *7999*
Wiebe, Edward: Kindergarten manual, *1828*
Wiener, Alexander S.: Rh factor discovery, *4835*
Wiener, Leo: Dog hotel, *2436*
Wiggins, Leonard A.: Glider pilot's license, *1598*
Wiggins, Mary E.: Gallstone operation, *5079*
Wigglesworth, Edward: Divinity professor at a college, *3266*
Wignell, Thomas: Play by an American writer to be successfully presented by an established company, *1246*
Wilbur, James H.: Boarding school on a Native American reservation, *3063*
Wilcox, L.S.: Tung trees, *1021*
Wilde, Francis E.J.: Electric flashing sign, *2351*
Wilder, L. Douglas: Governor who was African-American, *7621*
Wildey, Thomas: Odd Fellows lodge, *5719*
Wildman, Ernest Atkins: Camp for conscientious objectors, *5221*
Wiles, Andrew: Mathematical proof of Fermat's last theorem, *6761*
Wiley, David: Agricultural journal, *4703*
Wiley, Herbert Victor: Glider released from an airship, *1548*
Wilkes, Charles: Scientific expedition fitted out by the federal government, *6723*
Wilkinson, David: Nuts and bolts factory, *7918*
Wilkinson, Jeremiah: Nails, *7907*
Willard, Charles Foster: Aviation meet, *7292*
Willard, Emma Hart: School for the higher education of women, *3079*
Willard, Frances Elizabeth: College president who was a woman, *2971*
Statue of a woman installed in the Capitol's National Statuary Hall, *5409*
Willard, Samuel: Book of folio size, *1734*
Willerup, Christian B.: Scandinavian Methodist Episcopal church, *6566*
Willet, Edward: Monkey trained to perform, *1139*

Williams, Bert: Movie featuring an African-American actor, *5554*

Williams, Charles, Jr.: Telephone for domestic use, *7712*

Williams, Daniel Hale: Surgery society (national), *5047*
Suture of the human heart, *5090*

Williams, Edward Christopher: Librarian who was African-American, *4674*

Williams, Elkanah: Ophthalmology course at a college, *3137*

Williams, George Washington: History of African-Americans, *1871*

Williams, Henry J.: Publishing society, *1785*

Williams, Horatio Burt: Portable electric stethoscope, *4946*

Williams, Isaac: Neutrality regulation enacted by Congress that governed the actions of citizens, *3978*

Williams, J.A.: Welsh magazine, *4743*

Williams, Jesse: Cheese factory of consequence, *3859*

Williams, Jesse Lynch: Pulitzer Prize for drama, *1708*

Williams, John: Medal of Honor awarded to a member of the Naval Service, *1671*

Williams, John Foster: Federal revenue cutter, *6857*

Williams, Jonathan: Army academy, *3194*
Army engineer corps, *5178*

Williams, Kathlyn: Serial movie with installments longer than one reel, *5550*

Williams, Lorraine: Role-playing game, *4014*

Williams, Richard F.: Hospital and asylum for African-Americans, *4874*

Williams, Robley Cook: Virus separated into component parts, *5062*

Williams, Roger: Baptist church, *6543*
Earthquake description, *2861*
Native American dictionary, *1796*
Religious refuge for people of all faiths, *5923*

Williams, Samuel: Astronomical expedition to record an eclipse of the sun, *6662*

Williams, Samuel Wells: Chinese language and literature lectureship at a college, *3116*

Williams, Terry: College to offer athletic scholarships to women, *3004*

Williams, Thomas Robinson: Felt manufacturing mechanical process, *7867*

Williams, Thomas W.: Steam whaler, *6885*

Williams, Vanessa: Beauty pageant to be held nationwide, *3628*

Williams, Walter: Journalism school at a college, *3102*

Williamson, James De Long: Community trust charity, *5742*

Williamson, John Ernest: Photographs taken under the sea, *5821*

Williamson, Walter: Homeopathy college, *3163*

Willich, Anthony Florian Madinger: Agricultural encyclopedia, *1831*

Willing, Thomas: Bank chartered by Congress, *3757*

Willis, Nathaniel Parker: Illustrated weekly magazine, *4715*

Willis, Sophia: American flag flown over a schoolhouse, *1126*

Williston, Mrs. Samuel: Cloth-covered buttons, *2288*

Willkie, Wendell Lewis: Political convention to be televised, *3342*

Willoughby, Frances Lois: Doctor in the regular Navy who was a woman, *5291*

Wills, Chris: Hang-gliding national championships, *7300*

Wills, Maury: Baseball player to steal more than 100 bases in a season, *7154*

Willson, Thomas Leopold: Carbide factory, *4438*

Wilson, Allen Benjamin: Sewing machine to sew curving seams, *4355*

Wilson, Carrie: National union for women, *4610*

Wilson, Debra Lee: Coast Guard officers who were women who served aboard ships, *5214*

Wilson, Edmund Beecher: Biology course offered at a college, *3240*

Wilson, Edward O.: Pulitzer prize awarded to a science book, *1718*

Wilson, Henry: Military service by African-Americans to be authorized by Congress, *5145*

Wilson, James: Globe factory, *4798*
Supreme Court of the United States, *2742*

Wilson, Kemmons: Holiday Inn, *2432*

Wilson, Philip Duncan: Bone bank, *4837*

Wilson, S. Clay: Underground comic book of note, *4739*

Wilson, Thomas Leopold: Acetylene gas, *4437*

Wilson, William Bauchop: Senate election in which neither candidate was seated after a recount, *2630*

Wilson, William "Bill W.": Twelve-step rehabilitation program, *2662*

Wilson, William Powell: Commercial museum, *5580*

Wilson, Woodrow: Ancient and modern history chair at a college, *3095*
Bill of $100,000 denomination, *5394*
Bird protection international treaty, *3747*
Dish set made in America for the White House, *6256*
Mother's Day, *4243*
President buried in Washington, *6197*

Wilson, Woodrow —*continued*

President to receive a passport while in office, *6232*

President to visit Europe, *6233*

Research society (national), *6793*

Skyscraper higher than 750 feet in height, *2099*

Winans, Ross: Locomotive with six or eight driving wheels, *6353*

Railroad car with a center aisle, *6371*

Winchester, Boyd: International copyright agreement, *4631*

Winchester, Oliver Fisher: Shirt factory, *2266*

Wing, Simon: Socialist Labor Party of North America national convention, *3360*

Wingate, George Wood: International rifle tournament of consequence, *7473*

Wingfield, Edward Maria: Battle between English colonists and Native Americans, *5908*

Colonial council, *5906*

Episcopal church service in an English colony, *6547*

Slander proceedings, *2767*

Winslow, Alan Francis: Pilots in American units to participate in air combat in World War I, *8043*

Winslow, Edward: Cattle to be imported, *1076*

Wedding of colonists in New England, *4813*

Winslow, Josiah: Governor of a colony who was born in America, *7609*

Winslow, Samuel: Patent granted by a colony, *4646*

Winsor, Frederick: Country day school, *3066*

Winsor, Justin: Library association (national), *4688*

Winters, Jonathan: Video recording on magnetic tape televised coast-to-coast, *7847*

Winthrop, James: Astronomical expedition to record an eclipse of the sun, *6662*

Winthrop, John (astronomer): Astronomer of note, *6659*

Scientific expedition sponsored by a colony, *6661*

Winthrop, John (colonist): Apples, *3892*

Colonial government federation, *5926*

Election held in a colony, *3310*

Fork, *4365*

Winthrop, John, Jr.: Ironworks that was successful, *4446*

Winthrop, John (miner): Copper mine, *5316*

Wirt, William: Anti-Masonic Party convention, *3348*

School to use platoon organization, *3067*

Wirz, August Herman: Collapsible tube machine, *7927*

Wirz, Henry: Trial of a war criminal by the federal government, *7969*

Wisden, J.: International cricket tournament, *7273*

Wise, Isaac Mayer: Rabbinical college for the Reform Jewish movement, *3274*

Wise, John: Airmail dispatched from a post office in a balloon, *6014*

Airship, *1512*

Airship bombing plan, *8100*

Aviation book, *1987*

Transatlantic crossing attempted by a balloon, *1538*

Wistar, Caspar: Anatomy book, *1896*

Wistar, Isaac Jones: Anatomy research institute, *5055*

Witherell, Warren: Water skier to jump 100 feet, *7593*

Withers, C. Clark: Radio broadcast from a submerged submarine, *6268*

Withers, Clark: Two-way radio conversation between a submerged submarine and another vessel, *7760*

Wittenmyer, Annie T.: Temperance society for women (national), *2678*

Wolcott, Alexander S.: Commercial photography studio, *5812*

Wold, Peter Irving: Speaker to address an organization by television, *7831*

Wolf, Donald: Cloning of a primate from an embryo, *6754*

Wolf, Ludwig Martin Nicolaus: Sewing machine lamp holder, *4359*

Wolfe, Richard: Church without theology, creed, or dogma, *6602*

Wolff, Julius: Sardine cannery, *3888*

Woll, Frederick Albert: Optometry courses at a college, *3153*

Wollstonecraft, Mary: Book advocating voting rights for women, *2012*

Wong, Delbert E.: Judge of Chinese ancestry, *2728*

Wood, Abraham: Expedition of Englishmen to cross the Allegheny Mountains, *5927*

Wood, Charles Raymond, Jr.: Ramjet helicopter, *1564*

Wood, Edward Stickney: Medical chemistry course at a college, *3145*

Wood, Elizabeth A.: Picturephone commercial service, *7750*

Wood, George Bacon: Pharmaceuticals book, *1929*

Wood, Harold L.: Charting of the Northwest Passage, *6734*

Wood, Henry Alexander Wise: Automatic plate-casting and finishing machine for stereotype printing, *5796*

Laborsaving machine approved by a labor union, *4616*

Wood, John: Rotogravure press, *5781*

Wood, John Jethro: Plow with interchangeable parts, *1042*

Wood, R.F.: Airship filled with helium gas, *1519*

Wood, Sally Sayward: Women's club, *5732*

Wood, Walton J.: County public defender, *4639*

Wood, William M.: Naval militia established by a state, *5255*

Woodbridge, William: Education association, *3223*

Woodhouse, James: Chemistry laboratory manual, *1980*
Chemistry society, *6777*

Woodhull, Victoria Claflin: Brokerage office owned by women, *3818*
Equal Rights Party convention, *3363*
Presidential candidate who was a woman, *3405*

Woodland, N.J.: Bar code scanner, *2373*

Woodruff, Hiram: Harness horse race at night, *7389*

Woodruff, Robert: Speeding driver law enacted by a state, *4221*

Woods, Leslie G.: Soldiers in the American army killed in combat in World War I, *8038*

Woods, Tiger: Golf champion of African-American and Asian descent, *7370*

Woods, William: Cast steel for plows, *4491*

Woodward, Artemas: Brushes, *4267*

Woodward, George B.: Bicycle club, *7184*

Woodward, Orator Frank: Gelatin dessert, *3966*

Woodward, Robert Burns: Chlorophyll, *4997*
Synthetic quinine, *4999*

Woodward, Samuel B.: Psychiatry association (national), *5035*

Woodworth, John Maynard: Surgeon general, *4213*

Wooldridge, William O.: Sergeant major of the Army, *5174*

Woolley, Leonidas G.: Electric locomotive headlight, *6425*

Woolman, Mary Schenck: Trade school for girls, *3291*

Woolworth, Frank Winfield: Five-cent store, *2496*

Worden, Alfred Merrill: Astronauts to ride a vehicle on the moon, *7042*

Worden, John Lorimer: Ironclad turreted vessel in the Navy, *6923*
Naval battle between ironclad vessels in the Civil War, *7961*

Workman, Sonny: Horse to win a $100,000 purse in one race, *7410*

Worthington, Henry Rossiter: Independent single direct-acting steam power pump, *4397*

Worthington, John: Health board established by a city, *4172*

Worthylake, George: Lighthouse, *4123*

Wouves, P.R.: Cryptography chart, *4797*

Wozniak, Steven: Personal computer, *2537*

Wren, Mr. and Mrs. Edward: Distinguished Service Cross awarded to an animal, *1664*

Wren, Solomon: Marine Corps commando raid, *5231*

Wright, Arthur Williams: Doctor of Philosophy degree, *2977*

Wright, Carroll Davidson: Vending machine to dispense postage stamps, *2394*

Wright, Elizur: Life insurance nonforfeiture law enacted by a state, *4545*

Wright, George: Baseball team whose players received a regular salary, *7162*

Wright, George Green: Anthrax vaccine for human immunization, *4924*

Wright, James: Child abuse prevention organization, *5737*

Wright, James Hood: Electric light from a power plant in a residence, *3495*

Wright, Jonathan Jasper: Justice of a state supreme court who was African-American, *2720*

Wright, Orville: Airplane accident that was fatal, *1387*
Airplane endurance flight exceeding one hour, *1427*
Airplane flight, *1426*
Airplane purchased by the federal government, *1389*
Intercity airplane flight by a U.S. military officer, *1428*

Wright, Silas: Customs fee stamps, *7649*
Political machine, *3347*

Wright, Wilbur: Airplane flight, *1426*
Airplane purchased by the federal government, *1389*

Wright, William Hammond: Movie showing another planet, *6687*

Wu, Maw-Kuen: Superconducting material that operated at relatively high temperatures, *6823*

Wunderlich, Frieda: Dean of a university graduate school who was a woman, *2974*

Wyatt, Francis: Alcohol prohibition enforcement officers, *2672*
Alcohol temperance law enacted by a colony, *2674*

Wyatt, James: Waxworks museum, *5575*

Wye, Thomas E.: Factories operated by the federal government in peacetime, *4387*

Wyeth, Jamie: Christmas postage stamp regular issue, *6094*

Wyman, George A.: Transcontinental motorcycle trip, *5492*

Wyman, Jane: Made-for-TV movie, *7789*
President who had been divorced, *6202*

Wyman, Jeffries: Allergy book, *1916*

Wyman, Walter: Tuberculosis hospital established by Congress, *4902*

Wyman, Walter Scott: Floating electric power plant, *3481*

Wynne, Arthur: Crossword puzzle, *4010*
Wynne, Jim: Motorboat ocean race, *7218*
Wythe, George: Law school at a college, *3121*

Y

Yalden, James: Accounting society (national), *3754*
Yale, Linus, Jr.: Pin-tumbler cylinder lock, *2133*
Yamada, Masao: Army chaplain of Japanese ancestry, *5204*
Yannas, Ioannis V.: Transplant of artificial skin, *5102*
Yate, Esther: National water skiing tournament, *7592*
Yeager, Charles Elwood "Chuck": Airplane to fly faster than the speed of sound, *1468*
Yeager, Jeana: Round-the-world nonstop airplane flight without refueling, *1482*
Yeaton, Hopley: Navy officer commissioned, *5278*
Yepremian, George: Football game to last longer than 80 minutes, *7335*
Ying Shing Wen: West Point graduates who were Chinese nationals, *3201*
Yolton, John Maloney: Airship with an enclosed cabin, *1522*
Yost, Charles Woodruff: United Nations Security Council resolution vetoed by the United States, *3981*
Youmans, Edward Livingston: Popular science magazine, *4773*
Young, Achsah: Execution for witchcraft, *2793*
Young, C.C.: Sheep of the Karakul breed, *1086*
Young, Edna Earle: Navy personnel in the regular Navy who were women, *5266*
Young, Ella Flagg: Sex education program for high schools, *3088*
Young, John Richardson: Gastroenterology treatise, *1898*
Young, John W.: Reusable manned spacecraft, *7087*
Young, Lee Roy: State police, *4134*
Young, Leo C.: Radar detection of airplanes, *7676*
Young, Mahonri: Monument to a bird, *5411*
Young, Perry H.: Pilot on a scheduled passenger line who was African-American, *1604*
Young, Robert A. "Bob": Judge who had served time in prison, *2731*
Young, Samuel Baldwin Marks: Army war college, *3200*
Young, William G.: Ice cream freezer, *3862*

Yount, Harry: National park, *3735*
Yulee, David Levy: Senator who was Jewish, *2647*
Yung Wing: Chinese graduate of an American college, *3011*

Z

Zacharie, Issachar: Chiropody book, *1913*
Zachos, John Celinergos: Stenotype device, *2361*
Zachow, Otto: Brake for four-wheeled cars, *5439*
Zaharias, Babe Didrikson: Golfer born in America to win the British Women's Amateur Golf Tournament, *7363*
Zahm, Matthew: Christmas tree, *4254*
Zakrzewska, Marie Elizabeth: Infirmary for women staffed by physicians who were women, *4877*
Zamenhof, Lazarus Ludwig: Esperanto club, *5717*
Zane, Ebenezer: Sale of federal land to an individual, *5950*
Zeisberger, David: Protestant church west of the Alleghenies, *6519*
Zeiss, Carl: Contact lenses, *5073*
Zenger, John Peter: Algebra book, *1883*
Medicine advertisement in booklet form, *2318*
Political newspaper, *5632*
Trial in which freedom of the press was upheld, *5633*
War map, *4794*
Zentzytzki, Stanislaus: Bobsled run, *7581*
Zerega, Antoine: Macaroni factory, *3913*
Zettlein, George: Baseball game in which a team made no runs in nine innings, *7117*
Zieber, George B.: Sewing machine manufacturer, *4352*
Ziegler, Walter E.: Veterinary hospital established by a city, *5125*
Zinzendorf, Benigna von: School for Protestant girls, *3050*
Ziolkowski, Korczak: Monument to a Native American, *5417*
Zobian-Lindahl, Lisa: Sports bra, *2281*
Zoll, Paul M.: Pacemaker, *4952*
Zoller, Frederick: Installment finance company, *3805*
Zworykin, Vladimir Kosma: Electron microscope, *6800*
Electron tube, *3437*
Electronic road system, *6632*
Television, *7771*

Geographical Index

The following is a listing of key locations in the main body of the text, arranged alphabetically by state and city. To find an entry in the main body of the text, please go to the italicized number.

ALABAMA

Antitrust law enacted by a state, *2520*
Boycott law enacted by a state, *2310*
Coin bearing the likeness of a living person, *5377*
Dental surgeons to be licensed by a state, *4936*
Educational television network that was state-wide and state-supported, *7806*
Tugboat with a diesel-electric engine, *6889*

Auburn

Surgical operation on a bull to correct a sperm block, *5124*

Cahawba

Vice president sworn in on foreign soil, *6246*

Clarke County

Battle between Native Americans and European soldiers, *5894*

Enterprise

Monument to an insect, *5412*

Fairhope

Enclave, *2195*

Florence

Composer of jazz music, *1331*

Fort Rucker

Helicopter refueling flight, *1577*

Huntsville

Army general who was a Russian immigrant, *5149*

Mobile

Confederate paper money, *5384*
Parade held by a mystic society, *3659*
Parade with float tableaux, *3662*

Transatlantic airplane flight carrying 100 people, *1472*

Montgomery

Attorney general to be incarcerated, *6127*
Battle flag, *1128*
Confederate congressional session, *7947*
Mass boycott by civil rights protesters, *2259*
Night flight in an airplane, *1429*
Silver wire suture, *4955*

Pratt City

Navy enlisted man killed in World War I action, *8035*

Prattville

Birth registration uniform numbering system, *2162*

Sylacauga

Meteorite known to have struck a person, *6682*

Tuskegee

Postage stamp depicting an African-American, *6090*

Wakefield

Former vice president to be arrested, *6241*

ALASKA

American territory occupied by the Japanese in World War II, *8080*
State admitted to the Union that had no border with another state, *7607*
Territory annexed by the federal government that was noncontiguous, *5968*

Anchorage

Transpacific nonstop jet airplane flight, *1475*

Kodiak Island

Russian Orthodox mission, *6495*

ALASKA—Kodiak Island—*continued*
Russian settlement, *5943*

Little Diomede Island

Swimmer to cross the Bering Strait, *7522*

Metlakahtla

President to visit Alaska and Canada while in office, *6234*

Nenana

Railroad operated by the federal government, *6343*

Point Barrow

Crossing of the North Pole underwater by a submerged submarine, *6993*

ARIZONA

Airplane disaster involving more than 100 persons, *1404*
Exploration of the Grand Canyon of the Colorado, *6725*
Movie of feature length made outdoors, *5558*
State supreme court chief justice who was a woman, *2730*

Apache Pass

Medal of Honor action, *1670*

Ashfork

Steel dam, *3606*

Flagstaff

Moon of Pluto to be observed, *6684*
Planet found beyond Neptune, *6680*

Marana

Solar-powered long-distance airplane flight, *1481*

Naco

Airplane bombing raid by a mercenary soldier, *2781*

Phoenix

Pilot to receive the Congressional Medal of Honor, *1658*
Surgical facility outside a hospital, *5089*

Prescott

Old age home for pioneers, *5975*
Rodeo for roping and tying steers, *3690*

Tsaile

College on a Native American reservation, *2969*

Tucson

Airport owned by a city, *1503*
House with solar heating and radiation cooling, *2129*

Yuma

Soldier's Medal awarded to a woman, *1663*

ARKANSAS

Teacher testing requirement to be enacted by a state, *3071*

Benton

Fuller's earth, *5334*

Hot Springs

Military hospital, *5013*

Lonoke

Army officer to receive the three highest decorations, *1665*

Murfreesboro

Diamonds in actual rock, *5340*

Wilmar

Gas turbine to pump natural gas, *3521*

CALIFORNIA

Cartel of corporations, *2524*
Congressional representative of Indian ancestry, *2614*
Congressional representative who had been an actress, *2612*
Corrupt election practices law enacted by a state, *3316*
District attorney who was a woman, *2714*
Docks owned by a state, *2481*
Father and son to become commercial airline pilots, *1602*
Health maintenance organization, *4540*

Kwanzaa celebration, *4249*
Locomotive to use oil for fuel, *6358*
Motor vehicles powered by natural gas, *5508*
National park to contain an active volcano, *3737*
Negative election campaign run by media specialists, *3323*
No-fault divorce law enacted by a state, *4810*
Oyster cocktail, *2669*
Quarantine law for plants enacted by a state, *4211*
Resale price maintenance law enacted by a state, *2313*
Right-to-die law enacted by a state, *2843*
State on the Pacific coast to be admitted to the Union, *7604*
Sweet potato, *1020*
Telecast transmitted by satellite to Japan, *7855*
Transcontinental telegraph line, *7700*
Visitor to open the New York Stock Exchange, *3829*

Alameda

Hydrogenated peanut butter, *3950*
Swimmer to cover 100 meters freestyle in less than one minute, *7516*

Apple Valley

Triple jet ace, *1621*

Bakersfield

Airport owned by a county, *1505*

Berkeley

Airship disaster, *1513*
Bevatron, *6805*
Campus takeover by student protesters, *3015*
Cyclotron, *6798*
Intercollegiate football game to attract 100,000 spectators, *7325*
Medal of Honor awarded in the Korean War, *1684*
Museum to install refrigerated vaults, *5586*
National women's figure skating four-time winner, *7434*
Neptunium, *6817*
Plutonium, *6818*
Pole vaulter to clear the bar at 15 feet, *7560*
Private hydroponic garden, *1037*
Radioactive isotope medicine, *4995*
Radioactive substance produced synthetically, *6816*
Synchrotron, *6802*
Virus separated into component parts, *5062*
Vitamin E reduction to alpha tocopherol, *3972*

Buena Vista

Grape vines planted in California for wine-making, *2668*

Burbank

Airline to install rear-facing passenger seats, *1419*
Grammy awards for musical recordings, *1629*
Jet-propelled fighter plane, *1489*
Movie that was entirely computer-animated, *5539*

Calaveras County

Frog-jumping jubilee, *1151*

Camp Parks

Coast-to-coast telecast by satellite, *7852*

Camp Selfridge

Airplane flight to the deck of a carrier, *1434*

Capitola

Commercial production of plants in water, *1038*

Chico

Public locker plant, *2366*
Tung trees, *1021*

Coloma

Gold discovered in California, *5329*

Coronado

Airplane refueling attempt in midair, *1496*

Culver City

Radar for commercial and private planes, *7681*

Cupertino

Interactive multimedia authoring program, *2553*

Davis

Genetically altered food, *3840*

Downey

Gas-turbine propeller-driven airplane, *1400*

Duarte

Medicine produced using recombinant DNA, *5004*

CALIFORNIA—*continued*

El Segundo

Barbie doll, *2152*

Ellwood

Bombing raid on the continental United States in World War II, *8075*

Emeryville

DNA chain polymerization, *5065*
Dog racetrack to use an imitation rabbit, *7278*

Folsom

Sawmill driven by electricity, *4412*

General Grant National Park

National Christmas tree, *4258*

Hawthorne

Bomber plane with the Flying Wing design, *1491*
Rocket airplane for military use, *1490*

Hollywood

Humanist association, *5746*
Movie in Cinemascope, *5562*
Movie of feature length made in Hollywood, *5551*
Movie star who was a weapons inventor, *5527*
Oscar awarded to a performer who was African-American, *1633*
Oscar for best picture, *1630*
Oscar for best picture awarded to a movie that was independently produced, *1637*
Oscar for best picture awarded to an X-rated movie, *1638*
Oscar movie awards ceremony to be telecast, *1636*
Oscar winners who were father and son, *1634*
Oscar winners who were husband and wife, *1635*
Oscars for best acting, *1631*
Oscars for best movie director, *1632*
Radio show sponsored by a cooperative of commercial advertisers, *2338*

Honey Lake

Movie of a solar eclipse taken from an airplane, *6688*

Inglewood

Electric starting gate for horse races, *7401*

Horse to win $1 million in races, *7411*

La Habra

Citrons, *3905*

La Jolla

Astronaut to converse with an aquanaut, *7033*
Oceanography institution, *6713*
Transatlantic undersea radio conversation, *6283*

Lake County

Borax, *5331*

Lassen Peak

Volcanic eruption for which a date can be estimated, *2864*

Loma Linda

Heart transplant using a baboon heart, *5104*

Loomis

Judge who had served time in prison, *2731*

Los Angeles

Airmail and express service by helicopter, *6031*
Airplane race of importance in which both men and women were contestants, *7298*
Airport fog disposal unit, *1509*
Animated feature-length cartoon in Technicolor, *5536*
Animated three-dimensional cartoon in Technicolor, *5537*
Athlete who was African-American to win the James E. Sullivan Memorial Trophy, *1720*
Aviation meet, *7292*
Bank to be automated, *3800*
Baseball player to steal more than 100 bases in a season, *7154*
Bicyclist from the United States to win the Tour de France, *7199*
Buddhist temple, *6438*
Catholic cardinal whose see was west of the Rockies, *6477*
Chinchilla farm, *1074*
Circular office building, *2066*
Commercial television station west of the Mississippi River, *7797*
Congressional representative to give birth while holding office, *2620*
Coptic Orthodox Church bishop, *6500*
County public defender, *4639*
Discotheque, *3631*
Editor of a major daily newspaper who was a woman, *5622*

Electric guitar, *1325*
Emmy awards for excellence in television, *1628*
Football with a rubber covering, *7313*
Free agents in major league baseball, *7158*
Gas-turbine propane-fueled locomotive, *6369*
General-purpose computer network, *2544*
High jump over seven feet, *7563*
Highway interchange structure with four levels, *6633*
Judge of Chinese ancestry, *2728*
Liner equipped with a gyrostabilizer, *6899*
Lung tumor operation in which the patient was under hypnosis, *5086*
Mobile telephone commercial service, *7735*
Movie to earn $1 billion, *5515*
Movie to gross $50 million, *5513*
Movie version of a Shakespeare play to be made in the United States, *5549*
Night coach, *5422*
Orca, *1161*
Parachute jump from an airplane by a woman, *1582*
Photograph of genes, *4909*
Photographer to receive the John Simon Guggenheim Memorial Foundation award, *1627*
Pilot from the United States to establish an airplane altitude record, *1594*
Pilot to bail out of an airplane flying at supersonic speed, *1592*
Postage stamp issued jointly by two countries, *6069*
Presidential campaigner to be assassinated, *3416*
Round-the-world flight over the North Pole on a regularly scheduled air route, *1479*
Shot-put toss over 60 feet, *7562*
Sodium reactor, *3550*
Subway service in Los Angeles, *6414*
Super Bowl football game, *7333*
Telecast images received in an airplane, *7832*
Theater to show movies, *3704*
Three-dimensional telecast, *7844*
Trackless trolley system, *6404*
Transcontinental bus service, *5421*
Transcontinental eastbound airplane flight made in stages, *1440*
Transcontinental foot race, *7557*
Transcontinental jet airplane passenger service, *1422*
Transcontinental nonstop airplane flight by a woman, *1456*
Transcontinental nonstop eastbound airplane service, *1420*
Transcontinental nonstop two-way airplane service, *1421*
Veterinary hospital established by a city, *5125*
Video recording on high-definition magnetic tape, *7818*

March Field

Transcontinental round-trip airplane flight made within 24 hours, *1465*

Mare Island

Electrically propelled naval ship, *6930*
Submarine expressly designed and built to fire guided missiles, *6975*

Mariposa County

Fifty-dollar gold pieces, *5367*
Private mint authorized by the federal government, *5352*

Merced

Mother and son to enlist simultaneously in the Army, *5175*
Round-the-world nonstop flight by a jet airplane, *1480*

Montebello

Commercial hydroponicum, *1039*

Monterey

Army chaplain who was Catholic, *5194*
Consul to California, *3987*
Rock music festival, *1372*
Ship from the Atlantic coast to anchor in a California port, *6858*

Mount Hamilton

Movie showing another planet, *6687*
Observatory on a mountaintop, *6666*
Seismograph, *6712*

Mount Palomar

Telescope lens 200 inches in diameter, *6671*

Mount Toro

Television stations to share the same frequency, *7802*

Mount Wilson

Astronomer to measure the size of a fixed star, *6668*

Muroc

Airplane to fly faster than the speed of sound, *1468*

CALIFORNIA—Muroc—*continued*

Airplane with a delta wing, *1402*

Astronaut who was a woman to live in a space station, *7054*

Astronaut who was a woman to pilot the space shuttle, *7053*

Pilot of an airplane to qualify as an astronaut by attaining a 50-mile altitude, *1623*

Reusable manned spacecraft, *7087*

Rocket plane for manned supersonic flight, *1492*

Rocket-powered car to break the sound barrier on land, *5461*

Round-the-world nonstop airplane flight without refueling, *1482*

Newport Bay

Airplane round-trip flight over water, *1441*

Oakland

Bird refuge established by a state, *3743*

Commercial power laundry, *2440*

Hotel at an airport, *2431*

Tennis champion to win the Grand Slam, *7536*

Orange

Septuplets, *2178*

Otay

Glider flight, *1546*

Palm Springs

Movie to be shown simultaneously on pay television and in movie theaters, *5519*

Palo Alto

Basketball leagues for women to attract significant attendance at games, *7178*

College graduate in geology who was a woman, *3241*

Computer mouse, *2535*

Factoring of a 100-digit number, *6760*

Graphical user interface for a commercial computer, *2547*

Photographs showing action, *5818*

Presidential nomination ceremony broadcast on radio, *3412*

Palomar

Quasar to be observed, *6683*

Pasadena

Antimatter to be observed, *6815*

Cosmic ray to be discovered, *6679*

Human-powered aircraft, *1406*

Newsreel in color, *5699*

Nobel Prize winner to receive awards in two different categories, *1699*

Photograph taken on Mars, *6705*

Pilot of a jet fighter to win a dogfight in the Korean War, *7981*

Tournament of Roses, *7318*

Petaluma

Coin-operated locker, *2369*

Playa del Rey

Speedway with a board track, *7508*

Point Arguello

Weather satellite to provide high-resolution cloud-cover photographs at night, *7072*

Redwood City

Concrete seagoing ship, *6876*

Tape recorder built in the United States for commercial use, *7014*

Video tape recorder for sounds and pictures, *7821*

Richmond

Grant-in-aid enacted by Congress to help the states build roads, *6626*

Riverside

Air Force Medal of Honor for action in the Korean War, *1667*

Forest Service aerial patrol, *3730*

Oranges of the seedless navel variety, *3903*

Sacramento

Camel race, *1146*

Robot to perform surgery, *3449*

Store with fixed prices, *2495*

Transplant of a major organ into a person with mental retardation, *5107*

Union catalog of books in a state library, *1776*

San Bernardino

Boxing referee who was a woman, *7244*

San Diego

Airplane loop-the-loop, *1443*

Catholic mission in California, *6454*

Double-deck streetcar, *6401*
Exploration of land on the Pacific coast by a European, *5896*
Hydroplane, *1391*
Hydroplane flight to and from a ship, *1436*
Jet-propelled landing on an aircraft carrier, *1464*
Lighthouse on the Pacific Coast, *4128*
Navy officer who was a woman to hold a major command, *5297*
Photograph taken from an airplane, *5820*
Ship with a floating scientific instrument platform, *6717*
Swimmer who was a woman to swim the English Channel in both directions, *7519*
Tennis champion who was a woman to win the Grand Slam, *7537*
Transcontinental airplane flight made within 24 hours, *1447*
Transcontinental glider tow, *1551*
Transcontinental nonstop helicopter flight, *1578*
Transpacific sailboat crossing by a woman, *6999*
Twin-engine pressurized airplane, *1401*

San Fernando

Glider entirely built of plywood and plastic, *1553*
Powered soaring glider commercially licensed, *1556*

San Francisco

Airline flight attendant who was a woman, *1412*
Army language school, *3204*
Bank of importance to lease personal property, *3798*
Be-In, *3668*
Bed that could be hidden, *4330*
Bicycle track of wood, *7191*
Blue jeans, *2268*
Boxing match timed by automatic timer, *7235*
Bridge with piers sunk in the open sea, *3593*
Cable car put into service, *6398*
Chinese immigrants to America, *5964*
Chinese laundry, *2439*
Chinese newspaper, *5668*
Chinese restaurant, *2455*
Chinese theater, *3699*
Chinese theatrical performance, *1250*
Christian religious service in English on the Pacific Coast, *6501*
Condom commercials on television, *6843*
District attorney who was African-American, *2716*
Dugong, *1158*
Dynamite, *4423*
Electric company organized to produce and sell electricity, *3457*

Equal Rights Party convention, *3363*
Federal treaty signed by a woman, *4006*
Fifty-dollar gold pieces minted by the federal government, *5376*
Flea laboratory, *6749*
Giant panda, *1154*
Hospital for patients of Chinese ancestry, *4891*
Jetway, *1510*
Jukebox, *7007*
Labor union label, *4612*
Law school where the entire faculty was 65 years of age or over, *3125*
Military expeditionary force to be sent beyond the Western Hemisphere, *8009*
Military think tank, *5128*
Minister who was openly homosexual, *6837*
Modern dancer, *1234*
Municipal streetcars, *6405*
Naval ship with a plural name, *6936*
Newspaper reproduced commercially and regularly by radio facsimile, *5658*
Nylon, *7877*
Occupation of federal territory by Native American protesters in the modern era, *5977*
Opera house established by a city, *1351*
Phase-contrast cinemicrography film to be shown on television, *5565*
President and First Lady to die during the term for which he had been elected, *6196*
Public school for Chinese-American children, *3062*
Rat extermination throughout an entire city, *4183*
Rock and roll broadcast on FM radio, *1371*
Round-the-world bicycle trip, *7201*
Round-the-world flight by a commercial airplane, *1462*
Round-the-world steamboat passenger service, *6888*
Slot machine, *3635*
Stadium operated by a city, *7506*
Steamboat to employ electric lights successfully, *6873*
Stock exchange to specialize in mining securities, *3816*
Telephone exchange for Chinese-American subscribers, *7733*
Tong organized crime gang, *2777*
Transcontinental air race, *7295*
Transcontinental airmail flight, *6018*
Transcontinental car trip, *5471*
Transcontinental motorcycle trip, *5492*
Transcontinental nonstop balloon flight, *1544*
Transcontinental solo trip on horseback by a woman, *1183*
Transcontinental telecast received on the East Coast, *7840*
Transpacific airmail flight, *6025*
Transpacific radio conversation, *6267*
Transpacific sidewheeler steamer, *6871*

CALIFORNIA—San Francisco—*continued*
Transpacific telegraph cable, *7703*
Transport airplane designed for transoceanic service, *1414*
Underground comic book of note, *4739*
World Series disrupted by an earthquake, *7137*
X-ray three-dimensional stereo fluoroscopic system, *4911*

San Gabriel

Flying disk for use in throwing games, *7585*

San Jose

Navy pilot shot down and captured in North Vietnam, *8015*
Physical manipulation of individual atoms, *6824*

San Leandro

Steam tractor, *1054*

San Luis Obispo

Human-powered helicopter, *1571*
Motel, *2429*

San Pedro

Canned tuna, *3889*
Ship to pass both ways through the Northwest Passage, *7001*

Santa Barbara

Avocado, *3902*
Oil spill with disastrous consequences, *3544*
Oil wells successfully drilled in the ocean, *3535*

Santa Clara

Medical college on the Pacific Coast, *3165*
Microprocessor, *3446*

Santa Cruz

Loganberry, *3904*

Santa Monica

Car-airplane combination, *5447*
Cyber cafe, *2467*
Pen with truly erasable ink, *8155*
Transcontinental air derby for women, *7297*
Transcontinental bicycle trip made in less than three weeks, *7204*

Soquel

Patent on a number, *6764*

South Pasadena

Ostrich farm, *1071*

Squaw Valley

Artificial ice skating rink of Olympic size, *7435*

Stanford

Acoustic microscope, *6750*
Astronaut who was a woman to fly in space, *7048*
Computer modem that was practical, *2534*
Holographic data storage system, *2540*
Human antibodies produced artificially, *5005*
Microscopic cantilever, *6825*
Quark to be observed, *6821*
Radar signal bounced off the sun, *7683*

Stockton

Runner from the United States to run a mile in less than four minutes, *7564*

Sunnyvale

Video game, *4013*

Sylmar

Hang-gliding national championships, *7300*

Tassajara Springs

Zen Buddhist monastery, *6439*

Tulare County

Animal disease of American origin, *5122*

Vallejo

Streamlined submarine, *6968*

Vandenberg

American flag to orbit the earth, *1131*

Vandenberg Air Force Base

Satellite with a nuclear reactor to orbit the earth, *7074*
Space capsule recovered from an orbiting satellite, *7062*

Van Nuys

Plastic bonded airplane, *1398*

Washington

Salmon cannery, *3887*

Yosemite

State park, *3734*

Yosemite National Park

Conservationist of note, *3712*

COLORADO

Abortion legalized by a state as a medical procedure, *6835*
Baby carrier, *2154*
Child delinquency law enacted by a state, *2147*
Mineral segregation by oil flotation, *5335*

Boulder

Optical computer, *2539*

Boulder City

Hydroelectric power plant to produce a million kilowatts, *3485*

Canon City

Hanging railroad bridge, *3585*

Castlewood

Dam filled with rocks, *3605*

Colorado City

Intercity trucking service, *2484*

Colorado Springs

Air Force academy, *3190*
Air Force Academy cadets who were women, *3193*
Air Force Academy graduate who was Native American, *3191*
Air Force Academy graduates who were African-American, *3192*
Rack-rail diesel-electric locomotive, *6366*

Danbury

Hat factory, *2293*

Denver

American Bar Association member who was a woman, *4640*

Birth to be televised for the public, *2164*
Centralized refrigeration service, *4436*
Church without theology, creed, or dogma, *6602*
Comprehensive digital atlas of the human body, *4913*
Liver transplant, *5097*
Opera broadcast over the radio in its entirety, *1350*
Pronghorn antelope, *1148*
Ship transported overland across the Rocky Mountains, *6935*
Snow goose, *1167*
Tampon to be mass-produced, *4061*
Train to run 1,000 miles nonstop, *6432*
Tuberculosis hospital for needy patients, *4903*
Veterans of Foreign Wars of the United States meeting, *5311*
Zoo habitat constructed of simulated rock formations without bars, *1188*

Gilman

Underground mill for the separation of zinc and lead, *5343*

Golden

College diploma made of silver, *2980*

Grand Junction

Election using the preferential ballot system, *3320*

North Canaan

Hail insurance, *4510*

Telluride

Power transmission installation using alternating current, *3467*

CONNECTICUT

Aviation law enacted by a state, *1384*
Bicycle with a rotary crank, *7181*
Boiler inspection law enacted by a state, *4106*
Branding law enacted by a colony, *1065*
Dental hygienists to be licensed by a state, *4941*
License plates for vehicles, *4226*
Pounds for stray livestock, *1066*
Purple Heart, *1656*
Speeding driver law enacted by a state, *4221*
Steel, *4490*

Ansonia

Copper refinery furnace, *4474*

CONNECTICUT—*continued*

Avon

Sewing machine lamp holder, *4359*

Berlin

Government contract authorized by Congress for pistols, *8092*
Tinware manufacturers, *4291*

Bridgeport

Electric socket operated by a pull chain, *4344*
Handheld rocket launcher, *8133*
Helicopter commercially designed, *1558*
Steam car, *5425*
Trading stamp, *2327*

Bristol

Brass clock works, *7900*
Fishing rod of telescoping steel tubes, *7932*
Spring manufacturer, *4400*

Centerbrook

Comb made of ivory, *4066*

Danielson

Dentist who was a woman, *4861*

Derby

Industrial school, *3282*
Machine for manufacturing pins, *4350*
Sheep of the Merino breed, *1085*

Easton

Meteorite whose landing was recorded, *6677*

Fairfield

Helicopter hoist rescue, *1563*

Farmington

Cattle club to promote Guernsey cattle, *1092*

Georgetown

Wire sieves, *4370*

Glastonbury

Bible translation by a woman, *1970*

Granby

Copper coins, *5354*

Copper mine, *5316*

Greenwich

Squash rackets champion who was a woman, *7502*

Groton

Diesel engine in a submarine, *6965*
Nuclear-powered submarine, *6973*
Nuclear-powered submarine with turbine-electric drive, *6978*
Submarine equipped with ballistic missiles, *6976*
Submarine from the United States destroyed in World War II, *8066*
Submarine to have two complete crews, *6977*
Submarine to remain submerged for two weeks, *6974*

Gurleyville

Silk dyers, *7888*

Hamden

Rubber shoe manufacturer, *2301*

Hartford

Accident insurance company, *4504*
Aircraft liability and property damage insurance, *4516*
Aluminum used commercially in a transmission conductor, *3471*
Anesthetic in dentistry, *4829*
Aviation department of a state government, *1385*
Baseball catchers' chest protector, *7106*
Belting, *4392*
Bicycle factory, *7183*
Boiler insurance company, *4505*
Book manuscript that was typewritten, *1751*
Brick machine, *2057*
Car insurance policy, *4519*
Children's magazine, *4695*
Constitution to declare that "the foundation of authority is in the free consent of the people", *1099*
Cookbook by an American author, *1847*
Copyright law enacted by a state, *4627*
Cryptography book, *2017*
Electric alternator, *3469*
Electrical transmission of three-phase alternating high-frequency current, *3468*
Elliptical office building, *2096*
Free public art museum in continuous existence, *5595*
Genealogy of an American family, *1864*
Gyroscopes for use as toys, *2142*

Hydroelectric power plant to use a storage battery, *3470*
Intercollegiate lawn tennis match, *7528*
Law book of federal laws, *1876*
Mercury boiler turbine, *3477*
Neutrality regulation enacted by Congress that governed the actions of citizens, *3978*
Parachute jump using a nylon parachute, *1591*
Pay telephone, *7715*
Pay television dramatic program, *7787*
Pneumatic tires, *5495*
Prayers in sign language, *6528*
President to ride in a car, *6223*
School for deaf students, *3032*
Secession convention during the War of 1812, *7635*
Silver plating factory, *4466*
Steam turbine operated by a public utility to produce electricity, *3472*
Teachers' institute, *3261*
Underwater torpedo operated by electric current, *8098*
Watch made by machinery, *7901*
Worsted mill operated by waterpower, *7893*

Hebron

Historical hoaxes, *3645*

Huntington

Tungsten and tellurium, *5322*

Ivoryton

Comb-cutting machine, *4067*

Kensington

Monument to commemorate the Civil War, *5400*

Killingworth

Gem-cutting machine, *5317*
Type foundry, *5801*

Litchfield

Anthology of American literature, *1740*
Law report, *1874*
Law school operated privately, *3122*

Litchfield County

Temperance organization, *2675*

Mansfield

Silk mill, *7887*

Silk thread, *4362*

Marion

Nuts and bolts factory, *7918*

Meriden

Player piano that was completely automatic, *1317*
Stainless steel flatware, *4375*

Middlebury

Lathe, *7914*

Middletown

Agricultural experiment station operated by a state, *1003*
Education association, *3223*
Elastic webbing, *7869*
Factory standardization to federal government specification, *4381*
Teaching methodology course at a college, *3262*

Milford

Camp for boys, *2143*

Mystic

Ironclad seagoing naval warship, *6922*

New Haven

Acidophilus milk, *3876*
Applied chemistry professor at a college, *3234*
Arbitration law enacted by a colony, *2353*
Baseball batting and fielding cage, *7108*
Blotting paper, *5755*
Building in all-Gothic architecture, *2071*
Caster for bedsteads, *4323*
Chinese graduate of an American college, *3011*
Chinese language and literature lectureship at a college, *3116*
Class photograph, *5813*
College art museum, *5594*
College course in the contemporary novel, *3101*
College daily newspaper, *5646*
College magazine, *4699*
College to feature rowing as a sport, *7467*
Continental coin, *5357*
Dictionary of the English language compiled by an American, *1800*
Doctor of Philosophy degree, *2977*
Doctor of Philosophy degree awarded to an African-American scholar, *2978*
Fine arts department in a college, *2902*

CONNECTICUT—New Haven—_continued_
Football dummy, _7311_
Football uniforms worn in a game, _7310_
Geography book, _1978_
Geology society (national), _6778_
Hamburger, _3940_
Intercollegiate football championship, _7317_
International championship figure skating tournament, _7431_
International football game, _7316_
Knights of Columbus meeting, _5724_
Map of the United States, _4795_
Music magazine, _4694_
National Basketball Association commissioner, _7172_
Paleontology chair at a college, _3237_
Pay station telephone service, _7731_
Penalty rule in football, _7304_
Physiology laboratory, _4926_
Pituitary hormone, _4996_
Planetarium built in America, _6660_
Political history book, _1868_
Sabbath laws published by a colony, _6509_
Sprinkler head, _4108_
Stone crusher, _5332_
Tape measure, _7926_
Telephone directory, _1818_
Theater and dramatic criticism course at a college, _3105_
Tornado of record, _2863_

New London

Capture of a British frigate in the War of 1812, _8023_
Circumnavigation of the earth by a submerged submarine, _6996_
Coast Guard Academy graduates who were women, _3211_
Episcopal bishop, _6549_
Eye infirmary, _4871_
Marine engagement in battle, _7994_
Mine barrage, _8090_
Navy nuclear submarine division, _5306_
Patented pills, _4981_
Steam whaler, _6885_
Submarine emergency air supply container, _6967_
Submarine escape training tank, _6969_
Submarine to surface at the North Pole, _6995_
Submarine to travel under the North Pole from the east, _6994_
Toothpaste tube, _4073_

New Milford

Automatic streetlight system, _2217_

North Windham

Fourdrinier papermaking machine, _5750_

Northfield

United Church of Christ ordination of a woman in which all the principal roles were filled by women, _6536_

Putnam

Nontwisted sewing thread, _4364_

Riverton

Chair factory, _4321_

Rocky River

Hydroelectric power plant to use water pumped into a reservoir, _3479_

Salem

Music school authorized to confer degrees, _2899_

Salisbury

Children's library, _4664_

Seymour

Screw auger, _7911_

Simsbury

Detonating fuse of the Cordeau-Bickford type, _4424_
Safety fuse, _4422_
Textile-wrapped detonating fuse, _4426_

South Norwalk

Derby hat, _2295_

Stamford

Ambulance ship for first aid to boaters and pleasure craft, _4827_
Crane, _4408_
Electric shaver, _4060_
Portable typewriter, _2387_
Postage meter, _6008_
Railroad signal system with automatic electric block, _6422_
Shoe measuring stick, _2299_
Telegraph code converter, _7710_

Stanfield

Cider mill, _3841_

Stonington

Discovery of Antarctica by an American, _6722_

DELAWARE—Wilmington—*continued*
Synthetic fiber, *7876*
Synthetic rubber for manufacture, *4489*
Teflon created in a laboratory, *4482*
Thread as strong as steel, *7880*
Toothbrush with synthetic bristles, *4074*

DISTRICT OF COLUMBIA

Washington

Admiral of the Navy, *5271*
Aerial photograph in natural colors, *5826*
African-American history trail, *5979*
African-American preacher to deliver a sermon in the House of Representatives, *2588*
Agricultural journal, *4703*
Agriculture bureau scientific publication, *1763*
Agriculture organization (national), *1089*
AIDS policy coordinator for the federal government, *4192*
Air attack on Germany by the Army Air Force in World War II, *8061*
Air bag requirement by the federal government, *4231*
Air Force chairman of the Joint Chiefs of Staff, *5136*
Air Force general who was a woman, *5140*
Air Force general who was African-American, *5135*
Air pollution law of importance enacted by Congress, *3718*
Airmail letter sheet, *6023*
Airmail pickup by an airplane without landing, *6024*
Airmail postal card, *6047*
Airmail stamps, *6063*
Airplane model to make a sustained flight under its own power, *1425*
Airplane to land on the White House lawn, *6255*
Airplane with ailerons, *1394*
Alcohol abuse programs required in schools by the federal government, *2679*
Alcohol prohibition law enacted by Congress, *2684*
Alcohol prohibition vote taken in Congress, *2682*
Ambassador from the United States who was a woman, *3991*
Ambassador to the United States who was a woman, *3990*
Ambassador who was an African-American woman, *3994*
American flag made of American bunting to fly over the Capitol, *1129*
American to hug the Queen of England, *6656*
Animated film inducted into the National Film Registry, *5538*
Antitrust law enacted by Congress, *2521*

Arbitration law enacted by Congress, *2356*
Architect and engineer who worked professionally, *1193*
Archivist of the United States, *4677*
Archivist training program at a college, *3107*
Army ambulance corps, *5011*
Army balloon corps, *5182*
Army chaplain who was African-American, *5201*
Army chief engineer, *5163*
Army corps for women, *5189*
Army dental corps, *5016*
Army engineer corps, *5178*
Army general to become an admiral in the Navy, *5150*
Army medical corps, *5008*
Army nurse corps for women, *5017*
Army nursing school, *3176*
Army officer to occupy both the nation's highest military post and the highest nonelective civilian post, *5153*
Army officer who was a woman, *5170*
Army organization under the Constitution, *5143*
Army Reserve Officers Training Corps units, *5183*
Army secret service bureau, *5181*
Army signal corps, *5180*
Army specialist corps for women, *5190*
Army veterinary corps, *5021*
Army war college, *3200*
Army War College graduates who were women, *3206*
Art museum devoted to work by women, *5599*
Artificial aortic valve, *5053*
Artist of renown who was African-American, *1209*
Astronaut international rescue agreement, *7037*
Astronaut to become a general, *7044*
Astronaut to become an admiral, *7043*
Astronomer employed in the Naval Observatory who was a woman, *6667*
Astronomical observations book, *1985*
Astronomy photographs in color to be published in a magazine, *6699*
Attorney general to plead guilty to a criminal offense, *6126*
Attorney general whose father also served as attorney general, *6125*
Auction of radio spectrum for satellite services, *6284*
Autogiro owned by the federal government, *1533*
Ban by Congress on importation of diseased cattle, *4210*
Ban on federal funding for human cloning research, *6755*
Ban on sex discrimination in wages enacted by Congress, *6834*
Bank deposit insurance law enacted by Congress, *3782*

DISTRICT OF COLUMBIA—Washington—
continued

Congressional opening session to be televised, *2571*

Congressional page who was female, *2590*

Congressional standing committee headed by an African-American, *2591*

Conscience fund, *2771*

Constitutional amendment proposal guaranteeing women the right to vote, *3432*

Constitutional amendment proposal mandating equal legal rights for women and men, *6830*

Constitutional amendment proposal to bear the signature of a president, *1108*

Constitutional amendment submitted to the states for repeal, *1109*

Consumer protection law enacted by Congress, *2311*

Copyright law on photographs enacted by Congress, *4630*

Corporation tax levied by Congress, *7653*

Corps badges systematically assigned to an entire army, *5224*

Corrupt election practices law enacted by Congress, *3319*

Crime insurance policy authorized by a state, *4518*

Daylight saving time program, *7896*

Dead letter office, *5989*

Demonstration in Washington against the Vietnam War, *8017*

Deportation of aliens authorized by Congress, *5864*

Design for the Great Seal of the United States, *1132*

Director of the Federal Bureau of Investigation, *4141*

Doctor commissioned in the regular Army who was a woman, *5172*

Draft law enacted by Congress during peacetime, *5220*

Draft law enacted by Congress during wartime, *5219*

Drawback legislation enacted by Congress, *2471*

Drinking straws, *4374*

Drug control chief appointed by the federal government, *2693*

Drug control law enacted by Congress, *2687*

Easter egg roll, *4239*

Election day for presidential voting held nationwide, *3387*

Election in the District of Columbia, *3325*

Election law granting African-American men the right to vote, *3428*

Electoral college members invited to a presidential inauguration, *3391*

Electric locomotive, *6356*

Electric range, *4293*

Emancipation proclamation, *2252*

Embargo act enacted by Congress, *2475*

Embargo act of the Continental Congress, *2470*

Endangered species list issued by the federal government, *3719*

Enemy saboteurs executed in the United States, *8058*

Execution of a woman by hanging by the federal government, *2798*

Exhibition of the *Mona Lisa* in the United States, *1231*

Export report by the federal government, *2473*

Fat substitute in prepared foods, *3886*

Father and son to occupy the same Cabinet post, *6109*

Father and son who were senators at the same session, *2644*

Federal administrator who was an African-American woman, *2257*

Federal aid program for primary and secondary schools, *3070*

Federal aid to libraries, *4678*

Federal government building built to withstand a nuclear attack, *2119*

Federal law exempting debtors from prison, *2814*

Federal law hostile to lotteries, *3642*

Federal law requiring radios on ships, *4222*

Federal marshals who were women, *4151*

Federal reserve banks, *3777*

Federal treasury surplus to be returned to the states, *7596*

Federal treaty rejected by the Senate, *4003*

Federally chartered bank owned and managed by women, *3789*

First Lady to be depicted on a monument to a president, *6134*

First Lady to pilot an airship, *6132*

First Lady who was also a federal official, *6133*

Foreign service school in a college, *3126*

Former president to address the Senate, *6175*

Former president to become chief justice of the Supreme Court, *6164*

Free mail delivery in cities, *5996*

Fugitive slave law enacted by Congress, *2247*

Gag rule in the House of Representatives, *2586*

Gaslight in the White House, *6253*

Gasoline tax levied by Congress, *7659*

General of the Armies of the United States, *5152*

General of the Armies of the United States with the rank of six stars, *5161*

General of the U.S. Army, *5151*

Genetically altered plants, *1028*

Genetically altered virus approved for use in a vaccine, *5066*

Geographer of the United States, *6707*

Geography magazine, *4775*

Geological survey authorized by Congress, *6710*

DISTRICT OF COLUMBIA—Washington—
continued

Navigation act enacted by Congress, *2472*
Navy admirals to wear the five-star insignia, *5273*
Navy bureau of medicine and surgery, *5009*
Navy chairman of the Joint Chiefs of Staff, *5293*
Navy Day, *4247*
Navy dental corps, *5019*
Navy mail service, *6005*
Navy–Marine Corps Medal for Heroism awarded to a woman, *1668*
Navy officer commissioned in the U.S. Naval Reserve who was a woman, *5287*
Navy officer to become an admiral, *5270*
Navy officer to become an engineer, *5282*
Navy personnel in the regular Navy who were women, *5266*
News dispatch by telegraph, *5602*
Newspaper advertisement scented with perfume, *2336*
Newspaper wrappers for mailing newspapers, *5995*
Newsreels showing presidential candidates, *5698*
Nickel five-cent piece, *5370*
Nobel Peace Prize awarded to an African-American, *1697*
Notes wholly engraved and printed at the Bureau of Engraving and Printing, *5390*
Observatory established by the federal government, *6665*
Officer to preside over both of the branches of Congress, *2565*
Olympic Games boycott, *7450*
Painting by an African-American artist to hang in the White House, *1221*
Paper money fractional currency, *5388*
Paper money issued by the federal government, *5385*
Paper money of the present small size, *5393*
Parcel post domestic air service, *6033*
Parcel post service, *6006*
Parent-teacher association (national), *3227*
Parking garage that was completely automated, *5485*
Passport fee, *5885*
Passport photographs, *5886*
Patent list, *2027*
Pension for presidents and their widows, *6172*
Pension granted to the widow of a president, *4584*
Pensions paid by the federal government to workers in private industry, *4588*
Phonograph that was practical, *7005*
Photograph bounced off the moon, *5830*
Photograph of the Senate in session, *2635*
Photograph showing air in motion across airplane wings, *5822*

Physician to Congress, *2569*
Picturephone commercial service, *7750*
Pilot to fly a regularly scheduled airmail transport who was a woman, *1600*
Piracy law enacted by Congress, *2772*
Plow for pulverizing the soil, *1049*
Poet laureate of the United States, *2034*
Police officer who was a woman to be killed in the line of duty, *4152*
Political asylum granted on grounds of sexual orientation, *5882*
Political asylum granted to avoid genital mutilation, *5883*
Polygamy ban enacted by Congress, *4807*
Pope to visit the White House, *4084*
Popular vote in a presidential election, *3386*
Post office in an airplane, *6040*
Postage stamp depicting a Jew, *6091*
Postage stamp depicting a living American, *6097*
Postage stamp depicting an African-American woman, *6100*
Postage stamp depicting an American woman, *6087*
Postage stamp depicting the American flag, *6082*
Postage stamp featuring a work of art in true color, *6093*
Postage stamp issued with perforations, *6054*
Postage stamp whose design was decided by popular vote, *6101*
Postage stamp with valuation of one dollar, *6060*
Postage stamps depicting the American eagle, *6079*
Postage stamps in coils, *6062*
Postage stamps of 50 different designs sold as a single sheet, *6098*
Postage stamps to feature paintings, *6086*
Postage stamps without a denomination, *6077*
Postal card, *6044*
Postal directory, *1816*
Postal savings bank, *3775*
Postcard, *6046*
Prefrontal lobotomy, *5087*
President buried in Washington, *6197*
President elected for third and fourth terms, *6170*
President elected for two nonconsecutive terms, *6162*
President inaugurated in the city of Washington, *6146*
President inaugurated on January 20, *6169*
President of a black African country to visit the United States, *4082*
President to be assassinated, *6193*
President to be censured by Congress, *6151*
President to be impeached, *6159*
President to be wounded in an unsuccessful assassination attempt while in office, *6207*

President to celebrate his silver wedding anniversary at the White House, *6191*

President to die in Washington, *6189*

President to fly in a helicopter, *6229*

President to invite the president-elect, *6165*

President to make a radio broadcast from the White House, *6212*

President to make a radio broadcast in a foreign language, *6216*

President to pitch a ball to open the baseball season, *6163*

President to read a veto message to Congress, *6168*

President to receive a passport while in office, *6232*

President to receive a presidential pardon, *6179*

President to reside in Washington, *6144*

President to resign, *6177*

President to review the military forces, *6147*

President to take the oath of office using a nickname, *6180*

President to use a radio, *6209*

President to use a telephone, *6161*

President to use the line-item veto, *6181*

President to visit a nation not recognized by the federal government, *6238*

President to visit Europe, *6233*

President who came to the office through appointment rather than election, *6178*

President who had been divorced, *6202*

President who was a bachelor, *6192*

President who was a Rhodes Scholar, *6206*

President who was Catholic, *6203*

President whose assassination was attempted, *6187*

President whose grandson became president, *6188*

President whose mother lived at the White House, *6195*

President whose son became president, *6184*

Presidential address televised from the White House, *6217*

Presidential airplane, *6227*

Presidential candidate nominated at a caucus, *3399*

Presidential Citizen Medal, *1644*

Presidential election in which a computer was used to predict the outcome, *3393*

Presidential election in which a loser won, *3385*

Presidential election in which candidates were nominated for the vice presidency, *3384*

Presidential election in which soldiers in the field were allowed to vote, *3389*

Presidential hot line, *6173*

Presidential inauguration to be broadcast on radio, *6213*

Presidential message to Congress that was broadcast on radio, *6211*

Presidential news conference filmed for television and newsreels, *6219*

Presidential news conference to be televised live, *6220*

Presidential pet to star in a movie, *6201*

Presidential press conference recorded on tape, *6218*

Presidential protest, *6152*

Presidential railroad car, *6225*

Presidential Unit Citation award in peacetime, *1643*

Presidential veto to be overridden by Congress, *6154*

Press censorship by military authorities, *5604*

Printing press for printing wallpaper in color, *5770*

Professional football championship game broadcast on radio, *7330*

Protection of Native American hunting grounds authorized by Congress, *5951*

Public service symbol of the federal government, *3714*

Pure food and drug law established by Congress, *4175*

Quarantine law for plants enacted by Congress, *4212*

Radar detection of airplanes, *7676*

Radar observations, *7675*

Radio broadcast from the Senate chamber, *2631*

Radio broadcast in which citizens telephoned the president, *6221*

Radio broadcast of a debate, *6269*

Radio broadcast of an open session of Congress, *2567*

Radio fax transmission to a moving train, *7673*

Radio network broadcast received on the Pacific Coast, *6274*

Radio news program sponsored by a cooperative of commercial advertisers, *2339*

Railroad safety law enacted by Congress, *4219*

Red Cross meeting, *5739*

Registered mail, *5991*

Registration of aliens by the federal government, *5872*

Reigning king to visit the United States, *6645*

Reservation for Native Americans established by the federal government, *5946*

Restrictions by Congress on immigration of Chinese laborers, *5866*

Revenue stamp printed by the Post Office Department, *7660*

Revenue stamps issued by the federal government, *7648*

Scientific evidence for life on Mars, *7027*

Sculptor to obtain a federal commission, *1207*

Seagoing radio broadcasting station, *5304*

Secession idea to be mentioned in Congress, *7634*

Secret Service agents who were women, *4170*

DISTRICT OF COLUMBIA—Washington—
continued

Secret service established by the federal government, *4169*

Secretary of state who was a woman, *6123*

Senate filibuster, *2627*

Senate hearing witness who was a woman, *2628*

Senate parliamentarian, *2632*

Senate proceeding to be shown on television, *2637*

Senate whip, *2629*

Senator to address the Senate in military uniform, *2648*

Senator to serve three states, *2645*

Service number issued by the Army, *5226*

Shoulder sleeve insignia issued by the Army, *5227*

Signal flares, *5242*

Sky marshals, *4150*

Skyjacking law enacted by Congress, *2785*

Smoking ban on airplane flights, *2700*

Soil conference, *1005*

Soldiers' homes established by Congress, *5309*

Special delivery mail service, *6001*

Speed limit for highway traffic established by Congress, *4230*

Spoils system of presidential patronage, *6150*

Standard time program, *7895*

Standardization of nomenclature for naval vessels, *5264*

State dinner televised from the White House, *6258*

Statue cast by the federal government, *5404*

Statue of a woman installed in the Capitol's National Statuary Hall, *5409*

Stealth aircraft, *1493*

Steamboat inspection service established by Congress, *4217*

Streamlined electric locomotive, *6365*

Strike settlement mediated by the federal Department of Labor, *4596*

Strike suppressed by federal troops in peacetime, *4594*

Supreme Court decision declaring a state law unconstitutional, *2748*

Supreme Court decision establishing the power of the federal government, *2747*

Supreme Court decision in a state boundary case, *2751*

Supreme Court decision voiding an act of Congress, *2746*

Supreme Court justice to be appointed chief justice, *2761*

Supreme Court justice to be impeached, *2757*

Supreme Court justice who was a woman, *2765*

Supreme Court justice who was Jewish, *2762*

Supreme Court nominee to die before taking office, *2760*

Surgeon general, *4213*

Surgeon general who was African-American, *4215*

Swimming pool in the White House, *6257*

Tariff commission established by Congress, *7666*

Tariff enacted by Congress to prevent the importation of obscene literature and pictures, *7665*

Tariff passed by Congress for protection, *7664*

Tax levied by Congress on excess profits of corporations, *7654*

Telecast of an object in motion, *7825*

Telecast of image and sound, *7827*

Telegraph appropriation by Congress, *7689*

Telegraph station, *7690*

Telephone recording devices, *7724*

Television license, *7794*

Ten Most Wanted list, *2783*

Territory annexed by the federal government, *5955*

Three brothers from one family to serve in the Senate, *2656*

Tobacco sales to minors to be restricted by federal regulations, *2701*

Trade dollars, *5371*

Transatlantic supersonic jet service, *1424*

Transcontinental radio fax transmission of a photograph, *7669*

Transpacific telephone service using the transoceanic cable, *7749*

Treasury notes bearing interest, *3814*

Treaty between the federal government and a foreign nation to provide for mutual reduction of import duties, *4004*

Treaty between the federal government and a South American nation, *4002*

Treaty between the federal government and an Asian nation, *4005*

Treaty to reduce the number of nuclear missiles, *4007*

Trial in which lawyers appeared on a Picturephone, *4625*

Trial of a war criminal by the federal government, *7969*

Umpire in organized baseball who was African-American, *7102*

Uniforms for mail carriers, *5998*

Union catalog of books in American libraries, *1775*

University for African-American students, *2951*

Use of "American" as an adjective, *1098*

Vaccination law enacted by Congress, *4919*

Vaccination program by the federal government to protect Native Americans against smallpox, *4920*

Veterans' Day, *4246*

Vice president chosen under the 25th Amendment, *6249*

Vice president elected by the Senate, *6244*

Vice president to die in office, *6242*

Vice president to succeed to the presidency after the death of a president, *6245*

Vice presidential candidate to decline the nomination, *3400*

Vice president's widow to receive a pension, *6247*

Vietnam War Moratorium Day demonstration, *8019*

Vote in the House of Representatives to be recorded electronically, *2594*

Vote in the House of Representatives to be tallied by machine, *2593*

Voting machines in congressional elections, *3328*

War bond issued by the federal government, *3813*

War that was predicted by pizza orders, *7972*

Warehouse legislation enacted by Congress, *2480*

Water pollution law enacted by Congress, *3716*

Wedding in the White House, *6252*

Wedding of a president in the White House, *4815*

Women's Army Corps member to be part of the Regular Army, *5171*

Work week of 40 hours to be required by Congress, *4567*

Workday of eight hours to be authorized by Congress, *4556*

Workers' compensation insurance law enacted by Congress, *4523*

Wound chevron issued by the Army, *5225*

Year in which exports exceeded imports, *2476*

Year in which the federal budget exceeded $1 trillion, *3752*

Year in which the prison population exceeded 1 million, *2832*

Year in which two presidents were elected, *3388*

Year when citizens of the District of Columbia could vote in a presidential election, *3434*

Zinc, *5325*

Zip codes, *6013*

FLORIDA

Artist to come to America, *1195*

Autopsy, *2847*

Catholic bishop to exercise episcopal functions, *6446*

Land mines, *8097*

Mailbox see-through locker, *5987*

Meteor shower on record, *6676*

Military prison on an island, *2821*

Swiss settlement in America, *5931*

Triplets born several weeks apart, *2179*

Anastasia Island

Alligator farm, *1072*

Apalachicola

Mechanical freezer patent, *4347*

Arcadia

Rattlesnake meat in cans, *3942*

Belle Glade

Kenaf fiber, *1027*

Bonita Springs

Coast Guard officers who were women who served aboard ships, *5214*

Cape Canaveral

Animal fired into space to orbit the earth, *7024*

Animals to survive a space flight, *7023*

Astronaut to be launched into space, *7029*

Astronaut to fly in space who was African-American, *7049*

Astronaut to orbit the earth, *7030*

Astronaut to orbit the earth on two trips, *7032*

Astronaut to walk in space, *7031*

Astronaut who was a civilian to orbit the earth, *7035*

Astronauts to die in a spacecraft, *7036*

Astronauts to fly free in space, *7050*

Astronauts to land on the moon, *7040*

Astronauts to orbit the moon, *7038*

Astronauts to participate in an international spaceflight, *7046*

Astronauts to rendezvous in space with another spacecraft, *7034*

Astronauts to retrieve a manmade object from the moon, *7041*

Astronauts to ride a vehicle on the moon, *7042*

Astronauts to transfer from one spacecraft to another while in orbit, *7039*

Color photograph of the earth taken from space, *6700*

Commercial satellite, *7069*

Communications satellite, *7063*

Communications satellite with signal reception and transmission equipment, *7065*

Geodetic satellite, *7070*

Geologist to reach the moon, *6718*

Geosynchronous satellite, *7071*

Husband and wife to fly in space together, *7052*

Intermediate-range ballistic missile, *8138*

International satellite, *7067*

Live telecast from space, *6691*

Manned docking of two spacecraft, *7082*

Multisatellite launching, *7061*

Navigational satellite, *7059*

Orbiting geophysical observatory, *7073*

Orbiting observatory, *6673*

FLORIDA—Cape Canaveral—*continued*

Orbiting solar observatory, *7066*

Photograph of a solar eclipse taken from the atmosphere, *6703*

Photograph of the earth taken from the moon, *6702*

Photographs of the moon in close-up, *6701*

Physician to practice as an astronaut in space, *7045*

Planetary probe to enter the atmosphere of Jupiter, *7092*

Postage stamp issued on the date of the event it commemorated, *6070*

President to attend the launching of a manned space flight, *6176*

President to witness the firing of a Polaris missile, *6174*

Robot to conduct a roving exploration of the surface of another planet, *7093*

Satellite from the United States to impact the moon, *7068*

Satellite placed in orbit by the United States, *7056*

Satellite repair in orbit, *7077*

Satellite to transmit colored photographs of the full earth face, *7075*

Satellite to transmit photographs of the earth, *7057*

Ship to fire a Polaris missile, *8140*

Space shuttle disaster, *7090*

Space station launched by the United States, *7085*

Spacecraft launched by the United States to dock with a Russian space station, *7091*

Spacecraft placed in solar orbit, *7078*

Spacecraft to carry a message intended to be read by living beings elsewhere in the universe, *7084*

Spacecraft to land on Mars, *7086*

Spacecraft to leave the solar system, *7088*

Spacecraft to transmit close-up photographs of Mars, *7081*

Spacecraft to transmit close-up photographs of the lunar surface, *7080*

Spacecraft to transmit data from Venus, *7079*

Spacecraft to transmit photographs from lunar orbit, *7083*

Spy satellite, *7060*

Submerged submarine to fire a Polaris missile, *8142*

Weather satellite to provide cloud-cover photographs, *7058*

Cocoa Beach

Ship motion simulator to aid in the development of ballistic missiles fired from shipboard, *8121*

Swimmer to swim the English Channel underwater, *7520*

Coral Gables

College to offer athletic scholarships to women, *3004*

Daytona Beach

Car to exceed the speed of 200 miles per hour, *5445*

Diesel engine speed record, *5482*

Gainesville

Transplant of human embryo tissue, *5108*

Hialeah

Electric-eye camera installed at a racetrack, *7400*

Hollywood

Transatlantic solo trip by rowboat, *6998*

Jacksonville

Colonial warfare between European powers in America, *5900*

Truce violation, *5901*

Key Largo

Undersea hotel, *2437*

Undersea park established by the federal government, *3739*

Key West

Airplane rescue at sea, *1435*

Cuban boatlift, *5881*

Hydroplane international service, *1409*

International airplane passenger station, *1506*

President to conduct religious services as commander-in-chief of the Navy, *6166*

President to travel underwater in a captured enemy submarine, *6228*

Telephone cable deep-sea service, *7736*

Kissimmee City

Tax on aviation levied by a city, *7652*

Lantana

Motorcycle trip from the United States to Tierra del Fuego by a woman, *5494*

Marineland

Porpoise, *1156*

Mayport Naval Auxiliary Station

Airmail by missile, *6034*

Miami

Atomic bomb explosion over enemy territory, *8086*
Attorney general who was a woman, *6128*
Bilingual report of a congressional committee, *2595*
Child born in an airplane, *2160*
First Lady to travel in an airplane to a foreign country, *6131*
Greyhound racing association, *7279*
Motorboat ocean race, *7218*
President to fly in an airplane, *6226*
President to visit a foreign country in wartime, *6237*
Savings and loan association established by the federal government, *3783*
Skyjacking of a commercial American airplane, *2784*
Totalisator to record racetrack bets and odds, *7399*
Transatlantic solo boat journey by a woman, *6990*

Miami Beach

Chairman of a major political party who was a woman, *3344*
Father and son team to win the national contract bridge championship, *4026*

Milton

Coast Guard airplane pilot who was a woman, *5213*

New Smyrna

Greek settlement, *5938*

North Fort Myers

Round-the-world journey on foot, *7590*

Orlando

Professional football game in which a woman participated, *7334*
Twin postage stamps, *6073*

Pensacola

Branding punishment by a federal court, *2818*
Naval air training school, *3217*
Naval battle in the Civil War, *7959*
Navy airship, *1516*

Ponte Vedra

Golf champion of African-American and Asian descent, *7370*

Port Canaveral

Ship to transport fresh orange juice in stainless-steel tanks, *2488*

St. Augustine

African slaves in America, *2238*
Aquarium for large marine animals, *1190*
Billiards, *4015*
Catholic holy orders, *6450*
Catholic mass, *6444*
Catholic parish, *6445*
Catholic priest born in America, *6448*
European settlement in America that was permanent, *5899*
Map of a city within the present limits of the United States, *4790*
Painting of an American scene by a European painter, *1211*
School run by missionaries in America, *3037*
Town built by free African-Americans, *2183*

St. Marks

Ships built by Europeans in America, *6846*

St. Petersburg

Hydroplane service, *1408*
Open-air post office, *6039*
Shuffleboard championship tournament, *7582*

Sanford

Marine Corps jet ace in Korea, *1619*

Sebastian

Bird reservation established by the federal government, *3745*

Tallahassee

Checkers champion of renown, *4011*

Tampa

Medal of Honor awarded in World War II, *1679*
Professional hockey player who was a woman, *7383*

Tortugas

Photographs taken under the sea in natural colors, *5825*

FLORIDA—*continued*

Venice

Circus clown training school, *3301*

West Palm Beach

Human-powered submarine race, *7219*

Winter Park

Book course at a college, *3104*
College to use the unit-cost plan, *2966*
Coxswain of a men's college varsity rowing
team who was a woman, *7471*

GEORGIA

Birth registration law enacted by a state, *2159*
Book censorship board established by a state,
1792
Coast Guard serviceman who was African-
American, *5209*
Election law lowering the voting age in a state
to 18, *3433*
Laws of entail and primogeniture to be abol-
ished by a state, *4620*
Lynching ban enacted by a state, *2256*
President to be born in a hospital, *6198*
Railroad safety law enacted by a state, *4218*
Senator elected by popular vote, *3329*
Senator who was a woman, *2651*

Americus

Telephone call on a commercial line using solar
energy, *7746*

Athens

State university, *2935*

Atlanta

Advertisement on a space vehicle, *2348*
AIDS epidemic, *2878*
Airplane instructor's license, *1601*
Black Power advocate, *2262*
Golf champion to hold the four highest golf ti-
tles, *7361*
Intercollegiate football game between African-
American colleges, *7323*
Minister who was a transsexual, *6844*
Movies with color, *5545*
Navy chaplain who was an African-American
woman, *5206*
Nursing school for African-American students,
3169
Official use of the "Coke" trademark, *3848*

Olympic gold medalist who was an African-
American woman, *7449*
Penitentiary building opened by the federal
government, *2826*
Pinball ban enacted by a city, *7455*
Prisoners in a federal penitentiary to be em-
ployed in industry, *2828*
Radio station owned and operated by African-
Americans, *6300*

Augusta

Airplane in actual military operation, *1485*
Steamboat patent, *6855*

Columbus

Aviator who was African-American, *1609*
Parachute fatality in the Army, *1590*

Crisp County

Hydroelectric power plant operated by a county, *3480*

Fort Benning

Army general who rose from draftee, *5155*
Army parachute battalion, *5188*

Grover's Island

Shipbuilding law enacted by Congress, *5263*

Jefferson

Anesthetic administered in childbirth, *4830*
General anesthetic, *4828*

La Fayette

Carpeting of tufted plastic, *4319*

Macon

Baptism in America, *6442*
College secret society for women, *2986*

New Echota

Native American newspaper, *5666*

Rome

Bauxite, *5336*

Savannah

Agricultural experiment farm, *1002*
Beef export, *3938*

Cattle to be exported, *1077*
Cotton gin, *1030*
Hospital and asylum for African-Americans, *4874*
Interfaith charity organization, *5730*
Iron sailing vessel, *6867*
Patent issued by the Confederate States of America, *4655*
Presidential appointment, *6138*
Protestant Sunday school, *6518*
Scouting organization for girls, *2148*
Silk export, *7886*
Transatlantic crossing by an American steamboat, *6979*

Toccoa

Weight lifter to lift more than 6,000 pounds, *7587*

Washington

Holes in one shot by a father and son in the same golf game, *7362*

HAWAII

Congressional representative of Japanese ancestry, *2616*
Island territory annexed by the federal government, *5974*
President to go through the Panama Canal while in office, *6167*
Senator of Chinese ancestry, *2657*
State admitted to the Union that was separated by a substantial body of water, *7608*

Hilo

President to visit Hawaii while in office, *6236*

Honolulu

Adjustable stadium, *7512*
Coronation, *6646*
Space capsule recovered in midair from an orbiting satellite, *7064*
Submarine disaster, *6966*
Transpacific radio fax transmission, *7670*
Transpacific solo airplane flight by a woman, *1460*
Volcanic eruption to be broadcast on radio, *2870*

Maui

Coast Guard ship commander who was a woman, *5215*

Mauna Kea

Telescope of importance with a compound objective mirror, *6674*

Oahu

Air hero in World War II, *1615*
Guided missile launched from a nuclear submarine, *8141*
Oceanographer of distinction who was a woman, *6719*

Pearl Harbor

American losses in the Pacific in World War II, *8067*
Circumnavigation of the world by a submarine, *6991*
Navy admiral killed in action in World War II, *8068*
Radar used to detect enemy airplanes, *7679*
Ship from the United States to sink a Japanese submarine in World War II, *8069*
Submarine from the United States sunk by an enemy submarine, *8083*

Waikiki

Surfer, *7579*

IDAHO

Governor who was Jewish, *7617*
Hydroelectric power plant built by the federal government, *3473*
State seal designed by a woman, *7599*

Arco

Electric power generated from nuclear energy to illuminate a town, *3547*

Boise

Air raid shelter for a community, *4090*

Idaho Falls

Deaths in an American nuclear reactor, *3553*
Electric power from nuclear energy, *3546*
Nuclear reactor fueled by plutonium, *3554*

Kellogg

Mimeographed daily newspaper, *5654*

Latah County

County created by federal law, *5973*

Twin Falls

Motorcycle jump across a river canyon, *3682*

Winimac

Product liability lawsuit to result in a criminal trial, *2315*

ILLINOIS

Ban enacted by a state on the employment of women in an occupation, *4559*
Ban on sex discrimination in employment enacted by a state, *6828*
Internal revenue collector for the federal government who was a woman, *7657*
Plumbing law enacted by a state, *2231*
Portrait of Abraham Lincoln, *6157*
Seat belt law enacted by a state, *4228*
Senator to act in the movies, *2659*
State aid to railroads, *6326*
State law to establish English as an official language, *5870*
Tax enacted by a state to support public schools, *3054*

Belleville

Airship transfer of mail to a train, *1523*
Pilot to die because of a lack of oxygen, *1614*

Brookfield

Forest horse, *1184*

Carthage

Presidential candidate to be assassinated, *3404*

Champaign

Nobel Prize winner to win twice in the same field, *1701*

Chicago

Adding machine absolutely accurate at all times, *2377*
Addressograph, *2365*
Air-conditioned railroad cars, *6386*
Air-to-ground public telephone service, *7748*
Airplane flight longer than 500 miles, *1444*
Airplane sleeping berths, *1413*
Airport runway illumination, *1504*
All-color television station to televise live local programs, *7805*
All-star football game, *7327*
All-star major league baseball game, *7130*
Ambulance service with an incubator, *4825*
American combatant to die in World War I, *8027*
American Derby horse race, *7393*
Anti-Monopoly Party convention, *3362*
Aquarium with an inland saltwater environment, *1187*
Armored car in commercial use, *5444*
Athlete to win the James E. Sullivan Memorial Trophy, *1719*
Automobile club, *5465*

Badminton championship tournament, *7584*
Ballet on an American theme by an American choreographer, *1236*
Baseball coach in the major leagues who was African-American, *7103*
Baseball game between an all-white team and an all-African-American team, *7116*
Baseball league for women, *7101*
Baseball manager to win pennants in both leagues, *7099*
Baseball pitcher to throw a curve ball, *7138*
Baseball player to hit a home run in an All-Star game, *7150*
Baseball players to win the Most Valuable Player award, *1722*
Baseball teams to go on a world tour, *7165*
Baseball with a cork center, *7109*
Bicycle tire made of cord, *7190*
Bifocal contact lenses, *5074*
Big-league football team to travel coast-to-coast, *7306*
Blood bank, *4834*
Book collection of importance on ultramicrofiche, *4687*
Bowling automatic scoring machine, *7230*
Bowling tournament sponsored by the American Bowling Congress, *7223*
Bread factory that was completely automatic, *3925*
Bridge table to shuffle and deal cards by electricity, *4024*
Cafeteria, *2459*
Canal made of concrete, *3602*
Car race, *7260*
Car radio, *6309*
Caterpillar Club member, *1584*
Catholic prelate named to the Roman Curia who was American-born, *6478*
Cellular telephone system, *7727*
Chinese person granted citizenship, *5874*
City founded by an African-American pioneer, *2187*
City law requiring reporting of premature births, *2161*
Clock movement to be electrically wound, *7902*
Coast-to-coast radio hookup, *6272*
Coin bearing the likeness of a foreign monarch, *5374*
College extension courses, *2997*
College varsity sports program, *2998*
Columbus Day, *4233*
Commemorative coin, *5373*
Commemorative postage stamps, *6084*
Communist Labor Party of America convention, *3374*
Communist Party of America convention, *3375*
Composer of gospel music, *1332*
Congressional representative who was a mother, *2610*

Decathlon champion from the United States, *7556*

Dental inlay made of gold, *4866*

Deodorant soap, *4062*

Department store to sell insurance, *2511*

Drive-in banking service, *3796*

Driver license board, *5469*

Dual-purpose postage stamp, *6066*

Electric elevated railroad, *6337*

Electric washing machine, *4276*

Envelope with a window, *5766*

Farmer Labor Party convention, *3376*

Fax transmission of movie film, *7672*

Ferris wheel, *3623*

Food processor, *4304*

Foreign car exhibited, *5427*

Forestry association (national), *6784*

Gasoline obtained from crude petroleum by the cracking process, *3536*

Greenback Labor Party convention, *3361*

Hospital open to all races as a matter of policy, *4886*

Hotel that was fireproof, *2424*

Jet airplane passenger trip, *1474*

Judge of a federal district court who was African-American, *2729*

Juvenile court, *2707*

Kapok, *7873*

Kidney transplant, *5095*

Labor activists to be executed, *4564*

Law school graduate who was a woman, *3124*

Life insurance group contract, *4549*

Livestock market paper, *5644*

Madstone, *3647*

Mail-order business, *2494*

Major league no-hitter baseball game on opening day, *7133*

Mobster convicted for tax evasion, *2782*

Modeling school, *3298*

Moving sidewalk, *6638*

National bone bank to acquire temporal bones for ear research, *4839*

National curling championship, *7277*

National political convention of a major party presided over by an African-American, *3337*

National political convention to propose African-Americans for the offices of president and vice president, *3343*

Naval militia of a state to have a hydroplane, *5256*

News reporter at a political convention who was a woman, *5614*

Newspaper circulation audit, *5652*

Nobel Peace Prize awarded to an American woman, *1695*

Nobel Prize for physics awarded to an American, *1691*

Nonfiction best seller, *1788*

Nuclear product for peacetime use, *3545*

Nuclear reactor built for private industrial research, *3549*

Opera composer who was a woman, *1334*

Optometry school, *3168*

Organized crime massacre, *2780*

Pay television system, *7799*

Physical education department at a college, *7452*

Pilot who was an African-American woman, *1597*

Pinball game machine, *7454*

Pipeless organ, *1324*

Planetarium open to the public, *6669*

Poet who was an African-American woman to win the Pulitzer Prize, *1715*

Poisoning of store merchandise, *2788*

Police bureau of identification, *4158*

Popcorn snack, *3962*

Portable electric stethoscope, *4946*

Portable movie projector, *5573*

Presidential candidate to accept his party's nomination in person, *3413*

Presidential election debates to be shown on television, *3394*

Progressive Party national convention, *3373*

Prohibition Party convention, *3356*

Propaganda course at a college, *3256*

Public school for children with disabilities, *3019*

Pullman sleeping car, *6375*

Pullman sleeping car that was comfortable, *6377*

Punchboards, *2368*

Radio broadcast of a livestock auction, *1075*

Radio receiver with an auxiliary solar-cell power unit, *6313*

Radio show with a plot, *6290*

Railroad car with an observation dome, *6388*

Railroad dining car, *6379*

Railroad dining car powered by electricity, *6389*

Railroad freight cars with compartments, *6390*

Railroad to run west out of Chicago, *6328*

Reply-paid card, *6045*

Rock and roll song, *1368*

Roller derby, *7465*

Rolling lift bridge, *3587*

Rotary Club meeting, *2451*

Round-the-world bicycle trip by a husband and wife, *7203*

Self-sustaining nuclear chain reaction demonstration, *6819*

Senator who was an African-American woman, *2661*

Serial movie with installments longer than one reel, *5550*

Sewer district established by a city, *2232*

Sex education program for high schools, *3088*

Sextuplets, *2171*

Skyscraper, *2098*

ILLINOIS—Chicago—*continued*

Skyscraper higher than 1,400 feet in height, *2102*

Slide fastener, *2291*

Snow cruiser for Antarctic research, *6716*

Soap opera on daytime television, *7781*

Social Democracy of America Party national convention, *3368*

Sociology professor at a college, *3252*

Softball game, *7497*

Solar energy battery to be manufactured commercially, *3559*

Solar-powered car, *5457*

Steel-frame building, *2080*

Surgical operation televised coast-to-coast, *5085*

Suture of the human heart, *5090*

Swimmer from the United States to make a round-trip crossing of the English Channel, *7521*

Taxidermy method of stuffing animals, *6746*

Teletypesetter, *5807*

Tennis champions who were brothers, *7535*

Trademark character, *2328*

Train with electric lighting, *6429*

Transcontinental daily railroad service, *6339*

Underground city sewer system, *2228*

Underwater highway tunnel, *3614*

Vacuum cleaner that used suction, *4272*

Vice presidential candidate who was an African-American woman, *3415*

Water supply tunnel for a city, *3615*

Web-fed four-color rotary printing press, *5780*

Wire recorder for sound recording, *5250*

Women's World Fair, *2413*

World championship professional football game, *7326*

World chess champion from the United States, *4033*

World Cup soccer tournament held in the United States, *7496*

Year-round railroad shipments of dressed beef, *2482*

Coal City

Golfer to shoot below his age, *7369*

Cook County

Fingerprint conviction in a crime, *4163*

Decatur

Company to pay a fine of $100 million for a price-fixing scheme, *2525*

Grand Army of the Republic post for veterans of the Civil War, *5310*

Presidential candidate to ride in a car, *3410*

Soybean processing plant, *1024*

De Kalb

Barbed wire commercial production, *4406*

Des Plaines

McDonald's restaurant, *2464*

Wedding on television, *4820*

East Peoria

Building built completely inside a factory, *2090*

Payment by the Federal Deposit Insurance Corporation, *3784*

Evanston

College degree awarded to a ventriloquist's dummy, *2981*

College president who was a woman, *2971*

Fort Chicago

West Point graduate killed in action, *3197*

Fort Sheridan

Court-martial of an officer for collaborating with his captors, *2741*

Freeport

Bicycle with a back-pedal brake, *7187*

Glencoe

Bottle with a screw cap, *4287*

Golf champion to win both the U.S. Open and the Professional tournaments, *7360*

Grand Detour

Steel plow with a steel moldboard, *1045*

Herrin

Massacre of strikebreakers by union members, *4597*

Kankakee

Circular school building, *2121*

La Salle

Coal, *3501*

Railroad land grant, *6330*

Lake Forest

Golf champion born in America, *7357*

Liberty

European king buried in the United States, 6654

McHenry County

Silo, 1051

Miller's Station

Glider with cambered wings, 1547

Moline

Flemish newspaper, 5680

Morrison

Time lock, 2135

Ottawa

Game preserve, 7424

Peoria

Armored car, 5432
Diesel-powered tractor, 1057

Quincy

Catholic priest who was African-American, 6467

River Park

Hearing aid, 5069

Rock Island

Railroad bridge across the Mississippi River, 3581
United Christian Party convention, 3370

Scott Air Force Base

Air Force Reserve officer who was a nun, 5138

Shelbyville

Dishwasher, 4274

Spring Grove

Haflinger horse, 1185

Springfield

Airplane accident involving a woman that was fatal, 1393

Congressional page who was African-American, 2592
Medical slang dictionary, 1810
President who had received a patent, 6156
Surgery society (national), 5047

Streamwood

Parade in which the marching music was supplied by transistor radios, 3670

Urbana

Betatron, 6801
Civic design chair at a college, 3254

Wheaton

Golf course with 18 holes, 7348
Radio astronomer, 6670

Williamson County

Airplane bombing raid by criminals, 2778

Wilmette

Baha'i house of worship, 6604

Winnetka

Correspondence school to offer instruction in Braille, 3029

INDIANA

Election campaign using radio, 3322
Gas conservation law enacted by a state, 3519
Governor to be granted almost dictatorial power, 7619
Interurban streetcar line, 6403
Naval bombardment of the Japanese homeland in World War II, 8085
Sterilization of humans by a state government as a matter of public policy, 6829
Tax on chain stores enacted by a state, 7658
Tornado disaster on a large scale, 2869

Alexandria

Rock wool insulation factory, 2047

Anderson

Automatic headlight control, 4227

Bloomington

Bacterium to be discovered that was visible to the naked eye, 6752

INDIANA—Bloomington—*continued*

Scientific survey of sexual behavior among Americans, *6831*

State university to grant equal privileges to women, *2953*

Vocational guidance chair at a college, *3295*

Bluffton

School to use platoon organization, *3067*

Brazil

Army pilot who was African-American to shoot down an Axis airplane in World War II, *8063*

Elkhart

Clarinet made exclusively of metal, *1319*
Fizzing cold remedy, *4994*
Railroad apprentice school, *3287*
Saxophone production, *1318*
Sousaphone, *1322*

Evansville

Gas refrigerator, *4348*
Soldiers in the American army killed in combat in World War I, *8038*
Vitamin to be commercially synthesized and manufactured, *3971*

Fort Wayne

Baseball game at night, *7121*
Computerized pump, *4417*
Elopement by airplane, *4809*
Gasoline pump, *4410*
Gasoline pump with price and gallon displays, *4418*
Sailor to reenlist in the Navy while under the North Pole, *5267*
Sawmill to use a band saw, *4404*

Gary

Nobel Prize in economic sciences, *1700*
Railroad freight yard that was fully automatic, *6346*

Greencastle

Sorority at a college, *2988*

Indianapolis

Car trip made with a diesel engine, *5474*
Death penalty authorized by federal law, *2802*
Driver who was a woman to compete in the Indianapolis 500, *7269*

Family of lawyers admitted simultaneously to practice before the Supreme Court, *4641*
Full-page magazine advertisement for a food product, *2329*
Gallstone operation, *5079*
Greenback Party convention, *3359*
Long-distance car race on a racetrack, *7267*
Millionaire who was an African-American woman, *2444*
Navy commissioned officer who was African-American, *5290*
Prison built for women and managed by women, *2823*
Quintuplets to survive infancy who were African-American, *2177*
Race-car driver to win $100,000, *7268*
Rapid-fire machine gun, *8107*
Socialist Party national convention, *3372*
Transistor radio receiver to be mass-produced, *6312*
Union passenger station used by several railroad companies, *6332*
White bread, *3926*

Lafayette

Commissioned officer in the Marine Corps who was African-American, *5239*
Olympic athlete from the United States to win 10 medals, *7442*

Martinsville

Goldfish hatchery, *1061*

Michigan City

Waterless natural gas storage tank, *3520*

New Harmony

Communistic settlement that was not religious, *2189*
Printing instruction at a school, *3284*

Richmond

Lawn mower, *7933*

South Bend

Automatic washing machine, *4281*
Seat belts in cars, *4229*
Shot fired by American infantry in World War I, *8037*

Vincennes

Department store, *2491*

Wabash

Electric streetlight installed in a city, *2216*

West Baden

Building with a large-scale clear-span dome, 2085

IOWA

Cigarette tax enacted by a state, 2699
Senator unseated after a recount, 3330
Soldier from the United States to land on French soil in World War II, 8060

Alleman

Corn-husking championship, 1025

Ames

Cornstone, 2051
Electronic digital calculator, 3438
Veterinary school established by a state, 3183

Cedar Rapids

Photograph bounced off a satellite, 5831
Radio sextant, 6960
Trampoline commercially manufactured, 7374

Davenport

Appendectomy, 5080
Carousel patent, 3620
Chiropractic school, 3172
Chiropractor, 4977
Portable movie camera, 5574

Des Moines

Army training camp for African-American officers, 5184
Car with an electric storage battery, 5426
Debate among party hopefuls for the presidential nomination to be shown on television, 3398

Fairfield

Electric power plant operated by a city, 3459

Fort Madison

Prison guard who was a woman to serve in a maximum security prison for men, 2831

Froelich

Gasoline tractor, 1055

Marion

Concrete cantilever bridge, 3590

Mount Pleasant

Lawyer who was a woman, 4636

Muscatine

Buttons of freshwater pearl, 2290

Onawa

Eskimo pie, 3867

Oskaloosa

Community to fingerprint its citizens, 4164

Sioux City

Joint stock land bank, 3778

Urbandale

Highway bridge with welded aluminum girders, 3596

KANSAS

Blue-sky laws enacted by a state, 2523
Chiropractic regulation law enacted by a state, 4940
Governor to be impeached and acquitted, 7613
Magazine in a Native American language, 4744
Senator who was Native American, 2650
Vice president who was Native American, 6248

Abilene

Cow town, 2192
Mechanized shooting gallery, 3622

Argonia

Mayor who was a woman, 2207

Atchison

Fuel alcohol plant, 3540
Transatlantic solo airplane flight by a woman, 1455

Bronson

International horseshoe pitching contest, 7578

Chapman

County high school, 3085

Dexter

Helium in natural gas, 6813

KANSAS—continued

Dodge City

Bullfight, 7258

Fort Riley

Army general who was African-American, 5154

Girard

Book series of small-size paperbacks, 1753

Greenleaf

Pilot wounded in Vietnam who was a civilian, 8013

Leavenworth

Carousel with a jumping horse mechanism, 3625

Demonstration of rapid aerial photography, 5823

Fingerprinting in federal penitentiaries, 4161

Lyon

Christian martyr on American soil, 6443

Manhattan

Farmers' institute sponsored by a college, 2894

Newton

Army generals who were brother and sister, 5160

Nicodemus

African-American town in continuous existence, 2193

Salina

Launching silos for Atlas F missiles, 8143

Sapling Grove

Wagon train to California, 5962

Topeka

Congressional representatives to marry each other, 2622

Coursing club, 7394

Marine general who was African-American, 5241

Small claims court, 2710

Victoria

Cattle of the Aberdeen-Angus breed, 1081

Wichita

Ace to fly a jet, 1620

KENTUCKY

Bourbon whiskey, 2666

Jockey to win more than $5 million in purses in one year, 7420

Senator to serve in contravention to the age limit, 2642

Senator who was returned to the Senate after being defeated for the presidency, 2646

State law abolishing imprisonment for debt, 2815

State nullification proceedings to obstruct federal legislation, 7595

Ashland

Steel mill to produce continuous sheets, 4497

Barbourville

Colonial settlement west of the Allegheny Mountains, 5935

Churchill Downs

Jockey who was a woman to ride in the Kentucky Derby, 7418

Covington

Horse race mutuel ticket to pay more than $1,000, 7397

Crab Orchard

Road appropriation of a specific sum by a state, 6614

Danville

Abdominal operation other than a cesarean section, 5076

Frankfort

Road authorization by a state, 6612

Harrodsburg

Cantilever bridge, 3583

Hodgenville

President born beyond the boundaries of the original 13 states, *6186*

Jefferson County

Health department of a county organized on a full-time basis, *4185*

Lexington

Drug treatment center for addicts established by Congress, *2688*
Vineyard, *1013*

Logan County

Camp meeting, *6525*
Duel in which a future president of the United States participated, *2809*

Louisa

Needle dam, *3607*

Louisville

Aluminum foil, *4340*
Baseball game that was a shutout, *7119*
Braille encyclopedia, *1834*
Coast Guard inland station, *5210*
Coin box for streetcars, *6396*
Filly to win the Kentucky Derby horse race, *7408*
Gas mask, *4402*
Jockey to win the Kentucky Derby five times, *7413*
Jockey to win the Triple Crown twice, *7412*
Kentucky Derby horse race, *7392*
Multiple common battery telephone switchboard, *7734*
President whose body was exhumed, *6208*
Presidential candidate who was Catholic, *3407*
Telegraph ticker to print type successfully, *7697*
Terra cotta factory, *2058*

Murray

Radio broadcast demonstration, *6262*

Rosine

Bluegrass musician of renown, *1335*

Troublesome Creek

Oil well, *3524*

LOUISIANA

Amphibious vehicle, *6943*

Congressional candidate elected while missing, *2619*
Governor who was Catholic, *7611*
Law code adopted by a state, *4621*
Price regulation law enacted by a state, *2522*
Prizefighting ban enacted by a state, *7234*
Quarantine board established by a state, *4209*
Senator to win a seat that had been occupied by his father and his mother, *2654*
Sugar cane to be imported, *3896*
Sulfur mine offshore, *5346*

Calcasieu Parish

Sulfur deposit, *5333*

Carville

Leprosy hospital, *4887*
Protestant church for lepers, *6533*

Ferriday

Exploration of the Mississippi River by a European, *5895*

Lake Charles

Catholic bishop who was an American-born African-American, *6480*

Lake Providence

Congressional representative to serve a single day, *2604*

New Orleans

Artificial-ice manufacturing plant, *4432*
Boxer to die from blows inflicted in a fight, *7250*
Boxing match under the Marquis of Queensberry rules, *7236*
Business economics course at a college, *2918*
Catholic convent, *6451*
Catholic nun, *6452*
Citizen of the United States to be hanged for treason, *2835*
College for women to affiliate with a university, *2956*
Confederate coin, *5368*
Confederate cruiser to raid Union commerce, *7944*
Craps, *3634*
Episcopal bishop deposed for heresy in the United States, *6552*
Gospel singer, *1337*
Greek Orthodox church, *6496*
Heavy water to be identified, *6814*
International chess champion from the United States, *4029*

LOUISIANA—New Orleans—*continued*

Levees, *3604*

Mardi Gras, *4234*

Methodist missionary, *6574*

Mosaic pavement, *6630*

Musician born in America to achieve fame in Europe, *1328*

Political science association (national), *6790*

Precanceled stamps printed on rotary presses, *6064*

President of a major medical society who was a woman, *5049*

Seatrain, *6890*

Senator who was Jewish, *2647*

Ship with a combined diesel and gas-turbine engine, *6946*

Siamese twins separated successfully by surgery, *2175*

Statue officially sanctioned by the Pope, *5407*

Sugar refinery, *3956*

Tieless streetcar tracks that were soundless and shockless, *6408*

University for African-American students founded as a Catholic institution, *2964*

Opelousas

Newspaper printed on bagasse newsprint, *5798*

Tangipahoa

Town founded by a woman, *2188*

Watson Brake

Human construction in North America, *5888*

Young's Point

News reporter tried as a spy, *5615*

MAINE

Child born of European parents on American soil, *2155*

European to set foot on the North American continent after the Vikings, *5893*

International commercial telephone service, *7732*

Senate election race in which both candidates were women, *2634*

Ship built by English colonists in America, *6848*

Survey of public lands, *5945*

Andover

Telephone call conveyed by a privately owned satellite, *7768*

Transoceanic telecast by satellite, *7853*

Augusta

Fur trading post, *5920*

Bangor

Chewing gum, *3959*

Bar Harbor

National park east of the Mississippi River, *3736*

Transatlantic radio fax transmission of a photograph, *7668*

Bath

Navy destroyer named for a Confederate officer, *6933*

Steel sailing vessel, *6874*

Turbine-propelled naval ship, *6928*

Bristol

Knighthood conferred on a person born in America, *6641*

Bucksport

Fish hatchery run by the federal government, *1060*

Floating electric power plant, *3481*

Calais

European settlement in the northeast after the Vikings, *5904*

Cape Porpoise

Exploration of the New England region by an Englishman, *5903*

Caribou

Transatlantic solo balloon flight, *1545*

Castine

Graduate of a four-year maritime school who was a woman, *3309*

Dixfield

Diving suit, *6709*

Eastern Egg Rock

Bird for which a definite crossing of the Atlantic was recorded, *1165*

Eastport

Sardine cannery, *3888*

Farmington

Earmuffs, *2270*

Gardiner

Technical institute, *3283*

Greenville

Forest fire lookout tower, *3729*

Kittery

Knighthood conferred on a soldier born in America, *6642*

Lewiston

International dogsled mail, *6010*

Limerick

Bank president of a national bank who was a woman, *3786*

Limestone

Transatlantic nonstop jet airplane eastward flight, *1476*
Transatlantic nonstop jet airplane flight, *1473*

Machias

Naval battle in the Revolutionary War, *7991*

Mount Desert

Colonial warfare between England and France in America, *5911*

New Harbor

Land sale by Native Americans to Europeans, *5918*

Norway

Snowshoe production, *2304*

Pemaquid

Road pavement, *6606*

Penobscot Bay

Astronomical expedition to record an eclipse of the sun, *6662*

Phippsburg

Thanksgiving worship service, *6503*

Portland

Oratorio by an American, *1289*

Skowhegan

Senator who was a woman who had previously served in the House of Representatives, *2653*

South Berwick

Blanket factory, *4264*
Waterpower development grant to a colonist, *5913*

Thomaston

Doughnut cutter, *4295*
Numbering system for patents, *4653*

Winthrop

Oilcloth factory, *7870*
Threshing machine to employ steam, *1046*

Wiscasset

Women's club, *5732*

York

City incorporated in the colonies, *2181*
Pile bridge, *3565*

MARYLAND

Autopsy with verdict of a coroner's jury, *2849*
Ban on cheap handguns enacted by a state, *4155*
Complete DNA sequencing of a free-living organism, *6757*
Congressional representative of Polish ancestry, *2623*
Czech settler in America, *5921*
Dog domestically bred, *1170*
First Lady who was not born in the United States, *6129*
Nail cutting and heading machine, *7908*
Naval battle between colonists, *5922*
Physician who was Jewish, *4962*
Public official of Italian ancestry, *5860*
Religious toleration law enacted by a colony, *6511*
Senator who was Catholic, *2638*
Silver deposit for coinage, *5364*
State to have a state sport, *7600*

MARYLAND—*continued*

Supreme Court justice who had been a representative in Congress, *2758*

Supreme Court justice who was African-American, *2763*

Woman in America to appeal for the right to vote, *3420*

Workers' compensation insurance law enacted by a state, *4522*

Abingdon

College founded as a Methodist institution, *2937*

Alberton

Wooden railroad bridge of a purely truss type, *3573*

Annapolis

Arbitration law enacted by a state, *2355*

Citizenship conferred by special grant, *5861*

Marine pilot, *5235*

Naval academy, *3213*

Naval Academy graduate to attain the rank of rear admiral, *3215*

Naval Academy graduate who was African-American, *3219*

Naval Academy graduate who was Japanese, *3214*

Naval Academy students who were women, *3221*

Navy admirals who were brothers, *5294*

Printer who was a woman, *5782*

Baltimore

Airplane used for newspaper reporting, *5606*

American expeditionary force to land in Africa in World War II, *8055*

Analytical chemistry course requirement for pharmacy students, *3146*

Anti-Masonic Party convention, *3348*

Automated tanker under the American flag, *6902*

Aviation medicine book, *1921*

Balloon flight, *1535*

Baseball player to win Most Valuable Player award in both major leagues, *1724*

Bottle cap with a cork crown, *4286*

Bowling with duckpins, *7222*

Cathedral, *6461*

Catholic African-Americans, *6458*

Catholic bishop appointed to serve in the United States, *6457*

Catholic bishop consecrated in the United States, *6460*

Catholic community of African-American nuns, *6462*

Catholic diocese and archdiocese, *6456*

Catholic nuns in a cloistered community, *6470*

Catholic parish church for African-Americans, *6464*

Catholic priest, *6459*

Catholic seminary, *3268*

City orchestra supported by taxes, *1362*

Civil War bloodshed, *7952*

Clipper ship, *6866*

Clock to strike the hours, *7897*

Coast Guard Academy graduate who was African-American, *3210*

College for women founded as a Catholic institution, *2958*

Constitutional Union Party convention, *3355*

Country day school, *3066*

Democratic Party national convention, *3349*

Dental college, *3162*

Double-deck railroad coaches, *6370*

Egyptian antiquities collection, *5578*

Electric streetcars commercially operated, *6400*

Gas streetlights throughout a city, *2214*

General medical clinic, *4843*

Health board established by a city, *4172*

History of medicine department at a college, *3157*

Horse racing magazine, *4782*

Human stem cells to be cultured in a laboratory, *5068*

Hygiene and public health school at a college, *3177*

Ice cream freezer, *3862*

Ice cream wholesale dealer, *3863*

Label patent, *4657*

Law magazine, *4700*

Liberty ship, *6894*

Linotype machine, *5805*

Local anesthetic, *4832*

Locomotive bid, *6351*

Locomotive with six or eight driving wheels, *6353*

Manual training school entirely financed by public taxes, *3290*

Methodist bishop, *6560*

Methodist minister who was African-American, *6559*

Monument to Christopher Columbus, *5396*

Monument to George Washington, *5397*

Museum especially constructed as a museum and art gallery, *5577*

National political convention to adopt the two-thirds rule, *3333*

Naval patrol bomber, *1488*

Night school for immigrants, *2887*

Odd Fellows lodge, *5719*

Ophthalmology book, *1905*

Ophthalmology course at a college, *3137*

Passenger locomotive, *6349*

Polo game played outdoors at night, *7461*

Postmaster who was a woman, *5982*

President to make a radio broadcast, *6210*
President who was a "dark horse" candidate, *3403*
Presidential candidate nominated at a national convention, *3401*
Professor at a first-class medical school who was a woman, *3151*
Psychology journal, *4759*
Psychology laboratory, *4927*
Race between a locomotive and a horse-drawn vehicle, *7388*
Radio telephone message from a submerged submarine to shore, *7755*
Railroad car with a center aisle, *6371*
Railroad for commercial transportation of passengers and freight, *6321*
Railroad station for both passengers and freight, *6320*
Railroad timetable advertised in a newspaper, *6323*
Railroad to run trains to Washington, *6327*
Railroad to use an electric engine, *6340*
Railroad union, *4608*
Refrigerator, *4345*
Silk sutures and ligatures, *4956*
Smallpox vaccine clinic, *4916*
Sociology society (national), *6791*
Stone arch railroad bridge, *3571*
Stratovision flight by an airplane during which a television signal was transmitted, *7839*
Submarine fitted with an internal combustion engine, *6963*
Sugar substitute, *3964*
Sunday newspaper, *5635*
Swedenborgian or New Church temple, *6524*
Tooth-wear gauge, *4867*
Union Reform Party convention, *3371*
University press, *2960*
Warship to capture an enemy ship after the Revolution, *8005*

Baltimore Harbor

Atomic-powered lighthouse, *4129*

Beltsville

Radio broadcast from a moving train, *6276*

Bethesda

Alternative medicine department in a federal research institution, *5067*
Computer software application on Digital Video Disc, *2555*
Cooperative store operated by women, *2503*
Gene therapy, *5118*
Identification of the AIDS virus, *5064*
Tissue bank, *4838*

Bladensburg

Duel between representatives in Congress, *2810*
President to face enemy gunfire while in office, *6148*

Bohemia Manor

Labadist community, *6514*

Catonsville

Military school operated by a church, *3186*

College Park

Airplane outfitted with a machine gun, *1484*
Army pilot to fly solo in an airplane, *1607*
Helicopter flight, *1572*

Cumberland

Highway built by the federal government, *6616*
Milk bottles, *4285*

Ellicott's Mills

President to ride on a railroad train, *6222*

Fort Meade

Army armored car unit, *5187*

Frederick

Carpet mill to make ingrain carpets, *4312*
Supreme Court chief justice who was Catholic, *2759*

Frederick County

Direct tax on Britain's American colonists without their consent, *7641*

Gaithersburg

Molecular measuring machine, *6811*

Glenross

Patent granted to an African-American inventor, *4652*

Hagerstown

Bookwagon traveling library, *4676*

Hyattsville

Satellite composite map of the United States, *4802*

MARYLAND—Hyattsville—*continued*

Single tax adopted by a city for local revenue purposes, *7651*

Laurel

Whooping crane, *1169*

Mount Savage

Fire brick to withstand high heat, *2055*
Railroad rails of iron, *6418*

Patuxent

Jury composed of women, *2734*

Poolesville

American to be recognized by Tibetan Buddhists as a reincarnated lama, *6440*

Prince Georges County

Painter to obtain a public commission, *1198*

Relay Post Office

Camp for conscientious objectors, *5221*

St. Johns

Shorthand account of a trial, *4619*

St. Mary's City

Catholic school, *3042*
Lead coffins, *2837*

St. Mary's Village

Catholics to settle in the English colonies in America, *6447*

Somerset

Semiautomatic rifle, *8118*

Sykesville

Railroad to carry troops, *6324*

Talbot County

Manual training courses offered in a school, *3281*

Towson

Electric hand drill, *7937*

Warburton Manor

Novel by an American writer to be translated into a foreign language, *1838*

Washington County

Elementary schools to use closed-circuit televisions in teaching, *3069*

Wheaton

Self-service post office, *6043*

MASSACHUSETTS

Accident reports by employers, *4563*
Aurora borealis display, *6765*
Ban on Jesuits to be enacted by a colony, *6449*
Ban on Quakers enacted by a colony, *6586*
Board of education established by a state, *3056*
Bookbinder, *1731*
Bridge, *3562*
Brothers to serve simultaneously as governors of their respective states, *7610*
Car insurance law enacted by a state, *4520*
Centennial celebration of the Revolution, *8006*
Child labor law enacted by a state that included an education requirement, *4573*
Child labor law enacted by a state that regulated hours of employment, *4574*
Christian worship services organized by African-American slaves, *6515*
Colonial law banning Christmas, *4253*
Colonial law requiring towns to hire teachers and construct schools, *3045*
Commercial telephone service using toll lines, *7730*
Compulsory education law enacted by a state, *3059*
Compulsory education law in a colony, *3043*
Congressional representative reelected after serving a prison term, *2615*
Congressional representative to serve 18 terms who was a woman, *2611*
Consul, *3986*
Continental money, *5347*
Credit union law enacted by a state, *3774*
Election held in a colony, *3310*
Execution for witchcraft, *2793*
Factory inspection law enacted by a state, *4383*
Fork, *4365*
Free trade policy by the federal government, *7662*
Gas commission established by a state government, *3518*
Geodetic survey, *6711*
Geological survey for a state government, *6708*
Health board established by a state government, *4177*

History of New England, *1860*
Horse racing ban by a colony, *7385*
Horses, *1174*
Household product made entirely of plastic, *4288*
Independence Day, *4232*
Insignia to designate state army regiments, *5222*
Insurance regulation enacted by a state, *4499*
Iron exportation, *4447*
Labor bureau established by a state, *4557*
Life insurance nonforfeiture law enacted by a state, *4545*
Lifesaving service for distressed mariners, *4116*
Literacy qualification for voting, *3426*
Loan by a colony, *3802*
Locomotive owned by an industrial company, *6360*
Marine insurance law enacted by a state, *4502*
Medal of Honor awarded to an African-American soldier in the Civil War, *1677*
Milk purity law enacted by a state, *4202*
Minimum wage law enacted by a state, *4577*
Missionary society organized in the English colonies, *6568*
Nautical school established by a state, *3305*
No-fault car insurance law enacted by a state, *4521*
Paper money, *5382*
Patent granted by a colony, *4646*
Physician in the New England colonies, *4960*
Poetry collection by an American poet, *1943*
President with a brother in the Senate, *6205*
Probation officer for juvenile delinquents to be hired by a state, *2822*
Quarantine law enacted by a colony, *4207*
Rebellion against the federal government, *5947*
Religious leader in the American colonies who was a woman, *6507*
Respirator known as the iron lung, *4947*
Roll-on-roll-off carrier, *6898*
School for children with mental disabilities, *3016*
Scientific expedition sponsored by a colony, *6661*
Semaphore telegraph system, *7684*
Senator to be censured, *2643*
Senator who was African-American to be elected by popular vote, *2658*
Settler heroine publicly rewarded, *5933*
Shoes to be manufactured, *2298*
Slavery ban enacted for a territory of the United States, *2246*
State law to end de facto segregation in schools, *2261*
State police officers who were women, *4144*
Vaccination law enacted by a state, *4918*
Vice president who had served in the House of Representatives, *6239*
Voting registration law enacted by a state, *3424*

Woodcut, *1222*

Abington

Shoe manufacturing machine, *2303*
Sprinkler system patent, *4107*

Albany

Colonial congress, *2572*

Amherst

Physical education and hygiene professorship at a college, *7451*

Auburn

Rocket flight using liquid fuel, *7017*

Beverly

Cotton mill, *7882*

Billerica

Leather-splitting machine, *4456*

Boston

Actor to receive curtain applause, *1275*
Adding machine to print totals and subtotals, *2376*
Aerial photograph, *5815*
Agricultural book, *1757*
Agricultural book distinctly American, *1758*
All-Star Game of the National Basketball Association, *7174*
Almanac with a continuous existence, *1766*
American gazetteer, *1814*
American history book of importance whose author was a woman, *1865*
Americans killed by British soldiers in the Revolution, *7986*
Annulment of a marriage by court decree, *4805*
Annunciator, *2358*
Antiquarian bookseller, *1784*
Antislavery book, *2023*
Apples, *3892*
Archeology organization (national), *6787*
Architecture department at a college, *2903*
Arithmetic book by an American-born author, *1882*
Arithmetic book printed in America, *1881*
Artist of importance to be born in America, *1200*
Arts and sciences organization (national), *5709*
Automobile school, *3292*
Bacteriology textbook, *1918*
Baseball book, *1998*

MASSACHUSETTS—Boston—*continued*

Baseball glove, *7105*

Baseball teams to travel abroad, *7163*

Basketball professional player who was African-American, *7173*

Bathhouses owned and operated by a city, *4195*

Bicycle club, *7184*

Bicycle magazine, *4784*

Bicycle trip of 100 miles sponsored by a club, *7200*

Bill depicting a battleship, *5392*

Boat race for fishermen, *7214*

Book auction catalog, *1779*

Book auction printed catalog, *1780*

Book catalog of a college, *1767*

Book of folio size, *1734*

Book of music by a composer born in America, *1936*

Book on Americanisms, *1745*

Book plate, *1737*

Botanical report on plant hybridization, *6735*

Bridge on a large scale, *3566*

Building heated by steam, *2074*

Burglar alarm, *2132*

Business manual, *1793*

Business organization for African-Americans (national), *2450*

Calico printery, *7859*

Camel, *1137*

Capture of a German ship by an American ship in World War II, *8049*

Caricature, *1213*

Carillon, *1305*

Carnegie Hero Fund Commission award granted to a woman, *1639*

Catalog of theological and biblical literature, *1952*

Catholic magazine, *4697*

Cattle of the Guernsey breed, *1079*

Chamber music ensemble, *1359*

Child to be killed in the Revolution, *7985*

Children's book, *1729*

Children's magazine with literary merit, *4708*

Chiropodist, *4970*

Christian Science church, *6600*

Coach of a professional basketball team who was African-American, *7177*

Coffee in a can, *3851*

Cold storage plant, *4407*

College program of study abroad, *2995*

Colonial copyright law, *4626*

Colonial government federation, *5926*

Concert with documentation, *1287*

Constitution adopted by a state, *1101*

Court tennis, *7524*

Craft union, *4603*

Cricket club, *7271*

Dealer in Oriental rugs, *4316*

Dental school to be associated with a medical school, *3167*

Dentist, *4854*

Designated hitter in a major league baseball game, *7157*

Discount clothing store, *2498*

Divorce, *4806*

Doctor of Philosophy degree awarded to a woman, *2979*

Draft law enacted by a colony, *5216*

Drinking water conduit to be built underwater, *2227*

Dwarf exhibited as a theatrical attraction, *3653*

Ecology book, *1991*

Economics journal, *4774*

Education book, *1827*

Educational association (national), *3224*

Electrotherapy book, *1914*

Encased postage stamps, *6055*

Engineering society, *3608*

Engraving of any artistic merit, *1223*

Engraving to achieve popularity, *1225*

Epidemiology report, *1888*

Episcopal church organized in New England, *6548*

Esperanto club, *5717*

Express delivery service, *2479*

Eye conservation class, *3028*

Federal dry docks, *6905*

Fire alarm system operated by electricity, *4104*

Fire engine, *4092*

Fire hose of rubber-lined cotton web, *4099*

Fire of serious consequence, *2879*

Fireboat with two-way radio equipment, *4112*

Fishing treatise, *1993*

Folding theater chair, *4326*

Football club, *7301*

Football stadium, *7505*

Foreign missionary society organized by women, *6578*

French grammar, *1857*

Gambling law for residents enacted by a colony, *3633*

General pharmacopoeia, *1930*

Glue factory, *4428*

Gold bullion deposit for coinage, *5365*

Golf tee, *7352*

Harpsichord, *1307*

Health insurance company, *4534*

Hebrew grammar, *1854*

High school, *3080*

High school for girls, *3081*

Historical print engraved in America, *1224*

Historical society (state), *5710*

History book by a Jewish author of ancient times, *1862*

History of science society (national), *6795*

Horse breeders' society, *7386*

Horse race pari-mutuel in which all the jockeys were women, *7417*

Horseriding exhibition, *3652*

Hotel recognized as a modern first-class hotel, *2422*

Hotel to install radio reception, *2430*

Hotel with safe deposit boxes, *2423*

Hygiene department in a public school district, *4182*

Hymnbook with music, *1972*

Ice exported, *3932*

Indoor ski school, *7486*

Inoculation against smallpox using material from human smallpox pustules, *4914*

Iron piano frame, *1308*

Jockey to win seven consecutive races in one day, *7414*

Kindergarten, *3073*

Latin grammar textbook, *1852*

Latvian newspaper, *5677*

Law book of federal laws then in force, *1880*

Lawyer disbarred, *4632*

Legislature of a colony to establish two chambers, *7623*

Leopard, *1143*

Library catalog in book form, *4660*

Lighthouse, *4123*

Limb reattachment, *5088*

Lion, *1136*

Logic book, *1975*

Long-distance telephone call, *7754*

Long-distance telephone call over underground cables, *7756*

Magazine for women, *4709*

Magic lantern book, *2018*

Magician of note, *3655*

Map made in America to be published in a book, *4792*

Marathon race held annually, *7552*

Marathon runner from the United States who was a woman, *7565*

Mason who was African-American, *5729*

Medal awarded by the Continental Congress, *1649*

Medical inspection of schoolchildren, *4180*

Medical pamphlet, *1886*

Medical school for women, *3164*

Medical society, *5029*

Medical society for women, *5037*

Medical society (state), *5030*

Medicine ball, *7574*

Military organization established by a colony, *5253*

Militia, *5252*

Milk inspection law enacted by a state, *4203*

Mineralogy textbook, *1982*

Miniature book, *1733*

Motorcycle endurance run, *7437*

Mule born in the United States, *1141*

Municipal subway, *6410*

Music book for children, *1939*

Music book printed with bars, *1932*

Music convention of singing teachers, *2901*

Music festival, *1283*

Music instruction in a public school, *2900*

Music printed in a magazine, *1280*

Mutual liability insurance company, *4513*

National Hockey League team from the United States, *7377*

Nautical almanac, *1765*

Naval action of importance in the War of 1812, *8021*

Naval militia established by a state, *5255*

Naval vessel to sail around the Cape of Good Hope, *6981*

News agency, *5623*

Newspaper advertisement, *2317*

Newspaper printed on wood-pulp paper, *5790*

Newspaper publisher, *5609*

Newspaper that was successful, *5630*

Nickel plating, *4471*

Novel by an African-American writer, *1845*

Novel by an American writer to be published in America, *1839*

Occupational therapy treatment, *5114*

Oratorio performance, *1288*

Orchestral song to be printed, *1378*

Organ transplant that was successful, *5096*

Pacemaker, *4952*

Painless surgery demonstration, *4831*

Patent medicine advertisement, *2316*

Patent medicine to achieve nationwide popularity, *4989*

Patriotic song by an American, *1376*

Performance of "America the Beautiful", *1380*

Peritonitis preventive, *4992*

Pharmacopoeia prepared by a medical association, *1928*

Phrenology book, *1908*

Physical education classes in elementary schools, *3060*

Physician who was an African-American woman, *4973*

Physiology journal, *4777*

Physiology society, *5033*

Pictorial postal cards, *6050*

Playground, *2144*

Poem to be printed in a newspaper, *1945*

Poem to win national acclaim, *1947*

Poetry collection by an African-American woman, *1946*

Poetry collection by an American poet who was a man, *1944*

Polar bear, *1138*

Politician who was openly homosexual to win an election, *6839*

Post office in a colony, *6035*

Poultry show, *1069*

Power printing press capable of fine book work, *5771*

Probation system for criminals of all ages, *2825*

Professional hockey player to score 50 goals in one season, *7379*

MASSACHUSETTS—Boston—_continued_

Professional hockey player who was African-American, *7380*

Public garage, *5483*

Public school with a continuous existence, *3040*

Quakers executed for their religious beliefs, *6587*

Quakers to arrive in America, *6585*

Railroad coach modeled after English coaches, *6373*

Railroad excursion rates, *6329*

Rat of record, *1140*

Recipes using standard measurements, *3878*

Religious magazine, *4693*

Religious tract society, *6570*

Rifled gun, *8094*

Road map for motorists, *4801*

Road map for public use, *4793*

Rocket-tracking ship, *6945*

Roller skates, *7462*

Round-the-world bicycle trip by a woman, *7202*

Round-the-world solo sailing journey, *6984*

Round-the-world solo sailing trip by an African-American, *7002*

Running shoes, *2306*

Sailcloth factory, *7862*

Savings bank life insurance, *4547*

School band, *1360*

School for blind students, *3023*

School for music teachers, *2898*

Schoolbook, *1823*

Science society, *6776*

Self-portrait, *1212*

Sermon to be printed, *1948*

Sewing machine manufacturer, *4352*

Ship to carry the American flag around the world, *1123*

Shirt factory, *2266*

Siamese twins, *2170*

Smallpox epidemic, *2873*

State legislators who were African-American, *7624*

Statistical society, *6779*

Steam-powered printing press, *5769*

Steel vessels of the Navy, *6925*

Supreme Court clerk, *2743*

Surgeon who was a woman, *4974*

Swimming school, *7514*

Symphonic work by an American composer, *1290*

Technical college for women, *2962*

Telephone conversation over outdoor wires, *7752*

Telephone message, *7751*

Telephone operator who was a woman, *7729*

Telephone switchboard or exchange, *7728*

Television theater to be licensed, *7775*

Theater lighted by electricity, *3701*

Theological school that was multisectarian, *3271*

Theological school to admit women as students, *3273*

Tobacco tax enacted by a colony, *2695*

Toothpick manufacturing machine, *4071*

Trademark for food, *2324*

Transplant of artificial skin, *5102*

Tuberculosis patients' home, *4897*

Turbine-propelled oceangoing merchant vessel, *6886*

Unitarian prayer book, *1956*

Vaudeville show, *3688*

Vending machine to dispense postage stamps, *2394*

Veterinary college, *3180*

Visible speech method of instruction for deaf students, *3034*

Vocal instruction book, *1933*

Vocational high school for girls, *3086*

War song, *1377*

Water supply system built for a city, *2224*

Whist rule book, *1999*

Window glass factory, *4036*

World Series baseball game, *7123*

Worsted mill for making wool yarn, *7892*

Yacht club, *7207*

Young Men's Christian Association, *5712*

Young Women's Christian Association, *5713*

Bradford

Foreign missionary society, *6572*

Brant Rock

Radio program broadcast, *6264*

Bridgewater

Textile machine, *7861*

Bristol

Pirate on the Atlantic seaboard, *2768*

Brookline

Indoor curling rink, *7276*

International tennis matches for the Davis Cup challenge trophy, *7531*

Cambridge

Aeronautical engineering course at a college, *3244*

Almanac, *1764*

Ancient and modern history chair at a college, *3095*

Artificial gene, *5063*

Astronomer of note, *6659*

Bachelor of Arts degree, *2976*

Bible concordance, *1960*

Bible translated into a Native American language, *1959*

Book privately printed, *1732*

Book published in America, *1728*

Bookseller, *1777*

Broad jump to reach more than 25 feet, *7555*

Bronze statue of full length, *5398*

Business history chair at a college, *2922*

Chemical laboratory at a college, *3235*

Climatology professor at a college, *3242*

College entrance requirement other than Greek, Latin, and arithmetic, *2941*

College founded in America, *2925*

College graduate who was Native American, *3006*

College orchestra, *1357*

College student to work his way through college, *3005*

Computer-aided manufacturing system, *4421*

Computer bug, *2527*

Computer game, *4012*

Computer graphics software, *2548*

Computer programming language for children, *2551*

Computing device with electronic components, *2526*

Cooperative store at a college, *2497*

Court-martial by the Army, *2739*

Dermatology chair at a college, *3144*

Divinity professor at a college, *3266*

Document known to have been printed in America, *1096*

Ecumenical synod, *6510*

Entomology professor at a college, *3238*

Fire prevention law enacted by a colony, *4091*

Football goalpost, *7309*

French instruction at a college, *3110*

Grand jury, *2733*

Greek play, *1254*

Gymnastics instruction at a college, *7372*

Hebrew instruction at a college, *3109*

Hebrew type, *5799*

Hygiene lectures at a college, *3136*

Hymnbook published in America, *1931*

Instrument for observing radiation in total darkness, *6807*

King born in the United States, *6649*

Law book of colonial laws, *1872*

Medical chemistry course at a college, *3145*

Military computer network, *2542*

Museum devoted exclusively to papermaking, *5589*

Music chair at a college, *2904*

Native American grammar, *1850*

Newspapers, *5629*

Nobel Prize for chemistry awarded to an American, *1692*

Patent on an animal, *6751*

Pathology chair at a college, *3139*

Photograph of a meteor, *6697*

Photograph of a star other than the sun, *6693*

Planetarium, *6658*

Play of note written by an American, *1240*

Player piano, *1316*

Political economy chair at a college, *3251*

Primer in a Native American dialect, *1851*

Printing lecture course in a college, *3294*

Printing press, *5767*

Protest by college students, *3007*

Pulitzer prize awarded to a science book, *1718*

Racing shell, *7469*

Semitic museum, *5583*

Spelling book, *1822*

Stroboscopic lamp for high-speed photography, *5841*

Surrogate birth experiment with an animal, *5123*

Synod held in America, *6508*

Synthetic quinine, *4999*

Theology school that was nonsectarian, *3269*

Thesis directory, *1811*

Urban planning instruction at a college, *3253*

Vaccination against smallpox using cowpox, *4915*

Vitamin K to be synthesized, *3973*

Voice reader, *2538*

Weather report delivered to the Army, *6768*

Windmill for grinding grain, *3909*

Cambridgeport

Achromatic lenses, *5833*

Canton

Congressional representative to be refused a seat, *2600*

Cape Ann

Schooner built in America, *6852*

Cape Cod

Balloon honeymoon, *4808*

Child born of English parents in New England, *2157*

Naval battle in the War of 1812, *8020*

Transatlantic radio broadcast, *6263*

Carver

Divided road, *6619*

Charlestown

Naval officers' training school, *3212*

Cheshire

Cheese factory cooperative, *3857*

MASSACHUSETTS—Cheshire—*continued*
Plate glass, *4040*

Chicopee

Newspaper whose contents were transmitted by a communications satellite, *5660*

Clinton

Gingham factory, *7871*
Paper bag manufacturing machine, *5757*

Colrain

American flag flown over a schoolhouse, *1126*

Concord

Pencil factory, *8148*
Pile driver, *4389*

Dedham

Canal for creating water power, *3599*

Dennis

Cranberry cultivation, *3900*

Dorchester

Chocolate mill, *3955*
Property tax established by a colony to support public schools, *3041*
School committee, *3044*
Singing contest, *1282*

Dover

House completely heated by solar energy, *2128*

East Walpole

Airship for private commercial operation, *1526*

East Watertown

Synthetic rubber, *4488*

Easthampton

Cloth-covered buttons, *2288*

Fairhaven

Japanese to enter the United States, *5961*

Fitchburg

Factory without windows, *4386*

Florence

Free kindergarten, *3075*

Framingham

Reformatory for women established by a state, *2824*

Franklin

Coffee percolator, *3850*

Gloucester

Frozen food for the mass market, *3949*
Modern carillon, *1323*
Universalist church services, *6520*

Great Barrington

Power plant using alternating current, *3464*

Greenfield

Architecture book distinctly American, *2015*
Cutlery factory, *4369*
Manual training institute, *3285*

Hamilton

Professional open golf championship match, *7344*

Holyoke

Volleyball, *7575*

Hopkinton

Shoe peg, *2300*

Lancaster

Genealogical collective work, *1869*
Industrial school for girls, *3286*

Lawrence

Mohair, *7872*
Water filtration system for bacterial purification of a city water supply, *2234*

Leicester

Geology textbook, *1983*

Lexington

Microwave oven, *4302*

Revolutionary War armed conflict, *7989*
Teacher training school established by a state, *3260*

Lowell

Belts of leather for transmitting power, *4393*
Cash carrier system, *2360*
Factory workers' magazine, *4714*
Machine gun, *8104*
Ornamented soda fountain for restaurants, *2456*
Rubber shoe heel, *2305*
Sprinkler system, *4101*
Swimmer from the United States to swim the English Channel, *7517*
Telegrapher who was a woman, *7694*
Turbine successfully operated by waterpower, *4399*

Lynn

Baseball catcher's mask, *7107*
Coinage dies, *5353*
Cooking pots made in America, *4290*
Ironworks that was successful, *4446*
Manufacturer of metal goods, *4461*
National union for women, *4610*
Pontoon bridge, *3568*
Welding by the electric process, *4435*

Malden

Movie projector patent, *5570*

Marblehead

Executive officer of a man-of-war who was a woman, *5300*
Warship to receive definite orders to attack the enemy, *7993*

Martha's Vineyard

Native American preacher of Christianity, *6513*

Maynard

Minicomputer, *2533*

Medfield

Brushes, *4267*
Writer to work professionally who was a woman, *2031*

Medford

Commercial fishery, *2416*

Melrose

Patent examiner who was a woman, *4656*

Methuen

Yogurt dairy, *3856*

Millbury

Lyceum for adult education, *2884*

Millville

Factories operated by the federal government in peacetime, *4387*

Milton

Children's church, *6535*
Hard water crackers, *3918*
Vaccination program offered by a city, *4917*

Minot's Ledge

Iron pile lighthouse, *4127*

Mount Greylock

Artificial snow from a natural cloud, *6774*

Nantucket

Lifeboat, *4118*
Nautical school, *3303*
Novel about whaling, *1842*
Prison, *2811*
Ship sunk by a whale, *2420*
Sperm whale captured at sea, *2418*
Whaling expedition, *2419*

Natick

Church for Native Americans in New England, *6512*

New Bedford

Coast Guard officers' training school, *3209*
Helicopter to deliver material across a picket line, *1562*

New Plymouth

Income tax levied by a colony, *7638*

Newburyport

Algebra book by an American-born author, *1885*
Coast survey book, *2014*
Cracker bakery, *3917*
Federal revenue cutter, *6857*
Pamphlet produced from a steel plate engraving, *1744*

MASSACHUSETTS—Newburyport—*continued*

Wool carding machine, *7894*

Newport

Pushball, *7573*

Newton Center

World figure skating champion from the United States, *7433*

North Beverly

Reindeer, *1152*

North Woburn

American woman to become a countess, *6644*

Northampton

Basketball played at a college, *7167*
Great Awakening of religious revival, *6517*
Gymnasium to offer systematic instruction, *7371*
Indelible pencil, *8152*
Sugar beet mill, *3958*
Theater operated by a city, *3703*
Volunteer unit made up of college women to serve overseas, *5185*
Whole-wheat bread, *3919*

Northfield

Youth hostel, *2150*

Orleans

Shots fired by German forces to land on American soil in World War I, *8045*

Pecoit

Gunpowder mill, *8088*

Pittsfield

Artificial lightning demonstration, *6770*
Broadcloth, *7863*
Cattle fair, *1078*
Intercollegiate baseball game, *7114*
Lightning observatory, *6771*

Plymouth

Cattle to be imported, *1076*
Chimes and bells, *1302*
Colonial treaty with the Native Americans, *5915*

Congregational church, *6505*
Duel, *2807*
Earthquake description, *2861*
Execution in America, *2792*
Forestry law enacted by a colony, *3722*
Former president who was elected to the House of Representatives, *6149*
Furs exported, *3740*
Governor of a colony who was born in America, *7609*
Greeting addressed to the Pilgrims by a Native American, *5914*
Hurricane of record, *2860*
Hydrophobia book, *1902*
Leather tanning, *4455*
Military leader of the English settlers, *5251*
Pension law enacted by a colony, *4581*
Popcorn, *3954*
Property tax levied by a colony, *7637*
Prostitute, *6826*
Thanksgiving Day, *4261*
Wedding of colonists in New England, *4813*

Provincetown

Corn found by English settlers, *3908*

Quincy

Cod-liver oil, *4980*
Deportation, *5857*
Franchise chain, *2463*
Granite, *5323*
Guided missile cruiser, *6940*
Minister to Great Britain, *3985*
Nuclear-powered cruiser, *6941*
Offshore radar warning station, *7682*
Photoengraving high-speed process, *5696*
Photograph of a former president, *6153*
Railroad accident, *6325*
Railroad with iron-plated wooden rails, *6318*
School to provide separate classrooms for each class, *3058*
Steel seven-masted schooner, *6875*

Rowe

Nuclear reactor operated commercially, *3552*

Rowley

Cloth mill, *7858*
Fulling mill for making wool cloth, *7891*
Toll bridge, *3563*

Roxbury

Kindergarten for blind children, *3027*
Nurse to receive formal training, *5023*
Rubber company, *4484*
Streamlined railroad train, *6428*

Rutland

Tuberculosis sanatorium established by a state, *4901*

Salem

Autopsy officially recorded, *2848*
Brick kiln, *2053*
Electric light for household illumination, *3490*
Naval vessel to display the American flag around Cape Horn, *1127*
News dispatch by telephone, *5605*
Pottery, *4308*
Yacht, *6859*

Saugus

Escalator patent, *2106*

Saxonville

Bunting manufacture, *7868*

Scituate

Quaker annual meeting, *6588*

Sheffield

Slave to be emancipated, *2245*

Shelburne

Bridge of flowers, *3592*

Shrewsbury

Birth-control pill, *6833*
Watchmaker, *7899*

Somerville

Brass and copper seamless tubes, *4467*
Pipe or screw wrench, *7929*
Telephone for domestic use, *7712*

South Boston

Olympic athlete from the United States to win a gold medal, *7441*

South Braintree

Manila paper, *5752*

South Hadley

Canal for boat transportation, *3600*
College for women, *2944*

Dinosaur fossils, *6739*
Gymnastics instruction at a college for women, *7373*

Southborough

Centrifugal cream separator, *3855*

Southwick

Reflecting telescope, *6663*

Springfield

All-metal roller skate, *7464*
Arsenal of the federal government, *5126*
Basketball game, *7166*
Basketball rules, *7168*
Car produced for commercial sale, *5429*
Farmers' institute sponsored by a state, *2893*
Friction matches, *4334*
Intercollegiate football association, *7303*
Kindergarten manual, *1828*
Meat packer, *3937*
Medal of Honor awarded to a Jewish soldier, *1675*
Metal gun cartridge, *8105*
Motorcycle with a built-in gasoline engine, *5489*
Muskets, *8091*
Shampoo commercially produced, *4069*
Twin-cycle motorcycle, *5490*
Wrench patent, *7916*

Sterling

Paper sewing patterns, *4357*

Stockbridge

Village improvement society, *2191*

Taunton

Silk power loom, *7889*

Uxbridge

Woman whose vote was recorded, *3421*

Waltham

Coal oil factory, *4431*
Cotton mill entirely powered by water, *7884*

Ware

Bedspring manufacturing patent, *4322*

Wellesley

Spectrophotometer, *6799*

MASSACHUSETTS—continued

West Boylston

Carpet power loom, *4313*

West Bridgewater

Steel shovel, *7906*

West Newbury

Comb factory, *4065*

Westborough

American "Robin Hood", *2769*
Reformatory for boys established by a state, *2820*

Westfield

Whips commercially manufactured, *7910*

Westover Air Force Base

Transatlantic helicopter flight, *1576*

Weymouth

Ball-point pen, *8154*

Whitman

Chocolate chip cookies, *3928*

Williamstown

College alumni association, *2991*
Fraternity house at a college, *2985*

Winthrop

Steam-driven motorcycle, *5487*

Woods Hole

Ship outfitted for hurricane research, *6775*

Worcester

Abrasive for commercial use, *4442*
Agricultural dictionary, *1799*
Bible in folio size to be illustrated, *1964*
Boxing arena, *7503*
Calliope, *1311*
Dictionary published in the United States, *1797*
Envelope folding and gumming machine, *5765*
Envelope folding machine, *5763*
Esperanto course at a college, *3117*

Geography school at a college, *3245*
Greek Testament, *1965*
Hair clipper, *4068*
Historical society (national), *5711*
History of printing, *1866*
Hospital for treatment of the mentally ill established by a state, *4873*
Intercollegiate billiard match, *4018*
Intercollegiate regatta, *7470*
Lawyer formally admitted to the bar who was African-American, *4634*
Paper twine machine, *5761*
Parkland purchased by a city, *3733*
Piano wire, *1310*
Pocket dictionary, *1798*
Psychology society (national), *5043*
Sewage disposal by chemical precipitation, *2233*
Silk loom, *7890*
Spring winding machine, *4411*
Wire gauge, *7920*

MICHIGAN

Ban on surrogate motherhood enacted by a state, *2168*
Fireworks law enacted by a state, *4113*
Interracial jury, *2735*
Labor cooperatives to be authorized by a state, *4609*
Medal of Honor winner to receive two awards, *1674*
Republican Party meeting, *3353*

Adrian

Seeding machine, *1047*

Ann Arbor

Bacteriology courses at a college, *3149*
Bibliography course at a college, *3098*
Book series microfilmed, *4683*
College entrance plan using certified schools, *2994*
Genetics clinic, *4848*
Honors program offered by a university, *2996*
Ice skater to cover 100 miles in less than six hours, *7436*
Microfilm editions of federal publications and documents, *4686*
Physician who was a Chinese woman, *4978*
Public speaking department at a college, *3100*
State university supported by a direct property tax, *2952*

Battle Creek

Bowler to earn $100,000 in one year in tournaments, *7232*

Cereal sold as a breakfast food, *3916*

Bay City

Wrecking crane, *4409*

Big Beaver Island

Community leader to exercise the authority of king and high priest, *5965*

Dearborn

Plastic car, *5451*

Detroit

Air-conditioned car, *5449*
Airplane diesel engine, *1498*
Billiard match to attain international fame, *4017*
Boxing match broadcast on radio, *7238*
Car factory, *5433*
Car fueled by methanol, *5463*
Car with an automatic transmission, *5450*
Car with front-wheel drive, *5459*
Car with the steering wheel on the left side, *5438*
Catholic magazine in English, *4702*
Cellulose sponge for medical and surgical use, *4951*
Championship heavyweight boxing title won in the first round, *7237*
Commercial radio station licensed, *6294*
Computer-aided design (CAD) software, *2549*
Concrete rural road, *6624*
Congressional representative who was a Catholic priest, *2601*
Corporation to own its own airplane, *1396*
Corporation with a net income of more than $1 billion in one year, *2406*
Daughters of the American Revolution member who was African-American, *5718*
Death by suicide machine, *2845*
Diesel cars to be mass-produced, *5460*
Electric car to be mass-produced, *5464*
Electric power substation with a rotary converter completely unattended, *3474*
Electric self-starter used in cars, *5442*
Free-piston car, *5458*
Gas-turbine bus, *5424*
Instantaneous phonograph recording, *7011*
Mitral valve corrective surgery, *5092*
Mobile home, *5505*
News program on radio, *5704*
Newspaper association, *5617*
Pneumatic hammer, *7934*
Pneumatic piano player, *1320*
Police officer who was a woman, *4136*
Prince of Wales to visit the United States, *4078*
Professional hockey player to reach a score of more than 1,000 points, *7381*

Public school classes for children with epilepsy, *3022*
Radio orchestra, *1364*
Refrigerated railroad car, *6378*
Sedan car, *5443*
Senator who had been a newspaper reporter, *2655*
Telecast from a foreign country, *7842*
Toy pinball game machine, *7453*
Vehicular tunnel to a foreign country, *3619*
Wedding broadcast over the radio, *4819*
Wedding by transatlantic telephone, *4821*
Year in which more than 1 million passenger cars of one make were produced, *5453*
Year in which more than 100,000 passenger cars were produced, *5440*
Zebra mussels, *1162*

East Lansing

Farriers' course at a college, *3299*
President of a major university who was African-American, *2975*

Flint

Sports car with a plastic laminated fiberglass body, *5455*

Fort Wayne

Subcompact car with front wheel drive, *5462*

Grand Rapids

Carpet sweeper, *4273*
Game warden to be paid a salary, *3744*
Hydroelectric power plant to furnish arc lighting service, *3458*
Water supply to be fluoridated, *2236*

Grosse Ile

Airship made completely of metal, *1524*

Hancock

Finnish college, *2959*

Hattiesburg

Naval Reserve flier who was African-American, *1618*

Holland

Antibiotic synthetically manufactured, *5002*

Houghton

Professional hockey team, *7375*

MICHIGAN—*continued*

Ishpeming

Ski club association, *7480*

Jackson

College commencement exercises in a prison, *2982*
Trimline telephone, *7725*

Kalamazoo

Dental drill powered by electricity, *4864*
Pedestrian shopping mall, *2513*

Lansing

Car exported from the United States, *5431*

Lenawee County

Fence made of woven wire, *1052*

Mendon

Electric locomotive headlight, *6425*

Mount Clemens

Airplane to fly faster than 200 miles per hour, *1448*
Transatlantic eastward flight by jet airplane, *1469*

Mount Vernon

Typewriter, *2384*

Olivet

College to dispense with credits, hours, points, and grades, *3001*

Plymouth

Air gun, *8111*

Pontiac

Curling club, *7275*
Movie of the sun, *6689*

Port Huron

Newspaper printed on a train, *5789*
Underwater railroad tunnel to a foreign country, *3617*

Trenton

Traffic lanes designated by painted lines, *4223*

Tupelo

Electric power contract between a city and the federal government, *3482*

Warren

Smog chamber for air pollution research, *3717*

Wyandotte

Bessemer steel converter, *4492*

MINNESOTA

Aerial ferry, *3589*
Blue Cross and Blue Shield plans, *4536*
Congressional representative elected by prohibitionists, *2606*
In-line roller skate that was commercially successful, *7466*
Intercollegiate basketball game, *7169*
Parental leave law enacted by a state that applied to both mothers and fathers, *4571*
Primary election law enacted by a state, *3318*
Telecast from the stratosphere, *7849*

Austin

Canned ham, *3941*
Sit-down strike, *4598*

Babbitt

Taconite production, *5342*

Chippewa Falls

Supercomputer, *2532*

Crosby

Balloon flight to rise higher than 100,000 feet, *1541*

Duluth

Canal incorporated into a seaway, *3603*

Edina

Enclosed climate-controlled suburban shopping mall, *2512*

Faribault

Episcopal cathedral, *6550*

Hutchinson

American expeditionary force to land in Europe in World War II, *8052*

Lake City

Water skis, *7591*

Minneapolis

American Legion convention of veterans of World War I, *5312*
Children's department in a library, *4672*
Delegates to a national political convention who were women, *3338*
Electric toaster, *4301*
Golfer to win both the U.S. Open and the U.S. Amateur in the same year, *7358*
Heart operation in which the deep-freezing technique was employed, *5093*
Immunology society, *5048*
Ink paste, *5787*
Milky Way candy bar, *3969*
Monthly cumulative index of books, *1774*
Navy–Marine Corps Medals for Heroism awarded to Marines, *1661*
Nursing school at a college, *3173*
Transfusion of artificial blood, *4840*
Vending machine that dispensed liquid automatically, *2393*

New Ulm

Catholic hillside shrine, *6466*

St. Paul

Cellophane transparent tape, *4339*
Forestry association (state), *6785*
Hospital for disabled children established by a state, *4889*
Radio facsimile newspaper, *5656*
Sound-absorbing material made of rigid insulating board, *2050*
Tape-recording machine for mass production of tapes, *7015*

Stillwater

Toaster, *4299*

MISSISSIPPI

State to ratify the Prohibition Amendment to the Constitution, *2683*
State to repudiate a debt, *7597*

Bay St. Louis

Catholic seminary for the education of African-American priests, *3278*

Camp Shelby

Army chaplain of Japanese ancestry, *5204*

Clarksdale

Cotton crop commercially produced entirely by machinery, *1035*
Jet airplane to transport mail, *6030*

Columbus

Decoration Day, *4236*
State college for women, *2954*

Edgewater Park

Bridge player to win more than 1,000 master points in one year, *4027*

Jackson

Lung transplant, *5098*
Pellagra experiment of note, *5058*
Transplant of an animal organ into a human being, *5099*

Meridian

Rabbi in the Reform movement who was a woman, *6490*

Natchez

Battleship to visit an inland city, *6987*
Pilot from the United States to shoot down a German fighter plane in World War II, *8059*
Senator who was African-American, *2649*

Pascagoula

Cargo ship fully automated and flying the American flag, *6901*

Rodney

Land grant college for African-American students, *2895*

Vicksburg

Warship sunk by an underwater torpedo mine, *7965*

MISSOURI

Bachelor tax enacted by a state, *7644*
Dental crown made of gold, *4863*
State west of the Mississippi River to be admitted to the Union, *7603*
Vice presidential candidate of a major political party to resign before the election, *3417*

Columbia

Journalism school at a college, *3102*

MISSOURI—*continued*

Crystal City

Building in which wrought-iron window sashes were installed, *2052*

De Soto

Newspaper published by soldiers in the field, *5641*

Florissant

Catholic school for Native Americans, *3053*

Glasgow

Railroad bridge entirely of steel, *3584*

Hannibal

Railroad post office, *6037*
Statue to commemorate literary characters, *5413*

Independence

Overland wagon road across the Rocky Mountains, *6617*

Jefferson Barracks

Army cavalry unit, *5179*

Kansas City

Baseball player to play all nine positions in one game, *7155*
Democratic Party convention between presidential elections, *3379*
Execution for kidnapping, *2801*
Football game to last longer than 80 minutes, *7335*
Helicopter rescue of an American pilot behind enemy lines, *7979*
National political convention at which a woman made a seconding speech, *3339*
Shopping center in a suburban business area, *2501*
Shopping mall, *2502*
Wedding by telegraph, *4816*
World War II veterans' society officially recognized by Congress, *5313*

Kirksville

Osteopathic physicians who were women, *4976*
Osteopathy journal, *4762*
Osteopathy school, *3170*

Liberty

Bank and train robbery gang, *2775*

Louisiana

Fruit tree patent, *1026*

Macon

Osteopathic physician, *4975*

Marshfield

Horse motel, *2435*

Newton County

National monument dedicated to an African-American, *5416*

Philadelphia

Masonic college, *2945*

St. Joseph

Pony Express mail, *5994*
Ready-mix food, *3947*

St. Louis

Adaptable railroad freight car, *6392*
Adding machine successfully marketed, *2378*
Airmail dispatched from a post office in a balloon, *6014*
Airship race, *7291*
Allergy journal, *4764*
Antibacterial mouthwash, *4072*
Babysitters' insurance policy, *4527*
Balloon cup race, *7288*
Baseball game in which a team made no runs in nine innings, *7117*
Baseball play-off series, *7134*
Bibliography organization (national), *4691*
Bohemian church, *6463*
Bowling tournament for women, *7225*
Catholic mass in English, *6479*
Cow flown in an airplane, *1153*
Diesel engine built for commercial service, *5479*
Electric power using municipal garbage as a boiler fuel, *3489*
Electron tube, *3437*
Evaporated milk, *3873*
Fiberglass sutures, *4957*
Garbage incinerator, *3713*
Genetically engineered product to appear in food, *3839*
Geodesic dome of substantial size, *2094*

Glider flight indoors, *1549*
Helicopter with a twin engine, *1559*
Ice cream cone, *3866*
International exchange of fingerprints, *4162*
Ironclad naval vessels, *6921*
Junior chamber of commerce, *2453*
Law school at a university to admit women, *3123*
Lung removal, *5081*
Mobile overseas telephone call from a moving vehicle, *7763*
Mobile telephone commercial service, *7740*
Nobel Prize shared by an American husband and wife, *1696*
Olympic Games held in the United States, *7443*
Olympic medalist who was African-American, *7444*
Orthodontia journal, *4763*
Orthodontists' society, *5045*
Parachute jump from an airplane, *1581*
Police department to adopt the fingerprinting system, *4160*
Public school kindergarten, *3074*
Railroad mystery excursion, *3667*
Ramjet helicopter, *1564*
School for blind students to adopt the Braille system, *3025*
Sewing machine to stitch buttonholes, *4354*
Silverite national convention, *3367*
Soccer team entirely made up of Americans, *7492*
Steel arch bridge, *3582*
Teacher training school principal who was a woman, *3264*
Train with fluorescent lights, *6434*
Transcontinental expedition to the Pacific coast, *6721*
Traveler's aid program, *5966*
Vacuum cleaner driven by a motor, *4275*

Sedalia

Sheet music to sell millions of copies, *1293*

Springfield

City in miniature, *2197*
Federal cemetery to contain graves of both Union and Confederate soldiers, *2853*

Tipton

Overland mail service, *5993*

Washington

Corncob pipe commercial manufacture, *2704*
Zither factory, *1313*

MONTANA

Congressional representative who was a woman, *2609*
Pension laws enacted by a state, *4587*

Fort Laramie

Native American to win territorial concessions from the federal government, *5970*

Poplar

Plastic oil pipeline, *3541*

Superior

Bibles in hotel rooms, *6579*

NEBRASKA

Arbor Day, *4238*
State legislature with a single chamber in the post-Revolutionary era, *7630*

Beatrice

Homestead law enacted by Congress, *5967*

Chadron

Horse race of 1,000 miles, *7396*

Grand Island

Interstate Commerce Commission Medal of Honor, *1654*

Lincoln

Industrial corporation course at a college, *2920*
Team to achieve a perfect score in the International Mathematical Olympiad, *3249*

North Platte

Wild West Show, *3689*

Omaha

Bowler to win $10,000 in a tournament, *7229*
Log-rolling national championship tournament, *7576*
Road paved with glasphalt, *6635*
Streamlined lightweight high-speed three-car passenger train, *6431*
Vending machine law enacted by a city, *2397*

Swan

Forest planting by the federal government, *3726*

NEVADA

Gambling permit stamp issued by the federal government, *7661*
Heavyweight boxing champion of the world who was African-American, *7252*
Narcotics ban enacted by a state, *2691*

Carson City

Execution by lethal gas, *2800*
Movie of a heavyweight championship boxing fight, *5546*

Frenchman Flat

Atomic bomb explosion to be shown on television, *8126*
Atomic bomb underground explosion, *8127*
Nuclear cannon, *8129*

Henderson

Titanium plant fully self-contained and fully integrated, *4477*

Lake Mead

Speedboat to exceed 200 miles per hour, *6953*

Las Vegas

Casino in Las Vegas, *3636*
Slot machine payoff of $275,000, *3639*

Reno

Congressional representative to attend college after his term of service, *2608*

Virginia City

Silver mill, *4469*

Yucca Flat

Nuclear warhead mounted on a rocket, *8131*

NEW HAMPSHIRE

Attorney of the United States, *2711*
Federal judge to be impeached, *2719*
Free public libraries authorized by a state, *4670*
Insurance board established by a state government, *4503*
Navy officer commissioned, *5278*
Paper bag machine, *4405*
Senate president pro tempore, *2625*
Senator elected on an antislavery ticket, *2250*
Ski lifts to be regulated by the state, *7487*

Workday of 10 hours to be mandated by a state, *4554*

Centre Harbor

Intercollegiate rowing race, *7468*

Concord

Alarm clock, *7898*
Forest fire drenched by artificial rain, *3732*
Melodeon patent, *1309*

Dartmouth

Educational computer programming language, *2550*

Derry

Potatoes to be cultivated, *3894*

Dover

Mass scalping of Native Americans by colonists, *5934*
Strike by women, *4592*

Franconia

Ski lift, *7484*

Grafton

Mica, *5321*

Laconia

Water skier to jump 100 feet, *7593*

Manchester

Credit union, *3773*

Meredith

Artificial leg patent, *5050*

Mount Washington

Botanic expedition, *6738*
Cog railroad, *6333*

Nashua

Tool factory, *7917*

New Castle

Revolutionary War incident, *7988*

Newington

Community forest, *3723*

North Conway

Skimobile ski lift, *7485*

Orford

Internal-combustion engine, *5477*

Peterborough

Free public library established by a city, *4668*

Portsmouth

Leaping submarine, *6972*
Naval ship of the line, *6913*
Navy yard, *5261*
Submarine to be refloated, *6970*
Submarine to make a submerged passage through the Northwest Passage, *6997*
Submarine with a pressure hull of high-tensile steel, *6971*

Portsmouth Harbor

American flag displayed on a man-of-war, *1119*

Troy

Horse blankets, *4263*

Walpole

Herbal book, *1927*
Novel published in America to be republished in England, *1840*

Washington Center

Adventist church to accept Saturday as the Sabbath, *6529*

Wolfeboro

Summer home, *2123*

NEW JERSEY

Artificial animal breeding cooperative organization, *1083*
Automatic steering gear for ships, *6958*
Book intended for circulation in the English colonies, *1730*
Coin to use *E pluribus unum* as a motto, *5356*
Congressional representative who was a grandmother, *2621*

Daily state lotteries with the same winning daily number, *3644*
Election law enacted by a colony granting voting rights to women, *3422*
Hammered iron, *4454*
Holding companies authorized by a state, *2404*
Labor union discrimination law enacted by a state, *4614*
Labor unions to be legalized by a state, *4613*
Medical licensing law enacted by a colony, *4935*
Movie with a plot, *5547*
Noise-control law enacted by a state, *3721*
Pear and peach trees, *3891*
Public defender hired by a state, *4642*
Supreme Court nominee who was rejected by the Senate, *2753*

Atlantic City

Airplane to fly higher than a mile in altitude, *1431*
Beauty pageant to be held nationwide, *3628*
Birth to be shown on closed-circuit television, *2163*
Boardwalk, *2063*
Building shaped like an elephant, *2079*
Casino outside the state of Nevada, *3638*
Disease research and treatment organization, *5046*
Rocket glider flight, *1552*
Transatlantic airship flight, *1515*
Transcontinental flight made by African-Americans in their own airplane, *1458*
Transcontinental group tour by car, *5473*

Bayonne

Relay race in a college track meet, *7550*

Belleville

Copper rolling mill, *4464*
Postage stamp depicting a nurse, *6099*

Belmar

Radar signal to the moon, *7680*

Beverly

Partridge propagation, *1067*

Bloomfield

Electric sterilamp, *4950*

Bordentown

Locomotive cowcatcher, *6417*

NEW JERSEY—*continued*

Brick Township

Trial of a surrogate mother for refusing to give up her baby, *2167*

Brotherton

Reservation for Native Americans established by a state, *5937*

Brunswick

Airport baggage scanning system, *1511*

Burlington

Mason, *5727*
Town trust fund for education, *3047*

Burlington County

Plow patent, *1041*

Caldwell

Parachute jump from an autogiro, *1588*

Caldwell Township

Synthetic mica, *5345*

Camden

Condensed soup, *3948*
Drive-in movie theater, *3709*
Ferryboat built exclusively to transport cars, *6911*
Nuclear-powered merchant ship, *6900*
Phonograph record of a stage performance by the original cast, *7008*
Phonograph with an automatic record changer, *7010*
Phonograph with an enclosed horn in the cabinet, *7009*
Railroad rails of T shape, *6416*
Steel pens, *8150*
Unscheduled event to be televised as it occurred, *5607*

Camp Kilmer

Aerocycle, *1570*

Cape May

Aviation unit of the military trained for overseas duty, *5132*

Carlstadt

Food-O-Mat, *2509*

Coytesville

Standard broadcast station to transmit a television image, *7795*

Elizabeth

Containerized shipping, *2487*
Flicker animation, *5530*
Miniature television tube, *7809*
Self-service supermarket, *2504*
Serviceman to die in Somalia, *7982*

Elizabethport

Cutlery shears, *4368*
Electric sewing machine, *4360*

Englewood

Figure skating champion from the United States to compete in the Olympic Games, *7432*
Transcontinental dial telephone service without the aid of operators, *7745*

Fort Monmouth

Coast-to-coast solar-powered two-way radio conversation, *6282*
Walkie-Talkie two-way radio device, *7722*

Freehold

Revolutionary War conflict in which American and British troops met on equal terms, *8002*

Greenville

Revolver shooting tournament, *7477*

Haddonfield

Dinosaur skeleton found in the United States, *6744*

Hadley Field

Airplane scheduled passenger flight at night, *1410*

High Bridge

Manganese steel, *4495*
Manganese steel for railroad tracks, *4496*

Hightstown

Parachute tower for training jumpers, *1589*

Hoboken

Baseball game, *7111*

Harness horse race at night, *7389*
Heavyweight championship boxing match broadcast on radio, *7241*
International cricket tournament, *7273*
Locomotive to pull a train on a track, *6347*
Mechanical engineering laboratory, *3561*
Tunnel construction using compressed air, *3616*
Zipper, *2292*

Holmdel

Computer operating system for multiple users, *2545*
Radio waves from space to be observed, *6681*

Jersey City

Armenian newspaper, *5675*
Boxing match to gross $1 million, *7240*
Cornstarch made commercially from maize, *3912*
Drinking water supply to be chemically treated with chlorine compounds, *2235*
Dry dock, *6904*
Moving sidewalk in a railroad station, *6639*
Physician with a mobile medical office, *4979*

Kearny

Linoleum manufacturing machine, *4317*

Lakehurst

Glider released from an airship, *1548*
Rigid airship, *1521*
Round-the-world airplane passenger race, *7299*

Maplewood

Transcontinental car trip driven entirely in reverse, *5475*

Margate

Commercial DNA bank, *6756*

Menlo Park

Incandescent lamp, *3492*
Incandescent lamp factory, *3494*
Mimeograph, *5784*
Phonograph, *7004*
Photograph taken by incandescent electric light, *5819*
Radio patent, *6305*

Millville

Retirement colony, *2198*
Uniforms for working women, *2275*

Moorestown

Percheron horse importation, *1179*

Morristown

Golfer to win the United States Women's Amateur Championship, *7356*
Telegraphic system in which dots and dashes represented letters, *7687*

Murray Hill

Encyclopedia of integer sequences, *6763*
Phototransistor, *3440*
Transistor, *3439*

Navesink

Naval radio station, *5301*

New Brunswick

Antibiotic, *4998*
Bandage with built-in adhesive, *4945*
Home screening kit for HIV infection, *4954*
Intercollegiate football contest, *7315*
Interstate telephone call, *7753*
Microbiology laboratory, *4932*
Plant patent, *1063*
Theology school, *3267*

New Sweden

Log cabins, *2069*

Newark

Beer in cans, *2671*
Business library supported by taxes, *4675*
Camera exposure meter, *5843*
Celluloid photographic film, *5838*
Fire extinguisher using vaporized chemicals, *4110*
Grand jury foreman who was a woman, *2737*
Jury school, *2736*
Malleable iron castings, *4451*
Motorboat with a storage battery, *6950*
Patent leather, *4458*
Puppet show to be televised, *1259*
Road pavement of sheet asphalt, *6621*
Socialist Labor Party of North America national convention, *3360*
State legislative hearing to be shown on television, *7633*
Synthetic fertilizer, *1016*
Toll collection machine, *6634*
Transcontinental autogiro flight by a woman, *1532*
Two-way telegraph, *7702*

NEW JERSEY—Newark—*continued*
Velvet carpeting and tapestry, *4314*

North Arlington

Steam engine for industrial use, *4388*

Pahaquarry Mines

Hard-surfaced road, *6609*

Passaic

Life insurance group policy, *4548*

Paterson

Industrial park, *4380*
Linen thread factory, *4363*
Locomotive steam whistle, *6355*
Revolver pistol, *8096*
Strike in which a militia was called out, *4593*

Paulsboro

Aviation gasoline obtained by the catalytic cracking method, *3539*

Perth Amboy

African-American to vote under authority of the 15th Amendment, *3429*

Pitman

Doctor in the regular Navy who was a woman, *5291*

Plainsboro

Rotating milking platform, *1056*

Princeton

College charter granted by a governor, *2928*
College literary society, *2990*
College skeet tournament, *7478*
Discus-throwing competition, *7551*
Electronic road system, *6632*
Intercollegiate lacrosse association, *7572*
Mathematical proof of Fermat's last theorem, *6761*
Mathematical theory of economic decision-making, *6758*
Radio impulse transmission, *6304*
Theology school graduate who was African-American, *3270*
Virus obtained in crystalline form, *5059*

Rahway

Haircloth, *7866*

Ridgewood

Submarine cable plow, *7709*

Riverton

Japanese beetle, *1023*

Sandy Hook

Transatlantic yacht race, *7211*
Yacht race broadcast on radio, *7215*

Sea Girt

State police class in which women completed training, *4153*

Sewell

Illuminated nine-hole regulation golf course, *7350*

Trenton

Actor to have an exclusive movie contract, *5524*
Army chaplain killed in action, *5195*
Chinaware for restaurant use, *4309*
Dish set made in America for the White House, *6256*
National conference on crime, *4147*
Open-hearth furnace for the manufacture of steel, *4493*
Pottery to make sanitary ware, *4041*
Railroad charter granted by a state, *6317*
State committee chairman of a major political party who was a woman, *3341*

Tuckerton

Stock order from a zeppelin, *3826*

Vineland

Intelligence test in a school for children with mental retardation, *3021*

West Orange

Alkaline dry cell battery, *3475*
Movie studio, *5543*
Movie to be copyrighted, *5544*

Whitehouse Station

Chicken pox vaccine, *4925*

Woodbridge

Fire brick, *2054*

NEW MEXICO

Native American map of record, *4791*
Senator who was a Latino, *2652*

Acoma

Settlement in America in continuous habitation, *5891*

Alamogordo

Jet drone target missile, *8137*
Rocket-driven sled on rails, *7021*

Alamogordo Air Base

Atomic bomb explosion, *8123*

Albuquerque

Artwork to incorporate lightning, *1220*
Commercial building with solar heating, *2067*
Personal computer, *2537*
Technical school for Native Americans, *3302*
Teraflop computer, *2541*
Transatlantic balloon flight, *1543*

Artesia

Underground school, *2122*

Clovis

Humans in America, *5887*

Fort Stanton

Tuberculosis hospital established by Congress, *4902*

Ruidoso

Horse race for a purse of more than $1 million, *7404*

Santa Fe

Anthropology laboratory, *6748*
Art museum of importance devoted to the work of an individual woman, *5600*
Nuclear reactor patent, *6806*

Silver City

Race between a horse and a bicycle, *7395*

White Sands

Ballistic missile, *8134*

Rocket to attain a 100-mile altitude, *7019*
Rocket to intercept an airplane, *8136*
Rocket to reach outer space, *7020*
Ultraviolet pictures of the sun, *6698*

NEW YORK

Ambulance air service, *4824*
Bank deposit insurance law enacted by a state, *3762*
Bank to establish a branch in a foreign country, *3776*
Bathhouses mandated by a state, *4196*
Blood testing laws enacted by a state, *4188*
Blood tests for marriage license applicants to be required by a state, *4190*
Blood tests for pregnant women to be required by a state, *4189*
Botanist of note who was a woman, *6737*
British marine corps of American colonists, *5228*
Canal of importance, *3601*
Chiropody school of note, *3174*
Circus to feature a car as an attraction, *3673*
Coastal shipping service, *2478*
Commercial corporation, *2402*
Concrete, *2041*
Congregational Church minister who was African-American, *6522*
Congressional medal awarded to a physician, *1652*
Congressional representative of Italian ancestry, *2605*
Congressional representative of Puerto Rican ancestry, *2618*
Credit insurance, *4512*
Cross-dresser of note, *6827*
Dental society of a city, *5032*
Dissection of a living animal to demonstrate anatomy and physiology, *5054*
Dog license law enacted by a state, *1172*
Domed sports stadium, *7511*
Education department at a college, *3265*
Environmental protection law enacted by a state in connection with advertising, *3711*
Fire escapes for tenements, *4105*
Forest reserve established by a state, *3724*
Golf clubs for hitting balls, *7351*
Great Lakes vessel, *6851*
Historical novel, *1841*
Horticultural society, *1088*
Installment sales law enacted by a state, *2314*
Justice on the federal bench who was a woman, *2725*
Labor antidiscrimination commission of a state government, *4568*
Labor mediation and arbitration board established by a state, *4561*
Labor union to nominate its own political candidates, *4604*
Landscape painter, *1203*

NEW YORK—*continued*

League of Native American nations, *5897*
Librarian who was African-American, *4674*
License plates for vehicles, *4220*
Lock-stitch sewing machine, *4349*
Major league baseball player killed in a game, *7148*
Margarine law enacted by a state, *3883*
Marine regiment to land in Europe in World War I, *8034*
Missionary to the Native Americans who was African-American, *6569*
Novel by a writer born in America, *1836*
Painting movement, *1204*
Pharmacists to be regulated by a state, *4939*
Pope to visit the United States before his election, *4081*
President to make a radio broadcast from a foreign country, *6214*
Presidential campaign manager who was a woman, *3392*
Prison matrons for guarding women prisoners, *2819*
Pure food and drug law enacted by a state, *4178*
Radio broadcast from a submerged submarine, *6268*
Radio navigation beacons, *6957*
States with populations of more than 1 million, *5849*
Steamboat with a twin-screw propeller, *6860*
Submarine built for use in war, *6961*
Superintendent of schools hired by a state, *3052*
Supreme Court chief justice, *2752*
Supreme Court decision in a commerce case, *2750*
Supreme Court decision in a matter between states, *2745*
Team sport played in America, *7094*
Telecommunication by deaf people that was both visual and oral, *7837*
Temporary insanity defense in a criminal case, *4622*
Transatlantic radio message of the regular westward service, *6265*
Transcontinental commercial telephone service, *7720*
Truancy law enacted by a state, *3061*
Truth-in-advertising law enacted by a state, *2330*
Turreted frigate in the Navy, *6920*
Underground burial of electric wires to be required by a state, *2222*
Vice president who was nominated specifically for that office, *6240*
Vice presidential candidate from a major political party who was a woman, *3419*
Voting machines, *3317*
War map, *4794*

Albany

Christmas cards, *4256*
Dutch settlement in America, *5912*
Dye plant, *4433*
Electric bell for electromagnets, *3452*
Electromagnet, *3451*
Electromagnetic telegraph, *7686*
Library society (state), *4690*
Medical jurisprudence treatise, *1879*
Paleontology report, *1974*
Patriotic song to achieve national popularity, *1374*
Perforated wrapping paper, *5758*
Political machine, *3347*
Remote television pickup, *7830*
Stamp collection magazine, *4727*
Steamboat to make regular trips, *6861*
Streamlined steam locomotive, *6364*
Sweet crackers, *3923*
Whig Party convention, *3350*

Albion

Santa Claus school, *4259*

Aqueduct

Jockey who was a woman to win a major stakes race, *7419*

Ardsley-on-Hudson

Intercollegiate golf association, *7343*

Armonk

Floppy disk, *2536*
Large commercial computer network, *2543*
Typewriter that could retype text automatically, *2392*
Typewriter without type arms, *2391*

Ashville

Fire department composed entirely of women, *4114*

Attica

National bank to fail, *3767*

Auburn

Execution by electrocution, *2799*
Key time recorder, *2381*
Prison organized into community groups, *2827*

Auriesville

Catholic beatification of a Native American, *6474*

Barcelona Harbor

Lighthouse fueled by natural gas, *4126*

Bayside

Television receiver and transmitter operated by laser beam, *7822*

Beacon

Psychodrama treatment for psychiatric patients, *5116*

Bentonsville

Circular saw, *7913*

Binghamton

Alcoholics' asylum, *4879*
Farm bureau, *1004*
Flight trainer for airplane pilots, *1500*

Bloomville

Milk pasteurized commercially, *3875*

Blue Mountain Lake

Hotel to install electric lights, *2426*

Boonville

Snowmobile to exceed a speed of 125 miles per hour, *7491*

Buffalo

Air conditioner for home use, *4333*
Air conditioner patent, *4413*
Architect who was a woman, *1194*
Bicycle champion who was a woman, *7197*
Bowler to roll two perfect games, *7226*
Bowler who was a woman to obtain a perfect score, *7227*
Cancer laboratory, *4930*
Catholic church to become a basilica, *6471*
Cellophane, *4338*
Desk with a roll top, *4325*
Domestic relations court, *2709*
Free Soil Party convention, *3352*
Grain elevator operated by steam, *1048*
Herd book for livestock, *1761*
Indoor ski slope, *7488*
Jet airplane, *1399*
Motorcycle that was practical, *5488*
Pacemaker to be implanted in a patient's body, *4953*
Paper made from wood pulp, *5754*

Skin grafting, *5077*
Steamboat on the Great Lakes, *6865*
Superintendent of schools hired by a city, *3055*
Telecast transmitted to Canada, *7843*
Timber dry dock, *6906*

Caldwell's Landing

Heavyweight boxing match to last longer than 100 rounds, *7233*

Canandaigua

Land office, *5948*

Canastota

Tire chains, *5497*

Cardiff

Prehistoric hoax, *3648*

Cato

School completely irradiated with germicidal lamps, *4191*

Chautauqua

Correspondence course of a serious nature, *2886*

College Point

Sugar-free soft drinks, *3847*

Corning

Heat-resistant glass, *4048*
Photosensitive glass, *4051*

Creedmoor

International rifle tournament of consequence, *7473*

Cuba

Oil spring, *3523*

East Fishkill

Handwriting teaching system widely used in schools, *3057*

East Rochester

Tract housing development, *2196*

Eastchester Township

Police radio system, *4146*

NEW YORK—*continued*

Elizabethport

Medal awarded to an American food producer, *1651*

Elmira

Automatic aircraft cannon, *8119*

Elmont

Horse stakes race ending in a triple dead heat, *7402*

Jockey who was a woman to win a Triple Crown race, *7421*

Elmont Park

Horse to win a $100,000 purse in one race, *7410*

Horse to win the Triple Crown, *7409*

Elmsford

Cocktail, *2665*

Hearing aid using transistors, *5071*

Fair Point

Chautauqua organization meeting, *2885*

Farmingdale

Bicycle racer to attain the speed of a mile a minute, *7193*

Fashion Race Course

Baseball game in which spectators were charged admission, *7112*

Baseball series, *7113*

Fayette

Mormon Church meeting, *6492*

Fayetteville

Natural cement rock, *2039*

Fishkill

Revolutionary War national veterans' organization, *5308*

Fort Ticonderoga

Revolutionary War military action, *7990*

Frankfort

Girder bridge of cast iron, *3574*

Franklin Square

Bank to issue a credit card, *3810*

Fredonia

Natural gas corporation, *3513*

Natural gas used as an illuminant, *3511*

Garden City

Airmail pilot, *6015*

Airplane with a fuselage of molded plywood, *1395*

College to offer courses to railroad commuters, *3003*

Fighter plane, *1486*

National wheelchair games, *7586*

Stabilized airplane in commercial use, *1397*

Transatlantic radio program received from Great Britain, *6271*

Genesee

Daredevil jumper of note, *3676*

Geneva

Abstract paintings, *1217*

College course without Greek or Latin, *2992*

Goshen

Telegraph used by a railroad, *7696*

Governors Island

Army nurse in modern times who was a man, *5173*

Greenpoint

Oil drill offshore rig, *3534*

Greenwood Lake

Airmail flight by rocket, *6026*

Motorcycle racer who was a woman, *7440*

Hammondsport

Airplane bombing experiment, *8113*

Airplane flying school, *3188*

Airplane race won by an American in Europe, *7290*

Airplane sold commercially, *1388*

Gyroscope, *1494*
Naval airplane, *1483*
Pilot licensed by the Aero Club of America, *1595*

Hartsdale

Transoceanic radio signal conveying a television image, *7828*

Hastings-on-Hudson

Photograph of a stellar spectrum showing the dark lines, *6695*

Hempstead Plains

Horse race run on a regular basis, *7384*

Hicksville

Car race for the Vanderbilt Cup, *7264*

Hudson

Comic magazine, *4698*
Medal of Honor awarded to a helicopter pilot, *1685*

Hyde Park

Presidential library, *6171*

Hydeville

Spiritualist, *6599*

Ilion

Revolver that was self-cocking, *8103*
Typewriter that was practical, *2385*

Ithaca

Editor in chief of a law review who was a woman, *3127*
Electrical engineering school at a college, *3239*
Forestry school at a college, *3076*
Graduate student who was a woman to receive a university fellowship, *3012*
Halftone printing plate, *5785*
Hotel administration course at a college, *3297*
Ice cream sundae, *3865*
Industrial and labor relations school at a college, *3257*
National college fraternity for African-American men, *2989*
Ptarmigan, *1166*
Quantum theory of electromagnetic radiation, *6759*

Screw caliper, *7928*
Veterinary department at a college, *3182*

Jerome Park

Steeplechase, *7391*

Johnstown

Ax factory, *7909*
Gloves, *2264*
Leather tanning by the oil tan method, *4457*

Jones Beach

National water skiing tournament, *7592*

Kinderhook

President born an American citizen, *6183*

Kings Point

Merchant marine academy, *3307*
Merchant Marine Academy cadets who were women, *3308*

Lake Placid

Auction duplicate bridge championship, *4023*
Dogsled race on an Olympic demonstration program, *7280*
International ski meet, *7482*
Olympic Games competition to be held in the winter, *7446*
Olympic gold medalist in both the Summer and Winter Olympics, *7447*

Lansingburg

Oiled silk patent, *7864*

Larchmont

Capture of an American ship captain by a German submarine in World War II, *8057*
Remote-controlled railroad passenger car, *6391*

Le Roy

Gelatin dessert, *3966*

Levittown

Planned suburban development, *2199*

Lewiston

Inclined railroad, *6315*

Little Falls

Balloon pilot who was a woman, *1539*

NEW YORK—*continued*

Lockport

Heating system to heat buildings from a central station, *2078*

Locust Grove

Bank to open a branch in a trailer, *3788*

Manhattan Beach

Motorcycle association, *7439*

Melville

Magnetic resonance image of a human body, *4912*

McGraw

Corset, *2271*

Mineola

Monoplane, *1390*

Mitchel Field

Air defense military organization, *5134*
Airplane flight between New York and Alaska, *1446*
All-blind airplane flight, *1451*
Parachute-jumping contest, *7296*

Monroe

Liederkranz cheese, *3860*

Monsey

Police officer who was a Chassidic Jew, *4157*

Montauk Point

Mobile telephone one-way communication, *7719*
Movie of a solar eclipse taken from an airship, *6686*

Monticello

Perfecta or Exacta horse race, *7403*
Softball game of 365 innings, *7498*

Mount Vernon

Professional Golfers Association tournament, *7345*

New Paltz

Adding machine to employ depressible keys, *2375*

New Russia

Organ with color display, *1315*

New York

Academic costume standardization for colleges, *2957*
Academic hall of fame, *5582*
Accounting society, *3753*
Accounting society (national), *3754*
Accounting society (state), *3756*
Actor to appear abroad, *1276*
Actors' union, *4615*
Acupuncture treatment center, *4852*
Adhesive postage stamps, *6051*
Advertising association to combat business abuses, *2452*
Advertising magazine, *4726*
Advertising show to be held annually, *2412*
Aerial camera with nine lenses for large-scale mapping, *5845*
African-American magazine, *4745*
Agricultural fair held annually, *1001*
Agriculture professor at a college, *2890*
Air-conditioned train, *6430*
Air rights lease, *2064*
Airline to carry 100 million passengers, *1423*
Airmail long-distance night service, *6020*
Airmail regular service, *6016*
Airmail service from ship to shore, *6022*
Airplane race between cities, *7293*
Airplane round trip, *1430*
Airship from the United States lost to enemy action in World War II, *8064*
Airship to land and take off from an oceangoing steamship, *1527*
Algebra book, *1883*
All-electric railroad, *6342*
All-fiction pulp magazine, *4731*
All-news radio station, *6303*
Allergy book, *1916*
Amateur athletic competition, *7547*
Amateur athletic games held indoors, *7543*
Amateur athletic games held outdoors, *7544*
Amateur open swimming championship meet, *7515*
Ambassador who was Jewish, *3989*
Ambulance equipped for mobile coronary care, *4826*
American flag displayed from the right hand of the Statue of Liberty, *1130*
Anesthesiology professor at a college, *3158*
Animal humane society, *5735*
Animated cartoon in color, *5533*
Animated cartoon made for television, *7782*

Animated cartoon made with cel animation, *5532*

Animated cartoon with sound, *5535*

Animation for technical purposes, *5534*

Antismoking law enacted by a colony, *2696*

Antitoxin laboratory established by a public health department, *4200*

Apartment house cooperative, *2126*

Apartment house to occupy a square city block, *2127*

Apartment house with a modern layout, *2125*

Aquatic play, *1249*

Arabic magazine, *4748*

Arbitration organization (national), *4645*

Arbitration tribunal, *2354*

Archival course at a college, *3106*

Arctic expedition by an American explorer, *6724*

Armenian Orthodox cathedral, *6499*

Army general to be consecrated a bishop, *5158*

Army medical book, *1895*

Art auction televised on a coast-to-coast circuit, *1230*

Art magazine, *4722*

Art museum to sell reproductions, *5596*

Artificial eyes, *5051*

Artificial insemination of a woman resulting in conception, *5113*

Artists' organization (national), *1205*

Arts and letters organization (national), *5716*

Astronomy photograph, *6692*

Atheist organization, *5745*

Athletic club, *7542*

Attack on British soldiers by civilians in the Revolution, *7984*

Attorney general of the United States, *6124*

Automatic electric stock quotation board, *3824*

Automatic plate-casting and finishing machine for stereotype printing, *5796*

Automaton, *3650*

Aviation correspondence school, *7289*

Aviation course in a high school, *3089*

Aviation magazine, *4776*

Aviation trophy, *1641*

Baby carriage, *2140*

Bacteriology diagnostic laboratory in a city health department, *4198*

Bacteriology laboratory, *4928*

Baking soda commercial production, *3934*

Ballet, *1232*

Ballet choreographer of international renown, *1235*

Ballet transmitted by satellite, *1238*

Balloon flight by an aeronaut born in America, *1537*

Bandwagon, *2326*

Bank clearinghouse, *3764*

Bank open day and night, *3792*

Bank robbery, *2773*

Bank to operate a window in a subway station, *3797*

Bank to provide movies for customers waiting in line, *3801*

Bank with resources exceeding $1 billion, *3780*

Bas relief of stainless steel in large size, *1219*

Baseball championship, *7122*

Baseball dyed yellow, *7110*

Baseball league, *7096*

Baseball pinch hitter, *7144*

Baseball pitcher to pitch a perfect no-hit, no-run, no-walk World Series game, *7153*

Baseball player who was African-American to win the Most Valuable Player award, *1723*

Baseball rules standardizing the game, *7095*

Baseball team, *7159*

Baseball team of African-American players to play professionally, *7164*

Baseball team to tour, *7160*

Baseball uniforms, *7104*

Basketball game at a large commercial sports arena, *7170*

Basketball game to be shown on television, *7171*

Battleship, *6926*

Beauty pageant to be shown on television, *3629*

Belgian immigrants, *5917*

Benefit performance of a play, *1244*

Bible for the blind in embossed form, *1968*

Bible society (national), *6573*

Bibliophile magazine, *4725*

Bicycle patent, *7180*

Bicycle race paced by a motorcycle, *7194*

Bicycle race to be shown on television, *7198*

Bicycle school, *7182*

Bicycles, *7179*

Billiard ball of composition material resembling ivory, *4019*

Billiards book, *2000*

Biological study of camouflage in nature, *6745*

Bird banding association (national), *6792*

Birth control clinic, *4844*

Boat club, *7206*

Bombing of a skyscraper by foreign terrorists, *2790*

Bonding company, *4511*

Bonds issued by the federal government, *3811*

Bone bank, *4837*

Book auction, *1778*

Book bound with preprinted offset cloth, *1755*

Book commercially bound in cloth, *1746*

Book fair, *1783*

Book jacket, *1748*

Book of Common Prayer in the Mohawk language, *1951*

Book of road maps, *4796*

Book-of-the-Month Club selection, *1789*

Book on the game of bridge, *2005*

Book on the game of bridge by a championship team, *2006*

NEW YORK—New York—*continued*

Book publishers' catalog, *1769*
Book review editor, *5613*
Book review newspaper supplement, *5650*
Book set by linotype, *1752*
Book set into type completely by electronic composition, *1756*
Book trade magazine, *4712*
Bookseller's guide, *1787*
Booksellers' organization, *1782*
Bowling magazine, *4786*
Bowling match, *7220*
Bowling match that used white balls on black lanes, *7228*
Bowling rule standardization, *7221*
Box spring, *4327*
Boxer to hold three titles simultaneously, *7253*
Boxer to win distinction in the ring, *7248*
Boxing match at which admission tickets sold at $100, *7245*
Boxing match broadcast on radio from ringside, *7239*
Boxing match to be shown on television, *7243*
Brassiere patent, *2276*
Brick building, *2068*
Bridge designed by computer, *3597*
Broadway play shown in a television version with its original cast, *1266*
Brokerage firm whose shares were traded by a major stock exchange, *3835*
Brokerage office owned by women, *3818*
Bronchitis treatise, *1911*
Building built to serve as a hotel, *2421*
Building constructed wholly of cast iron, *2076*
Building designed to be used by artists, *2062*
Building in which wrought-iron beams were used, *2077*
Building with a high steeple, *2097*
Building with caisson foundations, *2083*
Burglar alarm operated by ultrasonic or radio waves, *2136*
Burglar alarm system, *2134*
Burlesque show, *3687*
Bus with cross seats, *5420*
Bustle, *2269*
Cabinet, *6102*
Cabinet member indicted while in office, *6122*
Cancer hospital, *4885*
Cancer hospital established by a city, *4890*
Cancer prevention clinic for children, *4850*
Cancer research fund, *5056*
Canning book, *1849*
Canning of food, *3944*
Canoe club, *7212*
Cantorial school, *3280*
Car accident, *5466*
Car accident fatality, *5470*
Car driver who was a woman, *5467*
Car equipped with a two-way radio, *7717*
Car finance company, *3806*

Car magazine, *4788*
Car race from New York to Paris, *7265*
Car show, *5434*
Car to exceed the speed of a mile a minute, *5436*
Carbon microphone used in radio broadcasting, *6308*
Carrier for liquid bulk chemicals, *6897*
Cartoon showing the Democratic Party as a donkey, *5702*
Cartoon showing the Republican Party as an elephant, *5703*
Cartoon showing Uncle Sam, *5701*
Cartooning school, *2911*
Cat show, *1147*
Catalog of first American editions of American authors, *1773*
Catholic mass for night workers, *6469*
Catholic midnight mass to be televised, *6476*
Catholic priest from the United States to be made a cardinal, *6465*
Catholic saint who was a male American citizen, *6482*
Catholic saint who was born in America, *6481*
Cattle of the Afrikaaner breed, *1082*
Celluloid, *4480*
Census of the United States, *5848*
Certified public accountant, *3755*
Chain radio broadcast, *6270*
Chain store organization, *2493*
Chairman of the Joint Chiefs of Staff who was African-American, *5129*
Chamber of commerce established by a state, *2448*
Check photographing device, *3795*
Chemistry organization (national), *6786*
Chess tournament, *4028*
Child abuse prevention organization, *5737*
Child hygiene bureau, *4186*
Children's hospital, *4878*
Children's museum, *5581*
Chinese-American women's organization to be incorporated, *5726*
Chiropodists to be regulated by a city, *4937*
Chiropody book, *1913*
Cholera epidemic, *2876*
Chop suey, *3879*
Christmas tree decorated with electric lights, *4257*
Chrome tanning process, *4459*
Chromium plating process, *4476*
Church service in sign language to be televised, *6594*
Cigar bands of special interest, *2703*
Cigar-rolling machine, *2706*
Cigarette-manufacturing machine, *2705*
Circumnavigation of the globe by a warship, *6980*
Circumnavigation of the world by a cruise ship, *6989*

NEW YORK—New York—*continued*

Dental drill, *4856*

Dental journal, *4754*

Dental society (national), *5034*

Dentistry book, *1922*

Department store to hold a public art auction, *2507*

Department store to occupy a city block, *2492*

Design patent, *4654*

Detective who was a woman, *4140*

Diapers that were disposable, *2151*

Dictionary compiled by a woman, *1808*

Diesel-electric locomotive, *6363*

Dissection report, *1890*

District nurse, *5024*

Dog hotel, *2436*

Dog show, *1171*

Double-deck bridge, *3591*

Double-deck bus, *5419*

Double-deck elevator, *2112*

Double-header baseball games that were shut-outs, *7125*

Dow Jones Industrial Average to exceed 1,000 points, *3836*

Dow Jones Industrial Average to exceed 7,000 points, *3838*

Drama broadcast on radio from a regular stage, *1262*

Drama school, *2905*

Dried milk patent, *3870*

Driver arrested for speeding, *5468*

Drug treatment center for minors, *2690*

Dry ice manufactured commercially, *4441*

Dual sewer system for sewage and storm water, *2229*

Dutch Reformed church, *6506*

Dynamo that was successful, *3460*

Editorial to be broadcast over radio and television, *5707*

Educational magazine, *4706*

Educational television network operated as a nonprofit corporation, *7807*

Egg incubator, *1068*

Election in which returns were broadcast on radio, *3390*

Electric company, *3455*

Electric elevator successfully operated, *2109*

Electric flashing sign, *2351*

Electric light from a power plant in a residence, *3495*

Electric organ, *1314*

Electric power generated by cosmic rays, *3484*

Electric power station with a central source, *3461*

Electric printing press, *5774*

Electric sign of large dimensions, *2349*

Electric sign showing an animated cartoon, *2352*

Electric stove, *4298*

Electric streetcar run with current generated by a stationary dynamo, *6399*

Electric tabulating machine, *2364*

Electric tattoo machine, *4054*

Electric taxicabs, *5430*

Electrical hearing aid, *5070*

Electrical timing device for foot races, *7558*

Electricity journal, *4769*

Electronic watch, *7905*

Electrotype, *5803*

Elephant, *1142*

Elevated railroad, *6334*

Elevator, *2103*

Elevator in a hotel, *2107*

Elevator in an office building, *2108*

Elevator with a completely enclosed car, *2105*

Elevator with electronic signal controls, *2113*

Elevator with safety devices, *2104*

Elks meeting, *5722*

Embossing press, *5773*

Emergency 911 telephone system, *4087*

Enclosed baseball park, *7504*

English actor of note to perform in America, *1274*

English grammar by an American published in America, *1856*

Entomologist hired by a state, *6742*

Envelope manufacturer, *5762*

Epidemiologist, *4173*

Episcopal bishop who was African-American, *6551*

Etcher, *1206*

Ethical culture society, *5744*

European edition of an American newspaper, *5649*

Evening school for working children, *3046*

Execution by the Army, *2795*

Execution for slave trading carried out by the federal government, *2797*

Eye bank, *4836*

Eye hospital, *4872*

Factory with temperature and humidity control, *4384*

Fashion magazine, *4728*

Fashion show to be shown on television, *2414*

Federal election, *3380*

Felt hats for women, *2296*

Fiction writer to win the Pulitzer Prize twice, *1709*

Figure skater of note, *7429*

Film-developing machine, *5840*

Film professorship at a college, *2914*

Financial "corner", *3751*

Financial news agency, *5624*

Fire chief, *4094*

Fire department established by a city, *4093*

Fire department to be paid, *4095*

Fire engine with a steam boiler, *4100*

Fire of great destructive force, *2881*

Fireboats, *4097*

NEW YORK—New York—*continued*

Intercollegiate bicycle race, *7192*

Intercollegiate court tennis match, *7534*

Intercollegiate fencing championship competition, *7282*

Intercollegiate football game to be shown on television, *7329*

Intercollegiate indoor polo championship, *7460*

Intercollegiate track meet to be shown on television, *7559*

Intercollegiate transatlantic chess match by cable, *4030*

International federation of students, *3228*

International lifeboat race, *7217*

International postal card, *6049*

International radio broadcasting license, *6297*

International six-day bicycle race, *7189*

Interstate anticrime pact, *4133*

Investment trust, *3822*

Invisible-glass installation, *4050*

Irish magazine, *4742*

Ironclad turreted vessel in the Navy, *6923*

Italian newspaper, *5674*

Italian opera, *1346*

Jazz concert at Carnegie Hall, *1298*

Jazz record, *1294*

Jew to win full citizenship, *5858*

Jewish cemetery, *2851*

Jewish congregation, *6483*

Jewish prayer book, *1954*

Jewish prayer services to be televised in their entirety, *6595*

Jewish religious school for children, *6485*

Jewish synagogue, *6484*

Jews to arrive in America, *5892*

Joint meeting of the Senate and the House of Representatives, *2557*

Judge of the U.S. Court of Appeals who was an African-American woman, *2732*

Judge on the federal bench who was African-American, *2727*

Judge who was an African-American woman, *2726*

King and queen to be shown on television, *6653*

King cobra snakes, *1157*

Klieg light unit for movie production, *5572*

Knighthood conferred on American soil, *6643*

Labor newspaper, *5639*

Labor union for women, *4606*

Land sale swindle, *5919*

Landscape architect, *1192*

Large-type weekly newspaper, *5659*

Laryngology clinic, *4842*

Laryngology instruction at a college, *3142*

Laryngology journal, *4757*

Laryngophone, *5249*

Laser, *3443*

Law book containing laws enacted by more than one session of Congress, *1875*

Law instruction at a college, *3120*

Law text, *1877*

Lawn tennis, *7523*

Lawyers' society (state), *4643*

Laxative in candy form, *4991*

Letter to circumnavigate the world by commercial airmail, *6027*

Librarians' union, *4617*

Library for seamen, *4667*

Library journal, *4729*

Library newspaper room, *4671*

Library school at a college, *3099*

Library society (local), *4689*

Life insurance policy rated substandard, *4546*

Life preserver of cork, *4119*

Lifeboat of corrugated iron, *4120*

Lighting designer for the stage, *1265*

Line drawing to illustrate a newspaper article, *5685*

Linoleum, *4315*

Lipreading instruction for deaf people, *3035*

Liquor reform movement, *2673*

Loan to the United States, *3804*

Long-distance car race, *7263*

Long-distance dial telephone service, *7742*

Long-distance radio fax transmission of medical information, *7671*

Long-playing microgroove phonograph records, *7012*

Lutheran hymnbook, *1971*

Macaroni factory, *3913*

Macy's Thanksgiving Day Parade, *4262*

Magazine about recreational drugs, *4740*

Magazine for mechanics, *4768*

Magazine on microfilm offered to subscribers, *4685*

Magazine to contain a phonograph record, *4738*

Magic lantern feature show, *3692*

Magician's advertisement, *2319*

Major league baseball game to be shown on television, *7132*

Major league baseball player in the postwar era who was African-American, *7151*

Manufacturers' fair, *2408*

Margarine manufacturer, *3882*

Mariners' church, *6575*

Martini, *2670*

Mason jar, *4283*

Mass-market paperback book, *1786*

Master skyscraper antenna, *6314*

Mastoid operation, *5078*

Matzah made by machine, *3921*

Mayor of New York City who was African-American, *2212*

Measurement organization (national), *2449*

Mechanical engineering society (national), *3610*

Medical center devoted to teaching, treatment, and research, *3178*

Medical college founded as a Jewish institution, *3179*

Medical ethics book, *1892*
Medical journal, *4750*
Medical jurisprudence course at a college, *3134*
Medical licensing law enacted by a city, *4934*
Medical officer assigned to a naval vessel who was a woman, *5292*
Medicine advertisement in booklet form, *2318*
Mercantile library, *4666*
Mercury vapor lamp, *3496*
Methadone program, *2692*
Methodist preacher, *6557*
Metropolitan Opera orchestra conductor who was a woman, *1340*
Metropolitan Opera orchestra conductor who was African-American, *1339*
Metropolitan Opera singer who was African-American, *1338*
Micropaleontology course at a college, *3247*
Midwife to practice professionally, *4961*
Midwifery professor at a college, *3130*
Milk delivery in glass bottles, *3871*
Milk pasteurizing stations, *4204*
Milk sale regulations enacted by a city, *4205*
Millionaire with a fortune greater than $100 million, *2443*
Mineralogy journal, *4765*
Mines school at a college, *3236*
Minimum wage law established by a city for public contract work, *4580*
Minstrel show troupe, *3685*
Missionary training school, *3275*
Mobile computer center, *2531*
Mobile television unit, *7813*
Modern art exhibition, *1228*
Monkey trained to perform, *1139*
Monument to an American poet, *5402*
Motorboat magazine, *4789*
Motorboat pleasure craft, *6949*
Motorboat race under organized rules, *7216*
Motorcycle police, *4139*
Movie by a major company for an African-American audience, *5559*
Movie censorship board at the national level, *5540*
Movie entertainment shown on an airplane, *5514*
Movie exhibition, *5509*
Movie exhibition in a theater to a paying audience, *5511*
Movie in Esperanto, *5561*
Movie in Technicolor, *5555*
Movie photographed from an airplane, *5548*
Movie premiere festivities to be shown on television, *5517*
Movie premiered simultaneously in major cities throughout the world, *5520*
Movie recorded on film to be shown on a screen, *5510*
Movie sex shocker, *5553*

Movie showing the inside of a living heart, *4910*
Movie to premiere on television, *5518*
Movie trailer to be shown on television, *2343*
Movie with both sound and color, *5560*
Movie with scent, *5566*
Movie with sound recorded on the film, *5556*
Movie with sound to be released as a feature, *5557*
Municipal ferryboats, *6910*
Music book printed from type, *1935*
Music society for the protection of composers and song writers, *1286*
Music synthesizer powered by electricity, *1321*
Musical comedy to be shown on television, *1268*
Musical comedy written by African-Americans for African-American performers, *1256*
Musical comedy written for television, *1269*
Musical instrument capable of making any audible sound, *1326*
Musical to run for more than 3,000 performances, *1271*
Musical with an American theme and original score, *1252*
Musk ox, *1150*
Mutual life insurance company, *4544*
Nail machine, *7921*
Narcotics ban enacted by Congress, *2686*
National fencing league, *7281*
National labor congress, *4553*
Native American art exhibition, *1229*
Naturalization act enacted by Congress, *5862*
Nautical school established by a city, *3304*
Naval Reserve Nurse Corps nurse who was African-American, *5289*
Naval vessel equipped with a gyrostabilizer, *6929*
Navy chaplain who was Catholic, *5202*
Navy medical school, *3171*
Navy submarine contract, *6962*
Nazi death camp guard to be deported, *5880*
Neon advertising sign, *2350*
Neurasthenia book, *1919*
Neurological disease research institute, *5057*
Neurology textbook, *1915*
New York City Marathon, *7566*
New York Stock Exchange member who was African-American, *3834*
New York Stock Exchange seat owner of Chinese ancestry, *3837*
New York Stock Exchange seat owner who was a woman, *3833*
News dispatch by commercial telegraph, *5603*
News magazine featuring photographs, *4736*
News photographs of distinction, *5817*
Newsboy, *5648*
Newspaper advertisement across two columns, *2320*
Newspaper clipping bureau, *5625*

NEW YORK—New York—*continued*
Newspaper colored supplement, *5690*
Newspaper for African-American readers, *5664*
Newspaper for Jewish readers, *5663*
Newspaper index separately published, *5643*
Newspaper page set by linotype, *5793*
Newspaper premiums, *2325*
Newspaper printing plant to install electricity, *5792*
Newspaper rotogravure sections, *5692*
Newspaper syndicate, *5626*
Newspaper to store issues on microfilm, *4682*
Newspaper with a color page, *5689*
Newspaper with a full page of woodcut engravings, *5686*
Newsreel theater, *3707*
Night court, *2708*
Nobel Prize for physiology or medicine awarded to an American citizen, *1693*
Nudist organization, *7580*
Numerical system of insurance rating, *4514*
Nurse appointed to a college professorship, *5028*
Nursery school, *3072*
Nurses' training, *3133*
Nursing magazine, *4758*
Nursing society, *5040*
Obelisk to be brought to the United States, *5403*
Obstetrics book, *1900*
Ocean mail contracts, *5990*
Off-track betting operation, *3637*
Oil company, *3525*
Okapi, *1155*
One-way street, *6611*
Opera by an American composer, *1345*
Opera by an American composer to be performed at the Metropolitan Opera House, *1349*
Opera composed by a woman to be performed at the Metropolitan Opera House, *1348*
Opera of a serious nature, *1344*
Opera performed by a professional visiting troupe, *1342*
Opera prima donna who was African-American, *1333*
Opera produced at the Metropolitan Opera House, *1347*
Opera singer who was African-American to sing a white role, *1336*
Opera to be televised from the Metropolitan Opera House, *1353*
Opera written for television, *1354*
Ophthalmologist of note, *4972*
Ophthalmology clinic, *4846*
Opticians' journal, *4760*
Optometry courses at a college, *3153*
Optometry society (national), *5044*
Orchestra from the United States to make a European tour, *1363*

Orchestra in a theater, *1356*
Orchestra of international stature, *1358*
Organ school, *2907*
Organists' society (national), *1285*
Orphanage, *2137*
Orthodontia treatise, *1924*
Orthodox rabbi born in America to be ordained, *6488*
Orthopedic hospital, *4881*
Orthopedics chair at a college, *3143*
Outdoor scenes to be televised, *7829*
Paint ready-mixed, *7925*
Paired six-day bicycle race, *7195*
Panorama show, *3684*
Paper collar, *2285*
Paperback publisher, *1790*
Parachute jump from a balloon, *1580*
Parent-teacher assocation, *3226*
Parking meter enforcement division of a police department, *4149*
Passenger to circle the world on commercial airlines in less than 100 hours, *1477*
Passover seder to be shown on television, *6489*
Peace society, *5733*
Pediatric clinic, *4841*
Pediatrics book, *1920*
Pediatrics journal, *4756*
Pediatrics professor at a college, *3141*
Peep show using film in a vending machine, *3691*
Penny restaurant, *2460*
Pension fund for teachers, *4585*
Pensions paid by the federal government, *4583*
Performance by a British rock group, *1370*
Periodical index, *1771*
Permalloy, *7705*
Petroleum jelly, *4988*
Philology society (national), *6783*
Phonograph trade magazine, *4730*
Photoelectric cell, *3478*
Photoengraved magazine, *5786*
Photograph of a president in office, *6155*
Photographic type-composing machine, *5809*
Photographs used in surveying, *5810*
Photography book, *1986*
Photography magazine, *4719*
Photojournalist, *5618*
Phrenologist, *4969*
Physician who was a woman, *4971*
Physics association (national), *6789*
Physiology society (national), *5041*
Piggyback railroad operation, *6338*
Pilot licensed by the Aero Club of America who was a woman, *1596*
Pilot on a scheduled passenger line who was African-American, *1604*
Pilot to fire a gun from an airplane, *1608*
Pizzeria, *2462*
Plastic surgery professor at a college, *3156*
Plate glass produced on a large scale, *4042*

NEW YORK—New York—*continued*

Radio magazine, *4779*

Radio network for African-Americans, *6302*

Radio network program sponsored by commercial advertising, *2335*

Radio paging service, *7743*

Radio production course at a college, *2912*

Radio program simultaneously transmitted, *6280*

Radio receiver advertised, *6306*

Radio receiving contest, *6261*

Radio society, *6259*

Radio two-way broadcast from an airplane, *6273*

Radio variety show with a live studio audience, *6291*

Radium treatment for cancer, *5115*

Ragtime instruction book, *1941*

Railroad interlocking signal machine, *6424*

Railroad merger, *6331*

Railroad to be completely equipped with diesel-electric engines, *6344*

Railroad treatise, *2020*

Rap album to attract a mass audience, *1373*

Rapid-transit subway, *6411*

Ready-made clothing for children, *2273*

Rebellion of African-American slaves in a colony, *2241*

Reformatory for juvenile deliquents, *2817*

Refugee to arrive under the Refugee Relief Act of 1953, *5877*

Regatta, *7208*

Religion magazine printed in rotogravure, *4734*

Religious radio program broadcast by a husband and wife, *6596*

Religious service to be televised from a church, *6593*

Religious services to be shown on television, *6592*

Religious tract society (national), *6576*

Research society (national), *6793*

Retail store whose sales in one day exceeded $1 million, *2508*

Revolving gun turret for ships, *8106*

Rh factor discovery, *4835*

Rhinoceros, *1144*

Rhyming dictionary, *1803*

Rifle society (national), *7472*

Right-to-die society, *2840*

Rivet production, *2037*

Rock musical, *1272*

Rocket to break the sound barrier, *7018*

Roller coaster, *3621*

Roller coaster with a loop-the-loop, *3626*

Rotary printing press, *5777*

Rotary printing press with a continuous-roll feed, *5779*

Round-the-world commercial airplane service, *1416*

Round-the-world solo airplane flight, *1457*

Round-the-world telephone conversation, *7762*

Russian newspaper, *5681*

Russian Orthodox saint canonized in the United States, *6498*

Safe deposit vault, *2359*

Safety congress, *4184*

Safety pin, *4336*

Safety razor, *4056*

Saint Patrick's Day parade, *3651*

Salute fired by Great Britain in honor of an officer of the United States, *3976*

Salvation Army services, *6531*

Savings bank, *3759*

Savings bank with a deposit of half a billion dollars, *3781*

Savings group for children, *3769*

School for colonial children in America, *3038*

School nurses in public schools, *5027*

School of modern dance, *2908*

Science fiction course at a college, *3108*

Science fiction magazine, *4732*

Science journal, *4767*

Seagoing dredge with a hopper, *6884*

Secret service established in a colony, *4168*

Secretary of state, *6104*

Secretary of the treasury, *6103*

Self-service restaurant, *2458*

Senate journal, *4696*

Senate page who was African-American, *2636*

Serbian Orthodox cathedral, *6497*

Session of Congress, *2556*

Session of the House of Representatives, *2576*

Session of the Senate, *2624*

Settlement house in a poor city neighborhood, *2194*

Sewing machine equipped with a rocking treadle or double treadle, *4353*

Sex-change operation, *6832*

Sextuple newspaper printing press, *5795*

Sheep of the Karakul breed, *1086*

Sheet of souvenir postage stamps, *6065*

Ship from the United States sunk by a German submarine in World War II, *8048*

Ship-to-shore mobile telephone commercial service, *7739*

Ship-to-shore telecast, *7836*

Shoe pegging machine, *2302*

Shoot-the-chutes, *3624*

Sick-leave benefit funds for teachers, *4562*

Sightseeing bus, *5418*

Simultaneous radio broadcast on all three major networks, *6278*

Singer whose voice was broadcast over radio, *1330*

Singing telegram, *7708*

Single Tax League national conference, *7650*

Singles bar, *2466*

Sitcom television show, *7780*

Six-day bicycle race for women, *7186*

Skee-ball alley, *3627*

Skyscraper higher than 1,250 feet, *2100*
Skyscraper higher than 750 feet in height, *2099*
Skyscraper of bronze and glass, *2101*
Skywriting advertisement exhibition, *2334*
Skywriting advertisement written at night, *2337*
Sneakers, *2307*
Snow-melting apparatus, *2221*
Snow-melting apparatus using pipes embedded in the sidewalk, *2223*
Soap in liquid form, *4271*
Soap manufacturer to render fats in his plant, *4266*
Soccer player to score 12 points in one game, *7494*
Social organization for the hard of hearing (national), *5725*
Social register published, *1820*
Society of Automotive Engineers member who was a woman, *6794*
Soda water machine, *3844*
Solar energy battery, *3558*
Song popular in the Confederate States, *1381*
Soup company, *3946*
Spanish grammar, *1855*
Spanish newspaper, *5665*
Sparrows, *1164*
Sports book, *1994*
Sports event to be televised live, *7100*
Sports trainer to work professionally, *7548*
Spray can, *7939*
Squash tennis organization (national), *7500*
Squash tennis tournament, *7501*
Stamp auction, *6057*
Stamp collection society, *6056*
Stamped envelopes, *6053*
Statue presented to the United States by a foreign country, *5405*
Steam distribution plant, *3507*
Steam-propelled ferryboat, *6907*
Steam-propelled frigate, *6916*
Steamboat service to California around Cape Horn, *6883*
Steamboat to make an ocean voyage, *6862*
Steamship passenger line between American and European ports, *6882*
Steel-frame residence, *2082*
Stenotype device, *2361*
Stereo telecast, *7857*
Stereotyped book, *1743*
Stock brokerage concern of importance whose president was a woman, *3830*
Stock brokerage concern to use a telegraph ticker, *3817*
Stock exchange, *3812*
Stock exchange at which more than a million shares were traded in one day, *3820*
Stock exchange director who was a woman, *3831*
Stock quotation boards, *3821*

Stockholder meetings televised coast-to-coast simultaneously, *3832*
Stone pavement, *6608*
Street gangs, *2770*
Streetcar, *6394*
Streetcar company, *6393*
Strike by physicians against long working hours in hospitals, *4602*
Strike by workers, *4589*
Strike of postal employees, *4601*
Stuntman, *3680*
Submarine that was practical and submersible, *6964*
Subway, *6409*
Subway car with side doors, *6412*
Subway train to run automatically without conductors or motormen, *6413*
Sugar and glucose from cornstarch, *3961*
Suicidal person to jump off the Empire State Building and live, *2844*
Suits for men made of Dacron, *2279*
Sunday comics section in a newspaper, *5688*
Supreme Court of the United States, *2742*
Surgery manual, *1893*
Surgical elevation of the skull to treat epilepsy, *5082*
Surgical operation televised on a closed circuit, *5083*
Suspension bridge with steel towers, *3588*
Swedish magazine, *4747*
Swimmer who was an American woman to swim the English Channel, *7518*
Sword swallower, *3656*
Symphonic work to require an airplane propeller, *1296*
Symphony orchestra devoted exclusively to radio broadcasting, *1365*
Talking book for blind listeners, *2029*
Tariff legislation enacted by Congress, *7663*
Tattoo shop, *4053*
Tattooed man exhibited as a theatrical attraction, *3661*
Teddy bear, *2145*
Telecast from a submerged submarine, *7838*
Telecast originating live in three countries, *7846*
Telecast received from England, *7851*
Telecast using coaxial cable, *7833*
Telegraph cable, *7688*
Telegraph call boxes, *7701*
Telegraph company, *7695*
Telegraph message sent around the world by commercial telegraph, *7704*
Telegraph system, *7685*
Telegraph ticker to print letters of the alphabet, *7691*
Telephone concert held long-distance, *1291*
Telephone switchboard with Braille markings, *7738*

NEW YORK—New York—*continued*

Television camera lens to provide zoom effects, *7815*

Television commercial, *2341*

Television commercial in color to appear on a local show, *2346*

Television drama program regularly scheduled, *7778*

Television eyewitness allowed to testify in a federal court, *2715*

Television image using a split screen, *7816*

Television magazine, *4781*

Television network evening news program anchor who was a woman, *5621*

Television news commentator who was African-American, *5620*

Television newsmagazine, *5708*

Television production course at a college, *2913*

Television program in color, *7784*

Television receiver that showed two programs simultaneously, *7819*

Television show to be sponsored by a commercial advertiser, *2344*

Television variety talent show series, *7776*

Tenement house, *2124*

Tennis champion who was African-American, *7538*

Tennis society (national), *7525*

Tennis tournament of national scope, *7526*

Terra cotta, *2056*

Test for newborn health, *2165*

Theater built and named for a living actress, *3706*

Theater designed and built for the rear projection of movies, *3708*

Theater history, *1870*

Theater lighted by gas, *3697*

Theater ticket agency, *3700*

Theater ticket scalpers, *3698*

Theater to employ women as ushers, *3702*

Theatrical presentation sponsored by the federal government, *1263*

Theory of fair division, *6762*

Theosophical society, *5743*

Three-dimensional feature movie, *5563*

Three-dimensional feature movie in color, *5564*

Ticker-tape shower for a celebrity, *3666*

Tightrope performer who was a woman, *3657*

Tightrope walker to span two skyscrapers, *3669*

Tin can with a key opener, *4284*

Toilet paper, *5756*

Tourist guide for train travelers, *2024*

Tourist guide with train schedules, *2025*

Toy distribution center, *2138*

Trade school for girls, *3291*

Trade tokens, *5358*

Trading ship sent to China, *6879*

Traffic law enacted by a colony, *4216*

Traffic police squad, *4135*

Train of airplanes, *1459*

Traitor to the American cause during the Revolutionary War, *7998*

Transatlantic crossing attempted by a balloon, *1538*

Transatlantic mobile telephone call between two cars, *7765*

Transatlantic passenger line, *2477*

Transatlantic radio fax of a check, *3794*

Transatlantic radio fax of a drawing, *5694*

Transatlantic round-trip airplane flight from the United States, *1461*

Transatlantic steamboat service, *6881*

Transatlantic telephone call carried by the transoceanic telephone cable, *7767*

Transatlantic telephone service using the transoceanic cable, *7747*

Transatlantic trip by rowboat, *6985*

Transcontinental car race, *7266*

Transcontinental car trip by women, *5472*

Transcontinental daily air-rail passenger service, *1411*

Transcontinental demonstration of radio telephone operation, *7721*

Transcontinental express bus service, *5423*

Transcontinental journey on foot, *7589*

Transcontinental motorcycle trip by women, *5493*

Transcontinental Picturephone call, *7769*

Transcontinental Pullman sleeping car daily service, *6345*

Transcontinental regular airmail service, *6019*

Transcontinental telecast received on the West Coast, *7841*

Transcontinental telephone demonstration, *7718*

Transcontinental trip in a gas-turbine car, *5476*

Transoceanic newspaper, *5657*

Trial in which freedom of the press was upheld, *5633*

Triode for radios, *6307*

Troops from the United States to sail to Europe in World War I, *8033*

Trust company, *3761*

Tuberculosis laboratory established by a city, *4199*

Tuberculosis vaccine, *4921*

Tugboat powered by steam, *6880*

Turkish bath, *4194*

Twelve-step rehabilitation program, *2662*

Two-way radio conversation between a submerged submarine and another vessel, *7760*

Typesetting machine, *5804*

Typewriter to produce a line of writing visible as it was being typed, *2388*

Typewriting primer, *1829*

Typing school, *3289*

Ukrainian daily newspaper, *5683*

Underwater highway tunnel with twin tubes, *3618*

Underwater telegraph cable that was practical, *7693*

United Nations delegate who was African-American, *3992*

United Nations permanent ambassador who was a woman, *3993*

United Nations postage stamps in U.S. denominations, *6068*

United Nations Security Council resolution vetoed by the United States, *3981*

Universal chapel embracing eight faiths, *6437*

V-mail film, *6012*

Vacation fund to send poor children to the country, *2139*

Valentines commercially produced, *4235*

Vasectomy outpatient service, *4851*

Vedanta Center, *6601*

Vending machine for art, *2401*

Vending machine to dispense fresh flowers, *2400*

Veterinary college of importance, *3181*

Veterinary hospital, *5119*

Vice presidential candidate who was African-American, *3406*

Vichyssoise, *3880*

Video recording on magnetic tape televised coast-to-coast, *7847*

Visiting nurses, *5025*

Vulcanized rubber, *4486*

Warship propelled by electricity, *6932*

Washington news correspondent, *5611*

Water cures, *5112*

Waxworks museum, *5575*

Weather forecasting service by telephone, *6772*

Wedding during a parachute jump, *4822*

Welsh magazine, *4743*

Western series on television, *7779*

Woman to sell securities on the floor of the New York Curb Exchange, *3828*

Women's hospital, *4880*

Women's professional club, *5723*

Wood engraving made with an engraving tool, *1226*

Workers' compensation agreement, *4550*

Workers' library, *4665*

World heavyweight boxing champion to regain his crown, *7255*

World Series baseball game that was a shutout, *7124*

World Series baseball game to be shown on television, *7135*

World Series baseball games to gross $1 million, *7129*

World tour by a woman traveling alone, *6983*

World's fair, *2409*

Worldwide live television program, *7856*

Writer to win a Pulitzer Prize four times for drama, *1716*

Writer to win the Pulitzer Prize in both fiction and poetry, *1714*

Writer whose livelihood was obtained exclusively by writing, *2032*

X-ray machine exhibited in the United States, *3664*

X-ray movies of human organs in action, *4908*

X-ray of the entire body of a living person made in a single exposure, *4905*

Yacht from the United States to win an international yacht race, *7209*

Yeshivah for Jewish religious study, *3276*

Yiddish newspaper, *5670*

Yiddish professorship at a college, *3119*

Yiddish theater performance, *1255*

Young Men's Hebrew Association, *5714*

Young Women's Hebrew Association, *5715*

Zionist organization (national), *6487*

Zoning ordinance, *2205*

Newburgh

Botanist to become a prominent landscape gardener, *6741*

Cakes of soap of uniform weight and individually wrapped, *4268*

Double-deck ferryboat, *6909*

Ice skating champion, *7427*

Steel-hulled ferryboat, *6908*

Newhouseville

Fax transmission by a press syndicate direct to newspaper offices, *5627*

Newport

Pin-tumbler cylinder lock, *2133*

Newton Creek

Kerosene, *3527*

Niagara County

Fruit spraying, *1019*

Niagara Falls

Airplane flight under a bridge, *1437*

Daredevil to cross Niagara Falls on a tightrope, *3677*

Daredevil to go over Niagara Falls in a barrel, *3679*

Daredevil to go over Niagara Falls in a rubber ball, *3681*

Electricity generated by Niagara Falls waterpower, *3456*

King of Great Britain to visit the United States, *6652*

Photograph to gain world fame, *5814*

NEW YORK—Niagara Falls—*continued*

Railroad suspension bridge, *3580*

Two-handed shovel, *7940*

Utilization of Niagara Falls waterpower for industrial purposes, *4379*

North Elba

Bobsled run, *7581*

Norwich

Condensed milk, *3869*

Meat biscuit, *3920*

Olean

Natural gas for manufacturing, *3514*

Oneida

Steel animal traps commercially manufactured, *7922*

Oneida County

Fur-bearing animals raised commercially, *1070*

Ossining

Execution carried out by the federal government for the killing of an FBI agent, *2804*

Execution of an organized crime leader in the electric chair, *2803*

Peacetime death sentence for espionage, *2836*

State prison to take fingerprints, *4159*

Oswego

Screw-propelled steamboat on the Great Lakes, *6869*

Teacher training school at which students conducted practice classes, *3263*

Pearl River

Broad-spectrum antibiotic, *5000*

Catgut substitute, *4958*

Peekskill

Car hill-climbing contest, *7262*

First aid instruction, *4122*

Pelham Manor

Stained-glass window, *4039*

Plattsburg

College principally for war veterans, *2967*

Plattsburgh

Physiologist of note, *4967*

Pleasantville

Distinguished Service Cross awarded to an animal, *1664*

Poplar Ridge

Plow with interchangeable parts, *1042*

Port Chester

Frozen bread, *3929*

Port Washington

Seaplane glider, *1550*

Train operated exclusively by women, *6436*

Transatlantic airmail service, *6028*

Transatlantic commercial airplane service, *1415*

Poughkeepsie

Baseball teams for women, *7161*

Candy packaged in a factory, *3963*

Ice yacht, *7205*

Ice yacht club, *7210*

Medical insurance group policy for college students, *4537*

Pins manufactured with a solid head, *4351*

Richford

Billionaire, *2445*

Riverdale

Motorcycle hill-climbing contest, *7438*

Rochester

Business school, *2917*

Camera to use film rolls, *5837*

Car patent, *5428*

Card time recorder, *2383*

Check protectors, *3790*

Color film, *5844*

Communion cups for individuals, *6582*

Community chorus, *1361*

Copy machine, *2374*

Electrobasograph, *4949*

Filmpack camera, *5839*

Food stamps, *4086*

Goat show, *1073*

Infrared photograph, *5827*

Installment finance company, *3805*

Mail chute, *6000*

Milk station operated by a city government, *4206*

Photograph taken from an airplane at night, *5824*

Photographic copying machine, *2370*

Presidential nominee who was African-American, *3409*

Printed streetcar transfers, *6402*

Railroad tank car lined with glass, *6385*

Social-Democratic Party of America national convention, *3369*

Temperance society for women (state), *2677*

Transparent paper-strip photographic film, *5836*

Typesetting machine to dispense with metal type, *5808*

Vending machine to operate automatically, *2395*

X-ray photograph of the entire body of a living person taken in a one-second exposure, *4906*

X-ray photograph showing the complete arterial circulation in an adult human, *4907*

Rockaway

Transatlantic hydroplane flight made in stages, *1445*

Rockville Center

Bank to install an automatic teller, *3799*

Rocky Point

Transatlantic commercial telephone service, *7737*

Rome

Cheese factory of consequence, *3859*

Roosevelt Field

Stowaway on an aircraft, *1518*

Transatlantic solo airplane flight, *1450*

Transcontinental nonstop airplane flight, *1449*

Transcontinental solo airplane flight by a woman, *1453*

Rye

Tennis tournament to be shown on television, *7533*

Sackets Harbor

Chloroform, *4985*

Glucose from potato starch, *3957*

St. Regis

Prisoners captured in the War of 1812, *8022*

Saranac Lake

Tuberculosis research laboratory, *4929*

Tuberculosis sanatorium using modern treatment methods, *4899*

Saratoga

Banking association (national), *3768*

Economics association, *6788*

Intercollegiate athletic association, *7545*

Intercollegiate track meet, *7546*

Lawyers' society (national), *4644*

Saratoga Springs

Potato chips, *3960*

Schenectady

Air brake, *6420*

Automaton to operate by long-distance control, *3442*

College radio station, *6295*

Diathermy machine, *4948*

Drama broadcast on radio, *1257*

Drama school at a college, *2910*

Ductile tungsten, *5341*

Duplex compound locomotive, *6362*

Fluorescent lamp, *3500*

Glass that was nonreflecting, *4049*

Golf club with a steel shaft, *7353*

High-jump standards using electric eye detectors, *7561*

Industrial research laboratory, *4377*

Locomotive communications headlight, *6427*

Microscope with a radiation block, *6803*

Opera to be televised in its entirety, *1352*

Photograph of a beam of 1-billion-volt x-rays, *5829*

Photographic flashbulbs, *5842*

Play to be shown on television, *1260*

Radio broadcast heard in both the Arctic and the Antarctic regions, *6277*

Radio tube made of metal, *6311*

Round-the-world radio broadcast, *6275*

Social fraternity at a college, *2984*

Sodium vapor lamps, *3499*

Speaker to address an organization by television, *7831*

Stroboradiograph, *6808*

Television programs to be shown regularly, *7774*

Television sets to be installed in homes on an experimental basis, *7810*

Schuylerville

National day of thanksgiving, *4260*

NEW YORK—*continued*
Sea Cliff

American to sail to Europe to fight in World War I, *8025*

Seneca Falls

Bloomers, *2267*
Voting rights convention organized by women, *3425*

Sheepshead Bay

Radio broadcast sent from an airplane, *6266*
Transcontinental airplane flight made in stages, *1439*

Sloatsburg

Cotton twine factory, *4335*

South Butler

Minister who was a woman, *6530*

Southampton

Golf player in an official amateur tournament who was African-American, *7355*
International golf match, *7346*
Whaling industry established by a city, *2417*

Stony Point

Medal awarded by the Continental Congress to a foreigner, *1650*
Revolutionary War bayonet charge, *8003*

Suffern

Avon Lady, *4057*

Suffolk County

Hunting license required by a state, *7425*

Syracuse

Billiard match, *4016*
Citizenship and public affairs school at a college, *3255*
Dental chair, *4859*
Dial time recorder, *2382*
Electric portable typewriter, *2390*
Hambletonian harness horse race for three-year-olds, *7398*
Plank road, *6618*
Presbyterian minister who was a woman, *6584*

Ticonderoga

Graphite, *5328*

Tonawanda Reservation

American woman of European descent to be made a Native American chief, *6647*

Troy

Boy Scouts of America uniformed troop, *2149*
Collar factory, *2284*
Collar manufacturer, *2283*
Detachable collar, *2282*
Engineering college, *3233*
Horseshoe manufacturing machine, *1178*
Laundry, *2438*
Paper for printing made from rags and wood-pulp fiber, *5753*
Professional fraternity at a college, *2987*
Waffle iron patent, *4294*

Tupper Lake

Sermon preached from an airplane by radio, *6591*

Tuxedo Park

Building of pressed structural steel, *2086*
Outdoor museum with nature trails, *5585*
Tuxedo coat, *2272*

Uniondale

Goalie in a National Hockey League team to score a goal, *7382*

Upton

Nuclear reactor used in medical therapy, *5061*

Utica

Electric power line commercial carrier, *3476*
Five-cent store, *2496*
Fly casting tournament, *7285*
State nominating convention, *3315*

Waddington

Explosion of Thermit to break up ice jams, *4425*

Wallkill

Creamery for commercial production, *3854*

Warsaw

Liberty Party convention, *3351*

Watertown

Biscuits of shredded wheat, *3924*

Watervliet

Conscientious objectors, *5217*
Shaker religious community, *6521*

West Albany

Locomotive to attain a proven speed of 112.5 miles per hour, *6361*

West Hempstead

Lottery in which the top prize was $1 million, *3643*

West Milton

Electric power generated from nuclear energy to be sold commercially, *3548*

West Point

Army academy, *3194*
Blockade of enemy ships, *8001*
Intercollegiate Army–Navy football game, *7320*
Mechanics textbook, *1988*
Movie for training soldiers, *3203*
Seacoast gun carriage, *8102*
West Point cadet who was a woman to graduate at the top of her class, *3208*
West Point cadets who were women, *3207*
West Point graduate who was African-American, *3199*
West Point graduate who was Jewish, *3195*
West Point graduate who was Native American, *3198*
West Point graduates, *3196*
West Point graduates who were Chinese nationals, *3201*
West Point instructor who was a woman, *3205*

Westbury

Amateur golf championship tournament for women, *7342*

Westchester

Telephone directory with internet addresses, *1821*

White Plains

Freeze-dried coffee, *3853*

Yonkers

Amateur golf tournament, *7339*
Golf mixed foursome, *7354*
Thermosetting resin, *4440*

NORTH CAROLINA

Governor to be impeached and convicted, *7615*
Independent civil government in America, *5939*
National seashore, *3738*
Nurses to be registered by a state, *4938*
State denied admission into the Union, *7601*
Wolf to be reintroduced into the wild, *3750*
Written constitution adopted by a community of American-born freemen, *1100*

Asheville

Forest management on a professional scale, *3725*
Tuberculosis sanatorium, *4898*

Cabarrus County

Gold nugget, *5320*

Cape Hatteras

Radio distress signal resulting in an airship rescue, *6288*
Radio SOS call from an American ship, *6287*
Smokescreen for concealing the movement of troops and ships, *5247*

Chapel Hill

English grammar instruction at a college, *3113*
Marriage course at a college, *3103*
Observatory operated by a college, *6664*

Charlotte

Balloon flight powered by solar energy, *1542*
Civil rights sit-in, *2260*
Jewish mobile synagogue, *6491*
Teletypesetter circuit operated by a news agency, *5628*
Video recording on magnetic tape televised in color, *7850*

Davidson

X-ray photograph, *4904*

Fort Bragg

Army helicopter battalion, *5191*

Gastonia

Factory cooled by air conditioning, *4385*
Greek Orthodox college and orphanage, *3279*

Halifax

Declaration of independence by a colonial government, *1112*

NORTH CAROLINA—continued

Hatteras

Naval vessel from the United States to sink a German submarine in World War II, *8054*

Hatteras Island

Confederate forts to surrender in the Civil War, *7958*

Kill Devil Hills

Airplane flight, *1426*

Kinston

Billiard player to win a match in the first inning, *4020*

Lexington

Silver mine, *5327*

Manteo

First-day special cancellation of a postage stamp, *6067*

Newberne

Revolving gun, *8093*

Pamlico Sound

Union ship captured in the Civil War, *7960*

Pinehurst

Golfer to earn $100,000 in a contest, *7367*

Raleigh

Birth control clinic run by a state government, *4847*
Building with its roof supported by cables, *2092*
Magazine for and by deaf students, *4720*
Nuclear engineering course at a college, *3248*
Nuclear reactor privately operated, *6804*
School for blind African-American students, *3026*
Television station to regularly broadcast high-definition television, *7808*

Reidsville

Air Force ace in Vietnam, *1624*

Roanoke Island

Artist in the English colonies, *1196*

Beer, *2663*
Child born of English parents in America, *2156*
Letters written in English in America, *1095*
Native American to become a Protestant, *6502*
Surveyor in America, *5902*

Salem

Cottonseed hulling machine, *1031*

Spray

Acetylene gas, *4437*
Carbide factory, *4438*

Union County

President born after the death of his father, *6182*

Washington

Town named for George Washington, *2186*

NORTH DAKOTA

Bonding law enacted by a state, *4524*
Fire and tornado insurance fund enacted by a state, *4533*
Hail insurance law enacted by a state, *4515*
States admitted to the Union simultaneously, *7606*

Bismarck

Bank wholly owned and operated by a state, *3779*

Buelah

Synthetic fuels plant, *3522*

Devil's Lake

Clothes dryer, *4278*

Esmond

State speaker of the House who was a woman, *7628*

Minot

Pilot of a B-52 bomber who was a woman, *1626*

Portal

Absolute monarch to visit the United States, *6650*

OHIO

Battle fought by federal troops after the formation of the Union, *5144*
Coal pipeline, *3509*
Court-martial at which the judges included enlisted men, *2740*
Employment service established by a state, *4565*
History of African-Americans, *1871*
Land set-aside for schools authorized by the Continental Congress, *3051*
Land subsidy by Congress for road improvements, *6615*
Mother and son simultaneously elected to Congress, *2613*
Presidential candidate to make campaign speeches in a foreign language, *3408*
Presidential election in which votes were tallied electronically, *3395*
Sale of federal land to an individual, *5950*
Senator who had been an astronaut, *2660*
Telephone company answering service, *7744*
Trailer church, *6534*
Train robbery of a train in motion, *2776*
Working hours of women to be regulated by a state, *4555*

Akron

Airship to land on a roof, *1517*
Airship with an enclosed cabin, *1522*
Balloon tire production, *5501*
Clincher tire, *5496*
Cord tires, *5498*
Glider pilot's license, *1598*
Nonskid tires, *5500*
Oat-crushing machine, *3914*
Police patrol wagon, *4137*
Synthetic rubber tires, *5502*
Tubeless car tires, *5503*

Alliance

College summer school, *2993*

Ashtabula

Election using proportional representation, *3321*

Athens

Land grant university, *2940*

Barberton

Matchbooks, *4337*

Bellefontaine

Concrete road, *6622*

Canton

Football game in which referees were allowed to check television instant replays, *7336*
Professional football association, *7305*

Chillicothe

Book completed entirely by one man, *1754*
Cattle that were purebred shorthorns, *1080*

Cincinnati

Ambulance service for hospitals, *4823*
Anarchist, *4551*
Apprentice continuation school, *3293*
Astronomy magazine, *4770*
Bar code scanner, *2373*
Baseball game at night by major league teams, *7131*
Baseball players to hit home runs, *7141*
Baseball team whose players received a regular salary, *7162*
Battery to convert radioactive energy into electrical energy, *3488*
Caterpillar Club member who was a woman, *1586*
Clay pigeon target for trapshooting, *7474*
Dentist who was a woman to obtain a D.D.S. degree, *4862*
Extinction by humans of a native American animal, *3746*
Fire department to be paid a salary, *4103*
Fire engine that was practical, *4102*
Floating soap, *4055*
Forestry book, *1990*
High school night classes, *3082*
Hydrogenated vegetable shortening, *3885*
Liberal Republican convention, *3358*
Mail delivery car with the steering wheel on the right, *5454*
Miniature car, *5448*
Musical comedy broadcast on radio, *1264*
National manufacturing assocation, *4376*
National political convention to be addressed by a woman, *3336*
Peep show machine, *3686*
People's Party national convention, *3366*
Phonetic dictionary, *1806*
Rabbinical college for the Reform Jewish movement, *3274*
Radio license, *6293*
Railroad chapel car, *6381*
Railroad owned by a city, *6335*
Synthetic laundry detergent, *4279*
Toothpaste with fluoride, *4075*
Tuberculosis hospital for the poor established by a city, *4900*
Union Labor Party convention, *3364*
United Labor Party convention, *3365*
Wedding in a balloon, *4814*

OHIO—*continued*

Cleveland

Airplane flight over water, *1432*
Airship passenger transfer to an airplane, *1525*
Aluminum streetcar, *6407*
Animal humane society (national), *5738*
Automatic pilot on an airplane, *1499*
Automatic traffic light, *4225*
Baseball player who was African-American to hit a home run in a World Series, *7152*
Baseball player who was Native American, *7143*
Brick pavement on a rural road, *6623*
Car advertisement in a specialty magazine, *2331*
Community trust charity, *5742*
Dutch elm disease breakout, *3731*
Electric arc streetlights, *2215*
Electric traffic signal lights, *4224*
Fireworks law enacted by a city, *4111*
Fluorescent paint, *7938*
Fund-raising organization to sell stamps, *5734*
Health museum, *5590*
Heart operation for the relief of angina pectoris, *5091*
Heart operation in which the elective cardiac arrest technique was employed, *5094*
Ice cream cone rolling machine, *3868*
Judge to impose the death penalty who was a woman, *2722*
Kindergarten for children with disabilities, *3018*
Mail truck, *6003*
Major league baseball player to make seven consecutive hits in seven times at bat in the same game, *7156*
Mayor of a major city who was African-American, *2209*
Multigraph, *2367*
National Union for Social Justice national convention, *3377*
Paint prepared from standard formulas, *7930*
Political convention to be broadcast on radio, *3340*
School radio station on ultrahigh frequency, *6298*
State supreme court justice who was a woman, *2723*
Submachine gun, *8115*
Superconducting motor, *6810*
Temperance society for women (national), *2678*
Truck completely streamlined, *5506*
Unassisted triple play in a major league baseball game, *7126*
Unassisted triple play in a World Series baseball game, *7127*
Union Party convention, *3378*
Universal constant in physics to be measured by American scientists, *6812*
Valeteria, *2398*

Clyde

Navy officer killed in action in the Spanish-American War, *8008*

Columbus

Ace of Aces from the United States, *1611*
Ceramics school, *2906*
Gorilla, *1159*
Junior high school, *3087*
Labor Reform Party national convention, *3357*
Metric distance markers on a state highway, *6636*
Ornithopter that succeeded in flying, *1407*
Presidential candidate to make a campaign speech, *3402*
Shipment of merchandise by airplane, *2485*
State school for blind students, *3024*

Dayton

Airplane purchased by the federal government, *1389*
Cash register, *2363*
Ethyl gasoline to be marketed, *3538*
Fighter plane equipped with a cannon, *1487*
Hydrogen-cooled turbine generator, *3483*
Parachute known as the "free parachute", *1583*
Pilot to bail out of a disabled airplane, *1585*
Postage stamp with fluorescent tagging, *6071*
Pressure suit, *1386*
Soapbox derby, *7583*

Gambier

Tintype camera, *5834*

Greene County

State legislator who was African-American to represent a constituency with a white majority, *7625*

Jacobsburg

Hybrid seed corn shipment, *1022*

Kent

Forestry school operated privately, *3077*

Kings Mills

Shot tower, *8112*

Kirtland

Mormon temple, *6493*

Lima

Tank with a turbine engine, *8122*

Mansfield

Electronic range for domestic use, *4303*

Marblehead

Lifesaving medal awarded by the Treasury Department, *1653*

Marietta

Photograph of a lightning flash, *6696*

Milford

Police chief who was a woman, *4142*

Monroeville

Monument to commemorate the Spanish-American War, *5408*

Mount Pleasant

Abolition newspaper, *5637*

Nela Park

Electric light bulb frosted on the inside, *3498*

New Concord

Presidential candidate who had been an astronaut, *3418*

Newark

Fiberglass, *4052*

North Bend

Train robbery of a disabled train, *2774*

Oberlin

Aluminum pots, *4297*
Anti-saloon organization, *2680*
College graduate who was an African-American woman, *3010*
College to enroll women and men on equal terms, *2943*

Oxford

Beehive with removable frames, *1050*

Port Bucyrus

Airport manager who was a woman, *1507*

Put-in-Bay

Defeat of a British naval squadron in the War of 1812, *8024*

Ridgeway

Serviceman killed during the Bosnia conflict, *7983*

Riverside

Compressed fresh yeast, *3935*

Schoenbrunn

Protestant church west of the Alleghenies, *6519*

Solon

National skeet tournament, *7479*

Springfield

Baby show, *2141*
Bellows, *4395*

Steubenville

District land office, *5953*

Toledo

Airplane propeller blade of hollow steel, *1502*
All-glass windowless structure, *2089*
Automatic computing pendulum scale, *2380*
Balloon to land on a building, *1540*
Bowler to make a perfect score of 300, *7224*
Dress made of spun glass, *2274*
Funeral home operated on the cooperative plan, *2839*
Glass-blowing machine, *4044*
Major league baseball player who was African-American, *7142*
Officer killed in action in the Korean War, *7978*
Paint-spraying device, *7936*
Rectangular television tube, *7817*
Television receivers to project large images, *7820*

Toronto

Titanium mill, *4478*

Van Wert

County library, *4673*

Wilmington

Airplane human pickup, *1463*

Worthington

Catholic seminary under the supervision of the Pope, *3277*

OHIO—*continued*

Xenia

Cartridge-loading machinery, *8110*

Yellow Springs

College professor who was a woman, *2947*
Physiology and hygiene courses at a liberal arts college, *3140*

Zanesville

Bridge in a Y shape, *3569*
Stone breaking machine, *5324*

OKLAHOMA

Artificial insemination for women to be permitted by a state, *5117*
Lethal injection as a method of execution, *2805*
Oil and gas conservation law enacted by a state, *3537*

Duncan

Ambassador to the United Nations who was a woman, *3996*

El Reno

Church organized by Native Americans, *6603*
Distinguished Service Cross awarded in enemy-occupied territory, *1660*

Elk City

Community hospital, *4892*

Kingfisher

Wal-Mart store, *2514*

Oklahoma City

Automatic parking meter, *5446*
Bombing by domestic terrorists resulting in large loss of life, *2791*
Esperanto magazine, *4749*
Gas turbine used by an electrical utility company, *3487*
Mayor of a major city who was a woman, *2210*
Shopping cart, *2371*
Traveling cancer clinic, *4849*

Prague

Olympic athlete from the United States to win the pentathlon and decathlon, *7554*

Shawnee

Airplane flight to land at the North Pole, *6731*
Discovery of the North Pole, *6727*
Sergeant major of the Army, *5174*

Tahlequah

Principal chief of the Cherokee Nation who was a woman, *4085*

OREGON

Exploration by ship of the mouth of the Columbia River, *5949*
Gasoline tax levied by a state, *7655*
Husband and wife to be elected simultaneously to both chambers of a state legislature, *7632*
Litter law enacted by a state, *3720*
Paper money issued by the Native Americans, *5383*

Albany

Molybdenum centrifugal casting, *4479*

Beaverton

Cloning of a primate from an embryo, *6754*

Champoeg

Government on the Pacific Coast, *5963*

Lakeview

American civilians killed in the continental United States in World War II, *8084*

Oregon City

Hydroelectric power plant generating alternating current to operate over a long distance, *3466*
Newspaper published on the Pacific Coast, *5640*

Portland

Airplane takeoff from a hotel roof, *1442*
Commercial television station on ultrahigh frequency, *7800*
Plywood, *2049*
Ship completed in less than two weeks, *6878*
Swimsuit, *2277*
Victory ship launched, *6896*

Salem

State library to publish a master catalog, *4679*
University on the Pacific Coast, *2948*

PENNSYLVANIA

Agricultural college to be chartered by a state, *2891*
Child labor law enacted by a state that restricted the age of the worker, *4575*
Congressional representative who was Catholic, *2597*
Congressional representative who was Jewish, *2598*
Death penalty ban by a state, *2796*
Electoral vote cast contrary to instructions, *3382*
English patent granted to a resident of America, *4647*
Flag Day, *4240*
Governor of a state who had also been governor of a territory, *7614*
Inheritance tax enacted by a state, *7645*
Liquor stores run by a state government, *2505*
Locomotive to attain a speed of one mile in less than a minute, *6359*
Movie censorship board established by a state, *5541*
Natural gas pipeline constructed over a long distance, *3516*
Organs, *1303*
Printed ballot, *3314*
Railroad for freight transportation, *6316*
Rhodes Scholars, *2961*
Senate election in which neither candidate was seated after a recount, *2630*
Senate election that was contested, *3327*
Sex discrimination law enacted by a state that affected high school athletic competitions, *6840*
Speaker of the House, *2578*
Telephone with push buttons, *7726*

Allentown

Cement, *2044*
Homeopathy school, *3161*
Transistors produced commercially for a specific product, *3441*

Altoona

Railroad rails of steel, *6419*
Steel railroad passenger coach, *6382*

Amesland

Colonial law for the maintenance of an insane patient, *4171*

Ardmore

Car with a circulating lubrication system, *5437*
Shaft-driven car, *5435*

Auburn

Tunnel, *3611*

Avondale

Coal mine disaster, *3506*

Bedford

Truck driving school, *3300*

Bethlehem

Cottonseed oil, *3881*
Horse grooming products sold for human use, *4064*
Moravian settlement in America, *6540*
Oil drill seagoing rig, *3543*
Orchestra, *1355*
Postage stamps of four different designs sold as a single sheet, *6096*
Tax rebellion, *5952*
Trombone, *1306*
Vacuum-cast steel, *4498*
Water pumping plant, *2225*
Zinc commercial production, *5330*
Zinc sheet mill, *4470*

Braddock

Steel mill to install an electrical machine, *4494*

Brookville

Caterpillar Club members who were father and son, *1587*

Brownsville

Bridge of cast iron, *3572*

Bryn Mawr

Biology course offered at a college, *3240*
Dean of the faculty at a college, *2972*
Graduate school for women, *2955*
Student government at a college, *3013*

Butler

General purpose military vehicle, *5248*

Carbon County

Anthracite coal, *3502*

Carbondale

Locomotive for railroad use, *6348*

PENNSYLVANIA—*continued*

Carlisle

Christmas savings club at a bank, *3793*
Declaration of independence by citizens of an American colony, *1110*
School of prominence for Native American children, *3065*

Chambersburg

Straw paper, *5751*

Chester

Air Force chief master sergeant who was African-American, *5137*
All-welded self-propelled seagoing petroleum carrier ship, *6892*
Commercial ship to conquer the Northwest Passage, *7000*
Iron rolling mill, *4449*
Iron sloop yacht, *6872*
Merchant ship formally blessed at a launching ceremony, *6893*
Naval ship with a mixed company of male and female personnel, *6937*
Passenger ship with a diesel engine, *6877*

Chester County

Botany book by an American-born author, *1979*
College for African-American students, *2949*
Heating stove, *4331*

Coalport

Coal miner who was a woman to be killed in a mining accident, *3510*

Coatesville

Boiler plates, *4430*

Columbia

Newspaper vending machine to deliver a single copy, *2399*

Danville

Lithuanian settlement, *5971*

Delta

Slate used for roofing material, *2035*

Donora

Deaths from smog, *3715*

Downington

Apple parer, *4367*

Dusboro

Iron casting, *4448*

East Pittsburgh

Elevator with two cars, *2111*

Easton

Civil rights chair at a college, *3128*
Comparative philology chair at a college, *3115*
Model laboratory school at a college, *3259*
Soldering gun, *7941*

Eddystone

Heavy tank, *8120*

Emporium

Illegal television station, *7798*

Ensfield

Sugar beets, *3901*

Ephrata

Communistic settlement with a religious basis, *2182*

Erie

Gas-turbine-electric locomotive, *6368*
Iron vessel built for the Navy, *6917*

Essington

Lutheran church, *6555*

Fairmount

Wire suspension bridge for general traffic, *3576*

Falkner Swamp

Reformed Church meeting, *6516*

Fayette County

Iron mill to puddle and roll iron, *4450*

Fleetwood

Air raid shelter, *4088*

Frankford

Building and loan association, *3763*

Germantown

Bible printed in German, *1961*
Brethren, *6545*
German magazine, *4741*
Melons and cantaloupes, *3899*
Mennonite meetinghouse, *6538*
Mennonites to arrive in America, *6537*
Paper mill, *5747*
Protest against slavery, *2240*
School for Protestant girls, *3050*
Teaching methodology book, *1825*
Theological treatise, *1950*
Watermark in paper, *5748*

Gettysburg

Cabinet session held at a place other than the
seat of the federal government, *6116*

Hanover

Civil War bloodshed north of the Mason-Dixon
Line, *7967*

Harrisburg

Digest of American law, *1878*
National political convention to adopt the unit
rule, *3334*
Opinion poll, *5601*
Railroad sleeping car, *6372*
Raptor sanctuary, *3748*
Teletypewriter system employed by a police de-
partment, *4143*

Haverford

College cricket club team to tour England,
7274
College founded as a Quaker institution, *2942*
Cricket game played by a college team, *7272*

Huntingdon County

Coke used successfully as a blast furnace fuel,
3505

Johnstown

Ace in World War II, *1616*
Dam disaster of great consequence, *2868*
Railroad tunnel, *3613*

Kennet Square

Paper folding machine, *5764*

Kleinfeltersville

Evangelical Church conference, *6526*

Kobuta

Polystyrene, *4483*

Lancaster

Airship, *1512*
Airship bombing plan, *8100*
Ball bearing commercial installation, *2038*
Chocolate bars, *3965*
Christmas tree, *4254*
Conestoga wagon, *5936*
Crematory established by a state government,
2858
Electric watch, *7904*
Embossed inlaid linoleum, *4318*
Insulating brick, *2059*
Slicing machine, *4296*
Steamboat, *6853*
United Brethren in Christ meeting, *6541*

Latrobe

Professional football game, *7322*

Leechburg

Tin factory, *4473*

Lewisburg

College football player to score 50 points in
one game, *7307*

Lewiston Junction

Railroad signal system of continuous cab signals, *6426*

Lititz

Electric spinning reel, *7943*
Pretzel bakery, *3922*

Lock Haven

Test pilot who was a woman, *1603*

Mansfield

Football game at night, *7321*

Marcus Hook

Rayon, *7874*

Mauch Chunk

Iron blast furnace to use anthracite coal in
smelting, *4452*

PENNSYLVANIA—Mauch Chunk—*continued*
Mining tunnel on a large scale, *3612*

Middletown

Nuclear power plant to sustain a major accident, *3556*

Monongahela City

Carborundum, *5337*

Montgomery County

Bird banding, *6740*
Brick roofing tile, *2036*

Montoursville

Flashbulb device with multiple flashbulbs, *5847*

New Castle

Baseball player on a white team who was African-American, *7140*

Oil Creek

Commercial oil refinery, *3529*
Oil pipeline, *3531*
Oil pipeline of importance, *3533*

Peach Bottom

Nuclear commercial power plant licensed operator who was a woman, *3555*

Philadelphia

Abolition organization, *2243*
Academy, *2929*
Actor of American birth, *1273*
Actors' home, *1277*
Adhesive and medicated plaster, *4942*
Advertising agency, *2322*
Advertising school, *2921*
African Methodist Episcopal bishop, *6564*
African Methodist Episcopal church convention, *6563*
African Methodist Episcopal preacher who was a woman, *6565*
Agricultural encyclopedia, *1831*
Agriculture society, *1087*
Airmail regular delivery service by autogiro, *6029*
American flag to represent the United States, *1118*
American history chair at a college, *3096*
Amphibious seaplane glider, *1554*
Anatomy book, *1896*

Anatomy lectures, *3129*
Anatomy research institute, *5055*
Animal rights organization (national), *5740*
Animated photograph projection before a theater audience, *5529*
Anthracite coal used commercially, *3504*
Anti-aging skin cream, *4063*
Arabic daily newspaper, *5678*
Arcade, *2061*
Archery club, *7568*
Architecture book printed in America, *2009*
Arctic expedition to seek the Northwest Passage, *6720*
Army chaplain who was Jewish, *5200*
Art museum, *5593*
Articles of Confederation, *1102*
Artificial lens for cataract patients, *5052*
Astronomer to acquire international fame, *6657*
Automatic telephone system, *7713*
Autopsy performed by a woman physician on a male corpse, *2850*
Aviation book, *1987*
Aviation magazine devoted primarily to airplanes, *4780*
Balloon flight in which a presidential order was carried, *1536*
Bank chartered by Congress, *3757*
Bank of the United States, *3758*
Baseball game in which a team made no hits in nine innings, *7118*
Baseball game in which one team scored more than 100 runs, *7115*
Baseball player to play as a professional, *7139*
Baseball strike, *4595*
Basketball team to score more than 10,000 points, *7176*
Belt conveyor system, *4390*
Bible in Hebrew, *1967*
Bible printed in English, *1962*
Bible society, *6571*
Bible translated into English, *1966*
Bifocal eyeglasses, *5072*
Blood serum made of dried human blood, *4833*
Blowpipe, *6796*
Book advocating voting rights for women, *2012*
Book entered for copyright, *4629*
Book for the blind, *1747*
Book made with American paper, ink, and type, *1738*
Book on child-rearing, *2019*
Book on vellum, *1749*
Book showing photographs of movements in sequence, *1750*
Book with color plates, *1741*
Botanical garden, *6736*
Botany professor at a college, *3229*
Boxing match to attract 100,000 spectators, *7242*
Boxing referee in a heavyweight championship match who was African-American, *7246*

Brawl in the House of Representatives, *2583*
Brewery to remain in business for 200 years, *2664*
Bridge named for a woman, *3598*
Bubble gum, *3967*
Building erected in the United States for public use, *2115*
Business school at a college, *2919*
Cable car, *6395*
Car advertisement in a national magazine, *2332*
Carpet mill, *4311*
Catholic Bible in English, *1963*
Catholic church in the English colonies, *6453*
Catholic funeral attended by the Continental Congress, *6455*
Centennial exhibition, *2410*
Chemistry laboratory manual, *1980*
Chemistry magazine, *4766*
Chemistry professor at a college, *3230*
Chemistry society, *6777*
Chemistry textbook, *1976*
Chess book, *1995*
Chess computer to beat the world chess champion, *4034*
Chiropody school at a college, *3175*
Chlorophyll, *4997*
Chrome-tanned leather successfully marketed, *4460*
Circulating library, *4661*
Circus, *3672*
City directory, *1813*
Clearinghouse for stocks and bonds, *3819*
Coin bearing the likeness of a president, *5375*
Coin bearing the likeness of an American woman, *5381*
Coin to use the motto "In God We Trust", *5369*
Coins bearing dates other than the year of issue, *5380*
Coins manufactured for a foreign government, *5372*
Coins produced by steam power, *5366*
Collapsible tube machine, *7927*
College classes intended to combat the influence of communism, *3002*
College under Jewish auspices that was nonsectarian, *2963*
Comic opera written for the American stage, *1343*
Comic weekly, *4717*
Commemorative stamped envelopes, *6083*
Commercial artist, *1201*
Commercial museum, *5580*
Composer born in America, *1327*
Compressed pills or tablets, *4987*
Congressional apportionment of representatives, *2582*
Congressional eulogy for a president, *6185*
Congressional investigation, *2560*
Constitution of the United States, *1104*

Constitutional amendments, *1107*
Continental Congress assembly to be opened with prayer, *2575*
Continental Congress session, *2573*
Copley Medal awarded to an American, *1646*
Copper coins made by the U.S. Mint, *5359*
Copyright law enacted by Congress, *4628*
Cornmeal machine for grinding maize, *3910*
Cowboy hat, *2297*
Craft union contract, *4605*
Cranioscopy book, *1909*
Cricket magazine, *4783*
Croquet league, *7571*
Cryptography chart, *4797*
Daily newspaper, *5634*
Decalcomania pictures, *4307*
Decimal system of money, *5348*
Declaration of rights, *1111*
Delegate to a national political convention who was African-American, *3335*
Dental filling made of gold, *4860*
Dental hygienists' book, *1925*
Dental mallet, *4865*
Dental surgery textbook, *1923*
Department store sales demonstrations using television, *2342*
Department store to sell apartments, *2510*
Dermatology treatise, *1917*
Detective story, *1844*
Diamonds in a meteorite, *5338*
Dictionary of American law, *1805*
Distilling book, *1848*
Dollar marks, *5802*
Draft of civilians by Congress, *5218*
Drug mill, *4982*
Druggist, *4965*
Dynamo for a direct-current outdoor lighting system, *3454*
Editorial apology for false news to appear in a newspaper, *5631*
Electric cooking experiment, *3450*
Electric light in a store, *3491*
Electric motor using interpole direct current, *5481*
Electric turnstile with a rachet, *2362*
Electrical show, *2411*
Electrocution experiment, *2794*
Electron microscope, *6800*
Electronic computer, *2528*
Electronic computer for commercial use, *2529*
Electronic computer with solid-state components, *2530*
Electronic voice mechanism, *7723*
Embalming book, *1910*
Emergency first aid organization, *4117*
Encyclopedia compiled by American editors, *1832*
Encyclopedia printed in the United States, *1830*
Engineering book, *1977*
Entomology book, *1984*

PENNSYLVANIA—Philadelphia—*continued*
Entomology journal, *4772*
Episcopal catechism, *1955*
Episcopal priest who was a woman, *6553*
Escalator of the modern type, *2110*
Extradition treaty with a foreign country, *4001*
Federal government employees who were women, *5351*
Fiction best seller, *1781*
Fire insurance agent, *4528*
Fire insurance company to receive a charter, *4530*
Fire insurance joint-stock company, *4531*
Fire patrol to protect property during fires, *4098*
Fireworks book, *2021*
Fishing club, *7284*
Fishing magazine, *4785*
Fluorescent mineral exhibit, *6715*
Folding bed, *4328*
Foreign service committee, *3974*
Fox hunting club, *7422*
French newspaper, *5662*
Frigate, *6914*
Fruit culture treatise, *1759*
Fustians, everlastings, and coating, *7860*
Gaslights for display, *3654*
Gasoline-mechanical railroad cars, *6387*
Gastroenterology treatise, *1898*
Gazetteer of the world, *1815*
General of the Continental Army, *5146*
Geology book, *1981*
German book printed in America, *1953*
German instruction at a college, *3111*
German newspaper, *5661*
Glider commercial freight service, *1555*
Golfer to play 180 holes in one day, *7359*
Gymnastics book, *1996*
Health insurance clause in a labor contract, *4538*
Hebrew spelling book, *1858*
Hemophilia treatise, *1899*
High-speed newspaper printing and folding machine, *5791*
Highway bridge with concrete arches, *3586*
Homeopathic hospital, *4875*
Homeopathic medical society, *5031*
Homeopathic pharmacy, *4986*
Homeopathy college, *3163*
Horticultural magazine, *4711*
Hospital, *4868*
Hospital for insane patients operated privately, *4896*
Hospital to treat poor patients at no charge, *4869*
Hydrotherapy book, *1887*
Hymnbook compiled by an African-American editor, *1973*
Ice cream soda, *3864*
Ice skating club, *7428*

Influenza epidemic, *2874*
Insane patients' home, *4894*
Insurance book, *1794*
Insurance company owned by African-Americans, *4501*
Insurance journal, *4721*
Insurance law treatise, *1873*
Intercity stagecoach service, *2184*
Intercollegiate wrestling association, *7577*
Internal revenue tax levied by Congress, *7642*
Invisible ink, *8147*
Jewish magazine, *4746*
Judge to be impeached, *2718*
Know-Nothing (American) Party convention, *3354*
Labor Day, *4237*
Labor union to admit workers other than craft workers, *4611*
Lager beer, *2667*
Law history book, *1861*
Library association (national), *4688*
Library building, *4662*
Life insurance company, *4542*
Life insurance offered by a general insurance company, *4543*
Lightning demonstration, *6767*
Lightning rod, *4096*
Lipreading tournament held nationally, *3036*
Lithograph, *1214*
Locomotive with a cab, *6354*
Lottery held by the Continental Congress, *3641*
Lutheran services in English, *6556*
Macadam road, *6613*
Magazine containing a fashion plate, *4701*
Magazine for blind readers, *4713*
Magazine for patients with mental illness, *4716*
Magazine for professional printers, *4723*
Magazine published in America, *4692*
Marble building, *2070*
Marine band, *5230*
Marines, *5229*
Masonic book, *2007*
Masonic lodge, *5728*
Masonic magazine, *4705*
Maternity book, *2013*
Medal of Technology awarded to a woman, *1655*
Medical book by a navy medical officer, *1901*
Medical college, *3159*
Medical dictionary, *1804*
Medical education book, *1891*
Medical encyclopedia, *1833*
Medical record of an epidemic, *2875*
Medical research chair at a college, *3154*
Medical society (national), *5036*
Metal purchased for coinage, *5363*
Methodist churches for African-Americans, *6561*
Milestones between cities, *2185*
Military dictionary, *1802*

Military drill manual, *2011*
Military field strategy manual, *2010*
Military organization to oppose the British, *5254*
Mineral water bottler, *3842*
Minister plenipotentiary, *3984*
Mint of the United States, *5350*
Mobile electric power plant, *3486*
Mobile telephone conversation between the ground and an airship, *7761*
Mother's Day, *4243*
Music book by an author born in America, *1934*
Music publishers, *1281*
Musical instrument dealer, *1279*
Mustard, *3943*
Narrow-gauge locomotive, *6357*
National convention of African-Americans, *2248*
National tennis championship match for women, *7529*
Naval protection, *5259*
Naval vessel equipped to lay mines, *6931*
Navy doctor, *5276*
Navy officer to abolish corporal punishment on his ship, *5281*
Navy petty officer who was a woman, *5286*
Neutrality proclamation by the federal government, *3977*
News correspondent accredited to the White House, *5616*
Newspaper cartoon, *5684*
Newspaper to publish the Constitution, *1105*
Newspaper to publish the Declaration of Independence, *1115*
Newspaper with an aviation section, *5651*
Nursing school to award a diploma, *3166*
Oil tank railroad cars, *6376*
Organ built in the United States, *1304*
Passport, *5884*
Patent granted jointly to a father and son, *4650*
Patent recipient to obtain more than one patent, *4649*
Pathology textbook, *1907*
Pay television presentation of a sporting event, *7785*
Paymaster general of the Continental Army, *5164*
Pediatrics monograph, *1897*
Pencil with an attached eraser, *8151*
Penny daily newspaper, *5638*
Pension law enacted by Congress, *4582*
Performance of *The Stars and Stripes Forever*, *1292*
Petroleum exported to Europe, *3530*
Pharmaceuticals book, *1929*
Pharmacist who was a woman, *4963*
Pharmacist who was a woman to receive a degree from a pharmacy college, *3147*
Pharmacopoeia, *1926*

Pharmacy college, *3160*
Pharmacy journal, *4751*
Pharmacy professorship at a college, *3132*
Pharmacy society (national), *5038*
Philosophy book printed in America, *2008*
Phonetic Bible, *1969*
Phonograph record, *7006*
Photograph of a solar eclipse, *6694*
Photographic attempt to show motion, *5569*
Phrenology journal, *4753*
Physician to receive a Bachelor of Medicine degree, *3131*
Physician who was African-American, *4966*
Plate-glass insurance, *4507*
Play about a Native American, *1247*
Political convention to be televised, *3342*
Porcelain, *4038*
Postage stamp catalog, *2026*
Postmaster general under the Continental Congress, *5983*
Presbyterian presbytery, *6581*
Presidential amnesty issued to rebellious citizens, *6143*
Presidential candidate who was renominated after a defeat, *3414*
Presidential commission, *6142*
Presidential election debate between an incumbent president and a challenger to be televised, *3397*
Presidential veto of a congressional bill, *6141*
Printed copies of the Constitution, *1103*
Printer's ink, *5783*
Printing of the Declaration of Independence, *1114*
Printing press for polychromatic printing, *5776*
Printing press invented in the United States, *5768*
Prison reform society, *2812*
Prison to have individual cells for prisoners, *2813*
Professional football game in which 10 touchdowns were made, *7328*
Psychiatry association (national), *5035*
Psychiatry book, *1903*
Psychiatry textbook, *1912*
Psychology professor at a college, *3148*
Public exhibition of postage stamps, *6058*
Public reading of the Declaration of Independence, *1116*
Public telecast over telephone wires using the narrow-band system, *7848*
Publishing society, *1785*
Quadruplets delivered by cesarean operation, *2174*
Quarantine law enacted by Congress, *4208*
Quarterly magazine, *4704*
Quartermaster of the Continental Army, *5166*
Quinine, *4983*
Radio contest, *6260*
Railroad owned by a state, *6319*

PENNSYLVANIA—Philadelphia—*continued*

Railroad track that was practical, *6415*
Reclining chair, *4324*
Relief map, *4800*
Religious weekly newspaper, *5636*
Restaurant with an automatic arrangement for vending food, *2461*
Revolving door, *2081*
Rhubarb, *3897*
Rocking chair, *4320*
Root beer, *3846*
Rosicrucian Order lodge, *6598*
Rotogravure press, *5781*
Rough-dry laundry service, *2441*
Sandblasting process, *4434*
Savings bank to receive money on deposit, *3760*
Schwenkfelder to arrive in America, *6539*
Science society (national), *6780*
Secular song by a composer born in America, *1375*
Seed business, *1011*
Sheet-glass drawing machine, *4045*
Shorthand book, *1735*
Shorthand journal, *4718*
Sieve, *4366*
Signer of the Declaration of Independence, *1113*
Silver coins, *5362*
Slide rule book, *1884*
Sociology treatise, *1989*
Soda water, *3843*
Songbook of secular songs, *1937*
Songbook of secular songs by a composer born in America, *1938*
Special session of Congress, *2561*
Special session of the Senate, *2626*
Split-level buildings, *2073*
Squash rackets champion, *7499*
Standardization of weights and measures for customs, *2474*
State legislator who was an African-American woman, *7631*
Steam engine for industrial use that was practical, *4391*
Steam shovel, *4396*
Stereotype printing, *5800*
Stomach washing with a tube or syringe, *5111*
Stone arch bridge, *3564*
Story serialized in a newspaper, *1835*
Streamlined all-steel diesel-motor train, *6433*
Street-cleaning machine, *2220*
Street letter box, *5992*
Street-sweeping service, *2219*
Strike benefit by a union, *4590*
Sulfuric acid, *4427*
Supreme Court decision, *2744*
Surgical operation shown on a local television program, *5084*
Suspension bridge of iron wire, *3570*

Swimmer of note, *7513*
Symphonic concert to be shown on television, *1299*
Symphony on an African-American folk theme, *1297*
Tax levied by Congress directly on the states, *7643*
Teachers' organization (national), *3225*
Territory owned by the federal government, *5942*
Tetraploid flower, *1064*
Textbook printed in America, *1824*
Textile machinery patent, *7865*
Theater building of brick construction, *3695*
Theological college for Jews, *3272*
Therapeutics book, *1904*
Title guaranty insurance company, *4509*
Tobacco tax enacted by Congress, *2697*
Trade directory, *1812*
Trade union organization established in a city, *4607*
Translation of a classic, *1736*
Transportation report, *2022*
Trotting horse, *1177*
Tuberculosis research and prevention society, *5042*
Type specimen book from an American type foundry, *1742*
Unitarian church, *6523*
University legally designated as such, *2933*
Use of the name United States instead of United Colonies, *1097*
Varnish manufacturer, *4429*
Venetian blinds, *4306*
Voice synthesizer, *7711*
Wall and floor tiles, *2042*
Wallpaper, *4305*
Warship builder, *5260*
Warship with propelling machinery below the waterline, *6918*
Washing machine, *4270*
Waterworks system to use cast-iron pipes, *2226*
White lead manufacturer, *4462*
Wire glass, *4043*
World heavyweight boxing champion to retire undefeated, *7254*
Yellow fever vaccine for human immunization, *4922*
Zoo, *1186*

Phoenixville

Water gas plant, *3517*

Pittsburgh

Aluminum-faced building, *2091*
Aluminum in metallic form, *4475*
Angle iron, *2040*
Armored truck holdup, *2779*
Brown dwarf star to be discovered, *6685*

PENNSYLVANIA—*continued*

Shuman's Station

Timber trestle pier of lattice construction, *3575*

Skippack

Blackboards for use in schools, *3048*

South Bethlehem

Navy contract for armor plate, *5265*

Springfield

Artist of American birth to head the Royal Academy of London, *1202*

State College

Driving course in a high school, *3090*

Sunbury

Electric power plant with a three-wire central station, *3463*

Titusville

Oil well drilled by torpedoes, *3532*
Oil well that was commercially productive, *3528*

Troy

Pineapple cheese, *3858*

Uniontown

Battle in the French and Indian War, *7971*
Bloodshed in the French and Indian War, *7970*

Villa Nova

Cattle tuberculosis test, *5121*

Village Forks

Twin covered bridges, *3579*

Warren

Tractor with an endless chain, *1053*

Washington

Crematory, *2857*
Disciples of Christ meeting, *6527*

Waynesburg

Baseball league for children, *7097*

Westmoreland County

Suspension bridge, *3567*

Wildwood

Coal mine to be automated, *3508*

Wilkes-barre

Anthracite coal burned experimentally, *3503*

Willow Grove

Autogiro flown in America, *1529*
Autogiro licensed for commercial use, *1530*
Transcontinental autogiro flight, *1531*

York

Locomotive to burn coal, *6352*
Treaties entered into by the federal government, *3998*
Wrecking crane operated from a car, *4416*

PUERTO RICO

Commonwealth of the United States, *5976*

Fajardo

Surgeon general who was a woman, *4214*

San Juan

Governor of Puerto Rico to be elected, *3324*

RHODE ISLAND

Commander-in-chief of the Continental Navy, *5277*
Governor of Italian ancestry, *7620*
Health insurance law enacted by a state, *4539*
Oyster propagation, *1058*
State law prohibiting discrimination against soldiers, *5127*

Bellefonte

Screw factory, *7912*

Block Island

Marine officer killed in service, *5234*

Bristol

Circumnavigation of the North American continent by a ship, *6992*
Torpedo boat, *6924*

Conanicut Island

Portable church, *6532*

Cranston

Asphalt-covered racetrack, *7510*
Bridge hand in which each player was dealt a perfect hand, *4025*
Car race on a racetrack, *7261*

Cumberland

Nails, *7907*

Greenwich

Building known as a Quonset hut, *2117*

Newport

Bicycle organization (national), *7185*
Candle factory for making spermaceti candles, *4341*
Cattle club to promote Jersey cattle, *1090*
Court-martial in a colony, *2738*
Felt manufacturing mechanical process, *7867*
Gas streetlights, *2213*
Golf course with nine holes, *7347*
International polo series, *7458*
International professional tennis contest, *7530*
National championship stroke-play golf match, *7338*
National tennis championship matches, *7527*
Naval war college, *3216*
Naval War College president who was a former prisoner of war, *3222*
Naval War College students who were African-American, *3220*
Navy chaplain who was a woman, *5205*
Newspaper editor who was a woman, *5610*
Open golf championship tournament, *7341*
Parade of automobiles, *3665*
Post office building, *6036*
Roller skating rink open to the public, *7463*
Seventh Day Baptist Church, *6544*
Slave importation ban enacted by a colony, *2242*
Torpedo manufacturing station, *8109*
Transatlantic crossing by a submarine under its own power, *6988*

Pawtucket

Child labor in a factory, *4572*
Cotton mill to spin cotton yarn successfully, *7883*
Cotton thread, *4361*
Patent granted to an inventor who was a woman, *4651*
Strike in which women participated, *4591*

Toy action figure, *2153*

Providence

Animated picture machine, *5528*
Baptist church, *6543*
Building with an all-marble dome, *2084*
Catamaran, *7213*
Gas-powered streetcar, *6397*
Gold leaf, *5339*
Health laboratory established by a city, *4197*
Health laboratory established by a state to diagnose diseases by the examination of sputum, *4201*
Jewelers' supply house, *5319*
Lime, *5315*
Lunch wagon, *2457*
Mineralogy instruction at a college, *3231*
Mutual fire insurance company, *4532*
Native American dictionary, *1796*
Naval attack in the Revolutionary War, *7987*
Outdoor school for children with tuberculosis, *3020*
Post office fully mechanized, *6042*
Price regulation law enacted by a colony, *2517*
Religious refuge for people of all faiths, *5923*
Screw machine to make pointed screws, *7923*
Spinning jenny for cotton, *7881*
Straw hats, *2294*
Tap dancer of renown, *1233*
Unassisted triple play in organized baseball, *7120*

Quonset Point

Navy jet airplane squadron, *5303*

Warwick

Corrupt election practices law enacted by a colony, *3313*
Slavery emancipation law enacted by a colony, *2239*

SOUTH CAROLINA

Atlas issued by a state, *4799*
House of Representatives election that was contested, *3326*
Indigo crop, *1009*
Novel by an American to depict Native Americans in a realistic manner, *1843*
Secession act at the start of the Civil War, *7636*
Senate filibuster to last for more than 24 hours, *2633*
Senator elected by a write-in vote, *3331*
State to secede from the Union, *7945*
Supreme Court chief justice whose nomination was not confirmed, *2754*

SOUTH CAROLINA—continued

Vice president to resign, *6243*

Barnwell County

Workers' compensation lawsuit involving the rights of an injured servant against his master, *4552*

Beaufort

Justice of a state supreme court who was African-American, *2720*

Buford

Union regiment in the Civil War made up of African-American soldiers, *7966*

Chapin

Cotton fabric used on a road, *6629*

Charleston

Act inaugurating the Civil War, *7946*
Army major who was African-American, *5169*
Building of fireproof construction, *2072*
City college, *2936*
Civil rights anthem to achieve fame, *1383*
Confederate ship surrendered to the Union, *7963*
Cotton crop exported, *1029*
Cremation, *2856*
Earthquake of consequence to be recorded, *2867*
Fire insurance company, *4529*
Golf players' club, *7337*
Independent government in an American colony, *5940*
Jewish congregation in the Reform movement, *6486*
Library, *4659*
Locomotive illumination, *6350*
Music society, *1278*
Naval skirmish in the Civil War, *7950*
Navy Cross awarded to a Coast Guard officer in World War II, *1659*
Opera performed in America, *1341*
Photographs of combat, *5816*
Physician born in America who was graduated from a foreign medical school, *4964*
Police chief who was both African-American and Jewish, *4154*
Price sheet for commodities, *2321*
Public museum, *5576*
Rivetless cargo vessel, *6891*
Soldier killed in the Revolutionary War who was Jewish, *7996*
Submarine built in the United States to sink an enemy warship in actual warfare, *7968*

Weather observations to be systematically recorded, *6766*

Charlestown

American imprisoned as an enemy agent in the Tower of London, *8004*
Pastelist, *1197*

Columbia

Library building at a university, *4669*

Dewitt's Corner

Treaty between states after the Declaration of Independence, *7594*

Dillon

Paprika mill, *3952*

Fort Sumter

Civil War attack, *7949*

Georgetown

Congressional representative who was African-American, *2603*

Greenville

Secular song hit, *1379*

Parris Island

French to arrive in America, *5898*

Port Royal

Ship built in America to cross the Atlantic Ocean, *6847*

Silver Bluff

Baptist churches for African-Americans, *6546*

Sumter

City government using the manager plan, *2204*

Winnsborough

Hailstone shower of record that was fatal, *2866*

SOUTH DAKOTA

Native American Day, *4252*

Aberdeen

Grandmother to give birth to her own grandchild, *2169*

Quintuplets to live more than five years, *2176*

Brookings

Fluorescent electric lighting to be installed on every street of a city, *2218*

Custer

Monument to a Native American, *5417*

Rapid City

Aerial photograph showing the lateral curvature of the horizon and the beginning of the stratosphere, *5828*

Watertown

High school to fingerprint its students, *4166*

Wounded Knee

Armed occupation by Native American protesters in the modern era, *5978*

Yankton

Hutterites, *6542*

TENNESSEE

Alcohol prohibition law enacted by a state, *2676*

Cabinet member who had served as a Confederate officer, *6107*

Congressional representative to serve before his 25th birthday, *2599*

Election for governor in which two brothers were the opposing candidates, *7616*

Former president to become a senator, *6160*

Jim Crow law, *2255*

Senator to be impeached, *2641*

Senators elected but not seated, *2640*

State readmitted to the Union after the Civil War, *7605*

Chattanooga

Baseball pitcher who was a woman, *7149*

Medal of Honor of the Army, *1673*

Miniature golf course, *7349*

Clarksville

Athlete who was an African-American woman to win the James E. Sullivan Memorial Trophy, *1721*

Jackson

Medical journal published by an African-American, *4761*

Kingsport

Cellulose sponge for household use, *4280*

Knoxville

College that was nondenominational, *2939*

Dueling law enacted by a state, *2808*

Memphis

Airborne express delivery service, *2489*

Children's hospital for research and treatment of catastrophic childhood diseases, *4893*

Golfer to break 60 in a Professional Golfers Association tour, *7368*

Holiday Inn, *2432*

Keedoozle store, *2506*

Self-service grocery store, *2500*

Sewage-disposal system separate from the city water system, *2230*

Typewriter ribbon, *2386*

Nashville

Dogs trained to guide the blind, *1173*

FM radio transmitter to receive a commercial license, *6299*

Futurity horse race, *7390*

Postage stamp for balloon mail, *6059*

Showboat theater, *3696*

Oak Ridge

Labor dispute in which the Taft-Hartley Act was invoked, *4569*

Museum devoted exclusively to nuclear energy, *5591*

Radioactive isotopes exported, *6820*

Pulaski

Ku Klux Klan meeting, *2253*

Rogersville

Trade journal, *4710*

Shiloh

Army field hospital, *5010*

Sweetwater

Japanese high school in the United States, *3093*

Tuskegee

Native American language to be given a written form, *5959*

TENNESSEE—*continued*

Washington College

College named after George Washington, *2934*

TEXAS

Bowie knife, *8095*
Cave paintings, *1210*
Round-the-world helicopter flight, *1579*
State police, *4134*
State supreme court in which all the judges were women, *2724*

Abilene

Golfer to play 24 hours continuously on a regulation course, *7365*

Arlington

Belly-dancing course at a college, *2916*

Austin

Armored division transported by airplanes to a foreign country, *5193*

Beaumont

Oil journal, *4778*

Big Spring

Bullfighter who was a woman to fight professionally, *7259*

Brownsville

Cotton boll weevil, *1032*

College Station

Football game to be broadcast on radio with a play-by-play description, *7324*

Columbia

President of the Republic of Texas, *4077*

Corpus Christi

Welding machine for aluminum pipes, *4420*

Corsicana

Navy chaplain who was Jewish, *5203*

Crystal City

Monument to a comic-strip character, *5415*

Dallas

City radio station, *6296*
Correction fluid for typewriters, *2389*
Courtroom verdict to be televised, *2717*
Electronic pocket calculator, *3447*
Hospital insurance group plan, *4535*
Integrated circuit, *3444*
Murder to be shown live on television, *2786*
Newspaper printed on pine-pulp paper in color, *5797*
Sanitary napkin, *4059*
Two-way moving sidewalk, *6640*

Floydada

Payment by the Federal Crop Insurance Corporation, *1006*

Fort Bliss

Army ballistic missile operational unit, *5192*

Fort Worth

Airplane to fly with a load of 100,000 pounds, *1471*
Ballet technique course at a college, *2915*
Computer hacker to be convicted, *2789*
Helium plant, *6797*
Hotel to establish a heliport, *2433*
Laundromat, *2442*
Lightweight solo streetcar, *6406*
Round-the-world nonstop flight by an airplane, *1470*

Freeport

Latex paint, *7942*
Magnesium commercially produced from seawater, *5344*
Seawater conversion plant, *2237*

Galveston

City government using the commission plan, *2202*
Hotel built over a pier, *2434*
Newspaper delivery train, *5647*

Houston

Boxer to win world titles in five weight divisions, *7256*
Championship game of the American Football League, *7331*
Drive-up mailbox, *6009*
Educational television station, *7801*
Fullerenes to be observed, *6822*
Heart transplant using an artificial heart, *5101*

Long-distance car-to-car telephone conversation, *7764*

Oil refinery with a carbon monoxide boiler, *3542*

Space-to-ground news conference telecast, *5608*

Superconducting material that operated at relatively high temperatures, *6823*

Voting rights in space, *3435*

Wedding in an airplane, *4818*

Huntsville

Execution by lethal injection, *2806*

Indianola

Camels imported for military purposes, *1145*

Kelly Air Force Base

Air Force military engineer who was a woman, *5139*

Lampasas

Banking association (state), *3770*

Lufkin

Microwave television station, *7804*

Nueces County

Cotton acreage reduction payment, *1034*

Port Arthur

Cargo ship from the United States attacked by a German submarine in World War I, *8028*

Randolph Air Force Base

Space cabin simulator, *7022*

San Angelo

Air-conditioned public elementary school, *2120*

San Antonio

Air-conditioned office building, *2065*

Airplane accident in a solo military airplane that was fatal, *1392*

Airplane flying school operated by a woman, *7294*

Mayor of a major city who was of Mexican descent, *2211*

Schertz

Liver transplant from a live donor, *5105*

Temple

Road with a depressed trough, *6628*

Texarkana

Federal credit union, *3785*

Waco

Murder trial to be televised, *4624*

Quadruplets to graduate from college, *2173*

Weatherford

Mechanical cotton picker, *1033*

UTAH

Bird banding by federal authorities, *6747*

Game preserve appropriation by the federal government, *3749*

Senator to fly in space, *7051*

Shot fired by the Navy in World War I, *8031*

State senator who was a woman, *7626*

Fort Bridger

Cartridge belt patent, *8108*

Natural Bridges National Monument

Power plant using solar cells, *3560*

Promontory

Transcontinental railroad service, *6336*

Salt Lake City

Heart transplant using an artificial heart that was intended to be permanent, *5103*

Japanese newspaper in continuous publication, *5682*

Monument to a bird, *5411*

Mormon man ordained to the priesthood who was African-American, *6494*

Wendover

Motorcycle to exceed 200 miles per hour, *5491*

VERMONT

Absentee voting law enacted by a state, *3431*

Patent granted by the federal government, *4648*

Poliomyelitis epidemic, *2877*

Sculptor of renown, *1208*

Sit-down strikes to be outlawed by a state, *4599*

VERMONT—*continued*

Slavery emancipation law enacted by a state, *2244*

Sports bra, *2281*

State admitted to the Union after the ratification of the Constitution, *7602*

Trade monopoly, *2515*

Bradford

Globe factory, *4798*

Brandon

Electric motor using direct current, *3453*

Burlington

Factory heated by steam, *4382*

Concord

Teacher training school, *3258*

Dorset

Marble quarry, *5318*

Grandpa's Knob

Wind turbine, *3557*

Ludlow

Social security monthly payment, *4526*

Middlebury

College graduate who was African-American, *3009*

Horse farm operated by the federal government, *1182*

School for the higher education of women, *3079*

Montpelier

Dairy association (state), *1091*

Norwich

Civil engineering course at a college, *3232*

Military school, *3184*

Proctor

Company nurse, *5026*

Randolph

Morgan horse, *1176*

Rupert

Copper cents minted by a state, *5355*

St. Johnsbury

Platform scale, *2379*

Springfield

Sandpaper patent, *4394*

Stratton Mountain

Ski carousel, *7489*

Windsor

Election law enacted by a state to grant universal voting rights to freemen, *3423*

Woodstock

Ski tow made of rope, *7483*

VIRGINIA

Alcohol prohibition enforcement officers, *2672*

Alcohol temperance law enacted by a colony, *2674*

Ban on convicts holding public office, *3312*

Book written in America, *1727*

Boxer of fame who was African-American, *7249*

Breech-loading cannon, *8099*

Capture of an enemy warship by a commissioned American naval officer, *7995*

Chaplain of the U.S. Army, *5197*

Clerk of the House of Representatives, *2577*

Colonial badges issued to "friendly" Native Americans, *5929*

Congressional representative appointed to a presidential cabinet, *2596*

Crop limitation law enacted by a colony, *1007*

Crop surplus destruction ordered by a government, *1008*

Expedition of Englishmen to cross the Allegheny Mountains, *5927*

Former president to serve as an official of an enemy government, *6158*

Fungicide used medicinally, *5001*

Gambling law for ministers enacted by a colony, *3632*

Governor who was African-American, *7621*

Hemp to be exported, *1010*

History book of the colonial era, *1859*

Horse that was a thoroughbred, *1175*

Hunting law enacted by a colony, *3741*

Inheritance tax levied by a colony, *7640*

Irish to arrive in America, *5932*

Local radio network, *6301*

Lottery, *3640*

Medical regulations enacted by a colony, *4933*

Motorboat, *6948*

Naval expedition mounted by an English colony, *5910*

Physician in the colony of Virginia, *4959*

Potato, *3890*

Presbyterian church, *6580*

President of the Continental Congress, *2574*

President who had been a senator, *6139*

Rice to be imported, *3893*

Sabbath law enacted by a colony, *6504*

Senator appointed by a governor, *2639*

Silk culture, *7885*

Supreme Court chief justice to serve in a presidential cabinet, *2756*

Supreme Court chief justice who had been a congressional representative, *2755*

Supreme Court decision reversing the ruling of a state supreme court, *2749*

Tomatoes eaten in America, *3895*

Treason trial by a colony, *2833*

Voluntary sterilization regulation enacted by a state, *6841*

Accomack

Salt works, *3930*

Theatrical performance, *1239*

Alexandria

Motorboat to travel at a speed of more than 40 miles per hour, *6952*

Pilot to fly a million miles in a jet airplane, *1605*

Railroad coupler, *6423*

School for African-American children established by a state, *3064*

Supreme Court justice to participate in a television program, *2764*

Toll road, *6610*

Arlington

Building containing 6.5 million square feet of usable space, *2118*

Burial at the Tomb of the Unknown Soldier, *2854*

Foreign servicewomen interred in the Arlington National Cemetery, *2855*

President buried in the National Cemetery, *6199*

Transatlantic message over radio telephone, *7757*

Weather map to be telecast, *7826*

Arlington Heights

Airplane accident that was fatal, *1387*

Bull Run Creek

Civil War battle, *7957*

Cape Henry

Episcopal church service in an English colony, *6547*

Jet airplane to land on a ship, *1466*

Lighthouse built after American independence, *4124*

Charles City County

Breach-of-promise suit, *4804*

Charlottesville

Electoral vote for a woman, *3396*

Chesapeake Bay

Photographs taken under the sea, *5821*

Cobbs

Oral school for deaf students, *3031*

Craney Island

Lightship, *4125*

Danville

American woman to become a member of the British Parliament, *6648*

Edom

Cesarean operation, *5075*

Elizabeth City

Child born of African-American parents in America, *2158*

Fairfax

Confederate officer killed in the Civil War, *7955*

Falling Creek

Ironworks, *4445*

Lead, *5314*

Fort Eustis

Military heliport, *1569*

Fort Monroe

Army school for chaplains, *3202*

VIRGINIA—*continued*

Fort Myer

Airplane endurance flight exceeding one hour, *1427*

Airship ordered by the federal government, *1514*

Intercity airplane flight by a U.S. military officer, *1428*

Fortress Monroe

School for freed slaves, *2251*

Fredericksburg

Monument to a woman financed by women, *5406*

Gosport

Ship constructed by the federal government, *6915*

Greensville

Criminal convicted on the evidence of DNA matching, *4167*

Hampton

Astronauts trained by the United States, *7028*
Free school funded by an endowment, *3039*

Hampton Roads

Airplane bombing experiment to sink a battleship, *8117*

Airplane flight from a ship, *1433*

Airship filled with helium gas, *1519*

Circumnavigation of the globe by a fleet of warships, *6986*

Naval battle between ironclad vessels in the Civil War, *7961*

Navy chaplain killed in action, *5199*

Scientific expedition fitted out by the federal government, *6723*

Ship-to-shore conversation over radio telephone, *7758*

Harrison's Landing

Taps, *1382*

James City

Road construction law enacted by a colony, *6607*
Wolf bounty, *1135*

James River

Medal of Honor awarded to a Marine in the Civil War, *1672*

Jamestown

Battle between English colonists and Native Americans, *5908*

Bottle, *4282*

Colonial council, *5906*

Cyclone of record, *2862*

English settlement in America that was permanent, *5907*

Fireworks, *3649*

Game played in the English colonies in America, *4008*

Glass factory, *4035*

Landowner of substance who was African-American, *5928*

Legislative assembly of a colony, *7622*

Maize, *3907*

Massacre of settlers by Native Americans, *5916*

Poetry translation prepared in America, *1942*

Polish settlers in America, *5909*

Postage stamp depicting a Native American, *6088*

Prefabricated ship built in America, *6849*

Rebellion in the English colonies, *5905*

Sheep, *1084*

Slander proceedings, *2767*

Tobacco cultivation, *2694*

Wedding of colonists in Virginia, *4812*

Langley Field

Full-scale wind tunnel for testing airplanes, *1501*

Radio telephone communication from an airplane, *7759*

Wind tunnel for testing airplane parts, *1497*

Lexington

Journalism course at a college, *3097*
Military school established by a state, *3185*

Lorton

Train to transport passengers and their cars, *6435*

Lynchburg

Medal of Honor awarded to a conscientious objector, *1681*

Manassas

Balloonist to direct artillery fire, *7964*

Mathias Point

Union naval officer killed in the Civil War, *7956*

Mechanicsville

Army field telegraph used in warfare, *5243*

Mill Point

Chain-stitch single-thread sewing machine, *4356*

Monroe

Balloon carrier, *6919*

Mount Vernon

Army lieutenant general, *5148*
First Lady to receive free mail franking privileges, *6130*
President to receive the unanimous vote of the presidential electors, *3381*
President to tour the country, *6230*
Presidential election in which more than one candidate declared for the presidency, *3383*

Newport News

Aircraft carrier, *6934*
Aircraft carrier with an angle deck, *6939*
Maritime museum, *5587*
Navy captain who was African-American, *5296*
Nuclear-powered aircraft carrier, *6942*
Transcontinental airship flight, *1520*

Norfolk

Autogiro to land and take off from a ship, *1534*
Child born in the United States through in vitro fertilization, *2166*
Marine hospital established by Congress, *4870*
Naval ship with a crew of mixed nationalities, *6944*
Navy nuclear task force to circumnavigate the globe without refueling, *5307*
Navy school for chaplains, *3218*
Navy surgeon, *5280*
Radio compass on a naval airplane, *1495*
Super-giant locomotive, *6367*
Transcontinental round-trip solo flight between sunrise and sunset, *1478*

Petersburg

Electric blanket, *4265*
Interstate railroad, *6322*

Portsmouth

Naval hospital established by Congress, *5007*

Television station owned by a religious organization, *6597*

Richmond

Artmobile, *5598*
Bank for African-Americans operated by African-Americans, *3771*
Bank president who was a woman, *3772*
City manager, *2203*
Commander of a combat ship who was African-American, *5295*
Navy admiral who was African-American, *5274*
Sheriff who was an African-American woman, *4156*

Roanoke

Quids political faction, *3346*

Southampton County

Slave rebellion after the Revolution, *2249*

Upperville

Horse show, *1180*

Virginia Beach

Civic center with an aluminum geodesic dome, *2093*

Wallops Island

Rocket with an electrostatic (ion) engine, *7025*

Walnut Grove

Reaper machine that was practical, *1044*

Williamsburg

College charter granted by the Crown, *2926*
College proposed in America, *2924*
College to confer medals as prizes, *2930*
College to have a full faculty, *2927*
College to use the honor system during examinations, *2931*
College with an elective system of study, *2932*
Cookbook, *1846*
Emperor of Japan to visit the United States, *6655*
English grammar by an American, *1853*
Fencing book, *1992*
Hospital for insane patients established by a colony, *4895*
Italian instruction at a college, *3114*
Law school at a college, *3121*
Pleurisy book, *1889*

VIRGINIA—Williamsburg—*continued*

Political economy course at a college, *3250*
Scholastic fraternity at a college, *2983*
School for Native Americans to be permanently established, *3049*
School of modern history at a college, *3094*
School of modern languages at a college, *3112*
Statehouse, *2114*
Theater, *3693*
Work of satirical fiction, *1837*

Yorktown

Customhouse, *2469*

WASHINGTON

Forest canopy crane to be used in North America, *6753*
Mail franking privilege, *5984*
Postage stamps depicting a woman, *6085*
State named for a person born in America, *7598*
Trial of a teacher for violating a state ban on teaching the theory of evolution, *3068*
Volcano known to claim human life, *2871*

Bellevue

Educational multimedia CD-ROM, *2554*

Cape Disappointment

Settlers to reach the Pacific coast, *5957*

Lynnwood

Amateur boxing match for women, *7247*

Pasco

Airmail contractor, *6021*

Redmond

Ascent of Mount Everest by an American, *7588*

Renton

Jet airplane used for commercial transport, *1403*

Richland

Nuclear reactor for research and development, *6809*

Seattle

Basketball collegiate player to score more than 1,000 points in one season, *7175*

Battleship built on the Pacific coast, *6927*
Bridge with open-mesh steel flooring, *3594*
Commercial software for personal computers, *2552*
Employment office established by a city, *4566*
Fisheries school at a college, *3296*
Hockey team from the United States to win the Stanley Cup, *7376*
International airmail, *6017*
Jumbo jet, *1405*
Natural medicine clinic subsidized by a government, *4853*
Pontoon bridge of reinforced concrete, *3595*
Revolving restaurant, *2465*
Ship from the United States lost in World War I, *8026*
Steam-operated pressing machine, *4414*
Streamlined ferryboat, *6912*
Theater operated as part of a state school system, *3710*
World's Fair that was financially successful, *2415*

South Cle Elum

Medal of Honor awarded posthumously to a Coastguardsman killed in action in World War II, *1680*

Spokane

Eye wash commercially manufactured, *4990*
Father's Day, *4244*

Tacoma

School stadium, *7509*

Tenino

Wooden money, *5378*

Vancouver

Army field range, *5245*
Steamboat on the Pacific coast, *6868*

Walla Walla

College comprehensive senior examination program, *3000*
Dean of students at a college, *2973*
Settlers to cross the continent who were women, *5960*

Wenatchee

Transpacific nonstop airplane flight, *1454*

Woodland

Skyjacking in which the skyjacker disappeared, *2787*

Yakima Reservation

Boarding school on a Native American reservation, *3063*

WEST VIRGINIA

Belt conveyor more than four miles long, *4419*
Rural free mail delivery, *6002*
Sales tax enacted by a state, *7656*

Alderson

Prison established by the federal government for women, *2829*

Berkeley Springs

Spa at a mineral spring, *5109*

Charles Town

Jockey who was a woman to win on a regular parimutuel flat track, *7415*

Charleston

Brick pavement on a city street, *6620*
Salt well drilled west of the Alleghenies, *3933*

Chester

Jockey who was a woman to ride two winners in one day, *7416*

Colliers

Bareknuckle world heavyweight boxing champion, *7251*

Fetterman

Union soldier killed by enemy action in the Civil War, *7954*

Green Bank

Scientific program to search for extraterrestrial life, *6672*

Institute

Coal hydrogenation plant, *4444*

Kanawha

Trust, *2518*

Parkersburg

Vitrolite, *4047*

Parsons

Confederate general killed in the Civil War, *7953*

Skin Fork

Soldier killed in action in the Korean War, *7977*

Welch

City parking garage, *5484*

Wheeling

Double-deck steamboat, *6864*
Natural gas plant operated by a city, *3515*
Steel-cut nails, *7931*

White Sulphur Springs

Golfer to break 60 for 18 holes in a major tournament, *7364*

WISCONSIN

Congressional representative who was a Socialist, *2607*
Governor to be removed from office by a state supreme court, *7612*
Probate delay law enacted by a state, *2842*
Unemployment insurance act, *4525*

Appleton

Hydroelectric power plant to furnish incandescent lighting, *3462*

Beloit

College whose tuition fees were based on family income, *2970*

Cambria

Film rolls for cameras, *5835*

Cambridge

Scandinavian Methodist Episcopal church, *6566*

Chippewa Falls

Steel ski jump, *7481*

Clintonville

Brake for four-wheeled cars, *5439*

Green Bay

Football game to gross $1 million, *7332*

WISCONSIN—*continued*

Kewaunee

Naval ship to surrender in peacetime without a fight, *6947*

La Crosse

Book issued on microcards, *4684*

Lake Geneva

Bicycle corps of cadets, *3187*
Radio car for military use, *5246*

Madison

Animal husbandry professor at a college, *2896*
Dairy school at a college, *2897*
Dance major at a college, *2909*
Game management chair at a college, *3078*
Lightweight brick, *2060*
Milk butterfat tester, *3874*
State legislature to use an electric vote record-er, *7627*
Weather forecast broadcast on radio, *6769*

Milton

Monolithic concrete building, *2075*

Milwaukee

Brother and sister to win national tennis singles championships in the same tournament, *7539*
Duplicate whist tournament, *4022*
Major league baseball game in which the majority of the players on one team were African-American, *7136*
Mayor of a major city who was a Socialist, *2208*
Newspaper advertisement printed on aluminum foil, *2347*
Occupational therapy course at a college, *3155*
Outboard motor, *6951*
Presbyterian elder who was a woman, *6583*
Safety association (national), *4187*
Whist organization, *4021*

Muskego

Norwegian newspaper, *5667*

Neenah

Flour rolling mill, *3915*

Peshtigo

Forest fire of consequence, *2883*

Portage

Lie detector, *4623*

Racine

Bicycle traffic court, *7196*
Blow dryer for hair, *4070*
Bohemian dictionary, *1807*
Confectionary machine, *3968*
Continuation school for adults established by a state government, *2889*
Czech newspaper, *5669*
Electric blender, *4300*
Malted milk, *3872*
Strike to last longer than a year, *4600*

Sayner

Snowmobile patent, *7490*

Watertown

Quintuplets, *2172*

Waukesha

Newspaper advertisement that looked three-dimensional, *2345*

WYOMING

Cannibal, *2838*
Election law enacted by a state to grant voting rights to women after the adoption of the Constitution, *3430*
Governor who was a woman, *7618*
National forest, *3727*
National park, *3735*

Belle Fourche River

National monument designated by the federal government, *5410*

Cheyenne

Frontier Day, *4242*
Yellow pages telephone directory, *1819*

South Pass City

Justice of the peace who was a woman, *2721*

Warren Air Force Base

MX intercontinental ballistic missile base, *8144*

973
ANZ

Anzovin, Steven.

Famous first facts
about American
politics.

42141

$140.00